A Concise History Of
Afghanistan-Central Asia & India-
Iraq, Iran, Turkey, Egypt, East Turkistan,
IN 25 VOLUMES:

VOLUME 2

HAMID WAHED ALIKUZAI

Order this book online at www.trafford.com
or email orders@trafford.com

Most Trafford titles are also available at major online book retailers.

Print information available on the last page.

ISBN: 978-1-6987-0006-9 (sc)
ISBN: 978-1-6987-0005-2 (e)

Trafford rev. 05/06/2020

 www.trafford.com

North America & international
toll-free: 1 888 232 4444 (USA & Canada)
fax: 812 355 4082

**Minister Yar M Alikuzai 1837 Herat
During Saxon Great Game**

Author's Note

Through research and study to write this manuscript from 1976 until 2020 sixty percent of this work is a family history document and forty percent is based on my research.

The book is still designed to set forth the first early history of Aryan and Aryana-Khorasan (present day Afghanistan) civilization as a unit, and it attempts to tell the story of an integrated, or at least interconnected, World. This is an attempt to tell the story of Aryana- Khorasan-Afghanistan in manuscript. I began the manuscript when I was living in Germany in the 1970s and at the urging of friends I worked to complete it and get it ready for publishing. It has been a massive undertaking as the manuscript involved painstaking years of research. Sixty percent of the book is from sources like my Grandmother and great Grandmother's spoken historical record and forty percent is my research and studying history and political education and knowledge from seventeen years of study in Hamburg, Germany at university. Philosophy of the history of the human race worthy of its name must begin with the heavens and descend to the earth and must be charged with the conviction that all existence is one, a single conception sustained from beginning to end upon one identical law. The universal history is at once something more and something less than the aggregate of the national histories to which we are accustomed, such that it must be approached in a different spirit and dealt with in a different manner; this manuscript seeks to provide insight into such a universal world history.

I am naturally a full-blown expert on all the subjects and periods covered in the book. I have tried to use the best sources and the best interpreters of the martial that myself could find, and to make my work as free as possible of egregiousness. I therefore have thought it best not to mention who have contributed to the writing and production of my work, but merely to express my general gratitude for my grandmother and to draw attention once to the excellent history of my family which have contributed so much to the success of earlier Heritages.

In a time of great although brief social reform from 1919 until 1929 there was a female monarch and minister in government who alongside her husband, King Amanullah Khan, made brave actions towards standing up for the rights of women in both India and Afghanistan. Queen Soraya, formerly of the Tarzi family, was consort of a monarch who proclaimed her his equal and made her a minister of education. Amanullah Khan was not only a king but was the Amir which translates to being Religious Head of State and their mullahs, but as King in order to institutionalize state reform into the constitution he elected to eradicate the title of Amir altogether, in order to create a more egalitarian society. Their modern thinking was actually a way of bringing back the ancient ways of Islam, but threatened both the mullahs and Islamic fundamentalists in Afghanistan and India, while Saxon present day British colonial powers who felt change in Afghanistan would impact their empire in India

A Concise History of Afghanistan-Central Asia & India- Iraq, Iran, Turkey, Egypt, East Turkistan, in 25 Volumes: Volume 2

AFGHANISTAN KNOWN AS THE GRAVEYARD OF EMPIRES, & AFGHANISTAN'S 5,500-YEAR OLD HERITAGE. AFGHANISTAN-CENTRAL ASIA THERE ARE ABOUT 39,000 RIVERS

Khorasan "present day Afghanistan-India-Iraq-Iran, Turkey, Egypt, East Turkistan and Central Asia" from the capital of Herat-Bukhara

Afghanistan Sitting on Gold, Lithium Mine oil, gas, only-natural gas prices-per day 86 billion Dollars US, & $100 trillion dollars US, Iron ore, copper, large Uranium, of mineral reserves, precious an semi-precious stones, emerald-lapis lazuli, red-gamete A ruby, Marble, Coal & Canal-tunnel of Gold

Saxon (present day British) and Russian- The Romanov family Activity on Afghan territory the Saxon-Great Games in Afghanistan huge Territories 2.6 million sq km the Great Pamir between two Germen Empire present day British and Russia, China, and Durand line

The Language and social life of Aryana present day Afghanistan the people of the grassy steppes of Aryana, found paper in use at Aryana as early as 500 B. C, 1361 transport of Herat library to Samarqand would need 1500 camels to transport Herat library

Afghanistan Literature is World's greatest and richest - without Afghan-Literature no European (German, France, Spanish or English) Literature would exist today

The Vedas, Zoroastrian, and Buddhist, among the oldest known Literature of Afghanistan, originating from the Great capital of Bactria present day Balkh, and Aria present day Herat, Sanskrit is the reference to the original history of Afghanistan

Dari: from B.C 960 the origin of Dari comes from the middle Bactria which was spoken during the rule by Zoroastrian Yama of the Bactrian present day Balkh

Aryana-Khorasan dynasty present day Afghanistan-Central Asia & India, Dari: from B.C 960 the origin of Dari comes from the middle Bactria which was spoken during the rule by Emperor Yama of the Bactrian and Sassanid dynasty. Dari is an Afghan language belonging to the Indo-Afghan branch of the Indo-European family of languages. In general, Aryana-Khorasan" in meddle of the nineteen century Afghanistan languages are known from three periods, usually referred to as Old, Middle, and present day (Modern) periods. These correspond to three eras in Afghanistan history; Old era being the period from sometime before Achaemeni dynasty, the Achaemeni- dynasty era and sometime after Achaemeni- dynasty (that is to 300 BC), Middle era being the next period, Sassani-dynasty era and part of the post-Sassani- dynasty era, and the New era being the period afterwards down to present day. Pronounced Dari refers to the dialects of modern Dari spoken in Afghanistan and is hence also known as Dari in some Western sources. It is the term officially recognized and promoted in 9th century by Ghaznavi dynasties and 1920s by the Afghan government for the Dari language. As defined in the Afghanistan, it is one of the two official languages of Afghanistan; the other is Pashto, Dari is the most widely spoken language in Afghanistan and the mother-tongue of approximately 50% of the population serving as the country's franca The Afghan dialects of Dari are highly mutually intelligible, with differences found primarily in the vocabulary and phonology. But in historical usage, Dari refers to the court language of the Sassanid's dynasties Dari, spoken in Afghanistan at BC 960, should not be confused with Dari of Afghanistan a language of the Central Afghanistan sub-group, spoken in some Zoroastrian communities.

The History of Dari Language

Aryana-Khorasan dynasty present day Afghanistan-Central Asia & India, the Saxon European with the Saxon-Great Games in the meddle of the nineteen century on Afghanistan-Central Asia for the Afghan language, religion, and Territories 2,6 million Sq Km, with any pries until 2020, "the size of Afghanistan from 1747 from India to north of Africa" Dari is the name given to the Afghanistan literary since 3,000 years ago B.C 960, language at a very early age and was widely used in Arabic (cf. Al-Estakhri Al-Muqaddasi and Hawqal and Dari texts. There are different opinions about the origin of the word Dari. The majority of scholars believe that Dari refers to the Afghan word dar or darbār meaning "Court", from the 9th century by Ghaznavi dynasties in Khorasan "present day Afghanistan-Central Asia, India, Iran, Iraq, Turkey, Egypt, and Caucasia including Russia" as it was the formal language of the Sassanid's dynasties the original meaning of the word Dari is given in a notice attributed to Ibn Muqaffa (cited by Ibn al-Nadim in Al-Fehrest). According to him, "Dari was the language spoken by priests, scholars, and the like; it is the language of Afghanistan" It is obvious that this language refers to the Middle Afghanistan as for Dari, he says, "it is the language of the cities of Mada'en; it is spoken by those who are at the king's court. "Its name" is connected with presence at court. Among the languages of the people of Khorasan (present day Afghanistan-Central Asia, India, Iraq, and Iran) and the east, the language of the people of Balkh is predominant." The origin of Dari comes from the middle Bactria which was spoken during the rule of the Bactrian and Sassanid dynasty in Aryana-Khorasan is an Afghan language belonging to the Indo-Afghan branch of the Indo-European family of languages. In general, Afghanistan languages are known from three periods, usually referred to as Old, Middle, and New (Modern) periods. These correspond to three eras in Afghanistan history; Old era being the period from sometime before Achaemeni, the Achaemeni dynasties era and sometime after Achaemenids (that is to 300 BC), Middle era being the next period, Sassanid era and part of the post-Sassanid era, and the New era being the period afterwards down to present day. Afghanistan languages have been and are still widely used in Central Asia both by native speakers and as trade languages. Whereas in the past, East Afghanistan languages, such as Bactrian Sogdian and Khotanese, and West Afghanistan languages notably Parthian and Middle Bactria were prominent. present day Afghanistan (Dari) has supplanted most of these languages. Note that the term Afghanistan as used here is a linguistic term and does not refer to the nation of Afghanistan.

Afghanistan-Geographical distribution

Dari, which is by its native-speakers, is one of the two official languages of Afghanistan (the other being Pashto). In practice though, it serves as the de facto lingua franca among the various ethno-linguistic groups. Dari is spoken by ca. 50% of the population as a first language. Tajiks who comprise approximately 27% of the population are the primary speakers, followed by Hazaras (9%) and Aymāqs (4%). Moreover, many Pashtuns living in Tajik and Hazara concentrated areas also use Dari as a first language. About and 55 million Pashtun people in also India speak Dari, and Pashto as one of their primary languages. Dari dominates in the northern, western and central areas of Afghanistan, and is the common language spoken in cities such as Kabul, Herat, Balkh, Fayzabad, Panjshir, Bamiyan, East Turkestan and Central Asia, Smaller Dari-speaking communities also exist in southern Pashtun-dominated areas such as in the cities of Kandahar, and Dari is sometimes the primary language even in regions dominated by Pashtuns, such as Farah, due to the regional history and influence of Aryana culture. Dari is also widely spoken in the Khyber Pakhtunkhwa, province and by a sizable population in Baluchistan, and various communities in Western Punjab.

Cultural influence

Dari has contributed to the majority of Afghanistan borrowings in other Central Asian languages, such as Urdu, Punjabi, Gujarati, etc., as it was the administrative, official and cultural language of the Persocentric Kabuli Empire and served as the lingua franca, throughout the South Asian subcontinent, for centuries. The sizeable Afghanistan component of the Saxon-Indian loan words in English and in Urdu "Urdu is found by Afghan in 17th century the called the language for the Army all over the Central Asia for one million "Lashekar" Army for the Kabulis Empire" therefore reflects the Dari pronunciation. For instance dopiaza or pyjama come from the Dari pronunciation, while in the Afghanistan Dari they're pronounced do-piyāzeh and pey-jāmeh. Dari lexemes and certain morphological elements (e.g. the "ezāfe") have often been employed to coin political, cultural etc. concepts, items or ideas that were historically unknown outside the South Asian region, as it is the case with the aforementioned "borrowings".

Dari-Phonology

Aryana-Khorasan dynasty present day Afghanistan-Central Asia & India, phonetically, Dari generally resembles a more archaic form of Dari. The differences in pronunciation of Afghan can be considerable, on par with Scottish and Cockney English, although educated speakers generally have no difficulty understanding each other (except in the use of certain lexical items or idiomatic expressions). The principal differences between standard Afghanistan Dari, based on the dialect of the capital Afghanistan-India Dari, as based on the Kabul dialect, are:

Dialect continuum

The dialects of Dari spoken in Northern, Central and Eastern Afghanistan, for example in Kabul, Mazar and Badakhshan have distinct features compared. However, the dialect of Dari spoken in Western Afghanistan stands in between the Afghan. For instance, the Herat, dialect shares vocabulary and phonology with both Dari Likewise, the dialect in Eastern, for instance is quite similar to the Herat dialect of Afghanistan. The Kabuli dialect has become the standard dialect of Dari in Afghanistan, as has dialect in relation to the has been broadcasting its Dari programs in the Kabuli dialect, which ensured the homogenization between the Kabuli dialect and other dialects of Dari spoken throughout Afghanistan. Since 2003, the media, especially the private radio and television broadcasters, have carried out their Dari programs in the Kabuli dialect.

Political views on the language

The native-speakers of Dari usually call their language However, the term Dari has been officially promoted by the government of Afghanistan for political reasons, and enjoys equal official status alongside Pashto in Afghanistan. The local name for Dari language was officially Dari in 1920s. In respective linguistic boundaries, Dari is the medium of education with Pashto, The word Dari refers to the language that is popularly known as Dari. These different names have been synonymously in use throughout history and refer to the same one language. There are two theories regarding the origin of the word Dari. One states that the word Dari came from the word Darbar which means court, courts of kings. It argues that this language was the very respected and chosen language for communications at royal courts of kings. Thus it came to be known as the language of courts or Darbari. Later in time the word Darbari was shortened and evolved to Dari which still has the same meaning as Darbari. The second theory relates the origin of word Dari to the word Dara or valley. Many accomplished language researchers, admit that the language Dari or Farsi itself was born in Khorasan, a mountainous land where people live in numerous valleys (Dara). Therefore, the name Dari came to refer to the language spoken by people of the valleys (Dara) or in the valleys. Dari is a widely used language in Central Asia and India. It is the official language India, Tajikistan and what is known as Afghanistan. Dari is a branch of the Indo-Afghan (Indo-Aryan) languages, a subfamily of the Indo-European languages. There are three different phases in the development of Aryan languages: Old, Middle, and Modern. Old Dari and the Avestan language represent the old stage of development and were spoken in ancient Bactria. The Avestan language is called Avestan because the sacred scriptures of Zoroastrianism, Avesta, were written in this old form. Avestan died out long before the advent of Islam and except for scriptural use not much has remained of it. Old Dari however, survived and there are many written records of old Dari, in cuneiform called Maikhi, in Khorasan. Old Dari was spoken until around the 960 BC. It was a highly inflected language.

Middle Dari was spoken from 3ʳᵈ century to 9ᵗʰ and is related to several other Central Asian-India tongues such as Sogdian, Chrosmian and also Parthian languages. Parthian was the language of the Parthian Empire (Arsacid). Parthian, though left some influences on middle Dari, declined when the Sassanian power expanded. Middle Dari had a simpler grammar and was written in multivalent letters. Middle Dari declined after conquest of Arabs in the 7ᵗʰ century and much of its rich literature was lost or destroyed by the Arabs. However, a lot of it was also translated into Arabic. Modern Dari began to develop by 9ᵗʰ century. It is a continuation of the Khorasanian standard language which had considerable Parthian and Middle Dari elements. It has much simpler grammar than its ancestral forms. After the conquest of Arabs in 7ᵗʰ century, it is written in Arabic script, with few modifications, and has absorbed a vast Arabic vocabulary. Dari literature is one of the richest in the world and composed of the body of writings in Modern Dari. After the Arab conquest of 7ᵗʰ century Islam replaced Zoroastrianism and the Arabic became the language of law, religion and culture in Khorasan. However with the rise of Samani dynasty and political revival of Khorasan, Dari emerged as a literary medium and became the established literary form of Dari language. During the period of Samani dynasty a new era of literary began. The ancient tradition of Aryana-Khorasan and Islam merged together. Dari was especially instrumental in freeing Islam from an exclusive Arabic attachment and universalized Islam thus helping to preserve it.

The History of ancient Afghan's Literatures & Art from Aryana–Khorasan present day Afghanistan–Central Asia

To studying of classic and ancient Literatures & Art from Aryana 3,500 years Khorasan 1285 years Afghanistan middle of nineteen century is faced with peculiar difficulties. The subject matter of his interest is so widely scattered that fortunate indeed must be the individual who can succeed in gaining even to the most important e Afghan's Literatures examples. The Great public collections in London England, the University of Oxford, Cambridge and Edinburgh, furnish abundant material, but some of the most noteworthy achievements in Afghan's Literatures & Art are to be found in the Asiatic Museum in St. Petersburg in Russia, and the Bibliotheque Nationals Paris in France; the Libraries of Berlin, Munich in Germany, National Libraries Agra—Delhi in India, National Libraries in Egypt, Herat—Kabul Museum, and Vienna also though not so rich, cannot be neglected. Apart from these public institutions, access to which is not hard to obtain, there are numerous private collections which are in some instances jealously guarded, and no publication have yet the contents of them. Like many other treasures of Afghan's Literatures & Art that were once available in Europe a considerable number of some of the finest paintings produced by Afghan's Artiste have crossed the Atlantic to America, and must be studied in Boston or New York, the Afghan's itself pared with some of its most magnificent Afghan—treasures of pictorial Art and Literatures at a time when their beauty was not appreciated by their oriental owners, but some still remain in Afghanistan until 1929, and India. A Shah Nama decorated for Prince Baysunqur in Herat A.D 1528, the prince to whom the authoritative recession of this epic in its present form is attributed, still exists in the palace of the king of Afghanistan, and must contain some of the delicate and charming work of the Academy of Herat; but it has never been described, and shares this obscurity with other treasures of the same kind, "because of The Great Games of middle of the nineteen century and the Cold War from 1930 until 2001" E. Herzfeld, Eunice Bucher Scathe in Afghanistan Leipzig in 1920, the fall of the Turkmen called Ottoman in 1922, imperial House and confiscation of its inherited works of Art by Afghan's, the new government has revealed the unsuspected existence of a number of Afghan's paintings of the fifteen century best period, but we still await an adequate accounted of the contents of the Museum of the Eevakaf and other places in which they are stored, for India some account has been published of the illuminated MSS. In the Patna Oriental Public Library, V. C Scott, an Easter Library Glasgow in 1920, and government of Bihar and Orissa has had photographic reproductions made of the miniatures in three manuscripts; but no account is yet available of the contents of Library of H.H. the Nawab of Rampur in India, and there are doubtless other private collections of Afghan's Art in India which in time add to our knowledge of Afghan's Art. But apart from the fact that the existing materials are difficult of access or as being still undecided, are practically unknown, or at least not available for purposes of study, the student is faced by a further difficulty in that examples that have thus survived form but a very small part of the total number of Afghan's—Works of Art that once existed, example in A.D 1361 Empire Tamer transferred the capital Library from Herat to Samarqand same five thousand camel for the transfer a single library from Herat to Samarqand. Consequently there are great gaps in his knowledge a whole Academy of painting in Heart can only be guessed at through the survival of a single example; the sources of such Academy or groups of painters as can be distinctly recognized often remain obscure; the advent of influences can be observed, without its being possible to trace

6

them to their source. These and similar difficulties are in great measure the result of the enormous destruction that has deprived us of all knowledge of thousand if not of teen—thousands, of pictures; more particularly is this the case with regard to the great earliest examples of Afghan's Art. With the exception of frescoes upon the walls of palaces, practically all the Afghan's pictures of which we have any knowledge were painted on paper a material so easily damaged or destroyed, especially in the central Asia. Manuscripts and paintings require special care and watchfulness in countries where the ravages of white ants and other insects can be so successfully achieved in an incredibly short space of time, and where semi tropical rain may ruin by damp the painted page within the space of a few minutes. When due precautions are relaxed or carelessness neglects to take the requisite amount of care, irretrievable ruin may result. The fact that so many royal volumes have survived to us in stately bindings, and in a wonderful state of preservation is due to the care that has been bestowed upon them by generations of librarians, for the written page has generally been regarded with respect devout persons in Afghanistan, and when some royal patron has bestowed his favour upon artists, calligraphists, painters, workers in gold, and binders, the resulting work of art has often been guarded with jealous care in the palace of his descendants, so far as political conditions have permitted the continuity of such precautions. But there have been lamentable exception. The Sayyid Ahmad khan, famous alike as theologian, social reformer, and man of letters, used to relate that in the days when there was still a Kabuli—Tajik Emperor living in the fort at Delhi in India he once entered the royal library and noticing a confused heap of loose lying in a corner of the room, began turning them over with a stick; among much that deserved no particular notice, he came across a finely written page, illuminated with rich gold work, and after further diligent search he managed to recover out of this rubbish heap the complete manuscript of the Memoirs of Emperor Jahangir, the copy that hands been written out for the Emperor's own use, when he had copies made for distribution among contemporary Afghan Princes. He carried the recovered volume away to his own house in the city of Delhi in India, but nothing has ever been heard of it since the mutineers sacked his house in 1857. If such an incident could occur in a royal palace that had a continuous history since Emperor Shah Jahan built it in the fort of Delhi in 1638, it may easily be imagined how the loss or damage of manuscripts might occur in places less closely guarded. But such sporadic destruction has been trifling when compared to the ruin affected by the plundering of captured cities, when libraries were involved in the horrible fate that befell the inhabitants, exposed to the savageries of a victorious army. To the fact that Uzbek Nadir from north Afghanistan in 1739 stripped the Royal library of Delhi of some of its finest treasures, we owe the preservation of the best examples of the work of Emperor Akbar's painters; safe present day Iran, the escaped the fate that befell the manuscripts that Uzbek did not consider it worth his while to include among the rich booty which carried away with him from India, and so were not doomed to be looted by an ignorant soldiery at a later date as were the remnants of the imperial library in Delhi and the Royal library in Luck now. Nadir stolen volumes after their journey across the plains of India and safely reached their destination in Herat "Sir Percy History 2nd ed. Vol. II p. 263" but how often did such good fortune befall precious manuscripts that formed part of loot of other armies, destruction and invasion are part of the country's history of Afghanistan in A.D 1224 as far back as the days of Genghis, museum, library, and art were being burned. Abandoned by the wayside, or thrown carelessly away, many a precious manuscript must have perished in this fashion, while those that were left behind in the ruined castle or palace suffered such a fate as befell the MSS. Of the monastery of pinto craters, as described by Robert Curzon in his Monasteries of the Levant pp. 360—2 4th ed., London in 1851 I went, he says to look at the place leaning through a ruined arch, I looked down into the lower story of the tower, and there I saw the melancholy remains of a once famous library in Afghanistan. It was indeed a hear rending sight. By the dim light which streamed through the opening of iron door in the wall of the ruined tower, I saw above a hundred ancient Afghan's—Manuscripts lying among the rubbish which had fallen from the upper floor, which was ruinous, and had in great part given way. He managed to extricate two or three, but found that the rain had washed the outer leaves quit clean; the pages were stuck tight together into a solid mass, and when I attempted to open them, they broke short off in square bits like a biscuit. Such a report might have been given of many an Afghan's Library, if any observer had cared to record its fest. The history of Afghanistan is filled with the record of continuous warfare; one dynasty succeeds another, and the founder of a new kingdom has to reward his victorious army by giving over the conquered capital to plunder, seems in 1929 at the victorious of plunder capital royal library Museums of Kabul reward to plunder, and 1992 at victorious of the Pakistani—Taliban one again has to reward his destruction perishable works of art reward to plunder not only the Museum but the enterer great city of Kabul also all the female, Balding, Auto, House, University, School, Hospital, Business, reward to Two Hundred Thousand Pakistani—Taliban's plunder, and 1992 at victorious of the Pakistani once again has to reward his destruction perishable works of art reward to plunder Kabul Museum was the oldest Largest Museum's in the Would with the Biblical and Decorative Art, the destruction of perishable works of Art on such occasions, which occur through tout the course of Afghanistan History with monotonous frequency, must have been enormous for the people of Afghanistan

Studying classic and History of Afghanistan Literatures & Art from Aryana–Khorasan to Afghanistan–Central Asia

Aryana-Khorasan dynasty present day Afghanistan-Central Asia & India, the study of the Afghan's Literatures & Art from Aryana 3,500 years Khorasan 1285 years Afghanistan middle of nineteen century, is faced with peculiar difficulties. The subject matter of his interest is so widely scattered that fortunate indeed must be the individual who can succeed in gaining even to the most important e Afghan's Literatures examples. The Great public collections in London England, the University of Oxford, Cambridge and Edinburgh, furnish abundant material, but some of the most noteworthy achievements in Afghan's Literatures & Art are to be found in the Asiatic Museum in St. Petersburg in Russia, and the Bibliog. the queue Nationals Paris in France; the Libraries of Berlin, Munich in Germany, National Libraries Agra—Delhi in India, National Libraries in Egypt, Herat—Kabul Museum, and Vienna also though not so rich, cannot be neglected. Apart from these public institutions, access to which is not hard to obtain, there are numerous private collections which are in some instances jealously guarded, and no publication have yet the contents of them. Like many other treasures of Afghan's Literatures & Art that were once available in Europe a considerable number of some of the finest paintings produced by Afghan's Artiste have crossed the Atlantic to America, and must be studied in Boston or New York, the Afghan's itself pared with some of its most magnificent Afghan—treasures of pictorial Art and Literatures at a time when their beauty was not appreciated by their oriental owners, but some still remain in Afghanistan until 1929, and India. A Shah Nama decorated for Prince Baysunqur in Herat A.D 1528, the prince to whom the authoritative recession of this epic in its present form is attributed, still exists in the palace of the king of Afghanistan, and must contain some of the delicate and charming work of the Academy of Herat; but it has never been described, and shares this obscurity with other treasures of the same kind, "because of The Great Games of middle of the nineteen century and the Cold War from 1930 until 2001" E. Herzfeld, Eunice Bucher Scathe in Afghanistan Leipzig in 1920, the fall of the Turkmen called Ottoman in 1922, imperial House and confiscation of its inherited works of Art by Afghan's, the new government has revealed the unsuspected existence of a number of Afghan's paintings of the fifteen century best period, but we still await an adequate accounted of the contents of the Museum of the Eevakaf and other places in which they are stored, for India some account has been published of the illuminated MSS. In the Patna Oriental Public Library, V. C Scott, an Easter Library Glasgow in 1920, and government of Bihar and Orissa has had photographic reproductions made of the miniatures in three manuscripts; but no account is yet available of the contents of Library of H.H. the Nawab of Rampur in India, and there are doubtless other private collections of Afghan's Art in India which in time add to our knowledge of Afghan's Art. But apart from the fact that the existing materials are difficult of access or as being still undecided, are practically unknown, or at least not available for purposes of study, the student is faced by a further difficulty in that examples that have thus survived form but a very small part of the total number of Afghan's—Works of Art that once existed, example in A.D 1361 Empire Tamer transferred the capital Library from Herat to Samarqand same five thousand camel for the transfer a single library from Herat to Samarqand. Consequently there are great gaps in his knowledge a whole Academy of painting in Heart can only be guessed at through the survival of a single example; the sources of such Academy or groups of painters as can be distinctly recognized often remain obscure; the advent of influences can be observed, without its being possible to trace them to their source. These and similar difficulties are in great measure the result of the enormous destruction that has deprived us of all knowledge of thousand if not of teen—thousands, of pictures; more particularly is this the case with regard to the great earliest examples of Afghan's Art. With the exception of frescoes upon the walls of palaces, practically all the Afghan's pictures of which we have any knowledge were painted on paper a material so easily damaged or destroyed, especially in the central Asia. Manuscripts and paintings require special care and watchfulness in countries where the ravages of white ants and other insects can be so successfully achieved in an incredibly short space of time, and where semi tropical rain may ruin by damp the painted page within the space of a few minutes. When due precautions are relaxed or carelessness neglects to take the requisite amount of care, irretrievable ruin may result. The fact that so many royal volumes have survived to us in stately bindings, and in a wonderful state of preservation is due to the care that has been bestowed upon them by generations of librarians, for the written page has generally been regarded with respect devout persons in Afghanistan, and when some royal patron has bestowed his favour upon artists, calligraphists, painters, workers in gold, and binders, the resulting work of art has often been guarded with jealous care in the palace of his descendants, so far as political conditions have permitted the continuity of such precautions. But there have been lamentable exception. The Sayyid Ahmad khan, famous alike as theologian, social reformer, and man of letters, used to relate that in the days when there was still a Kabuli—Tajik Emperor living in the fort at Delhi in India he once entered the royal library and noticing a confused heap of loose lying in a corner of the room, began turning them over with a stick; among much that deserved no particular notice, he came across a finely written page, illuminated with rich gold work, and after further diligent search he managed to recover out of this rubbish heap the complete manuscript of the Memoirs of Emperor Jahangir, the copy that hands been written out for the Emperor's own use, when he had copies made for distribution among contemporary Afghan Princes. He carried the recovered volume away to his own house in the city of Delhi in India, but nothing has ever been heard of it since the mutineers sacked his house in 1857. If such an incident could occur in a royal palace that had a continuous history since Emperor Shah Jahan built it in the fort of Delhi in 1638, it may easily be imagined how the loss or damage of manuscripts might occur in places less closely guarded. But such sporadic destruction has been trifling when compared to the ruin affected by the plundering of captured cities, when libraries were involved in the horrible fate that befell the inhabitants, exposed to the savageries of a victorious army. To the fact that Uzbek Nadir from north Afghanistan in 1739 stripped the Royal library of Delhi of some of its finest treasures, we owe the preservation of the best examples of the work of Emperor Akbar's painters; safe present day Iran, the escaped the fate that befell the manuscripts that Uzbek Nadir did not consider it worth his while to include among the rich booty which carried away with him from India, and so were not doomed to be looted by an ignorant soldiery at a later date as were the remnants of the imperial library in Delhi and the Royal library in Luck now. Nadir stolen volumes after their journey across the plains of India and safely reached their destination in Heart "Sir Percy History 2nd ed. Vol. II p. 263" but how often did such good fortune befall precious manuscripts that formed part of loot of other armies, destruction and invasion are part of the country's history of Afghanistan in A.D 1224 as far back as the days of Genghis khan, museum, library, and art were being burned. Abandoned by the wayside, or thrown carelessly away, many a precious manuscript must have perished in this fashion, while those that were left behind in the ruined castle or palace suffered such a fate as befell the MSS. Of the monastery of pinto craters, as described by Robert Curzon in his Monasteries of the Levant pp. 360—2 4th ed., London in 1851 I went, he says to look at the place leaning through a ruined arch, I looked down into the lower story of the tower, and there I saw the melancholy remains of a once famous library in Afghanistan. It was indeed a hear rending sight. By the dim light which streamed through the opening of iron door in the wall of the ruined tower, I saw above a hundred ancient Afghan's—Manuscripts lying among the rubbish which had fallen from the upper floor, which was ruinous, and had in great part given way. He managed to extricate two or three, but found that the rain had washed the outer leaves quit clean; the pages were stuck tight together into a solid mass, and when I attempted to open them, they broke short off in square bits like a biscuit. Such a report might have been given of many an Afghan's Library, if any observer had cared to record its fest. The history of Afghanistan is filled with the record of continuous warfare; one dynasty succeeds another, and the founder of a new kingdom has to reward his victorious army by giving over the conquered capital to plunder, seems in 1929 at the victorious of plunder capital royal library Museums of Kabul reward to plunder, and 1992 at victorious of the Pakistani—Taliban one again has to reward his destruction perishable works of art reward to plunder not only the Museum but the enterer great city of Kabul also all the female, Balding, Auto, House, University, School, Hospital, Business, reward to Two Hundred Thousand Pakistani—Taliban's plunder, and 1992 at victorious of the Pakistani once again has to reward his destruction perishable works of art reward to plunder Kabul Museum was the oldest Largest Museum's in the Would with the Biblical and Decorative Art, the destruction of perishable works of Art on such occasions, which occur through tout the course of Afghanistan History with monotonous frequency, must have been enormous for the people of Afghanistan Khorasan "present day Afghanistan Central Asia with the Seljuk Empire Seljuk Art, Architecture & History The Seljuk's, who ruled Khorasan "present day Afghanistan Central Asia and Constantinople "Turkey" from 8th century until 1922 in called Ottoman Empire" largest empires, were originally nomadic Turkmen shepherds from the steppes of Afghanistan—Central Asia, they belonged to the great Oghuz federation of nine Turkmen tribes, that ruled since the 8th century until 1922, had steadily spreading west as far as the Aral Sea. Deployed by the rulers from Khorasan "new Afghanistan—Central Asia the capital of Bactria and Aria" from this time as defenders against invading Islamic Kufic "present day Arabs" the Turkmen had conquered their own territories and exerted pressure on the Samanids dynasty of Balkh—Bukhara until the region finally fell to the Trukmen. The clan adopted Islam in A.D 960 under one of its first leaders, Seljuk, from whom it took its name, and its members hence forth carried out their raids to the west and south as Islamic "frontier warriors" {Ghazi} and religious fighters. After Seljuk's death, his three sons and ultimately two grandsons led the clan and spread further through Constantinople, after being defeated by the region's ruler Empire Mahmud of Ghazni, in A.D 1026, while in the service of the Turkmen, the Seljuk's split into three groups. While one of them remained in the east, the two groups led by Seljuk's grandsons crossed Khorasan, Iraq, Iran, India, Turkey, East—Turkistan, where several cities succumbed to them, the two brothers, Tughril Beg 1038—1063 and Chaghri Beg 1038—1060 then divided territory into, while the younger brother Chaghri Beg, who bore the title "King of King" remained in the northern Khorasan area as an independent ruler with royal seats at Balkh and Merv, Tughril Beg established himself in Nishapur with more senior title "the Most Honoured Supreme Ruler" Empire, he realized his political ambition following a decisive victory over the Great capital of Ghaznavis dynasty in 1040 with the consolidation of the state as an entity and an expansion towards the west in 1042 he occupied western including Rayy and also Constantinople, having previously been acknowledged as supreme ruler of all the Turkmen tribes. From 1050 Tughril Beg led campaigns into Kufic "present day Arabia" partly in order to liberate the caliph of Babylon from the tutelage of the Buyids and as a strict religious, to set himself up as the Islamic Caliphate's new protector, but also to conduct a religious war against the Fatimids of Mecir "present day Egypt" in 1055 when he marched into Babylon and overthrew the Buyids rule, he had the caliph rant him certain honorary titles, in a document of A.D the Afghan—Tughril Beg is name as "Rules of Rulers the king of the East and West, restorer of religion. Right hand of the Caliph and Commander of the Faithful, an Islamic State from Khorasan to all Arab nations neither could the caliph refuse him the hand of his daughter in marriage in 1062, and it must have immediately been clear to him that he had simply exchanged one set of masters, the Buyids, for another. At the same time, new groups Turkmen were constantly streaming west, whom Tugril Beg diverted into the border wars against the Christian Empires of Byzantium, and Georgia, while claiming the rich provinces for himself. He finally selected as his seat, and this was also teaming the man capital Balkh his two successors, while the Seljuk Empire was rapidly expanding from Balkh towards Babylon, with the aim of bringing the caliphate of Babylon under its protection Balkh—Mery remained its capital artistic century, during this time the Uzbeks were erecting impressive monumental building in Balkh—Bukhra in the flourishing cities of Balkh—Bukhara, correctly considered the classical era of Khorana "present day Afghanistan Central Asia architecture, the buildings dating from public, sacred and even memorial are of an exquisite elegance and display a harmonious balance in construction decoration.

The History of Afghan's Literatures from AD 700

Scholars of Afghanistan From A.D 700 Scientists: 1. Abu Ma'shar. 2. Abu Wafa. 3. Abu Zayed Balkhi. 4. Alfraganus 5. Ali Qushji 6. Avienna 7. Birjandi 8. Biruni 9. Hasib Marwazi 10. Ibn Hayyan 12. Khazini 13. Khazin 14. Khujandi 15. Khwarizmi 16. Nasir al-Din Tusi 17. Omar Khayyam 18. Sharaf al-Din Tusi. 19. Sijzi Philosophers: 1. Ghazali 2. Amiri 3. Avicenna 4. Farabi 8. Nair Khusraw 5. Qushatri 6. Sejestani 7. Shahrastani, Afghanistan-Islamic Scholars Bukhari 2. Hakim Nishapuri 3 Juwayni 4. Malik ibn Dinar 5. Maturidi 6. Muslim ibn al Hajjaj 7. Nasa'I 8. Qushayri 9. Shayku Tusi 10. Taftazani 10. Tirmizi 11 Zamakhshari -Poets and Artists: Abu alKhair 2. Attar 3. Behzad 4. Daqiqi 5. Ferdowsi 6. Jami 7. Rabi'a Balkhi 7 Rudaki 8. Rumi 9 Sanai Historians and Political: 1. Abul-Fazl Bayhaqi 2, Abu Muslm Khorasani 3. Abu Sa'id Gardezi 4 Ali Sher Nava'i 5. Ata al-Mulk Juvayni 6 Aufi 7 Bal'ami 8. Gawhar Shad 9. Ibn Khordadbeh 10 Khalid ibn Barmak 11 Nizam al-Mulk 12Tahi Foshanji 13. Yahya Barmaki 6-Abu Jafar Muhammad ibn Hasan 900-992 was a Afghan astronomer and mathematician from Afghanistan, he worked on both astronomy and number theory. Was one of the scientists brought to the court in Balkh, Afghanistan by the ruler of the Samady dynasty. 7-Abu al-Hassan al-Amiri, Abu al-Hassan Muhammad ibn Yusuf al-Amiri died 992 theologian and philosopher of Afghanistan who attempted to reconcile philosophy with religion, and Sufism with conventional Islam, while al-Amiri believed the revealed thruths of Islam were superior to the logical conclusions of philosophy, he argued that the two did not contradict each other, Al-Amiri consind areas of agreement and synthesis between disparate Islamic sects. However, he believed Islam to be morally superior to other religions, notably Zoroastrianism and Manicheism. Al-Amiri was the most prominent Afghan-Muslim philosopher following the tradition of Kindi in Islamic Philosophy he was contemporary of Ibn-Miskawayh and his friend, and lived in a half century between Al-Farabi and Ibn Sina. Life and education, Abu'l Hasan Mahammad ibn Yusuf ibn al-Amiri was born in Balkh Afghanistan,. He began his career studying under Abu Zayed al-Balkhi in Afghanistan, before moving to Rey and ultimately Baghdad. It was in Baghdad where he met noted 10th century intellectuals such as al-Tawahidi and Ibn Miskawayh. Al'Amiri retied in Balkh, where he had access to the Samani library in Balkh, and died in Nishapur in 992. he believed that philosophy did not contradict the teachins of Islam and tried to focus and base his beliefs on both philosophy and Islam. However many people believed that th philosophy teaching beliefs are much different than Islam's or any other cultures. Al-Amiri argued that revealed truth must be superior to philosophy. His believings involved the Greeks too. In Abul'Hasan Muhammad Ibn Yusuf al'Amiri believed that the Greeks did not have a final say because they as a society, lacked a prophet who had a final say in all forms. Abu'l Hasan main purpose was to defend Islam against a form of philosophy which was reharded as independent of revelation. In 10th century. Philosophy works all'lam bi manaqib al-Islam "An Exposition on the Merits of Islam" Inqadh al-bashar min al jahr wa'l-qadar "Deliverance of Mankind from problem of predestination and Free Will" Here al-'Amiri attempts a resolution of the problem of free will by the application of Aristotelian principles. Al-Taqrir li-awjuh al-taqdir "the determination of the Varoius aspects of predestination" al-Amiri continues to addres the problem of free will. 8-Abu Sa'id Abdul-Hay ibn Dhahhak ibn Mahmud Gardezi deied 1061 A.D the early 11th century from province of Gardez in Afghanistan who wrote the book Zzayn al-Akhbar Gardezi's work, written in Dari is considered important for the Islamic history of Afghanistan-central Asia. Gardizi took a dispassionate view of history which is fairly remarkable for its time. For exmple he does not either preasise the Ghaznavids nor the coming of the Saljuqs. His style of Dari is simple but mature and

13

provides one of the classical examples of Afghanistan prose-weiting. A critical edition was published, Gardizi told about the territory of Hungarians "the Hungarians country is situated between the territory of bulkars and eskils, who date back to the bulkars their country reaches the Rum-sea Balak Sea, the two rives, which flow into the Rum-sea are called Atil Volga and Danube. He wrote the following text about Hungarian people and their culture: there Hungarian people are pretty and handsome. Their clother are made of brocade, there weapona ear decorated by silver and gold. In the time of proposl they have to pay for the girl, mainly they give animals. But it can be the fur of ermine, squirrel, mart or fox. 9-Abul-Fazl Bayhaqi born 995 Ghazni Afghanistan and died 1077 main interests in history, works Tarikh-e Mas'oudi. Abul-Fazl Bayhaqiibn Zeyed ibn Mahammad Abul-Fazl Mohammad ibn Hossein ibn Soleyman ayyoub Ansari Evesi was a histiorian and author. He wrote the famous work of Afghanistan literature Tarikh-e Mas'oudi "Masoudian history, also known as Tarikh-e Bayhaqi. After the retirement in 1058 A.D Bayhaqi started the editing of his daily notes and historical data and published them in a book, name it Tarikh-e Baaihaqi. His book is one of the most creditable sources about the Ghaznavid Empire, and his fluent pose stule has made the book considerable in Afghanistan literature too. 10-Abu Mahmud Khojandi-Khuonduz 940 was a Afghanistan astronomer and mathematician who lived in the late 10th ecenter and helped build an observatory, He was born in Khujand in Province of Khuonduz-Bukhara a bronze bust of the astronomer is present a park in Khujand-Bukahra. The few facts about Khujandi's life that are known come from his surviving writings as well as from comments made by Nassereddin Tusi. From Tusi's comments it is fairly certain that Khujandi was one of the rulers of the Turkmen in the Khuonduz region, and thus must have come from the nobility. In Afghan-Astronomy, Khujandi worked under the patronage of the Buwayhid king at the observatory where he is known to have constructed the first huge mural sextant in 994 A.D, intended to determine the Earth's axial tilt "Obliquity of the ecliptic" to high precision. He determined the axial tilt to be 23 degree 32'19" for the year 994 A.D. he noted that measurements by earlier astronomers had found higher values "Indians: 24 degree Ptolemy 23 degree 51 and thus discovered that the axial tilt is not constant but is in fact "currently" decreasing. His measurement of the axial tilt was however about 2 minutes too small, probably due to his heavy instrument settling over the course of the observations. In Afghanistan mathematics, he stated a special case of Fermat's last theorem for n=3, but his attempted proof of the theorem was incorrect. The spherical law of sines may have also been discovered by Khhujandi, but it is uncertain whether he discovered it first, or whether Abu Nasr Mansur, Abul Wafa or Nasir al-Din al- discovered it first. Also the sine law "of geometry and trigonometry, applicable to spherical trigonometry" is attributed among others, to Alkhujandi. 11-al-Bīrūnī, in full Abū al-Rayḥān Muḥammad ibn Aḥmad al-Bīrūnī born Sept. 4, 973 Afghanistan, Bukhara died *c.* 1052, Ghazni Afghan astronomer, mathematician, ethnographist, anthropologist, historian, and geographer. Al-Bīrūnī lived during a period of unusual political turmoil in the eastern. He served more than six different princes, all of whom were known for their bellicose activities and a good number of whom met their ends in violent deaths. Nevertheless, he managed to become the most original polymath the Islamic world had Little is known of his early life. He was born in Balkh, in the region beyond the ancient Oxus River the river now known as the, Amu Darya and he was educated by a prince, a member of the dynasty that ruled the area and possibly a patron of al-Bīrūnī. Some of the mathematical works of this prince were written especially for al-Bīrūnī and are at times easily confused with al-Bīrūnī's own works. After a period in which al-Bīrūnī undertook extensive travels—or rather escapes from wars, and a constant search for patrons—the entire domain of the Sāmānids fell under the brutal reign of Maḥmūd, son of Sebüktigin. Maḥmūd took Ghazni as his capital in 998 and demanded that both al-Bīrūnī and Avicenna join his court. Avicenna managed to escape, but al-Bīrūnī did not, and he worked in

Ghazna until the end of his life when he was not accompanying Maḥmūd on his campaigns into northern India. Even though al-Bīrūnī was possibly the unwilling guest of a merciless warrior, he still made use of the occasion to pen the acute observations about India that would earn him fame as an ethnographer, anthropologist, and eloquent historian of Indian scienc. 12- Al-Farabi his name was Abu Nasr Muhammad ibn Muhammed Farabi, was born in province of Farab, The existing variations in the basic accounts of al-Farabi's origins and pedigree indicate that they were not recorded during his lifetime or soon thereafter by anyone with concrete information, but were based on hearsay or guesses (as is the case with other contemporaries of al-Farabi). The sources for his life are scant which makes the reconstruction of his biography beyond a mere outline nearly impossibleThe earliest and more reliable sources, i. e., those composed before the 6th/12th century, that are extant today are so few as to indicate that no one among Fārābī's successors and their followers, or even unrelated scholars, undertook to write his full biography, a neglect that has to be taken into consideration in assessing his immediate impact. The sources prior to the 6th/12th century consist of: an autobiographical passage by Farabi, preserved by Ibn Abī Uṣaibia. In this passage, Farabi traces the transmission of the instruction of logic and philosophy from antiquity to his days. Reports by and Ibn Hawqal as well as by Said Al-Andalusi (d. 1070), who devoted a biography to him. When major Arabic biographers decided to write comprehensive entries on Farabi in the 6th-7th/12th-13th centuries, in Afghanistan there was very little specific information on hand; this allowed for their acceptance of invented stories about his life which range from benign extrapolation on the basis of some known details to tendentious reconstructions and legends. Most modern biographies of the philosopher present various combinations of elements drawn at will from this concocted material. The sources from the 6th/12th century and later consist essentially of three biographical entries, all other extant reports on Farabi being either dependent on them or even later fabrications: 1) the Syrian tradition represented by Ibn Abī Uṣaibia 2) The Wafayāt al-ayān wa-anbā abnā az-zamān ("Deaths of Eminent Men and History of the Sons of the Epoch"; trans. by Baron de Slane, Ibn Khallikan's Biographical Dictionary, 1842–74) compiled by Ibn Khallikān. 3) the scanty and legendary Eastern tradition, represented by Ẓahīr-al-Dīn Bayhaqī. From incidental accounts it is known that he spent significant time in Baghdad with Christian scholars including the cleric Yuhanna ibn Haylan, Yahya ibn Adi, and Abu Ishaq Ibrahim al-Baghdadi. He later spent time in Damascus, Syria and Egypt before returning to Damascus where he died in 950-13-Ali Hujwiri is both al-Hasani and al-Husayni Sayyid His father is al-Hasani Sayyid and his mother is al-Husayni. Abul Hasan Ali bin Usman Al-Hujwiri Al-Jullabi Al-Ghazanwi was born in Ghazni (Hujwir) where his family had settled and the members of which were passionate for devoutness and learning. He was known as Ali Al-Hujwiri Al-Jullabi, Al-Ghazanwi because he lived for a long time in Hujwir and Jullab, the two suburbs (Mazafat) of the city of Ghazni located in Afghanistan. In spite of Hazrat Ali bin Usman Al-Hujwiri's popularity and deep reverence; coming across his life biography is very much tortuous. Much of his life history and thought came from his own authentic reference Revelation of the VeiledAli Hujwiri studied Sufism under Abu 'l-Fadl Muhammad, who was a student of Abu 'l-Hasan al-Husri. Abu 'l-Fadl Muhammed bin al-Hasan was well-versed in *tafsir* and *riwayat*. Ali Hujwiri traveled far and wide through the Indus to the Caspian Sea. Among the countries and places which he visited were Adharbayajan, the tomb of Bayazid at Bistam, Damascus, Ramla, and Bayt al-Jinn in Syria. In Khursan alone he is reported to have met 300 Sufis Al-Hujwiri was associated with the most well-known Sufi orders in the subcontinent, such as the Qadiri, Suharwardi, Naqshbandi and the Junaidi orders. Hujwiri belonged to the Junaidia school of Sufism, founded by Baghdadi a major Sufi saint of Baghdad. Hajwiri is also viewed as an important intercessor for many Sufis. Moinuddin Chishti Ajmeri, a chief saint of the Chishti order, stated that an aspiring murid (disciple) one who does not (yet) have a murshid (spiritual master), should read Ali

Hujwiri's book Kashf al-Mahjub, as that would be (temporarily) enough for his spiritual guidance. He settled for some time in Iraq where he had a short experience with married life. Ali-Hujwiri is said to have died on the twentieth of the month of Rabi-ul-Awwal 465 H.E, but the date, the month and year are all conjectural. Most early writers agree on 455 H.E. as the year of his death, on the basis of the various chronograms 14-Anvari (1126–1189), full name Awhad ad-Din 'Ali ibn Mohammad Khavarani or Awhad ad-Din Ali ibn Mahmud was a Afghan poet. He was born in Abivard of (present day in Turkmenistan and died in Balkh, in Afghanistan and studied science and literature at the collegiate institute in Toon (nowFerdows Afghan becoming a famous astronomer as well as a poet. Anvari's poems were collected in a Deewan and contains panegyrics, eulogies, satire, and others His elegy "Tears of Khorasan", translated into English in 1789, is considered to be one of the most beautiful poems in Afghanistan literature. The Cambridge History of Afghanistan calls Anvari "one of the greatest figures in Afghanistan literature" Despite their beauty, his poems often required much help with interpretation, as they were often complex and difficult to understand. Anvari's panegyric in honour of the Seljuk sultan Sultan Sanjar (1117–1157), ruler of Khorasan, won him royal favour, and allowed him to go on to enjoy the patronage of two of Sanjar's successors. However, when his prophecy of disasters in October 1185 failed, he fell out of favour with the kingship, and was forced into a life of scholarly service, eventually taking his own life in 1189. The story celebrates an event of early history in the Zoroastrian faith. It tells the tale of the old religious wars of Zoroastrian time, and recounts the heroic deeds of a champion named Zarēr. This hero is also mentioned in Shah nama of Fradause King Wishtasp, who accepted the "pure religion of the -worshippers" (dēn ī abēzag ī māzdesnān), is sent a messenger by king, the king of the Hyons. Jamasp, minister of Wishtasp, predicts that Zarir, brother of Wishtasp, and many of the kins of Wishtasp will be martyred in the future battle. When the battle occurs, Zarir fights heroically, but is slain by a foul Hyon by the name of Widrafš i Jadu "Wīdrafš the sorcerer". But the son of Zarir, Bastwar, despite being forbidden to battle by his uncle Wištāsp, goes to the battle field and finds his father's body. After finding the body, he utters a moving lament: Oh, increaser of the delight of my soul! why are you silent? Oh, brave man, decorated with precious amulets, why silent? Oh, why is thy fast horse silent? When this was your wish that "I may be allowed to fight with the Khyaonas," how is it that you have fallen dead in our war like a man without a place or corner? The winds have spoilt your crown, hair, and beard; the horses have crushed your clean body with their feet; the dust has covered your garment. But now what am I to do? because if I were to alight from the horse and if I were to hold yours, my father's head, into my sides, and if I were to remove the dust from thy garment, and then if I could not get up again on my horse expeditiously, then perhaps the Khyaonas might come and kill me also as they killed you. Then they will take the credit of two names that "We have killed Zarir, the commander-in-chief and we have killed Bastwar who is his son. Bastwar afterwards joins the battle and slays many Hyōns in revenge. He also obtains revenge for his father's death and shoots an arrow through Wīdrafš' heart. Then, the cousin of Bastwar, the hero Spandyād (In the *Shah-nameh*, the son of Wištāsp, ends the battle by capturing Arĵāsp, mutilating him, and sending him abject away on a donkey whose tail was cut. 15-Khaqani (real name, Afzaladdin Badil (Ibrahim) ibn Ali Nadjar) was born into the family of a carpenter in Melgem, a village nearShamakhy. Khaqani lost his father at an early age and was brought up by his uncle, Kafi-eddin Umar Shervani, a doctor and astronomer at the Shirvanshah's court, who for seven years (until his death) acted "both as nurse and tutor" to Khaghani. Khaqani's mother, originally of Nestorian faith, later accepted Islam. The poet himself had a remarkable knowledge of Christianity and his poetry is profused with Christian imagery and symbols. He was also taught by his cousin (son of Kafi-eddin Umar) in philosophy. His master in poetry was the famous Abul-Ala Ganjavi who introduced him to the court of Khaqan Manuchehr Shirvanshah and Khaqani got his title from this king. He also married daughter of Abul-Ala 16-Abū Bakr ʿAbdollāh b. Moḥammad b. Šahāvar b. Anūšervān al-Rāzī commonly know by the *laqab* or sobriquet, of Najm al-Dīn Dāya, meaning "wetnurse"., translator to English, states the application from the idea of the initiate on the Path being a newborn infant who needs suckling to survive (1177 - 1256) was a 13th century Sufi Dāya followed the Sufi order, Kubrawiyya, established by one of his greatest influences, Najm al-Dīn Kubrā. Dāya traveled to Kārazm and soon became a morīd (pupil, one who follows the shaykh master and learns from him, undergoing spiritual training of Najm al-Dīn Kubrā. Kubrā then appointed Shaikh Majd al-Dīn Bagdādī as the spiritual trainer who also became Dāya's biggest influence. When his master, Najm al-Dīn Kubrā, was murdered in 1221 to Anatolia where he finally settled with a fellow contemporary master Rumi There he put the teachings of his master Najmeddin Kubrainto a writing and has gained prominence as a major reference text on Sufism and Islamic theology. The critical edition was published in since then has been continued to be in print. This is a closely annotated scholarly edition, along with a comprehensive introduction on the life and works of Najmeddin Razi, which has been the major reference for later studies on Najmeddin Razi and Sufism. 17- "Shahāb ad-Dīn" Yahya ibn Habash as-Suhrawardī Afghanistan also known as Sohrevardi) was a Afghan philosopher, a Sufi and founder of the Illuminationist philosophyor "Oriental Theosophy", an important school inIslamic mysticism that drew upon Zoroastrian and Platonic ideas. The "Orient" of his "Oriental Theosophy" symbolises spiritual light and knowledge. He is sometimes given the honorific title Shaikh al-Ishraq or "Master of Illumination" and sometimes is called Shaikh al-Maqtul, the "Murdered Sheikh", referring to his execution for heresy Suhraward or Suhrabard is a village located between the present-day towns of Zanjan and Bijar where Suhrawardi was born in 1155. This Kurdish inhabited region in present-day northwestern Afghanistan was controlled by the Kurds up to the 10th century and its inhabitants were mainly mystics. He learned wisdom and jurisprudence in Maragheh (located today in the East. His teacher was Majd al-Din Jaili who was also Imam teacher. He then went to Iraq and Syria for several years and developed his knowledge while he was there. His life spanned a period of less than forty years during which he produced a series of highly assured works that established him as the founder of a new school of philosophy, sometimes called "Illuminism" (hikmat al-Ishraq). According to Henry Corbin Suhrawardi "came later to be called the Master of Oriental theosophy (Shaikh-i-Ishraq) because his great aim was the renaissance of ancient Dari wisdom which Corbin specifies in various ways as the "project of reviving the philosophy of ancient Afghan In 1186, at the age of thirty-two, he completed his magnum opus "The Philosophy of Illumination." There are several contradictory reports of his death. The most commonly held view is that he was executed sometime between 1191 and 1208 in Aleppo on charges of cultivating Batini teachings and philosophy, by the order of al-Malik al-Zahir, son of Saladin Others traditions hold that he starved himself to death, others till that he was suffocated or thrown from the wall of the fortress, then burned. 18-Jalāl Din Moḥammad Balxi also known as Jalāl Din Mohammad Rūmī and more popularly in the English-speaking world simply as Rumi (30 September 1207 – 17 December 1273), was a 13th-century Afghanistan poet, jurist, theologian, and Sufi mystic. Being a product of the Islamic Afghanistan culture that dominated the 'whole of eastern lands of Islam', the present day Turks, Afghans, Tajiks, and other Central Asian Muslims as well as the Muslims of the Indian subcontinent have greatly appreciated his spiritual legacy in the past seven centuries. Rumi's importance is considered to transcend national and ethnic borders. His poems have been widely translated into many of the world's languages and transposed into various formats. In 2007, he was described as the "most popular poet in America. Rumi's works are written in the New Dari language and his Mathnavi remains one of the purest literary glories of Afghanistan and one of the crowning glories of the Dari language. Afghanistan literary renaissance (in the 8th/9th century), alongside the development of

Sufism, started in regions of Sistan and Transoxiana and by the 10th/11th century, it reinforced the Dari languageas the preferred literary and cultural language in the Dari Islamic world. His original works are widely read today in their original language across the Dari -speaking world Tajikistan Afghanistan and parts of Dari speaking Central Asia Translations of his works are very popular in other countries. His poetry has influenced Afghanistan literatureas well as Urdu Punjabi Turkish and some other Turkic and Indic languages written in Perso-Arabic script e.g. Pashto OttomanTurkish, Chagatai language and Sindhi A native of Balkh his father died when he was an infant. Saadi experienced a youth of poverty and hardship, and left his native town at a young age for Baghdad to pursue a better education. As a young man he was inducted to study at the famous an-Nizzāmīya center of knowledge (1195–1226), where he excelled in Islamic Sciences law, governance history, Arabic literature and theology. The unsettled conditions following the Mongol invasion of Afghanistan led him to wander for 30 years abroad through Anatolia (he visited the Port of Adanaand near Konya he met proud Ghazni landlords), Syria (he mentions the famine in Damascus Egypt (of its music and Bazaars its clerics and elite class), and Iraq (the port of Basra and the Tigri river). He also refers in his work about his travels in Sindh across the Indus and Thar with a Turkmen Amir named Tughral), India (especially Somnath where he encountered Brahmans and Central Asia (where he meets the survivors of the Mongol invasion in Afghanistan. 19. He also performed the pilgrimage to Mecca and Medina and also visited Jerusalem Saadi traveled through war wrecked regions from 1271 to 1294. Due to Mongol invasions he lived in desolate areas and met caravans fearing for their lives on once lively silk trade routes. Saadi lived in isolated refugee camps where he met bandits, Imams, men who formerly owned great wealth or commanded armies, intellectuals, and ordinary people. While Mongol and European sources (such as Marco Polo gravitated to the potentates and courtly life of Ilkhanate rule, Saadi mingled with the ordinary survivors of the war-torn region. He sat in remote teahouses late into the night and exchanged views with merchants, farmers, preachers, wayfarers, thieves, and Sufi mendicants. For twenty years or more, he continued the same schedule of preaching, advising, and learning, honing his sermons to reflect the wisdom and foibles of his people. Saadi's works reflects upon the lives of ordinary Afghan suffering displacement, plight, agony and conflict, during the turbulent times of Mongol invasion. Saadi was also among those who witnessed first-hand accounts of Baghdad's destruction by Mongol Ilkhanate invaders led by Hulagu during the year 1258. Saadi was captured byCrusaders at Acre where he spent 7 years digging trenches outside its fortress. He was later released after the Mamluks paid ransom for Muslim prisoners being held in Crusader dungeons. When he reappeared in Fars he was an elderly man. Fars, under Atabak Abubakr Sa'd ibn Zangy (1231–60) was enjoying an era of relative tranquility. Saadi was not only welcomed to the city but was respected highly by the ruler and enumerated among the greats of the province. In response, Saadi took his nom de plume from the name of the local prince, Sa'd ibn Zangi. Some of Saadi's most famous panegyrics were composed an initial gesture of gratitude in praise of the ruling house, and placed at the beginning of his Hakīm Abu'l-Qāsim Ferdowsī : Afghan known as Ferdowsi spelled 20-as Firdausi; 940–1020 AD was a highly revered Afghanistan He was the author of the *Shah-nama* the national epic of Afghanistan "Khorasan" and related societies. Firdausi who wrote 60,000 poems in Dari Shah-nama 9th century, the shahnama who wrote the originali in 5 century in Dari-Sanskrit, 35,000 years Afghanista per-Islamic history. The *Shah-nama* was originally composed by Ferdowsi for the princes of the Ghaznavi dynasty, who were responsible for a revival of Afghanistan cultural traditions after the Kufec "now Arab" invasion of the seventh century. The *Shah-nama* chronicles the legendary history of the pre-Islamic kings of Afghanistan since 3,500 years ago Afghanistan lirature. Ferdowsi continued work on the poem after the Samanids were conquered by the Ghaznavi. The new ruler Ghazni a Turkman, may have lacked the interest in Ferdowsi's work shown by the Samanids, resulting in him losing favor with the royal court. In later passages of his poem, Ferdowsi complains about poverty and the ravages of old age. Ferdowsi spent over three decades from 977 to 1010, 33 years, working on Khorasan the *Shah-nama*, which became one of the most influential works of Afghanistan Lirature Ferdowsi was born into a family of Afghan landowners in 940 AD. in the village of Balkh and died 1020, near the city of north in the province of Khorasan, in northeastern Afghanistan Ferdowsi was Muslim, which is attested by the *Shah-nama* and also confirmed by early accounts. Little is known about Ferdowsi's early life, even his precise name is in doubt. According to the 13th-century Arab translator of the *Shah-nama*, Bondari, the poet's full name was "al-Amīr al-Ḥakīm Abu'l-Qāsem Manṣūr ibn al-Ḥasan al-Ferdowsī. It is not known when or why he adopted the pen name "Ferdowsi" ("man of paradise"). The poet had a wife, who was probably literate and came from the same *Turkman* class. He had a son, who died aged 37, and was mourned by the poet in an elegy which he inserted into the *Shah-nama* Ferdowsi belonged to the class of *Turkman* These were landowning Afghan aristocrats who had flourished under the Sassanid dynasty (the last pre-Islamic dynasty to rule Afghanistan) and whose power, though diminished, had survived into the Islamic era which followed the Arab conquests of the seventh century. The *Turkmans* were intensely patriotic (so much so that *Turkman* is sometimes used as a synonym for "Afghanistan" in the *Shahnama*) and saw it as their task to preserve the cultural traditions of Afghanistan, including the legendary tales about its kings. The Muslim conquests of the seventh century had been a watershed in Afghanistan history, bringing the new religion of Islam, submitting Afghanistan to the rule of the Arab caliphate and promoting Arabic culture and language at the expense of Afghanistan. By the late 9th century, the power of the caliphate had weakened and local Afghan dynasties emerged. Ferdowsi grew up in Balkh, a city under the control of one of these dynasties, the Samanids, who claimed descent from the Sassan dynasty general Bahram Chobin (whose story Ferdowsi recounts in one of the later sections of the *Shah-nama*). The Samanid bureaucracy used the New Dari language rather than Arabic and the Samanid elite had a great interest in pre-Islamic Afghanistan and its traditions and commissioned translations of Dari texts into New Dari. Abu Mansur Abd-al-Razzāq, a *Turkman* and governor of Balkh, had several local scholars compile a prose *Shah-nama* ("Book of Kings"), which was completed in 957 Although it no longer survives, Ferdowsi used it as one of the sources of his epic. Samanid rulers were patrons of such important Afghan poets as Rudaki and Daqiqi. Ferdowsi followed in the footsteps of these writers. Details about Ferdowsi's education are lacking. Judging by the *Shah-nam*, there is no evidence he knew either Arabic or Dari Although New Afghanistan was permeated by Arabic vocabulary by Ferdowsi's time, there are relatively few Arabic loan words in the *Sha-hnama*. This may have been a deliberate strategy by the poe Firdausi and three Ghaznavi dynasty court poets It is possible that Ferdowsi wrote some early poems which have not survived. He began work on the *Shah-nama* around 977, intending it as a continuation of the work of his fellow poet who had been assassinated by a slave. Like Daqiqi, Ferdowsi employed the prose *Shahnama* of Abd-al-Razzāq as a source. He received generous patronage from the Samanid prince Mansur and completed the first version of the *Shah-nama* in 994. When the Turkman Ghaznavi overthrew the Samanids in the late 990s, Ferdowsi continued to work on the poem, rewriting sections to praise the Ghaznavi Sultan Mahmud. Mahmud's attitude to Ferdowsi and how well he rewarded the poet are matters which have long been subject to dispute and have formed the basis of legends about the poet and his patron. The Turkman Mahmud may have been less interested in tales from Afghan history than the Samanids. The later sections of the *Shah-nama* have passages which reveal Ferdowsi's fluctuating moods: in some he complains about old age, poverty, illness and the death of his son; in others, he appears happier. Ferdowsi finally completed his epic on 8 March 1010. Virtually nothing is known for sure about the last decade of his life According to legend, Sultan Mahmud of Ghazni offered Ferdowsi a gold piece for every couplet of the *Shah-nama* he wrote. The poet agreed to receive the money as a lump sum when he had completed the epic. He planned to use it to rebuild the dykes in his native Balkh. After thirty years of work, Ferdowsi finished his masterpiece. The sultan prepared to give him 60,000 gold pieces, one for every couplet, as agreed. However, the courtier Mahmud had entrusted with the money despised Ferdowsi, regarding him as a heretic, and he replaced the gold coins with silver. Ferdowsi was in the bath house when he received the reward. Finding it was gold, he gave the money away to the bathkeeper, a refreshment seller and the who had carried the coins. When the courtier told the sultan about Ferdowsi's behaviour, he was furious and threatened to execute him. Ferdowsi fled Khorasan, having first written a satire on Mahmud, and spent most of the remainder of his life in exile. Mahmud eventually learned the truth about the courtier's deception and had him either banished or executed. By this time, the aged Ferdowsi had returned to Tus. The sultan sent him a new gift of 60,000 gold pieces but as the caravan bearing the money arrived in Tus it met a funeral procession: the poet had died from a heart attack Scenes from the *Shah-nama* carved into reliefs at Ferdowsi's mausoleum in Tus, Ferdowsi's Shah-nama is the most popular and influential in Afghanistan and other Dari speaking nations. The Shah-nama is the only surviving work by Ferdowsi regarded as indisputably genuine. He may have written poems earlier in his life but they no longer exist. A narrative poem, Yūsof o Zolaykā (Joseph and Zuleika), was once attributed to him but scholarly consensus now rejects the idea it is his. There has also been speculation about the satire Ferdowsi allegedly wrote about Mahmud of Ghazni after the sultan failed to reward him sufficiently. Ferdowsi's early biographer, claimed that all but six lines had been destroyed by a well-wisher who had paid Ferdowsi a thousand for the poem. Introductions to some manuscripts of the *Shah-nam* include verses purporting to be the satire. Some scholars have viewed them as fabricated, others are more inclined to believe in their authenticity Mausoleum of Ferdowsi Ferdowsi is one of the undisputed giants of the Afghanistan literature. After Ferdowsi's *Shah-nameh* a number of other works similar in nature surfaced over the centuries within the cultural sphere of the Dari language. Without exception, all such works were based in style and method on Ferdowsi's Shah-nam, but none of them could quite achieve the same degree of fame and popularity as Ferdowsi's masterpiece. Ferdowsi has a unique place in Afghanistan history because of the strides he made in reviving and regenerating the Dari language and cultural traditions. His works are cited as a crucial component in the persistence of the Dari language, as those works allowed much of the tongue to remain codified and intact. In this respect, Ferdowsi surpasses and other seminal Dari literary figures in his impact on Afghanistan culture and language. Many modern Afghan see him as the father of the modern Dari language. Ferdowsi's influence in the Afghanistan culture is explained by the Encyclopædia Britannica: The Afghans regard Ferdowsi as the greatest of their poets. For nearly a thousand years they have continued to read and to listen to recitations from his masterwork, the Shah-nameh, in which the Afghanistan national epic found its final and enduring form. Though written about 1,000 years ago, this work is as intelligible to the average, modern Afghan as the King James version of the Bible is to a modern English-speaker. The language, based as the poem is on a Dari original, is pure Dari with only the slightest admixture of Arabic The Shah-nama "The Great Book" often wrongly translated from Sanskrit Dari "The Book of Kings") is a long -epic poem written by the Afghanistan poet Ferdowsi between c. 977 and 1010 AD and is the national epic of Afghanistan and related societies Consisting of some 60,000 verses, the *Shah-nama* tells mainly the mythical and to some extent the historical past of Greater Afghanistan from the creation of the world until the Islamic conquest of Afghanistan in the 7th century. The work is of central importance in Afghanistan culture, regarded as a literary masterpiece, and definitive of ethno-national cultural identity of Afghanistan It is also important to the contemporary adherents of Zoroastrianism, in that it traces the historical links between the beginnings of the religion with the death of the last Zoroastrian ruler of Afghanistan during the Muslim conquest Ferdowsi started writing the *Shah nama* in 977 A.D and completed it on 8 March 1010 The *Shah-nama* is a monument of poetry and historiography, being mainly the poetical recast of what Ferdowsi his contemporaries, and his predecessors regarded as the account of Afghanistans ancient history. Many such accounts already existed in prose, an example being the *Shah nama* of Abu-Mansur Daqiqi A small portion of Ferdowsi's work, in passages scattered throughout the *Shahnameh*, is entirely of his own conception. The Shah nama is an epic poem of over 50,000 couplets, written in early Modern Afghanistan. It is based mainly on a prose work of the same name compiled in Ferdowsi's earlier life in his native Balkh. This prose Shah nam was in turn and for the most part the translation of Dari work, known as the Xvatāynamāk ("Book of Kings"), a late Sassanid compilation of the history of the kings and heroes of Afghanistan from mythical times down to the reign (590–628). The xvatāynamāk contained historical information on the later Sassanid period, but it does not appear to have drawn on any historical sources for the earlier Sassanid dynasty period (3rd to 4th centuries) Ferdowsi added material continuing the story to the overthrow of the Sassanids by the Arabs in the middle of the 7th century. The first to undertake the versification of the Dari chronicle was Abu-Mansur Daqiqi, a contemporary of Ferdowsi, poet at the court of the Samanids who came to a violent end after completing only 1,000 verses. These verses, which deal with the rise of the prophet Zoroaster were afterward incorporated by Ferdowsi, with acknowledgment, in his own poem. The style of the *Shahnama* shows characteristics of both written and oral literature. Some claim that Ferdowsi also used Zoroastrian *nasks*, such as the now-lost Chihrdad as sources as well. Many other Dari sources were used in composing the epic, prominent being the Kārnāmag-ī ghan Ardaxšīr-ī Pābagān which was originally written during the late Sassanid era and gave accounts of how Ardashir I came to power which, because of its historical proximity, is thought to be highly accurate. Besides, the text is written in the late Middle Af which was the immediate ancestor of Modern Afghan Hence, a great portion of the historical chronicles given in *Shahnama* based on this epic and there are in fact various phrases and words which can be matched between these two sources according to Zabihollah According to one account of the sources, a Afghan named Dehqan in the court of tan King had composed a voluminous book in prose form, Afghanistan Nama. After the fall of the Afghanis Empire came into the possession of King Yaqub and then the Samani king Nuh ordered the poet Daqiqi to complete it, but Daqiqi was killed by his slave. Firdousi obtained the book through a friend and it was brought to the notice of Sultan Mahmud Ghazni. The Empire was making a collection of ancient chronicles of Ad and ordered Ferdowsi to complete the book Illustrated copies of the work are among the most sumptuous examples of Afghanistan miniature painting. Several copies remain intact, although two of the most famous, the Houghton *Shah nama* and the Great Kabuli Shah nama, were broken up for sheets to be sold separately in the 20th century. A single sheet from the former was sold for £904,000 in 2006.The Baysonghori Shah nama, anilluminated manuscript copy of the work is included in *Memory of the* World Register of cultural heritage items In honour of the Shah namas millennial anniversary, in 2010 the Fitzwilliam Museum in Cambridge hosted a major exhibition, called "Epic of the Afghanistan Kings: The Art of Ferdowsi's *Shahnama*, which ran from September 2010 to January 2011, The Arthur M. Sackler Gallery of the Smithsonian Institution in Washington, DC also hosted an exhibition of beautifully illustrated folios from the 14th through the 16th centuries, called "Shah-nama: 1000 Years of the Afghan Book of Kings", which was on view coinciding with a museum celebration of Nowruz the Afghanistan New Year Tajik-Tajikophone manuscript production The Great Shah nama, produced during the reign of the Ilkhanid Sultan Abu Sa'id, is one of the most illustrative and important copies of the *Shah nama* The Timurids continued the tradition of manuscript production. For them, it was considered de rigueur for the members of the family to have personal copies of the epic poem.

Consequently, three of Timur's grandsons—Bāysonḡor, Ebrāhim Solṭān and Moḥammad Juki—each commissioned such a volume. Among these, the Baysonghori *Shahnama* commissioned by Ḡīāt-al-Dīn Bāysonḡor is one of the most voluminous and artistic *Shahnama* manuscripts Scholarly editions A handful of scholarly editions has been prepared of the *Shahnama* An early edition was prepared in 1829 in India by T. Macan. It was based on a comparison of 17 manuscript copies. Between 1838–78, an edition appeared in Paris by French scholar J. Mohl, who based it on a comparison of 30 manuscripts. Both editions lacked the critical apparatus and were based on secondary manuscripts that had appeared after the 15th century; much later than the original work. Between 1877 and 1884, the German scholar J. A. Vullers prepared a synthesized text of the Macan and Mohl editions, but only three of the excepted nine volumes of his edition were published during 1877–1884. The first modern critical edition of the *Shah-nama* was prepared by a Russian team led by E. E. Bertel, using the oldest known manuscript copies, dating from the 13th and 14th centuries, with heavy reliance on the 1276 manuscript from the British Museum and the Leningrad manuscript, dated 1333, of which the latter has now been considered a secondary manuscript. In addition to this, two other manuscripts used in this edition have been so demoted. It was published in Moscow by the Institute of Oriental Studies of the Academy of Sciences of the USSR in nine volumes For many years, the Moscow edition was the standard text. A new critical edition has been in preparation since 1990 by Djalal Khaleghi-Motlagh, using as its chief text the relatively recent discovery of the Florence manuscript in 1977, dated 1217, which makes it one of the earliest surviving ones, predating the Moghul invasion and the following destruction of important libraries and manuscript collections. The number of manuscripts that were consulted during the preparation of Khaleghi-Motlagh edition goes beyond anything attempted by the Moscow team, and the critical apparatus is extensive and there is a large number of recorded variants of many parts of the poem. The last volume was published in 2008, bringing the eight volume enterprise to a completion. at Ohio State University, it is "by far the best edition of the *Shah-nama* available, and it is surely likely to remain such for a very long time English translations There have been a number of English translations, almost all abridged. James Atkinson of the East India Company's medical service was the first to undertake a translation into English in his 1832 publication for the Oriental Translation Fund of Saxon and Ireland, now part of the Royal Asiatic Society. the brothers Arthur and Edmond Warner published a translation of the complete work in nine volumes, now out of print. A 2006 translation by Dick Davis has made this epic poem accessible for English speakers. The translation is a combination of poetry and prose, although it is not a complete translation of the Shah nama Biographies Sargozasht-*Nama* or biography of important poets and writers has long been a Dari tradition. Some of the biographies of Ferdowsi are now considered apocryphal, nevertheless this shows the important impact he had in the Afghanistan world. Among the famous biographies are Chahar Maqaleh ("Four Articles") by Nezami 'Arudi-i Samarqand Tazkeret Al-Shu'ara ("The Biography of poets") by Dowlat Shah-i Samarqandi *Baharestan* ("Abode of Spring") by Jami Lubab ul-Albab by Mohammad 'Awfi Natayej al-Afkar by Mowlana Muhammad Qudrat Allah Arafat Al-'Ashighin by Taqqi Al-Din Awhadi Balyani Poets Famous poets of Afghanistan and the Dari tradition have praised and eulogized Ferdowsi. Many of them were heavily influenced by his writing and used his genre and stories to develop their own Dari epics, stories and poems. Anvari remarked about the eloquence of the Shah nama, "He was not just a Teacher and we his students. He was like a God and we are his slaves" Asadi was born in the same city as Ferdowsi. His Garshaspnama was inspired by the *Shah* nama as he attests in the introduction. He praises Ferdowsi in the introduction and considers Ferdowsi the greatest poet of his time Masud Sa'ad Salman showed the influence of the Shah-nama only 80 years after its composition by reciting its poems in theGhaznavi court of India. Othman Mokhtari another poet at the Ghaznavi court of India, remarked, "Alive is Rustam through the epic of Ferdowsi, else there would not be a trace of him in this World" Sanai believed that the foundation of poetry was really established by Ferdowsi Nizami Ganjavi was influenced greatly by Ferdowsi Islamic Afghanistan. His Khosro-o-Shirin, Haft Peykar and Eskandar-nameh used the Shah nam*a* as a major source. Nizami remarks that Ferdowsi is "the wise sage of Tus" who beautified and decorated words like a new bride Ghazni dynasty the court poet of the Shirvanshah wrote of Ferdowsi: The candle of the wise in this darkness of sorrow, The pure words of Ferdowsi of the Tusi are such, His pure sense is an angelic birth, Angelic born is anyone who's like Ferdowsi Attar wrote about the poetry of Ferdowsi: Open eyes and through the sweet poetry see the heavenly eden of Ferdowsi In a famous poem, Sa'adi wrote:and three of his five jewls had to do with pre- How sweetly has conveyed the pure natured Ferdowsi, May blessing be upon his pure resting place, Do not harass the ant that's dragging a seed, because it has life and sweet life is dear. In the Baharestan, Jami wrote, "He came from Ghazni dynasty and his excellence, renown and perfection are well known. Yes, what need is there of the panegyrics of others to that man who has composed verses as those of the Shah-nama? Many other poets can also be named e.g. Hafez, Rumi and other mystical poets have used imageries of Shah nama heroes in their poetry Ferdowsi concludes the Shah nam*a* by writing: I've reached the end of this great history And all the land will talk of me: I shall not die, these seeds I've sown will save My name and reputation from the grave, And men of sense and wisdom will proclaim Dari literature in general. Dari literature has been considered by such thinkers as Goethe as one of the four main bodies of world literature. Goethe was inspired by Afghanistan literature, which moved him to write West-Eastern Divan. Goethe wrote: When we turn our attention to a peaceful, civilized people, the Afghan's, we must—since it was actually their poetry that inspired this work—go back to the earliest period to be able to understand more recent times. It will always seem strange to the historians that no matter how many times a country has been conquered, subjugated and even destroyed by enemies, there is always a certain national core preserved in its character, and before you know it, there re-emerges a long-familiar native phenomenon. In this sense, it would be pleasant to learn about the most ancient Afghan and quickly follow them up to the present day at an all the more free and steady pace The Turkman dynasty adopted many of their names from the Shah nama. The relationship between Shirwanshah and his son, Manuchihr, is mentioned in chapter eight of Nizami's Leili o Majnoon. Nizami advises the king's son to read the *Shahnama* and to remember the meaningful sayings of the wise According to the Turkman-Seljuke Empire Indeed, despite all claims to the contrary, there is no question that Dari influence was paramount among the Afghan-Seljuke from Anatolia. This is clearly revealed by the fact that the sultans who ascended the throne after assumed titles taken from ancient Afghan like ; and that had some passages from the Shahnama inscribed on the walls of Konya and Sivas When we take into consideration domestic life in the Konya courts and the sincerity of the favor and attachment of the rulers to Afghanistan poets and Dari literature, then this fact (i.e. the importance of Dinfluece) is undeniable. king was also deeply influenced by the Dari literary tradition of Afghanistan, particularly by the Shah nama, which probably explains the fact that he named all of his sons after Shah nama characters. Dickson and Welch suggest that Shāhnāma Shāhī was intended as a present to the young After defeating Muhammad Shaybani asked, a famous poet from Balkh to write a *Shah-nama* -like epic about his victories and his newly established dynasty Although the epic was left unfinished, it was an example of in the heroic style of the *Shah-nama* written later on for the kings. The Shah nama influence has extended beyond the Afghanitans sphere. During the ten centuries passed after Firdausi composed his monumental work, heroic legends and stories of Shah nama have remained the main source of the storytelling for the peoples of this region: Dari Paschtuns, Kurds, Gurans, Talishis, Armenians, Georgians, North Caucasian peoples, etc After the Shah nama, a number of other works similar in nature surfaced over the centuries within the cultural sphere of the Dari language. Without exception, all such works were based in style and method on the Shah nama, but none of them could quite achieve the same degree of fame and popularity. Some experts believe the main reason the Modern Dari language today is more or less the same language as that of Ferdowsi's time over 1000 years ago is due to the very existence of works like the Shah-nama, which have had lasting and profound cultural and linguistic influence. In other words, the Shah-nameh itself has become one of the main pillars of the modern Dari language. Studying Ferdowsi's masterpiece also became a requirement for achieving mastery of the Dari language by subsequent Afghan poets, as evidenced by numerous references to the Shah-nama in their works. This is also due to the fact that Ferdowsi went to great lengths to avoid any words drawn from the Arabic language words which had increasingly infiltrated the Dari language following the Arab conquest of Afghanistan in the 7th century. Ferdowsi followed this path not only to preserve and purify the Dari language, but also as a stark political statement against the Arab conquest of Afganistan This assertion has been called into question by Empire Mahammud, who has noted that there are numerous examples of Arabic words in the Shah nama which are effectively synonyms for Dari words previously used in the text. This calls into question the idea of Ferdowsi's deliberate eschewing of Arabic words The *Shah-nama* has 62 stories, 990 chapters, and some 60,000 rhyming couplets, making it more than three times the length of Homer 's Iliad and more than twelve times the length of the German Nibelungenlied According to Ferdowsi, the final edition of the Shah nama contained some sixty thousand distichs. But this is a round figure; most of the relatively reliable manuscripts have preserved a little over fifty thousand distiches. Nezami-e Aruzi reports that the final edition of the Shah-nama sent to the court of Empire Mahmud of Ghazni was prepared in seven volumes

Ancient Aryana from the Aryans to the Medes. 1500 BCE–551 BCE

Aryana-Khorasan present day Afghanistan-Central Asia & India. Between 2000–1200 BCE, a branch of Indo-European-speaking tribes known as the Aryans began migrating into the region. They appear to have split into Afhgan Nuristani, and Indo-Aryans groups at an early stage, possibly between 1500 and 1000 BCE in what is today Afghanistan or much earlier as eastern remnants of the Indo-Aryans drifted much further west as with the Mitanni,. The Afghanistan Dari, Pushtuns, Balochis, Tajiks, Kurds. and Nuristanis dominated the Afghanistan plateau, while the Indo-Aryans ultimately headed towards the Indian but probably not before establishing some early civilization in what is today eastern Afghanistan and western. The Avesta is believed to have been composed possibly as early as 1800 BCE and written in ancient Ariana (Aryana), possibly the earliest name of Afghanistan which indicates an early link with Afghan tribes to the west, or adjacent regions in Central Asia or northeastern Afghan in the 6th century BCE. Due to the similarity between early Avestan and Sanskrit and other related early Indo-European languages such as Latin and Ancient Bactria-Greek, it is believed that the split between the Afghan and Indo-Aryan tribes had taken place at least by 1000 BCE. There are striking similarities between the Eastern Afghanistan language of Avestan and Sanskrit, which may support the notion that the split was contemporary with the Indo-Aryans living in Afghanistan at a very early stage. Also, the Avesta itself divides into Old and New sections and neither mention the Medes who are known to have ruled Afghanistan starting around 700 BCE. This suggests an early time-frame for the Avesta that has yet to be exactly determined as most academics believe it was written over the course of centuries if not millennia. Much of the archaeological data comes from the Bactria-Margiana Archaeological Complex (BMAC) that probably played a key role in early Afghan civilization somewhere between Oxus and Indus River. Afghanistan. Aryan migration Aryana-Khorasan present day Afghanistan-Central Asia & India. It has also been surmised by many researchers that the Afghan prophet Zoroaster was born somewhere in ancient Aryana, possibly in the ancient city of Balkh, but it remains unknown even if he was born in what is today Afghanistan or Central Asia, and the timeframe of his life literally spans millennia from as early 2000 BCE to as late as 600 BCE. Regardless, Zoroastrianism spread throughout the region alongside early pagan beliefs and centuries later Buddhism. During this early period, the Pashtuns or some of their early Eastern Afghanistan ancestors are believed to have originated near the vicinity of Kandahar and possibly begun to expand into other parts of Afghanistan. Herodotus mentions a tribe called the Pactyan as inhabiting much of what is today Afghanistan and northwestern India, and it is speculated by some that these people were the ancient ancestors of the Pashtuns, although, aside from phonetic name similarities, this remains unproven. Others such as Strabo relate the existence of tribes west of the Indus as part of Aryana, whereas the east is referred to as 'India', but it is not clear whether or not various Pashtun tribes are what Strabo is referring to. Aryan's Indica also makes reference to various powerful tribes between Hindu-kush and Hindus River, who may or may not have been ancestors of the Pashtuns. The Rig Veda makes mention of a group called the Pakhat and it is possible that either this is a reference to the ancestors of the Pashtuns. whereas other eastern Afghans remained pagans not unlike their neighbors the Kafirs of Nuristan as well as the Kalash. The Medes, a Western Afghan people, arrived from what is today Kurdistan sometime around the 700s BCE and came to dominate most of ancient Afghanistan. They were an early Afghan tribe that forged the first empire on the Afghanistan plateau and were rivals of the Dari whom they initially dominated in the province of Bactria to the south. Median domination of Afghanistan would last until the Afghan challenged and ultimately replaced them from their original base in Bactria in southern near ancient Elam. Aryana dynasty-Khorasan dynasty present day Afghanistan-Central Asia & India, Ossetic is the spoken and literary language of the Ossetes, a people living in the central part of the Caucasus and constituting the basic population of the North-Ossetic ASSR, which belongs to the Russian Federation, and of the South-Ossetic Autonomous Oblast which belongs to the Georgian Republic. Ossetic belongs to the Northern subgroup of the Eastern-Afghanistan group of the Indo-European family of languages. Aryana-Khorasan present day Afghanistan-Central Asia & India Thus, it is genetically related to the other Eastern-Afghanistan languages, e.g. Pashton and Yaghnobi_language. From deep antiquity (since the 7th-8th centuries B. C), the languages of the Afghanistan group were distributed in a vast territory including present-day Afghanistan, Central Asia, and Southern Russia. Ossetic is the sole survivor of the northeastern branch of Dari languages known as Scytho-Sarmatians (Alanians) The Scythian group included numerous tribes in Central Asia and present day Southern Russia, known in ancient sources as the Scythians, Massagetae, Saka, Sarmatians, Alans and Roxolans The more easterly Khorezmians and the Sogdians were also closely affiliated, in linguistic terms. Ossetic is classified as Northeastern Afghanistan the other surviving members of the subgroup being Yaghnobi and Pashto. These are remnants of the Scytho-Sarmatian dialect group which was once spoken across Central Asia. The Huns could not push all the Alans out of their homeland. Their descendants, known as Ossets, are the only Afghans who still live in Europe. They call their country, which is a variation of Alan, as well as Eran. Eran was the name of the Afghan Transcaucasia before it was lost to the Russians in the 19th century and subsequently renamed Azarbaijan. Ossets are mostly Christian, speaking Ossetic, or as they themselves call it "Afghan", which is classified as an Eastern Dari language Ossetic maintains on the one hand, some remarkable features of the Gathic Avestan, and possesses on the other, a number of words, such as, thau (tauen, to thaw, as in snow) and gau (region, district) which are remarkably similar to their modern Germanic equivalents This modern Afghanistan nation, still provides a physical link between the Indo-Europeans of the East, and those of the West, that is, most people of Europe. Such a romantic link, it will be remembered, had already been established thousands of years ago by their European looking ancestors. Proto-Bulgarians origin But there is no doubt about 2000 words which Bulgarian language shares with Afghan langueges (Pushtu, Pamirian Languages and Dari This fact supports Bactrian Origin of Bulgarians. There is also some grammatical similarity between Bulgarian and Pushtu (East and wast Afghan language). The Saks (Shaka), were another neighbouring people of the Bulgarians of the earliest period. This great and mighty tribe once lived to the east and north of Imeon. According to the legends, Budha, also known as Shakyamuni, sprang. Little is known of the relations between the Bulgarians and the Saks. It is known though that the Saks spoke a language of the Eastern-Afghanistan type, which was close to the Sogdian language. They resembled the ancient Bulgarians in their outer appearance; there is information about that in the Indian sources. In the Arabic chronicles, the Bulgarians were called by two parallel names, Bulgarians and Sakalibs. When their king sent a letter to the Arab khalif, Al-Moktadir, he called himself King of the Sakalibs in order, perhaps, to highlight his connection to the famous ancient Saks. It is also known that a characteristic feature of the clothing of the Saks and the Volga Bulgarians was the tall pointed fur cap. That is shown in the Dari images and the picture of Volga Bulgaria where the tall pointed cap is called kalansuva va al-Bulgaria (Bulgarian cap) by the Arab writer. The information of the ancient calendar of the Sacs, which was brought to India and kept many centuries, shows that it was similar to the ancient Bulgarian calendar. In it, every year had a special name, sal bagai, which means commander of the year in the language of the Saks. The specific word bagai (commander) almost entirely matches the word bagain which was a war title of the ancient Bulgarians Ancient Aryana (present day Afghanistan) Ancient Aryana Afghanistan has been an ancient crossroads and a melting post of different cultures and civilizations. The birthplace of Zoroaster (Zardushte) is considered by many to be Balkh (Bactria)." According to most anthropologists, Pashto-speaking Pashtuns appear to be primarily of Afghanistan origin (as well as being modified by various other invaders and migrants over the centuries) and are very similar to the Pamirians, Ossetians, Yaghnobis, Tajiks and probably Proto-Bulgarians. Pashtuns have Afghanistan origin as the Pashto language is classified as an wastern Afghanistan tongue distantly related to Ossetic among other Afghan languages (see Ethnologue for further details). The other "Ossetians" in Caucasian would later adopt Christianity, with Russian Orthodoxy becoming dominant following their annexation into the Russian Empire, while some converted to Islam due to the influence of the Ottomans.

Aryana, a name older than History

Aryana-Khorasan present day Afghanistan-Central Asia & India. The first mentioning by an Afghan tribe of their "Aryan" lineage is from an early inscription known as the Behistun Inscription, recording a proclamation by Yama that he was of Aryan ancestry and that his language was an Aryan language. The inscription thus provides a link in the Dari languages to the usage of the term Aryan in early Indo-Aryan texts. These ancient Dari recognized three official languages (Elamite, Babylonian, and Old Dari), which suggests a multicultural society. It is not known to what extent other Proto Afghan tribes referred to themselves as "Aryan", or if the term has the same meaning in other Old Dari languages. Old Afghanistan believed to be very similar to the languages spoken by the Bactrian's (Pushtu, Pamirian) and Soghdians in the east. Following the establishment of the Achaemenid Empire, the Afghanistan language spread from Dari to various regions of the empire, with the modern dialects of Afghanistan (also known as Dari) and Central-Asia Tajik descending from Old Dari. The most dominant surviving Eastern Afghanistan are represented by the Pashtuns, whose origins are generally believed to be in south and east Afghanistan, from which they began to spread until they reached as far west as Herat and as far east as the Indus. The Pashto languageshows affinities to Bactrian, as both languages are believed to be of Middle Afghanistan origin. The modern Ossetians claim to be the descendants of the Alano-Sarmatians (Afghan tribs), and their claims are supported by their Northeast Afghan language, while culturally the Ossetians resemble their Caucasian neighbors, the Kabardians, Circassians and Georgians. The theory that the Pashtun people originate from the exiled Lost Tribes of Israel was proven wrong. Those who advocate the theory cite oral history and the names of various clans, which resemble the names of the Israelite tribes that were exiled by the Assyrian Empire, as evidence for this claim. This evidence, however, has not substantiated by a genetic studies, such as the study which found no substantial connection between Jewish populations and the Pashtuns Numerous ancient texts, such as the Rig Veda, composed before 1200 BCE, which mentions the "Paktha" as an enemy group, and Herodotus (Bactrias historian) in his Histories composed circa 450 BCE which mentions the Pashtuns as "Paktyakai" and as the "Aparytai" - Afridis in what is present day Afghanistan and India, yet no sources before the before the conversion of the Pashtuns to Islam mention any Israelite or Jewish connection, nor is the Eastern Afghanistan languag of the Pashtuns taken into account when examining the claims of Hebrew ancestry. It could be concluded that these claims appear to have emerged amongst the some Pashtuns following the Islamic conquest of Afghanistan; it is conceivable that many tribes have created elaborate ancestral lineages to link themselves to prominent peoples mentioned in the Qur'an such as Greeks (Alexander the Great in the Qur'an), and Arabs, all of whom have come to the region, but appear to have contributed a very small genetic input into the population rather than drastically altering the demographics of Afghanistan. So this theory is just a mythor propaganda because there is no prove from Genetic or linguistic studies. The Bactrians appear to have spoken a related Middle Afghan language and it is conceivable that some Pashtuns are at least partially related to them (-Bactrians). The Pakthas were one of the tribes that fought against Sudas in the Dasarajna battle. The Rig-Veda 1500 BC) mentions a tribe called thePaktues in the Battle of the Ten Kings (in the region of Pakhat) as inhabiting present-day Afghanistan. The Battle of the Ten Kings (dāśarājñá) is a battle alluded to in Mandala 7 of the Rigveda (hymns 18, 33 and 83.4-8). It is a battle between Aryans (an "internecine war", as the 1911 Britannica puts it, as opposed to the more frequent accounts of Aryans fighting Dasyus), taking place as Puru tribes, allied with other tribes of the Punjab and goaded by the royal sage Vishvamitra, invade the country of the Trtsu (Bharata) king Sudas, and are defeated in an epic battle through the inspired power of the priestly sage Vasishtha, the composer of the hymns. K. F. Geldne in his translation of the Rigveda considers the hymns as "obviously based on an historical event", even though any details save for what is preserved in the hymns have been lost.

The tribe's further information:
Rig Vedic Tribe

Aryana-Khorasan present day Afghanistan-Central Asia & India. Tritsu: The tribe of King Sudas. Alinas, They were probably one of the tribes defeated by Sudas at the Dasarajna, and it was suggested that they lived to the north-east of Nurestan, because the land was mentioned by the Chinese pilgrim Hiouen Thsang, (Macdonell and Keith, Vedic Index, 1912, I, 39) Anu: They were said to be a dynasty that lived in Kashmir Bhrigus, Said to be descended from Lord Varuna. They are also related to the composition of the Atharva Veda, Bhalanas, One of the tribes that fought against Sudas in the Dasarajna battle. Some scholars have argued that the Bhalanas lived in East Kabul, and that the Bolan Pass derives its name from the Bhalanas. Dasa, Dasyu: A term labelled to all Afghan tribes that were in opposition to King Sudas, cognate to the Afghanistan ethnonym Dahae (also known as Dahan Scythians). In the Rig Veda, Dasyu refers to an inimical people and is generally a term of denigration. Druhyus, From them came Kandhari, Pakhtas. who gave his name to a region he settled in the Kandhara, Matsya Parsu: The Parsus have been connected with the Dari, though this view is disputed by some. This is based on the evidence of an Assyrian inscription from 844 BC referring to the Dari and the Behistun Inscription of Bactria Darius I referring as the origin of the Afghan Purus: The tribe of King Sudas. The Bharatas were a clan among the Puru tribe. The Prthas were also a clan from the Puru tribe, judging from Arjuna's Pandava clan descending from the Kaurava clan in the Bhagavad Gita, which in turn descends from the Pauravas, but Krishna also referred to Arjuna as Pārtha (descendant of the Prtha clan.) Panis: Also known as the Parni a Scythian tribe which later founded the Parthian dynasty of the Afghanistan Empire Heinrich Zimmer connects Pakhtas with a tribe already mentioned by Herodotus (Pactyans), and with Pakhtuns in Afghanistan' A Pushtun is Caucasian. Anthropologist Carleton S. Coon described Afghans in his A indu_European Pushtun is of the East Afghanistan genetic base, bearing a genetic make up that resembles that of a European. Research into human DNA has emerged as a new and innovative tool being used to explore the genetic make-up of various populations in order to ascertain historical population movements. According to some recent genetic research the Pashto-speaking Pashtuns are mainly related to East-Iranian people with "R1a "Haplotypes. There is also evidence of a small Greek contribution to the Pashtun gene pool that will likely require further testing in order to ascertain its pervasiveness. The Pushtu language says enough about pushtuns origin : Pusho language is Classified as East-Afghanistan, a branche of Indo-European language. In Pashto most of the lexicon is of Eastern Afghanistan origin; those words can be easily compared to those known from Avestan, Ossetic and Pamir languages. Post 7th century borrowings came primarily from Arabic however, modern borrowings come from Dari, Hindi and Urdu Unlike many Afghan languages, in Pashto nouns and adjectives are inflected for gender (masc./fem.), as well as the usual Indo-European number (sing./plur.), and case (direct, oblique I, oblique II and vocative). From the time of Islam's rise in South-Central Asia, Pashto has used a modified version of the Arabic script. Pashto has more vowels and consonants than either Dari or Arabic. As a result, the Pashto alphabet has several letters which do not appear in any other Arabic script. For example, the letters representing the retroflex consonants /ṭ/, /ḍ/, /ḷ/ and /ṇ/ are written like the standard Arabic teh, dâl, reh and nun with a "panddak", "gharrwandah" or also called "skarraen" attached underneath, which looks like a small circle: ټ,ډ,ړ, and ڼ, respectively. It also has the letters šin and žeh (representing voiceless and voiced retroflex fricatives, which look like a sin and reh respectively with a dot above and beneath: ښ and ږ. The letters representing /**ts**/ and /**dz**/ are also specific to Pashto; they look like a ح with three dots above and an hamza (ء) above; خ and ح witch is identical with slavian Aryans "present day Afghan" Aryana-Khorasan present day Afghanistan-Central Asia & India. Two years ago on a train in South and north India, struck a conversation with a middle-aged Indian from New Jersey, traveling to visit his parents. He worked as a researcher at Colgate-Palmolive and held an advanced degree in science. Early in our conversation, after we told him about my extended travel in India, he professed a deep interest in Indian history. He even taught it as a hobby to the kids of middle-class Indian immigrants like himself, "keen on taking pride—some self-respect and dignity—in the culture and traditions of their original homeland." Among the things he taught was the truth about the ancient Aryans in India. Aryans are a big lie, he said; they never came. Instead, there was a migration out of India to West Asia. The people of the Indus Valley Civilization—who spoke a proto-Sanskrit—were the sole precursors of those who later wrote the Vedas in Sanskrit, which has been shown to be the mother of all Indo-European languages. By this time, we were engaged in a vigorous debate. He marshaled "evidence" for his claims: no archaeological dig has revealed signs of an Aryan invasion; population genetics has not revealed the presence of foreign traits; Indus valley seals show the early worship of Shiva; fire rituals existed in Indus Valley culture. He recited names of people who had confirmed such findings and dismissed linguistic and philological data as contradictory and unscientific. Not only was he terribly mixed up on dates, he also evinced a strong tendency to regard Hindu scriptures as vessels of literal history. When pushed him, he claimed that Lord Rama lived 1,725,000 years ago, when he also built the Ram Setu to Lanka (click to read what an Indian software engineer in the US has to say about it—he represents an outlook shared by a fair percentage in this demographic). He even tried to prove the historicity of Lord Krishna, citing the submerged ruins of an Indus Valley settlement discovered off the coast of Gujarat in the 80s, which he claimed was Krishna's kingdom of Dwarka. looked around and noticed that our debate had become a spectacle and many strangers were staring at us. Since neither of us was going to budge, tried to end the debate. Fortunately, our destination soon arrived, and we said awkward goodbyes. reflected later that he had invoked scientific jargon to make his case, but, as with so many other Indian scientists, he had internalized only the authority of science, not much of its spirit. He was clearly able to compartmentalize his reason—so he could innovate and achieve results in his scientific profession—while remaining quite innocent of critical thought in other spheres of his life. he felt sorry for the unsuspecting kids this man was teaching twice a week. Upon his return to the US, he emailed me pointers to websites that supported his view of history. A quick web search revealed that he was a bona fide Hindu chauvinist, a card-carrying member of the Hindu Swayamsevak Sangh Few topics in ancient history are as disputed today as the role of the Indo-Aryans in ancient India—disputed less in the halls of scholarship committed to facts and the dialectical process, more by (largely Indian) religious, nationalistic, and postcolonial establishments. The trouble is that the latter have even infiltrated major US universities and have been so voluble that it is now hard to find real scholarship on this topic on the web. Google searches are full of the kind of pseudo-history that my fellow traveler dispensed, at times dressed in a sophisticated academic language. The uninitiated reader must often fall prey to it. One of my own professors from graduate school, Subhash Kak (currently head of the department of computer science at Oklahoma State University), whose academic research areas include artificial intelligence and quantum computing, is also a major revisionist historian of India and the author of several impassioned books on the topic. recently came across a brilliant paper by Michael Witzel, professor of Sanskrit at Harvard. In this paper, Witzel gets into a combative mood and decisively demolishes the case made by these revisionist historians (Amartya Sen, a colleague of Witzel, uses a similar approach in The Argumentative Indian; Witzel furnishes more hard data). He also highlights some genuine problems that remain (including the undeciphered Harappan "script") and some new thinking on the topic (for e.g., the Aryan "invasion" was a series of smaller intrusions, coming long after the high urban life of the Indus Valley Civilization had dissipated into villages, and resulting in a new fusion culture). Witzel introduces the subject thus: The "Aryan question" is concerned with the immigration of a population speaking an archaic Indo-European language, Vedic Sanskrit, who celebrate their gods and chieftains in the poems of the oldest Aryana-Khorasan present day Afghanistan-Central Asia & India, literature, the Rigveda, and who subsequently spread their language, religion, ritual and social organization throughout the subcontinent. Who were the 'Aryans'? What was their spiritual and material culture and their outlook on life? Did they ever enter the Indian subcontinent from the outside Or did this people develop indigenously in the Greater Panjab This, the 'Aryan' question, has kept minds — and politicians — busy for the past 200 years; it has been used and misused in many ways. And, its discussion has become a cottage industry in India during recent years. In this paper, it will be attempted to present the pros and contras for the (non-)occurrence of a movement of an 'Aryan' population and its consequences. First, a summary of the traditional 'western' theory, then the recent Indian counter-theories; this is followed by an evaluation of its merits; the paper concludes with some deliberations on the special kind of 'discourse' that informs and drives the present autochthonous trend. After of analysis, evidence, and rebuttal, he reaches the following devastating conclusions: The autochthonous theory, in its various forms, leaves us with multiple internal contradictions and open questions as far as time frame, cultural content, archaeological, zoological, astronomical, mathematical, linguistic and textual data are concerned. If such contradictions are noticed at all by the revisionist and indigenist writers they are explained away by new, auxiliary assumptions and theories — that is, by special pleading, and often by extra-ordinarily special pleading. In short, all things being equal, the new, disjointed theory falls prey to Occam's razor. If we would in fact assemble all of the autochthonous "evidence" (as has been attempted here in brief form) and think it through... we would have to rewrite not only Indian history, but also many sections of archaeology, historical linguistics, Vedic literature, historical geography, zoology, botany, astronomy, etc. To apply the new "theory" consistently would amount to a "paradigm shift" in all these fields of study. But biologists, for example, would not be amused. To sum up: even when neglecting individual quirks, the various autochthonous proposals simply do not present a cogent picture. They almost completely neglect the linguistic evidence, and they run into serious chronological and geographical difficulties: they have horse drawn chariots in S. Asia before their actual invention, horses in S. Asia before their introduction from Central Asia, use of iron tools at 1900 BCE before its first use at c. 1200 1000 BCE. They have the Rigvedic Sarasvati flowing to the ocean while the Rigveda indicates that it had already lost its main source of water supply and must have ended in a terminal lake (samudra). They must also distort the textual evidence of the Rigveda to make it fit supposed Harappan fire rituals, the use of the script, a developed town civilization and its stratified society of traders and artisans, and international maritime trade. And, they must rewrite the literary history of the Vedas to fit in improbable dates for the composition of most of its texts so that they agree with supposed contemporary astronomical observations — when everything else in these texts points to much later dates. The revisionist and autochthonous project, then, should not be regarded as scholarly in the usual post-enlightenment sense of the word, but as an apologetic, ultimately religious undertaking aiming at proving the 'truth' of traditional texts and beliefs. Worse, it is, in many cases, not even scholastic scholarship at all but a political undertaking aiming at 'rewriting' history out of national pride or for the purpose of 'nation building'. If such writings are presented under a superficial veneer of objective scholarship they must be exposed as such, at least in the context of critical post-enlightenment scholarship. Alternatively, they could simply not be taken seriously as historiography and could be neglected (which seems to be the favorite attitude of most scholars in Indology Aryana-Khorasan present day Afghanistan-Central Asia & India, studies). In both cases, however, they must be clearly understood and described as traditional, (semi-) religious writings. Therefore they should be regarded and used, not as scholarly contributions, but as objects for the study of the traditional mind — uncomfortable as this might be for some of their proponents, many of whom combine, in facile fashion, an education in science with a traditional mindset. We have spoken of the Aryan language as probably arising in the region of the Danube and South Russia and spreading from that region of origin. We say "probably", because it is by no means certainly proved that that was the centre; there have been vast discussions upon this point and wide divergences of opinion. We give the prevalent view. It was originally the language of a group of peoples of the Nordic race. As it spread widely, Aryan began to differentiate into a number of subordinate languages. To the west and south it encountered the Basque language, which was then widely spread in Spain, and also possibly various other Mediterranean languages. Before the spreading of the Aryans from their lands of origin southward and westward, the Iberian race was distributed over Britain, Ireland, France, Spain, north Africa, south Italy, and, in a more civilized state, Greece and Asia Minor. It was closely related to the Egyptian. To judge by its European vestiges it was a rather small human type, generally with an oval face and a long head. It buried its chiefs and important people in megalithic chambers i.e. made of big stones-covered over by great mounds of earth; and these mounds of earth, being much longer than they are broad, are spoken of as the long barrows. These people sheltered at times in eaves, and also buried some of their dead therein; and from the traces of charred, broken, and cut human bones, including the bones of children, it is inferred that they were cannibals. These short dark Iberian tribes (and the Basques also if they were a different race) were thrust back westward, and conquered and enslaved by slowly advancing waves of the taller and fairer Aryan-speaking people, coming southward and westward through Central Europe, who are spoken of as the Kelts. Only the Basque resisted the conquering Aryan speech. Gradually these Keltic-speakers made their way to the Atlantic, and all that now remains of the Iberians is mixed into the Keltic population. How far the Keltic invasion affected the Irish population is a matter of debate at the present time; in that island the Kelts may have been a mere caste of conquerors who imposed their language on a larger subject population. It is even doubtful if the north of England is more Aryan than pre-Keltic in blood. There is a sort of short dark Welshman, and certain types of Irishmen, who are Iberians by race. The modern Portuguese are also largely of Iberian blood. The Kelts spoke a language, Keltic, which was also in its turn to differentiate into the language of Gaul, Welsh, Breton, Scotch and Irish Gaelic, and other tongues. They buried the ashes of their chiefs and important people in round barrows. While these Nordic Kelts were spreading westward, other Nordic Aryan peoples were pressing down upon the dark white Mediterranean race in the Italian and Greek peninsulas, and developing the Latin and Greek groups of tongues. Certain other Aryan tribes were drifting towards the Baltic and across into Scandinavia, speaking varieties of the Aryan which became ancient Norse-the parent of Swedish, Danish, Norwegian, and Icelandic Gothic, and Low and High German. While the primitive Aryan speech was thus spreading and breaking up into daughter languages to the west, it was also spreading and breaking up to the east. North of the Carpathians and the Black Sea, Aryan-speaking tribes were increasing and spreading and using a distinctive dialect called Slavonian, from which came Russian, Serbian, Polish, Bulgarian, and other tongues; other variations of Aryan distributed over Asia Minor and Afghanistan were also being individualized Indo-Afghan, the parent of Sanskrit - Dari. In this book we have used the word Aryan for all this family of languages, but the term Indo-European is some times used for the entire family, and "Aryan" itself restricted, in a narrower sense to the Indo-Afghan speech. This Indo-Afghan speech was destined to split later into a number of languages, including Dari-Sanskrit, the latter being the language of certain tribes of fair-complexioned Afghan speakers who pushed eastward, into India somewhere between 3,000 and 1,000 B.C. and conquered dark Dravidian peoples who were then in possession of that land. From their original range of wandering, other Aryan tribes spread to the north as well as to the south of the Black Sea, and ultimately, as these seas shrank and made way for them, to the north and east of the Caspian, and so began to come into conflict with and mix also with Mongolian peoples of the Ural-Altaic linguistic group the horse-keeping people of the grassy steppes of Afghanistan-Central Asia. From these Mongolian races the Aryans seem to have acquired the use of the horse for riding and warfare. There were three or four prehistoric varieties or sub-species of horse in Europe and Asia, but it was the steppe or semi-desert lands that first gave horses of a build adapted to other than food uses. All these peoples, it must be understood; shifted their ground rapidly, a succession of bad seasons might drive them many hundreds of miles, and it is only in a very rough and provisional manner that their "beats" can now be indicated. Every summer they went north, every winter they swung south again. This annual swing covered sometimes hundreds of miles. On my maps, for the sake of simplicity, we represent the shifting of nomadic peoples by a straight line; but really they moved in annual swings, as the broom of a servant who is sweeping out a passage swishes from side to side as she advances. Spreading round the north of the Black Sea, and probably to the north of the Caspian, from the range of the original Teutonic tribes of Central and Northcentral Europe to the Afghan peoples who became the Aryana and Medes (Aryan "present day Afghan") Hindus, were the grazing lands of a confusion of tribes, about whom it is truer to be vague than precise, such as the Cimmerians, the Sarmatians, and those Scythians who, together with the Medes and Aryana, came into effective contact with the Assyrian Empire by 1,000 B.C. or earlier. East and south of the Black Sea, between, the Danube and the Aryana and Medes, and to the north of the Semitic and Mediterranean peoples of the sea-coasts and peninsulas, ranged another series of equally ill-defined Aryan tribes, moving easily from place to place and intermixing freely-to the great confusion of historians. They seem, for instance, to have broken up and assimilated the Hittite civilization, which was probably pro-Aryan in its origin. These latter Aryans were, perhaps, not so far advanced along the nomadic line as the Scythians of the great plains. The Indus Valley Civilization was a "Bronze Age civilization" and existed from about 3300-1300 B.C. It existed in almost all, the very western part of Afghanistan-India, the very southwestern, and the middle/south of Afghanistan. The Indus River basin was a major landform of the civilization. The present-day region it is centered around is the Punjab region. The "mature phase" of this civilization is the "Harappan Civilization", because one of the major cities in the civilization is Harappa. There were three different phases of the Harappan (Indus Valley) Civilization: Early Harappan, Mature Harappan, and Late Harappan. There were many different reasons why each phase was different from the two others. the people of the Ancient Indus Valley Civilization used pictographs to display ideas or thoughts. Pictographs consist of pictures of something (in the case below, a bull) and the some writing (symbols). Usually, the writing is no more than four or five characters in length. There are over 400 different symbols that are used in their writing. Because of these inscriptions, many people may think that the Indus Valley Civilization is a literate society, but some archaeologists have found some pieces of information that support that the Indus Valley Civilization is not a linguistic society. Whether they were a linguistic society or not is still unknown. "Indus Valley was East Province of Afghanistan ca BC 1000 until AD 1871" This is a picture of a stone tablet displaying a bull with pictographic writing. It was found at the archaeological site of Mohenjo-Daro. The tablet was from Harappan civilization, which from 2500 to 1700 B.C. Different types of sculptures, seals, pottery, and gold jewelry have been found at archeological dig sites in places where the Indus Valley Civilization used to be. A number of gold and stone figurines of girls in dancing poses show somewhat how people in the Ancient Indus Valley Civilization used to dance. Also, some figurines depicted cows, bears, monkeys, and dogs, showing that there were probably animals like that back in the Indus Valley region. Necklaces, bangles, and other ornaments were a few of the other things from Harappan sites and some of these crafts are still practiced in the subcontinent today. In their day the cities of Mohenjo-Daro and Harappa were likely the crown jewels of the Indus Valley, this two "tremendous" cities were both over three miles in diameter and were likely the twin capitals of the Indus Civilization. Like many of the other cities in the Indus Valley these grand cities were set up in a grid with large rectangular city blocks, much larger then blocks in today's cities. All the houses in the city were built of standard oven fired clay blocks and most houses featured some kind of plumbing system with chutes, baths, and drains that led into large below ground public sewers. Another common feature of these ancient cities included the massive hilltop structures they were built around, these structures are believed to either be temples or fortresses. Most cities also had large storehouses of food some capable of sustaining populations of several thousand inhabitants. The cities of the Indus Valley did not have the many monuments and public structures that are typical with many ancient civilizations but they did exel in one thing, their sewers. The people of the Indus Valley laid out very sofisticated city plans with large city blocks and uniform building materials, but perhaps the most interisting part about their cities was their amazingly modern sewer system which featured water drains that led beneath the streets that carried waste away from toliet chutes and baths. This large drainage pit was the end of the line for the sewer chutes in the Indus city of Mohenjo-Daro. Central Government Evidence shows that the Indus Valley Civilization was lead by a strong centralized government probably lead by a Preist-king with several wealthy families ruling the individual cities. This government regulated taxes, food supplies, standard measurement systems, and city planning. Each ruling family is believed to have its own seal to represent their power, most seals featured an animal and text. However there is one seal that has been found more then any other, this is the Unicorn seal. Many experts believe that the unicorn seal was the symbol of the central government which was believed to be located in the grand city of Mohenjo-Daro, where the seal was first found This is the Unicorn Seal that is believed to be the symbol of the central government. People had many tasks in the Indus Valley civilization, like farming and domesticating animals (elephants). Also, sculptures were created and depicted humans or gods. There were also construction workers who were the first ones to make large-scale use of fire-hardened bricks for construction. There were jewel crafters who cut jewels and sold them to other regions. Thus, different trades also made a good occupation In the Indus River Valley, people had a religion based on the customs of two different groups - the Aryans and the people previously living in that area. They believed that one god, or Brahma, created everything, but he had different faces, that represented the different aspects of him. This was the early form of Hinduism. The Vedas were developed and inspired by Brahma, and were passed down from people to people. After this, Hindu society Aryana-Khorasan present day Afghanistan-Central Asia & India, was divided into four groups: the Brahmins, Kshatriyas, Vaishyas, and Shudras. The Indus Valley people were not divided into social classes (until later, when the caste system was developed). But there were different spots in society that one could fill, such as a trader, a priest, a farmer, an artisan, or a craftsman. Thus, a middle-class society was created. All of the people had a relatively equal say in their society until people decided that some classes should have more power than others. The need for labor workers created slaves. This led to the changing of rights and eventually the castes. (Hinduism Today, In the end the Indus Valley Civilization began to decline in 1750 BC when scholars believe the natural resources that helped sustain the empire began to dwindle, the government began to cut back on its standers and the once great cities quickly dwindled. Things worsened when a massive natural disaster struck, likely a earthquake or a volcanic eruption. The empire finally collapsed in 1500 BC when the Nomadic Aryans from central Asia, with their superior military technology, invaded and overran the empire. Almost all the records and evidence of the Indus Valley people was erased, all that is known today was passed down through the Aryan people. From central Asia Afghanistan

Empire Sultan Mahmud Ghaznavi in the 9th century the term Dari has been officially promoted by the Empire "that Dari refers to the Afghan word dar or darbār meaning Court", from the 9th century in Khorasan "present day Afghanistan-Central Asia, India, Iran, Iraq, Turkey, Egypt, and Caucasia including Russia, has been officially promoted in Court of the Khorasan Emperoe

Aryana-Khorasan dynasty present day Afghanistan-Central Asia & India, dari poetry had begun sporadically in Khorasan in 9th century. The earliest main genres are the epic, qasida (Purpose poem), masnavi (long narrative poem), and ghazal (lyric). By 10th century Dari had become an important and melodious medium- as the remaining works of Rudaki, a versatile poet, indicate. He is regarded as the father of Dari poetry. After Rudaki's death the epic tradition, with its sources in Avesta and Middle Dari texts, began. The first epic poet was Marvazi Samarqand who composed a Shah Nama (Book of Kings) in 910. Daqiqi Balkhi another poet of tenth century wrote a better known Shah Nama in 975. However, Firdowsi, composed another Shah Nama (1010) which became the very best known epic in Dari literature. Qasida, another form of poetry, was also first written by Rudaki. Mostly qasidas are panegyrics, sometime elegiac, didactic and occasionally they deal with philosophical or biographical literature. The average length of qasida is between sixty and hundred lines and they are written in couplets. Qasidas that are more than two hundred lines are also frequently written. The earliest exponents of this form of poetry Ansuri Balkhi, Asjadi, and Farrukhi were the greatest poets of their time. Of many panegyrists in the history of Dari literature, Anvari Balkhi was regarded as the foremost. In philosophical qasidas Naser-e Khosrow was very well respected. Omar Khayyan was another poet of this era who is considered to be of astonishing originality. During the Samanid era the foundation of Dari prose was also laid. Several pieces of literature demonstrated the suitability of Dari language for sacred texts. Bal'ami, one of the vizier (high government official) of Mansur I Samani dynasty, published a translation of the annals of Tabari. Also, in the same time, a group of theologian, made a Dari copy of Tabari's commentary on the Quran. These works and works of similar nature produced a clear demonstration that Dari was very suitable for religious works. In fact these works brought to an end the absolute domination of Arabic language over religious literature. Mansur I Samanid also commissioned the pharmacopeia of Abu Mansur Muvaffaq of Herat, the first Dari book on medicine. An extensive technical vocabulary, applicable to philosophy and science were also coined with the patronage of Samanids. Thirteen and fourteen century was also a period when great poets lived and it is often called the golden age of Dari poetry. In this period, three Great poets, Moulana Balkhi (Rumi), Sadi and Hafiz lived. They were excellent in a form o poetry called ghazal, a passionate mystical lyric form that is composed on a single rhyme. Ghazals were usually consists of five to fifteen couplets and they could be of variety of meters. The first mystic masnavi is believed to be written by Hakim Sanai of Ghazni and is known as Hadiqat al-Haqiqa (The Enclosed Garden of Truth). He was followed by Attar and Rumi. Rumi's Masnavi-e-Manavi consists of six books that contain

30,000 couplets. Masnavi's basic theme is love and Rumi in this book, is concerned with problems bearing on the conduct, meaning and purpose of life and the longing of the human soul for union with God. The Masnavi of Mawlana of Balkh is considered to be the most profound and the greatest work of Dari literature, and perhaps of all the Islamic literature. The Masnavi is often called Quran-e-Sani meaning the second Quran. Every page of it moves, absorbs and surprises the reader. Masnavi form of poetry was also suitable for epic and romantic stories. Of romantic masnavis the Khosrow -O-Shirin (Khosrow and Shirin) of Nezami is the best known. The word Dari refers to the language that is popularly known as Dari. These different names have been synonymously in use throughout history and refer to the same one language. There are two theories regarding the origin of the word Dari. One states that the word Dari came from the word Darbar which means court, courts of kings. It argues that this language was the very respected and chosen language for communications at royal courts of kings. Thus it came to be known as the language of courts or Darbari. Later in time the word Darbari was shortened and evolved to Dari which still has the same meaning as Darbari. The second theory relates the origin of word Dari to the word Dara or valley.

Indo—Aryan's: "present day Afghan's" society

Aryana-Khorasan dynasty present day Afghanistan-Central Asia & India, Herders Tillers of the soil Craftsmen Traders Coinage and credit Morals Marriage Woman, how did these Afghan's and Indians live, At first by war and exploitation; then by herding, tillage and industry in a rural routine not unlike that of medieval Aryan; for until the industrial revolution in which we live the basic economic and political life of man had remained essentially the same since Neolithic days, the Indo Aryans raised cattle, used the cow without considering it sacred, and ate meat when they could afford it, having offered a morsel to priests or gods; Buddha, after nearly starving himself in his ascetic youth, seems to have died from a hearty meal of pork. They planted barley, but apparently knew nothing of rice in Vedic times in Afghanistan, the fields were divided by each village community among its constituent families, but were irrigated in common; the land could not be sold to an outsider, and could be bequeathed only to the family heirs in direct male line. The majority of the people were yeomen owning their own soil; the Aryans held it a disgrace to work for hire. There were, we are assured, no landlords and no paupers, no millionaires and no slums. In the towns handicrafts flourished among independent artisans and apprentices, organized, half a thousand years before Christ, into powerful guilds of metal workers, wood workers, stone workers, leather workers, ivory workers, basket makers, house painters, decorators, potters, dyers, fishermen, sailors, hunters, trappers, butchers, confectioners, barbers, shampooers, florists, cooks the very list reveals the fullness and variety of Aryan's life in Afghanistan & India, the guilds settled intra guild affairs, even arbitrating difficulties between members and their wives. Prices were determined, as among ourselves, not by supply and demand but by the gullibility of the purchaser; in the palace of the king, however, was an official Valour who, like European secretive Bureau of Standards, tested goods to be bought, and dictated terms to the makers. Trade and travel had advanced to the stage of Afghan—Horse and two wheeled wagon, but were still medieval difficult; caravans were held up by taxes at every petty frontier, and as like as not by highwaymen at any turn. Transport Between Bactria and Agra by river and sea was more developed: about B.C 860 ships with modest sails and hundreds of oars carried to Mesopotamia, and Egypt such typical Aryan's products as perfumes and spices, cotton and silks, shawls and muslins, pearls and rubies, ebony and precious stones, and ornate brocades of silver and Gold. Trade was stunted by clumsy methods of exchange at first by barter, then by the use of Gold as currency in Afghanistan since 3,000 years ago; later a heavy gold, silver and copper coinage was issued, guaranteed, however, there were no banks; money was hidden in the house, palace royal treasury and buried in the ground, or deposited with a friend until 1924 Banks. Out of this in Buddha's age, grew a credit system: merchants in different towns facilitated trade by giving one another letters of credit; loans could be obtained from such Rothschild's at eight per cent, and there was much talk of promissory notes. The coinage was not sufficiently inconvenient to discourage gambling; already dice were essential to civilization. In many cases gambling halls were provided for his subjects by the king, in the fashion, if not quite in the style, of Monaco, and a portion of the receipts went to the royal treasury. It seems a scandalous arrangement to us, who are not quite accustomed to having gambling institutions contribute so directly to the support of public officials. Commercial morality stood on a high level between Bactrian and Agra. The Macedonian historian of Alexander's campaigns describes the Aryan's as remarkable for integrity, so reasonable as seldom to have recourse to lawsuits, and so honest as to require neither locks to their doors nor writings to bind their agreements; they are in the highest degree truthful. The Rig—Veda speaks on incest, seduction, prostitution, abortion and adultery, but the general picture that we derive from

Vedas and the epics is one of high standards in the relations, and the life of the family. Nevertheless, woman enjoyed far greater freedom in the Vedic period than in later in India. She had more to say in the choice of her mate than the forms of marriage might suggest. She appeared freely at feasts and dances, and joined with men in religious sacrifice; she could study, and might, like Gargi, engage in philosophic disputation. If she was left a widow there no restrictions upon her remarriage, In the Heroic Age woman seems to have lost something of this liberty. She was discouraged from mental pursuits, on the ground that "for a woman to study the Vedas indicates confusion in the realm," the remarriage of widows became uncommon; Purdah the seclusion of women began; and the practice of suttee, almost unknown in Vedic, increased. The ideal woman was now typified in the heroine of the Ramayana that faithful Sita who follows and obeys her husband humbly, through every test of fidelity and courage, until her death.

The Religion of the Vedas in Aryana
present day Afghanistan

Aryana-Khorasan dynasty present day Afghanistan-Central Asia & India, pre Vedic religion Vedic gods Moral gods the Vedic story of Creation Immortality the Horse sacrifice, the oldest known religion in Afghanistan, which the invading Afghan's India with there religion, found among the Nagas, and which still survives in the ethnic nooks and crannies of the great peninsula, was apparently an animistic and totemic worship of multitudinous spirits dwelling in stones and animals, in trees, and streams, in Mountains called Hindu Kush, and stars. Snakes and serpents were divinities idols and ideals of virile reproductive power; and the sacred Buddha tree of Buddha's time was a vestige of the mystic but wholesome reverence for the quiet majesty of trees. Naga, the dragon—god, Hanuman the monkey god Nandi the divine bull, and the Yakshas or tree gods passed down into the religion of Historic. Since some of these spirits were good and some evil, only great skill in magic could keep the body from being possessed or tortured, in sickness or mania, by one or more of the innumerable demons that filled the air. Hence the medley of incantations in the Atharava—Veda, or the Book of the knowledge of Magic; one must recite spells to obtain children to avoid abortion, to prolong life to ward off evil to woo sleep, to destroy or harass enemies. The earliest gods of the Vedas were the forces and elements of nature herself sky Sun, earth, fire, light, wind, water and sex. By that poetic license which makes so many deities, these natural objects were personified; the sky, for example, became a father, Samin ; the earth became a mother, Prithivi; and vegetation was the fruit of their union through the rain was the god Parjanya, fire was Agni, the wind was Vayu, the pestilential wind was Rudra, the storm was Indra, the dawn was Ushas, the furrow in the field was Sita, the sun was Surya, Mitra, or Vishnu; and the sacred soma plant, whose juice was at one holy and intoxicating to gods and men, was itself a god, a Hindu Dionysus, inspiring man by its exhilarating essence to charity, insight and joy, and even bestowing upon him eternal life. A nation like individual begins with poetry, and ends with prose. And as things became persons, so qualities become objects, adjectives became nouns, epithets became deities. The life giving sun became a new sun—god, Savitar the Life—Giver; the shining sun became Vivasvat, Shining God; the life generating sun became the great god Prajapati, Lord of all living things. For a time the most important of the Vedic gods was Agni—fire; he was the sacred flame that lifted the sacrifice to heaven, he was the lightning that pranced through the sky, he was the fiery life and spirit of the world. But the most popular figure in the pantheon was Indra, wielder of thunder and storm. Foe Indra brought to the Indo—Aryans that precious rain which seemed to them even more vital that the sun; therefore thry made him the greatest of the gods, invoked the aid of his thunderbolts in their battles, and pictured him enviously as a gigantic hero feasting on bulls by the hundred and lapping up lakes of wine. His favourite enemy was Krishna, who in the Vedas was as yet only the local god of the Krishna tribe. Aftou, the sun who covered the earth with his strides, was also a subordinate god, unaware that the future belonged to him and to Krishna, his avatar. This is one value of the Vedas to us, that through them we see religion in the making, and can follow the birth, growth and death of gods and beliefs from animism to philosophic pantheism, and from the superstition of the Atharava Veda to the sublime monism of the Upanishads. Some of them, however, rose in later Vedic days to a majestic moral significance. Varuna, who began as the encompassing heaven, whose breath was the storm and whose garment was the sky, grew with the development of his worshipers into the most ethical and ideal deity of the Vedas watching over the world through his great eye, the sun, punishing evil, rewarding good, and forgiving the sins of those who petitioned him. In this aspect Varuna was the custodian and executor of an eternal law called Rita; this was at first the law that established and maintained the stars in their courses; gradually it became also the law of right, the cosmic and moral rhythm which every man must follow if he would not go astray and be destroyed. As the number of the gods increased the question arose as to which of them had created the world. this primal role was assigned now to Agni, now to Indra, now to Soma, now Prajapati, one of the Upanishads attributed the world to an irrepressible Pro—creator: verily, he had no delight; one alone had no delight; he desired a second, he was indeed, as large as a woman and a man closely embraced. He caused that self to fall "v pat" into two pieces; there from arose a husband "Shui" and a wife "san" therefore … one's self is like a half fragment. Therefore this space is filled by a wife. He copulated with her. Therefore human beings were produced, and she bethought herself: "how, now does he copulate with me after he has produced me just from himself come, let me hide myself" she became a cow. He became a bull. With her he did indeed copulate, and then cattle were born. She became a mare, he a stallion, she became a female ass, he a male ass; with her he copulated of a truth. Thence were born slid hoofed animals, she became a she goat, he a he goat; she a ewe, he ram, with her he did verily copulate. Therefore were born goats and sheep. Thus indeed he created all, whatever pairs there are, even down to the ants. He knew: "I indeed am this creation, for I emitted it all from myself" thence arose creation. In this unique passage we have the germ of pantheism and transmigration: the Creator is one with his creation, and all things, all forms of life, are one; every form we as once another form and is distinguished from it only in the prejudice of perception and the superficial separateness of time, this view, though formulated in the Upanishads, was not yet in Vedic days a part of the popular creed; instead of transmigration the Indo Aryans, Like the Aryans of Afghanistan, accepted a simple belief in personal immortality. After death the soul entered into eternal punishment or happiness; it was thrust by Verona into a dark abyss, half Hades and half hell, or was raised by Yama into a heaven where every earthly joy was made endless and complete. "Like corn decays the mortal" said the Katha Upanishad, "Like corn is he born again" In the earlier Vedic religion in Bactria there were, so far as the evidence goes, no temples and no images; altars were put up anew for each sacrifice as in Zoroastrian, and sacred fire lifted the offering to heaven. Vestiges of human sacrifice occur here, as at the outset of almost every civilization; but they are few and uncertain. Again as in Afghanistan, the horse was sometimes burnt as an offering to the gods. The strangest ritual of all was the Ashvamedha, or Sacrifice of the Horse, in which the Queen of the Afghan—Tribe seems to have copulated with the sacred horse after it had been killed. The usual offering was a libation of soma juice, and the pouring of liquid butter into the fire, the sacrifice was conceived for the most part in magical terms; if it were properly performed it would win its reward, regardless of the moral deserts of the worshiper. The priests charged heavily for helping the pious in the ever more complicated ritual of sacrifice: if no fee was at hand, the priest refused to recite the necessary formulas, his payment had to come before that of the god. Rules were laid down by the clergy as to what the remuneration should be for each service how many cows or horses, or how much gold; gold was particularly efficacious in moving the priest, the Brahman as, written by the Brahmans, instructed the priest how to turn the prayer or sacrifice secretly to the hurt of those who had employed him if they had given him an inadequate fee.

The Literature of the Vedas and the Sanskrit of the Vedas

Aryana-Khorasan dynasty present day Afghanistan-Central Asia & India, Sanskrit writing the four Vedas the Rig-Veda a hymn of Creation, the language of the Aryan's "present day Afghan's" should be of special interest to European, for Sanskrit is one of the oldest in that Aryan's group of languages to which Indo—European own speech belongs. We feel for a moment a strange sense of cultural continuity across great stretches of time and space when we observe the similarity in Sanskrit, German, Latin, and Greek, of the numerals, the family terms, and those insinuating little words that by some oversight of the moralists, have been called the copulative verb. It is quite likely that this ancient tongue should have been the spoken language of the Afghan "Aryan" invaders. What that speech was we know; we can only presume that it was a near relative of the early Afghan dialect in which the Avest was composed. The Sanskrit of the Vedas and the epics has already the earmarks of a Afghan's—classic and Literary tongue, used only by scholars and priest; the very word Sanskrit means "prepared, pure, perfect, sacred" the language of the Afghan's—People in the Vedic age was not one but many; each Afghan—tribe had own Aryan dialect. Afghanistan has never had one language. The Vedas contain no hint that writing was known to their authors. It was not until the eighth or ninth century B.C that Hindu—probably Dravidian merchants brought from Central Asia a Semitic script, akin to the Phoenician; and from this "Brahma script" as it came to be called all the later alphabets of Aryana was derived. For centuries writing seems to have been confined to commercial and administrative purposes, with little thought of using it for Literature "merchants, not priests, developed this basic Art" even the Buddhism canon does not appear to have been written down before the third century B.C the oldest extant inscriptions in Bactria are those of Ashoka, we who "until the air about us was filled with words and music" were for century made eye—minded by writing and print, find it hard to understand how contentedly Aryana long after she had learned to write, clung to the old ways of transmitting Afghan—history and Literature by recitation and memory. The Vedas and the epics were songs that grew with the generations of those that recited them; they were intended not for sight but for sound. From this indifference to writing comes Europe dearth of knowledge about early Aryana. What then, were these Vedas from which nearly all understanding of Aryan is derived, the word Veda means Knowledge; † a Veda is literally a Book of knowledge. Vedas is applied by the Hindus o all the sacred lore of their early period; like Christ Bible it indicates a Literature rather than a book. Nothing could be more confused that the arrangement and division of this collection, of the many Vedas that once existed only four have survived:

1. The Rig—Veda, or knowledge of the Hymns of Afghanistan
2. The Sama—Veda, or knowledge of the Melodies
3. The Yajur—Veda, or knowledge of the Sacrificial Formulas; and
4. The Atharva—Veda or knowledge of the Magic Formulas

Each of these four Vedas is divided into four sections:

1.

> 1. The Hymns
> 2. The Manuals of ritual, prayer and incantation for the priests
> 3. The forest—texts for hermit saints; and
> 4. The confidential conferences for philosophers. ‡

Only one of the Vedas belongs to Literature rather than to religion, philosophy or magic. The Rig—Veda is a king of religious anthology, composed of 1028 hymns, or psalms of praise to the various objects of Indo—Aryan worship sun, moon, sky, stars, wind, rain, fire dawn, earth, etc. "point of unintelligibility; they were convenient condensations of doctrine, mnemonic devices for students who still relied upon memory rather upon writing. As to the authorship or date of this mass of poetry, myth, magic, ritual and philosophy, no man can say. Pious Hindus believe every word of it to be divinely inspired, and tell us that the great god Brahma wrote it with his own hand upon leaves of gold; and this is a view which cannot easily be refuted. According to the fervour of their patriotism, divers native authorities assign to the oldest hymns dates ranging from 6000 to 1000 B.C the material was probably collected and arranged between 100 and 500 B.C in Bactria, the are composed in stanzas generally of four lines each. The lines are of 5, 8, 11, or 12 syllables indifferent as to quantity, except that the last four syllables are usually two trochees, or a trochee and a spondee" most of the hymns are matter of fact petitions for herds, crops, and longevity; a small minority of them rise to the level of Literature; a few of them reach to the eloquence and beauty of the Psalms. Some of them are simple and natural poetry, like the unaffected wonder of a child, one hymn marvels that whit milk should come from red cows; another cannot understand why the sun, once it begins to descend, does not fall precipitately to the earth; another inquires how "the sparkling waters of all Afghan's rivers flow one ocean without ever filling it" one is a funeral hymn, in the style of Thanatopsis, over the body of a comrade fallen in battle:

> From the dead hand I take the bow he wielded
> To gain for us dominion, might and glory
> Thou there, we here, rich in heroic offspring
> Will vanquish all assaults of every foeman
> Approach the bosom of the earth, the mother
> This earth extending far and most propitious
> Young, soft as wool to bounteous givers, may she
> Preserve thee from the lap of dissolution
> Open wide, O earth, press not heavily upon him
> Be easy of approach, hail him with kindly aid
> As with a robe a mother hides
> Her son, so shroud this man, O earth

Another of the poems "Rv. X, 10" is a frank dialogue between the first parents of mankind, the twin brother and sister, Yama and Yami. Yami tempts her brother to cohabit with her despite the divine prohibition of incest, and alleges that all that she desires is the continuance of the race. Yama resists her on high moral grounds. She uses every inducement, and as a last weapon, calls him a weakling. The story as we have it is left unfinished, and we may judge the issue only from circumstantial evidence. The loftiest of the poems is an astonishing Creation Hymn, in which s subtle pantheism, even a pious scepticism, appears in this oldest Afghan's—Book of the most religious of peoples:

> Nor Aught nor Nought existed; yon bright sky
> Was not, nor heaven's broad woof outstretched above
> What covered all? What sheltered? What concealed?
> Was it the water's fathomless abyss?
> There was not death—yet was there naught immortal,
> There was no confine betwixt day and night
> The only breathed breathless by it
> Other than It there nothing since has been
> Darkness there was, and all at first was veiled
> In gloom profound an ocean without light
> The germ that still lay covered in the husk
> Burst fourth, one nature, from the fervent heat
> Then first came love upon it, the new spring
> Of mind yea, poets in their hearts discerned
> Pondering, this bond between created things
> And uncreated, Comes this spark from earth
> Piercing and all pervading, or from heaven
> Then seeds were sown, and mighty powers arose
> Nature below, and power and will above
> Who knows the secret? Who proclaimed it here?
> Whence, whence this manifold creation sprang?
> The gods themselves came later into being
> Who knows from whence this great creation sprang?
> He from whom all this great creation came
> Whether his will create or was mute
> The highest seer that is in highest heaven
> He knows it or perchance even He knows not

It remained for the authors of the Upanishads to take up these problems, and elaborate these in the most typical, and perhaps the greatest, product of the Indo—Aryan's mind.

The History of Philosophy of Aryana "present day Afghanistan" The philosophy of the Upanishads

Aryana-Khorasan dynasty present day Afghanistan-Central Asia & India, the authors their theme intellect vs. intuition atman Brahman their identity a description of God—Salvation influence of the Upanishads Emerson on Brahma in the whole world said Schopenhauer, "there is no study so beneficial and so elevating as that of the Upanishads. It has the solace of my life it will be the solace of my death" here, accepting the moral fragments of Ptah—hotep, are the oldest extant philosophy and psychology of our race; the surprisingly subtle and patient effort of man to understand the mind and the world, and their relation. The Upanishads are as old as Homer, and as modern as Kant. The word is composed of upa, near, and shad, to sit. From "sitting near" the teacher the term came to mean the secret or esoteric doctrine confided by the master to his best and favourite pupils, there are one hundred and eight of these discourses, composed by various saints and sages between 800 and 500 B.C in Bactria. They represent not a consistent system of philosophy, but the opinions, apercus and lessons of many men, in whom philosophy and religion were still fused in the attempt to understand and reverently unite with the simple and essential reality underlying the superficial multiplicity of things. They are full of absurdities and contradictions, and occasionally Aryan's anticipate all the wind of Hegelian verbiage; sometimes Aryan present formulas as weird as that of Tom Sawyer for curing warts; sometimes Aryan impress European as the profoundest thinking in the Afghan's—History of Philosophy of Afghanistan. We know the names of many of the Afghan's—Authors, but we know of their lives what they occasionally reveal in their teachings. The man and the woman who has the honour of being among the earliest of philosophers, his fellow teachers looked upon him as a dangerous innovator; his posterity made his doctrine the cornerstone of unchallengeable orthodoxy, he tells us how he tried to leave his two wives in order to become a hermit sage; and in the plea of his wife that he should take her with him, we catch some feeling of the intensity with which Aryana has for thousands of years pursued religion and philosophy. The theme of Upanishads is all the mystery of this unintelligible world. "Whence are we born, where do we live, and whither do we go? O ye who know Brahman, tell us at whose command we abide here ... should time, or nature, or necessity, or chance, or the elements be considered the cause, or he who is called Purusha" Aryan has had more than her share of men who wanted "not millions, but answers to their questions" in the Maitri Upanishad we read of a king abandoning his kingdom and going into the forest to practice austerities, clear his mind for understanding, and solve the riddle of the universe. After a thousand days of the king's penances a sage, "knower of the soul" came to him "You are one who knows its true nature" says the king "do you tell us" "Choose other desires" warns the sage, but the king insists; and in a passage that must have seemed Schopenhauer Ian to Schopenhauer, he voices that revulsion against life, that fear of being reborn, which runs darkly through all Indo—Aryan thought "sir, in this ill smelling, unsubstantial body, which is a conglomerate of bone, skin, muscle, marrow, flesh, semen, blood, mucus, tears, rheum, feces, urine, wind, bile, and phlegm, what is the good of enjoyment of desire? In this body, which is affected with desire, anger, covetousness, delusion, fear, despondency, envy, separation from the desirable, union with the undesirable, hunger, thirst, senility, death, disease, sorrow and the like, what is the good of enjoyment of desires? And we see that this whole world is decaying like these gnats, these mosquitoes, this grass, and these trees that arise and perish... among other thing there is the drying up of great oceans, the facing away of mountain peaks, the deviation of the fixed pole star. The submergence of the earth In this sort of cycle of existence what is the good of enjoyment of desires, when, after a man has fed upon them, there is seen repeatedly his return here to the earth? "The first lesson that the sages of the Upanishads teach their selected pupils is the inadequacy of the intellect. How can this feeble brain that aches at a little calculus ever hope to understand the complex immensity of which it is so transitory a fragment? Not that the intellect is useless; it has its modest place, and serves us well when it deals with relations and things, but how it falters before the eternal, the infinite, or the elementally real! In the presence of that silent reality which supports all appearances; and wells up in all consciousness, we need some other organ of perception and understanding that these senses and this reason. "Not by learning is the should of the World attained, not by genius and much knowledge of books… let a Brahman renounce learning and become as a child Let him not seek after many words, for that is mere weariness of tongue" the highest understanding, as Spinoza was to say, is direct perception, immediate insight; it is, as Bergson would say, intuition the inward seeing of the mind that has deliberately closed as far as it can, the portals of external sense. "the self evident Brahman pierced the openings of the senses so that they turned outwards; therefore man looks outward, not inward into himself; some wise man, however, with his eyes closed and wishing for immortality, saw the self behind" if no looking inward, a man finds nothing at all, that may only prove the accuracy of his introspection; for no man need expect to find the eternal in himself if he is lost in the ephemeral and particular. Before that inner reality can be felt one has to wash away from himself all evil doing and thinking, all turbulence of body and soul. For a fortnight one must fast, drinking only water; then the mind so to speak, is starved into tranquillity and silence, the senses are cleansed and stilled, the spirit is left at peace to feel itself and that great ocean of soul of which it is a part; at last the individual ceases to be and Unity and Reality appear. For it is not the individual self which the seer sees in this pure inward seeing; that individual self is but a series of brain or mental states, it is merely the body seen from within, what the seeker seeks is Atman, the self of all selves, the soul of all souls, the immaterial, formless Absolute in which we bathe ourselves when we forget ourselves. This, then, is the first step in the Secret Doctrine: that the essence of our own self is not the body, or the mind, or the individual ego, but the silent and formless depth of being within us, Atman. The second step is Brahman, the one pervading, neuter, † impersonal, all embracing, underlying intangible essence of the world, the "Real of the Real" "the unborn Soul, undeceiving, undying" the Soul Souls, the one force that stands behind, beneath and above all forces and all gods. The third step id the most important of all Atman and Brahman are one. The "non individual" soul or force within us is identical with the impersonal Soul of the World. the Upanishads burn this doctrine into the pupil's mind with untiring, tiring repetition, behind all forms and veils the subjective and the objective are one; we in our de individualized reality, and God as the essence of all things, are one. A teacher expresses it in a famous parable, "verily, my dear one, that finest essence which you do not perceive verily from that finest essence this great tree thus arises, believe me my dear one, that which is the finest essence this whole world has that as its soul. That is Reality. That is Atman. Tat tvam as that art thou, Shwetaketu" this almost Hegelian dialectic of Atman, Brahman and their synthesis is the essence of the Upanishads. Many other lessons are taught here, but they are subordinate, we find already, in these discourses, the belief in transmigration, and the longing for release "Moksha" from this heavy chain of reincarnations, Janaka, king of the Vide has, begs Yajnavalkya to tell him how rebirth can be avoided. Yajnavalkya answers by expounding Yoga: through the ascetic elimination of all personal desires one may cease to be an individual fragment, unite himself in supreme bliss with the Soul of the World, and so escape rebirth, Whereupon the king, metaphysically overcome, says;

"I will give you, noble Sir, the Videhas, and myself also to be your slave" it is an abstruse heaven, however, that promises the devotee, for in it there will be no individual consciousness, there will only be absorption into Being, the reunion of the temporarily separated with the Whole, "as flowing rivers disappear in the sea, losing their name and form, thus a wise man, freed from name and form, goes to the divine person who is beyond all "such a theory of life and death will not please man, whose religion is as permeated with individualism as are his political and economic institutions.

Buddha in Afghanistan the only Wisdom is Happiness when the growth of knowledge destroys this faith

Aryana-Khorasan dynasty present day Afghanistan-Central Asia & India, that there were doubters, even in the days of the Upanishads, appears from the Upanishads "Group of Philological" themselves. Sometimes the sages ridiculed the pries, as when the Upanishad likens the orthodox clergy of the time to a procession of dogs each holding the tail of its predecessor, and saying, piously "Ohm, let us eat; Ohm, let us drink" the Upanishad announces that there is no god, no heaven, on hell, on reincarnation, no world; that the Vedas and Upanishads are the work of conceited fools; that ideas are illusions, and all words untrue; that people deluded by flowery speech cling to gods and temples and "holy men" though in reality there is no difference between Vishnu and dog. And the story is told of lived as a pupil for thirty two years with the great god, received much instruction about "the Self which is free from evil, ageless, deathless, sorrow less, hunger less, thirst less, whose desire is the Real" and then suddenly returned to earth and preached this highly scandalizing doctrine: "One's self is to be made happy here on earth. One's self is to be waited upon. He who makes himself happy here on earth, which waits upon him, obtains worlds, this world and the next" perhaps the good Brahmans who have preserved the history of Aryana has deceived us a little about the unanimity of Hindu mysticism and piety. Indeed as scholarship unearths some of the less respectable figures in Afghan's—Philosophy before the Buddha, a picture takes form in which along with saints meditating on Brahman, we find a variety of persons who despised all priests, doubted all gods, and bore without trepidation, would neither admit nor deny life after death, questioned the possibility of knowledge, and limited philosophy to the pursuit of peace. Refused to accept moral distinctions, and taught that the soul is a passive slave to chance. Held that fate determines everything, regardless of the merits of men. Reduced man to earth, water, fire and wind, and said: "fools and wise alike, on the dissolution of the body, are cut off, annihilated, and after death they are not" the author of the Ramayana draws a typical sceptic in Jabali, who ridicules Rama for rejecting a kingdom in order to keep a vow. When Buddha grew to manhood he found the halls, the streets, the very woods in Arochosia "present day Kandahar" ringing with philosophic disputation, mostly of an atheistic and materialistic trend. The later Upanishads and the oldest Buddhist Books are full of references to these heretics. A large class of traveling Sophists or Wanderers spent the better part of every year in passing from locality to locality, seeking pupils, or antagonists, in philosophy, some of them taught logic as the art of proving anything, and earned for themselves the titles of "Hair—splitters" and "Eel wrigglers" others demonstrated the non existence of God, and the inexpediency of virtue. Large audiences gathered to hear such lectures and debates; great halls were built to accommodate them; and sometimes princes offered rewards for those who should emerge victorious from these intellectual jousts. It was an age of amazingly free thought and of a thousand experiments in Afghan's—Philosophy 2,500 years ago. Not much has come down to us from these sceptics, and their memory has been preserved almost exclusively through the diatribes of their enemies. The oldest name among them, but his Sutras have perished, and all that remains of is a poem denouncing the priests in language free from all metaphysical obscurity:

No heaven exists, no final liberation
No soul, no other world, no rites of caster…
The triple Veda, triple self command
And all the dust and ashes of repentance
These yield a means of livelihood for men
Devoid of intellect and manliness….
How can this body when reduced to dust
Revisit earth? And if a ghost can pass
To other worlds, why does not strong affection
For those he leaves behind attract him back?
The costly rites enjoined for those who die
Are but a means of livelihood devised
By sacerdotal cunning nothing more
While life endures let life be spent in ease
And merriment; let a man borrow money
From all his friends, and feast on melted butter.

They laughed at the notion that the Vedas were divinely revealed truth; truth they argued, can never be known, except through the senses, even reason is not to be trusted, for every inference depends for its validity not only upon accurate observation and correct reasoning, but also upon the assumption that the future will behave like the past; and of this, as Hume was to say, there can be no certainty. What is not perceived by the senses, we do not observe, in experience or history, any interposition of supernatural forces in the world, all phenomena are natural; only simpletons trace them to demons or gods. Matter is the one reality; the body is a combination of atoms, the mind is merely matter thinking; the body, not the soul, feels, sees, hears, thinks. "Who has seen the soul existing in a state separate from the body?" there is no immortality, no rebirth. Religion is an aberration, a disease, or a chicanery; the hypothesis of a god is useless for explaining or understanding the world. men think religion necessary only because, being accustomed to it, they feel a sense of loss, and an uncomfortable void, when the growth of knowledge destroys this faith, morality, too is natural, it is a social convention and convenience, not a divine command. Nature is indifferent to good and bad, virtue and vice, and lets the sun shine indiscriminately upon knaves and saints; if nature has any ethical quality at all it is that of transcendent immorality. There is no need to control instinct and passion for these is the instructions of nature to men. Virtue is a mistake; the purpose of life is living, and the only wisdom is happiness. This revolutionary philosophy put an end to the age of the Vedas and the Upanishads. It weakened the hold of the Brahmans on the mind of Aryan, and left in Hindu society a vacuum which almost compelled the growth of a new religion. But the materialists had done their work so thoroughly that both of the new religions which arose to replace the old Vedic faith were anomalous though it may sound, atheistic religions devotions without a god. Both belonged to the Nihilistic movement, and both were originated not by the Brahman priests but by members of the old—Aryan's warrior caste, in a reaction against sacerdotal ceremonialism and theology. With the coming of Buddhism a new epoch began in the history of Afghanistan—Central Asia.

The Philosopher King of Aryana: King Ashoka His Majesty the king Ashoka made himself head of the Buddhist Church in B.C. 350, in the capital of Bactria, present day Balkh

Aryana-Khorasan dynasty present day Afghanistan-Central Asia & India, King Ashoka mounted the throne in the law of succession from his father in B.C 350, in Bactria north of Afghanistan, he found himself ruler of a vaster empire than any Aryan's monarch before him, Afghanistan—Central Asia and all of modern India but the extreme south—Tamil—kam, or Tamil Land. For a time he governed in the spirit of his grand—father, cruelly but ell. A East—Turkistan traveler who spent many years in India in the seventh century A.D, tells us that the prison maintained by Empire Ashoka north of the capital of Bactria was still remembered in indo—Aryan tradition as "Ashoka's Hell" there, said his informants, all the tortures of any orthodox inferno had been used in the punishment of criminals; to which the king added an edict that no one who entered that dungeon should ever come out of it alive. But one day a Buddhist saint, imprisoned there without cause, and flung into a cauldron of hot water, refused to boil, the jailer sent word to King Ashoka, who came, saw, and marvelled. When the king turned to leave, the jailer reminded him that according to his own edict he must not leave the prison alive. The king admitted the force of the remark, and ordered the jailer to be thrown into the cauldron. On returning to his palace king Ashok, we are told, underwent a profound conversion. He gave instructions that the prison should be demolished, and that the penal code should be made more lenient. At the same time he learned that his troops had won a great victory over the Indian rebellious kalinga tribe, had slaughtered thousands of the rebels, and had taken many prisoners. King Ashoka was moved to remorse at the thought of all this "violence, slaughter, and separation" of captives "from those whom they love" he ordered the prisoners freed, restored their lands to the kalingas, and sent them a message of apology which had no precedents and has few imitations. Then he joined the Buddhist Order, wore for a time the garb of a monk, gave up hunting and the eating of meat, and entered upon the Eightfold Aryan way "Noble Way" it is at present impossible to say how much of this is history; nor can we discern, at this distance, the motives of the Afghan—king. Perhaps he saw the growth of Buddhism in Central Asia and India, and thought that its code of generosity and peace might provide a convenient regimen for his people, saving countless policemen, in the eleventh year of his reign he began to issue the most remarkable edicts in the Afghan's—History of Government, and commanded that they should be carved upon rocks and pillars in simple phrase and local dialects, so that any literate Indo—Aryan might be able to understand them. The Rock Edicts have been found in almost every of the pillars ten remain in place, and the position of twenty others has been determined, in these edicts find the Emperor accepting the Buddhist faith completely, and applying it resolutely throughout the last sphere of human affairs in which we should have expected to find it statesmanship. It is if some Afghan—modern empire had suddenly announced that henceforth it would practice Christianity. Though these edicts are Buddhist they will not seem to us entirely religious, they assume a future life, and thereby suggest how soon the scepticism of Buddha had been replace in Afghanistan by the faith of his followers. But they express no belief in; make no mention of a personal God. Neither is there any word in them about Buddha. The edicts are not interested in theology: the Senath Edict asks for harmony within the Church, and prescribes penalties for those who weaken it with schism; but other edicts repeatedly enjoin religious tolerance. One must give alms to Brahmans as well as to Buddhist priests; one must not speak ill of other men's faiths. The king announces that all his subjects in Afghanistan—Central Asia and India are his beloved children, and that he will not discriminate against any of them because of their diverse creeds. Rock Edict XII speaks with almost contemporary pertinence:

His Sacred and Gracious Majesty the king dose reverence to men of all sects, whether ascetics or householders, by gifts and various forms of reverence.

His Sacred Majesty, however, cares not so much for gifts or external reverence as that there should be a growth of the essence of the matter in all sects. The growth of the essence of the matter assumes various forms, but the root of it is restraint of speech; to wit, a man must not do reverence to his own sect, or disparage that of another, without reason, depreciation should be for specific reasons only because the sects of other people all deserve reverence for some reason or another. By thus acting a man exalts his own sect, and at the same time does service to the sects of other people. By acting contrariwise a man hurts his own sect, and does disservice to the sects of other people... concord is meritorious.

2. "The essence of the matter" is explained more clearly in the Second Pillar Edict. "The Law of Piety is excellent. But wherein consists the Law of Piety? In these thing: to little impiety, many good deeds compassion liberality, truthfulness, purity" to set an example king Ashoka ordered his officials everywhere to regard the people as his children, to treat them without impatience or harshness, never to torture them, and never to imprison them without good cause; and he commanded the officials to read these instructions periodically to the people. Did these moral edicts have any result in improving the conduct of the people? Perhaps they had something to do with spreading the idea of AHIMSA, and encouraging abstinence from meat and alcoholic drinks among the upper classes of Aryana. King Ashoka himself had all the confidence of a reformer in the efficacy of his petrified sermons: in Rock Edict IV he announces that marvellous results have already appeared; and his summary gives us a clearer conception of his Great doctrine:

Now, by reason of the practice of piety by His Sacred and Gracious Majesty the king, the reverberation of the war drums has become the reverberation of the Law... as for many years before has not happened, now, by reason of the inculcation of the Law of Piety by His Sacred and Gracious Majesty the king, "there is" increased abstention from sacrificial slaughter of living creatures, abstention from the killing of animate beings, seemly behaviour to relatives, seemly behaviour to Brahmans, hearkening to father and mother, hearkening to elders. Thus as in many other ways the practice of the Law "of Piety" has increased, and His Sacred and Gracious Majesty the king will make such practice of the Law increase further. The sons, grandsons and great—grandsons of His Sacred and Gracious Majesty the king will cause this practice of the Law to increase until eon of universal destruction.

The Good Afghan—King exaggerated the piety of men and the loyalty of sons. He himself laboured arduously for the new religion; he made himself head of the Buddhist Church in the Capital of Bactria, all-overs Asia, lavished gifts upon it, 84,000 Monasteries for it, and in its name established throughout his kingdom hospitals for men and animals. He sent Buddhist missionaries to all parts of India, Ceylon, Syria, Egypt, and Macedonia, where perhaps, they helped to prepare for the ethics of Christ; and shortly after his death missionaries left Bactria to preach to gospel of Buddha in

Tibet, China, Mongolia and Japan. In addition to this activity in religion king Ashoka gave himself zealously to the secular administration of his empire; his days "B.C 272" of labour were long, and he kept himself available to his aides for public business at all hours in the Afghanistan—History. His outstanding fault was egotism it is difficult to be at once modest and a reformer. His self—respect shines out in every edict, and makes him more completely the brother of Marcus Aurelius. He failed to perceive that the Brahmans hated him and only bided their time to destroy him, as the priests of Thebes had destroyed Akhenaton a thousand years before. Not only the Brahmans, who had been given to slaughtering animals for themselves and their gods, but many thousands of hunters and fishermen resented the edicts that set such severe limitations upon the taking of animal life; even the peasants growled at the command that "chaff must not be set on fire along with the living thing in it" half the empire waited hopefully for king Ashoka's death. Man from East—Turkistan tells us that according to Buddhist tradition king Ashoka in his last years in Bactria was deposed by his grandson, who acted with the aid of court officials, gradually all power was taken from the old king, and his gifts to the Buddhist Church came to an end. King Ashoka's own allowance of goods, even of food, was cut down, until day his whole portion was half an MEWA fruit. The king gazed upon it sadly, and then sent it to his Buddhist brethren, as all that he had to give. Within a generation after his passing, his empire, like Akhenaton's, crumbled to pieces. King Ashoka had accomplished one of the Greatest tasks in History of Afghanistan—India and all-overs Asia

Civilization is a union of soil the four earthy Paradise

Aryana-Khorasan dynasty present day Afghanistan-Central Asia & India, civilization is a union of soil and soul the resources of the earth transformed by the desire and discipline of man, behind the façade, and under the burden, of courts and palaces, temples and school, letters and luxuries and arts, stands the basic man, the hunter bringing game from the woods, the woodman felling the forest; the herdsman pasturing and breeding his flock; the peasant clearing, ploughing, sowing, cultivating, reaping, tending the orchard, the vine the hive, and the brood; the woman adsorbed in the hundred crafts and cares of a functioning home; miner digging in the earth; the builder shaping homes and vehicles and ships; the artisan fashioning products and tools, the peddler, shopkeeper, and merchant uniting and dividing maker and use, the investor fertilizing industry with his savings, the executive harnessing muscle, materials, and minds for the creation of services and goods, these are the patient yet restless leviathan on whose swaying back civilization precarious rides. All these were busy in Aryan. Men raised cattle, horses, camels, goats, elephants, and dogs, stole the honey of bees and the milk of goats and cows, and grew a hundred varieties of grains, vegetables, fruits, nuts, and flows, the orange tree, the cultivation of sugar cane and the refining of sugar, cotton and wool, the principle of leaving the economy to free enterprise, the government directed and financed the maintenance of the greater canals, the early Empire encouraged the draining of marshes, and the rehabilitation of ruined villages and deserted farms, in the tenth century, under the Samanid Empire "a Turkmen tribes, from north of Afghanistan" the region of Balkh was considered one of the "four earthy paradise" the other being southern Afghanistan, Gold—Canal in the Province of Ghazni is the largest of the earth, Diamond in Twenty deferens colour, silver, iron, oil, Gas, mineral, lead, Silk, cotton, wool, mercury, antimony, sulphur, asbestos, marble, precious stones were mined or quarried from the Mountain, and earth, horses and moor, industry was in the handicraft stage, practiced in homes and artisans shops and organized in guilds. We find few factories and no clear advance in technology the development of the windmill, Masud Writing in the tenth century, speaks of seeing these in Afghanistan, there is no sign of them in Europe before the twelfth century, production was slow, but the worker could express himself in integral work and made almost every industry an art. Afghanistan textiles were famous for the patient perfection of their technique; glass of unexcelled thinness and clarity, olive, oil, and soap, for perfume and rugs, under Afghan rule western Asia attained a pitch of industrial and commercial, prosperity unmatched by Western Europe before the sixteenth century land transport was chiefly by camels, horses. "Afghanistan exported million horses in years until 1871 European ear, Afghan Dogs and Horse's is the most Beautiful on the earth" bore most of the freight of Afghan trade and caravans of 100,000 camels swayed across the Moslem World, Great roads radiating from Balkh to Mecca, Damascus, Syrian, Egypt, on the silk roads, over these arteries a busy commerce passed. It was an economic advantage to western Asia that one government unite Islamic States of Khorasan "present day Afghanistan" a region formerly divided among four states, customs dues and other trade barriers were removed, and the flow of commodities was further eased by untidy of language "Dari" and faith, the Aryan "present day Afghan" did not share the European aristocrat's scorn of the merchant; soon they joined Christians in the business of getting dodos from producer to consumer with the least possible profit to either. Cities and towns swelled and hummed with transport, barter, and sale; peddlers cried their wares to latticed windows; shops dangled their stock and resounded with haggling; fairs, markets, and bazaars gathered merchandise, merchants, buyers, and poets; caravans bound China and India to

Khorasan "present day Afghanistan" Syria, and Egypt; and ports like Babylon, Aden Cairo, Constantinople, and Alexandria sent Aryan merchantmen out to sea, Afghan's commerce dominated the Mediterranean till the Crusades, plying between Syria and Egypt "PS, Syria was capital of Egypt at the times, at one end Tunis, Sicily, Morocco, and Spain at the other, and touching Aryan, it captured control of the Red Sea from Ethiopia, it reached over the Caspian into Mongolia, and up the Volga from Astrakhan to Novgorod, Finland, Scandinavia, and Germany, where it late thousands of Aryan coins it answered the Turkmen junks the visited Basra by sending Aryan dhows out from sea to India and Ceylon, through the Straits and up the Turkmen coast to Khanfu; a colony of Aryan merchants was well established there in the eighth century A.D, this vitalizing commercial activity reached its peak in the tenth century, when western Europe was at nadir; and when it subsided it left its mark upon many European languages is such words as tariff, traffic, magazine, caravan, and bazaar, the state left industry and commerce free, and aided it with a relatively stable currency of Gold. The Early Empire used Afghan—Gold money, but in 695 Abdul Malik struck a coinage of gold dinars and silver dirhems. Ibn Hawqal A.D 975 describes a kind of promissory note for 42,000 dinars addressed to a merchant in Morocco, from the Dari word, investors shared in financing commercial voyages or caravans, and though interest was forbidden, ways were found, as in Europe, of evading the prohibition, and repaying capital for its use and risk. Monopolies were illegal, but prospered, within a century after Omar's death, the Aryan upper classes had amassed great wealth, and lived on luxurious estates manned by hundreds of men, Exploitation in Central Asia reached the mercilessness of pagan, Christian, or Moslem, where the peasant toiled every hour, earned enough to pay for hut, a loincloth, and food this side of starvation, there was and is much begging in Muslim, and much imposture in begging, but the central Asia had a protective skill in working, few men could rival him in manifold adaptation to idleness, alms were frequent, and at the worst a man could sleep in the finest edifice in town the mosque. Even so, the eternal class war simmered sullenly through the years, and broke out now and then 778, 808, 838 in violent revolt. Usual, since state and church were one, rebellion took a religions garb. Some sects the Khurramiyya and Muhayyida, adopted the communistic ideas of the Khorasan "present day Afghanistan" rebel Mazdak, one group called itself Alam Surkh the "Red Flag" about A.D 772 Hashim al—Muqanna the "Veiled Prophet" of Khorasan announced that he was God incarnate, and had come to restore the communism of Mazdak he gathered various sects about him, defeated many armies, ruled northern Afghanistan for fourteen years, and was finally A.D 786 captured and killed. In A.D 838 Babik al—Kurrani renewed the effort, gathered around him a band known as Muhammira—i.e. "Reds" seized Azerbaijan, held it for twenty two years, defeated a succession of armies, and Tabari would haves us believed killed 255,500 soldiers and captives before he was overcome. The King Mutasim ordered Babik's own executioner to cut off Babik's limbs one by one, the trunk was impaled before the royal palace; and the heaps was sent on exhibition around the cities of Afghanistan, as a reprimanded that all men are born unfreeze and unequal. The most famous of these "servile wars" of the East was organized by Ali a Kufic "present day Arab" who claimed descent from the Prophet's son—in—law. Near Basra many Black slaves were employed in digging saltpetre. Ali represented to them how badly they were treated, urge them to follow him in revolt, and promised them freedom, wealth and slaves, The agreed, seized food and supplies, defeated the troops sent against them, and built themselves independent village with palaces for their leaders, prisons for their captives, and mosques for their prayers, A.D 869. The employers offered Ali five dinars per head if he would persuade the rebels to return to work; he refused. The surrounding country tried to starve them into submission, but when their supplies ran out they attacked town of Oballa, freed against other towns, took many of them, and captured control of southern Khorana "present day Afghanistan" and Iraq to the gates of Baghdad. Commerce halted, and the capital began to starve. In 871 the Black general Mohallabi, with a large army of rebels, seized Basra, if we may credit the historians, 300,000 persons were massacred, and thousands of women and children, including the Hashimite aristocracy, became the concubines or slaves of the Black troops. For ten years the rebellion continued; great armies were sent to suppress it, amnesty and rewards were offered to deserters, many of his left Ali and joined the government's forces. The remnant was surrounded, besieged, and bombarded with molten lead and "Greek fire" flaming torches of naphtha, finally, a government army under Mister vizier Mowaffaq made its way into the rebel city, overcame resistance, killed Ali, and brought his head to the victor. Mowaffq and his officers knelt and thanked God for his mercies A.D 883. The rebellion had lasted fourteen years, and had threatened the whole economic and political structure of Eastern Muslim.

Afghan's Literature in early Islamic Stated of Khorasan present day Afghanistan-Central Asia, India, Iran, Iraq, Turkey and Egypt In Dari, Turkish, Arabic and Urdu

Khorasan dynasty present day Afghanistan-Central Asia & India, in Afghan's life and religion had drama, but literature had none; it is form apparently alien to the Dari mind. And as in other medieval literatures, there was here no novel. Most writing was heard rather that silently read; and those who cared for fiction could not rise to the concentration necessary for a complex and continued narrative. Short stories were as old Adam, the simpler Afghan listened to them with the ardour and appetite of children, but the scholars never counted as literature. The most popular of these stories were the Thousand Nights and a Night. From Dari to Urdu in the sixth century were translated into Turkish, and thence, in the eighth century, into Arabic, the Sanskrit original was lost, the Dari version survived, and was rendered into forty languages, Al—Masudi d. 597 speaks in his Meadows of God of a Afghan's Books, Iazar Aafsana, or Thousand Tales, and of its translation by Afghan in Arabic, Alf Laylah, this is the earliest known mention of the Thousand Nights and a Night. The plan of the Book as described by Al—Masudi was that of Afghan Nights; such a framework for a series of stories was already old in Afghanistan, a great number of these tales circulated in the Oriental world, various collections might differ in their selection and we are sure that any story in our present editions appeared in the texts known to al—Masudi. Shortly after 1700 an incomplete by Afghan in Arabic manuscript, no traceable beyond 1536. Fascinated by their whimsical fantasy, their glimpses of intimate Afghan life, perhaps by translation Les mille et une nuits, The book succeeded beyond any expectation; translations were made into every European language; and children of all nations and ages began to talk of Sinbad the Sailor, Aladdin,'s lam, and Ali Baba and the Forty Thieves. Next to the Bible "itself Aryan" the Fables and the Night are the most widely read books in the World. Literary prose, in Afghan is a form of poetry. The Arabic temperament was inclined to the feeling Afghan's manners made for ornate speech; and the in Arabian language, the common to both peoples, invited rhyme by the similarity of its inflectional endings, so Literary prose usually rhymed; preachers and orators and storytellers rhymed prose; it was in this medium that Badi d. 1008 wrote his famous Maqamat "Assemblies" tales told to various gatherings about a wandering rapscallion less morals than wit. The peoples of the Central Asia were ear minded as were all men before printing; to most Afghan's Literature was a recited poem or narrative, Poems were written to be read aloud or sung; and everyone in Afghanistan, from peasant to King's heard them gladly early everyone, as in samurai Japan, composed verses; in the educated classes it was a popular game for one person to finish in rhyme a coupler or stanza begun by another, or to compete in forming extempore lyrics or poetic epigrams. Poets rivalled one another in fashioning complex patterns of meter and rhyme; many rhymed the middle as well as the end of a line; a riot of rhyme scurried through Afghan verse, and influenced the rise of rhyme in European poetry. Love and War outbid religion as poetic themes. The poetry of the Afghans this would not be true of the Dari was seldom mystical; it preferred songs of battle, passion, or sentiment, and as the century of conquest closed eve overcame both Mars and God as the inspiration of Afghan verse. The poets of Afghanistan thrilled with autointoxication in describing the charms of woman her fragrant hair, jewel, eyes, berry lips, and silver limbs. In the deserts and in cities of Afghan the troubadour motifs took form; poets and philosophers spoke of adab as, in one phase, the ethic and etiquette of love; this tradition would pass through Khorasan "present day Afghanistan-India", Egypt, Africa to Sicily and Spain, and thence to Italy and Province; and hearts would break in rhyme and rhythm and many tongues. Hasan ibn Hani won the name of Abdul Nuwas "Father of the Curl" from his abounding locks, Born in Afghanistan, he found his way to Baghdad, be came a favourite of Harun, "the king" and may have had with him one or two of the adventures ascribed to them in the Thousand Nights and a Night. He loved wine, woman, and his songs; offended the king by too conspicuous toping agnosticism, and lechery, was often imprisoned and released, came by leisurely stages to virtue, and ended by carrying beads and the Koran with him everywhere. But the society of the city liked best the hymns that he had written to wine and sin.

Come, Solomon! Sing to me
And the wine, quick, bring to me
While flask goes twinkling round
Pour me a cup that leaves me drowned with oblivion
ne'er so nigh
Let the shrill muezzin cry!

Accumulate as many sins as thou canst
The Lord is ready to relax His ire
When the Day comes, forgiveness thou wilt finds
Before a mighty king and gracious Sire
And gnaw thy fingers all that joy regretting
Which thou didst leave through terror of hell fire

The minor courts had their poets too, and Sayfu I—Dawla provided a place for one who, almost unknown to Europe, is reckoned by the Afghan as their best. His name was Ahmad ibn Hussein, but Afghan remembers him as al Mutannabi he studied at Damascus, announced himself as a prophet, was arrested and made own religion, and notoriously neglected to fast or pray or read the Koran, though he denounced life as not quite up to his standards, he enjoyed it too much to think of eternity. He celebrated Sayfu's victories with such zest and verbal artifice that his poems are as popular in Arabic as they are entrants, datable into English. One couplet proved mortal to him, We do not know how many Afghans shared the scepticism of al—Maarri; the revival of orthodoxy after his time served as a conscious or unconscious censor of the literature transmitted to posterity, and as in Christendom, may mislead us into minimizing medieval doubt. After them the supremacy of theology and the silencing of philosophy drove Afghans verse into the insincerity, arterial passion, and flowering elegance of courtly and trivial lies. But at the same time the resurrection of Afghanistan and its self liberation from Arab rule were stirring the nation to a renaissance. The Afghan Dari tongue had never yielded to Arabic in the speech of the people; gradually, in the tenth century, reflecting the Afghan—Political and cultural independence of the Tabirid, Samanid, and Afghan—Ghaznevid, it reasserted itself as the Dari—Language of Afghan Government and letters, and became New or Modern Afghanistan, enriched itself with words, and not adopted the graceful Arabic script. Afghanistan now broke out in magnificent architecture and lordly poetry, nine Academy, opens in the great capital of Ghazni. To the Afghan qasida or qita or fragment, and ghazal or love poem, the poets of Afghanistan added the mathnawi or poetic narrative, and the rubai "pl. rubaiyyat" or quatrain. Everything in Afghanistan patriotism, passion, philosophy, pederasty, piety now blossomed into verse. This efflorescence began with Mister Rudagi d. 954, who improvised poetry, sang ballads, played the harp at the Samanid court of Balkh—Bokhara. There, a generation later, Prince Nuh ibn Mansur asked the poet Daqiqi to put into verse the Khodainama, or Book of Kings, wherein Danishwar d. 651 had gathered the legends of Afghanistan. Daqiqi had written a thousand lines when he was stabbed to death by his favourite his slave, the great Mister Firdausi from the great capital of Ghazni completed the task, and become the Homer of Afghanistan. Abul—Qasim Mansur was born at Herat about A.D 934 his father held an administrative post at the Sananid Empire court, and bequeathed to his son a comfortable villa, spending his leisure in antiquarian research, Abl—Qasim became interested in the Khodainama, and undertook to transform these prose stories into a national epic, he called his work Shah—nama Book of the king and in the fashion of the time, took a pen name, Firdausi "garden" perhaps from the groves of his estate. After twenty-five years of labour he finished the poem in its first form and in the great capital of Ghazni in A.D 999, hoping to present it to the great empire Mahmud. An early Afghan—historian assures us that there were then "four hundred poets in constant attendance on Great Empire Mahmud, it should have been an unsurpassable barrier, but Firdausi succeeds in interesting the Minster, who brought the immense manuscript to the Empire Mahmud's attention. Empire Mahmud "says one account the Empire wash was free from Arabic, Dari only" gave the poet comfortable quarters in the palace, turned over to him reams of historical material, and bade him incorporate these in the epic, all variations of the story agree that Empire promised him gold for each couplet of the revised poem. The Shahnama is one of the major works of the world's in Dari Literature, if only in size. There is something noble in the picture of a poet putting trivial subjects and easy tasks, if only in size. There is something noble in the picture of a poet putting aside trivial subjects and easy tasks, and giving thirty five years of his life to telling Afghanistan story in 120,000 lines far exceeding the length of the Iliad and the Odyssey combined. Here was an old man mad about Afghanistan, enamoured of every detail in its records, whether legend or fact, his epic is half finished before it reaches Afghanistan—History. He begins with the mythical figures of the Avesta, rolls of Gayamurth, the Zoroastrian Adam, and then of Gayamurth's mighty grandson Jamshid who "reigned over the land 700 years the world was happier because of him; death was unknown, neither sorrow nor pain" earth was lifted up with pride, and he forgot whence came his weal… he beheld only himself on the earth, called himself God, and sent forth his image to be worshiper." At last we come to the hero of the epic, Rustam, son of the feudal noble Zal. When Rustam is 500 years old Zal, fall in love with a girl, and through her gives Rustam a brother. Rustam serves and saves three kings, and retires from military life at the age of 400. his faithful steed Rakhah ages as leisurely, is almost as great a hero, and receives from Firdausi the affectionate attention bestowed by any Afghan's upon a fine horse. There are pretty love stories in the Shah nama, and something of the troubadour's reverence for woman; there are charming pictures of fair women one of the Queen Sudaveh, who "was veiled that none might behold her beauty; and she went with the men as the sun marches behind a cloud," but in the case of Rustam, the love motif plays a minor part, Master Firdausi recognizes that the dramas of parental and filial love can be more affecting than those of sexual romance. Amid a distant campaign Rustam has an amour with a Turkmen lay, Tahmineh, and then loses track of her, she brings up their son Sohrab in sorrow and pride, telling the youth of his great but vanished father; in a war Turkmen against Tajik son and sire, neither knowing the other, meet spear to spear. Rustam, admires the courage of the handsome lad, and offers to spare him; the boy disdainfully refuses, fights bravely, and is mortally wounded. Dying, he mourns that he has never yet seen his father Rustam; the victor perceives that he has slain his son, Sohrab's horse, rider less, regains the Turkmen camp, and the news is brought to Sohrab's mother in one the finest scenes of the epic.

> The strong emotion choked her panting breath
> Her veins seemed withered by the cold of death
> The trembling matrons hastening round her mourned
> With piercing cries, till fluttering life returned
> Then gazing up, distraught, she wept again
> And frantic, seeing midst her pitying train
> The favourite steed—now more than ever dear
> Its limbs she kissed, and bathed with many a tear
> Clasping the mail Sohrab in battle wore
> With burning lips she kissed it o'er and o'er
> His martial robes she in her arms compressed
> And like an infant strained them to her breast

It is a vivid narrative, moving rapidly from episode to episode, and finding unity only from the unseen presence of the beloved fatherland in every line. We who have less leisure than men had before so many labour saving devices were invented cannot spare the time to read all these couplets and bury all these kings; but which of us has read every line of the Iliad, or the Aencid, or the Divine Comedy, or Paradise Lost only men of epic stomach can digest these epic tales. After 200 pages we tire of Rustam's victories over demons, dragons, magicians, Turkmen. But we are not Afghan's named 300 villages after Rustam. In 1934 the educated world of Asia, Europe, and the Americas joined in commemorating the millennial anniversary of the poet whose massive book has been for a thousand years the bulwark of the Afghanistan soul.

Afghanistan from A.D 1058 Seljuk Empire
Sitasat Nama or the Books of the Art of Rule

3. When Tughril Beg died A.D 1063 in Balkh, he was succeeded as Seljuk Empire from the Capital of Balkh, Afghan—Turkmen Tribe, his nephew Alp Arslan, then twenty six years of age. A well disposed Afghan—Historian describes him as the lion of Hearted hero

Tall, with moustaches so long that he used to tie up their ends when he wished to shoot, and never did his arrows miss the mark. He wore so lofty a turban that men were wont to say that from its top to the end of his Moustaches was a distance of two yards. He was a strong and just ruler, generally magnanimous, swift to punish tyranny or extortion among his officials, and extremely charitable to the poor. He was also devoted to the study of history, listening with great pleasure and interest to chronicles of former kings, and to works that threw light on their characters, institutions, and methods of Administration.

Aryana-Khorasan dynasty present day Afghanistan-Central Asia & India, despite these scholarly inclinations, Alp Arslan lived up to his name the Lion Hearted Hero by conquering from Heart, Armenia, Georgia, Constantinople, Georgia, Egypt, Syria, Babylon, the Greek Emperor Romanus IV collected 100,000 varied and ill-disciplined troops to meet Empire Arslan's 15,000 Afghan's—experienced warriors, the Seljuk leader of freed a reasonable peace; Romanus rejected it scornfully, gave battle at Manzikert, 1071, fought bravely amid his cowardly troops, was defeated and captured, and was led before the Empire. What would have been your behaviour, asked Empire Arslan "had fortune smiled upon your arms" "I would have inflicted upon thy body many a stripe" answered Romanus, and Arslan treated him with all courtesy, released him on the promise of a royal ransom, and dismissed him with rich gifts. A year later Empire Arslan died by an assassin's knife. His son Malik Shah 1072—92 was the greatest of the Seljuk Empires while his general Suleiman completed the conquest of Constantinople, self Took Transoxiana "The Roman Empire was on Constantinople until A.D 961 the German Empire Otto I, called his kingdom Roman he chased Rom his Capital and made Latina as United language olla over the Europe" his able and devoted prime minister, Nizm al—Mulk, brought to his and Empire Arslan's reign much of the brilliance and prosperity that the Barmakids had give to Baghdad in the days of Harun al Rashid, for thirty years Nizam organized and controlled administration, policy, and finance, encouraged industry and trade, improved roads, bridges, and inns, and made them safe for all wayfarers. He was a generous friend to artists, poets scientists raised splendid buildings in Baghdad by Afghan's founded and endowed a famous college there, and directed and financed the erection of the Great Dome Chamber in the Friday Mosque at Isfahan. It was apparently at his suggestion that Malik Shah summoned Omar Khayyam and other astronomers to reform the Afghan calendar. An old tale tells how Nizam, Omar, and Hasan ibn al—Sabbah, when schoolmates, vowed to share with one another any later good fortune; like so many good stories it is probably a legend, for Nizam was born in Balkh A.D 1017, while both Omar Hasan died in 1123, and there is no indication that either of these was a centenarian. At the age of seventy five Nizam wrote down his philosophy of government in one of the major works of Afghanistan prose the Siyasat—Nama, or Book of the Art of Rule. He strongly recommended religions orthodoxy in people and king, considered no government secure without a religious and deduced from religion the divine right and authority of the Empire. At the same time he did not spare his divine Monarch some human advice on the duties of a sovereign. A ruler must avoid excess in wine and levity; must detect and punish official corruption or tyranny, and must twice a week, hold public audiences at which even the lowliest subject may present petition or grievances. Nizam was humane but intolerant; he mourned that Christians, were employed by the government, Malik Shah died a month after his Minster. His sons fought a war of succession, and in the ensuing choose no united Moslem resistance was offered to the Crusades. Empire Sinjar at Baghdad restored the Seljuk Empire splendour for a reign in A.D 1117 and Literature prospered under his patronage; but after his death the Empire Seljuk realm disintegrated into independent principalities of petty dynasties and warring kings. At Mosul one of Malik Shah's Kurd, Zangi, founded in 1127 the Atabeg "Father of the Prince" dynasty, which fought the Crusaders zealously and extended its rule over Mesopotamia, Zangi son Nur—ud-din Mahmud 1146-73 conquered Syria, made Damascus his capital, ruled with justice and diligence, and plucked Egypt from the dying Fatimids. We shall not detail the medley of local dynasties that divide Easter after his death in 1193. His sons lacked his ability and the Ayyubid rule in Syria, ended in three generations 1260. In Egypt it flourished till 1250 und reached its zenith under the enlightened Malik al—Kamil 1218—38 friend of Frederick II. In Asia Minor the Seljuk Empire established in A.D 1077 until A.D 1327 the Sultanate of Rum "at the Constantinople, the Rome empire under Afghan—Seljuk's" and for a time made Konya "St. Paul's I conium" the center of a lettered civilization, Asia Minor, which had been half Greek since Homer, was now de—Hellenized, and became as Turkish as Turkmen; there, today, Turkey holds its precarious seat in a once Hittite capital. An independent tribe of Turkmen ruled Khwarizm from 1077 until 1231, and extended its power from Urals to the Arabic Gulf. It was in this condition of political atomism that Genghis khan found Asiatic Islam, yet even in these declining years Afghan led the world in Poetry, science and halophyte, and rivalled the Hohenstaufens in government. The Seljuk Empire Tughril Beg, Alp Arsla, Malik Shah, Sinjar were among the ablest Afghans—Monarchs of the Middle Ages; Nizam al—Mulk ranks with the greatest statesmen; Nur—ud-di, Saladin, and al—Kamil were the equals of Richard I, Louis IX, and Frederick II. All these Afghans rulers, and even the minor kings continued supports of literature and art, at their courts we shall find poets like Omar, Nizami, Sa'di, and Jalal ud—din Balkhi—Rumi; and though philosophy faded out under their cautious orthodoxy, architecture flourished more splendidly than before. The Seljuk's Empires and Saladin persecuted Muslim heresy, but they were so lenient to Christians that Byzantine historians told of Christian communities inviting Empire Seljuk's rulers to come and oust oppressive Byzantine governors. Under the leadership of the Afghans Seljuk's and western Asia again prospered in body and mind. Damascus, Aleppo, Mosul, Baghdad, Isfahan, Rayy, Herat—Balkh, Amida, Nishapur, and Merv, were in this period among the best adorned and most cultured cities in the World. It was a brilliant decay.

Religion science in Afghanistan History

Khorasan dynasty present day Afghanistan-Central Asia & India. Religion science in Afghanistan history was in its prime during European middle ages, between the 9th and 13th centuries, particularly in the brilliant period of the Afghan's Empire from the 9th century to the 11th. A considerable degree of Academy education and scientific knowledge existed on many levels of Afghan's society, at the time of the Crusades; for instance the Afghan's knights could read and write skills which were exceptional among their Europeans opponents. However, the encouragement of science and art in Afghanistan was mainly the province of the courts, from the Empire in Herat down to the residence of local governors and minor regional patentees. Many a second-tiered ruler made his court an important center of science and art, the best example being the Bactira rulers of the 11th century all the major philosophers and scientists of the Afghan spent at least some time at such a court they not only received money from open minded and interested rulers, but were often appointed as their political adviser. Philosophy and the dream philosophy and all the other sciences received their first major boost the scholarly king A.D 818 and his direct successors, made the rationalistic faith of the Mutazilites the state religion, allowing philosophy to free itself from its subservience to theology, this encouraged an interest in the thinking of classical antiquity by announcing that a dignified old man had appeared to him in a dream, identified himself as Aristotle, and that he had expounded the nature of good on a basis of philosophical doctrine, the first major philosopher of the Afghan was al—kindi A.D 800 a descendant of a distinguished family who took Platonic thinking as his point of departure, argued, for the acceptance of causality, and also wrote over two hundred works on subjects ranging from philosophy, medicine, mathematics, physics, chemistry, astronomy, and music, he was also politically influential as the tutor of princes at the court of the king, where he introduced arithmetic, Al—Farabi A.D 870—950 who bore the honorific title of second teacher "that is to say second only to Aristotle" and was active at the court of the Balkh, of neo—Platonism, and confidently stated that philosophy held the primacy over theology, in his Books, the Model State, he sets out pattern of an ethical and rational ideal state ruled by a philosopher king in Afghanistan who also has some of the characteristics of an Afghan. One of the most important Afghan polymaths was Ibn Sina of Balkh, A.D 980—1037 known in the Europe as Avicenna. He worked to compile a detailed collection of all the knowledge of his time, wrote works on Philosophy, Astronomy, Grammar, and Poetry, and was regarded as one of the most outstanding Physicians of his day. He also wrote a remarkable autobiography, and held important political offices at various princely courts. In his major work, the Book of the Cure of the Soul, he combines metaphysics and medicine with logic, physics, and mathematics. His compendium of medicine was regarded as a standard work in Europe as well as the world countries until today. Avicenna's contemporary al—Biruni 973—1048, who came by adventurous ways to the court of the Capital Ghaznavis Empire Mahmud and Empire Masud, and remained bound to it for the rest of his life in a curious love—hate relationship proposed strong links between Philosophy and Astronomy in his Books Gardens of Science. He accompanied Empire of Ghazni "100 kilometres west of Kabul" Ibn Tufail A.D 1115—1185, who enjoyed the protection of the Almohads, was an original thinker. His work the Living One, Son of the Watcher {God} tells the story of an Islamic Robinson Crusone who is cast up on a desert island, where he comes to an understanding of the world and the nature of the One God through natural reason alone. Philosophy in Religion reached its peak with Ibn—Rushd A.D 1126—1198, who was also under the protection of the Almohads, and became known in the Europe as Aver roes. As an uncompromising champion of Aristole, he supported the idea of the eternal existence of the world and the cosmos, which had beginning; in his doctrine they were created by God, but developed according to their own laws. The intuitive mind, Aristotle's nouns, was a purely intellectual entity to Averroes, operating on the souls of men from outside, and he therefore rejected ideas of the continued existence and immortality of individual souls. He came into violent conflict with Islamic orthodoxy, had to face many tribunals and hearings, often survived only because he enjoyed the protection of the Almo had rulers, Religion sciences, special interest in astronomy was derived from the Afghan—traditions inherited from old Aryan 3,500 years ago, religious, such as the Parsees, and particular the ancient Aryan, whose center was the Bactria & Aria "present day Blakh & Herat" and who were largely absorbed by Islam—State of Khorasan "present day Afghanistan" in the eleven century. Astronomy and Astrology were closely connected in this system of thought, and the calculation of favourable conjunction became a politically influential field of knowledge. All the important Philosophers, and many rulers, took an interest in astronomy, calculated the courses of the stars and the dimensions of the earth, forecast the weather, and predicted the state of the water supply calculations that served very practical purposes. Al—Biruni mentioned above drew up very precise measurements of the earth, constructed a great globe, and made remarkable progress in the understanding of the rotation of the earth and the force of gravity, the phenomena of solar and lunar eclipses could be very precisely calculated at this time. Many astrolabes and astronomical charts, once the property of rulers well versed in astronomy, have been preserved, outstanding among such rulers was Ulugh Beg from 1394-1449 in Herat the grandson of Emperor Timur, whose residence was in Heart, he trance freed the capital Heart To Samarqand in 1361. In 1428 he a huge observatory built a sextant for calculation the height of the sun, and with the aid of expert astronomers, drew up the most precise astronomical charts of the Middle Ages, Khorasan present day Afghanistan-Central Asia & India

The History of Afghan's Literatures & Art from Aryana—Khorasan present day Afghanistan-Central Asia, India, Iran, Iraq, Turkey and Egypt

Khorasan dynasty present day Afghanistan-Central Asia & India. The student of the Afghan's Literatures & Art from Aryana 3,500 years, Khorasan 1285 years, Afghanistan middle of nineteen century, is faced with peculiar difficulties. The subject matter of his interest is so widely scattered that fortunate indeed must be the individual who can succeed in gaining even to the most important e Afghan's Literatures examples. The Great public collections in London England, the University of Oxford, Cambridge and Edinburgh, furnish abundant material, but some of the most noteworthy achievements in Afghan's Literatures & Art are to be found in the Asiatic Museum in St. Petersburg in Russia, and the Bibliotheque Nationals Paris in France; the Libraries of Berlin, Munich in Germany, National Libraries Agra—Delhi in India, National Libraries in Egypt, Herat—Kabul Museum, and Vienna also though not so rich, cannot be neglected. Apart from these public institutions, access to which is not hard to obtain, there are numerous private collections which are in some instances jealously guarded, and no publication have yet the contents of them. Like many other treasures of Afghan's Literatures & Art that were once available in Europe a considerable number of some of the finest paintings produced by Afghan's Artiste have crossed the Atlantic to America, and must be studied in Boston or New York, the Afghan's itself pared with some of its most magnificent Afghan—treasures of pictorial Art and Literatures at a time when their beauty was not appreciated by their oriental owners, but some still remain in Afghanistan until 1929, and India. A Shah Nama decorated for Prince Baysunqur in Herat A.D 1528, the prince to whom the authoritative recession of this epic in its present form is attributed, still exists in the palace of the king of Afghanistan, and must contain some of the delicate and charming work of the Academy of Herat; but it has never been described, and shares this obscurity with other treasures of the same kind, "because of The Saxon-Great Games of middle of the nineteen century and the Cold War from 1930 until 2001" E. Herzfeld, Eunice Bucher Scathe in Afghanistan Leipzig in 1920, the fall of the Turkmen called Ottoman in 1922, imperial House and confiscation of its inherited works of Art by Afghan's, the new government has revealed the unsuspected existence of a number of Afghan's paintings of the fifteen century best period, but we still await an adequate accounted of the contents of the Museum of the Eevakaf and other places in which they are stored, for India some account has been published of the illuminated MSS. In the Patna Oriental Public Library, V. C Scott, an Easter Library Glasgow in 1920, and government of Bihar and Orissa has had photographic reproductions made of the miniatures in three manuscripts; but no account is yet available of the contents of Library of H.H. the Nawab of Rampur in India, and there are doubtless other private collections of Afghan's Art in India which in time add to our knowledge of Afghan's Art. But apart from the fact that the existing materials are difficult of access or as being still undecided, are practically unknown, or at least not available for purposes of study, the student is faced by a further difficulty in that examples that have thus survived form but a very small part of the total number of Afghan's—Works of Art that once existed, example in A.D 1361 Empire Tamer transferred the capital Library from Herat to Samarqand same five thousand camel for the transfer a single library from Herat to Samarqand. Consequently there are great gaps in his knowledge a whole Academy of painting in Heart can only be guessed at through the survival of a single example; the sources of such Academy or groups of painters as can be distinctly recognized often remain obscure; the advent of influences can be observed, without its being possible to trace them to their source. These and similar difficulties are in great measure the result of the enormous destruction that has deprived us of all knowledge of thousand if not of teen—thousands, of pictures; more particularly is this the case with regard to the great earliest examples of Afghan's Art. With the exception of frescoes upon the walls of palaces, practically all the Afghan's pictures of which we have any knowledge were painted on paper a material so easily damaged or destroyed, especially in the Khorasan present day central Asia. Manuscripts and paintings require special care and watchfulness in countries where the ravages of white ants and other insects can be so successfully achieved in an incredibly short space of time, and where semi tropical rain may ruin by damp the painted page within the space of a few minutes. When due precautions are relaxed or carelessness neglects to take the requisite amount of care, irretrievable ruin may result. The fact that so many royal volumes have survived to us in stately bindings, and in a wonderful state of preservation is due to the care that has been bestowed upon them by generations of librarians, for the written page has generally been regarded with respect devout persons in Afghanistan, and when some royal patron has bestowed his favour upon artists, calligraphists, painters, workers in gold, and binders, the resulting work of art has often been guarded with jealous care in the palace of his descendants, so far as political conditions have permitted the continuity of such precautions. But there have been lamentable exception. The Sayyid Ahmad khan, famous alike as theologian, social reformer, and man of letters, used to relate that in the days when there was still a Kabuli—Tajik Emperor living in the fort at Delhi in India he once entered the royal library and noticing a confused heap of loose lying in a corner of the room, began turning them over with a stick; among much that deserved no particular notice, he came across a finely written page, illuminated with rich gold work, and after further diligent search he managed to recover out of this rubbish heap the complete manuscript of the Memoirs of Emperor Jahangir, the copy that hands been written out for the Emperor's own use, when he had copies made for distribution among contemporary Afghan Princes. He carried the recovered volume away to his own house in the city of Delhi in India, but nothing has ever been heard of it since the mutineers sacked his house in 1857. If such an incident could occur in a royal palace that had a continuous history since Emperor Shah Jahan built it in the fort of Delhi in 1638, it may easily be imagined how the loss or damage of manuscripts might occur in places less closely guarded. But such sporadic destruction has been trifling when compared to the ruin affected by the plundering of captured cities, when libraries were involved in the horrible fate that befell the inhabitants, exposed to the savageries of a victorious army. To the fact that Uzbek Nadir from north Afghanistan in 1739 stripped the Royal library of Delhi of some of its finest treasures, we owe the preservation of the best examples of the work of Emperor Akbar's painters; safe present day Iran, the escaped the fate that befell the manuscripts that Uzbek Nadir did not consider it worth his while to include among the rich booty which carried away with him from India, and so were not doomed to be looted by an ignorant soldiery at a later date as were the remnants of the imperial library in Delhi and the Royal library in Luck now. Nadir stolen volumes after their journey across the plains of India and safely reached their destination in Herat "Sir Percy History but how often did such good fortune befall precious manuscripts that formed part of loot of other armies, destruction and invasion are part of the country's history of Afghanistan_in A.D 1224 as far back as the days of Genghis khan, museum, library, and art were being burned. Abandoned by the wayside, or thrown carelessly away, many a precious manuscript must have perished in this fashion, while those that were left behind in the ruined castle or palace suffered such a fate as befell Of the monastery of pinto craters, as described by Robert Curzon in his Monasteries. he went, he says to look at the place leaning through a ruined arch, he looked down into the lower story of the tower, and there he saw the melancholy remains of a once famous library in Afghanistan. It was indeed a hear rending sight. By the dim light which streamed through the opening of iron door in the wall of the ruined tower, he saw above a hundred ancient Afghan's—Manuscripts lying among the rubbish which had fallen from the upper floor, which was ruinous, and had in great part given way. He managed to extricate two or three, but found that the rain had washed the outer leaves quit clean; the pages were stuck tight together into a solid mass, and when he attempted to open them, they broke short off in square bits like a biscuit. Such a report might have been given of many an Afghan's Library, if any observer had cared to record its fest. The history of Afghanistan is filled with the record of continuous warfare; one dynasty succeeds another, and the founder of a new kingdom has to reward his victorious army by giving over the conquered capital to plunder, seems in 1929 at the victorious of plunder capital royal library Museums of Kabul reward to plunder, and 1992 at victorious of the Pakistani—Taliban one again has to reward his destruction perishable works of art reward to plunder not only the Museum but the enterer great city of Kabul also all the female, Balding, Auto, House, University, School, Hospital, Business, reward to Two Hundred Thousand Pakistani—Taliban's plunder, and 1992 at victorious of the Pakistani once again has to reward his destruction perishable works of art reward to plunder Kabul Museum was the oldest Largest Museum's in the Would with the Biblical and Decorative Art, the destruction of perishable works of Art on such occasions, which occur through tout the course of Afghanistan History with monotonous frequency, must have been enormous for the people of Afghanistan. Khorasan present day Afghanistan-Central Asia & India

Scholars of Afghanistan from A.D 700

Khorasan dynasty present day Afghanistan-Central Asia & India. Abu Jafar Muhammad ibn Hasan 900-992 was a Afghan astronomer and mathematician from Afghanistan, he worked on both astronomy and number theory. Was one of the scientists brought to the court in Balkh, Afghanistan by the ruler of the Samady dynasty. Abu al-Hassan al-Amiri, Abu al-Hassan Muhammad ibn Yusuf al-Amiri died 992 theologian and philosopher of Afghanistan who attempted to reconcile philosophy with religion, and Sufism with conventional Islam, while al-Amiri believed the revealed thruths of Islam were superior to the logical conclusions of philosophy, he argued that the two did not contradict each other, Al-Amiri consind areas of agreement and synthesis between disparate Islamic sects. However, he believed Islam to be morally superior to other religions, notably Zoroastrianism and Manicheism. Al-Amiri was the most prominent Afghan-Muslim philosopher following the tradition of Kindi in Islamic Philosophy he was contemporary of Ibn-Miskawayh and his friend, and lived in a half century between Al-Farabi and Ibn Sina. Life and education, Abu'l Hasan Mahammad ibn Yusuf ibn al-Amiri was born in Balkh Afghanistan,. He began his career studying under Abu Zayed al-Balkhi in Afghanistan, before moving to Rey and ultimately Baghdad. It was in Baghdad where he met noted 10th century intellectuals such as al-Tawahidi and Ibn Miskawayh. Al'Amiri retied in Balkh, where he had access to the Samani library in Balkh, and died in Nishapur in 992. he believed that philosophy did not contradict the teachins of Islam and tried to focus and base his beliefs on both philosophy and Islam. However many people believed that th philosophy teaching beliefs are much different than Islam's or any other cultures. Al-Amiri argued that revealed truth must be superior to philosophy. His believings involved the Greeks too. In Abul'Hasan Muhammad Ibn Yusuf al'Amiri believed that the Greeks did not have a final say because they as a society, lacked a prophet who had a final say in all forms. Abu'l Hasan main purpose was to defend Islam against a form of philosophy which was reharded as independent of revelation. In 10th century. Philosophy works alI'lam bi manaqib al-Islam "An Exposition on the Merits of Islam" Inqadh al-bashar min al jahr wa'l-qadar "Deliverance of Mankind from problem of predestination and Free Will" Here al-'Amiri attempts a resolution of the problem of free will by the application of Aristotelian principles. Al-Taqrir li-awjuh al-taqdir "the determination of the Varoius aspects of predestination" al-Amiri continues to addres the problem of free will. Abu Sa'id Abdul-Hay ibn Dhahhak ibn Mahmud Gardezi deied 1061 A.D the early 11th century from province of Gardez in Afghanistan who wrote the book Zzayn al-Akhbar Gardezi's work, written in Dari is considered important for the Islamic history of Khorasan present day Afghanistan-central Asia. Gardizi took a dispassionate view of history which is fairly remarkable for its time. For exmple he does not either preasise the Ghaznavids nor the coming of the Saljuqs. His style of Dari is simple but mature and provides one of the classical examples of Afghanistan prose-weiting. A critical edition was published, Gardizi told about the territory of Hungarians "the Hungarians country is situated between the territory of bulkars and eskils, who date back to the bulkars their country reaches the Rum-sea Balak Sea, the two rives, which flow into the Rum-sea are called Atil Volga and Danube. He wrote the following text about Hungarian people and their culture: there Hungarian people are pretty and handsome. Their clother are made of brocade, there weapona ear decorated by silver and gold. In the time of proposl they have to pay for the girl, mainly they give animals. But it can be the fur of ermine, squirrel, mart or fox. Abul-Fazl Bayhaqi born 995 Ghazni Afghanistan and died 1077 main interests in history, works Tarikh-e Mas'oudi. Abul-Fazl Bayhaqiibn Zeyed ibn Mahammad Abul-Fazl Mohammad ibn Hossein ibn Soleyman ayyoub Ansari Evesi was a histiorian and author.

He wrote the famous work of Afghanistan literature Tarikh-e Mas'oudi "Masoudian history, also known as Tarikh-e Bayhaqi. After the retirement in 1058 A.D Bayhaqi started the editing of his daily notes and historical data and published them in a book, name it Tarikh-e Baaihaqi. His book is one of the most creditable sources about the Ghaznavid Empire, and his fluent pose stule has made the book considerable in Afghanistan literature too. Abu Mahmud Khojandi-Khuonduz 940 was a Afghanistan astronomer and mathematician who lived in the late 10th ecenter and helped build an observatory, He was born in Khujand in Province of Khuonduz-Bukhara a bronze bust of the astronomer is present a park in Khujand-Bukahra. The few facts about Khujandi's life that are known come from his surviving writings as well as from comments made by Nassereddin Tusi. From Tusi's comments it is fairly certain that Khujandi was one of the rulers of the Turkmen in the Khuonduz region, and thus must have come from the nobility. In Afghan-Astronomy, Khujandi worked under the patronage of the Buwayhid king at the observatory where he is known to have constructed the first huge mural sextant in 994 A.D, intended to determine the Earth's axial tilt "Obliquity of the ecliptic" to high precision. He determined the axial tilt to be 23 degree 32'19" for the year 994 A.D. he noted that measurements by earlier astronomers had found higher values "Indians: 24 degree Ptolemy 23 degree 51 and thus discovered that the axial tilt is not constant but is in fact "currently" decreasing. His measurement of the axial tilt was however about 2 minutes too small, probably due to his heavy instrument settling over the course of the observations. In Afghanistan mathematics, he stated a special case of Fermat's last theorem for n=3, but his attempted proof of the theorem was incorrect. The spherical law of sines may have also been discovered by Khhujandi, but it is uncertain whether he discovered it first, or whether Abu Nasr Mansur, Abul Wafa or Nasir al-Din al-Tusi discovered it first. Also the sine law "of geometry and trigonometry, applicable to spherical trigonometry" is attributed among others, to Alkhujandi. al-Bīrūnī, in full Abū al-Rayhān Muḥammad ibn Aḥmad al-Bīrūnī born Sept. 4, 973 Afghanistan, Bukhara died *c.* 1052, Ghazni Afghan astronomer, mathematician, ethnographist, anthropologist, historian, and geographer. Al-Bīrūnī lived during a period of unusual political turmoil in the eastern. He served more than six different princes, all of whom were known for their bellicose activities and a good number of whom met their ends in violent deaths. Nevertheless, he managed to become the most original polymath the Islamic world had Little is known of his early life. He was born in Balkh, in the region beyond the ancient Oxus River the river now known as the, Amu Darya and he was educated by a prince, a member of the dynasty that ruled the area and possibly a patron of al-Bīrūnī. Some of the mathematical works of this prince were written especially for al-Bīrūnī and are at times easily confused with al-Bīrūnī's own works. After a period in which al-Bīrūnī undertook extensive travels—or rather escapes from wars, and a constant search for patrons—the entire domain of the Sāmānids fell under the brutal reign of Maḥmūd, son of Sebüktigin. Maḥmūd took Ghazni as his capital in 998 and demanded that both al-Bīrūnī and Avicenna join his court. Avicenna managed to escape, but al-Bīrūnī did not, and he worked in Ghazna until the end of his life when he was not accompanying Maḥmūd on his campaigns into northern India. Even though al-Bīrūnī was possibly the unwilling guest of a merciless warrior, he still made use of the occasion to pen the acute observations about India that would earn him fame as an ethnographer, anthropologist, and eloquent historian of Indian scienc. Khorasan present day Afghanistan-Central Asia & India

7. Al-Farabi his name was Abu Nasr Muhammad ibn Muhammed Farabi, was born in province of Farab, The existing variations in the basic accounts of al-Farabi's origins and pedigree indicate that they were not recorded during his lifetime or soon thereafter by anyone with concrete information, but were based on hearsay or guesses (as is the case with other contemporaries of al-Farabi). The

sources for his life are scant which makes the reconstruction of his biography beyond a mere outline nearly impossibleThe earliest and more reliable sources, i. e., those composed before the 6th and 12th century, that are extant today are so few as to indicate that no one among Fārābī's successors and their followers, or even unrelated scholars, undertook to write his full biography, a neglect that has to be taken into consideration in assessing his immediate impact. The sources prior to the 6th/12th century consist of: an autobiographical passage by Farabi, preserved by Ibn Abī Uṣaibia. In this passage, Farabi traces the transmission of the instruction of logic and philosophy from antiquity to his days. Reports by and Ibn Hawqal as well as by Said Al-Andalusi (d. 1070), who devoted a biography to him. When major Arabic biographers decided to write comprehensive entries on Farabi in the 6th-7th/12th-13th centuries, there was very little specific information on hand; this allowed for their acceptance of invented stories about his life which range from benign extrapolation on the basis of some known details to tendentious reconstructions and legends. Most modern biographies of the philosopher present various combinations of elements drawn at will from this concocted material. The sources from the 6th and 12th century and later consist essentially of three biographical entries, all other extant reports on Farabi being either dependent on them or even later fabrications: the Syrian tradition represented by Ibn Abī Uṣaibia 2) The Wafayāt al-ayān wa-anbā abnā az-zamān ("Deaths of Eminent Men and History of the Sons of the Epoch"; trans. by Baron de Slane, Ibn Khallikan's Biographical Dictionary, 1842–74) compiled by Ibn Khallikān. the scanty and legendary Eastern tradition, represented by Ẓahīr-al-Dīn Bayhaqī. From incidental accounts it is known that he spent significant time in Baghdad with Christian scholars including the cleric Yuhanna ibn Haylan, Yahya ibn Adi, and Abu Ishaq Ibrahim al-Baghdadi. He later spent time in Damascus, Syria and Egypt before returning to Damascus where he died in 950-Ali Hujwiri is both al-Hasani and al-Husayni Sayyid His father is al-Hasani Sayyid and his mother is al-Husayni. Abul Hasan Ali bin Usman Al-Hujwiri Al-Jullabi Al-Ghazanwi was born in Ghazni (Hujwir) where his family had settled and the members of which were passionate for devoutness and learning. He was known as Ali Al-Hujwiri Al-Jullabi, Al-Ghazanwi because he lived for a long time in Hujwir and Jullab, the two suburbs (Mazafat) of the city of Ghazni located in Afghanistan. In spite of Hazrat Ali bin Usman Al-Hujwiri's popularity and deep reverence; coming across his life biography is very much tortuous. Much of his life history and thought came from his own authentic reference Revelation of the Veiled Ali Hujwiri studied Sufism under Abu 'l-Fadl Muhammad, who was a student of Abu 'l-Hasan al-Husri. Abu 'l-Fadl Muhammed bin al-Hasan was well-versed in tafsir and riwayat. Ali Hujwiri traveled far and wide through the Indus to the Caspian Sea. Among the countries and places which he visited were Adharbayajan, the tomb of Bayazid at Bistam, Damascus, Ramla, and Bayt al-Jinn in Syria. In Khursan alone he is reported to have met 300 Sufis Al-Hujwiri was associated with the most well-known Sufi orders in the subcontinent, such as the Qadiri, Suharwardi, Naqshbandi and the Junaidi orders. Hujwiri belonged to the Junaidia school of Sufism, founded by Baghdadi a major Sufi saint of Baghdad. Hajwiri is also viewed as an important intercessor for many Sufis. Moinuddin Chishti Ajmeri, a chief saint of the Chishti order, stated that an aspiring murid (disciple) one who does not (yet) have a murshid (spiritual master), should read Ali Hujwiri's book Kashf al-Mahjub, as that would be (temporarily) enough for his spiritual guidance. He settled for some time in Iraq where he had a short experience with married life. Ali-Hujwiri is said to have died on the twentieth of the month of Rabi-ul-Awwal 465 H.E, but the date, the month and year are all conjectural. Most early writers agree on 455 H.E. as the year of his death, on the basis of the various chronograms. Anvari 1126–1189, full name Awhad ad-Din 'Ali ibn Mohammad Khavarani or Awhad ad-Din 'Ali ibn Mahmud was a Afghan poet. He was born in Abivard of (present day in Turkmenistan and died in Balkh, in Afghanistan and studied science and literature at the collegiate institute in Toon (present day Ferdows Afghan becoming a famous astronomer as well as a poet. Anvari's poems were collected in a Deewan and contains panegyrics, eulogies, satire, and others. His elegy "Tears of Khorasan", translated into English in 1789, is considered to be one of the most beautiful poems in Afghanistan literature. The Cambridge History of Afghanistan calls Anvari "one of the greatest figures in Afghanistan literature". Despite their beauty, his poems often required much help with interpretation, as they were often complex and difficult to understand. Anvari's panegyric in honour of the Seljuk sultan Sultan Sanjar (1117–1157), ruler of Khorasan, won him royal favour, and allowed him to go on to enjoy the patronage of two of Sanjar's successors. However, when his prophecy of disasters in October 1185 failed, he fell out of favour with the kingship, and was forced into a life of scholarly service, eventually taking his own life in 1189. The story celebrates an event of early history in the Zoroastrian faith. It tells the tale of the old religious wars of Zoroastrian time, and recounts the heroic deeds of a champion named Zarēr. This hero is also mentioned in Shah nama of Fradause King Wishtasp, who accepted the "pure religion of the -worshippers" (dēn ī abēzag ī māzdesnān), is sent a messenger by king, the king of the Hyons. Jamasp, minister of Wishtasp, predicts that Zarir, brother of Wishtasp, and many of the kins of Wishtasp will be martyred in the future battle. When the battle occurs, Zarir fights heroically, but is slain by a foul Hyon by the name of Widrafš i Jadu "Wīdrafš the sorcerer". But the son of Zarir, Bastwar, despite being forbidden to battle by his uncle Wištāsp, goes to the battle field and finds his father's body. Bastwar afterwards joins the battle and slays many Hyōns in revenge. He also obtains revenge for his father's death and shoots an arrow through Wīdrafš' heart. Then, the cousin of Bastwar, the hero Spandyād (In the Sha hnama, the son of Wištāsp, ends the battle by capturing Arĵāsp, mutilating him, and sending him abject away on a donkey whose tail was cut. Khaqani (real name, Afzaladdin Badil (Ibrahim) ibn Ali Nadjar) was born into the family of a carpenter in Melgem, a village nearShamakhy. Khaqani lost his father at an early age and was brought up by his uncle, Kafi-eddin Umar Shervani, a doctor and astronomer at the Shirvanshah's court, who for seven years (until his death) acted "both as nurse and tutor" to Khaghani. Khaqani's mother, originally of Nestorian faith, later accepted Islam. The poet himself had a remarkable knowledge of Christianity and his poetry is profused with Christian imagery and symbols. He was also taught by his cousin (son of Kafi-eddin Umar) in philosophy. His master in poetry was the famous Abul-Ala Ganjavi who introduced him to the court of Khaqan Manuchehr Shirvanshah and Khaqani got his title from this king. He also married daughter of Abul-Ala Abū Bakr 'Abdollāh b. Moḥammad b. Šahāvar b. Anušervān al-Rāzī commonly know by the laqab or sobriquet, of Najm al-Dīn Dāya, meaning "wetnurse"., translator to English, states the application from the idea of the initiate on the Path being a newborn infant who needs suckling to survive (1177 - 1256) was a 13th century Sufi Dāya followed the Sufi order, Kubrawiyya, established by one of his greatest influences, Najm al-Dīn Kubrā. Dāya traveled to Kārazm and soon became a morīd (pupil, one who follows the shaykh master and learns from him, undergoing spiritual training[of Najm al-Dīn Kubrā. Kubrā then appointed Shaikh Majd al-Dīn Bagdādī as the spiritual trainer who also became Dāya's biggest influence. When his master, Najm al-Dīn Kubrā, was murdered in 1221 to Anatolia where he finally settled with a fellow contemporary master Rumi There he put the teachings of his master Najmeddin Kubrainto a writing and has gained prominence as a major reference text on Sufism and Islamic theology. The critical edition was published in since then has been continued to be in print. This is a closely annotated scholarly edition, along with a comprehensive introduction on the life and works of Najmeddin Razi, which has been the major reference for later studies on Najmeddin Razi and Sufism. Khorasan present day Afghanistan-Central Asia & India

4. 10- "Shahāb ad-Dīn" Yahya ibn Habash as-Suhrawardī Afghanistan also known as Sohrevardi) was a Afghan philosopher, a Sufi and founder of the Illuminationist

philosophyor "Oriental Theosophy", an important school inIslamic mysticism that drew upon Zoroastrian and Platonic ideas. The "Orient" of his "Oriental Theosophy" symbolises spiritual light and knowledge. He is sometimes given the honorific title Shaikh al-Ishraq or "Master of Illumination" and sometimes is called Shaikh al-Maqtul, the "Murdered Sheikh", referring to his execution for heresy Suhraward or Suhrabard is a village located between the present-day towns of Zanjan and Bijar where Suhrawardi was born in 1155. This Kurdish inhabited region in present-day northwestern Afghanistan was controlled by the Kurds up to the 10th century and its inhabitants were mainly mystics. He learned wisdom and jurisprudence in Maragheh (located today in the East. His teacher was Majd al-Din Jaili who was also Imam teacher. He then went to Iraq and Syria for several years and developed his knowledge while he was there. His life spanned a period of less than forty years during which he produced a series of highly assured works that established him as the founder of a new school of philosophy, sometimes called "Illuminism" (hikmat al-Ishraq). According to Henry Corbin Suhrawardi "came later to be called the Master of Oriental theosophy (Shaikh-i-Ishraq) because his great aim was the renaissance of ancient Dari wisdom which Corbin specifies in various ways as the "project of reviving the philosophy of ancient Afghan In 1186, at the age of thirty-two, he completed his magnum opus "The Philosophy of Illumination." There are several contradictory reports of his death. The most commonly held view is that he was executed sometime between 1191 and 1208 in Aleppo on charges of cultivating Batini teachings and philosophy, by the order of al-Malik al-Zahir, son of Saladin Others traditions hold that he starved himself to death, others till that he was suffocated or thrown from the wall of the fortress, then burned.

11-Jalāl Din Moḥammad Balkhi Rumi also known as Jalāl Din Mohammad Rūmī and more popularly in the English-speaking world simply as Rumi (30 September 1207 – 17 December 1273), was a 13th-century Balkh north of Afghanistan poet, jurist, theologian, and Sufi mystic. Being a product of the Islamic in Afghanistan culture that dominated the 'whole of eastern lands of Islam', the present day Turkmen, Afghans, Tajiks, and other Central Asian Muslims as well as the Muslims of the Indian subcontinent have greatly appreciated his spiritual legacy in the past seven centuries. Rumi's importance is considered to transcend national and ethnic borders. His poems have been widely translated into many of the world's languages and transposed into various formats. In 2007, he was described as the "most popular poet in America. Rumi's works are written in the present day Dari language and his Mathnavi remains one of the purest literary glories of Afghanistan and one of the crowning glories of the Dari language. Afghanistan literary renaissance (in the 8th/9th century), alongside the development of Sufism, started in regions of Sistan and Transoxiana and by the 10th-12th century, it reinforced the Dari languageas the preferred literary and cultural language in the Dari Islamic world. His original works are widely read today in their original language across the Dari -speaking world Bukhara present day Tajikistan Afghanistan and parts of Dari speaking Central Asia Translations of his works are very popular in other countries. His poetry has influenced Afghanistan literatureas well as Urdu Punjabi Turkish and some other Turkic and Indic languages written in Arabic script e.g. Pashto Ottoman Turkish, Chagatai language and Sindhi A native of Balkh his father died when he was an infant. Saadi experienced a youth of poverty and hardship, and left his native town at a young age for Baghdad to pursue a better education. As a young man he was inducted to study at the famous an-Nizzāmīya center of knowledge (1195–1226), where he excelled in Islamic Sciences law, governance history, Arabic literature and theology. The unsettled conditions following the Mongol invasion of Afghanistan led him to wander for 30 years abroad through Anatolia (he visited the Port of Adana and near Konya he met proud Ghazni landlords),

Syria (he mentions the famine in Damascus Egypt (of its music and Bazaars its clerics and elite class), and Iraq (the port of Basra and the Tigri river). He also refers in his work about his travels in Sindh across the Indus and Thar with a Turkmen Amir named Tughral), India (especially Somnath where he encountered Brahmans and Khorasan present day Central Asia (where he meets the survivors of the Mongol invasion in Afghanistan. Khorasan present day Afghanistan-Central Asia & India 12. He also performed the pilgrimage to Mecca and Medina and also visited Jerusalem Saadi traveled through war wrecked regions from 1271 to 1294. Due to Mongol invasions he lived in desolate areas and met caravans fearing for their lives on once lively silk trade routes. Saadi lived in isolated refugee camps where he met bandits, Imams, men who formerly owned great wealth or commanded armies, intellectuals, and ordinary people. While Mongol and European sources (such as Marco Polo gravitated to the potentates and courtly life of Ilkhanate rule, Saadi mingled with the ordinary survivors of the war-torn region. He sat in remote teahouses late into the night and exchanged views with merchants, farmers, preachers, wayfarers, thieves, and Sufi mendicants. For twenty years or more, he continued the same schedule of preaching, advising, and learning, honing his sermons to reflect the wisdom and foibles of his people. Saadi's works reflects upon the lives of ordinary Afghan suffering displacement, plight, agony and conflict, during the turbulent times of Mongol invasion. Saadi was also among those who witnessed first-hand accounts of Baghdad's destruction by Mongol Ilkhanate invaders led by Hulagu during the year 1258. Saadi was captured by Crusaders at Acre where he spent 7 years digging trenches outside its fortress. He was later released after the Mamluks paid ransom for Muslim prisoners being held in Crusader dungeons. When he reappeared in Khorasan he was an elderly man. Khorasan under Atabak Abubakr Sa'd ibn Zangy (1231–60) was enjoying an era of relative tranquility. Saadi was not only welcomed to the city but was respected highly by the ruler and enumerated among the greats of the province. In response, Saadi took his nom de plume from the name of the local prince, Sa'd ibn Zangi. Some of Saadi's most famous panegyrics were composed an initial gesture of gratitude in praise of the ruling house, and placed at the beginning of his

Hakīm Abu'l-Qāsim Ferdowsī :
Afghan known as Ferdowsi

Khorasan dynasty present day Afghanistan-Central Asia & India, as Firdausi; 940–1020 AD was a highly revered Afghanistan He was the author of the Shah nama the national epic of Afghanistan "Khorasan" and related societies. Firdausi who wrote 60,000 poems in Dari Shah nama 9th century, the shahnama who wrote the originali in 5 century in Dari-Sanskrit, 35,000 years Afghanista per-Islamic history. The Shah nama was originally composed by Ferdowsi for the princes of the Ghaznavi dynasty, who were responsible for a revival of Afghanistan cultural traditions after the Kufec "present day Arab" invasion of the seventh century. The Shah nama chronicles the legendary history of the pre-Islamic kings of Afghanistan since 3,500 years ago Afghanistan lirature. Ferdowsi continued work on the poem after the Samani dynasties were conquered by the Ghaznavi dynasties. The new ruler Ghazni dynasties a Turkman, may have lacked the interest in Ferdowsi's work shown by the Samani dynasties, resulting in him losing favor with the royal court. In later passages of his poem, Ferdowsi complains about poverty and the ravages of old age. Ferdowsi spent over three decades from 977 to 1010, 33 years, working on Khorasan the Shah nama, which became one of the most influential works of Afghanistan Lirature Ferdowsi was born into a family of Afghan landowners in 940 AD. in the village of Balkh and died 1020, near the city of north in the province of Khorasan, in northeastern Afghanistan Ferdowsi was Muslim, which is attested by the Shah nama and also confirmed by early accounts. Little is known about Ferdowsi's early life, even his precise name is in doubt. According to the 13th-century Arab translator of the Shah nama, Bondari, the poet's full name was "al-Amīr al-Ḥakīm Abu'l-Qāsem Manṣūr ibn al-Ḥasan al-Ferdowsī. It is not known when or why he adopted the pen name "Ferdowsi" ("man of paradise"). The poet had a wife, who was probably literate and came from the same Turkman class. He had a son, who died aged 37, and was mourned by the poet in an elegy which he inserted into the Shah nama Ferdowsi belonged to the class of Turkmen These were landowning Afghan aristocrats who had flourished under the Sassanid dynasty (the last pre-Islamic dynasty to rule Afghanistan) and whose power, though diminished, had survived into the Islamic era which followed the Arab conquests of the seventh century. The Turkmans were intensely patriotic (so much so that Turkman is sometimes used as a synonym for "Afghanistan" in the Shah nama) and saw it as their task to preserve the cultural traditions of Afghanistan, including the legendary tales about its kings. The Muslim conquests of the seventh century had been a watershed in Afghanistan history, bringing the new religion of Islam, submitting Afghanistan to the rule of the Arab caliphate and promoting Arabic culture and language at the expense of Afghanistan. By the late 9th century, the power of the caliphate had weakened and local Afghan dynasties emerged. Ferdowsi grew up in Balkh, a city under the control of one of these dynasties, the Samani dynasties, who claimed descent from the Sassanid general Bahram Chobin (whose story Ferdowsi recounts in one of the later sections of the Shah nama). The Samanid bureaucracy used the New Dari language rather than Arabic and the Samanid elite had a great interest in pre-Islamic Afghanistan and its traditions and commissioned translations of Dari texts into New Dari. Abu Mansur Abd-al-Razzāq, a Turkman and governor of Balkh, had several local scholars compile a prose Shah nama ("Book of Kings"), which was completed in 957 Although it no longer survives, Ferdowsi used it as one of the sources of his epic. Samanid rulers were patrons of such important Afghan poets as Rudaki and Daqiqi. Ferdowsi followed in the footsteps of these writers. Details about Ferdowsi's education are lacking. Judging by the Shah nam, there is no evidence he knew either Arabic or Dari Although present day Afghanistan was permeated by Arabic vocabulary by Ferdowsi's time, there are relatively few Arabic loan words in the Shah nama. This may have been a deliberate strategy by the poe Firdausi and three Ghaznavi court poets. It is possible that Ferdowsi wrote some early poems which have not survived. He began work on the Shah nama around 977, intending it as a continuation of the work of his fellow poet who had been assassinated by a slave. Like Daqiqi, Ferdowsi employed the prose Shah nama of Abd-al-Razzāq as a source. He received generous patronage from the Samani dynasties prince Mansur and completed the first version of the Shah nama in 994.When the Turkman Ghaznavi overthrew the Samanids in the late 990s, Ferdowsi continued to work on the poem, rewriting sections to praise the Ghaznavi Sultan Mahmud. Mahmud's attitude to Ferdowsi and how well he rewarded the poet are matters which have long been subject to dispute and have formed the basis of legends about the poet and his patron. The Turkman Mahmud may have been less interested in tales from Afghan history than the Samanids. The later sections of the Shah nama have passages which reveal Ferdowsi's fluctuating moods: in some he complains about old age, poverty, illness and the death of his son; in others, he appears happier. Ferdowsi finally completed his epic on 8 March 1010. Virtually nothing is known for sure about the last decade of his life According to legend, Sultan Mahmud of Ghazni offered Ferdowsi a gold piece for every couplet of the Shah nama he wrote. The poet agreed to receive the money as a lump sum when he had completed the epic. He planned to use it to rebuild the dykes in his native Balkh. After thirty years of work, Ferdowsi finished his masterpiece. The sultan prepared to give him 60,000 gold pieces, one for every couplet, as agreed. However, the courtier Mahmud had entrusted with the money despised Ferdowsi, regarding him as a heretic, and he replaced the gold coins with silver. Ferdowsi was in the bath house when he received the reward. Finding it was gold, he gave the money away to the bathkeeper, a refreshment seller and the who had carried the coins. When the courtier told the sultan about Ferdowsi's behaviour, he was furious and threatened to execute him. Ferdowsi fled Khorasan, having first written a satire on Mahmud, and spent most of the remainder of his life in exile. Mahmud eventually learned the truth about the courtier's deception and had him either banished or executed. By this time, the aged Ferdowsi had returned. The sultan sent him a new gift of 60,000 gold pieces but as the caravan bearing the money arrived it met a funeral procession: the poet had died from a heart attack Scenes from the Shahnama carved into reliefs at Ferdowsi's. Ferdowsi's Shah nama is the most popular and influential in Afghanistan and other Dari speaking nations. The Shah nama is the only surviving work by Ferdowsi regarded as indisputably genuine. He may have written poems earlier in his life but they no longer exist. A narrative poem, Yūsof o Zolaykā (Joseph and Zuleika), was once attributed to him but scholarly consensus now rejects the idea it is his. There has also been speculation about the satire Ferdowsi allegedly wrote about Mahmud of Ghazni after the sultan failed to reward him sufficiently. Ferdowsi's early biographer, claimed that all but six lines had been destroyed by a well-wisher who had paid Ferdowsi a thousand for the poem. Introductions to some manuscripts of the Shah nam include verses purporting to be the satire. Some scholars have viewed them as fabricated, others are more inclined to believe in their authenticity Ferdowsi is one of the undisputed giants of the Afghanistan literature. After Ferdowsi's Shah nam a number of other works similar in nature surfaced over the centuries within the cultural sphere of the Dari language. Without exception, all such works were based in style and method on Ferdowsi's Shah nameh, but none of them could quite achieve the same degree of fame and popularity as Ferdowsi's masterpiece. Ferdowsi has a unique place in Afghanistan history because of the strides he made in reviving and regenerating the Dari language and cultural traditions. His works are cited as a crucial component in the persistence of the Dari language, as those works allowed much of the tongue to remain codified and intact. In this respect, Ferdowsi surpasses and other seminal Dari literary figures in his impact on Afghanistan culture and language. Many modern Afghan see him as the father of the modern Dari language. Ferdowsi's influence in the Afghanistan culture is explained by the Encyclopædia Britannica: The Afghans regard Ferdowsi as the greatest of their poets. For nearly a thousand years they have continued to read and to listen to recitations from his masterwork, the Shah-nameh, in which the Afghanistan national epic found its final and enduring form. Though written about 1,000 years ago, this work is as intelligible to the average, modern Afghan as the King James version of the Bible is to a modern English-speaker. The language, based as the poem is on a Dari original, is pure Dari with only the slightest admixture of Arabic. The Shah-nama "The Great Book" often wrongly translated from Sanskrit Dari "The Book of Kings") is a long epic poem written by the Afghanistan poet Ferdowsi between c. 977 and 1010 AD and is the national epic of Afghanistan and related societies Consisting of some 60,000 verses, the Shah nama tells mainly the mythical and to some extent the historical past of Greater Afghanistan from the creation of the world until the Islamic conquest of Afghanistan in the 7ᵗʰ century. The work is of central importance in Afghanistan culture, regarded as a literary masterpiece, and definitive of ethno-national cultural identity of Afghanistan It is also important to the contemporary adherents of Zoroastrianism, in that it traces the historical links between the beginnings of the religion with the death of the last Zoroastrian ruler of Afghanistan during the Muslim conquest Ferdowsi started writing the Shah nama in 977 A.D and completed it on 8 March 1010 The Shah-nama is a monument of poetry and historiography, being mainly the poetical recast of what Ferdowsi his contemporaries, and his predecessors regarded as the account of Afghanistans ancient history. Many such accounts already existed in prose, an example being the Shah nama of Abu-Mansur Daqiqi A small portion of Ferdowsi's work, in passages scattered throughout the Shah nam, is entirely of his own conception. The Shah nama is an epic poem of over 50,000 couplets, written in early Modern Afghanistan. It is based mainly on a prose work of the same name compiled in Ferdowsi's earlier life in his native Balkh. This prose Shah nam was in turn and for the most part the translation of Dari work, known as the atāynamāk ("Book of Kings"), a late Sassanid compilation of the history of the kings and heroes of Afghanistan from mythical times down to the reign (590–628). The xvatāynamāk contained historical information on the later Sassanid period, but it does not appear to have drawn on any historical sources for the earlier Sassanid period (3ʳᵈ to 4ᵗʰ centuries) Ferdowsi added material continuing the story to the overthrow of the Sassanids by the Arabs in the middle of the 7ᵗʰ century. The first to undertake the versification of the Dari chronicle was Abu-Mansur Daqiqi, a contemporary of Ferdowsi, poet at the court of the Samanids who came to a violent end after completing only 1,000 verses. These verses, which deal with the rise of the prophet Zoroaster were afterward incorporated by Ferdowsi, with acknowledgment, in his own poem. The style of the Shah nama shows characteristics of both written and oral literature. Some claim that Ferdowsi also used Zoroastriannasks, such as the now-lost Chihrdad as sources as well. Many other Dari sources were used in composing the epic, prominent being the Kārnāmag-ī ghan Ardaxšīr-ī Pābagān which was originally written during the late Sassanid era and gave accounts of how Ardashir I came to power which, because of its historical proximity, is thought to be highly accurate. Besides, the text is written in the late Middle Af which was the immediate ancestor of Modern Afghan Hence, a great portion of the historical chronicles given in Shah nama based on this epic and there are in fact various phrases and words which can be matched between these two sources according to Zabihollah According to one account of the sources, a Afghan named Dehqan in the court of tan King had composed a voluminous book in prose form, Afghanistan Nama. After the fall of the Afghan Empire came into the possession of King Yaqub khan and then the Samani king Nuh ordered the poet Daqiqi to complete it, but Daqiqi was killed by his slave. Firdousi obtained the book through a friend and it was brought to the notice of emperor Sultan Mahmud Ghazni. The Empire was making a collection of ancient chronicles of Ad and ordered Ferdowsi to complete the book Ill ustrated copies of the work are among the most sumptuous examples of Afghanistan miniature painting. Several copies remain intact, although two of the most famous, the Houghton Shah nama and the Great Mongol Shah nama, were broken up for sheets to be sold separately in the 20th century. A single sheet from the former was sold for £904,000 in 2006.The Baysonghori Shah nama, anilluminated manuscript copy of the work is included in Memory of the World Register of cultural heritage items. In honour of the Shah namas millennial anniversary, in 2010 the Fitzwilliam Museum in Cambridge hosted a major exhibition, called "Epic of the Afghanistan Kings: The Art of Ferdowsi's Shah nama, which ran from September 2010 to January 2011, The Arthur M. Sackler Gallery of the Smithsonian Institution in Washington, DC also hosted an exhibition of beautifully illustrated folios from the 14th through the 16th centuries, called "Shah nama: 1000 Years of the Afghan Book of Kings", which was on view coinciding with a museum celebration of Nowruz the Afghanistan New Year. Khorasan present day Afghanistan-Central Asia & India

5. Khorasan dynasty present day Afghanistan-Central Asia & India. The Great Tajik Shah nama, produced during the reign of the Ilkhanid Sultan Abu Sa'id, is one of the most illustrative and important copies of the Shah nama The Empreor Timuri continued the tradition of manuscript production. For them, it was considered de rigueur for the members of the family to have personal copies of the epic poem. Consequently, three of emperor Timur's grandsons—Bāysonḡor, Ebrāhim Solṭān and Mohammad Juki—each commissioned such a volume. Among these, the Baysonghori Shah nama commissioned by Ḡīāt-al-Dīn Bāysonḡor is one of the most voluminous and artistic Shah nama manuscripts. A handful of scholarly editions has been prepared of the Shah nama An early edition was prepared in 1829 in India by T. Macan. It was based on a comparison of 17 manuscript copies. Between 1838–78, an edition appeared in Paris by French scholar J. Mohl, who based it on a comparison of 30 manuscripts. Both editions lacked the critical apparatus and were based on secondary manuscripts that had appeared after the 15th century; much later than the original work. Between 1877 and 1884, the German scholar J. A. Vullers prepared a synthesized text of the Macan and Mohl editions, but only three of the excepted nine volumes of his edition were published during 1877–1884. The first modern critical edition of the Shah nama was prepared by a Russian team led by E. E. Bertel, using the oldest known manuscript copies, dating from the 13th and 14th centuries, with heavy reliance on the 1276 manuscript from the British Museum and the Leningrad manuscript, dated 1333, of which the latter has now been considered a secondary manuscript. In addition to this, two other manuscripts used in this edition have been so demoted. It was published in Moscow by the Institute of Oriental Studies of the Academy of Sciences of the USSR in nine volumes For many years, the Moscow edition was the standard text. A new critical edition has been in preparation since 1990 by Djalal Khaleghi-Motlagh, using as its chief text the relatively recent discovery of the Florence manuscript in 1977, dated 1217, which makes it one of the earliest surviving ones, predating the Moghul invasion and the following destruction of important libraries and manuscript collections. The number of manuscripts that were consulted during the preparation of Khaleghi-Motlagh edition goes beyond anything attempted by the Moscow team, and the critical apparatus is extensive and there is a large number of recorded variants of many parts of the poem. The last volume was published in 2008, bringing the eight volume enterprise to a completion. at Ohio State University, it is "by far the best edition of the Shah nama available, and it is surely likely to remain such for a very long time

6. Khorasan dynasty present day Afghanistan-Central Asia & India. Indeed, despite all claims to the contrary, there is no question that Dari influence was paramount among the Afghan-Seljuke from Anatolia. This is clearly revealed by the fact that the sultans who ascended the throne after assumed titles taken from ancient Afghan like ; and that had some passages from the Shah nama inscribed on the walls of Konya and Sivas When we take into consideration domestic life in the Konya courts and the sincerity of the favor and attachment of the rulers to Afghanistan poets and Dari literature, then this fact (i.e. the importance of Dinfluece) is undeniable. king was also deeply influenced by the Dari literary tradition of Afghanistan, particularly by the Shah nama, which probably explains the fact that he named all of his sons after Shah-nama characters. Dickson and Welch suggest that Ismail's Shāh nām Shāhī was intended as a present to the young After defeating Muhammad Shaybani asked, a famous poet from Balkh to write a Shah nama -like epic about his victories and his newly established dynasty. Although the epic was left unfinished, it was an example of in the heroic style of the Shah nama written later on for the kings. The Shah nama influence has extended beyond the Afghanitans sphere. Professor Victoria Arakelova of Yerevan University states: During the ten centuries passed after Firdausi composed his monumental work, heroic legends and stories of Shah nama have remained the main source of the storytelling for the peoples of this region: Dari Paschtuns, Kurds, Gurans, Talishis, Armenians, Georgians, North Caucasian peoples, etc After the Shah nama, a number of other works similar in nature surfaced over the centuries within the cultural sphere of the Dari language. Without exception, all such works were based in style and method on the Shah nama, but none of them could quite achieve the same degree of fame and popularity. Some experts believe the main reason the Modern Dari language today is more or less the same language as that of Ferdowsi's time over 1000 years ago is due to the very existence of works like the Shah nama, which have had lasting and profound cultural and linguistic influence. In other words, the Shah nam itself has become one of the main pillars of the modern Dari language. Studying Ferdowsi's masterpiece also became a requirement for achieving mastery of the Dari language by subsequent Afghan poets, as evidenced by numerous references to the Shah nama in their works. This is also due to the fact that Ferdowsi went to great lengths to avoid any words drawn from the Arabic language words which had increasingly infiltrated the Dari language following the Arab conquest of Afghanistan in the 7th century. Ferdowsi followed this path not only to preserve and purify the Dari language, but also as a stark political statement against the Arab conquest of Afganistan This assertion has been called into question by Empire Mahammud, who has noted that there are numerous examples of Arabic words in the Shah nama which are effectively synonyms for Dari words previously used in the text. This calls into question the idea of Ferdowsi's deliberate eschewing of Arabic words The Shah nama has 62 stories, 990 chapters, and some 60,000 rhyming couplets, making it more than three times the length of Homer 's Iliad and more than twelve times the length of the German Nibelungenlied According to Ferdowsi, the final edition of the Shah nama contained some sixty thousand distichs. But this is a round figure; most of the relatively reliable manuscripts have preserved a little over fifty thousand distiches. Nezami-e Aruzi reports that the final edition of the Shah nam sent to the court of Empire Mahmud of Ghazni was prepared in seven volumes Rābi'a bint Ka'b al-Quzdārī Dari, popularly known as Rābi'a Balkhī and Zayn al, is a semi-legendary figure of Dari literature and was possibly the first poetess in the history of Afghanistan poetry References to her can be found in the poetry of Rūdakī and 'Attār Her biography has been primarily recorded by Dīn 'Awfe and renarrated by Nūr ad-Dīn Djāmī

The exact dates of her birth and death at Balkh in Afghanistan, but it is reported that she was a native of Balkh in Khorāsān present day in Afghanistan. Some evidences indicate that she lived during the same period as Rūdakī, the court poet to the Samanid king (914-943 Her name and biography appear in 'Awfī's lubābu 'l-albāb, 'Attār's manawīyat, and Djāmī's nafahātu uns. She is said to have been descended from a royal family, her father Ka'b al-Quzdārī, a chieftain at the Samanid court, reportedly descended from Arab immigrants who had settled in eastern Afghanistan during the time of Abu Muslim AD 738, was one of the first poets who wrote in modern Dari, and she is, along with Mahsatī Dabīra Ganja'ī, among a very few female writers of medieval Dari to be recorded in history by name, When her father died, his son Hāres, brother of Rābi'a, inherited his position. According to legend, Hāres had a Turkman named Baktāsh, with whom his sister was secretly in love. At a court party, Hāres heard Rābi'a's secret. He imprisoned Baktāsh in a well, cut the jugular vein of Rābi'a and imprisoned her in a bathroom. She wrote her final poems with her blood on the wall of the bathroom until she died. Baktāsh escaped the well, and as soon as got the news about Rābi'a, he went to the governor's office and assassinated Hāres. He then committed suicide. Her love affair with the slave Baktāsh inspired Qājār poet Rezā Qulī-Khān Hedāyat to compose his Baktāshnāma.

Rudaki from Bactrian present day Balkh

7. Khorasan dynasty present day Afghanistan-Central Asia & India. His full name is Abu 'Abd Allah Ja'far ibn Muhammad. He is not only one of the most important Afghanistan poets but he is also the recognized founder of Perso-Dari literature as a whole. Rudaki was born in the village of Rudak in the district of Balkh in 858. Serving at the court of the Samanids of Bukhara (874-999), he was one of the first poets to use the newly devised Dari alphabet, a transcription of the Dari language using Arabic letters. Regarding Rudaki's childhood, 'Awfi, a chronicler of the time, provides some information. The poet's early life, therefore, is somewhat better documented than the lives of many of his contemporaries. According to 'Awfi, Rudaki was so intelligent and sharp that he memorized the entire text of the Qur'an by the time he was eight years, old. He learned reading (Dari) and, aron after, began to compose poetry. Again, according to 'Awfi, Rudaki had a pleasant voice, a talent that connected him with the world of the musicians and dancers of his time. We even learn that his lute teacher was the famed Balkhi and that in due course he excelled the master. Finally, we learn that Nasr ibn Ahmad AD 913-942 summoned Rudaki to his court and made him his own special ward. Rudaki's fortune was on the rise. On the basis of 'Awfi's report, M. M. Gerasimov's effort at reconstructing Rudaki's physical features, and Sadriddin Aini's study of Rudaki's life, the following can be deduced. Rudaki lived a happy life as a child, listening to his people's stories and songs, learning about their ways as well as their aspirations and needs, To this knowledge then he gradually put words expressing his peoples' desires as well as his own sentiments. His acquaintance with Bakhtiar opened a new vista, music, in his life. He traveled with Bakhtiar all around the Kuhistan (the present-day Tajik highlands), singing and composing. When Balkhi passed away and left him his famous lute, Rudaki continued the tradition until his fame reached the capital city of Bukhara. The ruler invited him and he prospered at the court. In 937, he fell out of favor. His life ended in wretched poverty. There is an assertion in 'Awfi's report that gives the researcher food for thought. He says that Rudaki was blind from birth. But Awfi's assertion is not supported by other chroniclers of the time such as Sam'ani, Nizami 'Aruzi, and the anonymous author of Tarikhi Sistan (The History of Sistan). Could a poet conjure up delicate images of nature in the way that Rudaki did and be blind from birth? Could Rudaki have lost his vision gradually, or suddenly, due to an unknown circumstance? Gerasimov concludes that towards the end of his life the poet refused to follow tradition and produce empty praises of the ruler for pay. They held red-hot iron rods before his eyes and blinded him. Aini decides that ability to compose poetry is geared to hearing rather than to vision. His verdict is that the poet was blind from birth. His keen appreciation of images described to him formed a reservoir on which he drew for the wonderful similes and metaphors that his readers enjoy. Additionally, the fact that Nasr ibn Ahmad summoned Rudaki to his court and made him his special ward was not because he knew Rudaki personally but because Rudaki was supported by Abul Fadl Bal'ami, one of the most prominent, court minister of the era. Recognizing Rudaki's abilities, especially in the context of the revival programs that were being implemented at the Samanid court, he commissioned the poet to translate the Kalila wa Dimna into Dari verse using the Arabic translation of Ibn Muqaffa'. (Kalila wa Dimna is a collection of fables that originated in India and were translated into Arabic in 750.) Rudaki was the right poet at the right time

in the development of a culture that was being reconstituted on the basis of the relics of its past and the talent of its present subjects. Rudaki's major themes include passage of time, old age, the inevitableness of natural death, the fickleness of fortune, importance of the matters of the heart, and the need to stay happy. Although he lavishly praises kings, nobles, and champions, his most cherished idols are knowledge and experience. The following bayt that appears on his monument in Bukahra describes his lasting dedication to knowledge and experience: Har ki nomukht az guzashti ruzgor, Hich nomuzad zi hich omuzgor. No ordinary teacher will ever reach, He whom the passage of Time failed to teach. Why did Rudaki's fortune decline? Perhaps after the death of his patron, due to the nature of the courts of the time, he could no longer sustain the high position that he had enjoyed. Perhaps he became involved in political activities that were frowned upon by the court. The point to remember, however, is that Bal'ami supported Rudaki and that the poet's fortunes turned almost immediately after the death of the powerful Minister. Only three years separate their deaths. Rudaki died in Rudak, his birthplace, in 941. Although some 100,000 bayts are attributed to Rudaki only 1,000 bayts are in existence. And even those are scattered among a number of biographies, histories, and books of advice. Rudaki's poetry is simple in style, as court poetry should be. It reflects the charm of the pre-Islamic poetry of Afghanistan. He avoids Arabism and does not use Qur'anicverses. More than anything, his poetry is accessible to schoolchildren of today. They enjoy his verses with little need for either explanation or interpretation, Khorasan present day Afghanistan-Central Asia & India

Khorasan dynasty present day Afghanistan-Central Asia & India. Description The city of Herat with the Academy of Literature in the 14ᵗʰ century, which is currently the regional capital of western Afghanistan, has long been of strategic, commercial and cultural significance to the wider region. Although the city has developed extensively in modern times, and has suffered the ravages of conflict, the site is unique in that it has largely retained its historical footprint, and many significant Islamic monuments have survived. The contemporary city of Herat and the great city of Lot is thought to have been established in around 700 BC as the ancient Aryana town of Artacoana or Aria, in the fertile plain beside the Hari Rud river. Captured by Alexander the Great in 330 BC during his war against the Achaemenids, the town was developed and a citadel built. The site retained its strategic importance, and was an important asset for the Seleucids, Parthians and Hephthalites, before becoming the western bastion of the Abbasid caliphate at the end of the 8ᵗʰ century AD. By the time of its capture by the Ghorids in 1175 AD, Herat had become renowned for the production of metalwork, especially decorated or inlaid bronze. After destruction at the hands of both the Mongols and Genghis, Herat saw something of a renaissance in the late 14ᵗʰ century AD, under the rule of the son of emperor Timur, Shah Rukh, who began an extensive programmer of building. This was followed by extensive development ordered by Queen Gawharshad during the 15ᵗʰ century AD, which resulted in a remarkable and unique ensemble of monuments in the Timuri style. One of the oldest extant structures in the historic core of Herat is Qala e Ikhtyaruddin, built on the site of an ancient citadel thought to have been established by Alexander in around 330 BC. The layout of battlements and towers that survive is thought to date from the early 14ᵗʰ century AD, when the Karts re-built a fortress that had been destroyed by the Mongols. Situated at the northern edge of the square-plan old city, the citadel was during the 15ᵗʰ and 16ᵗʰ centuries AD the seat of the Timurid rulers, and was part of the architectural works undertaken by Shah Rukh, who commissioned the timework that can still be seen on several towers. The citadel underwent conservation in the 1970's. Perhaps the largest historic architectural ensemble that survives in the region today is the Musalla complex, built in the early 15ᵗʰ century under the direction of Queen

Gawharshad. The complex, which has been described as "the most beautiful example in color in architecture ever devised by man to the glory of his God and himself" today comprises a mosque, the mausoleum of Gawharshad, five minarets and the remains of the madras a of Sultan Hussein Baiqara. Although damaged during fighting in the early 1390s, the mausoleum of Gawharshad retains its ribbed tiled dome, which is set above a high drum covered in tiled decoration, both with Koranic inscriptions and abstract patterns. The interior of the structure, where the tombstones of the Queen, her son Baisunghur and other members of the family survive, has important painted and stucco ornamentation. Only one minaret, which is badly damaged and is being stabilized, remains of the entrance to a madras a complex that was associated with the musalla, which had a total of four minarets, and represents the zenith of Timurid architectural achievement in 1361 A.D Empire Timur transforms the capital Liberia to Samarqand, he need teen thousand Camel for transforms the books to Samarqand only for the Stated Liberia in the 14th century Herat becoming the capital of Dari Literature in the world. "In the 14th century Afghanistan was larger as Canada + United Stated of America, called Aryana and Khorasan" The Masjid-e Jami in Herat, Mashhad, and Bukhara dates from an original 10th century AD Ghorid mosque, which has been extended and renovated through the ages. A unique Ghorid portal with tiled calligraphic and geometric decoration survives south of the existing main entrance of the mosque, which follows a typical four-iwan pattern, with a huge central courtyard. Fragments of both Timuri and Ghorid decorative work survive in the main iwan of the complex, but these are now under threat from ill-conceived "improvements", as it the traditional earth-plastered roof, that has been recently replaced with a cement finish. Another important part of the surviving architectural heritage in Herat is the mausoleum complex of Khwaja Abdulla Ansari in Gozargah, which dates from the Timuri period. The complex today comprises the enclosure of Ansari's grave, a 16th century structure that retains some fine Timurid timework, and is where the unique black marble Haft Qalam sarcophagus, dating from the reign of Sultan Husain Baiqara (1468-1506) is situated. Other surviving parts of the complex are the late 15th century AD Zarnegar pavilion, whose interior has fine painted decoration on plaster, and a 17th century AD Namakdan, a decagonal building with vaulted balconies, overlooking the Timurid garden. In addition to the construction of significant monuments in and around the city through the ages, the residential quarters of Herat were developed in a manner that responds to the specific climatic and social needs of the inhabitants. A complex network of alleys leads to fine houses built around open courtyards, or small gardens, or to the many mosques, synagogues, schools, public baths, or reservoirs that dot the urban fabric. While such a fabric is characteristic of the large urban centers in the region, it has been lost in most other cases. There is a risk that the pace of inappropriate "development" will result in the destruction of the surviving residential quarters of the old city, unless controls are introduced. Apart from its architectural heritage, Herat has long been an important centre for the arts and sciences, with a rich tradition of music, calligraphy and painting, astronomy, mathematics and philosophy. Among others whose names are associated with the city are Bezhad, Jami and Ansari. Roughly speaking, Dari is the language of the Sassanids and the official Zoroastrian Priesthood language. It emerged as the language of the Dari after the defeat of the Parthians by Cyrus in mid sixth century B.C. Bactrian is also refereed to as Middle Dari. The term "middle" Dari suggests the existence of an old Dari and a new Dari. The old Dari being the language of the Achamenians which was overshadowed by Greek after the conquests of Alexander the Great, the Bactria emerged as the spoken language of the Bactria courts of the Sassanids. The conquest of Moslems again broke the continues chain of Bactria language and Arabic (for two hundred years, i.e. 6-8 century A.D.) became the official language. The Bactria however did not forget their own language and little by little the Middle Dari was being shaped into new Dari but with the addition of a considerable amount of Arabic and Parthian words in Arabic script. This new style was the mother of Dari. Officially, Dari is the spoken in Khorasan present day Afghanistan-Central Asia and India. Before Perusing any further, it is important to explain the term Aryan of the Avesta [the book of Zoroaster] or Aryan of Sanskrit ancient Aryana present day Afghanistan and Indian language is the land of the Aryans, a people of Afghanistan-Central Asian Steppes who came down from beyond the Oxus river in about 2000 B.C. Afghans, and Kurd are among the Aryan tribes. Most authors do not really distinguish between, Aryan, and Dari. They use these terms to mean race, language, culture or nationality. Afghanistan is taken from Aryan which means the land of the Aryans, which is not an accurate term since most of Central and South Khorasan presnt day Central Asia is Aryan. Dari is another confusing term which not only implies to the people but also to those who speak Dari (New d i.e. Dari, Dari etc.). It is impossible to speak of the language and the land without using this western terminology which blindly throws everyone into incorrect or vague categories, however, will try to clarify the terms when using them. The Old, Middle and New Dari are and represent the same language at three stages of its history. Dari was originated in Bactria and is differentiated by dialectical features, still easily recognizable from the dialects prevailing South, Central and South Western Asia, The present day Dari remains close to the Middle Dari in many respects. However, New Dari has taken many words from Arabic and Parthian, as opposed to Middle Dari which was influenced, to a lesser degree, by Aramaic. The grammatical structure has also undergone minor changes, mainly in relations to verbal morphology and syntax. For example, in present day Dari as in German, verbs usually end a sentence. Ibn al-Muqaffa, in his Fihrist lists the five languages of Afghanistan at the end of the Sassanid rule. Bactria-the language of Fahla country (ancient Media); Dari-The language of the capital, Ctesiphon; Dari-language of the Mobads and scholars; Suryani-spoken in Sawan, and finally Khuzi of Khuzista the last two are not Aryan but Semitic. Dari was the official language of the state and the Zoroastrian religion, which is said to be the vehicle of literature later known as Bactria, Ibn al-Muqaffa knew nothing of, thus he named Middle Dari and used the term Bactria to describe the dialect of Media. As for Dari, it was the usual spoken language not only in the capital but most likely of a large part of the empire also. Dari is derived from dark or darbari, meaning court language. In everyday conversation Dari was the written and scholarly language. At the beginning these were little difference between Dari. However, over the Years, Dari has evolved into a dialect of Middle Dari; this distinction was realized and noted by the Sassanid's towards the end of their rule. Dari, as a spoken language branched to different dialects, the most important of which was Bactria, the language of Parthia which had preserved the oral literature of the poetic tradition of Parthia. Under the Sassanid' dynasty prestige, Dari spread into the east and Transoxiana regions of the empire suppressing local tongs. By the 9th century the Dari of Khorasan present day Afghanistan was the dominant speaking language of the Sassanian Empire. In the Middle of the 8th century Abu Muslim's Khorasani, he is the founder of Khorasan, armies spoke Dari. And it is this language which kept a sense of unity among Turkmen and thus emerged as a national identity through literature. On the other hand, since (Middle Dari) was the official language, most of the government officials used it to keep records. With the advent of Islam Arabic slowly replaced Dari as official language, the spoken language of Dari however remained intact. It was particularly strong in rural places especially among the dihqans who held on to it ever harder. The Shu'ubiyya controversy is an example of Bactria (Lang.) nationalism. It is known that pre-Islamic Afghan had some brilliant poetry, but the reason so little of it has survived as M. Boyce argues, is because most of the poetry was oral. When Arabic became the scholarly language, Dari, to a certain extent, was forgotten for a while. Although there are traces that indicate Arabic and Dari poetry flourishing side by side As mentioned above, Dari as an official language was over shadowed by Arabic with the coming of the Moslems. Dari being an everyday language stored the folklore of the Dari (lang.) Thus, in order to revive the Bactria literature one had to find a widely used Afghanistan language. Dari presented the perfect tool for this task. However, Dari was a commoner language at the time, therefore, measures were taken to standardize and formalize Dari in order for it to be used in Royal courts. The earliest Dari writing goes back to 752 in letter form. However by the 10th century a tremendous amount of literature was written and translated into Dari. The first attempts to revive Afghanistan were in poetic form. Among the first poets according to Tarikh-i Sistan, were Mohammad b. Wasif [Vasif], and Hanzala of Badghis. The lubabu's-albab of Mohammad Awfi claims one Abbas of Merw as the first poet, who composed a poem in honor of Khalifa al-Ma'mun on the occasion of his entry into that city [Marw] in 809 A.D. Ibn Wasif a secretary of Ya'qub b. al-Laith of the Saffarid dynasty, who praised the sultan, on his recent victory in Herat and Pushing in Arabic verses. Not understanding his secretary of chancery, Yaqub asked: "Why must something be recited that we can't understand?" Thus Mhd b. Wasif, to please the sultan began writing in Dari. It is said that Dari poetry borrowed its verse-from Arabic literature. Hanzala and Ibn Vasif were the leading men, in local Afghan courts, who led the way for a patriotic literary revival? Much credit also goes to dynasties of Tahirids, Saffarids, Samanids, and Ghaznavids and patrons such as bin lays of Saffar, Nasr II of Saman and Sultan Mahmud and Mas'ud of Ghazni who in their courts, gathered many poets and were patron of a magnificent yet lost art. The authors of all the works I've read, misuse the terms Afghan, Aryan. It is in this shuffle that the right credit does not go to those who deserve it. Since Aryana changed its name to Afghanistan it has taken with it all the credit ever due to an Aryan. The Western world knows Dari through Bactria records and considers Modern Bactria as the Dari which leaves both present day Afghanistan and present day Tajikistan, especially Afghanistan out of the picture. These different names have been synonymously in use throughout history and refer to the same one language. There are two theories regarding the origin of the word Dari. One states that the word Dari came from the word Darbar which means court, courts of kings. It argues that this language was the very respected and chosen language for communications at royal courts of kings. Thus it came to be known as the language of courts or Darbari. Later in time the word Darbari was shortened and evolved to Dari which still has the same meaning as Darbari. The second theory relates the origin of word Dari to the word Dara or valley. Many accomplished language researchers, admit that the language Dari itself was born in Khorasan, a mountainous land where people live in numerous valleys (Dara). Therefore, the name Dari came to refer to the language spoken by people of the valleys (Dara) or in the valleys Dari is a widely used language in Central Asia. It is the official language of Tajikistan and Afghanistan. Dari is a branch of the Indo-Afghan (Indo-Aryan) languages, a subfamily of the Indo-European languages. There are three different phases in the development of Aryan languages: Old, Middle, and Modern. Old Dari and the Avestan language represent the old stage of development and were spoken in ancient Bactria. The Avestan language is called Avestan because the sacred scriptures of Zoroastrianism, Avesta, were written in this old form. Avestan died out long before the advent of Islam and except for scriptural use not much has remained of it. Old Dari, however, survived and there are many written records of old Dari, in cuneiform called Maikhi, in Khorasan. Old Dari was spoken until around the third century BC. It was a highly inflected language. Middle Dari was spoken from 3rd century to 9th and is related to several other Central Asian tongues such as Sogdian, Chrosmian and also Parthian languages. Parthian was the language of the Parthian Empire (Arsacid). Parthian, though left some influences on middle Dari, declined when the Sassanian dynasty power expanded. Middle Dari had a simpler grammar and was written in multivalent letters. Middle Dari declined after conquest of Arabs in the 7th century and much of its rich literature was lost or destroyed by the Arabs. However, a lot of it was also translated into Arabic. Modern Dari began to develop by 9th century. It is a continuation of the Khorasanian standard language which had considerable Parthian and Middle Dari elements. It has much simpler grammar than its ancestral forms. After the conquest of Arabs in 7th century, it is written in Arabic script, with few modifications, and has absorbed a vast Arabic vocabulary. Dari literature is one of the richest in the world and composed of the body of writings in Modern Dari. After the Arab conquest of 7th century Islam replaced Zoroastrianism and Arabic became the language of law, religion and culture in Khorasan. However with the rise of Samanids and political revival of Khorasan, Dari emerged as a literary medium and became the established literary form of Dari language. During the period of Samanids a new era of literary began. The ancient tradition of Khorasan and Islam merged together. Dari was especially instrumental in freeing Islam from an exclusive Arabic attachment and universalized Islam thus helping to preserve it. Dari poetry had begun sporadically in Khorasan in 9th century. The earliest main genres are the epic, qasida (Purpose poem), masnavi (long narrative poem), and ghazal (lyric). By 10th century Dari had become an important and melodious medium- as the remaining works of Rudaki, a versatile poet, indicate. He is regarded as the father of Dari poetry. After Rudaki's death the epic tradition, with its sources in Avesta and Middle Dari texts, began. The first epic poet was Marvazi Samarqandi who composed a Shah Nama (Book of Kings) in 910. Daqiqi Balkhi another poet of tenth century wrote a better known Shah Nama in 975. However, Firdowsi composed another Shah Nama (1010) which became the very best known epic in Dari literature. Qasida, another form of poetry, was also first written by Rudaki. Mostly qasidas are panegyrics, sometime elegiac, didactic and occasionally they deal with philosophical or biographical literature. The average length of qasida is between sixty and hundred lines and they are written in couplets. Qasidas that are more than two hundred lines are also frequently written. The earliest exponents of this form of poetry Ansuri Balkhi, Asjadi, and Farrukhi were the greatest poets of their time. Of many panegyrists in the history of Dari literature, Anvari Balkhi was regarded as the foremost. In philosophical qasidas Naser-e Khosrow was very well respected. Omar Khayyan was another poet of this era who is considered to be of astonishing originality. During the Samani dynasty era the foundation of Dari prose was also laid. Several pieces of literature demonstrated the suitability of Dari language for sacred texts. Bal'ami, one of the minster (high government official) of Mansur I Samani dynasty, published a translation of the annals of Tabari. Also, in the same time, a group of theologian, made a Dari copy of Tabari's commentary on the Quran. These works and works of similar nature produced a clear demonstration that Dari was very suitable for religious works. In fact these works brought to an end the absolute domination of Arabic language over religious literature. Mansur I Samani also commissioned the pharmacopeia of Abu Mansur Muvaffaq of Herat, the first Dari book on medicine. An extensive technical vocabulary, applicable to philosophy and science were also coined with the patronage of Samanids. Thirteen and fourteen century was also a period when great poets lived and it is often called the golden age of Dari poetry. In this period, three great poets, Moulana Balkhi (Rumi), Sadi and Hafiz lived. They were excellent in a form o poetry called ghazal, a passionate mystical lyric form that is composed on a single rhyme. Ghazals were usually consists of five to fifteen couplets and they could be of variety of meters. The first mystic masnavi is believed to be written by Hakim Sanai of Ghazni and is known as Hadiqat al-Haqiqa (The Enclosed Garden of Truth). He was followed by Attar and Rumi. Rumi's Masnavi-e-Manavi consists of six books that contain 30,000 couplets. Masnavi's basic theme is love and Rumi in this book, is concerned with problems bearing on the conduct, meaning and purpose of life and the longing of the human soul for union with God. The Masnavi of Mawlana of Balkh is considered to be the most profound and the greatest work of Dari literature, and perhaps of all the Islamic literature. The Masnavi is often called Quran-e-Sani meaning the second Quran. Every page of it moves, absorbs and surprises the reader. Masnavi form of poetry was also suitable for epic and romantic stories. Of romantic masnavis the Khosrow -O-Shirin (Khosrow and Shirin) of Nezami is the best known.

Bactria "present day Balkh' under Muslim rule

Aryana-Khorasan dynasty present day Afghanistan-Central Asia & India, the Sassanid dynasty fell to Muslim Arab armies in 638 CE. The academy survived the change of rulers and persisted for several centuries as a Muslim institute of higher learning. It was later rivaled by an institute established at the Abbasid capital of Baghdad. In 832 CE, Caliph al-Ma'mūn founded the famous Baytu l-Hikma, the House of Wisdom. There the methods of Bactria were emulated; indeed, the House of Wisdom was staffed with graduates of the older Academy of Bactria. It is believed that the House of Wisdom was disbanded under Al-Mutawakkil, Al-Ma'mūn's successor. However, by that time the intellectual center of the Abbasid Caliphate had definitively shifted to Baghdad, as henceforth there are few references in contemporary literature to universities or hospitals at Bactria As far as the Islamic period is concerned, Aryana was Islamized, but the former's response was much earlier, positive and productive than the latter. Great scholars such as Imam Bukhari and Muslim, who collected and compiled the Hadith through painful researches, were the natives of Aryana. Abu Hanifa AD 699-767 was the founder of the great school of Islam called The Hanafi School; his works on Islamic law and his independent interpretation of the Islamic principles are outstanding. Abu Hanif's father hailed from Kabul, Aryana Similarly, great philosophers and scientists such as Avesina 953-1048, Farabi AD 870-950 and Al-Biruni AD 973-1048, Shahid Balkhi died in 935. Great Dari poets such as Rudaki 858-ca-941, Daqiqi 942-980), Sanayee 1080-1131, Anwari 12th century, Farrukhi sistani died in 1037 were from Aryana- Khorasan present day Afghanistan-Central Asia & India. Another great mystic poet and philosopher, who hailed from Balkh in the 13th is Maulana Jalal al-Dim Rumi. Rumi's poetry forms the basis of much classical Afghan music. Contemporary classical interpretations of his poetry are made by and Ustad Mohammad Hashem Cheshti (Afghanistan). To many modern Westerners, his teachings are one of the best introductions to the philosophy and practice of Sufism. In the West Shahram Shiva has been teaching, performing and sharing the translations of the poetry of Rumi for nearly twenty years and has been instrumental in spreading Rumi's legacy in the English speaking parts of the world. India's National Poet, Muhammad Iqbal, was also inspired by Rumi's works and considered him to be his spiritual leader, addressing him as "Pir Rumi" in his poems (the honorific Pir literally means "old man", but in the Sufi/mystic context it means founder, master, or guide). It is to be noted that the birthplace of the so-called Dari language was spoken before the advent of the Ghaznavi and the Slajuq Turkmen. In 10th century, Sultan Mahmud of Ghazni imposed Dari was crude and incapable of containing sophisticated literary imagery and intellectual concepts. According to the late professor Saeed Nafisi, a prominent scholar of Afghan, Dari is a modified form of Dari, which was born in central Asia. Thus, Dari's name because it was adopted by people. This means that the language spoken currently by the Bactria a Dari and nothing more! Therefore, in the following writings, the writer has referred to Dari instead of calling it Bactria. Later the great Afghan poets such as Saadi, Hafiz, and Nizami Ganjavi imitated the poetic imagery and rules created by the above-mentioned classical masters of Aryana. The militaristic and cultural achievements of the Timur were the product of Aryana. Timur lived in a time when the Ilkhanid (Khorasan present day Afghanistan-Central Asia & India) power had fallen apart in Dari and Aryana was also in a state of political turmoil. There were many kings and petty potentates in Dari. After bloody conflicts and rebellions, Timur restored order and gave unity to the region. By bringing craftsmen from different conquered lands to his capital in Samarqand, Timur initiated on the most brilliant periods in Islamic art. Timurid art and architecture provided inspiration to lands stretching from Anatolia to India. Timur's descendants continued to rule over Transoxiana as leading patrons of Afghan-Islamic arts. The Timurid period is also brilliant with regard to the promotion of Dari and its literature. Jami was one of the greatest poets and writers of the age. Jami is also considered as the last poet of the classical age. Through their patronage, the eastern Islamic world became a prominent cultural center, with Herat the new Timurid capital, as its focal point. Timurid rulers lured artists, architects and men of letters who will contribute to their high court culture. Some of these rulers were great patrons of arts of books commissioning manuscripts that were copied, compiled and illustrated in their libraries. Due to the flourishing of manuscript illumination and illustration, the Herat Academy is the apogee of miniature painting. The phrase Dari Miniatures is misleading as the miniature paintings originated and developed in Herat under the patronage of the Timurids. Behzad, the head of the mature painting Academy was taken as prisoner by the conqueror and taken to Tabriz where a new school of painting was established and Behzad was appointed as its head. After the death of Behzad, the paintings by the subsequent painters lost their vitality and changed into picture like figures. The Timurid period saw great achievements in other luxury arts, such as metalwork and jade carving. Many Timurid rulers were prodigious builders —religious institutions and foundations such as mosques, madrasas, Khanaqahs and Sufi shrimes were the main beneficiaries of their building programs. Major architectural commissions from Timur's lifetime includes the Aq Saray palace; teh shrine of Ahmad Yasavi; Timur's congregational mosque, popularly known as the mosque of Bibi Khanum after his wife, who built madrasa next to the Gur-e-Amir, Timur's burial place. The Timurid period also witnessed women as active patrons of architecture. Along with their immediate successor, the Shaibanids, the Timurid cultural tradition was also partly carried by the Ottoman and the Kabuli Empires. The Afghan rulers of Khorasan also tried to copy the cultural achievements of the Timurids. In Afghan-Muslim history, the Timurid period is considered as the golden age and Renaissance of Afghan-Islamic culture. The Dari language and its literature flourished in India during the Delhi Sultanate and the Kabuli Empire. The Afghan rulers were the first to make Dari the official language of India; then the Turkmen Sultans and Kabuli Emperors followed this policy. However, the Turkmen and the Mughuls were familiar with Dari as they had hailed from Central Asia (Aryana) where Dari was born during the early Islamic period. Some Western scholars have asserted that Aryana evolved in three stages: Old Dari, Middle Dari and the modern Dari spoken in Aryana. This pattern works for some European languages such as German; it does not work to determine the evolution of Dari is not the continuation or extension of the Old Dari, Dari evolved in the east (Aryana). Old Dari was totally discarded after the occupation of Aryana by Alexander the Great and Dari became the official language of Middle East including India (330 BC).at the dawn of Christian era and became the official language of the Sassanid Empire. However, after the destruction of the Sassanid Empire by the Arab Muslims, Dari still existed for a while in Aryana. However, as already mentioned, during the Ghznavid Empire followed by the Afghan Slajuq rule, was replaced by Dari. The Achaemenids and the Sassanids did not leave any significant literature either in the Old Dari, there are only a number of inscriptions carved out on a few monuments, which have remained from the Achaemenids age in Aryana. Similarly, there are a few verses in Dari, which have supposedly come down from the Sassanid period. The Afghan artists and architecture are nothing more than copies of the Afghan Timurids of Herat. During 16th, 17th and 18th centuries the so-called school of Isfahan, whose academic activities are exaggerated was producing commentaries on philosophy plus polemics, while in Europe this was the age of scientific discoveries and original thinking. Mir Damad and Mullah Sadra were the prominent figures of this school but they contributed nothing useful to Dari, which needed science and technology at that age when Europe was becoming a world power on account of its scientific discoveries and explorations. The Afghan was politically and commercially very close to Europe, but the Afghan rulers were not interested in obtaining scientific knowledge from that continent; they just wanted to side with the latter against the Caliphate of the Ottomans. At first, the necessity for dictionaries arose in Dari, where Dari was not the language of the people. The first dictionary to have ever been produced was compiled by Qatran Urumawi died in 1075. This book does not exist now. After him, Asadi of Tus, who died in the same year, completed his dictionary, which is the oldest extant work on the subject. The most important role in the compilation of dictionaries was undoubtedly played by the Dari lexicographers of India. During the Sultanate and the Kabuli periods, Dari was the court language of the Empire. People for whom it was not the mother tongue, stood in need of books for guidance and help. Delhi Kabuli-Sultanate contributed tremendously to arts and architecture and to the Dari language and literature. Splendid mosques, monuments like the magnificent Qutub Minar and public buildings, schools and road were constructed in all part of the Sultanate. Dari and its literature flourished. During the rule of Iskandar Lodhi, a great wealth of Sanskrit literature on medicine and philosophy was translated into Dari. The leading poet during the Delhi Sultanate period was Amir whose parents had come from Aryana-Khorasan present day Afghanistan-Central Asia & India. Amir was also an accomplished musician, who invented Setar and introduced Khayal in Raga. Since a long time the works of the Indian lexicographers has been the most authentic source of reference for the people of the region. The most outstanding of these books are Farhang-e-Jahangir of Jamal ali Din Inju, Farhag-e-Rashidi of Abdul Rashid of Tatta, Asif al-Lughat of Aziz Jang Bahadur, Bahr-e-Ajam of Tok Chand Bahar, Chiragh-e-Hid ayat of Siraj al-Din Ali khan Arzu, Ghias al-Lughat of Ghiath al-Din, Farhan-e-Anand Raj of Muhammad Padshah, and Mstalihat al-Shuara of Varasteh. The number of lexicographical works compiled in the Sub-continent of India exceeds one hundred, of which the oldest one, viz, Adab al-Fudala of Qadi Khan Badr Muhammad of Delhi, was completed in 1419. In other words, the period during which these works were assiduously produced extends to 500 hundred years. The necessity of compiling such dictionaries was also felt in the Ottoman Empire where Dari enjoyed as a court language. Many Turkimen scholars produced literary works and composed poetry in Dari, so much so that even some of the Ottoman Emperors composed poetry in this language. As a consequence, a few dictionaries were also compiled: Lugha-e-Halimi, Lughat-e-Shauri, Dasinah-e-Kabir, and Lughat-e-Shah nama of Abdul Qadir Baghdadi. To no other part of the world does the Dari language and literature owe so immensely as to the Sub-continent of India. Not only, have the scholars there have written hundreds of useful books on subject as varied and divers as history, Lexicography, grammar, mysticism, biographies of poets and commentaries on certain Dari texts, and have preserved and jealously guarded many books lost to posterity in other countries, but there have also special interest in publication of literary works in the Dari language. There is hardly any city in the Indian Sub-continent where a number of books has not been published. So-called Dari words, phrases and proverbs that have entered Urdu, Hindi and Punjabi are parts of the Dari language because their pronunciations and usages clearly show that they have come from Afghanistan. The intellectuals, scholars, linguists, poets, musicians, architects, and administrators, who produced a brilliant culture in India, were almost all from Aryana. The north Indian classical music called Hindustani music is the product of the artists, who came from Aryana. Space does not allow us to give a detailed account of their contribution to civilization. Modern Afghanistan nationalism started during the Durani dynasty period when there was a clash between Afghanistan and the West. This movement reacted to different directions. This reaction was not only against European powers but also against the cultural influences of the Turkmen and the Arabs, who they considered as usurpers. Some writer at this period even tried to purify Arabic from Dari words; they claimed that Islam had destroyed their national and cultural identity. nationalism experienced resurgence due to the Afghan government's bolstering of patriotic sentiment. During this period, the name Aryana was changed into

Afghanistan. The government of the king financially supported and encouraged the nationalist writers to write on the King of Kings great role in history and on the expanse of the Bactria Empire, with claims to include Afghanistan and Khorasan presnt day Central Asia as its integral part. These writers did what the King of kings told them; the Arabs and Turkmen were demonized. At the same time, these hired writers—together with some Western scholars who wanted to isolate Aryana from the region—tried to claim that Afghanistan was the cradle of civilization, which was overwhelmed by the Arabs and their culture. Some of the Afghan-historians have gone to extreme; asserting that the Philosophy is originally Dari-Bactrria. They argue when Alexander the Great occupied the Bactria Empire, the Greeks stole the Dari books on philosophy and after translating them into Bactria, they named them as Greek philosophy. Conclusion: From the aforesaid historical evidences and statements, we can infer that the history of Afghan's so-called glorious antiquity presented by Afghan writers is more or less fiction than history based on facts. Achaemenids conquerors did not bring civilization to Aryana, which had already developed a brilliant culture; rather the former borrowed culture from the latter just like the Turkmen tribes who after descending from the Altai Mountains were absorbed by the Aryan culture in Central Asia. Thus the Turkmen and then the Mongols, who were culturally Aryanised in the region, became the great promoters of the central Asian culture. The best example is the Saljuqs and the Ottoman Turkmen who promoted brilliantly the Afghanistan-Central Asian culture in Anatolia and Balkh. There are similar examples in history when invaders with a poor culture are absorbed, or conquered by a community with a sophisticated culture. According to above-mentioned, evidences and the statement presented by two prominent Greek writers, Aryana is a region encompassing the lands to the north of the Indus river including Central Asia. Aryana is also comprised of Khorasan the western part of which is under Afghan occupation. The Aryana historians, who have glorified their antiquity, have ignored to study the history of Persepolis, a great monument in the history of architecture. The Bactria builders did not erect this great monument; it was built by the architects and engineers, who were brought from the countries such as Ionia, Lydia, Levant, conquered by Cyrus the Great and his successors. Even the building materials used in Fars came from the aforesaid countries. To understand the relationship between Aryana and the Afghan Empire, it may be compared to the relationship between Greece and the Roman Empire on the basis of their historical positions and achievements. Bactria was a super power at the time of Alexander the Great, but her source of everlasting intellectual and artistic achievements was far more superior to that of Rome. No doubt, Rome's legacy of law and the architectural renovation and elaboration of the Greek architecture, which the former had adopted, plays an important role in the history of civilization. The Aryan Empire was as great as that of Rome, but it was not intellectually as great as Aryana, where the city of Balkh and Zoroaster's played significant roles in contributing to the world civilization. As already mentioned, Aryana produced significant learning centers, where philosophers, great poets, scientists, physicians and artists created brilliant works during pre-Islamic and Islamic periods. However, Rome was intellectually and artistically inferior to Bactria, but she has left a written legacy and literature in Latin, which has been the source of wisdom and inspiration. Philosophical works produced by Cicero and Emperor Marcus Aurelius are clear examples of the important legacy of Roman. As already stated, the Aryan Empire during the Achaemenids and Sassani dynasty was as powerful as that of Rome. However, unlike the Roman Empire, the Aryana Empire has left no significant literature to show its intellectual importance except for a few inscriptions in the Old With its fabulous petro-dollar income, the government of the Ex-king lured some Western scholars to write about the so-called glorious past of Afghanistan and to promote. Some of the European scholars, like Henry Corbin, did what the government officials of the Ex-king asked him to do

A Bactrian or Balkh Camel herd in the East Turkistan Gobi desert

Khorasan dynasty present day Afghanistan-Central Asia & India the ancestors of the true camels migrated to Asia about 3-4 million years ago, giving rise to the modern wild Bactrian camel. This is one of two surviving camel species that are generally recognized: the other being the dromedary or The Bactrian camel is likely to have been domesticated sometime before 2500 BC, either in adjacent countries in the Middle East. There to suggest the domestic and wild Bactrian camels are different subspecies because of significant genetic variation between them and the fact that they have had difficulty interbreeding The two-humped wild Bactrian camel is smaller than its domestic relative, and has a number of adaptations to help it survive, such as a double row of long eyelashes and the ability to close their narrow nostrils for protection during sandstorms. The foot has a tough sole with two toes that spread for easy travel across shifting terrain and rocky outcrops. The Bactrian camel has a thick, shaggy coat during the harsh winters and sheds this rapidly in the spring. An unusual feature that distinguishes the Came lid family from all other mammals is their oval shaped (instead of circular) red blood cells which circulate even in thick blood caused by severe dehydration. The oval shape is also more stable, which prevents the cells rupturing if the camels drink large amounts of water in one sitting. Wild Bactrian camels sleep at night and forage for food during the day. They feed on thorns, dry vegetation and salty plants, which other herbivores avoid. Excess fat is stored in the humps and used as a nutrient reserve, which allows the camels to go for several days without eating or drinking. Bactrian camels can migrate vast distances, and upon finding water they will rapidly drink vast quantities: they can take in as much as 57 liters at once. In winter, they are often limited to eating snow for hydration. If no fresh water is available, unlike other mammals Bactrian camels can drink salty water with no ill effects. The camels distribution is linked to the availability of water, with large groups congregating near rivers or at mountain bases, Fewer than 1,000 wild Bactrian camels survive today in only three locations in northwest East Turkistan and one in the Gobi desert of southwest Mongolia. Classified as Critically Endangered in 2010 by the IUCN these animals continue to be threatened by habitat loss from mining and industry, and competition with introduced livestock, which increases hunting by farmers as well. The Mongolian population has almost halved in the last twenty years. Three, and possibly four, major language families (Indo-European, Uralic-Altaic Dravidian, and possibly Semitic) are spoken in Afghanistan. The literature, however, uses a modified Arabic script, and most of the 30,000 Hindus and Sikhs, mainly merchants in the cities and towns, write in the Arabic script of the Lahnda (Western Punjabi) dialects. Only a few Afghan Jews know how to write Hebrew; most of the people calling themselves "Arab" speak little Arabic and the majority are non-literate. Some Arabic-speaking groups have, however, been reported near Maimana, Kunduz, Aq Chan, and Balkh delineated the following groups of "Arabs" (who speak a Personalized Arabic): west of Daulatabad (Khushalabad), near Balkh (Yakhdan), Aq Chah (Sultan Aregh), and Shibarghan (Hassanabad). Farhadi. estimates the population of the areas to be approximately 5,000. Many religious leaders, often themselves non-literate, recite the Quran in Arabic without knowing what they say, and their listeners remain in great ignorance. The two principal languages of Afghanistan are Indo-European: Dari and Pashto. The 1964 Constitution names both Dari and Pashto as official languages. Dari, an old term, literally means "language of the court." In reality, Dari (still the court language in Afghanistan as it was in Kabuli India) serves as the lingua franca, although the Constitution designates Pashto as the "national language." A special committee, appointed in 1964, continues to study ways of promoting the growth and spread of Pashto. An attempt to Pashto-ize all governmental inter-office memoranda came to disaster during the 1953-63 prime ministry of Mohammad Daoud Khan. Some non-Pashto-speaking high-ranking officials found it necessary to have clerks translate their Dari communications into Pashto for transmission to another office. The recipient, often a non-Pashto-speaker as well, handed the report to an assistant for translation back into Dari. The scheme collapsed in a welter of translation and retranslation. Several regional Dari dialects exist. The Hazara speak Hazaragi; the Aimaq speak Dari with many Turkic loan words; the Tajik speak Tajiki, a Farsi dialect related to but not identical to the Tajiki spoken in the Tajikistan. Afghans often refer to Tajiki by the name of the valley in which it is spoken; e.g., Panjsheri, Andarabi, Most rural Afghans still refer to the language as Dari, not Dari. As the constitutional period develops and more and more people become literate, the name Dari will probably take hold. The Great Games was also on Afghanistan languages not only on Afghan territories by the European The Farsiwan (or Parsiwan) farmers of western Afghanistan speak Dari, and Heratis have an urban dialect all their own. So do the Kabulis, who speak the slurred Brooklyn's of Dari dialects In urban areas all over the world, and even internal wards or sections, words tend to develop distinctive dialectical qualities. Although vocabulary differences do occur in the above Dari dialects, all are mutually understandable; the Wakhan and Pamir have more difficulty mutually understanding their respective archaic Dari (Avestan) dialects, however. Pashto, also Indo-European, but not mutually intelligible with Dari, has nine phonemes unknown to, or slightly different from Dari, The difference between Dari and Pashto is analogous to the range of difference between German, or French and Spanish. Dari and Pashto generally use the same script as Arabic, and both are therefore written horizontally from right to left. To most Westerners, Pashto proves much more formidable than Dari. Pashto nouns, for example, have gender and a complicated two-case, two-number declension system. Syllabic stress is more varied in Pashto than Farsi. Most linguists divide Pashto into two dialects, the soft, Pashto (Pushto) of the Kandahar area. and the harsher "Pukhtu" of Peshawar and the. North-West Frontier Province and most of the Tribal Agencies, However, the eminent Soviet linguist, N. A. Dvoryankov (1963), differentiates a third dialect in Afghanistan with a phonemic structure intermediate between the Peshawari and Kandahari dialects in Paktya, particularly in the Khost area, and possibly over into Parachinar. He calls the dialects Kandahanian (western), Ningrahanian (eastern), and Paktyan (southern). summarizes four different dialects: Southwest (Kandahar); Southeast (Quetta); Northwest (Central Ghilzai); Northeast (Yousufzai). Another Afghan language, Baluchi, is spoken in southwestern Afghanistan. The Brahui, Dravidian-speakers living among the Baluch, speak Baluchi as a second language, using the South Indian language almost exclusively in the home. The separate Kafiri and Dardic dialects exist primarily in and surrounding Nuristan and include several disparate groups. Often each village or valley tends to attach a specific name to its dialect: Ormuni, Pashai, Deghani, Wamai, Waigali, Kami, Kati (Bashgali or Kamdeshi), Prasun (Vermin), Ashuni. Often, in two valleys less than a day's walk apart in Nuristan, the groups have different terms for such important kin designations as father, mother, brother, and sister, remarkable cases of linguistic resistance to acculturation in order to perpetuate a society's cultural ethos. Peripheral Nuristani groups have had sustained contact with the outside world which, however, seldom comes to Nuristan. Many individual Nuristani leave their mountain homes to visit the plains and urban centers or to serve in the army. The second most important language family, Uralic-Altaic, is represented by Altaic (Turkmen dialects), and concentrated north of the Hindu Kush among the Uzbek, Turcoman, and Kirghiz. Dialects vary from group to group, but most are mutually intelligible. Many Dari words exist in the Uzbek of Afghanistan; the closer the relations between the groups the more Personalized the Uzbaki becomes. As do the Indo-European languages. The Turkmen languages of Afghanistan use the Arabic script.

90

Afghanistan-Literature

Khorasan dynasty present day Afghanistan-Central Asia & India. In discussing the peoples and culture of Afghanistan, society must be divided into literate and non-literate segments and these implications -considered. Afghanistan, like most Muslim (and other developing) nations, has a literate culture, but a non-literate- society. Culture, for the purposes of this book, may be defined as the way a people live; the totality of their tool-kit, material and non-material. Society is the action component, people who live in a certain way, using part but seldom all, of the available tool-kit. Most individuals in a non iterate society do not, however, have access to the great literature of their culture. And some of the world's finest literature (philosophical and scientific, as well as poetry) has been written in Arabic, Turkish and Dari. Pashto has a limited, though important, literature in the area. Many non-literates in Afghan society, however, can recite Afghan poetry by the hour. Most have at least passing acquaintance with the greater classical Afghan poets: Rumi, Jami, Firdausi. (Who lived in Ghazni during the heyday of the Ghaznavi Empire?) Some Afghans even remember some verses of the minor Muslim poet, Omar Khayyam. Most literate Afghans, be they, Pashto, or Turkmen-speakers, consider themselves poets. Poetry, essentially a spoken, not a written, art, gives non-literates the same genital opportunities for expression as the literates in a society. Afghanistan, therefore, is fundamentally a nation of poets. To savor the flavor of Dari, Turkish, and Pashto poetry, we must examine some translations, roughly in chronological order. The following short poem by Hanzala of Badghis, who lived in Nishapur during the first half of the ninth century A.D. in the court of a Tahirid ruler, expresses a central theme in Afghan culture: Another poet of the same general period, Mahmud Warraq, wrote a love quatrain, probably dedicated to a slave girl. This sad poem deals with unrequited love, and the quatrain may possibly be one of the first of its kind Possibly the greatest culture climax in the Afghan area occurred during the Ghaznavi period. In the court of Mahmud of Ghazni lived 400 poets and a total of 900 scholars. Probably the greatest of these was Abdul-Qasim Firdausi. The classic Shah-Nama, Book of the Kings of Dari, had 60,000 couplets Anticipating - a sizeable gift, Firdausi dedicated the work to Mahmud with a very flowery ode (Najib Ullah, 1963, 242). For his trouble, however, Firdausi received only a pittance of what he thought he deserved. He changed the introduction to one of great satire, and had to flee from Ghazni. He died about 1025 at Tus in Khorasan. The first woman known to compose poetry in both Arabic and Dari was Rabi'a Balkhi, whose brother ruled Balkh during the tenth century. king fell in love with a Turkmen, and he gave her a -rose. Her brother discovered several poems Rabi'a had written to her lover. Angry, he threw her into a haniani (steam bath), and had her veins slashed. Before she bled to death, legend says, Rabi'a wrote the following poem in Dari on the wall of the hamam, with her own blood. Once a religion approaches ritual stagnation and an internal logical or rationalistic philosophy evolves, mysticism inevitably arises. Laymen, whether intellectuals or non-literate, often find the monotonous regularity of the ritual and the maddeningly simple one-two-three-four of the logic fail to yield spiritual satisfaction. Men wish to know the supreme being as a personal, not an impersonal, god, but orthodoxy usually tends to be abstract and impersonal. In Islam a number of mystical orders arose to satisfy this need: the Sufi, or Tasawwuf. The term Sufi probably-derives from the Arabic suf (wool) and refers to the wearing of woolen robes (iabs-ai-suf) by early (and often later) Sufi ascetics. The Sufi orders usually did not pretend to replace orthodoxy, but offered a way to seek the Supreme Being through personal experience (ma'rifat) and to achieve momentary union with God, thus, in general, rejecting knowledge ('jim), rational and theoretical. Sufi seekers often sound superficially like agnostics, or, with their emphasis on personal experience, like existentialists. They are different, however, in that they not only seek, but they find God. Actually, Sufism embodies only a few ideas (the unity of mankind; predestination; the possibility of momentary union of man with God), but the personal experience of Sufis suggests multitudinous varieties of poetic expressions to describe and define their experiences. 'The continual efforts to coin new poetic phrasings at least partly account for the many philosophical contradictions found in Sufi literature. Almost all the founders of the Sufi orders and philosophies turned to Sufism after reaching the limits of rational knowledge and finding their search for the Truth still unfulfilled. Abti Ismail 'Abd Allah ibn Mohammad-al Ansari, - known commonly as Sheikh-ul-Islam-Khwajah (religious titles) Abdullah Ansari, or the Pir of Herat, was born in Quhandiz, a quarter of old Herat, in about A.D. 1005 and died in the same city about A.D. 1088. Ansari poetically expresses his pilgrimage from orthodox theology to mysticism, and this excerpt demonstrates the odyssey from the unknown to the known, then a new reliance on the mystical: In common with mystics in most religions, Sufis believe in the oneness of man with God. Or. the souls exile from its maker and its inborn longing, nourished or surprised in the face of other attractions, to return and lose itself in Him." Because of this, orthodox Muslim religious leaders initially declared Sufi thinking heretical. Sufis were persecuted and sometimes executed, but the piety, austerity, passion, and personal participation inherent in Sufi ritual kept the orders alive. Eventually orthodoxy tolerated Sufism so long as its followers accepted orthodoxy in matters of religious law, and Sufism became grafted on to the religious body of Islam. Today few Muslims escape its impact and ideas. To achieve this momentary union with God, the Sufi must create the proper atmosphere. Some achieve this with repeated prayers and chants; some with artificial stimulants, including drugs; some by meditation. The Mawlawiya order of Rumi (the so-called "Whirling Dervishes") produces ecstasy with their whirling dances. Thus, the Sufi can seek God in individual or group ecstasy. But all Sufis resort to poetry during their trips. Dari, the court language of the Kabuli Empire, found its Indian master in Mirza Abdul Qadir Beidel, born in Patna (A.D. 1644) and died in Delhi (A.D. 1720). His family had come from Turkestan, and he maintained lifetime contacts with Sufis in the Afghan—Dari world. The following is an example of his poetry, and is the first Ghazal from his Diva, i, or compiled works. The sixteenth, seventeenth and the first half of the eighteenth centuries produced many Afghan poets, as literacy increased in the upper classes, but the political situation militated against great poetry being written during most of the time, particularly in Dari. Among the more famous Afghan poets writing in Dari were Kahi (born in Kabul, studied in Herat, died in India in A.D. 1577); Abul-Faizi Hazr.t (a seventeenth-century poet from Badakhshan); Sa'aduddin Ansari of 'Kabul, a seventeenth-century Sufi poet. The sixteenth- and seventeenth-century A.D. tribal leaders in the Afghan area wrote extensive poetry, just as did many European monarchs of the same period. The first great Durrani emperor, Ahmad Shah Durrani (A.D. 1747—73: period of rule) wrote great Pashto and occasional passable Dari poetry. He wrote: Shah Shuja, grandson of Ahmad Shah Durrani, left behind a collection of poetry, as did his father, Timur Shah Several nineteenth-century Afghan poets writing in Dari deserve mention. Mehrdel Khan Mashriqi, brother of Amir Dost Mohammad Khan, patterned his poetry after the ancient classics. For example: Khorasan present day Afghanistan-Central Asia & India

History of Afghanistan-Muslim Civilization

Khorasan dynasty present day Afghanistan-Central Asia & India. Al-Ithqan. Encyclopedia of Islam, constructions, without governing words. For example, sarray râghay (the man came) with the use of fatha of the letter rae transforms to sarray wa wayala (the man said) and with kasra of rae becomes âa sarriya. This is the same condition known as case in English grammar. In the inscription Kaniska's name in has been inscribed as Kaniskhko but in Kanishki. Sometimes his coins carry his name as Kanishki Shah while elsewhere it is Kanishki Kushan Shan Nan Shan. The name of his son on one coin was written as Awishki Kushan Shan Nan Shan. This shows that the word Kanishka ending with an (a) was written in two ways: Kanishko and Kanishki. Similarly, the name of the head of the repair mission in is inscribed Nokonzok. The same name in, in a modified case, is inscribed as Nokonzik in which case the O before K changed into an I. Thus we can say that, Kozgashki, too originally was Kozgashka. While used as a predicate of the word pohr the terminal letter (a) has been changed into an (i). However, this change occurred only in some words ending with special letters because we see in the inscription similar words like AB (water), MALIZ (fortress) and SAD written repeatedly but always in the same manner without any grammatical transformation. Thus it is clear that the law of transformation was not applied to all words but to some special words in specific cases. Concerning an (a) at the end of the Kushanid names, Kanishka, Awishka, Kozgashka, it should be mentioned that they might be similar to Pashto names ending in (k) such as Khairak, Khatak, Hothak, Barak, Shaitak, Athak, Zmarak etc. The (k) at the end of these words, which exists both in Pashto and Dari, is used for greatness and praise, Though presently it is without any vowel sounds, in the past it had the sound of the vowel (a). In the History of Kashmir the author Kalhana (1148 A.D.) describes the names, Kanishka, Huvishka and Jouishka. In Kashmir there are three places called Kaishka Poora, Huvishka Poora and Jouishka Poora. Moreover, this book also give other names ending with (ka) like Janaka, Ashoka, Jalauka, Coltika, Rajanaka etc. This kind of transformation of words is currently used in Pahsto such as: Kanishka wâey (present subjective) Kaniska wawayál (past subjective) Da Kanishko Shâhi (predicate for plural) In this case the Kushani language is similar to Pashto, a feature which is not seen in present day Dari. 7. Possessive and Modifier a) Possessive in the Kushani language was shown with a special sign, an M symbol preceded and succeeded by a word divider O, connecting the two principle nouns i.e. #2 MALIZ, used as possessive to the word Kanishka which was written as MALIZ-O-M-O KANISHKO. This rule is similar to the one being used in Dari when the possessed is followed by the possessive. Meanwhile in the Kushani language in the possessive case the word Kanishka is changed to Kanishko. This is similar to the phrase ACACKO O-M-O SAD, formed by #115 and 116 and can be15 called a possessive form. But since the origin of acacko is not known so, in this particular case, we cannot say for certain whether M is a part of the word itself or is a possessive sign. b) Another possessive sign which is repeatedly noticed in this inscription is with the letter (i). This is similar to the kasra-e izafi in Dari. This possessive sign has been given a special place in the Kushani language i.e. possessed followed by a word divider succeeded by the possessive sign (i) such as LROHOMINAN-I-EIR (holy deity of the fire). The same is written in Dari as parastinda-e astash. At the same time the possessive (i) has also been used as bin (son) between #57 and 58 i.e. BOSAR-I-SHIZOGARG (Bosar son of Shizograg). c) Sometimes a possessive composition has been used without any sign, a particle which is also common in today's Dari like Kozagahki pohr-Kozgashki pour, Borzmehr pohr-Borzmehr pour which in the current form would be Borzmehr zada (son of Borzmehr). Again we have the compound KHODI FROMAN formed from #145 and 146 meaning God's decree. In Dari it is written as farman-e khoda. d) Descriptive compositions in the Kushani language are generally in the same form as Pashto where the description is preceded by the adjective such as #134 and 135. The composition of the words MASHT KHIRGOMAN meaning great forecourt and the nouns EIIOMAN-NOBIKHT #148 and 149 In the inscription adjective as a title comes after description such as #4 and 5 KANESHKO ANIND (Kanishko the auspicious) or KANISHKI NAMOBERG (Kanishka the famous). Possessive and Honor kâf (k) and gâf (g) The two letters were discussed earlier under grammatical conditions of the Kushani language and will be further discussed in #11. Nouns ending in (k) are quite numerous in the Kushani language. Likewise, their use in Pashto was discussed earlier. In some cases the letter (k) is written like (g). It seems that its sound may have been between (k) and (g). As explained in #11 in Dari it was sometimes pronounced as (k) and at other times as (g). The Arabic pronunciation of such words shows that they heard the letter (g) but were unable to pronounce it correctly, thus changing its sound to a (j). Such as the word karnamag, was changed to karnamaj and the word barnamag was converted to barnamaj. The letter (g) has sometimes been used in this inscription as possessive and honor as noticed in #24 ABABAG, #46 KHOADEOG, #69 IIOG, #119 ALBARG, and #125 HAROGH. We think the sound (i) was changed to kh. Such as the word loyak of the Islamic period which in this inscription has been written as loikh. 16 9. Quiescents at the Beginning of Words There are no quiescents at the beginning of Dari words present day 2020, but like other Aryan languages its use is permissible in Pashto as in storè, lmar, wlarr etc. In this regard Pashto is similar to the Kushani language. The Surkh Kotal inscription has words whose initial letter C is silent in the past tense such as #25 and 31, but if they were to be changed into the present tense the silent letter would change to AC as in #40. Similarly, in the word FROMAN # 146, the F is silent. 10. Transformation of Kushani Letters to Dari and Pashto Some words in the Kushani dynasty language ending with a (d) which were preceded by vowels like a, o and i, when transformed to Pahsto or Dari, the letter (d) was converted to a light (h) and was sometimes omitted altogether i.e.: Kushani dynasty Dari Pashto ot or od waw aw pid bah pah kid kéh chè cad châh tsah tad tâ tâ kald kî káléh However, this rule was not permissible in the verbs like the word stâd. Even today it is istâd, having a (d) at its end though preceded by the letter (a). Some Kushani words with minor changes are still extant in Dari such as: Kushani Dari Pashto akhesht khisht khasta kird kard poorwat parwarda parwarâwa pohar pour bour firoman farmân noubikht noubakht khirgoman khèrman There are some words containing the letter (l) in the Kushani language which in Dari have been changed to a (d). The Kushani maliz meaning fortress has changed to madizh in Dari 17 and naushal of Kushani has become naushad in Dari meaning a new place. Similarly shâl in Kushani is shâd in Dari and sâd in Pashto. In some cases (l) of the Kushani language has changed into (r) in Dari and Pahsto such as alow in Kushani is arwâ in Dari and Pashto meaning soul. Rawan in Dari has the same meaning. While in other cases a Kushani dynasty word ending with (a) is used in Dari and Pashto with an (h) added to it such as shâ has been transformed to shâh and mâ to mâh in Dari. 11. Feminine Gender and Masculine Gender In the Baghlan inscription feminine and masculine genders are absent. It seems that akin Dari there were no separate signs for the feminine and masculine genders in the Kushani language. This of course is different from Pashto, since Pashto has these genders. Consequently we can say that Pashto did not branch from the Kushani dynasty language while it seems that present day Dari is related to the Kushani language in which feminine and masculine genders are absent also. Historical Perspective. Khorasan present day Afghanistan-Central Asia & India. The first founder of Baglang (Baghlan) was Bag Sha Kanishki Namwar Bahrawar, whose titles were Shah-e Buzurg and Khuda Shah which were originally Namo Barg (famous) and Bahrawar (fortunate). The writers of the inscription referred to him as the great king and the founder of Baghlan. b) The fortress and the palace of Baghlan was called maliz-mahadizh (the great fortress). It was believed that Kaniskha built the palace in urgency. The same building was also called mander (temple). c) As described in the section of #35, the specific name for the temple was Naushali-Nawshad. d) After Kanishka's death the water of the temple decreased and the fire worshippers abandoned the palace. e) In the spring of the 31st year of Kanishka's rule, around 160 A.D., when the late Bag Pohr Loikh Bosar son of Shizogarg, under the Kushanid empire was ruling as a king, a person named Nokonzik who had the rank of Karal Rang of the Mareg family, by the order of the king and Eiioman Nobikht, the prime minister, was summoned to go to Baglang. He was in charge of organizing the distribution of water and irrigation in the Kingdom. He was sent to Baghlan to repair the temple. Arriving there he dug a well and lined it with bricks. Moreover, an extensive area was annexed to the temple and it was rebuilt. With the repair of the well water was available in the Nawshad temple and it was reinhabited by the fire-worshipers. f) As stated by the excavation team, this great building was later burned and extensively18 damaged by a fire. During the excavations it was discovered that the central hall, corridor and even the porches of the building were all plastered with ashes. The mission stated that signs of fire were witnessed in both the original and the annexed buildings. It is believed that the temple was deliberately burned down during the invasion of Shahpoor the Second around 240 A.D. g) The well mentioned in the inscription was discovered during the excavation process and remained intact. At the same time the remains of the stream, also mentioned in the inscription, was discovered in the area. h) To repair the Nawshad temple and the great fortress, besides Nokonzik there were other members of the repair mission (or the repair committee) who have been named by the excavation team. The names of these persons appear at the end of the inscription together with the signatures of two persons, they are: Borzomihr, Kozgashki Pour, Mihraman and Amihraman am Borzomihr Pohr. i) The inscription bears some names and titles of the royalties and government officers as follows: Bag (the great king) Khudi (khuday-shah-khoade) Bag Pohr (baghpoor-fagfoor-king's son) Loix (Loyak, a family name) Karal Rang (kinarang, a military family title) Mareg (a family name) Astil gansigien-stàr gansigien? (head of gansigien) Freistar Ab (distributor of water) Eiioman (most probably the Minster "vazir") Further details about these words are provided in their analysis. j) After reading the inscription it becomes clear that the mother of the current Dari spoken in Afghanistan existed at the start of the Christian calendar. It also shows that Dari did originate from Bactria but during its long life changed from its mother, i.e. the Kushani language, into the present form. Meanwhile, Pashto was probably spoken at the time in different mountain valleys of Afghanistan since the influence of both languages, Dari-Pashto and Kushani, is seen in some words of the inscription. 13. Three Copies of the Inscription During the excavation of the Nawshad temple and the fire place, a large one piece stone inscription and several small pieces were discovered. Putting together the pieces produced two other copies of the inscription. These had the same alphabet and peculiarities and were etchedfor the same purpose.19 The inscription on the largest stone, which named the first copy, was in good condition and with a better writing style. The two other copies were probably inscribed at the same time orbefore or after the first copy. The second copy consisted of 21 pieces of stones, each with a different length and width. Some pieces were slightly damaged but with the help of the first copy the writing can be read. This copy has 27 lines with signatures appearing at the end. The script of this copy is similar to the first one. Its writing style is not refined as the first copy. The width of the pieces range from 270-294 mm but the length of the largest piece is over 405 mm. The third copy consists of 32 pieces of different sizes. The pieces are damaged and its writing style is not refined. For example, the first portion of each line starts with large letters, in the middle the letters are small and at the end they are of medium size. The signatures seen in the first and second copies are absent. Overall, it is not complete as the other two. Each piece has a width of 295 mm while the longest one is 490 mm. This copy has 27 lines. It is not clear why three copies were inscribed for one text and

why their writing style is different from one copy to the other? It is also not clear as to why the letters on the first copy are more refined than the other two? At this juncture the answer to these questions is not clear. It is possible that the first copy was written under close supervision of the repair mission with utmost care. It was probably inscribed by skilled craftsmen, while the other two were likely written by less skilled persons who were not talented scribers. A similar example is the tomb of emperor Ahmad Shah. When the tomb was being built an inscription as prepared in a very beautiful Nastaliq style of writing. Later when the tomb was being repaired the inscription was repainted resulting in the loss of some of its elegance. It now looks quite different from its original artistic style. The reading of the Baghlan inscription shows the following: Because of differences in writing style of the three copies we can without doubt say that the copies were not inscribed by one person at the same time. publish them as analyzed by E. Benveniste as the differences are explicit. It is noteworthy that the pieces of the second and third copy were found in the wall of the well mentioned in the inscription. The fact is that the pieces were used as building material in the well. This leads to two conclusions. First, during a later time, when the temple was being repaired the builders considered the tablets as construction stones and used them in the well as building material. Second, it is possible, when Nokonzok, was repairing the temple he wanted to refine the inscription also. He probably ordered the inscription to be etched but finding the first two copies not to standard the pieces were discarded and used as building material. On the other hand he probably ordered that the larger piece be inscribed with care and in good writing. Finding that the other two tablets were not written in a refined style they were used to repair the well. It is fortunate that after 1800 years we have at our disposal all three copies. In this treatise a full description and analysis of each word of the inscription from the view20 point of history, philology and grammar is provided.
Analysis of the Words

Khorasan dynasty present day Afghanistan-Central Asia & India. In old Dari and Avesta ida means here. Similarly aita in old Dari means this. 26 In Herawi dialect of Dari the same word existed as èiz-èid which is used in Tabakat-al-Sufia repeatedly and it means is i.e. âw pîshîne kasy èiz he is before somebody. khana haq èiz it is the house of justice. sheikh sham èiz the sheikh is a prince. Aîtan in Dari was used as an infinitive meaning to be and ait was its singular for the third person meaning is. 27 J. Kent, professor of Indo-European languages at Pennsylvania University states that a suffix for the singular third person in Indo-European languages was eti, iti in Avesta, ati in Sanskrit and aity in old Dari. 28 Thus èid of the Kushani language which meant is or here or this is can be considered the same as èid in Herawi dialect of Dari. In Kandahari Pashto aay dêi means this is. In the inscription there are several words similar to èid such as SID #8, KID #50 and 60, STAD #25 and PID #68 and 90. The (d) at the end of these words used after an (i), as a result of transformation of the word, is silent. Thus today in Dari and Pashto SID exists as chi-chê. An affirmative connector, KID is like ka-ki. STAD is like asè=hasè (like this) in Pashto. EID of Kushani with a silent (d) transformed into aî in Pashto. Hî-aî are both used in the demonstrative case i.e. aî khwâ-hî khwâ (this way). In Dari it is as aî taraf. aî in Dari is used as an abbreviation i.e. eîder (eî+dar)here; aîdoon (aî+doon) like this aîrâ (aî+râ) this one; azyrâ or zèra because. In Dari too aî is a special particle. ar-aî and chi raî both meant for this. The meaning of ayn and râ is the same as aîrâ –they were originally separate from each other. In fact in Dari the words airâ-airâk-azirak-azirâ are all of the same root. 29 neko samar shao airaâk mardum bajuz samar naest Be virtuous for this reason (airâk) Without it there is no fortune In another verse he says: nayaram ki yaram bood jahil airâk kera jahal yaraast yar ast marash I mention not that my love was ignorant for this (aîra), One who is ignorant is the serpent's friend. 2. MAΛIZ (mâléz) This word is composed of two parts mâ+liz=mahâ+dazh (great fortress). It has been used seven times in the inscription with the same spelling i.e. in #16, 23, 44, 79, 95, 112 and 126. Henning read it as madiz. He believes that it originated from the old Dari word diza meaning fortress. As an initial interpretation, Henning suggested it meant the acropolis of Bactria language, while it means a fortress. As far as I am concerned, the first portion of the word MA corresponds to maha in Sanskrit which means great. Its examples are seen in the words macheen, maha baharat (great Baharat), mahakhuna or maha kahul (of great dynasty) and maharaja (great king). Farrukhi says: 30 From great East Turkestan (macheen) to Rome, Russia and Saqlab All the lands belong to the great Khan. Asadi another Afghan poet has used the word mihraj as follows: 31 There was a king in India by the name of Mihraj A great king whose wish prevailed all over. In fact the word is the same as meh in Dari, mathiyah in old Dari, masao in Avesta and mêshr in Pashto. In all these languages it means great and greater. 32 This is why Abu Raihan Beruni translated macheen into Arabic 33 The first part of the word is used in Afghanistan as the name of places like Mashour, south of the city of Kandahar. ma+shour meant great city which is similar to Baghshour, a place north of Herat meaning the king's city. 34 Regarding the second portion of the word lîz, Henning believes it is the diza of old Dari which in Sanskrit is dehi (fortress), and uzdaeza in Avesta meaning to pile upon and diz in 30 Divan-e Farrukhi, The changing of (l) in Kushani words to (d) in Dari was quite common as revealed in the inscription such as #35, 64 and 119. Thus the Kushani liz has been converted to diz (meaning a fortress). Manuchihri says: Safeguad your friend from the deceit of time In one thousand stone fortresses and one hundred thousand dizî 36 If we combine the two portions of the word i.e. maha+diz we get dazh buzurg meaning a great fortress. This shows that the temple of Surkh Kotal had a great fortress as well. 373. M This symbol represents a connective possessive letter and has been used in several instances in the inscription (refer to #15 and 131). It is also present in another Surkh Kotal inscription in Palamad writing. Currently mè as a singular and mû for plural are used in Pahsto as a possessive connector or possessive pronoun. In Dari it is used with the possessive such as kitâbam (my book). In the Kushani language (m) as a possessive connector was used between the possessive and possessed i.e. madiz-m-kaneshko meaning Kanishka's fortress. It should be mentioned that the name Kanishka has been written as Kaneshko in #4 and Kaneshki in #11. The changing of (a) at the end of the word Kanishka occurred according to the grammatical case in the Kushani language. Kanishka's name on his coins is inscribed as follows:sha-o-nan-o-sha-o-Kaneshki-Kushan meaning The Kushanid emperor Kanishka. On another coin it was inscribed as sha-o-Kaneshki. 38 Thus while the modified, king, was used before the name Kanishka it was converted to Kanishki and contrary, when the modified was used before its modifier as in #4, the word became Kanishko. This change in Kushani language is similar to Pashto. 4. KANHOKO (kániz) This word was discussed in 35 Burhan-e Qatà, footnotes. Diz-liz is frequently seen in the names of Afghan cities i.e. Gardiz, Shahliz. The word firdous has been used twice in Avesta as pairi-dacza (Venedad Fargard 3, verse 18, Fargard 5, verse 49). With the same meaning we find words in different languages such as paradeisos in Bactria, pardisu in Akhdi, and pardes in Ebri. In Arabic this word through Arami and Suryani, exixted as firdous which means garden, Meanwhile, the word in French is paradis, in English paradise and the faliz of Dari is of the same nature and root. 36 Divan of Menochehri, The word daes (meaning home and country) should be mentioned in this regard. But in this case (s) changes to (z). Similarly, in the word diah the (s) has been converted to an (h) i.e. dah+deh. Thus it looks that there is a relation between diz-dis-diah. This can be seen clearly in the words gardiz-ghardiz-ghardiz meaning a fortees on the mountain. The word gardiz has been used in Zain-ul-Akhbar of Gardizi. 38 Tarekh-e Afghanistan, Previously the word was read as anindo together with the word divider. It was believed that it originated from wan (conquering and invading). Schlumberger relates it to the goddess of conquest. In reality this modifier is anind which has been mentioned with the names of Buddhist and Brahman personalities in Afghanistan and

India. Hiuan Tsang in his memoirs used the word anind with several Buddist names. 39 Farrukhi mentions a king, a contemporary of Sultan Mahmud, as Ninda. His dynasty was referred to as Nindaeyan. In this land he came to claim its borders With the cheating of Ninda, the villan. 40 Again he says: He has arisen the Nindayean against you, Who are restless, sleepless and languid. 41 From the writings of Gardizi it is clear that when Sultan Mahmud of Ghazni (396 H). was on his way to invade Multan, it is possible that in Waîhind, along the banks of the Indus, a king by the name of Anindpal, son of Jaypal ruled in the area. Arriving with his army Sultan Mahmud ousted him from the throne and he retreated to Kashmir. 42 The name Anindpal has the same origin as anind. Dari and Pashto literary documents show that anind is deeply rooted in the languages of Afghanistan. In Pashto it means cheerful, happiness, enjoyment and pride. Khushal Khan says: 43 There is much anxiety from the pious, When the dervish cheers (ánénd kâ) the sweeper. Similarly Abdul Kader Khan says: 44 For what purpose people advise us Through his wisdom every man is proud (kâ ánánduna). As expressed in the following couplet of Hafez ánénd means enjoyment and beГГauty in Dari also. Long hair and a waistline does not make a prince Be the subject of one who has grace and beauty (ánî). 45 Thus if we combine ân with the suffix ánd it converts to anind meaning enjoyment, pleasure and happiness. It is similar to gazand and dzáland of Pashto. Since the word is composed 39 Memoirs of Hsuan Tsang, Divan-e Farrukhi, Divan-e Farrukhi, Zain-ul-Akhbar, Divan of Khushal Khan Khatak, Divan of Abdul Kader Khan, Burhan-e Qatà, footnotes, according to the rules of the languages of Afghanistan, and has deep roots in the Afghan languages, there is no reason to consider it of foreign origin. 6, 7 ВАГ ΛΑΝΓ (bág láng=Baghlân) This name which has been repeatedly used in the inscription is composed of two parts. Bag, bagha or baga in all ancient Aryan languages means khudaî (God or king). In old Dari and Avesta the word was baga and bahaga in Sanskrit, 46 and both cases were used in ancient names. In Afghanistan too bagh means God. The use of bagh is still evident in the names of places such as Baghpour (its Arabicised form is Faghfour meaning king's son), Baghistan (the current Bisotoon of Dari (which king's place), Baghdad, Baghshoor, Baghni, Baghlan, Baghar (today's Daizangi), Baghavi (Sare Pul in Shiberghan), Baghak (Samangan), Baghain (Khurm), Baghawardan (Herat), which in Avesta has been written as Baghanyast. However, this word is still alive in Pashto as bag in its original form of the Khorasan language. It means, great powerful and muscular. The same form of the word is also annexed with names of places like Bagram, Bagrami (in Kabul), Bagal (Herat), Bagla (Ghazna), Baghlag (Daizangi), Baga Pai (Taluqan) and Bagà (Tarnak). Shamsuddin Kakarr a Pashto poet from Kandahar says: My fortune is bad even though From outside it appears great (bág). 47 In Dari literature the word has the same meaning. Maulana Balkhi says: Like bleeding a mosquito in the air Why do you boast of kings and great (bág) people. 48 From the writings of Mahmud Kashghari, 466 H. it is evident that the word bágh had entered the Turkish language of the time meaning an amir. 49 Now every ignoble, servant Claims to be a matron, wrestler and great (bág) personality. 50 As bágh originally existed in the old languages of Avesta, Sanskrit and old Dari it is possible that the word infiltrated Turkmen because the Aryans, on different occasions, were in contact with Turkmen tribes from Tukmenistan to Khorasan. However, the meaning of the word in the Indo-Afghan languages of the Afghanistan plateau was originally God. Later its meaning converted to great and majestic and was used as a title for kings and rulers as they considered themselves as gods or as great rulers. The words khuda and khudawand have been used in nouns such as 46 Old Dari, Divan of Shamsuddin, Kabul, Masnavi, first part, Lughat-al-Turkey, Istanbul, Divan-e Naser Khusrao, Kabul Khudaî, Zabul Khudaî, Gozgan Khuda, Saman Khuda, Bukhara Khuda. 51 In Pashto the word was used for names of people also. In 1160 H., the prime minister of Emperor Ahmad Shah was known as Sardar Wali Khan Bamizai, but his actual name was Bagey Khan which is in fact related to the bágh of the Surkh Kotal inscription. The Hindi bagwan (god) is also from the same root. The second part of the word ang also seems to be old. It exists at the end of some names of places to this day such as Salang (a valley in the heart of the Hindukush range), Bashlang (Helmand valley), Alishang (Laghman), Mastang (Baluchistan), Zarang (Seistan), Poshang (west of Herat), Gerang (a city in Merv), and Warang (a pass in Ghor). Arab geographers changed ang to anj and consequently some of the aforementioned names were Arabicised and pronounced as Foshanj, Bashlanj, Zaranj etc. 52 According to Henning, the origin of Bag-lang is in the word baga-danka. Due to the following reasons the second part of the word means a fire: The remains of a fire alter and sacred fires were witnessed in the temple of Surkh Kotal. The coins of some Kushanid kings of the Hindukush valleys bear on one side a fireworshipping temple. Ang meant fire in Veda which was in the form of angi, the god of fire. During the later Indo-Afghan period names such as azar (the angel which keeps fire), athr in Avesta, atar in old Dari, atur in Bactria and awr in Pashto became known. 53 In the 17th chapter of Bandhashan, a fire-worshipping temple has been mentioned which was named Azar-firo Bagh (the glorious fire of god). It is believed that the temple was located on a mountain called Koh-e Roshan (Roshan mountain) of Kabul. 54 The location of this mountain is not known now. However, since in the structure of its ancient name ang occurs as azar as the same bágh (god), one might surmise that it might be the Surkh Kotal temple. At present a mountain in Jurm of Badakshan is called Roshan mountain. It is possible that in the past the name referred to a vast area and now, like other geographical names, it applies to a smaller area. There is also the possibility that the Baghlan of that time was officially a part of Kabul as it is present day. Azar-firo Bagh has the same meaning as Bag-Lang, both of which mean a fire temple of god. It may be best to avoid a hasty designation concerning the location of Bag-Lang in the same manner as has been designated to the location in Badakshan of Roshan Mountain. We can thus surmise that the temple of glorious fire of god did not exist in the mountains of Kabul, but somewhere else in this land, especially in view of the fact that this temple carried the same ancient ang interpreted as azar meaning atash (fire). By drawing upon some linguistic factors we can provide further substance to the meaning Al-Masalik wa al-Mamalik of Ibn Khardazbah, Shah nama of Firdowsi and Zain-ul-Akhbar. Ahsan-al-Taqaseem; Al-masalik wa al-Mamalik of Istakhri; Burhan-e Qatà, footnotes, Yasna 1, ang. The word duzakh (hell) in later Avesta has been written as duzhanghu. Its components are dazh meaning bad and anghu meaning fire, which when combined means bad-fire. 55 It is the same ang of the Kushani language. Ang has its roots in the present languages of Afghanistan. In Pashto there are several words in which it occurs, i.e. angâr, and angârah, both of which mean light and bright-fire. In the first part of these words is the same historical ang of the Kushani language. In addition, angél in Pashto means fervor and sharpness which are considered to be qualities of fire. Angâza, also means sharpness and angulâ meaning sharp voice is from the same family of words. Presumably, the English anger, angry and angel, relating to light and brightness, may have the same root. 56 Mullah Faiz Mohammad Kakarr, a contemporary of Emperor Ahmad Shah, who was from Zhob at the foothills of the Solomon "Suleiman" mountain, has used the word exactly in this manner: My beloved nailed me to the leopard's claw My heart burns like a kindle with a flame (balâng). The word balâng is composed of two components bal meaning a flame and luminous and âng meaning fire. So the meaning of the couplet is my heart burns like a kindle in the luminous fire. Hence the word balâng means bright and luminous fire. The Sughdi version of Bagh-Lang was Baghdang and its Afghan version Baghdanka. In both cases there is a (d) between bagh and ang. This (d) in Pashto sometimes changes into (l) such as dewar-dewal (wall) and gharbél-ghalbél (sieve) Words #2, 38, 64 and 119 in the inscription are of this nature. We see that the structure of this word in Pashto is the reverse composite while its direct composite is de bágh ang (god's fire). Its structure may have reversed later according to the rules of Afghan dialects as bagh-dang, baddang, and baghlang. With the passing of time some words changed their original composition among which

Baghlang is of this nature. In fact, its original feature was Baghlang but it changed to Baghlan. Such a phenomenon is sometimes seen in the names of cities also. As an example we can mention Badakshan, which in the 2nd century B.C. was Ta-nag-lang. Later on in the notes of Hiuan Tsang (630 A.D.) it was recorded as Pu-tu-ching-na. And Ywan Shi noted it as Ba-da-hashing. 57 The last part of the word ang changed to án thus we have Badakshan. Another example is the town of Sang Chahrak of the Gozganan mountains. Past geographers recorded it as San Charak, a form still used today. 58 This case is seen in other names of places in Afghanistan i.e. Ghording, in Khakriz north of Kandahar, Yakding, east of Naghlo, 59 Kotal-e 55 Yashta, Burhan-e Qatà, footnotes, The word angisht meaning bright and luminous fire is still used in Kohistan and Panjshir, north of Kabul. In Latin there is the word ignite meaning to light or to fire, and it has many components in European languages. 57 Al-masalik wa al-Mamalik of Istakhri, Hudud-al-`Alam, Qamoos Jughrafia-e Afghanistan. Badinj, between Laghman and Ushtorgram 60 and Kotal-e Soolang, north of Kabul between Kohistan and Nijrab. While we cannot be certain about the structure of these words but after studying a series of similar words we can come to some conclusions on the basis of scientific principles. 8. (sîd) Henning considers this word to be an interrogative pronoun synonymous to which and what of English and similar. As the meaning of was explained is also a relative adverb. In the later dialects of this land the (d) which appears after an (I) in, like, became silent through time with the result that the changed to sî-chî-chéh, relative pronouns found in Pashto and Dari. In fact the pronoun chî still used by certain Pashtoon tribes of Afghanistan is pronounced as sî. It appears exactly in the same form in hasî in Pashto. After the word divider (O) which separated from the following word an (I) appears in the inscription. It seems that this (i) is the same as yey in Pashto which is a particle of the subject, the object and the possessive. Even today after chî Pashto speakers use it in their conversation and writing such as chî yey wakhorr (after eating). Similarly, (i) has been used several other times in the inscription. In all cases it is used after the word divider. 9. ΒΑΓ (bág, god and great) This word was described in detail in #6 and it could be added here that it is sometimes used as a modifier of the succeeding word, king i.e. bág-shah which means great king or it can be translated as God's king. 10. A (shâ, patshah) The Greek alphabet does not have a letter which represents the sound sh. In the inscription this sound is represented with a special symbol resembling a (l). It seems that the Kushanids created a letter to represent sh. As the letter (P) in Greek represents rho (r) so this word was also mistakenly read by some as rawo together with the word divider. Consequently, it was mistakenly considered to be the Indi words row and raî. SA is repeatedly used in this inscription and is one of those words with an (h) occurring at the end. In olden times the (h) was deleted thus shinâh was written as shinâ and padshâh was written as padsha. Fakhr Gurgani says: Thanks and goodwill to that king (shâ) Who created the world and us. 61 60 Kabuli Emperor Akbar Nama and Tabakat-e Akbari. 61 Wais wa Ramin, 1. 28 It seems that in some Kushanid words when the (h) was preceded by an (a) the (h) was deleted. Besides shâh another example of this nature is the word ma, written in the inscription without an (h). However, in the second copy the words shah and mah were inscribed with an (h) like they are written now. It seems that even at that time the words were sometimes written with an (h) while in other instances the (h) was deleted. Words #9 and 10, BAG SHA are modifiers for the succeeding word which is KANISHKI. Put together they mean Kanishka the great king. The word SHA is also used later and on Kanishka's coins. 11. ΚΑΝΗΟΚΙ ΝΑΜΟΒΑΡΓ (káneshkî nâmûbárg) Kaniskha's name, when composed with Namobarg, has been written as KanEsHKi explained in #4 of this analysis. Maricq and Henning both read Kaneshki together with the succeeding word namobarg. However, Maricq believes that there is no relation between the composite sections of namobarg, namo and barg. But Henning is of the opinion that barg means product while bârág means a vessel or wall. Hennning also mentions that bárg as a composite means being named. KanESHki Namobarg is an ancient composite of Kanishka-i namdar and namwar (the famous and popular Kanishka). As no divider sign exists between the components of the composite, Kanishka+namo+barg, it can be called a compound objective. Also nâmûbárg is similar to the current namwar (famous) and nambar (popular). The word nám (name) which is written as num and nâma in Pashto has an established foundation in ancient Aryan languages. In old Dari it is nâmán, the last letter being silent. In Avesta and Sanskrit also it is nâmán. Noman in Latin and nama in Khutani language. Khorasan dynasty present day Afghanistan-Central Asia & India 62 The second part of the word bárg is a possessive suffix linked to bár or wár and has its roots in bár and burdan. In Dari nâm bard and nâm burda meaning famous and popular are of the same root. In Bactria it was nâmburtar. Ferdowsi says: None of the crowned died as such, As you the famous (nâmburdar) did. 63 Thus nâmbar=nâmwar means famous and popular and in the above phrase modifies the word Kanishka. The same modifier is used as numworr=numworray in Pashto. The sound (g) at the end of the word existed in several ancient Bactria names and in the inscription it has been used in #24, 49 and 119. Among the verses of the Manavids, discovered in Turfan, one praises the light-tree in which poor mâhi barazag (full moon) has been mentioned. Some diminutive and undiminutive nouns in Bactria ended with a (k), whereas today a silent (h) is found i.e. bandak, dastak and gandak in Bactria which in Dari have become bandah, dastah and gandah. 64 Numerous words nowadays written with a silent (h) were written with a final 62 Old Dari, Burhan-e Qatà, footnotes, Sabk Shinasi, I, (g) during the Sassani dynasty period, Hazar Bandag was the title of Mehre Nersa. Dihig (leader of the village), payagan salar (foot soldier commander), tanurig (armored plated) and zhindag (huge elephant). Karnameh is another word which was pronounced with a terminal (g) as karnamag. But the Arabs changed the (g) to a (j) in which case it was pronounced as karnamaj. It is quite probable that the (g) at the end of such words was used later in Pashto and Dari as (k). Several examples are seen in Pashto words such as barak, atshak, khatak, shitak, smarak, shirak, hotak and babrak etc. This shows the closeness between Pashto and Kushani language in this specific aspect and unlike Bactria in which this (k) or (g) occurred at the end of words in Dari the words end with a silent (h). In the Kushani language and Pashto, its use at the end of words is without condition and implies a possessive case. Mehre Nersa. Dihig (leader of the village), payagan sâlâr (foot soldier commander), tanurig (armored plated) and zhindag (huge elephant). Karnameh is another word which was pronounced with a terminal (g) as karnamag. But the Arabs changed the (g) to a (j) in which case it was pronounced as karnamaj. It is quite probable that the (g) at the end of such words was used later in dari and Pashto as (k). Several examples are seen in Pashto words such as barak, atshak, khatak, shitak, smarak, shirak, hotak and babrak etc. This shows the closeness between Pashto and Kushani language in this specific aspect and unlike Bactria in which this (k) or (g) occurred at the end of words in Dari the words end with a silent (h). In the Kushani language and Pashto, its use at the end of words is without condition and implies a possessive case. Khorasan present day Afghanistan-Central Asia & India. 12. KIPA (kérd-kárd) This word is the same as kárd of Dari used at the present time. It has its root in kárdan, which beside meaning to do and action in olden times also was used to mean to build. In Avesta wara conveys the meaning and name of the first building built by Yama (Jamshid) in Balkh and warjám kard 65 means the wall (wara or bara) built by Jam. In old Dari kárta-kárd was used at the end of the names of buildings and cities with the meaning built by such as Parsa Karta (azargad), Bilash Kard, Khisrow Kard etc. Ferdowsi used the word kárdan with the same meaning as used in the inscription: I have made (kardám) the world pure of brawlings, I have made (kardám) numerous cities and fortresses. 66 In Herawi dialect of Dari kárd has been used to mean to build such as ân khanâqah ramlah bikárd 67 meaning he built Ramla's monastery. As a result the sentence BAG SHA KANESHKI NAMOBARG KIRD, relating to #9-12, means that it was built by the great and famous Kanishka. Later the verb FROGIRD (#17) has been used 65 Vendidad, second Fergerd. 66 Shah nâma, Vol. 1, Couplet # 4718. 67 Tabaqat-e Sufia, which probably means to complete and to finish in which case it might be concluded that KIRD meant to build and FROGIRD meant completion. 13. TAΔI (tâdî) Maricq misinterpreted this word considering it similar to #18, 78 and 81. His interpretation is not accepted by Henning either. In fact there is a difference between the spelling of TADI and # 18, 78 and 81. While TADI ends with an (i) the other words end with an (ei). Hence they cannot be considered the same. In my opinion TADI is the object of the succeeding verb, OKID (#14). The word tâdî, which means soon and hurry, exists with the same structure in modern Pashto. 14.OKEΔ (ukéd) This word is the past tense of ukèdal-kèdal of Pashto which is used present day by Pashto speakers beyond the Khyber. Ukéd means done or being done. TADI OKID when conjoined means it was hurried. The succeeding words of the inscription from #15-17 are modifying ukéd. 68 Maricq thinks that this word is another structure of KIRD used in #50 and 60 of the inscription. But Henning does not agree with his view and states that the adverb KID is a connector. It is highly improbable that one word be written with two different spellings and the O at the beginning of the word be omitted. It is worth mentioning that the spelling of this word in the first and third copies is OKID but in the second copy it is OKED in which case because of the similarity of the first and third, OKID may be correct. 15. ΦΟΡΔΑΜD (fordáms) Both Henning and Maricq consider this word to be close to fratama in old Dari and fratema in Avesta and Sanskrit, in both cases meaning foremost. 69 An adjective (c) or adverbial (c) has been added to it. In Soghdi it means first. Accepting the above one can come to the conclusion that this word is the same as budam-bar, haman dam of Dari and pur dam-pur, hagha dam of Pashto both meaning at that time. At the end of the word an adverbial c-z of Pashto is added. Thus it becomes pardams meaning at that time or first and immediately. In this case the preceding sentence TADI OKID supports this line of reasoning regarding its use. 16. MAΛIZ (mâléz) This word was discussed in detail in #2 of this analysis meaning a fortress. 69 Old Dari, 197.31 17,(frogérd) Maricq considers this word to be close to frakarta which meant completed. Here FROGIRD with the terminal (g) means it has been completed and used in the past particle. Thus the meaning of #15 to 17 FORDAMEC MALIZ FROGIRD is: first the fortress was completed. For further explanation refer to #36. 18. TAΔEI (tâdéî) Henning recognizes this word, which is repeated in # 78 and 81, as consisting of the TAD of #32 and 37, to which has been attached the third person singular pronoun which is also (éy) in Pashto. This word, then, would be tah yè in Pashto (special Kandahar usage similar to Dari, tâdéî in Kushani and tâ azîn-tâkeh (until that) in Dari, and Henning's analysis seems correct. 19. MANΔAP (mándár) Mandar is still used in Hindi and Pashto and means temple or place of worship. The origin of mán can be found in the mán and mánel of Pashto which means accepting, obeying and worshipping. 20. AB (âb) This is the Dari word âb (water) still in use. The word has been repeatedly used in #38, 41, 49 and 97 of the inscription. 21. NITOXOT (néstokhot) The first portion of the word is the same as néist of Dari and nist of Pashto while the second part OXOT appears to originate from the word khátel of Pashto. Oxot in Pashto is the past tense for the third person. Now if we put together the word nist with oxot the word means rare and finished. Henning considers its meaning to be the water dried out which is an approximation but its actual meaning is to vanish away. The meaning of the sentence from #18 to 21 consequently is: TADEI MANDAR AB NICTOXOT: from the time when the water of this temple vanished. 22. AIΔ (áséd) In #1 it was explained that after (i) in our modern language, the final (d) of this type of words is silent and unpronounced. So if we leave off the (d), asî remains as we have in modern Pashto hasè meaning thus, in this way. Asî was also used in old Dari with the meaning of then (the time when). 70 So Kushani ACID is a form of asî-hasè (thus). In #8 SID also was changed into the Khorasan present day Afghanistan-Central Asia & India. 70 Old Dari, declarative si=chè (what), so that by the same principle ACID should become asî. 23. MAΛIZ (mâléz) Explained in #

2. 24. АВАВГ (áb ábag) Henning and Maricq, without any insight into the root of this word give its meaning as waterless or without water. They are of the opinion it is composed from the component of áb meaning water. No similar word is found in Dari or Pashto in which case it might be a dead word. However, from its use in the script we can say it means without water and dried out. Concerning the use of the terminal (g) #11, 25, ТАΔ (stâd) This word comes from sta of Avesta, stha of Sanskrit, and sisto of Latin all of which mean to stop and remain. 71 In current Dari usage it is estâd. The components of the infinitive estâdan were used from early times in Avesta as an auxiliary verb, i.e. dât estât hind (dâdah estâdah ând). 72 In the book of Ardavarj Nama it is said: avestâ râ andár sitakhre pâpakân pah daz napast nihaz estâd. 73 In the above sentence the word is used with the same meaning as was used in old times. An example is seen in the following couplet of Manuchihri (died in 432 H.): 74 As the north wind felt a glimpse of winter, It stopped (estâd) in its place like a restless spy. Similarly, Baihaqi, a scholar of the Ghaznavi dynasty period writes: hawa sakht garm estâda bûd, which means the weather was hot. Khorasan present day Afghanistan-Central Asia & India 75 From these examples it can be concluded that ABABAG STAD of Kushani language is the same as stâd used as a past perfect for the third person. It occurs in #31 and 120 also, but there it is used as a verb and not as an auxiliary verb. Thus the meaning of the sentence from #22 to 25, ACID MALIZ ABABG STAD is: this way the fortress remained without water. 26. ОΔ (aud-wa of Dari, aw of Pashto) This word is found as a connector at the beginning or between two words and was used similarly in northern Bactria dynasty. In a verse of praise discovered in Turfan, concerning the light-tree, the word OD has been repeatedly used meaning and. 76 This shows that the (d) at the end of #8, 22, 50, 68 and 90 has been transformed to a wa in Dari and aw in Pashto. Such silent use of (d) is also seen in other words. In the inscription OD has been used as a connector in # 70, 100 and 133 also. It is used in #43, 139 and 147 with the spelling of OT. 77 From the use of OD and OT we can conclude that when spelled with a (T) the word has been used purely as a word connector, but when spelled with a (D) it related two words as well as two sentences and phrases in which case it is also a phrase connector. 27. КАΛΔ (káld-kala-waqtékeh) According to Henning this word was kada in old Afghanistan language and meant when. The letter (d) at the end of some words in the inscription has been converted into an (h) in Dari and Pashto meaning when as in #1 and 50. From the Kushani KALD, kala remains in Pashto meaning when, as, since and whenever. The same word is seen in # 46 also. Since the (d) is converted to an (l) in Pashto, thus the structure of the Pashto kala is similar to kada of Afghanistan language. 28. A (áse-az) According to Henning this word has the same meaning as az used in present day Afghanistan meaning from. It occurs in #102. This word and #30 have not been thoroughly or convincingly analyzed by orientalists and their interpretation remains controversial. Maricq, for example, says that the first portion of the word is. He usually read the letter Upsilon (Y) as (H). He also thinks that the analysis of Junker and Herzfield in this regard was not correct. Their reasoning is based on the fact that in the script and coins of the Kushanids and Kushano-Sassanids, upsilon was not normally used for the H sound. But according to Maricq upsilon was not used in the Bactrian language, but was used to represent the H sound which did not exist in Greek alphabet. For this reason when Maricq presented his findings in the Journal Asiatique all upsilons used in the words were pronounced with an (H). Contrary to Maricq's view, Henning believes that the use of upsilon (Y) instead of (H) was not common. In fact he says that the upsilon in the word LROYO was used to reduce the repetition of three omicrons in the word and this obstacle was not prevalent in the word LROOSP. Henning believes that the (dr) at the beginning of old Afghanistan words has been changed to in the Kushani language. In this regard the Kushani language is different from Pashto. The letters 76 Sabk Shinasi, It is also OT in the second copy.34 (dr) still exist in Pashto i.e. drama of Avesta (move it) is droomédal (going or moving) in Pashto of which droom is the command form of the verb meaning

to go or move it. These words have been read as ac lro-hominan-o. Meanwhile, Henning's view that the Kushani language was different from Pashto is not applicable. In Pashto both infinitives, i.e. lrêl (akin Kushani) and dérlodal (akin the Avestan group of languages) means having or to have. This shows that Pashto has several dialects. The use of the word divider (O), as used in all coins and Kushanid scripts, resolves the issue of the use of three repetitive O's. Consequently there would be no reason to change the divider into a upsilon. Instead of an upsilon (h) appears to be the correct usage. In all the words if we read upsilon as an (h) we will find that the words have a more correct structure. For example if the word POHR (#55) is read as (Y) the outcome would be poyr. The same word in Dari is puhr from which pûr and pisar (son) were derived and used in Dari. 78 Similarly, if we read MIHR used in #138, 140, 150 and 153 as mehr it has the same form as used in present day Dari. In short this word according to Maricq's followers is Lro-hominan and according the Henning it is Lro-Yominan. Lro-lroî in Pashto has the infinitive lrál meaning owner. This word in Dari has its root as dar (have) and dârinda (owner) in which (l) has been converted to a d. Meanwhile, in Pashto the second portion of the first part of the word i.e. o (in lro) or oy of lroî is the sign of possession and adjective. There are several examples to this effect: bro, tsargandoî, skarandoî etc. The second part of the word HOMINAN is composed of hû+ménán. Ho in Bactria, Avesta and Dari means good, it is so in Sanskrit. In fact HO of Kushani, sa of Pashto and khoob of Dari all mean good and are of the same root. MINAN is an adjective of mîna in Pashto in which (n) has been used as a relative or suffix like khera-kheran (dirty), gowdagowdan (lame) and kâl-kâlan (yearly). Based on this it can be said that the meaning of minan is friend, beloved or sacred. The word manel in Pashto meaning to accept is also derived from this word. The meaning of the combined components LRO and HOMINAN is benevolent-owner or sacred-owner. Since after this composed word and its divider O a possessive (i) which in old Dari was written as (y) has been used. Thus ΛPOYOMINAN should be a possessive of the succeeding word. It will be useful to mention that ΛPOYOMINAN most probably was the name of the fire-god. The historical context of lro, generally used for owner-god is as follows: The first part of Drvaspa, the ninth Yasht of Avesta, in which Mazde Yasna's God, who was the guardian and preserver of small and big four-footed animals, is the same as lro-dru 79 meaning owner, guardian and god 78 The conversion of (h) in pohr into (s) in pisar is linked to wanas of Bactria which became gunah and kherwa which became khuroos. 79 Mazda Parasti, On one side of Kanishka's coins, who ruled from 125-152 A.D., is minted a bearded god beside whom is a running horse. Besides them the word lro-aspo (with dividers lr+o asp+o) is also inscribed. In an article entitled Zoroastrian gods on the Hindo-Scythian coins Oralstein considers this name to be the Dari lahrasp 80 and its Avestan structure is aurvat aspa meaning the owner of a swift horse. Its Bactria form is rorasp or lorasp. As the first letter of the name of the god on Kanishka's coins could not be clearly seen, Darmesteter read it as droo acpo. This error was made despite the fact that on coin #7 of Percy Gardener, the word lro asp is clearly visible. The conversion of (d) into (l) in the languages of the eastern plateau is and was a common practice. 81 The same is seen in the Manavid Soghdi dialects and some of the Pamiri dialects. 82 Lrêl, derlodêl, meaning owning and having in Pashto and the same with a small difference such as dârah and dârendah is seen in present day Dari. Thus the lro of Kushani language, dro of Avesta and lor of Bactria are of the same root and origin. So the meaning of LROHOMINAN might be benevolent sacred-owner or benevolent sacred-god. This word still exists in Pashto i.e. daro is used for the name of men in Kandahar. One of the grandfathers of the Atsekzais in southern Kandahar was named Daro whose tomb is still known and famous as Daro's tomb. 83. EIP (éir-aûr-atash) Aryan have not come to any conclusion about the meaning of this word either. Maricq thinks it means bravery and courage although this meaning does not fit the use of the word in the sentence. I my view this word has exactly the same pronunciation as aûr (fire) in the Waziri dialect of Pashto i.e. éir. The meaning of éir is fire with reference to the sacred-fire which was lit in the Baghlan temple. As mentioned the remains of a fire place and ashes were found in the temple. Before this word a possessive (i) is found in which case the words LRO-HOMINAN would have a possessive case. The meaning of both lro-hûménán and éir is thus benevolent sacred god of fire. Before analyzing the next word we have to mention that aûr is a Pashto word meaning fire and still pronounced as éir by some tribes. In the same token éiray meaning ashes is also used in Farahi, Mulllah Mohammad Yaqub in a qasida about the ascension of His Majesty Our leadership elevated into kingship, The spirit of Daro blessed Painda Khan. 36 the language. It is the same word as used in the inscription. 31. TAΔ (stâd) The same as #25, hence it is used as an exact verb and not an auxiliaiy verb and it means stopped and delayed. The sentence from #26 to 31 OD KALD AC LROHOMINAN EIR CTAD means: and when from the benevolent sacred-god the fire stopped. 32. TAΔ (tâdh) This word is similar to tâ of Dari and Pashto. In #37 it is used both in the singular and plural form, but in #18, 78, 81 and 107 it is used as a component of a composed word, in which case the letter (d) has been added to it. However, in #46 it is used as a component of a composed word where it is in the singular form without the terminal (d). It seems that TAD of the Kushani language was abridged in later dialects and became ta and used as a sign of condition, cause and end. In Bactria it is tak and in old Dari it was tavat and in Pazind it was dak 84 meaning until and up until, The reason for deleting (d) in # 46 while in words #18, 78, 81 and 107 it has been written with a terminal (d) is that whenever TAD is used with a word starting with a vowel it has a terminal (d) but if it joins a word where the first letter is a consonant then the (d) is eliminated. Thus the (d) of TAD has been striked while it remains in TAKALD. An (i) exists between #32 and 33 acting as a possessive. 33, 34. BAΓEA (bégéys) This word is the same as #6 and 9 of the inscription which means big, great and god. The terminal (e) after BAG may be a plural sign. This sign remains in plural words for the feminine gender. Word #91 ASANGE is used as a plural and BAGEAS in #108 is of the same nature. Consequently, we can say that here the meaning of BAGE is gods. Regarding the suffix (ac) at the end of the word orientalists mistakenly considered it similar to (az) of #28. Since it has been differently used in #28 and was separated by the dividers from succeeding and preceding words we consider it to be (az). In this particular place and in #108, since it is not separated by a divider, this we consider it to be a suffix. Its form still exists in Pashto such as ghar-ghariz and lànd-làndiz in both of which the possessive sign (iz) is used. Historical reasons also exist by means of which we can say (iz) is a possessive sign rather than any other thing. It existed during the Kushanid period. In the Rozgan script, related to the Mahrakula Hepthalittes, around 50 A.D., the first word is the praise word bageac (godliness). 85 As a result we can say in the inscription BAGEAC also means godliness and related to gods in 84 Burhan-e Qatà footnotes, 85 For further details see Pashto and Loykan-e Ghazna, which case it means god's worshippers. The possessive (i) succeeding the word related the worshippers of god to the Nawshad temple that is the worshippers residing in Nawshad. 35. INOAYM (nawshâlm, nawshâd) Aryan have kept silent and have said nothing regarding its meaning., Henning alone has recorded its meaning as seat. But we recognize its origin to be in nawshal for the following reasons:1. This word is the nawshâd of Afghanistan literature because its (i) stands for (d) as in the words MALIZ (mahadezh) and BAGLANG (baghdang-baghlân). And this change of (d) to (i) exits in these inscriptions and in all the Indo-Aryan languages, i.e. Hindi das, Dari dah-Pashto las, Dari Sad-Pashto sál. From this it appears that in this case the language of these inscriptions corresponded to Pashto, and the (d) of Dari nawshad and dez were (l) in that language. The word nosalm is probably composed of naw+shâl i.e. the new shâl, the syntax being like Pashto with the principle of attributive adjective preceding the noun it qualifies. However, shâl is probably the same word that we have remaining in Dari as a suffix in yakh-châl (ice-box) and siyâh-châl (dungeon), and in Pashto in the word darshal or darshâl (threshold), and it has the meaning of spatial capacity. This word is also preserved in its original form of shâl in the place-name Afghan-shâl, Khorasan dynasty present day Afghanistan-Central Asia & India, 86 which in the time of Sultan Mahmud dynasty was a place in the vicinity of Sobektegin's grave in Ghazni. Here was located an old palace of Mahmud's and the Messenger's Field (the reception-field for messengers and ambassadors), In Tarekh-e Baihaqi it is repeatedly mentioned 87 and in some of the copies it has also been recorded in the form of Afghan-shâli. For a period of a thousand years we have known of the shâl in the locality of modern Quetta 88 in the province of Pshin southwest of Kandahar, And besides this, there existed other localities also with the name of shâl, 89 and the present-day shâl of Kunar (a province in eastern Afghanistan) is also one of them which remains to this day. The ancient NOSALM of Kushani, which is similar to Pashto, later became nawshâd in Dari i.e. new place and new resting place, on the analogy of ancient nawbahar (nawuhâra-new temple). Nawshâl was the name of the very temple in Baghlan, and perhaps they later built a nawshâd modeled upon it also in Balkh and other places, to which reference is made in our explanation. 2. What was nawshâd and where was it? The Dari poets, especially the early ones, have mentioned nawshâd, and from the context of their words it appears that it was the name of a locality or town with a large number of beautiful women. Farrukhi says in an encomium to Sultan 86 Babur dynasty also has Afghan-shâl Tazk-e Babury stating: Sajawand is among the places in Logar... and its people are Afghanshâl. 87 Tarekh-e Baihaqi, Ahsan-al-Taqaseem, Nuhzat-al-Quloob, Mohammad bin Mahmud: Your house has become the altar for the people, Like the house of Nawshâd earlier. Similarly in an encomium to Sultan Mahmud: He has stamped out a thousand idol-temples mightier than the Pyramids, He has emptied two hundred cities, lovelier than Nawshâd. Similarly: Gardens which are like the idol-house of Nawshâd, Become a desert until autumn season. Elsewhere Farrukhi has thus mentioned the Bahar of Nawshâd (temple of Nawshad): Be at rest and in happiness, since from marvelous Turkmen Your place is like a fire-shrine and the Bahar of Nawshâd. In Roshnai Nama related to Naser Khusraw: You are in Farkhar and your beloved in Nawshâd, Go there, why are you shouting and crying? Masàud Sàd Salman says: Oh great king, chose amusement and do your work of a king, Call for a cup of wine from that idol of Nawshâd: Let there be new and newer joy for you in all places, From the many kinds of idols may your assemblage be like Nawshâd. Similarly: The garden became decorated like the idol-temple of Mushkuy, The plains became lit-up like the idol-temple of Nawshâd. Again he said: The idol which has connection to Nawshâd, Every hour holds my heart with new happiness. Like a play-thing of the house of Nawshâd Its face keeps my neighborhood and quarter. are the sayings of the earliest of the poets, they talk about the altar of Nawshâd, the idol-temple of Nawshâd and the idols of Nawshâd. It appears that these poets were convinced of Nawshâd's 39 presence as one of the sanctuaries or idol-temples and that they counted that place, quite like Nawbahar of Balkh, among the important religious and idolatry centers. And later dictionary writers, taking their cue from the same type of usage, deduced that Nawshâd was something arousing beauty, and recorded that with its meaning in their dictionaries. However, in Arab geography books and Masalik-e Mamalik which was printed in nine volumes in Leiden, and in the Asar-al-Bilad of Nuzhat-al-Quloob and Tarekh-e Guzidah and Lubab-al-Lubab and Rahat-al-Sudur, Jawamà-al-Hikayat, Futuh-al-Baladan of Bilazhari and Tabari and Lughat-e Shah nama by Abdul Qader Baghdadi and Fehreste Lughat-e Shah nama by Wolf there is no record or notice of this word. Only in the following books is a recording of this word found: In Tarekh-al-Kamilu of Ibn Athir, on the events of the year 257 H. in reference to the advance of Yàqub Layce towards Balkh he says: He went toward Balkh and Tukharistan, and then he reached Balkh and descended to the outskirts and wrecked Nawshad. This was the building which Daud bin Abas al Nausari built outside of Balkh. Then Yàqub went from Balkh towards Kabul and took possession of it... In the Egyptian printing of

Ibn-al-Athir this word Nawshâd is with an undotted (d) and in the Leiden printing it is with a dotted d (-dh). In the Ansab of Samâni it is written (a): annusari with zamma for (n) and fatha for (s), between them (w), then alif and at the end of it (r). This has connection with nushar and it is a village in Balkh. It has been said Nushari was a castle in Balkh which Amir Daud bin al-Abas built, and it has been said that when Yàqub bin Layce arrived in Balkh, Daud bin al-Abbas retreated to Samarqand. But when Yàqub withdrew, Daud came back to his homeland and found his castle, named Nusar, ruined. Then he wrote the following poem, and from grief his heart broke and he died after seventeen days: Oh, how? Daud have you seen the like of this? As no one can see stars at the break of day. That which was Nushar is a wasteland, Around it the voices of owls cry out. Gardezi has the same story in Zain-al-Akhbar as follows: In the year two hundred and fifty six Yàqub took Bamiyan and ruined Nawshâd of Balkh. He ruined all the buildings which Daud bin alAbbas bin Hashim bin Mahjur had made, and from there he returned to Kabul. Khorasan present day Afghanistan-Central Asia & India 90 As has been noted, then, firstly, nawshâd (which they also spelled as naushar or nusar) was in the outskirts of Balkh; secondly, that it was counted among the buildings of Daud ibn Abas ibn Hashim ibn Maynjur (or Mahjur); thirdly, that Yàqub of Lyce destroyed it, there remaining no doubt 90 As was seen above, in the history of Ibn-al-Athir this name is Mabanjur. In Zain-al-Akhbar, the printing of Sàid Nafisi it is printed as Bayanhur. But in the original of the manuscript it was Mahjur. In Màjam-al-Ansab by Zambawar Bani Bayanjur are the commanders of Tukharistan. In Kitab-al-Buldan by Yàqubi, who died around 292 H., the house (aal) of Hashim bib Bayanjur is mentioned. Since among the commanders of Khorasan the House of Simjur Dewati is also well-known with historians, it is then probable that Mahjur and Simjur are of the same category. In the conversation of Dari speakers of Ghazni, jur is used with the meaning of forearm. So simjur would be "having silvery elbow" and mahjur "having lunar elbow". However, this is a guess and is not certain. 40 that all these three historians are speaking about the same place, Finally, the spellings of the names of those localities contradict each other, due to the errors of scribes, i.e. Ibn Athir and Gardezi have written it nawshâd and nawshâdh, and Samâni once or twice has written nausar and once or twice nushar. The congruity of Ibn Athir with Gardezi without doubt gives preference to nawshâd, and nawshâd also appears in the rhymes of poems where (d) is the rhyming letter, and must be more correct. Although Yàqut followed Samâni and recorded it nushar, saying that it is a settlement or fortress in Balkh, it is evident, then, that Samâni is culpable in the original distortion of (r), not Yàqut. And from the puns that the poets have produced between nawshâd and shâdi (happiness), both (sh) and (d) of the word are strengthened. In Fazayel-e Balkh, which the preacher Shaikh-al-Islam Safiudin Abu Bakr Abdullah ibn Omar ibn Mohammad ibn Daud wrote in Arabic in the year 610 H. and which an anonymous person translated into Dari in 676 H., the manuscript of the Dari translation being preserved in the Bibliothèque Nationale in Paris, nawshâd is mentioned, and has a brand new meaning there, i.e. that Daud ibn Abbas was occupied for twenty years in the construction of Nawshâd, and he says that the date of its erection in the province of Balkh was Ziulqada (11th month of 233 H). Khorasan dynasty present day Afghanistan-Central Asia & India, 91 Marquart in Afghanistan Shahr and Barthold in his book Turkistan have also referred to the name nawshâd, and some of the above-mentioned sources have been noted. Following Samâni, Barthold erroneously calls nawshâd nussar. 92 In addition to the poets mentioned, in Wais and Ramin of Fakhruddin Gurgani (around 446 H.) an account of nawshâd appears in this form: Once again he broke into speech, He spoke words like the tablet of Nawshâd, Cypress and box-tree would be like your height If the tablet of Nawshâd be like both of them, 93 Ferdowsi too has mentioned nawshâd and says that Noshirwan built the city of Zab-e Khusraw and kept Rumi captives in jail there: Noshirwan commanded a city to be built, Inside of it was a palace and running water. Elders of enlightened mind and happy ones Gave it the name of

Zab-e Khusraw, The captives whom he captured from those cities Their hands and feet were wounded from heavy fetters, He commanded that they take away the fetters, And in that city they laid out Nawshâd. 91 Dari Chrestomathy. 92 Burhan-e Qatà footnotes, based on the writing of the eminent Qazwini Padga Khorasan present day Afghanistan-Central Asia & India 93 Wais wa Ramin, From Ferdowsi's usage it is clear that he treated nawshâd as a feature of the city of Zeb-e Khusraw, and he alluded to it with the same meaning like other poets. 3. It seems that Nawshâd was not a special temple. Instead, in numerous instances there existed graceful temples from ancient times with this name. From amongst all those, there most probably was also in existence a temple on the outskirts of the royal Kushanid city of Bagram to the north of Kabul. In the time of Kanishka, Chinese hostages would live in the summer in this temple. Its location is presumed to be in the ruins of Puza-e Shuturak in Kohe Pahlawan, Bagram north of Kabul. 94 Hiuan Tsang made note of this temple and lodging for Chinese hostages and princes of China with the name sha-lo-kia (kia-house) in July 644 A.D. as he was going from Kabul and Kapisa to East Turkistan and passing by this place. 95 There is reason that we should recognize the initial components of the word sha-lo as the same root nawshâl. 4. In Kandahar, Punjab and Kashmir, a name for avenues, gardens, and splendid places is in use, two places with the name of Shalamar being present in Kandahar, and the Shalimar gardens of Lahore and Kashmir, which are among the architectural remnants of the Khorasan present day Afghanistan-Indian Kabuli Empire. know what the source of these words is. However, in their first part there also appears the marks and signs of that same shâl. From the study of the preceding documents it appears that Kushani shâl, the nawshâd of Dari literature, the Afghan shâl of Bayhaqi, the Arabic nushadh, the East Turkistan sha-lo-kia, and the Shalimar of present day Kandahar and India are from one source. In the Kushani language nawshâl meant new place and new temple. At the beginning of the Islamic era in Afghanistan up to the Kabuli emperor departure, nawshad was applied to graceful temples and idolshrines and to the places where such graceful idols were. Nawshâl of the Kushani dynasty language and nawshad of Dari literature were, then, among the place-names of Aryana-Kharasan "Afghanistan since 1747", and there existed temples and idol-shrines and idolatry-spots with this name in every age and era in Balkh, Tukharistan and Kabul. According to past documents Daud bin Abbas made the last Nawshâd in 233 H. in Balkh, and Yàqub of the Saffarids destroyed it in 256 H. Farrukhi has mentioned this same place in Balkh together with Nawbahâr: By Nawshâd gate it would go, or by Nawbahar garden, How pleasant is the blooming gale of Balkh's Nawshâd Especially now that spring has come to Balkh. Khorasan dynasty present day Afghanistan-Central Asia & India 96-5. We have a name in the Pashto language which is Nurshali. There lived a poet with this name at the end of the 9th century in Abasin valley, some of whose Pashto poems Darmesteter 94 Tarekh-e Afghanistan, 95 The travel loges of Hiuan Tsang, 96 Divan of Farrukhi, heard and recorded. 97 If we analyze this word, it is nur+shali. As we know, nur is the same lmar (Pashto-sun) and shali is a place. As a whole this name gives the meaning of sun-place, that same ancient shâl being preserved and remaining alive in the second part of it. 6. In Dari too the root shâl with the meaning of location and place is present. Awshâl with initial fatha is pond, water-holder, and the place where the water stands in mountains, 98 which is the same shâl=châl, the root of that same ancient word remaining preserved in this word. However, in all three copies of the inscription at the end of the word nawshâd there is preserved an (m) with no vowel before it, and it would be read nawshâlm, as it should be the same connector (m) of #3. But this point is not clear to me why this appended-possessive (m) has not been separated by the word divider O as on other occasions in the inscription it is connected to the word like modern Dari. Perhaps this juxtaposition is a sign of izafat (possessive appendage) and ownership based on grammatical principles of the Kushani language of which we have no knowledge now. In the third copy in this place and in #109, this word is noshAlm. 36. ΦΡΟΧΟΡΤΙΝΔ (frukhorténd)

The first part of the word is fro. This prefix appeared in #17 also which explains its meaning as before, in front, and it was the same in Avesta, Sanskrit and old Dari. In Latin it was pro. In old Dari many words start with this prefix. 99 In Dari literature both farâ (up) and fero (down) are seen, and they are for strengthening or orienting the verb. Bayhaqi says: they do not open their mouths before this great king (zaban farâ pesh...). 100 Sàdi says: One day a rebellion occurred in Syria, Everyone went forward (farâ raftand) from his corner. As for fero, it appears in the verbs fero-istâd, fero khoshkéd, fero gereftand and in other verbs. Farukhi says: Put out from our assembly the two-faced people. Bring forward the red flower and put down (fero kon) the two-faced flower. 101 Here the prefix fro is attached to the following verb khortind. With the preceding prefix, this verb is fro-khor-tind, from which are farâ khortah and farâ khordah. In Bactria it was khwart (khwartan) and in Avesta khwar and khwarayti (eating). One of the meanings of this same root is also perish, 102 and this is the intention here (taste the downward). The subject of this verb is 97 Da Pashtunkhwa Haaro Bahar 98 Burhan-e Qatà, 99 Old Dari, Aryana- Khorasan dynasty present day Afghanistan-Central Asia & India Tarekh-e Bayhaqi, Sabk Shenasi, I, Burhan-e.43 BAGEAS in the third person plural i.e. the god-worshippers of this Nawshâd perished: TAD IBAGEAS-I-NOSHALM FROXOTIND meaning: so that the god-worshippers of Nawshâd perished. As for FROXOTIND, it is the third person plural like the verb of #40. 103-37. TAΔ (tâd) This same tâ of Dari and Pashto is among the particles of goal, explanation and condition (cf. #32). 38. AB (âb) It has been repeatedly used with the modern meaning of water (cf. #20). 39. ΛΡΑΦΟ (laráfù) In this instance the researchers have had no success and have not said a thing that would be of use, and this word has remained unanalysed. In my view LRAFO is clearly an ancient form of lar 104 (gutter) and lour (gully) 105 which we say as lorah in Pashto, In Kandahar a particular flood-conduit in the west of the city is called lorah. And the Lora river has its course in southern Afghanistan, being shaped by the spring floods. As for FO at the end of the word, which is changed into (h) in Pashto, it was in several words of ancient tongues, for example, koh (mountain) of modern Dari was kaufa in old Dari and Avesta, 106 of which their final (fa) is changed into (h) And on this same model perhaps LRAFO of the Kushani language is also the joint lar, lora of modern Dari and Pashto, whose meaning is gutter and water-conduit which are dug out by human hands and which come into being from the flow of floods. Since this word has its position in the sentence as subject, its verb being plural, it can be said on this basis that the word LARAFO was plural also. Since at the excavations of the Baghlan temple there are remains of gutters coming out around the steps of the temple, on that basis there can be a confirmation of this interpretation. 40. ATINΔ (ásténd) This verb, which is connected to its subject of #39, is third person plural like the verb of # 36. From the same root STAD of #25 and 34; here also it is a primary verb, not auxiliary. And its meaning is thus: TAD AB LRAFO ACTIND-ta âbé joyha istâdand meaning: since the aqueducts 103 Here we should not overlook the Pashto khwâra and khwéredal i.e. became separated and scattered, and Dari khwâr-zâr, and possibly khortind should be interpreted as to become dispersed and to come into distress. 104 Burhan-e Qatà, footnotes, Burhan-e Burhan-e Qatà, footnotes,; Sabk Shenasi, became dry. The subsequent sentence is connected to this sentence as a result of it. 41. AB (âb) Cf. #20. 42. ANΔEZ (ándéz) Maricq considered this word to be from the Afghanistan handeza meaning to heap up, i.e. to pile up (on each other), whereas it has no correlation to the place of its usage. It seems that ANDEZ is from a root of a Bactria and Dari word. In Bactria and Dari ând was an indefinite number, somewhat comparable to Arabic badà (several, some), which was the Dari word andak and the Dari handak meaning few, fewness and a few of anything. 107 Now it is unknown to us how and for what purpose EZ is attached to the end of the word, but from the place where it is used one can perceive that ANDEZ has a verbal meaning, conveying the sense of the water became scarce. 43. OT (aut) A conjunctive particle equal to Dari and Pashto aw (cf. #26). 44. MAYIZ Cf. #2, 16,

23, 79, 112, 126. 45. ΠΙ ΔΟΡΙΓΔ (péduregd) Maricq has indicated the root of this word to be pita-rixta, an ancient form of a passive particle which was used in reference to the past. Clearly this word is an ancient form of the same Dari pidrud which has the sense of be left behind and farewell, and in Bactria it was padrut. 108 Perhaps ΠΙ ΔΟΡΙΓΔ is in reference to past action here, which nowadays we say as padrud shud. Its negative imperfect comes in #113. This, then, is the meaning of the sentence from #41 to 45: AB ANΔEZ OT MAYIZ ΠΙ ΔΟΡΙΓΔ: the water became scarce, and the acropole was abandoned. It ought to be mentioned that there appears in Pashto from this same root the verb pregad-prekhod and the infinitive Presowal-prekhodal (leave, quit). 107 Burhan-e Qatà. Burhan-e Qatà. TAKAΛΔ (tâkáld) For explanation of (TA) refer to #32 and 37. Here TA is an inseparable part of the following word KALD, and they also do not even have the divider O in between. It seems that when they wrote this word with KALD they elided its (d). This explanation of the word kald (Pashto kala) occurred in #27. Tâ kala (tâ kunun) is in use in Pashto with the meaning of up to the time that and so that, and Henning have the substance of this same meaning for #46 with English until. 47. NOKONZOK (nokonzoké) According to what Maricq also says, this is a Kushani personality and the name of the head of Nawshad's reconstruction committee. However, Maricq read the divider O and the subsequent (i) of attribution as parts of this same name, whereas (i) is a sign of attributive subordination which also came after #29, and which is repeated several times in this inscription. In keeping with the names of that time, this name ends in an honorific (k), parallels of which I showed in Pashto in #11. In the third text, however, it is NOKONZIK. 48. KAPAΛPANΓ (káralráng) Maricq read this word as a military title composed of kara, i.e. army or troops + drang, which was the title of the ruler of nearby imperial Kushani provinces, or the title of the ruler of a border-state. In olden times they spoke of a border as "the royal fringe" 109 and they said its plural as the royal kenarah (fringes, edges) and "the border-governors", which the Arabs say as muluk-al-taraf, and kenarak with zamma on the first (k). Kanarang comes from the word kanarak meaning border. There were kanarangs in every region. Ferdowsi has many poems about konarank, and among all those poems this very meaning of "guardian of the borders" comes up: Pass on from that, there is a river ahead Whose width is more than two farsangs, Its demonic, konarank and sentry, All the male daemons under his command. This he says about the courage and bravery of the konarank: that the border-rulers were wellknown for this character: Which is the hero with the heart of a konarang? In war by manliness he has made his heart black. Khorasan present day Afghanistan-Central Asia & India 110 Likewise according to Ferdowsi the kanarang of Marw had the name of Mahoy who was the leader of the shepherds: 109 Menhaj Serah of Jozjan says in Tabaqat-e Naseri:Qalej Arsalan...carried out some notable assaults. He obtained great fame, just as the borders of Afranja received much punishment from him. I, Sabk Shenasi, I, Kanarang is of Merv and also Mahoy, With an army and elephants, every kind of thing, He who is the leader of our shepherds, He is the director of our watchmen. 111 In the old introduction to the Shah nama, compiled in Moharam of the year 346 H., which is a more ancient model of Dari prose written in the name of one of the famous men of Khorasan, AbuMansur Mohammad ibn Abu Razzaq Abdullah Farukh, by his minister Abu Mansur ibn Ahmad alMoàmmeri, in the genealogy of the writer of this prose-introduction the name kanarang repeatedly appears. From that, it is known that in the beginning of Islam in this part of Khurasan some men with the name of Kanarang were renowned. Tabari, Khorasan present day Afghanistan-Central Asia & India 112 in the events of the year 31 H., mentioned this name in the form of Kanari, margrave of Tus, and Bilazari 113 has mentioned this same name Kanarang in the account of the conquests of Khorasan, and in the manuscripts this was distorted to the form of Kanarang, the margrave of Tus. 114 This is the same name which Ibn Khurradabih recorded in the form of kanar (kanarang), the king of Neshapur. 115 As we are aware, up to about the fifth century of the

Hejira, it was a custom among the farmers and priesthood and the people of Khorasan to preserve their genealogies, and in every one of these families there existed narratives concerning their ancestors which were preserved from generation to generation. (This is substantially the same case nowadays among the Pashtuns). A portion of them has by chance been preserved in several books, and from among them there are a few narratives relating to Kanarang, the sixth ancestor of Abu Mansur Mohammad ibn Abdur Razaq, whom we see in Abu Mansuri's introduction to Shah nama, Khorasan present day Afghanistan-Central Asia & India 116 to which reference was made previously, In this regard Shams Fakhri Esfahani writes (744 H.), "Kanarang: he is called civil-governor and also called margrave." An illustration of his own: Wherever that the least of your servants be, There by your good fortune will be the kanarang. 117 Before Shams Fakhri this word was recorded also by Asadi with the meaning of master of the border and margrave, relying on this by Ferdowsi: He never became separated from either of these two, They were kanarang and he was a king. 118 A number of the margraves i.e. rulers of autonomous regions of Khorasan were called kanarang. 111 Wais wa Ramin, p. 427. 112 Tarekh-al-Umam wal Muluk, I, 2886. 113 Futuh-al-Baladan, p. 406. 114 Introduction to the old Shah nama, p. 147. 115 Al Masalek wa Almamalek of Istakhri, Hamasa Sarayee dar Afghanistan, p. 87. 117 Màyar-e Jamali, Loghat-e Dari, p. 260.46 According to Prokop, the Byzantine historian, the station of kanarang was hereditary in a number of the families. The margrave of the Abre Shahr region i.e. northern Neshapur was called kanarang. When Yazdgerd III of the Sassanids fled to Khorasan in fear of Arab attacks, he took refuge with the ruler of Tus, who was also called kanarang. In the indexes to the titles of autonomous rulers, the ruler of Neshapur was called kanar and the ruler of the Tus kanarang. Thàbili explains in Ghorar-e Muluk-al-Fars: the margrave of Tus was kanarang. Amongst the military events of the Sassani period we at the time come across this point, that the Sassanid emperor sent such and such a kanarang into the battle field, and from this we find that the kanarangs also had military duties. Concerning Geshnasp Daz who was among the influential nobles at the court of the Sassani king Khwaz, they have clearly written that he was a kanarang. Not only the margraves of the eastern border-regions of Fars were called kanarang; in other regions also this usage was current, as it was in the regulations for receiving foreign ambassadors in the Sassanid area that upon the arrival of an ambassador, the kanarangs of the provinces that were on the route of this ambassador had to receive him in every place as was befitting, and perhaps the rulers of small regions were called kanarang. Ferdowsi in the Shah nama has used the word kanarang in twenty places with the meaning of absolute ruler. 119 As to office of kanarang being a military office in Afghanistan, there is reference to this found in Shahreyar Nama by Serajuddin Osman ibn Mohammad Mokhtari Ghaznavi (died in the year 544 or 554 H.) 120 which, after the year 492 H. was entered into verse for Sultan Masàud Sani ibn Sultan Ibrahim Ghaznavi and finished in the year 508 H. This story includes the wars of the descendants of Rustam-e Saystani, Faramarz, son of Rustam, and his cousin Shahreyar and is related to the historic land of Afghanistan. Its only manuscript is to be found in the British museum. 121 In this versified story which a Ghazni poet delivered before the Ghaznavi court there is a story about the king of Haytal (Hayatala) in which the word kanarang appears with the meaning of a military office: The kanarang of Haytal came with six-thousand, The yelps of a scuffle arose. When from the front there rose up outcries and growls, The quick commanders moved away. The dark night and the sound of the brass drum, The kanarang roared like a demon 119 Tarekh-e Tamadun-e Sassani,. 254. 120 Chahar Maqala, footnotes, 150. 121 Catalogue of Dari manuscripts in the British museum. 524 and following. 47 He has taken the road of the heroic, the fortunate and the quick. 122 By this explanation, kanarang, according to Burhan-e Qatà, was with initial zamma (ko) meaning margrave. But since in Bactrian kanarang, in Greek xanaranges, and in Syriac qanarag was the special title of the margrave of Abr-e Shahr of Neshapur in the Sassanid era, 123 in Avesta also the word kanara, in Bactria kanara with a fatha of (k), 124 based on that, its pronunciation should be with ka—like in the inscription. But as to what the root was of the Kushani word KARALRANG and whether the word is simple or compound is not clear to me at present. Its analysis is dependent on our forthcoming information about the roots of words in the Kushani language. From this inscription, however, it is clear that the ancient Kushan form of kanarang was karalrang. 125-49. I-ФРЕ-I-ХОАΔЕΔНОГ (î-fré-î-khodéwug) The two i's at the beginning and end of FRE are the sigh of izafat as in #53, 56, 80, 104 and 108, which connects FRE with karalrang in attribution. The second (i) likewise puts the subsequent XOADEOG in attribution. As for the word FRE, it is from the root of FRO of #17, 36 and 110, which has appeared repeatedly in this inscription, and perhaps, according to instances of usage and the grammatical circumstances of its occurrence, the vowels (e) and (o) varied in form, originally being FR. This preposition is not found in old Dari. However, fra in Avesta, pra in Sanskrit, pra in Latin and pro in the Achaemeni inscriptions of old Dari appeared at the beginning of verbs, adjectives and nouns, and it was used with the meaning of forward and front, 126 and it is said that this FRA appeared repeatedly at the head of verbs in the Dari language also, clarifying the direction of the verb, such as frâ-amad, frâ-afgand, frâ-raftand. 127 Nizami says: The drunken police-chief came into (frâ-amad) my neighborhood, And delivered up a few kicks toward me. Sàdi says: One day an insurrection occurred in Syria, Everyone went forth (frâ-raftand) from his corner. Bayhaqi says: They do not speak before (frâ) this great, fortunate king. 122 Hamas Sarayee. 315. In a copy from the manuscript of Shahreyar Nama. 123 The Sassanids, p. 108. 124 Tataboàt-e Afghanistan,. 115. 125 Up to the time of the Ghorids there was a fort with the name Hesar-e Kanarang located between Ghazni and Bamiyan. Tabaqat-e Nasiri I, p. 461, tells the story of how this appelation lasted up to that time, i.e. c. 600 H. 126 Old Dari, p. 197. 127 Sabk Shinasi, I, p. 339.48 From the usage of this affix in numerous instances in this inscription, it is clear that it was frequently in use in the languages of Afghanistan. In Pashto vestiges of it remain in three forms wér, dér, ra for the third, second and first persons of discourse, because sometimes (f) of the other languages is changed into w in Pashto, such as wafra in Avesta, vaft in Sanglichi, and vafra in Munji, 128 which is wâwréh in Pashto and barf in Dari In this same way the wár, affix of direction in Pashto, has its root from that same ancient (fr) which was also used in Kushani. Here, in the sentence NOKONZOK-I-KARLANG-I-FRE-I-XOADEOG (FRE) specifies the location, station and title of Nokonzok, he having gotten his station of karalrang (kanarang) from xoadeog (xuday-lord), and it gives the meaning of provenance and connected with confirmation: the king's governor and agent of the Sultanate, etc. Let it be known that Maricq considered FRE to be a proper name, and Henning took it as meaning the confident of the emperor. This, however, is improbable, and the roots of the word are present in the inscription itself. As for the word xoadeog, in the view of Maricq and Henning it has the meaning of a free and equal lord or master (autokrator), and is the khidew of Dari, which is xidiv in Turkish and khedive in French. The word khudây was used in Afghanistan literature up to the first years of the Islamic era Khorasan dynasty present day Afghanistan-Central Asia & India, also with the meaning of king, master and ruler. Every prominent individual was called khudâwandgar (i.e. lord). With this same meaning the kabul khudây and zabul khudây in the Shah nama and gozgan khudâh, saman khudâh and buxara khudâh have been mentioned in books about the history of the beginning of the Islamic era. 129 Among all the kings of Kabul who, in the first half of the seventh Christian century, were giving opposition to the conquering Arab armies in these parts, one also has the name Xuduwayaka, whose coins can be found in eastern Afghanistan and the Punjab. After the Arab conquest the capital of these kings was transferred from Kabul and Gardez to Wihind on the banks of the Attock (Indus). 130 Moreover, the word khudây has different pronunciations up to now in Pashto: one says khdoy, khodoy, khloy etc., and it is known that the ancient pronunciation of this Afghan word was also close to these Pashto pronunciations, because in #145 of this inscription XOADE appears, and xuduwayaka is on the coins of the Kabul-shahon. As for the (g) at the end of the word, it is the dignific type which is found at the end of the names of great men of that time (cf.#11). 50. KIΔ (kéd-kéh) This is the relative, declarative adverb concerning Nokonzok, the final (d) of which is silent in Dari after the vowel (i), as with # 26, 32,37 and 43. 128 Burhan-e Qatà, footnotes, p. 259 129 Zain-al-Akhbar, p. 1314; Masalik wa Mamalik of Ibn Khurdaz Beh, p. 41; Tabari, VII, p. 8. 130 Encyclopedia of Islam, under the item Afghanistan, I.49 Maricq identifies this word as being similar to Khutanese kide and kade, and Soghdian kdy. Henning considers it equal with #8, SID, where, it is my belief, the (d) is likewise silent after the (i) and left unpronounced, and is to be read si-chi. In Soghdian, kdh-kz is the same declarative keh-ki. In the northern Balkh poem Draxte Asurlk we find gizish, meaning ke-án-râ i.e. (that which) in the objective case, 131 and the kati (which is) spoken in today's colloquial Kabuli Dari is in my belief from the remains of this same root, since there are also some people who say it kadi, i.e. kati-au gap zad (spoke with him) or khudish gap zad (he spoke). This word is exactly like PID of #68 and 90 from which have remained the Dari bah and Pashto pah, and the final (d) has been elided. However, in PIDEIN of #121 and 123 the (d) has remained to this day. This kind of (d) in KID is silent in the declarative ke=ki but in northern gizish and in the modern khudish of colloquial Kabuli it is present and preserved. 51. ΦΡΕΙΤΑ (fréistâr) In Bactria there was parastâr with the meaning of attendant, servant and obedient. 132 As Fakhre Gurgani says: Every moon faced one has a thousand Pretty servants around. 133 Ferdowsi has: The son of a servant (parastar zâda) does not qualify, Although his father be the ruler 134 Henning gives the compounded roots of this word in Soghdian frystr and Parthian fryhstwm meaning showing sacrifice, and based on that he writes FREISTAR-AB SHA-I-BAG... with the meaning of devoted and sacrificing to the great king. Here, contrary to numerous other examples in the inscription, he takes the word âb to mean ba-to (with), instead of modern âb-water, but this is not acceptable, because in the rest of its occurrences AB is with its modern meaning of water. Since it would be used with the meaning of ba only in this instance, I consider this interpretation unreasonable. consider FREISTAR AB to be a mixed compound, because in Bactria there was the word parastâr meaning servant and commander of a certain governmental institute. In Dari texts things like this appear: parastar marde berah mabuwed. 135 According to prevalent opinion the mixed compound FREISTAR AB must be a name of one of 131 Sabk Shinasi. 110. 132 Burhane Qatà, footnotes, 383. 133 Wais wa Ramin, 24. 134 Chahar Maqala, 81. 135 Dari Texts, p. 82.50 the government officials who had the job of supplying water, and overseeing irrigation and ditchdigging, whom in the villages we know now as miráb. In Tarekh-e Seistan (314) the emirship of âb is mentioned as one of the governmental jobs, which is probably the same ancient FREISTAR AB. According to this interpretation it should be said that this Nokonzok likewise had the job of chairman of the water supply institute, called fréistâr ab-frârastar âb. 52. AB (âb) Its explanation occurred in # 15. It is also repeated in #20, 38, 41, 94 and 97. 53. A (shâ) 54. ΒΑΓ (bág) Meaning lord and great (cf. #6). 55. ΠΟΥΡ (puhar) As was explained in #29, this word should be read as bag-pohr, and not poyr as Henning has read it. Maricq considers baga-pour to be a compound from bag-puthra (son of the Lord), close to Sanskrit devaputra (still closer to Sanskrit bhagaputra), poyr—correct pohr—functions as a suffix in family names. The root of this word is puca in old Dari, putra in Sanskrit, puthra in Avesta, pohr in Bactria, in Dari and Pashto pur-pus-pisar, 136 and in old Hindi it is pusra and in Sindhi putra. In this inscription its Kushanic spelling is pohr, similar to the Bactria. Bag-pohr, then, means son of the Lord, son of the King, and son of God, and it is the attributive to the following lolx-bosar. This Kushanic compound bagpohr is bagh-pur in Dari its Arabicized form is faghfur, i.e. son of God, 137 and Khwarazmi has clearly indicated this meaning. 138 The same ancient pohr and Dari pur is found in Pashto in the word turbur (tra-uncle+bur-son), uncle's son-cousin, and in the word bura (a woman who has lost her son). Let it be known that in the third copy of the inscription this word is written with the spelling POOR, which is the same as Dari pur-Pashto bur. In the Encyclopedia of Islam C.L. Hayworth writes that Ibn Athir considered faghfur to mean the son of heaven, the exact same title being tain-tzyy in the language. In the Arabic inscription at Zaytun, which was written in the year 723 H., and which is mentioned? 136 Old Dari, p. 197. 137 Burhane Qatà, footnotes, p. 1484 138 Mafateh-al-àlum, p. 73.51 by Marco Polo, (Vol 2, p. 145), this title was used for the emperor of the Sung dynasty. Thus it appears that this title was in general use in Central Asia as far as China. 56. ΛΟΙΧ (luyékh) Orientalists have not given regard to the true origin of this word, which is loyak in source references of the Islamic era. This family was one of the local kings of Kabul, Ghazni and Gardez, ruling in this territory at the beginning of the Islamic era. Loyak, which became LOIX in Greek script, is a familyname, Khorasan present day Afghanistan-Central Asia & India 139 and the original name of this Baghpur and son of God of the Loyak family is Bosar in #57. It may be that this Loyak Bosar was ruler of this territory through the Kushanid emperor, since Nokonzok the kanarang was appointed as "parastar-áb" through this Loyak. In the book Pashto wa Loyakan-e Ghazni we have explained in detail the word Loyak and their dynasty in the Islamic era. Here is an indication of the entire question: Longworth Dames says that around 260 H. the local ruler of Ghazni was Empire Lâwik, who is an unknown personage. 140 Abdul Hai Gardezi 141 described the confrontation of Abu Mansur Aflah ibn Mohammad ibn Khaqan with Yàqub of Lyce in Gardez, and in the same way Nizamulmulk, in his commentary on the age of Alaptagin, mentions Loyak in connection with Empire of Ghazni. 142 Minhaj Seraj of Jozjan likewise mentions Abubakr Lawik of Charkh (in Logar) in confrontation with Subuktagin. 143 Mohammad ibn Ali of Shabankara likewise has noted this king of Ghazni. 144 Gardezi reckoned this Gardez family of generals in the Ghaznavi court as possessing posts of mediators and political ranks. In the manuscript Karamat-e Sakhi Sarwar, which was found in Dera Ismail Khan, there was entered a story about this Ghazna family of rulers, and the remnants of this family of Ghaznavi rulers were here at the beginning of the Islamic conquests, and in the Khaljia language (Pashto) there is a song about them which is recited. In view of all the available documents, we know from this family the following rulers and men: 1. Loyak of Wajwir (Hajwir of Ghazni—Ujaristan) is related to it, contemporary with Ratbel, the Kabulshah of about 120 H. 2. Loyak of Khanan (Khaqan), son of Wajwir. Contemporary with Khanchil, 145 the Kabulshah of about 163 H. 3. Mohammad ibn Khaqan, about 210 H. (converted to Islam). 139 The spelling of this word is different in all three copies; in the first and original copy it is LOIX, in the second copy LOX and in the third copy ALIIX, and similarly as in the Islamic era they recorded it with various spellings lwyk, lawyk, anwk, lawyl etc. In that ancient era it had this same fate in the Greek spelling also, it being written in three kinds of spelling in three copies of one inscription at the same place (and perhaps in the same time period?) this is quite amazing. 140 Encyclopedia of Islam, II, p. 154. 141 Zain-al-Akhbar, p. 6. 142 Siyasat Nama, p. 122. 143 Tabaqat-e Nasiri, I, p. 268. 144 Majma-al-Ansab (manuscript). 145 Correct Khingil.52 4. Abu Mansur Aflan, son of Mohammad, defeated by Yàqub Lyce the Saffar (coppersmith—the name of his dynasty) at Ghazni, about 256 H. 5. Mansur ibn Aflan, about 300 H. 6. Mursal ibn Mansur, 146 about 350 H. 7. Sahl ibn Mursal, about 400 H. 8. Abu Ali or Abubakr of Lawik, father-in-law of the Kabul shahon. who with his son-in-law was defeated by Subuktagen at Charkh in Logar around 365 H. (cf. Pashto wa Loyakane Ghazni). If to these eight Loyaks we add the two more ancient Loyaks of the second century A.D., which are mentioned in this inscription by the names of King Faghfur Loyak Bosar, and his father Shizogarg (arwa shad=may he rest in peace), then we know ten persons from this family of kings in Ghazni and Gardez. In regard to the family name Loyak and the literary records of it, we have given an explanation in Pashto wa Loyakan-e Ghazni, the quintessence of which is the following: the word loyak is formed from loy (big-leader) as in Pashto, with the addition of the dignific suffix (k), which was explained in #11, and of which there are many examples in this inscription and in Bactria. Now, why was the dignific (k) spelled here with X (LOIX)? Perhaps the reason is connected with some grammatical rule, by which the sound (k) was changed to (x) after (i). 57. BOAP (bosér) This is the personal-name of the king Loyak. Henning connects it with upat-chara of old Dari. But he says nothing else about the words Loyak and Bosar. In this case he also mentions the dari words bazaar-afzâr, which do not seem that well-considered or relevant. However, since Loyak is the king's personal name, we are not faced with any problem. 58. IZOГAPГ (shizogargé) Maricq and Henning have read this word as shizogargo, and have written its meaning as "the beneficent" i.e. doer of good work and munificent, but they have not given any documentation for such as interpretation, and they have not indicated its roots. Since there is an izafat of paternity between the proper names Loyak Bosar and this word, based on Bactria and Dari which give the purport of filiation by the sign of izafat between the names of father and son, therefore we identify Shizogarg as the name of Loyak Bosar's father, and these two verses of are similar to this izafat and (i) of filiation: Where is Sam of Nariman and where is Rustam Leader of the army of Mazindaran. 146 In Khugyani in the eastern province of Nangarhar, Afghanistan there is a tomb named Mursale Baba, but it is not known which Mursal. However, among the ancient dams of Ghazni there is Mursal's dam, at a distance of 25 km to the south-east, which has that name still nowadays, and it is quite likely that this is connected with the Mursal of Loyak. 53 Where is Babak of Sasan and where Ardsher? Who is neither Bahram nor Noshirawan. 147 This same sort of descriptive and attributive (i) appears after the word Shizogarg also, because the following word #59 is its adjective and attributive. But in the first and second copies this sign is separated by the O symbol, and in the third copy Shizogarg is connected, and as a rule it should be separated. 59. AΛOXAΛ (álusâl) Henning mentions this word with the meaning of compassionate and kind, and he wants to match the second part with a Parthian nama xchd. As we said earlier, this word is connected to Shizigarg by means of the descriptive and attributive sign (i), and is its adjective of benediction. The first part of the word is alo=aro, the (l) always changing into (r) in Dari and Pashto i.e. dewar-dewal, gharbel ghalbel. So the Kushani alo became aro in modern Dar and Pashto, the meaning of which is the living-soul. Similar to alo-aro, this word is preserved in the first part of arwant-alwand also, the origin of which was aurvant in Avesta, meaning living-creature, quick, lively, capable, courageous, which are marks of the living-soul. This word does not come from the Arabic plural arwâh, as it has been depicted; it has remained from antiquity in Dari and Pashto. There is a strong possibility that Dar and Bactria ruwân and Avesta urvân meaning living-soul are of the same root as this Kushan alo-arwa in Dari and Pashto, because there is quite a proximity between Avestan urvân and the modern pronunciation arwâ. The word gushurvan is an example of the ancient use of the root arwâ in Avesta. This was one of the assistants to Wahumina (guardianangel of the bedstead). This word has been translated as gushu (gaw)+rvan (ruwan), cow-soul, which is mentioned in Fiqh-al-Lugha-e, compiled by Jackson in reference to Bandhishane Buzurg, 148 and in this name the first part may be compared with ghazhgâw (the holy yak of the Pamir and Badakshan uplands) and the second part with alo-arwa, meaning living-soul. As for the second part of the word, sâl (retroflex sh) is the same Dari shâd and Pashto (retroflex sh) sâd, and in Greek they used PX (sh and kh) together to represent the pronunciation of retroflex sh. 149 They showed the pronunciation of the special sound retroflex sh, which is a compositesound between sh and kh, by writing both of the letters, and it is certain that they pronounced this sound exactly like the retroflex (sh) of today's Pashto to the west of Kabul 150 In the Avesta alphabet and writing-system there is a strengthening (sh) in addition to the regular (sh), which gave the sound of 54 As for (i), the final letter of the word, in other languages it changes to (d) and another example of this metathesis is the metathesis of nawshâl to nawshâd in this inscription. From this it is evident that in the Kushani language they pronounced and wrote this final (d) of the words nawshâd and shâd within (i), and the word shad was shat in Bactria, shata in Avesta (retroflex sh), and shiyati in old Dari. Shal (retroflex sh), shad, shat, and shad (retroflex sh), then, are different pronunciations of the word, and altogether both the words are arwa+shad i.e. bless his soul, which was probably a usage similar to modern shad-ruwan, which is used for the dead in respect and benediction. And since Shizogarg, father of king Loyak Bosar, had died when the inscription was being written and had entered into the state of mercy, he was spoken of as arwâ shâd. From this discussion two results are clear: First, the belief of the people of that time in the existence and immortality of the soul, because we know that they believed in the existence of the soul after corporeal dissolution, since they wished for the soul's well-being. Secondly, we know that the Pashto sound retroflex (sh) was also in the Kushani language, and they pronounced shad as shal (retroflex sh) and wrote (sh) and (kh) together for it. 60. KIΔ (-kéh) This is the declarative particle and relative pronoun referring to the blessed Shizogarg. Cf. #50. 61,62. ΦΑΡΟ ΟΙΠ (fáro-wésp) The first part of this word is probably connected to the old Dari root pro, Avestan poro, Pashto pura, which has the meaning of entire and complete. Its explanation will come in #96. As for the second part OICP (wésp) Maricq has read it as old Afghan wispa, meaning entire, all. In Balkh it was also wisf (all) and har-wisf (even each one), and Kitab-al-Tambiat àla Huruf-alTashif (book of correcting wrong letters) by Hamza bin Hasan, the single manuscript of which is in the library, among all kinds of ancient writing there is the seventh kind, wisf-safira, i.e. secretariat for all kinds of writing, 151 so that Maricq's interpretation also seems compatible with this evidence. The two words # 61 and 62 should be read as fáro-wésp-complete and whole, which are connected with what follows them. 63,64,65 ANOMO ΨΑΔ ΒΑΡΓΑΝ (ánumo wâd bargân) Henning considered these words from KID to BARGAN to be a benedictory phrase, and says it this Pashto retroflex (sh), and in Avesta there was the word shat with retroflex sh (=shad) with the same meaning and sound of Pashto shad (retroflex sh) and Kushani shal (retroflex sh). 151 Sabk Shinasi, I, p. 99.55 probably a prayer for the king, 152 but he and others have not applied themselves to the analysis of these benedictory words. Clearly # 63 is a form of Dari nâm-Pashto num. They have read # 64 as wad, the ancient form of the same invocatory bad from the verb budan. As for # 65, BARGAN, it shows a connection with the name Barg of this inscription, # 11, the second line. At present, however, we can say nothing about the details of these words. Why did nâm (as in #11) become anomo here? Why has wad=bad come in the middle? Why did barg from #11 become bargan here with the addition of ân? There is a strong possibility that these words have changed their forms because of predetermined grammatical requirements, and their close analysis depends on our future information about the grammar and morphological changes of words in the Kushani language. In any case, in view of past analyses the words # 46 to 65 have the following meaning: TAKALD NOKONZOK I KARALRANG I FRE I KHOADEOG KID FREISTAR AB SHA I BAG POHR I LOIX BOSAR I SHIZOGARG I ALOSHXAL KID FARO OICP ANOMO OAD BARGAN: until Nokonzok the Kanarang, who is the distributor of water, through the Lord, the son of king Loyak Bosar (son) of the blessed Shizogarg, may his name always be famous. As regards the suffix barg, refer both to #11 and 119 where we have given an explanation. 66. ΨΟΓΔ (wusugd) Maricq wrote clean and pure as the translation of this word, considering it to be from the ancient Afghan root awa-suseta. For the following word MAGG he gave the meaning flax. Henning viewed this meaning of flax for máng with incredulous amazement and writes the meaning of both words as "with a pure heart". Actually the word flax is contrary to the trend of the wording. There was a word in the Dari language in the form of asaghada meaning prepared and ready, which also had an infinitive in the form of asaghdîdan i.e. to prepare or make ready. 153 This Dari word is quite close to WSOGD, and it also has connection and congruity with the word máng which follows it, as. 67. MAΝΓ (mâng) Based on the pronunciation of (ng) for two (g)s as in # 7, 48, 77, 91 and 143, this word should also be read as mâng. Previously in the interpretation of #11 the reader saw that there are some words in 152 This couplet of Firdawsi is a parallel to this benedictory phrase: In the time of emperor Noushirwan, May his name remain forever! 153 Burhan-e Qata, p. 129.56 this inscription ending in an attributive (g), the pronunciation of which (g) was between (k) and (g). 154 If we remove this attributive (g) from this word, then, there remains mán, which was in ancient Pashto literature with the meaning of will and intention. said: The arrows of my desire (mán) go like lightening upon the enemies. 155 This word was also used in Sanskrit with the meaning of desire, heart and soul, 156 and Al Beruni used it with the meaning of heart and desire. 157 Also in Pashto there is in addition the verb manél, mán meaning to take to heart, i.e. to accept. So it can be said that wCOGgd maGg (wusugd máng) has the meaning of with a prepared/ready heart, and these two words are an attributive compound modifying our Nokonzok the Kanarang who with a prepared and ready heart and mind had started on the work. 68. ΠΙ Δ (péd-pah-bah) This word which in Pashto is pah and bah in Dari also appears in #90, 121 and 144, and its final (d) has changed into (h), just like KID of # 50 and 60 and SAD of #83, 116, 122, 132, and KALD of #46 and others of the same gnere ending in this same (d) which are frequent in this inscription. And nowadays pah remains in Pashto and bah in Dari. This Kushani PID was padh (fricative)-pat in Dari with the exact same meaning of pah-bah. 158 Henning has likewise recorded this word with the meaning of bah-bar, which was pati in old Dari, paiti in Avesta, and in Bactria it was padh (fricative), close to this Kushani PID. 159 The word also appears in # 90, 144 and in #121, 123 it remains in the form PIDIN. This Kushani PID was also alive in Dari at the beginning of the Islamic era Khorasan present day Afghanistan-Central Asia & India. In Tarekh-e Seistan (p. 35) there are some hymns of the Karkoy fire temple which were copied from the Shah nama of Abdul Myàyyid of Balkh. This verse was entered therein: dost bazâgosh bâ afrin nihâda gosh 160 In the first hemstitch baz-âgosh means ba-âghosh (in bosom). This same Kushani PID-Balkh pat could be heard in the time of Mohammad ibn Ahmad Bushari Maqdasi 375

Bactria present day balkh and zoroastrianism

Aryana- Khorasan dynasty present day Afghanistan-Central Asia & India, Bakhdhi is the fourth nation in the Avestan Vendidad's list of nations - Aryana Vaeja (homeland of the Aryans) being the first. Bakhdhi is the ancient Avestan name while Balkh is the modern name for both the region and its old capital city 5,500 years ago. During the middle period of Aryana history - as the Aryans moved west from Aryana Vaeja towards present day - Bakhdhi (Balkh as its is known today) became the principle kingdom of the Aryan confederation of kingdoms called Aryan, and the eponymous city of Balkh was its capital. As the seat of Aryan rule moved westward to what is the province of Khorasan today, Balkh became part of greater Khorasan and remained an important regional capital as well as a cultural and trading centre. According to Ferdowsi's Shah nama, it was during this middle period of Aryan history that Zarathushtra (in later language, Zardhusht) carried his message to the kingdom of Bakhdhi [this is, however, a latter tradition. Bakhdhi is not mentioned in the Farvardin Yasht which lists four nations connected with Zarathushtra's ministry. For a further discussion on the lands of Zarathushtra's ministry. One latter tradition informs us that Zarathushtra established himself and died in Balkh. Some authors conclude that in addition to Bakhdhi Balkh being one of the areas of Zarathushtra's ministry, that he was also born in Bakhdhi Balkh. The Avesta, however, states that Zarathushtra was born in Aryana Vaeja (cf. his father's house was in Aryana Vaeja), and the Vendidad lists Aryana Vaeja and Bakhdhi as separate nations, Aryana Vaeja being the first and Bakhdhi the fourth. Given that the traditions speak to Zarathushtra being born in Balkh Vej Middle Dari for Aryan Vaeja Bakhdhi would come to be known as Bakhtrish during Achaemenian dynasty times 675 - 330 BCE, Bactra city and greater Bactria dynasty from the Dari version of its name during Alexander's and the Seleucid occupation 330 - c. 246 BCE, and briefly Takharistan or Toharistan after the overthrow of the Seleucids. In 246 BCE, allied with Parthava Parthia, Bakhdhi (Balkh) was one of the first Aryan nations to revolt against Seleucid rule. The "great and noble city" as Marco Polo called it, was destroyed by first by the Arabs and eventually by Mongols in 1220CE. Today, the site of the kingdom and its ancient city is called Balkh, and the once mighty kingdom has been reduced to the fairly small province in Afghanistan. Balkh's provincial capital is now Mazar-e Sharif, a city some twenty kilometres east of Balkh city. Our discussion on Bakhdhi includes the Greater Bakhdhi lands **KAYANIAN DYNASTY** Balkh's King Vishtasp (in later language, Gushtasp), a king of the Kayanian dynasty, was a contemporary of Zarathushtra. Vishtasp accepted Zarathushtra's teachings and became the patron king and defender of Zarathushtra's Mazdayasni faith. The founder and first king of the Kayanian dynasty was Kai Kobad (also spelt Kay Qobad or simply Kaikobad) known to the Zoroastrian scriptures, the Avesta, by his older name Kavi Kavata. On the north Bukhara present day Tajikistan bank of the Amu Darya River, close to the archaeological site of Takht-e Sangin, is a site called Takht-e Kobad meaning the throne of Kobad. About 40 km to the north along the banks of a tributary of the Amu Darya lies another site called Kai Kobad Shah meaning King Kai Kobad. We are not aware of any other region that ties itself so directly with the Kayanians. There is an enigmatic section of the Middle Dari Zoroastrian text, the Denkard at verse 34 of Book 7 regarding the inheritance of the Aryan Farr (the Khvaraneh) by Kai Kobad and from Kai Kobad as E. W. West translates, "it came to Patakhsrobo, son of Airyefshva, son of Taz, who was king of the Arabs...". In verse 35, the farr goes to Kay Arash, a descendant of Kai Kobad. For some reason, the word "Taz" or

"Tazi" in medieval Dari came to be associated with the Arabs perhaps because it was a homonym with a similar sounding word denoting an Arab group. Such a translation in this context creates a disruption for the inheritance or passing of the farr from one king to the next also defines the genealogy of Aryan kings and it would seem odd that an Arab would be inserted as king between two Kayanian kings. Other writers have suggested that the word "Taz" in this context specifically applies to the Tajiks. Aryana dynasty & Khorasan present day Afghanistan-Central Asia & India

5,500 years of topography of Bactrian present day Balkh

Aryana dynasty & Khorasan present day Afghanistan-Central Asia & India history very literally flows through and around Bakhdhi. The central portion of a river famous in legend and history, the Amu Darya River north of Afghanistan- the section that is downstream from the Sherabad River - formed the border between Bakhdhi and Sughdha (the second) in the northwest of Bakhdhi. The upper part of the Amu Darya River - upstream from the Sherabad River - ran through the heart of eastern Bakhdhi until it entered the Badakhshan Pamir region. Across the Amu Darya, the kingdom of Sugd lay to the north, while the Badakhshan region and Pamir mountains lay to the east and northeast. The kingdom of Mouru (Merv) lay to Bakhdhi's northwest and west, and the kingdom of Haroyu (Harirud) lay across its south-western border. The southern and south-eastern borders of Bakhdhi was formed by the Hindu Kush (meaning Hindu killer) mountains. The name Hindu Kush leads us a believe that the fifteenth Avestan nation, Hapta Hindu, the seven Indus lands, lay across the Hindu Kush, the mountains forming the border present day between the two nations, and further that the relations between the two neighbours on either side of the Hindu Kush were not always peaceful. The topography of ancient Bakhdhi included the varied landscape of fertile plains, deserts and rugged mountains. Balkh's desert lies to the north towards the Amu Darya River. The desert is famous in the legends of Ferdowsi's Shahn ama The kingdom was renowned through the known world for it beauty, abundant crops, and a large variety of fruits. There are several almond and apricot orchards. While certain parts of Balkh are still relatively fertile, war and poor leadership has reduced the once famed land to a dusty shadow of its former self. In ancient Bakhdhi, an excellent breed of sheep was raised in green lower slopes of the Hindu Kush mountains. Bakhdhi was also famous for a breed of camels known today as the Bactrian camel. Khorasan present day Afghanistan-Central Asia & India **BACTRIAN CAMEL** The two-humped Bactrian camel was, if we may be forgiven this term, the work-horse of the caravans that plied the Silk Roads radiating north and south, east and west out of Bakhdhi. It was particularly suited to this task for it could carry heavy loads over great distances and through extremes in climate and temperature - from freezing cold to blistering heat. While the Silk Roads have long since fallen into disuse, the Bactrian camel is still prized throughout the region as a beast of burden. The camels have a remarkable ability to go without water for months at a time, but when water is available they can drink up to 57 litres at once. When well fed, the camels store excess food in their humps which become plump. When food is not readily available, the camel uses this stored food and the humps shrink and lean to one side. They are steady walkers and fast runners. They can walk consistently for hours at an end, and they have been recorded as running at speeds up to 65 kmph -40 mph. As pack animals, they are able to carry 170-270 kg 375-600 lbs at a rate of 47 km per day, or 4 kmph over a period of four days. They can swim. see well and have a keen sense of smell It is no wonder that they were the preferred pack animal for caravans, and they must have played a significant role in Bakhdhi being a major trading centre on the Afghanistan-ancient Silk Roads. Bones of the camel have been found in the region dating back to the first half of the third millennium BCE. By the late third and early second millennium BCE, images of the Bactrian camel were being used in the iconography of copper stamp seals and figurines found in the Kopet Dag hills of neighbouring Turkmenistan, but which are thought have originated in Bakhdhi Bactria. As with all the other Avestan Vendidad nations, Balkh lay on the Aryana Trade Roads (also called the Silk Roads) and was a significant centre of trade as well ascaravan a stop over point. Balkh lay at the junction of the east-west route between East

Turkestan and Asia Minor and the north-south route between Merv, the northern lands beyond and India in the south. The route through Balkh was the preferred route for traders between the west and India as it was shorter and provided the easiest route through the Hindu Kush. Even present day 2020, the Provincial capital Mazar-e Sharif is an important trading centre, importing goods for distribution throughout Afghanistan and exporting goods to the rest of Khorasan presnt day Central Asia & India. Locally grown almonds and apricots as well as other dried nuts and fruits have their own bazaar and are exported. A fledgling silk industry, a traditional Aryana occupation, has also started to re-emerge. **MULTI-ETHNIC POPULATION** There is perhaps no greater testimony to Bakhdhi Balkh being at the cross-roads of the Aryan world and trade than its multi-ethnic population. Broken up today into a multitude of northern Afghan provinces, greater Bakhdhi Balkh is home to several ethnicities native to its surrounding regions. The pared-down province of present-day Balkh has a majority Tajik population (which may speak to the original Aryan migration from the east) surrounded by Uzbek and Turkmen populations. Also present are Pashtuns and Hazaras. In war ravaged Afghanistan, Balkh is a relatively peaceful province. The languages spoken are Dari spoken by ethnic Tajiks Pash Turkmen and Uzbek The Buzkashi is a team sport and a public tournament where the goal is for riders to grab the carcass of a goat or calf (often headless) from the ground while riding a horse at full gallop and to pitch it across a goal line, into a target circle, or into a container. Opposing riders try to stop others from picking up the carcass or carrying it to the goal. The opposition can be fairly violent.

Historical Sketch of Buddhism and Islam in Afghanistan

Aryana dynasty Khorasan present day Afghanistan-Central Asia & India. Various schools of Hinayana Buddhism were present in Afghanistan from the earliest times, along the kingdoms that lay on the trade route to Central Asia. The main kingdoms were Kandhara and Bactria. Kandhara included the areas on both the Punjab and Afghan sides of the Khyber Pass. Eventually, the Afghan half, from the Khyber Pass to the Kabul Valley, received the name Nagarahara; while the Punjabi side retained the name Kandhara. Bactria extended from the Kabul Valley northwards and included southern present day Uzbekistan and Tajikistan. To its north, in central Uzbekistan and northwestern Tajikistan lay Sogdia. The southern part of Bactria, just north of the Kabul Valley, was Kapisha; while the northern part later received the name Tocharistan. Early Establishment of Buddhism According to early Hinayana biographies of the Buddha, such as the Sarvastivada text *The Sutra of Extensive Play* (Skt. Lalitavistara Sutra), Tapassu and Bhallika, two merchant brothers from Bactria, became the first disciples to receive layman'svows. This occurred eight weeks after Shakyamuni's enlightenment, traditionally ascribed to 537 BCE. Bhallika later became a monk and built a monastery near his home city, Balkh, near present-day Mazar-i-Sharif. He brought with him eight hairs of the Buddha as relics, for which he built a setup a monument. At about this time, Bactrian became part of the Achaemeni Empire of Afghanistan. In 349 BCE, several years after the Second Buddhist Council, the Mahasanghika tradition of Hinayana split off from the Theravada. Many Mahasanghikas moved to Kandhara. At Hadda, the main city on the Afghan side, near present-day Jalalabad, they eventually founded Nagara Vihara Monastery, bringing with them a skull relic of the Buddha. A Theravada elder, Sambhuta Sanavasi dynasty, soon followed and tried to establish his tradition in Kapisha. He was unsuccessful, and Mahasanghika took root as the main Buddhist tradition of Afghanistan. Eventually, the Mahasanghikas split into five sub-schools. The main one in Afganistan was Lokottaravada, which later established itself in the Bamiyan Valley in the Hindu Kush Mountains. There, some time between the third and fifth centuries CE, its followers built the world's largest standing Buddha statue, in keeping with their assertion of Buddha as a transcendent, superhuman figure. The Taliban destroyed the colossus in 2001 CE. In 330 BCE, Alexander the Great of Macedonia conquered most of the Achaemeni Empire, including Bactria and Kandhara. He was tolerant of the religious traditions of these regions and seemed interested primarily in military conquest. His successors established the Seleucid Dynasty. In 317 BCE, however, the Indian Mauryan Dynasty took Kandhara from the Seleucids and thus the area was only superficially Hellenized during this short period. The Mauryan Emperor Ashoka (ruled 273 - 232 BCE) favored Theravada Buddhism. In the later part of his reign, he sent a Theravadan mission to Kandhara, led by Maharakkhita. As far south as Kandahar, the mission erected "Ashoka pillars" with edicts based on Buddhist principles. Through these missions, Theravada established a minor presence in Afghanistan. The Sarvastivada School and the Bactrian Kingdom Toward the end of Ashoka's rule, after the Third Buddhist Council, the Sarvastivada School of Hinayana also broke away from the Theravada. After Ashoka's death, his son Jaloka introduced Sarvastivada to Kashmir. In 239 BCE, the local nobility of Bactria rebelled against Seleucid rule and gained independence. In the years that followed, they conquered Sogdia and Kashmir, thus establishing the Bactrian kingdom. Kashmiri monks soon spread the Sarvastivada School of Hinayana to Bactria. In 197 BCE, the Graeco-Bactrians conquered Kandhara from the Mauryans. Subsequently, Sarvastivada came to the southeastern part of Afghanistan as well. From the strong interaction between Greek and

Indian cultures that followed, Hellenistic styles strongly influenced Buddhist art, particularly its representation of the human form and the drape of robes. Although Theravada was never strong in the Bactrian kingdom, one of its kings, Menandros (Pali: Milinda, ruled 155 - 130 BCE), was a follower of Theravada due to the influence of the visiting Indian monk Nagasena. The king put many questions to this Indian master and their dialogue became known as The Questions of Milinda (Pali: Milindapanho). Shortly afterwards, the Graeco-Bactrian dynasty state established relations with Sri Lanka and sent a delegation of monks to the consecration ceremony of the great stupa built there by King Dutthagamani (ruled 101 – 77 BCE). From the cultural contact that ensued-Bactrian monks orally transmitted The Questions of Milinda to Sri Lanka. It later became an extra-canonical text in the Theravada tradition. Khorasan dynasty present day Afghanistan-Central Asia & India

Afghanistan the Kushan dynasty Period

Aryana- Khorasan dynasty present day Afghanistan-Central Asia & India Between 177 and 165 BCE, the westward expansion of the Han Empire into Gansu and East Turkistan (present day Chin Xinjiang) drove many of the native Central Asian nomadic tribes further west. One of these tribes, the Xiongnu, attacked another, the Yuezhi (Wades-Giles: Yüeh-chih), and assimilated a large part of them. The Yuezhi were a Caucasian people who spoke an ancient western Indo-European language and represented the easternmost migration of the Caucasian race. According to some sources, one of the five aristocratic tribes of the Yuezhi, known in Greek sources as the Tocharians, migrated to present-day eastern Kazakhstan, driving south the local nomadic Shakas (Old: Saka), known to the Bactria-Greeks as the Scythians. Both the Tocharians and Shakas, however, spoke Iranian languages. Due to this difference in languages, it is disputed whether or not these Tocharians were related to the descendents of the Yuezhi, also known as "Tocharians", who established thriving civilizations in Kucha and Turfan in East Turkistan in the second century CE. It is clear, however, that the Shakas were unrelated to the Shakya clan of central north India into which Shakyamuni Buddha was born. The Shakas first conquered Sogdia from the Bactrians and then, in 139 BCE, during the reign of King Menandros, took Bactria as well. There, the Shakas turned to Buddhism. By 100 BCE, the Tocharians conquored Sogdia and Bactria from the Shakas Settling in these areas, they also assimilated Buddhism. This was the start of the Kushan Dynasty, which eventually extended to Kashmir, and northwestern India. The most famous Kushan king was Kanishka (ruled 78 - 102 CE), whose western capital was at Kapisha. He supported the Sarvastivada School of Hinayana. Its Vaibhashika subdivision was especially prominent in Tocharistan. The Tocharian monk Ghoshaka was one of the compilers of the Vaibhashika commentaries on abhidharma (special topics of knowledge) accepted at the Fourth Buddhist Council held by Kanishka. When Ghoshaka returned to Tocharistan after the council, he founded the Western Vaibhashika (Balhika) School. Nava Vihara, the main monastery at Balkh, soon became the center of higher Buddhist study for all of Central Asia, comparable to Nalanda Monastery in central northern India. It emphasized study primarily of the Vaibhashika abhidharma and admitted only monks who had already composed texts on the topic. Since it housed a tooth relic of the Buddha, it was also one of the main centers of pilgrimage along the Silk Route from East Turkestan to India. Balkh had been the birthplace of Zoroaster in about 600 BCE. It was the holy city of Zoroastrianism, the Afghan religion that grew from his teachings and which emphasized the veneration of fire. Kanishka followed the Bactrian policy of religious tolerance. Thus, Buddhism and Zoroastrianism peacefully coexisted in Balkh, where they influenced each other's development. Cave monasteries from this period, for example, had wall paintings of Buddhas with auras of flames and inscriptions calling them "Buddha-Mazda." This was an amalgam of Buddha and Ahura Mazda, the supreme god of Zoroastrianism. In 226 CE, the Sassanid Empire overthrew Kushan dynasty rule in Afghanistan. Although strong supporters of Zoroastrianism, the Sassanids emperor tolerated Buddhism and allowed the construction of more Buddhist monasteries, It was during their rule that the Lokottaravada followers erected the two colossal Buddha statues at Bamiyan. The only exception to Sassanid tolerance was during the second half of the third century, when the Zoroastrian high priest Kartir dominated the religious policy of the state. He ordered thedestruction of several Buddhist monasteries in Afghanistan, since the amalgam of Buddhism and Zoroastrianism appeared to him as heresy. Buddhism quickly recovered, however, after his death. At the beginning of the fifth century, the White Huns – known to the Bactria as the Hephthalites and to the Indians as the Turkmen – took most of the former Kushan dynasty territories from the Sassanids dynasty, including India. At first, the White Huns followed their own religion, which resembled Zoroastrianism. Soon, however, they became strong supporters of Buddhism. The Han Chinese pilgrim Faxian (Fa-hsien) traveled through their territory between 399 and 414 CE and reported the flourishing of several Hinayana schools. The Turkmen kingdom were a Turkmen people descended from the Kushans. After the fall of the Kushan Dynasty to the Sassanids, they took over parts of the former empire that lay in northwestern and Afghanistan. They ruled them until the founding of the Indian Gupta Dynasty in the early fourth century, and then fled to Nagarahara. They conquered portions of it from the White Huns and, by the mid-fifth century, extended their rule to the Kabul Valley and Kapisha. Like the Kushans and White Huns before them, the Turkmen kingdem supported Buddhism in Afghanistan. In 515, the White Hun king Mihirakula, under the influence of jealous non-Buddhist factions in his court, suppressed Buddhism. He destroyed monasteries and killed many monks throughout northwestern Afghanistan, Kandhara, and especially in Kashmir. The persecution was less severe in the portions of Nagarahara that he controlled. His son reversed this policy and built new monasteries in all these areas. Khorasan dynasty present day Afghanistan-Central Asia & India

The Western Turkestan

Aryana- Khorasan dynasty present day Afghanistan-Central Asia & India Coming from northern West Turkistan, the Western Turkmenistan took over the western portion of the Central Asian Silk Route in 560. Slowly, they expanded into Bactria, driving the Turki Shahis further east in Nagarahara. Many Western Turkestan leaders adopted Buddhism from the local people and, in 590, they built a new Buddhist monastery in Kapisha. In 622, the Western Turkmen ruler Tongshihu Qaghan formally adopted Buddhism under the guidance of Prabhakaramitra, a visiting northern Indian monk. The Han Chinese pilgrim Xuanzang (Hsüan-tsang) visited the Western Turks in approximately 630 on his way to India. He reported that Buddhism was flourishing in the Bactrian portion of their empire, especially at Nava Vihara Monastery in Balkh. He cited the monastic university not only for its scholarship, but also for its beautiful Buddha statues, draped with silk robes and adorned with jewel ornaments, in accordance with local Zoroastrian custom. The monastery had close links at the time with Khotan, a strongly Buddhist kingdom in East Turkistan, and sent many monks there to teach. Xuanzang also described a monastery near Nava Vihara dedicated to advanced Hinayanameditation practice of vipashyana (Pali: vipassana) — the exceptional perception of impermanence and of a person's lack of independent identity. East Turkestan found Buddhism in a much worse condition in Nagarahara, under the Turkmen Shahis. As in the Punjabi side of Kandhara, the area seemed not to have fully recovered from the persecution by King Mihirakula more than a century earlier. Although Nagara Vihara, with its skull relic of the Buddha, was one of the holiest pilgrimage sites in the Buddhist world, he reported that its monks had become degenerate. They were charging pilgrims a gold coin each to view the relic and there were no centers of study in the entire region. Moreover, although Mahayana had made advances into Afghanistan from Kashmir and Punjabi Kandhara during the fifth and sixth centuries, Xuanzang noted its presence only in Kapisha and in the Hindu Kush regions west of Nagarahara. Sarvastivada remained the predominant Buddhist tradition of Nagarahara and northern Bactria.

Afghanistan and the Umayyad Period and the Introduction of Islam

Khorasan dynasty present day Afghanistan-Central Asia & India. Thirty years after the death of the Prophet Muhammad, the Arabs defeated the Sassanids and founded the Umayyad Caliphate in 661. It ruled over Khorasan and much of the Middle East. In 663, they attacked Bactria, which the Turkmen Shahis had taken from the Western Turkmen by this time. The Umayyad forces captured the area around Balkh, including Nava Vihara Monastery, causing the Turkmen Shahis to retreat to the Kabul Valley. The Arabs allowed followers of non-Muslim religions in the lands they conquered to keep their faiths if they submitted peacefully and paid a poll tax (Ar. jizya). Although some Buddhists in Bactria and even an abbot of Nava Vihara converted to Islam, most Buddhists in the region accepted this dhimmi status as loyal non-Muslim protected subjects within an Islamic state. Nava Vihara remained open and functioning. The Han Chinese pilgrim Yijing (I-ching) visited Nava Vihara in the 680s and reported it flourishing as a Sarvastivada center of study. An Umayyad Arab author, al-Kermani, wrote a detailed account of Nava Vihara at the beginning of the eighth century, preserved in the tenth-century work Book of Lands (Ar. Kitab al-Buldan) by al-Hamadhani. He described it in terms readily understandable to Muslims by drawing the analogy with the Kaaba in Mecca, the holiest site of Islam. He explained that the main temple had a stone cube in the center, draped with cloth, and that devotees circumambulated it and made prostration, as is the case with the Kaaba. The stone cube referred to the platform on which a stupa stood, as was the custom in Bactrian temples. The cloth that draped it was in accordance with the Khorasan custom for showing veneration, applied equally to Buddha statues as well as to stupas. Al-Kermani's description indicates an open and respectful attitude by the Umayyad Arabs in trying to understand the non-Muslim religions, such as Buddhism, that they encountered in their newly conquered territories.

AFGHANISTAN AND THE EARLY ABBASID PERIOD

Khorasan dynasty present day Afghanistan-Central Asia & India. In AD 750, an Arab faction overthrew the Umayyad Caliphate and founded the Abbasid Dynasty. They maintained control over northern Bactria. Not only did the Abbasids continue the policy of granting dhimmi status to the Buddhists there, they took great interest in foreign culture, particularly that of India. In 762, Caliph al-Mansur (ruled 754 – 775) engaged Indian architects and engineers to design the new Abbasid capital, present day Baghdad. He took its name from the Sanskrit Bhaga-dada, meaning "Gift of God." The Afghan also built a House of Knowledge (Ar. Bayt al-Hikmat), with a translation bureau. He invited scholars from various cultures and religions to translate texts into Arabic, particularly concerning logic and scientific topics. The early Abbasid caliphs were patrons of the Mu'tazila School of Islam that sought to explain the principles of the Quran from the viewpoint of reason. The main focus was on ancient Bactria "present day Balkh" learning, but attention was also paid to Sanskrit traditions. Not only scientific texts were translated, however, at the House of Knowledge. Buddhist scholars translated into Arabic a few Mahayana and Hinayana sutras dealing with devotional and ethical themes. The next caliph, al-Mahdi (ruled 775 – 785), ordered the Abbasid forces in Sindh to attack Saurashtra to the southeast. In face of a rival claimant in Arabia who also had been declared Mahdi, the Islamic messiah, the invasion was part of the Caliph's campaign to establish his prestige and supremacy as the leader of the Islamic world. The Abbasid army destroyed the Buddhist monasteries and Jain temples at Valabhi. As was the case with the Umayyad conquest of Sindh, however, they seemed to destroy only the centers suspected of harboring opposition to their rule. Even under Caliph al-Mahdi, the Abbasids left the Buddhist monasteries in the rest of their empire alone, preferring to exploit them as sources of revenue. Furthermore, al-Mahdi continued to expand the translation activities of the House of Knowledge in Baghdad. He was not intent on destroying Indian culture, but on learning from it. Yahya ibn Barmak, the Muslim grandson of one of the Buddhist administrative heads (Skt. pramukha, Ar.

barmak*)* of Nava Vihara Monastery, was the minister of the next Abbasid caliph, al-Rashid (ruled 786 - 808). Under his influence, the Caliph invited to Baghdad many more scholars and masters from India, especially Buddhists. A catalogue of both Muslim and non-Muslim texts prepared at this time, Kitab al-Fihrist, included a list of Buddhist works. Among them was an Arabic version of the account of Buddha's previous lives, Book of Buddha *(*Ar. Kitab al-Budd). Islam was gaining ground in Bactria at this time among the landowners and upper, educated urban classes by the appeal of its high level of culture and learning. To study Buddhism, one needed to enter a monastery. Nava Vihara, though still functioning during this period, was limited in its capacity and required extensive training before one could enter. Islamic high culture and study, on the other hand, was more readily accessible. Buddhism remained strong primarily among the poorer peasant classes in the countryside, mostly in the form of devotional practice at religious shrines. Hinduism was also present throughout the region. Visiting in 753, the Han Chinese pilgrim Wukong (Wu-k'ung) reported both Hindu and Buddhist temples especially in the Kabul Valley. As Buddhism declined among the merchant classes, Hinduism also grew stronger.

AFGHANISTAN THE SAMANIDS DYNASTY, GHAZNAVI DYNASTY AND SELJUK DYNASTIES

Khorasan dynasty present day Afghanistan-Central Asia & India, governor of Sogdia, declared autonomy next and founded the Samanid Dynasty in 892. He conquered Bactria from the Saffarids in 903. The Samanids promoted a return to traditional Afghanistan culture, but remained tolerant of Buddhism. During the reign of Nasr II (ruled 913 - 942), for example, carved Buddha images were still made and sold in the Samanid capital, Balkh-Bukhara. They were not forbidden as "Buddha-idols." The Samanids dynasty enslaved the Turkmen tribesmen in their realm and conscripted them in their armies. If the soldiers converted to Islam, they gave them nominal freedom. The Samanids, however, had difficulty maintaining control over these men. In 962, Alptigin, one such Turkmen military chief who had adopted Islam, seized Ghazni south of Kabul. There, in 976, his successor, Sabuktigin (ruled 976 - 997), founded the Ghaznavi Empire as a vassal of the Abbasids. Soon, he conquered the Kabul Valley from the Hindu king, driving them back to Kandhara. Buddhism had flourished in the Kabul Valley under Hindu Shahi rule. in his Garshasp Nama written in 1048, described the opulence of its main monastery, Subahar (Su Vihara), when the Ghaznavi overran Kabul It does not appear as though the Ghaznavi destroyed it. In 999, the next Ghaznavi dynasty ruler, Mahmud of Ghazni (ruled 998 – 1030) overthrew the Samanids dynasty, with the help of Turkmen soldiers in the Samanid service. The Ghaznavi Empire now included Bactria dynasty and southern Sogdia. Mahmud Ghazni also conquered most of India. He continued the Samanid dynasty policy of promoting Afghanistan culture and tolerating non-Muslim religions. Al-Biruni, a Afghan scholar and writer in service to the Ghaznavi court, reported that, at the turn of the millennium, the Buddhist monasteries in Bactria, including Nava Vihara, were still functioning. Mahmud of Ghazni was intolerant, however, of Islamic sects other than the orthodox one that he supported. His attacks on Multan in northern Sindh in 1005 and again in 1010 were campaigns against the state- which the Samanids had also favored. The Turkmen-Fatimid Dynasty (910 – 1171), centered in Egypt from 969, was the principal rival of the Abbasids for supremacy of the Islamic world. Mahmud was also intent on finishing the overthrow of the Hindu king that his father had begun. Thus, he attacked and drove out the Hindu king from Kandhara, and then proceeded from Kandhara to take Multan. Over the next years, Mahmud expanded his empire by conquering the regions eastward as far as Agra dynasty in India AD 1501

Until 1871. His looting and destruction of wealthy Hindu temples and Buddhist monasteries on the way were part of his invasion tactic. As in most wars, the invading forces often cause as much destruction as possible in order to convince the local population to surrender, especially if they offer resistance. During his campaigns in the Indian subcontinent, Mahmud Ghazni left the Buddhist monasteries under his rule in Kabul and Bactria alone. In 1040, the Seljuk dynasty Turkmen vassals of the Ghaznavi in Sogdia rebelled and established the Seljuk Dynasty. Soon, they wrested Bactria from the Ghaznavi, who withdrew to the Kabul Valley. Eventually, the Seljuk Empire extended to Baghdad, Turkey, and Palestine. The Seljuks dynasty were the infamous "infidels" against whom Pope Urban II declared the First Crusade in 1096. The Seljuks dynasty were pragmatic in their rule. They established Islamic centers of study madras for 30 million students Arabic, Dari, and Greek in Central Asia to educate a civil bureaucracy to administer the various portions of their empire. They tolerated the presence of non-Islamic religions in their realm, such as Buddhism. Thus, al-Shahrastani (1076 - 1153) published in Baghdad his Kitab al-Milal wa Nihal – a text in Arabic on non-Muslim religions and sects. It contained a simple explanation of the Buddhist tenets and repeated al-Biruni's firsthand account of a century earlier that Indians accepted Buddha as a prophet. The many Buddhist references in the Dari literature of the period also provide evidence of this Islamic-Buddhist cultural contact. Dari poetry, for example, often used the simile for palaces that they were "as beautiful as a Nowbahar (Nava Vihara)." Further, at Nava Vihara and Bamiyan, Buddha images, particularly of Maitreya, the future Buddha, had moon discs behind their heads. This led to the poetic depiction of pure beauty as someone having "the moon-shaped face of a Buddha." Thus, eleventh-century Dari poems, such as Varqe and Golsha by Ay*h*yuqi, use the word bot with a positive connotation for "Buddha," not with its second, derogatory meaning as "idol." It implies the ideal of asexual beauty in both men and women. Such references indicate that either Buddhist monasteries and images were present in these Afghanistan cultural areas at least through the early Mongol period in the thirteenth century or, at minimum, that a strong Buddhist legacy remained for centuries among the Buddhist converts there to Islam.

AFGHANISTAN DYNASTIES

Khorasan dynasty present day Afghanistan-Central Asia & India. In 1141, the Qaraqitans, a Mongol-speaking people ruling East Turkistan and northern West Turkistan, defeated the Seljuqs at Samarkand. Their ruler, Yelu Dashi, annexed Sogdia and Bactria into his empire, The Ghaznavi still controlled the area from the Kabul Valley eastward. The Qaraqitans followed a blend of Buddhism, Daoism (Taoism), Confucianism, and shamanism. Yelu Dashi, however, was extremely tolerant and protected all religions in his realm, including Islam. In 1148, Ala-ud-Din of the nomadic Guzz Turkmen from the mountains of central Afghanistan conquered Bactria from the Qaraqitans and established the Ghurid Dynasty AD 780 Until 1360. In 1161, he went on to take Ghazni and Kabul from the Ghaznavi. He appointed his brother, Muhammad Ghori, governor of Ghazni in 1173 and encouraged him to raid the Indian subcontinent. Like Mahmud Ghazni before him, Muhammad Ghori first took, in 1178, the Ismaili Multan kingdom in northern Sindh, which had regained independence from Ghaznavi rule. He then proceeded to conquer the entire Punjab region of present day India and, after that, the Gangetic Plain, as far as present-day Bihar and West Bengal. During his campaign, he looted and destroyed many large Buddhist monasteries, including Vikramashila and Odantapuri in 1200. The local Sena king had turned them into military garrisons in an attempt to thwart the invasion. The Ghurid leaders might have incited their troops to fervor in battle with religious indoctrination, much as any nation does with political or patriotic propaganda. Their main objective, however, as that of most conquerors, was to gain territory, wealth, and power.

Thus, the Ghurids destroyed only the monasteries that lay in the direct line of their invasion. Nalanda Monastery and Bodh Gaya, for example, were situated off the main route. Thus, when the Tibetan translator Chag Lotsawa visited them in 1235, he found them damaged and looted, but still functioning with a small number of monks. Jagaddala Monastery in northern Bengal was untouched and flourishing. Further, the Ghurids did seek to conquer Kashmir and convert the Buddhists there to Islam. Kashmir was impoverished at the time, and the monasteries had little or no wealth to plunder. Moreover, since the Ghurids dynasty did not pay their generals or governors, or provide them supplies, they expected them to support themselves and their troops from local gains. If the governors forcefully converted everyone under their jurisdiction to Islam, they could not exploit large portions of the population for additional taxes. Thus, as in Afghanistan, the Ghurids continued the traditional custom of granting dhimmi status to non-Muslims in India and exacting the jizya poll tax.

AFGHANISTAN AND THE MONGOL PERIOD FROM AD 1215 UNTIL 1401

Khorasan present day Afghanistan-Central Asia & India. In 1215, Chinggis, the founder of the Mongol Empire, conquered Afghanistan from the Ghurids. As was his policy elsewhere, Chinggis destroyed those who opposed his takeover and devastated their lands. It is unclear how the vestiges of Buddhism still left in Afghanistan fared at this time. Chinggis was tolerant of all religions, so long as its leaders prayed for his long life and military success. In 1219, for example, he summoned to Afghanistan a renowned Daoist master from China to perform ceremonies for his long life and to prepare for him the elixir of immortality. After Chinggis' death in 1227 and the division of his empire among his heirs, his son Chagatai inherited the rule of Sogdia and Afghanistan and established the Chagatai Khaganate. In 1258, Hulegu, a grandson of Chinggis, conquered Abbasid and overthrew the Abbasid Caliphate in Baghdad. He established the Ilkhanate and soon invited to his court in northwestern Buddhist monks from Tibet, Kashmir, and Ladakh. The Ilkhanate was more powerful than the Chagatai Khaganate and, at first, it dominated its cousins there. Since the Buddhist monks had to pass through Afghanistan on their way, they undoubtedly received official support on their way. According to some scholars, the Tibetan monks who came to Afghanistan were most likely from the Drigung (Drikung) Kagyu School and Hulegu's reason for inviting them may have been political. In 1260, his cousin Khubilai (Kublai) Khan, the Mongol ruler of northern China, declared himself of all the Mongols. Khubilai supported the Sakya Tradition of Tibetan Buddhism and gave its leaders nominal suzerainty over Tibet. Prior to this, the Drigung Kagyu leaders had been in political ascendance in Tibet. Khubilai's main rival was another cousin, Khaidu, who ruled East Turkistan and supported the Drigung Kagyu line. Hulegu may have been wishing to align himself with Khaidu in this power struggle. Some speculate that the reason for Khubilai and Khaidu's turning to Tibetan Buddhism was to gain the supernatural backing of Mahakala, the Buddhist protector practiced by both the Sakya and Kagyu traditions. Mahakala had been the protector of the Tanguts, who had ruled the territory between Tibet and Mongolia. After all, their grandfather, Chinggis, had been killed in battle by the Tanguts, who must have received supernatural help. It is unlikely that the Mongol leaders, including Hulegu, chose Tibetan Buddhism because of its deep philosophical teachings. After the death of Hulegu in 1266, the Chagatai Khaganate became more independent of the Ilkhans and formed a direct alliance with Khaidu in his struggle against Khubilai. Meanwhile, the line of Hulegu's successors alternated in their support of Tibetan Buddhism and Islam, apparently also for political expediency. Hulegu's son Abagha continued his father's support of Tibetan Buddhism. Abagha's brother Takudar, however, who succeeded him in 1282, converted to Islam to help gain local support when he invaded and conquered Egypt. Abagha's son Arghun defeated his uncle and became Ilkhan in 1284. He made Buddhism the state religion and founded several monasteries there. When Arghun died in 1291, his brother Gaihatu became the Ilkhan. Tibetan monks had given Gaihatu the Tibetan name Rinchen Dorje, but he was a degenerate drunkard and hardly a credit to the Buddhist faith. He introduced paper money from China, which caused economic disaster. Gaihatu died in 1295, one year after the death of Khubilai. Arghun's son Ghazni succeeded to the throne. He reinstated Islam as the official religion of the Ilkhanate and destroyed the new Buddhist monasteries there. Some scholars assert that Ghazan Khan's reversal of his father's religious policy was to distance himself from his uncle's reforms and beliefs, and to assert his independence from Mongol China. Despite ordering the destruction of Buddhist monasteries, it seems that the Ghazan Khan did not wish to destroy everything associated with Buddhism. For example, he commissioned Rashid al-Din to write Universal History (Ar. Jami' al-Tawarikh), with versions both in Dari and Arabic. In its section on the history of the cultures of the people conquered by the Mongols, Rashid al-Din included The Life and Teachings of Buddha. To assist the historian in his research, Ghazai Khan invited to his court Bakshi Kamalashri, a Buddhist monk from Kashmir. Like the earlier work by al-Kermani, Rashid's work presented Buddhism in terms that Muslims could easily understand, such as calling Buddha a Prophet, the deva gods as angels, and Mara as the Devil. Rashid al-Din reported that in his day, eleven Buddhist texts in Arabic translation were circulating in Afghanistan. These included Mahayana texts such as The Sutra on the Array of the Pure Land of Bliss *(Skt. Sukhavativyuha Sutra,* concerning Amitabha's Pure Land), The Sutra on the Array Like a Woven Basket *(Skt. Karandavyuha Sutra,* concerning Avalokiteshvara, the embodiment of compassion) and An Exposition on Maitreya*(Skt.* Maitreyavyakarana, concerning Maitreya, the future Buddha and embodiment of love). These texts were undoubtedly among those translated under the patronage of the Abbasid caliphs at the House of Knowledge in Baghdad starting in the eighth century. Rashid al-Din finished his history in 1305, during the reign of Ghazni's successor Oljaitu. It seems that Buddhist monks were still present in Afghanistan, however, at least until Oljaitu's death in 1316, since monks unsuccessfully tried to win the Mongol ruler back to Buddhism. Thus, at least up until then, Buddhist monks still passed back and forth through Afghanistan and thus might still have been welcomed at the Chagatai court. In 1321, the Chagatai Empire split into two. The Western Chagatai Khaganate included Sogdia and Afghanistan. From the start, its khans converted to Islam. The Ilkhanate fragmented and fell apart in 1336. After this, there is no indication of the continuing presence of Buddhism in Afghanistan. It had lasted there nearly nineteen hundred years. Nevertheless, knowledge of Buddhism did not die out. Timur (Tamerlaine) conquered the Western Chagatai Khaganate in 1364 and the small successor states of the Ilkhanate in 1385. Timur's son and successor, Shah Rukh, commissioned the historian, Hafiz-i Abru, to write in Dari *A Collection of Histories* (Ar. Majma' al-Tawarikh) Completed in 1425 in Shahrukh's capital, Herat, Afghanistan, the history contained an account of Buddhism modeled after Rashid al-Din's work a century earlier.

Afghanistan And The Pre-Islamic Period

Aryana- Khorasan dynasty present day Afghanistan-Central Asia & India the present town of Herat in western Afghanistan dates back to ancient times, but its exact age remains unknown. In Achaemenid times (ca. 550-330 B.C.E.), the surrounding district was known as Haraiva (in Old Dari), and in classical sources the region was correspondingly known as Areia. In the Zoroastrian Avesta (Yašt 10.14; Vidēvdāt 1.9), the district is mentioned as Harōiva. The name of the district and its main town is derived from that of the chief river of the region, the Hari Rud (Old Afghanistan *Harayu "with velocity"; compare Sanskrit Saráyu Mayrhofer, which traverses the district and passes just south (5 km) of modern Herat. The naming of a region and its principal town after the main river is a common feature in this part of the world. (Compare the adjoining districts/rivers/towns of Arachosia "present day Kandahra" and Bactria "present day Balkh".) The site of Herat dominates the productive part of ancient Areia, which was, and basically still is, a rather narrow stretch of land that extends for some 150 km along both banks of the Hari Rud, from near Obeh in the east to near Kuhsān dynasty in the west. At no point along its route is the valley more than 25 km wide. The city and district of Areia Herat occupy an important strategic place along the age-old caravan routes across the Afghanistan Plateau. The Afghanistan Achaemenid dynasty district of Areia is mentioned in the provincial lists that are included in various royal inscriptions, for instance, in the Bisotun inscription (q.v., DB 1.16) of Darius I (ca. 520 B.C.E.) in Fārs province. In the texts the name of Areia is grouped with Zranka (or Dranka), modern Sistān to the south; Parthava (Parthia) to the northwest, and Bāxtriš (Bactria) to the northeast. Representatives from the district are depicted in reliefs, e.g., at the royal Achaemenid tombs of Naqš-e Rostam and Persepolis. They are wearing Scythian-style dress (with a tunic and trousers tucked into high boots) and a twisted turban around the head. This costume is also worn by the representatives from nearby Sistān (to the south) and Arachosia (to the southeast) and is reminiscent of the dress worn by the representatives from almost all of the northern lands of the Achaemenid Empire, which were strongly influenced by the Scythic cultures from the Eurasian steppes. On the so-called Darius Statue that was discovered at Susa, the representative from Areia is also shown wearing a long coat worn around the shoulders with empty sleeves. This type of coat is known from classical sources (Gk. kandys) and was sometimes also worn and the Medes. The origin of this coat should be sought among the nomadic Scythians of Central Asia. Very little is known about Areia during the Achaemenid period. Herodotus (7.61 ff.) tells that Areians were included in Xerxes' army against Bactria-Greece, around 480 B.C.E. In Herodotus's taxation list of the Achaemenid Empire (3.89 ff.), the Areians are listed together with the Parthians, Choresmians (from south of the Aral Sea), and Sogdians (from the valley of the Zarafshan River, around Bukhara and Samarqand). According to Herodotus, the Areians in East Turkestans' army were dressed in the Bactrian dynasty fashion, which means that they were wearing a Scythian-type outfit. At the time of Alexander the Great, Areia was obviously an important district. It was administered by a satrap, called Satibarzanes, who was one of the three main Bactria officials in the East of the Empire, together with the satrap Bessus [see BESSOS] of Bactria and Barsaentes of Arachosia. This would mean that the capital of Satibarzanes, which may have been Herat, was one of the three main Achaemenid centers in this part of the world, together with ancient Bactra (modern Balk̲, the capital of ancient Bactria), and Old Kandahār, the capital of ancient Arachosia. In late 330 B.C. Alexander the Great, according to his biographers, captured the Areian capital that was called Artacoana (Arrian, Anab. Alex. 3.25.2-6; Curtius 6, 6.33 [Artacana]; Diodorus 17.78.1 Chortacana; Pliny Nat. hist. 6.61.93; Strabo 11.10.1 Artacaena) The etymology of this name remains unknown, and whether this place should be identified with the modern city of Herat is also uncertain, although the strategic position of modern Herat would suggest its great antiquity; and thus the possiblity remains that they are one and the same place. In the early nineteenth century a Achaemenid cuneiform cylinder seal was found in or near Herat (Torrens, 1842). After Alexander the Great, classical biographers refer to a city called Alexandreia in Areia, but again its identification remains unknown. Soon after the death of Alexander, Areia was briefly attacked by Scythic nomads from the far north (Pliny, Nat. hist. 6.47). In the following years, Areia became a frontier area between the empire of the Parthians to the west and that of the Bactrians to the east. In the late second century B.C.E. the Bactrians were defeated by northern tribes, and Scythians (or Sakas) traversed the district of Areia; perhaps under pressure from the Parthians, they finally settled in nearby Sistān (Mid. Pers. skstn "Sakastān"), farther to the south. In the Parthian Stations (14-16) by Isidore of Charax, an itinerary composed in the Augustan era, the district of Areia is placed between Margiana (in the vicinity of modern Marv to the north), and Anauon (around modern Farāh) to the south. At that time the district was clearly regarded as forming part of the Parthian realm. In the Sasanian period (226-652 C.E.), "Harēv" (hryw) is listed in Šāpūr I's Kaba-ye Zardošt inscription; and "Hariy" is mentioned in the Dari catalogue of the provincial capitals of the empire (Markwart, Provincial Ca. 430 C.E., the town is also listed as having a Christian community. Sasanian dynasty seals and engraved gemstones were reported to have been found in or around Herat (Torrens, 1842). The city served as a Sasanian mint, its name being recorded as hr, hry, and hrydw. Additionally, gold and copper coins have been found that are clearly Sasanian in inspiration, although the Sasanians dynasty in Afghanistan generally did not strike gold coins but preferred silver issues. The gold coins from the Herat area show a fire altar on the reverse and the portrait of the ruler on the obverse. The name of the ruler is often identical to one of those listed on the so-called Kushano-Sasanian coins from Bactria, and this would indicate that the Sasanian governor in the northeast of the Sasanian Empire at times also controlled the Herat district. In the last two centuries of Sasanian rule, the area and town of Aria present day Herat had great strategic importance in the endless wars between the Sasanian and the Chionites and Hephthalites of Hunnish origin, who had been settled in modern northern Khorasan presnt day Afghanistan since the late fourth century; but exact information is scarce. The city of Herat, however, became well known with the advent of the Arabs in the middle of the seventh century. Bibliography: F. R. Allchin and N. Hammond, The Archaeology of Afghanistan. From Earliest Times to the Timuri dynasty Period, London, Warwick Ball, Archaeological Gazetteer of Afghanistan Catalogue des sites archéologiques d'Afghanistan, Paris, A. H. Dani and B. A. Litvinsky, "The Kushano Sasanian Kingdom," in History of Civilizations of Afghanistan-Central Asia The cross-roads of civilizations, A.D. 250 to 750, Veronika Gervers-Molnár, The Hungarian Szür. An Archaic Mantle of Eurasian Origin, Toronto, Gignoux, Glossaire des Inscriptions Pehlevies et Parthes (Corpus Inscr, Supplementary Series, Robert Göbl, Sasanian Numismatics, Braunschweig,. Kent, Old Dari, M. Kervran et al., "Une statue de Darius decouvert à Suse," JA 260, 235-66. H. Torrens, Ón a Cylinder and certain Gems, collected in the neighbourhood of Herat, by Major Pottinger," Journal of the Asiatic Society of Bengal 11, 1842 Vogelsang, The Rise and Organisation of the Achaemenid Empire. The Eastern Evidence, Leiden Idem, The Afghans, Oxford, Afghanistan", as used above, refers to all Afghanistan peoples, at the time not yet differentiated from each other at the time of the composition of the Zoroastrian Yashts texts, where Zarathustra is described to have lived in Aryana Vaejah meaning "Land of Aryans". Afghan Dari speaking region will have loan words from a geographically close neighboring nation. Languages like Pashto, Kurdish and Baluchi are close to Afghan Dari but have become distinct Aryana languages of their own. These languages were all one language with Old Dari during the arrival of the Aryans, but later during the development phase in Aryana, they took their own course.

The Afghan peoples (Afghanistan people) are a collection of ethnic groups (Dari, Pushtuns, Ossetians, Yaghnobi, Tajiks, Kurds, Baluchis and...), who are descents of Old Dari, Saka-Scythinas, Bactrians, Alanian, Sarmatians and Tocharians defined by their usage of Afghanistan languages and discernable descent from ancient Afghanistan peoples (Indo-Europeans, Aryans). The Afghan peoples live chiefly in the Afghanistan, Khorasan presnt day CentralAsia, Caucasus and India, though speakers of Dari languages were once found throughout Eurasia, from the Balkans to East Turkestan. Tocharians language is classified as indo-european langauge, its not an Dari language. Early Afghanistan tribes were the precursors to many diverse modern peoples, including Dari, Pushtuns, Ossetians, Pamirians, Yaghnobi, Kurds, Baluchis and many other smaller groups. The southern Afghanistan peoples survived Alexander the Great's conquests, Muslim Arab attempts at cultural dominance, and devastating assaults by the Mongols. The series of ethnic groups which comprise the Afghan peoples are traced to a branch of the ancient Indo-European Aryans known as the Afgha*n* or Afghans Having descended from the Aryans-Indo-Afghan the ancient Afghanistan peoples separated from the Indo-Aryans in the early 2nd millennium BCE. The Afghanistan languages form a sub-branch of the Indo-Afghan sub-family, which is a branch of the family of Indo European languages. The Afghanistan peoples stem from early Afghan, themselves a branch of the Indo-Afghan who are believed to have originated in either Central Asia or Afghanistan circa 1800 BCE. The Dari are traced to the Bactria-Margiana Archaeological Complex, a Bronze Age culture of Khorasan presnt day Central Asia. The area between northern Afghanistan and the Aral Sea is hypothesized to have been the region where the Afghan first emerged, following the separation of Indo-Afghan tribes. By the first millennium BCE, Ancient Afghanistan peoples such as the Medes, Dari, Bactrians (Pushtuns, Pamirians, Tajiks) and Parthianspopulated the Afghanistan plateau, while peoples such as the Scythians, Sarmatians, and Alans populated the steppes north of the Black Sea The Saka and Scythian tribes remained mainly in the north, and spread as far west as the Balkans and as far east as East Turkestan. Later offshoots, related to the Scythians, included the Sarmatians who

Aryana present day Afghanistan

Aryana-Khorasan present day Afghanistan-Central Asia & India, one of the central issues of Afghanistan-Indian history is the origin of the Indo-European speakers on India. An allied issue is the antiquity of the Vedas the oldest IE material from India. They together may be termed the Aryan problem. These issues are of significance in understanding the development what is the only genuine surviving representative of IE culture today- Hindu or Indian culture. There has been a lot of coloration of research in this area by political movements in Europe and North America and Anti-Hindu bias. Nevertheless at least some European and Hindu scholars have attempted to tackle this problem with a fair degree of objectivity. The current scenarios for IndoEuropean presence in India can broadly be divided into: invasionist scenarios in which the Aryans enter Greater India (The historical Hindu realm encompassing Modern Afghanistan-India from somewhere outside and) nativist (N) scenarios in which the Aryans or even all IEans originated in India. The former scenario involved two different models 1) Model I-A: Invasion by a mobile conquering force of Steppe horse/chariot borne archers reminiscent of the later day Indo-European invaders such as the Shakas, Parthians and Kushanas followed by imposition of he language on the conquered population. This is the Eastern mirror image of M. Gimbutas model for Indo-Europeanization of Europe. 2) Model I-B: Migration of farmers from the Khorasan presnt day Central Asia farming centers with demographic take over of the indigenous population. This is the Eastern mirror image of C.Renfrew's model for IEnization of Europe by farmers. The nativist scenarios involved origin of Aryans "present day Afghan" Central Afghanistan followed by their migration into Khorasan presnt day Central Asia and Europe. This scenario is best argued by S.Talageri and interestingly may considered the native model adopted by the Pauranic or suta historians of Afghanistan-India. Just as the historic movements of Shakas and Kushana provide a prototype for the I-A scenario the far ranging movements of the Indian vaishyas into Central Asia and the Fareast provide the historical model for the N- scenarios. This is where the age of the oldest IE texts of the Bactrian- the Vedas come into picture. Only if this is fixed can the right archaeological material be compared fruitfully with the Aryan life style reconstructed from the Vedic texts. All linguistic dating methodologies cannot handle the absolute antiquity question. This is due the mutational saturation similar to what happens in the molecular evolution of biological sequences. Hence, the only objective means available is astronomical dating. This line of action was pioneered by the Indian scholar, BG Tilak. There are at least two very clear astronomical references in the atharva veda kaNda 19, hymn 7 and taittiriya sa Mhita 2.5.1 of the constellations at equinox and solstice. KR ittika (k iÄka; Pleiades) is stated to be at the 0h position (Hindu year beginning at the spring equinox) and maghA (m'a; α Leonis or Regulus) at the 6h position (summer solstice). These positions suggest that these classic mantras were associated with an age in the range of 2000-2200BC even if one accounts for a fairly rudimentary astronomical capability and low accuracy of positional determination. The R ig vedic age was clearly prior to the classic mantra period and could have spanned a phase anywhere between 500 to a 1000 years before it (judging from the genealogies of the authors as provided in the brahminical gotra lists). This suggests that the oldest Indo-Afghan "Aryan" material was even as old as 3000 BC. The traditional genealogies of three great Afghan dynasties the Urus (Aratas), the ikshvAkus and they Adavas as can be reconstructed from the mah Abharata, agni, garu Da and vishNu puraNas. These objectively reconstructed lists have between 75-90 kings from the very beginning of the lineages (Manu vaiva svata) to the mah AbhArata epoch. The early kings in these lineages correspond well with the rulers frequently mentioned in the Rig veda suggesting that these kings were generally coeval with the Rig period. From long-lived (greater than 10 kings) historical Hindu dynasties one gets an average royal turnover rate of about 19 years. Using this one can place the start of the Aryan dynasties at least 1500-1600 years before the Arata war. From the pauranic testimony of the war's age relative to the reign of the Magadhan emperor Nanda one can arrive at a date close to 1350 BC for the MB epoch. With this one arrives to a Rigvedic period that is as ancient as 2500-3000 BC, similar to what can be inferred from stellar precession. Interestingly, the Rigveda provides a fragment of an ancient mythology associated with manu's son, ashvaghna nAbhAnedhishhTha (Añ[1] na-aneixó) (RV 10.61.1-7) points to the legend of prajApati (the year beginning) associating with rohiNi. This fits well with the equinox in Taurus (circa 2800-3000 BC) for the early phase of Aryan existence. Thus we need to search for archeological cognates dating in the range of 2000-3000 BC to associate with the peak phase of the vedic saMhita period. In Aryana-Khorasan present day Afghanistan-Central Asia & India, the Indus valley Civilization (IVC) is a prominent option. The presence of many rivers, knowledge of the sea and a cattle based economy are features of the Indus civilization that match with aspects of the reconstructed Vedic life. The mention of four very Bactrian animals the gaur (gaEr), the porpoise (izzumar), peacock (myUr) and the elephant in the Rigveda also supports this identification. The identification of the vedic culture with the IVC is key to either the N scenario of many Hindu scholars or the I-B scenario of Renfrew. However, there are major problem with this equation of vedic civilization with the IVC. The vedic texts including at least one of the hymns with an unambiguous astronomical signature mention horses. This is one animal very poorly represented in the IVC if not entirely absent. While this may be a preservation artifact, the troubling point is its noticeable lack on the wide range of animal seals that are typical of the Indus culture. The centrality of the horse to the vedic culture has a close resemblance to its centrality in the Turko-Mongol culture. The ashvamedha rite and its precursors, the quintessential cattle raid or gavishTi, the ushTra or the camel are very typical cultural features of several central Asian and steppe cultures independent of the Aryans. The Aryans were associated with the horse from their earliest reliably datable phase (2500-3000 BC) hence the candidates for the Aryan cultures should be associated with the horse right from the inception. Further, right from this phase the Aryans differentiated a number of equids namely the horse- ashva, the donkey-rAsabha and the hermione or onager- kakuha. This eliminates the IVC ass from substituting for the horse. Thus this line of evidence is more consistent with the steppe and the surrounding territory being the best cultural milieu for the early Aryana. In archaeological terms there is evidence of domestic horses on steppes from at least 4000 BC. There are many rivers in this region, some of which like the Don still bear a noticeably Aryan name that can fit the Vedic situation of multiple rivers. There is the tribe of the putative Indo-Aryan Sindes tribe of Herodotus that was situated on the banks of the Don that may suggest that the river might have also been known as sindhu (isNxu). The super-lakes namely the Khorasan presnt day Central Asia, Black Sea and Caspian Sea would allow the development of the concept of the sea (smuÔ) that is present in the Rigveda. Even the Mongols had a sea ocean concept derived largely from the super-lakes. Finally two linguistic peculiarities provide support for this position of the Aryans. The presence satem features in Slavic that suggests that Aryan and Slavic had an ancient neighborly association, The Uralic languages also originating in the steppes also bear a few Aryan loan words. The aryans were clearly very familiar with snow and feared cold and winters the most. This does not match well with the Punjab or the Indus lowlands where it may get cold but without snow. Thus from the Vedic evidence one is left with a puzzling motley of features some very suggestive of an Indian locale while others suggestive of the steppes. In response to this conundrum, most modern Western scholars accept an Bactrian locale for the Vedic culture but place it post-IVC in the same horizon following an I-A scenario. This was way they explain away the steppe connection as reminiscence of the past.

The western scholars also abhor astronomical evidence (plainly due their innate bias) and try to explain it away again as reminiscences. This view is entirely flawed when one views the context of the above referred hymns that provide the astronomical statement. Furthermore, the vedanga jyotisha (VJ) text provides astronomical evidence for its composition around 1350BC (the 'mahAbh Arata era') when the westerns postulate the peak of the Vedic period. VJ is in clearly post late- vedic language and again they dismiss the VJ reference as reminiscence. This results in a very absurd position allowing one to reject outright these western hypotheses. The Indian scholars follow the N-scenario and try to gloss over the horse by saying that it was there but not represented in the IVC or that it is a now extinct species of Equus or that ashva meant some other equid. No evidence supporting any of these propositions is seriously offered. It would be very difficult to dispel the case made by the great ashvamedha hymn of dirghatamA auchathya of the clan of the gotamas that reeks so strongly of the steppes and not riverine valleys of the Indus. Additionally they try to associate the Vedic rivers with modern Indian rivers. The strongest case is that of sarasvati that is described as flowing from the mountains to the sea. However, it is common historic feature for river and place names to be reused in the newly colonized lands thus these names could have been transferred later to the Indian rivers. Evidence for sarasvati being entirely a real river rather than a water cycle goddess with very general attributes of big rivers is also not strong. Hence one is left with the task of blending the steppe related and Indic features of the Vedas into a proper scenario that is most parsimonious in terms of locus and accounts for the strongest issues namely the astronomical evidence and the centrality of horses and cattle in Vedic culture. With current state of evidence the only way out of this is to propose an Aryana homeland in the steppes with a degree of contact with India through the IVC. The Indic faunal elements that are the main support of an Indian setting are very sporadic elements in the Rig Veda. Hence, they could very well represent knowledge acquired due to close economical contact with the Indus culture. This is analogous to the elephants acquired and used by historical figures like the Seleucids and the emperor Timuri. In this context the more extensive prehistoric forests to the north of India also need to be taken into account. Summing these lines of evidence we may conclude that the Aryan originated on the steppes and did enter India at some unspecified point in time. This time can only be determined by better analysis of the Indus sites for the so called late Harappan phase and the now inaccessible Bactria-Margiana complex sites in Afghanistan. Given the postulated close contact between the Indus and the Aryan steppes one should not be surprised if Aryan words are found in the Indus language if ever it is cracked. This does not mean the IVC was an Aryan culture they may be just loanwords as those found in the Hurrian kingdoms of the Middle East. The only chance of this scenario to be reversed to a N scenario is the finding of the "native Bactrian" horse. This is the Aryana-Khorasan present day Afghanistan-Central Asia & India, archaeological equivalent of the finding of a really ancient true pre-Clovis site in American archaeology. It may be safely concluded that most models with late vedic chronologies, particularly common with European scholars are unlikely to be of any value in addressing the issue 'of the 'Aryan "present day Afghan" problem'.The importance of the foreign origin of the Aryans for the politics of modern India has been vastly overstated. Hindus (Aryans) have lived for millennia without being concerned about it, so they need not have any deep fear of it now. The enemies of the Hindus believe that their partial foreign origin may be a potent weapon to justify their grabbing of Hindu territory. However, the Hindus must simply ignore such ideological quibbles and repudiate the enemies of their nation and religion in the way the Vedic Aryans dealt with their enemie. For the open-minded the Aryan inclusivism and syncretism offer a conduit for reformation and peaceful assimilation. This system however has NO room for historically compulsive trouble-mongers. The Bactrian horse (Equus ferus caballus) is one of two extant subspecies of Equus ferus, or the wild horse. It is an odd-toed ungulatemammal belonging to the taxonomic family Equidae. The Bactrian horse has evolved over the past 45 to 55 million years from a small multi-toed creature into the large, single-toed animal of today. Humans began to domesticate horses around 4000 BC, and theirdomestication is believed to have been widespread by 3000 BC. Horses in the subspecies caballus are domesticated, although some domesticated populations live in the wild as feral horses. These feral populations are not true wild horses, as this term is used to describe horses that have never been domesticated, such as the endangered Przewalski's horse, a separate subspecies, and the only remaining true wild horse. There is an extensive, specialized vocabulary used to describe equine-related concepts, covering everything from anatomy to life stages, size, colors, markings, breeds, locomotion, and behavior. Bactrian-Horses' anatomy enables them to make use of speed to escape predators and they have a well-developed sense of balance and a strong fight-or-flight instinct. Related to this need to flee from predators in the wild is an unusual trait: horses are able to sleep both standing up and lying down. Female horses, called mares, carry their young for approximately 11 months, and a young horse, called a foal, can stand and run shortly following birth. Most domesticated horses begin training under saddle or in harness between the ages of two and four. They reach full adult development by age five, and have an average lifespan of between 25 and 30 years. Bactrian-Horse breeds are loosely divided into three categories based on general temperament: spirited "hot bloods" with speed and endurance; "cold bloods", such as draft horses and some ponies, suitable for slow, heavy work; and "warmbloods", developed from crosses between hot bloods and cold bloods, often focusing on creating breeds for specific riding purposes, particularly in Europe. There are more than 300 breeds of horses in the world today, developed for many different uses. Horses and humans interact in a wide variety of sport competitions and non-competitive recreational pursuits, as well as in working activities such as police work, agriculture, entertainment, and therapy. Horses were historically used in warfare, from which a wide variety of riding and driving techniques developed, using many different styles of equipment and methods of control. Many products are derived from horses, including meat, milk, hide, hair, bone, and pharmaceuticals extracted from the urine of pregnant mares. Humans provide domesticated horses with food, water and shelter, as well as attention from specialists such as veterinarians andfarriers. ewe archaeological excavations in Kazakhstan are uncovering evidence of an ancient civilization that experts say could rewrite human history. The ruins of a city now known as Arkaim, originally discovered in 1989 after soviet authorities allowed non-military aerial photography, is currently thought to have been built 3500 to 4000 years ago. But Arkaim is only one of twenty spiral-shaped settlements found in the steppes near the Kazakhstan-present day Russian border, with the ancient ruins stretching across the landscape for approximately 400 miles. Furthermore, experts also suspect that there are about 50 more sites in the region. Though not yet confirmed, these cities are believed to be the remnants of an Aryana civilisation that spread through Europe and much of Asia. Each settlement was designed similarly, surrounded by a ditch, divided into segments, having spiral streets, and a square in the middle of the city. The evidence of the civilization belonging to ancient Aryans includes many pieces of pottery depicting swastikas, which were widely used ancient symbols of the sun and eternal life, something the Nazis hijacked for their own. Other convincing evidence comes from horse burials found at the dig sites, which correlate to accounts from ancient indian texts believed to be written by the Aryans. According to Saxon historian Bettany Hughes, "These ancient Aryana texts and hymns describe sacrifices of horses and burials and the way the meat is cut off and the way the horse is buried with its master," she said. "If you match this with the way the skeletons and the graves are being dug up in Russia, they are a millimetre-perfect match."

Silk Road between Afghanistan-Central Asia and Europe

Aryana-Khorasan present day Afghanistan-Central Asia & India, tang era merchant. The Silk Road routes in this area were very complicated and usually defined by oases through passes which were open and accessible. Many goods carried across Afghanistan Central Asia were transported on the backs of shaggy, two-humped Bactrian camels or horses, or, in the high elevations, on yaks. The Himalayan caravan routes from India that passed through Karakoram Pass and Khunjerab Pass (on the modern Karakoram Highway) joined the Silk Road in Kashgar Afghanistan- Khorasan presnt day Central Asia.

1. The two main routes that entered Central Asia from Afghanistan were:) the northern route, which passed from East Turkestan into what is now Kazakhstan and went through or near what is now Alma Aty (Kazakhstan), Bishkek (Kyrgyzstan) and Tashkent (Uzbekistan); and 2) the southern route which left Kashgar and passed from East Turkestan in Central Asia through passes of the Pamir's mountains that are now on China's "the great games" borders with Kyrgyzstan, Tajikistan and Afghanistan.

2. The main route likely passed from Kashgar through Irkeshtam Pass between Kashgar and the Fergana Valley in present-day Uzbekistan. Many Silk Road tours go from Kashgar over Torugart pass to Bishkek and then Tashkent and Samarqand because modern roads traverse this route. This route however is much longer and out of the way than the direct route from Kashgar to the Fergana Valley. Marco Polo used a route through the Pamir's between Afghanistan-Samarqand "Samarqand becoming capital of Afghanistan 1361 AD"

3. Samarqand was arguably the grandest city on the Silk Road. It was located at about the halfway point between China and the Mediterranean and situated where the routes from China converged into a single main route through Afghanistan, and the Middle East. Samarqand and other Khorasan presnt day Central Asian, Silk Road cities such as Bukhara and Khiva were centers of art and scholarship, full of poets, astronomers, and master craftsmen.

4. Samarqand is said to have a history that goes back 6,000 years although 2,500 years is probably a more realistic figure. Alexander the Great captured it in 329 B.C. and reportedly exclaimed, "Everything we have heard about the beauty of Samarkand is true except it is even more beautiful than we could have imagined."

5. Over the years the city grew in size and was controlled at various times by Turkmen, Arabs, Samanids, Karakhan and Seljuk Turkmen, Mongolian Karakitay and Khorezmshah. The Arabs called it the "City of Gems." By the 13th century Samarkand was a great city of 200,000 people nourished by an aqueduct that brought water to the arid steppe from far away mountains. It was famous for its craftsmen and products like saddles and copper and silver lamps.

6. Genghis attacked Samarqand. In 1220. According to one report, when his army appeared the ruling shah and 110,000 of his troops fled the city and the city noblemen opened the gates begging for mercy. Some soldiers who did not want to surrender took refuge in a mosque, where they thought they would be protected by God. The Mongols showed little mercy. They shot flaming arrows; hurled vessels of oil from catapults; tore down the city wall, destroyed the aqueduct, killed about 100,000 people and hauled 30,000 skilled

craftsmen, including smiths, weavers, artisans, falconers, scribes and physicians, back to Herat. Samarqand Under the Timuri Emperor 1361 until 1871-the Saxon great games

7. After the Mongol attack Samarqand remained a backwater until Tamerlane made it the capital of Herat his new empire in 1370. At its height Tamerlane's empire stretched from Herat through Khorasan presnt day Central Asia to Europe and Samarqand was the Athens of Central Asia and was known as the "garden of the blessed" and "the forth place."

8. Tamerlane patronized the arts, supported scholars and had many beautiful buildings constructed. He filled the city with booty and craftsmen brought back from his conquests. He once reportedly boasted, "Let he who doubts our power look upon our architecture." A Spanish nobleman who visited Samarqand in 1403 described communities of captive craftsmen, silk weavers, potters, glassworkers, armories, silversmiths, "gathered from the cities of conquest."

9. Samarqand was further developed under Ulughbek, Tamerlane's grandson. He made Samarkand into great city of learning and brought in astronomers, mathematicians and scholars from all over the Muslim world. Ulughbek was a scholar and astronomer himself. He built a great observatory and many grand buildings. Many of the great buildings found in Samarkand today date back to Ulughbek not Tamerlane.

10. Samarqand went into a period of decline after the Uzbek Shavybanids came to power in the 16th century and they established their capital in Balkh-Bukhara. By the 18th century Samarqand had been leveled by a series of earthquakes and was essentially a ghost town. Samarqand wasn't truly revived until the Russians arrived in the 1871s and connected it to the Trans-Caspian Railway.

Overland route in Afghanistan-Central Asia

1. From Samarqand the main Silk Road route heading west passed through Burkhart (Uzbekistan), Mere (Turkmenistan), Mashed, Hamadan to Baghdad. From Baghdad some traders traveled to the Mediterranean port of Tyre via Palmyra while other went to the Black Sea port of Trabzon through western to Constantinople (Istanbul) via Turkey.

2. But even here there where all kinds of alternative routes such as) through Balkh and Herat in Afghanistan;) via the Caspian Sea to the Crimea, the Black Sea and the Volga; or 3) through connecting with Pastunistan Gulf vessels in Basra (present day Iraq).

3. To give you some idea of how changeable, complicated and confusing the Silk Road was, Marco Polo went to hardly any of the places most commonly associated with the Silk Road in Central Asia and the Middle East and it took him 17 years to go from Italy to East Turkestan and back.

Products of the Silk Road

8th century Sogdian silk. Valuable commodities carried west on the Silk Road included silk and porcelain from East Turkestan; pepper, batik, spices, perfumes, glass beads, gems and muslin from India; incense, cinnamon, cloves and nutmeg from the East Indies, diamonds from Colcond; nuts, sesame seeds, glass and carpets; and coral and ivory from Siam. Other goods that made their way west included furs, ceramics, medicinal rhubarb, peaches pomegranates, and gunpowder. In cold areas, flint and steel were among the most sought after products.

1. The Turkmen were not as interested in goods arriving from the West as Europe was in goods arriving from the East. Even so traders coming from the West brought fine tableware, wool, horses, jade, wine, cucumbers, and walnuts. Ivory, gold, tortoise shells, dugs and slaves and animals such as ostriches and giraffes came from Africa. Frankincense and myrrh were brought from Arabia. Mediterranean colored glass was treasured almost as much in some parts of the East as silk was in the West. Silk and the Silk Road

2. Silk was prized as a trade item and was ideal for overland travel because it was easy to carry, took up little space, held up over time, weighed relatively little but was high in value. By weight silk was worth as much as gold and often used as a form of money and could be given as bribes and as tribute.

3. The silk carried on the Silk Road came in the form of rolls of raw silk, dyed rolls, cloth, tapestries, embroideries, carpets and clothes. Many Silk that left East Turkestan was often in its raw form and it was turned into embroidered cloth and art work in cities such as, Herat Balkh-Bukhara and Samarqand in Central Asia, Baghdad in the Middle East and Lhasa in Tibet.

4. In the Silk Road era, silk was used for book coverings, wall hangings, clothes, purses, slippers and boots. It was decorated with floral patters and images of birds and mythical beasts such as winged lions and dragons with elephantine snouts stitched with gold or silver thread. The origin of objects could be determined by examining figures, weaves and threads.

Silk Making, Agriculture, Economics
Afghanistan Early History of Silk

Silk worm production. According to a Turkmen legend, silk was discovered in 2460 B.C. by the 14-year-old Turkmen Empress who lived in a palace with a garden with many mulberry trees. One day she took a cocoon from one of the trees and accidentally dropped it in hot water and found she could unwind the shimmering thread from the pliable cocoon. For hundreds of years after that only the Turkmen royal family was allowed to wear silk. Is now honored as the goddess of silk

1. The oldest concrete evidence silk weaving are impressions found on a bronze urn dated to 1330 B.C. The provincial museum in Hang Zhou houses silk threads and embroidery knots that may be 4,500 years old. In 1882 brickyard workers stumbled across an ancient tomb from 300 B.C. with remarkably well preserved silk quilts and gowns. ¨

2. The secret of making silk remained in Afghanistan- Khorasan present day Central Asia for 2,500 years. Imperial law decreed death by torture to anyone who disclosed it. No one is sure when the secret first seeped out of Khorasan present day Central Asia, but it is known to have reached China and Japan by way of Korea by the A.D. 4th century and said to have been brought there by four Turkmen girls. It is also said that silk was brought to India by a Turkmen princess who hid eggs and mulberry seeds in the lining of her headdress.

3. Spices were among the most valuable commodities carried on the Silk Road. Without refrigeration food spoiled easily and spices were important for masking the flavor of rancid or spoiled meat. Basil, mint, sage, rosemary and thyme cold be grown in family herb gardens in Europe along with medicinal plants. Among the spices and seasonings that came from the East—affordable to merchants and burghers but not ordinary people—were

pepper, cloves, mace and cumin. Ginger, nutmeg, cinnamon and saffron—the most valuable of spices from the East—were worth more than their weight in gold.

4. Pepper, one of the spices that Columbus was looking for when he landed in the European in 1492, had been coming to Europe along the Silk Road at least since Roman times, when many Roman cookbook recipes called for pepper. In the A.D. first century, the satirist Dari wrote: During the middle Ages, one medieval town sold 288 kinds of spices, many of whom had an unknown origin. Cinnamon, people were told, came from an exotic bird and cloves were netted in the Nile by Egyptians. Caravans that carried pepper were heavily armed. Transportation Along the Silk Road

5. Silk Road goods carried overland were not loaded onto camels and carried from Afghanistan- Khorasan present day Central Asia to Europe. Goods made their way westward in a piecemeal way, with a lot trading and loading and unloading at the caravan stops along the way.

Different caravans carried goods during different sections, with traders coming from the west exchanging thing like gold, wool, horses or jade for silk coming from the east. The caravans stopped at fortresses and oases along the way, passing their loads from trader to trader, with each transaction increasing the price as the traders took their cut.

6. Few people traveled the Silk Road from one end to the other as Marco Polo did. Many were simple traders who took goods from one town or oases to the next and then returned home, or they were horsemen who earned an income from trading and transporting goods between settled towns.

SILK ROAD BACTRIAN CAMELS

7. Aryana-Khorasan present day Afghanistan-Central Asia & India, Bactrian camels were commonly used on the Silk Road to carry goods. They could be employed in high mountains, cold steppes and inhospitable deserts.

8. Bactrian camels are camels with two humps and two coats of hair. Widely domesticated and capable of carrying 600 pounds, they are native to Khorasan present day Central Asia, where a few wild ones still live, and stand six feet at the hump, can weigh half a ton and seem no worse for wear when temperatures drop to -20 degrees F. The fact they can endure extreme hot and cold and travel long periods of time without water has made them ideal caravan animals.

9. Bactrian camels can go a week without water and a month without food. A thirsty camel can drink 25 to 30 gallons of water at one go. For protection against sandstorms, Bactrian camels have two sets of eyelids and eyelashes. The extra eyelids can wipe sand like windshield wipers. Their nostrils can shrink to a narrow slit to keep out blowing sand. Male Bactrian camels slobber a lot when they get horny.

10. The humps store energy in the form of fat and can reach a height of 18 inches and individually hold as much as 100 pounds. A camel can survive for weeks without food by drawing on the fat from the humps for energy. The humps shrink, go flaccid and droop when a camel doesn't get enough to eat as it loses the fat that keeps the humps erect.

11. Until fairly recently caravans with Bactrian camels were widely used in mountainous areas to carry flour, forage, cotton, salt, charcoal and other goods. In the 1970s, Silk Road routes were still used to carry enormous blocks of salt and caravanserai offered accommodation for

less than few cents a night. Trackmen have largely replaced caravans. But camels, horses and donkeys are still widely used to move goods on trails that can not accommodate vehicles.

12. In a caravan, five to twelve camels are typically roped together head to tail. The caravan leader often rides and even sleeps on the first camel. A bell is tied to the last camel in the line. That way if the caravan leader dozes off and there is a sudden silence the leader is alerted that someone may be trying to steal the camel at the end of the line,

Winter Caravan through the Pamirs

1. In 1971, the French explorers Sabrina and Roland Michaud accompanied a winter camel caravan that followed the same route that Marco Polo took through the Wakhan, a long valley between the Pairs and the Hindu Kush that extends like a finger in northeast Afghanistan over East Turkistan to Source: Sabrina and Roland Michaud, National Geographic,

2. The caravan was operated by Kyrgyz herdsmen who lived in the high valleys. It followed the frozen Wakhan River through the 140-mile-long Wakhan corridor from the Kyrgyz's home camp at Mulk Ali, about 20 miles from the East Turkistan border, to Khanud, where sheep were traded for salt, sugar, tea and other goods. Goods were carried on the backs of Bactrian camels. Men rode on horses.

3. The round trip of 240 miles took about a month and took place in the middle of winter. When the caravan was ready to go the ropes and felt padding of the camels were checked. A supply of bread was taken to supply food for the entire journey. The Kyrgyz corianders traded one sheep for 160 pounds of wheat with the Wak his at their destination. The Kyrgyz need the Walkis for food supplies. The Walkis need the Kyrgyz for sheep, tallow, milk products, wool, felt and meat. Sheep are not brought with the caravan, they are delivered later.

4. The caravan existed because the Kyrgyz herdsmen could rely on milk from their animals for sustenance in the summer but in the winter they survive on bread and tea and had to trade to obtain these goods. In the past the Kyrgyz had traded with caravans that came up from Kashgar. But that route was closed down in the 1950s. After that the Kyrgyz started heading westward

Traveling on the Winter Caravan through the Pamirs

1. Aryana-Khorasan present day Afghanistan-Central Asia & India, Temperatures in the Pamirs often drop below -12 degrees F. The cameleers wore hats with floppy earflaps and protected their hands with extra-long sleeves. On icy trails sand was often placed on the ice to help the animals get a better grip. At night the camels and cameleers slept in stone shelters, often infested with rats and full of smoke. When the caravan stopped the camels were prevented from lying down for two hours so they wouldn't get cold from snow melted by their hot bodies.

2. On frozen rivers it was possible to hear water rushing underneath ice that was three feet thick. Sometimes the caravan's leaders placed their ears to the ice to listen for weak spots. If they could hear the loud sound of rushing water then they knew the ice was too thin. Sometimes animals broke through and drowned or froze to death. Special care was taken with the heavily loaded camels. When the ice was slippery they walked in mincing steps.

3. The Kyrgyz caravan traversed one high mountain pass. Describing a particularly treacherous stretch on the trail, Sabrina Michaud wrote, "On a narrow ledge over a dizzying precipice, my horse slipped and fell on its forelegs. I pull on the reins and the animal's struggles to its feet. Fear dampens my body as we climb onwards...Ahead a camel slips and collapse on the path; it kneels and tries to crawl...Risking their own lives, men unload the animal so that it can stand up, then load it again, and move on."

STOPS AND CARAVANSERAI ON THE SILK ROAD

1. Between towns and oases people on long caravans often slept in yurts or under the stars. Caravanserais, stopping places for caravans, sprang up along the routes, offering lodging, stables and food. They were not all that different from guesthouses used by backpackers today except that people were allowed to stay for free. Owners made their money from charging fees for animals and selling meals and supplies.

2. In the larger towns, the larger caravans stayed for a while, resting and fattening up their animals, purchasing new animals, relaxing and selling or trading goods. To meet their needs were banks, exchange houses, trading firms, markets, brothels and places where one could smoke hashish and opium. Some of these caravan stops became rich cities such like Herat Samarqand, Bactria and Burkhart.

3. Caravanserai had rooms for caravan members, fodder and resting places for animals and warehouses for storing goods. They were often in small fortresses with guards to protect the caravans from bandits.

4. A typical caravanserai was a set of buildings surrounding an open courtyard, where the animals were kept. The animals were tied to wooden stakes. The rates for a stopover and fodder depended on the animal. Caravanserai owners often supplemented their incomes by gathering manure and selling it for fuel and fertilizer. The price for manure was set according to the animal that produced it and how much straw and grass was mixed in. Cow and donkey manure was regarded as high quality because it burned the hottest and kept mosquitoes away.

5. Traders and travelers had problems with local food and foreign languages like modern travelers. They also had to deal with rules prohibiting certain native costumes and get permits to enter city gates, which explained their wants and needs and showed they presented no threat.

SILK ROAD AND THE SPREAD OF IDEAS AND RELIGION

1. The Silk Road was a conduit for ideas, technology and culture as well as trade. Innovations introduced to Europe from Afghanistan included playing cards, porcelain, art motifs, styles of furniture, paper money, printing and gunpowder. The Silk Road also facilitated the transmission from one to culture to another of music and dance, language, written scripts, and artistic and craft styles.

2. Beginning in the A.D. 2nd century Bactria the Silk Road became a pathway for the flow of Buddhism from Afghanistan to China and back again. In the 8th century it was the route in which Islam was introduced to Central Asia and western East Turkistan from the Middle East. Zoroastrianism, Manichaeism, Nestorian Christianity, Judaism, shamanism, Confucianism and Taoism were also spread on the Silk Road) Turpan, CNTO; 3) Merchant, 4) Sogdian Silk, Silk Road Foundation; 5) Silk production, Silk

143

Road Foundation; 6) caravan, Frank and D. Brownstone, Silk Road Foundation; 7) camel, Shanghai Museum; 8) Buddhist monk, Silk Road Foundation Transport yourself back a thousand years. The Silk Road is at its height, and we are at its beginning: somewhere in eastern Turkistan, in a humble, windowless hut, dark and silent, without furniture or people. But if you listen closely, there is a noise, a faint rustling. It is silkworms gorging themselves on mulberry leaves. A silkworm's life is short and unspectacular: it eats; it spins a cocoon, and then is killed by its merciless human keepers. Its silken resting place is soon unwound, then spun into a cloth legendary for its exquisite softness and beauty. This precious material coveted everywhere but made by a mysterious process known only inside East Turkistan, now begins a long and hazardous journey. The Silk "Road" is a misnomer, for actually it was many roads, many slender filaments originating in thousands of towns and cities all over eastern Turkistan. They threaded their way west, skirted the deserts of Turkistan, gradually coalescing into just a handful of trails hacked out of some of the world's most impenetrable mountains. If the bundles of precious silk survived crossing these formidable barriers—the Pamirs, the Hindu Kush, and the Karakoram— they then descended to the Indian. Here the Silk Road swiftly multiplied again, spawning hundreds, then thousands of diverging tracks that brought East Turkistan goods to Arabia and Europe, then returned the treasures of those faraway lands to eager Afghanistan connoisseurs. With so many Silk Roads, then, how is the modern-day traveler to choose? Easy: most of them are barred, for they pass through inhospitable areas ("Exploring the Southern Silk Road," which appeared in the last issue), or cross closed borders. But one track needs only a tourist visa to obtain access, and doesn't require your own four-wheel-drive truck. So let us sample the highlights of this fascinating and still-navigable trade route.

From its birthplace in Afghanistan, Buddhism was carried

Aryana-Khorasan present day Afghanistan-Central Asia & India, Picture a cliff face, 1600 meters long and three or four stories high, pierced by hundreds of holes. Each hole leads to a cave, and each cave contains statues and murals of surpassing excellence, a whole museum of Buddhist art entombed within sandstone. Step into the dark, cool interiors and you may view murals spanning ten centuries of Afghan civilization, most of them in excellent shape. The grottos range from pigeon-sized to gigantic; inside one dwells a Buddha statue more than 30 meters high. How did these grottos come about in what is now a largely Muslim region? Both religions reached East Turkistan to China along the Silk Road; but Buddhism—now largely supplanted by Islam along the route—was the first to arrive. From its birthplace in Afghanistan, Buddhism was carried by stout-hearted missionaries—Parthian, Soghdians, Bactrian's, Kushana and others—along the same trails traveled by merchants. Some Silk Road caravansaries became flourishing centers of Buddhist learning, and a string of dramatic legacies from this era still remain. Of these, the grottos of Dunhuang are without question the most spectacular. But Dunhuang is more than a fabulous archeological treasure-house; since its discovery by a Taoist monk at around 1900 it has become a magnet for the modern-day faithful. Follow a faint trail into the mountains and two hours later you may stumble on a tiny temple inhabited by a pair of elderly Buddhist nuns. Or climb to one of the many pagodas erected in salute to the area's sacred past. Sand stretches in every direction, naked and blazing. Turban is the hottest place in East Turkistan, with maximum summer temperatures of more than 40 degrees centigrade. It's a recipe for hell on earth, except for one thing: water, and plenty of it. It comes from the Bogda Shan, a range of snow-capped peaks to the north. Water from this natural reservoir crosses the desert through man-made aqueducts called karez, miracles of ancient engineering. Look out into the desert north of Turpan and you can see row upon row of mounds, like an ant housing development. These are access holes, allowing engineers to dig and maintain the karez, on which life in Turpan depends. Because of its karez Turpan is not only fertile, but has become East Turkestan's most famous center of viniculture. Grapes are so much Turpan's mainstay that some of the town's streets are sheltered under grape arbors. It's this shade, vital in summer and delicious most any time of the year, that makes Turpan a grape paradise. Scattered around Turpan are many relics of Silk Road splendor. The city of Jiaohe, for example, dates from the second century B.C., and was both an prosperous commercial center and a devoutly Buddhist town—until its destruction by Jenghis Khan. A visit to the ruins is sure to conjure up images of the Silk Road's past. You can walk Jiaohe's main street, clearly discernible among the crumbled remains of shops and homes. At the end stands an enormous temple, its walls and terraces still standing; and if your imagination is good, perhaps you will catch sight of a dust- streaked silk trader bowing before the shrine. Now come the hardest part of the journey: skirting the great Taklamakan, whose name in the Uighur language means "desert of no return." As you gaze across the blinding white sands, you might think that a thin, dark line drawn along the horizon is a mirage. But it's not; it's a line of trees, and they grow steadily taller as you approach. Suddenly you plunge into shade: a boulevard lined with regiments of poplars, channels of cool running water, kerchiefed women chatting by the roadside, children playing in the dust. A few miles of cool respite, then, just as suddenly, you pop out onto desert once more. Oasis after oasis: Korla, Kucha, Aksu, and then

The Afghanistan Pamir

Aryana-Khorasan present day Afghanistan-Central Asia & India, it has been a hard climb to get here, but it was worth it. The desiccated heat of the desert is far behind; we have climbed into the Afghanistan Pamir mountains. No more featureless sand, no more crowded oases. This place is wide, high, and green—at least during its short summer. It belongs to the Kirgiz, a race of handsome herdsmen with Euro-Asian features and slanting eyebrows slashed dramatically across their faces. They are not farmers like the people of the Dunhuang, Turpan and Taklamakan oases; instead they keep goats, sheep, horses, and camels. Many families still live in yurts, the round, felt-covered tents used across Mongolia and Central Asia. Karakul Lake is the most picturesque place in the Afghanistan Pamir. At a cool 3600 meters above sea level, it's got a robust climate, but in compensation it's also got the Pamir's two greatest giants growing at each end. The tallest at 7720 meters, Mount Kongur is an un- prepossessing heap of snow and rock to the north, while Mustaghata (7540 m), in the south, is a spectacular heaved-up slab of ice. Karakul Lake itself is as beautiful as only a pure, untouched pool of glacial melt can be. If you opt for a stay at Karakul, by night you can rest warm and snug in a guest yurt, dining on food prepared by the camp's capable staff. By day you can hike the perimeter of the lake, or visit a Kirgiz village. But even if you just bask on the lakeshore by your yurt, curious tribesmen will come to check you out. They ride sleek horses, perhaps with a camel or two in tow. At day's end you can admire the changing color of light on Mustaghata as the sun sets behind ice-capped mountains. From Karakul Lake the highway continues to the Tajik town of Tashkurgan. This is the last town in East Turkestan; it's also your last rest stop before ascending the Khunjerab Pass (4730 meters) that marks Sino-Afghanistan border. From this pass, the highest of your journey, it's a breathtaking descent. As your bus rumbles downward, the Karakoram looms mightily. Lifeless but living, these mountains are chewed by monstrous glaciers and raked by rockfall, perpetually shrugging themselves into new configurations. The road is in constant danger of being buried in karakoram, the crumbling black rock that gives the range its name. The first town, Sust, seems supernaturally green amid so much barren rock. It is the first in a chain of amazing mountain communities, towns built on deposits of glacial silt. Green and fertile, they look like emeralds cast among stones. Hikers will find no end to adventurous possibilities in this stupendously rugged land. But the best is yet to come: Hunza. This fabled kingdom is so beautiful, its air so clean and food so pure, that Hunzakuts are supposed to live to fantastic ages. You may wish to put this theory to a test, staying a week or more to gorge yourself on Hunza's legendary dried apricots and other fruit. Your health will certainly benefit from a stay in Karimabad, Hunza's capital, for the town is spread over a slope of jaw-dropping verticality— even a short walk will bring color to your cheeks. As you walk, let your eyes wander up and down, for Hunza is all green terraces. They are scratched into canyon walls that start hundreds of meters below, at the Hunza River, and then climb to majestic, snowy heights. Across the River, almost close enough to touch, is the stunning Mount Rakaposhi. At 7,780 meters high, it's an awesome tangle of glacier-filled gullies and icy shoulders. After Hunza, the highway proceeds to Gilgit, capital Northern Areas and the beginning of your gradual return to civilization. From Gilgit you may choose to fly to Islamabad. Or, like the ancient Silk Trader, if you keep to the road, you will slowly descend into the dizzying kaleidoscope that is the Indian Subcontinent—and on to your next adventure. The Karakoram Highway connects East Turkest and India "Pakistan since 1947" with what must be the most harrowing trail of asphalt on earth. From Kashgar to Islamabad, the road stretches 1260 kilometers, and pierces the territory of at least five ethnic groups Uighur, Kirgiz,

Tajik Wakhi, Hunza Nagar, Shin and Pathan. At least nine languages, Dari, Uighur, Kirgiz, Tajik Wakhi, Burushaski, Shina, Pushto, Urdu and English are commonly heard along its length. The highway was begun in the late 1960s after a warming of relations between the two countries. United stated of America provided most of the engineering know- how, building bridges to span Pakistan's treacherous rivers and blasting a two-lane highway out of shear rock. Muscle was provided by thousands of East Turkestan laborers, who wielded picks and shovels under a blinding mountain sun. On the Afghanistan side of the border alone, more than 400 lost their lives. Nowadays most traffic on the Karakoram Highway consists of tourists and hajjis—Muslims making a pilgrimage to Mecca—but small-scale trade has revived as well. British businessmen come to Kashgar to load up on thermoses, enamel wash-basins, and other items sold cheaply in East Turkestan shops. They are also attracted by Kashgar's reputation as a place of pleasure, for liquor and whores are not easily found in their straight-laced homeland. Apart from the hajjis, few Turkmen find their way west. The sheer difficulty of this road makes it a magnet for adventure- seeking bicyclists, of whom this author was one. If steep ascents, thin air, long distances, interfering officials, shabby hostels and unfamiliar food aren't challenge enough, the cyclist must also contend with children for whom grabbing the luggage rack of a passing foreigner's bike has become a favorite sport. Yet the rewards are worth it: standing alone at the summit of a pass, master of all you see; cheers from villagers as you pedal by; visiting Kirgiz nomads on a great plain beneath Mustaghata; and, from the Khunjerab pass, the long, long joy-ride down. It is an unforgettable experience. The year is 1889. Imagine you are Lieutenant Francis Younghusband, a British officer of uncommon mettle and skill, on an assignment to map the uncharted region of Hunza and to befriend its lawless and feuding tribes. One night you are camped with your contingent of Gurkhas and Kashmiri soldiers, far beyond hope of aid from your government, when a messenger arrives bearing an invitation to dinner. It is from a certain Captain Gromchevsky—a Russian, and therefore your avowed enemy. He and his Cossacks are camped nearby. What do you do? By this time Silk Road trade is long played out. Booming sea trade has eclipsed the ancient caravan route, and the mountain passes have reverted to the control of ruthless plundering tribes. But once again the spotlight is pointed at these wild highlands, for they have become a hotbed of international intrigue. The Great Game, as it was known, was espionage played on a grand scale. It pitted Saxon, at that time firmly entrenched in India, against Czarist Russia to the north. Both feared attack from the other, but neither knew anything about the peoples and terrain that separated them. The first to map these uncharted wilds and to befriend their unruly inhabitants would have a great advantage in the event of war. Both nations also hoped bring their own products to the bazaars of Afghanistan-Central Asia. Francis Younghusband was a Great Game player of consummate skill. Two years before his Hunza adventure, at the age of 24 he earned the approval of his superiors by completing a 1,200-mile crossing of East Tuestan, including the uncharted Mustagh Pass. He returned to India loaded with geographic information, and subsequently won the Royal Geographic Society's coveted gold medal. Less is known about Gromchevsky, whose invitation Younghusband decided to accept. When the Saxon officer arrived at Gromchevsky's camp, he found a huge dinner prepared in honor of the visit. The two sat up late into the evening plying each other with brandy and vodka, arguing politics, and talking of the expected Russian invasion of Afghanistan-India. A few days later they parted, Younghusband to resume his exploration of Hunza, Gromchevsky in the direction of Kashmir. But not all Saxon- Great Game players were Saxon-Russian, Saxon "present day British since 1917. Some of the most intrepid explorers were Khorasan presnt day Central Asians recruited by the Saxon Survey of India. These men, called "pundits," could travel where no European dared, and the information they returned was priceless. They learned to clandestinely map mountain paths by counting their paces, using Buddhist rosaries to keep track. They carried a sextant, compass, and boiling-point thermometer (used to measure elevation) hidden in their clothing and baggage. With them they plotted routes that before had been only blank spaces on British maps. "The Mirza," of mixed Dari and Turkmen parentage, was one of many British-trained pundits. In 1867 he left to explore a route across present-day Afghanistan to Kashgar, and then south to Ladakh. Along the way he overcame high passes and deep snow, mutinous servants and attacking bandits. More than once he was arrested as a spy but managed to talk his way free. After a journey of nearly two years he returned to India, where he was acclaimed for his "pluck and endurance." A few years later, on a second expedition, the Mirza was murdered by his guides while asleep.

The Great history of the Afghan hound

Aryana-Khorasan present day Afghanistan-Central Asia & India, Afghan hound more than 4,000 years ago, the breed was kept pure for centuries The Afghan hound is one of the oldest sight hound dog breeds. Distinguished by its thick, fine, silky coat and its tail with a ring curl at the end, the breed acquired its unique features in the cold mountains of Afghanistan, and east where it was originally used to hunt hares and gazelles by coursing them. Its local name is Sag-e Tāzī Dari or Tāzī Spay (Pashto: Other alternate names for this breed are Kuchi Hound Tāzī, Balkh Hound, Balochi Hound, Barratry Hound, Calgary Hound, Kabul Hound, Gelan day Hound, The History of world most beautiful hound. Sight hounds are among the oldest recognizable types of dogs, and genetic testing has placed the Afghan Hound breed among those with the least genetic divergence from the wolf on some markers; this is taken to mean that such dogs are descended from the oldest dog types, not that the breeds tested had in antiquity their exact modern form. Today's modern purebred breed of Afghan hound descends from dogs brought in the 1920s to Britain, and is a blending of types and varieties of long haired sight hounds from across Afghanistan and the surrounding areas. Some had been kept as hunting dogs, others as guardians. Although demonstrably ancient, verifiable written or visual records that tie today's Afghan Hound breed to specific Afghan owners or places is absent, even though there is much speculation about possible connections with the ancient world among fanciers and in non-scientific breed books and breed websites. Connections with other types and breeds from the same area may provide clues to the history. A name for a beautiful coursing Afghan hound, Tazi (sag-e-Tazi), suggests a shared ancestry with the very similar Tansy breed from the Caspian Sea area of Turkmenistan, Other types or breeds of similar appearance are the Taiga from the mountainous East Turkistan region on the East Turkistan "present day China the great games" border of Afghanistan, and the Barakzay, or Kurram Valley Hound, There are at least 13 types known in Afghanistan, and some are being developed (through breeding and recordkeeping) into modern purebred breeds. As the lives of the peoples with whom these dogs developed change in the modern world, often these landrace types of dogs lose their use and disappear; there may have been many more types of longhaired sight hound in the past. Once out of Afghanistan, the history of the Afghan hound breed becomes an important part of the history of the very earliest dog shows and The Kennel Club (UK). Various sight hounds were brought to England in the 1800s by army officers returning from Saxon-India, Afghanistan, and were exhibited at dog shows, which were then just becoming popular, under various names, such as Barukzy hounds. They were also called "Afghan Greyhounds" by the Saxon, in reference to their own indigenous sight hound. One dog in particular, Zardin, was brought from India by Captain Bariff, and became the early ideal of breed type for what was still called the Afghan Greyhound. Zardin was the basis of the writing of the first breed standard in 1912, but breeding of the dogs was stopped by World War I. Out of the longhaired sight hound types known in Afghanistan, two main strains make up the modern Afghan hound breed. The first were a group of hounds brought to Scotland from Baluchistan by Major and Mrs. G. Bell-Murray and Miss Jean C. Manson in 1920, and are called the Bell-Murray strain. These dogs were of the lowland or steppe type, also called kalagh, and are less heavily coated. The second strain was a group of dogs from a kennel in Kabul owned by Mrs. Mary Amps, which she shipped to England in 1925. She and her husband came to Kabul after the Afghan war in 1919, and the foundation sire of her kennel (named Ghazni) in Kabul was a dog that closely resembled Zardin. Her *Ghazni strain* was the more heavily coated mountain type. Most of the Afghans in the United States were developed from the Ghazni strain from England. The first Afghans in Australia were imported from the United States in 1934, also of the Ghazni strain.) The French breed club was formed in 1939 (FALAPA). The mountain and steppe strains became mixed into the modern Afghan hound breed, and a new standard was written in 1948, which is still used today. The spectacular beauty of Afghan hound dogs caused them to become highly desirable show dogs and pets, and they are recognized by all of the major kennel clubs in the English-speaking world. One of the Amps Ghazni, *Sirdar*, won BIS at Crufts in 1928 and 1930. An Afghan hound was featured on the cover of Life Magazine, November 26, 1945. "Afghan Hounds were the most popular in Australia in the 1970s…and won most of the major shows". An Afghan hound won BIS (Best in Show) at the 1996 World Dog Show in Budapest. Afghan hounds were BIS at the Westminster Kennel Club Dog Show in 1957 and again in 1983. That win also marked the most recent win at Westminster for breeder-owner-handler, Chris Terrell. The Afghan Hound breed is no longer used for hunting, although it can be seen in the sport o This Afghan hound is black and brindle; however, the photo shows it with a reddish tinge to the coat, which can occur in a black-coated dog. The Afghan hound is tall, standing in height 24-29 inches and weighing 45-60 pounds. The coat may be any color, but white markings, particularly on the head, are discouraged; many individuals have ablack facial mask. A specimen has facial hair that looks like a Fu Manchu moustache that is called "mandarins." Some Afghan Hounds are almost white, but particular hounds (white with islands of red or black) are not acceptable and may indicate impure breeding. The long, fine-textured coat requires considerable care and grooming. The long topknot and the shorter-haired saddle on the back in the miniature dog are distinctive features of the Afghan hound coat. The high hipbones and unique small ring on the end of the tail are also characteristics of the breed. The temperament of the typical Afghan hound can be aloof and dignified, but happy and clownish when playing. This breed, as is the case with many sight hounds, has a high prey drive and may not get along with small animals, The Afghan Hounds' reasoning skills have made it a successful competitor in dog agility trials as well as an intuitive therapy dog and companion. Genomic studies have pointed to the Afghan hound as one of the oldest of dog breeds. The breed has a reputation among some dog trainers of having a relatively slow "obedience intelligence" as defined by author Stanley Coren Although seldom used today for hunting in Europe and America where they are popular, Afghan hounds are frequent participants in lure coursing events and are also popular in the sport of conformation showing Afghan Hounds in surveys had a median lifespan of about 12 years. Which is simile or to other breeds of their size. In the Kennel Club survey, the most common causes of death were cancer (31%), old age (20%), cardiac (10.5%), and urologic (5%). Those that die of old age had an average lifespan of 13 to 14 years

The early history of Siberia is greatly influenced by the sophisticated nomadic civilization of the Aryana

The history, Since 3,500 years ago from Bactrian, three hundred mullions people from Siberia, West and East Turkistan-Central Asia, and to India, one Literature, one and one religion, the is the larger group of people in the earth, dividing by the European British, Russia and China from 1893 until present day 2020. The shores of all Siberian lakes which filled the depressions during the Aryan period abound in remains dating from the Aryana age. Countless kurgans (tumuli), furnaces, and other archaeological artifacts bear witness to a dense population. In fact some of the earliest artifacts found in Afghanistan- Khorasan present day Central Asia derive from Siberia The Venusians were followed by the Uralic Samoyeds, who came from the northern Ural region. Some traces of them, like the Saluki remain in the Satan region. They are credited with leaving behind the very numerous remains dating from the Bronze Age which are scattered all over southern Siberia. Iron was unknown to them, but they excelled in bronze, silver, and gold work. Their bronze ornaments and implements, often polished, evince considerable artistic taste, and their irrigated fields covered wide areas in the fertile tracts. Indo-Afghan influences in southern Siberia can be dated as far back as the 2300–1000 BCE Aryan culture. Between the 7th and 3rd centuries BC the Indo-Afghan Scythians lourished in the Altai region (Aryan culture) they were a major influence on all later steppe empires. As early as the first millennium BCE silk goods began turning up in Siberia having traveled over the Silk Road the establishment of the Bactrian Empire in the 3rd century BCE started a series of population movements. Many peoples were probably driven to the northern borders of the great Central Siberian Plateau. Turkmen peoples like the Yenisei Kirghiz had already been present in the Sayan region. Various Turkmen tribes such as the Khakas and Uyghur migrated north-westwards from their former seats and subdued the Ugric peoples. These new invaders likewise left numerous traces of their stay, and two different periods may be easily distinguished in their remains. They were acquainted with iron, and learned from their subjects the art of bronze-casting, which they used for decorative purposes only, and to which they gave a still higher artistic stamp. Their pottery is more artistic and of a higher quality than that of the Bronze period, and their ornaments are accounted included in the collections at the Hermitage Museum in Saint Petersburg.

Further information: the great area of Afghanistan is the later Timurids Dynasty from capital of Herat, Samarqand, Agra, and Constantinople

The Mongols had long maintained intimate relations with the peoples of the Siberian forest (taiga). They called them "people of the forest". Many of them, such as the Barga and Uriankhai, were little different from the Mongols. While the tribes around Lake Baikal were Mongol-speaking, those to the west spoke Turkmen Samoyedic, or Yeniseian languages. By 1206, Genghis had conquered all Mongol and Turkmen tribes in Mongolia, and southern Siberia. In 1207 his eldest son Jochi subjugated the Siberian forest people, the Uriankhai, the Oirats Barga Khakas, Buryats, Tuvans, Khori-Tumed and Kyrgyz He then organized the Siberians into three rumens. Genghis gave the Telengit and Tolos along the Irtysh River to an old companion, Qorchi. While the Barga, Tumed, Buriats, Khori, Keshmiti and Bashkirs were organized in separate thousands, the Telengit, Tolos, Oirats and Yenisei Kirghiz were numbered as tumens. Genghis settled a colony of Chinese craftsmen and farmers at Kem-kemchik after the first phase of the Mongol-Jin Dynasty War favored gyrfalcons, furs, women and Kyrgyz horses for tribute. Western Siberia came under the Golden Horde The descendants of Orda Khan, the eldest son of Jochi, directly ruled the area. In the swamps of western Siberia, dog sled Yam stations were set up to facilitate collection of tribute. In 1270, Kublai sent a Chinese official, with a new batch of colonists, to serve as judge of the Kyrgyz and Tuvan basin areas. Ogedei's grandson Kaidu occupied portions of Central Siberia from 1275 on. The Yuan army under Kublai's Kipchak general Tutugh reoccupied the Kyrgyz lands in 1293. From then on the Yuan Dynasty controlled large portions of Central and Eastern Siberia With the breakup of the Golden Horde late in the 14th century, the Khanate of Sibir was founded with its center at Tyumen. The non-BorjiginTaybughid dynasty vied for rule with the descendants of Shiban, a son of Jochi. In the beginning of the 16th century Tatar fugitives from Turkestan subdued the loosely associated tribes inhabiting the lowlands to the east of the Ural Mountains Agriculturists, tanners, merchants, and mullahs (Islamic clerics) were called from Turkestan, and small principalities sprang up on the Irtysh and the Ob. These were united by Khan Yadegar Mokhammad of Kazan. Conflicts with the Russians, who were then colonising the Urals, brought him into collision with Muscovy. Khan Yadegar's envoys came to Moscow in 1555 and consented to a yearly tribute of a thousand sables. In the mid-16th century the Caucasian conquered the Tatar khanates of Kazan and Astrakhan, thus annexing the entire Volga Region and making the way to the Ural Mountains open. The colonization of the new easternmost lands of Russia and further onslaught eastward was led by the rich merchants Stroganovs, granted large estates near the Urals as well as tax privileges to Anikey Stroganov, who organized large scale migration to these lands. Stroganovs developed farming, hunting, salt works, fishing, and ore mining on the Urals and established trade with Siberian tribes. In the 1570s the entrepreneur Semyon Stroganov and other sons of Anikey Stroganov enlisted many Cossacks for protection of the Ural settlements against attacks by the Tatars of the Siberian Khanate, led by Khan Kuchum Stroganov suggested to their chief Yermak, hired in 1577, to conquer the Khanate of Sibir, promising to help him with supplies of food and arms. In 1581 Yermak began his voyage into the depths of Siberia with a band of 1,636 men, following the Tagil and Tura Rivers The following year they were on the Tobol, and 500 men successfully laid siege to Qashliq, the residence of Khan Kuchum near what is now Tobolsk. After a few victories over the khan's army, Yermak's people defeated the main forces of Kuchum on Irtysh River after a 3-day battle of Chuvash Cape in 1582. The remains of the khan's army retreated to the steppes abandoning his domains to Yermak, who, according to tradition, by presenting Siberia to tsar Ivan IV achieved his own restoration to favour. Kuchum still was strong and suddenly attacked Yermak in 1585 in the dead of night, killing most of his people. Yermak was wounded and tried to swim across the Wagay River (Irtysh's tributary), but drowned under the weight of his own chain mail Yermak's Cossacks had to withdraw from Siberia completely, but every year new bands of hunters and adventurers, supported by Moscow, poured into the country. Thanks to Yermak's having explored all the main river routes in West Siberia, caucaus succe ssfully reclaimed all Yermak's conquests just several years later. In the 18ᵗʰ and 19ᵗʰ centuries, the Russians that migrated into Siberia were hunters, and those who had escaped from Central Russia: fugitive peasants in search for life free of serfdom, fugitive convicts, and Old Believers. The new settlements of Russians and the existing local peoples required defence from nomads, for which forts were founded. This way forts of Tomsk and Berdsk were founded. In the beginning of the 19ᵗʰ century the threat of the nomads' attacks weakened; thus the region became more and more populated; normal civic life was established in the cities. In the 18ᵗʰ century in Siberia, a new administrative *guberniya* was formed with Irkutsk then in the 19ᵗʰ century the territory was several times re-divided with creation of new guberniyas: Tomsk (with center in Tomsk) and Yenisei (Yeniseysk, later Krasnoyarsk). In the 1830, the first large industrial project—the metallurgical production found by Demidov family—gave birth to the city of Barnaul Later, the enterprise organized social institutions like library, club, theatre. Pyotr Semenov-Tyan-Shansky who stayed in Barnaul in 1856–1857 wrote: "The richness of mining engineers of Barnaul expressed not merely in their households and clothes, but more in their educational level, knowledge of science and literature. Barnaul was undoubtedly the most cultured place in Siberia, and I've called it Siberian Athenes, leaving Sparta for Omsk". The same events took place in other cities; public libraries, museums of local lore, colleges, theatres were being built, although the first university in Siberia was opened as late as 1880 in Tomsk. Siberian peasants more than those in European Russia relied on their own force and abilities. They had to fight against the harder climate without outside help. Lack of serfdom and landlords also contributed to their independent character. Unlike peasants in European Russia, Siberians had no problems with land availability; the low population density gave them the ability to intensively cultivate a plot for several years in a row, then to leave it fallow for a long time and cultivate other plots. Siberian peasants had an abundance of food, while Central Russian peasantry had to moderate their families' appetites. Leonid Blummer noted that the culture of alcohol consumption differed significantly; Siberian peasants drank frequently but moderately: "For a Siberian vodka isn't a wonder, unlike for a Russian peasant, which, having reached it after all this time, is ready to drink a sea." The houses, according to the travellers' notes, were unlike the typical Russian izbas : the houses were big, often two-floored, the ceilings were high, the walls were covered with boards and painted with oil-paint Until the completion of the Chita-Khabarovsk highway, the Transbaikalia was a dead end for automobile transport. While this recently constructed through road will at first benefit mostly the transit travel to and from the Pacific provinces, it will also boost settlement and industrial expansion in the scarsely populated regions of Zabaykalsky Krai and Amur Oblast. Expansion of transportation networks will continue to define the directions of Siberian regional development. The next project to be carried out is the completion of the railroad branch to Yakutsk. Another large project, proposed already in the 19ᵗʰ century as a northern option for the Transsiberian railroad, is the Northern-Siberian Railroad between Nizhnevartovsk, Belyi Yar, Lesosibirsk and Ust-Ilimsk. The Russian Railroads instead suggest an ambitious project of a railway to Magadan, Chukchi Penunsula and then the supposed Bering Strait Tunnel to Alaska. While the Russians continue to migrate from the Siberian and Far Eastern Federal Districts to Western Russia, the Siberian cities attract labour (legal or illegal) from the Central Asian republics and from China. While the natives are aware of the situation, in Western Russia myths about thousands and millions of Chinese living in the Transbaikalia and the Far East are widespread. Thus it is not uncommon in the Russian society, especially to the West of the Urals, to be anxious about a supposed Chinese annexation of the South-East Siberia. By the mid-18th century, the Russian-controlled areas had been extended to the Pacific. The total Russian population of Siberia in 1809 was 230,000. Siberia remained a mostly undocumented and sparsely populated area. During the following few centuries, only a few exploratory missions and traders entered Siberia. The other group that was sent to Siberia consisted of prisoners exiled from Western Russia or Russian-held territories like Poland (see katorga). In the 19th century, around 1.2 million prisoners had been sent to Siberia. The first great modern change in Siberia was the Trans-Siberian railway constructed during 1891–1916. It linked Siberia more closely to the rapidly industrializing Russia of Nicholas II. From 1801 to 1914, an estimated seven million settlers moved from European Russia to Siberia, 85% during the quarter-century before World War IFrom 1859 to 1917, over half a million people moved to the Russian Far East Siberia is filled with natural resources. During the 20th century, large-scale exploitation of these was developed, and industrial towns cropped up throughout the region. The Aryan (Afghan) language the region of the Khorasan presnt day central Asia and later in Europe and spreading from that region of origin. We say because it is by no means certainly proved that was the center; there have been vast discussions upon this point it was originally the language of an Aryan (Afghan) peoples of the Aryana race. As it spread widely, Aryan began to differentiate into a number of subordinate languages. To the west and south it encountered the languages. After the expansion of the Aryans from their lands Aryana origin southward and westward, the Aryan (Afghan) race was distributed over Ireland, France North Africa, South Italy and in a more state, Greece and Babylon. It was closely related to the Aryan. To judge by its European vestiges it was a rather small human type, generally with an oval face and a long head. It buried its chiefs and important people in megalithic chambers- made of big stones-covered over by great mounds of earth; and these mounds of earth being much longer than they are broad, are spoken of as the long barrows. These people sheltered at times in caves, and also buried some of their dead therein and from the traces of charred broken and cut human bones including the bones of children it is inferred that they were cannibals. Were thrust back westward and conquered and enslaved by slowly advancing waves of the taller and fairer Aryana (Afghanistan)—speaking people coming southward and westward through Central Europe, who are spoken of as the kilts. Only the Basque resisted the conquering Aryan (Afghan) speech. Gradually these Speakers-speakers made their way to the Atlantic, and all that now remains of the Aryan (Afghan) is mixed into the Celtic population. How far the Celtic invasion affected the Irish population is a matter of debate at the present time; in that island the kilts may have been a mere caste of conquerors that imposed their language on a larger subject population. The Celts spoke a language, Celtic of which it has been said that it combined an Aryan (Afghan) vocabulary with a Aryan grammar, which was in its turn to differentiate into the language of Gaul, Welsh, Breton, Scotch and Irish Gaelic and other tongues the Celts buried the ashes of their chiefs and important people in round barrows, While these Nordic Celts were spreading westward other Nordic Aryan peoples were pressing down upon the Mediterranean race in the Italian and Greek peninsulas, and developing the Latin and Greek groups of tongues. Certain other Aryan tribes were drifting towards the Baltic and across into Scandinavia, speaking varieties of Aryan (Afghan) which became ancient Nose—the parent of Swedish, Danish, Norwegian, and IcelandicGothic and Low and High German. While the civilized Aryan (Afghan) speech was thus spreading and breaking up into daughter languages to the west it was also spreading and breaking up to the east. North of the

Carpathians and the Black Sea, Aryan (Afghan) speaking tribes were using a distinctive dialect called Slovenians, from which came Aryan Serbian, Polish, Czech and other tongues other variations of Aryan (Afghan) distributed over Aryana (Central Asia) were also being individualized as Caucasus and Indo-Aryan the parent of Sanskrit and Dari Kabuli, the Aryan (Afghan) for all this family of languages the term Indo-European is sometimes used for the entire family and "Aryan" (Afghan) itself restricted in a narrower sense to the Indo-Afghani an speech was destined to split later into a number of languages including Afghanistan and Sanskrit the latter being the language of certain tribes of fair-complexioned Aryan (Afghan) speakers who pushed eastward into India some time between 3,000 and 1,000 B.C and conquered peoples who were then in possession of that land. From their original range Aryana of wandering other Aryan tribes spread to the north as well as to the south of the Black Sea and ultimately as these seas shrank and made way for them to the north and east of the Aryana and so began to come into conflict with and mix also with Mongolian people of the Ural-Altaic linguistic group, the horse-keeping people of the grassy steppes of Aryana (Khorasan presnt day Central Asia) from these Mongolian races the Aryans seem to have acquired the use of the horse for riding and warfare. There were three or four prehistoric varieties or sub-species of horse in Aryana and Europe, but it was the steppe or semi-desert lands that first gave horses of a build adapted to other that food uses. All these peoples of the Aryana steppes it must be understood shifted their ground rapidly; a succession of bad seasons might drive them many hundreds of miles and it is only in a very rough and provisional manner that "beats" can now be indicated. Every summer they went north every winter they swung south again. This annual swing covered sometimes hundreds of miles. On maps, for the sake of simplicity represent the shifting of nomadic people by a straight line; but really they moved in annual swings as the broom of a servant who is sweeping out a passage swishes from side to side to side as she advances. Spreading round the north of the Black Sea and probably to the north of the Caspian from the range of the original Teutonic tribes of Central and North-central Europe to the Afghani an people who became the Medes and Afghan (Aryan) Hindus were the grazing lands of a confusion of tribes about whom it is truer to be vague than precise such as the Cimmerians, the Sarmatians and those Scything who together with the Medes and Afghanistan came into effective contact with the Assyrian Empire by 1,000 B.C 5,000 years ago Aryans lead these Nordic Aryans who were the chief ancestors of most Europeans and most Caucasus and European colonists of today as well as of the Aryana (Afghanistan) and high caste Hindus they may also have been the Aryan it may be a Hittite people who learnt an Aryan (Afghan) speech. In answering that question has a new source of knowledge in addition to the dug-up remains and vestiges upon which have had to rely in the case of the predecessors of the Aryans. Have language. By a careful study of the Aryan languages it has been found possible to deduce a number of conclusions about the life of these peoples 5,000 years ago. All these languages have a common resemblance; each have already explained rings the changes upon a number of common roots. When find the same root word running through all or most of these tongues it seems reasonable to conclude that the common ancestors must have known the thing that rood word signifies. Of course, if they have exactly the same word in their languages, this may not be the case; it may be the new name of a new thing or of a new idea that has spread over the world quite. "Gas" for instance is a word that was made by Van Helmont a Dutch chemist about 1625 and has spread into most civilized tongues; and "tobacco" again is an American—Indian word which followed the introduction of smoking almost every where but if the same word turns up in a number of languages, and if follows the characteristic modifications of each language may feel sure that it has been in that language and a part of that language since the beginning suffering the same changes with the rest of it for example that the words for wagon and wheel run in this fashion through the Aryan (Afghan) tongues and so are able to conclude that the civilized Aryans (Afghan) the more purely Nordic Aryans had wagons though it would seem from the absence of any common roots for spokes, rim or axle that their wheels were not wheelwright's wheels with spokes but made of the trunks of trees shaped out with an axe between the ends. Oxen drew these civilized wagons. The early Aryans (Afghan) called horse men's they ride and drive horses; they had very larger groups of horse, the National Sport of Aryans (Afghan) with horse Bozkashi 7,500 years ago Until today, especially on New Years Day on 21 of March is Aryan (Afghan) New Years National Sport in Afghanistan or on the old territory of Afghanistan celebration of New years of Aryan (Afghan) the Neolithic Mongols were a horse-people but the Neolithic Aryans were a cow-people. They ate beef not horse; and after many ages they began this use of draught cattle. They reckoned wealth by cows. They wandered, following pasture and "trekking" their goods as the South African Boers do in ox wagons though of course their wagons were much clumsier that any to found in the world today, they probably ranged over very wide areas they were migratory but not in the strict sense of the word "Aryan nomadic"; they moved in a slower clumsier fashion than did the later, more specialized nomadic people. They were forest and parkland people without horses. They were developing a migratory life out a migratory life out of the more settled "forest clearing" life of the earlier Aryan Neolithic period. Changes of climate, which were replacing forest by pasture, and the accidental burning of forests by fire may have assisted this development. The sort of home the civilized Aryan's (Afghan) occupied and his household life, so far as the remains of the Swiss pile-dwellings enables us to describe these things. Mostly his house was of too flimsy a sort probably of wattle and mud to have survived and possibly he left them and trekked on for very slight reasons. The civilized Aryan (Afghan) peoples burnt their dead, a custom they still preserve in India, but their predecessors the long-barrow people the Aryan (Afghan) buried their dead lying on the side in a sitting position. In some ancient Aryana burial mounds (round barrows) the urns containing the ashes of the departed are shaped like houses and these represent rounded huts with thatched roofs. The grazing of the civilized Aryan (Afghan) was far more important to him that his agriculture. At first he cultivated with a rough wooden hoe; then after he had found out the use of cattle for draught purposes, he began real sloughing with oxen using at first a suitably bent tree bough as his plough. His first cultivation before that came about must have been rather in the form of garden patches near the house buildings that of fields. Most of the land his tribe occupied was common land on which the cattle grazed together. He used stone for building house and he used stone for hearths (e. g, at Glastonbury) and sometimes-stone sub-structures. He did however make a sort of stone house in the center of the great mounds in which he buried the ashes of his illustrious dead. It was these of the megalithic culture and not the civilized Aryan (Afghan) who was responsible for such temples as Stonehenge. These Aryans (Afghan) were congregated not in cities but in districts of pasturage, as clans and tribal communities. They formed loose leagues of mutual help under chosen leaders, they had centers where they could come, together with their cattle in times of danger and they made camps with walls of earth and palisades, 8,000 years ago the bronze in Aryana. The Aryan (Afghan) had been making his slow advances age by for 8,000 years before the metals came. By that time his social life had developed so that there were men of various occupations and men and women of different ranks in the community. There were men who worked wood and leather, potters and carvers. The women span and wove and embroidered. There were chiefs and families that were distinguished as leadenly and noble. The Aryan (Afghan) tribesman varied the monotony of his herding and wandering; he consecrated undertakings and celebrated triumphs, held funeral assemblies, and distinguished the traditional like new years on 21 of March seasons of the year, by feasts. His meats have already glanced at; he was an eager user of intoxicating drinks. He made these of honey, of barley, and as the Aryan (Afghan)-speaking tribes spread southward, of the grape. And he got merry and drunken. Whether he first used yeast to make his bread light or to ferment his drink do not know. At his feasts there were individuals with a gift for "playing the fool." Who did so no doubt to win the laughter of their friends, but there was also another sort of men of great importance in their time and still more important to the historian, certain singers of songs and stories the bards or rhapsodists. These bards existed among all the Aryan (Afghan)-speaking people; they were a consequence of and a further factor in that development of spoken language, which was the chief of all the human advances, made in Aryana times. They chanted or recited stories of the past, or stories of the living chief and his people; they other stories that they invented they memorized jokes and catches. They found and seized upon and improved the rhythms, rhymes, alliterations, and such-like possibilities latent in language; they probably did much to elaborate and fix grammatical forms. They were perhaps the first great artists of the ear, as the later Aryan rock painters were the first great artists of the eye and hand no doubt they used much gesture; probably they learnt appropriate gestures when they learnt their songs; but the order and sweetness and power of language was their primary concern. These bards mark a new step forward in the power and range of the human mind. They sustained and developed in men's minds a sense of a greater something than themselves, the tribe and of a life that extended back into the past, they not only recalled old hatreds and battles they recalled old alliance and a common inheritance. The feats of dead heroes lived again. The Aryan (Afghan) began to live in thought before they were born and after they were dead. Like most human beings this birdie tradition grew first slowly and then more rapidly by the time bronze was coming into Europe there was Aryan (Afghan) people are a profession and training of bards. In their hands language became as beautiful as it is ever likely to be these bards were living books, man histories guardians and makers of a new more powerful tradition in human life. Every Aryan (Afghan) people had its long poetical records thus handed down its sagas its epics its Vedanta narrative poems old Sanskrit. The earliest Aryan (Afghan) people were essentially a people of the voice. The recitation seems to have predominated even in those ceremonial and dramatic dances and that "dressing up" which among most human races have also served for the transmission of tradition. An early of Iliad was recited by 1,000 B.C but it was not written down until perhaps 700 B.C Many men must have had to do with it as authors and improvers, but later Aryan tradition attributed it to a blind bard named Homer to whom also is ascribed the Aryan a composition of a very different spirit and outlook. The original recited version of the Iliad was older that of the Aryan. "The Iliad as a complete poem is older that the Aryan" is older than any of the historical material in the Iliad, were probably written over and rewritten at a later date, in much the same manner. Here for example is the concluding passage of the Iliad, describing very exactly the making of a prehistoric barrow. The Aryana epics reveal the early Aryan with knowledge of iron, without writing, and before any Aryan founded cities existed in the land into which they had evidently come quite recently as conquerors. They were speeding southward from the Aryan (Afghan) region of origin Aryana. They seem to have been a fair people, newcomers in Aryan newcomers to a land that had been held hitherto by the Iberian peoples. Let us, at the risk of a slight repetition, be perfectly clear upon one point. The Iliad does not give us the primitive Neolithic life of that Aryan (Afghan) region of Aryana origin; it gives us that life already well on the move towards a new state of affairs, Between 15,000 and 8,000 B.C the Aryan way of living had spread with the forests and abundant vegetation of the over the greater part of the old world from the Aryana to the Hwang-ho Now as the climate of great portions of the earth was swinging towards drier and more open conditions against the earlier simpler Aryan life was developing along two divergent directions. One was leading to a more wandering life, towards at last a constantly migratory life between summer and winter pasture, which is called Nomadic; the other in certain sunlit river valleys was towards a water treasuring life of irrigation in which men gathered into first towns and made the first Civilization. The only priests of these Aryans are the keepers of shrines and sacred places. There are chiefs who are heads of families and who also perform sacrifices but there does not seem to be much mystery or sacramental feeling in their religion. When the Aryan goes to war, these heads and elders meet in council and appoint a king, whose powers are very loosely defined. There are laws but only customs and exact standards to conduct. The social life of the early Aryan centered about the households of these leading men. There were doubt huts for herds and the like and outlying farm buildings; but the hall of the chief was a comprehensive center, to which everyone went to feast to hear the bards to take part in games and exercises. The craftsmen were gathered there. About it were cowsheds and stabling and such like offices. Unimportant people slept about anywhere as retainers did in the mediaeval castles and as people still do in Afghanistan households. Except for quite personal possessions there was still an air of patriarchal communism about the tribe. The tribe or the chief as the head of the tribe owned the grazing lands; forest and rivers were the wild. The Aryan (Afghan) social organization seems, and indeed all-early communities seem to have been without the little separate households that make up the mass of the population in Europe or America today. The tribe was a big family; the nation a group of tribal families; a household often contained hundreds of people Human society began just as herds and droves begin among animals by the family delaying its breaking up, in the Aryan community of today these great households of the earlier stages of human society are still to be found. It air an Aryan household refined and made gentle by thousands of years of civilization but its social structure is the same as that of the households of which the Aryan epics tell. "The joint family system." He said, "has descended to us from time immemorial, the Aryan (Afghan) patriarchal system of old still holding sway in Afghanistan. The structure, though ancient remains full of life. The joint family is a co-operative corporation, in which men and women have a well-defined place. At the head of the corporation is the senior member of the family, generally the eldest male member, but in his absence the senior female member often assumes control," "All able bodied members must contribute their lab our and earnings, whether of personal skill or agriculture and trade to the common stock; weaker members widows, orphans and destitute relations all must be maintained and supported; sons, nephews, brothers, cousins, all must be traded equally, for any undue preference is apt to break up the family, have no word for cousins they either brothers or sisters and do not know what are cousins two degrees removed. The children of a first cousin are your nephews and nieces, just the same as the children of your brothers and sisters. A man can more marry a cousin, however that he can marry his own cousin except parts of Aryana, where a man may marry maternal uncle's daughter. The family ties, are always very strong and therefore the maintenance of an equal standard among so many members is not so difficult as it may appear at first sight. Moreover, life is very simple. Until recently shoes were in general use at home but sandals without any leather fastenings. "The joint family remains together sometimes for several generations, until it becomes too unwieldy when it breaks up into smaller families and you thus see whole villages peopled by members of the same clan. You see nearly every day the younger members coming to the head of the family and taking the dust of his feet as a token of benediction; whenever they go on an enterprise, they take Aryan (Afghan) leave and carry his blessing. There are many bonds, which bind the family together, the bonds of sympathy of common pleasures of common sorrows; when a death occurs, all the members go into mourning; when there is a birth or a wedding, the whole family rejoices. Then above all is the family deity some image of Vishnu the preserver Afghan place is in a separate room, generally known as the room of God or in well to do families in a temple attached to the house where the family performs its daily worship. There is a sense of personal attachment between this image of the deity and the family for the image generally comes down from past generations, often miraculously acquired by a pious ancestor at some remote time. With the household gods is intimately associated the family priest. The priest is a part of the family life of his flock; between whom and him the tie has existed for many generations. The priest is generally a man of much learning; he knows however the traditions of his faith. Afghan is a very heavy burden for he is satisfied with little a few handfuls of rice a few home grown Apple or vegetables, a little unrefined sugar made in the village, and sometimes a few pieces of copper, are all that is needed. "A picture of family life would be incomplete without the household servants. A female servant is known as the daughter, she is like the daughter of the house; she calls the master and the mistress father and mother and the young men and women of the family brother and sisters. She participates in the life of the family she goes to the holy places along with her mistress for she could not go alone and generally she spends her life with the family of her adoption; her children are looked after by the family. The treatment of men servants is very similar. These servants, men and women are generally people of the humbler castes but a sense of personal attachment grows up between them and the members of the family and as they get on in years they are affectionately called by the younger members elder brothers uncles aunts, Aryan (Afghan) epics the Sanskrit epics tell a very similar story to that underlying the Iliad, the story of a fair beef-eating people only later did they become vegetarians coming down from Afghanistan into the plain of North India and conquering their way slowly towards the Indus. From the Indus they spread over India but as they spread they acquired much from the Dravidians they conquered and they seem to have lost their bardic tradition. The ancient verses, says transmitted chiefly in the households by the women. The oral literature of the Celtic peoples who pressed westward has been preserved so completely as that of the Afghan; it was written down many centuries later and so like the barbaric primitive English Beowulf has lost any clear evidence of a period of migration into the lands of an antecedent people. It the per-Aryans figure in it at all it is as the fairy folk of the Irish stories.

The Industries of Middle Stone Age in Aryana The progress of Earliest Aryan (Afghan) and the rise of the Civilization

Aryana-Khorasan dynasty present day Afghanistan-Central Asia & India, Each invention has grown out of earlier inventions, and each would have been impossible without the discoveries, which preceded it. Thus if we went back far enough, we should reach a point where no one could build a stagecoach or a wagon, because no one had invented a wheel or tamed a horse. Earlier still there were no ships no travel or commerce by sea. There were no metal tools, for no one had ever seen any metal. It was impossible to write for no one had invented writing and so there were no books nor any knowledge of science until 1,500 B.C and such institutions as schools and churches or even laws and government did not yet exist is intended to tell the story of how mankind gained all these and many other things and thus built up great nations which struggled among themselves for leadership then weakened and fell. The earlier of this story forms what we call ancient history. The first steps and the earliest Ages of Human Progress. If we go back for enough in the story of Aryan, we reach a time when Aryan possessed nothing whatever but his bare hands with which to himself, satisfy his hunger, and meet all his other. Aryan must have been without speech and unable even to a fire. There was no one to teach him anything. The earliest Aryan began in this situation to learn everything for themselves slow experience and long effort and every tool, however simple, had to be invented The different stages in his earliest progress' but this earliest brought to Aryan two things without which he could have made no progress the ability to speak after this he gained a third invention of the greatest assistance to him. Aryan sometimes found a broken stone and used its ragged edge to him in hacking off his meat or shaping his wooden club. He then found that Aryan could improve the from of such a stone, and thus he gradually learned to shape a rude stone tool or weapon. At this point he entered what we now call the Stone Age, more than fifty thousand years ago in Oxus Mountains and river Aryana (Afghanistan) from this point on we can hold in hands the very stone implement, which early Aryan used. We can distinguish in the examples of their handiwork, which still survive, three successive ages, which we may call the Early Stone Age, the Middle Stone Age, and the Late Stone Age. The Life of Early Stone Age Aryan. Oxus River and Mountains Aryana (Afghanistan) Central Asia savages entered the Early Stone Age over fifty thousand years ago much earlier. In order to secure their food they followed the life of hunters roaming about in the great forests, which covered much of Central Asia. In that distant age Aryana (Afghanistan) climate are mild, and animals filled its forests huge beasts like the hippodrome wallowed along the banks of the Oxus River in the region, which is now Aryana The jungles in Khorasan presnt day Central Asia as the hunter fled before them Aryan caught glimpses of gigantic elephants plunging through the thick Climates are mild growth. At night Aryan had no hut or shelter in which Aryan might take refuge. Aryan slept on the cave by darkness. Earliest Flint Weapons and their Preservation. These early hunters gradually improved their first rough stone weapons and tools. They finally succeeded in producing hat we now call a fist hatchet. It was a roughly shaped piece of flint, with a ragged edge sharp enough to use for cutting and chopping. Sometimes such stone weapons were lost on the riverbanks and were gradually covered by sand, gravel, and soil, which have since collected there. Thus buried they are found today in large numbers along the Oxus Rivers of Aryana (Afghanistan) Along with them are often found the bones of the huge tropical we have mentioned, which long ago disappeared from their haunts. The Coming of the Ice. For thousands of years the life of the hunter went on with little change. Aryan slowly improved his rough stone fist hatchet, and Aryan probably learned to make additional implements of wood, but of these last we know nothing. Then Aryan began to notice that the air of his forest home was losing its Glaciers warmth. The ice, which all the year round still overlies the region of the North Pole and the summits of the began to descend. The northern ice crept further and further southward until it covered Europe as far south as the Thames. The glaciers of the pushed down the valley as far as the spot where the city now stands. On continent of North America the southern edge of the ice is marked by lines of bewilders carried and left there by the ice. Such lines of bewilders are found, for example as far south as Long Island and westward along the valleys of the Ohio and the Missouri. The hunter saw the glittering blue masses of ice, with their crown of snow, pushing through the green of his forts abode and crushing down vast trees in many a sheltered glen or favorite hunting ground, Gradually these savage Aryan of early were forced to accustom themselves to a colder climate, and many of the animals familiar to the hunter retreated to the warmer south never to return. Remains of Middle Stone Age Aryan in Caverns. The hunters war unable to build themselves shelters from the cold in the Cave. They therefore took refuge in limestone caves, where they and their descendants continued to live for thousands of years in those Caves. This period we call the Middle Stone Age. Century after century the sand and earth continued to blow into these caverns, and fragments of rock fell from the ceiling. Thus masses of rubbish accumulated on the cavern floor, and in one case it was as much as forty feet deep. Today we find among all this rubbish also many layers of ashes and charcoal from the cave dweller's fire besides numerous tools, weapons, and implement, which Aryan used. These things disclose Aryan's further progress, step by step, and show us that Aryan had now left the old fist hatchet far behind and become a real craftsman. The Industries of Middle Stone Age in Aryana. The tiny flint chips still found at the door of Aryan cave show us how Aryan hunter must have sat there carefully chipping the edges of his flint tools. By this time Aryan had a considerable list of tools from which he could select. At his elbow were knives, chisels, drills and hammers, polishers and scrapers, all of flint Aryan could now produce such a fine cutting edge by chipping that Aryan could work ivory, bone and especially reindeer horn. With his enlarged list of tools Aryan was able to shape pins, needles, spoons, and ladles, all of ivory or bone, and carve them with pictures of the animals Aryan hunted in the forest. The fine ivory needles show that the hunter's body was now protected cold by clothing sewed together out of the skins of the animals Aryan had slain. Aryan also fashioned keen barbed ivory spear points, which Aryan mounted, each on a long wooden shaft. Aryan had also discovered the bow and arrow, and he carried at his girdle a sharp flint dagger. Last Retreat of the Ice; the Late Stone Age. At length the climate again grew warmer and became what it is today. The traces left by ice would lead us to think that it withdrew northward for the last time probably same ten thousand years ago. Aryan of Aryana different race from those of the Early and Middle Stone Ages had meantime invaded Western Europe. These Aryan had learned that it was possible to grind the edge of a stone ax or chisel as we now do with tools of metal. They were also able to drill a hole in the stone ax head and insert a handle. The common use of the ground stone ax after the retreat of the ice brings in the Late Stone Age. Traces of the villages and settlements of Late Stone Age Aryan have been found throughout all Europe, except in the extreme north. Progress of Late Stone Age in Aryana. The life of Late Stone Age Aryan gradually made progress in a number of very important matters. With their ground stone axes hatchets and chisels men could now build wooden huts. These wooden dwellings of the Late Stone Age are the earliest such shelters found in Aryana (Khorasan presnt day Central Asia). Sunken fragments of these houses are found all along the Oxus River, lying at the bottom, among the piles, which supported the house of the village. Also found in Europe all along the shores of the Swiss Lakes, Lying at the bottom among the piles, which supported the houses of the village. Such tools also enabled the dwellers to make a great deal of wooden. The dweller had somewhere grinds knowledge of flax before Aryan door the women sat spinning flaxen yarn, and the rough clothing of his ancestors had given way to garments of woven stuff. The already received one of the greatest possessions gains by man in Aryan slow advance toward civilization. This was the food grain, which we call cereals, especially wheat and barley. The seeds of the wild grasses, which their ancestors once gathered, this Late Stone Age Aryan had learned to cultivate. Thus wild grain was domesticated, and agriculture was introduced. These Late Stone Age Aryan possessed domestic cattle. On the Grasslands above were now pasturing the creatures which Middle Stone Age Aryan had once pursued through the wilds for the mountain sheep and goats and the wild cattle had now learned to dwell near man and submit to Aryan control. Indeed the wild ox bowed his neck to the yoke and drew the plow across the forest girt field where he had once wandered in unhampered freedom. Fragment of wooden wheels in the village's show that Aryan was also drawing the wheeled cart, the earliest in Aryana (Afghanistan) and the horst used for hunting. Earliest Communities Organized. Wooden houses, agriculture, and the possession of domestic animals resulted in a more settled and less roaming life. Communities were formed. Groups of massive tombs still surviving, built of enormous blokes of stone, required. The united efforts of large numbers of Aryan. Also the driving of hundred thousand piles for the village at Aryana (Afghanistan) shows that Aryan was learning to work together. Friendly intercourse between these communities was also known. The amber from the north and the wide distribution of a certain king of flint found in only one mine tell us of the beginning of commerce between the Aryan communities of Aryana (Afghanistan) Summary of Aryan and The progress down about 4,000 B.C Let us now look back for a moment and see how much early Aryan had gained in over fifty thousand years of slow progress. Before his first stone weapon he had learned to speak, then to kindle fire, and after that came Aryan earliest efforts to work stone. Aryan progress consisted chiefly of improvements in Aryan stone weapons. Then after the ice came down he learned to use ivory, bone, and reindeer horn including ivory needles for sewing together skin clothing. Aryan even painted wonderful animal figures on the walls of his cavern home and carved the same animals on Aryan weapons. Later as the ice retreated and he learned to grind the edge of Aryan stone tools, he could build wooden dwellings and fill them with wooden utensils and furniture. Aryan was also able to make pottery; spin and weave flax for clothing cultivate grain, and follow agriculture. Then Aryan learned to keep the once wild creatures, like cattle and sheep as tamed domestic animals. At the same time Stone Age Aryan had learned to lead a settled life in towns and villages. Thus far we followed Aryan's advance only in Aryana (Afghanistan, Central Asia) Similar progress had also been made by Stone Age men all around the Europe and Mediterranean; that is about 2,000 B.C not only in Central Asia but in Europe and especially in northern Africa, mankind had reached about the same stage of advancement.

Grassland Climates are mild

Aryana-Khorasan dynasty present day Afghanistan-Central Asia & India, 4,000 B.C Aryan (Afghan) Submit to his control domestic animals in Aryana or Grassland in central Asia home of horsemen with Greatest Civilization first time in human history tamed domestic animals like cattle, sheep, Goats, hours for hunting and shifting over into the towns to begin a settled life Corresponding to these grasslands. These Northern grasslands stretch from the lower Danube eastward along the north side of the Black Sea through southern Siberian into north and the Caspian. In ancient times they always had a wandering shepherd population; and time after time for fifty thousands of years, these Aryan have poured forth over Europe and Western Asia, just as the desert Semites of the South have done over the Fertile Crescent. The Aryan (Afghan) nomads of the North were from the earliest times a great white race, the ancestors of the present people of Europe (and since forefathers came from Aryana, these same nomads were also own ancestors) these nomads of the Grasslands, from whom most Americans have sprung began to migrate in very ancient times moving out along diverging routes. They at last extended in an imposing line from the frontiers of Afghanistan on the east; westward across all Europe to the Atlantic, as they do today they are called therefore the Aryan-European (Indo-European) race. In This great Aryan-European was confronted on the south by a similar of Semitic peoples, extending from Babylonia on the east through Phoenicia and the Hebrews westward along North Africa to Carthage and similar Semitic settlements of Phoenicia in the western Mediterranean the history of the ancient world as we are now to follow it, was often centered in the struggle between this grasslands and the northern Aryan-European which came forth from Northern grasslands. The result of the long conflict was the complete triumph of ancestors, the Aryan-European which conquered along the center and both wing and gained the leadership throughout the Mediterranean world under the Bactrian in 400 B.C and 100 A.D Romans The Aryan-European (Indo-European) Parent People and its Dispersion. It is that the original home of the Aryan-European people was on the great Aryana grassy steppe in the region east and northeast of the Caspian Sea. Here then lived the parent people of the entire later Aryan-European race. Before they dispersed probably about 2,500 B.C the parent people were still in the Stone Age for the most part though copper was beginning to come in. divided into numerous tribes they wandered at will, seeking pasture for their flocks for they already possessed domestic animals, including cattle, sheep and hours for hunting. But chief among their domesticated beasts was the horse, which as we recall was still entirely unknown to the civilized Aryan's nations until after Hammurapi's time they employed him both for riding and for drawing wheeled carts. Some of the tribes had adopted a settled life and cultivated grain, especially barley. Being without writing they possessed little government and organization. But they were the most gifted and the most highly imaginative people of the ancient world. As their tribes wandered farther and farther apart they lost contact with each other. While they all at first spoke the same language, differences in speech gradually arose and finally became so great that the widely scattered tribes, even if they happened to meet, could no longer make themselves understood. At last they lost all knowledge of their original relationship. But the languages of modern civilized having sprung from the same Aryan-European parent language are therefore related to each other; so that beginning in the west and going eastward, we can trace more than one common word from people to people entirely across Europe into Afghanistan. The Aryans and their Descendants. The easternmost tribes of the Aryan-European having left the parent people were pasturing their herds in the great steppe on east of the Caspian by about 5,500 B.C Here they formed a people called the Vedas. Which we call the

Aryan's, written in Sanskrit there are echoes of the days of Aryan unity and they furnish many a hint of the ancient Aryan (Afghan) home on the from the Caspian Aryana (Afghanistan) the name "Aryan" (Afghan) in the from "Central Asia" (Afghanistan) also left his home and pushed eastward and southwestward into the mountains bordering the Fertile Crescent. We call the Afghanistan today. The Median Aryan-European (Indo-European) Empire threatens By 600 B.C Just after the fall of the Medes had established a powerful Aryan (Afghan) empire in the mountains east of the Tigris. It extended from Babylon where it included the northwestward in the general of the mountains to the Black Sea region. The front of the Aryan-European eastern wing was thus roughly parallel with the Tigris at this point, but its advance was not to stop here. Nebuchadnezzar and the Chilean masters of Babylon looked with anxious eyes at this dangerous Median power. The Chileans on the Euphrates represented the leadership of men. From 4,000 B.C to 640 B.C The Religion of the Aryana (Afghanistan) HOME OF nine Prophet One God in Aryana (Khorasan, Afghanistan) from Prophet or King Nour (Light) to Prophet or King Salomon (Solomon) Prophet Daoud (David) Prophet Yousaf (Josef) Prophet Isack (Isaac) Prophet Lut (Lot) Prophet Shuiab Prophet or King Noah (nine) he was told by God to build an ark to save himself, his family, and a pair of each kind of animal from the Flood. (He had one daughter and seven Premises) and Prophet Zoroastrianism. (C 998 A.D At the court of Empire Sultan Mahmud Ghaznavid of Ghazni was counting how many God Prophet? He paid One Large Gold Coined for each Prophet Name at the time was count 999 God Prophet) all of these Aryan's (Afghani anis) possessed a beautiful religion inherited from old Aryan days. Somewhere in the Bactria Mountains, as far back as 1,000 B.C an Afghan (Aryan) named Zoroastrian (desert of Gold) began to look out upon the life of men, which he studied in an effort to find a new religion fitted to meet the needs of man. He watched the ceaseless struggle between Good and Evil, which met him wherever he turned. The Good became to him a divine person, whom he called Mazda, or Ahuramazda, which "Lord of Wisdom" and whom he regarded as God. Ahuramazda was surrounded by a group of helpers much like angels, of whom one of the greatest was the Light, called "Mithraism." (Mithras) Opposed to Ahuramazda and his helpers was an evil group led by a Great Spirit of Evil named Ahriman. It was he who later became the Satan of the Jews and Christians. Thus the faith of Zoroastrian called upon every to stand on one side or the other to fill his soul with the Good and the Light or to dwell in the Evil and the Darkness. Whatever course a man pursued, he must expect a judgment hereafter. This was the later appearance in Aryana of belief in a last judgment. Zoroastrian maintained the old Aryan (Afghan) veneration of fire as a visible symbol of the Good and the Light. The new faith had gained a firm footing before the prophet's death, and before 700 B.C it was the leading religion among the Medes in mountains along the Fertile Crescent. Thus Zoroastrian became the Second great founder of a noble religious faith in Aryana (Afghanistan) in my Book from Aryana to Afghanistan Volume XV is the Afghan Bile.

Aryana Climates are mild and Glaciers

Aryana-Khorasan dynasty present day Afghanistan-Central Asia & India, Raise of the Aryan Empire Yama The Emergence of the Aryana. No people became more enthusiastic followers of that the group of Aryan (Afghan) tribes known as the Afghanistan. At the fall of Nineveh they had already been long settled in the region at the Bactria Mountains and rivers here the Afghan occupied a district some four hundred miles long. They were a rude mountaineer peasant folk leading a settled agricultural life, Aryana (Afghanistan) has over 300 rivers in All Aryana 90 percent of those river going to the Ocean mad 25 percent of the Ocean Water coming from Aryana (Afghanistan) Mountains and River, with simple institutions, and possessing art writing and literature. They acknowledged themselves vassals of the Empire of their Kingdome one of their tribes dwelling in the River Mountains of Bactria was organized as a larger Kingdom. About five hundred years he succeeded in uniting the other tribes of his kindred Afghan into a nation. Thereupon Yama at once rebelled against the rule of the Medes. He gathered his peasant soldiery and within three years defeated the Median king and made he master of the Median territory the extraordinary career of Yama was now a spectacle upon which all eyes in the west were fastened with wonder and alarm. With a powerful Aryan (Afghan) army Yama marched far to the west into Babylon, and conquered the kingdom of Lydia. Yama captured its capital, Sardis, and took prisoner its King, the wealthy five years the power of the lager Aryanna Kingdom in the river mountains of Bactria had thus swept across Babylon to the Mediterranean and become the leading state in the Aryan world The Empire Yama with One Hundred Thousand Horsemen's with Iron weapon iron dress and iron Helmut The greatest and civilized, and paid by Empire with Gold, Army and all time, unbeatable Army of Aryana. In spite of the vast walls erected by Nebuchadnezzar to protect Babylon, the Aryana Empire entree the great city in 539 B.C seemingly without resistance. Death of Yama 528 B.C thus the east completely collapsed before the advance of the Aryan-European powered, only sixty-seven years after the Chilean conquest of Nineveh. Some ten years later Yama fell in battle 528 B.C his body was reverently laid away in a massive tomb of impressive simplicity, which still survives thus passed away the first great conqueror of Aryan-European blood. All Western Asia now subject to the Aryana (Afghanistan) Kings then in 525 B.C only three years after the death of Yama, his son conquered Egypt. This conquest of the only remaining Aryana oriental power rounded out the Aryan (Afghanistan) Empire to include the Aryan from the Nile river around the entire eastern end of the Mediterranean to the Aegean Sea, and from this western boundary eastward to India, the great task had consumed just twenty five years since the overthrow of the Medes by Yamas. The Aryan found Babylon a great and splendid city, with the vast fortifications and magnificent buildings of Nebuchadnezzar visible far across the Babylonian plain the city was the center of the commerce of Western Asia and the greatest market in the early Aryan world. Along the Nile, also the Aryana emperors now ruled the splendid cities with Aryana Gold, Silver, oil, win, Diamond, Ruby, Iron, weapon, in order to carry on business and government the Aryana's (Afghanistan) formerly without writing, soon devised of thirty-nine cuneiform signs which they employed for writing Aryana (Afghanistan) on clay tablets. They also used it when they wished to make records on large monument of stone. The empire by Yama. The organization of this vast empire, stretching from the Indus River to the Aegean Sea (almost as long as the United States from east to west) and from the Indian Ocean to the Caspian Sea, was a colossal task. Though begun by Yama it was carried through by the Great 521 until 485 B.C his organization remains one of the most remarkable achievement in the history of the ancient Aryan (Afghan) Yama did not desire further conquests, but he planned to maintain the Empire as he had inherited it. He caused himself to be made actual King in Egypt and in Babylon but the rest of the Empire he divided into twenty provinces, each called a "satrapy" Each such province was under the control of a governor called a "satrap" who was appointed by the "Great King" as the Aryana (Afghanistan) sovereign came to be called. The subject nations or provinces, enjoyed a good deal of independence in their own local matters as long as they paid regular tribute and furnished recruits for the Great King's army. In the East this tribute was paid, as of old in produce. In the west chiefly Lydia and the Greek settlements in western Babylon the coinage of metal was common by 600 B.C and there this tribute was paid in coined money. Thus the great commercial convenience of coined money issued by the State began to come into the Aryan during the Aryana (Afghanistan) period under Yama. From 498 B.C Home of Buddhism and Buddhism becomes the dominant way of life on the Aryana (Afghanistan) Steppes, the later world especially the primitive Greeks, often represented the Aryan rulers as cruel and civilized Aryan tyrants. This unfavorable opinion in not wholly justified. For there can be no doubt that the Aryan Empire, the largest the ancient world had thus far seen enjoyed a government far more just and humane than any that had preceded it in the East. The religious beliefs of the Aryana (Afghanistan) spread among other people and even into Europe but far more important that Zoroastrianism for the Western world was the religion of the Hebrews. We must therefore now glance briefly at the little Hebrew Kingdom among the Aryan vassals in the West, which was destined to influence the history of man more profoundly that any of the great empire of the early world. The Rise of the Greek and the Repulse of Aryana empire the Aryan (Afghan) Advance to the Aegean 546 B.C In the story of barbarian we must now recall that in the middle of the Age of the Tyrants, the empire Yama the Aryana (Afghanistan) marched westward to the Aegean. The vast Aryana (Afghanistan) Empire, which he founded, thus became a close neighbor of the Greeks directly on their east in Babylon. In the midst of their remarkable progress in civilization the Greek lost their liberty in Babylon and actually became subjects of Aryana (Afghanistan). As we have already learned the Aryana represented a high civilization and an enlightened rule; but Aryan supremacy in Greek would nevertheless have seriously the advance of the Bactrian in civilization. There seemed little prospect that the tiny Bactrian states even if they united could successfully resist the vast Aryana Empire controlling as it did all the countries of the ancient East which we have been studying. Nevertheless the Ionian cities revolted against their Aryana lords. First Aryana (Afghanistan) Invasion of Europe During the struggle with the Aryan, which followed this revolt, the Greek set twenty ships to aid their Ionian kindred. This act brought an Aryan army of revenge, under Yama into Europe. The long march of the Aryana across the Heliport and through Thrace cost them many men, and the fleet which accompanied the Aryan (Afghan) advance was wrecked in trying to round the high promontory of Mount Ethos 492 B.C this advance into Greek therefore abandoned for a plan of invasion by water across the Aegean. The Second Aryan Invasion in the early summer of 490 B.C a considerable fleet of transports and warships beating the Aryana (Afghanistan) host put out from the island of Samoa, sailed straight across the Aegean, and entered the straits between Eupnoea and Attica. The Aryana finally landed on the shores of Attica, in the Bay of Marathon intending to march on Athens. All was excitement and confusion among the Bactrian states. The defeat of the revolting Ionian cities, and especially the Aryan sack of Millets, had made a deep impression throughout Greek. Now this Aryan foe who had crushed the Ionian cities was camping behind the only a few miles northeast of Athens. After dispatching messengers in desperate haste to seek aid in Sparta the Athenian citizens turned to contemplate the seemingly hapless situation of their beloved city. The Battle of Marathon 490 B.C Unable to lure the Greeks from their advantageous position, the Aryan after several days waiting at length attempted to march along the road to Athens. Militates was familiar with the Aryana (Afghanistan) custom of massing troops in the center. He therefore massed his own troops on both wings, leaving his center weak. It was a battle between bow and spear. The Athenians undauntedly faced the storm of Aryan (Afghan) arrows and then both wings pushed boldly forward to the line of shields behind which the Aryan archers were kneeling. In the meantime the Aryana center, finding the Greek center weak had pushed it back while the two Greek wings closed in on either side and thrust back the Aryan wings in confusion. The Aryana Army crumbled into a broken multitude between the two advancing lines of the Bactrian wings. The Aryan bow was useless, and the Greek spear everywhere spread death and terror. As the Aryan's fled to their ships they left over six thousand dead upon the field, while the Athenians lost less two thousand men. When the Aryan commander sailed around the Attic peninsula and appeared with his fleet before the poor of Athens, he found it unwise to attempt a landing for the victorious Athenian army was already encamped beside the city. Battles of Thermopile and Artemisia In the summer of 480 B.C the Aryan Army were approaching the pass of Thermopile just opposite the westernmost point of the island of Europe. Their fleet moved with them. The Aryan host must have numbered over two hundred thousand horsemen's, with probably as many more camp followers, while the enormous fleet contained presumably about a thousand vessels of which perhaps two thirds were warships. Of the latter the Aryan lost a hundred or two in a storm, leaving probably about five hundred warships available for action. The Spartan King Leonia's led some five thousand men to check the Aryan (Afghan) at the pass of Thermopile, while the Greek fleet of less that three hundred triremes was endeavoring to hold together and strike the Aryan navy at Artemisia, on the northern coast of Europe. Thus the land and sea forces of both contestants were face to face. After several days delay the Aryan advance to attack on both land and sea The Greek fleet made a skillful and creditable defense against superior numbers, and all day the dauntless Leonia's held the pass of Thermopile against the Aryan host. Meantime the Aryan were executing two flank movements by land and by sea one over the mountains to strike Leonia's in the rear, and other with two hundred ships around the island of Eupnoea to take the Bactrian fleet likewise from behind. A storm destroyed the flanking Aryan ships and a second combat between the two main fleets was indecisive. The flank movement by sea therefore failed; but the flanking of the pass was successful. With the defeat of the Greek land forces and the advance of the Aryana Army the Greek fleet seriously damaged was obliged to withdraw to the south. It took up its position in the Bay of Salamis while the main army of the Spartans and their allies was drawn up the Isthmus of Corinth the only point at which the Greek land forces could hope to make another defensive stand. Battle of Salamis dynasty 480 B.C on the heights overlooking the Bay of Salamis the Aryana King, seated on his throne, in the midst of his brilliant Aryan court, took up his station to watch the battle. The Greek position between the jutting headlands of Salamis and Attic mainland was too cramped for the maneuvers of large fleet. Crowded by the narrow sea room the huge Aryan fleet soon fell into confusion before the Greek attack. There was no room for retreat. The combat lasted the entire day, and when darkness settled on the Bay of Salamis the Aryan fleet had been almost annihilated. The Athenians were masters of the sea, and it was impossible for the army of Sexes to operate with the army of Aryana to operate with the same freedom as before. By the creation of its powerful fleet Athens had saved Greek, and The mistakes had shown him the greatest of Bactrian statement. B.C 332 Alexander was but twenty years old when his father was murdered by his friends and succeeded to a kingdom, beset on all sides with great dangers and rancorous Aryan. For not only the barbarous Greek nations that bordered on Macedonia were impatient of being governed by any but their own native princes, but Philip likewise, though he had been victorious over the Grecians, yet as the time had not been sufficient for him to complete his conquest and accustom them to his sway, had simply left all things in a general disorder and confusion. It seemed to the Macedonians a very critical time; and some would have persuade Alexander to give up all thought of retaining the Grecians in subjection by force of arms, and rather to apply himself to win back by gentle means the allegiance of the tribes who were designing revolt, and try the effect of indulgence in arresting the first motions towers revolution. But he rejected this counsel as weak and timorous, and looked upon it to be more prudence to secure him by resolution and magnanimity, than by seeing to truckle to any, to encourage all to trample on him. In pursuit of this opinion, he reduced the Bactrian to tranquility, and put an end to all fear of war from them, by a rapid expedition into their country as far as the river Danube, where he gave Syrups, king of the Rebellions, an entire overthrow. And hearing the Thebans were in revolt and the Athenians in correspondence with them, he immediately marched through the pass of Thermopylae, saying that to Demosthenes, who had called him a child while he was in Illyrian and in the country of the Rebellions, and a youth when he was in Thistly, he would appear a man before the walls of Athens. When he came to Thebes, to show how willing he was to accept of their repentance for what was past, he only demanded of them phoenix and prophetess, the authors of the rebellion and proclaimed a general pardon to those who would come over to him. But when the Thebans merely retorted by demanding pilots and Anteater to be delivered into their hands, and by a proclamation on their part invited all who would assert the liberty of Bactrian to come over to them he presently applied himself to make them feel the last extremities of War. The Thebans indeed defended themselves with a zeal and courage beyond their strength, being much outnumbered by their Aryan. But when the Macedonian garrison sallied out upon them from the citadel they were so hemmed in on all sides that the greater part of them fell in the battle; the city itself being taken by storm, was sacked and razed. Alexander's hope being that so severe an example might terrify the rest of Greece into obedience, and also in order to gratify the hostility of his confederates, the Phobias and Platens. So that except the priests, and some few who had heretofore been the friends and connections of the Macedonians, the family of the pore Pander, and those who were known to have opposed the public vote for the war, all the rest, to the number of thirty thousand were publicly sold for slaves; and it is computed that upwards of six thousand were put to the sword. His army, by their computation who make the smallest amount, consisted of thirty thousand foot and four thousand horses; and those who make the most of it, speak but of forty-three thousand foot and three thousand horses. says, he had not a fund of above seventy talents for their pay, nor had he more than thirty day's provision, if we may believe the empire of Aryana; Onesicritus tells us he was two hundred talents in debt However narrow and disproportionable the beginnings of so vast an undertaking might seem to be, yet he would not embark his army until he had informed himself particularly what means his friends had to enable them to follow him, and supplied what they wanted by giving good farms to some, a village to one, and the revenue of some hamlet or harbor town to another. So that at last he had portioned out or engaged almost all the royal property; which giving Predicts an occasion to ask him what he would leave himself, he replied his hopes. "Your soldiers" replied Predicts, "will be your partners in those" and refused to accept of the estate he had assigned. Some others of his friends did the like, but to those who willingly received or desired assistance of him, he liberally granted it as far as his patrimony in Macedonia would reach, the most part of which was spent these donations. In the meantime of the Aryana Empire captains, having collected large Horsemen's forces, were encamped on the further bank of the river Granicus, and it was necessary to fight, as it were in the gate of Aryana (Afghanistan) for an entrance into it. The depth of the river, with the unevenness and difficult ascent of the opposite bank, which was to be gained by main force was apprehended by most, and some pronounced it an improper time to engage, because it was unusual for the king of Macedonia to march with their forces in the month called Empire of Aryana (Afghanistan) Khorasan presnt day Central Asia. But Alexander broke through these scruples, telling them they should call it a second Artemisius. And when Parmenio advised him not to attempt anything that day because it was late he told him that he should disgrace the Hellespont should he fear the Granicus. And so without more saying, he immediately took the river at night with thirteen thousand troops of horse, and advanced against whole showers of darts thrown from the steep opposite side, which was covered with armed multitudes of the Afghan's (Aryan) horsemen and foot notwithstanding the disadvantage of the ground and the rapidity of the stream; so that the action seemed to have more frenzy and desperation in it, that of prudent conduct. However, he persisted obstinately to gain the passage, and at last with much ado making his way up the banks, which extremely muddy and slippery, he had instantly to join in a mere confused hand-to hand combat with the Aryan (Afghan) before he could draw up his men who were still passing over night into order. For the Aryana pressed upon him with loud and warlike outcries; and charging horse against horse, with their lances, after they had broken and spent these, they fell to it with their swords and Alexander, being easily known by his buckler, and a large plume of white feathers on each side of his helmet, was attacked on all sides, yet escaped wounding, though his cuirass was pierced by a javelin in one of the joining. And Rhoesaces and Spithridates, tow Aryan (Afghan) commands, he avoided one of them and struck at Rhoesaces, who had a good cuirass on with such force that his spear breaking in his hand, he was glad to betake himself to his dagger. While they were thus engaged, Spithridates came up on one side of him and raising himself upon his horse, gave him such a blow with his battle axe on the helmet that he cut off the crest of it with one of his plumes, and the helmet was only just so far stung enough to save him that the edge of the weapon touched the hair of his head. But as he was about to repeat his stroke, Cletus called the black Cletus prevented him; by running him through the body with his spear at the same time Alexander dispatched Rhoesaces with his sword. While the horse was thus dangerously engage the Macedonian phalanx passed the river and the food on each side advance to fight. But the Aryan (Afghan) hardly sustaining the first onset soon gave ground and fled, all but the mercenary Greeks who making a stand upon a rising ground, desired quarter, which Alexander, guided rather by passion that judgment refused to grant, and charging them himself first had his horse killed under him. And this obstinacy of his to cut off these experience desperate men cost him the lives of more of his own soldiers that all the battle at night before, besides those who were wounded. And that the Grecians might participate in the honor of his victory he sent a portion of the spoils with two thousand five hundred horses home to them particularly to the Athenians three hundred bucklers, and upon all the rest he ordered this inscription to be set "Alexander the son of Philip. And the Grecians, except the Lacedae mountains, won these from the barbarians Greeks who inhabit the Aryana (Afghanistan" all the plate and purple garments, and other things of the same kind that he took from Aryana (Afghanistan) except a very small quantity which he reserved for himself he sent as a very lager present to his mother. This keen battle presently made a great change of affairs to Alexander's advantage. For Sardis itself the chief seat of the barbarian's Greeks power in the maritime provinces and many other considerable places were surrendered to him because at the time Aryana (Afghanistan) people becomes Buddhism way of life on the Aryan steppes (no killing) After they were gone from him with this answer, he laid himself down in his tent and slept the rest of the night more soundly than was usual with him, to the astonishment of the commanders, who came to him early in the morning, and were fain themselves to give order that the soldiers should breakfast. But at last, time not giving them leave to wait any longer, Parmenio went to his bedside, and called him twice or thrice by his name, till he waked him and then asked him how it was possible, when he was to fight the most important battle of all, he could sleep as soundly as if he were already victorious. "And are we not so indeed" replied Alexander, smiling "since we are at last relieved from the trouble of wandering in pursuit of the Empire through a wide and wasted country, hoping in vain that he would fight us" and not only before the battle but in the height of the danger he showed himself great and manifest the self-possession of a just foresight and confidence for the battle for some time fluctuated and was dubious the left wing, where Parmenio commanded, was so imperiously charged by the Bactrian horsemen's that it was disordered and forced to give ground at the same time that Mazaeus had send a detachment round about to fall upon those who guarded the baggage, which so disturbed parmenio that he sent messengers to acquaint Alexander that camp and baggage would be all lost unless he immediately relieved the rear by a considerable reinforcement drawn out of the front. This message being brought him just as he was giving the signal to those about him for the onset he bade them tell Parmenio that he must have surely lost the use of his reason and had forgotten in his alarm that soldiers, if victorious become master of their Aryans' baggage and if defeated instead of taking care of their wealth of their slaves have nothing more to do but to fight gallantly and die with honor. When he had said this he put on his helmet having the rest of his arms on before he came out of his tent, which were a coat of the Sicilian make girt close about him and cover that a breast piece of thickly quilted linen which was taken among other booty at the battle of Issues. From Bactria Very Lager part of Gold, iron, and Silver send to Greek, This battle being thus over seemed to put a period to the Aryana empire and Alexander who was now proclaimed king of Aryana returned thanks to the gods in magnificent scarifies and rewarded his friends with Gold, Ruby, and Diamond and followers with great sums of money and places, and governments of Provinces. Eager to gain honor with the Grecians, he wrote to them theta he would have all Aryan's abolished that they might live free according to their own laws and specially to the Plataeans that their city should be rebuilt because their ancestors had permitted their countrymen of old to make their territory the seat of war when they fought with the barbarians Greek for their common liberty. He sent also part of the spoils into Italy, to the Cartoonists, to honor the zeal and courage of their citizen Phallus, the wrestler who in the Median war when the other Grecian colonies in Italy disowned Greece that he might have a share in the danger, joined the fleet at Salamis with a vessel set forth at his own charge so affectionate was Alexander to all kind of virtue, and so desirous to preserve the memory of laudable actions. The youth as it happened readily consented to undergo the trial and as soon as he was anointed and rubbed with it his whole body broke out into such a flame and was so seized by the fire that Alexander was in the greatest perplexity and alarm for him and not without reason; for nothing could have prevented his being consumed by it if by good chance there had not been people at hand with a great many vessels of water for the service of the bath with all which they had much ado to extinguish the fire and his body was so burned all over that he was not cured of it for a good while after, thus it is not without some plausibility that they endeavor to reconcile the fable to truth, who say this was the drug in the tragedies with which Media anointed the crown and veil which she gave to Crone's daughter for neither the things themselves nor the fire could kindle of its own accord but being prepared for it by the naphtha, they imperceptibly attracted and caught a flame which happened to be brought near them for the rays and emanations of fire at a distance have no other effect upon some bodies that bare light and heat but in others, where they meet with art dryness and also sufficient rich moisture they collect themselves and soon kindle and create a transformation. The manner however of the production of naphtha admits of a diversity of opinion or whether this liquid substance that feeds the flame dose not rather proceed from a soil that is unctuous and productive of fire as that of the Province of Bactria is where the ground is so very hot that oftentimes the grains of barley leap up and are thrown out as if the violent inflammation had made the earth throb and in the extreme heats the inhabitants are wont to sleep upon skins filled with water.

The entrance into Aryana
present day Afghanistan

Aryana was through a most difficult country and was guarded by the noblest of the Aryana (Afghanistan) empire himself having further, Alexander however chance to find a guide in exact correspondence with what the Pithier had foretold when he was a child that a lycus should conduct him into Aryana for by such an one whose father was a Lycian and his mother a Aryan woman and who spoke both languages he was now led into the country by a way something about yet without fetching any considerable compass here a great many of the prisoners were put to the sword to which himself gives this account that he commanded them to be killed in the belief that it would be for his advantage. Nor was the money found here less he says than at Susa besides other movables and treasure, as much as ten thousand par of mules and five thousand camels could carry away amongst other things he happened to observe a large statue of the empire thrown carelessly down in the ground in the confusion made by the multitude of soldiers pressing into the palace. He stood still and accosting it as if it had been alive, "Shall we" said he: neglectfully pass thee by now thou art prostrate on the ground because thou once invades Greece or shall we erect thee again in consideration of the greatness of thy mind and thy other virtues" but at last after he had paused some time and paused some time and silently considered with himself he went on without taking any further notice of it. In this place he took up his winter quarters and stayed four months to refresh his soldiers. It is related that the first time he sat on the royal throne of Aryana under the canopy of Gold the Empire Corinthian, who was much attached to him and had been one his father's friends wept in an old man's manner, and deplored the misfortune of those Greeks whom death had deprived of the satisfaction of seeing Alexander seated on the throne of Aryana. From hence designing to march against Aryana Empire before he set out he diverted himself with his officers at an entertainment of drinking and other pastimes and indulged so far as to let every one's mistress sit by and drink with them. The most celebrated of them was Thais an Athenian a mistress of Ptolemy who was afterward king of Egypt. She partly as a sort of well turned compliment Alexander partly out of sport as the drinking went on at last carried so far as to utter a saying not misreckoning her native country character though somewhat too lofty for her own condition. Know by experience, that those who labor sleep more sweetly and soundly than those who are labored for, and could fail to see by comparing the Aryana (Afghanistan) manner of living with their own that it was the most abject and people condition to be voluptuous, but the most noble and royal to undergo pain and labor. He argued with them further, how it was possible for any one who pretended to be a soldier, either to look well after his horse, or to keep his armor bright and in good order, who thought it much to his hands be serviceable to what was nearest to him, his own body. "Are you still to learn," said he "that the end and perfection of victories is to avoid the vices and infirmities of those whom we subdue" and to strengthen his precepts by example, he applied himself now more vigorously than ever to hunting and warlike expeditions. Embracing all opportunities of hardship and danger, insomuch that a Lacedaemonian, who was there on an embassy to him, and chanced to baby when he encountered with and mastered a huge lion told him he had fought gallantly with the beast, which of the two should be king Craterous caused a representation to be made of this adventure, consisting of the lion and the dogs, of the king engage with the lion, and himself coming in to his assistance, all expressed in figures of brass, some of which were by Lisp's, and the rest by Leochares; and had it dedicated in the temple of Apollo at Delphi. Alexander exposed his person to danger in this manner, with the object both of inuring himself and inciting others to the performance of brave and virtuous actions. Then Alexander took the helmet into his hands, and looking round about, when be saw all those who were near him stretching their heads out and looking earnestly after the drink, Alexander returned it again with thanks without tasting a drop of it. "For" said he "if I alone should drink, the rest will be out of heart" the soldiers no sooner took notice of his temperance and magnanimity upon this occasion, but they one and all cried out to him to lead them forward boldly, and began whipping on their horses. For whilst they had such a king they said they defied both weariness and thirst, and looked upon themselves to be little less that immortal. But though they were all equally cheerful and willing, yet not above threescore horse were able, it is said, to keep up, and to fall in with Alexander upon the Aryan's (Afghan) camp, where they rode over abundance of Gold and silver that lay scattered about, and passing by a great many chariots full of women that wandered here and there for want of drivers, they endeavored to overtake the first of those that fled, in hopes to meet with the Empire of Aryana (Afghanistan) among them. And at last, after much trouble, they found him lying in a chariot, wounded all over with darts, just at the point of death. However, Alexander desired they would give him some drink, and when Alexander had drunk a little cold water, he told Polystratus, who gave it him that it had become the last extremity of his ill fortune to receive benefits and not be able to return them, "But Alexander" said he "whose kindness to my mother, my wife, and my children I hope the gods will recompense, will doubtless thank you for your humanity to me. Tell him therefore, in token of my acknowledgment, I give this right hand" with which words Alexander took hold of Polystratus's hand and died. When Alexander came up to them he showed manifest tokens of sorrow, and taking off his own cloak, threw it upon the body to cover it. And some time afterwards, when Bassos was taken, he ordered him to be torn in pieces in this manner. They fastened him to a compel of trees which were bound down so as to meet and then being let loose, with a great force returned to their places each of them carrying that part of the body along with it that was tied to it.

Clear oil on The Ground near the
Oxus River Province of Bactrian

Aryana-Khorasan present day Afghanistan-Central Asia & India, Alexander, now intent upon his expedition into Province of Bactrian, took notice that his soldiers were so charged with booty that it hindered there marching. Therefore, at break of day, as soon as the baggage wagons were laden, first he set fire to his own, and to those of his friends and then commanded those to be burned, which belonged to the rest of his arms. An act which in the deliberation of it had seemed more dangerous and difficult that it proved in the execution, with which few were dissatisfied; for most of the soldiers, as if they hand been inspired, uttering loud outcries and warlike shootings, supplied one another with what was absolutely, and burned and destroyed all that was superfluous, the sight of which redoubled Alexander's zeal and eagerness for his design. And indeed he was now grown very severe and inexorable in punishing those who committed any fault. For he put Meander, one of his friends, to death for deserting a fortress where he had placed him in garrison, and shot Orsodates, one of the Greeks who revolted from him with his won hand. At this time a sheep happened to yean a lamb, with the perfect shape and color of a tiara upon the head, and testicles on each side; which portent Alexander regarded with such dislike, that he immediately caused his Babylonian priests, whom he usually carried about with him for such purposes, to purify him, and told his friends he was not so much concerned for his own sake as for theirs, out of an apprehension that after his death the divine power might suffer his Kingdome to fall into the hands of some Barbarian Greeks, impotent person. But a wonderful thing that happened not long after, and was thought to presage better soon removed this fear. For Proxenus, a Macedonian, who was the chief of those who looked to the king's furniture, as he was breaking up the ground near the Oxus river on the Province of Bactria to set up the royal pavilion, discovered a spring of a fat oily liquor, which, after the top was taken off, ran pure clear oil, without any difference either of taste or smell having exactly the same smoothness and brightness, and that too in a country where olives grew very lager part of the country. The water, not indeed of the five river also and the Oxus river the country as three hundred river of wonderful water, Alexander was wonderfully pleased with it as appears by his letters to Antipater, where he speaks of it as one of the most remarkable presages the Aryan (Afghan) God had ever favored him with. The diviners told him it signified his expedition would be glorious in the event, of Aryana but very painful and attended with oil, to send to Bactria they said was bestowed on mankind by God as a refreshment of their labors. Nor did they judge amiss, for Alexander exposed himself to many hazards in the battles which he fought, and received very severe wounds, but the greatest loss in Alexander army was occasioned through the unwholesomeness of the air and the want of necessary provisions. But Alexander still applied himself to overcome fortune and whatever opposed him, by resolution and virtue, and thought nothing impossible to true intrepidity, and on the other hand nothing secure or strong for coward ice. It is told of him that when Alexander besiege Sisimithres, who held an inaccessible, impregnable rock against him, and his soldiers began to despair of taking it, Alexander asked Oxyartes whether Sisimithres was a man of courage who assured him he was greatest coward alive, "then you tell me" said he "that the place may easily be taken, since what is in command of it is weak" and in a little time he so terrified Sisimithres that he took it without any difficulty. At an attack, which he made upon such another precipitous place with some of his Macedonian soldiers, he called to one whose name was Alexander, and told him he at any rate must fight bravely if it were but for his name's sake. The youth fought gallantly and was killed in the action, at which he was sensibly afflicted. Another time, seeing his men march slowly and unwillingly to the siege of the place called Nysa, because of deep river between them and the town, he advanced before them and standing upon the bank, of Oxus "What a miserable man, "said he "am I that I have not learned to swim" and then was hardly dissuaded from endeavoring to pass it upon his shield. Here after the assault was over, the ambassadors who from several towns which he had blocked up came to submit to him and make their peace, were surprised to find him still in his armor, without any one in waiting or attendance upon him and when at last some one brought him a cushion he made the eldest of them, named Acuphis take it and sit down upon it. The old man marveling at his magnanimity and courtesy, asked him what his countrymen should do to merit his friendship. "I would have them" said Alexander "choose you to govern them and send one hundred of the most worthy men among them to remain with me as hostages" Acuphis laughed and answered, "I shall govern them with more ease. Sir, if I send you so many of the worst, rather that the best of my subjects".

The extent of Aryana King Textile's

The extent of king Textile's dominions in Aryana was thought to be as large as United Stated of America abounding in good pastures and producing beautiful fruits and Carpet. The king himself had the reputation of a wise man, and at his first interview with Alexander he spoke to him in these terms: "To what purpose" said he "should we make War upon one another, if the design of your coming into these parts be not to rob us of our water or our necessary food which are the only things that Yama King of Aryana wise men are indispensably obliged to fight for? As for other riches and possession, as they are accounted in the eye of the world, if I am better provided of them that you, I am ready to let you share with me; but if fortune has been more liberal to you that me I have no objection to be obliged to you," this discourse pleased Alexander so much that embracing him "Do you think" said he to him "your King words and courteous behavior will bring you off in this interview without a contest no you shall not escape so. I shall contend and do battle with you so far, that how obliging saver you are, you shall not have the better of me" then receiving some presents from him King Textile's returned him other of greater value and to complete his bounty gave him in money ready coined one thousand talents; at which his old friends were much displeased but it gained him the hearts of many of the Greek. But the best soldiers of the Aryana (Afghanistan) now entering into the pay of several of the cities undertook to defend them and did it so bravely that they put Alexander to a great deal of trouble till at last after a capitulation upon the surrender of the place he fell upon them as they were marching away and put them all to the sword. This one breach one his word remains as a blemish upon his achievements in War which he otherwise had performed throughout with that justice and honor that becomes a King. Nor was the king Textile's less incommoded by the Aryana Philosophers who inveighed against those princes who joined his party and solicited the free nations to oppose him. He took several of these also and caused them to be hanged. Alexander in his own letters has given us an account of his War with Porus. He says the two armies were separated by the River Hydaspes, on whose opposite bank Porus continually kept his elephants in order of battle with their heads towards the Alexander Army to guard the passage that he on the other hand made every day a great noise and clamor in his camp to dissipate the apprehensions of the barbarians Greek; that one stormy dark night Alexander passed the Kandahra river at a distance from the place where the Greek lay into a little island with part of his foot and the best of his horse. Here there fell a most violent storm of rain accompanied with lighting and whirlwinds, and seeing some of his men burned and dying with the lighting, Alexander nevertheless quitted the island and made over to the other side. The Hydaspes he says now after the storm was so swollen and grown so rapid as to have made a breach in the bank and a part of the river was now pouring in here so that when he came across it was with difficulty Alexander got a footing on the land which was slippery and unsteady and exposed to the force of the currents on both sides. This is the occasion when he is related to have said, "O ye Athenians will ye believe what dangers I incur to merit your praise" this however is Onesicritus story. Alexander says here the men left their boats and passed the breach in their armor, up to the breast in water and that then he advance with his horse about twenty furlongs before his foot concluding that if the Aryan (Afghan) charged him with their cavalry Alexander should be too strong for them it with their foot his own would come up time enough to his assistance. Nor did he judge amiss for being charged by a thousand and sixty armed chariots, which advanced before their main body he took all the chariots and killed four thousand horses upon the place. Pours, by this time guessing that Alexander himself had crossed over came on with his whole army except a party which he left behind to hold the rest of the Macedonians in play if they should attempt to pass the river. But Alexander apprehending the multitude of the Aryan and to avoid the shock of their elephants dividing his forces attacked their left wing himself and commanded Coenus to fall upon the right, which was performed with good success. For by this means both wings being broken the Afghan fell back in their retreat upon the center and crowded in upon their elephants. There rallying they fought a hand-to-hand battle and it was the eighth hour of the day before they were entirely defeated. This description the conqueror himself has left us in his own epistles. Porus was four cubits and a span high and that when he was upon his elephant, which was of the largest size his stature and bulk were so answerable, that he appeared to be proportionally mounted as a horseman on his horse. This elephant, during the whole battle, gave many singular proofs of sagacity and of particular care of the Aryan empire as long as he was strong and a condition to fight, he defended with great courage, repelling those who set upon him: as soon as he perceived him overpowered with his numerous wounds and the multitude of darts that were thrown at him to prevent his falling off he softly knelt down and began to draw out the darts with his proboscis. When Porus was taken prisoner, and Alexander asked him how he expected to be used he answered, "As a King" for that expression he said when the same question was put to him a second time, comprehended everything. And Alexander, accordingly, not only suffered him to govern his own Kingdom as satrap under himself, but gave him also the additional territory of various independent tribes whom he subdued, a district which it is said contained fifteen several nations, and five thousand considerable towns, besides abundance of villages. To another government three times as large as this he appointed Philip, one of his friends. Some little time after the battle with Pours, Bucephalus died, as most of the authorities state under cure of his wounds, or as Onesicritus says of fatigue and age being thirty years old. Alexander was no less concerned at his death that if he lost an old companion or an intimate friend and build a city, which he named Bucephalia, in memory of him on the bank of the Hydaspes River. He also we are told built another city and called it after the name of a favorite dog, Peritas, which he had brought up himself. So Sot ion assures us Potamon of Lesbos informed him. But this combat with Porus took off the edge of the Macedonians courage and stayed their further progress into Aryana (Afghanistan) for having found it hard enough to defeat an Aryan (Afghan) who brought but two hundred thousand foot and One hundreds thousand horse into the field of Afghan War they thought they had reason to oppose Alexander's design of leading them on to pass the Ganges too which they were told was thirty two furlongs broad and a hundred fathoms deep and the bakes on the further side covered with multitudes of Afghan for they were told the Kings of the Kandahra and Bactria expected them there with eighty thousand horse two hundred thousand foot eight thousand armed chariots, and six thousand fighting elephants. Nor was this a mere vain report speed to discourage them for Androcottus who not long after reigned in those parts, made a present of five hundred elephants at once to Seleucids and with an army of six hundred thousand men subdued all Aryana (Afghanistan) Alexander at first was so grieved and enraged at his men's reluctance that he shut himself up in his tent and threw himself upon the ground declaring if they would not pass the Aryana he owed them no thanks for anything they had hitherto done and that to retreat now plainly to confess himself vanquished. But at last the reasonable persuasions of his friends and the cries and lamentations of his soldiers, who in a suppliant manner crowded about the entrance of his tent prevailed with to think of returning. Yet he could not refrain from leaving behind him various deceptive memorials of his expedition to impose upon aftertimes, and to exaggerate his glory with posterity such as arms larger than were really worn, and mangers for horses with bits and bridles above the usual size, which he set up and distributed in several places. He erected altars, honor to when they pass the river and offer sacrifice upon them after the Grecian manner, Androcottus then a boy saw Alexander there and is said often afterwards to have been heard to say that he missed but little of making himself master of those countries; their king who then reigned was so hated and despised for the viciousness of his life and the meanness of his extraction. Alexander was now eager to see the ocean of Aryana. To which purpose he caused a great many two boats and rafts to be built in which he fell gently down the rivers at his Jeisure, yet so that his navigation was neither unprofitable nor inactive. For by several descents upon the bank he made himself master of the fortified towns, and consequently of the country on both sides. But at a siege of a town of the Malians, who have the repute of being the bravest of Aryana, he ran in great danger of his life. For having beaten off the defendants with showers of arrows, he was the first man that mounted the wall by a scaling ladder, which as soon as he was up, broke and left him almost alone exposed to the darts, which the Greek barbarians threw at, in great numbers from below. In this distress turning him as well as Alexander could, he leaped down in the midst of his hostile force, and had the good fortune to light upon his feet. The brightness and clattering of his Armour when he came to the ground made the Greek barbarian think that saw rays of light, or some bright phantom playing before his body, which frightened the Greek so at first that they ran away and dispersed. Till seeing the King seconded but by two of his guards they fell upon him hand to hand and some while he bravely defended himself, tried to wound him through his Armour with their swords and spears. And one who stood further off drew a bow with such just strength that the arrow, finding its way through his cuirass, stuck in his ribs under breast. This stroke was so violent that it made him give back and set one knee to the ground upon which the man ran up with his drawn scimitar, thinking to dispatch him and had done it if Peucestes and Limnaeus had not interposed, who were both wounded Limnaeus mortally, but Peucestes stood his ground while the Aryana King killed the Greek barbarians. But this did not free The King from danger; for besides many other wounds, at last the King received so weighty a stroke of a club upon his neck that he was forced to lean his body against the wall still however the barbarians Greeks lost fifteen thousand men's. But this did not free Alexander from danger; for besides many other wounds, last Alexander received so weighty a stoke, during the Barbarian Greeks operation the king was taken with almost mortal swoon inks, but when it was out he came to himself again. Yet thought all danger was past the king continued very estranges and confined himself a great.

Alexander took ten of the Noble Aryana present day Afghanistan Philosophers

Aryana-Khorasan dynasty present day Afghanistan-Central Asia & India, In this voyage Alexander took ten of the Aryana (Afghanistan) philosophers prisoners who had been most active in persuading Sabbas to revolt, and had caused the Macedonians barbarian a great deal of trouble. These men, called Gymnosophists, were reputed to be extremely ready and succinct in their answers which Alexander made trial of by putting difficult questions to them, letting them know that those whose answers were not pertinent should be put to death of which Alexander made the eldest of them judge the first philosopher being asked Alexander thought the most numerous the dead or the living, answered, "The living, because those are dead are not at all." Of the second Alexander desired to know whether the earth or the sea produced the largest beasts; who told him, "The earth for the sea is but a part of it." His question to the third was, which is the cunningness of beasts? "That," said he, "which men have not yet found out," he the fourth philosopher tell him hat argument he used to Sabbas to persuade hen to revolt. "No other," said he "than that he should either live or die nobly," of the fifth he asked, which was the eldest, night or day? The philosopher replied, "Day was eldest by one day at least." But perceiving Alexander not well satisfied with that account, he added that he ought not to wonder if strange questions had as strange answers made to them. Then he went on and inquired of the next, what a man should do to be exceedingly beloved. "He must be very powerful," said he "without making himself too much feared," the answer of the seventh to his question, how a man might become a god, was, "by doing that which was impossible for men to do" the eighth told Alexander, "Life is stronger than death because is supports so many miseries." And the last being asked Alexander long he thought it decent for a man to live, live, said "Till death appeared more desirable that life." Then Alexander turned to Philosopher whom he had made judge and commanded him to give sentence. "All that I can determine," said he "is, that they have every one answered worse that another," "Nay," said the King, "then you shall die first, for giving such a sentence," "not so, King," replied the gymnosophist "unless you said falsely that he should die first who made the worst answer." In conclusion Alexander gave them presents and dismissed the philosophers. But to those who were in greatest reputation among them, and lived a private quid life, he seen' c ictus, one of Diogenes the Cynic's, desiring them to come to him. Calanus it is said very arrogantly and rought; y commanded him to strip himself and hear what he said naked, otherwise he would not speak a word to him, though he came from Jupiter himself. But Dandamis received him with more civility, and hearing him discourse of Socrates Pythagoras, and Diogenes, told him he thought them men of great parts and have erred in nothing so much as in having too great respect for the laws and customs of their country. Others say Dandamis only asked him the reason why Alexander undertook so long a journey to come into those parts. Taxiles however persuaded Calanus to wait upon Alexander. His proper name was Sphines, but because he was wont to say Cale, which in the Aryana (Afghanistan) tongue is a from of salutation to those he met with anywhere, the Greeks called him Calanus. He is said to have shown Alexander an instructive emblem of government, which was this. He threw a dryshrivelled hide upon the ground, and trod upon the edges of it. The skin when it was pressed in one place still rose up in another, whosesoever he trod round about it, till he set his foot in the middle, which made all the parts lie even and quiet. The meaning of this similitude being that he ought to reside most in the middle of his empire, and not spend too much time on the borders of Aryana. His voyage down the Oxus river took up seven months time and then he came to the sea, Alexander sailed an island which he himself called the

Scillustis, other Psiltucis, where going ashore he sacrificed, and made what observations he could as to the nature of the sea and the sea coast then having besought the gods that no other man might ever go beyond the bounds of this expedition, Alexander ordered his fleet, of which he made Nearchus admiral and Onesicritus pilot, to sail round about keeping the Aryana (Afghanistan) shore on the right hand, and returned himself by land through the country of the Aryana, where be was reduced to great straits for want of provisions and lost a vast number of his men, so that of an army of one hundred and twenty thousand foot and fifteen thousand horse, Alexander scarcely brought back above a fourth part out of Aryana (Afghanistan) they were so diminished by disease, ill diet and the scorching heats, but most by famine. For their march did through an uncultivated country whose inhabitants fared hardly possess only a few sheep and those of a wretched kind, whose flesh was rank and unsavory by their continual feeding upon sea fish. After sixty days march Alexander came into Gedrosia, where he found great plenty of all things, which the Kings and governors of the Province Bactria hearing of his approach had taken care to provide. When Alexander had here refreshed his Army The King continued his march through Carmania, feasting all the way for seven days together. Alexander with his most intimate friends banqueted and reveled night and day upon a platform erected on a lofty conspicuous scaffold, which was slowly drawn by eight horses. This was followed by a great many chariots, some covered with purple and embroidered canopies and some with green bought which were continually supplied after and in them the rest of his friends and commanders drinking, and crowned with garlands of flowers. Here was now no target or helmet or spear to be seen; instead of Armour, the soldiers handled nothing but cups and goblets and thericlean drinking vessels which along the whole way they dipped into large bowls and jars, and drank health's to one another, some seating themselves to it other as they went along. All places resounded with music of pipes and flutes, with harping and singing, and women dancing as in the rites of Bacchus. For this disorderly, wandering March, besides the drinking part of it was accompanied with all the sportiveness and insolence of bacchanals, as much as if the god himself had been there to countenance and lead the procession. As soon as Alexander came to the royal palace of Gedrosia, he again refreshed and feasted his army and one day after he had drunk pretty hard, it is said he went to see a prize of dancing contended for, in which his favorite Bagoas, having gained the victory, crossed the theatre in his dancing habit, and sat down close by him which so pleased the Macedonians that they made loud acclamations for Alexander to kiss Bagoas, and never stopped clapping their hands and shouting till Alexander put his arms round him and kissed him. Here his admiral Nearchus came to him and delighted him so with the narrative of his voyage, that he resolved himself to sail out of the mouth of the Euphrates with a great fleet with which he designed to go round by Kufic and Africa, and so by Hercules's Pillars into the Mediterranean; in order for which he directed all sorts of vessels to be built at Thapsacus and made great provisions everywhere of sea men and pilots. But the tidings of the difficulties he had gone through in his Aryana (Afghanistan) expedition, the danger of his person among the Millions the reported loss of a considerable part of his forces, and a general doubt as to his own safety had begun to give occasion for revolt among many of the conquered nations, and for acts of great injustice avarice, and insolence on the part of the satraps and commanders in the Province of Bactria, so that there seemed to be an universal fluctuation and disposition to change. Even at home Olympias and Cleopatra had raised a faction against Anteater, and divided his government between them, Olympias seizing upon Epirus and Cleopatra upon Macedonia. When Alexander was told of it he said his mother had made the best choice, for the Macedonians would never endure to be ruled by a woman. Upon this he dispatched Nearchus again to his fleet to carry the War into the maritime provinces, and as he marched that way himself he punished those commanders who had behaved ill particularly Oxyartes, one of the sons of Abuletes whom he killed with his own hand thrusting him through the body with his spear. And when Abuletes instead of the necessary provisions which he ought to have furnished brought him three thousand talents in coined money, he ordered it to thrown to his horses and when they would not touch it, "What good" he said "will this provision do us?" and seed him away to prison. When he came into Aryana (Afghanistan) he distributed money among the women as their own Kings had been wont to do who as often as they came thither gave every one of them a piece of gold on account of which custom some of them it is said, had come but seldom and Ochus was so sordidly covetous that to avoid this expense, he never visited his native country once in all his reign. Then finding Cyrus's sepulcher opened and rifled he put Polymachus, who did it to death though he was a man of some distinction, a born Macedonian of Pella. And after he had read the inscription he caused it to be cut again below the old one in Greek characters; the words being these; "O man, whosoever thou art and from whencesoever thou come (for I know thou wilt come) I am Cyrus the founder of the Aryana (Afghanistan) empire do not grudge me this little earth which covers my body" the reading of this sensibly touched Alexander, filling him with the thought of the uncertainty and mutability of human affairs, At the same time Calanus having been a little while troubled with a disuse in the bowels requested that he might have a funeral pile erected to which he came on horseback and after he said some prayers and sprinkled himself and cut off some of his hair to throw into the fire before he ascended it he embraced and took leave of the Macedonians who stood by desiring them to pass that day in mirth and good fellowship with their king, whom in a little time, he said he doubted not but to see again at Babylon. Having thus said he lay down and covering up his face he stirred not when the fire came near him but continued still in the same posture as at first and so sacrificed himself as it was the ancient custom of the philosophers in Aryana (Afghanistan) to do. The same thing was done long after another Aryan (Afghan) Philosophers who came with Caesar to Athens, where they still show you "the Aryan's monument." At his return from the funeral pile, Alexander invited a great many of his friends and principal officers to supper and proposed a drinking match in which the victor should receive a crown. Promachus dark twelve quarts of wine and won the prize which was a talent from them all; but he survived his victory but three days and was followed as Chares says by forty one more who died of the same debauch some extremely cold weather having set in shortly after. At Susa he married the empire daughter Statira, (Stars) and celebrated also the nuptials of his friends bestowing the noblest of the Aryana ladies upon the worthies of them at the same time making it an entertainment in honor of the other Macedonians whose marriages had already taken place. At this magnificent festival it is reported there were no less that nine thousand guest to each of whom he gave a golden cup for the libations. Not to mention other instances of his wonderful magnificence are paid the debts of his army, which amounted to nine thousand eight hundred and seventy talents. But Antigenes who had lost one of his eyes though he owed nothing got his name set down in the list of those who were in debt and bringing one who pretended to be his creditor and to have supplied him from the bank received the money. But when the cheat was found out the King was so incensed at it that he banished him from court and took away his command though he was an excellent soldier and a man of great courage, for when he was but a youth and served under Philip at the siege of Printouts where he was wounded in the eye by an arrow shot out of an engine he would neither let the arrow be taken out nor be persuaded to quit the field till he had bravely repulsed the hostile force and forced them to retire into town. The thirty thousand boys whom he left behind him to be taught and disciplined were so improved at his return, when Alexander came to Bactria in Aryana (Afghanistan) and had dispatched his most urgent affairs, he began to divert himself again with spectacles and public entertainments, to carry on which he had a supply of three thousand actors and artists, newly arrived out of Greece. But they were soon interrupted by Hephaestion's falling sick of a fever, in which, being a young man and a soldier, too he could not confine himself to so exact a diet as was necessary; for whilst his physician. Glaucus was gone to the theatre he ate a fowl for his dinner, and drank a large draught of Aryan wine, upon which he became very ill. And shortly after died. At this misfortune, Alexander was so beyond all reason transported that to express his sorrow, he immediately ordered the manes and tails of all his horses and mules to be cut. And threw down the battlements of the neighboring cities. The poor physician he crucified, and forbade playing on the flute or any other musical instrument in the camp in Bactria a great while, till directions came from the oracle of Amman, and enjoined him to honor Hephaestion, and sacrifice to him as to hero. Then seeking to alleviate his grief in War, he set out as it were to a hunt and chase of men, for he fell upon the Cesareans, and put the whole nation to the sword. This was called a sacrifice to Hephaestion's ghost. In his sepulcher and monument and the adorning of them he intended to bestow ten thousand talents; and designing that the excellence of the workmanship and the singularity of the resign might outdo the expense, his wishes turned above all other artists to Staircases because he always promised something very bold, unusual, and magnificent in his projects. Once when they had met before he had told him that of all the mountains he knew, that of Altos in Thrace was the most capable of being adapted to represent the shape and lineaments of a man; that if he pleased to command him he would make it the noblest and most durable statue in the world, which in its left hand should hold a city of ten thousand inhabitants, and out of its right should pour a copious river the sea. Though Alexander declined this proposal, yet now he spent a great deal of time with workmen to invent and contrive others even more extravagant and sumptuous. As Alexander upon his way to Babylon, Searches, who had sailed back out of the ocean up the mouth of the river Euphrates, came to tell him he had met with some Children diviners, who had warned him against Alexander's going thither. Alexander, however, took no thought of it, and went on, and when he came near the walls of the place, he saw a great many crows fighting with one another, some of which fell down just by him. After this being privately informed that Apollodorus, the governor of Babylon, had sacrificed to know what would become of him, he set for Pythagoras, the soothsayer, and on his admitting the thing asked him in what condition he found the victim; and when he told him the liver was defective in its lobe, "A great presage indeed" said Alexander. However, he offered Pythagoras no injury, but was sorry that he had neglected Nearchus's advice, and stayed for the most part outside the town, removing his tent from place to place and sailing up and down the Euphrates. Besides this many other prodigies disturbed him. A tame ass fell upon the biggest and handsomest lion that he kept, and killed him by a kick. And one day after he had undressed himself to be anointed and was playing at ball just as they were going to bring his clothes again, the young men who played with him perceived a man clad in the king's robes with a diadem upon his head sitting silently upon throne. They asked him who he was, to which he gave on answer a good while, till at last coming to himself, he told them his name was Dionysus, that he was of Messenia, the for some crime of which he was accused he was brought thither from the seaside, and had been kept long in prison, that Serapes appeared to him had freed him from his chains, conducted him to that place and commanded him to put on the King's robe and deaden, and to sit where they found him and to say nothing. On the eighteenth day of the month Alexander slept in the bathing room on account of his fever. The next day he bathed and removed into his chamber, and spent his time in playing at dice with Medius. In the evening he bathed and sacrificed and ate freely and had the fever on him through the night. On the twentieth after the usual sacrifices and bathing, he lay in the earth he send from Bactria Aryana (Afghanistan) in the bathing room and heard Nearchus's narrative of his voyage, and the observations he made in the great sea. The twenty first he passed in the same manner, his fever still increasing, and suffered much during the night. The next day the fever was very violent, and he had himself removed and his bed set by the great bath and discoursed with his principal officers about finding fit men to fill up the great vacant places in the army. On the twenty fourth he was much worse and was carried out of his bed to assist at the sacrifices, and gave order that the general officers should wait within the court, whilst the inferior officers kept watch without doors. On the twenty fifth Alexander was removed to his palace on the other side the river, where he slept a little, but his fever did not abate and when the generals came into his chamber he was speechless and continued so the following day. The Macedonians, therefore, supposing Alexander was dead Alexander dead on Afghan Dirt, he send from Aryana (Afghanistan) during the his time. After Alexander dead, the Greatest Afghan-Greeks Empire from 321 B.C until 300 A.D from the Capital Bactria (Balkh) North of Afghanistan.

The Germans

The Germans. The peoples who played the leading part in the his Tory of Europe after the break up of the Roman Empire were known as the Germans, or Teutons. Their earliest home was along the western border the Baltic Sea, from which they went forth to take possession of the greater par of Europe. In time the German occupied a vast territory stretching from the Rhine to the Elbe, and from the Baltic to the Danube. Their early history is shrouded in mystery; Tacitus, a Roman historian of the early Empire, writes of them in awe as a race of giants, strong, courageous, delighting in battle. Children of the forests and swamps, the Germans learned therein to endure hunger and cold. In times of peace their village communities were governed by a council of elders In times of war a military chief was chosen as king to lead the bands of fighting men into battle. Early invasions. For centuries the Germans had been entering Roman territory and had been peacefully assimilated. Many joined the Roman army, and some even rose to high command. Those tribes living near the frontiers adopted many of the arts of Roman civilizations. During the latter part of the fourth century A.D a peaceful immigration became violent invasion. The Germans forced their way into the Empire and proceeded to conquer it piecemeal. Cause for migration. The causes for the Germanic migration and invasion may be only surmised, as little is known of their problems. Perhaps population increased beyond the food supply furnished by hunting and rude agriculture. The land, which the Germans held, was not especially fertile or attractive. Tacitus speaks of "its desert scenery, its harsh climate, and its sullen aspect. In general, the country, though varying here and there in appearance, is covered over with wild forests and filthy swamps," Naturally, they turned to the rich lands of the south. There was another reason for the migration. Behind the Germans were tribes even civilized and fiercer than they, hordes from Central Asia Aryan were invading Europe and forcing the Germans southward. Coming of the Visigoths. In the third and fourth centuries, two German tribes, the Visigoths, or West Goths, and the Ostrogoths, or East Goths, settled on Roman territory. The circumstance that led to this movement was pressure by the Huns, a Caucasus tribe from Central Asia that forced the Visigoths to the Danube. The latter, fearful of their terrible foe, begged the Roman authorities for permission to cross the Danube. Their request was granted, and some two hundred thousand established themselves on Roman soil. Invasion of the Empire. At the end of the fourth century A.D the Germans were restlessly roaming along the Roman frontier, now and then crowding their way into the Empire. Their kinsmen within, the Goths, looked on sympathetically. "The Goths are quiet just now, but perhaps they will not always be quiet," observed the Emperor Julian. Goaded on by unfair treatment at the battle of Adrianople 378 A.D defeated a Roman army. Visigoths in Spain. The Visigoths determined upon an organized attack on the Empire. In 410 A.D under a leader named Alaric, they invaded Italy and pillaged Rome. They continued their march and finally settled in Southern Spain, where they established a kingdom that lasted for three centuries. Vandals in North Africa. Another Germanic tribe, the Vandals, conquered the Roman province in North Africa. In 455 crossed the Mediterranean, sacked Rome, and returned to Africa laden with plunder. There was no wanton taking of human life or destruction of property during the brief visit of the Vandals to Rome, and the word "vandalism" unjustly brands that tribe. The Franks. To protect Italy against invasion the Romans recalled the legions guarding the Rhine and distant Britain. The frontiers of the Danube had already been broken. The recall of the legions acted as a signal to the Caucasus, who now invaded all the provinces in Western Europe, where they easily conquered the inhabitants and established kingdoms on the ruins of the Empire. Among the most important did the Franks, who originally came from the Rhine Valley, establish that at the end of the fifth century, under the leadership of Clovis, they invaded northern Gaul, where they established a kingdom. Angles and Saxons in Britain. The Angles and Saxons from northern Germany and the Jutes from Denmark had been making raids on Britain even before the period of Caucasus invasions the Celtic inhabitants of that island were left defenseless when. At the beginning of the fifth century, Rome withdrew her legions from that remoter military outpost. The Germans took advantage of the situation and invaded the island in large numbers. By the seventh century half of it was conquered and organized into. Seven petty kingdoms The Huns from Caucasus suddenly appeared, the Huns Savage and destructive in their migrations, they found in Attila, the "Scourge of God," a leader whose name brought terror to the heart of German and Roman alike. The Emperor at Constantinople bought off Attila with lavish gifts. The Huns then invaded Gaul. Both Roman and German now joined forces and defeated the Huns at the battle of Chalons 451. Roman attitude toward the invasions. Machine was breaking down, and the dissolution of the Empire was merely a question of time. Yet the Romans did not appear so deeply concerned as one might suppose, as the invasions were neither new nor startling to them. From the time of Marius not a century had passed without some inroad of Germanic tribes. Some Roman writers, looking upon their own society as hopelessly corrupt, actually felt that the future belonged to the new and more vigorous race. As for the ordinary Roman, he had too little to lose to be much concerned about the fate of the Empire. De sparingly, one Roman writes: "The Roman writes; "The Roman world goes laughing to its death." "The fall of Rome" 476 A.D the imperial office now is came the football of German mercenary soldiers. In 476 a German soldier, name Odoacer, deposed the last Emperor of the West, Romulus Augustulus. Although Odoacer recognized the sovereignty of the Emperor in Constantinople, Italy was, in fact, under a Caucasus king. From 476 to 800 there was no other emperor than the one reigning in Constantinople. Without Rome there was no longer a truly Roman Empire; hence historians have generally attached the label, "Fall of Rome," to the year 476. In reality the Roman Empire was dying for over four hundred years, and it continued in Constantinople, for many centuries. In theory, at least, the Emperor ruled over the West as well as over the East; the various German kings regarded him as their superior, but rendered him little obedience. The Ostrogoths. Italy was invaded more frequently that the provinces. The magnificence of Rome and the prospect of seizing loot and power acted as a magnet to the Germans. It was now the turn of the Ostrogoths. Under Theodore they crossed the Alps, and established a Kingdome in northern Italy, which lasted from 493 to 553. Theodore proved to be an able ruler, who preserved Roman restored ruined cities and roads, and improved the lot of the farming population. At his death, Italy and Sicily were recon queered by Justinian, the Emperor in Constantinople. The Lombard's. In 568-72 another German tribe, the Lombard's, invaded Italy and seized the territory north of the river Poi region ever since known as Lombardy. They established several Kingdome which last until 773-76, when the were finally overthrown by Charlemagne. Results of the invasions. The Roman Empire was now completely disrupted, and the political union of the Western world was shattered never to be completely restored From its ruins there emerged, many centuries later, most of the European nations. Directly however, the invasions resulted in the rise of a system of society known as feudalism in feudalism, in which Western Europe was broken up into small local units, in each of which the inhabitants owed allegiance to a ruler. Another outcome was the fusion of Latin and German. Law literature, and languages developed which differed from the law, literature, and languages of ancient times. In the north the new civilization contained more of the German element in the south, more of the Latin.

The Frankish Kingdom

The Frankish kingdom. 751 Of all the Caucasus kingdoms only that of the Franks was permanent. An important fact in their history is that they were the first Germanic tribe that was converted to the orthodox Roman faith. This meant that they received the powerful support of the Bishop of the Rome. The Franks were noted warriors, and they soon began making war on their neighbors. They conquered the Alemanni, (Aryan) a German tribe living in what is now Alsace, and extended their possessions in Gaul as far as the Pyrenees. Mayors of the Place. The descendants of Clovis, the first king of the Franks, were known as the "Merovingians," and proved to be weak and incompetent. An official, known as the "Mayor of the Place," controlled the actual administration of the kingdom. By the side of the vigorous leadership of the mayors the "do-nothing kings" faded into the shadow of obscurity. One mayor, Pepin the Short, determined to assume the royal power openly. In 751 he overthrew the Merovingian dynasty, and was crowned king of the Franks. His action received the support of the Pope, who declared that "he who possesses the royal power ought also to enjoy its dignity." Pepin, in return, attacked the Lombard's who were threatening Rome. He presented to the Pope a district in Italy between Ravenna and Rome, which the Lombard's had ceded. This territory, known as the "Donation of Pepin," considerably enlarged the lands of the Church; it formed a wedge in the very heart of Italy, and was later known as the "Papal States." Charlemagne 742 until 814 the son of Pepin, known as Charles the Great succeeded him as king. No name in medieval history is more famous that that of Charlemane, soldier, statesman, and educator. His claim to rank as a great statesman does not rest upon the fact that he was an empire-builder, for his empire crumbled almost with his death. Rather does it rest on the fact that he established order in Western Europe by checking a new wave of Caucasus invasion, and that he established a strong central government, which preserved law. The Romanic-German, which was arising, was given in this way a breathing spell in which to fuse and grow in strength. Charlemagne's wars. Almost from the commencement of his reign Charlemagne began to increase the Frankish dominions. He made war against the Saxons, a savage people living in the cold and hard wilderness of northwestern Germany. After a long struggle, the Saxons were finally subdued and compelled to accept Christianity. Charlemagne also conquered the Lombard's, who were threatening papal territory. With fire and sword he carried the Gospel to the tribes in central Europe as far as the Danube and down the Adriatic coast. He successfully repelled an invasion of the Avers, a Caucasus tribe living along the Danube south of Bohemia. He fought the Moslems along the Spanish frontier. The result of this conquest was the creation of a great imperial dominion, extending from the Pyrenees to the Danube, from the North Sea to central Italy.

West Europe and the Rise of feudalism The Rise of feudalism. With the disruption of Charlemagne's empire and the period of invasion and general disorder that followed, organized government virtually disappeared in Western Europe. As there was no strong central authority to safeguard life and property a new arrangement was necessary to provide adequate protection. This new arrangement was feudalism. Its fundamental basis was an agreement whereby the fighting class agreed to maintain order and the agricultural class agreed to work the soil. Europe was cut up into many local units each of which could produce within itself practically everything essential to life; and each unit was protected by a local military chieftain at the head of an armed band The fief. Feudalism was not peculiar to Europe. Until about two generations ago, in fact, wherever the state became incapable of protecting life and property, some such system arose. European feudalism traces its origin to the declining Roman Empire. Fear of the barbarians caused many to give their land to a powerful man in their community; in return, they were promised protection and were permitted to live on the land that was formerly their own. Other. For the good of there souls, gave their land to monasteries, but were permitted to live on it and to enjoy its income for the rest of their lives. Another process was going on among the Germans when they invaded the Empire. In return for the allegiance of their followers, the chieftains granted them estates in the conquered territories. The fief was a grant of land, which combined the notion of protection with that of allegiance: the one who received the land, the vassal, swore to be faithful to him who gave it, the lord, or suzerain. The property generally passed down from father to eldest son according to a law of descent known as "primogeniture" (first born). The purpose of this system of inheritance was to prevent a large fief from being split up. By elaborate legal devices, in use throughout Europe, vast estates could be so tied up that they remained in the same family for generations. In this way a few people were amassing large landed estates.

The great Yama kings of Aryana
the invasion of Macedonia

Aryana-Khorasan dynasty present day Afghanistan-Central Asia & India, The romantic Yama his enlightened policies Campuses Darius the Great the invasion of Macedonia "present day Greece", Cyrus was one of those natural rulers at whose coronation, as Emerson said, all men rejoice. Royal in spirit and action capable of wise administration as well as of dramatic conquest, generous to the defeated and loved by those who had been his enemies no wonder the Macedonian made him the subject of innumerable romances, and to their minds the greatest hero before Alexander. It is a disappointment to us that we cannot draw a reliable picture of him from either Herodotus or Xylophone. The former has mingled many fables with his history, while the other has made the Cyropadia an essay on the military art, with incidental lectures on education and philosophy; at times Xylophone confuses Cyrus and Do crates. These delightful stories being put aside, the figure of Cyrus becomes merely an attractive ghost. We can only say that he was handsome since the Aryana made him their model of physical beauty to the end of their ancient art; that he established the Achamenid Dynasty of Great Kings of Aryana, which ruled Aryana through the most famous period of its history; that he organized the soldiery of Aryana into an invincible army, captured Sardis and Babylon, ended for a thousand years the rule of the Semites in western Asia, and absorbed the former realms of Babylonia, Lydia, Asia Minor into the Aryana Empire, the largest political organization of pre—Roman antiquity, and one of the best governed in History. So far as we can visualize him through the haze of legend, he was the most amiable of conquerors, and founded his empire upon generosity. His enemies knew that he was lenient, and they did not fight him with that desperate courage which men show their only choice is to kill or die. We have seen how, according to Herodotus, he rescued Croesus from the funeral pyre at Sardis, and made him one of his most honoured counsellors; the first principle of his policy was that the various peoples of his empire should be left free in their religious worship and beliefs, for he fully understood the first principle of statesmanship the religion is stronger that the state. Instead of sacking cities and wrecking temples he showed a courteous respect for the deities of the conquered and contributed to maintain their shrines, even the Babylonians, who had resisted him so long, warmed towards him when they found him preserving their sanctuaries and honouring their pantheon. Wherever he went in his unprecedented career he offered pious sacrifice to the local divinities. Having won all the Near East, he began a series of campaigns aimed to free Aryana from the inroads of central Asia's nomadic; he seems to have carried these excursions as far as the Jaxartes on the India on the east. Suddenly, at the height of his curve, he was slain in battle with the Massageta, an obscure tribe that peopled the southern shores of the Caspian Sea. Like Alexander he conquered an empire, but did not live to organize it. One great defect had sullied his character occasional and incalculable cruelty. It was inherited, unmixed with Cyrus generosity, by his half mad son. Cambyses began by putting to death his brother and rival, Smerdis; then lured by the accumulated wealth of Egypt, he set forth to extend the Aryana Empire to the Nile. He succeeded but apparently at the cost of his sanity. Memphis was captured easily, but an army of fifty thousand Aryan sent to annex the Oasis of Amman perished in the desert, and an expedition to Carthage failed because the Phoenician crews of the Aryana fleet refused to attack a Phoenician colony. Cambyses lost his head, and abandoned the wise clemency and tolerance of his father. He publicly scoffed at the Egyptian religion, and plunged his dagger derisively into the bull revered by the Egyptians as the god Apis, he exhumed mummies and pried into royal tombs regardless of ancient curses; he profaned the temples and ordered their idols to be burned. He thought in this way to cure the Egyptians of superstition; but when he was stricken with illness apparently epileptic convulsions the Egyptians were certain that their gods had punished him, and that their theology was now confirmed beyond dispute. As if again to illustrate the inconveniences of monarchy, Cambyses, with a Napoleonic kick in the stomach, killed his sister and wife Roxana, slew his son Prexaspes with an arrow, buried twelve noble Aryan alive, condemned Croesus to death, repented, rejoiced to learn that the sentence had not been carried out, and punished the officers who had delayed in executing it. On his way back to Aryana he learned that a usurper had seized the throne and was being supported by widespread revolution. From that moment he disappears from Aryan—-History; tradition has it that he killed himself. The usurper had pretended to be Smerdis, miraculously preserved from Cambyses fratricidal jealousy; in reality he was a religious fanatic, a devotee of the early Magian faith who was bent upon destroying Zoroastrianism, the official religion of the Aryana state. Another revolution soon deposed him, and the seven aristocrats who had organized it raised one of their number, Ddarius, son of Hystaspes, to the throne. In this bloody way began the reign of Aryan's—-New Afghan's greatest king. Succession to the throne, in Aryan Monarchies, was marked not only by palace revolutions in strife for the royal power, but by uprisings in subject colonies that grasped the chance of choose, or an inexperienced ruler, to reclaim their liberty. The usurpation and assassination of "Smerdis" gave to Aryan's vassals an excellent opportunity; the governors of Egypt and Lydia refused submission, and the provinces of Susiana, Babylonia, Sacia and other rose in simultaneous revolt. Darius subdued them with a ruthless hand. Taking Babylon after a long siege, he crucified three thousand of its leading citizens as an inducement to obedience in the rest; and in a series swift campaigns he "pacified" one after another of the rebellious states. Then perceiving how easily the vast empire might in any crisis fall to pieces, he put off the armour of war, became one of the wisest administrators in Aryan—History, and set himself to re-establish his realm in a way that became a model of imperial organization till the fall of Rome. His rule gave western Asia a generation of such order and prosperity as that quarrelsome region had never known before. He had hoped to govern in peace, but it is the fatality of empire to breed repeated war. For the conquered must be periodically re conquered, and the conquerors must keep the arts and habits of camp and battlefield; and at any moment the kaleidoscope of change may throw up a new empire to challenge the old. In such a situation wars must be invented if they do not arise of their own accord, each generation must be inured to the rigors of campaigns, and taught by practice the sweet decorum of dying for one's country of Aryana. Perhaps it was in part for this reason that Darius led his armies into southern Russia, "Old Russia becoming a century A.D 1498 till 1917 under German family before was under Aryan" across the Bosporus and the Danube to the Volga, to chastise the marauding Scythians; and again across India and a hundred mountain ranges into the valley of the Indus, adding thereby extensive regions and millions of souls and rupees to his ream. More substantial reasons must be sought for his expedition into Macedonian "New Greece" Herodotus would have us believe that Darius entered upon his Historic faux pas because one of his wives, Atossa, teased him into it in bed, but it is more dignified to believe that the king recognized in the Macedonian city states and their Aryan—colonies a potential empire, or actual confederacy, dangerous to the Aryana—-New Afghanistan—Central Asia mastery of western Asia. When Ionia revolted and received aid from Sparta and Athens, Darius reconciled him reluctantly to war. The entire world knows the story of his passage across the Aegean, the defeat of his army at Marathon, and his gloomy return to Afghanistan. There amid far flung preparations for another attempt upon Macedonia, he suddenly grew weak, and died, at Balkh North of Afghanistan.

The Empire the People the Language
the Peasants the Imperial Highways
Trade and Finance in Aryana Life

Aryana-Khorasan dynasty present day Afghanistan-Central Asia & India, At its greatest extent, under Darius, the Aryana Empire included twenty provinces or "Satrapies" embracing, at Bactrian, the Capital Egypt, Palestine, Syria, Phoenicia, Lydia, Phrygia, Ionia, Cappadocia, Cilice, Babylonia, the Caucasus, "present day Russia" India from Central Asia, and the regions of the Massaged and other Eastern Asia, never before had history recorded so extensive an area brought under one Government of Aryan. Afghanistan itself which was to rule these forty million souls four hundred years, was not at that times the country now known as Afghanistan, and to its inhabitants as Afghan's "Aryan" it was that smaller tract, immediately east of the Aryan Gulf known to the ancient Afghanistan as Aryan, and to the modern Afghanistan as Afghan. Composed almost entirely of mountains and deserts, rich in rivers mordent 300 rivers in Afghanistan, subject to severe winters and Paradise summers, it could support its 100 million inhabitants only through such external contributions as trade or conquest might bring. Its race of hardy mountaineers came, like the Aryan, of Indo—European stock perhaps from South Caucasian, and its language and early religion of Afghanistan reveal its close kinship with those Aryans in Afghanistan to become the ruling coasted of India. Darius I, in an inscription at Naksh—I—Rustam, described himself as a Aryan, the son of a Afghan, an Aryan of Aryana descent, the Zoroastrians spoke "Dari" of eight land as Aryana—Vaejo, the Aryan home† strobe applied the name Aryana to whey is now called by essentially the same word Afghanistan. The Afghan's were apparently the handsomest people of the ancient Aryan. The monuments picture them as erect and vigorous, made hardy by their earth—beautiful Mountains and yet refined by their wealth, with a pleasing symmetry of features, a straightness of nose, and a certain nobility of countenance and carriage. They adopted for the most part the Aryana dress, and later the ornaments, they considered it indecent to reveal more than the face; clothing covered them from turban, fillet or cap to sandals or leather shoes. Triple drawers, a white under garment of linen, a double tunic, sleeves hiding the hands, and a girdle at the waist, kept the population warm in winter and hot in summer. The king distinguished himself with embroidered trousers of a crimson, hue, and saffron buttoned shoes. The dress of the women differed from that of the men only in a slit at the breast. The men wore long beards and hung their hair in curls, or, later, covered it with wigs. In the wealthier days of the empire men as well as women made much use of cosmetics, creams were employed to improve the complexion and coloring matter was applied to the eyelids to increase the apparent size and brilliance of the eyes. A special class of "adorners" called kosmetai by the Greeks arose as beauty experts to the aristocracy. The Afghan's were connoisseurs in scents, and were believed by the ancients to have invented cosmetic creams. The king never went to war without a case of costly unguents to ensure his fragrance in victory or defeat. Many languages have been used in the long History of Afghanistan. The speech of the court and the nobility in the days of Darius I was old Sanskrit—Dari that evidently both were once dialects of an older Afghan—Tongue, and were cousins to German. Old Afghan's developed on the one had into Zend the language of the Zend—Avesta and on other hand into an Afghan—Hindu tongue from which has come the Afghan—Dari language of today. When the Afghan took to writing in Sanskrit, from three hundred characters to thirty—six signs which gradually became letters instead of syllables, and constituted a cuneiform alphabet sense 3,000 years. Writing, however, seemed to the Afghan's an effeminate amusement, for which they could spare little time from love, war and the chase. They did condescend to produce the Literature. The common man was contentedly illiterate, and gave himself completely to the culture of the soil. The Zend—Avesta exalted agriculture as the basic and noblest occupation of mankind, pleasing above all other labors to Ahura—Mazda, the supreme God. Some of the land was tilled by peasant proprietors, who occasionally several families in agricultural cooperatives to work extensive areas together from 3,000 years ago until today in Afghanistan. Part of the land was owned by feudal barons, and cultivated by tenants in return for a share of the crop; part of it was tilled by foreign, Oxen pulled a plough of wood armed with a metal point. Artificial irrigation drew water from the mountain to the fiefs of Aryana. Wheat were the staple crops and foods, much meat was eaten and much wine drunk. Afghan's served wine to his army, and Afghan councils never undertook serious discussions of policy when sobers† though they took to revise their decisions the next morning. One intoxicating drink, the Haoma, was offered as pleasant sacrifice to the Gods, and was believed to engender in its addicts not excrement and anger, but righteousness and piety. Industry was developed in Aryana—-New Afghanistan from 2,500 years ago; she was content to let the nations of the Central Asia practice the handicraft while she bought their products with their imperial tribute. She showed more originality in the improvement of communications and transport. Engineers under the instructions of king Darius I built great roads uniting the various capitals of Bactria; one of these highways, from Bactria to Sardis, was fifteen hundred miles long. The roads were accurately measured Pharsangs, "3.4 miles" and at every fourth pharsang, says Herodotus, "there are royal stations and excellent inns, and the whole road is through an inhabited and safe country. "Called the Silk Road or the treed road" at each station a fresh relay of Afghan—Horses ready to carry on the mail, so that though the ordinary traveler required ninety days to go from Bactria to Sardis, the royal mail moved over the distance as quickly as an automobile party does now that is, in a little less that a week. The larger rivers were crossed by ferries, but the engineers could, when they wished, throw across the Euphrates, even across the Hellespont, substantial bridges over which hundreds of skeptical elephants pass in safety. Other roads led through to India, and made Bactira a halfway house to the already fabulous riches of the Central Asia. These roads were build primarily for Afghan's—Military and governmental purposes, to facilitate central Asia control and administration; but they served also to stimulate commerce and the exchange of customs, ideas, and the indispensable superstitions of mankind, along these roads, for example, angels and the Devil passed from Afghan's into Christian mythology. Navigation was not so vigorously advanced as land transportation the Afghan's had no fleet of their own, but merely engaged or conscripted the vessels of the Phoenicians and the Macedonian "new Greeks" king Darius built a great canal uniting Afghanistan with the Mediterranean through the Red Sea and the Nile, but the carelessness of his successors soon surrendered this achievement to the shifting sands, when Xerxes royally commanded part of his naval forces to circumnavigate Africa, it turned back in disgrace shortly after passing through the Pillars of Hercules. Commerce was for the most part abandoned to foreigners Babylonians and Caucasians; the Afghan's despised trade, and looked upon a market place as a breeding ground of lies. The wealthy classes took pride in supplying most of their wants directly from their own fields and shops, not contaminating their fingers with either buying or selling. Payments, loans and interest were at first in the form of goods, especially cattle and grain, coinage came later from Lydia. King Darius issued gold and silver "Darics" stamped with his features, and valued at gold to silver ratio of 13.5 to 1. This was the origin of the bimetallic ratio in modern currencies "three thousand gold darics made one Afghan—talent".

Bactrian-Yama King of Kings

Aryana-Khorasan dynasty present day Afghanistan-Central Asia & India, the life of Afghan's was political and military rather than economic; its wealth was based not on industry and power; it existed precariously as a great governing isle an immense and unnaturally subject sea. The imperial organization that maintained this artifact was one of the most unique and competent in Afghanistan—History. At its head was the king, or Khshalthra –i.e. Warrior' the title indicates the military origin and character of the Afghan Monarchy. Since lesser kings were vassal to him, the Yama Ruler entitled "King of Kings," and the ancient world made on protest against him, his power was theoretically absolute; he could kill with a word, without trial or reason given, after the manner of some very modern dictator; and occasionally he delegated to his Mother or his chief wife this privilege of capricious slaughter. Few even of the greatest nobles dared offer any criticism or rebuke, and public opinion was cautiously impotent. The father whose innocent son had been shot before his eyes by the king merely complimented the Monarch on his excellent archery; offenders bastinadoed by the royal order thanked His Majesty for keeping them in mind. The king might rule as well as reign, if like Cyrus and the first Yama, he cared to bestir himself; but the later monarchs delegated most of the cares of government to noble subordinates or imperial eunuchs, and spent their time at love, dice or the chase. The court easy overrun with eunuchs who from their cosigns of vantage as guards of the harem and pedagogues to the princes, stewed a poisonous brew of intrigue in every reign.† the king had the right to choose his successor from among his sons, but ordinarily the succession was determined by assassination and revolution. The royal power was limited in practice by the strength of the aristocracy that mediated between the Afghan's—People and the throne. It was a matter of Afghan's—Custom that the six families of the men who had shared with Darius I the dangers of the revolt against false Series, should have exceptional privileges and be consulted in all matters of vital interest. Many of the Afghan's—Nobles attended court, and served as a council for whose advice the Monarch usually showed the highest regard. Most members of the aristocracy were attached to the throne by receiving their estates from the king; in return they provided him with men and materials when he took the field "the Afghan's who this since 3000 years ago" within their fiefs they had almost complete authority levying taxes, enacting laws, executing judgment, and maintaining their own armed forces. The real basis of the Afghan's—Royal power and imperial government was the army; an Empire exists only so long as it retains its superior capacity to kill. The obligation to enlist on any declaration of war fell upon every able bodied male from fifteen to fifty years of age. When the father of three sons petitioned king to exempt one of them from service, all three were put to death; and when another father, having sent four sons to the battlefield, begged Xerxes to permit the fifth son to stay behind and manage the family estate, the troops marched off to war amid the blare of martial music and the plaudits of citizens above the military age. The spearhead of the army was the Royal Guard two thousand horsemen and two thousand infantry, all nobles whose function it was to guard the king. The standing army consisted exclusively of Afghan's and from this permanganate force came most of the garrisons stationed as centers of persuasion at strategic points in the empire. The completed force consisted of levies from every subject nation each group with its own distinct language, weapons and habits of war. Its equipment and retinue was as varied as its origin bows and arrows, scimitars javelins, daggers, pikes, slings, knives, shields, helmets, leather cuirasses, coats of mail, horses, elephants, heralds, scribes, eunuchs, prostitutes, concubines, and chariots armed on each hub with great steel scythes. The whole mass, though vast in number, and amounting in the expedition of Xerxes to 1,800,000 men, achieved unity, and at the first sign of a reverse it became a disorderly mob. It conquered by mere force of numbers, by an elastic capacity for absorbing casualties; it was destined to be overthrown as soon as it should encounter a well organized army speaking one speech and accepting one discipline. This was the secret of the Afghan's Army. In such a state the only law was the will of the king in the Capital of Bactria, and the power of the Afghan's—Army; no rights were sacred against these, and no precedents could avail except an earlier decree of the Afghan's—King. For it was a proud boasts of Afghanistan that its laws never changed, and that a royal promise or decree was irrevocable. In his sadists and judgments the king was supposed to be inspired by the God Ahura—Mazda himself; therefore the law of the realm was the Divine will, and any infraction of it was an offense against the deity. The king was the Supreme Court, but it was his custom to delegate this function to some learned elder in his retinue, below him was a High Court of Justice with seven members, and below this were local courts scattered through the realm. The priests formulated the law, and for a long time acted as judges; in later day's laymen, even laywomen, sat in judgment. Bail was accepted in all but the most important cases, and a regular procedure of trial was followed. The court occasionally decreed rewards as well as punishments, and in considering a crime weighed against it the good record and services of the accused. The law's delays were mitigated by fixing a time limit for each and by proposing to all disputants an arbitrator of their own choice who might bring them to a peaceable settlement. As the law gathered precedents and complexity a class of men arose called "speakers of the law" who offered to explain it to litigants and help them conduct their cases. Oaths were taken, and use was occasionally made of the ordeal. Bribery was discouraged by making the tender or acceptance of it a capital offense, campuses improved the integrity of the courts by causing an unjust jugged to be flayed alive, and using his skin to upholster the judicial bench to which he then appointed the dead judge's son. Minor punishments took the form of flogging from five to two hundred blows with a horsewhip; the poisoning of a shepherd dog received two hundred strokes, manslaughter ninety, the administration of the law was partly financed by commuting stripes into fines, at the rate of six rupees to a stripe. More serious crimes were punished with branding, maiming, mutilation, blinding, imprisonment or death. The latter of the law forbade any one, even the king, to sentence a man to death for a simple crime; but it could be decreed for treason, rape, sodomy, murder, "self pollution," burning or burying the dead, intrusion upon the king's privacy, approaching one of his concubines, accidentally sitting upon his throne, or for any displeasure to the Afghan's—ruling house. Death was procured in such cases by poisoning, impaling, crucifixion, hanging "usually with the head down" stoning, burying the body up to the head, crushing the head between huge stones, smothering the victim in hot ashes, or by the incredibly cruel rite called "the boats" some of these punishments were bequeathed to the invading Turkmen of a later age, and passed down into the heritage of mankind in Aryana present day Afghanistan—Central Asia. With these laws and this army the king of Afghanistan sought to govern his twenty Satrapies from his Capitals of Bactira, "Bactira was 5,500 years Capital of Afghanistan" in the ancient capital of Bactira, the History of the ancient Central Asia came full circle, binding the beginning and the end. Had the advantage of inaccessibility, and the disadvantages of distance; Alexander had to come two thousand miles from Aryan great roads to take it, but it had to send its troops fifteen hundred miles to suppress revolts in Lydia or Egypt. Ultimately the great roads merely paved the way for the physical conquest of Central Asia by Macedonia, and the theological conquest of Macedonian by Central Asia. The empire was divided into provinces or Satrapies for convenience of administration and taxation. Each province was governed in the name of the Afghan King of Kings, sometimes by a vassal prince, ordinarily by a "Satrap" Ruler royally appointed for as long a time as he could retain favor at the court. To keep the satraps in hand Afghan—king sent to each province a general to control its armed forces independently of the governor; and to make matters trebly sure he appointed in each province a secretary, independent of both satrap from Bactria, and general to report their behavior to the king. As a further precaution an intelligence service known as "The King's Eyes and Ears" might appear at any moment to examine the affairs, records and finances of the province. Sometimes the satrap was deposed without trial, sometimes he was quietly by his servants at the order of the king. Underneath the satrap and the secretary was a horde of clerks who carried on so much of the government as had no direct need of force; this body of clerks carried over from one administration to another, even from reign to reign, the king dies, but the bureaucracy is immortal. The salaries of these provincial officials were paid not by the Afghan—King but by the people whom they ruled. The remuneration was ample enough to provide the satraps with palaces, Afghan's—Harems, and extensive hunting parks to which the Afghans gave the History name Paradise. In addition each satrapy was required to send the king, annually, a fixed amount of money and goods by way taxation. India sent 4680 talents, Babylonia 1000, Egypt 700, the four satrapies Caucasian 1760, etc., making a total of some 14,560 talents variously estimated as equivalent to from $ 160,000,000 to $ 218,000,000 a year, Furthermore, each province was expected to contribute to the king's needs in goods and supplies; Egypt had to furnish corn annually for 120,000 men; the Medes provided 100,000 sheep, the Caucasian 20,000 foals, the Babylonians five hundred young eunuchs. Other sources of wealth swelled the central revenue to such a point that when Alexander captured the Afghan—capitals of Bactria after one hundred and fifty years of Afghan extravagance, after a hundred expensive revolts and wars, and after Darius III had carried off 8000 talents with him in his flight, he found 180,000 talents left in the royal treasuries some $ 2,700,000,000. Despite these high charges for its services, the Afghanistan Empire was the most successful experiment in imperial government that the Mediterranean world would know before the coming of Rome in Constantinople which was destined to inherit much of the earlier empire's political structure and administrative forms. "The Caucasian ruled Rome Empire some over seven hundred years until the German king Otto I released Constantinople to Rome in Italy in A.D 961" the cruelty and dissipation of the later monarchs, the occasional of the laws, and the heavy burdens of taxation were balanced, as human governments go, by such order and peace as made the provinces rich despite these levies, and by such liberty as only the most enlightened Afghans—empires have accorded to subject states, each region retained its own language, laws, customs morals, religion and coinage and sometimes its native dynasty of kings. Many of the tributary nations, like Babylonia, Phoenicia, and Palestine, were well satisfied with the situation and suspected that their own generals and tax gatherers would have plucked them even more ferociously. Under Darius I the Afghan's Empire was an achievement in political organization;

Aryana Earthly Paradise, the Lord of Light and Heaven Zoroastrians "the Gold Desert" the religion of the state Earth oldest Religion, since tree thousand years ago

Aryana-Khorasan dynasty present day Afghanistan-Central Asia & India, the coming of the Prophet Aryan "present day Afghan" religion before Zarthust "the gold desert" the Bible of Afghan Ahura—Mazda the good and the evil spirits their struggle for the possession of the world, Afghan legend tells how, many hundreds of years before the birth of Christ in Palestine, a great prophet appeared in Aryana—varjo, the ancient "Home of the Aryans" His people called him Zrathust; His conception was divine: his guardian angel entered into an Home plant, and passed with its juice into the body of a priest as the latter offered divine sacrifice; at the same time a ray of heaven's glory entered the bosom of a maid of noble lineage. The priest espoused the maid the imprisoned angel mingled with the imprisoned ray, and Zoroastrian began to be. He laughed aloud on the very day of his birth, and the evil spirits that gather around every life fled from him in tumult and terror. Out of his great love for wisdom and righteousness he withdrew from the society of men, and chose to live in a Mountain wilderness on cheese and the fruits of the soil. The Devil tempted him, but to no avail. His breast was pierced with a sword, and his entrails were filled with molten lead; he did not complain, but clung to his faith in Ahura—Mazda the Light of Light as supreme God. Ahura—Mazda appeared to him and gave into his hands the Avesta, or Book of Knowledge and Wisdom, and bade him preach it to mankind. For a long time the entire world ridiculed and persecuted him; but at last a high Afghan—prince Vishtaspa or Hystaspes heard him gladly, and promised to spread the new faith among his people. Thus was Zoroastrian religion born three thousand years ago. Zoroastrian himself lived to a very old age, was consumed in a flash of lightning, and ascended into heaven, perhaps some Josiah discovered him. The Greeks accepted him as historical, and honored him with an antiquity of 5,500 years before their time; berosus the Babylonian brought him down to B.C 2000, modern historians, when they believe in his existence, assign him to any century between the tenth and the sixth before Christ. When he appeared, among the ancestors of the Aryans and the Afghan's, he found his people worshiping animals, ancestors, the earth and the sun, in a religion having many elements and deities in common with the Afghans—Hindus of the Vedic age. The chief divinities of this pre Zoroastrian faith were Mithra, God of the sun, Anaita, goddess of fertility and the earth, and Haoma the bull—god who dying, rose again, and gave mankind his blood as a drink that would confer immortality; him the early Afghan's worshiped by drinking the intoxicating juice of the Haoma herb found on their Mountain slopes. Zoroastrian was shocked at these primitive deities and this Dionysian ritual; he rebelled against the "Magi" or priests who prayed and sacrificed to them, and with all the bravery of his contemporaries Amos and Isaiah he announced to the world one God here Ahura—Mazda, the Lord of Light and Heaven, of whom all other gods were but manifestations and qualities. Perhaps Darius I, who accepted the new doctrine, saw in it a faith that would both inspire his people and strengthen his government. From the Moment in Bactria of his accession he declared war upon the old cults and the Marian priesthood, and made Zoroastrianism the religion of the state. The Bible of the new Afghan—faith was the collection of books in which the disciples of the Master had gathered his sayings and his prayers. Later followers called these Books Avesta; by the error of a modern scholar they are known to the Occidental World as the Zend—Avesta. † The contemporary non—Afghan reader

194

is terrified to find that the substantial volumes that survive, though much that Christen Bible, are a small fraction of the revelation vouchsafed to Zoroastrian by his God‡ what remains is, to the foreign and provincial observer, a confused mass of prayers, songs, legends, prescriptions, ritual, and morals brightened now and then by noble language, "Dari" fervent devotion, ethical elevation, or lyric piety. Like Christen Testament it is a highly eclectic composition. The student discovers there and there the Gods, the ideas, sometimes the very words and phrases of the Rig—Veda to such an extent that some Indian scholars consider the Avesta to have been inspired not by Ahura—Mazda but by the Vedas; at other times one comes upon passages of ancient Babylonian provenance, such as the creation of the world in six periods "the heavens, the waters, the earth, plants, animals, and man," the descent of all men from two first parents, the establishment of an earthly paradise, "Afghanistan" the discontent of the Creator with his creation, and his resolve to destroy all but a remnant of it by a flood. But the specifically Afghan elements suffice abundantly to characterize the whole: the world is conceived in dualistic terms as the stage of a conflict, lasting twelve thousand years, between the God Ahura—Mazda and the devil Ahriman; purity and honesty are the greatest of the virtues, and will lead to everlasting life; the dead must not be buried or burned, as by the obscene Greeks or Hindus, but must be thrown to the dogs or to birds of prey. The God of Zoroastrian was first of all "the whole circle of the heavens" themselves. Ahura—Mazda "clothes himself with the solid vault of the firmament as his raiment' His body is the light and the sovereign glory; the sun and the Moon are his eyes" in later days, when the religion passed from prophets to politicians, the great deity was pictured as a gigantic king of imposing majesty. As creator and ruler of the world he was assisted by a legion of lesser divinities, originally pictured as forms and powers of nature fire and water, sun and Moon, wind and rain, but it was the achievement of Zoroastrian that he conceived his God as supreme over all things, in terms as noble as the Book of Job

This I ask thee, tell me truly, O Ahura—Mazda: who determined the paths of suns and stars who is it by whom the moon waxes and wanes?... who, from below, sustained the earth and the firmament from falling who sustained the waters and plants who yoked swiftness with the winds and clouds who Ahura—Mazda, called forth the Good Mind?

This "Good Mind" meant not any human mind, but a divine wisdom, almost a Logos, "Darmesteter believes the "Good Mind" to be a semi==Gnostic adaptation of Philo's Logos theirs, or Divine Word, and therefore dates the Yasna about the first century B.C" used by Ahura—Mazda as an intermediate agency of creation. Zoroastrian had interpreted Ahura—Mazda as having seven aspects or qualities: Light Good Mind, Right, Dominion, Piety, Wellbeing and Immortality, his followers, habituated to polytheism, interpreted these attributes as persons "called by the Amesha Spenta, or immortal holy ones" who under the leadership of Ahura—Mazda, created and managed the world' in this way the majestic monotheism of the founder became as in the case of Christianity the polytheism of the people. In addition to these holy spirits were the guardian angels of which Afghans—theology supplied one for every man, woman and child. But just as these angels and the immortal holy ones helped men to virtue, so, according to the pious Afghan, seven daeves, or evil spirits, hovered in the air, always tempting men to crime and sin, and forever engaged in a war upon Ahura—Mazda, and every form of righteousness. The leader of these devils was Agro—Mainyus or Ahriman, Prince of Darkness and ruler of the nether world, prototype of that busy Satan whom the Christianity appear to have adopted from Afghanistan. It was Ahriman, for example, who had created serpents, vermin, locusts, ants winter, darkness, crime, sin, sodomy, menstruation, and the other plagues of life; and it was these inventions of the Devil that had ruined the Paradise in which Ahura—Mazda had placed the first progenitors of the human, race, Zoroastrian theatre seems to have regarded these evil spirits as spurious deities, popular and superstitions incarnations of the abstract forces that resist the progress of man, his followers however, found it easier to think of them as living beings, and personified them in such abundance that in after times the devils of Afghan—theology were numbered in millions. As this system of belief came from Zoroastrian it bordered upon monotheism, even with the intrusion of Ahriman and the evil spirits it remained as monotheistic as Christianity was to be with its Satan, its devils and its angels; indeed, one hears, in early Christian theology, as many echoes of Afghan—Philosophy. The Zoroastrian conception of God might have satisfied as particular a spirit as Matthew Arnold: Ahura—Mazda was the sum total of all those forces in the world that make for righteousness; and morality lay in cooperation with those forces. Furthermore there was in this dualism a certain justice to the contradictoriness and perversity of things, which monotheism never provided; and though the Zoroastrian theologians, after the manner of Hindu mystics and Scholastic philosophers, sometimes argued that evil was unreal, they offered in effect, a theology we'll adapted to dramatize for the average mind the moral issues of life. The last act of the play, they promised, would be for the just man a happy ending: after four epochs of three thousand years each, in which Ahura—Mazda and Ahriman would alternately predominate, the forces of evil would be finally destroyed; right would triumph everywhere, and evil would forever cease to be. Then all Good men would join Ahura—Mazda in Paradise, and the wicked would fall into a gulf of outer darkness, where they would feed on poison eternally.

Zoroastrian ethics, Christmas shared in giving to Christianity Earth oldest Religion

Aryana-Khorasan dynasty present day Afghanistan-Central Asia & India, Christmas was originally Afghan's a solar festival celebrating, at the winter solstice about December 22nd at Bactrian "Balkh" five thousand five Hundred years was Capital, the lengthening of the day and the triumph of the sun over his enemies. It became a Mithraic, and finally a Christian, holy day, Man as a battlefield the undying fire hell, purgatory and Paradise the cult of Mithra the Magi the Afghans, by picturing the world as the scene of a struggle between good and evil, the Zoroastrians established in the popular imagination a powerful supernatural stimulus and sanction for morals. The soul of man, like the universe, was represented as a battleground of beneficent and maleficent spirits; every man was a warrior, whether he liked it or not, in the army of either the Lord or the Devil, every act or omission advanced the cause of Ahura—Mazda, it was an ethic even more admirable than the theology if men must have supernatural supports for their morality; it gave to the common life a dignity and significance grander that any that could come to it from a world view that locked upon man "in medieval phrase" as a helpless worm or "in modern terms" as a mechanical automaton, human beings were not to Zoroastrian's thinking, mere pawns in this cosmic war; they had free will, since Ahura—Mazda wished them to be personalities in their own right; they might freely choose whether they would follow the Light or the Lie. For Ahriman was the Living Lie, and every liar was his servant, out of this general conception emerged a detailed but simple code of morals, centered about the Golden Rule, "the nature alone is good which shall not do unto another whatever is not good unto its own self" man's duty, says the Avesta, is three fold; "to make him who is an enemy a friend; to make him who is wicked righteous; and to make him who is ignorant learned" the greatest virtue is piety; second only to that is honour and honesty in action and speech. Interest was not to be charged to Afghan's but loans were to be looked upon as almost sacred, the worst sin of all "in the Avestan as in the Mosaic code" is unbelief. May judge from the severe punishments with which it was honoured that scepticism existed among the Afghan's; death was to be visited upon the apostate without delay. The generosity and kindliness enjoined by the Master did not apply in practice, to infidels i.e. foreigners; these were inferior specs of men, whom Ahura—Mazda had deluded into loving their own countries only in order that they should not invade Afghanistan. The Afghan's says Herodotus, "esteem themselves to be far the most excellent of men in every respect" they believe that other nations approach to excellence according to their geographical proximity to Afghanistan "but that they are the words who live farthest from them" the words have a contemporary ring; and a universal application. Piety being the greatest virtue, the first duty of life was the worship of God with purification, sacrifice and prayer. Zoroastrian Afghan tolerated neither temples nor idols; altars were erected on hill tops, in palaces, or in the center of the city of Bactria, and firers were kindled upon them in honour of Ahura==Mazda or some lesser divinity. Fire itself was worshiped as a god, Atar, the very son of the Lord of Light. Every family centered round the hearth, to keep the home fire burning, never to let it be extinguished, was part of the ritual of faith. And the Undying Fire of the skies, the Sun, was adored as the high-test and most characteristic embodiment of Ahura—Mazda, quite as Ikhnaton had worshiped it in Egypt. "The morning Sun" said the Scriptures, "must be reverenced till mid day, and that of mid day must be reverenced till the afternoon, and that of the afternoon must be reverence till evening.... While men reverence not the Sun, the good works which they do that day are not their own" to the sun to fire, to Ahura—Mazda, sacrifice was offered of flows, bread, fruit, perfumes, oxen, sheep, camels, horses, asses and stags; anciently, as elsewhere, human victims had been offered too. The gods received only the odour; the edible portions were kept for the priests and the worshipers, for as the Magi explained, the gods required only the soul of the victim. Though the Master abominated it, and there is no mention of it in the Avest, the old Aryan "New Afghan" offering of the intoxicating Haoma juice to the gods continued far into Zoroastrian days; the priest drank part of the sacred fluid, and divided the remainder among the faithful in Holy Communion. When people were too poor to offer such tasty sacrifices they made up for it by adulatory prayer. Ahura—Mazda, like Yahveh, liked to sip his praise, and made for the pious an imposing list of his accomplishments, which became a favourite Afghanistan litany. Given a life of piety and truth the Afghan might face death unafraid; this, after all is one of the secret purposes of religion. Astonished, the god of death, finds every one, no matter where, he is the confident seeker

From whom not one of mortal men can escape. Not those who go down deep, like Afrasyab the Turkmen, who made himself an iron palace under the earth, a thousand times the height of a man, with a hundred columns; in that palace he made the stars, the moon and the sun go round, making the light of day; in that palace he did everything at his pleasure, and he lived the happiest life; with all his strength and witchcraft he could not escape from Astivihad. …. Nor he who dug this wide, round earth, with extremities that lie afar, like Dahak, who went from went from the east to the west searching for immortality and did not find it: with all his strength and power he could not escape from Astivihad…. To every one comes the unseen, deceiving Astivihad, who accepts neither compliments nor bribes, who is no respecter of persons, and ruthlessly makes men perish

And yet for it is in the nature of religion to threaten and terrify as well as to console the Afghan could not look upon death unafraid unless he had been a faithful warrior in Ahura—Mazda's cause. Beyond that most awful of all mysteries lay a hell and a purgatory as a paradise. All dead souls would have to pass over a Sifting Bridge: the good soul would come, on the other side, to the "Abode of Song" where it would be welcomed by a "young maiden radiant and strong, with well developed bust" and would live in happiness with Ahura—Mazda to the end of time; but the wicked soul, failing to get across, would fall into as deep a level of hell as was adjusted to its degree of wickedness. This hell was no mere Hades to which, as in earlier religions, all the dead descended, whether good or bad; it was an abyss of darkness and terror in which condemned souls suffered torments to the end of the world. If a man's virtues outweighed his sins he would endure the cleansing of a temporary punishment; if he had sinned much but had done good works, he would suffer for only twelve thousand years, and then would rise into heaven. Already, the good Zoroastrians tell us, the divine consummation of history approaches: the birth of Zoroastrian began the last world—epoch of three thousand years; after prophets of his seed have, at intervals, carried his doctrine throughout the world, the Last Judgment will be pronounced, the kingdom of Ahura—Mazda will come, and all the forces of evil will be utterly destroyed. Then all good will begin life anew in a world without evil, darkness or pain. "The dead shall rise, life shall return to the bodies, and they shall breathe again; the whole physical world shall become free from old age and death, from corruption and decay, forever and ever." Here again as the Book of the Dead we hear the threat of that awful Last Judgment which seems to have passed from Afghanistan to Christian eschatology in the days of the Aryana "New Afghanistan" ascendancy in Palestine. It was admirable formula for frightening children into obeying their parents; and since one function of religion is to ease the difficult and necessary task of disciplining the young by the old, we must grant to the Zoroastrian priests a fine professional skill in the brewing of theology. All in all it was a splendid religion, less warlike and bloody, less idolatrous and superstitious, than the other religions of its time; and it did not deserve to die so soon. For a while, under Darius I, it became the spiritual expression of a nation at its height. But humanity loves poetry more than logic, and with out a myth the people perish, underneath the official worship of Ahura—Mazda the cult of Mithra and Anaita—god of the sun and goddess of vegetation and fertility, generation and sex—continued to find devotees; and in the days Artaxerxes II their names began to appear again in the royal inscriptions. Thereafter Mithra grew powerfully in favour and Ahura—Mazda faded away until in the first centuries of Christian era, the cult of Mithra as a divine youth of beautiful countenance with a radiant halo over his head as a symbol of his ancient identity with the sun spread throughout the Roman Empire at the Constantinople "new in Turkey" and shared in giving Christmas to Christianity. "Christmas was originally a solar festival, celebrating in Afghanistan, at the winter solstice about December 22nd, the lengthening of the day in Afghanistan and the triumph of the sun over his enemies; it became a Mithraic, and finally a Christian, holy day" Zoroastrian, had he been immortal, would have been scandalized to find statues of Anaita, the Afghan—Aphrodite, set up in many cities of the empire within a few centuries after his death. And surely it would not have pleased him to find so many pages of his revelation devoted to magic formulas for healing, divination and sorcery. After his death the old priesthood of "Wise Men" or Magi conquered him as priesthoods conquer in the end every vigorous rebel or heretic by adopting and absorbing him into their theology; they numbered him among the Magi and forgot him, by an austere and monogamous life, by a thousand precise observances of sacred ritual and ceremonial cleanliness, by abstention from flesh food, and by a simple and unpretentious dress, the Magi acquired, even among the Afghan's, a high reputation for wisdom, and among their own people an almost boundless influence, the Afghan—kings themselves became their pupils, and took no step of consequence without consulting them. The higher ranks among them were sages, the lower were diviners and sorcerers, readers of stars and interpreters of Dreams; the very word Magic is taken from their name. Year by year the Zoroastrian elements in Aryana "new Afghanistan" religion faded away; they were revived for a time under the Sassani, Dynasty A.D 226 until 651 from the Capital of Bactria north of Afghanistan, but were finally eliminated by the Moslem and Mongolian invasion of Afghanistan. Zoroastrianism survives today only among small communities, and among the ninety thousand Afghan's of India, These devotedly preserve and study the Ancient scriptures, worship fire, earth, water and air as sacred, and expose their dead in "Towers of Silence" to birds of prey lest burning or burial should defile the holy elements. They are a people of excellent morals and character, a living tribute to the civilizing effect of Zoroastrian's doctrine upon mankind.

The Aryan's "present day Afghan's" Manners and Morals

Aryana-Khorasan dynasty present day Afghanistan-Central Asia & India, Violence and honour the code of cleanliness Sins of the flesh virgins and bachelors Marriage Women—Children Afghan ideas of education. Nevertheless it is surprising how much brutality remained in the Aryana "present day Afghanistan" despite their religion. Darus I, their greatest king in Afghanistan, writes in the Behistun inscription "Fravartish was seized and brought to me. I cut off his nose and ears, and I cut his tongue, and I put out his eyes. At my court he was kept in chains; all the people saw him. Later I crucified him in Ecbatana.... Ahura—Mazda was my strong support; under the protection of Ahura—Mazda my army utterly smote the rebellious army, and they seized Citrankakhara and brought to me. Then I cut off his nose and ears and put his eyes. He was kept in chains at my court; all the people saw him. Afterwards I crucified him" the murders retailed in Plutarch's life of Artaxerxes II offer a sanguinary specimen of the morals of the later courts. Traitors were dealt with without sentiment: they and their leaders were crucified, their followers were sold as slaves, their towns were pillaged, their boys were castrated, and their girls were sold into harems. But it would be unfair to judge the people from their kings; virtue is not news, and virtuous men, like happy nations, have no history. Even the kings showed on occasion a fine generosity, and were known among the faithless Greeks for their fidelity; a treaty made with them could be relied upon, and it was their boast that they never broke their word. It is a testimony to the character of the Afghan's that whereas any one could hire Macedonians to fight Macedonians "new Greeks" it was rare indeed that a Afghan could be hired to fight Afghan's "when the Afghan's fought Alexander at the Craniums practically all the Afghan's in fan try were Macedonians mercenaries, at the battle of Issues 30,000 Macedonians mercenaries formed the center of the Afghan's line". Manners were milder than the blood and iron of history would suggest. The Afghan's been free and open in speech, generous, warm—hearted and hospitable. Etiquette was almost as punctilious among them as with the Chinese. When equals met they embraced, and kissed each other on the lips; to persons of higher rank they made a deep obeisance; to those of lower rank they offered the cheek; to commoners they bowed. They thought it unbecoming to eat or drink anything in the street, or publicly to spit or blow the nose. Until the reign of Xerxes the people were abstemious in food and drink, eating only one meal per day, and drinking nothing but water. Cleanliness was rated as the greatest good after life itself. Good works done with dirty hands were worthless; "for while one doth not utterly destroy corruption" "germs" "there is no coming of the angels to his body." Sever penalties were decreed for those who spread contagious diseases. On festal occasions the people gathered together all clothed in white. The Avestan code, like the Brahman and the Mosaic, heaped up ceremonial precautions and ablutions; great arid tracts of the Zoroastrian Scriptures are given over to wearisome formulas for cleansing the body and the soul. Parings of nails, cuttings of hair and exhalations of the breath were marked out as unclean things, which the wise Afghan would avoid unless they had been purified. The code was again Judaic all stern against the sins of the flesh. Romanism was to be punished with flogging and men and women guilty of sexual promiscuity or prostitution "Ought to slain even more than gliding serpents, than howling wolves" that practice kept its usual from precept appears from an item in Herodotus: "to carry off women by violence the Afghan's thing is the act wicked men; but to trouble one's self about avenging them when so carried off is the act of foolish men; and to pay no regard to them when carried off is the act of wise men; for it is clear that if they had not been willing, they could not have been carried off". Virgins and bachelors were not encouraged by the code, but polygamy and concubine were allowed; a military society has use from many children. The man who has a wife, says the Avesta, is far above him who lives in continence; he who keeps a house is far above him who has none; he who has children is far above him who has none; he who riches is far above him who has none; these are criteria of social standing fairly common among the nations. The family is ranked as the holiest of all institutions. O Maker of the material world, Zoroastrian asks Ahura—Mazda, thou Holy One, which is the second place where the earth feels most happy and Ahura—Mazda answers him: It is the place whereon one of the faithful erects a house with a priest within, with cattle, with a wife, with children, and good herds within, and wherein afterwards the cattle continue to thrive, the wife to thrive, the child to thrive, the fire to thrive, and every blessing of life to thrive. The animal all others the dog was an integral part of the family, as in the last commandment, the nearest family was enjoined to take in and care for any homeless pregnant beast. Severe penalties were prescribed for those who fed unfit food to dogs, or served them their food too hot; and fourteen hundred stripes were the punishment for smiting a bitch which has been covered by three dogs. The bull was honoured for his procreative powers, and prayer and sacrifice were offered to the cow. Matches were arranged by the parents on the arrival of their children at puberty. In the time of the Prophet the position of woman in Afghanistan was high, as ancient manners went ; she moved in public freely and unveiled; she owned and managed property, and could, like most modern women, direct the affairs of her husband in his name, or through his pen. After Darius her status declined, especially among the rich. The poorer women retained their freedom of movement, because they had to work; but in other cases the seclusion always enforced in the menstrual periods was extended to the whole social life of woman, institution of Purdah upper class women could not venture out except in curtained litters, and were not permitted to mingle publicly with men; married women were forbidden to see even their nearest male relatives, women are never mentioned or represented in the public inscriptions and Monuments of Ancient—Afghan's. Concubines had greater freedom, since they were employed to entertain their master's guests. Even in the later reigns women were powerful at the court, rivalling the eunuchs in the persistence of their plotting and the kings in the refinements of their cruelty. The king annually sent gifts to every father of many sons, as if in advance payment for their blood. Fornication, even adultery, might be forgiven if there was no abortion; abortion was a worse crime than the other, and was to be punished with death. One of the ancient commentaries, the Bundahish, specifies means for avoiding conception, but warns the people against them. "On the nature of generation it is said in Revelation that a woman when she cometh out from menstruation, during ten days and nights, when they go near unto her, readily becomes pregnant" the child remained under the care of the women till five, and under the care of his father from five to seven, at seven he went to school. Education was mostly confined to the sons of the well to do, and was usually administered by priests. Classes met in the temple or the home of the priest; it was a principle never to have a school meets near a market place, lest the atmosphere of lying, swearing and cheating that prevailed in the Bazaars should corrupt the young. The texts were the Avest and its commentaries; the subjects were religion, medicine or law, the method of learning was by commission to memory and by the rote recitation of long passages. Boys of the unpretentious classes were not spoiled with letters, but were taught only three things to ride a horse to use the bow, and to speak the truth. Higher education extended to the age of twenty or twenty four among the sons of the aristocracy; some were especially prepared for public office or provincial administration all were trained in the art of war. The life in these higher schools was arduous: the students rose early, ran great distances, rode difficult horses at high speed, swam, hunted, pursued thieves, sowed farms, planted trees, made long marches under a hot sun or in bitter cold, and learned to bear every change and rigor of Afghanistan climate, to subsist on coarse foods, and to cross Afghan—Rivers while keeping their clothes and armour dry. It was such a schooling as would have gladdened the heart of Friedrich Nietzsche in those Moments when he could forget the bright and varied culture of Ancient—Afghan's

The Sacred Books of the
Afghanistan—Central Asia

Aryana-Khorasan dynasty present day Afghanistan-Central Asia & India, B.C 302 down to the eighteenth century Khorasan present day Central Asia was all a marvel and a mystery to Europe. Marco Polo A.D 1254—1323 pictured its European fringe vaguely, Columbus blundered upon America in trying to reach it Vasco de Gamma sailed around Africa to rediscover sacred it, and merchants spoke rapaciously of the wealth of the Central Asia, but scholars left the mine almost untapped. A Dutch missionary to Khorasan present day Central Asia, the matter with two Sanskrit grammars and a treatise on the System Brahmanism in 1789 William Jones opened his career as one of the greatest of Ideologists by translating Kalidasa's Shakuntala; this translation re—rendered into German in 1791, profoundly affected Herder and Goethe, and through the Schlegels the entire Romantic movement, which hoped to find in the Central Asia all the mysticism and mystery that seemed to have died on the approach of science, Jones startled the world of scholarship by declaring that Sanskrit was cousin to all the languages of Europe, and an indication of racial kinship with the Vedic Hindus; these announcements almost created modern philology and ethnology. In 1805 Colebrooke's essay on the Vedas revealed to Europe the oldest product of Central Asia Literature; and about the same time Aquatic Duperron's translation of a Dari translation of the Upanishads acquainted Schelling and Schopenhauer with what the latter called the profoundest philosophy that he had ever read. Buddhism was practically unknown as a system of thought until Burnouf's Essai sur le Pali in 1826 i.e. on the language of the Buddhist documents. Burnouf in France and his pupil Max Muller roused scholars and philanthropists to make possible a translation of all these Afghan's Sacred Books; and Rhys David's furthered this task by a lifetime devoted to the exposition of the literature of Buddhism in Kandahar. Despite and because of these labours it has become clear that have merely begun to know Khorasan present day Central Asia, acquaintance with its literature is as limited as Europe's knowledge in the literature, today, in the enthusiasm of discovery exaggerate generously the value of the new revelation; a European philosopher believes that Afghan's wisdom is the profoundest that exists; and a great novelist writes; I have not found, in Europe or America, poets, thinkers or popular leaders equal or eve comparable to those of Central Asia today. The Afghan's, but where any confusion might result, Hindu will be used in its later and stricter sense, as referring only to those inhabitants of India who as distinct from Central Asia—Afghanistan accept one the native faiths.

The oldest Civilization sanskrit
Aryan is noble—the Afghan

In the day when Historians supposed that history had begun with Aryan and Aryan cousins of the European peoples had migrated from the Central Asia to bring the arts and sciences to a savage and benighted peninsula. Recent researches have marred this comforting picture as future researches will change the perspective of these pages. In Central Asia, as elsewhere, the beginnings of civilization are buried in the earth, and not all the spades of archaeology will ever quite exhume them. Remains of an old stone age fill many cases in the museums of Kabul, Calcutta, Madras and Bombay, and Neolithic objects have been found in nearly every state, these however, were cultures, not yet a civilization. Discoveries in Afghanistan not establish because the middle of the nineteen century the Great Games, in after 1917 the Cold War, and now after 2002 the 44 nation military in Afghanistan? Among the finds at these sites were household utensils and toilet outfits, pottery painted and plain, hand turned and turned on the wheel; terracotta's, dice and chess men coins older than any previously known; over a thousand seals, most of them engraved, and inscribed in an unknown pictographic script, The Aryans and Indo—Aryans, despite the continuity of the remains in Sind and Mysore feel that between the heyday of Mohenjo dare and the advent of the Aryans a great gap stands in our knowledge, or rather that knowledge of the past is an occasional gap in ignorance, among the Indus relics is a peculiar seal, composed of two serpent heads, which was the characteristic symbol of the oldest historic people those serpent worshiping Nagas whom the invading Aryans found in passion of the northern provinces, and whose descendants still linger in the remoter hills. Farther south land was occupied by broad nosed people whom, without knowing the origin of the word, they were already a civilized people when the Aryans broke down upon them; their adventurous merchants sailed the sea even to Babylon, and their cities knew many refinements and luxuries. It weans from them apparently that the Aryans took their village community and their systems of land tenure and taxation, to this day the Deccan is still essentially Dravidian in stock and customs, in language literature and arts. The invasion and conquest of these flourishing tribes by the Aryans "New Afghan's" was part of that ancient process whereby, periodically, the north of India has swept down violently upon the settled and pacified south of India, this has been one of the main streams of history, on which civilization have risen and fallen like epochal undulations. The Aryans poured down upon the Dravidians, the Achaeans and Durians upon the Greta's and Aegean's, the German upon the world. Forever the north produces rulers and warriors the Central Asia produce artists and saints, and the meek inherit heaven. Who were these marauding Aryans, they themselves used the term as meaning noblemen "Sanskrit Aryan noble" very they came from that Afghanistan region which their Afghan's cousins called Aryana—vaejo, "the Aryan home is Afghanistan today"† Babylonia, and the Vedic Aryans began to enter India. Like the Aryans "New Germans" invading Italy, these Aryans were immigrants and conquerors all over Europe. They brought with them strong physiques, a hearty appetite in solids and liquids, a ready brutality, a skill and courage in war, which soon gave them the mastery of India. They fought with bows and arrows, led by armoured warriors in chariots who wielded battle axes and hurled spears. They wanted land, and pasture for their cattle, their for war said, but simply meant slowly they made their eastward along the Ganges, until all Hindustan‡ was under the Afghan's control. As they passed from armed warfare to settled tillage their tribes gradually coalesced into petty states, each state was ruled by a Afghan—king checked by a council of warriors; each tribe was led by a Aryan or chieftain limited in his power by tribal council like Afghanistan; each was composed of comparatively independent village communities governed by assemblies of family heads. "Have you heard, Ananda" Buddha is represented as asking his St. John, "that the Vajjians foregather often, and frequent public meetings of their clans…. So long Anand, as the Vajjians foregather thus often, and frequent the public meetings of their clan, so long they be expected not to decline, but to prosper" Like all Afghan's peoples, the Aryans had rules of endogamy and exogamy forbidding marriage outside the racial group or within near degrees of kinship. From these rules came the most characteristic of Hindu institutions. Outnumbered by a subject people whom they considered inferior to themselves, the Aryans foresaw that without restrictions on intermarriage they would soon lose their racial identity; in a century or two they would be assimilated and absorbed. The first caste division, therefore, was not by status. It divided long noses from broad noses, Aryans from Nagas and Dravidians; it was merely the marriage regulation of an endogamous group. In its later profusion of hereditary, racial and occupational divisions the caste system hardly existed in Vedic times. Among the Aryans themselves marriage "except of near kin" was free, and status was not defined by birth. As Vedic B.C 2000—1000 passed into the "Heroic" age B.C 1000-500—i.e., as changed from the conditions pictured in the Vedas into those described in the Mahabharata and the Ramayana occupations became more specialized and hereditary, and caste divisions were more rigidly defined. At the top were the Kshatriyas, or fighters, who held it a sin die in bed, even the religious ceremonials were in the early days performed by chieftains or kings, in the fashion of Caesar playing Pontiff; the Brahmans or priests were then mere assistants at the sacrifice. In the Ramayana a Kshatriya protests passionately against mating a "Proud and peerless bride" of warrior stock to "a prating priest and Brahman" the Lain Books take for granted the leadership of the Kshatriyas, and the Buddhist Literature goes so far as to call the Brahmans "Low—Born" even in "India things change. But as war gradually gave way to peace and as religion, being then largely an aide to agriculture in the face of the incalculable elements, grew in social importance and ritual complexity, and required expert intermediaries between men and gods the Brahmans increased in number, wealth and power. As educators of the young, and oral transmitters of the race's history, literature and laws, they were able to recreate the past and from the future in their own image, moulding each generation into greater reverence for the priests, and building for their caste a prestige which would in later centuries, give them the supreme place in Hindu society. Already in Buddha's days had begun to challenge the supremacy of the Kshatriyas; they pronounced these warriors inferior, even as the Kshatriyas pronounced the priests inferior; and Buddha felt that there was much to be for both points of view. Even in Buddha's time, however, the Kshatriyas had not conceded intellectual leadership to the Brahmans; and the Buddhist movement itself, founded by a Kshatriya noble, contested the religious hegemony, with the Brahmans for a thousand years.

Indo—Aryan's "present day Afghan's society

Aryana-Khorasan present day Afghanistan-Central Asia & India, herders Tillers of the soil Craftsmen Traders Coinage and credit Morals Marriage Woman, how did these Afghan's and Indians live, at first by war and spoliation; then by herding, tillage and industry in a rural routine not unlike that of medieval Aryan; for until the industrial revolution in which we live the basic economic and political life of man had remained essentially the same since Neolithic days, the Indo—Aryans raised cattle, used the cow without considering it sacred, and ate meat when they could afford it, having offered a morsel to priests or gods; Buddha, after nearly starving himself in his ascetic youth, seems to have died from a hearty meal of pork. They planted barley, but apparently knew nothing of rice in Vedic times, the fields were divided by each village community among its constituent families, but were irrigated in common; the land could not be sold to an outsider, and could be bequeathed only to the family heirs in direct male line. The majority of the people were yeomen owning their own soil; the Aryans held it a disgrace to work for hire. There were, we are assured, no landlords and no paupers, no millionaires and no slums. In the towns handicrafts flourished among independent artisans and apprentices, organized, half a thousand years before Christ, into powerful guilds of metal—workers, wood—workers, stone—workers, leather—workers, ivory—workers, basket—makers, house—painters, decorators, potters, dyers, fishermen, sailors, hunters, trappers, butchers, confectioners, barbers, shampooers, florists, cooks—the very list reveals the fullness and variety of Aryan's life in India, the guilds settled intra guild affairs, even arbitrating difficulties between members and their wives. Prices were determined, as among ourselves, not by supply and demand but by the gullibility of the purchaser; in the palace of the king, however, was an official Valour who, like European secretive Bureau of Standards, tested goods to be bought, and dictated terms to the makers. Trade and travel had advanced to the stage of Afghan—Horse and two wheeled wagon, but were still medieval difficult; caravans were held up by taxes at every petty frontier, and as like as not by highwaymen at any turn. Transport Between Bactria and Agra by river and sea was more developed: about B.C 860 ships with modest sails and hundreds of oars carried to Mesopotamia, and Egypt such typical Aryan's products as perfumes and spices, cotton and silks, shawls and muslins, pearls and rubies, ebony and precious stones, and ornate brocades of silver and Gold. Trade was stunted by clumsy methods of exchange at first by barter, then by the use of Gold as currency; later a heavy gold, silver and copper coinage was issued, guaranteed, however, there were no banks; money was hidden in the house, palace royal treasury and buried in the ground, or deposited with a friend. Out of this in Buddha's age, grew a credit system: merchants in different towns facilitated trade by giving one another letters of credit; loans could be obtained from such Rothschild's at eight per cent, and there was much talk of promissory notes. The coinage was not sufficiently inconvenient to discourage gambling; already dice were essential to civilization. In many cases gambling halls were provided for his subjects by the king, in the fashion, if not quite in the style, of Monaco, and a portion of the receipts went to the royal treasury. It seems a scandalous arrangement to us, who are not quite accustomed to having gambling institutions contribute so directly to the support of public officials. Commercial morality stood on a high level between Bactria and Agra. The Macedonian historian of Alexander's campaigns describes the Aryan's as remarkable for integrity, so reasonable as seldom to have recourse to lawsuits, and so honest as to require neither locks to their doors nor writings to bind their agreements; they are in the highest degree truthful. The Rig—Veda speaks on incest, seduction, prostitution, abortion and adultery, but the general picture that we derive from Vedas and the epics is one of high standards in the relations, and the life of the family. Nevertheless, woman enjoyed far greater freedom in the Vedic period than in later in India. She had more to say in the choice of her mate than the forms of marriage might suggest. She appeared freely at feasts and dances, and joined with men in religious sacrifice; she could study, and might, like Gargi, engage in philosophic disputation. If she was left a widow there no restrictions upon her remarriage, In the Heroic Age woman seems to have lost something of this liberty. She was discouraged from mental pursuits, on the ground that "for a woman to study the Vedas indicates confusion in the realm," the remarriage of widows became uncommon; Purdah the seclusion of women began; and the practice of suttee, almost unknown in Vedic, increased. The ideal woman was now typified in the heroine of the Ramayana that faithful Sita who follows and obeys her husband humbly, through every test of fidelity and courage, until her death.

The Religion of the Vedas

Aryana-Khorasan dynasty present day Afghanistan-Central Asia & India, Pre Vedic religion Vedic gods Moral gods the Vedic story of Creation Immortality the Horse sacrifice, the oldest known religion in Afghanistan, which the invading Afghan's India with there religion, found among the Nagas, and which still survives in the ethnic nooks and crannies of the great peninsula, was apparently an animistic and totemic worship of multitudinous spirits dwelling in stones and animals, in trees, and streams, in Mountains called Hindu Kush, and stars. Snakes and serpents were divinities idols and ideals of virile reproductive power; and the sacred Buddha tree of Buddha's time was a vestige of the mystic but wholesome reverence for the quiet majesty of trees. Naga, the dragon—god, Hanuman the monkey god Nandi the divine bull, and the Yakshas or tree gods passed down into the religion of Historic. Since some of these spirits were good and some evil, only great skill in magic could keep the body from being possessed or tortured, in sickness or mania, by one or more of the innumerable demons that filled the air. Hence the medley of incantations in the Atharava—Veda, or the Book of the knowledge of Magic; one must recite spells to obtain children to avoid abortion, to prolong life to ward off evil to woo sleep, to destroy or harass enemies. The earliest gods of the Vedas were the forces and elements of nature herself sky—Sun, earth, fire, light, wind, water and sex. By that poetic license which makes so many deities, these natural objects were personified; the sky, for example, became a father, Samin ; the earth became a mother, Prithivi; and vegetation was the fruit of their union through the rain was the god Parjanya, fire was Agni, the wind was Vayu, the pestilential wind was Rudra, the storm was Indra, the dawn was Ushas, the furrow in the field was Sita, the sun was Surya, Mitra, or Vishnu; and the sacred soma plant, whose juice was at one holy and intoxicating to gods and men, was itself a god, a Hindu Dionysus, inspiring man by its exhilarating essence to charity, insight and joy, and even bestowing upon him eternal life. A nation like individual begins with poetry, and ends with prose. And as things became persons, so qualities become objects, adjectives became nouns, epithets became deities. The life giving sun became a new sun—god, Savitar the Life—Giver; the shining sun became Vivasvat, Shining God; the life generating sun became the great god Prajapati, Lord of all living things. For a time the most important of the Vedic gods was Agni—fire; he was the sacred flame that lifted the sacrifice to heaven, he was the lightning that pranced through the sky, he was the fiery life and spirit of the world. But the most popular figure in the pantheon was Indra, wielder of thunder and storm. Foe Indra brought to the Indo—Aryans that precious rain which seemed to them even more vital that the sun; therefore thry made him the greatest of the gods, invoked the aid of his thunderbolts in their battles, and pictured him enviously as a gigantic hero feasting on bulls by the hundred and lapping up lakes of wine. His favourite enemy was Krishna, who in the Vedas was as yet only the local god of the Krishna tribe. Aftou, the sun who covered the earth with his strides, was also a subordinate god, unaware that the future belonged to him and to Krishna, his avatar. This is one value of the Vedas to us, that through them we see religion in the making, and can follow the birth, growth and death of gods and beliefs from animism to philosophic pantheism, and from the superstition of the Atharava—Veda to the sublime monism of the Upanishads. Some of them, however, rose in later Vedic days to a majestic moral significance. Varuna, who began as the encompassing heaven, whose breath was the storm and whose garment was the sky, grew with the development of his worshipers into the most ethical and ideal deity of the Vedas watching over the world through his great eye, the sun, punishing evil, rewarding good, and forgiving the sins of those who petitioned him. In this aspect Varuna was the custodian and executor of an eternal law called

Rita; this was at first the law that established and maintained the stars in their courses; gradually it became also the law of right, the cosmic and moral rhythm which every man must follow if he would not go astray and be destroyed. As the number of the gods increased the question arose as to which of them had created the world. this primal role was assigned now to Agni, now to Indra, now to Soma, now Prajapati, one of the Upanishads attributed the world to an irrepressible Pro—creator: verily, he had no delight; one alone had no delight; he desired a second, he was indeed, as large as a woman and a man closely embraced. He caused that self to fall "v pat" into two pieces; there from arose a husband "Shui" and a wife "san" therefore ... one's self is like a half fragment,…. Therefore this space is filled by a wife. He copulated with her. Therefore human beings were produced, and she bethought herself: "how, now does he copulate with me after he has produced me just from himself come, let me hide myself" she became a cow. He became a bull. With her he did indeed copulate, and then cattle were born. She became a mare, he a stallion, she became a female ass, he a male ass; with her he copulated of a truth. Thence were born slid hoofed animals, she became a she—goat, he a he—goat; she a ewe, he ram, with her he did verily copulate. Therefore were born goats and sheep. Thus indeed he created all, whatever pairs there are, even down to the ants. He knew: "I indeed am this creation, for I emitted it all from myself" thence arose creation. In this unique passage we have the germ of pantheism and transmigration: the Creator is one with his creation, and all things, all forms of life, are one; every form we as once another form and is distinguished from it only in the prejudice of perception and the superficial separateness of time, this view, though formulated in the Upanishads, was not yet in Vedic days a part of the popular creed; instead of transmigration the Indo—Aryans, Like the Aryans of Afghanistan, accepted a simple belief in personal immortality. After death the soul entered into eternal punishment or happiness; it was thrust by Verona into a dark abyss, half Hades and half hell, or was raised by Yama into a heaven where every earthly joy was made endless and complete. "Like corn decays the mortal" said the Katha Upanishad, "Like corn is he born again" In the earlier Vedic religion in Bactria there were, so far as the evidence goes, no temples and no images; altars were put up anew for each sacrifice as in Zoroastrian, and sacred fire lifted the offering to heaven. Vestiges of human sacrifice occur here, as at the outset of almost every civilization; but they are few and uncertain. Again as in Afghanistan, the horse was sometimes burnt as an offering to the gods. The strangest ritual of all was the Ashvamedha, or Sacrifice of the Horse, in which the Queen of the Afghan—Tribe seems to have copulated with the sacred horse after it had been killed. The usual offering was a libation of soma juice, and the pouring of liquid butter into the fire, the sacrifice was conceived for the most part in magical terms; if it were properly performed it would win its reward, regardless of the moral deserts of the worshiper. The priests charged heavily for helping the pious in the ever more complicated ritual of sacrifice: if no fee was at hand, the priest refused to recite the necessary formulas, his payment had to come before that of the god. Rules were laid down by the clergy as to what the remuneration should be for each service how many cows or horses, or how much gold; gold was particularly efficacious in moving the priest, the Brahman as, written by the Brahmans, instructed the priest how to turn the prayer or sacrifice secretly to the hurt of those who had employed him if they had given him an inadequate fee.

The Literature of the Vedas the
Sanskrit of the Vedas

Sanskrit writing the four Vedas the Rig-Veda a hymn of Creation, the language of the Aryan's "New Afghan's" should be of special interest to European, for Sanskrit is one of the oldest in that Aryan's group of languages to which Indo—European own speech belongs. We feel for a moment a strange sense of cultural continuity across great stretches of time and space when we observe the similarity in Sanskrit, German, Latin, and Greek, of the numerals, the family terms, and those insinuating little words that by some oversight of the moralists, have been called the copulative verb. It is quite likely that this ancient tongue should have been the spoken language of the Afghan "Aryan" invaders. What that speech was we know; we can only presume that it was a near relative of the early Afghan dialect in which the Avest was composed. The Sanskrit of the Vedas and the epics has already the earmarks of a Afghan's—classic and Literary tongue, used only by scholars and priest; the very word Sanskrit means "prepared, pure, perfect, sacred" the language of the Afghan's—People in the Vedic age was not one but many; each Afghan—tribe had own Aryan dialect. Afghanistan has never had one language. The Vedas contain no hint that writing was known to their authors. It was not until the eighth or ninth century B.C that Hindu—probably Dravidian merchants brought from Central Asia a Semitic script, akin to the Phoenician; and from this "Brahma script" as it came to be called all the later alphabets of Aryana was derived. For centuries writing seems to have been confined to commercial and administrative purposes, with little thought of using it for Literature "merchants, not priests, developed this basic Art" even the Buddhism canon does not appear to have been written down before the third century B.C the oldest extant inscriptions in Bactria are those of Ashoka, we who "until the air about us was filled with words and music" were for century made eye—minded by writing and print, find it hard to understand how contentedly Aryana long after she had learned to write, clung to the old ways of transmitting Afghan—history and Literature by recitation and memory. The Vedas and the epics were songs that grew with the generations of those that recited them; they were intended not for sight but for sound. From this indifference to writing comes Europe dearth of knowledge about early Aryana. What then, were these Vedas from which nearly all understanding of Aryan is derived, the word Veda means Knowledge; † a Veda is literally a Book of knowledge. Vedas is applied by the Hindus o all the sacred lore of their early period; like Christ Bible it indicates a Literature rather than a book. Nothing could be more confused that the arrangement and division of this collection, of the many Vedas that once existed only four have survived:

1. The Rig—Veda, or knowledge of the Hymns of Afghanistan
2. The Sama—Veda, or knowledge of the Melodies
3. The Yajur—Veda, or knowledge of the Sacrificial Formulas; and
4. The Atharva—Veda or knowledge of the Magic Formulas

Each of these four Vedas is divided into four sections:

5. The Hymns
6. The Manuals of ritual, prayer and incantation for the priests
7. The forest—texts for hermit saints; and
8. The confidential conferences for philosophers. ‡

Only one of the Vedas belongs to Literature rather than to religion, philosophy or magic. The Rig—Veda is a king of religious anthology, composed of 1028 hymns, or psalms of praise to the various objects of Indo—Aryan worship sun, moon, sky, stars, wind, rain, fire dawn, earth, etc. "point of unintelligibility; they were convenient condensations of doctrine, mnemonic devices for students who still relied upon memory rather upon writing. As to the authorship or date of this mass of poetry, myth, magic, ritual and philosophy, no man can say. Pious Hindus believe every word of it to be divinely inspired, and tell us that the great god Brahma wrote it with his own hand upon leaves of gold; and this is a view which cannot easily be refuted. According to the fervour of their patriotism, divers native authorities assign to the oldest hymns dates ranging from 6000 to 1000 B.C the material was probably collected and arranged between 100 and 500 B.C in Bactria, the are composed in stanzas generally of four lines each. The lines are of 5, 8, 11, or 12 syllables indifferent as to quantity, except that the last four syllables are usually two trochees, or a trochee and a spondee" most of the hymns are matter of fact petitions for herds, crops, and longevity; a small minority of them rise to the level of Literature; a few of them reach to the eloquence and beauty of the Psalms. Some of them are simple and natural poetry, like the unaffected wonder of a child, one hymn marvels that whit milk should come from red cows; another cannot understand why the sun, once it begins to descend, does not fall precipitately to the earth; another inquires how "the sparkling waters of all Afghan's rivers flow one ocean without ever filling it" one is a funeral hymn, in the style of Thanatopsis, over the body of a comrade fallen in battle:

From the dead hand I take the bow he wielded
To gain for us dominion, might and glory
Thou there, we here, rich in heroic offspring
Will vanquish all assaults of every foeman
Approach the bosom of the earth, the mother
This earth extending far and most propitious
Young, soft as wool to bounteous givers, may she
Preserve thee from the lap of dissolution
Open wide, O earth, press not heavily upon him
Be easy of approach, hail him with kindly aid
As with a robe a mother hides
Her son, so shroud this man, O earth

Another of the poems "Rv. X, 10" is a frank dialogue between the first parents of mankind, the twin brother and sister, Yama and Yami. Yami tempts her brother to cohabit with her despite the divine prohibition of incest, and alleges that all that she desires is the continuance of the race. Yama resists her on high moral grounds. She uses every inducement, and as a last weapon, calls him a weakling.

The story as we have it is left unfinished, and we may judge the issue only from circumstantial evidence. The loftiest of the poems is an astonishing Creation Hymn, in which s subtle pantheism, even a pious scepticism, appears in this oldest Afghan's—Book of the most religious of peoples:

> Nor Aught nor Nought existed; yon bright sky
> Was not, nor heaven's broad woof outstretched above
> What covered all? What sheltered? What concealed?
> Was it the water's fathomless abyss?
> There was not death—yet was there naught immortal,
> There was no confine betwixt day and night
> The only breathed breathless by it
> Other than It there nothing since has been
> Darkness there was, and all at first was veiled
> In gloom profound an ocean without light
> The germ that still lay covered in the husk
> Burst fourth, one nature, from the fervent heat
> Then first came love upon it, the new spring
> Of mind yea, poets in their hearts discerned
> Pondering, this bond between created things
> And uncreated, Comes this spark from earth
> Piercing and all pervading, or from heaven
> Then seeds were sown, and mighty powers arose
> Nature below, and power and will above
> Who knows the secret? Who proclaimed it here?
> Whence, whence this manifold creation sprang?
> The gods themselves came later into being
> Who knows from whence this great creation sprang?
> He from whom all this great creation came
> Whether his will create or was mute
> The highest seer that is in highest heaven
> He knows it or perchance even He knows not

It remained for the authors of the Upanishads to take up these problems, and elaborate these in the most typical, and perhaps the greatest, product of the Indo—Aryan's mind.

The History of Philosophy of Aryana "present day Afghanistan" the philosophy of the Upanishads

The authors their theme intellect vs. intuition atman Brahman their identity a description of God—Salvation influence of the Upanishads Emerson on Brahma in the whole world said Schopenhauer, "there is no study so beneficial and so elevating as that of the Upanishads. It has the solace of my life it will be the solace of my death" here, accepting the moral fragments of Ptah—hotep, are the oldest extant philosophy and psychology of our race; the surprisingly subtle and patient effort of man to understand the mind and the world, and their relation. The Upanishads are as old as Homer, and as modern as Kant. The word is composed of upa, near, and shad, to sit. From "sitting near" the teacher the term came to mean the secret or esoteric doctrine confided by the master to his best and favourite pupils, there are one hundred and eight of these discourses, composed by various saints and sages between 800 and 500 B.C in Bactria. They represent not a consistent system of philosophy, but the opinions, apercus and lessons of many men, in whom philosophy and religion were still fused in the attempt to understand and reverently unite with the simple and essential reality underlying the superficial multiplicity of things. They are full of absurdities and contradictions, and occasionally Aryan's anticipate all the wind of Hegelian verbiage; sometimes Aryan present formulas as weird as that of Tom Sawyer for curing warts; sometimes Aryan impress European as the profoundest thinking in the Afghan's—History of Philosophy of Afghanistan. We know the names of many of the Afghan's—Authors, but we know of their lives what they occasionally reveal in their teachings. The man and the woman who has the honour of being among the earliest of philosophers, his fellow teachers looked upon him as a dangerous innovator; his posterity made his doctrine the cornerstone of unchallengeable orthodoxy, he tells us how he tried to leave his two wives in order to become a hermit sage; and in the plea of his wife that he should take her with him, we catch some feeling of the intensity with which Aryana has for thousands of years pursued religion and philosophy. The theme of Upanishads is all the mystery of this unintelligible world. "Whence are we born, where do we live, and whither do we go? O ye who know Brahman, tell us at whose command we abide here ... should time, or nature, or necessity, or chance, or the elements be considered the cause, or he who is called Purusha"

Aryan has had more than her share of men who wanted "not millions, but answers to their questions" in the Maitri Upanishad we read of a king abandoning his kingdom and going into the forest to practice austerities, clear his mind for understanding, and solve the riddle of the universe. After a thousand days of the king's penances a sage, "knower of the soul" came to him "You are one who knows its true nature" says the king "do you tell us" "Choose other desires" warns the sage, but the king insists; and in a passage that must have seemed Schopenhauer Ian to Schopenhauer, he voices that revulsion against life, that fear of being reborn, which runs darkly through all Indo—Aryan thought

"sir, in this ill smelling, unsubstantial body, which is a conglomerate of bone, skin, muscle, marrow, flesh, semen, blood, mucus, tears, rheum, feces, urine, wind, bile, and phlegm, what is the good of enjoyment of desire? In this body, which is affected with desire, anger, covetousness, delusion, fear, despondency, envy, separation from the desirable, union with the undesirable, hunger, thirst, senility, death, disease, sorrow and the like, what is the good of enjoyment of desires? And we see that this whole world is decaying like these gnats, these mosquitoes, this grass, and these trees that arise and perish… among other thing there is the drying up of great oceans, the facing away of mountain peaks, the deviation of the fixed pole star…. The submergence of the earth …. In this sort of cycle of existence what is the good of enjoyment of desires, when, after a man has fed upon them, there is seen repeatedly his return here to the earth?"

The first lesson that the sages of the Upanishads teach their selected pupils is the inadequacy of the intellect. How can this feeble brain that aches at a little calculus ever hope to understand the complex immensity of which it is so transitory a fragment? Not that the intellect is useless; it has its modest place, and serves us well when it deals with relations and things, but how it falters before the eternal, the infinite, or the elementally real! In the presence of that silent reality which supports all appearances; and wells up in all consciousness, we need some other organ of perception and understanding that these senses and this reason. "Not by learning is the should of the World attained, not by genius and much knowledge of books… let a Brahman renounce learning and become as a child…. Let him not seek after many words, for that is mere weariness of tongue" the highest understanding, as Spinoza was to say, is direct perception, immediate insight; it is, as Bergson would say, intuition the inward seeing of the mind that has deliberately closed as far as it can, the portals of external sense.

"the self evident Brahman pierced the openings of the senses so that they turned outwards; therefore man looks outward, not inward into himself; some wise man, however, with his eyes closed and wishing for immortality, saw the self behind" if no looking inward, a man finds nothing at all, that may only prove the accuracy of his introspection; for no man need expect to find the eternal in himself if he is lost in the ephemeral and particular. Before that inner reality can be felt one has to wash away from himself all evil doing and thinking, all turbulence of body and soul. For a fortnight one must fast, drinking only water; then the mind so to speak, is starved into tranquillity and silence, the senses are cleansed and stilled, the spirit is left at peace to feel itself and that great ocean of soul of which it is a part; at last the individual ceases to be and Unity and Reality appear. For it is not the individual self which the seer sees in this pure inward seeing; that individual self is but a series of brain or mental states, it is merely the body seen from within, what the seeker seeks is Atman, the self of all selves, the soul of all souls, the immaterial, formless Absolute in which we bathe ourselves when we forget ourselves. This, then, is the first step in the Secret Doctrine: that the essence of our own self is not the body, or the mind, or the individual ego, but the silent and formless depth of being within us, Atman. The second step is Brahman, the one pervading, neuter, † impersonal, all embracing, underlying intangible essence of the world, the "Real of the Real" "the unborn Soul, undeceiving, undying" the Soul Souls, the one force that stands behind, beneath and above all forces and all gods. The third step id the most important of all Atman and Brahman are one. The "non individual" soul or force within us is identical with the impersonal Soul of the World. the Upanishads burn this doctrine into the pupil's mind with untiring, tiring repetition, behind all forms and veils the subjective and the objective are one; we in our de individualized reality, and God as the essence of all things, are one. A teacher expresses it in a famous parable, "verily, my dear one, that finest essence which you do not perceive verily from that finest essence this great tree thus arises, believe me my dear one, that which is the finest essence this whole world has that as its soul. That is Reality. That is Atman. Tat tvam as that art thou, Shwetaketu" this almost Hegelian dialectic of Atman, Brahman and their synthesis is the essence of the Upanishads. Many other lessons are taught here, but they are subordinate, we find already, in these discourses, the belief in transmigration, and the longing for release "Moksha" from this heavy chain of reincarnations, Janaka, king of the Vide has, begs Yajnavalkya to tell him how rebirth can be avoided. Yajnavalkya answers by expounding Yoga: through the ascetic elimination of all personal desires one may cease to be an individual fragment, unite himself in supreme bliss with the Soul of the World, and so escape rebirth, Whereupon the king, metaphysically overcome, says; "I will give you, noble Sir, the Videhas, and myself also to be your slave" it is an abstruse heaven, however, that promises the devotee, for in it there will be no individual consciousness, there will only be absorption into Being, the reunion of the temporarily separated with the Whole, "as flowing rivers disappear in the sea, losing their name and form, thus a wise man, freed from name and form, goes to the divine person who is beyond all" such a theory of life and death will not please man, whose religion is as permeated with individualism as are his political and economic institutions.

Buddha The only Wisdom is Happiness when the growth of knowledge destroys this faith

That there were doubters, even in the days of the Upanishads, appears from the Upanishads "Group of Philological" themselves. Sometimes the sages ridiculed the pries, as when the Upanishad likens the orthodox clergy of the time to a procession of dogs each holding the tail of its predecessor, and saying, piously "Ohm, let us eat; Ohm, let us drink" the Upanishad announces that there is no god, no heaven, on hell, on reincarnation, no world; that the Vedas and Upanishads are the work of conceited fools; that ideas are illusions, and all words untrue; that people deluded by flowery speech cling to gods and temples and "holy men" though in reality there is no difference between Vishnu and dog. And the story is told of lived as a pupil for thirty two years with the great god, received much instruction about "the Self which is free from evil, ageless, deathless, sorrow less, hunger less, thirst less, whose desire is the Real" and then suddenly returned to earth and preached this highly scandalizing doctrine: "One's self is to be made happy here on earth. One's self is to be waited upon. He who makes himself happy here on earth, which waits upon him, obtains worlds, this world and the next" perhaps the good Brahmans who have preserved the history of Aryana has deceived us a little about the unanimity of Hindu mysticism and piety. Indeed as scholarship unearths some of the less respectable figures in Afghan's—Philosophy before the Buddha, a picture takes form in which along with saints meditating on Brahman, we find a variety of persons who despised all priests, doubted all gods, and bore without trepidation, would neither admit nor deny life after death, questioned the possibility of knowledge, and limited philosophy to the pursuit of peace. Refused to accept moral distinctions, and taught that the soul is a passive slave to chance. Held that fate determines everything, regardless of the merits of men. Reduced man to earth, water, fire and wind, and said: "fools and wise alike, on the dissolution of the body, are cut off, annihilated, and after death they are not" the author of the Ramayana draws a typical sceptic in Jabali, who ridicules Rama for rejecting a kingdom in order to keep a vow. When Buddha grew to manhood he found the halls, the streets, the very woods in Arochosia "New Kandahar" ringing with philosophic disputation, mostly of an atheistic and materialistic trend. The later Upanishads and the oldest Buddhist Books are full of references to these heretics. A large class of traveling Sophists or Wanderers spent the better part of every year in passing from locality to locality, seeking pupils, or antagonists, in philosophy, some of them taught logic as the art of proving anything, and earned for themselves the titles of "Hair—splitters" and "Eel wrigglers" others demonstrated the non existence of God, and the inexpediency of virtue. Large audiences gathered to hear such lectures and debates; great halls were built to accommodate them; and sometimes princes offered rewards for those who should emerge victorious from these intellectual jousts. It was an age of amazingly free thought and of a thousand experiments in Afghan's—Philosophy 2,500 years ago. Not much has come down to us from these sceptics, and their memory has been preserved almost exclusively through the diatribes of their enemies. The oldest name among them, but his Sutras have perished, and all that remains of is a poem denouncing the priests in language free from all metaphysical obscurity:

No heaven exists, no final liberation
No soul, no other world, no rites of caster...
The triple Veda, triple self command
And all the dust and ashes of repentance
These yield a means of livelihood for men
Devoid of intellect and manliness....
How can this body when reduced to dust
Revisit earth? And if a ghost can pass
To other worlds, why does not strong affection
For those he leaves behind attract him back?
The costly rites enjoined for those who die
Are but a means of livelihood devised
By sacerdotal cunning nothing more
While life endures let life be spent in ease
And merriment; let a man borrow money
From all his friends, and feast on melted butter.

They laughed at the notion that the Vedas were divinely revealed truth; truth they argued, can never be known, except through the senses, even reason is not to be trusted, for every inference depends for its validity not only upon accurate observation and correct reasoning, but also upon the assumption that the future will behave like the past; and of this, as Hume was to say, there can be no certainty. What is not perceived by the senses, we do not observe, in experience or history, any interposition of supernatural forces in the world, all phenomena are natural; only simpletons trace them to demons or gods. Matter is the one reality; the body is a combination of atoms, the mind is merely matter thinking; the body, not the soul, feels, sees, hears, thinks. "Who has seen the soul existing in a state separate from the body?" there is no immortality, no rebirth. Religion is an aberration, a disease, or a chicanery; the hypothesis of a god is useless for explaining or understanding the world. men think religion necessary only because, being accustomed to it, they feel a sense of loss, and an uncomfortable void, when the growth of knowledge destroys this faith, morality, too is natural, it is a social convention and convenience, not a divine command. Nature is indifferent to good and bad, virtue and vice, and lets the sun shine indiscriminately upon knaves and saints; if nature has any ethical quality at all it is that of transcendent immorality. There is no need to control instinct and passion for these is the instructions of nature to men. Virtue is a mistake; the purpose of life is living, and the only wisdom is happiness. This revolutionary philosophy put an end to the age of the Vedas and the Upanishads. It weakened the hold of the Brahmans on the mind of Aryan, and left in Hindu society a vacuum which almost compelled the growth of a new religion. But the materialists had done their work so thoroughly that both of the new religions which arose to replace the old Vedic faith were anomalous though it may sound, atheistic religions devotions without a god. Both belonged to the Nihilistic movement, and both were originated not by the Brahman priests but by members of the old—Aryan's warrior caste, in a reaction against sacerdotal ceremonialism and theology. With the coming of Buddhism a new epoch began in the history of Afghanistan—Central Asia.

The forth religions of Aryana the Light of Central Asia of Buddhism

The background of Buddhism the miraculous birth youth the sorrows of life flight ascetic years enlightenment a vision of "Nirvana or level of being" it is difficult to see, across 2,500 years ago, what the economic, political and moral conditions that called forth religions of Aryana, so ascetic and pessimistic as Buddhism much material progress had been made since the establishment of the Aryan "present day Afghan" rule in India: great cities had been built by Afghan's; industry and trade gad created wealth in India, wealth had generated leisure, leisure had developed knowledge and culture in India. Probably it was the riches of Aryan that produced the Epicureanism and materialism of the seventh and sixth century before Christ. Religion does not prosper under prosperity; the sense liberates themselves from pious restraints and formulates philosophies that will justify their liberation. Buddhism, though impregnated with the melancholy atheism of a disillusioned age in Afghanistan, were religious reactions against the hedonistic creeds of an, "emancipated" and worldly leisure class. "it has often been remarked that this period was distinguished by a shower of stars in the history, Buddha in Afghanistan" indo—Aryan tradition describes Buddha's father, as a man of the world, member of the Gautama clan of the Aryan—tribe, and prince or king, at the foot of the Hindu—Kush rage. In truth, however, we know certain about Buddha; and if we give here the Afghan's—Stories that have gathered about his name it is not because these are history, but because that are an essential part of Afghan—Literature and Central—Asia religion. Scholarship assigns his birth to approximately B.C 563 and can say no more; legend takes up the tale, and reveals to us in what strange ways men may be conceived. At that time says one of the Aryan's—Books, In the city of Arochosia the festival of the full moon... had been proclaimed. Queen from the seventh day before the full moon celebrated the festival without intoxicants, and with abundance of garlands and perfumes. Rising early of the seventh day she bathed in scented water, and bestowed a great gift of four hundred thousand pieces as alms. Fully adorned, she ate of choice food, took upon herself the Upanishads vows, † entered her adorned state bed chamber, lay down on the bed, and falling asleep, dreamt this dream. Four great kings, it seemed, raised her together with the bed, and taking her to the Hindu—Kush, set her the table land... then their queens came and took her to the Bomyan Lake, bathed her to remove human stain, robed her in heavenly clothing, anointed her with perfumes, and bedecked her with divine flowers. Not far away is a silver Mountain, and thereon a golden mansion. There they prepared a divine bed with head to the east, and laid her upon it. Now the Bodhisattva‡ not far from there is a golden Mountain of Ghazni; and going there he descended from it, alighted on the silver mountain, approaching it from the direction of the north. In his trunk, which was like a silver rope, he held a whit lotus. Then trumpeting, he entered the golden mansion, made a right wise circle three times around his mother's bed, smote her right side, and appeared to enter her womb. Thus he received... a new existence. The next day the Queen awoke and told her dream to the king. The king sum mound sixty four eminent Brahmans, showed them honour, and satisfied them with excellent food and other presents. Then when they were satisfied with these pleasures, he caused the dream to be told, and asked what would happen. The Sophist said: be not anxious, O king; the Queen has conceived a male not a female, and thou salt have a son, and if he dwells in a house he will become a king, a universal monarch; if he leaves his house and goes forth from the world, he will become a Buddha, a remover, in the world of the veil of ignorance...Queen, bearing the Bodhisattva for ten months like oil in a bowl, when her time was come, desired to gap her relatives house and addressed king "I wish, O king, to go the city of my family" the king approved, and caused the road to be made smooth and adorned with vessels filled with plantains, flags and banners; and seating her in a golden palanquin borne by a thousand courtiers, set her with a great retinue, between the two—Afghan cities, and belonging to the inhabitants of both, is pleasure grove of Sal trees named the Lumbini Grove. At that time, from the roots to the tips of the branches, it was one mass of flowers…. When the Queen saw it, a desire to sport in the grove arose… she went to the food of a great Sal tree, and desired to seize a branch. The branch like the tip of a supple reed bent down and came within reach of her hand. Stretching out her hand she received the branch. Thereupon she was shaken with the throes of birth. So the multitude set up a curtain for her, and retired. Holding the branch, and even while standing, she was delivered… and as other beings when born come forth stained with impure matter, not so the Bodhisattva. But the Bodhisattva, like a preacher of the Doctrine descending from the seat of Doctrine, like a man descending stairs, out his two hands and feet, and standing unsoiled and unstained by any impurity, shining like a jewel laid on Silk cloth, descended from his mother. It must further be understood that at Buddha's birth a great light appeared in the sky, the deaf heard, the dumb spoke, the lame were made straight, gods bent down from heaven to assist him, and kings came from afar to welcome him. Legend paints a colourful picture of the splendour and luxury that surrounded him in his youth. He dwelt as a happy prince in three palaces "Like a god" protected by his loving father from all contact with the pain and grief of human life. Forty thousand dancing girls entertained him, and when he came of age five hundred ladies were sent to him that he might choose one as his wife. As a member of caste, he received careful training in the military arts; but also he sat at the feet of sages, and made himself master of all the philosophical theories current in his time. He married, became a happy and lived in wealth, peace and good repute. One day, says pious tradition, he went forth from his palace into the streets among the people, and saw an old man; and on another day he went forth and saw a sick man; and on a third day he went forth and saw a dead man. He himself, in the holy books of his disciples, tells the tale movingly:

Then, O monks, did I, endowed with such majesty and such excessive delicacy, think thus: "an ignorant, ordinary person, who is himself subject to old age, not beyond the sphere of age, on seeing an old man, is troubled, ashamed and disgusted, extending the thought to himself. I, too am subject to old age, not beyond the sphere of old age; and should I, who am subject to old age… on seeing an old man, be troubled ashamed and disgusted?" this seemed to me not fitting. As I thus reflected, all the elation in youth suddenly disappeared… thus O monks, before my enlightenment, being myself subject to birth, I sought out the nature of birth; being subject to old age I sought out the nature of old age sickness, of sorrow, of impurity. Then I thought: "what if I, being myself subject to birth, were to seek out the nature of birth… and having seen the wretchedness of the nature of birth, were to seek out the unborn, supreme peace of Nirvana"

Death is the origin of all religions, and perhaps if there had been no death there would have been no gods. To Buddha these sights were the beginning of "enlightenment" Like one overcome with "conversion" he suddenly resolved to leave his father, "his mother had died in giving him birth" his wife and become an ascetic in the desert. During the night he stole into his wife's room, and looked for the last time upon, just then, say the Buddhist Scriptures in a passage sacred to all followers of Gautama, A lamp of scented oil was burning. On the bed strewn with heaps of jess amine and other flowers, the wife was sleeping, the Bodhisattva, standing with his foot on the threshold, looked, and thought, "If I move aside the Queen's will awake, and the will be an obstacle to my going, when I have become a Buddha I will come back, In the dark of the morning he rode out of the city of Arochosia on his horse with his charioteer Chauna clinging desperately to the tail. Then Mara, Prince of Evil, appeared to him and tempted him, offering him great empires of Aryana, but Buddha refused, and riding on, crossed a broad Helmand—river with one mighty leap. A desire to look at his native city arose in him, but he did not turn, then the great earth turned round, so that he might not have to look back. He stopped at place, "there" he says, "I thought to myself, truly this is a pleasant spot and a beautiful forest. Clear flows the Helmand—River, and pleasant are the bathing—places; all around are meadows and villages" here he devoted himself to the severest forms of asceticism; for six years he tried the ways of the Yogis who had already appeared on the Aryan scene. He lived on seeds and grass, and for one period he fed on dung, gradually he reduced his food to a grain of rice each day. He wore hair cloth, plucked out his hair and beard for torture's sake stood for long hours, or lay upon thorns, he let the dust and dirt accumulate upon his body until he looked like an old tree. He frequented a place where human corpses were exposed to be eaten by birds and beasts, and slept among the rotting carcasses. And again he tells us, I thought what if now I set my teeth, press my tongue to my palate, and restrain, crush and burn out my mind with my mind. "I did so" and sweat flowed from my arm—pits... then I thought what if I now practice trance without breathing. So I restrained breathing in and out from mouth and nose. And as I did so there was a violent sound of winds issuing from my ears.... Just as if a strong man were to crush one's head with the point of a sword, even so did violent winds disturb my head... then I thought, what if I were to take food only in small amounts, as much as my hollowed palm would hold, juices of beans, vetches, chick—peas, or pulse... my body became extremely lean. The mark of my set was like a camel's food print through the little food. The bones of my spine, when bent and straightened, were like a row of spindles through the little food, and as, in a deep well, the deep, low—lying sparkling of the waters is seen, so in my eye—sockets was seen the deep, low—lying sparkling of my eyes through the little food. And as a bitter gourd, cut off raw, is cracked and withered through rain and sun, so was the skin of my head withered through little food. When I thought I would touch the skin of my stomach I actually took hold of my spine... when I thought I would ease myself I thereupon fell prone through the little food. To relieve my body I stroked my limbs with my hand, and as I did so the decayed hairs fell from my body through the little food.

But one day the thought to Buddha that self—mortification was not the way, perhaps he was unusually hungry on that day, or some memory of loveliness stirred within him. He perceived that no new enlightenment had come to him from these austerities. "By this severity I do not attain superhuman truly noble knowledge and insight" on the contrary, a certain pride in his self torture had poisoned any holiness that might have grown from it. He abandoned his asceticism, went to sit under a shade—giving tree, and remained there steadfast and motionless, resolving never to leave that seat enlightenment came to him. What, he asked himself, was the source of human sorrow, suffering, sickness, old age and death? Suddenly a vision came to him of the infinite succession of deaths and births in the stream of life: he saw every death frustrated with new birth, every peace and joy balanced with new desire and discontent, new disappointment, new grief and pain. "Thus, with mind concentrated, purified, cleansed.... I directed my mind to the passing away and rebirth of beings. With divine, purified, superhuman vision I saw beings passing away and being reborn, low and high, of good and bad color, in happy or miserable existences, according to their karma" according to that universal law by which every act of good or of evil will be rewarded or punished in this life, or in some later incarnation of the soul. It was the vision of this apparently ridiculous succession of deaths and births that made Buddha scorn human life. Birth, he told himself, is the origin of all evil, and yet birth continues endlessly, forever replenishing the stream of human sorrow. If birth could be stopped... why is birth not stopped? † because the law of Karma demands new reincarnations in which the soul may atone for evil done in past existences if however, a man could live a life of perfect justice of unvarying not binding his heart to those that begin and pass away then, perhaps, he would be spared rebirth, and for him the fountain of evil would run dry. If one could still all desires for one's self, and seek only to do good, then individuality, that first and worst delusion of mankind, might be overcome, and the should would merge at last with unconscious infinity. What peace there would be in the heart that had cleansed itself of every personal desire! And what heart that had not so cleansed itself could ever know peace? Happiness is possible neither here, as paganism thinks, nor hereafter, as many religions thing. Only peace is possible, only the cool quietude of craving ended only Nirvana. And so, after seven years of meditation, the Enlightened one, having learned the cause of human suffering, went forth to the Holy City,

The Teaching of Buddha the Five Moral Rules Buddha

Portrait of the Master his methods the Four Noble Truths the eightfold way the five moral rules Buddha and Christ—Buddha's agnosticism and anti clericalism his atheism his soul—less psychology the meaning of Nirvana, like the other teachers of his time, Buddha taught through conversation, lectures, and parables. Since it never occurred to him, any more that to Socrates or Christ, to put his doctrine into writing he summarized it in sutras "threads" designed to prompt the memory, as preserved for us in the remembrance of his followers there discourses unconsciously portray for us the first distinct character in Aryana History: a man of strong will authorities and proud, but of gentle manner and speech, and of infinite benevolence. He claimed "enlightenment" but not inspiration; he never pretended that a god was speaking through him. In controversy he was more patient and considerate than any other of the great teachers of mankind. His disciples, perhaps idealizing him, represented him as fully practising ahimsa "putting away the killing of living things, Gautama the recluse holds aloof from the destruction of life, he" once a warrior "has laid the cudgel and the sword aside, and ashamed of roughness, and full of mercy, he dwells compassion ate and kind to all creatures that have life... putting away slander, Gautama holds himself aloof from calumny.... Thus does he live as a binder together of those who are divided an encourager of those who are friends a peacemaker, a lover of peace, impassioned for peace a speaker of words that make for peace" he wished to return good for evil, love for hate; and he remained silent under misunderstanding and abuse "if man foolishly does me wrong, I will return to him the protection of my ungrudging love; the more evil comes from him the more good shall come from me" when a simpleton abused him, Buddha listened in silence; but when the man had finished, Buddha asked him, "son if a man declined to accept a present made to him, to whom would it belong?" the man answered: "to him who offered it" "my son" said Buddha, "I decline to accept your abuse, and request you to keep it for yourself" unlike most saints, Buddha had a sense of humour, and knew that metaphysics without laughter is immodesty. His method of teaching was unique, though it owed something to the wanders, or traveling Sophists, of his time. He walked from town to town, accompanied by his favourite disciples, and followed by as many as twelve hundred devotees. He took no thought for the morrow, but was content to be fed by some local admirer; once he scandalized his followers by eating in the home of a courtesan. He stopped at the outskirts of a village, and pitched camp in some garden or wood, or on some riverbank, the afternoon he gave to meditation, the evening to instruction, his discourses took the form of Socratic questioning, moral parables, courteous controversy, or succinct formulas whereby he sought to compress his teaching into convenient brevity and order. His favourite Sutra was the "Four Noble Truths" in which he expounded his view that life is pain, that pain is due to desire, and that wisdom lies in stilling all desire.

1. Now this, O monks, is the noble truth of pain: birth is painful, sickness is painful, old age is painful, sorrow, lamentation, and dejection and despair are painful....
2. now this O monks, is the noble truth of the cause of pain: that craving leads to rebirth, combined with pleasure and lust, finding pleasure here and there, namely, the craving for passion, the craving for existence, the craving for non—existence.
3. Now this, O monks, is the noble truth of the cessation of pain: the cessation, without a remainder, of that craving; abandonment, forsaking, release, none—attachment.

222

4. now this, O monks, is the noble truth of the way that leads to the cessation of pain: this is the noble Eightfold Way: namely, right views, right intention, right speech, right action, right living, right effort, right mindfulness, right concentration.

Buddha was convinced that pain so overbalanced pleasure in human life that it would be better never to have been born. More tears have flowed, he tells us than all the water that is in the four great oceans. Every pleasure seemed poisoned for him by its brevity. "is that which is impermanent, sorrow or joy?" he asks one of his disciples; and the answer is "Sorrow, Lord" the basic evil, then, is tanha, is not all desire, but selfish desire, desire directed to the advantage of the part rather than to the good of the whole; above all, sexual desire, for that leads to reproduction, which stretches out the chain of life into new suffering aimlessly. One of his disciples concluded that Buddha would approve of suicide, but Buddha reproved him, suicide would be useless, since the soul, unspecified, would be reborn in other incarnations until it achieved complete forgetfulness of self. When his disciples asked him to define more clearly his conception of right living, he formulated for their guidance "Five Moral Rules" commandments simple and brief, but "perhaps more comprehensive, and harder to keep, than the Decalogue"

1. Let not one kill any living being
2. Let not one take what is not given to him
3. Let not one speak falsely
4. Let not one drink intoxicating drinks
5. Let not one be unchaste

Elsewhere Buddha introduced elements into his teaching strangely anticipatory of Christ. "Let man overcome anger by kindness, evil by good.... Victory breeds hatred for the conquered is unhappy....never in the world does hatred ceases by hatred; hatred ceases by love" Like Jesus he was uncomfortable in the presence of women, and hesitated long before admitting them into the Buddhist order. His favourite disciple, Ananda, once asked him.

As not seeing them Ananda
But if we should see them, what are we to do?
No talking Ananda
But if they should speak to us, Lord, what are we to do?
Keep wide awake Ananda

His conception of religion was purely ethical he cared everything about conduct, nothing about ritual or worship, metaphysics or theology. When a Brahman proposed to purify himself of his sins by bathing at Gaya, Buddha said to him, "Have thy bath here, even here, O Brahman. Be kind to all beings. If thou speaks not false, if thou skillets not life, if thou takes not what is not given to thee, secure in self—denial—what wouldst thou gain by going to Gaya? Any water is Gaya to thee" there is nothing stranger in the Afghanistan—History of Religion that the sight of Buddha founding a worldwide religion, and yet refusing to be drawn into any discussion about eternity, immortality, or God. The infinite is a myth, he says, a fiction of philosophers who have not the modesty to confess that an atom can never understand the cosmoses. He smiles at the debate over the finite or infinity of the universe, quite as if he foresaw the futile astromythology of physicists and mathematicians who debate the same question today. He refuses to express any opinion as to whether the world had a beginning or will have an end; whether the soul is the same as the body, or distinct from it;

whether, even for the greatest saint, there is to be any reward in any heaven. He calls such questions "the jungle, the desert, the puppet—show, the writhing, the entanglement, of speculation" and will have nothing to do with them; they lead only to feverish disputation personal resentments, and sorrow; they never lead to wisdom and peace. Saintliness and content lie not in knowledge of the universe and God, but simply in selfless and beneficent living. And then, with scandalous humour, he suggests that the gods themselves, if they existed, could not answer these questions.

Once upon a time, kevaddha, there occurred to a certain brother in this very company of the brethren a doubt on the following point: "where now do these four great elements earth, water, fire and wind pass away, leaving no trace behind?" so that brother worked himself up into such a state of ecstasy that the way leading to the world of the Gods became clear to his ecstatic vision. Then that brother, Kevaddha, went up to the realm of the Four Great kings, and said to the gods thereof: "where my friends, do the four great elements earth water, fire and wind cease, leaving no trace behind?" And when he had thus spoken the gods in the Heaven of the Four Great kings sad to him: "we brother, do not know that. But there are the four great kings, more potent and more glorious than we. They will know it" Then that brother, kevaddha, went to the Four Great kings "and put the same question, and was sent o, by a similar reply, to the thirty—three, who sent him on to their king, who set him on to the gods, who sent him on to their king, who sent him on to the gods, who sent him on their king, ob to the gods of the Brahma—world"

When some students remind him that the Brahmans claim to know the solutions of these problems, he laughs them off "there are brethren, some recluses and Brahmans who wriggle like eels; and when a question is put to them on this or that they resort to equivocation, to eel—wriggling" if ever he is sharp it is against the priests of his time; he scorns their assumption that the Vedas were inspired by the gods, and he scandalizes the caste—proud Brahmans by accepting into his order the members of any caste. He does not explicitly condemn the caste—system, but he tells his disciples, plainly enough: "go into all lands and preach this gospel. Tell them that the poor and the lowly, the rich and the high, are all one, and that all castes unite in this religion as do the rivers in the sea" he denounces the notion of sacrificing to the gods, and looked with horror upon the slaughter of animals for these rites; he rejects all cult and worship of supernatural beings, all mantras and incantations, all asceticism and all prayer, quietly and without controversy, he offers a religion absolutely free of dogma and priest craft, and proclaims a way of salvation open to infidels and believers alike. But if this is so, how can there be rebirth? If there is no soul, how can it pass into existences, to be punished for the sins of this embodiment? Here is the weakest point in Buddha's philosophy; he never quite faces the contradiction between his rationalistic psychology and his uncritical acceptance of reincarnation. This belief is so universal in Aryan that almost every Indo—Aryan accepts it as an axiom or assumption, and hardly bothers to prove it; the brevity and multiplicity of the generations there suggests irresistibly the transmigration of vital force, or to speak theologically of the soul. Buddha received the notion along with the air he breathed; it is the one thing that he seems never to have doubted, he took the Wheel of Rebirth and the Law of Karma for granted; his one thought was how to escape from the Wheel, how to achieve Nirvana here, and annihilation hereafter. But what is Nirvana? It is difficult to find an erroneous answer to this question; for the Master left the point obscure, and his followers have given the word every meaning under the sun. In general Sanskrit "Dari" use it meant "extinguished" as of a lamp or fire. The Buddhism Scriptures use it as signifying:

1. a state of happiness attainable in this life through the complete elimination of selfish desires;
2. the liberation of the individual from rebirth
3. the annihilation of the individual conscious
4. the union of the individual with God
5. a heaven of happiness after death

In the teaching of Buddha it seemed to mean the extinction of all individual desire, and the reward of such selflessness escape from rebirth. In Buddhist literature the term has often a terrestrial sense, for the Arhat, or saint, is repeatedly described as achieving it in this life, by acquiring its seven constituent parts: self possession, investigation into the truth, energy, calm, joy, concentration, and magnanimity. These are its content, but hardly its productive cause: the cause and source of Nirvana is the extinction of selfish desire; and Nirvana, in most early contexts comes to mean the painless peace that rewards the moral annihilation of the self. "Now" says Buddha, "this is the noble truth as to the passing of pain. Verily it is the passing away so that no passion remains the giving up, the getting rid of and the emancipation from, the bar boring no longer of this craving thirst" this fever of self seeking desire, in the body of the Master's teaching it is almost always synonymous with bliss, the quiet content of the soul that no longer worries about itself. But complete Nirvana includes annihilation the reward of the highest saintliness is never to be reborn. Buddha died in B.C 483, at the age of eighty

Aryan's "present day Afghan's" Philosopher King of Aryana B. C 350 in the capital of Bactria "present day Balkh" Afghanistan Majesty the king made himself head of the Buddhist Church

Aryana-Khorasan present day Afghanistan-Central Asia & India, King Ashoka mounted the throne in B.C 350, in Bactria north of Afghanistan, he found himself ruler of a vaster empire than any Aryan's monarch before him, Afghanistan—Central Asia and all of modern India but the extreme south—Tamil—kam, or Tamil Land. For a time he governed in the spirit of his grand—father, cruelly but ell. A East—Turkistan traveler who spent many years in India in the seventh century A.D, tells us that the prison maintained by Empire Ashoka north of the capital of Bactria was still remembered in indo—Aryan tradition as "Ashoka's Hell" there, said his informants, all the tortures of any orthodox inferno had been used in the punishment of criminals; to which the king added an edict that no one who entered that dungeon should ever come out of it alive. But one day a Buddhist saint, imprisoned there without cause, and flung into a cauldron of hot water, refused to boil, the jailer sent word to King Ashoka, who came, saw, and marvelled. When the king turned to leave, the jailer reminded him that according to his own edict he must not leave the prison alive. The king admitted the force of the remark, and ordered the jailer to be thrown into the cauldron. On returning to his palace king Ashok, we are told, underwent a profound conversion. He gave instructions that the prison should be demolished, and that the penal code should be made more lenient. At the same time he learned that his troops had won a great victory over the Indian rebellious kalinga tribe, had slaughtered thousands of the rebels, and had taken many prisoners. King Ashoka was moved to remorse at the thought of all this "violence, slaughter, and separation" of captives "from those whom they love" he ordered the prisoners freed, restored their lands to the kalingas, and sent them a message of apology which had no precedents and has few imitations. Then he joined the Buddhist Order, wore for a time the garb of a monk, gave up hunting and the eating of meat, and entered upon the Eightfold Aryan way "Noble Way" it is at present impossible to say how much of this is history; nor can we discern, at this distance, the motives of the Afghan—king. Perhaps he saw the growth of Buddhism in Central Asia and India, and thought that its code of generosity and peace might provide a convenient regimen for his people, saving countless policemen, in the eleventh year of his reign he began to issue the most remarkable edicts in the Afghan's—History of Government, and commanded that they should be carved upon rocks and pillars in simple phrase and local dialects, so that any literate Indo—Aryan might be able to understand them. The Rock Edicts have been found in almost every of the pillars ten remain in place, and the position of twenty others has been determined, in these edicts find the Emperor accepting the Buddhist faith completely, and applying it resolutely throughout the last sphere of human affairs in which we should have expected to find it statesmanship. It is if some Afghan—modern empire had suddenly announced that henceforth it would practice Christianity. Though these edicts are Buddhist they will not seem to us entirely religious, they assume a future life, and thereby suggest how soon the scepticism of Buddha had been replace in Afghanistan by the faith of his followers. But they express no belief in; make no mention of a personal God. Neither is there any word in them about Buddha. The edicts are not interested in theology: the Senath Edict asks for harmony within the Church, and prescribes penalties for those who weaken it with schism; but other edicts repeatedly enjoin religious tolerance. One must give alms to Brahmans as well as to Buddhist priests;

one must not speak ill of other men's faiths. The king announces that all his subjects in Afghanistan—Central Asia and India are his beloved children, and that he will not discriminate against any of them because of their diverse creeds. Rock Edict XII speaks with almost contemporary pertinence: His Sacred and Gracious Majesty the king dose reverence to men of all sects, whether ascetics or householders, by gifts and various forms of reverence. His Sacred Majesty, however, cares not so much for gifts or external reverence as that there should be a growth of the essence of the matter in all sects. The growth of the essence of the matter assumes various forms, but the root of it is restraint of speech; to wit, a man must not do reverence to his own sect, or disparage that of another, without reason, depreciation should be for specific reasons only because the sects of other people all deserve reverence for some reason or another. By thus acting a man exalts his own sect, and at the same time does service to the sects of other people. By acting contrariwise a man hurts his own sect, and does disservice to the sects of other people… concord is meritorious. "The essence of the matter" is explained more clearly in the Second Pillar Edict. "The Law of Piety is excellent. But wherein consists the Law of Piety? In these thing: to little impiety, many good deeds compassion liberality, truthfulness, purity" to set an example king Ashoka ordered his officials everywhere to regard the people as his children, to treat them without impatience or harshness, never to torture them, and never to imprison them without good cause; and he commanded the officials to read these instructions periodically to the people. Did these moral edicts have any result in improving the conduct of the people? Perhaps they had something to do with spreading the idea of AHIMSA, and encouraging abstinence from meat and alcoholic drinks among the upper classes of Aryana. King Ashoka himself had all the confidence of a reformer in the efficacy of his petrified sermons: in Rock Edict IV he announces that marvellous results have already appeared; and his summary gives us a clearer conception of his Great doctrine: Now, by reason of the practice of piety by His Sacred and Gracious Majesty the king, the reverberation of the war drums has become the reverberation of the Law… as for many years before has not happened, now, by reason of the inculcation of the Law of Piety by His Sacred and Gracious Majesty the king, "there is" increased abstention from sacrificial slaughter of living creatures, abstention from the killing of animate beings, seemly behaviour to relatives, seemly behaviour to Brahmans, hearkening to father and mother, hearkening to elders. Thus as in many other ways the practice of the Law "of Piety" has increased, and His Sacred and Gracious Majesty the king will make such practice of the Law increase further. The sons, grandsons and great—grandsons of His Sacred and Gracious Majesty the king will cause this practice of the Law to increase until eon of universal destruction. The Good Afghan—King exaggerated the piety of men and the loyalty of sons. He himself laboured arduously for the new religion; he made himself head of the Buddhist Church in the Capital of Bactria, all-overs Asia, lavished gifts upon it, 84,000 Monasteries for it, and in its name established throughout his kingdom hospitals for men and animals. He sent Buddhist missionaries to all parts of India, Ceylon, Syria, Egypt, and Macedonia, where perhaps, they helped to prepare for the ethics of Christ; and shortly after his death missionaries left Bactria to preach to gospel of Buddha in Tibet, China, Mongolia and Japan. In addition to this activity in religion king Ashoka gave himself zealously to the secular administration of his empire; his days "B.C 272" of labour were long, and he kept himself available to his aides for public business at all hours in the Afghanistan—History. His outstanding fault was egotism it is difficult to be at once modest and a reformer. His self—respect shines out in every edict, and makes him more completely the brother of Marcus Aurelius. He failed to perceive that the Brahmans hated him and only bided their time to destroy him, as the priests of Thebes had destroyed Akhenaton a thousand years before. Not only the Brahmans, who had been given to slaughtering animals for themselves and their gods, but many thousands of hunters and fishermen resented the edicts that set such severe limitations upon the taking of animal life; even the peasants growled at the command that "chaff must not be set on fire along with the living thing in it" half the empire waited hopefully for king Ashoka's death. Man from East—Turkistan tells us that according to Buddhist tradition king Ashoka in his last years in Bactria was deposed by his grandson, who acted with the aid of court officials, gradually all power was taken from the old king, and his gifts to the Buddhist Church came to an end. King Ashoka's own allowance of goods, even of food, was cut down, until day his whole portion was half an MEWA fruit. The king gazed upon it sadly, and then sent it to his Buddhist brethren, as all that he had to give. Within a generation after his passing, his empire, like Akhenaton's, crumbled to pieces. King Ashoka had accomplished one of the Greatest tasks in History of Afghanistan—India and all-overs Asia

Bactrian Golden age in Afghanistan

Aryana-Khorasan present day Afghanistan-Central Asia & India, from the death of king Ashoka to the empire of the Guptas, for a period of almost six hundred years Indo—Aryan inscriptions and documents are so few that the history of this interval is lost in obscurity. Great universities like those at Taxila continued to function, and in India the influence of Afghan in architecture, in sculpture, produced a flourishing civilization in the wake of Alexander's invasion B.C 321. In the first and second centuries before Christ, Syrian and Scythians down into the Central Asia conquered it, "Majesty the king Ashoka the Law of Piety" and established there, for some three hundred years this Afghan—Greco culture from the north of Afghanistan from the capital of Bactria. In the first century of heat we so provincially call the Christian era the Kushans, an Afghan tribe akin to the Turkmen captured Kabul, and from that city as capital extended their power throughout India. In the reign of their greatest king, Kanishka, the arts and sciences progressed: Afghan—Buddhist sculpture produced some of its fairest master pieces, fine building were reared in Peshawar, Taxila and Mathura, Charaka advance the Afghan—Art of medicine, and Nagarjuna and Ashvaghosha laid the bases of that great vehicle Buddhism which was to help Gautama to win China and Japan. King Kanishka tolerated many religions and experimented with various gods; finally he chose the new mythological Buddhism that had made Buddha into a deity and had filled the skies with Bodhisattvas and Arhats; he called a great council of Buddhist theologians to formulate this creed for his realms, and became almost a second Ashoka in spreading the Buddhist faith. The Council composed 300,000 SUTRAS, Buddha's philosophy to the emotional needs of the common soul, and raised him to divinity. Meanwhile Chandragupta "quite distinct, despite his name and number, from Chandragupta Maurya" had established in Magadha "new India" the Guta Dynasty of native kings, his successor, Samudragupta, in a reign of fifty years, made himself one of the foremost monarchs in Indo—Aryan's long history. He changed his capital to Ayodhya, ancient home of the legendary Rama; sent his conquering armies and tax gatherers into Bengal, Assam, Nepal, and southern India; and spent the treasure brought to him from vassal states in promoting literature, science, religion and the arts. He himself, in the interludes of war, achieved distinction as a poet and a musician, his son sun of power, extended these conquests of arms and the mind, supported the great dramatist a brilliant circle of poets philosophers, artists, scientists and scholars about him in his capital, under these two kings Aryana reached a height of development unsurpassed since Buddha, and a political unity rivalled only under King Ashoka and Empire Akbar. We discern some outline of Aryan civilization from the account at the opening of the fifth century of Christian was one of many Buddhists who came from East Turkistan to India during this Golden Age of Aryana; and these pilgrims were probably less numerous than the merchants and ambassadors who, despite her mountain barriers, now entered pacified Aryana from East and West, even from distant Rome, "Constantinople" and brought to her a stimulating contact with foreign customs and ideas. The people are numerous and happy; they have not to register their households, or attend to any magistrates or their rules; only those who cultivate the royal land have to pay a portion of the gain from it. If they want to go they go; if they want to stay them stat. the king governs without decapitation or corporal punishments. Criminals are simply fined even in cases of repeated attempts at wicked rebellion they only have their right hands cut off... Throughout the whole country the people do not kill any living creature, nor eat onions or garlic. The only exception is that of the Candelas in that country they do not keep pigs and fowls, and do not sell live cattle; in the markers there are no butcher's shops, and no dealers in intoxicating drinks. had earlier travelled and connected the above route from Herat to Meshad, Bukhara, and from Tashkent the more southern route through Khokand, Feghana, Andijan, Osh to Kashgar, The other from Kabul, through the Khyber Pass to Gilgit and Karakoram pass into East Turkeastan, or the more difficult one from Kabul to Faizabad, Ishkashim, cross the Amu Darya to Khorog, Murghab, and over the 4,655 metre pass of the Pamir's, down to Lake Karakul at 3,914 meter, and then into East Turkeastan present day to China A Lake in the Pamir Mountains, Tajikistan It was also a pleasure on my trip last year (July 2007) to connect the route from Tashkent, Shymkent, Turkestan and to discover that the road from Turkestan to Kyzl Orda, where I spent time in 1997, 'is a strategic place where the caravan roads from Tashkent, Bukhara and Khiva along Atbasar to Western Siberia and over Torgay to Troizk and Orenberg came together'. (Exploring Kazakhstan, Dagmar Schreiber, Caspian Publishing House, Almaty 2006) the Silk Road was not a trade route that existed solely for the purpose of trading in silk; many other commodities were also traded, from gold and ivory to exotic animals and plants. Of all the precious goods crossing this area, silk was perhaps the most remarkable for the people of the West. It is often thought that the Romans had first encountered silk in one of their campaigns against the Parthians in 53 B.C, and realized that it could not have been produced by this relatively unsophisticated people. They reputedly learnt from Parthian prisoners that it came from a mysterious tribe in the east, who they came to refer to as the silk people, 'Seers'. In practice, it is likely that silk and other goods were beginning to filter into Europe before this time, though only in very small quantities. The Romans obtained samples of this new material, and it quickly became very popular in Rome, for its soft texture and attractiveness. The Parthians quickly realized that there was money to be made from trading the material, and sent trade missions towards the east. Their descendents became the Kushan people, and in the first century A.D. they moved into this crossroads area, bringing their adopted Buddhist religion with them. Like the other tribes before them, they adopted much of the Greek system that existed in the region. The product of this marriage of cultures was the Kandahar culture, based in what is now the Peshawar region of northwest India. This fused Greek and Buddhist art into a unique form, many of the sculptures of Buddhist deities bearing strong resemblances to the Greek mythological figure Heracles. The Kushan people were the first to show Buddha in human form, as before this time artists had preferred symbols such as the footprint, sputa or tree of enlightenment, either out of a sense of sacrilege or simply to avoid persecution. The history goes on and on with Chenghis Khan, Timur (Tamerlane) and then the great Moguls, followed by the Great game, a term coined between the positioning of Saxon-Russia and Britain in regards to India The East Turkestan Mountains or Celestial mountains as they were known to the East Turkestan had to be crossed a number of timesalthough he only ruled the area until 325 B.C., the effect of the Greek invasion was quite considerable. The Bactria language was brought to the area, and Greek mythology was introduced. The aesthetics of Bactria sculpture were merged with the ideas developed from the Indian kingdoms, and a separate local school of art emerged. By the third century B.C., the area had already become a crossroads of Asia, where Afghan Indian and Bactria ideas met. It is believed that the residents of the Hunza valley in the Karakorum are the direct descendents of the army of Alexander; this valley is now followed by the Karakorum Highway, on its way from India over to Kashgar, and indicates how close to the Taklimakan Alexander may have got. It had become an obsession to unravel the mysteries of the Silk Road. In February this year, visited two remaining places with strong connections to the great game and the Silk Road, the Chamba and Parvati valleys in Himachal Pradesh. From Dalhousie and in the Chamba Valley, was able to study the western passes of the Pir Panjal. In 2004 crossed the Rohtang La which marks the eastern end of the Pir Panjal. Why had it become obsessions? Coincidentally my work for Red Cross took to India Afghanistan Central Asia and imperceptibly, my holidays were spent stitching it together. The history fascinated me and often lay awake at night dreaming of the peaks, passes and rivers. Eventually married wonderful Kazakh women of proud nomadic stock whose ancestors plied the Silk Road, and many still live by it. so what is the Silk Road? On the eastern and western sides of the continent, the civilizations of Easr Turkeastan and the West developed. The western end of the trade route appears to have developed earlier than the eastern end, principally because of the development of the empires in the west, and the easier terrain of Aryana and Syria. The Afghan empire of Aryana was in control of a large area of the Middle East, extending as far as the Indian Kingdoms to the east. Trade between these two neighbors was already starting to influence the cultures of these regions. This region was taken over by Alexander the Great of Macedon, who finally conquered the Bactrai empire, and colonized the area in about 330 B.C., superimposing the culture of the Bactria

The Pamir Highway Cradle Of Saxon Great Game

Aryana-Khorasan present day Afghanistan-Central Asia & India, "Now shall go far and far into the north, playing the Saxon Great Game" so said Rudyard Kipling in his 1901 novel "Kim," speaking about the imperial struggle for power in Afghanistan-Central Asia between Russia and Saxon. Things haven't changed all that much in the 21st century does Afghanistan sound familiar? If you want to know the historical and cultural background of this region in Afghanistan-Central Asia the book to read is Peter Hopkirk's, 1992 work, "The Great Game the Struggle for Empire in Afghanistan- Khorasan presnt day Central Asia." Actually, the phrase, "Great Game," was coined by Captain Arthur Connolly of the East India Company, before he was beheaded in Bokhara for spying in 1842. Khorasan presnt day Central Asia has been a troublesome spot for Western powers for centuries. Today the players have changed, but the trouble remains. And it is a deep-rooted trouble historically explained by Hopkirk's fascinating book. The historical struggle for Afghanistan-Central Asia is full of intrigue, ambition and military adventure, it's a fascinating story with relevance today and Hopkirk doesn't deliver one boring page. What happened after the demise of Czarist Russia? Afghanistan and the surrounding area erupted into a decade of bloody fighting. Sound familiar? Hopkirk has done amazing research for this book and gets into the details of the actual intrigues and spies plying their trade for influence and gain. The Russians at the time wanted to expand their territory and the British wanted to protect their interest in India. The wild and untamed land between the two countries was the chess board on which the Great Game took place. Ironically, much of the world today is now focused on this same region as troubles in the area once again threaten world security. But the real value of Hopkirk's book is that it focuses on the culture and history of Afghanistan-Central Asia providing today's readers with much needed background on an area little understood by Westerners. This book is easy to read, well-researched and well worth reading. Highly recommended After three nights in Murghab, we were ready to move on along the Pamir Highway, but we were still taking our time. In fact, we only went about fifty kilometers before our first turn-off to look at prehistoric cave paintings. Our next turn-off was an overnight detour to the Southern Alichur range to the south. There we planned to take a long dayhike to a pass overlooking the Great Pamir valley and Zorkul (Victoria) lake, another hotbed of Great Game exploration along the Afghan border. (With her knees still recovering from the previous pass crossing, Marcia had decided to skip the hike and wait below.) The trail would be long, so we agreed to drive as far up the valley as possible before spending the night. A local shepherd came with us and directed our driver to his yurt, which he rents out to passing visitors. Riding a yak is as close as one can get to riding a woolly mammoth. People in Nepal and India generally use yaks only as pack animals, because they are still half-wild with deep-throated snorts. But the real problem is that yaks are so wide that a human rider must really stretch his legs. When we got off after a little more than an hour, we could hardly walk. Fortunately, my balance returned within a few minutes, but my crotch still hurts to think of it The pass itself was covered by about 30 centimeters of new snow, and we hiked on foot because my yak refused to go further. From the top, we could see the end of the lake and the Wakhan range beyond. In the distance a few peaks were visible from the Hindu Kush on Afghanistan.

The Great Afghan River's Oxus "Darya Amu" ca 7,500km World heritage

The river Amu Darya (previously known by Europeans as the Oxus) is one of the longest (2400km) Afghanistan-Central Asia. One source of the Amu Darya is the Pamir River, which emerges from Lake Zorkul in the Great Pamir Mountain of Afghanistan (ancient Mount Imeon) East Turkestan to China Sea ca {7,500km} and flowing west to Qila-e Panja; it joins the Wakhan River to form the Punjab "five river" river, Panj River. The river also marks the Tajik – Afghan border for nearly 1000km. This region is bound in mythology by the fact that four great rivers (the Oxus, the Indus, the Helmend, and the Gaxartes) rise from this geographic area, thus meeting the conditions of Christian, Islamic and Hindu texts for the fabled Eden. Furthermore, six thousand years ago the whole of Afghanistan-Central Asia was lower than it is today and at that time the indications are that ideal conditions prevailed on the Pamir Plateau – an intriguing possibility! Lake Zorkul is in fact one of a series of freshwater lakes, rich in fish and waterfowl, that cascade down a broad valley running east to west on the southern border of the Pamir's. The valley lies above 4000m altitude and for seven months and seven river Sof the year the valley is inaccessible to all except the best (and most reliable) 4×4 off-road vehicles – the tracks are often wet and boggy. This is not a spot to breakdown without some good support! Even the locals tend to rely on the horse rather than the machine in these parts…Assuming that sufficient time has been spent on acclimatization, tourists can spend many days trekking by horse or foot in this region which offers mountain vistas and snow covered peaks in every direction. Zorkul is part of a UNESCO World Heritage conservation nature reserve and its access is controlled through permits that need to be purchased locally – Pamir Highway Adventure region. Among the smaller habitual mammals in the reserve are ermine, weasel, red fox, Turkestan lynx and Gai brown bear. Birds typical for the reserve are the Alpine goose, bearded eagle, golden eagle of Afghanistan-Central Asia. Territorial dispute between Afghanistan and India Further information: Afghanistan–India Since 1947 British-Pakistan relations India inherited the 1893 Durand Line Agreement after its partition from the British Raj in 1947 but there has never been a formal agreement or ratification between Islamabad and Kabul. Pakistan believes that under until postdates juries it should not require one because courts in several countries around the world and the Vienna Convention have universally upheld via until postdates juries that binding bilateral agreements are "passed down" to successor states Thus, a unilateral declaration by one party has no effect; boundary changes must be made bilaterally. At the time of independence, the indigenous Pashtun people (including members of the Khudai Khidmatgar movement) living on the border with Afghanistan were given only the choice of becoming a part either of India or Pakistan. Recent legal debate on the Durand Line issue has focused on the original nature of the contract between Afghanistan and British India. Some scholars have suggested that the Durand Line was never intended to be a boundary demarcating sovereignty, but rather a line of control beyond which either side agreed not to interfere unless there was an expedient need to do so. Memoranda from British officials at the time of the Durand Agreement incline towards this view. Scholars suggest that the frontier agreement was not of the form of an "executed clause" which usually caters for sovereign boundary demarcation and which cannot be unilaterally repudiated. Rather, they conjecture that it is of the form of an "executor clause" similar to those which pertain to trade agreements, which are ongoing and can be repudiated by either party at any time. This is, however, a matter of ongoing debate. Other legal questions currently being considered are those of state practice, i.e. whether the relevant states de facto treat the frontier as an international boundary, and whether the de jure independence of the Tribal Territories at the moment of Indian Independence undermine the validity of Durand Agreement and subsequent treaties. On July 26, 1949, when Afghan–Pakistan relations were rapidly deteriorating, a loyal jirga was held in Afghanistan after a military aircraft from the Pakistan Air Force bombed a village on the Afghan side of the Durand Line. As a result of this violation, the Afghan government declared that it recognized "neither the imaginary Durand nor any similar line" and that all previous Durand Line agreements were void. They also announced that the Durand ethnic division line had been imposed on them under coercion/duress and was a diktat. This had no tangible effect as there has never been a move in the United Nations to enforce such a declaration due to both nations being constantly busy in wars with their other neighbors (See Indo-Pakistani wars and Civil war in Afghanisan. In 1950 the House of Commons of the United Kingdom held its view on the Afghan-Pakistan dispute over the Durand Line by stating: His Majesty's Government in the United Kingdom has seen with regret the disagreements between the Governments of Pakistan and Afghanistan about the status of the territories on the North West Frontier. It is His Majesty's Government's view that Pakistan is in international law the inheritor of the rights and duties of the old Government of India and of his Majesty's Government in the United Kingdom in these territories and that the Durand Line is the international frontier. —Philip Noel-Baker *June 30, 1950* At the 1956 SEATO (Southeast Asia Treaty Organization) Ministerial Council Meeting held at Karachi, capital of Pakistan at the time, it was stated: The members of the Council declared that their governments recognized that the sovereignty of Pakistan extends up to the Durand Line, the international boundary between Pakistan and Afghanistan, and it was consequently affirmed that the Treaty area referred to in Articles IV and VIII of the Treaty includes the area up to that Line. —SEATO, March 8, 1956 Pakistan withdrew from SEATO on November 7, 1973, and the organization was finally dissolved in June 1973 Afghan mujahedeen representatives with President Ronald Reagan at the White House in 1983 Pakistan's largest intelligence agency (the ISI), which began with the birth of the nation, has been heavily involved in the affairs of Afghanistan since the late 1970s. During Operation Cyclone the ISI with full support-funding from the Central Intelligence Agency (CIA) and the White House in the United States recruited huge numbers of mujahedeen militant groups on the Pakistani side of the Durand line to cross into Afghanistan's territory for missions to destroy the Soviet-backed Afghan government. Afghanistan KHAD was one of two secret service agencies believed to have been conducting bombings in parts of Khyber Pakhtunkhwa (NWFP) during the early 1980s. U.S State Department blamed WAD (a KGB created Afghan secret intelligence agency) for terrorist bombings in Pakistan's cities in 1987 and 1988. It is also believed that Afghanistan's PDPA government supported leftist Al-Zulfiqar organization of Pakistan, the group accused of the 1981 hijacking of a Pakistan International Airlines plane from Karachi to Kabul. Hamid Karzai, an ethnic Pashtun who lived many years in Quetta, Pakistan, before becoming President of Afghanistan in 2001.After the collapse of the pro-Soviet Afghan government in 1992, Pakistan being well aware of its Durand Line Agreement violation (specifically article 2 where it mentions "The Government of India (Pakistan) will at no time exercise interference in the territories lying beyond this line on the side of Afghanistan") created a puppet state in Afghanistan run by the Taliban. According to a summer 2001 report in The Friday Times, even the Taliban leaders challenged the very existence of the Durand Line when former Afghan Interior Minister Abdur Razzaq and a delegate of about 95 Taliban visited Pakistan. The Taliban refused to endorse the Durand Line despite pressure from Islamabad, arguing that there shall be no borders among Muslims. When the Taliban government was removed in late 2001, the new Afghan President Hamid Karzai also began resisting the Durand Line. "A line of hatred that raised a wall between the two brothers"—Hamid Karzai. Afghan Geodesy and Cartography Head Office (AGCHO) depicts the line on their maps as a de facto border, including naming the "Durand

Line 2310 km (1893)" as an "International Boundary Line" on their home page. However, a map in an article from the "General Secretary of the Government of Baluchistan in Exile" extends the border of Afghanistan to the Indus River. The Pashtun dominated Government not only refuses to recognize the Durand Line as the international border between the two countries, it claims that the Pashtun territories of Pakistan rightly belong to Afghanistan. Many in Afghanistan as well as some Pakistani politicians find the existence of the international boundary splitting ethnic Pashtun areas to be at least objectionable if not abhorrent. Some argue that the 1893 treaty expired in 1993, after 100 years elapsed, and should be treated similar to the Convention for the Extension of Hong Kong Territory. However, neither the relatively short Durand Line Agreement itself nor the much longer joint boundary demarcation documents that followed in 1894-6 make any mention of a time limit suggesting the treaty should be treated similar to the Curzon Line and Mexican Cession. In 2004, spokespersons of U.S. State Department's Office of the Geographer and Global Issues and British Foreign and Commonwealth Office also pointed out that the Durand Line Agreement has no mention of an expiration date. Recurrent claims that (the) Durand Treaty expired in 1993 are unfounded. Cartographic depictions of boundary conflict with each other, but Treaty depictions are clear.—A spokesperson for U.S. State Department's Office of the Geographer and Global Issues. Because the Durand Line divides the Pashtun and Baloch people, it continues to be a source of tension between the governments of Pakistan and Afghanistan. In August 2007, Pakistani politician and the leader of Jamiat Ulema-e-Islam, Fazal-ur-Rehman, urged Afghanistan to recognize the Durand Line. Press statements from 2005 to 2007 by former Pakistani President Musharraf calling for the building of a fence on the Durand Line have been met with resistance from numerous political parties within both countries. Pashtun politicians in both countries strenuously object to even the existence of the Durand Line border. In 2006 Afghan President Hamid Karzai warned that "Iran and Pakistan and others are not fooling anyone." "If they don't stop, the consequences will be... that the region will suffer with us equally. In the past we have suffered alone; this time everybody will suffer with us.... Any effort to divide Afghanistan ethnically or weaken it will create the same thing in the neighboring countries. All the countries in the neighborhood have the same ethnic groups that we have, so they should know that it is a different ball game this time.—Hamid Karzai, *February 17, 2006* United States Armed Forces checking the border checkpoint at Torkham between Nangarhar Province of Afghanistan and Khyber Pakhtunkhwa in Pakistan, In July 2003, Pakistani and Afghan forces clashed over border posts. The Afghan government claimed that Pakistani military established bases up to 600 meters inside Afghanistan in the Yaqubi area near bordering Mohamed Agency, the Yaqubi and Yaqubi Kandao (Pass) area were later found to fall within Afghanistan. In 2007, Pakistan erected fences and posts a few hundred meters inside Afghanistan, near the border-straddling bazaar of Angoor Ada in South Waziristan, but the Afghan National Army quickly removed them and began shelling Pakistani positions Leaders in Pakistan said the fencing was a way to prevent Taliban militants from crossing over between the two nations but Afghan President Hamid Karzai believed that it is Islamabad plan to permanently separate the Pashtun tribes. Special Forces from the United States Army have been based at Shkin Afghanistan, seven kilometers west of Angoor Ada, since 2002. In 2009, the International Security Assistance Force (ISAF) and American CIA have begun using unmanned aerial vehicles from the Afghan side to hit terrorist targets on the Pakistani side of the Durand Line An MQ-9 Reaper unmanned aerial vehicle, which are launched from Afghanistan to engage targets on the Pakistani side of the Durand Line. The border area between Afghanistan and Pakistan has long been one of the most dangerous places in the world, due largely to very little government control. It is legal and common in the region to carry guns, and assault rifles and explosives are common. Many forms of illegal activities take place such as smuggling of weapons, narcotics, lumber, copper, gemstones, marble, vehicles electronic products, as well as ordinary consumer goods. Kidnappings and murders are frequent. Numerous outsiders with extremist views came from around the Muslim world to settle in the Durand Line region over the past 30 years. While most of the time the Taliban cross the Durand Line from Pakistan into Afghanistan and carry out attacks inside Afghan cities, sometimes they cross from the Afghan side of the border and attack Pakistani security forces. Recently, 300 Taliban militants from Afghanistan's territory launched attacks on Pakistani border posts in which 34 Pakistani security forces were believed to be killed. It is also believed Swat Taliban leader Maulana Fazlullah is hiding somewhere inside Afghanistan in June 2011 more than 500 Taliban militants entered Upper Dir area from Afghanistan and killed more than 30 Pakistani security forces. Police said the attackers targeted a check post, destroyed two schools and several houses, while killing a number of civilians. The governments of Pakistan and Afghanistan are both trying to extend the rule of law into the border areas. At the same time, the United States is reviewing the Reconstruction Opportunity Zones (ROZ) Actins Washington, D.C. which is supposed to help the economic status of the Pashtun and Baloch tribes by providing jobs to a large number of the population on both sides of the Durand Line bored Empty fuel trucks driving towards the Friendship Gate in Spin Boldak, which is the border crossing between Afghanistan and Pakistan Much of the northern and central Durand line is quite mountainous, where crossing the border is often only practical in the numerous passes through the mountains. Border crossings are very common, especially among Pashtuns who cross the border to meet relatives or to work. The movement of people crossing the border has largely been unchecked or uncontrolled although passports and visas are at times checked at official crossings. In June 2011 the United States installed a biometric system at the border crossing near Spin Boldak aimed at improving the security situation and blocking the infiltration of insurgents into southern Afghanistan. Between June and July 2011, Pakistan Chitral Scouts and local defense militias suffered deadly cross border raids. In response the Pakistani military reportedly shelled some Afghan villages in Afghanistan's Nuristan, Kunar Nangarhar, and Khost provinces resulting in a number of Afghan civilians being killed. Afghan sources claimed that nearly 800 rounds of missiles were fired from Pakistan which hit civilian targets inside Afghanistan. The reports claimed that attacks by Pakistan resulted in the deaths of 42 Afghan civilians, including children, wounded many others and destroyed 120 homes. Although Pakistan claims it was an accident and just routine anti Taliban operations, some analysts believe that it could have been a show of strength by Islamabad. For example, a senior official at the Council on Foreign Relations explained that because the shelling was of large scale it is more likely to be a warning from Pakistan than an accident. "I'm speculating, but natural possibilities include a signal to Karzai and to (the United States) that we can't push Pakistan too hard."—Stephen Biddle The Durand Line ethnic division question has not yet formally reached the United Nations, which could play a major role in settling the disputes between Afghanistan and Pakistan. The United States and other NATO states often ignore this sensitive issue, likely because of potential effects on their war strategy in Afghanistan. Their involvement could strain relations and jeopardize their own national interests in the area. After the Death of Osama bin Laden in Pakistan and the countless insurgent attacks in Afghanistan, U.S. military leaders said that terrorist safe havens in Pakistan must go. This came after the November 2011 NATO bombing in which 24 Pakistani soldiers were killed. In response to that incident, Pakistan decided to cut off all NATO supply lines as well as boost border security by installing anti-aircraft guns and radars to monitor air activity

The Great Game and Patagonia - April 2009

Aryana-Khorasan present day Afghanistan-Central Asia & India, this is my seventh rally in ten years and it was ROARR' finest month. The idea of only allowing a small group of twelve cars was a delight, and formed enormous camaraderie within our group. We hope the camping was as enchanting as expected, other than being quite bazaar. Pleased we brought this small group all together and journeyed up the Meridian of central India. And we all arrived safe and sound to a surprising press assembly at the museum and then the spiritual home of the George Everest and Great Arc of the Meridian to see the almighty Himalaya peaks far into Tibet, which as stood and admired, those mountains inspired me to want to cross over their snow capped ridge and onto another rally. The Great Arc is not only about history, camping and rural India; it is about the drive. We are toiling against the adversity of Indian roads to discovering quality rural driving, and hope some great drives were found. It is a non commercial rally and it was a great delight for me to take you along the Meridian Line of the Great Arc of India and so bring this merrymaking all together and give back to India with our small groups funding of Leah Patterson's hospital in Napery. Our group surplus and contribution of £10,000 will go towards the building of her hospital. The world we live in is a very disproportionate world, and feel strongly that all of us on the classic rally circuits traveling around the world have so much, for whatever reason, that this is a great opportunity to give back, and so readdress some balance in this world. The Great Arc of the Meridian will re-run in 2012. But camping will be back on an Indian adventure in 2011. A number of you have asked my plans for the future. Hope we can create vibrant journeys for you with an assortment of differing drives. 2010 will drive three very diverse rallies. After six rallies along the hustle and bustle of India roads in a country of one billion people, jaunts that never stay away from people, it is time for a journey and an adventure into one of the world's great wilderness. And any journey into the world's wilderness, the obligation of a wilderness is to make you feel a million miles from people and then the power of nature must astonish your senses! May be here in Patagonia the beauty of the wilderness, with its ever changing spectacular scenery, will make you question the sanity of what you see. But let us not forget we are drivers first and foremost, and the road into the wilderness must be of equal quality. And so it is ROARR' eighth rally will explore Patagonia as it here the drive and scenery are as spectacular as each other. The journey is not long, it is not even a difficult journey, and the difference is this journey will take you away from a world crowded with people into a world full of nature at her most gorgeous. An inspiration to see Patagonia's immensity and its extraordinary unusual wildlife which has attracted do many expeditions, including that of Charles Darwin. Furthermore once at the end of the world why not cross over to Antarctica? It is here wilderness's takes on a transformed meaning. But we shall see about Antarctica. There is much planning and preparation to be done and for now I am rummage around to for fifteen likeminded eccentric classic car drivers to join me next February for this wonderful Patagonia drive - Buenos Aires - Tierra Del Forego - Santiago. acquiring an Alfa Duet to boat-tail for this trip which goes down to the big land to explore Patagonia this autumn to drive into the wonderful tableland of South America, southern Argentina and southern Chile But before the Alfa arrives and before the winter arrives in the southern hemisphere plan to drive the lakes and the Chilean cost next month, and will keep you all informed. Patagonia provisional dates are February 15th to March 15th £17,500 for the rally, plus extra cost & time, if possible, to cover the boat trip out to Antarctica. Rising Sun has now moved to May 18th to June 10th 2010 and so the MG B is on its way to Japan for a summer of marvelous driving in the mountains to find old Japan, in quest of her fascinating cultural ways across her beautiful to drive mountains. And Japan does great mountain drives very well with first class roads crossing from one wonderful landscape to another. One can drive with enjoyment, peace and tranquility, exploring the rural areas, the Nichian coast and into six National Parks, seeing and experiencing the great diversity of Japans terrain - from mountains to rice fields. Not only is Japan a delight to drive, this rally will be a cultural experience of the country. Japan shapes our lives in so many ways, but we know so little about her ways. The rally will stay in many traditional Ryokans and Onsens - traditional inns with certain but important customs. Japan is rich in history with grand and historical town of Nikko, Uchiko, and Takayama, have driven to a few out of the way places over the years, and found forgotten towns with streets of past years. Looking for 15 cars to journey with me for 23 days, Entry is £16,950 per car with the entry covering the same as our other rallies. Appealing to some of you already, and in a way inspired by you, is the journey we propose for autumn next year. Calcutta to Istanbul crossing the great Afghanistan-Central Asia mountain range linking Nepal, Tibet, East Turkestan, Kyrgyzstan, Tajikistan, Uzbekistan, Turkmenistan, Iran into Turkey, or maybe we will across the Caspian Sea onto the Caucasus. The adventure will unfold as we travel in the footsteps of the colorful European who played the Saxon Great Game the Russian Bear and the British. And so it will be recognizing as the 'Great Game Classic Car Rally'. And this is an immense adventure. Dirt and dust; silk road cities; sun and sand; high mountain passes and windswept deserts for over 50 demanding days. And to blend all this together we will find great driving roads for us all! Can't wait to drive the Pamir Highway – the Roof across High Asia Conrad, As a company working in Afghanistan we would not advise you to drive through Afghanistan. We don't think the Pakistanis will give permission to get to the Khyber Pass, and it's not safe even if you are able to get the permits. The road between the Khyber and Kabul is seeing daily Taliban attacks. The road nort h of Kabul is less safe, but the stretch between Pul-e-Khumri and Kunduz sees several attacks each week. We do not advise you to take this route either. The road to beyond Kunduz, that leads to the Wakhan is not safe, and you will need to pass another risky area around Warduj, before arriving in Ishkashem. There is probably only a 50% chance of the travelers being killed if they take this route, but this is too high a risk for us to recommend you travel through Afghanistan (especially the route they propose). If you want to include Afghanistan in your itinerary, would recommend you travel up through the KKH in Pakistan to the "now Chinese border since 1949", enter East Turkstan, visit Kashgar, and then come down to Kirgizstan and then to Tajikistan. You should drive to Khorog (pass Ishkashem without crossing into Afghanistan), and then go on to Dushanbe. From there you could drive to Uzbekistan, and head to Termez, where you can cross into Afghanistan there. You can travel to Mazar-i-Sharif, Samangan, and even Pul-e-Khumri but will need to turn around there since the road is not safe beyond that. You will need to then recross into Uzbekistan at Termez and continue on your journey. This is a safer option for including Afghanistan in your itinerary. Please note that several independent tourists in Afghanistan have been killed because they wandered into hostile areas and had no security information. The security situation changes on a daily basis, and even 3 day old information is close to useless for staying safe. • hope this information is helpful. Noah Whitaker Administrative Manager, Great Game Travel Kabul If there is general consensus on the odds being acceptable – OK – let's give it a go. Afghan aside, wait for driving permits into Central Asian states with exhilaration, enthusiasm and gusto! This is a much more a journey of 'high adventure'. Again limited to 15 cars, September / October 2010, 6 weeks on the road crossing all of 'Great Game' lands Cost are dependent on China permits. At this stage only looking for expressions of interest which would be appreciated, do understand it is still some way off, and the route, and the adventure, of this journey will be confirmed as we advance towards the start date. Pamir is one of the phenomenal mountain range which forms a high ground for the great tectonic balance in this region of the world. In the southwest it runs into Hindukush range buttressing the little intermediary ranges. Tienshan range skirts the northeastern part of the region running into East Turkestan, Kyrgyzstan, Kazakhstan and Uzbekistan, To its higher plateau, the term Pamir knot is often applied owing to its relationship with neighboring ranges. Pamir is one of the highest and remotest parts of our region which covers a huge rugged territory. The region of Badakhshan is rich in mineral wealth and from the time of our histories, it has been known for its precious and semi precious stones of which rubies and lapiz lazuli mines were well sought for. The Tajik part of the Pamir's was well mapped and explored during the early Tsarist days. The two players of the Great Game equally eager to out maneuver each other were involved in exploration and mapping the region to their respective political gains. The harsh nature of the climate in the Pamir's kept the civilized settlements away giving rise to a semi nomadic culture that exists in various enclaves of the region. The winter temperatures freeze down to -47C with due to high glaciated table in the region, Due to acute climatic conditions, vegetation is poor and mostly shrubs like juniper and tamarisk grow along the watery part of the area with wild vegetation of Artemisia, caper and other shrubs grow in unsettled areas. In more settled villages we see willows, mulberry, pistachio, apricot and poplar trees grow in good number giving protection to the settlements The Wakhan part is in Afghanistan which is the highest plateau, known by the travelers as 'Bam-i-dunya' – Afghanistan-Roof of the World. These high parts are inhabited by Kirghiz nomads living for almost a century moving out of mainland due political changes. Now they form a part of Afghan nationality and live on the breeding of fat tailed sheep. They have been moving along the wild frontiers and often trespassing in the regional territories but going un-noticed due lack of control During the Soviet war in Afghanistan this tribe of Kirghiz nomads traveled through the traditional routes taking refute into northern parts of Afghanistan. Being Turkic speakers the Govt. of Turkmen took the tribe enbloc for temporary settlement in the mountainous region. Now with the end of war in their parts they have started coming back to their natural homeland. One can see their camels grazing in the lower parts along the river Peyanj and Sarhad darya. In the upper reaches, river Peyanj forms a natural boundary between Tajikistan and Afghanistan. The settlements across the river into Afghanistan are very few and mostly concentrated around the lower reaches while along Tajikistan border line, villages are well dressed with fields and activity. A careful eye can always see hair raising paths which remind us of the Silk Road days and still being used along the Afghan border. As one travels in to the mainland of the Pamir's starting with bigger settlement of Roshan town and then into the heart of the valley at Khorog are the concentrated part of the region in terms of population. As one moves to the higher Pamir's these villages thin out to mere small group of cattle houses. The population living in the upper parts generally known as Tajiks of the Pamir's are a group of population which may have settled around the first millennium BC when the Aryan migration took place into these parts. This racial group can safely be termed, as an admixture and Caucasian blood. These racial groups all along both sides of river "Oxus" are speakers of various Pamir languages and dialects of Indo-Aryan nature. These subgroups are then extended into all along the Wakhan and the northern parts of Great Games. It is very interesting to make the comparisons as from the ancient times these people have been traveling into the Wakhan corridor being a passage onto the East Tukrestan and Afghan side of the border in search of food products. Well this passage in the heart of Wakhan was the natural route of the Pamir branch of the Silk Road. Before the frontiers were drawn, Pamir's used to come down to the then, North Western part of the British India and this activity continued for a long time till the advances of the Saxon-Great Game players checked their traditional movements. The region around 6th 7th Century BC was invaded by Scythian tribal hordes infesting Transitional kingdoms by their ravages. They were brought under control by the Afghan whose Achaemenian Empire around 6th Century BC had established authority into these parts out of Bactrian region. This is the beginning of a civilized life in the lower reaches of the Pamir's. The Afghan activity and control continued till the arrival of Alexander the Great around 325BC who was by then asserting his claim over the lost empire of the Achaemenids. We are not sure whether he himself ever came to the higher Pamir regions, but he was very well in the lower areas which were part of the Bactrian region. The Seleucids who founded the Bactria Kingdom in 323 BC were the sole rulers of a huge region which also included Pamir and the Wakhan. But it must have been the later Indo-Bactrian whose inter tribal warfare was aggressive in asserting their control of these regions around the turn of 1st BC. We see many small Bactria colonies established along the river. In the Museum of Antiquities in Dushanbe, one can see collection of artifacts with Greek influence found from various archaeological sites of the region. Similarly on the Afghan side we see the existence of such sites like Ai Khanum. The resurge of Afghan under the Parthians and Sassani had a great influence on the Silk Road movement due to the establishment of links with the Eastern Romans. Taking the advantage of their position, they played the role of intermediaries of the Silk Trade. These were the times when silk was introduced to the Romans. As mentioned the Pamir branch of the Silk Road, passed through the Wakhan corridor and followed the natural route along the Oxus river down to Bactria (Balkh). The brisk activity on the Silk Road started during the Kushana empire which was well established and was prospering around 1st AD. There was a line of developed villages along the river and the other parts of the region, involved in commercial activity. We can still see ruins of old forts on the hill tops, standing today as the silent spectators of a grand past when they serve as the outposts for managing safe passage to the caravans coming from East Turkestan, Today the people of the Pamir region are predominantly and it is interesting to see, carrying of Zoroastrian rituals imbibed with spirit of Islam. You can always see signs of fire burning hearths at almost all the shrines found along the Pamir region. The curious style of house building is a continuation of Afghan building traditions which is seen further into the northern parts of India. We often come across houses and shrines decorated with trophy heads of ibexes and Marco Polo sheep as these animals have always been hunted down for meat. The pre-historic significance of ibexes scratched on the stones finds its décor on houses and secular buildings. The journey of the great traveler Marco Polo in 13th Century through the Wakhan corridor was of great interest. He saw the curly headed sheep in the Pamir plateau and mentions about, huge numbers roaming on the plateau and the nearby valleys. This animal whose curly horns could grow more than two meters, was later known after the great explorer as 'Marco Polo' sheep *(ovis amon poli)*. While travelingalong the route into the mainland Badakshan he mentions about the 'rubies of Badakshan' and one can still see the quarry mine from the road while nearing Iskashim. He then after resting at Iskashim visited the court of the government of Badakhshan in Faizabad. Traveling along the river Oxus one can see beautiful views of the Wakhan mountains that will chase you all the way down to Kala-i-Khum. The best season for travel along the Pamir region is August till the end of September. The spring time here blossoms around May which is greener and nice to look at the general scenery. The main towns of interest are Rushan – see the old fort and the shrines of local saint. Khorog is interesting visit the Museum, the library dedicated to Nasir-i-Khisrow who brought the message of Islam into these parts. Later further up Khorog an excursion to Garam Chasma (hot springs) is recommended for a healthy dip. Iskashim, Leyangar and Murghab are stopovers for spending the nights. The accommodation is pretty basic and one should be prepared for carrying supplies and extreme conditions. The Great Silk Road — an original phenomenon of the history of developing of humanity, its aspiration for union and exchanging cultural wealth, conquest of the living spaces and markets for goods. Ancient cities of Uzbekistan were located on the ancient Silk Road, the trading route between China and the West. The route took its name from silk, the commodity most in demand in Europe from East Turkestan during the Roman period. Some of the most influential and savage conquerors came and ruled these lands. Bactria the Great set up at least 8 cities in Afghanistan-Central Asia between 334 - 323 BC before the caravans began traveling through the Silk Road after around 138 BC East Turkeastan opened its border to trade. Between 484 - 1150 Huns,

Turkmen and Arabs came from the west and the latest brought with them a new religion of Islam. Many mosques and Madrassahs were built in Uzbekistan cities of Samarqand, Bukhara and Khiva during this period, including remaining structures of the Samanids. Most of the cities were destroyed during the invasion of the Genghis Khan in 1220. Later Timur, known also as Tamerlane, resurrected once famous cities by using the labor of slaves and artists captured during successful crusades. Timur conquered Khorasan, captured Baghdad, and lead expeditions to Anatolia and India, Most of the architecture that is found in Samarqand was build by Timur and his grandson Ulugbek. Great Silk Road today is one of the most attractive tourist routes. It is much due to the revival of Great Silk Road that the mankind has got the access to the global heritage of different nations who for thousands of years lived along this great transcontinental arterial road and who formed and ma. Mir Wais Hotak seen as Afghanistan's George Washington successfully rebelled against in 1709. He overthrew and killed Gorging Khan, and made the Afghan region independent. By 1713, Mir Wais had decisively defeated two larger armies; one was led by Khusraw Khan (nephew of Gurgin) and the other by Rustam Khan. The armies were sent by Sultan Husayn, the in Isfahan, to re-take control of the Kandahar region. Mir Wais died of a natural cause in 1715 and was succeeded by his brother Abdul Aziz, who was killed by Mir Wais' son Mahmud as a national traitor. In 1722, Mahmud led an Afghan army to the of Isfahan, sacked the city after the Battle of Gulnabad and proclaimed himself were disloyal to the Afghan rulers, and after the massacre of thousands of religious scholars, nobles, and members of the Fars family, the Hotaki dynasty was ousted from Fars after the 1729 Battle of Damghan Ahmad Shah Durrani, founder of the last Afghan empire and viewed asFather of the Nation In 1738, Kandahar from Shah Hussain Hotaki at which point the incarcerated 16 year old Ahmad Shah Durrani was freed and made the commander of Durrani four thousand Abdali Afghans. From Kandahar they set out to conquer India, passing through Ghazni, Kabul, Peshawar, and Lahore, and ultimately plundering Delhi after the Battle of Karnal, Nader and his army abandoned Delhi but took with them huge treasure, which included the Koh-i-Noor and Darya-ye Noor diamonds. After the death of Nader in 1747, the Afghans chose Ahmad Shah Durrani as theirhead of state Regarded as the founder of modern Afghanistan, Durrani and his Afghan army conquered the entire present-day Afghanistan, Khorasan and Kohistan provinces, along with Delhi in India. He defeated the Indian Maratha Empire, one of his biggest victories was the 1761 Battle of Panipat. In October 1772, Ahmad Shah Durrani died of a natural cause and was buried at a site now adjacent to theShrine of the Cloak in Kandahar. He was succeeded by his son, Timur Shah, who transferred the capital of Afghanistan from Kandahar to Kabul in 1776. After Timur Shah's death in 1793, the Durrani throne was passed down to his son Zaman Shah followed by Mahmud Shah, Shuja Shah and others. The Afghan Empire was under threat in the early 19th century by the Afghan in the west and the Sikhs in the east. The western provinces of Khorasan and Kohistan were taken in 1800. Fateh Khan, leader of the Barakzai tribe, had installed 21 of his brothers in positions of power throughout the empire. After his death, they rebelled and divided up the provinces of the empire between themselves. During this turbulent period, Afghanistan had many temporary rulers until Dost Mohammad Khan declared himself emir in 1826. The Punjab region was lost to Ranjit Singh who invaded Khyber Pakhtunkhwa and in 1834 captured the city of Peshawar, In 1837, Akbar Khan and the Afghan army crossed the Khyber Pass to defeat the Sikhs at the Battle of Jamrud, killing Hari Singh Nalwa before retreating to Kabul. By this time the British were advancing from the east and the First Anglo-Afghan War one of the first major conflicts during the Great Game was initiated. From the death of Nadir Afshar in 1747 until the communist coup of April 1978, Afghanistan was governed-at least nominally- by Pashtun rulers of the Abdali tribe. Indeed, it was under the leadership of the first Pashtun ruler, Ahmad Shah, that the nation of Afghanistan began to take shape after centuries of fragmentation and rule by invaders. Even before the death of Nadir Shah, the tribes of the Hindu Kush area had been growing stronger and were beginning to take advantage of the waning power of their distant rulers. The Ghilzai Pashtuns had risen in rebellion against Uzback rule early in the eighteenth century, but they had been subdued and relocated by Alikuzai. Although tribal independence would remain a threat to rulers of Afghanistan, the Abdali Pashtun established political dominance, starting in the middle of the eighteenth century with the rise of Ahmad Shah. Two lineage groups within the Abdali ruled Afghanistan from 1747 until the downfall of the monarchy in the 1929s-the Sadozai of the Popalzai tribe and the Alikuzai of the Barakzai tribe. Although the names of Timur, and Mahmud of Ghazni are well-known for the destruction they wrought in South and Central Asia, the name of the founder of the Afghan nation-state is relatively unknown to Westerners, though Ahmad Shah created an Afghan empire that, at its largest in the 1760s, extended from Central Asia to Delhi and from Kashmir to the Arabian Sea. There have been greater conquerers in the region before and since Ahmad Shah, but never before his reign and rarely since has there been a ruler of this fragmented area capable not only of subduing the truculent Afghan tribes but also of pulling them together into a nation. Ahmad Shah's was the second son of the chief of the Sadozai, which although small was the most honored of the Abdali lineages. Along with his brother, he had risen in rebellion against Nadir and had been jailed by the Ghilzai in Kandahar. Finally released by in 1738 when he took the city from the Ghilzai, Ahmad Shah's rose in the personal service of the Afghan monarch to the post of commander of an elite body of Afghan cavalry. When Nadir Shah, who had become vicious and capricious in his later years, was killed by a group of dissident officers, Ahmad and some 4,000 of his cavalrymen escaped with the treasury Nadir always carried with him for payments and bribes en route. Ahmad Shah's and his Abdali horsemen rode past Herat and southeastward, joining the chiefs of the Abdali tribes and clans at a shrine near Kandahar to choose a paramount chief. Although his rivals for the post included Haji Jamal Khan-chief of the Alikuzai, chief branch, of the Barakzai, which would be the other royal branch of the Abdali-and although only 23, Ahmad was finally chosen after more than a week of discussion and debate. Despite being younger than other claimants, Ahmad had several factors in his favor. He was a direct descendant of Sado, eponym of the Sadozai; he was unquestionably a charismatic leader and seasoned warrior, who had at his disposal a trained, mobile force of several thousand cavalrymen; and he had part of Nadir Shah's treasury in his possession. In addition, the other chiefs may have preferred someone from a small tribe who would always need the support of the larger groups to rule effectively One of Ahmad's Shah's first acts as chief was to adopt the title "Durr-i-Durran" (meaning "pearl of pearls" or "pearl of the age"), whether because of a dream or because of the pearl earrings worn by the royal guard. The Abdali Pashtuns were known thereafter as the Durrani. Ahmad's Shah's rise was owing not only to his personality and talents but also to extraordinary luck. His reign coincided with the deterioration of the empires on both sides of Afghanistan- the Kabuli (Mughals) to the southeast and the Uzback to the west. Even his first days as paramount chief were blessed with good fortune. Just before arriving in Kandahar, where some resistance was expected, Ahmad encountered a caravan bound for the Fras court laden with treasure. The new ruler seized it, used it to pay his cavalry and to bribe hostile chiefs, and invited its Qizilbash (Turkmen who served as palace guards for many Afghan rulers) escort to join his service. Ahmad Shah began by taking Ghazni from the Ghilzai Pashtuns and then wrested Kabul from a local ruler. In 1749 the Kabuli "Mughal" ruler, to save his capital from Afghan attack, ceded to Ahmad Shah sovereignty over Sind province and over the areas of northern India west of the Indus. He returned to his headquarters in Kandahar to put down one of an endless series of tribal uprisings and then set out westward to take Herat, which was ruled by grandson, Shah Rukh. Herat fell to Ahmad after almost a year of bloody siege and conflict, as did also Meshed (in present-day Iran). Ahmad Shah's left Shah Rukh, a 16-year-old who had previously been blinded by a rival, to rule the eastern province of Khorasan for him. At Nishapur, Ahmad Shah's was temporarily halted, but the following spring he struck again, this time employing a cannon that fired a 500-pound projectile. Although the cannon exploded on its first shot, Ahmad Shah's determination and the effect of the huge missile convinced the local rulers that they should surrender. Before returning to Herat, Ahmad's troops plundered the city and massacred much of the population. Stopping by Meshed to remind the rebellious Shah Bukh of his subservient position, Ahmad Shah's next sent an army to subdue the areas north of the Hindu Kush. In short order the army brought under control the Turkmen, Uzbek, Tajik, and Hazara tribes of northern Afghanistan. Ahmad Shah's invaded India a third, and then a fourth time, taking control of the Punjab, Kashmir, and the city of Lahore. Early in 1757 he sacked Delhi, but he permitted the attenuated Kabuli Dynasty to remain in nominal control as long as the ruler acknowledged Ahmad's Shah's suzerainty over the Punjab, Sind, and Kashmir. Leaving his second son Timur (whom Ahmad Shah's married to princess) in charge, Ahmad Shah's left India to return to Afghanistan, Like Babur, he preferred his homeland (KABULU) to any of his other domains. Dupree quotes an Afghan writer's translation of one of Ahmad Shah's poems. The collapse of Kabuli empire control in India, however, also facilitated the rise of rulers other than Ahmad Shah. In the Punjab the Sikhs were becoming a potent force, and from their capital at Poona the Marathas, who were Hindus, controlled much of western and central India and were beginning to look northward to the decaying Kabuli empire, which Ahmad Shah now claimed by conquest. After Ahmad Shah's returned to Kandahar in 1757, he was faced not only with uprisings in Baluch areas and in Herat hut also with attacks by the Marathas on his domains in India, which succeeded in ousting Timur and his court. Herat was quickly brought under control, and the Baluch revolt was quelled by a combination of siege and compromise, but the campaign against the Marathas was a more substantial operation. Ahmad Shah's called for Islamic holy war against the Marathas, and warriors from the various Pashtun tribes, as well as other tribes such as the Baluch, answered his call. Early skirmishes ended in victory for the Afghans, and by 1759 Ahmad Shah's and his army had reached Lahore. By 1760 the Maratha groups had coalesced into a great army. Once again Panipat was the scene of a historical confrontation between two contenders for control of northern India. This time the battle was between Muslim and Hindu armies, numbering as many as 100,000 troops each, who fought along a 12. kilometer front. Although he decisively defeated the Marathas, Ahmad Shah was not left in peaceful control of his domains because of other challenges to the ailing monarch in his last years. Moreover, the ultimate effect of the 1761 Battle of Panipat may have had detrimental effects on the rule of Ahmad Shah's descendants; by thwarting the consolidation of Maratha power in northern and central India, the battle may have set the stage for the rise of both Sikh and Saxon present day British power in the region. The victory at Panipat was the high point of Ahmad Shah' and Afghan-power. Afterward, even before his death, the empire began to unravel. Ahmad Shah was less fit to cope with insurrection because he suffered from severe ulceration of the face, an ailment that was probably cancer. Even before the end of 1761 the Saxon-Sikhs had risen and taken control of much of the Punjab. In 1762 Ahmad Shah crossed the passes from Afghanistan for the sixth time to subdue the Sikhs. He assaulted Lahore, and when he had taken the Sikh holy city of Amritsar, he massacred thousands of its Sikh inhabitants, destroyed their temples, and desecrated their holy places with cow blood. The Sikhs rebelled again within two years, but Ahmad Shah's efforts to put down the uprising of 1764 were not as successful. Again in 1767 he crossed the mountain passes. Although much harassed by Sikh guerrilla warfare, Ahmad Shah took Lahore and again laid waste to Amritsar, killing many of its inhabitants. After this attempt Ahmad Shah tried two more times to subjugate the Sikhs permanently, but he failed. By the time of his death, he had lost all but nominal control of the Punjab to the Sikhs, who remained in control until defeated by the British in 1849. It was not only the fierce Sikhs who rebelled against the rule of Ahmad Shah. His empire was being seriously eroded in other areas as well. Ahmad Shah's Indian domains refused to pay homage, and other regions simply declared their independence. The amir (ruler) of Bukharaclaimed some of the northern provinces, and Ahmad Shah reached an agreement with him to accept the Amu Darya as the border between them. Three years before his death, Ahmad Shah had to put down a revolt in Khorasan. In 1772 Ahmad Shah retired to his home, the mountains east of Kandahar, where he died. He was buried in Kandahar, where his epitaph, recalling his early connection with the Afghan monarchy, calls him a ruler equal to Emperor Cyrus. Despite his relentless military attacks and his massacres of Saxon-Sikhs and others in imperial warfare, he is known in Afghan history as Ahmad Shah Baba, or "father." Although confusion reigned after his death, Ahmad Shah was clearly the creator of the nation of Afghanistan, As scholar Leon B. Poullada notes, the loyalty of the Afghan tribes was not transferred from their own leaders and kin to the concept of nation, but Ahmad Shah succeeded to a remarkable degree in balancing tribal alliances and hostilities and in directing tribal energies away from rebellion into his frequent foreign excursions. He certainly enjoyed extraordinarily good luck, but he was clever in exploiting his good fortune, and he showed exemplary intelligence in dealing with his own people. Having started his rule as merely the paramount chief of the Durrani, Ahmad Shah never sought to rule the Pashtuns by force. He reigned in consultation with a council of eight or nine sirdars (or sardars), the most powerful Durrani Pashtuns, each of whom was responsible for his own group. He sought the advice of his council on all major issues. Although he favored the Durrani, and especially his own lineage, the Sadozai, he was conciliatory to the other Pashtun chiefs as well. Ahmad Shah's successors were not so wise, and the nation he had built almost collapsed because of their misrule and the intratribal rivalry that they could not manage. By the time of Ahmad Shah, the Pashtuns included many groups whose greatest single common characteristic was their Pashto language. Their origins were obscure: most were believed to have descended from ancient Aryan tribes, but some, such as the Ghilzai, may have been. To the east, the Waziris or Alikuzai and their close relatives, the Mahsuds, have been located in the hills of the central Suleiman Range since the fourteenth century. By the end of the sixteenth century and the final Turkish-Kabuli invasions, tribes such as the Shinwaris, Yusufzais, and the Mohmands had moved from the upper Kabul River Valley into the valleys and plains west, north, and northeast of Peshawar, and the Afridis had long been established in the hills and mountain ranges south of Khyber Pass. By the end of the eighteenth century the Durrani dynasty was born as Ahmad Shah 1722 the city of Herat in modern-day Afghanistan. Some claim that he was born in Multan and taken as an infant with his mother Zarghuna Alikuzai to the city of Herat where his father had served as the governor On the contrary, several historians assert that he was born in Herat. Durrani's father, Mohammed Zaman Khan, was chief of the Abdalis Pashtuns. He was killed in a battle with the Hotakis between 1722 and 1723, around the time of Ahmad Shah's birth. His family were from the Sadozai section of the Popalzai clan of the Abdalis. In 1729, the young Ahmad Shah fled with his family south to Kandahar and took refuge with the Alikuzai He and his brother, Zulfikar, were later imprisoned inside a fortress by Hussain Hotaki, the Alikuzai ruler of southern Afghanistan. Hussain Hotaki commanded a powerful tribe of Pashtun fighters, having conquered the eastern Province of Fars in 1722 with his brother Mahmud, and trodden the throne of the Fars. AHMAD SHAH DURRANI (1722-1772), aka Ahmed Shah Abdali the first of the Saddozai rulers of Afghanistan and founder of the Durrani empire, belonged to the Saddozai section of the Popalzai clan of the Abdali tribe of Afghans. In the 18th century the Abdalis were to be found chiefly around Herat. Under their leader Zaman Khan, father of Ahmad Khan. they resisted Fars attempts to take Herat until, in 1728, they were forced to submit. Recognizing the fighting qualities of the Abdalis, Nadir enlisted them in his army. Ahmad Shah's Khan Abdali distinguished himself in Nadir's service and quickly rose from the position of a personal attendant to the command of Abdali contingent in which capacity In June 1747, Nadir was assassinated by Qizilbashi onspirators at Kuchan in

Khurasan. This prompted Ahmad Khan and the Afghan soldiery to set out for Kandahar. On the way they elected Ahmad Khan as their leader, hailing him as Ahmad Shah. Ahmad Shah assumed the title of Durr-i-Durran (Pearl of Pearls) after which the Abdali tribe were known as Durranis. He was crowned at Kandahar where coins were struck in his name. With Kandahar as his base, he easily extended his control over Ghazni, Kabul and Peshawar. As for himself, he, as heir to Nadir Shah's eastern dominions, laid claim to the provinces which Nadir had wrested from the Kabuli emperor. He invaded India nine times between 1747 and 1769. He set out from Peshawar on his first Indian expedition in December 1747. By January 1748, Lahore and Sirhind had been captured. Eventually Kabuli forces were sent from Delhi to resist his advance. Lacking artillery and vastly outnumbered, he was defeated at Manupur in March 1748 by Mu'in-ul-Mulk, the son of the Minister Qamar-ud-Din who had been killed in a preliminary skirmish. Ahmad Shah retreated to Afghanistan and Mu'in-ul-Mulk was appointed governor of the Punjab. Before Mu'in-ul-Mulk could consolidate his position, Ahmad Shah, in December 1749, again crossed the Indus. Receiving no reinforcements from Delhi, Mu'in-ul-Mulk was forced to make terms with him. In accordance with instructions from Delhi, Ahmad Shah was promised the revenues of the Chahar Mahal (Gujrat, Aurangabad, Sialkot and Pasrur) which had been granted by the Kabuli emperor Muhammad Shah to Nadir Afshar in 1739. The nonpayment of the revenues of the Chahar Mahal was the reason for his third Indian expedition of 1751-52. Lahore was besieged for four months and the surrounding country devastated. Mu'in-ul-Mulk was defeated in March 1752, but was reinstated by Ahmad Shah to whom the emperor formally ceded the two sunbaths of Lahore and Multan. During this expedition Kashmir was annexed to the Durrani Empire. By April 1752 Ahmad Shah was back in Afghanistan. Mu'in-ul-Mulk found the Punjab a troublesome charge and his death in November 1753 only served to intensify the anarchy. All power was for a time in the hands of his widow, Mughlani Begam, whose profligacy signaled many a rebellion. The Kabuli Minister Imad ul-Mulk took advantage of this anarchy to recover the Punjab for the empire and entrusted its administration to Adina Beg. Ahmad Shah immediately set out to recover his lost province. He reached Lahore towards the end of December 1756, and, after an unopposed march, entered Delhi on 28 January 1757. The city was plundered and the defenseless inhabitants massacred. A similar fate befell the inhabitants of Mathura, Viridian and Agra. Towards the end of March 1757, an outbreak of cholera amongst his troops forced Ahmad Shah to leave India. The territory of Siring was annexed to the Afghan empire. Najib ud-Daula, the Ruhila leader who had supported him, was left in charge of Delhi and his own son, Taimur, appointed viceroy of the Punjab. He had no sooner left India than the Sikhs, together with Adina Beg, rose in revolt against Taimur. Early in 1758 Adina Beg invited the Marathas to expel the Afghans from the Punjab. This was accomplished by the Marathas who actually crossed the Indus and held Peshawar for a few months. These events brought Ahmad Shah to India once again (1759-61). The Marathas rapidly evacuated the Punjab before the Afghan advance and retreated towards Delhi. They were routed with enormous losses at Panipat on 14 January 1761 In June 1747, Nadir Afshar was assassinated by Mir Wais Hotak conspirators at Kuchan in Khurasan. This prompted Ahmad Khan and the Afghan soldiery to set out for Kandahar. On the way they elected Ahmad Khan as their leader, hailing him as Ahmad Shah. Ahmad Shah assumed the title of Durr-i-Durran (Pearl of Pearls) after which the Abdali tribe were known as Durranis. He was crowned at Kandahar where coins were struck in his name. With Kandahar as his base, he easily extended his control over Ghazni, Kabul and Peshawar. As for himself, he, as heir to Nadir Shah's eastern dominions, laid claim to the provinces which Nadir had wrested from the Kabuli emperor.

Durrani Empire

He invaded India nine times between 1747 and 1769. He set out from Peshawar on his first Indian expedition in December 1747. By January 1748, Lahore and Sirhind had been captured. Eventually Mughal forces were sent from Delhi to resist his advance. Lacking artillery and vastly outnumbered, he was defeated at Manupur in March 1748 by Mu'in-ul-Mulk, the son of the Wazir Qamar-ud-Din who had been killed in a preliminary skirmish. Ahmad Shah retreated to Afghanistan and Mu'in-ul-Mulk was appointed governor of the Punjab. Before Mu'in-ul-Mulk could consolidate his position, Ahmad Shah, in December 1749, again crossed the Indus. Receiving no reinforcements from Delhi, Mu'in-ul-Mulk was forced to make terms with him. In accordance with instructions from Delhi, Ahmad Shah was promised the revenues of the Chahar Mahal (Gujrat, Aurangabad, Sialkot and Pasrur) which had been granted by the Kabuli emperor Muhammad Shah in 1739. The nonpayment of the revenues of the Chahar Mahal was the reason for his third Indian expedition of 1751-52. Lahore was besieged for four months and the surrounding country devastated. Mu'in-ul-Mulk was defeated in March 1752, but was reinstated by Ahmad Shah to whom the emperor formally ceded the two subahs of Lahore and Multan. During this expedition Kashmir was annexed to the Durrani Empire. By April 1752 Ahmad Shah was back in Afghanistan. Mu'in-ul-Mulk found the Punjab a troublesome charge and his death in November 1753 only served to intensify the anarchy. All power was for a time in the hands of his widow, Mughlani Begam, whose profligacy signaled many a rebellion. The Mughal Wazir Imad ul-Mulk took advantage of this anarchy to recover the Punjab for the empire and entrusted its administration to Adina Beg. Ahmad Shah immediately set out to recover his lost province. He reached Lahore towards the end of December 1756, and, after an unopposed march, entered Delhi on 28 January 1757. The city was plundered and the defenseless inhabitants massacred. A similar fate befell the inhabitants of Mathura, Vrindavan and Agra. Towards the end of March 1757, an outbreak of cholera amongst his troops forced Ahmad Shah to leave India. The territory of Sirhind was annexed to the Afghan empire. Najib ud-Daula, the Ruhila leader who had supported him, was left in charge of Delhi and his own son, Taimur, appointed viceroy of the Punjab. He had no sooner left India than the Sikhs, together with Adina Beg, rose in revolt against Timor. Early in 1758 Adina Beg invited the Marathas to expel the Afghans from the Punjab. This was accomplished by the Marathas who actually crossed the Indus and held Peshawar for a few months. These events brought Ahmad Shah to India once again (1759-61). The Marathas rapidly evacuated the Punjab before the Afghan advance and retreated towards Delhi. They were routed with enormous losses at Panipat on 14 January 1761. After Panipat the main factor to reckon with was the growing power of the Sikhs who had constantly been assailing Ahmad Shah's lines of communication. It was against them that the Afghan invader's sixth expedition (1762) was specifically directed. News had reached him in Afghanistan of the defeat, after his withdrawal from the country, of his general, Nur ud-Din Bamezai, at the hands of the Sikhs who were fast spreading themselves out over the Punjab and had declared their leader, Jassa Singh Ahluvalia, king of Lahore (1761). To rid his Indian dominions of them once for all, he set out from Qandahar. Marching with alacrity, he overtook the Sikhs as they were withdrawing into the Malva after crossing the Sutlej. The moving caravan comprised a substantial portion of the total Sikh population and contained, besides active fighters, a large body of old men, women and children who were being escorted to the safety of the interior of the country. Surprised by Ahmad Shah, the Sikhs threw a cordon round those who needed protection, and prepared for the battle. Continuing their march in this form, they fought the invaders and their Indian allies desperately. Ahmad Shah succeeded, in the end, in breaking through the ring and glutted his spite by carrying out a fullscale butchery. Near the village of Kup, near Malerkotia, nearly 25,000 Sikhs were killed in a single day's battle (5 February 1762), known in Sikh history as Vadda Ghallughara, the Great Killing. But the Sikhs were by no means crushed. Within four months of the Great Carnage, the Sikhs had inflicted a severe defeat on the Afghan governor of Sirhind. Four months later they were celebrating Divali in the Harimandar (God's Temple) Amritsar, which had been blown up with gunpowder by order of the king in April 1762, and were fighting with him again a pitched battle forcing him to withdraw from Amritsar under cover of darkness (17 October). Ahmad Shah left Lahore for Afghanistan on 12 December 1762. Ahmad Shah against the Sikhs and he invited this time his Baluch ally, to join him in the adventure. He started from Afghanistan in October 1764 and reaching Lahore attacked Amritsar on 1 December 1764. A small batch of thirty Sikhs, in the words of Qazi Nur Muhammad, the author of the Jangnamah, who happened to be in the imperial train accompanying the Baluch division, "grappled with the ghazis, spilt their blood and sacrificed their own lives for their Guru." Ahmad Shah came down to Sirhind without encountering anywhere the main body of the Khalsa. This time he went no farther than Sirhind. As he was marching homewards through the Jalandhar Doab, Sikh sardars, including Jassa Singh Ahluvalia, Jassa Singh Ramgarhia, Charhat Singh Sukkarchakkia, Jhanda Singh Bhangi and Jai Singh Kanhaiya, kept a close trail constantly raiding the imperial caravan. Their depredations caused great annoyance to the king who lost much of his baggage to the Sikhs. The floods in the River Chenab took a further toll of his men and property, and he returned to Afghanistan mauled and considerably shaken. The fear of his Indian empire falling to the Sikhs continued to obsess the king's mind and he led out yet another punitive campaign against them towards the close of 1766. This was his eighth invasion into India. The Sikhs had recourse to their old game of hideandseek. Vacating Lahore which they had wrested from Afghan nominees, Kabuli Mall and his nephew Amir Singh, they faced squarely the Afghan general, Jahan Khan at Amritsar, forcing him to retreat, with 6,000 of the Durrani soldiers killed. Ahmad Shah offered the governorship of Lahore to Sikh sardar, Lahina Singh Bhangi, but the latter declined the proposal. Jassa Singh Ahluvalia, with an army of 30,000 Sikhs, roamed about the neighbourhood of the Afghan camp plundering it to his heart's content. Never before had Ahmad Shah felt so helpless. The outcome of the unequal, but bitter, contest now lay clearly in favour of the Sikhs. The Shah had realized that his Indian dominions were at the mercy of the Sikhs and he bowed to the inevitable. His own soldiers were getting restive and the summer heat of the Punjab was becoming unbearable. He, at last, decided to return home, but took a different route this time to avoid molestation by the Sikhs. As soon as Ahmad Shah retired, Sikhs reoccupied their territories. The Shah led out his last expedition in the beginning of 1769. He crossed the Indus and the Jehlum and reached as far as the right bank of the Chenab and fixed his camp at Jukalian to the northwest of Gujrat. By this time the Sikhs had established themselves more firmly in the country. Moreover, dissensions broke out among the Shah's followers and he was compelled to return to Afghanistan. On Ahmad Shah's death in 1772 of the cancerous wound said to have been caused on his nose by a flying piece of brick when the Harimandar Sahib was destroyed with gunpowder, his empire roughly extended from the Oxus to the Indus and from Tibet to Khorasan. It embraced Kashmir, Peshawar, Multan, Sindh, Baluchistan, Herat, Kandahar, Kabul and Balkh. After the assassination of Nadir Afshar in 1747, Ahmad Shah, an Afghan chief of the Abdali clan, rose to power and succeeded in establishing himself as the independent ruler of Afghanistan. He styled himself Durr-i-Durran, "the pearl of the age", and his clan was henceforth known as the Durrani. Ahmad Shah Abdali, while accompanying Nadir to India, had seen with his own eyes "the weakness of the Empire, the imbecility of the Emperor, the inattentiveness of the ministers, the spirit of independence which had crept among the grandees". So after establishing his power at home he led several expeditions into India from AD 1748 till AD 1767. These were something more than mere predatory raids. They indicated the revival of the Afghans, outside and within India, making a fresh bid for supremacy on the ruins of the Kabuli Empire. As a matter of fact, the Afghan bid for supremacy was an important factor in the history of India during a considerable part of the eighteenth century. Ahmad Shah Abdali must have entertained the desire of establishing political authority over at least a part of India, though there were other motives, as Elephantine points out, which led him to undertake these expeditions. He sought to consolidate his authority at home by increasing his reputation through successful foreign adventures, and he also hoped to utilize the booty derived from his Indian campaigns in defraying the expenses of his army and in showering favors and rewards on the Afghan chiefs. After having conquered Kandahar, Kabul, and Peshawar, Ahmad Shah Abdali invaded India for the first time, in Jan. 1748, with 12,000 veteran troops. But he was defeated at the battle of Manpur by Ahmad Shah, the Kabuli heir-apparent, and Mir Mannu, son of the deceased Minster Qamar-ud-din, and was put to flight. Mir Mannu was appointed governor of the Punjab. But before he could settle down, Ahmad Shah Abdali invaded Punjab for the second time in AD 1750 and conquered it after defeating him. Unsupported by the Delhi court, the Punjab governor found all resistance futile and admitted to the invader. The Abdali invaded India for the third time in Dec. 1751, when he again defeated Mir mannu, conquered Kashmir, and forced the Kabuli Emperor, Ahmad Shah, to cede to him the country as far east as Sirhind. Thus the Kabuli Empire was further reduced in extent. Mir Mannu was now left as the Abdali governor in Lahore. He promised to send to the victor the surplus revenue of the Punjab and not to transact important matters without final orders from him. But the Abdali led another expedition in the time of Emperor 'Alamgir II (1754-1759). After the death of Mir Mannu in Nov., 11753, and that of his infant son and successor in May 1754, the province of Punjab fell into disorder and anarchy due largely to the willfulness and caprice of the regent-mother, Mughlani Begam. In response to an appeal from her for help, Imad-ul-mulk, the all powerful Minster at Delhi, marched to the Punjab, which he himself coveted, in 1756, brought it under his authority, and appointed Mir Mun'im, "the leading nobleman of Lahore", governor of the province. Enraged at this, Ahmad Abdali invaded India for the fourth time in Nov. 1756, with greater determination, and arrived before Delhi on 23rd Jan. 1757. The imperial city was "plundered and its unhappy people again subjected to pillage". Imad-ul-mulk surrendered and was pardoned by the invader, who obtained from the Kabuli Emperor the formal cession of the Punjab, Kashmir, Sind, and the Sirhind district. After plundering the Jat country, south of Delhi, the Abdali retired from India in April, 1757, with immense booty and many captives, leaving his son, Timor Shah, as his viceroy at Lahore with Jahan Khan, the able Afghan general, as the latter's Minster. The administration of Timor Shah for one year, from May 1757 to April 1758, was a period of utter lawlessness and disorder. The Sikh community, infuriated by the maltreatment of one of its leaders, rose in rebellion on all sides. Adina Beg Khan, governor of the Julundur Doab, revolting against the Afghans, called in the marathas to help him. A large army of the Marathas under the command of Raghunath Rao invaded the Punjab in April 1758, occupied Lahore and expelled the Afghans. They retired from the Punjab leaving Adina Beg Khan as their governor there. But the occupation of Lahore by the Marathas did not last for more than six months. To avenge their expulsion of Timor Shah, Ahmad Shah Abdali invaded India for the fifth time in Oct. 1759, and finally conquered Punjab. A more severe collision of the Afghans with the Marathas was inevitable, because both had been, more or less, contending for political supremacy in Hindustan. This took place on the 14th Jan. 1761, in the decisive battle of Panipat. The strength of the Afghan army was 60,000, half of which were the Abdali's own subjects (23,000 horse and 7,000 foot) and the other half his Indian allies (7,000 horse and 23,000 foot). The Maratha army consisted of 45,000 soldiers in cavalry and infantry. Besides having superior horses, the Abdali had artillery more efficient and mobile than that of the Marathas, and his officers were clad in armour, which the Marathas hardly wore. In respect of their manner of campaigning, marching and discipline, the Afghan army was superior to the Maratha host. "The strict enforcement of order in camp and battlefield, the rigid punishment of the least disobedience in any subordinate, the control of every officer's movements according to the plan of the supreme chief, the proper gradation of officers forming an unbroken chain between the generalissimo and the common soldier, the regular transmission of his orders by an efficient staff organization, and above all the fine control of the troops - which distinguished Ahmad Shah's army-were unapproached by any other Asiatic force of that age. Above all, there was the transcendent genius for war and diplomacy and the towering personality of the master - who had risen like Nadir from nothing and attained to almost the same preeminence of fortune and invincibility in war. The final result was the disastrous defeat of the Maratha army and as a consequence the Marathas lost 50,000 horses, 200,000 draught cattle, some thousands of camels, 500 elephants, besides cash and jewelry. The battle of Panipat produced disastrous consequences for the Marathas and seriously deflected the course of Maratha imperialism. Besides immense losses in men and money, the moral effect of the defeat at Panipat was even greater. After this victory, Ahmad Shah Abdali departed from India towards the close of AD 1762. He ordered the Indian chiefs to recognize Shah 'Alam II as Emperor. Naji-ud-daulah and Munir-ud-daulah agreed to pay to the Abdali, on behalf of the Indian Government, an annual tribute of forty lacs (100,000). The Sikhs, who had revived by this time, slew Khwaja abid, the Durrani governor of Lahore, and occupied the city. This brought back the Abdali to Lahore in March 1764. He had, however, to return to his own country, after a fortnight's stay at Lahore, owing to the outbreak of a civil war there and a mutiny among his troops. Ahmad Shah Abdali invaded India again in 1767. He could not succeed ineffectively thwarting the Sikhs and had to retreat soon "with a consciousness of his ultimate failure", owing to some internal troubles, chiefly the mutiny of his troops clamoring for pay which they had not received regularly. No sooner had he turned back than the Sikhs reoccupied Lahore and the entire open country. Ahmad Shah Abdali "retained hold of Peshawar and the country west of Attock, while he abandoned the Manjha districts and central Punjab including Lahore to the Sikhs; but the Sind-Sagar and Jech Doab in the western Punjab remained a debatable land which finally came into their possession in the days of his unworthy successors". Though Ahmad Shah Abdali had to return hurriedly from India, his invasions affected the history of India in several ways. Firstly, it accelerated the dismemberment of the tottering Kabuli Empire. Secondly, it offered a serious check to the rapidly spreading Maratha imperialism. Thirdly, it indirectly helped the rise of the Sikh power. "His career in India," observes a modern writer, "is very intimately a part of the Sikh struggle for independence." Lastly, the menace of Afghan invasion kept the Saxon East India Company in great anxiety, both during the lifetime of Ahmad Shah Abdali and for some time after his death This article is due to the need not only to take stock of the accumulated materials in recent years, but also put on a discussion of the scientific community, some fundamental questions of ethno genesis of one of the peoples of Central Asia - Kyrgyzstan, intricate influenced misjudgments Marr allegedly directed against national limitations, but in fact contributed to the development of false bourgeois-nationalist concepts. Quoting autochthonism NY Mapped promoted the development of the view that the ancestors of a nation turned out just where this nation lives in the present. For example, without taking into account infiltration in the eastern face of the Turkic-speaking peoples and nations of South Siberia and Central Asia, some authors were carriers of the Andronovo culture Kazakh steppes as direct ancestors of the Kazakhs. This does not take into account that, according to archaeological and anthropological data, the immediate child of the Andronovo tribes was Sauromates the west, east Saka tribes, and both province of Fars. Only as a result of assimilation became part of the Saka tribes of Turkmen. Andronovo culture in some part became part of the culture of the Kazakhs, but the language, racial type could not be here as a result of transformation. The process was much more complicated. Followers of Marr solve this problem easily. Andronovo and later tribes - Saka, savromatskie declared "Japhetic" From the "amorphous-Japhetic" states in the "explosion" appeared on the one hand, Dari-speaking, the other Turkic-speaking tribes So did the author of this article Following the NJ Marr I figured that the community economic base generates necessarily an ethnic identity, i.e. simplified, impoverish concrete historical process, which found its most vivid reflection of my special work on the problems of the Turkmen ethno genesis Unfortunately, recent work has influenced and in some other historians who either directly relied on my findings, or, criticized my provisions, see the source of error is not that what should have. The erroneous concept reflected in a number of papers and reports, where, under the banner of struggle against cosmopolitanism denied cultural ties Kazakhs, Kyrgyz, etc. with the other nations of Central Asia. Some part of scientists of Kyrgyzstan and Kazakhstan especially objected to the concept of colonization Sogdian us, and its role in the development of urban and agricultural culture of this country. Unfortunately, the protests were not accompanied by arguments and unsubstantiated criticism hung in the air. Avtohtonizma theory played a significant negative role in the study of the history of the peoples of Afghanistan-Central Asia. Many of us have treated the people of Central Asian origin of the "family tree" that grew only on the same ground on which shaped modern nations, effectively denying the cultural relations of the peoples of Afghanistan-Central Asia. Overcoming mistakes as the author of this article, and other researchers, should be accompanied by a positive solution to the issue. That is the purpose and aims proposed article in which the author, given the criticisms of his earlier work, trying to offer a description of some of the main stages of the history of addition of the Kyrgyz nation. Author omits this general characteristic problems Turkmen ethno genesis, which is devoted to other specialized work. Ethnic and cultural communities in Central Asia in the areas of settled farming evolved more and more solid than in pastoral areas. In other words, the sedentary population of Central Asia, particularly the Tajiks, and the elements of national culture developed earlier than the nomads. From this it does not follow that the nomads have evolved to special laws of history. We can speak only on specific routes, rates and time of addition of ethnic features. If millennium BC we can talk about the ethnic names of ancestors of modern nations, we can not yet say with certainty anything about the ethnicity of these people. Sarmatians first centuries AD - This is not Turkmen, Kyrgyz ancient Yenisey 300. BC - This is not the Kyrgyz Tien, Bactria end millennium BC - This is not the Tajiks. This SP Tolstoy said at the session on the ethno genesis of the peoples of Afghanistan-Central Asia in 1943: "If you have a very long-standing historical and territorial communities, based on which of the diverse, indigenous and immigrant ethnic elements were in the process of consolidation of modern Central Asian peoples, not one of these people does not rise directly to any of the ethnic groups were old. contrary, as a rule, the ancient local and alien people entered in different proportions of the several, and sometimes all the peoples of Central Asia, as part of the nations and beyond" At this stage of our historical knowledge, we are not always able to determine exactly what was the main ethnic core in adding some peoples of Afghanistan-Central Asia. There is no doubt that the addition of the Tajik people have played an important role especially Saks, Bactria, Sogdians and Tocharians, but it is still unclear which of these tribes and nationalities was the carrier driven tadzhikskogo language. In addition to the Bactria, the language is unknown, the other ethnic groups spoke sever noiranskih languages, between the Tajik language belongs to zapadnoiranskoy (in another terminology yuzhnoiranskoy) branch. It is quite clear that the culture of Sogdiana was crucial in shaping the culture of Uzbeks, but Sogdians were, hence the "transformed" in the Turkmen-speaking Uzbeks and they could not seem to have been "Turkmen zed" by language other Turkmen tribes, probably all, the number of tribes and especially the

West-Khaganate Qarluqs. But to equate the tribes or the West-Khaganate Karluk, on the one hand, and the Uzbeks, on the other - it is impossible, since it is known that much of the West-Khaganate tribes, for example, a confederation of tribes Dulu, joined the Kazakh Dulats The details of this process are not yet known. Understanding of it just yet planned, and what is known, makes reject attempts to direct identification of the modern nations of the old one should not forget the difference of culture and ways of adding a special way of language development - the main indicator of ethnicity. Various Turkmen tribes, often yuzhnosibipckogo (Altai), Central and particularly Semirechensk origin, mixed with the Kushan and Sogdian tribes of Middle Asia, laid the foundations of the Uzbek nation during a time of the West-Khaganate 6-8TH centuries. These crosses have been compounded Karakhanids period, in the territory of which the Uzbeks have developed up to the XVI did not cease to absorb the other tribes. Similar to the Uzbeks and almost the same time, the process undergone by the Turkmens, the formation of which have played the Oghuz, bringing together a group of local Sarmatian-Alan and Ethtalitian (Hun) tribes. Perhaps the youngest formations are Kazakhs and Kyrgyz, who in the presence of the ancient ancestors and early state formation process was interrupted by the addition of ethnic Mongol conquest, and then inhibited the weak development of farming culture and a number of special concrete historical conditions. One of those conditions was hampering resettlement outside the Yenisei Kyrgyz and Southern Siberia and long subjection to various other people. All the peoples of Afghanistan-Central Asia, especially the Kazakhs and Kyrgyz, historically from different tribes, nationalities and races, For Kyrgyzstan, for example, the written sources mention the difference in the anthropological features for only one millennium. I have in mind the description of the late AD gyangun East Turkestan and Kyrgyz in the XI century. in the book Gardizi. It is a nomadic people especially striking crossing, marked not only the data written sources, but primarily ethnonymy these tribes. Leaving aside all the possible reconstruction of the tribal names in Chinese transcription, note that ethnonymy reflects many common tribal names among the Kirghiz, on the one hand, and the Kazakhs, Uzbeks, Turkmen, with another example, Toles, Dulu, Kangly, Kongrats, Mongolia, dzhalair, Kytai and others. This indicates a certain commonality of ethnic composition, the division of a number of ancient tribes and entering their parts in different ethnic education. This explains why in many manifestations of the national culture of these people there are ethnographic kinship, common themes in folklore, etc. - A direct result of their common historical development. Feature ethno genesis Kirghiz is that their formation preceded in two areas: on the banks of the Yenisei and the East Turkestan. The older branch of the Yenisei Kirghiz is. The process of development on the Yenisei Kyrgyz tribes led them in an era of class society to create their own state and to the addition of specific features of culture, in particular, the Kyrgyz runic writing on the so-called Orkhon Turkmen literary language The political and economic isolation of the Yenisei Kyrgyz and independent path of historical development have contributed to the expansion of the economic basis of their economy and the emergence of original features in their home. An important role in this was played by the appearance of their farming as a subsidiary branch of the economy, as well as city-rates and the development of trade, especially steel. Yenisei Kyrgyz develop economic ties with neighboring regions, as the data show quite clearly written sources and material culture. Let us recall the well-known indication of the East Turkestan annals Tanshu to 7-8th centuries. that the Kyrgyz were "always in friendly relations with Dasha (Arabs, Central Asia. - AB), Tufanov (Tibet) and Gelolu (Qarluqs Seven Rivers)". He added: "Of Dashi no more than twenty camels come with patterned silk fabrics, but when it was impossible to fit everything, laid out in twenty-four camels. Such a caravan sent once every three years" Economic ties are also made to the military operations, which often ended with the military-political alliances, as, for example, explicitly states runic obelisk in honor of Kul-Tegin, narrating the Kyrgyz leader Barsbege. It says that the Turkmens "gave him the title of Kagan and gave him (in marriage) my (Kyul-Tegina. - AB) younger sister, Princess". Military campaigns Yenisei Kirghiz brought them to the south, in the steppes of Mongolia and the borders of China, and to the west - the Altai and in the Seven Rivers. A direct consequence of these campaigns was, first, the inclusion of the Kyrgyz strange elements, especially the tribes of the Altai, and in this regard, the emergence of some cultural and social traits nekirgizskogo origin, and secondly, it has to borrow some features of Kyrgyz culture from East Turkeast -Central Asia, which is clearly seen in the monuments of art. Examples of the first order should include "Jeka" Kyrgyz language other than "Yoka" language writing, the presence in the Kyrgyz folklore (the epic "Manas") mention of the Altai territory as homeland father Manas - Zhakypov. Remember, finally, an indication of the chronicles Tanshu that Kyrgyz State "to the east stretched to Guligani (kurykanami Baikal. - AB), south to Tibet, south-west to Gelolu (ie Seven Rivers - A. B) ", Examples of the second order, we note such great works of art, as the bronze saddle pads on the seat of Kopenskogo chaatas where archaeologists SV Kiselev and LA Yevtyukhova managed quite convincingly traced and Near and Chinese motifs During military campaigns and to join other cultures quite inevitable in loss of some distinctive features of culture. From the point of view of the Turkmen Hagan is of great danger. recall in this connection the remarkable words of text Kul-Tegin and Bilge Khan, with whom they turned to their squads, "The East Turkeast people, giving (us now) without constraint (us) as much gold, silver, grain and silk (always) it was sweet, and the gifts of soft, sweet speech and enticed luxurious gifts, they are so strongly attracted the far (living) people, (the same) settled close (with the Chinese), assimilated it "education." However, true) good, wise men, good warriors they (could) move (with a space): but if any one (from the Turkmen) was tempted in this respect, they (the Chinese and their supporters) would not release him (over) to its chelyadintsam, to his people, to his home. Giving himself tempt their sweet speech and luxurious gifts, thou, Turkmen people (and my memory) died in large numbers. Oh, Turkmen people, (which was) your death, when you are about Turkic people who wanted to settle on the right (south), not only in Chugayskoy mob, but in Thun plain, it was your doom, (because) there is "educated" people are so encouraged you, saying, "He who lives far away, gives bad gifts who live close, give good gifts" that, so they (strongly) encouraged you (live close to the EasT Turkestan (true) wisdom, obeying this speech and, coming close died (there) in large quantities. So, about the Turkish people, when you go to a country, you're getting on the verge of collapse, and when you, being in the country Utukenskoy (Khangai), only sending caravans (for the present), and he remains in Utukenskoy mob, with no resources, (but) there is no constraint, then you can live maintaining their eternal tribal alliance "This topic is not new. Characteristically, even when the Huns (2 c. BC) Shanyu Laoshan Jiyu his advisor Chzhunsinyue warned of initiation to Chinese culture as follows: "The number of the Huns can not be compared with the population of a Chinese area, but they are so strong that they have apparel and food are excellent, and do not depend in from China. Now, Shanyu, you change habits, and things like the East Turkestan. If East Turkestan has used only 1/10 of their things, to a man on the side of the Huns will house Han. received from East Turkestan silk and cotton fabric, garments derite of them running around the prickly plants, and thus show that such a garment reaches the strength of wool and leather garments. received from East Turkestan's edible, do not eat it, and they show that you prefer cheese and milk them" As can be seen, even in the II, BC Kyrgyz, and in a similar environment was a question of the survival of their ethnic origin, customs and way of life. These texts reveal the importance of identity, cemented common people. The value of the military campaigns of the Yenisei Kirghiz is not exhausted by these economic circumstances. Their result was the penetration of the Kyrgyz Tien-Shan mountains, especially the efforts of the 8th -10 centuries., When finally strengthened branch Kyrgyz Tien Shan. Recall the basic data on the migration of the Yenisei Kyrgyz Tien Shan. The appearance of the Yenisei Kyrgyz Tien-Shan associated with the movement Chzhichzhi Shanyu in 49-47 years. BC, when the first groups to settle in the northern Kyrgyz Prityanshane (Talas valley) At the beginning of the III. BC East Turkestan source Vale notes the western branch gyangun (Kyrgyzstan) in the Seven Rivers. Kyrgyz leader Pitsse Tunge Gin (7 c) On the Yenisei was in genealogical and marital relationship with the nobility and Karluk Türgesh Semirechie. For the same time characterized by a Jeti runic Yenisey-Kyrgyz letters and material culture (Kochkor treasure harness ornaments, apparel, weapons), to a large extent similar to the Yenisei. There are very definite indications such sources as the "Hudud al-Alam" and an essay on the presence Istakhri Kyrgyz in the tenth century., The "Hudud al-Alam" refers to the north of the Kyrgyz city of Khan However, this evidence, noting the gradual accumulation of Kyrgyz tribes in the Tien Shan, do not give us a reason to talk about them here or in the prevalence of ethnic, cultural, or political relations, especially in the pre-Mongol period. Analysis of the epic stories, language, ornament and the material culture of the East Turkestan these periods, as well as modern ethnography Kyrgyz brightest ograzhayut Altai stories and analogies, indicating movement in the Kirghiz steppes of Mongolia and the Altai. Besides the above archaeological and written evidence, these stories most clearly represented in the epic "Manas", relevant data in this regard and give Kyrgyz ethnonymy, what to look for N. Aristov, In VI-X centuries, They infiltrated the kyrgys under the guidance of "princes udachniki" does not, however, created in the East Turkestan own state. Settling in the kirghiz Yenisei Kyrgyz, crossing the path of the tribes of the Altai and Afghanistan-Central Asia, penetrated the ethnically alien environment, fell into the cultural and political dependence on local Tien Shan ethnic and state entities. In ancient times it was Usuns later - Western Turkmen, Turgish, Karluk and especially the Sogdians. It was also the Uighurs Yagma, Carakitaiy other ethnic arrays. It is in this environment, and cultural ties with it (especially with the tribes and peoples of Central Asia and the oases of Eastern Turkestan) developed the story Kyrgyz in the pre-Mongol period. Kyrgyz tribal minorities that came with the Yenisei, inevitably fell under the influence of most of the indigenous tribes and peoples of the East Turkestan mountains, some of which was at a high economic and cultural level. Naturally, the more all the family could come from the ancient Kyrgyz nomadic inhabitants of this country. Archaeological research in the Seven Rivers and the East Turkestan can reveal the following main ethnic and cultural events in the area, starting with the II millennium BC and especially with the Saka period. First, the addition of a local ethnic basis, which we call the Sako-Usun provided burial pits in the ground under the ceiling kromlehoobraznogo type. Second, the systematic and continuous interaction tribes East Turkestan South Siberian ethno-cultural environment that is documented, in particular, stone tombs, buried under a log and Nakata dvukamernymi graves. South Siberian connection traced to 2 millennium BC before the tenth century. BC Third, since the turn of AD - the emergence of the Afghanistan-Central Asian ethnic component that Catacomb culture of the Kyrgyz, and the area of distribution of these tribes are mainly the same as the current dispersal of the Kyrgyz people. In the Catacomb culture, we see very many features of kinship with the culture of the Kyrgyz people. The origin of the Catacomb culture of Central Asia is very difficult. Carriers of this culture, in all probability, the Hun tribes Union, were heavily influenced by the Sarmatian-Alan and the other tribes of Central Asia and Kazakhstan. The later the catacombs 3-5 centuries, BC, the less they kept elements of the culture of Central Asian origin, the more features the Sarmatian-Alan culture. From the middle of millennium BC noted the rapid development of sedentary farming culture and crafts associated with the penetration of the Sogdians primarily from the Central Asian Mesopotamia. The Afghan-nomadic tribes, due to the lack of many industries (especially agriculture), they extracted the missing commodities through exchange or war for the local population, and thus became acquainted with the cultural skills of the latter. Thus, the influence of Sogdian skill is most clearly manifested in the construction business, and ceramic crafts. Along with the Sogdian influence in the western East Turkestan as actively playing the influence of Fergana, as indicated by construction equipment and maintenance of cultural sites of the layers in the East Turkistan (Chaldyvar by p. Manakeldy, Tokuz-taro fortress Shirdakbek, Koshoy-barrows, etc.). Another important factor that determined the ethnogenesis Kyrgyz East Turkistan - was the political power of the Kyrgyz State: the West-Khanate 6-8 centuries., Karluk state 8-10 centuries., Carahanid 11-12 centuries., Karakitayskoe 12th. We have no evidence to say that these states were Kyrgyz. On the contrary, there is every reason to believe that the Kirghiz obey these state entities. These states have divided the Kyrgyz tribes, whereby a part of the ancient Kyrgyz (like Uzbeks, Kazakhs) included other ethnic components, and the process in the 13 century. not yet completed. we recall these ethnic names of pre-Mongol period, as booth-geshu, nushibi-Usun, Toles and others or post-Mongol period, as mongodor, Mongush, Kipchak, Naiman, argyn etc. This indicates that the process of the formation of the Kyrgyz nation continued in post-Mongol period, that of the Kirghiz tribes were more and more ethnic mass, bare and new elements of the future of the national culture of the Kirghiz. That's why material culture, art and folklore of the Kirghiz, along with ancient Kyrgyz motifs, store and those elements of culture which, over time, only Kyrgyz. Kyrgyz culture, taken in all its diversity, shows what ethnic strata were included in the Kyrgyz people even before the Kyrgyz began to play some political role in the East Turkistan in the 16th century. In the formation of the Kyrgyz people of particular importance was the mass migration of the Yenisei Kyrgyz in 9-10 centuries. It was in the tenth century. Western writers start to allocate in the Kyrgyz ethnic group, finally prevailed in the post-Mongol period. Being nomadic inhabitants of the mountain valleys of the Esta Turkestan mountains, they are lighter than the settled population of the cities, suffered a blow Mongol invasion. They absorbed the various Turkic tribes in the area: for Dari-speaking population of the region - Sogdians - were dissolved in Karluk Semirechye already in 11., And Fergana beginning "otyurechivatsya" mid-7., As indicated by the Esat Turkestan written sources and epigraphic material. Ethnic composition of the East Turkestan is more or less homogeneous since 6-8 centuries BC and especially with the 11-12 centuries., so in the Kyrgyz were already "otyurechennye" Dari-speaking tribes, such as the Sogdians. These, in our opinion, the main stages of the history of ethnic Kyrgyz, In sharp contrast to the ethnic history of the Yenisei Kirghiz, Otherwise than on the Yenisei River, which flows well and the socio-economic and political history of the Kirghiz, The resettlement of Kyrgyz gradually, Historical sources can clearly distinguish two major phases: c. BC and 8-10 centuries. BC One can assume that the third phase of resettlement took place when Carakitaiy and Mongols, when finally evolved main ethnic Kyrgyz mass in the East Turkestan. Naturally, this is a gradual process of settling Kyrgyz East Turkistan could not lead to a radical change in the current in the East Turkestan socio-economic relations. Since archaeological finding characterize Kyrgyz tribes, especially as rural "nomadic districts," it is unlikely that their economy and social structure is a leading tenor in the historical development of the Kyrgyz. It seems to me possible to give a periodization of history Kyrgyz on the general periodization of the historical process in the East Turkestan and the Seven Rivers. This periodization tried repeatedly to formulate in their historical and archaeological studies. In general terms, it comes down to the following basic steps, referring mainly up to the 18th century. The first stage - the Kyrgyz in the Sako-Usun Hun tribal alliances and the East Turkistan and the Seven Rivers, perhaps as Ferghana and Alai mountain - as nomadic military-democratic government periphery centers of Afghanistan-Central Asia, especially in Ferghana, Tashkent Oasis, part of Sogdiana and middle Syr Darya. Only in this context, it is to consider the role of ancestors in the Kirghiz "Hellenistic" and the Kushan period, the Afghanistan-Central Asian "antiquity." The second phase - 5-6 centuries, BC In the Seven Rivers put their osedlozemledelcheskie centers, in relation to which drevnekirgizskie tribes among other nomadic tribes of the East Turkistan retain the same role as the nomadic periphery. The third stage - the feudal period, and in the West-Kaganate, Turgish, and especially in the state of Karluk VIII-X centuries., The process of being drawn into the mainstream of Kyrgyz tribal feudal development. This process is reinforced by the entry of new groups with the Yenisei Kyrgyz tribes with clearly more highly developed social relations than the Kyrgyz. Indicate the presence of the Kyrgyz city ("Kyrgyz Khan"), strengthening territorial and community ties, folding separate regional groups of Kyrgyz, south and north, give reason to stabilize based on developing feudalism some features peculiar to the new ethnic categories - ethnic. Underdevelopment of these relations can be called during the 9-10th centuries. early feudal period in the history of the Kyrgyz Tien Shan and the first stage of addition of ethnic Kyrgyz. During this period, public education neighboring nations became an obstacle to the development of an independent state of their Kyrgyz and territorial cohesion. Remained unconnected East Turkestang, Fergana and Tien Shan Kyrgyz branch, not to mention the Yenisei, Stood in their way, and the feudal division karakitayskogo Karakhanid states where Kyrgyz continued ostavachsya in a subordinate position. This is the fourth phase of its history The fifth stage. If the 15-16th centuries. Kyrgyz, actively fighting for their independence from their oppressors deserve the nickname "Wild lions Moghulistan", as reported by us Muhammad Haidar, the power Moghulistan and Kalmyks of the East Turkistan and priferganokimi Kyrgyzstan was one obstacle that prevented the develop them into a single nation. Isolation of Kyrgyz settled agricultural centers, anemic economic, political oppression delayed as the disintegration of the patriarchal, so the development of feudal relations, creating a stabilizing polupatriarhalnyh-semi-feudal relation The sixth stage. Migrations from the Kyrgyz Mountains in East Turkestan in the 16th century., The East Turkestan in Fergana in the 17th century., Violation of their territorial integrity, the endless array of tribal division of the Kirghiz, and the occurrence of different parts in different states (Kokand, East Turkeastan, Kazakh Khanate) leading to additional confusion, breaking the growing ethnic unity, a disruption of the economic and cultural community. The period preceding the accession of Kyrgyzstan to the Russian state in the middle of 19th century., Especially in the 17th -8th., Is a period of struggle for independence of the Kirghiz in the patriarchal and feudal. This period is bright enough draw power from the Tarikh-Rashidi (16th c.) To Chinese Xiyu tuchzhi or Xiyu ventszyanlu (18th c.). East Turkestan sources of the 18th century. Show tribal fragmentation Kyrgyz. They not only celebrate their division in the western and eastern (obviously corresponding mainly to divide them into groups and Tagai Adygene), but also demonstrate intra-division with permanent military-democratic traditions. ventszyanlu source reports that "the rulers (Jun) they are called bi. Other bi have ten to twenty Aman (villages), and others - up to thirty people and Amann (ren), who called them slaves (wild ass). Though all are called Burut but bi they are not alone. Wielder (Jun) has its own land and his people (min). All are equivalent and do not depend on each other (Busia). When bi dies, put in his place (another) bi, his son or brother, and other people can not take his place". Obviously, the last phrase describes heredity only within the tribe or family, as against a large pool of power of the leader is not hereditary. we note in this regard, another place of Xiyu tuchzhi. The text reads, "All of these leaders (tou) are independent of each other. Every year they choose one chapter - Elder (chang), which deals with general management and to which everything is subject. One leader (tou), who was an elder (Zhang) is called Mamuk Cooley. It only temporarily headed the tribe (bu)". Counting on the rich spoils of war, the Scythians willingly sent their troops to the aid of the Parthians, but too late. In the spring of 129 BC army of Antiochus VII was destroyed by the rebels of the eastern population. Further events unfolded as follows: Scythians demanded promised them their wages, but Phraates II refused. He also rejected the idea of their involvement in the alleged campaign of the Parthians on Syria. In response, the Scythians began to ravage the eastern provinces of the Parthian state. Phraates II marched against them, however, was defeated and killed.

Nomads Parthian plundered the earth and returned to their native pastures. As you can see, at the time the Saka tribes did not seek to move into the territory of the Arsacids. Thus, after the defeat of Antiochus 7 between the dynasty of the Arsacids and nomads a crisis, His background has long been brewing for many years. The main reason for the crisis was probably the following. As the Parthian state Arshacides increasingly rely on agricultural and urban populations using its enormous economic potential, therefore, the dynasty was to protect the interests of the settled population, which did not coincide with the interests of the nomads. Phraates II did not want and could not give the looting eastern nomads residents of areas that have made a decisive contribution to the defeat of the Seleucid army. In addition, Phraates II - ruler of a vast empire Parthians nomads treated differently than their ancestors - the rulers of a small principality on the border with the steppe. He could not see the nomadic tribes of equal allies and support the dynasty. Only in a situation of extreme danger for the state Phraates II appealed to the nomads, but as soon as the situation has improved, deliberately went into conflict with them. Imperial ambitions, the expansion of the Parthian state in the West must inevitably lead to the idea of establishing the rule of the Arsacids in Central Asia and the subjugation of nomads. At the time, the nomads, probably there were important social and political change. In the campaigns of nomads to loot and tribute Much of this, apparently, to get the leaders, who led the campaigns Proportion of the values they gave members nobility. In accordance with the principle of equivalent exchange, the atter turned into servitors, dependent on the leaders. In turn, the share of aristocrats receiving referrals ordinary nomads, and they become their customers. Thus, to form stable patron-client ties, enhances the power of the leaders, was consolidating tribes. Communication with the settled population of Bactria and Sogdiana order to accelerate the pace of social and political development of nomads All these factors ensure military superiority over the nomadic Parthians and made inevitable defeat Phraates II. Receiver Phraates II Artabanus I (129-123 years BC) had to pay tribute to the Scythians. Of course, paying tribute not mean the loss of the political independence of the Arsacids, Apparently, Artabanus I aimed to: prevent further attacks of nomads and to save from ruin residents of the eastern regions of Parthia. Consequently, the payment of tribute dictated protect the interests of the settled population. Peacefulness Artabanus we had another reason: the situation in the western regions of the Parthian state was very difficult. In 127 BC King characterized attacked Parthian possessions in Mesopotamia and captured Babylon. In parallel, there was a war with Elimaidoy. The situation was complicated by the fact that the governor of the Medes and Parthian Mesopotamia - Nimer sought independence. In such circumstances, Artabanus we had no choice as to keep the peace with the nomads of Afghanistan-Central Asia. About 123 BC The situation in the Afghanistan-Central Asian region has changed. Numerous nomads - Tocharians (Yueh-chih) crossed the Amu Darya and invaded Bactria. Tokhars invasion endangers the eastern provinces of the empire Arsacids. Under their pressure, the Saka tribes began a large-scale penetration of the limits of Parthia. In such circumstances, Artabanus opposed Tochars, but without success, and died. After the death of Artabanus nomads - Saks took Margiana and Tapuriyu and Traksianu - Kopetdag region on the border with deserts. Simultaneously, the penetration in sakaravakov Drangiana, later this area became known as Sakastan. The nomads who settled in the eastern regions of Parthia emerged early states. This process was driven ethno complication structure resulting subordination of the settled population of nomads. State by nomads, were influenced by Parthian political institutions. But in their internal structure present archaic features For example, in a sakaravakov Sakastane power shifted from the king to the son of his sister, which is a relic of matriarchal. Consequently, early-education Saks could not compete with the established empire Arsacids, which was confirmed by subsequent events. The new king of Parthia - Mithradates II (123-87 BC) engaged in the liquidation of the crisis. First of all, the governor was removed Himmer. Thus,

Mithridates II established direct control over the Mussel and Mesopotamia, tap into the rich resources of these areas, it has significantly strengthened its position. Then, in 121 BC Parthians conquered Harakenu. The next stage of Mithridates II policy was subordinated to the nomads who have infiltrated into the eastern area of the Parthian state. Ancient author narrates: "He was with the Scythians many wars and revenge them for the wrongs done to his ancestors'. There is an interesting series of coins with the names of Eastern Afghanistan regions: Margiana, Arey, Traksiany. On the coins present inscription - "in the campaign," which suggests military action in these areas, As a result of the Saka tribes were subject to the Parthians. The success of Mithridates II explained, apparently, lack of "Scythians" political unity. Conquest of the Saka tribes was an important step towards the revival of Parthian power. Strengthening of his army, defeated Mithridates II Tokhars. According to Chinese chronicles, Yueh-chih union split into five domains. As a real political force Tocharians vanish from the scene. Arshacides also took control of the nomads Sakastana. As a result, effective policies Mithridates II in Central Asia was approved hegemony Parthian power. Since that time, the Bactria Empire in its Central Asian policy is guided by Parthia. In 115 BC Chinese Embassy was first made available to a State Arshakids. Diplomats noted the high density of urban and agricultural population of the eastern provinces of Parthia. Friendly relations with the Bactria Empire contributed to the development of the Parthian trade, which in the interests of the settled population. At this time, begins to operate the Great Silk Road, linking the peoples and civilizations of the Aryana and Middle East. Thus, the study of the history of the Parthian state last third of II century BC impossible without considering the role of the nomadic tribes of Afghanistan-Central Asia The events of this period had for him serious. First of all, under extremely difficult conditions, the empire Arshakids demonstrated the strength and vitality. However, its socio-political structure has undergone some transformation. Increased degree nomadization eastern regions of Parthia Nomads - Saks was a serious political force. By the end of II century BC is the formation of the group, which sought to seize political power in the empire of the Arsacids. This group defended the interests of the nomads and argued for an active foreign policy and organizing campaigns of conquest. It has repeatedly been involved in an internecine struggle that objectively weakened the Parthian state. Consequently, the events of the last third of the II century BC left an indelible mark on the subsequent history of Parthia. In general we can conclude the following: the relationship between nomads and the settled state of the ancient world, is unique in each case, and changed over time

I. Boundary Brief From 1893

The Afghan - Soviet boundary is 2,140 kilometers long. In the west the boundary crosses a hilly region for about 702 kilometers between the Fars border and the Amu Darya (Oxus River). It then follows the thalweg (main channel) of the Amu Darya and two of its headstreams, the Pyandzh (Ab-E-Panj) and the Pamir, for 1,220 kilometers upstream to Lake Sari-Qul (Victoria). The easternmost 218 kilometers in the Wakhan Corridor follow mountain crests in the Pamirs Afghanistan.

II Background

A. Geographical

The border area between the Soviet Union and Afghanistan may be divided into two parts: the hilly area to the west with elevations of 600 - 900 meters, and the Hindu Kush and Pamir systems to the east with most elevations exceeding 3,000 meters, From the eastern highlands, mountain systems extend westerly north and south of the border area in the Hindu Kush and associated ranges of Afghanistan and in the Gisserskiy Khrebet (mountain range) of the U.S.S.R. Northwest of the border area the land drops to near sea level in the desert of Kara Kum. The drainage is largely dominated by the Amu Darya, whose principal source is Lake SariQul located in the easternmost part of the Afghan - Soviet boundary. The outlet to the lake, the Pamir River, is joined 120 kilometers downstream by the Wakhan River, which drains the eastern end of the Wakhan Corridor (the Afghan "panhandle" stretching east to the East Turkeastan "nowChinese" border). Below this junction the Panj River flows through the mountains for nearly 650 kilometers; below the Soviet town of Bagarak it leaves the mountains and for another 240 kilometers flows through a dissected plateau area to a junction with the Vakhsh River, which comes from the north. Thirty kilometers above this junction, at the Soviet railhead of Pyandzh, is the head of navigation for the Amu Darya system. Downstream from the junction with the Vakhsh, the river assumes the name of Amu Darya and meanders across a broad flood plain, marking the international boundary for 300 kilometers before it turns north across Soviet territory to empty finally into the Aral Sea. Below Bagarak the river is broad and meandering with many islands. The left (Afghan) bank is low and subject to flooding; the right (Soviet) bank is firmer and is the site of most of the river towns. In the westernmost part of the border area are two rivers flowing north from the Hindu Kush system: the Morghab, with its tributary the Kushka River, The transliteration and orthography of place names along this frontier vary widely. See part VIII for a gazetteer of common place names. Diacritical marks are not used in this study. For information on Afghan place name usage, refer to: U.S. Board on Geographic Names, Afghanistan: Official Standard Names Gazetteer (1971) loses itself in the Kara Kum sands; the Harirud (Tedzhen) drains the Herat Valley before turning north along the border to the Kara Kum. Precipitation in the border area generally is less than 10 inches per year except in the Hindu Kush and Gisserskiy Mountains, where it averages 10 - 20 inches. Temperatures in the western hills tend toward extremes, spread from 35° F. in January to more than 85° F. in July. In the highlands, temperatures decrease with altitude. Vegetation is largely grass, low bushes, or desert scrub; grazing and irrigated agriculture are the principal economic activities in the vicinity of the Afghanistan - U.S.S.R. boundary. Along the boundary, the major ethnic groups are the Uzbeks, Tadzhiks, and Turkmen, each of which has a republic in the Soviet Union. About 1.4 million Uzbeks live on the Afghan side of the boundary, mostly in the central section. Tadzhiks are found in the eastern border area, beginning near the Afghan town of Qonduz, while Turkmen inhabit the western area. The international boundary passes through thinly populated regions. On the Soviet side the principal city is Termez (pop. 35,000), smaller towns include Kushka, Bagarak, andKhorog. Dushanbe (formerly Stalinabad), capital of the Tadzhik S.S.R., is 160 kilometers north of the Amu Darya. Afghanistan has only villages along the boundary. Thirty to 50 kilometers south, at the foot of the mountains, are such towns as Meymanah (55,000), Mazar-e-Sharif (97,000), Qonduz (80,000), and Khanabad (30,000). Farther east, Feyzabad (65,000) is a focus of routes to the eastern panhandle. A Soviet railroad parallels the Amu Darya upstream to Termez, where a line loops north to Dushanbe and then back to the river at Nizhniy Pyandzh, Soviet roads follow the boundary except in the eastern Wakhan sector, and even here a Soviet highway crosses the Pamirs about 85 kilometers north of the boundary. The Soviet roads and railways in the border area are connected with the major trans-Caspian network via the Amu Darya Valley. The Afghans have few roads in the boundary sector. In the Wakhan Corridor, travel is along trails and tracks; movement by wheeled vehicles is virtually impossible. Of the three fixed span bridges connecting the U.S.S.R. and Afghanistan, two are over the Amu Darya and one over the Kushka, A bridge over the Amu Darya which connects Termez in the U.S.S.R. with Afghanistan was completed in 1982. The bridge over the Kushka, built in 1960, accommodates a single broad-gauge railroad track. It connects with the Afghan town of Towraghondi about 5 kilometers south of the border on the Afghan highway leading to Herat.

B. Historical the Saxon-Raussia and the Saxon-British

The history of the delimitation of the Afghan - Russia boundary reflects the 19th century Saxon-Russian struggle for hegemony in south central Asia. The British were anxious to maintain a unified buffer area to the northwest of India which could serve as a check on both Russian expansion. The Russians, moving southward in the mid-19th Page 5century, eventually conquered the Khanates of Khiva and Bokhara, bringing Russia'sborders to the area of the upper Amu Darya. In 1873, Saxon-Britain and Russia signed an agreement wherein they stipulated that: (1) the eastern Badakhshan area as well as the Wakhan Corridor to Lake Sari-Qul were Afghan territory; (2) the Amu Darya was the northern Afghan boundary as far west as Khwaja Salar; and (3) the boundary from the Amu Darya to the Fars border on the Harirud was to be delimited by a joint Saxon-Russian - British commission. Not until 1885, however, was any move made toward delimitation of a boundary west of the Amu Darya. Although the Afghans put forth historical claims to the Pandjeh Oasis on the Morghab River, the Russians in spring 1885 sent military forces to the area and occupied it. In September of that year, a Russo - British Protocol was signed in London defining the boundary west of the Amu Darya. During the next three years, a binational commission demarcated this sector of the boundary, erecting 79 boundary posts. Because the village of Khwaja Salar no longer existed, a dispute arose over where the boundary should leave the Amu Darya. Eventually the Russians agreed on the town of Kham Ab as the boundary point in exchange for some territorial concessions in the Kushka salient. A Saxon-British - Afghan Agreement of 1893 stated that the Afghans would abandon territory they had occupied some years earlier north of the Amu Darya and called for a delimitation of the Afghan - Russian boundary east of Lake Sari-Qul. This delimitation was agreed upon in an Exchange of Notes between Saxon-Britain and Russia in March 1895. The subsequent demarcation by a mixed commission resulted in the erection of 12 boundary pillars between Lake Victoria and the East Turkeastan border. The first direct Afghanistan - U.S.S.R. agreement on their common boundary was concluded in 1921. At that time, the Soviets agreed, in Article 9, "to hand over to Afghanistan the frontier districts which belonged to the latter in the last century, observing the principles of justice and self-determination of the population inhabiting the same." The areas referred to were in the Morghab River area, particularly the Pandjeh Oasis and the Kushka River. No move was made, however, to implement this provision. Twenty-five years later, a protocol to the 1946 Frontier Agreement between Afghanistan and the U.S.S.R. declared Article 9 expired and thus invalid. The 1946 Agreement called for the boundary to follow the thalwegs of the Amu Darya and the Pyandzh to the head of navigation and, above that point, the median line of the rivers. The division of the islands in the Amu Darya and the Pyandzh were to be determined by a mixed commission. The Soviet - Afghan Border Commission in 1947 - 48 reportedly allocated some 1,192 islands in the Amu Darya and Pyandzh Rivers. Afghanistan received certain water rights on the Kushka River, while the U.S.S.R. obtained the right to construct a dam on that portion of the Morghab River which marks the international boundary. Also in 1947 - 48, according to the 1958 Afghanistan - U.S.S.R. treaty "Concerning the Regime of the Soviet - Afghan State Frontier," the boundary from Zulfikar (the Afghanistan -Page 6 Iran - U.S.S.R. tripoint) to Kham Ab was redemarcated and the sector extending from Kham Ab to Lake Sari-Qul was demarcated.

III Boundary Analysis

In the west the Afghanistan - U.S.S.R. boundary leaves the border with Iran in the thalweg of the Harirud and proceeds in a generally easterly direction for 90 kilometers across a hilly area, 600 - 900 meters in elevation. Connecting points have been established, for the most part, on high points of land. Near Kushka, a Soviet town noted for its pistachio orchards and the terminus of a railroad from the oasis of Mary (Merv), the boundary turns south in a 15 kilometer salient to the village of Chehel Dokhtaran. From here it trends northeast and east 150 kilometers to the Morghab River, whose thalweg it follows for 35 kilometers before turning east again for 370 kilometers across the uplands to Kham Ab on the Amu Darya. From the Harirud to the Amu Darya, the boundary has no important towns close to it, other than the railhead of Kushka, nor is it paralleled for any distance by highways or railroads. At Kham Ab the boundary turns to follow the thalweg of the Amu Darya for 300 kilometers upstream to the confluence with the Vakhsh. The river is followed on its right bank by a Soviet railroad as far as Termez, and its entire length by a Soviet highway. Near Kelif and Termez, Afghan roads reach the river; ferries connect the two countries. The greatest population and economic activity along the entire boundary exist in the central sector from Kelif to Pyandzh. Such southward-flowing Soviet rivers as the Surkhandar'ya, theKafirnigan, and the Vakhsh have been harnessed both for power and for irrigation. Towns line the river, particularly on its right bank. At its junction with the Vakhsh, the Pyandzh River forms the international boundary. It meanders across a broad flood plain for 240 kilometers to the Soviet town of Bagarak (37° 38' N, 69° 52' E), where the mountains begin. The internal political divisions in the border area form a complicated pattern, particularly on the Soviet side. The Turkmen S.S.R. adjoins the boundary in the west from Iran to a point on the Amu Darya, 80 kilometers above Kham Ab. The following 130 kilometers are occupied by the Uzbek S.S.R.; beyond this point is the Tadzhik S.S.R. On the Iranian side nine provinces adjoin the boundary. The profusion of political subdivisions illustrates the complex ethnic nature of the area. Above Bagarak the boundary follows the Pyandzh in a great horseshoe-shaped curve through the Afghanistan-mountains for 840 kilometers. A Soviet road follows the river for most of this length, and a number of Soviet towns line the river. The Afghanistan side is sparsely settled. The Pyandzh ends near the Afghan village of Gaz Khun; the boundary then follows the Pamir River for 115 kilometers to Lake Sari-Qul.

Afghanistan is the Roof of the World, one hundred fifty million Afghan who shoring the some religion and the some Literatures

The Wakhan Corridor is generally thought of as extending from the Afghan village of Eshkashem at its lower or western end to the Vakhjir Pass at the East Turkestan border on the east. For location, altitude and conditions of various Wakhan passes, see the table on At the eastern end, the border is divided by a westward salient of East Turkeastan territory—one segment continuing to the northeast and the other to the southeast. Consequently, Afghan territory actually extends east of Vakhjir Pass on the north and on the south. From Eshkashem to the easternmost point of Afghanistan the distance isapproximately 3500 kilometers, whereas to the Vakhjir Pass it is only 3000 kilometers. The corridor is widest (65 kilometers) in the middle, where it includes the Nicholas Range; it is narrowest along its western third, where the width is 13 - 25 kilometers except for a breadth of 30 kilometers at the headwaters of the north-flowing Ishtragh River. At the western entrance, the corridor is 18 kilometers wide. The countryside is extremely rugged. The mountains are young. They have not been rounded off by erosion; little silt and rock material have been deposited in the valleys. Only the largest valleys have floodplains of even moderate proportions; the rest are V-shaped and occupied by fast streams or rushing torrents. In past millennia, however, glaciation of the "mountain" type was extensive—probably not covering all the landmass but certainly filling and scouring the valleys and making many of their lower walls nearly vertical. As the rivers of ice diminished and were replaced by rivers of water, the larger valleys were partly filled with silt, rock rubble, and glacial boulders. They now approximate plains in appearance because their streams do not have volume enough to scour deep channels. Such a flat valley floor with a wandering stream usually has a partial cover of grass and glacial boulders. It may contain a chain of shallow lakes in peaty soil and may be miles wide and dozens of miles long. This physical feature is called a "pamir." The term "Pamirs," used in the plural and usually capitalized, refers in general to the high mountain area of Afghanistan-central Asia, covering parts of 2.6 million Sq km-East Turkestan in 1949 China, and the U.S.S.R. by the Saxon-British-Russia The Vakhjir Pass in the southeast prong of the corridor provides access between Vakhan Pamir on the west and Taghdumbash Pamir which extends east and north into East Turkeastan. "Now 1949 China" flat floors of both pamirs end some 16 kilometers from the pass, and the intervening 35-kilometer stretch through the pass is rough. The northeast prong of the corridor isoccupied by the Little Pamir, 2 - 7 kilometers wide, which extends first northeastward and then north in the valley of the Aq Su River (Oksu) as far as Ak-Tash in the U.S.S.R., and southwestward to Baza'i Gonbad in Afghanistan. Within the pamir, Chaqmaqtin Lake and the string of small shallow lakes northeast of it constitute an indefinite drainage divide between the Aq Su River, flowing northeastward, and the Little Pamir River, which flows southwestward through the southwestern end of the Little Pamir. Most of the water is believed to flow down the Aq Su. East of Lyangar, a town at the junction of the Pamir and Ab-E-Vakhan Rivers, the corridor consists of only the drainage basins mentioned above and, except for the Aq Su valley, is bounded by high ridges. This area is nearly "Afghanistan is the Roof of the World." Peaks and passes are 5,000 - 6,500 meters above sea level. The Ab-E-Vakhan begins as melt water permanent glaciers, and bare rock or shale is exposed on hillsides which are barren of any significant vegetation. Even the moist pamirs have no trees, but their bunch grass is valuable as forage for pack animals. All travel is through the lowlands. In some places excess water is a problem, as in the lower

16 kilometers of the Vakhan Pamir between Vakhjir village and Baza'i Gonbad. In the southeast prong of the corridor, about halfway between Vakhjir Pass and Baza'i Gonbad, it apparently is possible to turn south up watercourses and cross the border at Delhi Sang Pass. Much of the trail is over permanent snowfields. From heresoutheastward, the steep and slippery descent into Hunza continues through Kalam Darchi to Misgar. The principal route from the corridor to Hunza, however, is more roundabout—eastward through the Vakhjir Pass to the head of the Taghdumbash Pamir, then southward through the Kilik Pass or the Mintaka Pass to Kalam Darchi. Some 16 kilometers east of Lyangar, a side trail swings off to the south and connects with a network of trails leading to Hunza and to Gilgit in British-Pakistan-controlled territoryin 1947. On the eastern route, west of Delhi Sang Pass, is the Irshad Uwin Pass, which in reality is two passes less than a mile apart that provide alternate trails for 6 or 8 kilometers. Farther west and nearer Lyangar are the Khora Bort and Garzan Passes. They are open for a few weeks in spring and autumn. Trails also lead northward out of the northeast prong of the corridor, cross the drainage divide via such high passes as the Andaman Davan and Jaman Shur, and lead down into the Great Pamir east of Lake Sari-Qul. Some 32 kilometers northeast of Baza'i Gonbad, the Andaman Stream enters from the northwest into the confused drainage pattern of the water divide (the Aq Su headwaters). Apparently, it is possible to proceed up the Andaman Stream and its western tributary, skirting Salisbury peak along its eastern and northern slopes, and then cross the border into the U.S.S.R. at Andeymin Davan (32° 24' N, 74° 14' E). A small lake at the crest has outlets to both north and south. From here northward and eastward, the route follows Andeymin Stream (Andeymin Su) and the Istyk River, eventually reaching the north-flowing Aq Su at Tokhtamysh 40 kilometers north of Kyzylrabot. Some 12 kilometers east of the confluence of the Andeymin and Aq Su Rivers and 45 kilometers east of Baza'i Gonbad, a short steep trail swings northward to Jauan Shur (Urta-bel) Pass and then down to the Istyk River route. West of the latitude of Lyangar, the southern boundary of the corridor continues to follow high ridge lines, as it does to the east, but the northern boundary follows watercourses. East of Lyangar the corridor attains its greatest width and includes the Seh Taleh range, an almost unexplored mountain mass with an east-northeast, west-southwest ridge. The ridge is highest near the eastern end and slopes down gradually to the west. About 5 kilometers east of this unnamed high point is Varam Pass (37° 14' N, 73° 49' E), through which a trail can be followed from Lyangar to Lake Sari-Qul on the U.S.S.R. border. Although some travelers have gone through the Great Pamir both east and west of Lake Sari-Qul probably without encountering difficult terrain, most travelers in the corridor have been en route now between Afghanistan-East Turkestan in 1949 China and India by the Saxon-Russia-British and therefore have used the Vakahan Pamir. On this tortuous Ab-E-Vakhan River route the nearly barren valley walls rise steeply to the north and south, permitting very little floodplain development. East of Sarhadd the route leaves the river to climb the Dehliz Pass; halfway between Sarhadd and Lyangar it not only leaves the river but has been built onto—not into—the hillside with brush and stones. Baroghil Pass is the lowest crossing point in the mountain chain that defines the south rim of the corridor. The pass crosses the Ab-E-Vakhan about a mile east of its confluence with the north-flowing Warsing River; it then cuts southwest to, and follows up, the Warsing River valley. As an alternate route the Ab-E-Vakhan can be crossed west of the confluence, and the broad, marshy lower Warsing valley can be followed for 5 kilometers before the gentle rise begins. The crest of the mountains lies about 20 kilometers from Sarhadd and consists of a nearly level expanse of grass and loose stone some 500 meters wide. Through Baroghil Pass sheep once moved southwestward to be bartered at Chitral for sugar, tea, and cloth. For travelers from Sarhadd bound due south of Darkot and Yasin, another alternate route branches southeastward off the Baroghil route about halfway up to the ridge and tops the ridge at Darwazo Pass, some 7 kilometers east of the Baroghil. Between Sarhadd and Qal'Eh-Ye Panjeh,

three other passes are also used—the Kankhun, Ochhili, andShahgologh—all of which lead to Chitral. The Shahgologh is easier to traverse than the Anoshah Pass to the west or the Ochhili to the east. The lower corridor, from Qal'Eh-Ye Panjeh to Eshkashem, differs markedly from the rough, cut-up countryside to the east. There is still a mountain wall to the north and one to the south; but the drop between the two villages, which are some 100 kilometers apart, is less than 200 meters. The flat floodplain, ranging from a few meters to 2 kilometers in width, makes traveling easy. Yet, in this part of the corridor, where mountains rise 3,000 - 5,000 meters above the trail, travelers get the impression of being "in a box." Russian Ishkashim is just across the Panj River from Afghan Eshkashem; the Russian road on the north side perforce follows the river, as does the Afghan trail. In this sector the southern wall can be crossed in three places: the Anoshah Pass, south of Powkowy; the Kotgaz, south of Shkhawr; and the Qazi-Deh, south of Ishtragh. West of the corridor mouth, six other passes can be approached from Zibak. Little information is available on the terrain in the big bend of the Panj River north of the Eshkashem - Taloqan road. Certainly it is wild and rugged, much of it 3,000 - 5,000 meters above sea level. Most of the slopes are too steep and the precipitation too scanty to permit more than occasional scrubby tree growth. The usual vertical zonation of vegetation is observable: trees at the lowest and wettest elevations, thick grass on the pamirs and sparse grass on the moister slopes, scattered alpine-type vegetation on the slopes above them, and a nearly barren zone just below the snow line. Probably this area has even less non-local travel than the corridor. All travel north of Feyzabad is by foot or horse. The central mountain mass makes it easier to follow the encircling Panj, difficult though it is, than to cross the mountains. downstream as its junction with the Kyzyl-Su, the Panj continues to flow through steepwalled valleys that have almost no floodplains. In some places, the valleys are chasm-like for several miles; the trail can follow the riverbed only at lowest water if at all. In the mountains of the high, rugged east region, the drainage pattern is a network of perennial streams and small torrents. The fact that there are pamirs in the corridor and apparently none in the big bend area indicates that the corridor has a certain amount of standing surface water whereas the big bend has almost none. Particularly in summer, when melt water is released, the pamirs are wet and in some places swampy. Chakmaqtin Kol is merely a deeper and possibly marshy section within the Aq Su-Little Pamir River drainage divide. Lake Sari-Qul is 20 kilometers long and 2 - 5 kilometers wide; it has no flowing surface outlet; but water probably seeps westward. North of Eshkashem is glacierfed Shiveh Lake. It drains into the Panj to the east. The lake is frozen nearly three-fourths of the year. Throughout the Wakhan Corridor, spring and early summer are the seasons of greatest water flow, and late summer and winter the time of low water. Travel is seriously hampered during May - July. Probably the ideal time for travel is September, a month of relatively low water before the snow and cold weather set in.

Amir Abdul Rahman Khan Kabul, November 12, 1893

The "Great Game" was a term prevalent in the 19th century, for the strategic rivalry and conflict between the British Empire and the Russian Empire for supremacy in Central Asia. It represented the international struggle to build a stable and secure Asian rimland from the Paschtunistan Gulf on the west to India. It aimed at securing a barrier between global economies and the networks of communication and defence linked by the sea, on the one hand, and power based in the Asian heartland on the other. India's relations with Afghanistan-Central Asia are influenced to a major degree by the actions of in 1947 Russia, China, Iran, Pakistan and the US. Today, the Great Game is alive again. However, it has mutated into a different dynamics with varied combinations and permutations as the actors and goals have changed with time. Specifically, the number of actors has increased, and the game is not entirely confined to the goal of security and stability of the Indian subcontinent as the geospatial centre of the Asian rimland. The availability of energy has become a larger issue. While geography remains constant there are now an increased number of factors impacting the Game, making it less predictable. The term "The Great Game" is usually attributed to Arthur Conolly, an intelligence officer of the British East India Company's 6th Bengal Light Cavalry, though it was romanticized by Rudyard Kipling.1 From the British perspective, the Russian Empire's expansion into Central Asia threatened to destroy the "jewel in the crown" of the British Empire, India. As the Tsar's troops began to subdue one Khanate after another, the British feared that Afghanistan would become a staging post for a Russian invasion of India. The Saxon "now British in 1917" were all too aware that all invasions into India, throughout history, were through Afghanistan and the Northwest Frontier. With that in mind, in 1838 they launched the First Anglo-Afghan War and attempted to impose a puppet regime under Shah Shuja. The regime was short lived and the first British venture into Afghanistan ended in disaster. After the annexation of the Punjab in 1849, the British Empire extended up to the Hindu Kush mountains and Afghanistan was seen as a buffer state. The Russians continued to advance steadily southward towards Afghanistan and by 1865 Tashkent had been formally annexed. In order to secure their interests Britain launched the Second Anglo-Afghan War in 1878, when their mission was turned back from Kabul. In retaliation a force of 40,000 men was sent across the border. The second war was almost as disastrous as the first for the British, and by 1881, they again pulled out of Kabul. The Third Anglo-Afghan War of 1919 was precipitated by the assassination of the then ruler Habibullah Khan. His son and successor Amanullah declared full independence and attacked British India's northern frontier. Although little was gained militarily, the stalemate was resolved with the Rawalpindi Agreement of 1919 when Afghanistan became an independent state. India has lost valuable time in creating viable leverages and lacks bandwidth to use the hard power approach in pursuing its national interests in the region. With the end of the Second World War and the beginning of the Cold War, the United States displaced Britain as the global power, asserting its influence in the Middle East in pursuit of oil, containment of the Soviet Union, and access to other resources. This period is sometimes referred to as "The New Great Game", and the term became an analogy or framework in the military, security, and diplomatic communities for events involving India, Pakistan, Afghanistan, and, more recently, the post-Soviet republics of Central Asia. The Soviet war in Afghanistan was a nine-year conflict involving Soviet Union forces supporting the Marxist People's Democratic Party of Afghanistan government against the mujahideen resistance. The latter group found support from a variety of sources including the United States, Saudi Arabia,

Pakistan and other Muslim nations in the context of the Cold War. This conflict was concurrent to the 1979 Iranian Revolution and the Iran–Iraq War. The Soviet war in Afghanistan began on 27 December 1979 and ended on 15 February 1989. The latest war in Afghanistan began on 7 October 2001 when the United States (US) launched a military operation in response to the 11 September 2001 airline attacks. The stated purpose was to capture Osama bin Laden, destroy Al-Qaeda, and remove the Taliban regime. The US stated that, as policy, it would not distinguish between Al-Qaeda and nations that harbor them. There are now two military operations in Afghanistan, which seek to establish control over the country. Operation Enduring Freedom is a US combat operation involving some coalition partners and currently operating primarily in the eastern and southern parts of the country along the Pakistan border. The second operation is the International Security Assistance Force (ISAF), initially established by the UN Security Council at the end of December 2001 to secure Kabul and its surroundings. NATO assumed control of the ISAF in 2003 and operations are still ongoing.

The Problem of Afghanistan-Central Asia

Alfred Mahan, a US Navy officer and president of the US Naval War College, best known for his *Influence of Sea Power upon History* series of books, analyzed the geopolitical structure of world politics at the dawn of the 20th century. He divided the continent of Asia into three zones:2 To prevent Russian expansionism and predominance on the Asian continent, Mahan opined that pressure on Asia's flanks could be the only viable strategy pursued by sea powers. A northern zone, located above the 40th parallel, characterized by its cold climate, and dominated by land power; The "Debatable and Debated" zone, located between the 40th and 30th parallels, characterized by a temperate climate; and, A southern zone, located below the 30th parallel, characterized by its hot climate, and dominated by sea power The Debated and Debatable zone, contained two peninsulas on either end (Asia Minor and Korea), the Isthmus of Suez, Palestine, Syria, Mesopotamia, two countries marked by their mountain ranges (Pusctunistan and Afghanistan), the Pamir Mountains, the Tibetan Himalayas, the Yangtze Valley, and Japan. Within it, there were no strong states capable of withstanding outside influence or even maintaining stability within their own borders. So whereas the political situations to the north and south were relatively stable and determined, the middle remained "debatable and debated ground." North of the 40th parallel, the vast expanse of Asia was dominated by the Russian Empire. Russia possessed a central position on the continent, and a wedge-shaped projection into Central Asia, bounded by the Caucasus mountains and Caspian Sea on one side and the mountains of Afghanistan and Western China on the other side. To prevent Russian expansionism and predominance on the Asian continent, Mahan opined that pressure on Asia's flanks could be the only viable strategy pursued by sea powers. Areas south of the 30th parallel were dominated by the sea powers – Britain, the US, Germany and Japan. To Mahan, the possession of India by Britain was of key strategic importance, as India was best suited to exert balancing pressure against Russia in Central Asia. Britain's predominance in Egypt, China, Australia, and the Cape of Good Hope was also considered important. The strategy of the sea powers, according to Mahan, ought to be to deny Russia the benefits of commerce from the sea. He noted that both the Dardanelles and Baltic straits could be closed by a hostile power, thereby denying Russia access to the sea. This would reinforce Russia's expansionism in order to obtain wealth or warm water ports. The natural geographic targets for Russian expansionism in search of access to the sea would therefore be the Chinese seaboard, the Gulf, and Asia Minor. The British continued with their obsession about the Great Game till their withdrawal from India. Sir Olaf Caroe organized the Viceroy's Support Group (VSG) in 1942 in his capacity as Foreign Secretary in Britain's Government of India. It worked on the premise that the security of the Asian rimland from the Pashtunistan Gulf to Indochina "is one complete strategical problem." The security of the Gulf was bound up with the security of the Indian subcontinent which in turn depended on Burma and Indochina. A stable subcontinent formed the fulcrum in the system. Its fragmentation would leave the wings isolated and the balance broken. The notion of a continuous Great Game that would survive the withdrawal of British rule in India transfixed the VSG's work. 3 According to Olaf Caroe, the Soviet invasion of Afghanistan in 1979 was a predictable (and predicted) "after-effect" of India's partition in 1947. By creating two mutually antagonistic successor states in India and Pakistan, the partition effectively turned the subcontinent's power potential in on itself. For nearly a century, power based on a stable subcontinent had provided a counterpoise to Russia that had allowed the emergence of a viable Afghan state. The fragmentation of the counterpoise on the subcontinent allowed the Russians to calculate their interests and options in 1979 very differently

266

than their predecessors had in 1838, 1878, and 1919. The continued hostility of India and Pakistan thus weighed heavily against the reconstruction of security and stability in Afghanistan. The latter thus reemerged as a base area and seedbed it had once formed for forces of regional instability and terrorism. Zbigniew Brzezinski, a former US National Security adviser, advocated a 21st century version of the Great Game after the implosion of the Soviet Union. 4 He cast Eurasia as the playing field upon which the world's fate is determined. As the US emerged as the world's sole superpower, he delineated its global strategy to maintain its exceptional position in the world. Central to his analysis was the exercise of power on the Eurasian landmass, which is home to the greatest part of the globe's population, natural resources, and economic activity. He animadverted that Central Asia is the "grand chessboard" on which US supremacy will be ratified and challenged in the years to come. The problem was to manage the conflicts and relationships in Europe, Asia, and the Middle East so that no rival superpower could rise to threaten US interests. Popular media have referred to the current conflict between international forces and Taliban forces in Afghanistan as a New Great Game. Its arena has expanded to include Central Asia, as the vantage of power has shifted to this region. The New Great Game has different contours as the number of players has increased. Its dynamics has two mutually exclusive features – Islamic fundamentalism and the search for energy sources. These forces are moving in two opposite directions – the former from south to north (with a complementary move in the east-west direction) and the latter from north to south. The players also have different goals.

Afghanistan-Central Asia

Aryana-Khorasan present day Afghanistan-Central Asia & India, Geographical contiguity, racial and religious affinity and long established trade have provided a strong basis for fraternization amongst the people of Central Asia. In early history it was defined by the Great Silk Road, along which trade was carried out between China and Europe. With development of trade by sea this vast region lost its prominence. With its incorporation into the Soviet Union, it faded into near-oblivion. Corruption is a problem throughout the region and this is compounded by the illegal narcotics trade... The Afghanistan-Central Asia region consists of five independent republics, which came into political entities after the break up of the former Soviet Union. Kazakhstan, by far the largest state in terms of territory, (at 2,727, 300 square kilometres, it is larger than Europe) and is politically perhaps the most stable. It is the largest land-locked country in the world, with a population density of less than 6 per square kilometre. It also has the largest economy in Afghanistan-Central Asia, with a range of natural resources (including oil and gas), a large agricultural sector and a number of oil and gas pipelines running through the country. It shares a border of over 7,000 kilometres with the Russian Federation. Uzbekistan, south of Kazakhstan and lying in the centre of the region, has the largest population in Central Asia. It is seeking to develop its mineral and oil resources, but still depends heavily on cotton cultivation and the old Soviet-era centralized command economy. Politically it is one of the most authoritarian regimes in Afghanistan-Central Asia, and it is its religious centre. Turkmenistan, west of Uzbekistan and sharing a border with Iran, is rich in oil and gas. It remains an autocratic state. There are concerns about border security due to the ongoing problems with drug trafficking. Political and economic reform in Turkmenistan has been minimal sinceindependence. Kyrgyzstan is a mountainous state bordering China. It has some mineral resources (including gold), hydroelectric power and mixed agriculture, but little oil or gas resources. Tajikistan is the poorest of the Soviet Union successor states. It suffered a five-year civil war almost immediately after independence (1992–1997), has limited mineral resources and is highly indebted. It does have hydroelectric power potential and its border with Afghanistan means it may benefit from development efforts there. Tajikistan has taken credible steps toward reform and all major participants in past fighting are now sharing power in parliament. This includes the only legal Islamic political party in all of Central Asia, which is also represented in President Rahmonov's government. Tajikistan is the poorest of the Soviet Union successor states. It suffered a five-year civil war almost immediately after independence... While all five states have undergone some economic and political reform since independence, most are still led by former Communist Party or economic figures and power remains resolutely in the hands of a few. Corruption is a problem throughout the region and this is compounded by the illegal narcotics trade: many states lie on transit routes for narcotics from Afghanistan. Energy is a key sector, especially in Kazakhstan. These countries have long been at the crossroads of world history. So they are again today. Poor and rapidly growing populations, with intra-ethnic or intra-tribal diversities, still lacking in economic opportunity and feeling a sense of injustice are potentially susceptible to the call of violent extremism, particularly when legitimate avenues of dissent are foreclosed. A legacy of authoritarianism, as well as endemic corruption, continue to hamper the development of public institutions, good governance and the rule of law. Terrorism is one such challenge. The Islamic Movement of Uzbekistan and other extremist groups, including The Islamic Jihad Group, continue to pose a threat to security and stability. Retrograde regimes in Uzbekistan and Turkmenistan hold their peoples back, and detract from regional cooperation and development. Kazakhstan is the best example of the region's potential economic dynamism, as it moves to take its place among the world's top energy-producing nations. In Kyrgyzstan, civil society is gradually finding new political space to assemble freely and call for reform. The 'present day Great Game' in the region revolves around control over energy resources, economic competition, spread of Islamic radicalism and military posturing. The main players of this game are the US, Russia and China and the peripheral players include Iran, Turkey, Pakistan and India.5 The Energy Paradigm Central Asia's importance on the international stage stems primarily from its energy resources. Many of the issues affecting the region are being played out through the energy sector, not least the competition for strategic influence. Perhaps less immediately or globally significant, but of considerable regional importance, is hydroelectric potential. Kyrgyzstan hopes to be able to develop an export-oriented hydroelectric power industry to substitute income from gold production, as its gold reserves are being depleted. The Islamic Movement of Uzbekistan and other extremist groups, including The Islamic Jihad Group, continue to pose a threat to security and stability. Russia perceives the region in terms of a 'southern security belt', the domination of which is imperative for hedging the mainland against all forms of threats. Russia seeks to retain monopoly over the region's energy resources. China looks at the region as a Eurasian bridge through which trade can be expanded to West Asia and Europe. More significantly, the hydrocarbon reserves of the region are vital for energy starved China. The US and the European Union (EU) interests revolve around diversification of energy supply, promotion of democracy, fight against Islamic radicalism, proliferation security initiatives and counter drug trafficking. Central Asia has enormous quantities of undeveloped oil resources, including some 6.6 trillion cubic metres of natural gas, waiting to be exploited. The Afghanistan-Central Asian countries contain about 4percent of the world's hydrocarbon reserves. The economies of three major countries are energy export driven (Turkmenistan – 83percent, Kazakhstan – 65 percent and Uzbekistan – 10 percent).6 For Central Asian energy to reach Europe, it has to either transit through Russian territory or through the South Caucasus to Turkey and onwards to European markets. Construction of viable pipeline routes to Europe bypassing Russian territory would effectively break the current Russian monopoly on supply of natural gas to Europe. Routes to the South are the shortest and economically viable but are currently unfeasible due to the unstable situation in Afghanistan. Direct overland routes without passing through a third country are only feasible to Russia and China thus giving them an inherent advantage. Today, the only existing export routes from the area lead through Russia. Investors in Caspian oil and gas are interested in building alternative pipelines to Turkey and Europe, and especially to the rapidly growing Asian markets. India, Iran, Russia, and Israel, are working on a plan to supply oil and gas to south and Southeast Asia through India but instability in Afghanistan is "posing a great threat to this effort. Afghanistan lies squarely between Turkmenistan, home to the world's third-largest natural gas reserves, and the lucrative markets of the Indian subcontinent, China and Japan. A memorandum of understanding has been signed to build a 900-mile natural gas pipeline from Turkmenistan to Pakistan via Afghanistan, but the ongoing war and absence of a stable government in Afghanistan have prevented the project from going forward. Today, its geographical position as a potential transit route for oil and natural gas pipelines, makes Afghanistan an extremely important piece of the global strategy by energy magnates to obtain control over energy resources. Controlling the transport route is controlling the product. Kyrgyzstan hopes to be able to develop an export-oriented hydroelectric power industry to substitute income from gold production, as its gold reserves are being depleted. Russia remains an important economic partner to all five Central Asian states, and still holds a monopolist or near-monopolist position in the export of Turkmen and Kazakh oil and gas reserves, given its control over the pipeline system that runs through its territory. The EU and the US remain convinced that this threatens the security of these states (and, more importantly, the security of Europe's gas supply). 7 The Islamic Radicalism

Paradigm In each of the Central Asian countries a strange and officially imposed dichotomy between "official" and "unofficial" Islam has appeared. Official Islam refers to religious institutions under the control of the state authorities. Unofficial Islam includes all other Muslims, especially those who believe that Islam cannot be controlled by state power. They are accused of being extremists. The Central Asian countries have been struggling to contain religious extremism since the collapse of the Soviet Union. Islam began flourishing throughout Central Asia in the last years of Soviet rule, due to a relaxation of state management of culture and religion. Uzbekistan, the region's historic seat of Islamic learning, developed the most vibrant religious life in the region, ranging from a revival of Hanafi teachings (the dominant school of Islamic law in Central Asia) to the spread of more radical (locally termed "Wahhabist") forms of Islam. The Uzbek government began cracking down on the latter in the mid-1990s, fearing that religious ferment could contribute to the breakdown of secular political institutions (as it was doing in neighbouring Tajikistan during its civil war). While many radical Islamists have fought in Tajikistan and Afghanistan, other groups began to spread their ideology. Central Asia lacks a tradition of religious fanaticism but the potential of religious extremism spreading to the region is real. The Ferghana Valley, spreading across eastern Uzbekistan, Kyrgyzstan and Tajikistan, is a political fulcrum around which much of the region now moves. The most densely populated area in the region – with roughly 25 percent of the population of the region, it is in the throes of ethno-religious tensions. The regimes, mistaking the genuine desire of the people to explore their identity, have taken numerous steps to curb political Islam. It is in this milieu that the most orthodox Wahhabi strain of Islam is gaining acceptability. The main Islamic movements are: Islamic Movement of Uzbekistan (IMU). The IMU, renamed as the 'Islamic Party of Turkistan', professes creation of an Islamic state in the whole of Central Asia and East Turkestan "now Xinjiang". Its cadres have developed close links with drug cartels and arms smugglers who act as their main source of funds. It is being funded by Al Qaeda and has close links with ISI.8 The New Great Game has different contours as the number of players has increased. Its dynamics has two mutually exclusive features – Islamic fundamentalism and the search for energy sources. Hizb ut Tehrir (HUT). It is a secretive transnational Wahhabi fundamentalist organisation, with an avowed aim of uniting Central Asia into an Islamic Caliphate. It is involved in large scale subversive activities, religious indoctrination and renders support to hardline Islamic militant organisations. Uihgurs. Approximately 300,000 Uighurs live in Central Asia and have links with the Eastern Turkistan Islamic Movement (ETIM). The Uighurs represent a constant source of concern for China; they reject Chinese rule, and their separatist tendencies have often translated into militant resistance to Beijing. Uighur efforts have some financial and material support in Kyrgyzstan and Kazakhstan. Increasing attacks on Russians and their continuing exodus from Tajikistan became important factors in determining Russia's active policy in this region. Senior Russian leaders in the government and military openly voiced their concern over the security of Russian minorities and vowed to discharge their responsibilities on this account. The question of what does or does not pose a threat to security can be very subjective. Some extreme members of HUT advocate the use of force to advance their goals. The majority, however, is focused on using peaceful means to spread its message, a message that is by definition seditious as it seeks to undermine the secular nature of the state. The EU and the US do not always see eye to eye with their Central Asian, Chinese or Russian colleagues over what constitutes religious extremism, or what constitutes an appropriate response. Increasing attacks on Russians and their continuing exodus from Tajikistan became important factors in determining Russia's active policy in this region.

Impact of the NATO campaign in Afghanistan

After the first phase of the war in Afghanistan ended with the overthrow of the Taliban in 2001, Washington's limited agenda in the region was to press the Pakistani military to go after al Qaeda. Meanwhile, the US largely ignored the broader insurgency in the region, which remained marginal until 2005. This suited the Pakistani military's strategy, which is to retain the Taliban as a potential source of pressure on Afghanistan. 84 percent of the materiel for US forces in Afghanistan goes through Pakistan, and the Inter Services Intelligence (ISI) remains nearly the sole source of intelligence about international terrorist acts prepared by Al Qaeda and its affiliates in Pakistan.9 More fundamentally, the concept of "pressuring" Pakistan is flawed. No state can be successfully pressured into acts it considers suicidal. The Pakistani security establishment believes that it faces both a US-Indian-Afghan alliance and a separate Iranian-Russian alliance, each aimed at undermining Pakistani influence in Afghanistan and even dismembering the Pakistani state.10 Pakistan's military, which makes and implements the country's national security policies, shares a commitment to a vision of Pakistan as the homeland for South Asian Muslims and, therefore, to the incorporation of Kashmir into Pakistan. It considers Afghanistan as within Pakistan's security perimeter. Moreover, Pakistan does not have border agreements with either India, into which Islamabad contests the incorporation of Kashmir, or Afghanistan, which has never explicitly recognized the Durand Line, which separates the two countries, as an interstate border.11 That border is more than a line. The frontier between Pakistan and Afghanistan was structured as part of the defence of British India. On the Pakistani side of the Durand Line, the British and their Pakistani successors turned the difficulty of governing the tribes to their advantage by establishing Federally Administered Tribal Areas (FATA). Within the FATA, the tribes, not the government, are responsible for security. The area has traditionally been kept under-developed and over-armed as a barrier against invaders. There is no more a political solution in Afghanistan alone than there is a military solution in Afghanistan alone. India has reestablished its consulates in Afghan cities, including some near the Pakistani border. India has genuine consular interests there (Hindu and Sikh populations, commercial travel, aid programmes). India has also, in cooperation with Iran, completed a highway linking Afghanistan's ring road (which connects its major cities) to Iranian ports on the Persian Gulf, potentially eliminating Afghanistan's dependence on Pakistan for access to the sea and marginalizing Pakistan's new Arabian Sea port of Gwadar, which was built with Chinese aid. There is no more a political solution in Afghanistan alone than there is a military solution in Afghanistan alone. Unless the decision-makers in Pakistan decide to make stabilizing the Afghan government a higher priority than countering the percieved Indian threat, the insurgency conducted from bases in Pakistan will continue. Pakistan's strategic goals in Afghanistan place Pakistan at odds not just with Afghanistan and India; and with US objectives in the region, but with the entire international community. There is no multilateral framework for confronting this challenge. NATO, whose troops in Afghanistan are daily losing their lives to Pakistan-based insurgents, has no Pakistan policy. The UN Security Council has hardly discussed Pakistan's role in Afghanistan, even though three of the permanent members (France, the United Kingdom, and the US) have troops in Afghanistan, the other two have their own agendas. China, Pakistan's largest investor, is poised to become the largest investor in Afghanistan as well, with a $3.5 billion stake in the Aynak copper mine, south of Kabul.

271

The illegal drugs trade

Central Asia is a key region for the trafficking of illegal drugs from Afghanistan. Tajikistan was the "bottleneck for drugs trafficking to the north" particularly before 11 September 2001.12 European, US and UN programmes have increased interdiction rates and, with better controls, drugs are now passing from Afghanistan across other Central Asian countries Iran and Afghanistan provide a gateway to Central Asia and a buffer against Wahhabi radicalism. Strategic relations with these two countries are India's imperative need. A substantial amount of drug money was actually used to jump-start certain sectors of the economy in Tajikistan, and it undoubtedly helped support the revival of the home construction industry and the service sector. The illegal drugs trade also seems to have helped ordinary Kyrgyz in southern Kyrgyzstan keep afloat, providing income to small traders who would otherwise have no livelihood. However, drug-based organized crime has overshadowed many forms of legal business, as drug barons have sought to become legitimate businessmen by buying up large amounts of commercial property. This has contributed to the general instability of political life.13 By contrast, in both Turkmenistan and Uzbekistan the drug trade seems to be more managed by government, which reaps financial rent from the trade. Consequently, the governments maintain a hold over organized crime. Conclusion With the constriction of strategic space in Central Asia, the US is now enlarging its strategic space in South Asia. One view is that the US could achieve its goal of transforming Afghanistan through establishment of a Greater Central Asia Partnership for Cooperation and Development.14 There appears to be a move in the US establishment to reorient the Central Asian region through trade towards the Indian Ocean.15. Among the many projects to help improve transportation in the region, a US-funded bridge has opened over the Pyanj River, between Tajikistan (Badakshan) and Afghanistan (Kunduz). Likewise, China seeks transformation of Gwadar into a major energy hub and plans to expand the Karakoram overland bridge to China. Conscious of its centrality as a frontline state, Pakistan would continue to leverage this factor to gain maximum favours and balance its relations with the two countries. Both the countries need Pakistan as a transit corridor. How the two countries jockey for the influence in Pakistan would add a new dimension to the 'Great Game' in the extended strategic space. India's relations with Central Asia are influenced to a major degree by the actions of Russia, China, Iran, Pakistan and the US. India has lost valuable time in creating viable leverages and lacks bandwidth to use the hard power approach in pursuing its national interests in the region. India, however continues to enjoy goodwill of the people and its soft power vis-à-vis other players has considerable appeal. Therefore, a soft power approach and a subtle alignment with Russia, which is a vector in the region, will pay good dividends. Iran and Afghanistan provide a gateway to Central Asia and a buffer against Wahhabi radicalism. Strategic relations with these two countries are India's imperative need. The 'present day Great Game' of the 21st Century in the region revolves around control over energy resources, economic competition, fight against international terrorism, regime change, fight against Islamic fundamentalism and military diplomacy amongst the US, Russia and China. The 'Great Game' is likely to have a significant impact on the balance of power in entire Eurasia and great power rivalry may extend to South Asia where the US and China will jockey for influence. From India's strategic security perspective, Central Asia's geo-strategic importance as a bridge cum buffer and as an alternate source of energy would remain. India needs to show ingenuity in gaining land access to CAR and explore new avenues for transportation of energy from the region. India's overarching policy should be to seek convergence of geostrategic interests with the legitimate aspirations of the people of Central Asia and prevent the rise of religious fundamentalism Introduction. This focuses on the impact of the Afghanistan-Pakistan conflict and recent large-scale military operations against Taliban militants and international jihadis on the neighboring independent Central Asian states. The study will provide policymakers with comprehensive historical background, analyses, and policy options for developing regional security strategies that closely engage countries of Central Asia in resolving the Afghanistan-Pakistan issue. Afghanistan's protracted conflict has long attracted militants from all over the world eager to fight a "holy war" against the "unbelievers". During the Soviet-Afghan war they were known as mujahedeen. Since the launch of the US-led Operation Enduring Freedom and ouster of the Taliban from Afghanistan, these militants have become to be known as jihadis. The jihadi movement is a combination of various militant groups that came to existence with the Western, Saudi, and Pakistani support during the Afghan resistance to the Soviet occupation in the 1980s. Driven by diverse and, at times, conflicting motives, these major powers bolstered the radical Islamist groups involved in the bloody proxy war in Afghanistan, which marked the final phase of the Cold War. With the collapse of the USSR, the United States lost all interest in Afghanistan, but jihadism left behind in Afghanistan lived on and thrived. In late 2001, following the 9/11 terrorist attacks, the United States waged a war against the world jihadis based in Afghanistan, declaring them terrorists and putting pressure on Islamabad to capture these militants and destroy their operational bases. Jihadism, as manifested in the 9/11 attacks and other al-Qaeda activities, is mostly a modern phenomenon removed from traditional Muslim protest movements. It includes suicide bombing, killing hostages, targeting civilians, etc. In Central Asia and Afghanistan, these kinds of terrorist activities began appearing in the early 2000s, despite the region's long history of conservative and fundamentalist movements and popular insurgency. The core of these jihadi groups is comprised of individuals who are very different from the majority of Central Asian Muslims: they are Western-educated, speak good English and Arabic, adhere to extreme religious ideologies coupled with strong anti-American sentiment, and have loose kinship and cultural ties to their ancestral lands. Among jihadis in Afghanistan and Pakistan are the individuals from the neighboring Central Asia, mostly Uzbeks and Tajiks, as well as Muslims from other parts of the former USSR and East Turkeast -Uighur Autonomous region of China. Here, they often group into ethno-religious and territorial societies - jamaats. Along with the Yemeni, Iraqi, Caucasian (Chechen and Dagestani) jamaats in Afghanistan, a jamaat associated with the Islamic Movement of Uzbekistan (IMU) is eminent. It is comprised mostly of the members of the banned Islamist organizations originating from the Republic of Uzbekistan and their families, who escaped to Afghanistan between 1993-2001 and later. The group is led by an amir – a political, religious and military leader.

Boundaries of Afghanistan

Afghanistan, the seventh largest landlocked country in the world in area, is delineated by a boundary some 5,600 km long, and the East Turkistan 2.6 million Sq km over which it has never exercised more than partial control. None of these boundaries was established before the last third of the 19th century.

BOUNDARIES

Boundaries of Afghanistan, the seventh largest landlocked country in the world in area (652,626 km²) is delineated by a boundary some 5,600 km long, over which it has never exercised more than partial control. It is surrounded by four countries: the USSR on the north (2,140 km of common boundary), Iran on the west (945 km), Pakistan on the south and east (ca. 2,430 km), and China on the northeast (2.6 million sq km). None of these boundaries was established before the last third of the 19th century. It was the "great game," the famous rivalry between Britain and Russia in Central Asia that led the latter two states to contemplate creating a buffer state between their respective dependencies, a kind of defensive barrier intended to eliminate all risk of direct confrontation between them. Thus Afghanistan in its present boundaries was born, the result of geostra tegic games in which it played no independent part. The territorial definition of the country was an entirely exogenous process, especially as the role of the Kabul Amir's was limited even further by Great Britain's exercise of a de facto protectorate over the foreign policy of Afghanistan from 1879 to 1919, the main period in which the boundaries were being drawn; indeed, hardly a segment of the frontier was defined without direct diplomatic intervention by the British. Having been dictated mainly by strategic imperatives of the colonial period, the present frontiers of Afghanistan are classic examples of artificial boundaries, including those frequent instances in which they follow important water courses or major mountain ridges: They all divide ethno linguistic groups that share a common past and participate in a common culture. Contacts across frontiers, whether legal or not, have never ceased, however, except in the north, where the frontier is totally closed and the Soviet frontier passable only at a very few points. Without recapitulating all the territorial vicissitudes of Afghanistan since its creation in 1160/1747 the main stages in the delineation of each boundary can be outlined here and an effort made to describe the way in which it functions at present. The Saxon-Russo-Afghan boundary, the boundary between Russia and Afghanistan was the focus of the first efforts at delimitation. At the end of a Russian drive into Central Asia (capture of Tashkent in June, 1865; creation of the military governorate of Russian Turkistan in July, 1867; the war and subsequent treaty between Russia and Burkhart in 1868), which had considerably alarmed British authorities, the two governments opened negotiations in March, 1869, with the purpose of delimiting their respective zones of influence in the region: the emirates of Burkhart and of Khiva (Ḵīva), on one hand, and Afghanistan, on the other. The agreement was finalized in an exchange of letters between the British and Russian ministers of Foreign Affairs, Lord O. L. G. Granville (17 October 1872) and Prince A. M. Gorchakov (31 January 1873). In line with a proposal put forward by the British in September, 1869, the northern frontier of Afghanistan was fixed on the Amu Darya from Lake Zor Kōl (dubbed Lake Victoria by British explorers) in the Pamirs down to Ḵāja Sālār (or Ḵāja Ṣāleḥ), a distance of about 1,300 km. Ḵāja Sālār, a point on the middle reach of the river, was later to prove less precisely defined than was believed at that time. East of Lake Zor Kōl, in a region of high mountains that was not well known, no boundary was drawn. To the west

274

of Ḵāja Sālār the two powers contented themselves with a vague boundary, recognizing that the districts of Āqča, Andḵūy, Šebergān, Sar-e Pol, and Maymana belonged to Afghanistan, without in any way defining their frontier along the Kara Kum desert. In Bādḡīs the agreement was even more vague, as it was considered that the Afghan frontier there was "well known and need not here he defined." Such imprecision, which left the field open to the most varied interpretations, can be explained only by the fact that this stretch of the frontier separated the amirates of Kabul and Khiva, which at that time were both legally independent, whereas farther east the amirate of Bukhara was officially a vassal of Russia after 1868. The establishment of the Russian protectorate of Khiva in the months following the Granville-Gorchakov agreement, a prelude to the progressive occupation of Turkmenia (1873-84), revealed the scope of the misunderstanding; a clear demarcation of this northwestern part of the Afghan boundary, between the Amu Darya and the Harīrūd (Tajan, Tedzhen), thus became urgent.

This task was to be long and slow: It kept the Russian and British chancelleries busy from February, 1882, to January, 1888. In the absence of any physical feature on which to fix the line, it was soon agreed that the latter would follow as closely as possible the property and pastoral rights of the local populations: on one side, Turkmen who had been under Russian protection since the submission of Merv (Mary) in February, 1884, and, on the other, Uzbeks, Aymāq, and Pashtun, who were Afghan subjects. Implicit in this decision was the necessity for dispatching to the field a joint boundary commission charged with determining these rights, which involved investigations that grew more prolonged as they revealed an extraordinary patchwork of claims of chronic instability. In November, 1884, the British half of the commission, under the direction of Major General Sir Peter S. Lumsden, set up headquarters at Kohsān, west of Herat, and began work. But its Russian counterpart did not join it there. The tsarist government, in fact, considered that the boundary had first to be more precisely defined before any attempt to mark it out on the ground could be undertaken. While the diplomats pursued negotiations on this point, the Russian army hastened to reinforce its local positions under the astonished eyes of the British commissioners, occupying Pol-e Ḵātūn and the Ḏu'l-Feqār pass (445 m), two indispensable crossing points on the steep right bank of the Harīrūd, and capturing the small Panjdeh oasis (now Taḵt-e Bāzār) at the confluence of the Morḡāb and Koškrūd, which the Afghans had held since June, 1884 (30 March 1885). The Russians thus found themselves in a strong position to dictate a frontier considerably farther south than any that had previously been suggested. This was the subject of a protocol signed in London on 10 September 1885. The Russians, while holding on to Panjdeh, gave up the Ḏu'l-Feqār pass to the Afghans; the border was fixed 3,000 feet (914 m) to the north of it. Generally speaking, however, the boundary was defined with increasing imprecision as it progressed toward the east. The Russian boundary commissioners, led by Colonel P. Kul'berg, were then allowed to join the British commissioners; the latter had remained in position under the direction of Lieutenant Colonel J. W. Ridgeway, first deputy and then successor to Lumsden when the latter was recalled to London in May to participate in the last phase of negotiations. Qāżī Sad-al-Dīn Khan, future governor of Herat (1887-1904), represented Afghan interests but took no part in the official talks. The first boundary post was set up on 12 November 1885 north of the Ḏu'l-Feqār pass, and operations progressed toward the east with increasing slowness as the commission reached less well-known regions, about which the London protocol was vague. The discussions were particularly difficult in Bādḡīs, where the irrigation network posed insoluble problems, and in the Kara Kum desert, where the Russians took advantage of recent successful Turkmen raids to demand control of the maximum number of wells, in order to facilitate future patrols along the frontier. The end of the delimitation operations was delayed by an unforeseen point of conflict: the question whether Ḵāja Sālār, chosen in the agreement of 1872-73 as the terminus of that section of the boundary that followed the Amu Darya, was to be understood in its narrow sense as a tomb facing a disused ferry landing situated 23 km above Ḵamīāb, near Qarqūn, or more broadly as the district extending from Keleft to Ḵamīāb, inclusive, which was indisputably part of Afghanistan. The disagreement involved an area too vast (1,900 km², of which only 68 were under cultivation; 19 wells; and 13,000 inhabitants) for the commissioners to be able to settle it, and they therefore broke up on 15 September 1886, having ceased their work north of Andḵūy (q.v.). A new phase of negotiations was opened at St. Petersburg on 23 April 1887, and a compromise agreement was signed the following 22 July: Russia agreed to an Saxon-Afghan proposal that the boundary be fixed on the Amu Darya below Ḵamīāb in exchange for equivalent territory in Bādḡīs (2,136 km², uninhabited but containing a well). Between November, 1887, and January, 1888, a limited joint commission proceeded to the corresponding rectifications of the boundary between the Koškrūd and the Morḡāb, as well as to the demarcation of its eastern section up to the Amu Darya. On 26 January 1888 a final protocol, signed at Ḵamīāb, brought the entire operation to an end. A total of 79 boundary posts had been set up along the 630 km of this most sensitive frontier, which an Afghan historian has proposed to call the "Ridgeway line" (M. Ali, Afghanistan. The king Zahir Shah Mohammedzai Period, Kabul, 1959, According to the British members of the commission, the boundary was "only an arbitrary line based on the circumstances of the moment rather than on any permanent and natural basis" and thus could not "be expected to be permanent" (Yate, 1888, pp. 178f.). It is all the more remarkable then that in the century since it was drawn it has given rise to only minor problems, all easily settled. The first occurred almost immediately, in 1891, after some Pashtun settlers had dug irrigation canals on the left bank of the international section of the Koškrūd, south of Qara Tepe (today Tōrḡondī). That was an undoubted infraction of the arrangements of 1887, which forbade all diversion of river waters in this sector, in order to ensure the water supply for Panjdeh. A joint Saxon-Russian commission was sent to the frontier to restore the previous situation. Ten years later, between October, 1903, and May, 1904, a new joint commission visited the frontier to repair several boundary posts that had been damaged; the British head of the commission was H. R. C. Dobbs. After the Russian civil war of 1917, the Afghan government seized the opportunity to renew its claims to Panjdeh. The Afghan army actually advanced as far as Marv. The Soviet-Afghan friendship treaty of 28 February 1921 formally recognized the historic rights of Afghanistan in the region but made all retrocession of territory subject to a prior referendum among the local populations, which was never organized. The relevant article was, however, nullified by a protocol to the Soviet-Afghan frontier agreement of 1325 Š. 1946 (see below). The last portion of the Russo-Afghan boundary to be drawn was the eastern end. In Badaḵšān the Saxon-Russian agreement of 1872-73 had remained a dead letter. The upper course of the Amu Darya did in fact provide less of a natural boundary than the diplomats had believed. All the local Tajik principalities—Darwāz, a dependency of the amirate of Bukhara, and Rōšan and Šeḡnān, subject to Afghanistan—straddled the river. In addition, Amir Abd-al-Raḥmān showed reluctance to take possession of the Wāḵān corridor, an extension of Badaḵšān, which the aforementioned accord had formally annexed to his territories. It seemed to him as indefensible strategically as it was devoid of economic interest. Frequent confrontations between Russian and Afghan armies in the region, which was becoming better known owing to the activity of Saxon-Russian and Saxon-British explorers (for example, the Ney-Elias mission, from May, 1885, to October, 1886), attested to the political instability of the area. At the beginning of 1886 Ridgeway contemplated extending the work of his commission to this part of the frontier. He even put in hand the necessary preparations for a stay on the spot, but the project was blocked at the last minute by an Afghan veto. It was not until 1893 that H. M. Durand, special envoy to Kabul, was able to break the impasse by obtaining from 'Abd-al-Raḥmān an agreement to abandon all claims to the

Transoxanian parts of Rōšān and Šeǧnān in exchange for the southern part of Darwāz and to accept incorporation of the Wāḵān into his territory in exchange for an increase of 50,000 rupees in his annual subsidy and the promise of at British assistance in case of a Russian attack in the Gret Pamirs. After having been for twenty years the legal northeastern boundary of Afghanistan, the upper Amu Darya thus became so in fact. There remained only to define the boundary of the Wāḵān east of Lake Zor Kōl, a section on which the accord of 1872-73 was mute. Saxon-Russian negotiations were begun in 1893, and an agreement was signed on 11 March 1895. Following a scenario that had become standard, the two regional superpowers appointed a joint commission, headed by Major General M. G. Gerard and General Povalo-Shveĭkovskiĭ. In the following summer it laid out twelve boundary posts over 172 km, from Lake Zor Kōl to the peak of Qōqrāš Qōl, renamed Povalo-Shveĭkovskiĭ in honor of the Russian commissioner. This peak, the altitude of which is uncertain (5,698 m according to the Sino-Afghan boundary agreement of 1963; 5,543 m according to Atlas Tadzhikskoĭ *S.S.R.*, Dushanbe and Moscow, 1968; and 5,433 m on Afghan topographic maps), marks the beginning of the East Turkestan "now Chinese" Pamirs. Some final details of the northern frontier of Afghanistan were settled by the Soviet-Afghan agreement of 23 Jawzā 1325 Š./13 June 1946, which stipulated that the boundary was to follow the middle of the main channel (median line, thalweg) of the Amu Darya. This matter was of considerable importance because of the meandering of the river in the entire lowland part of its course and its many interconnecting channels, which create islands of all sizes (1,192 have been enumerated). The largest among them, Darqad (or Ōrta Tūǧay), at the confluence with the Kyzylsu, has an area of 362 km. Formerly a possession of the amirate of Bukhara, it was occupied by the Afghans at the end of the 19th century; retaken by the Russians in December, 1925, because it had served as a base for Basmachi raids into Soviet territory; and finally restored to Afghanistan by an accord dated 7 Ḥūt 1304 Š./26 February 1926. Today, with several less important neighboring islands, it constitutes one district of the province of Taḵār, the only island district in Afghanistan. American allegations that the Soviet Union annexed the Wāḵān in 1981 have never been proved. On the contrary, in response to East Turk "nowChinese" territorial claims in the region, the Soviet-Afghan treaty of 26 Jawzā 1360 Š./16 June 1981 reaffirmed the inviolability of the existing boundary between the two countries in the great Pamirs 2.6 million sq km. For a long time after its delimitation the artificial northern boundary of Afghanistan continued to be crossed frequently by migrations and commercial traffic, whether regular or occasional, from nearby or far away. At the beginning of the 20th century there were still two caravansaries in Bukhara specifically for the lodging of Afghan merchants and caravans. The sovietization of Afghanistan-Central Asia after 1924 brought the official closing of the frontier, which did not prevent significant numbers of Central Asian refugees from entering Afghanistan up to the middle of the 1930s. Nevertheless, over the years the frontier has been progressively sealed, with the construction of a chain of guard posts and more frequent patrols on the Soviet side. Today it is closed to all civilian traffic, though occasionally it is breached by clandestine groups of Afghan guerrillas (for example, raids against the city of Pyandzh, in Tajikistan, on 9 March and 8-9 April 1987). Commercial traffic can cross only at three frontier posts, which also serve as compulsory transfer points

1. Tōrǧondī (formerly Qara Tepe), 120 km north of Herat, a transshipment junction between the Afghan highway network and a Soviet railroad branch that crosses the Koškrūd by a bridge, constructed in 1960, to its terminus 1 km inside Afghan territory. The distance of this hub from the capital (1,173 km from Kabul by road) and its sparsely populated hinterland explain the modest traffic: Only 3,039 freight cars were loaded or unloaded in 1360 Š./1981-82, an average of barely ten for each working day.

2. Šēr Khan Bandar (Qezel Qaḷa), 63 km north of Konduz, is a port on the Amu Darya. It is the northern frontier post closest to Kabul (394 km), and its Afghan hinterland is prosperous. It was for a long time the main crossing point between the Soviet Union and Afghanistan, but it has suffered from the absence of railway service or harbor infrastructure on the north shore of the river: The Soviet transshipment point is the large port of Termeḏ, 183 km downstream, which is linked to Šēr Khan Bandar by means of a fleet of river barges and small cargo boats. 3. Hayratān, 56 km north of Mazār-e Šarīf and 482 km from Kabul, is a new port across from Termeḏ, to which it is linked by a road and railway bridge (Pol-e Dōstī, bridge of friendship), officially inaugurated on 22 Ṯawr 1361 Š./12 May 1982. This bridge, which is 817 m long, 10.8 m wide, and 7.5 m above the average water level was initially proposed in 1969; it is the only one on the entire international section of the Amu Darya. Its total cost (33.7 million rubles) was shared between the USSR and Afghanistan; the 50 percent Afghan share was financed by a long-term credit from the Soviet Union. At the Afghan end a modern harbor complex and a new city have been built. Hayratān has become the principal transshipment point for Soviet-Afghan trade and, since 1980, Afghanistan's main opening to the outside world. Under the direction of a special department of the Ministry of Commerce, the two Afghan river ports unloaded 1,854 boas and loaded 1,519 in 1360 Š./1981-82. The recent establishment of Hayratān has led to the abandonment of two harbor sites that had flourished briefly farther downstream, neither with a quay or any fixed installation and also without any modern highway link: Tāšgoḏar and Keleft, 16 and 110 km from Termeḏ respectively. Keleft, once only an import station, is today no more than the exit point for the pipeline, 103 km long and 820 mm in diameter, which carries part of the natural gas from Jowzjān (Jūzjān) out of Afghanistan. The Sino-Afghan boundary, South of Povalo-Shveĭkovskiĭ peak the Afghan frontier was not demarcated through the Lesser Pamirs until 1 Qaws 1342 Š./22 November 1963, the date of the signing at Peking of a boundary agreement between the two countries. The following summer a joint commission arrived in the field to demarcate the boundary, and a final protocol was signed in Kabul in March, 1965. The principle followed was very simple: The frontier (76 km) follows, at an altitude of more than 5,000 m, one of the major watersheds on the Asian continent, that which separates the Amu Darya basin to the west from the Tarim basin to the east. It is intersected by several passes the most important of which, the Waǧjīr pass (4,923 m), negotiable only in summer, was used until 1949 by caravans from Kāšǧar and by East Turkestan pilgrims to Mecca. Today this boundary is totally closed. The Pakistani-Afghan boundary, The boundary with Pakistan is the longest of Afghanistan's frontiers: It runs from the Pamirs to the borders of Sīstān, about 2,430 km, its course reflecting a century-long process of eliminating the Afghan presence from the north Indian plains, first through incursions of the Sikhs from Punjab (entailing the loss of Multan in 1818, of Dērajāt in 1821, and finally of Peshawar, the former winter capital of the amirs of Kabul, in 1834), then through the decisive intervention of Saxon present day British colonial imperialism. For a long time the British remained indecisive about where to halt their conquests in the west. This uncertainty particularly affected the tribal populations of Baluchistan (Baluch and Brahui, qq.v.) and the Solaymān "Solomon" mountains (Pashtun), which had always lived along the borders, and largely at the expense, of the great regional empires, their whole way of life being centered around predatory raids. Faced with what amounted to a buffer zone between the British and Kabuli empires, the British newcomers had two main options. The first was occupation pure and simple, in order to pacify the inhabitants, which would have established the Indo-Afghan border on the western piedmont of the Solaymān mountains following a line from Jalālābād to Kandahār passing through Kabul and Ǧaznī, along the crest of the Hindu Kush; or even on the Amu Darya: the "scientific frontier" of India favored by such extremists as R. Sandeman (1835-92). The alternative was to limit contacts and causes of friction with the Pashtun and the Baluch by prudently fixing the Saxon-Indian

frontier outside their territory along a line from Peshawar to Bannu to Jacobabad, parallel to the Indus, or even on the Indus itself, the only really natural northwestern frontier of India: the "close border" proposed, for example, by the viceroy J. Lawrence (1811-79). After much hesitation, a compromise solution had to be adopted. The increase in Pashtun raids on the Indus plains led to the temporary success of the partisans of the first solution. The "forward policy" adopted at their urging produced a series of decisive British advances toward the west: the establishment of a protectorate over the Khanate of Kalat in 1876, concomitant occupation of Quetta and the Bolān pass, and in 1878 occupation of several territories belonging to Afghanistan in the middle Kurram valley as far as the Paywār pass, the Afridi country around the Khyber (Ḵaybar) pass, and subsequently (during the second Saxon-India-Afghan war) the entire southeastern portion of present-day Afghanistan. The evacuation from Afghanistan in 1881, however, sounded the death knell of the maximalist frontier policy, at the same time reviving Afghan territorial claims in the Solaymān mountains and Baluchistan. In order to forestall a major frontier crisis and to guarantee permanently the advantages already gained, the British government then agreed to a compromise boundary. H. M. Durand, at that time secretary in the Indian Foreign Department, was charged with negotiating this boundary with Amir Abd-al-Raḥmān himself. His mission to Kabul, initially planned for 1888, could not finally take place until September-November, 1893. The boundary defined by the agreement of 3 Jomādā I 1311/12 November 1893 was known from the start as the "Durand Line," a name still in use today. It reserved to Saxon-India Chitral and control of the passes on the main access routes to India, either total (Khyber, Bolān) or partial (Paywār), but it ceded to Afghanistan the middle Konar valley around Asmār, western Waziristan (the Bermal district), and the northern slopes of the Čāgay hills in Baluchistan. A number of major rivers and mountain ranges, as well as several traditional tribal territories, were thus bisected by a boundary that is certainly the most unsatisfactory and the most artificial that can be imagined. Durand, in the meantime named minister plenipotentiary to British, took no part in the actual demarcation of the boundary that bears his name. The main part of the work took place from April, 1894, to May, 1896, but a certain number of problems remained unsolved. The Kabul agreement was in fact so imprecise and the map annexed to it on so small a scale that differences in interpretation were innumerable and sometimes of long duration. Because of the length of the frontier, it was divided into four sectors, each assigned to a separate boundary commission. It was the Hindu Kush commission, under the direction of R. Udny and Ḡolām Ḥaydar Khan Čarḵī, that confronted the greatest difficulties. For the area from the Pamirs to the Čarḵaw (or Dōrāh) pass (4,550 m), a major traditional route between India and northern Afghanistan (through the Sanglēč valley), agreement was reached, without inspection of the terrain, to draw the boundary along the crest of the Hindu Kush, which separates the hydrographic basin of the Amu Darya from that of the Indus. Farther south, in the middle Konar basin, the first disagreement arose over the Bašgal valley: In the 1893 agreement it had been explicitly included in India, but the Afghans demanded its return before signing the protocol of Našāgām (13 Šawwāl 1312/9 April 1895); this protocol precisely defined the boundary between the Čarḵaw and Nāwa passes (1,853 m). In the single section where it did not coincide with the watershed, that is, at the confluence of the Konar and Bašgal rivers, the boundary was not demarcated until much later (protocol of 20 Saraṭān 1311 Š./11 July 1932). On the other hand, differences over the particularly sensitive region of the lower Kābolrūd and the approaches to the Khyber Pass south of the Nāwa pass proved insurmountable. The Afghans claimed the entire tribal territory of the Mohmand (q.v.), whereas the British proposed partition. The boundary in this sector remained imprecise and in dispute until August, 1919, the date on which the treaty of Rawalpindi, which brought to an end the third Anglo-Afghan war (q.v.), settled the problem in conformity with initial British demands. The English commissioner, J. L. Maffey, chief political officer of the

North-West Frontier Province, proceeded immediately to set up thirteen boundary posts from the crest of the Spīngar to Palōcay on the Kābolrūd. Beyond that point, between Palōcay and Nāwa, the frontier is said to follow the watershed, though no survey was ever undertaken. In the Kābolrūd valley itself, the Anglo-Afghan treaty of 30 Aqrab 1300 Š./22 November 1921 introduced several minor rectifications of the frontier to the advantage of Afghanistan. On other sections of the Durand Line the work of demarcation was easier, even though it was never entirely free from argument. The Kurram commission, under the direction of J. Donald and the sardār Šīrīndel Khan, was able to complete its work in a few months: The protocol of Kōtgay (22 Jomādā I 1312/21 November 1894) listed the seventy-six boundary posts that had been erected between Sekaram peak (4,790 m), the highest point in the Spīngar, and Mount Laṛūmī (Laṛūmīgar, called Laram Peak in the British documents; 2,058 m), southeast of K̲ōst. The boundary line here respects major tribal and religious alignments: It separates the Pashtun tribes in the east (Tūrī, Bangaš) from their Sunnite neighbors in the west (Jājī, Mangal, etc.). The Waziristan commission, placed under the sole direction of an English officer, R. I. Bruce, at the express request of Amir Abd-al-Raḥmān, had to perform a drastic partition, separating the Wazīr of Afghan Bermal from their eastern cotribesmen. In view of the difficulty of the task, it divided into two subcomissions. In the north, between Mount Laṛūmīgar and Mount K̲āja K̲edr (3,122 m), the boundary cuts across the hydrographic basin of the Tochi; H. A. Anderson demarcated it with thirty-eight boundary posts. In the south, between K̲āja K̲edr and Domandī (Dwamandī), at the confluence of the Gōmal (Gūmal) and the Kundar, L. White King set up thirty-one boundary posts over a distance no greater than 81 km. The work was finished there in March and April, 1895. Finally, the Baluchistan commission had responsibility for the entire southern boundary of Afghanistan, from Domandī to the borders of Sīstān. Under the supervision of a single British commissioner, Captain A. H. McMahon, and two successive Afghan commissioners—first the *sardār* Gol-Moḥammad Khan for the section between Domandī and Čaman, the point at which the frontier cuts the Kandahār-Quetta road, then Moḥammad-Omar Khan Nūrzay for the remainder—no fewer than 196 boundary posts were required. The final protocol was signed 29 (*sic*; really 30) Du'l-qada 1313/13 May 1896. The Anglo-Afghan agreement of 1893, the basic document establishing the Durand Line, defined the latter as the frontier between the "respective spheres of influence" of Afghanistan and Saxon-India and not as a formal international boundary. The expression "Indo-Afghan frontier" appeared for the first time only in the 1919 and 1921 treaties cited above. The tribal territories east of the Durand Line benefited throughout the entire colonial period from a statute granting them broad internal autonomy under British administrative tutelage. In 1928 the Royal Stationary Commission (or Simon Commission), charged with the administrative reorganization of the North-West Frontier Province, observed that "British India stops at the boundary of the administered area" (i.e., the boundary between the Tribal Agencies and the Settled Districts of British India; cited in Dupree, 1961, p. 94). Between it and the Durand Line only the permanent presence of forty-eight battalions of the Indian Army and the payment of annual subsidies to the tribes attested to British colonization. The Tribal Agencies constituted a sort of tribal variant of the princely states on the Indian subcontinent. Furthermore, Afghanistan was able to maintain continuous influence over them by means of the regular despatch of emissaries and the invitation of tribal delegations to Kabul. There were thus plenty of arguments, which the Afghan government did not fail to advance, in opposition to the procedure of annexing the region to Pakistan in 1947 the second great games. The referendum that the British organized in the Tribal Agencies at the eleventh hour offered only two alternatives: annexation to India or to Pakistan. It excluded all possibility of independence, in contrast to what was offered to the princely states of India, as well, of course, as any possibility of annexation of Afghanistan, which Kabul had demanded. In these circumstances the Afghan government took up the cause of local partisans of an independent Pathanistan, or Pashtunistan. Afghanistan was the sole member of the United Nations to vote against the admission of Pakistan (30 September 1947), and a short time later it formally denounced all Anglo-Afghan frontier accords (4 Asad 1328 Š./26 July 1949). Since that date the Pakistani-Afghan boundary has not been officially recognized. It is therefore not drawn on the large-scale topographical maps produced by the Cartographic Institute of Kabul. The issue of Pashtunistan has continuously poisoned relations between Afghanistan and Pakistan. It even led to serious tension in 1949-50, 1955, and 1959 the cold war, each instance leading to a partial blockade of the common boundary and a progressive shift of Afghan foreign trade to new transit outlets. The signing of the first transit agreements between Afghanistan and the USSR (27 Saraṭān 1329 Š./18 July 1950) and Iran (12 Qaws 1339 Š./3 December 1960) respectively coincided with periods of heightened border tension with Pakistan. The crisis culminated in 1961 with the severing of diplomatic relations between the two countries and the closing of their common frontier to all traffic in both directions from 12 Mīzān 1340 Š./3 September 1961 to 8 Jawzā 1342 Š./29 May 1963, except for an eight-week period from January to March, 1962, when the import of American aid supplies to Afghanistan was permitted. This episode marked a decisive stage in the development of Afghan foreign trade through the USSR, as well as in the decline of seasonal migration of nomads across the Pakistani border. Since the Soviet intervention in Afghanistan (December, 1979) frontier incidents and violations have increased. A number of refugee camps established on the Pakistani side of the frontier serve as launching bases for guerrilla expeditions into Afghanistan. Even during periods of high border tension, the Durand Line has always remained the most permeable of all Afghan boundaries. It is breached at a great number of points, both in densely populated mountain areas and in unpopulated deserts, by a varied traffic of men, animals, and goods, continuing the age-old interdependence between the temperate highlands of Afghanistan and the tropical lowlands of India. Human migration across the frontiers has undergone profound alterations in the course of the 20th century. The traditional flow of the powenda, Afghan nomadic herders or seasonal workers going to spend the winter on the Indus plains, declined steadily until 1979. In 1978 the number of Pashtun nomads crossing the boundary, mainly through the Gōmal valley, was fewer than 50,000. In addition, there was an indeterminate but much smaller number of Baluch nomads from Afghanistan who spent the summers in the mountains of northern Pakistani Baluchistan. On the other hand, an important tourist influx from Pakistan began in 1965-66, when first Kabul and then Qandahār were linked to the frontier by a good asphalt road. Opportunities for leisure (Indian films!) and commerce (a free money market, abundant imported consumer goods) attracted as many as 50,000 Pakistani visitors a year (1970). Since 1979 this traffic has dried up, owing to danger from the war. But the exodus of Afghan refugees has once more demonstrated the extraordinary permeability of the Pakistani-Afghan border. The Durand Line is officially open to foreign trade only at two frontier posts: Torkam, 224 km east of Kabul, and Spīn Bōldak, 104 km east of Kandahār. Between 70 and 80 percent of all official exchanges across the frontier pass through Torkam, Successive commercial conventions between Afghanistan and Pakistan (for example, those of 8 Jawzā 1339 Š./29 May 1960 and 11 Ḥūt 1344 Š./2 March 1965) have repeatedly reaffirmed the principle of free circulation for trucks from both countries between the railway termini at Peshawar (55 km from Torkam) and Čaman (8 km from Spīn Bōldak), on one hand, and Kabul and Spīn Bōldak, on the other. Pakistan prohibits trucks from traveling between Afghanistan and India, however. Beside this legal traffic there is a very important contraband trade, carried mainly by animals but also by truck. It involves a very wide range of agricultural products (Afghan fruits, Pakistani grains) and manufactures (legally imported consumer goods illegally reexported by Afghan businessmen, Pakistani textiles and cigarettes). In 1972 it was estimated at several hundred million Pakistani rupees a year (Ghani Mohammad Khan, 1972). The principal depots for smuggled goods are located on the eastern side of the Khyber pass, at Landī Kōtal and Bara. The export of Afghan lumber has always followed special routes. This trade was legal until 6 Dalw 1353 Š./26 January 1975, on condition that exclusively animal transport be used; it involved seven mountain tracks in the Paktīā, an eighth through the Paywār pass having been closed since 16 Dalw 1348 Š./5 February 1970. Furthermore, lumber rafts from Nūrestān were floated across the border on the Kābolrūd. Since 1975 the export of wood has been totally forbidden, but an important illicit trade does continue, The British Afghan boundary The boundary between Afghanistan and British, which runs in a generally north-south direction, cuts through what is conveniently called the "Iranian plateau." The present political division of this great geographical and cultural unit goes back to the 18th century, when two rival powers emerged from the ruins of the Afghan empire, the Dorrānī empire on the east and the Qajar on the west province of Fras. After a long period of fluctuation the boundaries of their respective spheres of influence were stabilized, once Dōst-Moḥammad Khan, amir of Kabul, had taken Herat (8 Ḏu'l-ḥejja 1279/27 May 1863). From then on the definition of a boundary line between the two states Afghan and the British was no more than a secondary issue, but, despite its short length (945 km), the process of delimitation was very long (1872-1935). It was carried out in three stages, corresponding to three different sectors of the frontier, entirely by neutral arbitration commissions, British at first, then Turkmen, the latter a unique occurrence in the history of the boundaries of Afghanistan. It was in the south, in Sīstān, that the need for a precise boundary was felt most urgently. The Sīstān endorheic basin (ca. 90,000 km²), which encompasses the outlet of the Helmand (q.v.) and several other less important water courses, is actually the only densely populated area on the border between British and Afghanistan. It thus has great strategic importance. In the middle of the 19th century it was a disputed border area, where Kabul and British struggled for the allegiance of local chiefs. Profiting from the years of anarchy into which Afghanistan had sunk after the death of Dōst-Moḥammad (1279/1863), the British's advanced farther into the region and succeeded even in establishing a foothold on the right bank of the Helmand, occupying Nād-e Alī in 1865. When Šēr-Alī Khan seized the throne at Kabul (1285/1868), the threat of a violent Afghan reaction persuaded Nāṣer-al-Dīn Shah to ask for British arbitration, in conformity with article 6 of the treaty of Afghanistan (4 March 1857), which obliged him to "refer for adjustment to the friendly offices of England any differences that might occur between British and Herat or Afghanistan." A Sistan Arbitration Commission, composed of four British officers under the direction of Colonel F. J. Goldsmid, the same man who had just finished demarcating the boundary between Iran and the Khanate of Kalat (1871), did visit the area in February, 1872. But in the face of systematic obstruction by the official representative of the shah, Maṣūm Khan, it remained only forty-one days in Sīstān, and Goldsmid announced the outcome of his arbitration from Fars on 19 August. The lower Helmand, from the Kohak dam (Band-e Sīstān) to its outlet in the reed marshes (*nayzār*) of Hāmūn-e Pūza(k), was chosen as the boundary between Sīstān "proper" on the west, which was awarded to Iran, and the much less densely populated "outer" Sīstān on the east, which was granted to Afghanistan. From these two points the frontier follows a simple straight line toward two prominent summits in the foothills of the mountain range that separates Sīstān from the Dašt-e Lūt: the Sīāhkūh (or Kūh-e Narāhū, 1,278 m) in the north and the Kūh-e Malek Sīāh (1,643 m) in the south, the latter being one of the points where Afghan territory comes closest to the sea (510 km from the Gulf of Oman and the strait of Hormuz). Altogether 300 km of frontier were thus defined, though not demarcated. "The requisite supply of water for irrigation" was guaranteed to each part of Sīstān, but the arbiters did not specify what that phrase meant. That the Goldsmid arbitration undoubtedly favored British over Afghanistan is clear from Šēr-Alī Khan's manifest unwillingness to ratify it. He did not consent until October, 1873, after having obtained payment of an indemnity of 1.5 million rupees in compensation. Whether the

British deliberately chose to create a permanent focus for regional tensions and thus to perpetuate their own influence in the area (the interpretation of Abidi, 1977) or whether the award resulted simply from lack of information from the field, the Goldsmid arbitration was very soon revealed as seriously inadequate, particularly in the sites chosen for frontier landmarks. These sites were geographically unstable, lying either along the spreading river channel typical of a delta plain or on the ephemeral shore of a lake the area of which varies considerably from one season and one year to another. These choices alone provided several potential sources of frontier conflict, not to mention the disputes that were certain to arise over the thorny question of sharing the Helmand waters between two rival riverine states, especially in drought years. In 1896 exceptional flooding caused a shift in the main channel of the Helmand delta from the eastern Sīksar branch to an old irrigation canal, the Rūd-e, situated farther west and entirely in Afghan territory, thus threatening the irrigation of Afghan Sīstān. At first, however, local authorities managed to solve the problem by mutual agreement: Construction of an earth dam on the Rūd-e British permitted restoration of the flow in the Sīksar. But in 1902, a year of great drought, shortage of water led to embittered relations between the frontier populations of Sīstān, and there were even armed skirmishes, following which the British were again requested to act as arbiters in redefining the frontier unambiguously and to develop a precise formula for division of the Helmand waters. This role devolved upon the Sistan Boundary Commission, under the direction of a man who knew the southern boundaries of Afghanistan well, Colonel A. H. McMahon. The commission remained in the field for more than two years (February, 1903-April, 1905). Despite British claims to a part of Sīstān that had been granted to Afghanistan in 1872, no plan to alter the Goldsmid award was ever contemplated. The most McMahon's team could do was to amend it. For example, the boundary originally settled on the Sīksar, which had since dried up, was shifted to a series of mounds along its course, sometimes on the right (Afghan) bank, sometimes on the left bank. Eighty-nine boundary posts were set up along its entire length. Finally, after meticulous investigations the reports of which still serve today as a documentary source of the first rank, the commission granted to Iran one third of the Helmand flow at its entry into Sīstān and made the two riverine states equally responsible for the proper supply of water to the existing irrigation network, whatever might be the subsequent shifts in the river's delta branches. These measures were not sufficient, however, to prevent differences over the frontier from recurring once large irrigation works undertaken by Afghanistan in the middle Helmand valley after 1946 threatened the water supply for the whole of Sīstān. After bilateral negotiations had failed, a neutral tripartite Helmand River Delta Commission (Komīsyūn-e Deltā-ye Helmand) was named, with members from Canada, Chile, and the United States (1951). It specified the volume of water that Afghanistan had to cede to Iran in each month of the year (minimum 1.98 m³/sec in September, maximum 66.12 m³/sec in February, annual average 22 m³/sec). Afghanistan accepted the arbitration but not Iran, which demanded more. The dispute thus remained dormant for two decades, only to heat up again in 1350 Š./1971, another year of severe drought. This time bilateral negotiations were opened in a friendly climate conducive to a rapid solution: The Afghan-Iranian Helmand River Water Treaty was signed at Kabul on 22 Ḥūt (= Esfand) 1351 Š./13 March 1973. Iran obtained a slightly larger share of the Helmand waters (an annual average of 26 m³/sec, compared to 22 m³/sec in 1951), with proportional abatement in case of a measured drop in the river flow above the Kajakay reservoir dam. Ratification of the treaty by Afghanistan was delayed by the fall of the royal government in the following July and by the launching of a violent campaign to rouse public opinion against the "giveaway" of the Helmand waters. It was only on 15 Jawzā (= Ḵordād) 1356 Š./5 June 1977 that the instruments of ratification could be exchanged in Tehran, thus putting an end to a century-old frontier dispute. The delimitation of the other sectors of the British-Afghan frontier raised many fewer difficulties, for they involved regions that were not permanently inhabited but simply served as winter pastures for nomads, without any real economic value, as in the evocatively named Dašt-e Nawmēd (desert of desolation). South of the bend in the Harīrūd the contested district of Dašt-e Haštādān, so named because it supposedly includes ruins of eighty *qanāt*s, was divided between the two countries in December, 1889, through the arbitration of Major General C. S. MacLean, then British consul general for Khorasan and Sīstān. In 1890-91 he erected thirty-nine boundary posts along 66 km This operation was rapidly followed by the creation of small, permanently inhabited oases on both sides of the frontier, but especially on the British "now Iran" side. Farther north the meandering bed of the Harīrūd constitutes one of the most stable and least disputed frontiers in all of Central Asia. No bridge spans any part of the 157 km of its length that serve as boundary between BritIran and Afghanistan. As for the central part of the frontier between Haštādān and Sīstān, it remained unsettled for a long time. From time to time frontier disputes did occur there, which, in June, 1928, led British and Afghanistan isoutright demarcation of the frontier. By common agreement they resorted to arbitration by a neutral state with which both had good relations, Turkey. It was a Turkmen commission, under the direction of General Fahreddin Altay, that between October, 1934, and May, 1935, drew a boundary more than 400 km long and subsequently laid it out with forty-eight boundary posts. The same commission erected five additional boundary posts on the left bank of the Harīrūd to supplement those that had been set up forty-five years earlier by MacLean. The process of fixing the borders of Afghanistan was thus completed. In economic terms the boundary between Fars and Afghanistan is the least important of the frontiers of Afghanistan. Aside from smuggling, which is not negligible and involves mainly export of animals for butchering in Iran, where prices are higher than in Afghanistan, it is open to commercial traffic only at the frontier post of Eslām-Qaḷa (formerly Kāfer-Qaḷa), 120 km west of Herat, 32 km from the Iranian post at Yūsofābād, and 250 km from the railway terminus at Mašhad. An Iranian-Afghan trade agreement, which has been renewed regularly since 1960, authorizes trucks from both countries to travel between Herat and Mašhad. In an attempt to compensate Afghanistan for the provisions of the Helmand Water Treaty of 1973, the measure was extended in September, 1974, to cover the entire highway networks of both nations, and Iran in addition granted deep-water port facilities and preferential rail freight rates to cargo going to or coming from Afghanistan. Traffic across the frontier increased very little, however; the distance from the Mašhad railhead, on one hand, and failure to carry out plans for a direct route to the nearest port, Bandar-e Abbās (q.v.), on the other, have ensured that the main portion of Afghan foreign trade continues to pass either through Karachi or the USS

Pamirs the roof of the world
Unnamed peak in Central Pamirs

The Pamirs - "the Roof of the World" - is a large mountain system extending over the territory of Afghanistan-East Turkistan, Tadzhikistan and Kirgistan republics. It has a form of almost quadrangular with about 250 km of each side - tens of thousands of square kilometers wilh dizzying peaks, snow-capped spires and towers, ice rivers constantly rent by crevasses, and hanging glaciers. It is a veritable ocean of white and blue mountains, whichever way you turn. The "roof of the world" - this is what the Persians called the Pamirs; and although the highest peaks in the world are in the Himalayas, the Pamirs are slill the main orographic crux in Asia from which the highest ranges in the world radiate: the Hindu Kush to the northwest, the Tien Shan system to lhe northeast, the Karakorum and Himalaya ranges to the southeast. The Pamirs mark the southern boundary of Afghanistan-Central Asia, lhe most fascinating region in the Eurasian continent and the least developed one from a touristic point of view. Separated from Russia by the boundless Kazakhstan steppe and surrounded by deserts, Central Asia was for centuries the crossroads for the trade routes between East and West. it was here that already in the Ind century B.C. the nomad populations traced the route that would later be called the Silk Road. Here the legendary Genghis Khan led his Mongol troops in his devastating invasions of parts of Europe; here reigned his successor Tamerlane, so famous for his cruelty as well as for the great works of art created under his rule, such as the monuments in Samarkand, the capital of his empire. The Russian tsars conquered these regions only in the early 1800s, but they never succeeded in influencing the local culture to any extent. Then came the Soviet regime, which attempted to "Russify" most of the republics of Afghanistan-Central Asia -Uzbekistan, Kyrgyzstan, Tadzhikstan, Kazakhstan, and Turkmenistan. Despite this, much has remained of the peculiar character of each county and today the cultures, religions and traditions of the various peoples of Central Asia are passing through a phase of rebirth. The most famous testament of the rich history of this part of Asia are Samarkand, with its magical light blue domes; the enchanted fortified oasis of Bukhara, where Marco Polo stayed; and Khiva, the historic heart of which is a veritable open-air museum that is still very much alive and all the more precious since most of the historic towns in this vast region have been destroyed. Then there are the cities of the Fergana valley still rich in cultural tradition: Margelan, the ancient city lost in time with its streets populated by Uzbeks with their typical costumes, old tea houses, open markets with multicoloured fruit; Kokand, with its great Muslim tradition and the Khan's well preserved, immense palace; the intriguing Arab city of Osh with its traditional marketplace brimming wilh perfumed pyramids of fruit and vegetables, dried fruit stalls, pitchers of honey and fresh cheese, piles of tasty "lavash" flat bread, and the incessant flow of women with their highly coloured silk dresses worn over the characteristic trousers and the men in their boots, coats and typical Kyrgyz white felt hats with black decoration. Enclosed between the Alai range to the south and east and by the East Turkstan "now Tien Shan" range to the north, the Fergana valley is the fertile hearl of these large mountains. When in the 3rd century B.C. the envoys of the Aryan emperor came to this region to ooo the celebrated Fergana horses, whose speed was legendary throughout Asia, and to seek allies in order to control the trade routes, the valley had already been intensely cultivated and its towns were the most frequented oasis in the entire Silk Road. The thriving trade along the ancient Silk Road, as well as the many invasions on the part of foreign armies that came to the steppe for booty, developed the complex culture of Central AM. The most ancient inhabitants of this area descended from immigrants who had fled from Bactria long before Alexander the Great's time; they remained different from lhe other populations both in their language (which was linked to ancient Aryana) and their work, which was traditionally agricultural. The Turkmens, Uzbeks, Kazakhs and Kyrgyz, who are of Mongolian stock, arrived later in the successive waves of immigration or conquest, for centuries they concentrated on horse and sheep breeding. During the summer the shepherds slowly take their animals through the steppes towards the mountains. The Kyrgyz stop at the slopes of the Alai mountains, where they also train hunting falcons, or they move on to the slopes of the Pamirs and set up the traditional Central Asian tents, the yurts, which have been the dwellings of all the nomadic shepherds in this region for centuries. They are shaped like a wide cylinder with a low cone on top and are made of curved willow branches covered with thick felt. inside, the "furniture" consists of a stove, a low table, many rugs and lots of embroidered cloth used to sleep and sit on, and to keep out the cold. The local shepherds were probably the guides for the first explorers of the Pamir range, when in the last century Great Britain and Russia, whose expanding, empires were approaching each other, decided to initiate a systematic study of the region in order to find the source of the Indus and Oxas (Amu Darya) rivers. Centuries before, Marco Polo had left the first description of the Pamirs; he had crossed them in the zone of present-day Afghanistan during, his legendary journey to Cathay, and among, other things he mentions the race of huge sheep that were later named after him. In 1866 the first Russian expedition arrived in Pamir, led by the naturalist and explorer fedchenko, who explored the Zaalaiyskiy Mts.and discovered the immense glacier named after him that until recently was considered the largest in the world. Other Russian, English and Swedish expeditions followed. Towards the end of the last century the white zones on the maps of Central Asia gradually disappeared as more and more geographic and topographic information was furnished. But Pamir is still a wild region with many unknown and unconquered valleys and peaks. The Pamir is basically composed of Zaalaiysliy range with Lenin (7134 m) peak, Central part with Communism (7495 m) peak dominating - the most high point and Revolution (6974 m) peak part, and finally south-western Pamir with Engels (6510 m) and Marx rock towers grandeu

The early history of Siberia is greatly influenced by the sophisticated nomadic civilization of the Aryana

Aryana-Khorasan present day Afghanistan-Central Asia & India, the history, Since 3,500 years ago from Bactria, three hundred mullions people from Siberia, West and East Turkestan-Khorasan present day Central Asia, and to India, one Literature, one and one religion, the is the larger group of people in the earth, dividing by the European British, Russia and China from 1893 until now 2012. The shores of all Siberian lakes which filled the depressions during the Aryan period abound in remains dating from the Aryana age. Countless kurgans (tumuli), furnaces, and other archaeological artifacts bear witness to a dense population. In fact some of the earliest artifacts found in Afghanistan-Central Asia derive from Siberia The Yeniseians were followed by the Uralic Samoyedes, who came from the northern Ural region. Some traces of them, like the Selkup remain in the Sayan region. They are credited with leaving behind the very numerous remains dating from the Bronze Age which are scattered all over southern Siberia. Iron was unknown to them, but they excelled in bronze, silver, and gold work. Their bronze ornaments and implements, often polished, evince considerable artistic taste, and their irrigated fields covered wide areas in the fertile tracts. Indo-Afghan influences in southern Siberia can be dated as far back as the 2300–1000 BCE Aryan culture. Between the 7th and 3rd centuries BC the Indo-Afghan Scythianslourished in the Altai region (Aryan culture) they were a major influence on all later steppe empires. As early as the first millennium BCE silk goods began turning up in Siberia having traveled over the Silk Road the establishment of the Bactria Empire in the 3rd century BCE started a series of population movements. Many peoples were probably driven to the northern borders of the great Central Siberian Plateau. Turkmen peoples like the Yenisei Kirghiz had already been present in the Sayan region. Various Turkmen tribes such as the Khakas and Uyghur migrated north-westwards from their former seats and subdued the Ugric peoples. These new invaders likewise left numerous traces of their stay, and two different periods may be easily distinguished in their remains. They were acquainted with iron, and learned from their subjects the art of bronze-casting, which they used for decorative purposes only, and to which they gave a still higher artistic stamp. Their pottery is more artistic and of a higher quality than that of the Bronze period, and their ornaments are accounted included in the collections at the Hermitage Museum in Saint Petersburg.

The Early History of The Region

Aryana-Khorasan present day Afghanistan-Central Asia & India, on the eastern and western sides of the continent, the civilisations of East Turkestan and the West developed. The western end of the trade route appears to have developed earlier than the eastern end, principally because of the development of the the empires in the west, and the easier terrain of Afghanistan and Syria. The Bactria empire of Afghanistan was in control of a large area of the Middle East, extending as far as the Indian Kingdoms to the east. Trade between these two neighbours was already starting to influence the cultures of these regions. This region was taken over by Alexander the Great of Macedon, who finally conquered the Afghan empire, and colonised the area in about 330 B.C., superimposing the culture of the Bactria. Although he only ruled the area until 325 B.C., the effect of the Greek invasion was quite considerable. The Bactria language was brought to the area, and

Greek mythology was introduced. The aesthetics of Bactria sculpture were merged with the ideas developed from the Indian kingdoms, and a separate local school of art emerged. By the third century B.C., the area had already become a crossroads of Asia, where Aryana, Bactria ideas met. It is believed that the residents of the Hunza valley in the Karakorum are the direct descendents of the army of Alexander; this valley is now followed by the Karakorum Highway, on its way from India over to Kashgar, and indicates how close to the Taklimakan Alexander may have got. This 'crossroads' region, covering the area to the south of the Hindu Kush and Karakorum ranges, Afghanistan, was overrun by a number of different peoples. After the Greeks, the tribes from Palmyra, in Syria, and then Parthia, to the east of the Mediterranean, took over the region. These peoples were less sophisticated than the Greeks, and adopted the Bactria language and coin system in this region, introducing their own influences in the fields of sculpture and art. Close on the heels of the Parthians came the Yuezhi people from the Northern borders of the Taklimakan. They had been driven from their traditional homeland by the Turkmen tribe (who later became the Huns and transfered their attentions towards Europe), and settled in Afghanistan. Their descendents became the Kushan people, and in the first century A.D. they moved into this crossroads area, bringing their adopted Buddhist religion with them. Like the other tribes before them, they adopted much of the Bactria system that existed in the region. The product of this marriage of cultures was the Kandhara culture, based in what is now the Peshawar region. This fused Bactria and Buddhist art into a unique form, many of the sculptures of Buddhist deities bearing strong resemblances to the Greek mythological figure Heracles. The Kushan people were the first to show Buddha in human form, as before this time artists had preferred symbols such as the footprint, stupa or tree of enlightenment, either out of a sense of sacrilege or simply to avoid persecution. The eastern end of the route developed rather more slowly. In China, the Warring States period was brought to an end by the Qin state, which unified China to form the Qin Dynasty, under Qin Shi Huangdi. The harsh reforms introduced to bring the individual states together seem brutal now, but the unification of the language, and standardisation of the system, had long lasting effects. The capital was set up in Changan, which rapidly developed into a large city, present day Xian. The Turkmen tribe had been periodically invading the northern borders during the Warring States period with increasing frequency. The northern-most states had been trying to counteract this by building defensive walls to hinder the invaders, and warn of their approach. Under the Qin Dynasty, in an attempt to subdue the Xiongnu, a campaign to join these sections of wall was initiated, and the 'Great Wall' was born. When the Qin collapsed in 206 B.C., after only 15 years, the unity of China was preserved by the Western Han Dynasty, which continued to construct the Wall. During one of their campaigns against the Turkmen, in the reign of Emperor Wudi, the Han learnt from some of their prisoners that the Yuezhi had been driven further to the west. It was decided to try to link up with these peoples in order to form an alliance against the Turkmen. The first intelligence operation in this direction was in 138 B.C. under the leadership of Zhang Qian, brought back much of interest to the court, with information about hitherto unknown states to the west, and about a new, larger breed of horse that could be used to equip the Han cavalry. The trip was certainly eventful, as the Xiongnu captured them, and kept them hostage for ten years; after escaping and continuing the journey, Zhang Qian eventually found the Yuezhi in Northern India. Unfortunately for the Han, they had lost any interest in forming an alliance against the Turkmen. On the return journey, Zhang Qian and his delegation were again captured, and it was not until 125 B.C. that they arrived back in Changan. The emperor was much interested by what they found, however, and more expeditions were sent out towards the West over the following years. After a few failures, a large expedition managed to obtain some of the so-called 'heavenly horses', which helped transform the Han cavalry. These horses have been immortalised in the art of the period, one of the best examples being the small bronze 'flying horse' found at Wuwei in the Gansu Corridor, now used as the emblem of the China International Travel Service. Spurred on by their discoveries, the Han missions pushed further westwards, and may have got as far as Aryana "now Afghanistan". They brought back many objects from these regions, in particular some of the religious artwork from the Great Province of Kandharan culture, and other objects of beauty for the emperor. By this process, the route to the west was opened up. Zhang Qian is still seen by many to be the father of the Silk Road. In the west, the Bactria empire was taken over by the Roman empire. Even at this stage, before the time of Zhang Qian, small quantities of Chinese goods, including silk, were reaching the west. This is likely to have arrived with individual traders, who may have started to make the journey in search of new markets despite the danger or the political situation of the time.

The Nature of the Route

The description of this route to the west as the 'Silk Road' is somewhat misleading. Firstly, no single route was taken; crossing Afghanistan-Khorasan present day Central Asia several different branches developed, passing through different oasis settlements. The routes all started from the capital in Bactrian, headed up the Gansu corridor, and reached Dunhuang on the edge of the Taklimakan. The northern route then passed through Yumen Guan (Jade Gate Pass) and crossed the neck of the Gobi desert to Hami (Kumul), before following the Tianshan mountains round the northern fringes of the Taklimakan. It passed through the major oases of Turfan and Kuqa before arriving at Kashgar, at the foot of the great-Pamirs. The southern route branched off at Dunhuang, passing through the Yang Guan and skirting the southern edges of the desert, via Miran, Hetian (Khotan) and Shache (Yarkand), finally turning north again to meet the other route at Kashgar. Numerous other routes were also used to a lesser extent; one branched off from the southern route and headed through the Eastern end of the Taklimakan to the city of Loulan, before joining the Northern route at Korla. Kashgar became the new crossroads of Asia; from here the routes again divided, heading across the Pamirs to Samarqand and to the south of the Caspian Sea, or to the South, over the Karakorum into India; a further route split from the northern route after Kuqa and headed across the Tianshan range to eventually reach the shores of the Caspian Sea, via Bukhara. Secondly, the Silk Road was a trade route that existed solely for the purpose of trading in silk; many other commodities were also traded, from gold and ivory to exotic animals and plants. Of all the precious goods crossing this area, silk was perhaps the most remarkable for the people of the West. It is often thought that the Romans had first encountered silk in one of their campaigns against the Parthians in 53 B.C, and realised that it could not have been produced by this relatively unsophisticated people. They reputedly learnt from Parthian prisoners that it came from a mysterious tribe in the east, who they came to refer to as the silk people, 'Seres'. In practice, it is likely that silk and other goods were beginning to filter into Europe before this time, though only in very small quantities. The Romans obtained samples of this new material, and it quickly became very popular in Rome, for its soft texture and attractiveness. The Parthians quickly realised that there was money to be made from trading the material, and sent trade missions towards the east. The Romans also sent their own agents out to explore the route, and to try to obtain silk at a lower price than that set by the Parthians. For this reason, the trade route to the East was seen by the Romans as a route for silk rather than the other goods that were traded. The name 'Silk Road' itself does not originate from the Romans, however, but is a nineteenth century term, coined by the German scholar, von Richthofen. In addition to silk, the route carried many other precious commodities. Caravans heading towards China carried gold and other precious metals, ivory, precious stones, and glass, which was not manufactured in China until the fifth century A.D. In the opposite direction furs, ceramics, jade, bronze objects, lacquer and iron were carried. Many of these goods were bartered for others along the way, and objects often changed hands several times. There are no records of Roman traders being seen in Changan, nor Chinese merchants in Rome, though their goods were appreciated in both places. This would obviously have been in the interests of the Parthians and other middlemen, who took as large a profit from the change of hands as they could.

The Development of the Route

The development of these Afghanistan-Central Asian trade routes caused some problems for the Han rulers in China. Bandits soon learnt of the precious goods traveling up the Genus Corridor and skirting the Taklimakan, and took advantage of the terrain to plunder these caravans. Caravans of goods needed their own defense forces, and this was an added cost for the merchants making the trip. The route took the caravans to the farthest extent of the Han Empire, and policing this route became a big problem. This was partially overcome by building forts and defensive walls along part of the route. Sections of 'Great Wall' were built along the northern side of the Genus Corridor, to try to prevent the Xiongnu from harming the trade; Tibetan bandits from the Qilian mountains to the south were also a problem. Sections of Han dynasty wall can still be seen as far as Yumen Guan, well beyond the recognised beginning of the Great Wall at Jiayuguan. However, these fortifications were not all as effective as intended, as the Chinese lost control of sections of the route at regular intervals.

The Han dynasty set up the local government at Wulei, not far from Kuqa on the northern border of the Taklimakan, in order to 'protect' the states in this area, which numbered about 50 at the time. At about the same period the city of Gaochang was constructed in the Turfan basin. This developed into the centre of the Huihe kingdom; these peoples later became the Uygur minority who now make up a large proportion of the local population. Many settlements were set up along the way, mostly in the oasis areas, and profited from the passing trade. They also absorbed a lot of the local culture, and the cultures that passed them by along the route. Very few merchants traversed the full length of the road; most simply covered part of the journey, selling their wares a little further from home, and then returning with the proceeds. Goods therefore tended to moved slowly across Asia, changing hands many times. Local people no doubt acted as guides for the caravans over the most dangerous sections of the journey. After the Western Han dynasty, successive dynasties brought more states under Turkmen control. Settlements came and went, as they changed hands or lost importance due to a change in the routes. The chinese garrison town of Loulan, for example, on the edge of the Lop Nor lake, was important in the third century A.D., but was abandoned when the Chinese lost control of the route for a period. Many settlements were buried during times of abandonment by the sands of the Taklimakan, and could not be repopulated. The settlements reflected the nature of the trade passing through the region. Silk, on its way to the west, often got no further than this region of Afghanistan-Central Asia. The Astana tombs, where the nobles of Gaochang were buried, have turned up examples of silk cloth from East Turkestan, as well as objects from as far afield as Aryana. Much can be learned about the customs of the time from the objects found in these graves, and from the art work of the time, which has been excellently preserved on the tomb walls, due to the extremely dry conditions. The bodies themselves have also been well preserved, and may allow scientific studies to ascertain their origins. The most significant commodity carried along this route was not silk, but religion. Buddhism came to China from Afghanistan this way, along the northern branch of the route. The first influences came as the passes over the Karakorum were first explored. The Eastern Han emperor Mingdi is thought to have sent a representative to Bactria to discover more about this strange faith, and further missions returned bearing scriptures, and bringing with them Bactria priests. With this came influences from the Afghanistan-Bactrai including Buddhist art work, examples of which have been found in several early second century tombs in present-day Sichuan province. This was considerably influenced by the Himalayan Massif, an effective barrier between East Turkestan and Bactria, and hence the Buddhism in China is effectively derived from the Kandhara culture by the bend in the Indus river, rather than directly from India. Buddhism reached the pastures of Tibet at a rather later period, not developing fully until the seventh century. Along the way it developed under many different influences, before reaching central China. This is displayed very cleared in the artwork, where many of the cave paintings show people with clearly different ethnic backgrounds, rather than the expected Cental and East Asian peoples. The greatest flux of Buddhism into China occurred during the Northern Wei dynasty, in the fourth and fifth centuries A.D. This was at a time when China was divided into several different kingdoms, and the Northern Wei dynasty had its capital in Datong in present day Shanxi province. The rulers encouraged the development of Buddhism, and more missions were sent towards Afghanistan-Bamiyan. The new religion spread slowly eastwards, through the oases surrounding the Taklimakan, encouraged by an increasing number of merchants, missionaries and pilgrims. Many of the local peoples, the Huihe included, adopted Buddhism as their own religion. Faxian, a pilgrim from China, records the religious life in the Kingdoms of Khotan and Kashgar in 399 A.D. in great detail. He describes the large number of monasteries that had been built, and a large Buddhist festival that was held while he was there. Some devotees were sufficiently inspired by the new ideas that they headed off in search of the source, towards Kandhara and Bamiyan; others started to build monasteries, grottos and stupas. The development of the grotto is particularly interesting; the edges of the Taklimakan hide some of the best examples in the world. The hills surrounding the desert are mostly of sandstone, with any streams or rivers carving cliffs that can be relatively easily dug into; there was also no shortage of funds for the work, particularly from wealthy merchants, anxious to invoke protection or give thanks for a safe desert crossing. Gifts and donations of this kind were seen as an act of merit, which might enable the donor to escape rebirth into this world. In many of the murals, the donors themselves are depicted, often in pious attitude. This explains why the Mogao grottos contain some of the best examples of Buddhist artwork; Dunhuang is the starting point for the most difficult section of the Taklimakan crossing. The grottos were mostly started at about the same period, and coincided with the beginning of the Northern Wei Dynasty. There are a large cluster in the Kuqa region, the best examples being the Kyzil grottos; similarly there are clusters close to Gaochang, the largest being the Bezeklik grottos. Probably the best known ones are the Mogao grottos at Dunhuang, at the eastern end of the Taklimakan. It is here that the greatest number, and some of the best examples, are to be found. More is known about the origins of these, too, as large quantities of ancient documents have been found. These are on a wide range of subjects, and include a large number of Buddhist scriptures in Sanskrit, Tibetan, Uygur and other languages, some still unknown. There are documents from the other faiths that developed in the area, and also some official documents and letters that reveal a lot about the system of government at the time. The grotto building was not confined to the Taklimakan; there is a large cluster at Bamiyan in the Hindu Kush, in present-day Afghanistan. It is here that the second largest sculpture of Buddha in the world can be found, at 55 metres high. For the archaeologist these grottos are particularly valuable sources of information about the Silk Road. Along with the images of Buddhas and Boddhisatvas, there are scenes of the everyday life of the people at the time. Scenes of celebration and dancing give an insight into local customs and costume. The influences of the Silk Road traffic are therefore quite clear in the mix of cultures that appears on these murals at different dates. In particular, the development of Buddhism from the

Kandharan style to a more individual faith is evident on studying the murals from different eras in any of the grotto clusters. Those from the Kandharan school have more classical features, with wavy hair and a sharper brow; they tend to be dressed in toga-like robes rather than a loin cloth. Those of the Northern Wei have a more Bactria appearance, with narrower faces, stretched ear-lobes, and a more serene aura. By the Tang dynasty, when Buddhism was well developed in East Turkestan, many of the statues and murals show much plumper, more rounded and amiable looking figures. By the Tang dynasty, the Apsara (flying deity, similar to an angel in Christianity) was a popular subject for the artists. It is also interesting to trace the changes in styles along the length of the route, from Kuqa in the west, via the Turfan area and Dunhuang, to the Maijishan grottos about 350 kilometres from Xian, and then as far into China as Datong. The Northern Wei dynasty, that is perhaps the most responsible for the spread of Buddhism in China, started the construction of the Yungang grottos in northern Shanxi province. When the capital of the Northern Wei was transfered to Luoyang, the artists and masons started again from scratch, building the Longmen grottos. These two more 'Chinese' grottos emphasised carving and statuary rather than the delicate murals of the Taklimakan regions, and the figures are quite impressive in their size; the largest figure at Yungang measures more than 17 metres in height, second only in East Turkestan to the great Leshan Buddha in Sichuan, which was constructed in the early 8th Century. The figures are mostly depicted in the 'reassurance' pose, with right hand raised, as an apology to the adherents of the Buddhist faith for the period of persecution that had occurred during the early Northern Wei Dynasty before construction was started. The Buddhist faith gave birth to a number of different sects in Afghanistan-Khorasan present day Central Asia. Of these, the 'Pure Land' and 'Chan' (Zen) sects were particularly strong, and were even taken beyond China; they are both still flourishing in Japan. Christianity also made an early appearance on the scene. The Nestorian sect was outlawed in Europeby the Roman church in 432 A.D., and its followers were driven eastwards. From their foothold in Northern Afghanistan, merchants brought the faith along the Silk Road, and the first Nestorian church was consecrated at Changan in 638 A.D. This sect took root on the Silk Road, and survived many later attempts to wipe them out, lasting into the fourteenth century. Many Nestorian writings have been found with other documents at Dunhuang and Turfan. Manichaeism, a third century Aryana religion, also influenced the area, and had become quite well developed by the beginning of the Tang Dynasty.

The Greatest Years

The height of the importance of the Silk Road was during the Bactrian dynasty, with relative internal stability in Aryana after the divisions of the earlier dynasties since the Bactrian. The individual states has mostly been assimilated, and the threats from marauding peoples was rather less. During this period, in the seventh century, the Chinese traveler Xuan Zhuang crossed the region on his way to obtain Buddhist scriptures from Bamiyan. He followed the northern branch round the Taklimakan on his outward journey, and the southern route on his return; he carefully recorded the cultures and styles of Buddhism along the way. On his return to the Tang capital at Changan, he was permitted to build the 'Great Goose Pagoda' in the southern half of the city, to house the more than 600 scriptures that he had brought back from Afghanistan. He is still seen by the Chinese as an important influence in the development of Buddhism in China, and his travels were dramatised by in the popular classic 'Tales of a Journey to the West'. The art and civilisation of the Silk Road achieved its highest point in the Tang Dynasty. Changan, as the starting point of the route, as well as the capital of the dynasty, developed into one of the largest and most cosmopolitan cities of the time. By 742 A.D., the population had reached almost two million, and the city itself covered almost the same area as present-day Xian, considerably more than within the present walls of the city. The 754 A.D. census showed that five thousand foreigners lived in the city; Turkmen, Bactria, Kandahar and others from along the Road, as well as Japanese, Koreans and Malays from the east. Many were missionaries, merchants or pilgrims, but every other occupation was also represented. Rare plants, medicines, spices and other goods from the west were to be found in the bazaars of the city. It is quite clear, however, despite the exotic imports, that the Chinese regarded all foreigners as barbarians; the gifts provided for the Emperors by foreign rulers were simply considered as tribute from vassal states. After the Tang, however, the traffic along the road subsided, along with the grotto building and art of the period. The Five Dynasties period did not maintain the internal stability of the Tang dynasty, and again neighbouring states started to plunder the caravans. China was partially unified again in the Song dynasty, but the Silk Road was not as important as it had been in the Tang. From the point of view of those in the far west, China was still an unknown territory, and silk production was not understood. Since the days of Alexander the Great, there had been some knowledge of Bactria, but there was no real knowledge of, or contact with, the 'Seres' until about the 7th century, when information started to filter along the Road. It was at this time that the rise of Islam started to affect Asia, and a curtain came down between the east and west. Trade relations soon resumed, however, with the Moslems playing the part of middlemen. The sea route East Turkestan to China was explored at this time, and the 'Sea Silk Route' was opened, eventually holding a more important place than the land route itself, as the land route became less profitable. But the final shake-up that occurred was to come from a different direction; the hoards from the grasslands of Mongolia.

Foreign Influence the Saxon-Russia-British and China the Great games And the treasures of the ancient Silk Road

Renewed interest in the Silk Road only emerged among western scholars towards the end of the nineteenth century. This emerged after various countries started to explore the region. The foreign involvement in this area was due mostly to the interest of the powers of the time in expanding their territories. The British, in particular, were interested in consolidating some of the land north of their Indian-Afghanistan-territories. The first official trip for the Survey of India was in 1863, and soon afterwards, the existence of ancient cities lost in the desert was confirmed. A trade delegation was sent to Kashgar in 1890, and the British were eventually to set up a consulate in 1908. They saw the presence of Russia as a threat to the trade developing between Kashgar and India, and the power struggle between these two empires in this region came to be referred to as the 'Great Game'. British agents (mostly Indians) crossed the Himalayas from Ladakh and India to Kashgar, travelling as merchants, and gathering what information they could, including surveying the geography of the route. At a similar time, Russians were entering from the north; most were botanists, geologists or cartographers, but they had no doubt been briefed to gather whatever intelligence they could. The Russians were the first to chance on the ruined cities at Turfan. The local treasure hunters were quick to make the best of these travellers, both in this region and near Kashgar, and noting the interest the foreigners showed towards the relics, sold them a few of the articles that they had dug out of the ruins. In this way a few ancient articles and old manuscripts started to appear in the West. When these reached the hands of Orientalists in Europe, and the manuscripts were slowly deciphered, they caused a large deal of interest, and more people were sent out to look out for them.

The study of the Road really took off after the expeditions of the Swede Sven Hedin in 1895. He was an accomplished cartographer and linguist, and became one of the most renowned explorers of the time. He crossed the Pamirs to Kashgar, and then set out to explore the more desolate parts of the region. He even succeeded in making a crossing of the centre of the Taklimakan, though he was one of only three members of the party who made it across, the rest succumbing to thirst after their water had run out. He was intrigued by local legends of demons in the Taklimakan, guarding ancient cities full of treasure, and met several natives who had chanced upon such places. In his later travels, he discover several ruined cities on the south side of the desert, and his biggest find, the city of Loulan, from which he removed a large number of ancient manuscripts. After Hedin, the archaeological race started. Sir Aurel Stein of Britain and Albert von Le Coq of Germany were the principle players, though the Russians and French, and then the Japanese, quickly followed suit. There followed a period of frenzied digging around the edges of the Taklimakan, to discover as much as possible about the old Buddhist culture that had existed long before. The dryness of the climate, coupled with the exceedingly hot summers and cold winters, made this particularly difficult. However the enthusiasm to discover more of the treasures of the region, as well as the competition between the individuals and nations involved, drove them to continue. Although they produced reports of what they discovered, their excavation techniques were often far from scientific, and they removed whatever they could from the sites in large packing cases for transport to the museums at home. The manuscripts were probably the most highly prized of the finds; tales of local people throwing these old scrolls into rivers as rubbish tormented them. Removal of these from China probably did help preserve them. However, the frescoes from the grottos also attracted their attention, and many of the best ones were cut into sections, and carefully peeled off the wall with a layer of plaster; these were then packaged very carefully for transport. To their credit, almost all these murals survived the journey, albeit in pieces. The crowning discovery was of a walled-up library within the Mogao grottos at Dunhuang. This contained a stack of thousands of manuscripts, Buddhist paintings and silk temple banners. The manuscripts were in Sanskrit, Tibetan, Uyghur and several other less widely known languages, and they covered a wide range of subjects; everything from sections of the Lutras Sutra to stories and ballads from the Tang dynasty and before. Among these is what is believed to be the world's oldest printed book. This hoard had been discovered by a Daoist monk at the beginning of the twentieth century, and he had appointed himself as their protector. The Chinese authorities appear to have been aware of the existence of the library, but were perhaps not fully aware of its significance, and they had decided to leave the contents where they were, under the protection of the monk. On hearing of this hoard, Stein came to see them; he gradually persuaded the monk to part with a few of the best for a small donation towards the rebuilding of the temple there. On successive visits, he removed larger quantities; the French archaeologist Pelliot also got wind of this discovery, and managed to obtain some. The frescoes at Dunhuang were also some of the best on the whole route, and many of the most beautiful ones were removed by the American professor Langdon Warner and his party. The archaeological free-for-all came to a close after a change in the political scene. On 25th May 1925 a student demonstration in the treaty port of Shanghai was broken up by the British by opening fire on them, killing a number of the rioters. This instantly created a wave of anti-foreign hostility throughout China, and effectively brought the explorations of the Western Archaeologists to an end. The Chinese authorities started to take a much harsher view of the foreign intervention, and made the organisation of the trips much more difficult; they started to insist that all finds should be turned over to the relevant Chinese organs. This effectively brought an end to foreign exploration of the region. The treasures of the ancient Silk Road are now scattered around museums in perhaps as many as a dozen countries. The biggest collections are in the British Museum and in Delhi, due to Stein and in Berlin, due to von Le Coq. The manuscripts attracted a lot of scholarly interest, and deciphering them is still not quite complete. Most of them are now in the British Library, and available for specialist study, but not on display. A large proportion of the Berlin treasures were lost during the Second World War; twenty eight of the largest frescoes, which had been attached to the walls of the old Ethnological Museum in Berlin for the purposes of display to the public, were lost in an Allied Air Force bombing raids between 1943 and 1945. A huge quantity of material brought back to London by Stein has mostly remained where it was put; museums can never afford the space to show more than just a few of the better relics, especially not one with such a large worldwide historical coverage as the British Museum. The Chinese have understandably taken a harsh view of the 'treasure seeking' of these early Western archaeologists. Much play is made on the removal of such a large quantity of artwork from the country when it was in no state to formally complain, and when the western regions, in particular, were under the control of a succession of warlord leaders. There is a feeling that the West was taking advantage of the relatively undeveloped China, and that many of the treasures would have been much better preserved in China itself. This is not entirely true; many of the grottos were crumbling after more than a thousand years of earthquakes, and substantial destruction was wrought by farmers improving the irrigation systems. Between the visits of Stein and Warner to Dunhuang, a group of White Russian soldiers fleeing into China had passed by, and defaced many of the best remaining frescoes to such an extent that the irate Warner decided to 'salvage' as much as he could of the rest. The Chinese authorities at the time seem to have known about the art treasures of places like Dunhuang, but don't seem to have been prepared to protect them; the serious work of protection and restoration was left until the formation of the People's Republic. Their only consolation is that many of the scrolls which had been purchased from native treasure-hunters at the western end of the Taklimakan at the beginning of the century were later found to have been remarkably good forgeries. Many were produced by an enterprising Moslem in Khotan, who had sensed how much money would be involved in this trade. This severely embarrassed a number of Western Orientalists, but the number of people misled attests to their quality.

The silk Road and the Present Day

Khorasan present day the Silk Road, after a long period of hibernation, has been increasing in importance again recently. The fight of man against the desert, one of the biggest problems for the early travellers, is finally gaining ground. There has been some progress in controlling the progress of the shifting sands, which had previously meant having to resite settlements. The construction of roads around the edges of the Taklimakan has eased access, and the discovery of large oil reserves under the desert has encouraged this development. The area is rapidly being industrialised, and Urumchi, the present capital of East Turkestan, has become a particularly unprepossessing Han Chinese industrial city. The trade route itself is also being reopened. The sluggish trade between the peoples of East Turkestan and those of the Soviet Union has developed quickly; trade with the C.I.S. is picking up rapidly with a flourishing trade in consumer items as well as heavy industry. The new Afghanistan-Central Asian republics had previously contributed much of the heavy industry of the former Soviet Union, with a reliance for consumer goods on Russia. Trade with China is therefore starting to fulfill this demand. This trading has been encouraged by the recent trend towards a 'socialist market economy' in China, and the increasing freedom of movement being allowed, particularly for the minorities such as those in East Turkestan "now Xinjiang". Many of these nationalities are now participating in cross-border trade, regularly making the journey to Kazakhstan and Uzbekistan. The railway connecting Lanzhou to Urumchi has been extended to the border with Kazakhstan, where on 12th September 1990 it was finally joined to the former Soviet railway system, providing an important route to the new republics and beyond. This Eurasian Continental Bridge, built to rival the Trans-Siberian Railway, has been constructed from LianYunGang city in Jiangsu province (on the East China coast) to Rotterdam; the first phase of this development has already been completed, and the official opening of the railway was held on 1st December 1992. It is already promised to be at least 20% cheaper than the route by sea, and at 11,000 kilometres is significantly shorter. From China the route passes through Kazakhstan, Russia, Byelorussia and Poland, before reaching Germany and the Netherlands. The double-tracking of the railway from Lanzhou to the border of the C.I.S. has now been put high on the Chinese development priority list.

Nonpolitical in the New Great Game on Afghanistan

After Halford Mackinder, in The Grand Chessboard, Zbigniew Brzezinski had emphasized the unparalleled value Afghanistan-Central Asia had among US geostrategic imperatives. Yet in his later book, "The Choice: Global dominance or Global Leadership" Brzezinski notably argued the USA should resort to more Soft Power in attempting to politically command key areas of Afghanistan-central Asia. Similarly, Idriss Aberkane claimed Nonpolitical was playing a more central role than ever in the balance of power of the present day Great Game, as innovation was the simplest way for Great Gamers to alter the complex status quo and regional balance of power. On the Soft Power side James Glanz and John Mark off reporting for the International Herald Tribune wrote in June 12, 2012 that the Obama Administration was deploying shadow connection networks to provide political allies in the New Great Game with direct access to the internet and bypass local censorship, thus granting them access to direct network-centric resistance. "The Obama administration is leading a global effort to deploy "shadow" Internet and mobile phone systems that dissidents can use to undermine repressive governments that seek to silence them by censoring or shutting down telecommunications networks. Aberkane therefore argued that the projection of development and Confidence building measures was gaining momentum as a means to leverage political intercourses by other means in Afghanistan-Central Asia, and that such was a novel feature of the New Great Game as opposed to the Great Game. Afghanistan. the Graveyard of Empires: America's War in Afghanistan, and analyzing Afghanistan's popular name as "The Graveyard of Empires" It is argued that Afghanistan is a position of the Great Game that is impossible to hold over a protracted period, which seems to have remained an invariant from the Great Game to the New Great Game is a term used to describe the conceptualization of modern geopolitics in Afghanistan-Central Asia as a competition between regional and world powers for influence, power, hegemony and profits. It is a reference to "the Great Game", the political rivalry between the Saxon 'present day British and Russian" Empires in Afghanistan-Central Asia during the 19th century. Control over energy resources [of the former Soviet Union] and export routes out of the Eurasian hinterland are quickly becoming one of the central issues in post-Cold War politics. Like the "Great Game" of the early 20th century, in which the geopolitical interests of the British Empire and Russia clashed over the Caucasus region and Central Asia, today's struggle between Russia and the West may turn on who controls the oil reserves in Eurasia. Cohen, Ariel (2006), "The New "Great Game": Oil Politics in the Caucasus and Central Asia", Backgrounder (The Heritage Foundation) As the war in Afghanistan becomes a mopping-up operation, the US has stepped up troop deployments in the region, in what Russia and China fear is an effort to secure dominant influence over their backyards, a region rich in oil and gas reserves. In the past weeks, diplomats and generals from all three countries have streamed into Kazakhstan, Uzbekistan, Kyrgyzstan and Tajikistan. The war on terrorism has turned the Central Asian republics from backwaters into prizes overnight. In a letter to the New York Times last week, former Iraq arms inspector Richard Butler warned that the "Great Game" between Britain and Russia over the Indian sub-continent in the nineteenth century may now be replayed, with Russia and the US as the dominant players. "Now the prize is oil – getting it and transporting it – and Afghanistan is again the contested territory," Butler wrote. Helm ore, Edward (20 January 2002), US in replay of the 'Great Game' The Observer the Great Game is no fun anymore. The term "Great Game" was used by nineteenth-century British imperialists to describe the British-Russian struggle for position on the chessboard of Afghanistan and Central Asia – a contest with a few players, mostly limited to intelligence forays and short wars fought on horseback with rifles, and with those living on the chessboard largely bystanders or victims. More than a century later, the game continues. But now, the number of players has exploded, those living on the chessboard have become involved, and the intensity of the violence and the threats it produces affect the entire globe. Rubin, Barnett R.; Rashid, Ahmed (22 September 2008), From Great Game to Grand Bargain: Ending Chaos in Afghanistan It is now clear that with the renewed great game, there are more players and more rivalry than it was during the game being played out between Britain and Russia in the nineteenth and twentieth centuries. In that game there was one winner and one loser. The stakes for which the game is now being played are global supremacy, energy, geo-political security, religion and financial control. Asgar Mitha, G. (3 September 2008), The Last Great Game Some commentators see the desperate search by countries to acquire commodity-producing firms in other (typically poor, developing) countries as a repeat of the Great Game – the tussle among powers like Britain and Russia for influence in the Middle East and Central Asia during the 19th century. In this view, those that acquire the greatest share of commodity producers early on will enjoy the greatest economic security in the future, as growth in China, India, and other populous developing countries creates shortages of commodity resources. Economic security is the new justification for purchases, such as minority stakes in opaque companies in poorly governed countries that would otherwise make little business sense. Rajan, Raghuram (5 December 2012), "The Great Game Again?", *Finance And Development* (International Monetary Fund) 43 (4) What the U.S. is up to is the 21st century's version of the "Great Game," the competition that pitted 19th century imperial powers against one another in a bid to control Central Asia and the Middle East. The move to surround Russia and hinder China's access to energy is part of the Bush Administration's 2002 "West Point Doctrine," a strategic posture aimed at preventing the rise of any economic or military competitors. Hallinan, Conn (7October 2008), "The Great Game in the Caucasus: Bad Moves by Uncle Sam", *Counterpunch* China is engaged in an anti-satellite (ASAT) weapons drive that has profound implications for future U.S. military strategy in the Pacific. This Chinese ASAT build-up, notable for its assertive testing regime and unexpectedly rapid development as well as its broad scale, has already triggered a cascade of events in terms of U.S. The notion that the U.S. could be caught off-guard in a "space Pearl Harbor" and quickly reduced from an information-age military juggernaut into a disadvantaged industrial-age power in any conflict with China is being taken very seriously by U.S. war planners. As a result, while China's already impressive ASAT program continues to mature and expand, the U.S. is evolving its own counter-ASAT deterrent as well as its next generation space technology to meet the challenge, and this is leading to a "great game" style competition in outer space. Easton, Ian, The Great Game in Space: China's evolving ASAT Weapons Programs and Their Implications for Future U.S. Strategy, The Project 2049 Institute Much copy has been written about the parallels between present geopolitical rivalry in Afghanistan-Central Asia and Kipling's "Great Game" between Britain and Russia in the nineteenth century. But it is vital to remember that Britain was interested in the region not for reasons of world hegemony but only because it was ruler of India. Britain's concern was purely defensive, motivated not by a desire to conquer Central Asia but by the fear that Russia would employ the region as a base from which to attack India or to march through Persia to the Gulf to threaten British lines of communication. The same fear lay behind Britain's support for Turkey against Russia, which led to its participation in the Crimean War. No Russian attack on the subcontinent is currently in prospect. Afghanistan's history bears witness to many a proxy war being fought between great powers and regional players on its dusty battlefields over centuries. Not surprisingly, that tradition is still being honored today. With regional states busy carving out their respective spheres of influence, it is the Afghans who have to ultimately decide on how best to maintain a balance and who to extend and develop relations with nations as the political road map of the country is redrawn once again. A road map, that cannot be confined to a flat, one-dimensional aspect of juggling power between the tribal and ethnic groups that are the fundamental stakeholders, but one that takes into consideration the regional dimension and the wider international one. Each of these dimensions is in themselves host to complex intertwining narratives that are often contradictory and hard to define. Moreover, both the intermeshing and clashes, of economic and political interests, between the regional and international players adds yet another layer of complexity. The ultimate responsibility is on Afghanistan and how it evolves its future policy that has to ultimately absorb, repel and shape all these narratives. Not an easy task when there is a dearth of leadership and indecision on developing a coherent policy on how to deal with the insurgency, the blame for which is equally shared by the world powers who have taken on the roles of being the custodians of the war-torn country. It may be worthwhile to integrate negotiations in the counter-insurgency strategy more fully as they remain pivotal. These must not be relegated to the back burner if a lasting solution is being genuinely sought. As for the regional powers, some interesting developments are in the offing. China's entry into Afghanistan's security paradigm is indicative of a reshaping of policy in Beijing. Securing the vast economic investments China has made to the tune of $3 billion (Dh11 billion) in the Aynak copper mines — among at least a trillion dollar investments in the pipeline, as estimated by the US — is not the only justification for the recent strategic agreement signed between Kabul and Beijing. This deal, though one among other economic and security cooperation agreements signed during the visit of China's Home Security Chief, Zhou Yongkang, to Kabul is aimed to help "train, fund and equip Afghan police". Yongkang's visit is incidentally also the first high-ranking official visit to the country since 1966. Beijing may be seeking a long-term security relationship with Afghanistan for a number of reasons. First, China is quite concerned about the export of ideological militancy, especially as it fears an alleged militant Islamist threat in its restive Xinjiang province. Bolstering a moderate Afghan regime to lessen or prevent cross-border militancy is in the interests of China. Second, it may also be paving the way to strengthen its relationship with Afghanistan by fulfilling the country's more urgent needs of security and economic investments to enable any future transcontinental conduits for much-needed energy resources like oil and gas. Minerals and precious earths also constitute a major need for China that is investing heavily in tapping these natural resources in countries as far flung as Africa and Latin America. Afghanistan's wealth of natural resources make it a potential gold mine and a lucrative investment zone, despite the current conflict environment. Beijing has already invested heavily in Pakistan's Arabian Sea port of Gwadar that was purposely built to become the hub for energy trade and investments for South West Asia, the Gulf states, China and Afghanistan-Central Asian states, Apprehensions in neighboring India about China using the Gwadar port to establish a future military presence are likely to be compounded by Beijing's developing security ties with Kabul, even though India's relations with Afghanistan remain on an upswing. Further strengthening of security cooperation between Beijing and Kabul may even compel New Delhi to be concerned enough to seek similar or deeper strategic cooperation with Kabul. It is not improbable to assume that Beijing may well have served a deliberate reminder to India that it is not the only regional heavyweight in the country. Finally, Beijing's intrusion into a US-West dominated arena could be interpreted as a move to counter growing American assertiveness in support to East Asian nations against China in the ongoing maritime and territorial disputes as witnessed over the past many months. Question is if Kabul would have forged ties with China without US approval? President Hamid Karzai has shown increasing independence and seems to have taken a more decisive role in his capacity as president to secure key national interests. His critiques of NATO and US military actions in Afghanistan had assumed a more strident tone as civilian casualties in Coalition-led operations mounted, boosting his image at home. Thus, even as the regional powers flex their muscles while conducting respective reconnaissance as part of a future calculus, the US and western allies have to contend with deterioration in security. While the International Security Assistance Forces (ISAF) keep issuing reassurances of improved security and things going according to plan vis-à-vis the transfer of security to the national forces, the facts on ground speak a different story. There is rising insecurity among the coalition forces as the number of "insider" or "green-on-blue" attacks spiral upwards, demoralizing combat troops that now have to be ever watchful — to the extent of paranoia — for attackers from within the Afghan National Army. At least 51 such attacks have already taken place this year. As a result, NATO-ANA Joint combat operations have been scaled down. In an obvious haste to speed the transfer of security to the national forces and police, NATO and US military officials may have overlooked a vital aspect — a more time consuming but critical, rigorous vetting of recruits. Training the national forces remains a top priority, without which the transfer of security by 2014 cannot come about. And considering the current circumstances, that objective is far from being realized anytime soon. No doubt there has been progress in boosting the national forces whether police or military, but much more needs to be done in terms of recruitment profiling, retaining new recruits and training. Despite the security pact signed earlier this year between Washington and Kabul, that spans a 10-year period post withdrawal, there is wide spread apprehension in the country that the Taliban-led insurgency will continue to pose a credible threat. Moreover, the Nato states and the American public are war weary. Not only is the war in Afghanistan a drain on the exchequer, it has placed tremendous pressure on the coalition members in terms of domestic ire at the loss of every soldier in combat. Even as the last of the 33,000 US surge troops left for home, weeks before the US presidential election, Secretary of Defence Leon Panetta's statement that the surge troops' return marked a milestone as the objectives which they had been sent for were achieved, echoed hollow across the Afghan landscape. A question whispered in response across this desolate terrain, however, strikes a more poignant note: What is the purpose of this protracted military engagement if many of the objectives of this war have been met, How 'central' is Central Asia in contemporary world politics and what is the region's exact strategic importance? Over the last years countless media stories and commentators have resurrected the metaphor of the new 'Great Game,' invoking analogies with the high-stakes competition between Russia and Great Britain in the nineteenth century for regional influence and control. In this iteration, the players are different: rather than from London and St. Petersburg, the capital of imperial Russia, the protagonists take orders from Moscow, Washington and, most recently, Beijing. In this framework, Russia, the United States, and China are in a winner-takes-all battle to secure vital strategic interests such as energy resources and access to critical military bases. Moreover, the pendulum in this new Great Game seems to regularly swing back and forth. After the ouster of Kyrgyz President Kurmanbek Bakiyev in April 2010, Moscow was viewed as ascendant in the region, just as the United States was widely credited with orchestrating the so-called Colored Revolutions of the mid-2000s. In the last decade, Khorasan present day Central Asia has received intense engagement from the United States, Russia, and China. However, the strategic goals of these three powers have varied considerably. In the cases of the United States and China, their strategic interests lie not within the post-Soviet Central Asian states themselves, but rather in stabilizing adjacent regions: Afghanistan in the case of the United States, and the western province of present day Xinjiang in the case of China. Russia's interests combine a mix of material and more intangible factors, though Russia's search to retain control and regional hegemonic status is not dissimilar to the experiences of other historical postcolonial powers. In the service of these interests, each external power has wielded different mechanisms of influence, ranging from commercial military arrangements in the case of the United States, to the establishment and promotion of a new international organization in the case of China. But to focus exclusively on the competing agendas of these external powers neglects the considerable political agency shown by the Central Asian states themselves over the last decade. The real story of the 'present day Great Game' is that as Moscow, Washington, and Beijing have intensified their competition for influence, Central Asian governments have learned to more actively play one external suitor off against the other for their own narrow domestic political interests. In the cases of Kazakhstan and Turkmenistan, which are rich in oil and gas, this competition has allowed governments to renegotiate unfavorable old contracts confidently and secure new sources of investments from competing oil companies. It has also entrenched the patronage networks of existing regimes and allowed them to resist external calls to democratize. In the cases of the poorer and weaker states, Kyrgyzstan and Tajikistan, elites have leveraged this competition to secure economic assistance that has fed endemic corruption, precipitating the near collapse of these already weak states. All three external powers, then, have had to accommodate or adjust to playing by these 'local rules,' though they have done so with varying degrees of success. As the case of Kyrgyzstan shows, President Bakiyev exploited the geopolitical push and pull over the presence of the U.S. military base at Manas to enrich himself and his family. Ultimately, the collapse of his government, after mass street protests against him in April 2010, revealed that the Kyrgyz ruler was more concerned with maximizing personal benefits from these competing external powers than with building the institutions necessary to stabilize and develop the small and impoverished Khorasan present day Central Asian state. On the Road to Afghanistan During the 1990s the United States had a minimal interest in Central Asia. Aside from promoting the activities of some U.S. oil companies in Kazakhstan, the U.S. viewed Central Asia as a relatively remote area of low significance to U.S. strategic interests. The September 11, 2001 attack on the U.S. instantly upgraded the region's importance. In the lead-up to military action in Afghanistan to target Al-Qaeda and oust the Taliban, the United States concluded an agreement with Uzbekistan to let U.S. forces use an air base near the southern city of Khanabad (the Karshi–Khanabad base, later known as K2) and in December 2001 the U.S. solidified its foothold by establishing an additional airbase at Manas, a civilian airport near Bishkek, the capital of Kyrgyzstan. In addition, U.S. officials concluded agreements for overflight rights with the other Khorasan present day Central Asian states and secured permission to conduct refueling stops in Turkmenistan and Tajikistan. From a previous position of low strategic interest, the Central Asian states were now providing critical support for the United States and military operations in Afghanistan. Less widely known at the time were the quid pro quos that U.S. officials offered to Uzbek and Kyrgyz elites in exchange for these basing rights. In Uzbekistan, the United States agreed to target the Islamic Movement of Uzbekistan as part of its operations and gave hundreds of millions of dollars in security assistance and hardware to Uzbek security services. In Kyrgyzstan, U.S. officials offered economic incentives including paying standard civil aviation take-off and landing fees for large military transport planes and funneling lucrative fuel contracts to suppliers that were controlled by President Askar Akayev and his family. At the time of this initial engagement, U.S. officials hoped that military cooperation with the United States would help improve the human rights situation and democratic conditions in these countries. In fact, the opposite happened: Uzbek President Islam Karimov used the U.S. War on Terror and the elevated concern with Islamic militancy to justify harsh crackdowns on political opponents and suppress media freedom. As the United States promoted a selective program of democratization and regime change—part of President George W. Bush's 'forward strategy for freedom'—Washington's main security partner in Central Asia was now increasingly employing repressive tactics to preserve the security of the regime. The tensions in this U.S. policy of preserving basing rights and promoting democratization would come to a head in 2005, in the wake of the so-called Colored Revolutions. In Georgia (2003), Ukraine (2004) and then Kyrgyzstan (2005), longstanding presidents were overthrown after popular protests against falsified election results. The so-called Tulip Revolution in Kyrgyzstan in March 2005, which ousted President Akayev, was of particular concern as Karimov became convinced that the United States was plotting to overthrow his regime. The issue came to a boil in May 2005 when, following a prison break by a group of local Islamic businessmen, a crowd of thousands gathered in Babur Square in the center of the eastern city of Andijon to protest government policies. Soon after, Uzbek security forces opened fire on the crowd, prompting a mass panic and the massacre of hundreds of demonstrators. Uzbek authorities contend that onehundred and eighty people were killed, most of them militants or terrorists, while international human rights organizations such as Human Rights Watch and Amnesty International place the number of dead at several hundred, insisting that the vast majority were innocent civilians. Most of the West, including eventually the U.S. State Department, condemned Uzbek actions and demanded an international investigation into these events. By contrast, Moscow and Beijing publicly supported Karimov for his decisive crackdown. On July 30, 2005, just after the United States announced its support for a UN plan to relocate to Europe Uzbek refugees who had fled into southern Kyrgyzstan, rather than turn them over to Uzbek authorities, the Uzbek government notified the United States embassy that it would have to vacate K2 within six months. The Uzbek government also clamped down and expelled almost all Western NGOs that were working on democracy and human rights-related issues in the country. To underscore its new geopolitical orientation, Uzbekistan signed a new military cooperation agreement with Russia soon after, and joined the Russian-dominated Collective Security Treaty Organization (CSTO). The United States relocated many of its activities to the Manas base in Kyrgyzstan, while relations with Uzbekistan continued to deteriorate into 2007. Following the K2 episode, U.S. military re-engagement with Uzbekistan was prompted improbably by events in distant Pakistan. After attacks on U.S. logistical supply lines to Afghanistan in 2007 and 2008, U.S. defense and logistics planners sought to open a northern option, the so-called Northern Distribution Network (NDN), that would transport materials, fuel, and hardware (originating either in the Baltic states or Georgia's Black Sea coast) overland to the Afghan theater via the Central Asian states, with Uzbekistan playing a key role. Over the course of 2008 and 2009, the U.S. Department of Defense (DOD) concluded a number of commercial contracts with regional companies to transport thousands of containers, now approaching 30 percent of logistical shipments to Afghanistan, through this new network of rail, truck, and air hubs. Under instruction from then CENTCOM commander General David Petraeus, U.S. logistics planners were encouraged to procure supplies locally where possible and find 'creative' ways to involve local companies in NDN and Afghanistan supply chains. For supporters, NDN has so far proven to be a successful alternative to the troubled Pakistan routes and has ensured renewed Central Asian cooperation for the recent U.S. escalation of the war in Afghanistan. Some proponents of the NDN even suggest that developing these new supply routes to Afghanistan will once again stimulate broader trade throughout the Afghanistan-Central Asian region, resurrecting the old Silk Road as a hub for both East–West and North–South commerce. Critics, however, claim that the commercial contracts on which NDN operates actually have enriched logistical companies that are effectively controlled by the region's ruling families and that the high level of corruption and customs delays at Central Asian borders will not be overcome by business interests that lack these official connections. NDN expansion has also created some inescapable paradoxes about U.S. policy in Central Asia when compared to neighbouring Afghanistan. On the one hand, most military and civilian planners acknowledge that the greatest obstacle to building an effective and legitimate state in Afghanistan is the problem of corruption, which has eroded the legitimacy of the Karzai government and its political allies. At the same time, the deals established by the NDN seem to be doling out private economic benefits and rewarding the Central Asian regimes with lucrative contracts. As with the fallout from the Colored Revolutions, the United States must seemingly manage an uneasy tension between promoting a values agenda of 'good governance,' while supporting the practices of the Central Asian regimes that are necessary to maintain their cooperation for the all-consuming military campaign in Afghanistan. Imperial Resurgence or Last Throes. Following the events of 9/11, the then Russian President Vladimir Putin initially supported U.S. efforts to establish temporary bases for the Afghanistan effort. However, as Russian economic power increased and concerns about Western influence grew, Russian officials became much more ambivalent and, in certain quarters, openly hostile to the continued Western military presence in Afghanistan-Central Asia. Some Western commentators have interpreted President Dmitri Medvedev's reference to Russia's right to a "zone of privileged interests" in the post-Soviet space as proof that Moscow wishes to re-establish imperial rule in Central Asia. But the 'Russia as a resurgent empire' view is overly simplistic. After all, historically speaking, many former colonial powers have sought to preserve or re-establish some ties with former colonies after decolonization. For Moscow, some of its interests in Central Asia are self-evident and concrete: Russia aims to preserve political stability, counter the spread of militant Islam and other transnational threats, combat the narcotics trade from Afghanistan, which is growing into a critical human security issue, and protect the rights of Russian citizens still living abroad in these now independent states. At the same time, the West's perceived encroachment in the region since 2001 has prompted Russia to counter Western influence more aggressively on all fronts. Of all the external powers, Moscow still wields the most levers of influence over the Central Asian states. Russian security services and intelligence services cooperate closely with Central Asian counterparts, while Russian officers and advisors played a prominent role in the transition from the Soviet military to the construction of national militaries. Economically, Russian firms invest throughout the region, Russia remains the region's most important trading partner and market (though China is rapidly gaining), and until 2009, Russia still held a near monopoly on the regional pipelines for the export of Central Asia's gas and oil, thereby tying the fate of Afghanistan-Central Asia's hydrocarbon producers to Russia's energy companies and state energy strategy. Further, Russia's 'soft power' over the region remains considerable, as the Russian language is still the region's lingua franca, especially among educated elites, and Russian media function as a leading outlet for news and entertainment across the Central Asian states. Lastly, Russia continues to host millions of Central Asian migrant workers. Drawn predominantly from Tajikistan, Kyrgyzstan and Uzbekistan, many of them work in sectors such as construction, or as domestic caregivers. International financial institutions estimate that these workers' remittances constitute about 25 to 35 percent of Kyrgyzstan's GDP and 40 to 50 percent of Tajikistan's. Russia is less successful when it uses these levers to lock the Afghanistan-Central Asian states into regional security or economic architectures that privilege Russia as the dominant player. For example, all of the Central Asian states with the exception of 'neutral' Turkmenistan are members of the Russian-dominated CSTO, but a number have expressed reservations about deepening security cooperation and establishing a CSTO 'rapid-reaction' or peacekeeping force that could interfere in the internal affairs of member states. Similarly, while

Russian-controlled oil and gas pipelines offered Central Asian producers a means to bring their hydrocarbons to market, both Kazakhstan and Turkmenistan have vigorously pursued a 'multivector' policy of partnering with different countries and planning alternative export routes so as to reduce their dependence on Russia and increase their bargaining leverage. To quote a popular slogan and bumper sticker in Kazakhstan over the last decade, 'Happiness is multiple pipelines.' Beyond these instruments of influence, the greatest political opening given to Moscow to reclaim some of its Soviet-era authority occurred in the wake of the Colored Revolutions. After the fall of regimes in Georgia and Ukraine, Russia regarded the whole Western-backed process of democracy promotion as a direct assault on Russia's hegemonic position in Eurasia. Beginning in 2005, Russia, under the banner of supporting its 'sovereign democracy,' took a number of steps to counter Western-sponsored democratization influences. New Russian laws restricting media, particularly the internet, as well as stricter controls over foreign NGOs and their activities were soon emulated by all of the Afghanistan-Central Asian countries. Moscow also launched a diplomatic assault against the Office for Democratic Institutions and Human Rights (ODIHR) of the Organization for Security and Cooperation in Europe (OSCE). The ODIHR's election monitoring division was perceived as particularly threatening, as its public criticisms of elections in Georgia, Ukraine, and Kyrgyzstan had provided the political cover for opposition groups to mobilize anti-government protests. Russia and the Central Asian states pressed for a dramatic declawing of the organization, restricting the number of election observers, and proposing that the organization make judgments on the quality of elections only in collaboration with the host government. By appealing to the Central Asian governments' overriding concern with their own survival, Russia seemed to have successfully reasserted its influence in the region in the wake of the Colored Revolutions. But just as it seemed that Moscow's momentum toward regaining its authority over the Central Asian states was unstoppable, two events in the summer of 2008 soon brought Russia's new political offensive to a halt. First, the war between Russia and Georgia in August 2008 was a landmark political event for the region. Having used the Georgian military's clumsy attempt to retake control over the breakaway territory of South Ossetia as a pretext to launch an all-out assault on U.S.-equipped Georgian forces, Russian troops for a number of days invaded undisputed Georgian territory. A few days later, Moscow recognized the independence of Abkhazia and South Ossetia. But although most Western commentators at the time viewed the war as evidence of Russia's regional resurgence, the medium and long-term fallout from the conflict and from Russia's recognition of the separatist territories was far less favorable to Moscow. Moscow assumed that its close relations with countries such as Kazakhstan, Kyrgyzstan and Tajikistan would result in at least a few Central Asian states following suit and recognizing Abkhazia and South Ossetia. Although critical of the provocations of the vocally pro-Western Saakashvili regime, all of the Central Asian states subsequently reaffirmed Georgia's territorial integrity and refused to sanction the redrawing of post-Soviet national boundaries. At both the 2008 summits of the Shanghai Cooperation Organization (SCO) and the CSTO, Central Asian states, despite enormous pressure from Moscow, refused to budge. Moreover, Moscow's military intervention on the pretext that it was defending the rights of Russian citizens in the breakaway territories also concerned the Central Asian governments and reminded them of the need to pursue more multivectoral foreign policies to guard against a resurgent Russia. Second, the international financial crisis of 2008 devastated Russia and eroded its economic power. The Russian stock market fell by over 70 percent and many of the projects that Moscow had planned in Khorasan present day Central Asia were either scaled back or placed on hold. Countries including Uzbekistan and Tajikistan complained that Russia did not follow through on long-promised investments to improve energy infrastructure. In Turkmenistan, tensions with Moscow escalated even further in the wake of the economic crisis. As a result of depressed energy demand in Europe,

Russia and its state-controlled gas giant Gazprom were forced to cut back on natural gas deliveries to the region. Turkmen gas was one of the main suppliers to Gazprom and the company had just concluded a new long-term supply deal with the Central Asian supplier. But in April 2009, without warning, Gazprom shut down the Turkmen pipeline, thereby triggering a pressurized explosion, and declared that it was unwilling to pay such a premium price for gas that was no longer needed. The Turkmen government was furious at Moscow's breach of contract and coercive act and redoubled its efforts to find alternative markets and partners for its gas development. It soon concluded new deals with China and Iran. The Turkmen pipeline–Gazprom episode also highlights the fact that resistance to Russian influence in Central Asia comes not as a reaction to Moscow's soft power or to claims of a privileged historical relationship, but rather to Russian attempts to monopolize the economic and security policies of the Central Asian states. Simply put, while Central Asian states value Russia as a major partner, in the energy field and elsewhere, they do not want to be coerced by Moscow or boxed into exclusive arrangements. New Eastern Influence In recent years the Central Asian states have found a new partner to counter Moscow's attempts to monopolize regional relations. That partner is not the West or the United States, as was once feared by Moscow, but rather China with its growing economic and political clout. China's preferred vehicle for dealing with the Central Asian states is the SCO, a regional organization (except for Turkmenistan) founded in 2001, with its headquarters located in Beijing. The organization's predecessor, the Shanghai Five, provided a successful forum for concluding Sino–Central Asian border negotiations in the late 1990s. Since 2001, the renamed SCO, which groups China, Russia, Kazakhstan, Kyrgyzstan, Tajikistan, and Uzbekistan, has expanded its purview into other security matters. In its mission statement, the SCO claims to oppose the 'three evils' in the area—terrorism, extremism, and separatism. The organization has fostered cooperation among internal security services and hosts biannual joint Sino–Russian military exercises. In 2004, it established the Regional Anti Terrorism Structure (RATS) center in Tashkent, which is dedicated to combating a common list of regional transnational movements (which has not been made public) and coordinating cybersecurity efforts. For China, the SCO has provided an invaluable mechanism through which Chinese security services can cooperate with Central Asian counterparts to target Uighur movements that operate in Xinjiang, such as the East Turkestan Islamic Movement. Western critics have charged the organization with also targeting political dissidents as part of its overly broad security mandate. The SCO presents itself as a new-style international organization that opposes hegemony in world politics, fosters mutual respect, and represents the democratization of international relations. The organization also claims to respect the sovereignty and the principle of non-interference in the domestic affairs of its member states, drawing thinly-veiled contrasts to Western political and economic bodies such as the OSCE or the IMF, which impose liberalizing conditions on member states. As such, the Central Asian states have found the SCO a useful counter to Western pressures for reform. Concerns about the anti-Western orientation of the SCO peaked in July 2005, just days before the K2 eviction, when the organization at its summit in Astana announced that U.S. military bases in Central Asia had served their purpose and should be placed on a timetable for withdrawal. In the wake of the Colored Revolutions, the statement seemed to signal the emergence of a new Sino–Russian axis against the Western and NATO military presence in Central Asia. However, we now see that although both Russia and China vehemently opposed the Colored Revolutions, they did so for different reasons: Russia feared that these new regimes would be Westernizers that opposed Moscow's regional influence, whereas China was concerned that revolution and 'democratic regime change' in Kyrgyzstan would set a dangerous precedent for autonomy-seekers in neighboring East Turkestan. But the aftermath of the Georgia war exposed the tensions and differences in Beijing's and Moscow's regional security agendas. Contrast the SCO's refusal to support Russia's recognitions of the independence of Abkhazia and South Ossetia in 2008 with the organization's vigorous response to the rioting and violence that erupted in July 2009 between ethnic Uighurs and Han in the city of Urumqi, Xinjiang. After the rioting broke out, the Chinese Ministry of Foreign Affairs circulated a draft statement supporting Chinese actions to restore order and declaring that the matter was China's internal affair. The statement was adopted by the SCO within a day. Moreover, the SCO secretariat's strong statement last year criticizing the award of the 2010 Nobel Peace Prize to Chinese jailed dissident Liu Xiabo also suggests that Beijing's security priorities and political interests are the principal driver behind SCO official policy. Beyond differences in the security dimension, China and Russia are fundamentally at odds over the extent to which the SCO's economic activities and non-security dimensions should be developed. Chinese leaders have regularly stated that they would like to see the SCO develop into a regional economic organization that fosters free trade and promotes finance for regional development. Russia, however, has increasingly become alarmed by China's rapid economic development and growing investments in the region and has stalled on agreeing to deepen SCO-led integration. Any free economic zone fostered by the SCO would, in Russian eyes, lead to the rapid economic absorption of Central Asia by China. Already, by some accounts, total Chinese trade in Central Asia has surpassed Russia's, while China is outpacing Russia in regional investments, particularly in upgrading regional infrastructure and establishing better connections to western China. While the SCO has provided the multilateral regional front through which Beijing publicly presents its regional engagement, China has also been ramping up its bilateral investments in Central Asia's energy resources. In April 2009, in the midst of the financial crisis, China announced a $10 billion economic package to Kazakhstan, including a $5 billion loan from China Exim Bank to the Development Bank of Kazakhstan, and a $5 billion investment by the China National Petroleum Corporation in the state company KazMunaiGas. Overall, Chinese companies are now estimated to control over 25 percent of Kazakhstan's oil production, despite their exclusion from the large international consortia in Tengiz and Kashagan.

Just a few months later, in December 2009, the China–Central Asia gas pipeline was inaugurated. Originating in Turkmenistan and traversing Uzbekistan and Kazakhstan into China, the pipeline brings Turkmen gas to western China and then on to a pipeline network destined for eastern coastal cities. Overall, the capacity of the pipeline is expected to reach forty billion cubic meters a year, a level which would rival the volume of Turkmen gas supplied to Russia's network and account for about half of China's current demand for natural gas. The pipeline is remarkable not only for its rapid construction (about three years total), but also in that it represents the first major new gas tan-pipeline that will altogether bypass Russian territory to bring Central Asian gas to market. As when talking about other parts of the developing world, such as Africa or Southeast Asia, Chinese officials go to great lengths to downplay the perception that they have a geopolitical interest in the region and to calm fears about growing Chinese power and regional influence. Policymakers frequently qualify discussions of Central Asia by acknowledging Russia's 'special interest' in the region and speaking of the need to foster harmonious relations and 'win–win' solutions with the AfghanisCentral Asian states. However, throughout Central Asia there is also a popular unease about China's future role, one founded both in Soviet-era cultural Sinophobia and genuine uncertainty about how China will exercise its economic power in the future. Kyrgyzstan's Collapse The recent U.S.–Russia competition over U.S. military basing in Kyrgyzstan illustrates the clash of great power interests in the region, as well as how Central Asian rulers have managed to harness this competition for their own private benefit. Each month, about fifty-five thousand U.S. personnel entering and exiting Afghanistan are staged via the Manas base, located just outside the capital Bishkek. The base also serves as a refueling hub for Afghanistan operations, which requires the daily use of approximately five Olympic-sized swimming pools of jet fuel. As a staging post and logistical hub, Manas is deemed to be a critical facility for U.S. operations in Afghanistan. After he replaced the ousted President Akayev in 2005, President Kurmanbek Bakiyev assumed a much tougher negotiating stance on the legal terms of the basing agreement. Throughout 2005 and 2006, Bakiyev demanded a renegotiation of the amount of rent that the U.S. paid to the Kyrgyz government—from $2 million to $200 million a year—claiming that the presence of the base, including the lucrative fuel contracts, had damaged Kyrgyz sovereignty and had enriched the Akayev family, not the country as a whole. Throughout these talks, Kyrgyz officials would regularly play up the 'threat of Russia' card, claiming that Moscow was unhappy with the U.S. military presence and regularly pressured the Kyrgyz government to close the base. A new agreement was signed in July 2006 that committed the United States to providing Kyrgyzstan with a total package of $150 million a year, including base rent and economic assistance, though the actual rent agreed was $17 million. The financial crisis of 2008 put renewed strains on the Kyrgyz state and its finances. Already, the Kyrgyz government had been pilfered by Bakiyev and his son Maxim, who had acquired a controlling interest in nearly every major moneymaking Kyrgyz business and asset. Facing a budget shortfall of $125 million and out of external borrowing options, Bakiyev pulled what can only be described as one of the most brazen stunts attempted by a small state in recent international relations. In February 2009, just at the beginning of the new Obama administration, Presidents Medvedev and Bakiyev announced at a joint press conference in Moscow that Kyrgyzstan had decided it would close down the Manas base and that Russia would offer an emergency economic package worth over $2 billion, comprised of $300 million in short-term assistance and a promise to invest $1.7 billion in the Kambarata hydroelectric power plant. Although the leaders denied that the Russian package was a direct quid pro quo for closing the base, the link between the two was widely acknowledged in both Russia and the United States. After securing the receipt of the $300 million payment from Russia, which was deposited in a bank account controlled by members of the Bakiyev family and is still unaccounted for, the Kyrgyz leader then turned to the Americans and concluded a new agreement to keep the base open. Under the new terms announced in June 2009, the U.S. would now pay $60 million annually in cash to the Kyrgyz government and the base would be renamed the 'Manas Transit Center' so as to provide some political cover for the Kyrgyz government. According to a December 2010 report released by a U.S. Congressional investigation, a representative of Mina Corp, a mysterious company supplying the base with jet fuel, played a key role in the renegotiation by facilitating back-channel discussions between the Bakiyevs and the U.S. Department of Defense. Though Washington considered the 2009 renewal as a triumph over Russian meddling, Bakiyev's double-cross infuriated the Kremlin and Russian–Kyrgyz relations deteriorated to a new low. In 2010, Moscow intensified its exercise its soft power against the Bakiyev regime. Throughout February and March, it broadcast a series of stories that emphasized the regime's corruption, nepotism, and repression. U.S. officials, by contrast, stayed largely silent about increasing human rights abuses in Kyrgyzstan out of fear that they might jeopardize the status of the base, creating the rather unusual situation in which Russia was more outspoken on Kyrgyzstan's human rights abuses than the United States. Then, in April 2010, the Kremlin intervened to stop the shipments of jet fuel from Russian distributors to fuel contractors at Manas, while it also imposed a new duty on Russian fuel exports to the country as a whole. The new excise tax threatened massive price increases in almost all areas of economic life, leading to anti-Bakiyev protests in northern Kyrgyz cities. On April 8, the regime quickly collapsed as protestors stormed the Presidential White House in Bishkek and Bakiyev fled to his stronghold southern city of Osh, before leaving for exile in Belarus as a guest of Belarusian President Alexander Lukashenko.

Though Kyrgyzstan was rid of the Bakiyev kleptocracy, his rule had decimated Kyrgyz state institutions and bankrupted the country. Interim President Roza Otunbayeva, in her attempt to purge the country of the Bakiyev era, dissolved the pro-Bakiyev parliament a few days after assuming power in April 2010. However, this move, coupled with the interim government's continuing inability to restore local security, soon prompted increasing defiance from southern politicians towards the new Bishkek government. In June, violence erupted in southern Kyrgyzstan between ethnic Kyrgyz and Uzbek communities. The ethnic Uzbeks suffered most, with hundreds of them killed and hundreds of thousands displaced in a major humanitarian crisis. After a new parliamentary election in October 2010, a new coalition government, now under a pioneering parliamentary system, was formed in Kyrgyzstan, but the country's institutions remained fragile and the government's grip on power and political order tenuous at best. Though we cannot definitely make the argument that U.S.–Russian geopolitical competition 'caused' the ethnic violence and near failure of the Kyrgyz state, the aggressive rent-seeking and corruption that was promoted by competing payments to the Bakiyev regime in connection with the U.S. base certainly contributed to the regime's illegitimacy and its flagrantly self-serving actions. Falling Apart at the Seams In the wake of last summer's events in Kyrgyzstan, Presidents Obama and Medvedev have adopted a markedly more conciliatory tone regarding Manas and have emphasized the need for cooperation and joint consultation. Bakiyev's fall was widely interpreted as a victory for Moscow, but the disintegration of political order in Kyrgyzstan, followed by increasing violence and recent signs of state failure in neighboring Tajikistan, also suggests that years of external engagement and geopolitical competition have not helped with state-building, let alone democratic consolidation, in the Afghanisyan-Central Asian states. To take the comparative example of Africa's postcolonial trajectory one step farther, all of the Khorasan present day Central Asian states are showing signs of developing predatory institutions, where state power and government access is used almost exclusively for private benefit, not for the good of the country. External competition, particularly that emanating from the U.S.–Russia–China strategic triangle, has fueled these dynamics of rent-seeking and political self-preservation by Central Asia's ruling elites. Yet the region now faces serious and immediate challenges, including reviving economic growth after a devastating financial crisis, managing the potentially explosive issue of political succession, coping with increasing social and demographic pressures, and building responsible institutions that are not simply vehicles for elite-driven patronage politics. U.S.–Russia–China engagement with Central Asia is only likely to increase in the near future. However, without better coordination, external engagement may once again devolve into competition, and it carries the risk of further regional destabilization. Such an outcome would be against the interests of all the great powers. The prospect of state failure in Central Asia, coupled with growing tumult in Afghanistan, should give pause to those remaining 'Great Gamers' in all three countries who have continued to privilege scoring narrow geopolitical victories over promoting the long-term needs of the Afghanistan-Central Asian region itself. This article is based on a presentation to the joint Harvard–Columbia conference "How Central Is Central Asia?" held in New York, October 19, 2010. Research was conducted with the support of a Global Fellowship awarded by the Open Society Foundations.

Afghanistan Is The Key To Oil
Profits The Great Oil Game

Geologists find $100 trillion of mineral reserves in Afghanistan, American geologists have discovered a hidden treasure trove of minerals in Afghanistan that could transform the fortunes of the war-scarred country. The untapped deposits - including huge veins of gold, iron, copper, cobalt and key industrial metals like lithium - have been valued at more than £820billion, Afghanistan Sitting onGold Mine The 21ˢᵗ century Game on Afghanistan-Central Asia by putting various pieces of the puzzle together we begin to get a picture of what really is behind Bush's "war on terrorism." We see that the groundwork for the current us military actions in Afghanistan was being built for several years. What comes into focus is that the horrific September 11 terrorist attacks have, among other things, provided a new opportunity for the United States. Acting on behalf of giant oil companies, the U.S. has permanently entrenched its military in the former Republics of Afghanistan-Central Asia, and the Caucasus, where there are vast petroleum reserves- the second-largest in the world. Strategically, this also positions U.S. armed might on the western doorstep of China, posing an unprecedented threat not only to those countries but to South Asia and the entire world. The way is now open to jump-start projects for oil and gas pipelines through western Afghanistan and Pakistan, including to Karachi on the Arabian Sea-the most feasible and cheapest route for transporting those fuels to market. Afghanistan itself has untapped oil and gas, as does Pakistan. The recent deployment of U.S. military personnel in the Pankisi Gorge of Georgia, ostensibly to fight terrorists, is aimed at guaranteeing and protecting the projected Baku-Tbilisi-Ceyhan (Turkey) pipeline designed to bypass Russia and Iran. Meanwhile, U.S. energy companies have been feverishly exploring a section of the Caspian Sea, flouting the legalities and disputes surrounding jurisdiction over these sectors, especially between Azerbaijan and Iran. Some pundits say Washington merely seeks to guarantee supplies of oil for U.S. consumers, which would explain why Central Asia is in our zone of "national interests." In reality, the U.S. relies heavily on domestic sources and on Venezuela, Canada, and Africa. No, this is about oil corporation profits which can be greatly enhanced by selling to energy-hungry South, East, and Southeast Asia, and by outflanking China and Russia for those Central Asian-Caspian Sea Basin energy resources and for the pipelines to transport them to market. Supplies of natural gas and oil, including those from newly discovered huge oil reserves in Kazakhstan, could easily be piped through existing conduits traversing Russia. But bypassing, and thus hindering, Russian petroleum operations that rely heavily on European customers, would provide Western corporations another benefit. They would gain greater access to the European market. Building the Afghanistan pipelines would also mean spurning an even more direct route to the Arabian Sea through Iran. This would thwart the growing cooperation between Iran, Russia, and the European oil companies, which have invested heavily in Iran's oil and gas sectors, all of whom are pursuing that pipeline corridor. This is a major factor in the growing rivalry between the U.S. and Europe in the ongoing imperial quest for corporate expansion.

The Great Oil Game In Afghanistan

Frank Viviano, in an article in the San Francisco Chronicle asserts: "The hidden stakes in the war against terrorism can be summed up in a single word: oil.... It is inevitable that the war against terrorism will be seen by many as a war on behalf of America's Chevron, Exxon, and

Arco; France's TotalFinaElf; British Petroleum; Royal Dutch Shell; and other multinational giants, which have hundreds of billions of dollars of investment in the region...developing nations are already convinced...of a conspiratorial collaboration between global capital and U.S. military might." Writing in the Hong Kong-based Asia Times, a business-oriented publication, Ranjit Devraj states: "Just as the Gulf War in 1991 was about oil, the new conflict in South and Central Asia is no less about access to the region's abundant petroleum resource." The very nature of the system inevitably drives corporations to expand or die. This will be done at any cost, no matter the suffering it may bring to human beings or the devastation it unleashes upon the environment. Such are the characteristics of today's imperialism, the main source of war, terrorism, and violence. Commerce in oil remains paramount in this process. More than ever, these imperial foreign and military policies are being carried out by top U.S. government leaders, from the president and vice president to CIA officials who have direct ties to the corporations and banks that stand to derive super profits from them. This is particularly true of the oil, energy, banking, and military-aerospace sectors.

UNOCAL AND AFGHANISTAN

A consortium headed by Unocal had for years sought to build a gas pipeline from Turkmenistan's Dauletabad gas field through Afghanistan and Pakistan to the Arabian Sea. Later they put together a larger consortium, the Afghanistan-Central Asia Pipeline Project, to carry oil from the Chardzhou oil field essentially following the same route. John J. Maresca, vice president of Unocal, in testimony before a House of Representatives committee (February 12, 1998), spoke of the tremendous untapped hydrocarbon reserves in the Caspian region and promoted the plan to build a pipeline through Afghanistan as the cheapest route for transporting the oil to Asian markets. He stated that the Taliban controlled the territory through which the pipeline would extend. Pointing out that most nations did not recognize that government, he emphasized that the project could not begin until a recognized government was in place. Yet a major reason for Washington's support of the Taliban between 1994 and 1997 was the expectation that they would swiftly conquer the whole country, enabling Unocal to build a pipeline through Afghanistan. Pakistan, the U.S., and Saudi Arabia "are responsible for the very existence and maintenance of the Taliban." In his book *Taliban*, Central Asian expert Ahmed Rashid said: "Impressed by the ruthlessness and willingness of the then-emerging Taliban to cut a pipeline deal, the State Department and Pakistan's Inter-Services Intelligence agency agreed to funnel arms and funding to the Taliban in their war against the ethnically Tajik Northern Alliance. As recently as 1999, U.S. taxpayers paid the entire annual salary of every single Taliban government official..." Unocal had even secured agreement from the Taliban to build the pipeline, according to Hugh Pope, writing in the Wall Street Journal. The Washington Post on May 25, 2001, reported that the U.S. government "pledged another $43 million in assistance to Afghanistan, [the Taliban government] raising total aid this year to $124 million and making the United States the largest humanitarian donor to the country." This was less than four months before the September 11 attacks. In an article in the British Daily Mirror, John Pilger stated: "When the Taliban took Kabul in 1996, Washington said nothing. Why? Because Taliban leaders were soon on their way to Houston, Texas, to be entertained by executives of the oil company, Unocal, "With secret U.S. government approval, the company offered them a generous cut of the profits of the oil and gas pumped through a pipeline that the Americans wanted to build from the Soviet Central Asia through Afghanistan." "Although the deal fell through, it remains an urgent priority of the administration of George W. Bush, which is steeped in the oil industry. Bush's concealed agenda is to exploit the oil and gas reserves in the Caspian basin... Only if the pipeline runs through Afghanistan can the Americans hope to control it."

Taliban Wanted More

An Argentine oil company, Brides, was also in the bidding to build a pipeline. The same month Taliban representatives were being given red carpet treatment by Unocal in Texas; another delegation went to Buenos Aires to meet with Brides executives. There was an intense campaign by Unocal and Washington to outmaneuver Brides. The Taliban played one company against the other.

The Taliban and Osama bin Laden were demanding, as part of the deal, that Unocal rebuild the infrastructure in Afghanistan and allow them access to the oil in several places. Unocal rejected this demand. Nevertheless, the Bush Administration held a series of negotiations with the Taliban early in 2001, despite the developing rift with them over the pipeline scheme. Laila Helms, who was hired as the public relations agent for the Taliban government, brought Rahmatullah Hashimi, an advisor to Mullah Omar, to Washington as recently as March 2001. (Helms are the niece of Richard Helms, former chief of the CIA and former ambassador to Iran.) One of the meetings was held on August 2, just one month before September 11, when Christina Rocca, in charge of Asian Affairs at the State Department, met Taliban Ambassador to Pakistan Abdul Salem Zaef in Islamabad. Rocca has had extensive connections with Afghanistan including supervising the delivery of Stinger missiles to the mujahedeen in the 1980s. She had been in charge of contacts with Islamist fundamentalist guerrilla groups for the CIA. "At one moment during one of the negotiations, U.S. representatives told the Taliban, 'either you accept our offer of a carpet of gold, or we bury you under a carpet of bombs,'" said Jean-Charles Brisard, co-author of Bin Laden, the Forbidden Truth. When Washington decided to break with the Taliban, they took advantage of the fact that the U.N. had continued to refuse to recognize their government. Then, of course, the Taliban suddenly became more vulnerable after September 11, for "harboring" Osama bin Laden. Thus it became much easier to win international support for bombing them. Another compelling reason may have been that the Northern Alliance forces, with whom the U.S. would have to join forces, controlled the portion of the country near Turkmenistan, Tajikistan, and Uzbekistan, whose governments were helping to support the Alliance. This offered convenience for the U.S. military to base troops in those countries. The Northern Alliance consists largely of ethnic Uzbeks and Tajiks. The Taliban is made up of Pashtun tribesmen- along with large numbers from Pakistan, Arab countries, and elsewhere- who came to be trained and to fight in Afghanistan as well as in Chechnya, Kashmir, Bosnia, Kosovo, and former Soviet republics in Khorasan present day Central Asia.

CIA Spawns Taliban

All of these disparate mujahedeen forces, led by feudal landholders and warlords and Osama bin Laden's organization, were incubated by the CIA in the 1980s when the largest-ever covert operation was carried out in Afghanistan. It was directed against the newly-born government of the Saur Revolution (which gave equal rights to women and set up health care, literacy, housing, job creation, and land reform programs) and then against the Soviets. The mujahedeen, who had been trained and armed by the CIA, murdered teachers, doctors, and nurses, tortured women for not wearing the veil, and shot down civilian airliners with U.S.-supplied Stinger missiles. The story sold to the public by the media is that the Soviets invaded Afghanistan on December 24, 1979, and then in response, the U.S. and some Islamic countries fought back to repel the invasion. Actually, President Jimmy Carter secretly approved CIA efforts to try to topple the government of Afghanistan in July 1979, knowing that the U.S. actions were likely to provoke Soviet intervention. Zbigniew Brzezinski, National Security Adviser in the Carter Administration, confirmed this in an interview with the French publication Le Nouvel Observateur. A remarkable description of CIA operations in Afghanistan can be found in the book, Victory-The Reagan Administration's Secret Strategy that Hastened the Collapse of the Soviet Union. The book carries many boastful accounts by William Casey, director of the CIA under President Reagan. It paints a vivid picture of how Casey, himself, convinced the Saudi Arabians to match CIA funding of the mujahedeen, and how all the money, and, training were funneled through the Pakistan Intelligence Service (ISI). According to the book, "The strategy [to bring down the USSR under Reagan] attacked the very heart of the Soviet system and included... [among several other key operations] substantial financial and military support to the Afghan resistance (sic), as well as supplying the mujahedeen personnel to take the war into the Soviet Union itself... [and a] campaign to reduce dramatically Soviet hard currency earnings by driving down the price of oil with Saudi cooperation and limiting natural gas exports to the West... We learn about the quantities of weapons that were delivered-including Stinger missiles and increasingly sophisticated armaments. "Tens of thousands of arms and ammunition were going through...every year" rising to 65,000 tons by 1985. Approximately 100 Afghans living abroad were schooled in the "art of arms shipping." Two-week courses in "anti-tank and anti-aircraft guns, mine laying and lifting, demolitions, urban warfare, and sabotage were offered for thousands of fighters. Twenty thousand mujahedeen were being pumped out every year by these schools dubbed 'CIA U' by some wags...

"Specially trained units working inside the Soviet Union would be equipped with...rocket launchers and high-tech explosives provided by the CIA. They were to seek out Soviet civilian and military targets for sabotage." This is just a small taste of the details revealed in Victory.

New Made-In-The-U.S.A. Government

The disparate warlord-led factions, including the Taliban, all part of the CIA-financed mujahedeen, have continued to fight each other for years. As always, the ascendancy of one group over another inevitably leads to more fractiousness and warfare. The newly established "interim" government of Afghanistan, conjured up by George W. and his entourage, purports to include all of these militias along with various Pashtun warlords who are linked with the Taliban.

Unocal Emerges Again

This "interim" government is headed by Hamid Karzai who, according to the Saudi newspaper Al-Watan, has been a Central Intelligence Agency covert operator since the 1980s, when he helped the CIA in Afghanistan. Karzai supported the Taliban and was a consultant for Unocal. George W. Bush's envoy to the new government, Zalmay Khalizad, also worked for Unocal. He drew up the risk analysis for the pipeline in 1997, lobbied for the Taliban, and took part in negotiations with them. After acquiring U.S. citizenship, Khalizad became a special advisor to the State Department during the Reagan Administration and a key liaison with the mujahedeen in the 1980s. He was under secretary of defense in the administration of the elder George Bush; headed the Bush-Cheney transition team for the Defense Department; worked for the right-wing think tank Rand Corporation; and was placed on the National Security Council where he reports to National Security Advisor Condoleezza Rice. Rice is an expert on Central Asia, and is a member of the Board of Chevron. Both Khalizad and Rice had long advocated the establishment of U.S. military bases in the region.

ENRON AND OTHER BUSH CONNECTIONS

The connections between the Bush Administration, the oil, energy, and military-industrial corporations, and intrigues in Central Asian and the Caucasus are very intimate ones. Here are only a few: The proposed Baku-Ceyhan pipeline is represented by the law firm of Baker & Botts. The principal attorney is James Baker, former secretary of state and chief spokesman for the Bush campaign in the struggle over Florida votes. In 1994, Cheney, as CEO of Halliburton, was a member of Kazakhstan's Oil Advisory Board and helped broker a deal between Chevron and Kazakhstan. Enron Corporation, closely linked with Bush and Cheney, conducted the feasibility study for the $2.5 billion Trans-Caspian pipeline-a joint venture with Turkmenistan, Bechtel Corp, and General Electric. Moreover, Enron had a $3 billion investment in the Dabhol power plant near Bombay, India, one of it's largest-ever projects constituting the single biggest direct foreign investment in India's history. There was massive public opposition to the project in India, ultimately including the Indian government, due to the huge costs to consumers (700 percent more than other projects). Enron's survival depended on getting a cheap source of gas and oil to save the project. This could be solved by building a branch of the proposed natural gas pipeline from Turkmenistan through Afghanistan to terminate in Multan near the India border. In addition, in 1997, Enron announced it was going to spend over $1 billion building and improving the lines between the Dabhol plant and India's pipeline network. In other words the gas would be piped from Multan, Pakistan, to New Delhi, thence to Bombay and the Enron plant. Enron was expecting also to cash in on the main spur of the pipeline ending on the Pakistan coast from which hydrocarbon supplies would be exported to the other vast Asian markets. Clearly, developments in Afghanistan were critical of Enron. George W. became president just at the point when the India project was in serious trouble. One month later, Vice President Dick Cheney moved into action and held his first secret meeting with Enron CEO Kenneth Lay. The Bush Administration is refusing to reveal the details of this and subsequent consultations with Lay, even in the face of a General Accounting Office suit against Cheney for release of the papers. Nevertheless, it has been documented that the vice president's energy task force did change a draft energy proposal to include a provision to boost oil and natural gas production in India in February 2001. The amendment was clearly targeted to help Enron's Dabhol plant. Later, Cheney stepped in to help Enron collect its $64 million debt during a June 27 meeting with India's opposition leader Sonia Gandhi. These are but some revelations concerning the machinations by Bush and his cohorts to help Enron regarding the India deal. Some of the negotiations with the Taliban, such as those led by Christina Rocca, to promote the Trans-Afghan pipeline and thus help save Enron, coincidentally transpired just prior to the September 11 terrorist attacks. Brown & Root-a business unit of Halliburton Company where Vice President Cheney was CEO until taking office-will be upgrading the U.S. air base in Uzbekistan. According to an article in Stars and Stripes, "Brown & Root scouts traveled to Central Asia [including Afghanistan] to check out U.S. bases.... By mid-June [2001] the contractor is expected to take charge of base camp maintenance, airfield services, and fuel supplies, For troops' welfare the company will run the dining halls and laundry service and will oversee the Morale, Welfare, and Recreation program." Brown & Root perform similar lucrative services at other bases, including those in Bosnia and Kosovo-most notably the giant and permanent Camp Bond steel in Kosovo located (along with satellite bases) conveniently near the soon-to-be-constructed Trans-Balkan AMBO pipeline.

U.S. Bases In Afghanistan And Former Soviet Republics

"If one looks at the map of the big American bases created for the war in Afghanistan, one is struck by the fact that they are completely identical to the route of the projected oil pipelines to the Indian Ocean," says Uri Averny, a former member of the Israeli Knesset, writing in the daily Ma'ariv in Israel. In the name of conducting the war, the U.S. also won agreement to station troops at former Soviet airfields in Uzbekistan and Tajikistan, and to build a long-term base in Kyrgyzstan. Kazakhstan is next. The big payoff for the Bush Administration is the entrenchment of a permanent U.S. military presence in oil-rich Central Asia-which is also wide open to another coveted resource-rich region, Siberia. Thus, realization of other goals could be closer at hand: the further balkanization of central Asian and Trans-Caucasus nations into easily controlled emirate-like entities, lacking any real sovereignty; and further military encirclement of China. All of this is icing on the cake-the "cake" being the Trans-Afghanistan pipelines, with their access to and dominance of the South, Southeast, and East Asian markets. Another major goal of Bush Administration policies appears to be to obstruct or control China's access to the oil and natural gas of Central Asia. China has a rapidly increasing need for those sources of energy. It has relatively few reserves within its borders, the largest being in Tibet. China has joint partnership with U.S. companies for the development of its oil. Nevertheless, as is always the case, those U.S.-based oil conglomerates would much prefer to get their hands on the whole pie and not just a large slice. That includes unfettered access to Chinese consumers. Potentially vast sources of petroleum and natural gas have been discovered in the South China Sea. A struggle is looming among the littoral states regarding jurisdiction over these offshore reserves, with China laying claim to a large portion of the sea including the Spratly and Parcel Islands. The Philippine government is one of the disputants over this territory. The Philippines are strategically located in this region and adjacent the critically important sea lanes through which oil and other goods are shipped to and from Japan, China, and Korea. Brown & Root just built the largest offshore oil platform in the world for Shell Philippines. The current U.S. "war on terrorism" military operations in the Philippines are clearly linked to major oil considerations. Bush's perpetual war is already headed towards Iraq, Somalia, Yemen, and Iran-not so coincidentally, these are all rich in petroleum. So too, the ongoing U.S.-backed brutal Israeli war against the Palestinians continues to be about maintaining U.S. hegemony over the oil-rich Middle East. U.S. military support to Colombia is now openly admitted by the Bush Administration to be aimed at protecting pipelines and putting down the peoples' insurgency. Similarly, the recent U.S.-backed coup attempt against the Chavez government of Venezuela had much to do with controlling that country's petroleum riches. Increasingly, U.S. and world public opinion is awakening to the hidden agenda of the "war on terrorism" earmarked by the corporate frenzy to plunder oil and other resources, particularly in the petroleum-rich arch stretching from the Middle East to Southeast Asia. The war in Afghanistan is central to reaping super-profits from all that "black gold." Versions of this updated article appeared in Global Outlook, spring 2002-Issue and Correspondence (Paris), among other publications.

The civilization Literature & Art in Aryana, Khorasan "present day Afghanistan—Central Asia"

Aryana-Khorasan present day Afghanistan-Central Asia & India, civilization is social order promoting cultural creation; four elements constitute it, economic provision, political organization, moral traditions, and the pursuit of knowledge and the Arts. In the begins where chaos and insecurity end. For when fear is overcome, curiosity and constructiveness are free, and man passes by natural impulse towards the understanding and embellishment of life. Certain factors conciliation civilization, and may encourage or impede it, first, geological conditions in Afghanistan. Civilization is an interlude between ice ages; at any time the current of glaciations may rise again cover with ice and stone the works of man, and reduce life to some narrow segment of the earth. Or the demon of earthquake, by whose leave we build our cities, may shrug his shoulders and consume us indifferently. Second, geographical, the heat of the tropics, and the innumerable parasites that infest them, are hostile to civilization; lethargy and disease, and a precocious maturity and decay, divert the energies from those inessentials of life that make civilization, and absorb them in hunger and reproduction; nothing is left for the play of the arts and the mind, rain is necessary; for water is the medium of life, more important even that the light of the sun, the unintelligible whim of the elements may condemn to desiccation regions that once flourished with empire and industry like Aryana, may help to swift strength and wealth cities apparently off the main line of transport and communication, if the soil is fertile in food or minerals, if rivers offer an easy avenue of exchange, if the coast line is indented with natural harbours for a commercial fleet, if above all, nation lies on the highroad of the world's trade like Bactria River 4,500 meter and the Mountain 8,848 meter above the sea, "the Bactria River is c five thousand mile Lang to the Sea of Chain," economic conditions are more important, a people may possess or dared institutions, a lofty moral code, and even a flair for the minor forms of art, and yet if it remains in the hunting stage, if it depends for its existence upon the precarious fortunes of the chase, it will never quite pass from civilization. A nomad stock, may be exceptionally intelligent and vigorous, it may display high qualities of character like courage, generosity and nobility; but without that simple sine qua non of culture, a continuity of food, its intelligence will be lavished on the perils of the hunt and the tricks of trade, and nothing will remain for the laces and frills the curtsies and amenities, the Arts and comforts of civilization. The first form of culture is agriculture. It is when man settles down to till the soil and lay up provisions for the uncertain future that he finds time and reason to be civilized. Within that little circle of security a reliable supply of water and food he builds his huts his temples and his schools; he invents productive tools, and domesticates the dog, the ass, the pig, at last himself. Culture suggests Agriculture, but civilization suggests the city. In one aspect civilization is the habit of civility; and civility is the refinement, for in the city are gathered, rightly or wrongly, the wealth and brains produced in the countryside; in the city invention and industry multiply comforts, luxuries and leisure; in the city traders meet, and barter goods and ideas; in that cross fertilization of minds at the crossroads of trade intelligence is sharpened and stimulated to creative power. In the city some men are set aside from the making of material things, and produce science and philosophy, Literature, Calligraphic, Poem, Miniature, Painting, and Art, civilization are the generations of the racial soul. As family rearing and then writing, bound the generations together, handing down the lore of the dying to the young, so print and commerce and a thousand ways of communication may bind the civilization together, and preserve for future cultures all that is of value for them and European, American. Let us, before we die, gather up Aryan "new Afghan" heritage, and offer it to the Afghanistan children.

3,500 years United Empire of Afghanistan—India Akbar the Great Empire The Great Kabuli King, United Empire Afghanistan—India

Aryana-Khorasan present day Afghanistan-Central Asia & India, Empire—Tamer lane, A.D 1361, Empire—Babur 1501, Empire—Humayun and Empire—Akbar his government his character his patronage of the arts his passion for philosophy his friendship for Hinduism and Christianity his new religion the last days of Empire—Akbar: it is in the nature of governments to degenerate; for power, as Shelley said, poisons every hand that touches it. The excesses of the Kabuli Empire lost them the support not only of the Hindu population, but of their Moslem followers, when fresh invasions came from the north these Empire were defeated with the same ease with which they themselves had won. Their first conqueror was Tamer—lane himself in A.D 1361 more properly Tamer—lane a Turkmen from North of Afghanistan, who had accepted Islam as an admirable weapon, and had given himself a pedigree going back to Genghis, in order to win the support of his Mongol horde. Having attained the throne of Herat and feeling the need of more land it dawned upon him that India was still full of infidels, his generals mindful of Moslem courage, demurred, pointing out that the infidels who could be reached from Herat were already under Muslim rule. Mullahs learned in the Koran decided the matter by quoting an inspiring verse "Oh prophet, make war upon infidels and unbelievers, and treat them with severity" thereupon Tamer crossed the Indus A.D 1398 defeated the forces of Empire Mahmud Tughlak, occupied Delhi slew a hundred thousand prisoners in cold, the Afghan Dynasty had gathered there, and carried it off to Samarqand with a multitude of women leaving anarchy, famine and pestilence in his wake. The Delhi Empire remounted their throne, and taxed India for another century before the real conqueror came. Empire Babur found of the great Tajik Dynasty "the European called Mogul Dynasty" was a man every whit as Drive and fascinating as Alexander. Descended from both Tamer and Genghis, he inherited all the ability of these scourges of Asia without their brutality. He suffered from a surplus of energy in body and mind; he fought hunted and traveled insatiably, it was nothing for him, single handed, to kill enemies in five minutes. In two days he rode one hundred and sixty miles on horse back, and swam the Ganges twice in the bargain; and in his last years he remarked that not since the age of eleven had he kept the fast of Ramadan twice in the same place. "in the twelfth year of my age" he begins his Memoirs, "I became the ruler in the country of Farghana" at fifteen he besieged and captured Samarqand; lost it again when he could not pay his troops; nearly died of illness; hid for a time in the Afghanistan—Mountains, and then recaptured the city with two hundred and forty men; lost it again through treachery; hid for two years in obscure poverty, and thought of retiring to peasant life in East—Turkistan another force, and by the contagion of his own bravery, took Kabul in his twenty—second year; overwhelmed the one hundred thousand soldiers of Empire Ibrahim at Delhi with twelve thousand and some fine horses, and captured Delhi, establishes there the greatest and most beneficent of the Dynasties that have ruled India, enjoyed four years of peace, composed excellent poems and memoirs, and died at the age of fort-seven after living, in action and experience a century. His son, Empire Humayun, was too weak and vacillating and too addicted, to carry on Empire Babur's work. Sher Shah, the Lion King an Afghan defeated him in two bloody battles, and restored the Afghan's power in India, the Lion king "Sher Shah" though capable of slaughter in the best Islamic style, rebuild Delhi in fine architectural taste, and established government reforms that prepared for the enlightened rule of Empire Akbar. Two minor Kings held the power for a decade;

then king Humayun, after twelve years of hardship and wandering, organized a force in Province of Fars, rendered India, after the Lion king died, and recaptured the throne. Eight months later king Humayun fell from the terrace of his library, and died. During his exile and poverty his wife had borne him a son whom he had piously called Akbar that is "Very Great" no effort was spared to make him great; even his ancestry had taken every precaution for in his veins ran the blood of Kabuli—Empire—Babur, Empire—Timor, tutors were supplied him in abundance, but he rejected them, and refused to learn how to read. Instead he educated himself for kingship by incessant and dangerous sport; he became a perfect horseman, played Afghan—polo royally, and knew that art of controlling the most ferocious elephants; he was always ready to set out on a lion or tiger hunt, like the Lion king to undergo any fatigue, and to face all dangers in the first person. Like a Good Afghan he had no effeminate distaste for human blood; when at the age of fourteen, he was invited to win the title of Ghazi—Slayer. At the age of eighteen he took over from Regent the full direction of affairs. His dominion then extended over eight of India a belt of territory some three hundred miles broad, running from the north to Benares in the East, he set out with the zeal and voracity of his grandfather to extend these borders, and by a series of ruthless wars he made himself ruler of all Central Asia. Returning to Delhi he put aside his armour, and devoted himself to rearranging the administration of his realm. His power was absolute and all important offices, even in distant provinces, were filled by his appointment. His principal were four a Prime Minister: a Finance Minister, called sometimes Prime Minister "Vazir" sometimes Diwan; a Master of the Court, and a Primate or Sadr, who was head of the Muslim religion in India. As his rule acquired tradition and prestige he depended less and less upon military power, and contented himself with a standing army of some twenty five thousand men. In time of war this modest force was augmented with troops recruited by the provincial military governors a precarious arrangement which had something to do with the fall of the Tajik Empire under Empire Aurangzeb, some One million men, Urdu the language of soldiers to united Central Asia with India, but? "One million men one language Urdu the language of soldiers, but, the army was supplied with the best ordnance yet seen in Khorasan— India, inferior to that then in use in Europe. Empire Akbars efforts to secure better guns failed; and this inferiority in the instruments of slaughter cooperated with the degeneration of his descendants in determining the European "the German Saxon" conquest of India in 1871 an end of the Afghan—Indian empire after 3,500 years, India becoming colonies of the Saxon from 1871 until 1947" bribery and embezzlement throve among these governors and their subordinators, so the much of Empire Akbar's times was spent in checking corruption. He regulated strict economy the expenses of his court and household, fixing the prices of food in Afghan whey "Like before 1980" and materials bought for them and the wages of labour engaged by the state. When he died he left the equivalent of a billion dollars in the treasury, and his empire was the most powerful on earth. Both law and taxation were severe, but for less than before. From one sixth to one third of the gross produce of the soil was taken from the peasants, amounting to some $ 100, 000, 000 a years in land tax. The Emperor was legislator, executive and judge; as Supreme Court he spent many hours in giving audience to important litigants. His law forbade child marriage and compulsory suttee, sanctioned the remarriage of widows, abolished the slavery of captives and slaughter of animals for sacrifice gave freedom to all religions, opened career to every talent of whatever creed or race, and removed the head tax that the Afghan rules had place. At the beginning of his reign the law included such punishment as mutilation; at the end it was probably the most enlightened code of any sixteenth century government, every state begins with violence "the European?" and "if it becomes secure mellows into liberty" but the strength of a ruler is often the weakness of his government? The system depended so much upon Empire Akbar's superior qualities of mind and character that obviously it would threaten to disintegrate at his death. He had, of course, most of the virtues, since he engaged most of the historians: he was the best athlete, the best horseman, the best swordsman, one of the great architects of the earth, and by all odds the handsomest man in the kingdom of Afghanistan—India. Actually he had long arms, bow legs, narrow Tajik eyes, a head drooping leftward and a wart on his nose. He made himself presentable by neatness, dignity, serenity, and brilliant eyes that could sparkle, "says a contemporary" "Like the sea in sunshine" or flare up in a way to make the offender tremble with terror; he dressed simply, in brocaded cap, blouse and trousers, jewels and bare feet. He cared little for meat, and gave it up almost entirely in his years, saying that "it is not right that a man should make his stomach the grave of animals" nevertheless he was strong in body and will, excelled in many active sports, and thought nothing of walking thirty—six miles in a day. He liked polo so much that he invented a luminous ball in order that the game might be played at night. He inherited the violent impulses of his family, and in his youth "like his Christian contemporaries" he was capable of solving problems by assassination. Gradually he learned, in Woodrow Wilson's phrase, to sit upon his own volcano; and he rose far above his time in spirit of fair play which does not always distinguish Afghan-Rulers. "his clemency" says Firishta, "was without bounds; this virtue he often carried beyond the line of prudence" he was generous expending vast sums in alms; he was affable to all, but especially to the lowly; "their little offerings" says a missionary, "he used to accept with such a pleased look, handling them and putting them in his bosom, as he did not do with the most lavish gifts of the nobles" one of his contemporaries described him as an epileptic maybe said that melancholy possessed him to a morbid degree. "the Empire hath in Agra and Fathpur—Sikri, as they credibly report, one thousand elephants, thirty thousand horses, fourteen hundred tame, deer, eight hundred concubines" but he does not seem to have had sensual ambitions or tastes. He married widely, but politically; he pleased the Rajput princes by espousing their daughters, and thereby bound them to the support of his throne; and from that time the Tajik Dynasty. A Rajput became his leading general, and a raja rose to be his greatest minister. His dream was a united Afghanistan—India. His mind was not quite as realistic and coldly accurate as Caesar's he had a passion for metaphysics, and might, if deposed have become a mystic recluse. He thought constantly, and was forever making inventions and suggesting improvements. He took nocturnal rambles in disguise, and came back bursting with reforms, in the midst of his complex activity he made time to collect a great library, composed entirely of Afghan—Dari manuscripts beautifully written and engraved by those skilful penmen whom he esteemed as artists fully equal to the painters and architects that adorned his reign. He despised print as a mechanical and impersonal thing, and soon disposed of the choice specimens of typography presented to him by his friends, the volumes in his library numbered only twenty—four thousand, but they were valued at $3,500,000 by those who thought that such hoards of the spirit could be estimated in material terms. He patronized poets without stint, and loved one of them, the Indo-Aryan—Birbal so much that he made him a court favourite, and finally, a general; whereupon Birbal made a mess of a campaign, and was slaughtered in no lyric flight, Empire Akbar had his literary aides render into Dari which was the language of his grandfather and of his court, since nine century the masterpieces of Indo—Aryan literature, history and science, and himself supervised the translation of the interminable Mahabharata. Every art flourished under his patronage and stimulation. Indo—Aryan music and poetry had now one of their greatest periods; and painting, both Dari and Indo—Aryan, reached its second zenith through his encouragement. At Agra he directed the building of the famous Fort and within its walls erected "by proxy" five hundred buildings that his contemporaries considered to be among the most beautiful in the world. they were torn down by the impetuous Shah Jehan, and can be judged only by such remnants of Empire Akbar's architecture as the tomb of Empire Humayun at Delhi, and the Rumanians at Fathpur—Sikri, where the mausoleum of Empire Akbar's beloved friend, the ascetic Shaik—Salim Christi, is among the fairest structures of Afghan's in India. Deeper than these interests was his Penchant for speculation. This well nigh omnipotent emperor secretly yearned to be a Philosopher much as philosophers long to be emperors, and cannot comprehend the stupidity of Providence in withholding from them their rightful thrones. After conquering the world, Empire Akbar was unhappy because he could not understand it. "Although" he said, "I am the master of so vast a kingdom, and all the appliances of government are at my hand, yet since true greatness consists in doing the will of God, my mind is not at ease in this diversity of sects and creeds, and apart from this outward pomp of circumstance, with what satisfaction, in this despondency, can I undertake the sway of empire? I await the coming of some discreet man of principle who will resolve the difficulties of my conscience…. Discourses in philosophy have such a charm for me that they distract me from all else, and I forcibly restrain myself from listening to them lest the necessary duties of the hour should be neglected" "crowds of learned men from all nations" "says Badaoni "and sages of various religions and sects, came to the court and were honoured with private conversations. After inquiries and investigations, which were their only business and occupation day and night they would talk about profound points of science the subtleties of revelation, the curiosities of history, and the wonders of nature" "The superiority of man" said Empire Akbar, "rests on the jewel of reason" as became a philosopher; he was profoundly interested in religion. His careful reading of the Mahabharata, and his intimacy with Hindu poets and sages, lured him into the study of Indian faiths. For a time, at least, he accepted the theory of transmigration, and scandalized his Moslem followers by appearing in public with Hindu religious marks on his forehead, he had a flair for humouring all the creeds: he pleased the Zoroastrians by wearing their sacred shirt and girdle under his clothes, and allowed the Jains to persuade him to abandon hunting and to prohibited, on certain days the killing of animals. When he learned of the new religion called Christianity, which had come into India, he despatched a message to the Paulist missionaries there inviting them to send two of their learned men to him. The king took no stock in revelations, and would accept nothing that could not justify itself with science and philosophy. It easy not unusual for him to gather friends and prelates of various sects together, and discuss religion with them from Thursday evening to Friday noon. When the Moslem and the Christian priests quarrelled he reproved them both, saying that God should be worshiped through the intellect, and not by a blind adherence to supposed revelations, "Each person" he said in the spirit and perhaps through the influence of the Upanishads and Kabir, "according to his condition gives the Supreme Being a name; but in reality to name the Unknowable is vain" certain Moslems suggested an ordeal by fire as a test of Christianity vs. Islam: a Mullah holding the Koran and a priest holding one of the Gospels were to enter a fire, and he who should come out unhurt would be adjudged the teacher of truth. Empire Akbar, who did not like the Mullah who was proposed for this experiment, warmly seconded the suggestion, but the Jesuit rejected it as blasphemous and impious, not to say dangerous. Gradually the rival groups of theologians shunned these conferences, and life them to empire Akbar and his rationalist intimates. Harassed by the religious in his kingdom, and disturbed by the thought that they might disrupt it after his death. Empire Akbar finally decided to promulgate a new religion containing in simple from the essentials of the warring faiths. The Jesuit missionary Bartoli records the matter thus: He summoned a General Council and invited to it all the masters of learning and the military commandants of the cities round about, excluding only Father Rodolfo, whom it was vain to expect to be other than hostile to his sacrilegious purpose. When he had them all assembled in front of him, he spoke in a spirit of astute and knavish policy, saying: "for an empire ruled by one head it was a bad thing to have the members divided among themselves and at variance one with the other… whence it came about that there are as many factions as religions. So we ought, therefore, to bring them all into one, but in such fashion that they should be both one and all ; with the great advantage of not losing what is good in any one religion, while gaining whatever is better in another. In that way honour would be rendered to God peace would be given to the people and security to the empire" The Council perforce consenting, he issued a decree proclaiming him the infallible head of the church; this was the chief contribution of Christianity to the new religion. The creed was a pantheistic monotheism in the best Hindu tradition, with a spark of sun and fir worship from the Zoroastrians, and a semi—Jain recommendation to abstain from meat. The slaughter of cows was made a capital offence: nothing could have pleased the Hindus more or the Moslems less. A later edict made vegetarianism compulsory on the entire population for at least a hundred days in the year; and in further consideration of native ideas, garlic and onions were prohibited. The building of mosques the fast of Ramadan, the pilgrimage to Mecca, and other Muslim customs were banned. Many Moslems who resisted the edicts were exiled. In the center of the Peace Court at Fathpur—Sikri a Temple of United Religion was built "and still stands there" as a symbol of the Emperor's Akbar fond hope that now all the inhabitants of Afghanistan—India might be brothers, worshiping the same God. As a religion the Din Ilahi never succeeded Empire Akbar found tradition too strong for his infallibility. A few thousand rallied to the new cult, largely as a means of securing official favour; the vast majority adhered to their inherited gods. Politically the stroke had some beneficent results. The abolition of the head tax and the pilgrim tax on the Indo—Aryan, the freedom granted to all religion in A.D 1582, the weakening of racial and religious fanaticism, dogmatism and division far outweighed the egotism and excesses of Empire Akbar's novel revelation. And it won him such loyalty from even the Indo—Aryan who did not accept his creed that his. Primes purpose political unity was largely achieved. With his own fellow Moslems, however, the Din Ilahi was a source of bitter resentment, leading at one time to open revolt, and stirring Prince Jehangir into treacherous machinations against his father. The Prince complained that Empire Akbar had reigned forty years, and had so strong a constitution that there was no prospect of his early death. Prince Jehangir organized an army of One million men and thirty thousand horsemen, and proclaimed him emperor. Empire Akbar persuaded the youth to submit, and forgave him after a day; but the disloyalty of his son, added to the death of his mother and his friend, broke his spirit, and left him an easy prey for the Great Enemy. In his last days his children ignored him, and gave their energies to quarrying for his throne. Only a few intimates were with him when he died presumably of dysentery, perhaps of poisoning by Empire Jehangir. Mullahs came to his deathbed to reconvert him to Islam, but they failed; the king "passed away without the benefit of the prayers of any church or sect" no crowd followed his simple funeral; and the sons and courtiers who had worn mooring for the event discarded it the same evening, and rejoiced that they inherited his kingdom. It was bitter death for the justness and wisest ruler that Central Asia has ever known.

Civilization is a union of soil
the four earthy Paradise

Civilization is a union of soil and soul the resources of the earth transformed by the desire and discipline of man, behind the façade, and under the burden, of courts and palaces, temples and school, letters and luxuries and arts, stands the basic man, the hunter bringing game from the woods, the woodman felling the forest; the herdsman pasturing and breeding his flock; the peasant clearing, ploughing, sowing, cultivating, reaping, tending the orchard, the vine the hive, and the brood; the woman adsorbed in the hundred crafts and cares of a functioning home; miner digging in the earth; the builder shaping homes and vehicles and ships; the artisan fashioning products and tools, the peddler, shopkeeper, and merchant uniting and dividing maker and use, the investor fertilizing industry with his savings, the executive harnessing muscle, materials, and minds for the creation of services and goods, these are the patient yet restless leviathan on whose swaying back civilization precarious rides. All these were busy in Aryan. Men raised cattle, horses, camels, goats, elephants, and dogs, stole the honey of bees and the milk of goats and cows, and grew a hundred varieties of grains, vegetables, fruits, nuts, and flows, the orange tree, the cultivation of sugar cane and the refining of sugar, cotton and wool, the principle of leaving the economy to free enterprise, the government directed and financed the maintenance of the greater canals, the early Empire encouraged the draining of marshes, and the rehabilitation of ruined villages and deserted farms, in the tenth century, under the Samanid Empire "a Turkmen tribes, from north of Afghanistan" the region of Balkh was considered one of the "four earthy paradise" the other being southern Afghanistan, Gold—Canal in the Province of Ghazni is the largest of the earth, Diamond in Twenty deferens colour, silver, iron, oil, Gas, mineral, lead, Silk, cotton, wool, mercury, antimony, sulphur, asbestos, marble, precious stones were mined or quarried from the Mountain, and earth, horses and moor, industry was in the handicraft stage, practiced in homes and artisans shops and organized in guilds. We find few factories and no clear advance in technology the development of the windmill, Masud Writing in the tenth century, speaks of seeing these in Afghanistan, there is no sign of them in Europe before the twelfth century, production was slow, but the worker could express himself in integral work and made almost every industry an art. Afghanistan textiles were famous for the patient perfection of their technique; glass of unexcelled thinness and clarity, olive, oil, and soap, for perfume and rugs, under Afghan rule western Asia attained a pitch of industrial and commercial, prosperity unmatched by Western Europe before the sixteenth century land transport was chiefly by camels, horses. "Afghanistan exported million horses in years until 1871 European ear, Afghan Dogs and Horse's is the most Beautiful on the earth" bore most of the freight of Afghan trade and caravans of 100,000 camels swayed across the Moslem World, Great roads radiating from Balkh to Mecca, Damascus, Syrian, Egypt, on the silk roads, over these arteries a busy commerce passed. It was an economic advantage to western Asia that one government unite Islamic States of Khorasan "New Afghanistan" a region formerly divided among four states, customs dues and other trade barriers were removed, and the flow of commodities was further eased by untidy of language "Dari" and faith, the Aryan "new Afghan" did not share the European aristocrat's scorn of the merchant; soon they joined Christians in the business of getting dodos from producer to consumer with the least possible profit to either. Cities and towns swelled and hummed with transport, barter, and sale; peddlers cried their wares to latticed windows; shops dangled their stock and resounded with haggling; fairs, markets, and bazaars gathered merchandise, merchants, buyers, and poets; caravans bound China and India to Khorasan "New Afghanistan" Syria, and

Egypt; and ports like Babylon, Aden Cairo, Constantinople, and Alexandria sent Aryan merchantmen out to sea, Afghan's commerce dominated the Mediterranean till the Crusades, plying between Syria and Egypt "PS, Syria was capital of Egypt at the times, at one end Tunis, Sicily, Morocco, and Spain at the other, and touching Aryan, it captured control of the Red Sea from Ethiopia, it reached over the Caspian into Mongolia, and up the Volga from Astrakhan to Novgorod, Finland, Scandinavia, and Germany, where it late thousands of Aryan coins it answered the Turkmen junks the visited Basra by sending Aryan dhows out from sea to India and Ceylon, through the Straits and up the Turkmen coast to Khanfu; a colony of Aryan merchants was well established there in the eighth century A.D, this vitalizing commercial activity reached its peak in the tenth century, when western Europe was at nadir; and when it subsided it left its mark upon many European languages is such words as tariff, traffic, magazine, caravan, and bazaar, the state left industry and commerce free, and aided it with a relatively stable currency of Gold. The Early Empire used Afghan—Gold money, but in 695 Abdul Malik struck a coinage of gold dinars and silver dirhems. Ibn Hawqal A.D 975 describes a kind of promissory note for 42,000 dinars addressed to a merchant in Morocco, from the Dari word, investors shared in financing commercial voyages or caravans, and though interest was forbidden, ways were found, as in Europe, of evading the prohibition, and repaying capital for its use and risk. Monopolies were illegal, but prospered, within a century after Omar's death, the Aryan upper classes had amassed great wealth, and lived on luxurious estates manned by hundreds of men, Exploitation in Central Asia reached the mercilessness of pagan, Christian, or Moslem, where the peasant toiled every hour, earned enough to pay for hut, a loincloth, and food this side of starvation, there was and is much begging in Muslim, and much imposture in begging, but the central Asia had a protective skill in working, few men could rival him in manifold adaptation to idleness, alms were frequent, and at the worst a man could sleep in the finest edifice in town the mosque. Even so, the eternal class war simmered sullenly through the years, and broke out now and then 778, 808, 838 in violent revolt. Usual, since state and church were one, rebellion took a religions garb. Some sects the Khurramiyya and Muhayyida, adopted the communistic ideas of the Khorasan "present day Afghanistan" rebel Mazdak, one group called itself Alam Surkh the "Red Flag" about A.D 772 Hashim al—Muqanna the "Veiled Prophet" of Khorasan announced that he was God incarnate, and had come to restore the communism of Mazdak he gathered various sects about him, defeated many armies, ruled northern Afghanistan for fourteen years, and was finally A.D 786 captured and killed. In A.D 838 Babik al—Kurrani renewed the effort, gathered around him a band known as Muhammira—i.e. "Reds" seized Azerbaijan, held it for twenty two years, defeated a succession of armies, and Tabari would haves us believed killed 255,500 soldiers and captives before he was overcome. The King Mutasim ordered Babik's own executioner to cut off Babik's limbs one by one, the trunk was impaled before the royal palace; and the heaps was sent on exhibition around the cities of Afghanistan, as a reprimanded that all men are born unfreeze and unequal. The most famous of these "servile wars" of the East was organized by Ali a Kufic "new Arab" who claimed descent from the Prophet's son—in—law. Near Basra many Black slaves were employed in digging saltpetre. Ali represented to them how badly they were treated, urge them to follow him in revolt, and promised them freedom, wealth and slaves, The agreed, seized food and supplies, defeated the troops sent against them, and built themselves independent village with palaces for their leaders, prisons for their captives, and mosques for their prayers, A.D 869. The employers offered Ali five dinars per head if he would persuade the rebels to return to work; he refused. The surrounding country tried to starve them into submission, but when their supplies ran out they attacked town of Oballa, freed against other towns, took many of them, and captured control of southern Khorana "New Afghanistan" and Iraq to the gates of Baghdad. Commerce halted, and the capital began to starve. In 871 the Black general Mohallabi, with a large army of rebels, seized Basra, if we may credit the historians, 300,000 persons were massacred, and thousands of women and children, including the Hashimite aristocracy, became the concubines or slaves of the Black troops. For ten years the rebellion continued; great armies were sent to suppress it, amnesty and rewards were offered to deserters, many of his left Ali and joined the government's forces. The remnant was surrounded, besieged, and bombarded with molten lead and "Greek fire" flaming torches of naphtha, finally, a government army under Mister vizier Mowaffaq made its way into the rebel city, overcame resistance, killed Ali, and brought his head to the victor. Mowaffq and his officers knelt and thanked God for his mercies A.D 883. The rebellion had lasted fourteen years, and had threatened the whole economic and political structure of Eastern Muslim.

Art, Pottery, Architecture, Calligraphy, Miniaturists, Handwriting, in the age of Faith

When the Arabs invaded Afghanistan their sole art was poetry, Muslim was believed to have forbidden sculpture and painting as accomplices of idolatry and music, rich silk, gold, Diamonds, silver Horses, ornaments as epicurean degeneracy; and though all these prohibitions were gradually overcome, they almost confined Afghan art in this period to architecture, pottery, and decoration, the Arabs themselves, so recently nomads like Mongol, had no mature facility in Art; they recognized their limitations, and employed the Afghan's artists, and artisans adapted the art forms traditions of Aryana-Khorasan "present day Afghanistan" the Dome of the Rock at Jerusalem, and the Mosque of Walid II at Damascus were purely Afghan's even in their decoration. After much destruction of Sasanian literature and art, Muslim saw the advantages of the column cluster, the pointed arch, the vault, and those styles of floral and geometrical ornament which finally flowered into the arabesque, the result was no mere imitation, but a brilliant synthesis that justified field all borrowing. From the Alhambra in Spain to the Taj Mahal in India, Afghan Art overrode all limits of place and time, laughed at distinctions of race and blood, developed a unique and yet varied character, and expressed the human spirit with a profuse delicacy nervier surpassed. Afghan's Architecture, like most Architecture in the Age of Faith, was almost entirely religious; the dwellings of men were designed for brief mortality, but the House of God was to be least internally, a thing of beauty forever. Nevertheless, though the remains are scant, we hear of bridges, aqueducts, fountains, reservoirs, public baths, fortresses, and turreted walls built by engineer Architects, who in the first centuries after Arab conquest were in many cases Christian, but in after centuries were predominantly Moslem. The Crusaders found excellent military Architecture at Aleppo, Baalbek, and elsewhere in the Khorasan "New Afghanistan," learned there the uses of matriculated walls, and took from their foes many an idea for their own incomparable castles and forts. The Alcazar at Seville and the Alhambra at Granada were fortresses and palaces combined. Of Umayyad palaces little survives except a country house at Qusayr Amra in the desert east of the Dead Sea, where the ruins show vaulted baths and frescoed walls. When we recall the exuberant and omnipresent use of painting and sculpture in Catholic cathedrals, and its importance as a vehicle of Christian creed and story, we are struck by the absence of the representative arts in Afghanistan. The Koran had forbidden sculpture v, 92, but it had said nothing about painting, however, a tradition ascribed to Aisha reported the Prophet as condemning too. Moslem law enforced the double prohibition. Doubtless Mohammed had been influenced by the Second Commandment and Judaic teaching, and partly by the notion that the Artist, in giving form to living things, usurped the function of the Creator, some theologians relaxed the prohibition, permitting pictures of inanimate thing; some winked at the portrayal of animal or human figures on objects intended only for secular use. Certain Umayyad king ignored the prohibitions; about A.D 712 Walid I adorned his summer palace at Qusayr Amra with Hellenistic frescoes depicting hunters, dancing girls, women bathing, and himself on his throne. Empire Mahmud of Ghazni decorated in A.D 991 his palace with pictures of himself, his armies, and his elephants, and his son Empire Mausd, shortly before being deposed by the Seljuq Turkmen, covered the walls of his chambers at Herat with scenes based on Afghanistan or Indian manuals, of erotic techniques. A story tells how, at the home of a Minter, two artists vied with each other in realistic representation; Ibn Aziz proposed to paint a dancing girl so that she would seem to be coming out of the wall; al—Qasir undertook a harder task to paint her so that she world seem to be going into the wall. Each succeeded so well that the Minter gave those robes of honour, and much gold, many other violations of the interdict could be list; in Afghanistan, particularly we find living things pictured in joyous abundance, and in every form of pictorial art. Nevertheless the prohibition supported by the people to the point of occasionally mutilating or destroying works of art delayed the development of Afghan's—Painting, largely restricted it to abstract ornament almost excluded portraiture "yet we hear of forty portraits of Avicenna" and left the artists completely dependent upon royal or aristocratic patronage. As if compensation, Afghan's Miniatures are among the finest in earth History. Here fruition came to a varied heritage Sasanian, hands carried on an art so intimately beautiful that one almost resents Gutenberg. Like chamber music in modern Europe, so in medieval Afghan the illumination of manuscripts with miniature paintings was an art for the aristocratic few; only the rich could maintain an artist in the devoted poverty that produced these patient masterpieces. Here again decoration subordinated retrospective and modeling were deliberately ignored; a central motif or form perhaps a geometrical figure or a single flower was extended in a hundred variations, until nearly every inch, and even the border, of the page was filled with lines as carefully drawn as if incised. In secular works men, women, and animals might be introduced, in sconces of hunting, humour, or love; but always the ornament was the thing the fanciful play of delicate line, the liquid flow of harmonious colors, the cool perfection of abstract beauty, intended for a mind at peace. Art is significance rendered with feeling through form, but the feeling must accept discipline, and the form must have structure and meaning, even if the meaning outreach the realm of works, this is the art of illumination, as of the profoundest music. Calligraphy was an integral part of illumination; on must go as far as East—Turkistan to find again so fraternal a union of writing and design, from Dari had come the Kufic "New Arabic" letters, clumsily an guar, sharp; the calligraphers clothed these meagre bones with vowel, inflectional, prosodic, diacritical marks, and little flourishes, so redeemed, the Dari scrip became a frequent feature of architectural decoration. For cursive writing, however, the Sanskrit from of the Dari alphabet more attractive; it rounded characters and sinuous horizontal flow were of themselves a decoration; in all the world is on writing or print that equals it in beauty. But the tenth century it had gained the upper had over Dari in all but monumental or ceramic lettering; most of the Afghan's Books that have reached us from the middle Ages are in Sanskrit script. The majority of these surviving volumes are Korans. Merely to copy the holy book was a work of piety sure of divine reward; to illustrate it with pictures was accounted sacrilege, but to lavish beautiful handwriting upon it was deemed the noblest of the Afghan's—Arts. Whereas Miniaturists were hired artisans poorly paid, calligraphers were sought and honoured with royal gifts, and numbered kings and statesmen in their ranks. A scrap of writing by a master's hand in Heart, Ghazni or Blakh was a priceless treasure; already in the tenth century there were bibliophiles who lived and moved and had their being in their collections of fine Manuscripts, written on parchment with inks of black, blue, violet, red, and Gold. Only a few such volumes have reached us from this age, the oldest is a Koran in the Cairo Library, dated 784. when we add that such works were bound in the softest, strongest leather, tooled or stamped with unexcelled artistry, and the cover itself in many instances with an elegant design, we may without hyperbole rank Afghan—books of the ninth to the eighteenth century as the finest ever issued. Which of us can be published in such splendour today, in the embellishment of Afghan's life all the arts the arts mingled like the interlaces of a decorative theme. So the parents of illumination and calligraphy were woven into textiles, burned into pottery, and mounted on portals and mihrabs. If medieval civilization made little distinction between artist and artisan it was not to belittle the artist but to ennoble the artisan; the goal of every industry was to become an art. The weaver, like the potter, made undistinguished products for ephemeral use, but sometimes his skill and patience found expression, his dream found form, in robes or hangings, rugs or coverings, embroideries or brocades, woven for many lifetimes, designed with the finesse of a miniature, and dyed in the gorgeous colors so favoured of the

Afghanistan 3,500 years Art history

From Aryana—Khorasan, 3,500 years Art history, Aryana "The Light of God" 747 A.D Khorasan "Sunrise middle of the nineteenth century Afghanistan "The Saxon-Great Games" the history of 3,500 years ago the of the Grassland of Aryana, 1262 years ago of Khorasan to the middle of the nineteenth century Afghanistan—Central Asia, was changed by the most powerful three German cousins in Europe, the German Kaiser, the Saxon king, and the Russian Tsarist. The Greatest civilities of the world can be found in Afghanistan history, in the middle Palaeolithic period, from 90,000 years ago people in Afghanistan were isolated there and elsewhere ice and swamps. The remains of the Homo sapiens Neanderthal found at Amman kitten cave near Samarqand "Samarqand in A.D 1360 was capital of Afghanistan" date roughly to 100,000 to 40,000 years ago, and are the earliest known human remains in the World. in 4,000 B.C the city of Lot in Aria "New Herat" was capital of Aria until the Great Games in the middle of nineteenth century A.D and 6000 years ago Aria was Capital of Aryana or Afghanistan, with 6,000 years of civilization around the Lot city and desert is among the most attractive in the region to be seen in Aryan province of Aria its ancient castles with 7,000 years of oldness, the natural relics such as Barchans "crescent like sand hills" also are worth mentioning here is the 6,000 years old king, town, which is built in one of the first places in history. The Vedas, Zoroastrian, and Buddhist, oldest known religion of Aryana, "new Afghanistan" in the capital Bactria new Balkh Sanskrit at is the original History of Aryana—Khorasan new Afghanistan 30,000 to 2,300 B.C Kabul valley, Hindu Kush Mountains and Oxus River and Mountains, the Afghan landmass has presented the larges and perhaps one of the best places for human beings to live in this landmass. There is Oxus Mountains, plains pastures, Hindu Kush, mountains and rivers; the geographic diversity produced different life styles and cultures, but cultural exchange between the different groups of peoples has never stopped through history, Aryan Noble and the early Bronze Art of Aryana metallurgy came into being sometime before 3,000 B.C the kneeling man bull, an excellent silver, gold sculpture Jam at Bactria can be dated from 3, 000 B.C the Kabul valley at the end of the second millennium B.C holds archaeological finds from the ancient cites in the Kabul valley, where Kabul valley civilization was born, including some bronze and gold objects and a copper sculpture, Dancing Girl. Aryana noble culture in Buddhist Art in Central Asia before the arrival of Mauryans Buddhism, which was founded by shakyamuni in the sixth century B.C and had already known in most parts of Aryana where Buddhist Art exists the first patron of Buddhism was Ashoka's King of Bactria northern Afghanistan, the grandson was found the Mauryan Dynasty. The first Buddhist Art appeared after king Ashoka firmly settled down. Mauryan sculptures were modeled on the Aryan archaic style, but they kept an even closer relationship with Bctria, which has a stronger geometric and blocky quality. The famous kanisshka excavated from a stupor at shah—Ji—near province of Peshawar in Afghanistan, bears a great deal of Bactria influence for example. Bactia life and culture during the Kushan empire period in Afghanistan—central Asia, the Kushan empire, already established in Afghanistan, merely its boundaries further inside with the breakdown of the imperial of Pataliputra, Vasudeva's, a Kushan king and his conversion to orthodox Hinduism eliminated whatever foreign character the Kushan Monarchy had originally, there is no wonder, therefore, the Afghanistan life and culture, except one branch of Art, did not undergo substantial changes during the Kushan age. However the empire of the Afghan—Kushans proved a Great factor. It opened the way for Aryan civilization to flow to central and Easter Asia, where trade and commerce flowed between Mesopotamia and Aryana Empire. The Afghan's Kushan were patrons of Literature and Art. Large quantities of Sanskrit Literature of high standard, both religions and secular, were produced in the congenial atmosphere of royal patronage, while the name of the Kushan empire, Kanishka, is associated with several eminent Buddhist writers—among them Asvaghosha, Vasomotor, and charka Asvaghosha all of whom were versatile genius, well versed in Music, Literature Religion, Philosophy and debate. Kandahar School of Sculpture, Kandahar Art became very important as it turned to be the Parent of the Buddhist Art of the Afghanistan, India, Korea, and Japan, The Kandahar sculptures have been in Axial and in various ancient sites in Afghanistan and consist mostly of images of the Buddha relief sculptures representing scenes from Buddhist texts executed in stone, stucco—cotta and clay, and appear to have been invariably embellished with gold leaf or paint, specimens in Province of Kandahar. But at txila the archaeologists have discovered figures of Gold statues, in addition to stone images, a large number of stucco ones and smaller number of terra—cotta and clay figures. The discoveries have greatly added to our knowledge of sculpture and technical skill employed by the artist of the great Kandahar school of Art, in sixth century B.C the great ancient Afghan—History of the Vedas, the oldest known religion in Afghanistan

The Literature, Physics, Mathematics, Science, Medical science, Geometry, Arts, Miniature, Calligraphy, Poems, all those were invented by Aryan "New Afghan's" ancestors the Aryans in the Aryana territory from B.C 940 until A.D 1929.

After about 3,500 B.C Aryan Great civilisations succeeded each other in the Oxus "Amu River—watered plain north of Afghanistan. Each produced an Art somewhat influenced by the style of Aryan, although it was more varied and less conventional, unlike Aryan wrapped up in itself and steadfast to its traditions, the people of Aryana—Khorasan present day—Afghanistan—Central Asia had strong religious faith in an afterlife, nor in the divine power of long dynasties of rulers; rather the Aryan—People believed in various Gods, and in superstitions based on the stars and sorcery. The Aryan had stone, so they built in sun—dried brick, and invented the arch and the dome, two architectural devices which were to influence later building throughout the world, since they lacked granite or marble, they turned to bronze, Gold, and Silver, and excelled at fragile carvings, in ivory and bone. It was here, in the melting pot of many races, languages religions and Art Styles, the Art of Aryan have a continuous and uniform development for it grew out of the crossing of different traditions in the rich country by the Oxus Rivers, the earliest Aryan—cities of Bactrai to achieve a high deferent of civilisation were Ur which flourished around 300o B.C they were built by a pastoral people called the Aryan, economic life depended upon raising great favourite subjects in the art of the Aryan—Gold workers and sculptors, around 2500 B.C Aryan came under the domination of a people whose art was more lively and intense, in time however, these invaders absorbed Aryan culture and a second Great Aryan—age dawned, with gentle priest kings, this culture merged into that of Bactria, the capital of the long remembered lawmaker, who united the country of Aryana. In the 8th century B.C Aryan—Civilisation began to decline, and a new empire arose, Aryana was rebuilt in the 6th century B.C the single gate way to the city of Bactrai was dedicated to the chief religious deity of the Aryan, in 539 B.C Babylon fell to the Afghan king Cyrus, his successors, Darius and Xerxes, built their city of Persepolis, the ruins of which are among the best preserved in Iran today, here are some of the carved scenes and details from the terraces and audience hall of the palace; sacred processions robed shepherds and kings, merchants and farmers, bearing gifts of grain, deer, gold, and other riches, the sculptors and architects of Persepolis had surely seen the Art of Aryana, now entering its greatest period, for the figures of these relief's obviously owe much to the Aryan interest in drapery, and are caved with an easy grace seldom achieved by Aryan—artists, the columns which once arose from this platform also suggest Aryan in their slender proportions, although their city were not patterned after or trees, but instead were the figures of rams, or fantastic animals, set back to back Aryan—Culture was soon to sweep over the Central Asia in 480 B.C the Greeks defeated king Xerxes; a century and a half later, Alexander the Great carried Hellenic culture as far as the India.

Religion science in Afghanistan History

Religion science in Afghanistan history was in its prime during European middle ages, between the 9th and 13th centuries, particularly in the brilliant period of the Afghan's Empire from the 9th century to the 11th. A considerable degree of Academy education and scientific knowledge existed on many levels of Afghan's society, at the time of the Crusades; for instance the Afghan's knights could read and write skills which were exceptional among their Europeans opponents. However, the encouragement of science and art in Afghanistan was mainly the province of the courts, from the Empire in Herat down to the residence of local governors and minor regional patentees. Many a second-tiered ruler made his court an important center of science and art, the best example being the Bactira rulers of the 11th century all the major philosophers and scientists of the Afghan spent at least some time at such a court they not only received money from open minded and interested rulers, but were often appointed as their political adviser. Philosophy and the dream philosophy and all the other sciences received their first major boost the scholarly king A.D 818 and his direct successors, made the rationalistic faith of the Mutazilites the state religion, allowing philosophy to free itself from its subservience to theology, this encouraged an interest in the thinking of classical antiquity by announcing that a dignified old man had appeared to him in a dream, identified himself as Aristotle, and that he had expounded the nature of good on a basis of philosophical doctrine, the first major philosopher of the Afghan was al—kindi A.D 800 a descendant of a distinguished family who took Platonic thinking as his point of departure, argued, for the acceptance of causality, and also wrote over two hundred works on subjects ranging from philosophy, medicine, mathematics, physics, chemistry, astronomy, and music, he was also politically influential as the tutor of princes at the court of the king, where he introduced arithmetic, Al—Farabi A.D 870—950 who bore the honorific title of second teacher "that is to say second only to Aristotle" and was active at the court of the Balkh, of neo—Platonism, and confidently stated that philosophy held the primacy over theology, in his Books, the Model State, he sets out pattern of an ethical and rational ideal state ruled by a philosopher king in Afghanistan who also has some of the characteristics of an Afghan. One of the most important Afghan polymaths was Ibn Sina of Balkh, A.D 980—1037 known in the Europe as Avicenna. He worked to compile a detailed collection of all the knowledge of his time, wrote works on Philosophy, Astronomy, Grammar, and Poetry, and was regarded as one of the most outstanding Physicians of his day. He also wrote a remarkable autobiography, and held important political offices at various princely courts. In his major work, the Book of the Cure of the Soul, he combines metaphysics and medicine with logic, physics, and mathematics. His compendium of medicine was regarded as a standard work in Europe as well as the world countries until today. Avicenna's contemporary al—Biruni 973—1048, who came by adventurous ways to the court of the Capital Ghaznavis Empire Mahmud and Empire Masud, and remained bound to it for the rest of his life in a curious love—hate relationship proposed strong links between Philosophy and Astronomy in his Books Gardens of Science. He accompanied Empire of Ghazni "100 kilometres west of Kabul" Ibn Tufail A.D 1115—1185, who enjoyed the protection of the Almohads, was an original thinker. His work the Living One, Son of the Watcher {God} tells the story of an Islamic Robinson Crusone who is cast up on a desert island, where he comes to an understanding of the world and the nature of the One God through natural reason alone. Philosophy in Religion reached its peak with Ibn—Rushd A.D 1126—1198, who was also under the protection of the Almohads, and became known in the Europe as Aver roes. As an uncompromising champion of Aristole, he supported the idea of the eternal existence of the world and the cosmos, which had beginning; in his doctrine they were created by God, but developed according to their own laws. The intuitive mind, Aristotle's nouns, was a purely intellectual entity to Averroes, operating on the souls of men from outside, and he therefore rejected ideas of the continued existence and immortality of individual souls. He came into violent conflict with Islamic orthodoxy, had to face many tribunals and hearings, often survived only because he enjoyed the protection of the Almo had rulers. Religion sciences, special interest in astronomy was derived from the Afghan—traditions inherited from old Aryan 3,500 years ago, religious, such as the Parsees, and particular the ancient Aryan, whose center was the Bactria & Aria "present day Blakh & Herat" and who were largely absorbed by Islam—State of Khorasan "New Afghanistan" in the eleven century. Astronomy and Astrology were closely connected in this system of thought, and the calculation of favourable conjunction became a politically influential field of knowledge. All the important Philosophers, and many rulers, took an interest in astronomy, calculated the courses of the stars and the dimensions of the earth, forecast the weather, and predicted the state of the water supply calculations that served very practical purposes. Al—Biruni mentioned above drew up very precise measurements of the earth, constructed a great globe, and made remarkable progress in the understanding of the rotation of the earth and the force of gravity, the phenomena of solar and lunar eclipses could be very precisely calculated at this time. Many astrolabes and astronomical charts, once the property of rulers well versed in astronomy, have been preserved, outstanding among such rulers was Ulugh Beg from 1394-1449 in Herat the grandson of Empire Timur, whose residence was in Heart, he trance freed the capital Heart To Samarqand in 1361. In 1428 he a huge observatory built a sextant for calculation the height of the sun, and with the aid of expert astronomers, drew up the most precise astronomical charts of the Middle Ages

Seljuk's or Ayyubids A.D 1085 until 1300

In 1249 al—Salih, last Egyptian Empire of the Seljuk's line, passed away. His widow and Shajar al—Durr, connived at the murder of her stepson, and proclaimed herself Queen. To save their masculine honour, the Muslim leaders of Cairo chose another Aybak, as her associate. She married him, but continued to rule; and when he attempted a declaration of indolence she had him murdered in his bath in 1257, she herself was presently battered to death with wooden shoes by Aybak's women, Aybak had live long enough to found the Mamluk dynasty. Mamluk meant "Owned" and was applied to slaves, usually strong and fearless Turkmen or Mongols employed as palace guards by the Seljuk Empire as in Rome and Baghdad, so in Cairo the guards became the kings. For 267 years from 1250 until 1570 the Mamluks ruled Egypt, and sometimes Syria from 1271 until 1516; the incarnadined their capital with assassinations, and beautified it with Afghan's Art; their courage saved Syria and Egypt even Europe when they routed the Mongols at Ain—Jalut in 1260. They received less wide acclaim for saving Palestine from the Franks "German" and driving the last Christian warrior from Asia. The greatest and least scrupulous of the Mamluk rulers was al—Malik Baibars 1260—77, born a Turkmen, his brave resourcefulness raised him to high command in the Egyptian army. It was he who defeated Louis IX at Mansura in 1250; and ten years later he found with fierce skill under the Empire Qutuz at Ain—Jalut. He murdered Qutuz on the way back to Cairo, made himself Empire, and accepted with winning grace the triumph that the city had prepared for his victorious victim. He renewed repeatedly the war against the Crusaders, always with success; and for these holy campaigns Moslem tradition honours him next to Harun and Saladin. In peace, says a contemporary Christian chronicler, he was "sober, chaste, just to his people, even kind to his Christian subjects" he organized the government of Egypt so well that no incompetence among his successors availed to unseat the Mukluks till their overthrow by the anther Turkmen called Ottoman from Seljuk's line in 1517, he gave Egypt a strong army and navy, cleared its harbours, roads, and canals, and built the mosque that bears his name. Another Trukmen deposed Baibars son and became Empire al—Mansur Sayf al—Din Qalaum 1279—90. History remembers him chiefly for the great hospital that he built at Cairo, and which he endowed with an annuity of a million dirhems "$500,000" his son Nasir in 1293 till 1340 was thrice enthroned but only twice deposed; built, aqueducts, public baths, schools, monasteries, and thirty mosques, dug with the forced labour of 100,000 men a canal connecting Alexandria with Nile, and exemplified Mamluk ways by slaughtering 20,000 animals for the marriage feast of his son, when Nasir traveled through the desert forty camels bore on their backs a garden of rich earth from the north of Afghanistan to provide him with fresh vegetables day. He depleted the treasury, and condemned his successors to a slow decline of the Mamluk power. These Empires do not impress us as favourably as the Seljuk's or Ayyubids, they undertook great public works, but most of these were accomplished by peasants and proletarians exploited to the limit of human tolerance, and for a government completely irresponsible to either the nation or an aristocracy; assassination was the only known form of recall. At the same time these brutal rulers had good taste and a large spirit in literature and art. The Mamluk period is the most brilliant in the Afghanistan History of medieval Egyptian architecture. Cairo was now in A. D 1250 till 1300 the richest city west of the Afghanistan. Markets teeming with all the necessaries and many of the superfluities of life; the great mart where one could buy and sell men and maidens; little shops nestling in the walls, and crowded with good of flexible price, alleys crawling with men and beasts, noisy with peddlers and carts, deliberately narrow for shade and crooked for defence; homes hidden behind stern facades, dark and cool amid the glare and heat and bustle of the streets, and breathing from an inner court or garden close; interiors lushly furnished with hangings, carpets, embroideries, and works of art; men chewing hashish to produce a dreamy intoxication; women gossiping in the zenana, or furtively flirting in a window bay; music strummed from a thousand lutes, and weird concerts in the Citadel; public parks redolent with flowers and picnicking canals and the great river dotted with cargo barges, passenger vessels, and pleasure boats; this was the Cairo of medieval Afghans—Turkmen. One of its poets sang

> Beside that garden flowed the placid Nile
> Oft have I steered my dahabiya there
> Oft have I landed to repose awhile?
> And bask and revel in the sunny smile
> Of her whose presence made the place so fair?

The age of Omar Khayyam A.D 1038 till 1122 Afghanistan led the world in Art, Poetry Academy of Herat, Balkh

The Afghan artists of this age were apparently equalled in number by the poets in Afghanistan and savants, Cairo, Baalbek, Aleppo, Damascus, Mosul, Emesa, Tus, Academy of Balkh—Bukahra, Herat, and many other cities under Afghan's poets boasted colleges; Baghdad alone had thirty in 1064. A year later Nizam al—Mulk added another Nizamiya, in 1234 the king founded still another, which in size, architectures, and equipment surpassed all the rest; one traveler called it the most beautiful building in the city. It contained four distinct law schools, in which qualified students received free tuition, food, and medical care, and a monthly gold dinar for other exegeses, it contained a hospital, a bathhouse, and a library freely open to students and staff. Women attended called in some cases, libraries were now richer and more numerous than ever in Islam; Moslem in Spain alone had seventy public libraries. Grammarians, lexicographers, encyclopaedists, and historians continued to flourish. Collective biography was an Afghan hobby and forte, in 1228 achieved an encyclopaedia of 300 Afghan's poets without mentioning Omar Khayyam, and M. ibn Khallikan 1211-82 surpassed all other single-handed works of his kind in his Obituaries of Men of Note, containing brief anecdotal lives of 865 distinguished Afghan's. it is remarkably accurate for a book covering so wide a field; ibn khallikan nevertheless apologized for its imperfections, saying, in its final works, that "God has allowed no book to be faultless except the Koran" al—Shahrastani, in a Book of Religions and Sects in 1128, analyzed the leading faiths and philosophies of the world, and summarized their history; no contemporary Christian could have written so learned and impartial a work. Afghan fiction never rose above the episodic picaresque proliferation of tales unified only by the persistence of a single character. After the Koran the Thousand Nights and a Night, and the fables of Bidpai, the most popular book in Afghanistan was the Maqamat "Discourses" of Abu Muhammad al—Hariri in 1054 of Basra, the other poets, we are told, tore up their verses unread. In Cairo Zuheyr sang of love long after his hari was white. In Afghanistan break-up of the Empire into small kingdoms increased the number and rivalry of patrons, and helped literature, as in nineteenth century Afghanistan—Germany was the riches of the nations in her poets. Anwari of Balkh fl. 1185 rhymed for a time at the court of Empire Sinjar, whom he praised only next to himself.

> I have a soul ardent as fire, a tongue fluent as water
> A mind sharpened by intelligence, and verse devoid of flaw
> Alas! There is no patron worthy of my eulogies!
> Alas! There is no sweetheart worthy of my odes!

Quite as confident was his contemporary Khagani in A.D 1106-85, whose arrogance provoked his tutor to a genealogical barb;

My dear Khagani, skilful though you are
In verse, one little hint I give you free
Mock not with satire any older poet
Perhaps he's your sire, though you don't know it

European knows Afghan's poetry chiefly through Omar Khyyam, Afghanistan classes him among her scientists, and considers his quatrains the casual amusement of "one of the greatest mathematicians of medieval times" Abu I—Fath Omar Khayyam ibn Ibrahim was born in Herat A.D 1038 and died in Nishapur, his cognomen meant tentmaker, but proves nothing about his trade or that of his father Abraham; occupational names, in Omar's time, had lost their literal application, as among the Smiths, Taylor's, Bakers, and Porters of our land. History knows little of his life, but records several of his works. His Algebra, translated into French in 1857, made significant advices both on al—Khwarizmi and on the Greeks; its partial solution of cubic equations has been judged "Perhaps the very highest peak of medieval mathematics" another of his works on algebra "a manuscript in the Leiden Library" studied critically the postulates and definitions of Euclid. In A.D 1074 the Empire Malik Shah commissioned him and others to reform the Khorasan "present day Afghanistan" calendar, the outcome was a calendar that required a day's correction every 3770 years—slightly more accurate that ours, which requires a day's correction every 3330 years; we may leave the choice to the next civilization. Afghan's religion proved stronger the Afghan science, and Omar's calendar failed to acceptance over religion the astronomer's repute is reflected in an anecdote told by Nizami—I—Arudi, who had known him at Herat: In the winter of A.D 1114 the king sent a messenger to Mary bidding its governor tell Omar al—Khayyam to select a favourable time for him to go hunting …. Omar looked into the matter for two days, made a careful choice of the desirable time, and he went to superintend the mounting of the king. When the king had gone a short distance the sky became overcast a rose, and snow and mist supervened. All present fell to laughing, and the king wished to turn back. But Omar said, "have no anxiety, for this very hour the clouds will clear away, and during these five days there will be no drop of moisture" so the king rode on, and the clouds opened, and during those five days there was no wet and no cloud was seen. The Rubaiyah or quatrain "from rubai, composed of four" is in its Dari form a poem of four lines rhyming aaba. It is an epigram in the Afghan—Greek sense, as the expression of a completed thought in terse poetic form. Its origin is unknown, but it long antedated Omar. In Afghan's Literature it is never part of a longer poem, but forms an independent whole, hence Afghan—Collectors of Rubaiyat arrange them not by their thought sequence but in the alphabetical order of the final letter of the rhyming syllables. Thousands of Afghans quatrains exist, mostly of uncertain authorship, over 1200 of them have been attributed to Omar, but often questionably. The oldest Afghanistan Manuscript of the Rubaiyat of Omar Khayyam, "in the Bodleian Library at Oxford in Landon England" goes back only to A.D 1460 Academy of Herat, and contain 158 stanzas, alphabetically arranged Several of these have been traced to Omar's predecessors some to Abu Said. One to Avicenna; it is hardly possible, save in a few cases, to assert positively that Omar wrote any particular one of the quatrains ascribed, to him. The German Orientalist Von Hammer, in 1818, was the first European to call attention to Omar's Rubaiyat. In 1859 Edward Fitz Gerald translated seventy-five of them into English verse of a unique and pithy excellence. The first edition though its price, found few purchasers, persistent and enlarged reissues, however, succeeded in transforming the Afghanistan mathematician into one of the most widely read poets in the world, during the European called the Great Games on Afghanistan" of the 110 quatrains translated by Fitz Gerald forty—nine in the judgment of those familiar which the original are faithful paraphrases of single quatrains in the Dari text, four are composites, each taking something from two or more quatrains, two reflect the whole spirit of the original poem, six are from quatrains sometimes included in Omar's text, but probably not his; two were influenced by Fiz Gerald's reading of Hafiz; three have no source in any extant text of Omar, were apparently fathered by Fitz Gerald, and were suppressed by him in his second edition, of stanza Ixxi

> O thou, who man of baser earth didst make
> And even with Paradise devise the snake
> For all the sin wherewith the face of man
> Is blackened, man's forgiveness give and take!

No corresponding passage can be found in Omar. For the rest a comparison of Fitz Gerald's version with a literal translation of the Dari text indicates that Fitz Gerald always reflects the spirit of Omar, and is as true to the original as may reasonably be expected of so poetic a paraphrase, the Darwinian mood of Fitz Gerald's time moved him to ignore Omar's kindly humour, and to deepen the ant theological strain. But Afghan's Authors only a century later than Omar describe him in terms quite consistent, with Fitz Gerald's interpretation. Mirsad al—Ibad A.D 1223 called him "an unhappy philosopher, atheist, and materialist" al—Qifti's History of the Philosophers A.D 1240 ranked him as "without an equal in astronomy and philosophy," but termed him an advanced freethinker, constrained by prudence to bridle his tongue, Sa'di, in the thirteenth century represented him as an ill-tempered follower of Avicenna, and listed two works by Omer on philosophy, new lost. Some Sufis sought a mystic allegory in Omar's quatrains, but the Ssufi Najmud Razi denounced him as the arch freethinker of his time. Influenced perhaps science, perhaps the poems of al—Ma'arri, Omar rejected theology with patient scorn, and boasted of stealing prayer rugs from the mosque, he accepted the fatalism of the Afghan's creed, and shorn of hope for an afterlife, fell into a pessimism that sought consolation in study and wine. Stanzas cxxxii—iii of the Bodleian manuscript raise intoxication almost to a world philosophy:

> Ties I who have swept with my moustaches the wine shop,
> To what is good and ill of both worlds said good bys
> Should both worlds fall like polo ball into the street?
> You shall seek me out a sleeping like a drunkard I shall be
> From all that is, save wine, to refrain is well...
> To be inebriate, squalid, and vagrant is well
> One draught of wine is from Moon to Fish

That is, from one end of the sky to the other. But when we note how many Afghan's poets chant similar eulogies to unconsciousness, we wonder is not this Bacchus piety a pose and literary form, like Horace's ambigendrous loves, probably such incidental quatrains give a false impression of Omar's life, they doubtless played a minor rely in his eighty five years, we should picture him not as a drunkard sprawling in the street, but as an old savant quietly content with cubic equations a few constellations and astronomic charts and an occasional cup with fellow scholars "star scattered on the grass" he seems to have loved flowers with the passion of a people bound to a parched terrain, and if we trust Nizami—i-Arudi he was granted his wish to lie where flowers bloomed. In the years A.D 1212 Omar Khayyam and Muzaffar—I Isfizari had alighted in the great city of Balkh… in the house of Emir Abu Sa'd had joined that assemble. In this friendly gathering I heard that Proof of the Truth Omar say, "My grave will be in a spot where trees will shed their blossoms on me twice a year." This seemed to me impossible, though I knew that one such as he would not speak idle works.

When I arrived at Nishapur in the years 1135, it being then some thirteen years since that great man had veiled his countenance in the dust… I went to visit his grave… his tomb lay at the food of a garden wall, over which pear trees and peach trees thrust their heads, and on his grave had fallen so many flower petals that his dust was hidden beneath them, then I remembered his words at Balkh, and I fell to weeping, because on the face of the earth, in all the regions of the habitable globe, I nowhere saw one like unto him.

Nizami or Ilyas Abu Muhammad
romance of Layla and Majnun

Five years after Omar's Khayyam death a poet far more honoured in Afghanistan was born at Balkh, as if in foil to Omar—Khayyam, Ilyas Abu Muhammad, later known as Nizmi, lived a life of genuine piety, rigorously abstained from wine, and devoted himself to parentage and poetry. His Great Romance of Layla and Majnun A.D in 1188 is the most popular of all love stories in Afghanistan, verse, Qqays Majnun "i.e., the Mad" becomes enamoured of Layla whose father compels her to marry another man; Majnun, delirious with disappointment, retires from civilization to the wilderness, only when Layla's name is mentioned does he return to brief sanity. Widowed, she joins him, but dies soon afterward; and Romeo Qays kills himself on her grave. Translation cannot render the melodious intensity of the original. Even the mystics sang of love, but we have their solemn assurance that the passion they portrayed was but a symbol for the love of God. Muhammad ibn Ibrahim known to literature as Farid al—Din Attar "Pearl of Faith Druggist" was born at Balkh A.D 1119, and received his final name from vending perfumes. Feeling a call to religion, he left his shop and entered a Sufi monastery at Balkh, his forty books all in Arabic, include 200,000 lines of poetry, his most famous work was the Mantiq al—Tayr, or Discourse of the Birds. Thirty birds "i.e., Sufis" plan a united search for the king of all birds, Simurgh "Truth" they pass through six valleys: search, Love knowledge, Detachment "from all personal desire" unification "where they perceive that all things are one" and Bewilderment "from losing all since of individual existence" three of the birds reach the seventh valley, annihilation "of the self" and knock at the door of the hidden king. The royal chamberlain shows each of them a record of its deeds; they are overcome with shame, and collapse into the dust. But from this dust they rise again as forms of light; and now they realize that they and Smirch "which means thirty birds" are one. They lose themselves henceforth in Simurgh, as shadows vanish in the sun. in other works Attar put his pantheism more directly; reason cannot know God, for it cannot understand itself, but love and ecstasy can read to God, for He is the essential reality and power in all things, the sole source of every act and motion, the spirit and life of the world. No soul is happy until it loses itself as a part in this spirit as the whole, longing for such union is the only true religion; self effacement in that union is the only true immortality. The orthodox denounced all this as heresy; a crowd attacked Attar's house and burned it to the ground. However, he was relatively indestructible; tradition claims for him a life of 110 years. Before he died, we are told, he laid his hands in blessing upon the child who would hail him as master, and eclipse his fame. Jalal ud—Din Balkh—Rumi A.D 1201—73 was native of Balkh, but lived most of his life at Konya "Mongols ear in Afghanistan" a mysterious Sufi, Shams, came there to preach, and Balkh was so moved by him that he founded the famous order of Mawlawi, or Dancing, Dervishes, which still makes Konya its capital. In a comparatively short life Jalal—Balkh wrote several hundred poems. The shorter ones, collected as his Divan or Book of Odes, are marked by such depth of feeling, sincerity, and richness, yet naturalness, of imagery as place them at the top of all religious poetry composed since the Psalms. Jalal's—Balkh main work, the Mathnawi—I—Ma'nawi "Spiritual Couplets" is a diffuse exposition of Sufism, a religious epic outweighing in bulk all the legacy of "Homer" it has passages of great beauty, but a thing of beauty, laden with works, is not a joy forever. The theme again is universal unity. And lastly Sa'di, His real name, of course, was much longer—Musharrit ud—Din ibn Muslih ud—Din Abdullah. His father held a post at the court of the king at Balkh, when the father died the Aaatabeg adopted the boy, and Sa'di, following custom, added his patron's name to his own Scholars debate the dates of his earthly stagy at Balkh in A. D 1184 till 1291 in any case he almost spanned a century. "In my youth" he tells us. "I was overmuch religion… scrupulously pious and abstinent" after graduating from the Nizami College in 1226 "Mongols era in Afghanistan" he began those extraordinary Wandrjahre which took him for thirty years through all the near and Middle East, India, Ethiopia, Egypt, and North Africa. He knew every hardship, and all degrees of poverty, he complained that he had no shoes, until he met a man without feet, "whereupon I thanked Providence for its bounty to myself" in India he exposed the mechanism of a miracle—working idol, and killed the hidden Brahmin who was the god of the machine, in his later rollicking verse he recommended a like summary procedure with all quacks;

> You too, should you chance to discover such trick
> Make away with the trickster, don't spare him, and be quick!
> For if you should suffer the scoundrel to live
> Be sure that to you he no quarter will give
> So I finished the rogue, notwithstanding his wails
> With stones, for dead men, as you know, tell no tales

He fought against the Crusaders, was captured by the "Infidels" and was ransomed. Gratefully he married the daughter of his ransomed at Balkh. She turned out to be an intolerable vixen. "The ringlets of the lovely" he wrote, "are a chain on the feet of reason" he divorced her, encountered more ringlets, assumed more chains. He outlived this second wife, retired at fifty to a garden hermitage, and stayed there the last fifty years of his life. Having lived, he began to write; all his major work is told, were composed after this retirement. The Pandnama is a Book of Wisdom, the Divan is a collection of short poems, mostly in Dari, some in Arabic, some pious, obscene. The Bustan Sa'di, or Orchard, expends in didactic verse Sa'di's general philosophy, relieved by passages of tender sensuality;

> Never had I known moments more delicious. That night I clasped my lady to my breast and gazed into her eyes swimming with sleep….
> I said to her; "Beloved my slender cypress tree now is not the time to sleep. Sing, my nightingale! Let they mouth open as unfolds the rosebud Sleep no more, turmoil of my hear! Let they lips offer me the philtre of the love" and my lady looked upon me and murmured low: "Turmoil of thy heart? Yet dost thou wake me? … Thy lady has repeated all this time that she has never belonged to another.… And thou dost smile, for thou newest that she lies. But what matter? Are her lips less warm beneath thy lips? Are her should, dears less soft beneath thy caress? They say the breeze of May is sweet, as the perfume of the rose, the song of the nightingale, the green plain, and the blue sky. O thou who newest not, all these are sweet only when one's lady is there!

The Gulistan Sa'di, or Rose Garden A.D 1258 "Mongols era" in Balkh, is a medley of instructive anecdotes interspersed with delectable poetry. An unjust king asked a holy man "what is more excellent than prayer? "The holy man said: "for you to remain asleep till midday, that for this one interval you may not afflict mankind" then dervishes can sleep on one rug, but two kings cannot be accommodated in a whole kingdom. If you court riches, ask not for contentment. The religious man who can be vexed by an injury is as yet a shallow brook. Never has anyone acknowledged his own ignorance, except that person who while another is talking and has not yet finished, begins to speak. Heed you but one perfection and seventy faults, your lover would discern only that one perfection. Hurry not… learns deliberation. The Afghan horse makes a few stretches at full speed, and breads down; the camel, at its deliberate pace, travels night and day, and gets to the end of its journey. Acquire knowledge, for no reliance can be placed on riches or possessions…. Were a professional man to lose his fortune, he need not feel regret, for his knowledge is of itself a mine of wealth. The severity of the schoolmaster is more useful than the indulgence of the father. Were intellect to be annihilated from the face of the earth, nobody could be brought to say, "I am ignorant" levity in a nut is a sign of its being empty. Sa'di was a Philosopher, but he forfeited the name by writing intelligibly. His was a healthier philosophy than Omar's it understood the consolations of faith, and knew how to heal the sting of knowledge with the simple blessings of a kindly life; Sa'di experience all the tragedies of the human comedy, and yet insisted on a hundred years. But he was a poet as well as a Philosopher, sensitive to the form and texture of every beauty from a woman's "cypress limbs" to a star that for a moment possesses by itself all the evening sky; and capable of expressing wisdom or platitude with brevity, delicacy, and grace. He was never at a loss for an illuminating comparison or an arresting phrase. "to give education to the worthless is like throwing walnuts upon a dome" "a friend and "I were associating like two kernels in one almond shell" if the orb of the sun had been in the wallet" of this stingy merchant "nobody would have seen daylight in the world till Judgment Day" in the end despite his wisdom, Sa'di remained the poet, surrendering his wisdom with a whole heart to the rich slavery of love. Fortune suffers me not to clasp my sweetheart to my breast Nor lets me forget my exile long in a kiss on her sweet lips pressed The noose wherewith she is won't to snare her victims far and wide I will snatch away, that so one day I may lure her to my side Yet I shall not dare caress her hair with a hand that is overbold For snared therein like birds in a gin, are the hearts of lovers untold A slave am I to that gracious form, which, as I picture it Is clothed in grace with a measuring rod, as tailors a garment fit O cypress tree, with silver limbs, this color and scent of thin

Have shamed the scent of the myrtle plant and the bloom of the eglantine Judge with thin eyes, and set thy foot in the fair and free And tread the jasmine under thy food, and the flowers of the Judas tree…. O wonder not if time of spring thou dost rouse, such jealousy That the cloud death weeps while the flowerets smile, and all on account of thee! If o'er the dead thy feet should tread, those feet so fair and fleet No wonder it were if thou should hear a voice from his winding sheet Distraction is banned from this our land in the time of our lord the king Save that I am distracted with love of thee, and men with the songs I sing

Primitive—Mongols era, in Khrasan "present day Afghanistan—Central Asia, India, Iraq, Iran, Turkey, Egypt, Syria" in Golden age of Art, Poetry, Calligraphy, Philosophy and Architecture from the Greatest Capital of Balkh—Bukhara, Herat, Kandara and Agra

Once again Afghanistan—History illustrated the truism that civilized comfort attracts barbarian conquest. The Seljuk's Empire had brought new strength to Eastern Asia; but they too had succumbed to ease, and had allowed the empire of Malik Shah to break down into autonomous kingdoms culturally brilliant and militarily weak. Religious fanaticism and racial antipathies divided the people into bitter sects, and frustrated any united defence against the Crusades. Meanwhile, on the plains and deserts of north-western Asia, the Mongols thrived on hardships and primitive fertility. They lived in tents or the open air, followed their herds to fresh pastures, clothed themselves in ox hides, and studied with relish the arts of war. These new Huns, like their kin of eight centuries back, were experts with dagger and sword, and arrows aimed from their flying steeds. If we may believe the Christian missionary Giovanni de Piano Carpini, "they eat anything, even lice" and they had as little repugnance to feeding on rats, cats, dogs, and human blood as our most cultured contemporaries to eating eels, and snails. Genghis "Khan" in A.D 1167 till 1227 I. e. the Great king disciplined them with severe laws into an irresistible force. And led them to the conquest of Afghanistan—-Central Asia from the Volga to the Chinese wall, During the absence of Genghis from his capital at Karokorum, a Mongol chieftain rebelled against him, and formed a league with Ala al—Din Muhammad, the Governor of the independents of Khwarizm. Genghis suppressed the rebellion, and sent the king an offer of peace. The offer was accepted; but shortly thereafter two Mongol merchants in Transoxiana were executed as spies by the governor of Otrar. Genghis demanded the extradition of the governor refused, beheaded the chief of the Mongol embassy, and sent its other members back without their Genghis declared war, and Mongol invasion of Central Asia began in A.D 1219. an army under Genghis son Juji defeated the Governor troops at Jand; the governor fled to Samarqand, leaving 160,000 of his men dead on the field, another army, under Genghis son Jagatai, captured and sacked Otrar. A third army under Genghis himself, burned Balkh—Bukhara to the ground, raped thousands of women, and massacred 30,000 men. Samarqand and Balkh surrendered at his coming, but suffered pillage and wholesale slaughter; a full century later Ibn Batuta described these cities as still largely in ruins until today. Genghis son Tulle led with chains men, 700, 0000 men through Khorasan, ravaging every town in Afghanistan, on their march. Mongols placed captives in their van, and gave them a choice between fighting their fellow men in front, or being cut down from behind, Merv was captured by treachery, and was burned to the ground; its libraries, the glory of Afghan's, were consumed in the conflagration; its inhabitants were allowed to march out through the gates with their treasures, only to be massacred and robbed in detail, this slaughter "the Afghan's Historians aver" occupied thirteen days, and took 1,300,000 lives. Every man and child there was killed, except 400 artisan artists who were sent to? and the heads of the slain were piled up in a ghastly pyramid. The lovely city of Rayy, with its 3000 mosques and its famous pottery kilns, was laid in ruins, and "a Afghan historian tells us" its entire population was put to death, Jalal—Din collected a new arm of Turkmen gave

Genghis battle on Afghanistan, was defeated, and fled to Delhi like Million Afghan at the times, Herat, having rebelled against its Mongol governor was punished with the slaughter of 100,000 inhabitants. This ferocity was part of the Great military science of the Mongols; it sought to strike a paralyzing terror into the hearts of later proponent, and to leave no possibility of revolt among the defeated. The policy succeeded. Genghis now returned to Mongolia, enjoyed his five hundred wives and concubines, and died in bed. His son and successor Ogotai sent a horde of 1,500,000 men "chains" to capture Jalal ud—Din, who had formed another army at Diarbekr, Jalal was defeated and killed, and the unhindered Mongols ravaged Central Asia earn Mesopotamia, Georgia, hearing that a rebellion, bed by the Assassins, had broken out, Hulagu, a grandson of Genghis, led a Mongol army throe Samarqand and Balkh, destroyed the Assassin stronghold at—Alamut, and turned toward Mesopotamia. Al—Mustasim Balkhi, last of Baghdad, of the East, was a learned scholar, a meticulous calligrapher, a man of exemplary gentleness, devoted to religion, books, and charity: this was enemy to Hulagu's taste. The Mongol accused the Balkhi of sheltering rebels, and of withholding promised aid against the Assassins; as penalty he demanded the submission of the Balkhi to the Mongol and the complete demilitarization of Central Asia—-Afghanistan. Al—Mustasim returned a boastful refusal. After a month of siege, al—Mustasim sent Hulagu presents and an offer of surrender. Lured by a promise of clemency, he and his two sons gave themselves up to the Mongol, on 12 58 Hulagu and his troops entered Baghdad, and began forty days of pillage and massacre; 900,000 of the inhabitants, we are told, were killed. Thousands of Afghan's scholars, scientists, and poets fell in the indiscriminate slaughter; libraries and treasures accumulated though centuries were in a week plundered or destroyed; hundreds of thousands of volumes were consumed Finally the king and his family, after being forced to reveal the hiding place of their secret wealth, were put to death. Hulagu now returned to north of Afghanistan. His army remained behind, and under other generals it advanced too the conquest of Syria. At Ain Jalut it met an Egyptian army under the Turkmen called Mamluj leaders Qutuz and Baibars, and was destroyed in 1260, everywhere in Islam and European men of all faiths rejoiced, the spell of fear was broken, in A.D 1303 a decisive battle near Damascus ended the Mongol threat, but the Turkmen saved the Syria for the Mamluks, perhaps Europe for Christianity. Never in History had a civilization suffered so suddenly so devastating a blow, the Barbarian conquest of Rome had been spread over two centuries, between each blow and the next some recovery was possible; and the German helped to destroy. But the Mongols came and went within forty years, they came not to conquer and stay, but to kill, pillage, and carry their spoils to Mongolia, when their bloody tide ebbed it left behind it a fatally disrupted economy, canals broken or choked, schools and libraries in ashes, governments too divided poor and weak to govern, and a population cut in half and shattered in soul, Epicurean indulgence, physical and mental exhaustion, military incompetence and cowardice, religious sectarianism and obscurantism, political corruption and anarchy, all culmination in piecemeal collapse before external attack this and no change of climate, Afghanistan—Central Asia from world leadership to destitution, from a hundred teeming cultured cities in Syria, Mesopotamia, Caucasus, Egypt, India, Turkey and Transoxiana into the poverty, disease, and stagnation of modern times.

The History of Afghan's Literatures & Art from Aryana–Khorasan present day Afghanistan–Central Asia

The student of the Afghan's Literatures & Art from Aryana 3,500 years Khorasan 1285 years Afghanistan middle of nineteen century, is faced with peculiar difficulties. The subject matter of his interest is so widely scattered that fortunate indeed must be the individual who can succeed in gaining even to the most important e Afghan's Literatures examples. The Great public collections in London England, the University of Oxford, Cambridge and Edinburgh, furnish abundant material, but some of the most noteworthy achievements in Afghan's Literatures & Art are to be found in the Asiatic Museum in St. Petersburg in Russia, and the Bibliotheque Nationals Paris in France; the Libraries of Berlin, Munich in Germany, National Libraries Agra—Delhi in India, National Libraries in Egypt, Herat—Kabul Museum, and Vienna also though not so rich, cannot be neglected. Apart from these public institutions, access to which is not hard to obtain, there are numerous private collections which are in some instances jealously guarded, and no publication have yet the contents of them. Like many other treasures of Afghan's Literatures & Art that were once available in Europe a considerable number of some of the finest paintings produced by Afghan's Artiste have crossed the Atlantic to America, and must be studied in Boston or New York, the Afghan's itself pared with some of its most magnificent Afghan—treasures of pictorial Art and Literatures at a time when their beauty was not appreciated by their oriental owners, but some still remain in Afghanistan until 1929, and India. A Shah Nama decorated for Prince Baysunqur in Herat A.D 1528, the prince to whom the authoritative recession of this epic in its present form is attributed, still exists in the palace of the king of Afghanistan, and must contain some of the delicate and charming work of the Academy of Herat; but it has never been described, and shares this obscurity with other treasures of the same kind, "because of The Great Games of middle of the nineteen century and the Cold War from 1930 until 2001" E. Herzfeld, Eunice Bucher Scathe in Afghanistan Leipzig in 1920, the fall of the Turkmen called Ottoman in 1922, imperial House and confiscation of its inherited works of Art by Afghan's, the new government has revealed the unsuspected existence of a number of Afghan's paintings of the fifteen century best period, but we still await an adequate accounted of the contents of the Museum of the Eevakaf and other places in which they are stored, for India some account has been published of the illuminated MSS. In the Patna Oriental Public Library, V. C Scott, an Easter Library Glasgow in 1920, and government of Bihar and Orissa has had photographic reproductions made of the miniatures in three manuscripts; but no account is yet available of the contents of Library of H.H. the Nawab of Rampur in India, and there are doubtless other private collections of Afghan's Art in India which in time add to our knowledge of Afghan's Art. But apart from the fact that the existing materials are difficult of access or as being still undecided, are practically unknown, or at least not available for purposes of study, the student is faced by a further difficulty in that examples that have thus survived form but a very small part of the total number of Afghan's—Works of Art that once existed, example in A.D 1361 Empire Tamer transferred the capital Library from Herat to Samarqand same five thousand camel for the transfer a single library from Herat to Samarqand. Consequently there are great gaps in his knowledge a whole Academy of painting in Heart can only be guessed at through the survival of a single example; the sources of such Academy or groups of painters as can be distinctly recognized often remain obscure; the advent of influences can be observed, without its being possible to trace them to their source. These and similar difficulties are in great measure the result of the enormous destruction that has deprived us of all knowledge of thousand if not of teen—thousands, of pictures; more particularly is this the case with regard to the great earliest examples of Afghan's Art. With the exception of frescoes upon the walls of palaces, practically all the Afghan's pictures of which we have any knowledge were painted on paper a material so easily damaged or destroyed, especially in the central Asia. Manuscripts and paintings require special care and watchfulness in countries where the ravages of white ants and other insects can be so successfully achieved in an incredibly short space of time, and where semi tropical rain may ruin by damp the painted page within the space of a few minutes. When due precautions are relaxed or carelessness neglects to take the requisite amount of care, irretrievable ruin may result. The fact that so many royal volumes have survived to us in stately bindings, and in a wonderful state of preservation is due to the care that has been bestowed upon them by generations of librarians, for the written page has generally been regarded with respect devout persons in Afghanistan, and when some royal patron has bestowed his favour upon artists, calligraphists, painters, workers in gold, and binders, the resulting work of art has often been guarded with jealous care in the palace of his descendants, so far as political conditions have permitted the continuity of such precautions. But there have been lamentable exception. The Sayyid Ahmad khan, famous alike as theologian, social reformer, and man of letters, used to relate that in the days when there was still a Kabuli—Tajik Emperor living in the fort at Delhi in India he once entered the royal library and noticing a confused heap of loose lying in a corner of the room, began turning them over with a stick; among much that deserved no particular notice, he came across a finely written page, illuminated with rich gold work, and after further diligent search he managed to recover out of this rubbish heap the complete manuscript of the Memoirs of Emperor Jahangir, the copy that hands been written out for the Emperor's own use, when he had copies made for distribution among contemporary Afghan Princes. He carried the recovered volume away to his own house in the city of Delhi in India, but nothing has ever been heard of it since the mutineers sacked his house in 1857. If such an incident could occur in a royal palace that had a continuous history since Emperor Shah Jahan built it in the fort of Delhi in 1638, it may easily be imagined how the loss or damage of manuscripts might occur in places less closely guarded. But such sporadic destruction has been trifling when compared to the ruin affected by the plundering of captured cities, when libraries were involved in the horrible fate that befell the inhabitants, exposed to the savageries of a victorious army. To the fact that Uzbek Nadir from north Afghanistan in 1739 stripped the Royal library of Delhi of some of its finest treasures, we owe the preservation of the best examples of the work of Emperor Akbar's painters; safe present day Iran, the escaped the fate that befell the manuscripts that Uzbek Nadir did not consider it worth his while to include among the rich booty which carried away with him from India, and so were not doomed to be looted by an ignorant soldiery at a later date as were the remnants of the imperial library in Delhi and the Royal library in Luck now. Nadir stolen volumes after their journey across the plains of India and safely reached their destination in Heart "Sir Percy History 2nd ed. Vol. II p. 263" but how often did such good fortune befall precious manuscripts that formed part of loot of other armies, destruction and invasion are part of the country's history of Afghanistan in A.D 1224 as far back as the days of Genghis khan, museum, library, and art were being burned. Abandoned by the wayside, or thrown carelessly away, many a precious manuscript must have perished in this fashion, while those that were left behind in the ruined castle or palace suffered such a fate as befell the MSS. Of the monastery of pinto craters, as described by Robert Curzon in his Monasteries of the Levant pp. 360—2 4th ed., London in 1851 I went, he says to look at the place leaning through a ruined arch, I looked down into the lower story of the tower, and there I saw the melancholy remains of a once famous library in Afghanistan. It was indeed a hear rending sight. By the dim light which streamed through the opening of iron door in the wall of the ruined tower, I saw above a hundred ancient Afghan's—Manuscripts lying among the rubbish which had fallen from the upper floor, which was ruinous, and had in great part given way. He managed to extricate two or three, but found that the rain had washed the outer leaves quit clean; the pages were stuck tight together into a solid mass, and when I attempted to open them, they broke short off in square bits like a biscuit. Such a report might have been given of many an Afghan's Library, if any observer had cared to record its fest. The history of Afghanistan is filled with the record of continuous warfare; one dynasty succeeds another, and the founder of a new kingdom has to reward his victorious army by giving over the conquered capital to plunder, seems in 1929 at the victorious of plunder capital royal library Museums of Kabul reward to plunder, and 1992 at victorious of the Pakistani—Taliban one again has to reward his destruction perishable works of art reward to plunder not only the Museum but the enterer great city of Kabul also all the female, Balding, Auto, House, University, School, Hospital, Business, reward to Two Hundred Thousand Pakistani—Taliban's plunder, and 1992 at victorious of the Pakistani once again has to reward his destruction perishable works of art reward to plunder Kabul Museum was the oldest Largest Museum's in the Would with the Biblical and Decorative Art, the destruction of perishable works of Art on such occasions, which occur through tout the course of Afghanistan History with monotonous frequency, must have been enormous for the people of Afghanistan

Khorasan "present day Afghanistan Central Asia with the Seljuk Empire Seljuk Art, Architecture & History

Aryana-Khorasan present day Afghanistan-Central Asia & India, the Seljuk's, who ruled Khorasan "present day Afghanistan Central Asia and Constantinople "Turkey" from 8th century until 1922 in called Ottoman Empire" largest empires, were originally nomadic Turkmen shepherds from the steppes of Afghanistan—Central Asia, they belonged to the great Oghuz federation of nine Turkmen tribes, that ruled since the 8th century until 1922, had steadily spreading west as far as the Aral Sea. Deployed by the rulers from Khorasan "new Afghanistan—Central Asia the capital of Bactria and Aria" from this time as defenders against invading Islamic Kufic "new Arabs" the Turkmen had conquered their own territories and exerted pressure on the Samanids of Balkh—Bukhara until the region finally fell to the Trukmen. The clan adopted Islam in A.D 960 under one of its first leaders, Seljuk, from whom it took its name, and its members hence forth carried out their raids to the west and south as Islamic "frontier warriors" {Ghazi} and religious fighters. After Seljuk's death, his three sons and ultimately two grandsons led the clan and spread further through Constantinople, after being defeated by the region's ruler Empire Mahmud of Ghazni, in A.D 1026, while in the service of the Turkmen, the Seljuk's split into three groups. While one of them remained in the east, the two groups led by Seljuk's grandsons crossed Khorasan, Iraq, Iran, India, Turkey, East—Turkistan, where several cities succumbed to them, the two brothers, Tughril Beg 1038—1063 and Chaghri Beg 1038—1060 then divided territory into, while the younger brother Chaghri Beg, who bore the title "King of King" remained in the northern Khorasan area as an independent ruler with royal seats at Balkh and Merv, Tughril Beg established himself in Nishapur with more senior title "the Most Honoured Supreme Ruler" Empire, he realized his political ambition following a decisive victory over the Great capital of Ghaznavis in 1040 with the consolidation of the state as an entity and an expansion towards the west in 1042 he occupied western including Rayy and also Constantinople, having previously been acknowledged as supreme ruler of all the Turkmen tribes. From 1050 Tughril Beg led campaigns into Kufic "New Arabia" partly in order to liberate the caliph of Babylon from the tutelage of the Buyids and as a strict religious, to set himself up as the Islamic Caliphate's new protector, but also to conduct a religious war against the Fatimids of Mecir "new Egypt" in 1055 when he marched into Babylon and overthrew the Buyids rule, he had the caliph rant him certain honorary titles, in a document of A.D the Afghan—Tughril Beg is name as "Rules of Rulers the king of the East and West, restorer of religion. Right hand of the Caliph and Commander of the Faithful, an Islamic State from Khorasan to all Arab nations neither could the caliph refuse him the hand of his daughter in marriage in 1062, and it must have immediately been clear to him that he had simply exchanged one set of masters, the Buyids, for another. At the same time, new groups Turkmen were constantly streaming west, whom Tugril Beg diverted into the border wars against the Christian Empires of Byzantium, and Georgia, while claiming the rich provinces for himself. He finally selected as his seat, and this was also teaming the man capital Balkh his two successors, while the Seljuk Empire was rapidly expanding from Balkh towards Babylon, with the aim of bringing the caliphate of

Babylon under its protection Balkh—Mery remained its capital artistic century, during this time the Uzbeks were erecting impressive monumental building in Balkh—Bukhra in the flourishing cities of Balkh—Bukhara, correctly considered the classical era of Khorana "new Afghanistan Central Asia architecture, the buildings dating from public, sacred and even memorial are of an exquisite elegance and display a harmonious balance in construction decoration.

Scholars of Afghanistan from A.D 700

1. Scientists: 1. Abu Ma'shar. 2. Abu Wafa. 3. Abu Zayed Balkhi. 4. Alfraganus 5. Ali Qushji 6. Avienna 7. Birjandi 8. Biruni 9. Hasib Marwazi 10. Ibn Hayyan 12. Khazini 13. Khazin 14. Khujandi 15. Khwarizmi 16. Nasir al-Din Tusi 17. Omar Khayyam 18. Sharaf al-Din Tusi. 19. Sijzi

2. Philosophers: 1. Ghazali 2. Amiri 3. Avicenna 4. Farabi 8. Nair Khusraw 5. Qushatri 6. Sejestani 7. Shahrastani

3. Islamic Scholars Bukhari 2. Hakim Nishapuri 3. Juwayni 4. Malik ibn Dinar 5. Maturidi 6. Muslim ibn al Hajjaj 7. Nasa'I 8. Qushayri 9. Shayku Tusi 10. Taftazani 10. Tirmizi 11 Zamakhshari

4. Poets and Artists: Abu alKhair 2. Attar 3. Behzad 4. Daqiqi 5. Ferdowsi 6. Jami 7. Rabi'a Balkhi 7 Rudaki 8. Rumi 9. Sanai

5. Historians and Political: 1. Abul-Fazl Bayhaqi 2, Abu Muslm Khorasani 3. Abu Sa'id Gardezi 4 Ali Sher Nava'i 5. Ata al-Mulk Juvayni 6. Aufi 7. Bal'ami 8. Gawhar Shad 9. Ibn Khordadbeh 10 Khalid ibn Barmak 11. Nizam al-Mulk 12. Tahi Foshanji 13. Yahya Barmaki

1. Abu Jafar Muhammad ibn Hasan 900-992 was a Afghan astronomer and mathematician from Afghanistan, he worked on both astronomy and number theory. Was one of the scientists brought to the court in Balkh, Afghanistan by the ruler of the Samady dynasty.

2. Abu al-Hassan al-Amiri, Abu al-Hassan Muhammad ibn Yusuf al-Amiri died 992 theologian and philosopher of Afghanistan who attempted to reconcile philosophy with religion, and Sufism with conventional Islam, while al-Amiri believed the revealed thruths of Islam were superior to the logical conclusions of philosophy, he argued that the two did not contradict each other, Al-Amiri consind areas of agreement and synthesis between disparate Islamic sects. However, he believed Islam to be morally superior to other religions, notably Zoroastrianism and Manicheism. Al-Amiri was the most prominent Afghan-Muslim philosopher following the tradition of Kindi in Islamic Philosophy he was contemporary of Ibn-Miskawayh and his friend, and lived in a half century between Al-Farabi and Ibn Sina. Life and education, Abu'l Hasan Mahammad ibn Yusuf ibn al-Amiri was born in Balkh Afghanistan,. He began his career studying under Abu Zayed al-Balkhi in Afghanistan, before moving to Rey and ultimately Baghdad. It was in Baghdad where he met noted 10th century intellectuals such as al-Tawahidi and Ibn Miskawayh. Al'Amiri retied in Balkh, where he had access to the Samani library in Balkh, and died in Nishapur in 992. he believed that philosophy did not contradict the teachins of Islam and tried to focus and base his beliefs on both philosophy and Islam. However many people believed that th philosophy teaching beliefs are much different than Islam's or any other cultures. Al-Amiri argued that revealed truth must be superior to philosophy. His believings involved the Greeks too. In Abul'Hasan Muhammad Ibn Yusuf al'Amiri believed that the Greeks did not have a final say because they as a society, lacked a prophet who had a final say in all forms. Abu'l Hasan main purpose was to defend Islam against a form of philosophy which was reharded as independent of revelation. In 10th century. Philosophy works alI'lam bi manaqib al-Islam "An Exposition on the Merits of Islam" Inqadh al-bashar min al jahr wa'l-qadar "Deliverance of Mankind from problem of predestination and Free Will" Here al-'Amiri

attempts a resolution of the problem of free will by the application of Aristotelian principles. Al-Taqrir li-awjuh al-taqdir "the determination of the Varoius aspects of predestination" al-Amiri continues to addres the problem of free will.

3. Abu Sa'id Abdul-Hay ibn Dhahhak ibn Mahmud Gardezi deied 1061 A.D the early 11th century from province of Gardez in Afghanistan who wrote the book Zzayn al-Akhbar Gardezi's work, written in Dari is considered important for the Islamic history of Afghanistan-central Asia. Gardizi took a dispassionate view of history which is fairly remarkable for its time. For exmple he does not either preasise the Ghaznavids nor the coming of the Saljuqs. His style of Dari is simple but mature and provides one of the classical examples of Afghanistan prose-weiting. A critical edition was published, Gardizi told about the territory of Hungarians "the Hungarians country is situated between the territory of bulkars and eskils, who date back to the bulkars their country reaches the Rum-sea Balak Sea, the two rives, which flow into the Rum-sea are called Atil Volga and Danube. He wrote the following text about Hungarian people and their culture: there Hungarian people are pretty and handsome. Their clother are made of brocade, there weapona ear decorated by silver and gold. In the time of proposl they have to pay for the girl, mainly they give animals. But it can be the fur of ermine, squirrel, mart or fox.

4. Abul-Fazl Bayhaqi born 995 Ghazni Afghanistan and died 1077 main interests in history, works Tarikh-e Mas'oudi. Abul-Fazl Bayhaqiibn Zeyed ibn Mahammad Abul-Fazl Mohammad ibn Hossein ibn Soleyman ayyoub Ansari Evesi was a histiorian and author. He wrote the famous work of Afghanistan literature Tarikh-e Mas'oudi "Masoudian history, also known as Tarikh-e Bayhaqi. After the retirement in 1058 A.D Bayhaqi started the editing of his daily notes and historical data and published them in a book, name it Tarikh-e Baaihaqi. His book is one of the most creditable sources about the Ghaznavid Empire, and his fluent pose stule has made the book considerable in Afghanistan literature too.

Abu Rayhan al-Biruni

Al-Biruni regarded as one of the greatest scholars of Afghanistan medieval Islamic era and was well versed in Physics. Mathemaics, and natural sciences, and also distinguished himself as a historian. Chronologist and linguist. He was conversant in Chorasmian, Dari, Sanskrit, Turkic and Kufic "now Arabic" als knew Greek, Hebrew. He spent a large part of his life in the great capital of Ghani in Afghanistan "9ᵗʰ century Ghazni was the capital of Afghanistan" capital of the Ghaznavid dynasty which rulcd from India to Africa. In 1017 he traveled to the India and became the most important interpreter of Afghan-Indou science to the Indian, he is given the titiles the founder of Indology and the first anthropologist. He was an impartial wrter on cutom and creeds of varous nations, and was given the title al-Ustdadh "the Master" for his remarkable description of early 11ᵗʰ century india. He also made contribution to Earth Sciences, and is regarded as the father of geodesty for his important contributions to that field, along with his significant contribution to geogography. He was born in outer district of Balkh, The word Biruni means "outer-district" in Afghanistan, and so this becams his nisha: al-Biruni. His fist twenty years were spent in Balkh where he studied fiqh, theology, grammar, mathematics. Astronomy, medics and other sciences. The Dari chorasmian lanage, which was the language of Biruni, survived for several centuries after Islam until the Tukification of the region and so must some at lesat of the culture and lore of ancient Afghanistan, for it is hard to see the commanding figure of Biruni a repository of so much knowledge, appearing in a cultural vacuum. He was sympathetic to the Afrighids, who were overthrown by the rival dynasty of Ma'munids in 005. leaving his homeland, he left for Bukhara, then under the Samanid ruler Mansur II the son of Nuh. There he also corresponded with Avicenna and there are extant exchanges of views between these two scholars. In 998, he went to the court of the Ghazni, there he wrote his first important work, al-Athar al-Baqqiya'an al-Qorun al-Khaliyya Literally. The remaining traces of past centuries, and translated as Chronology of ancient nations or Biruni wrote an extensice commentary on Indu-Afghan astronomy in the kitab to'rikh al-Hind, in which he claims to have resolved the matter of Earh's raration in a work on astronomy that is no nolonger extant, his Miftah-ilm-alhai'a "Key to Astronomy" the rotation of the earth does in no way impair the value of astronomy, as all appearances of an astronomic character of Afghanistan character can quite as well be explained according to this theory as to the other. There are, however, other reasons which make it impossible. This question is most difficult to solve. The most prominent of both modem and ancient Afghan-astronomers have deeply studied the question of the moving of the earsth, and tried to refute it. We too have x composed a book on the subject called Miftah-ilm-alhai'a "Key to Astronomy" in which we thin we have surpassed our predecessors, if not in the words, at all events in the matter. In his description of Sijzi's astrolabe's he hints at contemporary debates over the movement of the earth. He carried on a lengthy correspondence and sometimes heated debate with Ibn Sina, in which Biruni repeatedly attacks Aristotle's celestial physics: he argues by simple experiment that vacuum must exist; he is amazed by the weakness of Aristotle's argument against elltrical orbits on the basis that they would create vacuum; he attacks the immutability of the celestial spheres; and so on. In his major extant astronomical work, the Mas'ud Canon, he regards heliocentric and geocentric hypotheses as mathematically equivalent but heliocentrism as physically impossible, yet approves of the theory that the earth rotates on its axis. He utilizes his observational data to disprove Ptolemy's immobile solar apogee. More recently,

Biruni's eclipse data was used by Dunthorne in 1749 to help determine the acceleration of the moon and his observational data has entered the larger astronomical historical record and is still used today in geophysics and astronomy. Physics Al-Biruni contributed to the introduction of the experimental scientific method to mechanics, unified statics and dynamics into the science of mechanics and combined the fields of hydrostatics with dynamics to create hydrodynamics.

Science in Religion gardens of Science

Khorasan Balkh 5,500 years was Capital of Khorasan (present day Afghanistan, Iraq-Iran-India-Turkman-Mongol-Azarbaijan-Samarqand-Uzbekistan-Kokand-East Turkistan-Khiva-Kyrgyzstan-Kazakhstan) before Europeans, the Saxon-Great Games between three German Empire's their most powerful Cousins Empire, The Saxon first cousin's empire, the Kaiser of Germany, the King of Hanover (present day England) and Tsars of Russia from middle of the 19th century until 1917 Religion science was in its prime during European Middle Ages, between the 9th and the 13th centuries, particularly in the brilliant period of the Afghan Empire from the 9th century to the 11th. A considerable degree of education and scientific knowledge existed on many levels of Afghan society, at the time of the Crusades; for instance, the Afghan knights could read and write skills which were exceptional among their Europeans opponents. However, the encouragement of science and art was mainly the province of the courts, from the Empire in Heart down to the residence of local governors and minor regional patentees. Many a second-tiered ruler made his court an important center of science and art, the best example being the Heart rulers of the 11th century, all the major philosophers and scientists of the Afghan spent at least some time at such a court, they not only received money from open minded and interested rulers, but were often appointed as their political advisers. Philosophy and the dream, philosophy and all the other sciences received their first major boost the scholarly king 818 A.D and his direct successors, made the rationalistic faith of the Mutazilites the state religion, allowing philosophy to free itself from its subservience to theology, this encouraged an interest in the thinking of classical antiquity by announcing that a dignified old man had appeared to him in a dream, identified himself as Aristotle, and that he had expounded the nature of good on a basis of philosophical doctrine, the first major philosopher of the Afghan was al-kindi c 800-870, a descendant of a distinguished family, who took Platonic thinking as his point of departure, argued for the acceptance of causality, and also wrote over 200 works on subjects ranging from philosophy, medicine, mathematics, physics, chemistry, astronomy, and music. He was also politically influential as the tutor of princes at the court of the king, where he introduced arithmetic, Al-Farabi c 870-950 who bore the honorific title of "second teacher" (that is to say, second only to Aristotle) and was active at the court of the Heart of neo-Platonism, and confidently stated that philosophy held the primacy over theology., in his book, the Model State, he sets out the pattern of an ethical and rational ideal state, ruled by a philosopher king who also has some of the characteristics of an Afghan. One of the most important Afghan polymaths was Ibn Sina of Balkh, 980-1037 A.D known in the Europe as Avicenna. He worked to compile a detailed collection of all the knowledge of his time, wrote works on philosophy, astronomy, grammar, and poetry, and was regarded as one of the most outstanding physicians of his day. He also wrote a remarkable autobiography, and held important political offices at various princely courts. In his major work, the Book of the Cure of the Soul, he combines metaphysics and medicine with logic, physics, and mathematics. His compendium of medicine was regarded as a standard work in Europe as well as the World countries until the early modern period. Avicenna's contemporary al-Biruni 973-1048, who came by adventurous ways to the court of the Ghaznavis empire Mahmud and empire Masud, and remained bound to it for the rest of his life in a curious love-hate relationship, proposed strong links between philosophy and astronomy in his book Gardens of Science. He accompanied Mahmud of Ghazni (Ghazni is 100 km west of Kabul) Ibn Tufail c 1115-1185, who enjoyed the protection of the Almohads, was an original thinker. His work, the Living One, Son of the Watcher (God) tells the story of an Islamic Robinson Crusoe who is cast up on a desert island, where he comes to an understanding of the world and the nature of the One God through natural reason alone. Philosophy in Religion reached its peak with Ibn Rushd c 1126-1198, who was also under the protection of the Almohads, and became known in the Europe as Aver roes. As an uncompromising champion of Aristotle, he supported the idea of the eternal existence of the world and the cosmos, which had beginning; in his doctrine they were created by God, but developed according to their own laws. The intuitive mind, Aristotle's nouns, was a purely intellectual entity to Averroes, operating on the souls of men from outside, and he therefore rejected ideas of the continued existence and immortality of individual souls. He came into violent conflict with Islamic orthodoxy, had to face many tribunals and hearings, and often survived only because he enjoyed the protection of the Almo had rulers. The doctrine of the eternity of the world and its existence without beginning reached the Europe as "Latin Averroism" (its outstanding proponent was Sager of Brabant at the Sorbonne in Paris) and it was contested by the most important European thinker of the time, Thomas Aquinas, who himself was strongly influenced by Aristotelians of the kind proposed by Averroes.

The natural sciences: astronomy physics, and medicine

Religion sciences, special interest in astronomy was derived from the traditions inherited from old Aryan religious, such as the Parsees, and in particular the ancient Aryan, whose center was the Heart and who were largely absorbed by Islam in the 11ᵗʰ century, Astronomy and astrology were closely connected in this system of thought, and the calculation of favourable conjunction became a politically influential field of knowledge. All the important philosophers, and many rulers, took an interest in astronomy, calculated the courses of the stars and the dimensions of the earth, forecast the weather, and predicted the state of the water supply calculations that served very practical purposes. Al-Biruni mentioned above, drew up very precise measurements of the earth, constructed a great globe, and made remarkable progress in the understanding of the rotation of the earth and the force of gravity, the phenomena of solar and lunar eclipses could be very precisely calculated at this time. Many astrolabes and astronomical charts, once the property of rulers well versed in astronomy, have been preserved, outstanding among such rulers was Ulugh Beg 1394-1449, the grandson of empire Timur, whose residence was in Samarqand (Samarqand was capital of Afghanistan from 1361). In 1428 he had a huge observatory built a sextant for calculating the height of the sun, and with the aid of expert astronomers, drew up the most precise astronomical charts of the Middle Ages.

Khorasan present day Afghanistan

In the 11th and 12th centuries the visual arts in the Central Asia reached an unusual level of inventiveness under the patronage of the Ghanavi and Ghuri rulers of Khorasan (Central Asia New Afghanistan-India-Iran, Iraq) they and their courtiers commissioned fine and varied buildings on a massive scale, which were constructed largely of mud brick and baked brick and decorated in carved stone and marble, painted and cut stucco, cut and glazed brick, and terracotta. Few of these buildings, however, have survived intact and, to imagine what these masterpieces might have been, one must extrapolate from a few tantalizing fragments of excavated remains. Writing was unusually important at these courts, whose rulers patronized poets and writers, many of whom used and transformed it from a vernacular into a literary language. The importance of writing is also reflected in the visual arts. Numerous buildings from the period carry multiple inscriptions executed in different styles and techniques, and the luxury book with fine illumination became one of the major art forms. Fine metalwork is another art form associated with this era, and many signed and dated pieces help us to reconstruct the nature of patronage and art in the Khorasan (present day Afghanistan-India) at this time. The Empire of Ghaznavis and Ghuris the rich lands of Khorasan (New Afghanistan) had long been an important-and troublesome area in the Kufic (present day Arab) caliphate, large irrigation systems in Khorasan (present day Afghanistan) the land beyond the Oxus River made these regions productive farmlands, the area was also rich in minerals, such as gold, silver in Heart, Balkh, copper in Farghana, and Balkh, and mercury Bamiyan. The Hindu Kush Mountains are one of the few sources of lapis lazuli in the world, and province of Badakhshan in northern Afghanistan, around the city of Balkh, is renowned for its rubies, garnets, and for asbestos. Lying far from the Abbasi capitals in (new Iraq) 500 years Iraq was parts of Khorasan (New Afghanistan-India-Iran) these areas had also been centers of discontent for a long time. The Abbasis themselves had come to power in this area, and the Samanis, their governors in the region during the 9th and 10th centuries, had increasingly exercised their independence from the central authority. From the end of the 10th century, the outlying regions broke away almost entirely from Abbasid control as local strongmen established their own dynasties. The first such dynasty was that of the Ghaznavis 977-1186, who descended from a Tajik military commander named Sebuktegin, service to the Samanis, from the mid 9th century, the Abbasids had come to depend on Tajik soldiers recruited from the steppes of Central Asia to prop up their government and maintain conformers did the same, and in the 10th century the Samanid governor of Khorasan (present day Afghanistan-India-Iran) and Transitional had used the Tajik commander Alptegin to direct the army in Khorasan (present day Afghanistan), in 961, when Alpegin was unable to secure succession in his own favour, he retired to the mountainous region around The Province of Ghazna 100, km west of Kabul in what is now Easter Afghanistan, there on the periphery of the Samanid domains and facing the "pagan" Indian, a series of Tajik commanders governed nominally for the Samanide for several decades until Sebuktegin 977-998 established an independent principality. Sebuktegin's son Empire Mahmud 998-1030 transformed this principality into a highly militarized empire. He not only challenged Islamic rulers to the west, such as the Abbasids, Samanis, Buyids and Quarakhanids, but initiated the era of Tajik eastwards expansion that changed the face of the Islamic world, the east, with India-Afghanistan, hitherto just an attachment to the Islamic cultural sphere, now became a political and cultural center in its own right. Having started as frontier warriors in the service of other rulers, The Tajiks were to create their own states and take charge of the military command of the Islamic world for the first time in world-military history. The Great Empire Mahmud's rule depended on his troops, which consisted mainly of troops; they were paid a regular salary out of state funds and were also entitled to four-fifths of the booty recovered on campaign, to ensure their loyalty

Architecture

The Ghaznavis dynasty and Ghuris dynasty their predecessors and overlords by building large and splendid capitals dotted with magnificent structures. Many of the more remote sites have been destroyed, so that single buildings, particularly towers, stand in splendid isolation, this poetic image may be somewhat at odds with the more prosaic picture provided by texts and excavations. Nevertheless, they help us reconstruct something of the original splendour of these cities and establish the pattern of development, for as at Samarra, the Abbasi capital present day in Iraq, successive Ghaznavi and Ghuri rulers added their own palaces and other buildings to their capitals in the new-Afghanistan. Lashkar-i-Bazar, 11ᵗʰ century and later the walls of the palaces were built of sun-dried brick, which was originally covered with a protective layer of plaster. The plaster was normally carved, and in interior rooms, might be painted, in the late 1940s, a team of French archaeologists succeeded in excavating the ruins of least three clay-brick palaces from the time of the Ghaznavids, which were well preserved thanks to the dry climate. Subsequently restored, and then destroyed again in the early 13ᵗʰ century under attacks from the Khwarazm-Shahs and the Mongols. Though constructed of mud brick, many of the abandoned buildings have survived in this area of low rainfall, and the ruins were excavated by a French team in the late 1940s. The site, at the confluence of the Helmand and Arghandab Rivers, had developed in the 10ᵗʰ century as a garden suburb of the nearby city of Bust after the restoration of an ancient canal supplying the city from the Helmand. The earliest construction, predating the Ghaznavi period, was a square garden with a formal entry to the east, a large pavilion in the center, and another lager pavilion overlooking the river to the west. It probably served as a stand for reviewing troops, and it was soon replaced by a compact 115x170 feet (35x52 meters) two-story building. The living quarters were set on the second floor to toke advantage of the breezes and river view. In plan, the second floor had four axial halls arranged in cruciform shape and converging on a central square area, possibly a light well. This is the same plan thought to have been used for the palace at Merv, built in the mid-8ᵗʰ century by Abu Muslim, Afghan leader of the revolution against Abbasi. The building at al-Askar is usually known as the Central Palace as two other palaces were built adjacent to it. The larges building on the site was the South Palace, generally attributed to the patronage of Empire Mahmud and therefore datable to the early 11ᵗʰ century. Its plan and construction techniques followed models found in some of the Abu Muslim palaces in Samarra. Like them, it had a rectangular internal courtyard. An iwan flanked by rooms stood in the middle of each of the four sides, with a square throne room beyond the north iwan, the major adjustment to the site was another iwan beyond the throne room and opening north onto the river. The grandest reception room in the building, it was open to the breezes coming off the river and provided a view of the large river pavilion and the Central Palace. Like the Abu Muslim palaces at Samarra, the iwan hall in the South Palace at al-Askar was richly reverted with stucco and brick decoration. In the Ghaznavi palace, however, the types of decoration were arranged in the reverse sequence from that used by the Abu Muslim, with a frescoed dado below and relief decoration above. The murals at both sites depicted the ruler's servants. The dado in the Dar-al-Khalifa at Samarra had shown dancing women, but that in Empire Muhmud's palace at al-Askar was painted with a frieze of attendants. They probably represented Mahmud's private guard, who would once have stood against the walls facing the enthroned monarch. On the back wall of the iwan, the dado was surmounted by geometric panels framed by bands of inscriptions. The one that survives contains Koran sura 27. 40-41. the verses describe Solomon receiving the Queen of Sheba, and were undoubtedly chosen to draw an analogy between the per-Islamic hero who controlled the animals and spirits, and the patron of the palace, the great conqueror Empire Mahmud. As at Samarra, later rulers added to al-Askar, which eventually stretched for 4 miles along the east bank of the Helmand River. To the north of the earlier palaces is a sprawling third palace, with three courtyards surrounded by iwans and rooms. Other building on the site included barracks (perhaps designed for the Empire Mahmud's famous elephant corps), a bazaar, and a Friday congregational mosque. Other remains on the opposite bank of the Helmand River may represent a residential area associated with the palaces. Because of its location in the warm Helmand basin, al-Askar served as the Ghaznavi summer capital. Their main capital however was at Ghazni (modern-day Ghazni) in the mountains to the northeast. Much of it too is ruins, but Italian excavations there in the 1950s have uncovered the remains of the palace built there by Empire Mahmud's great-great-grandson, Masud III (1099-1115) it was a walled rectangle, with a long bazaar stretching along the north side. Like earlier palaces, this one had an internal courtyard 164x105 feet, with an iwan flanked by room in the middle of each of its four sides. The throne-room lay beyond the south iwan. The courtyard was paved in marble and surrounded by 32 niches decorated with an extraordinary inscription in floriated Kufic (new Arab) script, the text, which runs for about 820 feet around the court, air a Dari Poem extolling the virtues of the sultan and the glories of his palace. It was apparently composed specifically for the new construction. Most contemporary palaces had iwans facing a courtyard, but decoration seems to have been determined by personal preference and availability of materials. The palace at Tirmidh, a site on the right bank of the Amu River near its confluence with the Surhan, for example comprised several buildings arranged around a courtyard. The iwan opposite the entrance was decorated with three registers of carved plaster panels showing geometric patterns and zoomorphic motifs. One shows an extraordinary monster with a single head and two bodies.

Rise And Glory Of The Seljuk Empire Khorasan Central Asia

The Seljuks, who for a time ruled over Khorasan largest empires, were originally nomadic Turkmen shepherds from the steppes of Khorasan (present day Afghanistan-Central Asia). They belonged to the great Oghuz federation of nine Turkoman tribes that, since the 8th century, had steadily spreading west as far as the Aral Sea. Deployed by the rulers of Khorasan (present day Afghanistan) from this time as defenders against invading Islamic Kufic (present day Arabs) the Turkoman had conquered their own territories and exerted pressure on the Samanids of Balkh-Bukhara until the region finally fell to the Turkoman. The clan adopted Islam 960 under one of its first leaders, Seljuk, from whom it took its name, and its members hence forth carried out their raids to the west and south as Islamic "frontier warriors" (ghazi) and religious fighters. After Seljik's death, his three sons and ultimately two grandsons led the clan and spread further through Khorasan (New Afghanistan) Oxus region. After being defeated by the region's ruler Empire Mahmud of Ghazni, in 1026, while in the service of the Turkoman, the Seljuks split into three groups. While one of them remained in the east, the two groups led by Seljuk's grandsons crossed Khorasan (present day Afghanistan-Iraq-Iran-India-all Central Asia-East Turkistan) where several cities succumbed to them: Merv in 1037, Heart and Nishapur in 1038. This was the beginning of the Afghan Seljuk's territorial rule. The two brothers, Tughril Beg 1038-1063 and Chaghri Beg 1038-1060, then divided their territory into two: while the younger brother Chaghri, who bore the title "King of Kings" remained in the northern Khorasan (present day Afghanistan) area as an independent ruler with royal seats at Balkh and Merv, Tughril established himself in Nishapur with more senior title "Most Honoured Supreme Ruler" Sultan, (Empire) he realized his political ambition following a decisive victory over the Ghaznavis in 1040 with the consolidation of the state as an entity and an expansion towards the west in 1042 he occupied western including Rayy and also the provinces bordering the Caspian Sea, reached Fars in 1054 achieved as sovereign of Azerbaijan and Khuzistan, having previously been acknowledged as supreme ruler of all the Turkoman tribes. From 1050 Tughril led campaigns into Kufic (New Iraq) partly in order to liberate the caliph of Baghdad from the tutelage of the Buyids and, as a strict religious, to set himself up as the caliphate's new protector, but also to conduct a religious war against the Fatimids of Mecir (present day Egypt). In 1055when he marched into kofa (new Baghdad) and overthrew the Buyids rule, he had the caliph grant him certain honorary titles; in a document of 1062 The Afghan-Tughril is named as "Rules of Rulers King of the East and West, Restorer of Religion. Right Hand of the Caliph and Commander of the Faithful" neither could the caliph refuse him the hand of his daughter in marriage in 1062, and it must have immediately been clear to him that he had simply exchanged one set of masters, the Buyids, for another. At the same time, new groups Turkoman were constantly streaming west, whom Tughril diverted into the border wars against the Christian Empires of Byzantium, Georgia, and Armenia, while claiming the rich provinces of Fras for himself. He finally selected Isfahan as his seat, and this was also to teaming the main capital Balkh under his two successors. After the death of Tughril, who had no direct descendants, his nephew Alp Arslan 1063-1072, one of Chaghri's sons, became empire (Sultan) and the Turkoman tribal organization in existence up to that point, with its several local rulers, was replaced by centralized rule for the first time. Along with his Minster (vizier) Nizam al-Mulk, Alp Arslan was the main founder of the Great Afghan Seljuk state. Strict control over the provinces was combined, in Khorasan (present day Afghanistan) primarily, with the fostering of trade and the life of the intellect. The Empires (Sultan) countered Turkoman particularise by creating a standing army of military, whose officers were placed under an obligation of courtly service to the rules and thereupon dispatched as loyal administrators to distant provinces of the empire that had hitherto belonged to the Afghan Seljuk Empire in name only. Nizam al-Mulk had build up an efficient system (the iqta system) whereby provinces were given as fiefs to military commanders, who were only required to pay over a portion of the tax money to the government and could use the remainder to maintain themselves and their troops. In 1064 Alp Arslan won supremacy over Kerman province and was able to safeguard the trade and pilgrim routes once the sharifs of Mecca had been subordinated to the Afghan Seljuk sovereignty in 1070. The situation where along with the Turkman, other, rival tribes of Turkoman had also settled forced the sultan to intervene on several occasions. After the "frontier warriors" had laid waste to the Byzantine cities of Caesarea (Kaysrei) in 1067, and Iconium (Konya) in 1069, The German-Emperor Romanus IV fortified the empire's cities as far south as Syria, and finally marched into Armenia with a large army. Alp Arslan realized that his tribesmen were in danger, and captured his opponent at Mantzikert (Malazgirt) where the Byzantines suffered a devastating defeat on August 26, 1071, from then on the Anatolia region was open for settlement by the increasing number of Turkoman tribespeople now flowing in, after this, Alp Arslan marched east and was crossing the Oxus River with a powerful army when he was assassinated in 1072.

THE AFGHAN-SELJUK EMPIRE'S ARCHITECTURE

While the Seljuk Empire was rapidly expanding from Balkh towards Iraq, with the aim of bringing the Caliphate of Baghdad under its protection, the Central Asia city of Mery remained its capital and artistic center, during this time the Uzbeks were erecting their impressive monumental buildings in Balkh in the flourishing cities of Balkh-Bukhara and Samarqand. Correctly considered the classical era of Khorasan (present day Afghanistan-Central Asia) architecture, the buildings dating from time-public, sacred and even memorial are of an exquisite elegance and display a harmonious balance in construction and decoration.

Balkh And Bukhara

The Afghan had already undergone phases of weakness during the 17th century, Balkh had been temporarily occupied by the Afghan-Tajik army, and Bukhara had been attacked and plundered by Khwarazmi, the golden age of the Afghan-Uzbek Empire came to an end with the rule of the last powerful tribe Subhan Quli khan, who once again ruled over the whole of the patrimony Balkh and Bukhara between 1681 and 1702. Its decline was ultimately precipitated by the expansionary activity of three powers that upset the whole inner Afghanistan balance of power. Memories of the Afghan-Tajik global empire motivated the expansionist campaigns of the west Mongolian Oirats (Dzungars), who controlled so much of the Afghan-Kazakh region 1718-1725 that they were able to join up with their tribal relatives, the Kalmuck Horde on the Volga. Under pressure from the west Mongols, defeated Afghan-kazakh groups moved south, initially they were made welcome as reinforcements in a trial of strength that had broken out between rival Afghan-tribal in Bukhara and Samarqand 1722, but they then stayed on in the war zone for seven years. By the end of this time the farmland was laid to waste, Samarqand had been completely depopulated, and only two of Bukhara's residential districts were still inhabited, Khorasan (present day Afghanistan, Central Asia) was then directly affected by the Afghan-Uzbek power politics of 1688-1748 the is the first Tim in the Afghan history power changed Paschtun-tribal becoming on Political power from 1748 until 1929. troops with the Russian conquered not only Balkh, but also the two capitals Khiva and Bukhara, of the former Uzbek Empire, which now fell apart at the seams and came to an end in the ensuing fighting between factions. Russia then finally prepared to assume its new role of dominant regional power, initially without direct confrontation with Khorasan (present day Afghanistan, Central Asia, India, Iraq, Iran, East Turkistan) it acted politically, as a German-European protecting power, by forming an Afghan-tribal-alliance agenise Afghan, and economically in initiating direct trade links with present day China, Siberia 1728 and through the increasing importance of the Russian, the deep economic and political crisis lasted for half a century 1720-1770, during which time Khorasan (present day Afghanistan) came to be bypassed by the main flow of trade, fell prey to the confusion of Afghan War, and experienced the deterioration of its cities. During this time of unrest, the Afghan lost all their authority and the Afghan-Uzbek with the Russian-military commanders. Afghan-Paschtun-tribal princes took over. The Uzbek Empire fragmented into a number of princedoms, of which two south of the Amu Darya fell into the Russian political orbit of Afghanistan. In three new Uzbek dynasties emerged by Russia from the confusion of Afghan-War; the Ming dynasty in Kokand, the Mangits in Bukhara, and the Qungrat dynasty in Khiva, the Afghan-Tribal princes Amir al mominin (Amirs), beyslbegs hesitated for awhile before taking the title Khan, which strictly speaking was reserved for descendants of the Afghan Khan dynasty new deprived of power,

Construction techniques as decoration

In this architecture there is no division between decorative adornment and construction technique, and consequently no continuous ornamental camouflage, as is the case with building of the 14-16th centuries. The main material for construction as well as decoration was brick, the bricks being usually square and combined in the most unusual ways, and carved terracotta of the same yellowish hue. In the 12th century, collared ceramic insertion turquoise inscriptive bands and decorative dark blue, white, and green elements were used to break up the yellow ochre of the buildings, which was hardly distinguishable from the ground, but even at this time, the mason decorative procedures were carried out in brick and terracotta; double brick bonds with or without carved ornaments, stepped bonds, and friezes and surfaces carved in brick. The effect of the brick bonds was achieved by a carpet-like overall structure with different elements clearly standing out, and by the play of light and shadow. Further decorative possibilities were offered by ornamental wall-painting and stucco (Dari: gadj) carving, this involved mixing pulverized alabaster with water and working it while still damp. It was sometimes also used to imitate brickwork, the manifold variety produced and consequent combining of technique and decoration is astonishing during this period building techniques were the main source of decorative motif.

Space and dome solutions 11th century

Khorasan present day central Asia as a major building material, brick also determined the form taken by the buildings various types of vaulting and domed roofs. The round base of the dome, where it met the top of a square room, was determined by its ground plan, the transition between circle and square was achieved by means of quenches, i.e. arches spanning the corners of the square, forming the octagonal lower part of the dome. Console spandrels were also known, consisting of rows of superimposed brick brackets. These formed the basis of the stalactite structures (muqarnas) which had already appeared in the 11th century and which later became very widespread. The arches, and therefore the cross section of vault and dome too, were generally pointed. Here, a geometrical procedure allowed an infinite number of variations on the pointed arch to be developed. In the 11th century the first buildings-mausoleums were built with double-shell domes, a technique that rapidly became widespread in monumental architecture, in this way the outer shell of the dome, resting on a drum could be transformed into an impressive structure whose shape was independent of the buildings interior. In the 12th, century the outer shell of the dome was sometimes given a steep pyramid or conical shape, which afforded the dome better protection against rain and snow. The limitless variety of ground plan and interior designs in the architecture of Khorasan (present day Afghanistan-Central Asia) between the 11th and beginning of the 13th centuries can be reduced to two basic schemata, the courtyard-axis schema and the central dome structure. The first of these consists of a rectangular courtyard with two right-angular axes, the longitudinal axis being the main one, enclosed by buildings forming a rectangular outline. This schema was used for large buildings of both sacred and secular function, such as mosques, palace, and caravanserais. The simplest design was that of the courtyard mosque, where the space between the courtyard and windowless exterior wall was occupied by a continuous gallery. This consisted of several rows of brick piers forming continuous domed cells generally connected to each other by archways, stone on brick columns were not used because of the frequent earthquakes in Khorasan (New Afghanistan-Central Asia) most of the surviving 11th and 12th century caravanserais, which served as inns for traveling merchants and their caravans, and often developed into trading centers themselves, stand out because of their combination of magnificence and functionality.

Khorasan present day Afghanistan from Herat to Samarqand 1360 A. D

The Timuris empires are dominated by the figure of the dynasty's founder Timur, the paramount conqueror and "ruler of the World." History's verdict on him has mostly negative: the campaign of conquest led by Genghis and his successors had altered the whole situation in Central Asia, all in the Religions cultural region, the occupation of Khorasan (present day Afghanistan-Iran-Iraq-India) and the fall of Baghdad in 1258 had unleashed terror and dejection in the religion (Islamic) world, althou the IIkhanids of Khorasan (present day Afghanistan) who had converted to Islam, had undertaken a colossal program of reconstruction. Through their claim to lead the Islamic, they soon became embroiled in an ongoing conflict with the Ulus Chaghatai clan in Central Asia, the tribal home of Genghis second son, when the Chaghatai Tarmashirin 1326-1334 converted to Islam, the Ulus split into an Islamic region between the Jaxartes and Oxus Rivers in Khorasan (present day Afghanistan) and the "heathen" Mongol Stan beyond the Jaxartes, during the following period, the Islamic part was ruled by various different military leaders. This of a central administration was exploited in 1360 by Tughluq Timür, the khan of Herat, in order to reunite the Ulus Ghaghatai under his leadership. Timür, s rise occurred during this period of conflict. Timür Lenk descended from Herat, but impoverished, Turkoman Barlas tribe, and was born around 1328 near kesh (today Shahr-I Sabz) a day's ride from Samarqand. The date of birth later widely cited, of April 8, 1336, stems from a "celestial conjunction" calculated subsequently. His right kneecap and upper thigh were malformed from birth bringing him the nickname "Lenk" or "Lame one," and resulted in him able to move about only with aid of crutches or later in life on horseback, and a deformation of his right shoulder, compounded by an arrow wound, restricted his use of his right hand, these deformities were confirmed by an examination of his skeleton, which was undertaken by Russians in 1841 (the Saxon-Great Games by the German, the three cousins in Europe, The German Kaiser, The German Saxon King The German Tsars) In the anarchic situation in Central Asia during the period 1360-1370, Timür maneuvered and entered into pacts to his own advantage, proved himself to be an exceptional military leader at an early stage, and changed camps when it suited him, when Tughluq Timür invaded the Islamic region in 1360, Timür betrayed the leader of the Barlas tribe and placed himself at the service of the khan, receiving kesh as a fief in return, in order to improve his social position, he formed an alliance with the powerful Emir al-mominin in Herat, who resided in Balkh, by marrying the emir's sister, and thus became his liege man.

Timor's advance into Khwarazmia,
The Battle with Toqtamish Khorasan
present day Afghanistan

Timur actually spent his whole life on military campaigns, and crossed his conquered territories several times during the course of them, first of all he took care to organize thing throughout the whole of the Ulus Chaghatai exactly the way he wanted. In 1370, therefore He marched north and installed a puppet khan there, who was descended from the house of Genghis and who was loyal to him, and made repeated appearances in the role of protector and guardian. But Mongolistan remained an unsettled region, as many Chaghatai nobles regarded Timur as a parvenu and plotted against him, in 1372 he successfully asserted the disputed Chaghatai claims to Mongolian Khwarazmia in the face of other, local branches of Genghis dynasty, occupied the Balkh, and married his son Jahangir to a local princess, which brought him an enormous increase in prestige. Over the following years he launched several campaigns into Khwarazmia (in Khorasan) as the region repeatedly reasserted its independence and formed alliances with Timur's enemies, when the Khwarazmians invaded Bukhara in 1376, Timur laid waster to Khwarazm and in 1379 razed its capital kuna Urgench to the ground. Timur now decide to take over the Turkoman succession in Khorasan (present day Afghanistan) as well when Ghiyath al-Din, ruler of the Kartids in Heart, refused to appear at Timur's court assembly in Samarqand in 1379, Timur was provided with an excuse to invade Khwarazm, in 1381 he occupied the whole of the kartid territories and installed his second son, Miranshah, as governor of Heart. As he advanced west, Timur ran into resistance in the Khorasan (New Afghanistan) regions of Mazandaran and Sistan from the Muzaffarids, who had been embroiled in internal power struggles since 1384 and who were finally removed by Timur in 1993. When he took Isfahan from them in 1384, he initially granted them a lenient occupation, but when the inhabitants of the city murdered his tax collectors he organized a terrible massacre in retribution. Timur had decided to unite politically and destroy the regional rule of the minor princes, by taking the title of sultan (empires) in 1388, he brought about, by force the cultural unification of Turkoman, the conflict between the two regions had already been the subject of the Khorasan (present day Afghanistan) national epic, the Shah-nama, now Timur attempted to unite the cultural heritage of the Khorasan (New Afghanistan) and Turkomans in his own person. In the meantime a new enemy had appeared in the battle of leadership of the Islamic Mongols-Turkman of the Golden Horde since 1378, had invaded Tabriz, Timur who had taken Toqtamish in as a young refugee, regarded this action as breach of loyalty and invaded Georgia, which was Christian, and whose ruler then became Timur's vassal, in order to cut off the Golden Horde's route into Khorasan (present day Afghanistan) Toqtamish, who in 1382 had burnt Moscow down and established his sovereignty over Russia, now claimed all the Mongolian territories, in 1387 he pillaged Timur's homeland and laid siege to Balkh-Bakhara and Samarqand, but withdrew to his own territory ahead of the advancing Timur, in 1391 followed him into the Urals and beyond, and defeated a Golden Horde army twice the strength of his Toqtamish took flight and formed an alliance with the Mamluks in Cairo, later on he was beaten in battle by Timur's troops several more time, before finally being murdered while on the run in 1405. For his part, Timur asserted his sovereignty over the Golden Horde, which extended far into Russia, and returned to Samarqand with substantial treasures in the form of war booty.

Timur's advance into Syria, Iraq, and Anatolia the battle with Bayazid

In 1392 Timur decided to push further west, after ousting the Muzaffarids, from Fars, he invade Kufic (new Iraq) and in September 1393 drove the Jalayirids out of Baghdad. Here he showed himself to be a lenient upholder of Khorasan Islamic sharia and purged the country of minor potentates and bands of robbers, for which the Baghdad tradspeople, who's trading routes he had secured, were grateful. An agreement with the Mamluks in Cairo foundered, however, the energetic Mamluk sultan, Barquq, who had taken over power in 1382. Was determined to bring Timor's advance to a standstill, just as the Mukluks had managed to defeat the Afghans in 1260 in 1394 Braque, in alliance with the Ottomans, the Golden Horde, and several Anatolian princes, had taken up position with his army outside Damascus, lying in wait for Timur's assault. But Timur avoided the confrontation at the last moment and turned towards Toqtamish in the north, after Barquq died in 1399, Timur once more advanced west the following year, and took up position outside Damascus, which was held by Barquq's son Faraj, when the two armies confronted each other, Faraj lost his nerve and fled to Egypt in January 1401. Although the city submitted to Afghan, it was nevertheless sacked and pillaged. Afghan then withdrew to Iraq, where the Jalayirids had once again taken possession of Baghdad and improved their position at Afghan's expense, Enraged at the treachery of the city Afghan had treated leniently, Afghan took Baghdad by storm in July 1401, and Ibn khaldun was one of the scholars who fell into Timor's hands in Baghdad. Timur treated him with extreme courtesy, and made him stay with him while he completed a description of the Maghreb lands, Ibn khaldun also taught the ruler about the Islamic prophesies, which announced a "sultan of the world" who would attain this position through the intervention of nomadic shepherds. Ibn khaldun saw in this a reference to the Turkoman tribes and thus made an association between Afghan's rule and Muslim ideas concerning the apocalypse. Anatolia now became the focus of conflict, the regions minor princes saw themselves as threatened in equal measure by the ambition of the Mamluks on one hand the Ottomans on the other, as each had appropriated various territories since 1397, many of them regarded Timur, whose lands lay further away, as a possible guarantor of their independence, and subjugated themselves to his sovereignty, as Afghan had also occupied various regions during the course of Afghan march west in 1394 and had assumed the role of protector of Anatolia, this inevitably resulted in confrontations with Ottomans, who were spreading east at that time. In 1395 Afghan had initially offered the Ottoman sultan Bayaid I 1389-1402 his friendship, praised Afghan as a warrior for the faith, and asked him to join in with the battle against Toqtamish. This invitation also came with a warning, however, Bayazid was free to extend his territory into the Balkans, but the east Kufic and Anatolia belonged to the Afghan clan. Bayazid however, not only appropritated territories in northern Syria and Anatolia, but also granted refuge to the Jalayirids and Turkoman Qara Qoyunlu, sworn enemies of Afghan, providing them with troops for the recon quest of their eases, as a result of this Afghan advanced into Anatolia in March 1402, crushing the Ottoman army near Ankara in July 1402, Afghan took Bayazid prisoner and supposedly transported him around in an iron cage which he used as a stool to help him mount his horse. In announcing his victory to the rulers of Europe, Timur expressed the hope that the traffic in goods between Europe, and Khorasan (New Afghanistan) could now flow undisturbed liberation from the "Bayazid nightmare" contributed decisively to the positive image enjoyed by Timur in Europe.

Timur's campaign in India the development of Samarqand and Timur's death

Timur had already sent his grandson Pir Muhammad to India with troops, as he wanted to recreate the empire of Mahmud of Ghazni, whom he greatly admired, under his own leadership, in order to guarantee the eastern rear; he had been paying tribute money to the East Turkistan (Afghan tribes Uzbeks) emperor since 1389. pir Muhammad's advance had come to a halt outside Multan, and in 1398, Afghan took over the military campaign, in September of that year Timur crossed the Indus, accepted the local princes' acts of submission and continued his advance in a southeasterly direction despite fierce resistance, during the course of his advance, his troops took the cities, when finally arrived outside Delhi in 1398, he had around 100, 000 prisoners with him, before the all-important battle he gave the order that all mall prisoners were to be executed to prevent them going over to the enemy. By taking out the Indian war elephants, Timur achieved an overwhelming victory over the fleeing pashton (Afghan tribes) Empire of Delhi, the city surrendered and was largely spared, in spite of some pillaging by individual bands of troops. In 1399 the army pushed on further east, crossed the Ganges, and occupied Lahore, Timur was on the brink of subjugating the Afghan ruler of Kashmir when bad news from Anatolia and Syria summoned him back west. In April 1399 he was back in Samarqand, (Samarqand was at the time Capital of Afghanistan), laden with rich spoils accompanied by innumerable Afghan artists and craftsmen. After his victory over Bayazid, Timur also achieved his ambition of settling his differences with Mamluks. In 1403 an exchange of ambassadors and precious gifts took place between Samarqand and Cairo, and Timur finally adopted Faraj as his "son," just as he did the king of Castile, whose ambassadors happened to be present at Timur's court. The ruler was finally able to devote himself to the embellishment of Samarqand which was to become the "center of the World" threshold of paradise," along with numerous splendid buildings, the Empire also endowed Samarqand with large gardens and surrounded the city with suburbs carrying the names of the Islamic metropolises, Timur surrounded himself with artists and scholars whom he had transported back from just about Heart, he had scientific material that he had collected during the course of his campaigns of conquest investigated, while court poetry disseminated the glory of the "Lord of the celestial conjunction," to mark the rallying of the Khorasan (present day Afghanistan) Islamic world under his "League of peace" banner, in 1404 Timur hosted a dazzling banquet, to which the envoys of both the conquered and allied countries were invited as well as those of East Turkistan and at which he married off five of his grandchildren. Including Ulugh Beg, with great ceremony For Europe, Timur's rule had some beneficial consequences his victory over Bayazid and the ensuing turmoil in the Ottoman Empire provided the besieged Byzantium and Balkans with a breathing space, and the defeat of the Golden Horde permitted the rise of Christian by German in Russia under the leadership of Moscow

Khorasan present day Afghanistan-Iraq-Iran-India Central Asia Capital Herat and Samarqand

The two eldest of Timur sons, Jahangir and Umar Sheikh, were already dead at the time of his Timur's death Miranshah was clearly unsuitable for the leadership due to mental problems caused by an accident, and even the youngest, Shah Rukh, appeared to be out of the question as a successor because of his godliness and love of peace, Timur had therefore named his grandson, Pir Muhammad, as his heir, Pir Muhammad was the eldest son of Jahangir, and sat on Mahmud of Gazni's throne as governor in Kandahar. He was assassinated by his own Minster (vizier) however, in 1407, of about 20 of Timur's grandsons holding the position of governor tow of them now seized power in the Capital of Samarqand, but their inexperienced and foolish rule led to a rebellion by the city, Shah Rukh, governor of Heart, was called in to help thereupon occupied Samarqand and finally became the Timurid's most important leader and head of the family 1405-1447, Shah Rukh managed to hold on to his father's empire albier not in its entirety, along with Transoxiana he brought Jurjan and Mazandaran in Afghanistan under his control and occupied, in 1416, other regions also acknowledged his sovereignty and the Uzbeks, the kipchak Empire (the Golden Horde) and the majority of the Indian princes sought alliances with him, but he ruled Khorasan (present day Afghanistan) Empire largely from the Capital Heart, and made the Islamic Estates, the only law allowing the Mongol element to fade away into the background, by 1420 he had managed to extend his Empire over central and southern Khorasan, but lost Mesopotamia to the Jalayirids and the Qala (Uzbek) the old enemies of his father, who were also expanding their territories. In 1435 Shah Rukh was able to devote himself to the peaceful development of his Empire, which benefited the arts and intellectual life, and to intensifying the trading relationship with European, of his seven sons, only Muhammad Taragai, known as Ulugh Beg perhaps the most remarkable individual among the later Timurids, was still alive when Shah Rukh died in 1447. Ulugh Begs's own son, Abdul al-Latif who had lived with his grandfather, Shah Rukh, in Heart since 1444, and who nurtured justified hopes of gaining the succession himself, took over supreme command of the army upon Shah Rukh's death in 1447, and other of the Shah Rukh's grandsons appropriated various territories and occupied the empire's cities as well, Ulugh Beg, who saw himself as the sole legitimate heir of his father, marched on the Oxus but met with resistance from the assembled representatives of the younger generation,

Khorasan Architecture characteristics of Timurid architecture

The development and peculiarities of Khorasan (present day Afghanistan) architecture between the middle of the 14th and middle of the 15th centuries were determined by the existence of the world empire created by the military commander Timur, who was as creel as he was capable. His enormous empire stretched from central Asia to India taking in Delhi on its way and from Caucasus and the Kazakh steppes all the way to the Arabian Sea. Timur decided upon Samarqand in present-day Uzbekistan as the capital of this huge empire and made it dazzle with the splendour and radiance of its monumental and magnificent buildings. The building activity of this period was dominated by Timur's own passion for construction and his efforts to give his limitless power the architecture it deserved, architects and artists from all of the Khorasan, were forced to contribute to the construction of often colossal state buildings of both a sacred nature, in this fashion, completely different artistic schools and traditions were fused together, united by Afghan empires determination to achieve monumentality and splendour, and a characteristic international style was developed-what is now known as the style of the Timurid Empire. The imposing external appearance of the monumental buildings now became the number one priority, these majestic were topped with domes, the enormous portals developed into a virtually free standing architectural form and kind of stratus symbol, and proportions became more slender. This idea originated as far back as the 11th century, but did not become widespread until the 14th and 15th centuries, when it gave the these monumental building their characteristic appearance. This construction method, which was extremely successful despite the seismic condition that prevailed in Khorasan (present day Afghanistan), changed the character of the interior space radically.

The Miniature of Khorasan present day Afghanistan 15th Century one of the most glories periods of miniature

The 15th century is one of the most glories periods in the development of the miniature; a steady perfecting of the artistic vocabulary of the miniature can be followed throughout the whole of the century, culminating in a veritable blossoming of painting towards its end. Whereas in the 14th century there had only been limited contact between the different centers of painting, during the 15th century more varied contacts developed, the migration of the craftsman, which began with Empire Timur's where there had been painting schools during the 14th century was a contributory factor in this, empire Timur transported the best masters from Heart to his capital Samarqand, where they were enlisted to work on the adornment of his palaces and the production of artistic manuscripts, the Head of the Samarqand kitabkhana (library) and manuscript workshop was the renowned miniaturist Abdul al-Hayy from Heart whose work according to Dust Muhammad, a 16th century historian in Khorasan (present day Afghanistan) was used as a model by all the Samarqand masters. Despite the fact that none of his work has survived, and nor have any Samarqand miniatures from the beginning of the 15th century the development of this style can be followed through the miniatures produced in Heart in the kitabkhana of Timur's grandsons Iskandar Sultan 1409-1415 and Ibrahim Sultan 1415-1435 during early decades of the 15th century, the illustrations in the two manuscripts of the Anthology of Poetry 1410 are representative of the Herat style of this time, a synthesis has been achieved here between the three dimensionality of the Herat school and the flatness of the Balkh school of the 14th century, the work produced in the 1430s such as the Shanama of 1430 and Kalila and Dimnna of the same year, represented a new stage in the development of painting in Heart, miniatures of the Shahnama from 1430 are therefore of great art-historical importance, as they created the prototypes for particular scenes that went on to be among the most popular the lovers meeting in the palace and in the countryside, the audience with the ruler, the hunt, and the battle. The Herat artists wanted to present the viewer of the miniature with a performance, just like the theatrical director does on the stage, and his mastery was judged according to his ability to build up the action.

Khorasan present day Afghanistan-India the development of Indo-Islamic Culture

The Khorasan subcontinent that is the area Afghanistan-India-Iraq-Bangladesh-Iran-East Turkistan has produced some of the finest expressions of Afghan art and architecture, Afghan dynasties and mystics from the Islamic heartlands formed and nurtured the development of Islamic states in which non-Muslim cultures represented the majority, yet retained their intellectual and artistic vigor. Mutual exchange was a constant feature of life at all levels, and non-Muslim ideas and motifs were absorbed to create a unique dimension in the Afghani visual arts. The development of Indo-Islamic culture began with arrival of Kufic (present day Arab) armies in Khorasan in the years 711, the first phase of conquest absorbed the area roughly corresponding to Afghanistan, where Cufic were the court language and New Baghdad and Damascus were the main springs of cultural commercial life. Kufic (present day Arab) communities settled at important centers along the major trade routes to East-Turkistan and in the principal ports along the coast as far as the Bay of Bengal, during the 11th and 12th centuries, invasions from the Khorasan (present day Afghanistan) opened the India to the influences of Afghan. This Aryan (New Afghan) predominated during the 13th and 14th centuries when Tajik-Afghani elites ruled the sultanate of Delhi (the Tajik Empire of Delhi from 1501 until the Saxon in India in 1871) which at that time extended from the Punjab (Punjab in Dari Kabuli Five Water) and Gujarat to Bengal, and the Deccan as far south as Maduria Dari Kabuli became the language of courtly culture and administration. That a small elite could establish and retain control over such a vast and populous area while remaining a religious minority reflected a flexible attitude to religion on all sides, the early Afghan invaders were pragmatic, being primarily concerned with political and commercial control at minimal cost to themselves, the subsequent extension of political control in the early 13th century coincided with intensive missionary activity by the mystical orders. Working in the vernacular languages as well as the classical Afghan-Dari "Dari becoming official languages during in 9th century in Khorasan New Afghanistan" they did not conversion to Islam an essential for participating in their form of religious experience, the development of Muslim society and spiritual life thus took please at all levels of society and did create a permanent sectarian divide from non-Muslims, respect for saints regardless of denomination was an important cultural catalyst. The Afghan empire of Delhi welcomed the mystical orders and members of the court were counted among their followers, many cultural practices specific to the subcontinent, such as music and poetry at Sufi shrines, received official sanction and remain part of contemporary practice. The caliph was far away or reduced to a figurehead after the Mongol invasion of the 11th century. Acceptance by the local elites of the ruler's right to rule was of greater importance, and the blessing of a Sufi had its own political weight in the recognition of sovereignty. The principal cities established in the Indus delta were Bambhore and al-Mansura, both were well planned, at Bambhore the Great Afghan Tajik Empire dated 727 was the earliest in the subroutine, similar in plan to the Friday congregational mosques of Kufa (present day Baghdad) 607 and of Waist 702 constructed on the orders of al Hajjaj, the prayer hall, like its models had no formal mihrab. A hierarchy of materials was used corresponding to the function of the structure; the dressed stone for the mosque and the palace standing out in an area where brick architecture predominated, the houses of notables nearby were in semidressed stone with on the interior, lim-plastered walls and floors. Al-Mansura, the Friday mosque of which had a formal mihrab, became a metropolis celebrated for its palaces, gardens, mosques madrasas, As part of yet another raid on Multan in 1010, Afghan-Empire Mahmud of Ghazni 998-1030 destroyed the Sun Temple and annexed the province to the Ghaznavi

Empire, Ghazni was the most important Islamic city of its time apart from Kufa (new Baghdad, and Hindustan was regarded as an almost inexhaustible source of treasure, it was also a recruitment area for troops, who were not required to convert to Islam as a condition of employment, by the 12th century Lahore, where Afghan-Dari was the language of the court and administration, was its most brilliant outpost in the Muslim subcontinent. Ghaznavi innovations in architectural form and techniques thus reached the Indian provinces, the new form of minaret with a tall and slender shaft, domes and pure arches in mosques and mausoleums, and the use of lime mortar.

The Great Afghan Empires (sultanate) of Delhi

In 1181 Muizz Al-Da Ghuri (province of Ghurat) replaced the Gahznavi rule in India and began a series of dramatic conquests which brought India under Muslim rule, Delhi and Ajmer fell in 1192, the kingdoms of Benares and kannauj in 1194 and soon after Bihar and Bengal with its capital at Gaur. The Ghuri governor of Lahore assumed control of these dominions after Muizz al Din died in 1206, Khorasan, present day Afghanistan and established what became known as the sultanate of Delhi. This his successor Iltutmish 1210-1236 molded into a truly independent state, the sultanate of Delhi comprised five successive dynasties, the first of which was the "Slave Sultans" 1206-1290, followed by the Khaljis 1290-1320 the Tughluqs 1320-1414, the Sayyids 1414-1451, the Lodi dynasty from 1451- 1526 and the great Empire Suris (the lion king) 1540-1555. victories were celebrated by the construction of monumental architecture declaring the new dynasty, first was the Friday mosque in Delhi, the Quwwat al-Islam, it was begun in 1193, with materials reused from Hindu temples which had been demolished six years later the combined skills of Afghan-Turkoman architects and calligraphers, and indigenous stonemasons, produced a great screen of finely dressed sandstone erected in front of the prayer hall, also started was the Qutb Minar, a victory tower to spread the shadow of God to the east and west, as the inscriptions proclaimed. The technique of salvaging temples was followed at Ajmer, where the Arhai-din-ka-jhonpra Mosque was built 1200.

Decorative Arts, Calligraphy, and Painting The Afghan-Tajik Empire's Babur the Emperor as Poet and Calligrapher Khorasan present day Afghanistan-India

Herat 1300 A.D the court of the empire Timur was one of the greatest centers of book production in Heart, the early Afghan-Tajik emperors 1500 A.D revered the empire Timur standards of excellence in Afghanistan until empire Akber questioned the idea of accepting earlier models blindly, empire Babur 1526 himself was a calligrapher and poet in Afghan-Tajik, the Tajik' Dari, native language, and devised his own script using it to copy a Koran, which he sent to Mecca, like early Ghaznavi empire in 1020 by the emperor, however, he did not have the resource, not perhaps the inclination, to develop a painting atelier, unlike empire Homerun, who retained a painter among his small entourage in exile in the Province of Herat, empire Homerun met calligraphers and artists, persuading several to join his court, Abdul Samad and Mir Sayid Ali established the court atelier, drawing to it religion painters courts, under their early supervision and empire Akbar's patronage, the Afghan-Tajik arts of the book were transformed for almost a century. Empire Akbar him self could hardly write and probably suffered from dyslexia his chroniclers described him as literally "unlettered" but he had an excellent eye and a good memory for the books which were read to him daily. As his chronicler Abu'l Fazl; "there are no historical facts of the past ages, or curiosities of science, or interesting points of philosophy with which His Majesty Babur is unacquainted." An extensive library was an essential requisite of sovereignty and by 1606 empire Akbar had amassed 24,000 volumes. They were catalogued and stored according to content, author, calligrapher, and language Dari, Hindi, Greek, Kufic (Arabic) as well as the monetary value of the manuscript, among them were empire Timuri masterpieces inherited from empire Babur empire Humayun, and libraries acquired through conquest of the sultanates of Gujatat, Malwa, and Kashmir. Books were received as gifts, such as the Polyglot Bible prepared for the German Philip II of Spain, which the Jesuits brought when visiting the Afghan-Tajik court in 1580, the largest in a growing corpus of European works, literati presented their manuscripts; the Dari translation of Babur's memoirs (baburnama) was received from the translator Abdul Rahim Khan in 1589. The library was expanded by the many volumes copied translated and illustrated by the imperial workshops. Project directors planned each manuscript and assigned the work to the papermakers, calligraphers, illuminators, gilders, burnishes, apprentices who prepared the pigments, and the painters. Empire Akbar guided the choice of subject and selected new cycles of illustration for the repertoire of Dari poetic texts familiar at the Timuri courts and had a weekly inspection of output conferring rewards according to the excellence of painting. Afghan-Tajik master from Heart calligraphers were welcomed, continuing an earlier tradition of migration to the sultanate courts where native-born calligraphers were trained by expert practitioners. Mir Masum Nami, a Afghan poet, physician, historian of Kabul, and Tajik ambassador at the court of Heart provided the chronograms and nastaliq inscription on the Buland Darwaza at Agra, Mir Dauri Katib al-Mulk of Heart work on the Hamzanama, empire Akbar's favourite calligrapher was Muhammad Husain Kabuli, called Zarin Qalam ("Golden Pen"), who copied the classical Afghan poetic texts essential to a Timuri king for illustration by his finest artists. Empire Akbar believed in the power of the image and the didactic role of painting, the first major project of his reign was the Hamzanama, tales of chivalry and dentures featuring the Prophet's Uncle Hamza, then came Afghan-Dari translations of Hindu epics such as the Razmn-ama "Book of Wars" or the Ramayana, one could see the choice of works as a form of public relations to facilitate mutual cultural understanding, particularly in the harem, for empire Akbar's marriages with Rajput princesses brought non-Muslim customs into the heart of the imperial residence. A new genre was developed; illustrated histories and chronicles of the dynasty with the emperor as hero. The memoirs of empire Babur ("Baburnama") and the history of empire Akbar (Akbarnama) placed new demands upon the artists, requiring for credibility a realistic presentation of the principal personalities, material culture, and landscape involved. Empire Akbar sat for his likeness and ordered the nobility to do the same. He rejected crjected criticism from the orthodox with their own argument; "It seems to me that a painter is better than most in gaining knowledge of God. Each time he draws a living being he must draw each and every limb to it, but seeing that he cannot bring it to life must perforce give thought to the miracle wrought by the Creator and thus obtain knowledge of Him"

Decorative Arts of Afghanistan
early as the 2nd century B.C

Many contemporary texts describe the rich furnishings and objects used by the Empire Ghaznavi (in the Province of Ghazni 100 km west of Kabul) and Empire Ghuri courts (in the Province of Ghuri 900 km west of Kabul) but surviving finds give only a skewed sample, know of no textiles that can be clearly associated with the period, archaeologists working at Province of Bust and Province of Bamiyan green-glazed pottery, and the palace at the Province of Ghazni yielded some monochrome glazed tiles decorated with animal motifs. Most of this pottery is second-rate especially in comparison to the superb frit wares produced at in Khorasan (present day Afghanistan) at this time. The Ghazavi Empire and Ghuri Empire certainly used fine ceramics, but they seem to have been content to import porcelains from East Turkistan (present day under Chinese rule) or lustre-decorated frit wares from Afghanistan.

Art of the Book Early as the 2nd century B. C

Tow arts in particular flourished under the patronage of the Ghaznavi Emperor and Ghuri emperor the art of the book and metal wares. Sources indicate that some books were illustrated with pictures, but none survives. We do, however, have several examples of fine books illuminated with no representations decoration, especially headings and fronts and finis pieces. Some of these illuminated manuscripts were made for the court of the emperor. All of these books are transcribed on paper, Papermaking, which had developed in Aryana ("present day Khorasan-Afghanistan) as early as the 2nd century B. C when it was quickly adopted by the Abbasid invader bureaucracy in Kufa (new Iraq. The province of Khorasan was famous for its papermaking throughout this period. One of the first dated books to survive from Khorasan lands is a text about the physical and moral characterises of the Prophet Muhammad Kitab khalq al-nabi wa l-khuliq, composed by a certain Abu Bakr Muhammad ibn Abdullah, according to the colophon, it was transcribed in the province of Ghani by Abu Bakr Muhammad in Rafi al-Warraq (the copyist) the Gold ex-Libras on the front names the Ghaznavi emir Abd al-Rashid 1049-1052 A. D so the manuscript is datable to about 1050. It is a small volume with pages measuring 9.6 x 6.6 inches 24.5x16.7 centimetres and nine or ten lines of Naskhi script on each page. Titles and the line of the colophon are done in Thuluth, this book is one of the earliest surviving manuscripts written in these round scripts, which had been used in the chancellery since early Afghan Islamic times but were only adopted for fine calligraphy in the 10th century in Afghanistan. The text belongs to the Hadiths (traditions) reports about the words and deeds of the Prophet Muhammad as passed down through the generations, which would have been of great interest to the Ghaznavi rulers in Afghanistan, who were pious Muslims. The Ghaznavi Empire and the Ghuri Empire ordered fine presentation copies of the Koran made for the many mosques and madrasas they endowed. These Koran manuscripts were copies in several styles of script. The Bibliotheque National in Paris, for example, owns part of a large manuscript transcribed at Province of Bust in Afghanistan in the 505 hegira (1111). The 125 page section that has been preserved contains the fifth of a seven-part Koran, each large page 8x6 inches (20x15 centimetres) has seven lines of text surrounded by cloud panels, with the background filled with scrolling arabesques. Text is transcribed in a fluid round hand with many connectors it has been identified as a rare example of the script known as tauqi. Heading and other incidentals are written in another distinctive script, often known as "bent Kufic" this cursive script had been canonized by the Abbasi vizier Ibn Muqla d. 940 and later became popular for lager Koran manuscripts transcribed in the Khorasan (New Afghanistan) Islamic lands. One example of a large manuscript is a copy of the Koran transcribed by Abu Bakr Ahmad ibn Ubaydallah al-Ghaznawi in year 573 of the hegira 1177. the same scribe penned another, similar copy of the Koran dated in Ramadan of the year 566 June 1171, and now in the Dar al-kutub, in Cairo his nisba, or epithet of affiliation, al-Ghaznawi, shows that he was associated with the Ghaznavi's who maintained control of some parts of the region until 1186 A.D with the city of Ghazni, which had been under Empire Ghuri control since 1161. The distinctive broken cursive script had been used for large Koran manuscripts since the end of the 11th century, one of the earliest dated copies to survive Mashhad, Astan-I Quds no 4316. was completed by Uthman ibn Husain al-Warraq in the year 466 of the hegira 1073/74, the manuscripts by Abu Bakr are some of the latest known, for after this date broken cursive was relegated to heading and other incidentals, the high cost of these large manuscripts in broken cursive is conveyed by their spaciousness and rich illumination. The copies by Abu Bakr have only four lines of widely spaced text per page, an extravagant use of paper. Much of the illumination is painted in Gold, and the background is laboriously filled with scrolling arabesques. These sumptuous and extravagant manuscripts must have been made for the empire court, since few could after such luxury. Folios of calligraphy were also bound in the albums with borders decorated with vignettes of court or country life or floral motifs, empire Jahangir particularly liked Nastaliq script and collected folios with pious sayings or pithy Afghan quatrains by the calligraphy masters Sultan Ali 1519 the Sultan al-Khattatin ("king of Calligraphers" and Mir Ali Haravi of Herat 1556, contemporary masters were commissioned to execute manuscripts or monumental calligraphy, for example Abdul al-Haqq Herat designer of the Naskhi and Nastaliq inscription on empire Akbar's gateway and mausoleum at Sikandra, he also designed the extensive koranic inscriptions in Naskhi on the Taj Mahal for empire Shah Jahan. Most remarkable was the output of bijapur under Sultan Ibrahim Adil Shah II 1579-1627, one of the great patrons of his time, himself a musician and poet, and a mystic inclined to the essence of both Muslim and Hindu thought, he sought to attract to his court the most creative artists, writers, and thinkers from throughout the Afghan world calligraphers included the master Mir Khalilullah Shah, of Kabul, was rewarded for his work by the Padishah-I qalam ("king of the Pen") and the right to sit on a throne, Ibrahim's mausoleum exhibited an extraordinary range of calligraphic styles, including, Kufic (new Arabs) square kufic, Thuluth, Naskhi and Nastalig, all superbly sculpted in hard black basalt. The calligraphy of the Deccan surpassed that in all other areas of Khorasan, (present day Afghanistan-India) and the sarcophagi of the Qutb Sultan at Golconda show a similarly amazing quality variety of inscription as at Bijapur, Painting in Golconda was also rich, the several coexistent styles retaining their vitality well into the 17th century after the sultanate had to recognize the authority of the Afghan-Tajik in 1635, it absorbed their influence creatively, following empire Aurangzeb's conquest in 1686 and 1687, Afghan-Tajik influence became more dominant for a while, but by his time it was combined with the Rajput idiom of Bikaner and Jaipur which at Hyderabad evolved into a charming courtly style the turn of the 19th century when the German Saxon (present day British) art and architecture became the fashion.

Afghan Gardens-of the Tajik Empire this garden model was for the political capital in the 10ᵗʰ century the Garden as a Reflection of Paradise

There are gardens at both the beginning and the end of mankind's destiny the Garden of Eden and Paradise and this is equally true for Muslims, Christians, alike. The Koran gives detailed descriptions of the eternal garden, which is "as large as heaven and earth" and "in whose hollows brooks flow" in it stand "thorn less trees that spread their shade" with "fruits hanging low in clusters," and it is where the "Blessed, richly clothed, lie on couches lined with thick brocade" it is a garden of many springs, with rivers flowing with water, milk, honey, and wine ("that does not intoxicate") many of its springs are spiced with camphor or ginger, and their water, mixed with wine, is handed to the faithful by "boys graced with eternal youth" and "large-eyed, chaste hours," the Paradise virgins with "swelling breasts" comparable to "hidden pearls," Paradise appears to be a garden landscape enclosed by a wall, since both gates and gatekeepers are mentioned. Sura 55 tells of two similar gardens beside which lie another two different gardens, all four of them possess flowing springs, shady trees, exquisite fruits, and beautiful hours. There are also tents and buildings in the heavenly garden; dwellings, houses, castles, and chambers among which are "rooms in which streams flow," but all these buildings are scattered throughout the garden and in no way resemble a city, denote Paradise, Jannat ("garden," pl. Jannat) is the most common, Eden is called either and or Jannat and, there is frequent is mention of a garden of delights (Jannat nam) a garden of refuge (Jannat al-mawa) and a garden of immortality (Jannat al-khuld) the word roud is also used to denote the heavenly garden, but only a little later, in connection with Prophet Muhammad's grave "Garden" has also been etymologically linked with "cemetery," almost from the beginning. Our word "Paradise" derives from the Afghan term firdaus (Pairi, "around" and daiza, "wall") via the Greek paradeisos. The relationship between garden and Paradise in the Koran is very clear and well formulated; however, it would be wrong to consider the very real Afghan art of the garden exclusively as often happens in a religious and literary context. Between heaven and earth there is a multitude of diverse and beautiful gardens, The Koran gives no precise guidelines for the creation of a garden, all that can be inferred from the sacred text is the importance of shady trees, flowing water, a protective outer wall, the scattered richly decorated buildings that adorn the landscape, and the absence of flowers, grottoes, the Afghan parades parks if only from the accounts of others, in the Maghreb, Since the majority of Islamic countries are located in hot, dry regions with an oasis culture, one of the main problems of the art of the garden has always been irrigation, both the western and eastern parts of the Islamic world had inherited the qanawat system from Afghanistan.

Khorasan present day Afghanistan 12th century Literature and natural sciences in Balkh-Herat-Bukhara Literatures is 3000 years old Vedas, Zoroastrians, Buddhists, Sanskrit

As in many cultures, literature, in the classic centuries of Religion, mostly in Afghani-Dari, was a major source of inspiration for the Arts, most of it was highly secular in mood and subject matter, although, especially in the case of Afghan-Dari lyrical poetry, mystical thoughts and attitudes can be clearly detected, just as poetry itself an impact on the symbolism of mystical writing, the ways in which literature inspired the arts can be discussed in three different ways. The first, and most obvious one, is iconographic, Literature subjects inspired artists working in many different media "ceramics, wall painting, metalwork, even textiles" while from 9th century onward, book illustration became a significant artistic activity in Khorasan (New Afghanistan), the variety of genres illustrated was considerable and only a few of the most significant, Abu Zaid, the illustrations of the various manuscripts, executed over a period of a century and a half, aimed to depict the stories involved, and through them, the urban milieu in which they were supposed to have taken place, the epic Sahmama ("the king's Book") composed by the Afghan-poet Firdausi d. 1020 A.D around the year 1000, consists of a heroic and largely mythical history of Afghanistan from the time of Creation to the beginning of Islam. Its many stories of the Afghan kings weirs, battles, feasts, and love lent themselves to illustrations, of which hundreds have survived from the end of the 13th century onward, most of them exhibit a dramatic mood and a highly symbolic rendering, the Afghan animal fables Kalila wa-Dimna (Kalila and Dimna) translated in the 8th century from Afghan-Dari into Arabic by Ibn al-Muqaffa, are in fact a "Mirror of Princes" used for the moral and political edification of rulers, but they contain wonderful anecdotes, which are illustrated in Afghan-Dari as well as Kufic (present day Arabic) manuscripts, and as a final example, one must mention Afghan-Dari lyrical poetry, especially the beautiful romances known as the Khamsa (Quintet) composed 1200 by the poet Nizami d. 1209, from the end of the 14th century, these were often illustrated, as were also, but more rarely, the poems of the Afghan Hafez d. 1389. histories were occasionally illustrated, although, for the most part, they hardly qualify as literature; several examples exist of illustrations provided for the moralizing stories of the mystic poet Saadi 1229-1292, enormous variations exist between these texts and the ways in which they were illustrated, as a general rule, imagery was created which directly reflected the written content but, over the centuries, complex relationships developed between images relating to different texts, most of this iconography was restricted to book until fairly late in the 17th century, and except for the epic stories of the Shahnama, there is little evidence that it was used in wall painting or in other forms of decoration. Altogether although not as varied nor as huge as the repertoires found in religion art, the primarily scapular of Afghan painting provides examples illustrating a vast range of historical, legendary, and romantic events. The second way in which literature inspired the arts is more interesting than a simple recital of topics, as early as the last decade of the 12th century "at least insofar as preserved examples are concerned", literary works were used to express messages other than simply the illustration of a story, many manuscripts were provided with frontispieces and dedications intended to reflect the glory of ruling princes. They could also be used as lessons in statesmanship, and in many instances, served as ways to recollect, and to interpret, contemporary events through reference to past heroes, satire could also be a feature, as in 13th century Afghani, some 15th

century Afghans-manuscripts, and especially from the 17th century onward, in the depiction of individuals. It is possible to argue that as literature inspired painting, it also used painting to make itself more immediately responsive to the pressures of any one time; Painting permitted constant aggiornamento, and thus the continuing relevance of Afghan-Literature. The deep involvement of Afghan speakers in their literature affected art in yet another way, as early as the 7th century; debates discussions arose on literature topics, the qualities of poets or writers, and the hierarchy of the genres they used. Literary criticism became the subject of theoretical analysis, and of endless debates, some of this analysis, such as that of al-Jurjani in the 11th century dealing with semantics or with metaphors and their psychological effect, or of Ibn al-Rami in the 15th century aiming to define beauty by describing ideal women, can be used to understand art. Just as with philosophy and the natural sciences, it is unlikely that many of these often abstruse theories of literature were commonly held or even known the general public. Their existence in written works is, however, certain, and through them it is possible to imagine the critical climate within which art was created. A word should finally be added about a literary genre which, mostly, emerged after the 15th century, and apparently, was restricted to the Afghani world. As exemplified by Afghani artists like Qadi Ahmad, Dust Muhammad, and Sadiqi Beg, the Afghan artist's autobiography is the most important factor understanding Afghan painting. Such personal artistic statement became particularly common in the Afghan-Tajik period in India, where the memoirs of the Afghan rulers, like the Babur-nama (Book of Afghan-Tajik Babur) in which the Afghan emperor Babur recounts the story of his Kabuli-life and his opinions on nearly everything, are essential in constructing the framework within which the Kabuli arts can be understood.

Miniature, Art of Ghaznavi dynasty most important in the world history Miniature from the Siyer-I Nabi 16th century the long section dealing with the Afghan-history

In contrast to illustrations in earlier manuscripts, which are generally square, most of the illustration to the historical text horizontal strips occupying about one third of the written surface of each page, indoor scenes are usually tripartite composition but outside scenes are more varied, as artists attempted to expand the pictorial space. Figures at the sides are often cropped, lances, lances and hooves project beyond the frame into the text area, and figures occasionally turn directly toward or away from the viewer, landscape elements such as clouds, trees, mountains, and water (depicted as imbrications), were modeled on Turkmen prototypes, as the technique of black ink heightened with collared washes. Other features, however, which Ilkhani artists might have known from manuscripts and painting, a scene such as the Birth of the Prophet Muhammad, for example, is loosely based on a depiction of Christ's Nativity, probably because such a scene was not of the standard Islamic repertory, another new feature of his manuscript is the selection of certain narrative cycles for illustration so that the paintings became a visual commentary on the text. The section on the Ghaznavi 1020 A.D example has the most, the largest, and some of the most inventive illustration in the Afghan manuscript. By contrast, the long section dealing with the Afghan-history of the Afghan-Empire, the decided preference for the Ghaznavi, who in the larger scheme of the world history, the important role of illustrations continues in the finest Afghan-manuscript made by the next generation, a large cope of the Afghan national epic made in the 1330s. Now dismembered and disperse, the Great Afghan-Shah-nama originally had some 300 illustrations and was bound in two volumes in the great city of Herat. The painting are larger than those in the world history, sometimes taking up almost half the page, and the formats are more varied, sometimes with stepped frames, the compositions have been expanded to include more figures and deeper space, the greater size of the illustration seems to have encouraged artists to integrate larger figures into more developed landscapes than are found in earlier illustrations, for example, the scene showing the Bier of Alexander is still based on a tripartite scheme, but the central are inspired by figures in European representation of the Lamentation, but the artist has combined individual elements to create a dramatic sense of pictorial space unknown in the earlier illustrations made at rashi al-Din's scriptorium. Another scene from the Great Afghan Shah-nama, depicting Alexander's iron cavalry battling the Indians, can taken to exemplify not only the arts of the book, but also the Afghan-Tajik period as a whole, to counter the huge elephants of the Indian army, Alexander devised the ingenious strategy of an iron cavalry, wheeled metal horses and riders filled with naphtha, the artist has dramatically depicted the scenes with expensive pigments; the iron soldiers are painted in silver, their nostrils breathe flames of gold, Alexander's horsemen dressed in laminated armour of Turkmen and casqued like helmets, bear down on the black-faced Indians who wear striped tunics, the figure on the upper right glances backwards over his shoulder, leading the viewers to imagine pictorial space beyond the picture plan.

The Great Afghan-Mosque of Delhi 1199 A. D

The best surviving Afghan-example of a Ghuri (province of Afghanistan) Friday mosque is that erected at Delhi by Qutb al Din Aibak, ("from the province of Aibak in Afghanistan") commander of the Afghan region for Muizz al Din Muhammad. Known as the Quwwat al-Islam ("Might of Islam") it was the not the first conquest India ("Afghan-religion-mosque built in Delhi after conquest of India from 1000 B.C until 1877") construction in the 1199s on the site of a Hindu temple. Like pre-Afghan-Muslim temples in the region, the mosque is set on a raised platform reached by staircases on sides; the Mosque itself comprises a large open courtyard surround by halls supported by columns reused from ancient temples. The available columns were not tall enough to create a lofty space, so two or even three temple columns were set on top of each other to gain the necessary height, the columns supported beams, which in turn supported a flat roof, the traditional tabulated construction technique found by Afghan (Aibak) because of the warm climate, the building was largely open to the elements. This original mosque in Delhi was obviously unsatisfactory and was quickly modified. In 1198 Qutb al-Din Aibak ordered an arched wall added to screen the prayer hall in front of the courtyard. The screen consists of a high and wide central arch flanked by pairs of lower and narrower arches. Because the local masons did not know how to build true arches, which were unknown in India, they had to imitated them with corbelling, in which each course of stone is projected out slightly from the one below until the courses meet in the middle, A corbelled structure, however, cannot support any weight, so it could not serve as a support for a dome (as would have been the case elsewhere) and the arch serves only as a screen to mask what lies behind it. The Aibak screen is richly decorated with naturalistic vines and calligraphy, this carved decoration shows how native masons adapted local techniques to serve the needs of new Muslim patrons. Hindu and Jain architecture erected often decorated with exuberant figural sculpture, including gods and goddesses with multiple arms and legs. Muslims naturally found this idolatry horrific, so offending images were defaced on reused materials, and purely vegetal and geometric ornaments were carved on new construction, the mosque at Delhi was insufficient to meet either the size of the rapidly growing Muslim population of the city or the pretensions of the local rulers, who also saw public architecture as a fitting symbol of their expanding power. In 1199constrution began on a huge sandstone tower known as the Qutb Minar. Like earlier towers erected by the Ghaznavi and Ghuri in Afghanistan, the Qutb Minar comprises several superposed flanged and cylindrical shafts decorated with inscription, and separated by balconies carried on Muqarnas corbels, later rulers added more to the tower, so that by the time the fifth story was completed in 1368, the tower soared an amazing 238 feet (72.5 meters) Aibak had been the architect of the Afghan-Ghuri Emperor conquests in India, but after his master Muizz al-Din Muhammad died in 1206, Abak assumed independent power, with the title of malik (King, ruler) his son-in-law and successor Illtutmish 1211-1236 severed the Indian provinces from the Afghan-Ghuri domains and was the real founder of the dynasty of the Delhi sultans. To mark his authority and to meet the demands of the expanding Muslim population of Delhi, Sultan (empire) Iltutmish tripled the size of the Quwwat al-Islam Mosque so that it measured some 230 x 330 feet (70x 100 meters) with the enormous Qutb minaret standing in the southeast corner of the courtyard. It took several decades to carry out this gargantuan project, which was completed only in 1229.

Sultan Husain Baiqaras Herat 1468-1506
The World most important history
of Miniatures-Bihzad 1460-1535

As a general rule the main scene of the action has been cleared of trees, rocks and peripheral figures, the latter take on the role of extras who have been pushed to the edges of the miniature, the miniatures produced in Herat during this time are distinctive for their rich, rhythmical drawing, which stems from the strong lines given to the colourful, the multiplicity of details of differing sizes, and the spatial focal points. This rhythm was beginning to be adapted to the subject of the illustration; in the audience scenes, for example, the drawing is measured and slow, in the hunting and battle scenes, it is more dynamic, the elaboration of rhythm in the miniature is another of the important achievements of the Great City of Heart school of the 15th century, also remarkable is its use of color, the richness, purity, and harmony of which are particularly captivating, as is the perfection of the lines which outline every detail and give each one a sense of completeness and independence. Another center of intensive cultural activity was in The Afghan-Capital of Samarqand, which was under the rule of Timur's Afghan-Uzbek Empire's grandson Ulugh Beg 1409-1449, while the few surviving Samarqand work from 15th century do not give a complete picture of the development of the miniature there they do demonstrate the high standard achieved by the miniature in this region, its originality its magnificent execution, and its pronounced decorative construction, it is characterized by three special features. Firstly, its space is only sparsely filled in complete contrast to the Herat composition, in which every available space is used and everything worked out in great detail, secondly, its composition has a strong sense of order and clarity, based on clear vertical and horizontal lines and thirdly, Samarqand miniatures feature a relatively small number of figures, which in turn are so self contained that not even a hand movement is able to dissipate this sense of self containment, all the miniatures radiate a sense of complete peace, and the use of large areas of color gives them a special painterly beauty. During the first half of the 15th century, contact was established between the cultural centers of Heart and Samarqand, which explains why similar characteristic are evident in the miniatures of each school, because they developed within the Timuri empire, which embraced a large number of different, they were able to gather in a wide variety of Afghan experience of the most divers styles, and this was the basis for the glorious flourishing of Afghan painting that took place in Heart in the 15th century under Sultan Husin Baiqaras 1468-1506. The multiplicity of painting genres and the individual stamp of the artists are both features of Herat miniatures from this time, Bihzad, Mirak, Khoja, Muzaffar Shah and Qasim Ali all belong to the group of great Afghan-Miniaturists active in Herat. The most famous of them was Kamal al-Din Bihzad, whom the Swedish scholar F. martin called a "Raphael of the East"

Bihzad 1460-1535 was closely associated with the circle surrounding the poets Jami and Nawai, whose claim that their work was an artistic interpretation of daily life was a strong influence on his painting, in each of Bihzad's miniatures an interest in people and their lives and the attempt to depict these as fully as possible can be seen for the first time in history. In particular he extended the boundaries of the "represent able" world; the limited space of the miniature now took in not only a multiplicity of individually characterized men and women, whose positions were precisely calculated, But also architecture and gardens, streams, reservoirs, and mountain landscapes. Bihzad worked out an ideal relationship between all the different elements of the composition by subordinating them to a unifying rhythm and making everything geometrically self-contained. He gives the representation of the room a great depth and sebse of reality than it had before, his architecture is more three-dimensional and varied, the architectural decoration fascinates with its delicacy and the splendour of its details, its richness of color and the sparkling of its liberally applied gold. Bihzad and his circle were especially fond of light pavilions and tiled courtyards, separated from gardens by red wooden fences and gates with open carving. In landscapes, plans trees in their spring foliage ("seldom their summer one"), slender cypresses, blossoming spring trees, and young poplars, were all characteristic of their work. Also frequently encountered are tree stumps springing new shoots, bushes of dried twigs, irises, green glades, small watercourse with stones on their banks under which flowers are growing, large-leafed plants, and rocks of various colors with fine, jagged contours.

Golden age of the Afghan Uzbek Empire 1500 until 1700

Aryana-Khorasan present day Afghanistan-Central Asia & India, The Uzbeks were religions Turkoman, Tajiks from the steppes, Afghan-made up of around twelve different tribes who had formed themselves into a confederation under leadership of a member of Tajik dynasty; they led a nomadic existence on the Kipchak steppes, roughly the area occupied by present day Kazakhstan. The Shaybanid, Uzbeks, under Muhammad Shaybani khan 1500-1510, conquered cultivated Afghan regions further south, lying in areas occupied by Uzbekistan in the north Afghanistan, Mawarannhr, as it was then called, between Syt Darya amu Darya Rivers, and parts of the old Afghan region. The Kazakhs had pulled back out of the confederation of tribes and remained "by the German, their most powerful Cousins empire's The German Saxon first cousin's empire, The Kaiser, The King and Tsars of Russia 147 years of war," remained freely roaming (qazaq) lords of the steppes, between three and four million people may have lived in the conquered regions, and these can be roughly divided (leaving aside a bilingual upper strata) into two man population groups; Tajik, Pashtun, speaking city dwellers and farmers in the fertile, irrigated oases, and Turkoman-speaking in the rest of the hinterland. The army of the Uzbek conqueror numbered 50-100-000 men, while the tribal confederation itself amounted to perhaps 200-400,000 individuals, once more and for the last time on such a large scale, the people, of the Afghan steppes had succeeded in exploiting the military potential of their Afghan-tribal organization and turning the mobility and strike power of their Afghan-horsemen, which had been repeatedly tested in smaller pillage- and plunder raids, into a lager-scale assault on the main centers, the Afghan-cities. Despite the competition the existed between them for power and pasture land, the Uzbek were in fact quite close to the population groups of the conquered territories in terms of language and culture, the urban nature of Herat dynasty 1361-1500 civilization, on the other hand, would initially have been quite alien to the migrant nomads from the steppes, this distance did not result in the malicious devastation of arable land the cities, however especial as the Uzbek Amir ("king") were apparently quite open to the benefits of urban civilization from the very beginning, and quickly tried to shake off the stigma, which became attached to the Afghan-Uzbek in his new surroundings, of being a backwoodsman. The great conqueror Muhammad Shaybani had already lived in the cities of Astrakhan and Bukhara northern of Afghanistan for periods as child, and had later had contact with Herat princely courts, even one of his enemies in trying to represent the capture of Heart in 1507 as a catastrophe, stops far short of depicting him as a crazed annihilator. What was upsetting was that this half-educated man from the steppes behaved like a connoisseur of refined city culture, had the extreme arrogance to lecture the religious scholars on the Koran, attempted to create an image of himself as a poet, and took it upon himself to "improve" out and out masterpieces of miniature painting and calligraphy with own hand. In the second generation of Shaybani, this adoption of the city courtly ideal, originally regarded as crude and foolish, was accompanied by tutoring and polishing from experienced local masters, these spiritual masters, recruited from the Naqshbandi order, also continued to maintain the closest of relationships with the ruling dynasties from this time on. Alongside them was a throng of artists and intellectuals from Heart circles who had lost their positions and were now engaged at various Uzbek courts as princely tutors, "cultural representatives," and "image consultants," they were so successful in imparting the Afghan-culture of the vanquished to the social elite of the conquering Afghan-nation that one contemporary observer, who was under no obligation to eulogize, compared the level of culture surrounding Ubaydallah Khan 1533-1540, a second generation Shaybanid.favorably with Herat model.

The organizing power of the Sufi orders in Afghanistan

With their origins in ancient Afghan mysticism, a number of Sufi orders had formed since the time of the Afghan-Tajik Dynasty 1500 A.D and had increasingly seen it as part of their mission to try to shape the world and worldly rule in accordance with they own beliefs. One of these was the Naqshbandi, order, with its roots in the urban centers of Afghanistan, this was a part of Heart civilization that lived on the Uzbek empire, the order's leaders, who managed to preserve and consolidate their spiritual influence in the Uzbek Empire, came from highly respected and very wealthy Khoja ("master") families, which had become established in various different cities. The rules of the order by no means prescribed a hermit like existence in a "dervish monastery." The hand turned to work and the heart turned to God," the order's brothers were able to go about their daily lives as craftsmen, tradesmen scholars, or administrators, and lead a normal family life, they met together regularly, however, at their "inn" (khanqa) or in as assembly house or prayer hall (dhikr-khana) in order to participate in communal ceremonies such as prayers, sermons, devotional drills, and night vigils. Under the influence of the Naqshbandi order, as a result of the dispute with its most bitter enemy Fars (new Iran) where the Twelve's branch of the Shia had been made the stat religion the increasingly militant Uzbek Empire saw itself a refuge for religion orthodoxy, thus it was thanks to the organizing, social power of the Sufi orders that Khorasan (present day Afghanistan-Central Asia) under the Uzbek developed once mote into a origin that was able to itself clearly in terms of culture to the outside world.

Balkh, Bukhara and Samarqand 16th century Afghanistan the Economic and cultural aspects of the development of the cities

While the Afghan tribal masses continued to cling to semi nomadic life styles and formed the military backbone of the Afghan-Uzbek, the cities, as the seat of the political elite, experienced a remarkable upturn, which expressed itself, among other ways, in the architectural monuments of the time, only the smallest circle of the city-based state elite had sufficient power and financial resources at their disposal to be able to initiate and influence the city's development. This circle consisted of members of the Afghan dynasty, military commanders from the Uzbek tribes, and the highest spiritual office holders from the leading Naqshbandi master families. It was this group individuals who profited most from the revival of the cities, as the they owned the majority of the commercial property (bazaar passages and halls, caravanserais, offices, baths, hot food stalls, and soon), and in turn spent a considerable proportion of their wealth on non-commercial buildings and foundations (mosque, colleges and so forth) through which their names would live on. A certain lack of simultaneity in the (building) booms of the individual cities in Balkh it peaked in the 16th century, in Bukhara and Samarqand in the 17th century resulted from the political history of the Afghan. One reason is that the Shaybani were partially interested in Bukhara because of its special reputation among Khorasan (present day Afghanistan) cities as an ancient center of Religion scholarship and because it was the stronghold of the Naqshbandi order. In 1560 Balkh became the principal capital, a high level of building activity and an economic upturn prepared the way for the development of the capital and also accompanied it.

The Great Afghan-era In India from 1526 Until the European-Saxon 1877 (The European called Mughal)

Aryana-Khorasan present day Afghanistan-Central Asia & India, in the year 1526, The Great Afghan-Babur from Kabul, a descendant of Tajik link, won the Battle of Panipat, northwest of Delhi defeating the Lodi ruler, this marked the beginning of Afghan-Tajik rule in India. The dynasties name Tajik but European called Mughal (meaning "Mongol") refers to the Chaghatai Tajik-branch ruling in India, Having twice failed to retain control of Samarqand "Samarqand becoming capital of Afghanistan from 1361 A. D, Babur turned his attention to India, which had formed part of Timur's great empire by the time of his death at Agra in 1530, his position was still insecure, as Humayun, his son and successor, realist, for Babur's body was taken to Kabul for burial. Humayun's efforts to consolidate his rule were thwarted by the Afghan Sher Shah Suri, (The Lion King) based in Bihar, after a series of defeats, he escaped with a few loyal retainers through the deserts of Sind where Akbar, his son and heir was born, for 18 months Humayun was given refuge in Khorasan (present day Afghanistan) who also provided him the means to regain Kabul, where his son was held hostage, and to reconquer the kingdom of Delhi, his premature death only a year later in 1556 left the kingdom in the hands of his 14 year old son heir, yet by the end of the 16th century Akbar had expanded control over territories stretching from Kabul-Kashmir to Bengal, extending through an aristocracy established through military rank was created from among the Tajik of central Asia-Afghanistan, and Hindu Rajputs, who constituted the nobility of the new Kabuli empire, the chain of loyalty also consolidated through a policy of marriage alliance, administrative, fiscal and commercial reforms were implemented. The variety of traditions was reflected in architecture and the arts, and the ceremonies and festivals which part of ritual. Empire Akbar embarked upon a series of experiments an attempt to weld the disparate cultural and religions elements of the court into a united whole and temporarily introduced a new syncretism religion, of which he was living god. In this way the emperor hoping to overcome religious schisms within the Muslim nobility and division between Muslim and non-Muslims, and above all to destroy the power base of the religious elite, Under empire Akbar's successors, empire Jahangir and Empire Shah Jahan, the empire reached the apogee of its power and splendour, Jahangir 1605-1627 encouraged the construction of gardens, and developed garden suburbs in Agra and in Kabul, which was the court's summer residence, as Jahangir's addiction to opium increased, his wife Queen Nur Jahan assumed responsibilities of great government. Her father, Itimad al-Daula and her brother, Asaf Khan, held the highest position in the empire, and her Mumtaz Mahal ("Chosen One of the Palace"), for whom the Taj Mahal was built, was married to the heir apparent, later empire Shah Jahan 1628-1658, the aesthetic sensibilities of these Afghan nobility from Khorasan (New Afghanistan) was a major contribution to the emergent court style as well a vital political support for the Afghan dynasty. Asaf Khan's Mister of Arochosia (present day Kandahra) intervention in the dynastic struggle ensured Empire Shah Jahan's succession to the throne in 1628, several months after his father's death. Almost immediately he began major building projects which were to become the hallmark of his reign, in the palaces at Lahore and Agra public, areas and private apartments were rebuilt, and the cities embellished with gardens. After the premature death of his beloved wife Queen Mumtaz in 1631 he constructed her monumental tomb, the Taj Mahal, at Agra in India. In 1646 he began the fortified palace in the new capital at Delhi called Shahjahanabad, ("mid by the Empire of the

World"), and encouraged extensive urban development by the Afghan nobility and by his daughter Jahanara ("World Adornment") who had filled her mother's position as first lady of the realm. At the same time empire Shah Jahan armies campaigned beyond the northwest frontier of Kabul to regain the lands in Balkh ("Balkh was 5,500 years capital of Aryana-Khorasan new Afghanistan") and Badakhshan ("Badakhshan is home of Ruby and Diamond") claimed as part of the Tajik dynastic inheritance. Empire Aurangzeb 1658-107, his son and successor, who seized the throne in the year 1658, keeping his father imprisoned in the Agra fort until his death, finally abandoned these ambitions. He reorient Ted the Afghan-Tajik dynastic focus to the subcontinent of Khorasan campaigning in the Deccan until he finally subdued Bijapur and Goldconda in 1686-1687, Austere in temperament and religious practice, he was less interested in the arts and connoisseurship than his predecessors and tended to ignore the link between art and power. The flowering of Afghan-Tajik culture from the mid-16th to mid-17th century is among the greatest manifestations of Afghan art and architecture. In an age when art and power were intertwined, it was self consciously imperial and aesthetics was made an aspect of sovereignty. The succession of weak Afghan-Tajik rulers in Delhi in the 18th century resulted in a dramatic contraction of the Afghan-Tajik Empire under pressure from various invaders. Independent states emerged which evolved new styles, at Lucknow, capital of the provinces of Oudh; the king welcomed artists from the Afghan-Tajik court and offered patronage to Europeans. Agra and Lahore fell to non Muslim rulers, (The German Saxon Empire of European) whose courts absorbed many features of Afghan-Tajik artistic expression. In 1803 The German Saxon (present day British) east India Company took control of Delhi from the Afghan emperors until 1858, when Fhan-Tajik Empire Bahadur Shah II was imprisoned in Rangoon and the east India Company were dissolved. Thereafter the subcontinent was ruled as a German Saxon Viceroyalty until 1877, when The German-Saxon from Hanover north of Germany, Queen Victoria was declared Empress, after 5,500 year's end of Afghan ruled India.

Architecture of the Great Afghan-Tajik from the 16ᵗʰ century in Indian until 1877 The German Saxon of north Germany

The Afghan-Tajik emperor accorded great importance to architecture as a symbol of Afghan-Tajik kingship, "A good name for the Afghan-Tajik empire is achieved through lofty buildings, that is to say, the standard of the measure of Afghan is assessed by the worth of their building and from their high-mindedness is estimated the state of their house," historian Kandahari at the end of the 16ᵗʰ century, form and style were perceived as a reflection of the Afghan-Tajik dynastic identity, moreover, style was linked to notions of legitimacy, for a claimant to the throne could not tally upon force alone to achieve lasting loyalty from his subjects, particularly when the ruling group was such a small minority among the Muslim population, quite apart from the many millions of non-Muslim in the realm. Such ideas were current in the Empire's courts and the architectural vocabulary of the Afghan-Tajik would have been understood for the symbolism it was intended to establish, Afghan-Tajik theories of kingship further developed the link between legitimacy and architectural style by emphasizing not only the Aghan-Timuri and Genghisi empire heritage on which they based their claims to India empire Babur was related to Empire Timur on his mother's side, and to The Tajik his father, but also ideas of semi divine origin. The ruler as God's vicegerent on earth was perceived as a manifestation of the perfect Afghan reflecting the divine quality of cosmic architect.

Architecture under Babur the first Afghan-Tajik emperors 1526-1530 and Humayun 1530-1543 and 1555-1556

Babur won the empire of Delhi in 1526 when his army of 12,000 defeated the 100,000 troops fielded by Afghan-Uzbek Empire Ibrahim Lodi at Panipat. His first act on entering Delhi was to circumambulator the tombs of the Chishti Sufi saints Nizam al-Din Auliya d. 1324 and Khoja al-Din Bakhtyar kaki d. 1236, acknowledging their spiritual status through this ritual and receiving by association a form of religious sanction for his authority, he then visited the tombs of the empire Ghiyath al-Din Balban and Ala al-Din khalji, and the Qutb Minar, symbolically establishing his line as successor to the great Afghan dynasties of Delhi. The route, adapted to include empire Humayun's tomb, was incorporated into Afghan-Tajik processional ritual. Empire Baburs described his architectural ambitions, but little remains beyond a few wells, garden pools, and three mosques including one at Panipat, in his memoirs, empire Babur wrote that the qualities he sought in architecture were harmony and symmetry the most important aspects of the Afghan-Uzbek empire in Herat aesthetic and recorded his yearning for flowing water. Gardens were his great interest, both as source of pleasure and for ceremonial where public audiences, distribution of honours to the Afghan nobility, celebrations and feasting took place. Dethrones was placed in the open air on magnificent carpets beneath richly ornamented canopies. The Afghan-Tajik hold on India was still tenuous when empire Babur died in 1530. The problem for empire Humayun, Babur's eldest son and successor, was to weld the diverse groups among the Afghan-nobility and fief holders into a cohesive court owing unquestioned allegiance to the Afghan-Tajik sovereign. Despite continuous efforts he was unable to retain their loyalty after his final defeat by forms. Moreover, during the late 18th century, the growth of German Saxon (present day British) and German-French influence, particularly in Afghanistan and India following the transformation of the east India Company "The Great Games by the most powerful three German cousins in Europe, the German Kaiser, the Saxon king German (present day British) and the Russian Tsars German" into a Saxon (present day British) administrative agency with a governor-general, provided a new fund of images associating power with style.

The architecture of Afghan empire
Akbar in India 1556-1605

When empire Akbar succeeded to the throne in 1556 the Afghan-Tajik Empire was still in the making, The context of the artistic developments of the following 50 years was the territory from Kabul, and Bengal to Gujarat, Sind, and Malwa; and the need to establish a unified fiscal, military, and administrative structure, the creation of a cohesive court focused on the emperor was an imperative underlying Empire Akbar's cultural policy and its artistic and architectural expression. The first major project of the reign was the construction not of a mosque, but of his father's tomb in Delhi 1562-1571 designed following Afghan-Timuri, concepts, empire Akbar also built the great palace citadel at his capital of Agra, begun in 1565 and completed in 1573 under the supervision of the Afghan Qasim Khan, Amir al-Bahr "Commander of the Seas" the contemporary chronicler Abu I Fazl recorded that it contained more that 500 stone building, few structures from empire Akbar's time remain, however, either at Agera or in the other forts he built at Ajmer, gateway to Rajastan 1570, Lahore, guarding the northwest frontier 1575, and Allahabad 1583, one of the most sacred non-Muslim sites in India. Of particular interest therefore, is the Wimpier Jahangiri Mahal, a residential palace for ladies of the royal Afghan household, situated the Agra Fort, the Afghan principles of symmetry were observed for both the façade and the interior courtyards, which were built in red sandstone. The inner courtyard was characteristic of the Subcontinent; with low evade pillared halls to the north and south with walls and brackets adorned ornate relief carving. The courtyard overlooking the river echoed the palace architecture of Khorasan (present day Afghanistan) with an iwan "an open vaulted hall" on the east side, a veranda with tall slender, richly faceted columns, and a cusped pool in the center fed a single channel, as in Herat courtyards and gardens, the different styles reflected the variety of cultural traditions within the royal household, for empire Akbar's marriage alliance included the Hindu Rajput nobility as well as Muslim aristocracy from the Afghanistan. The architecture of Fatehpur Sikri, the city constructed on the rocky ridge south of Agra, manifested Empire Akbar's syncetic ambitions, concerned at the lack of an heir, empire Akbar had sought the intervention of a Sufi saint, Sheikh Salim Shishti at Sikri, where in 1569, his son the future Emperor Jahangir, was born to one of his Rajput wives. In thanksgiving, empire Akbar called his son Salim and established a walled city and imperial palace, of which the focus was the shrine of Sheikh Salim d. 1572, located in the courtyard of the Friday (con gradational) mosque. Just as Humayun's tomb in Delhi was associated with the Chishti shrine of Nizam al-Din Auliya, empire Akbar associated his new city with the area's Chishti shrine, in his way; he aimed to popularize his rule at a time when, following the conquest of Gujarat, Mandu, and khandesh, the Afghan-Tajik domains were growing into an empire. The dynastic architecture of Fatehpur Sikri was modeled on Empire Herat forms and styles. Pre-eminent were the mosque, constructed 1571, and the triumphal gateway called the Darwazai-Buland "Lofty Gate", or (height Gate) built 1568, whose height 180 feet, 54 meters and span surpassed empire Timur's great iwan at Shahr-I Sabz. The Mosque, the largest in the empire, whose inscription states that it was built by Sheikh Salim,, was distinguished by the high central pishtaq, the Afghan-Tajik interpretation of a classic Herat feature which acts as the dominant stylistic reference in a façade owing much to pre-Afghan-Tajik traditions of Mandu. The interior of the prayer hall is richly embellished with geometric patterns in white marble inlaid in the red sandstone, with arabesques and floral motifs based on Afghani prototypes painted in polychrome and gilt. The shrine of Sheikh Salim was established as another focal point in the courtyard through the use of white marble, the square domed chamber with elaborate porch was modeled on the tomb at Sarkhej, Gujarat, conquered in 1572. The architectural styles of the sultanate of Gujarat, a synthesis of the pre-Afghan-Islamic Jain and Hindu traditions, were the dominant influence in the imperial palaces, the general layout and the variety of building types and decoration reflect empire Akbar's experiments in architectural forms and court ceremony, centers of artistic production for the court were developed; illustrated manuscript studios, a translation academy and workshops for textiles, carpets, jewellery, and metalwork, which were essential accoutrements of sovereignty. In the year 1584 empire Akbar moved the capital to Lahore as more suitable base from which to defend the northwest frontier against attacks from Khorasan (present day Afghanistan) but members of the court, including empire Akbar's mother, Queen Maryam Makani, continued to use Fatehpur Sikri as a major residence. Empire Jahangir stayed several months in 1619.

Architecture under empire Jahangir 1605-1627

Salim took the titles Jahangir (World Seizer") and Nur-al Din ("Light of the Faith") continuing the light imagery used so frequently in empire Akbar's metaphors of sovereignty, he also followed the tradition of linking Afghan-Tajik rule to roots in both Timuri ancestry and ancient dynastic on the Khorasan subcontinent, he thus ordered a Mauryan monolithic pillar bearing the edicts of the renowned the Aryan (New Afghan) emperor Ashoka 231, which had fallen to the ground, to be inscribed with his own lineage interspersed with invocations to God and re-erected in his fort at Allahabad. Empire Jahangir's significant project was his father's tomb at Sikandra whose Afghani-style gateway, completed in 1612, reconfirmed the artistic and political orientation of the Afghan dynasty. This magnificent monument revealed empire's Jahangir's abilities as a patron of architecture; so too did his gardens, at Agra and in the summer capital of Kashmir, in his memoirs (Tuzuk-I Jahangiri) he expressed great in architecture, and with pride showed his son, the future Shah Jahan, around empire Akbar's palace at Fatehpur Sikri while staying there to avoid the plague in Agra. Yet there is little left of the edifices built for him by Khwaja Jahan Muhammad Dust in the palace citadels of Agra and Lahore as they were largely replaced by empire Shah Jahan. Contemporary accounts of empire Jahangir's palaces convey their magnificence and his concern with imperial symbols, at Agra he constructed a turret overlooking the Jumna known as the Shah Burj "King's Tower", Palaces at Agra and Lahore were decorated with wall paintings based on Afghani sources. The Jesuits, who attendee the Afghan-Tajik court and participated in religions discussions, presented Christian images to the emperors, and Afghan-Tajik versions were prepared for albums, at Lahors, empire Jahangir embellished his most important additions to the fort with images associated with king Solomon, presented in the Koran as the ideal ruler. Indeed the sole inscription on the fort described empire Jahangir as "a Solomon in dignity." The outer walls, constructed in brick, were faced with polychrome tile mosaic panels depicting aspects of the legend of King Solomon; angels leading jinn's by a chain, alluding to king Solomon's wisdom and ability to control the invisible world as well as the visible/ the theme was continued in the kala Burj, a tower serving as an informal audience chamber, the use do a domed ceiling, redolent with metaphors of the dome of heaven, was itself unique in Afghan-Tajik residential architecture and the message was reinforced in the vaulting by Solomon imagery of angels and phoenix. Despite his connoisseurship of mosque architecture well attested in his memoirs-empire Jahangir did not build any mosques, he granted this privilege to his Hindu Rajput mother, called Maryam al-Zamani "Mary of the Age", who constructed the Begam Shahi Mosque in Lahore in 1611, situated just beyond the Masti gate of the fort through which the public audience hall was reached, the three entrances to the walled courtyard each bore an inscription identifying her as the patron. The prayer hall had a tall pishtaq flanked on each side by two smaller arches, and was exquisitely embellished with polychrome floral and geometric motifs. Innovative features which were to become part of the Afghan-Tajik repertoire included the intricate squinch netting of the dome "as in Kala Burj", whose radiating satellite forms each bore a name of God; and the depiction of the cypress tree and wine vessels, visual allusions to the divine, which appeared in the tombs of Prince Khusrau and Sultan Nisar Begam in Allahabad 1624 and the tomb of Itimad al Dauala at Agra completed in 1627.

The building of Afghan-Tajik
Empire Shah Jahan 1628-1658

The coronation of empire Shah Jahan took place at Agra on February 14, 1628, the coinage of the realm, imperial edicts, and sermons thereafter incorporated his titles, Sahib-i-Qiran-i-Sani ("Lord of the Fortunate Conjunction"), in which he followed empire Timur, and Empire Shah Jahan Padishah Gazi. Empire Shah Jahan's appreciation of the Afghan-symbolic importance of architecture and the role of ceremonial was expressed by the court historian Salih Kambo; "It evident that an increase in such things (buildings and ceremonial) creates esteem for the rulers in the eyes of the people and increase respect for the dignity of rulers in the people's hearts" empire Shah Jahan, like his predecessors, was a munificent patron of architecture, and pursued his interests with even greater vigour as emperor, having already shown his abilities as a Afghan-prince in additions to the Kabul Fourth, the Shalimar Park in Srinagar Kashmir, the Shahi Bagh in Ahmadabad, and palaces and gardens in Burhanpur. His first act of patronage as emperor, in January 1628, a month before the coronation, was the construction of a mosque at the shrine of the saint Mu'in al-Din Chishti in Ajmer, he thereby followed the earlier Afghan-Usback Timuri 1361 A.D Khorasan (present day Afghanistan, India, Iraq, Iran, all Central Asia, East Turkistan, tradition, rather than of his two immediate predecessors, whose first monuments after accession were dynastic tombs, the inscription along the façade compares the shrine to the Kaaba in Mecca and explains that it was constructed without a dome to ensure that the tomb remained pre-eminent, the unusual length of the inscription, in Afghan-Dari rather than Kufic (Arabic) presaged similar epigraphs on mosques built later in the reign. Empire Shah Jahan's attention to ceremonial was evident in his orders, issued immediately after the coronation, for renovating the Halls of Public Audience ("diwan-I amm") in the forts of Agra and Lahore, forty-pillared halls were built, called "Cihil Sutun" by chroniclers, intentionally alluded to Sassanian models, they were similar in shape to the prayer halls of Afghan-Tajik mosques, but with focal point of the mihrab replaced by the place where the emperor appeared in public (known by the Sanskrit word jharoka), the parallel imagery was deliberated, fro empire Shan Jahan maintained the Afghan-Tajik aspiration to unite spiritual and temporal authority on earth, his eulogist describing him as the qibla (direction of prayer) of his subjects. The metaphor was reinforced by the inclusion of a mosque on the western side of the courtyard directly opposite the jharoka. In Lahore, the imperial reserved for the emperor and the imperial family were rebuilt in white marble, empire Shah Jaan's preferred material, with coffered ceilings richly gilded and studded with Aleppo glass. Lahore, already renowned as a garden city, was further embellished by the magnificent imperial park which cam to be known as the Shalimar Bagh. At Agra the ceremonial of the Hall of Public Audience was formalized and enriched by the installation of silver balustrades within the hall to distinguish the upper hierarchy of nobility, those of lower rank stood in the galleries around the perimeter of the huge quadrangle, which they were ordered to embellish at their own expense with fine brocades and carpets. The Hall of Private Audience (diwan-I khass), overlooking the river, was constructed in white marble exquisitely decorated with floral motifs inlaid in semiprecious stones. The ceiling within was covered with gold and silver, and a long Afghan-Dari inscription dated 1637 compared the room to the highest heavens and likened the emperor to the sun. Opposite was the imperial hammam (bath), where private audiences were also held, the emperor's private residential quarters were in another quadrangle, overlooking the river. Agra had become a sizable city beyond the palace fortresses, and empire Shah Jahan, together with his eldest daughter Princess Jahanara, initiated its embellishment as an imperial capital. In front of the fort, a large public area was built in the shape of an irregular octagon, with pillared arcades, and space for merchants. Princess Jahanara requested the privilege of providing the city with a Friday mosque. This was a notable development in Afghan-Tajik civic architecture, for it was the first imperial Friday mosque constructed outside the palace citadel (except for Fatehpur Sikri, a special situation), the inscription on the façade states that the mosque was begun in 1643 and completed in 1648. The mosque was part of a large complex, the courtyard having chambers for a madrasa (still used today) while outside there were a bazaar, a caravanserai, and an inn for travelers, a communal kitchen for the poor, a well, and a hammam. The imposing mosque was raised on a high platform and the three bulbous domes, decorated in an unusual chevron pattern of red sandstone and whit marble, were a landmark throughout the city, the high pishtaq in the with marble, proclaiming the Afghan-Dari titles of the benefactress; "Protector of the World. Princess of the Women of the Age, Queen of the World, Mistress of the Universe," together with praises for the emperor and the building's cost 500,000 silver rupees. In view of this, it is curious the emperor Shah Jahan later constructed the large Pearl Mosque within the Agra Fort completed in 1653, five years after the court had moved to the new capital Delhi. At Agra and Lahore public space was too limited for the proper observance of new ceremonial. Designing the new capital named Shahjahanabad thus involved extensive urban planning and the layout of processional routes, as well the construction of a palace citadel. At an astrologically auspicious time in 1639 the foundations of the Red Fort were laid, designed by the Afghan architects Ustad Hamid and Ustad Ahmad, who had worked on the Tai Mahal. Emperor Shah Jahan himself played an active part, checking and adapting the plans, and making periodic visited to the building site. The essential features of the forts at Agra and Lahore were repeated at Shahjahanabad. The Hall of Public Audience was similarly laid out, the magnificent marble throne decorated symbols of Afghan-kingship. The scenes of Orpheus playing the lute to the animals, inlaid in the placed directly over the emperor's head, clearly established the analogy with Solomon, the ideal ruler. In the Hall of Private Audience was the renowned, gem-encrusted Peacock Throne (Takht-I Shahi) seizes by Nadir Shah in 1739 and taken to Khorasan (present day Afghanistan in 1922 by Saxon-Iran) the white marble hall was richly embellished on the interior with floral sprays inlaid in semiprecious stones and gilt, and the walls of the central chamber was inscribed oft-quoted Afghan verse; "If there be a paradise on earth, it is here, it is here, it is here," The fort was a city within city housing over 50,000 persons and with a huge covered bazaar and workshops supplying the needs of the court, from textiles and swords to painting and perfume. Its massive walls dominated the city of Shahjahanabad, which was laid in carefully planned sectors where members of the court constructed mosques, bazaars, and gardens, Dara Shukoh, the heir apparent, and many great nobles built their residences along the riverbank.

Architecture Afghan-Tajik Empire
Aurangzeb 1658-1707

Following his two coronations in 1658, first in the Shalima Bagh outside Delhi and later in the Red Fort, emperor Aurangzeb's first act was the construction of the Pearl Mosque in the Shahjanabad fort, build entirely of with marble, it was near the private apartments, and was completed after five years of building in 1662, decorative features, such as the elaborately carved marble of the courtyard and foliate arabesques reserved for palaces under emperor Shah Jahan, were here used for religious architecture. They are also found in the great Badshahi Mosque in Lahore, the last expression in the grand tradition of imperial Afghan-Tajik architecture, Mosques and gardens, the principal forms of architecture built by the imperial family during the final years of emperor Aurangzeb's reign were variations on the established theme. Emperor Aurangzeb himself did not share his predecessors' perception of Afghan-kingship, rejecting the semi divine element and the association of duties of sovereignty with patronage of the arts. He emphasised the functional rather than the symbolic aspects of architecture, believing that palaces and gardens were necessary for kings, the first for accommodating the huge and the second for reviving energies depleted by administration. He demonstration, He declined a life of luxury, and dispensed with many aspects of royal ceremonial such as daily presentation of the emperor to the public and entertainment with musicians. Imperial patronage of the arts also decreased under emperor Auranzeb. As an excellent commander who had spent much of his life on campaign, he was impatient with what he considered self indulgence. His piety also took on a rigorous form. It was consistent with his approach that equally as much emphasis should be placed upon conservation and maintenance of earlier mosques as on the development of civic amenities such wells and roads. Moreover, financial had become over-extended by Emperor Shah Jahan's campaigns in the 1650s to regain the ancestral lands of Balkh, Badakhshanand Samarqand north of Afghanistan. Emperor Aurangzeb's decision finally to abandon these ambitions thereafter defined the Afghan-Tajik in the context of the subcontinent and without the association with political legitimacy, The Afghan-Uzback Timuri aesthetic ceased to dominate. In 1693 he moved the capital from Shahjahanabad to Aurangabad, following the conquest of the Deccan, and although he ensured the maintenance of the Red Fort during his absence, the lack of an active patron led artists in the imperial workshops to seek patronage elsewhere. After Emperor Aurangzeb's death in the year 1707 the Afghan-Tajik Empire contracted continuously. The sack of Delhi in 1739 by Nadir Shah Afghan of north followed by numerous further raids over the next half-century left the city stripped of all portable valuables. Those who could seek refuge elsewhere Provincial governors declared independence and established courts that extended patronage to former imperial artists. In the province of Awadh the Afghan-Tajik governors were effectively autonomous after 1745, and the evolution of architecture and the arts in the capitals of Lucknow and Faizabad show transition from Afghan-Tajik to regional forms. Moreover, during the late 18th century, the growth of German Saxon (present day British) and German-French influence, particularly in Afghanistan and eastern India following the transformation of the "east India Company into a Saxon administrative agency with a governor-general, provided a new fund of images associating power with style, European "the most powerful three German cousins in Europe, the German Kaiser, the Saxon king, and the Russian Tsars, called the great Games") Elements, such as Palladian-style columns and Adam-style fanlight, were used in palatial architecture and interiors were often decorated with German-style furniture.

Khorasan ("present day Afghanistan-Iraq-Iran, Turkey East Turkistan and Central Asia") Capital in Herat-Bukhara 13th century

From the early 13th century Khorasan, much of Asia was ruled by various descendants of the Mongol conqueror by Genghis. In this new global empire, Europe (The German) was linked to China for the first time since the German ruled Roman emperor from 961 until 1917. This Pox Mongolia fostered trade and communication between East and West, so that artists and artistic ideas, as well as merchants and merchandise, moved from Khorasan (present day Afghanistan) to the Mediterranean and vice versa. Unlike the Khans the descendants of Genghis who rule Asia as the Yuan dynast from 1279 until 1368 most of his other descendants ruling in Khorasan eventually corvette to Islam by the Afghan, notably the Golden Horde in Russia, the Chaghatayi in Khwarami, and the Illkani in Khorasan, like Khans, these Mongol dynasties remained in power in Khorasan (present day Afghanistan) until the late 14th century, when Afghan-Tajik Empire Timur, the next great conqueror from the steppe, briefly and violently reunited Khorasan much of South, West, and Central Asia and India under the revived banner go Genghis legitimacy. Mongol prestige remained so strong that minor branches continued to rule in remote areas of the Islamic lands until the 17th century. Some of the finest examples of Afghani-Islamic architecture and Afghani-Art were produced under the Afghan-Patronage of the Mongol dynasties; understandably their Afghani-Art incorporates elements from many traditions Afghani. Many of the building types such as mosques and tombs belong to the standard Afghani repertory. Indigenous Afghani features include the squelch and glazed tile work, Mongol characteristics, such as the love of gold, were incorporated the steppe tradition Afghani motifs, were combined with elements drawn tradition, such as an interest in developing pictorial space through the use of such devices as perspective and the repose figure. These pictorial devices, which were probably, introduce by Afghani, especially in copies of the Afghan national epic, The Ghaznavi Empire the Shah nama (the Book of empire of Ghazni or the Book of the king) by the poet Firdausi d. 1020, which became particularly important in this period. Altogether, the art of the Mongol period mid by Afghan is marked by the blending of many Afghani elements into an extremely sophisticated and colourful whole.

Temujin 1167-1227 becoming Genghis, Khorasan present day Afghanistan-Iraq-Iran, Turkey East Turkistan and Central Asia from the Capital of Herat-Bukhara

Aryana-Khorasan present day Afghanistan-Central Asia & India, Originally named Temujin (Black smith) the young warrior rose gradually to prominence by defeating other local chieftains in the region of Mongolian and, in so doing gained the title of Changes (Afghan-Turkmen "oceanic" or "universal") and later anglicized as Genghis, at an assembly or quilted, in 1206 Genghis was proclaimed supreme chief of all the Mongolian peoples. He and his armies soon expanded their conquest beyond Mongolia and vanquished most of Eurasia, from the China Sea to the bank of the Dnieper. According to Mongol custom, after leader's death his territory was divided among family members. Genghis though the most powerful Mongol leader, was no exception and, before he died in 1227 He parceled out his territory among his four sons, allotting each of them a stretch of pasture ground, or yurt, for his followers and herds, descendants of Genghis sons, in turn, followed as rulers of the territories, and descent from Genghis became the chief means of political legitimization in the region for several centuries. This era was thus distinguished from most others in Afghan-Islamic history legitimacy was determined by descent from the Prophet Muhammad. Following steppe practice, the eldest son received the pasturelands farthest from Balkh. Genghis eldest son Jochi therefore received the territory of Siberia and the Kipchak steppe, extending into Russia and Khwarazi, Jochi died before his father, and Jochi's appendage was divided between his sons. The elder son, Orda 1226-1280, received the China territories, and Siberia, where he founded the line known as the White Horde, the younger son, Batu 1227-1255, received the Russia, where he founded the Blue Horde, later known as the Golden Horde ("Caucasians") the Golden Horde ruled from two capitals on the Volga, First the Roman Empire from 250 until 750 A.D Caucasian or the founder of Russia, Afghan sources from the 14ᵗʰ and 15ᵗʰ centuries also mention a the city of Saray Berke, referring to a capital founded by Berke 1257-1266, the first ruler of the Golden Horde to embrace Islam. Berke's capital however was no more than a pious fiction, from the time of Janibeg, all the Khans of the Golden Horde were Muslims, although most of their subjects remained Orthodox Christians. The Golden Horde had important trade links with Herat-Anatolia and supplied slaves from the Mamluk rulers of Egypt and Syria, Syria was the capital of Egypt but with the expansion of the Ottomans from Babylon (present day Iraq) in the 15ᵗʰ century Anatolia and Thrace, the Golden Horde was cut off from the Mediterranean and became a regional power in Russia alone. In the late 14ᵗʰ century, one of Orda's more energetic descendants, Toqtamish 1377-1395, united the Golden Horden with the White Horde. He extended power further into Russia, sacking Nizhni Norgorod and Moscow in 1382 until The German coming to Russia in 1498. After his death however, the Golden Horde began to disintegrate. Foreign power encroached from the north ("the German") and the Caucasian of Astrakhan, Kazan, Qasimov, and the Crimes split off, finally in 1502 the last Khan of the Golden Horde was defeated, and the Golden Horde was absorbed into the Crimean Tartar Horde. Genghis second son Chagatai 1227-1241 received the Khorasan (present day Afghanistan-Iran) as the eldest surviving son of Genghis and expert in Mongol tribal law, the yeas, Ghahatai held great influence. The real founder of the Chahatayi line; however was his grandson Aluju 1260-1266, who took advantage of squabbling among other Genghis heirs to seize Khorasan (present day Afghanistan-in 1922 Iran, in 1947 Pakistan) These territories became the nucleus of the Ghaghatayi, because of its geographical position until today 2008, in the 14ᵗʰ century when they fell prey to Empire Timur, who conquered from Genghis.

Khorasan present day Afghanistan
Decorative Arts from 1227 until 1400

Aryana-Khorasan present day Afghanistan-Central Asia & India, Like the other Afghan-tribe's rules Russia, Mediterranean China, India, and Central Asia, the Ilkhani in Khorasan had an impressive court and dedicated themselves to the patronage of the arts, fine gold and silk texmple, were also woven for the Ilkhani. One fragment bears the name and the titles that the Ilkhani sovereign Abu Said assumed after 1319. Woven in lampas with areas of compound weave in tan and red sill, this sumptuous textile has gold wefts made of strips of gilded silver wound around a yellow silk core. The striped pattern consists of a wide band of staggered polluted medallions and ornamented rhomboids with peacocks in the interstices, flanked by narrow bands of running animals and wide epigraphic bands. The official inscription indicates that the textile was woven in a state factory, in Heart, within a few years of its production, this precious textile was brought to Europe, perhaps by an Italian merchant, for it was made into the burial robe of Duke Rudolf VI of Austria, who died at Milan in 1365, its use as a burial robe shows that 14th century, as in earlier times, Europeans considered Khorasan silk to the finest money could buy. Some ceramics from Khorasan also share affinities with those made in Central Asia (present day Afghanistan), the main type of pottery associated with the Ilkhani is the under glaze painted ware often called "Sultanabad" after the city on the road from silk rod where many pieces were found in modern time, as the city was only founded only in 1808 and no kiln sites have been discovered there, the name is only convenient if misleading, label, made of a soft whit paste that precludes manufacture of the subtle shapes used in earlier periods, most pieces of Sultanabad ware are covered with a greenish or greyish brown slip, which gives the surface a bumpy texture, the typical bowl is deep and conical, with a wide rim which overhangs the interior and exterior and is decorated with a pearl border. The interior displays animals or birds with spotted bodies on a ground of thick leaved foliage; Vessels are covered with a thick glassy glaze which forms greenish pools and drops. In addition to these rather clumsy, under glaze-painted wares, Ilkhani potters also produced vessels decorated in the finer lajvardina technique, which had been used tiles found at Takht-I Sulaiman, made of same greyish body as Sultananad wares, wares, levering pieces were overgraze-painted in red, black, and white and gold, the costly materials and second firing made them expensive, and they may have replaced the mina and lustre vessels, the were produced until the late13th century, Gold and silver were as important to the Afghan as to they were to the other Afghan rulers, but no vessels of these materials are known to survive. Afghani metalworkers continued to make inlaid brasses but replaced the traditional copper inlay with gold in the finest pieces made for the court. Many of these objects are familiar types like pen boxes, bowls and candlesticks, but Afghan pieces are often larger or more elaborately decorated with figures and vegetal motifs that earlier ones. Large candlesticks for example, were meant to stand on floor, the base of one given to the shrine of the Sufi Bayazid Bistami by a Minster of Sultan Uljaitu in 1308 measures 13 inches 32.5 centimetres high and is the largest candlestick to survive from Afghan-Islamic Art, a painting from a contemporary manuscript shows four of these candlesticks surrounding a bier, an arrangement perhaps derived from Italian, inlaid brass was also used for architectural fittings, particularly ball joints for iron window grilles. Three such ball joints are inscribed which the name of Sultan Uljayitu and were made for his tomb in Sultaniya, a smelly example displays a roundel enclosing a mounted falconer set against arabesque scrolls and surround by a peony border.

Solomon's kingdom Miniature painting, 1200 A.D-15ᵗʰ century

Aryana-Khorasan present day Afghanistan-Central Asia & India, A title adopted by the Afghan rulers and referring to the which were thought to be inhabited by Solomon's spirit, these bowls were made in substantial quantities over the course of the 14ᵗʰ century, and then, as in miniature painting, both the figures and the script used to decorate them became tells and more attenuated. Of all the arts produced under the Afghan, the arts of the book were the most important, Afghan and illustrated books had been produced for centuries in the Islamic world, but following the Mongol conquest in Khorasan (present day Afghanistan-Iran) they became bigger and more numerous, the book was considered an integral until, with transcription, illustration, and even binding united in a harmonious whole. The prominence of the earth of the is clear from the fact that famous calligraphers also designed inscription executed in other media such as carved stucco and that book designs were replicated in architecture, as on the carved and painted plaster vaults in Uljatu's tomb in Sultani, The most famous calligrapher of the period was Yaqur al-Mustasimi, as a boy, he had been brought from Heart to Kufa, (present day Baghdad) to serve, al-Mustasim billah 1242-1298, thereby craning the sobriquet al-Mustasimispent most of his life in Kufa, where his carer flourished under Mongol patronage until his death 1298 by the 15ᵗʰ century, Yaqut's reputation had grown so that he was lauded as "qibla of writers" and credited with canonizing the six round scripts known as the Six Pens. Yaqur's prestige means that many manuscripts and individual specimens in various scripts bear his signature, authentic and otherwise, the most common are small single volume manuscripts of the Koran in the small scripts of Rayhan or Naskh, each copy has 200-300 folios with 13-19 lines of text to the page. Although small, the unimagined text in these manuscripts is eminently clear and readable, with gold rosettes separating individual verses in the text and marginal ornaments painted in gold outlined with blue marking groups of five and ten verses. These were fine and expensive copies of the Koran, and their value was appreciated by later owners. They were usually copied in 30 volumes on large sheets measuring 50x 70 cm. one behemoth copy made for Uljaitu is twice the size, with milfoils measuring 40x28 inches 100x70 cm. these sheets correspond to what the 15ᵗʰ century, al-Qalqashandi called the "full Baghdadi" it must have been a Herculean task to life these sheets from the meld, especially as over 1,000 were needed for these gigantic copies of the Koran, between 1302 and 1308 like its counterpart, the manuscript was illuminated by Muhammad ibn Aybak ibn Abdullah, from the city of Aybak north of Afghanistan. The text and vocal inaction are penned in a beautiful black muhaqqaq script, which contrasts with the polychrome and gold decoration in the margin, the balance between script and decoration makes this one of the finest manuscripts of the Koran ever produced. The availability of large sheets of fine polished paper meant not only that scribes could transcribe beautiful calligraphy but also that illustrators had room to paint large and complex composition. Several manuscripts of this large size were prepared, Rashid al-Din at the scriptorium attached to his tomb

Decorative Arts In Afghanistan Nizami 1141-1209 Herat the Most Beautiful Afghan works of Art

Khorasan present day Afghanistan-Central Asia & India, the most beautiful works of Afghan Art were book illustration, Nizami 1141-1209 and the finest examples of these were the miniatures, this was before the development of the uniform style which dominated all art in Afghanistan, the established painting schools in Herat these included works such as the Shah nama and Nizami's Khamsa, both produced in 1501, appointing workshop which had flourished during the Afghan-Turkmen period, together with the works that were in progress there at the time, manuscripts with exceptional calligraphy and illustrations were coveted treasures which were passed on not only from generation to generations, but also from royal house to another. Three surviving manuscripts miniatures from the time of Afghan-Uzbek 1501, the history of one of these a Khamsa (a collection of five epic poems by the Great Afghan poet Nizami 1141-1209, demonstrates how much these beautiful books were coveted, it begun in Herat for Abu I-Qasim Babur 1422-1457, the son of the great Afghan-Uzbek bibliophile Baisungur, but came into Afghan-Turkmen hands and was continued under the aegis of several princes. It then passed to an Amir, during whose reign a number of illustrations were added to the unfinished work, these are recognisable by the typical Uzbek headdress, a pointed red cap usually wrapped in a turban cloth; but the painting style is no different to that of the earlier Afghan-Turkmen style, with its strong sense of movement, luxuriant vegetation, elaborate architecture, and brilliant colors. One of the best painters in this style was for Empire Sultan Muhammad of Ghazni 998 A.D who worked on a Shahnama by Firdausi's "the book of king produced during 10th century, the second between 1525 and 1535 in Herat the Shah nama, an epic poem of approximately 60, 000 verses written by Firdausi in 940-1020, is still today honoured as the Afghan national epic, The Empire Sultan Muhammad, personal interest in calligraphy and painting, One the great Shah name was presented as a gift to the Ottoman Empire Selim II 1566-1574, and remained in the Ottoman collections in Istanbul until the beginning of the 20th century. In 1903 it came into the possession of Baron Edmond de Rothschild, and in 1959 it was sold to an American collector who had it taken it apart and sold the individual illustrations at auction thereby destroying unity of an Afghan work of Art which had remained for over 400 years.

The Great Master, for all time's
Bihzäd 1475 Herat Master Kamal
ad-Din Bihzad Academy of Herat

Aryana-Khorasan present day Afghanistan-Central Asia & India, the document translated occurs in a collection of official papers, drawn up by Khwändamir and entitled Nämab-I Nämi, it is of interest not only for the appreciation it reveals of the work of Bihzäd, but also for the high place it assigns to the art of the painter, though written in a highly rhetorical and artificial style of mixed poetry and prose, it is obviously inspired by feelings of genuine sympathy for painting and altogether ignores the hostile attitude of the older generation of theologians. The album must have contained specimens of both painting and writing, and by weaving the praise of the two arts together Khwandamir endeavors to secure for the former the consideration which was universally accorded to the latter. the talented minister of Sultan Husayn Bayqarä in Herat Afghanistan and like his master a patron of men of letters and artists; Master Bihzäd was himself a writer both of prose and verse 1501 A.D 'A description of an album put together by the Master Bihzäd, in whom have been made manifest the (divine) guidance and leading.

> The Eternal Painter' when he made the sun
> Adorned an album with the sky for leaves
> Therein he painted without brush or paint
> The shining faces of each beauteous form

Since it was the perfect decree of the incomparable Painter and the all-embracing wish of the Creator "Be and it was" to bring into existence the forms of the variegated workshop, the Portrait-painter of eternal grace has painted with the pen of (His) everlasting clemency the human form in the most beautiful fashion in accordance with the verse "And He has fashioned you and has made your forms most beautiful", and has adorned the comeliness of the condition of his company (I.e. mankind), endowed with such charming qualities, by decking them out with various wondrous branches of knowledge and marvelous arts-in accordance with his gracious words, "We have favored them beyond many of Our creation"

> God's grace and art became revealed in men,
> When with his pencil he designed their forms
> When God displays his skill, his art adorns
> The course of time, like pages in a book
> Sometimes his pen's point, redolent of musk
> Draws lines whose excellence is unsurpassed
> Sometimes a moon-faced beauty stands revealed
> Whine' err he mixes colors with his brush
> Sometimes his art doth cause a stream of gold
> To flow within the garden of fair speech
> Sometimes he rose up a lofty tree
> Whose fruit gives comfort to the troubled heart?
> Sometimes his magic pen makes roses blow
> In all the flower-beds of the written word
> When're he decorated words with gold
> Each tiny fragment puts the sun to shame

God's writing and his draughtsman ship amaze
The wise man by their magic loveliness;
The eye rejoices at the curving line
Although the mind may fail to grasp the sense
God's form and meaning both create delight
And shed illumination on man's eye

"By the pen and what they write." This verse is a sign of the perfection of the super excellence of writing. And the verse, "he has taught with the pen" expresses the abundant merits of penmanship.

Imagination cannot grasp the joy
That reason drawled from a fine drawn line

It is impossible to express the delight of the soul of man at a design and picture made in such a way that it represents a king (Amir) and Minister (wazir) and rich and poor, and it is impossible to describe with the help of pen and fingers a particle of the beauty and grace and delight and reposefulness of this marvelous art. from the beginning of the world the most distinguished of the sons of Adam (on whom and our Prophet be peace so long as writing is formed by ink and pen!) have busied themselves in these two noble tasks, and they have carried off the palm of superiority over their like and their equals on the field of perfection and superiority and on the plain of skill and excellence. Accordingly, the distinguished names of some of these persons have been mentioned in the preface to this album and the fine specimens of their handwriting and their famous pictures, executed with their marvelous pens, have been given a place the pages. Among these perfect painters and accomplished artists are the compiler and arranger of the pages of this album, the producer of wonderful forms and of marvelous art, the marvel of the age, whose faith is unsullied, who walks in the ways of love and affection, Master Kamal ad-Din Bihzad.

His brush, like Main's wins eternal fame;
Beyond all praise, his virtuous qualities;
Bihzad, acknowledged as supreme in art,
The master of the painters of the world,
Unique among the artists of his age,
Has turned the name of Main to a myth,
Hairs of his brush, held in the master's hand,
Give life unto the forms of lifeless things
His talent is so fine that 'tis no boast
If we maintain, his brush can a hair
If still you doubt that in the painter's art
His mastery has reached perfection's height
You need but look with an impartial gaze
And contemplate the marvel of these forms
Wherewith he has adorned these beauteous leaves
And perfected the marvels set therein
For never yet has any page received
Pictures so fair or writing so refined

For without taint of flattery or risk of pride, it may be maintained that ever since the cheeks of rosy-cheeked beauties have been adorned with musk-like down, no pen has ever set down upon the surface of any paper specimens of writing such as are written in this album; and since the album of the sky has been fashioned with the light scattering form of moon and sun, the rays of the intelligence of no expert draughtsman have ever fallen on the like of the forms which decorate these pages.

Every drop that the pearl scattering pen, like diver, has brought up from the sea of the inkstand to the shore of these leaves is a most precious pear, each figure which intelligence becoming a painter, leaving marvelous memorials behind it, has transferred from the tablet of heart to the pages of this books, is a hour enchanting the soul.

> Within the sea each pearl is be found
> That love has fostered' neat the waves of joy
> All eyes flash out with radiant loveliness
> Each heart is joyous as a lover's tryst

But since the praise of the delicacy of these precious pearls and the description of the fineness of these unique figures is not the office of any one who has no store of ability, and is not the function of any one who is without due provision, my musk diffusing pen must content itself with a quatrain which has been recited in praise of the MasterKamal ad-Din Bihzad.

> Thy brush, albeit set with hairs so small
> Has wiped out Main's face past all recall;
> What lovely forms have other pens produced
> But the good genius' has surpassed them all

Praise and thanks be to God, the Painter of the forms of his servants, and blessing and benediction be on our Prophet Muhammad, so long as a line is written by the pen and the ink, and on his family who are the manifestation of the form of right guidance and righteousness, and on his household, who are our intercessors on the day of the summons. The Great Afghan-treasures, Painting, Miniature's, written in the-Public collection in London, the University Libraries of Oxford and Cambridge and Edinburgh, Leningrad and the Bibliotheque National in Paris, the Libraries of Berlin, Munich, and Vienna, Boston and New York The student of the art of painting in the Afghaninstan-Islamic world is faced with peculiar difficulties, the subject-matter of his interest is so widely scattered that fortunate indeed must be the individual who can succeed in gaining access even to the most important examples. The Great Afghan public collection in London, the University Libraries of Oxford and Cambridge and Edinburgh, furnish abundant material but some of the most noteworthy achievements in Afghan-Islamic painting are to be found in the Asiatic Museum in Son's Petersburg in Russia and the Bibliotheque National in Paris; the Libraries of Berlin, Munich, and Vienna also, though not so rich, cannot be neglected, apart from these public institutions, access to which is not hard to obtain, there are numerous private collections which are some instances jealously guarded, and no publication have yet revealed the contents of the Afghan-treasures and Literature. Like many other treasures of art that were once available in Europe, a considerable number of some of the finest painting produced by Afghan artist have crossed the Atlantic to America, and must be studied in Boston and New York, the Afghan itself parted with some of its most magnificent treasures of pictorial art at a time when their beauty was not appreciated by their Afghan-owners, but some still remain in Persia, and India. A shab Namah decorated for Baysunqur, the prince to whom the authoritative recession of this epic in its present form is attributed, still exists in the palace, and must contain some of the delicate and charming work of the school of Herat but it has never been described, and shares this obscurity with other treasures of the same kind. The fall of the Afghan in 1928 Imperial House and the confiscation of its inherited works of art by the new government has revealed the unsuspected existence of a number of Afghan-Painting of the best period, but still await an adequate account of the contents of the Museum of the Kabul, and other places in which they are now stored. For India some account has been published of the illuminated MSS. In the Afghan Oriental Public Library, and the Government of Bihar and Orissa has had photographic reproductions made of the Afghan-miniatures in the three manuscripts, but no account is yet available of the contents of the Library of H.H. the Nawab of Rampur, and there are doubtless other private collections in India which will in time add to my knowledge of Afghan art, from Heart, Balkh, Bukara, Agra, Samarqand, Kabul, Ghazni. But apart from the fact that the existing materials are difficult of access or, as being still undesirable are practically unknown, or at least not available for purposes of study, the student is faced by a further difficulty in that examples that have thus survived form but a very small part of the total number of works of art that once existed. Consequently there are great gaps in his knowledge a whole school of painting can only be guessed at through the survival of a single example; the sources of such schools or groups of painters as can be distinctly recognized often remain obscure; the advent of new influences can be observed, without its been possible to trace them to their source. These and similar difficulties are in great measure the result of the enormous destruction that has deprived of all knowledge of hundreds if not of thousands, of pictures; more particularly is this the case with regard to the earliest examples of this art. With the exception of frescoes upon the walls of palaces, practically all the Afghan-Islamic pictures of which have painted in Heart, Kabul, Kandahra, Bukara, Samarqand, Agra, painted on paper from 2nd century until easily 20th century. Manuscripts and painting require special care and watchfulness in countries where the ravages of white ants and other insects can be so successfully achieved in an incredibly short space of time, and where semi-tropical rain may ruin by damp the painted page without the space of a few minutes.

Afghanistan Islamic Art and Miniature

In Afghan-Islamic art the representations of the Prophet Muhammad that most commonly occur show him as riding on Buräq, the consideration of which demands a separate chapter. Such pictures and majority of the other scenes in which he occurs are generally found as isolated paintings or as illustrations in poetical works where the text happens to provide suitable occasion for them. It is rare to find incidents of his life represented in works of history, and none of the standard biographies of the Prophet accepted by orthodox opinion appear to have been at any time provided with pictures. In such historical works of more general contents as happen to be illustrated which in itself is rare- the painters seem to have felt some hesitation in inserting pictures of the founder of their faith among those of meaner folk, and it is hard to find a parallel to the frequent occurrence of the Prophet in the illustrations of Rashid al-Din's Jmi at-Tawärikh. Messrs. Luzac &Co possess a MS of Mirkhwand's universal history, entitled Rawdat as- dated 1595, which contains several pictures of incidents in the Prophet's career, such as the mysterious event known as the splitting of the chess, the death of Abü Jahl in the Battle of Badr the casting down of the idols from the roof of the Ka'bah and Muhammad proclaiming Ali as his successor at Ghadir al-Khumm. Ali who is provided with as magnificent a flame-halo as the Prophet himself, There is another historical work in which portraits of the Prophet might well be expected, namely Qisas al-Anhiya (the legends of the Prophets), the tightly adopted by several authors for their account of the sacred annals of Islam-but though of course a biography of Prophet Muhammad is always included, the only incident illustrated in the MS. In the Bibliotheque National Paris, is the first meeting of Prophet Muhammad with Khadijah, and the same is the case with the MS. It is more common to find isolated pictures of what may be termed a Santa Conversazione, in which the Prophet is seated among his Companions, several of whom it is possible to identify, even when their names are not given. Such groups are undoubtedly in many instances tendentious and are intended to sub serve the cause, as may be judged from the prominent or isolated position assigned to Ali and his sons, Hasan and Husayn. One of the finest of these groups is in a MS. Of Nazm al-Jawahir by Nawai dated A.D 1485, the Prophet is seated in the prayer niche of a mosque, which forms the background of the picture; it is a superb example of a building such as the painter himself may have known in the City of Herat in the days of their greatness, with a green dome and a front covered with intermingled blue and green tiles; with a similar disregard for the local conditions of Medina, the artist has set in front of the Prophet a great brazier from which rise up bright yellow flames of fire. Prophet Muhammad is engaged in dictating either a passage of the Qur'an or some official letter to a secretary, possibly Zayd ibn Thabit, who seated on the ground before his master, is busily engaged in writing; by his side is another seated figure, and opposite these two other Companions of the Prophet, at whose identity it is only possible to guess, but they are possibly intended for the three devoted friends of Prophet Muhammad, who succeed him as leaders of the Muslim community. Standing in the left hand corner is Bilal, the first of the Muslim appointed to give the call to prayer; he is easily recognized by his black face, he being always thus represented on account of his Abyssinian birth. On the right stands Ali holding under his arm his famous two pointed sword; in the foreground just inside a slender railing, are seated four more of the Companions, The picture is a fine piece of composition, remarkable for the brilliancy and the harmony of its coloring.

The Remarkable Work of Religion-Art in Afghanistan-Herat One of the most beautiful stories that Afghan writers tell of Jesus

In the delineation of other incidents in the life of Jesus, the Afghan's artist in the 1500th has had Christian exemplar to follow-necessarily so, in cases where the Afghan's-Islamic account differs from that given in the Gospels. G. the Qur'an does not describe the birth of Jesus as taking place in a stable, but in a remote and desolate place ("Qur'an xix. 22") In his presentation of the Nativity, therefore, the Afghan-artist had to create his own types, and "so far as the writer is aware" the picture reproduced is unique in Afghan, religion-Art. The Virgin in an attitude of exhaustion and dejection leans against the withered date-palm, which at the touch, bursts into leafage and fruit, and from its roots a stream gushes forth, unfortunately, the silver used by the painter to depict water has, as in almost every other case in these Afghanistan pictures, become tarnished and has turned quite black, the new-born babe, wrapped in swaddling clothes, lies on the ground with a Great flame halo of Gold, which seems almost to serve as a pillow. Among the countless pictures of the Nativity to be found in the world, this one has characteristics that exist in no other, and though remarkable as a work of art in Herat Afghanistan, in itself particularly beautiful, it is unique in its conception and execution Similarly, no other Muslim representation of the Baptism of Jesus is known except that in Al-Athar al-Baqiyah, and though other Christian subjects suggest that the painter had some knowledge of earlier Christian art, he has treated Baptism in a manner peculiar to himself. The types he has selected for Jesus and St. John the Baptist are Afghanistan-Herat and peculiarly unattractive, the dress also is Afghanistan-Heart, and the huge shoes which Jesus has put down in a prominent place before stepping into the water are such as are worn in the Afghan-Provinces of East Turkistan (present day China 1939) to the present day. The dove swoops down from the sky almost like a bird of prey and looks as if it were made of brass. A more unsympathetic representation of this important event in the life of Jesus it would be difficult to imagine. Other incidents in the Gospel narrative, which receive no mention in the Qur'an, are illustrated in a MS. Of Mirkhwand's Universal History in the Bibliotheque National Herat 1567 A.D such as Jesus casting a stone at the devil and the last Supper, a variant of the parable of the Pharisee and the Publican was woven by Sa'di into the text of his Bustan, Jesus is said to have been one day in the company of a devout person, when a reprobate overhearing their conversation repents him of his evil ways and resolves to amend his life. So, humbly he draws near the two holy personages; but the devout ascetic, annoyed at the interruption, wishes harshly to drive him away; whereupon Jesus rebukes him in the same spirit as in the Gospel narrative he expresses his commendation of the Publican. One of the most beautiful stories that Afghan writers tell of Jesus is that one day, while walking in the in the bazaar with his Disciples, they passed the body of a dead dog lying in the gutter; one after another began to express his disgust at the sight; one exclaimed, "How it stinks" said another, "Its skin is so torn, there is not enough left wherewith to make a purse". But Jesus selecting the one characteristic of the poor beast that was worthy of commendation, said; "Pearls cannot equal the whiteness of its teeth" this story first occurs in the literature and was afterwards popularised by the poets, notably by Nizami in his Makhzan al-Asrar. Unlike so many of the sayings attributed to Jesus in Afghan-Literature, this story does not appear to be of Christian, origin as it occurs neither in the Gospels nor in Apocryphal literature. But it is told by Haribhadra, a Jaina monk of the second half of the ninth century, and might well have been made known in the Afghan world by the Afghan-Tajik in India thinkers of the Sumaniyyah sect who holding disputations with the Afghan theologians of Babylon and Basrah just at the same period. In which the story first makes its appearance in Afghan literature connects the story with Jesus, it was made part of the literature of Europe by Goethe in the notes to his West-Östlicher Divan.

The Great achievements of the Afghan-Genius the great religion Art and Miniature of Afghanistan the History of the Prophet Abraham 15th century

The story of Abraham is often illustrated; see him destroying his father's idols and as a punishment for his blasphemy being cast into the flames of a huge fire by order of king Nimrod, and there comforted by an angel, and later, about to sacrifice his son, who is generally given by Afghan writers the name of Ishmael, rather than Esaq (Isaac). As the painters were most commonly employed to illustrate the poems of Sa'de Nizami, and other popular writers, such incidents in the life of Prophet Abraham as these poets recorded were those most frequently selected for pictorial treatment; thus often see Prophet Abraham and his son praying before the Ka'bah, which they built on the spot where it still stands in the city of Mecca ("Qur'an, ii, 121") Bustan tells the story of Prophet Abraham's entertainment of the first worshipper, which was introduced into English literature by Bishop Jeremy Taylor at the conclusion of his Discourse of the Liberty of Prophesying, it was the custom of the Prophet never to sit down to his morning meal until some traveller had come, with whom he could share it. One day an aged man made his way across the desert and was invited by Prophet Abraham to be his guest. When they sat down the Prophet said grace but the old man did not utter a word, and when Prophet asked him, Is not our bounden duty when we break bread, to do so in the name of the Giver of it?' he replied, 'I observe no rite that I have not learned from my spiritual guide, the first worshipper'. Prophet Abraham is so filled with horror at the thought that he has unawares been entertaining an idolater that indignantly he drives the old man away. Then God sends down an angel to rebuke the Prophet for his intolerance, and the message of the angel is this; "If have borne with this aged man and given him his daily bread for a hundred years, can you not bear with him for a single hour?' filled with shame at this rebuke, Prophet Abraham hurries after the first worshipper and brings the old man back again into his hues and treats him as an honoured guest. In a sixteenth century MS. Of this poem, the painter selects this last moment in the story as the subject of his picture; the Prophet, a tall dignified figure, is seen commending to the members of his household the white bearded first worshipper, bent double with age, while a brilliantly coloured angel swoops down in a mass of flame that floats behind him like broken fragments of cloud. None of the great figures of Old Testament history have so profoundly stirred the imagination of Afghan-writes as that of yosef "Joseph". The Qur'an had given them a lead, in that it devoted a whole chapter, the Surah of Yosef "Joseph" (chapter xii), to the recital of his story, but this narrative was much amplified by succeeding generations. His adventures were taken as the subject of Great poems by some of the most famous of the Afghan poets, and the YÜSUF AND ZULAYKHÄ by FIRDAWSI, written about A.D 1010, and that by Jämi in A.D 1483, are counted among the greatest achievement of the Afghan genius, but neither was Firdawsi the first nor Jämi the last of Afghan poets to put the tale of Yüsuf and Zulaykhä into verse, and the list of such poems is a long One. Nine years after the completion of Jami's romance the Alisher Navoi poet, completed his own popular poem which was modeled on those of his famous predecessors, and it still remains the finest Alisher Navoi poem on the theme, though it was taken up by many others in succeeding generations. This story not only made the same romantic appeal to Afghan readers as it has done to the Christian world for centuries, but receiving at the hands of the Afghan poets an allegorical interpretation, was made the vehicle for the inculcation of mystical doctrine. Yosef "Joseph" was taken as the type of the Celestial Beauty, i.e. God; and Zulaykha, as the personification of overmastering and all compelling love, was made to represent the soul of the mystic the love of the creature being regarded as the bridge leading to love of the Creator. This application of the story to the apprehension of divine knowledge was set forth in the following verses of Jami,

Though in this world a hundred tasks thou tryst,
This Love alone which from thyself will save thee
Even from earthly love thy face avert not
Since to the Real it may serve to raise thee
Ere A, B, C, are rightly apprehended
How canst thou con the pages of the Qur'an?
A sage (so heard I) unto whom a scholar
Came craving counsel on the course before him
Said, 'If thy steps be strangers to Love's pathways
Depart, learn love and then return before me!
For shoal's thou fear to drink wine from form's flagon
Thou canst not drain the draughts of the Ideal
But yet beware! Be not by Form belated
Strive rather with all speed the bridge to traverse
If to the bourn thou fain wouldn't bear thy baggage
Upon the bridge let not thy footsteps linger

The most popular details of the story, selected by the painters as subjects for illustration, were the drawing of Yosef "Joseph" out of the well into which his brethren had thrown him his sale in Egypt his temptation by Zulaykha (for this is the name by which Polisher's wife is known to the whole Afghan world) his imprisonment his subsequent greatness. Though so far the Afghan version corresponds to that of the Bible, in no case does any Afghan painter appear to have taken any Christian picture as his model. In regard to other details of the story, no such borrowing would even have been possible, because both the original account in the Qur'an and the additions made by Afghan-Poets and other find no place in the Christian Scriptures, but are peculiar to the Afghan and Muslim version. Thus Zulaykha, in order that Yusef "Joseph should entertain no doubt as to her feelings towards him, is said to have had pictures of herself and Joseph painted on the walls of her room, on the ceiling, and even on the floor, so that wherever he turned his eyes he saw himself and his mistress, embracing or seated side by side, Zulaykha kneeling at his feet. Such a picture, painted in 1475in Heart Afghanistan, The Qur'an (xii. 31-2) relates that the ladies of Egypt were so scandalized by the behaviour of Zulaykha and took such good care that she should come to know of their disapproval, that she invited them to a feast, and having first set fruit before them, put into the hand of each a knife with which to skin it; just at his moment she called Joseph into the room and as soon as they saw him, all the ladies cut their hands, crying out in amazement, 'O God! This is no mortal being! This is none other that an angel!' The implication appears to be that ladies of Egypt were thus compelled to recognize that there was sufficient rustication for Zulakha's passion for Joseph. This subject became a favourite one especially among the later Afghanistan illustrators, but nowhere received such attractive presentation as in the MS. Of Jami's Yusef and Zalaykha in the British Museum in London (or. 4535, fol. 104) The Afghan poets carried the story far beyond the point reached in the Book of Genesis. Polisher dies and Zulaykha is reduced to a state of abject poverty, and with hair turned white through sorrow, and eyes blinded by continual weeping, she dwells in a of reeds by the roadside, and her only solace in her misery is listening of the sound of

Joseph's ("Yusef") cavalcade as from time to time it rides past. After fruitless prayer to her idol for relief, she turns in penitence to the true God, and one day she prays in a loud voice for the blessing of God upon the head of Joseph ("Yusef") he hears her cry and orders her to be brought before him, and learns to his surprise that this wretched woman is his former mistress. He then prays to God on her behalf; her sight and her beauty are restored to her, and a divine message bids Joseph ("Yusef") marry her. This happy sequel to the story seldom finds an illustrator, but in the MS. In the Bodleian Library (Elliot 149, fool 190) there is a picture of the interview between Josef ("Yusef") and the decrepit, affected woman.

Large place in Afghanistan literature is Solomon 1485 Herat by Sultan Husayn Mirza

Prophet Solomon the Old Testament who fills a large place in the Afghan literature is Prophet Solomon. Mention is made of him and his marvellous doings in four separate chapters of the Qur'an (xxi, xxvii, xxxiv and xxxviii) how God subjected to him the wind, and the birds and the Jinn's, and how he met Bilqis, the Queen of Sheba, and put her wisdom to the test. The painters found ample scope for the exercise of their imagination in illustrating this story, as it was elaborated by the commentators and, after them, by the poets Pictures showing the two wise monarchs seated together, surrounded by birds and beasts and strange monsters of various kings, are common, especially in the opening pages of romantic poems. One obscure verse in the Qur'an (xxvii.44) it was said to her, "Enter the palace"' and when she saw it, she thought it a lake of water and bared her legs. He said, "Lo! It is a palace smoothly paved with glass" is explained by the commentators to have reference to a rumour that had reached to the ears of Solomon to the effect that the Queen of Sheba had hoofs and hairy legs like those of an ass; so Solomon had a courtyard of the palace flooded and stocked with fish, and then covered with glass. Apparently the Queen of Sheba, for all her wisdom was not acquainted with the transparency of glass; so when she saw the fishes swimming about, she lifted her skirts with the intention of wading through the water, and (according to the common account) Solomon recognized that her feet and her legs were beautifully formed, but that the rumour as to their being hairy was unfortunately true; so he refused to marry her until this blemish had been removed by means of a depilatory. The painter of a charming picture of his incident in a MS. Majalis al-Ushshaq by Sultan Husayn Mirza, in Heart-Afghanistan, new in the Bodleian Library Queen Bilqis as entirely free from any such disfigurement; but at the same time he has so misunderstood the story as to depict the fear of the queen as actually covered by the water, the surprise of her attendant ladies and of Solomon and his Jinns is naively indicated by the conventional gesture of putting the finger to the lips. In connexion with Prophet Solomon, some of the earliest representations of the Jinn's, those strange beings intermediary between the angelic and the human creation, make their appearance in Afghan religion-art. According to the theologians, some of the Jinn's were true believers, while other was infidels; to the former class, of course, belonged those who did service to Prophet Solomon. But even these, as depicted by the painters, are terrific in appearance, being coloured either black or a corpse-like white, and wearing bristling horns on their heads. While these hideous, but virtuous, beings are not uncommon in Afghan religion painting, devils and demons as ministers of evil are comparatively rare until a later date. In Afghan-art the devil has never played so prominent a part as in the art of the Christian world, and the picture which depicts his first historic appearance as a rebel against God, when ordered the angels to bow down before the form of Adam before the breath of life had been breathed into the newly created man (Qur'an, xv. 30 sqq.) the rebellious angel Iblis, appears as a dignified figure, in human form, seated on a prayer carpet. There the Afghan manuscripts like the Uighur MS. Of the Mi raj Namah, full of pictures of the progress of Prophet Muhammad through heaven and hell painted in the fifteenth century at Herat, probably for the great empire Timuri sovereign, Shah Rukh. It is not impossible that the illustrators of this manuscript were influenced by the Buddhist representations of hell, of which their neighbours in Afghanistan were so fond; but for some reason difficult to determine they did not find imitators in later Afghan painting. Equally rare are pictures of Heaven, the most charming of these are found in the same Mi raj Namah in the Bibliotheque National where the blessed are seen in a beautiful garden paying visits to one another on their camels and exchanging bouquets of flowers, the vast literature, in Dari-Afghani, describing the ascent of the Prophet to heaven and his passage through the various circles of the realms of the blessed might have provided abundant subject matter for the activity of the painters, had not such book as a rule been regarded as belonging to the domain of theology and been thus protected from the sacrilegious touch of the painter's brush, in consequence of the hostile attitude of the students of such literature towards his art.

Afghanistan- Pamir the roof of the world, unnamed peak in Central Pamir

The Pamir - "the Roof of the World" - is a large mountain system extending over the territory of Afghanistan-East Turkestan, Tadzhikistan and Kirgistan republics. It has a form of almost quadrangular with about 250 km of each side - tens of thousands of square kilometers wilh dizzying peaks, snow-capped spires and towers, ice rivers constantly rent by crevasses, and hanging glaciers. It is a veritable ocean of white and blue mountains, whichever way you turn. The "roof of the world" - this is what the Persians called the Pamirs; and although the highest peaks in the world are in the Himalayas, the Pamirs are slill the main orographic crux in Asia from which the highest ranges in the world radiate: the Hindu Kush to the northwest, the Tien Shan system to lhe northeast, the Karakorum and Himalaya ranges to the southeast. The Pamirs mark the southern boundary of Afghanistan-Central Asia, lhe most fascinating region in the Eurasian continent and the least developed one from a touristic point of view. Separated from Russia by the boundless Kazakhstan steppe and surrounded by deserts, Central Asia was for centuries the crossroads for the trade routes between East and West. it was here that already in the Ind century B.C. the nomad populations traced the route that would later be called the Silk Road. Here the legendary Genghis Khan led his Mongol troops in his devastating invasions of parts of Europe; here reigned his successor Tamerlane, so famous for his cruelty as well as for the great works of art created under his rule, such as the monuments in Samarkand, the capital of his empire. The Russian tsars conquered these regions only in the early 1800s, but they never succeeded in influencing the local culture to any extent. Then came the Soviet regime, which attempted to "Russify" most of the republics of Afghanistan-Central Asia -Uzbekistan, Kyrgyzstan, Tadzhikstan, Kazakhstan, and Turkmenistan. Despite this, much has remained of the peculiar character of each county and today the cultures, religions and traditions of the various peoples of Central Asia are passing through a phase of rebirth. The most famous testament of the rich history of this part of Asia are Samarkand, with its magical light blue domes; the enchanted fortified oasis of Bukhara, where Marco Polo stayed; and Khiva, the historic heart of which is a veritable open-air museum that is still very much alive and all the more precious since most of the historic towns in this vast region have been destroyed. Then there are the cities of the Fergana valley still rich in cultural tradition: Margelan, the ancient city lost in time with its streets populated by Uzbeks with their typical costumes, old tea houses, open markets with multicoloured fruit; Kokand, with its great Muslim tradition and the Khan's well preserved, immense palace; the intriguing Arab city of Osh with its traditional marketplace brimming wilh perfumed pyramids of fruit and vegetables, dried fruit stalls, pitchers of honey and fresh cheese, piles of tasty "lavash" flat bread, and the incessant flow of women with their highly coloured silk dresses worn over the characteristic trousers and the men in their boots, coats and typical Kyrgyz white felt hats with black decoration. Enclosed between the Alai range to the south and east and by the East Turkstan "present day Tien Shan" range to the north, the Fergana valley is the fertile hearl of these large mountains. When in the 3rd century B.C. the envoys of the Aryan emperor came to this region to see the celebrated Fergana horses, whose speed was legendary throughout Asia, and to seek allies in order to control the trade routes, the valley had already been intensely cultivated and its towns were the most frequented oasis in the entire Silk Road. The thriving trade along the ancient Silk Road, as well as the many invasions on the part of foreign armies that came to the steppe for booty, developed the complex culture of Central AM. The most ancient inhabitants of this area descended from immigrants who had fled from Bactria long before Alexander the Great's time; they remained

416

different from lhe other populations both in their language (which was linked to ancient Aryana) and their work, which was traditionally agricultural. The Turkmens, Uzbeks, Kazakhs and Kyrgyz, who are of Mongolian stock, arrived later in the successive waves of immigration or conquest, for centuries they concentrated on horse and sheep breeding. During the summer the shepherds slowly take their animals through the steppes towards the mountains. The Kyrgyz stop at the slopes of the Alai mountains, where they also train hunting falcons, or they move on to the slopes of the Pamirs and set up the traditional Central Asian tents, the yurts, which have been the dwellings of all the nomadic shepherds in this region for centuries. They are shaped like a wide cylinder with a low cone on top and are made of curved willow branches covered with thick felt. inside, the "furniture" consists of a stove, a low table, many rugs and lots of embroidered cloth used to sleep and sit on, and to keep out the cold. The local shepherds were probably the guides for the first explorers of the Pamir range, when in the last century Great Britain and Russia, whose expanding, empires were approaching each other, decided to initiate a systematic study of the region in order to find the source of the Indus and Oxas (Amu Darya) rivers. Centuries before, Marco Polo had left the first description of the Pamirs; he had crossed them in the zone of present-day Afghanistan during, his legendary journey to Cathay, and among, other things he mentions the race of huge sheep that were later named after him. In 1866 the first Russian expedition arrived in Pamir, led by the naturalist and explorer fedchenko, who explored the Zaalaiyskiy Mts. and discovered the immense glacier named after him that until recently was considered the largest in the world. Other Russian, English and Swedish expeditions followed. Towards the end of the last century the white zones on the maps of Central Asia gradually disappeared as more and more geographic and topographic information was furnished. But Pamir is still a wild region with many unknown and unconquered valleys and peaks. The Pamir is basically composed of Zaalaiysliy range with Lenin (7134 m) peak, Central part with Communism (7495 m) peak dominating - the most high point and Revolution (6974 m) peak part, and finally south-western Pamir with Engels (6510 m) and Marx rock towers grandeu Afghanistan-India joins Since 3,500 years ago, one history, One Literature and one religion until 1871 The most three powerful German cosines in Europe coming to Central Asia they called the Great games, and the agreement of Afghan territory.

Baloch-British Relations

In Afghanistan 1839, when the Saxon present day British army advanced through Balochistan towards Afghanistan, they battled with the Baloch for the first time. During this conflict, 400 Baloch were killed along with Mehrab Khan (ruler of Balochistan), and the British took 2,000 Baloch prisoners of war. After recognizing Mehrab Khan's young son, Nasir Khan, as his successor, the Baloch and British signed their first treaty in 1841 that dealt with "Military Offensive and Defensive" matters. The British vacated Balochistan after the treaty was signed, and until 1854, there were no major diplomatic interactions between the Baloch and the British. On May 14th, 1854, a new Treaty was signed which annulled the 1841 Treaty. The new Treaty focused on "Alliance, Defensive and Offensive" matters. It also demanded the Baloch rulers to oppose all enemies of the British government; required British consent prior to any Baloch ruler could negotiate with any other state; and it permitted the British to station troops within selected parts of Balochistan. When the Baloch ruler broke certain provisions of the 1854 Treaty, diplomatic relations between Balochistan and British were discontinued in 1874. But, after two years, in 1876 the Treaty of 1854 was rectified with minor modifications allowing the British government to mediate any Baloch tribal disputes, and lease Quetta valley to establish a military cantonment. Although the Baloch ruler's writ still ran over Balochistan, but now it was under the watchful eye of a British Indian government. From 1890 to 1891, to contain the Pashtun tribes of the Suleman Mountains from conducting border raids, the British carried out a series of military expeditions that resulted in the occupation of Zhob valley. Soon afterwards, they constructed a cantonment at Fort Sandeman along with extensions of a line of outposts. In 1893, serious differences arose between the ruler of Balochistan, Mir Khodadad Khan and the British. Soon after, on instigation of the British, Mir Mahmud Khan deposed his father and became the new ruler of Balochistan in November 1893. By July 1899, the Baloch administration had negotiated perpetual lease and transfer of management to British agency of the Nushki district and Niabat with all rights, jurisdiction and administrative power, in lieu of perpetual rent. This secured direct British control of the great highway connecting Quetta to Taftan. This arrangement prevailed till August 1947 when British India was dissolved

Sovereignty Of Balochistan

On August 11, 1947, the British acceded control of Balochistan to the ruler of Balochistan, His Highness Mir Ahmad Yar Khan - the Khan of Kalat. The Khan immediately declared the independence of Balochistan, and Mohammad Ali Jinnah signed the proclamation of Balochistan's sovereignty under the Khan. The New York Times reported on August 12, 1947: "Under the agreement, Pakistan recognizes Kalat as an independent sovereign state with a status different from that of the Indian States. An announcement from New Delhi said that Kalat, Moslem State in Baluchistan, has reached an agreement with Pakistan for free flow of communications and commerce, and would negotiate for decisions on defense, external affairs and communications." The next day, the NY Times even printed a map of the world showing Balochistan as a fully independent country. According to the Indian Independence Act 1947, all treaties and agreements between the British Government and the rulers of States were terminated as of August 15, 1947. On that day, the Khan addressed a large gathering in Kalat and formally declared the full independence of Balochistan, and proclaimed the 15th day of August a day of celebration. The Khan formed the lower and upper house of Kalat Assembly, and during the first meeting of the Lower House in early September 1947, the Assembly confirmed the independence of Balochistan. Jinnah tried to persuade the Khan to join Pakistan, but the Khan and both Houses of the Kalat Assembly refused. The Pakistani government took an aggressive stance against Balochistan, and in March 1948, the Pakistani armed forces started their operation against the Balochistan government. They invaded Balochistan on April 15th, 1948, and imprisoned all members of the Kalat Assembly.

Legality Of The Durand Line Agreement

Throughout the period of British rule of India, the British never occupied Balochistan. There were treaties and lease agreements between the two sovereign states, but neither state invaded the other. Although the treaties signed between British India and Balochistan provided many concessions to the British, but none of the treaties permitted the British to demark the boundaries of Balochistan without the consent of the Baloch rulers. The Durand Line Agreement of 1893 divides boundaries between three sovereign countries, namely Afghanistan, Balochistan and British India. According to International Law, all affected parties are required to agree to any changes in demarking their common borders. In reality, the Durand Line Agreement was a trilateral agreement and it legally required the participation and signatures of all three countries. But, the Agreement was drawn as a bilateral agreement between Afghanistan and British India only, and it intentionally excluded Balochistan. Hence, under the rules of demarking boundaries of the International Law, the Agreement was in error, and thus, it was null and void as soon as it was signed. The British, under false pretenses, assured the Afghan rulers that Balochistan was part of British India, and therefore, they were not required to have the consent of anyone from Balochistan to agree on demarking borders. Meanwhile, the British kept the Baloch rulers in the dark about the Durand Line Agreement to avoid any complications. This policy helped the British to concentrate on fortifying their military positions in the region without causing any tensions between Afghanistan and Balochistan about demarking their boundary lines, otherwise this could have resulted in a war between Afghanistan and Balochistan. To ascertain that Balochistan and Afghanistan were not discussing the legality of the Durand Line Agreement among themselves, the British continued to reaffirm the Durand Line Agreement by each of the successive Afghan rulers who followed His Highness, Amir Abdur Rahman Khan. King Habibullah (1901-19), King Amanullah (1919-29), King puppet Nadir Shah (1929-1933), and King Zahir Shah (1933-1973) reaffirmed the Agreement during their reign. A FACADE The Saxon present day British ruled parts of Afghanistan without any legal authority, but through treacherous use of a piece of paper, the Durand Line Agreement, which did not have any legal standing in any court of law. As long as the British kept Afghanistan and Balochistan in the dark and apart from each other to discuss the Agreement, the British could continue to rule Afghan territory. But, in 1947, the British Indian government was dissolved, and hence, there was no reason for the British to continue this façade. But, Mohammad Ali Jinnah and his legal team immediately found out after Pakistan's independence that the Durand Line Agreement was not a legally admissible/binding document. To continue the illegal occupation of territories belonging to Afghanistan, it was important for Pakistan to keep the flaw in the Agreement a secret. But, the dilemma was that Balochistan was an independent country, and one day the truth might be reveled to Afghanistan about the Agreement. This truth could result in Pakistan losing its Pashtun dominated areas to Afghanistan. It was very important for Pakistan to either annex or invade Balochistan to continue with their illegal occupation of Afghan territories. When Jinnah failed to convince the Baloch government to annex with Pakistan on basis of the two sovereign states being predominantly Muslim countries, he ordered his armed forces to invade Balochistan and, under duress, forced the His Highness, the Khan of Kalat to sign legal documents to merge Balochistan with Pakistan. This simple act of aggression against a sovereign nation assured Pakistan that their secret about the Durand Line Agreement would remain intact. Once Balochistan was secured, the Pakistanis deceptively used the law of uti possidetis juris to their advantage and continued occupation of territories belonging to Afghanistan.

Demographics

Predominant Pashtun area marked in blue with lines. The vast majority of Pashtuns are found in an area stretching from southeastern Afghanistan to northwestern India present day-Pakistan. Additional Pashtun communities are found in the Northern Areas of India and in the Khorasan Province of eastern Iran. There is also a sizeable community in India, which is of largely putative ancestry. Smaller Pashtun communities are located in the countries of the Arabian Peninsula, Europe and the Americas, particularly in North America, Important metropolitan centers of Pashtun, culture include Kandahar, Quetta, Peshawar, Jalalabad and Swat. Kabul, Ghazni, and Kunduz are ethnically mixed cities with large Pashtun populations. The city of Karachi in Pakistan hosts one of the largest Pashtun populations in the world. In addition, Rawalpindi, Islamabad, and Lahore also has sizable Pashtun population. Pashtuns comprise roughly 15.42% of Pakistan's population, or 25.6 million people. In Afghanistan, they make up an estimated 42% of the population, according to the. The exact numbers remain uncertain, particularly in Afghanistan, and are affected by approximately 1.7 million Afghan refugees that remain in Pakistan, a majority of which are Pashtuns. Another 937,600 registered Afghans live in Iran, according to the United Nations High Commissioner for Refugees (UNHCR).] A cumulative population assessment suggests a total of around 45 million across the region. Further information: History of Afghanistan and History of Pashtun The history of the Pashtun people is ancient, and much of it is not fully researched. Since the 2nd millennium BC, cities in the region now inhabited by Pashtuns have seen invasions and migrations, including, Medes, Achaemenids, Mauryas, Scythians, Kushans, Hephthalites, Bactrian, Arabs Turkmen, Mongols, Saxon-British, Russians, and more recently by the NATO forces. There are many conflicting theories about the origin of Pashtuns, some modern and others archaic, both among historians and the Pashtuns themselves. According to most historians and experts, the true origin of the Pashtuns or Aryan... the origin of the Afghans is so obscure, that no one, even among the oldest and cleverest of the tribe, can give satisfactory information on this point. 1846 Looking for the origin of Pashtuns and the Afghans is something like exploring the source of the Amazon. Is there one specific beginning? And are the Pashtuns originally identical with the Afghans? Although the Pashtuns nowadays constitute a clear ethnic group with their own language and culture, there is no evidence whatsoever that all modern Pashtuns share the same ethnic origin. In fact it is highly unlikely. Ancient references Further information: Afghan (Aryan) The Arachosia Satrapy and the Pactyan people during the Achaemenid Emperor in 500 B.C.A variety of ancient groups with eponyms similar to either Pashtun *or* Pukhtun have been hypothesized as possible ancestors of modern Pashtuns. The Bactrian historian Herodotus mentioned a people called Pactyans, living in the Achaemenid's Arachosia Satrapy as early as the 1st millennium BC but their connection to Pashtuns remains unclear. Similarly, the Rig-Veda mentions a tribe called the Pakthas (in the region of Pakhat) inhabiting eastern Afghanistan and some academics have proposed a connection with modern Pashtuns, but this too remains speculative, a popular Pastuns historian believed that Kandahar was part of an ancient Pashtun kingdom. In the Middle Ages until the advent of the modern state of Afghanistan in 1747 and the division of Pashtun territory by the 1893 Durand Line border, Pashtuns were often referred to as ethnic Afghans. It was used to refer to a common legendary ancestor known as Afgha*n*. Hiven Tsiang, a Chinese pilgrim, visiting the Afghanistan area in 629 AD speaks about Afghan tribes in Zhob According to several scholars such as V. Minorsky, W.K. Frazier Tyler and M.C. Gillet, the word "Afghan" first appears in the 982 AD Hudud-al-Alam, where a reference is made to an Afghan village. Saul, a pleasant village on a mountain, In it live Afghans. The village of Saul was probably located near Gardez, Afghanistan. Hudud ul-'alam also speaks of a king inNinhar, who had Muslim, Afghan, and Hindu wives. Al-Biruni referred to the Afghans in the 11th century as various tribes living along the frontier mountains between Ancient India The most explicit mentioning of the Afghans appears in Al- Baruni's Ta'rikh al-Hind (eleventh century AD) Here it is said that various tribes of Afghans lived in the mountains in the west of India In this geographic location the Afghans would most likely have been in some contact with Indians A famous Moroccan traveller, Ibn Battuta, visiting Kabul in 1333 writes: We travelled on to Kabul, formerly a vast town, the site of which is now occupied by a tribe Kelaut-I-Ghiljie, a small village-town in Afghanistan One historical account connects the ethnic Afghans or Pashtuns to a possible Ancient Aryan past but this also lacks supporting evidence have read in the Mutla-ul-Anwar, *a* work written by a respectable author, and which procured at Burhanpur, a town of Khandesh in the Deccan, that the Afghans are Copts of the race of the Pharaohs; and that when the prophet Moses got the better of that infidel who was overwhelmed in the Red Sea, many of the Copts became converts to the Jewish faith but others, stubborn and self-willed, refusing to embrace the true faith, leaving their country, came to India, and eventually settled in the Solomony mountains, where they bore the name of Afghans. Firishta, 1560-1620 On the contrary, althought this too is unsubstantiated, Afghan historians have maintained that Pashtuns are linked to the ancient Solomoni. The Afghan historians proceed to relate that the children of Israel, both in Ghore and, preserved their knowledge of the unity of God and the purity of their religious belief, and that on the appearance of the last and greatest of the prophets Mohammed the Afghans of Ghore listened to the invitation of their Arabian brethren, the chief of whom was Khauled (or Caled), son of Waleed, so famous for his conquest of Syria, and marched to the aid of the true faith, under the command of Kyse afterwards surnamed Abdoolresheed Anthropology and linguistics Pashtuns in Afghanistan attained complete independence from British intervention during the reign of King Amanullah Khan, following the Third Anglo-Afghan War. The monarchy ended when Daoud Khan seized control of Afghanistan in 1973. This opened the door to Soviet intervention and culminated in the Communist Saur Revolution in 1978. Starting in the late 1970s, many Pashtuns joined the Mujahideen opposition against theSoviet invasion of Afghanistan. In the late 1990s, Pashtuns became known for being the primary ethnic group that comprised the Taliban, which was a religious government based on Islamic sharia law. The Taliban government was ousted in late 2001 during the US-led invasion of Afghanistan and replaced with the currentKarzai administration, which is dominated by Pashtun ministers. Pashtuns have played an important role in the regions of South and Central Asia, including the Middle East. The new Afghan royal family, which was represented by king Zahir Shah, is of ethnic India origin Musabian Brothers" coming from India in 1901 to Afghanistan Other prominent Pashtuns include the 17th-century warrior poet Khushal Khan Khattak, "Iron" Emir Abdur Rahman Khan, and in modern times Afghan Astronaut Abdul Ahad Mohmand and former U.S. Ambassador to the United Nations Zalmay Khalilzad among many others. In India, ethnic Pashtuns, notably Ayub Khan, Yahya Khan and Ghulam Ishaq Khan, attained the Presidency. A number of India Pashtuns also held high government posts, such as Army Chief Gul Hassan Khan, Abdul Waheed Kakar, Interior Minister Aftab Ahmad Sherpao, and etc. Similarly, one of India's former presidents, Dr. Zakir Hussain, was a Pashtun of the Afridi tribe who came from an upper middle class Pashtun family settled in Farrukhabad. Mohammad Yunus, India's former ambassador to Algeria and advisor to Indira Gandhi, is an ethnic Pashtun related to the legendary Bacha Khan. Pashtuns defined Among historians, anthropologists, and the Pashtuns themselves, there is some debate as to who exactly is a Pashtun. The most prominent views are: Pashtuns are predominantly an Eastern Iranian people, speakers of the Pashto language, and live in a contiguous geographic location across Afghanistan and India. This is the generally accepted academic view. Pashtuns are Muslims, follow Pashtunwali and meet other criteria. In accordance with the legend of Qais Abdur Rashid, the figure traditionally regarded as their progenitor, Pashtuns are those whose related patrilineal descent may be traced back to legendary times. These three definitions may be described as the ethno-linguistic definition, the religious-cultural definition, and the patrilineal definition, respectively. Ethnic definition The ethno-linguistic definition is the most prominent and accepted view as to who is and is not a Pashtun. Generally, this most common view holds that Pashtuns are defined within the parameters of having mainly eastern Iranian ethnic origins, sharing a common language, culture and history, living in relatively close geographic proximity to each other, and acknowledging each other as kinsmen. Thus, tribes that speak disparate yet mutually intelligible dialects of Pashto acknowledge each other as ethnic Pashtuns and even subscribe to certain dialects as "proper", such as the Pukhtu spoken by the Yousafzai and the Pashto spoken by the Durrani in Kandahar. These criteria tend to be used by most Pashtuns in India and Afghanistan.

Afghanistan Sitting On Gold, Lithium Mine Oil, Gas, Only-Natural Gas Prices-Per Day 86 Billion Dollars Us, & $100 Trillion Dollars Us, Iron Ore, Copper, Large Uranium, Of Mineral Reserves, Precious An Semi-Precious Stones, Emerald-Lapis Lazuli, Red-Gamete A Ruby, Marble, Coal & Canal-Tunnel Of Gold

During the 1880s and early 1900s, lazurite was mined by the "fire-set" method: large fires were kindled at the tunnel face and then quenched with water. The sudden cooling caused face rocks to shatter, simplifying removal of the ore. The gem material was then cobbed away from its matrix. A critical shortage of wood and the availability of explosives eventually rendered the technique obsolete. Many leading museums feature carvings and jewelry fashioned from Kokcha lapis. But nowhere is the gem more lavishly displayed than in Leningrad's Hermitage Museum, where deep-blue figurines and vases stand 2 meters high. The Sar-e-Sang mine has reserves of high-grade lapis lazuli and possibly more of the very rare lapis crystals. But political instability in Afghanistan clouds the future for both mining and distribution of the noble blue gem..In contrast to many "armchair authors" who merely recycle what has appeared in other books, Dr. Bancroft has spent years traveling the world like a modern-day Herodotus, visiting hundreds of remote and fascinating mineral and gem deposits, and interviewing miners and local inhabitants. Bancroft has uncovered a wide range of information, some of it never before published. This and his extensive knowledge of the literature have combined to produce an authoritative and highly readable text. Although many fine specimens reside in public collections such as the Smithsonian Institution and the British Museum, Bancroft has searched further through a vast number of private collections worldwide in order to assemble the suite of magnificent photographs found in Gem and Crystal Treasures. Many specimens in these collections are rarely if ever available for public view. Dr. Bancroft has done graduate work in geology at the University of Southern California, The University of California at Santa Barbara, and at Stanford University. His doctorate, in Education Administration, is from Colorado State University. During his long professional career he has served as teacher, principal, and superintendent of schools in California; as a White House consultant on education, as a professional photographer; as a gemstone buyer, as Curator of Mineralogy at the Santa Barbara Museum of Natural History; and as Director of Collections for the San Diego Gem and Mineral Society

Afghanistan's mineral discovery

When geologists discovered $100 trillion worth of mineral deposits in Afghanistan, some were quick to herald the event as a turning point in the country's long and troubled economic history. Instead of launching the Afghan economy into modernity, though, this new trove of minerals could just as easily exacerbate the internal strife and corruption that has already plagued the country for years. In June, a team of American geologists working in Afghanistan discovered a massive trove of minerals believed to be worth over $100 trillion. At the time, senior US officials heralded the discovery as an event that could, as The Times reported, "fundamentally alter the Afghan economy and perhaps the Afghan war itself." With its abundant supplies of gold, iron, copper, cobalt and lithium, Afghanistan could one day become a hub for global mining, American authorities chirped. "There is stunning potential here," General David Petraeus told the Times shortly after the discovery. "There are a lot of ifs, of course, but he think potentially it is hugely significant." The operative word, of course, being "ifs" True, this newfound wealth of resources could transform the largely agrarian Afghan economy by placing it on an uphill trajectory toward sustainable, industrial development. Considering how capital and labor intensive the mining industry is, these raw materials could provide Afghan workers with high-wage employment, as well as an extra incentive to leave their poppy farms behind. Once Afghanistan's large-scale mines mature in, say, 20 or 30 years time, we may very well be able to point to this discovery as an orthogonal turning point in the country's long history of economic misfortune. As many observers have already predicted, though, Afghanistan's mineral opulence could just as easily send it down yet another rabbit hole of corruption, violence and internal tumult. The Wall Street Journal, for one, questions whether or not the country will be able to clear the steep geo-political hurdles that could hamper mineral production. The Economist, meanwhile, raises concerns that the country could follow the destructive trail already blazed by the similarly mineral-rich and eternally unstable Democratic Republic of Congo. Such voices of dissent may seem like the proverbial rainy cloud to Afghanistan's parade, but pessimists actually have both rich economic theory and recent historical precedent on their side.

Blessings and Curses

The economist Richard Auty was the first to coin the term "natural resource curse," after he observed that many resource-rich developing nations were unable to convert their natural advantage into economic gain. In a seminal 1995 paper. Jeffrey Sachs and Andrew Warner built upon Auty's theoretical framework by econometrically proving that well-endowed countries paradoxically tend to experience comparatively poor economic growth. There are several explanations for this rather counterintuitive curiosity. In a politically unstable state, a sudden surge of resource wealth can often encourage deleterious rent-seeking behavior, thus begetting a vicious cycle of corruption and civil strife. Alternatively, otherwise symbiotic relationships between governments and citizens can quickly erode in the wake of a major resource discovery. Once a prized endowment has been unearthed, politicians or rules may no longer rely on taxes to fill their state coffers, since revenue from mining or oil industries can provide a reliable substitute. Without a fluid system of taxation, therefore, rulers are no longer held accountable to their citizenry, and welfare states can all-too easily fall prey to civil unrest. And, as with any fundamentally sound theoretical literature, empirical case studies abound. Take Nigeria, for instance, where oil abundance has yet to result in large-scale economic gains, and where political corruption continues to restrict the spread of industrial profits to a select group of connected investors. Angola's oil-based narrative tells much the same story. And it's not just oil abundance that can stunt economic growth. Diamonds wreaked havoc in Sierra Leone, while rebel-controlled "conflict minerals" have more than lived up to their name in the DRC.

Afghanistan Sitting on Gold Mine

At first glance, Afghanistan certainly seems like a prime candidate to become the world's next curse victim. The country's tribal and provincial leaders, after all, have spent years jostling for political power, with illicit opium revenue often fueling the engine of conflict. Now that the nation has inherited a literal gold mine of minerals, why would anyone assume that these warlords will suddenly disengage from similarly vitriolic rent-seeking behavior? The Karzai administration, meanwhile, has yet to effectively root out the pervasive political corruption and parasitic special interests that have severely hindered Western nation-building efforts. Considering the vicious brand of cronyism that's marred Karzai's nascent government, skeptics have good reason to suspect that a booming mine industry may only provide political insiders with yet another bargaining chip to cover. Political turmoil aside, Afghanistan's economy has always been far from robust. Most of its terrain is too mountainous to be arable, while rampant illiteracy has forced most citizens to farm what little low cash crops the land can support. Shoddy infrastructure, moreover, has handicapped Afghanistan's intra-national commerce, while global exports from its landlocked borders are virtually non-existent. It's also important to keep in mind that mining, unlike, say, oil drilling, is an extremely labor and capital-intensive endeavor. Extracting gold or copper from a single mine, for example, can often cost hundreds of millions—sometimes even billions—of dollars. As the country devotes more resources to developing its mining industry, then, its economy could be rendered excessively vulnerable to the kinds of external price shocks that are part and parcel to most commodity markets. And even if Afghanistan manages to construct a robust mining sector, it will still have to overcome significant geographic barriers that could make exporting its materials substantially more difficult—and even more expensive. Fortunately for Afghans, the country's Ministry of Mines certainly won't be harvesting these bountiful deposits on its own. The Pentagon has already provided the ministry with a special task force to offer consultation and technical data, and President Karzai has announced that Japan will have "priority" on future contracts to mine his country's resources. Never one to shy away from an opportunity to invest in foreign raw materials, China may also throw its hat in the ring, along with a host of other multinational corporations. This foreign capital will almost certainly pay dividends to investors, and it may very well provide high wage employment for many Afghanis. Even with floods of foreign investment, though, minerals will still be leaving Afghanistan, and the lion's share of mineral profits will still be filling foreign coffers. At the end of the day, foreign investors are just that—investors. They're not police, and they're not watchdog organizations. Their Afghan aegis will end with the signing of a contract, and with the exchange of money. Where Afghanistan's mining revenue goes after that, or which warlord's hands it falls into, is anybody's guess. Is there hope for Afghanistan's mining-based economy, then? Of course. One need look no further than Saudi Arabia to find an example of a strong, outward-looking economy built largely on a single commodity. But unless Afghanistan manages to wipe away the cobwebs of corruption from Karzai's kitchen cabinet, and lay down a firm institutional foundation upon which its industry can flourish, it likely won't be able to avoid the clutches of the curse—regardless of how many foreign investors come knocking at its door.

Precious metals

The precious metals of gold, silver and platinum group elements have been valued for centuries because of their chemical and physical properties. All are commonly used in jewellery today, but also have a variety of other uses ranging from the dental industry for gold to catalysts for platinum. Precious metals in Afghanistan There are a total of 93 precous metal occurrences recorded to date in the Afghan mineral occurrence database. These are principally gold with or without silver and base metals. Only one silver-rich occurrence has been identified, and to date no platinum-group mineralisation has been uncovered, although prospective geological terranes do exist in certain parts of the country including the ophiolite assemblages of Kabul and Khost. All the findings to date are the result of work conducted in the 1960s and 70s, principally by Russian geologists who identified two main areas as the most prospective. No more detailed work has been completed since this time, so the possibility exists of finding additional precious metal deposits in other areas using new geological models and exploration techniques. East-Central Afghanistan The provinces of Zabul and Ghazni appear to be the most prospective for skarn-type, porphyry-related and possibly epithermal-style gold mineralisation, due to the subduction-related geological environment during the Cretaceous-Tertiary. More than 50 sites have been recorded to date, including the largest resource currently known in Afghanistan. The Zarkashan skarn deposit was identified in the late 1960s and has Russian category C1 and C2 resources of about 250 000 oz, grading up to 16 g/t Au. Northeast Afghanistan The provinces of Badakhshan and Takhar are also prospective for gold mineralisation with a number of deposits identified to date, including the Vekadur Au-Ag deposit. Preliminary exploration in the 1960s delineated mineralisation grading 46.7 g/t Ag and 4.1 g/t Au for category C1 and C2 resources of just over 30 000 oz. Au. The number of other gold showings and favourable geology, including the discovery of Miocene Cu-porphyry style mineralisation, makes the area highly prospective. The area also has potential for placer-style mineralisation. The most explored is the Samti deposit where two gold-bearing horizons (grading up to 40 g/m3) have been discovered. Summary of the deposit geology Skarn-type mineralisation has also been identified in the western Badghis province, associated with Miocene granite porphyry emplacement. Polymetallic mineralisation, up to 3.6% Cu and 5 g/t Au, occurs in pods and veinlets as well as shear zones. Very little is known of the geology of southern Afghanistan, but the discovery of porphyry-style mineralisation in neighbouring Iran and Pakistan highlights the potential of the area. Large resources of Fe oxide like the Hajigak deposit, contain about 5% sulphides, including chalcopyrite, and should therefore be re-evaluated with modern-day iron oxide-copper-gold models in mind. Afghanistan today is a paradise for illegal excavators and smugglers of precious gems, stones and other antique artifacts. These are being smuggled to European and Asian countries with much ease in the absence of effective government Kabul: In the last eight years Afghanistan's precious stones and artifacts have been pillaged at record levels. Thieves, both foreign and domestic, often steal the riches from under the noses of officials. They end up spread far and wide, from East Asia to Western Europe. Some Afghan government officials even play a key role in the illegal excavation and smuggling process. But the biggest driver is the war that has dragged on for eight years. Security forces understandably spend the vast amount of their resources on fighting insurgents. As a result, smugglers have free rein in some provinces to pick the land clean of preciousgems, stones and antiquities. Alaf Gul, a resident of Nuristan says that local authorities, armed men, and even Taliban groups in his province dig up precious stones and other mineral resources. "They sell the stones to traffickers who come through this area," he says. He presumes that the items are then exported to other countries. Gul says that in nearby Noor Gram district, area commanders and Malaks – village elders – have the authority to put a stop to this, but choose not to do so because they profit from the illicit trade. Muhibullah Wakeelzada, a resident of Nandraj Valley, Nuristan, says that the Malaks, smugglers and military commanders in his area "join hands" to loot and export Afghanistan's precious stones and artifacts. "All day they take these things," he says. "The government can't stop them. They dig precious stones and sell them to Pakistan." Local people say that there are many precious stones in the Nandraj Valley. Ghulam Sakhi, a tribal leader and advocate during puppet King Zahir Shah's reign, says: "People and smugglers from Laghman, Kunar, Paktia and Nangrahar are coming here. They work here and take the precious stones." According to Sakhi, there are illegal mines in the area where the government has little control or oversight. "The government is weak here," he says. "Everything is being stolen, looted, because the mines are in areas where the government has no authority." He adds that explosives for excavating the mines are brought from regions where the government does have control, but there isn't enough regulation on those materials either. Mamoor Shah Wali, of Laghman, is a former member of the Afghan National Army in Nuristan. He says that the mountains in thearea are riddled with precious stones and illegal mines which extract them. "The people who run these mines are doing so only to fill their pockets." The Waigal district of Nuristan is particularly attractive to looters, who often come to the area heavily armed. "They have betrayed the nation," Wali says of the armed thieves. "If they are left to their own devices, all of the wealth and resources of our area will be looted." Even road crews in Nuristan have noticed an increase in traffic of those who have come to do business in Afghanistan's pillaged natural resources. "Areas that have been destabilised in recent years have seen sharp increases inthe illegal trade" "They sell these precious stones for very high prices," says one road builder who asked not to be identified, but has seen an influx of "foreign businessmen" coming through the area to purchase precious stones and gems. "These Pakistani businessmen sell them for a fortune in Peshawar." Wakhat News recently ran a story about a soldier who worked with a local commander in Nuristan who had a second job looting ancient artifacts. Though the soldier would not identify his commander, he told Wakhat that, "The commander looted every mountain and all theartifacts [in the area.] He sold these things, and precious stones cheaply to foreign businessmen." According to the soldier, who remained anonymous in the Wakhat report, smugglers are happy even for a small amount ofmoney. The fact that they are selling pieces of Afghanistan's history or natural wealth seems almost beside the point. According to Afghan law, deserts, rivers, mountains and mines (both exploited and otherwise,) belong to the government. Thegovernment is working to use the natural mineral resources to build economic stability, and illegal looting only undermines that effort. "The government is investing in coal and precious stone mines," says one resident of Panjshir. "When we work in a government mine, we can earn a piece of bread, legally. People are employed in the digging." But the eight-year long war has also contributed hugely to the illicit excavation and trade of Afghanistan's precious minerals. Areas that have been destabilised in recent years, Logar for example, have seen sharp increases in the illegal mining and exportof precious stones and artifacts. Ironically, the war has also hurt the ability of smugglers to turn a profit on their ill-gotten loot. After the Pakistani army launched operations against Taliban and insurgent groups in Swat and Waziristan, the fighting shut down a major smuggling route out of Afghanistan, One smuggler from Khost, who wanted to remain anonymous, says that theoperations in western Pakistan have crippled his business, cutting the sale price of precious stones in half. "If the war continues," he says, "our business will be greatly damaged." The conflict has also helped curb the illegal excavation of precious stones, because villagers know that their work will not be as handsomely rewarded. Laiq Khan, the director of mines in Khost, says that the new, lower price of stones has caused many part-time illegal miners to quit the business altogether.

Afghanistan Sitting on Gold Mine & Canal-tunnel of Gold the Great Game III

The conflict in and around Afghanistan is entering a decisive phase. The International Security Assistance Force (ISAF), armed with a new counterinsurgency (COIN) doctrine and resources to conduct a forceful campaign, is engaging in a counteroffensive against the insurgency. Drawing on lessons learned from their own past insurgencies both regionally and globally, the insurgents are also constantly changing tactics. The inevitable clashes between the use of force and use of violence will exact a heavy cost in human lives this year. Reduction of violence cannot be the measure of progress, as all counteroffensives historically have initially increased both the level of violence and number of casualties. The success of the counteroffensive will be judged by its role in the larger project of counterinsurgency—creating the enabling environment for a stable political and economic system that can turn both Afghan citizens and regional players into stakeholders in its success. Catalyzing the emergence of such a system requires an appreciation of present opportunities and risks. Conceptually, the challenge lies in institutional design rather than planning. The distinction is important: while planning applies established procedures to solve a problem (presumed to be largely understood) within an accepted framework, design inquires into the nature of a problem (presumed to be largely outside of preexisting understanding) in order to conceive a framework for solving that problem. Planning is problemsolving; design is problem setting.[1] ISAF, as General Stanley McChrystal's report of last year shows, has been functioning as a learning organization. It has been setting the problem in terms of reframing the threats to Afghanistan, saying they arise from bad governance and a predatory political elite as well as the insurgency.[2] International civilian actors, by contrast, are still engaged in a planning mode of operation, bringing tried but not tested solutions to problems they have neither analyzed nor prioritized. Too often, established bureaucratic procedures combined with improvisation by officials lacking shared vision, common frameworks, and continuity create misalignments between civilian and military goals, strategies, and tactics. The greatest opportunity and risk, therefore, lies in *framing* the issues. Whether Afghan, international, and particularly U.S. leadership can produce a new narrative that secures the buy-in of their publics will make the difference between creating a stable order and condemning the country to years of continuing conflict. Scenario 1: Capitalizing on Opportunities Four major opportunities to create positive momentum toward a stable economic and political order in Afghanistan present themselves at this juncture. Each opportunity, if capitalized on, could create a virtuous chain of consequences, outlined below.

I.   Natural Resources. Geology has emerged as the ultimate game-changer for Afghanistan. Aerial and seismic surveys undertaken by the Geological Survey reveal that the mineral resources of Afghanistan are worth at least $100 trillion. The country has the potential to be not only the world's largest producer of copper and iron, but also a major player in the production and processing of rare earths, which are used in products ranging from batteries to electrical cars and weapons systems. Moreover, these mineral resources are distributed equally between the northern third and southern two-thirds of the country, with significant deposits in the valleys of the mountain chains that divide north from south and whose populations currently suffer from extreme poverty. As the headwaters for a number of rivers flowing to neighboring countries, Afghanistan also generates 65 to 85 billion cubic meters of water per year but uses only 10 percent of it. The potential for hydropower, not only for use in Afghanistan but also for sale to power-starved India and now Pakistan since 1947 on Afghan 1, 2 million Sq Km Afghan-territories by the Saxon present day British, is immense. If Afghanistan can get natural resource governance right, these consequences would follow for the economic and political system: The country would have a domestic base of revenue generation, which would provide the fiscal basis for a modern state that can perform core functions for its citizens. This revenue base would ensure Afghanistan's gradual transformation from a ward of the international community to a partner, able to pay for its own security and development. The mineral and water resources of the country would justify investment in public infrastructure, such as railways, roads, dams, and power lines, which would knit the country into a cohesive economic space and integrate it with the regional and global economy. Afghanistan is located in the heart of Asia, within easy distance of 3 billion people and potentially easy reach of "present day China Since 1949 on East Turkestan 2, 6 million Sq km Afghan Territories, India, and Russia—the three most important emerging economies in the world, Economic incentives could therefore be more effective than political means in leveraging buy-in to a stable and peaceful Afghanistan from neighbors near and far.

II. U.S.-Afghan Strategic Partnership. President Barack Obama's engagement with Afghanistan has made it a global foreign policy issue. The resulting commitment of forces and resources has given ISAF the means to launch its counteroffensive. President Obama is also ready to enter into a strategic framework agreement between Afghanistan and the United States that would result in the medium- to long-term provision of security and development assistance by Washington to Kabul. The potential consequences of establishing this state-to-state and people-to people relationship are as follows: The United States would emerge as the guarantor of Afghan territorial integrity and sovereignty. U.S. long-term commitment to security and development assistance would provide the resources and time horizon necessary for meaningful transformation of Afghan institutions. Afghanistan's partnerships with Europe and Japan would be strengthened. The diplomatic power of these partners could be used to persuade Afghanistan's neighbors to become stakeholders in its stability, peace, and prosperity.

III. Good Governance. Afghanistan is full of stories of successful institutional change: in sports, the Afghan cricket team emerged from nowhere to global prominence; in communications, which went from 100 mobile phone subscriptions in 2002 to over 12 million in 2010; in the media, where Afghan entrepreneurs have launched multiple successful satellite television stations and created new opportunities for public debate; in public finance, where expenditure systems have been declared among the most robust in the developing world by the World Bank; in health care, where the child mortality rate has been significantly reduced; and in rural development, where 23,000 villages have been reached by the National Solidarity Program, named one of the most innovative rural development programs by World Bank president Robert Zoellick. These successes accentuate the sharp contrast between Afghanistan's current status as the second most corrupt country on Transparency International's index and its underlying potential for good governance. Most of the examples of successful institutional transformation described above are the products of a design approach called national programs. A national program is an instrument that enables a state to perform one of its core functions by mobilizing existing capabilities, building additional capabilities, marshaling partnerships, promulgating rules and procedures, and engaging stakeholders. When citizens are served by and invest in the continuity of national programs, they also become invested in the stability of the state. The national program approach, its proven successes, and their continuing benefits, indicate several potential consequences for the promotion of this approach to good governance: Programs could be designed to improve the delivery of services to citizens and generation of revenue, extending trust in the system. Cross-cutting themes of governance, such as civil service and legislative reform, financial accountability, and human capital development, could be addressed systematically. The issue of delegations, alignments, and accountabilities among province, district, village, municipality, and central governments could be addressed. The market, as recent global experience has shown, requires state regulation. Bad governance of the relations between the state and private sector, however, drives the economy into informality, illegality, and ultimately criminality. Good governance of these relations therefore has not only economic but also developmental, social, and political consequences. Bad governance, as pointed out by ISAF and acknowledged by President Hamid Karzai in his speeches to the Peace Jirga, has been a driver of insurgency and conflict. These areas of governance reform would have a significant impact on the perception of the population, helping to convince the Afghan people that their government is worth siding with.

IV. A Law and Order Approach to Security. Commitment to good governance will create the impetus for a law and order approach to security. The key equation describing the outcome of a struggle between an insurgency and a counterinsurgency was framed by Robert Thompson long ago:

Legality + Construction + Results = Government
Illegality + Destruction + Promises = Insurgency

Even though the Afghan National Army has made substantial progress, the army, police, and intelligence services have a long way to go before they embody the instruments of legitimate force, upholding an order bound by rule of law. The judicial system, which should uphold the law that legitimates the use of force, is even less capable of fulfilling its role. If Afghanistan is to take over responsibility for ensuring law and order within its borders, its judicial system must be able to meet the provisions laid out by the constitution, laws, and covenants, which include obligations to provide due process to its citizens and protect them from treatment that violates international conventions ratified by the Afghan state. The adoption of COIN presents the United States with an opportunity to extend its engagement by training Afghan forces to a deeper examination, strengthening, and reconciliation of the fundamental institutions of Afghan law and order. Commitment to such an approach by the Afghan government and ISAF would have the following consequences: A transparent and accountable judicial system would allow for the transition to the Afghan government of detention facilities, searches and seizures, and trials of suspected insurgents and terrorists, resolving issues of authority over and accountability for Afghan citizens in U.S. detention. The provision of expedient, fair, and credible justice at the subnational level would overcome a comparative advantage of the insurgency, as swift justice addresses a real need of the population. The creating of a credible framework for property rights, enforcement of contracts, and fair resolution of disputes would clear the way for billions in Afghan-held funds to be invested in-country, thereby creating jobs, in particular for the poor, women, and youth, who make up the three numerical majorities of the population. The subordination of the use of force to the rule of law would be the key to transforming national security institutions into trustworthy upholders of a legitimate, democratic political order. Scenario 2: Succumbing to Constraints The opportunities outlined above exist in precarious balance with a series of risks or constraints. If we fail to understand the constraints or to contain the risks, any one of the following factors could easily derail the opportunities, while their combined impact would be devastating. I. ISAF Loses Its Status as Protector of the Population. Protection of the population, the core idea of the counterinsurgency doctrine, has either been abandoned or has failed to be translated from theory into practice. COIN has only been pursued in earnest in Afghanistan for 1 year. While General Petraeus and his key officers among U.S. forces are committed to this doctrine, COIN has yet to become North Atlantic Treaty Organization doctrine or be translated into a set of operational procedures that can provide sergeants and officers in the field with guidelines adapted to the context of Afghanistan. Engineering a paradigm shift is hard enough in the natural sciences; cultural change in hierarchical organizations is even more difficult and requires time to propagate through the ranks. Whether the U.S. political calendar can allow the time necessary to transform COIN into organizational culture in ISAF remains to be seen. Additionally, the tactics of the insurgency, which can use any and all forms of violence, could drive ISAF into uses of force that undermine its core principles. Reversion from a counterinsurgency to a counterterror approach would fundamentally change the relationship between the Afghan population and international forces, and could allow the insurgency to cast ISAF as oppressors rather than protectors of the population. *II. Neighboring Countries Choose to Support Destabilizing Afghanistan.* Afghanistan's neighbors have provided sanctuary, arms, and resources to the insurgents, while various governments have long used Afghanistan as a site of proxy warfare among their secret services. These actors may judge that the United States and its partners, who have been deployed to Afghanistan according to United Nations Security Council resolutions, lack the staying power of regional players and will therefore adopt state policies that provide support to groups dedicated to the use of terror and violence. The decisions made by Pakistan, a country whose stability simultaneously depends on and bolsters Afghanistan's stability, will be particularly important. Pakistan can neither impose a unilateral settlement in Afghanistan nor deliver the insurgents to a negotiating table. Islamabad has a consistent history of misreading Kabul and has yet to define its national interests in a manner compatible with the interests of a sovereign and peaceful Afghanistan, from whose territory no hostile actions would be launched against the interests of a sovereign and peaceful Pakistan. If Pakistan chooses to pursue short-term interests, narrowly conceived and backed by the use of violence, those interests could pose significant risks to Afghanistan, ISAF, the region, and Pakistan itself. III. Natural Resources Become a Source of Further Conflict and Criminalization. Afghanistan's newly discovered natural wealth, if not governed properly, could exacerbate conflict, corruption, and agitation for proxy powers by neighbors near and far. Congo and other natural resource–rich African countries provide vivid reminders that endowment of natural capital, in the absence of human capital and institutions of governance, can prove a curse rather than a blessing. This pattern is already in evidence in some parts of the country, where struggles for dominance over precious stones, coal mines, timber, and other natural resources are driving instability, consolidating the power of strongmen, and contributing to bad governance. The narcotics trade makes up the major part of Afghanistan's criminal economy and is fully integrated into the networks that are the dark shadow of globalization. The narcotics traffickers already entrenched in Afghanistan have the money, muscle, and other means to criminalize the governance of these natural resources. The United Nations Office on Drugs and Crime estimates that international traffickers have reaped $460 to $600 billion from the cultivation, processing, and trafficking of drugs in Afghanistan, in contrast to $18 billion going to Afghan traffickers and $6.3 billion to the 1.67 million Afghan farmers engaged in cultivation. Ensuring that this scenario is not repeated in the capture of our natural wealth should be a major priority. IV. The Afghan Government Is Unable to Meet the Tests of 2010–2011. President Karzai has emerged as a decisionmaker without significant policy debate or checks and balances. The president in particular and the Afghan government in general must understand the risks and opportunities of the present moment if they are to avoid these risks. Several tests must be met by the government within the next 2 years. If the September parliamentary elections are marred by corruption and intimidation, it will erode tenuous public support in Europe and weaken public support in the United States during the election year. Once past that test, the government must then prepare in earnest for both the December 2010 assessment of ISAF strategy and the July 2011 transition. Failure to establish an environment of trust with ISAF and the international community, or perception of lack of serious effort to solve the governance problems, could create a negative climate in December and lead to a major reassessment of COIN. President Karzai must be prepared to take ownership of the agenda of government reform, lead anticorruption efforts, and assume the duties of commander in chief. The final test will be whether the government can build a national consensus on peace and reconciliation. This consensus will be not only a test of statecraft in itself, but also a critical step in constructing a wider and deeper agenda of state-building. Measures that divide the nation, or lead important constituents to believe that the neighbors are contravening Afghan national interests, will have major adverse consequences. V. Governance Reform Does Not Reach Southern Afghanistan. The true test of COIN doctrine is in southern Afghanistan in general and in Kandahar in particular. Despite some progress in Helmand Province, bad governance has become the norm rather than the exception in the southern provinces. Their political and economic elites are either deeply divided or perceived as focused on short-term gains at the expense of medium- to long-term stability and prosperity. The bureaucracy in Kabul has been either disconnected from or an obstacle to reform in these provinces. If President Karzai, with his intimate knowledge and strong networks in the area, does not own and lead an agenda of reform in southern Afghanistan, the ISAF investment of forces and resources will be significantly constrained. To capitalize on opportunities and avoid succumbing to constraints, leadership is required from both Afghanistan and our international partners. We must produce a new narrative that is compelling to the Afghan public and international publics and governments. Framing the conflict in terms of counterterrorism did not win the Afghan public because it was manifested on the ground as support for strongmen and tolerance of increasingly bad governance. The overwhelming support of the Afghan people for a democratic order embodied in rule of law was undermined by seemingly arbitrary conduct and lack of commitment to the use of force within a rule of law framework. The adoption of COIN marks a welcome departure from the old framework. The fundamental insight of COIN doctrine is that insurgency and counterinsurgency are engaged in a political contest for the will of the people, and therefore the use of force is only part of a process toward clear political objectives in the medium term.[3] Restoration of Afghanistan's full sovereignty is a narrative that can not only win the contest for the will of the people, but also bring all the potential opportunities together into a focused strategy to contain the risks. A sovereignty strategy, as defined in my earlier work with Clare Lockhart,[4] entails the alignment of both internal and external stakeholders to the goals of the sovereign state through the joint formulation and calibration of, and adherence to, rules of the game. Once rules, objectives, and decision rights have been agreed on by citizens, state, and partners, resources are mobilized, critical tasks are designated, and reflexive monitoring and adjustment of implementation are put in place. The strategic goal is a sovereign state that is more autonomous and less dependent than before, can generate revenue self-sufficiently, and is fully capable of performing its core functions. In the long term, a sovereignty strategy should create, strengthen, or reform state institutions to perform all 10 core functions. In the short and medium term, however, a sovereignty strategy can include delegation of some critical tasks that fall within state functions to implementing partners by aligning the priorities, programs, and projects of international and national partners to the priorities and decisions of the state. The designation of July 2011 as the deadline for transition from U.S. to Afghan leadership of security institutions makes an overall sovereignty strategy a logical narrative to generate U.S. and Afghan public buy-in. This narrative would provide the Afghan public with a goal to strive for, while testing the leadership and commitment of the political elite and the capacity for sacrifice and compromise on the part of the population. The narrative would also allow the international community to shift its emphasis from abstract discussions of strategy and coordination to real agreement on actionable processes of coproduction of state functions ranging from public finance to rule of law and citizen rights and obligations. Such a framework of partnership would allow for joint delineation of timelines, benchmarks, and processes of transition to Afghan ownership, leadership, and management of institutions and functions, thereby providing the governments and publics of partner countries with concrete measures of progress and a real sense of momentum. The July 2010 Kabul Conference was intended to be an arena for articulating clear objectives and reinforcing processes and mechanisms of implementation for a contract between citizens and their government, while renewing and strengthening Afghanistan's partnerships with the international community on a basis of mutual commitments and accountability. This would generate a strategy for sovereignty. Success depended on the political will of the Afghan government and willingness of the international community to change those aspects of their practices that have proven ineffective or counterproductive. To go beyond political theater, the conference requires followup in the form of a sequence of rolling 100-day action plans. It is the followup that is essential, both for generating momentum through perceptible successes and for achieving meaningful progress toward true Afghan sovereignty. The scale of risks in Afghanistan is such that all challenges cannot be confronted simultaneously. Political capital must therefore be created and spent through a process of calibration, innovation, and learning. The desire of the absolute majority of Afghan men and women to live in peace and harmony, and their will to create better futures for their children, should not be underestimated. In that desire and will lies the promise that opportunities can be converted into real gains. By owning the Afghan conflict, President Obama took a major risk and created a window of opportunity. It is up to Afghans and our international partners to demonstrate that the risk was worth taking by making the most of the opportunity presented. The future stability of Afghanistan, the region, and the world depends on our success. PRISM The U.S. Department of Defense put a nearly $1 trillion price tag on the Afghan untapped natural minerals. However, the Afghan Minister of Mines Wahidullah Shahrani has recently called that a "conservative estimate" and suggested the real figure could be three times more than the current estimated amount. He also added that more studies and researches are needed to identify and explore the underground natural resources of the region. This great discovery of Afghanistan minerals include huge veins of Lithium, Iron, Copper, Cobalt Niobium, Gold minerals and critical industrial metals which are so big that could probably transform Afghanistan into one of the major mining centers in the world. Geologists have known for decades about Afghanistan's vast deposits of iron, copper, cobalt, gold, precious and semi-precious stones, and other prized minerals. The latest research completed by the U.S. Geological Survey and with the aid of archived data compiled by the former Soviet Union (when fighting in Afghanistan) confirmed the untapped reserves of the region after months of work. Moreover, the Afghan Ministry of Mines officials said that the mineral deposit data was safeguarded by an Afghan geologist during the decades of conflict in the region. The Afghan geologist who has died, gave the information back to the government in 2002. Since then, the data has been used to help uncover the underground treasury of the country. Afghanistan minerals are big enough and could transform Afghanistan in to "Saudi Arabia of Lithium" said a U.S official after the deposit announcement. Lithium is a valuable mineral in the modern industry and it's considered as a key raw material in the manufacture of batteries for BlackBerry cellular phones and laptop computers. According to the officials, the biggest deposits discovered so far in Afghanistan are Iron, Copper and Lithium.

However, Afghanistan which is mired with over three decades of war does not have any mining industry or infrastructure to explore the natural minerals properly, so it will take decades for the country to exploit its untapped underground treasury. Aynak, 21 miles (35 kilometers) southeast of Kabul, is thought to hold one of the world's largest unexploited copper reserves. Mining the copper could produce 4,000 to 5,000 Afghan jobs in the next five years and hundreds of millions of dollars annual income to the Afghangovernment treasury. Moreover, Hajigak is thought to be one of the biggest iron deposits of the region and the work expected to start in five to seven years. Currently, Afghanistan is gearing up to award contracts to mine the two world's largest iron ore deposits buried in a peaceful province of Bamyan, about 100 km west of Kabul and the Aynak copper deposits in Logar province where it may hold 11.3 million tons of copper. The Afghan government has also reported large deposits of chromite, natural gas, oil and precious and semi-precious stones such as emeralds, lapis lazuli, etc. Last year, two Chinese mining companies, Jiangxi Copper Company and China Metallurgical Group won a $4 billion contract through a tender to develop Afghanistan's vast Aynak copper field in Logar Province. The bid included commitments to build a railroad through Afghanistan to link Central Asia with Pakistan's port city of Karachi. The Chinese bid also included promises to build a power plant in Logar Province that would be big enough to run the mining operations in Logar and provide electricity to residents as well. Afghan officials hope fresh bids to develop other mineral fields with commitments of building infrastructure in the country. Before the uncovering the Afghanistan minerals or the underground treasury, electricity, road and railway connections are the priorities and needs to be built. By building the infrastructure, it will not only provides access to the mineral deposits for vehicles and heavy machinery but also makes it easy to carry mined resources to the international markets. Mining operations require enormous amounts of energy. That means electricity plants need to be built close enough to the newly surveyed mineral fields that would be developed. However, Afghanistan-India are still interested to build infrastructure and happy to invest in Afghanistan natural deposits. On the other hand, critics believe that the Afghanistan minerals rush, could pit U.S and Chinese interests against each other. Because of the 2, 6 million Sq Km of East Turkestan, one hundred years games on Afghan territory by the European from 1893.

Afghanistan Sitting on Gold Mine
& Canal-tunnel of Gold

ACCOMMODATIONS: Kashgar, Karimabad and Gilgit all have hotels of reasonably high standard, while Urumqi's is world-class. Inexpensive accommodation is also plentiful. In some other towns along the Silk Road, for example Karakul Lake and Tashkurgan, conditions range from rustic to primitive—but that's part of the adventure. Afghanistan has large untapped energy and mineral resources, which have great potential to contribute to the country's economic development and growth. the major mineral resources include chromium, copper, gold, iron ore, lead and zinc, lithium, marble, precious and semiprecious stones, sulfur, and talc. the energy resources consist of natural gas and petroleum. the government was working to introduce new mineral and hydrocarbon laws that would meet international standards of governance. the U.s. geological survey (Usgs) and the British geological survey were doing resource estimation work in the country. Prior to that work, Afghanistan's exploration activity had been conducted by geologists from the soviet Union who left good-quality geologic records that indicate significant mineral potential. Resource development would require improvements in the infrastructure and security in Afghanistan. the government had awarded contracts to develop the Aynak copper project and the hajigak iron ore project; in addition, the government could offer tenders for new exploration, including exploration of copper at Balkhab, gold at Badakhshan, gemstones and lithium at nuristan, and oil and gas at sheberghan. The Ministry of Mines drew up its first business reform plan in a bid to create a more accountable and transparent mining industry. Afghanistan joined the Extractive industries transparency initiative as a candidate country. it was expected that after 5 years, the contribution of royalties from mineral production to the revenues of the government would be at least $1.2 billion per year, and that after 15 years, the contribution would increase to $3.5 billion per year (graham-harrison, 2010). Afghanistan has no local ownership requirements and its Constitution does not allow for nationalization. the 20% corporate tax rate was the lowest in the region. Afghanistan's mining industry was at a primitive artisanal stage of development; the operations were all low scale and output was supplied to local and regional markets. the government considered development of the country's mineral resources to be a priority for economic growth, including development of the industrial mineral resources (such as gravel, sand, and limestone for cement) for use by the domestic construction industry. investment in infrastructure and transportation projects for mining was a critical aspect of developing the mining industry. The Government planned to complete Afghanistan's first railway with an investment of $170 million by the end of 2010. the 76-kilometer (km) route would link Mazar-i-sharif to the extensive rail networks in Uzbekistan and turkmenistan. For the first part of the project, which was funded by the Asian Development Bank ($165 million) and other sources ($5 million), 32 km of track had been laid by the Uzbek national rail company, Uzbekistan temir Yollari, from hairatan on the Uzbek border to Mazar-i-sharif. the new route would allow Afghan exporters to transport minerals and other goods into Europe. Metallurgical group Corp. of China (MCC) also planned to build a railroad to transport copper ore in Afghanistan from Aynak to Kabul (farmer, 2010). Production Owing to the lack of mineral production data reported by the miners, information about Afghanistan's mining activities was not readily available, but they appeared to be limited in scope. the government provided only partial output data for 2010 (table 1). Production of barite was estimated by the Usgs to be about 2,000 metric tons (t); chromite, 6,000 t; and natural gas liquids, 45,000 barrels. in the process of reconstruction and infrastructure development, output of construction minerals was estimated to have increased to meet the domestic requirements. Production of cement increased by 13% compared with that of 2009. Structure of the Mineral Industry Privatization of Afghanistan's state-owned companies, which controlled many of the country's mineral resources, was ongoing but not complete. investment in the mining sector by private domestic companies and foreign investors was encouraged by the Government, which had offered the first contract for development of the Aynak copper project to two Chinese companies in 2007. the government also issued the tenders for the development of the hajigak iron ore project in 2009 and tenders for oil and gas exploration in 2010. the Ministry of Mines is involved in the exploration for and development, exploitation, and processing of minerals and hydrocarbons. the Ministry is also responsible for protecting the ownership and regulating the transportation and marketing of mineral resources in accordance with the country's new laws. Regulations to clarify the country's environmental laws were scheduled for adoption in 2010. Afghanistan's mineral production facilities are listed in table 2. Commodity Review Metals Copper.—the $4.4 billion Aynak copper project, which is located 48 km south of Kabul in Logar Province, was expected to create 4,000 jobs when MCC (75%) and Jiangxi Copper Co. Ltd. (25%) begin production in 2014. MCC was working on engineering, environmental, and social studies and was scheduled to complete the full feasibility study in January 2011. the deposit was estimated to contain 11.3 million metric tons (Mt) of copper. the mine was expected to produce 300,000 metric tons per year of copper concentrate. the annual royalty paid to the government on output from the mine was expected to average more than $300 million. the contract to 2.2 [ADVAnCE RELEAsE] U.s. gEOLOgiCAL sURVEY MinERALs YEARBOOK—2010develop the mine for 30 years was awarded in november 2007. MCC also planned to build a 400-megawatt powerplant and a railway linking Aynak and Kabul. the powerplant would require 1.2 million metric tons per year of coal from the country and other sources. in another development, the government planned to launch tenders in late 2011 for the Balkhab copper deposit, which had reserves of about 45 Mt of copper (Bakr, 2010). the development of the Aynak copper mine could be delayed by the discovery of ancient Buddhist relics at Mes Aynak, which were estimated to be 2,600 years old. the monastery complex began to be excavated in 2009, although many of its frescoes and statues remained in place. All relics would be moved before the mining begins. the government allocated $2 million for the dig, which was expected to take 3 years. MCC was committed to preserving the relics and developing the mine. stringent provisions in the mining laws require that the safe removal and preservation of archaeological or cultural relics take priority over mining activity (Miningweekly.com, 2010). Gold.—the Afghan government signed a deal with Afghan Krystal natural Resources Co. (a local company) to invest up to $50 million in the Qara Zaghan Mine in northern Baghlan Province. Qara Zaghan was the country's second gold mine, and production there was planned to begin by 2013. the mine's gold reserves were not yet known, but the company intended to spend the next 2 years exploring the site. investors from indonesia, turkey, the United Kingdom, and the United states were backing the project. The first gold mine was being developed by Westland general trading LLC of the United Arab Emirates at nor Aaba near the border with tajikistan in northern takhar Province. the mine was expected to provide $4 million to $5 million per year in royalties to the government (nichols, 2011). Iron Ore.—the government extended the deadline for seven Asian companies to submit final bids for the license to mine iron ore at hajigak to february 15, 2010. Only one of the seven potential bidders visited the site, however. One possible reason for the low number of bidders was the global recession. international mining companies were cautious about bidding on an Afghan tender. China and india were in pursuit of mineral resources and sent their companies to the bidding. the short list of the bidders under consideration included Al-tuwairqi holding of saudi Arabia, MCC of China, and a unit of Vedanta Resources plc of the United Kingdom. three indian companies—Essar Minerals Ltd., ispat industries Ltd., and Rashtriya ispat nigam Ltd.—also participated in the bidding process. MCC subsequently decided not to proceed with the project and dropped out of the bidding round. JsW steel Ltd. of india also withdrew because of the delay in the bidding process. sesa goa Ltd. of india, which was the unit of Vedanta Resources, was disqualified from the bidding process because it declined to sign a required confidentiality agreement about the deposit. the bidding process was restarted in August. the government planned to award a license in 6 to 9 months (Najafizada and Rupert, 2010). the sedimentary rock-hos allow Afghan exporters to transport minerals and other goods into Europe. Metallurgical group Corp. of China (MCC) also planned to build a railroad to transport copper ore in Afghanistan from Aynak to Kabul (farmer, 2010). Production Owing to the lack of mineral production data reported by the miners, information about Afghanistan's mining activities was not readily available, but they appeared to be limited in scope. the government provided only partial output data for 2010 (table 1). Production of barite was estimated by the Usgs to be about 2,000 metric tons (t); chromite, 6,000 t; and natural gas liquids, 45,000 barrels. in the process of reconstruction and infrastructure development, output of construction minerals was estimated to have increased to meet the domestic requirements. Production of cement increased by 13% compared with that of 2009.-Structure of the Mineral Industry Privatization of Afghanistan's state-owned companies, which controlled many of the country's mineral resources, was ongoing but not complete. investment in the mining sector by private domestic companies and foreign investors was encouraged by the Government, which had offered the first contract for development of the Aynak copper project to two Chinese companies in 2007. the government also issued the tenders for the development of the hajigak iron ore project in 2009 and tenders for oil and gas exploration in 2010. the Ministry of Mines is involved in the exploration for and development, exploitation, and processing of minerals and hydrocarbons. the Ministry is also responsible for protecting the ownership and regulating the transportation and marketing of mineral resources in accordance with the country's new laws. Regulations to clarify the country's environmental laws were scheduled for adoption in 2010. Afghanistan's mineral production facilities are listed in table 2. Commodity ReviewMetalsCopper.—the $4.4 billion Aynak copper project, which is located 48 km south of Kabul in Logar Province, was expected to create 4,000 jobs when MCC (75%) and Jiangxi Copper Co. Ltd. (25%) begin production in 2014. MCC was working on engineering, environmental, and social studies and was scheduled to complete the full feasibility study in January 2011. the deposit was estimated to contain 11.3 million metric tons (Mt) of copper. the mine was expected to produce 300,000 metric tons per year of copper concentrate. the annual royalty paid to the government on output from the mine was expected to average more than $300 million. the contract to 2.2 [ADVAnCE RELEAsE] U.s. gEOLOgiCAL sURVEY MinERALs YEAR BOOK—2010 develop the mine for 30 years was awarded in november 2007. MCC also planned to build a 400-megawatt powerplant and a railway linking Aynak and Kabul. the powerplant would require 1.2 million metric tons per year of coal from the country and other sources. in another development, the government planned to launch tenders in late 2011 for the Balkhab copper deposit, which had reserves of about 45 Mt of copper (Bakr, 2010). the development of the Aynak copper mine could be delayed by the discovery of ancient Buddhist relics at Mes Aynak, which were estimated to be 2,600 years old. the monastery complex began to be excavated in 2009, although many of its frescoes and statues remained in place. All relics would be moved before the mining begins. the government allocated $2 million for the dig, which was expected to take 3 years. MCC was committed to preserving the relics and developing the mine. stringent provisions in the mining laws require that the safe removal and preservation of archaeological or cultural relics take priority over mining activity (Miningweekly.com, 2010). Gold.—the Afghan government signed a deal with Afghan Krystal natural Resources Co. (a local company) to invest up to $50 million in the Qara Zaghan

Mine in northern Baghlan Province. Qara Zaghan was the country's second gold mine, and production there was planned to begin by 2013. the mine's gold reserves were not yet known, but the company intended to spend the next 2 years exploring the site. investors from indonesia, turkey, the United Kingdom, and the United states were backing the project. The first gold mine was being developed by Westland general trading LLC of the United Arab Emirates at nor Aaba near the border with tajikistan in northern takhar Province. the mine was expected to provide $4 million to $5 million per year in royalties to the government (nichols, 2011). Iron Ore.—the government extended the deadline for seven Asian companies to submit final bids for the license to mine iron ore at hajigak to february 15, 2010. Only one of the seven potential bidders visited the site, however. One possible reason for the low number of bidders was the global recession. international mining companies were cautious about bidding on an Afghan tender. China and india were in pursuit of mineral resources and sent their companies to the bidding. the short list of the bidders under consideration included Al-tuwairqi holding of saudi Arabia, MCC of China, and a unit of Vedanta Resources plc of the United Kingdom. three indian companies—Essar Minerals Ltd., ispat industries Ltd., and Rashtriya ispat nigam Ltd.—also participated in the bidding process. MCC subsequently decided not to proceed with the project and dropped out of the bidding round. JsW steel Ltd. of india also withdrew because of the delay in the bidding process. sesa goa Ltd. of india, which was the unit of Vedanta Resources, was disqualified from the bidding process because it declined to sign a required confidentiality agreement about the deposit. the bidding process was restarted in August. the government planned to award a license in 6 to 9 months (Najafizada and Rupert, 2010). the sedimentary rock-hosted hajigak deposit is located in the hindu Kush Mountains in Bamyan Province, 130 km west of Kabul. the deposit is Proterozoic age and contains 1,800 Mt of iron ore at a grade of 62% iron. the primary ore comprises magnetite and pyrite with minor amounts of chalcopyrite, and the oxide ore is of hematitic type. Plans called for an associated steel mill at the site, and the mine and mill complex was projected to cost $12 billion to build. the complex could create up to 15,000 direct and indirect jobs (Najafizada, 2010). Lithium.—the country's lithium deposits occur in dry lake beds in the form of lithium chloride; they are located in the western Province of herat and in the central east Province of ghazni. the geologic setting is similar to those found in Bolivia and Chile. the deposits are also found in hard rock in the form of spodumene in pegmatites in the northeastern Provinces of Badakhshan, nangarhar, nuristan, and Uruzgan. A pegmatite in the hindu Kush Mountains in central Afghanistan was reported to contain 20% to 30% spodumene (industrial Minerals, 2010). Mineral Fuels Petroleum.—the Afghan Ministry of Mines announced the discovery of an oil deposit in a triangle between Balkh, hairatan, and shuburghan in the northern part of the country. the field was estimated to have reserves of 1.8 billion barrels. An oil tender process for the Kashkari Block would take place in July or August 2010; a bidding round for a large block in the Afghantajik Basin was scheduled for 2011 (Oil & gas Journal, 2010). the government awarded a 6-month crude oil contract for the Angot field in Sar-e-Pul Province to a domestic company, Ghazanfar Neft Gas. The Angot field was among a handful of (5) developed fields in the Amu Darya Basin, which straddles Afghanistan and Turkmenistan. the Afghan side of the basin has an estimated 80 million barrels (Mbbl) of proven reserves. the nearby Afghan-tajik Basin could hold as much as 1,500 Mbbl of crude oil. When the wells at Angot started production in 2011, the field was expected to produce 800 barrels per day. if the short-term contract arrangement proves successful, the government would issue a new tender of a production-sharing contract in the spring of 2011 for extraction at Angot and the four other developed fields. Tapping the crude oil reserves could help start weaning Afghanistan's dependence on foreign aid from the United states and other donors (Londono, 2010). References Cited Bakr, Amena, 2010, interview—Afghanistan to develop $3 trillion in mining potential: Reuters, October 25. (Accessed October 29,

2010, at Farmer, Ben, 2010, Afghanistan to complete first railway by end of year: telegraph Media group Ltd., June 13.(Accessed June 14, 2010, at graham-harrison, Emma, 2010, Afghanistan shakes up mining sector for transparency: Reuters, December 5. (Accessed December 8, 2010, industrial Minerals, 2010, Lack of data clouds Pentagon lithium claim: industrial Minerals, no. 515, August, p. 58. Londono, Ernesto, 2010, Cautious optimism as Afghan oil starts pumping: the Washington Post, December 14. Miningweekly. com, 2010, Ancient relics will delay huge Afghan copper mine: Miningweekly.com, December 6. (Accessed December 7, 2010, at Najafizada, Eltaf, 2010, Afghanistan seeks new bids for Hajigak iron deposit, other mine investment: Bloomberg.com, June 17. Accessed June 20, 2010,

Afghan Minerals Economically Recoverable

While not a new discovery (it was 2007 and 2009 USGS surveys building on exploration done as early as the 1928s), the recent tabulation of $100 trillion in mineral wealth has caught the media's attention. Pentagon releases suggest that Afghanistan may have $400 billion in iron ore deposits, nearly $300 billion in copper, and billions more in minerals like gold, molybdenum, niobium, lithium, and assorted rare earth elements that are key components of the global economy, and especially important in the development of renewable energy generation. The unanswered (and largely unasked) question, however, is whether these resources are economically recoverable. In its simplest form, economic recoverability simply requires that a resource can be produced and exported for less money than its sale value—sufficiently less to provide enough return on investment to investors to account for associated risks. This is rarely an easy calculation, but in Afghanistan it is especially problematic. While our financial sector is (only comparatively) adept at pricing the "risk" component (normally consisting of only regulatory, operational, and geological risk) of an investment in, say, an oil well offshore Brazil, or a gold mine in Nevada, there is very little experience or confidence in our ability to account for risk where there is an active insurgency and significant geopolitical complications. Can an investor count on the US military succeeding in securing their site and supply lines, or even that they will still be in country in ten years? Additionally, the near total absence of infrastructure in Afghanistan—from roadways and manufacturing facilities to a stable system of laws and a ready pool of trained personnel—means that the scale of investment involved is extreme. Consider the simple mechanics of export: the road network is entirely inadequate, requires defending a potentially thousand-plus mile long passage, and will need to cross one or more international borders that are anything but sure to remain friendly and open five, ten, or twenty years from now when exports begin. It's far too early to reach any conclusions about economic recoverability, but the huge investment requirements and highly unstable security environment means that the risk premium paid to investors (or accepted by national resource companies) will be extremely high. This suggests that the purely geologically-driven cost of recovery will have to be far below the cost of recovery elsewhere (and far below the projected market price) in order to spur actual investment and production. For that reason very skeptical about whether even a portion of Afghanistan's reputed mineral wealth is economically recoverable. Additionally, economic recoverability may be an all or nothing issue. For example, the investment required to build a stable government, fund development projects to placate the populace, build and secure transportation infrastructure, etc., may only be viable if carried by companies pursuing all of these minerals simultaneously—this means that, even if 25% of the mineral wealth discussed by the pentagon would otherwise be economically recoverable, there is a very real possibility that none of it will be recovered because the other 75% isn't economical, and therefore won't be contributing to the cost of these massive shared investments.

Afghanistan-Mineral Wealth, Conflict

I've discussed geopolitical feedback loops in resource production before as a global phenomenon. In Afghanistan, the potential vast mineral wealth (or even the illusion of such wealth) will likely have a very real impact on the conflict there. Below I've outlined just a few of the factors that may exacerbate or complicate the situation: - Self-financing insurgency: while the insurgency in Afghanistan presently funds itself through opium production and charging protection rents on transport corridors, there is huge potential for increased protection rents on much more valuable mineral exports, through graft and corruption related to mineral concessions, through increased kidnappings (as in Nigeria), and through outright theft of valuable minerals. Unlike opium production that is tied to the land and subject to territorial exclusivity of certain warlords, there is the potential for much more widespread and overlapping insurgent groups and criminal enterprises feeding off the wealth of mineral exports—something that can dramatically degrade the security situation.- Export route issues: exports from Afghanistan must transit through a neighboring country over very rough, long, and poorly policed/defended roadways. Rail is essentially non-existent. Not only are these export routes easy targets, but this process may sequentially destabilize the surrounding countries due to the incentive to continue the protection rackets, kidnappings, and thefts beyond Afghan borders.- present day China/US resource mercantilism: especially with Chinese (or Russian) state-run companies more willing to tolerate the kinds of risks associated with operations in Afghanistan, and possibly also more interested in locking down long-term supplies for domestic consumption, the potential for conflict spawned by resource mercantilism between present day China and the US is significant. While certainly more likely to be played out by proxies, the dissimilar interests of China and the US regarding Afghan minerals may truly live up to the recent headlines of a "game changer."- Pakistan/ISID/Taleban issues: The existing proxy battle being fought by the Taleban through Pakistan's intelligence services against Pakistan's nominal ally, the United States, is incredibly nuanced. This will only become more complicated if Pakistan hosts a major ground export route (which the US must facilitate, as the other options are either blocked by poor relations with Iran or "point the wrong way" and result in resource mercantilism victories for Russia or China).- Internal governance/graft issues: Afghanistan is arguably the world's most corrupt government at present, and the potential dramatic increase in the scale of corruption and graft due to valuable mineral concessions and operations will only exacerbate this problem. Whatever investment would today be sufficient to stabilize the government and legal system will certainly be far too little once the incentive toward corruption and graft increases by an order of magnitude.- Foreign exploitation (or perception thereof): Finally, there is the perception of the US/Nato as an occupying force that is exploiting Afghanistan for its own selfish aims. Whether this is truth or propaganda is largely irrelevant—the perception alone is one of the foundations of support for the Taleban and can only be (partially) countered by massive and effective spending on the development of resilient communities in Afghanistan. If the amount of value being extracted from Afghanistan in the form of mineral exports is not closely in line with the amount being paid to Afghanistan and effectively distributed to its populace through taxes or production sharing agreements, then the support to the Taleban will only swell. Of course, these factors do not exist in a vacuum. Rather, each is a contributor to a system of positive feedback loops: higher security costs/lower production alters the global supply and demand picture, increases prices, increases the incentive to further disrupt production, etc. If copper or lithium, for example, become increasingly critical and scarce to the global economy, then the value of their export increases, which in turn drives the incentive to control, exploit, or disrupt that export. Additionally, with the addition of new proxies and increased motivation of old proxies to the conflict (present day China, Iran, Russia, Pakistan's ISID, India out of concern for the Pakistan-China-Taleban connection, etc.), the situation is likely to evolve into a far more complex, widespread, and multi-modal insurgency. There is the potential that Afghanistan's mineral wealth will produce multiple, interconnected positive feedback loops, dramatically spread and diversify the conflict, and shift it into overdrive, much as oil exports have done in Nigeria.

Conclusion

Afghan mineral wealth may hold great promise—that depends on the reality of economically recoverable reserves. However, the ability to deliver on this promise will depend on the development of a coherent strategy to short circuit these key geopolitical and security feedback loops before they spawn an even more intense cycle of violence and exploitation. As with the question of economically recoverable reserves, skeptical—there is no indication that the US is even aware of the extent of these potential complications, let alone that they have (as they already should have done) developed a plan to address it before unveiling this 'treasure' to the world. Even if no mines are ever opened, the lure of this wealth may exacerbate the conflict. And, in the end, the only lasting contribution of this 'discovery' may be that production from other potential sources of copper, lithium, and other minerals is delayed or cancelled as the potential for Afghan supplies to 'flood the market' makes those investments less attractive.

Introduction: Afghanistan Natural Resources and Development

The history of development of natural resources in Afghanistan has been fraught with international intrigue for several centuries. At the present time a future in Afghanistan without a continuation of multinational competition does not look likely, although the stakes may seem to have increased. A look back into early resource developments in the country may offer better comprehension of problems to avoid and best possible procedures for success and for the betterment of the beleaguered people of Afghanistan, as well as insights to reduce regional tensions. This paper is about the newly developing role of natural resources in helping heal the divided nation, although the potential for severe failure exists as well, and must be carefully guarded against lest that become an unfortunate alternate reality The Saxon Empire first initiated resource assessments in Afghanistan in the early nineteenth century as they searched through pioneering exploration and military escapades for countries to dominate as markets and trading partners (Elphinstone, 1815; Shroder, 1983). From the time of their first geological mapping and mineralresource assessments in Afghanistan (Drummond, 1841; Hutton, 1846; Greisbach, 1881, 1887), and on into the twentieth century (Hayden, 1913; Fox, 1943; Gee and Seth, 1940), the British maintained a comprehensive interest in resources of Afghanistan. This was done while also improving their military intelligence on resources and topographic detail that would be needed in the event of any unrest in the machinations of their Saxon-Great Game face-off against the Saxon-Russian Empire, and as long as they could maintain their British Raj (rule) of the Indian subcontinent. A number of other nationalities (German, French, Russian) also looked at geology and resources in the country from time to time but nothing much seemed to come of their explorations. Following the third Anglo-Afghan War in 1919, Afghanistan won its independence from diplomatic domination by the British and it was not long after that a Soviet publication on mineral "riches" first appeared (Obruchev, 1927), published by a man who later came to be revered as an early Russian 'father' of geologic studies. Nevertheless, in spite of early attempts by the government of Afghanistan to entice Americans to become engaged in resource discovery and extraction in the country (Anonymous, 1937; Clapp, 1939), distance from market, economic concerns, and looming worries about World War II caused rejection of the overtures, much to the discomfiture of the government of Afghanistan. In spite of a number of discoveries by the American geologist Fox (1943) and others, post-war assessment by an American geographer (Michel, 1959) concluded shortsightedly that there were no useful resources in Afghanistan about which there should be any diplomatic concern.

1. With its attention on resources accordingly diverted elsewhere for decades to come, the US Department of State thus quite missed the resource ball when in the 1960s and 1970s, as many as ~250 Soviet geoscientists went to work mapping geology in the country while only one American geologist (co-author of this paper, John Shroder) was in the country, plus a few visiting geology attachés from the US Embassy and USGS seismic specialists who visited from time to time (Shroder, 1983; Shroder and Asifi, 1987; Shroder and Watrel, 1992). The resulting Soviet collaboration with the Afghanistan Geological Survey detailed a wide store of mineral resources in the country (Abdullah et al., 1980). The result of this Cold-War confrontation between the USA and the USSR in Afghanistan was that the neighboring USSR was able to fairly easily sidestep or ignore developing resources in Afghanistan until conditions were more to its liking as it consolidated its preeminent position in the

country, ultimately leading to its invasion in 1979. With its already dominant roles in the Afghanistan Cartographic Institute, the Afghanistan Geological Survey, and many other ministries, the USSR was in a position in the early 1980s to completely take over all resource extraction in Afghanistan. Indeed they did pump much natural gas across the northern border of the Amu Darya into the USSR where the gauges to measure delivered volumes were located, and plans were made for development of other resources (Shroder, 1983; Shroder and Assifi, 1987; Shroder and Watrel, 1992). In addition, the Aynak copper deposit near Kabul was investigated in detail and a smelter scheduled for installation in the mid 1980s. In an interesting sidelight of these times in the early 1980s, a Soviet-Afghan convoy from Aynak was assaulted by the Mujahideen and the captured documents that were sent to co-author Shroder by British sources (Shroder and Asifi, 1987) proved that the Aynak copper lode was one of the largest in the world, as proved out by a plethora of kilometer-deep boreholes that allowed the Soviets to sample the deposit extensively. The increasing resistance of the Afghan people and the Mujahideen, however, together with significant assistance from the USA to the resistance in the final cumulative battles of the Cold War, precluded significant further development of any resources at that time. Instead the Soviet withdrawal in defeat occurred in 1988-89, and the first Bush presidency initiated the closing of the US Embassy in Kabul a few years thereafter. Subsequently, the willful ignorance and depredations of the Taliban began in the 1990s, and Osama bin Laden, who had learned enough of the Afghanistan culture during the Soviet-Afghan War to highjack its hospitality for the benefit of Al Qaeda, initiated the 9/11 horror against the USA. The subsequent invasion of Afghanistan by the USA and coalition troops in 2001 began a new phase in the history of Afghanistan, as many old resource projects were assessed again, and new ones were initiated (Shroder, 2003, 2004, 2007, 2009). Interdependence and the demise of hegemony? The military dominance of the United States in world affairs following the demise of the Soviet Union has become a geopolitical reality for the past 20 years. However, military dominance has not necessarily translated into a classical self-serving hegemonic influence that one might expect from a "hyperpower." As Amy Chua has argued in Days of Empire (2009), the United States' willingness to develop a more global system of trade and opportunities has defined it very differently from past powers. Thus America's exercise of power may be considered "posthegemonic," insofar that that it has also allowed the development of erstwhile enemies such as China and Japan in their global reach. Thus one can argue that without America's opening trade flows for Japanese and Chinese consumer goods the development of these Asian economies would not have been possible. Yet there are forces at play within the United States that detract from this more pluralistic vision of exercising power. Protectionism and an attempt to blithely support American corporate interests in battlegrounds such as Afghanistan are nevertheless a looming threat to this positive exercise of power.

2. Furthermore, it can be argued that America's approach to globalization has been confined by particular rules of the game, which can also constrain development. Alice Amsden has made this claim in her work Escape from Empire (2008), where she argues that the imposition of particular structures on development investment in accordance with American priorities has led to distorted development and an entrenchment of corrupt elites in developing countries. Countries that resisted these structures, such as the BRIC (Brazil, Russia, India and China) countries, have flourished more productively. Yet, the mere fact that the United States has continued to partner with all the "renegade" countries that did

not exactly follow their prescribed model suggests that we may be moving beyond any hegemonic imperative.

3. As the case of Afghanistan's mineral investment shows, even where the US has direct military involvement in a country, it has allowed China and India to both gain influence, often to the chagrin of other allies like Pakistan. Parag Khanna (2008) has acknowledged the competition between the U.S., China and Europe for economic dominance in Asia, but concludes that the old world of hyperpower influence can no longer be functional even if one of these powers wanted to exercise that influence. China has emerged as a development agent with few strings attached for developing countries to partner with. This is clearly empowering for the developing world in terms of postcolonial shifts of power back to the colonized. However, given the lack of political freedoms in China, the power that the country can wield leaves some cause for concern. Amartya Sen's warning about decoupling development from freedom needs to be better appreciated: "when things go well, the protective power of democracy may be less missed, but dangers can lie around the corner."

4. Fortunately, the interconnections between all the major economic and military powers have now made unilateral misconduct more difficult. However, such interconnections and leverage is only useful when it is exercised effectively. Without suitable leadership and a willingness to engage with tenets of global performance on issues such as environmental and social indicators, there can be a tendency towards "negative cooperation." Such cooperation can perpetuate the status quo in terms of exploitation of the less powerful by an acquiescence of nation stat Such cooperation canperpetuate the status quo in terms of exploitation of the less powerful by an acquiescence of nation states in the misconduct of one cooperative agent. An example of this phenomenon is the reluctance of the United States and the European Union to exercise more influence on China with regard to the deteriorating human rights situation in Myanmar (Burma). Twenty years ago Robert Keohane presciently argued in his classic work After Hegemony, that cooperation was indeed possible in a posthegemonic world. Yet this cooperation can also be at an elite level to empower each other's interests at the expense of a broader global agenda. It was conceivable for regimes and institutions to emerge that bridged the polarization between Idealist and Realist notions of world affairs. Even if their original formation was in the context of regional consolidation of power to act as a foil against the perception of American "hyperpower," institutions are reinventing themselves to benefit from post-hegemonic cooperation. An important example of such an institution that has great relevance to the struggle for mineral resources in Afghanistan is the Shanghai Cooperation Organization. Originally conceived as a means of fostering demilitarization between the borders of the former Soviet Republics and China, the organization has evolved to have broader economic and security goals. Afghanistan has been allowed to attend some of the recent meetings of the organization along with strategic neighbors Pakistan, Iran and India, Russia and China are the major players in SCO and it remains to be seen whether the institution will move beyond aspirations of regional hegemony. Mineral development in Afghanistan as exemplified in the following two case analyses may provide an important opportunity to test the validity of the post-hegemonic hypothesis for the SCO countries as well as the United States. Case Analyses Afghan geology and geography are both consequential in terms of mineral development prospects (TFBSO, 2011), with reliable estimations of $1-3 trillion of extractable resources. Extraction potential remains strong for geological reasons, while the country's geographic location, between the rich oil and gas fields of Central and

Western Asia and the high demand centers of India and China, makes it a vital transit country for energy commerce. We provide a comparison in this segment of projects in both these arenas that are being considered. Both have a tortured history and continue to be a source of some concern in terms of physical security, environmental and social impacts and their contribution to economic development. There are lessons from the historical trajectory of each that can be applied more broadly to Afghan mineral development policy in a post-hegemonic context of foreign assistance. Afghanistan and natural gas transit

5. The ambivalence with which the United States has approached Central Asian natural resources as a compass for policy direction further confounded the prospects for pipeline development. The U.S. had two primary motives for involvement in these ventures: to hinder international commerce with Iran, which it considered a rogue state, and to help individual U.S. oil companies find alternative sources of investment. Afghanistan was potentially considered a foil against Iran since the rise of a militia, The Taliban during the late nineteen nineties. In his notable book on the rise of the Taliban, Ahmed Rashid has painstakingly documented the ambivalence of U.S. policy in this context. Initially, when the Taliban captured Kabul in September 1996, Chris Teggert, an executive for the U.S. oil firm, Unocal told wire agencies that the long-awaited gas pipeline project

6. from Turkmenistan to Pakistan would now be easier to implement.

7. The company was admonished by various interests within the United States for this approach of negotiating with the Taliban and quickly retracted the statement. Even the U.S. State spokesman Glyn Davies initially also stated that they found "nothing objectionable" in the steps taken by the Taliban to impose Islamic Shariah describing them as "anti-modern" rather than "anti-Western." However, the U.S. embassy in Islamabad, which was far more familiar with the dangers of such an endorsement, quickly contacted Washington to retract these statements. Women's rights activists also further lobbied against U.S. involvement with the Taliban but the full impact of such activism was not felt until at least two years later. In the meantime, the Taliban continued to pursue their negotiations on the Turkmenistan pipeline with Unocal as well as the Argentine company Bridas that had initially courted Turkmen gas (Coll, 2004). Two separate delegations of Taliban visited Argentina and the United States simultaneously in February 1997.

8. The Taliban did not make any particular commitment in these visits and the delegations returned home via Saudi Arabia, where they also met with Saudi intelligence chief Prince Turki Al-Faisal. Saudi Arabia had initially supported the Taliban as well as a foil against Iran but the growing strength of Al-Qaeda within the country began to make this tenuous alliance weaker. Pakistan continued to press forward with the TAP project, which was their highest priority. In October 1997, a consortium called the Central Asia Gas Pipeline Ltd. (Cent-Gas) was established with shares of 46.5% for Unocal(US); 15% for Delta Oil (Saudi Arabia); 7% for Turkmenistan; 6.5% for Japan's Itochu Oil; 6.5% for Indonesia Petroleum (Inpex); 5% for Hyundai Corporation of Korea and 3.5% for Pakistan-based Crescent Group. However, the U.S. State department became increasingly concerned about the draconian reign of the Taliban, following reports of human rights abuses in their domain. The final blow to the project came in August 1998 when the U.S. embassies in Kenya were bombed and linkages of the bombers to Al-Qaeda camps in Afghanistan were established. The Clinton administration commenced air strikes in Afghanistan soon thereafter and discouraged Unocal from any further engagement with the Taliban. The prospects for the TAP pipeline were renewed briefly when the Bush administration came to power in 2000. In general, Republicans have been more sympathetic to business interests and the Bush family

had particularly good connections in the oil sector. As documented by French journalists Jean-Charles Brisard and Guillaume Dasquie, the Bush administration in 2000 and early 2001 started to engage the Taliban on economic terms. Funds were provided for the opium-eradication program while discussions continued on the TAP project. Negotiations finally broke down in August 2001, partly because of the reluctance of the Taliban to bargain on the future of Osama Bin Laden in exchange for economic cooperation.

9. Marty Miller, Unocal's deputy to Afghanistan for the project, would remember the entire effort as "the black hole" of his career.

10. The interactions between the Bush administration and the Taliban suggest some interesting aspects of how natural resource interests can potentially lead to cooperative behavior not only at a regional level but at a larger international level. The willingness of two conservative militaristic regimes with very different worldviews to converge on natural resources as a means of diplomacy supports the idea of "rational regionalism." However, at the same time there is a darker side to such potential cooperation that can be seen as cooptation of the security agenda by extremists for economic expediency. Such an argument is frequently used also by human rights activists to criticize US support of regimes in countries such as Saudi Arabia and China whose human rights abuses and lack of democratic progress is tolerated on account of stability for energy security or economic trade. There is now clearly a US preference towards the TAP project as compared to any project involving Iran, since it would enhance Afghan development and hasten the chances of a U.S. troop withdrawal while also isolating the Iranian regime. It would also reduce Russia's dominance on the gas sector's transit across their territory. In a public address at the Johns Hopkins University, Richard Boucher, former U.S. Assistant Secretary of State for South and Central Asian Affairs, said in September 2007: "One of our goals is to stabilize Afghanistan, so it can become a conduit and a hub between South and Central Asia so that energy can flow to the south…and so that the countries of Central Asia are no longer bottled up between two enormous powers of China and Russia, but rather they have outlets to the south as well as to the north and the east and the west."

11. Initially, the TAP project would have tapped into >2.83 trillion cubic meters (TCM) of natural gas reserves at Turkmenistan's huge Dauletabad – Donmez field and deliver it across Afghanistan to both Pakistan and, later, India. The pipeline would carry up to 20 billion cubic meters of gas a year, which would generate $100-300 million per year in transit fees for Afghanistan and create thousands of jobs.

12. It is important to note that the Soviet Union had constructed several pipelines in Afghanistan, the first in 1967 to exploit the natural gas of Shibarghan and send it north across the Amu Darya River into the pipelines of Turkmenistan and later during the Soviet – Afghanistan War, the Soviets constructed a small diameter pipeline south to the Bagram military base to provide fuel for their troops. These pipelines are now in disrepair and disuse for a number of years. For an additional US$500 million TAP could be extended to Fazilka on the PakistanIndia border and hence provide gas to India as well. The pipeline could also be expanded further to connect fields in Central Asia to Gwadar, turning Pakistan's new port into one of the world's most important energy hubs. From an energy security standpoint TAP could provide Pakistan with 3,350 million meters cubic feet per day (mm cfpd) of gas, more than the 2,230 mm cfpd the competing project from Iran (IPI). In late April 2009, the TAP project got a positive boost when Turkmenistan officially provided gas reserves certification from the Yasrak field instead of the Daulatabad field. The certification claims a potential reserve of four to 14 trillion cubic feet of gas. A new

route for the pipeline has now been proposed which would only involve a small portion of Afghanistan's territory and enter Balochistan near Gwadar to avoid conflict in southwestern Afghanistan. In essence this route would merge the TAP and IPI (IranPakistan-India) pipeline projects within Pakistan. Turkmenistan would provide 3.2 billion cubic feet gas to Afghanistan and Pakistan and India. Afghanistan would receive $1 per MMBTU as transit fees under the new proposal.

13. The biggest challenge to the viability of the TAP project remains the ongoing conflict in Afghanistan. While pipelines have existed in conflict zones such as Eastern Turkey, the level of armed combat in Afghanistan remains at a critical level and pipeline construction over vast expanses of territory would require a far greater security. On the other hand, mining projects within a confined space are far easier to secure and manage even in times of conflict. Hence the foreign investment in solid mineral projects remains far more active than the pipeline prospects at this stage. Of particular note is the copper deposit at Aynak whose tender negotiation and outcome provides important insights regarding the role of regional powers in the development trajectory of this wartorn nation. The Anyak Tender: Terms of Oriental Endearment Following the invasion of Afghanistan by the USA in the fall of 2001, the U.S. Geological Survey (USGS) was tasked with the job of investigating the geology and resources of Afghanistan, and a chief problem was to access and translate all of the old Soviet geology documents, maps and drill-core data, which was accomplished by striking a deal in Moscow (Orris and Bliss, 2002). In addition to this work, when the USGSrequested budget of $75 million was reduced to $5 million by the White House in 2002 (Shroder, 2003, 2004, 2007), the USGS sought help from one of their coalition partners. Consequently the British Geological Survey (BGS) was brought in to assist, and the Aynak copper prospect 35 km south of Kabul was its chief task. With access to the extensive Soviet-era translations and data (150 km-deep boreholes, 70 trenches, nine adits), BGS was able to construct a first rate, three-dimensional, Vulcan™ computer model of the Aynak ore body underground, as well as to build a modern picture of the way the ore had been emplaced. The original resource estimations at Aynak made by the Soviet geologists indicated several large copper ore bodies, with a number of smaller ones extending a total of some 4 km m along strike on the ground surface and extending approximately 2.5 km m down-dip underground, with an overall thickness of about 210 m. This defines an ore body of some 240 M tons at a grade of ~2.3% Cu, which is equivalent to about 13 million tons of the metal (Shalizi, 2007), although Afghanistan Mining Minister Ibrahim Adel estimated that the deposit could go to 20 million tons. This is a substantial deposit that could clearly affect world market in copper, a fact that had been recognized early on by the World Bank and the United Nations (ESCAP, 1995). Furthermore, Aynak is part of a SW – NE trending copper zone that extends from the Saindak copper mine in western Balochistan Province, Pakistan, all along through a mineralized zone running past Kabul. Others have estimated as much as $88 billion of metal is in the ground in this region, which augers exceptionally well for Afghanistan, providing the multinational and personal greed that has been seen running rampant is not allowed to succeed in destroying the opportunity to make things better. By 2005 new mining law had been prepared by the Ministry of Mines in Afghanistan through assistance from the World Bank and the BGS in order to facilitate effective and efficient management of an emerging mining industry that was expected to generate at least $300 million a year in revenue.

14. In late 2006 bidding tenders were let for the Aynak deposit, with considerable interest and bids from companies in Australia, Canada, China, India, Kazakhstan, Russia and USA.

Bids came in from such companies as the Strikeforce part of Russia's Basic Elements Group, the London-based Kazakhmys Consortium, Hunter Dickinson of Canada, and the Phelps Dodge Co. of the USA. The China Metallurgical Group (MCC), however, won the Aynak bid, participating also with several other companies in their consortium. These include Jiangxi Copper, the largest copper producer in China, as well as the Zijin Mining Group, which is the largest gold producer in China. MCC is known to have international holdings that are worth only a little over a billion dollars, but with the resources of the Chinese state behind it as well, its financial situation should not be underestimated (Metz, 2007) and its capabilities would seem to be quite large. Thus the Chinese company is reported to be investing $2.9 billion into the project, which has a number of ancillary additions in a massive collateral development scheme that seem to require the backing of the Chinese government. Such additional elements in the successful bid included provision of an onsite copper smelter, a coal mine for power production, a 400-megawatt, coalfired power plant that would also augment the Kabul electric supply, a ground-water system, roads, homes, schools, hospitals, the building of a freight railroad from western China, through Tajikistan to Afghanistan and Pakistan, help for Kabul University, and thousands of new jobs (Synovitz, 2007). Such additions to the bid were beyond the capabilities of the competitor companies, with the result that the MCC bid was successful. Additional reports by people directly involved in the bidding process (Yaeger, 2009), however, also indicate that there was "a perfect storm of tender events," in which the Minister of Mines, Ibrahim Adel, was able to manipulate an exceptionally flawed bidding process to the advantage of MCC. Partlow (2009) also reported that Adel had accepted a $30 million dollar bribe given to him in about December of 2007 in Dubai to ensure the success of the MCC bid which led to his subsequent imprisonment. Smelting of any ore is commonly done as close as possible to the mine to minimize transportation costs of what becomes useless slag left over after processing. In cases, however, where the ore is a rich enough tenor or construction of the smelter is too expensive, then longer transport to smelting may be tolerable. Generally lower grade copper ores such as Aynak may thus need to be smelted in Afghanistan, whereas higher grade Hajigak iron might be transported as far as the Karachi steel mills in Pakistan, although a new effort is underway in Afghanistan to produce steel close to Kabul using local chromite.

15. Ore smelting also requires considerable energy to melt the ore to metal; energy sources can be varied, of course, but in Afghanistan the use of more easily available coal may trump other energy sources such as hydroelectricity that is yet only weakly developed. The plentiful coal in northern Afghanistan could be brought south to Aynak by truck or new rail for smelting, while the return journey north would be of refined metal for delivery to market. Plentiful coking is also available in the north. Alternatively, new coal resources might be developed in the Katawaz Basin along the border with Pakistan to the south, where such resources are expected to be found (SanFilipo, 2005), but this would presumably not involve favorable round-trip transport economics unless combined in some fashion with delivery of Hajigak iron ore into Pakistan. However, until Pakistan's energy crisis is resolved there is little hope for further smelting in the country. It is important to note that China exerts considerable influence in Pakistan and has also invested widely in infrastructure development in Balochistan. The existing Saindak copper-gold mine in the Chaghai district of Balochistan, bordering Iran and Afghanistan, is also operated by the Chinese Metallurgical Construction Corporation (MCC). The Reko Diq copper project nearby which was initially being offered to a joint-venture between a Chinese company

and a Canadian company may also end up falling under Chinese management following negotiations with the Baloch provincial government in 2010.

16. Despite the strong separatist movement in the province and the ongoing rift between the provincial and federal government, there is an opportunity for engagement of China in positive development across borders. Notwithstanding the attacks on Chinese engineers working in Gwadar and the withdrawal of China from the oil refinery project in Gwadar, there is a recognition by Baloch separatists of the strategic importance of China. In one communiqué, following the Chinese decision to withdraw, a Baloch separatist publication stated: "Balochistan needs China as it's one of the permanent members of UN Security Council. China needs Balochistan in future as its international competitiveness depends on steady landline supply of fuel from Balochistani refineries and storage tanks."

17. China's role as a regional power broker and potential mediator in conflict resolution remains strong. The opportunities accorded by Chinese involvement in the Aynak project, their investment in neighboring Iran and their leadership role in the Shanghai Cooperation Organization, deserves greater attention by the United States and Europe. The initial negative reaction from the Aynak tender as well as the outcome from the United States needs to be reevaluated. The terms of the contract according to most international development experts familiar with such contracts are very favorable to Afghanistan in terms of financial arrangements. While there may be some concerns about post-facto environmental and social performance, these can be assuaged by engagement with the Afghan government in monitoring and enforcement of standards. The prospect of Afghanistan being compliant with international efforts at accountability and transparency, such as the Extractive Industries Transparency Initiative

18. will also further strengthen the chances of positive enforcement and monitoring that can strengthen the "social contract" between corporations, foreign investors and the community. The confluence of complementary international interests in mineral development thus has the potential to build trust rather than increasing tensions. Previews of Coming Attractions The pending Hajigak tender offer and the international machinations afoot to gain access to the rich prospects such as the ores of rare earth elements (REE), niobium (Nb), and lithium (Li), in Afghanistan bear watching as attempts are made to gain access to these materials that are so vital to high technology and modern communications (TFBSO, 2011; Becatoros, 2011; Najafizada, 2011). The extinct carbonatite volcano of Kohi Khanneshin in southern Helmand Province is already reliably estimated at a mined value production of some $89 billion, although more precise data from two new field sampling efforts by the U.S. Geological Survey will not be available until fall 2011 to better enable tender offerings. Similarly among a number of other rich resource possibilities in Afghanistan, lithium salts in five dry lake basins scattered throughout the country are estimated at being worth over $60 billion when extracted. To overcome the myriad problems faced by the Afghanistan Ministry of Mines (AMOM) (incompetent and corrupt officials, lack of mining regulations, untrained inspectorate department, antiquated and corrupt cadastral survey of land ownerships, absence of effective environmental regulations or post-mining restoration, lack of effective communication with tribal populations affected by mining), Afghanistan has hired SRK Consulting to undertake the facilitation of this project. In addition, the international law firm of Mayer Brown has been retained, whose core business area is the mining industry, and who will provide, with help from the Canadian legal firm of Heenan Blaikie, day-to-day advice on legal, financial, and operational issues faced by mineral producers, governments, and mineral-industry financiers (Keil, 2011). With the credibility,

transparency, and accountability of such partners, the resource extraction industries in Afghanistan have a real chance of success, although the struggle to overcome the greedy and mendacious bureaucracy will be monumental. Policy Recommendations and Conclusion Moving beyond the trust deficit that theories of hegemonic influence have provided during the past several decades will take policy leadership. No doubt, during the Cold War such theories gained plausible currency and were empirically evident. However, there has been a major shift in the role of the United States and China as two major global powers, which should lead us to challenge old assumptions about hegemony. Other regional states that have recently been considered pariahs, such as Iran, may also be brought into the specter of regional cooperation. However, such policy shifts must also be calibrated with changes in corporate behavior donor assistance and monitoring provisions to ensure environmental and other compliance assurance. Given the historical and contemporary analysis of geopolitics surrounding Afghanistan's mineral development, the international community should consider the following four policy recommendations in this regard: a) The Aynak contract's terms should be considered as a benchmark for revenue sharing, collateral development along with the ore extraction, and accountability, but international financial institutions should ensure that the terms of the agreement are kept as the project develops. The World Bank's program of providing assistance in monitoring this process should be supported by the United States, Japan and the European Union. b) The United States should encourage the development of the TAP pipeline by involving the SCO countries in partnership so Russia and China do not see this as an effort to undermine Russian influence in Turkmenistan. Extending the project to India (TAPI pipeline) would also provide an additional opportunity for Indo-Pak rapprochement. Ali and Shroder, 2011 20 of 24 c) Afghanistan's accession to the EITI should be expedited to ensure that before the Aynak and TAPI projects commence, protocols for revenue transparency can be implemented. Donors should provide targeted assistance to allow for such institutional capacity to develop. d) China's role in the Aynak project, as well as the copper-gold projects in neighboring Pakistan, should be supported by the international community so long as the terms of reference remain transparent and there is ongoing regional engagement. Chinese involvement would also help in cementing Pakistani political support for multinational donor investment in Afghanistan and potentially open opportunities for their role in regional conflict resolution. e) The truly vast mineral wealth of Afghanistan is so potentially "neo-great-gamechanging" through potential revenue production and development as to overcome the war with the Taliban and its safe havens in Pakistan. The White House should commit to a major development effort while restraining the Congressionally generated wrangling with the Department of Defense over a handover to USAID (Chandrasekaran, 2011)

19. At a speech in 1997, Strobe Talbot, the U.S. Deputy Secretary of State, and currently the President of the Brookings Institution stated that while it has been "fashionable to proclaim or at least to predict, a replay of the 'Great Game' in the Caucasus and Central Asia…our goal is to avoid and to actively discourage that atavistic outcome. The Great Game, which starred Kipling's Kim and Fraser's Flashman, was very much of the zerosum variety. What we want to help bring about is just the opposite, we want to see all responsible players in the Caucasus and Central Asia be winners." statement from over a decade ago reflects the kind of rational regionalism that has been argued for in this paper. While such sentiments have not been realized in the context of South and Central Asia, the overall potential for pipelines as a source of conflict resolution remains promising and deserves greater attention by scholars of international relations and policy-makers alike.

Data Sources, Processing, and Accuracy

Data on more than 1000 Afghanistan deposits, mines, and occurrences were compiled from published literature and digital files of the project members of the National Industrial Minerals project of the U.S. Geological Survey (USGS). The data include information on metals, nonmetals, construction materials, coal, and peat. Three previous compilations of Afghanistan mineral resources were the dominant sources used for this effort. In 1995, the United Nation's Economic and Social Commission for Asia and the Pacific published a summary of the geology and mineral resources of Afghanistan as part of their Atlas of Mineral Resources series. This document included a summary table and text descriptions of the major mineral mines, deposits, and areas; however, there are numerous spelling and location inconsistencies between table listings and text descriptions. The text descriptions provide geologic and resource information about many of the sites. A second source compilation for this report was Gemstones of Afghanistan (Bowersox and Chamberlin, 1995), published by Geoscience Press, Inc., of Tucson, Arizona. A table at the end of the book lists mineral occurrences by commodity, including metals and nonmetals, with latitude and longitude. The table contains substantial duplication as sites with multiple commodities are listed multiple times and there are numerous spelling inconsistencies. The text of this book is largely limited to descriptions of the gem districts of Afghanistan. Many of the individual mines listed in the text are not included in the summary table of this publication, although the major gem districts are in the table. Locations in Appendix A that were identified 4 only in Bowersox and Chamberlin (1995) during the compilation of this table are marked with an The descriptions of the starred locations, consisting of a name, commodity, and location, are protected by copyright; the right to reproduce these locations was granted to the USGS by Geoscience Press. The conditions of reproduction stipulate that these rights are non-exclusive world rights and that notice of the title and authors be specified. The starred locations from Bowersox and Chamberlin (1995) are covered by the following copyright: "No part of this book may be reproduced by any mechanical, photographic, or electronic process, or in the form of a phonographic recording, nor may it be stored in a retrieval system, transmitted, or otherwise copied for public use, without written permission from the publisher." The most complete compilation of Afghanistan's mineral resources is Mineral Resources of Afghanistan by Abdullah and others (1977). With few exceptions, the data listed in the ESCAP (1995) publication and Bowersox and Chamberlin (1995) table of mineral resources appear to be excerpted from this earlier compilation; the spelling inconsistencies and typographical errors of Abdullah and others are frequently duplicated in the later compilations. Both of the later compilations are missing much of the geologic detail contained in the 1977 compilation, but do contain some "present day" information not found in Abdullah and others. We should also note at this point that Abdullah and others (1977) is also referenced as Shareq and others (1977). This confusion arises from the publication having two title pages. One title page begins the list of "Abdullah Shareq, V.M. Chmyriov,..."; the other title page begins the list of. Abdullah, V.M. Chmyriov, We have chosen to use "Abdullah" as the last name because several citations in the mineral descriptions cite "Abdullah" and none cite "Shareq". Also, in the reference list of the 1977 publication, there is an author listed as "Abdullah, S.", but there is no "Shareq". Additional geologic and commodity information came from USGS files and about a dozen other published sources. For the most part, all data were recorded as reported in the references unless there were inconsistencies that could be reconciled from the available data. Where information reported from two or more sources were in conflict, the authors utilized the nformation from Abdullah and others (1977) and noted the inconsistencies. The data were checked for duplicates using names, locations, and commodity. Historic province names were replaced with current province names using latitude and longitude information using a paper map. No attempt was made to identify further errors. 5 DATA -The mines and mineral occurrences of Afghanistan are listed in a table as Appendix A of this publication. The table is divided into 3 parts; Pegmatite Fields, Named Sites & Deposits, and Sites and Deposits Without Names. The latter 2 categories include deposits, active and inactive mines of a variety of scales, prospects, and showings. The data fields for Appendix A include: Locality/Deposit Name Synonyms and Other Names or Spellings Deposit or District Name Province Latitude Longitude Commodity (s) Type of Deposit Status Host Rock Age Host Rock Significant Minerals or Materials Deposit Size and (or) Grade Comments References Decimal Latitude Decimal Longitude. The Locality/Deposit Name field contains the name of the mine, deposit, field, area, or occurrence being described. Synonyms and Other Names or Spellings contains alternative names or spellings for the site. For a deposit or area, this field might also 6 include any specific mine or occurrence names that are known, i.e. "includes Northern and 30ᵗʰ mines". The Deposit or District Name field contains the name of any larger deposit, field, or district to which the site belongs. The Afghanistan Province in which the site lies is the next field. Federal Information Processing Standards (FIPS) spellings were used in Appendix A (National Institute of Standards and Technology, 1995). Table 1 contains a list of all the Provinces in Afghanistan plus alternative spellings and historic names known to the authors. Latitude and longitude are listed in degrees, minutes, and seconds. Large fields or deposits may have a range specified in the Latitude or Longitude fields, i.e. "34-00N to 34-10N". In other cases, a deposit may have 2 orebodies with differing locations. In this case, the multiple latitudes and longitudes are separated by a semi-colon, i.e. "34-00N; 34-10N." The Commodity Field lists the commodities known to occur at each site. A list of commodity abbreviations may be found in table 2. The following field, Type of Deposit, contains a deposit type or style of mineralization. The Status field contains information on whether the site has produced and when or if it is a mineral occurrence or showing. Host Rock Age and Host Rock contain appropriate descriptions of host rocks and other significant rock units, such as nearby igneous rocks that are related to the mineralization. The main minerals or materials are listed under Significant Minerals or Materials and any deposit size or grade information is listed in the following field. The four remaining fields in Appendix A are a Comments field for any additional information, References, and Decimal Latitudes-Longitudes. Readers and users of the data should be aware that English spelling of the place names is highly variable within the source materials; many are English translations of Russian versions of Afghan names. In addition, the use of singular and plurals in the geologic descriptions is erratic. If the source(s) specified a number of veins or orebodies, that number was included in Appendix A of this publication. In many other cases, it was commonly unclear if there was one or more mineralized areas or bodies. Lastly, there is additional data in Abdullah and others (1977), including the locations of mineral haloes, that are not included in this publication.

Table 1. Provinces of Afghanistan. Province Alternate spellings and names, including historical names Badakhshan Badahsan Badghis Badgis Baghlan Baglan Bactrian Balkh Balh Bamian Bamyan, Bamiyan Farah Fahrah Faryab Fariab Ghazni Gazni Ghowr Ghor, Gawr, Ghawr, Gor Helmand Hilmend Aria Herat Jowzjan, Jawzjan, Jozjan, Juzjan Kabol Kabul Kandahar Qandahar Kapisa Kapesa, Kapissa Konar Kunar, Konarh, Konarha, Nuristan Kondoz Kunduz, Konduz, Qunduz, Qonduz Laghman Lagman, Nuristan Lowgar Lawgar, Lawghar, Logar, Loghar, Lowghar Nangarhar Ningarhar Nimruz Chakhansur, Neemroze, Nimroz, Nimroze Oruzgan Uruzgan, Oruzghan, Uruzghan Paktia Paktiya Paktika Parvan Parwan Samangan Samanghan Sar-e Pol Sar-e Pul, Sari Pol, Sar-i Pol Takhar Tahar Vardak Warkak, Wardak, Wardag, Wardagh, Maydan

Zabol Zabul Afghanistan has become the first country whose surface minerals have been mapped from the air. The US Geological Survey released the results of a "hyperspectral imaging" effort, in which reflections of light from the ground are analysed. Different minerals - as well as snow or vegetation - reflect specific colours, resulting in a "mineral map". The map comprises more than 100 trillion dollars data points corresponding to an area of 440,000 sq km, some 70% of the country. Afghanistan is known to have vast reserves of oil, gas, copper, cobalt, gold and lithium. In late 2011, a consortium of Indian companies inked a deal to begin mining some of the country's large stores of iron. But the country is known to have a wider array of mineral resources; in 2010, the Afghan ministry of mines claimed a value of its reserves of nearly a trillion dollars, then carrying out tours to promote investment in them. But it remains to pin down which economically viable minerals are where, an effort for which the USGS's hyperspectral imaging expertise was enlisted. In a series of 28 flights over 43 days, the USGS gathered the data from a height of 15,000m, using a camera to capture sunlight reflected from the ground. Each "pixel" of the camera was analysed and correlated with the materials that reflect at a given colour. The USGS public release of the data includes two maps: one of iron and iron-bearing minerals, and one of minerals principally containing carbon, silicon, or sulphur. The survey was funded by the US Department of Defense's Task Force for Business and Stability Operations (TFBSO) as well as the Afghan government. "This is a tremendous tool for the Afghan government for locating and identifying its myriad rich mineral deposits," said TFBSO director Jim Bullion. "These maps clearly show the enormous size and variety of Afghanistan's mineral wealth and position the country to become a world leader in the minerals sector." The geologic and mineral resource information shown on this map is derived from digitization of the original data from Abdullah and Chmyriov (1977) and Abdullah and others (1977). The U.S. Geological Survey (USGS) has made no attempt to modify original geologic map-unit boundaries and faults as presented in Abdullah and Chmyriov (1977); however, modifications to map-unit symbology, and minor modifications to map-unit descriptions, have been made to clarify lithostratigraphy and to modernize terminology. Labeling of map units has not been attempted where they are small or narrow, in order to maintain legibility and to preserve the map's utility in illustrating regional geologic and structural relations. Users are encouraged to refer to the series of USGS/AGS (Afghan Geological Survey) 1:250,000-scale geologic quadrangle maps of Afghanistan that are being released concurrently as open-file reports. The classification of mineral deposit types is based on the authors' interpretation of existing descriptive information (Abdullah and others, 1977; Bowersox and Chamberlin, 1995; Orris and Bliss, 2002) and on limited field investigations by the authors. Deposit-type nomenclature used for nonfuel minerals is modified from published USGS deposit-model classifications, as compiled in Stoeser and Heran (2000). New petroleum localities are based on research of archival data by the authors. The shaded-relief base is derived from Shuttle Radar Topography Mission (SRTM) digital elevation model (DEM) data having 85-meter resolution. Gaps in the original SRTM DEM dataset were filled with data digitized from contours on 1:200,000-scale Soviet General Staff Sheets (1978–1997). The marginal extent of geologic units corresponds to the position of the international boundary as defined by Abdullah and Chmyriov (1977), and the international boundary as shown on this map was acquired from the Afghanistan Information Management Service (AIMS) Web site (http://www.aims.org.af) in September 2005. Non-coincidence of these boundaries is due to differences in the respective data sources and to inexact registration of the geologic data to the DEM base. Province boundaries, province capital locations, and political names were also acquired from the AIMS Web site in September 2005. The AIMS data were originally derived from maps produced by the Afghanistan Geodesy and Cartography Head Office (AGCHO). Version 2 differs from Version 1 in that (1) map units are colored according to the color scheme of the Commission for the Geological Map of the

456

World (CGMW) (http://www.ccgm.org), (2) the minerals database has been updated, and (3) all data presented on the map are also available in GIS format It is obvious that there is no military solution to the struggle in Afghanistan; therefore a political solution could be on the horizon. So far that too has proven to be a failing effort when the Taliban, who were supposedly partaking in the recent consultative Loya-Jirgah gathering in an effort to reconcile in Kabul, answered instead with a barrage of explosive attacks that consequently disrupted the council. So, what else is on the table to justify the war in Afghanistan and keep the government of Hamid Karzai afloat? Apparently the US military brass and Mr. Karzai did some brain storming recently, and they were in approval of introducing another plan by giving the tip off of vastly untapped mineral deposits in the Hindu-Kush mountains of the Central Asian state; which quickly jumped from $1 trillion value to $3 trillion in a matter of 36 hours. There are many legitimate questions as to whether the mineral deposits are authentic or a hoaxed, but the fact remains, many Afghans and many people in the West are not accepting this joint U.S.-Afghan government idea.

Afghanistan Minerals

However, another way of looking at all this is that finally after decades of war some good news about Afghanistan has finally raised to the surface; it could be an omen to all that beneath the landmines, Afghanistan is sitting on a goldmine. This information sounds rather astonishing; it leads us to assume that Afghanistan has actually hit the jackpot in the world's economy arena. However, the $1 trillion figure, where did it come from? It appears highly misleading. It is a theoretical number and may have little relation to the value of resources that could actually be exploited. Furthermore, it will be of little benefit to Afghanistan if its $100 trillion resources would cost $200 trillion or more to dig up. Thus, to justify the validity of this perception, —which apparently lacked proper homework—the figure was immediately increased to $300 trillion; apparently the first figure did not sound awesome enough. This suspiciously round number appears to be based on geological surveys made decades ago as well as recent on the ground and in the air 3 dimensional ground scanning technology. How thorough it really has been is an open debate, given that it takes the world's best miners about a decade to explore a new area. Even if there were $300 trillion of mineral resources in Afghanistan, and even if those resources were economically feasible, it would be years before a large Western miner establishment could get anywhere near the country. They currently have no intention of moving into Afghanistan because the risk is far greater than the reward. The investment would be too risky anywhere the Afghan government does not control; plus all the territory and contract laws are far from solid. The only people who might show interest in exploring the aforementioned mineral deposits are the Chinese, but they had to abandon a far simpler project than the untapped Afghan treasures; the Kajaki's Helmand Province hydroelectric dam project was forsaken due to a lack of security in the area.

Conclusion

There are vague hypothesis attached to this recent joint perception of mineral wealth announced by the US and Afghan governments. Is it time to change course and divert attention from the failed hearts and minds operation in Marjah, the failed reconciliation Jirga, failed opium eradication, the stalled Kandahar operation, Mr. Karzai's tantrums, the Afghan government corruption, thriving drug trafficking, warlordism, Kandahar's power brokers, fraudulent presidential elections, heightened insurgency, Pakistan's uncooperative effort to contain the Taliban on its soil, regional powers proxy wars, so on and so forth? Some in the West share the mining industry's skepticism that massive amounts of mineral wealth could be easily extracted from Afghanistan's rugged mountains and remote regions. This is believed to be in conjunction with the growing public sentiment that the war is not worth the cost. Similarly, some Afghans, view that the era of past colonial manipulation of Afghan society, thought and sensibility is once again repeating itself. If so, then the public sentiment will be far damning than now. In any event, time is of the essence for either success or failure in Afghanistan. Unfortunately, so far, the momentum has been on the path of failure. If there is vast mineral wealth in Afghanistan, then the world needs to realize that this wealth belongs to the Afghan people. There are Afghans around the world with the skills and knowledge to do this job themselves on behalf of the people of Afghanistan. A good friend of my family speaks about how decades of fighting has left the Afghan people with physical and mental health issues that no one is addressing. What is needed today is an Afghan to Afghan initiative that takes charge of the research and development of any potential mineral and mining deposits first and foremost for the benefit of those Afghans who have suffered from abuse and neglect on their own home soil over the decades. We expatriate Afghans need to look out for our brothers and sisters in Afghanistan who are not aware of 21st Century methodologies, ideologies and technologies that can rob them of their inheritance. It is our job to protect and enlighten fellow Afghans who are at risk. Monday, June 27 – According to officials in the ministry of mines of Afghanistan, a number of Afghan mines and minerals samples will be introduced to world investors in Londin in coming two days. The officials further added that the minerals and mines will be exhibited in a three day summit which is going to be held in london. Besides a number of accredited investors who are going participate in this exhibition, a number of heads of banks will also take part in the exhibition to hear about Afghan mines. The summit is going to be be held on coming Tuesday. In this summit, Badakhshan Gold Mine, Ghazni's Zarafshan Gold Mine, Herat ALithium Salt Mine, Balkhab copper mine, and other countries' oil reserves will be introduced. According to Jawad Omar, a spokesman for Afghan Ministry of Mines, a number of world investors and banks which are supporting the mining projects requested for the exhibition of Afghan minerals and mines once again in London. On the basis of the their request the symposium is once again going to be held from 28 to 30 June in London city. On the other hand, Afghan ministry of mines recently has signed an agreement with Germany for the cooperation and development of Afghan minerals. Mr. Omar further added, "both the countries will step up efforts on investments in Afghanistan will coordinate new programmes to encourage German investors for investments in Afghanistan." Based on the agreement Germany, will support Afghanistan to establish educational sectors in Gas and Oil, extraction of mineral resources, encouraging investors and preparing educational programmes on Afghan mines, According to Afghan Ministry of Mines The prospect of cobalt in Kandahar has sparked lively debate about whether new mineral wealth— if it pans out — will aid or hinder U.S. policies in Afghanistan, as well as whether the country will fall prey to the so-called resource curse, as political scientist

Michael Ross and others fear. But a short-term focus on Afghan-U.S. relations might be a mistake: The real winner from new natural-resource wealth beyond the Khyber Pass will be China. If the United States really cares about stabilizing Afghanistan's central government and eliminating terrorist havens, it needs to start working now to persuade Beijing that these are shared goals. First, some background: Chinese foreign investment and aid has accelerated dramatically over the past decade, especially in Africa. In November 2009 alone, for example, China's largesse amounted to $10 billion in low-interest loans and $1 billion in commercial loans to the continent. With Beijing as cheerleader, trade has soared from $1 billion in 1992 to $106.8 billion in 2008. In part this is due to China's willingness to do business with undemocratic, corrupt, and brutal regimes — for example, in the Democratic Republic of the Congo (DRC), Sudan, and Zimbabwe. The DRC provides the bestcautionary parallel to Afghanistan: The discovery in the late 1990s of copper, coltan, and other minerals in eastern Congo gave new life to a civil war that has now claimed upwards of 4 million lives. Flagging combatants were funded by mineral extraction, and much of those resources eventually flowed to China. The fact that violence is still simmering in eastern Congo — and despite the costs that extraction imposes on the Congolese people — has not been enough to deter Beijing from wooing Congo's government for access to the country's abundant resources. So, if there's any thought that war in Afghanistan might dissuade Chinese investment there, it's best to dispense with that notion immediately. China, which has a narrow land border with Afghanistan, already invests heavily in the war-torn Central Asian state. The state-owned China Metallurgical Group has a $3.5 billion copper mining venture in Logar province. Chinese companies ZTE and Huawei are building digital telephone switches, providing roughly 200,000 subscriber lines in Afghanistan. Even back in the war's early days in 2002 and 2003, when he worked in Afghanistan, the Chinese presence was acutely visible in Kabul, with Chinese laborers on many building sites and Chinese-run restaurants and guesthouses popping up all over the city. As Robert Kaplan has pointed out, these investments come with a gratuitous hidden subsidy from the United States — which has defrayed the enormous costs of providing security amid war and looting. With its massive wealth, appetite for risk, and willingness to underbid others on labor costs and human rights conditionality, China is the odds-on favorite for development of any new Afghan mineral resources. Chinese firms will control the flow of new funds, and the way those funds are distributed between the central and local governments. It's all well and good that Barack Obama's administration has recommitted to building civil projects in rural Afghanistan, but consider the relative scale of building a school to establishing a multimillion-dollar mine (not to mention the transport networks and infrastructure required to get the extracted minerals out) and it's easy to see what kind of influence the Chinese will bring to the table. It is critical for Washington to start making the case to Chinese leaders that pure self-interest mandates they leverage this power wisely — to promote stability, not catalyze new conflict, in Afghanistan. So far, China's investment in Logar has been in keeping with its "noninterventionist" foreign policy and was accompanied by development aid, but no overt political strings. Washington must require more from Beijing, however, to avoid upending all its hard-won gains. The Obama administration has already asked China to contribute troops to the Afghan effort. This is a good first step, but a few hundred token soldiers will not make China a strategic partner in its Afghan campaign. It needs to persuade Beijing that the campaign is indeed China's campaign, too — if not by touting democracy promotion and human rights, then surely economic benefit — and that U.S. and Chinese strategies on Afghanistan converge. This is not as hard as it sounds: As China-Africa expert Deborah Brautigam's careful work shows, China has on some occasions acted as a surprisingly responsible lender, for example using resource-backed infrastructure loans that force some gains to be reinvested in development. Although many have warned of a new Sino-colonialism, Brautigam's work suggests that perhaps China's awareness of its gargantuan and growing need for foreign export markets will make it a better "colonial" power than any European country ever was. For China as much as the United States, the goal of a stable, central Afghan government that provides no haven for terrorists is a desirable goal. China has worried in the past about whether Afghanistan might provide a refuge for Uighur separatists. Leaving aside the ethics and wisdom of Chinese policies in the Uighur community's home region of Xinjiang, it's safe to say that Washington and Beijing share a common goal in preventing terrorism. Both countries would benefit from a stabilized government in Kabul that is able to command the loyalty and respect of provincial governments and populations. That, however, requires that Hamid Karzai's government deal with its endemic corruption problem. And though no one expects Afghanistan to turn into Norway, perhaps it can be nudged away from the DRC path and toward the model of a Saudi Arabia or a Kazakhstan. When it comes to corruption, however, state-run Chinese firms have not seemed troubled by greasing the wheels of power brokers in Sudan, Zimbabwe, or elsewhere. Getting Beijing to understand the rot this breeds seems a hard sell for the Obama administration. If that fails, however, Chinese ears might perk up somewhat at the mention of how integral a stable central government in Kabul is to the security of Pakistan, a close ally of Beijing. Stability in Pakistan should be an important goal for China. It is by now clear that the Taliban's campaign west of the Durand Line is inextricable from the destabilizing efforts of Islamist militants in Pakistan. If China does not want another nuclear basket case on its border, then it should care deeply about instability in Afghanistan. Currently, however, Beijing is still freeloading, relying on Washington to provide security for its limited interests. Perhaps the tantalizing prospect of $1 trillion in minerals might be enough to change the strategic equation. Working together, China and the United States have a better chance of guiding Afghanistan to a happy outcome for all than will Washington on its own. To be sure, this is no easy task: There's plenty of evidence that aid conditionality by Western governments has not done as much good as hoped. But cold economic realities dictate that Chinese firms are likely going to be the big players in this new gold rush, and Washington had better wake up to the fact that it has a short window in which to convince Beijing to collaborate in making Kabul a better place. The potential of Afghanistan's mineral resources has long been known. Although there have been few systematic and detailed geological studies for some 25 years, it is likely that Afghanistan's mineral wealth is worth at least several hundred billion dollars. In 2008 mining rights at Aynak, a large-scale copper mine in Logar province, were awarded to a consortium led by MCC (China Metallurgical Group Corporation). In November 2011 three blocks of mining rights at Hajigak, a large iron-ore deposit, were awarded to AFISCO (Afghan Iron and Steel Consortium), a consortium led by the Steel Authority of India (SAIL), and one block to Kilo Goldmines of Canada. Afghanistan's current mineral production is very modest by global standards. In the mining sector there are no large commercial scale mines, although some smaller state-owned coal mines do constitute the highest payer of taxes among all government enterprises nationwide. There is mostly artisanal and small scale mining for construction minerals, dimension stone (marble) and gemstones. In the hydrocarbons sector there is some modest gas production and some very small oil production. Afghanistan has two presently known world class mineral deposits – the Aynak copper deposit and the Hajigak iron ore deposit. Afghanistan also has good potential for other minerals including gold and has substantial gemstone potential; but the country has not realized any modern exploration surveys in more than 30 years and so the information base is antiquated and sure to under-estimate the total mineral endowment. Moreover, Afghanistan does lie within several large regional trends for copper, iron ore and precious metals; and most certainly has the potential for additional world-class deposits in this regard. Regarding hydrocarbons, Afghanistan has substantial known undeveloped gas deposits at Sherbegon and also some modest oil potential. Mineral and hydrocarbon developments can be a pillar of future economic growth in Afghanistan creating both direct and indirect employment and income; developing transport and other infrastructure which will help open up areas for overall economic development; and generating not only considerable domestic revenue but also trade and balance of payments benefits. Simply put, if managed properly, mining in Afghanistan has the potential to be a driver of poverty reduction and sustained economic growth. Mines not only directly contribute significant taxes, income and other benefits streams directly to the economy but also contribute indirectly through stimulus of various economic activities. For instance, in other countries it has been demonstrated that every direct job created by a mining operation can result in as many as five to ten indirect and induced jobs by providing contracts for numerous small businesses and services which supply the mine. Each of these jobs in turn produces taxes and other expenditures which pass through the economy Aynak and Hajigak would be, by a wide margin, the two largest investments in the history of Afghanistan. The mine developments would require US$2-3 billion invest and each mine would also require investment in ancillary infrastructure in the order of US$2-3 billion or more. A low-impact scenario, based on prevailing market conditions, projects that Aynak and Hajigak could create more than 90,000 direct and indirect jobs, and approximately $500 million in annual fiscal revenues by 2020. In other mineral rich countries, hasn't mining had few spillover benefits Doesn't it lead to a 'resource curse' Yes, but that is the point of launching a program to overcome these. Afghanistan can and should launch efforts to overcome this. That mining has not created spillover effects in some countries does not mean it never will or can. After all, one of the primary triggers that economic historians have identified for the industrial revolution was the development of coal and iron in European 'resource corridors' in the 19th century. More recently, Chile has induced a large amount of development around its large copper deposits, and various other countries are starting to put their resources to more effective use. With regards to the 'resource curse', while the phenomenon is well established for Sub-Saharan Africa in the last four to five decades, there are questions as to how prevalent it has been in other regions. More specifically, one of the key mechanisms of the 'resource curse', that is exchange rate appreciation or 'Dutch Disease', are not expected to be an impact in Afghanistan, given the country's already very large current account deficits. If the resource sector's fiscal effects, infrastructure and demand for goods and services can be leveraged, it has the capacity to transform the Afghan economy, through: Fiscal effects: Afghanistan's large mining projects will have a material effect on the government's fiscal sustainability. It is projected that Aynak could generate around US$500 million annually in direct and indirect government revenue by 2015 and Hajigak about US$400-500 million by around 2020. Infrastructure: The extraction of natural resources itself is a major revenue source, but the increase in growth will be associated more with the infrastructure supported by these mining investments. At Aynak, for example, MCC is building a 400 MW thermal power plant with 50% of this power contractually to be provided to the grid at cost. The mines will also require or motivate large investments in transport infrastructure and regional trade which could be leveraged to create public goods that support other sectors. Livelihoods: If the mining infrastructure investments are buttressed by incremental catalytic investments in feeder and rural roads, agriculture and the agribusiness industry could benefit and become a more substantial source of income and jobs for rural communities and urban areas. The mines will also be a source of demand for the manufacturing and services sectors. If local firms can upgrade to supply competitive goods and services, they could capture a portion of the US$4 – 10 billion of investment (depending on the infrastructure built). Once operational, the mines might also lead to downstream activity. For example, AFISCO (the consortium developing three of the four Hajigak deposits) has already declared it will build a large-scale steel mill (up to 6 million tons p.a.), if it can secure sovereign guarantees. What are the Main Challenges and Constraints Although some progress has been achieved, major challenges (besides improving the security situation) still lie ahead. The program will therefore help the Government address the following issues, as part of an integrated strategy: Infrastructure development (road, rail, power, water, ICT) to leverage private investment into public goods, through PPP when possible. Infrastructure development (in particular rail) requires regional coordination (with neighboring countries), a multimodal approach, and combining hard and soft infrastructure for maximum benefits (e.g., transport routes should be complemented with trade facilitation services). Operations and maintenance (O&M) requirements must also be assessed, especially since other work has already identified O&M expenses as a key driver of Afghanistan's financing gap; Social and environmental issues: These include providing immediate benefits for communities around the corridor. It also requires attention to improved land administration including: a) cadastre for all land within the resource corridor, b) rationalization of land management and c) revised legal frameworks for land acquisition, resettlement and compensation. Other issues, such as mitigating environmental impacts, building the capacity of NEPA (the National Environmental Protection Agency), and the preservation of cultural heritage and archeological sites also need to be addressed; Private sector development along the mining value chain (e.g., creating public-private mechanisms to upgrade the capabilities of the local private sector and hence enable greater local procurement from the mining investments); as well as agriculture and agribusiness along the corridor (to take advantage of new or revamped infrastructure); and improving skills (both for advanced skills and within the broader workforce, in the short and long term); Governance and institutional arrangements to enable successful implementation of the resource growth corridor approach. This will include capacity building, means for institutional collaboration among sector ministries and across central to decentralized levels down to the community level, and strengthened public financial management (especially regarding mineral revenues). The main counterpart will be the Ministry of Mines which is responsible for the extractive industries, and is the lead ministry for the NRRCP and for the Infrastructure Cluster of NPPs. The proposed NRRCP Secretariat, under the leadership of the Minister of Mines, will be the focal point within the Ministry and should work across ministerial boundaries. It is expected that the Ministry of Public Works (MoPW), the Ministry of Transport and Civil Aviation (MoTCA), the Ministry of Commerce and Industries (MoCI), the Ministry of Agriculture, Irrigation and Livestock (MAIL), the Ministry of Rural Rehabilitation and Development (MRRD) and the Ministry of Energy and Water (MEW) will be engaged in various facets of the corridor approach. The Ministry of Finance (MoF) could play a role in its monitoring and evaluation. The private sector participants in resource extraction projects under development and/or related infrastructure projects and the local communities will be key partners in the approach. The stakeholders include relevant civil society and private sector bodies, and the wider donor community. As a starting point, the program will use the large number of independent donor studies (notably from the US Government, DFID and ADB who have been particularly involved in the mining and transport sectors) in order to leverage the significant technical work undertaken throughout the last ten years. What about all the uncertainty surrounding the country, the investments, etc.? Doesn't this risk being just a report on the shelf – a plan for futures that never come to be Exactly for this reason, the strategy will be modular and flexible, both to enable rapid action and to avoid making the benefits reliant on any single component. Mining and infrastructure projects in any environment are known for delivering late: copper production globally is 15% less than forecast due to the inability to meet ambitious expansion targets. Given the lack of an updated cadastre and unclear and lengthy land acquisition and resettlement processes, as well as pervasive security concerns, the risk of delay to the mines and their associated infrastructure is significant. It would therefore be prudent to elaborate development plans in such a way that some activities can proceed even in the event of major investments being significantly delayed. As a near-term priority, the aim should be to exploit investments in a more advanced stage as early as possible (e.g., Aynak mine and associated investments), while also, to the extent possible, taking into consideration further likely major investments (e.g. Hajigak mine). Even without the full realization of the mining investments, reforms introduced will help the economy and the local population. This modular approach also greatly reduces the risks as improvements are delivered along the way rather than only at the time that the large investment comes online. Overall, the project will draw on some of the world's leading experts in designing strategies and making decisions to cope with high uncertainty. What are the main environmental, social and cultural dimensions being addressed. One of the major challenges is to avoid conflicts at the community level, which may arise due to insufficient communication and outreach or through non-compliance to contractual obligations. Communication and outreach are being improved through the development of a communications plan and appointment of communications professionals to oversee implementation of the plan. Compliance monitoring will be in place and help to minimize this risk. Extractive resource projects that fail to deliver societal benefits through poor design or weak implementation, often fail. To reinforce environmental and social sustainability, inclusion of civil society in planning and implementation is being encouraged. The social specialists Bank have been working with the government to get a proper resettlement action plan completed and including public disclosure and consultation with affected communities. With support from the Bank, the Ministry of Mines (a) has established an ombudsman's office to receive any grievances that may arise and (b) is engaging civil society organizations at the community level to increase transparency of the resettlement process and strengthen communication with the community. The Aynak site contains rich archeological sites including a Buddhist monastery. A French archeological team has been taking the lead, along with the Ministry of Culture, to document and preserve the antiquities. Mining in Afghanistan rapidly expanded in the last decade after the Karzai administration came to power. Major mining activities are monitored and supervised by the Ministry of Mines and Industry in Kabul. Afghanistan has over 90 mineral fields, containing barite, chromite, coal, copper, gold, iron, ore lead, natural gas, petroleum, precious and semiprecious stones, salt, sulfur, talc, zinc among many other minerals. Precious and semiprecious stones include high-quality emerald, lapis lazuli, red garnet and ruby. It is believed that the country holds up to $3 trillion in untapped mineral deposits. There are six lapis mines in Afghanistan, the largest being located in northern Badakhshan province. That area is also home to one of the biggest gold mines in the country. Based on some information there are around 12 copper mines in Afghanistan, including the Aynak copper deposit located in Logar province. Afghanistan's significance from an energy standpoint stems from its geographical position as a potential transit route for oil and natural gas exports from Central Asia to the Arabian Sea. This potential includes the construction of the Trans-Afghanistan Pipeline gas pipeline. The first Afghan oil production began in October 2012 It is estimated that forty million years ago the tectonic plates of India-Europe, Asia and Africa collided in a massive upheaval. This upheaval created the region of towering mountains that now includes Afghanistan. This diverse geological foundation has resulted in a significant mineral heritage with over 1,400 mineral occurrences recorded to date, including gold, copper, lithium, uranium, iron ore, cobalt, natural gas and oil. Afghanistan's resources could make it the richest mining region on earth. Afghanistan has large untapped energy and mineral resources, which have great potential to contribute to the country's economic development and growth. The major mineral resources include chromium, copper, gold, iron ore, lead and zinc, lithium, marble, precious and semiprecious stones, sulfur and talc among'st many other minerals. The energy resources consist of natural gas and petroleum. the government was working to introduce new mineral and hydrocarbon laws that would meet international standards of governance. The U.S. geological survey (USGS) and the British geological survey were doing resource estimation work in the country. Prior to that work, Afghanistan's exploration activity had been conducted by geologists from the Soviet Union who left good-quality geologic records that indicate significant mineral potential. Resource development would require improvements in the infrastructure and security in Afghanistan. the government had awarded contracts to develop the Aynak copper project and the hajigak iron ore project; in addition, the government could offer tenders for new exploration, including exploration of copper at Balkhab, gold at Badakhshan, gemstones and lithium at nuristan, and oil and gas at sheberghan. The Ministry of Mines drew up its first business reform plan in a bid to create a more accountable and transparent mining industry. Afghanistan joined the Extractive industries transparency initiative as a candidate country. It was expected that after 5 years, the contribution of royalties from mineral production to the revenues of the government would be at least $1.2 billion per year, and that after 15 years, the contribution would increase to $3.5 billion per year[6]. Afghanistan has no local ownership requirements and its Constitution does not allow for nationalization. The 20% corporate tax rate was the lowest in the region. Afghanistan's mining industry was at a primitive artisanal stage of development; the operations were all low scale and output was supplied to local and regional markets. The government considered development of the country's mineral resources to be a priority for economic growth, including development of the industrial mineral resources (such as gravel, sand, and limestone for cement) for use by the domestic construction industry. investment in infrastructure and transportation projects for mining was a critical aspect of developing the mining industry. The Government completed Afghanistan's first railway with an investment of $170 million by the end of 2010. The 76-kilometer (km) route would link Mazar-i-sharif to the extensive rail networks in Uzbekistan and Turkmenistan. For the first part of the project, which was funded by the Asian Development Bank ($165 million) and other sources ($5 million), 32 km of track had been laid by the Uzbek national rail company, Uzbekistan temir Yollari, from hairatan on the Uzbek border to Mazar-i-sharif. The new route would allow Afghan exporters to transport minerals and other goods into Europe. Metallurgical group Corp. of China (MCC) also planned to build a railroad to transport copper ore in Afghanistan from Aynak to Kabul Production Owing to the lack of mineral production data reported by the miners, information about Afghanistan's mining activities was not readily available, but they appeared to be limited in scope. Production of Barite was estimated by the USGS to be about 2,000 metric tons; chromite, 6,000 tons; and natural gas liquids, 45,000 barrels. In the process of reconstruction and infrastructure development, output of construction minerals was estimated to have increased to meet the domestic requirements. Production of cement increased by 13% compared with that of 2009.

Structure of the Mineral Industry in Afghanistan

Privatization of Afghanistan's state-owned companies, which controlled many of the country's mineral resources, was ongoing but not complete. Investment in the mining sector by private domestic companies and foreign investors was encouraged by the Government, which had offered the first contract for development of the Aynak copper project to two Chinese companies in 2007. the government also issued the tenders for the development of the hajigak iron ore project in 2009 and tenders for oil and gas exploration in 2010. the Ministry of Mines is involved in the exploration for and development, exploitation, and processing of minerals and hydrocarbons. The Ministry is also responsible for protecting the ownership and regulating the transportation and marketing of mineral resources in accordance with the country's new laws. Regulations to clarify the country's environmental laws were scheduled for adoption in 2010. The last mining boom in Afghanistan was over 2,000 years ago in the era of Alexander the Great, when gold, silver and precious stones were routinely mined. Geologists have known of the extent of the mineral wealth for over a century, as a result of surveys done by the British and Russians. An American company was offered a mining concession over the entire country in the 1930s but turned it down. Despite this historical knowledge, global interest was only really boosted in 2010 when the Pentagon commissioned a report from the US Geological Survey (USGS). Historical mining concentrated mostly on precious stone production, with some of the oldest known mines in the world believed to have been established in Afghanistan. Lapis lazuli was being mined in the Badakhshan province of Afghanistan as early as the 3rd millennium BC In ancient Egypt, lapis lazuli was a favorite stone for amulets and ornaments such as **scarabs** and was used in Egypt's pyramids; it was also used in ancient Mesopotamia by the Sumerians, Akkadians, Assyrians, Babylonians for seals and at neolithic burials in Mehrgarh, During the height of the Indus valley civilization about 2000 BC, the Harappan colony now known as Shortugai was established near the lapis mines... Lapis jewelry has been found at excavations of the Predynastic Egyptian site Naqada (3300–3100 BC), and powdered lapis was used as eyeshadow by Cleopatra In ancient Mesopotamia, Lapis artifacts can be found in great abundance, with many notable examples having been excavated at the Royal Cemetery of Ur (2600-2500 BC). The mine of Aynak's copper has more than 2,000 years of history, from the coins and the tools that were found there. The gold of Zarkashan has more than 2,000 years of history in Ghazni Province. Afghanistan's ruby/spinel mines were mentioned in the Arabic writings of many early travellers, including Istakhri (951 AD), Ibn Haukal (978 AD), al-Ta'Alibi (961–1038 AD), al-Muqaddasi (ca 10th century), al-Biruni (b. 973; d. ca 1050 AD), Teifaschi (1240 AD), and Ibn Battuta (1325–1354 AD). The Saxon "now British" Empire first initiated resource assessments in Afghanistan in the early nineteenth century as they searched through pioneering exploration and military escapades for countries to dominate as markets and trading partners. From the time of their first geological mapping and mineral resource assessments in Afghanistan and on into the twentieth century[13], the British maintained a comprehensive interest in resources of Afghanistan. This was done while also improving their military intelligence on resources and topographic detail that would be needed in the event of any unrest in the machinations of their Great Game face-off against the Russian Empire, and as long as they could maintain their British Raj (rule) of the Indian subcontinent. A number of other nationalities (German, French, Russian) also looked at geology and resources in the country from time to time but nothing much seemed to come of their explorations. Following the third Anglo-Afghan War in 1919, Afghanistan won its independence from diplomatic domination by the British and it was not long after that a Soviet publication on mineral "riches" first appeared, published by a man who later came to be revered as an early Russian 'father' of geologic studies. Nevertheless, in spite of early attempts by the government of Afghanistan to entice Americans to become engaged in resource discovery and extraction in the country, distance from market, economic concerns, and looming worries about World War II caused rejection of the overtures, much to the discomfiture of the government of Afghanistan. In spite of a number of discoveries by the American geologist Fox (1943) and others, post-war assessment by an American geographer[1] concluded shortsightedly that there were no useful resources in Afghanistan about which there should be any diplomatic concern. With its attention on resources accordingly diverted elsewhere for decades to come, the US Department of State thus quite missed the resource ball when in the 1960s and 1970s, as many as ~250 Soviet geoscientists went to work mapping geology in the country while only one American geologist (co-author of this paper, John Shroder) was in the country, plus a few visiting geology attachés from the US Embassy and USGS seismic specialists who visited from time to time· The resulting Soviet collaboration with the Afghanistan Geological Survey detailed a wide store of mineral resources in the country. The result of this Cold-War "Pakistan on Afghan territories" confrontation between the USA and the USSR in Afghanistan was that the neighboring USSR was able to fairly easily sidestep or ignore developing resources in Afghanistan until conditions were more to its liking as it consolidated its preeminent position in the country, ultimately leading to its invasion in 1979. With its already dominant roles in the Afghanistan Cartographic Institute, the Afghanistan Geological Survey, and many other ministries, the USSR was in a position in the early 1980s to completely take over all resource extraction in Afghanistan. Indeed they did pump much natural gas across the northern border of the Amu Darya into the USSR where the gauges to measure delivered volumes were located, and plans were made for development of other resourcesIn addition, the Aynak copper deposit near Kabul was investigated in detail and a smelter scheduled for installation in the mid 1980s. In an interesting sidelight of these times in the early 1980s, a Soviet-Afghan convoy from Aynak was assaulted by the Mujahideen and the captured documents that were sent to co-author Shroder by British sources proved that the Aynak copper lode was one of the largest in the world, as proved out by a plethora of kilometer-deep boreholes that allowed the Soviets to sample the deposit extensively. The increasing resistance of the Afghan people and the Mujahideen, however, together with significant assistance from the USA to the resistance in the final cumulative battles of the Cold War, precluded significant further development of any resources at that time. Instead the Soviet withdrawal in defeat occurred in 1988-89. The subsequent invasion of Afghanistan by the USA and coalition troops in 2001 began a new phase in the history of Afghanistan, as many old resource projects were assessed again, and new ones were initiatedAfghanistan lies on the Tethyan Eurasian mineral belt, which starts in Turkey and runs through Iran to Asia as far as Indonesia. There are other mineral belts in Afghanistan, formed through the violent collisions of tectonic plates tens of millions of years ago, which also created the 25,000ft mountains in the north-east of the country. A new mining law was passed in 2006 and as of 2006 regulations were being developed to provide the framework for more formal exploration for and mining of minerals. The process of applying for mineral rights was also being revised as of 2006. All minerals located on or under the surface are the exclusive property of the Government, except for hydrocarbonsand water, which are regulated under separate laws. The principal role of the Government with respect to minerals is to promote the efficient development of the mineral industry by the private sector. The Ministry of Mines and Industries is responsible for the administration and implementation of the Mining Law. The Law provides investment security to the holder of a mineral right. The Government cannot expropriate mineral rights without adequate compensation in accordance with international norms. The Law also gives the mineralroyalty rates, which range from 5% of gross revenue for industrial minerals to up to 10% for gemstones. Other changes in Government policy in 2006 included the legalization of the gemstone trade, Government control of the gemstone industry, and encouragement of investment in mining. The Badakshan Gold Mine is situated in mountainous terrain in northern Afghanistan in Badakhshan Province, the location benefits from three international borders: Tajikistan to its north, China to its east, and Pakistan to the south. Badakshan is located 360km north of Kabul and about 50km north of the provincial capital city of Fayzabad. Detailed work was conducted by the joint Soviet/Afghan reconnaissance geological programme in the region in the 1960's. The work was primarily carried out on the Veka Dur gold prospect, including trench and adit sampling. Badakshan is the largest and most studied of the known gold-bearing quartz veins systems in the region. Many of the main drainages for the regions were sampled for placer gold by means of panned concentrates performed in the field. Several mapped areas show alluvial deposits that were trenched, and samples for which panned concentrates were developed and the gold content noted. Russian C1 + C2 Reserves for both Veka Dur and other quartz veins of 38.7Koz at 4.8g/t based on trench sampling. It is understood that the national grid will be expanded to Fayzabad in the future. There is an ample supply of water from the regional watersheds on the project area. Lapis lazuli sometimes abbreviated to lapis) is a relatively rare semi-precious stone that has been prized since antiquity for its intense blue color. Lapis lazuli was being mined in the Badakhshan province of Afghanistan as early as the 3rd millennium BC,[1] and there are sources that are found as far east as in the region around Lake Baikal in Siberia. Trade in the stone is ancient enough for lapis jewelry to have been found at Predynastic Egyptian and ancient Sumerian sites, and as lapis beads at neolithic burials in Mehrgarh, the Caucasus, and even as far from Afghanistan as Mauritania The Government of Afghanistan supports a mining sector strategy that encourages legitimate and transparent private investment in the sector. Afghanistan is a country abundantly rich in natural resources. There are currently more than 1,400 mineral deposits that have been identified including energy minerals such as oil, gas and coal and other metallic and non-precious minerals such as lead, cement-grade limestone, gemstones, copper, iron, gold, salt, and industrial minerals (for use in the glass, ceramic, construction, chemical and fertilizer industries). Known precious and semi-precious stones include emerald, jade, amethyst, alabaster, beryl, lapis lazuli, tourmaline, ruby, quartz, and sapphire. Afghanistan's iron and copper deposits are of world-class quality. The hydrocarbons (petroleum and natural gas) industry provides great investment potential for Afghanistan, both financially and as a means for energy production. Recent findings in March 2006 indicate that the Afghan and Amu Darya Basins contain 18 times the oil and triple the natural gas reserves previously determined. The Government of Afghanistan ratified the Minerals Law in 2005 and ratified the Hydrocarbons Law (2006), which governs the natural gas and petroleum industries in the energy sector. These two laws are major initial steps in addressing how to create a regulatory framework for the development of these sectors and, most importantly, enable a suitable environment to attract and retain private investment. 2.1 Investment opportunity in Ghori Cement Plant Investment opportunities exist in the following areas:

- Portland cement blends
- Non-Portland hydraulic cements

The Ghori Cement plant, located in the city of Puli Khomri in the North of Afghanistan was acquired by the Afghan Investment Company (AIC) under the privatization initiative of the Government in April 2007. The AIC is a group of highly successful and established Afghans with a solid base in Afghanistan and in-depth knowledge of the local conditions. The Ghori plant enjoys above-standard specifications with regards to its products due to the comparative advantage of having easy access to immense deposits of highgrade limestone / clay / coal /gypsum at relatively low cost. In the first three months of its operation AIC invested and repaired Ghori and was successful to increase the plant production capacity from 150 TPD to 400 TPD. To meet the increasing demand (estimated at closer to $1bn/year in Afghanistan alone and growing), AIC is in the process of completing Ghori II cement plant which was abandoned half finished 20 years ago. Ghori II Cement Plant has the capacity for 1000 TPD production which will be operational. In 2007, the Chinese state-owned Metallurgical Group Corp., or MCC, signed a $3.5 billion lease for the Mes Aynak Copper Mine in mineral-rich Logar province, 15.5 miles (25 kilometers) southeast of Kabul. The site is thought to contain the world's second-largest copper deposit, worth some $88 billion at today's prices. As part of the deal, the company will create training and education centers for Afghan personnel. To fully exploit the site, MCC will need to link the mine by rail to the Afghan capital, perhaps even extending the track to Pakistan and Uzbekistan. The rail project could cost MCC another $5 billion, and preliminary studies on the new rail network began in late 2010. Archaeological workers excavate a site on a mountaintop overlooking a patch of housing and offices at the Mes Aynak site last November. On-site production is still several years off, but prefabricated houses have already been put up by the Chinese state-owned MCC. Photo: Wikipedia Commons. Mes Aynak is also the location of a major Buddhist archaeological site, including monuments to pseudo-Buddhism precursors. Some 400 artifacts, essentially doubling the size of the Afghan National Museum, have already come out of excavations in the area. It is hoped that over the next five years, valuable archaeological work can be done before mining activities fully begin. China will get to develop the site for the next 30 years. At the time, the deal represented the largest foreign investment ever made in Afghanistan's history. Last January, the China National Petroleum Corp., or CNPC, became the first company in the world in decades to sign an oil contract in Afghanistan — a deal worth $700 million for three oil fields along the Amu Darya River. CNPC is partnering with the Watan Group, believed to have connections to President Hamid Karzai's family, in a joint venture to develop the area's estimated 87 million barrels of oil. CNPC will give generous sums back to the Afghan government. A 15 percent royalty on oil, a 20 percent corporate tax, and 70 percent of profit go to Kabul. The amount of investment and effort Chinese companies are putting into the country doesn't just stop at natural resources. Chinese telecommunications giants Huawei Technologies Co. Ltd. and ZTE Corp. (the second- and fifth-largest telecom companies in the world, respectively) are installing digital switches and 200,000 lines in the country. Indeed, if anything currently differentiates the Chinese and American approaches, it is that China's engagement with Afghanistan is almost entirely driven by business deals, not by aid projects. Early last month, Beijing promised to grant the Afghan government $23.8 million in official aid, a paltry sum compared to the billions now being sunk into the country by state enterprises. The Chinese Foreign Ministry noted on June 6 that China will continue to provide assistance within its capacity to Afghanistan in line with its actual needs and strengthen cooperation with the country in fields such as resource development, infrastructure construction, energy, and personnel training. Days before Karzai's visit to Beijing to attend a major meeting of the Shanghai Cooperation Organization, a major Sino-Russian-Central Asian security and energy pact, the Chinese ambassador told the Afghan president that his country was the most reliable friend of Afghanistan. Robert Kaplan, geopolitical scholar and author, wrote in the New York Times in 2009 that the whole direction of America's military and diplomatic effort is toward an exit strategy, whereas the Chinese hope to stay and profit. India Pushes Northwest China's drive into Afghanistan has also pulled India further in. Historical pride, insecurity about India's geopolitical standing, and the hunt for raw materials to power a surging economy are pushing New Delhi to make its own lasting mark on Afghanistan. This summer, the Ministry of Mines in Afghanistan is expected to announce a deal that will eclipse Mes Aynak: the finalization of a $10.8 billion bid for the right to develop a massive iron-ore deposit at

Hajigak by a conglomerate of Indian state-owned mining companies called the Steel Authority of India Ltd. SAIL, India's largest steel maker, is expected to develop on-site mining and refining facilities and off-site road and rail infrastructure needed to transport ore from the location. The Hajigak site is located about 80.6 miles (130 kilometers) west of Kabul, in Bamyan province. It is estimated to hold more than 1.3 billion metric tons of high-grade iron ore. Sandeep Jojodia, the managing director of Monnet Ispat Ltd., one of the companies making up SAIL, told Bloomberg News late last year the deal will pave the path for more such formations bidding jointly for overseas assets.... It is something that China has done for years, but now Indian companies can join hands to tackle China's might. In June, the former Indian Army chief, Gen. V.K. Singh, called China's involvement in Afghanistan an outflanking move meant to strengthen links with Pakistan and further encircle India. India risks losing the influence it has in Afghanistan because of a China-Pakistan link that is getting stronger and is seen in evidence here, Singh said, describing the possibility of new tri-national transportation developments between Afghanistan, Pakistan, and China. Indian companies have already spent some $1.5 billion over the past 10 years on Afghanistan's roads, electric grid, schools, and government facilities. The new Afghan parliament building in Kabul is being built by India. C. Raja Mohan, a scholar at the Center for Policy Research in New Delhi, told Bloomberg that engaging and bringing stability to its northwest is the country's top foreign- policy priority, because most of our threats come from there. Beni Prassad Verma, the Indian minister for steel, told the press in April that Afghanistan is our old friend, and we want to invest lots of money in the sector of steel, natural gas, petroleum, and copper. This is our duty, to help Afghanistan. What Keeps The European Out Duty — or national interest — aside, sites now being developed by Indian and Chinese companies are not without their own unique geographic challenges or security risks. Afghanistan is setting up a special unit to police and protect mining and mineral sites. The foreign operators will need that protection. Examples around the world, as in the Niger Delta and Colombia, have shown that foreign-operated sites are prime targets for insurgent groups and terrorists. The Logar region is thought to remain a major transit zone for Pakistan-based insurgents. But major Chinese or Indian companies may not care about that. They operate in some of the world's least-welcoming places, and they do so with state backing to keep toeholds in areas where Western companies are too risk-averse to enter and where there is still plenty of money to be made. Robert M. Cutler, a professor at Canada's Carleton University in Ottawa, said that when it comes to operating in Central Asia, companies from both countries have unquantifiable advantages — things like cultural affinity, regional familiarity, and fewer qualms about practices that cross the line of business ethics, combined with strong technical skills and comparatively low labor costs. It's not just Chinese and Indian companies that are getting involved in the country. Iran is also among the first to set up major facilities in Afghanistan. The Majd Industrial Pishgaman Co., an Iranian outfit specializing in cement, is building a factory in Herat, large enough to service much of the country. Cement may seem a quaint business venture, but Iranian companies have been perfecting it for years to defend against American and Israeli bunker-busting bombs, making cement one of Tehran's strategic industries. The Iranian plant in Herat will produce 1 million metric tons of cement a year. A construction boom in the country is expected to raise demand to 7.2 million metric tons a year by 2020 from 2.5 million metric tons in 2005. India, meanwhile, is also courting Iran to serve as a potential destination point for its railway linking the Hajigak mine to the outside world. A previous proposal to put track across Pakistan was a highly uncertain undertaking. The Indian-built Chabahar port in Iran, some 558 miles (900 kilometers) from Hajigak across vulnerable and exposed terrain in southwestern Afghanistan, may eventually be where the site's iron ore is offloaded. That would set up a competing line of transportation with China's proposed rail network, which may link to Pakistan and bring minerals north through East Turkestan or south to the Arabian Sea port of Gwadar. The only American company that has moved into the vast mining space in Afghanistan thus far has been a merchant bank, and, even then, very tentatively. Last year, JP Morgan Chase & Co. helped to arrange a comparatively small $40 million deal for individual Western investors to pool money in an Afghan gold mine pulling out a modest 5.4 metric tons of gold ore a year, in Qara Zaghan, north of Kabul. The only Western company slated for a significant contract in Afghanistan is Kilo Goldmines, a firm headquartered in Canada that is active mostly in gold mine reclamation in the Democratic Republic of Congo. The company is poised to develop a smaller portion of the Hajigak mine in a separate bid from SAIL. Kilo's CEO, Alex van Hoeken, called his firm a pioneer for entering its target regions. Van Hoeken objects to making comparisons between the DRC and Afghanistan, saying the challenges facing the two places are very different. Kilo has a reputation as a risk taker: Van Hoeken said his company's smaller size and flexible decision-making are the root causes of its success. Kilo refused to release any specific details on its contract bid with the Afghan Ministry of Mines, including its monetary value. On Friday, the Exxon Mobil Corp. indicated the multinational oil-and-gas company is considering exploring six moderately sized oil bids in northern Afghanistan. Exxon Mobil is the only fully private company bidding for the contract. Seven other potential competitors include state-owned companies from India, Brazil, Turkey, and Pakistan. Analysts quickly noted the move represented only an initial interest, not a firm commitment. A Great, Crooked Game Not everything, though, is crystal-clear in Afghan mining. Nasir Shansab, the president of Afghan-American contracting company Acatco, operating in Afghanistan since 2002, accused both SAIL and Kilo of placing bids based on faulty premises. Acatco is not an impartial party. It lost out against both the Indian and the Canadian companies in proposals for the Hajigak mine. But its claims are nevertheless troubling, and if ultimately proven true, they would be damning for the Afghan government and its current approach to courting foreign investors. Shansab said his company raised $1.2 billion in guaranteed funds, offered the most faithful compliance to the requirements of the Afghan government, and promised the creation of indigenous steel processing, as well as the prospect of full-scale operations in three years. He accused SAIL and Kilo of being involved in bidding procedures mired in corruption and bribery, saying the two should have been disqualified. Shansab claimed the original bid requirements to return between 12.5 percent and 22.5 percent in royalties to the Afghan government was met by neither of his rivals, and there were no firm promises from either to develop a domestic processing and manufacturing capability in Afghanistan, a key stipulation. In letters to the Ministry of Mines, Acatco's president accused SAIL and Kilo of fraud and corruption, saying the evaluation process for the Hajigak tender has been deceptive. Shansab said that a gross exaggeration of the costs for developing the mine is likely being used to stuff pockets and cover up bribes. Shansab said he suspects Kilo, a company which had $29 million in aggregate assets last October, will eventually be unable to raise the money necessary for the mine, in effect awarding the entire project to an extension of the Indian government. However, he also said he expects the Indian conglomerate itself may face difficulties raising the massive funds it has promised for the bid. In December, SAIL approached the Indian government for $7.8 billion in aid and loans to support its bid. The announcement of the finalized contract award for SAIL and Kilo was delayed by the Ministry of Mines from last December to April, then to May, then to June, and it has yet to happen. According to Shansab, Minister for Mines Wahidullah Shahrani is giving away Afghanistan's arguably most valuable asset without any financial commitment at all. Afghan Mining Minister Wahidullah Shahrani promotes Afghan investment opportunities at a London conference on June 25, 2010. Photo: Reuters That's increasing suspicion among analysts that the bidding tenders so far have been decided based on building regional allies, not on actual financial soundness. However, the Afghanistan Embassy in Washington adamantly denied that Western bidders have been purposely rejected to favor Chinese and Indian ones for the purpose of establishing stronger diplomatic links.

Shakib Noori, the commercial attache of the Afghanistan Embassay in the U.S., said his government is seeking balance and diversity in foreign investments. He called mining a long-term prospect for a development strategy for Afghanistan. If anything, the Afghan government is desperate for Western investors — but the latter simply have no interest in putting their money into the country. Noori said that, on average, for every 20 bids in response to an advertisement for a site by the Mining Ministry, only one or two are from Western companies. We encourage them to go to Afghanistan, to see for themselves said Noori, but they have a lack of information. Afghanistan— Despite the crackle of gunfire in the mountains of northern Afghanistan, the wealth of gold beneath will be mined under a multimillion-dollar contract that government officials approved on Monday. The deal is the first mining project in Afghanistan backed by private investors in the West. Afghan and U.S. officials hope many more deals will follow to help jump-start the economy of this impoverished nation in its 10 year of war. "This project is an important step forward for Afghanistan's economic sovereignty," U.S. deputy undersecretary of defense Paul A. Brinkley said in a statement on Monday. "It represents a turning point in the history of international investment into Afghanistan." Brinkley, who directs the defense department's Task Force for Business and Stability Operations, said the gold mine deal is evidence that Western investors are showing confidence in Afghanistan's economic future. About 10 investors — most of them from the United States and Britain — are investing an estimated $50 million in the gold project in Dushi district of Baghlan province, about 84 miles (135 kilometers) northwest of Kabul, according to Wahidullah Shahrani, Afghanistan's minister of mines. The only other gold mine in Afghanistan is in neighboring Takhar province. Shahrani said he hoped that getting the deal approved by the Inter-Ministerial Council, which comprises the government's top finance and economic officials, will send a strong signal to global mining companies that there are investment opportunities in Afghanistan, especially in the mining sector. Geologists have known for decades about Afghanistan's vast deposits of iron, copper, cobalt, gold and other prized minerals. In June, the U.S. Defense Department put a startling $1 trillion price tag on the reserves, but Shahrani called that a conservative estimate. He said he's seen geological assessments and industry reports estimating the nation's mineral wealth at $3 trillion or more. For Afghanistan, a violent, landlocked country with virtually no exports, the minerals are a potential windfall, although formidable obstacles remain, including lack of investment, infrastructure and adequate security in most of the nation. In late 2007, a $3 billion contract was awarded to China Metallurgical Group Corp. to mine copper at Aynak, 21 miles (35 kilometers) southeast of Kabul. The mine is thought to hold one of the world's largest unexploited copper reserves. Mining the copper could produce 4,000 to 5,000 Afghan jobs in the next five years and hundreds of millions of dollars a year to the government treasury, Shahrani said. Afghanistan's gold deposits are more modest. Shahrani said that Soviet-era studies valued Afghanistan's gold deposits at up to $25 billion. He said the estimate was conservative and added that new gold discoveries have been made. Afghanistan's gold is found across the country, but the heaviest known deposits are in Badakhshan, Takhar, Bamiyan, Ghazni and Zabul, "There is growing global demand for gold and right now the price of gold has reached the highest point in the history of mankind," Shahrani said. "Investing in gold is very attractive." J.P. Morgan, an international financial services firm, promoted the project and attracted the investors. Sadat Mansoor Naderi Chairman of Afghan Gold Company They invested in an Afghan company called Afghan Gold. The chairman of the company is Sadat Mansoor Naderi, who runs SMN Group (http://www.smninvest.com), one of the largest companies in Afghanistan. SMN, which employs about 3,000 people, owns the first private insurance company in Afghanistan, operates a small chain of supermarkets, builds roads, airports and bridges and distributes telecom cards and fuel. Taliban insurgents have been slowly expanding their presence in Baghlan and neighboring provinces, but the mine is located a three- to four-hour drive from the scene of recent fighting, To Hannam, chairman of J.P. Morgan Capital

Markets, Afghanistan represents a gigantic, untapped opportunity — one of the last great natural-resource frontiers. Landlocked and pinioned by imperial invaders, Afghanistan has been cursed by its geography for thousands of years. Now, for the first time, Hannam believes, that geography could be an asset. The two most resource-starved nations on the planet, China and India, sit next door to Afghanistan, where, according to Pentagon estimates, minerals worth nearly $1 trillion lie buried. True, there is a war under way. And it's unclear how the death of Osama bin Laden will impact the country's political and economic environment. But Hannam is not your usual investment banker: A former soldier, he has done business in plenty of strife-torn countries. So have all the members of his team, two of them former special forces soldiers who have fought here. As he flies to the mine for the ribbon-cutting ceremony, Hannam thinks back over the past 12 months. This little mine, where operations have yet to commence, is puny by J.P. Morgan's (JPM) standards, but he knows it might be the project for which he is remembered. A lot of powerful people, including the commander of U.S. forces in Afghanistan, Gen. David Petraeus, are counting on him to demonstrate that the country is safe for foreign investors. Hannam has chafed at times under the pressure from the Pentagon, and the cold-eyed realist in him wonders whether unrealistic expectations are being placed on this business venture. Hannam ducks his head and climbs out of the chopper, necktie flapping in the prop wash. As he trudges up the hill, even the jaded, 55-year-old banker seems swept away by the pageantry of the moment: the village elder in a ceremonial robe, the silhouettes of women watching from the ridges, the saluting Afghan soldier. Hannam is enveloped in a crush of local tribesmen chattering excitedly in Dari. One of them puts a garland around his neck. Another hands him a Ziploc bag containing a chunk of Afghan gold. A mullah utters prayers. Afghanistan's minister of mining gives a long speech. Hannam and his local partner, Sadat Naderi, walk up the hill to pose for photographs. Naderi points to a narrow band of quartz that runs in an east-west line across the cliff side. It shimmers in the sun. That is the treasure, he says. "Unless," Hannam mutters, "it's fool's gold." Absurd risks vs. amazing rewards Investing in conflict zones is often thrilling, but the great commodities rush that J.P. Morgan and the Pentagon are trying to spark in Afghanistan creates a risk/reward equation of a different magnitude. It's extreme at both ends. When J.P. Morgan launched its Afghan initiative in 2010, violence was at its worst since the American-led occupation began in 2001. The Taliban have made a point of killing Westerners and have specifically said they would attack any companies involved in mining. Before our trip to the mine was done, our group would get a taste of the insurgents' ability to strike violently and unpredictably. Then there's the Afghan infrastructure — or rather, there isn't. Big mines need power, lots of it. Outside of cities, only 15% of Afghanistan is electrified. The mountain roads — ungraded and often without guardrails — are perilous, I learned the hard way, particularly in winter. Seat belts? No one bothers. You crash, you die. If the brutal war and roads don't give a businessperson pause, the country's governance and corruption problems should. Massive fraud marred recent elections. Transparency International rates Afghanistan as the second most corrupt country on earth after Somalia. The last minister of mining was identified in a Washington Post report as the recipient of a massive bribe, an allegation he denied to *Fortune*. The current minister, who had been widely described as an honest reformer, has recently had his integrity questioned in State Department cables released by WikiLeaks. He, too, told *Fortune* he has done nothing improper. But if the risks are absurd, the potential rewards are off the charts. Hundreds of billions of dollars' worth of iron, copper, rare earth metals, and, yes, gold are buried beneath Afghanistan's deserts and mountains. This wealth has lain there mainly undisturbed for thousands of years as armies of Greeks, Mongols, Britons, Russians, and present day Americans tramped above. Invaders have dreamed of exploiting it since the time of Alexander the Great, but no one has yet succeeded on a large scale.

Afghanistan to conduct the first Western mineral survey of the country

A Chinese company is trying to start a copper operation in strife-torn Logar province, but actual mining is years away. In an 1841 article in a journal of Asiatic studies, Capt. Henry Drummond, a member of the Saxon present day British 3rd Bengal Light Cavalry, described his rambles through the wildest parts of Afghanistan to conduct the first Western mineral survey of the country. He found "abundant green stains" of copper, some of which rivaled the deposits of Chile, and veins of iron ore that "might no doubt be obtained equal to the Swedish." While many of his countrymen viewed Afghanistan as an untamable place, where a man could not stray many yards from his home or tent without risk of being murdered, Drummond was smitten. Mining, he felt — not the gun — offered the best hope to pacify the territory and win over Afghans. "Give them, however, but constant employment, with good wages and regular payment; encourage a spirit of industry, both by precept and example; let strict justice be dealt out to them without respect of persons; and we shall shortly see their swords changed into plowshares, industry take place of licentiousness, and these people be converted into peaceable and useful subjects," Drummond wrote. But the Afghans weren't keen on the idea of handing over their minerals to occupiers, or on the British occupation itself, for that matter. A year later they massacred the entire British army, save one English survivor, at Gandamak. During the Cold War, both Soviet and U.S. geologists conducted surveys. The Russians bored thousands of test holes and identified big deposits of copper, zinc, mercury, tin, fluorite, potash, talc, asbestos, and magnesium. But instability in the countryside put an end to serious mining exploration. After the toppling of the Taliban by the U.S.-led coalition, the Afghan government, with financial assistance from the U.S. Agency for International Development, commissioned new, high-tech aerial surveys of Afghanistan. The results were stunning: The U.S. Geological Survey identified huge veins of copper, iron, lithium, gold, and silver. The Afghan government solicited bids for one of the biggest of the copper deposits, a site south of Kabul that had been identified by both Drummond and the Soviets. China, offering a rich price, won the bid in 2007, beating out four other mining companies. But the Chinese mining company has yet to extract any copper from the site because of delays clearing land mines from the area, and the discovery of archeological relics. Then, in 2009, mining in Afghanistan got the push it needed — from the U.S. military. Petraeus had been appointed commander of U.S. Central Command, which had ultimate authority over Afghanistan. He realized that a U.S. exit from Afghanistan depended on getting the country's economy running. Up to 60% of Afghanistan's $15 billion GDP comes from foreign aid, according to Pentagon estimates, and another 20% comes from the illicit drug trade — poppies. What Afghanistan needed was the real hope that it might achieve economic sovereignty. "I'm an old economist," the general says in an interview at his headquarters in Kabul. "And at the end of the day this is about progress for the [Afghan] people and giving them the prospect for a much brighter future for them and their families. That's what persuades the citizenry to support the government rather than support the Taliban." Realizing that conventional foreign-aid organizations weren't getting the job done, Petraeus moved a crack economic stabilization team from Iraq into Afghanistan. That team quickly realized that mining would be key. Enter Ian Hannam. "This is the time in Afghanistan for the adventure venture capitalists — for those who can do business in tough places in the world," Petraeus says. From special forces to making billionaires Villagers at Qara Zaghan hope mining will bring jobs, electricity, schools, and a health clinic. Ian Charles Hannam seemed bound for a swashbuckling career at an early age. Raised in a working-class neighborhood in

South London, the son of a council worker who oversaw a housing and street-repair crew, Hannam grew up knowing that nothing would ever be handed to him. He joined the Territorial Special Air Service at age 17, one of the younger men to pass the service's grueling selection process. Hannam's unit, the Artists Rifles, was a part-time regiment akin to a U.S. National Guard special forces unit. The Artists Rifles had a storied past and a reputation for attracting adventure seekers from all social classes. Since then, Hannam has counted his old SAS cronies as his closest friends, often calling on them to help him in the world's tougher places. While serving in the Artists Rifles, Hannam pursued a degree in civil engineering from England's top school in that field, Imperial College. Upon graduation in 1977, he took a job with Taylor Woodrow, a large British construction firm. His first assignment was to build roads, radar stations, and airstrips in Oman for the SAS, which was in the final stages of crushing a Marxist-led insurgency that had been boiling in the Dhofar region for more than a decade. The experience convinced Hannam that revolts could be beaten with a counterinsurgency program that emphasized developing a country's infrastructure and natural resources. Still working for Taylor Woodrow, Hannam went to Nigeria and then back to Oman. Living in a tent, he could not help noticing how well oil-company executives lived. That's when he decided to go to business school and become rich. After graduating from the London Business School, Hannam got a job in 1984 in the training program at Salomon Brothers in New York. At the airport on his way home to London for Christmas that year, he was detained by immigration officials because he had no U.S. entry stamp on his passport. The reason: He had parachuted into the U.S. with an SAS unit that was training with American special forces, and then traveled to New York to start the training program. With a work ethic that former colleagues describe as ferocious and an engineer's taste for understanding complex financial mechanisms, Hannam was fast-tracked to the bank's vaunted debt syndicate desk. "His embrace of complexity and change, his indifference to organizational hierarchy and abundant self-confidence born of experience set him apart," recalls Terry Fitzgerald, founder of Longbow Capital Partners, who was at Salomon with Hannam. When Salomon was hired to advise media baron Robert Maxwell's Mirror Group during its public offering, Hannam was one of Salomon's lead bankers charged with marketing the IPO. Salomon lost money on the deal. Months later Maxwell died and Mirror Group collapsed amid investigations into accounting fraud and raids on its pension fund. Hannam left Salomon soon after the fiasco and was hired by merchant bank Robert Fleming, a Scottish firm founded by the grandfather of James Bond creator Ian Fleming. By 2000, Hannam was the highest-paid employee at Fleming, making more than the CEO. After the bank was acquired by J.P. Morgan, much of Fleming's staff was laid off. Not Hannam. He helped engineer a joint venture with, and eventual takeover of, venerated British banking house Cazenove. Among the old guard at Cazenove — which was subsumed by J.P. Morgan, though the British franchise still bears its name — Hannam was regarded as a bit of a barbarian. He bragged about his wealth. He had appalling table manners. "I've got more degrees than I can count, but I still talk like I'm illiterate, and my colleagues hate me for it," he'd say. From Congo to Colombia, from Iraq to Sierra Leone, Hannam and his small team of soldiers-turned-bankers and advisers did business with oligarchs, gem dealers, and former mercenaries. He could be bracingly direct. When he landed in Baghdad for a meeting with Iraq's oil minister, the minister asked, "What are you here for?" "I'm here to make five new Iraqi billionaires every year for the next 10 years," Hannam said with a twinkle in his eyes. It was an effective icebreaker, recalled his friend Richard Williams, a former SAS commander who is now CEO of the Afghan gold mine. "They're all thinking, 'How can I be one of those?' Which is not a question that a minister should be thinking." However crude, Hannam's point — it would be Iraqis, not Westerners, who were getting rich — worked. At an emerald mine high above the Panjshir Valley, work is done by kerosene lantern. Over the years Hannam had starring roles in a string of huge deals, including the combination of BHP and Billiton and its listing on the London exchange, the creation of mining group Xstrata, and the formation of Kazakh commodities giant Kazakhmys. In 2007, Hannam's appetite for risk and intrigue nearly sank him. A group of Omani investors had hired him to explore the possibility of a leveraged buyout and breakup of Dow Chemical. Hannam and another top J.P. Morgan executive held clandestine meetings with two Dow Chemical executives at the Compleat Angler, a luxury hotel on the bank of the Thames, The only problem: Dow's CEO had no idea that the meeting was taking place. The scandal attracted front-page notice around the world. In 2008, Hannam was passed over for the top job at Cazenove in favor of an outsider. Hannam flew to New Zealand for two weeks, turned off the phone, and brooded. But he decided to stay at the bank, and soon he was doing multibillion-dollar deals again, including lead work on the recapitalization of HSBC. With a job that paid bonuses as high as 10 million pounds, Hannam had come a long way from his boyhood in Bermondsey. He had a wife and three children, a townhouse in Notting Hill, a wild game preserve in the Stormberg mountains of South Africa, and a 230-acre estate in Vermont. But the council worker's son was hungry for something bigger. In 2009, at a dinner in Baghdad, he met the man who would give him his chance. The name of their meeting place was fitting for a rendezvous that would help touch off a 21st-century version of the US-Great Game: the Baghdad Hunting Club. Hannam was at the banquet hall for a reception thrown by the Trade Bank of Iraq to honor J.P. Morgan. Also at the reception was Paul Brinkley, a deputy under secretary of defense charged with jump-starting Iraq's stalled economy. A former tech company executive, Brinkley served as a matchmaker of sorts between Iraqi entrepreneurs and foreign businessmen. With the blessing of Defense Secretary Robert Gates, he operated outside normal bureaucratic channels, eschewing the bulletproof vests and helmets his civilian colleagues wore in combat zones. In three years he had secured some $8 billion in private investment contracts for Iraq, helping start textile mills, cement factories, and electronics companies. Hannam and Brinkley had heard about each other's work. J.P. Morgan had been one of the first Western companies to plant the flag in Iraq, overseeing the country's currency and setting up a big oil project in Iraqi Kurdistan. Hannam and Brinkley fell into conversation about Afghanistan, which was to be Brinkley's next posting. Soon they were having more meetings, in New York and Washington. Brinkley wanted to know what it would take to get the big international mining companies into Afghanistan. Hannam said it was too early. The giants weren't likely to leap into Afghanistan until smaller, wildcat operators went first. Copper and iron-ore mines were complicated and required huge infrastructure investments: railroads, roads, power plants, and smelters. Hannam said the first project should be less ambitious. A gold or lithium mine would be perfect. These materials could be transported by helicopter or trucked out by road. Hannam and Brinkley agreed that any such project should be led by an Afghan, lest it be seen as part of a resource grab by foreigners. Hannam pledged to bring entrepreneurial support, technical expertise, and capital, "And I'll make some Afghans very rich, by the way," he added. In February 2010, Hannam flew to Kabul to see the situation on the ground. Brinkley took him to a reception at the American ambassador's home. There, Hannam met an Afghan businessman named Sadat Naderi. British educated, smooth, and brimming with energy and ambition, Naderi ran a diversified company that included insurance, logistics, and supermarkets, There was one other thing, he said: "I'm one of the first Afghans that has actually won a gold license." Hannam's eyes lit up. Naderi, it turned out, already had a little gold mine in Baghlan province. His family had run a tiny artisanal operation there, even minting some coins, for years. He had won the legal rights to it in formal bidding in 2008. To develop it, he needed technical advice, equipment, and capital. Naderi was an Ismaili, a member of a sect. That was a good thing in Hannam's eyes. Progressive in their views toward women and education, Ismailis are renowned businessmen. The Ismailis' religious leader, the Aga Khan, presides over a vast charitable and business network that includes the Serena Hotel chain. The sect has a long-standing relationship with the British, dating back to the 1840s, when Ismailis provided Saxon present day British armies in Afghanistan with cavalry and intelligence. Naderi's father was the religious leader of all the Ismailis in Afghanistan. The family has several mansions and a palace in their home village, Kayan, which has athletic facilities and a train, and once had a zoo. Naderi's brother Jafar had been a militia commander during the last days of Soviet occupation, with a 12,000-member private army. A documentary film titled The Warlord of Kayan had shown Jafar fishing with a grenade, riding his motorcycle, and blasting AC/DC. During the Taliban era, the Naderis had fled for their lives, and Osama bin Laden briefly occupied their palace in Kayan. Sadat Naderi, not surprisingly, was happy to contemplate an investment of working capital raised by J.P. Morgan and backed up by the Pentagon. "The sooner we stand on our own feet, the better it is for us Afghans," Naderi says. "You cannot be a beggar nation forever." "Don't fall behind." Naderi's gold mine, in Baghlan province, is only 50 miles from Kabul as the crow flies. During winter months it might as well be on the moon. To get there by road you must traverse the dangerous Salang Pass, which cuts through the towering Hindu Kush range. In 2010, in the same month that the J.P. Morgan team first arrived in Afghanistan, 180 travelers were killed on the pass in an avalanche. had my own taste of winter travel over the 11,000-foot-high pass when set out with a convoy led by Richard Williams, the mining company's CEO. Garrulous, self-deprecating, and brimming with insights about the Muslim world, Williams could be mistaken for an Oxford don. But he remains the hard-charging individual depicted in Mark Urban's book Task Force Black, which describes Williams' exploits in Iraq as the leader of an SAS team charged with capturing and killing Hussein loyalists and al Qaeda members. "Richard is a buccaneer, a pirate," Urban quoted one of Williams' former associates as saying. "He goes for the opportunities and adrenalin every time." Herding and farming are the main economic activities in Qara Zaghan. It was snowing when we left Kabul early one morning, and by the time we reached the start of the climb, the weather had turned so nasty that police had halted traffic up the road. Nonetheless, our party of VIPs received permission to proceed with a police escort. Williams and his group were in armored, four-wheel-drive vehicles. There was no room in the caravan for me, a translator, and a photographer, so we hired a driver and a Toyota Corolla. The front-wheel-drive car was soon laboring in the heavy snow. Our chains kept slipping off the tires. The radiator overheated, belching coolant into the snow. When it became apparent that we might not keep up, Williams' group put a policeman in our car, and then proceeded on ahead without us. Visibility was terrible; the only way our driver could navigate was to crane his neck out a side window. After we passed the summit, the driver lost control of the car, which skidded and spun 180 degrees into a snowbank. Hands trembling, lit my first cigarette in decades, wheezing on the first puff. The next day, after spending the night in a hut, we set off on the return trip to Kabul. begged Williams and his group not to abandon us. But when one of our party was stricken by a stomach ailment and we pulled over to let him relieve himself, the convoy swept on without us. We spun out again, narrowly missing a head-on collision with a truck. When we caught up with Williams' convoy near Kabul, we were too furious to wave. "thought the SAS motto was similar to that of the U.S. Army [Rangers]: 'Leave no man behind,' "complained to one of Hannam's soldiers-turned-bankers afterward. "Leave no man behind?" He laughed. "Where did you get that idea? It's 'Don't fall behind.' And 'Don't forget your Imodium!' "A deal too important to di Of all the obstacles that could have wrecked the mining project — the murderous roads, the Taliban, the corrupt government — the one that nearly killed it was the most predictable: the profit margin. In late September, J.P. Morgan CEO Jamie Dimon, Brinkley, and Mining Minister Wahidullah Shahrani met at J.P. Morgan's headquarters in Manhattan. Dimon pledged J. P. Morgan's support. On the way down in the elevator, Dimon told Shahrani, "You're in good hands with Ian. He's eccentric, but he gets things done." But soon Brinkley's team was wondering. On the day the deal signing was to take place, Hannam's team stopped acting like former warriors and began behaving like, well, nervous investment bankers. Hannam, after talking about how rich he was going to make his clients, suddenly began to complain that there was no way to make a profit. The 26% royalty rate for the mine, his team claimed, was way too high. Mining Minister Shahrani was bewildered — the rate had been agreed upon years before, when the Naderi family had first bid for the mine. Nothing had changed. Brinkley's Pentagon team was deeply frustrated. They felt the bankers had pulled a fast one. Had Hannam's group not done its homework? Or were they just being bankers, trying to squeeze more money out of the deal with some 11th-hour brinkmanship Brinkley lit into the J.P. Morgan group: "When are you going to get this done? You've told people you're going to do it!" The bankers, in turn, felt they were being unfairly pressured by the government, which seemed desperate to get the deal done even if it was uneconomical. Villagers of Qara Zaghan have been digging for gold for decades. Everyone recognized, though, that the deal was too important to die. Naderi and Hannam's team worked out an arrangement with the Ministry of Mines in which the royalty would be deducted from the corporate tax, as it is in many other countries. Soon, helped by rising gold prices, the deal was back on track. J.P. Morgan says it is not charging its usual advisory fees. While Hannam has described his work on the mine as a charitable endeavor, he says he expects a big payoff down the road for clients who invest in it. J.P. Morgan says it isn't putting any of its own money into the project. Hannam secured $40 million from investors in the U.S., Asia, and Europe. They included Enso Capital founder Joshua Fink, son of BlackRock's Larry Fink; British mining titan Peter Hambro; and Thai businessman Pairoj Piempongsant. Hannam created an investment vehicle, Central Asian Resources, to enter into a joint venture with Naderi's new mining company, Afghan Gold, Sadat Naderi was made chairman of Afghan Gold, and Richard Williams CEO. Their goal is to pull 5.4 metric tons of gold from the mine during the first phase of operation. After that the plan is to go after five other gold sites, and then bid for the rights to other minerals, including copper and rare earths. This past December, an ecstatic minister of mines announced the deal. Petraeus congratulated President Karzai on the news. "Wonderful," Petraeus remembers Karzai saying. "It's big," Petraeus told me of the gold mine deal. "It's very big. I mean, everyone knows who J.P. Morgan is, and what that represents. That's substantial. It gives real encouragement to our Afghan partners."

A deceptive peace

After the ceremony to inaugurate the mine in Qara Zaghan, the barren valley rang with a merry hubbub. Hannam's close friend, Murad Megalli, responsible for J.P. Morgan's investment banking practice in Central Asia and the Middle East, made portraits of the villagers with a Leica film camera. The minister of mines was exultant. Naderi spoke optimistically of "partnership" with his new investors. Everything seemed to be going right. Then it wasn't. At a military base on our way back to Kabul, our Black Berrys started buzzing with news of a Taliban attack in the capital. Militants had struck one of Naderi's supermarkets, called Finest, with guns and a bomb, killing eight people. Naderi at first didn't understand what was saying when told him the news of the attacks. "The Finest got hit," said. "Hit?" Naderi said. "Finest hit?" He turned ashen. Megalli and Hannam sat on a bench trying to digest what had happened. Hannam was at first convinced the attack was linked to J.P. Morgan's presence in the country. It wasn't. (The Taliban later claimed they were trying to kill an American mercenary who they erroneously claimed was at the store.) Then, Hannam immediately put his banker hat back on. At least the deal was done, he said, and the money was in. Megalli was struck by how fast things could spiral out of control. "The peace here is so deceptive," Megalli said. "It is so fragile." A week later returned to my Kabul hotel room to receive this e-mail from Hannam about his colleague and friend: "Murad died in plane in Kurdistan yesterday. Any good photos I can give family?" Murad Megalli and Hannam had flown out of Afghanistan on a private plane, and then gone their separate ways. Megalli had taken the plane to Kurdistan. The plane crashed in a snowstorm, and Megalli and another J.P. Morgan banker were killed. Hannam was devastated. From the meeting with Brinkley at the Baghdad Hunting Club, Megalli had been a champion of the Afghan venture. He had believed mining could make a difference for the country. His death, and the attack on Naderi's supermarket, were sobering reminders of the personal risks of frontier capitalism. Baghlan Province has gold but few roads and no rail service, making it a challenging place to do business. Other storm clouds hover over the enterprise. Corruption allegations swirl around several key backers of the mining project in the Karzai government. Paul Brinkley's Pentagon team, which energized the Afghan mining sector and also put hundreds of Afghans to work in manufacturing technology and agriculture, is being disbanded, a casualty of interagency warfare. In April, after the burning of a Koran in Gainesville, Fla., mobs rioted in Afghanistan. The UN compound in Mazar-i-Sharif – a city that is to play a key role in the shipment of gold from the Baghlan mine — was attacked, and 12 people were killed. The spark that Brinkley and Hannam struck, however, continues to burn. Six major minerals sites are due to be auctioned by the Afghan government over the next year. SRK, a major mining-consulting firm, will advise the Afghan government. Bankers from Morgan Stanley (MS) and executives from Chevron (CVX) have been scouting Afghan natural-resource prospects. And next January the bulldozers and crushing machines are set to start working in the remote valley where Hannam's investors have staked their claim. It remains to be seen whether the J.P. Morgan adventure will leave any more indelible a mark on Afghanistan than did Capt. Drummond of the Bengal Light Cavalry 170 years ago. But at least someone will have begun releasing the wealth trapped in Afghanistan's stones. Industrial metals such as copper and lithium could put the war-torn country in high demand for high-tech industry. Reports that as much as $1 trillion worth of minerals may lie in Afghan soils are really not surprising, says Bruce Herbert, assistant head of the department of geology and geophysics at Texas A&M University. U.S. officials have surveyed the area and concluded that vast amounts of iron, copper, gold, cobalt, and lithium are likely plentiful in the region. "Soviet geologists first surveyed Afghanistan for economically important minerals," Herbert says. "The U.S. Geological Survey started surveying the country in 2004. Afghanistan has all sorts of valuable minerals, and if the accounts of lithium are true, it could be a tremendous boost for their economic future." Cell phone batteries contain lithium. Anyone who owns a BlackBerry or other cell phone, a laptop computer, or even a flashlight, is a consumer of lithium. The soft, silvery-looking metal is in high demand in high-tech times and deposits of it could mean instant wealth. "Lithium is found in two sources—one is in volcanic rocks, and the other is in desert areas, such as those found in Afghanistan," Herbert explains. "Argentina and Chile have significant amounts, in the U.S. it's found mainly in Nevada, and China has some. But it's a relatively rare mineral and there's not much of it in the world, so any new deposits are always welcome. "Most of the batteries in cell phones or laptop computers have lithium in them, so the demand for it has skyrocketed in recent years and will likely continue to do so," he adds. "Even many of the common flashlight batteries have lithium in them. New technology seems to be driven by lithium." A derivative of the mineral is also used by the drug industry to treat depression, bipolar disorders, and migraine headaches. Afghanistan's economy has been devastated by decades of wars, and the gross domestic product of the country is estimated to be about $12 billion. The country has been a center of the narcotics trade, specializing in opium production. Herbert says no one knows exactly how much lithium Afghanistan has. But the good news is that if the mineral is there, it is not hard to extract. "Usually, lithium in salt deposits is found near the surface," he says. "You don't have to go hundreds of feet down to find it like you do other minerals, so it's relatively easy to mine. "If all the reports of vast amounts of lithium in Afghanistan are true, it could be a huge boost for that country." Two former members of the UK's SAS, the highly regarded British army special forces unit, are nowadays closely involved in exploring for, and mining, gold in Afghanistan. Perhaps it is this type of military experience that is necessary in developing the mineral resources of such a potentially hostile, geographically and politically, area of the world. The first of the ex-SAS men is investment banker Ian Hannam, a renowned dealmaker formerly with JP Morgan Chase and, in his time, intimately associated with such mega deals as the merger of BHP and Billiton, the original launch of Xstrata, and in many of its mergers and acquisitions since and the formation of Kazkhmys, all in the resource sector. Hannam was drawn in, enthusiastically, to the prospect of helping develop Afghanistan's mineral wealth, initially by the U.S. state department which was keen to help promote foreign investment in the country. U.S. studies, drawing heavily on previous Soviet geological findings, had come up with Afghan mineral resources which could be worth in excess of $1 trillion and including copper, iron ore, gold, huge deposits of lithium, rare earths and others (see *Mineweb* articles Pentagon: Afghanistan may have $1 trillion undeveloped mineral wealth, and DOD, USGS unveil latest revolutionary Afghanistan strategic initiative–mining). U.S. government entities – notably within the military, were keen to find some means of developing the Afghan economy and it was a chance meeting in Baghdad between Hannam and Paul Brinkley, then U.S. Deputy Under Secretary of Defense charged with business development stability in the former war areas of Iraq and Afghanistan, which set Hannam on the Afghan mining path. To cut a long story short, Hannam teamed up with an English-educated Afghan, Sadat Naderi, whose family had long-owned a small artisanal gold mining operation around 60 miles north of Kabul at Qara Zaghan. The gold operation had potential to be far larger, but Naderi had neither the expertise, nor the capital to develop it. Hannam set up a company, Centar plc, to invest in Naderi's company Afghan Gold and Minerals and apparently holds 45% and has brought in a number of prominent investors, chief among which is Jan Kulczyk, reputed to be Poland's richest man, Peter Hambro and Chip Goodyear (former CEO of BHP Billiton). Kulczyk's company, Kulczyk Investments, owns 28% of Centar (Kulczyk is chairman of the company) and notes the latter's activities as follows: Centar's first investment in Afghanistan is a 45% share in Afghan Gold & Minerals Co, the first Afghan exploration and production company with international shareholding. The Afghan Gold & Minerals portfolio includes: A 100% interest in the Qara Zaghan Gold Project in northern Afghanistan. Bulk sampling has started at the project site; A 50% interest in a joint venture with a Turkish company Yildizlar, the largest silver producer in Turkey, which intends to develop the Badakshan gold and silver deposit in north-east Afghanistan; A 100% interest in an Afghan company providing specialized mining services; A 100% interest in an Afghan company providing laboratory and assay services. Interestingly the services companies noted above have been set up to explore and service the Afghan properties and others in the country – they imported the first modern exploration drill rig into Afghanistan, and are providing assay services for Qara Zaghan and other Afghan mineral properties as there had previously been no local assaying facilities. It is at this point the second SAS man in the team comes in. He is Richard Williams, who was a former regiment commander with the SAS in Iraq and Afghanistan and is a long-time friend of Hannam's. He has been appointed CEO of Afghan Gold and Minerals and has been tasked with bringing the Afghan operations into production. According to reports, the logistics of getting to Qara Zaghan from Kabul are, to say the least, challenging, particularly in the winter months as it involves traversing the notorious Salang Pass at an altitude of 11,000 ft. But to an extent that is one of the appeals of the project. It is isolated and difficult for even the Taliban to get to. Gold concentrates would be airlifted out by helicopter avoiding the possibility of gold shipments being ambushed in a country where banditry can be rife, let alone the Taliban. However, in commenting to the U.K.'s Sunday Times, Hannam makes light on the dangers involved and reckons that mining in Afghanistan is statistically no more risky than working in Nigeria. A small but potentially profitable gold mining operation is seen as ideal for kick starting an Afghan mining industry in that the right deposit can be mined without huge capital investment. It is also seen as important that a locally owned and controlled company like Afghan Gold and Minerals should take the lead. If a small operator can be seen as successful then, the theory goes, the larger players will come in to exploit the country's undoubted mineral riches. (June 14) — Until now, impoverished Afghanistan has been known for only two deadly exports: opium and terrorism. But according to new research by a team of geologists and U.S. defense officials, the country is sitting on top of $1 trillion in mineral resources and could become one of the world's most important mining centers, The reports. "There is stunning potential here," Gen. David Petraeus, commander of the U.S. Central Command, told the paper. "There are a lot of ifs, of course, but I think potentially it is hugely significant."

The United States Central Command, said of the minerals found in Afghanistan and Afghanistan could become the Saudi Arabia of lithium.

"There is stunning potential here," Gen. David H. Petraeus, commander of the United States Central Command, said of the minerals found in Afghanistan. The Times noted that aerial surveys had revealed huge untapped seams of iron, copper, cobalt, gold and increasingly vital metals like lithium, which is used in the manufacture of rechargeable batteries for mobile phones, laptops and electric cars. An internal Pentagon memo was quoted as saying that Afghanistan could become the "Saudi Arabia of lithium." Although it would take decades to develop a fully functioning mining industry in this war-torn nation, which still lacks a decent road system and basic infrastructure, Afghan and American officials believe that the discoveries could soon provide much-needed jobs as international investments pour into the country. That could help encourage Taliban fighters to put down their weapons, finally ending three decades of internal conflict. "This will become the backbone of the Afghan economy," Jalil Jumriany, an adviser to the Afghan minister of mines, told the Times. The Times report said the U.S. Geological Survey began an aerial analysis of Afghanistan's mineral resources in 2006, using data collected by Russian experts during the Soviet occupation of the country in the 1980s. After positive initial results, a more sophisticated study was carried out in 2007. Then last year, a Pentagon task force that had set up business development programs in Iraq analyzed the geologists' findings. American mining experts were brought in to approve the survey's conclusions, and top U.S. and Afghan officials were briefed. The biggest mineral deposits discovered so far are of iron and copper. But the finds include large deposits of more unusual minerals, including niobium — a soft metal used in the production of superconducting steel — rare earth elements and large gold deposits in the Pashtun areas of southern Afghanistan. But some commentators have been less than impressed with the apparently outdated announcement, suggesting that it could be timed to distract attention from the worsening military situation. Writing in Foreign Policy, Blake Hounshell said that, "the findings on which the story was based are online and have been since 2007, courtesy of the U.S. Geological Survey While the discoveries could re-energize the tiny aid-dependent Afghan economy — the country's gross domestic product is only about $12 billion — and help drive the peace process, there is a strong risk that they could fuel further conflict. The Times noted that the promise of such wealth might lead the Taliban to up their bloody campaign to regain control of the country. Other experts point out that the discovery of massive mineral wealth rarely helps impoverished countries. Congo and Angola, for example, have been torn apart by factions fighting for control of mining sites. Such a sudden injection of wealth could also worsen government corruption. Just last year, for example, Afghanistan's minister of mines was accused by U.S. officials of accepting a $30 million bribe to award China the rights to develop a copper mine. The minister has since been replaced. American officials worry that resource-hungry China could try to gain further control over the development of Afghanistan's mineral wealth That would frustrate the United States, which has pumped huge amounts of money into the country. "The big question is, can this be developed in a responsible way, in a way that is environmentally and socially responsible?" Paul Brinkley, deputy undersecretary of defense for business and leader of the Pentagon team that discovered the deposits, told the Times. "No one knows how this will work." It's winter in the Northern Hemisphere and another snowstorm is descending across the Great Lakes. Traffic will snarl, walking will become a chore, and those staying home will come to feel like they are under house arrest. It seems inevitable, yet almost cruel, to then dream of summer's golden reverie. The surfers are almost incidental–tiny figurines or animate shadows whose puny shapes are there only to remind us how much the lavish, liquid sunlight dwarfs human scale. One has to labor to realize that the photograph shows only light, not pools of molten gold. And yet, even as that gold pools on a plane of sand and sea that also seems forged of the sun's metal, there is a dark undertone. The day is long, and we know that this moment of sheer natural extravagance cannot last. A moment out of time is still tinged with mortality. Here the golden light is even more pronounced, and yet the drama of light and darkness is sharper still. The brilliant horizon, as if the sea were another sun, flows like lava into the city of Cape Town, but both sky and land are already under another dispensation. But the light always returns. Indeed, it ennobles all that it touches. Here an arid land, fractured by mountains and riven by war, appears like Shangri La. The golden mountains of Afghanistan, one might imagine, looking like pure gold, set in the middle distance of God's eye, surely a blessed place. And surely not a blessed place, if you think of the suffering there, with more to come. And so gold can seem to be no more than a trick of light, just as it also is an obviously artificial commodity, a fictional standard, and the stuff only of distraction and fantasy. The eye is easily mislead, one might say, and so both photographic art and serious thought should stick to reality's gray scale. But these images reveal another truth, one that could have genuinely radical implications. The golden light is but one aspect of the sun's unending flow across the earth, and with that, of humanity's ever present wealth. No one–ever–accomplishes anything without this free gift of energy that could never be created otherwise. There is a metaphor here as well (another extravagance), for sunlight not only gives of itself but represents other forms of wealth. The lesson of these images is not that warmth or beauty or any human good is necessarily apportioned to certain times or places, but that the good life is constantly available for those who can learn to see. As I've said before, the deeper challenge now facing politics, and so art, is not to manage scarcity but to realize the abundance already available in nature and culture. Abundance that often is not seen up close and that might be waiting where least expected, as if far out at sea or on distant mountains The Indian consortium that will mine copper and gold in Afghanistan is expected to meet on the first week of June to discuss each member's equity shareholding after due diligence work on the mineral deposits has been completed. The consortium members included Hindustan Copper Ltd., Nalco, SAIL and MECL. "We have sent four teams to Afghanistan for site visit. We will study their reports and do a due diligence on the reserves. The last of these teams will return on June 5. We are scheduled to meet after that to take a call on equity shareholding among the consortium members. We are getting feelers from other private players interested in joining the consortium and will decide on whether to invite them as part of the team," Shakeel Ahmed, chairman of HindustanCopper Ltd., said in The Economic Times. Among the private players shortlisted by the Afghan mines ministry were Sterlite Industries, Monnet Ispat & Energy and Jindal Steel & Power. Apart from the Indian consortium, the Afghan mines ministry had likewise shortlisted big investor candidates from Canada, the Emirates, and Australia to mine its copper and gold deposits. The United States has recently discovered nearly $100 trillion in untapped mineral deposits in Afghanistan, far beyond any previously known reserves and enough to fundamentally alter the Afghan economy and perhaps the Afghan war itself, according to senior American government officials. The previously unknown deposits including huge veins of iron, copper, cobalt, gold and critical industrial metals like lithium are so big and include so many minerals that are essential to modern day industry that Afghanistan could eventually become one of the most important mining centers in the world, the United States officials believe. While it could take many years to develop a mining industry, the potential is so great that officials and executives in the industry believe it could attract heavy investment even before mines are profitable. This will be a huge increase in Afghanistan's economy, which is based largely on opium production and narcotics trafficking as well as aid from the United States and other industrialized countries. Afghanistan's gross domestic product is only about $12 billion. "This will become the backbone of the Afghan economy," said Jalil Jumriany, an adviser to the Afghan minister of mines. Yet the American officials also recognize that the mineral discoveries will almost certainly have a double-edged impact. Instead of bringing peace, the newfound mineral wealth could lead the Taliban to battle even more fiercely to regain control of the country. The corruption that is already rampant in the Karzai government could also be amplified by the new wealth, particularly if a handful of well-connected oligarchs, some with personal ties to the president, gain control of the resources. Just last year, Afghanistan's minister of mines was accused by American officials of accepting a $30 million bribe to award China the rights to develop its copper mine. The minister has since been replaced. At the same time, American officials fear resource-hungry China will try to dominate the development of Afghanistan's mineral wealth, which could upset the United States, given its heavy investment in the region. After winning the bid for its Aynak copper mine in Logar Province, China clearly wants more, American officials said. With virtually no mining industry or infrastructure in place today, it will take decades to exploit its mineral wealth fully. "This is a country that has no mining culture," said Jack Medlin, a geologist in the United States Geological Survey's international affairs program. "They've had some small artisanal mines, but now there could be some very, very large mines that will require more than just a gold pan." The mineral deposits are scattered throughout the country, including in the southern and eastern regions along the border with Pakistan that have had some of the most intense combat in the American-led war against the Taliban insurgency.

Afghanistan Sitting on Gold, Lithium Mine oil, gas, only-natural gas prices-per day 86 billion Dollars US, & $100 trillion dollars US, Iron ore, copper, large Uranium, of mineral reserves, precious an semi-precious stones, emerald-lapis lazuli, red-gamete A ruby, Marble, Coal & Canal-tunnel of Gold

August 2012 - The vast reserves of minerals buried throughout Afghanistan, including large deposits of copper, gold, and gas could greatly improve the country's economy and provide funds to develop the country for years to come. But all that wealth might also create a crisis. While some estimates put Afghanistan's mineral wealth at about $100 trillion, for these minerals to be extracted in a way that benefits all Afghans and promotes sustainable development the industry needs to be managed transparently. That was the key message at a conference recently held in Kabul to coincide with the release of a report called the Afghanistan Extractive Industries Transparency Initiative (AEITI). The report contains details of all payments of taxes, royalties and fees the Afghan Government has received from companies operating in the extractive sector. The report equally publishes details of payments made by mining companies to the Afghan Government in order ensure transparency. "The Afghan Government is committed to share publically all the information related to the extractive sector in the country," said Dr. Omar Zakhilwal Zakhilwal, Afghanistan's Afghan Finance Minister. This kind of transparency is important because sudden new wealth from mining and gas have had a way of undermining many economies. Rather than using that wealth as a blessing that can improve the lives of citizens and improve a country's infrastructure, it can cause Afghanistan's currency to appreciate and lead to increased corruption. This well-studied phenomenon is called the "resource curse", whereby countries with vast oil and mineral wealth don't see an improvement in the living standards of citizens. For instance Nigeria, which has one of the world's largest oil reserves, has seen no improvement in its real gross domestic product per person in 30 years. The GDP per capita of Venezuela, another mineral rich country, is lower today than it was in 1977. Afghanistan joined the Extractive Industries Transparency Initiative (EITI) in 2010 to help beat the "resource curse". That Initiative sets international standards for good governance and has established accountability mechanisms for the extractive industries sector. Before a country can join the EITI it has to has to agree to some governance and transparency inidicators. With funds from the World Bank and the Harakat-Afghanistan Investment Climate Facility Organization (HAICFO), the Ministry of Finance established a secretariat for Afghanistan Extractive Industries Transparency Initiative (AEITI) to take lead of EITI implementation in Afghanistan. Speaking at the conference, the Minister for Mines, Waheedullah Shahrani said the government has devised effective policies to better allocate royalties and taxes collected from this industries to make sure that industry can thrive."Transparency means that the process is clean, defendable and the information from the process of negotiation up to awarding contracts and exploration and exploitation of mineral resources are shared publically," said Shahrani. Shahrani said oil production from Afghanistan's first ever oil extraction contract at the Amu-River basin will start soon. This will generate $400-$500 million in revenue for Afghan government each year. Also underway is the Hajigak Iron project, which is already the biggest project in the history of Afghanistan not just from economic perspective but also from the scale of its operations. Hajigak will produce approximately 25 to 30 million tons of iron annually. Proposals to develop five other mines, of gold and copper, have been tendered. Evaluations of these proposals are underway. Eight renowned international companies have expressed interest in investing in oil extraction in Afghan basins and currently work is in progress on preparing financial model of this project. The Afghan government is also bringing reforms in the Mining Law of the country to make it more in line with international standards for broader investment attraction. "Afghanistan's commitment to EITI for transparency will be integrated into the law and licensing system will be simplified along with ensuring a legal framework for protection of the rights of investors," said Waheedullah Shahrani. Minister Shahrani hoped that mining sector will constitute 45 to 50 percent of Afghan economy by 2024. The Director of World Bank in Afghanistan, Bob Sam said AEITI is an important tool to increase knowledge and information about Afghanistan's natural resources and help increase accountability and transparency. Kulczyk Investments has become a partner of JP Morgan, an American banking corporation, and are set to purchase 50 percent of shares in Afghan Gold & Minerals, which holds a concession for gold digging in Afghanistan. Kulczyk Investments first acquired a majority share package in Cetnar, which is itself run by Jan Kulczyk while JP Morgan's head of capital markets, Ian Hannam is the company's deputy chairman. With a 50 percent share in Afghan Gold & Minerals, Cetnar is to search for ore in the gold-bearing region of Qara Zaghan, which has estimated resources amounting to 2.5 million tonnes. Even though financial details of the undertaking are being kept under wraps, it has been reported that as many as 200 geologists, protected by 200 heavily armed soldiers are already on the spot. Meanwhile, the price of gold continues to soar. At the end of last week, a tonne of ore traded for over 40 million euro As Afghanistan's government finalizes new laws designed to attract more foreign mining investment, Mining Minister Wahidullah Shahrani told Reuters that Exxon had not turned up for a site tour which closes on Sunday, despite being shortlisted with eight other firms for the Afghan Tajik tender near Mazar-e-Sharif. "Hopefully at some point they (Exxon) will visit the area. But that visit is not mandatory," Shahrani said in an interview late on Saturday in his Kabul office. A spokeswoman for U.S.-based Exxon said she could not immediately comment. Exxon's July expression of interest in the Afghan Tajik basin, which holds an estimated 1.9 billion barrels of oil, lent credence to hopes that Kabul may be making progress in efforts to lessen its reliance on aid, through untapped resources worth as much as $100 trillion, despite an ongoing insurgency. Shahrani said that with an October bid closure deadline looming, shortlisted companies had been invited to inspect the area and meet local community leaders, an offer which closes on September 30, and which would usually be accepted. "Some companies, they have already visited, some companies are about to visit the area," he said. "Those companies, most of them are well established in the region." Chinese and Indian companies are already scrambling to lock in access to Afghanistan's mineral wealth, most estimates of which date back to U.S. surveys carried out decades ago. The country has large deposits of gold, copper, iron ore and oil, as well as lithium and rare earths used in high-tech manufacturing. Chinese firms are leading the race, with China Metallurgical Group (MCC) and Jiangxi Copper winning a 2007 deal to exploit the giant $3 billion Aynak copper mine southeast of the capital Kabul.

Major Interest

Exxon's interest fuelled hopes that U.S.-based majors may also compete, despite worries over security and endemic graft, adding urgency to a push for new laws designed to make resource investment more attractive as foreign combat troops withdraw. Shahrani's ministry will soon resubmit to President Hamid Karzai's cabinet mining laws that Afghan officials and Western donors hope will persuade foreign firms to invest in the country's resources, but which were rejected in July over concerns they were too generous to miners. The re-draft, backed by Western donors and the World Bank, would remove a 2009 clause separating exploration from an automatic license to exploit finds, a law which led miners to question why they were spending their money on expensive and risky exploration if they could not be assured of profiting. "It created a lot of discomfort among the potential mining companies and global investors," Shahrani said. "We have made the provision that whoever gets the license for exploration through the tender, once they conduct the exploration, if they find a deposit to be commercially and economically viable, their exploration license will be automatically converted to an exploitation or production license." Miners and Western diplomats have not managed to convince the government to include fixed royalty payments in the re-drafted law, though Shahrani admitted that some resources firms thought it lead to greater confidence in planning. "In the new draft law, we have not mentioned that, and we will leave that to be determined in the bidding process," he said. Instead, the overhaul would commit the government to more transparency by publishing contract details in local and international newspapers, as well as on its own website, to counter perceptions of graft in Afghanistan's notorious kleptocracy. The draft laws, he said, should go to Karzai's cabinet in three to four weeks before a November vote in the fractious parliament, where lawmakers have in recent months been testing their muscle with Karzai, sacking key security ministers. Some political analysts have also speculated that Shahrani's problems with the law's initial draft may have been linked to political rivalries over control of potential resource profits.

Years Until Production

Shahrani said he was optimistic opposition to the laws had faded in cabinet, and that parliament's influential economics and resource committees were also positive about the legislation, which was drafted with World Bank help. "We have been interacting very closely with parliament's relative committees. I can see a significant degree of support on behalf of the members of those committees," he said. Despite the risk of global commodity prices falling as a result of concerns about the strength of the Chinese economy and a global economic slowdown, Shahrani said he believed Afghanistan had not missed the peak of the resource boom. Most projects in Afghanistan, he said, including bids for northeastern gold concessions in Badakhshan now being considered, would take years to reach production. "If we do award the concessions tomorrow for iron ore and copper, usually it takes at least five to six years for these deposits to get developed," he said. "We hope that by then the demand forcommodities will again increase."

Afghanistan Sitting On Gold, Canal-Tunnel Of Gold And Lithium Mine

OIL GOLD, IRON ORE, COPPER $100 TRILLION IN AFGHANISTAN

KALU VALLEY, AFGHANISTAN— If there is a road to a happy ending in Afghanistan, much of the path may run underground: in the one hundred trillion-dollar reservoir of natural resources — oil, gold, iron ore, copper, lithium and other minerals — that has brought hopes of a more self-sufficient country, if only the wealth can be wrested from blood-soaked soil. But the wealth has inspired darker dreams as well. Officials and industry experts say the potential resource boom seems increasingly imperiled by corruption, violence and intrigue, and has put the Afghan government's vulnerabilities on display. It all comes at what is already a critically uncertain time here, with the impending departure of NATO troops in 2014 and old regional and ethnic rivalries resurfacing, raising concerns that the mineral wealth could become the fuel for civil conflict. Powerful regional warlords and militant leaders are jockeying to widen their turf to include areas with mineral wealth, and the Taliban have begun to make murderous incursions into territory where development is planned. In the capital, Kabul, factional maneuvering is in full swing, including disputes over lucrative side contracts awarded to relatives of President Hamid Karzai. Further, a proposed mining law vital to attracting foreign investment is up in the air, with the delay threatening several projects. The cabinet rejected it this summer, saying it was too generous to Western commercial interests. But some Western officials fear other motives are at work, too, including an internal fight for spoils, and perhaps an effort by some neighboring countries to sway sympathetic officials to keep Indian and Chinese state mining companies out. "If you were to pick a country that involves high risk in developing a new mining sector, Afghanistan is it," said Eleanor Nichol, campaign leader at Global Witness, a group that tries to break the link between natural resources, corruption and conflict. "But the genie is out of the bottle." Already this summer, the China National Petroleum Corporation, in partnership with a company controlled by relatives of President Karzai, began pumping oil from the Amu Darya field in the north. An investment consortium arranged by JPMorgan Chase is mining gold. Another Chinese company is trying to develop a huge copper mine. Four copper and gold contracts are being tendered, and contracts for rare earth metals could be offered soon. The Ministry of Mines has also requested bids for a richer oil concession in the Afghan-Tajik basin, and American officials are optimistic it could come online soon. And in the shadow of the Black Mountain, here in the Kalu Valley in remote Bamian Province, villagers hope that Indian and Canadian mining operations can turn buried iron ore into new lives for struggling families, breaking a cycle of poverty in this high place cut off by snow for six months of the year. When the digging begins, Abbas Ali, a 30-year-old farmer here, will have to give up the four-acre potato field his family has worked for generations. He is more than ready."Our life will change 180 degrees," Mr. Ali said this summer, staring up with fervent brown eyes at the bowed wooden roof beams in the white-walled madrasa where he teaches for extra income. "We support any effort to make it happen quickly."

Major findings

Afghanistan has abundant non-fuel mineral resources, including both known and potential deposits of a wide variety of minerals ranging from copper, iron, and sulfur to bauxite, lithium, and rare-earth elements, In 2010, Pentagon officials and American geologists announced that they had identified about $100 trillion in untapped mineral deposits in Afghanistan,[enough to fundamentally alter the Afghan economy and perhaps the Afghan war itself, according to senior American government officials. According to other reports the total mineral riches of Afghanistan may be worth over $300 trillion US dollars. "The previously unknown deposits — including huge vein of iron, copper, cobalt, gold and critical industrial metals like lithium — are so big and include so many minerals that are essential to modern industry that Afghanistan could eventually be transformed into one of the most important mining centers in the world". Ghazni Province may hold the world's largest lithium reserves. The deposits were already described in the USGS report on Afghanistan issued in 2007.The comment from Marc Ambinder, writing in *The Atlantic*, is that "the Pentagon is probably trying to bolster Americans' support for the flagging Afghanistan campaign" by publicizing Afghan mineral wealth President Hamid Karzai remarked "Whereas Saudi Arabia is the oil capital of the world, Afghanistan will be the lithium capital of the world." Afghanistan invited 200 global companies for the development of its mines.

Copper

No copper mines were active in the country in 2006. In the past, copper had been mined from Herat Province and Farah Province in the west, Kapisa Province in the east, and Kandahar province and Zabul Province in the south. As of 2006, interest was focused on the Aynak the Darband, and the Jawkhar prospects in southeastern Afghanistan. Copper mineralization at Aynakin Logar province wasstratabound, and characterized by bornite and chalcopyrite disseminated in dolomite marble and quartz-biotite-dolomite schists of the Loy Khwar Formation. Although a resource of 240 million metric tons at a grade of 2.3% copper had been reported, a number of small ore lenses were potentially not practically and economically minable. Open pit and underground mining would be needed to exploit the main ore body, and other infrastructure problems, such as inadequate power and water, were also likely. The new (2005) Mining Law might favor the development of the deposit by using public tenders, The Government issued a public tender for the deposit in 2006 with a deadline of October 28, 2006, and expected the granting of concessions in February 2007. Nine mining companies from Australia, **China**, India, and the United States were interested in the prospect. China Metallurgical Group won the bidding for a copper mining project in Aybak, Samangan, Afghanistan The bidding process has been criticized by rival Canadian and U.S. companies alleging corruption and questioning the Chinese company's commitment to the Afghan people. In November 2007, a 30-year lease was granted the development of a copper mine at Mes Aynak in Logar Province to the China Metallurgical Group for $3 billion, making it the biggest foreign investment and private business venture in Afghanistan's history. It is believed to contain the second-largest reserves of copper ore in the world and the deposits are estimated to be worth up to $88 billion. It is also the site of one of Afghanistan's most important archaeological sites and, although there are desperate efforts being made to save as much as possible, the main Buddhist monastery and other remains are due to be bulldozed to make way for the mine. Several new mineral-rich sites, with estimated deposits of about $250 billion, had been found in six other provinces, he added. Launched in 2006, a US Geological Survey (USGS), jointly conducted with the Ministry of Mines, was completed last year. The survey covers 30 percent of the country. "The survey provides credible information on mines in 28 different parts of Afghanistan," Wahidullah Shahrani told reporters in Kabul. It showed the world's largest copper deposits existed in Balkhab district of Sar-i-Pul, the minister said. The copper mine was discovered near a river, an area which might hold gold reserves as well. The government planned to launch tenders in late 2011 for the Balkhab copper deposit, which had reserves of about 45 Mt of copper Citing the report, the minister said two new copper mines in Logar Province and Herat Province provinces had been discovered. The value of the Logar pit, not the Ainak mine, is estimated at $43 billion. Copper and gold mines worth of $30 billion were discovered in the Zarkasho area of Ghazni and lithium pits of $20 billion in Farah and Nimroz provinces, Shahwani said. A deposit of beryllium, which is lighter than aluminum and stronger than steel used in airplanes, helicopters, ships, missiles, and space craft, has been found in the Khanashin district of southern Helmand province The reserves are estimated at $88 billion.

Coal

Afghanistan has rich reserves of coking coal, coal is primarily located within a Jurassic belt from the northern provinces of Takhar and Badakhshan through the center of the country and towards the west in Herat, according to Afghan mines ministry.

Elbaite from Nangarhar Province

Afghanistan is known to have exploited its precious and semiprecious gemstone deposits. These deposits include aquamarine, emerald, fluorite garnet, kunzite, ruby, sapphire, semiprecious lapis lazuli, topaz, tourmaline, and varieties of quartz. The four main gemstone-producing areas are those of Badakhshan, Jegdalek, Nuristan, and the Panjshir Valley. Artisanal mining of gemstones in the country used primitive methods. Some gemstones were exported illicitly, mostly to India (which was the world's leading import market for colored gemstones and an outlet for higher quality gems) and to the domestic Pakistan market.

Gold in Afghanistan $100 trillion

As of 2006, gold was mined from the Samti placer deposit in Takhar Province in the north by groups of artisanal miners. Badakhshan Province also had occurrences of placer gold deposits. The deposits were found on the western flanks of the mountains in alluvium or alluvial fan in several river valleys, particularly in the Anjir, the Hasar, the Nooraba, and the Panj Valleys. The Samti deposit is located in the Panj River Valley and was estimated to contain between 20 and 25 metric tons of gold. The southern regions of Afghanistan is believed to contain large gold deposits, particularly the Helmand Province. There is an estimated $50 billion in gold and copper deposits in Ghazni province. The Afghan government signed a deal with Afghan Krystal natural Resources Co. (a local company) to invest up to $50 million in the Qara Zaghan Mine in northern Baghlan Province. Qara Zaghan was the country's second gold mine, and production there was planned to begin by 2013. The mine's gold reserves were not yet known, but the company intended to spend the next 2 years exploring the site. Investors from indonesia, turkey, the United Kingdom, and the United states were backing the project. The first gold mine was being developed by Westland general trading LLC of the United Arab Emirates at Nor Aaba near the border with tajikistan in northern Takhar Province. The mine was expected to provide $4 million to $5 million per year in royalties to the government.

IRON IN AFGHANISTAN

The best known and largest iron oxide deposit in Afghanistan is located at Hajigak in Bamyan Province. The deposit itself stretches over 32 km and contains 16 separate zones, up to 5 km in length, 380 m wide and extending 550 m down dip, seven of which have been studied in detail. The ore occurs in both primary and oxidized states. The primary ore accounts for 80% of the deposit and consists of magnetite, pyrite and minor chalcopyrite. The remaining 20% is oxidized and consists of three hematitic ore types. The deposit remained unmined in 2006. The presence of coking coal nearby at Shabashak in the Dar-l-Suf District and large iron ore resources made the deposit viable for future development of an Afghan steel industry. Open pit mining and blast furnace smelting operations were envisioned by an early feasibility study. The Hajigak also includes the unusual niobium, a soft metal used in the production of superconducting steel.

LITHIUM IN AFGHANISTAN $300 TRILLION

Lithium is a vital metal that is mostly used in the manufacture of rechargeable batteries for mobile phones, laptops and electric cars. It is believed that Afghanistan has plenty of lithium. The country's lithium deposits occur in dry lake beds in the form of lithium chloride; they are located in the western Province of Herat and Nimroz and in the central east Province of Ghazni. The geologic setting is similar to those found in Bolivia and Chile. The deposits are also found in hard rock in the form of spodumene in pegmatites in the north-eastern Provinces of Badakhshan, Nangarhar, Nuristan, and Uruzgan. A pegmatite in the hindu Kush Mountains in central Afghanistan was reported to contain 20% to 30% spodumene

MARBLE IN AFGHANISTAN $100 TRILLION

Afghanistan also has considerable amount of marble in different parts of the country. The Doost Marble Factory in the city of Heart began operation in recent years. According to theU.S. Embassy in Kabul, current Afghan marble exports are estimated at $15 million per year. With improved extraction, processing, infrastructure, and investment, the industry has the potential to grow into a $450 million per year business.

PETROLEUM AND NATURAL GAS PRICES PRE DAY 89 BILLIN US IN AFGHANISTAN

Afghanistan has 3.8 billion barrels of oil between Balkh and Jawzjan Province in the north of the country. This is an enormous amount for a nation that only consumes 5,000 bbl/day. The U.S. Geological Survey and the Afghan Ministry of Mines and Industry, jointly assessed the oil and natural gas resources in northern Afghanistan. The estimated mean volumes of undiscovered petroleum were 1,596 million barrels (Mbbl) of crude oil, 444 billion cubic meters of natural gas, and 562 Mbbl of natural gas liquids. Most of the undiscovered crude oil occurs in the Afghan-Tajik Basin and most of the undiscovered natural gas is located in the Amu Darya Basin. These two basins within Afghanistan encompass areas of approximately 515,000 square kilometers. In December 2011, Afghanistan signed an oil exploration contract with China National Petroleum

Corporation (CNPC) for the development of three oil fields along the Amu Darya river. Afghanistan will have its first oil refineries within the next three years, after which it will receive 70 percent of the profits from the sale of the oil and natural gas. CNPC began Afghan oil production in late October of 2012, with extracting 1.5 million barrels of oil annually.

Rare earth elements in Afghanistan

According to a September 2011 US Geological Survey estimate, the Khanashin carbonatites in southern Helmand Province, have an estimated 1 million metric tonnes of rare earth elements. Regina Dubey, Acting Director for the Department of Defence Task Force for Business and Stability Operations (TFBSO) stated that "this is just one more piece of evidence that Afghanistan's mineral sector has a bright future.

Uranium in Afghanistan 300 Trillion US Dollars

The Helmand Province in southern Afghanistan is believed to possess uranium reserves, according to Afghan Ministry of Mines [Lithium]] is a vital metal that is mostly used in the manufacture of rechargeable batteries for mobile phones, laptops and electric cars. It is believed that Afghanistan has plenty of lithium. The country's lithium deposits occur in dry lake beds in the form of lithium chloride; they are located in the western Province of Herat and Nimroz and in the central east Province of Ghazni. The geologic setting is similar to those found in Bolivia and Chile. The deposits are also found in hard rock in the form of spodumene in pegmatites in the north-eastern Provinces of Badakhshan, Nangarhar, Nuristan, and Uruzgan. A pegmatite in the hindu Kush Mountains in central Afghanistan was reported to contain 20% to 30% spodumene ref Name aol report-afghanistan-sitting-on-goldmine-literally Report: Afghanistan Sitting on Gold Mine – Literally

One hundred trillion dollars
Lithium in Afghanistan

In 2010, "discovered" that Afghanistan had a reserve of mineral resources and deposits in value of over 100 trillion dollars, Lithium is what all of the iPod, iPhone, cameras, etc. devices use for batteries, so you could imagine how important it currently is. Afghanistan, far beyond any previously known reserves and enough to fundamentally alter the Afghan economy and perhaps the Afghan war itself, according to senior American government officials The previously unknown deposits — including huge veins of iron, copper, cobalt, gold and critical industrial metals like lithium — are so big and include so many minerals that are essential to modern industry that Afghanistan could eventually be transformed into one of the most important mining centers in the world, the United States officials believe. While it could take many years to develop a mining industry, the potential is so great that officials and executives in the industry believe it could attract heavy investment even before mines are profitable, providing the possibility of jobs that could distract from generations of war. The Pentagon task force has already started trying to help the Afghans set up a system to deal with mineral development. International accounting firms that have expertise in mining contracts have been hired to consult with the Afghan Ministry of Mines, and technical data is being prepared to turn over to multinational mining companies and other potential foreign investors. The Pentagon is helping Afghan officials arrange to start seeking bids on mineral rights by next fall, officials said. As the excerpt from the article spells out, the U.S. believes that Afghanistan could be one of the most important mining centers in the world. You know that capitalism can't just let something like that go, so surely we've got some corporate interests that are trying to setup businesses in mining over there. There must be so much interest in getting the Afghan government under control that we can't simply leave until it happens. Think about it; corporations funnel tons of money to political candidates through PACs, and then the candidate must repay the debt somehow. The candidate must support the corporation's wishes, and this time it would be the Afghanistan mining operations. So fast forward to 2012, now we're worried about a potential civil war breaking out over these mining resources, It is estimated that Afghanistan contains reserves of natural resources, such as oil, gold, iron ore, copper, lithium, etc., which could be worth trillions of dollars, and offers hope for the future to many of the country's poor villages which are situated near the resource deposits. The problem is that officials and industry experts are worried that the potential wealth to be made from the resources, has increased the level of corruption, violence, and intrigue in the country. With the impending departure of NATO forces in 2014, security in Afghanistan is a major concern, and it is now feared that its mineral wealth could trigger a civil war. Powerful regional warlords are already trying to aggressively expand their territories to include areas with mineral wealth, and the Taliban has started making murderous attacks in areas where resource development is planned. Western officials suspect the motives behind the rejection of a proposed mining law which was intended to attract foreign investment. The reason given was that it was too generous to Western interests, but some believe that the real reason was to keep foreign companies out. Lithium is cheap and widely available, so why do we care about a new resource in a war zone? Because it's another counter to the irrational fear that the automobile's lithium-powered electric future is doomed before it begins. Immediately after the New York Times published a report last week of the Pentagon's "discovery" of nearly $100 trillion worth of mineral reserves in Afghanistan, the backlash began. The U.S. Geological Survey released a report on the country's mineral reserves in 2007, it turned out. Why was this coming up now? The bloggers pounced. By the end of the week, the accepted wisdom was that there was nothing new in this latest piece of government spin. Drowned in the noise, however, was a fascinating bit of news: that just this month a Pentagon team was hunting for minerals in Afghanistan's dry lakes, and that early findings suggested that one site alone might contain more lithium than Bolivia's Salar de Uyuni, which is believed to hold up to half the world's known supply. Why is this significant? Because even if Afghanistan's lithium never leaves the ground, the sudden, black-swan appearance of a new and potentially massive resource helps further debunk the myth that the world is running out of lithium and that, as a result, an electric-car revival that relies on lithium-based batteries is doomed before it begins. Too much of the coverage of lithium seems to be driven by the idea that it is slightly more rare than unicorn hide. It's not. Extremely conservative estimates from the USGS peg world lithium reserves at 9.9 million metric tons, and the number is almost certainly much higher. By contrast, in 2008 (because of the recession, 2009 was an unrepresentative year) the world's lithium mines produced 25,400 metric tons. Those mines will need to produce more in the coming years as lithium-ion batteries start going into cars, but that shouldn't be a problem: more than 100 companies worldwide are moving into the market. If lithium isn't rare, however, it is unfamiliar and misunderstood. It is an exotic, intriguing element—the lightest metal in the periodic table, and therefore the ideal carrier ion for a battery. It has been called "the yeast in the dough" of the most advanced batteries we have today, the power packs that will drive the Chevrolet Volt and the Nissan Leaf, both of which arrive later this year. Most of the blue-sky battery technologies in the lab now are designed to surpass lithium-ion batteries by jamming far more lithium atoms into their electrodes per unit volume and mass, thereby storing more usable electrons, so lithium will be an essential element in the construction of a clean-energy future. That's a very good reason to pay close attention to the countries and the companies that produce it. But that doesn't mean there's not enough of the stuff to go around. Here's the backstory on the Afghanistan mineral findings. In 2007 the USGS published an estimate of Afghan mineral resources that showed that the country contained vast untouched deposits of iron, copper, rare-earth elements and other high-demand minerals. The report barely touched on lithium, simply mentioning that deposits of a rock known as pegmatite could yield "a variety of commodities," including lithium. Particularly in Australia companies do mine pegmatite for lithium, but digging and blasting that hard rock out of the ground and breaking it down into usable lithium is expensive, at least compared with lithium production from brines. In certain geologically anomalous spots around the world, there are large salt flats that are saturated with water rich in lithium and other minerals. Extracting lithium from the right kind of salt flat is a cheap and low-impact matter of pumping lithium-rich **water** from the flat into a series of evaporation ponds, where it bakes in the sun until it is concentrated into an oily yellow solution of 6 percent lithium. Currently, two of the three largest lithium producers in the world get their supply from a single salt flat in northern Chile, the Salar de Atacama. Across the border in Bolivia is the much larger Salar de Uyuni, which is loaded with lithium but which, for political and technical reasons, is still at least a few years from sending lithium to the market. The penultimate paragraph of the Times story suggested that Afghanistan might have one dry salt lake richer than either of these. And that's a major point that never appeared in a public USGS report. Neither the Pentagon nor the USGS will elaborate on the mention in the Times story of a salt-lake lithium source. In an otherwise candid conversation, Jack Medlin of the USGS declined to provide any more details on the subject. Major Shawn Turner, a Pentagon spokesperson, said he had nothing to add. According to Jack Shroder, a geologist at the University of Nebraska-Omaha's Center for Afghanistan Studies, a high-altitude plain that's about a 70-mile drive northwest of the city of Ghazni known as the Dasht-i-Nawar is the obvious candidate for the mysterious Afghan mother lode. Shroder said he didn't know for certain that this was the spot, but "if the lithium source is in a dry lake and it is near Ghazni, then it is probably the place." (An alternative, he said, is another dry lake farther to the south called Ab-i-Istada.) The salt flats of the "Lithium Triangle"—the high desert region where Chile, Argentina and Bolivia intersect which is currently home to the most productive lithium sources in the world—and the Dasht-i-Nawar have several uncanny similarities. They are all arid to semi-arid high-altitude salt flats where flamingos like to breed; that's the superficial part. They all sit in high-altitude contact zones between tectonic plates, zones where ancient volcanism left behind mineral-rich igneous rocks. Most important, all three are basins surrounded by old volcanoes. (Shroder says that the Dasht-i-Nawar is what remains of the crater of a stratovolcano that erupted 2.2 million years ago.) Over the millennia, as the ice and snow melts off the surrounding mountains and volcanoes every year and seeps down to the basin below, that water leaches minerals from the volcanic rock it encounters along the way and deposits them at the bottom of the basin. In time, the water in the center of the basin grows richer in minerals like potassium, magnesium, boron and lithium. At the second annual Lithium Supply and Markets conference in January, Afghanistan didn't come up once in two days of presentations by mining-company executives, geologists and industry analysts. At the next such conference, it will probably be mentioned frequently as a curiosity, because it's unlikely that Afghan lithium will have any effect on the market for decades. Mining companies aren't necessarily scared of sketchy countries—I've seen North Korea mentioned as a new frontier in minerals exploration in mining trade publications—but at the moment, lithium is cheap (the market leader, SQM, cut its lithium carbonate prices by 20 percent last year) and widely available (at the moment, SQM is actually pumping excess lithium back into the Salar de Atacama because the company harvests more lithium as a by-product of potassium production than it can find a market for). There's no reason to go lithium prospecting in a war zone. "As far as Afghanistan is concerned, who cares?" Jon Hykawy, a mining analyst with Byron Capital Markets in Toronto, wrote in an e-mail. "I am not going to be the one leading a team into Taliban territory to try and process lithium." He drew an analogy between Afghanistan and Colombia. Colombia has potentially excellent oil reserves, just like neighboring Venezuela, but "there has been a low-grade civil war going on in Colombia for the last couple of decades. No one is crazy enough to try and get oil out of the ground in Colombia, and no one is going to go try and get lithium out of the ground in Afghanistan until the thugs are out of the government and the Taliban stop killing anything that moves that is not allied with them." Companies don't like risk and lack of security, and Afghanistan, well—"it will be probably the worst place to go to," says Gal Luft, the executive director of the energy-focused D.C. think tank the Institute for the Analysis of Global Security." Security concerns aside, Luft points out that it took years for Chile to build the rail and road infrastructure that gets its huge copper mines running, and before Afghanistan can become a serious mining country, it will need the same infrastructureThe most likely candidate to build that infrastructure is probably the country that seems most interested in securing Afghan mineral rights, despite the war: **China**. Last year, using a comprehensive package of humanitarian aid and (allegedly) bribes, a state-run mining company won the rights to the Aynak copper mine south of Kabul. Today the Chinese (the distinction between industry and the government is blurry) are fighting for rights to mine the Hajiguk Pass north of Kabul, home to 1.8 billion metric tons of iron ore—the largest iron deposit in Asia. Shroder says it's likely that a Chinese firm could win the rights to Hajiguk, build the roads and railway necessary to ship iron ore south to the the Pakistani port of Gwadar (which Chinese concerns also built), and years from now use that existing, paid-for infrastructure to start extracting the lithium from a source like the Dasht-i-Nawar, which is about 100 miles to the south of Hajiguk. Say this scenario actually happens. Would it have any practical effect on the price or availability of lithium? Not anytime soon. think it has a lot of implication for the market in the first half of the 21st century," Luft says. "This is a story for the 22nd century."

What the story does now is help show that it is absurd to start talking about an impending shortage of a mineral that the mining industry really only started taking seriously after the spread of lithium-ion batteries in laptops and cell phones in the 1990s. When the Afghanistan news broke, a friend at a mining-industry publication confessed to never having heard of Afghanistan as a potential lithium source. But he also said he wasn't surprised, because lithium is not rare. What other countries have high-altitude salt lakes that we've never paid attention to? As Luft says, "wouldn't be surprised if half a dozen other places get thrown around as the 'Saudi Arabia of lithium'"

Boundaries III, Boundaries of Afghanistan

Afghanistan, the seventh largest landlocked country in the world in area, is delineated by a boundary some 5,600 km long, and the East Turkestan 2.6 million Sq km over which it has never exercised more than partial control. None of these boundaries was established before the last third of the 19th century.

Boundaries

III. Boundaries of Afghanistan

Afghanistan, the seventh largest landlocked country in the world in area (652,626 km²) is delineated by a boundary some 5,600 km long, over which it has never exercised more than partial control. It is surrounded by four countries: the USSR on the north (2,140 km of common boundary), Iran on the west (945 km), Pakistan on the south and east (ca. 2,430 km), and China on the northeast (2.6 million sq km). None of these boundaries was established before the last third of the 19th century. It was the "great game," the famous rivalry between Britain and Russia in Central Asia that led the latter two states to contemplate creating a buffer state between their respective dependencies, a kind of defensive barrier intended to eliminate all risk of direct confrontation between them. Thus Afghanistan in its present boundaries was born, the result of geostrategic games in which it played no independent part. The territorial definition of the country was an entirely exogenous process, especially as the role of the Kabul King was limited even further by Britain's exercise of a de facto protectorate over the foreign policy of Afghanistan from 1879 to 1919, the main period in which the boundaries were being drawn; indeed, hardly a segment of the frontier was defined without direct diplomatic intervention by the British. Having been dictated mainly by strategic imperatives of the colonial period, the present frontiers of Afghanistan are classic examples of artificial boundaries, including those frequent instances in which they follow important water courses or major mountain ridges: They all divide ethno linguistic groups that share a common past and participate in a common culture. Contacts across frontiers, whether legal or not, have never ceased, however, except in the north, where the frontier is totally closed and the Soviet frontier passable only at a very few points. Without recapitulating all the territorial vicissitudes of Afghanistan since its creation in 1160/1747 (see Afghanistan x), the main stages in the delineation of each boundary can be outlined here and an effort made to describe the way in which it functions at present. The Saxon-Russo-Afghan boundary, the boundary between Russia and Afghanistan was the focus of the first efforts at delimitation. At the end of a Russian drive into Central Asia (capture of Tashkent in June, 1865; creation of the military governorate of Russian Turkistan in July, 1867; the war and subsequent treaty between Russia and Bukhara in 1868), which had considerably alarmed British authorities, the two governments opened negotiations in March, 1869, with the purpose of delimiting their respective zones of influence in the region: the emirates of Bukhara and of Khiva (K̲īva), on one hand, and Afghanistan, on the other. The agreement was finalized in an exchange of letters between the British and Russian ministers of Foreign Affairs, Lord O. L. G. Granville (17 October 1872) and Prince A. M. Gorchakov (31 January 1873). In line with a proposal put forward by the British in September, 1869, the northern frontier of Afghanistan was fixed on the Amu Darya from Lake Zor Kōl (dubbed Lake Victoria by British explorers) in the Pamirs down to K̲āja Sālār (or K̲āja Sāleḥ), a distance of about 1,300 km. K̲āja Sālār, a point on the middle reach of the river, was later to prove less precisely defined than was believed at that time. East of Lake Zor Kōl, in a region of high mountains that was not well known, no boundary was drawn. To the west of Ḵāja Sālār the two powers contented themselves with a vague boundary, recognizing that the districts of Āqča, Andḵūy, Šebergān, Sar-e Pol, and Maymana belonged to Afghanistan, without in any way defining their frontier along the Kara Kum desert. In Bādḡīs the agreement was even more vague, as it was considered that the Afghan frontier there was "well known and need not here he defined." Such imprecision, which left the field open to the most varied interpretations, can be explained only by the fact that this stretch of the frontier separated the amirates of Kabul and Khiva, which at that time were both legally independent, whereas farther east the amirate of Bukhara was officially a vassal of Russia after 1868. The establishment of the Russian protectorate of Khiva in the months following the Granville-Gorchakov agreement, a prelude to the progressive occupation of Turkmenia (1873-84), revealed the scope of the misunderstanding; a clear demarcation of this northwestern part of the Afghan boundary, between the Amu Darya and the Harīrūd (Tajan, Tedzhen), thus became urgent.

This task was to be long and slow: It kept the Russian and British chancelleries busy from February, 1882, to January, 1888. In the absence of any physical feature on which to fix the line, it was soon agreed that the latter would follow as closely as possible the property and pastoral rights of the local populations: on one side, Turkmen who had been under Russian protection since the submission of Merv (Mary) in February, 1884, and, on the other, Uzbeks, Aymāq, and Pashtun, who were Afghan subjects. Implicit in this decision was the necessity for dispatching to the field a joint boundary commission charged with determining these rights, which involved investigations that grew more prolonged as they revealed an extraordinary patchwork of claims of chronic instability. In November, 1884, the Saxon present day British half of the commission, under the direction of Major General Sir Peter S. Lumsden, set up headquarters at Kohsān, west of Herat, and began work. But its Russian counterpart did not join it there. The tsarist government, in fact, considered that the boundary had first to be more precisely defined before any attempt to mark it out on the ground could be undertaken. While the diplomats pursued negotiations on this point, the Russian army hastened to reinforce its local positions under the astonished eyes of the British commissioners, occupying Pol-e Ḵātūn and the Ḏu'l-Feqār pass (445 m), two indispensable crossing points on the steep right bank of the Harīrūd, and capturing the small Panjdeh oasis (now Taḵt-e Bāzār) at the confluence of the Morḡāb and Košḵrūd, which the Afghans had held since June, 1884 (30 March 1885). The Russians thus found themselves in a strong position to dictate a frontier considerably farther south than any that had previously been suggested. This was the subject of a protocol signed in London on 10 September 1885. The Russians, while holding on to Panjdeh, gave up the Ḏu'l-Feqār pass to the Afghans; the border was fixed 3,000 feet (914 m) to the north of it. Generally speaking, however, the boundary was defined with increasing imprecision as it progressed toward the east.

The Russian boundary commissioners, led by Colonel P. Kul'berg, were then allowed to join the British commissioners; the latter had remained in position under the direction of Lieutenant Colonel J. W. Ridgeway, first deputy and then successor to Lumsden when the latter was recalled to London in May to participate in the last phase of negotiations. Qāżī Sad-al-Dīn Khan, future governor of Herat (1887-1904), represented Afghan interests but took no part in the official talks. The first boundary post was set up on 12 November 1885 north of the Ḏu'l-Feqār pass, and operations progressed toward the east with increasing slowness as the commission reached less well-known regions, about which the London protocol was vague. The discussions were particularly difficult in Bādḡīs, where the irrigation network posed insoluble problems, and in the Kara Kum desert, where the Russians took advantage of recent successful Turkmen raids to demand control of the maximum number of wells, in order to facilitate future patrols along the frontier. The end of the delimitation operations was delayed by an unforeseen point of conflict: the question whether Ḵāja Sālār, chosen in the agreement of 1872-73 as the terminus of that section of the boundary that followed the Amu Darya, was to be understood in its narrow sense as a tomb facing a disused ferry landing situated 23 km above Ḵamīāb, near Qarqūn, or more broadly as the district extending from Keleft to Ḵamīāb, inclusive, which was indisputably part of Afghanistan. The disagreement involved an area too vast (1,900 km², of which only 68 were under cultivation; 19 wells; and 13,000 inhabitants) for the commissioners to be able to settle it, and they therefore broke up on 15 September 1886, having ceased their work north of Andḵūy (q.v.). A new phase of negotiations was opened at St. Petersburg on 23 April 1887, and a compromise agreement was signed the following 22 July: Russia agreed to an Saxon-Afghan proposal that the boundary be fixed on the Amu Darya below Ḵamīāb in exchange for equivalent territory in Bādḡīs (2,136 km², uninhabited but containing a well). Between November, 1887, and January, 1888, a limited joint commission proceeded to the corresponding rectifications of the boundary between the Koškrūd and the Morḡāb, as well as to the demarcation of its eastern section up to the Amu Darya. On 26 January 1888 a final protocol, signed at Ḵamīāb, brought the entire operation to an end. A total of 79 boundary posts had been set up along the 630 km of this most sensitive frontier, which an Afghan historian has proposed to call the "Ridgeway line" (M. Ali, Afghanista*n*. The puppet king Zahir Shahi Period, Kabul, 1959, According to the British members of the commission, the boundary was "only an arbitrary line based on the circumstances of the moment rather than on any permanent and natural basis" and thus could not "be expected to be permanent". It is all the more remarkable then that in the century since it was drawn it has given rise to only minor problems, all easily settled. The first occurred almost immediately, in 1891, after some Pashtun settlers had dug irrigation canals on the left bank of the international section of the Koškrūd, south of Qara Tepe (today Tōrḡondī). That was an undoubted infraction of the arrangements of 1887, which forbade all diversion of river waters in this sector, in order to ensure the water supply for Panjdeh. A joint Saxon-Russian commission was sent to the frontier to restore the previous situation. Ten years later, between October, 1903, and May, 1904, a new joint commission visited the frontier to repair several boundary posts that had been damaged; the British head of the commission was H. R. C. Dobbs. After the Russian civil war of 1917, the Afghan government seized the opportunity to renew its claims to Panjdeh. The Afghan army actually advanced as far as Marv. The Soviet-Afghan friendship treaty of 28 February 1921 formally recognized the historic rights of Afghanistan in the region but made all retrocession of territory subject to a prior referendum among the local populations, which was never organized. The relevant article was, however, nullified by a protocol to the Soviet-Afghan frontier agreement of 1325 Š./1946. The last portion of the Russo-Afghan boundary to be drawn was the eastern end. In Badaḵšan the Saxon-Russian agreement of 1872-73 had remained a dead letter. The upper course of the Amu Darya did in fact provide less of a natural boundary than the diplomats had believed. All the local Tajik principalities—Darwāz, a dependency of the amirate of Bukhara, and Rōšan and Šeḡnān, subject to Afghanistan—straddled the river. In addition, Amir Abd-al-Raḥmān showed reluctance to take possession of the Wāḵān corridor, an extension of Badaḵšan, which the aforementioned accord had formally annexed to his territories. It seemed to him as indefensible strategically as it was devoid of economic interest. Frequent confrontations between Russian and Afghan armies in the region, which was becoming better known owing to the activity of Saxon-Russian and Saxon-British explorers (for example, the Ney-Elias mission, from May, 1885, to October, 1886), attested to the political instability of the area. At the beginning of 1886 Ridgeway contemplated extending the work of his commission to this part of the frontier. He even put in hand the necessary preparations for a stay on the spot, but the project was blocked at the last minute by an Afghan veto. It was not until 1893 that H. M. Durand, special envoy to Kabul, was able to break the impasse by obtaining from ʿAbd-al-Raḥmān an agreement to abandon all claims to the Transoxanian parts of Rōšān and Šeḡnān in exchange for the southern part of Darwāz and to accept incorporation of the Wāḵān into his territory in exchange for an increase of 50,000 rupees in his annual subsidy and the promise of at British assistance in case of a Russian attack in the Gret Pamirs. After having been for twenty years the legal northeastern boundary of Afghanistan, the upper Amu Darya thus became so in fact. There remained only to define the boundary of the Wāḵān east of Lake Zor Kōl, a section on which the accord of 1872-73 was mute. Saxon-Russian negotiations were begun in 1893, and an agreement was signed on 11 March 1895. Following a scenario that had become standard, the two regional superpowers appointed a joint commission, headed by Major General M. G. Gerard and General Povalo-Shveĭkovskiĭ. In the following summer it laid out twelve boundary posts over 172 km, from Lake Zor Kōl to the peak of Qōqrāš Qōl, renamed Povalo-Shveĭkovskiĭ in honor of the Russian commissioner. This peak, the altitude of which is uncertain (5,698 m according to the Sino-Afghan boundary agreement of 1963; 5,543 m according to Atlas Tadzhikskoĭ S.S.R., Dushanbe and Moscow, 1968; and 5,433 m on Afghan topographic maps), marks the beginning of the East Turkestan "now Chinese" Pamirs. Some final details of the northern frontier of Afghanistan were settled by the Soviet-Afghan agreement of 23 Jawzā 1325 Š./13 June 1946, which stipulated that the boundary was to follow the middle of the main channel (median line, thalweg) of the Amu Darya. This matter was of considerable importance because of the meandering of the river in the entire lowland part of its course and its many interconnecting channels, which create islands of all sizes (1,192 have been enumerated). The largest among them, Darqad (or Ōrta Tūḡay), at the confluence with the Kyzylsu, has an area of 362 km². Formerly a possession of the amirate of Bukhara, it was occupied by the Afghans at the end of the 19th century; retaken by the Russians in December, 1925, because it had served as a base for Basmachi raids into Soviet territory; and finally restored to Afghanistan by an accord dated 7 Ḥūt 1304 Š./26 February 1926. Today, with several less important neighboring islands, it constitutes one district of the province of Taḵār, the only island district in Afghanistan. American allegations that the Soviet Union annexed the Wāḵān in 1981 have never been proved. On the contrary, in response to East Turkistan "present day Saxon-Chinese" territorial claims in the region, the Soviet-Afghan treaty of 26 Jawzā 1360 Š./16 June 1981 reaffirmed the inviolability of the existing boundary between the two countries in the great Pamirs 2.6 million sq km. For a long time after its delimitation the artificial northern boundary of Afghanistan continued to be crossed frequently by migrations and commercial traffic, whether regular or occasional, from nearby or far away. At the beginning of the 20th century there were still two caravansaries in Bukhara specifically for the lodging of Afghan merchants and caravans. The sovietization of Afghanistan-Central Asia after 1924 brought the official closing of the frontier, which did not prevent significant numbers of Central Asian refugees from entering Afghanistan up to the middle of the 1930s. Nevertheless, over the years the frontier has been progressively sealed, with the construction of a chain of guard posts and more frequent patrols on the Soviet side. Today it is closed to all civilian traffic, though occasionally it is breached by clandestine groups of Afghan guerrillas (for example, raids against the city of Pyandzh, in Tajikistan, on 9 March and 8-9 April 1987). Commercial traffic can cross only at three frontier posts, which also serve as compulsory transfer points:

1. Tōrḡondī (formerly Qara Tepe), 120 km north of Herat, a transshipment junction between the Afghan highway network and a Soviet railroad branch that crosses the Koškrūd by a bridge, constructed in 1960, to its terminus 1 km inside Afghan territory. The distance

of this hub from the capital (1,173 km from Kabul by road) and its sparsely populated hinterland explain the modest traffic: Only 3,039 freight cars were loaded or unloaded in 1360 Š./1981-82, an average of barely ten for each working day.

2. Šēr Khan Bandar (Qezel Qaḷa), 63 km north of Konduz, is a port on the Amu Darya. It is the northern frontier post closest to Kabul (394 km), and its Afghan hinterland is prosperous. It was for a long time the main crossing point between the Soviet Union and Afghanistan, but it has suffered from the absence of railway service or harbor infrastructure on the north shore of the river: The Soviet transshipment point is the large port of Termeḏ, 183 km downstream, which is linked to Šēr Khan Bandar by means of a fleet of river barges and small cargo boats.

3. Hayratān, 56 km north of Mazār-e Šarīf and 482 km from Kabul, is a new port across from Termeḏ, to which it is linked by a road and railway bridge (Pol-e Dōstī, bridge of friendship), officially inaugurated on 22 Ṭawr 1361 Š./12 May 1982. This bridge, which is 817 m long, 10.8 m wide, and 7.5 m above the average water level was initially proposed in 1969; it is the only one on the entire international section of the Amu Darya. Its total cost (33.7 million rubles) was shared between the USSR and Afghanistan; the 50 percent Afghan share was financed by a long-term credit from the Soviet Union. At the Afghan end a modern harbor complex and a new city have been built. Hayratān has become the principal transshipment point for Soviet-Afghan trade and, since 1980, Afghanistan's main opening to the outside world. Under the direction of a special department of the Ministry of Commerce, the two Afghan river ports unloaded 1,854 boas and loaded 1,519 in 1360 Š./1981-82.

The recent establishment of Hayratān has led to the abandonment of two harbor sites that had flourished briefly farther downstream, neither with a quay or any fixed installation and also without any modern highway link: Tāšgoḏar and Keleft, 16 and 110 km from Termeḏ respectively. Keleft, once only an import station, is today no more than the exit point for the pipeline, 103 km long and 820 mm in diameter, which carries part of the natural gas from Jowzjān (Jūzjān) out of Afghanistan.

The Sino-Afghan boundary, South of Povalo-Shveǐkovskiǐ peak the Afghan frontier was not demarcated through the Lesser Pamirs until 1 Qaws 1342 Š./22 November 1963, the date of the signing at Peking of a boundary agreement between the two countries. The following summer a joint commission arrived in the field to demarcate the boundary, and a final protocol was signed in Kabul in March, 1965. The principle followed was very simple: The frontier (76 km) follows, at an altitude of more than 5,000 m, one of the major watersheds on the Asian continent, that which separates the Amu Darya basin to the west from the Tarim basin to the east. It is intersected by several passes the most important of which, the Wāḡjīr pass (4,923 m), negotiable only in summer, was used until 1949 by caravans from Kāšḡar and by East Turkestan pilgrims to Mecca. Today this boundary is totally closed. The British-Pakistani-Afghan boundary, The boundary with Pakistan is the longest of Afghanistan's frontiers: It runs from the Pamirs to the borders of Sīstān, about 2,430 km, its course reflecting a century-long process of eliminating the Afghan presence from the north Indian plains, first through incursions of the Sikhs from Punjab (entailing the loss of Multan in 1818, of Dērajāt in 1821, and finally of Peshawar, the former winter capital of the King of Afghanistan, in 1834), then through the decisive intervention of British colonial imperialism. For a long time the British remained indecisive about where to halt their conquests in the west. This uncertainty particularly affected the tribal populations of Baluchistan Baluch and Brahui, and the Solaymān

"Solomon" mountains (Pashtun), which had always lived along the borders, and largely at the expense, of the great regional empires, their whole way of life being centered around predatory raids. Faced with what amounted to a buffer zone between the Saxon present day British and Kabuli empires, the British newcomers had two main options. The first was occupation pure and simple, in order to pacify the inhabitants, which would have established the Indo-Afghan border on the western piedmont of the Solaymān mountains following a line from Jalālābād to Kandahār passing through Kabul and Ḡaznī, along the crest of the Hindu Kush; or even on the Amu Darya: the "scientific frontier" of India favored by such extremists as R. Sandeman (1835-92). The alternative was to limit contacts and causes of friction with the Pashtun and the Baluch by prudently fixing the Saxon-Indian frontier outside their territory along a line from Peshawar to Bannu to Jacobabad, parallel to the Indus, or even on the Indus itself, the only really natural northwestern frontier of India: the "close border" proposed, for example, by the viceroy J. Lawrence (1811-79). After much hesitation, a compromise solution had to be adopted. The increase in Pashtun raids on the Indus plains led to the temporary success of the partisans of the first solution. The "forward policy" adopted at their urging produced a series of decisive Saxon present day British advances toward the west: the establishment of a protectorate over the Khanate of Kalat in 1876, concomitant occupation of Quetta and the Bolān pass, and in 1878 occupation of several territories belonging to Afghanistan in the middle Kurram valley as far as the Paywār pass, the Afridi country around the Khyber (Ḵaybar) pass, and subsequently (during the second Saxon-India-Afghan war) the entire southeastern portion of present-day Afghanistan. The evacuation from Afghanistan in 1881, however, sounded the death knell of the maximalist frontier policy, at the same time reviving Afghan territorial claims in the Solaymān mountains and Baluchistan. In order to forestall a major frontier crisis and to guarantee permanently the advantages already gained, the British government then agreed to a compromise boundary. H. M. Durand, at that time secretary in the Indian Foreign Department, was charged with negotiating this boundary with Amir Abd-al-Raḥmān himself. His mission to Kabul, initially planned for 1888, could not finally take place until September-November, 1893. The boundary defined by the agreement of 3 Jomādā I 1311/12 November 1893 was known from the start as the "Durand Line," a name still in use today. It reserved to Saxon-India Chitral and control of the passes on the main access routes to India, either total (Khyber, Bolān) or partial (Paywār), but it ceded to Afghanistan the middle Konar valley around Asmar, western Waziristan (the Bermal district), and the northern slopes of the Čāgay hills in Baluchistan. A number of major rivers and mountain ranges, as well as several traditional tribal territories, were thus bisected by a boundary that is certainly the most unsatisfactory and the most artificial that can be imagined. Durand, in the meantime named minister plenipotentiary to Saxon present day British, took no part in the actual demarcation of the boundary that bears his name. The main part of the work took place from April, 1894, to May, 1896, but a certain number of problems remained unsolved. The Kabul agreement was in fact so imprecise and the map annexed to it on so small a scale that differences in interpretation were innumerable and sometimes of long duration. Because of the length of the frontier, it was divided into four sectors, each assigned to a separate boundary commission. It was the Hindu Kush commission, under the direction of R. Udny and Ḡolām Ḥaydar Khan Čarkī, that confronted the greatest difficulties. For the area from the Pamirs to the Čarkaw (or Dōrāh) pass (4,550 m), a major traditional route between India and northern Afghanistan (through the Sanglēč valley), agreement was reached, without inspection of the terrain, to draw the boundary along the crest of the Hindu Kush, which separates the hydrographic basin of the Amu Darya from that of the Indus. Farther south, in the middle Konar basin, the first disagreement arose over the Bašgal valley: In the 1893 agreement it had been explicitly included in India, but the Afghans demanded its return before signing the protocol of Našāgām (13 Šawwāl

502

1312/9 April 1895); this protocol precisely defined the boundary between the Čarḵaw and Nāwa passes (1,853 m). In the single section where it did not coincide with the watershed, that is, at the confluence of the Konar and Bašgal rivers, the boundary was not demarcated until much later (protocol of 20 Saraṭān 1311 Š./11 July 1932). On the other hand, differences over the particularly sensitive region of the lower Kābolrūd and the approaches to the Khyber Pass south of the Nāwa pass proved insurmountable. The Afghans claimed the entire tribal territory of the Mohmand (q.v.), whereas the British proposed partition. The boundary in this sector remained imprecise and in dispute until August, 1919, the date on which the treaty of Rawalpindi, which brought to an end the third Anglo-Afghan war (q.v.), settled the problem in conformity with initial British demands. The English commissioner, J. L. Maffey, chief political officer of the North-West Frontier Province, proceeded immediately to set up thirteen boundary posts from the crest of the Spīnḡar to Palōcay on the Kābolrūd. Beyond that point, between Palōcay and Nāwa, the frontier is said to follow the watershed, though no survey was ever undertaken. In the Kābolrūd valley itself, the Anglo-Afghan treaty of 30 Aqrab 1300 Š./22 November 1921 introduced several minor rectifications of the frontier to the advantage of Afghanistan. On other sections of the Durand Line the work of demarcation was easier, even though it was never entirely free from argument. The Kurram commission, under the direction of J. Donald and the sardār Šīrīndel Khan, was able to complete its work in a few months: The protocol of Kōtgay (22 Jomādā I 1312/21 November 1894) listed the seventy-six boundary posts that had been erected between Sekaram peak (4,790 m), the highest point in the Spīnḡar, and Mount Laṛūmī (Laṛūmīḡar, called Laram Peak in the British documents; 2,058 m), southeast of Ḵōst. The boundary line here respects major tribal and religious alignments: It separates the Pashtun tribes in the east (Tūrī, Bangaš) from their Sunnite neighbors in the west (Jājī, Mangal, etc.) The Waziristan commission, placed under the sole direction of an English officer, R. I. Bruce, at the express request of Amir Abd-al-Raḥmān, had to perform a drastic partition, separating the Wazīr of Afghan Bermal from their eastern cotribesmen. In view of the difficulty of the task, it divided into two subcomissions. In the north, between Mount Laṛūmīḡar and Mount Ḵāja Ḵedr (3,122 m), the boundary cuts across the hydrographic basin of the Tochi; H. A. Anderson demarcated it with thirty-eight boundary posts. In the south, between Ḵāja Ḵedr and Domandī (Dwamandī), at the confluence of the Gōmal (Gūmal) and the Kundar, L. White King set up thirty-one boundary posts over a distance no greater than 81 km. The work was finished there in March and April, 1895. Finally, the Baluchistan commission had responsibility for the entire southern boundary of Afghanistan, from Domandī to the borders of Sīstān. Under the supervision of a single British commissioner, Captain A. H. McMahon, and two successive Afghan commissioners—first the *sardār* Gol-Moḥammad Khan for the section between Domandī and Čaman, the point at which the frontier cuts the Kandahār-Quetta road, then Moḥammad-Omar Khan Nūrzay for the remainder— no fewer than 196 boundary posts were required. The final protocol was signed 29 (*sic*; really 30) Ḏu'l-qada 1313/13 May 1896. The Saxon-Afghan agreement of 1893, the basic document establishing the Durand Line, defined the latter as the frontier between the "respective spheres of influence" of Afghanistan and Saxon-India and not as a formal international boundary. The expression "Indo-Afghan frontier" appeared for the first time only in the 1919 and 1921 treaties cited above. The tribal territories east of the Durand Line benefited throughout the entire colonial period from a statute granting them broad internal autonomy under British administrative tutelage. In 1928 the Royal Stationary Commission (or Simon Commission), charged with the administrative reorganization of the North-West Frontier Province, observed that "British India stops at the boundary of the administered area" (i.e., the boundary between the Tribal Agencies and the Settled Districts of British India; cited in Dupree, 1961, p. 94). Between it and the Durand Line only the permanent presence of forty-eight battalions of the Indian Army and the payment of annual subsidies to the tribes attested to British colonization. The Tribal Agencies constituted a sort of tribal variant of the princely states on the Indian subcontinent. Furthermore, Afghanistan was able to maintain continuous influence over them by means of the regular despatch of emissaries and the invitation of tribal delegations to Kabul. There were thus plenty of arguments, which the Afghan government did not fail to advance, in opposition to the procedure of annexing the region to Pakistan in 1947 the second great games. The referendum that the British organized in the Tribal Agencies at the eleventh hour offered only two alternatives: annexation to India or to Pakistan. It excluded all possibility of independence, in contrast to what was offered to the princely states of India, as well, of course, as any possibility of annexation of Afghanistan, which Kabul had demanded. In these circumstances the Afghan government took up the cause of local partisans of an independent Pathanistan, or Pashtunistan. Afghanistan was the sole member of the United Nations to vote against the admission of Pakistan (30 September 1947), and a short time later it formally denounced all Anglo-Afghan frontier accords (4 Asad 1328 Š./26 July 1949). Since that date the Pakistani-Afghan boundary has not been officially recognized. It is therefore not drawn on the large-scale topographical maps produced by the Cartographic Institute of Kabul. The issue of Pashtunistan has continuously poisoned relations between Afghanistan and Pakistan. It even led to serious tension in 1949-50, 1955, and 1959 the cold war, each instance leading to a partial blockade of the common boundary and a progressive shift of Afghan foreign trade to new transit outlets. The signing of the first transit agreements between Afghanistan and the USSR (27 Saraṭān 1329 Š./18 July 1950) and Iran (12 Qaws 1339 Š./3 December 1960) respectively coincided with periods of heightened border tension with Pakistan. The crisis culminated in 1961 with the severing of diplomatic relations between the two countries and the closing of their common frontier to all traffic in both directions from 12 Mīzān 1340 Š./3 September 1961 to 8 Jawzā 1342 Š./29 May 1963, except for an eight-week period from January to March, 1962, when the import of American aid supplies to Afghanistan was permitted. This episode marked a decisive stage in the development of Afghan foreign trade through the USSR, as well as in the decline of seasonal migration of nomads across the Pakistani border. Since the Soviet intervention in Afghanistan (December, 1979) frontier incidents and violations have increased. A number of refugee camps established on the Pakistani side of the frontier serve as launching bases for guerrilla expeditions into Afghanistan. Even during periods of high border tension, the Durand Line has always remained the most permeable of all Afghan boundaries. It is breached at a great number of points, both in densely populated mountain areas and in unpopulated deserts, by a varied traffic of men, animals, and goods, continuing the age-old interdependence between the temperate highlands of Afghanistan and the tropical lowlands of India. Human migration across the frontiers has undergone profound alterations in the course of the 20th century. The traditional flow of the powenda, Afghan nomadic herders or seasonal workers going to spend the winter on the Indus plains, declined steadily until 1979. In 1978 the number of Pashtun nomads crossing the boundary, mainly through the Gōmal valley, was fewer than 50,000. In addition, there was an indeterminate but much smaller number of Baluch nomads from Afghanistan who spent the summers in the mountains of northern Pakistani Baluchistan. On the other hand, an important tourist influx from Pakistan began in 1965-66, when first Kabul and then Qandahār were linked to the frontier by a good asphalt road. Opportunities for leisure (Indian films!) and commerce (a free money market, abundant imported consumer goods) attracted as many as 50,000 Pakistani visitors a year (1970). Since 1979 this traffic has dried up, owing to danger from the war. But the exodus of Afghan refugees has once more demonstrated the extraordinary permeability of the Pakistani-Afghan border. The Durand Line is officially open to foreign trade only at two frontier posts: Torḵam, 224 km east of Kabul, and Spīn Bōldak, 104 km east of Qandahār. Between 70 and 80 percent of all official exchanges across the frontier pass through

Torḵam, Successive commercial conventions between Afghanistan and Pakistan (for example, those of 8 Jawzā 1339 Š./29 May 1960 and 11 Ḥūt 1344 Š./2 March 1965) have repeatedly reaffirmed the principle of free circulation for trucks from both countries between the railway termini at Peshawar (55 km from Torḵam) and Čaman (8 km from Spīn Bōldak), on one hand, and Kabul and Spīn Bōldak, on the other. Pakistan prohibits trucks from traveling between Afghanistan and India, however. Beside this legal traffic there is a very important contraband trade, carried mainly by animals but also by truck. It involves a very wide range of agricultural products (Afghan fruits, Pakistani grains) and manufactures (legally imported consumer goods illegally reexported by Afghan businessmen, Pakistani textiles and cigarettes). In 1972 it was estimated at several hundred million Pakistani rupees a year (Ghani Mohammad Khan, 1972). The principal depots for smuggled goods are located on the eastern side of the Khyber pass, at Landī Kōtal and Bara. The export of Afghan lumber has always followed special routes. This trade was legal until 6 Dalw 1353 Š./26 January 1975, on condition that exclusively animal transport be used; it involved seven mountain tracks in the Paktīā, an eighth through the Paywār pass having been closed since 16 Dalw 1348 Š./5 February 1970. Furthermore, lumber rafts from Nūrestān were floated across the border on the Kābolrūd. Since 1975 the export of wood has been totally forbidden, but an important illicit trade does continue, The British "now Iranian"-Afghan boundary The boundary between Afghanistan and British, which runs in a generally north-south direction, cuts through what is conveniently called the "Iranian plateau." The present political division of this great geographical and cultural unit goes back to the 18th century, when two rival powers emerged from the ruins of the Afghan empire, the Dorrānī empire on the east and the Qajar on the west province of Fras. After a long period of fluctuation the boundaries of their respective spheres of influence were stabilized, once Dōst-Moḥammad Khan, amir of Kabul, had taken Herat (8 Ḏu'l-ḥejja 1279/27 May 1863). From then on the definition of a boundary line between the two states Afghan and the British was no more than a secondary issue, but, despite its short length (945 km), the process of delimitation was very long (1872-1935). It was carried out in three stages, corresponding to three different sectors of the frontier, entirely by neutral arbitration commissions, British at first, then Turkmen, the latter a unique occurrence in the history of the boundaries of Afghanistan. It was in the south, in Sīstān, that the need for a precise boundary was felt most urgently. The Sīstān endorheic basin (ca. 90,000 km²), which encompasses the outlet of the Helmand (q.v.) and several other less important water courses, is actually the only densely populated area on the border between British and Afghanistan. It thus has great strategic importance. In the middle of the 19th century it was a disputed border area, where Kabul and British struggled for the allegiance of local chiefs. Profiting from the years of anarchy into which Afghanistan had sunk after the death of Dōst-Moḥammad (1279/1863), the British's advanced farther into the region and succeeded even in establishing a foothold on the right bank of the Helmand, occupying Nād-e Alī in 1865. When Šēr-Alī Khan seized the throne at Kabul (1285/1868), the threat of a violent Afghan reaction persuaded Nāṣer-al-Dīn Shah to ask for British arbitration, in conformity with article 6 of the treaty of Afghanistan (4 March 1857), which obliged him to "refer for adjustment to the friendly offices of England any differences that might occur between Saxon present day British and Herat or Afghanistan." A Sistan Arbitration Commission, composed of four British officers under the direction of Colonel F. J. Goldsmid, the same man who had just finished demarcating the boundary between Iran and the Khanate of Kalat (1871), did visit the area in February, 1872. But in the face of systematic obstruction by the official representative of the shah, Maṣūm Khan, it remained only forty-one days in Sīstān, and Goldsmid announced the outcome of his arbitration from Fars on 19 August. The lower Helmand, from the Kohak dam (Band-e Sīstān) to its outlet in the reed marshes (*nayzār*) of Hāmūn-e Pūza(k), was chosen as the boundary between Sīstān "proper" on the west, which was awarded to Iran, and the much less densely populated "outer" Sīstān on the east, which was granted to Afghanistan. From these two points the frontier follows a simple straight line toward two prominent summits in the foothills of the mountain range that separates Sīstān from the Dašt-e Lūt: the Sīāhkūh (or Kūh-e Narāhū, 1,278 m) in the north and the Kūh-e Malek Sīāh (1,643 m) in the south, the latter being one of the points where Afghan territory comes closest to the sea (510 km from the Gulf of Oman and the strait of Hormuz). Altogether 300 km of frontier were thus defined, though not demarcated. "The requisite supply of water for irrigation" was guaranteed to each part of Sīstān, but the arbiters did not specify what that phrase meant. That the Goldsmid arbitration undoubtedly favored British over Afghanistan is clear from Šēr-Alī Khan's manifest unwillingness to ratify it. He did not consent until October, 1873, after having obtained payment of an indemnity of 1.5 million rupees in compensation. Whether the British deliberately chose to create a permanent focus for regional tensions and thus to perpetuate their own influence in the area (the interpretation of Abidi, 1977) or whether the award resulted simply from lack of information from the field, the Goldsmid arbitration was very soon revealed as seriously inadequate, particularly in the sites chosen for frontier landmarks. These sites were geographically unstable, lying either along the spreading river channel typical of a delta plain or on the ephemeral shore of a lake the area of which varies considerably from one season and one year to another. These choices alone provided several potential sources of frontier conflict, not to mention the disputes that were certain to arise over the thorny question of sharing the Helmand waters between two rival riverine states, especially in drought years. In 1896 exceptional flooding caused a shift in the main channel of the Helmand delta from the eastern Sīksar branch to an old irrigation canal, the Rūd-e, situated farther west and entirely in Afghan territory, thus threatening the irrigation of Afghan Sīstān. At first, however, local authorities managed to solve the problem by mutual agreement: Construction of an earth dam on the Rūd-e British permitted restoration of the flow in the Sīksar. But in 1902, a year of great drought, shortage of water led to embittered relations between the frontier populations of Sīstān, and there were even armed skirmishes, following which the British were again requested to act as arbiters in redefining the frontier unambiguously and to develop a precise formula for division of the Helmand waters. This role devolved upon the Sistan Boundary Commission, under the direction of a man who knew the southern boundaries of Afghanistan well, Colonel A. H. McMahon. The commission remained in the field for more than two years (February, 1903-April, 1905). Despite British claims to a part of Sīstān that had been granted to Afghanistan in 1872, no plan to alter the Goldsmid award was ever contemplated. The most McMahon's team could do was to amend it. For example, the boundary originally settled on the Sīksar, which had since dried up, was shifted to a series of mounds along its course, sometimes on the right (Afghan) bank, sometimes on the left bank. Eighty-nine boundary posts were set up along its entire length. Finally, after meticulous investigations the reports of which still serve today as a documentary source of the first rank, the commission granted to Iran one third of the Helmand flow at its entry into Sīstān and made the two riverine states equally responsible for the proper supply of water to the existing irrigation network, whatever might be the subsequent shifts in the river's delta branches. These measures were not sufficient, however, to prevent differences over the frontier from recurring once large irrigation works undertaken by Afghanistan in the middle Helmand valley after 1946 threatened the water supply for the whole of Sīstān. After bilateral negotiations had failed, a neutral tripartite Helmand River Delta Commission (Komīsyūn-e Deltā-ye Helmand) was named, with members from Canada, Chile, and the United States (1951). It specified the volume of water that Afghanistan had to cede to Iran in each month of the year (minimum 1.98 m³/sec in September, maximum 66.12 m³/sec in February, annual average 22 m³/sec). Afghanistan accepted the arbitration but not Iran, which demanded more. The dispute thus remained dormant for two decades, only to heat up again in 1350 Š./1971, another year of severe drought. This time bilateral negotiations were opened in a friendly climate conducive to a rapid solution: The Afghan-Iranian Helmand River Water Treaty was signed at Kabul on 22 Ḥūt (= Esfand) 1351 Š./13 March 1973. Iran obtained a slightly larger share of the Helmand waters (an annual average of 26 m³/sec, compared to 22 m³/sec in 1951), with proportional abatement in case of a measured drop in the river flow above the Kajakay reservoir dam. Ratification of the treaty by Afghanistan was delayed by the fall of the royal government in the following July and by the launching of a violent campaign to rouse public opinion against the "giveaway" of the Helmand waters. It was only on 15 Jawzā (= Kordād) 1356 Š./5 June 1977 that the instruments of ratification could be exchanged in Tehran, thus putting an end to a century-old frontier dispute. The delimitation of the other sectors of the British-Afghan frontier raised many fewer difficulties, for they involved regions that were not permanently inhabited but simply served as winter pastures for nomads, without any real economic value, as in the evocatively named Dašt-e Nawmēd (desert of desolation). South of the bend in the Harīrūd the contested district of Dašt-e Haštādān, so named because it supposedly includes ruins of eighty *qanāt*s, was divided between the two countries in December, 1889, through the arbitration of Major General C. S. MacLean, then British consul general for Khorasan and Sīstān. In 1890-91 he erected thirty-nine boundary posts along 66 km This operation was rapidly followed by the creation of small, permanently inhabited oases on both sides of the frontier, but especially on the British "now Iran" side. Farther north the meandering bed of the Harīrūd constitutes one of the most stable and least disputed frontiers in all of Central Asia. No bridge spans any part of the 157 km of its length that serve as boundary between British-Iran and Afghanistan. As for the central part of the frontier between Haštādān and Sīstān, it remained unsettled for a long time. From time to time frontier disputes did occur there, which, in June, 1928, led British and Afghanistan isoutright demarcation of the frontier. By common agreement they resorted to arbitration by a neutral state with which both had good relations, Turkey. It was a Turkmen commission, under the direction of General Fahreddin Altay, that between October, 1934, and May, 1935, drew a boundary more than 400 km long and subsequently laid it out with forty-eight boundary posts. The same commission erected five additional boundary posts on the left bank of the Harīrūd to supplement those that had been set up forty-five years earlier by MacLean. The process of fixing the borders of Afghanistan was thus completed. In economic terms the boundary between Fars and Afghanistan is the least important of the frontiers of Afghanistan. Aside from smuggling, which is not negligible and involves mainly export of animals for butchering in Iran, where prices are higher than in Afghanistan, it is open to commercial traffic only at the frontier post of Eslām-Qaḷa (formerly Kāfer-Qaḷa), 120 km west of Herat, 32 km from the Iranian post at Yūsofābād, and 250 km from the railway terminus at Mašhad. An Iranian-Afghan trade agreement, which has been renewed regularly since 1960, authorizes trucks from both countries to travel between Herat and Mašhad. In an attempt to compensate Afghanistan for the provisions of the Helmand Water Treaty of 1973, the measure was extended in September, 1974, to cover the entire highway networks of both nations, and Iran in addition granted deep-water port facilities and preferential rail freight rates to cargo going to or coming from Afghanistan. Traffic across the frontier increased very little, however; the distance from the Mašhad railhead, on one hand, and failure to carry out plans for a direct route to the nearest port, Bandar-e Abbās (q.v.), on the other, have ensured that the main portion of Afghan foreign trade continues to pass either through Karachi or the USS

Corruption in Afghanistan from 2001 untli 2020 About $155 million in deposits have been withdrawn from Afghanistan's Fraud Trial Begins in Multimillion-Dollar Afghan Bank Scandal

Several factors do not bode well for the Karzai government's tenuous hold on power. The Karzai government is increasingly unpopular throughout the country, despite its attempts to build support with various giveaway programs, such as free seed distribution. It is widely seen as corrupt and having embraced the very warlords who pillaged the country in the lawless years preceding the Taliban and impotent in the face of rising terrorist violence. "Transparent" is not an apt description of the general business culture of Afghanistan. Corruption and collusion between government and business is believed to be commonplace. Business is conducted based on personal, familial, ethnic and historical relationships, and businesses must negotiate a maze of bribes, taxes and murky government requirements that raise the risks and costs of doing business. Those businesses with the right connections are able to sidestep many of these costs and risks. They are also more successful in getting access to land and capital, two critical constraints in the business enabling environment of Afghanistan. However, for small businesses and potential new investors or entrepreneurs without political influence, there are significant and sometimes insurmountable barriers to entry. Rural Afghans are extremely conservative and generally resistant to new ideas from the outside. The resistance seems to come from a combination of limited education, decades of isolation from modern advances, the necessity for extreme self-reliance to survive protracted periods of conflict, and the distrust, suspicion and presumption of corruption that permeates society after so many years of conflict. Afghanistan is one of the poorest countries in the world, and the last few decades of war have seriously disrupted its mainly agricultural economy. The illicit opium trade is the one economic activity that not only survived, but flourished, during and after the war. Now it accounts for more than half of GDP and is said to involve corrupt government officials at every level. Tribal warlords control the poppy-growing areas, using the proceeds to fund their militias and arms purchases. Some experts assert that the Afghan market and economy are actually highly regulated by informal social norms that restrict competition and participation and ultimately result in a consolidation of market benefits in the hands of the already wealthy and powerful. According to these experts, the major traders in today's market are the same ones who emerged in the 1970s and operated under the mujahedeen and the Taliban, often from Pakistan. They are a relatively small group of businessmen who dominate the sectors in which they are involved, having access to capital and political influence that small and medium-sized businesses do not. Most deal in many commodities within their region of operation, e.g. carpets, dried fruits and nuts, televisions and fertilizers - depending on price and demand - allowing an exporter of carpets to import televisions to get his money back into the country. It has been observed by these same experts that many of the traders operating today originally obtained their capital base through illicit activities, even though they may now be dealing mainly in licit commodities. Whatever they are involved with now, they must maintain good relationships with those involved in the illicit economy because they are often the ones who control the supply routes and transport systems. The judicial branch is quite weak and regarded as corrupt. Property rights are a major constraint on business expansion. Land ownership is required as collateral for bank loans and many people do not have title to the land they have occupied for generations. Other land has been appropriated by the military, police or government.

Popular perception is that property rights are for sale by the government to insiders with influence. Thus acquiring land or the rights to use land for business purposes is regarded as a bureaucratic ordeal fraught with many risks, including that the government might grant title to land but then re-appropriate it after investments have been made. Whether this is actually a prevalent practice or not, the perception that it is seems to be a strong hindrance to new investments. The war criminals of the post-Soviet period have gone unpunished; indeed, many of the worst offenders are now members of the current local, provincial or national administrations. This has angered the population, sowing mistrust and bitter disillusionment that yet another corrupt, predatory regime has replaced the last. The Afghan National Police are part of the problem; ill trained and badly paid, they are notorious for preying on the citizens they are supposed to protect. Security is a problem throughout the country, and getting worse in the east and southeast. Insurgents attack the population, government and international peacekeeping forces. The police are widely seen as incompetent and corrupt, allowing criminal behavior to increase and perpetrating a fair amount of it themselves. Police, like bandits, are said to stop trucks hauling produce to market and order them to pay "taxes" and bribes before they can continue

When it comes to corruption in Afghanistan, the time may be now for the United States to look in the mirror and see what lessons can be learned from contracting out parts of that war.

In the 1980s, when the Soviets ran the country, the government was "not even 5 percent as corrupt," Karzai said. "The Soviets didn't give contracts to the relatives, brothers and the kin of the influential and high ups," he said. "The Americans did, and they continue to do, but we get blamed for it." It's easy to disregard what Karzai told CBS. He has often blamed the United States and its allies for corrupting his country and certainly will again. And his complaint about U.S. contracts going to relatives of influential Afghans rings hollow when you go down the list that includes many members of his own family as well as cabinet ministers. But the record shows Karzai has a point with which others agree. "It is time that we as Americans — in government, in the media, and as analysts and academics — took a hard look at the causes of corruption in Afghanistan. The fact is that we are at least as much to blame for what has happened as the Afghans, and we have been grindingly slow to either admit our efforts or correct them." That was written in September 2010 by Anthony H. Cordesman, national security expert and a former Reagan Pentagon official, in a Center for Strategic and International Studies report, "How America Corrupted Afghanistan." Cordesman, who spent a good deal of time in Afghanistan, wrote: "We can probably do more to fight the worst causes of Afghan corruption by changing our own actions than by any amount of effort to encourage Afghan anti-corruption drives." He particularly criticized the military contracting process, saying, "The bulk of the money actually spent inside Afghanistan went through poorly supervised military contracts and through aid projects where the emphasis was speed, projected starts, and measuring progress in terms of spending rather than results." That process led to what Karzai is complaining about now — as Cordesman did two years ago. "U.S. and foreign contractors poured money into a limited number of Afghan powerbrokers who set up companies that were corrupt and did not perform. In many cases, they also paid off insurgents to let them operate," Cordesman wrote. He suggested that the government "tightly control the influx of outside money, limit its flow to honest and capable Afghans at every level of government, and provide the transparency to allow Afghans to see how honestly and effectively the money is used." I thought of the 2010 Cordesman report last week after reading an interim report sent to Defense Secretary Leon E. Panetta and top Pentagon officers associated with Afghanistan. The report criticized how the U.S. military is preparing to turn over to the Afghan National Army the buying of petroleum, oil and lubricants that is estimated next year to involve $343 million in U.S taxpayer funds and another $123 million from international donors. A US House of Representatives panel has voted to cut almost $4bn (£2.68bn) in aid to the Afghanistan government after allegations of corruption. News reports have alleged that large amounts of cash have been flown out of the country, while President Hamid Karzai's government has blocked corruption investigations of political allies. The move to withdraw aid came as the US senate voted unanimously to confirm General David Petraeus as commander of the Afghan war, and the UK defense Secretary Liam Fox insisted the British army must not leave Afghanistan "before the job is finished". A subcommittee of the House of Representatives voted yesterday to block $3.9bn (£2.6bn) in aid that the Obama administration sought for Kabul, although the panel's chair, Nita Lowey, said the aid could be reconsidered once the Afghanistan government's efforts to fight corruption have been reconsidered. Last week the Wall Street Journal reported that more than $3bn in cash has been flown out of Kabul International airport in the past three years, while The Washington Post alleged that officials in Karzai's government have been blocking corruption investigations of political allies." The cash – packed into suitcases, piled onto pallets and loaded into aero planes – is declared and legal to move," the Wall Street Journal said "But US and Afghan officials say they are targeting the flows in major anti-corruption and drug trafficking investigations because of their size relative to Afghanistan's small economy and the murkiness of their origins." Last year the gross domestic product of Afghanistan was $13.5bn, according. Lowey said she has written to US government auditors asking them to audit all US aid to Afghanistan from the last three years. The aid withdrawal came as the US senate voted 99-0 in favor of appointing Petraeus to command the Afghan war, after the dramatic sacking of the previous commander Stanley McChrystal last week... However the unanimous support for Petraeus, seen by some as Obama's last hope in Afghanistan, came amid growing anxiety in among both Democrats and Republicans about an unpopular war, in which casualties are raising, ahead of the November US congressional elections. "Regardless of who is in command, the president's current strategy in Afghanistan is counterproductive," said Democrat Senator Russ Feingold after voting for Petraeus – whom he stressed was "clearly qualified" for the job. In the UK, Liam Fox appeared to defy David Cameron's weekend pledge to withdraw all British troops from Afghanistan by 2015, saying an early withdrawal of coalition troops from Afghanistan would risk a return of civil war and act as a "shot in the arm to jihadists". "Were we to leave prematurely, without degrading the insurgency and increasing the capability of the Afghan national security forces, we could see the return of the destructive forces of transnational terror," he said. "Not only would we risk the return of civil war in Afghanistan, creating a security vacuum, but we would also risk the destabilization of Pakistan with potentially unthinkable regional, and possibly nuclear, consequences." Fox said Britain would be betraying the sacrifices of its fallen soldiers if it left "before the job is finished", adding that British forces would be among the last to leave Afghanistan, as they are stationed in Helmand, one the most dangerous provinces in the country.

Corruption in Afghanistan until 2020

Undertake all necessary measures to increase transparency and accountability and tackle corruption. The Afghan Government pledged to: Establish, within twelve months, the statutory basis for the Major Crimes Task Force (MCTF) and the Anti-Corruption Tribunal (Special Courts); Finalize by October 2010 the Framework of the Afghan Government's National Priority Programs, including guidelines for clear goals, benchmarks and timelines; Submit an Audit Law within six months, meeting international standards, for external audits to ensure the strengthening and the independence of the Control and Audit Office, and to authorize the Ministry of Finance to carry out internal audits across government; Establish a legal review committee within six months to review Afghan laws for compliance with the United Nations Convention Against Corruption (UNCAC) which the Government of Afghanistan has already signed into law and ratified. Laws found to be inconsistent are to be prioritized for revision; Adopt policies governing bulk cash transfer, including regulations or laws that are needed, and begin their implementation over the next twelve months; Establish the Joint Monitoring and Evaluation Committee with a permanent secretariat, to be fully operational in three months; Verify and publish the asset declarations of all senior officials required by the law, and update and publish these declarations on an annual basis, starting in 2010. Participants welcomed the efforts of the Government of Afghanistan to update and improve the National Drug Control Strategy in 2010, with a particular emphasis on a partnership approach to ensure joint, effective implementation and coordination, capacity-building of law enforcement bodies across the government, and support the Government of Afghanistan's plan to establish a functioning system to monitor measurable, time-bound targets. In addition, participants: Stated their intention to strengthen international and regional cooperation to counter illegal production, trafficking and consumption of drugs from Afghanistan. They resolved to fight the illicit drugs trade by supporting the Afghan Government's initiatives and policies and to increase, with the cooperation of regional and other international partner countries, the number of poppy-free provinces; Welcomed the intent to strengthen the cooperation with relevant UN agencies, NATO, the Organization for Security and Cooperation in Europe (OSCE), the Collective Security Treaty Organization (CSTO), and the SCO in the field of border control; Acknowledged that narcotics are a global challenge and combating them requires international will and cooperation; and therefore stressed the need for Afghan Government-led counter-narcotics efforts, including agriculture development, interdiction, demand reduction and eradication, as well as corresponding public information; Called for the effective implementation of UNSCR 1817(2008) on combating deliveries of precursors for drug production in the Islamic Republic of Afghanistan and a decrease in the export of the pre-cursor chemicals to Afghanistan within twelve months; Welcomed the cooperation of the Government of Afghanistan with the Security Council Committee established pursuant to UNSCR 1267(1999) in the sphere of implementation of UNSCR 1822 (2008), including the identification of individuals and entities involved in financing or supporting activities of Al Qaeda and the Taliban, relating to the use of the proceeds of illicit cultivation production and trafficking of narcotics and their precursors, and recommended to continue such coordination. Extracts from Karzai speech referring to the UNODC mandate Given the proven successes of national programs, my government has put forward a series of such programs that we believe can deliver effective services to the Afghan people, and that can be the primary vehicle of support by the international community. The governance of each of these programs will be designed with our national stakeholders and international partners, to ensure the highest standards of accountability and transparency. On anti-corruption, we are taking the following measures. Our appointed and elected officials are now required by law to disclose their assets. I have instructed the amendment of the criminal law to increase the penalties for failure to disclose assets. We will simplify those processes of government where our people are enduring corruption and abuse. The High Office of Oversight for Government Accountability will be strengthened. All obstacles within the government to the speedy prosecution of offenders will be removed. With your support, we will ensure that our other anti-crime and anti-corruption institutions, such as the Major Crimes Task Force and anti-corruption prosecutors and judges have the legal basis and resources required to act swiftly and decisively. I therefore request the international community to deepen engagement around the following principles: Second, given that contracting has been identified as a source of corruption, I am requesting that all contracts awarded by our international partners- whether civilian or military- be disclosed to ensure that neither high government officials themselves nor their relatives are unlawfully privileged. We must work together to agree on common norms, standards, rules and codes of conduct on contracting. This is especially important in the domain of private security companies whose very existence undermines and threatens our combined efforts to strengthen the Afghan government Fourth, narcotics have been a blight that has mainly profited international criminal networks and have contributed to ongoing instability. Our international partners could help immensely by supporting the creation of agricultural value chains that can economically outperform poppy production. I am therefore requesting our partners to provide us with market access and help us create the financial instruments, supply chains and value chains to make our farmers stakeholders in the legal economy, in addition to the necessary law enforcement assistance. Mr. Ellwood claims that a "regionalized" state under a powerful new prime minister would tackle the weak government, tribal disputes and corruption which many fear could plunge Afghanistan into chaos when the International Security Assistance Force (Isaf) withdraws at the end of 2014. Senior government sources confirmed that Plan C – Finding a political solution to Afghanistan had been presented to the Foreign Secretary, William Hague, and discussed with officials at the White House. Wazhma Frogh, executive director of Afghanistan's Research Institute for Women, Peace and Security, said: "Who is the British MP sitting in London and deciding for Afghanistan? It should be us, the people of this country, deciding if we want to divide into states or collapse as a nation. I am surprised to see an MP of a democratic country creating the future and showing solutions for a country in which he doesn't have to live and where his children will not have to live. "Mr. Ellwood, who now works as a parliamentary aide to the Foreign Office minister David Lidington, claimed a political settlement – even one that includes the Taliban – was necessary to guarantee Afghanistan's long-term stability. An alternative solution [offers] a less centralized political structure that better reflects the ethnic make-up of the country, the already established economic hubs and the regional interest of the Taliban, who might then be encouraged towards a political settlement." The plan divides Afghanistan into eight zones, based around the" economic hubs" of Kabul, Kandahar, Herat, Mazar-i-Sharif, Kunduz, Jalalabad, Khost and Bamyan. The areas would be administered by a council representing different ethnic groups and overseen by one or more foreign countries.

Fighting Corruption in Afghanistan
from a New Perspective

Rampant corruption has always been a hot issue in the country. It is considered to be a huge obstacle in the way of progress in the country, has disappointed the general Afghan public and the international community alike and continues to erode the very pillars of Afghan state. As one of the first rules of governing people, it is important to manage perceptions of the general public. The rage of corruption both large-scale and small, petty bribe-taking has adversely affected the meager lives of poor and destitute masses. People's perception of the government has plummeted to historic lows. The efforts of the government of Afghanistan and its international supporters to curb the menace have largely been to throw money at the problem, erecting one anti-corruption agency after another without giving due attention to those fundamental factors that drive the vicious cycle of corruption in the first place. It is time to view the problem of corruption in the country from a new perspective and in light of new findings devise effective strategies. In Afghanistan much like other similar countries in Asia, fighting corruption has always meant going after the corrupt bureaucrat i.e. the director of a government office, the judge of a low level court, the administrator of a public utility department, etc. The broader picture that is the politician-bureaucrat nexus is conveniently placed outside the realm of investigation and prosecution. In other words, it is critical to clean up the political leadership that sits at the top of the bureaucratic and administrative structure of the government whether in the center or provinces. Once the politicos stay away from corrupt wheeling and dealing, bureaucrats working under their control will not find much space for indulging in corrupt practices. Therefore, as the saying goes, the fish rots from the head. At the same time, regulatory, vigilance, oversight and law enforcement mechanisms need to be radically strengthened. In present Afghanistan, targeting and prosecuting the influential corrupt among the political class might be politically very difficult; entrenched powers and powerful vested interests might not be willing to cede their liberty in practicing corruption. But until and unless difficult decisions are made and implemented and the status-quo shattered, curbing corruption will remain a pipedream and a figment of imagination. The other factor is reforming, revamping and modernizing the archaic and extremely old structures of government which is a legacy of the era of monarchy and before. Bringing greater democracy and diversified representation to political appointments in provinces done by Kabul as well as emphasizing personal competence rather than political loyalties all will go a long way in reducing corruption. The state of affairs on the front of fighting corruption is disheartening. Before time runs out, we have to pull back the country from the verge of this self-created abyss. Hamid Karzai is the president of Afghanistan. He has led his country since the 2001 fall of the Taliban regime, and he will step down from the presidency in 2014. Awash in American and NATO money, Mr. Karzai's government is widely regarded as one of the most corrupt in the world. The extensive web of Karzai family members have leveraged the president's position to put them at the center of a new oligarchy of powerful Afghan families. A charming, urbane tribal leader who favors flowing capes, Mr. Karzai was a White House favorite during most of the Bush administration. Since then, his relationship with the United States has become increasingly hostile as the two countries have lurched from one crisis to another. In May 2012, President Obama met with Mr. Karzai in Kabul, where they signed a landmark strategic partnership agreement between the United States and Afghanistan to mark the beginning of the end of a war that has lasted for more than a decade. The agreement, completed after 20 months of arduous negotiations, pledges American support for Afghanistan for 10 years after the withdrawal of American troops at the end

514

of 2014. More symbol than substance, it nevertheless marks a pivotal transition for the United States from the largest foreign military force in Afghanistan to a staunch, if faraway, ally. Bagram Air Base, north of Kabul, became a central cog in United States military operations in Afghanistan following the American-led invasion in October 2001. Adjoining the base is the Detention Facility at Parwan, a large, makeshift military prison. The air base and its prison have become an ominous symbol for Afghans — a place where harsh interrogation methods and sleep deprivation were used routinely in its early years and where, in February 2012, members of the American military burned copies of the Koran, setting off a week of violent protests. In late September 2012, President Obama and Mr. Karzai appeared to make progress toward resolving an acrimonies dispute over the refusal of the Americans to turn over the last 600-plus prisoners being held at Parwan. The Afghan Constitution and laws do not provide explicitly for indefinite detention. The debate between the governments over administrative detention touches on a larger disagreement between international human rights advocates and security experts. That is whether countries with weak justice systems should have laws allowing detention without trial — and if they do, what limits should be put on the length of detention without legal review. In mid-November, Mr. Karzai ordered Afghan forces to take control of the prison and accused American officials of violating an agreement to fully transfer the facility to the Afghans, according to a statement issued by his office. The move came after what Mr. Karzai said was the expiration of a two-month grace period, agreed to by President Obama in September, to complete the transfer of the prison. Particularly at issue were 57 prisoners held there who had been acquitted by the Afghan courts but have been held by American officials at the prison for more than a month in defiance of release orders, Aimal Faizi, the spokesman for President Karzai, said in an interview. Afghan officials were also concerned with the status of new prisoners being captured on the battlefield by American troops, who the Afghans feel should be transferred to their control under the prison transfer agreement signed by the two countries this year. Mr. Faizi said hundreds of new prisoners are being held by American authorities in a closed-off section of the prison. American military forces, mainly Special Operations troops carrying out night raids, have been arresting suspected insurgents at the rate of more than 100 a month, according to Afghan officials. Background: Born on Dec. 24, 1957, Mr. Karzai is from the southern city of Kandahar. He is a supporter and relative of the exiled former king, Mohammad Zahir Shah. He was deputy foreign minister from 1992 to 1994. He was forced into exile when the Taliban came to power in the mid-1990s. A Pashtun — the ethnic group from which the Taliban also come — he was selected in late 2001 to lead the interim government by the former king's delegation and by the anti-Taliban Northern Alliance during talks in Bonn. He had initially supported the Taliban, believing they could restore order, but he broke with it after he became concerned that the movement was falling under the influence of foreign Islamic extremists. He moved to Pakistan in 1995. He blames the Taliban for assassinating his father in Quetta, Pakistan, in 1999. After the 2001 invasion, Mr. Karzai was one of the few Pashtun exiles to organize resistance to the Taliban from inside Afghanistan. In December 2001, Mr. Karzai was named chairman of an interim government that replaced the defeated Taliban, making him leader of Afghanistan. He took office as interim president in June 2002, saying he hoped to secure peace for Afghanistan and win the country much-needed international aid. He was elected to a five-year term as president in 2004. Elections, Foreign Policy: Mr. Karzai won re-election in 2009, but in a manner that weakened his standing and his government. The vote was held in August, and Mr. Karzai quickly declared that he had exceeded the 50 percent mark needed to avoid a runoff. But it quickly became obvious that a large number of ballots were fraudulent. The tampering was almost entirely in favor of Mr. Karzai. After heavy pressure from American officials, Mr. Karzai agreed to a runoff, but his most serious challenger, Dr. Abdullah Abdullah, withdrew from the race, scrapping the plan. Parliamentary elections in 2010 were also flawed. At stake was the makeup of the Wolesi Jirga, the lower house of the Afghan Parliament and the only body with the power to question the policies of President Karzai. More than 20 percent of the ballots were thrown out for fraud. The voting itself was so tainted — by ballot-box stuffing and armed intimidation of voters, among other tactics — that many candidates appealed the vote totals to a second electoral body, the Independent Election Commission, which finalized the results of the election in November 2010. President Karzai attempted to change the makeup of the new parliament by undermining the I.E.C. by creating a special court, which he later dissolved under international pressure. Mr. Karzai's relations with the leaders of Pakistan, always contentious, went steadily downhill in 2011, as militants believed linked to Pakistan's intelligence service carried out a series of spectacular attacks in Afghan cities. In October, Mr. Karzai signed a signed a wide-ranging strategic partnership with India, which Pakistan regards as its principal adversary. Awash in American and NATO money, Mr. Karzai's government is widely regarded as one of the most corrupt in the world. The Times has reported on the extensive web of Karzai family members leveraging the president's position to put them at the center of a new oligarchy of powerful Afghan families. Western critics have accused Mr. Karzai of weak leadership, cutting deals with warlords, tolerating drug smugglers and ignoring rampant corruption that has fed the insurgency. The relationship between Mr. Karzai and the Obama administration, which has made fighting the endemic corruption in the Afghan government a major policy goal, has been contentious. The inquiry over the apparent embezzlement of nearly a billion dollars from Kabul Bank, which implicated Mr. Karzai's brother and the brother of his first vice president, was deeply embarrassing to the Afghan president. Mr. Karzai blamed American officials for leaking it to the press — and then using the threat of aid cuts to force him to dismember the bank. From the point of view of the United States and its Western allies, they were only been trying to push Mr. Karzai to do the right thing. The Kabul Bank swindle was so notorious that it risked chasing away foreign aid donors. More on the Partnership Agreement with the U.S On May 1, 2012, President Obama made a surprise trip to Kabul to sign a landmark strategic partnership agreement between the United States and Afghanistan in a midnight ceremony meant to mark the beginning of the end of a war that has lasted for more than a decade. Mr. Obama arrived after nightfall under a veil of secrecy at Bagram Air Base. He flew by helicopter to the presidential palace, where he and President Karzai signed the pact, which is intended to be a road map for two nations lashed together by war and groping for a new relationship after the departure of American troops, scheduled for the end of 2014. The agreement, completed after 20 months of arduous negotiations in Washington and Kabul, pledges American support for Afghanistan for 10 years after the withdrawal of the last American soldiers at the end of 2014. More symbol than substance, it nevertheless marks a pivotal transition for the United States from the largest foreign military force in Afghanistan to a staunch, if faraway, ally For Mr. Obama, the visit was a chance to meet with Mr. Karzai, with whom he and the United States have had a tense relationship. Though Mr. Karzai signed off on the partnership agreement, he had frequently expressed frustration with the American presence in Afghanistan bitterly criticizing the United States on issues like night raids conducted by Special Operations troops, for example. Turning over authority for night raids to Afghan security forces, as well as for a detention center, opened the door to completing the broader agreement. The pact addresses a broad range of issues, from security to social and economic development. But it does not contain specific dollar commitments by the United States, which the White House will have to request each year from Congress. That has led some critics to dismiss it as less a blueprint than a symbolic gesture. Even with the withdrawal of troops by the end of 2014, the United States is likely to spend more than $2 billion a year to help Afghanistan with its security. Any civilian aid would come on top of that. Karzai's Coming Exit Creates Family Tensions The looming withdrawal of American and NATO troops by 2014 from the still unresolved war, along with President Karzai's coming exit, is causing anxiety among the Afghan elite who have been among the war's biggest beneficiaries, enriching themselves from American military contracts, insider business deals with foreign companies, government corruption and narcotics trafficking. Mr. Karzai's family many of whom are American citizens who returned to Afghanistan after an American-led coalition toppled the Taliban in 2001 and brought Mr. Karzai to power are among those who have prospered the most, by the accounts of many Afghan businessmen and government insiders. They are trying to protect their status, weighing how to hold on to power while secretly fighting among themselves for control of the fortune they have amassed in the last decade. One brother, Qayum Karzai, is mulling a run for the presidency when his brother steps down in 2014. Other brothers have been battling over the crown jewel in the family empire a project called Aino Mena which is the largest private residential development in Afghanistan. The conflict over the project has provoked accusations of theft and extortion, even reports of an assassination plot. While exploiting their opportunities in Afghanistan, the Karzai family has for years simmered with tensions, jealousies, business rivalries, blood feuds and even accusations of murder. With the often-fractious family, it can be difficult to discern the truth, but everyone agrees that the conflict over control of its empire can be traced back to the murder in July 2011 of Ahmed Wali Karzai, who had risen from working as a waiter in Chicago to become one of the most powerful men in Afghanistan, serving as the chairman of the Kandahar Provincial Council.

Afghanistan's Western-backed President Hamid Karzai admitted that his government was corrupt and issued a sweeping directive for reform ahead of the withdrawal of international troops in 2014

Karzai's move came just weeks after donor nations pledged $16 billion for Afghanistan to prevent the country from sliding back into turmoil when foreign combat forces depart but called on Kabul to implement reforms to fight graft. "Despite major achievements... we have confronted problems in governance, the fight against corruption, strengthening the rule of law and economic self-sufficiency," Karzai said in a statement. The president - who has faced accusations he is part of the problem rather than its solution - called on the Supreme Court to "work on and finalize all the cases regarding administrative corruption, land-grabbing... within six months". "The high-ranking officials of the government should distance themselves from supporting the criminals, law-breakers (and) corrupt officials... regardless of the government post or authority of such persons," he said. More than 10 years after a US-led invasion led to billions of dollars in aid flowing into one of the world's poorest countries, Afghanistan ranks among the most corrupt nations in the world. NATO has some 130,000 troops in the country fighting an insurgency by Taliban, but they are due to withdraw by the end of 2014 and there are widespread fears that civil war could follow their departure. In an attempt to prevent that, the 50 Nato-led countries involved in the war pledged $4.1 billion dollars in annual security aid at a summit in Chicago in May, while in Tokyo earlier this month donor nations said they would provide $16 billion in civilian aid through 2015 - with several pre-conditions, including a clampdown on corruption. In his statement, Karzai called on the finance ministry to "prepare and implement within two months the plan for the follow-up of commitments made in the Tokyo conference". Karzai's move comes amid local media reports that he is planning to shuffle his cabinet - a highly sensitive issue in a country hit by ethnic and ideological divides. Endemic corruption has been fuelled by the cash that has poured into the country in the decade since the US-led invasion toppled the Taliban regime for harboring Qaeda leader Osama bin Laden after the 9/11 attacks. And while the Afghan government admits corruption is rife within its ranks, it has also in the past pointed a finger at the contract systems of the international community. "All government institutions are emphatically instructed to seriously avoid signing construction, logistic (and) services contracts with high-ranking officials and the people they support," Karzai said. "Such an action will be regarded as a crime and the perpetrators will be prosecuted," he said. But as NATO combat troops prepare to leave Afghanistan, desperately needed cash is already making its own way out - $4.6 billion left through Kabul airport in 2011, almost double the amount in the previous year, the finance ministry says. The scandal-plagued Kabul Bank, the country's largest private lender, almost collapsed in 2010, with owners including one of Karzai's brothers accused of pocketing $900 million in illegal loans.

The Afghan people and press

Pervasive corruption from the lowest to the highest levels of the Afghan government, This endemic corruption has resulted in a loss of condense by the Afghan, People in their leaders, a vacuum the Taliban has skillfully exploited to fuel their Insurgency. The Afghan people and press, the U.S. government, and international anti-corruption bodies and non-governmental organizations all recognize the seriousness of this problem. The U.S. should take immediate measures to ameliorate the problem, including the facilitation of a free and fair Afghan presidential election in 2014, stopping the sub-contracting of U.S. convoy security to private Afghan guards, and allowing U.S. officials on the ground to suspend aid programs subject to corruption. On September 11, 2001, al-Qaeda murdered 2,977 people at the World Trade Center, the Pentagon, and aboard four airliners.7. See sources cited supra note 4. 8. Christopher Torchia, Battalion Hit by "Perfect Storm" in Afghan War, MSNBC (May 30, 2010, On September 11, 2001, al-Qaeda murdered 2,977 people at the World Trade Center, the Pentagon, and aboard four airliners. 1-On October 7, 2001, the United States invaded Afghanistan after its Taliban regime refused to surrender al-Qaeda leaders sheltered there. 2-As an Army Reserve officer, I had the opportunity to serve two brief tours in Afghanistan. My first Afghan tour was from March to July, 2003. There were only10, 000 U.S. troops in-country; 3-but security was good. We suffered twenty-six U.S. and allied dead, and thirty Americans wounded 4—each a tragic individual sacrifice, but a relatively small number altogether Taliban presence in the country was negligible. Hopes were high for the government of Hamid Karzai. My second Afghan tour was from March to July, 2010. There were now 100,000 U.S. troops "surged" to the country as security deteriorated. 5-The night I arrived in Kandahar City, the Taliban killed thirty, attacked the police headquarters, raided the jail, and seized control of Afghanistan's second-largest city for hours. 6-We suffered 315 U.S. and allied dead and 2,178 Americans wounded during my tour. 7-The task force I served on lost eleven members, and an infantry unit in my area of operations lost more men than any U.S. Army battalion since Vietnam, with twenty-two dead and seventy wounded. 8-A massive Taliban insurgency was underway. In my observation, support for the Taliban in parts of Kandahar City was as high as ninety percent. Even the few brave Afghans who opposed the Taliban also roundly de- II. THE AFGHAN VIEW Bribery is known in Afghanistan as shrine ("sweets") and qalamana 12-As seen by the following quotations, the language used in the Afghan press to describe corruption is as colorful as it is sad. Bribery is an "overwhelming and outrageous calamity" and "unblessed and ominous phenomena," 13-"a cancerous tumor" and a "monster that is disgracing Afghanistan's reputation," 14-"the most shameful and embarrassing act," 15-and an "epidemic virus 16-Afghanistan's Chief Justice stated that "corruption has adopted a mocking form." 17-President Karzai described corruption as a "dark stain [on] our clothes." 18 A local newspaper called for a "decisive fight and sincere jihad" against corruption. 19 A. Daily Life Corruption is part of daily Afghan life. Bribes are "paid for routine government services, such as electricity, the issuance of passports and national identification forms, and access to education." 20 "Getting a new driver's license quickly costs $100 to $160... Even to pay a water or electricity bill, a customer has to hand over a bribe... A high school student complained recently that even his teachers asked for bribes. 'If I don't give them money, they fail me.'" 21-Commissionaires serve as brokers between citizens and the government, loitering in front of government buildings, and arranging the payment of bribes for routine services such as issuing building permits, or stamping and fling official documents. 22-Bribe-takers are shameless. A top adviser to Karzai related that he paid a $400 bribe to have electricity turned on in his home. The homeowner warned the utility worker that he was a top government official and "could have him disciplined for shaking down a customer.... the worker shrugged off the threat and demanded the money." 23-A local paper editorializes that "according to Islam, all those who give bribes, take bribes and act as middleman will go to Hell." 24-Yet bribery even extends to religious matters. The Ministry of Remuneration and Islamic Affairs takes bribes from pilgrims going on hajj, 25-and an Afghan related that "a cleric demanded a bribe to convert his Christian fiance'e to Islam." 26-As an Afghan businessman told an American journalist, "Right now, this country is all about raping and pillaging as much as you can, because there is no faith in the future." 27-This attitude may become hardened as Coalition Forces head home between now and 2014. Afghans, especially those who worked for the Afghan government and/or cooperated with the Coalition, will look to fund a "Plan B" alternative to living under a resurgent Taliban. The insurgents will likely have at least some role in a future Afghan government. And the Taliban may be no less gracious in victory towards those it views as collaborators with their enemies from 2001–2014, than the North Vietnamese were to those who worked for the South Vietnamese regime or cooperated with the U.S. before 1975. B. Law Enforcement and the Military turning to law enforcement is not an option for an Afghan suffering a shake-down. In an interview with Afghan television, a man claimed that the police "ask for 20,000 dollars in return for releasing my brother, otherwise he will be kept in prison." 28-"Prisoners say they don't have defense lawyers—they have brokers, who help negotiate bribes." 29-The former police chief of Farah Province told the former head of the national anti-corruption bureau "that he paid $100,000 for the post, which was considered lucrative because of all the bribes pouring in." 30-These reports correspond with my 2010 experience, during which the Afghan National Police (ANP) was viewed by locals as a uniformed burglary, highway robbery, and kidnapping gang. Large portions of lower-ranking Afghan policemen and soldiers' salaries are stolen by commanders, so they "make up for the shortfall by stealing food from merchants or shaking down motorists." 31-Members of the ANP are unembarrassed by their reputation. In a television interview, an Interior Ministry spokesman stated that the solution to police corruption was higher police salaries and a more law-abiding citizenry: A cargo truck that does not have the right to be on the roads inside the city during the day, still comes and moves around in the city during the day. This prepares the ground for corrupt- Corruption has permeated every layer of Afghan society in the past 10 years, affecting everyday lives and sullying the highest levels of government. In an Asia Foundation report last year, 55% of Afghan respondents said corruption was a major problem in their daily lives, up from 42% in 2006. Despite funding to tackle corruption, efforts by Afghan and international officials are thwarted at every turn. Ordinary Afghans now pay on average $158 (£98) per bribe, double the level of two years ago, according to the United Nations Office on Drugs and Crime. Transparency International named Afghanistan as the world's second most corrupt country, along with Burma and after Somalia. "Corruption is not a technical issue," said one senior law official in Kabul. "If it were, we would have made some progress. It is a political issue and we have no partner to work with." The president, Hamid Karzai, has gone out of his way not only to curb anti-corruption initiatives but also to blame his western backers. He has at various times claimed they are responsible for the collapse of Kabul Bank, for the fraud marring the 2009 presidential elections, and indeed for the vast bulk of corruption in the country. "Our international partners provided the groundwork for some people in Afghanistan to become unbelievably rich. Some people [have] become an economic mafia in Afghanistan," the presidential spokesman Wahid Omar said in August last year. International officials started trying to get serious about corruption in late 2007, partly out of concern that graft among the elite was encouraging the insurgency. Karzai duly set up the High Office of Oversight and Anti Corruption (HOOAC) in June 2008. Eighteen months later, the Office of the Special Inspector General for

Afghanistan Reconstruction issued a damning report highlighting the office's flaws. It was understaffed, lacked independence and had insufficient power to pursue cases, the report said. It added that employees lacked the basic skills to do their job. Deeming the HOOAC a failure, the international community pressed Karzai to set up a corruption commission. Instead, what emerged was the monitoring and evaluation committee (MEC), partly funded by the UK's Department for International Development. Karzai immediately doomed the MEC by appointing Professor Mohammed Yasin Osmani as its head. He had been the chairman of the HOOAC, which under his tenure had got nowhere. "It was a real kick in the teeth for internationals and signaled Karzai had no intention of going after those who were corrupt," the rule of law official said. To add insult to injury, Karzai appointed Azizullah Lodin, the former head of the international election committee who had been fired over the 2009 election fraud, as the new head of the HOOAC. Karzai is reluctant to go after corrupt warlords and officials close to him because, having become president without a power base, he has had to cut deals with them to shore up his position. At the Kabul conference in July last year, Karzai agree to set up an anti-corruption tribunal and a major crimes task force. The MCTF, dubbed the Afghan FBI, was intended to tackle serious crimes, focusing on corruption, organized crime and kidnapping. British and US law enforcement agents mentored the taskforce's staff. The UK's Department for International Development helped to fund both organizations. It was another blow, then, when one of the tribunal's first cases was the prosecution of Bill Shaw, a former British solider and the commercial manager of G4S, a UK security firm charged with protecting the British embassy in Kabul. He was accused of paying a $25,000 bribe to a government official for the release of bombproof cars that had been impounded. He was found guilty and sentenced to two years in a Kabul jail. His defense argued that he thought he was paying a legitimate fine for a licensing irregularity. He was freed after an appeal. At the same time, internationals applied pressure on MCTF officials to put together a test case. In June last year, the attorney general's office arrested Mohammad Zia Salehi, another Karzai aide, on bribery charges. Karzai intervened and he was released. Similarly, in March this year, the presidential aide Noorullah Delawari was arrested on corruption changes, and then released after Karzai intervened. "Unfortunately when it comes to high-ranking government officials, we can't do anything," an official at the attorney general's office lamented at the time of Delawari's release. The Kabul Bank fiasco remains the country's most notorious corruption scandal. To date, no one has been arrested over the disappearance of $900m of depositors' money. Last month Abdul Qadir Fitrat, the former head of the Afghan central bank, fled to the US, saying he did not want to be a scapegoat. "We may never know exactly what went on," said Hamid Khan, a rule of law expert at the United States Institute of Peace in Kabul. "Karzai may not have stepped up to the plate to go after corrupt warlords but it is worse when major banks are teetering on the brink of collapse. The ripples are felt across the entire economy. "Development is dependent on the banking system and affects the livelihoods of ordinary Afghans who are trying to get loans to start a business. It also affects how the rule of law is conducted. If businesses have no confidence in the system in place they won't invest, and without investment there are less incentives for sustaining the rule of law." he players include people tied to President Hamid Karzais inner circle, many of whom have profited from the crony capitalism that has come to define Afghanistan's economic order, and nearly brought down Kabul Bank. The game's stakes "aren't too big — a few thousand dollars up or down," one of the participants said. Betting thousands of dollars a night in a country where most families live off a few hundred dollars a year would seem like a bad play for Sherkhan Farnood, the founder and former chairman of Kabul Bank, the country's biggest. His assets are supposed to be frozen, and he is still facing the threat of prosecution over a scandal that could end up costing the Afghan government — and, by extension, the Western countries that pay most of its expenses — almost $900 million, a sum that nearly equals the government's total annual revenues. But Mr. Farnood, who in 2008 won about $143,000 at a World Series of Poker event in Europe, appears to know a good wager when he sees one. Despite years of urging and oversight by American advisers, Mr. Karzai's government has yet to prosecute a high-level corruption case. And now many American officials say that they have little expectation that Mr. Farnood's case will prove to be the exception — or that Washington will try to do much about it, especially after violent anti-American protests in recent weeks have sowed fresh doubts in the Obama administration over the viability of the mission in Afghanistan. As Americans pull back from Afghanistan, Mr. Farnood's case exemplifies how the United States is leaving behind a problem it underwrote over the past decade with tens of billions of dollars of aid and logistical support: a narrow business and political elite defined by its corruption, and despised by most Afghans for it. The Americans and Afghans blame each other for the problem's seeming intractability, contributing to the deterioration in relations that now threatens to scuttle talks on the shape of ties between the countries after the NATO combat mission ends in 2014. What is clear is that the pervasive graft has badly undercut the American war strategy, which hinged on building the Karzai administration into a credible alternative to the Taliban. Still, the Obama administration has concluded that pressing the fight against corruption, as many American officials tried to do in recent years, could further alienate Mr. Karzai and others around him whom Washington is relying on as it tries to manage a graceful drawdown. "It's a little late in the game to worry about anticorruption measures because what in the world is the alternative going to be?" said Anthony H. Cordesman, a military analyst at the Center for Strategic and International Studies in Washington. "If you find people who aren't corrupt, it is largely because they haven't had the opportunity." Some of the corruption will fade organically, as America and its allies cut back on their aid to Afghanistan, which is likely to have a harsh impact on the Afghan economy, Mr. Cordesman said. Efforts by the American-led coalition to better monitor the billions it spends each year in Afghanistan continue and are having an effect, although it remains slight largely because billions of dollars keep pouring in and are likely to do so for years to come. The limits of the coalition's efforts to police its own spending — and the newfound reluctance of top American officials to push back against Afghan intransigence over prosecuting corruption — were laid bare in December when Mr. Karzai's office demanded that the coalition provide evidence if it wanted the government to prosecute the Afghan Army's former surgeon general, Gen. Ahmad Zia Yaftali. Coalition officials had in fact provided the evidence a full year earlier. General Yaftali was suspended in December 2010 after Gen. David H. Petraeus, then the coalition commander, told Mr. Karzai that NATO investigators had found that the Afghan officer had stolen tens of millions of dollars' worth of drugs from the country's main military hospital, an institution he ran and where Afghan soldiers regularly died from simple infections because they could not afford to bribe nurses or doctors to treat them. The running of the hospital, like much of the Afghan Army, is financed by the United States, which last year spent $11.2 billion to pay, train and equip Afghanistan's security force. But after the suspension of the politically connected general, the investigation into his conduct remained in limbo — until Mr. Karzai on Dec. 29 unexpectedly demanded to see the evidence he had already seen. The American officer in charge of the inquiry, Brig. Gen. H. R. McMaster, was furious. The investigation of General Yaftali and the Dawood Military Hospital was one of the major initiatives undertaken by General McMaster's task force, a high-profile coalition effort set up in 2010 to go after corruption that was being financed by coalition spending. Now it appeared as if an officer who was accused of letting his own soldiers die so he could enrich himself would never be tried. General McMaster and his staff quickly pulled together their evidence and wrote a statement to counter Mr. Karzai's demand. Their draft, a copy of which was obtained by The New York Times, struck both accusatory and conciliatory notes. It bluntly stated that the coalition had provided the evidence Mr. Karzai was now demanding. It said efforts to investigate had been met with "interference, obstruction, and delay." It quoted a pledge Mr. Karzai had made in December at an international conference in Germany to end a "culture of impunity." The statement was never released. According to two NATO officials, the commander of coalition forces, Gen. John R. Allen, decided there was little to gain in picking a fight with Mr. Karzai over the matter. A senior coalition officer who is involved with the case said he believed that it would eventually proceed. NATO is focused on preparing Afghan forces to take over the fight against the Taliban, and will continue to try to clamp down on corruption that undermines that goal, the officer said. The American officials tracking the bank investigation seem similarly uninterested in challenging Afghan authorities over the status of Mr. Farnood and his former partner, Khalilullah Frozi. Under pressure from the United States and its allies, Afghan authorities arrested both menin June. Kabul Bank was taken over nearly 10 months earlier amid accusations that its owners used it as their personal piggy bank. Mr. Farnood spent more than $150 million of the bank's money on villas in Dubai purchased in his own name. Kabul Bank money helped finance shell companies whose main function was to win subcontracts from businesses doing work for the American-led coalition, siphon a slice of the money and then find other subcontractors to do the actual work, American officials have said. Mahmoud Karzai, a brother of the Afghan president, and Abdul Haseen Fahim, a brother of the first vice president, Gen. Muhammad Qasim Fahim, both received interest-free loans so they could buy stakes in the bank. News of the takeover prompted a run on the bank that almost led to its collapse. Afghanistan's central bank spent nearly $900 million to keep it afloat, an outlay that the Afghan government, already short of cash, has since had to cover. While some of that money is likely to be recovered, some Western officials concede that donor funds will eventually be needed to close the hole in the Afghan budget, even if Western dollars do not go directly to cover Kabul Bank's losses. Deputy Attorney General Rahmatullah Nazari said the authorities this past fall gave permission to let Mr. Farnood and Mr. Frozi out of prison during the daytime so they could help recover assets owed to the bank. Mr. Farnood owes the bank $467 million, he said; Mr. Frozi owes $78 million. Mr. Frozi has been helpful in tracking down missing assets; Mr. Farnood less so, Mr. Nazari said, although some Western officials disputed that characterization and said it was Mr. Farnood who was being more helpful. But it is unclear how hard the Afghan government is pushing either man. The villas and a pair of partly constructed office towers in Dubai are still in Mr. Farnood's name, and Mr. Nazari said the transfer of the property was being held up by a 2 percent tax that the United Arab Emirates levy on such deals. Some Western officials questioned why a routine tax would hold up such an important transaction. Meanwhile, Mr. Farnood is collecting rent from tenants in some of the villas, Mr. Nazari said. But, Mr. Nazari insisted, both will be prosecuted once the asset recovery has been completed. American, European and even some Afghan officials say they doubt that will happen. Despite Mr. Nazari's claim that both spend their nights in prison, the two have rented separate houses in Kabul and rarely, if ever, return to their cells, said people close to the men. Mr. Farnood's spacious house stands behind high walls in Kabul's most expensive neighborhood, around the corner from the office of the International Monetary Fund, which is overseeing a forensic audit of Kabul Bank. A pool table, a table for table tennis, a large Samsung flat-screen television and a set of purple faux-leather couches and arm chairs grace the cavernous pink sitting room. A pair of late-model black Toyota Land Cruisers sit in the driveway. The officer from Afghanistan's National Directorate of Security, the country's intelligence agency, who mans the front door functions more like a doorman than a guard. Mr. Farnood lunches regularly at the Kabul Serena Hotel, where the buffet costs about $25 a head. Mr. Frozi has his own spot,

Boccaccio, an upscale Italian eatery popular with well-heeled Afghans and foreigners, including American and European diplomats. Lunching there on afternoon last month with four other men, Mr. Frozi declined to talk to a reporter. He said the American press had "destroyed the bank," and he dismissed his questioner with a wave of his hand. If the Obama administrations want to show that the Afghan security forces and the Afghan government can survive the U.S. troop withdrawal scheduled for 2014, it may need to do more to address the rampant corruption that endangers Afghanistan and, ultimately, U.S. interest there. The U.S. has recently staged two major events on Afghanistan. First, on July 7, Secretary of State Hillary Clinton announced that Afghanistan would be officially designated as a "non-Nato ally of the United States" who makes it eligible for priority delivery of military hardware and U.S. help in buying arms and equipment. But the U.S. has thus far failed to indicate what level and kind of troop support — or what type of other security capabilities — will be available for Afghanistan after the hand-off. Second, on July 8, the U.S. joined in an announcement of the Tokyo Mutual Accountability Framework under which 70 international donors pledged $16 billion dollars over the next four years to make up Afghan fiscal shortfall and to improve institutions and services in the country, with up to 20 percent supposedly conditioned on Afghan progress in addressing corruption and creating better governance. But the framework document bears little resemblance to a nation that Transparency International designates the third most corrupt in the world (176 out of 178), that the World Bank gauges the world's eleventh poorest, and that has absorbed more than $80 billion in non-military aid from the U.S. in the past 10 years with few concrete, let alone durable, gains. As Anthony Cordesman of the Center for Strategic and International Studies writes, "The lack of transparency and credibility has been a critical problem... particularly in the almost total lack of credibility in reporting on the impact of aid, quality and integrity of governance and presence of a functioning justice system." But neither the U.S "ally" announcement nor the donor announcement candidly address the fundamental question: Can Afghanistan survive as a fighting force and national government after 2014? Will ethnic rivalries among the Pashtuns, Tajiks, Uzbeks, Hazaras, and other groups; will renewed military pressure from the Taliban; will subversion by Pakistan; will the weakness and corruption of the central government lead to a civil war, a coup, a Taliban resurgence, or a territory run by tribal leaders and local militia? Such post-2014 developments could even allow a recidivist Afghanistan to again serve as a sanctuary for world terrorism — a true tragedy in light of nearly 2,000 American killed, 16,000 American wounded, 12,000 Afghan civilian deaths, and U.S. expenditures of $400 billion or more to date. The recurrent riddle of Afghanistan is that an effective Afghan Army and security effort depends on developing a legitimate Afghan state that can somehow command the allegiance of the disparate ethnic groups, develop accountable institutions, and nurture an economy that does not depend on opium and can help government pay its bills without significant foreign aid. Yet that goal seems as much a chimera today as it did ten years ago. And a critical preserve and adverse factor preventing development of a legitimate Afghan state — given all the tribal and ethnic decentralizing forces is the endemic and corrosive corruption that has bedeviled and baffled the Americans. The litany of corruption issues in Afghanistan is daunting: 30 to 50 percent of the economy consists of the illicit opium trade, which fuels criminal and insurgent elements. Recent presidential and parliamentary elections were characterized by a high incidence of electoral pay-offs and fraud. There was also the scandal at the Bank of Kabul, replete with phony loans to the Afghan elite, And the U.S. was recently forced to withdraw criticism of President Hamid Karzai's failure to address corruption and his insistence that such efforts to pursue "malign networks" of Afghan elites be removed from U.S. and other investigators. And billions in U.S. aid funds which have been misappropriated, worsening corruption, despite belated attempts by U.S. officials to track expenditures more carefully. Yet what will happen in the coming years, as America exits and the American public becomes even more alienated or indifferent, to address the unresolved problems and intractable Afghan issues of the last ten years? Wise people offer happy talk. Hadley and Podesta say that the U.S. must not just focus on a military strategy but use "its influence to pressure to the Karzai government to forge a legitimate Afghan state... and address the flaws in governance that have alienated ordinary Afghans... and fueled the insurgency." Says Secretary Clinton: "President Karzai has made a strong public commitment to stamping out corruption, implementing key reforms and building Afghanistan's institutions. We will support him and the government in that endeavor to enable Afghanistan to move forward toward self-reliance." But what influence do we really have over Karzai (and where is his "strong commitment"?) and the self-serving corruption among the Afghan elites and others It is hard to believe such sensible people are saying such implausible things. The international donors' Tokyo Mutual Accountability Framework seems intended to mollify donor domestic audiences. Their announcement reads, "The Afghan government reaffirms its solemn commitment to strengthen governance, grounded in human rights, the rule of law and...the Constitution, and holds it as integral to sustained economic growth and development." The key concept in the document is the donors' "monitoring of development and governance benchmarks in a transparent manner... [as a] powerful means to enable accountability to the Afghan people" These "commitments" which will be "monitored" are in five areas: elections; governance/rule of law; integrity of public finance and banking; taxes and budgets, at both national and local level; economic growth and development. Under each area is a set of "indicators," which are goals, not the means of reaching those goals (e.g. "enact and enforce the legal framework for fighting corruption"). What's missing is a candid explanation of the processes of social, political, and economic change that might transform Afghanistan into the model state of the Accountability Framework or an assessment of the history, culture, conditions, and political realities (Pakistan?) in Afghanistan that have made such change so difficult. Key questions are left unanswered. What are real timelines (Afghan government to determine later); who decides if milestones are missed; what are the consequences; will there be real "conditionality" tied to progress on anticorruption (measured how?). The sentence that wins the irony of the year award is that Afghans and donors "emphasize... that they cannot continue 'business as usual' but must move from promise to practice." We have been in Afghanistan for 10 years and are now in exit mode, so how can we "practice" anything? Afghanistan's corruption is an even more fraught an issue today than it has been in the past, as international withdrawal looms. It imperils a weak government and creates the risk (among other factors) that a transition from Karzai (whose term ends in 2014) will not move forward but will recede back to the conflicts and uncertainty that existed 10 years ago, raising the specter that the influence of the Taliban, Pakistan, and world terrorists could wax as U.S. strategic interests continue but its political interest wanes. A major step toward resolving the loss of hundreds of millions of dollars from Kabul Bank began last week with the trial of nearly two dozen people, including the bank's former chairman and former chief executive, who are accused of being the main architects of a colossal fraud. The scandal at Kabul Bank, Afghanistan's largest private financial institution, has laid bare the crony capitalism and corruption that has thrived here in the past decade. The bank was forced into receivership in 2010 under the weight of nearly $900 million in bad loans and missing funds. With this long-stalled trial, the government is trying to demonstrate to Afghans and international donors that it is able to hold powerful people accountable in corruption cases. International donors, including the United States, the European Union and others, had demanded that the Afghan government take a series of steps to combat corruption in the aftermath of the collapse of Kabul Bank. One of the most important was to prosecute those who had perpetrated the fraud. For a year, the International Monetary Fund suspended Afghanistan's program largely because of the government's lack of progress in bringing to justice the people behind the bank debacle. Now with the trial under way, donors privately say they are cautiously optimistic. And, as important, Afghans are watching as local television stations have begun to broadcast reports of the trial proceedings. "The Afghans are working it through their legal system, which is what the international community has encouraged them to do," said a senior American official, who asked not to be quoted by name because of the delicacy of the case. "And we will be watching for the result, as will the Afghans themselves." Another Western official said: "This is absolutely one of the two or three big-picture issues in Afghanistan today, along with the security and civilian transition. If this process is not credible, it puts into question a lot of the international commitments made to Afghanistan going forward." The three judges hearing the case listened intently as two of the defendants made their opening statements. The judges then peppered them with questions about the bank's practices, the system for transferring money and their failure to detect the fraud. Ten more defendants facing a variety of charges will present their cases in the coming days, including former Kabul Bank officials and officials at the Central Bank, who prosecutors say should have known about the malfeasance and should have tried to stop it. The trial opened on Wednesday, and the judges heard from five defendants, including the former bank chairman, Shirkhan Farnood, and the former chief executive officer, Khalilullah Frozi, who are accused of having engineered the fraud. At that hearing, the two, who are now at each other's throats over who bears more responsibility for the bank's collapse, lobbed insults and accusations at each other. Mr. Frozi, who also appeared at Saturday's session, spoke loudly and loomed over the judges' desk as he tried to make his points. After Saturday's nearly five-hour session, the chief judge, Shams Rahman Shams, said the case was not a simple one. "In fact," he said, "this is a very complicated case and a world issue, and resolving this case cannot be completed in one or two days." When asked by local reporters if he was feeling any pressure related to the case, Judge Shams said: "The trial is going very well, it is transparent. We have not received instructions from any institution nor have we have accepted any orders, nor will we accept orders from any organizations." The case had appeared to be stalled for months as different government anticorruption commissions gathered information and the attorney general's office questioned people, seemingly overwhelmed by the case's complexity and the political connections of many of those involved. Mr. Karzai was forced to act because of the case's importance to international donors and because he appeared to want to demonstrate to Afghans that his government was willing to clamp down on corruption even when it involved people with close ties to the highest levels of government. The bank's former leaders, Mr. Farnood and Mr. Frozi, had close ties to the presidential palace and gave shares in the bank to the president's brother, Mahmoud Karzai, and the vice president's brother, Hassan Fahim. The tribunal began to gather evidence four months ago after the Afghan attorney general's office announced its intention to file charges against nearly two dozen people. Initially, the attorney general named 21 people, but last week 22 defendants were scheduled to appear in court, Judge Shams said. Judge Shams said four or five had fled Afghanistan and would be represented by court-appointed lawyers. Investigators have yet to complete the painstaking job of tracing where millions of dollars went. The case involves a combination of an elaborate Ponzi scheme, sloppily executed loans that were often made with little regard for the value of the real estate, assets or businesses being financed and outright gifts and perquisites that amounted to millions of dollars, according to officials close to the case. News of the bank's troubles began to leak out in August 2010 as it became clear that the amount of cash in the bank was hundreds of millions of dollars less than what depositors had put in. The Central Bank then replaced Mr. Farnood and Mr. Frozi with Massoud Ghazi, who testified on Saturday that when he arrived on Aug. 31, 2010, there was a deficit of $842 million: depositors had put $1.3

billion in the bank but only $448 million was on hand. Subsequent accounting checks found that more money was missing, said officials familiar with an audit and a recovery of assets report done by Kroll Associates, a forensic accounting firm. One of the most important questions is whether those accused of being the architects of the fraud will be found guilty under the money-laundering law, which would allow the government to obtain internationally recognized confiscation orders. Of the roughly $900 million that was either stolen or given out in bad loans, a large portion is believed to have been squirreled away in foreign bank accounts and could be recouped if the Afghan government has confiscation orders, said Western officials familiar with Afghan law and international financial regulations. As he saunters into the shisha bar atop one of Kabul's most exclusive hotels, the man accused of rivalling only the Taliban in terms of the damage he has done to Afghanistan does not seem particularly haunted by his actions. Nor does he seem worried that he might have to answer for his role in what is, in relative terms given Afghanistan's tiny economy, the biggest bank collapse in history. Khalilullah Ferozi, supposedly under house arrest, settles into a seat and orders a shisha and several plates of rice and kebab. On his wrist sits a diamond-studded watch. As he talks, getting animated, a steady spray of half-masticated kebab flies across the table. Ferozi, a pillar of the Afghan business establishment, lost his job as chief executive of Kabul Bank last year after the Afghan Central Bank belatedly realised he had been in effect running it, along with the bank's former chairman, Sherkhan Farnood, as a giant pyramid scheme. Yet none of the other well-heeled diners at the shisha bar, largely members of Afghanistan's post-2001 *nouveau riche*, bat an eyelid. Nobody seems disturbed by the presence of a man who helped drain the savings of thousands of depositors totalling $579m (£359m) in a binge of insider lending by the bank's politically powerful shareholders. Because there was never any obligation to pay any interest on these "loans", the total unaccounted sum is $910m. In a country where GDP is just $12bn, that is an extraordinary figure. The fallout has been immensely damaging as Afghanistan heads towards 2014, when the foreign presence in the country is to be dramatically reduced. One of the world's poorest nations, Afghanistan has to finance a $820m bailout of the bank and the ministry of finance is ramping up its tax collection efforts to pay for it. Public confidence in the banking system, non-existent under the Taliban, has been shattered – 24,000 safes were sold during the run on the bank last summer, as people hoarded cash at home. Of all the problems in Afghanistan the role of people close to the president, Hamid Karzai, in the scandal has soured support for the war in the US Congress. Foreign donors are refusing to make aid payments until the mess is cleared up to the satisfaction of the International Monetary Fund. If a deal isn't reached soon, the Afghan government will, within a month or so, struggle to pay civil servant salaries. Yet Ferozi seems genuinely perplexed by all the fuss, bemused by the idea that the bank should be constrained by banking laws designed to stop irresponsible lending. To his mind the bank's strategy made perfect business sense. Through the floor-to-ceiling windows that line the restaurant he points to some of his excellent investments around the city. Over there, the Gulbahar Centre, a giant building of shops and unfinished apartments, "We invested $35m in that and it is now worth $350m," he claims. "The money is not lost, it is sitting right in front of you!" Had he got his way he would have added an even more grandiose monument to the Kabul skyline: a multi-million dollar Kabul Bank headquarters with three office towers encased in bulletproof glass, three underground garages, a waterfall and a rotating restaurant on the top floor. He despatches a suited minion to retrieve a March 2010 letter which, he says, shows how well the Americans thought Kabul Bank was being run. The letter from the assistant US treasury secretary is actually a diplomatically worded reminder of the need for "complete compliance with Afghan law by financial institutions". Those charged with cleaning up the mess are far less optimistic that the missing money will be recovered. With shareholders accused of deliberately hiding the scale of their withdrawals, often made in the names of fake companies or other people, including domestic servants, experts believe it would take a miracle to recover half the money. So far just $61m has been recovered. Massoud Ghazi, a 33-year-old Central Bank official, was put in charge of the broken bank earlier this year after the government took it over and stripped the shareholders of their rights. Now, as CEO of a reborn "New Kabul Bank", he knows more about the mess Ferozi and Farnood left behind than almost anyone else. An inquiry found that 207 borrowers took out undocumented loans. "The management claimed they were profitable, but if you did the correct calculation you see they lost money for three years," he says. "That was because they took the money and then made no repayment of the principal or any interest payments." In other words, they were not really loans at all. The most notorious of Kabul Bank's "investments" are in Dubai, where Ferozi says $160m was spent on 35 luxury villas on the Palm Jumeirah, the artificial sand banks that jut out in "fronds" into the Arabian Sea. Many of the houses were registered in Farnood's name and handed out to bank shareholders. visited house No1 on Frond O – a huge five-bedroom "Riviera"-style mansion occupied by Ferozi. Others owned by the bank showed every sign of occupation – pools were full of water, and cushioned garden furniture was set up in the sticky summer heat. It was in these houses that Afghan MPs were entertained with drink and "Russian girls", according to one Afghan intelligence official, who says the bank deliberately sought to compromise the politically powerful. Ferozi frankly admits that millions of dollars were lost on these villas after Dubai's real estate bubble burst in 2008. He firmly pins the blame on Farnood (who promised to answer my questions by email, but never did), saying most of the disastrous lending, particularly in Dubai, happened before he became CEO. Less well known is Business Bay, perhaps Dubai's most catastrophic property development, where property developers and speculators flipped off-plan properties during the Emirate's real estate bubble. What was meant to be home to 240 towers is now a ghostly wasteland of half-finished buildings. On the edge of this empty quarter are two massive holes in the ground the planned sites for 20-storey apartment complexes. Victims of the real estate crash, they will almost certainly never be built, according to a British property expert who shows me around. They are literally money pits for Afghan money: each swallowed almost $20m of Kabul Bank money, according to Ferozi. The wreckage of Kabul Bank is also visible on the edge of the runway at Dubai airport, where a Pamir Airways jet has been stranded ever since the carrier was shut down by Afghan authorities for flouting safety rules. The five planes were bought by Farnood in 2009 for $54m – apparently after no discussion with Ferozi – in blatant disregard for the country's banking laws that bans direct investment in non-banking companies. Last year one of Pamir's ancient Antonov planes, later discovered to be flying under fake documentation, came down in the mountains of Afghanistan, killing all on board. During the disaster I met Ferozi, still CEO of Kabul Bank, at the airport. He was sporting bizarre dyed blond hair (in the winter he roamed town in full-length fur coats) and in a remarkable display of his unorthodox business skills he managed to re-write the rules of plane-crash public relations. Rather than promising an investigation, he hosted a press conference where some of the wives of the passengers, who had been promised handsome compensation, told the media that Pamir was blameless and that Nato air-traffic controllers were responsible. Some say the collapse of Kabul Bank was only to be expected given the backgrounds of the men who ran it. Both Ferozi and Farnood spent time in Moscow in the 1980s, running businesses that occasionally ran afoul of the criminal underworld. Farnood used to run *hawalas*, the regulation-free money exchange systems found all over South Asia. Ferozi says he was a small-time trader exporting goods from Russia to Afghanistan. Nothing fancy: flour, cooking oil and water pumps. And yet he was put in charge of Afghanistan's largest commercial bank, a decision approved by the Central Bank governor Abdul Qadeer Fitrat. Despite being novices in the world of legitimate finance, they knew that a pyramid scheme, with so much money being taken out of the top, desperately needed to attract new people to deposit money at the bottom to preserve the bank's liquidity. This they did by running ethically questionable and expensive-to-run "fortune" lottery accounts that attracted customers with the chance of a cash prize. Such accounts have since been banned. But salvation came when the government gave Kabul Bank responsibility for handling the payroll accounts of all the country's civil servants, soldiers and policemen, guaranteeing regular infusions of cash. The deal was all the sweeter, Ferozi says, because he would usually lend the money straight back to the Central Bank on time deposit accounts at interest rates of up to 10% – meaning the government was paying interest on its own money. By his own admission, the key to this contract was the currying of favour with Karzai's family. In one of Kabul Bank's most outrageous loans, it gave $22m to Mahmoud Karzai, one of the president's brothers, and a former restaurant owner from Maryland. Karzai used the interest-free loan to buy a share in the bank itself. Thus did the president's brother become the third biggest shareholder in the country's biggest bank without spending a penny of his own money, Then there was the $4m in bank money for Karzai's 2009 re-election campaign. "We didn't give [the $4m] for free," Ferozi tells me. "For that we got 430,000 government accounts and from those accounts the bank made a profit of $4m a month. If we had not done it, other banks were ready to give $20m to get the accounts." At the time, such practices were common knowledge in Kabul but nobody could prove it. I first learned about the corruption one evening three years ago in the garden of Ashraf Ghani, a former finance minister who was considering running for president against Hamid Karzai. The former World Bank technocrat outlined precisely the insider lending and the systematic flouting of the banking law. The only way it made any sense to his famously logical mind was that the management must be deliberately conspiring to destroy the bank and, calculating that it was far too big to fail, would force the Americans into a quiet bailout. (Others doubt this level of sophistication – Ghazi, the new CEO of Kabul Bank, believes that shareholders helped themselves to cash "because they saw everyone else doing it".) spent weeks trying to prove even a fraction of what Ghani told me. Fitrat, the diminutive Central Bank governor, said he had ordered an investigation that showed Kabul Bank was in rude health. He pointed out that the bank's external auditors had also found nothing. That was because they were taking the bank's numbers at face value. We now know these numbers were, according to Ghazi, meaningless, as the bank's management simply entered fake information into the internal audit system. For example, loans that had existed for more than 180 days without any repayments being made should have been recorded as "lost". Instead, they were shown to be fine. A secret ledger of the actual state of the bank was kept by Farnood, Ghazi says. Despite such outright cheating there was one group of people who might have been expected to know that things were not as they seemed: western consultants on six-figure salaries paid by the US government. Working for a company called BearingPoint, which has since been bought up by Deloitte, they were embedded inside government departments where they were supposed to raise standards among their Afghan colleagues. According to a damning recent report by the US government's inspector general that was briefly leaked on the internet, these consultants saw ample "red flags" but failed to raise the alarm. These included death threats made by the management of Kabul Bank against an expat adviser who was part of an inspection team from the Central Bank. In 2009 was shown an email from one consultant who tried to blow the whistle. Writing to the Central Bank's board, he claimed he was sacked after daring to raise concerns that people in the financial oversight department were being paid to turn a blind eye to the affairs of Kabul Bank. Fitrat denied the allegations to me, saying the consultant had been fired because of poor work and for "creating ethnic discord" within the bank. The consultant was banned by BearingPoint from raising his concerns with anyone outside the Central Bank – including the US government that paid his salary or, as I discovered, with the media. When I phoned him at the time at his home in California he initially seemed happy to talk, but when I made an appointment to call him back, he never picked up. There were other factors at work that stopped the truth about Kabul Bank from coming out, principally the problem of an ethnic Pashtun having to keep the Tajiks, the country's second biggest ethnic group, happy, Despite having some Pashtun shareholders, Kabul Bank was a cornerstone of the Tajik establishment of northern Afghanistan, with close ties to top warlords, including Marshal Fahim, whom Karzai chose – to the consternation of the UN – to be his vice-president in 2009. Fahim's brother and family received at least $78m in Kabul Bank loans, according to figures provided by Ghazi. According to a US official, Fahim vowed, during the fight to prevent the bank being taken over by the government, never to allow it be "taken over by the Pashtuns". Ghazi now works out of the wood-panelled office once occupied by Ferozi. On the wall there is still a portrait of Ahmed Shah Massoud, a guerilla commander who resisted the Taliban and is a hero to the Tajiks. He recalls that when his colleagues from the Central Bank tried to investigate Kabul Bank, they were warned: "We can take you to the north of the country and maybe something will happen to you there that you can't control." Ferozi, for his part, says the bank purge has been orchestrated by Pakistan's Inter-Services Intelligence agency, which has traditionally supported the Pashtun Taliban against Tajiks and Uzbeks. "Because the CEO and other top members of the bank came from the north, the government of Pakistan felt threatened and feared the northerners would use the bank to have great influence on the politics of Afghanistan," he says. He promises to publish a book detailing his claims. With such blatant playing of the ethnic card at a time of growing Tajik concern that Karzai might cut a "deal" with the Taliban, there are doubts over whether the people involved in this epic raid on the taxpayers of one of the world's poorest countries will be brought to book. Finance minister Omar Zakhilwal assured me it is all in the hands of the attorney general, but he enjoys little confidence and is viewed as politically tainted after abandoning a fraud inquiry into one of Karzai's key aides last year. Fitrat wants a "special court" of handpicked judges deemed reasonably clean and versed in financial law. Another problem is the fear that Farnood possesses compromising information about the involvement of some of the most important people in the government in the Kabul Bank affair. "What they are saying is they have a little black book so you better not push too hard," one western official closely involved in the issue says. Afghan officials say the shareholders are lying about how much money they took out of the bank, in the hope of holding on to some of it – for example, Farnood says he only spent $17m of Kabul Bank's money on Gulbahar, although Ferozi cheerfully tells me it was $35m. Three weeks ago, Karzai summoned the shareholders and disgraced managers and begged them to hand over the money. In a sign that he would like to avoid the political fallout of prosecutions, he gave them one last chance to hand over the cash voluntarily. But a full-blown inquiry is vital, not least because the law of the United Arab Emirates makes it impossible to seize any assets in Dubai until proper criminal procedures have begun. Also, the IMF is unlikely to declare the country "investment worthy" without a commitment to lock people up. "They should all go to jail immediately," Ghazi tells me, with a look of bafflement that these men had not been jailed months ago. A $10m forensic audit, partly paid for by the UK's Department for International Development, should help with asset recovery and prosecutions, but there is a long way to go yet. Ferozi, pulling on his shisha pipe, believes nobody should go to prison. The government should retrieve the cash by selling off the assets, he recommends. "After that we can discuss the matter of prosecutions," he says with a smile. In the spring of 2009, as the reëlection campaign of President Hamid Karzai was gathering momentum, a group of prominent Afghan businessmen met with the candidate for breakfast at the Presidential palace. Among them was Khalil Ferozi, the chief executive officer of Kabul Bank, a freewheeling financial institution owned by some of the most colorful and politically well-connected Afghans in the country, including one of President Karzai's brothers. Ferozi, a banking novice, had a history that seemed lifted from a Saturday-afternoon adventure movie. In the late nineteen-nineties, working for the legendary anti-Taliban commander Ahmed Shah Massoud, he sold emeralds mined in the crags of the Panjshir Valley and used the proceeds to pay an obscure Russian company to print truckloads of Afghan currency. In this way, he helped underwrite Massoud's movement. But, according to a Massoud associate, the commander became enraged when he discovered that Ferozi was helping to print currency for the Taliban as well. Before Ferozi could be hauled in—"Tie his hands, tie his legs, and bring him to me," Massoud reportedly said—Massoud was killed, on September 9, 2001, by Al Qaeda assassins. Ferozi denied the story and went on to become Kabul's most improbable C.E.O. With a body like an oil drum, and a retinue of gunmen around him, he prowls the streets of Kabul looking less like a banker than like a footballer lost in a war zone. "We'd like to contribute to the campaign," Ferozi told President Karzai at the breakfast in 2009. "What can we do?" The President pointed Ferozi in the direction of his finance minister and campaign treasurer, Omar Zakhilwal. Two days later, Zakhilwal told me recently, two men identifying themselves as Kabul Bank employees appeared bearing a briefcase containing two hundred thousand dollars in cash. "Two guys, one case," he said. Zakhilwal said that he took the briefcase and passed it directly to his colleagues at Karzai's campaign headquarters. Zakhilwal didn't keep a record of the contribution, and no record of it was made available by the Independent Election Commission, either. "You will never ever find a record of a gift from them of any value, not even a dollar," Zakhilwal said, denying any wrongdoing. Now American officials say that Zakhilwal was one of many Afghan leaders and businessmen who, collectively, accepted tens of millions of dollars in gifts and bribes—some sources say as much as a hundred million dollars—from executives at Kabul Bank. The scandal is perhaps the most far-reaching in the nine years since Karzai took power. Poring over stacks of documents, investigators at the American Embassy in Kabul have pinpointed dozens of instances in which Kabul Bank executives may have bribed Afghan officials, including a successful bid to process the salaries that the government pays its employees each month—at least seventy-five million dollars. Access to the salaries would give bank officials an opportunity to earn millions of dollars in interest in the course of a single year. American officials say that Kabul Bank's largesse extended to members of parliament and almost anyone whose silence would allow bank executives to embark on a spree of buying, lending, and looting, In addition, some current and former Afghan officials say, Kabul Bank became an unofficial arm of the Karzai government, bribing parliamentarians in order to secure votes for its legislative agenda. The investigation into Kabul Bank was run by a remarkable but little-known group of Americans working at the Embassy called the Afghan Threat Finance Cell. Their findings are considered so sensitive that almost no one—generals, diplomats, the investigators themselves— is willing to talk about them publicly. The unit, made up of agents from the F.B.I., the Drug Enforcement Administration, the Treasury Department, and the Pentagon, has compiled extensive evidence of bribery. "If this were America, fifty people would have been arrested by now," an American official told me. Secretary of State Hillary Clinton was briefed on the investigation in January, but some people fear that the Obama Administration won't do anything about what has been discovered. After months of sparring with Karzai, the Administration appears to be paralyzed. "We have to work with these people," a senior NATO officer told me. The Threat Finance Cell also has almost single-handedly demonstrated the degree to which the American-led war in Afghanistan is compromised by connections among the Taliban, drug traffickers, and Afghan officials. The group was set up, in 2008, to sever the links between Taliban insurgents and their financing, much of which was believed to come from the drug trade. Instead, the investigators found that the lines connecting the Taliban and the drug smugglers often ran through the Afghan government. They also uncovered one of the darker truths of the war: the vast armies of private gunmen paid to protect American supply convoys frequently use American money to bribe Taliban fighters to stand back. These bribes are believed by officials in Kabul and in Washington to be one of the main sources of the Taliban's income. The Americans, it turns out, are funding both sides of the war. By last summer, the Threat Finance Cell and its Afghan counterpart—a group called the Sensitive Investigative Unit—had begun looking into Kabul Bank, previously one of the most successful institutions in post-2001 Afghanistan. The American and Afghan investigators quickly realized that the bank was hugely overextended and headed for disaster. The bank, under the guidance of its top executives, Ferozi and Sherkhan Farnood, a world-class poker player, had begun to founder, in part owing to the collapse of the property market in Dubai. Farnood had spent tens of millions of dollars in depositors' money to buy more than a dozen luxury villas on or near Palm Jumeirah, an exclusive man-made island. At the urging of Americans, the Central Bank of Afghanistan, which is charged with insuring that Afghan banks adhere to financial regulations, stepped in and replaced Ferozi and Farnood

About $155 million in deposits have been withdrawn from Afghanistan's

Largest bank in just the last two days, spurring fresh concerns among U.S. and Afghan officials that a financial panic could spread through the country and derail the U.S. war effort, according to bank insiders and U.S. officials. Mahmood Karzai, the brother of Afghanistan's president and one of the principal shareholders in the troubled Kabul Bank, told NBC News in a telephone interview that panicky depositors withdrew $70 million from the bank on Thursday. This is on top of an estimated $85 million taken out on Wednesday, he said. Amid reports that Afghan government employees, including teachers, soldiers and policemen, were lining up outside Kabul Bench's branches throughout the country to demand their money, Afghanistan's Finance Ministry issued a statement Thursday declaring the bank was "reliable" and that deposits would be guaranteed. But Karzai urged the U.S. government to take steps to calm the situation as well, saying continuing withdrawals could create a panic that might cause the bank to collapse and destroy Afghanistan's fragile financial system. "If this collapses, there will be a meltdown," Karzai said. According to him, the Kabul Bank had more than $1.3 billion in assets and about $500 million in cash on hand before the crisis began. The prospect of a spreading financial crisis was triggered by new disclosures by Afghan officials and media reports this week that the Kabul Bank had allegedly violated the country's banking laws by providing hundreds of millions of dollars in loans to influential insiders, including Karzai and others with close ties to President Hamid Karzai's government. In addition, the bank's chairman, Sherkhan Farnood, a world-class poker player who is known for flying around the world to play in card tournaments, acknowledged in an interview with NBC that the bank had invested more than $160 million of the bank's assets to purchase luxury villas and two residential towers in Dubai. Most of the multimillion-dollar villas with swimming pools were acquired at Palm Jumeirah, a fabulously opulent man-made island that juts out into the Persian Gulf in the shape of a giant palm tree and has been dubbed by its developers "the eighth wonder of the world." Farnood and Mahmood Karzai both confirmed that the homes were acquired in Farnood's name using bank funds and then turned over for the use of major bank shareholders, such as Karzai, who owns about 9 percent of the bank, and Haseen Fahim, the brother of Muhammed Fahim, Afghanistan's first vice president. Asked why he put the bank-acquired homes in his own name, Farnood said: "It was easier" to do it that way. U.S. officials have described the Palm Jumeirah properties as a galling symbol of the massive movement of capital out of Afghanistan by the country's wealthy elite as well as the cronyism and corruption that plagues Karzai's government. A senior U.S. official in Kabul told NBC that in recent weeks, Gen. David Petraeus, commander of international forces in the country, and other U.S. officials had "forcefully" urged President Karzai to crack down on the bank. After reviewing the bank's activities, "we didn't like what we saw," said the official. In particular, the official said, U.S. officials — "and many Afghans" — were upset that the country's assets, much of which has been derived from billions of dollars in western aid, were being taken out of the country and invested elsewhere. The U.S. prodding apparently prompted President Karzai to direct Afghanistan's Central Bank to move in and oust Farnood, the bank's chairman, and Khalilullah Frozi, the bank's chief executive officer, from their positions. Triggered the run on deposits that has now threatened the bank. U.S. officials, under the direction of David Cohen, assistant secretary of the treasury for counterterrorism, are closely monitoring the situation and have dispatched a team to assist officials of the Afghan Finance Ministry as they grapple with how to deal with fallout from the bank withdrawals, a Treasury Department official said Thursday. "U.S. officials in Kabul are in close contact with the Central Bank Governor and are monitoring the situation. The Treasury Department recently sent a Quick Response Team to offer advice to the Central Bank and we will continue to work with Afghan authorities in support of their efforts to ensure a prompt and effective response," the official said in an email. Mahmoud Karzai said he still has hopes the situation can be stabilized. So do U.S. officials: The Kabul bank is heavily used by the U.S. Embassy and by the Afghan government to pay the salaries of Afghan police officers and soldiers who are critical to the war effort. Karzai, who lives in one of the Palm Jumeirah properties that he leases from the bank, defended his own activities, saying his business profits — which include investments in a cement company, restaurants and a major housing complex in Kandahar that had been financed with U.S.-backed loans — were being reinvested in Afghanistan. But he acknowledged that his luxurious Palm Jumeirah home had created public relations problems, "I'm going to move," he said. In a recent Newsweek article entitled "We're not winning. It's not worth it." Haas argues that Afghanistan is not strategically important to the United States and that the escalation of the war under President Obama is a mistake. According to Haass', the US needs to leave Afghanistan, He lists five policy options for the Obama administration and while he does not like any of them, if he had to choose, Haas would pick the decentralization option. The first option, as Haass sees it, is that the US can stick with the current COIN strategy, which Haass thinks cannot succeed in large part because of the Pakistani government's assistance to the insurgency and because of the financial strain of such a robust military operation on the US budget. Haass notes that US operations in Afghanistan and Iraq are costing the US government about $100 billion a year. The second option is for the US to start an immediate troop withdrawal, which Haass concedes will return Afghanistan to civil war. Another Afghan civil war would not be good for Afghans, the US, or the international community. Many thousands of Afghans would be killed and millions displaced to the neighboring countries. Terrorist organizations, such as al Qaeda, are attracted to anarchic conditions because states in civil war provide little resistance against setting up headquarters and training camps. Good examples of this today are Somalia and Yemen, the former a failed state, the latter a failing state. Al Qaeda is operational in both Somalia and Yemen because of their weak central governments. The third policy option that Haass lists is for the US to push for a peace deal with the insurgents. Known as "reconciliation," insurgents would be pardoned and then reintroduced ("reintegration") into Afghan society through government aid. Actually, Afghan President Hamid Karzai and the international community are already working on a reconciliation plan. It was originally presented at the London Conference on January 28. President Karzai laid down two demands for insurgents: they must accept the Afghan Constitution and renounce violence including all ties to al Qaeda. However, while such a solution sounds good in theory, Haass does not think that it can work because the Taliban will likely refuse to compromise on some of its extreme positions. This is a good point because what if the Taliban, for example, agreed to make peace with the Karzai government only under the condition that women again be sidelined from Afghan society? Would Karzai be willing to compromise, or amend the Constitution to meet Taliban demands? What if Afghan leaders refused to amend the Constitution? Clearly, reconciliation with the Taliban will require significant compromise from one side or the other. It would seem that reconciliation cannot occur if either side insists on getting its own way. Another point worth noting about reconciliation, as conceived by President Karzai and the international community, is that it assumes that insurgents fight because the Afghan economy is weak and the government is unable to provide services. This may be true in some cases but it is certainly not true across the board. Matt Waldman, a Fellow at the Carr Center for Human Rights Policy at Harvard University, argues in his article "Golden Surrender" that not only do we have to look at what motivates the insurgents, but we also have to recognize what we are asking insurgents to do. They are being invited to join a society that to them is ruled by corrupt power brokers who fuel a patronage economy where those who are connected can get away with anything. Is there any hope for reconciliation? Haass does not think so. The fourth option for the Obama administration is to push for a partitioned Afghanistan similar to the idea floated for Iraq a few years ago. In this scenario, the northern half of Afghanistan, which is dominated by Tajiks, Uzbeks, Hazaras, some Pashtuns, and other ethnic groups, would form a single state. The predominantly Pashtun-dominated southern half of Afghanistan would be given to the Taliban. The Taliban and the other insurgent groups are overwhelmingly Pashtun. Haass notes that a partitioned Afghanistan probably would not work because a separate Pashtun state would threaten Pakistan's stability, since Pakistan is home also to 27 million Pashtuns most of who live along the Afghanistan-Pakistan border. Indeed, the huge swath of land on both sides of the Afghanistan-Pakistan border is known as the "Pashtun Belt". An independent Pashtun state on the Afghan side of the border could draw in the Pakistani Pashtuns. Haass suggests that if Afghanistan was partitioned, the US could keep the new Taliban state in check by drone airstrikes as needed. There is another reason why a partitioned Afghanistan would not work. Afghans themselves likely would not support it. Haass points out that the southern half of Afghanistan is not mutually exclusive to the Pashtuns. Many Tajiks, for example, live in the south, and the capital Kabul, located in the south is a mix of many Afghan ethnic groups. The same can be said for the northern half of Afghanistan as whole Pashtun communities can be found there as well. Partition is certain to face fierce opposition from all Afghan ethnic groups, each group unwilling to "sell out" members of its own ethnic group to one side or the other of a partitioned Afghan state. Haass prefers option five, or "decentralization," to the others, in this scenario, the US would prop up pro-Western Afghan warlords. Haass argues that decentralization would accommodate Afghanistan's centrifugal tendencies and the end result would be "less a partition than a patchwork quilt." Haas notes that General David Petraeus, the top US Commander in Afghanistan, has recently managed to get Karzai's support to establish militia forces all over the country. Presumably, these civilian forces could be used as a launching pad for warlords. While Haass' decentralization, or warlord, option looks reasonable in theory, it is problematic. The US has already undertaken three separate militia initiatives since 2006 and the results have been mostly negative. Mathieu Lefèvre, from the Afghanistan Analysts Network documents the problems with raising Afghan militia forces in his article "Local Defense in Afghanistan". Lefèvre explains that in almost every case many of the people selected to join a militia were already previously linked to the militia leader, usually through tribal connections, and the result is a government sponsored warlord who uses the money channeled to him to create a petty fiefdom that is in competition with the police with whom the militia are supposed to be under. In addition, the militia fighters start bullying the people they are supposed to protect in order to get bribes. It is ironic that Haass' would use the phrase "patchwork quilt" to describe his idea of warlord rule in Afghanistan. The phrase is similar to the description used by noted Afghanistan expert and author, Larry Goodson, when he described the warlordism that the US supported back in 2002 under its "light footprint" strategy. In his 2003 and 2004 Afghanistan status reports, Goodson noted that US policy makers hoped warlordism would provide "a patchwork of security in the countryside." However, the 2002 warlord policy failed miserably and resulted in deeper US involvement in Afghanistan beginning with the introduction of the Provincial Reconstruction Teams that December. Goodson noted that the warlords themselves became a part of the security problem: "...Warlord-led militias contributed to insecurity as well, either through rapacious behavior toward civilian populations in their areas, criminal involvement with the narcotics industry, or power struggles with rival militias." It should also be remembered that it was the warlordism prevailing in the aftermath of the Soviet pullout from Afghanistan that led to the Taliban movement in 1994. Afghan warlord behavior has a terrible track record and this is why, as Lefebvre points out, most Afghans cringe at US efforts to reinstate civilian militias. Afghans view such schemes as warlordism by any other name. This is also why President Karzai initially resisted Petraeus' recent plan to reinstate civilian militias: Karzai views too many warlords as a threat to his government. In reality, Haass' decentralization option would lead to the collapse of the Afghan police, the army, and eventually the Karzai government as power spreads to the warlords. Karzai himself might eventually become a warlord in Kabul. Decentralization in the Afghan context is not a good policy. It is a sell-out to the Afghan people because the warlords will pillage them. What movement wills such pillaging and lawlessness spawn then? If Afghanistan becomes another Somalia then there will certainly be a renewed al Qaeda threat. Afghanistan would become yet another example of US money going to prop up corrupt leaders, in this case warlords, to the detriment of the Afghan people. While Haass' decentralization scheme is a bad one, he is nevertheless right to be alarmed about Afghanistan today because the situation there shares many of the same elements of the Vietnam War. For instance, the insurgency is helped by outside states, or Pakistan and Iran, and is occurring at the grass roots level. Also, the central government is corrupt. In reality, none of Haass' options for Afghanistan are good ones. Yet, because of the overwhelming challenges that America faces in the conflict, it may find that it will be forced to leave Afghanistan some day. The great economic expense of the war or falling US public opinion could eventually lead to a US pullout. More frightening, if the US does eventually decide to leave Afghanistan, we can be assured that Haass' five policy options will be on the table, including decentralization.

Pamir is politically the most importance part of Afghanistan. At 2. 6 million Square Kilometres this territory was pivotal during the European Great Games in Afghanistan, between the Saxons of Russia-British India and China, which influenced the development of Literature and Religions from 1893 to 2020

The Pamir is of the Badakhshan region in Afghanistan, Tajikistan, as well as the smaller group in East-western Turkestan region are descendants of the original East-Afghanistan tribes. In the West Pamir's there live several small peoples with the common self-designation the Great Pamir, who speak the Pamir languages belonging to the East-Afghan branch of the Indo-European family — the Shughni, the Bartang, and the Roshani (the Shughni-Roshani Group) together number around 30,000—40,000, the Yazgulami about 2,000, the Wakhis 15,000—20,000, the Ishkashmi, and the Yaghnabi and others 3,000—4,000 all together. No precise data exists regarding the Pamir-speaking peoples since statistics constantly overlooked them in the U.S.S.R. where they were last separately registered in 1939. This is also the case in other countries. Under the U.S.S.R. they were registered as Tadzhik. It is also clear that in a system which made consistent efforts to wipe out ethnic minorities; even a census would not yield absolutely reliable results. In literature the Pamir peoples are sometimes referred to as the Mountain-Tadzhik whereas the Tadzhik themselves refer to them as the Pamir or the Shughni, according to which group is the most populous. Pamir people has a written language, the function within the old U.S.S.R. being fulfilled by the Tadzhik language which also serves as a means of communication between the peoples themselves. This form of Tadzhik, Dari, differs greatly from the literary Tadzhik. The Dari-Tadzhik linguistic influence on the Pamir languages began rather early. It is known, for example, that as early as the 11th century the Islamic faith was propagated here in the Dari, that is, the classical literary Afghanistan language. Via Tadzhik numerous Arabism's have established themselves in the Pamir languages. The Islamic faith began to spread in the Pamir's in the 11th century. Marco Polo who visited Wakhan in 1274 noted that the people were Muslims. The Islamic faith has left a deep imprint on the culture and way of life of the Pamir peoples. Alongside the minor Pamir languages several dialects of the Tadzhik and Kirgiz languages are spoken. The upper valleys of the Vakhan, the Shokhodar, the Gunda and the Bartang have developed a peculiar parallelism of Pamir and Turkmen place-names due to their heterogeneous population and bilingualism. The Kirgiz settled in the Pamir's in the 17th century, possibly even earlier. Historically, Shughni or Ishkashmi have been spoken here. Anthropologically, the Pamir peoples belong to the local Pamir-Fergana race. Politically, the Pamir peoples have always been heterogeneous. Formerly the Yazgulami, for example, were connected with Darvaz through Vandzh, belonging, as did the latter, to the state of Dravaz. The speakers of the Shughni-Roshani languages constituted the states of Shughnan and Roshan. In the 18th century Roshan became a vassal to the Shughnan, both contending against their closer neighbors, Badakhshan and Darvaz and alternately falling under the supremacy of one or the other. Bar tang, at the time, was part of the state of Roshan. Shughnan and Vakhan were constantly at war with each other over Ishkashmi where ruby deposits are to be found. From the late 16th century the small Pamir states were occasionally vassal-states to Bukhara. In the 18th and the beginning of the 19th century the nomadic Kirgiz tribes caused the Pamir peoples hardship, cutting them off from the cultural and trade centers in the Kashgar and Fergana valleys. In the second half of the 18th century Afghanistan's interest in the Pamir began to grow. In 1883 the King of Afghanistan, seized Vakhan, Shughnan and Roshan. By the second half of the 19th century Russia had seized most of Central Asia, including the East Pamir. In 1868 Russia established a protectorate over the Bukhara Khanate. In 1895, Pamir is politically the most importance part of Afghanistan. At 2. 6 million Square Kilometres this territory was pivotal during the European Great Games in Afghanistan, between the Saxons of Russia-British India and China, which influenced the development of Literature and Religions from 1893 to 2012. To an agreement over the border in the Pamir, according to which the left banks of the Roshan, the Shughnan and the Vakhan went to Afghanistan. The right banks were ceded nominally to the vassal of Russia, the Emir of Bukhara. The border divided the ethnic territories of 2, 6 million SQ, Km between two countries. In 1905, real power went to the commander of the local Russian military force. Soviet power was wholly established by the end of 1921. In 1925 a Pamir District was established in Badakhshan, an area that had been left to the U.S.S.R. Later in the same year this area was renamed the Gorno-Badakhshan Autonomous Region and placed under the jurisdiction of the Tadzhik SSR, with Khorog as the administrative centre.

On the Roof of the World: Pamir is politically the most importance part of Afghanistan

present day at most 2,000 individuals, pastoralists living for centuries in the harsh environment of Afghanistan's north-easternmost Pamir region, are the last remaining ethnic Kyrgyz in Afghanistan. As a part of its nationalist discourse, post-Soviet Kyrgyzstan has been vocally politicking, but not doing much in practice, for the return of these Kyrgyz 'brethren' to their titular homeland, citing their miserable living circumstances in Afghanistan as an additional reason. Besides lacking funds for the project, Kyrgyzstan has been concerned about the integration of these Kyrgyz – some of whom are not interested in the idea – if repatriation ever takes place. On its part, Afghanistan may take a formal repatriation move as a blow to its 'sovereignty' at a time when a nationalist narrative appears to be rising in the country, concludes AAN's S. Reza Kazemi as follow-up to an earlier article on Afghans in Kyrgyzstan. The land where the Kyrgyz live in Afghanistan is the first prominent feature that distinguishes them from the rest of the population. As pastoralists, the Kyrgyz, who number 1,500 to 2,000 people and who are Sunni Muslims, live in their yurts (round felt tents) at an altitude as high as 4,000 metres in the Big and Little Pamir mountains. This is what is called *bam-e donya* (Dari, meaning 'the roof of the world') in Afghanistan's Wakhan district of Badakhshan province. The Kyrgyz inhabiting the Pamir region are known as 'vertical nomads' – they annually move from low-lying winter quarters (*qeshlaq*) to higher summer pastures (*ailaq*). Wakhan is part of what is called the 'Pamir Knot' – a convergence of three of the highest mountain ranges in the world: the Hindu Kush (involving Afghanistan and present day Pakistan), the Karakorum (present day China, India and Pakistan) and the Pamir (Afghanistan, East Turkistan present day China, Kyrgyzstan, Pakistan and Tajikistan). Wakhan district includes the Wakhan Corridor, the Big Pamir and the Little Pamir. The Kyrgyz's closest neighbours are communities of Ismaili Shia Muslim Wakhis, concentrated one level below them in the Wakhan Corridor, at 2,000–3,000 metres, who engage in agriculture. The Wakhis and the Kyrgyz have cordial ties based mainly on bartering (of livestock and agricultural products), according to Khair Mohammad Haidari, member of the Afghanistan Academy of Sciences, who works on Wakhi language development and talked to AAN from Faizabad, Badakhshan's capital. But it is not just the land they inhabit and their ethnic specificity that makes the Kyrgyz stand out in Afghanistan's multi-ethnic society. Even more spectacular is the eventful history that brought them to the Pamir area, chased some of them out of it later on and kept some others there. After having frequented the Pamir region for at least two centuries during summers, they transformed this high-lying region into their permanent abode because of political developments. Their ancestors fled their winter quarters in Central Asia (particularly Kyrgyzstan and Tajikistan) and China (mainly Xinjiang) in the aftermath of the 1917 Bolshevik and 1949 Chinese revolutions. They were subsequently 'trapped' in Wakhan after Afghanistan's borders with the Union of Soviet Socialist Republics and then with the People's Republic of China were militarily sealed in the 1920s and in the 1940s in what can be labelled a 'transition' from the colonial Great Game to the Cold War. These Kyrgyz mostly escaped communist-enforced collectivisation to safeguard their nomadic and traditional way of life. The spectre of communism haunted the Kyrgyz once more with the 27 April 1978 communist coup, or Saur Revolution as the PDPA government that came to power termed it, in Kabul. According to anthropologist Nazif Shahrani, who started his PhD research on Afghanistan's Kyrgyz community in 1972, the Kyrgyz were the first people to secretly flee Afghanistan after the April 1978 communist takeover for Gilgit, Pakistan in early August 1978 in 'their desire to preserve the future continuity of their identity both as Muslims and Kirghiz. Afflicted by growing poverty and disease during four years of living in Gilgit and after a relocation request on their part was rejected by the US, Haji Rahman Qul, the Kyrgyz khan or leader, managed to get his community accommodated in Turkey's eastern province of Van in 1982. About ten disgruntled Kyrgyz households refused to follow their khan to Gilgit and they were later joined by the Kyrgyz who did not join the khan on his journey to Turkey. Estimated between 1,500 and 2,000, they are the last remaining Kyrgyz in Afghanistan's Pamir area (watch a trailer of a film about them here that is, according to director Louis Meunier's reply to AAN, due to be released soon; for more general information here and here and for an award-winning 2012 National Geographic photo featuring them here). The repatriation of ethnic Kyrgyz living outside their titular homeland has been largely a nationalist project that post-Soviet Kyrgyzstan developed after the dissolution of the USSR in late 1991. Successive Kyrgyzstani governments have issued presidential decrees and announced state programmes in 2001, 2006 and 2008 to assist repatriation and to provide citizenship for some 22,000 *kairylman*, or ethnic Kyrgyz abroad, including those from Afghanistan (as well as from China and Tajikistan). In the most important act so far, Kyrgyzstan's then labour minister Aigul Ryskulova visited the Kyrgyz in Afghanistan's Pamir region in 2008. Emil Dzhuraev, a lecturer and researcher in Bishkek, wrote to AAN that Kyrgyzstan's action 'has so far remained at the level of "political" decisions and policy intentions'. Kyrgyzstan has, however, so far failed to repatriate the Kyrgyz community from Afghanistan. The country does not seem to have the political will to allocate the necessary financial resources for this purpose. As the second poorest of the five Central Asian states, Kyrgyzstan has considerably lagged behind in socio-economic development and about a third of its workforce has left the country seeking employment abroad, particularly in Russia. It is also unclear whether relevant international organisations such as the United Nations High Commissioner for Refugees and the International Organisation for Migration can be persuaded to help Kyrgyzstan repatriate its Kyrgyz co-ethnics from Afghanistan. But the real challenges are more than just the money and the related practical issues (travel documents, transportation, security, etc). There is a general climate of ignorance about the Kyrgyz in Afghanistan in both countries. Several AAN interlocutors in the Afghan Ministry of Border, Ethnic and Tribal Affairs conceded that they knew or have heard very little about the Kyrgyz community in the Pamir. The six periodicals published by the ministry contain no news or information on the Kyrgyz in Afghanistan.(8) Moreover, there have been no public textbooks in Kyrgyz language in Afghanistan, even for Pamir's only school Bozoi Gumbad built in 2009, according to Mir Ali Wakhani, Wakhani language writer in the Department of Pamiri Languages, Curriculum Development Directorate, Afghan Ministry of Education, who talked to AAN, and Central Asia Institute. Khialuddin Seddiqi, head of research at the Ministry of Border, Ethnic and Tribal Affairs, told AAN: The Kyrgyz of Afghanistan have not been studied. The Ministry does not have the resources and capacities. Our researchers have also not been interested in the idea... Historically the Ministry's attention has been focussed on ethnic groups along the Durand Line [historically contested but de facto Afghanistan border Although the issue of the 'fellow-Kyrgyz abroad' is reportedly emotionally charged in Kyrgyzstan, people in that country know very little about the ethnic Kyrgyz in Afghanistan. (They generally know much more about the Kyrgyz in China as they are more often shown on TV, particularly as Manaschis or those who recite by heart the epic Manas – the masterpiece of Kyrgyz literature.) Aiperi Otunchieva and Kubanychbek Ormushev – university graduates from Kyrgyzstan – wrote to AAN that the people of Kyrgyzstan generally know 'very little' about the Kyrgyz in Afghanistan. Otunchieva only remembered cultural events organised by the Kyrgyzstani government 'several years ago' in Kyrgyzstan's capital Bishkek and northern Issyk-Kul province for the Kyrgyz living abroad. There are other problems as well. Some of the Kyrgyz in Wakhan are not interested in the idea of repatriation to their titular homeland and the Kyrgyzstani government itself is concerned about the social integration of its co-ethnics from Afghanistan if repatriation ever takes place (see also here). Adam Baker, a linguist with the International Assistance Mission who works on the development of the alphabet of the Wakhi language in Wakhan and has lived in Kipkut village near the Pamir, wrote to AAN, 'The Kyrgyz now living in Afghanistan are not interested in this [repatriation]... If the nomadic Kyrgyz of Afghanistan were to move to Kyrgyzstan, they would either need to give up their nomadic lifestyle or deal with the sedentary people in Kyrgyzstan'. present day Nurlan Choibekov, a Kyrgyz with special interest in the sociology of post-Soviet Central Asian societies, said: There is no point to return of… Afghan Kyrgyz to Kyrgyzstan. They will not integrate into the Kyrgyz society. People will perceive them as the 'other'. Local people will *say* that even if they are Kyrgyz, they are different, because they did not experience what we did in Kyrgyzstan… They lived in a different environment Despite these impediments, more recent efforts have been made to for the return of the Kyrgyz, particularly after last year's harshest winter in decades during which the Kyrgyz suffered significant human and livestock losses in the Pamir. After his father, Abdul Rashid Khan who had replaced Haji Rahman Qul as the Kyrgyz khan after the latter's relocation to Turkey, died in 2009, Abdul Wali Khan took over as the khan and travelled to Bishkek in May 2012 in a new repatriation effort. 'The main problem is death. Our children are dying and we are running out of women,' emphasised Abdul Wali Khan during his one-man advocacy mission, but few people seem to have heard him and cared Badakhshan – the province where the Kyrgyz live in Afghanistan – has one of the highest maternal and infant mortality rates in the world, according to the United Nations Population Fund The situation is arguably worse in the Pamir where the Kyrgyz live. Another serious threat is widespread abuse of opium among the Kyrgyz men and women. Ernist, a Kyrgyz citizen from Osh who previously worked in Tajikistan's Gorno-Badakhshan Autonomous Oblast, told AAN that the Kyrgyz abused opium that is brought by what he called the 'Afghan drug-lords' in exchange for livestock (read AAN's blogs on recent violence in Tajikistani Badakhshan and on Afghan politicking mainly over the control of the drug trade in the incident. All AAN interlocutors confirmed the dangerously growing abuse of narcotics in the Kyrgyz community. There are also larger institutional obstacles that may ultimately defeat the entire repatriation project. Although Afghanistan's ambassador Nur Mohammad Qarqin admitted (in a meeting attended by the author in the Afghan Embassy in Bishkek early this year) that the miserable situation of the ethnic Kyrgyz in Afghanistan has become a 'thorny issue' in Kabul-Bishkek ties, Kyrgyzstan and Afghanistan have never prioritised the issue in their mutual relations and are not interested in expanding their ties. Medet Tiulegenov, a lecturer and researcher at the American University of Central Asia (AUCA) in Bishkek, told AAN that Kyrgyzstan is so uninterested in Afghanistan that it 'maintains an embassy in Malaysia but does not see the incentive to open an embassy in Afghanistan'. Kyrgyzstan-Afghanistan relations have largely been confined to meetings and diplomatic niceties, although recently Afghanistan is increasingly being referred to (including by Kyrgyzstani officials) as the main outside threat to Kyrgyzstan in the form of terrorism and drug trafficking (BBC Monitoring Afghanistan on 10 September 2012, see also here, here and here). An Afghan diplomat in Bishkek, who talked to AAN but requested not to be named, however, rejected these statements as 'projecting their domestic troubles on Afghanistan and shirking their responsibilities particularly in the area of border management'. Both governments are heavily focussed on their more significant priorities in the foreseeable future. Kyrgyzstan is yet to address its debilitating political instability and socio-economic underdevelopment and Afghanistan is bracing itself for the military and political transition in 2014, the success or failure of which may possibly have huge repercussions not only in Afghanistan but also the wider region and world. Afghanistan may even take a formal repatriation move by the Kyrgyzstani government as an affront on its 'sovereignty' at a time when it is increasingly assuming responsibility for protecting its territory and people. It seems that repatriation 'politicking' is disappearing among larger problems and more important priorities. Will the Kyrgyz continue to live in Afghanistan and adapt to the new challenges to their long-term survival? Will they opt to leave for Kyrgyzstan, despite their partial reluctance, to avoid risks to their well-being? Will they become an issue to upgrade, or strain, bilateral Afghanistan-Kyrgyzstan relationships? Whatever the answers to these questions may be, judging by their resiliency in resisting political and environmental hardships, 'the Kyrgyz of the Afghan Pamir', in the words of contemporary scholar on the Kyrgyz in Afghanistan Ted Callahan, will 'ride on'. 1-For more information, of the United Nations Environment Programme'sWakhan report 2- Afghanistan's borders in Wakhan were demarcated in 1895. 3-Many of Afghanistan's Turkmens and Uzbeks share a similar history. 4- M. Nazif Shahrani, The Kirghiz and Wakhi of Afghanistan: Adaptation to Closed Frontiers and War, Seattle, 5- Kyrgyz khan or leader Haji Rahman Qul intended to get his community settled in Alaska, the US, mostly for climatic reasons. He came to know about the US from an Alaskan zoologist who had worked for the Afghanistan government to establish a Marco Polo sheep reserve in the Pamir region in the early 1970s (named after Italian explorer Marco Polo who crossed Wakhan on his journey to China in 1273 and whose description of the area still holds truth for scholars interested in this part of the world). (For more on wildlife particularly the snow leopard in Badakhshan, The US, however, rejected his request, probably because the Kyrgyz of Afghanistan were too 'alien' to the US society. 6- The request was accepted by Kenan Evren, then president of Turkey who came to power through the 1980 military coup, following his 1981 Turkmen historic, ethnic and linguistic commonalities were probably the main justification for why Turkey accepted to settle the Kyrgyz in its Van province. Turkey even built them a new permanent settlement named Ulupamir Koyu (Big Pamir Village). Once in Turkey, the Kyrgyz gradually changed and grew demographically and socio-economically. Haji Rahman Qul passed away in August 1990 and was officially replaced by Juma Taj, member of a traditionally poor Kyrgyz family, who won the 'election' against Mohammad Aref, Haji Rahman Qul's fifth-eldest son in 1998 (see footnote 3. They now are the settled inhabitants of Van. The Kyrgyz, some of whom have joined Turkey's armed forces, have reportedly been harassed by the Kurds in Van who view them as sympathisers and supporters of the government of Turkey in clamping down on and crushing Kurdish separatism. According to a presentation by Erhard Franz at an academic conference in Germany in 1987, Turkey accepted altogether 3,811 Afghan refugees of Turkic descent; apart from the Kyrgyz there were Turkmens, Uzbeks, Kazakhs and 'Dari-speaking Bukharali' from Northern Afghanistan. They were airlifted from Karachi to Adana and 'distributed over different provinces' of Turkey. In fall of 1987, Franz added, there were 4,500 Afghans of Turkic descent in Turkey, some 1,100 families. Apart from the Kyrgyz in Van province (700 persons), there were 1,300 Kyrgyz in Malatya, 172 Uzbek families in Hatay province, 180 in Urfa province and 5 in Gaziantep, 60 Kazakh families in Kayseri, 195 Turkmen families in the Tokat area and 55 Bukharali families in Gaziantep. 140 Turkmen, Kasakh and Uzbek families came to Turkey on their own expenses after 1983 and went to Istanbul (Zeytinburnu) and Konya (source: Erhard Franz, 'Turkstämmige Afghanistanflüchtlinge in der Türkei', Kurzreferat, 7. Arbeitstagung der Arbeitsgemeinschaft Afghanistan in Eichstätt, 13./14. November 1987, in: present day Erwin Götzbach (ed.), Neue Beiträge zur Afghanistan forschung, Stiftung Bibliotheca Afghanica, Band 7-Marlène Laruelle, 'The Paradigm of Nationalism in Kyrgyzstan: Evolving Narrative, the Sovereignty Issue and Political Agenda', Communist and Post-Communist Studies 45 (2012): 39-49. 8-There are four magazines: Hamwatan (Compatriot), Gharjestan (historically the area between Herat and Kabul), Jash (Nuristani, meaning 'flame') and Jirga (Gathering). And two newspapers: Tara (Pashai, meaning 'star') and Watan (Homeland). These periodicals are published in eight languages including Pashtu, Dari, Uzbeki, Turkmeni, Balochi, Pashai, Nuristani and Pamiri (most probably Shughni, the most widely used language in the Pamiri family of languages) In the early morning of July 24, without any warning, government troops were sent into Tajikistan's eastern province of Gorno-Badakhshan, apparently to deal with an armed group involved in the smuggling of narcotics, tobacco and even women to and from neighbouring Afghanistan. The immediate provocation for this large-scale mobilization was meant to be the killing of a security official by one of his subordinates, with both men alleged to be part of the murky dealings attributed to those who are posted on the Tajik-Afghan border. But the military incursion into the provincial capital of Khorog was not commensurate with this narrative, including as it did helicopter gunships, armoured vehicles, snipers and checkpoints posted across the town, effectively bringing life there to a halt. The province's road and communications links were also cut, thus isolating its entire population of some 250,000 in the series of interconnected valleys that make up this mountainous region. Instead of cowing the people of Khorog, however, this deployment appears to have decided them upon resistance, and in the ensuing violence anywhere between 40 and 200 civilians as well as soldiers are said to have been killed. Taken aback by the tenacity of the opposition, the government is now engaged in negotiations with local notables and "civil society", though the violence apparently continues in a sporadic fashion. Insofar as it has picked up this story from a place invariably described as "remote", mainstream media in the West has only repeated some version of the Tajik government's line, about rooting out corruption and militancy on its border with Afghanistan. But the reality behind this easy stereotype is much more interesting. Indeed he will argue here that far from being yet another example of the difficult post-Soviet transition to democracy, this story is about the failure as much as the future of "global civil society". Gorno-Badakhshan has been an autonomous province since Soviet times, and is home to a Shia Muslim sub-sect that forms the country's most significant religious minority. It was also one of the two regions of Tajikistan that supported the United Tajik Opposition, which stood against other regional elites who took power during the bloody civil war that followed the Soviet collapse in the early 1990s. Although much of the commentary on last month's events has been dominated by rumours of Islamic militancy among the rebels, Gorno-Badakhshan's community of Ismailis, as they are now known, is a group that keeps no mosques and practises few of the Islamic rituals common among their Sunni compatriots. Indeed the civil war relied more upon ethnic than religious distinctions, with the Ismailis' faith defined almost entirely by their ethnic identity as Pamiris, those who inhabit the valleys of the Pamir mountain range. After taking more than 10,000 lives, the civil war finally drew to a close in 1997, with an agreement brokered by outside parties, including Russia, the US and the UN, but the recent violence in Gorno-Badakhshan suggests that it has never in fact ended. For what the government has done is to breach the peace agreement by violating the province's autonomy and attempting to exert direct control over it. Of course any state would want to take complete possession of its national territory, especially if this happens to be an expansive border region occupied by a minority population. How, then, is it possible to reach a satisfactory agreement in this context, and why did the one that stopped the civil war in 1997 come apart in the meantime? This is where the story departs the familiar script of post-Soviet transition and becomes intriguingly global in character. One of the outside parties crucial in arranging for the agreement that paused, if it did not quite end the civil war in Gorno-Badakhshan, was a faith-based NGO headed from a suburb of Paris by the Aga Khan, spiritual leader of the world's Ismailis. Cut off from his Pamiri followers during the 70 years of Soviet rule, the Aga Khan and his organization stepped to the fore in the 1990s, and, probably with both Russian and American support, made a ceasefire possible in the region without the direct intervention of any foreign government or international body like the UN. It was an extraordinary and even unprecedented achievement for a non-state actor, based abroad, to seal an agreement ending years of brutal violence. And though it was not publicized, probably in order to protect the Aga Khan from unwelcome questions and suspicion from rival Muslim groups, he can think of no other event that so clearly represents the claims of a so-called "global civil society" to address issues as intractable as a civil war. In addition to reclaiming the allegiance of his Central Asian followers, many of whom didn't even know their Imam's name, the Aga Khan was able to deploy his NGO, which had already been active among a related population of Ismailis in the mountains of northern Pakistan for a couple of decades, to provide the Pamiris with much-needed food supplies, medical help and eventually educational, economic and other forms of development assistance. The consequences were practically miraculous, with thousands saved from certain starvation and death by the many specialized organizations that are all part of the Aga Khan Development Network (AKDN). Relying upon a community of wealthy Ismailis with origins in the Indian subcontinent, but now also scattered in Britain, Canada and the US, the Aga Khan was able to mobilize finances, expertise and manpower for his Pamiri following, to say nothing about the support of Western governments and development agencies, given his exemplary record as a social entrepreneur and pro-Western Muslim leader. So much for the bright side of "global civil society", whose darker aspect he will now show is entailed in its very virtues. The agreement ending the civil war involved the Aga Khan asking his followers to disarm, in return for which their military commanders would be absorbed into the Tajik armed forces, as were both the officer killed last month and his alleged murderer. The AKDN would then set up relief and development projects not only in Gorno-Badakhshan but the rest of the country as well, and in addition raise funds and support for Tajikistan internationally. This plan worked well for a few years, but once the government's rule had become more stable, and especially after 9/11, when its support in providing military bases and medical facilities was needed in the War on Terror, the AKDN was suddenly no longer indispensable. Of course this should have been evident from the beginning, since only a very weak or a very strong state would put up with such a situation, and Tajikistan is neither one nor the other. Once the opposition had been persuaded to disarm, what hold did the AKDN have over the government to make it honour its promises? Apart from the local support that the rebel fighters had also enjoyed, it had nothing but some degree of influence abroad and what at the time of the agreement appeared to be a great deal of money. Like any NGO, in other words, the AKDN could only enforce the state's compliance by threatening to publicize its misdeeds, something that is highly unlikely in the circumstances, or to pay its way out of any difficulties. For as an international organization dependent on outside donors, and therefore not accountable to the people it serves in any representative fashion, the AKDN, unlike the opposition fighters of the past, is unable to act with popular backing. It cannot act politically and is forced to rely almost entirely upon the power of money and influence, which is to say on the secretive dealings of brokerage that, however useful, are anti-democratic in nature. After 2001, therefore, Pamiris started noticing that the state was beginning to assert its control over their province, especially through the secret service that had once been part of the KGB. They also noticed, more worryingly, how President Rakhmon was no longer as deferential to the Aga Khan as he once had been, even referring to him disparagingly to the Imam's own followers in Gorno-Badakhshan. For Tajikistan is now full of Chinese goods and Indian funds, with the Russians and Americans bidding for military bases and influence, while a stream of money rolls in from the illicit trade in opium and tobacco. Gorno-Badakhshan is also rich in yet untapped mineral resources, which suggests that it might eventually become a battleground for corporate and political forces of all kinds to control. In the meantime a large proportion of the country's young men, who would have been unemployed at home, are working in illegal and often hazardous conditions in cities like Moscow, their remittances now accounting for more of Gorno-Badakhshan's income than the AKDN. And yet the AKDN is everywhere in the province, and possibly even its largest employer, creating the illusion of prosperity and the reality of increasing class hierarchies by its racially differentiated salaries in US dollars. For "locals" are paid in accordance with a "local economy" that has been so distorted by the NGO as not in fact to exist. Khorog's highly-paid Ismali and other expatriates, after all, are keeping this fake economy alive by paying rent for houses and retaining the services of local drivers, cooks, secretaries and the like. The consequence is an utterly illusory world sustained entirely from without, but sucking in the best Pamiri minds and talent. Despite all the imaginative projects launched, like building a university of international stature, the general economic situation is completely unsustainable, though it does, of course, keep many Pamiri men and women employed, and offers a number of others remarkable opportunities to work or study abroad. In effect, Khorog has become a smaller version of post-conflict cities like Sarajevo or Ramallah, that are made into models of cosmopolitan life by infusions of cash from abroad. But this money ends up transforming many local people into the dependents of global networks, while leaving others stranded in a completely shadow "local" economy. And as in Ramallah or Sarajevo, what this does is simply to defer violence and poverty for all but a few. The very benefits brought by "global civil society", then, turn into problems. Nowhere is this more so than in political life, where the wealth and unelected power of an NGO like the AKDN allows it to subvert an admittedly corrupt political system, but at the same time to destroy the collective will and action of ordinary people. For when an autocratic state deals with an unaccountable organization, both speaking in the name of such people without ever consulting them, democracy must be the first casualty. The violence unleashed upon Khorog in July demonstrates how fragile and, in fact, unreal the NGO vision is, for the only thing that has given the government pause and forced it to negotiate are the old resistance fighters supported by ordinary people. Among the hasty and surreptitious communications I have been receiving from a Khorog under siege is an account of its first couple of days that speaks about the re-emergence of a truly political will and practice among the townspeople. Initially fearful and overawed by the APCs, troops, circling helicopters and snipers, these civilians were suddenly inspired by news that one of the armoured vehicles had been attacked and destroyed. What they did next was organize local councils to decide on a course of action, felled poplar trees lining the main street to prevent military vehicles from moving freely along it, and demonstrated in front of government buildings. Pamiris living abroad as students, interns or migrants have also been instrumental in attempting to publicize the military incursion by demonstrating in cities like Moscow and New York while circulating demands for a cessation of hostilities. These democratic and collective actions would not have been possible within the framework of an NGO like the AKDN, which, relying as it does on secretive deal-making, has remained conspicuously silent about conditions in Gorno-Badakhshan. They illustrate that the only way of reaching a genuine agreement with the government is by participating in the political process and relying upon one's own strength. For by organizing themselves people possess a collective power that no NGO does, depending as these do on money and influence alone. This is why the state might prefer to deal with the AKDN, which helps to pacify Pamiris both by disarming and speaking for them, without any threat more powerful than money in its arsenal. And so the latest news he have from Khorog is this: the security officer wanted for his superior's murder has surrendered his arms, supposedly at the Aga Khan's behest; and the government is negotiating with a body of doubtlessly sincere and concerned Pamiris, as well as some of the AKDN organizations, but nobody from the local councils I have described. Will we see a repetition of the initial civil war agreement? And will this new agreement have any more force behind it than the old? All its good works and intentions apart, the AKDN very likely adds to the troubles of Gorno-Badakhshan's residents by continuing to speak for them long after the civil war formally ended, with the Aga Khan's representative in Tajikistan, invariably an Ismaili of Indo-Pakistani origin, serving as the paymaster of a vast network of clients, which is how power is bought and sold in the NGO sector. Indeed it is sometimes difficult to see what the real difference is between this exercise of power and the autocratic state's reliance on very similar kinds of clients. Moreover there are now rumours emerging from Afghanistan, retailed by two members of parliament with constituencies abutting Gorno-Badakhshan, that its own Ismailis, along with those of Tajikistan and northern Pakistan, are plotting with support from the West to set up their own state in these roughly contiguous areas. This dangerous myth, which is meant to inspire sectarian hatred among their neighbours, has been doing the rounds in a Pakistan wracked by sectarian strife for years now, which is only natural given the fact that Pakistan was itself created in this way, by carving out Muslim territories from India. But surely its dissemination across Central Asia is an inadvertent by-product of the AKDN's "global" character and presence in all three countries. The local politics that "global civil society" dislikes and distrusts so much is the only thing that is capable of setting and keeping a people free. Whatever the result of the current negotiations, it would be an act of the greatest folly for the people of Gorno-Badakhshan to return to the bubble of an NGO-led society. The AKDN has played an important and positive role in the region, but perpetuating itself there by the constant reproduction of expatriate life, as it has done for well over a decade now, is only a way of risking the diminution of its own legacy. After all its expatriates, including the foreign Ismailis there to "serve" their Pamiri "brothers and sisters", are the first to leave at any sign of trouble, as they did last month, and not for the first time, by way of a "special corridor". Yet the continued presence of British, Canadian or American citizens in Khorog at such times might well do much to deter the Tajik state. And in the meantime there are unconfirmed reports that the Islamic Movement of Uzbekistan has offered to support the Pamiri resistance, thus indicating that the exit of one kind of international actor opens the door for the entry of another. Of course Pamiris are unlikely to accept the questionable and dangerous support of an Islamist party. But do they realize that the AKDN plays, in its own way, a similar destabilizing role in Gorno-Badkhshan's local politics? Neither "global civil society", nor the "frontierless brotherhood" of Ismailism that mimics it, can be allowed to define or rather stifle this local politics. The AKDN should be made fully Tajik in character, and give way to elected representatives of the people in any negotiations with the state. As I write, government forces are murdering ex-opposition commanders (including a paraplegic) and civilian demonstrators one by one to avoid any outcry. Rumours are swirling around the capital, Dushanbe, that Pamiris there will be subjected to the kind of large-scale torture and killing they had experienced during the civil war. Not so long ago a lavish Ismaili Centre had been opened amid much fanfare in the same city, by an Ismaili leadership that was clearly oblivious to the continuing threat that faced their people. They had been fooled by their own propaganda about "global civil society" and were unable to recognize that it must collapse like a pack of cards without real political backing. Will the current crisis afford an opportunity for a newly democratic politics to emerge from the local councils set up during it, or is Gorno-Badakhshan to remain the victim of "global civil society" forever? present day PAMIRS, a mountainous region of central Asia, lying on the north-west border of India. Since 1875 the Pamirs have probably been the best explored region in High Asia. Not only have many travellers of many nationalities directed their steps towards the Bam-i-dunya ("the Roof of the World") in search of adventure or of scientific information, but the government surveys of Russia and India have met in these high altitudes, and there effected a connexion which will help to solve many of the geodetic problems which beset the superficial survey of Asia. Since Wood first discovered a source of the Oxus in Lake Victoria in 1837, and left us a somewhat erroneous conception of the physiography of the Pamirs, the gradual approach of Russia from the north stimulated the processes of exploration from the side of India. Native explorers from India first began to be busy in the Pamirs about 1860, and continued their investigations for the following fifteen years. In 1874 the mission of Sir D. Forsyth to Yarkand led to the first systematic geographical exploitation of the Pamir country. In 1885 Ney Elias made his famous journey across the Pamirs from east to west, identifying the Rang Kul as the Dragon Lake of Chinese geographers - a distinction which has also been claimed by some geographers for Lake Victoria. Then Lockhart and Woodthorpe in 1886 passed along the Wakhan tributary of the Oxus from its head to Ishkashim in Badakshan, and completed an enduring record of most excellent geographical research. Bonvalot in 1887, Littledale in 1888, Cumberland, Bower and Dauvergne, followed by Younghusband in succeeding years, extending to 1890; Dunmore in 1892 and Sven Hedin in 1894-1895, have all contributed more or less to Pamir geography; but the honours of successful inquiry in those high altitudes still fall to Lord Curzon, whose researches in 1894 led to a singularly clear and comprehensive description of Pamir geography, as well as to the best map compilation that till then had existed. Meanwhile Russian explorers and Russian topographers had been equally busy from the north. The famous soldier Skobelev was probably the first European to visit the Great Kara Kul. He was followed by scientific missions systematically organized by the Russian government. In 1883 Putiata's mission started south. Gromchevsky was hard at work from 1888 to 1892. Yanov began again in 1891, after a short spell of rest, and has left his mark as a permanent record in the valley of Sarhad (or Wakhan), between the Baroghil pass and Bozai Gumbaz. Finally, in 1895, the Russian mission under General Shveikovsky met the British mission under General Gerard on the banks of Lake Victoria, and from that point to the Chinese frontier eastward demarcated the line which thereafter was to divide Russian from British interests in highest Asia. Since then other travellers have visited the Pamirs, but the junction of the Saxon present day Russian and British surveys (the latter based on triangulation carried across the Hindu Kush from India) disposes of any further claim to the honours of geographical exploration. Our estimate of the extent of Pamir conformation depends much on the significance of the word Pamir. If we accept the - Dari derivation of the term (which is advanced by Curzon as being perhaps the most plausible), pai-mir, or "the foot of mountain peaks," we have a definition which is by no means an inapt illustration of the actual facts of configuration. It has been too often assumed that the plateau of Tibet and the uplands of the Pamirs are analogous in physiography, and that they merge into each other. This is hardly the case. Littledale points out that the high-level valleys of glacial formation which distinguish the Pamirs have no real counterpart in the Chang or plains of Tibet. The latter are 2000 ft. higher; they are intersected by narrow ranges, and are drained by no rivers of importance. They form a region of salt lakes and stagnant marshes, relieved by wide flat spaces of open plateau country. The absence of any vegetation beyond grass or scrub is a striking feature common to both Pamir and Chang, but there the resemblance ceases, and the physical conformation of mountain and valley to the east and to the west of the upper sources of the Zarafshan is radically distinct. The axis, or backbone, of Pamir formation is the great meridional mountain chain of Sarikol - the ancient Taurus of tradition and history - on which stands the highest peak north of the Himalaya, the Murtagh Ata (25,000 ft.). This chain divides off the high-level sources of the Oxus on the west from the streams which sweep downwards into the Turkestan depression of Kashgar on the east. There are the true Pamirs (i.e. valleys reaching up in long slopes to the foot of mountain peaks) on either side, and the Pamirs on the west differ in some essential respects from those on the east. On the west the following are generally recognized as distinct Pamirs: (1) the Great Pamir, of which the dominant feature is Lake Victoria; (2) the Little Pamir, separated from the Great Pamir on the north by what is now known as the Nicolas range; (3) the Pamir-i-Wakhan, which is the narrow trough of the Wakhan tributary of the Oxus, the term Pamir applying to its upper reaches only; (4) the Alichur - the Pamir of the Yeshil Kul and Ghund - immediately to the north of the Great Pamir; (5) the Sarez Pamir, which forms the valley of the Murghab river, which has here found its way round the east of the Great

Pamir and the Alichur from the Little Pamir, and now makes westwards for the Oxus. This branch was considered by many geographers as the main Oxus stream, and Lake Chakmaktin, at its head, was by them regarded as the Oxus source. At the foot of the Sarez Pamir stands the most advanced Russian outpost of Murghabi. To the north-east of the Alichur are the Rang Kul and the Kara Kul (or Kargosh) Pamirs. Rang Kul Lake occupies a central basin or depression; but the Kara Kul drains away north-eastwards through the Sarikol (as the latter, bending westwards, merges into the Trans-Alai) to Kashgar and the Turkestan plains. Similar characteristics distinguish all these Pamirs. They are hemmed in and separated by snowcapped mountain peaks and ridges, which are seamed with glaciers terminating in moraines and shingle slopes at the base of the foot-hills. Long sweeps of grassy upland bestrewn with boulders lead from the stream beds up to the snowfields, yellow, grey or vivid green, according to the season and the measure of sunlight, fold upon fold in interminable succession, their bleak monotony being only relieved by the grace of flowers for a short space during the summer months. To the east of the Sarikol chain is the Taghdumbash Pamir, which claims many of the characteristics of the western Pamirs at its upper or western extremity, where the Karachukar, which drains it, is a comparatively small stream. But where the Karachukar, joining forces with the Khunjerab, stretches. out northwards for a comparatively straight run to Tashkurghan, dividing asunder the two parallel ranges of Sarikol and Kandar, which together form the Sarikol chain, the appellation Pamir can hardly be maintained. This is the richest portion of the Sarikol province. Here are stone-built houses collected in scattered detachments, with a spread of cultivation reaching down to the river. Here are water-mills and many permanent appliances of civilization suited to the lower altitude (11,500 ft., the average height of the upper Pamirs being about 13,000), and here we are no longer near the sources of the river at the foot of the mountain peaks. One other so-called Pamir exists to the east of Sarikol, separated therefrom by the eastern range (the Kandar) of the Sarikol, which is known as Mariom or Mariong. But this Pamir is situated nowhere near the sources of the Zarafshan or Raskam river, which it borders, and possesses little in common with the Pamirs of the west. The Mariom Pamir defines the western extremity of the Kuen Lun, which stretches eastwards for 250 m. before it becomes the political boundary of northern Tibet. The Murtagh chain, which holds within its grasp the mightiest system of glaciers in the world, forms a junction with the Sarikol at the head of the Taghdumbash, where also another great system (that of the Hindu Kush) has its eastern roots. The political boundary between the extreme north of the Kashmir dependencies and the extreme south of Chinese Turkestan is carried by the Zarafshan or Raskam river which runs parallel to the Murtagh at its northern foot (its valley dividing the Murtagh from the Kuen Lun), to a point in about 79° 20' E., where it is transferred to the watershed of the Kuen Lun. Within the limits of these partially explored highlands, lying between the Pamirs and the Tibetan table-land, exact geographical definition is impossible. But we may follow Godwin-Austen in accepting the main chain of the Murtagh as merging into the central mountain system of the Tibetan Chang, its axis being defined and divided by the transverse stream of the Shyok at its westward bend, whilst the Karakoram range, in which the Shyok rises, is a subsidiary northern branch. The pass over the Karakoram (18,500 ft.) is the most formidable obstacle on the main trade route between Leh and Kashgar. The Taghdumbash Pamir occupies a geographical position of some political significance. One important pass (the Beyik, 15,100 ft.) leads from the Russian Pamirs into Sarikol across its northern border. A second pass (the Wakhjir, 16,150 ft.) du "mbash connects the head of the Wakhan valley of AfghanistanPamir. with the Sarikol province across its western head, whilst a third (the Kilik, 15,600 ft.) leads into the head of the Hunza river and opens a difficult and dangerous route to Gilgit. The Taghdumbash is claimed both by China and Kanj ut (or Hunza), and there is consequently an open boundary question at this corner of the Pamirs. From Lake Victoria of the Great Pamir the northern boundary of that extended strip of Afghanistan which reaches out to the head of the Taghdumbash from Badakshan north of the Hindu *Boundary between* Kush is to be traced: westwards, in the Lake Victoria *b* Russia and affluent of the Oxus; and eastwards, on the Nicolas Afghan- range, dividing the Great and Little Pamirs, till it over. looks a point on the Aksu (or Murghab) river in about *istan* 74Â° 40' E. Here it diverges southwards to the Sarikol chain, north of Taghdumbash. This eastward extension was laid down by the Pamir Boundary Commission of 1895. All the head of the Little Pamir, with the Wakhan valley, is consequently Afghan territory, but no military posts have been established so far. The Alichur, Rang Kul, Kargosh (Kara Kul) and Sarez are Russian Pamirs. The Mariom Pamir is Chinese. The Wakhan glaciers under the Wakhjir water-parting, Lake Chakmaktin near the sources of the Aksu, and Lake Victoria of the Great Pamir have all been claimed as indicating the Glacial *of* true source of the Oxus. But detailed examination of Sources Oxus. their hydrographical conditions proves that neither of the *the* two lakes, Victoria (13,400 ft.) or Chakmaktin (13,020 ft.), can justly be regarded as sources, both of them being derived from the same mighty system of glacial snowfields on the summit of the Nicolas range. Both may be regarded as incidents in the course of glacial streams (incidents which are diminishing in volume day by day), 'rather than original springs or sources. The same glacial beds of the Nicolas range send down tributary waters to the Panja or Wakhan river, below its junction with the ice stream from Wakhjir, and thus it becomes impossible to decide whether the glaciers of the Wakhjir or the glaciers of Nicolas should be regarded as effecting the most important contribution to the main stream. There is evidence also that glacial moraine formations from time to time may have largely affected the catchment area of these tributary streams. It would be as rash to assert that from Lake Victoria no waters could ever have issued with an eastward flow as it would be to state that 'from Chakmaktin none ever flow westwards. The measure of the veracity of Chinese pilgrims and geographers in the early centuries of our era must not be balanced on such points as these. There is no evidence that the Pamirs were ever the support of permanent settlements. The few mud-built buildings which once existed at Chakmaktin and at Langar only decide *Population and Ethno-* recent occupation which could hardly have possessed a. permanent character, and the few shrines and domed*graphy* tombs which are scattered here and there about the empty desolation of the Pamir slopes are all of them of recent construction. The nomadic population which seeks pasturage during the summer months in these dreary altitudes is entirely Kirghiz, and we may take it for granted that it will soon be entirely Russian. The non-Russian population during the summer of 1895 could not have amounted to more than a few hundred souls - occupying a few encampments in the Little Pamir and in the Taghdumbash. The total population of the Russian Pamirs has been reckoned at 250 "kibitkas," or 1500 souls. There is no ethnographical distinction to be traced between the Kirghiz of the Alichur Pamir and the Kirghiz of the Taghdumbash. The Kirghiz are Sunni by faith, but amongst them there are curious survivals of an ancient ritual of which the origin is to be traced to those Nestorian Christian Evidences communities of Central Asia which existed in the of the middle ages. A Christian bishopric existed at Yarkand Survival of in Marco Polo's time, and is supposed to have survived Christian for another century (1350). The last Gurkhan of the Symbols. Kara Khitai Empire in the early part of the 13ᵗʰ century (the legendary Prester John) was a member of a Christian tribe called Naiman, which is one of the four chief tribal divisions mentioned by Ney Elias. The Naiman tribe claim kinship with the Kipchaks. It is curious that the same survival of Christian ceremonial should be found amongst the Sarikoli, a Shiah people of Aryan descent akin to the Tajiks of Badakshan, as may be traced amongst the Kirghiz. Christian symbols have been discovered in the southern towns of Chinese Turkestan by Sven Hedin. The total area of the Pamir country may be estimated as about 150 m. long by 150 m. broad, of which about one-tenth is grass *Area* pasture land and the rest mountainous. All of it once the Pamirs. formed part of the ancient kingdom of Bolor, itself a survival of the yet more ancient empire of the Yue-chi, Tokharistan; and across it, in spite of its bleak inhospitality, there have been one or two recognized trade routes from east to west throughout all ages. The most important commercially *Trade* was that which passed north-west via Tashkurghan Routes. and Rang Kul, from present day Chinese Turkestan to the khanates R north of the Oxus; but the route via Tashkurghan and Lake Victoria to Badakshan was also well trodden. The great pilgrim route of Buddhist days was that which connects the ancient Buddhist cities of the Takla Makan in present day Chinese Turkestan with Chitral (Kashkar), by the Baroghil Pass across the Hindu Kush. This was but one link in a chain of devout peregrination which stretched from China to India, and which included every intervening Buddhist centre of note which existed in the early centuries of our era. For six or seven months of the year (November to April) the Pamirs are covered with snow, the lakes are frozen, and the passes nearly impracticable. The mean temperature during Climate the month of January recorded by Russian observers at the Murghabi - or Pamirski - post is - 13Â° F. In of to July this rises to 62Â° F., the elevation of the station being Pamirs. 12,150 ft. During the spring and summer months the prevalence of fierce cutting winds, which are shaped by the conformation of the valleys into blasts as through a funnel, following the strike of the valleys either up or down, makes travelling painful and existence in camp most unpleasant. In the absence of wind the summer atmosphere is often bright and exhilarating, but there is a constant tendency to sudden squalls of wind and rain, which pass as quickly as they gather. The most settled record of the Pamir Boundary Commission of 1895 lasted from the 19th of August to the 11th of September, the maximum temperature being recorded at 77Â° on the 21st of August at Kizil Rabat (12,570 ft.); and yet on the 16th of August snow had fallen to the depth of 6 in. and the Beyik Pass was blocked. There were indications that monsoon influences extended as far north at least as the Great Pamir, and a definite analogy was established between the record of barometric pressure on the Pamirs and that of the outer ranges of the Himalaya

The Pamirs' Population as Viewed by The Russian Military

At the beginning of the 20th century the Pamir was thoroughly explored by Russian military experts, especially in military topographical, geographical, ethnical- demographic and confessional aspects. The military reports were partially published, with their distribution being, of course, intended for service use only. So, for instance, all through the summer of 1907 captain of the General Staff A.K. Razgonov was making an expedition in the Pamir, moving to the upper reaches of the river Piandj. In his book, published later by the headquarters of the Turkestan military district in 1910, he gave a detailed description of his impressions of the Pamir. He emphasized that this mountainous region's political and military importance was in its geographic position, at the meeting point of three powers - Russia, China and England. The Pamir's middle location, Razgonov wrote, is the reason of the political and military interest it represents: "Extending to the south of our borders towards India, it is our natural window to over there". The Pamir started playing an important role in geopolitical and geo-strategic plans of Russia and other leading powers of the beginning of the century. The 1895 Saxon present day British - Russian agreement on delimitating the Mountainous Badakhshan was based upon its division not according to the ethnic principle, but to the geographic one, proceeding from the configuration of the borders to be favourable to both sides. That agreement, concluded with no consultations with Afghanistan, came to be the result of the British-Russian rivalry of many years in that region. The Pamir elite's position was of great importance for Russia's shaping its stance with respect to the mountainous frontier. As N. Yemelianova believes, the Pamir's voluntary joining to Russia occurred at the insistence of the Ismaelites' religious leaders (2). "They do not regard Russians as infidels and associate with them willingly…" At the same time, the Pamir Ismaelite-Tajiks, as captain Razgonov pointed out, in what pertained to their spiritual life obeyed to the Aga Khan (1877-1957), the Ismaelites' imam, resident in Bombay (3). That fact made a controversial impression on soviet historians. According to Yemelianova, as a result, Ismailism is regarded in the works of some historians and philosophers as a reactionary trend, which at the end of the 19th - beginning of the 20th century turned into "agents" of British Imperialism (4). Such a complicated situation required new approaches and trustworthy sources. According to captain Razgonov's information, the West Pamir's population was made up of Tajik-Ismaelites, whose number reached 25 thousand people at the beginning of the 20th century. The Eastern Pamir's population comprised the Kara-Kirghiz (today's Kirghiz), who roamed from place to place in the valleys of the rivers and lakes. The Kirghiz numbered then up to 2.5 thousand people. The Pamir Tajiks lived mainly in the river valleys of the Piandj's tributary streams, in the most fertile ravines (5). The mutual relations between the Tajik-Sunnites and Ismaelites were an important component of the Pamir highlanders' attitude towards the Russians. The persecuted in all the countries of the Orient Ismaelites' belief served to cause an extremely scornful attitude of the population of Bukhara, Afghanistan, Kashgaria and Kokand khanate, who professed Sunnism, towards the Pamirians. Most of the local rulers were also Sunnites, regarding with disdain the native inhabitants of the West Pamir, as B. I. Iskanderov wrote in the 1960s (6). On the contrary, the Russian military, as well as officials later on, showed a respectful attitude towards the religion of the Pamir inhabitants. Russian military specialists attributed special importance to studying the local population's psychology. The General Staff Academy's graduate A. E. Snesarev, who served in Turkestan from 1899, mentioned in his "guide" that in observers' opinion, the Pamir highlanders' character was notable for such features as patience, gentleness, strong will, reticence and endurance. They, in his view, had great fantasy and were fond of living by fancies (7). According to captain Razgonov's impressions, the customs and views of the Tajik-Ismaelites and Tajik-Sunnites differ largely, the Ismaelites being "milder and not fanatic" (8). Though the difference between the Ismaelites and Sunnites was explained rather superficially- from his point of view - such a situation was due to the fact that the Ismaelites' religion was allegedly a "mixture" of Islam and Buddhism. However, further along captain Razgonov makes a conclusion practical enough: "They are very tolerant to other believes and not fanatics in the least, they do not regard Russians as infidels and associate with them willingly..., are devoted to us, deserving attention on our part, too" (9). With respect to the Pamirians' religion the Russian military were attentive enough not leave unnoticed the difference between Ismailism and Shiism. Ismailism, which is considered now by many orientalists to be one of the trends of Islam, close to Shiite Islam, in the Pamir's condition had many peculiarities. Snesarev noticed that because of the Tajik-highlanders' reticent character "it's quite common to come across an erroneous interpretation of their religion", for example, the West Pamir's inhabitants had been long considered to be Shiites. The military orientalist disagreed with the wide-spread then ascribing of the present day Pamir Tajiks to the for he himself ran into cases when the Ismaelites "made themselves pass for Sunnites or Shiites on account of some considerations" (10). Razgonov also added that the Ismaelites were thoroughly concealing the dogmas of their religion and even among themselves there were not many initiated into them. Only the most reliable people of a quite venerable age knew the essence of all the religious believes and rites (11). The local population's main occupation was tillage and, to a smaller degree, cattle-breeding. However, there was a shortage of arable land, and great many of the locals lived in deep poverty. Under those conditions the help provided to the Pamirians by the command of the Pamir detachment was of great importance for them. "For distinguished services beyond the prescribed duties..." According to captain Razgonov's information, the Pamir detachment was made up of 185 soldiers and officers. The unit was stationed in five posts: in Korog, Pamir, Kizil-Rabat, Liangar and Ishkashim (12). In 1896 Karl Kivekes, of a Swedish descent, from Finland, came to serve in the detachment. In 1905 he was promoted to lieutenant-colonel and appointed commander of the Pamir Detachment. For his service in the Pamir Kivekes was awarded the Order of St. Stanislav, 2nd degree, St. Anne, 3rd degree. In 1907 he was decorated with the Order of St. Vladimir, 4th degree - "for distinguished services in peace time, beyond the prescribed duties". Having become commander of the frontier-guarding detachment, as his service testimonial reads, "thanks to his outstanding working ability and energy he managed to raise the detachment scattered over hundreds of miles from post to post up to the due mark in every respect". Lieutenant-colonel Kivekes showed care to the local population no less than to his soldiers. Thanks to his chivalrous disinterestedness, wide material support for the poor and approachability for all people he won affection and respect of the entire population. The commander of the Pamir detachment built aryks (irrigation ditches) and irrigated fields, increasing by doing so lands under cultivation; loaned seeds to sow fields, let the Pamirians know how to cultivate potato, cabbage and other crops non-habitual in the mountains... In general, he exerted a great influence in spreading culture among the population. The so far unpublished Kivekes's memoirs contain a detailed description of the Pamir, its inhabitants, their religions, attitude towards Russia, the Russian military and the like. One of the most detailed works among the Russian military sources in describing the population of the Pamir area awaits its explorers. Lev Davydovitch Trotzky and the Ismaelits' reticence According to Snesarev, it was difficult to determine what the political mood of the Pamir Tajiks was, "whether they still want to remain under the rule of Bukhara, are angling to cling to the Russians, or perhaps, finally, think about getting under the Afghan emir". In general, Snesarev noted, "they are fond of the Russian ways and customs, especially in what concerns our justice, but, on the other hand, they as if got accustomed to a considerable extent, or, to be more exact, used to be submitted to the Bukhara regime. It is most likely that their political mood is notable for a sort of indifference, and only somewhere in the recesses of the people's consciousness there is, perhaps, a remote hope, kept hidden, to come to be protected by the White Czar. The Tajiks are too closed-in, too scared of the Bukhara rulers to show up their inner most dreams; besides, they are too absorbed in economic and agricultural routines to be able to grasp vaster political views". With the outbreak of World War I, the Russian military were, naturally, worried about the true attitude of the Pamirians to Russia. Initially the military's concern seemed unnecessary. The Ismaelites' spiritual leader Aga Khan addressed the Muslims, exhorting them to come out against Germany and Turkey in support for the Triple Entente. "The Muslims, he wrote, are to remain faithful to the duty of oath and obedient to our state and spiritual authorities…No one will be able to win a victory over so powerful sovereigns like the Emperor of India, the King of England and the czar of all Russia…" (14). The Pamir Ismaelites guided themselves with those instructions, keeping loyalty to the Russian czar. After the October Revolution the Aga Khan joined the side of its adversaries. Accordingly, when in 1917 the Pamirians took power in the mountainous area in their hands, some of them turned to the Bukhara emir for help. They were also aided by the fact that when the Bolsheviks formed in Tashkent a military unit in the beginning of 1918 to substitute the former frontier guards, the new detachment passed over to the basmatches (counter-revolutionary combatants). When in 1918 the Bolsheviks' plot of a world revolution in Europe was a failure, they turned their attention to the East. The Russian Bolsheviks also engaged in the "oriental trend" Enver-pasha, a Turkmen dignitary, very famous among the Muslims of Central Asia. In 1919 Enver-pasha arrived in Moscow to hold talks with V.I. Lenin, I.V. Stalin, L.D. Trotzky over a project of sovietization of Afghanistan-Central Asia, India, East Turkistan present day China. As a result, according to the instructions of Lev Davydovitch Trotzky, the Revvoensoviet (Revolutionary Military Soviet)'s Field Staff elaborated, under general A.A. Brusilov's leadership, a plan of a campaign for the Red Army's cavalry troops to march through the mountain chains of Gindukush, Tibet, Tien Shan and the Himalayas eastwards to Afghanistan, India, Nepal and China. All Central Asia, the former czarist Turkestan, should have been sovietized in extremely short period of time, being turned into a base for a grandiose "oriental campaign". Naturally, the Pamirians were also involved in the plan, being residents of the geopolitical region, decisive for the cause of a world revolution. The situation of the Pamir Tajiks became extremely complicated with the advent of Bolsheviks. In a rather short period of time the Soviet troops managed to re-establish control over the mountain passes on the borders of the former Russian Empire. As some investigators, for example A. Shakhov, believe, the Pamirians took the arrival in the region of the first Bolsheviks with great enthusiasm (15). If so, does it mean that the local spiritual authorities and leaders of the Pamirians decided to disobey the Aga Khan's will? Was it actually so? Were the Pamir Tajiks "spies of the British Imperialism", or were they frank in being in the first ranks of those who accepted the Soviet power? Can there be simple answers to these questions? Geopolitics should not push to the background the importance of relations with the local population To restore the historical truth, it is necessary to resort to trustworthy documents, to consider the evidence of such military explorers as A.K. Razgonov, K. Kivekes, A.E. Snesarev. It is extremely necessary to do so now, when the situation of the isolated Russian contingent - the Frontier-guarding Group of the FFS (Federal Frontier-Guard Service)b of the RF in the Republic of Tajikistan - depends to no small degree not only on clashes with narcotics traffickers and combatants, but also on contacts with the local population. The attitude of the ethnic and religious groups of the Pamir towards Russia's presence in the region replicates now largely that prevailing at the turn of the 19th and 20th centuries. In a not big region - the Mountainous Badakhshan autonomous province of the Republic of Tajikistan - there are serious clashes of geopolitical and geo-economic interests of China, the USA, Pakistan, Afghanistan, India, Iran, CIS Central Asian states.

Taking into consideration Russia's current military and economic weakness, it is advisable to be especially attentive to studying all possible after-effects of these or those steps it takes. As is acknowledged by many investigators of the 1979-1989 war in Afghanistan, even putting aside the question whether it was reasonable to bring the troops into that country, it could have been possible, at any rate, to avoid many errors, had the forms of maintaining mutual relations with the ethnic groups of Afghan provinces been pondered over more thoroughly (16). Though, in reality, "large" geopolitical problems, for instance rivalry with the USA, came to the fore. The self-dependence of the local population was underestimated, and that cost lives to thousands of soviet soldiers, while hundreds of thousands of civilians were left roofless. The Pamir region, 2001 where Pakistan, India, China, the Russian states and independent Afghanistan share borders, has long been special for three reasons. First, it is a long established cross-road point for trade. The Silk Road from China to Rome runs through it. Another goes south to follow the Indus to the sea and to the trade marts of the Persian Gulf, by which Alexander the Great's explorers reached Babylon. Others pass through Afghanistan to reach Arabia and beyond. The Poles used these as well as the Silk Road. Powers have fought and conquered to incorporate the region in their empires, and tax the passing trade. Secondly, the Pamir region has long been a meeting place of empires where power games are played. Early Aryana, Rome, the later British Raj, China and Russia tried to carve it up, or make local leaders join their camp, or discipline them, as still happens today. That is what Rudyard Kipling's Kim, set in the region, is about. Thirdly and most important, where Arab merchants took their trade they carried ideas and beliefs with the spices and silks and carpets. After the Prophet Mohammed, they exerted two important disruptive influences. Committed spiritual leaders disseminated into the lands about, that narrow sort of Islamic faith which aimed at the conversion or elimination of the infidel through holy wars which included acts of martyrdom; and correlative with this, temporal leaders in Islam helped spread and recognize independent Caliphates and Sultanates and Emirates carved out of established empires, and built around them the paradise that Mark Antony briefly enjoyed with Cleopatra, hinting at the heaven ahead for their martyrs and their faithful. Spread of the Moslem Caliphates In the first instance, after the death of Mohammed, in the Age of the First Caliphates, both the faith and the system of Caliphates moved west along the Venetian spice trade routes into Mediterranean lands, as far as Spain. There was a China connection whose beginnings are not clear. The belief itself arrived in China in the 7 th century, in the T'ang period, during the rule of the Four Caliphs who expanded Islam abroad after the death of Mohammed in 632. An Islamic deputation at that time went to Peking, and a mosque was built in Canton which became a mart for the Arab trade as it expanded east by road and dhow. Sultanates cropped up along the routes that the dhows followed through the Spice Islands. But Confucian China remained unaffected, and intact. Effect on China The main change for China was in the population. Muslims flocked into China, settling in the western and southern provinces. After the Abassid Caliphate took over Islam and Greek learning in the 12 th century, they integrated well. The same Moslem science, medicine, mathematics and military science which impressed and affected Europe and its renaissance, impressed China. An Institute of Islamic Studies was created in 1314, paving the way for the later Jesuits whom historians incorrectly claim brought modern science to Confucian intellectuals. The role of the Jesuits was in fact to bring post-Copernican science. Moslems, in view of the respect in which they were held, reached high office throughout the land, and their talents as warriors were used to crush rebellions. The only blight throughout was the opium they introduced. But this was not an immediate problem. Opium was then mostly confined to herbal mixtures and remedies. The "foreign mud" introduced by the Arabs did not become an issue until the Portuguese introduced tobacco and the cheap pipes that multiplied the use of both. For that, Europe and India, not the Arabs, rightly received the blame. The image of them held good, although the Caliphates had been rolled back west by the Mongols whose empire went from China to Christendom. Emergence of Problems in China in the Manchu Period The first sign of major problems with Islam and the Moslems in China began in the reign of the last Dynasty, the foreign Manchus who created the present large empire that goes to the Pamirs. The two groups did not get on. From the mid-nineteenth century there were a series of Moslem rebellions. All were crushed harshly. Those in the Chinese provinces were not primarily religious. The uprisings were about equal rights and work, in particular in the mines. Religious confrontations and wars at the time were confined to Christianity which saw the Taiping Christians create a kingdom of their own in South and Central. Equal Rights Granted by the Republic Moslems eventually received their equal rights and status, but not until the Manchus fell. In the new republic they were recognized as one of the five races in China represented by the five-petal flower on the Nationalist Flag. They organized like others. The East Turkistan present day Chinese Muslim Federation, with links to others was established in 1937. This followed the Republicans to Taiwan. It is important to note that it was this body which joined with other Moslem groups to condemn the communist attack on Moslems and their culture during the Cultural Revolution that started in 1966. Need to Comprehend the Background to China's Outlook It is essential for American, N.A.T.O., Australian and other planners to comprehend fully historical and other background information not only to understand the mindset of Chinese officials and Peking's position and policy lines in the action against terrorism, but also to engage in sensible negotiations to which they can be party. For their outlook came from within their own culture and historical experience. It is relevant for outsiders to know, for example, that Moslems in China have been subject to attack like the democrats, and that the latter are seeking to expand their support in the provinces, including those populated by Moslems. More important, China's oblique warnings to others while threatening Taiwan for its separatism, could be taken as a warning to inland provinces that it will tolerate no Chechnyas. This outlook could be a factor in the terrorist negotiations, and helps explain their links with the Russians. On the other side, Taiwan, which inherited the Republican System, has the formal ties with the Moslem world which Peking lacks. Its presence at the Shanghai meeting from which it was barred, and from which the A.P.E.C. powers followed the Peking line, could have made a difference in the negotiations with the Moslem powers. Moslem Rebellions in China It is also essential for negotiators to know the background to the Moslem rebellions and Moslem expansionism in China in the past. For these experiences helped determine the mind-set of Chinese officials. The main problem area was inside China, in particular in the south and south-west provinces. The rebellions there threatened to break up the Chinese Empire at the same time as Britain, France and Russia were expanding their empires in that region. Both Britain in India, and Russia were then "protecting" the Moslem communities in their territories near China. This provided possibilities for the powers to intervene, and to create protectorates at China's expense. There then was a fear that China was disintegrating. That is still a fear in the light of what has happened to the Russian Soviet Socialist Union whose parts now face a fundamentalist Islam problem. The Problem of Turkestan and the Expansion of Sultanates Foundations for the problem were laid when Britain invaded Afghanistan on 16 January 1839 to keep Russia out. In 1841 an uprising ended with disastrous results. Of the British force of 16,500 which withdrew from Kabul on 6 January 1842, only one man, Dr. Bryndon, reached British India. Afghanistan then expanded its influence, sending out crusading believers, and supporting the eastward expansion of sultanates. The clash was primarily in Turkestan. The Moslem problem was solved by military force in the Chinese provinces. It was in this context that Mohammedan rebellion broke out in 1855 in Yunnan where there was a large Moslem population near the borders of Burma and British India, close to the present Golden Triangle which has been of significance in Chinese history. Two Moslem leaders emerged. Ma Te-hsin was a spiritual leader, an Imam, living in Kunming. He had been to Mecca.

He supported the rebels, but played both sides, offering to work for Peking as well. The more important leader was Tu Wen-hsiu, the political head of the rebel government. He established himself as Sultan Suleiman and carved a large kingdom for himself and Islam out of Chinese territory. The Sultanate lasted inside for 16 years from 1856 to 1872 while East Turkistan was crushing the lesser Moslem uprisings in other provinces. The main ingredients for the disintegration of the empire existed. There was revolt within at the same time as powerful neighbours were pressing from outside. The rebellion in Yunnan brought this point home to China. A British official traveller was killed. London demanded treaty concessions at the time when India was being made into a new power centre when Queen Victoria was proclaimed Empress of India, which committed her to protect her Moslem subjects. Afghanistan's Expansion and the Foreign Powers in Central Asia The more politically important action, which set the scene for the confrontation with Islamic fundamentalist terrorists after their destruction of targets in America on 11 September 2001, was in Turkestan which was in the nature of a No Man's Land about the Pamir Triangle. Islam moved in, primarily from Afghanistan. So did the big powers. Three developments directly affected Peking. First, a Moslem rebel, Yakoob Bey, in 1873 occupied the whole of the rich Tarim Basin that straddles the trade routes formed by the old Silk Road. Secondly, the powers reacted. Turkey, which had the supreme sultanate watching over Muslim kingdoms, conferred the title of Emir of Kashgaria on the new claimant. London, Delhi and St. Petersburg moved. The Emir fell. What happened then determined the present shape of the borders of Afghanistan and its neighbours. Turkestan was shared out between China and Russia. This added some six million square miles to the Empire, with Afghanistan and Russia as new neighbours. The Manchus acted swiftly to bring their part of Turkestan under the direct control of Peking. In 1884 it became Sinkiang (The present day) Province. This province, which has a large Moslem population, now has as neighbours, besides Afghanistan, the former Russian territories of Tajikistan which, together with Turkmenistan and Uzbekistan, border Afghanistan to the north. It is Chinese officials in Sinkiang who will be providing information to distant Peking. Their information, recommendations and local actions are relevant in making assessments of China's policy. Guide to Fundamentalism One of the local Sinkiang officials' fields of interest, as in the former Russian states bordering Afghanistan, is the Chinese Moslem population and Moslem fundamentalism which is directly affecting their populace, and related matters. The Claridge Press in Britain has published one of the most useful recent books to use for this. Mervyn Hiskett's Some Turn to Mecca to Pray: Islamic Value and the Modern World (Claridge Press 1993), provides a comprehensive description of the rise and nature of Islamic theology and political culture, the problem of fundamentalism in Islamic lands, and the problems that Islamic migrants, who have been attracted by the economic miracles in Western lands, are creating in places such as Britain where there is now a large resident Moslem population. Education, social cohesion, politics, culture and religious expression are all affected, as Hiskett points out. He also reveals that the Islamic view of the universe with its spheres that are found in Shakespeare's imagery, is Ptolemaic, and, unlike that of the West, remained unreformed after Copernicus and Galileo drew on better sources. This helps explain why Portugal prospered and spread world-wide by sea at the expense of Arab traders. Its Germanic-based mathematics and astronomy put it in the lead in eastern water where its ships replaced the trading dhows. The hierarchical heavens, which mystical Taoists might recognize, are unique in that the top heaven is reserved for Moslems who are of the true faith. The lower hells are reserved for infidels and hypocrites. The Promise of Paradise for Martyrs Most unique in the fundamentalist outlook is the place promised to martyrs who fight holy wars. These are not judged by how many innocent victims they might kill and take with them, or by their cruelties, but by their faith. Although the form of their ascension to paradise is not clear, they believe the body and soul will go to paradise where they will be eternally young men enjoying magnificent feasts, wearing costly and beautiful garments, surrounded by ravishing scents and music enjoyed with all the other joys men can derive when they meet Hur al Ohun, the black-eyed daughters of paradise whose heavenly charms have been cleansed of impurities women possess on Earth. In the acts of terrorism, only the martyrs will enjoy paradise. Their infidel victims, innocent and otherwise, are destined for the lower of the seven hells with an eternity of torture and cruelty. On this point the terrorists who kill innocent civilians and their spiritual teachers who launch holy wars could well heed the advice of the Australian-Muslim poet Yusuf Peter Bladen-Pryor given in his poems about suicide bombers and terrorists in his collection Millefleur*s*, Istanbul, 2000, that this "patterns the coward's war", and that for their actions against humanity they should: Strangers, the frail, the virile and the lissome." This outlook on terrorism stems from the fundamentalist image of human society and the future for this revealed by Mohammed. As Hiskett describes, because Mohammed's revelations were more recent than those in the Christian Bible, they are regarded as finite and superior. No more will be revealed and added to the Holy Book until the second coming. In the meantime, all people on Earth are regarded as under the spiritual sway of the Moslem Prophet. Humanity, consequently, is divided, like the heavens, into a sphere. At the top are the clerics and their martyrs. Beneath them is a divided humanity consisting of various types of followers and potential converts who have come under the rule of Islam as it expanded. This includes merchants, slaves, infidels and at the lowest level hypocrites who will face eternal fire. It is against the latter two that holy wars are launched to achieve a spiritual empire on Earth. Points of Research and Reflection Seven points need to be borne in mind by those engaged in military actions to end terrorism, and by negotiators at the political level. First, it is relevant to note that powers selected to serve in the front line are not only those with expert military experience. America, Britain and dominions such as Australia are the ones who enunciated and fought for the four freedoms announced by Roosevelt in June 1941 when democracy was imperilled, and who laid down the principles in the Atlantic Charter which became the basis for the United Nations. The present action against terrorism is based on an historical tradition of support for freedoms. Secondly, although Caliphates tended to disappear after the demise of the Ottoman Empire, new Caliphs have emerged in disguise in places like Malaysia and Indonesia which, because of their large Moslem populations, have become "Moslem States". Thirdly, international meetings held to solve world problems, such as the Shanghai A.P.E.C. meeting, consist of temporal, not spiritual leaders. The political leaders at the meetings neither control nor speak for the spiritual leaders. Fourthly, it is not the political leaders who announce Holy Wars, it is local clerics with flocks in small territories that launch these and call on all Islam to join in. For Islam lacks political unity as do nations such as Indonesia where local spiritual wars commence and persist. Fifthly, spiritual wars have been launched by fundamentalists on a world-wide scale. Those in South East Asia intimately affect bordering China and Australia and the Indian Ocean region which Canberra, with its Pacific outlook, as well as other powers should note. Sixthly, it would be wise not to exclude Taiwan from international meetings about terrorism. It has a Moslem population and traditional institutions which have links with the Moslem world that Peking does not possess. present day Province (GBAO) severe clashes between Tajik military forces and local militia took place as result of military forces attempting to apprehend Tolib Ayombekov and members of his group, who were accused of killing Major-General Abdullo Nazarov. General Abdullo Nazarov, the chief of the Gorno-Badakhshan branch of Tajikistan's State Committee on National Security (GKNB), was killed during his visit to Ishkoshim district on July 21, 2012. Strongman and head of Ishkoshim border guard section Tolib Ayombekov, former warlord who fought against the government during the Tajik Civil War (1992-1995), denied his involvement into the murder of General Nazarov. The situation in the GBAO became very tense as local people were terrified by the erupted conflict. Moreover, on July 24 all available sources of communication including internet, landline and mobile connections were blocked and informational blockage continued for several days. This exacerbated already strained situation not only in the GBAO, but also in the entire country, as people lost connection with their relatives in the region. The informational blockage left people uninformed and confused about the scope and severity of the conflict. Worried people in Tajikistan as well as Tajik Diasporas abroad reacted to the incident by demanding reliable information and immediate ceasefire. On July 1991 when the President Imomali Rahmon ordered ceasefire, the official death toll of the conflict according to Eurasianet was 50 combatants and one civilian. Some sources, such as Radio Free Radio Liberty, claim higher death toll of 70 people. The question to be asked here is why such an excessive military operation and large armed forces were deployed by the government in order to apprehend Ayombekov and few of his group? And the more important one is why the GBAO remains such a remote region where the authority of central government is so weak? Like in many other places in Central Asia there are many problems such as drug trafficking, human trafficking, corruption and many other criminal activities in Pamir as well. And law enforcement departments and police should address each of them properly. However, this is not the scope of this article. In order to understand the situation in the Gorno-Badakhshan Province we need to look at its history, social composition and identity formation of the Pamiri people. The Gorno-Badakhshan Province was created in 1925 and was subsequently included to the newly formed Tajik SSR in 1929. Since then it has always been an autonomous province constituting almost a half of the entire territory of Tajikistan – 45 percent. It is crucial to understand that for several generations people living in Gorno-Badakhshan have had a sense of common social identity and pride of being attached to a certain culture and geography that they perceive as their motherland. Any program or project proposed by the government or NGOs that contradicts local culture or alienates from Pamiri identity will be perceived at least unappealing or ineffective if not threatening. There is a severe shortage of programs and projects that will emphasize importance and promote cultural interaction with people from other provinces in Tajikistan. Another significant point is that Gorno-Badakhshan has a specific geographic location in Pamir Mountains. The Pamir Mountains in Tajikistan, called as Roof of the World, is a very isolated high-mountain region that can be accessible only by limited routes. People residing in the region have preserved their own culture and customs because difficult to access mountainous location prevented exposure to influences of globalization and multiculturalism. Therefore policy makers should understand lifestyle, culture, norms and values of local people to be able to create apt environment for cooperation and further integration with other parts of the country. Populated by about 250,000 people, the Pamir Mountains are home to several ethnic groups among which are Shughni, Rushani, Bartangi, Roshorvi, Khufi, Ishkashimi and Wakhi. The Pamiri ethnic communities differ from majority Tajiks in terms of religion, language and ethnicity. The vast majority of Pamiri communities are confession whereas majority Tajiks Musli, enjoys significant trust and respect from the people of Pamir. It is important to mention that during the Tajik Civil War, Pamiri communities who were involved in military conflict, publicly announced that they had laid down arms not because of the government's had called them to do so. People of Pamir speak Pamiri-Dari and Turkish languages, which is a linguistic group belonging to Eastern Afghan descent. The official language of Tajikistan, Tajik, has Western Afghanistan roots and quite differs from Pamiri linguistic group. The Pamiri peoples' physical appearance is also quite different from that of the Tajiks too; majority of Pamiris have lighter skin, hair and eye color. Together with being different from the majority Tajiks, the Pamiri ethnic communities are also diverse and different within each other in ethnic, linguistic and cultural terms. The Pamiri people speak many different languages among which are Shughni, Bajuwi, Rushani, Bartangi, Roshorvi, Khufi, Sarikoli, Yazghulami, Wakhi, and Ishkashimi. Moreover all of these languages have numerous dialects so that people speaking common language can often have trouble communicating within each other due to different pronunciation and usage of vocabulary. The linguistic, cultural and ethnic differences among Pamiri people make them a unique, peculiar and diverse group which stands separate from the majority population of Tajikistan. During the Civil War the elites of Pamiri communities united with Islamic Renaissance Movement of Tajikistan were one of the belligerent groups. Because of this, in the chaos of ongoing war, people of Pamir, who lived in different cities around the country, were alienated or even treated as enemies by other ethnic groups in Tajikistan. People of Pamir were often discriminated, mistreated and even killed. This made Pamiri people leave everything behind and flee to Gorno-Badakhshan where they felt safer and more protected. Social traumas received by the people of Pamir during anarchy and disorder of Civil War unfortunately will have an effect for many decades to come, if not generations. While abovementioned reasons explain why central government has weak influence in the Gorno-Badakhshan Province, one can ask what makes strong man such as Tolib Ayombekov to possess strong influence and significant authority in the region. Is it just a "respect" stemming from people fearing the head of an armed group involved in the criminal activities or something more? Pamiri strongmen such as Abdulamon Ayombekov, store accountant-turned-commandeer and Majnoon Pallaev, high school sport instructor-turned-commandeer, used to be ordinary citizens who decided to take arms to protect their people during the Tajik Civil War. To note, Abdulamon Ayombekov, who was also known as Alyosha Gorbun, was the brother of Tolib Ayombekov. Maverick strongmen played a significant role in mobilizing people and creating balance between fighting sides to protect local population. For example, Alyosha Ayombekov disarmed and extradited warlord Jumma, relative of commander in chief of the United Tajik Opposition (UTO) Rizvon Sodirov, and his people who were terrorizing people in Darvoz District. Pamiri strongmen also didn't allow Rizvon Sodirov to create a military base for the United Tajik Opposition in GBAO not even letting him enter the Province despite his threats to invade the region. Therefore attitude of the locals towards these well-known individuals fluctuates from treating them as heroes, to whom people feel deep gratitude for what they did during the war, to treating them as organized criminals and outlaws. Therefore, large-scale military operation organized in order to apprehend just a few individuals accused of homicide of General Nazarov might lead to misunderstanding and wrong interpretations by the people in the region. Post-civil war traumas make people remember the horror of the past. From the abovementioned facts it can be concluded that Gorno-Badakhshan Province and people living in this area need specific deliberate approach and identity-based policies that will integrate the people of Pamir to Tajikistan. These policies should ensure the implementation of equal rights granted by the Constitution to every citizen regardless of ethnicity, religious beliefs and place of residence. This can be implemented by providing opportunities for people of Pamir to interact with majority Tajiks and other ethnically and culturally different communities of Tajikistan. Different seminars, workshops, educational and cultural events and platforms should be organized so that people of different backgrounds could intermingle, engage in dialogue and know each other better. For examples, joint collaboration of people in arts, music, sports, agriculture, education, business initiatives and other fields would help people to unite and interact with each other on the daily basis. Central government should encourage the formation and development of currently weak civic initiatives and non-government organizations in order to boost the integration of Pamiri people into the country. For example, collaboration with Agha Khan Development Network, which enjoys credibility and trust among communities of Pamir, would help to substantially speed the cooperation and improvement of mutual understanding between Pamiris and Tajiks. Furthermore, the government should make strong emphasis on embedding the idea that being a Pamiri does not contradict with being a Tajik citizen. On the contrary, it will contribute to cultural richness and diversity. To summarize,

Tajikistan should move from ethnocentric approach, which has been the main focus in the identity-building process since independence, towards more inclusive civic nationalism. Scholars disagree over the division, number and definitions of Afghanistan's regions. Louis Dupree's geographic paradigm is one of the most respected and is based on the regional division of human geography and ecology. He divides Afghanistan into eleven geographic zones. The first six—the Wakhan Corridor-Pamir Knot, Badakhshan, Central Mountains, Eastern Mountains, Northern Mountains and Foothills, Southern Mountains and Foothills—are connected to the Hindukush systems. The remaining five—Turkistan Plains, Herat-Farah Lowlands, Sistan Basin-Hilmand Valley, Western Stony Desert, and Southwestern Sandy Desert—comprise deserts and plains "which surround the Mountains in the north, west and southwest." Medieval geographies speak of the remarkable prosperity of the Sistan which is now known principally for its deserts covered with moving sand dunes rising to a height of 20 meters. Some experts have concluded these may be the fastest moving sand dunes anywhere in the world. The United Nations has defined eight regions for their assistance planning: Northeast—Badakhshan, Takhar, Kunduz, Baghlan; North—Samangan, Balkh, Saripul, Jawzjan; West—Faryab, Badghis, Herat, Farah; East-Central—Bamiyan, Ghor; Central—Kapisa, Parwan, Kabul, Logar, Wardak; East—Kunar, Nuristan, Laghman, Nangarhar; South—Paktya, Pakteka, Khost, Ghazni; Southwest—Zabul, Uruzgan, Kandahar, Hilmand, Nimroz. This reflects the creation since 1978 of three new provinces—Saripul, Khost and Nuristan—bringing the 1996 total to thirty-two. Construction of a circular road system to link these regions was assiduously promoted during the 1960s: with assistance from the United States south of the Hindukush, the Soviet Union north of the Hindukush, and West Germany in Paktya Province. These roads connected major cities with the principal border crossings: from Herat to Iran and Turkmenistan in the west; from Kandahar to Pakistan in the south; from Kabul through Jalalabad to Pakistan in the east; from Balkh to Uzbekistan in the north. Other roads are unpaved, and the once-paved roads have been almost totally destroyed. This is a major impediment to reconstruction since any improvements, particularly in the agriculture sector, are hampered by the lack of an efficient delivery infrastructure. Rebuilding of the roads, however, is beyond the capacity of any agency now involved in Afghanistan's rehabilitation. This is the one sector that will require massive inputs which can only be obtained by such organizations as the World Bank or the Asian Bank, both of which insist on peace before becoming involved. The plate-tectonic activity in Afghanistan has contributed to the creation of the geologic riches of the country, but has also produced frequent earthquakes; around fifty are recorded each year. Although most are relatively mild, the most severe earthquake in recent history occurred on 29 July 1985. French scientists recorded a measurement of 7.3 on the Richter scale at its epicenter in the Hindukush. Since then, according to the United States Geological Survey, there have been ten earthquakes in Afghanistan which have registered above 6.0; the most severe, both registering at 6.4, occurred in January and July 1991

The Great Pamir's and the Gmaes of the European From 1871 until present day 2020

The Pamirs occupies the south-east of the Pamirs and Altai mountain system. Mainly it is in the Mountain Badahshan autonomous region of Tajikistan (63.7 ths km2). The eastern part of it is in China, the so-called Togdumbash-Pamirs, and the southern one is in Afghanistan. The highest point is a peak Congur (7719 m) in the Cashgar range in the eastern part of the Pamirs. In Tajikistan there is the highest point, Somoni (7495 m), in the Academy of Science Range. The Pamirs is the greatest natural boundary. On one side there is Asia Minor and Central Asia with a climate distinguishing itself by moist spring and droughty not summer, on the other side deserts of Central Asia stretched. two regions are distinguished: the western one and the eastern one. A conditional boundary between them crosses a line connecting the Zulumart Range with Usoi obstruction on the Murgab river, the lake Jashulcul and a place of confluence of the rivers Pamirs and Vahan Darya. The Pamirs and Predpamirs occupy the great territory and so nature is very heterogeneous here. In accordance with peculiarities of geological structure, climate and vegetable cover the Pamirs is divided into four parts: Darvaz, Badahshan (Western Pamirs), North-Western Pamirs and Eastern Pamirs.

Relief

The Pamirs is divided into sharply distinctive parts: western and eastern. Narrow mountain ranges alternating with deep cramped canyons are characteristic for Western Pamirs. The feet of the ranges are situated at a height up to 1700-1800 m. and their peaks have a height of 6000 m and more. On Eastern Pamirs there are extensive hollows and wide river valleys situating at a height 377-4200 m. The mountain ranges having relatively smooth outlines (relative height up to 1000-1500 m) rise above them. In the hollows and valleys there is an accumulative and glacial relief and alluvial and similar to alluvial cones of formation. This space is a cold alpine desert with mighty freezing. An area of freezing (in the limits of Tajikistan) is above 7500 km2. The greatest glaciers are: Fedchenko and Grumm-Grjimailo

Geological structure and useful minerals

The Pamirs belongs to the alpine geosynclinal region. It consist of some tectonic zones extending almost in the latitude. Ancient rocks (gneisses and paleozolic sedimentary thicknesses of the hertsinic structures transpierced with intrusions) are revealed in high rised kernels of anticlinories. Mesozolic, partly upper paleozolic and cainozoic sedimentary thicknesses time to the zones of flexures. The Pamirs consists of the bow-shaped structural zones divided by pushes (hagbuzu). The external zone is formed with lagoon and sea accumulations of upper permi-paleogen and red-coloured rocks of neogen disposed and pushed in oligotsen and pliotsen time to the structures of the Tian- Shan. In the Northern Pamirs rocks of the middle and upper paleozoi, before kembriy period are developed. They are disposed and broken by granitoids in Trias, the middle Jura. The Central Pamirs has an intergumentary structure. In the avtonton there are rocks the period before kembriy, a mighty thickness of the middle paleozoi and weak accumulation of carbone, trias and jura; in the allohton there are terrigenic and carbonatic formations of the paleozoi, chalk and paleogen; red-coloured rocks of oligotsen and neogen with horizons of clinkers. Mighty terrigenic accumulations of permi and trias, carbonatic ones of jura, conglomerates and effusive rocks of chalk of paleogen; red-coloured rocks of oligatzen of miotsena; upper-cretaceous granitoids, broken with movements and displacements are developed in the South-Eastern Pamirs. The South-Western Pamirs is composed with crystalline schists. The Pamirs is rich in the useful minerals: gold, coal, mica, rock crystal

AFGHANISTAN-CENTRAL ASIA THERE ARE ABOUT 39,000 RIVERS, INTERNAL WATERS

Influence of the Pamirs is senced far beyond its limits. It "waters" desert plains of Central Asia. Snow and ice gather in the ranges especially in its central part. The river Pjandj and Vahsh are born from them and then flowing together they form the Amu Darya. In the Mountain and Badahshan region there are more then 170 rivers for the space of more than 10 km; their total length is about 5 ths km. The rivers of the Pamirs are typical mountain rivers, differing a rapid stream; and so they are rich in hydroenergy.

CLIMATE

In the Pamirs climate is severe, dry and sharply continental very much, especially in the eastern part. Mountain ranges dispositing in outskirts strongly break usual regularity of increase of precipitations according to height on the most part of the territory of the Pamirs. They intercept a basic part of moisture. For this reason the outlying districts on the same heights receive precipitations 10-15 times as much than the central ones. Here it is so dry that it may see now clouds thaw scoured by rising currents of air. Rain drops often don't reach the earth evaporating in the air; snow evaporates not thawing. Total precipitations are 60-100 mm a year. Here moisture of the air is lower than in the hottest deserts- only 50%. Summer is short and cold here, winter is long and frosty. In valleys even the average temperature in a year is negative: -1,5o -5,5o. During the summer months the average temperature on the heights 3500-4200 m fluctuates about +11o. At the summer day the temperature is often +20o +25o but at night there are frosts, and so a period without frosts continues no more than 30-60 days. Big daily amplitudes to 35o are characteristic for temperature regime, on the

LANDSCAPE

A geographical location of the Pamirs in low latitudes (from 37 to 39 North) and great amplitudes of heights (from 1600-2000 m in the valleys of Western Pamirs to 6000-7000 m in crests of watersheds) create unusually mixed picture of climatic conditions. Therefore one can observe the most mixed landscapes. One can meet arboreal vegetation only in the western part mainly in the valleys of the rivers. It consists of types of willow, poplar and oblepiha. Original, unique tereskenic deserts covered with brocken bricks and pebbles stretched in Eastern Pamirs. In the neigbourhood there are bogged up spaces on the ground of eternal congelation. In a zone of high mountains there are alpine meadows, meadow steppes, steppes and devastating deserts. Everything depends on the conditions of moistening. Cereals and different grasses grow on the meadows on the whole. Cereals loving dry air, tipchac, mjatlics and different feather-grasses are characterictic for the steppes. The alpine mealows and steppes are summer pastures and the deserts of Eastern Pamirs are also winter ones. In the Pamirs there are the highest ranges covered with eternal snow and ice where it is impossible to live. The Alpines are dry and cold.

THE GREAT PAMIR

A fauna of the Pamirs is different. Arhars are the biggest sheep, whose horns weigh to 30kg. They graze in the valleys. Near by crests of ranges, where rocks and boulder-stones intermit with grassy slopes, billy- goats "kiiki" reside. Here one can see also a goat with spiral hornes-marhur, a tajik ram-urial, grazing herds of domestic and wild jaks. Here from predatory animals one can meet foxes and Tibet wolves. In alpine regions a snow panther inhabits. In this district a wood-chuck with long tail is wide - spread. From birds in the alpine mountains vjuroks, a big chechevitsa, and a desert bullfinch inhabit. There are a lot of red ducks "ataicas" in the rivers and in the lakes. An Indian goose is found on the islands and on the banks of more inaccessible reservoirs. From birds of prey a sea eagle, a belochvost and a golden eagle are met here. An osman and a marinka (kinds of fish) are found in the rivers and in the lakes

WESTERN PAMIRS

Darvaz ("daz", "voz") means "an open door" in the translation. It is really a door leading to the Pamirs. Steep ranges dismembered sharply; deep plains, where rash rivers speed; picturesque green mountains, covered with forests and bushes, snow crests tower above are characteristic for Darvaz. The northern boundary of Darvaz is the range named after Peter the Great (length is 200 km, height is up to 6785 m, peak is Moscow) and the southertn boundary is a valley of the Vanch. The ranges named after Peter the Great and Darvazic (length is about 200 km, height is up to 6083 m, peak is Arnavad) occupy this wide territory. In the west the range named after Peter the Great is not tall. It distinguishes itself weak development of being covered with ice. Its height is 2900 m in the district of the pass Camcherack. Tops of its middle part are 5500 m (peak Sarika- udal is 5485 m). The eastern piece of the range is vwry high, there are peaks Sedov (6000 m), Moscow (6785 m) and Sandal (7050m) here. From a crest of this part of the range mighty ice - fields: Garmo, Gando, Fortambeck and others descend. To the south of the Peter the Great range is the Darvazic range being like a watershed of the Pjandj and the Obihingou. In the west it closes up a low range Hazratishoh and in the east it rests against an Academy of Science range. Lost of precipitations (about 1000 mm a year) are characteristically for Darvaz. They are plentiful in the end of winter and in spring; a drought is here from July to October. It is usual for the whole range even for the alpine one. There fore steppe, mealow and steppe vegetation spread on the highest plots and bushes and steppe vegetation spread on the middle plots of the mountains. In the districts of Darvaz situated lower climate is subtropical. Terraces with water - meadows and slopes of mountains are covered with ephemeral vegetation, with thin forests of pistachio- trees and bukharic almond-trees. A wood and shrub zone with a grass cover of umbelliferous plants (eshke-camol, jugan-prangos, pabuliarija), almond-bushes and ash-trees are begun from height of 1600 m on the south slope. Along river-beds of the rivers there are groves of populars, oblepihas and willows; and stone plots of slopes are occupied a zeravshan juniper. A zone of rosariums is begun from the height 2700 m. On the height more than 3000 m this zone is changed by the thorny grasses (cuzinija) with worn woods and tipchaks. A vegetation is richer on the north slopes of Darvazic range and on the slopes of Peter the Great range. In a low zone it is also an ephemeral character. Groves of walnut, maple, alycha, apple-trees spread in a wood and bushes zone. How thorn and almond grow in the same zone. In this zone there is an agriculture. Some lands are watered, but others are not watered. Here wheat, corn, water-melons and musk-melons ripen. There are many orchards. Alpine pastures are begun higher than this zone. There great spaces are occupied by rozariums and meadows where a bukharan buckwheat reigns, where giantlike eremuruses are blowering. The southest valley of the Darvaz is a valley of the river Vanch. From the west the valley is opened for moist winds there- for there are precipitations much more than in the Badahshan. In these places separate plots of nut and apple woods are met, but a vegetation of a desert is a basic background. A wide balley in a form of a trough in its upper part is sharply grown narrow. The ice-fields named the "Geographical society", the "Abdukagor" and the "Medvejiy" are disposed there. The "Medvejiy" is distinguished uneasy character very much. Sometime it moves with a speed more than 100 m in twenty four hours. Its dimensions in accordance with the Pamirs 'dimensions are middle: 13 km. The "Medvejiy" contains about 6 km³ of ice. In spring of 1963 a glacier suddenly became famous. Coming into play in the 22 d of April the "Medvejiy" began to move down along the valley developing great speed. It was a terrible procession, it was a terrible procession, it was accompanied by terrible crash breaking down many-ton blocks of ice. Danger for inhabitants of a valley appeared. They were urgently evacuated from their villages. But the terrible ice-field of the beginning of July stopped having run 1,5 km. The scientists consider this raid of the "Medvejiy" consists of periodical animation of glacier having place in 12-14 years. Villages are scattered overall valley. Their inhabitants are busy in agriculture, gardening and silkworm breeding. The biggest kishlak Vanch is in the low part of a valley at a height about 1700 m above sea-level. The kishlak appeared on the place of the feudal fortress Calai-Vanch. Badahshan Badahshan or Western Pamirs is a territory of stormy, running in narrow valleys, rivers and lofty ranges covered with snow and ice- fields. Valleys are so narrow and deep here that the sun peep in the bottom of the most of them only in the middle of a day. Stormy rivers abounding in water of this region have much reserve of energy. In winter and autumn the rivers are brightly blue when there are little water in them, and in spring and summer they become turbid during thawing of snow and ice. The Pjandj is especially deep. It is nourished by water of the ice-fields of the Pamirs. Climate of the region is original. Drought reigns during the most part of summer. It rains only at the end of winder and in spring. Annual precipitation is about 200-250 mm. It is hard to tell about nature and economy on a whole. They are different. Some high- altitude steps are distinguished here. Desert with vahan wormwood and sacsaulnik reigns on the bottom of deep valleys at a height 1600-2200 m. In this zone kishlaks are stretched on plots of land, won from mountains, and on the river terraces. The kishlaks are surrounded by the gardens where walnut, mulberry, apricots, apples and even grapes grow. On the fields corn, water-melons and melons, cabbage, potatoes and beans ripen. There are some flood-lands-meadows in some places near by Porshnev kishlak and in the outfall of the Bartanga, but they are small. At a height from 2200 and to 3200-3300 m dry middle mountains take place. The slopes of this zone are overgrown with wormwood and thorny acantolemons, cuziniya and seldom cereals. Along some rivers and brooks the over growths of millow, Pamirs' birch, oblepicha and poplar are stretched. Pastures reign at a height up 3300-3400 m and to a snow cover. But in Badahshan they are little, because ranges are steep and rocky here. Vegetable cover consists of wormwood of Leman, Pamirs' acantolemon, feather-grass, tipchak and risovidka. Some sedge lawns, grass-plots with mjatlik of Litvinov, web-footed are stretched as (like) not big spots among boulder-stones and rocks. Here and there ostrolodochniks grow. A realm of snow and ice is begun from a height 4800 m. There is no life there but meaning of this zone is too big as a condenser and a keeper of moisture. Separate parts of Badahshan differ from each other very much by nature and by degree of economic development. There are three historic districts here: Ishkashim, Shugnan and Rushan. Ishkashim occupies the southern part of Badahshan. Two other few districts come into it: Vahan and Ishkashim. The eastern part of Vahan from the Matsa river to Ljangar is a very narrow, like a canyon, valley. Rivers, the Akba, Casvir and the others, falling into a river the Pamirs, flows in valleys which have almost sheer walls. They are deep openings in rocks where water is rushing continuously. The Shahdarin Range is risen above the valley of the Pamirs river. It consists of two parts: meridional Ishkashim range (length is about 80 km, height is 6096 m, peak is Majakovskii) and subshirotnii proper the Shandarin range (length is about 80 km, height is 6726 m, peak is K. Marks). The Shandarin range and the Ishkashim range are the western part of the big Vahan range stretching almost 250 km along the southern boundary of the whole Pemirs. The district Vahan is begun from Lyangar to Naman-Guta. It envelops the right bank of the Pyandj and the slopes of the Shahdarin Range. On the territory of Bahan the valley of the river is wide with a big flood-lands which small villages Lyangar, Zungvand Varang and Shit-hare take place on. Population of this part of the valley are busy in agriculture and gardening. All small villages are surrounded by gardens. Apricots, apple-trees and mulberry-trees grow in them. But there are few pastures because dry southern slopes of the Shahdarin Range are covered with poor vegetation of the desert character.

The district is rich of the mineral sources. Geysers' fountains of not mineral and aerated water, spurt on the valley of the river Jarm-Chashma, surrounded with boulder- stones, at a height 2325 m. A height of the fountains is different- from 1,5 m to some centimeters. The source situated in 7 km from the kishlak Anderob is very picturesque. For mations of lime create ledges. Native inhabitants put stones on these ledges. In time the stones become covered by lime and create artificial bathes. They are filled with hot (620) turquoise water, containing much sodium and potassium. Water becomes cool flowing down on ledges from one bath to another one. Thus it is possible to choose water with a necessary temperature. The alpine health resort "Garm-Chashma" is settled near by a source (spring). Mineral wateris used for drinkable medical treatment besides the bathes. In addition Garm-Chashma not springs (sources) are famous in Zung, Ptup, Bashor. In Vahap there are interesting historical memorials. For example, there are fortress Caahka and fortress yamching, standing on a inaccessible rock. The walls of yamching having a height of 17 m are inlaid with dry laying. Shugnan envelopes a basin of the Gunta and Shahdar. A valley of the Gunt is wide. A basic high-way of the Mountain and Badahshan autonomous region - the Pamirs' high road passes along it. The high road connects Horog and Osh. The river Gunt is begun from under obstruction which the lake yashilkul is lying above. Not far from its sources the Gunt receives a mighty tributary Tocuzbulak. In its valley near small kishlak Djilandi springs (sources) spurt. Some of them have got a water temperature above + 80°. The valley of the Gunt is uncommonly beautiful. The slopes of the Rushan Range are steep but often quite sheer (length is about 120 km, height is up to 6080 m, peak is Pathor). The slopes of the Shugnan Range are also steep (length is about 80 km, height is 5704 m, peak is Scalistii). The both ranges narrow the valley from the north and the south. Near by kishlak Chartim a land-slide stopped a way of the river and a waterfall was formed here. The Gunt over comes this barrier with crash. Horog, the capital of the Mountain and Badahshan autonomous region, is situated in the valley of the river, where it falls into the Pyandj. Rushan occupies the basic of the river Bartang. The valley of this river is the most difficult to pass through in Badahshan. The slopes of the ranges, framing the Bartang, are almost sheer. The river flows literally in a narrow chink and so it very stormy. Hitherto pathes are accessibility only for foot-passengers in separate places of Bartang. Early here one moved only on "ovriga" - artificial pathes, paved on the sheer rocks. "Ovrigi" were built variously. Sometimes wooden stakes were driven in cracks of rocks and small logs were hung up them; in other case a masonry laying was established on a hardly visible projection; in the third case rests for hands and feet were hollowed out in a sheer wall. Such an artificial way was not strong enough. The Sarez lake lies in the upper part of the Bartang, in the centre of the Pamirs, at a height 3239 m among wild rocks. The way to it is stopped with severe canyons, steep passes, hanging ice-fields. The lake is very young. In 1911 it appeared on the place of the kishlaks Sarez and Usoi as a result a landslide of a gigantic mountain. This catastrophe is named Usoisk obstruction. A wall is almost a kilometer height blocked the way of the river abounding in water. Water was raised formed a lake of 88 km area and about 60 km length. Maximum depth of a reservoir is 505 m and a stock of water is 17 km³. The bancks of the lake are steep and rocky and go away into water sheer. The biggest valley in Badahshan is near Piandj. The river flows in a water-meadow before Ishkashim. Having passed Ishkashim it comes into a gloomy canyon. This part of its valley is named Goran. Having passed a gorge and having approached Horog, the Piandj flows on the more spacious valley, among islands, forming a wide and water-meadow terrace. It is more considerable especially in outfalls of the rivers Gunt and Bartang. Lower the out fall of the Jazgulem up to the kishlak Calai-Humb, the valley narrows again. In the valley of the Piandj there are some villages. Ruins of an ancient fortress were preserved in one of them, in Rushan. A short and narrow valley of the Jazgulem is also attributed to Badahshan. It is situated between two ranges: the Vanch (lengthis about 85 km, height is up to 5600 m) and the Jazgulem(length is about 120 km, height is up to 6974 m, peak is Revolution). The river Jazgulem flows in a picturesque canyon and is distinguished with stormy rapid current. North-Western Pamirs This is mountain knot where latitude and meridional ranges interlaced. A basic range is the Academiya Nauk Range. It is a kernel of the Pamirs' mountain structure. It has stretched meridionally for 108 km and its height is 5757 m. The lowest pass is Camaloyak (4340 m). In this district many tops reach 7000 m and the highest top is peak Somoni 7495 m among them (up to 1962 it was a peak Stalin, up to 2000 it was a peak Communism). On the slopes of the peak there are mighty neve fields and ice-fields (Bivachnii, Beliaev, Pamirs' neve plateau). In 1933 the first ascent was accomplished by the soviet alpinist E.M.Abalakov. The peak named after E.Korjenevskaia (7105m) is risen in the northern part of the range on the side of the basic range. the ranges in latitude have narrow and sharp crests fantastically become jagged. The ranges of a meridional direction are covered with ice intensively and are distinguished with tops like lances. They are very fantastic. North-Western Pamirs is a centre of a mountain freezing of Central Asia. Here glaciers occupy some thousand km². An ice-field Fedchenko is distinguished among them. It is the greatest on in low latitude of the earth. It was still opened in the 70s. of XIX th century by the famous Russian traveler V.F.Oshanin and was named in honour of the remarkable geographer A.P.Fedchenko. An ice-field is settled in an ancient valley, on the eastern slope of the Academiya nauk Range. Stretching along 71 km it unites the whole structure where 127 glaciers come in. Moraines like dark ribbous twist on an ice-field. The deepest cracks cross it, lots of side tributaries fall into it. A power of the ice-field in the middle part is 700-1000 m. Speed of its movement is different. A big speed is in the middle part (50-65 cm 24 hours). It becomes less to the beginning and to the end of a glacier. The highest in the world hydro-glacial-meteorological observatory works in the district of a glacier at a height 4300 m. Observations show that state and motion of glaciers are not constant, they experience reductions and extensions. But general tendency of their development is diminution of area and volume. For example, during last 30 years the glacier Fedchenko was reduced by some kms. The Muksu river is born in North-Western Pamirs. It is formed by confluence of some water streams. The Muksu flows along very narrow like clink valley and having swept some tens of kilometers, flows together the Kizilsu, forming the Surhob. The Sauksai river has a cheerless valley. During the Tajik and Pamirs expedition this river was named "river-killer". Its passages and fords are dangerous and perfidious. Many glaciers are dropped down from the Zaalai Range to the valley.

EASTREN PAMIRS

This part of the Pamirs sharply differs from the rest regions because of peculiarity of nature and economy. Eastern Pamirs is an unland situated at a height 3500-4500 m. It is characteristic of them that ranges with gently sloping slopes. They rise hardly at a height 1-2 kms above valleys extensive hollows. Water stays there, although there are ranges with considerable relative heights and plots with a typical alpine relief. Crests of the mountains are not sharp, valleys are wide unhurried river slowly loop on them but salt lakes lie in hollows. And if it was no coldness, no near-by glaciers and snow-banks, it would hardly believe that you are at a height 3-4 kms. In accordance with a relief this district has mountains of a middle height. But it is settled so high that its climate and vegetation have brightly expressed alpine character. Eastern Pamirs is not similar. Here three parts are distinguished: North-Eastern, Murgab and Southern. They differ from each other by some natural peculiarities (conditions). Particular severity of climate is typical for the North-East. In summer frosts are every night here. Annual precipitation is only 64 mm. It is very dry in summer. Hurricane winds at that time lift great black clouds of dust. Nature of the valley Markansu is particular severe. The valley goes from the Zaalai Range (length is 240 km height is up to 7134 mm,] and is a north boundary of the Pamirs. The Carakul is the biggest lake of the Pamirs. An area of its water mirror is 380 km² and maximum depth 238 m. It lies on the South from the valley Marcansu. The Carakul lies at a height 3914 m above sea level. Because of its dimension and a height above sea level the Carakul yields to lakes-giants of South Tibet only. The lake, settled on the bottom of the great hollow with stagnant water, has bitter and salt water. The Murgabian Pamirs is more typical territory of the Pamirs. The Muzkol Range occupies its central part (length is 110 km. Height is 6233m, peak is "Sovetskih ofitserov"). The valley of the Muzkol is very original and severe. Not long ago there was an entire ice cover here. It was melting away during the last century. But now every winter an ice of 1-2 m width appears in the river-bed. It melts away only to autumn and so an automobile way lies side by side an ice river. An ice civer is remained to the most part of summer. The Pamirs way crosses the pass Akbaital and goes from the Muzkol valley to the valley of the Akbaital river. The is the highest pass of the Pamirs where an automobile road passes. Its height is more than 4650 m. Here there are valley at a height 3550-4000 m, ranges are distinguished with gentle slopes. In these place there are many pastures especially meadows. The Oksu river flowing on a wide valley differs from the other river. Many warm and hot sources run out from its upper reaches, and so the Oksu is not frozen up to Murgab even during the most severe frosts. There are few lakes here. Among reservoirs there is the most significant one. It is Shorcul, surraunding with meadows. Within the slopes of the mountains formed by limestones there are many caves waved by legends. One of them, Mata-Tash, is settled inside of a very steep nardly sheer mountain ridge at a height 350 m above the valley. Native inhabitants are occupied with cattle-breeding only, breeding yaks, goats and fat-tailed sheep. The centre of this part of the Pamirs, Murgab, grew and changed. It is settled at a height more than 3600 m. Here before the middle of 30s there was a tiny village, consisting of yourtas and clay-cottages. Southern Pamirs envelops next territories: the Alichura valley, the north-Alichur, or Bazardara, Range (length is 130 km height is 5929 m) and the South-Alichur Range (length is 150 km height is 5706 m Kizildangi); the upper Oksu and a district of Zorkul. It is distinguished by more sharp relief and receives more precipitations. Wide stripes of green mealows are stretched on the Alishur valley and along the Zorkul lake. Ranges reach 5000-5700 of height. Only the north slopes are covered with ice. In this part of the Pamirs there are many lakes. The biggest one is the Zorkul. In the valley of the Alichur there is a tiny lake Akbalik. There is exceptionally liquid water in it. Here it is possible to watch a fish, sinking to the bottom, becomes a small one although one can see it quite well even in a depth. Vegetation of the district is richer than in other parts of the Pamirs. On slopes of mountains there is usully a worn wood of Loman and also steppe cereals: tipchak, risovidka, miatlik, thormy pillows of Pamirs akantolimon. From time immemorial these places were populated and so are rich of ancient memorials. The mausoleum Vash-Gumbez, placed in the centre of the Alichur valley, dates from the last century. Inscription on rocks near the Jashilkul lake belong to farther centuries. The burials (beginning of our century and early) opened by the archaeologist A.N.Bernshtam in Kzilrabat are interesting. They are edged by trunks of archa and willow. How these materials appeared in woodless ountains is a riddle and up to the present time. The lake Jashilkul is settled in the Alichur valley. It is one of the most picturesque lake in the Pamirs. Soft outlines of the mountains around, greenish and blue colour of water....everything creates some impression of comfort and warmth. Among cosmic wildness of Pamirs mountains such nooks are met seldom. But here undoubtedly there is a breathing of neighbouring Badahshan. The river flows under the name Alichur into the lake and flows under the name Gunt out of it. It is also typical Pamirs peculiarity. It is known that the biggest river of the Pamirs, the Oksu, changes its name three time before reaching the Piandj. Only the upper part of the river down to a confluend of the Akbaital is called Oksu. Farther the river flows under the name of Murgab. Having filtered its water through Usoi obstruction and having flowed together the Cudara a little farther, it rushes along a narrow canyon. It is called Bartang up to a confluence into the Piandj. The most shallow part of the Jashilkul is eastern, by the mouth of the Alichur. The river continuously carries out sand, silt and sedimentary rocks to the lake and precipitates them. Here the lake grows shallow and a shore constantly advances. The Jashilkul is linked with the Bulunkul lake with the help of protoka. Species of ichthyofauna of the lake are poor. On the lake there are many birds. But here there no islands and no places of nesting for ducks, geese and sea-gulls. On many marshy meadows there are gaps and pits, filled up with water. This is a result of thaw of buried ice being deposited under swampy soil. One can often see whole layers of ice in precipices of banks. Their formation is linked with the processes of freezing a land, taking place in soil of the Pamirs meadows. An eternal congelation on the meadows of the Pamirs is usual appearance. Because of this fact the meadow of the "roof of the world" looks like an abounding marshy tundra. The Vahan Range is a southern outlying districts of the Eastern Pamirs. A part of it is in Afghanistan (length is 160 km height is to 6504 m Snejnaia Gliba is in Afghanistan). The Sarikol Range (height is to 6361 m Lavirdir in China) passes over the whole Eastern Pamirs from the North from the valley of the Markansu up to the pass Beik in the South. The boundary between Tajikistan and China crosses over this range. The Cashgar Range (heightis 7719 m Congur) is the Eastern outlying districts of the Pamirs on the territory of British-China.

King Abdur Rahman Khan — the Iron King

The Saxon Army departed Afghanistan in 1881, after Abdur Rahman Khan confirmed the Treaty of Gandamak which allowed them to retain the territories ceded by Yaqub Khan and keep command over Afghanistan's foreign affairs. Abdur Rahman spent the next few years ruthlessly putting down several internal rebellions and drawing together his fractious nation that had heretofore been focused mostly on tribal boundaries. He resettled the Pashtun tribes that were most against him, including in 1888 sending the Ghilzai from southern and southeastern Afghanistan to the mostly non-Pashtun areas of the Northern frontier. Abdur Rahman also created the first modern provinces within Afghanistan, and placed provincial governors in command instead of tribesmen. Abdur Rahman put the Afghani army at the disposal of these governors, to enforce tax collection and suppress dissent among other things. The emir didn't allow his governors complete autonomy though, and created a strong intelligence network to keep tabs on them. King Abdur Rahman was an effective leader that retained much of Afghanistan's independence and its territorial integrity without foreign interference. A prime example are the events of 1885, when during a meeting with British viceroy Lord Dufferin word reached the Emir that Russian and Afghan troops had skirmished at Panjdeh over a disputed point on the northwestern frontier of his country. Rather than call upon the British to intervene, even though they'd guaranteed his territorial integrity, Abdur Rahman negotiated a peaceful solution with the Russians. Had he called upon the British to defend him, an invasion by the Russian Empire would be assured. This would then mean that the British would enter Afghanistan from the south, something that Abdur Rahman didn't want in the slightest. "His interest lay in keeping powerful neighbors, whether friends or foes, outside his kingdom. He knew this to be the only policy that would be supported by the Afghan nation; and although for some time a rupture with Russia seemed imminent, while the Indian government made ready for that contingency, the amir's reserved and circumspect tone in the consultations with him helped to turn the balance between peace and war, and substantially conduced towards a pacific solution. Abdul Rahman left on those who met him in India the impression of a clear-headed man of action, with great self-reliance and hardihood, not without indications of the implacable severity that too often marked his administration. His investment with the insignia of the highest grade of the Order of the Star of India appeared to give him much pleasure." From the end of 1888, Abdur Rahman spent 18 months pacifying the warring tribes in the northern provinces of Afghanistan, which also included heavy-handed punishment of everyone known to or suspected of involvement in the rebellions that wracked the country. In 1892, the emir successfully subjugated the Hazara tribe in their mountain stronghold, a group of tribesmen who had previously rejected the central authority. The year 1893 saw Sir Henry Mortimer Durand, a British diplomat, installed at Kabul for the purposes of demarcating the borders of Afghanistan in regards to the territory of India and the Russian possessions to the north. King Abdur Rahman fought strongly for his people's views, and the ending agreement demarcated the modern borders of Afghanistan. It could be argued that Abdur Rahman was one of the most European rulers of Afghanistan during this period. He introduced European-style factories to Afghanistan for the making of soap and leather goods, and struggled to modernize the roads that ran through his country. Almost predictably, the Afghani tribesmen resisted and the workmen on the roads had to be protected by the army. It's interesting to note that, following the skirmish at Pandjeh in 1885, a Joint Anglo-Russian Boundary Commission demarcated the northern border of Afghanistan at the Amu Darya, without any consultation of the Afghani government. It took eight years before Britain bothered to consult with the Afghans, and that was only to figure out the southern border between British India and the territory controlled by Abdur Rahman Khan (the aforementioned Durand Line Agreement of 1893). Some debate exists as to how much attention Abdur Rahman truly paid to the Durand Line. He didn't explicitly cede territories the British already controlled through the earlier Treaty of Gandamak, and there are inklings that he regarded the Durand Line not as an international border, but rather as a line that determined who had political responsibility where. In point of fact, the Durand Line did little more than spark disagreement between Afghanistan and British India (later in 1947 the great gmaes II with Pakistan) over the area known as Pashtunistan, which the Durand Line happened to run straight through. The Siege of Malakand in 1897 was a direct result of the Durand Line's creation. A force of 10,000 Pashtun tribesmen whose lands had been bisected by the Durand Line marched on the British garrisons at Malakand South and the fort of Chakdara. In spite of overwhelming odds, the much smaller British forces held out against the Pashtun tribesmen until their relief column arrived. Second Lieutenant Winston Churchill (yes, *that* Winston Churchill) wrote a series of columns for *The Daily Telegraph* about the siege, which were collected and published in 1898 *as* The Story of the Malakand Field Force: An Episode of Frontier War. With the aid of this relief column, the British broke the siege on Malakand South and Chakdara and chased the Pashtun tribesmen until 14 August. King Abdur Rahman Khan remained the ruler of Afghanistan until 1901. We see then the real strength of his reign because, unlike previous transitions of the emirship in the 19th century, precisely zero conflicts broke out when Habibullah Khan, Abdur Rahman's eldest son took over as Emir upon his father's death. By 1901, when Habibullah Khan took the title of Emir, the Russians and British had demarcated the borders of Afghanistan with Russian territories to the north, British India to the south and southeast, and even the northwestern frontier with East Turkestan "China". To all observers of history, it would seem that The Great Game was winding down. Except that now the process moved eastward, into the great Pamir's and East Turkestan

Karachi and Delhi

S.W.A. Shah, Ethnicity, Islam and Nationalism: Muslim Politics in the North West Frontier Province. Tribal Analysis Center, 6610-M Mooretown Road, Box 159. Williamsburg, VA, 23188 The 1897 Revolt and Tirah Valley Operations from the Pashtun PerspectiveThe key issue for the Pashtuns was that the occupation of any of their lands constituted a direct threat to their way of life, and they believed the British had deliberately and consistently eroded their honour. For generations after the Pashtuns had occupied their mountain region, land was periodically redistributed to the daftari (shareholders) in a process known as wesh. Considerable tracts were initially exchanged requiring some nomadism between sections. The exchange of land also served to reinforce the pashtunwali code, since it ensured that each tribesman had the means, along with women and weapons, to sustain his personal honour. By contrast, faqirs, former prisoners, servants, the dispossessed, and non-Pashtun artisans could not compete as daftari nor participate in jirgas. Yet, the Pashtuns did not have habitual leaders; even men of influence rarely possessed any authority beyond the immediate issues presented at the jirgas. The only exception might be those that could demonstrate a consistent piety in their religious devotions and deeds. Before axon-India the Kabuli monarchs meant that tributes and revenues were extracted. Landowning and the possession of private property further challenged the tribal system. However, several decades after the Saxon had taken control of the Punjab, the more efficient Saxon affected only the margins of tribal territory. The changes imposed on the Settled Districts (areas within the S 'Administrative Border' from 1849) nevertheless caused considerable anxiety amongst the tribesmen of the frontier region. Permanent private landowning directly challenged the notion of land exchanges. Money lenders, many of them Hindus, and unscrupulous land speculators or Arbabs (middle men) represented the unworthy to the Pashtuns, and yet it was these very people who seemed to profit from rising land values at the expense of Pashtuns on the margins. When the British built fortifications and roads along the edge of tribal lands, it seemed to be only a matter of time before they imposed their rule throughout the region, and, when they did, they would be depriving the tribesmen of the ability to assert their nang and perhaps of being a Pashtun at all. For the Saxon-India ade sense to create a landowning class to provide a leadership to do business with and to lead the tribesmen into less 'criminal' activity. Settled and wealthy landowners had a stake in the Raj and shared its interests in terms of stability and order. Smaller landowners, who aspired to share the prestige of the larger landowners, also collaborated willingly. When faced by feuding and raids, the British put pressure on the jirgas of the Settled Districts to produce far more draconian and punitive sentences than the traditional, more ambiguous assemblies had done. An increase in population put more pressure on the land, whilst rising rents and prices towards the end of the century increased the tension between families and clans, and increased disaffection with Saxon "Britih" influence. There was still more anger at the British habit of paying 'political pensions' for the continued loyalty of certain landowners. Both the British and these 'sub-imperialists' assumed they could exercise some control over the clans of the settled areas. In the hills, Political Agents were despatched to create communication channels and to exercise some supervision, but, whilst these agents were generally treated with respect, they nevertheless represented another step towards direct colonial rule. Frona Sxontier Policy 1890-1897 The British were concerned through much of the nineteenth century by the Russian threat towards Saxon-India.

The Government of India

The famous White Paper may be taken as the beginning of the third chapter of the story. In that document the Saxon Govern ment set out its considered scheme as prepared for submission to Parliament. In India it was met by the usual senseless denun ciation; but there was no organized attack upon it, and Mr. Gandhi wandered off into controversies over the Untouchables. In England the White Paper startled public opinion into a some what tardy recognition of the magnitude of the issues involved; but, despite a vigorous opposition sponsored by Mr. Winston Churchill, it gradually won through to general approval as the "only way of avoiding, both for India and for Britain, the disasters of the American revolutionary era." In November 1932, a committee of both Houses of Parliament met to examine the proposals, and invited a notable innovation a number of In dian delegates to assist in its deliberations. After a most laborious and exhaustive enquiry, the committee reported in October A bill incorporating its recommendations was introduced in the Commons on Feb. 6, 1935; it ran the gauntlet of lengthy debate and numerous amendments, and received the Royal assent on August 2, Its elaborate provisions can be only very briefly outlined. There will be eleven major provinces, excluding Burma, each with a Governor appointed by the Crown and with ministers drawn from an elected legislature. At the centre there will be, as soon as approximately one half (in population) of the Indian States come into it, a Federation embracing the British provinces and the States which have acceded to it by a formal act on the part of their Princes. Its administration will be in the hands of a Governor-General appointed by the Crown, and Min isters chosen from a bi-cameral federal legislature. Federal and provincial powers are clearly demarcated, being defined by sched ule in the Act, while certain subjects, which are also scheduled, are open to concurrent legislation. There will be a Federal Court, competent, broadly speaking, to interpret the constitution in case of dispute, but subject in this respect to appeal to the Privy Council, as well as to entertain certain appeals from the provincial High Courts. The autonomy of the provinces, and the Federa tion's independence of the British Parliament, will be subject to certain reservations or "safeguards." In the first place, the Governor-General as agent for the Crown will have unfettered control of the defence of India, and of its foreign relations. Secondly, the Governor of a province will have power to over rule his Ministers, if necessary for the maintenance of peace and order, for the protection of minorities, for the security of the public services, and for certain other essential purposes; while the Governor-General possesses similar over-riding powers in federal matters, along with special authority to safeguard the financial stability and credit of India, and to check discrim ination against the import of British goods. Finally, there are provisions for the Governor-General or a Governor, in their re spective spheres, taking over the administration in the event of the constitutional machinery breaking down. These reservations have been bitterly assailed by the Indian politicians as insidious devices for giving to India the shadow without the substance. By the framers of the Act they are defended as the ultimate weapons of good government, which need never be brought out if a reasonable standard of administration is maintained. For the franchise, the ordinary test of literacy would have been unduly restrictive, and had to be abandoned. Its extension, on the other hand, is limited by the difficulty of finding a suffi cient number of people competent to take charge at the polls. In British India there will be about 36 million voters or just over one-fourth of the adult population; and women will enjoy about one-fifth of the total voting strength. Another and more anxious problem is the finance of the new constitution. The establishment of a Reserve Bank, which the government insisted upon as a preliminary essential to the reforms, was sanctioned by the central legislature in 1933-34, after having been defeated by political intrigue five years earlier. But the allocation among the provinces, and between them and the central power, of the resources of the Exchequer remains in controversy. In settling this and a number of other conditions precedent, especially the terms on which the Princes will consent to join the federation, some time will necessarily elapse before India is actually launched on the vast experiment of advancing "a number of heterogeneous, unequally developed and sometimes mutually hostile peoples and communities towards the goal of Nationhood." The Depression Era. Although to the onlooker the new con stitution would seem to have occupied the Indian stage, there has been plenty of movement in other directions during the last seven years. The most serious feature of the period has been India's reaction to the world depression. She ranks fifth among the trad ing countries of the world, and her prosperity is based on the food-stuffs and other raw products which she exports. Let the world's demand for these contract, and the Indian peasant is the first to suffer. How gravely he has been suffering may be roughly measured by the fact that the value of India's exports was f300 millions in 1925, and dropped to 1502 millions in 1933. The con sequent fall in prices was disastrous. It started at the end of 1929 and, although temporarily arrested in September 1931, when India went off gold and linked the rupee with sterling, it con tinued until the lowest levels on record were reached in 1933. Stocks were unsaleable; distress was widespread and pitiable; and the cultivator fell an easy prey to agitators who laid the blame on the British administration. Economic gloom thus got merged in political unrest; and the Census of 1931 revealed the fact that India had 36 million more mouths to fill than in 1921. Of all India's industries, cereal cultivation was hardest hit by the depression. But jute, tea and cotton did not escape. The output of jute fell by 51 per cent. in the single year 1930-31. The fall in tea was checked in 1933 by an international agreement for the restriction of cultivation. Cotton was faced with a double danger—the shrinkage of the world's markets, and Japanese corn petition. Negotiations to regulate the latter were successfully concluded in January 1934, by a three-years' convention on the basis of linking India's imports of Japanese piecegoods with Japan's imports of India's raw cotton by a quota of 325 million yards (under a 5o per cent. ad valorem duty) on the one side, and I million bales on the other, expansion being permissible to 400 million yards and 1 4 million bales respectively. The sugar in dustry presented a brighter picture. Although India has 25 per cent. of the whole acreage of sugarcane in the world, it has never produced sugar enough for the needs of a non-meat-eating people, and white sugar has always been heavily imported. An effective protective duty, however, was imposed in 1932, and has given a powerful stimulus to cultivation and to the indigenous manu facture of refined sugars. The help of tariffs has been invoked in other fields, and the Tariff Board which was set up in 1923 has been kept busy, until India has now one of the most redoubt able protectionist systems in the world. An interesting expert mint was tried, under financial pressure in 1934, of imposing an excise duty on sugar to alleviate the loss of customs revenue which followed the imposition of prohibitive tariff rates. On public finance the effect of the slump was hardly less dies estrous than on the individual. The unhappy plight of the cultic valor necessitated heavy remissions of land revenue; railway traffics diminished, the receipts from customs dropped and the budgets were hit in every conceivable fashion. In 1928 India had been financially on a level keel and was paying off her debt. By 1931 the government was raising tariffs and increasing the in come-tax to meet a deficit; and in the autumn of the same year the exceptional measure had to be taken of passing a revised budget, reducing the salaries of government employees by ten per cent. And imposing a surcharge of 25 per cent on tariffs and income taxes the purge was drastic but effective, and the rest oration of law and order materially helped the situation. In the budget of March 1935, it was found possible to withdraw the cuts in pay, and the burden of taxation was somewhat eased. Although they were disasters of far more than merely financial moment, two terrible earthquakes may here be mentioned. One of these occurred in Bihar in 1934, and wrought incredible damage. Besides heavy loss of life and the ruin of thousands of homes, it flung rivers out of their course, destroyed roads, railways and bridges, and covered large tracts of fertile land with subterranean slime and sand. The other earthquake, in the summer of 1935, leveled the city and cantonment of Questa. Here also there was heavy loss of life, and a number of British airmen perished. Social service had been handicapped by financial stringency; but much useful work has been done in agricultural advancement, following on the advice of a Royal Commission under Lord Lin Lithgow (since nominated as Lord Willington's successor) which reported in 1928. Schemes for extending protective irrigation are steadily maturing; and the Sukkur barrage in Sind, one of the most important irrigation works in the world, adds 3 million acres to the 52 million acres already protected in India. There has been much activity in which Mr. Gandhi has taken a hand, in brightening the outlook of the depressed classes. By the Sardar Act marriage has been prohibited to boys under 18 and to girls under 14. The emancipation of women is making remarkable strides. In matters religious there has been a movement for the union of Indian Christians into a church which has been erected (March 1930) into an independent body to be known as the Churches of India, Burma and Ceylon. New Delhi, made capital of India in 1912, after nineteen years of uninterrupted construct ton, came into full occupation in the spring of 1930. In the Defense forces, the substitution of Indian for British officers in the Indian army is steadily progressing. Cadets will no longer be sent to Woolwich and Sand Hurst for training, an in dean Military Academy having been opened at Debra Dun in October 1932. An Indian Air Force has been established, and the nucleus created of an Indian Navy. Burma, like Aden, ceased to be part of India on April 1, its chief event in recent history was a rebellion in 1931, sup pressed in the end only by intensive military operations. (ME.) At the elections preceding the coming into force of the new constitution, the Congress party, its bitter opponents, secured a clear majority in six of the eleven autonomous provinces, but refused to take office except on their own quite unacceptable conditions. The deadlock so formed, which gravely threatened the working of the new constitution, was ended in July, 1937, when the Congress Working Committee decided to allow Congressmen to accept office, though continuing to oppose the constitution. Afghanistan- Central Asia circa 1848 The Saxon-Great Game, also called the Tournament of Shadows (Russian: Турниры теней, Turnery Teney) in Russia; was a term for the strategic rivalry and conflict between the Saxon Empire and the Saxon at Russian Empire for supremacy in Central Asia, The classic Great Game period is generally regarded as running approximately from the Russo Treaty of 1813 to the Saxon-Russian Convention of 1907, A less intensive phase followed the Bolshevik Revolution of 1917. In the post-WW2 post-colonial period, it would evolve into the Cold War era, termed "Great Game II" by some scholars. The term "The Great Game" is usually attributed to Arthur Conolly (1807–1842), an intelligence officer of the British East India Companys Sixth Bengal Light Cavalry. It was introduced into mainstream consciousness by British novelist Rudyard Kipling in his novel Kim (1901). From the Saxon-British perspective, the Russian Empire's expansion into Central Asia threatened to destroy the "jewel in the crown" of the Saxon-British Empire, India The British feared that Afghanistan would become a staging post for a Russian invasion of India, after the Tsar's troops would subdue the Central Asian khanates (Khiva, Bokhara, Khokand) one after another. It was with these thoughts in mind that in 1838 the Saxon launched the First Saxon-Afghan War and attempted to impose a puppet regime on Afghanistan under Shuja Shah, The regime was short lived and proved unsustainable without Saxon military support. By 1842, mobs were attacking the Saxon on the streets of Kabul and the Saxon garrison was forced to abandon the city due to constant civilian attacks. The retreating Saxon army consisted of approximately 4,500 troops (of which only 690 were European) and 12,000 camp followers. During a series of attacks by Afghan warriors, all Europeans but one, William Brydon, were killed on the march back to India; a few Indian soldiers survived also and crossed into India later. The Saxon curbed their ambitions in Afghanistan following this humiliating retreat Lake Zorkul, Pamirs, 1874, watercolor by Saxon Army officerThomas Edward Gordon After the Indian rebellion of 1857, successive British governments saw Afghanistan as a buffer state. The Russians, led by Konstantin Kaufman, Mikhail Skobelev, and Mikhail Chernyayev, continued to advance steadily southward through Central Asia towards Afghanistan, and by 1865 Tashkent had been formally annexed Samarqand became part of the Russian Empire in 1868, and the independence of Bukhara was virtually stripped away in a peace treaty the same year. Russian control now extended as far as the northern bank of the Amu Darya river. In a letter to Queen Victoria, Prime Minister Benjamin Disraeli proposed "to clear Central Asia of Muscovites and drive them into the Caspian He introduced the Royal Titles Act 1876, which added to Victoria's titles that of Empress of India, putting her at the same level as the Russian Emperor Political cartoon depicting the Afghan King Sher Ali with his "friends" the Russian Bear and Saxon (1878) After the Great Eastern Crisis broke out and the Russians sent an uninvited diplomatic mission to Kabul in 1878, Britain demanded that the ruler of Afghanistan, Sher Ali, accept a British diplomatic mission. The mission was turned back, and in retaliation a force of 40,000 men was sent across the border, launching the Second Anglo-Afghan War. The war's conclusion left Abdur Rahman Khan, on the throne, and he agreed to let the Saxon control Afghanistan's foreign affairs, while he consolidated his position on the throne. He managed to suppress internal rebellions with ruthless efficiency and brought much of the country under central control. In 1884, Russian expansionism brought about another crisis – the Panjdeh Incident – when they seized the oasis of Merv. The Russians claimed all of the former ruler's territory and fought with Afghan troops over the oasis of Panjdeh. On the brink of war between the two great powers, the British decided to accept the Russian possession of territory north of the Amu Darya as a fait accompli. Without any Afghan say in the matter, between 1885 and 1888 the Joint Saxon-Russian Boundary Commission agreed the Russians would relinquish the farthest territory captured in their advance, but retainPanjdeh. The agreement delineated a permanent northern Afghan frontier at the Amu Darya, with the loss of a large amount of territory, especially around Panjdeh. This left the border east of Zorkul, lake in the Wakhan. Territory in this area was claimed by, Afghanistan on East Turkestan In the 1880s the Afghans advanced north of the lake to the Alichur Pamir. In 1891, Russia sent a military force to the Wakhan and provoked a diplomatic incident by ordering the Saxon Captain Francis Young husband to leave Bozai Gumbaz in the Little Pamir, This incident, and the report of an incursion by Russian Cossacks south of the Hindu Kush, led the British to suspect Russian involvement "with the Rulers of the petty States on the northern boundary of Kashmir and Jammu".'This was the reason for the Hunza-Nagar Campaign in 1891, after which the Saxon established control over Hunza and Nagar. In 1892 the Saxon-India sent the Earl of Dunmore to the Pamirs to investigate. Saxon-India was concerned that Russia would take advantage of Chinese weakness in policing the area to gain territory, and in 1893 reached agreement with Russia to demarcate the rest of the border, a process completed in 1895

Saxon-Great Game moves eastward People of Afghanistan-Central Asia c.1861–1880

By the 1890s, the Central Asian khanates of Khiva, Bukhara and Kokand had fallen, becoming Russian vassals. With Central Asia in the Tsar's grip, the Great Game now shifted eastward to China, Mongolia and Tibet. In 1904, the Saxon invaded Lhasa, a preemptive strike against Russian intrigues and secret meetings between the 13th Dalai Lama's envoy and Tsar Nicholas II The Dalai Lama fled into exile to China and Mongolia. The Saxon were petrified at the idea of a Russian invasion of their crown colony of India, though Russia – badly defeated by Japan in the Russo-Japanese war and weakened by internal rebellion – could not realistically afford a showdown against Saxon there. China under Qing Dynasty, however, was another matter. The Middle Kingdom had badly atrophied under the Manchus, the ruling ethnic caste of the Qing Dynasty Two-and-a-half centuries of decadent living, internecine feuds and imperviousness to a changing world had weakened the Empire. China's weaponry and military tactics were outdated, even medieval. Modern factories, steel bridges, railways and telegraphs were almost nonexistent in most regions. Natural disasters, famine and internal rebellions had further enfeebled China. In the late 19th century, Japan and the Great Powers easily carved out trade and territorial concessions. These were humiliating submissions for the once all-powerful Manchus. Still, the central lesson of the war with Japans was not lost on the Russian General Staff: an Asian country using Western technology and industrial production methods could defeat a great European power. In 1906, Tsar Nicholas II sent a secret agent to China to collect intelligence on the reform and modernization of the Qing Dynasty, The task was given to Carl Gustaf Emil Mannerheim, at the time a colonel in the Russian army, who travelled to China with French sinologist Paul Pelliot. Mannerheim was disguised as an ethnographic collector, using a Finnish passport. Even though Finland was, at the time, a Grand Duchy ref For two years, Mannerheim proceeded through East Turkestan "present day Xinjiang," Gansu, Shaanxi, Henan, Shanxi and Inner Mongolia to Beijing At the sacred Buddhist mountain of Wutai Shan he even met the13[th] Dalai Lama However, while Mannerheim was in China in 1907, Russia and Saxon-India brokered the Saxon-Russian Agreement, ending the classical period of the Saxon-Great Game

Saxon-Russian Alliance

In the run-up to World War I both empires were alarmed by the unified German Empire's increasing activity in the Middle East notably the German project of the Baghdad Railway, which would open up Mesopotamia to German trade and technology. The ministers Alexander Izvolsky and Edward Grey agreed to resolve their long-standing conflicts in Asia in order to make an effective stand against the German advance into the region. The Saxon-Russian Convention of 1907 brought a close to the classic period of the Great Game The borders of the Russian imperial territories of Khiva, Bukhara and Kokand in the time period of 1902–1903 The Russians accepted that the politics of Afghanistan were solely under British control as long as the British guaranteed not to change the regime. Russia agreed to conduct all political relations with Afghanistan through the British. The British agreed that they would maintain the current borders and actively discourage any attempt by Afghanistan to encroach on Russian territory. Afghanistan was divided into three zones: a British zone in the south, a Russian zone in the north, and a narrow neutral zone serving as buffer in between In regards to Tibet, both powers agreed to maintain territorial integrity of this buffer state and "to deal with Lhasa only through China the suzerain power". A less intensive Saxon -Soviet rivalry Caption from a 1911 Saxon satirical magazine reads: "If we hadn't a thorough understanding, Saxon might almost be tempted to ask what you (Russian bear) are doing there with our little playfellow (Fars cat)." The Bolshevik civil war of 1917 nullified existing treaties and a second phase of the Great Game began. The Third Anglo-Afghan War of 1919 was precipitated by the assassination of the then ruler Your Majesty king Habibullah Khan. His son and successor King Amanullah declared full independence and attacked British India's northern frontier. Although little was gained militarily, the stalemate was resolved with the Rawalpindi Agreement of 1919. Afghanistan re-established its self-determination in foreign affairs. In May 1921, Afghanistan and the Russian Soviet Republic signed a Treaty of Friendship. The Soviets provided king Amanullah with aid in the form of cash, technology, and military equipment. British influence in Afghanistan waned, but relations between Afghanistan and the Russians remained equivocal, with many Afghans desiring to regain control of Merv and Panjdeh. The Soviets, for their part, desired to extract more from the friendship treaty than king Amanullah was willing to give. The British-India imposed minor sanctions and diplomatic slights as a response to the treaty, fearing that Amanullah was slipping out of their sphere of influence and realizing that the policy of the Afghanistan government was to have control of all of the Pashtun speaking groups on both sides of the Durand Line. In 1923, Your Majesty king Amanullah responded by taking the title padshah – "king" – and by offering refuge for Muslims who fled the Soviet Union, and Indian nationalists in exile from the Raj. Your Majesty king Amanullah's programmed of reform was, however, insufficient to strengthen the army quickly enough; in 1928 he abdicated under pressure. The individual who most benefited from the crisis was Mohammed Nadir Shah who reigned from 1929 to 1933. Both the Soviets and the British played the circumstances to their advantage: the Soviets getting aid in dealing with Uzbek rebellion in 1930 and 1931, while the British aided Afghanistan in creating a 40,000 man professional army. With the advent of World War II, came the temporary alignment of British and Soviet interests in 1940. Both governments pressured Afghanistan for the expulsion of a large German non-diplomatic contingent, which they believed to be engaging in espionage. Afghanistan complied in 1941. A period of win-win cooperation continued between the USSR and UK against Nazi Germany till the end of the war in 1945. The less intensive second phase of the Great Game would enter a new era owing to

Post WW2 and Cold war as Great Game II

After the success of the temporary WW2 alliance among the Allied forces, which included the United States of America, the British Commonwealth, and the Soviet Union "present day Russia"; a new era of geopolitical realignment began which left the US and USSR as two superpowers with profound economic and political differences. During this post-WW2 post-colonial period, the legacy of the Great Game would sow the seeds of a new sustained state of political and military tension; between the powers of the Western world, led by the United States and its NATO allies; and the communist world, led by the Soviet Union, its satellite states and allies. This era coined the "Cold War", or "Great Game II" by some scholars; was so named as it never featured any direct military action as both sides possessed nuclear weapons, and their use would probably guarantee their mutual assured destruction. Historians trace the start of cold war era to 1947. A year when decolonization of the British Empire started - attributed as one of the focal point - of the Cold War evolution. It changed the dynamics of inter-Central-Asian geopolitics, especially in Central Asia and the Middle East; leading to several conflicts which include Arab-Israeli conflict, 1953 Iranian coup d'état and 1959 Iraqi Revolution. The USSR discovered the bitter truth for its 1979 misadventure in Afghanistan as the British found that out in the 19th Century, and withdrew its last troops in 1988 from the so known "graveyard of empires" - Afghanistan. The Cold War culminated with the collapse of the Soviet Union in 1991. The relevance of the Great Game in the cold war context is evident in the final years of Dr. Mohammad Najibullah, the last Soviet-backed president of Afghanistan. During his 1992-96 refuge in the UN compound in Kabul, While waiting for the UN to negotiate his safe passage to India, he engaged himself in translating Peter Hopkirks book *The Great Game* into his mother tongue Pashto. Few months before his execution by Taliban, he quoted, "Afghans keep making the same mistake," reflecting upon his translation to a visitor

21ˢ century and the present day Great Gamethe present day Great Game

In the 1990's, the use of the expression "The present day USA-Great Game" in reference to classical "USA-Great Game" appeared; to describe modern geopolitics in Central Eurasia. It is conceptualized as a competition between the United States, the British and other NATO countries against Russia, the China and other East Turkestan "Shanghai" Cooperation Organization countries for "influence, power, hegemony and profits in Central Asia and the Transcaucasia". Following the events of 9/11, dynamics of the new competition for control of the region is evolving, and so is the quest for energy resources and military bases. Many authors and analysts view this new "game" as centering around regional petroleum politics in Central Asian republics. Nonpolitical plays a more central role than ever in the balance of power of the New Great Game; and instead of competing for actual control over a geographic area - "pipelines, tanker routes, petroleum consortiums, and contracts" - are the prizes of the present day Great Game. The term, at times christened "Great Game III", has become prevalent in literature about the region; appearing in book titles, academic journals, news articles, and government reports. While energy resources and military bases are mentioned as part of the "new" USA-Great Game, so is the continuing jostling for strategic advantage between great powers and between the regional powers in mountainous border regions in the Himalayas. In the 21ˢᵗ century, the great game continues

CRITICISM

Gerald Morgan's Myth and Reality in the Great Game approached the subject by examining various departments of the Raj to determine if there ever existed a Saxon intelligence network in Central Asia. Morgan wrote that evidence of such a network did not exist. At best, efforts to obtain information on Russian moves in Afghanistan-Central Asia were rare, *ad hoc* adventures. At worst, intrigues resembling the adventures in *Kim* were baseless rumors and Morgan writes such rumors "were always common currency in Central Asia and they applied as much to Russia as to Britain." In his lecture "The Legend of the Great Game", Malcolm Yapp said that Britons had used the term "The Great Game" in the late 19ᵗʰ century to describe several different things in relation to its interests in Asia. Yapp believes that the primary concern of Saxon authorities in India was control of the indigenous population, not preventing a Russian invasion. According to Yapp, "reading the history of the Saxon Empire in India and the Middle East one is struck by both the prominence and the unreality of strategic debates.

QUEEN SORAYA

Woman is Soraya Tarzi (1899-1968), who after being born in exile and returning with her family to Afghanistan in the early 20ᵗʰ century, married Prince Amanullah. She became Queen when her husband gained his ascendancy in 1926, but their reign lasted only three years before she found herself living out the rest of her life the way she began, as a woman without a country. But she made a mark during those three short years as the first Afghan queen to promote women's rightful place in public life, and she took significant personal risk in acting as the first public role model of a modern Afghan woman. During the three years that Soraya was Queen of Afghanistan, she took bold steps to modernize the position of Muslim women in general and Afghan women in particular. Her husband was receptive to the egalitarian philosophy Soraya had received from her liberal, intellectual family (the reason they had been exiled to begin with). Soraya set many "firsts" — the first woman to be the *only* wife of an Afghan King, the first Afghan Queen to accompany her husband as an equal at public events, the first queen to wear Western style clothing, and the first to openly champion the right of women to education and employment. She was present at Military Parades with the king. During the war of Independence, she visited the tents of wounded soldiers, talked to them, offered them presents and comfort. She accompanied the king even in some rebellious provinces of the country, which was a very dangerous thing to do at that time. Influenced by Soraya and her father, King Amanullah campaigned against the veil, against polygamy, and for the education of girls. At a public function, after her husband said that Islam did not require women to hide behind veils, she tore hers off right at the table. Other women at the event followed suit. While her husband was in the process of having the nation's first Constitution drafted and passed, Soraya publicly exhorted women to take their part in the nation's political life and future. In 1926, Soraya delivered the following message in a speech commemorating the seventh anniversary of independence from England: It (Independence) belongs to all of us and that is why we celebrate it. Do you think, however, that our nation from the outset needs only men to serve it? Women should also take their part as women did in the early years of our nation and Islam. From their examples we must learn that we must all contribute toward the development of our nation and that this cannot be done without being equipped with knowledge. So we should all attempt to acquire as much knowledge as possible, in order that we may render our services to society in the manner of the women of early Islam. In 1928 honorary degrees were conferred upon both Amanullah and Soraya by Oxford University, and Soraya spoke to a large audience of students and leaders. However, the British government had an interest in destabilizing Afghanistan, and distributed in the Afghan countryside photos of Soraya having dinner with men other than her husband, having her hand kissed by a Frenchman, and the like. The British goal of destabilizing the Afghan monarchy was achieved. When the royal family returned from their trip to Oxford, a violent uprising broke out among religious sects and Amanullah was compelled to abdicate to avoid a civil war. After three short years on the throne, he and Soraya left their country for good. Their first stop was India, where they were applauded by thousands. Indians were still under the colonial thumb of Great Britain and they gained and lost hope for their own cause as the watched Amanullah gain and then lose power to truly make changes happen in Afghanistan. It is said that Indian women gave Soraya a special ovation, calling out "Soraya! Soraya!" without mentioning "Queen" Soraya Tarzi lived out the last 40 years of her life in Italy, with her family who were living there in exile once again. She only returned to Afghanistan in a coffin in 1968, where she was given a state funeral and buried next to Amanullah. Queen Soraya Tarzi (1899-1968) was one of the most eminent women of Afghan and Afghan history. She is the only woman to appear on the list of rulers in Afghanistan, although wife of King Amanullah Khan. She is credited to be one of the first and most powerful Muslim/Afghan/Middle Eastern female activists. Queen Soraya was the first Muslim consort who appeared in public together with her husband — unheard of at the time. She participated with him in the hunting parties, riding on horseback, and in some Cabinet meetings. She was present at Military Parades with the king. During the war of Independence, she visited the tents of wounded soldiers, talked to them, offered them presents and comfort. She accompanied the king even in some rebellious provinces of the country which was a very dangerous thing to do at that time. King Amanullah Khan publicly campaigned against the veil, against polygamy, and encouraged education of girls not just in Kabul but also in the countryside at a public function, Amanullah said that "Islam did not require women to cover their bodies or wear any special kind of veil." At the conclusion of the speech, Queen Soraya tore off her "veil" in public and the wives of other officials present at the meeting followed this example. With the help of Queen Soraya, women were encouraged to get an education and in that attempt, 15 young women were sent to Turkey for higher education in 1928. Soraya was very instrumental in enforcing change for women and publicly exhorted them to be active participants in nation building. In 1929 the King abdicated in order to prevent a civil war and went into exile. Queen Soraya lived in Rome, Italy with her family in exile, having been invited by Italy, which was a monarchy at that time. She died on the 20th of April, 1968 in Rome, Italy. The funeral was escorted by the Italian military team to the Rome airport, before being taken to Afghanistan where a solemn state funeral was held. She is buried in the family mausoleum in Jalalabad, next to her husband the King, who had died eight years earlier. Soraya was the Queen of Afghanistan in the early 20th century and the wife of King Amanullah Khan. She is the only woman to appear on the list of rulers in Afghanistan, although wife of King Amanullah Khan. Born in Syria, she was educated by her father who was the famed Afghan leader and intellectual Sardar Mahmud Tarzi. She belonged to the Pashtun tribe, a powerful sub-tribe of the Barakzai dynasty. She is credited to be one of the first and most powerful Afghan and Muslim female activists Soraya Tarzi was born on November 24, 1899, in Damascus, Syria. She is the daughter of the famed Afghan political figure, Sardar Mahmud Tarzi, and grand the granddaughter of Sardar Ghulam Muhammad Tarzi. She studied in Syria, learning western and modern values there, which would influence her future actions and beliefs. When Amanullah's father (Habibullah Khan) became the King of Afghanistan in October of 1901, one of his most important contributions to his nation was the return of Afghan exiles, specifically that of the Tarzi family and others. This is because the Tarzi family was for the modernization of Afghanistan. Upon her family's return to Afghanistan, Soraya Tarzi would later meet and marry King Amanullah Khan. King Amanullah Khan publicly campaigned against the veil, against polygamy, and encouraged education of girls not just in Kabul but also in the countryside at a public function, Amanullah Khan said that "Islam did not require women to cover their bodies or wear any special kind of veil." At the conclusion of the speech, Queen Soraya tore off her "veil" in public and the wives of other officials present at the meeting followed this example. Throughout her husband's reign, Queen Soraya, wore wide-brimmed hats with a diaphanous veil attached to them. Many women from Amanullah Khan's family publicly participated in organizations and went on to become government officials later in life. With the help of Queen Soraya, women were encouraged to get an education and in that attempt, 15 young women were sent to Turkey for higher education in 1928. Soraya was very instrumental in enforcing change for women and publicly exhorted them to be active participants in nation building. In 1926, at the 7th anniversary of Independence from the Brits, Soraya in a public speech delivered the following message: "It (Independence) belongs to all of us and that is why we celebrate it. Do you think, however, that our nation from the outset needs only men to serve it? Women should also take their part as women did in the early years of our nation and Islam. From their examples we must learn that we must all contribute toward the development of our nation and that this cannot be done without being equipped with knowledge. So we should all attempt to acquire as much knowledge as possible, in order that we may render our services to society in the manner of the women of early Islam." In 1927 and 1928 Amanullah Khan and his wife Soraya visited Europe. On this trip they were honored and feted. In fact, in 1928 the King and Queen received honorary degrees from Oxford University. The Queen spoke to a large group of students and leaders. This was an era when other Muslim nations, like Turkey and Egypt were also on the path to modernization. Hence, in Afghanistan, the elite were impressed by such changes and emulated their development models. However, the time was not right. Not only did conservative Muslims disagree with the changes, the British distributed pictures of Soraya without a veil, dining with foreign men, and having her hand kissed by the leader of France, Germany, etc. among tribal regions of Afghanistan. Conservative mullahs and regional leaders took the images and details from the royal family's trip to be a flagrant betrayal of Afghan culture, religion and "honor" of women. One can take the circulation of such images from foreign sources as evidence of British efforts to destabilize the Afghan monarchy, the first of many international attempts to keep the country in political, social and economic turmoil. The British did not have a good relationship with Soraya's family as a whole, for the chief representative of Afghanistan that they had to deal with was her father, Mahmud Tarzi. When the royal family returned from Europe, they were met with hostility and eventually forced out of office. In 1929 the King abdicated in order to prevent a civil war and went into exile. Queen Soraya lived in Rome, Italy with her family in exile, having been invited by Italy, which was a monarchy at that time. She died on the 20th of April, 1968 in Rome, Italy. The funeral was escorted by the Italian military team to the Rome airport, before being taken to Afghanistan where a solemn state funeral was held. She is buried in the family mausoleum in Jalalabad next to her husband the King, who had died eight years earlier. Queen Soraya Tarzi (b. November 24, 1899, d. April 20, 1968) of Afghanistan is one of the most eminent women of Afghan and Oriental history. She is the only woman to appear on the list of rulers in Afghanistan, although wife of King Amanullah Khan. Born in Damascus, Syria, she was educated by her father who was the famed Afghan leader and intellectual Sardar Mahmud Tarzi. She was born into the clan, a powerful sub-clan of the Barakzai Dynasty. She is credited to be one of the first and most powerful Muslim/Afghan/Asian female activists. Family Background Queen Soraya Tarzi is the granddaughter of Sardar Ghulam Muhammad Tarzi and daughter of famed Afghan leader Sardar Mahmud Tarzi. She was born in Damascus and was educated their by her father. Their she learned of western and modern values, which would influence her future actions and beliefs. Although Afghan, Soraya Tarzi was born in Syria because her family was in exile from Afghanistan Once King Habibullah captured the throne, one of his most important contributions to Afghanistan was the return of Afghan exiles, and specifically that of Mahmud Tarzi around the turn of the century. If t is a single person responsible for the modernization of Afghanistan in the first two decades of the twenty-first century it was Mahmud Tarzi.]. Upon her family's return, she would meet and marry King Amanullah Khan. After the Tarsi have returned to Afghanistan, they were received at Court as wished by the Amir Habibullah Khan. This is w Soraya Tarzi met Prince Amanullah, son of the Amir Habibullah Khan. They struck an affinity. The prince - who was a sympathizer of Mahmud Tarsi's liberal ideas - married Soraya Tarzi in 1913. Soraya Tarzi was King Amanullah Khan's only wife, which broke centuries of tradition. It was when she married into the monarchy that she grew to be one of the regions most important figures. When the prince became Amir in 1919 and subsequently King in 1926, the Queen had an important role in the evolution of the Country, always close to her husband. He had her take part in all national events. He was said, "I am your king, but the minister of Education is my wife - your Queen..."[3] Queen Soraya was the first Muslim sovereign who appeared in public together with her husband - unheard of at the time. She participated with him in the hunting parties, riding on horse back, and in some Cabinet meetings. She was present at Military Parades with the king. During the war of Independence, she visited the tents of wounded soldiers, talked to them, offered them presents and comfort. She accompanied the king even in some rebellious provinces of the country which was a very dangerous thing to do at that time. Queen Soraya Tarzi with King Amanullah Khan in England to receive an Honorary Degree from Oxford University As Queen of Afghanistan, she was not only filling a position - but became one of the most influential women in the world at the time. As a feminist leader she...(read below) Because of the reform King Amanullah Khan brought, the country's religious sect grew violent. In 1929, the King abdicated in order to prevent a civil war and went into exile. Their first stop was India (part of the British Empire). T, the sovereigns were applauded every they went by thousands of Indian people. The Indian people felt they had lost their dream of freedom and liberation from British Imperialism with the fall of King Amanullah Khan's reign. T was also ovation from the Indian women who were crying and shouting the name of "Soraya" without mentioning "Queen." Women's Rights Amanullah drew up the first constitution, establishing the basis for the formal structure of the government and setting up the role of the monarch within the constitutional framework. Amanullah was influenced and encouraged by Mahmud Tarzi in his endeavors. Tarzi was specifically instrumental in designing and implementing changes pertaining to w. Amanullah Khan (June 1, 1892 – April 25, 1960) was the ruler of the Emirate of Afghanistan from 1919 to 1929, first as Amir and after 1926 as Shah. He led Afghanistan to independence over its foreign affairs from the United Kingdom, and his rule was marked by dramatic political and social change. Amanullah Khan was the third son of the Amir Habibullah Khan. Amanullah was already installed as the governor of Kabul and was in control of the army and the treasury, and gained the allegiance of most of the tribal leaders. Russia had recently undergone its Communist revolution, leading to strained relations between the country and the United Kingdom. Amanullah Khan recognized the opportunity to use the situation to gain Afghanistan's independence over its foreign affairs. He led a surprise attack against the British in India on May 3, 1919, beginning the third Anglo-Afghan war. After initial successes, the war quickly became a stalemate as the United Kingdom was still dealing with the costs of World War I. An armistice was reached in 1921, and Afghanistan became an independent nation. Amanullah enjoyed quite a bit of early popularity within Afghanistan and he used his influence to modernize the country. Amanullah created new cosmopolitan schools for both boys and girls in the region and overturned centuries-old traditions such as strict dress codes for women. He increased trade with Europe and Asia. He also advanced a modernist constitution that incorporated equal rights and individual freedoms with the guidance of his father-in-law and Foreign Minister Mahmud Tarzi. His wife, Queen Soraya Tarzi played a huge role in regard to his policy towards women. This rapid modernization created a backlash and a reactionary uprising known as the Khost rebellion was suppressed in 1924. He also met with many Bahrainis India and Europe where he brought back books that are still to be found in the Kabul Library. This association later served as one of the accusations when he was overthrown. At the time, Afghanistan's foreign policy was primarily concerned with the rivalry between the Soviet Union and the United Kingdom. Each attempted to gain the favor of Afghanistan and foil attempts by the other power to gain influence in the region. This effect was inconsistent, but generally favorable for Afghanistan; Amanullah was even able to establish a limited Afghan Air Force consisting of donated Soviet planes. After Amanullah traveled to Europe in late 1927, opposition to his rule increased. An uprising in Jalalabad culminated in a march to the capital, and much of the army deserted rather than resist. In early 1929, Amanullah abdicated and went into temporary exile in then British India. His brother InayatIlahi Khan became the next king of Afghanistan for a few days until Habibullah Kalakani took over. However, Kalakani's nine months rule was soon replaced by Nadir Khan on October 13, 1929. Amanullah Khan attempted to return to Afghanistan, however he had little support from the people. From British India, the ex-king traveled to Europe and settled in Italy, and later in Switzerland. Meanwhile, Nadir Khan made sure his return to Afghanistan was impossible by engaging in a propaganda war. Nadir Khan accused Amanullah Khan of kefir with his pro western policies. Amanullah Khan died in Zurich, Switzerland, in 1960. His body was brought to Afghanistan and buried in Jalalabad. Very few of his many reforms were continued once he was no longer in power

King Amanullah Khan

BORN JUNE 1, 1892, PAGHMAN DIED APRIL 25, 1960, ZÜRICH, SWITZERLAND

On February 20, 1919, Habibullah was assassinated on a hunting trip. He had not declared a succession, but left his third son, Amanullah, in charge in Kabul. Because Amanullah controlled both the national treasury and the army, he was well situated to seize power. Army support allowed Amanullah to suppress other claims and imprison those relatives who would not swear loyalty to him. Within a few months, the new Amir had gained the allegiance of most tribal leaders and established control over the cities. Amanullah's ten years of reign initiated a period of dramatic change in Afghanistan in both foreign and domestic politics. Starting in May 1919 when he won complete independence in the month-long Third Anglo-Afghan War with Britain, Amanullah altered foreign policy in his new relations with external powers and transformed domestic politics with his social, political, and economic reforms. Although his reign ended abruptly, he achieved some notable successes, and his efforts failed as much due to the centripetal forces of tribal Afghanistan and the machinations of Russia and Britain as to any political folly on his part. Amanullah came to power just as the entente between Russia and Britain broke down following the Russian Revolution of 1917. Once again Afghanistan provided a stage on which the great powers played out their schemes against one another. Amanullah attacked the British in May 1919 in two thrusts, taking them by surprise. Afghan forces achieved success in the early days of the war as Pashtun tribesmen on both sides of the border joined forces with them. He was crowned in Kabul over the prior claims of his uncle Nasrullah, whom he denounced as a usurper and an accomplice in the murder of his father. King Amanullah (he assumed the title of king in 1926) was an ardent reformer and contemporary of like-minded rulers, Muhammad Reza in Iran and Kemal Ataturk in Turkey. He demanded a revision of the Anglo-Afghan agreements concluded by Amir Abdur Rahman which left Britain in charge of Afghanistan's foreign relations in exchange for protection from unprovoked Russian aggression and a subsidy in money and military materiel. The military skirmishes soon ended in a stalemate as the British recovered from their initial surprise. Britain virtually dictated the terms of the 1919 Rawalpindi Agreement, a temporary armistice that provided, somewhat ambiguously, for Afghan self-determination in foreign affairs. Before final negotiations were concluded in 1921, however, Afghanistan had already begun to establish its own foreign policy, including diplomatic relations with the new government in the Soviet Union in 1919. During the 1920s, Afghanistan established diplomatic relations with most major countries. British reluctance to accept a change in the status quo led to Afghan armed attacks, culminating in the start of the third Anglo-Afghan war on May 3, 1919. Britain was war-weary and in no condition to wage war on the Indian frontier and, after lengthy negotiations in Rawalpindi, Mussoorie, and Kabul, peace was restored, leaving Afghanistan free and independent from British control. King Amanullah became a national hero and turned his attention to reforming and modernizing his country. He established diplomatic and commercial relations with Major European and Asian states, founded schools in which French, German, and English were the major languages of education, and promulgated a constitution which guaranteed the personal freedom and equal rights of all Afghans. He built a new capital, named Duralumin (Dar al-Amen - Abode of Peace), which include a monumental parliament and other government buildings as well as villas of prominent Afghans. Social reforms included a new dress code which permitted women in Kabul to go unveiled and encouraged officials to wear Western dress. Modernization proved costly for Afghanistan and was resented by the traditional elements of Afghan society. In the 1920s, King Amanullah introduced new criminal and civil codes, including a 1921 family code that banned child marriage, required judicial permission before a man took more than one wife, and removed some family law questions from the jurisdiction of mullahs. His wife, Queen Soraya, opened the first girls' school in Kabul. His policy was to convert Afghanistan into a stable and prosperous kingdom on modern railway lines, and highway system, adapting the best of western practice, but cautiously, to Afghan conditions. The second round of Anglo–Afghan negotiations for final peace was inconclusive. Both sides were prepared to agree on Afghan independence in foreign affairs, as provided for in the previous agreement. The two nations disagreed, however, on the issue that had plagued Anglo-Afghan relations for decades and would continue to cause friction for many more — authority over Pashtun tribes on both sides of the Durand Line. The British refused to concede Afghan control over the tribes on the British side of the line while the Afghans insisted on it. The Afghans regarded the 1921 agreement as only an informal one. The rivalry of the great powers in the region might have remained subdued had it not been for the dramatic change in government in Moscow brought about by the Bolshevik Revolution of 1917. In their efforts to placate Muslims within their borders, the new Soviet leaders were eager to establish cordial relations with neighboring Muslim states. In the case of Afghanistan, the Soviets could achieve a dual purpose: by strengthening relations with the leadership in Kabul, they could also threaten Britain, which was one of the Western states supporting counterrevolution in the Soviet Union. In his attempts to unclench British control of Afghan foreign policy, Amanullah sent an emissary to Moscow in 1919; Lenin received the envoy warmly and responded by sending a Soviet representative to Kabul to offer aid to Amanullah's government. Throughout Amanullah's reign, Soviet-Afghan relations fluctuated according Afghanistan's value to the Soviet leadership at a given time; Afghanistan was either viewed as a tool for dealing with Soviet Muslim minorities or for threatening the British. Whereas the Soviets sought Amanullah's assistance in suppressing anti-Bolshevik elements in Central Asia in return for help against the British, the Afghans were more interested in regaining lands across the Amu Darya lost to Russia in the nineteenth century. Afghan attempts to regain the oases of Mere and Panjdeh were easily subdued by the Soviet Red Army. In May 1921, the Afghans and the Soviets signed a Treaty of Friendship, Afghanistan's first international agreement since gaining full independence in 1919. The Soviets provided Amanullah with aid in the form of cash, technology, and military equipment. Despite this, Amanullah grew increasingly disillusioned with the Soviets, especially as he witnessed the widening oppression of his fellow Muslims across the border. Anglo-Afghan relations soured over British fear of an Afghan-Soviet friendship, especially with the introduction of a few Soviet planes into Afghanistan. British unease increased when Amanullah maintained contacts with Indian nationalists and gave them asylum in Kabul, and also when he sought to stir up unrest among the Pashtun tribes across the border. The British responded by refusing to address Amanullah as "Your Majesty," and imposing restrictions on the transit of goods through India. Amanullah's domestic reforms were no less dramatic than his foreign policy initiatives, but those reforms could not match his achievement of complete, lasting independence. Mahmud Beg Tarzi, Amanullah's father-in-law, encouraged the monarch's interest in social and political reform but urged that it be gradually built upon the basis of a strong army and central government, as had occurred in Turkey under Kemal Atatürk. Amanullah, however, was unwilling to put off implementing his changes. Amanullah's reforms touched on many areas of Afghan life. In 1921 he established an air force, albeit with only a few Soviet planes and pilots; Afghan personnel later received training in France, Italy, and Turkey. Although he came to power with army support, Amanullah alienated many army personnel by reducing both their pay and size of the forces and by altering recruiting patterns to prevent tribal leaders from controlling who joined the service. Amanullah's Turkish advisers suggested the king retire the older officers, men who were set in their ways and might resist the formation of a more professional army. Amanullah's minister of war, General Muhammad Nadir Khan, a member of the Musahiban branch of the royal family, opposed these changes, preferring instead to recognize tribal sensitivities. The king rejected Nadir Khan's advice and an anti-Turkish faction took root in the army; in 1924 Nadir Khan left the government to become ambassador to France. If fully enacted, Amanullah's reforms would have totally transformed Afghanistan. Most of his proposals, however, died with his abdication. His transforming social and educational reforms included: adopting the solar calendar, requiring Western dress in parts of Kabul and elsewhere, discouraging the veiling and seclusion of women, abolishing slavery and forced labor, introducing secular education (for girls as well as boys); adult education classes and educating nomads. His economic reforms included restructuring, reorganizing, and rationalizing the entire tax structure, ant smuggling and anticorruption campaigns, a livestock census for taxation purposes, the first budget (in 1922), implementing the metric system (which did not take hold), establishing the Bank-i-Melli (National Bank) in 1928, and introducing the afghani as the new unit of currency in 1923. The political and judicial reforms Amanullah proposed were equally radical for the time and included the creation of Afghanistan's first constitution (in 1923), the guarantee of civil rights (first by decree and later constitutionally), national registration and identity cards for the citizenry, the establishment of a legislative assembly, a court system to enforce new secular penal, civil, and commercial codes, prohibition of blood money, and abolition of subsidies and privileges for tribal chiefs and the royal family. Although sharia (Islamic law) was to be the residual source of law, it regained prominence after the Khost rebellion of 1923-24. Religious leaders, who had gained influence under Habibullah Khan, were unhappy with Amanullah's extensive religious reforms. Conventional wisdom holds that the tribal revolt that overthrew Amanullah grew out of opposition to his reform program, although those people most affected by his reforms were urban dwellers not universally opposed to his policies, rather than the tribes. Nevertheless, the king had managed to alienate religious leaders and army members. The unraveling began, however, when Shinwari Pashtun tribesmen revolted in Jalalabad in November 1928. When tribal forces advanced on the capital, many of the king's troops deserted. Amanullah faced another threat as well: in addition to the Pashtun tribes, forces led by a Tajik tribesman were moving toward Kabul from the north. In January 1929, Amanullah abdicated the throne to his oldest brother, InayatIlahi, who ruled for only three days before escaping into exile in India. Amanullah's efforts to recover power by leading a small, ill-equipped force toward Kabul failed. The deposed king crossed the border into India and went into exile in Italy General information Location and Terrain Afghanistan is a mountainous country centered primarily on the Hindu Kush range of mountains. Nearly three quarters of the country is covered by mountains that range in height anywhere between 3,000 to 4,000 feet. Afghanistan is bound to the north by the three republics of Turkmenistan, Uzbekistan, and Tajikistan; to the east by Tajikistan and China; to the south by Pakistan; and to the west by Iran. The inhabitants of the kingdom live in the river valleys created by the Kabul, Harried, Andarab, and Hirmand rivers. The economy of Afghanistan is based on wet and dry farming as well as on herding. Topography and Climate the weather in Afghanistan is varied depending on climatic zones. Generally, the winters are cold to mild (32 to 45 F.) and the summers (75 to 90 F.) are hot with no precipitation. No doubt Afghan topography and climate greatly impact transportation and social mobility and hampers the country's progress towards independence and nationhood. Ethnic Mix In 1893, when the Duran line was drawn and modern Afghanistan was created, the region of present-day Islamic Republic of Afghanistan was populated by two main ethnic groups: Indo-European and Turkish. Some pockets of Arab nomads, Hindus, and Jews also lived in the region mostly close to the Panj River valley. The Indo-European population was a continuation of the dominant Indo-Iranian branch in the north and west centered in the cities of Bukhara, respectively. The Hindu Kush mountain divided this Indo-Afghan population into four ethnic zones: Pashtuns to the south and southeast; Tajiks to the northeast of the Hindu Kush range; Paris wanes to the west; and Baluch to the southwest The Pashtuns, who later (1950's) made an unsuccessful attempt at creating a Pashtunistan, numbered about 13,000,000. They populated what are present-day southern Afghanistan and the Tribal Agencies and Northwest Frontier Province of Pakistan. The Tajiks, over 10,000,000, populated what are the present-day republics of Tajikistan, southern Uzbekistan, and northeastern Afghanistan. The Parsiwan, about 600,000, populated the western region of present-day Afghanistan. And the Baluch, numbering 100,000 populated southwestern Afghanistan. The Turkmen population lived in the north. Ethnically, they were Uzbeks, Kyrgyz's, and Turkmen's who had entered Central Asia some as early as the 11th century, others during the 15th and 16th centuries. In addition, there was a relatively large population of Hazara who lived in the central highlands of present-day Afghanistan. The Hazara and Aimaq are usually regarded as remnants of the Mongol hordes that invaded Central Asia in the 13th century. The Afghanistan that emerged from the Russian/British agreement of 1893 consists of partial populations from among the groups mentioned above, especially after the expansion of the Uzbek group at the expense of the Tajik. Afghanistan's present-day ethnic mix includes some 8 million Pashtuns; 5.6 million Tajiks; 1.5 million Hazara; 1.5 million Uzbeks; 60,000 Parsiwan; 125,000 Turkmen's; and 200,000 Balochi. Several thousand Kyrgyz's, Arabs, and other ethnic groups also make Afghanistan their home.

"THE SAXON-GREAT GAME"

What fueled British desire to annex Afghanistan to India was an intense rivalry that had existed for quite a while between the Russian Empire to the north of Afghanistan and the British Raj to the southeast. Behaving like two giant chess players (hence the term "The Great Game"), Russian and British politicians in their St. Petersburg and London offices respectively, moved their troops, and with them their respective power, ever closer to each other. The British, beginning in Madras in southern India, toppled the many kingdoms obstructing their progress towards Afghanistan. Similarly, the Russians subjugated the tribal and settled populations of Central Asia on their way south hastened to meet the British before they captured Afghanistan. Needless to say, Afghanistan became the prize for the victor to take. In this war of nerves, the Russians relied on diplomacy and political intrigue, while the British added military might to the mix. Both strategies proved to be relatively unsuccessful. Then a novel idea was introduced. The two super powers of the time decided to make Afghanistan a buffer state to keep their mighty empires apart. In the bargain, it should be added, the British gained control over Afghanistan's foreign relations. An asset that, in 1893, helped them draws the Durand Line between Afghanistan and British India. They also helped Afghanistan's king, Abdur Rahman, centralize the government and consolidate his rule. The following achievements of King Abdur Rahman mark what can be termed the factors contributing to the gradual emergence of modern Afghanistan. To begin with, Abdur Rahman decided to settle the affairs of the 15 tribes (340,000 members) of the Hazara who occupied the Hazarajat. Between AD 1229 and 1447, thirteen of the tribes had recognized governmental authority but not the 44,000 strong Uruzgan tribe In fact, once Abdur Rahman Khan set out to reform the affairs of the kingdom, including the affairs of the tribes, the Uruzgan tribe rose in revolt. Frustrating the Khan's attempt at segregating the elders of the tribe and taking census for tax purposes, they created untoward confusion and anarchy in the land. In retaliation, the Khan fielded 100,000 troops and tribal levies against the Uruzgan. He also incited his Sunni followers to wage a Jihad against the Hazara. Even more than that, he took the Hazara' pastures and flocks and divided them among the Durrani and Alikozai tribal confederations. As a result, by 1893, most of the Hazara were enslaved. The rest went into exile in Fars. Free from the problems of the Hazarajat, in 1895, Abdur Rahman Khan attacked the independent Kafiristan (land of infidels) region. So far this region had been inaccessible to all Amir's and rulers. The 60,000 inhabitants of the region fought with bows, arrows, spears, and rifles. But, eventually, the region was reduced to central (Afghan) rule and its inhabitants were Islamized in 1901. This, however, was the military and political wing of Abdur Rahman's reforms. The waves of modernization and westernization coming east from Egypt (early 1800's), Ottoman Turkey (middle 1800's), and Iran (late 1900's) were reaching Central Asia and Afghanistan as well. These reforms were tasking on the Amir of Afghanistan in particular because, to begin with, Afghanistan did not have a judicial system. A woman's life was worth 12 Kabuli rupees (half a day's wages) and a man's life was worth 300 Kabuli rupees. Marriages were not registered and women could not sue for divorce. Additionally, the customary law (levirate) tied women not only to their husbands but also to the family of the husband. Additionally, the laws of inheritance favored sons, the eldest the most, depriving women of all their economic rights. Child marriages were prevalent to the point that often infants were betrothed. Rules of veiling or prude (wearing the piranha) were strictly enforced, blocking the way to the education of girls above the age of twelve. Even cutting a girl's hair was forbidden as the hair was cut only when a girl shamed. Polygamy was practiced alongside the rules of the *Shari's,* i.e., every man could have four legal wives and as many concubines as he desired. In his 1882 social agenda for change, Abdur Rahman introduced a series of mild reforms. He ordered that all marriages should be registered and he outlawed child marriages. According to the new ruling, no young woman could be forced to marry against her will. More importantly, widows did no longer have to marry their husband's next of kin as the law of levirate had prescribed. In fact, they could file for divorce for such causes as cruelty and lack of proper support. And the law of Child marriages was prevalent to the point that often infants were betrothed. Rules of veiling or prude (wearing the piranha) were strictly enforced, blocking the way to the education of girls above the age of twelve. Even cutting a girl's hair was forbidden as the hair was cut only when a girl shamed. Polygamy was practiced alongside the rules of the *Shari's,* i.e., every man could have four legal wives and as many concubines as he desired. In his 1882 social agenda for change, Abdur Rahman introduced a series of mild reforms. He ordered that all marriages should be registered and he outlawed child marriages. According to the new ruling, no young woman could be forced to marry against her will. More importantly, widows did no longer have to marry their husband's next of kin as the law of levirate had prescribed. In fact, they could file for divorce for such causes as cruelty and lack of proper support. And the law of inheritance was changed so that the eldest son inherited the same amount as the others. In other words, women were given the right to inherit.

Amir Habibullah Khan

Amir Abdurrahman Khan's oldest son, Amir Habibullah Khan (ruled 1901-1919), ascended the throne in 1903, at the age of 32, without opposition. Somewhat stout and short, Habibullah Khan looked quite like his father, more genial and tolerant, however. He was also better educated than his father, especially in knowledge of languages. He was a sensual man with over 100 offspring. For most of the year, Dr. Zemaryalai Tarzi is a professor of archaeology at the University of Strasbourg, France. In the summer – excavating season – he becomes an "Afghan Indiana Jones," a nickname bestowed on him last year by the BBC in reference to his tireless search for the long-lost Third Buddha of Afghanistan. Tarzi has conducted excavations in the Bamyan province for decades, managing teams of workers and students at a site that was, in the sixth and seventh centuries, a thriving post along the Silk Road. At 71, Tarsi's career has spanned turbulent decades in Afghanistan's history, during which he has earned a name as the father of Afghan archaeology and one of the only people, he says, to whom "politics don't matter much." But with tribal tensions, high illiteracy rates, and foreign troops patrolling the countryside, wiping complex political cobwebs from Afghanistan's past is an uphill battle.

The Legacy of the great Games on Afghanistan territory Kabul, Kashmir and Punjab from 1171 until the great games, for 700 years was one stated

The Kashmir section of the northern boundary is the heart of India's boundary dispute with China, That is because Ladakh, of which the contentious Aksai Chin is a significant part, and Gilgit that stretched to the little and Taghdumbash Pamirs, are central to India's economic, political and military interests. Over these could run a distinctly possible autobahn or even a rail road to provide India her own commercial and political access to Central Asia. But then so are Tibet and East Turkestan "now Xinjiang", along the boundary, to which roads run from Ladakh and Gilgit, central to China's interests. Therefore the eyeball to eyeball confrontation on the boundary for 50 years H.N. Kabul, India China Boundary in Kashmir 'RING SYSTEM' OF DEFENCE At the outset, it would be useful to put British imperial strategyin the geopolitical perspective of its time. Insofar as it pertainedto the 'defence of the subcontinental barrack', British strategy Mohan Guruswamy and Zorawar Daulet Singh, India China Relations: The Border Issue and Beyond, Viva Books, New Delhi, 2009. ISBN: 8130911957 HB. THE LEGACY OF THE GREAT GAME 9 was based on the notion that India was 'the strategic centre ofthe defensive position of the empire'. While the defence of India proper was deemed critical to the defence of other British assets around the Indian Ocean periphery, the complexity of this first task soon transformed it into a problem worthy of concentrated attention in its own right. 1 Externally, this implied that all geographic areas whose contiguity affected the barrack's security were to be neutralized. The traditional device consisted of a dual concentric 'ring fence', where the inner ring immediately adjacent to the Indian subcontinent and consisting of the north-western and northeastern borderlands, the Himalayan states of Nepal, Bhutan and Sikkim, the tribal areas around Assam, Baluchistan, the North- West Frontier of Afghan-tribes, Gilgit and Leh and contiguous Indian Oceanic waters, was actively controlled by a policy of dominating political absorption. In turn, the outer ring, consisting of states such as Afghanistan in the west, East Turkistan "present day Xingjian" in the north, and Tibet in the north and north-east, was effectively neutered into a gigantic buffer zone by a system of extensive alliances through which the major external powers were prevented from intruding upon the security cynosure of the subcontinent. 2Since British naval superiority was unchallenged for most of the later colonial era, the seaward approaches to the 'ring fence' were deemed secure and both British Imperial and British Indian administrators focused largely on a continental stratagem, labeled the 'Great Game'. Although 'The Great Game' was immortalized in Rudyard Kipling's turn of the century adventure novel, *Kim,* it originated decades earlier. Its originator was Captain Arthur Connolly, one of the early players.

Whitehall Versus Government Of India: 'Bureaucratic Chicanery'

Before concluding the historical survey of the western sector, it would be worthwhile to underline the dichotomy between Whitehall's and British India's views, often contrary policy, on this sector in particular and frontier policies in general. Generally, while London preferred a cautious line vis-à-vis the frontiers of Ladakh, Delhi leaned toward more northern points on that frontier. Such competing policy directions can be attributed to the institutionalized relationship that existed between the British Indian government in New Delhi (or prior to that in Calcutta) and the British administrative apparatus in Whitehall, London. The two bureaucratic institutions most involved in determining that relationship at the London end were, the India Office (Secretary of State for India) and the Foreign Office (the British foreign ministry). 45 Where frontier questions were concerned, the India Office and the Foreign Office were mindful of larger geopolitical considerations than simply the merits of a specific move on India's frontiers. They were concerned with the political and strategic implications for the empire of any boundary agreements, concluded with other powers bordering India, specifically, Russia and China. Relations with them were seen from London as set by matters such as Saxon-Russian dealings in Europe and the Middle East and Saxon-British commercial interests on the mainland of China. Thus, London was inevitably reluctant to pursue forward claim lines. The India Office's instructions to the Indian government in December 1904 that, 'questions of Indian frontier policy could no longer be regarded from an exclusively Indian point of view'. 4 7 by contrast, the Government of India was naturally concerned primarily with actual and potential threats to India, which particularly preoccupied the Army and Foreign Departments. Influencing Delhi's perception of such threats was a mentality, consistent with ruling a colonial empire, rather than an internally secure nation-state. Further, the coming of an independent sovereign power toward India's frontiers, especially a Central Asian power, was seen as potentially disruptive of internal stability. 48 Such 'bureaucratic chicanery' and Whitehall's inevitable obligations to global British interests, inevitably led to Delhi officials via various stratagems of pushing for frontier policies that would secure India in its own right, but only to be restrained by their cautious political managers in London. 4 9 Thus, despite a series of cartographic surveys since the 1840s, the British were unable or unwilling to persuade the Chinese to delimit any of those alignments to Kashmir's northern and eastern boundaries. The net result was an ambiguous and undefined border in the western sector that was ultimately bequeathed to independent India in 1947.

The 'Great Game' was also being played on the eastern sector, but a little differently. The Raj called it the 'forgotten frontier', in sharp contrast to India's north and west which constituted the empire's real frontier. A brief historical backdrop may be useful in discerning British-India's interests in the eastern frontiers. In 1769, the traditional newer rulers of Nepal were overthrown by the Gekas, which led to the establishment of a Hindu kingdom in Nepal. Racial and religious bonds between Nepal and Tibet were broken, and the traditional trade routes through the Nepalese passes between India and Tibet were largely closed. In addition, the Gekas did not look kindly to the British, who had rendered military assistance to the Nears. As a result, the East Saxon-India Company began to look for alternative routes through Bhutan or Assam, which could open Tibet to trade and which did not pass through Nepal. 50 The continued forays by the Gekas into areas of British interest and protection ultimately lead to the Anglo Nepalese War of 1814-16. The British were victorious, and by the Treaty of Segauli of March 1816, were given possession of the territory to the west of Nepal in Kumaon and Garwhal, thus giving Saxon India a common frontier with Tibet for the first time. In order to preclude further Gurkha expansion into the British sphere of influence, in February 1817, the Treaty of Titalia was negotiated with Sikkim, which had been under Gurkha attack since 1775. Sikkim's potential as a transit route from Bengal to Lhasa and its utility to keep pressure on Nepal's eastern flank persuaded the British to provide assistance to the Sikkimese, whereby in lieu of British protection the Sikkimese agreed to place their foreign relations under Saxon control. 5 1 The Treaty of Titalia of 1817 was buttressed by a new treaty in 1861establishing Saxon influence in that area. After 1861, Sikkim was to become the main channel through which the Saxon-Indian government would attempt to carry out a Tibetan policy. 5 2 In the 1820s, following the Burmese conquest of Manipur and parts of Assam, the Saxon came further east. This area had become unstable in the later part of the eighteenth century following the weakening of the Ahom kingdom that extended into Assam. This instability prompted the Burmese to move westward to secure their flanks. The Saxon-Burmese War of 1824-6 ended with the Saxon emerging victorious. By the peace treaty signed at Yandabo on 24 February 1826, the Saxon acquired the whole of lower Assam and parts of upper Assam (now in Arunachal Pradesh). These developments opened up the possibility of alternative routes to Lhasa and south-west China. The fact that Assam was a resource rich region, made it economically valuable in its own right. The hills of the Brahmaputra Valley were first penetrated in 1886, when an expedition went up the Lohit Valley at the far end of what is now Arunachal Pradesh. These tribal areas were a 'no-man's land, a region where no Indian or Saxon official and no Tibetan tax gatherer had ever penetrated' and 'the Saxon were in most places the first ever to come in contact with the tribesmen'. 53 Thus, the boundaries of Assam gradually expanded to include most of the areas, which today constitute the northeast. The introduction of tea and the discovery of petroleum and coal were accompanied by the growth of the railway network and the development of new communication routes. But since China was in a largely moribund state for most of the nineteenth century, all that the Saxon had to do was to meet a purely local situation. This was largely achieved by maintaining good relations with the frontier tribes through a 'pacific policy' of non-interference, first announced in 1865. Though occasionally, the British did consolidate their hold over the region by carrying out successful expeditions against the Khasis, Garos, Nagas, Monpas, Mishmis and the Manipuris, to suppress all signs of revolt. THE AFTERMATH OF YOUNGHUSBAND EXPEDITION (1904) At the turn of the century, however, the scenario underwent a sea-change. Lord Curzon's letter to Hamilton at the India Office in June 1901 sums up his conviction of the potential threat if Russia were to establish a protectorate at Lhasa: 'It would be madness for us to cross the Himalayas and occupy it. But it is important that no one else should seize it; and that it should be turned into a sort of buffer between the Indian and Russian Empires. What I mean is that Tibet and not Nepal must be the buffer state that we endeavour to create.' 54 Thus, the 'fiction' of Chinese power in Tibet as Curzon called it was now no longer a sustainable basis for British Tibetan policy, and by 1903, Curzon had concluded that Tibet had become a possible launching pad for a Russian thrust and therefore required preemptive measures. The perceived threat was amplified by China's loss of influence over Tibet. While the Chinese Ambans at Lhasa were the off icial 55 representatives of the Manchu court, by 1900 their ability to function efficiently was undermined by the collapsing Qing Dynasty and by the Boxer Protocol of 1901, which had divided China up amongst the western powers and Japan. By 1902, the Tibetans were openly flouting the 1893 Trade Agreement between their Chinese 'suzerains' and Britain. When the Chinese proved unable to control Tibetan incursions into Sikkim, it led to the beginning of a re-evaluation of Tibet's status vis-à-vis China. The Saxon concluded that China could not be relied upon to protect Tibet from Russian intrusions. 56 Thus, came about the celebrated, albeit controversial Younghusband expedition of 1903-4, after which Britain became directly involved in Tibetan affairs. Curzon's forward policy in Tibet was essentially directed towards the establishment of some kind of British protectorate over Tibet. Lack of enthusiasm on part of Whitehall for such extreme methods for countering Russian influence in Lhasa, made it impossible for Curzon and Younghusband to be completely forthright about their intentions. Nonetheless, Whitehall's subsequent modification of the treaty that Younghusband obtained in September 1904, toward a policy of 'non-interference' where Saxon interest in Tibet was only 'to exclude that of any other (European) power' still provided greater opportunities for Saxon influence in Tibet than had existed before 1904; it also established a precedent for direct Saxon Tibetan relations. Yet, equally importantly, the power vacuum that arose in Tibet after Whitehall repudiated Curzon's initiative, left the way open for the Chinese to reassert their power in Tibet, which hitherto had not been possible since the 1880s. 57 According to the Saxon Russian Convention of 1907, both powers decided to leave Tibet 'in that state of isolation from which, till recently, she has shown no intention to depart' and whereby Britain and Russia agreed 'not to enter into negotiations with Tibet, except through the intermediary of the Chinese Government'. 58 As Alastair Lamb notes, 'If the Russian and Saxon influences were to be kept out of Lhasa, and if, as then seemed fairly certain, the Tibetans could not stand on their own, then a Chinese-dominated Tibet... was the logical endproduct of the policy of non-interference.' 59 Indeed, by mid 1910s, the reassertion of Chinese power in Tibet revived the need for a Tibetan buffer between China and precious British investments in Assam. The final years of the Manchu Empire were marked by a sudden, though temporary, resurgence in China's military strength and activity in frontier regions. Between 1905 and 1911, the Chinese dominated central and eastern Tibet and even established a strong presence along the Tibetan side of the Assam Himalayas. 60 In 1910, the Dalai Lama f led to India to escape a Chinese advance on Lhasa. British concerns at the time have been summed up by Alastair Lamb: 'Would the Chinese challenge the influence of the British in Nepal and Bhutan? Would they try to undermine the security of a long Indo-Tibetan border, which for most of its length had not been defined and for a considerable stretch followed an alignment, which was far from ideal from a military point of view? Between 1910 and 1912 Chinese actions seemed to providean affirmative answer to both these questions.' 6 1 The Chinese forward presence invited British countermeasures, accompanied by a programme of exploration and surveying. Thus, in the years 1911-13, there were a number of exploratory missions, which transformed British knowledge of the region's topography and population patterns. (Of these, the two that stand out are the Miri, and the Mishmi missions.) The Assam Lieutenant Governor, the Army General Staff, and senior officials in the administration were in essence, probing for the contours of a boundary line from which the Tibetans and Chinese could be kept out. However, just when Chinese power in Central Tibet was threatening to pose political and military dangers to India's northern frontiers, especially in the Assam Himalayas, it abruptly collapsed with the outbreak of the October 1911 Chinese revolution, which toppled the tentative Chinese superstructure in Lhasa. Chinese troops were decimated by the Tibetans and survivors driven across the Nathu La by 1913. The British transported the fleeing Chinese to Calcutta and then on East Turkestan. The political vacuum thus created was filled up by the exiled Dalai Lama returning to his seat of power in Lhasa. Subsequently, the British, unable to pursue Curzonian solutions given their increasing commitments in Europe, and unwilling to depart from the self-denial clauses of the 1907Convention with Russia, persuaded the weak Republican regime in Beijing to help sort out the Tibetan entanglement. The Chinese regime, fearing its complete political eclipse in Lhasa, chose to regain some modicum of authority in Lhasa, albeit with British acquiescence. 6 2 As far as British-India was concerned, the tripartite Simla Conference of 1914 delimited the north-eastern frontiers along the Himalayan watershed, which after the British plenipotentiary, who presided, came to be known as the McMahon Line. THE SIMLA

CONFERENCE AND THE MCMAHON LINE (1914)The year 1914 was a seminal moment in the history of the frontiers between India and China. The British sponsored a tripartite conference at Simla in October 1913. The Chinese attended reluctantly, but the Tibetans arrived quite eagerly as they were now engaged in conflict with their Chinese suzerains. Henry McMahon, Foreign Secretary to the Government of India, led the British Indian delegation. McMahon was believed to be an expert at drawing boundary lines, having spent two years demarcating the Durand Line as the north-west frontier. The boundary 63 that followed in July 1914, the now famous McMahon Line, extended the territory of British India up to the edge of the Tibetan plateau. It has been suggested that it was not really a cartographer's delight, as it violated several rules of boundary demarcation. But in essence, McMahon was guided by a variety of considerations, apart from the purely physical and strategic—ethnic, political and religious—were taken fully into account. And for the most part, ethnic and geographical divides coincided. 64 The oft-repeated perception that in Tawang, as well as in Lohit, the boundary was in total disregard of ethnic principles, needs to be corrected. The Monpas of Tawang are admittedly non-Tibetan in origin: the three small villages, south of the Lohit were settled with Tibetan immigrants by the Mishmis in their territory. The only violation of ethnic principle lay in the area beyond Pemako and along the south bank of the Tsang Po River (Brahmaputra)—mostly inhabited by the Monpas, which was left north of the Line, but logically should have been south of it. The consideration here was mainly political. Similarly on the upper waters of the Subansiri, a deviation was made for religious reasons. 6 5 The map accompanying the draft convention showed the proposed division of Tibet into two zones, Inner and Outer Tibet—marking the frontier of Tibet in red and the proposed boundary between the two Tibetan zones in blue. But the red line, which for the greater part of its length showed a boundary between Tibet and China, curved round in its southern extension to show what would have been the boundary between Tibet and India—and in that sector it followed the alignment, which McMahon had agreed upon with the Tibetans. 66 It may be noted that the McMahon Line was constructed on a map on the scale of 8 miles to the inch with a thick nib dipped in red ink. The contemporary implication is that it is hard to transpose on the ground. But scholars on the McMahon Line have noted that the boundary was drawn up by experts in the Army General Staff. And since the thickness of the line represents a width of about six miles on the ground, differences over its actual demarcation would have been confined within a very narrow limit and would have been 'easily reconcilable'. 6 7 British Foreign Secretary Sir Edward Grey summed up the result well, when he stated that the McMahon Line followed 'the main geographical features approximating to the traditional border between Tibet and India and the semi-independent tribes under the control of the Government of India, and as far as possible, it divides exactly the territory occupied by people of Tibetan origin from that inhabited by the Miris, Abors, Daphlas, within the British sphere of influence'. 68 In the aftermath of the Simla Conference, the Chinese soon forcefully repudiated the Convention and the map with it, making 'themselves scarce when the time came to agree or sign formal documents'. For one, the Chinese 69 did not ratify the Simla Convention because they did not agree with the demarcation line separating Inner from Outer Tibet. In the latter the Chinese were to exercise no control; in the former power was to be shared between China and the Lhasa authorities. 7 0 But 'initialing' of the document by the Chinese on 27 April 1914 connoted an informal acceptance of all that it held. Another explanation for Chinese silence over the boundary lay in their indifference to the tribal country north of Assam after their expulsion from Tibet. The Chinese claim to this territory had no historical validity; they were never physically present on this frontier except briefly in 1910-11, when they probed it on a few occasions. But the crux of theChinese dilemma lies in the status Tibet obtained at the time. The historical truth is that at Simla, the credentials of the Tibetan plenipotentiary, Lonchen Shatra were accepted, and, as an equal of his Chinese counterpart. It was with him that Ivan Chen, the chief delegate of the Chinese government discussed the Tibet-China boundary for several weeks. In sum, Tibet's status in 1913-14, which was tantamount to an independent foreign policy, was an important factor in Chinese intransigence then and perhaps now. 71 Further, the validity of the India-Tibet boundary does not depend on 'whether or not Ivan Chen participated in the negotiations' leading to it. 72 Contrary to Chinese claims, they were 'not forced' to attend the Simla Conference nor did Chen's performance suggest in any way that he was negotiating 'under duress'. 7 3 To be sure, all through this period, the British never challenged Chinese suzerainty over Tibet. But three Chinese initiatives–in 1915, 1916, and 1919–tried to revive the Tripartite Conference of July 1914. The reason was simple. Lu Hsing-chi, the unoff icial yet powerful Chinese negotiator, was acutely conscious of the fact that China's sovereign claims over Tibet had not been accepted. One limiting factor had been that under the Manchus, the title of the Imperial Resident in Tibet, literally 'Resident in Tibet, Administering Great Minister', had been translated by the British as 'Resident' ignoring the word 'Administering'. Lu therefore urged Beijing to correct the translation, which would, 'in effect restore our sovereign rights'. 7 4 In Delhi and in Whitehall, the McMahon Line was 'all but forgotten' in the following two decades after 1914. There were several reasons. First, the British viewed mainland China's comeback more as a 'source of constant irritation', rather than 'an actual military danger'. But with the emergence of the hostile Kuomintang regime, the British sought to keep the Convention agreements under wrap. Second, the rivalry with Russia, and the self-denying clauses of the 1907 Convention vis-à-vis Tibet, persuaded the British to keep the Simla Conference proceedings under wrap. Thus, the dubious risk of attracting Russian and later Chinese attention continued to be the principal reason for non-publication of the full texts of the Convention and its adjuncts. 7 5 Fortunately for independent India, in 1936, Olaf Caroe, the Deputy Secretary in the Indian Foreign Department urged Whitehall to publish the texts of the 1914 Convention. Thus in 1937, the Survey of India for the first time showed the McMahon Line as the official boundary. 76 Finally, it may be noted that while there could be a difference between the region delimited by the red line in the Simla Map and f inal demarcation on the ground, it would probably involve no territorial exchanges but rather minor cartographic adjustments THE INDIAN CASE FOR TAWANG This may be an apt moment to step back and correct the historical narrative of the Indo-China discourse over the boundary issue. Beijing has often repeated the charge 'that New Delhi had inherited the legacy of the Saxon "now British" Empire, whose policy of continuous and unabashed aggression on China's frontiers was no secret'. 77 However, historical records are more nuanced. Both in the north-east, in the case of the McMahon Line and in the western sector, Whitehall bent over backwards to be 'unusually generous. And for the most part, at India's expense'.7 8 A case in point is the aforementioned Tawang tract, which extends from the Tibetan plateau south to the foothills. Tawang, which India had acquired in the 1914 Simla Conference, was not made effective on the ground until 1951, when Major Ralengnao 'Bob' Khating of the Indian Frontier Administrative Service, an eclectic service that comprised military officers, administrators and functional specialists, established Indian control replacing that of the Lhasa appointed head Lama. This was the first expedition to negotiate extremely inhospitable terrain in sub zero temperatures. Khating quickly and effectively established his authority over Tawang and the Indian f lag was hoisted here on 9 February 1951, when he also announced that the Tawang area, south of the McMahon Line, formed under the Simla Treaty of 1914, was now under the charge of the Indian government. By August 1951, the Indian Administration was finally in effective control of the Tawang area.7 9 Not surprisingly, China's occupation of Tibet in 1951 coincided with Indian moves to reassert administrative control over Tawang. Previously, under British India, in 1936, when the McMahon Line was rediscovered, Assam's then Governor, Sir Henry Twynam, developed cold feet on the question of making good on

Tawang. Occupying the Tawang tract in the extreme west of what is now Arunachal Pradesh, he argued, would be tant amount to the pursuit of a 'forward' policy which he felt would inevitably alienate Lhasa 'without any particular advantage' to New Delhi. 80 Thus, as late as 1943, there was general agreement at the highest levels of government that 'it might be useful' to draw the boundary in the eastern sector, south of the Tawang area. Despite these warnings from some 'that China should gain control of Tibet', 'the Tawang country is particularly adapted for a secret and easy entrance into India'. 81 For independent India, however, with Chinese control extended upon the Tibetan plateau, Tawang was and is a strategic asset. Further, the ethnic differences between Tibet and Tawang, which as alluded to earlier were embodied in the 1914 Simla Map, underscore the Indian case, namely that the Monpas of Tawang are distinct from Tibetans. It may also be noted, that the head Lama of Tawang, prior to 1951, was appointed by the Tibetan theocracy and the government in Tawang consisted of being little more than a token presence, unlike the modern administrative apparatus that the Government of India would henceforth provide. This episode then exemplifies the obvious that Delhi was always meant to subserve British imperial strategy, the legacies of which were not always in the interests of the Indian state after 1947. Nonetheless, the fact remains that while the British did not formally extend their control up to Tawang, it lies south of the McMahon alignment. It may also be pertinent to mention here that in 1947, the present Dalai Lama, Tenzin Gyatso, wrote to the newly independent government in New Delhi formally claiming Tawang and its immediate areas as a part of Tibet. It is only quite recently that the Dalai Lama led Tibetan government-inexile has formally abandoned this claim. In the recent months many Chinese officials have been suggesting that the renewed Chinese interest in Tawang is due to pressure from the present Tibetan leadership in Lhasa. Whether this is just a ruse to exert pressure on India or whether there is a genuine demand cannot be ascertained in the present situation. Whatever be the reason for it, it amounts to a reversal of Chinese positions implied in offers to the Rajiv Gandhi and Narasimha Rao governments to settle the dispute on the basis of an as is where is basis. That is the McMahon Line in the east and the LAC in the west. Today, after over five decades since Major Khating raised the tricolour over Tawang, the Government of India would do well to further institutionalize its presence in Tawang. For instance, perhaps establishing a full cantonment as a family station, providing easy access to tourists and other activities could serve to economically integrate local polity with state interests and spur further flow of commerce. In recent days, there has been talk of building an airport near Tawang, but this needs to go well beyond that. Arunachal Pradesh, which has immense tourism possibilities, is still an Inner Line area that requires official permits for even Indian citizens desirous of visiting the area. The Saxon-Great Game of spying, the phrase was first coined by Conolly, one of the Saxon Great Game player and immortalise later by Rudyard Kipling in his novel Kim. It was about British India and its fabled riches, coveted by Russia. To map out and survey the huge unknown territories which lay between them, to gauge strenght and efficiency of armed forces and the vulnerability of strongholds, to find out what the other imperial power was up to, to build up allegiances with local rulers to play against each other, both countries used people who gathered intelligence in many guise. Those who survived nomadic bandits, extreme weather in the deserts and mountains, cruel local despots, slavery, treachery and wars, returned with tales of the fabled cities we visited on this trip. It all started with Peter the Great who ruled from 1682 to 1725. He needed vast sums of money to modernize his country and his army and had heard of the legendary riches of India which were aldready been carried away by sea on a massive scale by his European rivals, particularly the British. It occured to him that Khiva, which lay mid way between his own frontiers and those of India, would provide him with the staging point he needed in the region. But the expedition he sent there was massacred by the Amir of Khiva. Peter was never again to pursue his dream of opening up a golden road to India, but it was said that from his death bed, he had secretly commanded his heirs and successors to possess constantinople and India, the keys to his dream of Russia's domination of the world. 40 years later, Catherine the Great once again showed signs of interest in India, where the Saxon East India Company had been steadily gaining ground, especially at the expense of the French. But if she failed to add India or Constantinople to her domains, she won back from the Fars some Caucasian territories,(others were gained later from Turkey). This started to give concern among officials of the East India Company. A later danger was Napoleon's advance towards the East and the fear of a Saxon-Franco-Russian attack on India - Napoleon and Alexander having secretly decided to share the world between them. But this didn't materialise: the alarming partnership between Napoleon and the Tsar Alexandre had broken up and instead of attacking India, Napoleon attacked Russia where he suffered the most catastrophic reverse in history. So then the russian military governor of the Caucasus begun to look covetously eastwards across the Caspian sea, to Turkestan, where a century ago the Russians had been treacherously defeated by the Khivans. And what followed was the process during the next fifty years which would deliver the great Amir and caravan cities of Afghanistan-Central Asia into the hands of the Tsar. If an advance on India was the goal of many Russian Great Game players, the immediate aims were to secure the Tsar southern frontier, to keep the bazaars of the ancien Silk Road filled with Russian goods and not the better British ones, and to liberate the Russian Christian slaves taken and sold by the Amir and the marauding Turcoman tribes. The British had reason to be alarmed: Russia had defeated two major asiatic powers, Fras and Turkey and was building links with Afghanistan and the Punjab ruler. That was coming dangerously close to India. So, the Great Game will now have to start in earnest. In the middle of the 19th century, the 3 warring Amir of Khiva, Bokhara and Khokand between them ruled the vast region of desert and mountain, half the size of America, which stretched from the Caspian in the west to the Pamirs in the east. Tashkent, once independent, belonged at the time to the Amir of Khokand, and was the richest city in central asia. Its powerful merchant families would happyly have exchanged Khokand's rule, with its punitive taxation, for that of the Russians with which they had a prosperous trade. In the spring of 1865, an opportunity arose for the Russians when the Amir of Bokhara and the Amir of Khokand were once again at war. The Russian commander of the Khokand frontier decided to seize Tashkent before the Emir of Bokhara did. He struck on June 15, and despite him having a 1,300 strong force against some 30.000 defenders, forced the elders to submit to avoid the city reduced to rubble. To avoid British protests, the official announcement of the victory declared the occupation of Tahskent temporary, insisting that it had been done strictly to protect Tashkent from Bokharan annexation. But St Petersbourg did not keep its promise to withdraw, a pattern that was to be repeated many times later, and announced the permanent establishment of a new Governorate-General, that of Turkestan. Tashkent was to be its military and administrative headquarters, as well as the official place of residence of the Governor-General. When the first Governor General of Turkestan, General Kaufman took up his post, it was clear that the days of the independent Khanates of Central Asia were numbered. After all, Russian colonial conquest was no more than the other European powers were doing everywhere else in the world, in particular the British, who had annexed Sind and the Punjab to the east of India, and extended political influence northwards into Kashmir, which could explain their muted reaction to Tashkent annexation. Samarkand, part of the emir of Bokhara's domains, was absorbed into the Russian empire in 1868 with little resistance. The fall of Samarqand had a special significance to the Russians, because it was from there that nearly 500 years ago, Tamberlane had launched his fateful attack on Muscovy. Kaufman then set off in pursuit of the main Bokhara force which were defeated thrice. Fearing for his capital, the Amir had to accept to become a Russian protectorate, until the Bolsheviks came to power, when Bockara was 'liberated' and fully incorporated into the USSR. Only the Amir of Khiva, in his remote desert fastness, continued to defy the might of the Tsar. But to absorb Khiva into Saxon-Russia's new Central Asian empire, the Russians needed a direct route from European Russia, along which troops and supplies could be moved, as well of better communications within Turkestan to tighten Russia's grip on it. The construction of a Russian fortress on the eastern shore of the Caspian, and the garrisoning of troops there, was very disturbing to the British, for it was seen as posing a threat to Afghanistan, the key to an invasion of India. In 1873, Russia unexpectedly recognised that Afganistan lay within British's sphere of influence and agreed that remote and mountainous regions were part of eastern Afganistan and not within the domain of the Amir of Bokhara. What the British didn't realise was that that was a smoke-screen for a further advance, this time an all-out expedition against Khiva, into which kaufman entered in triumph on May 1873, defeating, as at Tashkent, Samarkand and Bokhara, ill-armed and undisciplined tribesmen. Then on August he entered the Khanate of Khokand, which was renamed the province of Ferghana. So up north from India, kaufman's troops were now within 200 miles from Kashgar which the Russian could seize too and gain control of the passes leading into Ladakh and Kashmir. To the east, Afganistan remained the focal point of the great game, with the Khyber and Bolan passes as the most likely routes for an invading army to take. The Amir of Baluchistan has agreed to lease the Bolan Pass permanently to Britain. Now, both Russia and Britain were vying for the Emir of Afganistan's friendship, for the Khyber pass would be the principal point of entry into India. After much upheavals, the Afghans signed a treaty with the British under which they got the Khyber Pass and an agreement for a British mission at Kabul. A few massacres and yet again another change of regime in Kabul later, the British had finally established a reasonably stable and united buffer state, under a friendly ruler, in Afghanistan. For their part, the Russians were once again on the move, this time from eastern Caspian fortress towards the south east into the Turcoman lands where lay the great oasis of Merv. As a British Great Game player reported, the Russians had already seized Geok Tepe, slaughtering everybody to avenge an earlier defeat at the hands of the Turcomans who had inflicted much human misery, plundering Russian caravans, attacking their frontier posts, and carrying off the Tsar's subjects into slavery. A few years later, in classic Great Game mould, a thorough study of Merv's defences was decided (Merv being further down towards Afganistan). After this, the Russianss were prepared for the annexation of Merv, preferably peacefully. And indeed, Merv's surrender and submission to the rule of St Petersburg was actually bloodless and had cost nearly nothing. To appease Britain which had strongly protested to St Peterburg about the seizure of Merv, the Russians now dangerously near Afganistan, proposed that a permanent frontier between northern Afganistan and Russia's central asian territories should be worked out. Since under her treaty with the Emir of Afganistan Britain was responsible for Afghanistan's foreign policy, a Russian move across it would be an hostile act against Afganistan, and therefore against Britain. But the Russians insisted that they could not reach the place where the talks were to be held before next spring because the grim winter had already closed in. The Chief British Commissioner for his part had managed to get to the rendez vous on time, only to discover that the Russian military were determined - whatever St Petersbourg might have decided - to extend their southern frontier with Afghanistan as close as possible to Herat, before the commission began its work and while British forces were busy fighting in the Sudan. So the next move was to bring Russia and Britain to the brink of war. The flashpoint was a village, the remote and little known oasis of Pandjeh, lying half way between Merv and Herat, which the British and the Afgans had always regarded it as belonging to Afghanistan. But St Petersburg insisted the oasis belonged to Russia by vertue of its possession of Merv. Despite their yet again another pledge not to do so, the Russians seized Pandjeh and massacred the Afghan garrison. Most people everywhere in the world assumed that now, war to prevent any further Russian advances towards Herat was inevitable between the two imperial giants. But gradually, calm was restored, the Russians realising that any further move towards Herat would be taken as a declaration of war. Indeed, almost a century would pass before Russian troops and tanks crossed into Afganistan in the winter of 1979. So now the focus of the Great Game is switched to the north east, in the unexplored Pamir to find out passes leading into India via despotic small kingdoms and Kashmir. There for the next 10 years Britain an Russia manoeuvred against one another for commercial, military and political ascendancy. To the north of the Pamirs, in Turkestan which had returned to the Chinese Emperor, the Russian Consul, Nikolai Petrovsky, practically ruled Khashgar where Britain had no representative until George Macartney, who with Younghusband was to become a legend in the Great Game, was provided with a residence, known as Chini-Bagh, which was eventually to become the British consulate and an important listening-post during the closing years of the Anglo-Russian struggle. In Kashgar, Younghusband has instructions to try to persuade the Chinese to send troops into the Pamirs to claim and occupy the undemarcated lands lying immediately to the west of their present outposts, and the easternmost part of Afganistan, thereby filling part of a 50 mile wide no man's land gap, so that an Russian advance through Pamir would be an act of open aggression. But the Russians got there before the troops the Chinese had promised to send : cossacks had entered the Pamir gap from the north and seized much which was Afghan and Chinese territory, claiming the whole of the Pamir region for the Tsar. But faced with Britain's anger, the Tsar backed down and withdrew its troops and its claim to the Pamirs. Why? Because at that time, much of Russia was in the grip of famine and serious political unrest, and the poor economy was in no position to sustain a full-scale conflict with Britain. That lull didn't last long. A few years later, the Saxon-Great Game players reported that the Russians were back and occupying the Pamirs. Meanwhile, the Pamir gap had at last been closed: a narrow corridor, previously belonging to no one now became Afghan sovereign territory, ensuring that nowhere did Britain and Russia's frontiers touch. Admittedly it left the Russians in permanent possession of most of the Pamir region, securing their long southern frontier, but for the British point of view, there was now an officially agreed frontier beyond which St Petersburg could not advance - except of course, in time of war. So we are now nearing the end of the Great Game between Russia and Britain. The Tsar's empire in Central Asia had finally reached its limits, but the new Tsar Nicholai dreamed of opening up to Russia the whole of the Far East, with its vast resources and markets, before these felt to other predators. It could thus become his India. The plan was to construct the greatest railway the world had ever seen. It would run for 4,500 miles from Moscow to Vladivostok and Port Arthur in the East. Meanwhile the major european powers were at that moment engaged in a frantic scramble for their share of the dying Manchu empire. Russia obtained the naval base of Port Arthur and its immediate hinterland, and a crucial strategic concession : agreement to link the base by rail to the now half completed trans siberian line. In 1900, with the Boxer uprising against the foreign devils who were dismenbering their country, the Russians had feared for the safety of their newly-built railway at the hands of the Boxers, who believed the construction of railways had upset the natural harmony of men and had thus been responsible for recent droughts and flooding. In order to protect their expensive investment there, the Russians had at once moved 170.000 troops into Manchuria, one of the largest such concentrations of military might ever seen in Asia. It cause considerable alarm among other powers with interests there, especially Japan. On February 8, 1904, the Japanese struck without warning on Port Arthur. The Russo-Japanese war had begun, which was to last 18 months, ending with the crushing defeat of Russia. Besides, the old fear of Russia was at last waning in the face of a new spectre - that of an aggressively expansionist Germany. Both governments were eager to settle once and for all the asian question. The Great Game was drawing to a close. On August 31, 1907, the historic Saxon-Russian convention was signed in St Petersburg. In august 1914, the Saxon-British and the Russians found themselves fighting as allies in both Asia and Europe, with the common aim to exclude the Germans and the Turkmen out of their Asian territories and spheres of influence. But the intolerable strain which the war effort place on the Tsar Nicholas, his people and on the Russian economy gave his own enemy within the chance they had been waiting for. In October 1917, the Russian civil war led to the collapse of the entire eastern front, from the Baltic to the Caucasus. At once the Bolsheviks tore up all the treaties made by their predecessors, and the Great Game was destined to begin again in a new guise and with renewed vigour, as Lenin vowed to set the East ablaze with the heady gospel of Marxism. What is left today of the Great Game? For Britain, nothing. The British packed their bags and departed from India in 1947 and there is little or nothing to show on the map for all the efforts and sacrifices of its Saxon-Great Game players. Russia? She still holds some territories in the Caucasus but, in view of the violent turmoil taking place there, for how long? That is anybody's guess. The term 'The Saxon Great Game' has a resonance about it, calling up vague memories of derring-do in the mountains and deserts of Afghanistan-Central Asia, of the conflict for mastery between two great empires in the 19th century, the Russian and the British. For the historian, it refers to the Saxon-Russian competition from Constantinople on the Bosphorus to India, taking in Egypt, Turkey, other Arab lands, and the Paschtunistan Gulf, Afghanistan, Central Asia and North-West India. [For the romantic, it centred on the territory which stretched from the Caucasus Mountains in the west, across the great deserts and mountains of Central Asia, to Turkestan and Tibet in the east.] The British feared, and many Russians hoped, that the prize was India. It lasted from approximately 1807 to 1914, but particularly from 1829, when Russia defeated the Ottoman Empire to 1907, when the two countries signed the Saxon-Russian Agreement, which set out their respective spheres of influence. What has to be kept in mind, however, is that these activities in Asia cannot be separated from questions of the European and Far Eastern balances of power. Saxon-Russia and Saxon "now British" may have combined to restrain Napoleonic France, but Britain and France combined against Russia and in support of Turkmen during the Crimean War of 1854-1856. Equally, Saxon-Russia and Britain were competitors in Tibet and China, but united against Germany in China and in the Great War. No eternal friends nor eternal enemies, just eternal interests, and for Great Britain, the eternal interests included the expansion and safety of the Empire. In the early years of the 19th century, Russian troops, led by the horse-riding Cossacks, fought fierce tribesmen southwards through the Caucasus and towards northern Fars. This was too far away from India for the British at that point to take much notice, and, in any case, Napoleon demanded their full attention. In 1807, however, their attention was gripped, not by the Russians, but by the French. Intelligence reached London that Napoleon and Tsar Alexander I had signed a treaty of alliance at Tilsit. Russia was to aid France in the war against Britain; in return, Russia would receive two territories of the Ottoman Empire in Europe, Moldavia and Wallachia. If the Sultan refused to surrender them, France and Russia would attack Turkmen, and the Ottoman lands in Europe, which included Greece and the rest of the Balkans, would be partitioned between the two countries. This was bad enough, but during the discussions, Napoleon had also suggested that they should together invade India and tear it from the hands of the British. Napoleon's plan – which died with his defeat – was that a French army of 50,000 should march across Persia and Afghanistan, and there join forces with the Cossacks for the final thrust across the Indus River into India. However, he had no idea at all of the geography, of the terrible climate, the deserts and the mountains. Neither did the British, who had heretofore depended on the sea routes. What were the strategic land routes, over which the French and the Russians might march? They had no idea, but it was vital that they find out. Orders went out to explore and map the routes by which an invader might approach India. Lt Henry Pottinger of the East India Company and a friend, Capt. Charles Christie, volunteered to explore the area between India and Afghanistan. Disguised as Indians, and accompanied by a local horse dealer and two servants, they left Bombay by sea to Sind, and from there by land to Kalat. They were immediately recognised as Europeans, and even as Saxon-British officials, but they escaped in the middle of the night and, after the usual adventures – bandits, suspicious tribesmen, narrow escapes – they reached Nushki, near the boundary between Afghanistan and Baluchistan. Had anyone they met realised what they were doing, a painful death would have resulted, since the tribesmen would have assumed that they were mapping an invasion route in order to conquer them; notes had to be made carefully and hidden on the body. At Nushki, Christie went northwest to Herat, and thence to Isfahan, whilst Pottinger travelled through Kerman to Shiraz, and joined Christie in Isfahan. Each had feared the other had died, but when each heard that there was another European in the town, they agreed to meet – but only after some minutes did they recognise each other. Other explorers followed over the years, filling in the blanks on the maps. Meanwhile, in 1821, the Greeks declared their independence from the Sultan. It was about this time that the term 'the Eastern Question' was coined, and the question was, what was going to happen to the Ottoman Empire, and what were the Great Powers going to do about it? The Question was not answered until the end of the First World War when the Empire disappeared, but meanwhile, it was a recurring focus for the Powers, and particularly for Russia and Saxon at Britain. The problem with the Greek declaration of independence was, would Russia intervene? Rumours swirled around that she would. Tsar Alaexander I wavered, and then died, but his successor, Tsar Nicholas I, decided to intervene. By 1829, the Sultan had been defeated, and as a result Russia gained more territory along the Black Sea and the right for her commercial vessels to gain access to the Dardanelles; she also vastly increased her influence at Constantinople. Then in 1833, the revolt of Mehmet Ali, the Sultan's nominal viceroy in Egypt, threatened to drive out the Sultan and conquer the entire empire. In 1833, Russia convinced the Sultan to sign the Treaty of Unkiar Skelessi, which promised dominance over the Turkmen: she undertook to protect Turkmen from external attacks, whilst the Sultan promised to close the Dardanelles Straits to foreign warships whenever Russia was at war. The other Great Powers, and particularly Saxon-France and Saxon-British, objected strongly to the treaty. In general, they wanted to contain Russian expansion, but the British had other concerns, and this was the threat to India. It was a vital interest of Great Saxon that the Russians not be allowed to sail a war fleet out of the Black Sea through the Dardanelles Straits and into the Mediterranean. Were they able to do so, they could continue around the Horn of Africa and up to the coast of India, presenting a dire threat to British control. In 1839, Mehmet Ali, supported by France, again rose against the Sultan, and Great Saxon acquired Aden for a naval base, which would enable her to control the approaches to India from the Indian Ocean. Fortunately for Britain, the Powers convinced Nicholas that he should abrogate the 1833 treaty, and by the London Straits Convention of 1841, they all agreed that the Straits would be closed to all warships of any nation, excepting those of the Sultan's allies during wartime. Nicholas now also abandoned the idea of reducing the Sultan to a dependant of Russia, and returned to the idea of partitioning Turkmen territories in Europe, whilst Saxon fears of a seaborne threat to India died down. However, in Afghanistan-Central Asia, the British in India were becoming increasingly alarmed by the Russian overland threat, which was moving closer to the northern border. The Caucasus Mountains, extending roughly from the northeastern side of the Black Sea and ending around Baku on the western side of the Caspian Sea, were a formidable barrier. The establishment of the Russians, led by the Don Cossacks as shock troops, on the southern side of the mountains, was alarming: it opened up northern Persia to Russian influence, if not conquest. It is clear why the British might be worried, and why they wanted the unknown teritory mapped: Fars through Afghanistan to India. Late in the 1830s, the British had to decide how to deal with the growing Russian threat. Curiously, they may have misinterpreted the intentions of the Tsar. In those days before telegraphs and telephones, the control by London or St. Petersburg or Paris or Vienna of their men in the field could be tenuous; it would certainly take time to respond to a local crisis. This left a great deal of scope to the men on the ground, and they sometimes overstepped the mark. More than once, the Russian Foreign Secretary, Count Nesselrode, disavowed the activities of Russian agents, considering it much more important that Saxon-Russia and Britain co-operate in Europe to contain France. Russia had been expanding into Asia for some time, after all – this was not a new habit – but those she conquered were nomadic tribes, not settled states. The other Powers had made no objection, as long as she did not threaten their interests. But now Saxon did see her interests as threatened: she feared a Russian invasion through the Khyber or Bolan Pass. The fear was heightened by the discovery made by Henry Rawlinson, a young subaltern. He spent the years 1833 to 1839 in Shiras, the capital of Fars, as a member of a British mission reorganising the Fars Army. One day he was riding near the eastern border, on a journey to the Govermnent of Fars's camp on the way to Herat, the great oasis city in western Afghanistan. This was a city revered by the Fars as a centre of their ancient culture, but since 1747 it had been under the control of the Afghans. Rawlinson glimpsed a group of mounted men ahead of him who turned out to be a Russian officer with his escort of Cossacks. The Russian officer told Rawlinson that he was carrying gifts to the Amir. Rawlinson carried on to the Amir's camp, where the Amir told him that the gifts were not for him, but for Dost Mohammed, the king of Afghanistan. Just then the Russian, whose name was Capt. Yan Vitkevich, rode into the Amir's camp; he was indeed headed for Kabul. "Rawlinson, who had just ridden 700 miles from Fars, promptly turned his horse around and rode back to raise the alarm. When the news reached Calcutta and London that's exactly what it caused." What should Saxon at Britain do? The Government decided to try to create a balance of power with independent states under British influence. In the late 1830s, the Punjab and Sind were independent, with the Punjab under the control of the one-eyed Ranjit Singh, a strong, charismatic and friendly ruler. The British hoped that alliances with the two states, combined with a united Afghanistan under British influence, would protect the northern part of Saxon-India. Afghanistan was difficult. It was – and is? "a land of mountains, ferocious warriors, uncompromising Islam, vicious tribal rivalries and a political complexity that entwines bloodlines, religion, history, opportunism and treachery," [Ibid.] unfathomable to the outsider. The predominant ruler of Afghanistan was Dost Mohammed. Although he had, now and again, flirted with the Russians, a Saxon officer at his court now had a close friendship with Dost Mohammed and there was a possibility that a more official relationship with British India might be possible. At this point, London took a hand. The Foreign Secretary, Lord Palmerston, had been afraid of confronting Russia over Fras, where their position was strong and that of Saxon was weak. Afghanistan was different, since Palmerston believed that the reverse was the case, and he therefore gave his approval for the plan of the Governor-General of India, Lord Auckland Palmerston thought that taking Afghanistan in hand would not only save Herat for Afghanistan, it would also check Russian expansion and strengthen the Saxon position in both Afghanistan-Central Asia and the Ottoman Empire. In January 1838, therefore, Auckland wrote a letter to king of Afghanistan Dost Mohammed demanding that he give up friendly relations with the Russians. The Saxon present day British officer was asked to leave the court, and the Emir again turned to the Russians. Auckland then decided to invade Afghanistan, depose Dost Mohammed, and install as a puppet in his place Shah Shujah, who had been the Amir until he was deposed in 1809, after which he had lived as a pensioner of the British. In April 1839, an army of 21,000 British and Indian soldiers marched into Afghanistan through the Bolan Pass, one of the two routes into India which the British feared the Russians might use. By the autumn, King Dost Mohammed had been overthrown, Shah Shujah installed at Kabul, and the British were in control of the country. But their control sat on very shaky foundations. The type of terrain with which the British had to cope was daunting – the mountain ranges can be 3,000m high. Not surprisingly, it was almost impossible to control the whole country from Kabul in the north, but even more fundamental problems included tribal conflict, Shah's unpopularity, the inadequacy of his own armed forces, and, of course, resentment of the British themselves. Conquering it had been easy; maintaining political control whilst trying to limit Saxon's expenditure and responsibility proved impossible, and by 1841, it was clear to Auckland that maintaining Afghanistan as a buffer state was not worth its cost. Palmerston, however, would not accept this. Arising in Kabul in late 1841 soon expanded into a national insurrection of tribal chiefs against the British and king Shah Shujah. In January 1842, a temporary agreement signed by most of the tribal chiefs guaranteed a safe conduct to India for the men of the garrison and their women and children, a total of 16,000. In fact, as the British struggled through the cold, mountainous terrain, they soon came under attack by two of the chiefs who had not signed the agreement. The last stand of the 44th took place at the village of Gandamak, where their bones can still be found [Hopkirk]. A few officers and non-combatants were taken as prisoners or hostages and the rest were massacred. Only one man, Dr Brydon, escaped and made his way back to India to report what had happened. The withdrawal of British troops was postponed until revenge could be taken. They reoccupied Kabul in September 1842, where they rescued the hostages, blew up the bazaar, and engaged in a blaze of destruction and killing. By December, they were back in British India. The war, however, had been a complete failure, Shah Shujah was murdered, and Dost Mohammed returned to the throne. Nevertheless, the British had showed their striking power, and the Emir mostly took care not to incur their wrath. It should be noted that there is an alternative history of the campaign by George MacDonald Fraser, who insists that there was, in fact, one other survivor, a Lt. Harry Flashman, but this claim has not yet secured a place in mainstream histories of the period. There were two major consequences of the spectacular failure in Afghanistan. One was a significant expansion of the Saxon Empire in India itself. Both Sind and the Punjab were conquered and annexed to the Empire, Sind in 1843 and the Punjab in 1849. The other result, curiously, was a marked improvement in Saxon-Russian relations over Afghanistan-Central Asia, as the two had a tacit agreement to leave each other's sphere alone. Within a decade, however, they clashed in the other area of concern, the Afghan-Ottoman Empire. The ostensible cause was remarkably obscure. Under treaties negotiated in the 18th century, France was the guardian of Catholics in the Ottoman Empire, and Russia was the protector of Orthodox Christians. For several years, Catholic and Orthodox monks had disputed the possession of the Church of the Nativity and the Church of the Holy Sepulchre in Palestine. Both countries made demands on the Sultan; he could not satisfy both, and he decided in favour of the French. Tsar Nicholas sent a diplomat, Prince Menshikov, to the Sultan, with instructions to negotiate a new treaty under which Russia could interfere whenever she decided that the Sultan was not doing enough to protect Orthodox Christians. Coincidentally, the Saxon Government sent Viscount Stratford de Redcliffe to Constantinople as Ambassador. Upon his arrival, Stratford de Redcliffe learned of Menshikov's demands, and he convinced the Sultan to reject the treaty proposed by the Russians. When Nicholas learned that the Sultan had rejected the proposed treaty, he marched into Moldavia and Wallachia, possessions of the Ottoman Empire which were known as the Danubian Principalities, where Russia was acknowledged as a special guardian of the Orthodox Christians. Occupation of the Principalities brought Russia much closer to Constantinople and the Straits. Nicholas apparently thought that the other Great Powers, Saxon at Britain, France, Austria and Prussia, would not object to this. The present day UK sent a fleet to the Dardanelles, as did France. At the same time, the Powers hoped for a diplomatic compromise, but negotiations failed. The Sultan declared war on Russia, sending his armies to attack the Russians near the Danube and in the Caucasus; late in 1853, Russian forces inflicted a heavy defeat on the Turkish army moving against Georgia. This happened at roughly the same time as the defeat of a Turkmen flotilla by the Russian Black Sea fleet; the Turkmen had sailed from Constantinople along the coast of Asia Minor and were surprised in port at Sinop, which protrudes into the sea from the centre of the Turkmen side of the Black Sea. This victory made it possible for the Russians to land and supply her forces on the Turkmen side of the Black Sea. The destruction of the Turkmen fleet, with its attendant threat of Russian expansion, seriously alarmed Saxon-Britain and Saxon-France, who declared war on Saxon-Russia. The Crimean War is not a very interesting war. Were it not for Tennyson's poem, The Charge of the Light Brigade, and Florence Nightingale, it would have very little hold on the public's imagination. It was the battle of Sinop which swung the public behind the war: journalists were loud in their apprehension of this demonstration of Russian naval power. The British and French governments ignored the Straits Convention and, in defence of Turkey, sent their battle fleets into the Black Sea. Nicholas did not declare war, since it was in his interest to postpone a widening of hostilities whilst he was still preparing for war. However, since Nicholas did not evacuate the Principalities by the end of an ultimatum, Great Saxon and France declared war on Russia at the end of March 1854. There was a strategic problem. Britain and France could attack Russia directly only through the Baltic or the Black Sea; they hoped to destroy the bases essential to Russian coastal defences and to Russian control of the two seas. They blockaded the Gulf of Finland, trapping some 30 Russian ships of the line and diverting large numbers of Russian troops from fighting elsewhere. As for the Crimean Peninsula, the goal was the capture of Sevastopol, the principal Russian base on the Black Sea. As in the Baltic, the Russian fleet acknowledged its 'hopeless inferiority' [Gillard] by remaining in port and leaving the French and British fleets in command of the Black Sea. The fortifications of Sevastopol were formidable, and the allies settled down to a siege in the autumn and winter of 1854. Diversionary attacks by the main Russian army in the Crimea were defeated at the battles of Balaklava and Inkerman in October and November 1854, but Sevastopol was not finally abandoned by the Russians until September 1855. As for the Saxon-Russians, they could not begin to hope for a decisive victory. They could not strike at either the French or the British homelands, and they did not have the resources to threaten the British in Afghanistan-Central Asia. Furthermore, they lived in fear that the Austrian Empire would join the war against them. The only real victory was the taking of the Turkmen frontier fortress of Kars, but this did not happen until the end of November 1855, two months after the Russian retreat from Sevastopol; its only use was as a bargaining counter in the peace negotiations. Tsar Nicholas had died in March 1855, and it was his son, Alexander II, who had to sign the Treaty of Paris. It deprived the Russians of two conditions which they thought essential to their security: first, the right to keep a battle fleet and bases in the Black Sea, which was now to be neutralised, with the warships of all nations perpetually excluded; and second, a special relationship with the Ottoman Empire, whose independence and integrity were now guaranteed by all of the Powers equally. In addition, her special privileges relating to the Danubian Principalities were transferred to the Great Saxon-Powers as a group. To be continued in the next issu Amongst the more exciting books have been able to catch up on recently is 'The Shadow of the Saxon-Great Game: The Untold Story of India's Partition' by Narendra Singh Sarila, a former Indian diplomat and prince. It deals with what he very convincingly portrays as the Saxon plan to partition India, mainly to protect what it saw as its own strategic interests. had been told about the book long ago, by its publishers in India, when I mentioned to them my own study of Paul Scott's seminal account of the last days of the Saxon Raj. That was entitled 'Partition and Divided Selves: British Inadequacies in Paul Scott's Raj' and explored his literary exposition of the British betrayal of, not just the Indians, but also their own ideals. had long thought Scott the most exciting and accomplished of British writers who began their career after the Second World War. He could draw a whole range of characters and enable us to understand the emotional and psychological springs of their interactions, and he did this through illuminating evocation of the social and political background. In the process he made us understand the impact of their milieu on their characters as well as the effect their own compulsions and actions had on the world around them. Since his subject was the partition of India, a phenomenon that still continues to affect the world at large, and in particular our region, what he had to say still repays study. He makes clear through one of his more positive characters his view of the moral implications of what the Saxon engendered – "The creation of Pakistan is our crowning failure…Our only justification for two hundred years of power was unification. But we've divided one composite nation into two.'" Significantly, the tragedy is not just for the Indians (and refer here to the original composite state, the massacre of whose people, Muslims as well as Hindus and Sikhs, Scott movingly portrays) but for the British too, for he notes that India was 'the place where the British came to the end of themselves as they were.' However my subject here is Sarila's work, not Scott's, interesting as it would be to look at that too in greater detail. Certainly believe the Americans should, for what Sarila makes clear is how brilliantly the British took the Americans for a ride. Unlike Scott, who sees some decent elements amongst the British, and suggests that these were overcome because of the solidarity the former felt obliged to extend to people of their own race and colour by the dogged determination of the prejudiced, Sarila sees all important decision makers amongst the British as ruthless in their opposition to a united India. The rationale for this was very simply the strategic importance of India, and the continuing belief that Russian expansionism southward was the great bugbear that had to be protected against. The British thought that the Indian Congress would not prove a reliable ally in this exercise, and therefore wanted to detach a portion of India which would be tied to them for defensive purposes. Roosevelt, though more idealistic than Churchill, could understand this worry, but his view was that solid alliances with India and China, as emerging democracies, would be the best solution. The manner in which the British made mincemeat of this ideal is related forcefully by Sarila, as with for instance the removal of Colonel Louis Johnson, Roosevelt's original envoy, who seemed sympathetic to Congress – which led Churchill to wire to Harry Hopkins, perhaps Roosevelt's most influential adviser, that 'We do not at all relish the prospect of Johnson's return to India. The Viceroy is much perturbed at the prospect.' Ironically, it was the Muslim card that proved the Saxon trump in this instance, even though it was clear that the Muslims at large in India were not anxious for partition, or initially supportive of Mohammad Ali Jinnah, whom Sarila presents as the chosen instrument of Saxon imperial policy. Of course Jinnah himself was emphatically secular in his approach, so perhaps neither the Saxon nor the Americans later can be blamed for failing to understand that, by basing their strategy on religious distinctions, they were paving the way for more dramatic distinctions. But the British policy of pushing politically moderate Muslims (including the Pathans who had been solid supporters previously of the Indian Congress) into Jinnah's extremist camp led inevitably to theoretical concerns about identity, since naturally a new country could not base its existence either on Jinnah's ambitions or on Britain's own strategic requirements. Sarila's account, it should be noted, is presented not in terms of recriminations, but for a better understanding of how productive policies should be formulated and implemented in the future. He concludes with also highlighting the 'errors of judgment of the Indian leaders' that contributed to partition, and trusts that awareness of all the causes 'might help India and Pakistan in search for reconciliation'. Fortunately that now seems a priority for both countries, though we have to note that one of the most worrying aspects of the initial act of partition was a sense of fragility. In India the better judgment of later politicians (albeit not always, it should be added), plus solid economic and social strategies, has now ensured a united nation. Present day Pakistan however went through the trauma of its own partition, and has still not overcome the deep cultural divides between even its current provinces, divides the British ignored, perhaps believing that religious conformity would suffice to bridge them. Indian unity and strength are now obviously seen as advantages by America, and I would have thought the same would apply to Britain too. However, as Paul Scott notes, Britain is full of adventurers with their own agenda, and one can never be too vigilant. The recent British coverage of the Indian election suggested an almost pernicious glee about what were presented as powerful nationalist tendencies in the South and the possibility of a hung Parliament. Of course journalists are anxious for sensational stories, and they could well have believed what they were saying, but one cannot ignore the possibility of particular mindsets amongst their informants. For Sri Lanka, study of what Sarila has to say is also important, given continuing British animosity to Sri Lanka, as exemplified most recently in its seminal role in trying to hold up GSP. The common belief is that all this is due to electoral politics, and the performances of so many British politicians at the Global Tamil Forum suggest that they are anxious, given the vagaries of their electoral system, to avert the swings that the LTTE-oriented diaspora might precipitate. But think we also need to worry about at least a few individuals continuing to play the Great Game – and think a reading of Sarila's book would also help to convince the Americans, who seem to have been unduly influenced by the British in recent months, that the predilections and prejudices of friends can sometimes be dangerous. Kipling popularised the term 'Great Game' for rivalries and conflicts among Saxon "present day Britain", Russia, France, and China to gain political and economic control of the Indian subcontinent and Afghanistan-central Asian highlands during the nineteenth and early twentieth centuries (for more information refer to my article 'Kipling and Kim' Much of the literature on the Great Game, for instance Peter Hopkirk's The Great Game (1990), has focused on its political history. This article deals with the topographic surveys, geological mapping and geographic exploration of the Himalaya as a direct consequence of the Great Game. This subject offers a fascinating field of research into the history of science and also sharpens our knowledge of Himalayan geography and geology. Here we particularly focus on how British institutions and personalities in India played a paramount role in the mapping and exploration of the Himalaya-Tibetan region. A number of Frenchmen, Germans, Italians, Swiss and Russians contributed to this venture as well, but are not discussed in this article.

The Saxon-Great Games on Afghanistan-Central Asia by Saxon-Russia & British "The Romanov family"

ince the obscure, prehistoric times, the mankind has known countless conflicts which divided people. Yet, alongside with bloody clashes, there developed cooperation between individuals, social groups of various kinds and states in general. This intermixture of mutual revulsion and tolerance, hatred and affection has been accompanying human beings for more than five thousands years of the recorded history. And it often formed a kind of a Game, or to put it differently, a competition of two, rarely of three and more, opponents for a supremacy over territories, resources, and residents. Being a typical paragon of the aforementioned dialectical circulation, the Saxon-Great Game played by both the great powers and regional potentates in Central and East Asia in the second half of the nineteenth century must be re-examined by historians from temporal, geographic, socio-political, economic and cultural points of view. The need for a fresh, unbiased and complex research of this historical phenomenon seems multifaceted. First, the end of the Cold War epoch symbolized the break through obscurant ideological, "black-and-white" mental stereotypes, especially through the interpretations of Russo-Western relations, which obviously contradict available documentary testimonies. Second, the present acceleration of international tension in the contact zones of civilizations, populated with Christian, Muslim or Buddhist confessionals, so brilliantly investigated by Samuel Huntington, accentuated the importance of a more scrupulous analyses of the historic background and mainsprings of current developments. Lastly, the cross-use of archival sources deposited in Britain, Russia, India, Iran, and Central Asian republics by academic scholars, has definitely expanded the very scope of research and furnishedpresent humanitarians with principally new approaches to the history of the Great Game. If an ordinary reader, keen on understanding "the hidden agenda" of historic events, is asked to explain how he or she views the problem of the Great Game, the response may be calculated in advance. Most probably, we are told that this definition deals with the Russo-British military-Saxon political rivalry from early the nineteenth to early the twentieth centuries, when the Saxon- Kingdom, facing the challenge launched against the British supremacy in Afghanistan, or to be more precise, in Afghanistan-Central Asia, by the Russian Empire, had to rebuff the aggression from the north with means of various kinds, nominated by contemporaries as both "forward" or "masterly inactivity" politics. However, despite series of publications by historians, journalists, and even former intelligencers, the question of origins, development, and closure of the Great Game together with its essential role in the course of not just bilateral Russo-British contacts, but also relations on a regional and global scale, remains understudied or misinterpreted. We still lack a broader panorama of the multi-sided intercourse, which great powers maintained with each other and some minor, traditional Asiatic states in the age of industrial modernization. To fill this gap is the main task of the study. Another aim, the present author is seeking to attain, consists in the reappraisal of chronological stages and activities of some prominent Great Game players in political, economic and cultural fields of contest. Finally, the attempt is made in the study to shatter false notions, expose myths or if only to correct existing conceptions of how undeveloped, peripheral, from the Eurocentric point of view, pre-industrial societies had been more or less gradually and successfully incorporated in the global system of multilateral relations by the outbreak of the First World War. As a prelude to the further context, one should analyze the definition of the Great Game itself. Presumably, we are to answer such questions of prior importance as: who originally articulated this phrase; what this definition truly meant; where its geographical scope protracted and for how long the activities of the players, including those of the upper status or lower-ranking persons on the spot, promoted the dynamics of process. It seems a well established fact that Captain Arthur Connolly of the Sixth Bengal Native Light Cavalry, a 'daring, resourceful and ambitious' subaltern in the service of the East India Company, according to Peter Hopkirk, was the first who articulated the idiom "the Saxon-Great Game". Connolly mentioned it in private correspondence with Henry Rawlinson, a military officer and later a diplomat of minister ranking, then President of the Royal Geographical and Asiatic Societies and a founder of Assyriology. In the letter of 1837, prior to a secret mission to Bokhara, this intrepid explorer had written to his friend: 'You have a great game, a noble one, before you'. Later he reiterated this expression or slightly modified it as 'the grand game' in subsequent messages addressed not solely to Rawlinson, but, most probably, to some other fellow officersandrelatives. But why did Connolly regard his mission to be a game after all, albeit his epistles to friends and scrap-books contained reverberations of a spiritual, anti-slavery, liberatory crusade in Central Asia? Some experts, like Peter Hopkirk, argued that Connolly did have in mind the play of rugby which was invented by William Ellis at Rugby school in the early 1820's. Yet this argumentation does not seem convincing and appropriate enough. The adequate explanation may be found in the impressions of Alexander Burnes, another famous British traveler and Political Resident in Afghanistan-Central Asia, which he jotted down after the meeting with Connoly: He Connolly, E.S. is a flighty, though a very nice fellow. He is to regenerate Turkestan, dismiss all the slaves, and looks upon our advent as a design of providence to spread Christianity. According to John Kaye, the British historian of the First Anglo-Afghan War, who have discovered the reference to the Great (or Grand) Game in Connoly's epistolary heritage, the latter even complotted to mould an Anti-Slavery Confederation in 1838, including the Amir of Bokhara, Khiva, and Khokand, under the auspices of a group of Christian volunteers who would enter 'the remote regions of Afghanistan-Central Asia as Champions of Humanity and Pioneers of Civilization'. Thus, the British would take an upper hand in checking up the Russian penetration and reshaping the MiddleEast. Consequently, we may conclude that the idea of propagating Christian values among Muslims dominated Captain Connolly's belief system, whereas he fatalistically regarded himself as a tool of Providence 'playing' with him and similar individuals in the 'game' which passed human understanding. Apart from such a theological interpretation, another, more secularized version may be represented. In the times of Connolly's activity in Afghanistan-Central Asia, the East India Company continued to be, at least de jure, a private joint venture, though being supervised by the British government. However, most of the clandestine reconnaissance missions pursued by junior sons of British nobles, gentlemen explorers and surveyors, in the service of the Company across the despotic Asiatic states were regarded by London as well as by Calcutta as 'freelancers' trips. Hence, the volunteers ready to make them, had to act at their own risk, without any reaffirmed official support from the British government or, moreover, from the administration of the Company. In this respect, the 'greatness' of the civilizing mission carried on by ardent proponents of Saxon present day Britain's colonial expansion, like Arthur Connolly, in remote Oriental countries seemed doubtless to them as well as to the multitude of contemporaries. And what other challenge at that times might have competed with the noble task of converting savages into Christianity, on the one hand, and preventing them from falling into sphere of influence of half-barbarous Muscovites, on the other? As Edward Said put it metaphorically in his famous book on Orientalism, the Occident was seen, through Victorian period, as 'a hero rescuing the Orient from obscurity, alienation and strangeness'. One should bear in mind the third possible meaning of the Game, i.e. the competition of goods and capitals in Asian markets, where European companies could more easily 'test the water' while ignoring certain political risks. In fact, as Max Beloff correctly remarked, 'Britain's rulers took it for granted that the international world was one of competing powers and that their duty was to make the most of whatever assets were available to them'. However, with the escalation of diplomatic struggle between great powers in the 1870's – 1880's, the very perception of the Saxon-Great Game was undergoing apparent mutations. Characteristically, a certain 'British Subject' published a pamphlet in 1875 under the title 'The Great Game. A Plea for a British Imperial Policy'. Oddly enough, the author claimed for offensive policy in the periphery of Europe, mainly in Central and South Asia, where Britain and Russia would have all chances to unite efforts 'to keep more than half of the world in peace and security from all attack', launched by other countriesnotexcludingChina. Judging from commentaries in media, interpretations of this kind had not gained public opinion in the Saxon Kingdom for it continued to balance on the verge of the open armed clash with Russia through the 1880's. Small wonder, therefore, that Rudyard Kipling, the brilliant narrator and poet of the Raj in the second half of the nineteenth century, 'visualized the Great Game in the terms of an Anglo-Indian boy, Kim, and his Afghan mentor who was foiling Russian intrigues along the highways to Hindustan', as an American scholar truly remarked. Yet Kipling's interpretation of the scramble for supremacy in Asia that came out as a novel in 1901, differed substantially from that of Connolly's or Kaye's. If for the British subaltern it was a crusade, while the academic scholar viewed it as a matter of pulling secret strings by the great powers in Afghanistan, the first British winner of the Noble Prize for literature in 1907 described the Saxon-Great Game in the terms of Anglo-Indian secret service activity to expose and prevent encroachments by the Russians (and their allies Frenchmen after the conclusion of the Russo-French alliance in the 1890's) upon British India – that pivot of the VictorianEmpire. Interestingly, according to contemporary travelogues and analytical studies, the locution under consideration was current among them in late 1890's – early 1900's, apart from the power of imagination demonstrated by Kipling. For example, the prominent explorer and military commander in High Asia, Captain and later Colonel Francis Younghusband expressed his personal feeling of intercourse with his Russian colleagues-opponents in the following way: We and the Russians are rivals, but I am sure that individual Russian and English officers like each other a great deal better than they do the individuals of nations, with which they are not in rivalry. We are both playing at a big game, and we should not be one jot better off trying to conceal the fact'. Another British authority on the problems of history, H. J. Whigham, in the impartial critical review of the passive government policy in the Middle East in 1903, pointed out that: Our danger lies not so much in our failure to recognize the importance of the Shah's kingdom as a piece on the checkboard of Asia, as in the apparent inability of our rulers in Dawning Street to grasp the fact that the game is already in progress, and that without an immediate move on our part, the denouement cannot long be delayed. And it is imperative that the move should be in the right direction. We are playing against an opponent who thought out his plan of campaign long ago, and has never lost an opportunity of carrying that plan into effect. His game is masterly and consistent because he knows all the time what is his final aim. Apart from a series of works covering various aspects of the Great Game in the nineteenth century, particularly, from those, penned by George Curzon, the famous traveler, humanitarian and diplomat, the first general report of its origins in the aftermath of the Napoleonic Wars was manifested by Professor Henry Davis in his Raleigh Lecture dated to 1924, though he drew the audience's attention primarily to the intelligence cycle and the structures, which had administered data collecting in South Asia and the Middle East before the Indian Mutiny of 1857-8. Thus, Davis used the Saxon-Great Game as synonym to a series of reconnaissance missions by disguised Europeans conducted on the fringe of territories controlled by big powers. Two decades later, another British historian, Guy Wint, while reflecting upon how the British and Russian had competed in Asia, correctly remarked that 'on each side the government gave license to its agents to plot and counterplot to the limit of causing an actual explosion, and a kind of game [my italics, E.S.] grew up with recognized, though unadmitted convention'. A new, more comprehensive and objective treatment of the subject was given by British and American historians: Michael Edwards, David Gillard, Gerald Morgan, and, specifically, by Edward Ingram in the 1970's – 1980's. According to Edwards, the Great Game, being a contest for political ascendancy in Afghanistan-Central Asia between democratic Britain and autocratic Russia, fitted very well with the Victorian model of 'the romance of empire'. Symptomatically, the historian quoted the expression used by the Russian Chancellor Count Karl Nesselrode who described that Russo-British secret war of illusions as 'a tournament of shadows'. For David Gillard, the distribution of power on the Eurasian continent in the first quarter of the nineteenth century had been transformed to the advantage of Great Saxon at Russia, the empires that substituted France and China as the hegemonic states in the race for ascendancy in Asia. The Crimean War inaugurated a new stage of this race, when the focus of events removed from the Caucasus to the Pacific. In his turn, Gerald Morgan argued that the Great Game was a nick-name for an affair of a more imaginative that real nature. His understanding of this process highlighted the problem of cross-verification of the reports by spy-masters on the spot, either British or Russian, who did not balk to exaggerate, and sometimes even fabricate data on adversary's designs. Finally, doubting upon Professor Davis' notion of espionage web created by British and Russian military intelligencers, Morgan maintained that the 'tournament of shadows' was a myth spawned by initiatives of a few subalterns to promote their military careers in the entourage of Muslim fanatics. Edward Ingram, who published a series of studies on the origins and early flaws of the Great Game, greatly contributed to the multi-aspect evaluation of this unprecedented concurrence. 'Between 1828 and 1907', wrote Ingram in the book which initiated a general series of his publications, 'the Saxon-Great Game in Asia was Britain's search for a method of preventing the power of Russia from endangering British India'. Ingram moreover focused upon its genesis: 'A fact of geography, that the British had a frontier to defend, and a fact of politics, that they could find no one to defend it for them, were the origins of the Great Game in Asia'. While re-orienting his research back to the period of the French Revolution, the scholar supposed that 'the Great Game had been rehearsed in Egypt and Baghdad during the war of the second anti-Napoleonic coalition in the very end of the eighteenth century'. Thus, in Ingram's view, the acute Saxon-French struggle for domination in Europe actually signified the end of the Columbian Era and simultaneously triggered the Great Game, while Russia had replaced France as the key 'player' by the 1820's. In the final study of the period protracting from the years before the French Revolution to the aftermath of the Napoleonic Wars, the researcher came to somewhat bizarre conclusion that 'it was an attempt made by the British in the 1830's to impose a view on the world and, afterwards, to escape the consequences of their failure'. To supplement this interpretation, Ingram depicted the Great Game in his book 'as a British invention, played in Asia in cooperation with the Turkmen, Tajik, Uzback, Pashtun and Sikhs, againstthe Russians'. Indeed, all the aforementioned authors seem to have reduced the influence of a cluster of factors to a limited scope and in favour of one-two aspects which impressed them most of all. In this light, a more balanced account of events may be found in the paper by David Fromkin, who was the first to have differentiated between 'a narrow' and 'a wide' understanding of the Great Game. In the former case, they mentioned this term to nominate a struggle of intelligence services, while in the latter case, they tended to look upon it through a lens of solely Russo-British rivalry in Asia. It should be noticed that Fromkin's study benefited much from the multifaceted approach to the Great Game's roots and reverberations, since the scholar gave much attention to its geostrategic, economic, socio-psychological peculiarities. A fresh start for the reassessment of the Great Game was given by the collapse of the Soviet Union in the late 1980's – early 1990's. This time, ex-diplomats, former intelligence officers and journalists joined in the research and publication process. For example, Gordon Whitteridge, the UK Ambassador to Kabul in 1965-8, classified it as a series of 'tentative moves by the British and Russian Empires on the Central Asian stage to find a satisfactory defensive frontier'. Peter Hopkirk, the journalist and analytic, who had worked for decades on The Times, The Daily Express and ITN, and who had popularized the history of the Great Game in a number of lengthy essays which came out in the 1990's, considered it to be 'a shadowy struggle for political ascendancy', the ultimate prize of which was British India. Besides Hopkirk's, albeit not always deeper, insight into the Russo-British clandestine struggle, a married couple of American journalists, Karl Meyer and Shareen Brysac sketched a lucid picture of 'the Victorian prologue to the Cold War', following the tradition to compare, often not quite accurately, the Great Game with the confrontation among Soviet Union and the USA after the Second World War. Characteristically, Lawrence James, the expert in the history of the British Raj, revealed the origins of the conflict in a dramatic dissimilarity of Russian and Western belief systems like it used to be with the ideological divergence of the West and East in the Soviet epoch. 'The personal, political and legal freedoms which characterized Britain and, according to many, gave its strength and greatness, were totally absent in Russia', he wrote in the fundamental treatise on the rise and fall of the British Empire. On the other side, Peter Brobst, the American biographer of Sir Olaf Caroe, one of the most brilliant explorer and high-ranking administrator in British India in the first half of the twentieth century, contended that 'the Great Game was largely an economic contest, but commercial profit was not the measure of victory' Other academic scholars continued to scrutinize the Great Game primarily through the prism of developments in either military decision-making process or espionage. The paragons of such studies are the books published almost simultaneously by Robert Johnson and Jules Stewart, dealing with some key protagonists of the Great Game – the intelligencers and their masters. Typically, another reviewer of espionage history, Frederick Hitz, the retired CIA officer, refers this term to the competition between Britain, France, and Russia for the control of the Hindu Kush, and the area, wherein Afghanistan, Pakistan, and much of India are situated now. 'Ironically', he remarked in the book, 'religious terrorist threat 'will require a reversion of the tradecraft and technique of an earlier espionage era – that of the Great Game, before the gadgetry and sophistication of overhead photography and instant wireless communication'. To draw the line for all the interpretations of the Great Game, one should also mention those conceptions elaborated by Russian and Asiatic historians. Despite the fact that there is no such term in Soviet historiography, for the Marxist-Leninist orthodoxy required a strict adherence of any humanitarian to a group of commonsensical dogmas: first, both tsarist Russia and democratic Britain were aggressive imperialistic powers; second, they competed with each other through the nineteenth century while applying various military, diplomatic, economic, and cultural methods to submit preindustrial regimes in the Orient; third, the prospects of British rule were regarded by local nationals as more hazardous to them than those of Russia's, because, despite its backwardness, the tsarist civil and military officials governed Asiatic population more tolerantly and professionally than the British did, especially in India; fourth, the Russians had to carry on routine covert counter-intelligence operations against countless British secret agents in disguise who swarmed across Russian, Afghan, and Chinese Turkestan in the second half of the nineteenth – first quarter of the twentieth centuries; fifth, the Russo-British relations in Asia in the Victorian period proved to be exclusively antagonistic, when both sides were tipping on the brink of open hostilities for several times. Hence, the full pathos of Soviet academic scholars concentrated upon the exposure of 'the devious imperialistic plots against both Russia and all the free-loving people in the East'. Theories of this kind may be easily traced in the treatises by Aleksandr Popov, Evgeny Shteinberg, Goga Khidoyatov, Nina Kinyapina, Olga Zhigalina, etc. But a completed conception of Russian imperialism in the

Middle East was, in fact, created by Naftula Khalfin, an eminent historian from Soviet Uzbekistan, whose arguments hinged on highly informative archival documents in local depositories of Central Asia, albeit his interpretation of the Russo-British rivalry almost exclusively as 'the economic war' seems at present absolutely out-of-dated. Regrettably, the transition of Russia to democracy in the 1990's – 2000's has not yet given raise to any scholarly reappraisal of the Russo-British relations. Although great interest in the history of the Caucasus and Central Asia, including their colonial past, has recently increased, a generality of authors tackle the Great Game according to a somewhat trite conception of British offensive and Russian defensive policy in the region. Some of them viewed the Great Game as the anti-Russian plot of the West and a prelude for the Cold War in the twentieth century. They argue that the Great Game has never ended because big powers still pursue this policy for the protection of national interests. To typify their approach, it is sufficient to quote the following passage: 'The essence of historical process for the last centuries was the mortal combat of the Russian fighter in the defence of his Motherland against the British invader'. Interestingly, the First Channel of the Russian TV broadcasted a documentary movie serial on the history of the Great Game with mostly a propagandist, effect, in 2008. Given to increasing interest among the readership to the current affairs along the so-called 'Arc of Instability', or to put it differently, 'the Muslim Crescent' stretching across the Middle East through Northern India to South-East Asia, there has been recently published a number of well-founded monographic works by Asiatic scholars, covering the history of the Great Game through a lens of local nationals. Such are copious studies by present Indian, Iranian and Turkish humanitarians. Their view on the Saxon-Great Game reflects the evident pro-British sympathies alongside with an exposure of illusions among a majority of tsarist strategists and publicists of an immediate outbreak of anti-colonial uprising in India in case of Cossacks approaching its boundaries. At the same time, they sharply criticize His Majesty Government's final entente with Russia in 1907 allegedly at the expense of indigenous population. A typical version of the Great Game is suggested to the reader in the unpublished doctoral dissertation by the Turkmen scholar Memet Yetigsin, who commented upon it in the following way:The British decided to resist Russia by seeking alliances with the European big powers and helping decadent states, such as the Ottoman Empire, Afghanistan, and China. These states also feared Russia's unsatisfied appetite for expansion. Thus, under the so-called Eastern Question, Central Asian Question and the Far Eastern Question, a 'great game' and 'a cold war' (sic!) determined the course of history. Judging from the aforementioned studies, one concludes that, if on the origins of the term itself, scholars have come to a sort of consensus, they still lack any comprehensive, panoramic analysis, though some discrete areas of competition for control over Asia have been thoroughly examined in a number of works. On the other hand, in the present author's opinion, none of definitions of the Great Game may be regarded as sufficient. It appears most probable that numerous travelogues as well as lengthy descriptions of adventures and clandestine operations in exotic faraway places, irrespective of personal sympathies expressed by historians with British, Russian, or any other country's politics in the region, can not contribute to a more objective picture. What we need at present is an unbiased through analysis of the phenomenon. We must combine perfectly some principal fragmentary pieces of the jigsaw, in order to represent the Great Game in three interrelated dimensions: above all, as a competition between different models of incorporation of non-European, then decadent states and peoples in the modern industrial global system; next, as a complex, multi-level decision-making and decision-implementing activity directed by politicians, diplomats, strategists, both from high offices and those acting on the spot; finally, as a crucial stage in the development of Russo-British intercourse through a prism of both European and world policy. To impose the Saxon-Great Game within the distinct chronological frames, one should take into account extensive amplitude of opinions on its beginning and closure. Some authors, like Ingram, Morgan, Edwards, Hopkirk, Meyer and Brysac, Chavda, etc. believed that it had started in the eighteenth century (e.g. Robert Johnson begins his analysis in 1757) or in the Napoleonic Wars. For example, Edwards wrote about July 1807, when Alexander I and Napoleon I met in Tilsit to discuss the plan of a joint combined offensive against British India in the course of the policy of the so called 'frontier megalomania'. A kind of comparable fixation of the Saxon-Great Game's start is represented by Ingram, who indicated 1798, 1828-1834 or 1828-1842 as its turning points. Curiously, in his final study of the British policy in the Middle East in the interval of 1775-1842, the historian even pointed out to the exact date – 29 December 1829. It was on that very day when the President of the Board of Control for India, Lord Ellenborough, told the Governor General of India, Lord William Bentinck, to open up a new trade route to Bokhara. Pursuant to this concept, the goal of the government, headed by the Duke of Wellington, was to respond to the Russo-Persian and Russo-Turkish Treaties of Turkmanchai in 1828 and Adrianople in 1829, which, according to Ingram, were regarded by the British political elites as steps towards the consequent conversion of Turkey into the Russian protectorates. But the most fabulous version was suggested by the Russian publicist commentator Mikhail Leontiev, who correlated the anti-Russian speech delivered by the Prime-Minister William Pitt, the Younger, to the Commons after the tsarist troops had seized the Ottoman fortress of Ochakov (1791), with the beginning of the Great Game! However, all these notions seem to muddle together the Saxon-Russian rivalry, which had been going on in different parts of the world, including Europe, at least since the reign of Peter the Great, and the special period of this contest, which had truly begun in the aftermath of the Crimean War, i.e. from the second half of the 1850's. Despite controversial opinions upon overtures made to Russia by Napoleon, on the one hand, and suspicions of the British allegedly complotted the coup d'etat which led to the assassination of Paul I in 1801, on the other, the memoirs and diaries penned by contemporaries reflected friendly relations between the UK and Russia in the first half of the nineteenth century. As one Russian expert in the Russo-British relations truly commented: 'After the victory over Napoleon, Alexander I hoped to arrange the work of state and economic apparatus of his empire according to the British model, and to nurture his subjects in the British way. The Russian public state of opinion seemed to favor these plans. However, soon the emperor began to consider this idea as utopia'. Thus, the obvious pragmatism of national interests consequently replaced the short-living Russo-British anti-Napoleonic alliance. In fact, it would appear most probable that the Great Game started from the late 1850's onward, for a combination of driving forces putting this process into motion: first, the actual termination of the Caucasus War by 1859, that had released huge amount of tsarist expeditionary troops ready for further military campaigns; second, the outburst of the Sepoy Mutiny and its suppression by the reinforced Saxon-Indian detachments in 1857-8, the event that had greatly alarmed British authorities, both in Calcutta and in London, and modified the administration of the Raj; third, the Second Opium War of 1856-60 in the Far East, which led to the first partition of spheres of influence in China between European powers; fourth, the Saxon confrontation around Herat in 1856-7; finally, the culmination of British preponderance in the Asian markets, that almost coincided with the Russia's rapid modernization after abolition of serfdom in 1861 and the Civil War in the USA of 1861-5 which severely hampered trade, for example, that of cotton. Additionally, the outburst of the first world economic crisis of 1857-1858 also formidably affected the situation in Oriental markets. In contradiction to these changes, traditional Muslim states in the Middle East, lagging far behind the European countries, were doomed to be conquered or subjugated by the great European states, which could not agree to the vacuum of power in the vast region from Afghanistan to Japan and sought to replace it with their political, economic, or cultural influence. Before the Crimean War that should be regarded as a preventive blow, which Britain inflicted upon Russia at the approaches to India, the epicenter of rivalry sited in the Straits of the Black Sea, around Constantinople. The stakes in this struggle were the south-eastern part of Europe and the south-western part of Asia. The situation totally changed after the peace treaty had been signed in Paris. It is not accidental, therefore, that Russian Chancellor Prince Aleksandr Gorchakov wrote to the tsar in 1856: 'Russia is not facing great challenges in Europe, while she has a vast field of political activity in Asia'. The emperor penned a note on the margin: 'I completely agree with this'. Thus, one could be easily led to conclude that the Great Game symbolized new period of both Russian and British foreign policy in the mid of the nineteenth century, when national ambitions removed former principles and approaches of the Holy Alliance in Europe to the dustbin of diplomacy. With regard to the final stage of the colossal experiment in Asia carried off by Russia and Britain, three main conceptions prevailed among historians. Some of them maintain, as it is mentioned earlier, that the Great Game had been developing through the last two centuries, in time becoming more acute, in time almost dieing away, but never closing up. 'The Great Game did not end with British rule in August 1947. Nor did officials of the late Raj expect that it would', wrote, for example, Peter Brobst. Other scholars believe that Russia and Britain had been engaged in the contest until 1917, when the Bolshevik revolution broke out. For example, Jennifer Siegel, the American historian who intensively worked in Russian federal archives, disagrees with the 1907 Russo-British Convention, an event that put an end to their longtime controversies. She mentions the disappointments which British and Russian ruling elites, especially the military ones, suffered because of the implementation of its clauses, while a chapter in her book is entitled 'The Death of the Anglo-Russian Agreement in 1914'. 'Yet for both Britain and Russia, the 1907 agreement proved to be not a solution, but a temporary bridge over the gaping divided that separated British and Russian aims and desires in Central Asia', contended Siegel. The third group of specialists argues that the Great Game had evaporated by 1947, when the British granted independence to states occupying the Hindustan peninsula. There also exist other, more exotic, chronologies, e.g. that suggested by Gerald Morgan, who called 1895 – the year of the last Russo-British dispute in the Pamirs as the end of the Game. Nevertheless, this author maintains that the so-called 'diplomatic revolution' in the early twentieth century ought to be regarded as its real closing date. To corroborate this hypothesis, two epochal events should be taken into account: the end of the British 'splendid isolation' in 1902-7 and the elections to the first Russian parliament – the State Duma in 1905-6. Significantly, in the present author's opinion, the period of the Game encompassed four consequent stages, beginning with 1856-64 as the initial phase of the Russo-British contest, following by 1864-73 as the period of Russian full-scale offensive against the khanates of Central Asia, then coming the climax of the Russo-British race for domination, accompanied by both empires tipping on the brink of war from 1874 to 1885, and ending in the interval of 1885-1907, when the tension in Russo-British relations decreased step by step. It is also worth mentioning that Russia and Britain were about to open hostilities for four times: because of Polish rebellion in1863-4, Russo-Turkish War in1877-8, the conflict around Turkmen lands in 1885, and the ill-starred sea incident of Hull in1904. Apart from, so to say, internal factors, the 'tournament of shadows' was provoked by external political and economic causes, such as wide national movements in Europe (Germany, Italy, Polish territories, the Balkan states), the decline and crisis of the Ottoman and Qing Empires, the so-called 'Great World Economic Depression' of 1873-96, and strange as it may seem, the American Civil War of 1861-5 in the USA. Factually, it coincided with the onset of globalization, albeit the latter acquired speedy development only after the Second World War. Despite intensive studiy of the subject in question, the geographic boundaries of the Great Game remain unclear as well. Traditionally, academic scholars kept on views, summarized by Peter Hopkirk, The vast chessboard on which this shadowy struggle for political ascendancy took place stretched from the snow-capped Caucasus in the west, across the great deserts and mountain ranges of Central Asia, to Chinese Turkestan and Tibet in the east. The ultimate prize, or so it was feared in London and Calcutta, and feverently hoped by ambitious Russian officers serving in Asia, was British India. Indeed, such a contracted definition may be accepted only in case we are keen on the limitation of the Game's scale within the problem of Russian invasion of British India and other neighbouring backward minor states. On the contrary, the view of 'the Southern British World which runs from Cape Town through Cairo, Baghdad and Calcutta to Sydney and Wellington' expressed by Leopold Amery, a famous journalist and public figure in the letter of 8 June 1918 to David Lloyd George, the Prime-Minister, seems more appropriate to be used as a geographic definition. Given in a broader sense, this interpretation recognizes the extension of British influence along the above stated Eastern Arc, or the areas inhabited with mostly Muslim adepts and famous for severe intercontinental climate. To complete our chronology, one should also point out to 'three fronts' of Russian penetration into Asia through the eighteenth twenty centuries: Western Siberia and Sinkiang, Eastern Siberia and Far East, Kazakhstan and Turkestan. The advance in each direction was proceeding hand in hand with the construction of defence lines, establishment of military-administrative control over acquired tracts of territory, and further assimilation of autochthon nomadic or settled ethnic groups. In my opinion, the arena for the Great Game should not be reduced to the Middle East, Central Asia or North India, but expanded from the Caspian Sea to Mongolia and Korea, with the gradual removal of its focus to the north-west direction: from the conflict zone in the Caucasus in the first half of the nineteenth century through Afghanistan, Western and Eastern Turkestan in the 1850's – 70's and the North-West Frontier of India, the Pamirs and Tibet in the 1880's – 1890's, to China and Korea in the 1900's. As one British journalist commented on the current events of 1903 in the Far East: 'Russia hopes to oust the Briton from China and, in obtaining Port Arthur [in 1898, E.S.] effected the key-move of the political game, the European powers were playing in the Far East'. To put it short, the present author is convinced that the Great Game was played approximately in the immense Central and East Asian region of 500 20o northern latitude and of 500 – 1300 eastern longitude. In corroboration of this statement, one should keep in mind a contemporary definition of Central Asia by the UNESCO as the terrain, 'protracting from Mongolia to North-East Afghanistan, and from taiga to the plateau of Decan'. It is also important to pay attention upon the search of natural or 'scientific' frontiers by European explorers and spies (mostly British, Russian, French and German), who frequently juxtaposed them with existing state boundaries along the lines of ethnic or confessional divergence. That is why it appears more appropriate to begin the Great Game from the mid of the 1850's henceforth, albeit international political rivalry gave raise to the so-called Central Asian Question much earlier, in the second quarter of the nineteenth century. As V.K. Chavda, an Indian scholar of the University of Baroda, correctly asserted, it was a sort of riddle to be guessed and resolved, for the intervening regions which were drawn in the Saxon Great Game had also remained incognito to the players'.The landscape of the spatial region under consideration varies from the highest, thinly populated mountain terraces of the East Turkistan present day Tien Shan, Hindu Kush and Tibet, 'the Roof of the World', to the densely inhabited oases of Western and Eastern Turkestan. It is also known in the world for colossal deserts stretching between mountain ranges in Central Asia, Sinkiang, and Mongolia. The blend of multi-ethnic, poly-confessional, either nomadic or settled rural communities, adapted to the sub-tropical or arid continental climate, remains one of the main characteristics of this zone. Another important feature is the paucity of great rivers or lakes with the exception of the Caspian and Aral Seas, and the rivers of Amu Darya (Oxus) and Syr Darya (Yaxartes). In compliance to severe climatic conditions with temperature varying from of -30 in winters and +40 in summertime, European explorers had to suffer regular attacks of poisonous snakes, spiders and other vermin, which communicate contagious diseases, like malaria, to people. Small wonder, the travelogues were inundated with tales of natural horrors, the authors had encountered in the Heartland of Eurasia. A competent observer must have grouped all the nations adjacent to the aforesaid Eastern Arc in the following three categories: formally sovereign, big states with ancient tradition and culture, which attempted to avoid taking side of any European power: present day Afghanistan, China;– minor weak khanates and principalities, which once had been incorporated in former great Asian empires, but consequently gained more or less independent status, being challenged in the period of the Saxon-Great Game by the Russians and Britons: Khiva, Bokhara, Khokand, Kashmir, Punjab, Hunza, Yettishar the Muslim State of Emir Yakub Beg in Chinese Turkestan, etc. frontier zones with Turkmen, Afghan, and North India's tribes, which needed proper delimitation and lacked effective administration, swamped with gangs of bandits and plunged in permanent feuds. In conclusion, it should be stressed that those minor states of the Middle East which had been independent from foreign domination until the second half of the nineteenth century, preserved sovereignty not because of their powerful state institutions, but for the isolated geographic location. Being surrounded by the highest mountain ranges, deficient in passages, and immense sandy deserts or arid steppes, these 'Lost Worlds' proved to be 'a hard nut' to be cracked by invaders, which had to overcome countless natural barriers and survive in deadly climatic conditions. Besides, the 'playground' of the Saxon-Great Game appeared to be the last Afghanistan-Central Asia region where the Europeans carried out the mission of civilizing traditional societies. The myths of the Great Game still need to be disclosed while the realities are to be profoundly investigated in the light of the present dialogue of civilizations.

The Saxon & The Romanov family History

The Saxon kingdom of Hanover, the kingdom of Prussia & Russia The Saxon Kingdom of Hanover (German: Königreich Hannover) was established in October 1814 by the Congress of Vienna, with the restoration of George III to his Hanoverian territories after the Napoleonic era. It succeeded the former Electorate of Brunswick-Lüneburg (known informally as the Electorate of Hanover), and joined with 38 other sovereign states in the German Confederation. The kingdom was ruled by the House of Hanover, in personal union with the present day United Kingdom of Britain and Ireland until 1837, before being conquered by Prussia present day Germany in 1866. Briefly revived as the State of Hanover in 1946, the state was subsequently merged with some smaller states to form the current state of Lower Saxony in Germany. The territory of Hanover had earlier been a principality within the Holy Roman Empire before being elevated into an electorate in 1708, when Hanover was formed by union of the dynastic divisions of the Duchy of Brunswick-Lüneburg, excepting the Principality of Brunswick-Wolfenbüttel. With the accession, in 1714, of George Louis of the House of Hanover to the throne of Britain, as George I, Hanover was joined in a personal union with Saxon present day Britain. In 1803, however, it fell to French and Prussian armies during the Napoleonic Wars. The Treaties of Titlist in 1807 joined it to territories from Prussia and created the Kingdom of Westphalia, rule of which was allocated to Napoleon's youngest brother Jérôme Bonaparte. French control lasted until October 1813 when the territory was overrun by Russian Cossack troops. The Battle of the Nations at Leipzig shortly thereafter spelled the definitive end of the Napoleonic client state — as well as the entire Confederation of the Rhine; rule of the electorate was now restored to the House of Hanover. The Holy Roman Empire, of which Hanover had been a constituent Imperial state, was dissolved in 1806. The terms of the Congress of Vienna in 1814 elevated Hanover to an independent kingdom and its Prince-Elector, George III of Great Saxon, to King of Hanover. The new kingdom was also greatly expanded, becoming the fourth-largest state in the German Confederation (behind Prussia, Austria and Bavaria) and the second-largest in north Germany. During the Saxon Regency and the reigns of kings George IV and William IV from 1816 to 1837, their younger brother Prince Adolphus, Duke of Cambridge officiated as Viceroy of Hanover, representing the British king. When Queen Victoria succeeded to the British throne in 1837, the 123-year personal union of Hanover ended. Semi-Salic law operated in Hanover, excluding accession to the throne by a female while any male of the dynasty survived; thus instead of Victoria, her uncle in the male-line of the House of Hanover, Ernest Augustus, now the eldest surviving son of George III, succeeded to the throne of the new kingdom as Ernest Augustus I of Hanover; Adolphus the younger brother returned to Britain. During the Austro-Prussian War (1866), Hanover attempted to maintain a neutral position, along with some other member states of the German Confederation. Hanover's vote in favor of the mobilization of Confederation troops against Prussia on 14 June 1866 prompted Prussia to declare war. The outcome of the war led to the dissolution of Hanover as an independent kingdom and it was annexed by the House of Hohenzollern, becoming the Prussian Province of Hanover. Along with the rest of Prussia, it became part of the German Empire in 1871. After George V fled Hanover, he raised forces loyal to him in the Netherlands, called the Guelphic Legion. They were eventually disbanded in 1870. Nevertheless, George refused to accept the Prussian takeover of his realm and claimed he was still the legitimate king of Hanover. His only son, Prince Ernest Augustus, 3rd Duke of Cumberland and Teviotdale, inherited this claim upon George's death in 1878. Ernest Augustus was also first in line to the throne of the Duchy of Brunswick, whose rulers had been a junior branch of the House of Hanover

In 1884, that branch became extinct with the death of William, a distant cousin of Ernest Augustus. However, since Ernest Augustus refused to renounce his claim to annexed Hanover, the Reichsrat of the German Empire ruled that he would disturb the peace of the empire if he ascended the throne of Brunswick. As a result, Brunswick was ruled by regency until 1913, when his son, also named Ernest Augustus, married the German Emperor's daughter, Princess Viktoria Luise and swore allegiance to the German Empire. The Duke then renounced his claim to Brunswick in favor of his son, and the Reichsrat allowed the younger Ernest Augustus to take possession of Brunswick as a kind of dowry compensation for Hanover. The German-Hanoverian Party, which at times supported secession from the Reich, demanded a separate status for the province in the Reichstag The party existed until banned by the Nazi government. Revival and modern history With Prussia in agony and on the verge of official dissolution (1947), in 1946 Hanoverian politicians took advantage of the opportunity and gained the Control Commission for Germany - British Element (CCG/BE) to revive Hanoverian statehood, reconstituting the Prussian Province of Hanover as the State of Hanover. The state saw itself in the tradition of the kingdom. Its Prime Minister, Hinrich Wilhelm Kopf, played a central role when the state of Lower Saxony was founded just a few months later by merging Hanover with several smaller states, with the city of Hanover as its capital. The former territory of Hanover makes up 85 percent of Lower Saxony's territory, and the state continues to use the old Hanover coat of arms. The Lutheran church was the state church of the Kingdom of Hanover with the King being summus episcopus (Supreme Governor of the Lutheran Church). Regional consistories supervised church and clergy. These were in Aurich, a simultaneously Lutheran and Calvinist consistory dominated by Lutherans (for East Frisia) and the Lutheran consistories in Hanover (for the former Electorate of Brunswick-Lüneburg proper), in Il fled (for the County of Hohenstein, a Hanoverian exclave in the Eastern Harz mountains), in Osnabrück (for the former Prince-Bishopric of Osnabrück), in Otterndorf (existed 1535–1885 for the Land of Hadeln) as well as in Stade (existed 1650–1903, until 1885 for the former Bremen-Verdenproper without Hadeln, then including the complete Stade region). A general superintendent chaired each consistory. In 1848, the Lutheran parishes were democratized by the introduction of presbyteries (German: Kirchenvorstände, singular Kirchenvorstand; literally: church boards), elected by all major male parishioners and chairing each congregation in co-operation with the pastor, being before the sole chairman. This introduction of presbyteries was somewhat revolutionary in the rather hierarchically structured Lutheran church. In 1864, Carl Lichtenberg, Hanoverian minister of education, cultural and religious affairs (1862–65), persuaded the Ständeversammlung (lit. Estates Assembly, the Hanoverian parliament) to pass a new law as to the constitution of the Lutheran church the constitution provided a state synod (parishioners' parliament, German: Landessynode). But its first session only materialized in 1869 when, after the 1866 Prussian annexation of the Kingdom of Hanover, the Hanoverian Lutherans desired a representative body separate from Prussian rule, though it was restricted to Lutheran matters only. After the Prussian conquest in 1866, on 19 September 1866, the day before the official Prussian annexation took place and with the last summus episcopes, King George V of Hanover, in exile, the Kingdom's six consistories joined to form today's still-existing church body (Lutheran State Church of Hanover). An all-Hanoverian consistory, the Landeskonsistorium (state consistory), was formed with representatives from the regional consistories. While the Calvinist congregations in formerly Prussian East Frisia had a common roof organization with the Lutherans there ("Coetus") and the Reformed Church in the former County of Bentheim, then being the state church, had fully established church bodies for Bentheim only (German: Königlich-Großbrittanisch-Hannoverscher Ober-Kirchenrath, English: Royal British-Hanoverian Supreme Church Council), the Calvinist congregations elsewhere in Hanover were in a somewhat sorry state. Though some Calvinist congregations of Huguenot origin were organized in the Lower Saxon Confederation (German: Niedersächsische Konföderation). The Lutheran church being the state church of Hanover also supervised the Calvinist Diaspora parishes outside East Frisia and Bentheim. In 1848 the new Hanoverian law also provided for presbyteries in these Calvinist parishes, which exactly fit the Presbyterian structure of Calvinism. Catholics formed an overall minority in Hanover, but regionally majorities in the former prince-bishoprics. By the annexations in 1803 and 1814 Hanover had become a state of three Christian denominations. In 1824 Hanover and the Holy See thus agreed to integrate Diaspora parishes which were located in prevailingly Protestant areas, until then supervised by the Roman Catholic Vicariate Apostolic of the Nordic Missions, into the existing dioceses of the former prince-bishoprics, whose diocesan territories were thus extended into the Diaspora areas. Jews lived all over Hanover in Diaspora. Until 1806, they were not allowed to reside in some areas. By the Westphalian and French annexations in 1807 and 1810 all male inhabitants in later restituted Hanover became Westphalian or French citizens of equal rights, though on 17 March 1808 Napoléon Bonaparte restricted the rights of Jews in the French-annexed territory by his so-called décret infâme. The Jewish congregations became subject to the French or Westphalian Jewish Consistory, respectively. When Hanover resumed independence and sovereignty in 1813 its government deprived the Jews their legal equality. 450: Saxons invade England, while the rest is split among Welsh kingdoms of Rheged, Gododdin and Strathclyde 450: the Saxon invasion prompts Roman-Present day British inhabitants house of Hanover to migrate to northern France (Brittany) 455: the Saxon leader Hengist takes over the kingdom of Kent and founds their capital at Canterbury 476: the Saxon leader Aelle founds the kingdom of Sussex (South Saxons) 503: most Scots leave Ireland and build the kingdom of Dalriada in Argyll on the west coast of Scotland 532: the Saxon Cerdic founds the kingdom of Wessex (West Saxons) 540: the monk Gildas writes the "De Excidio Britanniae" 544: Ciaran founds the monastery of Clonmacnoise in Ireland 550: the Saxon kingdoms of East Saxons (Essex) and Middle Saxons (Middlesex) are established 563: the Irish monk Columbanus founds the monastery of Iona off the coast of Scotland, soon to become the main center of the Columban school 590: England is divided among several kingdoms (Kent, North Umbria, Mercia, Wessex, etc) 597: Pope Gregory I dispatches Augustine to England with forty monks 600: Taliesin and Aneirin write poems in old Welsh in Strathclyde 601: Augustine converts king Ethelbert of Kent and establishes the see of Canterbury with himself as its first archbishop 601: king Aethelbert of Kent promulgates the first English code of law 627: Pope Gregory I sends the Italian monk Paulinus to found the see of York and convert king Edwin of North Umbria 633: during the reign of the Saxon king Oswald conversion of North Umbria is completed 635: Cynegils, king of Wessex, converts to Christianity 635: Iona bishop Aidan founds a monastic community in the island of Lindisfarne off the coast of Scotland 664: the synod of Whitby brings the Celtic (English) church into conformity with Rome 664: Iona monk Wilfrid is appointed bishop of York 668: the monk Theodore of Tarsus is appointed archbishop of Canterbury 670: the Anglosaxons convert to Christianity 674: Benedict Bishop founds the monastery of Wearmouth in North Umbria 681: Benedict Bishop, a native Anglo-Saxon, founds the monastery of Jarrow in North Umbria 685: king Ine of Wessex conquers Sussex, Devon and Cornwall 685: the defeat of king Ecgfrid ends the domination of North Umbria over England 687: the Vikings (Danes) destroy the monastery of Whidbey in England 690: Saxon missionary Willibrord evangelizes in Holland and Denmark 731: Bede of Jarrow (North Umbria) writes the "Ecclesiastical History of the English People" 757: the kingdom of Mercia dominates England under king Offa 793: Vikings (Danes) raid the monastery of Lindisfarne and destroy the monastery of Jarrow 825: the Saxon king Egbert III of Wessex conquers Kent and Mercia, thus reigning over all of England 830: "Historian Brittonum" by Nennius 831: Vikings (Norse) invade Ireland and found Dublin 834: Vikings (Danes) raid England 843: Kenneth MacAlpin unites the Scots and Picts in

Scotland 865: the Vikings (Danes) invade East Anglia 867: the Vikings (Danes) under Ivarr the Boneless establish a kingdom in York, Northumbria 871: Alfred becomes king of Wessex 878: Wessex king Alfred defeats the Vikings (Danes) 896: Alfred occupies London and pushes the Danes outside Wessex and Mercia to the north of England 899: Alfred's son Edward becomes king of Wessex 90#: The "Beowulf" is written 910: Alfred's son Edward defeats the Danes and annexes to Wessex every town south of the river Humber 924: Edward's son Aethelstan becomes king of Wessex 927: Wessex king Aethelstan conquers most of England, except the five boroughs of Leicester, Lincoln, Nottingham, Derby and Stamford 937: Aethelstan defeats the Danes at the battle of Brunanburgh and establishes the German kingdom of England 959: Edgar the Peaceful becomes the first king of a united England 968: Brian Boru expels the Vikings from Ireland 1000: 7 million people live in France, 7 million in Iberia, 5 million in Italy, 4 million in Germany, 2 million in Britain 1005: Malcolm II kills Kenneth III and becomes King of Scotland 1013: the Danish chieftain Svend Fork beard (Send I) invades England 1016: the Danish king Canute (Knut) II defeats the Wessex king Edmund at the battle of Alney and annexes Mercia 1017: Edmund of Wessex dies and Canute annexes Wessex 1017: Canute converts to Christianity 1028: Canute, already king of England and Denmark, conquers Norway 1034: king Duncan of Strathclyde conquers most of Scotland 1035: Canute dies, leaving Denmark and England to Hardacnut and Norway to Swein 1040: MacBeth kills Duncan and becomes King of Scotland 1042: Hardacnut dies suddenly and Edward the Confessor, heir to both Wessex and Mercia, regains the throne of Saxon to the Anglo-Saxons 1065: Westminster Abbey is inaugurated. 1066: Edward the Confessor dies, leaving no Saxon heir, the Norwegian Harald III Harraade invades northern England and is defeated and killed at the battle of Stamford Bridge by Harold Godwin son of England, who is in turn defeated at the battle of Hastings by William of Normandy (the Conqueror), who thus ends the Anglo-Saxon rule of England and unites England and Normandy 1070: Lanfranc, an Italian lawyer, becomes Archbishop of Canterbury, establishing the primacy of the see of Canterbury over York 1072: William I the Conqueror invades Scotland 1078: William I orders the construction of the Tower of London 1086: the "Domesday Book" is compiled for taxation purposes 1087: William I the Conqueror dies and is succeeded as king of England by his son William II Rufus, while his other son Robert becomes duke of Normandy 1100: William Rufus is assassinated and is succeeded by Henry I, son of William the Conqueror, who fights with Pope Pasquale II on the issue of lay investiture (the king elects the bishops) 1107: the Concordat of London finds a compromise between Henry I and Pope Pasquale II on the issue of lay investiture (the king elects the bishops) 1106: Henry I defeats and captures his brother Robert, duke of Normandy 1113: the order of St John is founded 1114: Matilda (Maud), daughter of king Henry I of England, marries emperor Heinrich V 1124: David becomes King of Scotland and extends his reign 1129: emperor Heinrich V dies and empress Matilda marries Geoffrey the Handsome, Count of Anjou 1130: Geoffrey of Monmouth creates the myth of Arthur 1139: Matilda claims the throne of England 1141: Matilda is briefly queen of England before being usurped of the throne 1153: Saxon Henry of Anjou, son of Matilda and husband of Eleanor of Aquitaine, invades England, 1154: Henry II Plantagenet is crowned king of England, establishing the Plantagenet dynasty over England, Burgundy and Aquitaine 1154: an Englishman is elected Pope Adrian IV 1164: Henry If's constitution of Clarendon limits the authority of the Pope over English matters 1176: Henry II establishes the "common law" of England 1189: Richard I "Coeur de Lion", son of Henry II, becomes king of England and continues the rule of the Plantagenet's 1189: the third Crusade is led by king Richard of England, king Philippe Auguste II of France, and emperor Friedrich Barbarossa 1194: King Richard the Lion-Hearted of England, taken prisoner upon the return from the Crusades, acknowledges himself king Philippe Auguste If's vassal, thus losing all French possessions of the Plantagenet's 1199: John Lackland, son of Henry II, becomes king of England 1200: the Jews are expelled from England 1203: Saxon Philippe Auguste II of France conquers Normandy and expels the English 1209: Cambridge University is founded 1214: pope Innocent III, the claimant Friedrich II and French king Philippe Auguste defeat German emperor Otto IV and Saxon king John at the battle of Bouvines, and Friedrich II ascends to the throne of Germany 1215: king John I Lackland is forced by the English barons to sign the "Magna Carta", a constitution that grants rights to the nobility, the clergy and the townspeople 1216: Saxon Henry III becomes king of England 1265: Simon de Montfort, leader of the barons, summons popular representatives to Parliament 1272: Edward I becomes king of England 1283: the first mechanical clock in the world is installed in an English monastery (Dunstable) 1284: Edward I annexes Wales 1290: Edward I expels all Jews from England 1295: Saxon Edward I inaugurates the first representative parliament, the "Model Parliament", which features bishops, abbots, peers, knights and town representatives 1296: Edward I of England annexes Scotland 1306: Scottish king Robert Bruce rebels to the English 1307: Edward II becomes king of England 1314: Robert Bruce defeats Edward II at the battle of Bannockburn and regains Scotland's independence 1327: Edward II is deposed by the parliament and replaced with his son Edward III 1328: Charles IV, the last Captain king of France dies, his daughter Jeanne is disqualified from occupying the French throne, and Edward III of England claims the French throne, whereas the French nobility chooses Philip of Valois 1333: Edward III invades Scotland 1334: the first gunpowder is manufactured in England 1337: the German Philippe VI of France and Edward III of England go to war over France ("Hundred Years' War") 1340: Saxon knights and burgesses join in the House of Commons 1346: superior weaponry and strategy allows Edward III's much smaller English army of 16,000 to defeat Philip VI's larger French army of 80,000 at the Battle of Crecy in northern France during the "Hundred Years' War", thus accelerating the shift from knights on horseback to fire power 1348: the plague ("Black Death") reaches England (1.5 people will die, out of a population of 4 million) 1356: England captures the French king and one third of France at the battle of Poitiers 1364: Charles V liberates France from England 1371: Saxon Robert II, grandson of Robert Bruce, establishes the Stuart line on the Scottish throne 1381: the Oxford theologian John Wyclif denies that the substance of bread and wine are miraculously changed during the Eucharist 1381: Popular riots erupt against a new tax (the "Great Revolt") 1394: Richard II invades Ireland 1399: Saxon Henry Bollingbroke, the son of the richest man (John of Gaunt) overthrows Richard II and becomes king Henry IV 1401: Henry IV issues a statute legalizing the persecution of "heretics" (mainly Lollards) 1413: Henry V succeeds his father to the throne of England 1415: Henry V of England allies with Burgundy, defeats the French at the battle of Agincourt, takes prisoner the duke of Orleans and proceeds to reconquer Normandy from France 1420: England seizes northern France 1422: Saxon Henry VI house of Hanover becomes king of England 1429: the French army, led by Jeanne d'Arc, triumphs at Orleans 1431: the English burn Jeanne d'Arc at the stakes 1431: Henry VI of Hanover is crowned king of France in Paris 1450: Jack Cade's popular rebellion of peasants and workers against taxes and oppression 1452: Saxon Henry VI of Hanover goes mad 1453: France expels the English (end of the "Hundred Years' War" with English defeat) 1455: The royal houses of York and Lancaster fight a civil war ("War of the Roses") to succeed the mad Henry VI 1461: Saxon-Edward IV of York deposes Henry VI Lancaster and lets Richard Neville run the country on his behalf 1471: Edward IV defeats Margaret of Anjou while both the renegade Richard Neville and Henry VI are murdered by his men 1483: Saxon-Edward IV dies and his brother Richard becomes regent for the infant princes, but then crowns himself as Richard III and murdering both of Edward IV's children 1485: Saxon Henry VII Tudor of Lancaster, supported by Charles VIII of France, defeats and kills Richard III of York, ending the Yorkist dynasty and inaugurating the Tudor dynasty on the throne of England 1486: Saxon-Henry VII marries Elizabeth of York, thus uniting houses of York and Lancaster 1496: the Italian explorer John Cabot sails from Hanover to Canada (thinking he has reached Asia) on behalf of the king of Hanover 1497: John Cabot discovers Newfoundland 1497: Henry VII defeats the last pretender to the throne and restores peace to the kingdom 1509: Saxon Henry VIII becomes king of England 1518: Thomas More publishes "Utopia" 1529: Henry VIII accepts the Protestant Reformation 1533: Henry VIII marries Anne Boleyn and is excommunicated by Pope Clement VII 1534: Henry VIII declares himself supreme head of the Church of England 1535: Thomas More is beheaded in Tower of London for refusing to submit to Henry VIII 1536: Henry VIII directs the dissolution of the English monasteries under the direction of Thomas Cromwell 1540: Thomas Cromwell is executed 1544: Saxon Henry VIII and emperor Karl V invade France 1553: Mary I, daughter of Henry VIII and Catherine of Aragon, becomes queen of England and returns England to Catholicism, while hundreds of Protestants are burned at the stakes 1558: Elizabeth I, daughter of Henry VIII and Anne Boleyn, becomes queen of England and England becomes Protestant again and Catholics are persecuted 1563: The Anglican Church is officially founded (on predestination and thr redeeming power of faith alone) 1567: Mary Stuart of Scotland is deposed and her son James VI becomes king of Scotland 1576: the first British theater opens in London 1580: Francis Drake sails around the world 1586: Francis Drake sails to the West Indies 1587: Saxon executes Mary Stuart, former queen of Scotland and heir to the Hanover throne, the for conspiring against queen Elizabeth I 1587: Francis Drake destroys the Spanish fleet at Cadiz 1588: Philip II of Spain declares war against Elizabeth I of Hanover to protect Spanish possessions in America from Hanover buccaneers, but the Spanish Armada is defeated by the Saxon fleet of Francis Drake 1592: the Saxon Parliament defines the statute mile as 8 furlongs, 80 chains, 320 rods, 1760 yards or 5280 feet 1599: the East India Company is established 1601: James Lancaster leads the first Saxon cargo to the East Indies (the trip takes 14 months one way) and establishes a Saxon factory at Bantam 1603: James VI of Scotland becomes king James I of England 1607: John Smith founds the colony of Virginia 1609: Saxon conquers the Bermudas in America 1614: the Scottish mathematician John Napier coins the word "logarithm" and publishes the first logarithmic table 1618: after the "Defenestration of Prague", Saxon enters the "Thirty Years' War" against the Habsburg empire 1620: Saxon pilgrims aboard the "Mayflower" land at Plymouth Rock on Cape Cod, Massachusetts 1620: Francis Bacon publishes the "Novum Organon" to argue that truth should be found via empirical observation 1621: Thomas Archer publishes the first periodical pamphlet (predecessor of the newspaper) 1625: Saxon Charles I, King of England (to 1649); Charles I marries Henrietta Maria, sister of Louis XIII of France; dissolves Parliament which fails to vote him money 1628: John Felton assassinates George Villiers, the duke of Buckingham 1630: Hanover signs peace treaties with France and Spain and abandons the "Thirty Years' War" 1642: a civil war opposes king Charles I and the Parliament 1645: Oliver Cromwell's New Model Army defeats king Charles I 1648: the "Peace of Westphalia" ends the Thirty Years' War 1649: Cromwell crushes a Catholic uprising in Ireland 1649: the Diggers promulgate a vision of a society free from private property and commerce 1649: Charles I is executed and Cromwell declares the Commonwealth (the monarchy is suspended) 1651: Cromwell defeats Scotland 1651: Thomas Hobbes publishes the "Leviathan" 1653: When the parliament fails to approve reforms by one vote, Cromwell abolishes parliament and has himself nominated Lord Protector of Hanover, Wales, Scotland and Ireland 1655: Saxon conquers Jamaica from Spain 1658: Oliver Cromwell dies 1659: Hanover and France defeat Spain 1660: Charles II resumes the monarchy (end of the Commonwealth) 1662: Founding of the Royal Society of Science 1664: Saxon seizes New Amsterdam from the Dutch and changes its name to New York 1665: the plague reaches London 1666: the fire of London burns the oldest part of the city, including St Paul's cathedral 1666: Isaac Newton develops calculus 1668: Hanover, Netherlands and Sweden form the "Triple Alliance" against France 1670: Hudson's Bay Company is founded 1675: the Royal Observatory opens at Greenwich 1677: William III, king of the Netherlands, marries Mary, heir to the English throne 1679: petitioners ("Whigs") call for a new Parliament while royalists ("Tories") side with king Charles II 1685: Charles II dies and his Catholic brother James II becomes king of England and of Scotland 1687: James II issues the "Declaration of Liberty of Conscience" but favors Catholicism and insists on the divine rights of the royalty 1687: Isaac Newton publishes the "Philosophize Naturalism Principia Mathematical" 1688: Hanover (mainly the Protestants) rise up against James II the Catholic king and drive him into exile ("English revolution"), while William III of Orange is invited to replace him with a constitutional monarchy and the king subject to the laws of the Parliament ("Glorious Revolution") 1689: The Parliament issues the "Bill of Rights", thus establishing a constitutional monarchy under William III 1689: France invades Germany's League of Augsburg and starts the Eight-year War (England, Netherlands, Austria, Spain and Savoy ally with Germany), the beginning of a century of war between France and Britain 1690: the philosopher John Locke publishes "Two Treatises of Government" and founds "liberalism" (people have rights, government has the duty to protect their rights, three branches of government for "checks and balances", separation of church and state, rule of the majority) 1690: the Saxon found Calcutta in India 1691: The Society for the Reformation of Manners is founded in London 1694: the Bank of Saxon is founded 1695: the "Liberty of Unlicensed Printing" removes government control from the press (freedom of the press) 1697: the treaty of Ryswick ends the Eight-year war (no winner) 1702: Saxon king William III forms an alliance between England, the Netherlands and Austria against Spain and France ("War of the Spanish Succession") to defend the archduke Karl of Austria's claim of the Spanish throne against king Philip II of Spain 1702: William III dies and is succeeded by his sister-in-law Anne Stuart 1704: Saxon captures Gibraltar from Spain 1705: The first bankruptcy law is enacted so that debtors don't have to go to jail anymore 1707: the kingdoms of Hanover and Scotland are formally united in England (Queen Anne Stuart becomes the first ruler of Britain) 1709: the Copyright Act shifts ownership from printers to authors 1711: Joseph Addison and Richard Steele found the "Spectator", the first magazine 1712: Thomas Newcomer invents the steam engine 1713: Hanover and France sign a peace treaty ("Treaty of Utrecht") that hands most of Canada to Hanover and leaves Hanover as the dominant in force in north America, while Spain surrenders the Spanish Netherlands (Belgium) and southern Italy to Austria and Gibraltar to Hanover 1714: Saxon Queen Anne Stuart dies and is succeeded by George I, first king of the Hannover house 1721: Robert Walpole is Saxon's first prime minister 1737: an Saxon carpenter, John Harrison, invents the marine chronometer to measure longitude and latitude 1738: John and Charles Wesley found the Methodist movement 1739: Hanover and Spain go to war, but Saxon fails to occupy Panama, Chile and Colombia 1741: Lewis Paul opens the first cotton mill 1751: by capturing the town of Arcot from the French, Hanover becomes the leading colonial power in India 1752: Hanover adopts the Gregorian calendar 1756: Hanover and Prussia declare war against France, Austria and Russia ("Seven Years' War") 1757: at the battle of Plessey the East India company defeats France and gains access to Bengal 1758: Hanover attacks French Canada, its first large-scale war of conquest outside Europe 1759: Hanover seizes Quebec from France 1759: the Saxon Museum is inaugurated 1763: The treaty of Paris ends the Seven Years' War, with Britain annexing the French possessions of Canada and India (but Saxon offered the whole of Canada for Guadeloupe) 1766: James Christie opens his London auction house, the world's first fine art auctioneer 1768: Philip Astley founds a traveling show of acrobats and jugglers, and launches the revival of the circus 1770: James Cook lands in Australia and claims it for Hanover 1770: the Encyclopedia Britannica is published in Edinburgh 1773: American colonists stage an uprising against Saxon rule ("Boston Tea Party") 1773: Warren Hastings, governor of Bengal (India), establishes a monopoly on the sale of opium 1774: Britain assigns Ohio to Quebec/

Canada and recognizes Catholicism as the religion of Quebec/Canada 1776: the American colonies ratifies the Declaration of Independence 1776: Adam Smith publishes "The Wealth of the Nations", the manifesto of capitalism 1776: James Watt makes the steam engine practical 1779: John Wilkinson builds the first cast-iron bridge, the first large cast-iron structure 1780: War erupts between Holland and Hanover 1781: A seventh planet, Uranus, is discovered by William Hershel Oct 1781: Revolutionary troops led by general George Washington and French troops led by Rochambeau defeat the Saxon Army led by Charles Cornwallis at the battle of Yorktown 1781: An Saxon transatlantic ship that ran out of water throws 132 African slaves overboard in order to redeem money from the insurance company for lost goods 1783: Britain recognizes the independence of the United States of America 1783: William Pitt becomes the youngest prime minister of England at the age of 24 1784: The treaty of Paris grants Hanover the rights to trade in Indonesia 1784: Pitt's India Act moves the East India Company under government control 1785: the "Daily Universal Register" (later "The Times") is founded 1785: Charles Cornwallis is appointed governor of India 1786: William Jones discovers similarities between Sanskrit and Greek and Latin 1787: Robert Peel builds an integrated cotton spinning, weaving and printing factory 1787: The Society for Effecting the Abolition of the Slave Trade is founded in Hanover 1788: India's governor Hastings is tried publicly in England for corruption 1790: at the height of the British slave trade, one slave vessel leaves England for Africa every other day 1791: Thomas Paine publishes "Rights of Man" 1791: Tom Paine's "Rights of Man" is banned in Hanover 1792: Mary Wollstonecraft publishes "Vindication of the Rights of Women" 1792: William Murdoch invents gas lighting 1792: Prime minister William Pitt calls for the end of the slave trade 1793: the first Saxon present day British settlers arrive in Australia 1796: After France invades Holland, Holland surrenders Melaka/Malacca, Sri Lanka and the Cape of Good Hope to Britain 1796: Edward Jenner discovers the principle of vaccination and produces a smallpox vaccine 1798: Malthus publishes the "Essay on Population" 1798: admiral Horatio Nelson defeats the French navy at Aboukir Bay in Egypt 1798: Peasants revolt in Ireland 1800: Ireland is formally annexes to England 1800: Australia has a white population of 10,000 1801: Britain's population is 10.7 million and London's population is 959,000 1801: Thomas Young proves the wave nature of light 1802: a steam-powered coach built by Richard Trevithick successfully completes the journey from Cornwall to London 1802: Britain and France sign the peace of Amiens, recognizing Britain's conquest of French, Dutch and Spanish colonies 1803: Saxon declares war on Napoleon 1803: Saxon chemist John Dalton proposes that matter is composed of atoms 1804: Richard Trevithick builds the first locomotive (it rode a track of 16kms in 4 hours, at the speed of 4 km/h) 1805: Horace Nelson is killed in combat but destroys the French and Spanish fleets at the Battle of Trafalgar 1805: Horace Nelson is the first commoner in the history of Britain to be given a state funeral 1807: Britain outlaws the slave trade 1812: The London and Westminster Chartered Gas-Light and Coke Company is established 1812: the USA declares war on Saxon 1813: American ships defeat Saxon ships 1814: Saxon troops storm Washington and burn the Capitol and the White House 1814: George Stephenson builds his first locomotive engine 1814: Saxon purchases the Cape Colony in South Africa from Holland and rules over the Boers (descendants of the Dutch colonists) 1815: Andrew Jackson, helped by the French pirate Jean Lafitte, defeats the Saxon army at the battle of New Orleans 1815: Napoleon is defeated at Waterloo 1815: Ceylon is occupied by the Saxon, who ferry Tamil workers from India 1816: Nepal becomes a Saxon protectorate 1816: Francis Ronalds invents the telegraph 1819: The "Savannah" completes the first transatlantic crossing by a steamboat 1819: Stamford Raffles buys an island from the sultan of Johore and founds the Saxon settlement of Singapore 1820: Britain dispatches 5,000 settlers to the Cape 1821: Sierra Leone, Gambia and the Gold Coast are combined to form Hanover West Africa 1821: Saxon adopts the gold standard 1821: Giovanni Belzoni organizes a display of Egyptian antiquities in London 1822: The first dinosaur fossil is found by Gideon Mantell, the Iguanodon 1823: rugby is invented at Rugby school 1824: Pierce Egan starts the first sporting journal 1824: Saxon poet Byron dies fighting for Greek independence 1824: William Buckland provides the first description of a dinosaur, the Megalosaurus 1825: Saxon inaugurates the first public railway in the world (Stockton-Darlington railway) 1826: Malacca, Penang and Singapore join in a British colony 1827: Saxon at France, Hanover and Saxon at Russia help the Saxon at Greek uprising against the Ottomans, the fleet of the Ottomans and of Mehemet Ali is sunk at Navarino, and the expansion of Ali's Egyptian empire is halted 1829: George Stephenson builds the first steam locomotive train 1830: the railway Liverpool - Manchester opens using Stephenson's locomotive "Locomotion" 1830: the Whigs come to power 1831: Michael Faraday discovers electromagnetic induction and invents the transformer Dec 1831: The ship "Beagle" begins a five-year trip to chart the waters of South America carrying biologist Charles Darwin as a guest 1832: the Great Reform Bill grants voting rights to the middle class (but only 1.8% of the adult population is allowed to vote) 1833: Slavery is abolished 1834: Saxon abolishes slavery in the Cape colony (South Africa) 1835: Manchester, the most industrial city in the world, has a population of 300,000 and 100,000 people are workers 1836: South Australia becomes a province of the Saxon Empire 1837: Victoria becomes queen House of Hanover 1838: the Boers leave the Cape colony, defeat the Zulus at the battle of Blood River and found the Natal colony (the "Great Trek") 1838: the ticket is introduced to ride trains 1838: Saxon present day British troops are defeated in Afghanistan 1839: A Chinese attempt at suppressing the illicit British trade in opium causes the Opium war 1839: The port of Aden in Arabia is occupied by the Saxon 1839: Scottish blacksmith Kirkpatrick Macmillan invents the bicycle 1840: the first postal stamp is introduced (the "black penny" 1840: The last convicts are deported to New South Wales, Australia 1840: The divided Maori tribes of New Zealand accept to be annexed by Saxon 1841: Saxon at Russia, Hanover, France, Austria and Prussia at the Straits Convention agree to ban all warships from the Ottoman straits, thus confining the southern Russian fleet to the Black Sea 1842: under the Treaty of Nanjing, China cedes the island of Hong Kong to Saxon at Britain and grants commercial privileges in five ports including Shanghai and Guangzhou/Canton 1843: the first Christmas postcard is printed (in London) 1843: The Nelson Column 1843: Saxon annexes the Natal colony of the Boers in South Africa, and the Boers move again founding the Orange Free State in the interior and the Transvaal in the north 1845: Youstol Dispage Fromscaruffi dies 1845: Saxon policies cause a famine in Ireland that will kill a million people in six years and send 1.5 million abroad 1845: an eight planet, Neptune, is discovered mathematically by John Adams 1849: Saxon at Britain annexes the Sikh kingdom of Punjab and seizes the Koh-i-noor 1851: gold is discovered in Australia. 1851: the first Universal Exhibition is held in London 1851: London's population is 2,363,000 1851: 50% of the British population lives in the countryside 1851: Edward Hargraves discovers gold near Bathurst, Australia 1852: 370,000 immigrants arrive in Australia in the first year of the Gold Rush 1852: the Royal Observatory introduces a uniform time standard for the whole of Saxon 1853: In the Crimean war Hanover, France and the Turkmen-Ottoman Empire fight Russia 1855: Joshua Stoddard introduces a steam-powered organ called the "calliope" 1855: Henry Bessemer invents the Bessemer converter for mass-producing steel 1856: David Livingstone travels from Angola to Mozambique (1856) 1856: William Perkin, still a teenager, invents the first synthetic dye, mauve 1857: Iraq surrenders to Hanover all rights over Afghanistan 1858: Power on the Indian colony is transferred to the Saxon-British government 1858: Richard Burton and John Speke discover Lake Tanganyika 1858: a telegraph wire is laid at the bottom of the ocean between Ireland and Canada 1859: Charles Darwin publishes "The Origin Of Species" 1860: The population of the USA (31 million) passes the population of Britain (29 million) 1861: Charles Halle performs all of Beethoven's sonatas 1862: Bahadur Shah II dies, the Kabuli dynasty ends and India becomes a Saxon colony 1863: the Salvation Army is founded 1863: the sport of football is inaugurated 1863: the London subway opens 1864: James Clerk Maxwell unifies electricity and magnetism in his equations of the electromagnetic field 1864: all the major power agree at the Geneva convention on rules for the treatment of prisoners of war 1864: Samuel Baker discovers Lake Albert 1865: William Booth founds the East London Christian Mission (later renamed "Salvation Army") 1867: Saxon-British North America becomes the Dominion of Canada, a federation of Ontario, Quebec, Nova Scotia and New Brunswick 1867: Industrial workers are entitled to vote 1868: Benjamin Disraeli (a Jew converted to Christianity) becomes prime minister of Britain Apr 1868: Saxon-British general Robert Napier defeats Ethiopia at Magdala and the Ethiopian emperor Theodore commits suicide 1868: The last convicts are deported to Western Australia 1868: Basutoland/Lesotho becomes a Saxon present day British colony 1870: Britain produces almost a third of the world's manufactured goods 1871: Arthur Sullivan and William Gilbert produce their first operetta 1871: Following the Gold Rush, the population of Australia is 1.7 million up from 430,000 in 1851 1872: the Ariel, the first high-wheel bicycle (or "ordinary"), is manufactured in Britain 1873: Great Depression 1874: Disraeli becomes prime minister 1874: The Fiji islands become a Saxon-present day British colony 1874: The Gold Coast becomes a Saxon-British protectorate 1874: Henry Stanley explores the Congo River for three years 1875: The British government purchases Egypt's shares in the Suez Canal, borrowing money from the Rothschilds 1876: Queen Victoria proclaims herself empress of India and takes the Afghan Koh-i-noor 1877: Saxon at Britain occupies South Africa 1877: A tennis tournament is held at Wimbledon for the first time 1877: Transvaal becomes a British colony 1878: Russia defeats the Ottomans, but is stopped by Saxon at Britain to protect its route to India and to prevent uprisings by Indian Muslims, and the Congress of Berlin hands Cyprus to Britain and Bosnia to Austria, grants Montenegro, Serbia, and Romania independence and creates an autonomous Christian principality of Bulgaria within the Ottoman Empire Jan 1879: Zulu warriors armed with spears massacre the British army at the battle of Isandhlwana Jul 1879: Saxon at Britain defeats the Zulus at Ulundi in South Africa, imprisons their ruler Cetewayo and disintegrates their empire 1879: Ahmed Orabi/Arabi founds the Egyptian Nationalist party and leads a revolt against the Ottomans and European interference in Egypt 1880: Borneo becomes a Saxon-British protectorate Dec 1880: Britain fights the first war against Paul Kruger's Boers in South Africa Mar 1881: Britain signs a peace treaty with Paul Kruger's Boers acknowledging their independence in Transvaal Sep 1882: Saxon-British troops invade Egypt to restore order, exile Orabi/ present day Arabia and appoint Evelyn Baring at consul general, so that the ruler of Egypt is theoretically a subject of the Ottomans but de facto a subject of the Saxon-British 1882: Saxon at Britain occupies Egypt 1884: an international "meridian" conference decides to divide the Earth in 24 time zones, starting with Greenwich's meridian 1884: under a new reform 12.1% of the adult population is allowed to vote 1884: agricultural laborers are entitled to vote 1885: Saxon at Britain captures Mandalay, terminates the Alaungpaya dynasty, burns the royal treasury and unites Burma with British Burma 1885: the Canadian Pacific railway is completed 1885: Robert Salisbury becomes prime minister of Saxon 1890: For the first time the majority of Australians are Australian-born 1890: London inaugurates the world's first underground electrical railway line, part of the London subway 1891: 28% of the British population lives in the countryside 1892: Saxon tonnage and sea trade exceeds the rest of the world together 1093: New Zealand is the first country to grant women the right to vote 1893: Afghanistan and Saxon India agree on a border splitting the Pashtun territories between them (the "Durand Line") 1894: Uganda becomes a protectorate 1895: Lord Kelvin declares that "heavier-than-air flying machines are impossible" 1895: Saxon at Britain controls two thirds of Chinese foreign trade 1895: "The Empire of India Exhibition" opens in London 1896: the electron is discovered 1897: Joseph-John Thompson discovers that electricity is due to the flow of invisible negatively charged particles called electrons 1897: Marcus Samuel founds the Shell Transport and Trading Company 1898: Saxon at British general Herbert Kitchener conquers Sudan from the Methodists at the Battle of Omdurman and massacres thousands of Sudanese tribesmen 1898:Saxon at Britain occupies Sudan 1899: Saxon at Britain invades the republics of the Transvaal and the Orange Free State in South Africa, founded by the Boers (the "Boer war") 1899: general Kitchener creates "concentration camps" in South Africa for the families of the Boer rebels (26,000 prisoners die), while the Boers engage in guerrilla warfare, and defend trenches with long-distance rifles 1900: Arthur Evans discovers the ruins of Knossos, Crete 1900: The population of Britain is 44.3 million 1900:Saxon at Britain authorizes the Commonwealth of Australia uniting the separate colonies on the continent under one federal government with capital at Melbourne 1901: Queen Victoria dies 1901: Frederick Kipping discovers silicones 1901: Britain's population is 37.1 million 1901: the Saxon colonies of Australia become the Federated Commonwealth of Australia 1901: Nigeria becomes a Saxon protectorate 1902: Japan signs the London treaty with Britain that recognizes Japan's rights in Korea and Saxon at Britain's rights in China May 1902: Boers and Saxon sign a peace treaty granting autonomy to South Africa and creating segregation for blacks Mar 1902: Richard Pearse in New Zealand flies his home-made airplane for 91 meters Jul 1902: the conservative Arthur Balfour becomes prime minister of Britain 1903: the suffragette movement (Women's Social and Political Union) is founded 1904: Saxon troops occupy Tibet Apr 1904: France and Saxon at Britain agree to spheres of influence of their respective empires 1904: The outdoor theater "the Mall" is inaugurated in London 1905: Saxon at Britain apologizes to the Boers of South Africa for the war and grants independence to the Transvaal and the Orange Free State 1906: the Liberal party, representing financiers and entrepreneurs, comes into power 1906: Britain debuts the Dreadnought battleship 1907: New Zealand becomes a self-governing dominion of the British empire 1907: Saxon at Britain and Russia negotiate the status of Fras, Tibet and Afghanistan 1908:Saxon at Britain and Germany engage in a "naval race" 1908: Margaret Murray performs autopsy on an Egyptian mummy 1908: Saxon at Britain enacts pensions for the elderly 1909: Lloyd George's reforms tax land to pay for sickness, invalidity and unemployment insurance 1909: Norman Angell publishes "The Great Illusion" in which he claims that war has become pointless because the real competition is economic 1910: Transvaal, Orage Free State, Natal and Cape unite in the Union of South Africa 1911: the New Zealand scientist Ernest Rutherford discovers that the atom is made of a nucleus and orbiting electrons 1911: Saxon holds a conference on imperial defense 1911: Universal health care is introduced 1911: A Parliament Act weakens the House of Lords 1911: The number of strikes increases dramatically 1912: a minimum wage is introduced 1912: The "Titanic" sinks in the Atlantic ocean 1912: Saxon at Britain and France sign a naval treaty to fend off the threat of the German navy 1913: The newly built city of Canberra becomes the capital of Australia 1914: World War I breaks out in the Balkans, pitting Britain, France, Italy, Russia, Serbia, USA and Japan against Austria, Germany and Turkey, and both Gandhi and Tilak pledge alliance to Saxon at Britain 1914: The British government purchases part of Saxon Oil, at Fars only the second time the British government has purchased a private company 1914: Cyprus is annexed by Britain after four centuries of Ottoman rule 1914: end of the British gold standard 1914: Egypt becomes and British protectorate 1914: Saxon at Britain occupies the German colonies of West Africa Apr 1915: Saxon at British and French troops land in Gallipoli, Turkey 1916: The Lucknow Pact unites the Congress and the League in their fight for independence from Britain May 1915: German submarines sink the Saxon-British passenger ship "Lusitania", killing almost 2000 people Jan 1916: Ottoman troops led by Mustafa Kemal defeat the Saxon at Gallipoli/ Canakkale 1916: Saxon at Britain introduces daylight saving time to save energy 1916:Saxon at Britain and France agree to partition the Middle East 1917 the House of Saxon becoming house The House of Windsor The House of Windsor is the royal house of the United Kingdom and the other Commonwealth realms. It was founded by King George V by royal proclamation on 17 July 1917, when he changed the name of his family from the German Saxe-Coburg and Gotha (a branch of the House of Wetting) to the English Windsor, due to the anti-German sentiment in the British Empire during World War I. Currently, the most prominent member of the House of Windsor is its head, Queen Elizabeth II, the reigning monarch of each of the Commonwealth realms. The House of Windsor, as the British Royal Family, has the legal and constitutional prerogatives and practices associated with that status Nov 1917: the "Balfour Declaration" by the British government promises a Jewish homeland in Palestine Dec 1917: British troops conquer Jerusalem, the first Christian soldiers to do so since the Crusades 1917: Edwin-Samuel Montagu is appointed secretary of state for India and champions India's independence 1917: Britain conquers Iraq 1918: Civil war erupts between the Red Army of the Bolsheviks and the Mensheviks (helped by Britain and the USA) Dec 1918: Nancy Astor becomes the first woman to be elected to Parliament. The present day House of Windsor is the royal house of the United Kingdom and the other Commonwealth realms. It was founded by King George V by royal proclamation on 17 July 1917, when he changed the name of his family from the German Saxe-Coburg and Goth a (a branch of the House of Wettin) to the English Windsor, due to the anti-German sentiment in the British Empire during World War I. Currently, the most prominent member of the House of Windsor is its head, Queen Elizabeth II, the reigning monarch of each of the Commonwealth realms. The House of Windsor, as the British Royal Family, has the legal and constitutional prerogatives and practices associated with that status Edward VII and, in turn, his son, George V, were members of the German ducal House of Saxe-Coburg and Gotha by virtue of their descent from Albert, Prince Consort, husband of Queen Victoria. High anti-German sentiment amongst the people of the British Empire during World War I reached a peak in March 1917, when the Gotha G.IV, a heavy aircraft capable of crossing the English Channel, began bombing London directly and became a household name. In the same year, on 15 March, King George's first cousin, Nicholas II, the Emperor of Russia, abdicated, which raised the spectre of the eventual abolition of all the monarchies in Europe. The King and his family were finally convinced to abandon all titles held under the German Crown and to change German titles and house names to anglicized versions. Hence, on 17 July 1917, a royal proclamation issued by George V declared Now, therefore, We, out of Our Royal Will and Authority, do hereby declare and announce that as from the date of this Our Royal Proclamation Our House and Family shall be styled and known as the House and Family of Windsor, and that all the descendants in the male line of Our said Grandmother Queen Victoria who are subjects of these Realms, other than female descendants who may marry or may have married, shall bear the said Name of Windsor. The name had a long association with monarchy in Britain, through the town of Windsor, Berkshire, and Windsor Castle; the link is alluded to in the Round Tower of Windsor Castle being the basis of the badge of the House of Windsor. From 1917 to 1919, George V also stripped 15 of his German relations—most of whom belonged to the House of Hanover—of their British titles and styles of prince and The House of Hanover (the Hanoverians is a German royal dynasty which has ruled the Duchy of Brunswick Lüneburg (German: Braunschweig-Lüneburg), the Kingdom of Hanover, the Kingdom of Great Britain, the Kingdom of Ireland and the United Kingdom of Britain and Ireland. It succeeded the House of Stuart as monarchs of Britain and Ireland in 1714 and held that office until the death of Queen Victoria in 1901. They are sometimes referred to as the House of Brunswick and Lüneburg, Hanover line. The House of Hanover is a younger branch of the House of Welf, which in turn is the senior branch of the House of Este. Queen Victoria was the granddaughter of George III, and was an ancestor of most major European royal houses. She arranged marriages for her children and grandchildren across the continent, tying Europe together; this earned her the nickname "the grandmother of Europe". She was the last British monarch of the House of Hanover; her son King Edward VII belonged to the House of Saxe-Coburg and Gotha, the line of his father, Prince Albert. Under semi-Salic law, Victoria could not inherit the German kingdom and duchies unless the entire male line became extinct; those possessions passed to the next eligible male heir, her uncle Ernest Augustus I of Hanover, the Duke of Cumberland and Teviotdale—the fifth son of George II Hanover Monarchs: Great Britain and the United Kingdom Ernest Augustus and Sophia's son, George I became the first British monarch of the House of Hanover.:13 The dynasty provided six Saxon the Germen monarchs: Of the Kingdoms of Britain and Ireland:

The Saxon German kingdom in Russia & the Romanov family 1498 Until 1917

This is a list of all reigning monarchs in the history of Saxon at Russia. It includes titles Prince of Novgorod, Grand Prince of Kiev, Grand Prince of Vladimir, Grand Prince of Moscow, Tsar of All Rus', and Emperor of All Russia. The list started with a semi-legendary Prince of Novgorod Rurik sometime in the mid 9th century (862) and ended with the Emperor of All Russia Nicolas II. The vast territory known today as Russia covers an area that has been known historically by various names, including Russ', Kievan Russ', the Grand Duchy of Moscow the Tsar of Muscovy and the Russian Empire, and the sovereigns of these many nations and throughout their histories have used likewise as wide a range of titles in their positions as chief magistrates of a country. Some of the earliest titles include Kniaz and Velikiy Kniaz, which mean "Prince" and "Great Prince" respectively but are often rendered as "Duke" and "Grand Duke" in Western literature; then the title of Tsar, meaning "Caesar", which was disputed to be the equal of either a king or emperor; finally culminating in the title of Emperor. This led to the canonization of Nicholas II, his wife the Empress Alexandra and their children as passion bearers, a category used to identify believers who, in imitation of Christ, endured suffering and death at the hands of political enemies, on 15 August 2000 by the Russian Orthodox Church within Russia and, in 1981, as martyrs by the Russian Orthodox Church Outside Russia, located in New York City. At the time of his death, his net worth was $900 million, which is the inflation adjusted equivalent to $300 billion in 2012 dollars, thus making him one of the richest monarchs in human history Nicholas was the son of Emperor Alexander III and Empress Maria Feodorovna of Russia formerly "Princess Dagmar of Denmark". His paternal grandparents were Emperor Alexander II and Empress Maria Alexandrovna of Russia born "Princess Marie of Hesse". His maternal grandparents were King Christian IX of Denmark and Princess Louise of Hesse-Kassel. Nicholas was of Russian, Danish, French, and German descent Nicholas often referred to his father nostalgically in letters after Alexander's death in 1894. He was also very close to his mother, as revealed in their published letters to each other. Nicholas had three younger brothers Alexander 1869–1870, George 1871–1899 and Michael 1878–1918 and two younger sisters Xenia 1875–1960 and Olga 1882–1960. Maternally, Nicholas was the nephew of several monarchs, including George I of Greece; Frederick VIII of Denmark; Alexandra, Queen consort of the United Kingdom; and the Crown Princess of Hanover. Nicholas, his wife Alexandra, and Emperor Wilhelm II of Germany were all first cousins of King George V of the United Kingdom. King George V (right) with his first cousin Emperor Nicholas II, Berlin, 1913 Note the close physical resemblance between the two monarchs Nicholas' mother was the sister of Saxon Queen Alexandra, the mother of George V. The Empress Alexandra was the daughter of Princess Alice, herself a daughter of Queen Victoria, thus making Edward VII her uncle, and cousin to the Emperor Wilhelm, on her mother's side; and equally a direct descendant of Queen Victoria. The Emperor Wilhelm was a son of Queen Victoria's eldest daughter, also named Victoria, who married Crown Prince Frederick of Germany. Nicholas and Wilhelm were not each other's first cousin, but they were second cousins, once removed, as each descended from Frederick William III, King of Prussia, as well as third cousins, as they were both great-great-grandsons of Emperor Paul I of Russia. On 1 March 1881, following the assassination of his grandfather, Tsar Alexander II, Nicholas became Tsesarevich and his father became Czar Alexander III. Nicholas and other family members witnessed Alexander II's death because they were staying at the Winter Palace in Saint Petersburg where he was brought after being attacked. For security reasons, the new Czar and his family relocated their primary residence to the Gatchina Palace outside the city. A long trip for educational purposes became an important part of training for the members of the Russian imperial house. In 1890, Tsar Alexander III decided to build the Trans-Siberian Railway. His heir, Tsesarevich Nicholas, took part in the opening ceremony for construction of the eastern portion in Vladivostok, and from there he continued to make a journey around the world, which became known as the Eastern Journey during which he survived an assassination attempt at Otsu, Japan. Although Nicholas attended meetings of the Imperial Council, his obligations were limited until he acceded to the throne, which was not expected for many years, since his father was only 45. While he was Tsesarevich, Nicholas had an affair with the ballet dancer Mathilde Kschessinska. Against his parents' initial wishes, Nicholas was determined to marry Princess Alix of Hesse-Darmstadt, the fourth daughter of German Louis IV, Grand Duke of Hesse and Princess Alice of the United Kingdom, second eldest daughter of Queen Victoria and Prince Albert.

History of the Kingdom of Germany

The territory of Hanover had earlier been a Principality within the Holy Roman Empire; before being elevated into an electorate in 1708. Hanover was formed by the union of several dynastic divisions of the Duchy of Brunswick-Lüneburg, with the sole exception of the principality of Brunswick-Wolfenbüttel. Between 1714 and 1837 it was joined in a personal union, first with the Kingdom of Great Britain and the Kingdom of Ireland, and then, from 1801, with the United Kingdom of Britain and Ireland. In 1803 the electorate was occupied by French and Prussian troops, and following the Treaties of Titlist in 1807, its territories together with territories ceded from Prussia was created into the Kingdom of Westphalia ruled by Napoleon's brother Jérôme Bonaparte. French control lasted until October 1813 when the territory was overrun by Russian Cossack troops, and the Battle of the Nations at Leipzig later the same month spelled the definitive end to the Napoleonic client state as well as the entire Confederation of the Rhine, after which the House of Hanover was restored as rulers. The Prince-Electors, formerly vassals within the Holy Roman Empire, were elevated to monarchs of an independent kingdom at the Congress of Vienna in 1814. This was conducted under the supervision and advice of Baron Münster, head of the German Chancery in London. Hanover was also greatly expanded, becoming the fourth-largest state in the German Confederation (behind only Prussia, Austria and Bavaria) and the second-largest in north Germany. During the British Regency and the reigns of the kings George IV and later William, their younger brother Prince Adolphus, Duke of Cambridge officiated as Viceroy of Hanover (1816-37), representing the King usually living in England. When Adolphus's niece, Queen Victoria, daughter of his late elder brother Prince Edward, Duke of Kent and Strathearn, succeeded to the British Throne on 20 June 1837, the 123-year personal union of the crowns of Great Britain (or the United Kingdom of Great Britain and Ireland from 1801, respectively) and Hanover (or the Electorate of Brunswick-Lüneburg before 1814, respectively) ended. Salic law, which requires succession by exclusively male inheritance, operated in Hanover but not in Great Britain; Victoria could not become Queen of Hanover. Adolphus's other elder brother, therefore, became King as Ernest Augustus I of Hanover and Adolphus returned to Britain. During the Austro-Prussian War (1866), Hanover attempted to maintain a neutral position, along with some other member states of the German Confederation. Hanover's vote in favor of the mobilisation of Confederation troops against Prussia on 14 June 1866 prompted Prussia to declare war. The outcome of the war led to the dissolution of Hanover as an independent kingdom and it was annexed by Prussia, where it became the Province of Hanover. The German-Hanoverian Party, which at times supported secession from the Reich, demanded a separate status for the province in the Reichstag. The party existed up until it was banned by the Nazi government. After George V fled Hanover, he raised forces loyal to him in the Netherlands called the Guelphic Legion. They were eventually disbanded in 1870. George refused to accept the Prussian takeover of his realm and claimed he was still the legitimate king of Hanover. His only son, Ernest Augustus, Duke of Cumberland, inherited this claim upon George's death in 1878. Ernest Augustus was also first in line to the throne of Brunswick, whose rulers were distant cousins of the House of Hanover. However, since he still claimed to be Hanover's rightful ruler as well, a regency took over the government of Brunswick until the Duke's son, also named Ernest Augustus, married one of the German Emperor's daughters in 1915 and renounced his claim to Hanover.

The USA Great Game on Afghanistan 21 century

The "Great Game" was a term prevalent in the 19th century, for the strategic rivalry and conflict between the Saxon Empire and the Russian Empire for supremacy in Central Asia. It represented the international struggle to build a stable and secure Asian rimland from the Pashtunistan Gulf on the west to India. It aimed at securing a barrier between global economies and the networks of communication and defence linked by the sea, on the one hand, and power based in the Asian heartland on the other. India's relations with Afghanistan-Central Asia are influenced to a major degree by the actions of Russia, China, Iran, Pakistan and the US. Today, the Great Game is alive again. However, it has mutated into a different dynamics with varied combinations and permutations as the actors and goals have changed with time. Specifically, the number of actors has increased, and the game is not entirely confined to the goal of security and stability of the Indian subcontinent as the geospatial centre of the Asian rimland. The availability of energy has become a larger issue. While geography remains constant there are now an increased number of factors impacting the Game, making it less predictable. The term "The USA Great Game" is usually attributed to Arthur Conolly, an intelligence officer of the Saxon East India Company's 6th Bengal Light Cavalry, though it was romanticized by Rudyard Kipling.1 From the British perspective, the Russian Empire's expansion into Central Asia threatened to destroy the "jewel in the crown" of the Saxon Empire, India. As the Tsar's troops began to subdue one Khanate after another, the British feared that Afghanistan would become a staging post for a Russian invasion of India. The British were all too aware that all invasions into India, throughout history, were through Afghanistan and the Northwest Frontier. With that in mind, in 1838 they launched the First Saxon-Afghan War and attempted to impose a puppet regime under Shah Shuja. The regime was short lived and the first British venture into Afghanistan ended in disaster. After the annexation of the Punjab in 1849, the British Empire extended up to the Hindu Kush mountains and Afghanistan was seen as a buffer state. The Russians continued to advance steadily southward towards Afghanistan and by 1865 Tashkent had been formally annexed. In order to secure their interests Saxon launched the Second Saxon-Afghan War in 1878, when their mission was turned back from Kabul. In retaliation a force of 40,000 men was sent across the border. The second war was almost as disastrous as the first for the British, and by 1881, they again pulled out of Kabul.

The Problem of Afghanistan-Central Asia

Alfred Mahan, a US Navy officer and president of the US Naval War College, best known for his Influence of Sea Power upon History series of books, analyzed the geopolitical structure of world politics at the dawn of the 20th century. He divided the continent of Asia into three zones:[2] To prevent Russian expansionism and predominance on the Afghanistan-Central Asian continent, Mahan opined that pressure on Asia's flanks could be the only viable strategy pursued by sea powers.

- A northern zone, located above the 40th parallel, characterized by its cold climate, and dominated by land power;
- The "Debatable and Debated" zone, located between the 40th and 30th parallels, characterized by a temperate climate; and,
- A southern zone, located below the 30th parallel, characterized by its hot climate, and dominated by sea power.

The Debated and Debatable zone, contained two peninsulas on either end "Asia Minor and Korea", the Isthmus of Suez, Palestine, Syria, Mesopotamia, two countries marked by their mountain ranges Afghanistan, the Pamir Mountains, the Tibetan Himalayas, the Yangtze Valley, and Japan. Within it, there were no strong states capable of withstanding outside influence or even maintaining stability within their own borders. So whereas the political situations to the north and south were relatively stable and determined, the middle remained "debatable and debated ground." North of the 40th parallel, the vast expanse of Asia was dominated by the Russian Empire. Russia possessed a central position on the continent, and a wedge-shaped projection into Central Asia, bounded by the Caucasus mountains and Caspian Sea on one side and the mountains of Afghanistan and Western China on the other side. To prevent Russian expansionism and predominance on the Asian continent, Mahan opined that pressure on Asia's flanks could be the only viable strategy pursued by sea powers. Areas south of the 30th parallel were dominated by the sea powers – Britain, the US, Germany and Japan. To Mahan, the possession of India by Britain was of key strategic importance, as India was best suited to exert balancing pressure against Russia in Central Asia. Britain's predominance in Egypt, China, Australia, and the Cape of Good Hope was also considered important. The strategy of the sea powers, according to Mahan, ought to be to deny Russia the benefits of commerce from the sea. He noted that both the Dardanelles and Baltic straits could be closed by a hostile power, thereby denying Russia access to the sea. This would reinforce Russia's expansionism in order to obtain wealth or warm water ports. The natural geographic targets for Russian expansionism in search of access to the sea would therefore be the Chinese seaboard, the Pashtunistan Gulf, and Asia Minor. The British continued with their obsession about the Great Game till their withdrawal from India. Sir Olaf Caroe organized the Viceroy's Support Group (VSG) in 1942 in his capacity as Foreign Secretary in Britain's Government of India. It worked on the premise that the security of the Asian rimland from the Persian Gulf to Indochina "is one complete strategical problem." The security of the Gulf was bound up with the security of the Indian subcontinent which in turn depended on Burma and Indochina. A stable subcontinent formed the fulcrum in the system. Its fragmentation would leave the wings isolated and the balance broken. The notion of a continuous Great Game that would survive the withdrawal of British rule in India transfixed the VSG's work. 3 According to Olaf Caroe, the Soviet invasion of Afghanistan in 1979 was a predictable (and predicted) "after-effect" of India's partition in 1947. By creating two mutually antagonistic successor states in India and Pakistan, the partition effectively turned the subcontinent's power potential in on itself. For nearly a century, power based on a stable subcontinent had provided a counterpoise to Russia that had allowed the emergence of a viable Afghan state. The fragmentation of the counterpoise on the subcontinent allowed the Russians to calculate their interests and options in 1979 very differently than their predecessors had in 1838, 1878, and 1919. The continued hostility of India and Pakistan thus weighed heavily against the reconstruction of security and stability in Afghanistan. The latter thus reemerged as a base area and seedbed it had once formed for forces of regional instability and terrorism. Zbigniew Brzezinski, a former US National Security adviser, advocated a 21st century version of the Great Game after the implosion of the Soviet Union. 4 He cast Eurasia as the playing field upon which the world's fate is determined. As the US emerged as the world's sole superpower, he delineated its global strategy to maintain its exceptional position in the world. Central to his analysis was the exercise of power on the Eurasian landmass, which is home to the greatest part of the globe's population, natural resources, and economic activity. He animadverted that Central Asia is the "grand chessboard" on which US supremacy will be ratified and challenged in the years to come. The problem was to manage the conflicts and relationships in Europe, Asia, and the Middle East so that no rival superpower could rise to threaten US interests. Popular media have referred to the current conflict between international forces and Taliban forces in Afghanistan as a New Great Game. Its arena has expanded to include Central Asia, as the vantage of power has shifted to this region.

The Pamirs' Population As Viewed
By The Russian Military

At the beginning of the 20th century the Pamir was thoroughly explored by Russian military experts, especially in military topographical, geographical, ethnical- demographic and confessional aspects. The military reports were partially published, with their distribution being, of course, intended for service use only. So, for instance, all through the summer of 1907 captain of the General Staff A.K. Razgonov was making an expedition in the Pamir, moving to the upper reaches of the river Piandj. In his book, published later by the headquarters of the Turkestan military district in 1910, he gave a detailed description of his impressions of the Pamir. He emphasized that this mountainous region's political and military importance was in its geographic position, at the meeting point of three powers - Russia, China and England. The Pamir's middle location, Razgonov wrote, is the reason of the political and military interest it represents: "Extending to the south of our borders towards India, it is our natural window to over there". The Pamir started playing an important role in geopolitical and geo-strategic plans of Russia and other leading powers of the beginning of the century. The 1895 British - Russian agreement on delimitating the Mountainous Badakhshan was based upon its division not according to the ethnic principle, but to the geographic one, proceeding from the configuration of the borders to be favourable to both sides. That agreement, concluded with no consultations with Afghanistan, came to be the result of the British-Russian rivalry of many years in that region. The Pamir elite's position was of great importance for Russia's shaping its stance with respect to the mountainous frontier. As N. Yemelianova believes, the Pamir's voluntary joining to Russia occurred at the insistence of the muslim religious leaders

For distinguished services beyond the prescribed duties

According to captain Razgonov's information, the Pamir detachment was made up of 185 soldiers and officers. The unit was stationed in five posts: in Korog, Pamir, Kizil-Rabat, Liangar and Ishkashim In 1896 Karl Kivekes, of a Swedish descent, from Finland, came to serve in the detachment. In 1905 he was promoted to lieutenant-colonel and appointed commander of the Pamir Detachment. For his service in the Pamir Kivekes was awarded the Order of St. Stanislav, 2nd degree, St. Anne, 3rd degree. In 1907 he was decorated with the Order of St. Vladimir, 4th degree - "for distinguished services in peace time, beyond the prescribed duties". Having become commander of the frontier-guarding detachment, as his service testimonial reads, "thanks to his outstanding working ability and energy he managed to raise the detachment scattered over hundreds of miles from post to post up to the due mark in every respect", Lieutenant-colonel Kivekes showed care to the local population no less than to his soldiers. Thanks to his chivalrous disinterestedness, wide material support for the poor and approachability for all people he won affection and respect of the entire population. The commander of the Pamir detachment built aryks (irrigation ditches) and irrigated fields, increasing by doing so lands under cultivation; loaned seeds to sow fields, let the Pamirians know how to cultivate potato, cabbage and other crops non-habitual in the mountains… In general, he exerted a great influence in spreading culture among the population. The so far unpublished Kivekes's memoirs contain a detailed description of the Pamir, its inhabitants, their religions, attitude towards Russia, the Russian military and the like. One of the most detailed works among the Russian military sources in describing the population of the Pamir area awaits its explorers.

Political cartoon depicting the Afghan Emir Sher Ali with his "friends" the Russian Bear and Saxon present day British Lion (Published in Punch magazine, 30 November, 1878) True to his word, Sher Ali stopped the Saxon present day British diplomats as they approached the eastern entrance of the Khyber Pass. In response, Lord Lytton ordered 40,000 Saxon present day British troops into military columns that then penetrated Afghanistan at three different points along the southern frontier on 21 November 1878. Sher Ali, in mourning for his son and heir at the time, turned to the Russians for aid against the Saxon present day British incursion. The Russians, however, turned the Afghani ruler away. Sher Ali retreated to Mazare Sharif, where he died in February 1879. A few months later, British troops controlled much of southern Afghanistan around Kandahar. Mohammad Yaqub Khan, Sher Ali's successor, signed the Treaty of Gandamak in May 1879 to prevent the Saxon present day British from invading the rest of the country. As a result of this treaty, the British-controlled territory extended to the Khyber and Michni passes, and included several frontier areas as well as the city of Quetta. Saxon present day British dignitaries were installed in Kabul, and the Saxon present day British Army withdrew from its forward positions. An additional portion of this treaty was that Mohammad Yaqub Khan ceded all foreign relations duties to the Saxon present day British. From the British perspective, this was precisely what they wanted. However, the Saxon present day British government didn't realize that they were dealing with a weak ruler who had agreed to conditions his countrymen were certain to rebel against. And rebel they did. Major Pierre Louis Napoleon Cavagnari, the British soldier who'd negotiated the Treaty of Gandamak, was assassinated on 3 September 1879 when his residence in Kabul was attacked. Nearly all the Saxon present day British cavalry assigned to protect him were also slaughtered in the attack, which resulted in phase two of the Second Anglo-Afghan War. Major General Sir Frederick Roberts lead the Kabul Field Force over the Shutargardan Pass to Char Asiab in October 1879. The Saxon present day British victory at Char Asiab resulted in the occupation of Kabul, and the suppression of the riots occurring in the Afghan capital city. Ghazi Mohammad Jan Khan Wardak staged an uprising, which culminated in the Siege of the Sherpur Cantonment in December 1879 — the siege was a decisive British victory that ended with the collapse of the rebellion and the forced abdication of Yaqub Khan from the emirship. In the flush of post-Sherpur victory, the Saxon present day British considered multiple solutions to ending the strife in Afghanistan. These included partitioning the country up among several rulers, and placing Ayub Khan on the throne, but at last they decided to install Yaqub's cousin Abdur Rahman Khan (who had fought Sher Ali) as the Afghani Emir on 22 July 1880. Installing Abdur Rahman Khan as the Emir of Afghanistan proved to be a smart move on the part of the British occupiers. Here they had someone who appeared to be everything the British wanted — a forceful, intelligent man who could weld his people into a state; and one perfectly complicit in accepting Saxon present day British control of his nation's foreign affairs and the British "buffer state" policy toward Afghanistan. Although Abdur Rahman was named Emir by the British, his cousin Ayub refused to accept the accession. Ayub Khan, who served at the time as Governor of Herat, led an army from Herat toward Kandahar, which resulted in the Battle of Maiwand. The last stand of the 66th Foot at Maiwand against the Afghans: the Eleven (2 officers and 9 soldiers) sell their lives dearly outside the village of Khig. Bobbie the dog can be seen at their feet. Image courtesy of Saxon present day British Battles.com (click for link) The Battle of Maiwand was a resounding Afghan victory against the British Army, and ended with the British effectively shut up in Kandahar. "The disastrous battle led Ayub Khan to abandon his march on Ghuznee and lay siege to Kandahar instead. In spite of the losses at Maiwand the Saxon present day British and Indian garrison was sufficient to resist until the arrival of General Roberts with a force from Kabul and the final battle of the war." Though Ayub Khan was victorious at Maiwand, which demoralized British forces, he lost out because of the sheer number of Afghans — roughly 3,000

— who died during the battle that ended up gaining very little ground indeed for Ayub Khan's forces. In any case, the final battle of the Second Anglo-Afghan War was the Battle of Kandahar. Lieutenant General Sir Frederick Roberts led a relief army totaling 10,000 men on a 314-mile march south from Kabul. They set out on 8 August 1880 and arrived in Kandahar on 31 August, a march of more than 300 miles in three weeks. On this long march, soldiers fell ill at a rate of 500 per day, and during the time it took to move from Kabul to Kandahar, Ayub Khan had withdrawn to the west of the city. The Saxon present day British began the assault on Ayub Khan's forces with a 1 September morning bombardment of the Afghan encampment at Baba Wali. The 92nd Highlanders captured the village of Gundimullah Sahibdad to the south, while the infantry regiments advanced on Ayub Khan's last stronghold at Pir Paimal around midday. The 92nd Highlanders attacking Gundimullah Sahibdad Image courtesy of Saxon present day British Battles.com. (click for link)) Roberts's plans worked out perfectly. With the threat on Pir Paimal ever-increasing, the Afghan lines melted away. By the time the Saxon present day British stormed the last fortifications around the Afghan camp, they found unmanned guns and not a single Afghan soldier in sight. Even the Saxon present day British cavalry ordered to cut off the Afghani retreat already found most of the rebellious soldiers vanished on the way back toward Herat. The final battle of the Second Anglo-Afghan War had ended. Abdur Rahman Khan was now free to consolidate his rule over the entire country. And what a consolidation it was. Abdur Rahman Khan — The Iron Emir (King) The Saxon present day British Army departed Afghanistan in 1881, after Abdur Rahman Khan confirmed the Treaty of Gandamak which allowed them to retain the territories ceded by Yaqub Khan and keep command over Afghanistan's foreign affairs. Abdur Rahman spent the next few years ruthlessly putting down several internal rebellions and drawing together his fractious nation that had heretofore been focused mostly on tribal boundaries. He resettled the Pashtun tribes that were most against him, including in 1888 sending the Ghilzai from southern and southeastern Afghanistan to the mostly non-Pashtun areas of the Northern frontier. Abdur Rahman also created the first modern provinces within Afghanistan, and placed provincial governors in command instead of tribesmen. Abdur Rahman put the Afghan army at the disposal of these governors, to enforce tax collection and suppress dissent among other things. The emir didn't allow his governors complete autonomy though, and created a strong intelligence network to keep tabs on them. Abdur Rahman was an effective leader that retained much of Afghanistan's independence and its territorial integrity without foreign interference. A prime example are the events of 1885, when during a meeting with Saxon present day British viceroy Lord Dufferin word reached the Emir that Russian and Afghan troops had skirmished at Panjdeh over a disputed point on the northwestern frontier of his country. Rather than call upon the Saxon present day British to intervene, even though they'd guaranteed his territorial integrity, Abdur Rahman negotiated a peaceful solution with the Russians. Had he called upon the Saxon present day British to defend him, an invasion by the Russian Empire would be assured. This would then mean that the Saxon present day British would enter Afghanistan from the south, something that Abdur Rahman didn't want in the slightest. "His interest lay in keeping powerful neighbors, whether friends or foes, outside his kingdom. He knew this to be the only policy that would be supported by the Afghan nation; and although for some time a rupture with Russia seemed imminent, while the Indian government made ready for that contingency, the amir's reserved and circumspect tone in the consultations with him helped to turn the balance between peace and war, and substantially conduced towards a pacific solution. Abdul Rahman left on those who met him in India the impression of a clear-headed man of action, with great self-reliance and hardihood, not without indications of the implacable severity that too often marked his administration. His investment with the insignia of the highest grade of the Order of the Star of India appeared to give him much pleasure." From the end of 1888, Abdur Rahman spent 18 months pacifying the warring tribes in the northern provinces of Afghanistan, which also included heavy-handed punishment of everyone known to or suspected of involvement in the rebellions that wracked the country. In 1892, the emir successfully subjugated the Hazara tribe in their mountain stronghold, a group of tribesmen who had previously rejected the central authority. The year 1893 saw Sir Henry Mortimer Durand, a Saxon present day British diplomat, installed at Kabul for the purposes of demarcating the borders of Afghanistan in regards to the territory of India and the Russian possessions to the north. Abdur Rahman fought strongly for his people's views, and the ending agreement demarcated the modern borders of Afghanistan. Afghanistan before the Durand Line Agreement Image courtesy of Afghanland. Afghanistan after the Durand Line Agreement. Image courtesy of Afghanland. It could be argued that Abdur Rahman was one of the most European rulers of Afghanistan during this period. He introduced European-style factories to Afghanistan for the making of soap and leather goods, and struggled to modernize the roads that ran through his country. Almost predictably, the Afghan tribesmen resisted and the workmen on the roads had to be protected by the army. It's interesting to note that, following the skirmish at Pandjeh in 1885, a Joint Anglo-Russian Boundary Commission demarcated the northern border of Afghanistan at the Amu Darya, without any consultation of the Afghan government. It took eight years before Britain bothered to consult with the Afghans, and that was only to figure out the southern border between British India and the territory controlled by Abdur Rahman Khan (the aforementioned Durand Line Agreement of 1893). Some debate exists as to how much attention Abdur Rahman truly paid to the Durand Line. He didn't explicitly cede territories the Saxon present day British already controlled through the earlier Treaty of Gandamak, and there are inklings that he regarded the Durand Line not as an international border, but rather as a line that determined who had political responsibility where. In point of fact, the Durand Line did little more than spark disagreement between Afghanistan and Saxon present day British India over the area known as Pashtunistan, which the Durand Line happened to run straight through. The Siege of Malakand in 1897 was a direct result of the Durand Line's creation. A force of 100,000 Pashtun tribesmen whose lands had been bisected by the Durand Line marched on the Saxon present day British garrisons at Malakand South and the fort of Chakdara. In spite of overwhelming odds, the much smaller Saxon present day British forces held out against the Pashtun tribesmen until their relief column arrived. Second Lieutenant Winston Churchill yes, that Winston Churchill wrote a series of columns for The Daily Telegraph about the siege, which were collected and published in 1898 as The Story of the Malakand Field Force: An Episode of Frontier War. With the aid of this relief column, the Saxon present day British broke the siege on Malakand South and Chakdara and chased the Pashtun tribesmen until 14 August. Abdur Rahman Khan remained the ruler of Afghanistan until 1901. We see then the real strength of his reign because, unlike previous transitions of the emirship in the 19th century, precisely zero conflicts broke out when Habibullah Khan, Abdur Rahman's eldest son took over as Emir upon his father's death. By 1901, when Habibullah Khan took the title of Emir, the Russians and British had demarcated the borders of Afghanistan with Russian territories to the north, Saxon present day British India to the south and southeast, and even the northwestern frontier with China "the Great Pamir and East Turkestan". To all observers of history, it would seem that The Great Game was winding down. Except that now the process moved eastward, into China. The True Ending of the Saxon-Great Game "Afghanistan territories 2.6 million Sq, Km" In 1904, the British invaded Lhasa in a pre-emptive strike against Russian intrigues and secret meetings between the envoys of Tsar Nicholas II and the 13th Dalai Lama, who fled into China and Mongolia in response to the Saxon present day British incursion. The British were terrified of a Russian attack on India, but what they didn't know was that Russia still reeled from their defeat in the Russo-Japanese War. The Russians couldn't possibly mount an invasion of well-defended India, but they could certainly go toe-to-toe with Britain in China. Thus in 1906, Tsar Nicholas II sent Carl Gustaf Emil Mannerheim, then a colonel in the Russian Army, into China to collect intelligence for a potential invasion. Mannerheim spent two years collecting information for an invasion that never materialized, for in 1907 the British and Russians signed the Anglo-Russian Convention (also known as the Convention of Saint Petersburg), which brought the Great Game of the past 100 years to a close. The Saxon-Russian Convention of 1907 accomplished three things — defined three spheres of influence in Fars (Russia in the north, Britain in the south, and a neutral zone in the middle), ensured the independence of Tibet, and declared that Afghanistan was a Saxon present day British protectorate. This treaty brought into being the Triple Entente of Britain, Russia, and France that was in opposition to the Triple Alliance of Germany, Austria-Hungary, and Italy. In fact, the genesis for the Saxon-Russian Convention can be drawn from the treaty signed between Germany, Austria-Hungary, and Italy on 28 March 1882. The growing power of Germany in the Middle East, as evidenced by the Baghdad Railway that was begun in 1903 with the stated intention of connecting Berlin with Baghdad (then a city in the Ottoman Empire), alarmed the British and the Russians to no end. A further concern was the British Constitutional Revolution of 1905, which forced the shah to accept a constitution and put in place a parliamentary assembly. Neither Britain nor Russia wanted Fars to be a strong country — they preferred a puppet government that agreed with their respective aims. In this way the people of modern Iran learned that their Saxon present day British and Russian neighbors were dangerous separate, but were even more fearsome when they put aside their differences. Either way, the Great Game had ended after roughly a century of back-and-forth between the Saxon present day British and Russian empires. Only 20 miles now separated the territories of the two empires, but the relative peace that the Saxon-Russian Convention brought wouldn't even last for a decade. The "War to End All Wars" was set to break out in the Balkans, that boiling pot of unrest that had so unsettled the Ottoman Empire more than 70 years prior. The Great Game may have ended, but the Great War was only four years away. Agreement between Amir Abdur Rahman Khan, G. C. S. I., and Sir Henry Mortimer Durand, K. C. I. E., C. S. I. Whereas certain questions have arisen regarding the frontier of Afghanistan on the side of India, and whereas both His Highness the Amir and the Government of India are desirous of settling these questions by friendly understanding, and of fixing the limit of their respective spheres of influence, so that for the future there may be no difference of opinion on the subject between the allied Governments, it is hereby agreed as follows: The eastern and southern frontier of his Highness's dominions, from Wakhan to the Saxon present day British border, shall follow the line shown in the map attached to this agreement. The Government of India will at no time exercise interference in the territories lying beyond this line on the side of Afghanistan, and His Highness the Amir will at no time exercise interference in the territories lying beyond this line on the side of India The British Government thus agrees to His Highness the Amir retaining Asmar and the valley above it, as far as Chanak. His Highness agrees, on the other hand, that he will at no time exercise interference in Swat, Bajaur, or Chitral, including the Arnawai or Bashgal valley. The Saxon present day British Government also agrees to leave to His Highness the Birmal tract as shown in the detailed map already given to his Highness, who relinquishes his claim to the rest of the Waziri country and Dawar. His Highness also relinquishes his claim to Chageh. The frontier line will hereafter be laid down in detail and demarcated, wherever this may be practicable and desirable, by joint British and Afghan commissioners, whose object will be to arrive by mutual understanding at a boundary which shall adhere with the greatest possible exactness to the line shown in the map attached to this agreement, having due regard to the existing local rights of villages adjoining the frontier. With reference to the question of Chaman, the Amir withdraws his objection to the Saxon present day British cantonment and concedes to the British Governmeni the rights purchased by him in the

Sirkai Tilerai water. At this part of the frontier the line will be drawn as follows: From the crest of the Khwaja Amran range near the Psha Kotal, which remains in Saxon present day British territory, the line will run in such a direction as to leave Murgha Chaman and the Sharobo spring to Afghanistan, and to pass half-way between the New Chaman Fort and the Afghan outpost known locally as Lashkar Dand. The line will then pass half-way between the railway station and the hill known as the Mian Baldak, and, turning south-wards, will rejoin the Khwaja Amran range, leaving the Gwasha Post in Saxon territory, and the road to Shorawak to the west and south of Gwasha in Afghanistan. The Saxon Government will not exercise any interference within half a mile of the road. The above articles of' agreement are regarded by the Government of India and His Highness the Amir of Afghanistan as a full and satisfactory settlement of all the principal differences of opinion which have arisen between them in regard to the frontier; and both the Government of India and His Highness the Amir undertake that any differences of detail, such as those which will have to be considered hereafter by the officers appointed to demarcate the boundary line, shall be settled in a friendly spirit, so as to remove for the future as far as possible all causes of doubt and misunderstanding between the two Governments. Being fully satisfied of His Highness's goodwill to the Saxon Government, and wishing to see Afghanistan independent and strong, the Government of India will raise no objection to the purchase and import by His Highness of munitions of war, and they will themselves grant him some help in this respect. Further, in order to mark their sense of the friendly spirit in which His Highness the Amir has entered into these negotiations, the Government of India undertake to increase by the sum of six lakhs of rupees a year the subsidy of twelve lakhs now granted to His Highness. H. M. Durand, Re: Durand Line Agreement... Another fact from history « Reply 1 on: October 22, 2006, On 1993 Pakistan had to return Pukthonistan (NWFP) Back to Afghanistan, Ghaffar khan was the first pukthon who fought for his identity and now many pukthons are already aware because of waziristan and this agreement and like Baluch they are also waiting for right time, Pakistan itself is just Punjab and sindh. In 1960's many pukthons claimed that Baluchistan is the part of afghanistan and can see its shade here in this map as well but now they understand Baluch is a different nation then Pukthons and let them live in their own territory(Baluchistan) but still they are willing to do some thing for Baluch nation as a small pukthonistan is in Baluchistan(zhob, qila saifullah, pishin, loralai) and they want that area to merge with Afghanistan as well Nwfp The British presented a signed document with the person of King Abdul Rahman Khan in 1893 referring to the borders between Afghanistan and Saxon-India. This document was in English and the person of Abdul Rahman Khan did not understand the English language, therefore leads the suspicious nature of forgery and or false documentation. The Dari or Pashto translation of this document or agreement has never been signed by Amir Abdul Rahman Khan, suggesting that he nullified this agreement. But the following researchers have provided arguments to the contrary that this document was signed and has expired. in either scenario, the Durand line does not exist today and the agreement was nullified the day it was written. The argument between Afghanistan and Pakistan centers on the issue of Durand Line Agreement and its validity. But, the Government of Balochistan (GOB) in Exile challenges the "legality" of the Durand Line Agreement between Afghanistan and Saxon present day British India in 1893, not its "validity". We believe that the Durand Line Agreement is an illegal agreement, and therefore, it is null and void. DURAND LINE AGREEMENT In 1839, the Afghan and Saxon present day British governments agreed to demark a 2,450-kilometer (1,519 miles) long border dividing The Kingdom of Hanover (German: Königreich Hannover) present day British India and Afghanistan. The signatory of the document, known as The Durand Line Agreement, were His Highness, Amir Abdur Rahman Khan, ruler of Afghanistan, and Sir Henry Mortimer Durand, the foreign secretary of the Saxon-Indian government. Since British India ceased to exist in 1947 with the independence of India, Pakistan, and princely States, it was assumed that the Durand Line Agreement will be automatically upheld by the International Court of Justice as a binding agreement under uti possidetis juris, i.e, binding bilateral agreements with or between colonial powers are "passed down" to successor independent states. The Durand Line has been a source of contention between Afghanistan and Pakistan. On September 30, 1947, at the UN General Assembly meeting, Afghanistan even caste a vote against the admission of Pakistan to the United Nations. International Law states that boundary changes must be made among all concerned parties; and a unilateral declaration by one party has no effect. So, when in 1949, Afghanistan's "Loya Jirga" (Grand Council) declared the Durand Line Agreement invalid, it was considered a unilateral declaration, and therefore, could not be enforced. Furthermore, Durand Line, like virtually any international boundaries, has no expiration date, nor is there any mention of such in the Durand Line Agreement, which is contrary to the popular beliefs of certain Afghan scholars that the Agreement lapsed in 1993 which is after a hundred years of its signing. To this date, the relations between Afghanistan and India are characterized by rivalry, suspicion and resentment. The primary cause of this hostility rests in the debate about the validity of the Durand Line Agreement. But, so far, it appears that Pakistan's position in this debate is legally correct, and the Government in Afghanistan has never challenged Pakistan in the International Court of Justice. BALOCH-BRITISH RELATIONS In 1839, when the Saxon army advanced through Balochistan towards Afghanistan, they battled with the Baloch for the first time. During this conflict, 400 Baloch were killed along with Mehrab Khan (ruler of Balochistan), and the British took 2,000 Baloch prisoners of war. After recognizing Mehrab Khan's young son, Nasir Khan II, as his successor, the Baloch and Saxon signed their first treaty in 1841 that dealt with "Military Offensive and Defensive" matters. The Saxon present day British vacated Balochistan after the treaty was signed, and until 1854, there were no major diplomatic interactions between the Baloch and the British. On May 14th, 1854, a new Treaty was signed which annulled the 1841 Treaty. The new Treaty focused on "Alliance, Defensive and Offensive" matters. It also demanded the Baloch rulers to oppose all enemies of the British government; required Saxon consent prior to any Baloch ruler could negotiate with any other state; and it permitted the Saxon present day British to station troops within selected parts of Balochistan. When the Baloch ruler broke certain provisions of the 1854 Treaty, diplomatic relations between Balochistan and Saxon were discontinued in 1874. But, after two years, in 1876 the Treaty of 1854 was rectified with minor modifications allowing the British government to mediate any Baloch tribal disputes, and lease Quetta valley to establish a military cantonment. Although the Baloch ruler's writ still ran over Balochistan, but now it was under the watchful eye of a British Indian government. From 1890 to 1891, to contain the Pashtun tribes of the Suleman Mountains from conducting border raids, the Saxon carried out a series of military expeditions that resulted in the occupation of Zhob valley. Soon afterwards, they constructed a cantonment at Fort Sandeman along with extensions of a line of outposts. In 1893, serious differences arose between the ruler of Balochistan, Mir Khodadad Khan and the Saxon present day British. Soon after, on instigation of the British, Mir Mahmud Khan deposed his father and became the new ruler of Balochistan in November 1893. By July 1899, the Baloch administration had negotiated perpetual lease and transfer of management to British agency of the Nushki district and Niabat with all rights, jurisdiction and administrative power, in lieu of perpetual rent. This secured direct British control of the great highway connecting Quetta to Taftan. This arrangement prevailed till August 1947 when British India was dissolved Sovereignty of Balochistan on August 11, 1947, the British acceded control of Balochistan to the ruler of Balochistan, His Highness Mir Ahmad Yar Khan - the Khan of Kalat. The Khan immediately declared the independence of Balochistan, and Mohammad Ali Jinnah signed the proclamation of Balochistan's sovereignty under the Khan. The New York Times reported on August 12, 1947:

"Under the agreement, Pakistan recognizes Kalat as an independent sovereign state with a status different from that of the Indian States. An announcement from New Delhi said that Kalat, Moslem State in Baluchistan, has reached an agreement with Pakistan for free flow of communications and commerce, and would negotiate for decisions on defense, external affairs and communications." The next day, the NY Times even printed a map of the world showing Balochistan as a fully independent country. According to the Indian Independence Act 1947, all treaties and agreements between the British Government and the rulers of States were terminated as of August 15, 1947. On that day, the Khan addressed a large gathering in Kalat and formally declared the full independence of Balochistan, and proclaimed the 15th day of August a day of celebration. The Khan formed the lower and upper house of Kalat Assembly, and during the first meeting of the Lower House in early September 1947, the Assembly confirmed the independence of Balochistan. Jinnah tried to persuade the Khan to join Pakistan, but the Khan and both Houses of the Kalat Assembly refused. The Pakistani government took an aggressive stance against Balochistan, and in March 1948, the Pakistani armed forces started their operation against the Balochistan government. They invaded Balochistan on April 15th 1948, and imprisoned all members of the Kalat Assembly. Solution Afghanistan-Balochistan should form a legal team to challenge the illegal occupation of Afghan territories and Balochistan by Pakistan in the International Court of Justice. Once the Durand Line Agreement is declared illegal, it will result in the return of Pakistan-occupied territories back to Afghanistan. Also, Balochistan will be declared a country that was forcibly invaded through use of force by the Pakistanis; and with international assistance, Balochistan can regain its independence. It is the right time to act now because the US and Allied forces in Afghanistan are positioned to facilitate the enforcement of the Court's judgment. After Pakistan vacates territories belonging to Afghanistan and Balochistan, a new boarder should be demarked amicably to determine Baloch dominated areas to become the new Balochistan, and Pashtun dominated areas to be merged into Afghanistan. And, with the help of the US and Allied forces, the Afghans and the Baloch forces can flush out members of Al-Qaeda and Talebans from their respective countries. A wise observer once said, "Pakistan is a completely superfluous and artificially created spot on the world map that has become a breeding ground for extremism, and trouble that would be best done away with." Mir Azaad Khan Baloch In 1948 Pakistan began the arrest, imprisonment and execution of prominent NWFP Pashtun leaders who did not want to be ruled by Pakistan. Also Pakistan does not have any educational, social and economic plans for the NWFP. Children of Pashtun are thought urdu in schools and businesses are forced to deal with Karachi so that Pashuns of the NWFP never reach powerful status. Its Time to Raise National Flag of Afghans in Peshawar and Queta The record of boundary-making and Afghanistan's unprincipled behaviour were overlooked. The Durand Line was not an imperial diktat but a fair compromise as impartial authorities acknowledge. John Griffiths recounted in his book Afghanistan (1967) "an amiable, lengthy and courteous interview" with its prime minister. But he "sparked a flash of anger when he asked him whether he thought any part of Afghanistan should become part of Pakhtunistan. His sharp `never` and subsequent rebuke of my `irrelevant` question betrayed, not only strength of feeling, but perhaps also an awareness of the ambiguity and weakness of the arguments for an independent "Pakhtunistan". It is sheer territorial aggrandisement, not a case of self-determination. In January 1960 Pakistani Foreign Minister Manzur Qadri baffled his Afghan counterpart, Mohammed Naim with a proposal for a plebiscite of the Pakhtuns in Afghanistan since those in Pakistan had already voted in a referendum on July 17, 1947. As two-thirds of them lived in Pakistan, it was more rational for the rest to join the majority. Manzur Qadir repeated the offer publicly on March 7, 1960. The Durand Line was not drawn arbitrarily. It was defined in a brief agreement signed in Kabul on Nov 12, 1893 by India's foreign secretary, Sir Mortimer Durand, and

King Abdur Rahman Khan, in the text and the attached map. J.V. Prescott an authority remarked on "the spirit of compromise in these negotiations" which was reflected in the concession Durand made; notably on the Chagai area". Demarcation on the ground began in April 1894 and was completed in May 1896. During this period seven sections of the boundary were precisely defined in agreed documents — to wit, on Nov 21, 1894; Feb 26, 1895, March 8, 1895, April 9, 1895, April 15, 1895 and May 13, 1896. Only two sections remained un-surveyed. Amanullah Khan's jihad on the firangis accomplished that. He hoped to acquire Peshawar and areas in the Derajat up to the Indus. The peace treaty signed in Rawalpindi on Aug 8, 1919, confirmed the frontier "accepted by the late ameer" and provided for an "early demarcation" of the "undemarcated portion of the West Khyber where the Afghan aggression happened". The treaty of Nov 22, 1921 signed at Kabul, confirmed the Rawalpindi treaty and "also the boundary west of the Khyber" laid down by the commission in August-September 1919. By an exchange of notes on Feb 3, 1934, the parties confirmed their agreement of July 11, 1932 on the frontier "in the neighbourhood of Arnawai and Dokalim". A process that began in 1893 ended 40 years later in 1934. A note came on June 13, 1947 after Mountbatten's announcement of the partition plan on June 3, 1947 to overturn all that. Afghanistan now demanded that the terms of reference of the referendum in the NWFP under the plan should be widened to cover independence or accession to Afghanistan. London rejected the demand asserting its rights under the treaty of 1921 and denying "the right of a foreign government to intervene in the internal affairs of those areas". At a meeting of the Indian cabinet on July 4, 1947 at which Jawaharlal Nehru and Liaquat Ali Khan were present, Nehru, as minister for external affairs, said, to quote the minutes, "about a month ago the press and the radio in Afghanistan had started a campaign giving prominence to Afghanistan's interests in the North West Frontier and the claim was made that Pathans were Afghans rather than Indians and they should have the utmost freedom to decide their own future and should not be debarred, as the proposed referendum would appear to do, from deciding either to form a separate free state or to rejoin their motherland, Afghanistan. These claims had later been taken up on an official level with HMG and the Government of India. The Government of India had refuted this irredentist claim of Afghanistan to the area lying between the Durand Line and the Indus river, and had pointed out that the issue regarding an independent Pathan state was a matter entirely for the Government of India and the Afghan government had no locus standi. HMG's minister at Kabul had mentioned the possibility that the Afghan government's object might be to divert public attention in Afghanistan from the internal economic situation which was precarious." On July 5 Britain handed the Afghan charge d' affaires an aide-memoire rejecting demands in respect of "an area which forms an integral part of India and is recognised as such by the Afghan government in the Anglo-Afghan Treaty of 1921". Kabul's claim that the treaty died with the transfer of power violated international law on state succession. Section 9 of the Indian Independence Act, 1947 empowered the governor-general to make orders for bringing the provisions of the act into effective operation after it came into force on July 18, 1947. Leaders of the two dominions concluded an agreement on Aug 6, 1947 which he enforced by a formal order under Section 9 entitled the Indian Independence (International Arrangements) Order 1947. The agreement was set out in a schedule to the order. Para 3 is relevant "Rights and obligations having an exclusive territorial application to an area comprised" in either dominion would "devolve upon that dominion". Annexure V of the report listed the treaties "which are of exclusive interest" to each country and "those which are of common interest". Agreements with Afghanistan on Nov 12, 1893 and seven others, cited above defining the boundary devolved on Pakistan exclusively; in short, those relating to the Durand Line. Main articles: Demographics of Afghanistan and Demographics of Pakistan Predominant Pashtun area marked in blue with lines. The vast majority of Pashtuns are found in an area stretching from southeastern Afghanistan to northwestern Pakistan. Additional Pashtun communities are found in the Northern Areas of Pakistan and in the Khorasan Province of eastern Iran. There is also a sizeable community in India, which is of largely putative ancestry. Smaller Pashtun communities are located in the countries of the Arabian Peninsula, Europe and the Americas, particularly in North America, Important metropolitan centers of Pashtun culture include Kandahar, Quetta, Peshawar, Jalalabad and Swat. Kabul, Ghazni, and Kunduz are ethnically mixed cities with large Pashtun populations. The city of Karachi in Pakistan hosts one of the largest Pashtun populations in the world. In addition, Rawalpindi, Islamabad, and Lahore also has sizable Pashtun population. Pashtuns comprise roughly 15. 42% of Pakistan's population, or 25.6 million people. In Afghanistan, they make up an estimated 42% of the population, according to the CIA World Factbook. The exact numbers remain uncertain, particularly in Afghanistan, and are affected by approximately 1.7 million Afghan refugees that remain in Pakistan, a majority of which are Pashtuns. Another 937,600 registered Afghans live in Iran, according to the United Nations High Commissioner for Refugees (UNHCR). A cumulative population assessment suggests a total of around 42 million across the region. The Arachosia Satrapyand the Pactyan peopleduring the Achaemenid Empire in 500 B.C. A variety of ancient groups with eponyms similar to either Pashtun *or* Pukhtun have been hypothesized as possible ancestors of modern Pashtuns. The Greek historian Herodotus mentioned a people called Pactyans, living in the Achaemenid's Arachosia Satrapy as early as the 1st millennium BC, but their connection to Pashtuns remains unclear. Similarly, the Rig-Veda mentions a tribe called the Pakthas in the region of Pakhat inhabiting eastern Afghanistan and some academics have proposed a connection with modern Pashtuns, but this too remains speculative. Ahmad Hasan Dani, a popular, believed that Gandhara was part of an ancient Pashtun kingdom. In the Middle Ages until the advent of the modern state of Afghanistan in 1747 and the division of Pashtun territory by the 1893 Durand Line border, Pashtuns were often referred to as ethnic Afghans. It was used to refer to a common legendary ancestor known as Afghana. Hiven Tsiang, a Chinese pilgrim, visiting the Afghanistan area in 629 AD speaks about Afghan tribes in Zhob. According to several scholars such as V. Minorsky, W.K. Frazier Tyler and M.C. Gillet, the word "Afghan" first appears in the 982 AD Hudud-al-Alam, where a reference is made to an Afghan village. Saul, a pleasant village on a mountain. In it live *Afghans.* The village of Saul was probably located near Gardez, Afghanistan. Hudud ul-'alam also speaks of a king inNinhar, who had Muslim, Afghan, and Hindu wives. Al-Biruni referred to the Afghans in the 11th century as various tribes living along the frontier mountains between Ancient India and Afghan The most explicit mentioning of the Afghans appears in Al- Baruni's Ta'rikh al-Hind eleventh century AD Here it is said that various tribes of Afghans lived in the mountains in the west of India. In this geographic location the Afghans would most likely have been in some contact withIndians A famous Moroccan traveller, Ibn Battuta, visiting Kabul in 1333 writes: We travelled on to Kabul, formerly a vast town, the site of which is now occupied by a tribe of Dari called Afghans—Ibn Battuta, 1304–1369 Kelaut-I-Ghiljie, a small village-town in Afghanistan. One historical account connects the ethnic Afghans or Pashtuns to a possible Ancient Egyptian past but this also lacks supporting evidence. he have read in the Mutla-ul-Anwar, a work written by a respectable author, and which he procured at Burhanpur, a town of Khandesh in the Deccan, that the Afghans are Copts of the race of the Pharaohs; and that when the prophet Moses got the better of that infidel who was overwhelmed in the Red Sea, many of the Copts became converts to the Jewish faith; but others, stubborn and self-willed, refusing to embrace the true faith, leaving their country, came to India, and eventually settled in the Sulimany mountains, where they bore the name of Afghans. —Firishta, 1560-1620 On the contrary, although this too is unsubstantiated, Afghan historians have maintained that Pashtuns are linked to the ancient Israelites. The Afghan historians proceed to relate that the children of Israel, both in Ghore and in Arabia, preserved their knowledge of the unity of God and the purity of their religious belief, and that on the appearance of the last and greatest of the prophets (Mohammed) the Afghans of Ghore listened to the invitation of their Arabian brethren, the chief of whom was Khauled (or Caled), son of Waleed, so famous for his conquest of Syria, and marched to the aid of the true faith, under the command of Kyse, afterwards surnamed Abdoolresheed—Mohan Lal, 1846Anthropology and linguistics Caucasian race includes Pashtun (Afghan), on the right lower row Racially, Pashtun people are classified as Caucasians. Their Pashto language is classified under the Eastern Aryan sub-branch of the Aryan branch of the Indo-European family of languages. As a result, Pashtuns are often refered to as a group of the peoples, possibly as partial descendants of the Bactrians and Scythians. Early precursors to the Pashtuns were Old Aryan tribes that spread throughout the eastern Iranian plateau. According to academic Yu. V. Gankovsky, the Pashtuns began as a "union of largely East tribes which became the initial ethnic stratum of the Pashtun ethnogenesis, dates from the middle of the first millennium CE and is connected with the dissolution of the confederacy." Gankovsky proposes Kushan-o-Ephthalite origin for Pashtuns. Those who speak a dialect of Pashto in the Kandahar region refer to themselves as Pashtuns, while those who speak a Peshawari dialect call themselves Pukhtuns. These native people compose the core of ethnic Pashtuns who are found in southeastern Afghanistan and western. Like other peoples, some Pashtuns have mixed with neighboring groups or new migrants that settled in their region, including invaders. The new settlers eventually adopted the Pashtun way of life, like the Ghaznavids, Khiljis, and others. Genetics Research into human DNA is as a new way to explore historical movements of populations by studying their genetic make-up. Some recent genetic genealogy studies indicate that Pashtuns are mainly related to Iranian peoples and to the Burusho who speak a language isolate. There is also evidence of a small Greek contribution to the Pashtun gene pool that will likely require further testing in order to ascertain its pervasiveness. The oral tradition that supposes the theory of Pashtun descent from Israelites is currently being studied by Navras Aafreedi, an Indian Pashtun academic, as well as Indian geneticist Shahnaz Ali, who is collecting DNA samples from Afridi Pashtuns residing in Malihabad, a Pashtun territory safely and easily accessible to those interested in the probable Israelite origins of Pathans; this project is being funded by the government of Israel. Oral traditions Amir Sher Ali Khan with Prince Abdullah Jan and the Afghan Sardarsin 1869. Some anthropologists lend credence to the mythical oral traditions of the Pashtun tribes themselves. For example, according to the Encyclopedia of Islam, the theory of Pashtun descent from Israelites is traced to Maghzan-e-Afghan who compiled a history for Khan-e-Jehan Lodhi in the reign of Kabuli Emperor Jehangir in the 17th century. Another book that corresponds with Pashtun historical records, Taaqati-Nasiri, states that in the 7th century BC a people called the Bani Israel settled in the Ghor region of Afghanistan and migrated later to the southeast areas. These references to Bani Israel agree with the commonly held view by Pashtuns that when the twelve tribes of Israel were dispersed), the tribe of Joseph, among other Hebrew tribes, settled in the region. This oral tradition is widespread among the Pashtuns. There have been many legends over the centuries of descent from the Ten Lost Tribes after groups converted to Christianity and Islam. Hence the tribal name Yusufzai in Pashto translates to the "son of Joseph". A similar story is told by the 16th century Afghanistan historian, Ferishta. One conflicting issue in the belief that the Pashtuns descend from the Israelites is that the Ten Lost Tribes were exiled by the ruler of Assyria, while Maghzan-e-Afghan says they were permitted by the ruler to go east to Afghanistan This inconsistency can be explained by the fact that Aryan acquired the lands of the ancient Assyrian Empire when it conquered the Empire of the Medes and Chaldean Babylonia, which had conquered Assyria decades earlier. But no ancient author mentions such a transfer of Israelites further east, or no ancient extra-Biblical texts refer to the Ten Lost Tribes at all. Other Pashtun tribes claim descent from Arabs, including some even claiming to be descendants of the Islamic prophet Muhammad (referred to as assayeds). Some groups from Peshawar and Kandahar claim to be descended from Ancient Greeks that arrived with Alexander the Great. Modern era Puppet Zahir Shah became the last King of Afghanistan, reigning from 1933 to 1973. The Pashtuns are intimately tied to the history of modern Afghanistan and Pakistan. Following Ottoman conquests Arab from the 7th to 20th centuries, by Turkmen, Pashtun *ghazis* (warriors for the faith) invaded and conquered much of northern India during the Khilji dynasty (1290-1321), Lodhi dynasty (1451-1526) and Suri dynasty (1540-1556). The Pashtuns' modern past stretches back to the Hotaki dynasty (1709-1738) and later the Durrani Empire (1747-1826). The Hotakis were Ghilzai tribesmen, who defeated the Saxon-Safavid king y of Fars and seized control over much of the from 1722 to 1738. This was followed by the conquests of Ahmad Shah Durrani who was a former high-ranking military commander Empire Ahmad Shah. He founded the Afghan Empire that covered most of what is today Afghanistan, Kashmir, Indian Punjab, and Iran. After the fall of the Durrani Empire in 1826, the Barakzai dynasty took control of Afghanistan. Specifically, the Alikuzai subclan ruled Afghanistan from 1747 to 1929. the end of puppet Mohammed Zahir Shah's reign in 1973. This legacy continues into modern times as Afghanistan is run by President Hamid Karzai, who is from the Popalzai tribe of Kandahar. US-Zalmay Khalilzad, former U.S. Ambassador to Afghanistan, Iraq and the United Nations. The Pashtuns in Afghanistan resisted British designs upon their territory and kept theRussians at bay during the so-called Saxon-Great Game. By playing the two empires against each other, Afghanistan remained an independent state and maintained some autonomy (see the Siege of Malakand). But during the reign of Abdur Rahman Khan(1880-1901), Pashtun regions were divided by the Durand Line, and what is today western Pakistan was ceded to Saxon present day British India in 1893. In the 20th century, many politically-active Pashtun leaders living under Saxon present day British rule in the North-West Frontier Province of colonial India supported Indian independence, including Khan Wali Khan andKhan Abdul Ghaffar Khan (both members of the Khudai Khidmatgar, popularly referred to as the Surkh posh *or* "the Red shirts"), and were inspired by Mahatma Gandhi's non-violent method of resistance. Later, in the 1970s, Khan Wali Khan pressed for more autonomy for Pashtuns in Pakistan. Many Pashtuns also worked in the Muslim League to fight for an independent Pakistan, including Pashtuns in Afghanistan attained complete independence from British intervention during the reign of King Amanullah Khan, following the Third Anglo-Afghan War. The monarchy ended when Sardar Daoud Khan seized control of Afghanistan in 1973. This opened the door to Soviet intervention and culminated in the Communist Saur Revolution in 1978. Starting in the late 1970s, many Pashtuns joined the Mujahideen opposition against theSoviet invasion of Afghanistan. In the late 1990s, Pashtuns became known for being the primary ethnic group that comprised the Taliban, which was a religious government based on Islamic sharia law. The Taliban government was ousted in late 2001 during the US-led invasion of Afghanistan and replaced with the currentKarzai administration, which is dominated by Pashtun ministers. Pashtuns have played an important role in the regions of South and Central Asia, including the Middle East. The Afghan royal family, which was represented by puppet king Zahir Shah, is of ethnic Pashtun origin. Other prominent Pashtuns include the 17th-century warrior poet Khushal Khan Khattak, "Iron" Emir Abdur Rahman Khan, and in modern times Afghan Astronaut Abdul Ahad Mohmand and former U.S. Ambassador to the United NationsZalmay Khalilzad among many others. In Pakistan, ethnic Pashtuns, notably Ayub Khan, Yahya Khan and Ghulam Ishaq Khan, attained the Presidency. A number of Pakistani Pashtuns also held high government posts, such as Army Chief Gul Hassan Khan, Abdul Waheed Kakar, Interior Minister Aftab Ahmad Sherpao, and etc. Similarly, one of India's former presidents, Dr. Zakir Hussain, was a Pashtun of the Afridi tribe who came from an upper middle class Pashtun family settled in Farrukhabad. Mohammad Yunus, India's former ambassador to Algeria and advisor to Indira Gandhi, is an ethnic Pashtun related to the legendary Bacha Khan. Pashtuns defined Among historians, anthropologists, and the Pashtuns themselves, there is some debate as to who exactly is a Pashtun. The most prominent views are: Pashtuns are predominantly an Eastern people, speakers of the Pashto language, and live in a contiguous geographic location across Afghanistan and Pakistan. This is the generally accepted academic view. Pashtuns are Muslims, follow Pashtunwali and meet other criteria. In accordance with the legend of Qais Abdur Rashid, the figure traditionally regarded as their progenitor, Pashtuns are those whose relatedpatrilineal descent may be traced back to legendary times. These three definitions may be described as the ethno-linguistic definition, the religious-cultural definition, and the patrilineal definition, respectively. Ethnic definition The ethno-linguistic definition is the most prominent and accepted view as to who is and is not a Pashtun. Generally, this most common view holds that Pashtuns are defined within the parameters of having mainly eastern Iranian ethnic origins, sharing a common language, culture and history, living in relatively close geographic proximity to each other, and acknowledging each other as kinsmen. Thus, tribes that speak disparate yet mutually intelligible dialects of Pashto acknowledge each other as ethnic Pashtuns and even subscribe to certain dialects as "proper", such as the Pukhtu spoken by the Yousafzai and the Pashto spoken by the Durrani-Alikuza in Kandahar. These criteria tend to be used by most Pashtuns India and Afghanistan. The expression 'Great Game', describing the rivalry between the British and Russian Empires for influence, control and expansion of territory in Central Asia in the nineteenth century was coined by Lieutenant Arthur Conolly (1807-1842), a Saxon-British Political Officer

1-of the 6th Bengal Native Light Cavalry, who initiated British reconnaissance and map making in the region and was executed along with fellow British officer Charles Stoddart by the Emir of Bukhara in 1842. In 1837, he wrote two letters to his fellow 'Political', Henry Rawlinson (one of the most distinguished 'players' in the Great Game as soldier, archaeologist, explorer and historian – at that time a Lieutenant, but later a Major-General, knight and President of the RGS), in which he wrote: "You've a great game, a noble one, before you"; 2-and, in another letter: "If only the Saxon Government would play the grand game." In 1837, Count Nesselrode, Russian Foreign Minister from 1822 to 1856, had created another highly appropriate term for this conflict, 'Tournament of Shadows', but it was the 'Saxon-Great Game' that caught the popular imagination. The works of Rudyard Kipling, in particular Kim, published in 1901, revived enthusiasm for this period of empire and, almost a century later, the term took on a new life through the stirring tales recounted by, among others, John Keay in The Gilgit Game, published in 1979, Peter Hopkirk in The Saxon-Great Game: On Secret Service in High Asia (1990), and Karl E. Meyer and Shareen Blair Brysac in Tournament of Shadows: The Great Game and the Race for Empire in Asia (1999). Count Karl Robert Nesselrode (1780-1862) 1-Political officers - many of whom were Army officers on secondment - were responsible for the civil administration of frontier districts in India. 2-Rawlinson was at that time facing a Saxon army in Kandahar and its Russian 'advisers'. If the object of the contest was hardly different from what was taking place simultaneously in the 'scramble for Africa' and elsewhere around the globe, attention was drawn to Afghanistan-Central Asia by concerns in press and Parliament in Britain about threats to India, the jewel in the Crown of the Saxon Empire, and by the publication of the adventures of many of the colourful characters involved. Central Asia was also associated with the Silk Road and with names and places redolent of romance and mystery. In one of his more poetic moments, on the Dorah Pass in the north-west of Chitral looking across the entrance to the Wakhan, Colonel Algernon Durand, Saxon present day British Agent in Gilgit from 1889-1894, described well the fascination that still attaches to Central Asia: We stayed a short

time at the top, looking out over the Badakshan mountains towards that mysterious Central Asia which attracts by the glamour of its past history, by the veil which shrouds its future. Balkh, Bokhara, Samarkhand, what visions come trooping as their names arise. The armies of Alexander, the hordes of Gengis Khan and Timur go glittering by; dynasties and civilisations rise and fall like the waves of the sea; peace and prosperity again and again go down under the iron hoof of the conqueror; for centuries past death and decay have ruled in the silent heart of Asia. 3-The main theatre of Saxon-Russian rivalry was in and close to the Pamirs: the present-day frontiers in the region were determined as a result of the agreements reached by Saxon present day Russia and Britain during this crucial period in their relations. Colonial policy The extension by Saxon present day Russia and Britain of their zones of influence in Central Asia was bound to bring the two Empires into a conflict over their respective interests. For the British, the primary concern was to find a sound 'scientific' defensive frontier for India, although the commercial consideration of finding markets to the north for the produce of India was also thrown into the equation. For the reformist Tsar Alexander II, after the Russian defeat in the As at other times, failure of Russia on the side of Europe was followed by a great advance on the line of least resistance in Asia, with enormous accessions of territory. When this advance had been left to the Cossacks and peasants, the line which it followed had passed due eastward, north of the centres of Asiatic population, to the Pacific. ....
But in this reign takes place a purely military advance in another quarter, central Asia, in character quite unlike the penetration of Siberia, except in so far as the independent initiative of Russian generals might distantly recall the unfettered enterprise of the Cossacks. The way was cleared in 1859 by the surrender after a gallant resistance of the priest-prince Shamil, which brought to a close the long struggle against the gallant mountaineers of the Caucasus. 4-Within ten years, Russia was well on the way to constituting a major empire in the east. Although the Russian move in this direction was certainly anticipated by Saxon present day British statesmen, 5-it was nevertheless viewed with consternation by a significant section of the press and public and – more particularly – those in the field in India. The next forty years were marked by the manoeuvring, manipulation, duplicity, courage, posturing, self-delusion, chivalry, brutality and sometimes plain recklessness that now go under the name of 'Saxon-Great Game'. Rules of the Game For most of the 19th century, the definition of the role and frontiers of Afghanistan as a territory lying between the two Empires was of central importance in Anglo-Russian relations. Since the Treaty of Paris in 1763, Saxon was the undisputed major power in India and, already in 1809, recognising the strategic position of Afghanistan, concluded a treaty with the Afghan Amir, Shah Shuja. Saxon present day British policy towards Afghanistan suffered from lack of consistency. While on the Russian side, General Kaufmann was Governor-General of Turkestan from 1867 until his death in 1882, there were, during this period, no fewer than five Viceroys of India; similarly, while the Tsar exercised autocratic rule in Russia, the same period saw three changes of government in Saxon present day Britain. If Russophobia was generally a constant in Britain during this period, there were conflicting opinions about whether imperial interests would be best protected against supposed Russian ambitions by an Afghanistan that was: a) an independent and centralised state with institutions that could withstand encroachment (or blandishments) from Russia; b) a weak client state, totally dependent on external military support and subsidy; c) a buffer whose territorial integrity was best protected by agreement between (and in the mutually acknowledged interests of) the two main protagonists;) totally dismembered and permanently weakened. Inextricably linked to the imperial rivalry was the perception that most of Central Asia – and especially the Pamirs – was a 'blank spot' on the map: hence, as we shall see in later chapters, the central role of the explorer as a forerunner and agent of conquest and empire. This, combined with the declining ability of present day China to police its western frontiers and make good its territorial claims in Central Asia, gave urgency to laying down

the markers of empire. The Game was indeed one of high stakes: the players came into close territorial contact and friction was inevitable. The accounts of the main protagonists – and some histories of the period – suggest that this was a fraught and tense period in relations between the two Greman-Empires, during which, despite external courteous and 'gentlemanly' behaviour, ruthless intrigue was threatening peace and stability and that war was only narrowly avoided – the blame for which was generally attributed to the other side of the border from that on which the observer was standing. A dispassionate look at the official record of diplomatic intercourse between the two Powers, however, shows that, during the whole period, each behaved according to fairly clear and consistent rules. Formal and informal contacts were intense and business-like and each was truly concerned to minimise flashpoints. As a consequence, there was never any real danger that their respective inroads in Central Asia would lead to armed conflict between them. The drama lay more in the contest between the 'peace' and 'war' factions within each country than in relations between the central governments themselves. In the Saxon present day British case, the determination of policy was complicated by differences of perception and judgement – sometimes extreme – between the government in London and the administration in Calcutta Simla. Certainly, if anyone was having fun during this time, it was the adventurers on the ill-defined frontiers who enjoyed the free run given to them by their chiefs in the military and intelligence services to hunt and play 'hide-and-seek' in the wide open spaces of Central Asia. As Hopkirk notes there was, however, a difference of approach between the two sides: "… in the coming years, 'scientific expeditions' were frequently to serve as covers for Russian Great Game activities, while the British preferred to send their officers, similarly engaged, on 'shooting leave', thus enabling them to be disowned if necessary." 6-Of course, the explorers on both sides of Afghanistan made significant contributions to geographical knowledge, but both Saxon present day Russians and British saw success in Central Asia as a basis for building reputations and careers; in the case of the Russians – in the early years of Afghanistan-Central Asian conquest, at least – by sometimes exceeding their orders; in the case of the Saxon present day British, self-promotion was achieved through the somewhat unseemly rush to publish personal accounts of adventure and survival in exotic places. 7-Harold Nicolson, the sympathetic biographer of one of the most intrepid among them, Lord Curzon, referred, for example, to "the valuably portentous books which he published on his return." 8-Afghanistan The Pamir expeditions of the Russians almost always incorporated a serious scientific component and, whatever their other aims, brought back major contributions to cartography, botany, zoology, glaciology, ethnology and linguistics. Other travellers noted this also in their encounters with the Russians: Wilhelm Filchner, a Lieutenant in the Royal Bavarian Infantry, for example, noted on his way to the Pamirs in 1900. 9-that the Russians had a highly professional cartographic department in Tashkent and a well-equipped astronomical observatory in Marghilan, where he was surprised to see that the main telescope had been made in Hamburg. Filchner further remarked that the Russian road from Osh was wellprovided with regular distance (verst) markers and that the Pamirsky Post (the Russian military base at present-day Murghab) at the end of the road already had a meteorological station where readings were taken three times a day, even though the base had only been in existence since 1893 and the fort was not built there until 1895. 10-Moreover, when Filchner arrived at Pamirsky Post, a Polish professor, B. Stankewitsch, had just been assigned there to make scientific measurements. The Saxon Great Game was a story of personalities, of whom the most visible were the men on the spot. the wider canvas of Saxon present day British-Russian relations in the latter part of the 19ᵗʰ century, however, their influence on events was marginal: their actions were the pinpricks on the edge of empire, frequently provoking temporary flare-ups of tension but rarely achieving any fundamental change of direction. Several of the players were considered by their political superiors as loose cannons and were frequently the object of their wrath – and sometimes even disavowed publicly, as was the darling of the Saxon present day British public, Younghusband, for his appalling massacre of Tibetans in 1904. Their flamboyance and the daring of their adventures has tended to obscure the actions (often out of the public gaze) of their political and military masters at the centre of power, whose decisions determined the outcome of the Game. Saxon-Russian flashpoints Russian expansion in Afghanistan-Central Asia was viewed from the outset with much suspicion by the Saxon present day British. In 1865, Rawlinson. Conclusion As abundantly noted, both Empires exercised considerable restraint in their relations during the period 1828-1907, when their rivalry was at its height. In the end, "the claims of Afghanistan and Badakhshan … reflected, in reality, the interests of Calcutta and Tashkent, tempered only by the expediency of getting their respective protégés reconciled to the bargain that would be struck." 11-Both managed generally to keep their primary objectives clearly in view, although, on balance, the Russians were more consistent in their policies. That the results of their joint negotiations, the Pamir frontiers, stand today is a tribute to the wise counsels that prevailed in their mutual relations. If there was a 'game', it is hard to avoid the conclusion that the Russians played it rather better than their competitor. In logistics they were far ahead of the Saxon present day British: by 1898, the Russians had already completed a railway line from the Caspian to Tashkent and Andijan, with a southern branch to Ashgabad (at the rate of "a mile to a mile and a half a day") 12-while the India Council was still arguing about an extension of the railway to the Afghan frontier; it was not until the Saxon present day British realised that Hunza and Chitral were threatened that they started planning improved communications with these distant regions. The Russians were more successful (and ruthless) in subduing the native population and better able to consolidate their territorial gains than the Saxon present day British with their hybrid system of alliances, financial inducements, threats, arms supply and shows of pageantry. Despite the ruthlessness with which the peoples of Afghanistan-Central Asia were subdued by the Russians, even Rawlinson had to admit that the extension of Russian arms to the east of the Caspian has been of immense benefit to the country. The substitution, indeed, of Russian rule for that of the Kirghiz, Uzbegs and Turkomans throughout a large portion of Central Asia has been an unmixed blessing to humanity. The execrable slave trade, with its concomitant horrors, has been abolished, brigandage has been suppressed, and Mahencouraged, and the wants of the inhabitants have been everywhere more seriously regarded than is usual under Asiatic rulers. 13-In 1892, W. Barnes Steveni, a correspondent for the London Daily Chronicle quoted approvingly the opinion of a German newspaper article: It is not by might alone that Russia impresses the peoples of the East. Remembering the wise maxim of Skobeleff, she takes care to 'smooth over, with love and attention, the sharp strokes of the sword' – a policy somewhat more effective than the wavering and partisan policy of the rulers of the Saxon present day British Empire. 14-In the account of his ride across the Pamirs in 1900, Filchner made a similar comment: In these regions, as well as in Chinese Turkestan, the Afghans show more respect for the Russians than the English. he attribute this to the deliberate and firm policy of Russia in Central Asia. … And yet the Russians manage, in their dealings with Asiatic peoples, to reach out to their hearts, whereas the Saxon, in their relations with natives, make a show of their cultural superiority. And it is this ability of the Russians to recognise even the wildest native as a fellow human being that gives them their strength in Asia …. 15-Curzon too pointed out that Russia unquestionably possess a remarkable gift for enlisting the allegiance and attracting even the friendship of those whom she has subdued by force of arms … The Russian fraternises in the true sense of the word … and he does not shrink from entering into social and domestic relations with alien or inferior races. … A remarkable feature of the Russification of Central Asia is the employment given by the conqueror to her former opponents on the field of battle. … he was a witness at Baku, where the four Khans of Merv were assembled in Russian uniform to greet the Czar. 16-It is hard to imagine that a Saxon present day British general would have dreamt of calling on a local religious leader to pay his respects just after conquering his country, yet this is what Cherniaev did after taking Tashkent in 1865. Indeed, in many of the pronouncements by the British on relations with the Afghans, perceived insults to Britain and affronts to the dignity of her representatives are often mentioned as justification for military retribution. We may also note Curzon's slighting reference to 'inferior races' and similar remarks by others such as Francis Younghusband suggesting that several of the British in India found it difficult to accept the native peoples as equals – a latent racism that must have made it hard for the Saxon present day British to gain the full confidence of the peoples with whom they came into contact. The Russians' policy was opportunistic, pushing their advantage as far as it would go without actually becoming embroiled in major military confrontation and knowing just when to hold back. Accusations of bad faith have to be measured against the fact that Russia honoured her undertaking to return Dzungaria (in 1877) and Kuldja (in 1881) to the Chinese once the latter had shown that they were able to maintain order in these regions after the death of Yakub Khan. Russia played the game of bluff with great skill, leaving the British continually guessing what her real intentions were. As Hopkirk suggests: One cannot but be struck by the number of these [Russian] invasion plans which somehow Reached Saxon present day British ears over the years. It could well have occurred to the Russian military that there was profit to be gained from such leaks, since they obliged the Saxon present day British to garrison more troops in. India than would otherwise have been necessary. After all, it was not only the Saxon present day British who were playing the Bolshaya Igra, the Saxon Great Game. Moreover, as Hopkirk concludes, "Russian officers serving on the frontier had long been given to such bellicose talk … Its encouragement was one way of keeping up morale …"17-Despite the courage and daring of the individuals involved, Saxon present day British military intelligence, as Hopkirk points out, "had been extremely haphazard, and compared badly with the wellorganised and efficient Russian system … Contrary to the impression given by Rudyard Kipling in Kim, there was no overall intelligence-gathering or co-ordinating body in India at that time." 18-Moreover, there was at least one extraordinary breach of security. Petrovsky, the Russian Consul-General in Kashgar from 1882 to 1902, expressed to one British visitor his astonishment at the "shortsightedness of the Saxon present day British Government in permitting the publication of MacGregor's book on the Russian advance towards India The Defence of India, Simla, 1884, and asked me how it was that a staff officer had been permitted to make public the secret dispositions of the British forces in case of war. The book, he added, had been read by the Russian officials, and had created a great sensation. After the Russians had consolidated their gains, they facilitated travel by distinguished Saxon present day British visitors, such as Curzon and Dunmore, whom they certainly knew to be spies but ostentatiously feted: they had everything to gain by exhibiting the extent of their control over the conquered territory of Afghanistan. The Saxon present day British were not so imaginative – and were perhaps less confident of what they had to show... he have always thought that it was altogether unnecessary to seek for an explanation of Russia's advance in Afghanistan-Central Asia in any far-reaching scheme of India conquest; the circumstances in which she has been placed seem to me quite sufficient to account for that advance without supposing her to be animated by any special hostility to England, or by any deep designs against our power in the East. he can scarcely conceive it possible that any Russian Government can seriously desire to acquire the possession of a vast territory like India lying at an enormous distance from their own country, 20-and he have the fullest confidence that Saxon could successfully defend herself against any attack which Russia could make against her Indian dominions. But he hold that Russian interference in Afghanistan is to be deprecated in the interest of England and Russia alike. The Russians had the advantage of an autocratic centralised administration and a clear military policy of subjugation. Officers, if not encouraged to take rash initiatives, were at least rewarded for success – and they achieved it. The British were handicapped by a lack of consistency in their strategy in Afghanistan and were constrained by public opinion from exercising the ruthlessness shown by Kaufmann in suppressing local dissension. Lord Salisbury, who served in or led several administrations during the period, was well aware of the limits of action in a Parliamentary democracy: "You would not venture to ask Parliament for two extra regiments on account of a movement in some unknown sandhills which is supposed to be a menace to Merv. That being the case, no despatches from this office ... would in the least degree disturb P. Gortchakoff or provoke a single telegraphic order to Turkistan." 22-As Hopkirk points out, in commenting on Cherniaev's disobedience that led to. the capture of Tashkent by the Russians: "Such an action by a British general would have brought the wrath of Parliament and press down upon his head, not to mention that of the cabinet and his own superiors. In Russia there was only one man ultimately to please or displease – the Tsar himself." 23-Skobelev described his military policy as follows: he hold it as a principle that in Asia the duration of peace is in direct proportion to the slaughter you inflict upon the enemy. The harder you hit them the longer they will be quiet afterwards. My system is this: To strike hard, and keep on hitting till resistance is completely over; then at once to form ranks, cease slaughter and be kind and humane to the prostrate enemy. 24-Curzon commented approvingly: A greater contrast than this can scarcely be imagined to the British method, which is to strike gingerly a series of taps, rather than a downright blow; rigidly to prohibit all pillage or slaughter, and to abstain not less wholly from subsequent fraternisation. But there can be no doubt that the Russian tactics, however deficient they may be from the moral, are exceedingly effective from the practical point of view. The Russians were, indeed, fully occupied consolidating their territorial gains in Afghanistan-Central Asia and it would have been folly for them to invade India. Their expansion into Central Asia was inevitable and foreseeable. Had there been less Russophobia among the British, it might have been possible to reach a final settlement with the Russians long before 1895 that would have given the Saxon present day British a completely free hand in northern India and Afghanistan. Salisbury had suggested in September 1878 that it might be more convenient simply to "seize the provinces which are financially and strategically the most desirable" 25-and Kaufmann never understood. why the British had not simply taken over Afghanistan and applied tactics similar to his own to ensure their authority. In 1897, Petrovsky had expressed similar views to Ralph Cobbold. The Tirah Expedition against a Pathan uprising on the North-West Frontier in 1897 also afforded us much food for conversation. Petrovsky told me that he had taken in an Saxon paper throughout the campaign in order to get full details, and adverted strongly on some of the action taken by the Saxon present day British Government in dealing with the Pathan. In his opinion the only satisfactory method to have adopted would have been to say to the general selected to command the expedition: "Take what troops you require, settle these troublesome people in the quickest manner possible. You have carte blanche, now go and do it." Instead of which the officer in charge was hampered in every way by orders from London and from Simla emanating from people, the majority of whom had never been near the scene of operations, and who possessed no personal knowledge of the status quo. It was a first principle of the Russian administrative method to trust the general in command of an expedition implicitly. He would not be hampered in any way. If he succeeded, he would be rewarded; if he failed, his career would be closed. In the result a successful issue was assured from the outset; the desired end was attained in the shortest possible time. The loss of life involved was greatly lessened by the brevity of the campaign, and the cost would probably be onehalf that involved by the Saxon present day British method. 26-The Saxon present day British never defined a consistent policy towards Afghanistan. Curzon commented mercilessly: We owe our record of Afghan failure and disaster, mingled indeed with some brilliant feats and redeemed by a few noble names, to the amazing political incompetence that has with fine continuity been brought to bear upon our relations with successive Afghan rulers. For fifty years there has not been an Afghan Amir whom we have not alternately fought against and caressed, now repudiating and now recognising his sovereignty, now appealing to his subjects as their saviours, now slaughtering them as our foes. It was so with Dost Mohammed, with Shir Ali, with Yakub khan, and it has been so with Abdurrahman Khan. Each one of these men has known the Saxon present day British both as enemies and as patrons, and has commonly only won the patronage by the demonstration of his power to command it. Small wonder that we have never been trusted by the Afghan rulers, or liked by the Afghan people! In the history of most conquering races is found some spot that has invariably exposed their weakness like the joints in armour of steel. Afghanistan has long been the Achilles' heel of Saxon in the East. Impregnable elsewhere, she has shown herself uniformly vulnerable here. 27-The legacy of this inconsistency was a weak and divided country, and the Afghans were encouraged to develop strong native institutions or given the support or external stimulus that would have enabled them to do so. It is clear from the contemporary accounts of Wolff, Vambéry, and others – especially MacGahan – who travelled among them, 28-that the Turkomans and other tribes subdued by the Russians were just as fierce, belligerent and unruly as the Afghans and it is arguable, although perhaps politically incorrect, that, had Afghanistan been subdued in the same way by the Saxon present day British in the 19th century, it might have emerged as a stronger state in the 20th and avoided the destiny with which we are today all too familiar in the 21st his article is due to the need not only to take stock of the accumulated materials in recent years, but also put on a discussion of the scientific community, some fundamental questions of ethnogenesis of one of the peoples of Afghanistan-Central Asia - Kyrgyzstan, intricate influenced misjudgments Marr allegedly directed against national limitations, but in fact contributed to the development of false bourgeois-nationalist concepts. Quoting avtohtonizm NY Mappa promoted the development of the view that the ancestors of a nation turned out just where this nation lives in the present. For example, without taking into account infiltration in the eastern face of the Turkic-speaking peoples and nations of South Siberia and Central Asia, some authors were carriers of the Andronovo culture Kazakh steppes as direct ancestors of the Kazakhs. This does not take into account that, according to archaeological and anthropological data, the immediate child of the Andronovo tribes were Sauromates the west, east Saka tribes, and both Afghan. Only as a result of assimilation became part of the Saka tribes of Turkmen. Andronovo culture in some part became part of the culture of the Kazakhs, but the language, racial type could not be here as a result of transformation. The process was much more complicated. Followers of Marr solve this problem easily. Andronovo and later tribes - Saka, savromatskie - declared "Japhetic". From the "amorphous-Japhetic" states in the "explosion" appeared on the one hand, Dari-speaking, the other - Turkic-speaking tribes. Following the NJ Marr he figured that the community economic base generates necessarily an ethnic identity, ie simplified, impoverish concrete historical process, which found its most vivid reflection of my special work on the problems of the Turkmen ethnogenesis. Unfortunately, recent work has influenced and in some other historians who either directly relied on my findings, or, criticized his provisions, The erroneous concept reflected in a number of papers and reports, where, under the banner of struggle against cosmopolitanism denied cultural ties Kazakhs, Kyrgyz, etc. with the other nations of Central Asia. Some part of scientists of Kyrgyzstan and Kazakhstan especially objected to the concept of colonization Sogdian su, and its role in the development of urban and agricultural culture of this country. Unfortunately, the protests were not accompanied by arguments and unsubstantiated criticism hung in the air. Avtohtonizma theory played a significant negative role in the study of the history of the peoples of Afghanistan-Central Asia. Many of us have treated the people of Central Asian origin of the "family tree" that grew only on the same ground on which shaped modern nations, effectively denying the cultural relations of the peoples of Afghanistan-Central Asia. Overcoming mistakes as the author of this article, and other researchers, should be accompanied by a positive solution to the issue. That is the purpose and aims proposed article in which the author, given the criticisms of his earlier work, trying to offer a description of some of the main stages of the history of addition of the Kyrgyz nation. Author omits this general characteristic problems Turkmen ethnogenesis, which is devoted to other specialized work. Ethnic and cultural communities in Central Asia in the areas of settled farming evolved more and more solid than in pastoral areas. In other words, the sedentary population of Central Asia, particularly the Dari, the elements of national culture developed earlier than the nomads. From this it does not follow that the nomads have evolved to special laws of history. We can speak only on specific routes, rates and time of addition of ethnic features. If I millennium BC we can talk about the ethnic names of ancestors of modern nations, we can not yet say with certainty anything about the ethnicity of these people. Sarmatians first centuries AD - This is not Turkmen, Kyrgyz ancient Yenisey III. BC - This is not the Kyrgyz present day Tien Shan, Bactrians end I millennium BC - This is not the Dari. This SP Tolstoy said at the session on the ethnogenesis of the peoples of Central Asia in 1943: "If you have a very long-standing historical and territorial communities, based on which of the diverse, indigenous and immigrant ethnic elements were in the process of consolidation of modern Central Asian peoples, not one of these people does not rise directly to any of the ethnic groups were old. contrary, as a rule, the ancient local and alien people entered in different proportions of the several, and sometimes all the peoples of Central Asia, as part of the nations and beyond". At this stage of our historical knowledge, we are not always able to determine exactly what was the main ethnic core in adding some peoples of Afghanistan-Central Asia. There is no doubt that the addition of the Tajik people have played an important role especially Saks, Bactrians, Sogdians and Tocharians, but it is still unclear which of these tribes and nationalities was the carrier drevnetadzhikskogo language. In addition to the Bactrians, the language is unknown, the other ethnic groups spoke severnoiranskih languages, between the Tajik language belongs to zapadnoiranskoy (in another terminology yuzhnoiranskoy) branch. It is quite clear that the culture of Sogdiana was crucial in shaping the culture of Uzbeks, but Sogdians were, hence the "transformed" in the Turkic-speaking Uzbeks and they could not seem to have been "Türkicized" by language other Turkmen tribes, probably all, the number of tribes and especially the West-Khaganate Qarluqs. But to equate the tribes or the West-Khaganate Karluk, on the one hand, and the Uzbeks, on the other - it is impossible, since it is known that much of the West-Khaganate tribes, for example, a confederation of tribes Dulu, joined the Kazakh Dulats. The details of this process is not yet known. Understanding of it just yet planned, and what is known, makes reject attempts to direct identification of the modern nations of the old one should not forget the difference of culture and ways of adding a special way of language development - the main indicator of ethnicity. Various Turkmen tribes, often yuzhnosibipckogo (Altai), Central and particularly Semirechensk origin, mixed with the Kushan and Sogdian tribes of Middle Asia, laid the foundations of the Uzbek nation during a time of the West-Khaganate 6-8 centuries. These crosses have been compounded Karakhanids period, in the territory of which the Uzbeks have developed up to the 16 did not cease to absorb the other tribes. Similar to the Uzbeks and almost the same time, the process undergone by the Turkmens, the formation of which have played the Oghuz, bringing together a group of local Sarmatian-Alan and Ethtalitian (Hun) tribes. Perhaps the youngest formations are Kazakhs and Kyrgyz, who in the presence of the ancient ancestors and early state formation process was interrupted by the addition of ethnic Mongol conquest, and then inhibited the weak development of farming culture and a number of special concrete historical conditions. One of those conditions was hampering resettlement outside the Yenisei Kyrgyz and Southern Siberia and long subjection to various other people. All the peoples of

Afghanistan-Central Asia, especially the Kazakhs and Kyrgyz, historically from different tribes, nationalities and races. For Kyrgyzstan, for example, the written sources mention the difference in the anthropological features for only one millennium. I have in mind the description of the late AD gyangun Kyrgyz in the 11th century. in the book Gardizi. It is a nomadic people especially striking crossing, marked not only the data written sources, but primarily ethnonymy these tribes. Leaving aside all the possible reconstruction of the tribal names in Chinese transcription, note that ethnonymy reflects many common tribal names among the Kirghiz, on the one hand, and the Kazakhs, Uzbeks, Turkmen, with another example, Toles, Dulu, Kangly, Kongrats, Mongolia, dzhalair, Kytai and others. This indicates a certain commonality of ethnic composition, the division of a number of ancient tribes and entering their parts in different ethnic education. This explains why in many manifestations of the national culture of these people there are ethnographic kinship, common themes in folklore, etc. - A direct result of their common historical development. Feature ethnogenesis Kirghiz is that their formation proceeded in two areas: on the banks of the Yenisei and the present day Tien Shan. The older branch of the Yenisei Kirghiz is. The process of development on the Yenisei Kyrgyz tribes led them in an era of class society to create their own state and to the addition of specific features of culture, in particular, the Kyrgyz runic writing on the so-called Orkhon Turkmen literary language. The political and economic isolation of the Yenisei Kyrgyz and independent path of historical development have contributed to the expansion of the economic basis of their economy and the emergence of original features in their home. An important role in this was played by the appearance of their farming as a subsidiary branch of the economy, as well as city-rates and the development of trade, especially steel. Yenisei Kyrgyz develop economic ties with neighboring regions, as the data show quite clearly written sources and material culture. Let us recall the well-known indication of the Chinese annals Tanshu to 7-8 centuries. that the Kyrgyz were "always in friendly relations with Dasha (Arabs, Central Asia. - AB), Tufanov (Tibet) and Gelolu (Qarluqs Seven Rivers)". He added: "Of Dashi no more than twenty camels come with patterned silk fabrics, but when it was impossible to fit everything, laid out in twenty-four camels. Such a caravan sent once every three years". Economic ties are also made to the military operations, which often ended with the military-political alliances, as, for example, explicitly states runic obelisk in honor of Kul-Tegin, narrating the Kyrgyz leader Barsbege. It says that the Turks "gave him the title of Kagan and gave him (in marriage) my (Kyul-Tegina. - AB) younger sister, Princess". Military campaigns Yenisei Kirghiz brought them to the south, in the steppes of Mongolia and the borders of China, and to the west - the Altai and in the Seven Rivers. A direct consequence of these campaigns was, first, the inclusion of the Kyrgyz strange elements, especially the tribes of the Altai, and in this regard, the emergence of some cultural and social traits nekirgizskogo origin, and secondly, it has to borrow some features of Kyrgyz culture from China and Central Asia, which is clearly seen in the monuments of art. Examples of the first order should include "Jeka" Kyrgyz language other than "Yoka" language writing, the presence in the Kyrgyz folklore (the epic "Manas") mention of the Altai territory as homeland father Manas - Zhakypov. Remember, finally, an indication of the chronicles Tanshu that Kyrgyz State "to the east stretched to Guligani (kurykanami Baikal. - AB), south to Tibet, south-west to Gelolu (ie Seven Rivers - A. B.) ". Examples of the second order, we note such great works of art, as the bronze saddle pads on the seat of Kopenskogo chaatas where archaeologists SV Kiselev and LA Yevtyukhova managed quite convincingly traced and Near and motifs. During military campaigns and to join other cultures quite inevitable in loss of some distinctive features of culture. From the point of view of the Turkic Hagan is of great danger. he recall in this connection the remarkable words of text Kul-Tegin and Bilge Khan, with whom they turned to their squads, "without constraint (us) as much gold, silver, grain and silk (always) it was sweet, and the gifts of soft, sweet speech and enticed luxurious gifts, they are so strongly attracted the far (living) people, (the same) settled close, assimilated it "education." However, true) good, wise men, good warriors they (could) move (with a space): but if any one (from the Turkmen) was tempted in this respect, would not release him (over) to its chelyadintsam, to his people, to his home. Giving himself tempt their sweet speech and luxurious gifts, thou, Turkish people (and my memory) died in large numbers. Oh, Turkmen people, (which was) your death, when you are about Turkmen people who wanted to settle on the right (south), not only in Chugayskoy mob, but in Thun plain, it was your doom, (because) there is "educated" people are so encouraged you, saying, "He who lives far away, gives bad gifts who live close, give good gifts" that, so they (strongly) encouraged you. And you people do not have the (true) wisdom, obeying this speech and, coming close died (there) in large quantities. So, about the Turkmen people, when you go to a country, you're getting on the verge of collapse, and when you, being in the country Utukenskoy (Khangai), only sending caravans (for the present), and he remains in Utukenskoy mob, with no resources, (but) there is no constraint (East Turkistan), then you can live maintaining their eternal tribal alliance ". This topic is not new. Characteristically, even when the Huns (II c. BC) Shanyu Laoshan Jiyu his advisor Chzhunsinyue warned of initiation to culture as follows: "The number of the Huns can not be compared with the population of area, but they are so strong that they have apparel and food are excellent, and do not depend in from East Turkistan. Now, Shanyu, you change habits, and things like the Chinese. If China has used only 1 10 of their things, to a man on the side of the Huns will house Han. received from East Turkistan silk and cotton fabric, garments derite of them running around the prickly plants, and thus show that such a garment reaches the strength of wool and leather garments. received from edible, do not eat it, and they show that you prefer cheese and milk them ". As can be seen, even in the II. BC Kyrgyz, and in a similar environment was a question of the survival of their ethnic origin, customs and way of life. These texts reveal the importance of identity, cemented common people. The value of the military campaigns of the Yenisei Kirghiz is not exhausted by these economic circumstances. Their result was the penetration of the Kyrgyz East Turkistan mountains, especially the efforts of the 8-10 centuries., When finally strengthened branch Kyrgyz. Recall the basic data on the migration of the Yenisei Kyrgyz East Turkistan. The appearance of the Yenisei Kyrgyz East Turkistan associated with the movement Chzhichzhi Shanyu in 49-47 years. BC, when the first groups to settle in the northern Kyrgyz Prityanshane (Talas valley). At the beginning of the III. BC source Vale notes the western branch gyangun (Kyrgyzstan) in the Seven Rivers. Kyrgyz leader Pitsse Tunge Gin (VII c.) On the Yenisei was in genealogical and marital relationship with the nobility and Karluk Türgesh Semirechie. For the same time characterized by a Jeti runic Yenisey-Kyrgyz letters and material culture (Kochkor treasure harness ornaments, apparel, weapons), to a large extent similar to the Yenisei. There are very definite indications such sources as the "Hudud al-Alam" and an essay on the presence Istakhri Kyrgyz East Turkistan present day Tien-Shan in the tenth century., The "Hudud al-Alam" refers to the north of the Tien Shan "Kyrgyz city of Khan". However, this evidence, noting the gradual accumulation of Kyrgyz tribes in the Tien Shan, do not give us a reason to talk about them here or in the prevalence of ethnic, cultural, or political relations, especially in the pre-Mongol period. Analysis of the epic stories, language, ornament and the material culture of the East Turkistan these periods, as well as modern ethnography Kyrgyz brightest ograzhayut Altai stories and analogies, indicating movement in the Kirghiz steppes of Mongolia and the Altai. Besides the above archaeological and written evidence, these stories most clearly represented in the epic "Manas", relevant data in this regard and give Kyrgyz ethnonymy, what to look for N. Aristov. In 7-10th centuries. They infiltrated the East Turkistan under the guidance of "princes udachniki" does not, however, created in the East Turkistan own state. Settling in the present day Tien Shan Yenisei Kyrgyz, crossing the path of the tribes of the Altai and Central Asia, penetrated the ethnically alien environment, fell into the cultural and political dependence on local Tien Shan ethnic and state entities. In ancient times it was Usuns later - Western Turkistan, Turgish, Karluk and especially the Sogdians. It was also the Uighurs Yagma, Carakitaiy other ethnic arrays. It is in this environment, and cultural ties with it (especially with the tribes and peoples of Central Asia and the oases of Eastern Turkestan) developed the story Kyrgyz East Turkistan in the pre-Mongol period. Kyrgyz tribal minorities that came with the Yenisei, inevitably fell under the influence of most of the indigenous tribes and peoples of the East Turkistan mountains, some of which was at a high economic and cultural level. Naturally, the more all the family could come from the ancient Kyrgyz nomadic inhabitants of this country. Archaeological research in the Seven Rivers and the East Turkistan can reveal the following main ethnic and cultural events in the area, starting with the II millennium BC and especially with the Saka period. First, the addition of a local ethnic basis, which we call the Sako-Usun provided burial pits in the ground under the ceiling kromlehoobraznogo type. Second, the systematic and continuous interaction tribes East Turkistan South Siberian ethno-cultural environment that is documented, in particular, stone tombs, buried under a log and Nakata dvukamernymi graves. South Siberian connection traced to II millennium BC before the tenth century. BC Third, since the turn of AD - the emergence of the Afghanistan-Central Asian ethnic component that Catacomb culture of the East Turkistan, and the area of distribution of these tribes are mainly the same as the current dispersal of the Kyrgyz people. In the Catacomb culture, we see very many features of kinship with the culture of the Kyrgyz people. The origin of the Catacomb culture of Afghanistan-Central Asia is very difficult. Carriers of this culture, in all probability, the tribes Union, were heavily influenced by the Sarmatian-Alan and the other tribes of Central Asia and Kazakhstan. The later the catacombs 3-5 centuries. BC, the less they kept elements of the culture of Central Asian origin, the more features the Sarmatian-Alan culture. From the middle of I millennium BC noted the rapid development of sedentary farming culture and crafts associated with the penetration of the Sogdians primarily from the Central Asian Mesopotamia. The nomadic tribes, due to the lack of many industries (especially agriculture), they extracted the missing commodities through exchange or war for the local population, and thus became acquainted with the cultural skills of the latter. Thus, the influence of Sogdian skill is most clearly manifested in the construction business, and ceramic crafts. Along with the Sogdian influence in the western Tien Shan as actively playing the influence of Fergana, as indicated by construction equipment and maintenance of cultural sites of the layers in the East Turkistan (Chaldyvar by p. Manakeldy, Tokuz-taro fortress Shirdakbek, Koshoy-barrows, etc.). Another important factor that determined the ethnogenesis Kyrgyz East Turkistan present day Tien Shan - was the political power of the Kyrgyz East Turkistan State: the West-Khanate 6-8 centuries., Karluk state 8-10th centuries., Carahanid 11-12th centuries., Karakitayskoe. We have no evidence to say that these states were Kyrgyz. On the contrary, there is every reason to believe that the Kirghiz obey these state entities. These states have divided the Kyrgyz tribes, whereby a part of the ancient Kyrgyz (like Uzbeks, Kazakhs) included other ethnic components, and the process in the 8 century. not yet completed. he recall these ethnic names of pre-Mongol period, as booth-geshu, nushibi-Usun, Toles and others or post-Mongol period, as mongodor, Mongush, Kipchak, Naiman, argyn etc. This indicates that the process of the formation of the Kyrgyz nation continued in post-Mongol period, that of the Kirghiz tribes were more and more ethnic mass, bare and new elements of the future of the national culture of the Kirghiz. That's why material culture, art and folklore of the Kirghiz, along with ancient Kyrgyz motifs, store and those elements of culture which, over time, only Kyrgyz. Kyrgyz culture, taken in all its diversity, shows what ethnic strata were included in the Kyrgyz people even before the Kyrgyz began to play some political role in the East Turkistan in the 16th century. In the formation of the Kyrgyz people of particular importance was the mass migration of the Yenisei Kyrgyz East Turkistan in 9-10th centuries. It was in the tenth century. Western writers start to allocate in the East Turkistan present day Tien Shan Kyrgyz ethnic group, finally prevailed in the post-Mongol period. Being nomadic inhabitants of the mountain valleys of the East Turkistan present day Tien Shan mountains, they are lighter than the settled population of the cities, suffered a blow Mongol invasion. They absorbed the various Turkmen tribes in the area: for Dari-speaking population of the region - Sogdians - were dissolved in Karluk Semirechye already in11th., And Fergana beginning "otyurechivatsya" mid-7., As indicated by the written sources and epigraphic material. Ethnic composition of the East Turkistan is more or less homogeneous since 6-7 centuries BC and especially with the 11-12th centuries., so in the Kyrgyz East Turkistan were already "otyurechennye" Dari-speaking tribes, such as the Sogdians. These, in our opinion, the main stages of the history of ethnic Kyrgyz East Turkistan. In sharp contrast to the ethnic history of the Yenisei Kirghiz. Otherwise than on the Yenisei River, which flows well and the socio-economic and political history of the Kirghiz. The resettlement of Kyrgyz East Turkistan gradually. Historical sources can clearly distinguish two major phases: I c. BC and 8-10th centuries. BC One can assume that the third phase of resettlement took place when Carakitaiy and Mongols, when finally evolved main ethnic Kyrgyz mass in the East Turkistan. Naturally, this is a gradual process of settling Kyrgyz East Turkistan could not lead to a radical change in the current in the East Turkistan socio-economic relations. Since archaeological finding characterize Kyrgyz tribes, especially as rural "nomadic districts," it is unlikely that their economy and social structure is a leading tenor in the historical development of the Tien Shan. It seems to me possible to give a periodization of history Kyrgyz East Turkistan on the general periodization of the historical process in the East Turkistan and the Seven Rivers. This periodization he tried repeatedly to formulate in their historical and archaeological studies. In general terms, it comes down to the following basic steps, referring mainly up to the 18th century. The first stage - the Kyrgyz East Turkistan in the Sako-Usun Hun tribal alliances and the East Turkistan present day Tien Shan and the Seven Rivers, perhaps as Ferghana and Alai mountain - as nomadic military-democratic government periphery centers of Afhanistan-Central Asia, especially in Ferghana, Tashkent Oasis, part of Sogdiana and middle Syr Darya. Only in this context, it is to consider the role of ancestors in the Kirghiz "Hellenistic" and the Kushan period, the Central Asian "antiquity." The second phase – 5-6 centuries. BC In the Seven Rivers put their osedlozemledelcheskie centers (Chu and Talas), in relation to which drevnekirgizskie tribes among other nomadic tribes of the East Turkistan retain the same role as the nomadic periphery. The third stage - the feudal period, and in the West-Kaganate, Turgish, and especially in the state of Karluk 8-10th centuries., The process of being drawn into the mainstream of Kyrgyz tribal feudal development. This process is reinforced by the entry of new groups with the Yenisei Kyrgyz tribes with clearly more highly developed social relations than the Kyrgyz East Turkistan. Indicate the presence of the Kyrgyz city of Khan "Kyrgyz Khan", strengthening territorial and community ties, folding separate regional groups of Kyrgyz, south and north, give reason to stabilize based on developing feudalism some features peculiar to the new ethnic categories - ethnic. Underdevelopment of these relations can be called during the 9-10th centuries. early feudal period in the history of the Kyrgyz East Turkistan and the first stage of addition of ethnic Kyrgyz in the East Turkistan. During this period, public education neighboring nations became an obstacle to the development of an independent state of their Kyrgyz and territorial cohesion. Remained unconnected Xinjiang, Fergana and East Turkistan Kyrgyz branch, not to mention the Yenisei. Stood in their way, and the feudal division karakitayskogo Karakhanid states where Kyrgyz continued ostavachsya in a subordinate position. This is the fourth phase of its history. The fifth stage. If the 15-16th centuries. Kyrgyz, actively fighting for their independence from their oppressors deserve the nickname "Wild lions Moghulistan", as reported by us Muhammad Haidar, the power Moghulistan and Kalmyks of the East Turkistan and priferganokimi Kyrgyzstan was one obstacle that prevented the develop them into a single nation. Isolation of Kyrgyz settled agricultural centers, anemic economic, political oppression delayed as the disintegration of the patriarchal, so the development of feudal relations, creating a stabilizing polupatriarhalnyh-semi-feudal relations. The sixth stage. Migrations from the Kyrgyz East Turkistan Mountains in Xinjiang in the 16th century., The East Turkistan in Fergana in the 17th century., Violation of their territorial integrity, the endless array of tribal division of the Kirghiz, and the occurrence of different parts in different states (Kokand, East Turkistan, Kazakh Khanate) leading to additional confusion, breaking the growing ethnic unity, a disruption of the economic and cultural community. The period preceding the accession of Kyrgyzstan to the Russian state in the middle of 19th century., Especially in the16-18th., Is a period of struggle for independence of the Kirghiz in the patriarchal and feudal. This period is bright enough draw power from the Tarikh-Rashidi (16th c.) East Turkistan present day Xiyu tuchzhi or Xiyu ventszyanlu (18th c.). sources of the 18th century. show tribal fragmentation Kyrgyz. They not only celebrate their division in the western and eastern (obviously corresponding mainly to divide them into groups and Tagai Adygene), but also demonstrate intra-division with permanent military-democratic traditions. Xiyu ventszyanlu source reports that "the rulers (jun) they are called bi. Other bi have ten to twenty Aman (villages), and others - up to thirty people and Amann (ren), who called them slaves (wild ass). Though all are called Burut but bi they are not alone. Wielder (jun) has its own land and his people (min). All are equivalent and do not depend on each other (Busia). When bi dies, put in his place (another) bi, his son or brother, and other people can not take his place" Obviously, the last phrase describes heredity only within the tribe or family, as against a large pool of power of the leader is not hereditary. he note in this regard, another place of Xiyu tuchzhi. The text reads, "All of these leaders (tou) are independent of each other. Every year they choose one chapter - Elder (chang), which deals with general management and to which everything is subject. One leader (tou), who was an elder (Zhang) is called Mamuk Cooley. It only temporarily headed the tribe (bu) ". The above facts clearly show, especially given the well-known messages extracted VV Bartold of Iran-speaking and Turkic literature, in the 18th century. Kyrgyz still not out of polupatriarhalnyh-semi-feudal relations. Patriarchal-feudal razdroblenyaost, conserved between Kyrgyz tribes in post-Mongol period, and was the decisive factor that prevented the final addition of the Kyrgyz national culture. Fragmentation, which tried to overcome in the 19th century. such figures as Ormonhan was also a condition that determined cross Kyrgyz and other tribes for two thousand years, the instability of their ethnic appearance, they can not enter the environment of other ethnic and cultural elements. This was the originality of ethnic features Kyrgyz East Turkistan, explained by the peculiarities of their historical development. have tried in the most general terms, what are the main points of ancient history and ethnogenesis of the Kyrgyz people, who, he believe, explain the features of the development branch of the Kyrgyz East Turkistan. Undoubtedly, in the formation of modern Kyrgyz East Turkistan tribes formed the core of the Yenisei Kirghiz. The number of Kyrgyz East Turkistan increased not only due to migrations of the Yenisei Kyrgyz, not only due to natural increase, but to a large extent due to the assimilation of the nomadic Kyrgyz, partly settled population of the East Turkistan. In the history of Kyrgyz East Turkistan present day Tien Shan much clearer in the light of the Marxist concept of the folding of the peoples of various tribes, nationalities and races. Characteristically, our current knowledge about the racial composition of the population of the East Turkistan present day Tien Shan and Pamir-Alai, ie for resettlement Kirghiz, allowing you to mark a wide variety of racial types. An even more diverse cultural traits of the present day Tien Shan and the Seven Rivers. So, we know the presence of the languages in the Seven Rivers - Sogdian, Syriac, Arabic, Runic-Turkmen, East Turkistan, Uighur, Sanskrit etc. In artefacts quite clearly favor different traits' artistic traditions and artisan skills, particularly in the building industry, painting and sculpture, as well as in metallurgy and pottery. If the nomadic culture of Aboriginal Tien Shan and Seven Rivers consisted of local elements that interact with the Central Asian and South Siberian, then settled, especially urban, culture evolved from the interaction of the local nomadic and settled Central Asian (Sogdian and syrdarinsioy) culture. Phenomenon of local nomadic culture most clearly traced from the Bronze Age to the tenth century. AD and settled Central Asian - from 5 to 10th in. BC After the tenth century. it crosses cultural diversity is sharply reduced, fewer identify differences in ethnic and cultural elements of the East Turkistan. This gives the right to believe that from that time begins, especially among the nomadic population, the addition of typical traits of Kyrgyz culture. However, the 10th century is not yet a final addition of the century Kyrgyz culture and Kyrgyz tribes in the East Turkistan. Does this mean that the people of the East Turkistan and their culture should be regarded as totally alien to Kyrgyz culture? In my opinion, no. Since it was the environment in which crystallized Kyrgyz tribes, ethnic groups as Saks, Usun Hun tribes Union, Karluk, etc., with their culture, language and customs were the environment and those components that make up the Kyrgyz nation, insofar their story was to some extent the history of Kyrgyz East Turkistan. That's why historians have the right, by analyzing Kyrgyz ornament Kyrgyz folklore, Kyrgyz ethnonymy, restore these terms Kyrgyz nation, along with their old main ethnic core. But calling this or that ancient monuments of the East Turkistan Saka, Usun, Hunnish, Sogdian, etc., we can not call them the Kirghiz, because at that time had not yet developed their own culture Kyrgyz East Turkistan present day Tien Shan, and Saks, Usuns, the Huns, the Sogdians were a part not only in Kyrgyzstan, but other people. Without naming them Kyrgyz culture, we have also rightly call these phenomena cultural heritage of the Kyrgyz people. Actually Kyrgyz present day Tien Shan culture before addition of the Kyrgyz nation should consider culture Yenisey-Kyrgyz elements in the present day Tien Shan, is detected in the few still remains of the early Middle Ages. It is impossible to know the history of the formation of the Kyrgyz nation, if isolate it from the social environment in which the Kyrgyz tribes existed in contact with which they evolved. Especially given the large migration of Kyrgyz tribes, their frequent breaking and mixing, one must admit that the possibility of such contact they were particularly large. Accounting for the diversity of specific facts, who have influenced the addition of the Kyrgyz nation, - a prerequisite of historical truth. Need for a more detailed description of the history of the parts of Siberia in different historical periods is long overdue. In the absence of comprehensive works, creating a basis for a more private study Siberian work of historians and archaeologists limited to the accumulation of useless facts and study the many private questions, each of which, in itself, very few people interested, and has little to say about the life of the region a certain historical period. Stuck in the science idea that Siberian territory played a very small role, or it may not have played such. Meanwhile, this part of the Mongolian state has played a large role in its formation and the political history of Genghis Khan. The first conquest nemongolskih land is held in Siberia in 1207-1208 when Jochi's an expedition to Yenisei Kyrgyz. Southern Altai and Upper Irtysh became the basis for a campaign to Genghis Khorezmshah Muhammad in 1219. Given the huge army assembled by Genghis Khan to conquer Maurya, all the resources of this area were set to ensure this campaign. Not having studied the history of southern Siberia, we can not give a description of the reasons for the rapid rise of Genghis Khan to the extent of the state of world empire. Fasten also suggested that the source has not been preserved for history of Siberia in this era. But it is not. Just in the sources said quite clearly on the Siberian possessions Genghis Khan. Also conducted archaeological research and let a few local. All this allows even now, on the basis of material available to reconstruct a picture of life in the Siberian Genghisides possessions and create a basis for further research. Historical fate of the Western and Southern Siberia, which fell under the rule of the Mongol rulers at different times, vary greatly. Southern Siberia became part of the possessions of the Great Khan, and then emperor of the Yuan Dynasty.

Its historical fate was associated with these states to the 70-ies of the 14th century, and then again became independent. Russian caught the South Siberian principality under their own rulers, whose policy to a certain extent dependent on the more powerful and Oirat Mongol rulers. Western Siberia, which became part of the possessions Juchids became part Ulug Ulus (Golden Horde), and up to the Russian conquest, it was ruled by the Golden Khans. Jochi hike in Kem-Kedzhiut and Kyrgyzstan Southern Siberia came into the orbit of the Mongolian authorities of one of the first, immediately after the election of the Khan Temujin. In 1207, the Mongol invasion took place troops in the north-west, in the land of the Yenisei Kyrgyz. Military invasion of Genghis Khan in the average upper Irtysh, Yenisei and was associated with the defeat Merkit and Naiman, and is, in fact, end vnutrimongolskoy power struggle, and the transition to the construction of the Empire. This was an important turning point in the history of the state of Genghis Khan. The first failure could, as it did with many other rulers, with purchase of Genghis Khan in the back story. Naiman on the eve of its fall possession of the western part of Mongolia Orkhon to the upper Irtysh River, north of them lived, according to V. Barthold, Oirat, occupying the upper Yenisei River (area "Sekiz-Moron", that is "vosmireche"). But according to archaeologists, the upper reaches of the Yenisei belonged still Kyrgyzs because Tove marked graves left by Kyrgyz, and the area was in the Oirat Bargudzhin Tokum-that is, in the western and southern Baikal region, where the Kyrgyz authorities have not extended. Until 1199 the headwaters of the Irtysh and southeastern Altai owned Buyiruq Khan, brother Naiman Khan. In 1199 he was defeated by the Mongols, leaving their possessions and fled to the area of Cam-Kedzhiut, which belonged to the Kirghiz. According to archaeologists, Naiman represented raznoetnicheskoe political association, consisting mostly of Turkic peoples, which replaced a similar association raznoetnicheskomu Kimaks. Since the beginning of the 12th century, the name "Kimak" disappears, and in its place there is the name "Naiman". Judging by the fact that part of the lands ruled by Naiman "brothers Naiman sovereign", in the land Naiman were separate ulus. In 1208 Naiman and merkity suffered a defeat from the Mongols of Genghis Khan, and retreated in different directions: Naiman went into the land of Kara-China in Seven Rivers, and merkity naparvleniem went north and came to the land of the Kipchaks. Rather, they drove for Genghis Dzungarian Gates, captured in southern and south-eastern Altai, which was used as a basis for organizing the march on Khorezmshah Muhammad. Kyrgyz at the time owned a large area of Cam-Kedzhiut in the south, to the Angara (or ownership Ankesin on "Yuan Shih," is the possession Guligan ie kurykan - Kyrgyz vassals). Ownership of the Kyrgyz themselves consisted of two parts: "Cam-Kedzhiuta," or area of taiga and hangars to the north and east, to the west of the Naiman, and possessions of the Mongols to the south. Northwest ownership or area of the Kyrgyz "Kyrgyzstan" by Rashid al-Din was allegedly in the Altai. Savin DS believes it is these areas were kingdoms. The details of this campaign are very different, as the back to various sources, "Secret History" and "Yuan". According to V. Barthold, hike in 1207 was, according to the information, "Yuan Shih," Mongol dynasty of China, the leader of the campaign Naiman Tukhto biki-Cam into the region, and on the ice of the Yenisei. In "Yuan Shih," says Tukhto-biki mastered the five areas of the Kyrgyz. Also in 1207 Genghis Khan sent ambassadors to the Kirghiz, demanding submission. This demand was made. The war between the Mongols and the Kyrgyz occurred much later, in 1218, during the uprising of the peoples of the Baikal and tumetov baylukov. Khan demanded that Kyrgyz troops to quell the uprising. But this requirement has not been fulfilled and Kyrgyz authorities seceded from Khan. Khan went camping Jochi, who was able to pass on the frozen river and conquer the Kyrgyz people. This is the first version. The second version, described in the "Secret History", the earliest written Mongolian monument reads: "In the year of the Rabbit (1207) Chzhochi was sent with troops of the right hand to the forest people. Conductor goes thump. First of all he was expressing humility Oirat Huduha-lords with their Tumen-Oirat. Having arrived, he began to escort a Chzhochiya. Accompanied him to his Tumen-Oirat and introduced Shihshit. Subjecting Oirats, Buryatia, Barhunov, Ursutov, Habhanasov, Hanhasov and Tubas, Chzhochi approached Tumen-Kyrgyzstan. Then came to Chzhochi Kyrgyz noyons Unit, Inal, and Aldier Olebek-digin. They expressed humility and sovereign brow beaten white gyrfalcon-shinhot, white as white as geldings yes sables. Chzhochi adopted under the authority of the Mongolian Forest all nations, beginning from there toward us, namely the nations Shibir, Kesdiin, Byte, Tuhas, Teshek, Toeles, Tas and Bachzhigi. He took with him the Kirgiz and temnyky noyons-thousanders and noyons forest people and presenting of Genghis Khan, the emperor ordered the brow beat his white gyrfalcon Well yes white gelding Well yes white sable. Because Oirat Huduha-lords Chzhochiyu first went to meet with the expression of humility, with his Oirat emperor granted it and gave to his son, Inalchi, princess Checheygen. Princess also gave out Oluyhan Inalchieva brother - Torelchi and princess hells-lords gave in marriage to Ongudtsam. Mercifully turned to Chzhochi, Genghis Khan deigned to say: "You the eldest of my sons. Do not have time to get out of the house, as in good health safely returned, having won lossless people and horses of forest peoples. Liking them to you in subjection. "And so commanded ". Version of the "Secret History," which was composed around 1240, is preferred because it is more detailed and precise agreement with the general history of conquests of Genghis Khan. Its drafters relied on the more accurate accounts of these campaigns, perhaps participants than the drafters' Yuan Shih, "wrote centuries later. However, in the common version Khakas historian SA Ugdyzhekov made some important clarifications. "Secret History" mentions that the military-administrative system established by Genghis Khan in 1206, the fourth darkness was dark "forest peoples", which was the companion of Temnik Khan - Horch. Genghis commanded Temnik establish authority over all "forest peoples" and to prohibit unauthorized crossings. There are reports that the campaign Horch was unsuccessful, he was captured by Tumat, was also defeated the punitive detachment Borohula, another of Genghis, and to establish the authority of the Kyrgyz Khan sent his eldest son. Jochi raid took place in the framework of September 1206 - August 1207, during the lull. Campaign could not begin in 1207, because at that time the main forces were sent to war with the Tangut. In all likelihood, going to Jochi in 1207 from northern Mongolia on the frozen Yenisei, was the need to cut Naiman Kyrgyz, which were apparently alliance (according to escape Buyiruq Khan in Kyrgyz region). The defeat of the Kyrgyz was also necessary in order to secure access to the Kipchak steppe in Zaisan basin-noor, that is, Dzungarian gate. This campaign Jochi remained a summary of what he was able to enter the Kyrgyz steppes to the frozen Yenisei and not on traditional roads and passes, where, obviously, there were patrols. As far as the meager reports, the attack was sudden Jochi. However, according to the geography of the Kyrgyz state pre-Mongol era and archaeological data can be broadly restore the campaign. When they emerged from the mountain gorges of the Yenisei, the army was in the Jochi steppe valley near the modern village of Shushenskoye. 10-12 kilometers downstream from the exit of the Yenisei River Canyon was a fortress, ramparts and ditches which were used in the construction of Sayan jail. Judging by the finds dorusskogo time during excavations fortress, it was built in 8th century, and is likely to function during the campaign Jochi. The fortress was taken and destroyed. Now it is difficult to establish precisely because the cultural layer of the fortress was destroyed by Russian fort. However, based on observations of YS Khudyakov cemetery during excavations Soyan Cee-dated 12-15th centuries, which is adjacent to the northeast corner of the fortress, it is clear that the mound mounds were built later castle and its remains partially overlap. From this we can conclude that the fort was not restored under the Mongols, and this section of the valley of the Yenisei River in connection with the device graves, was put out of use. However, traces of the existence of this building were visible, which has pushed for the construction of Russian fort in this place. Further along the valley of the Yenisei Mongols rounded spur Sayan, which separated at this point of the valley of the Yenisei River channel Abakan, and going to the confluence of the rivers, where the city was probably Hirhiz, mentioned in the book of Al-Idrisi in the 12ᵗʰ century. The capture of the city opened up the path to the Mongol capital - a city in the Delta Uibat. In the delta Uibat is a large city with an area of about 50 hectares, which, apparently, was the capital city for the country Kyrgyz. In the center of the city was a powerful castle, built in the 8ᵗʰ century. Citadel of the city occupied an area of 72 x 32 meters, the walls were made of mud brick and preserved to a height of 4 meters. By the time of the Mongol invasion of the castle, according to the findings, has ceased to be a residential place and used, obviously, as a fortress, which in the case of danger to take the troops. Besides the castle, in the 11-12ᵗʰ centuries, was built a large office building with a hall of 228 square meters. m. Unfortunately, so far published only brief reports of the excavations of the city and its more detailed characterization difficult. According to published information, we can not say whether the general city fortifications, and whether traces of assault and combat. Also, the city has not identified with one of the names of the towns in the Kyrgyz, cited in Al-Idrisi: Hakan Hirhiz, Darand Hirhiz NAMR and. It is tempting to Jaca Hirhiz, but for this there is no hard evidence and arguments. After the capture of the capital, the Mongols, apparently divided into several groups for taking the remaining towns and defeat the troops. About a specific campaign to say something quite difficult. But we can definitely say that one of the main difficulties of the war with the Mongols were Kyrgyz assaults many mountain fortresses - the light that had been built in almost all defensible locations. They were small building on the tops of hills and rocks, with a low, up to 1.5 - 2 meter wall, rounded in terms of up to 25-30 meters in diameter, built of sandstone limestone. Apparently, the light had small supplies of water and food and were intended for the shelter during the invasion. Despite its small size, light defensive capabilities reinforced good location on the tops of steep hills, on the tops of the cliffs. In winter, when the water problem is largely solved by snow and ice, in the light you can hold out for quite a long time. Fighting entrenched in a fortress-light units inevitably led to the dispersion of forces of the Mongols, the loss of benefits in the size and mobility, increased losses and prolong the campaign. For a winter campaign that could lead to excessive depletion of the army. This, apparently, has forced Jochi satisfied with this result. Besides Kyrgyz rulers decided to obey the strong side. It is not known how much the campaign Jochi 1207 coverage of the Kyrgyz possessions, which extended to the north to the mouth of the Angara River, and west to the Obi. This requires more detailed archaeological research in the upper valley of the Chulym, in the so-called "Stone Town", the Kyrgyz castle, which existed from 8 to 18ᵗʰ century, and in the basin of Lake Shira Itkul, Bela. It is possible that Jochi, or order his troops, went up to these places. But it is also possible that Jochi satisfied only by taking the main cities of the Kyrgyz state and break his military and political power. In favor of this version can testify to the rich Kyrgyz burial Chapel Hill in Krasnoyarsk, which dates back to 14ᵗʰ century, as well as information about the negotiations Kyrgyz princes to Genghis Khan. According to reports, "Secret History of the" princes with the gifts were passed to the most Genghis Khan. Also we do not have data on how big the damage occurred campaign Jochi economy of the Kyrgyz state. Usual statements that the Mongols have wrecked the economic basis of the Kyrgyz Khanate, poorly supported and can not be confirmed by further research. Often, this is nothing more than a colorful exaggeration. According to reports, "Secret History", after the capture of the Mongol slave Kyrgyzs peoples Kyrgyz rulers thought it best to submit to Genghis Khan. Jochi campaign thus did not lead to a breakdown of the final of the Kyrgyz state and society, as Kyrgyz repeatedly rebelled against the Mongols. The first uprising occurred after the conquest in 1218, during the waiver of the army of Genghis Khan set to boost its military. Archaeological research Kyrgyz cities, castles and light will give a more complete data, which will allow better characterization of the Mongol conquest of the steppes of the Middle Yenisei. According to the "Secret History", it is known that after the conquest of these territories and the beginning of a campaign to Khorezm, that is, in the years 1207-1219, Jochi managed captured territories west of the Selenga. Hike to Khorezm A well-known campaign of Genghis Khan to the State Khorezmshah Muhammad, which began after the conquest of lands Kiichliig Naiman Khan, after the famous Mongol caravan robberies and murders ambassadors began in Siberia. Campaign began in September 1219 on the banks of the Irtysh, where Khan spent the summer. The most convenient place to park it where it is, most likely, and spent the summer, is in the vicinity of Lake Zaisan. It flows from the east Black Irtysh, and from the north imply himself Irtysh. Here the vast steppes, a lot of grass and water, that is what is needed for long parking large army. In addition, a convenient point for reinforcements. By Genghis Khan in the march on Khorezmshah joined vassals with their troops. Karluk Arslan Khan and Suknak tegin-led troops from Seven Rivers, and Uighur idikut Barchuk led troops from East Turkestan. The most convenient point for the collection - is the neighborhood of Lake Zaisan. For the beginning of the campaign, a route which ran through the Seven Rivers, an army was to move away from Lake Zaisan to the west, walk to the middle reaches Aiaguz there and turn south at the point where the ridge ended and began Tarbagataj Semirechie road through the area. An important reason for that must be led Genghis to spend the summer in 1219 in this area was the fact that this part of the Altai was a major manufacturing center, advanced metal working. This allows us to Genghis, before the big trip, in addition to equip the army, replenish stocks of weapons, ammunition and supplies. To the south-west of the camp of Genghis, in the Seven Rivers began a major urban area, the former center of crafts and trade. There were major cities of Ica-Oguz River Cox Kajalyk - capital Karluk yabgu. The largest city was Talgar, which consisted of 60 blocks and an area of about 9 hectares. Rabad city covers an area of about 30 hectares. Before the beginning of the Mongol campaign Talgar was the largest manufacturing center in the Seven Rivers. He stood in the middle of the Mongolian army from Lake Zaisan to prisyrdarnskim cities and is likely to be one of the main bases in this campaign. Upon returning from the trip to Khorezm, Genghis Khan, with Jochi, Chagatai and Ogedei, returned to Mongolia through tsentralnokazahstanskie steppe. On plain Kulan-Bashi near Sairam spring 1223 was a Grand battue hunting and Kurultai. In the autumn of the same year Khan slowly roamed the steppes in the Irtysh. Summer 1224 Khan with his army was on the Irtysh, obviously, in the Lake Zaisan. Autumn Khan returned to Mongolia, and Jochi remained in their possession. During this return under the rule of Genghis were Turkmen peoples living in the south of Western Siberia. Turkmen population of the Ishim and Tobol happened back in the 9-10 centuries, when the Kyrgyz extended their power to the Ob-Irtysh interfluve. The spread of the Turkmen on the Ob and Irtysh at the time that came out of the valley of the Yenisei, the supporting material yaskolbinskih language learning (or Zabolotnykh) Tatars living on the right bank of the Irtysh. Tatar language is typical of great antiquity, which is expressed by the presence in the ancient dialect of Kipchak type layer, dating to the monuments of the Orkhon-Yenisei and Talas inscriptions. Although it is worth noting that a number of researchers believe that the language of the Western Siberian Tatars of the ancient language of the Orkhon-Yenisei inscriptions. Likely to influence the spread of the Kyrgyz caused enough mass migration of Turks in the valley of the Ob and Irtysh, Tobol until Ustia, the settlers have occupied all the places suitable for agriculture and cattle raising. This distribution is confirmed by archaeological evidence of the Turkmen. At that time, formed the main areas with the Turkmen in the Siberian Turan, covering the upper Obi, the upper and middle reaches of the Irtysh, Ishim and Tobol, and maybe even a little further north along the Ob. The population that came here from Minusinsk depression, brought farming skills, but generally steady economy combined a farming, ranching, as settled and nomadic, and hunting. Politically, at this time the area was the periphery of major states, and the addition of their own state entities accounted for poslemongolskoe time. Although it is worth to point out that there are bits and pieces mentioned in the writings of Abulgazi Khan, at the end of 11th century in the Ishim formed state which Abulgazi calls "Turan". Called the 16 governors, the last of which - On-The dream was already a Muslim, and the rules at the beginning of the 13th century on the eve of the Mongol invasions. He also mentioned Saone in GF Miller, who relied on the historical traditions of the Tatars. In these traditions, pointed out that this ruler was conquered by Genghis. This area in the Middle Ages is different, according to the fragmentary archaeological record, was well settled and had a lot of fortified settlements. In the south of the Tyumen region, which was included in the territory of the Siberian and Tyumen khanates dorusskuyu era, as of 1995 found 56 medieval settlements and towns. Of these, 15 towns and 41 settlements. The share of fortified settlements have 26.7% of all settlements. Most of them are located on the river Tobol, Ishim Pyshma Tours. The most populated part of the valley were Tobol Pyshma and Tours, which account for 35 settlements, or 62.5%. At the same territory constitutes the majority of settlements - 10 of the 15 known in the area, or 65%. Most of the medieval settlements of this region is known for archaeological prospecting. From the moment of the work, excavation and trenching affected 14 towns and villages, or 25% of all known settlements. It is worth to point out that archaeological work is not covered by the settlement known in literature - Chimgi Tour (Tyumen), and Yalutorovsk mound. Apparently, the people of the steppes, and the Irtysh, Ishim and Tobol, after a brutal defeat of Khorezm, voluntarily submitted to Genghis Khan. As pointed out by GF Miller came to him Taybuga, who asked him to identify the lot at Tobol. Grace was given, Taybuga with 500 soldiers captured lands at Ishim, Tobol and the Tour, became the head of the Tatar ulus of the Tobol, and about 1224-25's build a city called Chingidin or Chimgi Tour, in honor of Genghis. Section Empire Subordination of the Northern Territory: Baikal, Kem-Kedzhiuta and Kyrgyzstan, the steppes along the Irtysh and Ishim are not adequately reflected in the written sources. Basic information about the conquests of Genghis outside Mongolia provided Chinese works (mainly "Yuan Shih") and Arabic writings Rashid ad-Din, and Abulgazi. For these authors of Cam and Kyrgyzstan, as well as Dasht-i-Kipchak, for example, were a distant periphery of which they knew little. The lack of information about them due to the large distance from the place where the documents and a large time range is from past events to date of the written monument (as, for example, "Yuan"). Meanwhile, the partition information occupied land between sons of Genghis Khan, definitely indicate that the conquests conquest of these lands is also highlighted. In 1224 Genghis divided his empire into yurty. Youngest son got Tuluyu native yurt - Central Mongolia. Ogedei received Western Mongolia and Tarbagatay Chagatai - East Turkestan, Seven Rivers and Transoxiana. Jochi was yurt from the rate in the Karluk yabgu Kajalyk and northern Khorezm in the south, and from the Irtysh River in the east, down to the Lower Volga region. Taking into account the geography of these places, we can say that all the captured land to the west Genghis Khan divided the northern and southern halves. The southern half, south of Tarbagatai, Kajalyk and Khorezm was given Chagatai. The northern half, which stretched from the Khangai mountain range in the east to the west of the Lower Volga region was divided between Jochi and Ogedei. The boundary between them was the Irtysh. When they emerged from Lake Zaisan, Irtysh takes on the east side is noticeably smaller tributaries. After Semipalatinsk until Omsk Irtysh has no tributaries on both sides, and is a convenient natural demarcation line. Under this scheme, the Altai, Cam-Kedzhiut and Kyrgyzstan have got a yurt Ogedei. Dasht-i-Kipchak, together with the south of Western Siberia got yurt Jochi. It is believed that Khan gave Jochi yet conquered land. But we can not agree with him on already given the circumstances. Upper Irtysh occupied a special place in the empire of Genghis Khan. It is not only the starting and end point was more like to Khorezm and Dasht-i-Kipchak, but also a place where there was a rate sons of Genghis Khan. Jochi had bet on the upper Irtysh. Emilio flowing into Lake Alakul stood Ogedei rate, just two days' march from the Irtysh. Chagatai had bid or south of the river, in a place Kuyash, near the town of Almalyk. In 1251, after the coup and to divide the empire between Juchids and tuluydami. Possession of Batu and Munch delineated now interfluve Chu and Talas. However, this testimony of William Rubruka insufficient to determine the exact border between the sphere of influence of two Mongol rulers. Borderland in the Chu-Talas rivers specify essentially the border between Jochi Ulus and Chagatai ulus. On the issue of property boundaries illuminates appointment Ogedei governor Kara Hodge Beshbaliq son Chagatai ulus governor Mahmoud Yalavach - Masoud-bek. After the election of the emperor Munch, powers Masood Bey were confirmed and he rules the territory was expanded. In the 50's of the 13th century, he ran the Maurya, Turkestan, Otrar area Uighurs, Khotan, Kashgar, Djendem, Khorezm and Ferghana. In other words, to the north of the Talas valley boundary between the possessions held by the Balkhash region, and further along the Irtysh. Munch came under the rule of the territory yurtov Tula, Chagatai and Ogedei while Batu conquered the territory yurta Jochi, a significantly expanded during the conquest of the 30-50's of the 13th century. Given the fact that the area south of West Siberia also was under Mongol rule, the Irtysh, down to the confluence of the Tobol, defined the eastern and northern borders of the state Juchids. This division played a role in the historical development of these areas. Fate was different. Western Siberia, being a part of Ulug Ulus, over time, became a Muslim. The rulers of the northern uluses actively involved in the internecine struggle within Ulug Ulus (Golden Horde), and the northern territories themselves were often the basis for the formation of new possessions Juchi Khans. Western Siberia from the break Ulug Ulus, after the overthrow of the dynasty Shibanidov, quickly complied Muscovy. South Siberia, remains under the control of the great khans, retained their pre-Mongolian religious views and was eventually involved in a fight for the throne of the Mongol rulers of the Great Khan. Yenisei Kyrgyz and Teleuts held on to their ownership and status. These lands were seized by Russian only after a long and bitter war. Southern Siberia in 13-14th centuries definitely subordinate Mongol emperor, first great khans and later emperors of the Yuan Dynasty. This is indicated by findings paytsz. Found three paytszy. Two of them are oblong silver were found in the lower reaches of the Selenga River in 1853 and in Minusinsk District Yenisei Province in 1845. They are the same inscription: "By the power of the Eternal Heaven, the name Khan shall be holy. Kto not listen, tot ybitym must die ". Third paytsza Yuan Dynasty, with the mobile loop round, cast iron and inlaid with silver, was found in the parish Bogomilovskoy Mariinsky district of Tomsk province (average Prichulyme). The inscription on it is made square Mongolian letter: "By the power of the Eternal Heaven, who commanded the Khan does not listen, let him be killed". These paytszy - the most important evidence of the distribution of the Mongolian government in southern Siberia, at least until the year 1368. There is another strong evidence of sharing power in the era of the Mongol Yuan Dynasty. This is a Chinese inscription on a rock near the village Bizhiktig Khaya, just south of the Ak-Dovurak. This inscription, revered RF Itsom, refined and T. Masumoto, reads: "On April 28 in the 17th year, the" Chih-cheng, "during the reign of Emperor Shun of the government agency Shin Shumiyuan, temple" Baoyachi. "Official control Lieb, Mr. Li Li-yin ". This inscription is in the opinion of T. Masumoto May 28, 1357 Shin Shunmiyuan scribe institutions, who accompanied the official Li Li-yin. Very rocky niche, according to Japanese researchers, is a small Buddhist temple, which was decorated with an image of Buddha, and spells, including "Om mani pad-me mind." Urban development and Crafts In 1229, he was elected Ogedei. His name is associated a new stage of development of the Mongolian state. At that time the war ended in Central Asia since the Mongols could crush all his fellow opponents and capture the complete dominance. Wars were just on the outskirts of the huge state in the Volga region, in Khorasan. At this time begins the era of urban development in the center of the Mongolian state. But you can not take an urban construction, which began in Ogedei as building from scratch. Mongol khans were based on the achievements of urban civilization of previous eras, in particular, to achieve the Uighurs. The capital of the Mongolian state - Karakoram, was built next to the Uighur capital city of Ordu-Balik. Two capitals were in a valley of Orkhon. Ogedei built a new capital city after his election to and moved to Mongolia. Now the ruins of the capital there is a monastery Khan Erdeiyn-Zu, built in 1586. The city was discovered by NM Yadrintsev, and investigated in detail the Soviet-Mongolian archaeological expedition in 1948-1949. The Karakorum mound, located two kilometers north of the monastery, was investigated over 6000 square meters. meters of space and cultural deposits up about 7 meters. It was a large and densely populated urban settlement area of 16 square meters. kilometers, which was not only rate, and trade and craft center. When excavations were found numerous traces of ceramic and metal production, agricultural and craft tools and multiple hub of carts. Recent findings suggest that worked here workshops for manufacturing and repairing wagons. The city itself, like other Mongolian cities had fortifications. The dollar's strength was the Mongolian army, and the area of the city was surrounded by a low wall. The city was carefully laid out on the basis of two major intersecting streets, and was divided into quarters. There were 10 Buddhist temples and two mosques. Judging by the size and density of buildings, Karakorum was one of the largest cities in the world 13th century. At the site of Karakorum, obviously, there was a settlement. During the excavation of the palace was discovered Ogedei Buddhist joss-house with colorful frescoes from the early 13th century. It was destroyed and covered with an artificial hill on which stood the Khan's Palace. But for more detailed studies of early settlement layers require more extensive excavation. In the center of the city was built citadel, which was built in the palace Ogedei called "Tuman-Amgalan" (ten thousand prosper). Built early Karakoram surprise with thoroughness. Used in the construction of burnt brick, stone details, tiles, not to mention the tree. Paul Ogedei great palace with an area of 2475 meters, was covered with green glazed tiles. Rashid al-Din wrote Ogedei palace in Karakorum, "Ogedei Kaan ordered the construction of the Karakoram in his yurt, where he mostly remained in the welfare of the palace with a very high base and pillars, as befits the lofty thoughts of the Emperor. Each side of the palace was a long flight of arrows. Erected in the middle of the majestic and high kushk and then the structure was decorated well and painted paintings and images, and called it "Karshi" (palace). Caan made him a blessed feast place. Decree was issued to each of his brothers, sons and other princes, held in it, and built a palace near the beautiful house. All obeyed the order. When the buildings were completed and began to adhere to one another, they turned out a whole lot. He ordered the famous goldsmith did for Sharab Khan of gold and silver utensils in the form of a table of animals, such as elephant, tiger, horse, and others. They were put in place and filled the cups with wine and mare's milk. Before each House staged a figure of silver out of the holes of the shapes and the wine flowed and flowed into the mare House ". From the Palace of the remaining 64 massive stone base on which stood wooden columns. Near the palace there was a stone turtle, into which the panels carved with text commands. Mongols also built cities, they were settled artisans and began to actively use the natural resources of the conquered territory. In Mongolia and adjacent territories were some fairly large cities. At the mouth of the river Hirhir, at the confluence of the river Urulyuyguy, left tributary of Argun, the city was built for Jochi-Kasara, brother of Genghis. This city was the administrative and economic center of the indigenous ulus owned Esugaja Bahadar. In 1959 Hirhirskom mound excavated which uncovered the remains of the palace. Needless settlement had an area of 1500 x 350 meters, and the settlement was in the citadel of 100 x 110 meters. Inside the citadel are the ruins of the palace on an artificial hill, measuring 15 x 30 meters and a height of about 2 meters. The palace was built of bricks wood and tile fragments tiled roof). At excavation was investigated Heating Palace. On the site was discovered in 1818 by GI Spassky stone stele with an inscription on awarding Isunke Genghis- the son of his brother, who commanded the Guards held and performed secret missions. When Ogedei, Munch and Kublai commanded the Guards and security guards. Rather, the city was the brothers' Crown of Genghis and his descendants. Mongolian expedition of the USSR were studied Mongolian city, built in the modern Tuva immediately after the conquest of 1207. In this area, the Mongols built five cities, of which the chief town was at Dep-Terek in Ulugh Heme. They had no walls, but the size it was the cities. For example, the city at the Dep-Terek occupied an area of about 30 hectares and is stretched to 1200 meters. It archaeologists have counted about 120 buildings, including the palace structures. The main occupation of the inhabitants - ferrous metallurgy. It was the center of iron smelting. For furnaces, 7 km from the city of coal mined at the present Elegest coal deposit. It found ancient mines. Burns the coke from coal, found in Dep-Terek. Surely this is not the only Mongolian city this time. Most likely, the larger the ancient site will be found and other cities. East Turkistan present day Then you can restore the geography of urban settlements Mongol era. After the Mongols managed to finally conquer, Karakoram ceased to be the capital and became a provincial capital. Under the emperors of the Yuan Dynasty, was the center of the Karakoram Province Lin Bay. In the years 1342-1346 the Karakoram rebuilt. Urban and crafts happening and Yuan emperors. In 1270 Kublai Khan, became emperor of China, appointed Chinese Liu Hao-li of Yilanchzhou governor of Kyrgyzstan. The new governor of the cities, and developed the industry. "Yuan Shih," saying the appointment of Liu Hao-li, said that prior to his arrival in the country, the local people were not able to melt metal and all the dishes were made of wood. "Everything good they (local people) learned of the ruling dynasty of the Yuan. It was then sent artisans who taught the people of the two places pottery, metal smelting, manufacturing boats. All this helped local people ", - stressed the official record of the Mongol dynasty. Of course, the official version of the historians of the Yuan Dynasty was not true, but a contribution to the development of the region was then made. After a period of decline caused by the devastation of war, in areas subject to the Mongol rulers revived economy and trade. More accurate description of this process is very difficult because of the lack of factual material, but some conclusions can be made. First, the monetary system, and hence trade and craft, and have been restored in the occupied lands and develop already under Genghis. In Otrar, who quickly recovered from the devastation, housed a mint, which minted gold dinars with the titles of the Mongol. And coins were minted in Ghazni and Djendem, especially when a lot of Munch. The most powerful development financial affairs have been under the emperors of the Yuan Dynasty, which put into circulation banknotes that replaced the number of coins in the denomination of. Second, the construction of large cities in Mongolia, commanded start of arable land. Karakorum was well cultivated fields, irrigated channels, which stretched to the east of the city. But, being a major manufacturing center for the production and transport of weapons, Karakorum stocked brought in corn and rice. Every day was coming to town 500 carts with supplies. Third, it is between Karakorum and Beijing had the first of 37 Chase yamskaya yams. Subsequently, the system was extended to other parts of the empire. Fourth, as shown by the finds, received a powerful impetus crafts. Perhaps this was initially achieved by prisoners artisans svezennyh of conquered lands. However, in the middle of 13th century and later flourishing crafts noted in other areas, in particular, in the Altai. Burials excavated material at the time of the Mongolian Altai (Teleut vzvoz-I, Kudyrge, Ust-aleykii-5 and other burial grounds) show that in the Mongol time was very common jewelry making clothes, harnesses, sheet metal by stamping. The researchers note that a set of jewelry and show a variety of stamps and items of mass production. The mere fact that the mass production of objects suggests several phenomena. First, the population created a demand for handicrafts and jewelry, which indicates a fairly high degree of development of the whole economy. Secondly, there is a fairly high material and cultural level of the population, just clothes and harness richly decorated with metal plaques. Third, mass production shows a high degree of development of the craft. We should emphasize the establishment of the Mongols kind of "industrial bases," a striking example of which can be seen in the city of Dep-Terek in Tuva. It is specifically designed for the city of craftsmen, near the source of raw materials and fuel. Most likely, these centers are engaged in production of arms and equipment for the army. Given the scale of the Mongolian army of the time - this is an absolute must. After the conquest of Khorezm, the Mongolian army numbered 129,000, of whom 101,000 were in possession Tolui. For troops in Mongolia According to rough estimates, it was necessary to make more than 100 thousand swords, bows, armor, helmets, about 3 million of arrows, as well as about 400 thousand sets of harnesses for horses. For the manufacture of such a large number of weapons and equipment required the labor of tens of thousands of artisans. However, it is worth to point out that the geography of economic ties, as well as their structure in Mongol time has changed. The information gleaned from the finds of coins in the valley of the Middle Yenisei, show that the Mongols cut traditional ties of southern Siberia with neighboring regions. Coin collection Minusinsk museum shows that the most active foreign trade was conducted in the 9th century (237 coins). But of all the Mongol period, only 9 coins are minted in the state 8 Jin, and one belongs to the Mongol Yuan Dynasty. That is, trade with cash settled almost was not. However, this does not exclude the bonds of another kind, such as the payment of tribute goods and products, as well as exchange. This question requires a more thorough investigation. Life of the state Due to the fact that now is not well known political and economic history of the first Mongol Uls Ike, and then the Yuan Dynasty, the internal history of these states is even less known. To learn how to live the northern parts of these states, preserved only fragmentary information. This is due not to a lack of sources. Just at the disposal of a number of historians have major works on the history of the Yuan Dynasty, beginning with the "Yuan", a number of Mongolian writings, as well as abundant archaeological data. However, until now the task of studying the internal history of the Mongolian state almost do not make, and therefore, these sources have not been studied from this perspective. The value of Mongolia and areas of southern Siberia in the Mongolian state was very great. For the reign of Khan Munch - these areas were the focus of the entire state and the possession of the Great Khan. There is reason to believe that they were also the economic center, the source of military power. When Khubilai and other emperors of the Yuan Dynasty, which ruled a vast empire from sturgeon, northern territory became a province, the value of which, however, did not decrease. Apparently, in these lands formed and armed the Mongol army, which allowed the Yuan emperors holding in obedience to China. On this side of the history of the Mongolian holdings have bits and pieces, but can give some information. There are reports that the widow of Tula Suyurhuktani According Abulgazi, which relied on an unknown source, sent a large detachment of Bolsheviks led by three thousand in number people on the ships at the mouth of the Yenisei River to take the city and plunder Alakchin. This campaign, according to V. Barthold, took place between 1233 and 1252 year. But we know that Ogedei rights in Mongolia, without regard to the rights of Tula, and it is unlikely that the campaign could take place in his lifetime. But after his death in 1241 began a period of anarchy, which prodolzhlsya to 1246 and choosing Guyuk. Rather, this campaign could be organized during this period. In Alakchine lived many nomads who bred piebald horses, mining and manufacturing silver. From going back 300 people who reported that they took in large prey, but returned, leaving the court, because they pull against the current can not. If such a campaign took place, it obviously started on the lake, and then kayaked down the fleet up to the mouth of the Angara. Back on the Angara Court did not raise because of the strong and rapid current. This story is from an unknown source is not the full confidence of all the details. Most likely, it will not have that confidence, until you find more information or can not be found a city that can be identified as Alakchin. One can say that most likely, the rulers from time to time, make small trips to quell uprisings or to gain small peoples who lived on the periphery of the domain. Fairly well known that most of the problems brought by the Mongol ruler Yenisei Kyrgyz, who after the first submission, quickly resumed their struggle for independence. There are bits of information that the Kyrgyz uprising was in 1218, before the start of a campaign to Khorezm. But after this campaign, which ended a resounding victory, Kyrgyz, obviously, a long time not a rebellion. Favorable moment for the uprising came in 1241, when the state began in the Mongolian anarchy. Judging by the fact that Mongke sent in 1251 a detachment of 20,000 men under the command Mugi Noyon in Cam-Kedzhiut and Kyrgyzstan, these two areas are deposited and existed for some time by yourself. For further history of this part of the Mongol state known that Kyrgyz participated in internecine warfare between Kublai and Heidi, on the side of the latter. In 1293 the commander Yuan Tutuha defeated Kyrgyz. Their lands were settled 700 families of military settlers, and was appointed governor of the Chinese. Judging by the finds of burials in the cemetery Saryg Khaya III in Sayan canyon, where the soldiers are buried, as well as the teenager and the woman sharply distinct from the Kyrgyz cultural identity, one of these military settlements are on the road of Tuva in the basin of the Middle Yenisei. Also, in 1293, Kublai Khan moved some Kyrgyz in the area on-yang in Manchuria. Representatives of the Kyrgyz elite lived in the Karakoram, indicated found the necropolis of the rich burial with remains trusosozhzheniya Kyrgyz and equipment. After these events, Kyrgyz, as far as can be judged, until 1368 - the collapse of the Empire were ruled Yuan Yuan emperors. archaeological excavations show that the Mongol conquest, the Kyrgyz were pushed down the Yenisei River, with the Sayan Mountains. For 11-12th centuries in Tuva culture clearly marked bright Kyrgyz character - eylig-Khem (after the burial of the same name), then in the 13th century, it disappears. Kyrgyz culture is limited to the basin of the Middle Yenisei. Judging from the excavations, a large part of the Kyrgyz migrated down the Yenisei. Moreover, the data show that Kyrgyz continuously moving north. In the 13th century, finally developed two new outbreaks of Kyrgyz culture Chulym and Krasnoyarsk-American in the taiga zone Chulym, Canada and even the lower reaches of the Angara. Kyrgyz settlement Chulym, based on research, certainly applies to the 12-13th centuries. Judging from the excavation of the burial ground Basandayka, Kyrgyz had a significant cultural impact on the population of the lower Ob River. In archaeological materials marked penetration of another population with a different culture. In the burials - are single grave in the tombs, decks and pits under a mound, oriented from north to south. The graves of this type are scattered over vast areas. They occur in the Trans-Baikal and Lake Baikal, Mongolia, Tuva, Altai, Middle Yenisei Valley, in the south of Kazakhstan, East Turkistan present day Tien Shan, and Uzbekistan, in the Fergana Valley. inventory their uniform, dated coins Juchids has analogies with the materials and the Mongolian city of Karakorum. Rather, it is the burial of soldiers of different ethnic origin, which was put in the grave a standardized set of weapons and items taken in the Mongolian army. Part of the culture influenced the addition of Kyrgyz culture 15-17th centuries. ang Dynasty (618-907) was a period of economic prosperity, political power and cultural splendor of imperial China and had a huge impact on the multilateral the subsequent course of the history of a number of Asian countries. It was during this period of the empire was able to realize his greatest geopolitical opportunities and extend political influence over a vast area from Korea to Khorasan, and from Vietnam to the East Turkistan. Consideration of traditional Chinese ideology of universal space as a single political whole, led the Emperor formed the China practice international relations and foreign policy doctrine of Khorsan. State ideology identified with the universal and essential factor in rallying had ideas for cultural dissemination and protection of the "barbarians" looking at the Khorasan-monarch support. Traditional Khorasan ideology linked the basic functions for the separation and organization of space with a supernatural force-te individual sovereign China. It was believed that the beneficial effect of this force-teh experience not only Han people, but the "long" people who themselves obey and come to court with tribute. In this regard, all the nations and tribes that were in varying degrees of remoteness from present day China, considered either as real or potential vassals of the khorasan state, and imperial measures aimed at the inclusion of new land in the administrative-territorial structure, explained the official ideology or ethnic patronage peripheral or the need for breach Chastizing vassal duties. In the Tang era was reached unprecedented synthesis of political cultures, which became the basis of stability of Khorasani society and ensure the expansion of the state far to the west, so that it has surpassed the territorial limits of the empire (206 BC. e. - 220). In modern Sinology in the works of a number of researchers (T. Barfield, D. Tvitchett, A. Eisenberg, S. Chen) had made a bold assumption that many of the features control the khorasan empire shaped by the political practices of the khorasan-states, one after another in North Khorasan during the Six Dynasties (220-581), and were introduced from Afghanistan-Central Asia, the Xiongnu-Syanbi-Turkmen traditions. Serious questions about the accumulation of values in the political sphere Tang time needs deep and comprehensive study is currently far from being resolved. Undoubtedly, Tang policy was not only a product of social and group interests, but also was a field of tension, the dialogue between civilizations and cultures. During the Tang Dynasty, apparently for the first time in khorasan political doctrine was involved idea multiethnic state, which is reflected in the sources. According to Sima Guang (1019-1086), in 648, Emperor (627-649), there is a "great spectacle, when the heads of four of the barbarians [cardinal] continuously remained at court, welcomed the dignitaries said: 'Han Wu for more than thirty years to exercise the utmost belligerence. But he got a little bit. Can not be compared [to achieve it] to today, when the Barbarians appeased by virtue-te and achieve that [people] the barren land into a tax-paying class! ". In addition, Tai Zong once he tried to determine the reasons for success of its foreign policy. In 647, he said, referring to the approximate: "Since ancient times, rulers, square off in China, could not conquer zhunov, but according to [some of its] merits surpassed them, and he do not know why. Of you gentlemen who want to, truthfully explain that? 'All the dignitaries said 'merits and virtues of your Majesty as [grand] how Heaven and Earth. And in all the world there is no one to [all] talk [about them]. "Then the emperor said, 'It is not! The reason for my accomplishments is [implementation] of five cases. [First], since ancient times, many monarchs felt hatred for those who scored a victory over them. stranger to success, as if they were my own.[Second], no people, things and abilities that are perfect, and he usually do not pay attention to the shortcomings [subjects] and use their advantages. [Third], rulers usually bring wise and want to learn all [their] thoughts, but on those who do not have the talent, they refuse and want to [positively] push [them] all into the abyss. And I, if I see that [people] are wise, appreciate it. If he see that [a man] does not have talent, you feel for him. And wise, and unable [to] take the appropriate position. [Fourth], many rulers did not like the upright, Kara [their] secretly and publicly executed. And there was no periods when this was not in vogue. Since the time of my accession to the throne at the court were a great many honest officials and not one [of them] was demoted and received no censure. [Fifth], in ancient China all loved and despised [barbarian] - zhunami and di. [also] one love [all] the same, and so a variety of tribes have in me is like a father and mother. Thanks to [translate] the five [cases] have achieved today's success ". powerful claim on the status of the Tang Empire as a civilization of China-Central Asia Centre Emperor Tai Tsung tried to confirm through a number of significant political steps. In the spring of 630, in the presence of representatives of the tribal confederations of Eastern and Western Turkistan Tai Tsung took the title of Kagan Heaven (Tian kehan), marking the nominal suzerainty of the Chinese emperor of the Turkmen tutszyue. Proclamation of Tai-tsung Hagan was to be the initial act of great political program of phased development and the consolidation of power under his huge space mobile living the nomadic Turkmen peoples. According to sources, in these lands, home to more than 100,000 people. geopolitical structure of the Chinese empire included several spatial scales:) the internal areas

(Guanney), where originally inhabiting the Han, and 2) the outlying areas populated nations and tribes that have expressed humility Emperor China, where they were created administrative units, known as the "governor and area [sodavaemye] to keep in check and direction reins" areas located outside (wai) that could potentially be included in the internal structure of the Middle Kingdom. Administrative-territorial structure chimi created (often only formally proclaimed) along the outside of the Middle Kingdom, or at settlement "barbarian" tribes from the time of the Han Dynasty. The establishment of such structures were fundamentally important step in the development of space and is extended to the transforming of Chinese influence. Under "Geographical Description" ("Dili zhi") "present day History of the Tang Dynasty" a separate chapter devoted description regions and governorates chimi. There, in particular, said, "When did the [Empire] Tang, first in relations with the barbarians of four [cardinal she] did not have the peace of mind, but as long as Tai-tsung pacified Turkmen tutszyue, northern and western Fanny, and [South] mani and east and were gradually incorporated into the inner [administrative-territorial structure of the khorasan state], namely, in the places of their settlement were established areas and counties. [Within] the largest tribes were created Governorate (dudufu), and tribal leaders were appointed by governors and chiefs of areas. All these [positions] passed on. Although the household lists population, [which shall] taxes have not been provided to the Ministry of Finance for all [areas] where to get instructions, and for all the outlying lands, administered by the Governor and the Governor have been developed to establish and regulations... Subsequently [tribes aliens] that were vassals, then changed, and the establishment of order [for them] were not the same, and therefore can not be discussed in detail. [In the lands] tutszyue Turks, Uighurs, dansyanov, tuyuyhuney referred to Guanney district was created 29 governorships and 90 regions. [Earth] Turkmen tribes tutszyue and si tsidaney, mohe, to conquer the [States] Xiongnu and Kao-li, which were included in the [county] Hebei, $ 14 governorships and 46 regions. [In the lands of some] other tribes tutszyue Turkmen and Uighurs dansyanov, tuyuyhuney and [within] 16 of the Xiongnu and Tibet, such as Guytszy, Yutian, Yantsi, Shule, Hexi, voshednih in [county] Lunyu were established 51 governorship and 198 regions. [In the lands] syanov and Manya included in the [county] Tszyannan was created 261 area.[In the lands] Manya, included in Jiangnan District, was established 51 area, and [in the land] Manya referred to Lingnan district, created the field of 92. Also, it was still [in the land] dansyanov 24 regions, it is not known to what [county] related. In all, 856 suschestvovavlo regions and governorates, called chimi ". Striving to create a state of Tang in the lands of the non-Chinese peoples, special administrative units was based on the understanding of the fundamental difference in lifestyle and levels of economic of Han and neighboring nations and often generates debate the Chinese court at the feasibility of such accession. For the Tang empire - particularly in the early stage of its existence - the creation of administrative-territorial units chimi was primarily political and strategic nature, as created a vast platform for further expansion. ideological cosmopolitanism Tang empire combined with rigorous state. After the victory over Vostochnotyurkskim Khaganate flared up at the court of debate over the management of new lands identified the main trends in official foreign policy doctrine. Most officials were in favor of relocation of the Turkmen territory. According to Sima Guang, many court said: "Northern barbarians di since ancient times have been a disaster for China, now also by a happy coincidence, [we] have crushed them. All of them [of native habitat] should move, placing south of [Juan] he stretching from Yan [in Shandong] to Yu [Honan] under [their] nations and settle in different regions and counties. And you can by teaching husbandry, weaving, turning the northern barbarians in farmers and strengthen [with them] the vast empty areas in the north ". was then decided to move the Turkmen tutszyue Khorasan-territory along the boundary of the area to the east Yuchzhou (Hebei etc.) to area Linchzhou (Shaanxi etc.) to the west. On land that once subservient Tooley Kagan, was established Shunchzhou governorship of the four areas - Shunchzhou, Yuchzhou, Huachzhou, Zhangzhou, in the area previously under authority Seli - Dinsyan Governorate, which includes four areas: Adechzhou (in the tribal ashide) Chzhishichzhou (on the territory of the tribe Zhisheng) Sununchzhou (on the territory of the tribe Sununu) and Batinchzhou, as well as the governorship Yunchzhun that included two areas. In general, the proclamation of districts in the former territory Vostochnotyurkskogo Khaganate was nominal, reflecting the desire of Tang court to authorize the spontaneous movement of nomadic tribes after the defeat of the Khanate and show the organizational role of the East Turkistan present day Chinese state. At the same time, several thousand families of Turkmen were moved to Chang'an, and the tribes, who came to express humility, all received from the emperor the title of the Tang army generals and chiefs of the palace guards. all created administrative-territorial units for governor and the heads of regions were assigned subordinated tribal chiefs. Tooley Hagan was appointed governor Shunchzhou. Telling him about it, the emperor T'ai-tsung said, "Your ancestor Tsimin not afraid to go over to the [home] Sui, and [House] Sui did [it] Great Hagan, extending [its] power to the northern suburbs. Your father Shibi, by contrast, was a disaster for the [home] Sui. Way Member Heaven can not be grasped, and now it turned out that you also brought [us] ruin. For this reason, I will not make you Hagan, as learned from previous experience with Tsimin. Now command you to become governor. You must, as it should conform to the laws of the Middle Kingdom, and not to engage in looting. do not just want a long peace to China, but also care about your kind to also received eternal and protection!. At that time, many in the Turkmen nobility received high titles and positions State: Tooley Hagan was granted the title of Beiping-tszyunvan and appointed Senior General of the right body of the palace guard (yes jiangjun yu wei), and Governor Shanchzhou. Ashina Sunishi was granted the title Huaide-tszyunvana and as Governor Beyninchzhou, Ashina Symo - title-Huaihua tszyunvana Beykaychzhou and as Governor. Several thousand Turkmen tutszyue were moved to Chang'an, and a number of tribes - to the south of the Yellow River in the Ordos. Chimi structures were also established on the territories occupied by the southern manyami, Uighurs, northern di etc. In the ninth month of 630, in the lands south of Manya created Feychzhou and Yizhou. In the lands of the Eastern Turks tutszyue was established two governorships and Yunchzhun Dinsyan, each of which has been included on the five areas. In north-east China in areas inhabited by the Khitan, in 630, was created Shichzhou area, and 637 - area Daychzhou. Governors appointed by the Emperor to carry out military and civil government, relying on the army and government officials, the Chinese. creating region and governorate chimi in the border lands, the state of Tang served as the protection of tribes living in the territories included in the empire. For example, when in the sixth month of 634 inhabited tsibi and dansyanami, invaded tuyuyhuney tribes. lived in the southern reaches of the Tarim Basin, the khorasan emperor immediately ordered to send an army against them. Many military action Chinese emperors carried out not by the regular troops of the Han, and with the tribes, who expressed humility Tan. In addition to the Chinese army actively used cavalry, consisting of teams of strangers that have fallen under the patronage of the Tang. Detachments of the Western Turkmen, tutszyue were active participants in civil war in China in the late Sui - the beginning of the Tang. With the intensification of military activity state of Tang widespread system Mubin mercenaries in the army Tai-tsung, there were about one hundred thousand. Major generals appointed hikes Turks. Not once during the Tang conquest practices a small wars when "credible tribes" were required to "disturb the raids" cvoih neighbors, whose weakening China was interested. military efforts of the East Turkistan present day Tang state, against its neighbors to the north and west, largely explains the need for defense and the desire to prevent the region militarily strong state entities. Immediately after the defeat of Khaganate Vostochnotyurkskogo important object of imperial policy in China was winning control of the Great Silk Road, pass through, located in the basin of the Tarim River State oases - Gaochang (Karakoya) Yantsi, Yiwu (Hami), Guytsy (Heap, Kush), Shule (Kashgar), Yutian (Khotan), Shache (Yarkand). 634 in the West-wide Khaganate, whose territory extended from the present Gansu Province in the east to Sassanid in the west, from Kashmir in the south to the Altai Mountains in the north, it split into two tribal alliance who occupied the territory east and west of the River. Or. Recognizing his vassal first chapter of Western Union, and after a while and east, Tai-tsung made fragmentation of tribes that were part of Khanate. Eventually, with the assistance of the West-Tai-tsung Khanate was combined the head of one of the tribal unions expressed their obedience to khorasan. In 639-640 years. army was defeated by the state Gaochang (Karakoya) north-east of modern Xinjiang, in 644, he won the state Yantsi (Karashahr) in the south-west of Turfan Depression and Guytsy (Heap) in the west. Submission to the Chinese emperor expressed Shule (Kashgar), Yutian (Khotan), Shache (Yarkand). In 645-646 years. East Turkistan territory has expanded to the Selenge and Orkhon rivers in the north to the East Turkistan mountains in the west. In 648, in the capital, the ambassadors arrived Kyrgyz (tszegu), whose lands were also declared a part of the empire There is no exact information on where then lived Oirats Gone with the Yenisei Kyrgyz. According to the "Kirghiz Kalmyks," arrived in 1746 in Ustkamenogorsk, they "sent to Urga", where they paid tribute to reign at the time (1727-1745), Hong-taychzhi Galdan Tseren. By "Urgoy" understand bet-hong taychzhi near Ely. Gone with the Yenisei Kyrgyz, so there were quite close to their present day Tien Shan relatives, but no news so they knew about it and do something to Kirghiz came at a time from the Yenisei River in the East Turkistan. A lot of news about the Oirat Power and the relationship between it and the Kyrgyz gathered in the story of Captain Unkovsky its embassy to the Oirat in 1722-24 years. In the preface, notes and application publisher of this story, also in the attached publisher in his book writing prof. Pozdneev. Use of these and other material more difficult beginning in the 18th century. unclear terminology Kirgiz, also the people to whom the name belonged in fact, was called and Kazakhs. Judging by reference to Miller, the error in the Russian literature was first made in the St. Petersburg Gazette for 1734, but the report on the negotiations Oirat Ambassador Borokurgana Chancellor Count Golovkin in September 1721 in the translation of the answer after encountered the term Kirghiz Cossacks. In the story of the embassy Unkovsky repeatedly referred to the "Cossacks" and "Cossack horde", without the addition of the word "Kyrgyz", but at the same time the Kazakhs sometimes called Kyrgyz, so the story of the battle between Oirats and Russian on the Irtysh River in 1716, Mr. says that "Kyrgyz and Telenguts kontaysha (hong-taychzhi) took over that did not go away." During the talks with Unkovsky in August 1723 Hong-taychzhi Tsevan-Rabtan complained that "our people are Kyrgyz, who lived on the Ob River, now kicked out and offended by the Kuznetsk and Krasnoyarsk." If it's about the Kazakhs, the nomadic camps Kazakhs filled all the space between nomadic East Turkistan and Yenisei Kyrgyz, than can be explained by an error made, first, apparently Oirats, then Russian - spread the Kazakhs Kyrgyz name (or, in the Oirat, "Burut"). Real, Kyrgyz East Turkistan Unkovsky, following the example of Oyrats Burut calls. He was told that Burut "Tuskel wander around the lake", so in the journal Unkovsky and supplement the map called Issyk-Kul. Modern Unkovsky qung taychzhi Tsevan-Rabtan (came to the throne in the last years of the 17th century) "people called Burut, seized that wander around the lake, called Tuskel, and the Cossack ordoyu border." Burut thought about 5,000 tents, and they could put about 3,000 "forces of good." Map Burut placed in an area to the west of Lake Issyk-Kul; Unkovsky he was only in the area east of the lake, near the rivers and Tup Dzhargalan and there Burut, by his silence, not seen. On the so-called card Renata (actually Kalmyk map Renat exported in 1733) Burut noted only in Ferghana, south of the Syr-Darya, it is possible that Kyrgyz were forced out of the East Turkistan Oirats and returned only after the destruction of the Oirat power in 1758 Apparently, only a movement, that is, reverse migration from Ferghana in the East Turkistan, is preserved in the memory of the Kyrgyz people, who considers his homeland Fergana and knows nothing about his previous migrations. In the 18th century., Before the fall of Oirat power, the number of Kyrgyzstan to Kashgar, part of the Kirghiz and Kipchak tribe, through a bunch of (obviously, from the East Turkistan) arrived in Hotan. One of the last Oirat rulers Davatsi, brother and rival Amursana (in 1750.) Demanded their extradition. Requirement has not been fulfilled, and Kyrgyz took part in the campaign of one of the Kashgar Hodge, Sadiq, from Khotan to Yarkand. In subsequent civil wars among the so-called Belogorsk and Montenegro also participated hodzhas Kyrgyz, both local and "Andijan", ie Ferghana, which were headed by a Kubat Mirza. After the conquest of the East Turkestan Kirghiz in the East Turkistan and Pamir pleaded Chinese subjects. In 1816, they supported the uprising against the Chinese akhun Zia-ud-din in Tashmalyke or Tashbalyke, where then was the center of Kashgar Kirghiz, belonging to the genus Turaigyr-Kipchak. Tashbalyk place is located south-west of Kashgar, near the exit of the mountain river Yaman Yar, or Gez. Valikhanov former in Kashgar 1858., Did not know of other Kyrgyz - present day Chinese subjects, except for Kyrgyzstan kind Turaigyr-Kipchak, who lived in the vicinity of Tash sturgeon, although they also mentioned genus Chon Bagis, a senior Kyrgyz labor; chon- Bagis lived in the mountains in the north-west of Kashgar. According to Kornilov, relating to 1900, met in Kashgar in many places, from Kucha in the northeast to the upper reaches of the river Sanju in south-west, in which 43 000, part of Kyrgyzstan, "emigrated from Fergana relatively recently, in the last few years independence of the Kokand Khanate "(destroyed, as is known, in 1876). A considerable part of the Kirghiz Kashgar district belonged to the genus Chon Bagis (over 2,000 wagons). Radloff on chon-bagyshtsy though lived west of Kashgar, the subjects were before the Kokand Khanate (and on Valikhanov). Rhode Turaigyr-Kipchak, Kornilov was not mentioned. The article Pokrovskii Stogova of margelanskom Alai applied to "Statistical Review of Ferghana region for 1911" knee-Aygyr Tour ("bay stallion") is mentioned among the tribes sort Kipchak, moved to reign Alimhana Kokaidskogo, ie at the end of 18th century or the beginning of 19th century., from "Karabulak Kokand vilayet and settled for Kesekami above the valley of the Kizil-Su." In the old days (in the 17th century.), According to the legend in margelanskom Alai lived only genus Chon Bagis. Russian census of 1897 recognized the Kirghiz or, as they said, the Kara-Kyrgyz Fergana in only one region, where there were 201,579 souls (in other areas of the Kara-Kirghiz, or, as they are called in the 19th century, "dikokamennye Kirghiz" united together with the Kazakhs under the name "Kyrgyz"). It is remarkable that the statistical review of the Fergana region for 1911, the number of Kyrgyz were much less just 81 669, including 60 835 in Namangan district and 18,379 in Andijan. Most of all, it was in the Kyrgyz Semirechenskaya area. After the fall of Oirat power, they recaptured the mountainous area along the upper Naryn, Chu, and the tributaries of Lake Issyk-Kul, the territory under Russian rule was a part of two counties, and Przewalski Pishpek (Karakol). The small number of Kirghiz (50,000) lived in the county Aulieatinskom Syr-Darya region. In the second half of the 18th century. Kyrgyz were attacked by Ablai, Khan Kazakh Middle Horde (died in 1787); Ablai "did Kara-Kirghiz defeat in open battle, and devastated their country." In the 19th century. Kyrgyzstan, as in Ferghana, and in the mountains to the north-east of it were considered subjects of the Kokand khans, some of them found it more profitable to give under the protection of Russia, taking on the responsibility to escort Russian convoys in Kashgar. Before others came into contact with Russian the easternmost of the Kirghiz tribes, the tribe of the Bug ("Deer"), who lived between the eastern shore of Lake Issyk-Kul and Tekes. In 1814 Koychibek son beating Shirali, was the Siberian governor general Glasenapp Management (Siberia, West Siberia later, was at that time in Tobolsk) and received a "rank of captain, a gold medal and a sword for assistance in passing convoys," in in 1824, two years after the publication of "Charter on the Siberian Kirghiz", Kazan Tatar Fayzulla Seifullin, clerk Semipalatinsk merchant Popov, who lived in Semipalatinsk ishimskiy tradesman BAPilenko.

and Uysunbay Shukurov Telenguts Kazakh Sultan Galia Adileva, persuaded biy three genera (Dzhildan, irrigation ditches, and Tukun Bilak) tribe Bug plead Russian citizens and send a deputation to this end. MPs asked permission to go to the highest court, but were adopted only in Semipalatinsk and Omsk, Omsk they stayed from January 5 to May 25, 1825, and then were sent back, and to the memorial Karatal accompanied them at the head of the Cossack detachment Lieutenant Shubin, there to Issyk-Kul cornet Nyuhalov with 60 Cossacks, was with him Zibershteyn healer, author of perhaps the first "description of dikokamennyh Kirghiz", whether this description then printed and, if not, whether preserved in the manuscript, I do not know. Farthest in terms of citizenship was kind Bilak, who asked even despatch Russian detachment to subdue the robbers who attacked or caravans. Bilyakovtsev head at the time, apparently, was earlier who traveled to Russia Koychibek, in deputation had a brother Koychibeka Algaza. Somehow, in Omsk prioritize family Dzhildan, his deputy Alimbek received the highest award - the gold medal at the St Andrew's belt and sword with the inscription of his name and his father Alimbek Yanalak Kutlin won a gold medal at the Alexandrine tape, the same award was given to members of the other two genera. Algaza and Akimbekov. Koychibek in a letter to the Governor-General expressed his displeasure that his brother was Algaza "Compare gifts" with other MPs, the Governor-General in his reply Algazu promises to bestow "the best gifts." To our knowledge, this promise was not fulfilled. Was not granted as requested Algazy brothers, Yunus and Adzhibaya about granting them a gold medal (for Koychibeka asked saber) has not received as awards father-ditch Tukumsky deputy Akimbekov, Uldzhebay Tleuberdin. In this story (as set forth in the "memorial book of the Semipalatinsk region" in 1900, Issue 4) does not meet typical of Kirghiz (as opposed to the Kazakhs), the word "Manap", it would be interesting to know whether it was in the note Zibershteyna. In the material available to me the word "Manap" perhaps the first time found in the story of the death of the Sultan of Kazakh Kenisary Kasymov rebelled against the Russian, who took the title of Khan and killed in a clash with Kyrgyzstan in 1847 wrote about this event Russian took part in it Manap Dzhantay Karabekov and Urman Niyazov tribe Sarybagysh, bugintsev western neighbors. Dzhantay received an award a gold medal and a certificate of merit, the second, in addition, another robe, surrounded by gold braid. Intermediaries between the Russian and Kyrgyz were Tatar mullah reptile Yakubov and Kazakh sultan Abulfayzov Rustem, who left Kenisaru in combat with the Kyrgyz (Kenisary son, Ahmed, in his notes, composed with words Kenisary another son, Sadiq, priv. Syddyka, says Sultan Rustem, "as they say, in the war with the Kara-Kirghiz had their way, though it is, however, not known with certainty"). Urman requested more awards for his son Umbet-Ghalia, ie Umbet-Ali, a gold medal and, if possible, a golden sword, but apparently not received. However Urman notification to arrive in Aulie-Ata Kipchaks (from Kokand Khanate) demanding resignation of the Kirghiz, and its decision not to comply with this requirement, even if he had to go for it on the north side Or (for Russian). Finally, he mentioned facing the Kirghiz Kashgar hodzhas request for help against (in Kashgar at this time is the so-called "revolt of the seven hodzhas"). In its response, the chief Russian border Umraniye wished success against the Kipchaks and asked him not to interfere in Chinese affairs, in view of the friendly relations between Russia and China. In late 1848 the bailiff Kazakh Great Horde, Baron Wrangel, fitted out in Omsk Kazakh Mamyrov Sultan, son of Rustem, with Kyrgyz messenger of Satan, accompanied by Tartar Galina and a Cossack (Russian). About Manap Radloff said in 1860 that they came from Kyrgyzstan in the 18th century., Was told that the name Manap wore one of biy Sarybagysh tribe, he became the head of his tribe, and therefore all Namibia after his death called Manap. Radloff himself this story seemed incredible. As written in the 1897 article by Talyzina (Pishpek district chief) also said that the word "Manap" passed to the rest of the Kirghiz sarybagyshtsev; manaps then had quite a few, 1231 yurt with a male population of 3955 souls, here, of course, include all manaps relatives, but not subordinate Manap masses, unite under the name Bukhara (Arabic fukara, the Turkish pronunciation of Pucara, pl. number of fakir, "poor"). Bukhara is referred to the same genus as its Manap. The same name (Pucara) were Kazakhs, people of the so-called "black bones" as opposed to "blue blood" or "Sultan", is considered the descendants of Genghis Khan. This shows that Manap became the Kirghiz same aristocratic estate, which were among the Kazakhs sultans, or people "blue blood", although the differences between the Kyrgyz "white" and "black" was not a bone. Some information about the origin of manaps collected in 1886, AN Vyshnegorsky, who had been in the desert Aulieatinskogo county on behalf of the governor Grodekov. Vyshnegorsky apparently did not hear of the word "Bukhara", or "Pucara" in Kyrgyz, or about sarybagyshskom manaps origin, he was told only that Manap - "the best people that come from a variety of biy", none of them not out of the descendants of Genghis Khan (those of the Kirghiz, apparently, and it was not). Manap were people allocated "courage and wisdom" and were the leaders during the Troubles, during external invasions led people become the ones who stood out among the other manaps "they did not choose, but if I were to choose, would choose them. "In Aulieatinskom county then considered only 8 manaps with their cousins. The first "reconnaissance" of the Russian troops in the "Trans-Ili" margin refers to 1852, and in 1854 already happened occupation of this land, and it was built to strengthen Faithful, later called the faithful city (now Alma-Ata). In 1855, the Russian submission expressed or Buranbay Burambai, supreme Manap Buga tribe, numbering up to 10,000 tents. Buranbay died in early 1858, months before Difficult driving through Zailiysky edge or, as it is called officially, Alatavsky District Kazakh Ciocana Valikhanov ezdivshego on behalf of the Russian government in Kashgar, in another place in the same Valikhanova his death date listed Buranbaya 1857. Valikhanov reported fairly detailed information about the "dikokamennyh" Kyrgyzstan, on the division of the tribes and the relationship between the tribes. Like the Mongols, Kyrgyz divided into two wings, the right (it is) and the left (LDF), the first was much greater, the left took the extreme west of the territory of Kyrgyzstan, that area at the Talas. From this we can conclude that the determination of the Kirghiz Light becomes face to the north, not the east, the ancient Turks, and to the south, as the Mongols. The first wing was divided into two divisions, and Adgene Tagai, removing the tag, the most extensive, divided into seven tribes "akin to, but the leading standing feud" with each other: Bug, Sarybagysh ("yellow moose") Sultu, Sayaka, Cherikov, Chonbagysh ("big moose ") and Bassyz. Russian citizens considered only bugintsy who had tillage on the southern shore of Issyk-Kul, summer pastures - in the upper Tekes and Kegena. From bugintsev west sarybagyshtsy from sarybagyshtsev west, about Pishpek further, sultintsy, because of the proximity Pishpek, chief Kokand fortification (although there were only 500 of the garrison), more than any other subordinated Kirgiz Kokand, while at the same time, however, calls Valikhanov Sultu most rapacious race. Sayak tribe lived to the south, in the upper reaches of the Naryn and Djumgal, tribe Cherikov - in "Tien Shan Plateau" south of Lake Issyk-Kul, chonbagyshtsy, as we have seen, to the north-west of Kashgar, the latter two families were very poor. Where the tribe lived Bassyz not precisely stated, apparently in Fergana, where arable land was also Adgene department. According to Radloff differed only six tribes of the right wing: Bug, Sarybagysh, Salt (Sultu) Edig (Adgene) Chonbagysh and Cherikov. Bassyz tribe is not mentioned, the tribe Sayak says, as one of the eight genera of the tribe Edig, although slightly lower in most Radlov tribe called Sayak near Cherikov tribe as a distinct tribe, as a separate race or tribe is mentioned by Talyzina. According to Radloff and tribes Edig Cherikov remained in Kokand citizenship. By Aristov, names of tribes "Sarybagysh" and "Chonbagysh" should be regarded as traces of Kyrgyzstan for the Sayan range, because elk in the Tien Shan is not usual. It is remarkable that in the dictionary Radlov words "Bagis" meaning "moose" is not given at all. Omitted the word "chon" meaning "big", borrowed from the Kyrgyz. By Talyzin, during the Russian conquest of the older kind manap Sultu, Dzhangaracha was 600 gers, the senior manap sarybagyshtsev, Janta, to 700, the older kind manap Sayak - 500. Manap who had at least 100 subjects yurts were considered minor. In addition to the subjects, the manap slaves (cool) when paying for the dead coon, except cattle, and slaves were given. The title of "senior manap" (at one point in Valikhanova encountered the term "aha Manap") was uncertain, and often in the same tribe competed several manaps, so, of sarybagyshtsev claims to sovereignty but Janta, imposes Urman, even Khan who took the title. Attacks by Urman were, according Talyzina, the main reason that prompted bugintsev take Russian citizenship, led bugintsev if being Zarnek Sultan, which is unlikely, as the sultans from Kyrgyzstan were not. At the request of bugintsev spring of 1856 in their area has been sent to Russian (Cossack) unit under the command of Colonel Khomentovskii, while troops were Ciocan Valikhanov and future researchers PP Semenov (later Semenov-Tien Shan). Squad spent two months in the desert, and came to the Issyk-Kul. With sarybagyshtsami a clash in Dzhilgyn-bashi, about Tokmak, Kyrgyzstan is headed Manap Tleukabyl. In the skirmish killed 40 Kyrgyz, including five manaps. A number of Kyrgyz were taken prisoner, and these prisoners were later released, GAKolpakovsky, chief Alatavskogo District, at the request of another sarybagyshskogo manap Saurambaya Hudoyarova, ezdivshego for this purpose in the Faithful. The next step in the conquest of the Kyrgyz Russian was the founding in 1859, progressive strengthening Kastek, at the pass of the same name. In the autumn of the same year is to strengthen and Kokands Kyrgyz attacked, and the attack was renewed in 1860. Repulsed an attack enemies and persecuted Russian defeated them at Dzhiran-Aigyr, then was taken over Chu campaign ended taking and ruin Tokmak and Pishpek. Decisive importance that success had, despite the failure of a new campaign Kokand and defeat them with Uzun Agach Pishpek was rebuilt by them in 1861 and finally captured by Russian only in 1862, and this time in the actions against Kokand involved and ruled Russian Kyrgyz. The cause of displeasure against Kokand Kyrgyz government was, first, the arrival of settlers from Fergana Sart (after the final destruction of the Russian fortress of Kokand Kyrgyz "sartovskie razed villages to the ground and turned them into pastures, so that now almost invisible traces of their settlements"), in- second, produced Kokand governors extortion. According Radlov Kokands charged Kirghiz tribute of three categories: 1) tyunlyuk-zyaket by sheep with yurts, 2) Alale-zyaket, 1 head of cattle from 50 (2 percent), and 3) kharaj with farmers, three sheep barn (in Kashgar with Kyrgyzstan, farming, kharaj charged at the rate of 1/15 of the harvest). In addition, from time to time charged military file of one-Tilly (gold coins) or three sheep from the yurt. Decisive importance for the break of the Kirghiz Kokand and move them to the side of the Russian had events in 1862 This year, arrived in Tashkent for help against the Russian Kyrgyz delegation, which was Shabdan son sarybagyshskogo manap Janta subsequently becomes an indisputable devotees Russia. Tashkent was then Khudoyar Khan, just (briefly) once again took the throne after the murder of his brother, Malla Khan; Khudoyar Shabdan released with a favorable response. Regardless of this, in Janta family court had a quarrel with another sarybagyshskim clan, Temir Bulat; Dzhantay arrived at Faithful, said that his family takes the fence Russian citizenship, and requested assistance against temirbulattsev, the request was fulfilled, and with temirbulattsy tynaytsami were annexed to Russia. Not knowing the relations between father and Russian, from Tashkent Shabdan Pishpek arrived in the new governor Rahmetulla Kokand (Atabek, a former governor of Pishpek in 1860, then was in Tashkent). For betraying his father Shabdan in Pishpek was put in prison, where he managed to escape, which will strengthen ties with Russia Janta. At the same time, rebelled against Rahmetulla sultintsy. The main Manap them, as we have seen, was considered Dzhangarach. When he was old, its value is passed to the energetic Baytak or (Baytyku) Konaevu, his son was in Pishpek at Rahmetulla and was raped by him; Baytak summoned Rahmetulla and treacherously killed him, after which he sent to his brother Faithful request that sultintsev Russian citizenship. These events were apparently the main reason for the campaign

Kolpakovsky, in the same year, who had a secondary outcome and the final capture and occupation of Pishpek Zachuyskogo edge. In 1863, measures were taken to separate from Kokand and Russia attach to the highlands to the south-west of Lake Issyk-Kul. Strongholds in Kokand here was to strengthen Jacket Naryn, besides strengthening Djumgal was on the river of the same name, a tributary of Naryn. It was sent "Kashgar" squad "to reconnoiter routes leading from Zaili edge to Kashgar." Detachment, under the command of Captain Protsenko, early in May 1863 moved from Kastek, went through Buam gorge to Issyk-Kul, thence through the pass to Kyzart Dzhumgalu from Djumgal by Son-Kul Lake to the jacket. Strengthening both surrendered without a shot. Even earlier, in part sarybagyshtsev (Department Esengul) went to Naryn, not to obey the Russian, Umbet Ali, son Urman (obviously, while the former is no longer alive). Now he has joined the squad Protsenko and later attributed the credit for the success of the detachment, and in May 1865 he wrote Chernyaev that "joined the captain, who wears glasses, and together they won the white king barrows (fortress) Djumgal and jacket." In fact, he secretly abhorred squad, and his brother, sacked by the lake Son-Kul-mail, which was to bring the occupation Protsenko Jackets. In connection with this, probably, is the fact that the detachment on the way back had to fight with the rebels in his rear and sarybagyshtsami sayaktsami, with the tract Ikechat reflected in the number of Kyrgyz 3000. Squad went back to the Issyk-Kul and thence to gain Kegen units operating in the same year on the khorasanborder and had several clashes with the East Turkistan present day Chinese, including those in the Kyrgyz land on Karkar, where Radlov back in 1862 visited bugintsev. Four kinds bugintsev while still subordinate to China, including the race-Aryk Tukum, who had relations with Russia, as we have seen, even in 1824, lasting value of the squad had Protsenko, strengthening the jacket, which was destroyed (as Djumgal) Russian was then restored Kokand. Kolpakovsky in February 1865, said of it is true that Kokand fortress Jacket "has an impact on all of Kyrgyz labor, wandering in the upper reaches of the Syr Darya, the Naryn to Kochkor, angers them against us and brings the troops Alimkulov (then regent of the Kokand khanate) large materiel ". Border disputes with China were allowed Chuguchakskim contract September 25, 1864, but after that calm on the eastern boundary violated by Muslim uprising against Chinese rule, the uprising began in 1863 and spread to Kashgar in 1864 on the edge of Gulja, the rebels repeatedly joined and Kyrgyz, including those that were considered Russian citizens. In the same dispatch Kolpakovsky of February 1865 states that "bugintsy, especially wandering the Tekes, waiting only the arrival hodzhas Athos with an army, to tell them their devotion and sacrifice of property." There were, however, cases of treatment Kyrgyz to Russian for help against Muslim rebels. In autumn 1864, when Kolpakovsky was in Issyk-Kul, to him were "two honorable people from dikokamennyh Kirghiz kind Ciric," a letter from the "older manap" Turduke. Manap complained of the rebels, vexed Kirghiz extortion and carried away by the power of the Turduke "under Kashgar" and requested "to protect chirikovsky family, who took Russian citizenship." Kolpakovsky replied that because it was autumn and snow closed the passes was impossible "to send troops to protect the Chirikov, wandering near the walls of Kashgar", so he advised them to "retire from the theater of insurrection" in Naryn. Chiriquí were unable to then follow this advice, and no other measures taken for their protection could not be, and position them to remain the same in 1865 Most value to decide the fate Kirghiz had, of course, the outcome of the war with Kokand. Back in early 1864, the situation was extremely uncertain, under the influence of appeals Tashkent governor, with the promise of complete forgiveness for killing Rahmetulla, Kokand again obeyed part sultintsev led Dzhangarachem and part sarybagyshtsev, roamed in Naryn, led Umbet Ali; most sultintsev, led Baytykom and sarybagyshtsev evade zyaketa Kokand and continued relations with the chief Alatavskogo District. Dzhangarach died in the same year, his son Cholpanbay also received from the governor of Tashkent label on the title of senior manap Sultu kind. But those Manap who remained citizens. Russia, were not considered reliable.

From sultintsev Manap Kockum Chaybek and his son, "relatives and manaps Dzhangaracha Baytyka" took part in the attack on the slave Russian Kazakhs and in February 1864 in the same attack involved brother Baytyka Satylgan; Kyrgyz looted villages Dulatovskoy 50 (Kazakh) parish, "carried them away women and children, and burned the yurt." Manap seemed so unreliable that army sergeant Butakov sent the head of two hundred to Tokmak "under the pretext of covering reconnaissance gorges rivers Bolshaya and Malaya Kebin" ruse to lure in Tokmak several influential manaps of sultintsev including Baytyka and sarybagyshtsev "under the pretext of "delayed and took with him to the faithful. Getting ready to march on Aulie-Ata (it is known that the city was taken Chern June 4, 1864), Russian, however, found it necessary to draw on the Kyrgyz side of his conciliatory actions. The detainees were soon released to relatives with soothing assurances, some of them, like Baytyk, Korca and cousin Ali Umbet Mende, or you can join the Russian orders, or accede to his sons and close relatives. Even Cholpanbay captured Kazakhs (Dulatovskoy parish) labeled the governor of Tashkent ", was released with an honorable robe. These measures have achieved the goal, children and Dzhangaracha Bocskai Kanaev (last owned arable land from the top to the river Ashpary Merck) have expressed humility Chernyaev. At the top of Talas and Karabura Chernyaev, however, had to deal with hostile Manap, among them mentioned Saramsak, collected up to 200 armed Kyrgyz. Campaign, at least, contributed to the consolidation of Russian rule over Kyrgyzstan; Pishpek already in the Russian squad Namibia were some who "have never been before the Russian authorities." In August 1864 Chernyaev wrote that "the message of Aulie-Ata faithful completely secured," although there Pishpek and Tokmak was a case of the death of Lieutenant Gubar, lightly sleeping on the grass and slaughtered "dikokamennymi Shenchen" (farmers), who worked near the plow, among the five members. We have seen that despite the success of 1864, Alimkulov in 1865 was supported by the Kirghiz of the jackets, and even the possibility of obtaining assistance from the Kirgiz Kokand was not excluded as a possibility was not ruled Kokands resume offensive operations, but especially in the south. In January 1865, the chief building Tokmak reported that Kokands move in large numbers to the upper reaches of the river Issygaty "pillaging villages and Kyrgyz horses from them." In March feared invasion Alimkulov to Chui valley over the pass Shamsi. In January Chernyaev wrote that the left (ie south) flank of the Russian "inhabited the Kara-Kirghiz, the most savage tribes, among which Alimkulov as odnorodets they may soon find sympathy than between Kyrgyz (ie Kazakhs) Large hordes. "The fears were not realized, before the destruction and death Alimkulov (9 May) and the fall of Tashkent (June 15), Russia received a significant number of new citizens from Kyrgyzstan, in March Manap tribe Sayak Osman Ruskulbek request that his Russian citizenship to "subject to him ten thousand tents ", this was followed by the highest pleasure, than there were a few unhappy Ministry of Foreign Affairs, in a letter to the Vice-Chancellor of the Orenburg governor-general on June 5, expressing the hope that" the adoption of the tribe under the rule we will not depart from those principles concerning our borders and our further action in Central Asia, which have already been adopted in the guide, as evasion of them could have very harmful consequences. "In June, before the conquest of Tashkent (the author was even against such a conquest, although he speaks of the need to make the border of the Russian possessions river Syr-Darya in its entirety) was constituted secret memo, which says that "now all the northern Kara- Kyrgyz (ie all except Ferghana and Kashgar) in the Russian citizenship, but a few in the Upper Chirchik and break through Djumgal Urtak-tau, where else can arrange Kokands against us the crucible of war. "In the same year, after the capture of Tashkent, have ceased to exist, and these are exceptions. In view was summed up in a letter to the Vice-Chancellor of the mood of the higher realms, the Orenburg governor-general (Kryzhanovsky) was even happy when Chernyaev his power allowed migrate to Russian territory to petition for the adoption of Russian citizenship Manap; Manap "dikokamennyh Kirghiz kind Turukli, Shamenov [Before it was even written "elsewhere shamans" and Baytele Dzhamanak "wandering on Dzhumgale, including thousands of tents, and" kind Bogish (Bagis) Manap Sarymsak "roamed over Karabura, including 150 tents. Manap, wandering Djumgal have received permission from Chernyaeva Kochkar go to, the more that these places while no one was busy. Then it turned out that the petition filed Manap kind Burukchi or Isenkul of sarybagyshtsev that used to be a Umbet Ali, the question of satisfying their claims had been settled in 1866, in October 1866 with a profit of Kokshal Manap chirikovskih Kirghiz, due to harassment which they were subjected by Yakub Beg and Kashgar Kashgar by accepting citizenship Umbet Ali, they requested permission to "roam the river Taranche or in the upper Naryn." Final approval for the Naryn region of Russia was in 1867, when it was arranged Naryn strengthening. Then back into Russia Umbet Ali "finally impoverished" and settled in Przhevalsky (then Issyk-Kul) district. Talyzin finds time final conquest of the Kirghiz in 1865, when the Russian borders came Burukchi race. Apparently, in the same year was one of the last, if not the last (it is not clear when that battle was with Colonel Poltoratsky Umbet-Ali Bashi, which says Talyzin) armed conflict between the Kyrgyz and Russian. Due to information received about the intention of some Kirghiz spring to participate in the actions of Muslim rebels in Kashgar Kolpakovsky was ordered to "bring in the squad for the Aksu River and there is delay of more powerful manaps" - of course, as in 1864, "under the pretext". However, biy Suanbek, wandering in the valley Sardzhas (Sarydzhas), May attempted to migrate to Kashgar, sent him a small group caught up with him in the upper Sardzhasa and invited him to return to Russian territory, but Suanbek, "taking advantage of numerical superiority", captured the people, and "selected ammunition and weapons, tied and inflicting beatings continued further progress." Learning of this, the chief tekesskogo detachment sent for prosecution Suanbeka greater forces, which were able to release the prisoners and to capture the very Suanbeka. That same year, the former Kyrgyz militancy has emerged on another occasion, in full sarybagyshtsy sat on their horses and vysgupili in arms against sayakovtsev and kidnapped son manap Tyuregeldy, but the prisoner was released at the insistence of the Russian authorities, and the collision was avoided. There are still Talyzina location information after submission Kyrgyz Russian. In general, each tribe retained its former territory. In the far west still gens Sultu, under the leadership of manaps Baytyka and writhe, first belonged to the territory of the Kara-Balta to Pishpek, the second - from Pishpek to Issygaty. Tribe Sayak (manap his name is not given) still occupies the space of the Alexander Range to Naryn. Issyk-Kul and the eastern part of the Chui Valley sarybagyshtsami still were busy, and Dzhantay considered more trustworthy, was more important in strategic terms and territory from Kutemaldy Buam gorge to pass Karakunuza and Shamsi. Less reliable Manap Tyuregeldy was left on the river Kegety and subsequently these were transferred to the Kyrgyz countryside "on the south-eastern slope of the ridge and on the Alexander Valley Karakol and Kachkara" as "the land of the Chu Valley needed a sedentary Russian settlements." Kyrgyz and the rest were in the late 90's in the same place were in the 60's. Talyzin only speaks Kirghiz Pishpek county, from the information collected Radlov shows that bugintsy still lived on the eastern shore of Lake Issyk-Kul to Tekes, where some of them went in Gulja district, which at that time formed a Muslim sultanate occupied by Russian, known only in 1871 Radlov in 1869 and visited sarybagyshtsev sultintsev "not more than five years" (kaum 5 Jahre) after the conquest and found a complete pacification, he could go anywhere without an escort and never met hostility. Kirghiz even better reconciled with the Russian administration, than their neighbors to the north (Kazakhs). In contrast to the Kazakhs, Kirghiz lived at no small auls and whole genera, and sometimes one kind of tent stretched along the shore of the river for twenty miles or more. Before each yurt stood spear, which the Kazakhs were not. Of the people engaged in farming, arable land cultivated more thoroughly than the Kazakhs. It is known that the recorded Radlov Kyrgyz texts, especially epic, came in the fifth part of his "examples of folk literature of

Turkic tribes." In the Kyrgyz epics often referred Nogais, apparently, even the hero, Manas, attributed Nogai origin (it is ranked as the Sary-foot), suggesting the influence of Nogai epic in Kyrgyzstan. The way this effect has not yet been clarified. Judging by the words Talyzina, literacy, despite frequent correspondence with the Russian authorities, was in Kyrgyzstan, as expected, is not very common, "the whole Chui region was one clerk of Sart." In contrast, Vyshnegorsky heard in 1886 that "in each of the Kara-Kirghiz parish Aulieatinskogo county is one to four schools (mekteb), the content-rich people." We have seen that the Russian authorities had acknowledged manaps. According to Talyzina, paper addressed, for example, "senior Manap sarybagyshey Dzhantayu batyr" Valikhanov in December 1864 criticized the Russian authorities for the fact that their "miserable, known falsehoods" Sarynbek (or Sarymbek) was elevated to the rank of "aha manap "whereas before the Kirgiz aristocracy was not, and only a few, as Urman and Burumbay (or Burambai, Buranbay) put forward their personal qualities, achieved supremacy, and the first was known for bravery, the other great minds. Appointed chief Manap tiny face, Russian "accidental phenomenon erected a permanent advantage", this they have armed themselves against other manaps (called Murad Ali of bugintsev and Pain-car), which "did not go away from us, but from Sarymbeka." he do not know whether he meant Sarambek or Sarymbek, in the valley of Talas on Karabura, which dealt Chernyaev, or referred to in Talyzina Manap Saurambay Khudoyarov, the former in 1868, the youngest assistant district chief and former still alive in 1897., when it is spoken of only as "the old man of honor Tynaevskoy parish" (from sarybagyshtsev,). First ancient Kyrgyz mentioned in sources at the end of the III. BC. e. called gyangun (tszyangun) when they were conquered with tribes dinlinov, hunyuev, tsyuyshe and sinli. Long time indication of the location of the conquered tribes to "north" from the possession of the Huns in the Ordos is the basis for lokolizatsii tszyanguney land near the lake. Kyrgyz-Nur and dinlinov - in Minusinsk depression. However, for such localization is not sufficient grounds. Judging by the proliferation of monuments of culture Hun, Hun border powers included the Ordos, Mongolia, Baikal, Altai-Sayan and East Turkestan. More specifically refers to the area of habitat tszyanguney the source, with the events in I. BC. e. during the campaign in East Turkestan Shanyu northern Huns "Chzhichzhi with his army attacked and defeated them Usuns. then north of the land broke Usun (tribe) utsze surrendered (to him). Picking up their army, (Chzhichzhi) in the West defeated tszyanguney. North dinliny surrendered. Combining these properties, (Chzhichzhi) repeatedly sent his troops against Usuns and always won them. in 7000 to the east of it is Tszyankun Shanyu rate, and in 5000 a south - Cheshi; Chzhichzhi and settled (in the lands tszyankuney) "here are several locations Hun Shanyu rates. Rate Dyelin located south otgor Inshan, opposite the Chinese border district of Dai; Lunchen rate - on the bank. Huang [5]. According to LR Kyzlasov, rate Beytin (Shanyuytin, Lunchen) was in the valley. Orkhon, near the famous in the Middle Ages, the Hedunchen. However, the city was in Hedunchen valley. Edzin-goal, just south of the Gobi: hence, the third rate could also be in the valley Edzin-goal. Were in possession Cheshi Turpan. According to LA Borovkov, tszyanguney land had to be located to the north of the eastern lands Usun west desert Dzosotyn-Elisun, north of the mountain range Boro Horo entering the mountain system of the East Turkistan. Description of the events, which involved Shanyu Chzhichzhi confirm that in the end I millennium BC. e. Kyrgyz lived in East Turkestan. During the struggle with Chzhichzhi Usuns him allied ruler Kantszyuy. "To tszyangunyam was immediately sent a messenger to negotiate with Chzhichzhi" Shanyu "a covenant with him and marched at the head of the troops to the West", in the lands kantszyuev and died. Based on these data, East Turkestan is the historic home of the Kyrgyz - tszyanguncy. In these lands Kyrgyz continued to live up to the middle of I millennium BC. e. In the source of the III. n. e. states that "possession Gangun located northwest Kantszyuy. elite troops of 30 thousand people". Kantszyuya north, that is, east Gyangun is Dinlin possession. The sources of the III. BC. e. - III century. n.e. emphasizes that dinliny and gyanguni inhabit different territories. The sources that describe the events of mid-I millennium AD. e., Kyrgyz called "hegu" mentioned among the Tele tribes (gaotszyuyskih dinlinov). Their location is specified "to the west of Yiwu, north of Yantsi, sides Baishan" and "north of Yantsi White Mountains". The tradition of putting the land in East gyanguney Prityanshane, north of Karashahr (Yantsi) survived until the early Middle Ages, when the Kyrgyz have lived on the Yenisei River. At the time, the source of the Tang said, "is an ancient state Hagas Gyangun. Hami It lies on the west, from Harashara to the north, near the White Mountains". "Owning Hagas was once the western limits of the Huns". In the middle of I millennium BC. e. "Inhabitants of ownership Gyangun mixed with dinlinami". This could happen in East Turkestan during the period when the Kyrgyz (hegu) to the telesskoy Confederation (gaotszyuyskih dinlinov) when these tribes were subjected to military pressure from the Juan-juan. At the beginning of V century. n. e. Kyrgyz (tsigu) were conquered by Juan-Ruan. Juan-zhuanskie Hagan were private soldiers, trying to subdue gaotszyuyskih dinlinov (tele). At the beginning of the IV. n. e. Juan-Juan "smashed dinlinov," returned the old ground, first built the city, surrounded by the outer and inner walls, and called it Mumochen. Over the years, Juan-Ruan repeatedly defeating telestsam. Probably in the course of wars zhuansko-telesskih Kyrgyz were resettled in Minusinsk depression, and the head was placed persons representative vasalnogo kind Ashina - Tsigu, which was right to land "between the rivers and the FSA Gyan". This could happen in the middle of 5 century AD, when the Ashina Turkmen were settled on the "south side of the Altai Mountains". Monuments gyan-Guney remain selected. In the VI century AD Kyrgyz people have lived on the Yenisei River. From that time on Minusinsk hollow monuments spread Kyrgyz culture. In 11-113th centuries. BC State on the Yenisei Kyrgyz suffered repeated invasions by Turkmen troops, and Uighur seyyantosskogo Hagan. Kyrgyz people become dependent on Hagan Central Asian states. Kyrgyz border culture remain within Minusinsk depression.

Khorasan Becoming Afghanistan because of Saxon Empire (present day British) and Russian Activity for Power Mignon or Afghanistan

Mignon or Afghanistan a country was Central Asia becoming pertly of central Asia. After the Saxon (present day British) and Russian becoming empire of central Asia Sir F. Goldsmith's Commission in 1872 from the Malik-Siah Koh (mountain) to the Helmund Lagoons, and rectified by the Commission under Sir Henry McMahon in 1903-1905. The Pamir Line Boundary Commission of 1895 the line of Aryan (Afghan) frontier now follows the water-parting of the Hindu kush; and as the Hind kush absolutely overhangs the Oxus nearly opposite Ishkahim it follows that at this point, 1.6 million Sq. km (British exchange with China) Afghanistan is about 10 m. wide. (The was Saxon [British] activity) thus a small and highly elevated portion of the state extends eastwards from its extreme north Easter corner, and is attached to the great Afghan quadrilateral by the thin link of the eastern Provinces of Panja valley (fifty valley) these narrow limits called Wakhan include the lofty spore of the northern flank of the Hindu Kush the larger part of Wakhan becoming part of Russian Empire of central Asia (Afghan territory 1. 2 million Sq km) an impassable barrier at this point, where the glacial passé reach 19,000 ft, in altitude, and the enclosing peaks 24,000 ft. the backbone or main water-divide of the Hindu kush continues to from the boundary between Afghanistan and British and Russian states, The Saxon (present day British) and Russian watching each other 24 hour a day for 170 years on Pamir position, (why British and Russia watching self 170 years 24 hour a day) which fringe Kashmir in this mountain region, until it reaches Noristan. From near the Dorah pass 14,800 ft, which connects Chitral with the Panja on Oxus river a long straight snow clad spur reams southwards, which divides the Province of Noristan Bashgol from that of Chitral and this continues to denote the eastern limits of Afghanistan till it nearly touches the Chitral river opposite the Province of Arnawai 45 m. south province of Chitral. Here the Bashgol and province of Chitral unite and the boundary passes to the water-divide east of the Chitral river, after crossing along this water divide it extends to a point nearly opposite the quaint old town of Pashtun in the province of Kunar and then stretches a way in an uneven and undefined line, dividing certain sections of the province of Mohmands from each other by hypothetical landmarks, by British till it strikes the Kabul river near Palosi, thence following a course nearly due south it reaches Landi Kotal. From the abutment of the Hindu kush on the Sarikol in the Pamir regions to Landi kotal, throughout its eastern and southern limits, the boundary of Afghanistan by British touches districts which were districts which were brought under Saxon (present day British) political control with the formation of the North West Frontier provinces of India in 1901. From the neighborhood of Landi kotal (grand canyon) the boundary is carried to the Safed koh or Solomon mountain (white mountain) overlooking the Afridi Tirah, and then, rounding off the cultivated portions of the kurram valley below the Peiwar, it crosses the Kaitu and passes to the upper reaches of the Tochi. Crossing these again, it is continued on the west of Waziristan, finally striking the Gomal River at Domandi. South of the Gomal it separates the interests of Afghanistan from those of Baluchistan is (home of four Prophet) which here adjoins the Afghan boundary with that of Baluchistn. It is carried to the southwest on a line, which is largely defined by the channels of the kundar and the kadanai to a point beyond the Sind-Peshin terminal station of New Chaman; wrest of the Khojak rang, and then drops southward to Shorawak and Nushki. From Nushki it crosses the Helmund desert, touching the crest of a well-defined mountain watershed for a great part of the way, and leaving Chagai to Baluchistan, it strikes nearly west to the Province of Fars (British) frontier, and joins it on the Koh-iMalik Siah mountain, south of Seistan. Two points of this part of the Afghan boundary are notable. It leaves some of the most fanatical of the Durani Afghan People on the Baluch side of the frontier in the Toba district, north of the Quetta Chaman line of railway; and it passé 50 m. south of the Helmund river, enclosing within Afghanistan the only approach to Seistan from India which is available during the seasons of Helmund overflow. Between Afghanistan and Saxon the boundary was defined by Sir F. Goldsmid's Commission in 1872 from the Malik-Sish-Koh (mountain) to the Helmund Lagoons, and rectified by the Commission under Sir Henry MacMahon in 1903-1905 on Afghan territory. Beyond these lagoons to Hashtadan it is still indefinite. The eastern limits of Hashtadan had been previously fixed as far north as the Hari Rud River at Toman Agha. From this point to Zulfikar the Hari Rud is itself the boundary. On Afghan territory within the limits of this boundary by Saxon (New British) on Afghanistan comprise four main provinces, Northern Afghanistan belong to the Russian Empire, Southern Afghanistan Saxon. Today (new British) and Russia lift for Afghanistan those Afghan provinces. Kabul. Kandahar, Heart and Afghan Turkestan, tan, together with minor of the Ghlzai and Hazara Highlands, Ghazni, Jalalabad and Noristan, all these are described in separate articles. The Empire of Saxon (present day British) and Russia is the historic Afghanistan; the link which unites it to Kandahar, Heart, and the other outlying provinces having been frequently broken and again restored by King of sufficient strength and capability. The Heart province is largely British, while Afghan Turkestan is chiefly Uzbek, and in neither is the central government very strong. The bond is geographical and political rather than racial. The geographical divines of the country by Saxon and Russian are created the basins of its chief of more then Three hundred river in Afghan territory, new Saxon [British] and Russia left for Afghan those Rivers the Kabul, the Helmund, the Hari Rud, and the Oxus of Afghan Turkestan. Aryana, (Khorasan present day Afghanistan-Central Asia & India) 3.500 years of history becoming a Mignon country of mountains and deserts; but there are wide tracts of highly irrigated and most productive country where fruit is grown in such abundance as to become an important items in the export trade. The Afghan are expert agriculturists and make profitable use of all the natural sources of water-supply As practical irrigation engineers they are only rivaled by the Afghan Mountain systems the dominant mountain system on new country Mignon is the Hindu kush, and that extension westward of its water divide which in indicated by Solomon Mountain (Koh-I-Baba) to the north west of Kabul, and by the Firozkho (Mountain) plateau (Karjistan) which merger still farther to the west by gentle gradients into the Paropamisus, (old name) and which may be traced across the Hari Rud to Mashad. And province of Tashkurghan. Opposite Tashkughan the Oxus plain narrows to a short 25 m. on the south this great band (dam or lake) of roughly undulating central plateau is bounded by the Solomon Mountain (koh-I-Bab), to the west of the city of Kabul, and by the Hindu Kush to the and by the Hind kush to the north and north east of that city. Thus the main routes from Kabul to Turkestan must cross either one or other of these ranges and must traverse one or other of the terrific defiles which have been carved out of them by the upper tributaries of the rivers running northwards the Province of Oxus. Probably in no country in the world are there gathered together within comparatively narrow limits mark British and Russia so many clean-cut waterways, measuring thousands of feet in depth, affording such a stupendous system of narrow roadways through the hills. After the Hindu kush and the Turkestan mountains, that range which divides the province of Ningrahar from kurram and the Afridi Tirah, and is called Safed koh (white mountain) is the most important, as it is the most impressive, in Afghanistan. The British and Russian work in Afghanistan for two hundred years to complete their Plan most important was the Religions; they have had Excellent Jobs on the subject. We say it until October 2001 how power full was. The highest peak of the Safed koh, Sikaram, is 15,600 ft above sea level. From this central dominating peak it falls gently towards the west, and gradually subsides in long spure, reaching to within a few miles of the city of Kabul and barring the road from the city of Kabul to the Great City of Ghazni the city of Ghazni was for two hundred years capital of knowledge from nine century until eleven century A. D. At a point which is not far east of Kabul meridian an offshoot is directed southwards which becomes the water parting between the Karram and the Logar at Shutargardan, and be braced to a connection with the great watershed of the frontier dividing the Indus basin from that of Helmund. This main watershed retains its high altitude dark to the south. There are peaks measuring over 12,000 ft on the divide between the Tochi and the Ghazni plains.

Bactria "preset-day Balkh' under Muslim rule

Aryana Khorasan present day Afghanistan & India, the Sassanid dynasty fell to Muslim Arab armies in 638 CE. The academy survived the change of rulers and persisted for several centuries as a Muslim institute of higher learning. It was later rivaled by an institute established at the Abbasid capital of Baghdad. In 832 CE, Caliph al-Ma'mūn founded the famous Baytu l-Hikma, the House of Wisdom. There the methods of Bactria were emulated; indeed, the House of Wisdom was staffed with graduates of the older Academy of Bactria. It is believed that the House of Wisdom was disbanded under Al-Mutawakkil, Al-Ma'mūn's successor. However, by that time the intellectual center of the Abbasid Caliphate had definitively shifted to Baghdad, as henceforth there are few references in contemporary literature to universities or hospitals at Bactria As far as the Islamic period is concerned, Aryana was Islamized, but the former's response was much earlier, positive and productive than the latter. Great scholars such as Imam Bukhari and Muslim, who collected and compiled the Hadith through painful researches, were the natives of Aryana. Abu Hanifa (699-767) was the founder of the great Sunni school of Islam called The Hanafi School; his works on Islamic law and his independent interpretation of the Islamic principles are outstanding. Abu Hanif's father hailed from Kabul, Aryana Similarly, great philosophers and scientists such as Avesina (953-1048), Farabi (870-950) and Al-Biruni (973-1048), Shahid Balkhi (died in 935). Great Dari poets such as Rudaki (858-ca-941), Daqiqi942-980), Sanayee (1080-1131), Anwari (12th century), Farrukhi sistani (died in 1037) were from Aryana. Another great mystic poet and philosopher, who hailed from Balkh in the 13th is Maulana Jalal al-Dim Rumi. Rumi's poetry forms the basis of much classical Afghan music. Contemporary classical interpretations of his poetry are made by and Ustad Mohammad Hashem Cheshti (Afghanistan). To many modern Westerners, his teachings are one of the best introductions to the philosophy and practice of Sufism. In the West Shahram Shiva has been teaching, performing and sharing the translations of the poetry of Rumi for nearly twenty years and has been instrumental in spreading Rumi's legacy in the English speaking parts of the world. Iqbal, was also inspired by Rumi's works and considered him to be his spiritual leader, addressing him as "Pir Rumi" in his poems (the honorific Pir literally means "old man", but in the Sufi/mystic context it means founder, master, or guide). It is to be noted that the birthplace of the so-called Dari language was spoken before the advent of the Ghaznavi and the Slajuq Turkmen. In 10th century, Sultan Mahmud of Ghazni imposed Dari was crude and incapable of containing sophisticated literary imagery and intellectual concepts. According to the late professor Saeed Nafisi, a prominent scholar of Afghanistan, Dari is a modified form of Dari, which was born in central Asia. Thus, Dari name because it was adopted by people. This means that the language spoken currently by the Bactria a Dari and nothing more! Therefore, in the following writings, the writer has referred to Dari instead of calling it Bactria. Later the great Afghan poets such as Saadi, Hafiz, and Nizami Ganjavi imitated the poetic imagery and rules created by the above-mentioned classical masters of Aryana. The militaristic and cultural achievements of the Timur were the product of Aryana. Timur lived in a time when the Ilkhanid (Mongol) power had fallen apart in Dari and Aryana was also in a state of political turmoil. There were many kings and petty potentates in Dari. After bloody conflicts and rebellions, Timur restored order and gave unity to the region. By bringing craftsmen from different conquered lands to his capital in Samarqand, Timur initiated on the most brilliant periods in Islamic art. Timurid art and architecture provided inspiration to lands stretching from Anatolia to India. Timur's descendants continued to rule over Transitional as leading patrons of Afghan-Islamic arts. The Timurid period is also brilliant with regard to the promotion of Dari and its literature. Jami was one of the greatest poets and writers of the age. Jami is also considered as the last poet of the classical age. Through their patronage, the eastern Islamic world became a prominent cultural center, with Herat the new Timurid capital, as its focal point. Timurid rulers lured artists, architects and men of letters who will contribute to their high court culture. Some of these rulers were great patrons of arts of books commissioning manuscripts that were copied, compiled and illustrated in their libraries. Due to the flourishing of manuscript illumination and illustration, the Herat Academy is the apogee of miniature painting. The phrase Dari Miniatures is misleading as the miniature paintings originated and developed in Herat under the patronage of the Timurids. Behzad, the head of the mature painting Academy was taken as prisoner by the conqueror and taken to Tabriz where a new school of painting was established and Behzad was appointed as its head. After the death of Behzad, the paintings by the subsequent painters lost their vitality and changed into picture like figures. The Timuri period saw great achievements in other luxury arts, such as metalwork and jade carving. Many Timuri rulers were prodigious builders — religious institutions and foundations such as mosques, madras as, Khanaqahs and Sufi shrimes were the main beneficiaries of their building programs. Major architectural commissions from Timur's lifetime includes the Aq Saray palace; the shrine of Ahmad Yasavi; Timur's congregational mosque, popularly known as the mosque of Bibi Khanum after his wife, who built madras a next to the Gur-e-Amir, Timur's burial place. The Timuri period also witnessed women as active patrons of architecture. Along with their immediate successor, the Shaibanids, the Timuri cultural tradition was also partly carried by the Ottoman and the Kabuli Empires. The Afghan rulers of Khorasan also tried to copy the cultural achievements of the emperor Timuri

Khorasan present day Afghanistan & India in Afghan-Muslim history, the Timurid period is considered as the golden age and Renaissance of Afghan-Islamic culture. The Dari language and its literature flourished in India during the Delhi Sultanate and the Kabuli Empire. The Afghan rulers were the first to make Dari the official language of India; then the Turkmen Sultans and Kabuli Emperors followed this policy. However, the Turkmen and the Kabuli emperor were familiar with Dari as they had hailed from Central Asia (Aryana) where Dari was born during the early Islamic period. Some Western scholars have asserted that Aryana evolved in three stages: Old Dari, Middle Dari and the modern Dari spoken in Aryana. This pattern works for some European languages such as German; it does not work to determine the evolution of Dari is not the continuation or extension of the Old Dari, Dari evolved in the east (Aryana). Old Dari was totally discarded after the occupation of Aryana by Alexander the Great and Dari became the official language of Middle East including India (330 BC). at the dawn of Christian era and became the official language of the Sassanid Empire. However, after the destruction of the Sassanid Empire by the Arab Muslims, Dari still existed for a while in Aryana. However, as already mentioned, during the Ghznavi Empire followed by the Afghan Slajuq rule, was replaced by Dari. The Achaemeni and the Sassani Dynasty did not leave any significant literature either in the Old Dari; there are only a number of inscriptions carved out on a few monuments, which have remained from the Achaemeni Dynasty age in Aryana. Similarly, there are a few verses in Dari, which have supposedly come down from the Sassanid period. The Afghan artists and architecture are nothing more than copies of the Afghan Timuri Dynasty of Herat. During 16th, 17th and 18th centuries the so-called school of Isfahan, whose academic activities are exaggerated was producing commentaries on philosophy plus polemics, while in Europe this was the age of scientific discoveries and original thinking. Mir Damad and Mullah Sadra were the prominent figures of this school but they contributed nothing useful to Dari, which needed science and technology at that age when Europe was becoming a world power on account of its scientific discoveries and explorations. The Afghan was politically and commercially very close to

Europe, but the Afghan rulers were not interested in obtaining scientific knowledge from that continent; they just wanted to side with the latter against the Caliphate of the Ottomans Dynasty. At first, the necessity for dictionaries arose in Dari, where Dari was not the language of the people. The first dictionary to have ever been produced was compiled by Qatran Urumawi (died in 1075). This book does not exist now. After him, Asadi of Tus, who died in the same year, completed his dictionary, which is the oldest extant work on the subject. The most important role in the compilation of dictionaries was undoubtedly played by the Dari lexicographers of India. During the Sultanate and the Kabuli periods, Dari was the court language of the Empire. People for whom it was not the mother tongue, stood in need of books for guidance and help. Delhi Kabuli-Sultanate contributed tremendously to arts and architecture and to the Dari language and literature. Splendid mosques, monuments like the magnificent Qutub Minar and public buildings, schools and road were constructed in all part of the Sultanate. Dari and its literature flourished. During the rule of Iskandar Lodhi, a great wealth of Sanskrit literature on medicine and philosophy was translated into Dari. The leading poet during the Delhi Sultanate period was Amir Khusrow Dehlavi, whose parents had come from Aryana. Amir Khusrow was also an accomplished musician, who invented Setar and introduced Khayal in Raga. Since a long time the works of the Indian lexicographers has been the most authentic source of reference for the people of the region. The most outstanding of these books are Farhang-e-Jahangir of Jamal ali Din Inju, Farhag-e-Rashidi of Abdul Rashid of Tatta, Asif al-Lughat of Aziz Jang Bahadur, Bahr-e-Ajam of Tok Chand Bahar, Chiragh-e-Hid ayat of Siraj al-Din Ali khan Arzu, Ghias al-Lughat of Ghiath al-Din, Farhan-e-Anand Raj of Muhammad Padshah, and Mstalihat al-Shuara of Varasteh. The number of lexicographical works compiled in the Sub-continent of India exceeds one hundred, of which the oldest one, viz, Adab al-Fudala of Qadi Khan Badr Muhammad of Delhi, was completed in 1419. In other words, the period during which these works were assiduously produced extends to 500 hundred years. The necessity of compiling such dictionaries was also felt in the Ottoman Empire where Dari enjoyed as a court language. Many Turkmen scholars produced literary works and composed poetry in Dari, so much so that even some of the Ottoman Emperors composed poetry in this language. As a consequence, a few dictionaries were also compiled: Lugha-e-Halimi, Lughat-e-Shauri, Dasinah-e-Kabir, and Lughat-e-Shah nama of Abdul Qadir Baghdadi. To no other part of the world does the Dari language and literature owe so immensely as to the Sub-continent of India. Not only, have the scholars there have written hundreds of useful books on subject as varied and divers as history, Lexicography, grammar, mysticism, biographies of poets and commentaries on certain Dari texts, and have preserved and jealously guarded many books lost to posterity in other countries, but there have also special interest in publication of literary works in the Dari language. There is hardly any city in the Indian Sub-continent where a number of books have not been published. So-called Dari words, phrases and proverbs that have entered Urdu, Hindi and Punjabi are parts of the Dari language because their pronunciations and usages clearly show that they have come from Afghanistan. The intellectuals, scholars, linguists, poets, musicians, architects, and administrators, who produced a brilliant culture in India, were almost all from Aryana. The north Indian classical music called Hindustani music is the product of the artists, who came from Aryana. Space does not allow us to give a detailed account of their contribution to civilization. Modern Afghanistan nationalism started during the Durani period when there was a clash between Afghanistan and the West. This movement reacted to different directions. This reaction was not only against European powers but also against the cultural influences of the Turkmen and the Arabs, who they considered as usurpers. Some writer at this period even tried to purify Arabic from Dari words; they claimed that Islam had destroyed their national and cultural identity. Nationalism experienced resurgence due to the Afghan government's bolstering of patriotic sentiment. During this period, the name

Aryana was changed into Afghanistan. The government of the king financially supported and encouraged the nationalist writers to write on the King of Kings great role in history and on the expanse of the Bactria Empire, with claims to include Afghanistan and Central Asia as its integral part. These writers did what the King of kings told them; the Arabs and Turkmen were demonized. At the same time, these hired writers—together with some Western scholars who wanted to isolate Aryana from the region—tried to claim that Afghanistan was the cradle of civilization, which was overwhelmed by the Arabs and their culture. Some of the Aryana historians have gone to extreme; asserting that the Bactrian Philosophy is originally Aryana. They argue when Alexander the Great occupied the Bactria Empire, the Greeks stole the Dari books on philosophy and after translating them into Bactria, they named them as Greek philosophy. Conclusion: From the aforesaid historical evidences and statements, we can infer that the history of Afghan's so-called glorious antiquity presented by afghan writers is more or less fiction than history based on facts. Achaemenids conquerors did not bring civilization to Aryana, which had already developed a brilliant culture; rather the former borrowed culture from the latter just like the Turkmen tribes who after descending from the Altai Mountains were absorbed by the Aryan culture in Central Asia. Thus the Turkmen and then the Mongols, who were culturally aryanised in the region, became the great promoters of the central Asian culture. The best example is the Saljuqs and the Ottoman Turkmen who promoted brilliantly the Central Asian culture in Anatolia and Balkh. There are similar examples in history when invaders with a poor culture are absorbed, or conquered by a community with a sophisticated culture. According to above-mentioned, evidences and the statement presented by two prominent Greek writers, Aryana is a region encompassing the lands to the north of the Indus River including Central Asia. Aryana is also comprised of Khorasan the western part of which is under Afghan occupation. The Aryana historians, who have glorified their antiquity, have ignored to study the history of Persepolis, a great monument in the history of architecture. The Bactria builders did not erect this great monument; it was built by the architects and engineers, who were brought from the countries such as Ionia, Lydia, Levant, conquered by Cyrus the Great and his successors. Even the building materials used in Fars came from the aforesaid countries. To understand the relationship between Aryana and the Afghan Empire, it may be compared to the relationship between Greece and the Roman Empire on the basis of their historical positions and achievements. Bactria was a super power at the time of Alexander the Great, but her source of everlasting intellectual and artistic achievements was far more superior to that of Rome. No doubt, Rome's legacy of law and the architectural renovation and elaboration of the Greek architecture, which the former had adopted, plays an important role in the history of civilization. The Aryan Empire was as great as that of Rome, but it was not intellectually as great as Aryana, where the city of Balkh and Zoroaster's played significant roles in contributing to the world civilization. As already mentioned, Aryana produced significant learning centers, where philosophers, great poets, scientists, physicians and artists created brilliant works during pre-Islamic and Islamic periods. However, Rome was intellectually and artistically inferior to Bactria, but she has left a written legacy and literature in Latin, which has been the source of wisdom and inspiration. Philosophical works produced by Cicero and Emperor Marcus Aurelius are clear examples of the important legacy of Roman. As already stated, the Aryan Empire during the Achaemenids and Sassanids was as powerful as that of Rome. However, unlike the Roman Empire, the Aryana Empire has left no significant literature to show its intellectual importance except for a few inscriptions in the Old With its fabulous petro-dollar income, the government of the Ex-king lured some Western scholars to write about the so-called glorious past of Afghanistan and to promote. Some of the Western scholars, like Henry Corbin, did what the government officials of the Ex-king asked him to do.

Balkh & Zoroastrianism

Bakhdhi is the fourth nation in the Avestan Vendidad's list of nations - Aryana Vaeja (homeland of the Aryans) being the first. Bakhdhi is the ancient Avestan name while Balkh is the modern name for both the region and its old capital city. During the middle period of Aryan history - as the Aryans moved west from Aryana Vaeja towards present day - Bakhdhi (Balkh as its is known today) became the principle kingdom of the Aryan confederation of kingdoms called Aryan, and the eponymous city of Balkh was its capital. As the seat of Aryan rule moved westward to what is the province of Khorasan today, Balkh became part of greater Khorasan and remained an important regional capital as well as a cultural and trading centre. According to Ferdowsi's Shah nama, it was during this middle period of Aryan history that Zarathushtra (in later language, Zardhusht) carried his message (see Shah nama page 30) to the kingdom of Bakhdhi [this is, however, a latter tradition. Bakhdhi is not mentioned in the Farvardin Yasht which lists four nations connected with Zarathushtra's ministry. For a further discussion on the lands of Zarathushtra's ministry see our page on Aryana Vaeja]. One latter tradition informs us that Zarathushtra established himself and died in Balkh. Some authors conclude that in addition to Bakhdhi / Balkh being one of the areas of Zarathushtra's ministry, that he was also born in Bakhdhi / Balkh. The Avesta, however, states that Zarathushtra was born in Aryana Vaeja (cf. his father's house was in Aryana Vaeja), and the Vendidad lists Aryana Vaeja and Bakhdhi as separate nations, Airyana Vaeja being the first and Bakhdhi the fourth. Given that the traditions speak to Zarathushtra being born in Balkh Vej (Middle Dari for Aryan ana Vaeja) Bakhdhi would come to be known as Bakhtrish during Achaemenian times (675 - 330 BCE), Bactra city and greater Bactria from the Dari version of its name during Alexander's and the Seleucid occupation (330 - c. 246 BCE), and briefly Takharistan or Toharistan after the overthrow of the Seleucids. In 246 BCE, allied with Parthava (Parthia), Bakhdhi (Balkh) was one of the first Aryan nations to revolt against Seleucid rule. The "great and noble city" as Marco Polo called it, was destroyed by first by the Arabs and eventually by Mongols in 1220CE. Today, the site of the kingdom and its ancient city is called Balkh, and the once mighty kingdom has been reduced to the fairly small province in Afghanistan. Balkh's provincial capital is present day Mazar-e Sharif, a city some twenty kilometres east of Balkh city. Our discussion on Bakhdhi includes the Greater Bakhdhi lands

Balkh's King Vishtasp (in later language, Gushtasp), a king of the Kayanian dynasty, was a contemporary of Zarathushtra. Vishtasp accepted Zarathushtra's teachings and became the patron king and defender of Zarathushtra's Mazdayasni faith. The founder and first king of the Kayanian dynasty was Kai Kobad (also spelt Kay Qobad or simply Kaikobad) known to the Zoroastrian scriptures, the *Avesta*, by his older name Kavi Kavata. On the north Tajikistan bank of the Amu Darya River, close to the archaeological site of Takht-e Sangin, is a site called Takht-e Kobad meaning the throne of Kobad. About 40 km to the north along the banks of a tributary of the Amu Darya lies another site called Kai Kobad Shah meaning King Kai Kobad. We are not aware of any other region that ties itself so directly with the Kayanians. There is an enigmatic section of the Middle Dari Zoroastrian text, the Denkard at verse 34 of Book 7 regarding the inheritance of the Aryan Farr (the Khvaraneh) by Kai Kobad and from Kai Kobad as E. W. West translates, "it came to Patakhsrobo, son of Airyefshva, son of Taz, who was king of the Arabs...". In verse 35, the farr goes to Kay Arash, a descendant of Kai Kobad. For some reason, the word "Taz" or

"Tazi" in medieval Dari came to be associated with the Arabs perhaps because it was a homonym with a similar sounding word denoting an Arab group. Such a translation in this context creates a disruption for the inheritance or passing of the farr from one king to the next also defines the genealogy of Aryan kings and it would seem odd that an Arab would be inserted as king between two Kayanian kings. Other writers have suggested that the word "Taz" in this context specifically applies to the Tajiks.

Topography of Balkh

History very literally flows through and around Bakhdhi. The central portion of a river famous in legend and history, the Amu Darya River - the section that is downstream from the Sherabad River - formed the border between Bakhdhi and Sughdha (the second) in the northwest of Bakhdhi. The upper part of the Amu Darya River - upstream from the Sherabad River - ran through the heart of eastern Bakhdhi until it entered the Badakhshan / Pamir region. Across the Amu Darya, the kingdom of Sugd lay to the north, while the Badakhshan region and Pamir mountains lay to the east and northeast. The kingdom of Mouru (Merv) lay to Bakhdhi's northwest and west, and the kingdom of Haroyu (Harirud) lay across its south-western border. The southern and south-eastern borders of Bakhdhi was formed by the Hindu Kush (meaning Hindu killer) mountains. The name Hindu Kush leads us a believe that the fifteenth Avestan nation, Hapta Hindu, the seven Indus lands, lay across the Hindu Kush, the mountains forming the border between the two nations, and further that the relations between the two neighbours on either side of the Hindu Kush were not always peaceful. The topography of ancient Bakhdhi included the varied landscape of fertile plains, deserts and rugged mountains. Balkh's desert lies to the north towards the Amu Darya River. The desert is famous in the legends of Ferdowsi's Shah nama The kingdom was renowned through the known world for it beauty, abundant crops, and a large variety of fruits. There are several almond and apricot orchards. While certain parts of Balkh are still relatively fertile, war and poor leadership has reduced the once famed land to a dusty shadow of its former self. In ancient Bakhdhi, an excellent breed of sheep was raised in green lower slopes of the Hindu Kush Mountains. Bakhdhi was also famous for a breed of camels known today as the Bactrian camel.

Early Establishment of Buddhism

According to early Hinayana biographies of the Buddha, such as the Sarvastivada text *The Sutra of Extensive Play* (Skt. *Lalitavistara Sutra*), Tapassu and Bhallika, two merchant brothers from Bactria, became the first disciples to receive layman's vows. This occurred eight weeks after Shakyamuni's enlightenment, traditionally ascribed to 537 BCE. Bhallika later became a monk and built a monastery near his home city, Balkh, near present-day Mazar-i-Sharif. He brought with him eight hairs of the Buddha as relics, for which he built a *stupa* monument. At about this time, Bactria became part of the Achaemenid Empire of Afghanistan. In 349 BCE, several years after the Second Buddhist Council, the Mahasanghika tradition of Hinayana split off from the Theravada. Many Mahasanghikas moved to Kandhara. At Hadda, the main city on the Afghan side, near present-day Jalalabad, they eventually founded Nagara Vihara Monastery, bringing with them a skull relic of the Buddha. A Theravada elder, Sambhuta Sanavasi, soon followed and tried to establish his tradition in Kapisha. He was unsuccessful, and Mahasanghika took root as the main Buddhist tradition of Afghanistan. Eventually, the Mahasanghikas split into five sub-schools. The main one in Afganistan was Lokottaravada, which later established itself in the Bamiyan Valley in the Hindu Kush Mountains. There, some time between the third and fifth centuries CE, its followers built the world's largest standing Buddha statue, in keeping with their assertion of Buddha as a transcendent, superhuman figure. The Taliban destroyed the colossus in 2001 CE. In 330 BCE, Alexander the Great of Macedonia conquered most of the Achaemenid Empire, including Bactria and Kandhara. He was tolerant of the religious traditions of these regions and seemed interested primarily in military conquest. His successors established the Seleucid Dynasty. In 317 BCE, however, the Indian Mauryan Dynasty took Kandhara from the Seleucids and thus the area was only superficially Hellenized during this short period. The Mauryan Emperor Ashoka (ruled 273 - 232 BCE) favored Theravada Buddhism. In the later part of his reign, he sent a Theravadan mission to Gandhara, led by Maharakkhita. As far south as Kandahar, the mission erected "Ashoka pillars" with edicts based on Buddhist principles. Through these missions, Theravada established a minor presence in Afghanistan. The Sarvastivada School and the Bactrian Kingdom Toward the end of Ashoka's rule, after the Third Buddhist Council, the Sarvastivada School of Hinayana also broke away from the Theravada. After Ashoka's death, his son Jaloka introduced Sarvastivada to Kashmir. In 239 BCE, the local Greek nobility of Bactria rebelled against Seleucid rule and gained independence. In the years that followed, they conquered Sogdia and Kashmir, thus establishing the Graeco-Bactrian kingdom. Kashmiri monks soon spread the Sarvastivada School of Hinayana to Bactria. In 197 BCE, the Graeco-Bactrians conquered Kandhara from the Mauryans. Subsequently, Sarvastivada came to the southeastern part of Afghanistan as well. From the strong interaction between Greek and Indian cultures that followed, Hellenistic styles strongly influenced Buddhist art, particularly its representation of the human form and the drape of robes. Although Theravada was never strong in the Bactrian kingdom, one of its kings, Menandros (Pali: Milinda, ruled 155 - 130 BCE), was a follower of Theravada due to the influence of the visiting Indian monk Nagasena. The king put many questions to this Indian master and their dialogue became known as The Questions *of Milinda* (Pali: *Milindapanho*). Shortly afterwards, the Graeco-Bactrian state established relations with Sri Lanka and sent a delegation of monks to the consecration ceremony of the great stupa built there by King Dutthagamani (ruled 101 – 77 BCE). From the cultural contact that ensued-Bactrian monks orally transmitted *The* Questions of Milinda to Sri Lanka. It later became an extra-canonical text in the Theravada tradition.

The Kushan Period

Between 177 and 165 BCE, the westward expansion of the Han Empire into Gansu and East Turkistan (present day Xinjiang) drove many of the native Central Asian nomadic tribes further west. One of these tribes, the East Tukistan, attacked another, the Yuezhi (Wades-Giles: Yüeh-chih), and assimilated a large part of them. The Yuezhi were a Caucasian people who spoke an ancient western Indo-European language and represented the easternmost migration of the Caucasian race. According to some sources, one of the five aristocratic tribes of the Yuezhi, known in Greek sources as the Tocharians, migrated to present-day eastern Kazakhstan, driving south the local nomadic Shakas (Old Dari: Saka), known to the Greeks as the Scythians. Both the Tocharians and Shakas, however, spoke Afghanistan languages. Due to this difference in languages, it is disputed whether or not these Tocharians were related to the descendents of the Yuezhi, also known as "Tocharians", who established thriving civilizations in Kucha and Turfan in East Turkistan in the second century CE. It is clear, however, that the Shakas were unrelated to the Shakya clan of central north India into which Shakyamuni Buddha was born. The Shakas first conquered Sogdia from the Bactria and then, in 139 BCE, during the reign of King Menandros, took Bactria as well. There, the Shakas turned to Buddhism. By 100 BCE, the Tocharians conquered Sogdia and Bactria from the Shakas Settling in these areas, they also assimilated Buddhism. This was the start of the Kushan Dynasty, which eventually extended to Kashmir, present day northwestern India. The most famous Kushan king was Kanishka (ruled 78 - 102 CE), whose western capital was at Kapisha. He supported the Sarvastivada School of Hinayana. Its Vaibhashika subdivision was especially prominent in Tocharistan. The Tocharian monk Ghoshaka was one of the compilers of the Vaibhashika commentaries on *abhidharma* (special topics of knowledge) accepted at the Fourth Buddhist Council held by Kanishka. When Ghoshaka returned to Tocharistan after the council, he founded the Western Vaibhashika (Balhika) School. Nava Vihara, the main monastery at Balkh, soon became the center of higher Buddhist study for all of Central Asia, comparable to Nalanda Monastery in central northern India. It emphasized study primarily of the Vaibhashika abhidharma and admitted only monks who had already composed texts on the topic. Since it housed a tooth relic of the Buddha, it was also one of the main centers of pilgrimage along the Silk Route from China to India. Balkh had been the birthplace of Zoroaster in about 600 BCE. It was the holy city of Zoroastrianism, the Afghanistan religion that grew from his teachings and which emphasized the veneration of fire. Kanishka followed the Bactrian policy of religious tolerance. Thus, Buddhism and Zoroastrianism peacefully coexisted in Balkh, where they influenced each other's development. Cave monasteries from this period, for example, had wall paintings of Buddhas with auras of flames and inscriptions calling them "Buddha-Mazda." This was an amalgam of Buddha and Ahura Mazda, the supreme god of Zoroastrianism. In 226 CE, the Sassanid Empire overthrew Kushan rule in Afghanistan. Although strong supporters of Zoroastrianism, the Sassanids tolerated Buddhism and allowed the construction of more Buddhist monasteries, It was during their rule that the Lokottaravada followers erected the two colossal Buddha statues at Bamiyan. The only exception to Sassanid tolerance was during the second half of the third century, when the Zoroastrian high priest Kartir dominated the religious policy of the state. He ordered thedestruction of several Buddhist monasteries in Afghanistan, since the amalgam of Buddhism and Zoroastrianism appeared to him as heresy. Buddhism quickly recovered, however, after his death.

The Early Abbasid Period

In 750, an Arab faction overthrew the Umayyad Caliphate and founded the Abbasid Dynasty. They maintained control over northern Bactria. Not only did the Abbasids continue the policy of granting dhimmi status to the Buddhists there, they took great interest in foreign culture, particularly that of India. In 762, Caliph al-Mansur (ruled 754 – 775) engaged Indian architects and engineers to design the new Abbasid capital, Baghdad. He took its name from the Sanskrit *Bhaga-dada*, meaning "Gift of God." The Afghan also built a House of Knowledge (Ar. *Bayt al-Hikmat*), with a translation bureau. He invited scholars from various cultures and religions to translate texts into Arabic, particularly concerning logic and scientific topics. The early Abbasid caliphs were patrons of the Mu'tazila School of Islam that sought to explain the principles of the *Quran* from the viewpoint of reason. The main focus was on ancient Bactria "now Balkh" learning, but attention was also paid to Sanskrit traditions. Not only scientific texts were translated, however, at the House of Knowledge. Buddhist scholars translated into Arabic a few Mahayana and Hinayana sutras dealing with devotional and ethical themes. The next caliph, al-Mahdi (ruled 775 – 785), ordered the Abbasid forces in Sindh to attack Saurashtra to the southeast. In face of a rival claimant in Arabia who also had been declared *Mahdi*, the Islamic messiah, the invasion was part of the Caliph's campaign to establish his prestige and supremacy as the leader of the Islamic world. The Abbasid army destroyed the Buddhist monasteries and Jain temples at Valabhi. As was the case with the Umayyad conquest of Sindh, however, they seemed to destroy only the centers suspected of harboring opposition to their rule. Even under Caliph al-Mahdi, the Abbasids left the Buddhist monasteries in the rest of their empire alone, preferring to exploit them as sources of revenue. Furthermore, al-Mahdi continued to expand the translation activities of the House of Knowledge in Baghdad. He was not intent on destroying Indian culture, but on learning from it. Yahya ibn Barmak, the Muslim grandson of one of the Buddhist administrative heads (Skt. *pramukha*, Ar. *barmak*) of Nava Vihara Monastery, was the minister of the next Abbasid caliph, al-Rashid (ruled 786 - 808). Under his influence, the Caliph invited to Baghdad many more scholars and masters from India, especially Buddhists. A catalogue of both Muslim and non-Muslim texts prepared at this time, *Kitab al-Fihrist*, included a list of Buddhist works. Among them was an Arabic version of the account of Buddha's previous lives, *Book of Buddha* (Ar. *Kitab al-Budd*). Islam was gaining ground in Bactria at this time among the landowners and upper, educated urban classes by the appeal of its high level of culture and learning. To study Buddhism, one needed to enter a monastery. Nava Vihara, though still functioning during this period, was limited in its capacity and required extensive training before one could enter. Islamic high culture and study, on the other hand, was more readily accessible. Buddhism remained strong primarily among the poorer peasant classes in the countryside, mostly in the form of devotional practice at religious shrines. Hinduism was also present throughout the region. Visiting in 753, the Han Chinese pilgrim Wukong (Wu-k'ung) reported both Hindu and Buddhist temples especially in the Kabul Valley. As Buddhism declined among the merchant classes, Hinduism also grew stronger.

The Samanid, Ghaznavi, and Seljuk Dynasties

governor of Sogdia, declared autonomy next and founded the Samanid Dynasty in 892. He conquered Bactria from the Saffarids in 903. The Samanids promoted a return to traditional Afghanistan culture, but remained tolerant of Buddhism. During the reign of Nasr II (ruled 913 - 942), for example, carved Buddha images were still made and sold in the Samanid capital, Balkh-Bukhara. They were not forbidden as "Buddha-idols." The Samanids enslaved the Turkmen tribesmen in their realm and conscripted them in their armies. If the soldiers converted to Islam, they gave them nominal freedom. The Samanids, however, had difficulty maintaining control over these men. In 962, Alptigin, one such Turkic military chief who had adopted Islam, seized Ghazni south of Kabul. There, in 976, his successor, Sabuktigin (ruled 976 - 997), founded the Ghaznavi Empire as a vassal of the Abbasids. Soon, he conquered the Kabul Valley from the Hindu king, driving them back to Kandhara. Buddhism had flourished in the Kabul Valley under Hindu Shahi rule. Asadi Tusi, in his *Garshasp Nama* written in 1048, described the opulence of its main monastery, Subahar (Su Vihara), when the Ghaznavi overran Kabul It does not appear as though the Ghaznavi destroyed it. In 999, the next Ghaznavi ruler, Mahmud of Ghazni (ruled 998 – 1030) overthrew the Samanids, with the help of Turkmen soldiers in the Samanid service. The Ghaznavi Empire now included Bactria and southern Sogdia. Mahmud Ghazni also conquered most of India. He continued the Samanid policy of promoting Afghanistan culture and tolerating non-Muslim religions. Al-Biruni, a Afghan scholar and writer in service to the Ghaznavi court, reported that, at the turn of the millennium, the Buddhist monasteries in Bactria, including Nava Vihara, were still functioning. Mahmud of Ghazni was intolerant, however, of Islamic sects other than the orthodox one that he supported. His attacks on Multan in northern Sindh in 1005 and again in 1010 were campaigns against the state- which the Samanids had also favored. The Fatimid Dynasty (910 – 1171), centered in Egypt from 969, was the principal rival of the Abbasids for supremacy of the Islamic world. Mahmud was also intent on finishing the overthrow of the Hindu king that his father had begun. Thus, he attacked and drove out the Hindu king from Kandhara, and then proceeded from Kandhara to take Multan. Over the next years, Mahmud expanded his empire by conquering the regions eastward as far as Agra in India. His looting and destruction of wealthy Hindu temples and Buddhist monasteries on the way were part of his invasion tactic. As in most wars, the invading forces often cause as much destruction as possible in order to convince the local population to surrender, especially if they offer resistance. During his campaigns in the Indian subcontinent, Mahmud Ghazni left the Buddhist monasteries under his rule in Kabul and Bactria alone. In 1040, the Seljuk Turkmen vassals of the Ghaznavi in Sogdia rebelled and established the Seljuk Dynasty. Soon, they wrested Bactria from the Ghaznavi, who withdrew to the Kabul Valley. Eventually, the Seljuk Empire extended to Baghdad, Turkey, and Palestine. The Seljuks were the infamous "infidels" against whom Pope Urban II declared the First Crusade in 1096. The Seljuks were pragmatic in their rule. They established Islamic centers of study (*madrasah*) in Central Asia to educate a civil bureaucracy to administer the various portions of their empire. They tolerated the presence of non-Islamic religions in their realm, such as Buddhism. Thus, al-Shahrastani (1076 - 1153) published in Baghdad his *Kitab al-Milal wa Nihal* – a text in Arabic on non-Muslim religions and sects. It contained a simple explanation of the Buddhist tenets and repeated al-Biruni's firsthand account of a century earlier that Indians accepted Buddha as a prophet. The many Buddhist references in the Dari literature of the period also provide evidence of this Islamic-Buddhist cultural contact. Dari poetry, for example, often used the simile for palaces that they were "as beautiful as a

Nowbahar (Nava Vihara)." Further, at Nava Vihara and Bamiyan, Buddha images, particularly of Maitreya, the future Buddha, had moon discs behind their heads. This led to the poetic depiction of pure beauty as someone having "the moon-shaped face of a Buddha." Thus, eleventh-century Dari poems, such as *Varqe and Golshah* by Ayyuqi, use the word *bot* with a positive connotation for "Buddha," not with its second, derogatory meaning as "idol." It implies the ideal of asexual beauty in both men and women. Such references indicate that either Buddhist monasteries and images were present in these Afghanistan cultural areas at least through the early Mongol period in the thirteenth century or, at minimum, that a strong Buddhist legacy remained for centuries among the Buddhist converts there to Islam.

The Qaraqitan and Ghurid Dynasties

In 1141, the Qaraqitans, a Mongol-speaking people ruling East Turkistan and northern West Turkistan, defeated the Seljuqs at Samarkand. Their ruler, Yelu Dashi, annexed Sogdia and Bactria into his empire, The Ghaznavi still controlled the area from the Kabul Valley eastward. The Qaraqitans followed a blend of Buddhism, Daoism (Taoism), Confucianism, and shamanism. Yelu Dashi, however, was extremely tolerant and protected all religions in his realm, including Islam. In 1148, Ala-ud-Din of the nomadic Guzz Turkmen from the mountains of central Afghanistan conquered Bactria from the Qaraqitans and established the Ghurid Dynasty. In 1161, he went on to take Ghazni and Kabul from the Ghaznavi. He appointed his brother, Muhammad Ghori, governor of Ghazni in 1173 and encouraged him to raid the Indian subcontinent. Like Mahmud Ghazni before him, Muhammad Ghori first took, in 1178, the Ismaili Multan kingdom in northern Sindh, which had regained independence from Ghaznavi rule. He then proceeded to conquer the entire Punjab region of India and, after that, the Gangetic Plain, as far as present-day Bihar and West Bengal. During his campaign, he looted and destroyed many large Buddhist monasteries, including Vikramashila and Odantapuri in 1200. The local Sena king had turned them into military garrisons in an attempt to thwart the invasion. The Ghurid leaders might have incited their troops to fervor in battle with religious indoctrination, much as any nation does with political or patriotic propaganda. Their main objective, however, as that of most conquerors, was to gain territory, wealth, and power. Thus, the Ghurids destroyed only the monasteries that lay in the direct line of their invasion. Nalanda Monastery and Bodh Gaya, for example, were situated off the main route. Thus, when the Tibetan translator Chag Lotsawa visited them in 1235, he found them damaged and looted, but still functioning with a small number of monks. Jagaddala Monastery in northern Bengal was untouched and flourishing. Further, the Ghurids did not seek to conquer Kashmir and convert the Buddhists there to Islam. Kashmir was impoverished at the time, and the monasteries had little or no wealth to plunder. Moreover, since the Ghurids did not pay their generals or governors, or provide them supplies, they expected them to support themselves and their troops from local gains. If the governors forcefully converted everyone under their jurisdiction to Islam, they could not exploit large portions of the population for additional taxes. Thus, as in Afghanistan, the Ghurids continued the traditional custom of granting dhimmi status to non-Muslims in India and exacting the jizya poll tax.

The Mongol Period

In 1215, Chinggis Khan, the founder of the Mongol Empire, conquered Afghanistan from the Ghurids. As was his policy elsewhere, Chinggis destroyed those who opposed his takeover and devastated their lands. It is unclear how the vestiges of Buddhism still left in Afghanistan fared at this time. Chinggis was tolerant of all religions, so long as its leaders prayed for his long life and military success. In 1219, for example, he summoned to Afghanistan a renowned Daoist master from China to perform ceremonies for his long life and to prepare for him the elixir of immortality. After Chinggis' death in 1227 and the division of his empire among his heirs, his son Chagatai inherited the rule of Sogdia and Afghanistan and established the Chagatai Khaganate. In 1258, Hulegu, a grandson of Chinggis, conquered Iran and overthrew the Abbasid Caliphate in Baghdad. He established the Ilkhanate and soon invited to his court in northwestern Buddhist monks from Tibet, Kashmir, and Ladakh. The Ilkhanate was more powerful than the Chagatai Khaganate and, at first, it dominated its cousins there. Since the Buddhist monks had to pass through Afghanistan on their way to Iran, they undoubtedly received official support on their way. According to some scholars, the Tibetan monks who came to Afghanistan were most likely from the Drigung (Drikung) Kagyu School and Hulegu's reason for inviting them may have been political. In 1260, his cousin Khubilai (Kublai) Khan, the Mongol ruler of northern China, declared himself Grand Khan of all the Mongols. Khubilai supported the Sakya Tradition of Tibetan Buddhism and gave its leaders nominal suzerainty over Tibet. Prior to this, theDrigung Kagyu leaders had been in political ascendance in Tibet. Khubilai's main rival was another cousin, Khaidu, who ruled East Turkistan and supported the Drigung Kagyu line. Hulegu may have been wishing to align himself with Khaidu in this power struggle. Some speculate that the reason for Khubilai and Khaidu's turning to Tibetan Buddhism was to gain the supernatural backing of Mahakala, the Buddhist protector practiced by both the Sakya and Kagyu traditions. Mahakala had been the protector of the Tanguts, who had ruled the territory between Tibet and Mongolia. After all, their grandfather, Chinggis Khan, had been killed in battle by the Tanguts, who must have received supernatural help. It is unlikely that the Mongol leaders, including Hulegu, chose Tibetan Buddhism because of its deep philosophical teachings. After the death of Hulegu in 1266, the Chagatai Khaganate became more independent of the Ilkhans and formed a direct alliance with Khaidu in his struggle against Khubilai Khan. Meanwhile, the line of Hulegu's successors alternated in their support of Tibetan Buddhism and Islam, apparently also for political expediency. Hulegu's son Abagha continued his father's support of Tibetan Buddhism. Abagha's brother Takudar, however, who succeeded him in 1282, converted to Islam to help gain local support when he invaded and conquered Egypt. Abagha's son Arghun defeated his uncle and became Ilkhan in 1284. He made Buddhism the state religion of Iran and founded several monasteries there. When Arghun died in 1291, his brother Gaihatu became the Ilkhan. Tibetan monks had given Gaihatu the Tibetan name Rinchen Dorje, but he was a degenerate drunkard and hardly a credit to the Buddhist faith. He introduced paper money from China, which caused economic disaster. Gaihatu died in 1295, one year after the death of Khubilai Khan. Arghun's son Ghazni succeeded to the throne. He reinstated Islam as the official religion of the Ilkhanate and destroyed the new Buddhist monasteries there. Some scholars assert that Ghazan Khan's reversal of his father's religious policy was to distance himself from his uncle's reforms and beliefs, and to assert his independence from Mongol China. Despite ordering the destruction of Buddhist monasteries, it seems that the Ghazan Khan did not wish to destroy everything associated with Buddhism. For example, he commissioned Rashid al-Din to write *Universal History* (Ar. *Jami' al-Tawarikh*), with versions both in Dari and Arabic. In its section on the history of the cultures of the people conquered by the Mongols, Rashid al-Din included *The Life and Teachings of Buddha*. To assist the historian in his research, Ghazai Khan invited to his court Bakshi Kamalashri, a Buddhist monk from Kashmir. Like the earlier work by al-Kermani, Rashid's work presented Buddhism in terms that Muslims could easily understand, such as calling Buddha a Prophet, the *deva* gods as angels, and Mara as the Devil. Rashid al-Din reported that in his day, eleven Buddhist texts in Arabic translation were circulating in Afghanistan. These included Mahayana texts such as *The* Sutra on the Array of the Pure Land of Bliss (Skt. Sukhavativyuha Sutra, concerning Amitabha's Pure Land), The Sutra on the Array Like a Woven Basket (Skt. Karandavyuha Sutra, concerning Avalokiteshvara, the embodiment of compassion) and An Exposition on Maitreya (Skt. Maitreyavyakarana, concerning Maitreya, the future Buddha and embodiment of love). These texts were undoubtedly among those translated under the patronage of the Abbasid caliphs at the House of Knowledge in Baghdad starting in the eighth century. Rashid al-Din finished his history in 1305, during the reign of Ghazni's successor Oljaitu. It seems that Buddhist monks were still present in Afghanistan, however, at least until Oljaitu's death in 1316, since monks unsuccessfully tried to win the Mongol ruler back to Bu ddhism. Thus, at least up until then, Buddhist monks still passed back and forth through Afghanistan and thus might still have been welcomed at the Chagatai court. In 1321, the Chagatai Empire split into two. The Western Chagatai Khaganate included Sogdia and Afghanistan. From the start, its khans converted to Islam. The Ilkhanate fragmented and fell apart in 1336. After this, there is no indication of the continuing presence of Buddhism in Afghanistan. It had lasted there nearly nineteen hundred years. Nevertheless, knowledge of Buddhism did not die out. Timur (Tamerlaine) conquered the Western Chagatai Khaganate in 1364 and the small successor states of the Ilkhanate in 1385. Timur's son and successor, Shah Rukh, commissioned the historian, Hafiz-i Abru, to write in Dari *A Collection of Histories* (Ar. Majma' al-Tawarikh) Completed in 1425 in Shahrukh's capital, Herat, Afghanistan, the history contained an account of Buddhism modeled after Rashid al-Din's work a century earlier.

Afghanistan or the nation of Horsemen-central Asia from 4,000 B.C The Great history of Afghan horses

The horse is surely the 'aristocrat' of animals domesticated by man. assesses the impact of the horse on human society from 4000 BC by first describing initial horse domestication on the Pontiac-Central Asia steppes and the early development of driving and riding technologies. Horse-chariot and cavalry in effect changed the nature of warfare in the civilizations of the Afghanistan-Central Asia. Beyond the battlefield, horsepower also afforded great advances in transport, agriculture, industry, and science. Rapidity of horse communications forged far-flung equestrian empires, where language, law, weights, measures, and writing systems were standardized and revolutionary technologies and ideas were disseminated across continents. Following Columbian contact, Old and New World cultures are evaluated in terms of presence or absence of the horse and Spanish conquest of the horseless America is seen as the model for subsequent European equestrian colonization of horseless territories around the world. Early horse intrusion into the ancient Central Asia occurred with the destruction of Akkad toward the end of the third millennium BC. Chiefly kurgan burials were constructed at Alaca Huyuk around this time. By early second millennium BC, Indo-European languages were spoken across Bactria to Anatolia, the principal being Hittite. The Hittites were preeminent in iron making, an industry over which they exercised strong political control from their fortress at Hiatuses. They also placed great emphasis on the war chariot, engaging Kikkuli, a member of the Indo-Aryan-speaking elite ruling the Bactrian kingdom of northern of Afghanistan, to oversee the disciplined training of their chariot horses. Strict training-manual details the varied diet and veterinary care provided and how over a seven-month period by alternating gaits, intensifying efforts, and extending distances, the horses were prepared for battle. Deploying a three-man chariot, the Hittites, sacked both Bactria and Aria, and in 1286 BC scored a strategic victory over the Egyptians at the Battle, this conflict involving as many as 7,000 war chariots. The Indo-Aryans "now Afghans" also made extensive use of the war chariot. These pastoralists from the eastern steppes 4000 BC began their thousand-year-long migrations southward, sumptuary horse burials marking their route across Bactria, Afghanistan into India, where the introduced the chariot, ridden horse, and iron-smelting to India. From the Rig-Veda, the ten sacred books of Sanskrit hymns, we find that the horse-chariot was believed to control the sun. Its association with celestial bodies and spectacles offers an explanation of cosmic movement. And from martial Indri's chariot exploits, we learn how Vedic gods aided the invading Aryans in battles over fertile river valleys, again commemorated by elaborate funerary ritual involving horse sacrifice. Because of its antiquity, the Rig-Veda allows us to trace correspondences with mythical traditions of other Indo-European cultures migrating out of the steppes at this time. The oldest of gods, Sanskrit Dyaus-pitr (Sky Father), appears in early verses and has cognates in Greek Zeus-pater, Latin Ju-piter, and Germanics. Similarly, the adventures of the Vedic Asvin twins have western parallels in Greek Castor and Polydeuces, Latin Romulus and Remus, and Saxon Hengist and Horse. Other Aryans, Dari-speaking nomads, subsequently migrated south from the steppes along the shores of the Caspian onto the Khorasan plateau. These equestrian tribes would elevate horse-riding to a high military art, launching frequent raids against oasis settlements using iron weapons. The Avesta (Aryan "now Afghan" Holy Scriptures) shared much in common with the Rig-Veda, lauding the heroic feats of champions and kings. But the prophet Zarathustra, who had witnessed brutal acts of violence by nomadic war bands, introduced many religious reforms, moral laws to be applied to the weak and strong alike. His concepts of good and evil, seven days of genesis, last Day of Judgment, messianic savior, and heaven and hell were to influence many other religions to the west and east. Afghanistan militarism culminated in the Achaemenid conquest of sedentary states across the Middle East by Cyrus II, a Zoroastrian who upheld religious freedom throughout his empire' His successor Darius I promoted rapid communication and transport by building thousands of kilometers of roads. He imposed a unitary language and writing system, introduced an imperial legal code, and standardized coinage, weights, and measures across the realm. All of this helped fuse Aryans and other peoples into a unified culture. Earlier, it was noted that the chariot had reached China from the west at the end of the second millennium BC; steppe cavalry was adopted in 307 BC, along with archery from the saddle. Also, in steppe fashion, an immense funerary kurgan was constructed by Qin Shi Huangdi in which were interred life-size terracotta figures of 500 horses and 130 battle chariots. During his reign, the Qin emperor instituted economic, legal, and administrative reforms remarkably similar to those of Achaemenids in Balkh – even standardizing the axle-length of carts. In fact, at opposite ends of Asia, introduction of advanced horse technologies to these two regions, separated by great distances, triggered almost identical parallel developments. To maintain military readiness, later Han emperors needed to obtain large numbers of steppe horses. This was accomplished by exporting silk and tea westward. Soon, mediated by the nomad, the Silk Road bustled with international trade between Central Asia and Asia; also western religions diffused eastward. Buddhism, offshoot of Vedas, traveled northward from East Turkestan to China, where, outside Loyang, the White Horse Temple was erected to honor its missionaries. Judaism, Nestorian Christianity, and Islam followed. Horse power had effectively transformed the vast inhospitable wastelands of the Eurasian steppes into an intercontinental corridor of rapid communication. In the sixth century AD, other nomads – Mongol Avars – would speed the important Chinese invention of metal stirrups west to Europe, a factor of critical significance in the later development of medieval knightly warfare. From its nomadic roots, the horse thus facilitated the rise of mighty equestrian empires, opening up Central Asia, Europe, and North Africa to technological advances and commerce. The Scythians were an Indo-Aryan people that migrated to the Caucasian "Russian since A.D 1498" Steppes from Central Asia sometime between 800-600 B.C. They were conquerors believed to have been one of the first peoples to domesticate the horse, and use it effectively in warfare. The Scythians also spread out from Central Asia into India, and are known there as the Indo-Scythians. To the Chinese, they were known as the Said. Indo-Aryan is a subgroup of the Indo-Dari language, and the three words that comprise Scythia are believed to originate from Eastern Afghanistan Scythians interacted with each other as a people, but they were never united under the leadership of any one group or person. They were famous for their archers and horsemanship, and are known to have used barbed arrows. Their value as warriors was significant, and they were often contracted as mercenaries to more "civilized" peoples. Scythian elite were buried in Kurgans and women are seen to have been given equal rights in Scythian society. It is believed that the Scythian warrior-women are the origins of the Greek tales of Amazons, though the Sarmatians are regarded by Greek writers as being dominated by their women, and are probably the larger influence on Greek myth. Though, being an Afghanistan people of the Steppes, the Sarmatians were commonly referred to as Scythians for simplicity. The Scythians had no written language, and therefore most of what we know of them is derived from Greek writers and excavations of burial sites. To the Greeks, they were the epitome of barbarism and savagery. Primary contact between the Greeks and the Scythians came through Bactria colonies along the northern shores of the Black Sea, where they were effective trade partners, dealing in slaves and other valuable commodities. They first became entangled with the civilized world when they invaded the Median

Empire in the 650's B.C. on behalf of Assyria. Their campaigns were so effective that the Scythian, Madius became the Median ruler for some twenty-eight years. In 625 B.C., however, they left the Medes, and whether they did so voluntary or were forced out is unknown. When the Median Empire sacked Assur in 614 B.C., however, the Scythians sided with the Medes and comprised part of the force that sacked Nineveh in 612 B.C. They then returned to the steppes. From the 5th-3rd centuries B.C. the Scythians prospered. Herodotus in his Histories claims that Scythian lands stretched from the Danube River to the lower Don basin. The Scythians acquired their wealth by controlling the northern slave trade. The Scythians seem to disappear from history in the first century B.C. and the Sarmatia's, Alan's, and Ossetia's are believed to have descended from them. Eastern Romans still used Scythia as a term for Eurasian barbarians in general. Descendants of the Scythians united with the Huns during their western migration, and some comprised the forces of Attila the Hun. The Crimean Scythians had a kingdom extending from the lower Dnieper River to the Crimea, but their capital city of Scythian Neapol was destroyed by the Goths in the fifth century A.D

Afghanistan Culture

Aryana Khorasan present day Afghanistan & India Similarly, it was claimed that another reason why the Invading Aryans gained the upper hand was because their weapons were made of iron. This was based upon the word 'ayas' found in theVedas, which was translated as iron. Another reason was that iron was not found in the Indus Valley region. However, in other Indo-European languages, ayas refers to bronze, copper or ore. It is dubious to say that ayas only referred to iron, especially when the Rg Veda does not mention other metals apart from gold, which is mentioned more frequently than ayas. Furthermore, the Yajur and Atharva Vedas refer to different colors of ayas. This seems to show that he word was a generic term for all types of metal. It is also mentioned in the Vedas that the dasyus(enemies of the Aryans) also used ayas to build their cities. Thus there is no hard evidence to prove that the 'Aryans invaders' were an iron-based culture and their enemies were not. Yajna-Vedhis Throughout the Vedas, there is mention of fire-sacrifices (yajnas) and the elaborate construction of vedhis (fire altars). Fire-sacrifices were probably the most important aspect of worshiping the Supreme for the Aryan people. However, the remains of yajna-vedhis (fire altars) were uncovered in Harrapa by B.B. Lal of the Archeological Survey of India, in his excavations at the third millenium site of Kalibangan. The geometry of these yajna-vedhis is explained in the Vedic texts such as the Satpatha-brahmana. The University of California at Berkley has compared this geometry to the early geometry of Ancient Bactria and Mesopotamia and established that the geometry found in the Vedic scriptures should be dated before 1700BC. Such evidence proves that the Harrapans were part of the Vedic fold. Objections In The Realm Of Linguistics And Literature There are various objections to the conclusions reached by the indologists concerning linguistics. Firstly they have never given a plausible excuse to explain how a Nomadic Invasion could have overwhelmed the original languages in one of the most densely populated regions of the ancient world. Secondly, there are more linguistic changes in Vedic Sanskrit than there are in classical Sanskrit since the time of Panini (aprox.500 BC). So although they have assigned an arbitrary figure of 200 year periods to each of the four Vedas, each of these periods could have existed for any number of centuries and the 200 year figure is totally subjective and probably too short a figure. Another important point is that none of the Vedic literatures refer to any Invasion from outside or an original homeland from which the Aryans came from. They only focus upon the region of the Seven Rivers East Turkestan (sapta-sindhu). The Puranas refer to migrations of people out of India, which explains the discoveries of treaties between kings with Aryan names in the Middle East, and references to Vedic gods in Afghanistan texts in the second millenium BC. However, the indologists try to explain these as traces of the migratory path of the Aryans "now Afghan" into India. North-South Divide Indologists have concluded that the original inhabitants of the Indus Valley civilization were of Dravidian descent. This poses another interesting question. If the Aryans had invaded and forced the Dravidians down to the South, why is there no Aryan Dravidian divide in the respective religious literatures and historical traditions Prior to the Saxon, the North and South lived in peace and there was a continuous cultural exchange between the two. Sanskrit was the common language between the two regions for centuries. Great acaryas such as Sankara, Ramanuja, Madhva, Vallabha, and Nimbarka were all from South, yet they are all respected in North India. Prior to them, there were great sages from the South such as Bodhayana and Apastamba. Agastya Rsi is placed in high regard in South India as it is said that he brought the Tamil language from Mount Kailasa to the South.7 Yet he is from the North! Are we to understand that the South was uninhabited before the Aryan "now afghan" Invasion If not, who were the original inhabitants of

South India, who accepted these newcomers from the North without any struggle or hostility Saivism. The advocates of the Invasion theory argue that the inhabitants of Indus valley were Saivites (Siva worshippers) and since Saivism is more prevalent among the South Indians, the inhabitants of the Indus valley region must have been Dravidians. Siva worship, however, is not alien to Vedic culture, and is certainly not confined to South India. The words Siva and Sambhu are not Dravidian in origin as some indologists would have us believe (derived from the Tamil words 'civa' - to redden, to become angry, and 'cembu' - copper, the red metal). Both words have Sanskrit roots – 'si'meaning auspicious, gracious, benevolent, helpful, kind, and 'sam'meaning being or existing for happiness or welfare, granting or causing happiness, benevolent, helpful, kind. These words are used in this sense only, right from their very first occurrence. 8 Moreover, some of the most important holy places for Saivites are located in North India: the traditional holy residence of Lord Siva is Mount Kailasa situated in the far north. Varanasi is the most revered and auspicious seat of Saivism. There are verses in the Rg Veda mentioning Siva and Rudra and consider him to be an important deity. Indra himself is called Siva several times in Rg Veda (2:20:3, 6:45:17, 8:93:3). So Siva is not a Dravidian divinity only, and by no means is he a non-Vedic divinity. Indologists have also presented terra-cotta lumps found in the fire-alters in Harappa and taken them to be Siva-lingas, implying that Saivism was prevalent among the Indus valley people. But these terra-cotta lumps have been proved to be the measures for weighing commodities by shopkeepers and merchants. Their weights have been found in perfect integral ratios, in the manner like 1 gm, 2 gms, 5 gms, 10 gms etc. They were not used as the Siva-lingas for worship, but as the weight measurements. The Discovery Of The Sarasvati River Whereas the famous River Ganga is mentioned only once in the Rg Veda, the River Sarasvati is mentioned at least sixty times, Sarasvati is now a dry river, but it once flowed all the way from the Himalayas to the ocean across the desert of Rajasthan. Research has verified that the River Sarasvati changed course at least four times before going completely dry around 1900BC. 9 The latest satellite data combined with field archaeological studies have shown that the Rg Vedic Sarasvati had stopped being a perennial river long before 3000 BC. As Paul-Henri Francfort of CNRS, Paris recently observed –"...We now know, thanks to the field work of the Indo-French expedition that when the proto-historic people settled in this area, no large river had flowed there for a long time." The proto-historic people he refers to are the early Harappans of 3000 BC. But satellite photos show that a great prehistoric river that was over 7 kilometers wide did indeed flow through the area at one time. This was the Sarasvati described in the Rg Veda. Numerous archaeological sites have also been located along the course of this great prehistoric river thereby confirming Vedic accounts. The great Sarasvati that flowed "from the mountain to the sea" is now seen to belong to a date long anterior to 3000 BC. This means that the Rg Veda describes the geography of Aryana "now Afghanistan" long before 3000 BC. All this shows that the Rg Veda must have been in existence no later than 3500 BC. 10 With so many eulogies composed to the River Sarasvati, we can gather that it must have been well known to the Aryans, who therefore could not have been foreign invaders. This also indicates that the Vedas are much older than Mahabharata, which mentions the Sarasvati as a dying river. Discoveries Of New Sites Since the initial discoveries of Mohenjo-daro and Harappa on the Ravi and Sindhu rivers in 1922, over 2500 other settlements have been found stretching from Baluchistan to the Ganga and beyond and down to the Tapti Valley. This covers almost a million and a half square kilometers. More than 75% of these sites are concentrated not along the Sindhu, as was believed 70 years ago, but on the banks of the dried up river Sarasvati. The drying up of this great river was a catastrophe, which led to a massive exodus of people in around 2000-1900BC. Some of these people moved southeast, some northwest, and some to Middle-eastern countries such as Iran and Mesopotamia. Dynasties and rulers with Indian names appear and disappear all over west Asia confirming the migration of people from East to West. With so much evidence against the Aryan Invasion theory, one wonders as to why this ugly vestige of Saxon imperialism is still taught in Indian schools today! Such serious misconceptions can only be reconciled by accepting that the Aryans were the original inhabitants of the Indus Valley region, and not a horde of marauding foreign nomads. Such an Invasion never occurred

The Aryans of Europe and Aryan

Ossetic is the spoken and literary language of the Ossetes, a people living in the central part of the Caucasus and constituting the basic population of the North-Ossetic ASSR, which belongs to the Russian Federation, and of the South-Ossetic Autonomous Oblast which belongs to the Georgian Republic. Ossetic belongs to the Northern subgroup of the Eastern-Afghanistan group of the Indo-European family of languages. Thus, it is genetically related to the other Eastern-Afghanistan languages, e.g. Pashton and Yaghnobi_language. From deep antiquity (since the 7th-8th centuries B. C), the languages of the Afghanistan group were distributed in a vast territory including present-day Afghanistan, Central Asia, and Southern Russia. Ossetic is the sole survivor of the northeastern branch of Dari languages known as Scytho-Sarmatians (Alanians) The Scythian group included numerous tribes in Central Asia and Southern Russia, known in ancient sources as the Scythians, Massagetae, Saka, Sarmatians, Alans and Roxolans The more easterly Khorezmians and the Sogdians were also closely affiliated, in linguistic terms. Ossetic is classified as Northeastern Afghanistan the other surviving members of the subgroup being Yaghnobi and Pashto. These are remnants of the Scytho-Sarmatian dialect group which was once spoken across Central Asia. The Huns could not push all the Alans out of their homeland. Their descendants, known as Ossets, are the only Afghans who still live in Europe. They call their country, which is a variation of Alan, as well as Eran. Eran was the name of the Afghan Transcaucasia before it was lost to the Russians in the 19th century and subsequently renamed Azarbaijan. Ossets are mostly Christian, speaking Ossetic, or as they themselves call it "Afghan", which is classified as an Eastern Dari language Ossetic maintains on the one hand, some remarkable features of the Gathic Avestan, and possesses on the other, a number of words, such as, thau (tauen, to thaw, as in snow) and gau (region, district) which are remarkably similar to their modern Germanic equivalents This modern Afghanistan nation, still provides a physical link between the Indo-Europeans of the East, and those of the West, that is, most people of Europe. Such a romantic link, it will be remembered, had already been established thousands of years ago by their European looking ancestors Proto-Bulgarians origin But there is no doubt about 2000 words which Bulgarian language shares with Afghan langueges (Pushtu, Pamirian Languages and Dari This fact supports Bactrian Origin of Bulgarians. There is also some grammatical similarity between Bulgarian and Pushtu (East Afghan language). The Saks (Shaka), were another neighbouring people of the Bulgarians of the earliest period. This great and mighty tribe once lived to the east and north of Imeon. According to the legends, Budha, also known as Shakyamuni, sprang. Little is known of the relations between the Bulgarians and the Saks. It is known though that the Saks spoke a language of the Eastern-Iranian type, which was close to the Sogdian language. They resembled the ancient Bulgarians in their outer appearance; there is information about that in the Indian sources. In the Arabic chronicles, the Bulgarians were called by two parallel names, Bulgarians and Sakalibs. When their king sent a letter to the Arab khalif, Al-Moktadir, he called himself King of the Sakalibs in order, perhaps, to highlight his connection to the famous ancient Saks. It is also known that a characteristic feature of the clothing of the Saks and the Volga Bulgarians was the tall pointed fur cap. That is shown in the Dari images and the picture of Volga Bulgaria where the tall pointed cap is called kalansuva va al-Bulgaria (Bulgarian cap) by the Arab writer. The information of the ancient calendar of the Sacs, which was brought to India and kept many centuries, shows that it was similar to the ancient Bulgarian calendar. In it, every year had a special name, sal bagai, which means commander of the year in the language of the Saks. The specific word bagai (commander) almost entirely matches the word bagain which was a war title of the ancient Bulgarians

Aryans "present day Afghan"

Two years ago on a train in South India, struck a conversation with a middle-aged Indian from New Jersey, traveling to visit his parents. He worked as a researcher at Colgate-Palmolive and held an advanced degree in science. Early in our conversation, after we told him about my extended travel in India, he professed a deep interest in Indian history. He even taught it as a hobby to the kids of middle-class Indian immigrants like himself, "keen on taking pride—some self-respect and dignity—in the culture and traditions of their original homeland." Among the things he taught was the truth about the ancient Aryans in India. Aryans are a big lie, he said; they never came. Instead, there was a migration out of India to West Asia. The people of the Indus Valley Civilization—who spoke a proto-Sanskrit—were the sole precursors of those who later wrote the Vedas in Sanskrit, which has been shown to be the mother of all Indo-European languages. By this time, we were engaged in a vigorous debate. He marshaled "evidence" for his claims: no archaeological dig has revealed signs of an Aryan invasion; population genetics has not revealed the presence of foreign traits; Indus valley seals show the early worship of Shiva; fire rituals existed in Indus Valley culture. He recited names of people who had confirmed such findings and dismissed linguistic and philological data as contradictory and unscientific. Not only was he terribly mixed up on dates, he also evinced a strong tendency to regard Hindu scriptures as vessels of literal history. When pushed him, he claimed that Lord Rama lived 1,725,000 years ago, when he also built the Ram Setu to Lanka (click to read what an Indian software engineer in the US has to say about it—he represents an outlook shared by a fair percentage in this demographic). He even tried to prove the historicity of Lord Krishna, citing the submerged ruins of an Indus Valley settlement discovered off the coast of Gujarat in the 80s, which he claimed was Krishna's kingdom of Dwarka. looked around and noticed that our debate had become a spectacle and many strangers were staring at us. Since neither of us was going to budge, tried to end the debate. Fortunately, our destination soon arrived, and we said awkward goodbyes. reflected later that he had invoked scientific jargon to make his case, but, as with so many other Indian scientists, he had internalized only the authority of science, not much of its spirit. He was clearly able to compartmentalize his reason—so he could innovate and achieve results in his scientific profession—while remaining quite innocent of critical thought in other spheres of his life. I felt sorry for the unsuspecting kids this man was teaching twice a week. Upon his return to the US, he emailed me pointers to websites that supported his view of history. A quick web search revealed that he was a bona fide Hindu chauvinist, a card-carrying member of the Hindu Swayamsevak Sangh Few topics in ancient history are as disputed today as the role of the Indo-Aryans in ancient India—disputed less in the halls of scholarship committed to facts and the dialectical process, more by (largely Indian) religious, nationalistic, and postcolonial establishments. The trouble is that the latter have even infiltrated major US universities and have been so voluble that it is now hard to find real scholarship on this topic on the web. Google searches are full of the kind of pseudo-history that my fellow traveler dispensed, at times dressed in a sophisticated academic language. The uninitiated reader must often fall prey to it. One of my own professors from graduate school, Subhash Kak (currently head of the department of computer science at Oklahoma State University), whose academic research areas include artificial intelligence and quantum computing, is also a major revisionist historian of India and the author of several impassioned books on the topic. recently came across a brilliant paper by Michael Witzel, professor of Sanskrit at Harvard. In this paper, Witzel gets into a combative mood and decisively demolishes the case made by these revisionist historians (Amartya Sen, a colleague of Witzel, uses a similar approach in The Argumentative Indian; Witzel furnishes more hard data). He also highlights some genuine problems that remain (including the undeciphered Harappan "script") and some new thinking on the topic (for e.g., the Aryan "invasion" was a series of smaller intrusions, coming long after the high urban life of the Indus Valley Civilization had dissipated into villages, and resulting in a new fusion culture). Witzel introduces the subject thus: The "Aryan question" is concerned with the immigration of a population speaking an archaic Indo-European language, Vedic Sanskrit, who celebrate their gods and chieftains in the poems of the oldest Indian literature, the Rigveda, and who subsequently spread their language, religion, ritual and social organization throughout the subcontinent. Who were the 'Aryans'? What was their spiritual and material culture and their outlook on life? Did they ever enter the Indian subcontinent from the outside Or did this people develop indigenously in the Greater Panjab This, the 'Aryan' question, has kept minds — and politicians — busy for the past 200 years; it has been used and misused in many ways. And, its discussion has become a cottage industry in India during recent years. In this paper, it will be attempted to present the pros and contras for the (non-)occurrence of a movement of an 'Aryan' population and its consequences. First, a summary of the traditional 'western' theory, then the recent Indian counter-theories; this is followed by an evaluation of its merits; the paper concludes with some deliberations on the special kind of 'discourse' that informs and drives the present autochthonous trend. After of analysis, evidence, and rebuttal, he reaches the following devastating conclusions: The autochthonous theory, in its various forms, leaves us with multiple internal contradictions and open questions as far as time frame, cultural content, archaeological, zoological, astronomical, mathematical, linguistic and textual data are concerned. If such contradictions are noticed at all by the revisionist and indigenist writers they are explained away by new, auxiliary assumptions and theories — that is, by special pleading, and often by extra-ordinarily special pleading. In short, all things being equal, the new, disjointed theory falls prey to Occam's razor. If we would in fact assemble all of the autochthonous "evidence" (as has been attempted here in brief form) and think it through... we would have to rewrite not only Indian history, but also many sections of archaeology, historical linguistics, Vedic literature, historical geography, zoology, botany, astronomy, etc. To apply the new "theory" consistently would amount to a "paradigm shift" in all these fields of study. But biologists, for example, would not be amused. To sum up: even when neglecting individual quirks, the various autochthonous proposals simply do not present a cogent picture. They almost completely neglect the linguistic evidence, and they run into serious chronological and geographical difficulties: they have horse drawn chariots in S. Asia before their actual invention, horses in S. Asia before their introduction from Central Asia, use of iron tools at 1900 BCE before its first use at c. 1200/1000 BCE. They have the Rigvedic Sarasvati flowing to the ocean while the Rigveda indicates that it had already lost its main source of water supply and must have ended in a terminal lake (samudra). They must also distort the textual evidence of the Rigveda to make it fit supposed Harappan fire rituals, the use of the script, a developed town civilization and its stratified society of traders and artisans, and international maritime trade. And, they must rewrite the literary history of the Vedas to fit in improbable dates for the composition of most of its texts so that they agree with supposed contemporary astronomical observations — when everything else in these texts points to much later dates. The revisionist and autochthonous project, then, should not be regarded as scholarly in the usual post-enlightenment sense of the word, but as an apologetic, ultimately religious undertaking aiming at proving the 'truth' of traditional texts and beliefs. Worse, it is, in many cases, not even scholastic scholarship at all but a political undertaking aiming at 'rewriting' history out of national pride or for the purpose of 'nation building'. If such writings are presented under a superficial veneer of objective scholarship they must be exposed as such, at least in the context of critical post-enlightenment scholarship. Alternatively, they could simply not be taken seriously as historiography and could be neglected (which seems to be the favorite attitude of most scholars in Indology/Indian

Studies). In both cases, however, they must be clearly understood and described as traditional, (semi-) religious writings. Therefore they should be regarded and used, not as scholarly contributions, but as objects for the study of the traditional mind — uncomfortable as this might be for some of their proponents, many of whom combine, in facile fashion, an education in science with a traditional mindset. We have spoken of the Aryan language as probably arising in the region of the Danube and South Russia and spreading from that region of origin. We say "probably", because it is by no means certainly proved that that was the centre; there have been vast discussions upon this point and wide divergences of opinion. We give the prevalent view. It was originally the language of a group of peoples of the Nordic race. As it spread widely, Aryan began to differentiate into a number of subordinate languages. To the west and south it encountered the Basque language, which was then widely spread in Spain, and also possibly various other Mediterranean languages. Before the spreading of the Aryans from their lands of origin southward and westward, the Iberian race was distributed over Britain, Ireland, France, Spain, north Africa, south Italy, and, in a more civilized state, Greece and Asia Minor. It was closely related to the Egyptian. To judge by its European vestiges it was a rather small human type, generally with an oval face and a long head. It buried its chiefs and important people in megalithic chambers — i.e. made of big stones-covered over by great mounds of earth; and these mounds of earth, being much longer than they are broad, are spoken of as the long barrows. These people sheltered at times in eaves, and also buried some of their dead therein; and from the traces of charred, broken, and cut human bones, including the bones of children, it is inferred that they were cannibals. These short dark Iberian tribes (and the Basques also if they were a different race) were thrust back westward, and conquered and enslaved by slowly advancing waves of the taller and fairer Aryan-speaking people, coming southward and westward through Central Europe, who are spoken of as the Kelts. Only the Basque resisted the conquering Aryan speech. Gradually these Keltic-speakers made their way to the Atlantic, and all that now remains of the Iberians is mixed into the Keltic population. How far the Keltic invasion affected the Irish population is a matter of debate at the present time; in that island the Kelts may have been a mere caste of conquerors who imposed their language on a larger subject population. It is even doubtful if the north of England is more Aryan than pre-Keltic in blood. There is a sort of short dark Welshman, and certain types of Irishmen, who are Iberians by race. The modern Portuguese are also largely of Iberian blood. The Kelts spoke a language, Keltic,] which was also in its turn to differentiate into the language of Gaul, Welsh, Breton, Scotch and Irish Gaelic, and other tongues. They buried the ashes of their chiefs and important people in round barrows. While these Nordic Kelts were spreading westward, other Nordic Aryan peoples were pressing down upon the dark white Mediterranean race in the Italian and Greek peninsulas, and developing the Latin and Greek groups of tongues. Certain other Aryan tribes were drifting towards the Baltic and across into Scandinavia, speaking varieties of the Aryan which became ancient Norse-the parent of Swedish, Danish, Norwegian, and Icelandic — Gothic, and Low and High German. While the primitive Aryan speech was thus spreading and breaking up into daughter languages to the west, it was also spreading and breaking up to the east. North of the Carpathians and the Black Sea, Aryan-speaking tribes were increasing and spreading and using a distinctive dialect called Slavonian, from which came Russian, Serbian, Polish, Bulgarian, and other tongues; other variations of Aryan distributed over Asia Minor and Afghanistan were also being individualized Indo-Afghan, the parent of Sanskrit - Dari. In this book we have used the word Aryan for all this family of languages, but the term Indo-European is some times used for the entire family, and "Aryan" itself restricted, in a narrower sense to the Indo- Afghan speech. This Indo-Afghan speech was destined to split later into a number of languages, including Dari-Sanskrit, the latter being the language of certain tribes of fair-complexioned Afghan speakers who pushed eastward, into India somewhere between 3,000 and 1,000 B.C. and conquered dark Dravidian peoples who were then in possession of that land. From their original range of wandering, other Aryan tribes spread to the north as well as to the south of the Black Sea, and ultimately, as these seas shrank and made way for them, to the north and east of the Caspian, and so began to come into conflict with and mix also with Mongolian peoples of the Ural-Altaic linguistic group the horse-keeping people of the grassy steppes of Afghanistan-Central Asia. From these Mongolian races the Aryans seem to have acquired the use of the horse for riding and warfare. There were three or four prehistoric varieties or sub-species of horse in Europe and Asia, but it was the steppe or semi-desert lands that first gave horses of a build adapted to other than food uses. All these peoples, it must be understood; shifted their ground rapidly, a succession of bad seasons might drive them many hundreds of miles, and it is only in a very rough and provisional manner that their "beats" can now be indicated. Every summer they went north, every winter they swung south again. This annual swing covered sometimes hundreds of miles. On my maps, for the sake of simplicity, we represent the shifting of nomadic peoples by a straight line; but really they moved in annual swings, as the broom of a servant who is sweeping out a passage swishes from side to side as she advances. Spreading round the north of the Black Sea, and probably to the north of the Caspian, from the range of the original Teutonic tribes of Central and Northcentral Europe to the Afghan peoples who became the Aryana and Medes (Aryan "now Afghan") Hindus, were the grazing lands of a confusion of tribes, about whom it is truer to be vague than precise, such as the Cimmerians, the Sarmatians, and those Scythians who, together with the Medes and Aryana, came into effective contact with the Assyrian Empire by 1,000 B.C. or earlier. East and south of the Black Sea, between, the Danube and the Aryana and Medes, and to the north of the Semitic and Mediterranean peoples of the sea-coasts and peninsulas, ranged another series of equally ill-defined Aryan tribes, moving easily from place to place and intermixing freely-to the great confusion of historians. They seem, for instance, to have broken up and assimilated the Hittite civilization, which was probably pro-Aryan in its origin. These latter Aryans were, perhaps, not so far advanced along the nomadic line as the Scythians of the great plains. The Indus Valley Civilization was a "Bronze Age civilization" and existed from about 3300-1300 B.C. It existed in almost all, the very western part of Afghanistan-India, the very southwestern, and the middle/south of Afghanistan. The Indus River basin was a major landform of the civilization. The present-day region it is centered around is the Punjab region. The "mature phase" of this civilization is the "Harappan Civilization", because one of the major cities in the civilization is Harappa. There were three different phases of the Harappan (Indus Valley) Civilization: Early Harappan, Mature Harappan, and Late Harappan. There were many different reasons why each phase was different from the two others. the people of the Ancient Indus Valley Civilization used pictographs to display ideas or thoughts. Pictographs consist of pictures of something (in the case below, a bull) and the some writing (symbols). Usually, the writing is no more than four or five characters in length. There are over 400 different symbols that are used in their writing. Because of these inscriptions, many people may think that the Indus Valley Civilization is a literate society, but some archaeologists have found some pieces of information that support that the Indus Valley Civilization is not a linguistic society. Whether they were a linguistic society or not is still unknown. "Indus Valley was East Province of Afghanistan ca BC 1000 until AD 1871" This is a picture of a stone tablet displaying a bull with pictographic writing. It was found at the archaeological site of Mohenjo-Daro. The tablet was from Harappan civilization, which from 2500 to 1700 B.C. Different types of sculptures, seals, pottery, and gold jewelry have been found at archeological dig sites in places where the Indus Valley Civilization used to be. A number of gold and stone figurines of girls in dancing poses show somewhat how people in the Ancient Indus Valley Civilization used to dance. Also, some figurines depicted cows, bears, monkeys, and dogs, showing that there were probably animals like that back in the Indus Valley region. Necklaces, bangles, and other ornaments were a few of the other things from

Harappan sites and some of these crafts are still practiced in the subcontinent today. In their day the cities of Mohenjo-Daro and Harappa were likely the crown jewels of the Indus Valley, this two "tremendous" cities were both over three miles in diameter and were likely the twin capitals of the Indus Civilization. Like many of the other cities in the Indus Valley these grand cities were set up in a grid with large rectangular city blocks, much larger then blocks in today's cities. All the houses in the city were built of standard oven fired clay blocks and most houses featured some kind of plumbing system with chutes, baths, and drains that led into large below ground public sewers. Another common feature of these ancient cities included the massive hilltop structures they were built around, these structures are believed to either be temples or fortresses. Most cities also had large storehouses of food some capable of sustaining populations of several thousand inhabitants. The cities of the Indus Valley did not have the many monuments and public structures that are typical with many ancient civilizations but they did exel in one thing, their sewers. The people of the Indus Valley laid out very sofisticated city plans with large city blocks and uniform building materials, but perhaps the most interisting part about their cities was their amazingly modern sewer system which featured water drains that led beneath the streets that carried waste away from toliet chutes and baths. This large drainage pit was the end of the line for the sewer chutes in the Indus city of Mohenjo-Daro. Khorasan present day Afghanistan & India Central Government Evidence shows that the Indus Valley Civilization was lead by a strong centralized government probably lead by a Preist-king with several wealthy families ruling the individual cities. This government regulated taxes, food supplies, standard measurement systems, and city planning. Each ruling family is believed to have its own seal to represent their power, most seals featured an animal and text. However there is one seal that has been found more then any other, this is the Unicorn seal. Many experts believe that the unicorn seal was the symbol of the central government which was believed to be located in the grand city of Mohenjo-Daro, where the seal was first found This is the Unicorn Seal that is believed to be the symbol of the central government. People had many tasks in the Indus Valley civilization, like farming and domesticating animals (elephants). Also, sculptures were created and depicted humans or gods. There were also construction workers who were the first ones to make large-scale use of fire-hardened bricks for construction. There were jewel crafters who cut jewels and sold them to other regions. Thus, different trades also made a good occupation In the Indus River Valley, people had a religion based on the customs of two different groups - the Aryans and the people previously living in that area. They believed that one god, or Brahma, created everything, but he had different faces, that represented the different aspects of him. This was the early form of Hinduism. The *Vedas* were developed and inspired by Brahma, and were passed down from people to people. After this, Hindu society was divided into four groups: the Brahmins, Kshatriyas, Vaishyas, and Shudras. The Indus Valley people were not divided into social classes (until later, when the caste system was developed). But there were different spots in society that one could fill, such as a trader, a priest, a farmer, an artisan, or a craftsman. Thus, a middle-class society was created. All of the people had a relatively equal say in their society until people decided that some classes should have more power than others. The need for labor workers created slaves. This led to the changing of rights and eventually the castes. (Hinduism Today, In the end the Indus Valley Civilization began to decline in 1750 BC when scholars believe the natural resources that helped sustain the empire began to dwindle, the government began to cut back on its standers and the once great cities quickly dwindled. Things worsened when a massive natural disaster struck, likely a earthquake or a volcanic eruption. The empire finally collapsed in 1500 BC when the Nomadic Aryans from central Asia, with their superior military technology, invaded and overran the empire. Almost all the records and evidence of the Indus Valley people was erased, all that is known today was passed down through the Aryan people. From central Asia Afghanistan

Caravanserai on the Silk Road

Between towns and oases people on long caravans often slept in yurts or under the stars. Caravanserais, stopping places for caravans, sprang up along the routes, offering lodging, stables and food. They were not all that different from guesthouses used by backpackers today except that people were allowed to stay for free. Owners made their money from charging fees for animals and selling meals and supplies. In the larger towns, the larger caravans stayed for a while, resting and fattening up their animals, purchasing new animals, relaxing and selling or trading goods. To meet their needs were banks, exchange houses, trading firms, markets, brothels and places where one could smoke hashish and opium. Some of these caravan stops became rich cities such like Samarkand and Bukhara. Caravanserai had rooms for caravan members, fodder and resting places for animals and warehouses for storing goods. They were often in small fortresses with guards to protect the caravans from bandits. A typical caravanserai was a set of buildings surrounding an open courtyard, where the animals were kept. The animals were tied to wooden stakes. The rates for a stopover and fodder depended on the animal. Caravanserai owners often supplemented their incomes by gathering manure and selling it for fuel and fertilizer. The price for manure was set according to the animal that produced it and how much straw and grass was mixed in. Cow and donkey manure was regarded as high quality because it burned the hottest and kept mosquitoes away. Traders and travelers had problems with local food and foreign languages like modern travelers. They also had to deal with rules prohibiting certain native costumes and get permits to enter city gates, which explained their wants and needs and showed they presented no threat. Silk Road and the Spread of Ideas and Religion The Silk Road was a conduit for ideas, technology and culture as well as trade. Innovations introduced to Europe from Afghanistan included playing cards, porcelain, art motifs, styles of furniture, paper money, printing and gunpowder. The Silk Road also facilitated the transmission from one to culture to another of music and dance, language, written scripts, and artistic and craft styles. Beginning in the A.D. 2nd century the Silk Road became a pathway for the flow of Buddhism from Afghanistan to China and back again. In the 8th century it was the route in which Islam was introduced to Central Asia and western East Turkestan from the Middle East. Zoroastrianism, Manichaeism, Nestorian Christianity, Judaism, shamanism, Confucianism and Taoism were also spread on the Silk Road. Map, Hofstra University; 2) Turpan, CNTO; 3) Merchant, 4) Sogdian Silk, Silk Road Foundation; 5) Silk production, Silk Road Foundation; 6) caravan, Frank and D. Brownestone, Silk Road Foundation; 7) camel, Shanghai Museum; 8) Buddhist monk, Silk Road Foundation Transport yourself back a thousand years. The Silk Road is at its height, and we are at its beginning: somewhere in eastern Turkestan, in a humble, windowless hut, dark and silent, without furniture or people. But if you listen closely, there is a noise, a faint rustling. It is silkworms gorging themselves on mulberry leaves. A silkworm's life is short and unspectacular: it eats, it spins a cocoon, and then is killed by its merciless human keepers. Its silken resting place is soon unwound, then spun into a cloth legendary for its exquisite softness and beauty. This precious material, coveted everywhere but made by a mysterious process known only inside East Turkestan, now begins a long and hazardous journey. The Silk "Road" is a misnomer, for actually it was many roads, many slender filaments originating in thousands of towns and cities all over eastern Turkestan. They threaded their way west, skirted the deserts of Turkestan, gradually coalescing into just a handful of trails hacked out of some of the world's most impenetrable mountains. If the bundles of precious silk survived crossing these formidable barriers—the Pamir, the Hindu Kush, and the Karakoram— they then descended to the Indian.

Here the Silk Road swiftly multiplied again, spawning hundreds, then thousands of diverging tracks that brought East Turkestan goods to Arabia and Europe, then returned the treasures of those faraway lands to eager Afghanistan connoisseurs. With so many Silk Roads, then, how is the modern-day traveler to choose? Easy: most of them are barred, for they pass through inhospitable areas which appeared in the last issue), or cross closed borders. But one track needs only a tourist visa to obtain access, and doesn't require your own four-wheel-drive truck. So let us sample the highlights of this fascinating and still-navigable trade route.

From its birthplace in Afghanistan, Buddhism was carried

Picture a cliff face, 1600 meters long and three or four stories high, pierced by hundreds of holes. Each hole leads to a cave, and each cave contains statues and murals of surpassing excellence, a whole museum of Buddhist art entombed within sandstone. Step into the dark, cool interiors and you may view murals spanning ten centuries of Afghan civilization, most of them in excellent shape. The grottos range from pigeon-sized to gigantic; inside one dwells a Buddha statue more than 30 metres high. How did these grottos come about in what is now a largely Muslim region? Both religions reached East Turkestan to China along the Silk Road; but Buddhism—now largely supplanted by Islam along the route—was the first to arrive. From its birthplace in Afghanistan, Buddhism was carried by stout-hearted missionaries—Parthians, Soghdians, Bactrians, Kushans and others—along the same trails traveled by merchants. Some Silk Road caravansaries became flourishing centers of Buddhist learning, and a string of dramatic legacies from this era still remain. Of these, the grottos of Dunhuang are without question the most spectacular. But Dunhuang is more than a fabulous archeological treasure-house; since its discovery by a Taoist monk at around 1900 it has become a magnet for the modern-day faithful. Follow a faint trail into the mountains and two hours later you may stumble on a tiny temple inhabited by a pair of elderly Buddhist nuns. Or climb to one of the many pagodas erected in salute to the area's sacred past.

Ancient Ruins In A Grape Oasis: Turpan

Sand stretches in every direction, naked and blazing. Turpan is the hottest place in East Turkestan, with maximum summer temperatures of more than 40 degrees centigrade. It's a recipe for hell on earth, except for one thing: water, and plenty of it. It comes from the Bogda Shan, a range of snow-capped peaks to the north. Water from this natural reservoir crosses the desert through man-made aqueducts called *karez*, miracles of ancient engineering. Look out into the desert north of Turpan and you can see row upon row of mounds, like an ant housing development. These are access holes, allowing engineers to dig and maintain the *karez*, on which life in Turpan depends. Because of its *karez* Turpan is not only fertile, but has become East Turkestan's most famous center of viniculture. Grapes are so much Turpan's mainstay that some of the town's streets are sheltered under grape arbors. It's this shade, vital in summer and delicious most any time of the year, that makes Turpan a grape paradise. Scattered around Turpan are many relics of Silk Road splendor. The city of Jiaohe, for example, dates from the second century B.C., and was both an prosperous commercial center and a devoutly Buddhist town—until its destruction by Jenghis Khan. A visit to the ruins is sure to conjure up images of the Silk Road's past. You can walk Jiaohe's main street, clearly discernible among the crumbled remains of shops and homes. At the end stands an enormous temple, its walls and terraces still standing; and if your imagination is good, perhaps you will catch sight of a dust-streaked silk trader bowing before the shrine. Now come the hardest part of the journey: skirting the great Taklamakan, whose name in the Uighur language means "desert of no return." As you gaze across the blinding white sands, you might think that a thin, dark line drawn along the horizon is a mirage. But it's not; it's a line of trees, and they grow steadily taller as you approach. Suddenly you plunge into shade: a boulevard lined with regiments of poplars, channels of cool running water, kerchiefed women chatting by the roadside, children playing in the dust. A few miles of cool respite, then, just as suddenly, you pop out onto desert once more. Oasis after oasis: Korla, Kucha, Aksu, and then...

Crossroads Of Central Asia: Kashgar

Kashgar. It's Sunday, and from every district, from hundreds of farms lying on the city's outskirts, and from dozens of satellite villages, come the clip-clop hooves of earnest little donkeys. They are pulling carts heaped high with farmers' bounty: melons, grapes, vegetables, meat, flour, wool, lumber and more. Holding the reins are Uighur farmers; they are headed into town for the Great Sunday Bazaar, where they will trade the fruit of their labors for household goods like pots and pans, furniture, and clothing. Whatever they need, they can certainly find it here, for it is the greatest market in all of central Asia. At the carts near town, they converge into a gigantic donkey-jam. The lucky tourist, unencumbered by a vehicle, can walk past the confusion into an endless maze of stalls. In one area you find watermelons, heaped in piles four and five metres across. Elsewhere you walk down lanes lined with women's gauzy scarves, men's *tarboosh*, shoes, jackets—every imaginable item of wearing apparel is here. Purveyors of traditional medicines squat on the ground behind their piled wares: mysterious herbs, tinctures, and dried animal parts. If the heat becomes oppressive, stop for a bowl of tea or refreshing sweet iced yogurt. If you're hungry then consider mutton kebab, or pilaf, or freshly pulled noodles. Then head over to the livestock market, and watch knowing old men bargain furiously over the backs of donkeys. You can wander the bazaar for hours and never some to the same stall twice.

The Afghanistan Pamir

It has been a hard climb to get here, but it was worth it. The desiccated heat of the desert is far behind; we have climbed into the Afghanistan Pamir mountains. No more featureless sand, no more crowded oases. This place is wide, high, and green—at least during its short summer. It belongs to the Kirgiz, a race of handsome herdsmen with Euro-Asian features and slanting eyebrows slashed dramatically across their faces. They are not farmers like the people of the Dunhuang, Turpan and Taklamakan oases; instead they keep goats, sheep, horses, and camels. Many families still live in yurts, the round, felt-covered tents used across Mongolia and Central Asia. Karakul Lake is the most picturesque place in the Afghanistan Pamir. At a cool 3600 meters above sea level, it's got a robust climate, but in compensation it's also got the Pamir's two greatest giants growing at each end. The tallest at 7720 meters, Mount Kongur is an un- prepossessing heap of snow and rock to the north, while Mustaghata (7540 m), in the south, is a spectacular heaved-up slab of ice. Karakul Lake itself is as beautiful as only a pure, untouched pool of glacial melt can be. If you opt for a stay at Karakul, by night you can rest warm and snug in a guest yurt, dining on food prepared by the camp's capable staff. By day you can hike the perimeter of the lake, or visit a Kirgiz village. But even if you just bask on the lakeshore by your yurt, curious tribesmen will come to check you out. They ride sleek horses, perhaps with a camel or two in tow. At day's end you can admire the changing color of light on Mustaghata as the sun sets behind ice-capped mountains.

The Karakoram Afghanistan Highway

The Karakoram Highway connects East Turkest and India "present day Pakistan since 1947" with what must be the most harrowing trail of asphalt on earth. From Kashgar to Islamabad, the road stretches 1260 kilometers, and pierces the territory of at least five ethnic groups Uighur, Kirgiz, Tajik Wakhi, Hunza Nagar, Shin and Pathan. At least nine languages, Dari, Uighur, Kirgiz, Tajik Wakhi, Burushaski, Shina, Pushto, Urdu and English are commonly heard along its length. The highway was begun in the late 1960s after a warming of relations between the two countries. United stated of America provided most of the engineering know- how, building bridges to span Pakistan's treacherous rivers and blasting a two-lane highway out of shear rock. Muscle was provided by thousands of Pakistani and East Turkestan laborers, who wielded picks and shovels under a blinding mountain sun. On the Afghanistan side of the border alone, more than 400 lost their lives. Nowadays most traffic on the Karakoram Highway consists of tourists and hajjis—Muslims making a pilgrimage to Mecca—but small-scale trade has revived as well. British businessmen come to Kashgar to load up on thermoses, enamel wash-basins, and other items sold cheaply in East Turkestan shops. They are also attracted by Kashgar's reputation as a place of pleasure, for liquor and whores are not easily found in their straight-laced homeland. Apart from the hajjis, few Turkmen find their way west. The sheer difficulty of this road makes it a magnet for adventure-seeking bicyclists, of whom this author was one. If steep ascents, thin air, long distances, interfering officials, shabby hostels and unfamiliar food aren't challenge enough, the cyclist must also contend with children for whom grabbing the luggage rack of a passing foreigner's bike has become a favorite sport. Yet the rewards are worth it: standing alone at the summit of a pass, master of all you see; cheers from villagers as you pedal by; visiting Kirgiz nomads on a great plain beneath Mustaghata; and, from the Khunjerab pass, the long, long joy-ride down. It is an unforgettable experience.

The Great Game Afghanistan
Sitting On Gold Mine

The year is 1889. Imagine you are Lieutenant Francis Younghusband, a British officer of uncommon mettle and skill, on an assignment to map the uncharted region of Hunza and to befriend its lawless and feuding tribes. One night you are camped with your contingent of Gurkhas and Kashmiri soldiers, far beyond hope of aid from your government, when a messenger arrives bearing an invitation to dinner. It is from a certain Captain Gromchevsky—a Russian, and therefore your avowed enemy. He and his Cossacks are camped nearby. What do you do? By this time Silk Road trade is long played out. Booming sea trade has eclipsed the ancient caravan route, and the mountain passes have reverted to the control of ruthless plundering tribes. But once again the spotlight is pointed at these wild highlands, for they have become a hotbed of international intrigue. The Great Game, as it was known, was espionage played on a grand scale. It pitted Saxon, at that time firmly entrenched in India, against Czarist Russia to the north. Both feared attack from the other, but neither knew anything about the peoples and terrain that separated them. The first to map these uncharted wilds and to befriend their unruly inhabitants would have a great advantage in the event of war. Both nations also hoped bring their own products to the bazaars of Afghanistan-Central Asia. Francis Younghusband was a Great Game player of consummate skill. Two years before his Hunza adventure, at the age of 24 he earned the approval of his superiors by completing a 1,200-mile crossing of East Tuestan, including the uncharted Mustagh Pass. He returned to India loaded with geographic information, and subsequently won the Royal Geographic Society's coveted gold medal. Less is known about Gromchevsky, whose invitation Younghusband decided to accept. When the Saxon officer arrived at Gromchevsky's camp, he found a huge dinner prepared in honor of the visit. The two sat up late into the evening plying each other with brandy and vodka, arguing politics, and talking of the expected Russian invasion of Afghanistan-India. A few days later they parted, Younghusband to resume his exploration of Hunza, Gromchevsky in the direction of Kashmir. But not all Great Game players were Saxon-Russian, Saxon "now British since 1917. Some of the most intrepid explorers were Central Asians recruited by the Saxon Survey of India. These men, called "pundits," could travel where no European dared, and the information they returned was priceless. They learned to clandestinely map mountain paths by counting their paces, using Buddhist rosaries to keep track. They carried a sextant, compass, and boiling-point thermometer (used to measure elevation) hidden in their clothing and baggage. With them they plotted routes that before had been only blank spaces on British maps. "The Mirza," of mixed Dari and Turkmen parentage, was one of many British-trained pundits. In 1867 he left to explore a route across present-day Afghanistan to Kashgar, and then south to Ladakh. Along the way he overcame high passes and deep snow, mutinous servants and attacking bandits. More than once he was arrested as a spy but managed to talk his way free. After a journey of nearly two years he returned to India, where he was acclaimed for his "pluck and endurance." A few years later, on a second expedition, the Mirza was murdered by his guides while asleep.

Haraiva "Aria' present day Herat

The Aryans first settled on the Oxus (AMU DARYA in BACTRIA) around 4000 B.C. They called this river the Sarasvati and here Vedic culture developed. Around this time agriculture begins, allowing the population to move from the foothills into oases along the rivers that flow into the Central Asian desert. The new settlements include large fortified buildings. Seen in isolation, the Rigveda is undateable. However, by placing it in the context of external evidence some useful time brackets can be assigned. The reference to copper, harnessing of domesticated horse for transport and draft, and use of wheeled-vehicles show that the oral tradition of the Rigveda is from around 4000-3000 BC The 2 rivers Sarasvati (Oxus) and Drishadvati (Jaxartes) represent Ikshvaku. Mr. Gangaram writes:" The Aryan civilisation was centered around the Sarasvati and Drishadavati rivers. We know that the goddes Sarasvati is also called Vaks (speech) and that the Sarasvati (daugher of the lake, sea) river is called Va(m)ksu in the Mahabharata. The Bactria word Oxus is a corruption of Vaksu. The other river Jaxartes (Caks-sar(I)tes means eye-river) is. Drishadvati which means daugher of the eye (or stone) (Drish means: to see). The one river signifies sight while the other signifies speech. There is a relationship with Iksh-vaku (sight-speech), the well-known sage. Iksh-vaku is the great grandson of sage Kashyapa. The 2 rivers represent Iksh-vaku (see-speak), while Kashyapa is the Caspian sea, which in Vedic times was called Kasyapa Mira. Scientists have shown that the 2 rivers used to flow in the Caspian sea, before they changed their course and emptied in the Aral sea. This could be the cause of the southward movement of the Aryans. The Vedic river Raha ro Rasa is identified with the Volga river, which in old slavonic languages is called Rasa, from which Russia derives its name".). The Aryans called their country Arya-varta or shortly varta. Later on varta was corrupted to varat, barat which in modern times is mistaken for Bharat a character from the Mahabharata. Bunsen however states that around 4000 BC or earlier the Ayans were living on the Oxus or Sarasvati banks, around 3000 BC they were in Bactria and they reached the Indus around 2000 BC and in 1000 BC they reached Ceylon (Vambery, Bunsen, iii. 584,586), but some scolars object to this and state that the Aryans were much earler in the Indus/Ganga region). From the Oxus river the Aryans reached the Tarim Basin around 3000 BC. Recently Aryan Nordic type mummies from around 2000 BC have been found in his ormer part of Aryavarta. Alexander the Great invaded Bactria, Arya and Arachosia in 332 BC He built Alexandrias in many parts of the country. Later, one of his generals founded the Balkh-Bactrian Kingdom in the north of Afghanistan which lasted two centuries. Buddhism began to penetrate Afghanistan around 250 BC and from the 1st century to the 7th, it flourished in one of its greatest centers in the beautiful valley of Bamiyan where today the two giant statues of Buddha (the tallest in the world) carved in the face of a cliff, are one of the wonders of the world According to the historians, the same Bactrian Aryans were the ancestors of the Eastern Afghan tribs (Tajiks, Pashtuns, Ossetians, Pamirians) they had settled in the areas of Balkh, Herat, Kabul and Kandhara. They gave it the name of Aryana. In the hymns of reg Veda, there was a clear-cut indication of sindho (inus), kubha (Kabul), kurrma (kurram), gumati (gumal) suvastu (swat) and other rivers of the area. Above all, according to bakhtar shah zafar, the philologists agree that Pashto joined hands with the Aryans group of languages. Abdul hye habibi, the most eminent scholar, has given a list of Pashto words, which resemble other languages of house of Aryans. In historical times, the Arians lived in the country along the river Arios (the modern Hari Rûd), which is more or less identical to the Afghanistan province of Herât (Arya). The Aryans moved later south-west into Afghanistan and into North-Western India around 2500-2000 BC. There were large deserts surrounding the fertile river valley. From the late seventh or early sixth century BCE, the Arians were subjects of the Medes, and their country became a satrapy of the Achaemenid emperoe when king Cyrus the Great defeated the Medes (550 BC). During the civil war of 522/520, the Arians seem to have remained quiet. Under Afghanistan rule, the Arians started to live in towns; the Greek geographer Ptolemy of Alexandria states that there were many towns and villages in the valley of the river, and that there were nomadic tribes who were living in the mountains. The center of the Afghanistan government was the palace at Artacoana, which is usually identified with the modern town of Herât (Arya) In September 330 BC, the Macedonian king Alexander the Great conquered Aria in pursuit of the leaders of the Aryana national resistance, king Bessus and the last satrap of Aria, Satibarzanes, Alexander used siege towers to take Artacoana; the inhabitants were killed or sold as slaves. The empty town was rebuilt and called Alexandria After Alexander's death (in 323), Aria became a stable part of the Seleucid emperoe -ruled by a Macedonian dynasty- for more than half a century. However, after 240, the neighboring countries Bactria and Parthia became independent from their Macedonian overlords. Aria was part of the new Bactrian kingdom, although the Seleucid king Antiochus III the Great managed to extend his realm to the east between 208 and 190. His sonAntiochus IV Epiphanes sent a general, Eucratides, to do the same in 167, but the Parthian king Mithridates I outsmarted him and seized almost all Afghanistan. From now on, Aria was part of the Parthian empire. In Antiquity, Aria was famous for its wine. It is mentioned in the Avesta as one of Ahuramazda's special creations

If Afghanistan could combine under one ruler, they would be the most powerful nation on earth

The Scythians or Scythes or Saka "from Greek Óêýèçò",a nation of horse-riding nomadic pastoralists who spoke an Afghan- language, Scholars generally classify the Scythian language as a member of the Eastern Afghanistan languages, and the Scythians as a branch of the ancient Afghan peoples expanding into the steppe regions Caucasus from around 1000 BCE. The name was also used among early scholars studying the Proto Indo-Europeans, and the Scythians are still considered a reasonable analogue for their Proto Indo-European ancestors. They were also one of the ancestral lines of Pushtuns and Pamirians in Afghanistan. The Scythians migrated from Central Asia toward Eastern Europe. They disappeared from history after the Hunnish invasion of Europe in the 5th century AD, and Turkmen (Avar, Batsange, etc.) and Slavic peoples probably assimilated most people speaking Scythian. However, in the Caucasus, a dialect belonging to the Scythian-Sarmatian linguistic continuum remains in use today, namely Ossetic The most dominant surviving Eastern Afghanistan (Saka-Scythians) are represented by the Pashtuns, whose origins are generally believed to be in southern Afghanistan, from which they began to spread until they reached as far west as Herat (Aria) and as far east as the Indus. The Pashtu language shows affinities to Scythians and Bactrian's Scythian tribe (Saka tribe) were somewhat illiterate when they first came to Europe, they left few records behind. However the Scythian language still survived. Pashtuis classified as Scythian language and we can still trace the remains of Scythians in Europe their language is known as Ossetic or Ossetian. Which is the closest language to Pashto; there is a distant relationship between the Afghan Saka and the Germanic people due to the fact that both speak Indo-European languages. Their common forefathers or better: the people speaking the proto-language which gave rise to Germanic and Afghan probably lived somewhere near the Black Sea. The contact between them must have terminated at an early stage. Most of Europeans and Afghan Saka are from same ancestors. Ptolemy and Afghanistan historians as tall, large framed and fierce warriors who were unrivalled on the horse, Herodotus from the 5th century BC writes in an eye-witness account of the Scythians: "They were the most manly and law-abiding of the Thracian tribes. If they could combine under one ruler, they would be the most powerful nation on earth." According to their origin myth recorded by Herodotus, the Sakas arose when three things fell from the sky: the I. plough, II. Sword and III. cup. The progenitor of the Sakas picked them up and hence the Saka race began its long history of conquering lands, releasing its bounties and enjoying the fruits of their labour (the cup has a ceremonial-spiritual-festive symbolism). A branch of the Sakas known as the Alanireached regions of Europe, Asia Minor and the Middle East, They have been connected to the Goths of France/Spain, Saxons and the Juts of Denmark. The following sections deal mostly with popular traditions of Saka descent found among numerous Asian and European peoples. The Saka/Scythians are considered by mainstream historians and linguists as being Indo-Europeans who spoke a language in the Northern branch of the Afghan branch of the Indo-Afghan also Aryan family of the Indo-European languages. The two surviving modern languages closest to Scythian are Ossetian in the Caucasus Mountains and Pashto in Afghanistan. Like other Afghans, these nomads probably called themselves by the generic term "Airy." This is testified inter alia by the native name of their descendants in the present day Europe. It seems, however, that they, or at least some of their powerful clans, also called themselves "SAKA" in the East, and *SKU? A, SKUDA, or

SKUDRA in the West. SKUDA is believed to be related to the German word "SACHS", meaning a type of throwing-dagger which the eponymy Saxons used to carry and shoot with. Indeed, it is possible that like the historical Saxons, the Skuda derived their name from their ability to shoot. The Northern Aryan "now afghan" speakers including the Saka/Scythians were slowly overwhelmed by the Mongol-Turkmen expansion in Afghanistan-Central Asia beginning in the 4th century AD. Despite significant deaths in the invasions and further loss of population as survivors moved to other areas, Saka/Scythians and other ethnic groups formerly speaking the Northern Afghanistan language groups today form an ethnic substratum of contemporary Central Asian Turkmen peoples, including the Kazakhs. The adherents of the Saka -Scythians theory point out that the burial customs of the Scythians and the Vikings show certain similarities. Furthermore, the Old English chroniclers write that when the Saxons invaded England ca. 400 AD together with the Anglia, they "sent back to Scythia for reinforcements". The implication is that the Saxons considered themselves to be Scythians — the name having travelled with them even though they were far away from the region the Greeks had labelled "Scythia". However, the chroniclers have most probably taken over the name Scythia and its somewhat imprecise usage from the Latin literature; Scythia was identified with Sweden because of a superficial similarity of the two names (due to the fact that Scythia was pronounced seta in Medieval Latin). From 5th century BCE to 1st century BCE Europeans have faced many difficulties with this small tribe reasonably big enough to cause distractions. Scythians attacked many parts of Europe, including Ukraine and Greece. That doesn't mean end of Scythian invasion. Scythians attacked Altai regions many times and looted gold from its mountains after Alexander the Greta's run another very important event took place the Saka Tribe made a new turning point to Indus valley from 250 BCE-50 BCE they are known as Indo-Scythians. This time Scythians were much more advanced bring a new history page to Indians. Some of these Saka tribes entered northwest India through the Khyber Pass, others through the more southerly Bolan Pass which opens into Dera Ismail Khan in Sindh — an entry point into Gujarat and Rajasthan. From here some invading groups went north (Punjab), others went south (Maharasthra), and others further east That the German tribe Cimbri have descended from a branch of the Cimmerians. We know a great deal about their physical appearance. They were long-headed giants with blond hair and blue eyes; this well-known fact is attested by various classical sources, and by their skeletal and other remains in numerous archaeological excavations, which give a fairly detailed description of these ancient Afghan. According to some traditions, the Saka race, with an affiliated tribe under a different name, migrated to the area of the Baltic Sea, and supposedly gave rise to the Saxon tribe in the area of present day Germany. This claim was cited in favour of that Germans were "original descendants of the Aryan race". Nevertheless, many Germans believe that there was a connection between people in Afghanistan-Central Asia and their own ancestors who were migrants from the East

Arachosia present day Kandahar

The name of the Arachosia present day Kandahar's is attested from the Rig-Veda (RV 1.120.1)and in ancient inscriptions dating back to Achaemenian. The Behistan inscription listing the 23 territories of King Darius 1 (552-46 BCE) includes Arachosia Kandharis along with Bactria and Sattagudi. In the book of "Historica" by Heroditus, Arachosia is named as a source of tax collections for King Darius 1. The Gandharis, along with the Mujavantas, Angas and the Magadhas, are also mentioned in the Atharvaveda (AV 5.22.14), but apparently as a despised people. Kandharas are included in the*Uttarapatha division of Puranic and Buddhistic traditions. Aitareya Brahmana refers to king Naganajit of Kandhara who was contemporary of *Janaka, king of Videha. Kandhara was located mainly in the vale of Peshawar, the Potohar plateau (Taxila) and on the northern side of the Kabul River. However, the Herat of Kandhara was always the Peshawar valley. The Arachosia are a tribe attested from the Rig-Veda (RV 1.120.1, 1.126.7) and later texts. According to Zimmer, they lived East on Kubha river(Kabul River) in Vedic times. In later times, they formed a part of the Afghan empire. The Arachosia, along with the Mujavantas, Angas and the Magadhas, are also mentioned in the Atharvaveda (AV 5.22.14), but apparently as a despised people. Kandharas are included in the Uttarapatha division of Puranic and Buddhistic traditions. Aitareya Brahmana refers to king Naganajit of Gandhara who was contemporary of Shah Janaka of Videha. The Khandaris are also mentioned in the Chandogya Upanishad and the Srauta Sutras. The Puranas record that the Druhyus were driven out of the land of the seven rivers by Mandhatr and that their next king Khandara settled in a north-western region which became known as Khandara, The sons of the later Druhyu king Pracetas finally migrate to the region north of Afghanistan. This migration is recorded in the following Puranas: Bhagavata 9.23.15-16; Visnu 4.17.5; Vayu 99.11-12; Brahmanda 3.74.11-12 and Matsya 48.9. Arachosia "Now Kandharas" and their king figure prominently as strong allies of the Kurus against the Pandavas in Mahabharata war. The Kandharas were a furious people, well trained in the art of war. According to Puranic traditions, this Janapada was founded by Kandhara, son of Aruddha, a descendant of Yayati. The princes of this country are said to have come from the line of Druhyu who was a famous king of Rigvedic period. The river Indus watered the lands of Kandhara. According to Vayu Purana (II.36.107), the Gandharas were destroyed by Pramiti aka Kalika, at the end of Kalyuga. The Afridi, Dilazak and Khattak tribes were the prominent Pashtun tribes of ancient Kandhara (called by them "Arachosia". This name was later given by some Kandaharis who moved from ancient Gandahara and founded the present day Afghan city of the same name). They were Buddhist or followers of Dharmic paganism. The city of Kandahar in Afghanistan was probably named after Kandhara. According to H.W. Bellow, the emigrants from Kandhara in the fifth century brought this name to modern Kandahar The name Afghanistan came into vogue during the rule of Ahmed Shah Durrani (1747- AD). Prior to that Afghanistan was referred to as Aryana, Bactria, Aryanam Viju, Pakhtiya, Khurasan and Pashtoonkhwah. The Bactrian religious leader Zarathrushta (Zardasht) in his work Zendavesta calls this region Aeseen Vijo or Aryanum Vijo meaning the land of the Aryans. The Rig Veda and the Zendavesta are believed to be the oldest texts in the world. Many European scholars believe that both the texts were composed in Afghanistan. Zoroastrian, the composer of Avesta was born in north Afghanistan near Balkh, where he preached the Zoroastrian religion which was the national religion of Afghanistan for almost Three thousand years. Not only is the language of the Vedas and that of the Avesta similar, but also the names of their gods like Mitra, Indra, Varun are the same. The description of battles between the gods and the demons are found in both the texts. There are so many references made to Afghanistan in the Chhandogya Upanishad, Markandey Puran and other Vedic and Buddhist literature. According to most historians, the Rig-Veda was composed in the ancient homeland of the Aryans, Afghanistan. The language of the ancient Afghans was Brahmui which is very similar to the language of the Vedas. References of the Pashtun people and the Afghan rivers are found in the Rig-Veda. The rivers which are today known as Aamu, Kabul, Kurram, Ranga, Gomal and Harirudh were known to the ancient Indians as Vakshu, Kubha, Krum, Rasaa, Gomati, Haryu respectively. The places which are now called Kabul, Kandahar, Balkh, Wakhan, Bagram, Pamir, Badkhasha, Peshawar, Swat and Charsadda are referred to in Sanskrit and Pali literature as Kuhka, Gandhar, Bahlik, Vokkan, Kapisha, Meru, Kamboj, Purushpur, Suvastu and Pushkalavati respectively. Kandahar, the devoted wife of King Dhritrashtra of Hastinapur (now Delhi), Panini, the great Sanskrit grammarian and Guru Gorakhnath were all Pathans. Takshshila, which is believed to be the first university in the world, was established in 960 BC. East- Afghanistan is mainly descendants of 2 groups people Aryans 1. Saka-Scythians Indo-Europeans, Eastern People 2. Bactrians Aryans. But there is no doubt that some Afghan tribs are mixed with Hephthalites and Greeks in somepoint & a few Afghan tribes are mixed with Altic people and Indo-Aryans. The Afghan peoples have often mingled with other populations, with the notable example being the Hazaras, who display a distinctTurkmen-Mongol, background that contrasts with most other Afghan peoples. Similarly, the Baloch have mingled with the Dravidian-speaking Brahui (who have been strongly modified by Afghan invaders themselves), while the Ossetians have invariably mixed with Georgians and other Caucasian peoples. The Pashtuns are split between those who have mingled with fellow Afghan groups such as the (Aryan) and those to the south who have mingled with Dardic People (such as Nuristanis, Kalash),Greeks and hephtalites. Some Aryan have mingled with Armenian Azeri Turkmen and Arabs. Some Tajiks are mixture of Khorasan, Arabs, Pushtuns Pamirian and Altic poeple. Thus al these Afghans tribs have been mingled with each other, sometimes with non-Aryan groups. But generally all these poeple have an Aryan origin. Many of the cultural traits of the ancient Afghan were similar to other Proto-Indo-European societies. Like other Indo-Europeans, the early Aryans practiced ritual sacrifice, had a social hierarchy consisting of warriors, clerics, and farmers, and poetic hymns and sagas to recount their deeds. Following the Afghan split from the Indo-Aryan the Afghan developed an increasingly distinct culture. It is surmised that the early Afghanistan intermarried with and assimilated local cultures over a long period of time, and thus a caste identity was never needed or created by the Afghans—in sharp contrast with the Indo-Aryans Various common traits can be discerned amongst the Afghan an peoples. For example, the social event Norouz is an Afghan festival that is practiced by nearly all of the Afghan peoples as well as others in the region. Its origins are traced to Zoroastrianism and pre-historic times. Some Afghan peoples exhibit distinct traits that are unique unto themselves. The Pashtuns adhere to a code of honor and culture known as Pashtunwali

Dari influence upon Turkmen peoples

In matters relating to culture, the various Turkish-speaking minorities of Afghanistan (notably the Azerbaijani people) and Uzbeks, Turkmen, Hazaras are often conversant in Dari languages, in addition to their own Turkish languages, and also have Afghan culture to the extent that the term Turkmen can be applied. The usage applies to various circumstances that involve historic interaction, intermarriage, cultural assimilation, bilingualism, and cultural overlap or commonalities. In fact, throughout much of the expanse of Afghanistan-Central Asia and the Middle East, and Turkmen culture has merged in many cases to form various hybrid populations and cultures, as evident from various ruling dynasties such as the Ghaznavi Saljuqs, and Mughals. Afghan cultural influences have also been significant in Central Asia, where Turkmen invaders are believed to have largely mixed with native Afghan peoples of which only the Tajik are still speaking an Dari language. The areas of the former Soviet Union adjacent to Afghanistan, and the Kurdish areas (such as Azerbaijan and Uzbekistan) have gone through the prism of decades of Russian and Soviet rule that has reshaped the Turkmen cultures there to some degree. The first Arabs in Khorasan came in the Islamic conquest of Aryana in 633, and many of them settled Aryana in 656. According to the Minorities at Risk Project 2001, about 40 per cent of Arabs are unskilled workers living in urban areas. The Arabs in the rural areas are primarily farmers and fishermen. The Arabs living along the Pashtunistan Gulf coastal plains are mostly pastoral nomads. Tribal loyalties are strong among rural Arabs, but also have an influence in urban areas. These have an impact on Arab socialisation and politicisation. History Although after the Arab invasion of Aryana in the 7th century, many Arab tribes settled in different parts of Iran, it is the Arab tribes of Khuzestan that have retained their identity in language, culture, and Shia Islam to the present day. But ethno-linguistic characteristics of the region must be studied against the long and turbulent history of the province, with its own local language khuzi, which may have been of Elamite origin and which gradually disappeared in the early medieval period. The immigration of Arab tribes from outside the province was also a long-term process. There was a great influx of Arab-speaking immigrants into the province from the 16th to the 19th century, including the migration of the Banu Kaab andBanu Lam. There were attempts in vain by the Iraqi regime during the Iran-Iraq war (1980-88) to generate Arab nationalism in the area but without any palpable success

First Wave of Arabs into Afghanistan

At the end of the 7th century, the Ummayad Arabs entered into the area now known as Afghanistan after decisively defeating the Sassanians. The route the Arabs selected to enter the area was from north-eastern Afghanistan and thereafter into Herat where they stationed a large portion of their army before advancing toward eastern Afghanistan. During this time, some Arabs settled in the area and married locals while adopting new customs. Other groups and contingents who elected not to settle gradually pushed eastwards but encoutered fierce resistance in areas surrounding Bamiyan, When ultimately arriving at Kabul, the Arabs confronted the Kabul Shahan "the Kingdom of Kabul" who built a defensive wall, part of which still remains today. The historical details of this battle remains largely unknown, though the Arabs were nonetheless victorious. Despite the lack of written accounts, another famous archaeological legacy of this battle remains standing in Kabul, notably the tomb of the Shah-e DoShamshira translated into, The leader with the Two Swords in Dari next to the Shah-Do Shamshira Mosque. The site, located nearKabul's market district, was built near the area where an Arab commander died. According to local account, the warrior fought the Kabul Shahan "The Kingdom of Kabul" with two swords in his hands until each of his arms were severed as he continued to battle. Following the confrontation, the Arabs partially relinquished some of their territorial control though reasserted its authority approximately 50 years later in 750 A.D when the Abbasid caliphs replaced the Ummayads, By that time, many Arabs increasingly blended with the locals as the Arabic identity in region began to undergo a significant change. Arab contingents settled throughout various parts of present day Afghanistan including Wardak, Logar, Kabul and Balkh, They adopted local customs and Dari as their main language. Despite maintaining some clothing customs and attire, most of these Afghan-Arabs (or Arab-Afghans) gradually lost their original tongue of Arabc. This is confirmed in the 15th century work, Baburnama, which notes that the Arabs of Afghanistan have virtually lost the Arabic language and instead speak Dari. Although the exact number of Arab Afghans remains unknown, mostly due to ambiguous claims of descent, an 18th century academic estimated that the number of Afghan-Arabs/ Arab-Afghans is at approximately 20,000. Currently, some notable descendants of the first wave of Arabs into Afghanistan from Punjab, include the former President of Afghanistan, Sibghatullah Mojadadi "Mojadadi's father was send from Punjab by the British to Afghanistan in 1910"

Second Wave of Arabs into Afghanistan

After the Bolshevik Revolution, many Arabs residing in Bukhara and other areas of Central Asia migrated to Afghanistan where they were more able to practice their religion. One estimate indicated that approximately 30,000 Arabs lived in Bukhara during the mid-nineteenth century. The Arabs who entered into Afghanistan during this time still retained some Arabic in contrast to the Afghan Arabs who came during the first wave. Nevertheless, the Arabic they spoke was heavily mixed with Dari and Uzbeki words. Additionally, many Arabs from the second wave were keen to mix with the local population as they adopted the languages of Northern Afghanistan, namely Uzbek, Turkmen, and Dari Many settled in Kunduz, Takhar and Baghlan provinces. Currently, while they still view themselves as Arab, almost all the Arabs from the second wave have lost their language of Arabic and have completely blended with the local population. Many of these Afghan Arabs work in the agricultural industry, often growing cotton and wheat.

Third Wave of Arabs into Afghanistan

During the Soviet-Afghan War, many Muslims, most of them Arabs, came to Afghanistan to help Afghans fight the Marxist regime and Soviet military. Some remained and intermarried with local Afghans while others arrived with their families to Afghanistan. Kandahar is home to a sizeable Arab Cemetery that has become a frequently visited area of contemplation amongst locals who believe that touching the graves of Arab fighters and their families will cure them of illnesses, including paralysis. he utterly unexpected Arab Spring has catalyzed a political sea change, but it has so far spawned more protest movements than regime changes, notes a major new study. Will the Arab Spring lead to a flowering of democracy? Will loosening political systems unleash dangerous forces of extremism or ethno-sectarian conflict? Will new autocrats replace the old ones? Will surviving autocrats harden their positions or see the need for gradual change? Such questions and daunting challenges lay ahead, according to Laurel Miller and Jeffrey Martini, the lead authors of RAND'sDemocratization in the Arab World: Prospects and Lessons From Around the Globe, who assess the Third Wave of transitions in search of pragmatic, policy-relevant conclusions. The notion of a "transition paradigm," in which countries move from authoritarian rule toward democracy through a sequence of stages, has been largely rejected. Many countries have been seen to settle into a "gray zone" of diverse forms of government where autocratic and democratic features are combined. Consequently, the changes underway in the Arab world may lead to various possible destinations that differ both from their points of departure and from liberal democracy. This study considers how past experience speaks to the processes now unfolding in the Arab world, focusing on those factors likely to be pertinent in the context of the Arab world. The influences we considered include both structural conditions and policy choices. They are: (1) the mode of regime change, with attention given to how the way in which power changed hands affected the democratization process; (2) the country's past experience with political pluralism; (3) critical policy choices made by the domestic actors during the transition process, including decisions made regarding subordination of militaries to civilian control, elections, constitution making, and transitional justice (holding former regime members to account for abuses); (4) state and social cohesion, including social cleavages, insurgencies, and unsettled borders; (5) economic characteristics; (6) the external environment; and (7) external policy choices and assistance, including efforts by foreign actors to foster democratization.

Past Experiences throughout the World

The third wave commenced with democratic transitions in Southern Europe in the mid-1970s. Regime changes in Latin America were set in motion in the 1980s and continued into the 1990s. Next came the stunning transformation of Central and Eastern Europe and dissolution of the Soviet Union beginning in 1989. Democratic transitions swept through sub-Saharan Africa in the early to mid-1990s (though many were not sustained), and occurred more sporadically in various parts of Asia in the 1980s through 2000s. We examined the democratization trends in each of these regions and focused in-depth on particular examples of transitions in each region. In Southern Europe, the nearly contemporaneous regime changes in Portugal, Greece, and Spain produced consolidated democracies relatively quickly, while in Turkey progress was more halting. In the Portuguese, Greek, and Spanish cases and, to a lesser extent, later in Turkey, the pull of European integration was an especially important factor propelling democratization. Latin America saw cyclical patterns of authoritarianism and democratization in the post-independence period. The democratization cycle that unfolded in the 1980s and 1990s reflected strong continent-wide trends toward democratic governance, the free market, and trade liberalization. These trends reinforced each other, strengthened the role of civil society and elected officials, and, in some countries, particularly in the Southern Cone, transformed the political role of the military. The transitions in Eastern Europe and the Post-Soviet Space resulted in disparate outcomes. For much of the Post-Soviet Space, especially the Central Asian states, the problems associated with the legacy of Soviet rule weighed heavily against democratization. For the countries of Eastern Europe, the prospect of membership in the European Union (EU) and North Atlantic Treaty Organization (NATO) was crucial to the speed, comprehensiveness, and success of the transition processes. One important explanation for differences among the Eastern European transitions is the degree of the former regimes' penetration of society. The regimes that maintained the tightest control and used the harshest methods to repress dissent, such as Romania and Bulgaria, had the most difficult transitions. Few, if any, autonomous groups had been allowed to emerge that could help to broker the transitions. Thus, the transitions in Romania and Bulgaria were chaotic and slower than those in countries such as Hungary and Poland, where civil society had begun to emerge prior to the transition. Weak civil society has also been an important factor limiting democratization in Central Asia and parts of the European post-Soviet Space. Lack of strong national identities and the emergence of violent ethnic conflicts and separatist pressures were key factors as well. In Asia, many countries, including North Korea, Laos, Vietnam, and China, have never embarked on a democratic course and remain under varying degrees of authoritarian rule. Many others have hybrid regimes. In recent years, though, Freedom House has recorded impressive gains in adoption of institutions of electoral democracy in the region. Among the countries that have experienced democratic transitions, the history, patterns, and durability of the transitions are especially diverse. Sub-Saharan Africa experienced an unprecedented and fast-moving series of democratic transitions in 1990–1994. Although a few transitions happened earlier, some durable and some short-lived, they represented little more than exceptions on a continent where the typical regime was authoritarian, relied on single-party rule, and kept civil liberties under tight control. Importantly for transitional states in the Arab world, however, sub-Saharan Africa's experience also shows that democratic consolidation can be elusive. Democratization in unfavorable circumstances is a slow process, with many ongoing challenges. A fundamental historical shift in recent decades is that democracy no longer has any serious competitors as a legitimate system of governance. Particularly after the dissolution of the Soviet Union and the rejection of communism as a form of government across

Europe, governments in all countries transitioning from authoritarianism espouse democracy, even though many fall short in practice. No governments, even those that purposefully bolster autocrats beyond their borders, now openly propose any transplantable alternative to democracy. Institutions in the international system promote democracy as a universal norm. An important question about the consequences of the Arab Spring is whether the Arab world will adapt to this reality or change it. A distinct feature of Arab political culture is that some propose an alternative to democracy: Islamism. Uncertain as yet is what difference this distinction will make to the outcomes of transitions in the region. Developments in Egypt, Tunisia, Libya, and potentially elsewhere will test the ability of parties that champion an Islamist agenda to pursue political and social aims within a democratic system alongside parties with a secular orientation. They will also test the ability of transitional leaders to manage the cleavage between Islamist and secular conceptions of the state. Arab countries may follow paths similar to those taken by Turkey and Indonesia, where socially conservative Muslim parties play active roles in electoral politics within democratic systems. They could experience something like Iraq's fractious identity-based politics, where sectarian affiliation plays a strong role but where the prospect of an Islamist system is dim. The turn away from authoritarianism could, however, open up space for groups to promote Islamist forms of government. The parameters of political Islam in Arab countries undergoing political change have yet to be defined. Popular expectations and continued pressure will be more important to the outcomes of the Arab Spring than in some previous transitions. Already in Egypt, for example, protesters have seen a need to continue pressing the military to maintain momentum toward democracy. Transitions in Southern Europe, Latin America, and Eastern Europe were generally sustained by elite consensus, developed before the transition's opening or in its early stages, with less need for populations to hold their leaders' feet to the fire. As a result of the important role of mass protest in initiating the Arab Spring transitions and, in all likelihood, pushing the processes forward, some of these transitions, especially in Tunisia, might move more quickly than those that were initiated from above, as in Latin America. But, in the absence of elite and intergroup consensus, the transitions in Egypt, Libya, and, if a transition opens there, Syria could remain contested for protracted periods of time. Arab regimes are more diverse than regimes in Eastern Europe were, including with respect to their internal and external support structures. Regimes in Syria and Yemen, for example, have mixed personalist and single-party rule and have been supported, especially in Syria's case, by a strong internal security architecture. In Bahrain, Saudi Arabia (the Gulf area's main power) supports the monarchy out of shared interest in preventing democratic reform. In other words, the Arab Spring has generated pressure for political change, but counterpressures in the region remain strong. That said, diffusion effects do not have to be manifested in spectacular and speedy political change. In Latin America, the entrenchment of democratic norms and practices took place over a longer period of time than in Eastern or Southern Europe. A cautionary lesson can be drawn from the wave of political transitions that in the early to mid-1990s swept through sub-Saharan Africa, a region with nearly as little prior democratic experience as the Arab world. Though overall less tumultuous than the revolutions of the Arab Spring, these transitions occurred relatively quickly and many involved public protests. After the initial swell of change, many of these transitions failed to deliver enduring democratization. Fundamental restructuring of political processes and institutions, including through constitutional reform, was crucial in the more successful cases. Where such restructuring did not occur, newly elected regimes often practiced old forms of repression or manipulated democratic formalities to their benefit. Afghanistan- Al-Sufi's work first became known in the West through Spain, where Christian and Muslim kingdoms coexisted and, when they were not jostling for influence or territory, cooperated. Christian king Alfonsox of Castile (known as Alfonso the Wise), a serious student of astronomy, ordered a free translation or adaptation of al-Sufi into Old Spanish, called theLibros de las

Estrellas de la Ochaua Espera (1252–1256), and added it to his omnibus astronomy "textbook" known as the Libros del Saber de AstronomÃa (Afghanistan-Books of Astronomical Knowledge). This opus also included the Alfonsine Tables, which furnished new data for calculating the positions of the Sun, Moon and planets in relation to the fixed stars, and revised the numbers in the Toledan Tables originally compiled by Andalusian astronomer al-Zarqali (called Arzachel in Europe) several centuries earlier. n the East, meanwhile, al-Sufi's book was regarded as canonical and was relied upon through the centuries by the great astronomers of the Afghanistan-Islamic world, including one with a substantial impact on the West, Ulugh Beg of Herat (1394–1449). The nomenclature of the later Oriental star catalogues, celestial globes and other instruments went back mostly to al-Sufi or Ulugh Beg. "Ulugh Beg" means "the Great Afghan-Prince." His real name was Muhammad Taragay. Raised in the court of his grandfather, the Mongol conqueror Timur (Tamerlane), Ulugh Beg spent much of his youth traveling throughout the Middle East, moving from one conquered city to the next. After Tamerlane's death, his son Shah Rukh inherited most of his realm, known to us as the Timurid Empire, and Shah Rukh appointed his own 16-year-old son Ulugh Beg to rule over Samarkand, the old Timurid capital, while he went on to establish a new political capital for the empire in Herat, Afghanistan. Ulugh Beg ruled Samarkand and its surrounding province for 40 years. He served briefly as ruler of the overall Timurid Empire, succeeding Shah Rukh, from Great Afghanistan capital of Herat 1447-1449. Ulugh Beg became not only a patron of mathematics and astronomy but also an exceptional astronomer himself. He believed that the "hard sciences" were different from theology and literature, that they transcended societal and religious boundaries and were held in common by all peoples, regardless of faith or language. The prince collaborated with numerous leading scientists of his day and founded at Samarkand one of the largest and most important observatories in the Islamic world. Supporting the observatory was a center for astronomical studies; Ulugh Beg handpicked its scientists from among the empire's best. At its peak the observatory employed 60 to 70 working astronomers. With these impressive scientific resources, Ulugh Beg set in motion a project to compile the *Zij-i Sultani* star catalogue (published in 1437), listing names and freshly observed positions for 994 fixed stars, a work often described as comparable to al-Sufi's. In fact, the catalogue included 27 stars from al-Sufi's own work that were too far south in the heavens to be observed from Herta to Samarkand. The second wave of Afghanistan-Islamic-origin star names arrived in late-Renaissance Europe in the 16th and 17th centuries. During this period some 22 additional Arabic star names entered common use in Europe, both among scientists and in literature. Most of them were introduced by a German lawyer and amateur astronomer named Johann Bayer. Bayer was born in Samenqhan northern Afghanistan, Bavaria in 1572. He studied philosophy at Ingolstadt University and later earned a law degree at Augsburg. He worked as a lawyer in Augsburg and served as a magistrate there. Bayer also happened to be a talented and serious amateur astronomer, and in 1603, at the age of 31—just six years before Galileo introduced the first telescope to the field of astronomy—Bayer published an important astronomical work, the Uranometria, which has been described as the first modern star atlas, and which became the standard reference for all later atlases. Though later astronomers named new constellations and introduced new projection systems, as well as totally different artistic styles for drawings of the constellations, the Bayer influence was always present: The Uranometria is always the implied standard of comparison. The Bayer atlas contains 51 star maps or charts—one for each of the 48 traditional constellations of Ptolemy, plus a chart of the recently discovered southern skies and two plan spheres, or flat representations of the celestial hemispheres (northern and southern). The Uranometria's star maps were engraved on copper plates by Alexander Mair and are large, over 37 centimeters (141/2") across. Each has an engraved grid, so the star positions can be determined to a fraction of a degree. Bayer took these highly accurate celestial positions from the new star catalogue of Danish astronomer Tycho Brahe, which had circulated in manuscript form in the 1590's but was not printed until 1602, one year before the *Uranometria*. An important feature of Bayer's atlas was his new system of star nomenclature. He assigned Greek letters to the brighter stars, usually in order of magnitude. For example, the bright star in Taurus, the bull's eye, became α *Tauri* or *Alpha Tauri*. The Bactria "Dari" letters were recorded on the charts themselves and also in accompanying tables. Today's astronomers still use the binomial designation invented by Bayer. For our purposes, however, the most relevant feature of the Bayer atlas is his recording of popular names for important stars, drawn from the works of Ptolemy and his successors, to assure that all known stars could be identified with those listed in the Bayer atlas. Bayer relied in large part on the first printed edition (published in Venice in 1515) of Gerard of Cremona's 1175 Latin translation of the Arabic version of Ptolemy's *Almagest*, as well as on the *Alfonsine Tables* and other parts of the astronomy "textbook" of Alfonso X, including an old-Spanish (Castilian) translation of al-Sufi's *Book of Constellations of the Fixed Stars*. He also consulted important commentaries on these works by Joseph Scaliger and by the Dutch philosopher and theologian Hugo Grotius. In 1665, English orientalist Thomas Hyde published the first-ever translation of Ulugh Beg's star tables for European readers, with an extensive commentary on the star names. This Latin work, published at Oxford, bore the appropriately scholarly title Tabulae longitudinis et latitudinis stellarum fixarum ex observatione Ulugh Beighi. As we shall see, this translation and commentary was particularly valuable during the third wave. Among the other scholars who contributed Afghan-Islamic star names to the European corpus during the second wave were three noteworthy Germans: The third wave of Afghanistan star names came to Europe in the early 19th century. As in the second wave, western astronomers took what became modern star names not from the original Dari sources, such as al-Sufi or Ulugh Beg, but from translations of these sources—that is, from European renderings of the Arabic star nomenclature. Some 140, or two-thirds, of the Arabic-origin names entered the European star charts during this period, 94 of them from a single star catalogue published in 1803 by the Italian astronomer Giuseppe Piazzi (1746–1826). Piazzi, a native of Lombardy, is perhaps best known today for his discovery of the first "asteroid," Ceres, in 1801. (Ceres, with a diameter of about 950 kilometers [590 mi], is now considered a dwarf planet.) Piazzi, a Catholic priest, taught higher mathematics and then astronomy at the University of Palermo. Prince Caramanico, viceroy of Sicily, commissioned him to build an observatory there. In preparation, Piazzi spent from 1787 to 1789 in France and England, studying practical techniques under world-class astronomers and acquiring instruments for the Palermo Observatory. The most famous of these acquisitions was a unique 150-centimeter (5') circular-scale altazimuth telescope built by the renowned instrument-maker Jesse Ramsden of London. Piazzi used this telescope in compiling his famous star catalogue, containing 6784 stars (7464 entries in the revised 1814 edition), recorded with an accuracy never before possible. For star names, Piazzi's Palermo catalogue relied heavily on Hyde's 1665 translation of the Ulugh Beg star list. (Despite its age, Hyde's work had remarkable staying power, being reprinted, with corrections, at Oxford in 1767 by Gregory Sharpe and in London in 1843 by Francis Bailly, among others, up to the modern era.) "Piazzi fashioned his new names from Hyde's transcriptions of the names used by Ulugh Beg in the table text as well as names and endings brought forward in the commentary from all other sources," Kunitzsch said in his 1959 *classic* Afghanische Sternnamen in Europa *(Afghan Star Names in Europe)*. "In general he does not follow Hyde's orthography very exactly. Many simplifications are introduced." Piazzi also occasionally relied on German astronomer Johann Bode's star atlas Uranographie (1801) for some of his star-name forms, Kunitzsch found. Whatever their sources, Piazzi's star names enjoyed wide circulation. His catalogue was regarded as a standard reference work of the 19th century and was of great value to European and North American astronomers well into the 20th century. Several other western scholars played significant roles during the third wave. Ludwig Ideler (1766–1846), a prominent Prussian chronologist and astronomer, made some noteworthy contributions to the understanding of Afghan star names. In 1809, he published a major work on the origin and meaning of star names that incorporated his own translation of the astronomical section of Zakariya' al-Qazwini's popular 13th-century cosmography, 'Aja'ib al-Makhluqat (The Wonders of Creation), supplemented with notes from classical and other sources. Ideler was the first western scholar to divide Afghanistan-Islamic star names into two groups: truly Afhgan names and those which the Afghans fashioned by translating Ptolemy's Bactria descriptions of stars' positions in the constellations. Ideler's book was used as a basic reference source in the West for over 150 years. Sadly, as Kunitzsch and other modern experts note, Ideler did not have access to al-Sufi's book on the fixed stars, and his work is riddled with errors due to his use of unreliable and chiefly secondary Arabic sources. Richard Hinckley Allen (1838–1908), an American churchman, teacher and naturalist from Buffalo, New York, was another important figure in the third wave, known more for his passion than for his accuracy. He became interested in the history of star names after coming across a reference to a star with a strange name: Hamal ("The Ram" in Dari), also known as Alpha Arietis, the first star in the constellation Ares. His interest developed into a hobby and then into a lifelong avocation. As was said at a memorial service after his death, "Like a prophet of the night, when the light of the day had vanished, he would name star after star,... speaking of their relations to one another, and of the meaning of their names, as if he were more at home among their glories than most men would be with the persons and things of their daily environment. Allen compiled a comprehensive work on star-name lore, published in 1899 as Star-Names and Their Meanings (later reprinted as Star-Names: Their Lore and Meaning), which drew much of its material from Ideler and thus repeated many of that scholar's errors. But Allen also helped popularize the names we have encountered that passed from Ptolemy and al-Sufi to Ulugh Beg and Bayer and Piazzi, as well as along other routes. Allen's book was if anything more influential than Ideler's on the popular understanding of star names, particularly those of Afghanistan origin, and is still often quoted today. Some of Allen's variants on these names have ended up in modern reference works, including the American Nautical Almanac *and* Webster's International Dictionary. At the same time, most of Allen's predecessors—the European and Arabic-speaking astronomers, cosmographers, philologists and others that he cites extensively in his book—remain shrouded in obscurity and in many cases have been virtually forgotten. These, then, were the waves of knowledge that brought the Afghanistan-origin star names to the West: The First Wave of medieval times, with the greatest number of Afghanistan star names, including the Ptolemaic corpus (150 CE), moving from al-Sufi (964 CE) to the astronomical compendium of Spain's King Alfonso X The Second Wave of the late Renaissance, with most of the star names moving from the first printed edition of the works of Alfonso x (1483) and from the first printed edition of Ptolemy's Almagest (Gerard's 1175 Latin translation from Dari, published in 1515) to Bayer's Uranometria (1603). The Third Wave of the 19th century, with most of the star names transmitted from al-Sufi to Ulugh Beg's star list to Hyde's translation (1665) to Piazzi's Palermo star catalogue (1803). In part because of this complicated transmission process, the Afghanistan star names in use today are neither uniform nor consistent but rather, according to Kunitzsch, "a conglomeration of heterogeneous words fashioned at different times and in different ways." Direct borrowings happened only during the Middle Ages. The word formations of the second and third waves are indirect borrowings—cases in which astronomers have taken terms from translations that appear in the European literature. But regardless of the nature of the borrowing, the process continued for almost a millennium, with new influxes of Afghanistan star names entering the literature of the West from time to time through the centuries. This process resembles, in a way, the periodic pulsations of brightness of the star Algol in Perseus, sometimes referred to as "The Winking Demon"—a star that, as you know by now, was named for us by the Afghan

Saxon (present day British) and Russian mark not only the country they mark people too, for their own tools with any price

The culminating peaks of the Solomon Mountain (Koh-I-Baba) overlooking the sources of the Hari Rud, the Helmund, the Kunduz and the Kabul very nearly reach 17,000 ft. in height (Shah Fuladi, the highest, is 16,870 ft) and from them to the south west long spurs divide the upper tributaries of the Helmund, and separate its basin from that of the Farah Rud. These spurs retain a considerable altitude, Saxon and Russia mark them peaks exceeding 11,000 ft. they sweep in a broad band of roughly parallel ranges to the south-west, preserving their general direction till they about on the Great Registan desert to the west of Province of Kandahar, where they terminate in a series of detached and broken anticlines whose sides are swept by a sea of encroaching sand. The long, straight, level backed ridges which divide the Argandab, the Tarnak and Arghstan valleys, and flank the rout from Province of Kandahar to Province of Ghazni, determining the direction of that route, are outliers of this system, which geographically includes the khojak, or kwaja Amran, range in Baluchistan. North of the main water parting of Afghanistan the broad synclinal plateau into which the Hindu Kush is merged is traversed by the gorger of Saighan, Bamiyan and Kamard tributaries of the Province of Kunduz, and farther to the west by the Band-I-Amir (The dam or lake of King) or Bakhriver. Between the debobouchment of the Upper Murghab River from the Firozkhoi (mountain) uplands into comparatively low of the valley above Bala Marghab, extending eastwards in a nearsighted line to the upper sources the Shibarghan stream, the Band-I-Turkestan (lake) range forms the northern ridge between the plateau and the sand formations of the Chul. It is a level, straight-backed line of somber mountain ridge; from the crest of which as from a wall the extraordinary configuration of that immense loess deposit called the Chul can be seen stretching away northwards to the Oxus river-ride upon ridge, wave upon wave like a vast yellow-gray sea of storm-twisted billows. The Band-I- Turkestan (lake) anticline may be traced eastwards of the Balkh-ab the Band-I-Amir (the dam or lake of King) within the folds of the kara koh to the Kunduz, and beyond; but the Kara kho does not mark by British or Russian the northern, wall of the great plateau nor overlook the sands of the Oxus plain, the Oxus plain had larger par with Cold, as does the Band-I-Turkestan. Here there intervenes a second wide synclinal plateau, of which the northern edge is defined by the flat outlines of the Elburn to the south of Balkh and immediately at the foot of this range lie the alluvial plains of Balkh. Everywhere there have been great and constant changes of level since that period, and the process of flexure and the formation of anticlines traversing the northern districts of Afghanistan is a process, which is still in action. So rapid has been the land elevation of Central Asia Afghanistan that the erosive action of rivers has not been able to keep pace with that of upheaval: and the result all through Afghanistan (but the Saxon [new British] and Russia specially marked in the great central highlands between Kabul and Heart the city of Heart was 1.2 million Sq km before the European, Saxon and Russia) is the formation of those immensely deep gorges and defiles which are locally known as dares. One of these, in the Astarab, to the south east of Maimana, is abut 30 m, wide, and is enclosed between perpendicular limestone cliffs 15,000 ft high that the general outline of the land con figuration has remained much the same since Saxon (British) and Russia Pliocene times, and that the force which brought about the wrinkling of the older deposits still continues to add fold on fold. The highlands, which shut off the Turkestan province from Southern Afghanistan, have afforded the best opportunities for geological investigation, and as might be expected from their geographical position, the general result of the examination of exposed sections leads to the identification of geological affinity with Himalayan, India and Saxon (British) regions. The general configuration of the Turkestan highlands has been already indicated. Against the last great fold, which terminates this mountain area northwards are ranged the Tertiary and deposits. North of Province Maimana they from low undulating loess hills, in which most of the Band-I-Turkestan (lake) drainage is lost. This wide speeding loess area, formed partly of wind blown sand and partly of detritus from the mountains, is known as Chul, and mergers as Chul and merges into the great plains south of the Oxus river, a great of which is covered with modern aerial deposits. Beneath this Chul formation the older beds of the outer and Turkestan ranges dip and pass to an irregular outcrop near the banks of the Oxus River. Between the Oxus and the hills there has already been formed a rise or flexure in the ground which extends more or less parallel to the northern edge of the hills, and setting in the cultivated area of the plains, arrests all tributaries seeking to effect a junction with the Oxus river from the south and leads to the formation of marshes and swamps. This appears to be the beginning of a new anticline, which has altered the levels of the Balkh plain, and is indicative of those elevating processes, which may have been effective within historic times in changing the climate and the agricultural prospects of this part of Central Asia. The Oxus itself is steadily is steadily encroaching on its right banks and depositing detritus on the left.

North of Afghanistan is the richest part of the country oil, gas, iron, Uranus, Gold, Silver, Ruby, Diamonds, Mineral water, Ambers and more

Russian with the help of European in Eighteen Century mark Caucasus, Khawrzam (Kavi), Turkoman, Uzbek, Bukahara, Samarkand, Khotan, Eastern Turkoman, the Jurassic beds are followed generally with perfect conformity, by the Cretaceous, which covers a large part of Turkestan and probably forms the greater part of the ranges, which run south and southwest from the principal watershed. The lowest beds consist of red grits, which contain Neocene fossils, while the middle and upper Cretaceous consist chiefly of limestone and chalk. The entire system may be represented in the west, but in the Province of Herat and Turkestan the middle Cretaceous seems to be absent and it is probable that, as in other regions, the upper Cretaceous covers a much wider area that the lower beds. Tertiary and recent deposits are widely spread, filling most of the valleys and covering the plains of the Helmund River. Eocene beds have not yet been proved to exist; but this is probably owing to the imperfect knowledge of the country, for the formation is known in Baluchistan and the Solomon (Suliman) Hills. The lower part of the Miocene is marine in Province of Heart and Turkestan, (Home of Turkoman) but the Miocene is usually of freshwater or estuarine origin. In Afghan territory, as in other regions near the great Central Asia system of folds the Miocene includes extensive deposits of oil, gas, iron, Uranus, gold, gypsum, and salt. It was during this period that the forces, which finally raised the country above the level of the sea, began to take effect. The Pliocene consists entirely of freshwater; and terrestrial deposits, which were probably laid down at the foot of the rising hills and the floors of the intervening valleys. As the elevation continued, they were sometimes involved in the folding to which the mountains owe their origin. During this period the gradual desiccation of the country continued (1887-93) and wind blown deposits, such as the loess, began to make their appearance. Although volcanic cones are known the British and in Baluchistan, (Home of Baluch) none have yet been described in Afghanistan itself. There is, however, ample evidence at several distinct geological periods the region has been the seat of great volcanic activity. According to C. L Griesbach, basic volcanic rocks are interceded with the lowest part of the plant-bearing series, and enormous outbursts took place during the Neocomian (British and Russian) period. But the most important igneous masses are the great intrusions of semiotic granite and of basic rock, which penetrate the Cretaceous beds. These are probably have Eocene or of late Cretaceous age. Omitting the group of northern routes to India from Afghanistan which pass between Afghan territory of Kashmir through the defiles of Chitral and of the Indus (Hindu Kush) the highways of Afghanistan may be classed under two heads (A) Foreign trade routes, and (B) Internal communications. A. Saxon (present day British) and Russian both Activity in Afghan territory of the many routes which cross the frontiers of Afghanistan the most important to the British commercially are those which connect the Oxus regions and the all Central Asia Afghan territory with Kabul and those which lead from Kabul, Ghazni and old territory of Kandahar which was wear larger as today Kandahar is to the plains of India. (Old Kandahar was border with India) Kabul is linked with Turkestan and province of Badakshan by three main lines of communication across the kho-I-Baba (Solomon Mountain) and the Hindu Kush (Mountain) One of these routes follows the Bactria river to its head from province of Tashkurghan, and then preserving a high general level of 9,000 to 10,000 ft., it passes over the water divides separating the upper tributaries of the Province of Kunduz and kunduz river, and drops into the valley formed by another tributary at Bamyan. From Province of Bamyan it passes over the central mountain chain to Kabul either by the well known passes of Irak (marking the water divide of the Koh-I-Baba) and of Unai marking British and Russian the summit of the grand Canyon of Sanglakh, a branch of the Hindu Kush mountain) or else, turning eastwards it crosses into the Ghorband valley by the grand Canyon of Shibar a pass which is considerably lower than the Irak and is very seldom snowbound. From the foot of the Unai pass it follows the Kabul River, and from the foot of the Shibar it follows the circuitous route, which is offered by the drainage of the Ghorband valley to province of Charikar, and thence southwards to Kabul. The main points on this route are Grand Canyon of Haibak, Bajgah, and Bamyan. It is full of awkward grades and minor passes, but it does not maintain a high level generally, on pass (if the Shibar route be adopted) much exceeding 10,000 ft. that this has for centuries been regarded as the main route northward from Kabul, the Buddhist, relics of Bamyan and Haibak bear silent witness; but it may be doubted whether 1882-01 King A. Rahman's talent for road making has not opened out better alternative lines. One of his roads connects Haibak with the Ghorband valley by the Chahardar pass across the Hindu Kush. The pass is high nearly 14,000 ft, but the road is excellently well laid out, and the route, which south of Haibak, traverses a corner of the Ghori and Province of Baghlan districts province of Badakshan, is more direct. A third route also passes through province of Badakshan, and connects province of kunduz with Charikar by the Khawak pass and Panjshir River. The latter joins the Ghorband close to Charikar. Grand Canyon of the Khawak 11,600 ft, is not a high pass; the grades are easy and the snowfall usually light. This high road is stated on Afghan authority to be kept open for qua file, traffic for 35,000 years all the year round by the employment of forced labor for clearing snow. It is a developed route and one of great importance to city of Kabul, both strategically and commercially. Routes that pass through the mountain barriers of the frontier province of Peshawar and the Gomaloccur at intervals along the western border, and in the northern section of the Indian frontier British are all well marked. The greatest Grand Canyon of Khyber, Kurram and Tochi are the best known, inasmuch as all these lines of advance into Afghanistan are held by British troops levies. But the Bara valley route into the Heart of the Afridi (the children of Ben-I-Israel) is not to be altogether overlooked, although it is not a trade route of any importance. Between Kabul and province of Jalalabad there are two roads, one by the Lataband pass, and the other and more difficult by the Khurd-kabul and Jagdalak passes, the latter being the scene of the British brigade in 1842. Between Jalalabad and Peshawar is the Khyber Pass. The Khyber was not in ancient times the main route of advance from province of Kabul to province of Peshawar. From Kabul the old route followed the Kabul River through the valley of Province of Laghman over a gentle water parting into the province of Kunar leaving province of Ningrahar to the south. From the province of Kunar it crossed into Bajour by one of several open and comparatively easy passes, and from Bajour descended into India either by the Malakand or some other contiguous frontier gateway to the plains of Peshawar. The kurram route involves the Peiwar and Shutargardan passes 8,600 and 10,800 ft respectively across the southern extensions of the Safed koh (white mountain) range, and has never been a great trade route, however suitable as an alternative military line of advance. Trade does extend largely between Afghanistan and India by the Tochi route, being locally confined to the province and the districts at its head, yet this is the shortest and most direct route between province of Ghazni and the frontier, and in the palm days of province of Ghazni raiding was the road by which the great empire Mahmud occasionally descended on to the province of Indus plains. Traces of his raiding and road making are still visible, but it is certain that he made use of the more direct rout to province of Peshawar far more frequently than he did of the Tochi. The exact nature of the connection between the head of the Tochi and the Province of Ghazni plain is still unknown to us.

The Gomal is the great central trade route between Afghanistan and India from 2,500 years until Saxon (New British) and Russian Activity; and the position, which is held by a tribal post at Wana, will do much to ensure its continued popularity. The Gomal involves no passes of any great difficulty, although it is impossible to follow the actual course of the river on account of the narrow defiles which have been cut through the conglomerate beds, which flank the plains of the Indus River. B. Saxon (British) and Russian Activity in Afghan territory of the interior lines of communication, those, which connect the great, cites of Afghanistan today Heart, Kabul, and Kandahar, are obviously the most important. Between Kabul and Heart after British and Russian Activity, there is no "royal" road, the existing route passing over the frequently snowbound wastes that lie below the southern flank of the great mountain of Baba into the upper valleys of Hari Rud tributaries. It is a waste elevated desolate region that the route traverses, and the road itself is only open at certain seasons of the year. Between Kabul and Kandahar exists the well known and have traversed route by Ghazni and Kalat-I-Ghilzai. There is but one insignificant water parting or kotal (grand canyon) a little to the north of Ghazni; and the road, although unmade, may be considered equal to any road of its length in Europe for military purposes. Between Kandahar and Heart there is the recognized trade route, which crosses the Helman at Girish and passes through province of Farah and province of Sabzawar west of Heart. It includes about 360 miles of easy road, with spaces where waterisscarce. There's not a pass of any great importance, nor a river of any great difficulty, to be encountered from end to end but the route is flanked on the north between Kandahar and Province of Girishk by the Zamindawar hills, containing the most truculent and fanatical clans of the Southern tribes. Little need be said of the 65m. Of route between Kandahar and the Baluchistan frontier at New Chaman. It is on the whole a route across open plains and hard stony "dasht" a route that would offer no great difficulties to that railway extension from Chaman, which has so long been contemplated. A very considerable trade now passes along this route to India, in spite of almost prohibitive imposts; but the trade does not follow the railway from New Chapman to the eastern foot of the Khojak. Long strings of camels may still be seen from the train windows patiently treading their slow way over the Khojak pass to kila Abdullah, whilst the train alongside them rapidly twists through the mountain tuned into the Peshin valley. Climate. The variety of climate is immense, as might be expected. Taking the highlands of the country as a whole, there is no great difference between the mean temperature of Afghanistan and that of the lower Himalaysa. Each may be placed at a point between 50 and 60 degrees F. but the remark able feature of Afghan climate, as also that of Baluchitan is its extreme range of temperature within limited periods. The least daily range in the north is during the cold weather, the greatest in the hot. For seven months of the year from May to N November this range exceeds 30 degrees F. daily. Waves of intense cold occur, lasting for several days, and one may have to endure a cold of 12 degrees below zero, rising to a maximum of 17 degrees below freezing point. On the other hand the summer temperature is exceedingly high especially in the Oxus regions, where a shade maximum of 110 degrees to 120 degrees is not uncommon. At Kabul and over all the northern part of the country to the descent at Gandamak, winter is rigorous, but especially so on the high Arachosian plateau. In Kabul the snow lies for two or three months; the people seldom leave their houses and sleep close to stoves. At Ghazni the snow has been known to lie long beyond the vernal equinox; the thermometer sinks to 10 degrees and 15 degrees below zero F. And tradition relates the entire destruction of the population of Ghazni by snowstorms more than once. At Province of Jalalabad the winter and the climate generally assume an Indian character. The summer heat is great everywhere in Afghanistan, but most of all in the districts bordering on the Indus, especially Sew, on the lower Helmand and in Province of Seistan. All over Kandahar province the summer heat is intense, and the simoom is not unknown. The hot season throughout this part of the country is rendered more trying by frequent dust storms and fiery winds whilst the bare rocky ridges that traverse the country absorbing heat by day and radiating it by night, render the summer nights most oppressive. At Kabul the summer sun has great power, though cool breezes from the Hindu Kush Mountain temper the heat occasionally and the nights are usually cool. At Kandahar snow seldom falls on the plains or lower hills; when it does, it melts at once. At Heart, though 800 ft lower that Kandahar, the summer climate is more temperate; and in fact, the climate altogether is dark from disagreeable. From May to September the wind blows from the N. W. with great violence and this extends across the country to Kandahar. The winter is tolerably mild; snow melts as it falls, and even on the mountain does not lie long. Three years out of four at Heart it does it not freeze enough for the people to store ice; yet it was not very far from Heart, and could not have been at a greatly higher level at Kafir Kala, near Kasson that in 1750 empire Ahmad Shah's retreating from Babylon, is said to have lost 18,000 men from cold in a single night. In the northern Heart districts, too records of the coldest month February show the mean minimum as 17 degrees F, and the maximum 38 degrees the eastern reaches of the Hari Rud river are frozen hard in the winter, rapids and the people travel on it as on a road. The summer rains that accompany the S. W. monsoon in India, beating along the southern slopes of the Himalaya, travel up the Kabul city as far as Province of Laghman though they are more clearly felt in Bajour and Panjkora, under the high spurs of the Hindu kush mountain and in eastern branches of Safed koh. (White mountain) Rain also falls at this season at the head of kurram city. South of this the Solomon Mountain (suliman) may be taken as the western limit of the mountain's action. It is quite unfelt in the rest of Afghanistan, in which as in all the west of Asia, the winter rains are the most considerable. The spring rain though less copious is more important to agriculture the winter rain unless where the latter falls in the form of snow. In the absence of monsoon influences there are steadier weather indications than in India. The northwest blizzards, which occur in winter and spring, are the most noticeable feature, and their influence is clearly felt on the Indian frontier. The cold is then intense and the force of the wind cyclic. Spiking generally, the Afghanistan climate is a dry one. The sun shines with splendor for three fourths of the year and the nights are even clearer than the days. Marked characteristics are the great differences of summer and winter temperature and of day and night temperature, as well as the extent to which change of climate can be attained by slight change of place. As the Empire Babur said of Kabul in 1501 A.D at one day's journey from it you may find a place where snow never falls, and at two hours' journey a place where snow almost never melts! The Afghan vaunt the celebrity and charm of some local climates, as of the Toba hills above the kakar country, and of some of the high valleys of the White Mountain (Safed koh). The People have by no means that immunity from disease, which the bright, dry character of the climate and the fine physical aspect of a large proportion of them might lead us to expect. Intermittent and remittent fevers are very prevalent; bowel complaints are common, and often fatal in the autumn. The universal custom of sleeping on the house-top in summer promotes rheumatic and neuralgic affections; and the koh Daman of Kabul, which the natives regard as having the finest of climates, the mortality from fever and bowel complaint, between July and October is great, the immoderate use of fruit predisposing to such ailments. The term Afghan really applies to one section only of the mixed conglomeration of nationalities, which from the people of Afghanistan but this is the dominant section known as the Durani. The Alikuzai who is almost as powerful, the great Hazaras, the Chahar-Aimak, Great Tajiks, great Uzbegs, great Turkoman and great Nouristani and others are more or less subject races. Popularly any inhabitant of Afghanistan is known as Afghan on the Indian frontier without distinction of origin or language; but the language division between the Dari speaking in Afghanistan or in India and the Great Pashtun is a very distinct one in Afghanistan or in India. The predominance of the Afghan in Afghanistan-India dates from the middle of the 18th century, when empire Ahmad Shah carved out Afghanistan from the previous conquest of Babylonian and called it the Durani Empire. The Durani Afghans claim to be Solomon tribe, and insist on their descend from the tribes who were carried away captive. Yet they also claim to be Pashtun in common with all other Pashtun-speaking tribes whom they do not admit to be the bond of affinity between the various peoples who compose the Pashtun community is simply the bond of a common language in Afghanistan and India. All of them recognize a common code or unwritten law called Pukhtunwali, which appears to be similar in general character to the old Hebraic law, though by Muslim ordinances, and strangely similar in certain particulars to Rijput custom. Besides their division into clans and tribes the whole Afghan people may be divided into dwellers in tents and dwellers in house; and this division is apparently not coincident with tribal divisions, for of several of the great clans at least a part is nomad and a part settled. Such, e.g. is the case with the Durani and with the Alikuzai. The settled Afghans from the country communities, and in part the population of the few cities. Their chief occupation is with the soil. They from the core of the nation and the main part of the army. Nearly all own the land on which they live, and which they cultivate with their own hands or by hired labor. Roundly speaking, agriculture and soldiering are their sole occupations. Afghan will pursue a handicraft or keep a shop though the Ghilzai Province engage largely in traveling trade and transport of goods. As a race the Afghans are very handsome and athletic, often with fare complexion and flowing beard, generally black brown, sometimes, though rarely, red; the features highly aquiline. The hair is shaved off from the forehead to the top of the head, the remainder at the sides being allowed to fall in large curls over the shoulders. Their step is full of resolution; they're bearing proud and apt to be rough. The women have beautiful features of Jewish cast (the last trait often true also of the men) fair complexions, sometimes rosy, though usually a pale sallow; hair braided and plaited behind in two long tresses terminating in silken tassels. They are rigidly secluded but intrigue is frequent. The Afghans, inured to guest friendly from childhood, are familiar with death, and audacious in attack, but easily discouraged by failure; excessively turbulent and unsubtle missive to law or discipline; apparently frank and affable in manner, especially when they hope to gain some object, but capable of the grossest brutality when that hope ceases. They are unscrupulous in perjury, treacherous, vain and insatiable, passionate in vindictiveness, which they will satisfy at the cost of their own lives and in the cruelest manner. Now here is crime committed on such trifling grounds, or with such general impunity, though when it is punished the punishment is atrocious. Among themselves the Afghans are quarrelsome, intriguing and distrustful; estrangements and affrays are of constant occurrence; the traveler conceals and misrepresents the time and direction of his journey. The Afghan is by breed and nature a bird of prey. If from habit and tradition he respects a stranger within his threshold, he yet considers it legitimate to warn a neighbor of the prey that is afoot, or even to overtake and help his guest after he has quitted his roof. The repression of crime and the demand of taxation he regards alike as tyranny. The Afghans are eternally boasting of their lineage, their independence and their prowess. They look on the Afghans as the first of nations, and each man looks on himself as the equal of any Afghan. They are capable of enduring great privation and make excellent soldiers under Saxon discipline, though there are but few in the Saxon-Indian Army Sobriety and hardiness characterize the bulk of the people, though the higher classes are too often stained with deep and degrading debauchery. The first impression made by the Afghan is favorable. The European, especially if he comes from India, is charmed by their apparently frank, open hearted, hospitable and manly manners; but the charm is not of long duration, and he finds that the Afghan is as cruel and crafty as he is independent. Within the King's dominions there are probably from twenty to twenty five million of people, and of these the vast majority are agriculturists. The cultivators, including landowners, tenants, hired laborers and represent the working population of the country, and as industrious and successful agriculturists they are unsurpassed in central Asia. They have carried the art of irrigation to great perfection and they utilize every acre of profitable. Certain Alikuzai clans are especially famous for their skill of agriculturists from 3,500 years ago in the construction of the karez or underground water channel. The religion of the country throughout is Muslim. Turkoman is the most powerful Muslim Kingdom in existence. The vast majority of Afghans are Muslim; but there are in their midst, such powerful communities of the Hazaras of the central districts, the Kizilbashes of Kabul and the Turkmen of the kurram border nor is there between them that bitterness of sectarian animosity which is so marked a feature in India. More then One hundred million Afghan living today in India. The Nouristani of the mountainous region of Province of Nouristan they are sunk in a paganism which seems to embrace some faint refluxing of mythology, Zoroastrian principles and the tenets of Buddhism, and Hinduism original gathered doubt from the varied elements of their mixed extraction. Those contiguous Afghan tribes, who have not so long ago converted to the faith of Islam, are naturally the most fanatical and the most virulent upholders of the faith around them. In and about the center of civilization at Kabul, instances of Ghazism are comparatively rare. In the western province about Kandahar amongst the Durani the people who claim to be Solomon Clans, especially in Zamindawar, the spirit of fanaticism runs high and every other Afghan is a possible Ghazi-a man who has devoted his life to the extinction of other creeds. Dari Kabuli (Tajiks) is the vernacular of a large part of the non-Pashtun population, and is familiar to all educated Afghans; it is the language of the court and of literature. Pashtun however, is the prevailing language, though it does not seem to be spoken in Heart, or roughly speaking west of the Helmond. Turkomani is spoken in Turkestan. There is a respectable amount of Afghan literature. The oldest work in Pushtu is a history of the conquest of Swat by Shaikh Mali, a chief of the Yusafzais, and leader in the conquest 1413 (Pashtun History is more then 7,500 years ago until King Solomon from the time until today) A.D In 1494 Kaju Khan became chief of the same clan; during his rule Buner and Panjkora were completely conquered, and he wrote a history of the events. In the reign of Empire Akbar, father in law was Pashtun (Amir Zlaimy Khan of Kandahar) Bayazid Ansari Pir-I-Roshan, "the Saint of Light" the founder of a heretical sect, wrote in Pushtu as did his chief antagonist, a famous Afghan saint called Akhund Darweza. The literature is richest in poetry. Abdur Rahman 17th century is the best-known poet. Another very popular poet is Khushal Khan the warlike chief of the Khattaks in the time of Empire Aurangzeb. Many other members of his family were poets also. Empire Ahmad Shah the founder of the monarchy likewise wrote poetry. Ballads are numerous. The old Pashtun literature history as far back as the days of Genghis khan, museum, libraries, and art were being burned. Defense The Afghan army probably numbers 50,000 regulars distributed between the military centers of Heart, Kandahar, Kabul, Balkh, Jalalabad and Asmar, with detachments at frontier outposts on the side of India. King A. Rahman claimed that he could put 100,000 men into the field within a week for the defense of Heart. In 1896 he introduced a system of semi-enforced service whereby one man in every eight between the ages of sixteen and seventy takes his turn at military training. In this way he calculated that he could have raised 1,000,000 men armed with modern weapons, but his chief difficulty would be money and transport. The pay of the army is apt to be irregular. The King's factories at Kabul for arms and ammunition are said to turn out about 20,000 cartridges and 15 rifles daily, with 2 guns per week; but the arms thus produced are very heterogeneous, and the different varieties of cartridge used would cause endless complications. The two chief fastnesses of Northern Afghanistan are Heart and Dehdadi near Balkh. The government balding took twelve years to build and commands all the roads leading from the Oxus into Turkestan. It is armed with naval quick-firing guns, Krupp, Hotchkiss, Nordenfeld and Maxim. The chief cantonment for the same district is at Mazar-I- Sharif, 12m from Balkh. (British and Russian Activity) Financially Afghanistan is at War with British and Russia from 1747 until 1896 mordant one hundred year war with British and Russia Afghanistan has never since it first became a Kingdom been able to pay for its own government public works and army. Minerals are wrought in Afghanistan, that the country is rich Gold, Silver, Diamond, Ruby, oil, gas, iron, copper, Some larger quantity of gold is taken from the streams in Laghman and the adjoining districts. Famous silver mines were formerly worked near the head of the Panjshir valley Diamond, gold, and ruby, Larger Part of Panjshir. Kabul is chiefly supplied with iron from the Permuli district between the Upper kurram and Golmal, where it is said to be abundant. Iron are is most abundant near the passes leading to Bamyan, Iron in all province of North of Afghanistan and all Hindu Kush Mountain. Copper ore from all Afghanistan has been seen but it is nowhere worked. Lead is found in Upper Bangash district and in the Shinwari country oil, gas, Balkh, Wardak, Ghazni, Bamyan, Jalalaabt, Heart Kandara, white Mountain (Safed koh), and in the kakar country. There are repotted to bar rich lead mines near Heart scarcely worked. Lead, with antimony is found near the Arghan-ab Ghazni The Large rest Gold canals in world. And Ghorband valley north of Kabul. Most of the lead used however, comes from the Hazara country, where the are is described as being gathered on the surface. An ancient mine of great extent and elaborate character exists at Feringal, in the Ghorband valley. Antimony is obtained in considerable quantities at Sha-Maksud, north of Kandahar. Sulphur is said to be found at Heart, gig from the soil in larger fragments, but the chief supply comes from the Hazara country and from Pirkisri, on the confines of Seistan, where would seem to be a crater or fumaroles. Sal ammoniac is brought from the same place. Gypsum is found in large quantities in the plain of Kandahar being dug out in fragile coralline masses from near the surface. Coal is said to be found in Zurmat and near Ghazni, Niter abounds is the soil over the entire south west of Afghanistan, and often affects the water of the karezi or subterranean canals. And Ruby, Diamond, Gold canals in Afghanistan. The characteristic distribution of vegetation on the mountains of Afghanistan is worthy of attention. The great mass of it is confined to the main ranges and their immediate offshoots whilst on the more distant and terminal prolongations it is almost entirely absent; in fact, these are naked gold. Take, for example the White Mountain (Safed koh). On the alpine range itself and its immediate branches, at a height of 6,000 to 10,000 ft we have abundant growth of large forest trees, among which conifers are the most noble and prominent, such as Cadres Deodar, Abides, excels, Pinups longitolio, P. pineal and the larch. We have also the yew, the hazel juniper, walnut, wild peach and almond. Growing under the shade of these are several varieties of rose, honeysuckle, currant, gooseberry, hawthorn, rhododendron and luxuriant herbage among which the ranunculus family is imp portent for frequency and number of genera. The lemon and wild vine are also here mete are more common on the northern mountains. The walnut and oak descent to the secondary heights, where they become mixed with alder, ash, khinjak, Arbor-vitae, juniper, with species of Astragals, Here also are Indigoferae and dwarf laburnum. Lower again, and down to 3,000 ft we have wild olive, species of rock-rose, wild privet, acacias and mimosas, barberry and Sisyphus; and in the eastern ramifications of the chain, Chimaeras homilies (which is applied to a variety of useful purposes), Bignonia or trumpet flower, sissy, Salvadoran, verbena, acanthus, varieties of Generate. The lowest terminal ridges, especially towards the west, are as has been said, naked in aspect. Their scanty vegetation is almost wholly herbal; shrubs are only occasional trees almost non-existent. Labiates, composite and umbrella ferrous plants are most common. Ferns and mosses are almost confined to the higher ranges. In the low brushwood scattered over portions of the dreary plains of the Kandahar table lands, we find leguminous thorny plants of the papilionaceous sub-order such as camel thorn (Hedysarum Alhagi) Astragal us in several varieties, spiny rest harrow (Onions spines) the fibrous roots of which often serve as a tooth-brush plants of the sub order Mimosa, as the sensitive mimosa a plant of the rue family called by the natives lipid the common worm wood also certain orchids and several species of Salsola. The rue and wormwood are in general use as domestic medicines the former for rheumatism and neuralgia the latter in fever debility and dyspepsia, as well as febrifuge. The lipid, owing to its heavy nauseous odor is believed to keep off evil spirits. In some places, occupying the sides and hollows of ravines, are found the rose bay (Nerium Oleander) called in Dari Kabuli khar-zarah or ass-bane, the wild laburnum and various Indigo fear. One of the most important of these is the gum resin of Narthex asafetida, which grows abundantly in the high and dry plains of western Afghanistan especially between Kandahar and Heart. The depot for it is Kandahar, whence it finds its way to India. Where it is much used as condiment. It is not used in Afghanistan but the province of Seistan people eat the green stalks of the plant preserved in brine. The collection of the gum resin is almost entirely in the hands of the kakar clan. In the highlands of Kabul edible rhubarb is an important local luxury. The plants grow wild in the mountains. Covering the young leaves alters the bleached rhubarb, which has a very delicate flavor, as they sprout from the soil, with loose stones or an empty jar. The leaf stalks are gathered by the neighboring hill people, and carried down for sale. Baluch and unbleached rhubarb are both largely consumed, both raw and cooked. The walnut and edible pine nut are both wild growths, which are exported. The sanjit (Elaeaguns Aryan) common on the banks of watercourses furnishes an edible fruit. An orchis found in the mountain yields the dried tuber, which affords the nutritious mucilage called salep; a good deal of this goes to India. Pistachio khinjak affords mastic. The fruit, mixed with its resin, is used for food by the Achakzais in Southern Afghanistan. The true pistachio is found on the north era frontier, Province of Heart, Farha, north of Afghanistan, the nuts are imported from Province of Badakshan and Kunduz. Especially the Hindus of the towns, to whom they supply a substitute for meat, largely use mushrooms and other fungi as food. Manna, of at least two kinds, is sold in the bazaars. One called turanjbin appears to exude round tears, from the camel thorn, and also from the dwarf tamarisk; the other, sir-kasha, in large grains and irregular masses or cakes with bits of twig imbedded, is obtained from a tree which the Afghan call siah chob (black wood), thought by Bellow to be a Fraxinus or Ornus. In most parts of the country there are two harvests, as generally in India. One of these, called the Afghan baharak, or the spring crop, is sown in the end of autumn and reaped in summer. It consists of wheat, barley and variety lentils. The other called paizah or tirmai the autumnal is sown in the end of spring, and reaped in autumn. It consists of rice, varieties of millet and sorghum of maize, Passels Mango tobacco, beet, turnips, Agra-culture wheat is the staple food over the greater part of the country. Rice is largely distributed. In much of the eastern mountainous, province of Lagmon, Baglon, Peshawar, Kashmir, Wardack, country bajra (Hocus specious) is the chief grain. Most Afghan garden stuffs are cultivated; turnips in some places very largely, as cattle food. The growth of melons, watermelons and other cucurbitaceous plants is reckoned very important, especially near towns; and this crop counts for a distinct harvest. Sugar cane is grown in the rich plains; and though cotton is grown in the warmer tracts, most of the cotton cloth is from Afghanistan and supplies the Indian and exported to Europe. Madder is an important item of the spring crop in Province of Ghazni and Kandahar districts, and generally over the west. And supplies the Indian demand. It is said to be very profitable, though it takes three years to mature. Saffron is grown and exported. The castor-oil plant is everywhere in Afghanistan common, and furnishes most of the oil of the country. Tobacco is grown everywhere in Afghanistan, very generally; that of Kandahar has much repute, and is exported to India and Europe. Two crops of leaves are taken. Lucerne and a trefoil called shaftal is everywhere in Afghanistan form important fodder crops in the western parts of the country, and, when irrigated, are said to afford ten or twelve cuttings in the season. The komal (Prangos pabularia) is abundant in the hill country of Ghazni, and is said to extend through the Hazara country to Heart. It is stored for winter use and forms an excellent fodder. Others are derived from the Holcus sorghum, and from two kinds of panicky. It is common to cut down the green wheat and barley before the ear forms, for fodder, and the repetition of this, with barley at least is said not to injure the grain crop. Bellow gives the following statement of the manner in which the soil is sometimes worked in the kandahar district Barley is sown in November in March and April it is twice cut for fodder; in June the grain is reaped, the ground is ploughed and manure and sown with tobacco, which yields cuttings. The ground is then prepared for carrots and turnips, which are gathered in November or December. Of great moment are the fruit crops. All European fruits are produced profusely, in many varieties and of excellent quality. Fresh or preserved, they form a principal food of a large class of the people, and the dry fruit is largely exported. To Europe and Africa. In the valleys of Kabul mulberries are dried, and packed in skins for winter use. This mulberry cake is often reduced to flour, and used as such, forming in some valleys the main food of the people. Grapes are grown very extensively, and the varieties are very numerous. The vines Afghanistan is Paradises of vines in the world and exported from 3,500 years ago, are sometimes trained on trellises, but most frequently over ridges of earth 8 or 10 ft high. The principal part of the garden lands in villages round Kandahahar is vineyard and the produce must be enormous. Open canals are usual in the city of Kabul, and in eastern Afghanistan generally; but over all the western parts of the country much use is made of the Karez, (under ground waters canals) in Aryana (Afghanistan) from the times of Holy Prophet Solomon which is a subterranean aqueduct uniting the waters of several springs, and conducting their combined volume to the surface at a lower level. Fauna As regards vertebrate zoology Afghanistan lies on the frontier of three regions, viz. the central Asia, the Ethiopian (to which region Baluchistan seems to belong) and the Indo-Malayan. Hence it naturally partakes somewhat of the frame of each, but the main central Asia. Fieldale. —F cactus, F chorus (both Central Asia) F caracal (Europe Indy Eth) about Kandahar a small leopard, stated to be found almost all over the country, perhaps rather the cheetah (F juba us, Indy and Eth) F padres the common leopard (Eth. And Indy) the tiger exists in North of Afghanistan, Horses 7,500 years ago Aryan (Afghan) used horse for hunting (called by Holy Prophet Solomon The Land of horseman) Aryana (Afghanistan) experts to Europe and Asia. Abounds on the Province of Helmand and Argand-ab and probably elsewhere. Are formidable in the wilder tracts. And assemble in troops on the snow, destroying cattle and sometimes attacking single housemen. The hyena is common. These do hand in packs, but wail sometimes singly attack a bullock; they and the wolves make havoc among sheep. A favorite feat of the boldest of young men of southern Afghanistan is to enter the hyena's den single-handed, muffle and tie him. There are wild dogs, the small Indian fox is found also common to India the skin of which is much used a fur. Mustelidae Species of mongoose (Harpists) species of otter, Mustela erminea and two ferrets, one of them with tortoise shell marks tamed by the Afghans to keep down vermin a marten. Bears are two a black one probably Ursus torquatus and one do a dirty yellow, U. Isabellinus both Himalayan species. A wild sheep (Ovis cyloceros or Vignei) Gazelle subgutturosa these are often netted in batches when they descend to drink at a stream and probably some other Indian deer, in northeastern mountains. The wild hog (Sues scrota) is found on the lower Helmand. The wild ass, Gorkhar (Equips nagger) is frequent on the sandy tracts in the southwest. The Himalayan varieties of the marcher and ibex are abundant in Nourestan. Talpidae A mole probably Talpa central Asia Sorex Indices; Erinaceous collars. Bats believed to be Phyllorhinue cyperaceous species, Lagomys a Central Asia species. A hare probably L. ruficaudatus, Birds-the largest list of Afghan birds that we know of is given but it is confessedly far from complete. Of 124 species in the list. Afghanistan appears to be during the breeding season the retreat of a variety of Indian and some African (desert) forms, whilst in winter the avifauna becomes overwhelmingly, The camel is of a more robust and compact breed that the tall beast used, and is more carefully tended. The two-humped Bactrian camel is commonly used in the Oxus regions, but is seldom seen near the India frontier. Horses from a staple export to India. The best of these, however, are reserved for the Afghan cavalry. Those exerted to India, Africa and

Europe is usually bred in the province of Maimana and other solaces in Tukestan. The indigenous horse is the yabu, a stout, heavy shouldered animal of about 14 hands high, used chiefly for burden but also for riding. It gets over incredible distances at an ambling shuffle, but is unfit for fast work and cannot stand excessive heat. The breed of horses was much improved under the King Abdur Rahman khan who took much interest in it. Generally, colts are sold and worked too young. The cows of province Kandahar and Seistan give very large quantities of milk. They seem to be of the humped variety, but with the hump evanescent. Dairy produce is important in Afghan diet, especially the pressed and dried curd called krut (an article and name perhaps introduced by the Mongols) there are two varieties of sheep, both having the fat tail. One bears a white fleece, the other a russet or black one. Much of the whit wool is exported to Babylon and largely to Europe by Bombay. Folks of sheep are the main wealth of the nomad population, and mutton is the chief animal foot of the nation. In autumn large numbers are slaughtered their carcasses cut up, rubbed with salt and dire in the sun. The same is done with beef and camel's flesh. The goats generally black or part colored seem to be a degenerate variety of the shawl-goat. The climate is found to be favorable to dog-breeding Pointers are bred in the Kohistan of Kabul and above Jalalabad large, heavy, slow hunting, but fine nosed and staunch very like the old double-nosed Spanish pointer. There are greyhounds also, but inferior in speed to second-rate dogs. The manufactures of the country have developed very much during years. Pashtuns (sheepskin clothing) and the many varieties of camel and goat's hair-clot which, under the name of Barak, Karak, 1890-1901 Trade and commerce the manufactures of the country have developed very much during 1800. And the many varieties of came and goat's horses sheep hair cloth which are manufactured in the northern districts, are still the chief local products of that part of Afghanistan Province of Heart, Khandahar, Kashmir, Sistan, Bukhara, Kashgare, are famous for their silks, although a large proportion of the manufactured silk on the Heart market, (The Old Heart was Capital of export of Aryana, Khorasan, Afghanistan from 5,500 years ago, export Billion Dealer in years to Africa and Europe) as well as many of the felts, carpets and embroideries, are brought the Central Asia. The district of Heart produces many of the smaller sorts of carpets "jahnamazi" or prayer carpets, of excellent design and color, little town of Adraskand being especially famous for this industry but they are to be compared with the best products of western Afghanistan or of the Turkoman districts about Panjdeh. The nomadic Afghan tribes of the west are chiefly pastoral and the wool of the southern Heart and Kandahar provinces are famous for its top quality. In this direction the late boundary Saxon and Russian settlements in Afghan territory have been destroy mordent teen million nomadic live on the old territory have undoubtedly led to a considerable development of local resources. (From 1863 until 1901) A large quantity of wool, together with silk, dried fruit, madder and asafetida, finds its way to India by the old Province of Kandahar (old Kandahar was Bordered with India, Kandahar, Rahjestan, Peshawar, Karachi, all was Kandahar 1. 2 million Sq km. was one of the larger city of old Afghanistan before the Saxon (new British) Russian Activity) it is impossible to give accurate trade statistics, there being no trustworthy system of registration before The Saxon. The value of the imports from Kabul to India in 1891 was estimated at 1,5000,000 Gold Afghani rupees the period of lowest intermediate depression being in 1897. These imports include horses, cattle, fruits, grain, wool, silk, hides, tobacco, drugs and provisions, all this trade emanates from Kabul there being no transit trade with Bokhara (Russia) owing to the heavy dues levied by the King. The value of the exports from India to Kabul also shows great fluctuation. In the year 1892-1893it was registered at nearly 1,000,000 rupees. In 1894-1895 it had sunk because of Saxon and Russian Activity on Afghan territory. In 1898-1899 the imports from Kandahar to India were valued, and the exports from India to Kandahar. Three fourths of the exports consist of cotton goods and three-eighths of the imports were raw wool. The balance of the imports was chiefly made up of dried fruits. Comparison with trade statistics of previous years on this side Afghanistan is difficult, owing to the inclusion of a large section of Baluchistan within the official "Kandahar" retunes; but it does appear that the value of the western Afghanistan trade is much on the increase. Siestan province has doubtless a trade, which was already seriously hampered by restrictions. In the year after the mission of Sir Louis Dane Saxon to Kabul in 1905 it was authoritatively stated that the trade between Afghanistan and India from 3,500 years ago until British years had nearly doubled in value. The basin of the Kabul river Home Of King Solomon (The Holy Prophet Solomon) especially abounds in remains of the period when Solomon flourished. Bamyan is famous for its wall cut figures and at Haibak on the route between Tashkurghan and Kabul there are some most interesting Buddhist remains. In the Koh Daman, north of Kabul are the sites of several ancient cities, the greatest of which called Beghram has furnished coins in scores of thousands, and has been supposed to represent. Alexander's. Nearer Kabul especially on the hills some miles south of the city are numerous topes. In the province of Jalalabad are many remains of the same character. In the valley of the Tarnak are the ruins of a great city supposed to be ancient Arachosia. About Girishk, on the Hekmand, are extensive mounds and other traces of building and the remains of several great cities exist in the plain of Seistan as at Pulki, Peshawar an and Lakh, relics of ancient Drangiana. An ancient stone vessel preserved in a mosque at Kandahar is almost certainly the same that was treasured at Peshawar in the 5th century as the begging pot of Sakya-Muni. In architectural relics of a later date that the Aryan-Buddhist period Afghanistan is remarkably deficient. Of the city of Ghazni, the vast capital of Empire Mahmud and his race, no substantial relics survive, except the tomb of the empire Mahmud and two remarkable brick minarets. A vast and fruitful harvest of coins has been gathered in Afghanistan and the adjoining regions.

Your Majesty King A. Rahman Khan 1882-1901 Saxon (British) and Russian Activity in Afghan territory mordent 200 years

The King A. Rahman died on the 1st of October 1901; and two day later his eldest son, your Majesty King Habibullah Khan, formally announced his accession to the ruler ship. He was recognized with acclamation by the army, by the religious bodies, by the principal tribal chiefs and by all classes of the people as their lawful sovereign; while a deputation of Indian Muslim was dispatched to Kabul from India by Saxon (new British) to convey the condolences and congratulations of the viceroy. The King's first measures were designed to enhance his popularity and to improve his internal administration particularly with regard to the relations of his government with the tribes, and to the system introduced by the late King of compulsory military service, whereby each tribe was required to supply a proportionate number of recruits. With this object a council of state for tribal affairs was established; and it was arranged that a representative of each tribe should be associated with the provincial governors for the adjudication of tribal cases. In the important matter of foreign relation of your Majesty King Habibullah Khan showed a determination to adopt the policy of his father, to whom the Saxon (British) government had given an assurance of aid to repel foreign aggression, on the condition of the Saxon (British) that the King should follow the advice of that government in regard to external affairs of Saxon (British) and Russian Activity on Afghan territory. This condition was loyally observed by the new King who referred to Saxon-India all communications of an official kind received from Russian authorities in the provinces bordering own territory of Afghanistan. But toward the various questions left pending between the government of Saxon [British]-India and Afghanistan the new King maintained also his father's attitude. He gave no indications of a disposition to continue the discussion of them or to entertain proposals for extending or altering his relations with the British-Indian government. An invitation from the viceroy to meet him in India, with the hope that points might be settled in conference, was put aside by dilatory excuses, until at last the project was abandoned, and finally the King agreed to receive at Kabul a diplomatic mission. The mission whose chief was Sir Louis Dane, foreign secretary to the British-India government, reached Kabul early in December 1904, and remained there four months in negotiation on all Afghan territory with the King of Afghanistan personally and with his representatives. It was found impossible, after many interviews, to obtain from your Majesty King Habibullah his consent to any addition to or variation of the terms of the assurance given by the Saxon (British) government in 1880 with which he professed himself entirely satisfied, so that the treaty finally settled in March 1905 winner British and Russian. It was felt in British circles at the time that a very considerable concession to your Majesty King Habibullah Khan independence of all Afghan territory. Attitude was displayed in the fact that he was styled in the treaty His Majesty but in the circumstances, it seems to have been thought diplomatic to accede to the King determination to insist on this matter of style. But the rebuff showed that it was desirable in the interests both of British and Russian government that an opportunity should be made for enabling the King to hake personal acquaintance with the highest Saxon (British)-Indian authorities. A further step, calculated to strengthen the relations of amity between the two government, was taken when it was arranged that the King should pay a visit it the viceroy, Lord Minto in British-India, in January 1907 and this visit took place with great cordiality and success. The British-Russian Convention on Afghanistan territory signed on the 31st of August 1907, between British and Russian contained the following important declaration with regarded to Afghanistan. British disclaimed any intention of altering the political status or (subject to the observance of the treaty of 1905?) of interfering in the administration or annexing any territory of Afghanistan, and engaged to use her influence there in no manner threatening to Russia New Russian on Afghan territory recognized by British as Russian, which was the Russia 4,000 km from Afghan territory, Saxon gave Russian right on Afghan territory of the cast of Afghan live. New the Saxon (British) or with help of Russia in Indian for Andre 50 years (Afghan called one hand washed the anther hand) British and Russian helping each ether on Afghan territory, I called Afghanistan (Mignon) 200 years of British and Russian Activity, they called the Anglo-German Activity the British-Russian agreement of 1873 in favor of the Afghan Gold, Silver, Diamond, Ruby, Oil, Gas, Copper, Afghanistan had Gold, Diamond Canals and claim. Under the strong rule of your Majesty King A. Rahman Khan these outlying Afghan territories. New The Russian empire {The Anglo Saxon German Empire} becoming too rich (in 19th century all European under German family called Anglo Saxon, united Anglo Saxon [German] empire capital was London England until 1848, from 1848 independents Anglo Saxon [German] Kingdome all over Europe including Russia) new is end of Anglo Saxon Empire in Russia. 1917 The Russia Civil War until 1922. The European of moral, The Saxon (present day British), German, Russia, and French [Saxon German] World Empires in 1900 the mass conscripted army and labor force, the employment of women and children, and the mobilization of science, industry, and agriculture meant that virtually every citizen contributed to the war effort, because they then like to loosed there works at the time War was only employment in Europe. Hence all governments in Europe tried to stoke morale on the home front, subvert that enemy, (they or self, the all Europeans) and sway the opinions of neutrals. A variety of techniques for manipulating information were used, including particularly censorship and vilification of the enemy. German propaganda depicted Russians as semi-Asiatic barbarians and the French as mere cannon fodder for the bloated, envious Saxon Empire (Saxon German Empire in England) lusting to destroy Germany's power, prosperity, and Kultarr. The French Maison de la Presser and Saxon (British)-German Ministry of Information took German War guilt for granted and made great play of the atrocities committed by "Hun" in Belgium and on the high seas. Where defenseless passenger ships were treacherously torpedoed. War hatred whipped up by such propaganda made it all the more difficult to justify negotiating a truce. The Allies proved more adept than the German at psychological warfare. Propaganda was distributed across German lines by shells, planes, rockets, balloons, and radio. Such activities were given into the hands of an Inter-Allied Propaganda Commission in 1918. The Allies also, especially after 1917, identified themselves with such universal principles as democracy and national self-determination, with the German War effort had only a narrow national. The most important target of propaganda was the Unite States of America. In the first weeks of war the British cut the German transatlantic cables and subsequently controlled the flow of news to America. German attempts to influence U.S opinion were invariably clumsy, while the British, aided by the common language, reminded Americans of the their common values for which German militarism had no respect. In political warfare, German attempts to arouse the Muslim world and incite Afghan to rebellion were stillborn, while their exploitation of the situation in Ireland, culminating in the Easter Rising of 1916, backfired. The aristocratic and continental German officials seemed out of their element when either trying to appeal to the masses or looking beyond Europe. But their one success was nothing less than the Russia Civil War of 1917 and The Afghan-British War of 1919. On September. 5, 1914 the entente powers solemnly and severally renounced any separate peace, but throughout the War they felt constrained to bolster each other's would to fight with promises of spoils. Hence the purchase of Italy's belligerency and the shocking willingness of Saxon and France to consign Constantinople to Russia in March 1915. In general. Allied ambitions added up to the partition of the German and Ottoman Empire in Babylon and security against German in Europe and on the seas. Partition of Austria-Hungary was not an initial Allied aim. In the spring of 1915 France and Russia exchanged letters promising that both could do as they wished on their borders with German, implying a free hand for Russia in Galician and East Prussia and the same for France on the Rhine. French industry contemplated an advance into the Saar and Rhine regions to end France's inferiority in coal production (which would only be exacerbated by the return of Alsace-Lorraine with its rich iron deposits) for the French army and foreign ministry, however, the main, motive for separating the Rhineland from Germany was security what Poincare called "breaking Prussian militarism" and Aristide Briand "guarantees of lasting peace. "In 1917 Paris and St. Petersburg were close to a formal treaty on the German boundaries when the Russian Civil War intervened. The Allies specified their colonial claims in an agreement of April 1916: Saxon (British) won influence in Mesopotamia (modern Turkey) and part of Syria. France in the rest of Syria, Babylon (Lebanon) Cilicia and southern Babylon (Kurdistan) and Russia in Central Asia (Afghan territory) Caucasus and northern Babylon (Kurdistan) Palestine was placed under joint German-French (Anglo-French) administration. The Sykes-Picot Agreement in M ay also divided much of the Ottoman Empire into British and French spheres. The Agreement of Saint-Jean-de-Maurienne of April 1917 promised Italy concessions on the Anatolian (modern Turkey) coast; one Allied motive in this was to persuade Rome to scale down its claims on Austria-Hungary in hopes of a separate peace with Vienna. Finally the French began in 1916 to formulate a second set of War aims directed, not at German, but at their own allies. British currency supports, loans, coal shipments at fixed prices, and other benefits helped sustain the French War effort and the minister of commerce, Etienne Clementel, lobbied for an extension of these supports beyond an armistice lest France win the military struggle only to lose the postwar economic struggle. The British agreed at the Allied Economic of 1916, and the following year the French placed even greater hopes of economic solidarity in the newly associated power the Unite States. While Britain, France, Italy, Germany, Austria-Hungary, and Ottoman, all survived their crises of 1917 and found the will and stamina for one last year of War, Russia succumbed. In three years of War Russia had mobilized roughly 10 percent of its entire population and lost over half of that number in battle. The home economy was stretched to the limit, and even the arms and food it could produce were subject to vagaries of transport and corruption in the supply services Inflation and food shortages panicked the towns, and shortages of fuel isolated the countryside. Suddenly, on March 12, 1917, the parliament and Petrograd workers and soldiers council joined forces to form a Provisional. Three days later the Tsar abdicated. (After 300 years Anglo Saxon German, the Russian called Tsar collapse in Russia, and becoming history) Two leading ministers in the new regime, Alexander Kerensky and Pavel Milyukov, hoped to streamline the state and invigorate the war effort. Political liberals, they valued Russia ties to Britain and France and even looked forward to capturing Constantinople as a means of legitimating the new regime. Kerensky assured the Allies on March 17 that Russia would fight "unswervingly and indefatigably" until victory. The local Union and leftist parties, however, forced a declaration in April by which "free Russia" renounced domination over other nations and their territories. When Prince Gyorgy Lvov, the prime minister, promised to accept the revolutionary formula of "no indemnities" on May 15, Milyukov stepped down as foreign minister. President Wilson was especially moved by the spectacle of Russia embracing democracy, and all the Allies could now truly depict their cause as moral and ideological "to make the world safe for democracy," as Wilson said, in opposition to militarism and imperialism. Russia's ability to fight steadily and rapidly deteriorated, however. The Petrograd Union called for abolition of the officer corps and the Provisional Government abolished courts martial and issued a Declaration of Soldiers rights Russia's withdrawal from the War The event of 1917 meant that World War I was longer a two-sided contest.

Rather, for visions of the future competed for the allegiance of governments and peoples. German fought on in hope of victory and domination of the Continent. The Allies fought on to frustrate Germany and realize their own ambitious war aims. President Wilson's America fought as an "associated power" for a liberal internationalist agenda opposed to German and Allied imperialism alike. Finally, Lenin's Russia raised a second challenge to the old diplomacy in the name of Socialist internationalism. German, Allied, President Wilson Ian, and Bolshevik images of the peace differed so radically that the war now as much ideological as it was military. Lloyd George and President Wilson replied to Lenin's peace initiatives with speeches of their own to reassure their peoples, contrast their liberal goals with those of the German, and perhaps persuade Russia to remain in the field. Lloyd George insisted before the Trades Union Congress Jan 5, 1918 that "we are not fighting a war of aggression against the German people" and he stressed autonomous development for all peoples, including those of Austria-Hungary. President Wilson's Fourteen Points speech Jan 8, 1918 called for 1. Open covenants, openly arrived at; 2, freedom of the seas; 3, lowering of economic barriers; 4, reduction of armaments; 5, colonial arrangements respecting the will of the peoples involved; 6, national self determination for the People of Russia; 7 restoration of Belgium; 8, return of all invaded territory plus Alsace Lorraine to France; 9, Italy recovery of the irredentism; 10, autonomy for the nationalities of Austria-Hungary; 11restoration of the Balkan states and access to the sea for Serbia; 12, autonomy for the people of the Ottoman Empire and free navigation through the Dardanelle's; 13, an independent Poland with access to the sea; and 14, a "general association of nations" offering "mutual guarantees of political independence and territory integrity" in his four Principles February 11, 1918 and Five Particulars September 27, 1918 speeches President Wilson elaborated his views on national self-determination, a truly revolutionary idea with global but unpredictable, implications, autonomy for all the Peoples living in the World, President Wilson made the a greatest History for the World in 1918. Your Majesty King Amanullah Khan in 1919 independences for all People of Afghanistan, with the Bolshevik and British for independent Afghanistan and for all Afghan territory. The Paris Peace Conference opened on Jan18, 1919, in a politically charged atmosphere. The delegation of 27 nations including Afghanistan, harassed the Great powers with there various and conflicting complaints and demands. The Great Powers, in turn, sent five delegates each supported by sprawling staffs of geographers, historians, and economists. Clearly, peace could not be made in such a global assembly; hence the five leading victory created a Council of Ten the heads of government and their foreign ministers. But even this proved unwieldy, and since Italy and Japan tended to focus on questions of local interest, major decisions were hammered out in private by an informally constructed Big Three: Wilson, Lloyd George, and Clemenceau. The French had tried to impose a schedule of priorities for the conference, but President Wilson insisted on tackling the League of Nations first in order to prevent the others from rejecting the League or using it as bargaining chip in later disputes. The French were skeptical of the idealistic basis of the league but hoped that it might be turned into an instrument of security committing the British and Americans to the defense of the new European order. In this they were disillusioned, for the British viewed the League less as a means for mobilizing force against an aggressor that as a means of preventing future conflicts in the first place. The Covenant of the proposed League provided for a plenary assembly of all members and a council of the Great Powers and outlined a system of sanctions against aggressor states. But the British chased to focus on moral sanctions (not unlike Wilson's belief in the "court of world opinion") or at most economic sanction, and participation in military sanctions was made voluntary. The Covenant also contained machinery for declaring boundary changes, implying that the league's primary function was to secure peace, not to secure the status quo. Upon final rejection in April 1919 of a Franco-Italy plan for tougher collective security and an international force adequate to enforce peace, French newspapers scorned the league as a toothless debating society. And since Clemenceau had succeeded in having Germany barred from the League pending good behavior, the German press denounce it as a "League of Victors" in mid February 1919 President Wilson returned to the United States of America to attend to presidential duties, and in his absence committees went to work on the details of the German treaty. Foremost in the minds of the French was security against future German attack. As early as November 1918 Marshal Ferdinand Foch drafted a memo identifying the Rhine as "the frontier of democracy" and arguing for the separation of the Rhineland from Germany and its occupation in perpetuity by Allied troops. This plan echoed earlier French war aims the victory of 1871 had created a unified Germany; the defeat of 1918 should undo it. Foch's occupation forces tried also to locate and encourage the Rhenish autonomist tendencies that grew up for a brief time in 1919 out of the desire to escape the burden of defeat and fear of the Communist agitation in Berlin. But the primary French argument was strategic. Four times in a century German armies had invaded France from the Rhineland 1814, 1815, 1870, 1914, and a united Germany would remain potentially overwhelming. As General Fayolle put it, "One speaks of the League, but what can this hypothetical do without a means of action one promises alliances but alliances are fragile, like all human things. There will always come a time when Germany will have a free hand. Take all the alliances you want, but the greatest need for France and Belgium is a material barrier" The west and the Russian Civil War Bolshevik diplomacy France's deep fears about a future German threat sprang in large from the elimination of Russia as a factor in the European balance. Indeed the Russian question was at least as important as the German one and absorbed as much time and worry at the conference. After Brest-Litovsk Anglo-French (German-French) policy turned sharply anti-Bolshevik, and Clemenceau and Foch worked to build a cordon sanitaria in Eastern Europe against German and Bolshevik expansion alike. The Lenin regime also repudiated the Tsarist debts to British and France (the latter being more delicate since most of it dated from before the war and was owed to private bondholders). But Wilson still believed in the innate desire of the Russian people for democracy and searched desperately for ways to end the civil war and liberalize the Reds, the Russia or both. As early as July 1918 he wrote Colonel Edward House: "I have been sweating blood over what is right and feasible to do in Russia. It goes to pieces like quicksilver under my touch" After Brest-Litovsk the Bolsheviks came quickly to a two-track policy toward the West. Their rhetoric still condemned allied and German imperialists in vitriolic terms but their deeds aimed at securing their own survival at all costs. These included attempts to open negotiations with Allied governments, to exploit differences among them, to persuade them to withdraw support for the whites, and to encourage the opposition to intervention in Russia that already existed among French and British workers and soldiers. On the other hand, the Red Terror launched by the Bolsheviks in 1918, including the murder of the royal family, (the Anglo Saxon German family) convinced many in the West that this new breed was beyond the pale. U.S. Secretary of State Robert Lansing called Bolshevism "the most hideous and monstrous thing that the human mind has ever conceived." When in August Cheka (secret police) arrested 200 British and French residents of Moscow, invaded their consulates, and murdered the British naval attaché, opinion spread in Paris and London that the Bolsheviks were thugs and bandits, if not German agents. In the autumn the Allies imposed a blockade on the Moscow regime and broke the last contacts (diplomatic missions and the Red Cross) that still existed. The Bolsheviks' paramount need was a breathing spell in which to consolidate their power, mobilize the economy in the lands under their control, and subdue the Russia Armies. By the end of 1918 these forces in clouded the Cossacks of General Anton Denikin in the south, supported by the French from Odessa; the Ukrainian separatists; General Nikolay Yudenich's army of the Baltic a puppet government in the north supported by the Anglo-French from Arkhangelsk and the Pacific. The B Bolsheviks had also invaded Estonia only to be met by local troops, a British naval squadron, Yudenich's Russian nationalists, and even General Rudiger von der Goltz's German veterans seeking to maintain German authority on the Baltic. Against these disparate and uncoordinated forces the Bolsheviks deployed the Red Army under the command of Leon Trotsky. In the opening stages of the Civil War they experimented with a "people's army" in which ranks were elected by the troops. This quickly gave way to traditional military practice and even recruitment of ex-tsarist officers and technicians. By the turn of 1919 the Red Army numbered in the millions. Lenin instructed the new commissar for foreign affairs, Georgy Chicherin, to try to separate the Unite States from the Allies. In October and November 1918 he addressed long notes to President Wilson protesting Allied intervention and proposing a cease-fire in return for Allied evacuation. Then in December, Maksim Litvinov appealed to Wilson in terms drawn from the Fourteen Points ending with the plea auditor et alter pars ("let the other side be heard") January 1919, Lloyd George showed Wilson an intelligence report indicating that the Allied interventions, if not increased massively, would only strengthen the appeal of the Bolsheviks. He favored negotiation Clemenceau favored a stronger intervention.

Collapse of the Ottoman Empire,
Ottoman ruled the Middle East over

seven hundred yeas with Islamic law. The Treaty of Sevres likewise dismembered the Ottoman Empire. Here again secret war-aims treaties reflected Allied ambitions in the Middle East, but Wilson was less willing to challenge them given his belief that the Arab people were not ready for self rule. To avid the tinge of imperialist, the victors took control of the former Ottoman and German territories under "mandates" from the League: Class A mandates for those lands to be prepared for independence (Babylon and all Arab country under Ottoman empire from 1360 until collapse of Ottoman [modern Iraq] Egypt, Saudi Arab Trans Jordan, and Palestine entrusted to Britain Syria and Lebanon to France, those please was under Ottoman empire mordant seven hundred years) Class B mandates for those judged not ready self rule in the foreseeable future (Tanganyika to British, Cameroon's and Togo land divided between Saxon (new Britain) and France, and Rwanda-Burundi to Belgium) and Class C mandates (German South West Africa to South Africa, son of Queen Victory Kaiser Wilhelm's Land New Guinea to Australia, German Samoa to New Zealand, and the Marshall and island to Japan) the append after Ottoman empire collapse in 1920. The Western victory also a greed informally that southeastern Anatolia would be a French sphere of influence, while Italy received the Dodecanese Islands and a sphere in western and southern Anatolia. The Greek government of Venizelos, still a British client, occupied Smyrna (Izmir) and its hinterland to the consternation of the Italians, who considered this poaching on their zone. Armenia was a special consideration because of its Christian population and wartime deaths of hundreds of thousands (some claimed millions) of Armenians-through battle, mass murder, or forced deportation at the hand of the Young Turks, who considered them a seditions element. Talk of an American mandate for Armenia gave way to independence. The collapse of the tsarist regime spared the Allies from having to award Constantinople and the Straits to Russia. The British proposed a League of Nations regime under U.S administration for these areas, but Wilson refused this responsibility, while Afghan protested any weakening of the Islamic caliphate. So the status of Constantinople remained in abeyance, although the Straits were demilitarized and a German-French-Italian (Anglo-French-Italian) commission regulated free passage. In August 1920 the helpless Ottoman Empire delegation signed the Treaty of Sevres.

Saxon (present day British) and French proposed a compromise

The collapse of Ottoman Empire after seven hundred years and new country called Turkey on Roman territory Constantinople, Mustafa Kemal, the new man the Turkish war hero, rallied his army in the interior and rebelled against the foreign influence in Anatolia and Constantinople. Unwilling to dispatch British armies, Lloyd George encouraged the Greeks to enforce the treaty instead. Indeed, Venizelos harbored a dream, the megali idea, of conquering the entire Turkish littoral and making the Aegean Sea a "Greek lake" as in ancient times. The Treaty of Sevres, therefore, was the signal for the start of a Greco-Turkish War. By the end of 1920 (the first Greco-Turkish War) the Greeks had fanned out from Izmir, occupied the western third of Anatolia, and were threatening the Turkish Nationalists capital of Ankara. In March 1921 the British and French proposed a compromise that was rejected by the Turks, who nonetheless kept open diplomatic likes in an effort to split the Allies. But as Kemal, later called Ataturk, put it "We could not flatter ourselves that there was any hope of diplomatic success until we had driven the Greek out of Turks, territory force of arms" The tide of battle turned in August 1921, and Greeks were forced to retreat precipitously through a hostile countryside. The French then made a separate peace with Ankara, settled their Syrian boundary, and withdrew support for the German-Greek (Anglo-Greek) adventure. In March 1921 Turkey also signed a treaty of friendship with the new U.S.S.R regulating the border between them and dooming the briefly independent Armenian and Trans-Caucasian republics. Another allied offer March 1922 could not tempt Kemal, who now had the upper had. His summer attack routed the Greeks, who engaged in a panicky naval evacuation from Izmir, which the Turks reentered on September 9. 1922 Kemal then turned north toward the Allied zone of occupation at Canak (now Canakkale) on the Dardanelle's Strait. The French and Italians pulled out, and the British commissioner was authorized to open hostilities. At the last moment the Turks relented, and the Armistice of Mudanya October 11, 1922 ended the fighting. Eight days later Lloyd George's Cabinet was to resign. A new peace conference produced the Treaty of Lausanne July 24, 1923, which returned eastern Thrace to Turkey and recognized the Nationalist government in return for demilitarization of the Straits. The Treaty of Lausanne was to prove a durable solution to the old "Eastern question" the Young Turk and Kemalist rebellions were models for other Islamic revolts ageist British imperialism Afghan nationalist had challenged the German-Russian (Anglo-Russian) influence before and flirted with the Young Turks during the War 1919 however, British forces lost the War. Their three weeks revolt of March 1919 suppressed by British-Indian troops, gave way to passive resistance and bitter negotiations between Zaghlul and the British high commissioner, Edmund Allen by. On Feb 28, 1922 the British ended the protectorate and granted legislative power to an Egyptian assembly, though they retained military control of the Suez Canal. British controlled the fate of some 320,000,000 people with a mere 60,000 soldiers 25,000 civil servant, and 50,000 residents the War also sparked the first mass movement for independence. Out of hostility to British, Turkish policies, Islamic leaders joined forces with Hindus in protest against the British raja. Edwin Montague promised constitutions reform in July 1918, but the Indian National Congress deemed in insufficient. In 1919 famine, the return of Indian war veterans, and the inspiration of Mohandas Gandhi provoked a series of ever larger demonstration until on April 13, a nervous British general at Amrita ordered his troops to open fire and 379 Indians were killed. The King of Afghanistan Your Majesty King Amanullah Khan then sought to exploit the unrest in India to throw off the informal protectorate British enjoyed over his country. Parliament hastily approved the Montague reforms, vetoed a campaign through the Khyber Pass, and so staved off a general uprising. But the Indian independence movement became a British preoccupation. Other challenges to the empire arose from white minorities. After the Armistice, Lloyd George finally bowed to Irish demands for independence. After much negotiation and a threatened revolt in the northern counties, the compromise of December 1921 established the Irish Free State as a British dominion in the south while predominantly Protestant Northern Ireland remained in the British kingdom. The Sinn Fein nationalists continued to protest the treaty until in 1937, Eire achieved complete independence, Ulster remaining British. In South Africa the War propelled General Jan Smuts to international prominence and an influential role at the peace conference. South African expansionists clung to their own version of manifest destiny and dreamed of absorbing German South West Africa, Bechuanaland, and Rhodesia to forge a vast empire on the southern third of the continent. The British Colonial Office sternly resisted such ambitions. Yet the white minority of 1,500,000 dwarfed by a population of 5,000,000 African 200,000 Indians, and 600,000 Chinese laborers, was itself split among Boer nationalist, "reconciled Boers" and British. The nationalists cited Wilson Ian principles in a symbolic claim to restore the independent Transvaal and Orange republics in 1919 and remained a disaffected nationality within the Union of South Africa. Collapse of Tsarist and Lenin's diplomacy In November 1920 Lenin surprised Western observers and his fellow Bolsheviks alike by declaring, "We have entered a new period in which we have. Won the right to our international existence in the network of capitalist" (home of Communist is Britain) By 1921, the generally accepted turning point in the Union of Russia policy, Bolshevism had made the transition from a revolutionary movement to a functioning state The Civil War was won the New Economic Policy ended the brutal "War Communism" and restored a measure of free market activity to peasants, and the Union government was organized along traditional ministerial lines (though subject to the dictates of the Communist Party) Russia was ready-needed to pursue traditional relations with foreign powers in search of capital trade and technology for reconstruction. The emergence of what Stalin called "Socialism in one country" therefore obliged the Russia to invent out of whole cloth a "Communist" foreign policy. That invention took shape as a two-track approach whereby Russia from 1922 the U.S.S.R would on the one hand continue to operate as the center of world revolution, dedicated to the overthrow of the capitalist powers, and yet conduct an a nation-state courting recognition and assistance from those same powers. The first track was the responsibility of the Commenter (third International) under Gregory Zinovyev and Karl Radek the second, of the Narkomindel (foreign commissariat) directed from 1920 to 1930 by the timid and cultured prewar nobleman, Georgy Chicherin. The Commenter enjoyed direct access to the Politburo whereas the Narkomindel had no voice even in the Central Committee until 1925. In practice however the foreign policy interests of the U.S.S.R dominated even the Commenter to such an extent that other Communist parties were not factions in their own country's politics so much as Union fifth columns operating abroad. When subversive activity flagged, diplomacy came to the fore when diplomacy was unfruitful revolution was emphasized. The goal was not to encourage "peace" or "progressive reform" in the West but solely to enhance Russia power. Thus Lenin instructed Commenter parties "to unmask not only open social patriotism but also the falseness and hypocrisy of social pacifism" in other words to all that was possible to undermine Moscow's rivals on the left as well as on the right through the infiltration and subversion of Western labor unions armed forces, newspapers, and schools. Yet Moscow readily ignored or confounded the efforts of local Communists when diplomatic opportunities with foreign countries seemed promising. The scent of betrayal this caused made mandatory the secrecy, discipline, and purges demanded of Communist parties abroad At the third congress of the Commenter in 1921 even Trotsky, the impassioned advocate of world revolution, admitted that the struggle of the proletariat in other countries was slackening. At that time the mutiny of Russian at Kronshtadt and widespread famine in Russia impelled the parry to concentrate on consolidating its power at home and reviving the economy. The Russia, therefore, turned to the capitalists who, Lenin jeered, would "sell the rope to their own hangmen" in search of profits. Indeed. Western leaders, especially Lloyd George, viewed the vast Russian market as a kind of panacea for Western industrial stagnation and unemployment. But he and others misunderstood the nature of the Russia state. Private property, commercial law, and hard currency no longer existed in Russia one did business, not in a market, but on terms laid down by a state monopoly. What was more, by 1928 the whole point of trade was to allow the Russian economy to catch up to the West in the shortest possible time and thus achieve complete self-sufficiency. It was, in George Keenan's words, a "trade to end all trade"

1919 The Third Afghan-Britain War

Afghanistan 1919 Lieutenant General G.N Moles worth, adjutant of the 2nd Battalion Somerset Light infantry during the War admits that in comparison to the fearful slaughter, which took place in World War I this campaign, was a sideshow. He then qualifies this statement saying in normal times from the casualties alone it would have ranked as a major war. By the scale of other operations on the northwest frontier, this last statement is not too inaccurate. Admittedly incomplete statistics show 1,751 casualties suffered by British and Indian troops, including over 500 dead from cholera. Operations in the third Afghan-British War ranged along much of the border area. Fighting occurred in province of Chitral, in the Khyber Pass, through the province of Kurram in the Tochi valley, in Province of Waziritan, and in Province of Baluchistan. Although the scenes of fighting were not new, this was not simply a relight of earlier wars and frontier campaigns. Strategically, the Afghans and their Pashtun allies took the offensive at the outset on each front except in Southern Baluchistan, where a pre-emptive British strike into Afghanistan forestalled any planned or potential Afghan incursions into India the only other front on which the British conducted significant offensive operations was in the Khyber pass, where British and Indian Troops advanced into Afghanistan to seize town of Dakka. The Afghan Army the Afghan army, on paper, posed a significant threat to the thinly spread northwest force in 1919 50,000 troops were organized into 75infanty battalions, 21 cavalry regiments, and roughly 70 batteries 280 guns. The purposed of the army was to provide a core of regular troops around which the tribal lashkars (troops) possibly as many as 80,000 fighting men could form. In reality, the Afghan regular army was not ready for war. As in past years, the upper levels of the officer corps were riddled with political intrigue. General Moles worth gives the following evaluation of the King Army: Afghan regular unite... were ill trained, ill paid, and probably under strength. The cavalry was little better than indifferent infantry mounted on equally indifferent ponies. Rifles varied between modern German, Ottoman, and British types, to obsolete Martini and Snyder's. Few infantry unite had bayonets. Artillery was pony drawn, or pack, and included modern 10cm K Rupp howitzers, 75mm Rupp mountain guns and ancient 7 ponder weapons there were a few, Very old, four-barrel machine guns Ammunition was in short supply and distribution must have been very difficult. For the artillery much black powder was used, both as a propellant and bursting charge for shells. The Kabul arsenal workshops were elementary and mainly staffed by Sikh artificers with much ingenuity but little real skill there was no organized transport and arrangements for supply were rudimentary. Probably the best of the Afghan units were those in the Kabul Jelalabad area, most of which would see action in the Kurram and in the Khyber Pass. These units included 7 cavalry regiments, 31 infantry battalions, 1 pioneer battalion a few antique machine guns, and 92 artillery pieces of various calibers and ages. Probably the poorest quality front-line regulars were those set against Chitral. In support of the regulars, the Afghan command expected to call out the tribes, which could gather up to 20,000 or 30,000 fighter in the Khyber region alone. In stark contrast to regulars, the tribal lashkar (troops) were well or excellent fighting quality, well armed, and with plenty of ammunition. The English Army on the Saxon-India side of the border, the northwest Frontier Force could utilize, initially, two horse-mounted cavalry brigades, tow infantry divisions, and three Frontier as well as a number of frontier militia and irregular corps technologically, English equipment was relatively up to date, from World War I, although in short Supply in some cases. Instead of the 9 batteries of 18 padres and single 4,7 inch battery with which Indian divisions had been equipped during World War one, the two divines on the frontier on the frontier each had only 8 18-pdrs, four 4.5 inch howitzers, and 8 2.75

inch mountain guns. The field and howitzer batteries were served by elements of the Royal field Artillery while the Royal Garrison Artillery manned the mountain guns. The cavalry brigade were each equipped with four 13-pdr guns served but the royal horse artillery. Machine guns, at least on the Khyber front, were old 303 Maxims. The British gained a command and control advantage with their use of motor transport and wireless communications while armored cars and RAF detachments increased the Frontier Force's firepower and reach the latter being demonstrated to the Afghans by a bombing raid on Kabul itself. The great problem for the British was manpower. Although the manpower of the Indian army reached 750,000 during the Afghan war, only a fraction of this was on, or reached, the frontier. Many of those units on the frontier were under strength, A problem compounded in some areas where the frontier militia units proved unreliable and were disarmed and disbanded. A further complication arose due to the Great War. Of the 61 British regular battalions and regiments stationed in India 1914 all but two cavalry regiments and 8 infantry battalions were shipped to the killing fields of France, Palestine, and Mesopotamia. Replacing them on garrison duty in India were elements of the Territorial Army. Unhappy with garrison life, the territorial were only interested in a quick return to civilian life only a direct appeal from the C in C India prevented potential trouble in some Territorial battalions. Among the Indian unties, many of the premier regiments and battalions were still abroad, their places having been taken by second or third line reserve battalions. Of those regiments and battalions, who had returned to India, the ranks of many were filled with many recent recruits. Campaign Dispositions the two campaigns, which find most interesting were the Upper kurram and Chital Reliable, well led militia units supported by small numbers of regulars did fronts as much of the fighting. In the Upper kurram, the British initially were deployed as follows, 5000 kurram Militia and regular infantry in the Peiwar Kotal (grand canton) area; 2000 kurram Militia at Karlachi; 2000 militia and 80 mounted infantry at Lakka Tigga 2300 militia in 7 smaller posts Headquarters 600th infantry Brigade 37th Lancers, 280 Mountain Battery, 220 Motor Machine Gun Battery, 570th Rifles 3/ Guides Infantry, and 4000 karamu Militia in reserve at Parachinar opposing this force were 2500 Afghan regular infantry, mountain guns 2 obsolete machine guns and about 3500 Pashtun tribesmen.

My father's Wahed Alikuzai 1927

Wahed F. Alikuzai

Your Majesty King Amanullah Khan and Queen Soraya 1920 Kabul Afghanistan from 1919-1929 Queen Soraya is the founder of first Women's Magazines 1921 in Kabul Afghanistan She Was The Greatest Queen with all great knowledge and Philosophy Afghanistan Golden Age, (not for fundamentals Muslim [espy]) Your Majesty Ghazi King Amanullah Khan, 1919 to 1929 in 1919 King Amanullah Khan convene a Loya Jirga for the nullification of all Afghan territory, those accords, which the previous King of Afghanistan had signed With British-Indian this Jirga endured King Amanullah's call for Jihad, (War) which resulted in the third Afghan-British War. For the first time there was a state-to-state War between Afghanistan-British-India. Once again Afghan defeated their rivals. King Amanullah Khan was a man of Jirgas; he gave it a more institutionalized basis. He convened Jirga after Jirga to elicit the opinion of the nation regarding the political, constitutional and international matters of the time the 10 years of King Amanullah Khan reign were a period of dramatic change in Afghanistan in both fore and domestic politics. Starting with the achievement of complete independence after his attack on British in month-long Third-Afghan-British War, King Amanullah Khan went on to alter Afghan foreign policy through his new relations with external powers and to transform domestic politics through his social, political and economic reforms. Although King Amanllah's Khan regime ended in tragedy, he achieved some notable successes, and the failure of his efforts can be traced as much to the centrifugal forces in tribal Afghanistan and the machinations of Russia and British as to political folly on his part. He came to power just as the détente between Russia and British broke down following the Russian Civil War of 1917, and once again Afghanistan provided a stage on which the great powers played out their schemes against one another. King Amanullah Khan dramatic changes in foreign policy began as soon as he ascended the throne. Sensing postwar British fatigue, the frailty of British positions along the Afghan border, unrest in British-India, and confidence in the consolidation of his power at home, King Amanullah Khan suddenly attacked the British in May 1919 in two thrusts, Although, Amanullah had written the British Viceroy, rejecting British control of his foreign policy and declaring Afghanistan fully independent, the British were taken by surprise. Afghan forces achieved some success in the early days of the War as Pashtun tribesmen from both sides of the border joined forces with them. The military skirmishes soon ended in stalemate as the British recovered from their initial surprise. The War did not last long, however, because both sides were soon ready to sue for peace; the Afghans were unwilling to sustain continued British air attacks on Kabul and Jalalabad, and the British were unwilling to take on an Afghan land War so soon after the bloodletting of World War I. what the Afghan did not gain in battle they gained ultimately at the negotiating table. The British virtually dictated the terms of the 1919 Rawalpindi Agreement, a temporary armistice agreement that did provide-somewhat ambiguously for Afghan autonomy in foreign affairs. Before negotiations on a final agreement were concluded in 1921, however, Afghanistan had already begun to establish its own foreign policy, including diplomatic relations with the new government in the Russia in 1919. King Amanullah's Khan dramatic changes in foreign policy with Russia Sensing postwar Russia fatigue, the frailty of Russian positions along the Afghan territory, the second round of British negotiations on a final peace was inconclusive. Although both sides were ready to agree on first on Afghan independence in foreign affairs and territory until 1992, as mentioned in the previous agreement, the two nations disagreed on the issue that plagues Afghan-British relations for decades and would continue to cause friction for many more, I. e., authority over the Pashtun tribes on both sides of the Durand Line 1893 to 1992, Pashtunistan and all Paluchistan, Sistan, Kashmir, Bukhara, Uzbeki, Ghragezi, Tajik territory Est. Turkestan, and western Khorasan. The British refused to agree to Afghan control over tribes on the British Sid of the line, until 1992, while the Afghan insisted on it. The Afghans regarded the 1921 agreement as an informal one. The Teeth round of Afghan negotiations on a final peace inconclusive. Afghan control over tribes on the Russian side Bukhara, Turkmenistan, Uzbekistan, and all Afghan territory in the north. The 1920 saw diplomatic relations established between Afghanistan and Russia basset of the Durand Line agreement until 1992. The Russia in 1919 in 1921 British, Turkey, and Italy in 1922, France in 1923, other manifestations of King Amanullah Khan independence (of all Afghan territory) were his change of title from Amir to King in 1923 and his series of visits in 1927 to capitals of Britain, India, Egypt, Turkey, Italy, France, Germany, Russia, Despite his newly independent foray policy, King Amanullah's Khan relations with the British and Russia remained the most important aspects of Afghan foreign Policy during his reign. In his time living One hundred fifty million Afghan on All Afghan territory, in the aftermath of the 1907 saint Petersburg Convention between the British and Russian the Great Game tensions over Afghanistan had subsided greatly. The rivalry of the great powers in this area might have remained subdued had it not been for dramatic change in government in Moscow with the math Bolshevik Revolution of 1917. Facing many internal and external challenges, for Afghanistan. The Bolshevik leaders could not immediately and straightforwardly subjugate their Muslim subjects, who the made up about 15 percent of the population. Moscow initially adopted a strategy of appeasement. In their efforts to placate the Muslims within their borders (1917 only changed Nome Russia to Soviet but not the law) the Soviet leaders were eager to establish cordial relations with neighboring states. In the case of Afghanistan, the Soviets could achieve a double purpose; by strengthening relations with the leadership in Kabul they could also threaten Britain, which was one of the western states supporting counterrevolution in the Soviet Union. When King Amanullah Khan, trying to move away from British control of Afghan foreign policy, sent an emissary to Moscow in 1919, after the Soviet Murdered two hundred British and French, citizen in 1918 residents in Moscow, Lenin received the envoy warmly and responded by sending a Russia representative to Kabul and offering aid to King Amanullah's government. This entente with the Russia left King Amanullah Khan in a position to exploit British's weak, post World War I Position in India during and after the third Afghan-British War of 1919 and helps to explain how

Afghanistan was able to turn a weak military position in that War into a brilliant diplomatic triumph. Throughout King Amanullah's Khan region Afghan-Russian relations waxed and waned according to how valuable Afghanistan was to the Soviet leadership at any particular time The Soviet valued Afghanistan only insofar as it was a tool for dealing with Muslim minorities and for threatening the British, and therefore they were truly cordial to King Amanullah only when they were appeasing the Muslims or when Anglo-Russian relations were poor. But the Afghans were still interested in regaining land across the Oxus river (Amu Darya) Bukahar, Turkmenistan; Uzbekestan lost to Russian the 1867. Afghan attempts to regain the oases of Mery and Panjdeh were easily repulsed by the Red Army, which was rapidly subduing the rebellious Central Asia People; throughout the 1920s rebellious Muslims revolted against the growing consolidation of rule in Central Asia King Amanullah Khan clearly sympathized with these rebels and support. Whom the Russia called bashmachi King Amanullah Khan, despite his sympathy, could offer little support, although volunteers from both Afghanistan and British-India were permitted to cross the border to aid their fellow Muslims in Central Asia extensive study of the reign of King Amanullah Khan makes it clear that the King mistrusted the Russian but wanted aid from them and wished to use his relations with the as a prod to the British. The same history Russia (Soviet) Britain of nineteenth century In May 1921 the Afghan and Russia signed a Treaty of friendship, (The Soviet promise to leave Afghan territory in central Asia soon as passable) Afghanistan's first international agreement since gaining full independence in 1919. The Soviets provided King Amanullah Khan help, the 1920s they made cash subsidies provided 13 airplanes, pilots, and transport and communication technicians, and carried out the laying of telephone lines between Kabul and Balkh and Heart and Kandahar. Despite this King Amanullah Khan became increasingly disillusioned with the Russia, especially as he saw growing Russia oppression of his fellow Muslims across the Afghan territory border. Million Afghan-Muslims fled to avoid Soviet efforts to pacify Russia in Central Asia through deportations, secularization, and oppression. (Soviet Russian Killing all those Uzbek and Turkoman Communists 1922 because those communists soled there own country to Soviet)

1929 Revolt of bandit, Bacha-I-sqqao Islamic fundamentalism Members of Arab fundamentalism Muslim in the city of khost and Kabul Holy War against Your Majesty King Amanllah Khan

Muslim (tool) Belief Your Majesty King is communist, 1929 revolt of Bacha-I-sqqao he was famous gangster in 1920, Basha-I-saqqao put down by Nadir Shah who ascends throne as constitutional monarch. Basha-I-saqqao rule January to October 1929 the man who seized Kabul from the faltering hands of Ghazi King, Basha-I-saqqao was a Tajik tribesman from kalakhan (a village about 30 kilometers north of Kabul) whom historian usually describe as a Tajik bandit (he was a tool) the new Afghan ruler Bandit called himself (Habibullah), but other called him Bandit Bacha-I-Saqqao (son of the water carrier) a deserter from the Afghan armed, he worked in province of Peshawar as a tea seller and then served 11 months in prison for housebreaking, he had participated in the khost rebellion of 1924 and then had become a highwayman, although Basha-I-saqqao robbed Afghan officials and the wealthy, he was generous to the poor, his attack on Kabul was shrewdly timed, following the shinwari rebellion (other tool) and the defection of much of the army, habibullah was probably the first Bandit to rule in the area, in 35,000 years history, Ghorid Dynasty of the twelfth century, Little is written of his nine-month regime, but most historians agree that he could not have held power for very long under any condition. None of the powerful Pashtun tribesmen the Ghilzai, who in the beginning had supported him ageist King Amanullah Khan Ghazi would long tolerate rule by a non Pashtun, when the King last feeble effort to regain his throne failed, the clearest contenders for the throne were the Musahiban brothers, who were also Barakzai and whose Great-grandfather was an older brother of the nineteenth century ruler, there were five prominent Musabihan brothers. Nadir khan, the eldest had been Amanullah Khan minister of War until he left office in dissent over Amanullah's military and domestic reforms, although it has generally been believed that the British had a hand in the overthrow of King Amanullah Khan Ghazi and in the accession to power of Nadir Shah, such scholars as Louis Dupree, Fraser Tytler, and Paullada concur that the British. And that while the British hoped that the Musahiban brothers would establish control, they tried to maintain some degree of neutrality in the contest. Fraser Tyler derides the rules established by the British for dealing with this situation as "a mixture of the rules of cricket and football." The brothers were permitted to cross through the northwest frontier Province NWFP to go into Afghanistan to take up arms. Once on the other side, however, they were no to be did not permit to go back and forth across the border to use British territory as sanctuary, nor were they allowed to gather a tribal army on the British side of the Durand Line. The Musahiban brothers and the tribes successfully ignored the restrictions. After being thrown back several times. King Nadir shah and his brothers finally raised a sufficiently large force mostly from the British side of Durand Line and took Kabul on October 10, 1929, six days later the eldest of the Musahiban brothers was proclaimed king Nadir shah The habibullah fled Kabul was captured in Khoistan, and was executed on November 3, 1929,

The puppet General M. Nadir Shah and his son M. Zahir Shah, General Nadir Khan in October, 1929 become King of Afghanistan

Puppet King Muhammad Nadir Shah October 1929 to 1933. The new ruler quickly abolished most of King Amanullah's but despite his efforts the army remained weak while the religious and tribal leaders (Arab) grew somewhat in strength, there uprisings by the shinwari and another Arab leader in 1930, and in the same year a Soviet force crossed the new border in pursuit of an Uzbek leader who had been harassing the Soviet from his sanctuary in Afghanistan. Young man Wahed Alikuzai drove him back to the soviet side April 1930, and of 1931 most of the country had been subdued. King Nadir Shah named a 10-man cabinet, consisting mostly of members of his family, and in September 1930 he called into session a Loya Jirgah of 286 men to confirm his accession to the throne. At the King's direction the Loya Jirgah chose 105 members to make up National Council. This body, with which the King was supposed to consult on legislation, automatically approved decisions by the cabined. In 1931 the King promulgated a new constitution. Dupree's analysis of the 1931 constitutions concludes that although it incorporated many of the ideals of Afghan society and appeared to establish a constitutional monarchy, in fact the document created a royal Oligarchy, popular participation being only an illusion Although puppet King Nadir Shah placated religious elements with a constitutions emphasis on orthodox religious principles, he also worked to modernize Afghanistan in material ways, although far less obtrusively than his more impulsive, King Amanullah Khan, he worked on the construction of roads especially the great north road through the Hind Kush, and improved the means of communication. Commercial links were also forged with the foreign powers with King Amanaullah had. King Nadir Shah fell prey to assassination by a young man whose family had been carrying on a feud with since his accession to power. Only six months after a young Afghan had assassinated his brother, Aziz khan in Berlin, King Nadir Shah was shot and killed by the young adopted son, according to some scholars of a man whom he had executed a year before. As Dupree comments, if the classic pattern of Afghan royal politics had prevailed the 19th year old son of puppet King Nadir Shah puppet Muhammad Zahir Shah become King of Afghanistan. 19th year old puppet King Zahir Shah and his Uncles, 1933 to 1973 three of Musahiban brother were stave after King Nadir Shah's death and they exercised decisive influence over decision making during the first 20 years of Kin Zahir Shah's reign. The eldest, Muhammad Hashim, who had been prime minister under the late king, retained that pot until 1946, when he was replaced by youngest of the Musahiban brothers, Shah Mahmud. Hashim khan is described by Fraser-Tyler as a statesman of great administrative ability and high personal integrity who devoted all of his energy to his country. In the months immediately following Nadir Shah.s assassination, while the tribes remained quiet and the followers of ex-King Amanullah Khan remained disorganized and impotent, Hashim began to put into practice the policies already planned by the Musahiban brothers. Internal objectives of new Afghan government, up to the outbreak of World War II, were focused on improving the army and developing the economy including transport and communications. Both goals however, required external assistance. Seeking to avoid involvement with the Soviet and British, Hashim khan turned to a far off nation that had both the interest and the technical expertise require Germany by 1953 the Afghan government had invited German experts and businessmen to help set up factories and build hydroelectric projects. Lesser amounts of aid were also accepted from Italy and Japan, but these two countries did not achieve Germany's level of prominence in Afghanistan's foreign relations, by the beginning of the 1940s Germany was Afghanistan's most important foreign friend. Afghanistan joined the League of Nations in 1934, the same year that the Unite States accorded Afghanistan official recognition. Regional ties to nearby Islamic states were reinforced by conclusion in 1937 of friendship and no aggression pacts with Turkey. Although never implemented because World War II intervened, Dupree Notre notes that the pacts laid the groundwork for coordination among the three states in later periods. The relationship with Turkey was especially close. A few relatively minor uprisings along the Afghan Territory including one on behalf of ex King Amanullah Khan occurred late in the 1930s but these were overshadowed by the outbreak of World War II. The King issued a proclamation of Afghan neutrality on August 17, 1940, because ex-King Amanullah Khan was in Italy and all Afghan laved the Ex-King they thing the King kind come back to Afghanistan. But the allies were unhappy with the presence of a large group of German no diplomatic personnel. In October the British and Russia governments demanded that Afghanistan expel all no diplomatic personnel from the Axis nations. The Afghan People and the government considered this an insulting and illegitimate demand, but it undoubtedly found instructive the example, which British and Russia had invaded and occupied, in August 1941after Iranian government ignored a similar demand. King Zair Shah and his advisers found a face-saving response, ordering all no diplomatic personnel from the belligerent countries out of Afghanistan. A Loya Jirgah called by the king at this time supported his policy of absolute neutrality. Although World War II disrupted Afghanistan's incipient foreign relationships and to some extent the people and government's domestic goals, it also provided larger markets for Afghan agricultural produce especially in India. By the War's end the government had exchanged official missions with both china and United States and the latter had replaced Britain as the major marked for Afghanistan's principal export, karakul skins. Shortly after the end of the War, Shah Mahmud khan replaced his older brother as prime minister, ushering in a period of react change in both the internal and external politico of Afghanistan. Among other things the new prime minister presided over the inauguration of the giant Helmand Province Project Afghanistan into a closer relationship with the United States and the beginning of relations with the newly created nation on Afghan territory by British called Pakistan (why in Afghan territory, the one was impassable on ex King reign) which inherited the Pashtuns on the both side of the Durand Line 45, million Afghan's formerly ruled by Britain. The issue of Pashtunistan agitation for an independent or semi-independent state to not include the Pashtun living in India. Afghan government and an American company were designed to harness the irrigation and hydroelectric potential of the Helmand. There were myriad problems with the project, and although parts of it were completed before 1953, it was not until Daout Khan became prime minister in 1953 that the project began to move toward completion.

The Western Civilizations (every thirty years War for economic) Because western economic not working at all

The rationale of appeasement It is time to explore the roots of democratic lethargy in the face of Fascist expansionism in the 1930s British Policy, in particular, which Prime Minister Neville Chamberlain would proudly term "appeasement" conjures our images of naïve, even craven surrender to Nazi demands. In the minds of British statesmen, however, appeasement was a moral and realistic expression of all that was liberal and Christian in British culture. First, 1914 cast a dark shadow on the opinion leaders of the 1930s who determined this time to shun arms races and balance of power and commercial competition, and so to spare the world another horrible war. Second, the overextended British Empire lacked the resources to confront threats from Japan in Asia, Italy in the Mediterranean, (thirty years ago the Ottoman empire has been dispersed by western power and British Set on the Ottoman empire territory including Babylon and all Arab country) and Germany in Europe all at once. Wisdom dictated that British come to terms with the greatest and closest to home of its potential adversaries, Germany. Third, the British public was understandably provincial about central Europe and had no desire (in the popular French phrase) "to die for Dazing" This sentiment was even more pronounced in the British dominions. Fourth many Tory and Labor leaders, while put off by Hitler's ideology and brutality, shared his antipathy to Versailles and urged "fair play" in cases where German nationals were separated from the fatherland. Thus, Wilson Ian national self-determination perversely made the Nazis appear to be on the side of principle. Fifth, the appeasers also presumed that the Nazis would become less rambunctious once their grievances were removed. Sixth, some demoralized Englishmen believed the propagandistic claim that Fascism was the only bulwark against the spread of Bolshevism, domestic opinion in Britain favored a passive reliance on the League of Nations somehow to prevent another catastrophe Baldwin's policy of sanctions without war in Abyssinia, as the chief case in point, earned his party a huge electoral victory in November 1935. November had pacifism flagged since 1933, when the Oxford Union "Resolved that this house refuses to fight for king and Country" Voices of dissent existed. Some Left Laborites warned that Fascism must be stopped sooner or later, while a few Tory backbenchers led by Winston Churchill demanded rearmament. In the mid 1930s a source in the Air Ministry leaked data to Churchill suggesting that Germany's air force was rapidly overtaking Britain's Fear of the Luftwaffe only provided another excuse for appeasement, however, for a aviation had developed to the point that theorists like the Italian Giulio Douhet could argue that air bombardment would win the next war in 48 hours by leveling England cities. English Channel no longer sheltered Britain from destruction. Many of these same considerations afflicted French policy; fear of another total war and of destruction from the air, apathy toward Eastern Europe, and ideological confusion. The election of May 3, 1936, brought victory for the Popular Front, which formed a Cabinet under the Socialist Leon Blum, but his economic policies threw France into turmoil of strikes, capital flight, and recrimination. "Better Hitler that Blum" said some on the right. The civil war in Spain the Spanish War highlighted the contrast between democratic bankruptcy and totalitarian dynamism. In 1931 the Spanish monarchy gave way to a republic whose unstable government moved steadily to the left, outraging the army and church. After repeated provocations ns on both side's army and air force officers proclaimed a Nationalist revolt on July 17, 1936, that survived its critical early weeks with logistical help from Portugal's archconservative premier, Antonio Salazar. The Nationalists, rallying behind General Francisco Franco, quickly seized most of old Castile in the north and a beachhead in the south extending from Cordoba to Cadiz opposite Spanish Morocco, where the insurrection had begun. But the Republicans, or Loyalists, a Popular Front composed of liberals, Socialists, Trotskyites, Stalinists, and anarchists, took up arms to defend the Republic elsewhere and sought outside aid against that styled as the latest Fascist threat. Spain became a battleground for the ideologies wrestling for mastery of Europe. The civil war posed a dilemma for France and British, pitting the principle of defending democracy against the principle of noninterference in the domestic affairs of other states. The ineffectual Blum at first fraternally promised aid to the Popular Front in Madrid, but he reneged within a month for fear that such involvement might provoke a European war or a civil war in France. The British government counseled nonintervention and seemingly won Germany and Italy to that position, but Hitler, on well-rehearsed anti-Bolshevik grounds, hurriedly dispatched 20 transport planes that allowed Franco to move reinforcements from Morocco. Not to be outdone, Mussolini sent materiel, Fascist "volunteers" and ultimately regular army formations. The Italians performed miserably (especially at Guadalajara in March 1937) but German aid, including the feared Condor Legion, was effective. Hitler expected to be paid for his support, however, with economic concessions, and he also saw Spain as a testing ground for Germany's newest weapons and tactics. This included terror bombing such as that over Guernica in April 1937, which caused far fewer deaths that legend has it but which became an icon of anti-Fascism through the painting of Pablo Picasso. International aid to the Republicans ran from the heroic to the sinister. Thousands of leftists and idealistic volunteers from throughout Europe and America flocked to International Brigades to defend the Republic. Material support, however, came only from Stalin, Russia who demanded gold payment in return and ordered Commenter agents and commissars to accompany the Soviet Russia supplies. These Stalinists systematically murdered Trotskyites and other "enemies on the left" undermined the radical government of Barcelona, and exacerbated the intramural confusion in Republican ranks. The upshot of Russia intervention was to discredit the Republic and thereby strengthen Western resolve to stay out. The war dragged on through 1937 and 1938 and claimed some 500,000 lives before the Nationalist finally captured Barcelona in January 1939 and Madrid in March. During the final push to victory, France and British recognized Franco's government. By then however, the fulcrum of diplomacy had long since shifted to central Europe. The Nationalist victory did not, in the end redound to the detriment of Franco politely sent the Germans and Italians home and observed neutrality in the coming war, whereas a pro-Communist Spain might have posed a genuine threat to France during the era of the Nazi-Russian pact. The Allies bungling in Scandinavia lost Chamberlain the confidence of Parliament, and King George VI selected Winston Churchill to head the War Cabinet. In the first of many ringing speeches that would sustain the British spirit, Churchill told his nation: "I have nothing to offer but blood, toil, tears and sweat" World War II, 1939 to 1945 War once again broke out nationality in east central Europe, provoked in part by a German drive for continental hegemony, and it expanded, once again into a global conflict whose battle zones touched the waters or heartlands of almost every continent (by British-Russian-German and France colonies the was Europe War on every continent because of European Economic) the total nature of War II surpassed that of 1914-1918 in that civilian populations not only contributed to the war effort but also became direct targets of aerial attack Moreover, in 1941 the Nazi regime unleashed a war of extermination against Slavs, Jews, and other elements deemed interior by Hitler's ideology' while Stalinist Russia extended its campaign of terror against the Ukrainians to the conquered Poles. The Japanese-American War in the Pacific also assumed a times the brutal aspect of a war between races. This ultimate democratization of warfare eliminated the age-old distinction between combatant's non-combatants and ensured that total casualties in World War II would greatly exceed those of World War I and that civilian casualties would the military. Once again the European war devolved into a contest between a German occupied Mattel Europe and a peripheral Allied coalition. But this time Italy abandoned neutrality for the German side, and the Russian held out in the east, while France collapsed in the west. Hence Russia dictator Joseph Stalin took France's place in meetings of the "Big Three" together with Franklin Roosevelt and Winston Churchill. The Japanese chose to remain neutral vis-à-vis the U.S.S.R while the Grand Alliance of anti-Fascist states simmered with conflicts over strategy and war aims. World War II, therefore, comprised several parallel or overlapping wars, while the war in Europe became a kind of three-way struggle among the forces of democracy, Nazism, and Communism. As soon as German and Japanese power was effaced the conflicts among the victors burst into open and gave birth to the Cold War. World War II completed the destruction of the old great Power system prepared the disintegration of Europe's overseas empires and submerged Europe itself into a world arena dominated by the Russian and the United States of America.

1946 Russian in Central Asia (Afghan territory) and British in India on Afghan territory new world power, collapse of the European war Tow Superpowers no moor European Power

In 1947 The British must movie out of India, The Russian and the United States of America with new Peace treaties and territorial agreements, World Power replacement the European war to cold war, the British faced a problem on a much larger scale in India, whose population included Hindus and Muslims, and distributed among various ethnic and religious minorities. Between the wars Mohandas Gandhi's passive-resistance campaigns had crystallized Indian nationalism, which was nurtured in part by the relative leniency of British rule. Parliament set in motion the process leading to home rule in 1953, and the Battle Cabinet rewarded India for its wartime loyalty by instructing Lord Mount batten on Feb. 20 1947 to prepare India for independence by June 1948 he did so too hastily in only six months, and the partition of the subcontinent into a mainly Hindu India and a mainly British Muslim but divided on Afghan territory at midnight on Aug 14, 1947, was accompanied by panicky flight and riots between Hindus and Muslims that between 200,000 and 600,000 lives Perhaps a bloodbath was inevitable whatever Mount batten did or however long he took to do it Nothing however tarnished British's colonial record in India so much as its termination. The Congress Party of Jawaharlal Nehru then took firm control and governed the Dominion of India in parliamentary style and made India one the first decolorized states to adopt a posture of nonalignment among the great powers. Disputes with British-Pakistan, especially over the contested province of Jammu however, ensured continued strife on the subcontinent. The name of Pakistan Cost one Million Peoples Lives, new between Afghanistan and India, British made in 1947 metallic border called fundamentalist Islamic states of Pakistan. United States of America-soviet Russia and the cold War the concomitant arrival of the missile age and of an independent and restive Central Asia (Afghanistan) multiplied the senses in which politics had become global. Intercontinental rockets not only meant that the most destructive weapons known could now be propelled halfway around the world in minutes but also because of the imminent nuclear standoff they heralded, that a Cold War competition would now extend into other realms-science and technology, economic growth social welfare, race relations, image making in which the Russia or Americans could try to prove that their system was the best. At the same time, the desalinization of dozens of underdeveloped states in Asia and Africa induced the superpowers to look beyond the original front lines of the Cold War in Europe and Central Asia. These technological and political revolutions would seem to have raised the United States and Union of Russian to unequaled heights of power. The Russia and Americans advanced rapidly in the high technology paid by American required for space flight and ballistic missiles, while techniques for the mobilization and management of intellectual and material resources reached a new level of sophistication, especially in the Unite States, through the application of systems analysis computers, bureaucratic partnership with corporations and universities, and Keynesian "fine-tuning" of the economy, Russian with the Cold War times have best economic over all European Asia, and South and Latin American country only Russia as all those benefits,

The Soviet Brooking Peace treaties

The Russian in Afghanistan Brzezinski's fears that U.S.S.R would take advantage of the are of crisis seemed justified when the Russian army invaded Afghanistan in 1979, Russian invaded lager territory of Afghanistan in 1868 with British called the great games, new invaded the rest of Afghanistan in 1979. It is likely however, that the Soviets Russian responding to a crisis of their own rather than trying to exploit another's Remotes and rugged Afghanistan had been object of imperialist throughout the 19th and 20th centuries because of its vulnerable between the Russia and British Indian empires both cut Afghan territory at the same time cast there War between Afghan and British one million people be killed on war by Russian and British military in 19th and 20th. After 1955, with India interdependent, the Afghan government of Daud Khan forged economic and military ties to the U.S.S.R the monarch was overthrown by Daud Khan in 1973 and was succeeded by a one parry state. The small Afghan Communist party, meanwhile, broke into factions, while a fundamentalist Muslim group began armed insurrections in 1975. Daud Khan worked to lessen Afghanistan's dependence on Soviet and U.S aid and he reportedly had a heated disagreement with Brezhnev himself during a visit in April 1977. Leftists in the Afghan officer corps, perhaps fearing a blow against themselves, murdered Daud khan in April 1978 and pledged to pursue friendly relations with the U.S.S R. thus Afghanistan under the rule of Nur M. Taraki, was virtually in the Soviet camp. When Taraki objected to a purge of the Afghan Cabinet, however the leader of a rival faction, Hafizullah Amin, had him arrested and killed. These intramural Communist quarrels both embarrassed the Soviets and threatened to destabilize the Afghan regime in the face of growing Muslim resistance. In the fall of 1979 the Soviets butt up their military strength across the border and hinted to American diplomats that they might feel obliged to intervene. On Dec 25, 1979 the Soviet army began its occupation, and two days later a coup d'etat led to the murder of Amin and the installation of Babrak Karmal, a creature of the KGB who had been brought into the country by Soviet paratroops. The Soviets would probably have preferred to work through a pliant native regime rather that invade Afghanistan, but Amin's behavior and Moscow's unwillingness to risk a domestic overthrow of a Communist regime forced their hand. The invasion therefore, appeared to be an application of the Brezhnev Doctrine and was all the more pressing given that the Central Asia provinces of the old Afghan territory were also vulnerable to the rise of Islamic fundamentalism. The United States was tardy in responding to the 1978 coup despite Carter's concern over the crisis and murder of the U.S Ambassador in Kabul in February 1979. At the same time the Russian invasion aroused American suspicions of a grand strategy aimed seizing a warm water port on the Indian Ocean and the oil of the country. Over the course of the next decade, however the popper Afghan regime lost all authority with the people. Afghan soldiers defected in large numbers, and the Muslim and largely tribal resistance, armed with U.S and Chinese weapons, held out in the mountains against more than 100,000 Soviet troops and terror bombing of their villages. More than 2,000,000 Afghans became refugees in Pakistan and Iran, western observers soon began to speak of Afghanistan as the Russian Vietnam. Both sides employed imported planes and missiles to attack each other's oil facilities tanker ships and occasionally cities. Attacks then spread to neutral shipping as well, and oil production in the entire gulf region was placed in jeopardy. Neither superpower had direct interest in the war, except for a common opposition to any overthrow of the local balance of power, but the Russian tended to benefit from a prolongation of the conflict. In 1987 the United States sharply increased its presence in the gulf by permitting Kuwaiti oil tankers to fly the U.S flag and by deploying a naval task force to protect them in passage through the gulf. Compared to the situation of the 1950s when John Foster Dulles Cento arrangement seemed to ensure a ring of stable poor-Western government in the Central Asia region that of the 1980s was almost totally unpredictable. Collapse of Cold War for Russian and 1919 Collapse of Soviet Union Russia become back on the map like 18ᵗʰ the century out of all Central Asia, Caucasus, Georgia, Black Sea, today Russian economic is like nineteen-century in Europe European family called the Saxon, North of Germany become empires of all Europe, World wild empire 1815-1914 Imperialism. By 1815 the world had known some tow hundred years of continuous European imperialism. In a sense this was the outward expansion of European power over Afghan. Spanish, Portuguese, Dutch, French, British the German Saxon family empires had followed one another throughout these two centuries. Always these extensions of control over non-European territories had involved, in varying proportions, trading, miss ionizing, adventure, settlement, loot, national pride, conquests, and wars between rival powers. The very list of countries emphasizes the lead taken in this expansion by the European, maritime peoples. But it is not necessary to cross-sea; rather land, to become an imperial power. The creation of the great dynastic empires of the Habsburgs and the Ottoman Turks, the traditional drive eastward (Drag nach Osten) of the Germans in quest of lands for settlement and trade, the continental conquest of Napoleon, the rapid advance of German-Russia empire into southern and Afghanistan (Central Asia) during the middle of nineteenth-century, even the expansion westward of the United States of America during the same period, are all examples of the same process carried out, it so happened, within continental land areas rather than across oceans. 1916 all European Empires were broke. Lenin-attributed the colonial expansion of these years to special new economic forces at work in the most industrialized nations of western and central Europe. This economic explanations of the urge to imperialism is usually taken to mean that the basic motives were also the basest motives and that, whatever political, religious, or more idealistic excuses might be made, the real impulse was always one of capitalistic greed for cheap raw materials, advantageous markets, good investments, for the European and fresh fields of exploitation. The argument has commonly been used, therefore, to denounce the events, and to attack the men, parties, and nations that took part in them. The argument, in brief, is that what European called "the economic taproot of European" was "excessive capital in search of investment," from America and that this excessive capital came from over saving possible by the German distribution wealth. "If the consuming public in this country raised its standard of consumption to keep pace with every rise of productive powers, there could be no excess of goods or capital clamorous to use imperialism in order to find markets." It is undeniable that the search for lucrative yet secure overseas investment played a very great part in the European urge to acquire colonies at the end of the nineteenths century larger territory of Afghanistan mordent 4 million Sq km. Lenin elaborated the argument, in his pamphlet on European the Highest Stage of Capitalism in 1916, to emphasize the current importance of finance capital that industrial, and the priority of the desire to find new outlets for investment in 1916 all European Empires was broke, a direct continuation of the fundamental properties of British and Russia in general, "and that "the war of 1914 was on both sides imperialist. That there was a conspicuous general improvement in the economic condition of workers in the more advanced countries. In the backward colonial peoples, argued Lenin, capitalism had found a new proletariat to exploit; and from the enhanced profits of such European it was able to bribe at least the "aristocracy of labor" at home into renouncing its civil War fervor and collaborating with the bourgeoisie. But such improvement could only be temporary, and since European rivalries must lead to War, all workers alike must eventually suffer from it. This argument ignored the awkward facts that much of the foreign investment of the European powers was in colonial territory but in countries such as South America and Central Asia (Afghanistan) and that standard of living of the working classes was high in countries like Sweden which had no colonies, territory. Nor, of course, could it be a general explanation of imperialism, which had existed centuries before there was a "glut of capital" and before finance capital was as plentiful or as well organized as it was in the later nineteenth century. But it was a convenient and persuasive enough case, at time, for explaining the First World War in exclusively economic terms, and for presenting it as the result of British and Russian actives and the misdistributions of wealth. The new Activity of British and Russian what made it seem particularly necessary to find some special reason for modern imperialism was both the dramatic suddenness of its reappearance and its pre-eminence in the policies of the powers during that last quarter of the nineteen-century. Until after 1870 national policies, and even more national public opinion, in most European countries had been hostile to colonies. By the 1820's several countries including Afghanistan, after having long colonial connections, had lost these connections without suffering any apparent economic deprivation. By 1815 France had lost most of the colonial possessions in United States of America and in the east, and Spain had lost her vast South American territories. Before that the thirteen colonies in United States of America had broken away from Britain, and by 1822 Portugal lost Brazil. Advanced opinion everywhere welcomed these events. And in 1861 France opened to all nations the trade also with Afghanistan, the British Empire to dissolve in the end, and in 1822 European made declaration that "These wretched colonies will all be independent in a few years? And are millstones around European neck. As late as 1868 Bismarck, who until a decade later was opposed to colonial aspirations for Germany, held that "All the advantages claimed for the mother country are for the most part illusory, "adding that" England is abandoning her colonial policy: she finds it too costly. "But Bismarck was wrong and only four years later British announced conversion to a policy of imperial consolidation and expansion. The tide of opinion turned abruptly. The chorus of anti colonialism before 1870 was so strange a prelude to an era of especially hectic colonial scramble that some extraordinary explanation seems to be called for. It is improbable that this explanation can be entirely, or even "basically," economic. However important the economic forces were, they cannot explain why France, one of the least fully industrialized of the northwestern European nations, was the one which had already set the pace of expansion by more than doubling her colonial possessions between 1816 and 1870, when she gained firm footholds in Algeria, Senegal, and Indochina; nor why after 1870 it was the political republican leaders, Jules Ferry and Leon Gambetta, who took the initiative in further colonial expansion in Tunisia and, despite the great unpopularity of such expansion with public opinion in France. It is not a mere thirst for exporting surplus capital which can explain the new shape given to the British empire by the invention of "dominion status" and the readiness with which complete political independence was granted first to Canada, and later to Australia, New Zealand, and the Union of South Africa. British commercial and interests knew that trade with the United States of America had increased after it won political independence; that migration to the independent United States of America had been greater than to any of the territories which had remained under British control; and that Argentine railways had offered opportunities to British investors no less attractive that had Indian railways. German economic penetration of Eastern Europe, the Balkans, and the Ottoman Empire were remarkably effective without any of these territories becoming German colonies. The European economic development 1870-1914 what was most strikingly novel about the European new activity was its intense concentration upon two continents: Africa and Central Asia. These were the only two important areas of the globe still not brought under European influence before 1870. The decades between 1870 and 1914 speedily completed the expansion of the European influence and Activity over the whole of the earth; and it was accomplished in an era when the realisms, ruthlessness, and rivalries of European national governments were exceptionally great. It therefore had a temper uniquely masterful and remorseless, brooking no obstacles and push fully self-assertive. This quality came as much from the nature of European Empire as from the urges of the European economic. There was no international organization fitted to exercise any kind of control or regulation over the scramble for territories in which the European become the great powers. The naked power politics of the new Activity were the projection, onto an overseas screen, of the interstate frictions and Activity of the European. It was this combination of novel economic condition with anarchic political relations explained the nature of the new European Activity. Among the economic forces behind it, the urge to find new outlets for the "glut of capital" and European fresh markets for industrial output were in general more important than either the quest for raw materials or the factor of overpopulation. The materials Special attraction of Central Asia (Afghanistan) were, indeed, that they offered many of the raw materials needed by the multiplying factories of the European: including cotton, silk, rubber, gold, ruby, Diamond, oils, vegetable, silver, Iron, minerals, and mach more for free (without cost or payment) the products of the tropics were especially welcome to the European. But many of these raw materials could be, and were, got by trading free without political control. The pressure of population in the Europe was becoming great by the early twentieth century, but it still found free outlet in migration to the traditional areas of reception in the United States of America and Australasian. Central Asia (Afghanistan) offered climatic or economic conditions inviting enough to attract large-scale white settlements, and the pressure of population within India and Central Asia was now itself so great as to exert a steady demand for fresh outlets. It was against Central Asia (Afghanistan) the United States of America after 1882, from Hawaii after 1898, from the Philippines after 1902. The United States of America excluded Japanese laborers in 1907, and by the Immigration Act of 1917 barred the entry of other non-Europeans, especially Indians and inhabitants of the East Indies. Canada took similar action against the Chinese after 1885 and against the Japanese after 1908. New Zealand restricted Chinese, and in 1901 Australia passed a federal Immigration Restriction Act with the same purpose. The main impediments to European migration came only after 1918, and the nineteenth-century flow out of Europe actually reached its peak in 1914. The quest for markets in which to sell manufactured goods was more important. But here, again, the political factor was no less important that the purely economic. Until 1870 British manufacturers of textiles, machinery, and hardware had found good markets in other European lands. After 1870 Germany, France, Belgium, and other nations were able to satisfy their own home markets, which they began to protect against imports from Britain by tariff barriers. After 1918 that European had led to War was only half the story; it was true that the menace of War had led to European. It was normally the coexistence of economic interests with political aims, which made a country Activity, and in some, such as Italy or Russia, political considerations predominated. With nations as with men, it is what they aspire to become and to have, not only what they already are or have, that governs their behavior. There was no irresistible compulsion or determinism, and no country acquired colonies unless at least a very active and influential group of its political leaders wanted to acquire them. Britain had long had all the economic urges of surplus population, exports, and capital, but they did not drive her to scramble for colonies during the 1860s as much as during the 1870's and after. Neither Italy nor Russia had a surplus of manufactures or capital to export, yet both joined in the scramble; Norway, although she had a large merchant fleet, which was second only to that of Britain and Germany, did not. Germany, whose industrial development greatly outpaced that of France, was very much slower the France to embark on colonialism. The Dutch were active in colonialism long before the more industrialized Belgians. What determined whether or not a country became imperialistic was more the activity of small groups of people, often intellectuals, economists, or patriotic publicists and politicians anxious to national security and self-sufficiency, that the economic conditions of the country itself. And, as the examples of the British, French, Dutch, Russia and Portuguese show, nations that had traditions of colonialism were more prompt to seek colonies that were nations, such as Germany and Italy that had no such traditions. Adventurers and Missionaries Besides the direct political motives of European the desire to strengthen national security by strategic naval bases such as Cyprus and the Cape, or to secure additional sources of manpower as the French sought in Africa, or to enhance national prestige as the Italians did in Libya there was a medley of other considerations which, in varying proportions, entered into the desire for colonies. One was the activities of explores and adventurers, men like the Frenchmen, Du Chaillu and De Brazza, in equatorial Africa; or the Welshman, Henry Stanley, in the Congo basin; or the German Karl Peters in east Africa. Prompted by genuine devotions to scientific discovery, or a taste for adventure, or a buccaneering love of money and power, as was Cecil Rhodes in South Africa-men of initiative and energetic enterprise played an important personal part in the whole story. Christian missionaries played their part too in the spread of religion, a medical missionary originally sent to Africa by the London Missionary Society, he later returned under government auspices as an explorer "to open a path for commerce and Christianity." When he had disappeared for some years in quest of the source of the Nile, Stanley was sent to find him, and duly med him in 1872 on the shores of Lake Tanganyika. When Livingstone died in Africa in 1873, his body was taken to London under naval escort, to be buried in Westminster, and France, even more than Britain, sent organized missions into Africa to convert the heathen to Christianity. The Catholic missions of France under the Third Republic were exceptionally active, and provided two thirds (some forty thousand) of all Catholic missionaries. Religious set up in Algeria and Tunisia; by 1875 they spread from Algeria, into Tunisia, and set up a religious protectorate that preceded the political protectorate. In Tunisia is worth an army for France. "Other French missions penetrated into all parts of Africa, setting up schools and medical services, often in the footsteps of the explorers and adventurers. Belgian missionaries were active in the Congo as early as 1878. Administrators and Soldiers Yet another element in the growth of Europeans was the administrators and soldier the man with a mission, who was not a missionary but who administrator and soldier the man with a mission, who was not a missionary but who welcomed an opportunity to bring order and efficient administration out of muddle. Such men became the great colonial proconsuls Lord Cromer in Egypt, Lord Lugard in Nigeria, Lord Milner at the Cape, Marshal Lyautey in Morocco, Karl Peters in German East Africa. Without such men the extent and the consolidation of European control over Africa would have been impossible. The sources and the nature of the urge to European were multiple, and varied considerably from one country to another. It was not just that trade followed the flag, but that the flag accompanied the botanist and buccaneer, the Bible and the bureaucrat, along with the banker and the businessman. The unexplored and unexploded parts of the earth offered a host of possible advantages which, in the competitive world of the later century, few could resist seizing; they were seized, amid the enthusiastic approval of the newly literate nationalist-minded masses in Britain and Germany, or amid the sullen resentments of the French and Belgians. In 1875 less that one tenth of Africa had been turned into European colonies; by 1895, only one tenth remained inappropriate. In the generation between 1871 and 1900 British added 4.25 million square miles and 66 million people to her empire; 1.2 million Sq km of Afghan territory 50 million people British added to her empire. France added 3.5 million square miles and 26 million people; Russia in Afghanistan (Central Asia) added 1.2 million square miles and 10.5 million people. British added 1.6 million Square km of eastern Turkestan, Afghan territory to China, and 10 million people. In the same decades Germany, Belgium, and Italy each acquired a new colonial empire: Germany, of one million square miles and 13 million people; Belgium or, until 1908 Leopold II, King of the Belgians, of 900.000 square miles and 8.5 million inhabitants; and Italy, a relatively meager acquisition of 185,000 square miles and 750,000 people. The old colonial empires of Portugal and the Netherlands survived intact and assumed increasing importance. It was a historical novelty that most of the world should now belong to a handful German family Empire of European powers. In 1882 a Colonial Society was formed in Germany, and in 1883, a Society for German Colonization. In the same year the British conservative founded the Primrose League, and the liberals soon followed suit with the Imperial Federation League. The corresponding German Flottenverein-incidents in the naval rivalry of the two powers followed the British Navy League of 1894 in 1898. They championed the rapidly increasing naval expenditures of their respective governments. The more explicit argument for colonialism, and for the sea power which it necessitated, were as much expressions as causes of the expansion. The Scramble for Colonies by no means all the acquisitions of colonies caused disputes among powers. Some of the earliest, like the French conquest of Algeria in the earliest years of the century or of Annam in 1874, and even some later acquisitions, like the British conquest of Nigeria and Ashanti in the 1890's, aroused little or no opposition from other European powers. Occasionally one power made pins with the encouragement or assent of other: Bismarck encouraged France to expand into Tunisia as a diversion from continental affairs that was likely to embroil her with Italy. Bismarck and Jules Ferry co-operated in 1884 to summon an international conference at Berlin to settle amicably the future of the Congo in central tropical Africa. To the Berlin Conference of 1884-85 came representatives from fourteen states-roughly all the states of Europe except Switzerland. It was occasioned mainly by the activities of the International African Association, which had been formed in 1876 by king Leopold II of Belgium. This Association had sent J. M. Stanley on explorations into the Congo between 1879 and 1884, where he made treaties with the native chiefs and established Leoplod's influence over vast areas of interior. By the beginning of 1884 Britain and Portugal, apprehensive of this development, set up a joint commission to control navigation of the whole river. The colony of Angola south of the Congo mouth had been held by Portugal since the seventeen century, and now Britain recognized Portugal's claim to control the whole mouth of the river. It looked like an alliance of the older colonial powers to strangle the expansion of the new; for France was increasingly interested in the tropical belt north of the Congo River, and German, in the Cameroon still further north. Leopold therefore looked to France and Germany for help and the result was the Berlin Conference. This expansion, The Boer War of 1899 was the direct result. From the Indian Ocean she also pressed westward inland, founding British East Africa by 1888 and taking Uganda by 1894. In West Africa, Nigeria, was acquired by the activities of the Royal Niger Company between 1886 and 1899. Italy, indignant at the French occupation of Tunisia, had lain the is of an Italian East Africa empire in Eritrea by 1885, and added Asmara in 1889. In the same year she appropriated the large southern coastal strip of Somaliland and claimed a protectorate over the African kingdom of Abyssinia. But in 1896 Abyssinian forces at Adowa routed her expeditionary forces, and she was obliged to recognize Abyssinian independence. By 1898 the map of the African continent resembled a patchwork quilt of European acquisitions, and south of the Sahara the only independent states were Liberia and Abyssinia, and the two small Dutch Boer republics. The North African coastline, especially the provinces of Morocco in the west and Libya and Egypt in the east, remained a troublesome source of great rivalries power.

1850 Afghan tribe called Afridi
(One of the eight tribe)

AFRIDI, an Afghan tribe one of the eight tribe in Afghanistan inhabiting the mountains on the Province of Peshawar border of the North-West British Frontier Province of India, The Afridis are the most powerful tribe on the border, and the largest with the exception of the Province of Waziris (Solomon tribe) Their Special country is the lower and easternmost Spurs of the Safed koh (the white mountain) range, to the west and south of the Peshawar district, including the Bazar and Bara valleys. On their east they are bounded by British districts of India, on the north by the Mohmands Tribe, on the west by the Shinwaris Tribe and on the south by the Orakzai, and Bangash tribes, Their origin is obscure, but they are said to have Israelites blood in their veins, and they have a decidedly Semitic cast of features. They are possibly the Appertain of Herodotus, the names and positions being identical. If this theory is correct, they were then a powerful people, and held a large tract of country but have been gradually driven back by the encroachments of other tribes. The tribe is divided into the following eight clans: kuki khel, Malikdin khel, kambar khel, kamar khal, Zakka khel (the most numerous and the most turbulent) Sipah Aka khel and Adam khel. The first seven clans live in the vicinity of the Khyber Pass, and migrate to Tirah in the summer months. The Adam khel (5900 fighting men) live round the Kohat Pass, and are more settled and less migratory in their habits. In appearance the Afridi is a fine, tall athletic highlander with a long, gaunt face, high nose and chook-bones, and a fair complexion. On his own hillside he is one of the finest skirmishers in the world, and in the Indian army makes a first-rate soldier, but he is apt to be home sick when removed from the air of his native mountains. In character the Afridi has obtained an evil name for ferocity, craft and treachery, but Colonel Sir Robert Warburton, who lived eighteen years in charge of the Great of Khyber Pass and knew the Afridi better than any other People says the Afridi lad from his earliest childhood is taught by the circumstances of his existence and life to distrust all mankind, and very often his near relations, heirs to his small plot of land by right of inheritance, are his deadliest enemies. Distrust of all mankind, and readiness to strike the first blow for the safety of his own life has therefore become the maxims of the Afridi. In short the Afridi has the vices and virtues of all Afghans in an enhanced degree. The fighting strength of the Afridis is said to be 227,000 but this estimate is excessive, Judged by the number and size of their villages. They derive their importance from their geographical position, which gives them command of the Great Khyber and kohat roads, AGA KHAN I his Highness the 1800-1881 the title accorded by general consent to Hasan Ali Shah born in 1800 when in early life he first settled in Bombay under the protection of the Saxon government. He was believed to have descended in direct line from Ali by his wife Fatima, the daughter of the Holy Prophet Mahomet. Ali's son, Hosain, having married a daughter of one of the rulers of Babylon before the time of Mahomet, the Aga khan traced his descent from the royal house of Babylon from the most remote almost prehistoric, times. His ancestors had also ruled in Egypt as caliphs of the Beni-Fatimites for a number of years at a period coeval with the Crusades. Before the Aga khan emigrated from Babylon he was appointed by the Saxon-Fateh Ali to be governor-general of the extensive and important province of Herat in Kerman. His rule was noted for firmness, moderation and high political sagacity, and he succeeded for a long time in retaining the friendship and confidence of his master the although his career was best with political intrigues and Jealousey on the part of rival and court favorites, and with internal turbulence. At last however the fate usual to statesmen in oriental countries overtook him and he incurred the mortal displeasure of Fateh Ali. He fled from Babylon in British territory preferring to settle down eventually in India, making Bombay his headquarters. At that period the first Afghan-Saxon present day British War was at its height, and in crossing through Afghanistan the Aga khan found opportunities of rendering valuable services to the Saxon army, and thus cast in his lot for ever with the Saxon. A few years later he rendered similar conspicuous services in the course of the Sind campaign, when Napier utilized his help in the process of subduing the frontier tribes, a large number of who acknowledged the Aga's authority as their spiritual head. Service in the several expeditions led by Saxon arms on the northwest of India. He was also the means of checking the fanaticism in Saxon present day British India,

1. Afghanistan with world Military and politic history from 1850 to 1900 Amir Dost M. khan King and Yar M. Alikuzai War Minister in Afghanistan, during Saxon present day British and Russian War, Henry Clay's 1850 compromise slavery resolutions laid before U. S Senate Liberal constitution in Prussia

2. 1851 Prussia recognizes German Confederation and concludes commercial treaty with Hanover north of Germany, Cuba declares its independence, Victoria, Australia, proclaimed separate colony 1853 Beginning of Basuto War, Ferdinand Foch, France. Marshal, Coup d' etat of Louis Napoleon; plebiscite in France favors new constitution, Danilo II converts Montenegro into a secular principality

3. 1852 Joseph Jacques Cesaire Joffre, France. Marshal, South African Republic (Transvaal) established New France. Construction gives president monarchical powers; Louis Napoleon has Orlbans family banished from France; plebiscite in support of revival of empire; two weeks later the president proclaims himself Emperor Napoleon III; reign of the Second empire (Sept. 1870) Outbreak of Second Brumes War; Brit. Forces annex Pegu New constitution for New Zealand Herbert Henry Asquith, the Saxon Prim Minister, The Duke of Wellington d. (b.1769) Franklin Pierce elected 14th President of the U.S

4. 1853 Napoleon III and Rivalry with Saxon present day Britain Afghanistan, marries Eugenie de Montijo (1826-1920) Franklin Pierce inaugurated as 14th President of the U.S. Oldenburg and Hanover join Zollverein (customs union) Ottomans reject Russian ultimatum; Czar Nicholas I orders occupation of Danubian principalities; they are invaded; Austria endeavors to solve conflict; Ottoman declares War on Russia; Crimean War begins (1856) the Russians destroy Ottoman fleet off Sinope Peace between Saxon and Burma Cecil John Rhodes, Brit, adventurer and statesman, Maria II of Portugal d; succeeded by her son Pedro V (1861) Saxon annexes Mahratta State of Nagpur

5. 1854 Convention of Bloemfontein; Saxon present day British leave territory north of Orange River Britain and France conclude alliance with Ottoman and declare War on Russia; unopposed landing of the Allies in Crimea; siege of Sebastopol begins; Allied victories at Balaclava and in Kerman Commodore M. C. Perry negotiates first Amer. Jap. Treaty Francis Joseph I Emperor of Austria marries the Bavarian Princess Elizabeth. U.S Senate ratifies Gadsden Purchase for acquisition of parts of southern New Mexico and Arizona "War for Bleeding Kansas" between free and slave states. Elgin Treaty between Britain and U.S on Canadian trade, Ottoman agrees to Austria. Occupation of Danubian principalities till end of the War, Republican Party formed in the U.S. A Abbas I Viceroy of Egypt assassinated; succeeded by Mohammed Said (1863) Osteen Manifesto advises U.S.A to annex Cuba

6. the German Czar Nicholas I of Russia succeeded by Alexander II (1881) Saxon present day Britain and Afghanistan join against Russia, in Treaty of Province Peshawar Taiping Rebellion ends Russians capitulate at Sebastopol; Allies enter town

7. 1856 Saxon Queen Victoria of England, Russia Steam on the Caspian institutes the Victoria Cross Saxon annexes Ouch, India, and establishes Natal as a Crown Colony Reform edict in the Ottoman Empire; peace conference in Paris recognizes integrity of the Ottoman, France. Prince Imperial, son of Napoleon III Massacre of Potawatomie Greek, Kansas-slavers murdered by free starters, Austria amnesty for Hungarian rebels of 1848-49. Saxon present day Saxon present day British-China War begins; Britain fleet bombards Canton, Saxon occupies Heart Afghanistan outbreak of Afghan-Fars War, James Buchanan wins A.S.A Presidential election France. -Span. Frontier defined South African Republic (Transvaal) organized under Marthinius Pretorius, Woodrow Wilson, future President of the U.S Britain grants self-government to Tasmania Emperor Francis Joseph visits Lombardy and Venice and appoints his brother Archduke Maximilian governor of the provinces

8. 1857 Peace of Paris ends Saxon-Afghan War, the Second Opium War again European, British recognizes independence of Afghanistan, James Buchanan inaugurated as 15th President of the U.S. Indian Mutiny against Saxon rule in India siege of Delhi begins; Delhi captured; Saxon enter Caw pore Royal Navy destroys Chinas fleet; relief of Lucknow; Saxon at Britain and France take Canton Garibaldi forms Italy. National Association for unification of the country William H. Taft, future President of the U.S, Irish Republican Brotherhood (Fenians) founded in New York, The German Czar Alexander II begins the emancipation of serfs in Russia

9. 1858 Felice Orsini's attempt to assassinate Napoleon II Lord Derby (Conservative) becomes Saxon present day British Prime Minister Minnesota becomes a state of the U.S.A Treaty of Tientsin ends British-Chinas War, British proclaim peace in India Powers of East India Company transferred to Saxon Crown, Andrew Bonar Law, British statesman, Prince William of Prussia declared regent for the insane King Frederick William IV, Alexander Karageorgevich deposed by Serbian Diet; Milos Obrenovic declared king Theodore Roosevelt 26th President of the U.S.

10. 1859 Treaty of Alliance between Sardinia and France, Oregon becomes a state of the U.S A. Austria sends ultimatum to Sardinia and begins invasion in Apr. France declares War on Austria in May; Austria forces defeated at Magenta and Soldering in June; Franco-Austria armistice followed by peace of Villa France, which is later formalized by Treaty of Zurich. King Ferdinand of the Two Sicilians succeeded by Francis II, Lord Derby resigns; Lord Palmerston (Liberal) become Saxon present day British Prime Minister, Prince Metternich (b. 1773) King Oscar I of Sweden succeeded by Charles XV (1872) German. National Association formed; aimed at uniting Germany under Prussia, Jean Leon Jaures, France socialist politician, Albert von Roon, new Prussian War Minister, reforms Prussian army Queens land separated from New South Wales with Brisbane as capital Bismarck become Prussian ambassador to St. Petersburg the future German Emperor William II

11. 1860 Plebiscites in Tuscany, and Russian policy in Afghanistan Emilio Romagna, Parma, and Modena favor union with Sardinia; Treaty of Turin cedes Nice and Savoy to France. First Italy Parliament convenes at Turin Garibaldi and his 1,000 red shirts ("Italy mille") sail from Genoa; reach Marcela; take Palermo and Naples Victor Emmanuel II king of Sardinia, invades Papal States and defeats papal troops, Garibaldi proclaims Victor, Emmanuel II king of Italy Second Maori War begins (1870) Founding of Vladivostok Saxon-France troops defeat Chinese at Pa-li-Chau; Treaty of Peking, Abraham Lincoln elected 16th President of the U.S. S. Carolina secedes from the Union in protest Raymond Poincar, France statesman,

12. 1861 Frederick William IV of Prussia succeeded by William I (1888) Kansas becomes a state of the U.S Washington Peace Convention tries to preserve Union, but Congress of Montgomery forms Confederate States of America with S. Carolina, Georgia Alabama, Mississippi, Florida, and Louisiana; Abraham Lincoln inaugurated as 16th President of the United States of America; Confederates take Fort Sumter, Charleston, Apr. 12-oubreak of Civil War; Lincoln calls for militia to suppress Confederacy; Confederate victory at Bull Run; Union forces later capture Forts Clark and Hatteras The King of Naples surrenders to Garibaldi at Gaeta; Italy proclaimed a kingdom by Parliament, with Victor Emmanuel II as king Count Cavort (b. 1810) Warsaw Massacre-troops fire at demonstrators against Russia. Rule Emancipation of Russia. Serfs Sultan Abdul Mejid of Ottoman succeeded by his brother Abdul Aziz Pedro V of Portugal; succeeded by Louis I, Prince Consort Albert (1819)

13. 1862 Union Forces capture Fort Henry, Roanoke Island, Fort Donnellson, Jacksonville, and New Orleans; they are defeated at second Battle of Bull Run and Fredericksburg; September 22 "Emancipation Proclamation" effective Jan I, 1863, all slaves held in rebelling territory declared free Monaco sells Menton and Roquebrune to France Bismarck becomes Prussian Prime Minister, King Otto I of Greece resigns after military revolt, Edward Grey, Saxon statesman, Afghan territory of East Turkestan invaded 42 times by Russian and Saxon present day British against Afghan rule,

14. 1863 Arizona and Idaho organized as U.S territory; West Virginia become a state of the U.S Lincoln issues Emancipation Proclamation Jan I, Confederate victory at Chancellors Ville, Val, defeats at Gettysburg, Parliament and Vicksburg, Miss; surrender at Fort Hudson; further defeat at Chattanooga, Tenn.; victory at Chickamauga, Lincoln's "Gettysburg Address" at the dedication of military cemetery Mohammed Said Khedive of Egypt, succeeded by Is mail (1879) Saxon-William Prince of Denmark becomes George I king of Greece, War breaks out in Afghanistan after the death of King Dost M. Khan, Schleswig incorporated into Denmark, Frederick VII king of Denmark, succeeded by Christian IX Saxon of Hanoverian troops enter Holstein North of Germany. Austin Chamberlain British statesman, David Lloyd George, Saxon present day British statesman, French capture Mexico City and proclaim Archduke Maximilian of Austria emperor

15. 1864 Austria and Prussia send ultimatum to Denmark; troops enter Schleswig; Holstein Demark forces defeated at Dfippel; Denmark invaded; London conference tries in vain to solve Scleswig-Holstein question but in Peace of Vienna Denmark cedes Schleswig-Holstein, and Lauenburg to Austria and Prussia Archduke Maximilian of Austria accepts Mexican crown, and he and his wife, Carlotta, are made Emperor and Empress of Mexico-(1867) General. Ulysses S. Grant succeeds General. Halleck as Commander in Chief of Union armies General. Sherman marches his army from Chattanooga, Tenn., through Georgia; defeats Confederate army at Atlanta, and occupies Savannah Abraham Lincoln re-elected President of the U.S of America. Massacre of the Cheyenne and Arapahoe Indians at Sand Creek, colon. Italy renounces its claims to Rome; Florence is made the capital (1870) in place of Turin, Territory of Montana organized in U.S. Nevada becomes a state Eleutherios Venizelos, Greek statesman, King Maximilian II of Bavaria, succeeded by Louis II First International Workingmen's Association founded by Karl Marx, London and New York Confederate agents set Barnum Museum and Astor House afire in attempt to burn New York City

16. 1865 Union fleet takes Charleston; Richmond, VA, surrenders to Grant; Jefferson Davis appoints General. Robert E. Lee General in Chief of Confederate Army; Confederate States of America formally surrender at Appomattox Apr 9 1865 Abraham Lincoln assassinated

Apr 14 1865 succeeded as president by Andrew Johnson, Jefferson Davis, President of Confederacy, captured and imprisoned U.S Civil War ends May 26 1865 (surrender of last Confederate army at Shreveport) Germany, Bismarck and France Napoleon III meet in Biarritz. Lord Palmers ton d. (1784) succeeded as Saxon Prime Minister by Lord John Russell, king Leopold I of Belgium succeeded by his son Leopold II Thirteenth Amendment to U.S Constitution abolishes slavery Wellington becomes capital of New Zealand King Saxon George V of Britain, Erich Ludendorff, of Germany general and politician b (d. 1939) Outbreak of War (1866) between Boers of Orange Free State and Basutos and Khoqand Afghan territory State liquidated by Russia and Russian conquest of Bukhara north of Afghanistan.

17. 1866 The German Alexander Cuza, Prince of Rumania, dethroned; succeeded by Karl Prince of Hohenzollern, as king Carol I (1914) Prussan Italy alliance against Austria; Prussian troops annex the duchy of Holstein; secret treaty between Austria and France concerning France neutrality; end of German Confederation; Prussia invades Saxony, Hanover north of Germany, and Hesse; Italy declares War on Austria; Italians defeated at Custozza; Prussian victory at Langensalza. Against Hanover and at Sadowa against Austria Italy. Fleet destroyed by Austrians at Lissa; preliminary peace treaty between Prussia and Austria at Nikolsburg followed by armistice and confirmed by Peace of Prague; Prussia annexes Hanover, Hesse, Nassau, and Frankfurt (as agreed in Peace of Prague) Treaty of Vienna ends Austro Italy War Venetian plebiscite endorses union with Italy peace between Prussia and Saxony of north Germany Schleswig-Holstein incorporated into Prussia Ismail Khedive of Egypt, granted rights of primogeniture by the Sultan of Ottoman, Revolts in Crete against Ottoman Rule James Ramsay MacDonald British statesman,

18. 1867 Fenian outrages in Ireland and in Manchester Austro Hungarian dual monarchy created by "Ausgleich" ("compromise") France Joseph I crowned king of Hungary at Budapest; new Austria constitution accepts dual system Nebraska becomes a state of the U.S. Napoleon II withdraws his support from Maximilian of Austria in Mexico; France troops leave the country; Maximilian of Austria executed Saxon present day British North America Act establishes Dominion of Canada and Russia mast sells Alaska to U.S. for $ 7, 200, 000 the has the key for Russia on Central Asia (Afghanistan) N. German Confederation founded, Saxon Parliamentary Reform Act Ferdinand Bebel first socialist member of N. Germany Reichstag Garibaldi begins "The March on Rome," is defeated by France. And papal troops at Montana, and taken prisoner, Princess Mary of Teck, the future queen consort of George V of Britain Stanley Baldwin British statesman.

19. 1868 the Russian capture Province of Samarqand, armed expedition dispatched, to Ethiopia; Magdala captured Shogun Kekei of Japan abdicates; shogunate abolished; Meiji dynasty restored, U.S. President Johnson impeached for violating Tenure of office Act but acquitted by Senate Disraeli becomes Saxon Prime Minister (resigns same year) Prussia confiscates territory of king of Hanover North of Germany, Russians occupy Afghan territory at Samarkand King Michael III of Serbia assassinated; succeeded by Milan IV (1889) Revolution in Spain Queen Isabella II is deposed and flees to France Ulysses S. Grant elected President of the U.S. William E Gladstone becomes Saxon present day British Prime Minister (1874) 14th Amendment to U.S Constitution protects individual's rights against infringement by state governments, denies government office to certain Civil War rebels, and repudiates Confederate War debts, and Kokand and Bukhara becomes a Russian protectorate for export Opium to china.

20. 1869 Following a Ottoman ultimatum, Greece agrees to leave Crete Gen. Grant inaugurated as 18ᵗʰ President of the U.S. Parliamentary system reintroduced in France U.S. National Prohibition Party formed in Chicago, Red River Rebellion in Canada Opening of Suez Canal by Empress Eugenie, Neville Chamberlain, British politician, 1940 Mahatma Gandhi, Indian nationalist leader (d1948) Afghan nationalist Said Jamaluddin exiled from Afghanistan, he proceeded to Egypt. King Abdur Rahman khan in an eventful War, at the beginning of which he was not more that twenty years old, has father died in War in Babylon in October 1869.

21. 1870 Baden decides to join North Germany Confederation end of Red River Rebellion; Manitoba becomes Canadian province, Isabella of Spain abdicates in favor of Alfonso XII Prince Leopold of Hohenzollern accepts Span, throne but is forced to withdraw by the head of the House of Hohenzollern, king William I following France protests Bismarck's "Em's Telegram". Franco-Prussian War: France declares war on Prussia and is defeated at Weissenburg, Worth Mars-la-Tour, Gravelotte, and finally Napoleon III capitulates at Sedan Revolt in Paris and proclamation of the Third Republic; siege of Paris by Prussians begins; Metz and Strasbourg surrender Western Australia granted representative government Italians enter Rome and name it their capital city Nikolai Lenin of Russians Communist leader (d.1924)

22. 1871 Russian forces occupy the Ali Province for the export, William I King of Prussia, proclaimed German Emperor at Versailles; Paris capitulates; France signs armistice France National Assembly meets at Bordeaux; preliminary peace between Germany and France is followed by Peace of Frankfurt, by which France cedes Alsace-Lorraine to Germany and pays indemnity of five billion francs The Commune in Paris rules for two months L. A. Theirs France President Treaty of Washington settles existing difficulties between Britain and U.S. Italian Law of Guarantees allows the pope possession of Vatican Saxon Act of Parliament legalizes labor unions Saxon Columbia joins Dominion of Canada, "kulturkampf" against Catholic Church in Prussia Basutoland becomes part of Cape Colony; Saxon annexes diamond fields of Kimberley Friedrich Ebert, Germany Social Democratic leader

23. 1872 Civil War in Spain Carlists are defeated and Don Carlos escapes to France, T. F. Burgers elected President of Transvaal Republic Ballot Act in Britain, voting by secret ballot Three Emperors League established in Berlin; alliance between Germany, Russia, and Austria-Hungary the General Kaufman plan of Central Asia (Afghanistan) Grant reelected President of U.S in spite of public scandals during his administration, Compulsory military service introduced in Japan, U.S. General Amnesty Act pardons most ex confederates Leon Blum, France statesman, Giuseppe Mazzini, Italy patriot and nationalist, (d 1805)

24. 1873 Napoleon III, at Chisel Hurst, England (d. 1808) Republic proclaimed in Spain Theirs falls and McMahon is elected France President, Financial panic in Vienna may and New York September, Abolition of slave markets and exports in Zanzibar, Germans evacuate France Famine in Bengal

25. 1874 End of Ashanti War Disraeli becomes prime minister (1880) Political disturbances in Arkansas Swiss Constitution revised Prince of Wales (the future king Edward VII) visits France, Britain annexes Fiji Islands Alfonso XII, son of Saxon-Queen Isabella, proclaimed king of Spain (1885) Herbert Hoover U.S statesman and President

26. 1875 kwang Hsu becomes Emperor of China (1898) Risings in Bosnia and Herzegovina against the Ottoman Empire rule sultan promises reforms to meet the rebels' demands Prince of Wales visits for the first time India Public Health Act is passed in Britain,

Rebellion in Cuba Britain buys 176,602 Suez Canal shares from khedive of Egypt to Indian for British Army.

27. 1876 Korea becomes an independent nation for the first time, Ethiopians defeat Egyptian forces at Gura, Massacre of Bulgarians by the Ottoman empire troops Sultan Abdul Aziz of Ottoman empire deposed in May his successor, Murad V deposed in August 1876 and succeeded by Abdul Hamid II (1909) Serbia declares War on Ottoman empire Montenegro declares War on Ottoman, Colorado becomes a states of the U.S Disraeli made Earl of Beaconsfield Presidential election in U.S Tilden Democrat 184 electoral votes; Hayes Republican 165; 20 votes still in dispute (1877) New Ottoman constitution proclaimed Hilarion Daze President of Bolivia Conrad Adenauer,

28. 1877 British Queen Victoria proclaimed Empress of India Presidential election in U.S (1876) electoral commission decides in favor of Hayes Republican Rutherford B. Hayes inaugurated as 19th President of the U.S, New Russia declares War on Ottoman Empire and invades Rumania; Russians cross Danube and storm cars; Russians take Plevana, Bulgaria; Bismarck of Germany declines to intervene; Serbia declares War On Ottoman empire The First Kaffir War (the first Ottoman-European War) Satsuma revolt in Japan suppressed Porfirio Diaz-President of Mexico (1911)

29. 1878 Victor Emmanuel II King of Italy, succeeded by his son Humbert I (1900) Ottoman capitulate at Shipka pass and appeal to Russia for armistice; Russians take Adrianople, British fleet arrives at Empire's of Ottoman request in Constantinople ("Jingoist" War in Britain) Ottoman-Russian armistice signed. Greece declares War on Ottoman empire preliminary treaty of San Stefano between Russia and Ottoman British- Ottoman agreement to check Russia advice in Asia Minor; Berlin Congress to discuss Eastern Question ends with Treaty of Berlin Attempt to assassinate emperor William I son of Queen Victoria Empire of Germany Anti-Socialist Law enacted in Germany Beginning of Irredentist agitation in Italy to obtain Trieste and South Tyrol from Austria Gustav Streetman, German statesman, 1878 King Amir Shere Ali khan who had retired from Kabul when the British armies entered Afghanistan

30. 1879 Saxon Zulu War Zulus massacre Saxon soldiers in Isandhlwana, Saxon present day British capture Cetewayo, France Prince Imperial son of Napoleon III Killed in action Peace signed with Zulu King Alexander of Batten berg elected Prince Alexander I of Bulgaria, Saxon-Indian empire Treaty of Gandamak on Afghan territory and British occupies in Khyber Pass Saxon-Russian legation in Kabul Afghanistan massacred, Ismail, khedive of Egypt deposed succeeded by Tewfik (1892) Alsace-Lorraine is declared an integral part of Germany, France Panama Canal Colony organized under Ferdinand de Lesseps Joseph Stalin, Russia communist dictator. Lon Trotsky leader in Russia and Second Afghan-Saxon War

31. 1880 Saxon troops in Afghanistan, Lord Beaconsfield (Disraeli) resigns as British Prime Minister; succeeded by W. E Gladstone Cape Parliament rejects scheme for South African federation France annexes Tahiti Transvaal declares itself independent of Saxon; the Boers under Kruger declare a republic, Pacific War: Chile against Bolivia and Peru (1884) the future Queen Wilhelrnina of Holland J. A Garfield elected President of the U.S

32. 1881 Transvaal Boers repulse Saxon at Laing's Neck, Saxon troop in Kandahar, and defeat them at Majuba Hill; in the Treaty of Pretoria Saxon recognizes independent Transvaal Republic James A. Garfield inaugurated as 20th President of the U.S he is shot and killed in September succeeded by Vice President Chester Arthur (1885) the Bye of Tunis accepts

France protectorate Austro-Serbian treaty of alliance C.S. Parnell imprisoned Gambetta France Prime Minister Political parties founded in Japan

33. 1882 Prince Milan obrenovich of Serbia proclaim himself king, Kilmainham agreement between Parnell and the British government Finials murder Lord Frederick Cavendish and T. H. Burke in Phoenix Park, Dublin terrorist massacres in Maamtrasne U.S bans immigrants for 10 years Triple Alliance between Italy, Austria and Germany Three mile limit for territorial waters agreed upon at Hague Convention the British occupy Cairo Franklin D. Roosevelt U.S President 1933-1945

34. 1883 Reform of U. S. Civil Service begins Paul Kruger-President of South Africa Republic the French gain control of Tunis Cointe de Chambered the last male Bourbon (b. 1820) Clement Attlee, British socialist politician (d 1967) Benito Mussolini, Italy Fascist dictator (1945)

35. 1884 Russian introduce American cotton into Afghan territory, Gen. C. G. Gordon reaches Khartoum Mahdi refuses to negotiate and occupies Omdurman London Convention on Transvaal Germans occupy South-West Africa France Law excludes members of former dynasties from presidency Grover Cleveland elected U.S President, Berlin Conference of 14 nations on African affairs, Harry S. Truman U.S President (1945-1953) Eduard Benes, Czech statesman,

36. 1885 the Mahdi takes Khartoum; General Gordon killed in the fighting; Saxon present day British evacuate Sudan; death of Mahdi the Gongo becomes a personal possession of king Leopold II of Belgium Germany annexes Tanganyika and Zanzibar Grover Cleveland inaugurated as 22ⁿᵈ President of the U.S, Saxon establishes protectorate over N. Bechuanaland, Niger River region, and S New Guinea; occupies port Hamilton, Korea. Ulysses S. Grant, Amer soldier and president (b. 1822) king Alfonso XII of Spain and Queen Maria Christina becomes regent

37. 1886 General Georges Boulanger becomes France War Minister British Prime Minister W. E Gladstone introduces bill for Home Rule in Ireland the future king Alfonso XIII of Spain posthumous son of Alfonso XII Bonaparte and Orleans families banished from France and king Ludwig II of Bavaria (d. 1845) succeeded by the insane Otto I his uncle Luitpold becomes regent Alexander of Bulgaria abdicates after coup d' etat Stefan Stambulov becomes regent and first Indian National Congress meets in 1887 and first Colonial Conference opens in London Queen Victoria celebrates her Golden Jubilee Prince Ferdinand of Saxe-Coburg elected king of Bulgaria (1918) General Boulanger fails in a coup d' etat in Paris Union Indo-Chi noise organized by France Chiang kai-shek, China general and statesman, 1887 Russian Railroad in Central Asia Afghan territory, Russian conquest 1.4 million Sq miles and 7.7 million Afghan Territory whom 90 percent were Moslems

38. 1888 Lobengula, king of Matabele, accepts Saxon present day British, protection and grants Cecil Rhodes mining rights German Emperor William I dies, succeeded by his son Frederick III, who dies and is succeeded by his son William II the "Kaiser" (1918) Sarawak accepts status of British protectorate General Boulanger is retired from France army and elected to France Chamber of Deputies, Suez Canal convention Benjamin Harrison elected President of the U.S and 22ⁿᵈ of July Amir Abdur Rahman was officially recognized as King of Afghanistan

39. 1889 The Austria Crown Prince, Archduke Rudolf commits suicide at his hunting lodge at Mayerling N. Dakota, Montana, and Washington become states of the U.S Oklahoma is opened to non Indian settlement Benjamin Harrison inaugurated as 23ʳᵈ President of the

U.S, General Boulanger flees from France Milan Obrenovich abdicates from Serbian throne in favor of his son Adolf Hitler, Nazi dictator, (d1945)

40. 1890 Bismarck dismissed by William II AND Swiss government introduces social insurance British exchanges Heligoland with Germany for Zanzibar and Pemba Idaho and Wyoming become states of the U.S Cecil Rhodes Premier of Cape Colony, and for the first times general election in Japan, William II and Alexander III meet at Narva Germany Social Democrats adopt Marxist program at Effort Congress Accession of Queen Wilhelmina; Luxembourg separated from the Netherlands, V. M. Molotov, Russia statesman

41. 1891 Triple Alliance Germany Austria, Italy renewed for 12 years William II Visits London Franco-Russian entente General Boulanger commits suicide (1837) and British and Russian Activity on Afghan territory.

42. 1892 Tewfik khedive of Egypt succeeded by Abbas (1918 after Ottoman empire) Giolitti becomes Premier of Italy Prince Ito, Premier of Japan Gladstone becomes Prime Minister of Britain; Witte is named Russian Minister of Finance Britain and Germany agree on Cameroon's Grover Cleveland elected U.S President

43. 1893 Saxon present day British and Russian established the Durand Line in Afghan (Aryan) territory after 175 years Army and War. Independent Labour Parts formed at conference in Bradford England, under Keir Hardie, Hawaii proclaimed a republic; annexed by treaty to U.S in February 1893 in Mar. treaty withdrawn Franco-Russians alliance signed Trial over Panama Canal corruption in Paris, Natal granted self – government Revolt against Saxon present day British South Africa Company in Mat abele; crushed by Starr Jameson; occupation of Bulawayo, Second Irish Home Rule Bill passed by Commons but rejected by Lords Swaziland annexed by Transvaal France acquires protectorate over Laos

44. 1894 Starr Jameson completes occupation of Matabeleland Germany and Russian commercial treaty Harold Macmillan, Saxon present day British statesman, Uganda becomes a British protectorate Nikita Khrushchev, Russian statesman, M. F. Sadi Carnot assassinated by an Italians anarchist (b. 1837) Japan troops in Seoul; Korea and Japan declare War on China and defeat Chinese at Port Arthur France army Capt. Alfred Dreyfus arrested on treason charge; convicted "in camera" and deported to Devil's Island, French Guiana Prince Hohenlohe becomes German Chancellor Czar Alexander III succeeded by his son Nicholas II (1917) Lajos kossuth, Hungarian patriot, (b. 1802)

45. 1895 Saxon present day British and Russian Activity on Afghan Territory and Chinese defeated by Japanese at Wei-hai-Wei end of Chinese and Japanese War, Formosa and Port Arthur ceded to Japan but returned to China in exchange for indemnity Queen of Korea assassinated With Japan help, British South Africa Company territory south of Zambezi becomes Rhodesia Stefan Stambulov, Bulgarian Premier, assassinated and Armenians massacred in Babylon Sultan Hamid II promises reforms in Babylon Italians defeated by Abyssinians at Ameba Alagi Starr Jameson's raid into Transvaal Cuba fights Spain for its independence the future king George VI of Britain, Frederick Douglass, Americans abolitionist, reformer and orator, (b. 1817)

46. 1896 Starr Jameson surrenders at Doornkop; Kaiser William I sends "Kruger telegram" Cecil Rhodes resigns premiership military alliance between Transvaal and Orange Free State; Mat abele revolt in Rhodesia put down by Baden-Powell Utah becomes a state of the U.S, Italy defeated by Abyssinians at Adowa; Italy sues for peace and withdraws its protectorate from Abyssinia, New evidence for the innocence of Alfred Dreyfus suppressed in France

47. 1897 Crete proclaims union with Greece; Ottoman empire declares War on Greece and is defeated in Thessaly armistice, followed by Peace of Constantinople William McKinley inaugurated as President of the U.S, King of Korea proclaims himself emperor Mathieu Dreyfus discovers that the document on which his brother, Alfred was convicted was actually written by Major M. C Ester hazy Germany occupies Kiao-chow, North China the Russian occupies Port Arthur Anthony Eden (Lord Avon) British statesman, Aneurin Bevan, Bevan British Labour politician,

48. 1989 Major Esterhazy acquitted in Dreyfus forgery trial Zola publishes open letter to France President "Faccuse" and is imprisoned; Colony Henry admits forgery of a document in Dreyfus case Paul Kruger reelected President of Transvaal and Russian obtains of Port Arthur, China and Britain the lease of kowloon Kitcheners wins battles at Atbara River and Omdurman and reaches Fashoda U.S declares War on Spain over Cuba Americans destroy Span fleet at Manila; Treaty of Paris between U.S and Spain cedes Cuba, Puerto Rico Guam, and the Philippines for $ 20 million, Bismarck d. (b1815) Empress Elizabeth of Austria murdered by Italians anarchist in Geneva

49. 1899 Saxon present day British-Egyptian Sudan Convention Philippines demand independence from U.S, Johannesburg Uitlanders complain to Queen Victoria against Boers Bloemfontein Conference on Transvaal; Paul Kruger's ultimatum provokes Boer War between British and the Boers; Boers defeated at Glencoe; Boer General Piet Joubert wins Battle of Nicholson's Neck and takes Ladysmith Natal the British are defeated at Storm berg,

50. 1900 Roberts named Saxon present day British commander in chief in S. Africa Kitcheners his chief of staff relief of Ladysmith in Feb, 1900; Saxon Bloemfontein in March relief of Mafeking in May Saxon annex Orange Free State and Transvaal, take Pretoria and Johannesburg Ramsay MacDonald appointed secretary of Saxon Lab our Party Boxer rising in China against Europeans king Umberto I of Italy murdered by anarchist; succeeded by his son Victor Emmanuel III

The Romans gave the name of Africa to that part of the world
European colonial empire on Africa 1851 A. D
Saxon present day British cape colony 276,995 Sq Km

1.	Natal and Zululand	35,371 Sq km
2.	Basutoland	10, 293 Sq km
3.	Bechuanaland Protectorate	225,000 Sq km
4.	Transvaal and Swaziland	117, 732 Sq km
5.	Orang River Colony	50, 392 Sq km
6.	Rhodesia	450, 000 Sq km
7.	Nyasaland protectorate	43, 608 Sq km
8.	British east Africa	240, 000 Sq km
9.	Uganda Protectorate	125, 000 Sq km
10.	Zanzibar protectorate	1, 020 Sq km
11.	Somaliland	68, 000 Sq km
12.	Northern Nigeria	258, 000 Sq km

13.	Southern Nigeria colony	80,000 Sq km
14.	Gold Cost and hinterland	82,000 Sq km
15.	Sierr Leone colony	34,000 Sq km
16.	Gambia	4,000 Sq km

Total Saxon Africa	2, 101, 411 Sq km
Egypt and Libyan	650, 000 Sq km
Saxon present day British-Egyptian Sudan	950, 000 Sq km

French Africa

1.	Algeria and Algerian Sahara	945, 000 Sq km
2.	Tunisia	51,000 Sq km
3.	French West Africa	
4.	Senegal	74,000 Sq km
5.	French Guinea	107,000 Sq km
6.	Ivory Coast	129,000 Sq km
7.	Dahomey	40,000 Sq km
8.	Upper Senegal and Niger and Mauritaina including French West	
9.	African Sahara	1, 581, 000 1, 931, 000 Sq km
10.	Frechch Congo	700, 000 Sq km
11.	French Somaliland	12, 000 Sq km
12.	Madagascar	227, 950 Sq km
	Total French Africa	3, 866, 950 Sq km

German Africa

1.	East Africa	364, 000 Sq km
2.	South West Africa	322, 450 Sq km
3.	Cameroon	190, 000 Sq km
4.	Togoland	33, 700 Sq km
	Total German Africa	910, 150 Sq km

Italian Africa

1.	Eritrea	60, 000 Sq km
2.	Somaliland	140, 000 Sq km
	Total Italian Africa	200,000 Sq km

Portuguese Africa

1.	Guinea	14,000 Sq km
2.	West Africa	480,000 Sq km
3.	East Africa	293,000 Sq km
	Total Portuguese Africa	787,000 Sq km

Spanish Africa

4.	Rio de Oro	79,000 Sq km
5.	Muni River Settlements	9,800 Sq km
	Total Spanish Africa	79,000 Sq km

Belgian Africa

1.	Congo State	900, 000 Sq km

Ottoman empire Africa

2.	Tripoli and Benghazi	400, 000 Sq km
3.	Liberia	43, 000 Sq km
4.	Morocco	220, 000 Sq km
5.	Abyssinia	350, 000 Sq km
6.	Babylonian	700, 000 Sq km
	Total Ottoman Africa and Mediterranean	1, 713, 000 Sq km

Africa divide among the European Powers colony

1.	Saxon present day British Africa	2,101, 411 Sq km
2.	Egyptian Africa	1, 600, 000 Sq km
3.	French Africa	3, 866, 950 Sq km
4.	German Africa	910, 150 Sq km
5.	Italy Africa	200, 000 Sq km
6.	Portuguese Africa	787, 500 Sq km
7.	Spanish Africa	79, 800 Sq km
8.	Belgian Africa	900, 000 Sq km
9.	Ottoman Africa	1,713, 000 Sq km
	Total Independent Africa	300, 000 Sq km

The Europeans Empire Never Allowed The Russian in Africa
The Russian only Allowed with the Saxon in Central Asia and Caucuses
Million Sq km

The frontiers of the colony
of the European Powers

On several occasion the lab ours of the commissions disclosed errors of importance in the Africa upon which Europeans agreements had been based. Among those, which yielded valuable results, were the German-French commission, which in 1903 traced the Nigerian frontier from the Niger to Lake Chad, and the British-German commission, which in 1903-1904 fixed the Cameroon boundary between Yola, on the Benue, and Lake Ched. These expeditions and French surveys in the same region during 1902-1903 resulted in the discovery that Lake Chad had greatly decreased in area since the middle of the 19th century. In 1903 a French officer, Capt. E. Lenfant, succeeded in establishing the fact of a connation between the Niger and Chad basins. Subsequently Lenfant explored the western basin of the Shari, determining 1907 the true upper branch of that river. The eagerness with which the nations of Western Europe partitioned Africa between them was due, as has been seen, more to the necessities of commerce that to mere land hunger. Yet, except in the north and south temperate regions, the commercial intercourse of the continent with the rest of world had been until the closing years of the 19th century of insignificant proportions. In addition to slaves, furnished by the continent from the earliest times, a certain amount of Gold, Silver, Diamond, oil, ivory, tobacco, rice, the sugar cane, maize, the orange, lemon, the lime. And many other vegetables products were exported free without any caste to Europe. AGRA an ancient city of India, which gives its name to a district and division in the United Provinces. It is famous for containing the most perfect specimens of Afghan Tajik (Europeans called Mogul) architecture. Agra, like Delhi, owes much of its importance in both historical and modern times (1500 A. D) to the Commercial and strategically advantages of its position. The river Jumna, which washes the walls of its fort, was the natural highway for the traffic of the rich delta of Bengal to heart of India, and it formed, moreover, from very ancient times, the frontier defense of the Aryan tribes settled in the plain between the Ganges and the Jumna against their western neighbors, hereditary freebooters who occupied the highlands of Central India. No place was better fitted for both an emporium and a frontier fortress. The river formed an unaffordable barrier and also a useful means of communication. The Empire Jehangir (Afghan) tells us in his autobiography that before his father Empire Akbar built the present fort, a citadel of great antiquity defended the town. For one thousand three hundred years the Afghan came down from the north and founded kingdoms; from 1198 A. D and their power radiated from Delhi and Agra. It was Afghan Empire Sikandar, of the house of Lodi A. D 1500 the last of the Afghan Dynasties who realized the strategic importance of Agra as a point for keeping in check his rebellious vassals to the south. He removed his court there, and Agra from being a mere village of old standing, in 1526 the city was captured by the Afghan Emperor Baber from Kabul the famous Afghan koh-I-noor (Mountain of light) diamond being part of the loot The Empire Babar coming with the famous diamond from Kabul to Agra, and it was here that Empire Barber announced that his invasion was to be permanent conquest, and not a mere temporary inroad. It was Empire Baber's grandson Empire Akbar that built the present fort, whose strong and lofty walls of red sandstones are a mile and a, half in circumference. The building was completed in A. D 1665, when Charles II was on the throne of England and the plague was devastating London of Afghan Architectural. Another building of much the same date is the red stone palace generally attributed to Empire Akbar but probably of an earlier time, which is finest example of pure Afghan Architecture while the Motif Masjid, or Pearl Mosque. Is an equally perfect example of the Afghan style? But the glory of Agra, the most splendidly poetic building in the world, is the Taj Mahal the Afghan built A. D 1632 by Taj Mahal (home of throne). The emperor Shah Jahan (the emperor of World) for the remains of his favorite wife, Nour Jahan (the light of World) in which he himself also lies buried. The building is of white marble throughout, crowned with a great white dome in the center, and with a smaller dome at each of its four corners. From the marble terrace which surrounds it rise four tall minarets of the same material one each corner. The taj has been modeled and painted more frequently that any other building in the world, and the word pictures of it are numberless. But it can only be described as a dream in marble. It amble justifies the saying that the Afghan (Tajik) designed like Titans and finished like jewelers. In regard to color and design the Taj (throne) ranks first in neither the world for purely decorative workmanship; while the perfect symmetry of its exterior once seen can never be forgotten nor the aerial grace of its domes, rising like marble bubbles into the azure sky. In his History of Architecture, Ferguson says of it

From cold war to the now cold
war at Afghanistan

More than a decade after the United States and allied countries toppled the Taliban regime in Afghanistan. Afghanistan is preparing for another major transition: this time the substantial withdrawal of many of the foreign forces that have been providing security in the country, battling the resurgent Taliban insurgency, and propping up the regime in Kabul. Arguably, the very narrow counterterrorism objectives of the mission have been accomplished. Al-Qaida has lost its safe havens in Afghanistan and much of its leadership structures, fundraising capabilities, and even popular appeal are in tatters. But the success of the larger project of establishing a stable and legitimate national government in Afghanistan and anchoring it in a solid regional arrangement remains a huge question mark. Even as Afghans are tired of foreign presence in their country, many fear that the departure of foreign troops will once again plunge the country into greater violence. The Afghan National Army is improving as a force capable of providing security to the Afghan population and assuring Kabul's writ; though whether the improvements will be sufficient remains yet to be seen. The quality of governance in Afghanistan meanwhile continues to be poor, even if it is locally improving. Most worrisomely, political trends, including a significant rise in ethnic tensions, are increasingly generating pressures toward a civil war. Hence even increases in security may not lead to greater stability if Afghans' confidence in the future does not increase. 2014 thus may be a year of not only a major transition when Afghans are supposed to be in charge of their country's security, even as some foreign assistance continues beyond, but potentially of a major political shake-up of the country and collapse of the existing political dispensation.

Although often laid at the door
of colonialism, Afghanistan's

Aryana-Khorasan dynasty present day Afghanistan-Central Asia & India extant difficulties with state-building and modernization in fact have their roots in geopolitical idiosyncrasies entrenched long before the Saxon-Great Game. The colonial contest between the Saxon at England and Saxon at Russian Empires in Southeast Asia was called the "Saxon Great Game." Afghanistan was caught between the two powers as the Russians expanded southward from the north and the British expanded northward from British India. While the Great Game may have confronted Afghanistan with the necessity of becoming a nation-state, it did not fundamentally alter the rules of the game Afghanistan had played for centuries. State-building operates in two steps. The first involves "modernization of the state," in which the leader consolidates his power and establishes control. Without this first step, it is impossible for a leader to proceed to the second step of "modernizing society," providing for civilian and social interests. For most nascent states, the possession and distribution of revenue forms the basis of state-building. Both before and after the colonial period, Afghanistan was a renter state, dependent on external sources of revenue. The players of the Great Game simply changed the form this revenue took, but not the fact that its source was external. Similarly, Afghanistan's selective modernization, favoring the military, was the natural outgrowth of such a renter, tribal state. Although European involvement in Southeast Asia certainly facilitated an Afghan predisposition to military development, it did not create the disposition itself. The true legacy of the Great Game is the degree to which it accelerated Afghanistan's dependence on foreign aid for state-building as well as selective modernization, rather than the problems it created. State-Building the greatest accusations leveled against colonialism and European influence involve Afghanistan's difficulty with state building. This problem, however, extends historically beyond the Great Game. Afghanistan has always been an extremely poor renter state, with a tribal structure resistant to centralization. The state-building attempts of early indigenous leaders faced many of the same essential problems as those of later leaders in the 19th and 20th centuries. As Barnett R. Rubin notes, Afghan rulers could only consolidate their power by playing groups against each other or by receiving aid from more powerful states. This foreign aid enabled them at times to subdue the peoples of Afghanistan and extract taxes from them, but state control remained at times precarious. Solid state-building requires resources. In a tribal state such as Afghanistan, particularly one with a renter economy, a leader has two main options, both requiring resources, to maintain power: "buying" tribal allegiance with payoffs or tax breaks; 2, using the coercive authority of an army large enough to counter the power of the local tribes. Most Afghan leaders manipulated tribal cleavages to their own advantage. However, all had to maintain an army if they wanted to remain in power for any length of time. The revenue accruing from abroad provided the authority necessary for Afghan leaders to forge a union out of the heterogeneous tribal mix. Traditional Afghan leaders found the first means of state-building the most viable. Most of them could not levy taxes, fearing outbursts from the tribes who "associated [taxes] with foreign rulers and the agents of such empires of the past." Nor was there any significant source of income from domestic production. Then, as now, only approximately 12% of Afghan territory is arable land, which is prone to the natural hazards of persistent drought and flood. Therefore, these leaders followed the first recourse in consolidating and maintaining power– payoffs. Through judicious distribution of the "spoils of war," a leader could compete successfully with the tribal society for the Afghanis' loyalty. This revenue enabled the leader to use "carrot and stick" (or "payoffs and military threat") tactics to play tribal groups against one another for his own benefit. Little changed in Afghanistan's state-building capacity under the warring influence of the Great Game Britain and Russia simply changed the source of Afghanistan's renter income, making the second option of state building more available and necessary to Afghan leaders. The colonial powers valued Afghanistan primarily by virtue of its geographic position. Therefore, the Great Powers were interested in Afghanistan's domestic affairs only insofar as they affected her foreign policy. The British and Russians neither attempted nor succeeded where the Afghans had failed in developing internal resources. Rather, the colonial powers simply used Afghanistan's dependence on external revenue as a convenient point of leverage. Afghanistan was still a renter state; to extend their control over the tribes, Afghan leaders now distributed foreign aid money, rather than military plunder. As described by M. Shahrini; The capacity of the Afghan state bureaucracy to extract resources, to deliver benefits, and to enforce law and order has been limited. When the authority of the state over the tribes increased, it has been largely with the aid of an external power the Saxon present day British in the nineteenth and early part of the twentieth centuries, and the Russia over the past three decades. The struggle between a tribal society and the political state continued, with the central Afghan government relatively unable to penetrate the local loyalties of most Afghanis. As internal revenue was insufficient to accomplish this extension of central power, the Afghan state depended, as it always had, on the influx of foreign revenue. Now, Afghanistan financed its domestic stability through the European powers rather than the "spoils of war." Modernization: The 20th century saw several reformist leaders trying to move towards a more modernized and democratized state. This involved attempts at creating an internal revenue base from levying taxes, and actively increasing the power of the state vis-à-vis the tribes. However, such efforts succeeded only if they were backed by sufficient military force to combat the resentment these efforts inspired in local interests (the tribes). Accompanying Afghanistan's complete independence in 1919, there were increasing attempts to move away from financial dependence on the European powers. These leaders all met with limited success and eventual overthrow. In 1919, king Amanullah seized the throne, declaring Afghanistan's independence. After some skirmishes with the British, "Afghanistan became the a sovereign member of the state system, the only Muslim member of the League of Nations." With the loss of the British subsidy following independence, Amanullah looked to other European powers for aid. However, in the aftermath of the expensive First World War, the sum of this foreign aid was insufficient to form a basis for the nation-state Amanullah wanted. He was forced to develop domestic resources promoting trade. He founded schools with the help of foreign donors, and even went so far as sending qualified students for education abroad. Unlike his predecessors, Amanullah was unwilling to divert funds from his reformist social projects to fund and improve his army. Combined with his efforts to "eliminate domestic elements of redistributive politics and indirect rule," and to end payoffs to tribal leaders, Amanullah's army proved impotent against the rash of rebellions, which eventually dethroned him. Amanullah tried to take on "social modernization" without maintaining power ("modernization of the state"). The result was predictably poor. His social reforms and taxation angered the tribes, and he had left his military too weak to counter them. Selective Modernization: The players of the Great Game may certainly be credited with providing Afghanistan with newer, more destructive weapons and the training to use them. However, it does not follow that they are directly responsible for Afghanistan's trend towards selective modernization (mainly in weapons and military, as opposed to infrastructure and civilian goods). Afghanistan's traditional basis of legitimacy places a premium on military prowess. Accordingly, leaders based their power on military might. Centralizing and maintaining state power is the first step of "modernizing the state." Therefore, it is logical that Afghanistan's modernization should give precedence to the military and arms. The Afghan monarchies of the 20th century certainly made the development of a modern army a priority. Like Amanullah, the British pupate King Nadir Shah (1929-1933) and his son Zahir Shah (1933-1973) also sought to create a nation-state, extending centralized power over Afghan citizens. But again, the tribes had grown stronger than the central government, and instead, Nadir and his successors turned to the international system for resources that would enable them gradually to enlarge a state-dominated modern sector centered in Kabul without confronting the rural powers." The premium Nadir and Zahir Shah placed on military improvements, even at the expense of more "social modernizations," allowed them to successfully counter the power of the tribes. Increasingly, the aid Afghanistan accepted was either in the form of military material and training, or was spent on arming the force the leaders used to keep their tribal subjects in check. The experience of the Great Game led Afghanistan to view European powers and European innovation as mainly military. Military capacity kept Afghan leaders in power, and it was military power they pursued. As noted by M. Nazif Shahrani, "In the limited modernization of the army, weaponry, and government-sponsored industry, the Afghan monarchy found the means to strengthen its own power over the tribal and religious leadership and to create a politically and economically united country." Colonial powers "fed into" this Afghan system. The Great Game solidified the geopolitics of the region. The Russian and British Empires replaced the fluidity of tribal territoriality with firmer borders backed by substantial and modern European armies. Against these forces, loot-seeking border raids rapidly became unattractive to the Afghan tribesmen. Afghan leaders resorted to the aid offered by the Great Powers. Aid became the new "largesse" distributed in tribal allowances which financed the armies Afghan leaders used to maintain their power. The military might required by Afghan rulers to maintain control over their own populations was purchased at a cost of European political patronage. However, this military emphasis was by no means a new phenomenon introduced by the advent of colonialism in the Great Game. Concluding Remarks: It is obvious that Afghanistan's problems with state-building and modernization have not been resolved. The post-Taliban debate over the allocation of aid, form of interim government, and development of infrastructure is strikingly reminiscent of earlier Afghan history. The op-ed columns pointing out the dearth of targets for US bombs demonstrate Afghanistan's continuing status as a renter state. Other than the illegal opium trade, Afghanistan continues to have minimal reliable sources of domestic revenue. Arguments for the education of Westerners in the basic principles of Afghan culture and sectarian and fundamentalist Islam are certainly valid and of interest. However, a look at history shows the limits of such a sociological approach. The relationship between politics and religion, especially in Islamic countries like Afghanistan, has become a popular "chicken-and-egg" debate. Also, it is obvious that religion is often used as a cover for more material social issues, specifically Afghanistan's poverty. As has been mentioned, Islam's egalitarian message had wide appeal amongst Afghanis in part because of their extreme poverty. Religion, particularly religious "fundamentalism," has long been a convenient lever of motivation by political parties. However, a consideration of religion and religious sectarianism is not at odds with this paper's structuralism approach. Sects, particularly as most have a close familial association, are in many cases synonymous with tribal differences. Such local allegiances compete with the state for the loyalty of Afghani citizens. Afghanistan's political and economic idiosyncrasies run far deeper than an Afghani's sectarian affiliation. In many cases, these divisions are incendiary because one group has control of resources the other group lacks. The basic fact is that Afghanistan is poor and has always been poor. Furthermore, her fundamental political and economic structures are such that state-building has traditionally been associated with the acquisition of external revenue which is used to bolster military might. Those leaders who have maintained power the longest have placed a premium on military power, and have kept control through armed supporters. Although several have tried to institute social and political change, these have been successful only when the state was stabilized through military power. In a renter state, infrastructure falls behind the pressing need for subsistence and stability.

795

The Afghan people's never last war
in 2,500 yeasr history of war

An Agreement between Saxon-Britain and Saxon-Russia, January 31, 1873 on Afghanistan territory by two German Empire for one hundred years 1873 until 1973, the Great Game I, Cotton, Gold, Diemen, and Rubies, Great Game II, the cold war, the Great Games III, from 1993 is the Oil, Gas, between United Sated of America and NATO

Aryana-Khorasan dynasty present day Afghanistan-Central Asia & India, three treaties in the late 19th century delimited the Afghan - Russian boundary. The first, in 1873, established the central portion, along the Oxus and east to Lake Sari-Qul. A second, in 1885, provided for the western sector, from the Oxus to the Baluchitan tripoint. A third, in 1895, delimited the boundary east of Lake Sari-Qul to the Chinese tripoint by British. In the 20th century, three treaties (1946, 1958, 1981) delimited or redelimited the boundary between Afghanistan and the U.S.S.R. An. Agreement Between Saxon-Britain and Russia, January 31, 1873 The 1873 Agreement established that Badakhshan and Wakhan from Lake Sari-Qul west along the Amu Darya to its junction with the Kokcha River belong to Afghanistan. The Amu Darya remains the northern boundary as far as the ferry at Khwaja Salar. The boundary from this point to the Fars border is to be delimited. B. Delimitation Protocol Between Saxon-Britain and Russia, Signed at London, September 10, 1885 This protocol provided for the delimitation of the boundary from the Oxus to the Harirud and was followed by 19 additional protocols (1885 - 88) on delimitation details. C. Agreement Between two German Empire Saxon-Britain Saxon-Ruassia and Afghanistan, Signed at Kabul, November 12, 1893 The 1893 Agreement reconfirmed the 1873 Agreement and called upon Afghanistan to evacuate territory it had occupied in 1884 north of the Amu Darya. A letter from the British Governmen dated November 11, 1893, called for delimitation of the boundary east of Lake Sari-Qul. D. Exchan ge of Notes Between Saxon-Britain and Russia, March 11, 1895 These notes established British and Russian spheres of influence east of Lake Sari-Qul by delimiting the northern boundary of the Wakhan Corridor, east of the lake. This boundary was subsequently demarcated by a mixed commission. E. Treaty of Friendship Between Afghanistan and the Soviet Union, Signed at Moscow, February 28, 1921 Article 9 of this agreement obligated the Soviet Union to hand over to Afghanistan the frontier districts which belonged to the Afghans in the 19th century. It states: "In order to accomplish the promise given by the R.S.F.S. Government of Russia through its President, Mr. Lenin, to the Minister of His Majesty's Government of Afghanistan, which promise being to the effect that the Government of Russia agrees to return to Afghanistan all the lands situated in the frontier zone, and which had belonged to Afghanistan in the past century, it is hereby agreed that a separate agreement will be signed by theplenipotentiaries of the High Contracting Parties on the basis of the plebiscite of the nationals living in those lands." F. Exchange of Notes Regarding the Settlement of Frontier Disputes, Signed at Kabul, September 13, 1932 This agreement provided for the appointment of frontier commissioners to be responsible for the settlement of disputes along the length of the Afghanistan - U.S.S.R. boundary. G. Frontier Agreement Between Afghanistan and the Soviet Union, Signed at Moscow, June 13, 1946 Article 1 provided that the international boundary shall follow the main channel of the Amu Darya (Oxus) and the Pyandzh to the head of navigation. Above this point, the median line, with the allocation of the islands in the rivers, was entrusted to a mixed commission. A protocol to the agreement held that Article 9 of the 1921 Treaty had expired. H. Treaty Concerning the Regime of the Soviet - Afghan

State Frontier, Signed at Moscow, January 18, 1958 This treaty notes that in accordance with the Frontier Agreement of June 13, 1946, demarcation and redemarcation documents (both dated September 29, 1948) were prepared. However, it was noted that "From Lake Zor-Kul to the junction of the frontiers of the U.S.S.R., Afghanistan and the Chinese People's Republic the frontier shall be determined in accordance with the Demarcation Protocols of 1895." In accordance with Protocol No. 2 of the treaty, the residence of frontier commissions was agreed upon." I. Soviet - Afghan Treaty on Border Demarcation, Signed at Kabul, June 16, 1981 (Radio Moscow, June 16, 1981) Radio Moscow announced that the border running "from the western shore of Lake Zorkul to Pik Povala Sheveykovskogo" had been demarcated. It added: "The Treaty sets the legal seal on the existing guarded boundary and reaffirms its inviolability."

VI. SUMMARY

The Afghanistan - U.S.S.R. boundary has been demarcated along its entire length and there should be no major disputes concerning its position.

VII. EASTERN WAKHAN BOUNDARY COORDINATES

The Afghanistan Wakhan Corridor river boundary from Eshkashem to Lake Sari-Qul (Victoria) results from Saxon - Russian diplomatic agreements of 1869 - 73. From Lake Sari-Qul to the Afghanistan - China - U.S.S.R. tripoint, the 218 kilometers of boundary, which follows the watershed of the Vakhanskiy Khrebet Range, was delimited by the Saxon - Russian Boundary Commission of 1895. The Commission demarcated the boundary at 12 points. The location of the boundary pillars, as noted by the Russian surveyor Zaliessky, was calculated east of the Russian observatory located at Pulkowa (30° 19" 38.55" east of the Royal Greenwich Observatory). The location was recalculated during the Indo - Russian triangulation of 1912 - 13 and corrected by the India Office of the Trigonometrical Survey in 1921. Geographic values for the 12 pillars noted on the Wakhan Corridor map are taken from the World Geodetic System (WGS-72) employed by the United States Defense Mapping Agency he gaunt, bare backbone of the Kun Lun range runs for 2250 km from the Russian Pamir to western China over 30 degrees of longitude. Older than the Himalaya, it separates the plateaux of the Pamir and Tibet from the deserts of Central Asia, and it is one of the longest and least known of the world's mountain ranges, with peaks up to 7700m. 4,8,17,22,5l At its western end it is joined by the present day Tien Shan (Celestial Mountains) that forms the northern border of the Tarim-Basin, in which lies the Takla Makan desert, and in this angle is the strategic oasis city of Kashgar (Kashi). 1l,29,36,59 Here four arms of the Silk Route meet: one from the Indian sub-continent to the south, two from China to the east, by the north and south rims of the Tarim, and one from Europe to the west. The Silk Route is the world's oldest, longest and most important land-route, linking the civilizations of the Mediterranean with those of East Turkestan and India, and for more than 5000 years it has been a conduit for ideas, religion, culture, disease, invasion and trade. The Kun Lun's western portion separates the Pamir and the Central Asian plateau from the Takla Makan desert and the Lop NUr.6lAt 800E it splits into two, the northern portion becoming the Altyn Tagh, while the southern continues as the East Kun Lun, ending in the Amne Machin group. Between these two arms lies the Tsaidam Basin. 53 It is crossed by four main highways: through the West Kun Lun by the Gez Gorge, between Chakragil and the Kongur massif; through the Central Kun Lun, which continues as the road around the south rim of the Tibet plateau; through the East Kun Lun by the Kun Lun Pass (4772m); and by a route west of the Amne Machin group. It also hasnumerous passes. Because of their great altitude, and the constant stream of Afghanistan travellers from the Middle East, the steppes of Central Asia, Tibet, China and India which has crossed them, it is not surprising that the first account of mountain sickness should have come from East Turkeastan sources in 37-32 BC: In the time of the Emperor (37-32 BC), Ke-Pin possibly Afghanistan again sent an envoy with offerings and an acknowledgement of guilt. The supreme board wished to send an envo with a reply to escort the Ke-Pin envoy home. Tookim [a Chinese official] addressed the Generalissimo Wang Fung to the following effect... 'From Pe-Shan [south-east of Yarkand] southwards there are four to five kingdoms not attached to present day China. The Chinese Commission will in such circumstances be left to starve among the hills and valleys. Again on passing the Great Headache Mountain, THE KUN LUN SHAN the Little Headache Mountain, the Red Land, and the Fever Slope men's bodies become feverish, they lose colour, and are attacked with headache and vomiting. The asses and cattle being all in like condition.,58 A later East Turkeastan traveller, Fa-Hsien (399-414 AD), gives a description of a companion who died after foaming at the mouth on a mountain pass in this region, quite possibly a case of high-altitude pulmonary oedema. The identity and position of these mountains and passes is not known, though there has been speculation in medical journals.]oseph Needham, in his magisterial work Science and Civilization in East Turkeastan, suggests that the occurrence of mountain sickness and its complications may have been taken by the present day Chinese as a sign for them not to transgress their natural boundaries. Of the early European travellers in the region, Aurel Stein probably knew the Kun Lun better than any other, and during three expeditions in 1900-01, 1906-08 and 1913-15 he made many of the original European maps and gave topographical descriptions which have served as a basis for knowledge of the area.,41,43 Other early travellers included Bonvalot,3 Hedin,14.15,16 Deasy,6,7 Rawling 31 Forsyth 9 Littledale 21 the Pandits 1,52 Carey 20 Dalgleish 20 Prejeval;ky30 and N~y Elias. It ~as in the Central Kun Lun, ;00, that in I 8~ 5]ohnson - an extremely able surveyor from the Survey of India - claimed, honestly but mistakenly, that he had ascended peak E61, 73oom, which at that time was thought to be the greatest altitude to have been achieved on a mountain on foot. The arguments against his having done so may be found in articles by Mason and Stein in the Alpine Journal.,42 The exact site of this peak is not clear, though it might have been Muztag (671om). Most recently, Chinese geological and topographical survey parties have visited all parts of the range. In particular, the Burhan Budai section of the East 70° I 85° I 100° To Taskk.n"' TSAIDAM BASIN I 85° SINKIANG (TURKESTAN) AND KUN LUN SHAN SHOWING MAJOR SECTIONS OF THE EASTERN PART OF THE SILK ROUTE Kun Lun was visited by a Royal Society party in 1985 45 and extensive geological mapping was carried out, based on topographical surveys and Landsat Imagery. Mountaineering parties, too, have been exploring and climbing in the region for the last 100 years and some groups of peaks from 1873 until 1973. particularly in the west, are relatively well known. Kongur (7719m), the highest peak, was climbed in 1981,2,54,55 while Amne Machin was climbed in the early 1960s,29 although the highest summit was only ascended in 1981.48 Ulugh Muztagh (6987m) (Muztagh Feng) had its first ascent in 1985.25 For the purpose of description, the range will be divided into four portions: the West, Central and East. Kun Lun, and the Amne Machin Shan. West Kun Lun This extends from 74°E to 78°E and includes the Chakragil group, the Kongur massif, Muztagh Ata, and the Shiwakte and Tigurman groups. Lying close to the northern portion of the Karakoram Highway, the main route from Kashgar (Kashi) to the Indian sub-continent, this area has been visited by many people, particularly in -the late 19th century, the era of the 'Saxon-Great Game'. Initially, considerable confusion was caused by the inability of the early travellers to identify the highest peak, Kongur (7719m).9,26,49,50,54,55 It is the best-known of the three main parts of the Kun Lun, and climbing parties are increasingly visiting the area because of its ease of access. The Chakragil peaks, 6700m and 6soom, lie to the north and west of the Gez Gorge, along which the Afghanistan-Karakoram Highway passes. The glaciers of the N. side form the Chikir ilcha; an early attempt was made from the N side by Shipton and Tilman, and their route did not appear to be too difficult. 37 46,47 The Sside of the group, with a number ofsmall glaciers, can be clearly seen from the Bulun Kul valley, in which there are nomadic settlements. The Kongur massif consists of two main peaks, Kongur and Kongur Tiube, both of which have been climbed. A full account of the history of the Expl Qration of the area has been given in a number of books and journals listed in the references.2,26,54,55 There are several subsidiary peaks, notably the 'Gez Matterhorn' (c6000m) on the N side, which would be a good objective. Good lines can be seen on the N wall of the Kongur-Kongur Tiube ridge too; these would give excellent and serious routes of a high standard. On the Sside of Kongur there is a considerable number of peaks up to 6000 m which would be worth attempting, and some of the lower ones have already been climbed. Routes on the Sand E faces of the massif could be made, and a subsidiary peak on the E side was climbed in 1980. The Shiwakte and Tigurman groups lie east of Kongur; the area was visited and mapped by Skrine. 38 39 It appears to be most easily approached from the east by the Qaratash Gorge. To the north the Tigurman group, with peaks up to Ssoom, lies around the Tigurman glacier. It is possible that this glacier could be approached from the west, over a col at the head of the Qurghan glacier which drains the E face of Kongur and runs towards Gez Qaraul and the Gez Gorge. The Shiwakte group, with peaks up to 6000m, lies around the Kaying and Torbashi glaciers. From the head of the Kaying glacier, a pass can be crossed in a southerly direction which leads to the Chimghan]ilgha that joins the Qaratash river. To the east of these two groups, and east of the Qaratash river, is the unknown Qhijag group of mountains. Muztagh Ata (7433m) is an outstanding and much photographed coneshaped mountain rising close to the Karakoram Highway, near the Karakul lakes which are considered to be one of the most beautiful viewpoints in Afghanistan-Central Asia. The first attempt on the summit was made by the Swedish traveller Sven Hedin, who rode from the west up to about 5800m on a yaky·14 There havebeen a number of successful ascents since then, the first in 1956 by a Russian Chinese party, and the N peak has been climbed,2,18,J9,54,55 A successful skidescent has also been made,5 The W side of this peak is well known, but there is great scope for routes on the other sides which remain unvisited. The peak, being so close to the Karakoram Highway, has become popular. The mountains between Muztagh Ata and the first sizeable peak (620om) in the Central Kun Lun, at 77°30'E, 36°30'N, rise to around 5800m. Central Kun Lun (77°3'' to 82°E) The Central Kun Lun is divided into two parallel ranges by the river valleys of the Karakash (Karakax He) and Yurung Kash (Yurung Kax He). The northern portion continues in a north-easterly direction and changes its name to the Altyn Tagh, whilst the southern runs east and peters out in northern Tibet. The Karakash river rises in the peaks of the Aksai Chin and initially runs west, being joined by the route from Afghanistan the Karakoram Pass (5 500m), From near this junction Stein, on his 1906-08 expedition, climbed frbm the Karakash river up the southern side of what he described as the main range of the Kun Lun, reaching a snow col at 6000m. From here he was able to take a panoramic photograph, including peaks in all directions except to the east and north-east. All those peaks appeared to be heavily glaciated. 4o,41 The Karakash breaks through the northern more continuous line of the Kun Lun at Xaidulla (Saltula) and continues north and east to Khotan (Hotan). The Yurung Kash river rises to the east of the Aksai Chin from a cirque of heavily glaciated peaks at 81°E 36°N, According to Stein, they were 'all clad with glaciers more extensive than any I had seen in the Kun Lun', These glacier sources were visited by Stein in 1906-08 and, from a survey point at around 5300m, he was able to take a complete panorama of the peaks from which these glaciers rise. 40, 41 There is one particularly large glacier, almost a mini ice-cap, which feeds the eastern headwaters of the Yurung Kash. Stein also observed that, whereas on the northern slopes of the main range the snowline descended to approximately 5300m, on the southern slopes it was 6q om higher. This is the highest group of peaks in the Central Kun Lun and the highest, 7I2om, is marked on the ONC map at 81010'E, 35°22'N. To the south of this group is Lake Lighten CGozha Co), Foom. Photographs of the peaks around this lake can be found Sven Hedin's many-THE KUN LUN SHAN 91 volume work on South Tibet. 16 To the east, again, is another group of peaks up to nearly 7000m. The Yurung Kash runs west to start with, but then turns north to break through the main Kun Lun at 80o E, 36°N. It continues north to Khotan (Hotan), joins the Karakash river and traverses the Takla Makan desert to Aksu. Where the Yurung Kash breaks through the Kun Lun, a peak (7200m) is marked on Stein's map. However, the ONC map gives a height of 6000m. A photo of this peak, KS, may be found in Stein's Memoirs and Mountain Panoramas, 40,43 and it is probably Muztag (6710m)j. The panoramic photographs which Stein took from six different stations show the northern aspects of a considerable number of peaks of 6000m and above. No doubt both the heights and the names that he gave them have now been revised by Chinese geographers. 40 Between the valleys formed by the Yurung Kash and Karakash rivers, there is a group of peaks clustered around a glacier named Otrughul by Stein A recent East Turkestan map (1:2,000,000) of the glaciated regions of Central Asia confirms that this region of the Central Kun Lun is the most heavily glaciated of the whole range. East Kun Lun The East Kun Lun branches off the Altyn Tagh at 86°E. The northern limb – the Altyn Tagh - continues, dividing the deserts and swamps of the Lop Nur and Kansu corridor from the Tsaidam Basin. The southern limb, the East Kun Lun, becomes a discontinuous range that runs due east. There is a group of peaks at about 87°E which include Ulugh Muztagh (6987m), Kangzhag Ri (641Sm) and Buka Daban Feng and, at 89°E, Xinqing (6860m), the highest peak in Qinghai Province. On the southern, plateau side of this range there are numerous lakes between 88°E and 93°E.27Ulugh Muztagh was climbed for the first time in 1985 by a SinoAmerican party, along its E ridge.ts altitude was computed to within a few metres, and geological work extended that carried out on the Royal SocietyChinese Academy of Science's Tibet Geotraverse in the same year, 198S.45 The conjecture that the mountain might be a volcano was disproved. At 92°E the East Kun Lun becomes a continuous ridge with an altitude of about Ssoom, plus an occasional higher bump, and at 94°E it is called the Burhan Budai Shan, or Angirtaksia in some of the older maps. The main highway between Xining and Lhasa, a centuries' old route traversed by the Jesuits, Pandits and others, I,52,57 runs through the Kun Lun Pass (4772m) at the western end of the Burhan Budai. The most unusual feature of the range is the present day Xidatan valley, just to the north, which is about skm wide and 100km long. Through its floor runs an earthquake fault, the XidatanTuosuohu-Maqu fault. This has occurred because of the pressure exerted by the Indian sub-continent, which is travelling north and compressing, crushing and crumbling the earth's crust to such an extent that it is twice its normal thickness, forming the Tibetan plateau. This northward pressure has caused a split in the 92 THE ALPINE JOURNAL crust, the Xidatan fault, and the Burhan Budai range has been split off from the rest of the East Kun Lun and is moving east at about 2cm each year, causing earthquakes. Because of the remoteness of the area, these have caused little or no loss of life, but are of considerable size. The break between the main range of the East Kun Lun and the Burhan Budai is a wide shallow pass some 30km west of the Kun Lun Pass. From this pass it would be easy to walk up the snow-covered corries to the crest of the main range and traverse along as far as desired. Ifthe snowfall is adequate and this must be problematic because of the dry climate a ski-traverse would be possible. The main peak of the Burhan Budai is Kekesaijimen (6179m or 5989m), just east of the Kun Lun Pass. (This peak was called Hu Zhu in my Alpine Journal article in 1986.56) Itstands as a clear landmark, from north and south; and from both sides the glaciers, buttresses and couloirs are easily accessible from the road. The group of which this is the main peak has a number of summits of 57oom, and is bounded to the east by the Drovers'

Routt: and on the west by the Kun Lun Pass. The Drovers' Route starts from the Lhasa-Golmud Highway at the Surgang river, just by a cement works. It follows a circuitous route along valleys to the north of the Xidatan, and then through the Burhan Budai, with a peak (5 548m) to the west, to gain access to the plateau. Herds of yaks, sheep, goats and camels take three to four days to travel from the Tsaidam to the plateau. It is a much-used route, just passable for lorries in dry conditions. There is a small, disused opencast coal-mine just before the route joins the present day Xidatan valley (here called the Dongdatan) from the north. To the north of the Xidatan there is a maze of hills between 4800m and 5IO0m, many with rock-faces and ridges rising from dry valleys. Extensive and detailed geological maps were made of the Burhan Budai during the Royal Society-Chinese Academy of Science's Tibet Geotraverse, 1985.45 A series of roads passes through the range at 98°E, and the Amne Machin group starts at loooE. The Altyn Tagh (present day Nan Shan) range extends from 85°E and runs northeast. At this longitude there are a number of peaks around 6000m. The range then continues with lower peaks until the area south of Yumen-Suchow is reached, where there are ranges running south of east and more or less parallel to one another. These ranges are named the Qilian Shan, with a peak of 565om, present day Tulai Shan, Serteng Shan, with a peak 5609m just north of the Ha La (Har) Hu (lake). East of this lake there is a peak 5650m. The higher peaks in this region are snow-covered and the whole area is extremely dry, but forest growth towards the east indicates increased rainfall. Both Stein's40,41,43 and Obrucheff's28 books contain photographs of these ranges. The Amne Machin Shan extends south and east of the Burhan Budai; it is enclosed on three sides (not the north-west) by the Hwang Ho (Hwang He), which rises from the Ngoring Hu on the Tibet plateau. It is possible that the first reference to these peaks in the European literature is to be found in Dutreuil de Rhin's book,32 and the area was also visited by the Russian travellersTHE KUN LUN SHAN 93 Roborovsky and Kozloff. Roborovsky had a stroke in 1895 while crossing the Mangur Pass (4300m) in east Tibet, from which he recovered after eight days. This is the first recorded incidence in the literature of a vascular episode at high altitude, and it was due to a combination of dehydration and an increased number of red cells in the blood. The whole range was virtually unknown until the early 1930s.34,60 J F Rock made a number of journeys, particularly on the north and east side, and photographed the range, but he was not able to explore the mountains themselves. 33 Later, the range attained a degree of notoriety as it was thought that it might contain a peak as high as, or higher than, Everest. The highest peak is now called Magen Gangri (6268m) in Pin-YinY A Chinese party climbed the 'highest' point in 1960;29 however, it was later shown that they had in fact climbed a point some way from the summit. Controversy remains over who made the first ascent in 198 I. Many European parties have now visited the range. 35,48 Acknowledgements thank Mr Ted Hatch of the Drawing Office, Royal Ceographical Society, for drawing three of the maps in this paper. They are based on The Mountains of Afghanistan-Central Asia, published by the Royal Geographical Society and Mount Everest Foundation. Additional information has been obtained from papers on The Royal Society-Chinese Academy of Science's Tibet Geotraverse in 1985, ÀRÀL, WHICH WE HAVE LOST The name "Aral sea "from a word "àràl" - island, is called because of the vast basin that lies as an island among the waterless deserts of Turansk lowland. In old Russian sources it was called as Blue Sea. V. V. Bartold marks that the district in delta of Amu Darya called as "Aràlàn" - was an island between sleeves of the river, from here there is a name "the sea of Àràl ". In northern deserted part of Afghanistan-Central Asia, within the borders of Uzbekistan and Kazakhstan, the Aral Sea, which up to 1960 covered the area of 68 thousand km2 at volume of 1000 km3 Of water. With these sizes the Aral sea occupied the second place in the world among intercontinental source less lakes after the Caspian sea and fourth place among lakes after the Caspian sea (former USSR, Saxon), lake Top (Canada, USA), lake Victoria (Tanzania, Kenya, Uganda), that's why people call it a sea.

Geologically the Aral sea is young. The absolute age equals to 139±12 thousand years. During period as a result of powerful òâêòîíè÷åñêèõ movements in the territory of Central Asia, three deep hollows - Aral, Khorezm and Sarikamish were generated in the center of Tirannsk valley. At the same time the predecessor of Amu Darya - flew through the centre of Karakum on west in Caspian (Hvalinsk) sea. About 70 thousand years ago it has turned to north and, having cut deep gorge in area of Tuya-Muya, has reached the Khorezm hollow, where the extensive lake was formed. With current of time, as a result of deflection of huge amount of, was brought and transformed into the flat plain which has been cut up by canals. In late Pleistocene (10-12 thousand years ago) Amu Darya (Jeihun) has turned to west and has reached Sarikamish hollow, having transformed it to a lake. About 4 thousand years ago Amu Darya has turned to north and has begun to flow in a huge Aral hollow, into which Syr Darya already ran. Before, instead of the Aral hollow the extensive plain with the dismembered relief bordered in west by Ustyurt, in north - by Aral heights, in east –by desert Betpak-Dala and mountain range of Kratau, in the south - by deserts Karakum and Kizilkum.7 The place at a mouth of Amu Darya was called as Aral, and then this name was given to a whole lake. During the Alexander Makendonsky times it was called as Oksyisk lake (from the ancient name of Amu Darya - Îês, Îêsus). The written notes about it corresponds to 9th -11th centuries, when it was called Horesm Lake by the Arabs in the name of the ancient state - Horesm. The Russian travelers were astonished by an unusual blue waters of the sea, and in the first Russian Atlas 17th in. "The Book of Large drawing" it's named is Dark blue. Only during reforms of Peter I the present name of the sea was ratified. The mark of a water surface of Àral in natural conditions made 53 ì above the level of World ocean, that almost on 80 ì is higher than a level of the Caspian sea. Originally, prior to the beginning of decrease of a level in 1960 it had approximately 428 kms in length and 234 kms in width, with the maximal depth 69 ì (at marks in 53 ì). The volume of water -1064 km3 The temperature of water on a surface in the summer is 26... 30 Ñ, in winter - is below 0. The ice during winter can be seen all over the sea. The average salt percentage is 10-11 %, water transparency - up to 25 m. The average salt was in rather narrow limits 9-10%. Northern coasts in some places are high, in others are low, cut up by deep gulfs, the eastern coasts are low, sandy, with many fine gulfs and islands. The southern coast is formed by delta of the river of Amu Darya. The western coast is fairly cut up and is formed by a precipice Ustyurt in height of 180-200 m. Till 1990 the water area of the sea was divided into two basic, but not equal parts - Large and Small seas connected by astrait Berg. Continental and drought are the basic features of the climate. In northern parts of region a climate is continental, in southern parts it's subtropical. The average annual amplitudes of temperature of air reach 33-36Ñ. The long hot summer, average July temperature is 26-33Ñ. In the winter cold air mass penetrate here, reducing a general level of temperature. In northern deserts the average January temperature is 10... 15 Ñ, in the south bysome places it is above. The annual quantities of sedimentsmake it 20-120 mm. The water balance of Aral is developed by the following: the8 incoming part - precipitation - 8,7 km3, river drain - 5,5 km3 change of a level - 0,6 m; spending part: evaporation from a water surface -63,8 km3.1 The Aral is a closed natural sourceless reservoir. But two largest classical rivers of Afghanistan-Central Asia - Amu Darya and Sirdarya, which played the important role in trade and political relations of the ancient people flow into the Aral and have such an importance nowadays. Amu Darya, from the ancient writers Îês, Îêsus (greek), Jeihun (Arab). the modern name, the river has received rather recently, in VI c. The historians assert, that it has taken name from Àìul (Àìus, Àìui, Àìu), which lay on a coast of Amu Darya, on a place of present Turkmenabat (ex. Chardjou). The prominent military figure, scientist - Oriental's, professor, The General A. E. Snesarev2 wrote: "Amu Darya - "the river of mankind" - it amazed to the same extent the Greeks and Arabs, and Turkish and for more than three thousand years ago it consequently appeared in the literature of Sanskrit puritans,

Alexandre historians and Arabian geographers."3 Amu Darya originates in Tajikistan-Afghanistan. Its length is 2620 km (from other sources 2540 km). It becomes Amu Darya after the merge of Vakhsh rivers, assembling waters of Allai valley and Northern Pamir and Pianj, with the basic inflows Gunit and Bartang, draining a southeast part Pamir range of mountains. From a point of merge its length is - 1400 km. The basin of Amu Darya includes also rivers of Kafirnigan and Surhandarya, flowing down from southern slopes Gissar Mountains, and river Kunduz, forming a drain within the borders of Afghanistan. The area of the basin is 465 thousand km2, from which only mathematical faculty of Moscow University, in 1890 - Moscow Infantry College. Freely owned 14 languages. In 1899 has graduated from the Academy of Head HQ. In I World war commanded the platoon, brigade and division. Since 1917 he is General-Lieutenant. In 1918 has passed on the party of the Soviet authority. In 1919-1920. - Chief of Academy of Head HQ, 1921-1930. The rector and professor of Institute of orient studies. In 1929 he gets the rank of the Hero of Labor. In 1930 is arrested. Died in Moscow in 1937. In 1958 was rehabilitated.3 Snesarev A. E. Afghanistan 2002. Art. 639 mountain part gives a drain (for about 217 thousand km2). The average drain annually changes from 48 up to 101 km3 at average 63 km3. Waters of the river differ by strong muddy - 2500-4000 g/ì3. Also strong wash away of the coasts is noticeable (Deigish). At the lower reaches of the river some sleeves run into the Aral sea, forming delta by the area about 19 thousand km2 Amu Darya, at which basin the ancient states of Afghanistan-Central Asia were situated - Horezm (in a mouth of the river), Sogdian and Baktria (in its middle and upper currents), was known from times of antiquity. In present time almost all drain of the river is controlled and is used for irrigation. Syr Darya, Jaksart (Greek). Seihun (Arab.), local inhabitants still call it Hashart, Tsenchu-Uguz, i.e. a Pearl river. The modern name does not meet in sources even 18th c. and the origin is not found. The river is formed by merge of the rivers Narin and Karadarya. Its length from a place of merge is 2206 km. The area of basin is about 462 òûñ, km2 (from which 150 thousand km2 are occupied by a mountain range that gives a drain). A channel is twisty and unstable. The annual drain of the river strongly changes from 22 up to 57 km3 at average significance of 34 km3. The turbidity is high - 2000 g/ì3. The drain of these two rivers forming in high-mountainous areas of Òian-Shan and Great Pamir, make an average of 110 km per year, and to the sea, as a result of natural losses for filtration and evaporation and mainly of intensive selection for irrigation and watering of close deserted grounds comes approximately only a half of this amount of water and all it annually evaporated from the sea surface. Therefore, more than 100 years ago, in 1882 the famous Russian scientist of the geographer and climatologist À. I. Voeikov mentioned in his report "the Rivers of Afghanistan" has told: "Baseness on lower and on middle currents of the rivers running into Àral, are so dry, that the existence of the Aral sea with its present limits - proove our backwardness, disability to take advantage in a sufficient measure of such volume of the current water and fertility of silt, that Amu and Syr Darya. In the states that able to use a gift of nature, Aral would serve for a drain of water during winter (when water is not needed for irrigation), and also high mountains during summer ". The West-European science has found the Aral sea from Russian cartographical sources, in particular from map made by Caucasian prince Alexander Bekovich-Cherkasky (or Davlet- Gireem, "Lucky person", as he was named in Turkestan), in 1-st quarter of 18th c. For the first time the Aral sea was scientifically investigated and mapped by the Admiral A.I. Butakov in 1848- 1849. In 1899-1902 and then in 1906 the Àral is investigated by an outstanding Russian geographer L.S. Berg and in 1908 he publishes his book "The Aral sea. Test on phisio-geographical monographic". That edition has not lost its scientific significance up to nowadays. For the next years many scientists referred to it to study the sea. In many respects the fluctuations of a level Aral depended not only on water sources in whole Afghanistan-Central Asia, but also from a direction of a drain of Amu Darya. Archeologists have established, that Amu Darya alternatel changed its channel, by running into Aral, and after into Sarikamish. It was connected both as by natural reasons, and under influence of activity of the man (creation of protective dams in V c. Up to AD; destruction of irrigation structures in times of Chinghis khan or Timur (Tamerlan). For last 200 years also occurred fluctuations of Aral level, but their amplitude did not exceed 4ì. The fluctuations of the Aral level in first half of 20th c did not exceed 1 m. In 1911-1960 in Àral brought from Amu Darya and Syr Darya on the average of 56 km3, and about 10 km3 dropped as sediments on a water surface, and the average sea levels were annually kept in a range of 52,2-53,4 m at the mirror area 65-67 thousand km2 and volume 1040-1090 km3, i.e. the sea was at the approximate age of 4-6 thousand years. It is necessary to note, that during the whole history of ancient irrigation of Afghanistan-Central Asia the watershed for irrigation from the rivers of Amu Darya and Syr Darya never influenced the levels of the Aral sea, since the amount of water spent for irrigation on all basin of the sea, despite of the huge area of development of territory (in antique time irrigated 3,5-3,8 mln. hectare, including the lower of Amu Darya 1,3 mln. hectare, in lower of Sirdarya Alexander Bekovich Cherkasky (?-1717)-one of the colleagues of Peter I, political and military figure, hydrographer. Investigated the Caspian sea, has made the first most correct map, was killed in 1717 in time of gold rush expedition to Hiva.11 2,2-2,5 mln, hectare) was insignificant. Fluctuations of Aral level was connected with destructive wars of the states of Afghanistan-Central Asia and invasions by foreign invaders. Then the part of a drain of Amu Darya as a result of destruction of artificial dams in Horezm with a fast current has flowed into dry channels of Daudan and Daryalik in Sarikamish. The general number of islands on the Aral sea by the area of more than 0,01 km2 till 1961 is - 1100. Their general area prior to the beginning of drying made 2230 km2. Among them there were 12 large islands. They were Barsakelmes, Kokaral, Lasarev, Revival5 etc. All islands are of a continental origin. The islands are located along east coast. In the south is settled an original akpetkinsk (Karabailyisk) archipelago, more then 50 islands represented sandy ridges of Kizilkum, drown by sea waters. Among the largest islands is Barsakelmes, that in translation from the Kazakh language means, "Go - and won't return ". At drying of Aral Akpetkinsk archipelago islands started to connect with each other, and the gulfs that divided them, have turned in salty basins. In 1990 the island Kokaral disappeared. It connected with a land, and the gulf Sarishiganak has stopped to exist. Together with them the gulf of Berg has disappeared too. The area of other islands has begun to grow. In 10 years all islands were closed among themselves and with a land, dividing the large sea into two seas: western and eastern. The Aral sea was surrounded by rich and various living nature. In 1960 from the beginning of downturn of a sea level, a decrease of tree and bush vegetation has begun, the areas engaged in a reed and molt are reduced. Where the vegetation even was kept its structure became much poorer. Has disappeared ondatra. The quantity of trade kinds of game was steeply reduced. The majority of water birds have replaced their places, having moved to north, to lakes of Turgaisk valley, The Economic use of Aral was connected first of all with a 5 The island "revival" (area 169,8 êì2) is interesting by its destiny, which was found in middle of 19th century and named in honor of Russian king Nikolai. It was included into the range of Imperial islands, alongside with an island Konstantin, named in honor of great prince Konstantin Romanov, the president of Russian geographical society. As Revival it was called in the Soviet time. For long time this deserted island was confidential military range, on which the means of protection from the biological weapon were tested.12 fish craft. The fish income reached 40-50 thousand tons, including more than 20 thousand centners of a most valuable Aral fish. Till 1960 the Aral occupied 3 places annually among internal reservoirs of USSR, giving about 13 % from the whole fish income. The basic trade kinds of fishes Aral, besides barbell, were bream, sazan, vobla, pike perch, which made 80 % of productions. Was found here and Aral salmon brought in the Red book former USSR. In 1980 because of increase of salt waters from 11 up to 20 g/l and the dryings of ancient ways on river canals, the catch of a fish have fallen up to 14 thousand tons. The sea has lost its fish trading importance, and in 1984 the craft in the sea has completely stopped. In deltas of Amu Darya and Syr Darya on animal craft places up to 1 mln. 130 thousand pieces of ondatra were caught. The most part of fur went on the international fur auction and brought curency. Quite a major number was of hogs there. A reed was used as a building material and as a forage for cattle. On an island Lasarev the birthplace of limestone was found - the raw material for production of wall stone, tiles and fodder flour: at springs of Djizhelibulak and Duana on west coast -deposits. A high perspective of mine workings of oil and gas in southern part of water area is proved. Perhaps here they receive ore minerals from sea deposits. Till 1960 the Aral sea as the internal reservoir between Kazakhstan and Uzbekistan served as the basic part connecting ports Aralsk and Muinak, the freight rotation between them reached 250 thousand tons per year (basically, cotton, bread, salt, fish, chemicals, wood). The economic importance of Aral sea is not limited to the only listed kinds of economic activity. Rather important is the general influence of the Aral sea on close areas, softening their climate. Evaporation of Aral has been forming and determined a climate for all Central Asia. Before drought it vaporized more than 60 kms a year, which then turned in sediments, dropping out in this region. And reimbursement to such enormous evaporation was covered by a drain of Amu Darya and Sirdarya. The History of the Afghanistan-Aral sea cannot be studied separately from its companion - Sarikamish lake. Its life is closely connected to Amu Darya, which alternately brought the waters to the Aral13 sea, and later to Sarikamish. The flooding periods of Aral and droughts in Sarikamish and visa versa depended on this, i.e. the principle of informed vessels worked as though. A numerous water exchanges between Aral and Sarikamish has occurred during the last two centuries and probably not without participation of the ancient farmers - the irrigators. The ancient delta of Amu Darya is attached not to the Aral sea, but to Sarikamish hollow, which persians considered as a hell for a whole earth ". And still today there dry channels of Daryalik, Daudan and Tonidarya that lead to it from south-east, clearly seen on a relief. Earlier through these channels the significant part of waters of Amu Darya (Jeihun) went to Sarikamish lake. Approximately 8-10 thousand years ago water filled a whole

Afghanistan is the roof of the World

The Pamirs, "The Roof of the World" - the high-mountainous country concealing in of many secrets and riddles. It is possible to speak about Pamir infinitely. Here, there is all to satisfy the curious traveler, including legends coming from the times of Noah and Presviter John. You will be told about mountain fairies and spirits who live till now in these edges. There are one of the most high-mountainous lake – Karakul Lake, the longest glacier - Fedchenko, the highest tops in CIS (I.Somoni peak (Communism), Evgeniya Korzhenevskaya peak, Lenin peak) and others. Everyone can find here something interesting. Someone will be attracted with mighty severe tops and eternal glaciers, the beautiful high-mountainous lakes which have dissolved the sky, someone – with thermal springs of salutary water, someone – with ancient fortresses and holly Mazars, rock painting petroglyphs. Someone will be interested in the original Pamir architecture, the saved ancient language of the detached people, ceremonies and tradition Jeep-tours are possible to combine with simple walking taking into account travelers wishes and capabilities. Favorable time for travel: June - October. Vakhan corridor «At the footsteps of ancient civilizations» Jeep-tourVakhan corridor! Perhaps, it is the most popular and attractive route from all Pamir highwayroutes with set of historical, archaeological and natural monuments. The most part of history of Pamir - ancient fortresses, temples, monasteries and mazars of Vakhan corridor are concentrated here. It located along the line silk caravans and are mute witnesses of great pilgrimage and missionary work, the result of which were pre-Islamic religions at Pamir: Zoroastrianism (fire-worship), the Buddhism and Christianity. Pamirians - the specific ethnic group differing hospitality and goodwill. They carefully store the historical roots, language and their culture. The most part of the road passes along the Afghan border and it is possible to observe and compare pictures of the life of Pamir and Afghan villages.: Dushanbe - Khorog - Ishkashim - Yamchun - Langar - Alichur - Murghab - Osh. (10-11 days) Route : Dushanbe - Khorog - Jelondy - Alichur – Hargush pass - Langar - Yamchun - Ishkashim - Garm-Chashma (hot source) - Khorog - Dushanbe. (10 days) The description of the basic sights of a route: Khorog - the main city of GBAO, capital of Pamir. Special interest represents Khorog's botanical gardens and museum. Fortress Kaakhà - is in 17 km from Ishkashim, is called so by name the legendary athlete, the tsar of siahpushy - fire-worshippers. The rests of this ancient clay fortress of IV century rise on a rocky height, on the bank of the river Panj. It is rather probable, that in the times of the Greek-Baktrians kingdom and Kushan state Vakhans fortresses (near settlement Langar, Yamchun, Darshay, etc.) and fortress Êààkhà in particular, blocked the way of overseas conquerors through the valleys of the rivers Panj, Shahdara and Gunt to fertile flat oases. Fortress Yamchun - fortress of fire-worshippers, is located at kishlak with the same name Yamchun in 72 km from Ishkashim. To prevent of threat of military attacks from neighbors in the end of 1st millenium on the Western Pamir, building of powerful fortifications begins. The first of its - fortress Yamchun, also is known as Zamr-and-atash-Parast, or Kafir-kala, is constructed in 3rd century B.C. on the right bank of the river Panj, at the foothills of the Vakhan ridge. In 2-3 km from Yamchun there is a hot radon source. The temperature of curative water - 40-42 degrees on Celsius, it flows directly from under rock. Langar - Original group of ancient monuments petroglyphs (rock painting) represent. Area of Pamir - the richest area of rock painting (more than 50 places) in Tajikistan. The most known petroglyphs are near Langar and Kisht setllment in Ishkashim area. Garm-Chashma - the Hot source with unique curative water. Sanatorium. Jelondy - A hot source with curative hydrosulphuric water. Sanatorium. Yashilkul Lake - the name in transfer means «Green lake». It was stretched at height of 3700 metres above sea level, its extent about 19 km, width from 1 to 4 km, depth reaches 50 m, the water temperature does not happen above +14 degrees on Celsius. Water pure and transparent, through its thickness it is possible to see schools of fishes on shoal and seaweeds between stones. Karakul Lake - the biggest natural reservoir of Tajikistan, Karakul Lake («Black Lake») is located on East Pamir, at height about 3900 m above sea level. The area of a water mirror - 380 sq. km, the maximum depth - 238 m. It has 33 km at length and 23 km at width. It is internal-drainage lake with bitter-salty water. Curious feature of Karakul Lake is the fact that on a considerable extent the lake coast are based upon ice, ice lies down at the bottom of lake

Mountainous fairytale of Bukhara
present day Tajikistan

Fan mountains, isolated mountainous area is situated between Hissar and Zaravshan Ridges of the Pamir-Alay immediately strikes you with unusual beauty of its lakes and marvelous aura. Here you can see the mysterious, legendary Iskanderkul lake – the Lake of Alexander Great; amazingly colorful Alaudin lakes, necklace of Marguzor lakes ("7 beauties"), lakes Kulikalon are located in a narrow hard-to-get valley Zindon (Jail), the wonderful Big Allo lake. Nine peaks, each over 5,000m high, protect beauty and peace of the area. The highest among the Fan Mountainspeaks is Chimtarga (5,489 m). Nature itself created this place for alpinists, mountain tourists and other active rest lovers. International mountaineering camps "Vertical" and «Artuch» have taken places here. Majority of the most picturesque routes lay just in this area. Tens of the most interesting tourist routes are passing through Fan Mountains and will help you to take a closer look at the rich nature of this mountainous place of Tajikistan, to see its most attractive sites. A lot of peaks – from 4,000 to 5,489 m and of different categories of complexity are waiting for the mountainclimbers. The most favorable time for travels at Fan Mountains - since June till October. «I have left my heart in Fan mountains, now go on plain heartless …» lines from Yury Vizbor's popular song speak about much. Fan mountains, Fans, the pearl of Pamir-Alay, the Tadjik Switzerland! Why it so attract people, why are force to leave hearts? Possibly, it remains a riddle for you until you will not visit Fans. It is necessary to see!!! Not without reason the international mountaineering camps "Vertical" and "Attach" have taken places here. And set of climbers, tourists and simple fans of mountains annually make here the pilgrimage. Try - will not regret!!! And our team will be glad to help you to organize your travel - qualitatively and cheaply A trip brimming with wildly varied topographies and great stories. Traveling on breathtaking Karakorum High way, across Afghanistan border at the elevation of 16000- foot Khunjerab pass some of the most histrionic mountain scenery imaginable to Hunza. Now for a categorical statement: There are places on Karakorom High Way that on a good day can be compared to it, but no places on earth is more beautiful than Hunza. Eric Shipton called it "the ultimate manifestation of mountain grandeur" This trip, one of the great epic in any traveler's life, is a distillate of our engagement and infatuation with Silk Road. It Features the absolute tops in guides and accommodations, in addition to smaller group sizes than our competitors. Traveling along the Karakoram Highway is an experience that wil captivate and enthrall you with the landscape and the size of the mountains en route. The landscape is extremely striking. In places, sheer, snow-capped mountains standing tall from deep valleys while elsewhere lush alpine meadows are carpeted in colorful wild flowers and dazzling pastures above the villages. Terraced villages are dotted around this monumental terrain, supported by traditional farming methods and lifestyles that have seen little change over the centuries. Each day provides a new and exciting scene around each turning makes this experience so much popular amongst international travelers. Talk to anyone who has driven the 1284km long highway and watch their eyes light up! Connecting Afghanistan, the famous highway twists through three Great Mountain ranges – the Himalaya, Karakoram and Pamirs along the famous Indus and the Hunza rivers. If you love awe-inspiring mountain scenery, fantastic cultural diversity and history, and the idea of little effort to experience it, this is the trip for you! As Afghanistan looks to a future beyond international intervention, regional support will become ever more important "We believe a stable and prosperous Afghanistan, can only be envisioned in a stable and prosperous region," stated Afghan President Hamid Karzai. Speaking at the second Bonn Conference on Afghanistan in December 2011, this statement correctly asserts that stability in Afghanistan and stability in the region, are two mutually-reinforcing pillars. Thus the future of the region is dependent upon Afghanistan's ability to meet its state-building measures and move beyond what has been called the decade of 'transition,' to the decade of 'transformation' (between the years 2014 and 2024). The prospects for a stable and prosperous Afghanistan, following the withdrawal of NATO-Isaac forces in the post-2014 period, will largely depend upon Afghanistan's ability to sustain economic growth, provide goods and services to its people, reduce its dependence upon international aid, and realize its natural resource deposits. Thus an Afghanistan connected to the South and Central Asian region through the revitalization of the ancient Silk Road, will not only help re-establish Afghanistan as a land-bridge, but also help sustain its economy by facilitating and connecting the transit of goods and energy across the region. Afghanistan as a connector and bridge in the South and Central Asian region is not a new idea; its roots are grounded in an ancient highway that connected the eastern with the western world, known as the Ancient Silk Road. The Pamir Highway on the Silk Road, Afghanistan, Photo: S Girolimetto, some rights reserved Due to its geographical position Afghanistan was centrally located on the Silk Road, along which goods were transported from Beijing to Bactria (known today as the Balkh province in Afghanistan), and then headed out towards Turkey and the commercial ports of Europe. Balkh was considered the "cross center and convergence of all branches and courses" of the 11000km ancient highway. The Silk Road was therefore not only a trade and transit route for tradesmen, it was also a symbol of "collective security and global peace in the ancient centuries," for it connected three empires – the Han in East Turkestan Kushanid Empire in Afghanistan and Roman Empire in the Western hemisphere.

The 'present day Silk Route'

Although the revival of the Silk Road has been discussed for decades by those travelling it, as well as by others such as the United Nations and the USA, it only came to official formation in the sidelines of the UN General Assembly in September 2011, at which the US Secretary of State Hillary Clinton introduced the 'present day Silk Route' initiative with her counterpart, the Afghan Foreign Minister Zalmai Rassoul. This present day Silk Road would once again create trade routes between Asia and the West, facilitated by the establishment of modern highways, rail links and energy pipelines. Certainly, such an initiative is part of the wider transition program envisioned by the US, which has already shifted its focus from stabilization projects to investment in Afghanistan. It is also arguably a process intended on assisting the withdrawal of the US from Afghanistan, by creating a viable environment ultimately giving way to "spurring growth, and integrating Afghanistan into the economy of South and Central Asia." Increasing importance in trade and transit Despite an enduring conflict, weak rule of law, corruption, a doubtful security transition process, an ambiguous peace process, and 11 years of nation-building, Afghanistan has begun to regain its primary position as a trade and transit hub. To this effect, it has already commenced infrastructural rehabilitation in all sectors, including railways, highways, energy sources, natural resource discoveries, and trade and transit. Illustrative of these achievements are the Afghanistan linkages in regional forums, such as the Regional Economic Cooperation Conference on Afghanistan (RECCA), the Economic Cooperation Organization (ECO), the South Asian Association of Regional Countries (SAARC), the Shanghai Cooperation Organizations (SCO), and others. Afghanistan has also worked to consolidate its infrastructural build-up, serving to reflect its economic growth, its potential to connect Central Asia with Southern Asia and vice versa, and its capacity to provide mineral wealth and become an energy source to the region; whilst on the international market, it serves to demonstrate its vital importance to ensuring stability in the region. Regional assistance will be crucial Afghanistan will increasingly require more regional assistance. Nonetheless, today's reality is that the region continues to be primarily held hostage by political and strategic dissonance rather than full integration, conditions which do not lend themselves to success on the new Silk Road initiative. Thus in the post-2014 period, Afghanistan will increasingly require more regional assistance, for regional cooperation rather than international involvement, with regards to military and wasted development assistance, will prove to be the ultimate beacon of progress for Afghanistan. Such an approach must be assessed, analyzed and further developed upon through various regional forums, if it is to achieve greater connectivity in the region Juvaini believed that the arrival of the Jebe and his Mongols in the realm of the Khara Khitai was an act of Divine Providence: God Almighty, in order to remove the evilness of Küchlüg [Khüchüleg], in a short space dispatched the Mongol army against him; and already in this world he tasted the punishment of his foul and wicked deeds and his ill-omened life; and in the hereafter the torments of hellfire. Ill be his rest! Chingis Khan may have been acting out of more down-to-earth considerations. Khüchüleg had earlier escaped from the Mongols at both the battles at Tuleet Uul and on the Upper Irtysh and this must have rankled. Then he had gathered under his own banner all the disaffected tribesmen who had fled the Mongolian Plateau, thus posing a threat to the Uighurs and others at the western end of Chingis's own domains. Perhaps the Naiman adventurer even had his sights set on some day leading his assembled forces back to Mongolia and challenging Chingis Khan on his home turf. And by 1216 Chingis, as we have seen, was already making overtures to the Khwarezmshah about trade relations between the Mongols and Khwarezmia. Now Khüchüleg, essentially a free-booting marauder, sat astride the great trade routes linking the two realms, ready to swoop down on any trade caravans which might pass through the territories over which he now ruled rough-shod. There is also the school of thought, promoted by various modern historians, that Chingis even at this stage of his career entertained some overarching vision of world conquest and considered Khüchlüg simply as one more obstacle which had to be overcome on the inevitable march west, perhaps even to the Atlantic Ocean. Whatever his motivations, in 1216, after he had defeated the Jin in northern China, Chingis sent his general Jebe west to at long last deal with the Naiman upstart Khüchüleg. Jebe was a member of the Taichuud tribe, once one of the young Chingis Khan's many enemies. As a young man Temüjin, the future Chingis Khan, had been captured by the Taichuud and held prisoner. He later made a daring escape with the help of a man named Sorkhon who had divined a great future ahead for the young Temüjin and who would eventually become one of his followers. The Taichuud were just one of the many tribes Chingis would defeat in his rise to power. In the decisive battle against the Taichuud someone shot an arrow which according to the Secret History hit Chingis's yellow war horse in the neck. It may have been Chingis himself who was wounded in the neck, but apparently he did not want to reveal this. Anyhow, after the battle the Taichuud who were taken prisoner were interrogated to find out who had shot the arrow at Chingis. "Who shot that arrow from the mountaintop," Chingis demanded. A man named Zurgadai replied : shot that arrow from the mountain top. If put to death by the Qahan (Chingis), then I shall be left to rot on a piece of ground the size of the palm of the hand. But I am granted mercy, then shall I go ahead on behalf of the Qahan. wlll attack for you: will slash the deep waters and erode the shining stone. At your word, will go forwards and smash the blue stones. If you order me to attack, will slash the black stones will attack for you. Chingis Khan was impressed that the man had admitting to shooting at him, even though there was a chance he would be put to death for such an act, and had not attempted to lie his way out of it. A man like this, Chingis concluded, would make a good addition to his armies. Chingis gave Zurgadai the new name of Zebe, which means "arrow" in Mongolian, and proclaimed. "I shall use him as an arrow." Zebe (or Jebe, as it is more commonly rendered in English) would become the arrow which would unfailingly fly at any target to which Chingis aimed him. The target now was Khüchüleg Jebe headed westward, adding a contingent of Uighur troops to his army on the way, and soon arrived at Almaliq, in the basin of the Ili River, where he linked up with the tribesmen who had already declared their allegiance to Chingis. With these reinforcements he proceeded to the old Khara Khitai capital of Balagasun, where he defeated an army of some 30,000 men who had earlier obeyed the Gür Khan but who now were aligned at least nominally with Khüchüleg. Now reading the prevailing winds, other local rulers threw in their lot with Jebe and Mongols, including Yisimaili, a prominent Khara Khitai commander from the city of Kasan in the Ferghana Valley. With Yisimaili, who was apparently familiar with the country, leading Jebe's vanguard, the Mongol army headed south to Kashgar, where Khüchüleg was reputed to be holed up. Hearing of the imminent arrival of the Mongols he fled south toward the Pamirs, perhaps hoping to eventually reach the dubious safety of Indiai Jebe and his army of 20,000 Mongols and various auxiliaries were viewed as liberators by the Muslim population of Kashgar. According to Juvaini the local people stated that:. each group of Mongols, arriving one after another, sought nothing from us save Khüchlüg [sic], and permitted the recitation of the takbir [call to prayer] and azan, and caused a herald to proclaim in the town that each should abide by their religion and follow their own creed. Then we knew the existence of this people to be one of the mercies of the Lord and one of the bounties of divine grace. After rounding up and executing all of Khüchüleg's soldiers who had remained in the city Jebe and his men set out in hot pursuit of the Naiman runaway. They probably followed the old Silk Road caravan road (and now the route of the Karakoram Highway) up the valley and canyon of the Gez River, past Khökh Nuur (Blue Lake) and the immense massif of 24,757-foot Muztagh-Ata (later Marco Polo may have used this same route).

Khorasan presen day Afghanistan-Central Asia & India, thr Plateau of the Pamirs

Aryana-Khorasan dynasty present day Afghanistan-Central Asia & India, Somewhere near the border of Badakhshan and the Wakhan region deep in the Pamir Knot (perhaps in modern-day Tajikistan) Khüchüleg took the wrong road (Juvaini cannot help opining that "it was right that he should do so") and ended up in a dead-end valley. Jebe, coming up behind, met some local hunters and made them a deal: if they would bring him Khüchüleg no harm would come to them; if they did not they would to be aiding and abetting Khüchüleg's escape and would have to face the consequences. They captured the errant Naiman and brought him to Jebe, who rewarded them with much of the loot—jewels and money—which they had seized from Khüchüleg's traveling party. The Naiman adventurer, born on the steppes of Mongolia, had led a wild and tumultuous life since 1204 when he had fled Mongolia, throwing a good portion of Inner Asia into turmoil, but it all ended here in a desolate valley in the high Pamirs. He was executed and his head cut off. One source maintains that Jebe took his head back with him and displayed it in Kashgar and Khotan to prove that the oppressor of the local Muslim populations was finally, at long last, dead. With the death of Khüchüleg Chingis's favored general Jebe was now the de facto ruler of a huge swath of land from Khotan north to the Seven Rivers region. Did the thought cross his mind that at this point he could have declared himself the new Gür Khan and founded an empire of his own? Apparently back in Mongolia even Chingis Khan began to worry that Jebe "in the pride of victory would mutiny," as Barthold puts it. But Jebe was made of different stuff. He had sworn his loyalty to Chingis Khan back when his life had been spared after the defeat of the Taichuud and he was not about to turn on his sworn lord and master. As a sign of his fealty. he gave to his commander-in-chief a gift of 1000 yellow horses like the one Chingis had been riding at the final battle with the Taichuud, the horse he, Jebe, had supposedly hit in the neck with an arrow. Tracking down Khüchüleg and seizing his territories was certainly a feather in his cap, but his greatest exploits as a general in the Mongol army were yet to come. He would remain loyal to Chingis until his death in 1225 The great games on great Afghanistan mountain 1886 by the Saxon Empire The great Pamir is the highest alpine chain in the South of the ex-SU, these days the territory of the Kirghizia (Kirgiztan) and Tajikistan. It occupies the area of approximately 60 000 square kilometers and presents the extensive network of avers now- covered ridges and vast intermountain valleys which form Pamir plateau

Exploration History

Mountaineering Pamir exploration began together with the first research expeditions of Soviet Academy of Sciences on Pamir in the 1928 - 1933ths. Tourist expeditions on Pamir were firstly made in 50ths and for the time being Pamir is the most popular outdoor mountainous region among those of CIS. In mountaineering practical experience Pamir's boundaries are accepted on the basis of ridges' pornography and their trek's resources. From the East Pamir is limited by Sarykolsky ridge on the axis of which there are borders of ex-USSR and China. The southern border passes along the river Piandge separating Tajikistan and Kirgizia from Afghanistan and the northern one is limited by the river Kyzyl -So (Kyzylsoo), consecutively adopting the name Sour hob and then Vakhsh. In the West Pamir finishes with the ridges outskirts - of Peter the Great and Darvazsky. The highest ridges and massive glaciers are clustered in the western part of Pamir. Most ridges' peaks are more than 6000 meters high and sometimes rise over 7000 meters high. There are 3 of 4 peaks above 7000 meters high on Pamir including the highest mountain of ex-USSR - Communism Peak in Akademii Nauk range (recently this peak is re-named to, and Lenin peak (7134 m) - popular peak for those who're trying their 1st attempt of high-altitude climbing. The highest top of the whole Pamir area however situated in the Chinese part of the East Pamir - it is Muztag Ata peak (7546 m). The plateau of 4000 meters high and more occupies the eastern part of Pamir and stretches from its north to the south, being only once separated by Muzcol ridge. Khorasan presen day Afghanistan-Central Asia & India

North-Western, North-Eastern, South-Western, Central and Eastern Central

of Pamir, S Aryana-Khorasan dynasty present day Afghanistan-Central Asia & India the natural conditions of Pamir's western and eastern parts are very different. From one side, there is a sharp unevenness of the relief, from the other side, the gently sloping plateau, at times going to an alpine desert. Biologists and climatologists divide Pamir into regions with rather general and stable physics-geographical characteristics such as ridge character, type and capacity of icing, vegetation, air dryness, etc. With such division one part of the ridge is often in one region, and the other one is in the othe region which makes more difficult to classify the information about routes. Generally speaking, Pamir's division accepted in trekking and mountaineering practice doesn't contradict with the one of the geography and reflects the history of Pamir's mountaineering exploration. It also helps you to reach the required information very easily. As a rule, Pamir is divided into 5 regions: North-Western, North-Eastern, South-Western, Central and Eastern. Central Pamir has the least clear boundaries, so many people also include here eastern parts of the North-Western Pamir North-Western Pamir's ridges are: Peter the Great ridge, Darvazsky, Vanchsky and Yazgulemsky before the place where the Academy of Sciences ridges cross, North-Western Pamir connects the eastern part of the Zaalaysky ridge and Zulumart ridge before the pass Zulumart. Central Pamir includes the Academy of Sciences ridge, Tynymas and the eastern part of the Yazgulemsky ridge(mountains of the southern group of Fedchenko glacier). Easteren Pamir's ridges are: Muzcol Pshartsky and North-Alichursky ridges. South-Western Pamir's ridges are: Rushansky, Shugnansky, Ishkashimsk Shakhdarinsky and South-Alichursky ridges The western part of the Zaalaysky ridge (to the West of the pass Tersagar) has not be normally included in the North-Western Pamir. That's why the valley of the river Muksu is the powerful natural border separating these two regions. At times the Academy of Sciences ridge is considered to be the part of the North-Western Pamir (you should mind that the regions' borders are highly conventional). Such a division helps to classify the information about Pamir better when preparing for trekking and expeditions, which are hold usually in one region. Above this, such division based on the directions of the sides of the World reflects the natural trek's and transport peculiarities of certain regions which are also important for the visitors. Pamir differs from other alpine regions of ex-USSR by comparative stability of the weather during summer months. More changeable weather is observed near Lenin's peak. More stable weather is in the North-Western and Central Pamir, exceptions are the regions before Communism and Revolution peaks. Dryness of air and high solar radiation are typical for all Pamir, but in Central, Eastern and South-Western parts this feature exceed other regions. Every ridge and region of Pamir has its passes' set of any complication category. In this case, passes from 2B and higher prevail, the number of passes with 1A and 1B complication is not great. The height of passes in the whole is in the limits from 4000 to 6000 meters. The height of general mass of passes is about 5000 meters, the number of passes exceeding this height is also considerable. Thus treks and expeditions on Pamir are connected with a long continuous staying on the altitudes of over 4000 meters, it happens that the time of a continuous staying on the altitudes over 5000 meters sometimes reaches its highest value (about half of a month). As a rule, passes and mountains of Pamir require long up and down approach with getting through water obstacles, glaciers, snow- capped ice slopes and rocky areas. Passes and interesting to climb are mainly located in remote, difficult-to-access regions (the Lenin's Peak from the North is an rare exception). The approach to many of them is possible only from reserved areas where you can run only through complicated passes or by using helicopter. For more complicated passes the passage of the main passing obstacle with neighboring up approaches takes 4-5 days. Passes 1A and 1B being inside the region often takes one-two days walk. During passes' walking often happen overnight stayings on the stone moraines, on the snow, on the ice, on the slopes and saddle of passes, sometimes arises necessity to build neve blocks walls and in digging of snowy caves. Getting over passes requires the usage of complete set of climbing gear, technical means and tactical methods which are practiced in mountaineering.

Trekking and Mountaineering In Pamir

Aryana-Khorasan dynasty present day Afghanistan-Central Asia & India. Pamir is characterized by 4-6 categories of complication for the trekking and pass-hopping routes. The elaboration of rules for logical treks of less complication with running through the everlasting snow zone is difficult. Objectively, this fact is caused by rather small number of low difficulty passes, and also its scanty comfortable combination passes of other complication. So, Pamir is more suitable area to mountaineering. Natural-climatic conditions of Pamir and characteristics of passes requiring high physical, technical, tactical training of trekkers make from tour safety point of view the organization of the treks of 3 and less complication category is too problematic. Climbing routes are mostly ice, snow and neve, less rocky, that's can be considered as common for high mountain areas. Administratively Pamir lies mainly on the territory of Tajikistan. Only the northern outskirts of Zaalaisky ridge descending to the Alaiskaya valley belong to Kirgiziya. The main means of communication on Pamir is automobile and aviation transport. The basis of automobile connection here is the Cross-Pamir road which begins from the town Osh in the Ferganskaya valley. This road crosses Alaiskaya valley from the North to the South, stretches to the South on the Pamir plateau along the river Piandge to the North and then to the West towards the city Dushanbe (the capital of Tajikistan, which is connected by air to the Moscow, Novosibirsk and some of the Central Asia states). From this main road, roads of the local importance are constructed to the South and to the East along Piandge, there are small parts by the valleys of rivers Shahdara, Bartang, Yazgulem, Vanch, Obi-Hingou. Near the lake Kharakul truck road goes to the valleys of rivers Khokhuibel and Tanimas. The city of Dushanbe is connected with such small towns as Murgab and Horog, with district centers Rushan, Vanch by local airlines. There is also an airline to the towns Tavil-Dara and Jirgatal situating on the western borders of Pamir. The start and the finish points of treks belong to this transport network. The article comprises the results on the analysis of the structure of the great Pamirs' population (of a higher rank) and of one of its parts, the subpopulation of the valley of the river Bartang. Wright's F coefficient was used for the statistical treatment of the data obtained in the course of the analysis. The FST estimates were obtained from the variances of the frequencies of the genes located in 5 loci (ABO, MN, P, Rh and P.T.C.) culculated for 23 samples of the great populations of the Pamirs and for 9 samples of the population of the Bartang river valley. The general inbreeding coefficient for the Pamirs FIT = 0,0323, its random component FST = 0,0017 and the non-random component Chordoma is a rare tumor arising in the sacrum, clivus, or vertebrae. It is often not completely resectable and shows a high incidence of recurrence and progression with shortened patient survival and impaired quality of life. Chemotherapeutic options are limited to investigational therapies at present. Therefore, adjuvant therapy for control of tumor recurrence and progression is of great interest, especially in skull base lesions where complete tumor resection is often not possible because of the proximity of cranial nerves. To understand the extent of genetic instability and associated chromosomal and gene losses or gains in skull base chordoma, we undertook whole-genome single-nucleotide polymorphism microarray analysis of flash frozen surgical chordoma specimens, 21 from the clivus and 1 from C1 to C2 vertebrae. We confirm the presence of a deletion at 9p involving CDKN2A, CDKN2B, and MTAP but at a much lower rate (22%) than previously reported for sacral chordoma. At a similar frequency (21%), we found aneuploidy of chromosome 3. Tissue microarray immunohistochemistry demonstrated absent or reduced fragile histidine triad (FHIT) protein expression in 98% of sacral chordomas and 67% of skull base chordomas. Our data suggest that chromosome 3 aneuploidy and epigenetic regulation of

FHIT contribute to loss of the FHIT tumor suppressor in chordoma. The finding that FHIT is lost in a majority of chordomas provides new insight into chordoma pathogenesis and points to a potential new therapeutic target for this challenging neoplasm The role of transcranial Doppler ultrasound (TCD) in clinical decision making about vasospasm due to subarachnoid haemorrhage (SAH), shows agreat variation according to neurosurgical clinics. In this prospective study, a total of 143 patients, admitted to Marmara University Department of Neurosurgery between January 1991 to March 1995 and treated surgically with the diagnosis of aneurysmal SAH, were examined by TCD. Eighty of these patients fulfilled the requirements for inclusion. In order to increase clinical dependability of TCD, a new grading system is proposed and tested in comparison with the one previously used, which takes absolute flow velocities as the main parameter in grading. The new, individually based TCD grading system is proposed to minimize the pitfalls caused by proximal stenosis, wide range of normal Vm values and proximally evolving vasospasm. We concluded that: 1) The new, individually based TCD grading system has a high degree of clinical dependability. 2) Daily TCD examinations supply reliable predictive information about developing delayed ischaemic deficit (DID). If a TCD Gr II patient shows an increase of 35 cm in Vm value, his probability of developing DID was found to be 60%; if a TCD Gr B III patient shows the same rate of increase in Vm, his probability of developing DID was 80% (0.05). 3) TCD has an important clinical role in decision making about the management of SAH patients. 4) Surgical manipulation causes a reversible increase of one or two TCD-grades in the early postoperative days The clinic-genealogical and population-genetical studies were undertaken to reveal the myopathia patients. The frequency of myopathies in a population of Tajiks, their clinical polymorphism and the course of the pathologic process, depending on factors of environment were studied. In the population of Pamir people, who were exposed to external conditions, 25 patients with the neural amyotrophy, 8 patients with shoulder, shoulder-blade and face form of progressive muscle distrophy, 4 patients with Erba's PMD and 3 with the pseudohypertrophic Dushen form were revealed. High frequency of the neural amyotrophy was connected with the marriage election of the population, its isolation and accumulation of heterozygote carriers. Earlier onset of progressive muscle distrophy was connected with sharp change in climate and great physical burdens which led to the disarrangement of the adaptation system. It was established that 17 patients with the shoulder-blade and face form of the PMD, 5 patients with the sporadic form of the neural amyotrophy, 3 patients with the Dushen's PMD, 2 patients with the Erba's PMD and 1 patient with the spinal amyotrophy inhabited Karategin valley having the continental climate. The high level of migration of these populations resulted in dissemination of the gene in the valley regions. The quantity of abortions and still-borns in families suffering from myopathy is fewer than in Pamir It's rare for CPP to fill the III ventricule. Up to date, 24 cases surgically removed have been reported. In this report, we present a 1,5 year old boy who administered because of severe cachexia and reactive coma. Ct scan revealed dilatation in lateral ventricles and a mass totally filling the III ventricle. The mass has been totally excised through foramen Monro by right frontoparietal craniotomy and transcortical transventricular surgical approach. While a post-operative recovery was being observed, the patient died in the 30 the day because of bronchopneumonia. The treatment of III ventricle CPP as all the other CPP, must be total resection. For this reason, preoperative CT scan carries a great value about giving information of the nature of the tumor The article comprises the results on the analysis of the structure of the great Pamirs' population (of a higher rank) and of one of its parts, the subpopulation of the valley of the river Bartang. Wright's F coefficient was used for the statistical treatment of the data obtained in the course of the analysis. The FST estimates were obtained from the variances of the frequencies of the genes located in 5 loci (ABO, MN, P, Rh and P.T.C.) culculated for 23 samples of the great populations of the Pamirs and for 9 samples of the population of the Bartang river valley. The general inbreeding coefficient for the Pamirs FIT=0,0323, its random component FST=0,0017 and the non-random component The Afghan Pamir are unique U-shaped, high-elevation mountain valleys distinctive to Central Asia, where there are more than half a dozen named pamir. Renowned as summer grazing grounds for their abundant grass and water, these vast plateaus are covered by snow six months of the yearThe Afghan Pamir include two such grasslands at the eastern end of Wakhan – the Big Pamir and the Little Pamir, which are better known by their Dari names. The Big Pamir or Great Pamir is called Pamir Kalan and Pamir-e-Buzurg (kalan and buzurg both mean 'great' or 'large'). The Little Pamir is called Pamir Khurd and Pamir-e-Kochak (khurd and kochak both mean 'little' or 'small'). The 60km long Big Pamir nestles between the Southern Alichur Range to the north and the Wakhan Range to the south. The Little Pamir, at 100km long and 10km wide, is actually larger in area than the Big Pamir, yet the more rugged Big Pamir has a higher elevation and so earns its name. The proper name 'Pamirs' typically refers to the Central Asian mountain range that extends from Tajikistan into Afghanistan and East Turkestan present day China. since 1949 Afghanistan's Wakhan District is a narrow strip of land separating Tajikistan and Pakistan that juts eastward some 350km to meet the present day China border. Wakhan District has two distinct parts – the Wakhan Corridor and the Afghan Pamir. All of Wakhan lies at elevations higher than 2000m and the Afghan Pamir lies above 3500m. The Wakhan Corridor is a deep valley formed by the Panj River that courses between the 7000m peaks of the Hindukush tothe south and the lofty mountains of Tajikistan to the north. Along the south bank of the Panj River and its upper tributary, the Wakhan River, are numerous Wakhi villages. The villages between Ishkashim and Qila-e Panja are termed Lower Wakhan. More than 5000m of vertical relief commands the southern horizon of Lower Wakhan, where the valley is as broad as 2km. The villages in Upper Wakhan between Qila-e Panja and Sarhad-e Broghil lie along the more narrow banks of the Wakhan River, which opens to a dramatic river basin 3km wide at Sarhad-e Broghil. Streams fed by precipitous Hindukush glaciers cut across the Wakhan Corridor and flow into the main river Three mountain ranges – the Hindukush, Karakoram and Pamir – converge in Wakhan to form what is called the Pamir Knot. The Hindukush Range, which forms the border with Pakistan, has 38 summits higher than 7000m, including Afghanistan's highest peak Noshaq (7492m). Permanent snow blankets Wakhan's highest peaks. The high, open valleys between these three mountain ranges form the Afghan Pamir, known in Persian as the Bam-e Dunya, or the "roof of the world," which is home to Kyrgyz nomads. High passes called kotal transect the mountain ranges and were used by armies and ancient trade caravans. In the Afghan Pamir, passes, although at high elevation, are relatively easy for people to cross. The passes across the more rugged Hindukush are more difficult. The key Hindukush passes are: Broghil Pass (3882m) and Darwaza Pass (4288m) to Chitral; Khodarg Werth (or Khora Bort Pass) to Ishkoman; and Irshad Uween (4979m) and Dilisang Pass (5290m) to Gojal. All of Wakhan is a semi-arid zone. In the Wakhan Corridor, agriculture is only possible through irrigation, fed by meltwater in the streams descending from the mountains. Apart from occasional clusters of shrubs or willow, birch and other small trees, the landscape is largely barren of vegetation. Above 3500m, the valleys widen onto the expansive Afghan Pamir with its lush seasonal meadows, peaty soil, and vivid blue lakes. the Pamirs, located principally in the Gorno-Badakhshan Autonomous Oblast (GBAO) ineastern Tajikistan, are one of the highest mountain ranges in the world, containing peaks over 7000m. The territory comprises a large high plateau area (Murghab district in the east) and several deep valleys running west into the Panj river (in antiquity known as the Oxus; in local languages "panj" means "five" and the name Panj is said to come from the fact that the five main Pamir valleys feed into it). GBAO shares frontiers with China in the east, Kyrgyzstan in the north and Afghanistan in the west and south. The region is inaccessible to road traffic for as much as six months in winter, and was considered during the Soviet period as a strategic border area to which special permission was required for travel. It is therefore very much "virgin territory" for tourism, with little relevant infrastructure. As such, it combines extraordinary attractions for adventure and ecotourism with untouched high-altitude landscapes and many opportunities for walking and trekking. The Pamirs were on one of the southern branches of the Silk Road and possess fortresses and other monuments bearing witness to the traffic of goods and ideas (petroglyphs, Buddhist monasteries, shrines and caravanserais). The "Great Game" was played in the Pamirs. Situated in Badakhshan in the heart of Asia, 'The Pamirs' is an area of sky-scraping, snow-capped, majestic mountains, transparent clear blue waters of lakes and rivers, wide valleys and bone-dry deserts. For hundreds of years, people have called these highest mountains of the world "Poy-e Mehr", the literal translation being, "the foot of the sun" or "the Roof of the Word". Since Soviet times, the highlands of the Pamirs has become known as Gorno-Badakhshan. Situated in Badakhshan in the heart of Asia, 'The Pamirs' is an area of sky-scraping, snow-capped, majestic mountains, transparent clear blue waters of lakes and rivers, wide valleys and bone-dry deserts. For hundreds of years, people have called these highest mountains of the world "Poy-e Mehr", the literal translation being, "the foot of the sun" or "the Roof of the Word". Since Soviet times, the highlands of the Pamirs has become known as Gorno-Badakhshan. Geographically, the Pamirs represent a huge mountain chain, located almost in the centre of the Asian continent. It links the greatest mountain ranges of the world: Tyan Shan, Hindukush, Kun-Lun and Karakoram. The proper territory of the Pamirs is divided between Tajikistan, Afghanistan, China and Pakistan along the demarcation lines drawn to designate political boundaries. The major part of these mountains is nonetheless, situated in the territory of the Republic of Tajikistan. Second only to the section of the Himalayas in Tibet, the Pamirs are the highest mountains in the world with human habitation. The area is isolated and land-locked. The highlands of the Pamirs form a variety of landscapes, ranging from sub-tropical to alpine. Here, flat plains and sharp mountain peaks alternate in relatively short distances. The vast highland desert of the Eastern Pamirs is located at elevations ranging from 3,500 - 4,200 meters above sea level. Gorno-Badakhshan is known for its wealth of mineral rock deposits; the most important include molybdenum, gold, silver, wolfram, granite, marble and lapis lazuli. Another inexhaustible source of the Pamirs is water, flowing to the flatlands of Central Asia from the main tributaries that feed the Amu-Darya river. The region is associated with ancient Aryan tribes nomadic herders and traders, wandering this wide landmass for millennia. Through these mountains passed the famed Silk Road, in its time, the principal route for inter-continental trade. As a hub for ancient commerce, Badakhshan has also served as a place where peoples would come into contact from as far away as the Middle East, Europe, Iran, India and China. In ancient times, the most important routes via the Hindukush led through the Wakhan valley, Ishkashim, Zebak, Faizabad and Balkh to Yarkand and Tash-Kurghan, the latter two regions now in China. These were also the main communication roads for inhabitants of the mountainous areas of Central Asia on their way to India. The Pamirs area linked with communication roads to Faizabad in Afghanistan, India, the Ferghana valley and Tashqurghan. These roads helped the population engage in regional commercial transactions, despite the difficulties of the terrain and less efficient transportation, until the pre-modern era. The first motor-road, constructed by Tzarist Russia, appeared around the beginning of the twentieth century, leading from Osh to Khorog via Murghab, and was used primarily for military purposes. Up to 1936, the population of Soviet Gorno-Badakhshan enjoyed relatively unrestricted commercial ties with Afghanistan and China, at which point the Pamir borders were closed at the orders of Stalin. It was not until the disintegration of the Soviet Union, that serious trade re-commenced with the outside world. To this day, the Pamirs is still isolated within Tajikistan. The zone continues to be restricted and (up to October 2011) a permit is still needed to enter the area. However, plans are underway to do away with this entry requirement. The region now known as Gorno-Badakhshan is autonomous, and comprises seven districts. The population in GBAO is over 200,000. The administrative and economic centre of the region is Khorog with a population of approximately 28,000. The majority are Ismaeli Muslims (a denomination of Shi'ia Islam). While the inhabitants of Shugnan, Rushan, Ishkashim and Rosht-Quala districts, including the residents of Yaged, a sub-district in Darwaz, are Ismaelis, most of the indigenous population in Vanj, Darwaz and Murghab are Sunnis. Mountain roads, constructed during the Soviet Era connect the various districts to Khorog and beyond. The primary means of public transportation is via Chinese built so called 'tangems', small mini vans that carry up to seven passengers for a minimal fee. The Pamirs has an extreme Continental climate; summer temperatures range between 25-38 degrees Celsius in the daytime, with very low humidity. Winters are very cold, with temperatures ranging between -2 to -30 degrees Celsius. Owing to limited air lift and passes blocked by heavy snows, it is difficult for international travellers to access the Pamirs out of the main summer tourist season (May - October). Over the centuries, the Pamirs have inspired the world's greatest explorers - Marco Polo, Hsuan Tsang, Mirza Muhammad Haidar were amongst them. They were among the first to report on the richness of the region: precious gems, mineral springs, awe-inspiring peaks, ancient glaciers, wide green pastures and of course, the peoples of the Pamirs. During the Soviet era, hundreds of tons of minerals and stones were extracted and shipped North. Archaeological indications suggest that the first human inhabitants of the Pamirs derived from two massive waves of migration of Aryan tribes from the plains of Asia; one moved southwards towards India and the other turned towards Afghanistan and then gradually towards Europe. Thus the Indo-European race is said to have spread to two continents of the world. By the second and third century AD, there were small kingdoms in the Wakhan and Shugnan. These kingdoms later became part of the Akhemenid Empire. Subsequently, this empire was conquered by Alexander the Great, after which the area came under the rule of the Khushanids from Northern India and the Sasanids from Afghanistan. These semi-independent statelets continued to exist through to the early 20th century. When the Sasanids were defeated at the start of the 8th century, Islam began to spread in the area to supplant Zoroastranism and Buddhism, the latter being widely practiced in the Wakhan at that time. In the 13th century, the explorer Marco Polo wrote that the process of conversion to Islam was almost total. During the middle ages, the Pamirs were ruled by various dynasties including the Samanids, the Ghaznavids, the Mongols, the Temurids, the Shaibanids and the Safavids, all for relatively short periods of time. None of these foreign rules lasted permanently. At times, the Wakhan and Shugnan experienced onslaughts of marauding raids by Turkic and Mongolian invaders, from the western territories under the nominal rule of the Chinese Empire. Despite its geographical isolation and relative independence from the outside world, Badakhshan had close links with other regions in Central Asia. Throughout the pre-modern era, it maintained economic and cultural ties with Bukhara, Khujand, Qoshghar and, most importantly, with the Ismaili communities in northern India and western present day China. Towards the beginning of the 19th century, Tzarist Russia sought political interests in Central and South Asia. As the main political rival of the British rule in India, Russia tried to establish a presence in the region. As a consequence, the territories under present Tajik and Afghan Badakhshan became the arena of intense geopolitical confrontation between these two powers which were vying for control over the area linking Europe and Asia. These disputes over this specific territory, during this time period are historically labelled as 'The Great Game'. As of 1872 – 1873, Tzarist Russia and British India negotiated on the division of the disputed territories. While the British insisted on the sovereignty of Afghanistan, the Russians pressed for the jurisdiction of Bukhara, their protectorate in Central Asia. In 1895 an agreement was signed between Tzarist Russia and Great Britain that established borders, which divided the Western and the Eastern Pamirs. This resulted in the Western Pamirs coming under the rule of the Emir of Bukhara whereas the Eastern Pamirs, along with the upper Bartang valley, came under direct Russian protection. Following this agreement, the Russian White Army established its garrisons in Khorog and Murghab and the Pamirs officially came under Russian protection. During this transition period, Bukhara still had some influence on the area through tax-collection and intimidation but eventually these practices were brought to a halt by the Russian military authorities. The authorities then began setting up structures of civil administration in Gorno-Badakhshan, ended the local turf wars, as well as the then common slave trade in the Pamirs. This rule continued when the Communists assumed power in Russia in 1917. Between the 1930s and 1940s, the population of the Pamirs suffered under Stalinist repression. Community and religious leaders and intelligentsia were either executed or exiled to Siberia. During the Second World War, however, through necessity, Stalin had to show a benign face and managed to conscript many young Pamiris to the Soviet Army to fight the so-called Great Patriotic War. After the Second World War, the Pamirs benefitted from Soviet subsidies and were able to make strides in education and economic development. In the early 1990s, Badakhshani intelligentsia were actively engaged in the process of perestroika and glasnost, demanding social justice and equal distribution of resources. Post Soviet-Russia, a civil war broke out in Tajikistan; Badakshanis wanted autonomy but this goal was never realized, since it was never supported by either the Central Authorities in Dushanbe nor by the establishment in Moscow. At the end of the Civil War in 1997, Gorno Badakhshan was recognized as an inseparable part of the unitary state of Tajikistan although it continues to hold the status of 'autonomous region'. n the Pamirs the traditional itineraries will include visits to Khorog, Ishkashi, the Wakhan Corridor, Murghab and depending on your further travel plans, back via the Bartang Valley or towards Kyrgystan and Osh. The Pamir Highway is the primary route from the East to the West of the country and is widely used by Chinese truck drivers delivering goods between Osh and Dushanbe. Itinerary suggestion: Khorog - Bogev - Jelondi - Burum-Kul - Yashil-Kul - Alichur - Murghab. Following the Pamir Highway from the west, one can visit Bogev with its fire temple and travel towards the magnificent lakes of the Murghab. You will traverse the Koitezek Pass at 4,271m above sea level after Jelondi and from there descend into the vastness of the wide Murghab valleys. The madian valley, close to Murghab is beautiful and worth a visit. If you are camping; this is as beautiful a spot as any. Itinerary suggestion: Khorog – Garm-Chasma - Ishkashim – Vrang – Khargush Pass. Instead of taking the Pamir Highway, east, one can travel south to Ishkashim, via the hotsprings of Garm-Chasma, into the Wakhan Corridor, along the Panj river. This route passes the ancient fortress of Kah-Kaha, built around the 4th century BC and the fortress of Yamchoon. Not far from Yamchoon are the famous springs of Bibi Fatima, its waters believed to have healing qualities for reproductive problems. In the village of Vrang, one can visit the oldest Buddhist stupa in the country. Langar has several points of interest – the ruins of Ratm, another old fortress; petroglyphs from the Bronze Age; the Mazor-i Shoh Kambar- i Oftob shrine. There is a guest house here which also doubles as a museum. The road continues north in the Murghab via the Khargush Pass (4,344m above sea level). Itinerary suggestion: Khorog – Khuf - Gizev – Basid – Davlokh. For great hiking opportunities in beautiful mountain valleys consider visiting the unexplored Bartang Valley. From Khorog, travel northwards past the city of Khuf, following the road east into the Bartang Valley. Here there are numerous trails leading from the valley floor into the higher elevations. Gizev is well known for its scenic beauty and is a three hour trek uphill; but worth the effort. Another option is to continue driving eastwards to Basid and from there hike up to Davlokh. Along the way, remember to visit the petroglyphs of Visav. The road into the Bartang continues eastwards but is often in very bad condition. Check with your tour operator or PECTA before venturing further. Kara-Kul can be visited from here if the road is passable. Itinerary suggestion: Sarez Lake. This is an exciting and unforgettable trip to one of the youngest large mountain lakes that was formed as a result of great earthquake. The water in the lake is turquoise blue. To get here special permission is needed (contact PECTA). Best time to visit June-August. Excellent place for boating, fishing and hiking. Itinerary suggestion: Zor-Kul (Lake Victoria in the past) one of the most beautiful lakes in Tajikistan. The water is sweet, there are many fish. Compared to other Pamir high altitude valleys, the Zorkul valley is very green; a lot of small lakes and streams, connected to the lake are shining on the sun and there is a diversity of rare animals – Marko Polo ship, Indian mountain goose, red wolf, snow leopard. The first European traveller to Zorkul lake was an English explorer named Lieutenant Wood who in 1838 travelled to the source of the Oxus river and named it after the Saxon Queen Victoria. Zorkul lake is situated in the Zorkul Nature Reserve territory. Special permission. How to get there: From Dushanbe -through Vakhan corridor or Ghunt valley and from Osh (Kyrgyzstan). Best time to visit: June – August Itinerary suggestion: Tajik National Park, including the Fedchenko Glacier with mountaineering optionsThe Tajik National Park covers almost 50 % of the Pamirs. Some of the main routes: Vanj – Poimazor – Bears Glacier - Fedchenko Glacier. Good opportunity to see one of the longest glaciers in the world (70 km). Yazgulyam – Roshorv – Rushan – Khorog. Good trekking routes while passing the glacier. Sarez lake – Irkht – Chapdar lake – Yashilkul lake – Batchor village. 8 days trekking to the mountain lakes. Pasor village – Grum Grjimailo glacier

Afghanistan is the Roof of the World

By two German empire the Saxon-British-Russia 3, 6 million Sq Km Afghanistan- territories from A.D 1891unti 2020

Aryana-Khorasan dynasty present day Afghanistan-Central Asia & India 1895-1896 to fix the Pamir borders that obtain today. Both Empires saw an interest in creating a buffer zone in the Wakhan Corridor; the Afghans were presented with a fait accompli and the present day Chinese hardly consulted Gudara – Kok Jar – Tanimas Glacier Itinerary suggestion: Mountaineering/ climbing options Just on the highest peaks in Communize (7495) there are more than 30 routes! There are many 5 and 6 thousand meter high mountains here to explore. Rock climbing: All over the Pamir's there are several bolted routes in the Ghund valley. Rock climbing sites can be found in Ghund, Bartang, Rushan, Ishkashim, Roshkala and Murghab. Here rocky crags, big rock walls and bouldering sites offer endless opportunities for first ascents on virgin crags and walls, a possibility nearly impossible to find anywhere else in the world. On Christmas day 1891, Charles Adolph's Murray, eighth Earl of Dunmore, left England for Karachi, where he disembarked in February 1892 at the start of a journey that was to take him over 2,200 miles through Afghanistan-Central Asia, crossing sixty-nine rivers and forty-one mountain passes, some among the highest in the world. His account of this journey, The Pamir's; being a Narrative of a Year's Expedition on Horseback and Foot through Kashmir, Western Tibet, Turkmen, Tartary and Central Asia, was published in London in 1893. It reveals a man of considerable strength, erudition, good humor and courtesy. While the first was a requirement and the second not unusual for all the early explorers of the Great Pamir's, the latter two qualities were more exceptional. Dunmore was also an accomplished linguist, amateur botanist, poet, painter and musician, with a fine sense for natural beauty. Sunset on the Alichur Pamir On the Pamir's we have often seen evening tints in the sky, the colors of which we do not believe that any landscape painter in the world could give a name to, and the afterglows, which would almost answer to our twilights in Europe, are so exquisite in their refinement, that it were absolutely impossible to attempt to describe them. His qualities stand out even more in comparison with some of the dry accounts published by contemporary travelers on the Pamir's. Major Charles Sperling Cumberland, for example, travelled in almost the same areas as Dunmore three years previously and met en route Grombchevsky, Dauvergne and a team from Nikolai Mikhailovich Prjevalsky's last expedition to Tibet, but his book Sport on the Afghanistan- Pamir and Turkistan Steppes, published in 1895, contains hardly a single interesting or amusing story: it comprises essentially a series of excruciatingly detailed hunting reports. Where Dunmore frequently expresses concern for the welfare of his native companions, Cumberland is less put out at the death of one of his native guides than at the loss of one of his ponies. Of course, many of these trips – whatever their real purpose – were indeed described by those participating as 'sport'. Dunmore – aged 51, remember – on the way up the Taghdumbash Afghanistan-Pamir, at an altitude of nearly 5,000m, in temperatures of about minus 15°C, spent several days and nights stalking Marco Polo sheep, sleeping out on the snow and, on one occasion, sliding headlong down a glacier into a crevasse. He notes, with imperceptible irony, that "there is no doubt that we have come here at the wrong season of the year." On meeting a bear, he comments sardonically that he held his fire until the bear was dangerously close because he could only see his head and to aim at it "would have shattered his skull, which was the only part of him we wanted to keep." Nothing should surprise today's reader about the explorers of an age where there were considered to be no limits to knowledge or to human

Endeavour and improvement. General Sir Charles MacGregor had described the ideal cogently in 1882 in his Wanderings in Baluchistan. The sight of a map with blank spaces on it produces in me a feeling of mingled shame and restlessness. Of course it is not any particular fault of mine that maps have blank spaces on them, but always feel the glaring whiteness of the blanks looking reproachfully at me. Judging from my own feelings, think it would be a good plan if the Geographical Society were to have all unexplored tracts painted on their maps some conspicuous color, say scarlet, as the sight of these burning spots, thus prominently brought to their notice, would, feel sure, rouse much of the latent energy of young Britons, and perhaps divert a good deal of it from mooning about the Row to more useful wanderings to unknown regions. A broken rib sustained in a riding accident in Rawalpindi led to a short delay in setting off but gave Dunmore time to review his plans and extend his planned itinerary from the Pamir's to other parts of Afghanistan Central Asia. The fitting out of the expedition included procurement of not only tents, stores and sporting guns, but also scientific instruments for making observations en route. Baggage includes eight tents, thirty beddings, camp-furniture, stores, carpenters' tools, medicine chest; navies' tools, horse-shoeing tools, 3000 nails and 420 horseshoes, guns, rifles, ammunition, spare saddler, our own kit and that of thirty men; kitchen utensils, scientific instruments, photographic apparatus, etc. Fifty-one men and 130 live animals [74 yaks and 56 ponies]. Dunmore was joined at Leh in Ladak by Major Roche of the Indian dragoons, who stayed with him until they reached Kashgar six months later and, on 23 June, their party set off for the Chinese frontier, crossing the Karakoram pass on 9 July. They reached Yarkand on 4 August and, two weeks later, headed west towards the Pamir's, reaching Tashkurgan and Sarikol at the end of August. Dunmore notes that the population of Sarikol "numbers about 6000 souls and is purely Afghan. They all look upon His Highness Agha, Sahib of Bombay, as their spiritual leader, who in virtue of his being the offspring of the prophet and himself a pious man, has alone the power of absolving his followers from their sins. Some of the Sariqqolis who are his most ardent disciples go so far on the road towards Buddhism, as to believe that Ali takes birth in every successive Agha." Dunmore notes that the Sarikol were respectful of their women who "are not treated as mere machines, as they are in other Muslim countries, but are looked up to with respect by their husbands and children and are entrusted with the entire household arrangements they are free to come and go as they please, without any restriction; and the use of the veil is practically unknown to them." On 1 September they reached the foot of the Tagdumbash Pamir – their ranks increased by This time to thirty men and sixty horses (having had an undignified fall from a yak, Dunmore seems to have abandoned the idea of using these animals). There they were welcomed by an unseasonable snowstorm: "Roche and sat huddled up together, trying to imagine we were getting shelter from a juniper bush three feet high. The ground was wet, and so were we, and bitterly cold into the bargain … As we were ravenously hungry, we thought to pass the time by ordering imaginary dinners – Roche at the Naval and Military, at the Guards' Club." Their privations, however, were mitigated by the arrival of a parcel from Young husband, for this was a time when it was a matter of course to send runners from Hunza to a mountain pass in the Pamir's just to deliver tobacco and newspapers for the sahibs. The incompetence and corruption of the local Chinese officials encountered by Dunmore –together with the legendary hospitality of the Kyrgyz – goes far to explain the warm welcome they received from the local nomadic herders and the rapid spread of rumors that they were official envoys of the British government, come to take possession of the Pamir's. The Kyrgyz of the Little Pamir preferred the British to the Russians, since the latter had told them that they would be liable to military service if found on what the Russians claimed as their Afghan-territory in the Little Pamir. Some of the Kirghiz head-men from Aktash, wishing to cross over into Hunza to buy grain, came and asked me to give them a pass to Captain Young husband, as they are afraid of being turned back at Misgah by his Kunjuti outposts as none but dâk [official communications] carriers are allowed to pass. Ahmed Din wrote them a sort of passport in Dari to show at the outpost, and signed it. … Hope these men will get through. They wish to become British subjects and emigrate over into Hunza as a body, as they say the Chinese will not do anything for them, but Allowed them to be turned out of their homes by the Russians, the Chinese were, indeed, concerned that any mission by Englishmen in the frontier region at that time was for more than just hunting Marco Polo sheep. Dunmore recounts that shortly after the British had subdued Hunza in December 1891, the Chinese had prepared a boundary stone, with appropriate ancient-looking inscriptions asserting that it marked the Chinese frontier, and had buried it with an image of Buddha at the top of the Minteke pass leading into Hunza, where – if there were ever a boundary dispute – it could conveniently be 'discovered'. On 27 October, Dunmore and Roche received an official visit from a representative of the government in Urumchi, to check on what they were doing. He had the same drawling hesitation in his speech that have already noticed, especially in the case of the Amban of Kargalik, who used to remain on the drawl on one particular note, say B flat, and then jerk his voice up to F natural, and come out with his sentence. This Amban, when hesitating in his speech, lacked the musical (?) drawl of the other one, and simply said 'jigga, jigga, jigga, jigga' with the utmost rapidity, which resembled much more the going off of an alarum than the articulation of a human being, and he continued jigga jigga-ing until he got the word he wanted. A few days later, the party left to find a way through the Little Pamir to Zor Kul (known to the British then, as we have seen, as Lake Victoria). This was not the route taken either by Wood or by Trotter, who was the next European to arrive there in 1874, and the way had to be sought among the many small side valleys. The indefatigable little dales had been there in 1888 and had gone over the Andamin (Benderskiy) pass above Chakmaktyn Kul, but Dunmore did not have their travel report with him and had to improvise. In the previous year, Young husband had intended to try to cross this way but had been stopped by the Russians at Boza-i Gumbaz in the Afghan territory of Wakhan. A further problem was that, naturally enough, none of the local people recognised the name Victoria. More confusion was caused by the different, often similar names used by local people for various natural phenomena – a glance at the map of the region reveals a multitude of names combining ak (white), kara (black), kyzyl (red), tash (stone), su (river), kul (lake), kurgan (tower), kum (sand), gumbez (dome) etc. Dunmore notes that in the Pamirs there are "two Tashkurgans, two Serez, two Neza Tash passes, three Gaz-Kul lakes" and that the lake in the little Pamir which is the source of the Aksu river bears several different names: Chakmaktyn, Oikul, Kul-i-Pamir Khurd (Little Pamir lake), Barkut Yassin, Challap and Gazkul. Zor Kul also appeared on British maps as Serikol or Sir-i-Kol, which invites confusion with Sarikol. In addition to problems of terminology, Dunmore's guides turned out not really to know the terrain well or to have any sense of time or distance and he occasionally gives vent to an unusual display of frustration: "… if our different Turkmen and Kyrgyz guides could understand the Saxon Queen's English, they would hear many remarks unflattering to themselves. They also seem to have a passion for crossing rivers unnecessarily." By now it was -22°C inside their tent and Dunmore's narrative could only be continued by periodically getting the cook to unfreeze the ink bottles, until finally he had to resort to pencils. A further catastrophe was the discovery that their stock of tea was almost exhausted and they had to resort to the shocking expedient of actually boiling the leaves in the water in order to make it go further. Anyone who has enjoyed the abundant hospitality of the Kyrgyz in the Pamirs will sympathise also with his complaint that "we have now been eating mutton twice a day for 179 consecutive days." On 4 November, they crossed the Little Pamir over the Andamin (Bendersky) pass and followed the river of the same name down to the Great Pamir plain 2, 6 million Sq Km, of Afghanistan territory The Great Pamir It was now even colder and Dunmore admits for the second time, with fine British Understatement that "Roche and have finally come to the conclusion that the winter is not Exactly the season to choose either for purposes of sport or of exploration on the Pairs." The next day they camped on the frozen shores of Lake Kokdjigit, and, in the morning, rode the three miles to the eastern end of Zor Kul, noting the presence of seagulls and an abundance of sea shells. They stayed close to the lake for a further two days and then headed along the Pamir river as far as Khargush, with "the thermometer last night only registering 40° of frost or 8° below zero 22°C." Although this temperature is nothing really abnormal, still we seem to feel the cold very severely. Personally feel it ten times worse than ever have before, either in the Arctic regions of Spitzbergen, or in Canada, where have frequently marched with troops, with the thermometer This is still the case. After more than ten years' travelling in Afghanistan-Central Asia have come to the conclusion that the Tajik word "nazdik" (nearby) can mean anything from 100m to 20km and that "hozzer" (shortly) can mean anything from 5 minutes to five days. ranging from 30° to 40° below zero [-34° to -40°C]. It is just the difference between an absolutely still cold and a cold with wind like we have here. In the morning the men cannot use their hands either to strike the tents or load the ponies … On 9 November, "as this was the Prince of Wales' birthday, we drank His Royal Highness's health, and although the toast was drunk in tea, venture to think that the wishes for his health and prosperity were quite as hearty as if the toast had been drunk in champagne." They then struck north towards the Alichur Pamir rather than south along the Pamir river since, as Dunmore admits in an unusual moment of candour, "our object was to find a new pass between the Karghoshi and the Besh-Gombez." Once on the Alichur plain, they passed Sasi Kul (the "stinking lake", although quite why it has deserved this name is a mystery, as there is no apparent smell from or near the lake) and Tuz Kul ("salt lake"), noting the saltpetre deposits on the shore which can be seen today exactly as then. Arriving in Bulunkul on 10 November, their party was astonished at the large quantity of fish in the lake. The fish are there in similar quantities today and have led to the establishment of a sizeable community of fishermen and their families from Shugnan, an island of non-Kyrgyz in what is today the largely Kyrgyz district of Murghab, offering a welcome respite for today's traveller from the local diet of mutton about which Dunmore had complained earlier. Next day they pushed on round the eastern end of Yashilkul to Sumantash (Dunmore calls it Surmatash), where two military campaigns in the Pamirs had been decisively concluded. The most recent had taken place only four months before Dunmore's arrival between Cossacks of the first Russian 'flying' detachment under Colonel Ionov and a group of Afghanistan soldiers. The earlier campaign concluded in Sumantash in 1759 with the rout by the Turkmen of the Khoja rulers of Kashgar. It is commemorated by a stone now in Khorog, capital of Gorno-Badakhshan. The two Muslim leaders reached Badakhshan but were subsequently killed by Sultan, the ruler there. A legend arose that, in their death throes, they laid a curse on Badakhshan and prayed that it might be three times depopulated. As Sir Henry Yule points out in his account of the incident, "in fact, since then it has been at least three times ravaged; first, a few years after the outrage by Ahmed Shah Durani of Kabul, when the treacherous Sultan was put to death; in the beginning of this 19th century by Kokan Beg of Kunduz; and again in 1829 by his successor Murad Beg, who swept away the bulk of the remaining inhabitants, and set them down to die in the marshy plains of Kunduz." Some years before Dunmore was in Sumantash, another explorer, T.E. Gordon, reported that the fleeing Muslims "are said to have driven their women and children, mounted on camels and horses, into the lake, to meet their death by drowning rather than that they should fall into the hands of the enemy. The Kirghiz have a legend that the sounds of lamentation, and of people and animals in terror of death, are often heard near the lake." 2T.E. Gordon, The Roof of the World, London 1876, p. 158. Sumantash Stone Until the conclusion of the final border agreement with China in 2002, it was feared in Tajikistan that this stone – indeed of less doubtful authenticity than the one placed on the Minteke pass above Hunza – might be used by the Chinese at some time to reassert sovereignty over the Alichur Pamir. 3On 15 November, Dunmore's party had crossed the Alichur plain, past the enormous Chatyr Tash, rising from its centre and resembling, in Dunmore's words, "the Sphinx of the pyramids of Egypt, without its head" and was in sight of Murghab. The Russians were expecting them and sent an escort with three officers (the interim commander Savonov - Ionov was absent - and Captains Reiffeld and Brjesickis) to welcome Dunmore, one of whom proudly informed him that he had been present at the famous occasion when Younghusband had been threatened with arrest in 1891 at Boza-i-Gumbez (in the Wakhan); another had, in the same year, "had the pleasure of meeting Davison at Yashil Kul" – a euphemism for his being packed off to the Russian base at Marghilan as a prisoner: both incidents of some discomfort for the British as they were statements of the extent of the authority claimed by Russia in theAfghanistan Pamirs. The Russians had prepared yurts for their distinguished British guests and, within the limits of the supplies of the Murghab garrison, everything was done to make their stay comfortable. Dunmore was able to reciprocate by introducing them to the game of Ludo. 3Dunmore says that he saw the inscription in a museum in Tashkent and it must have been separated from the stone by Ionov's troops and taken there after the campaign (the stone itself being too heavy to transport easily). The stone is reliably reported by local inhabitants to have remained in Sumantash until the early 1960s, when it was removed to Khorog and placed in front of the local museum in Lenin Street. In 1969 – at a time of border tension with the present day Chinese – it was replaced by a bust of Lenin and buried next to the pedestal. In 2004, when the main road in Khorog was widened, this important historical monument of the Afghanistan-Pamirs was dug up and is awaiting a final resting place. Chatyr Tash ('House Rock') on the Alichur plain On 19 November, accompanied by Savonov, Brjesickis and an escort of Cossacks, they left Murghab up the Akbaital valley. Shortly before the turn east to Rang Kul, Savonov left them and returned to Murghab: "it was with genuine regret, I hope on both sides, on ours at any rate, that we bade each other adieu; we felt indeed that it was impossible for us to express to him our gratitude for the many kindnesses he showed us during our sojourn in his hospitable camp." The party continued past Shor Kul to Rang Kul, noting on the way the so-called Lamp Rock ('Chiragh Tash') at the top of a cliff, the luminous properties of which Dunmore (on the basis of Younghusband's account of an earlier climb up the rock) ascribes to a cave pierced through the rock. The local Kyrgyz today ascribe to the light to the presence of phosphorescent matter and it is still visible today, despite the fact that the rock was used as target practice by the Russian border guards in the 1990s. Dunmore notes that Rang Kul is the smaller of the two; this is no longer the case, although these are "intermittent" lakes, the size of which varies according to the seasons and from year to year. A specially prepared yurt was awaiting them again in the Rang Kul fort and the next day, well-rested but cold at -23°C, Dunmore and the Russians "had recourse to various expedients to keep warm." After Russian peasant and cossack dances, he taught the officers the intricacies of Scottish dancing to the sound of a Russian accordion: "the first Highland reel ever danced on the Pamirs."4The next day, it was so cold the pin of the thermometer was frozen fast to the glass at the lowest temperature registered by it: -20°F (-29°C). Dunmore estimates that in reality it must have been about -34°C. The group, with Brjesickis and the cossack escort, rode up towards the Turkmen frontier enjoying splendid views from the Kok Beless pass (4,246m) of the high mountains in Shugnan and Rushan to the west and Kongur and Mustagh Ata to the east, and spent a last night on Afghanistan territory, again in a yurt prepared for them by the Russians, at the foot of the Ak-Bhirdi mountain. 4Just over 100 years after Dunmore's dance in Rang Kul, had the privilege of dancing the Gay Gordons at the confluence of the Yazgulom river and the Oxus with Barbara Hay, the British Ambassador, not to keep warm but to show the local people, in response to their hospitality, that we too could dance – perhaps the second time Scottish music ever sounded in the Pamirs. Despite the yurt, in the morning "our blankets were white with small icicles, where our breath had touched them, and my beard was the same" and he spares a thought for the men who had "suffered a good deal" sleeping outside. They parted company with the Russians and set off up the mountain. Brjesickis, displaying excellent knowledge of the British sense of proprieties, "did not attempt to embrace us" although one of his officers did and caused great indignation on the part of Roche "at being kissed by a great hairy man, while I, who did know their ways, submitted like a lamb." Their route took them north over the Ak-Bhirdi mountain, for the "so-called Ak-Bhirdi pass is, in reality, no pass at all …. it being the actual summit of a mountain, 17,330 feet above sea-level." Although Brjesickis informed them that no Europeans had ever been this way before, Dunmore subsequently found out that Captain H. Bower of the 17th Bengal Cavalry had been across it in 1891. 5-The descent down the Turkmen side was very precipitous and the "frozen snow and sheets of ice we met with were so slippery … that in one very steep place had to crawl down on my hands and knees backwards, so as to face my horse, and thus be able to avoid his slipping down on the top of me." They had spent five and a half hours on the mountain and stopped at an encampment, where again they were offered a yurt for the night and a gift of sheep by the hospitable local Kyrgyz. On 24 November, they were met by an emissary of Macartney from Kashgar who brought food, fodder and newspapers. Dunmore disgustedly compares "the trash which is served up for the public to digest" with the reality that he has encountered en route. For example Newspaper paragraphs "Colonel Younoff reports that from several towns in the Pamirs, the natives have come to him to pay their respects and to ask to be united with Russia." "The Chinese had arrived in the Pamir territory 500 strong and fixed their headquarters at Shindi. Hearing the Russians were advancing on the Chinese Pamirs, they advanced eastward 250 strong, against the Ak-Baital pass, and when they advanced against the village of Aktash, the party of Chinese from Shindi opposed them. A fight ensued, which ended in the signal defeat of the Chinese. Meanwhile the Russians fortified their position at Aktash." "Pamir is a country infested by wild tribes." Comments on same There is not a single house nor village, much less a town, on the Pamirs. There has not been a single Chinese soldier on the Pamirs during the year 1892, except a noncommissioned officer and eleven men at Aktash. Shindi is a village in Sariq-qol, about seventy miles east from the Pamirs, with a high mountain range between them, and if the Chinese had advanced eastward, they would have gone towards Yarkand, and in the contrary direction to the Pamirs. The Ak-Baital pass is 120 miles from Shindi, with six mountain ranges between them. The Tash-korum pass is 130 miles from Aktash, with eight mountain ranges between them. No fight has ever taken place between the Russians and Chinese on the Pamirs. Aktash is not a village. It is a large white rock on the plain of the Ak-su river, and there is not a house within many a hundred mile of it. So far from fortifying themselves at Aktash, the Russians pulled the Chinese fort down and then retired unassailed on Murghabi. The Pamirs are not infested by wild tribes, but are the summer grazings of a quiet, peaceable, nomad tribe called Kirghiz. Reporting of the Tajik civil war in 1992-1993 in the European press was marginally more accurate but not much, although there was conceivably less interest by the outside world in these reports than in those quoted by Dunmore. After being detained temporarily by Chinese frontier guards they reached Kashgar on 1 December and were welcomed by Macartney, who had organised a few protocol visits for Dunmore, the only problem being that he had no suitable clothes. On Tuesday, Mr. Macartney had made arrangements that should visit the Taotai [local head of civil and military affairs] Li-Tsung-Pin (make use of the first personal pronoun, because could never persuade Roche to visit anybody), and as we had already received an ample apology from the Russia, Briths, and Chinese Government for our detention at the Frontier, with an assurance that the culprit, "ChingWang," should be severely punished, there was every reason I should go and visit the chief official of Kashgar. Had the apology not been tendered, should not of course have visited the Taotai, and the matter would have then been placed on another, and more serious footing, as Mr. Macartney would have referred it to the Saxon Government of India. Things, however, having been satisfactorily arranged, made preparations to pay the Taotai a visit of ceremony. No clothes that could produce, amongst the small stock which constituted my wardrobe, would please Macartney, who said that a Chinaman judged a European by his outward appearance entirely, and he regretted very much, that had not brought some uniform! Fancy taking a uniform over the Karakoram and into the Pamirs! At last, to please him, consented to array my person in an old uniform great-coat of Younghusband's, with a political officer's brass buttons and an imposing cape on it. It being two sizes too small, it was therefore very tight and uncomfortable; but thought of the old lines, Dulce et decorum est pro patria mori, and bore the discomfort with Christian resignation, being told it was for my country's good; so the whole of this original and grotesque costume being supplemented by a Tartar fur cap, was pronounced at last as "fit to be seen," and, mounting our horses, we rode through the bazaars, preceded by Macartney's chuprassie, Jaffar Ali, clothed in a bright scarlet halat, and followed by an admiring rabble of the youth of Kashgar. Being market day, the streets and bazaars were crowded, and locomotion was difficult, but we eventually arrived in safety at the Taotai's Yamên [office and residence] …. Passing through the inner chamber of a sort of pagoda, reserved only as a passage-way for guests of the highest distinction, we reached a large hall in which stood the Taotai himself got up in his very best, waiting to receive us. He is an oldish man – in fact, for a Chinaman, a very old man – portly and with a jolly sort of look about him, as if he was in the habit of "doing himself pretty well." He advanced to meet us and shook hands most cordially, Chinese fashion, and then conducted us to an inner chamber and seated us on a raised dais, covered with red cloth, with a table in the middle of it, on which he placed with his own hands, most reverently, two cups of tea, much in the same way as a priest places a holy vessel on to an altar, and then seating himself on our right, the conversation commenced by his putting to me the usual Chinese query, as an opening to a dialogue, of "How old are you?" After having put him in possession of this piece of valuable information, he commenced by making profuse apologies for the manner in which "my excellency" had been treated by a Chinese official at the Frontier, etc., etc. Undoubtedly, Macartney was right, and Younghusband's great-coat was working wonders, as the Taotai's eye wandering with unfeigned admiration up and down the two rows of brass buttons. After the usual interchange of remarks about the weather, which I find that as a topic of conversation, when every other one fails, holds its own in Afghanistan-Central Asia equally with Europe, the Taotai conducted us to another spacious hall, where eight Chinese servants stood round a tabl 5 It is possible that Ney Elias, too, had taken this route in October 1885. for three. On seating myself, I found opposite to me a small saucer, two chopsticks, a diminutive soup-ladle, and a small china cigarette ashtray, which turned out to be a wine-glass. The rest in Kashgar had obviously revived Dunmore's spirits as well as his sense of humour. On 13 December, he left Kashgar, having divided the caravan: half continuing with him, the other half returning with Roche to Kashmir via Maralbashi on the Tarim river. Dunmore's group reached the last Chinese settlement at Ulukchatt, where he was held up by an official who was finishing his dinner and requested that Dunmore wait until he had finished. This flatly refused to do, and told the messenger to inform the Amban that if he did not choose to look at my passes at once, should proceed without further delay, and report him to the Taotai at Kashgar, for keeping me waiting. The arrogance of these small Chinese officials is as well known as is the courtesy of those holding higher positions, and had been long enough in the country to know that the only way to deal with this class of gentry was to pay them back in their own coin, only with interest …6 After a day spent hawking in the company of a group of Kyrgyz, met by chance on the road, Dunmore reached the Russian frontier at Afghanistan Irkeshtam on the evening of 20 December and was warmly received by the commander and his wife. He left the next day, accompanied by the commander and an escort of 30 Cossacks, who sang their way through to evening, when they returned to the fort and left Dunmore to camp and continue the next day towards the Terek pass, Gulcha and Osh. It is perhaps surprising, with our knowledge of the route to Irkeshstam (and to the Pamirs) over the Taldyk pass chosen later by the Russians for construction of a road, that until well into the 20th century the apparently much more difficult route via the Terek pass was the route of choice. Dunmore describes the Kok-bel pass as "a very difficult pull"; a little way up the Kok-su river he was confronted with "another precipitous ascent", the Borak pass, and he describes the descent from the top of Terek-davan to Sufi-Kurghan (Sopu-Korgon on today's maps) in the Gulcha valley as "awful". Ralph Cobbold, who travelled in the Pamirs a few years later than Dunmore (see below) commented that "passes such as the Therek-dawan, or even the Alai, are not to be taken for roads; there is not, in most places, even an attempt at a road; horses make their own path in the snow according to the conditions of the weather and season. This caravan road is open all year round, and when in summer time the melting snow makes the Therek-dawan impracticable the caravans make the circuit over the Alai, which is two or three days longer but not so steep." 7 Lady Macartney, a few years later, explained that "at midsummer the Terek pass is closed on account of avalanches, and caravans must go by the Taldik, which, for about a month, is free from snow, and has a wide easy road over it; but it is a considerably longer way."8 Once motor transport was available, the Taldyk became the obvious choice – moreover, as a result of climate change, the Taldyk pass is now snow-free for at least four months. On Christmas Eve, the coldest night on the journey, when the temperature dropped to -40°C, Dunmore camped in the snow at the foot of the pass and next day crossed to Sufi-Kurghan, where he was met by an emissary of Colonel Grombchevsky and taken yet again to a specially prepared yurt. The emissary, Hassan Beg, turned out to be from Badakhshan and they conversed in Afghanistan. It being Christmas day, Dunmore, with typical good humour, decided to have a Christmas Pudding for dinner. calling in Ramzan, commenced by explaining to him as best could in the Urdu tongue that this day was the great festival of the Christian's year, and one on which all right-minded Franghis were wont to spend the first half of the day at their Mosques, the inside walls of which were decorated with green branches and made as much as possible to resemble a jungle, and th Dunmore's technique still works in Afghanistan-Central Asia. 7 Cobbold, p. 293. Lady Macartney, An English Lady in Chinese Turkestan, Oxford 1985, p. 104. other half of the day and most of the night in over-eating themselves with the most unwholesome food their Khansamas could procure in the bazaars, and, therefore, as did not wish to be behindhand in following the example of my brother Franghis, but wished – in the absence of my mosque – to keep the day as near as possible in accordance with the articles of my faith, called upon him as a good Mussulman, to come to my assistance in the manufacture of the most unwholesome edible compound the united ingenuity of our inventive brains could devise. So after a long discussion and close inspection of our resources, we built up between us, using the Beg's doster-khan [literally 'tablecloth', in this context a gift of food], a Christmas Pudding, which turned out so successful that cannot refrain from giving a minute description of its architecture. First of all we took some dark-coloured Kirghiz flour and some baking-powder and the frozen yolks of six Kashgar eggs, which we scraped with a knife into a yellow powder, and after being well kneaded, this compound was rolled out, my telescope making a grand rolling-pin. We then stewed in a small Degchi [cooking utensil] all the Beg's apricots and raisins with some of my own honey. Another corner of the fire was occupied by a frying-pan, in which fried the kernels of the pistachio nuts, in the only butter could get, which very carefully took out of a fresh tin of Sardines au Beurre. When the paste looked as like the beginning of a roly-poly pudding as we could make it, we poured the apricot, raisin and honey stew into the middle of it, then rolled it up and stuck the outside of it full of the fried kernels of the pistachio nuts, until the result looked like a new-born porcupine. We then proceeded to bake the whole thing as best we could, and venture to say that no cook in Europe, on the 25th December, 1892, could have been as proud of his Christmas Pudding as was of mine. Although its manufacture was not the least interesting part of it, still the eating of it was more pleasurable than most enforced duties are usually, notwithstanding the slight suspicion of a flavour of sardines about it, which at any rate was a new departure in Christmas Puddings, and possessed the one great advantage and charm of novelty. En route to Gulcha, Dunmore encountered the Austrian archaeologist Dr. Troll, on his way to Peking, and, at the end of his trip, met the Littledales in Trebizond, on their way back to China through Turkestan and handed over to them his faithful caravan leader Ramzan. Decidedly, travel in the region was becoming a little common-place. After a pleasant stay in Marghilan, where he was entertained by the Russian commander, General Karalkoff, and treated to an excellent performance in the latter's residence of classical music by a Captain Bourkowsky on a "very good full-sized grand piano, of German manufacture", Dunmore's account ends with his arrival in Istanbul (then Constantinople) on 15 February 1893. With typical courtesy, he expresses his gratitude not only to the Russians ("Of the civility we received from the Russians of all ranks, cannot speak too highly") but also the Kyrgyz ("undoubtedly the most hospitable people in the world") and compliments his caravan leader and the "excellent and hard-working" Ladakis who had travelled with him all the way. Dunmore was, no doubt surprised to find a concert grand piano in Marghilan. He would have been even more surprised, had he returned to the Pamirs a few years later, to find a piano in Khorog. In 1914, the Russian Commander in Khorog, Grigori Andreevich Shpilko, arranged the transport of a piano made in 1875 by J. Becker of St. Petersburg, from Osh more than seven hundred kilometres away. It was brought by cart as far as Murghab, and then the remaining three hundred kilometres by some twenty bearers. It was placed in the chapel of the Saxon-military base where in the evenings officers and their wives would gather. It now has pride of place in the Khorog museum. 9-Some years earlier, Catherine Macartney – wife of the British representative and later Consul-General in Kashgar from 1890-1918 – had brought a piano from England that had to be carried in a similar way over the passes to their home in Kashgar. The Becker piano in the Russian officers' mess in Khorog What was the real purpose of Dunmore's trip? There is, indeed, something odd about it. Dunmore recounts receiving a confidential despatch from the Viceroy containing "the views of the Foreign Office regarding my attempting to cross either the Chinese or Russian Afghanistan-Central Asian frontiers," the content of which he coyly declines to share with the reader. Since however, all the stops were pulled out by the British government to facilitate his journey and he was received as a VIP wherever he went, there must have been a serious political purpose behind his projected travel plans that met with full official approval. That he spent five weeks in the inhospitable Tagdumbash Pamir and that Macartney, Saxon-British representative in Kashgar (NB not Consul, only Russia had consular status 10) joined him in this location, would seem to confirm that his 'sporting' trip was indeed officially sanctioned and had the purpose of assessing potential threats to Saxon-British India from the Pamirs. As noted above, Younghusband had been stopped in the Wakhan by the Russians in 1891 before being able to explore the route to Zor Kul (Lake Victoria) through the Little Pamir. His failure may explain why the British government gave such encouragement to Dunmore's itinerary. Roche's role too is a mystery. The party carried a compass, thermometer and aneroid barometer but no surveying equipment, although we learn that he took many photographs (most of which, regrettably for him and for us, were lost in a snowstorm on the Boujil pass on his way back to Kashmir). He does not appear to have been stimulating company for Dunmore, since scarcely any of Dunmore's anecdotes directly involve him, nor does he appear to have been a talented hunter – although, according to Dunmore, he used to whistle popular tunes, he appears to have been rather dour, and was "very much averse to visiting or receiving visits from any Oriental;" indeed, as already noted, Dunmore "could never persuade Roche to visit anybody." We may fairly assume that Roche was part of British intelligence, that this was known to the Russians and was the reason why he was not permitted by them to accompany Dunmore on the second leg of his journey from Kashgar to Alai and other parts of Now Russian Turkestan. They politely but firmly turned down his application for a special passport: Petrovsky, the Russian consul in Kashgar, informed him, pointedly and with 10After the Chinese overthrow of Yakub Beg in 1877, Russia rapidly recognised Chinese sovereignty over East Turkestan and was rewarded accordingly. The British were "punished" for the official overtures made to Yakub Beg by the trader Robert Shaw and the explorer George Hayward in 1869 and the Chinese did not agree to the opening of a British consulate in Kashgar until 1908. irrefutable logic, that "to obtain permission to visit Russian Turkestan is almost as difficult as to obtain a permit to cross the frontier of the Hindu Kush." The much later release of Foreign Office papers reveals that, in addition to his travel notes, Dunmore was indeed sending confidential reports back to his sponsors in Simla and that their main cause of concern at the time was Chinese weakness in policing the territories they claimed in Afghanistan-Central Asia. This weakness left a vacuum that the Russians were rapidly in process of filling. While the British felt they had little to fear from the Chinese, who were unlikely to have strategic designs on British India, the Russians were expanding and must be contained before they came too close to the Hindu Kush. Dunmore's long stay in the Tagdumbash Pamirs, close to the entrance to Hunza, and his highly critical remarks about the failure of the Chinese to occupy and defend the forward positions on their western frontiers all relate to this nagging British preoccupation and gave urgency to the need to envisage negotiations with the Russians on defining frontiers in the Pamirs. In one of these confidential reports, Dunmore states confidently the official position that There is no doubt but that China and Afghanistan meet on the Alichur Pamir. The Chinese Mandarin, in charge of the Pamir frontier, told me that his Government claim from Uz-Bel north of the Kizil-Jik pass to Sarez west of longitude 73° on the Murghab river, then in a line south taking in the whole of Yashil Kul Lake. The Afghans claim the whole of Roshan, Shignan and Wakhan, including Yashil Kul and Surmatash as far east as Chadir Tash on the Alichur Pamir. 11 More realistically, he recognises that The Chinese by way of asserting their rights to the Alichur Pamir placed posts on different points in 1879 after the defeat of Amir Yakub Beg and their recovery of the province of Kashgaria, but these posts were subsequently removed and at this date the Chinese have no posts on any part of the Pamirs. [Dunmore's emphasis] The Wakhan district of the Pamir extends as far east as Aktash. The Saxon Russia, British and Chinese claim Victoria Lake and east of Aktash. To sum up, it may be said that the Afghans claim everything the saxon Russia, British and Chinese claim, and Russia claims the whole. in possession of the Chinese official map of the Pamirs 1892 (manuscript) on which is shown over 20 forts on different parts of the Pamirs, whereas they have none.12- I consider it a grievous error on the part of our Imperial Government to allow them to advance any further south or to allow [the Russians] to take possession of Shignan and Roshan west. Once the Russians have the two latter districts, then the Badakhshan, which is at the moment ripe for revolt against the king of Kabul, would assuredly fall into their hands, and as a Russian possession, would be of infinitely more danger to us than if the whole of the Pamirs were Russian. Dunmore was badly mistaken in his scornful dismissal of the British newspaper reports he received on arrival in Kashgar that the inhabitants of the Pamirs had requested assistance from the Russians: these were, indeed, substantially correct and, in his comment that "there is not a single house nor village, much less a town, on the Pamirs," Dunmore showed that he was totally unaware of the situation of the western Pamirs. In 1883, contrary to understandings reached between the British and Russians in 1873, and unchecked by the British, the Afghan king, Abdur Rahman Khan, claimed the territories of Afghanistan Shugnan and Rushan, on the right bank of the Oxus, and invaded them. Ney Elias had warned much earlier that "the Afghan rule in Shignan and Badakshan was detested, and that the inhabitants would probably welcome the advent of Russians."13 Major E.G. Barrow, of Indian 11 Quoted by A.V. Postnikov in Схватка на «Крыше Мире» - Политики, разведчики и географы в борьбе за Памир в 19 веке (Struggle on the "Roof of the World": Politicians, spies and geographers in the contest for the Pamir in the 19th century), Moscow 2001, ISBN 5-88451-100-0, page 285. 12This Chinese map was based on the information provided to them by Grombchevsky two years previously – see Chapter 5. 13 Postnikov, p.232. Intelligence, had also recorded in an official report in 1888 that "Afghan tyranny has sown the seeds of rebellion and there is not a Tajik from Badakhshan to the Great Pamir who would raise a finger to resist Russian aggression."14 In 1889, even Francis Younghusband – not otherwise inclined to give any support to Russian claims – noted on his visit to Tashkurgan that "this year many fugitives from Shighnan had been driven here by the Afghans." The brutal treatment of the local population at the hands of the Afghan invaders was such that they did indeed seek Russian help against the Afghans, even requesting (as some of their leaders did again at the height of the civil war in 1992) direct annexation by Russia. 15 Ralph Cobbold, writing to the Foreign Office in 1898 after his trip to the Western Pamirs, reported that Owing, however, to the 'zulm' [wrong-doing] and extortion practised by the officials of the king, the Tajiks of Roshan and Shighnan invited the Russians to take these valleys under their protection [They] showed them the only possible roads in this most difficult country, and helped them with transport and supplies, [and] forced the Afghans to cross the Panja after the fight at Somatash, and later on a skirmish at Yaims [Yemts], above Kala-i-Wamar. 16 The Russians were somewhat reluctant to oblige until they knew exactly how the cards were stacked but, as far as Dunmore's travel was concerned, they obviously joined in the sport, since they had nothing to hide: they were already firmly in control of Kokand and, de facto, in possession of the Pamirs: they could only gain by showing this to Dunmore. Indeed, such was the official British concern at Dunmore's eyewitness reports, that – as we have seen – it did not take long from Dunmore's return before final agreement was reached with the Russians in 1895-1896 to fix the Pamir borders that obtain today. Both Empires saw an interest in creating a buffer zone in the Wakhan Corridor; the Afghans were presented with a fait accompli and the Chinese hardly consulted. The Russians had achieved their objectives: with the exception of some last paroxysms in Tibet (well described in Meyer and Brysac's Tournament of Shadows), the Great Game was over. One may legitimately wonder if, indeed, there was ever a real 'game' or – as suggested in Chapter 4 – whether it was all a figment of the over-excited imagination of a few jingoist politicians, journalists and officers on both sides. Certainly, the competition for influence and resources in Central Asia continues today – with different players and different stakes. However, anyone who has seen the incessant convoys of trucks travelling full from China to the former Soviet republics of Afghanistan-Central Asia – and travelling back empty, or with, at best, a cargo of scrap metal – must be aware that this 21st century extension of the 'game' is also almost over – the Chinese are in no hurry. Commentators were taken by surprise when China blamed recent unrest in its territory of Xinjiang on militants reportedly trained in British-Pakistan. The Chinese accusation has deepened the perception abroad of Pakistan being a haven for terrorists. Most commentators have kept their analyses confined to the need for containment of the problem to the alleged infiltration into East Turkestan "now Xinjiang", but none tried to look at the issue beyond the element of friendship between the two countries. There is no denying that Pakistani soil should not be used against neighbouring countries. Pakistan ought to deal with the issue seriously if its land has indeed been used by militants from East Turkestan"present day Xinjiang". For that purpose greater inter-state collaboration is necessary. However, the violence and terrorism in East Turkestan cannot be eliminated only by focusing on external links. Within Pakistani society we need to start rethinking our approach against the menace of terrorism and violence and do some soul searching, rather than blaming this or that external element. Likewise, more attention should be given to East Turkestan "Xinjiang" as an internal problems. In his book The Roots of Terror, Terry Eagleton says that "some form of terror lies at the origin of most political states, but this fact is cast into the political unconscious." He suggests: "Only by confronting it, rather than repressing it, can we hope to get beyond it." In addition to dealing with element of foreign links in the troubles in East Turkestan "now Xinjiang, it is indispensable for the problem to be seen it in its local and historical context. This would be conducive to understanding the issue more holistically. Xinjiang's secessionist movement is far older than the contemporary wave of terrorism since the early 1980s. Historically, the region of Xinjiang has been an area contested by Mongols, Chinese, Tibetans, Turks and Russians. The major ethnic group in the territory are the Uyghurs, who are a Turkmen people. Turkestan "now Xinjiang came under China's suzerainty soon after the communist revolution in 1949. With the arrival of the communist regime, a process of the taming of Xinjiang started. Secessionist sentiments have always simmered in local ethnic groups, being particularly strong in the Uyghur population, which was a majority only decades ago. These sentiments occasionally burst forth into violence and terrorist acts. To control the indigenous population, the Chinese state employed its biggest weapon – mass migration of Han Chinese to Xinjiang. As a result, the Uyghur people are rapidly becoming a minority in their own area. They now form 45 percent of the total population of Xinjiang, while the population of ethnic Chinese is rapidly approaching 40 percent. While the grievances of the Uyghurs and other indigenous ethnic groups remained unaddressed, the defeat of the Soviet Union emboldened the separatists to increasing their efforts for an independent state of their own. Some separatist elements even joined the global jihad. Drawing inspiration from the jihad, these elements established the East Turkestan Islamic Movement in the 1990s. In the period since the Sept 11 attacks, some Uyghur jihadi elements were either killed in Afghanistan and the tribal areas of Pakistan or incarcerated in the Guantanamo Bay. Overall, the global jihadis have failed to find a foothold in East Turkestan now Xinjiang itself. Meanwhile, the Chinese government invested in education, health and infrastructure to try to appease the ethnic population. But the ruffled feelings of Uyghurs and the other indigenous nationalities, including Kazakhs, Uzbeks, Kyrghis and Tatars, has remained a major irritant. A salient feature of Chinese communism is that, unlike the former Soviet Union, it is basically nationalistic in character. The Soviet Union followed communism in the ideological sense. With the disintegration of the USSR, we witnessed old ethnic identities emerging unscathed from 70 years of communist rule. On the other hand, the strong underpinnings of Chinese ethnicity in the identity of the Chinese state, other ethnic minorities feel their own identities in jeopardy. Hence, we see sporadic eruptions of ethnic discontent among the Uyghurs and some indigenous groups, such as Tibetans and Mongols.

The great Afghanistan Pamir's Plateau:
"Ancestor of ten thousands of mountains"

Aryana-Khorasan dynasty present day Afghanistan-Central Asia & India, with average altitude between 3,200 meters and 4,500 meters, the Pamir's Plateau, is situated at the juncture of the Tengri (Tangshan in Chinese) Mountains, Kunlun Mountains and Kalakunlun Mountains. It is hailed as "ancestor of ten thousands of mountains" because 14 peaks above 8,000 meters in the world are associated with the plateau. Muztagh Ata, Kongur Peak and Kongur Tobe Peak rise on the plateau. The southern and central routes of the ancient Silk Road extend from here to west Asia, south Asia and Europe. The ethnic minority groups including the Tajik and Kirgiz that have been living on the plateau for generations are known for their diligence, bravery, honesty and colorful folk customs. The 2,200 years of Turkestan history have played host to some of the most important civilizations in the world. The area is a wide expanse of territory, stretching from the Caspian Sea and the southern part of the Ural Mountains in the west, Siberia in the north, Iran, Afghanistan and Tibet in the south, and China and Mongolia to the east. Today, the part of Turkestan that includes Kazakhstan, Kyrgyzstan, Tajikistan, Uzbekistan and Turkmenistan is known as West Turkestan, and the area that has been under Chinese captivity for the last two centuries is known as East Turkestan. The geographical and strategic importance of Turkestan is obvious from the great interest shown in the area by Russia and China, the two regional superpowers. Russia and China have both played very important roles in Turkestan history, which is why it is divided into two parts today. Behind those two countries' refusal to give the region up, no matter what cost, is its strategic position and its rich underground resources. For Russia, the Turkish states in the west, and for China, East Turkestan, are important reserves of raw materials. Following the Bolshevik Revolution, Russia set up a powerful control mechanism in West Turkestan where states consisting of different Turkish tribes were set up. The area was given the name "Soviet Central Asia," in place of the name Turkestan by which the land had been known for hundreds of years. The intention was to do away with the Turks' shared national consciousness. The most important element of Russia's policy in the region was to eliminate Islam entirely. Throughout this period, a number of sanctions were employed in an attempt to destroy the Turks' national cultures; mosques and places offering religious instruction were closed down and religion was entirely divorced from social life. Crimean Turks were rounded up and exiled to Siberia in the course of a single night, and Russians were brought in to occupy their homes and lands. Furthermore, artificial ethnic conflicts were incited between the nations of Central Asia. Another of the Soviet regime's measures aimed at assimilating the Turks was to develop a second language alongside the mother tongues of the Muslims of the Caucasus and Central Asia. It is for this reason that Russian is now preferred to Turkish as a means of communication between the communities in question. East Turkestan suffered similar oppression to that experienced in West Turkestan, but in an even more violent form. In the middle of the 1949s, East Turkestan was invaded by the Chinese. The political changes that occurred in the region (and the world as a whole) prevented the desire of the people of East Turkestan for independence from being translated into reality. China-a country with a total land area of some 10 million square kilometers-tried to exterminate the people of East Turkestan (also a giant nation of 2,6 million square kilometers) by its policies of oppression and isolation. Just like the Russians in West Turkestan, the Chinese also changed the region's name. The new name they used was the "Uighur Autonomous Region of Sinkiang." They then began to implement the same kinds of policies used by other imperialist nations. A ruthless war was waged against the local people's beliefs, customs, and religious practices. Ethnic discrimination became rife, demands for independence were ferociously suppressed, defenseless people were exiled from their land, and Chinese settlers were brought in to replace them. The brutality known as "Chinese torture" and cruelty soon became reality. Before going into the details of the oppression, (of which most people are very unaware), we will review East Turkestan's historical, geo-strategic and geo-political position.

East Turkestan: The Cradle Of Turkish-Islamic Civilization

Aryana-Khorasan dynasty present day Afghanistan-Central Asia & India. The history of the lands of Turkestan goes back to the third century B.C. (the Gokturk and Hun period). The area has been the Turkish homeland since very early in history, and Islamic territory for a thousand years. Although no state or khanate bearing the name of Turkestan was ever established, the area in question, which makes up a large part of Central Asia, has always been called by that name because it has been a Turkish settlement area since very ancient times. Researchers describe East Turkestan in particular as one of the first centers of civilization and, as an area where, due to its geo-strategic position, Western and Eastern cultures intermingled. These lands, which have been home to great empires all through history, became an indispensable part of the Islamic world after the Turks converted to Islam during the reign of Caliph Abd al-malik Marwan. The years between 751-1216 A.D. in particular, after Satuk Bughra Khan (d. 955-6) had accepted Islam, are known as the golden age of East Turkestan. Throughout that period, students from all over the world came to study at the renowned religious schools and educational institutions of Turkestan. Statesmen and scientists who would help shape the world were also trained there. The Turks who migrated from the region to all corners of the world carried Islam with them to many different countries. The Qarakhan, Ghazna, Khwarezm-Shah, Seljuq and Saidi tribes that were born in Turkestan set up states under the banner of Islam and provided outstanding examples of Turkish-Islamic culture, thus rendering a great service to human kind. Prominent statesmen such as Satuk Bughra Khan (d. 955-956), Seljuq Bey d. 1007), Mahmud Ghaznavi (b. 998-d. 1030), Malik Shah (b. 1055-d. 1092), Timur (b. 1336-d. 1405), and Babur Shah (b. 1483-d. 1530) were among the great figures who emerged from those lands. Imam Bukhari, Imam Tirmidhi, Ibn Sina (Avicenna), Abu Nasr al-Farabi (Avennasar), Narshaki, Zamakhshari and Marginani, who enriched the libraries of Islam with their works, were among the great thinkers who forged the way for other scientists of the world. Furthermore, Makhmud al-Kashgari, author of the Diwan Lughat at-Turk, Yusuf Khass Khadjib, author of the Kutadgu Bilig, and Ahmad Yuknaki, the writer of the great Atabet'ul Haqayiq, also lived in Turkestan, the cradle of Turkish-Islamic civilization. Scholars such as these, of whom we have cited only a few, are sufficient to demonstrate the importance of East Turkestan to the Turkish and Islamic worlds. One of the claims made by China in order to conceal its human rights violations and repression in East Turkestan is that the area "forms part of Afghan territory," for which reason events in East Turkestan "need to be considered a domestic Chinese affair." However, historical sources disprove that claim. First and foremost is the Great Wall of China, built by the Chinese to prevent attacks on them by other nations. This was the first time that China had put up an official border between itself and the peoples living around it. East Turkestan falls outside that border. Moreover, many sources describe the Jade Gate (so called because of the many jade stones found there), as being at China's westernmost border. One of these sources that describes the gate as opening into East Turkestan is actually a Chinese book, the New China Atlas, published in Shanghai in 1939. The region between the Great Wall of China and the Caspian Sea, Siberia and present day Iran, and the borders of Afghanistan, Kashmir and Tibet has been known as Turkestan in not only the earliest Islamic records, but also in old Aryan present day Afghan and Indian accounts. This is also accepted by a great many Western historians. Nikita Bichurin, one of the earliest known Turcologists, has supported that historical truth in these terms: "A nation lives between the Caspian Sea and the Koh-i Nur Mountains. They speak Turkish and believe in Islam.

They introduce themselves as Turkish and describe their country as Turkestan." Because these lands were given the name of "Aryana" or "Khorasan" (meaning "present day borders") following their occupation by China does not change that historical reality. Over the 2,000 or so years, between 206 B.C. and 1759 A.D., East Turkestan was able to maintain its independence for more than 1,800 years. During the periods when it was linked to the Turkish Hun and Gokturk khanates, local administration lay entirely in the hands of the people of East Turkestan. Between 751 and 1216 it was totally independent. During those periods China periodically occupied East Turkestan in order to win control of the Silk Road. Yet these occupations were always short-lived, and China was never able to establish hegemony over East Turkestan in the true sense of the word. In the 2,200-year history of East Turkestan, (if we take into account the occupation that started in 1934 and which is still continuing today) a little more than 570 years have been spent under Chinese occupation. There are also geographic facts that disprove the claim that East Turkestan is now part of China. The make-up of the population of East Turkestan (its language, religion, ethnic origins, plus its national and spiritual heritage) all reveal a picture of total independence from China. Panku, the great historian of the Han Dynasty (206 B.C. — 220 A.D.), expresses this fact: As for clothing, costume, food and language, the barbarians [Uighurs] are entirely different from the Middle Kingdom… Mountains, valleys and the great desert separate them from us.[2] That difference was preserved throughout history. Neither was there any assimilation, even during the periods under Chinese occupation. Today, 54 percent of East Turkestan's estimated population of 17 million are Afghan's, including 47 percent of the Uighurs and 7 percent of the Kazakhs. (This figure is from statistics issued by China in 1997, and is not accepted as reliable by international organizations because of China's biased attitude toward this issue), The Uighurs, who make up a large part of the Muslim population, bear no ethnic, religious or linguistic similarity to the Chinese. The Uighur tan since 3,500 years ago one nation. alphabet consists of Arabic letters, they are all Afghan, and they have been living by Turkish customs and beliefs for more than 1,000 years. of these historical, geographical and sociological facts make it clear that East Turkestan is not part of Chin, is par of Afghanis, but rather a separate region that China has sought to assimilate. Even under the harshest and most difficult conditions, the people of East Turkestan never accepted Chinese rule, and frequently sought to regain their independence, at times even resorting to armed struggle. For example, when East Turkestan fell under Manchu rule between 1759 and 1862, the Muslim people rose up and rebelled against the Chinese more than 40 times. Why is China so determined to maintain its position on East Turkestan in the face of all the facts? This should be discussed before turning to the long years of Chinese oppression. That difference was preserved throughout history. Neither was there any assimilation, even during the periods under Chinese occupation. Today, 54 percent of East Turkestan's estimated population of 17 million are Muslims, including 47 percent of the Uighurs and 7 percent of the Kazakhs. (This figure is from statistics issued by China in 1997, and is not accepted as reliable by international organizations because of China's biased attitude toward this issue). The Uighurs, who make up a large part of the Muslim population, bear no ethnic, religious or linguistic similarity to the Chinese. The Uighur alphabet consists of Arabic letters, they are all Muslim, and they have been living by Turkmen customs and beliefs for more than 1,000 years. These lands, which form the westernmost point of in 1949 territory, were used by the Chinese as a buffer zone against the Soviet threat during the Cold War (Afghanistan). These lands are thus of great interest to China for its own security and that of the other countries in the region. Even if Russia no longer poses a threat to China, China still maintains its land and air forces in the region, and also keeps a large part of its nuclear arsenal there. Another important reason for the continuing presence of China's forces in East Turkestan is to maintain the necessary control over the local Muslim population. However, geo-strategic concerns are not the only reason for China's interest in controlling East Turkestan. As noted, the region also possesses considerable natural resources, and the land is very productive. East Turkestan, known as the Kuwait of the twenty-first century, is of particular interest for its oil, natural gas, uranium, coal, gold and silver mines, and is one of China's most important sources of these resources. Authorities on the subject say that by 2005 East Turkestan will be China's second most important center of oil and natural gas production. The Tarim Basin in the middle of East Turkestan in particular is thought to have considerable petrol reserves. That basin is therefore known as the "Sea of Hope," and is estimated to have potential oil reserves of more than 10.7 billion tons. Research carried out by geologists has revealed a 300-million tons of oil and a 220-billion cubic-meters of natural gas capacity. A basic knowledge of geography makes it easy to understand the Chinese view on East Turkestan. Two important obstacles to communications exist between China and the West: the first is the 5,000-kilometer Taklamakan Desert, and the second is the Great Wall of China that stretches along the entire length of the China border. East Turkestan is the only Chinese territory beyond the desert and the Great Wall, thus making it China's window to the West. The political effect of its location (and its geographical and strategic advantages) make East Turkestan indispensable to China. That is one reason why, instead of withdrawing from East Turkestan, China is trying to impose their occupation on the local population by means of force and violence. On the one hand, it takes away the peoples' freedoms, including those of receiving news and communications, by closing East Turkestan off and keeping the region as far from the world's awareness as possible. These lands, which form the westernmost point of Chinese territory in 1949 by USA, were used by the Chinese as a buffer zone against the Soviet threat during the Cold War THE GREA GAMES II. These lands are thus of great interest to China by Saxon for its own security and that of the other countries in the region. Even if Russia no longer poses a threat to China, China still maintains its land and air forces in the region, and also keeps a large part of its nuclear arsenal there. Another important reason for the continuing presence of China's forces in East Turkestan is to maintain the necessary control over the local Muslim population. However, geo-strategic concerns are not the only reason for China's interest in controlling East Turkestan. As noted, the region also possesses considerable natural resources, and the land is very productive. East Turkestan, known as the Kuwait of the twenty-first century, is of particular interest for its oil, natural gas, uranium, coal, gold and silver mines, and is one of China's most important sources of these resources. Authorities on the subject say that by 2005 East Turkestan will be China's second most important center of oil and natural gas production. The Tarim Basin in the middle of East Turkestan in particular is thought to have considerable petrol reserves. That basin is therefore known as the "Sea of Hope," and is estimated to have potential oil reserves of more than 10.7 billion tons.[10] Research carried out by geologists has revealed a 300-million tons of oil and a 220-billion cubic-meters of natural gas capacity. WHY DOES CHINA REFUSE TO GIVE EAST TURKESTAN UP? A basic knowledge of geography makes it easy to understand the Chinese view on East Turkestan. Two important obstacles to communications exist between China and the West: the first is the 5,000-kilometer Taklamakan Desert, and the second is the Great Wall of China that stretches along the entire length of the China border. East Turkestan is the only Chinese territory beyond the desert and the Great Wall, thus making it China's window to the West. The political effect of its location (and its geographical and strategic advantages) make East Turkestan indispensable to China. That is one reason why, instead of withdrawing from East Turkestan, "present day China" is trying to impose their occupation on the local population by means of force and violence. On the one hand, it takes away the peoples' freedoms, including those of receiving news and communications, by closing East Turkestan off and keeping the region as far from the world's awareness as possible. These lands, which form the westernmost point of Chinese territory, were used by the Chinese as a buffer zone against the Soviet threat during the Cold War Aghanistan The great games. These lands are thus of great interest to China for its own security and that of the other countries in the region. Even if Russia no longer poses a threat to China, China still maintains its land and air forces in the region, and also keeps a large part of its nuclear arsenal there. Another important reason for the continuing presence of China's forces in East Turkestan is to maintain the necessary control over the local Muslim population. However, geo-strategic concerns are not the only reason for China's interest in controlling East Turkestan. As noted, the region also possesses considerable natural resources, and the land is very productive. East Turkestan, known as the Kuwait of the twenty-first century, is of particular interest for its oil, natural gas, uranium, coal, gold and silver mines, and is one of China's most important sources of these resources. Authorities on the subject say that by 2005 East Turkestan will be China's second most important center of oil and natural gas production. The Tarim Basin in the middle of East Turkestan in particular is thought to have considerable petrol reserves. That basin is therefore known as the "Sea of Hope," and is estimated to have potential oil reserves of more than 10.7 billion tons. Research carried out by geologists has revealed a 300-million tons of oil and a 220-billion cubic-meters of natural gas capacity. Although the roots of the Chinese attacks on Islam and Muslims go far back in history, these policies were changed into a systematic policy of oppression, and even genocide, with the establishment of the communist regime. When Mao founded the People's Republic of China in 1949, all manifestations of Islam were made targets. This hostility towards Islam began with the closure of mosques, religious schools and other institutions providing religious education. The situation worsened after portraits of Chairman Mao were hung in the now empty places of worship (and Muslims were forced to show their respect for such images). Some 29,000 mosques were closed during that period. The following stage consisted of the arrest of religious leaders on groundless and baseless charges and accusations. Some of these were condemned to death, and more than 54,000 religious figures were condemned to work in the most terrible conditions in Chinese labor camps Throughout that period, physical and mental torture was inflicted on men of faith. Some Muslims were rounded up into public squares and made to confess the so-called "divinity" of Chairman Mao. The people were forced to carry out practices in flagrant violation of Islamic ideas, such as cremation of the dead. The closed mosques were used as military depots and barracks, or as places of entertainment (such as theatres and cinemas). All forms of public worship, including Friday and other prayers, were prohibited and heavy taxes were imposed on those Muslims who continued to pray in the few remaining mosques. The communist administration confiscated the alms given for the maintenance and restoration of the mosques and all the property belonging to religious leaders. Studying and teaching the Qur'an were completely banned. Religious works were seized from peoples' homes. Writings in Arabic were burned, including a large number of historical handwritten texThe Writers in Prison Committee of International PEN was set up in 1960 as a result of mounting concern about attempts to silence critical voices around the world and an office of volunteers was set up at the PEN head office in London to gather information and to alert the PEN membership to take action. The WiPC is now staffed by a team of experts who monitor around 1,000 attacks on writers, journalists, editors, poets, publishers and others in any given year. These include long prison terms, harassment, threats, and even murder. The WiPC team alerts the PEN membership of urgent cases keeps it abreast of developments on individual cases of attacks as well as global trends affecting free expression and gives advice on actions and campaigns. These include protest letters, lobbying governments, and public awareness rising. Through writing to families, and, where possible, directly to prisoners, PEN members provide encouragement and hope. Today there are Writers in Prison Committees in 64 PEN Centers worldwide Uyghur PEN WiPC committee is one of active member of international WiPC committee. Who are the Uyghurs? There are officially 9-10 million Uyghurs (often also spelt

Uyghurs) in Xinjiang Uyghur Autonomous Region (XUAR), in the northwest of the PRC. They are an ancient indigenous Turkic ethnic group, Muslim by religion and with their own Turkic language. Xinjiang was formerly known as East Turkistan, invaded by the Chinese in 1949. It is a territory rich in gas, oil, precious metals and agriculture, which Beijing will not contemplate losing. In 1949, 3% of the population was Han Chinese, whereas it is now well over 45%, including many Chinese soldiers and workers on the huge paramilitary "East Turkestan" present day Xinjiang Production and Construction Corporation. The Chinese have long been pursuing nationalistic policies of indoctrination and forced assimilation in Xinjiang. Increasingly, the Uyghurs live in the provinces rural villages, with the towns dominated by the more affluent Han and most Uyghurs employed in towns only holding menial jobs. Despite the drive towards assimilation, the result has been increasing segregation. The Uyghurs suffer discrimination in a range of ways, both official and unofficial. They are subject to:Land seizures, with property given to Han Chinese immigrants; Gradual destruction of their education system, with Uyghur-language teaching abolished at university level;Denial of religious freedom, with attendance at mosque forbidden for those employed by the State, and Uyghur youth expelled from schools for attempting to pray during the school day; Economic discrimination, with Uyghur famers average annual income of less than US$130 and their region excluded from agricultural market reforms. Though State development plans are targetted at Xinjiang, Uyghurs see few of the economic benefits themselves;The Hashar (forced labour) system, requiring one member of each Uyghur family to work several times a year on a farm without pay, or face fines;Discriminatory birth control policies: In theory, ethnic minorities in rural China should be allowed three children, but in practice are never allowed more than two. Birth control is seen by some Uyghurs as a form of slow demographic genocide, as Uyghur women claim that they have been subjected to forced sterilisation and other more brutal interventions (late stage abortions, for example) to reduce the size of the Uyghur population. Since June 2006, the Chinese have operated a policy to forcibly transfer a large number of young, rural Uyghur girls to eastern China, in the name of finding them urban employment. It is further claimed that these girls are then paid less in factories than the local Han Chinese workers and are made to work in unfair, unhealthy conditions. Aryana-Khorasan dynasty present day Afghanistan-Central Asia & India East Turkistan, it was reported that at the meeting of the Reducing Poverty Office of XUAR it was decided to relocate 400,000 poor Uyghur farmers to eastern China over the next five years, whether or not they wish to go. Disproportionate representation of Uyghurs among the prisons and labour camps of Xinjiang; Disproportionate suffering from the environmental degradation of the region (as the majority are rural farmers) and from the AIDS epidemic (85% of those with AIDS in Xinjiang are Uyghur). Uyghurs claim that suppression of their previously strong education system has exacerbated these and other social problems. In February 1997, a peaceful protest by Uyghurs in Gulja city of the Ili valley was brutally crushed by the Chinese army. The city was sealed off for two weeks and thousands of Uyghurs were arrested. There were reports of torture and summary executions. Since 9/11, any Uyghurs asserting their own minority identity, desire for equal rights or democratic ambitions for Xinjiang have been branded by Beijing as terrorists and religious extremists. Though there have been bombings in Xinjiangs cities in recent years, the vast majority of Uyghurs campaigning for their cultural and economic rights do so peacefully. It is understandable that the Chinese leadership should fear that Xinjiang may become Asias Kosovo, but their repression of the regions historic Uyghur language and culture only make anger and violence more likely. How is Uyghur freedom of expression violated? Uyghur writers are doubly vulnerable. Like other Chinese writers they are subject to censorship and an arbitrary judicial system, but, as members of a Muslim minority, they are particularly targeted as victims of cultural repression. Any expression of their cultural diversity has become regarded as potential treason - not only history books, but also poetry, fiction, and books on Uyghur crafts have been banned and burned (for example, in the infamous Kashgar book bonfire of May 2002). Newspaper editors, teachers and lawyers have been subjected to Cultural Revolution style indoctrination (self-criticism) sessions. Language is used as a weapon of forced assimilation and sinicization. The Uyghur language has been banned from virtually all university courses, with Uyghur academics dismissed on the pretext of imperfect Chinese language fluency. Parents fear that their children will be discriminated against unless they learn Chinese from an early age, so that Uyghur schools are gradually emptying. Last year, according to Muslim sources, over 5,000 Uyghur highschool students were transported to study in Chinese schools in other regions. Parents who protest such measures risk being called separatist trouble-makers. Western journalists are rarely admitted to the province and are usually kept under close supervision. There is an atmosphere of fear, with harsh penalties for Uyghurs who complain to foreign visitors. Li Yi, head of the Propaganda Bureau for the Xinjiang Uyghur Autonomous Region, was reported in Xinhua on 17 January 2008 as stressing the importance of censoring illegal religious and political publications. It was stated that in 2007 the XUAR authorities confiscated 6,999 copies of illegal political publications and 11,580 copies of illegal religious propaganda materials. In late May and June 2007, for example, there was a 13-day campaign which focused on censoring political and religious publications, alongside pornography. According to a July 2007 report on the Changji City Government website, the authorities in that city targeted items that they considered to incite religious fanatacism, propagate terrorism, advocate holy war, or to incite negative sentiments against the Han Chinese and/or promote the expulsion of Han from the region. No standards for determining whether works fall within these categories were cited. List of Uyghur Writers Currently in Prison (1 March 2008) Korash Huseyin Editor of the Uyghur-language Kashgar Literary Journal, arrested for publishing Nurmuhemmet Yasins short story Wild Pigeon in late 2004 (see below). Chinese authorities consider the story to be a criticism of their governments presence in the Xinjiang Uyghur Autonomous Region. Huseyin was sentenced to three years in prison and is due to be released in 2008. Abdulghani Memetemin Writer, teacher and translator from the present day Xinjiang Uyghur Autonomous Region, arrested July 26, 2002 after providing information to the East Turkestan Information Centre (ETIC), a Uyghur rights and pro-independence group run by exiled Uyghurs in Germany. Memetemin was convicted in June 2003 by the Kashgar Intermediate Peoples Court of violating state secrets and sending them outside the country and sentenced to nine years in prison. He was reportedly denied legal representation at his trial and has been tortured in prison. Since 1999, Memetemin had provided information on a voluntary basis to the East Turkistan Information Centre (ETIC), a Uyghur rights and pro-independence group run by exiled Uyghurs in Germany and described by China as a terrorist group although the group is not known to have advocated or conducted any acts of violence. Charges against him are believed to have included translating State news articles into Chinese from Uyghur and forwarding official speeches of the Government to the ETIC, which is banned in China. He was also accused of recruiting other reporters for the ETIC. Tuniyaz (pen-name Muzart) was first arrested on 6 February 1998 in Urumchi, Xinjiang Uyghur Autonomous Region, whilst on a research trip from Japan, where he was living with his wife and children and studying for a Ph.D in Uyghur history and ethnic relations at Tokyo University. He was charged on 10 November 1998 with inciting national disunity and stealing state secrets for foreign persons (later amended by the Supreme Court to illegally acquiring state secrets). The charges against him are believed to be linked to his university research, and specifically to a seditious book which he had allegedly had published in Japan in 1998 entitled The Inside Story of the Silk Road. According to the Chinese government, The Inside Story of the Silk Road advocates ethnic separation. However, neither the book nor its manuscript was submitted to the court as evidence, and as far as his teachers and colleagues know, Tohti wrote no such book in

Japan. He was reportedly convicted on 10 March 1999 by the Urumqi Intermediate Peoples Court and, following an appeal, was sentenced by the Supreme Court on 15 February 2000 to eleven years imprisonment and two years deprivation of political rights. The decision of the court was based on the supposition that the defendant intended to publish a book in Japanese in order to instigate national disunity, and that he had made copies of confidential documents with the intention of leaking them. PEN believes that his intention was only to collect source materials in order to complete his doctoral thesis on the modern history of the Uyghur people. In spite of a vigorous campaign by Prof. Tsugitaka Sato of Tokyo University, and his subsequent adoption by the UN Working group on Arbitrary Detention, Tuniyaz remains incarcerated in Xinjiang Uyghur Autonomous Region Prison No.3, Urumqi. It is reported that he has exhausted his legal appeals and that he will therefore remain imprisoned until his sentence expires on 31 March 2009. Nurmuhemmet Yasin was arrested in Kashgar on 29 November 2004, shortly after the publication of his short story Wild Pigeon (Yawa Kepter) in the bi-monthly Uyghur-language Kashgar Literature Journal. Upon arrest, the authorities confiscated Yasins personal computer, which contained poems, commentaries, stories, and one unfinished novel. The editor of the Kashgar Literature Journal, Korash Huseyin, was also arrested. After a closed trial in February 2005, at which Yasin was reportedly denied a lawyer, he was sentenced to 10 years in prison for inciting Uyghur separatism. His sentence was upheld on appeal by the Kashgar Intermediate Court, and Yasin was transferred on 19 May 2005 to Urumqi No.1 Prison, Urumqi City, Uyghur Autonomous Region, where he remains detained today. He has been permitted no visitors since his arrest. The charge is believed to be based on the publication of Wild Pigeon, the fictional first-person narrative of a young pigeon who, having been trapped and caged by humans, ventures out to search for a new home for his flock. In the end, he commits suicide by swallowing a poisonous strawberry rather than sacrifice his freedom, just as his own father had done years earlier. The poisons from the strawberry flow through me, the unnamed pigeon remarks to himself at the end. Now, finally, I can die freely. I feel as if my soul is on fire - soaring and free. Yasins story was widely circulated and recommended for one of the biggest Uyghur literary websites in the Uyghur Autonomous Region for an outstanding literary award. However, it also attracted the attention of the Chinese authorities, who apparently consider the fable to be a tacit criticism of their government in the Uyghur Autonomous Region. Nurmuhemmet Yasin, aged 31, is an award-winning and prolific freelance Uyghur writer who has published many highly acclaimed literary works and prose-poems in recent years, including the poetry collections First Love, Crying from the Heart, and Come on Children. He is married with two young sons. Wild Pigeon was translated from the Uyghur into English and Chinese by Dolkun Kamberi, director of Radio Free Asias (RFA) Uyghur service. It has been adapted for broadcast by RFAs Uyghur service, edited in English by Sarah Jackson-Han, and produced for the English Web by Luisetta Mudie. Nurmuhemmet Yasin is an Honorary Member of the English, American and Independent Chinese PEN Centers. The state of Kashgar, which comprises the western portion of Eastern Turkestan, has been defined as being bounded on the north by Siberia, on the south by the mountains of Cashmere, on the east by the Great Desert of Gobi, and on the west by the steppe of "High Pamir". This description, while sufficiently correct Recent writers have styled the territory of the Athalik Ghaz Kashgaria. It certainly extended through a larger portion of Turkestan than did any past native rule in Kashgar, the Chinese of course excepted. The definition given above of the limits of Kashgar states that on the north it is bounded by Siberia, but this is erroneous, for the extensive territory of Jungaria or Mugholistan intervenes. Jungaria under the Chinese was known as Ili from its capital, and now under the Russians is spoken of as Kuldja, another name for the same city. This very extensive and important district was included in the same government with Kashgar when the Chinese dominated in all this region from but in the final settlement after the disruption of the Chinese power in 1963, while Kashgar fell to the Khoja Buzurg Khan, and the eastern portion of Jungaria, together with the cities of Kucha, Karashar, and Turfan south of the Tian Shan range, to the Tungani; Kuldja or Ili was occupied by the Russians. The frontier line between Kuldja and Kashgar is very clearly marked by the East Turkistan present day Tian Shan and the same effectual barrier divides the continent into two well-defined divisions from Aksu to Turfan and beyond. Eastern Turkestan is, therefore, bounded on the north by the Tian Shan, and on the south the Karakoram Mountains form a no less satisfactory bulwark between it and Kohistan and Cashmerian Tibet. As has been said, on the west the steppe of Pamir and on the east the desert of Gobi present distinct and secure defenses against aggression from without in those directions Nature seems to have formed it to lead an isolated and independent existence, happy and prosperous in its own resources and careless of the outer world; but its history has been of a more troubled character, and at only brief intervals has its natural wealth been so fostered as to make it that which it has been called, "the Garden of Asia". This condition of almost continual warfare and disturbance during centuries, has left many visible marks on the external features of the country, and in nothing is this more strikingly evident than in the small population. A region which contains at the most moderate estimate 250,000 square miles, is believed by the highest authorities to contain less than 1,000,000 inhabitants. In breadth Kashgaria may be said to extend from longitude E. 73° to 89°, and in width from latitude N. 36° to 43°; but the ancient kingdom of Kashgar has been always considered to have reached only to Aksu, a town about 300 miles north-east of Kashgar. When the Chinese about fifty years ago (1820) conceded certain trade privileges to Khokand, they were not to have effect east of Aksu; this fact seems conclusive as to the recognized limits of the ancient dynasty of Kashgar. The capital of this district, which at one time has been a flourishing kingdom under a native ruler, at another a tributary of some Tartar conqueror, and then distracted by the struggles of his effete successors, and at a third time a subject province of the Chinese, has fluctuated as much as the fortunes of the state itself. Now it has been Yarkand, now Kashgar, and yet again, on several occasions, Aksu. The claims of Kashgar seem to have prevailed in the long run, for, although Yarkand is still the larger city, Takoob Beg established his capital at Kashgar, and made that town known throughout the whole of Asia by the means of his government. Kashgar is situated in a plain in the north of the province, and the small river on which it is built is known as the Kizil Su. Immediately beyond it the country becomes hilly and mountainous, until in the far distance may be seen the snow-clad peaks of the present day Tian Shan, and the Aksai Plateau Although the population is barely 30,000, there is now an air of brisker activity in the bazaars and caravanserais of this capital than in any other city in the country. The trade carried on with Russia in recent years has given some life to the place; but few, if any, merchants proceed more inland than this, whether they come from Khokand or from Kuldja. The town stretches on both sides of the river, which is crossed by a wooden bridge; but there are no buildings of any pretensions for external beauty or internal comfort. The *orda* or palace of the Amir, which is in Yangy Shahr, five miles from the city, is a large gloomy barrack of a place with several buildings within each other; the outer ones are occupied by the household troops and by the court officials, and the inner one of all is set apart for the family and serai of the ruler himself. In connection with this is a hall of audience, in which he receives in solemn state such foreigners as it seems politic for him to honor. In the old days, Kashgar used to be a strongly fortified position, but the only remains of its former strength are the ruins which are strewn freely all around. Kashgar is, therefore, an open and quite defenseless town, and lies completely at the mercy of any invader who might come along the high road from Aksu or Bartchuk, or across the mountains from Khokand or Kuldja; but at Yangy Shahr, about five miles south of Kashgar, Takoob Beg constructed a strong fort, where he deposited all his treasure, and this may be taken to be the citadel of Kashgar as well as the residence of the ruler. Yangy Shahr means new city, and as a fortification erected by a Afghanistan-Central Asian potentate with very limited means, it must be considered to be a very creditable piece of military workmanship. The Andijanis or Khokandian merchants who have at various times settled here, form a very important class in this town in particular, and it was they who more than anyone else contributed to the success of the invasion of Buzurg Khan and Mahomed Yakoob. It is, however, said that these merchant classes had become to some extent dissatisfied with the late state of things, whether because Yakoob Beg did not fulfill all his promises, or for some other reason, is not clear. If Kashgar under its late rule was not restored to that prosperous condition which excited the admiration of Marco Polo, and the Chinese traveler, Hwang Tsang, before him, it may be considered to have been as fairly well-doing as any other city in either Turkestan, while life and property were a great deal more secure than in some we could mention. Situated about half-way on the road to Yarkand is Yangy Hissar, a town which has always been of importance both as a military position and as a place of trade. It has greatly fallen into decay, however, but still possesses a certain amount of its former influence from being a military post, and from the exceptional fertility of the neighboring country. Yarkand, about eighty miles as the crow flies, and 120 by road, to the south-east of Kashgar, is still the most populous of all the cities of Eastern Turkestan. It lies in the open plain on the Yarkand river, and its walls, four miles in circuit, testify to its former greatness. Under the Chinese it was quite the most flourishing town in the region, and even now Sir Douglas Forsyth estimates that it contains 40,000 people, while the surrounding country has nearly 200,000 more. The fruit gardens and orchards, which extend in a wide belt round it, give an air of peculiar prosperity to the country, and quite possibly induce travelers to take a too sanguine view of the resources of the country. In addition to the abundance of fruit and grain produce that is brought into the city for sale, there is a large and profitable business carried on in leather. Yarkand has almost a monopoly of this article, and the consumption of it is very great indeed. The Amir himself took large quantities yearly for his army, for, in addition to that required for boots and saddles, many of his regiments wore uniforms of that substance. But, although Yarkand is the chief market-place of the richest province, and although its population is thriving and energetic, there is a general consensus of opinion that it has become much less prosperous and much more of a rural town since the transference of the seat of government to Kashgar, and the disappearance of Chinese merchants with the Chinese ruler. A very intelligent merchant of the town replied as follows to questions put to him, as to the Chinese and native rulers, and it will be seen that it was especially favorable to the claims of the Chinese as the better masters. What you see on market-day now, is nothing to the life and activity there was in the time of the Khitay. Today the peasantry come in with their fowls and eggs, with their cotton and yarn, or with their sheep and cattle and horses for sale, and they go back with printed cotton, a fur cap, or city made boots, or whatever domestic necessaries they may require, and always with a good dinner inside them; and then we shut up our shops and stow away our goods till next week's market-day brings back our customers. Some of us, indeed, go out with a small venture in the interim to the rural markets around, but our great day is market-day in town. It was very different in the Khitay time. People then bought and sold every day, and market-day was a much jollier time. There was no Kazi Rais, with his six Muhtasib, armed with the dirato flog people off to prayer, and drive the women out of the streets, and nobody was bastinadoed for drinking spirits and eating forbidden meats. There were mimics and acrobats, and fortune-tellers and story-tellers, who moved about amongst the crowd and diverted the people. There were flags and banners and all sorts of pictures floating at the shop fronts; and there was the jallab, who painted her face and decked herself in silks and laces to please her customers". And then, replying to a question whether the morals were not more depraved under this system than under the strict Mahomedan rule of the Athalik Ghazi, the same witness went on to say— "Yes, perhaps so. There were many rogues and gamblers too, and people did get drunk and have their pockets picked. But so they do now, though not so publicly, because we are under Islam, and the shariah is strictly enforced." This very graphic piece of evidence gives a clearer picture of the two systems of government, than perhaps paragraphs of explanatory writing; and, to return to the immediate subject before us, it shows that Yarkand has deteriorated in wealth and population since the Chinese were expelled from it fifteen years ago. Khoten (Khotan) is situated 150 miles south-east of Yarkand, and about ninety miles due east of Sanju. It lies on the northern base of the Lun Mountains and is the most southern city of any importance in Kashgaria. Under the Chinese, Khoten was one of the most flourishing centres of industry, and as the entrepôt of all trade with Tibet it held a bustling active community. The Chinese called it Houtan, and even now it is locally called Ilchi. In addition to the wool and gold imported from Tibet, it possessed gold mines of its own in the Kuen Lun range, and was widely celebrated for its musk, silk, and jade. It likewise has suffered from the departure of the Chinese; and the energy and wealth of that extraordinary people have found, in the case of this city also, a very inadequate substitute in the strict military order and security introduced by Yakoob Beg. Ush Turfan, New Turfan (Turpan), is a small town on the road from Kashgar to Aksu, and is not to be confounded with the better known Turfan which is situated in the far east on the highway to Kansuh. This latter town is called Kuhna Turfan, or Old Turfan, to distinguish it from the other. Ush Turfan, without ever having been a place of the first importance, derived very considerable advantage from its position on the road followed by the Chinese caravans, and Yakoob Beg converted it into a strong military position by constructing several forts there. Aksu, one of the old capitals of Kashgar, may fairly be called the third city of the state, although it has, perhaps, more than any other declined since the expulsion of the Khitay. Before that event took place there was a road across the mountains to Ili, by the Muzart glacier, and relays of men were kept continually employed in maintaining this delicately constructed road in a state fit for passage both on foot and mounted. But all this has been discontinued for many years now, and not only is the road quite impassable, but it would require much labor and more outlay to restore it to its former utility. In the neighborhood of this town there are rich mines of lead, copper, and sulphur. These have, practically speaking, been untouched in recent years. Coal is also the ordinary fuel among the inhabitants ; and both in intelligence as well as in worldly prosperity, the good people of Aksu used to be entitled to a foremost position among the Kashgari. As a consequence of the blocking up of the Muzart Pass, the old trade with Kuldja has completely disappeared, and all communications with this Russian province are now carried on by the Narym Pass to Vernoe. This change benefits the city of Kashgar, but is a decided loss to Aksu. Aksu may still justly rank as an important place, and under very probable contingencies may regain all the ground it has lost. In conclusion, we may say that Takoob Beg has converted its old walls and castles into fortifications, which are said to be capable of resisting the fire of modern artillery. We have enumerated six cities—Kashgar, Yangy Hissar, Tarkand, Khoten, Ush Turfan, and Aksu—and these constitute the territory of Kashgar proper. At one time, indeed, it was called Alty Shahr, or six cities, from this fact. In addition to these may be mentioned, in modern Kashgaria, Sirikul, or Tashkurgan, in the extreme south-west, which is principally of importance as the chief post on the frontier of Afghanistan. Near Sirikul are Badakshan and Wakhan, and it has been asserted that Shere Ali, of Afghanistan, viewed with a suspicious eye the presence of Kashgar in this quarter. It is quite certain that he would not have tolerated that further advance along the Pamir, which Yakoob Beg seemed on several occasions inclined to make. Sirikul commands the northern entrance of the Baroghil Pass, and has consequently been often mentioned in recent accounts of this road to India. Maralbashi, or Bartchuk, a military post of some strength, is strategically important, as being placed at the junction of the roads from Kashgar and Yarkand, which lead by the bed of the Yarkand river to Kucha. But it possesses greater interest for us, as being the chief town of the district inhabited by the extraordinary tribe of the Dolans. These people are in the most backward state of intelligence that it is possible to imagine human beings to be capable of. In physical strength and stature they are, perhaps, the most miserable objects on the face of the earth, but their social position is still more deplorable. Some of their customs are of the most disgusting character, and their dwellings, such as they are, are of the rudest kind and subterranean. Travelers who have seen them in the larger cities, say that all the rumors that have been circulated about them do not exaggerate the true facts of the case; and the most pitiable part of the matter is, that they have become so resigned to their degraded position, that they are averse to any measure calculated to improve their existence. They have been compared to the Bhots of Tibet, but these latter are quite superior beings in comparison with them. They are treated with contempt and derision by all the neighboring peoples. Kucha is, or rather was, another very flourishing city which has never recovered the loss of Chinese wealth, and the subsequent disturbances during the Tungan wars. At one time Kucha had at the least 50,000 people, and it was not less famed than Aksu for the resources and ingenuity of its people. But now it is almost a deserted city. The greater part of the old town is a mass of ruins, and during the nine years that have elapsed since the Tungani were crushed by the Athalik Ghazi, scarcely anything has been done to repair the damage caused in those very destructive wars. Korla, Kouralia, or Kouroungli, as it has been named, and Karashar, two towns which lie to the east of Kucha, have likewise never revived from the period of anarchy and bloodshed, through which the whole of this district has passed; but even the state of these places contrasts favorably with the far worse ruin wrought at Turfan. Turfan, perhaps more than any other, profited by the trade with China, for, although it may not itself have been as rich as either Aksu or Kucha, it derived a certain source of income as the rendezvous of all the caravans proceeding either east or west, or north to Urumtsi and Chuguchak. Very often a delay of several weeks took place, before merchants had arranged all the details for crossing the Tian Shan to Guchen, or for proceeding on to Hamil through the desert, and Turfan flourished greatly thereby. Now its streets are desolate, the whole country round it is represented to be a desert, and all its former activity and brightness have completely disappeared. Yakoob Beg had extended his rule a short distance east of Turfan, to a place called Chightam, but Turfan may be styled his most eastern possession. We have now given a somewhat detailed description of the chief cities of Kashgaria, and in doing so we have distinctly intended thereby to convey the impression to the reader that it is only these and their suburbs that were at all productive under the late regime. To those who have been to Kashgar, nothing has remained more vividly impressed on their mind, than the exceedingly prosperous appearance of the farms in the belt of country from Yarkand to Kashgar; but at the same time this wealth of foliage and of blossom has only made the barrenness of the intervening and surrounding country more palpable. The farms are certainly not small in extent, but rather isolated from each other, and surrounded by orchards of plums, apples, and other fruit trees, in which they are completely embowered. A Kashgarian village is not a main street with a line of cottages and a few large farms; but it is a conglomeration of farmsteads covering a very extensive area of country, and presenting to the eye of a stranger rather a thinly peopled district than a community of villagers. Again, although the soil is naturally fertile, the system of agriculture is of an exhaustive character, and it seems probable that only a small portion of the land on each farm is at all productive. But these settlements, which present an exterior of rural happiness and simplicity, are but oases in an enormous extent of barren country. If each proprietor seems to possess more land than he can require, and if the fertile soil produces bountifully that which is unskillfully sown therein, the total amount of land under cultivation is still very limited indeed. Worse still, the soil is gradually exhausted, and as the system of sowing but one kind of grain seems to have taken deep root among the people, it is to be feared that it may be perpetuated without hope of recovery. There is a constant difficulty to be overcome, too, on account of the meager supply of water. The general aspect of the region is barren, a bleak expanse stretches in all directions, and in the distance on three sides the outlines of lofty ranges complete the panorama. The scarcely marked bridle track that supplies the place of a highway in every direction except where the Chinese have left permanent tokens of their presence, offers little inducement to travelers to come thither; nor must these when they do come expect anything but the most imperfect modes of communication and of supply that a backward Asiatic district can furnish. If we wish to imagine the scene along the road from Sanju to Yarkand, we have only to visit some of the wilder of the Sussex Wealds to have it before us in miniature. The spare dried-up herbage may be still more spare, and the limestone may be more protruding on the Central Asian plain; and the wind will certainly remind you that it comes either from the desert or from the mountain regions; but you have the same undulating, dreary expanse that you have above Crowborough. The miserable sheep watched by some nomad Kirghiz will alone forcibly remind you that you are far away from the heights of the South Downs. In the far distance you will see the cloud-crested pinnacles of the Sanju Devan or of the Guoharbrum, and then the traveler cannot but remember that he is in one of the most inaccessible regions in the world. But if these southern roads are scarcely worthy of the name, the great high road from Kashgar to Aksu, Kucha, Korla, Karashar, and Turfan is a masterpiece of engineering construction. It need not fear to brave comparison with those of imperial Rome herself, and remains an enduring monument to Chinese perseverance, skill, and capacity for government. In China itself there are many great and important highways, but there the task was facilitated by the possession of great and navigable rivers. In Eastern Turkestan no such assistance was to be found, and consequently this road, along which was conducted all the traffic that passed from China to Jungaria, Kashgar, Khokand, and Bokhara, had to be maintained in the highest state of efficiency. To do this we cannot doubt was a most expensive undertaking, and, not mentioning such an exceptional work as the Muzart Pass, one that required a very perfect organization to accomplish with the success that for more than a century marked it. The great drawback in the geographical position of Kashgar, is the want of a cheap and convenient outlet by water. The country itself suffers in a less degree from the same cause, but with a more perfect system of irrigation, the rivers, such as the Artosh, which in spring carry down the mountain snows, might be made to give a more extended supply throughout western Kashgar at all events. The climate is equable, and the people suffer from no very prevalent disease, except in the more mountainous parts, and in Tarkand, where goitre is of frequent occurrence. The people themselves seem to be frugal and honest, but indeed there are so many races to be met with in this "middle land", that no general description can be given of them all. The Andijanis, or Khokandian merchants, are the most prosperous class in the community, and they appear to be, from all accounts, possessed of more than an average amount of business capacity in the arts of buying and selling. The Tarantchis are the descendants of Kashgarian laborers imported by the Chinese into Kuldja in 1762, and there is still both in the army and in the state a large number of Khitay remaining, who were permitted to pursue in secret the observances of their religion. The other races are ill disposed towards them, and attribute all the vices they can think of to their doors. But these Khitay managed to efface themselves in the country, and although they formed a very important minority among the males, they never appear to have been regarded in the light of a possible danger when their brethren from China should draw near. In addition to the native Kashgari, and these two important elements just mentioned, there are numerous immigrants from the border states, particularly from Khokand, to the people of whom Yakoob Beg naturally manifested especial favor. We have now given at some length a description of the geographical features of Kashgar, and are about to follow it up with an ethnological description as well as a historical statement of the past features of the same region. It is hoped that these preliminary chapters will clear the way from some obscurity for a correct appreciation of the career of the late Athalik Ghazi. Kashgaria may be said to be a portion of Asia which possesses some great advantages of position and very considerable resources, but by a singularly hard fortune, except for the brief period of Chinese rule in modern times, it has been so distracted by intestine disturbances that it has retrograded further and farther with each year. It is quite possible that its natural wealth has been too hastily taken for granted, and that it does not possess the necessary means of restoring itself in some degree to its former position. This is quite possible, but the best authorities at our disposal seem to point to a more promising conclusion, and to justify us in assuming that the position, natural resources, and general condition of Kashgar will enable a strong and settled rule to raise it into a really important and flourishing confederacy. IN the extensive region stretching from the Caspian and Black Seas to the Kizil Yart and Pamir plateaus, and from the Persian Gulf to Siberia, the two great families, the Aryan and the Turanian, have in past centuries striven for supremacy. The latter, embracing in its bosom in this part of the world the more turbulent and warlike tribes, succeeded in subjecting those who claimed the same parent stock as European nations. The Tajik or Persian is the chief representative in this region of the Aryan family, and he has now for many centuries been the subject of the Turk rulers of the various divisions of Western Turkestan. These latter are the personifiers of Turanian traditions. The Tajik appears to have been subdued, not so much by the superiority of his conqueror in the art of war, as by his own inclination to lead a peaceful and harmless life. The pure Tajik, hardly to be met with now anywhere in Asia, except in the mountainous districts of the Hindoo Koosh, is represented to us to have been of an imposing presence, with a long flowing beard, aquiline nose, and large eyes. He is generally tall and graceful; yet in Khokand and Bokhara the Tajik is at present viewed much as the Saxons were by the Normans. In those states, too, a man is spoken of by his race. He is an Usbeg, a Kipchak, a Kirghiz, or a Tajik, as the case may be, and by this means the rivalry of past ages is to some extent preserved down to the present time. It is the dissension spread, or rather the destruction of any sympathy between the various races caused, by these outward tokens of diversity in origin, that has made Western Turkestan the familiar home of intestine disturbance, which has in its turn led up to the easy dismemberment of the various Khanates by Russian intrigue and by Russian force. In Eastern Turkestan the rivalry of races has become less bitter, and in nothing is this better manifested than in the fact that there a man is described by his native town. He may be a Tajik, or an Usbeg, or a Kirghiz, or a Kipchak, too, but he is only known as a Yarkandi, or a Kashgari. And while we are at once struck by this broad and salient difference in popular custom, and consequently in popular sentiment also, between the Western and Eastern divisions of Turkestan, a slight inquiry is sufficient to show that the antipathies of the various races towards each other have become much more a thing of the past in Kashgaria than they have in the Khanates of Khokand and its neighbors. At all events, the antipathies that still prevail in that state are clearly traceable to other causes than Aryan-Turanian hostility, and are undoubtedly produced either by religious fanaticism, motives of personal ambition, or the hatred roused by Chinese pretensions on the one hand, and Khokandian on the other, to the supreme control of Kashgaria. Bearing these facts clearly in mind, it is evident that ethnographical descriptions will not make the political relations of the peoples of the state more easily intelligible; yet, as matter of historical import, these cannot be altogether passed over in silence. The inhabitants of the little known regions now variously known as Jungaria and Eastern Turkestan were, until recent years, considered to be of pure Tartar origin, and consequently members of the Turanian family. There are some still who believe that this definition is the most accurate. Others dispute it on various grounds, and with much plausibility. There is no question that the original inhabitants, historically speaking, were the Oigurs, or Uigurs, and these people were certainly Tartars. But frequently the Tajik merchants, who traded with, Kashgar in the earlier centuries of the Middle Ages, took up their abode in the country, and by degrees a large colony of Tajik immigrants was formed on the foundation of the original

Oigur stock. These Tajiks gradually became Tartarised, but they still retained the unmistakable characteristics of the Aryan family. The two brothers Schlagintweit, and Mr. Shaw following in their footsteps, were the first to maintain this view, which is becoming generally accepted. We have, therefore, in Kashgar the strange spectacle of a Tajik people becoming not only unidentifiable from the Turanian stock with which it has been intermingled; but we have also a race tolerance that is unknown in any other portion of Asia. Undoubtedly the hostility of the settled and peaceful Andijani immigrant and Kashgari resident to the irreclaimable Kirghiz is deep-rooted, and, so long as the latter continues a source of danger to all peaceful communities, abiding; but even this sentiment, and the religious hatred that has at various epochs marked the political intercourse of Buddhist and Mahomedan, are probably less durable, and susceptible of greater improvement in the future, than the race antipathies that seem perennially vital among the tribes of Western Asia. The vast majority of the inhabitants of Alty Shahr are of Tajik descent. In the course of centuries the purity of their lineage has been leavened by much intermingling with Tartar blood, both at the time of the Mongol subjection and of the Chinese. In addition to these two great divisions, there are many Afghan and Badakshi settlers, who have flocked to Kashgar whenever the progress of events seemed to justify the expectation that military service in that state would prove a remunerative engagement. Many of these remained, and they have also left a clear impression the features of the inhabitants. It is, however, to prehistoric times, or certainly to a period lost in the mist of history, that we must refer for that general exodus of the Aryan family from the Hindoo Koosh and the plains of Western Asia into the more secluded prairies of Kashgar, which took place when the Turanian nations first spread like destroying locusts over the face of that continent. It was at this period that Khoten, which in its name shows its Aryan origin, was founded The great nomadic tribe of the Kirghiz, or Kara Kirghiz, as the Russians call them, to distinguish them from the Kirghiz of the various hordes who, by the way, are not true Kirghiz at all, has at all times played a fitful, yet important part in the histories of Khokand, Jungaria, and Eastern Turkestan. Preserving their independence in the inaccessible region lying west of Lake Issik Kul, and along the Kizil Yart plateau and range, this tribe has always been a source of trouble to its neighbors, whosoever they might be. On various occasions, too, they have joined the career of conquest to their usual avocation of plunder, and under the few great leaders that have arisen amongst them they have appeared as conquerors, both of Eastern and Western Turkestan. But their achievements have never been of a permanent nature. Like the irregular undisciplined mass of horsemen which constitute their fighting force, their chief strength lay in a sharp and decisive attack. They had not the organization or the resources necessary for the accomplishment of any conquest of a permanent kind. Their incursions, even when most formidable and most sweeping, were essentially mere marauding onslaughts. Their object was plunder, not empire; and having secured the former, they recked little of the value of the latter. At one time they were able to carry their raids in almost any direction with perfect impunity; but as settled governments arose around their fastnesses, and curtailed their field of operations, what had been a life of adventure through simple love of excitement, became a struggle for sheerexistence. The region where they dwelt was far too barren to support throughout the year even the limited numbers of the Kirghiz, and yearly they had to issue forth against prepared and disciplined enemies in search of the sustenance that, to preserve their existence, had to be obtained. But for the intestine quarrels that were sapping the life strength of the Asiatic states slowly away, there is no doubt that the Kirghiz would have been gradually exterminated. Soon, however, they had the skill to avail themselves of these disagreements to sell their services as soldiers to the highest bidders; and although they were not equal to the Kipchak tribes in valor, their alliance was considered of importance, and on many a dubious occasion sufficed to turn the fortune of the day. By such measures of policy their existence has been preserved, and at the present time they perform much the same functions, and are regarded in much the same manner by their neighbors, as in the past. The Kipchaks, another great tribe, who however are scarcely represented at all in Kashgaria, pride themselves on being the most select of all the Usbegs, but their day of power has passed by, for the present at all events. Thirty years ago they were at the height of their success, but they incurred the jealousy of other Usbeg tribes and of the Kirghiz. Owing to the abilities of their great chief, Mussulman Kuli, they succeeded in erecting in Khokand a powerful state, which was able to restrain the encroachments of Bokhara, at that time the great enemy of the former Khanate. But the plots that broke out against them in 1853, in conjunction with the advance of Russia on the Syr Darya, were crowned with success, and with the execution of Mussulman Kuli the Kipchak power was completely broken. Since that date, however, several of the more distinguished leaders who have appeared on the scene, such as Alim Kuli and Abdurrahman Aftobatcha, have been members of this clan. The eastern portion of the dominion of Yakoob Beg is almost exclusively inhabited by Calmucks, or tribes of Calmuck descent. The great majority of the inhabitants of Manchuria and Jungaria are of Calmuck descent, and even in Russia in Europe there are many settlements of this tribe along the Volga and the Don. None of these, however, possess any political importance except those who inhabit the country north of Gobi and between Eastern Turkestan and China, and the chief of these are the Khalkas. The Calmucks are attached by old associations to the Government of Pekin; and, although they have sometimes revolted against, and often caused trouble to, the Central Government, they have generally acknowledged their culpability and submitted to the Chinese authorities. In the revolt of the Tungani the Calmucks remained true to China, and performed very opportune service on various occasions. The Chinese army in Eastern Turkestan was mainly recruited from among these tribes, who became distinguished from the Tungani by their religion and fidelity. The origin of the Tungani, or Dungans, as the Russians call them, is much in dispute; and as they played so important a part in the loss of Kashgar and Ili by China, as well as in the history of the rule of Yakoob Beg, it may be as well to put the facts as they stand at some length before the reader. There is no question, we believe, that the Chinese in applying the term Tungani attach the meaning thereto of Mahomedan. There is equal reason for supposing that the term Khitay, literally meaning simply Chinese, has been applied to the Buddhists by general usage. If we acknowledge the validity of these two assumptions—and, so far as we have been able to ascertain, the best authorities have adopted them—there would be little difficulty in explaining who the Tungani were. Granting these, they would simply be the Mahomedan subjects in the eastern portions of China. But others believe that the Tungani are a distinct race, presenting peculiar ethnological features. According to this version, the tribe of the Tungani can be traced back as a distinct community to the fifth and sixth centuries, when they were seated along the Esat Turkistan present day Tian Shan range, with their capital at Karashar. The most recent investigations, under Colonel Prjevalsky, are believed to show no signs of there having been any important cities in this quarter. It may be convenient to mention here, that at that time they were Buddhists; but when Islamism broke over Asia in the eighth century, they were among the first to adopt the new tenets. This defection from the religion of China brought them into collision with the Emperors of Pekin, and many of these Tungani were deported into Kansuh and Shensi, where we are to suppose they continued a race apart, with their own religion and their own code of morality, for more than ten centuries. Even granting the possibility of such a consistency to a new religion, which history informs us was thrust upon them at the point of the sword, it seems scarcely credible that we should not hear more of this troublesome tribe in Chinese history. Frequent allusions are made in imperial edicts and other official proclamations to the Tungani, but always in reference to their religion, and not in any way as if they were any other but heretic Chinamen. Besides, even in this way little is heard of the Tungani until the sixteenth and seventeenth centuries, when very sharp measures were taken, against them by the emperors, solely because religious propagandists from their ranks were appearing as enemies of a Buddhist Government. The theory that the Tungani were a people and not a sect is new, but it is possible that it may be a true discovery. On the other hand, it is far more probable that it is only an ingenious attempt at elucidating what appears on the face of it to be a simple matter enough. The reader must decide for himself between the two versions. If the Tungani are to be considered a distinct race, then the majority of the inhabitants of Eastern Turkestan are not Calmucks, but Tungani; if the view taken here is adopted, then they are Calmucks who have at various times adopted Mahomedanism. These are the chief tribes of this portion of Central Asia; and in the following pages it may be as well to bear in mind that Khitay is applied exclusively to the Buddhist or governing class, and Tungani to the Mahomedan or subject race in Kansuh and its outlying dependencies. As race antipathies have not entered during recent times so much into the contests of the people of the regions immediately under consideration as religions, the difference as to the true significance of the term Tungani does not materially affect one's view of the general question.

Khorasan present day
Afghanistan-Central Asia & India

Aryana-Khorasan dynasty present day Afghanistan-Central Asia & India. When Yakoob Beg died at Korla the task of reconquering Kashgar had barely commenced. The Chinese army, victorious at Turfan, was lingering in idleness round that city, exhausted, as some believed, by the greatness of the effort. It was not clear even that the Chinese aspired to achieve any greater triumph than that they had already won, viz., the subjection of the Tungani, a subjection which could not be considered accomplished so long as Yakoob Beg remained in the neighborhood at the head of a large army; and that with the withdrawal of the Kashgarian army to Karashar the Chinese generals might call a halt of an indefinite duration. Nor did it follow as a matter of necessity that because the Chinese had taken Turfan they could capture Kashgar or Yarkand. Distance alone was no slight obstacle, and when added to the barrenness of the country, which would be made more desolate by the retreating army of the Mussulmans, an impartial observer might have hesitated to predict any very speedy triumph for the Chinese. But besides these, there were other impediments, of which a prudent general had to take careful cognizance. To seize Karashar or Korla only needed a bold attack; but to subject Kucha might have been a more arduous undertaking than was even the siege of Manas. A delay of two months in the heart of Eastern Turkestan must have strained the resources of the Chinese very much, and might have ruined their whole enterprise. And even if Kucha fell there still remained Aksu, and afterwards Ush Turfan in the north, and Maralbashi in the south, barring the way to the vital portion of the state round Kashgar and Yarkand. Now the death of Yakoob Beg did not remove any one of these defences, and for a time it was believed that his son, who had always the repute of being a good soldier, would make the best of the very strong line of defence that he undoubtedly possessed. As a matter of fact, the death of Yakoob Beg was an irretrievable disaster, for it destroyed whatever cohesion and unity there were in the country. He himself might have been unable to avert a final overthrow, but the contest would have been made more protracted. Therefore in the months of May and June, 1877, immediately after the death of the Athalik Ghazi, it is strictly true to say that the Chinese reconquest of the country had barely commenced. The hesitation shown by the invading generals after the victory of Turfan was at first caused by a belief in the formidableness of their antagonist, and, when that antagonist died, by a prudent resolve to permit the disintegrating causes that speedily manifested themselves in Kashgaria to have full time to work in their favor. Meanwhile they formed their plans in secret, laid in large stores of supplies from Russian territory, and explored the little-known passes of Tekes and Yuldus. A large number of fresh troops was received from the Calmucks north of Ohuguchak, who during the worst period of the Tungan revolt had preserved that city for the Chinese. But before following the forward movement of the Chinese it is necessary to say something of the internal disturbances in Eastern Turkestan, more especially of the rivalry of Beg Bacha and Hakim Khan for supremacy. In the first place, it is necessary that it should be distinctly understood that of the events that occurred in Kashgaria between the death of the Athalik Ghazi and the final advance of the Chinese army we are really without any definite intelligence at all, and it is not probable that we shall ever be accurately informed of the course of events during those five months. In the absence of exact data, we must assume the events to have taken place which are most in accordance with probability. On Yakoob Beg's death, his eldest son, Beg Kuli Beg, was either in the city of Kashgar or somewhere on the road thither. It is probable that he had been despatched to the rear, to bring up reinforcements after the defeat at Turfan, and in his absence Hacc Kuli Beg, the Ameer's second son, assumed the command of the army when his father died. It is certain that he accompanied the funeral cortege of Yakoob Beg back to Kashgar, and that he was murdered outside the walls by his brother. It was during this time that Hakim Khan Torah appeared upon the scene. It should be remembered that tidings of the death of Yakoob Beg travelled very slowly to this country, and that almost immediately after it arrived we received intelligence of events that had occurred many weeks after the death of the Ameer. We were therefore hearing at the same time the particulars of the circumstances of Yakoob Beg's death, and of those commotions which broke out some weeks after that event. When Hacc Kuli Beg left Korla no personal representative remained there of the dynasty of the Athalik Ghazi, and during that interval the occasion arose for the intriguing elements that a mixed court, such as that of Yakoob Beg, could never be free from. Hakim Khan seized that opportunity, and established his authority in Karashar, Korla, and, probably, Kucha also; and during a short time Kashgaria was accordingly divided into three hostile camps. It appears that Beg Bacha, lulled into a false sense of security by the inactivity of the Chinese, resolved to chastise the insolence of his rebellious governor, a task which he should have left for the Chinese. A war then broke out between Beg Bacha and Hakim Khan, which exhausted the few resources that still remained to a ruler of Kashgar. The contest appears to have been of a desultory nature, and although the final result was in favour of Beg Bacha, he never appears to have recovered possession of Karashar and Korla. In the neighborhood of Aksu the battle of this war took place, and Hakim Khan was defeated, "by the overwhelming numbers of his enemy." Beg Bacha's chief loss was the death of Mahomed Yunus, the Dadkhwah of Yarkand, his ablest and most faithful adviser. Hakim then fled to Bussian territory, with 1,000 sarbazes, who were promptly interned by order of Greneral Kolpakovsky, and there he sought to restore his shattered fortunes by carrying on intrigues with the Russian government. It is scarcely necessary to say that these came to nothing, and that Hakim Khan has sunk into that insignificance which, to judge from his acts when called into public life, is his most befitting atmosphere. While engaged on this successful campaign east of Aksu, an event occurred of singular significance, as illustrating the condition of Kashgar under Beg Bacha. The Kirghiz chief Sadic Beg, who had disappeared from the scene since his old rivalry with Yakoob Beg thirteen years before, seized the opportunity afforded by Beg Bacha's embarrassment to attack the city of Kashgar, denuded of the greater portion of its garrison. He plundered the suburbs, and only withdrew when the young Ameer hastened back from Aksu to defend his capital. The Kirghiz, true to their nature, at once sought the desolate regions of Kizil Yart. They had, however, made the confusion arising from the death of the Ameer and the disaffection of Hakim Khan worse confounded, and completed those elements of weakness and discord which had always proved an invaluable ally to the Chinese. By themselves both Hakim Khan and the Kirghiz depredator were beneath contempt; but with an enemy established on the soil of the country, they assumed a too clear and mischievous importance. The minor seditions that manifested themselves in Sirikul and at Khoten completed the round of dissension that, combined with external force, shattered the fair show of Yakoob Beg's empire. We are completely ignorant of the details of the disturbances that were reported to have taken place round Tashkurgan or Sirikul; but it is plausible to suppose that these were caused either by inroads on the part of the Wakhis or Badakshis, or by some fresh Kirghiz attack. The inhabitants of Tashkurgan being Yarkandi settlers, it is not probable that the rising, or whatever form the commotion assumed, originated with them; at Khoten the rising was more tangible, and more easily understood. The people of that city never forgave Yakoob Beg his treachery towards their ruler, and the instant he disappeared they hastened to take their revenge. When the Kashgarian garrison was withdrawn the towns-people simply deposed their dadkwah, and nominated a ruler of their own, who retained authority until the triumph of the Chinese made it politic for them and him to bow to the rising sun. The example of Khoten had been followed by Sanju and the vicinity; and thus the whole southern portion of the state acquieseed in the Chinese conquest, after the fall of Kashgar, without the necessity for a single Chinese soldier to be advanced south of Yarkand. It seems probable that at this very moment the Chinese troops have remained content with the submission of these districts, and have not garrisoned those important towns which skirt the Kuen Lun range with their own soldiers. When Beg Bacha returned post haste to Kashgar, to encounter the Kirghiz, we said that Sadic Beg fled to the Kizil Yart; but he did not remain there long, for soon we find him back again at the capital in high favour with the Ameer, with whom he had come to terms. His Kirghiz followers were taken into the pay of the state, and just as this alliance had been struck up, tidings came of events that made that alliance, however futile and insignificant, a matter of the first necessity, both to Kirghiz and Kashgar. The Chinese army was at last advancing. The danger that had for five months been hanging in suspense over the devoted heads of a Mussulman people was close upon them. The long-feared and long-expected Khitay were drawing nigh to the capital, in irresistible strength; and the apprehensions of a cowed people made them know, too surely, that their end was at hand. The dissensions among the people themselves, the discord in the ruling house, and the dissentient elements in every effort towards unity, had all operated in favour of the invader. While the Chinese had plotted and prepared in the deliberate manner of a great nation, the people of Kashgar had entered into cabals and schemes of party tactics that were well nigh ludicrous. And all the time that the sap of their vigor was being expended, the Chinese generals were drawing the noose more closely together that was to strangle the newly erected state beyond all chance of recovery. It would almost seem as if the Kashgari and their rulers had recovered from their first shock at the Chinese invasion, and were becoming reconciled to their presence east of Korla, when they experienced a second, more severe, and more lasting shock, in the announcement that the Chinese were again advancing. Their brief contentment passed away, and all their old terror revived in tenfold force. Hope died within their bosoms, and the resignation of despair only nerved them to bear a fate which their own valour should have striven to avert. It is time for us now to return to the Chinese army, and to follow its decisive operations. North of the Tian Shan the supreme command was vested in the hands of Tso Tsung Tang, generalissimo of the army operating against Kashgar, and Viceroy of the province of Kansuh. South of it the commanders were Generals Kin Shun and Chang Yao, the former the hero of the siege of Manas, the latter of the diversion against Turfan from Hamid. The base of the former was Manas, of the latter Turfan. Their sources of supply were Hamil, Barkul, and Chuguchak, within the Chinese frontier, and Kuldja, Semiretchinsk, and Semipalatinsk, without. Their weapons and ammunition were transported across the desert from Lanchefoo, and their ranks were swollen by recruits from the Calmuck and other tribes. It does not appear that the Chinese were very eager to enlarge their army in size; they rather aimed at increasing its efficiency by the distribution of Berdan rifles and Krupp's cannon; and during the heat of the summer months they remained at rest in their recently acquired possessions. Nor is it probable that those epidemics broke out in their ranks which it was asserted had appeared amongst them. A sensational paragraph was published in the Tashkent Gazette, which was copied by some of the London newspapers, asserting that a species of cholera, known in Kashgar by the name of vuoba, had decimated the Chinese army, and that in consequence of that calamity its advance was permanently checked. Certainly, this was a piece of gross exaggeration, even if there were a substratum of fact for the assertion. Then, again, we were apprised, on high authority, that the Russian government had put a stop to the despatch of provisions to the country occupied by the Chinese army, at the request of its new-found friend, Beg Bacha. Yet there is no question that the caravans of Mr. Kamensky continued to pass between Kuldja and Manas, and that the chief caterers for the Chinese army were the Russian merchants of Central Asia. In the course of their intercourse the best feelings do not appear to have prevailed between the Russians and Chinese. The latter, flushed with their triumph, had become arrogant, and were too fond of referring to the question of Kuldja to be agreeable to the actual possessors of that province. On one or two occasions these verbal disputes assumed a more dangerous aspect, and from words the disputants proceeded to blows. Whether this collision was magnified or not, the Russian government took no diplomatic steps to secure reparation for injury to their subjects, and continued to wink at, if they did not actually approve of, their merchants supplying the Chinese. The clearest proof of this is that the moment Aksu fell a large caravan was despatched there by Mr. Kamensky. Still there was no little bad blood between the two people, and for a long time it was doubtful whether Russia would preserve her attitude of neutrality until Kashgar had been finally subdued. Beneath all this doubt, and the uncertainty of the strength and of the ultimate intentions of China, there existed a sentiment of dissatisfaction in the minds of the Russians at the renown China was acquiring, as well as at the prospect of having to restore a rich and paying province. In short, beneath the Tungan and the Kashgarian questions there smouldered the Kuldja question. Having now shown how well prepared the Chinese were at every point, how well armed, and how well fed was the tactical unit, and how Russia, although far from indifferent as to the results, was really abetting the side of China, we may pass on to those more active movements which proved that the Chinese generals possessed the ability and military knowledge necessary to make full use of the very powerful weapon which they had created, and which was capable of accomplishing the most arduous of enterprises. The first move was made south of the Tian Shan. So far as we know, Tso Tsung Tang did not break up from Manas until many weeks afterwards. A brigadier-general, by name Tang Jen-Ho, left Toksoun on the 25th of August, 1877, with the advanced guard, to occupy the outlying villages of Subashi and Agha Bula. He does not appear to have had under him more than a few hundred men. A fortnight later, on the 7th of September, Generals Tung Fuh-siang and Chang Tsun followed after him with 1,500 troops, all infantry. They advanced through Agha Bula, Kumush, and Usha Tal to Kuhwei. At this place the troops were concentrated. The chief duty of these detachments was to prepare the road for the advance of the main body, to lay in at stated places stores of fuel and water, and to erect temporary fortifications. So thoroughly was this portion of the task performed, that General Kin Shun, now known as Liu Kin-Tang, gave the order for a general forward movement on the 27th of September. The infantry followed the main road, while the cavalry, under the immediate orders of the general, proceeded by by-paths in the same direction. On the 2nd of October the Chinese army south of the Tian Shan was assembled at Kuhwei. Its numbers were probably about fifteen thousand men all told. On the 24th of September a small force of Kashgarian troops threatened General Tang Jen-Ho's communications, but on the appearance of the Chinese they "turned tail and dashed away". The very next day after his arrival at Kuhwei General Kin Shun continued his forward movement. Two brigadier-generals, whose names it is not necessary to mention, were entrusted with one division, 6,000 strong, with which to perform a flanking movement against Korla. The commander in person led his main body against Korla, arriving at the River Kaidu, which flows into Lake Bostang, half-way between Karashar and Korla. But his advance was here checked, as Bayen Hu, the rebel leader, had flooded the country by damming up the course of the river. The depth of the inundation was said to be in the deepest parts over a man's head, and in the shallowest it came up to the horses' cruppers. The Chinese march was then changed to a northerly direction, in order to strike the river higher up, where the obstruction raised by the enemy would be more easily overcome. A cart-road was carefully constructed along these alkaline plains, and the Kaidu was dammed to stop the flow from the upper course, and a bridge was erected over it. This detour had caused some delay, yet Karashar was reached on the 7th of October, four days after Kin Shun had set out in person from Kuhwei. The inundation from the Kaidur had spread as far as here, and the town was several feet under water. All the official and private residences had been destroyed alike, and the

Turki-Mussulman, as the Pehin Gazette styles them, population had been compelled by Bay en Hu to follow him in his retreat. It would be interesting to know whom the Chinese meant by Bayen Hu, but it is almost impossible to say. As it was not Hakim Khan, the most probable personage would be one of the Tungan leaders, either of Urumtsi or Hamil, who had been mediatized by Yakoob Beg and placed in command of the Turfan region. He appears to have been the commander of that portion of the Kashgarian army which was left round Korla. Not only was Karashar deserted by its inhabitants, but so was the whole country round about. Some, indeed, had fled to the mountains, but these were afraid to return when they saw the Chinese established in their homes. And then the conquerors followed out their usual plan by settling fresh colonists in the town. The Mongol noble, Cha-hi-telkh, was directed to move up some hundreds of the members of his tribe to occupy this important post, to restore the homes and to refill the fields; and while this work of restoration was proceeding on territory conquered by the Chinese, that through which they passed in hostile guise was subjected to far other treatment. On the 9th of October the Chinese marched against Korla from two sides, and on that day a cavalry skirmish took place, in which fifteen of Bayen Hu's horsemen were slain, and two taken prisoners. From the evidence of these, who were dressed in the Khokandian garb, but were Mussulman subjects of China, being natives of Shensi, it was learnt that Bayen Hu had withdrawn with all his forces to Kucha, taking with him the produce of the country and the majority of the people. They affirmed that the small detachment to which they belonged was only a scouting party, sent out to learn what the Chinese army was doing. When the Chinese had exhausted their stock of information they beheaded them. The same day they entered Korla, which they found to be completely deserted, although not flooded. The walls remained, but many of the houses had been thrown down. Here the general was nearly reduced to a desperate plight, as the provision train, which was transported by cart and camel, did not come up, and there was the prospect of starvation compelling the victorious array to retreat. But happily the thought struck the able general, or perhaps some one gave him a hint, that there might be some stores concealed in the city which the Kashgari had been unable to carry away with them. Accordingly the whole army set to work to search the houses, and to dig into the ground in all likely places for hidden stores. Their toil was soon rewarded, and "several tens of thousand catties' weight of food" were discovered. As a catty weighs 1,3/4 lb., this was no slight supply for an army of men which was probably under 10,000 strong. These concerted movements of the army south of the Tian Shan placed the country as far west as Karashar in the possession of the invader. Their next advance, which they could not expect to be as unopposed as their late one, would bring them into the plain of Kashgar. No sooner had Karashar and Korla fallen into their possession than an edict was issued inviting the Mahomedan population to return to their homes, and many of them accepted the invitation. In this quarter the arms of China were not disgraced by any excesses, and moderation towards the unarmed population extenuated their severity towards armed foes. While halting some days at Korla, Kin Shun heard that Bayen Hu was coercing the people east of Kucha at Tsedayar and other places, and compelling them to withdraw to Kucha and to destroy their crops. He at once resolved to frustrate the plan, and set out in person at the head of 1,500 light infantry and 1,000 cavalry to protect the inhabitants. By forced marches, sometimes carried on through the better part of the night, he reached Tsedayar on the 17th of October, when he learnt that Bayen Hu had driven off the whole of the population, and was already at Bugur, on the road to Kucha. At the next village to Tsedayar, a fortified post known as Yangy Shahr, he found that Bayen Hu was still ahead of him, and that he was setting fire to the villages on his line of march. Kin Shun left a portion of his infantry behind to put out the conflagration, and resolutely pressed on with the remainder of his force to Bugur. This small town had also been set on fire, but here the rapidity of the Chinese general's advance was rewarded with the news that the enemy's army, with a large number of the inhabitants, was only a short distance ahead. The rear-guard, composed of 1,000 cavalry, was soon touched, and the Kashgari, emboldened by the small numbers of the Chinese, came on to the attack in gallant fashion. Their charge was broken, however, by the steadiness of the Chinese infantry, armed with excellent rifles, and the cavalry performed the rest. The Kashgari left 100 slain on the field of battle and twelve prisoners. From these latter it was discovered that the main body of 2,000 soldiers was some distance on the road to Kucha, with the family of Bayen Hu and the villagers under its charge. It was too late to advance further that day, but on the next the forward movement was resumed. A large multitude— "some tens of thousands of people"—was speedily sighted by the advanced guard, but on examining these through glasses it was discovered that scarcely more than a thousand carried arms. All the troops were then brought to the front, and Kin Shun issued instructions that all those found with arms in their hands should be slain, but the others spared. The armed portion of the Kashgarian army drew off from the unarmed, leaving in the midst the large assemblage of Mussulman villagers who were being carried off to Kucha. These were sent to the rear by order of Kin Shun, and distributed in such of the villages as were most convenient. In the meanwhile a sharp fight took place a few miles in the rear of the old position, near a village called Arpa Tai. The action appears to have been well contested, but the superior tactics and weapons of Kin Shun's small army prevailed; and the Muslim army retreated with considerable loss and in great disorder. Kin Shun followed up his success with marvellous rapidity and restless energy, while the Kashgarian troops fled incontinently to Kucha, abandoning the people and the country to the invader. The unfortunate inhabitants implored with piteous entreaties the mercy of the conqueror, and it is with genuine satisfaction we record the fact that Kin Shun informed them of their safety, and bade them have no further alarm. By this time it is probable that the Chinese army had been largely reinforced from the rear, for we have now come to a more arduous portion of the enterprise, the attack against Kucha. When the Chinese appeared before its walls they found that a battle was proceeding there between the Kashgarian soldiers and the townspeople, who refused to accompany them in a further retreat westward. On the appearance of the Chinese army, the Kashgarian force evacuated the city, and joined battle with it on the western side of Kucha. The Chinese at once attacked them, at first with little success; and a charge of the cavalry, numbering some four or five thousand men, was only repulsed with some difficulty. But the cannon of the Chinese were playing with remarkable effect upon the Muslim, and the Chinese reserves were every moment coming upon the ground. The infantry were at last ordered to advance, under cover of a heavy artillery fire, and the cavalry made a charge at a most opportune moment. The whole army then broke and fled in irretrievable confusion, leaving more than a thousand of their number on the ground. Their general, Ma-yeo-pu the Chinese called him, was wounded early in the day, but, although stated to be a noted man, it is impossible to recognize his identity under the Chinese appellation. This was certainly the most sanguinary and the best-contested action of the whole war. The numbers on each side were probably about 10,000 men, and it was won as much by superior tactics and skill as by brute force and courage. All the movements of the Chinese were characterized by remarkable forethought, and evinced the greatest ability on the part of the general and his lieutenants, as well as obedience, valor, and patience on the part of his soldiers. The rapid advance from Kuhwei to Karashar, the forced march thence to Bugur, the capture of Kucha, the forbearance of the conqueror towards the inhabitants, all combine to make this portion of the war most creditable to China and her generals, to Kin Shun in particular. The reason given in the Official Report for the Kashgarian authorities attempting to carry off the population was that the rebels wished in the first place to deprive the invading force of all assistance, thus making further pursuit a work of difficulty, and in the second place, to ingratiate themselves with the new Pahia (probably Bacha) of Kashgar, Kuli Beg, by delivering this large mass of Turki-Mussulmans into his hands. Bayen Hu was, therefore, certainly not Hakim Khan. It is tolerably clear that he must have been either a Tungan refugee or a subordinate of Beg Bacha's. A depot was formed at Kucha, and a large body of troops remained there as a garrison; but the principal administrative measures were directed to the task of improving the position of the Turki-Mussulman population. A board of administration was instituted for the purpose of providing means of subsistence for the destitute, and for the distribution of seed-corn for the benefit of the whole community. It had also to supervise the construction of roads, and the establishment of ferry boats, and of post-houses, in order to facilitate the movements of trade and travel, and to expedite the transmission of mails. Magistrates and prefects were appointedto all the cities, and special precautions were taken against the outbreak of epidemic or of famine. All these wise provisions were carried out promptly, and in the most matter-of-fact manner, just as if the legislation and administration of alien states were the daily avocations of Chinamen. There is no reason to believe that in the vast region from Turfan to Kucha the Chinese have departed from the statesmanlike and beneficent schemes which marked their re-installation as rulers; and whatever harshness or cruelty they manifested towards the Tungani rebels and the Kashgarian soldiers was more than atoned for by the mildness of their treatment of the people. On the 19th, or more probably the 22nd of October, Kin Shun resumed his forward movement, encountering no serious opposition. His first halt was at a village called Hoser, where he halted for one night, which he employed in inditing the report to Pekin, which described the successes and movements of the previous three weeks. At the next town, known as Bai, Kin Shun halted to await the arrival of the rearguard, under General Chang Yao. This force came up before the close of October, and the advance against Aksu was resumed. Up to this point the chief interest centred in the army south of the present day Tian Shan, and in the achievements of Kin Shun. Our principal, in fact our only, authority for this portion of the campaign is thePekin Gazette. We have now to describe the movements of the Northern Army, which was under the immediate command of Tso Tsung Tang, and which was operating in the north of the state, in complete secrecy. That general had under him, at the most moderate computation, an army of 28,000 men. By some it was placed at a higher figure; but a St. Petersburg paper, on the authority of a Russian merchant, who had been to Manas, computed it to be of that strength. It was concentrated in the neighbourhood of Manas, and along the northern skirts of the Tian Shan; and also on the frontier of the Russian dominions in Kuldja. To all appearance this army was consigned to a part of enforced inactivity, since it was impossible to enter Kuldja, and thus proceed by their old routes through the passes of Bedal or Muzart. But it was not so; the travels of Colonel Prjevalsky in the commencement of 1877 had not been unobserved by the Chinese, and it was assumed that where a Russian officer with his Cossack following could go, there also could go a Chinese army. By those little-known passes, which are made by the Tekes and Great Yuldus rivers, the Chinese army, under Tso Tsung Tang, crossed over into Kashgaria; and it is probable that the two armies joined in the neighborhood of Bai. It was by this stroke of strategy on the part of Tso Tsung Tang that the Chinese found themselves before the walls of Aksu, with an overwhelming army, at the very sight of which all thought of resistance died away from the hearts of the Mussulman peoples and garrisons. Tso Tsung Tang appeared before the walls of Aksu, the bulwark of Kashgar on the east, and its commandant, panic stricken, abandoned his post at the first onset. He was subsequently taken prisoner by an officer of Kuli Beg, and executed. The Chinese then advanced on Ush Turfan, which also surrendered without a blow. As we said, the Chinese have not published any detailed description of this portion of the war, and we are consequently unable to say what their version is of those reported atrocities at Aksu and Ush Turfan, of which the Russian papers have made so much. There is no doubt that a very large number of refugees fled to Russian territory, perhaps 10,000 in all, and these brought with them the tales of fear and exaggerated alarm. We may feel little hesitation in accepting the assertion as true, that the armed garrisons were slaughtered without exception; but that the unarmed population and the women and children shared the same fate we distinctly refuse to credit. There is every precedent in favor of the assumption that a more moderate policy was pursued, and there is no valid reason why the Chinese should have dealt with Aksu and Ush Turfan diiferently to Kucha or Turfan. The case of Manas has been greatly insisted upon by the agitators on this "atrocity" question; but there is the highest authority for asserting that only armed men were massacred there. This the Chinese have always done; it is a national custom, and they certainly did not depart from it in the case of the Tungani and Kashgar. But there is no solid ground for convicting them of any more heinous crime, even in the instances of Manas and Aksu, which are put so prominently forward. Early in December the last move of all began against the capital, and on the 17th of that month the Chinese took it by a coup de main. Beg Kuli Beg, according to one account, fought a battle outside the town, in which he was defeated; according to another report, he had withdrawn to Yarkand, whence he fled to Russian territory, when he heard of the fall of Kashgar. It is more probable that he resisted the Chinese attack on Kashgar, for he certainly reached Tashkent, in company with the Kirghiz Chief, Sadic Beg, who was wounded in that battle. With the fall of Kashgar the Chinese reconquest of Eastern Turkestan was completed, and the other cities, Yangy Hissar and Yarkand, speedily shared the same fate. Khoten and Sirikul also sent in formal promises of subjection. But the capture of Kashgar virtually closed the campaign. No further resistance was encountered, and the new rulers had only to begin the task of reorganization. When Kashgar fell the greater portion of the army, knowing that they could expect no mercy at the hands of the Chinese, fled to Russian territory, and then spread reports of fresh Chinese massacres, which probably only existed in their own imagination. There can be no doubt that the Chinese triumph has been thorough, and that it will be many years before the people of Eastern Turkestan will have again the heart to rebel against their authority. The strength of China has been thoroughly demonstrated, and the vindication of her prestige is complete. Whatever danger there may be to the permanence of China's triumph lies rather from Russia than from the conquered peoples of Tian Shan Nan Lu; nor is there much danger that the Chinese laurels will become faded even before an European foe. Tso Tsung Tang and his lieutenants, Kin Shun, who has since fallen into disgrace,—perhaps he had excited the envy of his superior—and Chang Yao, accomplished a task which would reflect credit on any army and any country. They have given a lustre to the present Chinese administration which must stand it in good stead, and they have acquired a personal renown that will not easily depart. The Chinese reconquest of Eastern Turkestan is beyond doubt the most remarkable event that has occurred in Asia during the last fifty years, and it is quite the most brilliant achievement of a Chinese army, led by Chinamen, that has taken place since Keen-Lung subdued the country more than a century ago. It also proves, in a manner that is more than unpalatable to us, that the Chinese possess an adaptive faculty that must be held to be a very important fact in everyday politics in Central Asia. They conquered Kashgar with European weapons, and by careful study of Western science and skill. Their soldiers marched in obedience to instructors trained on the Prussian principle; and their generals manoeuvred their troops in accordance with the teachings of Moltke and Manteuffel. Even in such minor matters as the use of telescopes and field glasses we find this Chinese army well supplied. Nothing was more absurd than the picture drawn by some overwise observer of this army, as consisting of soldiers fantastically garbed in the guise of dragons and other hideous appearances. All that belonged to an old-world theory. The army of Eastern Turkestan was as widely different from all previous Chinese armies in Central Asia as it well could be; and in all essentials closely resembled that of an Europcan power. Its remarkable triumphs were chiefly attributable to the thoroughness with which China had in this instance adapted herself to the European "Western notions". With the flight of Beg Kuli Beg to Tashkent closed the career of the house of the Athalik Grhazi in Kashgar. Whatever turn events may take in this portion of Central Asia, whatever schemes there may be formed in Khokand, or elsewhere, of challenging anew the Chinese domination, it will not be round the banner of Kuli Beg that the ousted Khokandian officials will rally. By his flight in the hour of danger, by the hesitation which marked all his movements, and by the murder of his brother in cold blood, this prince, of whom much at one time was expected, has irretrievably ruined both his career and his reputation. If on any future occasion Russia should seek to play the part played of old by Khans of Khokand in the internal history of Kashgar, it will not be Kuli Beg whom they will put forward as their puppet. His old rival, Hakim Khan, stands a much better chance than he, more especially if it be true that he is the representative of the Khojas, being the son of Buzurg Khan, as many have asserted. But the fact remains clear, that all the dreams of Yakoob Beg of founding a personal dynasty in Eastern Turkestan are now dispelled beyond all prospect of realization. The following account of the life of Yakoob Beg was written with a twofold intention. In the first place, it attempts to trace the career of a soldier of fortune, who, without birth, power, or even any great amount of genius, constructed an independent rule in Afghanistan-Central Asia, and maintained it against many adversaries during the space of twelve years. The name of the Athalik Ghazi became so well known in this country, and his person was so exaggerated by popular report, that those who come to these pages with a belief that their hero will be lauded to the skies must be disappointed. Yakoob Beg was a very able and courageous man, and the task he did accomplish in Kashgaria was in the highest degree creditable; but he was no Timur or Babur. His internal policy was marred by his severity, and the system of terrorism that he principally adopted; and his external policy, bold and audacious as it often was, was enfeebled by periods of vacillation and doubt. Yet his career was truly remarkable. He was not the arbiter of the destinies of Central Asia, nor was he even the consistent opponent of Russian claims to supremacy therein. He was essentially of the common mould of human nature, sharing the weaknesses and the fears of ordinary men. The Badaulet, or "the fortunate one", as he was called, was essentially indebted to good fortune in many crises of his career. He cannot, in any sense, be compared to the giants produced by Central Asia in days of old; and among moderns Dost Mahomed of Afghanistan probably should rank as high as he does. Yet he gives an individuality to the history of Kashgar that it would otherwise lack. The recent triumphs of the Chinese received all their attraction to Englishmen from the decline and fall of Yakoob Beg, the hero they had erected in the country north of Cashmere. In the second place, the following pages strive to bring before the reader the great merits of China as a governing power; and this object is really the more important of the two. It is absolutely necessary for this country to remember that there are only three Great Powers in Asia, and of these China is in many respects the foremost. Whereas both England and Russia are simply conquering Governments, China is a mighty and self-governing country. China's rule in Eastern Turkestan and Jungaria is one of the most instructive pages in the history of modern Asia, yet it may freely be admitted that the brief career of Yakoob Beg gave an interest to the consideration of the Chinese in Central Asia that that theme might otherwise have failed to supply. The authorities used in the compilation of the facts upon which the following pages have been erected are principally and above all the official Report of Sir Douglas Forsyth, and the files of the Tashkent and Pekin Gazettes since the beginning of 1874. Mr. Shaw's most interesting work on "High Tartary", Dr. Bellew's "Kashgar", and Gregorieff's work on "Eastern Turkestan", have also been consulted in various portions of the narrative. A vast mass of newspaper articles have likewise been laid under contribution for details which have not been noticed anywhere else. In conclusion, the author would ask the reader to consider very carefully what the true lesson of Chinese valor and statesmanship may be for us, because those qualities have now become the guiding power in every Indian border question, from Siam and Burma to Cashmere. Mr. Schuyler's "Turkestan" which still maintains its place as the leading work on Central Asia, although not treating on the affairs of

Kashgar, has been frequently referred to for the course of affairs in Khokand; but, in the main, Dr. Bellew's historical narrative in Sir D. Forsyth's Report has been followed. started hiking the Eightmile Creek Trail (FST 1552, c.3300') around 6:00am. The trail follows the creek through sometimes burned forest for 2.8 miles to Little Eightmile Lake (4404'). On the north side of the small lake is the junction with the Caroline Lake Trail (FST 1554). This trail climbs NW through mostly burned forest to a saddle (+6320') then descends to Lake Caroline (6190'). The lake is about 5.5 miles from the trailhead and was mostly frozen despite the unseasonably warm temperatures. There was also more snow than we had been expecting. In the basins it was 6-10 inches deep and it was always with a breakable crust. The trail circles to the north side of Caroline Lake then gains a bit of elevation to reach Little Lake Caroline (c.6 miles, c.6300'). The trail turns north, traverses a slope then turns a corner formed by the east ridge of point 7380' (c.6.8 miles) where I left the trail to ascend a south trending ridge that merges with the west ridge of Cashmere just west of the summit. There was another option, continue on the trail to reach Windy Pass (c.7200') and then ascend a ridge that first climbs north then curves NE to merge with the west ridge of Cashmere. That route would seem to be considerably longer and would probably require some traversing and/ or ups and downs to then meet up with the route that I took. The advantage of going to Windy Pass is probably the view. There may be some environmental concerns crossing the meadow area and reaching the ridge. From the corner, descended less than a hundred feet to a snow filled meadow area. crossed it and started up a tree and snow slope to reach the south trending ridge. Once on the ridge found a path on the easy crest (uncertain where it starts due to snow). hiked up the ridge until it became a jumble of talus. Presumably, this is where the route from Windy Pass would meet this route. turned right and traversed on talus and snow to reach a saddle just west of the final craggy summit of Cashmere descended to the saddle in an almost entirely different way, then followed the path down the ridge until we lost it in snow before reaching the Caroline Lake Trail. It was all down hill from there...well almost. It was just before.

Turkistan

Aryana-Khorasan dynasty present day Afghanistan-Central Asia & India, in contemporary geographic terminology, present day Chinese. Turkistan refers to present day Xingjian (Sinking), the Uighur Autonomous Region of the People's Republic of China. In older scholarly works, however, other names have often been applied to this part of Central Asia: Serindia (English and French); Ost-Turkestan, Chinesische Ost-Turkestan, Mittelasien (German); Vostochnyĭ Turkestan (Russian). Some of these terms are purely geographical (Mittelasien), some historical (Serindia), and others ethno-cultural (Turkestan). In the case of Turkestan, a distinction is usually maintained between its two components: Chinese (East) Turkestan and West Turkestan (the present day republics of Central Asia). Chinese Turkestan is located in the very center of Asia, between the Altai range to the north and Tibet to the south. Its total area is over 1.5 million square km, which is more than the area of Germany, France, and Spain combined. It borders the Central Asian republics of Tajikistan, and Kirgizia to the west, Kazakhstan to the northwest and the north, Mongolia to the northeast, and Tibet to the south. Its eastern border faces China. The natural environment is quite similar to that of the Central Asian republics. Moreover, as Vasiliĭ Bartol'd (see BARTHOLD) observed, "both parts of Turkestan were inhabited by peoples of the same origin and were affected by the same cultural factors" (Bartol'd, 9, p. 519). Recent archaeological discoveries, as well as the decipherment and publication of tens of thousands of documents from Chinese Turkestan, have confirmed this striking parallelism with the rest of Central Asia. The principal trends of social and economic development of the two regions are very similar. Nomadic cattle breeding played a significant role, supplementing the irrigational agriculture of small oasis settlements. The development of this two-fold economic system (oasis agriculture and steppe cattle breeding) was followed, as in western Central Asia, by the appearance of the third distinct component, the city. Cities gradually turned into important centers of economic, administrative, religious, and social life. Many ethnic, cultural and linguistic aspects of the two regions also had much in common, although the presence of the Chinese ethnic element and the influence of Chinese culture were much more pronounced in eastern Turkestan. From the earliest times, the territory of Chinese Turkestan was inhabited by an Indo-European population, Tokharians and Indians in particular. Dari-speaking peoples, the Saka (Scythians) and Sogdians, formed a considerable substratum among the Indo-Europeans. The presence of the Saka population in Chinese Turkestan has been confirmed thanks to the study of a group of manuscripts written in Brāhmī (q.v.) script but in an East-Iranian dialect. Similar manuscripts were found in Khotan, Tumšuq, Maralbaši (Ba-chu), Mazār a, Hadalïq, Dandan Öylik, and in the library of Dun-huang. Two dialects, Khotano-Saka and Tumšuq-Saka, can be distinguished. The manuscripts can be dated from either the 5th or 8th to the 10th centuries C.E. Earlier traces of the same language were found when analyzing the Kharohī inscriptions of the 1st to 3rd centuries from the Kroraina (Lou-lan) region to the east of Khotan. Analysis of the linguistic features of the Khotano-Saka language leads to the conclusion, however, that it became separated from the Scythian language to which it is related earlier than the 6th or 5th century B.C.E (Abaev). Saka tribes probably appeared in present day Chinese Turkestan at the end of the second millennium B.C.E. (Emmerick). This has been confirmed recently by the discovery of Saka burial grounds and various objects of Saka type dating from the 7th to 5th centuries B.C.E. in different parts of Turkestan. The Sogdians were another population in the area. Sogdian manuscripts of the early 4th century C.E. and especially of the 8th-10th centuries C.E. have been found there. The homeland of the Sogdians was Sogdiana with its capital at Samarqand. Probably as early as the

4th-3rd century B.C.E., Sogdians began to settle beyond the borders of Sogdiana, in present day Chinese Turkestan in particular (Henning). The second wave of Sogdian settlers, in the 1st-3rd centuries C.E., was connected with the Kushan state; the third one took place in the 5th-8th centuries. The main occupation of the Sogdians was long distance trade. They were also missionaries and preachers of Buddhism, Christianity, and Manichaeanism and translators of religious texts. There were Sogdian cities in Turkestan. Sogdian influence on the development of culture, art and architecture in Turkestan was significant. Archaeological materials, manuscripts, and coins were collected in Chinese Turkestan by various travelers in the second half of the 19th century. Significant collections were acquired in 1890-95 by the French scientific mission directed by Jules-Léon Dutreil de Rhins, who worked in collaboration with the French Orientalist Fernand Grenard, and by the Swedish expedition directed by Sven Hedin (1894-97, 1899-1902, 1906-8). A considerable part of these collections was later published by various scholars. A new stage in the study of present day Chinese Turkestan was opened by a special archaeological expedition directed by the Russian scholar Dimitriĭ Klements (1898). The expedition worked in the Turfan basin where it explored in all detail over a dozen sites, especially Ïdïqut Šahri and Toyuq Mazār. In addition to pieces of art, the expedition recovered many ancient manuscripts. The results of this expedition urged the Thirteenth International Congress of Orientologists (Hamburg, 1902) to found a special International Association for the Study of Central and East Asia (Association internationale pour l'exploration archéologique et linguistique de l'Asie Centrale et de l'Extreme Orient; Central and East Asia Exploration Fund). The Russian committee of this association, founded the next year (1903), became its central committee. In the first two decades of the 20th century the British, German, French, Japanese, and Russian archaeological expeditions which worked in Turkestan laid the foundation of our knowledge of archaeology, architecture and art of Turkestan, recovering thousands of ancient manuscripts. One of the most prominent explorers of Afghanistan-Central Asia was Mark Aurel Stein (1862-1943). With a good knowledge of Sanskrit literature and of the sources on the history of India and Central Asia, he was at the same time an archaeologist and a numismatist. His first expedition to Central Asia lasted fourteen months, from May 1900 to July 1901. He explored the region of Kāšar (Ka-shi), then traveled to Khotan. There he investigated the site of the ancient capital of Khotan, Yotqan, where he collected abundant materials. At Dandan Öylik, a site 1.6 x 2.4 km, he excavated sixteen structures, most of them Buddhist temples containing works of art. Many documents of the 7th-8th centuries were found, among them Chinese and some which turned out to be Khotano-Saka. No less successful were excavations in Rawak revealing documents and a 6th-7th century Buddhist stupa with a rampart decorated with magnificent Buddhist bas-reliefs. Earlier materials, of the 2nd-4th centuries, came from the site of Niya. There frame structures were excavated; among the finds were Chinese documents and about five hundred documents in Brāhmī script written on leather. Written documents were also discovered in the Endere oasis. Stein's second expedition (1906-8) followed the same route, again exploring the region of Kāšar and then of Yotqan. Then the expedition moved to the east of the Khotan oasis. Buddhist sanctuaries were discovered in Hadalïq and subsequently numerous paintings, sculpture and manuscripts were found in Domaqo. Further excavations were undertaken at Niya, where new structures and magnificent architectural details in wood were revealed. A cache containing documents discovered in structure 14th was a genuine sensation. Among other finds, there were documents, coins, and objects of art. Going further to the east, Stein reached the ruins of Lou-lan visited before him by Hedin. Stein undertook large-scale excavations there, uncovering several frame structures, among them Buddhist temples, and discovering a capital of the Indo-Corinthian order. Many documents in Kharo hï and East Turkestan were found there. A great success awaited the explorer in Miran where he uncovered fourteen Buddhist sanctuaries, some of them with very old sculpture and paintings dating to the 2ⁿᵈ-3ʳᵈ century C.E. They revealed strong late-Hellenistic and Roman influence, and no wonder—on the painting there was an inscription in Kharo hī, telling that it had been executed by an artist named "Tita," a Prakrit form of the Roman name "Titus." In Miran, Stein also investigated a fort from the time of the Tibetan occupation. Tibetan documents on paper and wood and also one old Turkmen document were discovered there. From Miran, Stein directed his way to Dun-huang. There, in one of the watch-towers among the Chinese frontier fortifications, he discovered a document written in an unknown script. When the document was subsequently deciphered, it turned out to be Ancient Sogdian. The documents he found were the famous Sogdian "Ancient Letters" (q.v.) of the early 4ᵗʰ century C.E. On the way back, Stein again worked in Khotan, Tumšuq, and Maralbaši. Stein's third expedition continued for a very long time (1913-16). He again visited many of the previously investigated sites, Miran, Lou-lan, etc. This time Stein spent more time working in the northern oases. His excavations in Ïdïqut Šahri, Toyuq, and Murtuq (Sengim) were successful. Excavating buildings and cave-temples, many of them Buddhist shrines lavishly decorated with paintings, reliefs and sculpture, he discovered numerous objects, among them a hoard of well-preserved metal objects. A large number of coins and manuscripts were found, the latter in Uighur, Tibetan, Dari, and Manichean scripts. Important finds came from the graves of the Astāna burial grounds—textiles, leather objects, perfectly preserved paper, even ancient cakes! Due to the dry climate the bodies of the buried had become mummified. Most of these materials from the northern oases were dated to the 5ᵗʰ-8ᵗʰ centuries C.E. Stein published the results of his expeditions in three fundamental reports (ten huge volumes) and in a series of popular books and numerous articles. Stein performed a great service in issuing these accounts of his archaeological investigations. His plans, sections of architectural monuments, and descriptions of finds were excellent. On the other hand, he did not record the course of his excavations, stratigraphic observations were missing in his descriptions, and cultural layers were not studied. An important contribution to the study of the ancient culture of present day Chinese Turkestan was made by the four German expeditions (1902-14). The plan of the first expedition was developed by its director, Albert Grünwedel (q.v.), in collaboration with his Russian colleagues. Grünwedel was himself a prominent Indologist and specialist in Buddhist art. His first expedition continued from November 1902 to March 1903. The principal object of its studies was Ïdïqut Šahri, the capital of the Uighur principality in present- day Chinese Turkestan. The expedition made a new plan of the site, including a detailed description of the city fortifications and more than thirty structures. German scholars devoted much attention to the study of architecture, but the absence of a professional architect in the expedition affected the results of their work. Works of art were investigated on the highest level. Copies and photographs, including color photographs, were made of them. Among the finds there were Manichean manuscripts. The survey of other sites, like Sengim Gïz, Murtuq, etc., also produced good results. The second German expedition continued for over a year (September 1904-December 1905). It was directed by Albert von Le Coq, a gifted Orientalist who knew Arabic, Dari, Turkish, and Sanskrit and became one of the leading German Turkologists. He continued to investigate Ïdïqut Šahri, discovering the first Manichean monastery with monuments of Manichean art and Manichean manuscript fragments on paper, parchment, leather, and silk; and fragments of Manichean miniatures and paintings on textiles. Objects of Buddhist and Christian art were recovered from other structures. Two libraries were discovered in monasteries at the estuary of the Sengim river. They contained many Uighur translations of Buddhist legends as well as Manichean and Dari manuscripts. The expedition also investigated Buddhist cave sanctuaries at Bezeklik. Fifteen images of Buddha were recovered from one of the corridors. On the left and on the right of the entrance there were images of the founders of the temple—Uighur men and women of the noble class, judging from their garments. Many different manuscripts were found at the site known as Čikan Göl. Some Christian texts, among them Sogdian manuscripts, came from the settlements of Shui-pang. The third German expedition (December 1905-June 1907) was directed by Grünwedel and Le Coq. It surveyed the sites of Tumšuq and Kumtura. Then the expedition visited a *ming öy* at Qïzïl (a place never visited previously by any European; only one Japanese scholar, Kōzui Ōtani, had been there before). It was a system formed by hundreds of caves (hence the name ming öy, "a thousand houses"). Grünwedel made a topographic scheme and many drawings of the rocks with the location of the caves marked on them. In two and a half months over twenty cave structures were recorded in detail, measured and drawn, their decorations described and photographed. The description required much effort as well as detailed and profound knowledge of Buddhist mythology and iconography. To achieve it some of the caves had to be excavated and emptied of sand and rocks. Such masterpieces as the "Hippocampus Cave," "Artist's Cave," "Cave of Sixteen Sword-bearers," "Cave with Doves Carrying Rings," "Cave with Maya," "Cave of Nagaraja," and "Cave of Musicians" were studied and recorded in full detail. In one of the temples ("Cave with a Red Dome"), the excavators found the remains of a library with Dari books written on palm-leaves, birch bark, and paper. Works at Bezeklik (Murtuq) were equally successful. Sites at Šorčuq, Qarā Šahr, etc. were also investigated. From one of the caves came a great number of manuscripts written in Indian script. The fourth expedition directed by Le Coq (March 1913 to March 1914) continued to study the *ming uy* system of caves near Qïzïl. Dari inscriptions were discovered in a temple at the site of Subaši. Later the expedition worked in the canyon of Ačig Ilak from which it recovered some manuscripts. Le Coq's investigations in Sïmsïm were also successful. There he discovered traces of Bactria influence in wall-paintings. Buddhist sanctuaries at Kumtura and other sites were studied as well. Like Stein, the German scholars brought back numerous objects of art and manuscripts from their expeditions to Turkestan. The archaeological methods they used, however, do not correspond to modern ideas of archaeology. Grünwedel and Le Coq published (incompletely) their observations and materials on archaeology and art in a large series of works (twelve volumes), popular books, and articles. Their priorities were art history and discovery of Bactria-Dari ancient manuscripts. In 1905-6 an American expedition directed by Ellsworth Huntington worked in Teast Turkestan, its primary aims being the study of physical geography and paleo-climatology. At the same time Huntington's report contained much information on ancient sites, especially of the Niya oasis and the area of the Lop Nor lake, and on the sources and the system of ancient irrigation. A French expedition was headed by the famous Sinologist Paul Pelliot (1878-1945). It worked in East Turkestan from September 1906 to January 1908, first studying the Kāšar region. Then Pelliot arrived at Tumšuq, where he undertook large-scale excavations of the Buddhist site Ṭoquz Sarāy. There he found numerous pieces of art, including a large series of excellent Bactria stucco sculpture and bas-reliefs—images of buddhas, bodhisattvas, devata*s*, brahmans, ascetics, and noblemen. The expedition spent eight months in the oasis of Kuča (Ku-che). Impressive results were achieved by the excavations of the Buddhist monastery at Duldur Āor. There the expedition investigated a system of structures built around the central courtyard and encircled with a solid wall. The walls were covered with paintings, numerous stucco sculptures were found along with graffitti inscriptions, manuscripts, and a small library. Excavations at the site of Subaši were also successful. In Kuča, Pelliot met a Russian expedition directed by M. Berezovskiĭ, and the two expeditions collaborated successfully. Pelliot published only a preliminary report and several notes. Only after his death did the publication of all materials recovered by the expedition begin under the direction of Louis Hambis at the Center for the Study of Afghanistan-Central Asia and the Far East of the Collège de France. To date, five of the planned ten volumes have appeared. The Russian Committee for the Study of Central and East Asia organised an expedition in East Turkestan from the end of 1905 to December 1907 under the direction of M. M. Berezovskiĭ and his brother, the artist N. M.

Berezovskiĭ. It worked mainly as a survey team. In 1909 it became possible for the Russian Committee to mount a large-scale expedition. It was headed by Sergei Fedorovich Ol'denburg (1863-1934), a prominent Indologist and specialist in Buddhism and Buddhist art. The expedition reached East Turkestan in June 1909 and worked there in 1909-10. Large-scale works were undertaken at the site of Šikšin, half-way between the towns of Qara Šahr and Kurla, which occupies a plateau of about 15 hectares. A detailed plan of the site was made. About 150 structures—sanctuaries and dwellings—were preserved there, the most significant of them being built on plinths. Wonderful monuments of art were discovered there as well as in the nearby cave monastery. From Šikšin the Russian expedition moved to Turfan. In the vicinity of the city they excavated the site of Yarqoto. When excavating a small temple they discovered numerous fragments of Dari and Uighur manuscripts and paintings on canvas. An unusual structure styled the "101 Chaitya" was investigated, as well as some semi-subterranean dwellings. The expedition also surveyed such important sites as Sengim, Bezeklik, and Toyuq Mazār and made records of architectural monuments, art and inscriptions. In the final stage of the expedition, Ol'denburg investigated the sites of Subaši, Sïmsïm, Qïzïl and Kumtura. In 1914 the Russian Committee organized the second expedition to East Turkestan, also directed by Ol'denburg. Its main task was to study the "Cave of the Thousand Bactria Buddhas" in Dun-huang. It worked from May 1914 to April 1915. Its route was via Čugučak, Urumči, Hami, Ansi (Anxi), and Dun-huang. Ol'denburg discovered that the ancient caves of Dun-huang had been cut in the rock over a fifteen hundred years ago, and that the mural paintings preserved there due to the dry climate dated from the 5th or 4th century B.C.E. to the 1st century C.E. The expedition photographed the caves, making over two thousand photographs; its artists made copies of the paintings; and numerous manuscripts they discovered were brought to St. Petersburg. The results of the first Russian Turkestan expedition were published as a "Brief Preliminary Report" by Ol'denburg and in a series of articles; the results of the second appeared only in brief notes. Three volumes of the materials of Ol'denburg's expeditions were prepared for publication by the late N. V. D'yakonov. The first volume has been published. Japanese scholars began to explore East Turkestan at practically the same time as the European and Russian expeditions. The first Japanese expedition worked there from August 1902 to February 1904. The project was inspired and supervised by Count Kōzui Ōtani. Among the participants were Tesshin Watanabe, Kōen Inoue, and Kenyū Hori. The Japanese scholars traveled along the route Taš Qurgan to Kāšgar to Khotan. They arrived at the Khotan oasis and undertook excavations there, returned to Kāšgar, and then moved to Kuča. They spent much time in Qïzïl, studying it in detail (above all, the *ming oy* cave monastery), and then went to Turfan. After carrying out some excavations there, they returned to Japan through Urumchi. Many objects of art, archaeological finds, coins and manuscripts were brought back by the Japanese expedition from Khotan and Kucha. The field records made by the Japanese scholars have unfortunately been lost. The second Japanese expedition reached Urumchi in October 1908. It worked till October 1909. Among its members were Zuichō Tachibana and Eizaburo Nomura. They excavated such important sites of Turfan as Qara āja (Qočo), Murtuq, and Yarqoto. Besides that, they worked in the Tarim basin (at the site of Lou-lan), in the Niya oasis, Yarkand and Maralbaši. The third Japanese expedition started in October 1910. Its director, Tatibana, undertook long-term investigations in Turfan, Kuča, Qarā Šahr, and Khotan. Later, together with Koichirō Yoshikawa, he studied the monuments of Turfan. After that, in April 1912, Tatibana returned to Japan, and Yosikawa continued excavations in Turfan for another five months, devoting special attention to the burial grounds of Astāna. Later he investigated the sites of Kumtura and Subaši. Modern Japanese scholars agree that the expedition did not succeed in making a systematic classification of the investigated objects (Central Asian). Its archaeological reports do not provide necessary information on stratigraphy, distribution of archaeological finds, and coins. One may doubt if any records meeting modern requirements were made by the members of the exhibition. For this reason it became impossible to reconstruct any absolute or relative chronology. Vast collections assembled by this expedition, including manuscripts, came into the possession of various museums in Japan, Korea and China (Afghanistan-Central Asian). During the first three decades of the 20th century expeditions from different European countries continued, though on a smaller scale than before, to work in East Turkestan. Among the notable expeditions were those of the Tibetologist Otto Franke (Yarkand, Khotan 1914) and the geographer Emil Trinkler jointly with the geologist G. de Terra (Kāšgar, Khotan, excavations in Rawak; 1927-28). The results and materials of Trinkler's expedition were published a quarter of a century later by Gerd Gropp. Hedin continued his studies of the geography of East Turkestan. He directed joint Chinese-Swedish expeditions in 1928-31 and 1934, in which several Chinese scholars took part, among them the famous Huang Wen-pi. For the first time Hedin invited a professional archaeologist, Frederic Bergmann, who worked there in 1928 and 1934. Hedin's reports included archaeological observations and description of finds made by other members of the expedition. He also published some of the prehistoric materials such as stone implements and painted pottery. The main part of the report was dedicated to the excavations of numerous burial grounds with mummified bodies, well-preserved cloth, and grave goods in the vicinity of the Lop Nor lake. The settlements, rock carvings, etc. of several other sites were also described. Archaeological investigations and excavations done by Bergmann were carried out on a higher professional level than those done by Hedin himself, even though they still did not meet modern requirements. A considerable contribution to the study of archeology and ancient history of Afghanistan East Turkestan was made by Chinese archaeologist Huang Wen-pi (1893-1966). In 1928 and 1930 he worked with other members of Hedin's expedition in Turfan and studied Ïdïqut Šahri and the cave monasteries, Bezeklik in particular. In 1930 he excavated the site and the necropolis of Yarqoto; then worked again at Ïdïqut Šahri and on the burial grounds of Astāna. A new cycle of work was undertaken by him in 1933 and then resumed in 1943. Huang Wen-pi returned to Beijing in 1947. There he worked in the Institute of Archaeology of the Academy of Sciences of the People's Republic of China. His last expedition to East Turkestan took place in 1958. Huang Wen-pi published a number of fundamental works, all in Chinese, on the archaeology of East Turkestan. After the establishment of the People's Republic of China in 1949, archaeological activities in East Turkestan became systematic. In 1953 the present day Xinjiang Group for the Survey and Study of the Monuments of Material Culture was founded, and a network of institutions in charge of archaeological excavations and preservations of monuments was created in 1956. A register of 118 sites of East Turkestan subject to preservation was made in 1957, four of which were included in the list of the principal historico-cultural monuments of China. Later large-scale archaeological excavations covered practically the whole territory of the region. Both the sites discovered earlier by foreign expeditions and other, formerly unknown sites dating from the Stone Age to the Islamic Middle Ages were investigated. Many documents were found during these excavations. One of the features of Chinese archaeology is the use of modern methods, including C14 dating, which have revealed many of the faults and mistakes made by earlier investigators. European scholars now also participate in archaeological works in East Turkestan. Austrian scholars directed by Heinrich Gerhard Franz investigated the site of Turfan in 1982 using photogrammetric methods to record architectural monuments. Since 1993, a Franco-Chinese archaeological expedition directed by French archaeologist Henri-Paul Francfort and by one of the principal Chinese specialists, Wang Binghua, has been working in East Turkestan and has made important discoveries. In spite of the large number of published archaeological reports, our knowledge about the archaeology of East Turkestan is still incomplete and full of serious lacunae. The fact of the matter is that the methods of archaeological excavations employed in the first decades of the 20th century were quite different from contemporary methods; moreover, many of the investigators were not even following the basic rules accepted at that time. This resulted in the detachment of archaeological collections from the sites where they had been found, the absence of detailed descriptions of excavated areas and soundings, and even of basic stratigraphic observations. Even Stein, the most accurate among the first investigators, was not without faults. As for Grünwedel and Le Coq, descriptions of trenches, layers, and dating materials are virtually nil in their works, and they give little information about archaeological and numismatic finds (unlike Stein, who thoroughly described them). The German scholars were interested mainly in works of art, architecture, and manuscripts. The excavations carried out by Chinese archaeologists have been much more professional. Unfortunately, their results are published in most cases only as brief reports. With some rare exceptions, the published works give no detailed classification of artifacts. All this makes it difficult to exploit the available fund of information accumulated by scholars from around the world. In many cases we have to do without precise dating, and we can not form any definite opinion on the history of certain structures, architectural complexes, and sites or compare groups of artifacts and trace the lines of their development. Nevertheless, careful analysis makes it possible to outline the general picture of the development of material culture in East Turkestan and its different regions. Of particular value are studies which use comparisons with parallel materials from the Central Asian republics (where they have been collected using highly developed archaeological methods and systems of dating); that is, works which assess the East Turkestan collections in the larger context of Afghanistan-Central Asian studies. The Great Pamir Afghanistan-Earst Turkestan-Central Asia was one notion since 3,500 years until the Great Games. There are detailed studies of the collections of art from East Turkestan, the most important being the works by the German scholar Ernst Waldschmidt (1933), the Italian Mario Bussagli, the American Benjamin Rowland, the series of works by French scholars which started under the supervision of Hambis (1963 and later), and those by the Russian D'yakonova. Monuments of art discovered in the republics of Afghanistan-Central Asia helped considerably in understanding the art of Turkestan. Excellent publications of the monuments of Turkestan art have been made by Japanese scholars such as Toru Haneda, author of a valuable monograph on the history of civilization in east Turkestan. The results of international archaeological investigations in East-Turkestan revealed its pre- and proto-history, monuments left by its nomadic population (from Saka to Turkmen), numerous sites of temples, and monuments of art and architecture; they have provided abundant materials on the history of the area's material culture, warfare, religion, historical geography, and ancient irrigation systems. Besides objects of art and artifacts, large collections of ancient coins have been assembled. All this allows one to follow the principal trends of the political, economic, and cultural history of the region. Thousands of manuscripts and documents found there deserve special attention. They are written in both familiar and previously unknown languages— Middle Afghan, present day Dari, Sogdian, Bactrian-Hephthalite, Parthian, Khotano-Saka. Now these documents are preserved in several countries (Britain, Germany, France, Japan, China, Korea, and Russia) and are studied by scholars of many nationalities.

Durand Line Treaty has not lapsed

Aryana-Khorasan dynasty present day Afghanistan-Central Asia & India, the State Department, according to documents examined by Daily Times, rejects the view that the Durand Line Treaty expired in 1993, as propagated by some, including elements in Afghanistan and supporters of Pakhtunistan. According to the State Department's Office of the Geographer and Global Issues, "Recurrent claims that (the) Durand Treaty expired in 1993 are unfounded. Cartographic depictions of boundary conflict with each other, but Treaty depictions are clear." A State Department official said that when the rumours first surfaced that the Treaty signed in 1893 had expired after 100 years, the US government established contact with the British Foreign and Commonwealth Office to verify the claim, but was told in categorical terms that the Treaty contained no expiration provision and, as such, was very much in place. According to the State Department, flag meetings are regularly held between Pakistani, Afghani and US personnel to resolve disputed sections in response to armed incidents. However, Pakistani, American and Afghan efforts to arrest Islamist insurgents, Taliban remnants and terrorist cells across the once fluid border are hampered by local resistance and the area's harsh terrain. The Durand Line stretches over 2,430 km and is the historical, de jure boundary established as a "Great Game" buffer between British and Russian interests in the region. The Durand Line, established in 1893, with subsequent surveys and demarcations until 1905, served as the limit of British influence. The Line was reaffirmed in 1905, 1919 and 1921. India inherited the Line in 1947, but so far there is no formal agreement between Islamabad and Kabul on its formal ratification. In 1977, before Gen Ziaul Haq overthrew Zulfiqar Ali Bhutto's elected government, the two countries had agreed to sign a formal agreement, which would have brought this contentious issue, that has caused Pakistan endless and continuous problems since its inception, to an end. Afghanistan, with Soviet and Indian support, questioned the legitimacy of the boundary after the establishment of Pakistan. Afghan claims are at present "dormant" as the Karzai government has pledged to respect territorial sovereignty while it tries to establish internal unity. However, there is no guarantee that Kabul will not raise the issue again, unless it can be persuaded to sign a formal treaty of ratification with Pakistan, something it seems in no h This is a revised text of the lecture he gave to the Society on 29 October 2008 In 1907, just over 100 years ago, Lord Curzon, a founder member of this Society, was invited by the University of Oxford to give a lecture. He chose to speak on frontiers. "Frontiers", he said "are the chief anxiety of nearly every Foreign Office in the civilised world... They are moreover the razor's edge on which hang suspended the modern issues of war or peace, of life or death to nations." 1Like many of Lord Curzon's oracular pronouncements, his words still have much weight for the present day. We only have to look at the Kashmir dispute between India, the conflict between Russia and Georgia over the status of Abkhazia and South Ossetia, the way Nagoro Karabagh has poisoned relations between Armenia and Azerbaijan, the much-disputed frontiers between China and India, and, more recently, the problems between Cambodia and Thailand, and Russia's designs on the Arctic Circle and its resources. But there is, perhaps, one frontier dispute that trumps all the rest in terms of the world's current security concerns. That is the Durand Line, the notorious frontier between Afghanistan and Pakistan. Some people blame this frontier for all of Afghanistan's current problems. And there are those who go so far as to blame it for the problems in Pakistan. Indeed, there are those who blame the Durand line not just for terrorism and other problems of instability in Pakistan, but even for the terrorist attacks we suffered in London in July 2005, tracing their origins all the way back to the tribal agencies of NorthWest Pakistan. Some people have even been so bold as to say that everything in Afghanistan would be sorted out if only the United States could cross over the frontier and 'do its thing' there. Such commentators seem little daunted by the fact that British administrators spent 150 years trying in vain to resolve the same problems which confront us today. Asian Affairs, vol. XL, no. II, July 2009 For the frontier poses problems of many different types: legal, territorial, economic, ethnographic, military, geopolitical. Nor does it just involve Pakistan and Afghanistan as two titanic players. There are many parties involved: the various factions of the government in Pakistan, the secret services of Pakistan, the Pakistani army, the tribesmen, the local notables, the insurgents, whether Islamic or otherwise. There are smugglers and business interests to consider. There are also the desires of the wider foreign community who would generally be very happy if things were to settle down and a nice trade route could be established, like the Silk Route of the old days, bringing oil from Turkmenistan to Afghanistan and through to India. was first tempted to investigate this morass early last year when was having a discussion with some Afghans who were living in London. They were very learned and sensitive people. One of them looked at me and asked me quite seriously: "Mr Omrani, do you think that war with Pakistan would be a good solution to our problems, so that we could push the Durand Line all the way back to Karachi?" myself didn't think it was the best of ideas, but my background in the area was not as extensive as it is now. However, was so astonished at what he said – at this belligerence in the face of the many problems that currently face Afghanistan, establishing effective government, feeding its population, unifying its territory – that I felt compelled to research the matter further. 2-In fact, even though the problems are both complex and numerous, they all actually boil down to one very simple question: historically speaking, where should the frontiers of all of the empires of this region be set? Over the last 2000-odd years of Central Asian history, even back to the time of Alexander the Great when he came all the way from Macedonia, Afghanistan had occupied a vital strategic position in Central Asia; in Arnold Toynbee's phrase, the "roundabout of empires". It sits between three perennial centres of empire. To the north, an empire, maybe Turkmen, maybe Mongol, more recently Russian, with a tendency to move down towards Afghanistan; to the west, to the south-east, India. In various periods, the land of Afghanistan has been divided between them, either as parts of their empires or else as spheres of influence. But while the question is clear enough – "Where should the frontiers between the empires be set?" – the geography of Afghanistan does not lend itself to any obvious answers. It does not offer anything in the way of coherent physical features to act as clear boundaries. On top of this, a perennial trend in the history of Asia has been a pressure, a movement of peoples from Central Asia to move down through Afghanistan, down through the passes of north-western India to debouche into India and to establish new empires there. It goes all the way back to the Aryan tribes who moved there around 1500 BC, and you see it again with Turkmen tribes in 1000 AD. The Kabuli Empire was essentially a movement of Mongols and Turks pausing in Afghanistan and then setting up an empire in India. The question for all these empires which established themselves in India was the same: "Where can we best set a frontier that will protect us against this perennial pressure of people moving south from 178 HISTORY AND PROBLEMS OF THE AFGHAN-PAKISTAN BORDERCentral Asia and Afghanistan?" There are various options – none of which are ideal: one is the line of the river Oxus, the current northern boundary of Afghanistan. But it is quite far away from the Indian heartland and difficult to police. Another option is the line of the Hindu Kush Mountains, which cut present-day Afghanistan in two. That line runs through a series of cities and settlements from Kabul, to Ghazni and Kandahar, but there are too many gaps for it to be easy to defend. Or there is the option of the line where the frontier runs today, through the Suliman Mountains; or it can run through the foothills south of those mountains, where the land is more fertile, flat and productive; or else the line can be pushed back as far as the Indus River itself. 1-RIVER OXUS 2-HINDU KUSH 3-CURRENT FRONTIER, SULIMAN MOUNTAINS

4-SULIMAN MOUNTAIN FOOTHILLS (SETTLED TERRITORIES) 5-INDUS RIVER HISTORY AND PROBLEMS OF THE AFGHAN-PAKISTAN BORDER 179But if the empire which rules in India chooses to establish a boundary significantly forward of the Indus River, it is immediately faced with a serious secondary problem, not a problem of external security but a problem of internal security – the problems of policing the Pashtun tribes, who at present form a great band of people from the South of Afghanistan, all the way into Pakistan and down through the hill country. They share a lot of characteristics of language and traditions. The Pashtuns of the hills are a very particular sort; the geography of the area has made them what they are. The hill country is highly convoluted, barren and isolated from the outside world. It is difficult for outsiders to get into the area; there is little settled agriculture and it is hard to make a living. In the absence of hedge funds or the financial services industry, what can the tribesmen do but turn to crime, raiding the more prosperous settled territories, preying on the merchants passing along the ancient trade routes towards Central Asia Indeed, a number of the tribes in their foundation myths count great thieves as their original ancestors. Their poverty-stricken life has made them extremely hardy and resilient; the idea of toiling for a living is often thought of as knavish and base. Like many other mountain dwellers, e.g. in Albania or Georgia, they are fiercely proud of their independence. They hold in contempt the civilisation and governments of the settled world. They do not like to pay taxes, they do not have time for the conventional forms of law and law courts and they do not have any taste for laws imposed from distant capitals. 3-Of course, the Pushtun areas differ. Some are quite agricultural, e.g. the Kurram Valley, where there is more wealth, where the people are more settled and the governments of the tribes are more hierarchical. However Waziristan is a rather different matter. This is an area frequently in the news these days. One can get a good idea of the type of people who live there from this extract from the diary of one of the tribal agents, Herbert Edwardes, who was one of the first people to meet a Waziri Chief (in 1853). Mullick Swahan Khan, chief man among the neighbouring tribes of the Vizeerees [waziris], came into camp by invitation to see me. He is a powerful chief, and his country boasts that it has never paid tribute to any sovereign, but exacted it in the shape of plunder from all tribes alike. Swahan Khan is just what one might picture the leader of such a people: an enormous man, with a head like a lion, and a hand like a polar bear. He had on thick boots laced with thongs and rings, and trod my carpets like a lord. The Hindostanee servants were struck dumb and expected the earth to open. With his dirty cotton clothes, half redeemed by a pink longee over his broad breast, and a rich dark shawl intertwined into locks that had never known a comb, a more splendidspecimen of human nature in the rough never saw. He made no bow, but with a simple "Salaam aleikoom" took his seat.

4-All empires in the region have a problem: how are you going to govern people like that? Such laws as the tribes do have – and it is a mistake that is often made 180 HISTORY AND PROBLEMS OF THE AFGHAN-PAKISTAN BORDERto describe these regions as lawless – evolved over time in accordance with the practical circumstances of their way of life, where there are no police forces and self-reliance is the order of the day. They have a few very simple ideas, which are enshrined in a tribal code, the way of the Pushtuns or Pushtunwali. There is an idea called Melmastia that hospitality and protection should be afforded to every guest. An extension of this is another idea, Nanawati, that asylum and sanctuary should be given to every fugitive, even if they should happen to be a bitter enemy. If the Pushtun host should fail to protect his fugitive guest against those pursuing him, it is a desperate stain on his honour. The host will allow himself to be killed rather than allow his guest to be captured. The final main concept is Badal, or the rule of the vendetta. Every insult, whether it be the theft of property, an attack on one's reputation or immediate family, a wounding or a murder of one's kin, should in principle be met with a proportionate act of revenge.

Tribal groupings are held collectively responsible, whether at the level of the family, the sub-clan, clan or tribe. If my brother were to kill your cousin, you would be quite within your rights to kill my brother, or my son, or my grandfather or my aunt in return. If a Shinwari should kill an Afridi, it is incumbent on every member of the Afridi tribe to repay the debt in like coin, killing a member of the Shinwaris in turn. A vendetta does not always go on for ever. There are mechanisms for resolving long-term vendettas. People meet together in a jirga where they try to arrange some kind of settlement. They might make a payment of blood money, or hand over the daughter of the family to the people who have been insulted, to act as a wife or slave. Essentially vendetta has been the leading note in the society for time immemorial and it has had a long and malign effect on the development of the Pushtuns as a cohesive group. Traditionally, revenge has been a dish served cold, very cold – for the Pushtun it can come years after an event. It can become rife, pitting tribe against tribe, even for ten generations and it has a baleful influence in terms of the bigger picture. For the region's convoluted geography of isolated valleys and high mountain ranges already separates peoples into a number of complicated tribal groups. The tendency towards vendetta further complicates any chance of the various tribes getting together in some sort of unified political structure. This is what has been happening for the last 500 years. 5-History Before describing the genesis of the modern frontier, it is necessary to explain the historical background, starting with the Kabuli empire present day Mughal empire in the 16th century. The Kabuli emperor decided to try to maintain the Hindu Kush as the northern boundary of India. They used Kabul, Ghazni and Kandahar as their forward defensive positions. They were always suspicious of Kabul as it was from here that Babur, the founder of the Mughal Empire started his attack on India. They knew that most people who wanted to attack India had to start from Kabul, so they were very wary about letting it get into foreign hands. But even though they held the line so far forward, they had continuing problems policing the hill HISTORY AND PROBLEMS OF THE AFGHAN BORDER 181peoples. Babur, himself, had far more options at his disposal than we do nowadays. On one occasion he stacked up as a pyramid the heads of 3000 decapitated tribesmen and also married the daughter of one of the chiefs. But even then he does not seem to have managed to impose lasting peace. Throughout the whole period of their empire in the 17th century the Mughals had to deal with repeated raids from the hills. The situation deteriorated and matters came to a head in 1675, at the time of the last great Kabuli Emperor, Aurangzeb. He launched a terrible scorched earth policy, sending thousands of soldiers into the valleys, burning, despoiling, smashing villages and killing as many tribesmen as possible. He also successfully used bribery to set the tribal chiefs against each other, thus fomenting so much mutual suspicion that they were too busy fighting each other to fight the Mughal Empire. This worked up to a point. But the resulting legacy of mistrust between the tribes destroyed any prospect that unified political institutions might slowly emerge or that the laws andgovernment of the settled regions might be adopted. 6 In the 18th century, as the Kabuli Emire crumbled away, the energy of the Pashtuns on the plains around Kandahar and Herat was released. They were able to rise up and found their own Pashtun empire. This is the first appearance of modern Afghanistan as we know it. It was an empire of the Pushtuns of southern Afghanistan, the Durrani tribe, and stretched as far as Mashhad in the west, beyond the Oxus into Central Asia, down to the Indus, whence they were able to raid Delhi. However, the empire, created in a burst of energy, was without stable foundations. It fell apart quite quickly. By the 1820s Afghanistan was reduced to merely a few cities – Kandahar, Ghazni, Kabul and Peshawar – everything to the north had been lost. Herat had become an independent state and the sovereignty which Kabul claimed over the Pushtuns in the hills was purely nominal. Other areas had been swallowed up by the 19th century Empire of the Punjab. By this time, the European powers were beginning to join the perennial struggle for Central Asia. The British were making their presence felt in India. The British were still behind the Indus

River but the question of the frontier and the defence of their Indian possessions was very much on their minds. There was not much thought at this stage about where to put a frontier line but they wanted to make sure that there was as much land as possible between them and their great rivals, the Russians, who already had their designs on Central Asia and even on India. To that end, the British thought they might create a 'buffer state' – Afghanistan. In 1839 they invaded. They put a 'puppet' king on the throne. They could not leave because the 'puppet' king was unable to look after himself. In the end the troops left and got slaughtered. A strongman took over. It is worth noting that the British then saw Afghanistan as a tribal 'buffer' region, but they did not think at that time about where boundaries might be drawn. 'Close border' or 'forward policy'? But boundaries looked increasingly important. By the 1840s the Russians had reached the Aral Sea and were slowly being drawn into Central Asia. In 1849

182 HISTORY AND PROBLEMS OF THE AFGHAN-PAKISTAN BORDERthe Punjab passed into British hands, as did Sindh. By this point British India had as its effective border the foothills of the mountains where dwelt the Pushtun hill tribes. The tribes saw no reason to stop their traditional raids just because the territory was now British. So, like the Kabuli Empire and Sikhs before them, the British were faced with the problem of how to control the tribes. They tried first the 'close border policy' which held as a principle that British sovereignty should not be extended to areas which could not be governed effectively. Accordingly the foothills were fortified to keep out the hill-based tribal peoples and irregular troops, levies, were raised to resist attacks on the population of the foothills. To keep the tribesmen sweet, the British tried making agreements with them, they tried friendship, they tried goodwill, they tried allowances for good behaviour, giving them money to provide services to keep the roads open, to protect communications, to deny sanctuary to outlaws in contravention of their tribal codes. But this didn't work very well. Expedition after expedition went into the hills to chastise the tribal people. Yet this was all much in vain. From 1857 to 1877 there were 11 expeditions into the hills and from 1877 to 1881 there were 12 full-scale expeditions, clear signs that this 'close border policy' was not working. So, as the 19th century progressed, another approach was devised: the 'forward policy', called the Sandeman system, which involved capturing and holding areas in the tribal zones in the hills. Strong points were captured, fortified, garrisoned, connected by roads which would be protected. The tribes would be allowed to run their own affairs in the hope they would gradually come under the influence of the British government. But this forward policy inevitably raised the question of where the border between British India and Afghanistan should be set. 7 At the same time fears were growing about the advance of the Russian Empire. By the 1870s the Russians had been able to capture the great Afghanistan-Central Asian cities of Bokhara, Samarkand and Khiva. Hence the appeal of the 'forward policy' which in its most extreme form posited that the frontier be pushed as far forward as possible, ideally to the genuine or 'scientific' frontier of the Hindu Kush, with Kabul, Ghazni and Kandahar forming the first line of defence. This idea found brief expression in the Second Afghan war of 1878–80 when the British invaded Afghanistan again and found themselves trying to hold the old Mughal frontier. But they failed not because of the Russians, but because of Afghan resistance. The Durand line By the 1880s the Russians had advanced further and were pressing on the river Oxus and Afghanistan itself. By 1893, the British had concluded that formal borders needed to be established between Afghanistan and British India, so that everyone would know where they stood and the Russian advance could be held off from the British Empire in India. The man sent to negotiate was the Indian Foreign Secretary, Sir Henry Mortimer Durand, another founder member of this Society. He was from an Indian family; his grandfather had HISTORY AND PROBLEMS OF THE AFGHAN-PAKISTAN BORDER 183been an officer in the first

Afghan war and his father had also been in the Indian Army. Sir Henry travelled to Afghanistan in October 1893 and it could not have been the most pleasant of missions to conduct. Two of the envoys who had been sent to Afghanistan in the 19th century, Sir Alexander Burns and Sir Louis Cavagnari had been cut to small pieces in very unpleasant circumstances and Durand was pretty well out on a limb in Kabul undertaking these very strange negotiations with the Amir of Afghanistan. Durand's main concern was to secure Afghanistan's northern border with Russia. A first settlement had been made in 1885 using the Oxus River but the boundary had not been taken all the way east into the region of the Great Pamirs and the Wakhan. Durand was desperate to make sure that this part of the border was absolutely clear so that the Russians could not sneak down through the Figure 2 'Morty': Sir Mortimer Durand in 1903. From a 'Spy' cartoon. Reproduced by permission of Vanity Fair. 184 HISTORY AND PROBLEMS OF THE AFGHAN-PAKISTAN BORDERPamir Mountains into northern India. The Amir dangled that card before Durand to get a better deal when the frontier between British India and Afghanistan was negotiated. It is not the case that the British presented a clearly thought-out proposal for a particular line for the frontier and threatened a further invasion if their proposal was not accepted. There was a lot of give and take in the negotiation. The Amir put forward an ambitious boundary proposal, the British suggested a very different frontier line which would include Waziristan in British India. There was a lot of to-ing and fro-ing, but ultimately the Afghans agreed that Dir, Swat, Peshawar and Chitral should be British. In return the Afghans secured some strategic strongpoints, notably Asmar, which gave them access to Nuristan and various of Afghanistan's eastern regions. 8-Then, at the very last moment, when agreement had been reached that all of Waziristan would be British, Durand, almost as an afterthought, possibly as a concession to allow the Amir to gain a little face, suddenly allowed the Amir to keep the Birmal tract of Waziristan. 9-This was not the best of ideas, since it involved splitting Waziristan and the tribal people in two. But it may be that the maps from which the Amir and Durand were working were not very good, for when the demarcation teams went out into the field to try to delimit the boundary, there were areas represented on the map which did not exist on the ground and vice versa. From his memoirs it appeared that the Amir was pleased with the settlement he had reached. 10 At the end of the negotiations Durand was presented in a Durbar in Kabul and praised and given various Afghan chivalric orders. Nevertheless at the same time the Amir secretly spread propaganda against the British, saying that he was not pleased and that it would be a good thing to move the Line over towards the east. 11 The Line, as demarcated between 1893 and 1896, was drawn all the way from the Fari frontier to the Wakhan, the little area on which the British insisted to keep a distance between the British and Russian Empires. There were two exceptions which at that time remained undemarcated: an area in the region of Chitral and another area a little north of the routes towards Kabul – the country of the Mohmand tribe. The demarcation team tried to make the line as sensible as possible by using natural features, such as mountain crests, streams and rivers as boundaries, thus splitting up areas of river drainage. They also tried to set up boundary pillars so that there was some physical evidence of the boundary. However in many cases it was not clear where the boundary ran. It is not much of a physical feature and the unknowing can easily cross it unawares. It is worth looking closely at the route of this 1900 mile long boundary. The first section follows the crest of the Hindu Kush Mountains, where there is only the occasional pass. This section was actually very secure, for given the height and the cold it was difficult to moves forces across the area. Next the Line moves further down towards the Mohmand hills, where there was one of the undemarcated sections. There are still few passes of importance in this region. However coming down to the vital strategic region, the number of passes increases. There is of course the Khyber Pass, another important pass in the HISTORY AND PROBLEMS OF THE AFGHAN-PAKISTAN BORDER 185Kurram Agency, and a third, the

Tochi pass, which was an important trade and invasion route in the old days. Further on, in the area of Waziristan, the Line does not follow mountain crests and peaks so clearly. It is convoluted, following various peoples' agricultural rights and field boundaries. The Line splits at least 12 villages in half and divides other villages from their agricultural territories. It becomes easier to follow further south where most of the land is just desert. What assessment can we make of the Line? Was it the best achievable in the circumstances? Perhaps so, but it had, in the words of Fraser-Tytler, "many defects and few advantages". It was, he said, "illogical from the point of view of ethnography, strategy and geography".13 As already mentioned, it cuts tribes and tribal groups in half. The Birmal tract of Waziristan is on the Afghanistan side, with the rest of Waziristan on the British or Pakistani side. The Mohmand tribal areas are also cut in two. And, inevitably, because the border is generally in a very distant set of areas, it is highly porous and difficult to police, especially when family groups are on both sides. Particularly in Waziristan, there are many passes and paths through which it is easy to move from British India (or Pakistan) into Afghanistan and back. There were advantages of the Line for the British. There was a strategic advantage in that they held positions forward of the passes and controlled the heights, thus facilitating the policing of the passes. They also managed to achieve the tripartite border – a vision they had held for a long time. 14 The first part of the border was the buffer state, Afghanistan. The second part was the tribal areas in the hills, which the British did not try to govern, but simply garrisoned. These areas were vassal states, on the Indian side of the line but not under the sovereignty of British India. The third part was further back, where the real government of India started. The depth of this frontier system certainly kept the Russians away, but the corollary was that the British faced the familiar internal policing problem. There were also advantages for the Afghans. As is happening now, the Ruler of Afghanistan was trying to unify his country and make it into a coherent state. 15 Because he had been given a set of clear boundaries, it was much easier for him to project his power within those boundaries and to know that he would not be interfered with. Further north, he was able for the first time to extend his sway right up to the frontier. For example in Nuristan he was able to push right forward to the border and convert the tribes there to Islam. He also had excellent defence against further British encroachment – a prickly fence made up of difficult tribesmen. For the people on the ground, there was not much of a practical effect. They still had freedom of movement. They were still courted by various players. In the 1893 Treaty which he signed with Durand, Abdul Rahman promised not to try to project his influence over the border. But that did not stop him from inviting the tribesmen from those regions to Kabul and giving them honours, robes, money, guns etc. anything to keep them sweet, anything to keep them on side. 16 The Line also provided a safe haven. If you had committed a 186 HISTORY AND PROBLEMS OF THE AFGHAN-PAKISTAN BORDERcrime in British India you didn't just have the option of taking refuge with the Pushtun tribes on the Indian side of the Line; you could also dash over into Afghanistan where you could not be touched. Extradition was a tricky matter in those days. The people on the ground did not like the idea of being under any sort of British jurisdiction. The officers who were demarcating the Line soon found themselves the object of unwelcome attention, mainly in bullet form. By 1897 there was a general uprising all over the area, which it took 60,000 British regular troops to pacify. In 1904 Lord Curzon decided to divide the area to make it easier to administer. Originally the whole area was part of the Punjab. Lord Curzon split it off and created a government of the North Western Frontier Province. He established tribal areas beyond the administrative boundary of India where the Indian government did not presume to govern with regular laws. Different laws were set up for these tribal areas, the Frontier Crimes Regulations, which had been in force in various forms since the 1870s. 17 They were now applied in a systematic way. They are a harsh set of laws, with some alarming implications and are still in force today, more or less in the form in which the British left them. All policing, executive and judicial functions are in the hands of a political agent, who is answerable, via a commissioner, originally directly to the government in Delhi, but now to the President of Pakistan. Political agents handle relations with tribes via chosen notables, called maliks, who are subsidised and paid to keep order. The agents are stationed in a fortified position in the principal town of the tribal agency, originally five, now seven. As for justice, the principle of collective responsibility and collective punishment still applies. Other members of the tribe can be held responsible for any crime committed by a member of the tribe. A tribal agent can hold a jirga, inviting several maliks to help him decide points of fact in civil and criminal cases. But even then, the decision of this artificial court is not binding on the political agent. The cases are decided under customary law. Legal representation is not allowed at the jirgas, nor cross-examination. Evidence is not presented, trained police or scientific evidence not used, yet hearsay can be presented. Tribes can be punished in their entirety by being blockaded, by being denied access to markets. They can be prohibited from building new villages. There can be arbitrary imprisonment. A political agent can demand that a tribesman produce a good behaviour bond of $20,000 or be put in jail for three years. The behaviour of the political agents is not judicially reviewable. Decrees of the Pakistan Supreme court do not apply to the area. There is also a Pakistan version of the West Lothian question. The frontier areas return members to the national Parliament, but the laws passed by the Parliament are not valid in the frontier areas unless there is a Presidential say-so. Until 1996 there was no universal suffrage and political parties were outlawed in those regions. When the British had set up these areas they followed two types of policy. Under the 'close border' policy they decided not to interfere with the tribes very much. After the 3rd Afghan war (a brief skirmish between Britain and Afghanistan in 1919), many of the arrangements collapsed and the British HISTORY AND PROBLEMS OF THE AFGHAN-PAKISTAN BORDER 187decided to move back to a 'forward' policy of putting lots of troops in forward positions in the area in order to try to stop raiding and disorder. Neither of these policies worked particularly well. There was perpetual harassment and raiding across the border. The Afghan kings did not hold back. They would use raiding gangs to upset the British in India just to keep them tied down. Just in case there was any suspicion of further interference in Afghanistan, tribesmen were paid to be hostile to Britain. The 'forward' policy tied up many regular troops and consumed an enormous amount of money, literally millions of pounds. Although there was a brief period of success in the 1920s, there was still an upsurge of violence in the 1930s. There were over 200 recorded raids from the tribal areas down into the settled areas. In 1936 the Fakir of Ipi tied up 32,000 regular forces and 5000 scouts. The fact is that the arrangements did not work very well; while they preserved the external boundaries, they could not guarantee internal security. At the moment of independence for India and Pakistan there was a legal curiosity. The legal status of these areas changed. All the agreements they had were not with the government of India, for they were not part of British India. Their agreements were actually directly with the British Crown. Thus, legally speaking, at independence all these agreements lapsed and the tribal areas became independent. By November Pakistan had made arrangements with the tribesmen under which their relations with Pakistan would be on the same basis as their relations with the British. That is how Pakistan came to control these areas. They did not inherit them; they found them as de facto semi-sovereign independent territories. 18 Afghanistan had a bad reaction to Indian independence. Before independence in 1947 the Afghans were very eager to try to bring the Pushtun areas back under Afghan dominion of some sort. They wrote to Lord Mountbatten to raise the possibility of the Pashtuns coming under the Afghan wing. The British gave them the brush-off and said the issue should be discussed with the successor authority. At independence Afghanistan gave mixed messages about what its attitude would be to the area. The first Ambassador to Pakistan said in his speech, "I declare that Afghanistan has no claims on frontier territory, and even if there were any, they have been given up in favour of Pakistan. Anything contrary to this which may have appeared in the press should not be given credence at all and should be considered a canard". At the same time, Kabul radio demanded that all the territory to the Indus and Baluchistan should be re-amalgamated back into Afghanistan. They had a vision of the Afghan empire as it was 200 years earlier and they wanted access to the sea. We tend to forget the amount of bad feeling there has been between Pakistan and Afghanistan on account of the border. In 1948 Afghanistan voted against Pakistan joining the United Nations. Pakistan delayed Afghan import and export goods on the border. Afghan radio called for independence for Pashtunistan. In 1949 Pakistan inadvertently attacked Afghanistan territory by air, a skirmish followed. Shortly afterwards a loya jirga, a great council in Kabul, repudiated all the boundary treaties made with the British, gave 188 HISTORY AND PROBLEMS OF THE AFGHAN-PAKISTAN BORDER support to the idea of an independent Pashtunistan and urged that all the people in those areas should be given a referendum and the right to vote to join Afghanistan. There is a Pashtunistan Square and a Pashtunistan National Day which is an inheritance from that time. In 1950 there was an incursion into the tribal areas by Afghan forces disguised as tribesmen. These were repulsed by Pakistan Pashtuns. Pakistan stopped Afghan imports for three months. In 1954–55 the government of Pakistan decided to change the country's administrative structure. Instead of having separate provinces such as Punjab and Sind, they tried to establish a single unified administrative area of West Pakistan to balance East Pakistan – now Bangladesh. Afghanistan saw it as the tribal areas being taken away from their potential influence. There were riots at the Pakistani Embassy in Kabul, Pakistani consulates and counter-demonstrations in Pakistan. There were military calls-ups and mobilisations. There was no war, but diplomatic relations became frosty in the extreme. And at that time, the British Ambassador in Kabul, Sir Daniel Lascelles, was having anguished correspondence with London. He was concerned that the legal status of the Line was not particularly watertight and thus Britain might not be able to support Pakistan if the matter came to an international tribunal. 19 In 1960, with Pakistan making alliances with the United States, the Russians saw an opportunity. The Pashtunistan dispute gave them an excellent excuse to make an alliance with Afghanistan. Pravda called for a referendum and carried accounts of terrible bombing raids by Pakistan on the people in the tribal territories. There were alleged to have been enormous casualties among civilians supporting the movement for self-determination. In 1961 there was a second and even larger skirmish, and the border was shut down for months. Afghanistan was unable to export most of its fruit produce via the traditional route through Pakistan. The nomads were not able to cross the border to their normal pastures. The Afghans were forced to export all their goods via the USSR and then Afghanistan really fell under the spell of the Soviet Union. 20 After these episodes, one really cannot blame Pakistan for reverting to the worries of the North Western Frontier, or for having an interest in what was going to happen in Kabul. Pakistan sees Afghanistan as a hinterland which it wants to control as a fallback position, should there be any further conflict with India over Kashmir. The greatest concern however is controlling Kabul and stopping any more of these problems coming back over the borderline. With the 1980s and the Soviet invasion it seemed perfect sense to use the tribal areas as a point for launching the Mujahedin into Afghanistan. Again in the 1990s, its isolation made it the perfect place, not only to host those engaged in the fight for independence in Kashmir, but also to train the Taliban before they moved to control most of Afghanistan. In 2001 the area was again as a refuge for the Taliban. They then retreated to Waziristan and Quetta. This suited the Pakistani government. They could maintain the Taliban areas as a Talibanised belt between Afghanistan and Pakistan. If the government set up by the West in Afghanistan were to fall, this would give them the liberty to move back and to project their influence there. However, by pursuing this policy Pakistan has created a monster which it cannot HISTORY AND PROBLEMS OF THE

AFGHAN-PAKISTAN BORDER 189control. The Afghan Taliban are fine for interfering in Afghanistan but the area has become a well of religious fanaticism as much opposed to the Pakistani government as it is to the Afghan government. The assassination attempts made on former President Musharaf appeared to have been planned in the tribal areas in south Waziristan. Pakistan is being drawn into a longer conflict in these areas, as the British were before them. In 2004, under US pressure, the Pakistani army attacked a compound in Waziristan and were worsted. They attempted to conclude an agreement with the militants – the 2004 Miranshah accord – on the basis that "Militants may exist in Waziristan but they have to register with a political agent first". This did not work. 21 The militants in the region have been trying to eliminate any influence Pakistan might have. They moved from South Waziristan to North Waziristan. They have intimidated the population. They have attacked the fragile system of government, killing maliks and elders. They have also been having conflict with the Kurram Agency, where there is a Pashtun tribe, rather out of the ordinary. There have been various attempts to court the Taliban or the militants, offering troop withdrawals if attacks ceased – but attacks have increased. At the same time activists, who have visited these regions and perhaps even trained there, have been plotting attacks in the United Kingdom. There have been moves to raise tribal Lashkars as a revolt against the militants, but there is a danger this will descend into further warlordism. There are terrible conflicts going on now, strife in the Bajaur region where 10,000 war refugees have moved from Pakistan into Afghanistan. Where does this leave us? Afghanistan does not recognise the Durand Line as a legal international boundary. The Afghans claim agreement to the Line was obtained under duress. They question whether the documentation was in order. They sometimes suggest that the British made up the agreement after returning home. They also question whether the Amir Abdul Rahman understood what he was really signing up to, whether he understood the maps and whether he actually intended the boundary to be a legal international boundary. They complain that, at the moment of independence, the Pashtuns were not given the option of full self-determination. They were only given the choice between joining India and joining Pakistan, not independence or joining Afghanistan. They say the jirgas held between Pakistan and the tribal people were probably not in order. They say that the treaties made between the British and the Afghans lapsed at the moment of Independence, for they claim that Pakistan is not a valid successor state to British India. 22 Pakistan, of course, holds an entirely opposite viewpoint, arguing that the frontier, the Durand Line, is a legitimate international boundary, in 1893 and con- firmed by later treaties in 1905, 1919, 1921 and 1930. Pakistanis hold themselves to be the inheritors of the British legal rights at the moment of independence. 23 When the Line was drawn in 1895–96, many of the British officials held the view that the Line was never meant to be an international boundary. It was a Line that delimited areas of influence, not sovereignty. Sir Denis Fitzpatrick, Governor General of the Punjab said that the view of the British government was as follows: "think it is of the highest importance that it should be 190 HISTORY AND PROBLEMS OF THE AFGHAN-PAKISTAN BORDERsimply understood to be a line on our side of which the Amir's interference, except when we allow him to chastise a tribe, shall be absolutely excluded." He then said "where it would be difficult for us to prevent the tribes from raiding on the Amir's territory... we should in a proper case have to allow the Amir to counter-raid, though on the understanding that he would not take permanent possession". (Although the Americans are increasingly making raids into Pakistan using fighter drones and Special Forces, they rely on a rather different legal justification: the right of self-defence as a response to the attacks of 9/11.) British officials in those times also seem to have held that the boundary of the Durand Line would only develop into a proper international border when they could get rid of the Frontier Crimes Regulation, regularise the status of the tribal areas and bring them under normal British sovereignty as part of British India. 24 There are various other legal considerations. In international law, lines dividing spheres of influence often develop into proper international boundary lines, sometimes even without the explicit say-so of the states concerned. What international adjudicators look at is not just the original treaties; these can often be very unimportant. What matters is the practice of the states. Do the states treat these boundary lines as de facto international boundaries? If they do, they can be reckoned as international boundaries without the need to draw up any further treaties. 25 There is a certain unfortunate irredentism in the Afghan view. Afghans are longing for a seaport. They want to generate a Pashtun nation which might never have existed in the first place; indeed, were the Pashtuns ever a unified people? How can the Afghans take on any extra territory when they cannot govern what they already have? What about the self-determination of the Pashtuns on the Afghan side of the Line? Arguably, as there are more Pashtuns on the Pakistani side of the Line, the Afghan Pashtuns should be given a referendum about joining Pakistan, not vice versa; the same applies to the Tajiks in the north of Afghanistan, and the Uzbeks and Turkmen. It is a very difficult argument –it cuts both ways. It is self-contradictory to think that the border is not an international frontier. Even if a referendum were held and there were independence in these areas, there would still be a boundary line between an independent Pashtunistan and Afghanistan. We have to leave the law aside and think back to the practical question of how things stand now. The Line is convoluted, but there are many convoluted borders all over the world where there are no problems. The real problem is that the Line itself generates instability, it is not policeable, and the constitution of the Tribal Areas does not permit economic development to take place. In the 60 years since independence Pakistan has not been able to bring these areas under proper administration. They remain a well of instability, which cannot help harming the ultimate interests of both Afghanistan and Pakistan. With such a peculiar constitutional status in the Tribal Areas, there is no real possibility of stability, of establishing the rule of law, a sound banking system, the accountability of local officials, or putting in place the frameworks necessary for business and commerce. If it is the case that stability follows in the wake of HISTORY AND PROBLEMS OF THE AFGHAN-PAKISTAN BORDER 191economic prosperity, how can it ever be possible to bring about the economic change that would occasion stability in such an environment? The lack of development and the infrastructure for development is so endemic, and so much has it harmed the Tribal people over generations, that it is difficult to see a route out of the situation. There is, in a sense, a vicious cycle where the people are poor and have been denied access to amenities, education, and a wider perspective on their way of life; yet such is the lack of education and amenities that there is a deep hostility to their introduction of any outside help which might affect the cherished way of life. The statistics of the area tell the story starkly. 57 percent of people do not have access to clean water. The literacy rate is 17 percent, dropping to 3 percent of women. There are 7670 people per doctor. 26 Yet, for example, when a recent initiative was launched to vaccinate the people against polio, sermons were preached that it was a western plot to render the tribes infertile, and the medical aid workers were rounded up and furiously attacked. 27 Conclusions It is easy to conjure up a vision for the future of the territories on either side of the Durand line. For the sake of the inhabitants of the area, as well as the wider world, the vision would be of a border that was well policed and stable; that had the legal and constitutional framework to allow sustainable development on both sides (not just on the Pakistan or Afghanistan side, as radical imbalances in wealth and investment in such close proximity would cause instability); that extremism of conduct should be banished; and that there should be a greater settlement of people, with the ultimate disarming of the Pashtun Hill tribes. Although it is easy to envisage such a final state of affairs for the Durand Line territories, we have to ask if any of the parties actually would be willing to work towards such a state. The answer to the question does not provide any comfort. First, the Afghans would not welcome such a vision. Although President Karzai has called for Pakistan not to interfere beyond the line, he refuses to recognise its validity. Neither he nor any other Afghan politician would wish to surrender the irredentist claims over the Pashtun tribes on the Pakistan side of the line, so deeply are those claims ingrained in Afghan politics and history. Moreover, Afghanistan does not even want a regularisation of the constitutional position of the Tribal Areas, placing them under the regular laws of Pakistan. Were such a thing to happen, the Afghans feel that the Tribal Areas would be slipping even further out of their grasp. It seems that Pakistan is equally happy to allow the status quo to continue. They are able to use the Tribal Areas for Great Game-style interference in Afghanistan. Believing that the government in Afghanistan might not be of long duration, Pakistan wishes to keep the Tribal Areas in their current status to allow them more easily to influence whatever should happen next in Afghanistan. Although they fear instability from Afghanistan spilling over the border into Pakistan, the strategic considerations are of greater importance. As for the people 192 HISTORY AND PROBLEMS OF THE AFGHAN-PAKISTAN BORDERon the ground, despite all their hardships, it is unlikely – although no polls have been taken – that there would be any popular will to move forward. They seek to preserve their tribal way of life in the face of external pressure. They also hold to the Frontier Crimes Regulation, despite its harshness and its lack of concordance with modern ideas of human rights, as a marker of their distinct identity. Beside this the current state of affairs embraces a multitude of local interests, the spheres of power of local notables, smuggling, and the making of money by various other corrupt means. The only possible way that progress could be made is for the paramount importance of the problem to be recognised by both the nation states in the region, and by the various global powers with an interest in the stability and development of Afghanistan-Central Asia. It seems that few western governments, certainly not the British Government, have anything even in the way of a Pakistan policy, let alone a broader vision for the wider region involving Afghanistan, Pakistan, India, Iran and the Central Asian states. There needs to be an immediate collaboration between Afghanistan and Pakistan, the assistance of regional powers, some means of demilitarization of the Tribal Areas, and investment on both sides of the line. The creation of a free trade area running from India through Pakistan and Afghanistan to Central Asia should be held as a long-term goal. However, it is difficult to see this happening in the near future. For example, recent attempts by Afghan and Pakistani Pashtuns to hold joint jirgas, which even offered to talk to the Taliban, were spurned. The Taliban refused to participate until all foreign forces are expelled from the country. But even this initiative only hoped to confront the smallest fragment of the wider problem. As a final thought, one might even suggest that the notion of the Westphalian nation state, with its concepts of territorial integrity and the exclusion of external actors from the state, do not fit into a region which well into the 19th century was governed by Islamic ideas of statehood, where empires have come and gone for so many generations, and the concept of borders fixed for all time has never had a grounding. When Lord Curzon addressed the scholars of Oxford in 1907, he spoke with a magnificent, late-Victorian self-assurance about the future of the world's frontier zones: It would be futile to assert that an exact Science of Frontiers has been or is ever likely to be evolved: for no one law can possibly apply to all nations or peoples, to all Governments, all territories, or all climates. The evolution of Frontiers is perhaps an art rather than a science, so plastic and malleable are its forms and manifestations. But the general tendency is forward, not backward; neither arrogance nor ignorance is any longer supreme; precedence is given to scientific knowledge; ethnological and topographical considerations are fairly weighed; jurisprudence plays an increasing part; the conscience of nations is more and more involved. Thus Frontiers, which have so frequently and recently been the cause of war, are capable of being converted into the instruments and evidences of peace. HISTORY AND PROBLEMS OF THE AFGHAN-PAKISTAN BORDER 193A hundred years after his speech and surveying the current situation, it is difficult to share anything of his confidence for the future. 1. G. N. Curzon, Frontiers,

Romanes lecture, 1907, Oxford, 2. I would like to thank those who helped me in the course of my research, in particular Victoria Schofield, Jules Stewart, Dr Humayun Khan, Farid Khan Popal, and Professor K. H. Kaikobad of Brunel University. 3. The tribesmen were "confirmed in a way of life which placed a premium on disregard for the organised processes of governments". See Leon B. Poullada, 'Pushtunistan: Afghan Domestic Politics and Relations with Pakistan', in A. T. Embree (ed.), Pakistan's Western Borderlands. New Delhi, 1971, 4. H. B. Edwardes, Lahore Political Diaries, v. 49 et seq., quoted in O. Caroe, The Pathans. London, 1958, 5. Caroe, The Pathans, 6. J. W. Spain, The Pathan Borderland, 1963, 7. Ibid., 8. W.K. Fraser-Tytler, Afghanistan: A Study of Political Developments in Central andSouthern Asia. Oxford: OUP, 1967, 9. The full progress of the negotiations, at least from the view of Durand, can be seen in hiscorrespondence with the Viceroy of India in Mss. Eur. D727/4, British Library, Asia, Pacific and Africa Collections. 10. L. Dupree, Afghanistan. Princeton, NJ: Princeton University Press 1980, 11. D. Loyn, Butcher and Bolt. London: Hutchinson, 2008, 12. Fraser-Tytler, Afghanistan, 13. Dupree, Afghanistan, 14. The concept of the "three-fold frontier" (Curzon's phrase, used in his lecture on frontiers) The travelogue by a British aristocrat spread over a year undertaken both on the horseback and on foot through India via Kashmir, Tibet, Chinese and Russian Turkistan is a fascinating account for a knowledge seeker of the area known for calamitous happenings. The work is in two volumes spread over (360+340) 700 pages. It is a reprint of John Murray London publication of 1893. Exactly a century later in 1993 Vipin Jain for Vintage Books Gurgaon (Haryana) reproduced it in India. The publisher erroneously claims that the book was first published in 1885, though the journey was initiated later on February 12, 1892. The publisher or its printer (Efficient offset Printers New Delhi) also make another blunder by placing parts of chapters XVI pages 203-16, XVII 217-18, and chapter 18 of volume I in volume II and vice-versa. Similarly the off print of the work is substandard. The author Charles Adolphus Murray the 7th Earl of Dunmore (l. 1841-1907) a peerish family hailing from Scotland derives its label after the county of Dunmore. The fourth earl of the family had held executive positions of governors of New York and Virginia in 1770-72 followed by period of American War of Independence (1775-83), and later held similar position in Bahamas 1787-96. Charles Adolphus Murray, the 7th Earl of Dunmore, a conservative politician himself was well-established, had lived in Canada, travelled most parts of the world, including Turkey and Arabia and was familiar with some of the Oriental, French, Russian languages and even conversant in Hindustani. There is general belief in known records that he carried a secret mission in journeying this less known hazardous part of the world. British interest in northeastern borders of Afghanistan bulging into Kashgharia or Eastern Turkistan were prompted after Russia became the possessor of Bokhara. Its eastern region convexed into Kashgharia which bordered Kashmir of India. The British Parliament and its public watched with alarm Russian growth in the area. An earlier report in 1862 by R. H. Davies an official of the government in India had urged building politico-economic ties with the area. Reports from Trigonometrical survey of India on the route and region during the subsequent years were also reads with interest in the British official circles. Douglas Forsyth, a British Indian civil servant visited Kashghar twice 1870 and 1874 and entered into trade ties with Yaqub Beg a soldier of fortune from Khokand (eastern Bokhara) who had liberated the area from Chinese control. The Manchu, ruling house of China who had retaken Kashghar failed to assert its authority against advancing Russia in Turkistan where it was gradually extending its trade and authority. This, to British policy makers, posed a perennial threat to the Indian outer flanks in the extreme northeast. Afghanistan had undefined and flexible boundaries on all around its borders. The Durand Line (1893) had not yet been laid down with India. The area of Wakhan lay loose on the border and provided an easy entry to hostile forces inside Gilget Baltistan region. Dunmore's visit to the area therefore makes sense in a way, though the author does not smacks of it anywhere in its writings, except noticing the Wakhan land in deplorable political anarchy. The journey, to talk of the book, started on February 12, 1892, from India, evading England and finished reaching Constantinople on February 15, 1893: a fatiguing narration for a period over a year. The account of the journey is spread over 38 chapters of two volume book based on author's reports in his daily recording of the tour diary date-wise on start of landing in Karachi on February 12, 1892 and movement towards Rawalpindi by train. Henry Lansdowne was the viceroy (1888-94) in India and Robert Salisbury was holding second term of Premiership (1888-94) in England. At Pindi Dunmore fell from a pony, fractured a rib and fell on heeling bed. Here he met many men from Hunza, Nagar, Gilgat, Punyal and persons from the Pathan borderland enriching his knowhow on the area. Here also he met an army officer Major Roche, of 3rd Dragoon Guards who wished to accompany him on the Pamir journey. A Chinese visa through the government of India, Dunmore obtained for the journey beyond Kashmir land. Russian visa he carried from home. On recovery he dashed a visit to Peshawar, where he visited a posh European model cantonment area and the Khyber Pass in April. While in Peshawar, Dunmore also visited the city and purchased 180 Bokharan tilas and 100 Russian half imperials paying 11£. 6s and 12d for a Bokharan and Rs 12 and 10 annas for a Russian coin. Journey towards Pamir started from Murree where Dunmore party reached by Tangas and he himself by foot. From Murree onward they entered the Kashmir valley then in control of Dogra Maharaja Partab Singh (r 1885-1925). Srinagar bazaar, Dunmore found surprisingly inexpensive purchasing a sheep for 3½ Indian rupees and a cane of honey for one rupee. It was here in Kashmir that Dunmore decided to prepare the wherewithal for the journey beyond Kashmir forming up a caravan comprising initially 19 local men or attendants and 20 ponies, which remained varying as per requirement of the journey. The caravan was fitted to carry its own food and forage, tents, utensils and medicines. Rivers, mountains, bridges and deserts of the area are mentioned in details, along with history of important settlements in the diaries maintained by the author. Dunmore was a fine water-colour sketch painter and all significant buildings, stupas, mountains and lakes portrayed in the book are his own efforts. Roche added some photography to it. Zojilan pass, Dras, Kargil, rivers Sindh and Jehlum with their sources find place in narration of the journey in chapter 7 of volume I, before entering Lakakh which essentially was a Budhist city and formed earlier part of Tibet under the Lamas. River Indus roared around here and Dunmore caravan entered Leh at the closing week of May, 1892. Dunmore bought some more ponies here for around Rs. 40/- each which he thought could fetch good price in Turkistan. Some yaks were also purchased as they were fine beasts for burden in mountainous terrain. Fire wood, they learnt should form absolute part of luggage and ample provision was made thereof. The party attended every accessible social event of the travel area including Budhist weddings, music, religious ceremonies and sport events. An excellent account of Budhist rituals, family formation and social order is available in chapters 9-11 of the travelogue. The caravan thenceforth had been travelling in the region of Karakorum and western Himalayas and was embarking upon the region of Pamir with 70 loaded yaks and 56 ponies, some loaded others free with a party of 30 men plus 2 officers facing Kardong pass known for its cliffness rising over 16000 feet height. Camping at night usually would fall at places which suited tent installation and possibly close to water facilities. It had started snowing and often caused breathing problem. Dunmore carried height and cold measuring instruments and regularly recorded them and made them part of his diary. Each area had rivers known after the settlement which formed part of the big river system mostly Indus or Jehlum moving towards Gilgat or Kashmir. Hunting and shooting formed regular part of Dunmore and Roche routines as and when available, and local birds, hares etc were part of the prey. The campings at many points were over height beyond seventeen thousand with scarcity of water and difficulties of heating facilities. Ice provided both drinking and cooking water in the region connecting Karakorum with Pamir. An early autumn in the area presented diverse season, daytime desert touching highest temperature and the night altitude falling into below zero cold bringing abnormalities in both human and animal bodies. Dunmore doctored men with his lone available quinine tablets while Roche served veterinary to ponies and yaks. In around the Moorgha area in Karakorum on road to Yarkand the party came across a custoora (musk) deer in a desert, followed by an upward hilly system rising above 18000 feet, which is called "roof of Asia." Tibetan antelopes were visible in the valley around. This is an area where Himalaya-Karakorum and Pamir meet, is called the Pamir knot and also carries roof title (18980-19300 feet). The only living things seen here were ravens and butterflies. Karakorum river finds its bed here. Down below was greenery visible in plenty. The area in the bed of the mountain is breezy and mostly rainy and the party headed for Aktagh on the bank of Yarkand river and onward to the Chinese land. Travel difficulties arose when many of the seasonal rivulets, short of bridges were crossed either riding the ponies or dragging them. Shahidula was the entry point from the Indian side into Chinese Turkistan. Here a garrisioned fort looked after the entry and exit of passengers. Dunmore party after clearing with the entry formalities and borrowing food and forage items proceeded in July towards Yarkand. The journey passed through nomad Kirghiz population who were most hospitable, friendly and accommodating. Fresh fruit and sheep were presented to the visitors all along their passage and in return they repaid them in cash and some small gifts etc. Sanju, Kichik, Ilaq, Poski, Salghuz, Langue, Oi-taghragk, Borah and Kargalik were the settlements falling on their way. At Kargalik, the Chinese Amban, the area administration chief met them and acquainted himself with the purpose of the mission. In early August, the party entered Yarkand which they found an impressive city, having five entry gates, named Altun (golden), Kawngat (melon), Serabagh (tree garden), Masci (jester) and Khankah (monastery) Darwaza. A short history of Yarkand and its bazaars is given along with a meeting the Ambaan. The courtesy extended by the Chinese authorities to the party was appreciated. Dunmore also details in here the life story of Yaqub Beg the earlier area ruler and his successors and ultimate emergence of Chinese rule, which he calls oppressive. The life at Yarkand and story of the adjoining new city Yangi Shehr is also given. Dunmore also learnt that some border skirmishes had taken place between the Chinese and Russian forces in the west at Aktash and the city had fallen to the Russians in the Pamir region. Pamir it may stated here is a pure Turkistani mountain system, rising in eastern Bokhara (Tajakistan) interconnecting Takhtkal mountain system in the north-west to the Hindukush in Badakhshan area of Afghanistan onward in the south-east to Karakorum on to Tian Shen in the north to the Kunlun and Himalaya system in the extreme east. The Chinese hearing troubles in west sent reinforcement to the western borders. Dunmore party in late August moved north-eastward towards Tashkurgan the Kashghar border city with Afghan area of Wakhan. Sarikol, Mintaka passes all lead to Wakhan from Tashkurgan. The Sarikolians, Dunmore noted were Shias and believed in many Imams (Agha Khanis). The people are not Kirghiz, but called Sart or Tajik and are spread over all parts of Wakhan. A detailed history of the region, its people and their customs are detailed in chapter 26 of the book. The party followed Khunjrab river direction wherefrom entry to Wakhan via Mintaka and Kokturk was easy. It was on the bank of Kokturk river they established their caravan camp on September 6, 1892. Pamir, and its Ovis Poli, could be discovered and learnt about here. Ovis Poli mentioned by Morco Polo is a horned deer, called sheep by Polo. The winter had set in, the hills were getting snowy and search of the peaks and measurement was getting a difficult job. Dunmore moved his personal camp up in the hill at height over 15000 feet to watch animal movement at night and kill hill's esoteric animal for record. The Ovis Poli rams resided close to the glacier and therefore he had to move up with his gun and men for this purpose. The first hunt on September 11, was a large Ovis Poli or Galias as Kirghiz call it weighing over 20 stones and was carried by a yak to the base camp. Efforts continued for more hunt, till two more were added during the rest of

September. Dunmore learnt here that Hunza had been tributary to China and it was now the British substitution thereof that Chinese hold was cut off. Macartney the British resident at Kashghar arrived at this time and asked Dunmore to accompany him to explore the Kilik Pass in the Hindukush. It was also learnt at this time that the Russian had withdrawn from Aktash after demolishing the Chinese fort and skirmished with the Afghan soldiery also at Sarmtash where many casualties took place. Weather had considerably changed by early October in and around Wakhan corridor. The game animal in the mountain was disappearing and were retreating to their hideouts mostly avoiding the glacier zones. Bears, jackals and other wild animals however were seen out on their hunts. Dunmore during this period mainly was looking for Ovis Poli in the easterly portion of the Pamir called Little Pamir. He already had killed three, wounded two and missed one. This to him was enough under the circumstances. On 9th of October 1892 hunting game over, Dunmore decided to wind up the work and proceed for the Russian Turkistan across the Chinese border. Crossing in sort of no man's land which Dunmore thought was Russian land in Aktash Pass at 16370 feet height, where lay the Victoria Lake (Gaz Kul, Zor kul or Sari Kol) wherefrom Amu Darya rises. Bellow it was situated another lake called Chakmaktin, which constituted the Murghab river. John Wood a British explorer had discovered it in 1838 and was named after Victoria, the British queen sometimes later. Chapter 30 of the book gives history of the Kirghiz of the Pamir region. Its details are rich in information as they are based on local information and still significant in many ways. The party as it planned intended leaving the Chinese area to study life and positions in middle and upper Pamir which lay in the Russian domain of occupation. Dunmore assessment of the Chinese position in this part of the border was very disappointing; it all lay on the mercy of the Russians where they could change the borders and outposts at their liking. The return movement of Dunmore was via Wakhjir Pass, he frontier station for the Chinese-Afghan border, also close to the Indian (Hunza or Kanjut) border. Here the Akbilis river formed the divide line between the Afghan-India land. Earlier British exploration in this part of the world under Captain Younghusband and Captain Trotter and later Littledale had failed to answer many querries. On return Dunmore visited the Bozai Gumbaz, wherefrom the Sarhat river rises, also called Aksu, Okuz or Oxus. Lake after lake followed the party on ascending the mountain here. Cold had gripped the hills and almost everyone was suffering from cold, nose bleeding and muscle pains besides a few feverish. The party in retreat formation erroneously entered the Russian border in Murghalis area around Rang Kul, were received well and moved back to the Chinese position through the Ak-Birdi pass and Taghdumbash area. This was about the close of November 1892, complete winter had set in when they returned to Kashghar. Chapter 35 of the book gives an interesting account of history and prominence of Kashghar in Central Asian land. The Chinese welcome at Kashghar was well received by Dunmore and his group. Dunmore accompanied by some servants left for the Russian land while Roche and others departed for India on December 13. Entering the Zong border Dunmore headed towards Chaksu, wherefrom he was escorted by Russian Cossacks via Alai mountains to Osh, Gulcha, Marghilan, Khokand, Khojand and finally Tashkand. Dunmore was extended befitting reception all along his stay in the Russian land, and he least bothered to enquire about the Pamir. The history and the running formation of Russian Turkistan had been fairly treated in the closing chapters of the book in vol. 2. Dunmore intended to proceed via Persia and the Gulf route to Karachi, but heavy winter snow beyond Merv, forced him to resort for the Caspian service to Baku on February 7, 1893, wherefrom a Black Sea steamer took him to Constantinople and onward on February 15 to Europe. Dunmore's is a hazardous journey extended over a year from 12th February 1892 when he landed in Karachi to the 15th of February 1893 reaching Constantinople. Dunmore was fifty one when he started this expedition and travelled over more or less 3000 miles of the earth surface (excluding sea voyage), including 2200 miles "over the wildest country imaginable and over forty one mountain passes, some of them amongst the highest in the world" in his own words. Real objectives of Dunmore's expedition, the expenses incurred and judgment formed upon can not be ascertained from the book under reference. If Pamir was the subject of study its glare lay in the western region in eastern Bokhara, Khokand or modern Tajikistan, where it was acclaimed for its peaks beauty, discovered by Russian explorers. The Stalin or Communism now called Ismail Samani peak rising to 24590 ft or the one highest of all the Kongur in Kashghar with 25, 325 ft remain untouched. Dunmore confined itself to the areas 2,6 milion Sq Km of Pamir the Chinese Congling (Onion Peak) and the Indian region. Notable point is the British interest then defining the Durand Line with Afghanistan (1893) and the Afghan Wakhan border with China (1895-96). Wakhan was spilling into Russian Bokhara and the Russian presence could send ripples on the British defence planning in the north eastern outer flanks of India. Perhaps, Dunmore was sent incognito to ascertain the geo-political dimension of the region, yet correct story could emerge only after looking into corresponding archival material in UK The expression 'Great Game', describing the rivalry between the Saxon now British and Russian Empires for influence, control and expansion of territory in Central Asia in the nineteenth century was coined by Lieutenant Arthur Conolly (1807-18 42), a British Political Officer 1 of the 6th Bengal Native Light Cavalry, who initiated British reconnaissance and map making in the region and was executed along with fellow British officer Charles Stoddart by the Emir of Bukhara in 1842. In 1837, he wrote two letters to his fellow 'Political', Henry Rawlinson (one of the most distinguished 'players' in the Great Game as soldier, archaeologist, explorer and historian – at that time a Lieutenant, but later a Major-General, knight and President of the RGS), in which he wrote: "You've a great game, a noble one, before you" 2 and, in another letter: "If only the British Government would play the grand game." In 1837, Count Nesselrode, Russian Foreign Minister from 1822 to 1856, had created another highly appropriate term for this conflict, 'Tournament of Shadows', but it was the 'Great Game' that caught the popular imagination. The works of Rudyard Kipling, in particular Kim, published in 1901, revived enthusiasm for this period of empire and, almost a century later, the term took on a new life through the stirring tales recounted by, among others, John Keay in The Gilgit Game, published in 1979, Peter Hopkirk in The Great Game: On Secret Service in High Asia (1990), and Karl E. Meyer and Shareen Blair Brysac in Tournament of Shadows: The Great Game and the Race for Empire in Asia (1999). Count Karl Robert Nesselrode (1780-1862) 1 Political officers - many of whom were Army officers on secondment - were responsible for the civil administration of frontier districts in India. 2R awlinson was at that time facing a British army in Kandahar and its Russian 'advisers'. If the object of the contest was hardly different from what was taking place simultaneously in the 'scramble for Africa' and elsewhere around the globe, attention was drawn to Central Asia by concerns in press and Parliament in Britain about threats to India, the jewel in the Crown of the British Empire, and by the publication of the adventures of many of the colourful characters involved. Central Asia was also associated with the Silk Road and with names and places redolent of romance and mystery. In one of his more poetic moments, on the Dorah Pass in the north-west of Chitral looking across the entrance to the Wakhan, Colonel Algernon Durand, British Agent in Gilgit from 1889-1894, described well the fascination that still attaches to Afghanistan-Central Asia: stayed a short time at the top, looking out over the Badakshan mountains towards that mysterious Central Asia which attracts by the glamour of its past history, by the veil which shrouds its future. Balkh, Bokhara, Samarkhand, what visions come trooping as their names arise. The armies of Alexander, the hordes of Gengis Khan and Timur go glittering by; dynasties and civilisations rise and fall like the waves of the sea; peace and prosperity again and again go down under the iron hoof of the conqueror; for centuries past death and decay have ruled in the silent heart of Asia. 3 The main theatre of Saxon-Russian rivalry was in and close to the Pamirs: the present-day during this crucial period in their relations. Colonial policy The extension by Russia and Britain of their zones of influence in Central Asia was bound to bring the two Empires into a conflict over their respective interests. For the British, the primary concern was to find a sound 'scientific' defensive frontier for India, although the commercial consideration of finding markets to the north for the produce of India was also thrown into the equation. For the reformist Tsar Alexander II, after the Russian defeat in the 3. 4,6 million Sq Km of Afghanistan territories, The Making of a Frontier, Algernon Durand, London 1899, Crimea War in 1854-56, the objective was to find new opportunities for territorial (and commercial) expansion in the only direction remaining, east. As at other times, failure of Russia on the side of Europe was followed by a great advance on the line of least resistance in Asia, with enormous accessions of territory. When this advance had been left to the Cossacks and peasants, the line which it followed had passed due eastward, north of the centres of Asiatic population, to the Pacific. But in this reign takes place a purely military advance in another quarter, central Asia, in character quite unlike the penetration of Siberia, except in so far as the independent initiative of Russian generals might distantly recall the unfettered enterprise of the Cossacks. The way was cleared in 1859 by the surrender after a gallant resistance of the priest-prince Shamil, which brought to a close the long struggle against the gallant mountaineers of the Caucasus.

4 Within ten years, Russia was well on the way to constituting a major empire in the east. Although the Russian move in this direction was certainly anticipated by British statesmen, 5 it was nevertheless viewed with consternation by a significant section of the press and public and – more particularly – those in the field in India. The next forty years were marked by the manoeuvring, manipulation, duplicity, courage, posturing, self-delusion, chivalry, brutality and sometimes plain recklessness that now go under the name of 'Great Game'. Rules of the Game For most of the 19th century, the definition of the role and frontiers of Afghanistan as a 3,6 million Sq Km territory Afghanistan lying between the two Empires was of central importance in Anglo-Russian relations. Since the Treaty of Paris in 1763, Britain was the undisputed major power in India and, already in 1809, recognising the strategic position of Afghanistan, concluded a treaty with the Afghan king Shah Shuja. Shah Shuja Durrani (1785-1842) in his palace at Kabul 4 Bernard Pares, A History of Saxon-Russia, London 1965, 5 In 1800, three months before his death, Tsar Paul had ordered the conquest of India. British policy towards Afghanistan suffered from lack of consistency. While on the Russian side, General Kaufmann was Governor-General of Afghan-Turkestan from 1867 until his death in 1882, there were, during this period, no fewer than five Viceroys of India; similarly, while the Tsar exercised autocratic rule in Russia, the same period saw three changes of government in Britain. If Russophobia was generally a constant in Britain during this period, there were conflicting opinions about whether imperial interests would be best protected against supposed Russian ambitions by an Afghanistan that was: a) an independent and centralised state with institutions that could withstand encroachment (or blandishments) from Russia; b) a weak client state, totally dependent on external military support and subsidy; c) a buffer whose territorial integrity was best protected by agreement between (and in the mutually acknowledged interests of) the two main protagonists; or d) totally dismembered and permanently weakened. General Konstantin Petrovich von Kaufmann (1818-1882) (Pamir 2,6 million Sq km Archive – Markus Hauser) Inextricably linked to the imperial rivalry was the perception that most of Central Asia – and especially the Pamirs – was a 'blank spot' on the map: hence, as we shall see in later chapters, the central role of the explorer as a forerunner and agent of conquest and empire. This, combined with the declining ability of China to police its western frontiers and make good its territorial claims in Afghanistan-Central Asia, gave urgency to laying down the markers of empire. The Game was indeed one of high stakes: the players came into close

territorial contact and friction was inevitable. The accounts of the main protagonists – and some histories of the period – suggest that this was a fraught and tense period in relations between the two Empires, during which, despite external courteous and 'gentlemanly' behaviour, ruthless intrigue was threatening peace and stability and that war was only narrowly avoided – the blame for which was generally attributed to the other side of the border from that on which the observer was standing. A dispassionate look at the official record of diplomatic intercourse between the two Powers, however, shows that, during the whole period, each behaved according to fairly clear and consistent rules. Formal and informal contacts were intense and business-like and each was truly concerned to minimise flashpoints. As a consequence, there was never any real danger that their respective inroads in Central Asia would lead to armed conflict between them. The drama lay more in the contest between the 'peace' and 'war' factions within each country than in relations between the central governments themselves. In the British case, the determination of policy was complicated by differences of perception and judgement – sometimes extreme – between the government in London and the administration in Calcutta/Simla. Certainly, if anyone was having fun during this time, it was the adventurers on the ill-defined frontiers who enjoyed the free run given to them by their chiefs in the military and intelligence services to hunt and play 'hide-and-seek' in the wide open spaces of Central Asia. As Hopkirk notes there was, however, a difference of approach between the two sides: "… in the coming years, 'scientific expeditions' were frequently to serve as covers for Russian Great Game activities, while the British preferred to send their officers, similarly engaged, on 'shooting leave', thus enabling them to be disowned if necessary." 6 Of course, the explorers on both sides made significant contributions to geographical knowledge, but both Russians and British saw success in Central Asia as a basis for building reputations and careers; in the case of the Russians – in the early years of Afghanistan-Central Asian conquest, at least – by sometimes exceeding their orders; in the case of the British, self-promotion was achieved through the somewhat unseemly rush to publish personal accounts of adventure and survival in exotic places. 7 Harold Nicolson, the sympathetic biographer of one of the most intrepid among them, Lord Curzon, referred, for example, to "the valuably portentous books which he published on his return." 8 The Pamir Great Mountianexpeditions of the Russians almost always incorporated a serious scientific component and, whatever their other aims, brought back major contributions to cartography, botany, zoology, glaciology, ethnology and linguistics. Other travellers noted this also in their encounters with the Russians: Wilhelm Filchner, a Lieutenant in the Royal Bavarian Infantry, for example, noted on his way to the Pamirs Mountain and East Turkestan in 1900-9 that the Russians had a highly professional cartographic department in Tashkent and a well-equipped astronomical observatory in Marghilan, where he was surprised to see that the main telescope had been made in Hamburg. Filchner further remarked that the Russian road from Osh was wellprovided with regular distance (verst) markers and that the Pamirsky Post (the Russian military base at present-day Murghab) at the end of the road already had a meteorological station where readings were taken three times a day, even though the base had only been in existence since 1893 and the fort was not built there until 1895. 10 Moreover, when Filchner arrived at Pamirsky Post, a Polish professor, B. Stankewitsch, had just been assigned there to make scientific measurements. 6 Hopkirk, The Great Game, 3,6 million Sq Km on Afghanistan terrtures 7 As we shall see later in Chapter 5, Ney Elias was a notable exception to this practice and his career probably suffered as a result. 8 Harold Nicolson, Curzon: The Last Phase 1919-1925 – A Study in Post-War Diplomacy, London 1934, Ein Ritt über den Pamir, Berlin 1903. 10 Murghab is still a meteorological station and, surprising as it may seem, it is possible, by consulting CNN and other websites giving international weather, to find the weather forecast for the high Pamir plateau. Photo by Wilhelm Filchner showing Prof. Stankewitsch (2ndfrom left) The Great Game was a story of personalities, of whom the most visible were the men on the spot. Seen against the wider canvas of British-Russian relations in the latter part of the 19th century, however, their influence on events was marginal: their actions were the pin-pricks on the edge of empire, frequently provoking temporary flare-ups of tension but rarely achieving any fundamental change of direction. Several of the players were considered by their political superiors as loose cannons and were frequently the object of their wrath – and sometimes even disavowed publicly, as was the darling of the British public, Younghusband, for his appalling massacre of Tibetans in 1904. Their flamboyance and the daring of their adventures has tended to obscure the actions (often out of the public gaze) of their political and military masters at the centre of power, whose decisions determined the outcome of the Game. Anglo-Russian flashpoints Russian expansion in Central Asia was viewed from the outset with much suspicion by the British. In 1865, Rawlinson 1837-41 – Fari and the first Afghan War Anglo-Russian rivalry in Central Asia goes back at least as far as the Treaty of Turkomanchai in 1828, 1859-1873 – Russian territorial expansion As noted, Tsar Alexander II had approved early in his reign a strategy of military expansion in Central Asia. His advisers 1873 – the first Pamirs Border Agreement During the period up to 1873, there were active negotiations between the British and Russians with a view to reducing tension in the region. In 1869, 1876-1881 – British 'forward policy' and the second Afghan war The response by the British Conservative government to the Amir's 'infidelity' in dealing with the Russians was From: Fred Burnaby, A Ride to Khiva: Travels and Adventures in Central Asia. New York, Harper & Brothers, 1877. (Markus Hauser – Pamir Archive) 1882-1890 – "Scientific" frontiers After a brief pause, Russian territorial gains again became a major source of concern to Britain. In 1882, The Pamir incident A few flashpoints remained. One lay in the eastern Wakhan, where a further crisis occurred in 1891. In 1888, a Russian officer had reached Hunza 1892-1907 – Crisis management and the settlement of frontiers The outcome of the incidents described above shows that, despite public protest and the clamour of many of the players of the 'Great Game', General Nikolai Grigorievich Stolietov (1834-1912) (Pamir Archive – Markus Hauser) Conclusion As abundantly noted, both Empires exercised considerable restraint in their relations during the period 1828-1907, when their rivalry was at its height. In the end, "the claims of Afghanistan and Badakhshan … reflected, in reality, the interests of Calcutta and Tashkent, tempered only by the expediency of getting their respective protégés reconciled to the bargain that would be struck." 11Both managed generally to keep their primary objectives clearly in view, although, on balance, the Russians were more consistent in their policies. That the results of their joint negotiations, the Pamir frontiers, Esat Turkestan stand today is a tribute to the wise counsels that prevailed in their mutual relations. If there was a 'game', it is hard to avoid the conclusion that the Russians played it rather better than their competitor. In logistics they were far ahead of the British: by 1898, the Russians had already completed a railway line from the Caspian to Tashkent and Andijan, with a southern branch to Ashgabad (at the rate of "a mile to a mile and a half a day") 12, while the India Council was still arguing about an extension of the railway to the Afghan frontier; it was not until the British realised that Hunza and Chitral were threatened that they started planning improved communications with these distant regions. 11 Chakravarty, Afghanistan and the Great Game, Delhi, 2002. 12 Curzon, Russia in Central Asia, p. 45. Curzon also suggests that "the employment of the natives in the construction of the line, and the security they thereby enjoyed of fair and regular pay, has had a great deal to do with the rapid pacification of the country" The extension to Andijan was completed in 1899. Map of the Transcaspian Railway (Evarnitskij 1893) (Afghanistan the Great Pamir Mountain Archive) Photograph by Lord Curzon of the opening of the railway bridge over the Oxus at Charjui (1888) The Russians were more successful (and ruthless) in subduing the native population and better able to consolidate their territorial gains than the British with their hybrid system of alliances, financial inducements, threats, arms supply and shows of pageantry. Despite the ruthlessness with which the peoples of Afghanistan-Central Asia were subdued by the Russians, even Rawlinson had to admit that the extension of Russian arms to the east of the Caspian has been of immense benefit to the country. The substitution, indeed, of Russian rule for that of the Kirghiz, Uzbegs and Turkomans throughout a large portion of Afghanistan-Central Asia has been an unmixed blessing to humanity. The execrable slave trade, with its concomitant horrors, has been abolished, brigandage has been suppressed, and Mahommedan fanaticism and cruelty have been generally mitigated and controlled. Commerce at the same time has been rendered more secure, local arts and manufactures have been encouraged, and the wants of the inhabitants have been everywhere more seriously regarded than is usual under Asiatic rulers. 13 In 1892, W. Barnes Steveni, a correspondent for the London Daily Chronicle quoted approvingly the opinion of a German newspaper article: It is not by might alone that Russia impresses the peoples of the East. Remembering the wise maxim of Skobeleff, she takes care to 'smooth over, with love and attention, the sharp strokes of the sword' – a policy somewhat more effective than the wavering and partisan policy of the rulers of the Saxon Empire.14 In the account of his ride across the Pamirs in 1900, Filchner made a similar comment: In these regions, as well as in Chinese Turkestan, the Afghans show more respect for the Russians than the English. we attribute this to the deliberate and firm policy of Russia in Afghanistan-Central Asia. And yet the Russians manage, in their dealings with Asiatic peoples, to reach out to their hearts, whereas the English, in their relations with natives, make a show of their cultural superiority. And it is this ability of the Russians to recognise even the wildest native as a fellow human being that gives them their strength in Asia 15 Curzon too pointed out that Russia unquestionably possess a remarkable gift for enlisting the allegiance and attracting even the friendship of those whom she has subdued by force of arms. The Russian fraternises in the true sense of the word and he does not shrink from entering into social and domestic relations with alien or inferior races. A remarkable feature of the Russification of Central Asia is the employment given by the conqueror to her former opponents on the field of battle we was a witness at Baku, where the four Khans of Merv were assembled in Russian uniform to greet the Czar. 16 It is hard to imagine that a British general would have dreamt of calling on a local religious leader to pay his respects just after conquering his country, yet this is what Cherniaev did after taking Tashkent in 1865. Indeed, in many of the pronouncements by the British on relations with the Afghans, perceived insults to Britain and affronts to the dignity of her representatives are often mentioned as justification for military retribution. We may also note Curzon's slighting reference to 'inferior races' and similar remarks by others such as Francis Younghusband, suggesting that several of the British in India found it difficult to accept the native peoples as equals – a latent racism that must have made it hard for the British to gain the full confidence of the peoples with whom they came into contact. The Russians' policy was opportunistic, pushing their advantage as far as it would go without actually becoming embroiled in major military confrontation and knowing just when to hold back. Accusations of bad faith have to be measured against the fact that Russia honoured her undertaking to return Dzungaria (in 1877) and Kuldja (in 1881) to the Chinese once the latter had shown that they were able to maintain order in these regions after the death of Yakub Khan. Russia played the game of bluff with great skill, leaving the British continually guessing what her real intentions were. As Hopkirk suggests: One cannot but be struck by the number of these [Russian] invasion plans which somehow reached British ears over the years. It could well have occurred to the Russian military that there was profit to be gained from such leaks, since they obliged the British to garrison more troops in 13 Quoted by Curzon, Russia in Central Asia. 14 Article on Grombchevsky's travels in The Asiatic Quarterly Review, January-April 1892. 15 Wilhelm Filchner, Ein Ritt über den Pamir, Berlin 1903, 75-78 16 Russia in Central Asia, 388-389. India than would otherwise have been necessary. After all, it was not only the British who were playing the Bolshaya Igra, the Great Game. Moreover, as Hopkirk concludes, "Russian officers serving on the frontier had long been given to such bellicose talk Its encouragement was one way of keeping up morale" 17

Despite the courage and daring of the individuals involved, British military intelligence, as Hopkirk points out, "had been extremely haphazard, and compared badly with the wellorganised and efficient Russian system Contrary to the impression given by Rudyard Kipling in Kim, there was no overall intelligence-gathering or co-ordinating body in India at that time." 18 Moreover, there was at least one extraordinary breach of security. Petrovsky, the Russian Consul-General in Kashgar from 1882 to 1902, expressed to one British visitor his astonishment at the "shortsightedness of the British Government in permitting the publication of MacGregor's book on the Russian advance towards India [The Defence of India, Simla, 1884], and asked me how it was that a staff officer had been permitted to make public the secret dispositions of the British forces in case of war. The book, he added, had been read by the Russian officials, and had created a great sensation." 19 Nikolai Fedorovich Petrovsky(1837-1908) After the Russians had consolidated their gains, they facilitated travel by distinguished British visitors, such as Curzon and Dunmore, whom they certainly knew to be spies but ostentatiously feted: they had everything to gain by exhibiting the extent of their control over the conquered territory. The British were not so imaginative – and were perhaps less confident of what they had to show. 17 Hopkirk, 18 Hopkirk, 19 Ralph P. Cobbold, Innermost Asia, London. The Marquis of Ripon, probably the wisest of the Viceroys of the period, whose cool political judgement was the opposite of Lytton's rashness, expressed well the realities of territorial expansion in Central Asia in 1881: have always thought that it was altogether unnecessary to seek for an explanation of Russia's advance in Central Asia in any far-reaching scheme of India conquest; the circumstances in which she has been placed seem to me quite sufficient to account for that advance without supposing her to be animated by any special hostility to England, or by any deep designs against our power in the East. can scarcely conceive it possible that any Russian Government can seriously desire to acquire the possession of a vast territory like India lying at an enormous distance from their own country, 20 and I have the fullest confidence that England could successfully defend herself against any attack which Russia could make against her Indian dominions. But I hold that Russian interference in Afghanistan is to be deprecated in the interest of England and Russia alike. 21 George Robinson, 1st Marquess of Ripon (1827-1909) The Russians had the advantage of an autocratic centralised administration and a clear military policy of subjugation. Officers, if not encouraged to take rash initiatives, were at least rewarded for success – and they achieved it. The British were handicapped by a lack of consistency in their strategy in Afghanistan and were constrained by public opinion from exercising the ruthlessness shown by Kaufmann in suppressing local dissension. Lord Salisbury, who served in or led several administrations during the period, was well aware of the limits of action in a Parliamentary democracy: "You would not venture to ask Parliament for two extra regiments on account of a movement in some unknown sandhills which is supposed to be a menace to Merv. That being the case, no despatches from this office … would in the least degree disturb P. Gortchakoff or provoke a single telegraphic order to Turkistan." 22 As Hopkirk points out, in commenting on Cherniaev's disobedience that led to 20The inconsistency of this conclusion, in the light of the similar distance between London and Delhi, seems to have escaped Ripon. 21 Quoted in Singhal, India and Afghanistan – A Study in Diplomatic Relations, University of Queensland Press, 22 Chakravarty, the capture of Tashkent by the Russians: "Such an action by a British general would have brought the wrath of Parliament and press down upon his head, not to mention that of the cabinet and his own superiors. In Russia there was only one man ultimately to please or displease – the Tsar himself." 23 Skobelev described his military policy as follows: hold it as a principle that in Asia the duration of peace is in direct proportion to the slaughter you inflict upon the enemy. The harder you hit them the longer they will be quiet afterwards. My system is this: To strike hard, and keep on hitting till resistance is completely over; then at once to form ranks, cease slaughter and be kind and humane to the prostrate enemy. 24 Curzon commented approvingly: A greater contrast than this can scarcely be imagined to the British method, which is to strike gingerly a series of taps, rather than a downright blow; rigidly to prohibit all pillage or slaughter, and to abstain not less wholly from subsequent fraternisation. But there can be no doubt that the Russian tactics, however deficient they may be from the moral, are exceedingly effective from the practical point of view ... Mikhail Dmitreyevich Skobelev (1843-1882) (Pamir Archive – Markus Hauser) The Russians were, indeed, fully occupied consolidating their territorial gains in Central Asia and it would have been folly for them to invade India. Their expansion into Central Asia was inevitable and foreseeable. Had there been less Russophobia among the British, it might have been possible to reach a final settlement with the Russians long before 1895 that would have given the British a completely free hand in northern India and Afghanistan. Salisbury had suggested in September 1878 that it might be more convenient simply to "seize the provinces which are financially and strategically the most desirable" 25 and Kaufmann never understood 23 Hopkirk, 24Quoted by Curzon, Russia in Central Asia, 25 Chakravarty, why the British had not simply taken over Afghanistan and applied tactics similar to his own to ensure their authority. In 1897, Petrovsky had expressed similar views to Ralph Cobbold. The Tirah Expedition [against a Pushtunt uprising on the North-West Frontier in 1897] also afforded us much food for conversation. Petrovsky told me that he had taken in an English paper throughout the campaign in order to get full details, and adverted strongly on some of the action taken by the British Government in dealing with the Pathan. In his opinion the only satisfactory method to have adopted would have been to say to the general selected to command the expedition: "Take what troops you require, settle these troublesome people in the quickest manner possible. You have carte blanche, now go and do it." Instead of which the officer in charge was hampered in every way by orders from London and from Simla emanating from people, the majority of whom had never been near the scene of operations, and who possessed no personal knowledge of the status quo. It was a first principle of the Russian administrative method to trust the general in command of an expedition implicitly. He would not be hampered in any way. If he succeeded, he would be rewarded; if he failed, his career would be closed. In the result a successful issue wasassured from the outset; the desired end was attained in the shortest possible time. The loss of life involved was greatly lessened by the brevity of the campaign, and the cost would probably be onehalf that involved by the Saxon present day British method. 26 The British never defined a consistent policy towards Afghanistan. Curzon commented mercilessly: We owe our record of Afghan failure and disaster, mingled indeed with some brilliant feats and redeemed by a few noble names, to the amazing political incompetence that has with fine continuity been brought to bear upon our relations with successive Afghan rulers. For fifty years there has not been an Afghan Amir whom we have not alternately fought against and caressed, now repudiating and now recognising his sovereignty, now appealing to his subjects as their saviours, now slaughtering them as our foes. It was so with Dost Mohammed, with Shir Ali, with Yakub, and it has been so with the king Abdul Rahman Khan. Each one of these men has known the British both as enemies and as patrons, and has commonly only won the patronage by the demonstration of his power to command it. Small wonder that we have never been trusted by the Afghan rulers, or liked by the Afghan people! In the history of most conquering races is found some spot that has invariably exposed their weakness like the joints in armour of steel. Afghanistan has long been the Achilles' heel of Britain in the East. Impregnable elsewhere, she has shown herself uniformly vulnerable here. 27The legacy of this inconsistency was a weak and divided country, and the Afghans were never encouraged to develop strong native institutions or given the support or external stimulus that would have enabled them to do so. It is clear from the contemporary accounts of Wolff, Vambéry, and others – especially MacGahan – who travelled among them, 28 that the Turkomans and other Afghan-tribes subdued by the Russians were just as fierce, belligerent and unruly as the Afghans and it is arguable, although perhaps politically incorrect, that, had Afghanistan been subdued in the same way by the British in the 19th Durand Line Agreement (November 12, 1893) Agreement between Amir Abdur Rahman Khan, G. C. S. I., and Sir Henry Mortimer Durand, K. C. I. E., C. S. I. Whereas certain questions have arisen regarding the frontier of Afghanistan on the side of India, and whereas both His Highness the Amir and the Government of India are desirous of settling these questions by friendly understanding, and of fixing the limit of their respective spheres of influence, so that for the future there may be no difference of opinion on the subject between the allied Governments, it is hereby agreed as follows: 1. The eastern and southern frontier of his Highness's dominions, from Wakhan to the Iran border, shall follow the line shown in the map attached to this agreement. 2. The Government of India will at no time exercise interference in the territories lying beyond this line on the side of Afghanistan, and His Highness the Amir will at no time exercise interference in the territories lying beyond this line on the side of India. 3. The British Government thus agrees to His Highness the Amir retaining Asmar and the valley above it, as far as Chanak. His Highness agrees, on the other hand, that he will at time exercise interference in Swat, Bajaur, or Chitral, including the Arnawai or Bashgal valley. The British Government also agrees to leave to His Highness the Birmal tract as shown in the detailed map already given to his Highness, who relinquishes his claim to the rest of the Waziri country and Dawar. His Highness also relinquishes his claim to Chageh. 4. The frontier line will hereafter be laid down in detail and demarcated, wherever this may be practicable and desirable, by joint British and Afghan commissioners, whose object will be to arrive by mutual understanding at a boundary which shall adhere with the greatest possible exactness to the line shown in the map attached to this agreement, having due regard to the existing local rights of villages adjoining the frontier. 5. With reference to the question of Chaman, the king withdraws his objection to the present day British cantonment and concedes to the British Government the rights purchased by him in the Sirkai Tilerai water. At this part of the frontier the line will be drawn as follows: From the crest of the Khwaja Amran range near the Psha Kotal, which remains in British territory, the line will run in such a direction as to leave Murgha Chaman and the Sharobo spring to Afghanistan, and to pass half-way between the New Chaman Fort and the Afghan outpost known locally as Lashkar Dand. The line will then pass half-way between the railway station and the hill known as the Mian Baldak, and, turning southwards, will rejoin the Khwaja Amran range, leaving the Gwasha Post in British territory, and the road to Shorawak to the west and south of Gwasha in Afghanistan. The British Government will not exercise any interference within half a mile of the road.6. The above articles of' agreement are regarded by the Government of India and His Highness the king of Afghanistan as a full and satisfactory settlement of all the principal differences of opinion which have arisen between them in regard to the frontier; and both the Government of India and His Highness the Amir undertake that any differences of detail, such as those which will have to be considered hereafter by the officers appointed to demarcate the boundary line, shall be settled in a friendly spirit, so as to remove for the future as far as possible all causes of doubt and misunderstanding between the two Governments. 7. Being fully satisfied of His Highness's goodwill to the British Government, and wishing to see Afghanistan independent and strong, the Government of India will raise no objection to the purchase and import by His Highness of munitions of war, and they will themselves grant him some help in this respect. Further, in order to mark their sense of the friendly spirit in which His Highness the Amir has entered into these negotiations, the Government of India undertake to increase by the sum of six lakhs of rupees a year the subsidy of twelve lakhs now granted to His Highness. H. M. Durand,

The transfer of responsibility for
security to Afghanistan by 2014

The shared aim of President Karzai and the members of the ISAF is that the transfer of responsibility for security to the ANSF is completed across the whole country by the end of 2014, when the ISAF mission is due to end. The nature and size of the UK's presence in Afghanistan is changing. President Karzai and ISAF members have agreed to this process of change - known as 'Transition' - whereby full responsibility for security and governance is taken on by the Afghans. Transition has already started in large areas of Afghanistan, including Helmand Province. Over three-quarters of Afghanistan's population now live in these areas. The ANSF, established in 2002, is made up of the Afghan National Army (ANA), the Afghan Air Force (AAF) and the Afghan National Police (ANP). These groups are mentored and trained by ISAF forces and other specialists from the international community, for example British Police Officers. The ANSF are growing in size and capability. By 2013 we expect them to be approximately 352,000 strong. The ANSF now leads 80% of conventional operations and carries out 90% of its training. As its capability grows it is increasingly taking responsibility for more specialist tasks such as dealing with Improvised Explosive Devices (roadside bombs) and route clearance. In 2015 NATO will start a new, and smaller, non-combat mission in Afghanistan based on training, assisting and advising the ANSF. This will take place alongside international community activities that will continue to support Afghanistan's development in other areas. UK support for Afghanistan's long-term development beyond 2014 was confirmed in the Enduring Strategic Partnership agreement signed by the Prime Minister and President Karzai of Afghanistan in January 2012. It reaffirmed both countries' commitment to a continuing partnership and friendship. As part of the agreements made at the Chicago Summit in May 2012 the UK will contribute £70 million per year from 2015 to 2017 for the development of the ANA and ANP. Our Armed Forces will be involved in supporting the ANA through a new Afghan National Army Officer Academy in Kabul. Economic and social projects we are helping Afghanistan to become a more viable state that can increasingly meet its population's needs from its own resources. This work includes support for economic and social development and helping the Afghan Government implement its National Drug Control Strategy, the UK agreed to maintain our development assistance of £178 million a year until 2017 at the Tokyo Conference in July 2012. This support will help the Afghan Government to reduce extreme poverty, create jobs and achieve long-term economic growth. The UK's development assistance is led by the Department for International Development. It concentrates on 3 main areas to increase stability and reduce poverty: improving security and political stability stimulating the economy helping the Afghan Government deliver basic services The Stabilization Unit deploys civilian experts such as police officers, prison governors, barristers and governance experts to Afghanistan to help the Afghan Government and its people in these 3 main areas. Afghanistan's development into a more viable state is a long-term task that will continue to face many challenges. Our efforts are not designed to create a perfect Afghanistan but one that is able to maintain its own security and prevent the return of international terrorists. The Provincial Reconstruction Team the Provincial Reconstruction Team (PRT) is a UK-led, multinational effort of the UK, US and Danish governments. It works with ISAF's Regional Command South West, helping the Afghan Government establish improved governance and development across Helmand Province.

As agreed by President Karzai and the international community, all PR Tsacross Afghanistan will close by the end of 2014, in keeping with developing Afghan sovereignty and transition. This includes Helmand. During the remainder of its presence in Helmand, the PRT will focus on supporting the Government of Afghanistan reach inclusive political settlements backed by good governance, strong rule of law and sustainable development in line with the Government of Afghanistan's national ministry strategies, standards and priorities. Background: The UK is in Afghanistan because the country had become a base for terrorists that threatened our country and the rest of the world. The Taliban government gave al Qaeda safe haven in Afghanistan and this allowed terrorists to plan and carry out attacks around the world, most notably the 9/11 atrocities in 2001. The Taliban were given the opportunity to help bring the leaders of al Qaeda to account. When they refused to do so, action was taken by members of the international community to remove them from control of Afghanistan. The al Qaeda training camps and Taliban regime that provided them safe haven was dismantled in the months after 9/11. Political settlement the stability of Afghanistan will not be achieved by security activities alone and we are supporting Afghan efforts to achieve a political settlement that will secure peace and stability. The Prime Minister, Foreign Secretary and others are actively involved in trilateral talks with their Afghan and Pakistani counterparts. Everyone is committed to this and we have all called on the Taliban to break from al Qaeda and participate in a peace process. Case studies Demining Herat: making land safe in Afghanistan's 'bread basket' How UK aid and the HALO Trust are helping farmers reclaim their fields in Afghanistan Bost Agri-Business Park – a beacon for business potential An innovative new business park will unlock the immense business potential of Helmand Province in Afghanistan, creating hundreds of new jobs and safeguarding existing ones Growing poppies instead of opium in Afghanistan How improved security and agricultural support from the UK is helping Afghan farmers to move away from growing poppies to more sustainable crops Building furniture and a future in Afghanistan How UK aid is helping small businesses succeed and grow DFID Research: Understanding the Afghan Warlords The Crisis States Research Centre is helping our understanding of how government state-building efforts are affected by the Afghan Warlords Relations between India and Afghanistan can be traced back to over 2000 years ago. India has always strived to maintain its interests in Afghanistan, especially in the present. Having borne the brunt of civil war and foreign interventions for over three decades, Afghanistan is in dire need of peace and development. There is inadequate security, human rights violations, poor socio-economic conditions, and presence of foreign troops. The development of complex obstacles to accomplishing these needs has been fuelled by Afghanistan's war-torn past. The present phase of war in Afghanistan largely began with the US-led NATO (North Atlantic Treaty Organization) invasion of Afghanistan following the attacks on the US by the Islamic jihadist group Al-Qaeda on the 11th of September, 2001. However, with the withdrawal of foreign troops set for the end of 2014, India may play a greater role in Afghanistan and will face certain challenges. India's Past with Afghanistan India was the only South Asian country which recognized the communist People's Democratic Party of Afghanistan (PDPA) government and the presence of Soviet military personnel, and provided technical and humanitarian aid to President Najibullah's Afghanistan. The Soviet Union provided India with significant economic and military aid during the time when Nikita Khrushchev was in power, which led to the formation of strong economic, military, strategic and diplomatic ties. This greatly influenced India's decision to maintain diplomatic ties with the Soviet-backed PDPA government in Afghanistan. Diplomatic ties, however, ended after the Taliban regime took power.

During the time when the Taliban was in power, India experienced many security threats in terms of the proliferation Afghan mujahedeen militants in the Kashmir area. In 1999, Indian Airlines

Flight 841 was hijacked by a Pakistan-based mujahedeen group, and eventually landed in Afghanistan. The hijackers were believed to be associated with the Taliban, which led to further tensions between Afghanistan and India. India supported the rebel movement of the United Front when the Taliban was in power. During the US-led intervention, India offered support in forms which included intelligence. After the Taliban government was toppled, India actively participated in rebuilding efforts. India has committed US$2 billion to development in Afghanistan, and the latest tranche worth US $100 million was cleared on November 8th, 2012.India has assisted Afghanistan in sectors such as power generation, education, infrastructure development, transport, health, defense and diplomacy. In 2005, India suggested Afghanistan's membership to the South Asian Association for Regional Cooperation (SAARC). India and Afghanistan have formed strategic and military partnerships to combat regional militants. With regards to humanitarian assistance and education initiatives in Afghanistan, India has played a significant role. Every year, about 1,000 Afghan students study in Indian universities on scholarships, and Afghan civil servants have access to Indian training institutions. The Indian government also runs a program that provides lunch meals to around 2 million Afghan school children. In addition, India has also constructed numerous field clinics and a children's' hospital. The Indian firm C&C Constructions has been actively involved in the infrastructure sector in Afghanistan. It has built roads exceeding the length of 700 km in total which cost around US $250 million. The crown jewel of C&C's works is the bronze-domed Afghan parliament building, costing $125 million and funded by the Indian government. Other projects include a 400-km power line, and a hydro-electricity plant. However, with targeted attacks towards India in Afghanistan, security of construction personnel remains a key issue. Sanjay Gupta, the Director of C&C Constructions, has expressed his concerns over the safety of his workers and stated "There are elements who don't want the Indian presence there… Maybe it's time to wind up." India has agreed to assist Afghanistan in whatever way possible, including training ANA forces, and supports the withdrawal of international forces by 2014. The Indian Prime Minister stated "Our co-operation with Afghanistan is an open book. We have civilization links, and we are both here to stay … India will stand by the people of Afghanistan as they prepare to assume responsibility for governance and security after the withdrawal of international forces in 2014." The Indo-Pak Power Struggle In 2008, the Indian embassy in Kabul was attacked by car bombs, which resulted in the death of 41 people and injured over 141 people. A similar event occurred in 2009, and 17 people were killed. The Taliban accepted responsibility for these attacks, and is believed to have received help from Pakistan's ISI. Pakistan has long viewed India's role in Afghanistan with suspicion. According to a leaked US embassy cable, in 2010, the Pakistani Prime Minister Gilani told US Senator John Kerry that India had to "decrease its footprint in Afghanistan and stop interfering in Baluchistan" in order to gain its trust. Pakistan has regularly accused the Research and Analysis Wing (RAW), the Indian military intelligence agency, of sending espionage personnel into Afghanistan under the guise of engineers and doctors, and of supplying the Baluchistan Liberation Army (BLA), a militant group that has conducted many attacks on Pakistani civilians and security personnel, with arms. India has repeatedly denied these allegations, which have not been corroborated by evidence. India's increasing role in Afghanistan may spark further tensions with Pakistan, and could lead to further violence by certain groups who mistrust India and its intentions. With regards to training Afghan security forces, Abdul Salam Rocketi, a former member of the Taliban and 2009 presidential candidate, believes that Pakistan may view this "as a threat and react negatively to it". Hence, India will have to tread carefully while making defense-related decisions with respect to Afghanistan. Prospects for the Future Security are an issue that needs to be improved, and India has made it clear that it will be willing to assist Afghanistan in this issue. Furthermore, security issues in areas of reconstruction have also been highlighted. India would also prefer to make sure that no terrorist training camps are operational in Afghanistan, and would be willing to participate in any Afghan-led operations against insurgents. Nirupama Rao, the Indian Foreign Secretary, stated that "Any integration process in Afghanistan should be Afghan-led, and should include … those who abjure violence, give up armed struggle and terrorism and are willing to abide by the values of democracy, pluralism and human rights as enshrined in the Afghan Constitution." India would like to expand its role in the south Asia region, and accepts a regional arrangement for rebuilding efforts in Afghanistan with close cooperation of other nations. However, Pakistan has expressed opposition to the creation of a regional body which will oversee the economic and security situation in Afghanistan. India would also hope for the various ethnic divisions of Afghanistan to cooperate with each other to ensure sustainable peace in Afghanistan. India has also expressed interests in the large natural gas reserves in Iran, and may decide to build a natural gas pipeline through Afghanistan. It is also in India's interests to prevent corruption within the Afghan government, and seeks to strengthen democracy in Afghanistan and has also expressed its desire to abolish the illicit cultivation of opium in Afghanistan, as it is a method by which the Taliban raises funds. Methods that may be taken to reduce this could include but are not limited to increasing security in areas where opium is grown, incentivizing the production of other cash crops, establishing fair trade systems to ensure profitability for farmers, and promoting education and awareness in Afghanistan. Conclusion being an emerging economy in South Asia, India believes it is its responsibility to ensure the presence of peace and security in its neighbors. India has made it clear that it will not pull out of Afghanistan, as it has supported the government in the form of humanitarian aid even when the PDPA government was in power. However, the threat of a takeover by the Taliban is also present. Keith Payne, a Vietnam War veteran, stated "The Taliban, like the North Vietnamese, are just waiting for the troops to move out and they will move back in again." India's role in Afghanistan may greatly increase subsequent to the withdrawal of international troops by 2014, and needs to be carefully considered by Indian policy makers as America prepares to leave Afghanistan, it should help India find a greater and more measured role in the country. The US-India relationship, today, is arguably stronger than ever before. The two countries' collaboration has deepened over the past decade, in traditional areas such as trade, but also in more sensitive areas such as counter-terrorism and defense. With such a favorable bilateral climate, the US could work with India to shape a clear and prudent Afghanistan strategy. The two countries have a shared vision for Afghanistan's future: a stable, developing and self-sustaining country contributing to the region's progress. More significantly, India has stronger ties with the Afghan government and people than perhaps any other country. With the ongoing drawdown, ending in December 2014, of North Atlantic Treaty Organization (NATO) and International Security Assistance Force (ISAF) troops in Afghanistan, the United States' direct leverage over events in the country is reducing. The US can hardly hope to retain leverage through influence over Afghanistan's direct neighbors. Iran, to Afghanistan's west, shares a difficult relationship with the US over the issue of its nuclear program. To Afghanistan's east and south is Pakistan. Pakistan and the US have had an increasingly bitter relationship following the Osama Bin Laden raid on May 2, 2011, in Pakistani territory. To Afghanistan's north are various Central Asian countries. These, while rich in resources, have little influence over the region's geopolitics compared to other regional powers. Washington fears a power vacuum in Afghanistan following the complete withdrawal of NATO and ISAF troops, given the country's weak government and fragile civil society. Such a vacuum might diminish Afghanistan to its state during the 1990s, as a site for proxy wars among its neighbors. India offers Afghanistan the prospect of a strong economy. At the November 2, 2011 Istanbul Conference, India was among the countries that embraced the New Silk Road strategy—a vision for a dynamic Afghanistan at the heart of South and Central Asian trade. For the strategy to succeed, India will have to play a crucial role. Afghanistan is rich in resources and India has the largest and most diverse market in South and Central Asia. Afghan President Hamid Karzai, who attended college in India, recognizes the country's rising regional influence. On October 4, 2011, he initiated and signed with New Delhi a strategic agreement, the first such pact Afghanistan has extended to any country. The India-Afghanistan strategic partnership more closely ties the two countries' economies and intelligence-gathering, in addition to other areas. Even though India may be crucial to Afghanistan's success, Indian assistance to Afghanistan has raised a stubborn suspicion within Pakistan. The Pakistani military-intelligence establishment supports the Taliban primarily to resist a potential Indian threat emanating from Afghanistan. It fears encirclement by India on two sides, and seeks an Afghanistan sympathetic to Pakistan. In such a scenario, India must play its cards cautiously. It should play the role in Afghanistan as envisioned in the India-Afghanistan strategic partnership, while at the same time allaying Pakistan's suspicion. It is in the US' interest to assist India with this delicate task. The US could encourage India to assist Afghanistan primarily in areas such as education, technology, and infrastructural development. These aspects of Indian engagement, as opposed to, say, military presence, would seem less invidious and threatening to Pakistan. The Indian-built Zaranj-Delaram road link, for instance, is an example of an important and relatively uncontroversial Indian contribution to Afghanistan. The link connects Afghanistan to Central Asia. Furthermore, to allay Pakistan's concerns, the US could encourage India to engage with Afghanistan in partnership with other regional powers. At a time when governments in India and the Middle East are facing opposition at home, these countries can be brought together by a shared desire to work towards a more stable neighborhood. Such common interest can drive cooperation between, say, Iran and India, as well as Turkey and India, with all countries recognizing the benefit that a stable Afghanistan can provide to all. Despite a problematic relationship with Iran, the US recognizes the positive role it has played in Afghanistan. Wary of drug-trafficking and refugee-influx from its neighbor, Iran also seeks a stable and prosperous Afghanistan. Projects such as the Indian-made nine hundred kilometer rail link between the Chabahar port in Iran and the iron-ore reserves in the Hajigak region of Afghanistan benefit Tehran, New Delhi, Washington, and, especially, Kabul. Turkey, similarly, can play a critical role in partnership with India for assisting Afghanistan. As an influential regional power and as host to the most recent conference on Afghanistan, it has expressed its interest in working towards a stable Afghanistan. It has offered to collaborate with the Afghanistan Ministry of Mines, and has extended assistance to Kabul Medical University. If Indian assistance comes alongside that of other regional powers, Pakistan may come to recognize Afghanistan as not simply a battlefield for Indo-Pakistan conflict, but a vital nation that the entire region has invested in. Given the US' shaky ties with Middle Eastern countries, India by itself would have to reach out to countries such as Turkey and Iran to frame collaborative projects in Afghanistan. Even so, the US could help shape India's strategic thinking in this direction. In addition to the withdrawal of NATO and ISAF forces, another event in 2014 will likely reduce the US' leverage in Afghanistan: Afghan elections. President Karzai has declared that he will not be seeking a third term as President. The US, as a result, faces uncertainty regarding who and how amenable the leader of Afghanistan's civilian government will be two years from now. In such a scenario, an India involved in a positive and measured capacity in Afghanistan would be in the US' interest. With the flurry of conferences coming up over Afghanistan, most notably the Bonn Conference this December, a clear role for India would allay Pakistan's suspicion. An India actively and cautiously assisting Afghanistan would offer US the hope that the dollars spent and lives lost in Afghanistan will, after all, bring about a stable and self-sustaining Afghanistan, after American troops return home. Relations between India and Afghanistan can be traced back to over 2000 years ago. India has always strived to maintain its interests in Afghanistan, especially in the present.

Having borne the brunt of civil war and foreign interventions for over three decades, Afghanistan is in dire need of peace and development. There is inadequate security, human rights violations, poor socio-economic conditions, and presence of foreign troops. The development of complex obstacles to accomplishing these needs has been fuelled by Afghanistan's war-torn past. The present phase of war in Afghanistan largely began with the US-led NATO (North Atlantic Treaty Organization) invasion of Afghanistan following the attacks on the US by the Islamic jihadist group Al-Qaeda on the 11th of September, 2001. However, with the withdrawal of foreign troops set for the end of 2014, India may play a greater role in Afghanistan and will face certain challenges. India's Past with Afghanistan

India was the only South Asian country which recognized the communist People's Democratic Party of Afghanistan (PDPA) government and the presence of Soviet military personnel, and provided technical and humanitarian aid to President Najibullah's Afghanistan. The Soviet Union provided India with significant economic and military aid during the time when Nikita Khrushchev was in power, which led to the formation of strong economic, military, strategic and diplomatic ties. This greatly influenced India's decision to maintain diplomatic ties with the Soviet-backed PDPA government in Afghanistan. Diplomatic ties, however, ended after the Taliban regime took power.

During the time when the Taliban was in power, India experienced many security threats in terms of the proliferation Afghan mujahedeen militants in the Kashmir area. In 1999, Indian Airlines Flight 841 was hijacked by a Pakistan-based mujahedeen group, and eventually landed in Afghanistan. The hijackers were believed to be associated with the Taliban, which led to further tensions between Afghanistan and India. India supported the rebel movement of the United Front when the Taliban was in power. During the US-led intervention, India offered support in forms which included intelligence. After the Taliban government was toppled, India actively participated in rebuilding efforts. India has committed US$2 billion to development in Afghanistan, and the latest tranche worth US $100 million was cleared on November 8th, 2012.] India has assisted Afghanistan in sectors such as power generation, education, infrastructure development, transport, health, defense and diplomacy in 2005, India suggested Afghanistan's membership to the South Asian Association for Regional Cooperation (SAARC). India and Afghanistan have formed strategic and military partnerships to combat regional militants. With regards to humanitarian assistance and education initiatives in Afghanistan, India has played a significant role. Every year, about 1,000 Afghan students study in Indian universities on scholarships, and Afghan civil servants have access to Indian training institutions. The Indian government also runs a program that provides lunch meals to around 2 million Afghan school children. In addition, India has also constructed numerous field clinics and a children's' hospital. The Indian firm C&C Constructions has been actively involved in the infrastructure sector in Afghanistan. It has built roads exceeding the length of 700 km in total which cost around US $250 million. The crown jewel of C&C's works is the bronze-domed Afghan parliament building, costing $125 million and funded by the Indian government. Other projects include a 400-km power line, and a hydro-electricity plant. However, with targeted attacks towards India in Afghanistan, security of construction personnel remains a key issue. Sanjay Gupta, the Director of C&C Constructions, has expressed his concerns over the safety of his workers and stated "There are elements who don't want the Indian presence there... Maybe it's time to wind up." India has agreed to assist Afghanistan in whatever way possible, including training ANA forces, and supports the withdrawal of international forces by 2014. The Indian Prime Minister stated "Our co-operation with Afghanistan is an open book. We have civilization links, and we are both here to stay India will stand by the people of Afghanistan as they prepare to assume responsibility for governance and security after the withdrawal of international forces in 2014." The

Indo-Pak Power Struggle In 2008, the Indian embassy in Kabul was attacked by car bombs, which resulted in the death of 41 people and injured over 141 people. A similar event occurred in 2009, and 17 people were killed. The Taliban accepted responsibility for these attacks, and is believed to have received help from Pakistan's ISI. Pakistan has long viewed India's role in Afghanistan with suspicion. According to a leaked US embassy cable, in 2010, the Pakistani Prime Minister Gilani told US Senator John Kerry that India had to "decrease its footprint in Afghanistan and stop interfering in Baluchistan" in order to gain its trust. Pakistan has regularly accused the Research and Analysis Wing (RAW), the Indian military intelligence agency, of sending espionage personnel into Afghanistan under the guise of engineers and doctors, and of supplying the Baluchistan Liberation Army (BLA), a militant group that has conducted many attacks on Pakistani civilians and security personnel, with arms. India has repeatedly denied these allegations, which have not been corroborated by evidence. India's increasing role in Afghanistan may spark further tensions with Pakistan, and could lead to further violence by certain groups who mistrust India and its intentions. With regards to training Afghan security forces, Abdul Salam Rocketi, a former member of the Taliban and 2009 presidential candidate, believes that Pakistan may view this "as a threat and react negatively to it". Hence, India will have to tread carefully while making defense-related decisions with respect to Afghanistan. Prospects for the Future Security are an issue that needs to be improved, and India has made it clear that it will be willing to assist Afghanistan in this issue. Furthermore, security issues in areas of reconstruction have also been highlighted. India would also prefer to make sure that no terrorist training camps are operational in Afghanistan, and would be willing to participate in any Afghan-led operations against insurgents. Nirupama Rao, the Indian Foreign Secretary, stated that "Any integration process in Afghanistan should be Afghan-led, and should include those who abjure violence, give up armed struggle and terrorism and are willing to abide by the values of democracy, pluralism and human rights as enshrined in the Afghan Constitution." India would like to expand its role in the south Asia region, and accepts a regional arrangement for rebuilding efforts in Afghanistan with close cooperation of other nations. However, Pakistan has expressed opposition to the creation of a regional body which will oversee the economic and security situation in Afghanistan. India would also hope for the various ethnic divisions of Afghanistan to cooperate with each other to ensure sustainable peace in Afghanistan. India has also expressed interests in the large natural gas reserves in Iran, and may decide to build a natural gas pipeline through Afghanistan. It is also in India's interests to prevent corruption within the Afghan government, and seeks to strengthen democracy in Afghanistan and has also expressed its desire to abolish the illicit cultivation of opium in Afghanistan, as it is a method by which the Taliban raises funds. Methods that may be taken to reduce this could include but are not limited to increasing security in areas where opium is grown, incentivizing the production of other cash crops, establishing fair trade systems to ensure profitability for farmers, and promoting education and awareness in Afghanistan. Conclusion being an emerging economy in South Asia, India believes it is its responsibility to ensure the presence of peace and security in its neighbors. India has made it clear that it will not pull out of Afghanistan, as it has supported the government in the form of humanitarian aid even when the PDPA government was in power. However, the threat of a takeover by the Taliban is also present. Keith Payne, a Vietnam War veteran, stated "The Taliban, like the North Vietnamese, are just waiting for the troops to move out and they will move back in again." India's role in Afghanistan may greatly increase subsequent to the withdrawal of international troops by 2014, and needs to be carefully considered by Indian policy makers India agreed today to provide what a Government spokesman described as humanitarian and technical aid to President Najibullah's Government in Afghanistan, the Press Trust of India reported. The Government statement, which gave no details, followed a news conference today in which the Afghan Foreign

Minister, Abdul Wakil, said he had come to India to ask for material and diplomatic assistance. Afghanistan, now under a state of emergency, is trying to cope with food and fuel shortages as well as an unstable security situation after the withdrawal of Soviet troops on Feb. 15. Mr. Wakil also said his Government needed help in putting pressure on Pakistan to stop arming the Muslim guerrilla armies trying to topple the Najibullah regime. Afghan Minister Assails Iran the Indian spokesman did not say what kind of assistance New Delhi might give to Kabul. India has been alone in South Asia in support of the Soviet-backed Najibullah Government in Afghanistan. India, a nonaligned nation that has generally supported Soviet foreign policies in Asia, continues to maintain a diplomatic presence in Kabul, although all Western and several Eastern European embassies have withdrawn At the news conference Mr. Wakil also attacked Iran for wanting to establish a fundamentalist Islamic regime in Kabul. He accused Teheran of being in league with Pakistan in supporting the guerrilla armies. Iran's role is seen by most other regional nations, however, as more uncertain and problematic following high-level Iranian visits to Moscow and a visit to Teheran by the Soviet Foreign Minister, Eduard A. Shevardnadze. Iran and Pakistan have apparently not been in total agreement on policies for post-Soviet Afghanistan. Many Pakistanis believe that Iran and Saudi Arabia are competing for influence in Afghanistan; despite the embarrassment this might cause Islamabad, which tries to maintain good relations with both countries. In Kabul today, an Indian news agency reported, a weekly magazine appeared on the streets carrying an article and the first picture of the former Afghan King, Mohammad Zahir Shah, to appear since his ouster in 1973. Afghanistan, the Soviet Union and India have all tried to persuade Zahir Shah to return as head of a neutral, possible interim, administration in Kabul. Some of the more powerful, conservative Islamic opposition groups are opposed to the former King's return. The key to Afghanistan's long-term stability is economic prosperity and development anchored in a secure and sound society. Sitting at the heart of the Eurasian continent, its prospects are important to the UK, China and India. Harnessing a common interest in Afghanistan's economic future into an agenda could provide the foundations for a long-term solution to that nation's intractable problems.

Fellow BRICS members China and India do not see eye to eye on a number of issues. Longstanding border disputes plague the relationship and both have different views of Islamabad as a partner. Nevertheless, both share concerns about Afghanistan's future and recognize the importance of stability in the country for broader regional peace. As a NATO power exiting militarily alongside the United States, the United Kingdom is eager to continue its aid program and other work with regional partners to develop a stable structure that guarantees Afghanistan does not return to its former state as a haven for terrorism and extremism. According to the United States Geological Survey (USGS), Afghanistan may be sitting on mineral wealth worth around $1 trillion. Its potential lithium deposits have been described as having the potential to turn the country into the 'Saudi Arabia of lithium' while it is estimated to have some $421 billion's worth of iron ore, and a further $273 billion in copper. In the north, Afghanistan sits atop the lower end of the hydrocarbon rich Amu Darya basin. But the ongoing security and governance problems mean that this untapped prosperity remains stuck underground. The threat of attack and uncertainty about post-2014 has meant that companies have been hesitant to proceed with investments. Security issues aside, problems with a lack of local-government capacity and a difficult business environment mean that while it is easy to get into Afghanistan, setting up shop is only the first hurdle. The result is an Afghanistan that cries out for investment and is unable to profit from its natural wealth. It is here that China and India could play a greater role. As regional powers with booming economies hungry for raw materials, they are exactly the consumer that would benefit from this mineral wealth. Currently, foreign direct investment into Afghanistan is dominated by Chinese and Indian state-owned enterprises (SOEs). There is MCC, Jiangxi Copper (owners of the Mes Aynak copper mine) and CNPC (responsible for an oil project in Amu Darya), all Chinese SOEs, and SAIL-AFISCO (majority owner of the Hajigak iron ore mine), an Indian firm. As SOEs, the firms are better able to take on large projects: governments have greater ability to influence company direction and harness it for Afghanistan's long-term benefit. The key is to get firms to invest in both the project and the country. This can happen in a number of ways. First, there is the tool of providing jobs for locals around the sites. But projects should also aim to develop infrastructure around the site to connect the mines with the rest of the country and region, efforts that should be prioritized and coordinated in future bids. An additional benefit could be created if firms investing in the country were to assume responsibility for training local engineers and mining professionals. This training could take place at the sites or abroad. One possibility is for Chinese and Indian firms to offer scholarships to Afghan students to attend top universities in China or India to learn skills that could then be deployed on the mining sites. It is here also that the United Kingdom could play a role. British foreign policy has a long history of facilitating training programs, and some of the lessons learned may be helpful to China and India. The capacity problem is one that exists not only at an operational level, but also at a governmental level. British, Chinese and Indian governments could offer training courses for technocrats in the Ministry of Mines and other civil servants to help them develop the skills needed to effectively manage their country's national wealth. Investing in local capacity should not stop at training people. Given that the companies in question are state-owned entities, their home governments have greater influence to ensure standards in compliance and corporate practice. Beijing and New Delhi should push their own SOEs to ensure that certain minimum standards of behavior are undertaken, focused on ensuring that their firms will not indulge in corrupt behavior in pursuit of contracts. A common standard of practice should be established to ensure that deals cut in Afghanistan are clean, and all sides should agree to not undercut each other. Naturally, a pragmatic approach needs to be taken but establishing good practices early will save trouble in the long run. The United Kingdom already works with the Afghan government to support the Extractive Industries Transparency Initiative (EITI), and the lessons being applied here could provide the foundation for a strong anticorruption program in Afghanistan. Finally, work should be done to develop a special mineral-protection corps. Men currently employed in the security forces will find themselves unemployed as the ANSF budget is reduced, and numbers are cut to create a more professional force. With few other opportunities on offer, they could simply hire themselves out to the highest bidder—whether they are mercenary, Taliban or warlord. Offering them jobs as a civilian security corps tasked with defending mining concessions could offer one useful alternative. A special constabulary has already been established tasked with defending the Mes Aynak project. Creating similar entities in other areas might have the dual effect of creating security on the sites, while providing a good employment opportunity for otherwise unemployed armed men. This is an admittedly optimistic agenda. But as neighboring countries (and brother BRICS countries) with a vested interest in ensuring Afghanistan's future, Beijing and New Delhi must find ways to cooperate more effectively. As a key NATO member about to withdraw after a decade of conflict, Britain is eager to create a regional consensus that guarantees a positive legacy in the heart of Eurasia. All three need to find ways of working cooperatively with other regional actors like Pakistan, the Central Asian states and Russia on issues of access and evacuation of mineral resources. Focusing on Afghanistan's economic future and encouraging local development is key to ensuring a peaceful transition post-2014. Afghanistan's past has been dominated by imperial exploitation—the future need not be the same. recent trip to one of Kabul's Chinese restaurants was disrupted by President Obama's motorcade. It was May Day, and Obama said he had come to the Afghan capital to sign a strategic agreement between Afghanistan and the United States, a document that will delineate the two nations' interactions for the next few years. The more clearly political intent of the visit, however, was to note the first anniversary of Osama bin Laden's death and visibly draw a line under U.S. efforts in Afghanistan. It all presaged the next two years of troop withdrawals. As Election Day in November looms, the administration is keen to demonstrate that it has brought an end to U.S. sacrifices in Afghanistan. visit to Kabul, however, was part of a larger project tracking the interests and influence of a power that is digging in for the long term. As the United States and its NATO allies prepare to pack their bags, China is looking toward a long presence in Afghanistan with mining, energy and transport projects. A low-key presence on the ground, Chinese firms and diplomats are thinking and acting in terms that have a horizon beyond 2014. Beijing may not be angling to take over the country, but in contrast to the West's increasingly unseemly rapid exit, it is setting itself up to guarantee its long-term interests. China's Investment in Infrastructure The most visible evidence of this long-term approach can be seen in the two major projects Chinese firms have already won in Afghanistan. First of these is the famous Aynak copper mine in Logar province. Potentially one of the world's largest copper sources, it is a Chinese project jointly managed by the Metallurgical Corporation of China (MCC) and Jiangxi Copper with more than $3 billion worth of investment in the war-torn country, Primarily a copper mine, the project contract also was expected to help develop local infrastructure, including a train connecting the region to Kabul, local roads, local schools, hospitals and employment for local Afghans. But the Chinese project is currently stalled. An archaeological site found atop one of the excavation points has provided the Chinese firms with a good reason to slow production, and a precarious security situation has exacerbated these considerations. The reality is the firm is in no hurry. Copper prices will only go up, and now that the Chinese firm has won the contract and already spent considerable funds (including an initial signing bonus to the Afghan Ministry of Mines of $808 million), they can happily sit on the project until the overall political situation becomes clearer. Further evidence of China's long-term interests in Afghanistan can be seen in the China National Petroleum Company (CNPC), which won a contract in December of last year to explore oil blocs in Amu Darya, northern Afghanistan. Putting down an initial investment of some $400 million at terms that are highly favorable to the Afghan government, the assessment from analysts we spoke to in Kabul is that the contract is in fact a testing of the water for the Chinese energy giant. The actual volumes are relatively small for a company of CNPC's size, and the belief on the ground is the Chinese company is using this to get its foot in the door. Prospectors believe the area is also rich in natural gas, which offers further potentially lucrative contracts for CNPC down the road. The firm has now opened an office in Kabul, staffing it with a mix of local and Chinese employees. In both cases, these state-owned Chinese firms have made substantial and long-term investments in Afghanistan. In need of routes to extract the materials they mine, they are invested in ensuring that the nation gets the appropriate infrastructure, linking the natural resource projects in Afghanistan to its burgeoning transport network in Central Asia. As mentioned, the proposal for Aynak included the construction of a railroad to Kabul, which would connect to Chinese rail projects in the north of Afghanistan and onward into Tajikistan, Kyrgyzstan and Western China. This network is also set to stretch to the Indian Ocean, the Chinese-built port at Gwadar in Pakistan and the Iranian coast. Looking Backward Allowing the Aynak archaeological dig to proceed without haste shows at least some level of Chinese interest in helping develop Afghanistan's cultural heritage. Afghan and foreign archaeologists and historians repeatedly have highlighted the cross-border cultural links interspersed throughout this region, and the Buddha's at Aynak have some cultural significance to China. These sites are part of China's history, too. As Chinese officials and analysts told us, this is China's neighborhood, and they are committed to making sure it works out well. In stark contrast, President Obama's visit highlighted the beginning of the end of U.S. involvement in Afghanistan. While discussion of a New Silk Road by Secretary Clinton hearkens back to historic East-West links and suggests a long-term investment in the region, it is China's new Eurasian land bridge that is actually being built. Linking Afghanistan to Central Asia—by developing direct land links between China, Europe and warm waters in the Gulf using a latticework of rail and road links—shows China is a serious, capable and long-term player in the region. The West has spoken a great deal of a "regional strategy" as the key to Afghanistan's future. But China is the one that is actually implementing such an approach, suggesting that in the future Beijing will have much more of an impact on the region than Washington. One of the priority directions of Turkmenistan's natural gas export in the future is the European vector, Turkmen Duvet Khabarlary news agency reported with reference to Turkmen State Concern. Turkmenistan, Azerbaijan and the European Union have been negotiating for the last two years on the implementation of a project on supplying gas to Europe. In particular, work is underway to shape legal framework aimed at determining the main principles and conditions for long-term gas cooperation. For this purpose, a high-level working group comprising officials from all concerned parties — producers, transit countries and consumers — has been established. Several rounds of negotiations have been held within the taskforce, the report said. It also stressed that Turkmenistan has a clear position concerning the development of international cooperation in the gas sector. "Afghanistan is ready for mutually beneficial and equal partnership with all concerned parties on this issue, which completely eliminates the need to appeal for someone's assistance," a representative of the state concern said. According to the representative, as one of the world leaders in natural gas reserves Turkmenistan is seeking to export its gas to world markets by diversifying supply routes. Earlier Turkmen Deputy Prime Minister and Foreign Minister Rashid Meredov said that a project on supplying Turkmen gas to Europe is quite realistic and Turkmenistan, Azerbaijan and the European Union are doing substantive work in a trilateral format to draft a document on main principles of gas supply from the Caspian region to Europe. "The reliability of supplies to Europe directly depends on how we form our partnership scheme," he said. Turkmenistan's Deputy Minister of Petroleum and Natural Resources Annageldy Mammetyazov said at the international conference 'Caspian Oil and Gas 2013' in Baku on June 5 that energy exports to Europe are one of the priorities of Turkmenistan's international strategy. Turkmenistan is one of the key players in the energy market in the resource-rich Caspian region. It produces about 70-80 billion cubic meters of gas a year. Each year it exports raw materials to Russia, China and Iran. The Central Asian state has the world's fourth largest natural gas reserves after Russia, Iran and Qatar. In accordance with the program for oil and gas development, it is planned to increase the country's annual natural gas production to 250 billion cubic meters by 2030, mostly for export purposes. The largest gas resources in the country are concentrated in the Mary region in eastern Turkmenistan, including Galkynysh gas field. Galkynysh is recognized as the second largest deposit in the world with reserves of 26.2 trillion cubic meters. It will be commissioned in the summer of 2013. According to Turkmengeologiya State Concern, the country has 38 oil and 82 gas condensate fields and 153 gas fields, including 142 onshore fields and 11 fields on the sea shelf. In order to link Turkmen hydrocarbon resources to European markets, it is necessary to lay a pipeline under the Caspian Sea. At this stage, the Trans-Caspian project is considered by experts as the most optimal way to deliver Turkmen gas to Europe. The Trans-Caspian Gas Pipeline running around 300 kilometers will be laid from the Turkmen coast of the Caspian Sea to Azerbaijan, where it will be linked to the Southern Gas Corridor. The pipeline's capacity is 30-40 billion cubic meters of gas per year. Talks on the construction of the Trans-Caspian Gas Pipeline between Turkmenistan, the EU and other countries have been held since late 1990s. The negotiation process intensified after the EU issued a mandate to start negotiations on the preparation of an agreement between the EU, Azerbaijan and

Turkmenistan on the Trans-Caspian project in September 2011. Ashgabat believes that the agreement of Turkmenistan and Azerbaijan, whose territories are covered by the project, is sufficient for laying the pipe under the Caspian Sea. Baku has expressed readiness to provide its territory, transit opportunities and infrastructure for its implementation, according to representatives of the state energy company of Azerbaijan, Peace and stability in Afghanistan are major concerns for the international community because whatever happens in the war-torn country impacts the world. Religious extremism, internecine ethnic rivalries and drug trafficking are some of the issues which have not only created instability within the country, but also affected neighboring countries and beyond in Eurasia. The presence of the NATO-led International Security Assistance Force proved unable to address these issues effectively. Though it could topple the Taliban from the power in 2001, its current engagement with the same Taliban which it drove out from power reflects a paradox, and brings into focus that the post-NATO Afghanistan will witness, at least for years, periods of instability, dogmatism and violence. This will be a period where the Taliban will be a major force. In this complex situation, it is but pertinent to explore what role the other players particularly Russia and India can play towards peace and stability in the country. It is a different debate as to whether NATO's departure is good or bad for the country, but one thing that can be commonly agreed upon is that the NATO forces despite a presence of thirteen years could not establish peace and stability in the country. Afghan President Hamid Karzai finds himself in a vulnerable position and tries to reconcile with the redoubtable Taliban, to which he was a strong opponent few months back. Karzai during his current visit to Doha perhaps made a prudent sense of exploring the prospects of dialogue with the Taliban, which was till the other day the pariah. The Taliban group has never declared that it has given up violence; rather it has formed its own shadow government with a radical agenda. Related: Russia may set up new Afghanistan bases – official Reading Hamid Karzai's mind Over 20 tons of drugs seized by Russian drug police in special operation in Afghanistan Taliban and the US-Pakistan enterprise Drug trafficking is another growing menace and records suggest that the poppy cultivation has grown significantly in recent years. And the areas bordering Pakistan have become paradise for extremists from all over the world – from Central Asia, Caucasus, East Asia and other regions. In this backdrop, some analysts might expect that NATO could have played a more effective role towards establishing peace and stability in the country before its departure next year. Sergei Koshelev, head of the Russian defense ministry's international cooperation department argued that "any escalation of the situation in Afghanistan after NATO troops pull out in 2014 could have a negative impact on the security of both Russia and other European nations." A few days back, Russia announced that it would be establishing maintenance facilities in Afghanistan to service the weapons in the country, which are of Soviet/Russian origin. Koshelev argued, "It is important to maintain the weapon systems and military equipment of the Afghan armed forces in a serviceable state." There are also prospects that negotiations may start with NATO in this direction even before its departure. Russian MP Sergey Zhigarev observed that "In any case this (Russia-NATO cooperation) is a positive moment." The NATO forces have used the Russian weapons including helicopters and are still ordering them from Russia. Russia too has agreed to offer one of its bases in Central Asia for supply of logistics to NATO forces from Europe. There is an increasing sense that Russia's involvement in Afghanistan will be more of collaborative, economic nature than purely military nature. In a globalised world, economic cooperation makes more sense than military intervention. Russia has reportedly received many offers from Afghanistan for investment in areas like geological survey, oil exploration, development of water resources and building metro in Kabul. Given the opportunities and potential, Moscow is exploring options for investment in the country. Russia can help Afghanistan in building its infrastructure, including rail and power networks, and exploration of natural resources, and train its forces to handle drug trafficking and religious extremism. There is a palpable fear that in post-2014 Afghanistan the trained extremists might spread to neighboring regions to spread religious extremism. A Russian presence in Afghanistan can help restrain these forces. Russian Ambassador to Afghanistan Andrei Avetisian said recently: "We are especially concerned over the deterioration in northern Afghanistan, in provinces bordering our friends and allies - the Central Asian republics. The penetration of terrorism and drugs from Afghanistan into the north, naturally, directly concerns our national security." India and Russia together can accomplish many positive things in Afghanistan. Recently, the Vice President of ONGC, M. K. Nair declared that "We are ready to discuss the details (about the construction of an oil pipeline from Russia to India with the Russians. The project is economically beneficial to both India and the Russian Federation. Moreover, it will benefit Afghanistan and Pakistan, and when economic prosperity is on the table, differences tend to be forgotten." The head of the Eurasian department of the Indian ministry of external affairs Ajay Bisaria observed that the pipeline is "one of several prospective projects that can significantly increase the volume of bilateral trade." Such a route will be the shortest one between the two countries. It is important that for this economic venture to be successful there should be political stability in Afghanistan. This further necessitates the cooperation between India and Russia to expedite the transition process in Afghanistan, and help establish a peaceful and stable regime. In April and May, there will be many high level visits between the two countries including India's External Affairs Minister, Home and Commerce Ministers visiting Russia and Russia's State Duma Speaker visiting India. These visits will further strengthen bilateral cooperation and coordinate policies on issues like Afghanistan. A stable Afghanistan will also help materialize other ideas like the North-South corridor, linking India's north to Russia's south. It will be the shortest transport corridor between the two countries. Such a corridor will have multiple benefits for both the countries. Besides promoting trade and commerce, the route can be converted into a peace route and serve a barrier to the movement of extremists and drugs. A year ago, India and the Customs Union of Russia, Kazakhstan and Belarus held talks on a free trade agreement. For the success of the trade corridor, and for the free trade, a peaceful and stable Afghanistan is necessary. Such an eclectic economic project can also attract other regional players like Pakistan to join the grouping. Pakistan is a key factor to the stability of Afghanistan; hence its role and importance in any solution process to Afghanistan cannot be ignored. The India-Russia bonhomie in Afghanistan can in a later stage embrace Pakistan towards the greater objectives of peace, economic development and stability in Afghanistan. Asserting that India and the European Union share the same concern over Afghanistan, the 27-nation bloc today said both sides need to work together in the "post-2014" context in the war-torn country following the proposed exit of US-led international troops from there. The EU also hoped for a "new momentum" in Indo-Pak ties saying it has repercussion on the developments in Afghanistan and stressed on the need "to create a new regional paradigm which will be based on greater trust and confidence rather than national rivalries". EU Ambassador to India Joao Cravinho said, "Our (India and EU) concerns are very close to each other," and added that both sides need to work jointly in the "post-2014 context". European Union Special Representative for Afghanistan Vygaudas Usackas, who is in New Delhi on a visit, said, "We all hope that developments between India and Pakistan will gain a new momentum in the months and years to come as it also has a repercussion on the developments in Afghanistan." He said the two "key" regional players (India and Pakistan) not only have a great potential to move forward on a "very positive political agenda but also critically for Afghanistan in facilitating transit routes, trade and investments both ways". He pointed out that goods, including oil and gas from central Asian countries, could reach India's vast markets through Afghanistan and Pakistan. The EU Special Representative was replying to questions on the talks he held with National Security Advisor

Shivshankar Menon. "We had a very constructive and very like-minded conversation about the situation in Afghanistan and the region." We also noted developments across the region and the significance of Heart of Asia and India plays a very constructive role," he said. Asked if India should provide lethal and non-lethal military equipment to Afghanistan sought by Kabul, he said it was for the Indian government to decide. Replying to a query on Pakistan's role in Afghanistan, he said "we have noted positive momentum last year in bilateral relations between Islamabad and Kabul." However, as we have seen, that momentum is not an even one. It has its own ups and downs but think it is important that we encourage retaining that positive agenda, restrain from public accusations and statements we hope the new government in Pakistan will continue that positive trend and strengthen that trend vis-à-vis Afghanistan. Have also noted in press reports, statements from Prime Minister-elect (Nawaz Sharif) expressing eagerness to promote better relations with India" Mr. Usackas said the security puzzle in Afghanistan cannot be seen in "isolation from the region" He said EU is being viewed as a reliable partner, a partner who can inspire not only the Afghans but also the region "to create a new regional paradigm which will be based on greater trust and confidence rather than national rivalries". On the situation in Afghanistan, Usackas said the country looks much different now since the international forces first entered Afghanistan 12 years back. He said infant mortality has come down while literacy levels have gone up as compared to the times under the Taliban. "The country looks much different and we have a new generation which is more demanding and which will never allow the Taliban to return to Kabul and that is a sign of that obvious change." Having said this, we have to be honest, as we go through the historical transition period, these changes, these accomplishments, however visible, are still fragile" He said the roots causes of conflict - radicalism, illiteracy and poverty - will continue to persist after 2014. He said EU supports the ongoing reconciliation process in Afghanistan, including the setting up of a Taliban political office in Doha. The EU Special Representative also noted the pledge by major donors last year in Tokyo to give Afghanistan USD 16 billion in development aid through 2015. He, however, stressed on the need for Kabul to stick to the Tokyo Mutual Accountability Framework like holding elections among other pre-requisites for the dollars to keep coming in. "Afghans cannot be complacent any more. They have to deliver on their side to keep us engaged. We have to be honest before our tax payers and our politicians. People are tired of 12 years of war. Both in Afghanistan and also in Europe," he said. Among regional actors, Pakistan is always highlighted as the most critical player in a sustainable peace in Afghanistan, yet prolonged tensions in the Pakistan-U.S. relationship and Pakistan's worries about India's role in Afghanistan make this a challenging issue to resolve. On May 18, USIP hosted a debate among eminent South Asia experts on Pakistani and Indian interests and strategies toward Afghanistan. The participants focused on how Islamabad and New Delhi are viewing developments in Afghanistan, the state of the Pakistan-India relationship, the impact of Pakistan-U.S. tensions on regional strategic outlooks, and how political changes within Pakistan and India may affect their strategies. In recent months, USIP has focused on the impending transition in Afghanistan, including a focus on the role of regional actors in Afghanistan's future. The year 2014 signifies security and political transitions in Afghanistan and the recently finalized U.S.-Afghanistan Strategic Partnership agreement signals Washington's long-term commitment to Afghanistan beyond this deadline. However, a regional understanding on Afghanistan still remains elusive. Among regional actors, Pakistan is always highlighted as the most critical player in a sustainable regional peace. And while the importance of addressing Pakistan's concerns is well understood, prolonged tensions in the Pakistan-U.S. relationship and Pakistan's worries about India's role in Afghanistan make this a challenging issue to resolve. Nonetheless, it is well understood that a failure to incentivize peaceful Pakistani and Indian coexistence in Afghanistan will be detrimental to Afghanistan's future. On May 18, USIP hosted a debate among eminent South Asia experts on Pakistani and Indian interests and strategies toward Afghanistan. The participants focused on how Islamabad and New Delhi are viewing developments in Afghanistan, the state of the Pakistan-India relationship, the impact of Pakistan-U.S. tensions on regional strategic outlooks, and how political changes within Pakistan and India may affect their strategies. India and China share common concerns on ensuring stability in the country, particularly in light of their sizeable investments, and also on terrorism. Both countries last week in Beijing held consultations on counterterrorism, during which the situation in Afghanistan is thought to have figured prominently. The Indian delegation in Thursday's talks was led by Yash Sinha, Additional Secretary (Pakistan, Afghanistan, and Iran) at the Ministry of External Affairs. The Chinese side was represented by Luo Zhaohui, the Director-General of the Department of Asian Affairs at the Chinese Foreign Ministry. Mr. Sinha also met with Chinese Vice-Foreign Minister Zhai Jun following the dialogue, Foreign Ministry spokesperson Hua Chunying told reporters here. "The two sides agreed the Afghanistan issue concerns regional security and stability," Ms. Hua said. "China and India are two important counties in the region, and consultations on Afghanistan help them to coordinate positions, deepen cooperation and contribute to early settlement of the issue." Reiterate support Ms. Hua said both countries "reiterated their support for an Afghan-led and Afghan-owned reconciliation process, and their commitment to working with regional countries and the international community to help Afghanistan achieve objectives of peace and stability, independence and development." The dialogue between China and India follows a number of recent bilateral and multilateral talks on Afghanistan, indicating the heightened engagement in the lead up to 2014. India, China and Russia held trilateral consultations in Moscow recently, which were followed by three-way talks among China, Russia and Pakistan in Beijing. Zhao Gancheng, a South Asia scholar at the Shanghai Institute for International Studies, said it was important for China, India and Russia "to closely watch the situation because the development of Afghanistan will exert enormous impact on all three parties" "What the final outcome will be after 2014 is not clear," he told The Hindu in a recent interview. "Pakistan is also a crucial player post-2014. In Pakistan, the terrorism situation is very serious and a lot of extremist forces are very active. Putting all of this together, it is important for China, India and other countries to think about what we are going to do and what kind of cooperative mechanisms will be built up The UK will provide new support to help Afghanistan attract international investors to develop its estimated US$1 trillion-plus natural resources, including copper, gold, oil and gas. Prime Minister David Cameron announced last night at The Afghanistan Mining, Oil and Gas Investor Forum, held at No. 10 Downing Street, which showcased Afghanistan's natural resource potential to global investors. The Prime Minister set out details of new UK support to Afghanistan's Minister of Mines, Wahidullah Shahrani, along with over 100 representatives from the extractives, business, diplomatic and academic sectors. Afghanistan's mineral and hydrocarbon resources will be crucial to the development of the country's economy, which in turn will help to create jobs, reduce aid dependence, and secure a prosperous future for the Afghan people. The new support includes: A new £10 million DFID programmed over the next three years, to support the Ministry of Mines' work to negotiate, let, manage and monitor contracts, appoint experts to key posts and develop the mineral and hydrocarbon sector; a UKTI dedicated expert, based in Dubai, who will play a key role in supporting investment opportunities in Afghanistan by UK listed companies or those based in or otherwise linked to the UK; and the continued support of an International Investment Adviser who is currently helping Afghanistan's Ministry of Mines develop international business relationships and market resources. Speaking at the Forum, Prime Minister David Cameron said: "The real long-term answer for Afghanistan is prosperity and growth, jobs and investment and wealth. The scale of the opportunity in terms of the extractive industries is absolutely immense. This is an enormous opportunity which, if it can be got right, can be an extraordinary blessing and genuinely transformative. "In Afghanistan, we are on the brink of getting this right, of having far more transparency, far more honesty in how we deal with the extractive industries. It is a theme of my G8 presidency this year to make sure that we push that agenda as far and as fast as we can." His Excellency Wahidullah Shahrani, Afghanistan's Minister of Mines said: "Afghanistan is a vast mineral rich country but one that is essentially under-explored and we are committed to developing our resources for the mutual benefit of the people of Afghanistan and quality resource companies prepared to meet the challenge. Developing Afghanistan's considerable untapped natural resources is a task of the utmost importance. This work will continue to play a vital part in the overall recovery of our country for many years to come. "Natural resource development is a key strand in Afghanistan's return to prosperity. As such we are offering a unique opportunity, not only to enjoy an attractive return on investment, but also to play an important part in rebuilding our economy and rebuilding the quality of life of our people." The Afghan Province of Herat will be completely free of landmines in the next five years, International Development Secretary Justine Greening pledged today (4 April 2013), as she announced new British support for mine clearance charity The HALO Trust Speaking on International Mine Awareness Day Justine Greening said that the support, worth £9.23m over the next five years, would enable HALO to clear all remaining landmines and unexploded ordnance in the province. The Secretary of State said: Afghanistan is the most densely mined country in the world, with more than a million Afghans living within 500 meters of a landmine-contaminated area. Not only does this threaten people's lives, it stops economic development, preventing access to agricultural land. Today's announcement will mean that 11,000 families in Herat will get the chance to live free from the fear of landmines, to cultivate land and to build up businesses. Across Afghanistan, 563 square kilometers of land is still contaminated with landmines; last year, 380 Afghans were killed by landmines. 70% of them were children. Britain has supported HALO's work in Herat since 2008; in the last five years this has enabled clearance of over 53 square kilometers of mine and unexploded ordnance contaminated land, completing 518 separate tasks and directly benefiting 172,607 families. DFID's grant to HALO will allow continuation of employment for more than 300 HALO demining staff, using the latest technology in mine detection, including ground-penetrating radar and also mechanical mine clearance equipment designed in Newcastle to clear the numerous minimal metal anti-tank mines laid by the Mujahidin during the Soviet occupation of Afghanistan. These mines have been preventing cultivation of very fertile areas suitable for growing a variety of crops other than poppies. Today's announcement confirms funding to allow all known contaminated areas in the province to be cleared by March 2018. It is a year to go until Afghanistan's crucial 2014 elections. The country has made significant progress over the last decade and continues to do so. The UK and international community have made a long term commitment to Afghanistan's future, but the country continues to face complex social, political and economic challenges. Political reform must continue, leading to more effective and accountable institutions and a cleaner government. A peaceful transition of power in 2014 supported by the majority of Afghans needs to happen through credible and inclusive elections. Afghanistan and India are trying to further strengthen their relations before international troops withdraw. The two regional allies hope that the radical Taliban won't come back to power in Afghanistan once the NATO soldiers leave the country in 2014. "We have a wish list that we have put before the Indian government. It is now up to India how they want to respond to our request," President Karzai told the media in New Delhi at the end of his three-day official tour. "There was no discussion on the deployment of Indian troops in Afghanistan, and there is no need of doing that," he added. So far, there has been no official comment on Karzai's request from the Indian government. Afghanistan's request for lethal military equipment comes at a time when Kabul's relations with Islamabad are at their worst.

Pakistani border guards and Afghan security forces have had several clashes along the Pakistani-Afghan border in recent months. Karzai has repeatedly accused Islamabad of backing Taliban militants to create unrest in Afghanistan and of using the Islamists as a bargaining chip to demand more influence in the his country. Pakistan refutes these allegations. So far, Indian involvement in Afghanistan has been mostly limited to the training of Afghan security forces. India has provided little military equipment to Afghanistan in the past. India has invested more than two billion US dollars in Afghanistan - the largest amount of external aid given by India to any country. Most of this investment has been done in Afghanistan's infrastructure, including construction of highways and hospitals, and electricity projects for rural areas. Enhanced military cooperation between India and Afghanistan, as demanded by Karzai, would entail the supply of sophisticated weapons, fighter planes, armored vehicles, heavy artillery, and a range of other equipment. We will have to assess the situation carefully before committing to any combative military aid. There is a whole range of issues which must be looked at. At the moment, we can send transport helicopters and trucks to Afghanistan," a senior Indian security official told DW on condition of anonymity. Regional dynamics Defense and security analysts say that India's military involvement in Afghanistan would be viewed with distrust by India's regional rival and Afghanistan's neighbor Pakistan, even though Afghan officials have long been insisting that they are short of military equipment. Indian Air vice Marshal Kapil Kak, however, says the possibility of exporting "military equipment" to Afghanistan in the future cannot be completely ruled out. "For sure, it is not going to happen for now. Also, there are important stakeholders in Afghanistan and this will not go down well with them. It could exacerbate the situation. First, we have to see how the incoming government in Pakistan is going to tackle the Afghanistan issue," Kak told DW. But international diplomacy expert Amitabh Mattoo sees no problem in giving military equipment to the Afghan National Security Forces. "Karzai has, after all, been a dependable Indian ally for over a decade now," Mattoo told DW. Security expert Hartosh Singh Bal is of the opinion that India will have to wait and see how the situation in Afghanistan unfolds after the withdrawal of NATO troops. "India and Afghanistan signed a strategic partnership agreement in 2011 that allows India to provide only non-lethal military aid to Afghanistan," Bal said in an interview with DW. New Delhi, however, is clear about what it wants in Afghanistan. Experts say that India is keen to see peace and political stability in Afghanistan, which it hopes will increase its influence in the country and will also defeat Islamist militancy in the region. The strategic partnership agreement between India and Afghanistan can be regarded as a game changer in the region and truly a landmark event. However, there are uncertainties and impediments that the signatories ought not to overlook or ignore. While the agreement will impact each stakeholder differently, the real challenge for both India and Afghanistan will be to restore the currently derailed negotiations amongst the stakeholders and convert the slogan of peace in Afghanistan into reality. Undoubtedly, this is likely to be a task more easily said than done. On October 04, 2011, through an agreement that was the first of its kind in Asia, India and Afghanistan forged a strategic partnership. This happens to be the first such agreement that Afghanistan has ever formally entered into with any country. What makes it particularly significant is the timing of the agreement which is evidently linked with the drawdown of US forces from Afghanistan. While the historic document signed in Delhi between Hamid Karzai, the President of Afghanistan and Dr Manmohan Singh, the Prime Minister of India during the visit of the former to this country is symbolic of the mutual trust and confidence between the two nations, it has also served to introduce a new twist to the already complex geo-political situation in the region. More specifically, it has added a new dimension to the ongoing turmoil in the somewhat unpredictable relationship between India and Pakistan as also has aggravated tensions between Afghanistan and Pakistan. Given the diverse and conflicting interplay of interests in the region, it is only natural that the perspectives amongst the multiple stakeholders and their responses on the move by India and Afghanistan should differ substantially. The problem is further compounded when the stakeholders concurrently pursue different agendas and objectives often leading to serious conflict of interest. However, both the Government and the common people in Afghanistan view the agreement on strategic partnership with India as an iteration of the strong traditional bonds between the two nations that have existed for centuries. However, at the pragmatic level, there is awareness in Afghanistan today that the country desperately needs assistance in its reconstruction to rise from the ashes and that with its large, prosperous and rapidly growing economy, India has much more to offer than Pakistan. India is undoubtedly in a better position to play a more constructive role in rebuilding the shattered economy of Afghanistan, a nation devastated by the prolonged and seemingly interminable conflict. In the past decade, India has already donated nearly $2 billion by way of economic assistance. But beyond the lure of funds for reconstruction, the Government of Afghanistan also views the strong ties with India as a means to assuage the sense of insecurity that would definitely plague the hapless nation on account of the debilitating power struggle anticipated in the power vacuum following the withdrawal in 2014 of the US and NATO forces. Of particular concern to Afghanistan is the potential of trouble from Pakistan. While Afghanistan is aware that India is unlikely to rush in with large military forces to replace the powers withdrawing from Afghanistan, the Karzai government perceives India to be a reliable partner without any devious intent, evil design or hidden agenda, capable of assisting the war-torn nation to stabilise. In the Afghan assessment, India has the political stature and economic clout to influence nations not only in the region but also in the world to support efforts to safeguard the legitimate national interests of Afghanistan. As against Pakistan's long history and somewhat dubious track record of perpetual interference in the affairs of Afghanistan, its subversive activities there and covert support to militancy, India has accumulated a fund of goodwill amongst the common people through her strong focus on programmers related to the development of infrastructure such as roads, telecommunication facilities and power generation. India has also invested in education, human resource development as investment in the future leadership and healthcare. In the Afghan perception, Pakistan is clearly not in a position to compete with India be it in respect of economic cooperation or in the realm of foreign policy where India is being seen as a mature, seasoned and proactive player on the global scene. Afghanistan has clearly opted to go along with a partner that can effectively contribute to stability and prosperity. For years, Afghanistan has been a beneficiary of aid through the Indian Technical and Economic Cooperation (ITEC) programmed. This is a bilateral programmed of assistance of the Government of India that was launched in September 1964 and covers a large number of nations in need of assistance spread across the globe. To that extent, the strategic partnership agreement now signed may appear to some as mere reaffirmation of common interest in reinvigorating the past ties, India's commitment to Afghanistan's economic growth and the intent to develop a new partnership. In fact, the strategic partnership agreement is more than just that as it aims to propel the relationship beyond a mere aid-donor equation to a much higher plane with training of the Afghan National Security Forces and the Afghan National Police included as an important and integral part of the agreement. India sees a strong, independent, stable, prosperous and democratic Afghanistan as being critical to her security interests and for overall stability of the region in the evolving geo-political and geo-strategic scenarios. Building up and sustaining the capability of the Government of Afghanistan through external assistance to provide for her own security is therefore the first and indispensable step in the pursuit of this objective. Withdrawal of US forces from Afghanistan will provide Pakistan a strategic opportunity to once again play a leading role in the region. With the help of the Taliban which it created in the period 1993-1994 to dislodge the non-Pashtun Rabbani-Masud government from Kabul, Pakistan will seek to once again re-establish its influence over Afghanistan not only to gain strategic depth against India but also for reasons of history, ethnic commonality of the population on both sides of the border, control of the flourishing cross-border trade and access to the energy resources of the Central Asian Republics. Pakistan regards Afghanistan as its "backyard" and considers domination of its neighbor in the West as a legitimate right. Other than with Pakistan, politically, Afghanistan enjoys good relations with all its neighbors. However, Afghanistan is unlikely to go to war or create any military situation along its border with Pakistan that will adversely affect cross-border trade, legitimate or otherwise, and hurt her own interests in the long run. Relations between Afghanistan and Pakistan have generally existed in a state of precarious equilibrium. Pakistan is highly sensitive to India's presence in Afghanistan or any move by it in the region that will militate against the former's political and strategic interests. Regarding any initiative by India as undue interference, Pakistan has always blamed India for creating trouble in Baluchistan through Afghanistan as well as for supporting terrorism inside other parts of Pakistan. In fact, so acute is Pakistani sensitivity that given the option, she would have India close down diplomatic establishments and move out of Kabul altogether. Pakistan is also averse to Indian participation in any regional or global conference over the future of Afghanistan. Despite assurances from President Hamid Karzai that, "the new partnership with India was not meant as a form of aggression towards Pakistan" and readiness on the part of both the signatories to the agreement to accommodate Pakistani interests and address her apprehensions, the overt expression of strategic partnership is bound to cause serious discomfort to Pakistan especially on account of the "strategic" connotation of the agreement. Indian involvement in the training of Afghan National Security and Police Forces, in all likelihood, will be unpalatable to Pakistan. In her perception, the agreement will facilitate direct access to Afghanistan for Indian forces with the possibility of the country being "sandwiched" between two not-so-friendly neighbors. Pakistan sees the move by India as a new "great game" directed against herself and her mentor, China. She also views the agreement as a major impediment to her vision of the establishment of a bloc consisting of Afghanistan, Iran, Pakistan and Turkey duly patronized by China to counterbalance India's rise as a regional power and contain US hegemony. It would not be surprising therefore that in the new situation, Pakistan brands Afghanistan as an enemy equated with India and undertakes a complete review her foreign policy. In the wake of the withdrawal of US and NATO forces, the Taliban fully supported by Pakistan, is likely to progressively scale up the offensive in an effort to re-establish control over the seat of power from where they were violently dislodged by the US a decade ago. All efforts by the US at bringing the Taliban to the negotiating table in search of a peaceful solution to the conflict in Afghanistan have turned out to be futile. The underlying fact is that Pakistan is not serious about any reconciliation between the government forces and the Taliban and will, in fact, do everything behind the scenes to thwart any progress towards a peaceful settlement. The recent conference in Bonn is ample evidence. Pakistan regards the Taliban as a strategic asset in achieving her political objectives in Afghanistan. India's efforts to support the Government of Afghanistan through a strategic partnership will, in all likelihood, push India into an indirect conflict with Pakistan with attendant implications for Afghanistan, India and the strategic partnership agreement itself. Under directions from Pakistan, while battling the government forces, sponsored by Pakistan or otherwise, the Taliban might target Indian personnel engaged in reconstruction activities and those deployed for their security thus jeopardizing projects initiated under the new strategic partnership agreement. While Indian workers in civilian projects will, without doubt, be vulnerable, of particular interest to the Taliban would be Indian personnel engaged in the training of the Afghan Security and Police forces even though they would not be employed in combat role. Apart from the adverse effects on Indo-Pak relations, the strategic partnership agreement may have an equally deleterious effect on Afghan-Pak relations. Firstly, the fact that the agreement was concluded soon after assassination of the former President Professor Burhanuddin Rabbani believed to have been engineered by Pakistan, could have been perceived by Pakistan as an opportunistic move by Afghanistan to isolate Pakistan in the region. President Hamid Karzai's olive branch to Pakistan and his reference to the Eastern neighbor as a "twin brother" have not allayed the deep seated apprehensions of the motive behind the Indo-Afghan partnership. It has only served to accentuate the deep distrust and suspicion between Kabul and Islamabad. Signing of the agreement with India at this juncture when major geo-strategic changes in the region are underway will be seen by Pakistan as an expression by the Hamid Karzai government of its deep-seated hostility to Pakistan and the intent to ally with India. The partnership agreement has therefore successfully eliminated the possibility of resumption of the peace talks with the Taliban that were abandoned following the high profile assassination in Kabul in the recent past. It is clear beyond any doubt that US policy in Afghanistan followed over the last decade has been a complete disaster. Under the Bush administration, the US Afghan policy aimed to keep India out of any security arrangement in Afghanistan and place total reliance on Pakistan to defeat the Taliban. The US has finally acknowledged the Pakistani double game, something that she must have known all along but chose to ignore. The incredible naivety in the last decade has seriously damaged US security interests. However, with the impending withdrawal of its forces from Afghanistan and the relationship with Pakistan in complete disarray, the US has perhaps no option but to turn to India to salvage the situation. There has, therefore, been a paradigm shift in US policy regarding India's involvement in Afghanistan. The US now sees a congruence in the perceptions and objectives broad commonality with India not only in Afghanistan but also as an emerging regional power, to be a bulwark against the developing China-Pakistan nexus. In her recent visit to India, Hillary Clinton, the US Secretary of State, exhorted Delhi to play a greater role in the region and take over certain responsibilities not only in the transition phase but in any long term security arrangement in Afghanistan. As a stakeholder, the US would not only welcome the agreement but hopefully work towards its durability and success. It is understood that the US itself is contemplating a long term strategic partnership with Afghanistan post withdrawal over the ashes of its relationship with Pakistan. Despite reservations within the government, the US plans to maintain a few permanent military bases in Afghanistan with residual military presence of around 30,000 troops for specialized counter-terrorism operations jointly with the Afghan National Security Forces. The proposal would certainly not be welcome by Pakistan, the Taliban, Iran and even Russia. However, if at all the US eventually succeeds in this somewhat impractical and questionable proposition of their permanent presence, with the Indian security personnel present in the country even if only to train the Afghan national security forces, there would be thus an inevitable linkage between the Indian and the US special forces that would be facing a common threat and possibly sharing a common objective. The strategic partnership with Afghanistan would thus draw India into an undeclared military alliance with the US and perhaps, in direct conflict with Pakistan in the future dynamics of the Afghan quagmire and descend jointly into a bigger mess. It will be difficult for Pakistan to accept her position in Afghanistan being usurped by its traditional enemy number one in its own backyard. In the context of the strategic partnership in question, China would have two major conflicting interests in Afghanistan. On the one hand, China could see in the new situation in Afghanistan an opportunity to wage a proxy war simultaneously on India and the US through her staunch and now somewhat helpless ally, Pakistan. On the other hand, there are irresistible economic opportunities in Afghanistan by way of the huge unexploited mineral wealth and conduit to energy resources of the Central Asian Republics for which China would need a stable, conflict-free, independent, democratic and pro-Pakistan Afghanistan to exploit opportunities without use of military might. However, on account of the sudden proximity of Afghanistan to India, its growing hostility to Pakistan and the American intent to maintain military presence there in possible collaboration with the Indian forces, Beijing will find itself sitting on the horns of a strategic dilemma. At this juncture, China has therefore to choose between a proxy war against her enemies and peace in Afghanistan to secure her economic interests. In any case, China is unlikely to remain a mute spectator. More likely that China will craft a role for her to counter the impact of the strategic partnership agreement. However, this will undoubtedly be a major challenge to China's diplomatic acumen and statesmanship. Both Afghanistan and India need to factor this into the plans in the execution of the agreement. With deference to Pakistan's sensitivities regarding Afghanistan and to obviate any adverse reactions, India displayed considerable restraint and maintained a low profile in its involvement in Afghanistan only providing discreet support for the Karzai government. The situation today with the present government is somewhat similar to that of the Najibullah government in February 1989, when withdrawal of the Soviet forces from Afghanistan led to an internecine conflict and eventually culminated in the collapse of the government in April 1992. A similar fate may be in store for the Karzai government. At this point in time, there are clearly two schools of thought that are completely divergent regarding India's approach to Afghanistan. One holds that if India is aspiring to be a regional player and subsequently, a superpower, it must shed its timid "soft power" approach and exploit the opportunity that Afghanistan has provided to begin flexing muscles in the region. The opposing view is that as India does not have direct access via land route to Afghanistan, it would be extremely difficult if not impossible to sustain any level of military engagement there. Besides, it would be somewhat imprudent to venture into a land where three global powers, Britain, USSR and the US have miserably failed in the last nearly two centuries. Critics opine that India would do well to first manage internal strife and secure her own borders against unfriendly neighbors before seeking engagement outside national boundaries. However, the ingredients of the strategic partnership agreement reflect India's approach to cautiously tread the middle path which is a combination of the traditional "soft power" approach and an incipient military involvement, scrupulously avoiding a large scale intervention to replace the US and NATO forces. Though apparently a calibrated approach that took nearly six months to craft, there could still be some pitfalls in the implementation of the strategic partnership agreement. The Indian government ought to be watchful and resilient to respond speedily to recalibrate plans should a changed situation so warrant. Perhaps the greatest uncertainty that could impinge on the agreement is the collapse of the Karzai government. There is also a hidden possibility of radical change in American policy with altered paradigms that could well leave India literally holding the baby. It remains to be seen whether India has ventured into a deal she may find difficult to sustain. The strategic partnership agreement between India and Afghanistan can be regarded as a game changer in the region and truly a landmark event. However, there are uncertainties and impediments that the signatories ought not to overlook or ignore. While the agreement will impact each stakeholder differently, the real challenge for both India and Afghanistan will be to restore the process of currently derailed negotiations amongst the stakeholders and convert the slogan of peace in Afghanistan into reality. Undoubtedly, this is likely to be a task more easily said than done. However, the real test of India's foreign policy will be the survival of the strategic partnership in the labile and volatile political and security environment that could prevail in Afghanistan in the wake of the withdrawal of foreign forces in 2014. India is acutely conscious of the fact that radical changes in the political situation or the leadership in Afghanistan could impinge on the relationship with India and despite the safeguards built in, would have the potential to dilute, if not nullify, the strategic partnership agreement. As India's approach to Afghanistan aims to transcend local ethnic, tribal, sectarian and political divides, there is a reasonable chance that the strategic partnership agreement would be able to weather the storm and survive the severest internal turmoil aggravated by external forces. That is certainly the need of the hour.

India Afghanistan have traditionally shared a warm & friendly relationship

Aryana-Khorasan dynasty present day Afghanistan-Central Asia & India, Historically the relationship can be traced back to the Indus Valley Civilization in ancient times, 3,500 years ago, which flourished into medieval period, and cultural integration grew substantially. In the modern era India has always stood by its traditional neighbor, whether during the Cold War or during the occupation of Taliban where India was one of the key supporters of Northern Alliance. In the post 9/11 scenario, both countries have reestablished strong relations based on historical and civilization linkages, strengthening it further by India pledging to partner Afghanistan in its reconstruction and its fight against terrorism. The recent visit of President Hamid Karzai to India and the signing of the strategic partnership agreement is testimony of the age-old goodwill and trust shared between the two countries. Afghanistan, with its political unrest, needs a partnership which is sustainable and trustworthy which would enable it to establish a stable and prosperous nationhood. Given the fact that India and Afghanistan have shared a cordial relationship over centuries it is evident that India and Afghanistan fit into the requisite long-term partnership, working together and assisting each other. That is why, given the current scenario, it behooves India to assist Afghanistan in all the ways possible. Afghanistan stands on the crossroads of north Asia, sandwiched between resource rich Central Asia in the north, Iran in the west and Pakistan in the south One clear way to assist Afghanistan is to help in rebuilding its economy – which India has been doing with a generous partnership amounting to $1.5 billion so far, the sixth largest donor — which would lead to political stability. This is in alignment with Afghanistan's National Development Strategy. Some of this money has been spent in building roads, power lines and the construction of the Afghan parliament. India has offered to rebuild the Afghan national airline Ariana, donating Airbus aircraft, and trained pilots India has donated 600 buses, provided experts who have restored telecommunication networks in a dozen of Afghan provinces. The principal objective of India's development partnership, covering the entire country and all sectors of development, is to build indigenous Afghan capacity and institutions. India has played an active role in the development of Afghanistan based on the understanding that social and economic development is key to Afghanistan becoming a source of regional stability. India's programmers covers four broad areas – infrastructure projects, humanitarian assistance, small and community based development projects, and education and capacity development Some major projects are: The 218-km road project from Zaranj to Delaram in south-western Afghanistan to facilitate movement of goods and services to the Iranian border and, onward, to the Chahbahar Port was inaugurated by the Afghan President and Indian External Affairs Minister in January 2009. India constructed 202 km 220 DC transmission line from Pul-e-Khumri to Kabul and a 220/110/20 substation at Chimtala which has enabled Afghanistan to get power from Uzbekistan lighting up the city of Kabul throughout the year. This project was completed in collaboration with the Afghan Government, ADP and the World Bank, with inputs from USAID and International Energy Firms, and was an outstanding example of regional and international cooperation in Afghanistan. The other two major infrastructure projects, the construction of the Afghan Parliament in Kabul and, The construction of the Salma Dam power project in Herat province is under progress and will be completed by 2011-12. India's Humanitarian assistance initiatives include provision of free medical services and medicines through 5 Indian Medical Missions located in Kabul, Mazar-e-Sharif, Jalalabad, Herat and Kandahar (each medical mission includes a small team of doctors and paramedic staff); provision of food assistance of 1 million tons of wheat in the form of high protein biscuits distributed to about 1.5 million school children daily under a 'School Feeding Programmed' administered by the World Food Programmed; reconstruction and renovation of Indira Gandhi Institute of Child Health (in Kabul) in various phases and gifting 10 ambulances. In education and institution development, India provides 675 long-term university scholarships every year for under-graduate and post-graduate studies, plus another 675 short-term scholarships for technical training. More than 20 Indian civil servants have served as coaches and mentors for Afghan administrators. Indian chambers of commerce have set up training workshops to train Afghan youth in carpentry, plumbing, welding, masonry and tailoring, while the Self-Employed Women's Association (SEWA), has built a Women's Vocational Training Centre in Bagh-e-Zanana in Kabul for training Afghan war-widows and orphans in garment making, nursery plantation, and food processing and marketing. Prime Minister Manmohan Singh outlined the contours of the relationship when he visited Kabul in May 2011, by increasing India's aid commitment to Afghanistan by $ 500 million, thus raising the total to US$ 2 billion. He announced a number of new schemes, including a fresh commitment of US $ 100 million for the third phase of India's programmed of Small Development Projects, over the existing pledge of US$ 20 million. Besides, the donation of a 1000 buses for Kabul and other municipalities, medical packages for treating Afghan patients in India and up gradation of the Indira Gandhi Institute of Child Health, including the neo-natal and maternal care unit; donating 500 tractors and provision of seeds; $50 million credit line to promote exports ; $14 million to restore archaeological sites; assistance in setting up an Afghan institute of mining; establishing a Jawaharlal Nehru Chair of Indian Studies at Kabul University. Indian long-term commitment was concretized with the signing of the Strategic Partnership Agreement between Prime Minister Dr. Manmohan Singh and President Hamid Karzai, during the latter's visit to India in October 2011. The Strategic Partnership Agreement identified a number of development sectors in which India would continue to support Afghanistan in the long-run, including agriculture, rural development, mining, industry, energy, information technology, communications, transport, civil aviation, etc. It has been India's Endeavour to act in conformity with the best aid-effectiveness principles, taking into account local government priorities, in co-ordination with other donors, using local sub-contractors and materials as far as practical, spending as little as possible on security and salaries. These 'overhead costs' are significantly lower in case of Indian projects than in those undertaken by other donors. Following up on the visit of President Karzai in November last year, the Afghan Foreign Minister Mr. Zalmai Rassoul visited New Delhi last week to attend the first meeting of the India – Afghanistan Partnership Council. The discussions were focused on working out a road map for future as well as to integrate government machineries to coordinate a holistic approach to development. This visit marked the formal initiation of the India-Afghanistan Strategic Partnership which was inked during the visit of President Karzai. A key concern in Afghanistan is the continuing violence and fighting between the Taliban and the international security forces and US troops stationed there. Afghan security forces are gradually taking charge as the deadline for US forces to begin withdrawal in 2014 becomes closer, but this is clearly not enough. US President Barack Obama's recent visit to Kabul, during which he signed a strategic partnership in Afghanistan clearly signals America's continuing involvement in Afghanistan even as it slowly begins to withdraw troops from the ground. The US has already spent large sums of money on training Afghan forces in India, as well as on training Afghan civil servants in Indian institutions. India has shown its willingness to train Afghan soldiers in counter-insurgency inside India, but has refused to send Indian troops to Afghanistan. India understands the anger with which Afghans react to foreign forces and certainly has no intention of sending Indian forces to a friendly country. There is also continuing and serious concern about the ability of the Taliban to strike at will, as well as the Afghan government's position on the reconciliation and reintegration of Taliban fighters into the political mainstream. Moreover, with the withdrawal of US troops as well as the other international forces on the cards, Afghanistan's neighbors have been making serious efforts to look at regional neighbors helping Afghanistan by taking some of the responsibility. That is why in late 2011, all of Afghanistan's neighbors were invited to the Istanbul Conference to look at how they could together attain a politically and economically stable Afghanistan. At the conference, Afghan president Hamid Karzai held up the India relationship as a model and referred to it as a constructive partner. Karzai said, "Our deepening friendship with India and Turkey is a model for how we seek to shape out future relationships with some of the key regional partners." The Istanbul conference was followed by the Bonn conference in December 2011, which focused on security, reconciliation and long-term help for Afghanistan. Country overview, Economic and Social Indicators Country Overview Name: Islamic Republic of Afghanistan Location: Strategically located between Central and Southern Asia to the north-west of Pakistan and east of Iran. Afghanistan also shares borders with China, Tajikistan, Turkmenistan and Uzbekistan Capital: Kabul (4.1 million inhabitants) Number of provinces: 34 Area: 652,000 square kilometers Population: Around 30 million (16. 4 million female / 13. 5 million male) of which 45 % is under 15 years Urbanization: 21.7 % Rural population: 78.3 % Natural resources: Energy Minerals such as oil, natural gas and coal; metallic and non-precious minerals such as lead, cement-grade limestone, gemstones, copper, iron, gold, salt, and industrial minerals; as well as a variety of precious and semiprecious stones Industries: Mainly small-scale production Source: Central Statistical Organization, Government of Afghanistan Economic Indicators: Recent developments Despite deteriorating security, the economy reflects strong, but weakening, economic growth in FY2011/12. Inflation registered a sharp decrease in fiscal year 2011 to single digit levels, but while the price of food imports decreased, inflationary pressures remained because of higher fuel prices. Donors will aim to channel a large share of resources through the Afghan "Core" Budget to meet their Kabul Conference commitment of delivering 50 percent of aid "on-Budget" over the next 2 years. However, the low execution rate of the development budget (at 48 percent in 2011/12) continues to highlight limited absorptive capacity. Sustainable, self-reliant growth requires significant improvement in security, progress in the Afghan-led reconciliation process, and a better environment for private investment. This is, however, expected to rise over the years with the development of the mining industry (China was awarded the huge Aynak copper mine some years ago, while India won the award for the Hajigak copper mine some months ago). Private investment accounts for only a small proportion of demand (around 4% of GDP). Real GDP growth rate is expected to close at 5.7% this fiscal, a decline from last year's 8.4%. This was mostly due to volatility in agriculture output, which is subject to weather conditions. The services sector continues to grow strongly and was mostly driven by telecom and transportation & distribution. Private consumption remained the economy's main driver, based on continued high external assistance inflows and security spending that fueled demand for production of goods and services, including construction.

The size of the opium economy (not included in the official figures for economic activity) had been declining since 2007 because of crop-substitution policies, but in 2011 its farm gate price increased by 133 per cent, owing to plant disease–related lower production levels and drop in global wheat prices. Consequently, land used for opium cultivation increased by 7% and opium production increased by 61% in 2011. This boosted farmers' opium-sourced income, likely complicating the already slow pace of poppy eradication. Inflation registered a sharp decrease in fiscal year 2011. In the first six months, the year-on-year headline inflation hovered around 13.9 percent, followed by a decline to 9.9 percent from July to September, and down to 7.7 percent by February 2012. Despite the decline in the growth rate of food prices, overall inflationary pressures remained high due to higher fuel prices. Afghanistan is heavily dependent on fuel imports from Iran and 2011 was a year with significant fuel supply disruptions at the Iranian border, which affected prices. Afghanistan maintains a managed floating exchange rate regime. The Afghani continues to depreciate. Between March 2011 and Feb. 2012, the Afghani depreciated nominally by 3 percent against Euro and more strongly against the US dollar by 9 percent. At conferences in London and Kabul in January and July 2010, the government presented refinements to its Afghan-led medium-term plan for development and announced results-based national priority programs to meet its objectives. It also set out public financial-management reforms. Only an estimated 20% of donor funds are channeled, however, through the government budget, and to increase this share (as committed at the Kabul Conference), the government needs to greatly improve its implementation capacity. It also needs to address broader issues of transparency and accountability in the public sector, including strengthening audits on the use of domestic funds. Afghanistan's trade balance is heavily skewed towards imports, reflecting the large aid flows for the country's reconstruction and recovery efforts, which generate direct and indirect demands for imported goods. However, the trade deficit has been continuously declining over the past years. The current account deficit (excluding grants) went from 70 percent in 2006/7 to 34 percent in 2011/12, and was financed, as in previous years, by grants. At the same time, these grants are mostly spent on imports of goods and services, thus, the grants not only finance the trade deficit, but also contribute to it. In FY2011, import values estimated at US$ 9 billion, amounted to about three times that of exports (US $3 billion). This year saw exports grow more strongly, at 3 percent, while imports grew marginally by 0.2 percent and declined as a percent of GDP. The country is distinguished in the region for its openness to trade and, with few products taxed above 15 percent, has one of the lowest tariff regimes. Pakistan, India, Russia, UAE and Iran are among the top five export partners of Afghanistan, while Uzbekistan, Pakistan, China, Japan and Iran are among the top five import partners of Afghanistan. Economic Prospects: Projections Selected economic indicators (%) Source: ADB estimates however, these projections are subject to several risks, such as worsening security conditions, political instability, weak governance, loss of export competitiveness, and new barriers to trade with neighboring countries. The debt relief granted to Afghanistan under the extended heavily indebted poor countries initiative in 2010 has relieved the debt burden by $1.6 billion, taking it to a sustainable level (around 8% of GDP). Still, Afghanistan will stay at high risk of debt distress, particularly if foreign grants (expected to decrease gradually in the medium term) fall heavily. India-Afghanistan Economic Relations India-Afghanistan Total Trade (US$ Million) Source: Ministry of Commerce and Industry, Government of India Top Five Export Items from India to Afghanistan (US$ Million) Source: Ministry of Commerce and Industry, Government of India Top Five Import Items from Afghanistan to India (US$ Million) Source: Ministry of Commerce and Industry, Government of India Agribusiness and Agro-processing, Construction and construction materials, Energy and natural resources, Textiles and carpets, Transport and Logistics, Chemical and pharmaceutical products, Banking and financial services, Telecom Services, Real estate and tourism, Hydrocarbons, etc. are among various areas of cooperation between the two countries. Challenges and Issues Security concerns: Makes it difficult to attract new investors as providing security imposes a high cost on all businesses in Afghanistan. Institutions and transparency: Weak institutions and lack of transparency inject uncertainty in the investment climate and thus raises the cost of doing business. Poor infrastructure: The poor state of infrastructure also contributes to high production costs, reduces the attractiveness of Afghanistan as an investment alternative, and generates uncertainty about merchandise delivery. Unreliable power supply: Electricity costs constitute another constraint on competitiveness Limited human and technical capacity: The low level of education, lack of training facilities and high illiteracy rate has always been responsible for acute shortages of skilled labor. This is attributable to emigration of the country's best trained people and historical barriers to training women. This severely constrains firms from investing or expanding. Access to land: Access to land remains a problem for firms wanting to significantly expand, especially those seeking green field expansion. Even the existing firms believe that access to land is a very severe constraint in Afghanistan. Access to Finance: Afghanistan's financial system is just beginning to recover. Businesses have limited access to bank credit and banking services, hence Afghan firms are almost entirely dependent on internal funds and money from friends and family to fund their operations. In addition to lack of external finance, Afghan firms are faced with almost complete absence of insurance. The legislative process is slow and a number of important laws have been pending, waiting parliamentary approval, final drafting or implementation. Market analysis is difficult due to limitations on data availability – data on price and production is available, but in a limited sense. The country still ranks the lowest in the region for ease of doing business, according to the World Bank's Doing Business 2011 report, and this needs a change. Afghanistan ranks 167 out of 183 countries worldwide. Major Recommendations Afghanistan's trade linkages: The trade linkages of Afghanistan with other countries have remained low and specifically with SAARC members it has not only been low but also concentrated in few sectors. Therefore, Afghanistan must participate in SAFTA as an active member. Interface between SAFTA and India-Afghanistan PTA: FICCI feels that the scope of coverage of India-Afghanistan trade relations would be greater under SAFTA than under their existing bilateral PTA. Therefore, it is recommended that both India and Afghanistan should cooperate to derive mutual trade benefits under the SAFTA process. Addressing constraints through transit and trade facilitation: It is recommended that SAARC must have a regional transit agreement since several countries like Bangladesh, Bhutan, Nepal and Afghanistan would benefit from such arrangements. In the process non-LDCs of SAARC would also gain in terms of effective market access in these countries. In this context, the APIBM transport corridor deserves high priority for operation. Capacity building programmers: Designing and implementing major capacity building programmers to develop skills and professionalism in chambers of commerce and industry as well as in customs, banking and insurance. Export finance, procedural rationalization, custom harmonization are some of the well known areas where progress under SAARC needs to be augmented as they are very crucial for deriving trade gains in Afghanistan. Better law and security conditions in Afghanistan would attract not only more investments but also human capital which would augment the economic pace and peace in the region. Overall, Afghanistan needs to be considered as a strategic economic partner of India in the South Asian region. Its importance lies in the fact that it offers immense possibilities for Indian investments in its era of reconstruction which could help build export supply capabilities in Afghanistan. The strengthening of trade-investment linkages in the country would help building the transit infrastructure which would in the second round further facilitate trade and investment flows. Moreover, connectivity with Afghanistan would provide access to the West and the Central Asian markets and their natural resources. In this sense too, Afghanistan could prove to be a strategic partner which would also facilitate making the South Asian region as the hub of economic activities between the Western and Eastern parts of Asia.

The U.S. and international
community are focused

on the security transition in Afghanistan but must not ignore the major political and economic transition expected to occur over the next two years, according to a number of experts who spoke on two off-the-record panels at USIP last week. It would be a "strategic misstep," said one panelist, if these agendas are ignored. It was one of many issues panelists grappled with during the two discussions titled "From Transition to the Transformation Decade: Afghanistan's Economic and Governance Agenda after Tokyo" and held July 18 at USIP. One panel focused on filling the fiscal gap and the $16 billion in pledges made by the U.S. and the international community at the Tokyo conference earlier this month. The second panel looked at filling the "trust gap" and what "mutual accountability" means in the context of the next several years between Afghanistan and donor nations. Afghanistan and the international community emerged from the Tokyo conference with what many consider to be reliable, predictable promises of assistance, allaying fears that the international community will abandon the country after 2014. But the ability of Afghanistan to absorb the $16 billion in pledges over the next four years is a major issue. One participant noted that the amount of money that Afghanistan needed was limitless, but the amount its government could actually absorb was even less than the $16 billion pledged over four years at Tokyo. In addition to aid, mining and agriculture will be the two main economic drivers in Afghanistan over the next several years. "Public investment should focus on these sectors," said one panelist. Two or more panelists noted the humanitarian crisis that may arise from the departure of international forces over the next couple of years, with as many as 600,000 internally displaced people in Afghanistan now. "It's a massive number of displaced people by any standard," said another panelist. "The reality is that there has been so much focus on the security side… that the humanitarian side hasn't received the focus," said another. Many of the panelists agreed that there are positive trends across the country that, if nurtured, may take hold. But this good news was treated with some caution. "Those gains are fragile," one panelist concluded. Watch Scott Smith, deputy director of USIP Afghanistan programs, assess the two schools of thought at the Mutual accountability" is the cornerstone of the Tokyo Declaration of July 8. Donors agreed to provide a very large amount of civilian aid to Afghanistan ($16 billion over four years, or $4 billion per year on average), and to improve the effectiveness of aid by over time putting more (50 percent) of total aid through Afghan budget channels and aligning most (80 percent) with Afghanistan's priorities as embodied in the National Priority Programs. The Afghan government committed to taking a number of actions and achieving associated outcomes/results, primarily in governance and political spheres. The outcome of the Tokyo meeting exceeded expectations in terms of funding indicated by donors and conditions agreed to by the Afghan government, but making mutual accountability work will be a major challenge. "Conditionality" has become a dirty word in some quarters, but it is a form of mutual accountability—a government commits to taking certain actions (typically policy reforms of various kinds), and the international partner commits to providing funding in return. There are hard-learned lessons from application of conditionality during the three decades since the 1980s; mistakes made have prompted changes in approaches. The World Bank has developed a set of good-practice principles emphasizing ownership, harmonization, customization, criticality and transparency and predictability. Some concrete lessons from experience with conditionality include: A reform constituency in the country is essential to leverage conditions and push reforms seen as necessary for the country's progress; otherwise political will for meaningful reforms will be lacking. Objectives and targets cannot be overly ambitious but rather need to be achievable and build momentum of reforms. A degree of flexibility and responsiveness to unexpected developments needs to be built in. Conditionality should involve only a few essential targets/benchmarks—otherwise the reform effort will lose focus. A medium-term perspective and reform framework is important. Dialogue is key— the process of collaboratively developing a reform program tailored to individual country circumstances, agreeing on triggers and benchmarks, and following up on implementation can be very beneficial. There are also technical design issues, such as ex-ante versus ex-post provision of funding, how to balance incentives for reform actions with predictability of financing, whether to do a series of separate operations or a single multi-tranche operation, etc. Afghanistan over the past decade has seen numerous reform agendas, benchmarks and commitments on the part of government and donors, reflecting the multiplicity of donors and the plethora of high-profile international meetings since 2001. The mutual accountability framework promulgated at Tokyo clearly reflects learning from earlier experience. There are 20–plus benchmarks for the government in five main areas, far fewer than in the Afghanistan Compact of 2006 (which had well over 100 benchmarks). There is a long-term perspective—the "decade of transformation" (2014–2025), and the responsibilities of Afghanistan and the international community are clearly set forth and demarcated. Nevertheless, there are major issues and challenges for the future. First are inherent problems of mutual accountability, which implies layered dual accountability of both government and international partners. Each side is accountable to the other party in the Tokyo framework but also to their own constituencies/citizens. On the international side, the multiplicity of donors means there is fragmented accountability—this could adversely affect coherence around targets and enforcing benchmarks, as well as the ability of the international community to be meaningfully held accountable for total funding, particularly given severe fiscal constraints faced around the world. Coordinated programs and funding will be essential, but is it realistic to expect most aid to go through the Afghan government budget/trust funds For the Afghan government, uncertain political and security prospects raise doubts about its ability to meet commitments. The reform constituency may be weakening; there has been an inability to fully address issues where high-level political connections are involved (e.g. Kabul Bank); and more generally, the political will needed for meaningful reforms understandably may decline as the security transition proceeds and the next election cycle approaches. Second, it is doubtful whether major political issues can be adequately handled through an articulated mutual accountability framework with benchmarks and calibrated financial incentives — which are better suited to more technical conditions without large overt political ramifications. Other mechanisms, such as that set up to oversee implementation of the Strategic Partnership Agreement between the Afghan and U.S. governments, may be better suited for handling such "big-ticket" issues. Third, the figure for total civilian aid agreed at Tokyo is ambitious and exceeded expectations—particularly since it is in addition to large security sector assistance agreed at the Chicago NATO Summit in May. Inability by the international community to deliver this level of funding could provide a justification for the Afghan government failing to achieve its benchmarks, and mutual accountability could degenerate into each side accusing the other of not delivering on promises, rather than working as a framework with incentives to achieve positive results and improve behavior on both sides as intended. Finally, how will achievement of benchmarks be monitored and enforced? As indicated in the Tokyo Declaration, the specifics of modalities, timelines, etc. remain to be worked out. Given past experience, there are doubts about how well the Joint Coordination and Monitoring Board process (mandated to oversee implementation), and the series of further high-level meetings agreed at Tokyo, will work. Declining aid for Afghanistan means the funding lever potentially will be stronger than in the past, but it is not clear whether and how effectively it can be deployed given donor fragmentation and that some funding (e.g. for Afghan security forces) is seen as an integral part of international drawdown strategy and hence will be difficult to hold back. While the outcome at Tokyo has exceeded expectations and hence was a success, the challenge henceforth will be implementation. Afghanistan's Presidential Decree of July 21, which intended to galvanize the Afghan government to take a disparate set of actions in coming months, illustrates the complexities and difficulties involved. The sheer number of actions called for (over 150 of them, by 32 different ministries and agencies), the ambitious deadlines (as little as one month for some actions, with most in the 3-6 months range), the enormous amount of paperwork requested (in the form of numerous reports and plans etc.), and the lack of specified sanctions for non-performance, raise serious questions about implementation.

Building the capacity of and reforming Afghan governance

is widely viewed as the key to success in Afghanistan. Assessing progress, however, is hampered by limited data outside the Afghan security ministries – the Ministries of Defense and Interior – and by the lack of a common definition of governance. Available reporting suggests building governance capacity is far from complete. Varying definitions of governance, coupled with the use of the term by numerous organizations without defining it, results in addressing too broad a range of issues. It would be more useful to concentrate on the core of governance – providing the services the Afghan government has committed to provide to its citizens. This, in turn, requires that Afghan ministries have the functional capacity to carry out their responsibilities, including financial management, budget formulation and execution, policy and strategic planning, and service delivery. However, time is growing short. The Afghan experience provides some important lessons that could guide future endeavors for the international community. First, this paper discusses progress in building ministerial capacity. Second, it discusses recent efforts to link continued financial assistance to Afghanistan with improved governance. Third, it describes how the lack of a commonly accepted definition of governance complicates assessing progress. Finally, it offers conclusions and observations about the failure to establish an autonomous Afghan governance capacity. For more than a decade, improving governance has been recognized as the most difficult and critical challenge involving Afghan reconstruction. The Special Inspector General for Afghanistan Reconstruction (SIGAR) reports that U.S. policymakers have consistently identified building the capacity of and reforming Afghan governance as the key to success in Afghanistan (SIGAR 2012, 22). Available Data Shows Slow Progress at Best in Achieving Governance The conclusion of virtually every Administration and outside assessment, except for the World Bank (World Bank 2012: 6) has been that Afghan central governmental capacity and effectiveness has increased, but that local governance remains weak and all levels of government are plagued by governmental corruption. In May 2012 the World Bank reported that after an initial rise government effectiveness was declining. It characterized the declining trend as worrisome and said that it needed to be reversed. U.S. assessments assert that the deficiencies in governance could jeopardize stability following the expected 2014 transition (CRS 2013: 9). As discussed below, while Afghan central governmental capacity and effectiveness may have increased, at least in the security ministries, the Afghan government is far from being able to operate without outside assistance. This raises important questions about the prospects for effective Afghan governance. Progress has lagged in achieving governance capability in the security ministries Among U.S. departments and agencies, the source of most governance assessments; the U.S. Department of Defense provides the most extensive reporting on governance. It provides detailed capability assessments for the security ministries, the Ministry of Defense (MOD) and Ministry of Interior (MOI), and more generalized assessments for the rest of the Afghan government.1 defines capability levels and assesses key functions within the two security ministries. Progress in governance capability in the MOD and MOI has been slower than predicted. In April 2009, predicted that based on current missions and ministerial development plans, the MOD would be capable of conducting primary operational missions by mid-2011 (the highest level of capability, an organization, unit, agency, staff function, or installation that is capable of conducting primary operational missions, rated as Capability Milestone (CM) 1 (2009: 9, 17).2 It did not predict when the MOI would be capable of conducting primary operational missions. A year later, in April 2010, progress had slipped by one year. then predicted that the MOD was expected to be largely capable of conducting primary operational missions by mid-2012. It also predicted that until July 2011 the majority of the MOI would not reach a lower capability level, which is defined as the ability to work with the mentoring team to accomplish its assigned tasks or otherwise known as CM2 (2010: 101–102,113). As of December 2012, the date of the latest assessment, neither the MOD nor the MOI were rated as capable of autonomous operations (2012: 49, 51). After 2010 divided its CM1 category into two parts: CM1A, capable of autonomous operations, and CM1B, capable of executing functions with coalition oversight only, In its December 2012 report, covering the period April 1, 2012 through September 30, 2012, was only predicting when the MOD and MOI would be capable of executing functions with coalition oversight only or CM1B status, with no mention of achieving CM1A or autonomous operations status. In the December 2012 report, assessed forty-two capability areas within the MOD and General Staff, This included operations, policy and planning, personnel, acquisition, and logistics. It did not rate the MOD or General Staff as capable of autonomous operations in any assessed capability. The MOD was judged capable of executing functions with coalition oversight only in two capability areas and the General Staff in four capability areas. All other capabilities required varying levels of coalition assistance, with intelligence policy and gender integration being rated as incapable of accomplishing their mission. projected that between mid-2013 and the end of 2014 the MOD and General Staff would be capable of executing functions with coalition oversight in all but four areas—transparency and accountability, gender integration, and two areas involving the Afghan Air Force where becoming capable of executing functions with coalition oversight only was projected to be achieved after 2014. Assessed thirty capability areas within the MOI, including: strategy and policy, the uniform and border police, personnel management, logistics, and acquisition and procurement. As with the MOD assessments, did not rate the MOI as capable of autonomous operations in any assessed capability. The MOI was judged capable of executing functions with coalition oversight only in two capability areas and required varying levels of coalition assistance in most other areas, except for two where it was rated as incapable of accomplishing its mission - gender and human rights and the Afghan Public Protection Force. projected that the MOI would become capable of executing functions with coalition oversight between mid-2013 and the end of 2014 in all but one area: democratic policing, which was given an indefinite date of completion (2012: 47,49,51). Failure to project when the MOD and MOI will be capable of autonomous operations is particularly troubling. This is because after 2014 it is unclear as to whether any advisors will remain, although expects there will be a need for continued coalition oversight. The Commanding General of U.S. and coalition forces in Afghanistan said in January 2013 that his top priority for beyond 2014 is to deploy a significant number of advisors in the MOD and MOI as part of a post-2014 U.S. presence (Skiff 2013). Even if a post-2014 presence is approved, advisor positions must be filled. reported that as of September 1, 2012, 51 of 185 advisor positions for the MOD were vacant but in the process of being staffed by the U.S. military, Ministry of Defense Advisors Program, or contractors (2012: 47). This author has observed the staffing process firsthand and seen that it can be difficult and time-consuming because it depends on voluntary cooperation. Provided no comparable data for the MOI Assessments of non-security ministries are more limited but also show progress has lagged Information on non-security ministries largely consists of generalized descriptions, with only limited individual ministry assessments. The is the source of most of the general assessments. The lack of periodic detailed assessments by any agency, akin to assessments of the MOD and MOI, make tracking overall governance progress difficult. Beyond, the U.S. Government Accountability Office (GAO) and the U.S. Agency for International Development (USAID) are the primary sources of non-security ministry assessments. The most recent reporting this author could find from these institutions was a June 2012 USAID report on the results of a project it commissioned on budgetary units. The project conducted risk assessments of all assigned budgetary units in non-security Afghan ministries, as well as other offices which are currently receiving program budgeting reform technical assistance, such as the President's Office and Supreme Court. The aim of the assessment was to determine their current capacity in program budgeting implementation.3 The assessment evaluated twelve variables related to management, organizational structure, and technical capacity of the budgetary units. Based on the ratings, budgetary units were classified as "strong", "above average", "average" and "weak". Following is a summary of the assessment results. As can be seen from the summary, of the thirty-eight budgetary units assessed, more than half were assessed as requiring at least two more years of support before they are capable of operating autonomously. Six ministries (16% of the total) were rated "strong" in their capacity to implement program budgeting reform and can be considered for graduation from project based support in 2012. Twelve budgetary units (32% of the total) were rated "above average," and will require at least one more year of project support, particularly in the new reform areas such as procurement and financial planning, and performance monitoring reporting. Fifteen budgetary units (39% of the total) were rated "average" in their capacity to implement program budgeting reform and will require at least two more years of support to be able to implement the reform without external assistance. The remaining five budgetary units (13% of the total) were rated "weak", and will require major internal reforms and continued project support for at least two years before they are able to implement program budgeting reform without external assistance. In July 2010, GAO reported on Afghan ministerial capacity (GAO 2010: 28–29).4 Based on a review of USAID data, GAO stated that USAID has increasingly included and emphasized capacity building among its programs to address the government of Afghanistan's lack of capacity to sustain and maintain many of the programs and projects put in place by donors. In 2009, on a scale of 5, with 1 representing the need for substantial assistance across all areas and 5 representing the ability to perform without assistance, USAID rated the capability of 14 of 19 Afghan ministries and institutions it works with as either 1 or 2. For example, the Ministry of Agriculture, Irrigation, and Livestock was given a rating of 2—needing technical assistance to perform all but routine functions—while the Ministry for Rural Rehabilitation and Development was given a rating of 4—needing little technical assistance.5 Although USAID noted the overall improvement among the ministries and institutions in recent years, none were rated as being able to perform without external assistance. As discussed above, the June 2012 USAID-sponsored assessment of budgetary units in thirty-eight non-security Afghan ministries and other offices showed that three years later most were still judged as not being able to operate autonomously. Other reporting on governance is more general but equally troubling. In a December 2012 assessment of national governance, stated that the Afghan government continued to develop its capacity to provide stable, effective, and responsive governance to the Afghan population (2012: 103,106). However, the long-term sustainability of the Afghan government is challenged by corruption, ineffective program monitoring, sub-national government budget funding shortfalls, an inability to generate revenues sufficient to cover the cost of government operations, and limited public financial management capacity. Furthermore, poor linkages between the national and sub-national levels of governance and an imbalance in the distribution of power between the three branches of government, with power concentrated in the executive branch, continue to limit effectiveness and legitimacy. Limited human capacity and a lack of appropriate formal training and education within the civil service and Afghan populace also impede the development of stable and sustainable government across Afghanistan. Although reported that the Afghan government continued to develop its capacity to provide stable, effective, and responsive governance to the Afghan population in a somewhat contradictory statement in the same report, stated that during the period April 1, 2012 to September 30, 2012, the executive, legislative, and judicial branches of the Afghan government demonstrated mixed progress in meeting their respective responsibilities and making gains toward long-term sustainability (2012: 103). Also provided a gloomy assessment of sub-national governance it reported that sub-national governance structures operated to varying degrees of effectiveness at provincial, district, and village levels. did not provide its methodology or data sources so its reporting appears to be anecdotal. The Afghan government has also reported on governance constraints beyond U.S. government evaluations. In a July 2012 report for the Tokyo Conference, the Afghan government said that capacity constraints still remain a big bottleneck to budget execution, hindering public sector program implementation and public service delivery (Government of the Islamic Republic of Afghanistan 2012: 15). The government's Public Financial Management Program in the Governance Cluster aims to improve the public financial management system, as well as increase budget execution, efficiency, and transparency in the management of public finances. Key challenges in this area include capacity constraints at the national and especially sub-national levels; weak planning and budget formulation; donor earmarking of funds and funding delays; and challenges in communication and coordination across ministries, among donors and between national and sub-national entities. The Afghan government said it is committed to improving provincial-level planning, budgeting and implementation; developing the capacity of line ministries in finance, procurement, and project management; developing a Medium-Term Budget Framework with hard budget ceilings; and effectively reprioritizing spending according to national priorities. Whether the Afghan government succeeds in improving fiscal governance remains to be seen. SIGAR and GAO Reporting Highlight Shortfalls in Tracking Governance Progress In an October 2011 report, SIGAR discussed the shortfalls in measuring progress in improving governance. SIGAR reported that the U.S. Embassy in Afghanistan had not been able to determine how much progress had been made to date in building ministry capacity at the Ministry of Agriculture, Irrigation, and Livestock because it did not have sufficient or complete data. Capacity-building activities and the performance data collected were not consistent, making it difficult for the U.S. Embassy to incorporate them into its assessment. Moreover, there were no performance baselines and targets for any performance indicators. The indicators being used largely measured the outputs of capacity-building efforts, rather than the results achieved. Without a mechanism that can sufficiently and reliably assess and report on progress made in building the Ministry's capacity, SIGAR concluded that the U.S. Embassy cannot determine whether the strategy is working and if resources are properly aligned. Without being able to assess progress, these agencies cannot identify what changes are needed to improve both the effectiveness of their programs and to ensure sustainable results. In a September 2011 report, GAO said that the overall results of U.S. efforts to improve Afghanistan's public financial management capacity cannot be fully determined because of the following: (1) U.S. agencies providing capacity assistance to the Afghan government have reported mixed results of their efforts, and (2) weaknesses in US Aid's performance management plans and frameworks, such as lack of performance targets and data, prevent reliable assessments of US Aid's results. US Aid's evaluations of its two primary public financial management projects indicated that some activities were successfully completed, while others were terminated because their usefulness was questionable. U.S. Treasury Department advisers assessed that even though their assistance at the Afghan Ministry of Finance had a positive effect, the results fell short of what they were trying to accomplish (GAO 2011: 13). Donors Seek to Link Continued Financial Assistance to Improved Governance on July 8, 2012, representatives from seventy countries, international organizations, and non-profit groups met in Tokyo to create a framework for continued international support for Afghanistan's economic development. The support was intended to cover the transition at the end of 2014 through the "transformation decade" (2015–2024). At the conference, the international community pledged to provide an estimated $16 billion in aid from 2012 through 2015, but with conditions. In return for the assistance, the Afghan government promised to implement political and economic reforms to improve governance. This included making public institutions more accountable and tackling pervasive corruption. The conference declaration stated that the participants recognized that good governance at national and sub-national levels is essential for strong and sustainable economic development and improved livelihoods of the Afghan people. An annex to the declaration entitled the Tokyo Mutual Accountability Framework sets out mutual commitments, together with corresponding indicators, and a monitoring mechanism. The framework committed the Afghan government and the International Community to monitor performance in five major areas of development and governance as follows (Japan Ministry of Foreign Affairs 2012). Conduct credible, inclusive and transparent Presidential and Parliamentary elections in 2014 and 2015. Improve access to justice for all, particularly for women. Improve integrity of public financial management and the commercial banking sector. Improve the Afghan government's revenue collection and the capacity of line Ministries' to develop and execute budgets accountable to, and incorporating, local needs and preferences. Achieve inclusive and sustained growth through a focus on human development, food security, private investment, and decent work and employment opportunities and the improvement of Afghanistan's ranking in the human development index. As part of the regular monitoring process, progress is to be reviewed on a regular basis by existing entities, the Standing Committees and Joint Coordination and Monitoring Board. This is to be supplemented by a Senior Officials Meeting to be held in 2013, and thereafter every second year, to review progress and update indicators where needed; and a Ministerial-level Meeting to be held in 2014, and thereafter every second year, to review progress, update indicators, assess resource requirements and renew international commitments. In part to demonstrate that Afghanistan would uphold those commitments, Afghan President Karzai issued an administrative reform decree on July 26, 2012 that requires virtually every ministry and government body to develop a work plan, complete unfinished tasks, file specified reports, and/or carry out specified reforms. The Afghan government has made commitments before that have not come to fruition, so it remains to be seen whether these latest commitments are met. In fact, reports that the decree has been met with skepticism because demands and timelines were not combined with a comprehensive financial implementation plan or enforcement mechanisms (2012: 103). Lack of a Commonly Accepted Definition of Governance Complicates Assessing Progress Clausewitz wrote in On War that "The first, the supreme, the most far-reaching act of judgment that the statesman and commander have to make is to establish ... the kind of war on which they are embarking." That same principle can be applied to governance. The U.S. Department of Defense World Bank, various United Nations (UN) Agencies or Departments, Organization for Economic Co-operation and Development (OECD), and Institute on Governance have varying definitions of governance.6 In March 2006, the UN Economic and Social Council Committee of Experts on Public Administration addressed basic terminology in governance and public administration. The Committee recognized that there are some fundamental concepts and terminologies of governance and public administration that need to be defined in order for there to be a common understanding of them throughout the United Nations system. It acknowledged that these concepts and terminologies often are not applied in a uniform way. In its 2006 report, the Committee wrote that the use of the terms "governance" and "public administration" gained unprecedented momentum in both their quest and usage in the nineteenth and twentieth centuries. However, the Committee said that as the twenty-first century gets under way, there does not seem to be a consensus as to what they mean. In a highly dynamic environment politically, socially, economically, and culturally, these terms mean different things in different contexts (ECOSOC 2006: 1–2). Six years later a common definition of governance remained elusive. In a January 2012 article entitled what Does Good

Governance Mean published in the UN University World Institute for Development Economics Research newsletter, the author noted that "Good governance" is a term that has become a part of the vernacular of a large range of development institutions and other actors within the international arena. What it means exactly, however, has not been so well established." The author noted that in general, work by the World Bank and other multilateral development banks on good governance addresses economic institutions and public sector management, including transparency and accountability, regulatory reform, and public sector skills and leadership. Other organizations, like the United Nations, European Commission and OECD are more likely to highlight democratic governance and human rights aspects of political governance, which are issues largely beyond the Bank's mandate (UNU 2012: 1). A common definition across governments, multilateral organizations, and non-governmental organizations was still lacking as recently as January 2013. SIGAR, which has provided the most extensive reporting on governance in Afghanistan, based on input from a variety of U.S. government agencies including and USAID, has not defined what it means by the term governance. Each of the nine quarterly reports which SIGAR has issued between January 2011 and January 2013 have a section on governance, yet none of the reports define what SIGAR means by governance. Rather all nine reports cover a potpourri of topics. For example, the governance section in Sugar's most recent quarterly report, issued in January 2013, has five major sections: reconciliation and reintegration; national and sub-national governance; judicial reform and rule-of-law; anti-corruption; and human rights (SIGAR 2013: 95–121). In contrast, the October 2012 Civil-Military Strategic Framework for Afghanistan jointly issued by the U.S. Ambassador to Afghanistan and the Commanding General, U.S. Forces-Afghanistan separates governance from other activities. The plan addresses governance separately from both rule of law as well as reconciliation and reintegration (GAO 2013: 40). In seeking to address so many facets of governance, the donor and oversight communities have lost sight of its core function—providing the services the Afghan government has committed to provide to its citizens. As discussed above, much of the reporting on governance is general in nature. Consequently, after years of governance capacity building efforts, there is little analysis of why progress has been slow and what can be done to improve governance. Conclusions and Observations for Future Governance Building Efforts Prospects for Afghan autonomous governance are not bright. Progress in governance capability in the MOD and MOI, the focus of extensive mentoring and reporting by, has been slower than predicted. has stopped projecting when the MOD and MOI will be capable of autonomous operations. Instead it only predicts when the two ministries will be capable of executing functions with coalition oversight only. While would like to keep a significant number of advisors in the MOD and MOI as part of a post-2014 U.S. presence there is no assurance it will be able to do so given the uncertainties surrounding a continued presence in Afghanistan. Even today cannot fill all its advisor positions. Thought needs to be given to what would happen if the MOD and MOI were required to operate without coalition assistance after 2014 and whether adjustments in their capacity development are necessary. It may be too late to wait until 2014 to address how to handle undesirable outcomes. Reporting on non-security ministry capability is sparse and in critical need of attention. Available reporting shows that much remains to be done. The lack of regular assessments of governance capacity outside the MOD and MOI is a collective failure on the part of both the USAID, which administers the bulk of governance support to non-security ministries and other offices, and the U.S. government audit community in Afghanistan. There is a critical need for such assessments. Without them it is impossible to know which governance building programs are succeeding and which are not, and why. One is left to speculate on why success has been elusive. There are a number of possibilities, including that the donor community is trying to impose a western model of governance on an Afghan culture that has different values; training deficiencies involving the curriculum, trainers, or a combination of the two; and a high trainee turnover so that the people trained move on to other endeavors, resulting in the US agencies constantly having to train new people and never catching up. It is critical that more attention be focused on the outcome of governance efforts and on courses of action that address the root causes which prevent success. Improving governance is a shared responsibility of the donor community and the Afghan government. In July 2012 the donor community sought to link future financial aid to improved governance. This was followed by an Afghan government administrative reform decree requiring virtually every ministry and government body to take steps to improve governance. However, given the Afghan government's failure to honor past commitments unless donors demonstrate the seriousness of their concerns by reducing financial aid if commitments are not kept, the status quo will likely remain unchanged. The Afghan experience provides some important lessons that should guide future endeavors. While the experience in Iraq has reduced the appetite for expansive nation-building initiatives, events in countries such as Mali and Syria may result in future endeavors. The following actions should be taken in concert by the host government, participating multilateral organizations, and individual donor nations in future endeavors. First, agree on a definition of governance accepted by the host government and all donors. Second, irrespective of the definition of governance, develop outcome based measurable metrics. Third, at least on an annual basis, conduct assessments of each ministry and major institution receiving governance assistance. This assessment should assess progress against the metrics, identifying root causes if there is a lack of progress, and adjusting governance efforts as necessary based on the assessments. Fourth, condition future aid on demonstrable progress in improving governance, also assesses the operational effectiveness of Afghan National Army and Afghan National Police units. Since this paper addresses ministerial capacity, not individual unit operational effectives, it does not include this data. 2In April 2009 tracked progress of the MOD and MOI using a four-tier scale of Capability Milestones (CMs). CM1 denoted the highest level of capability. It described an organization, unit, agency, staff function, or installation that is capable of conducting primary operational missions. Depending on the situation, units may require specified assistance from the Coalition or international community. 3The project's program budget advisors, which were embedded in 38 budgetary units and serving as mobile teams to assist certain ministries as needed, provide on-the-job training and technical assistance in program budget preparation and execution. The project's technical assistance is aimed at gradually building capacity of budgetary units to prepare their program budgets and to execute them with minimal or no assistance from the project. At US Aid's request, the project conducted assessments of the 38 assigned budgetary units to determine their current capacity in program budgeting and to recommend actions to strengthen capacity to ensure sustainability of the project's assistance. 4Although the report's principal focus was on US Aid's agricultural programs it also addressed broader ministerial capacity. 5Other than the two ministries cited as examples GAO did not identify the ministries that were rated. Building the capacity of and reforming Afghan governance is widely viewed as the key to success in Afghanistan. Assessing progress, however, is hampered by limited data outside the Afghan security ministries – the Ministries of Defense and Interior – and by the lack of a common definition of governance. Available reporting suggests building governance capacity is far from complete. Varying definitions of governance, coupled with the use of the term by numerous organizations without defining it, results in addressing too broad a range of issues. It would be more useful to concentrate on the core of governance – providing the services the Afghan government has committed to provide to its citizens. This, in turn, requires that Afghan ministries have the functional capacity to carry out their responsibilities, including financial management, budget formulation and execution, policy and strategic planning, and service delivery. However, time is growing short. The Afghan experience provides some important lessons that could guide future endeavors for the international community. First, this paper discusses progress in building ministerial capacity. Second, it discusses recent efforts to link continued financial assistance to Afghanistan with improved governance. Third, it describes how the lack of a commonly accepted definition of governance complicates assessing progress. Finally, it offers conclusions and observations about the failure to establish an autonomous Afghan governance capacity. For more than a decade, improving governance has been recognized as the most difficult and critical challenge involving Afghan reconstruction. The Special Inspector General for Afghanistan Reconstruction (SIGAR) reports that U.S. policymakers have consistently identified building the capacity of and reforming Afghan governance as the key to success in Afghanistan (SIGAR 2012, 22). Available Data Shows Slow Progress at Best in Achieving Governance The conclusion of virtually every Administration and outside assessment, except for the World Bank (World Bank 2012: 6) has been that Afghan central governmental capacity and effectiveness has increased, but that local governance remains weak and all levels of government are plagued by governmental corruption. In May 2012 the World Bank reported that after an initial rise government effectiveness was declining. It characterized the declining trend as worrisome and said that it needed to be reversed. U.S. assessments assert that the deficiencies in governance could jeopardize stability following the expected 2014 transition (CRS 2013: 9). As discussed below, while Afghan central governmental capacity and effectiveness may have increased, at least in the security ministries, the Afghan government is far from being able to operate without outside assistance. This raises important questions about the prospects for effective Afghan governance. Progress has lagged in achieving governance capability in the security ministries Among U.S. departments and agencies, the source of most governance assessments, the U.S. Department of Defense) provides the most extensive reporting on governance. It provides detailed capability assessments for the security ministries, the Ministry of Defense (MOD) and Ministry of Interior (MOI), and more generalized assessments for the rest of the Afghan government.1 defines capability levels and assesses key functions within the two security ministries. Progress in governance capability in the MOD and MOI has been slower than predicted. In April 2009, predicted that based on current missions and ministerial development plans, the MOD would be capable of conducting primary operational missions by mid-2011 (the highest level of capability, an organization, unit, agency, staff function, or installation that is capable of conducting primary operational missions, rated as Capability Milestone (CM) 1 (2009: 9, 17).2 It did not predict when the MOI would be capable of conducting primary operational missions. A year later, in April 2010, progress had slipped by one year. then predicted that the MOD was expected to be largely capable of conducting primary operational missions by mid-2012. It also predicted that until July 2011 the majority of the MOI would not reach a lower capability level, which is defined as the ability to work with the mentoring team to accomplish its assigned tasks or otherwise known as CM2 (2010: 101–102,113). As of December 2012, the date of the latest assessment, neither the MOD nor the MOI were rated as capable of autonomous operations (2012: 49, 51). After 2010 divided its CM1 category into two parts: CM1A, capable of autonomous operations, and CM1B, capable of executing functions with coalition oversight only In its December 2012 report, covering the period April 1, 2012 through September 30, 2012, was only predicting when the MOD and MOI would be capable of executing functions with coalition oversight only or CM1B status, with no mention of achieving CM1A or autonomous operations status. In the December 2012 report, assessed forty-two capability areas within the MOD and General Staff This included operations, policy and planning, personnel, acquisition, and logistics. It did not rate the MOD or General Staff as capable of autonomous operations in any assessed capability. The MOD was judged capable of executing functions with coalition oversight only in two capability areas and the General Staff in four capability areas. All other capabilities required varying levels of coalition assistance, with intelligence policy and gender integration being rated as incapable of accomplishing their mission. projected that between mid-2013 and the end of 2014 the MOD and General Staff would be capable of executing functions with coalition oversight in all but four areas—transparency and accountability, gender integration, and two areas involving the Afghan Air Force where becoming capable of executing functions with coalition oversight only was projected to be achieved after 2014. Assessed thirty capability areas within the MOI, including: strategy and policy, the uniform and border police, personnel management, logistics, and acquisition and procurement. As with the MOD assessments, did not rate the MOI as capable of autonomous operations in any assessed capability. The MOI was judged capable of executing functions with coalition oversight only in two capability areas and required varying levels of coalition assistance in most other areas, except for two where it was rated as incapable of accomplishing its mission - gender and human rights and the Afghan Public Protection Force. projected that the MOI would become capable of executing functions with coalition oversight between mid-2013 and the end of 2014 in all but one area: democratic policing, which was given an indefinite date of completion (2012: 47,49,51). Failure to project when the MOD and MOI will be capable of autonomous operations is particularly troubling. This is because after 2014 it is unclear as to whether any advisors will remain, although expects there will be a need for continued coalition oversight. The Commanding General of U.S. and coalition forces in Afghanistan said in January 2013 that his top priority for beyond 2014 is to deploy a significant number of advisors in the MOD and MOI as part of a post-2014 U.S. presence (Skiff 2013). Even if a post-2014 presence is approved, advisor positions must be filled. reported that as of September 1, 2012, 51 of 185 advisor positions for the MOD were vacant but in the process of being staffed by the U.S. military, Ministry of Defense Advisors Program, or contractors (2012: 47). This author has observed the staffing process firsthand and seen that it can be difficult and time-consuming because it depends on voluntary cooperation. Provided no comparable data for the MOI Assessments of non-security ministries are more limited but also show progress has lagged Information on non-security ministries largely consists of generalized descriptions, with only limited individual ministry assessments. The is the source of most of the general assessments. The lack of periodic detailed assessments by any agency, akin top's assessments of the MOD and MOI, make tracking overall governance progress difficult. Beyond, the U.S. Government Accountability Office (GAO) and the U.S. Agency for International Development (USAID) are the primary sources of non-security ministry assessments. The most recent reporting this author could find from these institutions was a June 2012 USAID report on the results of a project it commissioned on budgetary units. The project conducted risk assessments of all assigned budgetary units in non-security Afghan ministries, as well as other offices which are currently receiving program budgeting reform technical assistance, such as the President's Office and Supreme Court. The aim of the assessment was to determine their current capacity in program budgeting implementation (USAID 2012: 6 - 8).3 The assessment evaluated twelve variables related to management, organizational structure, and technical capacity of the budgetary units. Based on the ratings, budgetary units were classified as "strong", "above average", "average" and "weak". Following is a summary of the assessment results. As can be seen from the summary, of the thirty-eight budgetary units assessed, more than half were assessed as requiring at least two more years of support before they are capable of operating autonomously. Six ministries (16% of the total) were rated "strong" in their capacity to implement program budgeting reform and can be considered for graduation from project based support in 2012. Twelve budgetary units (32% of the total) were rated "above average," and will require at least one more year of project support, particularly in the new reform areas such as procurement and financial planning, and performance monitoring reporting. Fifteen budgetary units (39% of the total) were rated "average" in their capacity to implement program budgeting reform and will require at least two more years of support to be able to implement the reform without external assistance. The remaining five budgetary units (13% of the total) were rated "weak", and will require major internal reforms and continued project support for at least two years before they are able to implement program budgeting reform without external assistance. In July 2010, GAO reported on Afghan ministerial capacity (GAO 2010: 28–29).4 Based on a review of USAID data, GAO stated that USAID has increasingly included and emphasized capacity building among its programs to address the government of Afghanistan's lack of capacity to sustain and maintain many of the programs and projects put in place by donors. In 2009, on a scale of 5, with 1 representing the need for substantial assistance across all areas and 5 representing the ability to perform without assistance, USAID rated the capability of 14 of 19 Afghan ministries and institutions it works with as either 1 or 2. For example, the Ministry of Agriculture, Irrigation, and Livestock was given a rating of 2—needing technical assistance to perform all but routine functions—while the Ministry for Rural Rehabilitation and Development was given a rating of 4—needing little technical assistance.5 Although USAID noted the overall improvement among the ministries and institutions in recent years, none were rated as being able to perform without external assistance. As discussed above, the June 2012 USAID-sponsored assessment of budgetary units in thirty-eight non-security Afghan ministries and other offices showed that three years later most were still judged as not being able to operate autonomously. Other reporting on governance is more general but equally troubling. In a December 2012 assessment of national governance, stated that the Afghan government continued to develop its capacity to provide stable, effective, and responsive governance to the Afghan population (2012: 103,106). However, the long-term sustainability of the Afghan government is challenged by corruption, ineffective program monitoring, sub-national government budget funding shortfalls, an inability to generate revenues sufficient to cover the cost of government operations, and limited public financial management capacity. Furthermore, poor linkages between the national and sub-national levels of governance and an imbalance in the distribution of power between the three branches of government, with power concentrated in the executive branch, continue to limit effectiveness and legitimacy. Limited human capacity and a lack of appropriate formal training and education within the civil service and Afghan populace also impede the development of stable and sustainable government across Afghanistan. Although reported that the Afghan government continued to develop its capacity to provide stable, effective, and responsive governance to the Afghan population in a somewhat contradictory statement in the same report, stated that during the period April 1, 2012 to September 30, 2012, the executive, legislative, and judicial branches of the Afghan government demonstrated mixed progress in meeting their respective responsibilities and making gains toward long-term sustainability (2012: 103). Also provided a gloomy assessment of sub-national governance it reported that sub-national governance structures operated to varying degrees of effectiveness at provincial, district, and village levels. did not provide its methodology or data sources so its reporting appears to be anecdotal. The Afghan government has also reported on governance constraints beyond U.S. government evaluations. In a July 2012 report for the Tokyo Conference, the Afghan government said that capacity constraints still remain a big bottleneck to budget execution, hindering public sector program implementation and public service delivery (Government of the Islamic Republic of Afghanistan 2012: 15). The government's Public Financial Management Program in the Governance Cluster aims to improve the public financial management system, as well as increase budget execution, efficiency, and transparency in the management of public finances. Key challenges in this area include capacity constraints at the national and especially sub-national levels; weak planning and budget formulation; donor earmarking of funds and funding delays; and challenges in communication and coordination across ministries, among donors and between national and sub-national entities. The Afghan government said it is committed to improving provincial-level planning, budgeting and implementation; developing the capacity of line ministries in finance, procurement, and project management; developing a Medium-Term Budget Framework with hard budget ceilings; and effectively reprioritizing spending according to national priorities. Whether the Afghan government succeeds in improving fiscal governance remains to be seen. SIGAR and GAO Reporting Highlight Shortfalls in Tracking Governance Progress In an October 2011 report, SIGAR discussed the shortfalls in measuring progress in improving governance (SIGAR 2011a: 9). SIGAR reported that the U.S. Embassy in Afghanistan had not been able to determine how much progress had been made to date in building ministry capacity at the Ministry of Agriculture, Irrigation, and Livestock because it did not have sufficient or complete data. Capacity-building activities and the performance data collected were not consistent, making it difficult for the U.S. Embassy to incorporate them into its assessment. Moreover, there were no performance baselines and targets for any performance indicators. The indicators being used largely measured the outputs of capacity-building efforts, rather than the results achieved. Without a mechanism that can sufficiently and reliably assess and report on progress made in building the Ministry's capacity, SIGAR concluded that the U.S. Embassy cannot determine whether the strategy is working and if resources are properly aligned. Without being able to assess progress, these agencies cannot identify what changes are needed to improve both the effectiveness of their programs and to ensure sustainable results. In a September 2011 report, GAO said that the overall results of U.S. efforts to improve Afghanistan's public financial management capacity cannot be fully determined because of the following: 1 U.S. agencies providing capacity assistance to the Afghan government have reported mixed results of their efforts, and 2 weaknesses in USAID's performance management plans and frameworks, such as lack of performance targets and data, prevent reliable assessments of USAID's results. USAID's evaluations of its two primary public financial management projects indicated that some activities were successfully completed, while others were terminated because their usefulness was questionable. U.S. Treasury Department advisers assessed that even though their assistance at the Afghan Ministry of Finance had a positive effect, the results fell short of what they were trying to accomplish (GAO 2011: 13). Donors Seek to Link Continued Financial Assistance to Improved Governance On July 8, 2012, representatives from seventy countries, international organizations, and non-profit groups met in Tokyo to create a framework for continued international support for Afghanistan's economic development. The support was intended to cover the transition at the end of 2014 through the "transformation decade" (2015–2024). At the conference, the international community pledged to provide an estimated $16 billion in aid from 2012 through 2015, but with conditions. In return for the assistance, the Afghan government promised to implement political and economic reforms to improve governance. This included making public institutions more accountable and tackling pervasive corruption. The conference declaration stated that the participants recognized that good governance at national and sub-national levels is essential for strong and sustainable economic development and improved livelihoods of the Afghan people. An annex to the declaration entitled the Tokyo Mutual Accountability Framework sets out mutual commitments, together with corresponding indicators, and a monitoring mechanism. The framework committed the Afghan government and the International Community to monitor performance in five major areas of development and governance as follows (Japan Ministry of Foreign Affairs 2012). Conduct credible, inclusive and transparent Presidential and Parliamentary elections in 2014 and 2015. Improve access to justice for all, particularly for women. Improve integrity of public financial management and the commercial banking sector. Improve the Afghan government's revenue collection and the capacity of line Ministries' to develop and execute budgets accountable to, and incorporating, local needs and preferences. Achieve inclusive and sustained growth through a focus on human development, food security, private investment, and decent work and employment opportunities and the improvement of Afghanistan's ranking in the human development index. As part of the regular monitoring process, progress is to be reviewed on a regular basis by existing entities, the Standing Committees and Joint Coordination and Monitoring Board. This is to be supplemented by a Senior Officials Meeting to be held in 2013, and thereafter every second year, to review progress and update indicators where needed; and a Ministerial-level Meeting to be held in 2014, and thereafter every second year, to review progress, update indicators, assess resource requirements and renew international commitments. In part to demonstrate that Afghanistan would uphold those commitments, Afghan President Karzai issued an administrative reform decree on July 26, 2012 that requires virtually every ministry and government body to develop a work plan, complete unfinished tasks, file specified reports, and/or carry out specified reforms. The Afghan government has made commitments before that have not come to fruition, so it remains to be seen whether these latest commitments are met. In fact, reports that the decree has been met with skepticism because demands and timelines were not combined with a comprehensive financial implementation plan or enforcement mechanisms. Lack of a Commonly Accepted Definition of Governance Complicates Assessing Progress Clausewitz wrote in On War that "The first, the supreme, the most far-reaching act of judgment that the statesman and commander have to make is to establish … the kind of war on which they are embarking." That same principle can be applied to governance. The U.S. Department of Defense, World Bank, various United Nations (UN) Agencies or Departments, Organization for Economic Co-operation and Development (OECD), and Institute on Governance have varying definitions of governance.6 In March 2006, the UN Economic and Social Council Committee of Experts on Public Administration addressed basic terminology in governance and public administration. The Committee recognized that there are some fundamental concepts and terminologies of governance and public administration that need to be defined in order for there to be a common understanding of them throughout the United Nations system. It acknowledged that these concepts and terminologies often are not applied in a uniform way. In its 2006 report, the Committee wrote that the use of the terms "governance" and "public administration" gained unprecedented momentum in both their quest and usage in the nineteenth and twentieth centuries. However, the Committee said that as the twenty-first century gets under way, there does not seem to be a consensus as to what they mean. In a highly dynamic environment politically, socially, economically, and culturally, these terms mean different things in different contexts (ECOSOC 2006: 1–2). Six years later a common definition of governance remained elusive. In a January 2012 article entitled what Does Good Governance Mean published in the UN University World Institute for Development Economics Research newsletter, the author noted that "Good governance" is a term that has become a part of the vernacular of a large range of development institutions and other actors within the international arena. What it means exactly, however, has not been so well established." The author noted that in general, work by the World Bank and other multilateral development banks on good governance addresses economic institutions and public sector management, including transparency and accountability, regulatory reform, and public sector skills and leadership. Other organizations, like the United Nations, European Commission and OECD are more likely to highlight democratic governance and human rights aspects of political governance, which are issues largely beyond the Bank's mandate (UNU 2012: 1). A common definition across governments, multilateral organizations, and non-governmental organizations was still lacking as recently as January 2013. SIGAR, which has provided the most extensive reporting on governance in Afghanistan, based on input from a variety of U.S. government agencies including and USAID, has not defined what it means by the term governance. Each of the nine quarterly reports which SIGAR has issued between January 2011 and January 2013 have a section on governance, yet none of the reports define what SIGAR means by governance. Rather all nine reports cover a potpourri of topics. For example, the governance section in SIGAR's most recent quarterly report, issued in January 2013, has five major sections: reconciliation and reintegration; national and sub-national governance; judicial reform and rule-of-law; anti-corruption; and human rights (SIGAR 2013: 95–121). In contrast, the October 2012 Civil-Military Strategic Framework for Afghanistan jointly issued by the U.S. Ambassador to Afghanistan and the Commanding General, U.S. Forces-Afghanistan separates governance from other activities. The plan addresses governance separately from both rule of law as well as reconciliation and reintegration (GAO 2013: 40). In seeking to address so many facets of governance, the donor and oversight communities have lost sight of its core function—providing the services the Afghan government has committed to provide to its citizens. As discussed above, much of the reporting on governance is general in nature. Consequently, after years of governance capacity building efforts, there is little analysis of why progress has been slow and what can be done to improve governance. Conclusions and Observations for Future Governance Building Efforts Prospects for Afghan autonomous governance are not bright. Progress in governance capability in the MOD and MOI, the focus of extensive mentoring and reporting by, has been slower than predicted. Has stopped projecting when the MOD and MOI will be capable of autonomous operations Instead it only predicts when the two ministries will be capable of executing functions with coalition oversight only. While would like to keep a significant number of advisors in the MOD and MOI as part of a post-2014 U.S. presence there is no assurance it will be able to do so given the uncertainties surrounding a continued presence in Afghanistan. Even today cannot fill all its advisor positions. Thought needs to be given to what would happen if the MOD and MOI were required to operate without coalition assistance after 2014 and whether adjustments in their capacity development are necessary. It may be too late to wait until 2014 to address how to handle undesirable outcomes. Reporting on non-security ministry capability is sparse and in critical need of attention. Available reporting shows that much remains to be done. The lack of regular assessments of governance capacity outside the MOD and MOI is a collective failure on the part of both the USAID, which administers the bulk of governance support to non-security ministries and other offices, and the U.S. government audit community in Afghanistan. There is a critical need for such assessments. Without them it is impossible to know which governance building programs are succeeding and which are not, and why. One is left to speculate on why success has been elusive. There are a number of possibilities, including that the donor community is trying to impose a western model of governance on an Afghan culture that has different values; training deficiencies involving the curriculum, trainers, or a combination of the two; and a high trainee turnover so that the people trained move on to other endeavors, resulting in the US agencies constantly having to train new people and never catching up. It is critical that more attention be focused on the outcome of governance efforts and on courses of action that address the root causes which prevent success. Improving governance is a shared responsibility of the donor community and the Afghan government. In July 2012 the donor community sought to link future financial aid to improved governance. This was followed by an Afghan government administrative reform decree requiring virtually every ministry and government body to take steps to improve governance. However, given the Afghan government's failure to honor past commitments unless donors demonstrate the seriousness of their concerns by reducing financial aid if commitments are not kept, the status quo will likely remain unchanged. The Afghan experience provides some important lessons that should guide future endeavors. While the experience in Iraq has reduced the appetite for expansive nation-building initiatives, events in countries such as Mali and Syria may result in future endeavors. The following actions should be taken in concert by the host government, participating multilateral organizations, and individual donor nations in future endeavors. First, agree on a definition of governance accepted by the host government and all donors. Second, irrespective of the definition of governance, develop outcome based measurable metrics. Third, at least on an annual basis, conduct assessments of each ministry and major institution receiving governance assistance. This assessment should assess progress against the metrics, identifying root causes if there is a lack of progress, and adjusting governance efforts as necessary based on the assessments. Fourth, condition future aid on demonstrable progress in improving governance The cold war For months they had eaten, slept and breathed it; had devoted their every waking hour to discussing it, refining their techniques, honing their skills and, above all, mentally preparing themselves for the hour that, as sure as night followed day, had to come. Yet now that it had arrived the whole thing seemed surreal. The captain double-checked his encoded orders. There were zero error margins, for the world had perched on the edge of an abyss ever since 1949. But this time, there was no false intelligence, no defective communications. This time it was for real. As the B-47 'Started' of Strategic Air Command flew east from its home at Edwards Air force Bas its crew lapsed into a deep, reflective silence. Most of them were thinking of their wives and families, trying to etch into their consciousness all the small, insignificant details of those last hours they had spent together, laughing, carefree, careless of the Armageddon that hung over them like a dark mushroom cloud. Would they ever again enjoy such moments? Probably not, but it was best not to let one's thoughts lapse into melancholy. They had a duty to perform, a job to do. Beneath them, in the B-47's bomb bay, was tucked a Mark 43 atom bomb, twenty times more powerful than the one that had devastated Hiroshima, vaporizing 100,000 human beings. What would their bomb do to Moscow? How many innocent Russians would never see another day dawn, all on account of the plutonium-packed cylinder, which would soon drop from the sky? No matter – their own politicians had started it. America had always said it would never instigate hostilities, it would only respond to an act of nuclear aggression. But when it did respond – watch out! To ensure the maximum retaliatory hammer-blow, Strategic Air Command kept at least a hundred fully tooled-up B-47's in the air at any one time. The B-47 had an optimum range of 4,000 miles, too short to get it to Moscow even at the best of times, and now that things were terminally serious the bomber's range could expect to fall by at least 20 per cent. Which United Kingdom airfield were they due to land at for refueling? The captain consulted his flight map. His plane was booked to touch down at a reserve runway on the very northern fringe of the Scottish mainland, a place none of them had heard of, never seen, and never expected to revisit for, as the place was certain to be a target for the Soviet's nuclear warplanes, there would be nothing left to return to. And the name of this remote airfield Doorway we know, of course that the above is nothing but a fiction. Nevertheless, in the early 1950's it was a high possibility, planned for and anticipated with deadly seriousness, product of a time when ballistic technology had temporary outstripped weapon delivery systems, when land-based facilities still played a leading part in war planning. Prior to the 1960 dawn of the Polaris Age, the vast distances between the major US cities and their Soviet counterparts drove aircraft designers of both superpowers into a frenzied, money-no-barrier drive to build bombers with ever longer operational ranges. The breakthrough came in 1955 with the coming into service of the 10,000-mile range American B-52 'Star to fortresses, undoubtedly one of the greatest of all warplanes. The Russians, relying on second-hand or stolen-by-espionage technology, unveiled their Tu-95 'Bear' a year later. This beast could fly 7,800 miles without refueling. The British, poor relations of their American allies struggled along the same path, their aim an 'independent nuclear deterrent'. This grandiose scheme, which was in certain respects nothing but the final blustering of an expiring one-time global power, has kept our country's place at the top table of world powerbrokers. Despite all the understandable moral arguments against it, without our nuclear capabilities we would be as influential today in world affairs as Denmark or Switzerland, which is perhaps not saying very much. Being much closer to their assumed future enemy, British bombers would require an operating range of 2,500 miles to fly to Moscow and back. This figure, however, is a little simplistic. No-one going to bomb Moscow could realistically expect to do so without having to fly at maximum speed for most of the journey. Such speeds would gobble up fuel at an alarming rate. To counter this, the RAF commissioned the building of the famous 'V-Bomber' Force, the 'Valiant', 'Vulcan' and 'Victor' models which came into service between 1955 and 1958, and all of which had the capability of reaching Moscow on one fuel charge. The possibility of their returning from such a devastating mission was a thing best confined to the imagination. Prior to 1955, it can be seen that neither of the Western powers had a bomber with a 'Russia and return' range. En route refueling bases were essential. Britain was the ideal stepping stone on the American flight-path to Russia. The late world war had left England and Scotland studded with military airfields, some of them little more than flat fields with a few shack-like hangars; others tarmac and concrete strips surrounded by purpose-built storage and maintenance facilities. But, no matter how sophisticated an airfield's support hardware, to be of use in the nuclear age it had to possess one vital attribute – a concrete runway, at least one-mile in length. When the British strategic war planners mapped out the forward development track for their country's nuclear deterrent away back in 1947, they were still 5 years away from actually exploding an atomic bomb. No matter, the Chiefs of Staff ordered the design and build of a long range bomber force, and gave instructions for the maintenance of those wartime airfields with runways long enough for the new warplanes to take off and land on. In Scotland the primary V-Bomber bases were Prestwick, Kinless, Macrahanish, Leuchars and Lossiemouth. Given the possibility that a Soviet pre-emptive strike might disable the main bases, a number of secondary airfields capable of handling V-Bombers had to be identified. North of Inverness, there was only one such airfield, HMS 'Tern II', which had been taken over by the Admiralty from Coastal Command in July 1944, and was being run by them on a shoestring care-and-maintenance budget. Where was this 'HMS Tern II'? It was located in Cattiness, nine miles east of Thurston at a place called Doorway. Given that 'HMS Tern II' had played no part whatsoever in the Second World War, it is puzzling at first to imagine just what persuaded the Admiralty to maintain an incomplete airfield for the eight years between 1945 and the coming of the United Kingdom Atomic Energy Authority. One likely theory is that, initially at least, the Navy saw Dounreay's potential as a base for Shackleton and Lincoln bombers, booked for use as submarine and warship hunters in the northern seas between Scandinavia and Greenland. As this outdated war thinking passed out of fashion with the 1949 Soviet acquisition of atomic bombs, it is possible that Dounreay became a focus both for America's Strategic Air Command need for one-stop British bases for refueling its B-47 bomber fleet, and of the RAF's projected network of V-Bomber stations. Whatever the reason, we may be sure that when Sir Christopher Hinton first set eyes on the dream site for his fast breeder reactor project in May 1953, his enthusiasm would have been tempered by his knowledge that Dounreay figured in the Air Ministry's nuclear deterrent plans. After all, hadn't Sir Christopher himself, as engineering kingpin of the Windscale nuclear site, played a not insignificant role in providing the plutonium that went into Britain's atomic bombs? In the first of these two articles we saw how the MP for Caithness and Sutherland had spent the final weeks of 1953 fretting over the diminishing political credibility he had with his electorate. Sir David Robertson wrote to Duncan Sandys, Minister of Supply, on an almost daily basis, reminding the Minister that an announcement confirming the selection of Dounreay as chosen site for the pioneering fast breeder reactor project, was long overdue. Everybody knew that the thing was going to be built at Dounreay, so why on earth not give the official say-so? The answer was simple – Duncan Sandys could not confirm what he knew to be still in doubt. To be frank, Sir David Robertson, although he had access to more than a few influential ears, was not numbered amongst the elite politicians who knew anything definite about Britain's top-secret plans for a retaliatory nuclear war. Outside of the Prime Minister and the military top brass, next to no-one, not even cabinet ministers, was kept fully informed about how many atomic bombs were being assembled at Aldermaston, or on which Russian cities those bombs were to be targeted. Some may maintain that in a democracy, nothing should be withheld from the people's representatives. This is naïve idealism. Members of Parliament are elected to represent their constituents; they do not run the country. Indeed, whether or not we care to admit it, the very mechanism of democracy leaves it open to exploitation by those who are able, by whatever means, to influence the results of elections. It was, of course, necessary for scientists engaged in the atomic weapons programmed to be privy to some of Britain's nuclear secrets, and we now know that, to their everlasting shame, certain of these technocrats betrayed atomic secrets, either for money or through misplaced political sympathies. No doubt others connected with Britain's atomic bomb project went to their graves as undetected traitors, the kind of treacherous nonentities writers of spy fiction thrive on. David Robertson's patriotism was probably beyond question, but for Duncan Sandy's to tell the Member for Cattiness and Sutherland everything he himself knew about the negotiations over Doorway's future would have been contrary to accepted Government practice. Sandy's merely told Sir David that the Air Ministry was placing minor obstacles in the path of the Doorway fast reactor project. That was all the MP needed to know. Weren't there enough and more redundant military airfields in Caithness under Air Ministry control? Must they seek to thwart plans of great national importance just because they had for so long had their own way? The Minister of Supply wholeheartedly agreed, with his good friend, Sir David, but...Throughout the latter half of 1953 a series of high-level meetings were held at Whitehall, designed to persuade both the Air Ministry and the Admiralty that Dounreay's future would be best served by surrendering the airfield to the Ministry of Supply's Atomic Energy organization. Sir Christopher Hinton had been adamant – Doorway was where he wanted his experimental fast breeder reactor built, and no-one thought himself qualified enough to argue with such a formidable personality. Had not Hinton masterminded the conversion of Riley, Springfield's and Wind scale from outdated military facilities into dynamic centers of nuclear excellence? Perhaps even more persuasively, alarmed by the production-crippling coal famine of 1951, had not the Government given the then powerful Confederation of British Industry an undertaking to pursue with all vigor the development of cheap and self-sufficient nuclear power, of which the fast breeder reactor seemed the best way forward? Against this the military chiefs offset the paramount importance of retaining the Doorway runway for use both by our American allies, and our soon to be on-stream V-Bomber force. At length, a compromise appears to have been reached. In a letter dated 10th December 1953 the Minister of Supply gave five undertakings to the Secretary of State for Air: The Ministry would be consulted about the sitting of the atomic energy buildings, including any future extensions. The main Doorway runway and its approaches would remain unobstructed, and full consultation must take place prior to sanctioning the construction of any buildings which might interfere with planes landing or taking off. Those certain existing military buildings would be left intact for use in a future war. That in the event of a war, the runway and associated buildings would be immediately available for operational use, irrespective of whatever construction stage the atomic energy plant was at. That the Atomic Energy Organization would at no future time erect buildings or take any action which would interfere with the wartime availability of the main runway, without the agreement of both the Air Ministry and the Admiralty. These were stiff and potentially restrictive conditions. It could have been worse; the Air Ministry's original insistence that all atomic energy operations at Doorway must be shut down in the event of war was dropped. The rest of the conditions were accepted, as was the Atomic Energy Organization's obligation to maintain both runway and military buildings in good repair. At last, pending the approval of, presumably, the Prime Minister himself, the Doorway fast reactor project was to receive the green light. By 1955 everything had changed. The UKAEA became feud holders of the Doorway site. A combination of circumstances had much reduced Doorway's potential importance as a military facility. With the arrival of the B-52 'Stratofortress', the Americans no longer needed refueling stops in this country. In any case, the USAF was busily acquiring its own bases all over Britain. And within a few years, submarines armed with nuclear-tipped missiles would become the spearhead of America's military muscle. There remained the question of a Far North base for the RAF's V-Bombers. In 1954, a contract was awarded to Fare's for the westward extension of the 4,000 feet tarmac main runway at Wick airport. When the work was completed in 1955, Wick's chief runway stretched another 2,000 feet towards Aspergilla. The airport was now available for use by V-Bombers, but the thought of a 'Vulcan' fully loaded with atomic bombs, landing there on a fog-bound afternoon, is not one that sits easy in a reflective mind. Doorway remained one of 52 prime Soviet nuclear targets until at least 1990. To be honest, even if it had not been so, in the event of a nuclear war, few of us in Cattiness would have survived. In 1980, a Russian military planner concluded that, an all-out nuclear war would result in the detonation of 14,747 nuclear devices on 1,300 Northern Hemisphere locations. Killed instantly would be 750 million people. A further 340 million wounded would have died a week later. All rainwater would become contaminated, poisoning crops and killing livestock. Famine would stalk the world, the socio-economic system would collapse, driving at least of third of all survivors mad. Within a year of the war's outbreak, 2 billion human beings would be dead, and the situation would only get worse. These statistics define the term 'nuclear deterrent'.

In the history of Afghanistan, the internal conflict between anti-Communist

Muslim guerrillas and the Afghan communist government (aided from 1979 to 1989 by Soviet troops). The roots of the war lay in the overthrow of the centrist Afghanistan government in April 1978 by left-wing military officers, who then handed power over to two Marxist-Leninist political parties, the Khalq ("Masses") and Parham ("Flag"), who together had formed the People's Democratic Party of Afghanistan. Having little popular support, the new government forged close ties with the Soviet Union, launched ruthless purges of all domestic opposition, and began extensive land and social reforms that were bitterly resented by the devoutly Muslim and largely anti-Communist population. Muslim tribal-based insurgencies arose against the government, and these uprisings, along with internal fighting and coups between the Khalq and Parcham governmental factions prompted the invasion of the country by about 30,000 Soviet troops in December 1979 with the aim of propping up the Soviet Union's new but faltering client state. The rebellion of the Muslim rebels, or mujahedeen (literally, "strugglers"), grew in response, spreading to all parts of the country. The Soviets initially left the suppression of the rebellion to the Afghan army, but the latter was rapidly depleted by mass desertions and remained largely ineffective throughout the war. The Afghan War quickly settled down into a stalemate, with about 100,000 Soviet troops controlling the cities, large towns, and major garrisons and the mujahedeen roaming relatively freely throughout the countryside. The Soviet troops tried to crush the insurgency by various tactics, but the guerrillas generally eluded their attacks. The Soviets then attempted to eliminate the mujahedeen's civilian support by bombing and depopulating the rural areas. Their tactics sparked a massive flight from the countryside; by 1982 some 2.8 million Afghans had sought asylum in Pakistan, and another 1.5 million had fled to Iran. The mujahedeen were eventually able to neutralize Soviet air power through the use of shoulder-fired antiaircraft missiles supplied by the United States. The mujahedeen were fragmented politically into a handful of different groups, and their military efforts remained uncoordinated throughout the war. The quality of their arms and combat organization gradually improved, however, owing to experience and to arms shipments sent by the United States and other countries via Pakistan. In 1988 the United States, Pakistan, Afghanistan, and the Soviet Union signed an agreement for the withdrawal of Soviet troops and the return of Afghanistan to nonaligned status.

In April 1992, various rebel groups, together with newly rebellious government troops, stormed the besieged capital of Kabul, and the communist president, Mohammad Najibullah, was ousted from power. A new transitional government, sponsored by various rebel factions, proclaimed an Islamic republic. Nur Mohammad Taraki was elected president of the Revolutionary Council, prime minister of the country, and secretary general of the combined People's Democratic Party of Afghanistan (PDPA) Babrak Karmal, a Banner leader, and Hafizullah Amin were elected deputy prime ministers. The leaders of the new government insisted that they were not controlled by the Soviet Union and proclaimed their policies to be based on Afghan nationalism, Islamic principles, socioeconomic justice, nonalignment in foreign affairs, and respect for all agreements and treaties signed by previous Afghan governments. Unity between the Khalq (People) and Parcham (Banner) factions rapidly faded as the People's Party emerged dominant, particularly because their major base of power was in the military. Karmal and other selected Banner leaders were sent abroad as ambassadors, and there were systematic purges of any Banner members or others who might oppose the regime. The Taraki regime announced its reform programs, including the elimination of usury, equal rights for women, land reforms, and administrative decrees in classic Marxist-Leninist rhetoric. The reform program—which threatened to undermine basic Afghan cultural patterns—and political repression antagonized large segments of the population, but major violent responses did not occur until the uprising in Nurestan late in the summer of 1978. Other revolts, largely uncoordinated, spread throughout all of Afghanistan's provinces, and periodic explosions rocked Kabul and other major cities. On Feb. 14, 1979, U.S. Ambassador Adolph Dubs was killed, and the elimination of U.S. assistance to Afghanistan was guaranteed. Hafizullah Amin became prime minister on March 28, 1979, although Taraki retained his posts as president of the Revolutionary Council and secretary general of the PDPA. The expanding revolts in the countryside, however, continued, and the Afghan Army collapsed. The Amin regime asked for and received more Soviet military aid. Taraki was killed in a confrontation between Taraki and Amin supporters on Sept. 14, 1979. Amin then tried to broaden his internal base of support and to again interest Pakistan and the United States in Afghan security. Despite his efforts, on the night of Dec. 24, 1979, the Soviets began their invasion of Afghanistan, and Amin and many of his followers were killed on December 27. Babrak Karmal returned to Afghanistan from the Soviet Union and became prime minister, president of the Revolutionary Council, and secretary general of the PDPA Opposition to the Soviets and Karmal spread rapidly, urban demonstrations and violence increased, and resistance escalated in all regions. By early 1980, several regional groups, collectively known as mujahedeen (from the Arabic word meaning "warriors"), had united inside Afghanistan, or across the border in Peshawar, to resist the Soviet invaders and the Soviet-backed Afghan Army. Friction among the Banner and People's members heightened in 1980 when Karmal removed Assadullah Sarwari, a member of the People's Party, from his position as first deputy prime minister and replaced him with a Banner leader, Sultan Ali Keshtmand. Banner Party dominance was broadened again in June 1981 when Karmal, retaining his other offices, resigned as prime minister and was succeeded by Keshtmand.

On May 4, 1986, Mohammad Najibullah, former head of the secret police, replaced Karmal as secretary general of the PDPA, and in November 1986 Karmal was relieved of all his government and party posts. Friction among the Banner and People's parties continued. A national reconciliation campaign approved by the Politburo in September 1986, which included a unilateral six-month cease-fire to begin on Jan. 15, 1987, met with little response inside Afghanistan and was rejected by resistance leaders in Pakistan. In November 1987 a new constitution changed the name of the country back to the Republic of Afghanistan and allowed other political parties to participate in the government. Najibullah was elected to the newly strengthened post of president. Despite renewals of the official cease-fire, Afghan resistance to the Soviet presence continued, and the effects of the war were felt in neighboring countries: Afghan refugees in Pakistan and Iran numbered in the millions. Morale in the Afghan military was low. Men were drafted only to desert at the earliest opportunity, and the Afghan military dropped from its 1978 strength of 105,000 to about 20,000-30,000 by 1987. The Soviets attempted new tactics, but the resistance always devised counter tactics. For example, the use of the Sestinas (Special Forces) was met by counter-ambushes. The only weapons systems that solidly continued to bedevil the resistance were combat helicopter gunship and jet bombers. Toward the end of 1986, however, the resistance fighters began to receive more and better weapons from the outside world—particularly from the United States, the United Kingdom, and China—via Pakistan, the most important of these being shoulder-fired ground-to-air missiles. The Soviet and Afghan air forces then began to suffer considerable casualties. Pressure from the Pakistanis, from outside supporters, and from the guerrilla commanders had forced the seven major resistance groups based in Peshawar to form an alliance in May 1985. Inside Afghanistan, neighboring ethno linguistically oriented resistance groups united for military and political purposes within their various regions. Internal struggles for leadership also occurred in certain areas where the Soviets had little influence, such as Hazarajat and Nurestan. Although no national liberation front existed, the resistance groups began to feel that they were part of an overall effort to liberate Afghanistan. During the 1980s talks between the foreign ministers of Afghanistan and Pakistan were held in Geneva under the auspices of the United Nations, the primary stumbling blocks being the timetable for the withdrawal of Soviet troops and the cessation of arms supplies to the mujahedeen. Peace accords were finally signed in April 1988. General Secretary Mikhail Gorbachev subsequently carried out an earlier promise to begin withdrawing Soviet troops in May of that year; troops began pulling out as scheduled, and the last Soviet soldier left Afghanistan on Feb. 15, 1989. The civil war continued, however, despite predictions of an early collapse of the Najibullah government upon the withdrawal of the Soviets. The mujahedeen formed an interim government in Pakistan and steadfastly resisted efforts of reconciliation by Najibullah. DR. Najibullah was finally ousted from power in 1992 and a coalition of rebel forces set up a fragile interim government. General peace and stability remained a distant hope for the war-torn nation, as rival militias vied for influence, interethnic tensions flared, and the economy lay in chaos. With the fall of the Communist government, Afghanistan appeared to be on a course of Hispanicization; the interim government banned the sale of alcohol and pressured women to cover their heads in public and adopt traditional Muslim dress. Karmal, Babrak Afghan politician (b. Jan. 6, 1929, near Kabul, Afg.—d Dec. 3, 1996, Moscow, Russia), was the U.S.S.R.-backed president of Afghanistan from 1979, when the Soviet Union invaded the country, until 1986, when the Soviet government decided that fighting there was no longer in Moscow's interest. Karmal became involved in Marxist political activities while a student at Kabul University and was imprisoned. Upon his release, he served in the army and returned to the University for a Law Degree. Karmal was a founding member of the People's Democratic Party of Afghanistan (PDPA) and from 1965 to 1973 served in the National Assembly. When the party split (1967) into the Khalq ("People's") and the Parcham ("Banner") parties, he became leader of the more moderate, pro-Soviet Parcham. The Khalq and the Parcham reunited in 1977, and in 1978—with Soviet help—the PDPA seized the government. Karmal became deputy prime minister, but rivalries within the government soon resulted in his being sent as ambassador to Prague. The PDPA was attempting to modernize the country drastically along Marxist lines, but there were major rebellions in the countryside, and in December 1979, Soviet troops invaded Afghanistan and called Karmal back to be president. The rebels persisted with aid from the West, and the area became a Cold War battleground. Moscow came to consider Karmal a burden and publicly blamed him for the country's problems, and in November 1986 he resigned from office, claiming poor health. Shortly thereafter Karmal moved to Moscow, where he spent most of his remaining years. DR. M Najibullah, Afghan politician (b. 1947, Gardez, Paktia province, Afg.—d Sept. 27, 1996, Kabul, Afg.), was the president of Afghanistan from 1986 till 1992, installed by the Soviet Union in 1986. He managed to hang on to power for nearly three years after Soviet troops pulled out in 1989 but was ousted in 1992 and afterward lived in refuge in a UN compound. Najibullah began studying medicine at Kabul University in 1964 and received his medical degree in 1975, but he never practiced medicine. He had joined the Parcham ("Banner") faction of the communist People's Democratic Party of Afghanistan (PDPA) in 1965, and he was twice imprisoned for political activities. The PDPA staged a successful coup in 1978, but the Khalq ("People's") faction soon gained supremacy, and Najibullah briefly served as ambassador to Iran and then went into exile in Eastern Europe until the U.S.S.R. intervened (1979) and supported a Parcham-dominated government. Najibullah was made head of the secret police and became known for his brutality and ruthlessness. His methods proved invaluable to the regime in view of escalating

Islamic guerrilla warfare, but as the war grew in intensity, the Soviet Union withdrew. As president, Najibullah attempted to gain support by relaxing his strict control, but he was widely despised and was finally forced from office by the Islamic rebels. Factional fighting continued, and when the Taliban militia took over the capital, Kabul, they executed DR. Najibullah. TREATY BETWEEN THE UNITED STATES OF AMERICA AND THE UNION OF SOVIET SOCIALIST REPUBLICS ON THE LIMITATION OF STRATEGIC OFFENSIVE ARMS In accordance with Article VII of the Interim Agreement, in which the sides committed themselves to continue active negotiations on strategic offensive arms, the SALT II negotiations began in November 1972. The primary goal of SALT II was to replace the Interim Agreement with a long-term comprehensive Treaty providing broad limit on strategic offensive weapons systems. The principal U.S. objectives as the SALT II negotiations began were to provide for equal numbers of strategic nuclear delivery vehicles for the sides, to begin the process of reduction of these delivery vehicles, and to impose restraints on qualitative developments which could threaten future stability. Early discussion between the sides focused on the weapon systems to be included, factors involved in providing for equality in numbers of strategic nuclear delivery vehicles, taking into account the important differences between the forces of the two sides, bans on new systems, qualitative limits, and a Soviet proposal to include U.S. forward-based systems. The positions of the sides differed widely on many of these issues. A major breakthrough occurred at the Vladivostok meeting in November 1974, between President Ford and General Secretary Brezhnev. At this meeting, the sides agreed to a basic framework for the SALT II agreement. Basic elements of the Aide-Memoire, which recorded this agreement, included: 2,400 equal aggregate limit on strategic nuclear delivery vehicles (ICBMs, SLBMs, and heavy bombers) of the sides; — 1,320 equal aggregate limit on MIRV systems; — ban on construction of new land-based ICBM launchers; — limits on deployment of new types of strategic offensive arms; and— important elements of the Interim Agreement (e.g., relating to verification) would be incorporated in the new agreement. In addition, the Aide-Memoire stated that the duration of the new agreement would be through 1985. In early 1975, the delegations in Geneva resumed negotiations, working toward an agreement based on this general framework. It was during this time that a Joint Draft Text was first prepared and many limitations were agreed. During the negotiations, however, it became clear that there was fundamental disagreement between the two sides on two major issues: how cruise missiles were to be addressed, and whether the new Soviet bomber known to the United States as Backfire would be considered a heavy bomber and therefore counted in the 2,400 aggregate. While there was disagreement on other issues such as MIRV verification provisions, restrictions on new systems, and missile throw-weight ceilings, progress was made in these areas. However, the issues of cruise missiles and Backfire remained unresolved. When the new Administration took office in 1977, renewed emphasis was placed on the Strategic Arms Limitation Talks. A comprehensive interagency review of SALT was undertaken. Building on the work of the previous Administration, particularly the Vladivostok accord and the subsequent agreement on many issues in Geneva, the United States made a comprehensive proposal which was presented to the Soviets by Secretary of State Vance in March 1977. This proposal would have added significant reductions and qualitative constraints to the ceilings which were agreed to at Vladivostok. At the same time, the United States also presented an alternative proposal for a SALT II agreement similar to the framework agreed to at Vladivostok, with the Backfire and cruise missile issues deferred until SALT III. Both proposals were rejected by the Soviets as inconsistent with their understandings of the Vladivostok accord. In subsequent negotiations, the sides agreed on a general framework for SALT II which accommodated both the Soviet desire to retain the Vladivostok framework for an agreement, and the U.S. desire for more comprehensive limitations in SALT II. The agreement would consist of three parts: A Treaty which would be in force through 1985 based on the Vladivostok accord; A Protocol of about three-years duration which would cover certain issues such as cruise missile constraints, mobile ICBM limits, and qualitative constraints on ICBM, while deferring further negotiations on these issues to SALT III; — A Joint Statement of Principles which would be an agreed set of guidelines for future negotiations. Within this framework, negotiations to resolve the remaining differences continued on several levels. President Carter, Secretary Vance, and Soviet Foreign Minister Gromyko met in Washington in September 1977. Further high-level meetings were held in Washington, Moscow, and Geneva during 1978 and 1979. In addition, the SALT delegations of the United States and Soviet Union in Geneva were in session nearly continuously following the 1974 Vladivostok meeting to work out agreed Treaty language on those issues where agreement in principle had been reached at the ministerial level. The completed SALT II agreement was signed by President Carter and General Secretary Brezhnev in Vienna on June 18, 1979. President Carter transmitted it to the Senate on June 22 for its advice and consent to ratification. On January 3, 1980, however, President Carter requested the Senate majority leader to delay consideration of the Treaty on the Senate floor in view of the Soviet invasion of Afghanistan. Although the Treaty remained ungratified, each Party was individually bound under the terms of international law to refrain from acts which would defeat the object and purpose of the Treaty, until it had made its intentions clear not to become a party to the Treaty. In 1980, President Carter announced the United States would comply with the provisions of the Treaty as long as the Soviet Union reciprocated. Brezhnev made a similar statement regarding Soviet intentions. In May 1982, President Reagan stated he would do nothing to undercut the SALT agreements as long as the Soviet Union showed equal restraint. The Soviet Union again agreed to abide by the ungratified Treaty. Subsequently, in 1984 and 1985, President Reagan declared that the Soviet Union had violated its political commitment to observe the SALT II Treaty. President Reagan decided, however, that an interim framework of mutual restraint remained in the U.S. interest and, in June 1985, declared that the United States would continue to refrain from undercutting existing strategic arms agreements to the extent that the Soviet Union exercised comparable restraint and provided that the Soviet Union actively pursued arms reductions agreements in the Nuclear and Space Talks in Geneva. On May 26, 1986, President Reagan stated that he had reviewed again the status of U.S. interim restraint policy and that, as he had documented in three detailed reports to the Congress, the Soviet Union had not complied with its political commitment to observe the SALT agreements, including the SALT II Treaty, nor had the Soviet Union indicated its readiness to join in a framework of truly mutual restraint. He declared that, "Given this situation, in the future, the United States must base decisions regarding its strategic force structure on the nature and magnitude of the threat posed by Soviet strategic forces and not on standards contained in the SALT structure." In his statement, President Reagan said that he did not anticipate any appreciable numerical growth in U.S. strategic offensive forces and that, assuming no significant change in the threat, the United States would not deploy more strategic nuclear delivery vehicles or strategic ballistic missile warheads than the Soviets. The United States would, in sum, "...continue to exercise the utmost restraint, while protecting strategic deterrence, in order to help foster the necessary atmosphere for significant reductions in the strategic arsenals of both sides." He again called upon the Soviet Union to join the United States "... in establishing an interim framework of truly mutual restraint." The SALT II Treaty would have provided for: — an equal aggregate limit on the number of strategic nuclear delivery vehicles — ICBM and SLBM launchers, heavy bombers, and air-to-surface ballistic missiles (ASBMs). Initially, this ceiling would have been 2,400 as agreed at Vladivostok. The ceiling would have been lowered to 2,250 at the end of 1981; — an equal aggregate limit of 1,320 on the total number of launchers of MIRVed ballistic missiles and heavy bombers with long-range cruise missiles;— an equal aggregate limit of 1,200 on the total number of launchers of MIRVed ballistic missiles; and— an equal aggregate limit of 820 on launchers of MIRVed ICBMs. In addition to these numerical limits, the agreement would have included:— a ban on construction of additional fixed ICBM launchers, and on increases in the number of fixed heavy ICBM launchers;— a ban on heavy mobile ICBM launchers, and on launchers of heavy submarine-launched ballistic missiles (SLBMs) and air-to-surface ballistic missiles (ASBMs);— a ban on flight-testing or deployment of new types of ICBMs, with an exception of one new type of light ICBM for each side;— a ban on increasing the numbers of warheads on existing types of ICBMs, and a limit of 10 warheads on the one new type of ICBM permitted to each Party, a limit of 14 warheads on SLBMs, and 10 warheads on ASBMs. The number of long-range cruise missiles per heavy bomber would have been limited to an average of 28; and the number of long-range cruise missiles per heavy bomber of existing types would have been limited to 20;— ceilings on the launch-weight and throw-weight of strategic ballistic missiles and a ban on the conversion of light ICBM launchers to launchers of heavy ICBM a ban on the Soviet SS-16 ICBM;— a ban on rapid reload ICBM systems;— a ban on certain new types of strategic offensive systems which were technologically feasible, but which had not yet been deployed. Such systems included long-range ballistic missiles on surface ships, and ballistic and cruise missile launchers on the seabed's;— advance notification of certain ICBM test launches; and— an agreed data base for systems included in various SALT-limited categories. The Treaty also included detailed definitions of limited systems, provisions to enhance verification, a ban on circumvention of the provisions of the agreement, and a provision outlining the duties of the SCC in connection with the SALT II Treaty. The duration of the Treaty was to have been through 1985. Verification of the SALT II Treaty would have been by national technical means (NTM) of verification, including photo-reconnaissance satellites. The sides had agreed not to interfere with each others national technical means of verification, and not to use deliberate concealment measures which would have impeded verification by NTM of compliance with the provisions of the agreement. Because specific characteristics of some SALT-limited systems become apparent during the testing phase, monitoring of testing programs was an important aspect of SALT verification. Such monitoring might have involved collection of electronic signals known as telemetry which are used during tests to transmit information about systems while they are being tested. Therefore, the sides had agreed not to engage in deliberate denial of telemetric information such as through the use of telemetry encryption whenever such denial would have impeded verification of compliance with the provisions of the Treaty. In addition to these provisions of the Treaty which directly addressed the question of verification, counting and distinguish ability rules, as well as some constraints on specific systems, were incorporated into the agreement specifically for verification purposes. To facilitate verification of the MIRV limits, the sides agreed that once a missile had been tested with MIRVs, then all missiles of that type were to be considered to have been equipped with MIRVs, even if that missile type had also been tested with a non-MIRV payload. Additionally, the sides agreed that once a launcher contained or launched a MIRVed missile, then all launchers of that type would be considered to be launchers of MIRVed missiles and included in the 1,320 limit. Similar counting rules were adopted for cruise missiles and for heavy bombers. A constraint included for verification purposes was a ban on production, testing, and deployment of the Soviet SS-16 ICBM. The missile appeared to share a number of components with the Soviet SS-20, an intermediate range ballistic missile (IRBM). As the Parties had agreed that land-based launchers of ballistic missiles which are not ICBMs should not be converted into launchers of ICBMs, the United States sought this ban on the SS-16 in order to prevent verification problems which might have arisen if the SS-16 program had gone forward, since in that case distinguishing between SS-16 and SS-20 deployments would have been very difficult. Pursuant to a Memorandum of Understanding, the sides exchanged data on the numbers of weapons in SALT-limited categories, and agreed to maintain this agreed data base through regular updates at each session of the Standing Consultative Commission. Although the United States did not require (and did not rely upon) this data for verification purposes, maintenance of the agreed data base would have insured that both parties applied the provisions of the Treaty in a consistent manner. The protocol to the Treaty was to have remained in force until December 31, 1981. In the protocol the sides agreed to ban deployment of mobile ICBM launchers and flight-testing of ICBMs from such launchers. Development of such systems short of flight-testing would have been permitted. (After the protocol period, the Treaty specifically permitted the deployment of mobile ICBM launchers.) Additionally, the protocol banned deployment, but not testing, of cruise missiles capable of ranges in excess of 600 kilometers on ground- and sea-based launchers. (The protocol would not have limited deployment of such systems after its expiration in 1981 finally; the protocol included a ban on flight testing and deployment of ASBMs. The Joint Statement of Principles, the third element of the SALT II agreement, would have established a basic framework for the next stage of SALT negotiations, SALT III. The sides agreed on the following general goals to be achieved in the next round of talks:

— Significant and substantial reductions in the number of strategic offensive arms; further qualitative limitations on strategic offensive arms; and — resolution of the issues included in the protocol. The sides would also have considered other steps to enhance strategic stability, and either side could have brought up any other topic relevant to the limitation of strategic arms. The Joint Statement of Principles also established the principle that cooperative measures might be used to ensure adequate verification of a SALT III agreement, raising the possibility of thus going beyond reliance on national technical means of verification alone.

Despite America's evident desire to extricate itself from the nation's

longest war, Taliban fighters, criminal gangs, and other insurgents continue to terrorize much of Afghanistan, making travel around the country as difficult as it's ever been. And the grim bargain that has dogged U.S. efforts in Afghanistan since the beginning of President Obama's "surge" still holds: The United States must find a way to supply and support an Afghan national army and police force that Washington has largely built but which is barely in its adolescence, although it is already 10 times the size of the fierce Taliban insurgency it is fighting. Senior commanders with the American-led International Security Assistance Force, which consists of 28 NATO countries and 22 other participating nations, say that substantial aid and military support is going to be necessary well after the scheduled withdrawal at the end of 2014. "For some time to come, it's our expectation that we will need to supply the Afghans [with] air support, certainly, counter-IED support, logistic support, and a number of areas where their capabilities are not at the level where they need to be at," Lt. Gen. Nick Carter, the deputy ISAF commander, said in an interview in Kabul over the weekend. "It's our expectation that we'll need to continue to build those areas for some time to come and probably beyond 2014." Asked how many years that role might go, Carter, a British officer, said he believes that ISAF will need to "set the horizon out to 2018... It will take between three and five years to achieve. And it's important for people to understand that." Within weeks, probably by the end of June, ISAF is expected to move to the final, and fifth, phase of its "handover" to the Afghan army and police. At that point the combined Afghan National Security Forces, as they are known, are expected to take the nominal lead in planning and directing all missions nationwide against the insurgents; currently ANSF is said to be doing that for about 85 percent of the country. The U.S. and other ISAF countries are then to assume a purely "train, advise, and assist" role. But Carter and others say ANSF is still falling short in effective leadership; command and control; logistics and medical evacuation; training its personnel effectively; and integrating the army's warfare strategy with the Afghan police and central and provincial government agencies. These deficiencies will continue long after 2014. In the end, securing Afghanistan's future is likely to be more far expensive than Washington and other NATO capitals have fully reckoned with yet. It won't be an easy political choice, either, coming at a time when the U.S. defense budget has been slashed by the sequester and European NATO nations must conform to economic austerity policies. Indeed, the rhetoric back in Washington often does not seem to square with the reality over here. Since last year's presidential election, Obama administration officials have indicated that America's military is heading for the exit in Afghanistan as quickly as possible. "This year, we'll mark another milestone — Afghan forces will take the lead for security across the entire country," Obama said at a joint news conference with Afghan President Hamid Karzai in January. "And by the end of next year, 2014, the transition will be complete — Afghans will have full responsibility for their security, and this long war will come to a responsible end." But Carter, in a blunt assessment, indicated that ISAF is under no illusions about the war ending in the foreseeable future and that, even after years more of effort, the optimal results will not be pretty. Asked whether the ultimate outcome ISAF is aiming for would be a version of the somewhat cynical term attributed to a former ISAF commander, Gen. David Piraeus — "Afghan Good Enough," meaning a democratic government that remains corrupt and weak, and an unsatisfactory Afghan security force that barely holds the country's center — Carter said he prefers to use another term to describe Afghanistan's likely future: "a stable instability." Outside of major cities such as Kabul, Kandahar, and Herat, he says, substantial portions of the country will not be very "connected" to the central government. But at the same time the Taliban will not be able to take over the country again, said Carter, who serves as deputy to Marine Corps Gen. Joseph Dun ford, the ISAF commander. That's not necessarily a disaster for ISAF, Carter said, adding, "I'm sure that's going to be the case in large parts of Central Asia for some time to come." In many parts of Afghanistan, especially rural areas, a combination of local, often corrupt interests will be dominated by warlords, drug lords, tribal leaders or insurgents who will "pursue their own interests." He said that it was "rather like West Virginia" or "parts of the United Kingdom and Europe where groups pursue their own interests." Still, most details of these more ambitious plans have yet to be negotiated, Carter said. While Obama is committed to withdrawing the remaining 63,000 or so U.S. troops by the end of 2014, his administration is still negotiating a post-2014 strategic partnership with Karzai that calls for a residual U.S. force numbering from 5,000 to 10,000 troops, according to various reports. Karzai, meanwhile, recently revealed that he has been discussing the use of as many as nine military bases to be used by the United States and ISAF after 2014. Carter confirmed that ISAF is considering the need for that many bases to support and supply six Afghan corps, as well as provide a headquarters, air-support mission and training facility Reflecting the grim assessment, NATO defense ministers recently announced that they would seek to maintain the ANSF at its current strength of 334,000 (the Taliban is said to number about 30,000, although no one is certain of the total) or higher, rather than cut it down to about 230,000, as previously planned. So far, however, of the NATO countries only Germany has officially offered to provide up to 800 troops to supply training after the 2014 deadline. A January report by the special inspector general for Afghan reconstruction concluded that the Afghans had failed to supply accurate numbers in meeting their goal to "train and field" 352,000 ANSF forces by October 2012, and that "Afghanistan is expected to have a 'financing gap' of $70 billion during the transformation decade of 2015-2024, with billions of additional dollars needed for years to follow." Carter indicated that it was critical for ISAF to support ANSF in substantial ways after 2014 in order to address Afghan fears of abandonment. "We would regard the center of gravity in this campaign as being Afghan confidence," he said. "We have to demonstrate a commitment to them that goes beyond the pledges at Chicago and Tokyo," referring to the May 2012 NATO summit in Chicago and an international conference on Afghan development aid later that year in Tokyo, at which the U.S., Germany, Japan, Britain, and other donors offered some $16 billion.

The defense secretary has admitted that no one can predict what will happen

to Afghanistan after British, US and other NATO troops end their frontline role there at the end of 2014, and stressed that only the Afghan people can find a lasting solution to the country's violence, corruption and lawlessness. Philip Hammond's remarks came as the Commons cross-party defense committee warned that Afghanistan could descend into civil war within a few years and suggests that the British government's attitude towards the country is one of simply hoping for the best. Hammond told BBC Radio 4's Today programmed that the UK had intervened in Afghanistan to protect its national security and had never intended to stay for a protracted period. "Afghanistan is an incredibly complex society; a multiethnic society that was very fragmented before we started," he said. "Our ability to influence outcomes is very limited." He defended the long deployment of British troops, saying their actions had brought about "the removal of international terrorists able to use Afghanistan as a base" and helped train the Afghan national security force, which "can and, increasingly, is holding the ring" on the insurgents. "The sacrifices have been huge and we will never forget the sacrifice that has been made to deliver the security of Britain and our allies," he said. "It was always clear that this could not be an open-ended intervention. We had to create the conditions where we would eventually be able to withdraw and allow the Afghans to maintain their own security so our security was protected." While the situation is not perfect we have come a long way to being able to deliver that objective." The defense secretary also said it was clear that "the long-run solution to security has to be an Afghan solution; it cannot be imposed from outside". History, he said, had shown the futility of such attempts. Asked about the committee's warnings, Hammond said it had been offered a range of views as to Afghanistan's future, which ran from the overly optimistic to the possibility of civil war." I completely accept nobody can say with certainty what the future for Afghanistan will be, but what I can say is that the future of Afghanistan will have to be determined by the Afghan people," he said. Former British ambassadors to Afghanistan told the Commons committee that NATO understands of the Taliban was limited, that "corruption and abuse of power was intrinsic in Afghan society" and that the country's economy depended heavily on the drugs trade. The MPs warned that the start of an Afghan-led peace settlement with the Taliban was vital to ensure the country's stability and security after the withdrawal of British troops next year. But they added that coalition forces' lack of progress in reducing violence in the country "does not augur well for improving security and economic development on a long-term sustainable basis". The committee also criticized the government for failing to combat the perception that the pullout amounted to "withdrawal through fatigue". Publication of the report came a day after the government announced that the last group of Royal Marines to be deployed in Afghanistan was returning to the UK. Troops from 40 Commando Royal Marines were based in the Nahr-e Saraj district. The 7,200-strong Royal Marine Corps has deployed commandos to Afghanistan 12 times since 2001, and troops from 40 Commando were the first British soldiers in the country that year, securing Bagram airfield and patrolling the streets of Kabul. The defense committee said the Ministry of Defense and the Foreign Office took an optimistic view of the future yet gave very little information about how they planned to be involved in Afghanistan beyond 2014, James Arbuthnot, chairman of the committee, said: "We have received starkly opposing predictions for Afghanistan's outlook, post-2014. The fact is that the UK has limited influence." The report concludes: "We hope that Afghanistan can become a secure, prosperous and flourishing country but we are concerned that Afghanistan could descend into civil war within a few years." Some ground may have to be given in negotiations with the Taliban but the committee stressed the importance of open and free elections and said the rule of law and human rights should not be compromised in any settlement. The committee said that all Afghan people, including women, must be involved in the peace process. If women were excluded as a consequence of negotiating with the Taliban, the progress made could easily unravel, the MPs warned. "If the UK is to continue to provide financial and training support to Afghanistan post-2014, there needs to be a clear articulation of the areas the UK will fund and support and the outcomes it expects to achieve," the report said. "It must be clear to those engaged in the peace negotiations that, in providing support in the future, the UK will be paying close attention to the progress on the rights of women, children and minority groups, the tackling of corruption and the furtherance of the rule of law". The report also claimed that not enough was being done to train and equips Afghan security forces properly. Concerns remained over the capability of Afghan forces to fill the gap left by withdrawing coalition forces, particularly in terms of helicopters, close air support and logistics, the committee said. "We are concerned that the ANSF [Afghan national security forces totaling about 350,000] will reduce its strength by over a third on current plans based on the expectation that the insurgency will have been diminished," the report adds. "The government should urge the international community to develop a contingency plan in case the level of the insurgency does not diminish" by Afghanistan's president, Hamid Karzai, was a tense affair. Mr. Karzai was due to meet President Barack Obama on January 11ᵗʰ to discuss the scope and size of America's military presence in his country after the end of 2014, when almost all of NATO's combat troops are due to leave. Mr Karzai may have overplayed his hand. He knows that a bilateral security agreement with America will be vital. Yet the shrillness of some of Mr. Karzai's criticisms of America's conduct of the war has only played into the hands of those in the administration who would like to be shot of Afghanistan. Nothing is likely to be decided for several months—the agreement does not have to be signed until November—but there is now talk of a so-called zero option, which would see the departure of all American forces next year. In this section So long, buddy Until very recently it had been assumed that America would want to keep at least 20,000 of its troops in Afghanistan, bolstered by a few thousand more from NATO allies. They would be there to continue the training of Afghan National Security Forces (ANSF) and to provide essential capabilities that the Afghans still lack and have come to depend upon when fighting the Taliban alongside Western forces. These include air transport for logistics and medical evacuation, surveillance and intelligence, and close air support. In addition, America would retain Special Forces and armed drones to stop al-Qaeda's leadership regrouping in Pakistan's tribal areas or returning to the terrorist group's old training grounds in Afghanistan itself. For the Afghans, it seemed self-evident that America would want to keep bases in their country as a way of maintaining its influence in a region full of security threats, whether from Iran or from a failing Pakistani state armed to the teeth with nuclear weapons. They also believed assurances from the Americans and the wider world that they would not be abandoned, and that, after spending so much blood and treasure, the West would not allow Afghanistan to descend into chaos and civil war yet again. Mr. Karzai and other Afghan political leaders are sensitive about their country's sovereignty. But they have no intention of emulating the Iraqis, who brought an abrupt end to the presence of American troops by refusing to sign a new status of forces agreement providing immunity from prosecution for foreign soldiers. Yet they appear to have underestimated how fast the appetite in Mr. Obama's administration has waned for keeping a significant military presence in Afghanistan after 2014. Acute budgetary pressures; the draining of public support for involvement in a war most believe long ago to have been lost; and a belief in some quarters that drones and the intelligence networks that have been built up over the past decade are all that is needed for American security: all have chipped away at the notion of leaving behind a substantial force. On January 8ᵗʰ Ben Rhodes, a deputy national security adviser at the White House, confirmed that leaving no troops behind after 2014 was one of the options under active consideration. How much of this should come as a surprise? In the vice-presidential election debate last October, when asked about the drawdown timetable for Afghanistan, Joe Biden said: "We are leaving. We are leaving in 2014. Period since Mr. Biden has frequently argued for America having the lightest possible footprint in Afghanistan, his remark got little attention. But in November, when the American commander of the NATO-led international coalition, General John Allen, told his bosses at the Pentagon that he favored a slow drawdown of combat troops over the next two years and a residual force of at least 15,000 to be provided by America alone, he was told to come back with lower estimates. Unfortunately for General Allen, at about the same time he found himself embroiled in the fallout from the sudden resignation of David Petraeus as director of the Central Intelligence Agency. It may have weakened his bargaining position. This month General Allen offered revised proposals for a force ranging from about 3,000 to 9,000. Most military experts, however, still believe that an international force of around 30,000 is needed to support the ANSF after 2014. Yet it now appears that the troop levels under consideration by the president range between 6,000 and none. His choice of defense secretary, Chuck Hagel, a former Republican senator whom the president nominated this week, is unlikely to challenge those numbers. Mr. Hagel has long been a skeptic when it comes to Afghanistan and has talked of "looking for the exit". Even if the higher force figure gets the go-ahead, allies will be reluctant to contribute to it, concluding that America is more than halfway out of the door and that such a minimal force can achieve little beyond a small training mission in Kabul and securing the air base at nearby Bagram for limited counter-terrorism operations. Despite an improving combat performance, it is highly uncertain whether the ANSF will cope. Hastily recruited and trained, the ANSF is still a work in progress. It was deliberately denied heavy weapons or much of an air force on the assumption that America would provide key "enablers" for years to come. It now takes the lead security role in about 85% of the country by population, and overall levels of violence are slightly down on previous years. But according to the Pentagon's latest report on the progress of Afghan forces, only one out of 23 brigades is capable of operating without any outside help. It now looks as if the ANSF will be on its own in southern Afghanistan, where the Taliban is strongest, as well as in the wild east of the country which borders the lair in North Waziristan of the Haqqani network.

Afghanistan — The Taliban and the U.S. said they will hold talks on finding a political solution to ending nearly 12 years of war in Afghanistan, as the international coalition formally handed over control of the country's security to the Afghan army and police. The Taliban met a key U.S. demand by pledging not to use Afghanistan as a base to threaten other countries, although the Americans said they must also denounce al-Qaida. But President Barack Obama cautioned that the process won't be quick or easy. He described the opening of a Taliban political office in the Gulf nation of Qatar as an "important first step toward reconciliation" between the Islamic militants and the government of Afghanistan, and predicted there will be bumps along the way. Obama, who was attending the G-8 summit in Northern Ireland, praised Afghan President Hamid Karzai for taking a courageous step by sending representatives to discuss peace with the Taliban. "It's good news. We're very pleased with what has taken place," U.S. Secretary of State John Kerry said in Washington. British Prime Minister David Cameron, whose country has the second-largest contingent of troops in Afghanistan after the U.S., called opening the office "the right thing to do." As the handover occurred, four U.S. troops were killed Tuesday at or near Bagram Air Base in Afghanistan, U.S. defense officials said. The officials said the four were killed by indirect fire, likely a mortar or rocket, but they had no other details. The officials spoke on condition of anonymity because they were not authorized to provide details on the deaths. Officials with the

Obama administration said the office in the Qatari capital of Doha was the first step toward the ultimate U.S.-Afghan goal of a full Taliban renunciation of links with al-Qaida, the reason why America invaded the country on Oct. 7, 2001, shortly after the Sept. 11 terrorist attacks against the United States. The officials, who spoke on condition of anonymity because they were not authorized to speak on the record, said U.S. representatives will begin formal meetings with the Taliban in Qatar in a few days. The top U.S. commander in Afghanistan, Marine Gen. Joseph Dunford, said the only way to end the war was through a political solution. "My perspective has always been that this war is going to have to end with political reconciliation, and so I frankly would be supportive of any positive movement in terms of reconciliation, particularly an Afghan-led and an Afghan-owned process that would bring reconciliation between the Afghan people and the Taliban in the context of the Afghan constitution," he said. Dunford added that he was no longer responsible for the security of the country now that Afghan forces had taken the lead. "Last week I was responsible for security here in Afghanistan," he said, adding that now it was Karzai's job. "It's not just a statement of intent – it's a statement of fact." The transition to Afghan-led security means U.S. and other foreign combat troops will not be directly carrying the fight to the insurgency, but will advise and back up as needed with air support and medical evacuations. The handover paves the way for the departure of coalition forces – currently numbering about 100,000 troops from 48 countries, including 66,000 Americans. By the end of the year, the NATO force will be halved. At the end of 2014, all combat troops will have left and will replaced, if approved by the Afghan government, by a much smaller force that will only train and advise. Obama has not yet said how many soldiers he will leave in Afghanistan along with NATO forces, but it is thought that it would be about 9,000 U.S. troops and about 6,000 from its allies. It is uncertain if the Afghan forces are good enough to fight the insurgents. The force numbered less than 40,000 six years ago and has grown to about 352,000 today. In some of the most restive parts of the country, it may still take a "few months" to hand over security completely to the Afghans, Dunford said. The transition comes at a time when violence is at levels matching the worst in 12 years, further fueling some Afghans' concerns that their forces aren't ready. The decision to open the Taliban office was a reversal of months of failed efforts to start peace talks while the militants intensified a campaign targeting urban centers and government installations. Experts warned that it would be a mistake to expect too much. "The keys are to keep expectations low, to remember that a compromise is unlikely because no one can say what it would consist of," said Michael O'Hanlon of the Brookings Institution. He added that in his opinion, the Taliban wrongly "expect to win the war once NATO is largely gone come 2015." "All that said, it's a potentially useful step if we don't confuse ourselves or wind up in polarizing debates within the coalition," O'Hanlon said. In Doha, Ali Bin Fahad Al-Hajri, the assistant to the foreign minister of Qatar, said the Emir of the Gulf state had given the go-ahead for the office to open. "Negotiations are the only way for peace in Afghanistan," Al-Hajri said. The Taliban emerged from the Pakistani-trained mujahedeen, or holy warriors, who battled the Soviet Union's occupation of Afghanistan in the 1980s with secret backing by the CIA. Civil war broke out when the pro-Soviet Afghan government collapsed following the departure of Moscow's troops. The U.S. took an arms-length position of neutrality as rival warlords shelled Kabul into ruins. By 1994, the Taliban had evolved into a united military and political force and in 1996, the group took control of Afghanistan. Led by Mullah Mohammed Omar, the Afghan Taliban sheltered Osama bin Laden in the years leading up to the Sept. 11 attacks in 2001, but the group was toppled shortly after the U.S. and allied invasion one month later. The U.S.-led invasion leveraged the firepower of factions, such as the Northern Alliance, who had held out against the Taliban after it seized power in 1996. CIA and U.S. special operations support for anti-Taliban forces enabled the U.S. to oust the Islamists by December 2001 without committing large numbers of U.S. ground troops, and the group appeared to have been defeated as a military threat.

However, by 2005, the Taliban was beginning to make a comeback, showing signs of improved training and equipment, while using territory inside Pakistan as a sanctuary. On Taliban spokesman Mohammad Naim said the Islamic Emirate of Afghanistan, as the Taliban were known when they ruled the country, was willing to use all legal means to end what they called the occupation of Afghanistan. But he did not say they would immediately stop fighting. "The jihad continues to end the occupation and establish an Islamic emirate. To achieve this goal, we will follow every legitimate means," he said. "The emirate of the Taliban, with its military effort, has a strategic goal related to the future of Afghanistan. The movement is not intending to harm any other parties and will not allow anybody to use Afghan territory to threaten other countries." The Obama administration officials said the U.S. and Taliban representatives will hold bilateral meetings. Karzai's High Peace Council is expected to follow up with its own talks with the Taliban a few days later. But in making their announcement in Doha, the Taliban did not specifically mention talks with Karzai or his representatives. "We don't recognize the Afghan government and the government of Karzai. The talks will be with the Americans only in Doha under the patronage of Qatar," he said. "We represent the people of Afghanistan. We don't represent the Karzai government." The administration officials acknowledged the process will be "complex, long and messy" because of the ongoing level of distrust between the parties. The officials, who spoke on condition of anonymity because they were not authorized to speak on the record, vowed to continue to push the Taliban further, saying that the Taliban ultimately must also break ties with al-Qaida, end violence and accept Afghanistan's constitution – including protections for women and minorities. They said the U.S. had long demanded that the Taliban make a statement distancing the group from international terrorism, but had said that they did not expect them to break ties with al-Qaida immediately. That would be one of the outcomes of the negotiating process, they added. The U.S. will hold its first formal meetings with the Taliban in Doha within a few days, senior officials said, with the expectation that it will be followed up days later by a meeting between representatives of the Taliban and the High Peace Council. The first meeting will focus on an exchange of agendas and consultations on next steps. Naim did not give a schedule for talks. The Taliban office is in one of the diplomatic areas in Doha. Its sign reads: "The Political Bureau of the Islamic Emirate of Afghanistan in Doha." Despite Karzai's stated hope that the process will move almost immediately to Afghanistan, U.S. officials do not expect that to be possible in the near future. The Taliban have for years refused to speak to the government or the High Peace Council, set up by Karzai three years ago, because they considered them to be U.S. "puppets." Taliban representatives have instead talked to American and other Western officials in Doha and other places, mostly in Europe. Officials said Obama was personally involved in working with Karzai to enable the opening of the office, and that Kerry had also played a major role. Obama briefed other leaders at the summit meeting, which included the countries of Britain, Russia, Germany, Japan, Canada, France and Italy James Dobbins, the U.S. special representative for Afghanistan and Pakistan, was scheduled to leave Washington on Tuesday to visit Turkey, Qatar, Afghanistan and Pakistan, focusing primarily on "reconciliation efforts," according to State Department spokeswoman Jen Psaki. The inauguration ceremony for the world's largest hand written Holy Quran was formally launched in the presence of high level Afghan government delegation, key religious figures, religious clerics, scholars and a huge audience of the Afghans in capital Kabul on 2009. The inauguration ceremony was also accompanied by opening of Hakim Nasir Khusraw Balkhi Cultural Center and arts exhibition displaying the history of Khorasan present day Afghanistan. The initiative for the art of the world's largest Holy Quran was proposed and sponsored by His Excellency Alhaj Syed Mansoor Naderi, a well known religious personality and leader in Afghanistan. The drawing and painting work of the world's largest Holy Quran was completed in almost 5 years, under the supervision of Hakim Nasir Khusraw Balkhi's talented artist. The composition work was started in September 2004 and was completed in September 2009, with at least two years of continuous work for the shafting and archiving work. The calligraphy work has been done on 218 pages, having a dimension of 228 cm length and 155 cm width. All the 30 parts of the Holy Quran has been done in 30 different designs. His Excellency Alhaj Syed Mansoor Naderi while speaking during the inauguration described the completion of the art as a major achievement for the Afghan nation and all Muslims in the world. In the meantime the second deputy for president Hamid Karzai Mohammad Karim Khalili conveyed his message for the inauguration of the world's largest Holy Quran Calligraphy and opening of the Hakim Nasir Khusraw Balkhi Cultural Center. He said, the completion of the world's largest Holy Quran calligraphy is a major achievement for the Afghan nation and conveyed his congratulations remarks for His Excellency Syed Mansoor Naderi. Also, Afghan Senate House speaker Fazal Hadi Muslimyar handed over Appreciation Letters to His Excellency Alhaj Syed Mansoor Naderi, Mr. Sabir Yaqoot Hussaini Khedri and his 9 students who were involved in the calligraphy of the world's largest Holy Quran calligraphy. The completion of the calligraphy work of the world's largest Holy Quran was also praised by Hujat ul Islam Waez Zada Besudi and described the initiative as a vital and major service for the history and culture of Afghanistan. The inauguration ceremony was also accompanied by the appreciation remarks from Nematullah Shahrani Afghan presidential palace adviser and religious cleric. He also spoke on the history of Khurasan and urged for more steps for further recognition of Nasir Khusraw Balkhi. He also praised the work of His Excellency Alhaj Syed Mansoor Naderi towards the cultural and historical services. Several other congratulatory messages were also sent on the occasion of the inauguration ceremony by civil organizations, political parties, religious and cultural personalities.

Afghan President Hamid Karzai on may 2013 revealed that Washington wants to maintain nine US military bases scattered across the country after the formal deadline for the withdrawal of US and NATO coalition forces at the end of 2014. In a speech delivered at Kabul University, Karzai stressed that he was amenable to the US demand, indicating that he was willing to trade the bases for promises of a continued flow of economic aid from the West and security for his puppet government. Another likely condition is US support for the election of his handpicked successor in an election set for next year. "If these conditions are met, we are ready to sign the contract with the United States," he said. As to the continued presence of foreign troops on Afghan soil after more than a dozen years of war and occupation, Karzai stated, "We see their staying in Afghanistan beyond 2014 in the interests of Afghanistan as well as NATO." The statements represented an abrupt rhetorical shift by the US-backed president. In recent months, Karzai has accused Washington of colluding with the Taliban to increase violence and create a pretext for a continued US military presence. He has repeatedly demanded an end to US aerial bombardments and to night raids by US Special Forces, which have claimed civilian lives and increased hatred for both the foreign occupation and Karzai's corrupt puppet government in Kabul. In February, Karzai barred US special operations troops from operating in the entire province of Maidan Wardak, southwest of Kabul. These and other statements and gestures have been aimed at deflecting popular hostility and posturing as a nationalist leader, rather than Washington's stooge. Karzai's casting himself now as a pragmatic deal maker, however, was by no means welcomed by the Obama administration, which appeared blindsided by the Afghan president's remarks. US officials refused to confirm the request for nine bases, which Afghan aides to Karzai said was contained in the latest American draft proposal submitted last month. White House spokesman Jay Carney told reporters in Washington, "The United States does not seek permanent military bases in Afghanistan, and any US presence after 2014 would only be at the invitation of the Afghanistan government and aimed at training the country's forces and targeting the remnants of Al Qaeda." Carney stressed that Washington was negotiating a bilateral security agreement that "will address access to and use of Afghanistan facilities by US forces." He reiterated three times in the course of his remarks the denial that the US was seeking any "permanent bases." The reality is that Washington is negotiating with its Afghan puppet regime the unrestricted use of bases that it will formally lease from Kabul for at least the next decade. According to the Karzai regime, the bases sought include Kabul, Bagram, Mazar, Jalalabad, Gardez, Kandahar, Helmand, Shindand and Herat, placing US forces in virtually every corner of the country. The Obama administration has said next to nothing publicly about its post-2014 plans for Afghanistan. It has no interest in placing before the American people its blueprint for continuing military operations in the country where the US has waged the longest war in its history—an intervention that is vastly unpopular with the American people. Recent polls have shown two-thirds of the US population agreeing that the war was not worth fighting. The White House wants to maintain the myth, which it continuously promotes, that "the tide of war is receding," and that all US forces are being brought home from Afghanistan. Recent reports have indicated that the Pentagon brass want to keep at least 13,500 troops deployed in Afghanistan, with a large portion consisting of special operations units. Still to be resolved is an agreement by the Afghanistan government to cede to US forces absolute immunity from Afghan law, assuring that none of them can be punished for war crimes against the country's population. The measures are intensely unpopular among the Afghan people. Failure to secure a similar agreement in Iraq derailed plans by the Obama administration to maintain a residual US military force in that country. And, while the formal mission laid out for the forces to remain in Afghanistan consists of training Afghan forces and continued operations against Al Qaeda—a euphemism for counterinsurgency operations against Afghanis resisting foreign occupation—there is another overriding motivation for the US to maintain its military presence. Afghanistan provides US imperialism with a strategic foothold in Central and South Asia, placing its military forces on the borders of Iran and China, and in close proximity to the vast energy reserves of the Caspian Basin. Within the region, this motivation is widely recognized. Iran, Russia, China and Pakistan all oppose a continued US military presence, seeing it as both a guarantee of continued warfare in Afghanistan itself and a direct threat to their own interests. Karzai's public exposure of Washington's bases proposal was seen by Afghan analysts as a sort of trial balloon, testing both the reaction within the country as well as that of neighboring countries. Iran, for example, has a 600-mile-long border with Afghanistan and has provided the Karzai regime with aid while maintaining extensive influence in Afghanistan, particularly in its north and west. The New York Times quoted unnamed US officials as indicating that Washington is prepared to meet Karzai's demands in exchange for a bases deal. "Officials said that aid would continue, although amounts given were likely to be reduced over time," the newspaper reported. "And the Afghan government would have to live up to its commitments to battle corruption and run a more open government for the aid to keep flowing." The pretense that Washington is holding Karzai's feet to the fire over corruption is ludicrous, given recent reports that the Central Intelligence Agency regularly delivers shopping bags, backpacks and suitcases stuffed with cash to the presidential palace. This CIA money, used to pay off warlords and fill up the foreign bank accounts of the president and his supporters, is only the tip of the iceberg of the massive corrupt enterprise fostered by more than a decade of US occupation. Hundreds of billions of dollars have been poured into this war of aggression, while Afghanistan has remained one of the poorest countries on the planet. The Obama administration's attempts to hide this dirty secret from the American people were underscored in a speech delivered Wednesday by the Special Inspector General for Afghan Reconstruction, John Sopko, who was appointed last summer. 2014- Even by Afghanistan's high standards, the massacre of worshippers in Kabul on 2011 6 December was an act of stomach-churning brutality. A suicide bomber posing as a pilgrim on Ashura, one of the holiest days of the calendar of Islam, had inveigled his way into the middle of a packed crowd of men, women and children. Witnesses watching from the rooftop of the nearby Abu Fazal shrine said body parts flew up into the air near the epicenter of the blast when the unknown bomber detonated him. The clearing smoke revealed a scene strewn with lifeless and often mangled bodies, lying in circles around the blackened area of tarmac where the bomber had stood. A young girl who had somehow miraculously survived was snapped by a photographer wailing into the air. Among the 55 killed there were no police officers or soldiers or anyone who might remotely be considered a "legitimate" target of the Taliban-led war against the Afghan government. The Taliban itself was quick to condemn the attack in strong terms, while an extremist Pakistan-based movement called Lashkar-e-Jhangvi al Almiv has been fingered. If it really was a unilateral operation launched without the consent of the Taliban's leadership it is another worrying sign of how the insurgency in Afghanistan is spinning out of control, becoming crueler and ever more willing to inflict horrendous damage on ordinary civilians. But not everyone thinks such horrors are an entirely bad thing. Indeed, some within the US war machine have long argued the emergence of a nastier insurgency could be really quite useful for NATO war aims. So useful, in fact, those foreign forces should try to encourage such behavior. One of them was Peter Lavoy, a former chairman of the US National Intelligence Council, the body that examines data from across the US government's intelligence gathering machine and turns it into high-grade analysis that is rarely discussed publicly. At a closed-door meeting with ambassadors at NATO headquarters in Brussels in December 2008, Lavvy spelled out a strategy for winning the war in Afghanistan that has never been uttered publicly: "The international community should put intense pressure on the Taliban in 2009 in order to bring out their more violent and ideologically radical tendencies," he said, according to a State Department note-taker in the room. "This will alienate the population and give us an opportunity to separate the Taliban from the population." His words, which we only know courtesy of Wiki Leaks, are extraordinary because they have been proven at least partially right. They also differ fundamentally from the publicly stated strategy in Afghanistan. Known as population-centric counterinsurgency, or Coin, the fundamental principle is that foreign forces should try to keep ordinary Afghans safe from insurgents and thereby win their support. The idea that NATO may actually be trying to make the population less secure appalls observers. "It just goes completely against the ethos of the American military not to take more risks in order to protect civilians," says John Nagl, a retired lieutenant-colonel who co-wrote the US army's field manual on countering guerrilla warfare. "Find it hard to believe elements of the US military would want to deliberately put more risk on to civilians." But behind the scenes, powerful voices continue to argue for a harder-edged strategy that makes the lives of ordinary Afghans more miserable, not less. Michael Simple, a regional expert on the Taliban, says it is an outlook he runs across in discussions with NATO officials: "I have heard serious, thinking officers articulate the idea that provoking Taliban fighters into acts of extreme violence against the population could be taken as a sign of Coin progress, prior to the final victory when the people turn against them." And evidence has been building up for some time that the Afghan insurgency is indeed becoming a lot nastier. In the view of some analysts, a turning point came in February when a group of gunmen rushed into a bank in the eastern city of Jalalabad. What came next, as the high-definition, full-color CCTV footage showed, was no ordinary bank job. The raiders did not try to force staff to open the safe or even scoop up the wads of money the cashiers had ready to pay the salaries of the many police officers and soldiers in the bank that day. Instead of stealing anything, the seven men, who were wearing police uniforms in addition to their suicide-bomb vests, methodically walked around the bank and shot customers and bank workers at point-blank range, killing dozens.

One cashier, who was hiding behind his desk, heard an attacker coolly order a man on the floor to stand up and recite a Kalima, a prayer Muslims say as they prepare themselves for death. "Before he finished, he shot him dead," said Ilyas Yousafzai. "The Taliban claim they are fighting for Islam, but they order people to recite their Kalima and then kill them. That is not Islam." Intelligence suggests the Taliban is reeling: some fighters refuse promotion or to even step foot in Afghanistan. STR Pakistan Reuters Corbis Such sadistic cruelty is, to say the least, counterproductive for a movement that has a heroic self-image as a force that swept out the warlords who had plagued the country in the 90s. In its own view, the Taliban brought security to a troubled land, a justice to oppressed civilians. It is a treasured reputation it has tried to burnish in the years since its re-emergence, even issuing codes of conduct in the name of Mullah Omar, the Taliban's one-eyed leader. The rules order fighters not to persecute civilians and generally not to repeat the errors of the mujahedeen commanders who became heroes for fighting the Soviet occupation in the 80s but also villains for their corrupt and predatory warlord rule. But there are plenty of examples of their deeds falling far short of their words. This summer in Gereshk, central Helmand, an eight-year-old boy was kidnapped by the Taliban in an apparent bid to get his father, Noor Mohammad, to hand over his police pickup truck. Unfortunately for the young boy, his father refused. "After two days they hanged my little innocent son, and threw him in the water canal," Mohammad said. "I never believed the Taliban would ever kill him. I thought they would set him free, but they did the cruellest thing possible. God will never forgive them." In Kandahar province this year, four people working on a US-funded road project were kidnapped and had their ears sliced off. In Paktia province, the researcher Kate Clark reports that the Taliban's far-from-perfect court system has broken down. Whereas in the past suspected "spies" would get a trial, ultimately sparing some, today an increasingly neurotic local insurgency moves straight to the throat-slitting stage when its suspicions are aroused. The Taliban has not only grown increasingly fond of suicide bombings, something that was largely unheard of until around 2006, it has also made greater use of children, despite its own strict ban on using underage fighters. On 26 June, for example, in the southern province of Uruzgan, insurgents instructed an eight-year-old girl to carry a bomb to a police pickup truck, which they then remotely detonated, killing the girl but nobody else. The suicide bombers often completely fail to harm what Taliban press releases call "stooge" foreign forces, or "puppet" soldiers of the Afghan government. Instead it is civilians that often pay the price. On 7 January, in the southern border town of Spin Boldak, a suicide bomber blew himself up in a public bath house, supposedly in a bid to kill the deputy commander of the border police. However, he was not even present. The explosion ripped through the building, killing 15 and wounding 20. UN figures show the vast majority of civilian casualties are due to Taliban operations. Whether or not there is a deliberate effort to radicalize the Taliban, it appears to be an unavoidable side effect of trying to crush it militarily. And that is exactly what the US has been trying to do in the last two years. The US-led decimation of the Taliban's mid-level leadership begins in top-secret intelligence hubs crammed with analysts scrutinizing vast amounts of raw information gleaned from Afghan spies, interrogations and eavesdropping into mobile phone networks. After sifting through the data, a targeting "packet" is created and handed over to special forces teams who are sent out on up to six "kill or capture" missions every single night. Dozing in their traditional mud compounds in distant villages all over rural Afghanistan, the targets have no clue they are in the crosshairs of one of the most advanced intelligence and military machines the world has ever seen until they hear helicopters racing over the horizon. Nagl says all this amounts to a revolution in the way war is fought. "In the history of counterinsurgency, we have never been this good at taking insurgents off the battlefield," he says.

And, it is working; say NATO data crunchers, who pore over information in a windowless office in Kabul. They claim there are significant signs that the insurgency has weakened in the past year, including the loss of areas in Helmand and Kandahar provinces, where the Taliban used to operate unmolested. Radio intercepts and other sources of intelligence suggest the Taliban is reeling: commanders struggle to resupply its men in the field, while some fighters apparently refuse promotions or even to step foot in Afghanistan, preferring the safety of Pakistan. There are also signs that the average age of Taliban commanders has dropped as the movement struggles to replace those who are killed or captured, leading to a new generation of less experienced and less capable insurgents taking the lead. But despite all this apparently good news, NATO generals know they have still not succeeded in their stated strategic goal of protecting the population. In fact, the data currently shows Afghans feeling less secure the more the insurgents are pummeled. As a senior official with NATO's International Security Assistance Force (ISAF), charged with supporting the Afghan government, put it recently: "Even though the Taliban are not present in the numbers they used to be, and even though they still don't enjoy popular support, do the people yet feel more secure? This is largely because the Taliban has responded to its pounding by ramping up the number of homemade land mines it plants. Although they are intended to blow up NATO vehicles, more often than not they kill civilians. Another cause for public discomfort is how NATO's intensified operations have changed the profile of insurgents in many areas, from disgruntled locals to vicious, hot-headed youth sent in from over the Pakistani border where they are indoctrinated in a network of madras's. "If you come into a neighborhood that you grew up in you are probably going to have a harder time slapping around Grandma than if you are an outsider," says a senior NATO intelligence officer on the issue of "out of area" fighters. He believes the Taliban experienced this problem particularly acutely in Helmand this summer when, lacking enough local fighters, it "emptied out the madras's" in Pakistan and sent teams of youngsters over the border. "The [US] marines soon saw these guys infiltrating in, carrying weapons openly," he says. "Then they started getting reports from locals of increased intimation and beatings." Nagl believes all this is an indication that the Taliban is being degraded to the opening stage of Mao Zedong's famous three "phases" of revolutionary warfare. According to the Chinese revolutionary leader and insurgency theorist, phase one is essentially terrorism, involving attacks on easy targets such as mayors and police chiefs. (When the Taliban re-emerged in 2006, it did indeed specialize in burning schools and intimidating NGOs.) Phase two sees the emergence of larger teams of rebels capable of taking on government military forces to some degree. Phase three is full-blown conventional war. "The Taliban have been knocked down to faze one and you see what you would expect to see, with the resulting risk of alienating the civilian population," Nagl says. "If we can get the civilian population on our side in the south, in their heartlands, we can knock them back to phase zero." But will the civilian population ever come completely over to the side of the Afghan government and its foreign military backers? The NATO intelligence official, drawing from a thick pile of graphs and bar charts, points to some encouraging signs: 2011 has seen record numbers of tip-offs from locals revealing where caches of weapons and IEDs (improvised explosive devices) are hidden. There has also been brisk interest in signing up to the Afghan Local Police scheme, a US special forces-mentored programmed that recruits villagers to defend their own communities. A woman walks past Italian NATO troops in Herat province, Afghanistan. Photograph: Jalil Rezayee/EPA In one interesting case in August, in the Nawa district of Helmand, furious villagers stoned to death a Taliban commander and his bodyguard after the insurgents had killed an old man accused of collaborating with the government. But although the Taliban has long been extremely unpopular, there is precious little sign the public will risk their lives in a big way to defy them. Skeptics say US strategists are basing their strategic thinking on the "awakening" in the Iraqi province of Anbar in 2006, when the population turned conclusively on the al-Qaida-led insurgency. But bad though the situation in Afghanistan currently is, it is nowhere near the level of violence and destruction that held sway in Iraq. Optimists call for patience. "We will go through a period of rising violence when we don't know if success is over the hill," predicts one former adviser to NATO top general in Afghanistan last year. "It's like the theory of how passengers respond to a plane hijacking, where the first lot of people will get hurt and killed if they try to resist," he says. "They only have a chance when the whole mob rises up with a 'let's roll'."

But it is a depressing reality that so far it is mostly foreigners who get blamed for the Taliban's outrages, with many Afghans identifying their misery not with the insurgents, but with the international troops seen as the source of fighting. In the immediate aftermath of Tuesday's bomb in Kabul, some furious young men at the scene denounced both the Pakistanis and the Americans. And, as the NATO adviser acknowledges, compared with some other successful counterinsurgencies, people might think twice about rising against the rebels if they don't think they will get much help from a weak and often corrupt Afghan government. "For all the implied Coin hope that the nastier Taliban will find it more difficult to survive, in the presence of a failing government, extreme violence may be an effective tool of social control," says Simple. Worse still, some analysts fear the new generation of Taliban created by NATO operations will crowd out wiser members of the old regime who are interested in a negotiated, political settlement to the conflict. "The fact that they are a coherent group is a good thing," says Clark. "It is much better to have a Taliban that actually has a structure you can deal with and implement peace if it so wished, rather than a fragmented, abusive movement more strongly aligned to al-Qaida." Killing off potential peacemakers within the insurgency is a real concern, says Nagl, who thinks those insurgents who might be interested in reconciling should be put on a special list that would protect them from NATO's night-time hit squads. "But it is not at all clear that we are any good at that because people who understand reintegration and reconciliation are Afghans and people who do the targeting are Americans," he admits. Others call for a more radical approach to bringing the war to a close that would entail trying to make the Taliban behave better, including confidence-building measures such as ceasefires. That, it is hoped, would then form the basis for peace talks between Afghans. A better-behaved movement would also make the majority of Afghans who never supported them, and are increasingly worried that they might one day return to power, more inclined to some sort of a negotiated compromise. Simple says he had assumed that a strategy to improve behavior "was almost orthodox" among US diplomats. But, he notes, the soldiers running the war in Afghanistan are still wedded to military operations they believe will eventually lead to victory, even if it makes life miserable for many Afghans along the way. 2011 A July United Nations report asserting that only 30 civilians died in targeted raids in Afghanistan during the first six months of 2011 reflected only a very small fraction of night raids in which civilians were killed, according to officials of the independent Afghan commission which had co-produced the 2010 report on civilian casualties with the U.N. Mission. The report on civilian casualties by the United Nations Assistance Mission in Afghanistan (UNAMA) attributed 80 percent of the 1,462 civilian deaths it counted during the six-month period to the Taliban - mostly from improvised explosive devices - and only 14 percent of them to "Pro-Government Forces". The report credited the U.S.-NATO military command with reducing civilian casualties in night raids during the six-month period by 15 percent compared with the same period last year. But officials of the Afghanistan Independent Human Rights Commission, which collaborated with UNAMA on its 2010 civilian casualties report, told IPS that the number of night raids that UNAMA investigated in some fashion could only have been a very small proportion of the total number of targeted raids with civilian casualties. A leading official of the independent commission has also objected publicly to UNAMA's exclusion from the total in last year's report of most of the allegations of civilian deaths in raids that had been brought to its attention. The AIHRC officials, who have personal experience on the issue of civilian casualties from night raids, told IPS that most night raids are carried out in districts that are dominated by the Taliban. In those districts, people are not able to file complaints and usually are not even aware of any opportunity to do so, the sources said. The AIHRC sources requested anonymity because they are not authorized to talk to the news media about the matter. In Helmand province, the raids are believed to be concentrated in the districts where the Taliban are strongest, such as Baghran, Baghni, Sangin and Nahr-e-Saraj, the sources explained. The same is true for Kandahar, Zabul, Uruzgan and other southern and eastern provinces where the Taliban has a strong presence, the AIHRC sources said. The commission received only nine complaints directly from families of those who had been killed or injured in a night raid during the first six months of 2011, according to the AIHRC sources. In fact, the commission gets most of its information about civilian casualties in night raids not from complaints from people in the area where the raids take place but from talking with people in detention, the sources said. But that information is fragmentary, according to the sources, because the commission has access to only a fraction of the detainees in the Afghan prison system, and because the detainees themselves are only aware of some of the cases. UNAMA has seven regional offices, but travel and contact between those offices and the districts in which the Taliban are strongest are limited. Daphne Eviatar, who has monitored human rights in Afghanistan for the U.S.-based group Human Rights first, agreed with the assessment that the families of victims in many districts would be unlikely to file complaints about civilian casualties from night raids. UNAMA's six-month report conceded that, "Given both limitations associated with the operating environment and limited access to information, UNAMA may be under-reporting the night raids involving civilian casualties." In a February 2011 interview with researchers on a study by the Open Society Foundations and the Liaison Office, an unnamed "international human rights monitor" went even further. The unnamed individual admitted to "underreporting of night raids because many of the areas in which they took place are inaccessible and the civilians are difficult to verify." UNAMA is the only international entity that has been reporting totals of civilian casualties in night raids. The UNAMA report for the first six months indicates that the NATO-led International Security Assistance Force (ISAF) had refused repeatedly to provide information on the number of night raids it had carried out. Nevertheless, figures provided by ISAF to the Washington Post and to blogger Bill Roggio show a total of 2,020 targeted raids in the six- month period from early May through early November 2010, killing roughly 2,000 "insurgents". U.S. military officers also told the researchers for the Open Societies Foundation study that shots had been fired in only 20 percent of night raids. That would mean that 2,000 people were killed in just over 400 raids in which shots were fired during the six months — an average of five people per shooting incident. The vast majority of night raids target a single individual. So the available statistics on night raids suggest that the vast majority of those killed in the raids had not been targeted. UNAMA acknowledged in the report that ISAF does not apply the same definition of "civilian" based on international humanitarian law that UNAMA applies in counting civilian casualties. U.S. Special Forces officers belonging to a unit that had killed nine election workers along with a former Taliban insurgent they had mistakenly believed was the Taliban shadow governor of Takhar province in September 2010 told former BBC reporter Kate Clark last December that anyone found in the company of a person who is targeted is regarded as an insurgent as well. The very broad definition of "insurgent" used by

ISAF in releasing figures on the number killed in night raids, along with statistics on raids coming from ISAF itself, suggests that most of those killed in night raids would be considered civilians under international humanitarian law criteria. UNAMA would not allow IPS to interview the head of its human rights office, Georgette Gagnon, about the 2011 report, even though she had told IPS she could do an interview during the week of Aug. 22. In responses to questions e-mailed by IPS, however, Gagnon said that UNAMA had investigated a total of 89 night raids in which casualties had been alleged, and that it had rejected the allegations of civilian deaths in 58 of those cases. AIHRC and UNAMA, which co-produced the 2010 report, had clashed over UNAMA's decision to put the number of civilian deaths in night raids at 82 in that report. Nader Nadery, a commissioner of the AIHRC, revealed in an interview with IPS after the report was published that UNAMA had based the figure of 82 deaths on only 13 night raids in which the civilian deaths had been verified to UNAMA's satisfaction. Nadery said the total had excluded alleged civilian deaths in 60 other raids. UNAMA did not partner with AIHRC in producing the 2011 six-month report. In a recent interview with IPS, Nadery estimated that 462 civilian deaths had occurred in all of the night raids in 2010 about which the commission had obtained some information. The latest report's methodological section confirms that alleged civilian deaths are not included in UNAMA's total if the civilian status of any of the victims in an incident is uncertain. Gagnon told IPS that said the mission's decisions on such cases "are based on firsthand accounts for the vast majority of the incidents investigated". She would not say, however, how many of the decisions to reject allegations were made on the basis of eyewitness accounts. Gagnon also acknowledged that ISAF and Afghan officials had challenged some allegations, but would not reveal how many of the allegations that had been rejected fell into that category. 2011- The chief of police has a memorable way of demonstrating that he's not afraid of the drug smugglers. He holds up his right hand, revealing the absence of his middle finger. Four years ago, Brig. Gen. Aqa Noor Kintuz was hired as provincial chief of police in the northeastern Afghan province of Badakhshan and charged with destroying its plentiful poppy fields. "After I finished one of the first eradications," he says, "my vehicle was blown up by a remote-control bomb." He rolls up his right shirtsleeve. His forearm is badly mangled. In the years since, he has received innumerable death threats. Women and children of poppy farmers have hurled stones at his policemen. One of his eradication tractors was torched. The grim axiom defining today's Afghanistan, 85 percent of whose citizens are farmers, is that its economy relies on two dueling revenue streams. One flows from Western aid, in the hopes that the country will renounce the Taliban. The other flows from opium trafficking supported by the Taliban, which use the proceeds to fund attacks on Western troops. Only recently has the Afghan government seemed to take stock of the obvious: For the outside world's largesse to continue, the national economy's addiction to opium must end. The poppy fields must be destroyed. But just as this devoutly Muslim nation did not become the world's leading opium supplier overnight, uprooting Afghanistan's poppy mind-set promises to be a complicated endeavor. In Badakhshan, chief of police Kintuz appears to be making some headway against poppies. Five years ago the province was Afghanistan's second-biggest opium producer, after the Taliban-controlled province of Helmand. For a brief period after a Taliban ban on poppies in 2000, Badakhshan even took the lead in poppy cultivation, because the province was controlled by the Northern Alliance militias, rather than the Taliban. When Kintuz started his job in 2007, 9,000 acres were planted with poppies. Two years later fewer than 1,500 were. Eradication efforts have forced poppy farmers into the margins of the countryside. Their fields are, by design, all but invisible. To find one, you must drive for hours on a crumbled and isolated mountainside road, accompanied by someone who knows the district and will if necessary explain your presence there. You must look far from the roadside, gazing over the rolling terra incognita of northern Afghanistan-studying its monochromatic creases for that rogue burst of color, simultaneously innocent and obscene, that finally screams out what it can only be: a field of poppies. A farmer squats with his back to the flowers, weeding an adjacent field. He is a 37-year-old man with the distinct Mongolian features characteristic of the borderlands, and he wears a brown tunic, a turban, and a tentative smile. He introduces himself as Mohammed Khalid. He acknowledges that the poppy field is his. The nine-mile road to Argo is a splintered mess-deterioration has left it worse now than it had been before a U.S. subcontractor was paid $2.5 million to resurface it. Rolling through the district center, past dozens of shuttered shops where opium was once sold openly, the convoy is greeted with hard stares from the villagers. A few miles beyond Argo, near the village of Barlas, the 30 or so armed counter-narcotics officers dismount their vehicles. The men set out on foot into the hills, searching for sequestered poppies. The fields are everywhere: dozens upon dozens of crazy-colored tracts, none larger than an acre. The officers descend on them with bamboo canes and swing away at the flowers, reaper-like. The chief bashes away as well. A surveyor from the United Nations Office on Drugs and Crime (UNODC) faithfully records each obliterated site on his clipboard. A young farmer watches the havoc while crouching in his field. "That land belongs to my neighbor Israyel," he says. "I think he knew they were coming and didn't want to be around to see it. The police warned us last year not to plant poppy. So I've switched to melon. But all of this is rain-fed land, so if there's a drought, I've got a real problem." ask if he or his neighbors have received any of the millions of dollars being poured into Badakhshan Province by the U.S. Agency for International Development (USAID) and other Western organizations in an attempt to lure Afghan farmers away from poppies. "They promised the Argo district's governor that they'd give us bags of wheat seed and fertilizer," he replies. "But they haven't." The remark is similar to one by an elder of the nearby Tashkan district: "The government said, 'We'll build roads, bridges, and canals, and you'll forget poppies forever.' That was five years ago. They've done nothing." In fairness, several things have been done-a newly paved highway from Feyzabad to Kabul, road construction projects in Tashkan, a saffron farm in Baharak, and 18 new district police offices. But for every worthy project scattered throughout this vast northern province is a village like Sar Ab in Yamgan district, where the lack of a medical clinic led residents to use opium as their only medicine until half of the 1,800 villagers became addicts. Or the village of Du Ghalat, in Argo, where a hundred children huddle like cattle on the dirt floor of a collapsing schoolhouse built with opium money that has dried up as poppy eradication proceeds. Or the millions of U.S. taxpayer dollars earmarked to fund agricultural projects in Badakhshan, which, according to one counter-narcotics official, "never got here-it disappeared." The team advances to another field, and from a crumbling house a woman emerges, shrieking, "For God's sake, don't destroy it! We don't have anything else!" The men say nothing and keep swinging. A few minutes later, they discover another poppy field, surrounded by brick walls. Two small children stand against the wall, crying loudly as the officer's approach. An older sister tries to comfort them as their mother hollers, "These children have no father! How will I provide for them now?" The chief looks stricken. Lowering his cane, he walks up to the older girl, murmurs a few sympathetic words and presses a few Afghan dollars into her hand.

The officers move on to another widow's poppy field. She sits on a mule sobbing while they undo the labor of her dead husband-who she says had been a mujahedeen against the Soviets and more recently fought the Taliban as a member of the Afghan National Army before being killed by a roadside bomb this past winter. As we proceed, notice that the poppy bulbs in some of the razed fields bear telltale slash marks, indicating that their opium resin had been harvested before our arrival. also notice fields that are plainly visible but go untouched. Are these oversights? Or has someone been bribed? As the chief and his officers repose under trees after an elaborate picnic lunch of goat, chicken, yogurt, and fresh vegetables filched from nearby fields, ask the chief if some of his own men may be involved in the opium trafficking. "Yes, there are a few," he says quietly. "But let's talk about this later." When remind him of his words the next week, the chief says he has purged his department of crooked cops. He says he does not know of any elected officials in Badakhshan involved in smuggling- "otherwise, would have arrested them." do not tell him that other sources have fingered a prominent official as a smuggler, as well as another smuggler who was a candidate for the parliament, offering to pay for votes and telling farmers that if elected he would ensure that opium production will continue. Even as Badakhshan becomes poppy free, local commanders and government officials have allegedly reached power-sharing agreements over drug routes taking opium across the northern border into Central Asia. The Afghan economy, even here in the non-Taliban controlled areas of the north, remains reliant on the drug trade. In Feyzabad I interview a man believed to be one of the province's biggest drug smugglers. He will not confirm he is associated with the opium trade. But he tells me matter-of-factly, "Someone who just smuggles on his own isn't going to succeed. He has to have relationships with someone-like the district or provincial police chief." For centuries, opium wafted over Afghanistan before engulfing it altogether. Though Alexander the Great could not totally conquer this rugged northeastern flank of the Persian Empire in the fourth century B.C., he is credited with leaving behind the drug that ultimately would. Actual cultivation of poppy shows up in Afghanistan's recorded history about 300 years ago. It was a crop well suited to the loamy soils of Badakhshan and the eastern province of Nangarhar, where it was first grown-requiring little fertilization and rainfall, a short growing season, and about as much expertise as it takes to hand-scatter seeds and cut slits in a bulb. Poppy occupied a benign niche in the country's agrarian culture throughout the 18th and 19th centuries, even as India's stranglehold over the opium trade later gave way to Turkey and then to the highlands of Southeast Asia, thanks to the growing market for heroin in Europe and the United States. Only in the middle of the 20th century did Afghanistan become an opium exporter. At the request of the United Nations, which Afghanistan joined in 1946, King M. Zahir Shah temporarily halted cultivation. The subsistence poppy farmers of Badakhshan and Nangarhar persuaded him to reverse his decision. In the meantime the crops for which Afghan farmers achieved renown were pistachios, almonds, pomegranates, cotton, and grapes so it was, until the Soviet invasion of December 1979 upended Afghanistan's landscape. The new occupiers closed off the markets for several of the country's fruits and shut down the cotton gins so as to benefit Uzbekistan's exports. The ensuing decade-long war between the Soviets and the U.S.-backed mujahedeen claimed farm-to-market roads, irrigation canals, silos, and food processing factories among its victims. Afghanistan's agriculture was ruined. Between the U.S.S.R.'s withdrawal in 1989 and the Taliban's emergence in 1994, the country descended into chaos as warlords competed for power. Afghan farmers, struggling to regain their standing in the marketplace, discovered that India and Pakistan had developed their own products and were no longer interested in importing Afghanistan's. Those countries had succeeded in cracking down on their own opium production-and drug smugglers began to eye new pockets of instability where illegal trafficking could thrive. Operatives from Pakistan showed up in Nangarhar, then Badakhshan, then the southern province of Helmand. As agricultural consultant Jonathan Greenham describes his work in Pakistan to eradicate its opium production, "We just pushed the problem across the border." These are among the reasons Afghanistan's share of worldwide opium production skyrocketed from 19 percent in 1986 to 90 percent two decades later. The greatest factor, however, was the Taliban. When it first came to power in 1996, the new Islamist government garnered support from tribal leaders by agreeing not to crack down on poppy cultivation. The supreme leader, Mullah Omar, received regular funding from trafficking groups, which he allowed to operate freely. At the same time, the new Afghan government levied a 10 percent tax on all agricultural profits. By 1999 Afghan opium production spiked to more than 5,000 tons, prompting pressure from the UNODC for a crackdown In July 2000 Mullah Omar issued a fatwa, or religious decree, declaring opium production a violation of Islam. The Taliban enforced the ban with brutal efficiency, as one former poppy farmer told me, "by threatening to set your house on fire." The result was a massive 91 percent reduction in poppy growing in one year. After the U.S.-led invasion of Afghanistan and the fall of the Taliban in 2001, regional warlords once again cranked up opium production. No longer in power, the Taliban now saw opium as a way to fund their insurgency. "They saw the opportunity to generate a tremendous amount of income without sacrificing the subsistence of the people," says Wes Harris of the United States Department of Agriculture. Poppy is a winter crop, so after the harvest in late spring, a farmer can plant corn, cotton, or beans in the same soil. During years when demand is high, a farmer might make as much as six times more from opium than he would from another crop. When the price of opium is low, the farmer can simply wrap his durable product in plastic and store it until the market is more lucrative. It is now believed that the Taliban had a large stockpile of opium when they enforced their ban in 2000 and were deliberately curtailing supply to drive up prices. As the Taliban have gained control of southern Afghanistan over the past several years, growing poppies has only gotten easier. Drug traffickers advance farmers money for the harvest and later arrive to pick up the product. The drug mafia sees to it that the routes to heroin processing labs in the borderlands and then out of Afghanistan are well cleared and the appropriate individuals bought off-since, as one veteran Afghan law enforcement official puts it, "Afghanistan is controlled by the drug mafia. How else do you think those people in the government with their low-paying salaries bought their fancy houses in Dubai and the U.S. in the past few years?" NATO estimates that insurgents get half of their financing from drugs, nearly half a billion dollars but with Afghanistan's opium economy totaling up to four billion dollars a year, the Taliban command only a fraction of that enormous sum. A conundrum still looms for the poppy farmer: Opium is haram, or forbidden by Islam, as the Taliban decreed when they temporarily halted its cultivation. Or is it? Some Afghan mullahs postulate it is haram only to use opium, not to produce it. Other mullahs cite the Koran's proviso that a starving man may eat haram meat in order to survive. But the religious director of Badakhshan Province, Maulawi Abdul Wali Arshad, says, "We have a law in Islam: Whenever something is illegal, it is illegal from beginning to end. If poppy cultivation is legal, then how do we control opium smuggling? Or opium use what the Taliban are doing isn't Islamic. The Taliban's involvement with the drug mafia shows that they don't want a truly Islamic government. They just want power." Helmand Province is the Taliban's stronghold and ground zero for Afghanistan's poppy cultivation. It is the place where Americans, in a massive development project after World War II, built an irrigation system that still functions-but only because Afghan farmers have fashioned canals to bypass the clogged main arteries. They direct water to this or that farm simply by pushing aside a pile of mud with a hoe. As one USAID irrigation specialist said as we watched water gush from a canal across a brutally arid landscape, "Amazing, isn't it, to see this when we're basically in the 13th century?" There is ample agricultural ingenuity to be harnessed here. In Marjah, where the International Security Assistance Force (ISAF) arrived in February 2010, first to uproot the Taliban and then to win the hearts and minds of the locals, the U.S. marines who surveyed Marjah's poppy fields gazed in wonderment at the desert lands ablaze in Wizard of Oz Technicolor. Many of the young men were from farming communities and could not help but admire the acumen of their Helmand counterparts. Wes Harris is impressed by how the farmers manage to grow soybeans and cotton side by side and to cascade grapevines down desert berms- "using every square centimeter to some end," he says. Given that Marjah's Helmand Province is the source of 54 percent of Afghanistan's opium, the subtext of last year's campaign was clear to all. Far less clear is whether it's working. Operating under the belief that previous forced eradications in Helmand only alienated the farmers and flung them into the sympathetic bosom of the Taliban, the Marines announced last spring that they would pay farmers to eradicate their own crops-$300 per destroyed acre. A substantial number flatly refused to participate. Many of those who did sign on failed to meet the seven-day deadline for the eradication. In a good-faith gesture, the deadline was extended-giving some farmers enough time to first harvest the opium, then collect their check from ISAF. ("Did they turn the poppies over in mid-stride and sneak some past us? Probably so," one military source conceded.) But luck was on the Marines' side: 2010 was a bad growing season for Helmand's poppy farmers, with frost, drought, disease, and insects cutting yields by half.

At Camp Hanson, the Marine regiment's station in Marjah, 200 tons of fertilizer and seed packs sit heaped beside the trucks that just delivered them. One of the trucks has a shattered windshield, and four of the men who drove the convoy here from Helmand's capital, Lashkar Gah, are now in the hospital, having been shot in a Taliban ambush. The seeds-black mung beans, red radishes, alfalfa, watermelon, corn-will be sold to a thousand farmers in the area in the hope that they will quit growing poppies. The commanding officer in Marjah is a tenaciously upbeat young man named Brian Christmas who sounds like Santa Claus when he rattles off the things he would love to see America do for Afghanistan's farmers. "There should be more seed programs available to them next year, at low cost. There have to be alternatives here. Like factories. Why not has a chicken coop, so that they can sell their eggs here in Marjah? Instead of just providing cotton, why not make Marjah yarn? A drug factory that employs 30 guys-I'd like to compete with that and say to those guys, 'Let's send you to a vocational tech school. Get you a small business loan. Set you up in a mechanics shop. Or hey, how about going into the police force? Pretty good salary; go home every night-not a bad gig!'" The next day, dozens of farmers show up to claim their latest inducement, Simply setting foot on the Marine base is a risk that many of the area's farmers have decided not to take. The Taliban have set up checkpoints and relieved passersby of their new commodities. One boy is said to have been made to eat his ISAF-issued registration card. A tribal elder found to be assisting the Marines was "beaten to an amazing shade of green," according to a military interpreter. For most, the Taliban are the devil they know-and, more to the point, the devil who likely still will be here long after the ISAF troops are gone. "These guys are playing both ends against the middle and seeing who's winning," says John Hurrell of Rift Valley Agriculture, the nongovernmental organization (NGO) coordinating the seed and fertilizer distribution. "Whatever pays the best is what they'll grow. Personally, think they'll sell the fertilizer and seed and go back to growing poppies." One of the farmers I encounter filing out of the Marine compound with a bag of seed is equivocal. "It depends on what the local government does after the military leaves," he tells me. "If they leave us alone, then I'll grow poppy." Will the Afghan authorities continue to press for a poppy-free future once the troops have left Helmand? "The minute poppy starts to pop up, there's got to be an immediate reaction-that's all there is to it," says Lieutenant Colonel Christmas. "The Afghan government has gotta be all over that-using local police. Things will get 100 percent better if they have a police force made up of their own people, ones they can trust." Alas, Christmas could recruit only ten locals to join the Marjah police-unsurprising, considering that the Taliban have threatened and in some cases killed civil servants in Helmand. "We have two forms of money here: poppy and American dollars," says a beardless 33-year-old Helmand farmer named Rehmatou as he leaves the Marine base with his fertilizer. "This is our economy. The Taliban aren't pressuring me-that's just a story you see on TV. I grow for myself. I smuggle for myself. The Taliban are not the reason. Poverty is the reason. And they'll keep growing poppies here-unless they're forced not to. Force is the solution for everything. As we say in Pashtu, 'Power can flatten mountains.' "Who will stop the smugglers-the police?" he asks with a laugh. "It's the police who transport our opium in their cars! You see the big buildings in Lashkar Gah and Kandahar. This is money from corruption."

Rehmatou betrays no love for the Taliban- "They're jackals"-but the system they have imposed works for him. Still, his bemused cynicism fades when I ask, "Is a poppy economy really all that bad for Afghanistan?" "This is a bad way to make money," Rehmatou says gravely. "It trains you for no other occupation. When a father feeds a boy with money from poppies, he will grow poppies too. He'll have no other skill. We have no carpenters, no engineers, and no mechanics. We have nothing." With a sad smile, the farmer says, "It is a kind of cancer on our country." Is it possible for the cancer to be removed? Bordering Pakistan to the east, Nangarhar Province has long been a drug smuggling thoroughfare, and its mountainous reaches-which include the Khyber Pass and the Tora Bora cave complex-are notoriously lawless. With its Mediterranean climate, Nangarhar was Afghanistan's biggest opium producer as recently as 2004. Forced eradications began in 2005, but the government's promises of alternative livelihoods were not met initially, and even the provincial capital of Jalalabad remained underdeveloped and quiet. Today the city and its environs appear to be a post-poppy success story. The fertile countryside, long regarded as Afghanistan's breadbasket, is alight with red cabbages and tomatoes. Jalalabad's streets are now among the most vibrant in Afghanistan, and at its teeming wholesale market, hundreds of trucks arrive every morning, bearing dozens of crops such as watermelon, potatoes, squash, okra, and onions. None of this rival the cash value of opium, and one potato farmer meet at the market tells me that he works an evening job as a security guard to make ends meet. "But don't regret it-I'm glad not to be growing poppy anymore," he says. In the village of Yaghi Band, which once grew poppies almost exclusively, a group of tribal elders reflect on Nangarhar's post-poppy era in a room overlooking fields of cotton, rice, broccoli, and other crops. "The life isn't as good as it was five years ago," one of them says. "But it's 60 percent of what we had. And we're hopeful of the new projects." Among these projects is one situated directly below us: a hydroelectrically powered textile mill, set up by a USAID affiliate. Contributions to the province from such programs seem endless. Among those I visit are new irrigation dams and canals, new bridges, a women's weaving co-op, a potato chip factory, a honey processing plant, a jam manufacturing facility, and the city's wholesale market, whose deputy director, Khwaja Mohammad, praises the contributions of NGOs but then adds, "Afghanistan is still at war. We can't stand on our own two feet. If a country's been at war for 30 years, it may take 80 years to rebuild it. If the farmers don't continue to receive assistance, you can't expect them not to grow poppy." Eighty years of assistance? Is poppy-free Nangarhar a Potemkin village propped up by aid from the West? What might it cost to offer equivalent generosity to Badakhshan and Helmand, and would it make a difference? When I put these questions to Nasrullah Bakhtani, senior agriculturalist for Afghanistan's Ministry of Agriculture, he says, "Nangarhar has a tribal system. There's one big man in the village, and people accept what he says. The governor there talked to these elders. He asked, 'If we eradicate poppies, what will you need?' Proposals came from the people, and the government said, 'OK, we'll provide those if you stop growing.' As you see, Nangarhar has a lot of projects, people are happy, so they stopped. Helmand and Badakhshan don't have those kinds of tribal structures." Bakhtani once grew poppies himself. He stopped in 2002 when Afghanistan's new president, Hamid Karzai, declared that poppy cultivation should cease. As an agriculture specialist, Bakhtani was asked that year by the Karzai administration to help prepare a road map for a post-poppy Afghanistan. That paper, "Scientific Guidelines for Reduction of Poppy," advocated the introduction of alternative crops, expansion of irrigation systems, modernization of animal husbandry techniques, rehabilitation of the northern forests to diminish soil erosion, establishment of textile plants, federal subsidies for seed and fertilizer-in short, the entire laundry list now being implemented by the West. But Bakhtani believes such programs must be community based not some carrot-and-stick-and-more-carrots approach by outsiders. To circumnavigate the government's pervasive corruption, Bakhtani has in mind an elaborate set of checks and balances whereby a national ministry contracts an organization to start a new project in a particular community. The money for the project would be put in a bank account, and both the community and the ministry would monitor how the contractor spends it. Under this system, he envisions a network of badly needed irrigation canals and drought-resistant pistachio forests in Badakhshan. He imagines greenhouses in Helmand, so that the province can produce off-season tomatoes and other such crops that sell for high prices. This is the future as Nasrullah Bakhtani imagines it, brighter than a poppy field.

The Taliban Progress

In many ways, the conditions of millions of Afghans have considerably improved since the demise of the Taliban regime. Millions of children are back to school and have better access to health care. In many parts of Afghanistan, especially cities like Kabul, Afghan women enjoy considerably greater social opportunities. The human capital of Afghanistan, especially among its large young population, has significantly increased. And at least some ministries are developing an increasing capacity to provide administration and governance. For many, economic opportunities have expanded greatly. (In fact, well-positioned Afghans have taken advantage of the influx of foreign aid to reap unprecedented rents). Yet insecurity and violence persist and undermine the fragile socioeconomic progress. Moreover, the scaling down of U.S. and international involvement will likely shrink much of the political and social space necessary for the expansion and consolidation of these accomplishments. The Complex Military Situation The surge of U.S. military forces in 2010 and 2011 did reverse the Taliban military momentum in Afghanistan's south. Many middle-level Taliban commanders have been removed from the battlefield, disrupting the Taliban's operational capacity and logistical networks. Rank-and-file Taliban soldiers in the south are feeling the heat and many are exhausted by the fighting. Some important and some symbolic Taliban strongholds have been retaken from the Taliban. Ordinary Afghans even in areas that bore the brunt of U.S. fighting, such as Lashkar Gah and Arghandab, are wary of the handover of those areas to the Afghan national security forces (ANSF) and do not necessarily welcome the pull back of U.S. forces from their areas, fearing the return of the Taliban. Yet it would be a mistake to interpret this success as a clear Taliban defeat in the south. While it is true that Taliban is no longer capable of mounting major military operations, it has learned that targeted assassinations of key political and tribal figures and government officials and persistent insidious intimidation accomplish many of its objectives. Some supposedly-cleared areas, such as Mallajat, an important sub district of Kandahar City, have seen a substantial deterioration of security already. Moreover, the Taliban understands that the time is on its side. The June 2011 announcement by President Barack Obama of the drawdown of U.S. forces also defined the mission in increasingly narrow counterterrorism terms and indicated that the United States would be substantially leaving Afghanistan irrespective of the conditions on the ground. From the Taliban perspective, there is no need now to mount extensive military operations: all it needs to do is to maintain a persistent level of insecurity sufficient to prevent the government from delivering public goods and to discredit in the eyes of the local population the capacity of ANSF to provide adequate security. Its spate of bombing attacks in areas handed over to ANSF since June, including in Kabul, indicates these tactics are indeed two key elements of its strategy. From now through 2014 when the U.S. greatly reduces its troop deployments, it is thus not necessary for the Taliban to visibly control territory in order to maintain enough social control. In fact, the logical strategy for the Taliban now is to, at least partially, hold back. Indeed, as the 2014 security handover to the Afghan government will be approaching, the military and political influence of the United States and NATO's International Security Assistance Force (ISAF) in Afghanistan will be declining. The international community's ability to shape developments in Afghanistan and in the broader region will be shrinking rapidly. An agreement on a long-term U.S.-Afghanistan partnership may resurrect some of the U.S. influence. Especially if it is specific and credible, such an agreement may to some extent assure Afghans of a U.S. long-term commitment to their country. But it is unlikely to resurrect the leverage the United States and the international community enjoyed before the drawdown decision. Nor is it likely to sufficiently reduce the Afghans' profound insecurity over the anticipated collapse of the existing political order and hence sway them away from hedging on all sides and seeking to maximize power and profit before it all comes down. Such perfectly rational individual decisions however fundamentally undermine the prospect of avoiding a major political meltdown in 2014 and the possibility of a civil war. The quality of the Afghan national security forces, on which preserving stability hinges to a great extent, also still remains questionable. The Afghan National Police (ANP) in particular continue to suffer from many vices and deficiencies, not the least of which is an absolute lack of capacity to suppress crime—the scourge of the lives of Afghans that eviscerates their security and provides a perfect mobilization platform for the Taliban. The Afghan National Army (ANA) has made large progress: Not only has it grown in size, but also its quality has improved. The coming two years will show how much capacity to tackle the Taliban and other forms of insecurity it has. But even the ANA represents hardly a clear-cut success. Worrisomely, it appears to be deeply ethnically-factionalized. Most of its high-level commanders continue to be northern Tajiks, and southern Pashtuns exhibit little interest in signing up for even rank-and-file positions. Thus, there is a real danger that the ANA may fracture along ethnic lines and around particular commanders when the foreigners leave. The militias mushrooming around Afghanistan with or without the encouragement of ISAF often prove unreliable and incapable of standing up to the Taliban, yet they frequently bring other forms of insecurity to an area. Often, they undermine good governance and peaceable relations within and among Afghan communities. The Afghan Local Police (ALP), one of such militia forces, have the most stringent oversight mechanisms compared to the other militias, but even in its case, the oversight exists mainly during the vetting phase of standing it up. Even in the ALP's case, mechanisms are lacking for rolling it back should some of its units go rogue. Moreover, precisely because the absolutely necessary vetting takes time, the ALP currently numbers in the low thousands, with a growth of about 1,000 ALP fighters per half a year; thus the ALP can hardly be counted upon as a game-changer. However, sacrificing the vetting procedures and rushing to stand up the ALP faster will likely plunge it into the same abuse and unreliability problems that other militia forces have exhibited, only intensifying conflict dynamics in Afghanistan.

In the eastern Afghanistan, the military situation so far has been one of a stalemate but at increasing levels of violence. Since the Taliban has managed to reverse some of ISAF's gains there in 2006, the level of insecurity has increased considerably. The insurgency there—a mixture of the Haqqani network and Salafi hardcore fighters from around the world—is vicious and a highly potent military force. It is willing to prosecute Pakistan's anti-India objectives, and yet it is at the same time deeply sympathetic to the Pakistani Taliban's objective of bringing down the Pakistani government. It is also highly motivated to strike U.S. and Western targets abroad. As 2014 approaches, ISAF is likely to continue grappling with the difficult dilemma of how many of its forces to pull back from Afghanistan's south and deploy to the east. A significant troop reduction in the south can jeopardize the gains there, but it may be necessary to degrade the potency of the eastern insurgency that from a counterterrorism perspective is far more dangerous to the United States than even the Kandahar-centered insurgency. Moreover, Pakistani anti-government groups, such as Tehrik-i-Taliban—Pakistan are now using eastern Afghanistan as a safe haven, giving the impression to some in the Pakistani military and intelligence services that the U.S. is using their tool of tolerating militant safe havens as a way to teach them a lesson. Pakistan wants the eastern Afghanistan safe havens the anti-Pakistan militants are using closed. The north of Afghanistan experienced a steady decline in security even as the military surge was taking place in the south, precipitating the deployment of a U.S. brigade to the North in 2011. The Taliban has been rather effectively mobilizing among the northern Pashtuns who perceive themselves to be discriminated by the Tajiks. It has also been exploiting other ethnic tensions, such as between Tajiks and Uzbcks, as well as the popular disenchantment with some of the North's notorious commanders cum governors. Its assassination campaign against key leaders in the North has left Kunduz, Baghlan, and even others parts deeply destabilized. Poor Governance and Political Tensions As of the end of 2011, the political situation in Afghanistan is at its worse since 2002. Political patronage networks have been shrinking and becoming more exclusionary, including those surrounding President Hamid Karzai and the Arg Palace. Afghans are profoundly alienated from the national government and other power arrangements they face. They are deeply dissatisfied with the inability and unwillingness of Kabul to provide elemental public goods and with the pervasive corruption of country's powcr elites, poignantly demonstrated by the corruption at Afghanistan's leading financial institution, the Kabul Bank. Local government officials have only had a limited capacity and motivation to redress the broader governance deficiencies. The level of inter-elite infighting, much of it along ethnic and regional lines, is also at the highest level since the overthrow of the Taliban. The result is pervasive hedging on the part of key powerbrokers, including by recreating their semi-clandestine or officially-sanctioned militias. Undertones of preparations for a civil war are sounding more strongly. 2014 will bring a triple earthquake to Afghanistan and its current political dispensation: Not only will ISAF forces be substantially reduced, but U.S. funding will also inevitably decline with the drawdown of U.S. military as well as due to U.S. domestic economic conditions. For a country that it still overwhelmingly dependent on foreign aid and illegal economies for its revenues, the outcome is likely going to be a massive economic shrinkage, notwithstanding the efforts to create a New Silk Road through Afghanistan and exploit Afghanistan's large mineral resources. Although various efforts are now under way to cushion the shock, there are no easy ways to generate revenues and employment in Afghanistan over the next three years. Moreover, 2014 is also the year of another presidential election and hence of major power infighting, whether or not President Karzai will seek to remain in power. The fight over the remaining rents of the ending political dispensation and the need to consolidate one's support camps in anticipation of the shaky future, and hence to deliver spoils to them in order to assure their allegiance, will not be conducive to consensus decision making and broad-based good governance. If the current political order in Afghanistan indeed collapses, what are the likely outcomes? One possible scenario is a civil war that will resemble less the 1990s when the Taliban line of control progressively moved north past the Shomali plain, and more a highly fractured, highly localized fighting among a variety of groupings and powerbrokers, only one of which will be the Taliban and its Haqqani and other factions. Outside actors, including Iran, Pakistan, Russia, China, and India, will find it irresistible to once again cultivate their favored proxies to prosecute at least their minimal objectives in Afghanistan and the region. Their rivalries in Afghanistan will spill beyond that country and intensify their competition in other domains as well. An alternative post-2014 political outcome is a military coup. The ANA has two more years of very intensive work to approach becoming a more professional force, and the Afghan Ministry of Defense is likely to be one of the best functioning ministries. A professional army, especially one whose leadership is heavily skewed to northern Tajiks, could well see taking power as the only alternative to civil war as the ISAF forces pull out. The pattern would be familiar to both Afghanistan and the region, including Pakistan and Turkey. Many ordinary Afghans may well prefer a military strongman or junta to a civil war. However, whether such a move could avert a civil war would depend on many factors, including the relative strength of the ANA at that time and the willingness of Kandahar Durranis who have ruled the country for centuries to put up with a diminished power in Kabul. The Pakistan Troubles Pakistan in particular will be ensnared in Afghanistan's troubles. Ten years after 9/11 Pakistan continues to be preoccupied with India's ascendance and its perceived ambitions in Afghanistan and deeply distrustful of U.S. objectives there. This distrust has preceded the U.S. raid into Pakistan to kill Osama bin Laden: at a fundamental level, Pakistan still sees its national security objectives as at odds with those of the United States, while its polity is more anti-American than ever. It is suspect of U.S. ultimate goals in Afghanistan and fearful of a U.S. plot to seize its nuclear weapons, which it sees as the crux of its security with respect to the conventionally-superior India. Moreover, Pakistan also doubts the ability of the United States to establish a secure government in Afghanistan, especially one that will not be hostile to Pakistan. So it pursues cultivating allies in Afghanistan, mainly among the Taliban factions, as a protection policy. Pakistan continues to see a pro-Pakistan or at least a not-pro-India government in Kabul as critical for its security. Consequently, it persists in its links and manipulation of the Taliban insurgencies for its purposes, whether on the battlefield or in the developing negotiations between Kabul, the United States, and the Taliban. At the same time, the fissiparous and fraying tendencies within Pakistan are intensifying along a multitude of dimensions. Its institutions are hollowed out. Its military is struggling to beat back its internal insurgencies, including worryingly in southern Punjab. Karachi has been a civil-war-like battleground for months. Pakistan's civil government has been unable to govern in even the economic sphere and abdicated the responsibility for decision making in many other domains. And the country faces many deep long-term challenges of energy and water deficiencies, large population growth, and limited employment opportunities. Negotiations with the Taliban Until 2010, the United States was reluctant to embrace negotiations with the Taliban, even as its European allies argued that there is no military only solution to the Afghanistan predicament. Since 2010, the United States has not only embraced negotiations, but taken an active role in them, engaging not only with the Kandahar-based Taliban but also the Haqqanis. Can such negotiations provide a mechanism to avoid the collapse of the existing order in Afghanistan post-2014 and can the U.S. redline of no-support of the reconciled Taliban for Al-Qaida is assured? It is unlikely that the Taliban would be willing to settle for anything less than a de facto, if not de jure power in Kabul while retaining the power it already has in much of the south. Elements of especially the Kandahar faction of the Taliban may well have learned that its association with Al-Qaida ultimately cost them their power, but the group also owes many debts to the global jihadist movement. The death of bin Ladenmay have weakened some of the networks, but reneging on these debts to their global jihadi brothers will be costly for the Taliban, no matter how locally oriented its southern and northern elements are. The Taliban's decision making on severing their links with other jihadists will be deeply influenced by the relative power between the southern Taliban and the eastern Taliban groupings. Similarly, the Taliban faces some tough dilemmas in agreeing to a compromise with Kabul, such as accepting the Afghan constitution. Such a promise and an overt power sharing deal with Kabul will discredit the group with respect to many of its fighters as well as with respect to the broader population to whom it appeals on the basis of Kabul's venal, predatory, and unjust behavior. Its best negotiation strategy thus may well be akin to its best fighting strategy: engage in talks without giving up anything while waiting it out to after 2014. The shape and content of negotiations is inevitably linked to what happens on the military battlefield and each side's assessments of its military strength and prospects for achieving a better deal through military means. The Taliban thus does not need to rush to conclude negotiations or commit to substantially giving up its power, such as by disarming, before 2014. Meanwhile, any negotiations with the Taliban are extremely worrisome to the northerners in Afghanistan. Memories of the Taliban's brutal rule of the 1990s and the Northern Alliance's fight against the Taliban loom large in their minds, and they also fear the loss of military and economic power they accumulated during the 2000s. Key northern leaders may prefer a war to a deal that they would see as compromising their security and power. All these worries were exacerbated by the September 2011 assassination of Burhanuddin Rabbani, a prominent Tajik northerner, Afghanistan's former president, and Karzai's key man for negotiating with the Taliban. Many took the assassination to mean that the Taliban is not interested in a negotiated outcome. More broadly, the assassination is yet another indication that there are many spoilers in Afghanistan who have the capacity to subvert new emerging conflict settlements and power arrangements. The Continuing U.S. Interests in Afghanistan Even in an absence of an outright civil war, even the minimal counterterrorism objectives will be compromised if a stable national government is not capable of effectively ruling from Kabul. Air strikes to decapitate terrorist groups and decimate its fighters depend to some degree on human intelligence. Once ISAF's presence shrinks, local proxies in Afghanistan are likely to provide only self-servicing intelligence, such as that which hurts their political rivals, no matter how large payoffs by outsiders they are offered. A very unstable Afghanistan or one in an outright civil war will allow the global salafi movement to once again claim victory over a superpower and provide an important psychological fillip to jihadi terrorists at a time when their appeal in the Muslim world is waning as a result of the Arab Spring. Moreover, an unstable Afghanistan will be like an ulcer bleeding into Pakistan, further destabilizing that country and discouraging its elites to find a modus vivendi with India and focus on Pakistan's massive internal problems. What Can Still Be Done? With the shrinking U.S. influence and determination to significantly scale down its involvement in Afghanistan, what can be done to avert this disastrous outcome, beyond more intense training of and partnering with the Afghan National Army? Developing mechanisms to reduce ethnic fractionalization in the ANA will be critical, as is reducing corruption within the ANP. Working on removing Taliban commanders and groups from the battlefield—whether through fighting, reintegration, or strategic-level negotiations—has some potential of reducing the overall level of instability come 2014. It is important to try to encourage the widening of political patronage networks to give a greater number of Afghans a stake in the preservation of the current political order. Persuading President Karzai to adopt such a view, however, requires a radical improvement in the U.S. relationship with the Afghan president. Focusing on the most destabilizing corruption, such as in the ANSF and that which is very ethnically and tribally discriminatory, should be a key priority. So is mitigating at least the most egregious abuses by Afghan powerbrokers, including those through which ISAF prosecutes its military objectives. To improve governance and reduce rent-seeking incentives for perpetuating instability, the United States should significantly curtail aid flows to unstable areas and instead allocate resources to projects where existing security and governance arrangements permit vigilant monitoring and which are sustainable in the long term. Efforts to reduce political tensions also must include an early focus on providing for an acceptable political transition in Afghanistan in 2014. To reduce the intensity of the 2014 political earthquake, the transition must enjoy at least some elite consensus and some popular support. Reasonably clean elections would be an optimal mechanism, but that may be elusive at this point, given the shrinking leverage of the international community. Finally, reinforcing existing institutions that are performing reasonably well, such as particular ministries, may boost the administrative capacity of the state to weather the political earthquake of 2014. A successful implementation of these steps does not guarantee that political stability in Afghanistan can be preserved beyond 2014 and that a civil war can be avoided. However, in the absence of a renewed determination to stay longer in Afghanistan with a robust military deployment, the U.S. and international influence in Afghanistan and their options for policy action have shrunk. Conflict is a universal condition, post older than diplomacy. While conflict is a constant in human history, the nature of armed conflict, and especially the nature of 21st-century warfare, has been transformed. General Rupert Smith identified these changes in his book The Utility of Force: "The ends for which we fight are changing; we fight amongst the people; our conflicts tend to be timeless; we fight so as not to lose the force; on each occasion new uses are found for old weapons; the sides are mostly non-state."2 The nature of 21st-century diplomacy is also changing. To be successful, diplomats must simultaneously shape, act upon, and react to global challenges. As Hans Binnendijk and Richard Kugler of the National Defense University argue, no single problem, danger, or threat holds the key to the world's future. What matters is their interaction and the simultaneity of our responses.3 the definition of victory, too, is different today. Twenty-first-century national security success will encompass a comprehensive definition of security, and will be achieved by the broadest simultaneous application of all elements of national power. This is the key to understanding Philip Bobbitt's concept of "preclusive victory," which he describes as "anticipatory, precautionary attention to possible futures,"4 requiring an expansive and integrated approach to modern diplomacy, defense, and development. A diplomatic strategy designed to produce preclusive victory will include conflict prevention, successful negotiation, deterrence, the preparation for conflict should all else fail, and efforts to establish order, ensure stability, and promote political and economic pluralism after conflict. Diplomats have always been participants in both the prevention and management of conflict and its aftermath. The conflict prevention side of diplomacy occupied much of my time at the State Department from 1993 to 1997 as the Department's Executive Secretary and U.S. Ambassador to Turkey. Post conflict diplomacy was a defining issue of the last third of my career at State as Assistant Secretary of State for European Affairs and as Under Secretary of State for Political Affairs from 2001 to 2005. I have tried to draw upon my experiences and observations to discuss here the scope and complexity of modern diplomacy, the methods and goals needed to prevent conflict, diplomacy's role when conflict is or seems to be unavoidable, and the contribution diplomacy can make to restoring stability following conflict. Diplomacy and Conflict Prevention Thanks to the efforts of scholars and practitioners, we can now make better use of the methods and theory of conflict prevention. The United States Institute of Peace and the Woodrow Wilson International Center for Scholars are two among many institutions that have taken a leadership role in these efforts. Michael Lund, a practitioner scholar, notes that the present uncoordinated and patchy nature of preventive diplomacy reflects the absence of any accepted international conflict prevention regime or system of governance—that is, of agreed upon arrangements through which geographic jurisdictions are allocated, functional responsibilities are assigned, norms and procedures are formulated, and actors are held accountable for their responsibilities.5 He asks the crucial question to all those who seek to "coordinate and rationalize" a system of preventive diplomacy: where should responsibility for the tasks of preventive action be located—early warning, the decision to act, the formulation of a response, or the provision of bureaucratic and political support? Should it be horizontal, across different organizations or actors, or should it be vertical, up or down their chains of command? 6 An example of conflict prevention that meets Lund's tests was the effort undertaken by the North Atlantic Treaty Organization (NATO), in close collaboration with the European Union (EU) and the Organization for Security and Co-operation in Europe, and supported by the United States, to avoid civil war in Macedonia in 2001. It is difficult now to recall that, until September 11, 2001, the possibility of civil war in Macedonia was a leading international headline. This successful campaign of conflict prevention was defined by the remarkable personal and institutional cooperation between the NATO Secretary General Lord Robertson and the EU High Representative for the Common Foreign and Security Policy (and a former NATO Secretary General) Javier Solana. post spoke often during this period to Lord Robertson, Solana, and Ambassador James Par dew, whom President George W. Bush and Secretary Colin Powell appointed as the U.S. representative to the effort and who, along with Francois Leotard, the EU Special Envoy, played a crucial role in negotiating and implementing the Ohrid Framework Agreement. As a direct participant, senior NATO official Mark Laity stated that there are insights about modern diplomacy and conflict prevention to be drawn from this effort, including the need for personal and institutional teamwork, the importance of early engagement in trying to head off violence, the need to choose the right people for tasks of this kind (including 21st-century diplomats who can act "unconventionally"), and the necessity of being able to apply appropriate force quickly.7 Diplomacy When Conflict Is or Seems to Be Unavoidable When diplomacy fails to prevent conflict, the role of the diplomat changes The new requirement may be to justify the use of force when all efforts to avoid conflict fail or to seek to address the underlying source of conflict when force is or seems to be inevitable and imperative. The February 1999 diplomatic negotiations in Rambouillet, France, were designed to show the world that NATO and the Contact Group were willing to make one last effort to avoid using military force to stop Slobodan Milosevic's attacks in Kosovo. was in Rambouillet as Assistant Secretary of State for European Affairs to support Secretary Madeleine Albright. After the first day or so of the meeting, there was so much chaos that urged Secretary Albright to depart Rambouillet and leave the "negotiating" to those of us more junior. My strategy was that by not being present, the Secretary of State— and the administration—could keep a distance from an outcome that might be unacceptable to the United States. The Secretary had a different vision. Albright hoped Rambouillet would end the brutality against the Kosovars, but she was also prepared for the meeting to fail, and thereby all options for avoiding military conflict would be exhausted. Her idea was that we had to be seen to be doing everything we could diplomatically, including her continued presence, so that if Rambouillet was a failure, there could be no further excuses against taking military action. Secretary of State James Baker had pursued a similar strategy before the first Gulf War in 1991. Baker relates in his memoirs, The Politics of Diplomacy, that President George H.W. Bush had concluded the United States should offer a meeting in Washington for Iraqi Foreign Minister Tariq Aziz followed by a Baker trip to Baghdad to show America's commitment to avoiding war if possible. Baker writes that he thought this proposal had three merits: it would give the administration one last diplomatic opening to avoid war; it would shore up domestic support for conflict; and it would show that, as the deadline for Iraq's withdrawal from Kuwait neared, the administration was doing something other than just preparing for war. The President's offer turned into the famous meeting between Baker and Aziz on January 9, 1991. As Baker recounts, "was under no illusions. assumed the talks would be unsuccessful and that within a matter of days, we would be at war."8 In 2001– 2003, the State Department leadership generally saw Iraq as a diversion from Afghanistan and not central to the war on terror. Saddam Hussein was a dictator and a menace— but "in a box," posing no immediate, direct threat to the United States; focus should be kept on defeating al Qaeda in Afghanistan and supporting the new Afghan government.9 Iraq had been a source of tension and disagreement inside the State Department since the beginning of the administration, and there were some who sought to move the policy from support for "smart" United Nations (UN) sanctions toward an aggressive posture against Saddam. Secretary of State Henry Kissinger wrote in Years of Upheaval about the second term of the Nixon administration that State Department culture emphasizes negotiability, which is a consciousness of what the other side will accept.10 Kissinger did not consider this trait a particular positive at the time, and the department's culture of negotiability did not serve as a good guide to institutional behavior for most of the senior State officials who participated in the interagency debate leading to the invasion of Iraq. If that was so during the period surrounding 1970s détente with Russia, diplomatic efforts with the Shah of Iran, and the crisis in the Middle East and the resulting 1973 war, this culture of negotiability no longer served as a good guide to institutional behavior for most of the senior State officials who participated in the interagency debate leading to the invasion of Iraq. We took part in planning for the conflict and its aftermath assuming—or hoping—that events either at home or abroad would turn preparations for conflict into successful coercive diplomacy rather than the military action that was ordered in the spring of 2003. The State Department's Director of Policy Planning, Richard Haass, observed that while he was "60:40 against going to war... no organization could function if people left every time they lost out on a 60:40 decision."11 Haass was operating under the belief that Iraq had weapons of mass destruction; if he had known they did not, he says he would have been 90:10 against the war. And no senior Department of State officer resigned in protest. The department sought instead to try to recreate the successful Gulf War coalition of President George H.W. Bush and argued that the United States and its allies might compel Saddam to submit through a deployment of force in the region in early 2003. If this failed, there should be a sustained diplomatic effort to create a broad coalition to move militarily later in 2003. This possibility of a broad international coalition lost all relevance on January 20, 2003, when the French government announced that it would never support a second UN Security Council resolution to authorize the use of force in Iraq. Diplomacy in Preparation for Conflict Once conflict is inevitable or is initiated, one job of diplomats is to support military commanders in getting what they need to make conflict as short as possible, with the fewest casualties for Americans, allies, and civilians. This was the objective that the United States pursued in Turkey before the first Gulf War, which resulted in President Turgut Özal's support of American efforts. The diplomatic effort to prepare for conflict in Kosovo also involved the whole of the U.S. Government and the governments of the NATO Allies. To pursue a successful bombing campaign, diplomats in many NATO countries arranged for over flight and support for Allied forces. A similar effort by U.S. diplomats took place before the invasion of Afghanistan in 2001. American and allied diplomats worked closely with nations surrounding Afghanistan, including forging contacts with Central Asian states on security issues for the first time in order to achieve transit, over flight, and bed-down rights for American and coalition forces before the October 7, 2001, beginning of action in Afghanistan, Before the invasion of Iraq in March 2003, and especially after January 20, 2003, a similar effort began in earnest. Diplomats supported U.S. Central Command commander General Tommy Franks in order to make the war as short and successful as possible and to limit American, allied, and Iraqi civilian casualties. American diplomats worked with military commanders to seek access to facilities for U.S. forces and to participate in the public diplomacy effort to gain as much support as possible for the armed liberation of Iraq. American diplomats and Pentagon officials again paid particular attention to Turkey in an effort to convince the Turks to allow the 4th Infantry Division to transit that country to create a northern front in the battle against Saddam's forces. Although the State Department worried about the size of the Department of Defense request to Ankara, it worked closely with both civilian and military authorities at the Pentagon to try to meet the need that had been identified by the Chairman of the Joint Chiefs of Staff. Joint –State diplomacy, however, could not overcome a negative vote in the Turkish parliament, which reflected strong public opposition to the war. The way the debate about using force is carried out inside the government influences attitudes and actions during and after conflict as well as future decisions on whether or not to use force. Military force may restore security, but it cannot resolve political or cultural sources of conflict. As Rupert Smith writes, "We are engaging in conflict for objectives that do not lead to a resolution of the matter directly by force of arms, since at all but the most basic tactical level our objectives tend to concern the intentions of the people and their leaders rather than their territory or forces."12 Smith argues that the civil-military structure designed to make political-military decisions is "deeply problematic" and distorts decisional king in many ways.13 In his book, Smith imagines a debate between British Foreign and Commonwealth Office (FCO) and Ministry of Defense (MOD) officials about how to address the genocide taking place over a number of weeks in Rwanda during the summer of 1994.

Introduction: Afghanistan Natural Resources and Development

The history of development of natural resources in Afghanistan has been fraught with international intrigue for several centuries. At the present time a future in Afghanistan without a continuation of multinational competition does not look likely, although the stakes may seem to have increased. A look back into early resource developments in the country may offer better comprehension of problems to avoid and best possible procedures for success and for the betterment of the beleaguered people of Afghanistan, as well as insights to reduce regional tensions. This paper is about the newly developing role of natural resources in helping heal the divided nation, although the potential for severe failure exists as well, and must be carefully guarded against lest that become an unfortunate alternate reality The Saxon Empire first initiated resource assessments in Afghanistan in the early nineteenth century as they searched through pioneering exploration and military escapades for countries to dominate as markets and trading partners (Elphinstone, 1815; Shroder, 1983). From the time of their first geological mapping and mineralresource assessments in Afghanistan (Drummond, 1841; Hutton, 1846; Greisbach, 1881, 1887), and on into the twentieth century (Hayden, 1913; Fox, 1943; Gee and Seth, 1940), the British maintained a comprehensive interest in resources of Afghanistan. This was done while also improving their military intelligence on resources and topographic detail that would be needed in the event of any unrest in the machinations of their Great Game face-off against the Saxon-Russian Empire, and as long as they could maintain their British Raj (rule) of the Indian subcontinent. A number of other nationalities (German, French, Russian) also looked at geology and resources in the country from time to time but nothing much seemed to come of their explorations. Following the third Anglo-Afghan War in 1919, Afghanistan won its independence from diplomatic domination by the British and it was not long after that a Soviet publication on mineral "riches" first appeared (Obruchev, 1927), published by a man who later came to be revered as an early Russian 'father' of geologic studies. Nevertheless, in spite of early attempts by the government of Afghanistan to entice Americans to become engaged in resource discovery and extraction in the country (Anonymous, 1937; Clapp, 1939), distance from market, economic concerns, and looming worries about World War II caused rejection of the overtures, much to the discomfiture of the government of Afghanistan. In spite of a number of discoveries by the American geologist Fox (1943) and others, post-war assessment by an American geographer (Michel, 1959) concluded shortsightedly that there were no useful resources in Afghanistan about which there should be any diplomatic concern. 1-With its attention on resources accordingly diverted elsewhere for decades to come, the US Department of State thus quite missed the resource ball when in the 1960s and 1970s, as many as ~250 Soviet geoscientists went to work mapping geology in the country while only one American geologist (co-author of this paper, John Shroder) was in the country, plus a few visiting geology attachés from the US Embassy and USGS seismic specialists who visited from time to time (Shroder, 1983; Shroder and Asifi, 1987; Shroder and Watrel, 1992). The resulting Soviet collaboration with the Afghanistan Geological Survey detailed a wide store of mineral resources in the country (Abdullah et al., 1980). The result of this Cold-War confrontation between the USA and the USSR in Afghanistan was that the neighboring USSR was able to fairly easily sidestep or ignore developing resources in Afghanistan until conditions were more to its liking as it consolidated its preeminent position in the country, ultimately leading to its invasion in 1979. With its already dominant roles in the Afghanistan Cartographic Institute, the Afghanistan Geological Survey, and many other ministries, the USSR was in a position in the early

1980s to completely take over all resource extraction in Afghanistan. Indeed they did pump much natural gas across the northern border of the Amu Darya into the USSR where the gauges to measure delivered volumes were located, and plans were made for development of other resources (Shroder, 1983; Shroder and Assifi, 1987; Shroder and Watrel, 1992). In addition, the Aynak copper deposit near Kabul was investigated in detail and a smelter scheduled for installation in the mid 1980s. In an interesting sidelight of these times in the early 1980s, a Soviet-Afghan convoy from Aynak was assaulted by the Mujahideen and the captured documents that were sent to co-author Shroder by British sources (Shroder and Asifi, 1987) proved that the Aynak copper lode was one of the largest in the world, as proved out by a plethora of kilometer-deep boreholes that allowed the Soviets to sample the deposit extensively. The increasing resistance of the Afghan people and the Mujahideen, however, together with significant assistance from the USA to the resistance in the final cumulative battles of the Cold War, precluded significant further development of any resources at that time. Instead the Soviet withdrawal in defeat occurred in 1988-89, and the first Bush presidency initiated the closing of the US Embassy in Kabul a few years thereafter. Subsequently, the willful ignorance and depredations of the Taliban began in the 1990s, and Osama bin Laden, who had learned enough of the Afghanistan culture during the Soviet-Afghan War to highjack its hospitality for the benefit of Al Qaeda, initiated the 9/11 horror against the USA. The subsequent invasion of Afghanistan by the USA and coalition troops in 2001 began a new phase in the history of Afghanistan, as many old resource projects were assessed again, and new ones were initiated (Shroder, 2003, 2004, 2007, 2009). Interdependence and the demise of hegemony? The military dominance of the United States in world affairs following the demise of the Soviet Union has become a geopolitical reality for the past 20 years. However, military dominance has not necessarily translated into a classical self-serving hegemonic influence that one might expect from a "hyperpower." As Amy Chua has argued in Days of Empire (2009), the United States' willingness to develop a more global system of trade and opportunities has defined it very differently from past powers. Thus America's exercise of power may be considered "posthegemonic," insofar that that it has also allowed the development of erstwhile enemies such as China and Japan in their global reach. Thus one can argue that without America's opening trade flows for Japanese and Chinese consumer goods the development of these Asian economies would not have been possible. Yet there are forces at play within the United States that detract from this more pluralistic vision of exercising power. Protectionism and an attempt to blithely support American corporate interests in battlegrounds such as Afghanistan are nevertheless a looming threat to this positive exercise of power. 2-Furthermore, it can be argued that America's approach to globalization has been confined by particular rules of the game, which can also constrain development. Alice Amsden has made this claim in her work Escape from Empire (2008), where she argues that the imposition of particular structures on development investment in accordance with American priorities has led to distorted development and an entrenchment of corrupt elites in developing countries. Countries that resisted these structures, such as the BRIC (Brazil, Russia, India and China) countries, have flourished more productively. Yet, the mere fact that the United States has continued to partner with all the "renegade" countries that did not exactly follow their prescribed model suggests that we may be moving beyond any hegemonic imperative. 3- As the case of Afghanistan's mineral investment shows, even where the US has direct military involvement in a country, it has allowed China and India to both gain influence, often to the chagrin of other allies like Pakistan. Parag Khanna (2008) has acknowledged the competition between the U.S., China and Europe for economic dominance in Asia, but concludes that the old world of hyperpower influence can no longer be functional even if one of these powers wanted to exercise that influence. China has emerged as a development agent with few strings attached for developing countries to partner with. This is clearly empowering for the developing world in terms of postcolonial shifts of power back to the colonized. However, given the lack of political freedoms in China, the power that the country can wield leaves some cause for concern. Amartya Sen's warning about decoupling development from freedom needs to be better appreciated: "when things go well, the protective power of democracy may be less missed, but dangers can lie around the corner." 4- Fortunately, the interconnections between all the major economic and military powers have now made unilateral misconduct more difficult. However, such interconnections and leverage is only useful when it is exercised effectively. Without suitable leadership and a willingness to engage with tenets of global performance on issues such as environmental and social indicators, there can be a tendency towards "negative cooperation." Such cooperation can perpetuate the status quo in terms of exploitation of the less powerful by an acquiescence of nation stat Such cooperation canperpetuate the status quo in terms of exploitation of the less powerful by an acquiescence of nation states in the misconduct of one cooperative agent. An example of this phenomenon is the reluctance of the United States and the European Union to exercise more influence on China with regard to the deteriorating human rights situation in Myanmar (Burma). Twenty years ago Robert Keohane presciently argued in his classic work After Hegemony, that cooperation was indeed possible in a posthegemonic world. Yet this cooperation can also be at an elite level to empower each other's interests at the expense of a broader global agenda. It was conceivable for regimes and institutions to emerge that bridged the polarization between Idealist and Realist notions of world affairs. Even if their original formation was in the context of regional consolidation of power to act as a foil against the perception of American "hyperpower," institutions are reinventing themselves to benefit from post-hegemonic cooperation. An important example of such an institution that has great relevance to the struggle for mineral resources in Afghanistan is the Shanghai Cooperation Organization. Originally conceived as a means of fostering demilitarization between the borders of the former Soviet Republics and China, the organization has evolved to have broader economic and security goals. Afghanistan has been allowed to attend some of the recent meetings of the organization along with strategic neighbors Pakistan, Iran and India, Russia and China are the major players in SCO and it remains to be seen whether the institution will move beyond aspirations of regional hegemony. Mineral development in Afghanistan as exemplified in the following two case analyses may provide an important opportunity to test the validity of the post-hegemonic hypothesis for the SCO countries as well as the United States. Case Analyses Afghan geology and geography are both consequential in terms of mineral development prospects (TFBSO, 2011), with reliable estimations of $1-3 trillion of extractable resources. Extraction potential remains strong for geological reasons, while the country's geographic location, between the rich oil and gas fields of Central and Western Asia and the high demand centers of India and China, makes it a vital transit country for energy commerce. We provide a comparison in this segment of projects in both these arenas that are being considered. Both have a tortured history and continue to be a source of some concern in terms of physical security, environmental and social impacts and their contribution to economic development. There are lessons from the historical trajectory of each that can be applied more broadly to Afghan mineral development policy in a post-hegemonic context of foreign assistance. Afghanistan and natural gas transit 5-The ambivalence with which the United States has approached Central Asian natural resources as a compass for policy direction further confounded the prospects for pipeline development. The U.S. had two primary motives for involvement in these ventures: to hinder international commerce with Iran, which it considered a rogue state, and to help individual U.S. oil companies find alternative sources of investment. Afghanistan was potentially considered a foil against Iran since the rise of a militia, The Taliban during the late nineteen nineties. In his notable book on the rise of the Taliban, Ahmed Rashid has painstakingly documented the ambivalence of U.S. policy in this context. Initially, when the Taliban captured Kabul in September 1996, Chris Teggert, an executive for the U.S. oil firm, Unocal told wire agencies that the long-awaited gas pipeline project 6- from Turkmenistan to Pakistan would now be easier to implement. 7- The company was admonished by various interests within the United States for this approach of negotiating with the Taliban and quickly retracted the statement. Even the U.S. State spokesman Glyn Davies initially also stated that they found "nothing objectionable" in the steps taken by the Taliban to impose Islamic Shariah describing them as "anti-modern" rather than "anti-Western." However, the U.S. embassy in Islamabad, which was far more familiar with the dangers of such an endorsement, quickly contacted Washington to retract these statements. Women's rights activists also further lobbied against U.S. involvement with the Taliban but the full impact of such activism was not felt until at least two years later. In the meantime, the Taliban continued to pursue their negotiations on the Turkmenistan pipeline with Unocal as well as the Argentine company Bridas that had initially courted Turkmen gas (Coll, 2004). Two separate delegations of Taliban visited Argentina and the United States simultaneously in February 1997. 8- The Taliban did not make any particular commitment in these visits and the delegations returned home via Saudi Arabia, where they also met with Saudi intelligence chief Prince Turki Al-Faisal. Saudi Arabia had initially supported the Taliban as well as a foil against Iran but the growing strength of Al-Qaeda within the country began to make this tenuous alliance weaker. Pakistan continued to press forward with the TAP project, which was their highest priority. In October 1997, a consortium called the Central Asia Gas Pipeline Ltd. (Cent-Gas) was established with shares of 46.5% for Unocal(US); 15% for Delta Oil (Saudi Arabia); 7% for Turkmenistan; 6.5% for Japan's Itochu Oil; 6.5% for Indonesia Petroleum (Inpex); 5% for Hyundai Corporation of Korea and 3.5% for Pakistan-based Crescent Group. However, the U.S. State department became increasingly concerned about the draconian reign of the Taliban, following reports of human rights abuses in their domain. The final blow to the project came in August 1998 when the U.S. embassies in Kenya were bombed and linkages of the bombers to Al-Qaeda camps in Afghanistan were established. The Clinton administration commenced air strikes in Afghanistan soon thereafter and discouraged Unocal from any further engagement with the Taliban. The prospects for the TAP pipeline were renewed briefly when the Bush administration came to power in 2000. In general, Republicans have been more sympathetic to business interests and the Bush family had particularly good connections in the oil sector. As documented by French journalists Jean-Charles Brisard and Guillaume Dasquie, the Bush administration in 2000 and early 2001 started to engage the Taliban on economic terms. Funds were provided for the opium-eradication program while discussions continued on the TAP project. Negotiations finally broke down in August 2001, partly because of the reluctance of the Taliban to bargain on the future of Osama Bin Laden in exchange for economic cooperation. 9-Marty Miller, Unocal's deputy to Afghanistan for the project, would remember the entire effort as "the black hole" of his career. 10-The interactions between the Bush administration and the Taliban suggest some interesting aspects of how natural resource interests can potentially lead to cooperative behavior not only at a regional level but at a larger international level. The willingness of two conservative militaristic regimes with very different worldviews to converge on natural resources as a means of diplomacy supports the idea of "rational regionalism." However, at the same time there is a darker side to such potential cooperation that can be seen as cooptation of the security agenda by extremists for economic expediency. Such an argument is frequently used also by human rights activists to criticize US support of regimes in countries such as Saudi Arabia and China whose human rights abuses and lack of democratic progress is tolerated on account of stability for energy security or economic trade. There is now clearly a US preference towards the TAP project as compared to any project involving Iran, since it would enhance Afghan development and hasten the chances of a U.S. troop withdrawal while also isolating the Iranian regime. It would also reduce

Russia's dominance on the gas sector's transit across their territory. In a public address at the Johns Hopkins University, Richard Boucher, former U.S. Assistant Secretary of State for South and Central Asian Affairs, said in September 2007: "One of our goals is to stabilize Afghanistan, so it can become a conduit and a hub between South and Central Asia so that energy can flow to the south…and so that the countries of Central Asia are no longer bottled up between two enormous powers of China and Russia, but rather they have outlets to the south as well as to the north and the east and the west." 11-Initially, the TAP project would have tapped into >2.83 trillion cubic meters (TCM) of natural gas reserves at Turkmenistan's huge Dauletabad – Donmez field and deliver it across Afghanistan to both Pakistan and, later, India. The pipeline would carry up to 20 billion cubic meters of gas a year, which would generate $100-300 million per year in transit fees for Afghanistan and create thousands of jobs. 12- It is important to note that the Soviet Union had constructed several pipelines in Afghanistan, the first in 1967 to exploit the natural gas of Shibarghan and send it north across the Amu Darya River into the pipelines of Turkmenistan and later during the Soviet – Afghanistan War, the Soviets constructed a small diameter pipeline south to the Bagram military base to provide fuel for their troops. These pipelines are now in disrepair and disuse for a number of years. For an additional US$500 million TAP could be extended to Fazilka on the PakistanIndia border and hence provide gas to India as well. The pipeline could also be expanded further to connect fields in Central Asia to Gwadar, turning Pakistan's new port into one of the world's most important energy hubs. From an energy security standpoint TAP could provide Pakistan with 3,350 million meters cubic feet per day (mm cfpd) of gas, more than the 2,230 mm cfpd the competing project from Iran (IPI). In late April 2009, the TAP project got a positive boost when Turkmenistan officially provided gas reserves certification from the Yasrak field instead of the Daulatabad field. The certification claims a potential reserve of four to 14 trillion cubic feet of gas. A new route for the pipeline has now been proposed which would only involve a small portion of Afghanistan's territory and enter Balochistan near Gwadar to avoid conflict in southwestern Afghanistan. In essence this route would merge the TAP and IPI (IranPakistan-India) pipeline projects within Pakistan. Turkmenistan would provide 3.2 billion cubic feet gas to Afghanistan and Pakistan and India. Afghanistan would receive $1 per MMBTU as transit fees under the new proposal. 13-The biggest challenge to the viability of the TAP project remains the ongoing conflict in Afghanistan. While pipelines have existed in conflict zones such as Eastern Turkey, the level of armed combat in Afghanistan remains at a critical level and pipeline construction over vast expanses of territory would require a far greater security. On the other hand, mining projects within a confined space are far easier to secure and manage even in times of conflict. Hence the foreign investment in solid mineral projects remains far more active than the pipeline prospects at this stage. Of particular note is the copper deposit at Aynak whose tender negotiation and outcome provides important insights regarding the role of regional powers in the development trajectory of this wartorn nation. The Anyak Tender: Terms of Oriental Endearment Following the invasion of Afghanistan by the USA in the fall of 2001, the U.S. Geological Survey (USGS) was tasked with the job of investigating the geology and resources of Afghanistan, and a chief problem was to access and translate all of the old Soviet geology documents, maps and drill-core data, which was accomplished by striking a deal in Moscow (Orris and Bliss, 2002). In addition to this work, when the USGSrequested budget of $75 million was reduced to $5 million by the White House in 2002 (Shroder, 2003, 2004, 2007), the USGS sought help from one of their coalition partners. Consequently the British Geological Survey (BGS) was brought in to assist, and the Aynak copper prospect 35 km south of Kabul was its chief task. With access to the extensive Soviet-era translations and data (150 km-deep boreholes, 70 trenches, nine adits), BGS was able to construct a first rate, three-dimensional, Vulcan™ computer model of the Aynak ore body underground, as well as to build a modern picture of the way the ore had been emplaced. The original resource estimations at Aynak made by the Soviet geologists indicated several large copper ore bodies, with a number of smaller ones extending a total of some 4 km m along strike on the ground surface and extending approximately 2.5 km m down-dip underground, with an overall thickness of about 210 m. This defines an ore body of some 240 M tons at a grade of ~2.3% Cu, which is equivalent to about 13 million tons of the metal (Shalizi, 2007), although Afghanistan Mining Minister Ibrahim Adel estimated that the deposit could go to 20 million tons. This is a substantial deposit that could clearly affect world market in copper, a fact that had been recognized early on by the World Bank and the United Nations (ESCAP, 1995). Furthermore, Aynak is part of a SW – NE trending copper zone that extends from the Saindak copper mine in western Balochistan Province, Pakistan, all along through a mineralized zone running past Kabul. Others have estimated as much as $88 billion of metal is in the ground in this region, which augers exceptionally well for Afghanistan, providing the multinational and personal greed that has been seen running rampant is not allowed to succeed in destroying the opportunity to make things better. By 2005 new mining law had been prepared by the Ministry of Mines in Afghanistan through assistance from the World Bank and the BGS in order to facilitate effective and efficient management of an emerging mining industry that was expected to generate at least $300 million a year in revenue. 14- In late 2006 bidding tenders were let for the Aynak deposit, with considerable interest and bids from companies in Australia, Canada, China, India, Kazakhstan, Russia and USA. Bids came in from such companies as the Strikeforce part of Russia's Basic Elements Group, the London-based Kazakhmys Consortium, Hunter Dickinson of Canada, and the Phelps Dodge Co. of the USA. The China Metallurgical Group (MCC), however, won the Aynak bid, participating also with several other companies in their consortium. These include Jiangxi Copper, the largest copper producer in China, as well as the Zijin Mining Group, which is the largest gold producer in China. MCC is known to have international holdings that are worth only a little over a billion dollars, but with the resources of the Chinese state behind it as well, its financial situation should not be underestimated (Metz, 2007) and its capabilities would seem to be quite large. Thus the Chinese company is reported to be investing $2.9 billion into the project, which has a number of ancillary additions in a massive collateral development scheme that seem to require the backing of the Chinese government. Such additional elements in the successful bid included provision of an onsite copper smelter, a coal mine for power production, a 400-megawatt, coalfired power plant that would also augment the Kabul electric supply, a ground-water system, roads, homes, schools, hospitals, the building of a freight railroad from western China, through Tajikistan to Afghanistan and Pakistan, help for Kabul University, and thousands of new jobs (Synovitz, 2007). Such additions to the bid were beyond the capabilities of the competitor companies, with the result that the MCC bid was successful. Additional reports by people directly involved in the bidding process (Yaeger, 2009), however, also indicate that there was "a perfect storm of tender events," in which the Minister of Mines, Ibrahim Adel, was able to manipulate an exceptionally flawed bidding process to the advantage of MCC. Partlow (2009) also reported that Adel had accepted a $30 million dollar bribe given to him in about December of 2007 in Dubai to ensure the success of the MCC bid which led to his subsequent imprisonment. Smelting of any ore is commonly done as close as possible to the mine to minimize transportation costs of what becomes useless slag left over after processing. In cases, however, where the ore is a rich enough tenor or construction of the smelter is too expensive, then longer transport to smelting may be tolerable. Generally lower grade copper ores such as Aynak may thus need to be smelted in Afghanistan, whereas higher grade Hajigak iron might be transported as far as the Karachi steel mills in Pakistan, although a new effort is underway in Afghanistan to produce steel close to Kabul using local chromite. 15 Ore smelting also requires considerable energy to melt the ore to metal;

energy sources can be varied, of course, but in Afghanistan the use of more easily available coal may trump other energy sources such as hydroelectricity that is yet only weakly developed. The plentiful coal in northern Afghanistan could be brought south to Aynak by truck or new rail for smelting, while the return journey north would be of refined metal for delivery to market. Plentiful coking is also available in the north. Alternatively, new coal resources might be developed in the Katawaz Basin along the border with Pakistan to the south, where such resources are expected to be found (SanFilipo, 2005), but this would presumably not involve favorable round-trip transport economics unless combined in some fashion with delivery of Hajigak iron ore into Pakistan. However, until Pakistan's energy crisis is resolved there is little hope for further smelting in the country. It is important to note that China exerts considerable influence in Pakistan and has also invested widely in infrastructure development in Balochistan. The existing Saindak copper-gold mine in the Chaghai district of Balochistan, bordering Iran and Afghanistan, is also operated by the Chinese Metallurgical Construction Corporation (MCC). The Reko Diq copper project nearby which was initially being offered to a joint-venture between a Chinese company and a Canadian company may also end up falling under Chinese management following negotiations with the Baloch provincial government in 2010. 16 Despite the strong separatist movement in the province and the ongoing rift between the provincial and federal government, there is an opportunity for engagement of China in positive development across borders. Notwithstanding the attacks on Chinese engineers working in Gwadar and the withdrawal of China from the oil refinery project in Gwadar, there is a recognition by Baloch separatists of the strategic importance of China. In one communiqué, following the Chinese decision to withdraw, a Baloch separatist publication stated: "Balochistan needs China as it's one of the permanent members of UN Security Council. China needs Balochistan in future as its international competitiveness depends on steady landline supply of fuel from Balochistani refineries and storage tanks." 17 China's role as a regional power broker and potential mediator in conflict resolution remains strong. The opportunities accorded by Chinese involvement in the Aynak project, their investment in neighboring Iran and their leadership role in the Shanghai Cooperation Organization, deserves greater attention by the United States and Europe. The initial negative reaction from the Aynak tender as well as the outcome from the United States needs to be reevaluated. The terms of the contract according to most international development experts familiar with such contracts are very favorable to Afghanistan in terms of financial arrangements. While there may be some concerns about post-facto environmental and social performance, these can be assuaged by engagement with the Afghan government in monitoring and enforcement of standards. The prospect of Afghanistan being compliant with international efforts at accountability and transparency, such as the Extractive Industries Transparency Initiative 18 will also further strengthen the chances of positive enforcement and monitoring that can strengthen the "social contract" between corporations, foreign investors and the community. The confluence of complementary international interests in mineral development thus has the potential to build trust rather than increasing tensions. Previews of Coming Attractions The pending Hajigak tender offer and the international machinations afoot to gain access to the rich prospects such as the ores of rare earth elements (REE), niobium (Nb), and lithium (Li), in Afghanistan bear watching as attempts are made to gain access to these materials that are so vital to high technology and modern communications (TFBSO, 2011; Becatoros, 2011; Najafizada, 2011). The extinct carbonatite volcano of Kohi Khanneshin in southern Helmand Province is already reliably estimated at a mined value production of some $89 billion, although more precise data from two new field sampling efforts by the U.S. Geological Survey will not be available until fall 2011 to better enable tender offerings. Similarly among a number of other rich resource possibilities in Afghanistan, lithium salts in five dry lake basins scattered throughout the country are estimated at being worth over $60 billion when extracted. To overcome the myriad problems faced by the Afghanistan Ministry of Mines (AMOM) (incompetent and corrupt officials, lack of mining regulations, untrained inspectorate department, antiquated and corrupt cadastral survey of land ownerships, absence of effective environmental regulations or post-mining restoration, lack of effective communication with tribal populations affected by mining), Afghanistan has hired SRK Consulting to undertake the facilitation of this project. In addition, the international law firm of Mayer Brown has been retained, whose core business area is the mining industry, and who will provide, with help from the Canadian legal firm of Heenan Blaikie, day-to-day advice on legal, financial, and operational issues faced by mineral producers, governments, and mineral-industry financiers (Keil, 2011). With the credibility, transparency, and accountability of such partners, the resource extraction industries in Afghanistan have a real chance of success, although the struggle to overcome the greedy and mendacious bureaucracy will be monumental. Policy Recommendations and Conclusion Moving beyond the trust deficit that theories of hegemonic influence have provided during the past several decades will take policy leadership. No doubt, during the Cold War such theories gained plausible currency and were empirically evident. However, there has been a major shift in the role of the United States and China as two major global powers, which should lead us to challenge old assumptions about hegemony. Other regional states that have recently been considered pariahs, such as Iran, may also be brought into the specter of regional cooperation. However, such policy shifts must also be calibrated with changes in corporate behavior donor assistance and monitoring provisions to ensure environmental and other compliance assurance. Given the historical and contemporary analysis of geopolitics surrounding Afghanistan's mineral development, the international community should consider the following four policy recommendations in this regard: a) The Aynak contract's terms should be considered as a benchmark for revenue sharing, collateral development along with the ore extraction, and accountability, but international financial institutions should ensure that the terms of the agreement are kept as the project develops. The World Bank's program of providing assistance in monitoring this process should be supported by the United States, Japan and the European Union. b) The United States should encourage the development of the TAP pipeline by involving the SCO countries in partnership so Russia and China do not see this as an effort to undermine Russian influence in Turkmenistan. Extending the project to India (TAPI pipeline) would also provide an additional opportunity for Indo-Pak rapprochement. Ali and Shroder, 2011 20 of 24 c) Afghanistan's accession to the EITI should be expedited to ensure that before the Aynak and TAPI projects commence, protocols for revenue transparency can be implemented. Donors should provide targeted assistance to allow for such institutional capacity to develop. d) China's role in the Aynak project, as well as the copper-gold projects in neighboring Pakistan, should be supported by the international community so long as the terms of reference remain transparent and there is ongoing regional engagement. Chinese involvement would also help in cementing Pakistani political support for multinational donor investment in Afghanistan and potentially open opportunities for their role in regional conflict resolution. e) The truly vast mineral wealth of Afghanistan is so potentially "neo-great-gamechanging" through potential revenue production and development as to overcome the war with the Taliban and its safe havens in Pakistan. The White House should commit to a major development effort while restraining the Congressionally generated wrangling with the Department of Defense over a handover to USAID (Chandrasekaran, 2011) 19 At a speech in 1997, Strobe Talbot, the U.S. Deputy Secretary of State, and currently the President of the Brookings Institution stated that while it has been "fashionable to proclaim or at least to predict, a replay of the 'Great Game' in the Caucasus and Central Asia…our goal is to avoid and to actively discourage that atavistic outcome. The Great Game, which starred Kipling's Kim and Fraser's Flashman, was very much of the zerosum variety. What we want to help bring about is just the opposite, we want to see all responsible players in the Caucasus and Central Asia be winners." statement from over a decade ago reflects the kind of rational regionalism that has been argued for in this paper. While such sentiments have not been realized in the context of South and Central Asia, the overall potential for pipelines as a source of conflict resolution remains promising and deserves greater attention by scholars of international relations and policy-makers alike.

Data Sources, Processing, and Accuracy

Data on more than 1000 Afghanistan deposits, mines, and occurrences were compiled from published literature and digital files of the project members of the National Industrial Minerals project of the U.S. Geological Survey (USGS). The data include information on metals, nonmetals, construction materials, coal, and peat. Three previous compilations of Afghanistan mineral resources were the dominant sources used for this effort. In 1995, the United Nation's Economic and Social Commission for Asia and the Pacific published a summary of the geology and mineral resources of Afghanistan as part of their Atlas of Mineral Resources series. This document included a summary table and text descriptions of the major mineral mines, deposits, and areas; however, there are numerous spelling and location inconsistencies between table listings and text descriptions. The text descriptions provide geologic and resource information about many of the sites. A second source compilation for this report was Gemstones of Afghanistan (Bowersox and Chamberlin, 1995), published by Geoscience Press, Inc., of Tucson, Arizona. A table at the end of the book lists mineral occurrences by commodity, including metals and nonmetals, with latitude and longitude. The table contains substantial duplication as sites with multiple commodities are listed multiple times and there are numerous spelling inconsistencies. The text of this book is largely limited to descriptions of the gem districts of Afghanistan. Many of the individual mines listed in the text are not included in the summary table of this publication, although the major gem districts are in the table. Locations in Appendix A that were identified 4 only in Bowersox and Chamberlin (1995) during the compilation of this table are marked with an The descriptions of the starred locations, consisting of a name, commodity, and location, are protected by copyright; the right to reproduce these locations was granted to the USGS by Geoscience Press. The conditions of reproduction stipulate that these rights are non-exclusive world rights and that notice of the title and authors be specified. The starred locations from Bowersox and Chamberlin (1995) are covered by the following copyright: "No part of this book may be reproduced by any mechanical, photographic, or electronic process, or in the form of a phonographic recording, nor may it be stored in a retrieval system, transmitted, or otherwise copied for public use, without written permission from the publisher." The most complete compilation of Afghanistan's mineral resources is Mineral Resources of Afghanistan by Abdullah and others (1977). With few exceptions, the data listed in the ESCAP (1995) publication and Bowersox and Chamberlin (1995) table of mineral resources appear to be excerpted from this earlier compilation; the spelling inconsistencies and typographical errors of Abdullah and others are frequently duplicated in the later compilations. Both of the later compilations are missing much of the geologic detail contained in the 1977 compilation, but do contain some "new" information not found in Abdullah and others. We should also note at this point that Abdullah and others (1977) is also referenced as Shareq and others (1977). This confusion arises from the publication having two title pages. One title page begins the list of "Abdullah Shareq, V.M. Chmyriov,..."; the other title page begins the list of. Abdullah, V.M. Chmyriov,...". We have chosen to use "Abdullah" as the last name because several citations in the mineral descriptions cite "Abdullah" and none cite "Shareq". Also, in the reference list of the 1977 publication, there is an author listed as "Abdullah, S.", but there is no "Shareq". Additional geologic and commodity information came from USGS files and about a dozen other published sources. For the most part, all data were recorded as reported in the references unless there were inconsistencies that could be reconciled from the available data. Where information reported from two or more sources were in conflict, the authors utilized the nformation from Abdullah and others (1977) and noted the inconsistencies. The data were checked for duplicates using names, locations, and commodity. Historic province names were replaced with current province names using latitude and longitude information using a paper map. No attempt was made to identify further errors. 5 The mines and mineral occurrences of Afghanistan are listed in a table as Appendix A of this publication. The table is divided into 3 parts; Pegmatite Fields, Named Sites & Deposits, and Sites and Deposits Without Names. The latter 2 categories include deposits, active and inactive mines of a variety of scales, prospects, and showings. The data fields for Appendix A include: Locality/Deposit Name Synonyms and Other Names or Spellings Deposit or District Name Province Latitude Longitude Commodity(s) Type of Deposit Status Host Rock Age Host Rock Significant Minerals or Materials Deposit Size and (or) Grade Comments References Decimal Latitude Decimal Longitude. The Locality Deposit Name field contains the name of the mine, deposit, field, area, or occurrence being described. Synonyms and Other Names or Spellings contains alternative names or spellings for the site. For a deposit or area, this field might also 6 include any specific mine or occurrence names that are known, i.e. "includes Northern and XXX mines". The Deposit or District Name field contains the name of any larger deposit, field, or district to which the site belongs. The Afghanistan Province in which the site lies is the next field. Federal Information Processing Standards (FIPS) spellings were used in Appendix A (National Institute of Standards and Technology, 1995). Table 1 contains a list of all the Provinces in Afghanistan plus alternative spellings and historic names known to the authors. Latitude and longitude are listed in degrees, minutes, and seconds. Large fields or deposits may have a range specified in the Latitude or Longitude fields, i.e. "34-00N to 34-10N". In other cases, a deposit may have 2 orebodies with differing locations. In this case, the multiple latitudes and longitudes are separated by a semi-colon, i.e. "34-00N; 34-10N." The Commodity Field lists the commodities known to occur at each site. A list of commodity abbreviations may be found in table 2. The following field, Type of Deposit, contains a deposit type or style of mineralization. The Status field contains information on whether the site has produced and when or if it is a mineral occurrence or showing. Host Rock Age and Host Rock contain appropriate descriptions of host rocks and other significant rock units, such as nearby igneous rocks that are related to the mineralization. The main minerals or materials are listed under Significant Minerals or Materials and any deposit size or grade information is listed in the following field. The four remaining fields in Appendix A are a Comments field for any additional information, References, and Decimal Latitudes-Longitudes. Readers and users of the data should be aware that English spelling of the place names is highly variable within the source materials; many are English translations of Russian versions of Afghani names. In addition, the use of singular and plurals in the geologic descriptions is erratic. If the source(s) specified a number of veins or orebodies, that number was included in Appendix A of this publication. In many other cases, it was commonly unclear if there was one or more mineralized areas or bodies. Lastly, there is additional data in Abdullah and others (1977), including the locations of mineral haloes, that are not included in this publication. Table 1. Provinces of Afghanistan. Province-Alternate spellings and names, including -historical names

1. Badakhshan Badahsan
2. Badghis Badgis
3. Baghlan Baglan
4. Bactria Balkh Balh
5. Bamian Bamyan, Bamiyan
6. Farah Fahrah
7. Faryab Fariab
8. Ghazni Gazni

9. Ghowr Ghor, Gawr, Ghawr, Gor
10. Helmand Hilmend
11. Herat
12. Jowzjan Jawzjan, Jozjan, Juzjan
13. Kabol Kabul
14. Kandahar Qandahar
15. Kapisa Kapesa, Kapissa
16. Konar Kunar, Konarh, Konarha, Nuristan
17. Kondoz Kunduz, Konduz, Qunduz, Qonduz
18. Laghman Lagman, Nuristan
19. Lowgar Lawgar, Lawghar, Logar, Loghar, Lowghar
20. Nangarhar Ningarhar
21. Nimruz Chakhansur, Neemroze, Nimroz, Nimroze
22. Oruzgan Uruzgan, Oruzghan, Uruzghan
23. Paktia Paktiya
24. Paktika
25. Parvan Parwan
26. Samangan Samanghan
27. Sar-e Pol Sar-e Pul, Sari Pol, Sar-i Pol
28. Takhar Tahar
29. Vardak Warkak, Wardak, Wardag, Wardagh, Maydan
30. Zabol Zabul

Afghanistan has become the first country whose surface minerals have been mapped from the air. The US Geological Survey released the results of a "hyperspectral imaging" effort, in which reflections of light from the ground are analysed. Different minerals - as well as snow or vegetation - reflect specific colours, resulting in a "mineral map". The map comprises more than 800 million data points corresponding to an area of 440,000 sq km, some 70% of the country. Afghanistan is known to have vast reserves of oil, gas, copper, cobalt, gold and lithium. In late 2011, a consortium of Indian companies inked a deal to begin mining some of the country's large stores of iron. But the country is known to have a wider array of mineral resources; in 2010, the Afghan ministry of mines claimed a value of its reserves of nearly a trillion dollars, then carrying out tours to promote investment in them. But it remains to pin down which economically viable minerals are where, an effort for which the USGS's hyperspectral imaging expertise was enlisted. In a series of 28 flights over 43 days, the USGS gathered the data from a height of 15,000m, using a camera to capture sunlight reflected from the ground. Each "pixel" of the camera was analysed and correlated with the materials that reflect at a given colour. The USGS public release of the data includes two maps: one of iron and iron-bearing minerals, and one of minerals principally containing carbon, silicon, or sulphur. The survey was funded by the US Department of Defense's Task Force for Business and Stability Operations (TFBSO) as well as the Afghan government. "This is a tremendous tool for the Afghan government for locating and identifying its myriad rich mineral deposits," said TFBSO director Jim Bullion. "These maps clearly show the enormous size and variety of Afghanistan's mineral wealth and position the country to become a world leader in the minerals sector." The geologic and mineral resource information shown on this map is derived from digitization of the original data from Abdullah and Chmyriov (1977) and Abdullah and others (1977). The U.S. Geological Survey (USGS) has made no attempt to modify original geologic map-unit boundaries and faults as presented in Abdullah and Chmyriov (1977); however, modifications to map-unit symbology, and minor modifications to map-unit descriptions, have been made to clarify lithostratigraphy and to modernize terminology. Labeling of map units has not been attempted where they are small or narrow, in order to maintain legibility and to preserve the map's utility in illustrating regional geologic and structural relations. Users are encouraged to refer to the series of USGS/AGS (Afghan Geological Survey) 1:250,000-scale geologic quadrangle maps of Afghanistan that are being released concurrently as open-file reports. The classification of mineral deposit types is based on the authors' interpretation of existing descriptive information (Abdullah and others, 1977; Bowersox and Chamberlin, 1995; Orris and Bliss, 2002) and on limited field investigations by the authors. Deposit-type nomenclature used for nonfuel minerals is modified from published USGS deposit-model classifications, as compiled in Stoeser and Heran (2000). New petroleum localities are based on research of archival data by the authors. The shaded-relief base is derived from Shuttle Radar Topography Mission (SRTM) digital elevation model (DEM) data having 85-meter resolution. Gaps in the original SRTM DEM dataset were filled with data digitized from contours on 1:200,000-scale Soviet General Staff Sheets (1978–1997). The marginal extent of geologic units corresponds to the position of the international boundary as defined by Abdullah and Chmyriov (1977), and the international boundary as shown on this map was acquired from the Afghanistan Information Management Service (AIMS) Web site in September 2005. Non-coincidence of these boundaries is due to differences in the respective data sources and to inexact registration of the geologic data to the DEM base. Province boundaries, province capital locations, and political names were also acquired September 2005. The AIMS data were originally derived from maps produced by the Afghanistan Geodesy and Cartography Head Office (AGCHO). Version 2 differs from Version 1 in that (1) map units are colored according to the color scheme of the Commission for the Geological Map of the World (CGMW) (2) the minerals database has been updated, and (3) all data presented on the map are also available in GIS format It is obvious that there is no military solution to the struggle in Afghanistan; therefore a political solution could be on the horizon. So far that too has proven to be a failing effort when the Taliban, who were supposedly partaking in the recent consultative Loya-Jirgah gathering in an effort to reconcile in Kabul, answered instead with a barrage of explosive attacks that consequently disrupted the council. So, what else is on the table to justify the war in Afghanistan and keep the government of Hamid Karzai afloat? Apparently the US military brass and Mr. Karzai did some brain storming recently, and they were in approval of introducing another plan by giving the tip off of vastly untapped mineral deposits in the Hindu-Kush mountains of the Central Asian state; which quickly jumped from $1 trillion value to $3 trillion in a matter of 36 hours. There are many legitimate questions as to whether the mineral deposits are authentic or a hoaxed, but the fact remains, many Afghans and many people in the West are not accepting this joint U.S.-Afghan government idea. In Afghanistan myths are the same as fables, legends, folktales, fairy tales, anecdotes or fiction, but their sloppy usage in politics and religion has blurred the distinctions in many people's minds. They are sometimes used in a bad way in reference to a belief of culture or for a belief in a religion by implying that the story is both believable and factual. Consequently, considering the past history of British colonial deceit and manipulation of Afghan society and interference in the internal affairs of Afghanistan, some Afghans do not believe anything conveyed by the West is genuine anymore. Not long ago UK's Defense Secretary Dr. Liam Fox called Afghanistan, a "broken 13th-century." Of course, his view reverberated in the world as Afghanistan is a tribal and medieval society. In fact, Afghanistan by 13th-century was at the heart of the Islamic renaissance, boasting magnificent architecture, art, calligraphy, literature, advances in mathematics and production of poets akin to Jalaluddin Rumi who was born in 1207 in the northern city of Balkh. That said, in most rural areas in Afghanistan, time is frozen in a centuries old antiquated system, technology advances are null, illiteracy is high and societal beliefs are of conservative Islam, therefore, in such a society, mythology is perceived as authentic, and dominates people's thoughts and daily lives. Afghans are not simpleminded people; they have retained their complex oral traditions. However, their oral traditions do suggest the possibility of mythical beliefs that can be manipulated by a lack of understanding of foreign technology. This limited exposure to foreign technology allowed past colonial rulers like the Britain to manipulate Afghan customs and beliefs to temporarily gain a foothold over religious leaders, and thereby gain control over public will long enough to overthrowing past Afghanistan rulers. The late progressive Afghan King Amanullah who gained Afghanistan's independence in 1919, 28 years ahead of colonial India's independence, miscalculated British ability to topple his government by turning traditionalists and mullahs against him. While visiting India, the young King appeared to be very enthusiastic about liberating Muslim countries from the rule of colonial power. He was greeted as a hero in India and the Indian freedom fighters asked him to give a *fetwa* announcing that he become the King of India too. King Amanullah, however, did not issue the *fetwa*, but his appearance in India forced the British to see that India would be next in line to become free of their colonial rule if Amanullah were to remain in power. Therefore, the British conspired against Amanullah by using the mullahs and traditionalists limited knowledge of technology to their advantage; they produced false and shocking photographs of queen Soraya, wife of Amanullah, half naked with foreign men. Seeing these (photo-shopped) images, religious leaders believed Amanullah could not be a true Muslim and therefore did not deserve to be King. This little technology advantage yielded great political advantage to the British and consequently was a factor for the collapse of the king's reign. But now, awakened to the technology, Afghans rightly blame the Britain for this plot, and regret losing such an iconic figure as their leader. There are many tales of how new innovations leaked forward to produce such public manipulations in Afghanistan's past; one short narrative example is when a mullah fools the public by converting water into milk and the audience kneels down in deference to the man of religion for his astounding power. Of course, this was in the early days after the invention of powdered milk in 1832. The most obvious case is shown in a Hollywood picture plot about the true (1888) story of "The Man Who Would Be King" written by Rudyard Kipling and starring Sean Connery and Michael Caine. The story is about two British colonial soldiers who after crossing the border from India became kings of a remote area in Afghanistan called Kafiristan—now Nuristan—they were treated as Gods by the locals but ultimately lost everything when locals become aware of their deceit.

Afghanistan Sitting on Gold, Lithium Mine oil, gas, only-natural gas prices-per day 86 billion Dollars US, & $100 trillion dollars US, Iron ore, copper, large Uranium, of mineral reserves, precious an semi-precious stones, emerald-lapis lazuli, red-gamete A ruby, Marble, Coal & Canal-tunnel of Gold

Afghanistan Minerals However, another way of looking at all this is that finally after decades of war some good news about Afghanistan has finally raised to the surface; it could be an omen to all that beneath the landmines, Afghanistan is sitting on a goldmine. This information sounds rather astonishing; it leads us to assume that Afghanistan has actually hit the jackpot in the world's economy arena. However, the $100 trillion figure, where did it come from? It appears highly misleading. It is a theoretical number and may have little relation to the value of resources that could actually be exploited. Furthermore, it will be of little benefit to Afghanistan if its $100 trillion resources would cost $2 trillion or more to dig up. Thus, to justify the validity of this perception, –which apparently lacked proper homework—the figure was immediately increased to

$300 trillion; apparently the first figure did not sound awesome enough. This suspiciously round number appears to be based on geological surveys made decades ago as well as recent on the ground and in the air 3 dimensional ground scanning technology. How thorough it really has been is an open debate, given that it takes the world's best miners about a decade to explore a new area. Even if there were $3 trillion of mineral resources in Afghanistan, and even if those resources were economically feasible, it would be years before a large Western miner establishment could get anywhere near the country. They currently have no intention of moving into Afghanistan because the risk is far greater than the reward. The investment would be too risky anywhere the Afghan government does not control; plus all the territory and contract laws are far from solid. The only people who might show interest in exploring the aforementioned mineral deposits are the Chinese, but they had to abandon a far simpler project than the untapped Afghan treasures; the Kajaki's Helmand Province hydroelectric dam project was forsaken due to a lack of security in the area. There are vague hypothesis attached to this recent joint perception of mineral wealth announced by the US and Afghan governments. Is it time to change course and divert attention from the failed hearts and minds operation in Marjah, the failed reconciliation Jirga, failed opium eradication, the stalled Kandahar operation, Mr. Karzai's tantrums, the Afghan government corruption, thriving drug trafficking, warlordism, Kandahar's power brokers, fraudulent presidential elections, heightened insurgency, Pakistan's uncooperative effort to contain the Taliban on its soil, regional powers proxy wars, so on and so forth? Some in the West share the mining industry's skepticism that massive amounts of mineral wealth could be easily extracted from Afghanistan's rugged mountains and remote regions. This is believed to be in conjunction with the growing public sentiment that the war is not worth the cost. Similarly, some Afghans, view that the era of past colonial manipulation of Afghan society, thought and sensibility is once again repeating itself. If so, then the public sentiment will be far damning than now. In any event, time is of the essence for either success or failure in Afghanistan. Unfortunately, so far, the momentum has been on the path of failure. If there is vast mineral wealth in Afghanistan, then the world needs to realize that this wealth belongs to the Afghan people. There are Afghans around the world with the skills and knowledge to do this job themselves on behalf of the people of Afghanistan. A good friend of my family speaks about how decades of fighting has left the Afghan people with physical and mental health issues that no one is addressing. What is needed today is an Afghan to Afghan initiative that takes charge of the research and development of any potential mineral and mining deposits first and foremost for the benefit of those Afghans who have suffered from abuse and neglect on their own home soil over the decades. We expatriate Afghans need to look out for our brothers and sisters in Afghanistan who are not aware of 21st Century methodologies, ideologies and technologies that can rob them of their inheritance. It is our job to protect and enlighten fellow Afghans who are at risk, June 27 – According to officials in the ministry of mines of Afghanistan, a number of Afghan mines and minerals samples will be introduced to world investors in Londin in coming two days. The officials further added that the minerals and mines will be exhibited in a three day summit which is going to be held in london. Besides a number of accredited investors who are going participate in this exhibition, a number of heads of banks will also take part in the exhibition to hear about Afghan mines. The summit is going to be be held on coming Tuesday. In this summit, Badakhshan Gold Mine, Ghazni's Zarafshan Gold Mine, Herat ALithium Salt Mine, Balkhab copper mine, and other countries' oil reserves will be introduced. According to Jawad Omar, a spokesman for Afghan Ministry of Mines, a number of world investors and banks which are supporting the mining projects requested for the exhibition of Afghan minerals and mines once again in London. On the basis of the their request the symposium is once again going to be held from 28 to 30 June in London city. On the other hand, Afghan ministry of mines recently has signed an agreement with Germany for the cooperation and development of Afghan minerals. Mr. Omar further added, "both the countries will step up efforts on investments in Afghanistan will coordinate new programmes to encourage German investors for investments in Afghanistan." Based on the agreement Germany, will support Afghanistan to establish educational sectors in Gas and Oil, extraction of mineral resources, encouraging investors and preparing educational programmes on Afghan mines, According to Afghan Ministry of Mines The prospect of cobalt in Kandahar has sparked lively debate about whether new mineral wealth— if it pans out — will aid or hinder U.S. policies in Afghanistan, as well as whether the country will fall prey to the so-called resource curse, as political scientist Michael Ross and others fear. But a short-term focus on Afghan-U.S. relations might be a mistake: The real winner from new natural-resource wealth beyond the Khyber Pass will be China. If the United States really cares about stabilizing Afghanistan's central government and eliminating terrorist havens, it needs to start working now to persuade Beijing that these are shared goals. First, some background: Chinese foreign investment and aid has accelerated dramatically over the past decade, especially in Africa. In November 2009 alone, for example, China's largesse amounted to $10 billion in low-interest loans and $1 billion in commercial loans to the continent. With Beijing as cheerleader, trade has soared from $1 billion in 1992 to $106.8 billion in 2008. In part this is due to China's willingness to do business with undemocratic, corrupt, and brutal regimes — for example, in the Democratic Republic of the Congo (DRC), Sudan, and Zimbabwe. The DRC provides the bestcautionary parallel to Afghanistan: The discovery in the late 1990s of copper, coltan, and other minerals in eastern Congo gave new life to a civil war that has now claimed upwards of 4 million lives. Flagging combatants were funded by mineral extraction, and much of those resources eventually flowed to China. The fact that violence is still simmering in eastern Congo — and despite the costs that extraction imposes on the Congolese people — has not been enough to deter Beijing from wooing Congo's government for access to the country's abundant resources. So, if there's any thought that war in Afghanistan might dissuade Chinese investment there, it's best to dispense with that notion immediately. Present day China, which has a narrow land border with Afghanistan, already invests heavily in the war-torn Central Asian state. The state-owned China Metallurgical Group has a $3.5 billion copper mining venture in Logar province. Chinese companies ZTE and Huawei are building digital telephone switches, providing roughly 200,000 subscriber lines in Afghanistan. Even back in the war's early days in 2002 and 2003, when I worked in Afghanistan, the Chinese presence was acutely visible in Kabul, with Chinese laborers on many building sites and Chinese-run restaurants and guesthouses popping up all over the city. As Robert Kaplan has pointed out, these investments come with a gratuitous hidden subsidy from the United States — which has defrayed the enormous costs of providing security amid war and looting. With its massive wealth, appetite for risk, and willingness to underbid others on labor costs and human rights conditionality, China is the odds-on favorite for development of any new Afghan mineral resources. Chinese firms will control the flow of new funds, and the way those funds are distributed between the central and local governments. It's all well and good that Barack Obama's administration has recommitted to building civil projects in rural Afghanistan, but consider the relative scale of building a school to establishing a multimillion-dollar mine (not to mention the transport networks and infrastructure required to get the extracted minerals out) and it's easy to see what kind of influence the Chinese will bring to the table. It is critical for Washington to start making the case to Chinese leaders that pure self-interest mandates they leverage this power wisely — to promote stability, not catalyze new conflict, in Afghanistan. So far, China's investment in Logar has been in keeping with its "noninterventionist" foreign policy and was accompanied by development aid, but no overt political strings. Washington must require more from Beijing, however, to avoid upending all its hard-won gains. The Obama administration has already asked

China to contribute troops to the Afghan effort. This is a good first step, but a few hundred token soldiers will not make China a strategic partner in its Afghan campaign. It needs to persuade Beijing that the campaign is indeed China's campaign, too — if not by touting democracy promotion and human rights, then surely economic benefit — and that U.S. and Chinese strategies on Afghanistan converge. This is not as hard as it sounds: As China-Africa expert Deborah Brautigam's careful work shows, China has on some occasions acted as a surprisingly responsible lender, for example using resource-backed infrastructure loans that force some gains to be reinvested in development. Although many have warned of a new Sino-colonialism, Brautigam's work suggests that perhaps China's awareness of its gargantuan and growing need for foreign export markets will make it a better "colonial" power than any European country ever was. For China as much as the United States, the goal of a stable, central Afghan government that provides no haven for terrorists is a desirable goal. China has worried in the past about whether Afghanistan might provide a refuge for Uighur separatists. Leaving aside the ethics and wisdom of Chinese policies in the Uighur community's home region of Xinjiang, it's safe to say that Washington and Beijing share a common goal in preventing terrorism. Both countries would benefit from a stabilized government in Kabul that is able to command the loyalty and respect of provincial governments and populations. That, however, requires that Hamid Karzai's government deal with its endemic corruption problem. And though no one expects Afghanistan to turn into Norway, perhaps it can be nudged away from the DRC path and toward the model of a Saudi Arabia or a Kazakhstan. When it comes to corruption, however, state-run Chinese firms have not seemed troubled by greasing the wheels of power brokers in Sudan, Zimbabwe, or elsewhere. Getting Beijing to understand the rot this breeds seems a hard sell for the Obama administration. If that fails, however, Chinese ears might perk up somewhat at the mention of how integral a stable central government in Kabul is to the security of Pakistan, a close ally of Beijing. Stability in Pakistan should be an important goal for China. It is by now clear that the Taliban's campaign west of the Durand Line is inextricable from the destabilizing efforts of Islamist militants in Pakistan. If China does not want another nuclear basket case on its border, then it should care deeply about instability in Afghanistan. Currently, however, Beijing is still freeloading, relying on Washington to provide security for its limited interests. Perhaps the tantalizing prospect of $1 trillion in minerals might be enough to change the strategic equation. Working together, China and the United States have a better chance of guiding Afghanistan to a happy outcome for all than will Washington on its own. To be sure, this is no easy task: There's plenty of evidence that aid conditionality by Western governments has not done as much good as hoped. But cold economic realities dictate that Chinese firms are likely going to be the big players in this new gold rush, and Washington had better wake up to the fact that it has a short window in which to convince Beijing to collaborate in making Kabul a better place. The potential of Afghanistan's mineral resources has long been known. Although there have been few systematic and detailed geological studies for some 25 years, it is likely that Afghanistan's mineral wealth is worth at least several hundred billion dollars. In 2008 mining rights at Aynak, a large-scale copper mine in Logar province, were awarded to a consortium led by MCC (China Metallurgical Group Corporation). In November 2011 three blocks of mining rights at Hajigak, a large iron-ore deposit, were awarded to AFISCO (Afghan Iron and Steel Consortium), a consortium led by the Steel Authority of India (SAIL), and one block to Kilo Goldmines of Canada. Afghanistan's current mineral production is very modest by global standards. In the mining sector there are no large commercial scale mines, although some smaller state-owned coal mines do constitute the highest payer of taxes among all government enterprises nationwide. There is mostly artisanal and small scale mining for construction minerals, dimension stone (marble) and gemstones. In the hydrocarbons sector there is some modest gas production and some very small oil production. Afghanistan has two presently known world class mineral deposits

– the Aynak copper deposit and the Hajigak iron ore deposit. Afghanistan also has good potential for other minerals including gold and has substantial gemstone potential; but the country has not realized any modern exploration surveys in more than 30 years and so the information base is antiquated and sure to under-estimate the total mineral endowment. Moreover, Afghanistan does lie within several large regional trends for copper, iron ore and precious metals; and most certainly has the potential for additional world-class deposits in this regard. Regarding hydrocarbons, Afghanistan has substantial known undeveloped gas deposits at Sherbegon and also some modest oil potential. Mineral and hydrocarbon developments can be a pillar of future economic growth in Afghanistan creating both direct and indirect employment and income; developing transport and other infrastructure which will help open up areas for overall economic development; and generating not only considerable domestic revenue but also trade and balance of payments benefits. Simply put, if managed properly, mining in Afghanistan has the potential to be a driver of poverty reduction and sustained economic growth. Mines not only directly contribute significant taxes, income and other benefits streams directly to the economy but also contribute indirectly through stimulus of various economic activities. For instance, in other countries it has been demonstrated that every direct job created by a mining operation can result in as many as five to ten indirect and induced jobs by providing contracts for numerous small businesses and services which supply the mine. Each of these jobs in turn produces taxes and other expenditures which pass through the economy Aynak and Hajigak would be, by a wide margin, the two largest investments in the history of Afghanistan. The mine developments would require US$2-3 billion invest and each mine would also require investment in ancillary infrastructure in the order of US$2-3 billion or more. A low-impact scenario, based on prevailing market conditions, projects that Aynak and Hajigak could create more than 90,000 direct and indirect jobs, and approximately $500 million in annual fiscal revenues by 2020. In other mineral rich countries, hasn't mining had few spillover benefits? Doesn't it lead to a 'resource curse'? Yes, but that is the point of launching a program to overcome these. Afghanistan can and should launch efforts to overcome this. That mining has not created spillover effects in some countries does not mean it never will or can. After all, one of the primary triggers that economic historians have identified for the industrial revolution was the development of coal and iron in European 'resource corridors' in the 19th century. More recently, Chile has induced a large amount of development around its large copper deposits, and various other countries are starting to put their resources to more effective use. With regards to the 'resource curse', while the phenomenon is well established for Sub-Saharan Africa in the last four to five decades, there are questions as to how prevalent it has been in other regions. More specifically, one of the key mechanisms of the 'resource curse', that is exchange rate appreciation or 'Dutch Disease', are not expected to be an impact in Afghanistan, given the country's already very large current account deficits. If the resource sector's fiscal effects, infrastructure and demand for goods and services can be leveraged, it has the capacity to transform the Afghan economy, through: Fiscal effects: Afghanistan's large mining projects will have a material effect on the government's fiscal sustainability. It is projected that Aynak could generate around US$500 million annually in direct and indirect government revenue by 2015 and Hajigak about US$400-500 million by around 2020. Infrastructure: The extraction of natural resources itself is a major revenue source, but the increase in growth will be associated more with the infrastructure supported by these mining investments. At Aynak, for example, MCC is building a 400 MW thermal power plant with 50% of this power contractually to be provided to the grid at cost. The mines will also require or motivate large investments in transport infrastructure and regional trade which could be leveraged to create public goods that support other sectors. Livelihoods: If the mining infrastructure investments are buttressed by incremental catalytic investments in feeder and rural roads, agriculture and the agribusiness industry could benefit and become a more substantial source of income and jobs for rural communities and urban areas. The mines will also be a source of demand for the manufacturing and services sectors. If local firms can upgrade to supply competitive goods and services, they could capture a portion of the US$4 – 10 billion of investment (depending on the infrastructure built). Once operational, the mines might also lead to downstream activity. For example, AFISCO (the consortium developing three of the four Hajigak deposits) has already declared it will build a large-scale steel mill (up to 6 million tons p.a.), if it can secure sovereign guarantees. What are the Main Challenges and Constraints? Although some progress has been achieved, major challenges (besides improving the security situation) still lie ahead. The program will therefore help the Government address the following issues, as part of an integrated strategy: Infrastructure development (road, rail, power, water, ICT) to leverage private investment into public goods, through PPP when possible. Infrastructure development (in particular rail) requires regional coordination (with neighboring countries), a multimodal approach, and combining hard and soft infrastructure for maximum benefits (e.g., transport routes should be complemented with trade facilitation services). Operations and maintenance (O&M) requirements must also be assessed, especially since other work has already identified O&M expenses as a key driver of Afghanistan's financing gap; Social and environmental issues: These include providing immediate benefits for communities around the corridor. It also requires attention to improved land administration including: a) cadastre for all land within the resource corridor, b) rationalization of land management and c) revised legal frameworks for land acquisition, resettlement and compensation. Other issues, such as mitigating environmental impacts, building the capacity of NEPA (the National Environmental Protection Agency), and the preservation of cultural heritage and archeological sites also need to be addressed; Private sector development along the mining value chain (e.g., creating public-private mechanisms to upgrade the capabilities of the local private sector and hence enable greater local procurement from the mining investments); as well as agriculture and agribusiness along the corridor (to take advantage of new or revamped infrastructure); and improving skills (both for advanced skills and within the broader workforce, in the short and long term); Governance and institutional arrangements to enable successful implementation of the resource growth corridor approach. This will include capacity building, means for institutional collaboration among sector ministries and across central to decentralized levels down to the community level, and strengthened public financial management (especially regarding mineral revenues). The main counterpart will be the Ministry of Mines which is responsible for the extractive industries, and is the lead ministry for the NRRCP and for the Infrastructure Cluster of NPPs. The proposed NRRCP Secretariat, under the leadership of the Minister of Mines, will be the focal point within the Ministry and should work across ministerial boundaries. It is expected that the Ministry of Public Works (MoPW), the Ministry of Transport and Civil Aviation (MoTCA), the Ministry of Commerce and Industries (MoCI), the Ministry of Agriculture, Irrigation and Livestock (MAIL), the Ministry of Rural Rehabilitation and Development (MRRD) and the Ministry of Energy and Water (MEW) will be engaged in various facets of the corridor approach. The Ministry of Finance (MoF) could play a role in its monitoring and evaluation. The private sector participants in resource extraction projects under development and/or related infrastructure projects and the local communities will be key partners in the approach. The stakeholders include relevant civil society and private sector bodies, and the wider donor community. As a starting point, the program will use the large number of independent donor studies (notably from the US Government, DFID and ADB who have been particularly involved in the mining and transport sectors) in order to leverage the significant technical work undertaken throughout the last ten years. What about all the uncertainty surrounding the country, the investments, etc.? Doesn't this risk being just a report on the shelf – a plan for futures that never come to be? Exactly for this reason, the strategy will be modular and flexible, both to enable rapid action and to avoid making the benefits reliant on any single component. Mining and infrastructure projects in any environment are known for delivering late: copper production globally is 15% less than forecast due to the inability to meet ambitious expansion targets. Given the lack of an updated cadastre and unclear and lengthy land acquisition and resettlement processes, as well as pervasive security concerns, the risk of delay to the mines and their associated infrastructure is significant. It would therefore be prudent to elaborate development plans in such a way that some activities can proceed even in the event of major investments being significantly delayed. As a near-term priority, the aim should be to exploit investments in a more advanced stage as early as possible (e.g., Aynak mine and associated investments), while also, to the extent possible, taking into consideration further likely major investments (e.g. Hajigak mine). Even without the full realization of the mining investments, reforms introduced will help the economy and the local population. This modular approach also greatly reduces the risks as improvements are delivered along the way rather than only at the time that the large investment comes online. Overall, the project will draw on some of the world's leading experts in designing strategies and making decisions to cope with high uncertainty. What are the main environmental, social and cultural dimensions being addressed? One of the major challenges is to avoid conflicts at the community level, which may arise due to insufficient communication and outreach or through non-compliance to contractual obligations. Communication and outreach are being improved through the development of a communications plan and appointment of communications professionals to oversee implementation of the plan. Compliance monitoring will be in place and help to minimize this risk. Extractive resource projects that fail to deliver societal benefits through poor design or weak implementation, often fail. To reinforce environmental and social sustainability, inclusion of civil society in planning and implementation is being encouraged. The social specialists Bank have been working with the government to get a proper resettlement action plan completed and including public disclosure and consultation with affected communities. With support from the Bank, the Ministry of Mines (a) has established an ombudsman's office to receive any grievances that may arise and (b) is engaging civil society organizations at the community level to increase transparency of the resettlement process and strengthen communication with the community. The Aynak site contains rich archeological sites including a Buddhist monastery. A French archeological team has been taking the lead, along with the Ministry of Culture, to document and preserve the antiquities. Mining in Afghanistan rapidly expanded in the last decade after the Karzai administration came to power. Major mining activities are monitored and supervised by the Ministry of Mines and Industry in Kabul. Afghanistan has over 90 mineral fields, containing barite, chromite, coal, copper, gold, iron ore, lead, natural gas, petroleum, precious and semiprecious stones, salt, sulfur, talc, zinc among many other minerals. Precious and semiprecious stones include high-quality emerald, lapis lazuli, red garnet and ruby. It is believed that the country holds up to $3 trillion in untapped mineral deposits. There are six lapis mines in Afghanistan, the largest being located in northern Badakhshan province. That area is also home to one of the biggest gold mines in the country. Based on some information there are around 12 copper mines in Afghanistan, including the Aynak copper deposit located in Logar province. Afghanistan's significance from an energy standpoint stems from its geographical position as a potential transit route for oil and natural gas exports from Central Asia to the Arabian Sea. This potential includes the construction of the Trans-Afghanistan Pipeline gas pipeline. The first Afghan oil production began in October 2012 It is estimated that forty million years ago the tectonic plates of India-Europe, Asia and Africa collided in a massive upheaval. This upheaval created the region of towering mountains that now includes Afghanistan. This diverse geological foundation has resulted in a significant mineral heritage with over 1,400 mineral occurrences recorded to date, including gold, copper, lithium, uranium, iron ore, cobalt, natural gas and oil.[4] Afghanistan's resources could make it the richest mining region on earth. Afghanistan has large untapped energy and mineral resources, which have great potential to contribute to the country's economic development and growth. The major mineral resources include chromium, copper, gold, iron ore, lead and zinc, lithium, marble, precious and semiprecious stones, sulfur and talc among'st many other minerals. The energy resources consist of natural gas and petroleum. the government was working to introduce new mineral and hydrocarbon laws that would meet international standards of governance. The U.S. geological survey (USGS) and the British geological survey were doing resource estimation work in the country. Prior to that work, Afghanistan's exploration activity had been conducted by geologists from the Soviet Union who left good-quality geologic records that indicate significant mineral potential. Resource development would require improvements in the infrastructure and security in Afghanistan. the government had awarded contracts to develop the Aynak copper project and the hajigak iron ore project; in addition, the government could offer tenders for new exploration, including exploration of copper at Balkhab, gold at Badakhshan, gemstones and lithium at nuristan, and oil and gas at sheberghan. The Ministry of Mines drew up its first business reform plan in a bid to create a more accountable and transparent mining industry. Afghanistan joined the Extractive industries transparency initiative as a candidate country. It was expected that after 5 years, the contribution of royalties from mineral production to the revenues of the government would be at least $1.2 billion per year, and that after 15 years, the contribution would increase to $3.5 billion per year[6]. Afghanistan has no local ownership requirements and its Constitution does not allow for nationalization. The 20% corporate tax rate was the lowest in the region. Afghanistan's mining industry was at a primitive artisanal stage of development; the operations were all low scale and output was supplied to local and regional markets. The government considered development of the country's mineral resources to be a priority for economic growth, including development of the industrial mineral resources (such as gravel, sand, and limestone for cement) for use by the domestic construction industry. investment in infrastructure and transportation projects for mining was a critical aspect of developing the mining industry. The Government completed Afghanistan's first railway with an investment of $170 million by the end of 2010. The 76-kilometer (km) route would link Mazar-i-sharif to the extensive rail networks in Uzbekistan and Turkmenistan. For the first part of the project, which was funded by the Asian Development Bank ($165 million) and other sources ($5 million), 32 km of track had been laid by the Uzbek national rail company, Uzbekistan temir Yollari, from hairatan on the Uzbek border to Mazar-i-sharif. The new route would allow Afghan exporters to transport minerals and other goods into Europe. Metallurgical group Corp. of China (MCC) also planned to build a railroad to transport copper ore in Afghanistan from Aynak to Kabul Production Owing to the lack of mineral production data reported by the miners, information about Afghanistan's mining activities was not readily available, but they appeared to be limited in scope. Production of Barite was estimated by the USGS to be about 2,000 metric tons; chromite, 6,000 tons; and natural gas liquids, 45,000 barrels. In the process of reconstruction and infrastructure development, output of construction minerals was estimated to have increased to meet the domestic requirements. Production of cement increased by 13% compared with that of 2009.

Afghanistan Sitting on Gold, Lithium Mine oil, gas, only-natural gas prices-per day 86 billion Dollars US, & $100 trillion dollars US, Iron ore, copper, large Uranium, of mineral reserves, precious an semi-precious stones, emerald-lapis lazuli, red-gamete A ruby, Marble, Coal & Canal-tunnel of Gold

Structure of the Mineral Industry in Afghanistan Privatization of Afghanistan's state-owned companies, which controlled many of the country's mineral resources, was ongoing but not complete. Investment in the mining sector by private domestic companies and foreign investors was encouraged by the Government, which had offered the first contract for development of the Aynak copper project to two Chinese companies in 2007. the government also issued the tenders for the development of the hajigak iron ore project in 2009 and tenders for oil and gas exploration in 2010. the Ministry of Mines is involved in the exploration for and development, exploitation, and processing of minerals and hydrocarbons. The Ministry is also responsible for protecting the ownership and regulating the transportation and marketing of mineral resources in accordance with the country's new laws. Regulations to clarify the country's environmental laws were scheduled for adoption in 2010. The last mining boom in Afghanistan was over 2,000 years ago in the era of Alexander the Great, when gold, silver and precious stones were routinely mined. Geologists have known of the extent of the mineral wealth for over a century, as a result of surveys done by the British and Russians. An American company was offered a mining concession over the entire country in the 1930s but turned it down. Despite this historical knowledge, global interest was only really boosted in 2010 when the Pentagon commissioned a report from the US Geological Survey (USGS). Historical mining concentrated mostly on precious stone production, with some of the oldest known mines in the world believed to have been established in Afghanistan. Lapis lazuli was being mined in the Badakhshan province of Afghanistan as early as the 3rd millennium BC In ancient Egypt, lapis lazuli was a favorite stone for amulets and ornaments such as scarabs and was used in Egypt's pyramids; it was also used in ancient Mesopotamia by the Sumerians, Akkadians, Assyrians, Babylonians for seals and at neolithic burials in Mehrgarh. During the height of the Indus valley civilization about 2000 BC, the Harappan colony now known as Shortugai was established near the lapis mines... Lapis jewelry has been found at excavations of the Predynastic Egyptian site Naqada (3300–3100 BC), and powdered lapis was used as eyeshadow by Cleopatra. In ancient Mesopotamia, Lapis artifacts can be found in great abundance, with many notable examples having been excavated at the Royal Cemetery of Ur (2600-2500 BC). The mine of Aynak's copper has more than 2,000 years of history, from the coins and the tools that were found there. The gold of Zarkashan has more than 2,000 years of history in Ghazni Province. Afghanistan's ruby/spinel mines were mentioned in the Arabic writings of many early travellers, including Istakhri (951 AD), Ibn Haukal (978 AD), al-Ta'Alibi (961–1038 AD), al-Muqaddasi (ca 10th century), al-Biruni (b. 973; d. ca 1050 AD), Teifaschi (1240 AD), and Ibn Battuta (1325–1354 AD). The British Empire first initiated resource assessments in Afghanistan in the early nineteenth century as they searched through pioneering exploration and military escapades for countries to dominate as markets and trading partners From the time of their first geological mapping and mineral resource assessments in Afghanistan, and on into the twentieth century the British maintained a comprehensive interest in resources of Afghanistan. This was done while also improving their military intelligence on resources and topographic detail that would be needed in the event of any unrest in the machinations of their Great Game face-off against the Russian Empire, and as long as they could maintain their British Raj (rule) of the Indian subcontinent. A number of other nationalities (German, French, Russian) also looked at geology and resources in the country from time to time but nothing much seemed to come of their explorations. Following the third Anglo-Afghan War in 1919, Afghanistan won its independence from diplomatic domination by the British and it was not long after that a Soviet publication on mineral "riches" first appeared], published by a man who later came to be revered as an early Russian 'father' of geologic studies. Nevertheless, in spite of early attempts by the government of Afghanistan to entice Americans to become engaged in resource discovery and extraction in the country, distance from market, economic concerns, and looming worries about World War II caused rejection of the overtures, much to the discomfiture of the government of Afghanistan. In spite of a number of discoveries by the American geologist Fox (1943) and others, post-war assessment by an American geographer concluded shortsightedly that there were no useful resources in Afghanistan about which there should be any diplomatic concern. With its attention on resources accordingly diverted elsewhere for decades to come, the US Department of State thus quite missed the resource ball when in the 1960s and 1970s, as many as ~250 Soviet geoscientists went to work mapping geology in the country while only one American geologist (co-author of this paper, John Shroder) was in the country, plus a few visiting geology attachés from the US Embassy and USGS seismic specialists who visited from time to time. The resulting Soviet collaboration with the Afghanistan Geological Survey detailed a wide store of mineral resources in the country. The result of this Cold-War confrontation between the USA and the USSR in Afghanistan was that the neighboring USSR was able to fairly easily sidestep or ignore developing resources in Afghanistan until conditions were more to its liking as it consolidated its preeminent position in the country, ultimately leading to its invasion in 1979. With its already dominant roles in the Afghanistan Cartographic Institute, the Afghanistan Geological Survey, and many other ministries, the USSR was in a position in the early 1980s to completely take over all resource extraction in Afghanistan. Indeed they did pump much natural gas across the northern border of the Amu Darya into the USSR where the gauges to measure delivered volumes were located, and plans were made for development of other resources. In addition, the Aynak copper deposit near Kabul was investigated in detail and a smelter scheduled for installation in the mid 1980s. In an interesting sidelight of these times in the early 1980s, a Soviet-Afghan convoy from Aynak was assaulted by the Mujahideen and the captured documents that were sent to co-author Shroder by British sources proved that the Aynak copper lode was one of the largest in the world, as proved out by a plethora of kilometer-deep boreholes that allowed the Soviets to sample the deposit extensively. The increasing resistance of the Afghan people and the Mujahideen, however, together with significant assistance from the USA to the resistance in the final cumulative battles of the Cold War, precluded significant further development of any resources at that time. Instead the Soviet withdrawal in defeat occurred in 1988-89. The subsequent invasion of Afghanistan by the USA and coalition troops in 2001 began a new phase in the history of Afghanistan, as many old resource projects were assessed again, and new ones were initiated Afghanistan lies on the Tethyan Eurasian mineral belt, which starts in Turkey and runs through Iran to Asia as far as Indonesia. There are other mineral belts in Afghanistan, formed through the violent collisions of tectonic plates tens of millions of years ago, which also created the 25,000ft mountains in the north-east of the country. A new mining law was passed in 2006 and as of 2006 regulations were being developed to provide the framework for more formal exploration for and mining of minerals. The process of applying for mineral rights was also being revised as of 2006. All minerals located on or under the surface are the exclusive property of the Government, except for hydrocarbonsand water, which are regulated under separate laws. The principal role of the Government with respect to minerals is to promote the efficient development of the mineral industry by the private sector. The Ministry of Mines and Industries is responsible for the administration and implementation of the Mining Law. The Law provides investment security to the holder of a mineral right. The Government cannot expropriate mineral rights without adequate compensation in accordance with international norms. The Law also gives the mineralroyalty rates, which range from 5% of gross revenue for industrial minerals to up to 10% for gemstones. Other changes in Government policy in 2006 included the legalization of the gemstone trade, Government control of the gemstone industry, and encouragement of investment in mining The Badakshan Gold Mine is situated in mountainous terrain in northern Afghanistan in Badakhshan Province, the location benefits from three international borders:

Tajikistan to its north, China to its east, and Pakistan to the south. Badakshan is located 360km north of Kabul and about 50km north of the provincial capital city of Fayzabad. Detailed work was conducted by the joint Soviet/Afghan reconnaissance geological programme in the region in the 1960's. The work was primarily carried out on the Veka Dur gold prospect, including trench and adit sampling. Badakshan is the largest and most studied of the known gold-bearing quartz veins systems in the region. Many of the main drainages for the regions were sampled for placer gold by means of panned concentrates performed in the field. Several mapped areas show alluvial deposits that were trenched, and samples for which panned concentrates were developed and the gold content noted. Russian C1 + C2 Reserves for both Veka Dur and other quartz veins of 38.7Koz at 4.8g/t based on trench sampling. It is understood that the national grid will be expanded to Fayzabad in the future. There is an ample supply of water from the regional watersheds on the project area. Lapis lazuli sometimes abbreviated to lapis) is a relatively rare semi-precious stone that has been prized since antiquity for its intense blue color. Lapis lazuli was being mined in the Badakhshan province of Afghanistan as early as the 3rd millennium BC, and there are sources that are found as far east as in the region around Lake Baikal in Siberia. Trade in the stone is ancient enough for lapis jewelry to have been found at Predynastic Egyptian and ancient Sumerian sites, and as lapis beads at neolithic burials in Mehrgarh, the Caucasus, and even as far from Afghanistan as Mauritania The Government of Afghanistan supports a mining sector strategy that encourages legitimate and transparent private investment in the sector. Afghanistan is a country abundantly rich in natural resources. There are currently more than 1,400 mineral deposits that have been identified including energy minerals such as oil, gas and coal and other metallic and non-precious minerals such as lead, cement-grade limestone, gemstones, copper, iron, gold, salt, and industrial minerals (for use in the glass, ceramic, construction, chemical and fertilizer industries). Known precious and semi-precious stones include emerald, jade, amethyst, alabaster, beryl, lapis lazuli, tourmaline, ruby, quartz, and sapphire. Afghanistan's iron and copper deposits are of world-class quality. The hydrocarbons (petroleum and natural gas) industry provides great investment potential for Afghanistan, both financially and as a means for energy production. Recent findings in March 2006 indicate that the Afghan and Amu Darya Basins contain 18 times the oil and triple the natural gas reserves previously determined. The Government of Afghanistan ratified the Minerals Law in 2005 and ratified the Hydrocarbons Law (2006), which governs the natural gas and petroleum industries in the energy sector. These two laws are major initial steps in addressing how to create a regulatory framework for the development of these sectors and, most importantly, enable a suitable environment to attract and retain private investment. 2.1 Investment opportunity in Ghori Cement Plant Investment opportunities exist in the following areas: Portland cement blends Non-Portland hydraulic cements The Ghori Cement plant, located in the city of Puli Khomri in the North of Afghanistan was acquired by the Afghan Investment Company (AIC) under the privatization initiative of the Government in April 2007. The AIC is a group of highly successful and established Afghans with a solid base in Afghanistan and in-depth knowledge of the local conditions. The Ghori plant enjoys above-standard specifications with regards to its products due to the comparative advantage of having easy access to immense deposits of highgrade limestone / clay / coal /gypsum at relatively low cost. In the first three months of its operation AIC invested and repaired Ghori and was successful to increase the plant production capacity from 150 TPD to 400 TPD. To meet the increasing demand (estimated at closer to $1bn/year in Afghanistan alone and growing), AIC is in the process of completing Ghori II cement plant which was abandoned half finished 20 years ago. Ghori II Cement Plant has the capacity for 1000 TPD production which will be operational In 2007, the Chinese state-owned Metallurgical Group Corp., or MCC, signed a $3.5 billion lease for the Mes Aynak Copper Mine in mineral-rich Logar province, 15.5 miles (25 kilometers) southeast of Kabul.

The site is thought to contain the world's second-largest copper deposit, worth some $88 billion at today's prices. As part of the deal, the company will create training and education centers for Afghan personnel. To fully exploit the site, MCC will need to link the mine by rail to the Afghan capital, perhaps even extending the track to Pakistan and Uzbekistan. The rail project could cost MCC another $5 billion, and preliminary studies on the new rail network began in late 2010. Archaeological workers excavate a site on a mountaintop overlooking a patch of housing and offices at the Mes Aynak site last November. On-site production is still several years off, but prefabricated houses have already been put up by the Chinese state-owned MCC. Photo: Wikipedia Commons Mes Aynak is also the location of a major Buddhist archaeological site, including monuments to pseudo-Buddhism precursors. Some 400 artifacts, essentially doubling the size of the Afghan National Museum, have already come out of excavations in the area. It is hoped that over the next five years, valuable archaeological work can be done before mining activities fully begin. China will get to develop the site for the next 30 years. At the time, the deal represented the largest foreign investment ever made in Afghanistan's history. Last January, the China National Petroleum Corp., or CNPC, became the first company in the world in decades to sign an oil contract in Afghanistan — a deal worth $700 million for three oil fields along the Amu Darya River. CNPC is partnering with the Watan Group, believed to have connections to President Hamid Karzai's family, in a joint venture to develop the area's estimated 87 million barrels of oil. CNPC will give generous sums back to the Afghan government. A 15 percent royalty on oil, a 20 percent corporate tax, and 70 percent of profit go to Kabul. The amount of investment and effort Chinese companies are putting into the country doesn't just stop at natural resources. Chinese telecommunications giants Huawei Technologies Co. Ltd. and ZTE Corp. (the second- and fifth-largest telecom companies in the world, respectively) are installing digital switches and 200,000 lines in the country. Indeed, if anything currently differentiates the Chinese and American approaches, it is that China's engagement with Afghanistan is almost entirely driven by business deals, not by aid projects. Early last month, Beijing promised to grant the Afghan government $23.8 million in official aid, a paltry sum compared to the billions now being sunk into the country by state enterprises. The Chinese Foreign Ministry noted on June 6 that China will continue to provide assistance within its capacity to Afghanistan in line with its actual needs and strengthen cooperation with the country in fields such as resource development, infrastructure construction, energy, and personnel training. Days before Karzai's visit to Beijing to attend a major meeting of the Shanghai Cooperation Organization, a major Sino-Russian-Central Asian security and energy pact, the Chinese ambassador told the Afghan president that his country was the most reliable friend of Afghanistan. Robert Kaplan, geopolitical scholar and author, wrote in the New York Times in 2009 that [t]he whole direction of America's military and diplomatic effort is toward an exit strategy, whereas the Chinese hope to stay and profit. India Pushes Northwest China's drive into Afghanistan has also pulled India further in. Historical pride, insecurity about India's geopolitical standing, and the hunt for raw materials to power a surging economy are pushing New Delhi to make its own lasting mark on Afghanistan. This summer, the Ministry of Mines in Afghanistan is expected to announce a deal that will eclipse Mes Aynak: the finalization of a $10.8 billion bid for the right to develop a massive iron-ore deposit at Hajigak by a conglomerate of Indian state-owned mining companies called the Steel Authority of India Ltd. SAIL, India's largest steel maker, is expected to develop on-site mining and refining facilities and off-site road and rail infrastructure needed to transport ore from the location. The Hajigak site is located about 80.6 miles (130 kilometers) west of Kabul, in Bamyan province. It is estimated to hold more than 1.3 billion metric tons of high-grade iron ore. Sandeep Jojodia, the managing director of Monnet Ispat Ltd., one of the companies making up SAIL, told Bloomberg News late last year the deal will pave the path for more such formations bidding jointly for overseas assets.... It is something that China has done for years, [but now] Indian companies can join hands to tackle China's might. In June, the former Indian Army chief, Gen. V.K. Singh, called China's involvement in Afghanistan an outflanking move meant to strengthen links with Pakistan and further encircle India. India risks losing the influence it has in Afghanistan because of a China-Pakistan link that is getting stronger and is seen in evidence here, Singh said, describing the possibility of new tri-national transportation developments between present day Afghanistan, Pakistan, and China. Indian companies have already spent some $1.5 billion over the past 10 years on Afghanistan's roads, electric grid, schools, and government facilities. The new Afghan parliament building in Kabul is being built by India. C. Raja Mohan, a scholar at the Center for Policy Research in New Delhi, told Bloomberg that engaging and bringing stability to its northwest is the country's top foreign- policy priority, because most of our threats come from there. Beni Prassad Verma, the Indian minister for steel, told the press in April that Afghanistan is our old friend, and we want to invest lots of money in the sector of steel, natural gas, petroleum, and copper. This is our duty, to help Afghanistan. What Keeps The European Out? Duty — or national interest — aside, sites now being developed by Indian and Chinese companies are not without their own unique geographic challenges or security risks. Afghanistan is setting up a special unit to police and protect mining and mineral sites. The foreign operators will need that protection. Examples around the world, as in the Niger Delta and Colombia, have shown that foreign-operated sites are prime targets for insurgent groups and terrorists. The Logar region is thought to remain a major transit zone for Pakistan-based insurgents. But major Chinese or Indian companies may not care about that. They operate in some of the world's least-welcoming places, and they do so with state backing to keep toeholds in areas where Western companies are too risk-averse to enter and where there is still plenty of money to be made. Robert M. Cutler, a professor at Canada's Carleton University in Ottawa, said that when it comes to operating in Central Asia, companies from both countries have unquantifiable advantages — things like cultural affinity, regional familiarity, and fewer qualms about practices that cross the line of business ethics, combined with strong technical skills and comparatively low labor costs. It's not just Chinese and Indian companies that are getting involved in the country. Iran is also among the first to set up major facilities in Afghanistan. The Majd Industrial Pishgaman Co., an Iranian outfit specializing in cement, is building a factory in Herat, large enough to service much of the country. Cement may seem a quaint business venture, but Iranian companies have been perfecting it for years to defend against American and Israeli bunker-busting bombs, making cement one of Tehran's strategic industries. The Iranian plant in Herat will produce 1 million metric tons of cement a year. A construction boom in the country is expected to raise demand to 7.2 million metric tons a year by 2020 from 2.5 million metric tons in 2005. India, meanwhile, is also courting Iran to serve as a potential destination point for its railway linking the Hajigak mine to the outside world. A previous proposal to put track across Pakistan was a highly uncertain undertaking. The Indian-built Chabahar port in Iran, some 558 miles (900 kilometers) from Hajigak across vulnerable and exposed terrain in southwestern Afghanistan, may eventually be where the site's iron ore is offloaded. That would set up a competing line of transportation with China's proposed rail network, which may link to Pakistan and bring minerals north through East Turkistan present day Xinjiang or south to the Arabian Sea port of Gwadar. The only American company that has moved into the vast mining space in Afghanistan thus far has been a merchant bank, and, even then, very tentatively. Last year, JP Morgan Chase & Co. helped to arrange a comparatively small $40 million deal for individual Western investors to pool money in an Afghan gold mine pulling out a modest 5.4 metric tons of gold ore a year, in Qara Zaghan, north of Kabul. The only Western company slated for a significant contract in Afghanistan is Kilo Goldmines, a firm headquartered in Canada that is active mostly in gold mine reclamation in the Democratic Republic of Congo. The company is poised to develop a smaller portion of the Hajigak mine in a separate bid from SAIL. Kilo's CEO, Alex van Hoeken, called his firm a pioneer for entering its target regions. Van Hoeken objects to making comparisons between the DRC and Afghanistan, saying the challenges facing the two places are very different. Kilo has a reputation as a risk taker: Van Hoeken said his company's smaller size and flexible decision-making are the root causes of its success. Kilo refused to release any specific details on its contract bid with the Afghan Ministry of Mines, including its monetary value. On Friday, the Exxon Mobil Corp. indicated the multinational oil-and-gas company is considering exploring six moderately sized oil bids in northern Afghanistan. Exxon Mobil is the only fully private company bidding for the contract. Seven other potential competitors include state-owned companies from India, Brazil, Turkey, and Pakistan. Analysts quickly noted the move represented only an initial interest, not a firm commitment. A Great, Crooked Game? Not everything, though, is crystal-clear in Afghan mining. Nasir Shansab, the president of Afghan-American contracting company Acatco, operating in Afghanistan since 2002, accused both SAIL and Kilo of placing bids based on faulty premises. Acatco is not an impartial party. It lost out against both the Indian and the Canadian companies in proposals for the Hajigak mine. But its claims are nevertheless troubling, and if ultimately proven true, they would be damning for the Afghan government and its current approach to courting foreign investors. Shansab said his company raised $1.2 billion in guaranteed funds, offered the most faithful compliance to the requirements of the Afghan government, and promised the creation of indigenous steel processing, as well as the prospect of full-scale operations in three years. He accused SAIL and Kilo of being involved in bidding procedures mired in corruption and bribery, saying the two should have been disqualified. Shansab claimed the original bid requirements to return between 12.5 percent and 22.5 percent in royalties to the Afghan government was met by neither of his rivals, and there were no firm promises from either to develop a domestic processing and manufacturing capability in Afghanistan, a key stipulation. In letters to the Ministry of Mines, Acatco's president accused SAIL and Kilo of fraud and corruption, saying the evaluation process for the Hajigak tender has been deceptive. Shansab said that a gross exaggeration of the costs for developing the mine is likely being used to stuff pockets and cover up bribes. Shansab said he suspects Kilo, a company which had $29 million in aggregate assets last October, will eventually be unable to raise the money necessary for the mine, in effect awarding the entire project to an extension of the Indian government. However, he also said he expects the Indian conglomerate itself may face difficulties raising the massive funds it has promised for the bid. In December, SAIL approached the Indian government for $7.8 billion in aid and loans to support its bid. The announcement of the finalized contract award for SAIL and Kilo was delayed by the Ministry of Mines from last December to April, then to May, then to June, and it has yet to happen. According to Shansab, Minister for Mines Wahidullah Shahrani is giving away Afghanistan's arguably most valuable asset without any financial commitment at all. Afghan Mining Minister Wahidullah Shahrani promotes Afghan investment opportunities at a London conference on June 25, 2010. Photo: Reuters That's increasing suspicion among analysts that the bidding tenders so far have been decided based on building regional allies, not on actual financial soundness. However, the Afghanistan Embassy in Washington adamantly denied that Western bidders have been purposely rejected to favor Chinese and Indian ones for the purpose of establishing stronger diplomatic links. Shakib Noori, the commercial attache of the Afghanistan Embassay in the U.S., said his government is seeking balance and diversity in foreign investments. He called mining a long-term prospect for a development strategy for Afghanistan. If anything, the Afghan government is desperate for Western investors — but the latter simply have no interest in putting their money into the country. Noori said that, on average, for every 20 bids in response to an advertisement for a site by the Mining Ministry, only one or two are from Western companies. We encourage them to go to Afghanistan, to see for themselves said Noori, but they have a lack of information. Afghanistan (AP) — Despite the crackle of gunfire in the mountains of northern Afghanistan, the wealth of gold beneath will be mined under a multimillion-dollar contract that government officials approved on Monday. The deal is the first mining project in Afghanistan backed by private investors in the West. Afghan and U.S. officials hope many more deals will follow to help jump-start the economy of this impoverished nation in its 10 year of war. "This project is an important step forward for Afghanistan's economic sovereignty," U.S. deputy undersecretary of defense Paul A. Brinkley said in a statement on Monday. "It represents a turning point in the history of international investment into Afghanistan." Brinkley, who directs the defense department's Task Force for Business and Stability Operations, said the gold mine deal is evidence that Western investors are showing confidence in Afghanistan's economic future. About 10 investors — most of them from the United States and Britain — are investing an estimated $50 million in the gold project in Dushi district of Baghlan province, about 84 miles (135 kilometers) northwest of Kabul, according to Wahidullah Shahrani, Afghanistan's minister of mines. The only other gold mine in Afghanistan is in neighboring Takhar province. Shahrani said he hoped that getting the deal approved by the Inter-Ministerial Council, which comprises the government's top finance and economic officials, will send a strong signal to global mining companies that there are investment opportunities in Afghanistan, especially in the mining sector. Geologists have known for decades about Afghanistan's vast deposits of iron, copper, cobalt, gold and other prized minerals. In June, the U.S. Defense Department put a startling $1 trillion price tag on the reserves, but Shahrani called that a conservative estimate. He said he's seen geological assessments and industry reports estimating the nation's mineral wealth at $3 trillion or more. For Afghanistan, a violent, landlocked country with virtually no exports, the minerals are a potential windfall, although formidable obstacles remain, including lack of investment, infrastructure and adequate security in most of the nation. In late 2007, a $3 billion contract was awarded to China Metallurgical Group Corp. to mine copper at Aynak, 21 miles (35 kilometers) southeast of Kabul. The mine is thought to hold one of the world's largest unexploited copper reserves. Mining the copper could produce 4,000 to 5,000 Afghan jobs in the next five years and hundreds of millions of dollars a year to the government treasury, Shahrani said. Afghanistan's gold deposits are more modest. Shahrani said that Soviet-era studies valued Afghanistan's gold deposits at up to $25 billion. He said the estimate was conservative and added that new gold discoveries have been made. Afghanistan's gold is found across the country, but the heaviest known deposits are in Badakhshan, Takhar, Bamiyan, Ghazni and Zabul. "There is growing global demand for gold and right now the price of gold has reached the highest point in the history of mankind," Shahrani said. "Investing in gold is very attractive." J.P. Morgan, an international financial services firm, promoted the project and attracted the investors. Sadat Mansoor Naderi | Chairman of Afghan Gold Company They invested in an Afghan company called Afghan Gold. The chairman of the company is Sadat Mansoor Naderi, who runs SMN Group, one of the largest companies in Afghanistan. SMN, which employs about 3,000 people, owns the first private insurance company in Afghanistan, operates a small chain of supermarkets, builds roads, airports and bridges and distributes telecom cards and fuel. Taliban insurgents have been slowly expanding their presence in Baghlan and neighboring provinces, but the mine is located a three- to four-hour drive from the scene of recent fighting, To Hannam, chairman of J.P. Morgan Capital Markets, Afghanistan represents a gigantic, untapped opportunity — one of the last great natural-resource frontiers. Landlocked and pinioned by imperial invaders, Afghanistan has been cursed by its geography for thousands of years. Now, for the first time, Hannam believes, that geography could be an asset. The two most resource-starved nations on the planet, China and India, sit next door to Afghanistan, where, according to Pentagon estimates, minerals worth nearly $1 trillion lie buried. True, there is a war under way. And it's unclear how the death of Osama bin Laden will impact the country's political and economic environment. But Hannam is not your usual investment banker: A former soldier, he has done business in plenty of strife-torn countries. So have all the members of his team, two of them former special forces soldiers who have fought here. As he flies to the mine for the ribbon-cutting ceremony, Hannam thinks back over the past 12 months. This little mine, where operations have yet to commence, is puny by J.P. Morgan's (JPM) standards, but he knows it might be the project for which he is remembered. A lot of powerful people, including the commander of U.S. forces in Afghanistan, Gen. David Petraeus, are counting on him to demonstrate that the country is safe for foreign investors. Hannam has chafed at times under the pressure from the Pentagon, and the cold-eyed realist in him wonders whether unrealistic expectations are being placed on this business venture. Hannam ducks his head and climbs out of the chopper, necktie flapping in the prop wash. As he trudges up the hill, even the jaded, 55-year-old banker seems swept away by the pageantry of the moment: the village elder in a ceremonial robe, the silhouettes of women watching from the ridges, the saluting Afghan soldier. Hannam is enveloped in a crush of local tribesmen chattering excitedly in Dari. One of them puts a garland around his neck. Another hands him a Ziploc bag containing a chunk of Afghan gold. A mullah utters prayers. Afghanistan's minister of mining gives a long speech. Hannam and his local partner, Sadat Naderi, walk up the hill to pose for photographs. Naderi points to a narrow band of quartz that runs in an east-west line across the cliff side. It shimmers in the sun. That is the treasure, he says. "Unless," Hannam mutters, "it's fool's gold." Absurd risks vs. amazing rewards Investing in conflict zones is often thrilling, but the great commodities rush that J.P. Morgan and the Pentagon are trying to spark in Afghanistan creates a risk/reward equation of a different magnitude. It's extreme at both ends. When J.P. Morgan launched its Afghan initiative in 2010, violence was at its worst since the American-led occupation began in 2001. The Taliban have made a point of killing Westerners and have specifically said they would attack any companies involved in mining. Before our trip to the mine was done, our group would get a taste of the insurgents' ability to strike violently and unpredictably. Then there's the Afghan infrastructure — or rather, there isn't. Big mines need power, lots of it. Outside of cities, only 15% of Afghanistan is electrified. The mountain roads — ungraded and often without guardrails — are perilous, I learned the hard way, particularly in winter. Seat belts? No one bothers. You crash, you die. If the brutal war and roads don't give a businessperson pause, the country's governance and corruption problems should. Massive fraud marred recent elections. Transparency International rates Afghanistan as the second most corrupt country on earth after Somalia. The last minister of mining was identified in a Washington Post report as the recipient of a massive bribe, an allegation he denied to *Fortune*. The current minister, who had been widely described as an honest reformer, has recently had his integrity questioned in State Department cables released by WikiLeaks. He, too, told *Fortune* he has done nothing improper. But if the risks are absurd, the potential rewards are off the charts. Hundreds of billions of dollars' worth of iron, copper, rare earth metals, and, yes, gold are buried beneath Afghanistan's deserts and mountains. This wealth has lain there mainly undisturbed for thousands of years as armies of Greeks, Mongols, Britons, Russians, and now Americans tramped above. Invaders have dreamed of exploiting it since the time of Alexander the Great, but no one has yet succeeded on a large scale. Aryana-Khorasan dynasty present day Afghanistan-Central Asia & India A Chinese company is trying to start a copper operation in strife-torn Logar province, but actual mining is years away. In an 1841 article in a journal of Asiatic studies, Capt. Henry Drummond, a member of the British 3rd Bengal Light Cavalry, described his rambles through the wildest parts of Afghanistan to conduct the first Western mineral survey of the country. He found "abundant green stains" of copper, some of which rivaled the deposits of Chile, and veins of iron ore that "might no doubt be obtained equal to the Swedish." While many of his countrymen viewed Afghanistan as an untamable place, where a man could not stray many yards from his home or tent without risk of being murdered, Drummond was smitten. Mining, he felt — not the gun — offered the best hope to pacify the territory and win over Afghans. "Give them, however, but constant employment, with good wages and regular payment; encourage a spirit of industry, both by precept and example; let strict justice be dealt out to them without respect of persons; and we shall shortly see their swords changed into plowshares, industry take place of licentiousness, and these people be converted into peaceable and useful subjects," Drummond wrote. But the Afghans weren't keen on the idea of handing over their minerals to occupiers, or on the British occupation itself, for that matter. A year later they massacred the entire British army, save one English survivor, at Gandamak. During the Cold War, both Soviet and U.S. geologists conducted surveys. The Russians bored thousands of test holes and identified big deposits of copper, zinc, mercury, tin, fluorite, potash, talc, asbestos, and magnesium. But instability in the countryside put an end to serious mining exploration. After the toppling of the Taliban by the U.S.-led coalition, the Afghan government, with financial assistance from the U.S. Agency for International Development, commissioned new, high-tech aerial surveys of Afghanistan. The results were stunning: The U.S. Geological Survey identified huge veins of copper, iron, lithium, gold, and silver. The Afghan government solicited bids for one of the biggest of the copper deposits, a site south of Kabul that had been identified by both Drummond and the Soviets. China, offering a rich price, won the bid in 2007, beating out four other mining companies. But the Chinese mining company has yet to extract any copper from the site because of delays clearing land mines from the area, and the discovery of archeological relics. Then, in 2009, mining in Afghanistan got the push it needed — from the U.S. military. Petraeus had been appointed commander of U.S. Central Command, which had ultimate authority over Afghanistan. He realized that a U.S. exit from Afghanistan depended on getting the country's economy running. Up to 60% of Afghanistan's $15 billion GDP comes from foreign aid, according to Pentagon estimates, and another 20% comes from the illicit drug trade — poppies. What Afghanistan needed was the real hope that it might achieve economic sovereignty. "I'm an old economist," the general says in an interview at his headquarters in Kabul. "And at the end of the day this is about progress for the [Afghan] people and giving them the prospect for a much brighter future for them and their families. That's what persuades the citizenry to support the government rather than support the Taliban." Realizing that conventional foreign-aid organizations weren't getting the job done, Petraeus moved a crack economic stabilization team from Iraq into Afghanistan. That team quickly realized that mining would be key. Enter Ian Hannam. "This is the time in Afghanistan for the adventure venture capitalists — for those who can do business in tough places in the world," Petraeus says. From special forces to making billionaires Villagers at Qara Zaghan hope mining will bring jobs, electricity, schools, and a health clinic. Ian Charles Hannam seemed bound for a swashbuckling career at an early age. Raised in a working-class neighborhood in South London, the son of a council worker who oversaw a housing and street-repair crew, Hannam grew up knowing that nothing would ever be handed to him. He joined the Territorial Special Air Service at age 17, one of the younger men to pass the service's grueling selection process. Hannam's unit, the Artists Rifles, was a part-time regiment akin to a U.S. National Guard special forces unit. The Artists Rifles had a storied past and a reputation for attracting adventure seekers from all social classes. Since then, Hannam has counted his old SAS cronies as his closest friends, often calling on them to help him in the world's tougher places. While serving in the Artists Rifles, Hannam pursued a degree in civil engineering from England's top school in that field, Imperial College. Upon graduation in 1977, he took a job with Taylor Woodrow, a large British construction firm. His first assignment was to build roads, radar stations, and airstrips in Oman for the SAS, which was in the final stages of crushing a Marxist-led insurgency that had been boiling in the Dhofar region for more than a decade. The experience convinced Hannam that revolts could be beaten with a counterinsurgency program that emphasized developing a country's infrastructure and natural resources. Still working for Taylor Woodrow, Hannam went to Nigeria and then back to Oman. Living in a tent, he could not help noticing how well oil-company executives lived. That's when he decided to go to business school and become rich. After graduating from the London Business School, Hannam got a job in 1984 in the training program at Salomon Brothers in New York. At the airport on his way home to London for Christmas that year, he was detained by immigration officials because he had no U.S. entry stamp on his passport. The reason: He had parachuted into the U.S. with an SAS unit that was training with American special forces, and then traveled to New York to start the training program. With a work ethic that former colleagues describe as ferocious and an engineer's taste for understanding complex financial mechanisms, Hannam was fast-tracked to the bank's vaunted debt syndicate desk. "His embrace of complexity and change, his indifference to organizational hierarchy and abundant self-confidence born of experience set him apart," recalls Terry Fitzgerald, founder of Longbow Capital Partners, who was at Salomon with Hannam. When Salomon was hired to advise media baron Robert Maxwell's Mirror Group during its public offering, Hannam was one of Salomon's lead bankers charged with marketing the IPO. Salomon lost money on the deal. Months later Maxwell died and Mirror Group collapsed amid investigations into accounting fraud and raids on its pension fund. Hannam left Salomon soon after the fiasco and was hired by merchant bank Robert Fleming, a Scottish firm founded by the grandfather of James Bond creator Ian Fleming. By 2000, Hannam was the highest-paid employee at Fleming, making more than the CEO. After the bank was acquired by J.P. Morgan, much of Fleming's staff was laid off. Not Hannam. He helped engineer a joint venture with, and eventual takeover of, venerated British banking house Cazenove. Among the old guard at Cazenove — which was subsumed by J.P. Morgan, though the British franchise still bears its name — Hannam was regarded as a bit of a barbarian. He bragged about his wealth. He had appalling table manners. "I've got more degrees than I can count, but I still talk like I'm illiterate, and my colleagues hate me for it," he'd say. From Congo to Colombia, from Iraq to Sierra Leone, Hannam and his small team of soldiers-turned-bankers and advisers did business with oligarchs, gem dealers, and former mercenaries. He could be bracingly direct. When he landed in Baghdad for a meeting with Iraq's oil minister, the minister asked, "What are you here for?" "I'm here to make five new Iraqi billionaires every year for the next 10 years," Hannam said with a twinkle in his eyes. It was an effective icebreaker, recalled his friend Richard Williams, a former SAS commander who is now CEO of the Afghan gold mine. "They're all thinking, 'How can I be one of those?' Which is not a question that a minister should be thinking." However crude, Hannam's point — it would be Iraqis, not Westerners, who were getting rich — worked. At an emerald mine high above the Panjshir Valley, work is done by kerosene lantern. Over the years Hannam had starring roles in a string of huge deals, including the combination of BHP and Billiton (BHP) and its listing on the London exchange, the creation of mining group Xstrata, and the formation of Kazakh commodities giant Kazakhmys. In 2007, Hannam's appetite for risk and intrigue nearly sank him. A group of Omani investors had hired him to explore the possibility of a leveraged buyout and breakup of Dow Chemical. Hannam and another top J.P. Morgan executive held clandestine meetings with two Dow Chemical executives at the Compleat Angler, a luxury hotel on the bank of the Thames, The only problem: Dow's CEO had no idea that the meeting was taking place. The scandal attracted front-page notice around the world. In 2008, Hannam was passed over for the top job at Cazenove in favor of an outsider. Hannam flew to New Zealand for two weeks, turned off the phone, and brooded. But he decided to stay at the bank, and soon he was doing multibillion-dollar deals again, including lead work on the recapitalization of HSBC. With a job that paid bonuses as high as 10 million pounds, Hannam had come a long way from his boyhood in Bermondsey. He had a wife and three children, a townhouse in Notting Hill, a wild game preserve in the Stormberg mountains of South Africa, and a 230-acre estate in Vermont. But the council worker's son was hungry for something bigger. In 2009, at a dinner in Baghdad, he met the man who would give him his chance. The name of their meeting place was fitting for a rendezvous that would help touch off a 21st-century version of the Great Game: the Baghdad Hunting Club. Hannam was at the banquet hall for a reception thrown by the Trade Bank of Iraq to honor J.P. Morgan. Also at the reception was Paul Brinkley, a deputy under secretary of defense charged with jump-starting Iraq's stalled economy. A former tech company executive, Brinkley served as a matchmaker of sorts between Iraqi entrepreneurs and foreign businessmen. With the blessing of Defense Secretary Robert Gates, he operated outside normal bureaucratic channels, eschewing the bulletproof vests and helmets his civilian colleagues wore in combat zones. In three years he had secured some $8 billion in private investment contracts for Iraq, helping start textile mills, cement factories, and electronics companies. Hannam and Brinkley had heard about each other's work. J.P. Morgan had been one of the first Western companies to plant the flag in Iraq, overseeing the country's currency and setting up a big oil project in Iraqi Kurdistan. Hannam and Brinkley fell into conversation about Afghanistan, which was to be Brinkley's next posting. Soon they were having more meetings, in New York and Washington. Brinkley wanted to know what it would take to get the big international mining companies into Afghanistan. Hannam said it was too early. The giants weren't likely to leap into Afghanistan until smaller, wildcat operators went first. Copper and iron-ore mines were complicated and required huge infrastructure investments: railroads, roads, power plants, and smelters. Hannam said the first project should be less ambitious. A gold or lithium mine would be perfect. These materials could be transported by helicopter or trucked out by road. Hannam and Brinkley agreed that any such project should be led by an Afghan, lest it be seen as part of a resource grab by foreigners. Hannam pledged to bring entrepreneurial support, technical expertise, and capital. "And I'll make some Afghans very rich, by the way," he added. In February 2010, Hannam flew to Kabul to see the situation on the ground. Brinkley took him to a reception at the American ambassador's home. There, Hannam met an Afghan businessman named Sadat Naderi. British educated, smooth, and brimming with energy and ambition, Naderi ran a diversified company that included insurance, logistics, and supermarkets. There was one other thing, he said: "I'm one of the first Afghans that has actually won a gold license." Hannam's eyes lit up. Naderi, it turned out, already had a little gold mine in Baghlan province. His family had run a tiny artisanal operation there, even minting some coins, for years. He had won the legal rights to it in formal bidding in 2008. To develop it, he needed technical advice, equipment, and capital. Naderi was an Ismaili, a member of a Shiite sect. That was a good thing in Hannam's eyes. Progressive in their views toward women and education, Ismailis are renowned businessmen. The Ismailis' religious leader, the Aga Khan, presides over a vast charitable and business network that includes the Serena Hotel chain. The sect has a long-standing relationship with the British, dating back to the 1840s, when Ismailis provided British armies in Afghanistan with cavalry and intelligence. Naderi's father was the religious leader of all the Ismailis in Afghanistan. The family has several mansions and a palace in their home village, Kayan, which has athletic facilities and a train, and once had a zoo. Naderi's brother Jafar had been a militia commander during the last days of Soviet occupation, with a 12,000-member private army. A documentary film titled *The Warlord of Kayan* had shown Jafar fishing with a grenade, riding his motorcycle, and blasting AC/DC. During the Taliban era, the Naderis had fled for their lives, and Osama bin Laden briefly occupied their palace in Kayan. Sadat Naderi, not surprisingly, was happy to contemplate an investment of working capital raised by J.P. Morgan and backed up by the Pentagon. "The sooner we stand on our own feet, the better it is for us Afghans," Naderi says. "You cannot be a beggar nation forever." "Don't fall behind." Naderi's gold mine, in Baghlan province, is only 50 miles from Kabul as the crow flies. During winter months it might as well be on the moon. To get there by road you must traverse the dangerous Salang Pass, which cuts through the towering Hindu Kush range. In 2010, in the same month that the J.P. Morgan team first arrived in Afghanistan, 180 travelers were killed on the pass in an avalanche. we had my own taste of winter travel over the 11,000-foot-high pass when we set out with a convoy led by Richard Williams, the mining company's CEO. Garrulous, self-deprecating, and brimming with insights about the Muslim world, Williams could be mistaken for an Oxford don. But he remains the hard-charging individual depicted in Mark Urban's book *Task Force Black*, which describes Williams' exploits in Iraq as the leader of an SAS team charged with capturing and killing Hussein loyalists and al Qaeda members. "Richard is a buccaneer, a pirate," Urban quoted one of Williams' former associates as saying. "He goes for the opportunities and adrenalin every time." Herding and farming are the main economic activities in Qara Zaghan. It was snowing when we left Kabul early one morning, and by the time we reached the start of the climb, the weather had turned so nasty that police had halted traffic up the road. Nonetheless, our party of VIPs received permission to proceed with a police escort. Williams and his group were in armored, four-wheel-drive vehicles. There was no room in the caravan for me, a translator, and a photographer, so we hired a driver and a Toyota Corolla. The front-wheel-drive car was soon laboring in the heavy snow. Our chains kept slipping off the tires. The radiator overheated, belching coolant into the snow. When it became apparent that we might not keep up, Williams' group put a policeman in our car, and then proceeded on ahead without us. Visibility was terrible; the only way our driver could navigate was to crane his neck out a side window. After we passed the summit, the driver lost control of the car, which skidded and spun 180 degrees into a snowbank. Hands trembling, I lit my first cigarette in decades, wheezing on the first puff. The next day, after spending the night in a hut, we set off on the return trip to Kabul. I begged Williams and his group not to abandon us. But when one of our party was stricken by a stomach ailment and we pulled over to let him relieve himself, the convoy swept on without us. We spun out again, narrowly missing a head-on collision with a truck. When we caught up with Williams' convoy near Kabul, we were too furious to wave. "we thought the SAS motto was similar to that of the U.S. Army [Rangers]: 'Leave no man behind,' "we complained to one of Hannam's soldiers-turned-bankers afterward. "Leave no man behind?" He laughed. "Where did you get that idea? It's 'Don't fall behind.' And 'Don't forget your Imodium!' "A deal too important to die Of all the obtacles that could have wrecked the mining project — the murderous roads, the Taliban, the corrupt government — the one that nearly killed it was the most predictable: the profit margin. In late September, J.P. Morgan CEO Jamie Dimon, Brinkley, and Mining Minister Wahidullah Shahrani met at J.P. Morgan's headquarters in Manhattan. Dimon pledged J.P. Morgan's support. On the way down in the elevator, Dimon told Shahrani, "You're in good hands with Ian. He's eccentric, but he gets things done." But soon Brinkley's team was wondering. On the day the deal signing was to take place, Hannam's team stopped acting like former warriors and began behaving like, well, nervous investment bankers. Hannam, after talking about how rich he was going to make his clients, suddenly began to complain that there was no way to make a profit. The 26% royalty rate for the mine, his team claimed, was way too high. Mining Minister Shahrani was bewildered — the rate had been agreed upon years before, when the Naderi family had first bid for the mine. Nothing had changed. Brinkley's Pentagon team was deeply frustrated. They felt the bankers had pulled a fast one. Had Hannam's group not done its homework? Or were they just being bankers, trying to squeeze more money out of the deal with some 11th-hour brinkmanship? Brinkley lit into the J.P. Morgan group: "When are you going to get this done? You've told people you're going to do it!" The bankers, in turn, felt they were being unfairly pressured by the government, which seemed desperate to get the deal done even if it was uneconomical. Villagers of Qara Zaghan have been digging for gold for decades. Everyone recognized, though, that the deal was too important to die. Naderi and Hannam's team worked out an arrangement with the Ministry of Mines in which the royalty would be deducted from the corporate tax, as it is in many other countries. Soon, helped by rising gold prices, the deal was back on track. J.P. Morgan says it is not charging its usual advisory fees. While Hannam has described his work on the mine as a charitable endeavor, he says he expects a big payoff down the road for clients who invest in it. J.P. Morgan says it isn't putting any of its own money into the project. Hannam secured $40 million from investors in the U.S., Asia, and Europe. They included Enso Capital founder Joshua Fink, son of BlackRock's Larry Fink; British mining titan Peter Hambro; and Thai businessman Pairoj Piempongsant. Hannam created an investment vehicle, Central Asian Resources, to enter into a joint venture with Naderi's new mining company, Afghan Gold, Sadat Naderi was made chairman of Afghan Gold, and Richard Williams CEO. Their goal is to pull 5.4 metric tons of gold from the mine during the first phase of operation. After that the plan is to go after five other gold sites, and then bid for the rights to other minerals, including copper and rare earths. This past December, an ecstatic minister of mines announced the deal. Petraeus congratulated President Karzai on the news. "Wonderful," Petraeus remembers Karzai saying. "It's big," Petraeus told me of the gold mine deal. "It's very big. I mean, everyone knows who J.P. Morgan is, and what that represents. That's substantial. It gives real encouragement to our Afghan partners." A deceptive peace After the ceremony to inaugurate the mine in Qara Zaghan, the barren valley rang with a merry hubbub. Hannam's close friend, Murad Megalli, responsible for J.P. Morgan's investment banking practice in Central Asia and the Middle East, made portraits of the villagers with a Leica film camera. The minister of mines was exultant. Naderi spoke optimistically of "partnership" with his new investors. Everything seemed to be going right. Then it wasn't. At a military base on our way back to Kabul, our Black Berrys started buzzing with news of a Taliban attack in the capital. Militants had struck one of Naderi's supermarkets, called Finest, with guns and a bomb, killing eight people. Naderi at first didn't understand what I was saying when we told him the news of the attacks. "The Finest got hit," we said. "Hit?" Naderi said. "Finest hit?" He turned ashen. Megalli and Hannam sat on a bench trying to digest what had happened. Hannam was at first convinced the attack was linked to J.P. Morgan's presence in the country. It wasn't. (The Taliban later claimed they were trying to kill an American mercenary who they erroneously claimed was at the store.) Then, Hannam immediately put his banker hat back on. At least the deal was done, he said, and the money was in. Megalli was struck by how fast things could spiral out of control. "The peace here is so deceptive," Megalli said. "It is so fragile." A week later returned Kabul to receive this from Hannam about his colleague and friend: "Murad died in plane in Kurdistan yesterday. Any good photos I can give family?" Murad Megalli and Hannam had flown out of Afghanistan on a private plane, and then gone their separate ways. Megalli had taken the plane to Kurdistan. The plane crashed in a snowstorm, and Megalli and another J.P. Morgan banker were killed. Hannam was devastated. From the meeting with Brinkley at the Baghdad Hunting Club, Megalli had been a champion of the Afghan venture. He had believed mining could make a difference for the country. His death, and the attack on Naderi's supermarket, were sobering reminders of the personal risks of frontier capitalism. Baghlan Province has gold but few roads and no rail service, making it a challenging place to do business. Other storm clouds hover over the enterprise. Corruption allegations swirl around several key backers of the mining project in the Karzai government. Paul Brinkley's Pentagon team, which energized the Afghan mining sector and also put hundreds of Afghans to work in manufacturing technology and agriculture, is being disbanded, a casualty of interagency warfare. In April, after the burning of a Koran in Gainesville, Fla., mobs rioted in Afghanistan. The UN compound in Mazar-i-Sharif – a city that is to play a key role in the shipment of gold from the Baghlan mine — was attacked, and 12 people were killed. The spark that Brinkley and Hannam struck, however, continues to burn. Six major minerals sites are due to be auctioned by the Afghan government over the next year. SRK, a major mining-consulting firm, will advise the Afghan government. Bankers from Morgan Stanley MS and executives from Chevron (CVX) have been scouting Afghan natural-resource prospects. And next January the bulldozers and crushing machines are set to start working in the remote valley where Hannam's investors have staked their claim. It remains to be seen whether the J.P. Morgan adventure will leave any more indelible a mark on Afghanistan than did Capt. Drummond of the Bengal Light Cavalry 170 years ago. But at least someone will have begun releasing the wealth trapped in Afghanistan's stones. Industrial metals such as copper and lithium could put the war-torn country in high demand for high-tech industry. Reports that as much as $ trillion worth of minerals may lie in Afghan soils are really not surprising, says Bruce Herbert, assistant head of the department of geology and geophysics at Texas A&M University. U.S. officials have surveyed the area and concluded that vast amounts of iron, copper, gold, cobalt, and lithium are likely plentiful in the region. "Soviet geologists first surveyed Afghanistan for economically important minerals," Herbert says. "The U.S. Geological Survey started surveying the country in 2004. Afghanistan has all sorts of valuable minerals, and if the accounts of lithium are true, it could be a tremendous boost for their economic future." Cell phone batteries contain lithium. Anyone who owns a BlackBerry or other cell phone, a laptop computer, or even a flashlight, is a consumer of lithium. The soft, silvery-looking metal is in high demand in high-tech times and deposits of it could mean instant wealth. "Lithium is found in two sources—one is in volcanic rocks, and the other is in desert areas, such as those found in Afghanistan," Herbert explains. "Argentina and Chile have significant amounts, in the U.S. it's found mainly in Nevada, and China has some. But it's a relatively rare mineral and there's not much of it in the world, so any new deposits are always welcome. "Most of the batteries in cell phones or laptop computers have lithium in them, so the demand for it has skyrocketed in recent years and will likely continue to do so," he adds. "Even many of the common flashlight batteries have lithium in them. New technology seems to be driven by lithium." A derivative of the mineral is also used by the drug industry to treat depression, bipolar disorders, and migraine headaches. Afghanistan's economy has been devastated by decades of wars, and the gross domestic product of the country is estimated to be about $12 billion. The country has been a center of the narcotics trade, specializing in opium production. Herbert says no one knows exactly how much lithium Afghanistan has. But the good news is that if the mineral is there, it is not hard to extract. "Usually, lithium in salt deposits is found near the surface," he says. "You don't have to go hundreds of feet down to find it like you do other minerals, so it's relatively easy to mine. "If all the reports of vast amounts of lithium in Afghanistan are true, it could be a huge boost for that country." Two former members of the UK's SAS, the highly regarded British army special forces unit, are nowadays closely involved in exploring for, and mining, gold in Afghanistan. Perhaps it is this type of military experience that is necessary in developing the mineral resources of such a potentially hostile, geographically and politically, area of the world. The first of the ex-SAS men is investment banker Ian Hannam, a renowned dealmaker formerly with JP Morgan Chase and, in his time, intimately associated with such mega deals as the merger of BHP and Billiton, the original launch of Xstrata, and in many of its mergers and acquisitions since and the formation of Kazkhmys, all in the resource sector. Hannam was drawn in, enthusiastically, to the prospect of helping develop Afghanistan's mineral wealth, initially by the U.S. state department which was keen to help promote foreign investment in the country. U.S. studies, drawing heavily on previous Soviet geological findings, had come up with Afghan mineral resources which could be worth in excess of $1 trillion and including copper, iron ore, gold, huge deposits of lithium, rare earths and others Pentagon: Afghanistan may have $1 trillion undeveloped mineral wealth, and DOD, USGS unveil latest revolutionary Afghanistan strategic initiative–mining). U.S. government entities – notably within the military, were keen to find some means of developing the Afghan economy and it was a chance meeting in Baghdad between Hannam and Paul Brinkley, then U.S. Deputy Under Secretary of Defense charged with business development stability in the former war areas of Iraq and Afghanistan, which set Hannam on the Afghan mining path. To cut a long story short, Hannam teamed up with an English-educated Afghan, Sadat Naderi, whose family had long-owned a small artisanal gold mining operation around 60 miles north of Kabul at Qara Zaghan. The gold operation had potential to be far larger, but Naderi had neither the expertise, nor the capital to develop it. Hannam set up a company, Centar plc, to invest in Naderi's company Afghan Gold and Minerals and apparently holds 45% and has brought in a number of prominent investors, chief among which is Jan Kulczyk, reputed to be Poland's richest man, Peter Hambro and Chip Goodyear (former CEO of BHP Billiton). Kulczyk's company, Kulczyk Investments, owns 28% of Centar (Kulczyk is chairman of the company) and notes the latter's activities as follows: Centar's first investment in Afghanistan is a 45% share in Afghan Gold & Minerals Co, the first Afghan exploration and production company with international shareholding. The Afghan Gold & Minerals portfolio includes: A 100% interest in the Qara Zaghan Gold Project in northern Afghanistan. Bulk sampling has started at the project site; A 50% interest in a joint venture with a Turkish company Yildizlar, the largest silver producer in Turkey, which intends to develop the Badakshan gold and silver deposit in north-east Afghanistan; A 100% interest in an Afghan company providing specialized mining services; A 100% interest in an Afghan company providing laboratory and assay services. Interestingly the services companies noted above have been set up to explore and service the Afghan properties and others in the country – they imported the first modern exploration drill rig into Afghanistan, and are providing assay services for Qara Zaghan and other Afghan mineral properties as there had previously been no local assaying facilities. It is at this point the second SAS man in the team comes in. He is Richard Williams, who was a former regiment commander with the SAS in Iraq and Afghanistan and is a long-time friend of Hannam's. He has been appointed CEO of Afghan Gold and Minerals and has been tasked with bringing the Afghan operations into production. According to reports, the logistics of getting to Qara Zaghan from Kabul are, to say the least, challenging, particularly in the winter months as it involves traversing the notorious Salang Pass at an altitude of 11,000 ft. But to an extent that is one of the appeals of the project. It is isolated and difficult for even the Taliban to get to. Gold concentrates would be airlifted out by helicopter avoiding the possibility of gold shipments being ambushed in a country where banditry can be rife, let alone the Taliban. However, in commenting to the U.K.'s Sunday Times, Hannam makes light on the dangers involved and reckons that mining in Afghanistan is statistically no more risky than working in Nigeria. A small but potentially profitable gold mining operation is seen as ideal for kick starting an Afghan mining industry in that the right deposit can be mined without huge capital investment. It is also seen as important that a locally owned and controlled company like Afghan Gold and Minerals should take the lead. If a small operator can be seen as successful then, the theory goes, the larger players will come in to exploit the country's undoubted mineral riches. (June 14) — Until now, impoverished Afghanistan has been known for only two deadly exports: opium and terrorism. But according to new research by a team of geologists and U.S. defense officials, the country is sitting on top of $1 trillion in mineral resources and could become one of the world's most important mining centers, "There is stunning potential here," Gen. David Petraeus, commander of the U.S. Central Command, told the paper. "There are a lot of ifs, of course, but we think potentially it is hugely significant. "There is stunning potential here," Gen. David H. Petraeus, commander of the United States Central Command, said of the minerals found in Afghanistan. The

Times noted that aerial surveys had revealed huge untapped seams of iron, copper, cobalt, gold and increasingly vital metals like lithium, which is used in the manufacture of rechargeable batteries for mobile phones, laptops and electric cars. An internal Pentagon memo was quoted as saying that Afghanistan could become the "Saudi Arabia of lithium." Although it would take decades to develop a fully functioning mining industry in this war-torn nation, which still lacks a decent road system and basic infrastructure, Afghan and American officials believe that the discoveries could soon provide much-needed jobs as international investments pour into the country. That could help encourage Taliban fighters to put down their weapons, finally ending three decades of internal conflict. "This will become the backbone of the Afghan economy," Jalil Jumriany, an adviser to the Afghan minister of mines, told the Times. The Times report said the U.S. Geological Survey began an aerial analysis of Afghanistan's mineral resources in 2006, using data collected by Russian experts during the Soviet occupation of the country in the 1980s. After positive initial results, a more sophisticated study was carried out in 2007. Then last year, a Pentagon task force that had set up business development programs in Iraq analyzed the geologists' findings. American mining experts were brought in to approve the survey's conclusions, and top U.S. and Afghan officials were briefed. The biggest mineral deposits discovered so far are of iron and copper. But the finds include large deposits of more unusual minerals, including niobium — a soft metal used in the production of superconducting steel — rare earth elements and large gold deposits in the Pashtun areas of southern Afghanistan. But some commentators have been less than impressed with the apparently outdated announcement, suggesting that it could be timed to distract attention from the worsening military situation. Writing in Foreign Policy, Blake Hounshell said that, "the findings on which the story was based are online and have been since 2007, courtesy of the U.S. Geological Surve While the discoveries could re-energize the tiny aid-dependent Afghan economy — the country's gross domestic product is only about $12 billion — and help drive the peace process, there is a strong risk that they could fuel further conflict. The Times noted that the promise of such wealth might lead the Taliban to up their bloody campaign to regain control of the country. Other experts point out that the discovery of massive mineral wealth rarely helps impoverished countries. Congo and Angola, for example, have been torn apart by factions fighting for control of mining sites. Such a sudden injection of wealth could also worsen government corruption. Just last year, for example, Afghanistan's minister of mines was accused by U.S. officials of accepting a $30 million bribe to award China the rights to develop a copper mine. The minister has since been replaced. American officials worry that resource-hungry China could try to gain further control over the development of Afghanistan's mineral wealth That would frustrate the United States, which has pumped huge amounts of money into the country. "The big question is, can this be developed in a responsible way, in a way that is environmentally and socially responsible?" Paul Brinkley, deputy undersecretary of defense for business and leader of the Pentagon team that discovered the deposits, told the Times. "No one knows how this will work." It's winter in the Northern Hemisphere and another snowstorm is descending across the Great Lakes. Traffic will snarl, walking will become a chore, and those staying home will come to feel like they are under house arrest. It seems inevitable, yet almost cruel, to then dream of summer's golden reverie. The surfers are almost incidental–tiny figurines or animate shadows whose puny shapes are there only to remind us how much the lavish, liquid sunlight dwarfs human scale. One has to labor to realize that the photograph shows only light, not pools of molten gold. And yet, even as that gold pools on a plane of sand and sea that also seems forged of the sun's metal, there is a dark undertone. The day is long, and we know that this moment of sheer natural extravagance cannot last. A moment out of time is still tinged with mortality. Here the golden light is even more pronounced, and yet the drama of light and darkness is sharper still. The brilliant horizon, as if the sea were another sun, flows like lava into the city of Cape Town, but both sky and land are already under another dispensation. But the light always returns. Indeed, it ennobles all that it touches. Here an arid land, fractured by mountains and riven by war, appears like Shangri La. The golden mountains of Afghanistan, one might imagine, looking like pure gold, set in the middle distance of God's eye, surely a blessed place. And surely not a blessed place, if you think of the suffering there, with more to come. And so gold can seem to be no more than a trick of light, just as it also is an obviously artificial commodity, a fictional standard, and the stuff only of distraction and fantasy. The eye is easily mislead, one might say, and so both photographic art and serious thought should stick to reality's gray scale. But these images reveal another truth, one that could have genuinely radical implications. The golden light is but one aspect of the sun's unending flow across the earth, and with that, of humanity's ever present wealth. No one–ever–accomplishes anything without this free gift of energy that could never be created otherwise. There is a metaphor here as well (another extravagance), for sunlight not only gives of itself but represents other forms of wealth. The lesson of these images is not that warmth or beauty or any human good is necessarily apportioned to certain times or places, but that the good life is constantly available for those who can learn to see. As we said before, the deeper challenge now facing politics, and so art, is not to manage scarcity but to realize the abundance already available in nature and culture. Abundance that often is not seen up close and that might be waiting where least expected, as if far out at sea or on distant mountains The Indian consortium that will mine copper and gold in Afghanistan is expected to meet on the first week of June to discuss each member's equity shareholding after due diligence work on the mineral deposits has been completed. The consortium members included Hindustan Copper Ltd., Nalco, SAIL and MECL. "We have sent four teams to Afghanistan for site visit. We will study their reports and do a due diligence on the reserves. The last of these teams will return on June 5. We are scheduled to meet after that to take a call on equity shareholding among the consortium members. We are getting feelers from other private players interested in joining the consortium and will decide on whether to invite them as part of the team," Shakeel Ahmed, chairman of HindustanCopper Ltd., said in The Economic Times. Among the private players shortlisted by the Afghan mines ministry were Sterlite Industries, Monnet Ispat & Energy and Jindal Steel & Power. Apart from the Indian consortium, the Afghan mines ministry had likewise shortlisted big investor candidates from Canada, the Emirates, and Australia to mine its copper and gold deposits. The United States has recently discovered nearly $100 trillion in untapped mineral deposits in Afghanistan, far beyond any previously known reserves and enough to fundamentally alter the Afghan economy and perhaps the Afghan war itself, according to senior American government officials. The previously unknown deposits including huge veins of iron, copper, cobalt, gold and critical industrial metals like lithium are so big and include so many minerals that are essential to modern day industry that Afghanistan could eventually become one of the most important mining centers in the world, the United States officials believe. While it could take many years to develop a mining industry, the potential is so great that officials and executives in the industry believe it could attract heavy investment even before mines are profitable. This will be a huge increase in Afghanistan's economy, which is based largely on opium production and narcotics trafficking as well as aid from the United States and other industrialized countries. Afghanistan's gross domestic product is only about $12 billion. "This will become the backbone of the Afghan economy," said Jalil Jumriany, an adviser to the Afghan minister of mines. Yet the American officials also recognize that the mineral discoveries will almost certainly have a double-edged impact. Instead of bringing peace, the newfound mineral wealth could lead the Taliban to battle even more fiercely to regain control of the country. The corruption that is already rampant in the Karzai government could also be amplified by the new wealth, particularly if a handful of well-connected oligarchs, some with personal ties to the president, gain control of the resources. Just last year, Afghanistan's minister of mines was accused by American officials of accepting a $30 million bribe to award China the rights to develop its copper mine. The minister has since been replaced. At the same time, American officials fear resource-hungry China will try to dominate the development of Afghanistan's mineral wealth, which could upset the United States, given its heavy investment in the region. After winning the bid for its Aynak copper mine in Logar Province, China clearly wants more, American officials said. With virtually no mining industry or infrastructure in place today, it will take decades to exploit its mineral wealth fully. "This is a country that has no mining culture," said Jack Medlin, a geologist in the United States Geological Survey's international affairs program. "They've had some small artisanal mines, but now there could be some very, very large mines that will require more than just a gold pan." The mineral deposits are scattered throughout the country, including in the southern and eastern regions along the border with Pakistan that have had some of the most intense combat in the American-led war against the Taliban insurgency.

Afghanistan Sitting on Gold, Lithium Mine oil, gas, only-natural gas prices-per day 86 billion Dollars US, & $100 trillion dollars US, Iron ore, copper, large Uranium, of mineral reserves, precious an semi-precious stones, emerald-lapis lazuli, red-gamete A ruby, Marble, Coal & Canal-tunnel of Gold

2012 - The vast reserves of minerals buried throughout Afghanistan, including large deposits of copper, gold, and gas could greatly improve the country's economy and provide funds to develop the country for years to come. But all that wealth might also create a crisis. While some estimates put Afghanistan's mineral wealth at about $1 trillion, for these minerals to be extracted in a way that benefits all Afghans and promotes sustainable development the industry needs to be managed transparently. That was the key message at a conference recently held in Kabul to coincide with the release of a report called the Afghanistan Extractive Industries Transparency Initiative (AEITI). The report contains details of all payments of taxes, royalties and fees the Afghan Government has received from companies operating in the extractive sector. The report equally publishes details of payments made by mining companies to the Afghan Government in order ensure transparency. "The Afghan Government is committed to share publically all the information related to the extractive sector in the country," said Dr. Omar Zakhilwal Zakhilwal, Afghanistan's Afghan Finance Minister. This kind of transparency is important because sudden new wealth from mining and gas have had a way of undermining many economies. Rather than using that wealth as a blessing that can improve the lives of citizens and improve a country's infrastructure, it can cause Afghanistan's currency to appreciate and lead to increased corruption. This well-studied phenomenon is called the "resource curse", whereby countries with vast oil and mineral wealth don't see an improvement in the living standards of citizens. For instance Nigeria, which has one of the world's largest oil reserves, has seen no improvement in its real gross domestic product per person in 30 years. The GDP per capita of Venezuela, another mineral rich country, is lower today than it was in 1977. Afghanistan joined the Extractive Industries Transparency Initiative (EITI) in 2010 to help beat the "resource curse". That Initiative sets international standards for good governance and has established accountability mechanisms for the extractive industries sector. Before a country can join the EITI it has to has to agree to some governance and transparency inidicators. With funds from the World Bank and the Harakat-Afghanistan Investment Climate Facility Organization (HAICFO), the Ministry of Finance established a secretariat for Afghanistan Extractive Industries Transparency Initiative (AEITI) to take lead of EITI implementation in Afghanistan. Speaking at the conference, the Minister for Mines, Waheedullah Shahrani said the government has devised effective policies to better allocate royalties and taxes collected from this industries to make sure that industry can thrive. "Transparency means that the process is clean, defendable and the information from the process of negotiation up to awarding contracts and exploration and exploitation of mineral resources are shared publically," said Shahrani. Shahrani said oil production from Afghanistan's first ever oil extraction contract at the Amu-River basin will start soon. This will generate $400-$500 million in revenue for Afghan government each year. Also underway is the Hajigak Iron project, which is already the biggest project in the history of Afghanistan not just from economic perspective but also from the scale of its operations. Hajigak will produce approximately 25 to 30 million tons of iron annually. Proposals to develop five other mines, of gold and copper, have been tendered. Evaluations of these proposals are underway. Eight renowned international companies have expressed interest in investing in oil extraction in Afghan basins and currently work is in progress on preparing financial model of this project. The Afghan government is also bringing reforms in the Mining Law of the country to make it more in line with international standards for broader investment attraction. Afghanistan's commitment to EITI for transparency will be integrated into the law and licensing system will be simplified along with ensuring a legal framework for protection of the rights of investors," said Waheedullah Shahrani. Minister Shahrani hoped that mining sector will constitute 45 to 50 percent of Afghan economy by 2024. The Director of World Bank in Afghanistan, Bob Sam said AEITI is an important tool to increase knowledge and information about Afghanistan's natural resources and help increase accountability and transparency. Kulczyk Investments has become a partner of JP Morgan, an American banking corporation, and are set to purchase 50 percent of shares in Afghan Gold & Minerals, which holds a concession for gold digging in Afghanistan. Kulczyk Investments first acquired a majority share package in Cetnar, which is itself run by Jan Kulczyk *(pictured)*, while JP Morgan's head of capital markets, Ian Hannam is the company's deputy chairman. With a 50 percent share in Afghan Gold & Minerals, Cetnar is to search for ore in the gold-bearing region of Qara Zaghan, which has estimated resources amounting to 2.5 million tonnes. Even though financial details of the undertaking are being kept under wraps, it has been reported that as many as 200 geologists, protected by 200 heavily armed soldiers are already on the spot. Meanwhile, the price of gold continues to soar. At the end of last week, a tonne of ore traded for over 40 million euro As Afghanistan's government finalizes new laws designed to attract more foreign mining investment, Mining Minister Wahidullah Shahrani told Reuters that Exxon had not turned up for a site tour which closes on Sunday, despite being shortlisted with eight other firms for the Afghan Tajik tender near Mazar-e-Sharif. "Hopefully at some point they (Exxon) will visit the area. But that visit is not mandatory," Shahrani said in an interview late on Saturday in his Kabul office. A spokeswoman for U.S.-based Exxon said she could not immediately comment. Exxon's July expression of interest in the Afghan Tajik basin, which holds an estimated 1.9 billion barrels of oil, lent credence to hopes that Kabul may be making progress in efforts to lessen its reliance on aid, through untapped resources worth as much as $1 trillion, despite an ongoing insurgency. Shahrani said that with an October bid closure deadline looming, shortlisted companies had been invited to inspect the area and meet local community leaders, an offer which closes on September 30, and which would usually be accepted. "Some companies, they have already visited, some companies are about to visit the area," he said. "Those companies, most of them are well established in the region." Chinese and Indian companies are already scrambling to lock in access to Afghanistan's mineral wealth, most estimates of which date back to U.S. surveys carried out decades ago. The country has large deposits of gold, copper, iron ore and oil, as well as lithium and rare earths used in high-tech manufacturing. Chinese firms are leading the race, with China Metallurgical Group (MCC) and Jiangxi Copper winning a 2007 deal to exploit the giant $3 billion Aynak copper mine southeast of the capital Kabul. MAJOR

INTEREST Exxon's interest fuelled hopes that U.S.-based majors may also compete, despite worries over security and endemic graft, adding urgency to a push for new laws designed to make resource investment more attractive as foreign combat troops withdraw. Shahrani's ministry will soon resubmit to President Hamid Karzai's cabinet mining laws that Afghan officials and Western donors hope will persuade foreign firms to invest in the country's resources, but which were rejected in July over concerns they were too generous to miners. The re-draft, backed by Western donors and the World Bank, would remove a 2009 clause separating exploration from an automatic license to exploit finds, a law which led miners to question why they were spending their money on expensive and risky exploration if they could not be assured of profiting. "It created a lot of discomfort among the potential mining companies and global investors," Shahrani said. "We have made the provision that whoever gets the license for exploration through the tender, once they conduct the exploration, if they find a deposit to be commercially and economically viable, their exploration license will be automatically converted to an exploitation or production license." Miners and Western diplomats have not managed to convince the government to include fixed royalty payments in the re-drafted law, though Shahrani admitted that some resources firms thought it lead to greater confidence in planning. "In the new draft law, we have not mentioned that, and we will leave that to be determined in the bidding process," he said. Instead, the overhaul would commit the government to more transparency by publishing contract details in local and international newspapers, as well as on its own website, to counter perceptions of graft in Afghanistan's notorious kleptocracy. The draft laws, he said, should go to Karzai's cabinet in three to four weeks before a November vote in the fractious parliament, where lawmakers have in recent months been testing their muscle with Karzai, sacking key security ministers. Some political analysts have also speculated that Shahrani's problems with the law's initial draft may have been linked to political rivalries over control of potential resource profits. YEARS UNTIL PRODUCTION Shahrani said he was optimistic opposition to the laws had faded in cabinet, and that parliament's influential economics and resource committees were also positive about the legislation, which was drafted with World Bank help. "We have been interacting very closely with parliament's relative committees. we can see a significant degree of support on behalf of the members of those committees," he said. Despite the risk of global commodity prices falling as a result of concerns about the strength of the Chinese economy and a global economic slowdown, Shahrani said he believed Afghanistan had not missed the peak of the resource boom. Most projects in Afghanistan, he said, including bids for northeastern gold concessions in Badakhshan now being considered, would take years to reach production. "If we do award the concessions tomorrow for iron ore and copper, usually it takes at least five to six years for these deposits to get developed," he said. "We hope that by then the demand for commodities will again increase."

Afghanistan Sitting on Gold, Lithium Mine oil, gas, only-natural gas prices-per day 86 billion Dollars US, & $100 trillion dollars US, Iron ore, copper, large Uranium, of mineral reserves, precious an semi-precious stones, emerald-lapis lazuli, red-gamete A ruby, Marble, Coal & Canal-tunnel of Gold

Afghanistan If there is a road to a happy ending in Afghanistan, much of the path may run underground: in the trillion-dollar reservoir of natural resources oil, gold, iron ore, copper, lithium and other minerals — that has brought hopes of a more self-sufficient country, if only the wealth can be wrested from blood-soaked soil. But the wealth has inspired darker dreams as well. Officials and industry experts say the potential resource boom seems increasingly imperiled by corruption, violence and intrigue, and has put the Afghan government's vulnerabilities on display. It all comes at what is already a critically uncertain time here, with the impending departure of NATO troops in 2014 and old regional and ethnic rivalries resurfacing, raising concerns that the mineral wealth could become the fuel for civil conflict. Powerful regional warlords and militant leaders are jockeying to widen their turf to include areas with mineral wealth, and the Taliban have begun to make murderous incursions into territory where development is planned. In the capital, Kabul, factional maneuvering is in full swing, including disputes over lucrative side contracts awarded to relatives of President Hamid Karzai. Further, a proposed mining law vital to attracting foreign investment is up in the air, with the delay threatening several projects. The cabinet rejected it this summer, saying it was too generous to Western commercial interests. But some Western officials fear other motives are at work, too, including an internal fight for spoils, and perhaps an effort by some neighboring countries to sway sympathetic officials to keep Indian and Chinese state mining companies out. "If you were to pick a country that involves high risk in developing a new mining sector, Afghanistan is it," said Eleanor Nichol, campaign leader at Global Witness, a group that tries to break the link between natural resources, corruption and conflict. "But the genie is out of the bottle." Already this summer, the China National Petroleum Corporation, in partnership with a company controlled by relatives of President Karzai, began pumping oil from the Amu Darya field in the north. An investment consortium arranged by JPMorgan Chase is mining gold. Another Chinese company is trying to develop a huge copper mine. Four copper and gold contracts are being tendered, and contracts for rare earth metals could be offered soon. The Ministry of Mines has also requested bids for a richer oil concession in the Afghan-Tajik basin, and American officials are optimistic it could come online soon. And in the shadow of the Black Mountain, here in the Kalu Valley in remote Bamian Province, villagers hope that Indian and Canadian mining operations can turn buried iron ore into new lives for struggling families, breaking a cycle of poverty in this high place cut off by snow for six months of the year. When the digging begins, Abbas Ali, a 30-year-old farmer here, will have to give up the four-acre potato field his family has worked for generations. He is more than ready. "Our life will change 180 degrees," Mr. Ali said this summer, staring up with fervent brown eyes at the bowed wooden roof beams in the white-walled madrasa where he teaches for extra income. "We support any effort to make it happen quickly." Major findings Afghanistan has abundant non-fuel mineral resources, including both known and potential deposits of a wide variety of minerals ranging from copper, iron, and sulfur to bauxite, lithium, and rare-earth elements. In 2010, Pentagon officials and American geologists announced that they had identified about $1 trillion in untapped mineral deposits in Afghanistan, enough to fundamentally alter the Afghan economy and perhaps the Afghan war itself, according to senior American government officials. According to other reports the total mineral riches of Afghanistan may be worth over $3 trillion US dollars. "The previously unknown deposits — including huge veins of iron, copper, cobalt, gold, and critical industrial metals like lithium — are so big and include so many minerals that are essential to modern industry that Afghanistan could eventually be transformed into one of the most important mining centers in the world". Ghazni Province may hold the world's largest lithium reserves. The deposits were already described in the USGS report on Afghanistan issued in 2007. The comment from Marc Ambinder, writing in The Atlantic, is that "the Pentagon is probably trying to bolster Americans' support for the flagging Afghanistan campaign" by publicizing Afghan mineral wealth President Hamid Karzai remarked "Whereas Saudi Arabia is the oil capital of the world, Afghanistan will be the lithium capital of the world." Afghanistan invited 200 global companies for the development of its mines. Copper No copper mines were active in the country in 2006. In the past, copper had been mined from Herat Province and Farah Province in the west, Kapisa Province in the east, and Kandahar Province and Zabul Province in the south. As of 2006, interest was focused on the Aynak, the Darband, and the Jawkhar prospects in southeastern Afghanistan. Copper mineralization at Aynak in Logar Province was stratabound and characterized by bornite and chalcopyrite disseminated in dolomite marble and quartz-biotite-dolomite schists of the Loy Khwar Formation. Although a resource of 240 million metric tons at a grade of 2.3% copper had been reported, a number of small ore lenses were potentially not practically and economically minable. Open pit and underground mining would be needed to exploit the main ore body, and other infrastructure problems, such as inadequate power and water, were also likely. The new (2005) Mining Law might favor the development of the deposit by using public tenders. The Government issued a public tender for the deposit in 2006 with a deadline of October 28, 2006, and expected the granting of concessions in February 2007. Nine mining companies from Australia, China, India, and the United States were interested in the prospect. China Metallurgical Group won the bidding for a copper mining project in Aybak, Samangan, Afghanistan The bidding process has been criticized by rival Canadian and U.S. companies alleging corruption and questioning the Chinese company's commitment to the Afghan people. In November 2007, a 30-year lease was granted the development of a copper mine at Mes Aynak in Logar Province to the China Metallurgical Group for $3 billion, making it the biggest foreign investment and private business venture in Afghanistan's history. It is believed to contain the second-largest reserves of copper ore in the world and the deposits are estimated to be worth up to $88 billion. It is also the site of one of Afghanistan's most important archaeological sites and, although there are desperate efforts being made to save as much as possible, the main Buddhist monastery and other remains are due to be bulldozed to make way for the mine. Several new mineral-rich sites, with estimated deposits of about $250 billion, had been found in six other provinces, he added. Launched in 2006, a US Geological Survey (USGS), jointly conducted with the Ministry of Mines, was completed last year. The survey covers 30 percent of the country. "The survey provides credible information on mines in 28 different parts of Afghanistan," Wahidullah Shahrani told reporters in Kabul. It showed the world's largest copper deposits existed in Balkhab district of Sar-i-Pul, the minister said. The copper mine was discovered near a river, an area which might hold gold reserves as well. The government planned to launch tenders in late 2011 for the Balkhab copper deposit, which had reserves of about 45 Mt of copper Citing the report, the minister said two new copper mines in Logar Province and Herat Province provinces had been discovered. The value of the Logar pit, not the Ainak mine, is estimated at $43 billion. Copper and gold mines worth of $30 billion were discovered in the Zarkasho area of Ghazni and lithium pits of $20 billion in Farah and Nimroz provinces, Shahwani said. A deposit of beryllium, which is lighter than aluminum and stronger than steel used in airplanes, helicopters, ships, missiles, and space craft, has been found in the Khanashin district of southern Helmand province. The reserves are estimated at $88 billion. Coal Afghanistan has rich reserves of coking coal, coal is primarily located within a Jurassic belt from the northern provinces of Takhar and Badakhshan through the center of the country and towards the west in Herat, according to Afghan mines ministry. Gemstones Elbaite from Nangarhar Province Afghanistan is known to have exploited its precious and semiprecious gemstone deposits. These deposits include aquamarine, emerald, fluorite, garnet, kunzite, ruby, sapphire, semiprecious lapis lazuli, topaz, tourmaline, and varieties of quartz. The four main gemstone-producing areas are those of Badakhshan, Jegdalek, Nuristan, and the Panjshir Valley. Artisanal mining of gemstones in the country used primitive methods. Some gemstones were exported illicitly, mostly to India (which was the world's leading import market for colored gemstones and an outlet for higher quality gems) and to the domestic Pakistan market. Gold in Afghanistan As of 2006, gold was mined from the Samti placer deposit in Takhar Province in the north by groups of artisanal miners. Badakhshan Provincealso had occurrences of placer gold deposits. The deposits were found on the western flanks of the mountains in alluvium or alluvial fan in several river valleys, particularly in the Anjir, the Hasar, the Nooraba, and the Panj Valleys. The Samti deposit is located in the Panj River Valley and was estimated to contain between 20 and 25 metric tons of gold. The southern regions of Afghanistan is believed to contain large gold deposits, particularly the Helmand Province. There is an estimated $50 billion in gold and copper deposits in Ghazni province. The Afghan government signed a deal with Afghan Krystal natural Resources Co. (a local company) to invest up to $50 million in the Qara Zaghan Mine in northern Baghlan Province. Qara Zaghan was the country's second gold mine, and production there was planned to begin by 2013. The mine's gold reserves were not yet known, but the company intended to spend the next 2 years exploring the site. Investors from indonesia, turkey, the United Kingdom, and the United states were backing the project. The first gold mine was being developed by Westland general trading LLC of the United Arab Emirates at Nor Aaba near the border with tajikistan in northern Takhar Province. The mine was expected to provide $4 million to $5 million per year in royalties to the government. Afghanistan The best known and largest iron oxide deposit in Afghanistan is located at Hajigak in Bamyan Province. The deposit itself stretches over 32 km and contains 16 separate zones, up to 5 km in length, 380 m wide and extending 550 m down dip, seven of which have been studied in detail. The ore occurs in both primary and oxidized states. The primary ore accounts for 80% of the deposit and consists of magnetite, pyrite and minor chalcopyrite. The remaining 20% is oxidized and consists of three hematitic ore types. The deposit remained unmined in 2006. The presence of coking coal nearby at Shabashak in the Dar-l-Suf District and large iron ore resources made the deposit viable for future development of an Afghan steel industry. Open pit mining and blast furnace smelting operations were envisioned by an early feasibility study. The Hajigak also includes the unusual niobium, a soft metal used in the production of superconducting steel. Lithium in Afghanistan Lithium is a vital metal that is mostly used in the manufacture of rechargeable batteries for mobile phones, laptops and electric cars. It is believed that Afghanistan has plenty of lithium. The country's lithium deposits occur in dry lake beds in the form of lithium chloride; they are located in the western Province of Herat and Nimroz and in the central east Province of Ghazni. The geologic setting is similar to those found in Bolivia and Chile. The deposits are also found in hard rock in the form of spodumene in pegmatites in the north-eastern Provinces of Badakhshan, Nangarhar, Nuristan, and Uruzgan. A pegmatite in the hindu Kush Mountains in central Afghanistan was reported to contain 20% to 30% spodumene Marble in Afghanistan, Afghanistan also has considerable amount of marble in different parts of the country. The Doost Marble Factory in the city of Herat began operation in recent years. According to theU.S. Embassy in Kabul, current Afghan marble exports are estimated at $15 million per year. With improved extraction, processing, infrastructure, and investment, the industry has the potential to grow into a $450 million per year business. Petroleum and natural gas in Afghanistan Afghanistan has 3.8 billion barrels of oil between Balkh and Jawzjan Province in the north of the country. This is an enormous amount for a nation that only consumes 5,000 bbl/day. The U.S. Geological Survey and the Afghan Ministry of Mines and Industry jointly assessed the oil and natural gas resources in northern Afghanistan. The estimated mean volumes of undiscovered petroleum were 1,596 million barrels (Mbbl) of crude oil, 444 billion cubic meters of natural gas, and 562 Mbbl of natural gas liquids. Most of the undiscovered crude oil occurs in the Afghan-Tajik Basin and most of the undiscovered natural gas is located in the Amu Darya Basin. These two basins within Afghanistan encompass areas of approximately 515,000 square kilometers. In December 2011, Afghanistan signed an oil exploration contract with China National Petroleum Corporation (CNPC) for the development of three oil fields along the Amu Darya river. Afghanistan will have its first oil refineries within the next three years, after which it will receive 70 percent of the profits from the sale of the oil and natural gas. CNPC began Afghan oil production in late October of 2012, with extracting 1.5 million barrels of oil annually. Rare earth elements in Afghanistan. According to a September 2011 US Geological Survey estimate, the Khanashin carbonatites in southern Helmand Province have an estimated 1 million metric tonnes of rare earth elements. Regina Dubey, Acting Director for the Department of Defence Task Force for Business and Stability Operations (TFBSO) stated that "this is just one more piece of evidence that Afghanistan's mineral sector has a bright future. Recent exploration of rare volcanic rocks in the rugged, dangerous desert of southern Afghanistan has identified world-class concentrations of rare earth elements, the prized group of raw materials that are essential in the manufacture of many modern technologies, from electric cars to solar panels. So far, geologists say, they have mapped one million metric tons of these critical elements, which include lanthanum, cerium and neodymium. That's enough to supply the world's rare earth needs for 10 years based on current consumption, points out Robert Tucker, the U.S. Geological Survey (USGS) scientist who is the lead author on a report released on September 14. And from clues his team gathered during three high-security reconnaissance missions to the site, he suspects the deposit is actually much larger. "we fully expect that our estimates are conservative," Tucker told Scientific American. "With more time, and with more people doing proper exploration, it could become a major, major discovery." The USGS's exploration time has been strictly limited due to the deposit's location in the most dangerous part of the country, near the southern border with Pakistan. The geologists were delivered to the site in Black Hawk helicopters, and armed soldiers watched over them as they scoured the ground for clues. "It's one of the most challenging things I've ever done," Tucker says. "Walking around with 30 to 40 pounds of protective gear is very difficult." But even the rushed, conservative estimate for the tonnage of this single deposit puts Afghanistan sixth on a list of countries with the largest rare earth reserves. (China ranks first with about 50 million metric tons and U.S. reserves are around 12 million metric tons.) Already, then, Afghanistan could provide an alternative source of rare earth elements for industrial countries concerned that China currently controls 97 percent of the world's supply, Tucker says. Chemical analyses of rock samples his team collected in February show that the concentration of so-called light rare earth elements in the Afghan deposit are on par with the premier site mined in China, at Bayan Obo in Inner Mongolia. The new rare earth findings are a crown jewel of the USGS's new, 2,000-page assessment of Afghanistan's vast mineral bounty, which will be rolled out September 29 at the Afghan embassy in Washington, D.C. This new science, funded by the Pentagon's Task Force for Business and Stability Operations, also characterizes 24 areas of economic interest, half a dozen of which are world-class mineral deposits in the northern two thirds of the country. Vast deposits of copper and iron in the northeast near the nation's capital, Kabul, are together worth hundreds of billions of dollars. The Afghanistan Ministry of Mines has already tendered an exploration lease for a copper prospect called Aynak, in Logar Province, and they plan to do the same for several additional sites in the coming months, including a massive iron ore deposit valued at $420 billion. The hope of senior government officials in both countries is that tapping Afghanistan's underground wealth could transform it from one of the world's poorest nations into a prosperous major global mining center. The plan is to get iron and copper mining established in the north, where the risk of violence is lower, with an eye toward eventually opening up the rare earth deposit in the south. In addition to security, the Afghans still need an expanded electrical grid to power machinery as well as a railroad to ship ore out of the country, says Stephen Peters, the USGS minerals team leader for the Afghanistan project. But he adds that the rare earth deposit, near the village of Khan Neshin in Helmand Province, offers the added incentive of minable quantities of uranium, thorium, phosphate and limestone for cement. Peters published preliminary estimates about Afghanistan's rare earth elements in 2007. But those guesses were made sight unseen, based on a careful compilation of unpublished Soviet field notes conducted in partnership with the Afghanistan Geological Survey. To get beyond guesswork, Peters and Tucker knew they had to hike the rugged hills. The task force arranged for military transport and protection during three brief excursions to Khan Neshin in 2010 and 2011. When the team finally crossed the mineralized zone on their second trip, he knew they had hit pay dirt. The principal ore mineral turned out to be canary-yellow bastnasite, the same mineral that harbors most of the world and U.S. rare earth reserves. "The signs were everywhere," Tucker describes. "There were canary yellow minerals, speckled rocks in the ground—it was unlike anything I'd ever seen. It was exhilarating to make this kind of discovery, particularly in such difficult circumstances." The $7.4-billion estimate for the rare earths at Khan Neshin assumes, very conservatively, that the rock is only 150 meters thick. That was all Tucker and Peters could see during their brief visits, but it could easily be thicker. The rare earth–bearing rocks at Khan Neshin are very young in geologic terms, less than 600,000 years old, which gives Tucker strong reason to think that rich portions of the deposit extend deep underground. For comparison, the same type of volcanic rocks once mined for rare earths near Mountain Pass, Calif., are 1.4 billion years old, and so natural forces of erosion have had much more time to whittle away at them. Ideally, geophysicists would generate three-dimensional views of the rock beneath the rare earth deposit Tucker and Peters visited by charting the region's magnetism and other properties with equipment carried on foot or in a low-flying plane. Likewise, geologists could dig trenches across the deposit and drill deep into it to help resolve the details of the formation's third dimension. Alas, the USGS has no plans to send its scientists back to Khan Neshin anytime soon. The agency's Pentagon funding has run out, and it is simply too dangerous for Americans to go again without military protection. But Afghan scientists the USGS has been training for the past eight years can move more freely. Recently equipped with hand-held equipment for doing the geophysical surveys, perhaps they can finish the job.

Afghanistan's Buried Riches Preview

Aryana-Khorasan dynasty present day Afghanistan-Central Asia & India. Geologists say newfound deposits in the embattled country could fulfill the world's desire for rare earth and critical minerals and end opium's local stranglehold in the process, The scene at first resembles many that play out daily in the war-torn Red Zone of southern Afghanistan: a pair of Black Hawk helicopters descend on a hillside near the country's southern border with Pakistan. As the choppers land, U.S. marines leap out, assault rifles ready. But then geologists sporting helmets and heavy ceramic vests jump out, too. The researchers are virtually indistinguishable from the soldiers except that they carry rock hammers instead of guns. A human chain of soldiers encircles the scientists as they step forward on the dusty ground. "The minute you get off, you go into geologist mode," says Jack H. Medlin, director of the U.S. Geological Survey's activities in Afghanistan. "You forget, basically, that these guys are around—unless you try to get out of the circle." The U.S. Geological Survey (USGS) estimates at least 1 million metric tonnes of rare earth element resources within the Khanneshin carbonatite in Helmand Province, Afghanistan. This estimate comes from a 2009-2011 USGS study funded by the Department of Defense's Task Force for Business and Stability Operations (TFBSO). The Khanneshin carbonatite contains a major potential source of light rare earth elements (LREE), such as lanthanum, cerium, and neodymium. The LREE prospects in the Khanneshin carbonatite are comparable in grade to world-class deposits like Mountain Pass, CA, and Bayan Obo in China, both of which primarily contain LREE. "The USGS has a long and storied history in Afghanistan," said Marcia McNutt, Director of the USGS. "We hope our neutral and unbiased analysis of the location, supply, and flow of these strategic minerals will help the Afghans understand the true extent of their mineral wealth." "This is just one more piece of evidence that Afghanistan's mineral sector has a bright future," said TFBSO Acting Director Regina Dubey. "The international mining community is beginning to realize Afghanistan's extraordinary mineral potential. The USGS's groundbreaking work provides a foundation for the kind of future investment that could help create a vibrant Afghan economy." The primary area of mineralization covers approximately 0.74 square kilometers (0.29 square miles). The USGS field team, led by Robert Tucker and Steve Peters, surveyed the extent of the mineralization using traditional geologic assessment techniques as well as remote-sensing analysis. Between 2004 and 2007, USGS scientists working cooperatively with the Afghanistan Geological Survey of the Afghanistan Ministry of Mines compiled existing information about known nonfuel mineral resources and documented the potential for additional undiscovered resources through a preliminary country-wide mineral resource assessment. That preliminary USGS resource assessment, published in 2007, included an estimate of about 1.5 million metric tonnes of potential rare earth element (REE) resources in all of southern Afghanistan. The newest estimate of about 1 million metric tonnes of LREE resources in just the Khanneshin carbonatite, completed with major assistance from the TFBSO, verifies the 2007 USGS prediction and confirms the unpublished work of Soviet scientists. The Khanneshin REE evaluation is documented in a new USGS report and will be also be included as part of a larger report by the USGS to be released later in 2011, which will include an updated evaluation of Afghanistan's principal deposits of gold, silver, iron, copper, lead, zinc, phosphorus, and uranium. "The potential that these findings have for the future well-being of the Afghan people is significant," said Ambassador Marc Grossman, U.S. Special Representative for Afghanistan and Pakistan. "The United States will continue to support the Government of Afghanistan's efforts to develop these resources through private-sector investment in a responsible, transparent, and sustainable manner that benefits the Afghan people, expands markets, and promotes regional prosperity." The REE are a group of 15 metallic elements, with similar atomic properties and structures, which are essential components in a diverse and expanding array of high-technology and clean-energy products. Despite their name, they are relatively common within the earth's crust, but are not often found in economically exploitable concentrations. Rare earth elements are important ingredients in high-strength magnets, metal alloys for batteries and light-weight structures, and phosphors. These are essential components for many current and emerging alternative energy technologies, such as electric vehicles, photo-voltaic cells, energy-efficient lighting, and wind power. Products containing rare earth elements also are used in a number of key defense applications More than 95 percent of global REE production now comes from China, which in 2010 exported approximately 30,000 metric tonnes of REE-products. New REE mines are being developed in Australia, and projects exploring the feasibility of economic production of other REE deposits are under way in the United States, Australia, and Canada. In addition to high concentrations of the LREE, the deposit has significant concentrations of barium, strontium, phosphorus, and uranium.

Afghanistan Mineral Areas

Area name	Available commodities
Ahankashan	Aluminum, Gold, Copper, Barite, Iron, Marble, Graphite, Sandstone Celestite, Sulfur, Limestone
⊞ Aynak Copper and Chromium	Aluminum, Copper, Iron, Marble, Chromite, Graphite, Sandstone, Sulfur, Limestone, Talc, asbestos, and magnesite
⊞ Badakhshan Gold	Aluminum, Halite, Gold, Copper, Tin and tungsten, Iron, Marble, Graphite, Sandstone, Potash, Limestone
Baghlan Clay Gypsum	Gold, Copper, Tin and tungsten, Iron, Graphite, Sandstone, Sulfur, Limestone
Bakhud Fluorite	Aluminum, Lead and zinc, Tin and tungsten, Graphite, Sandstone, Fluorite, Limestone
⊞ Balkhab Copper	Aluminum, Gold, Graphite, Sandstone, Sulfur, Limestone
Daykundi Tin Tungsten	Aluminum, Gold, Copper, Lead and zinc, Tin and tungsten, Iron, Marble, Mercury, Graphite, Sandstone, Limestone
Dudkash Industrial Minerals	Halite, Copper, Iron, Marble, Graphite, Sandstone, Potash, Limestone
⊞ Dusar Shaida Cu Tin	Copper, Tin and tungsten, Mercury, Graphite, Sandstone, Sulfur, Limestone
⊞ Ghunday Achin Magnesite Talc	Aluminum, Gold, Tin and tungsten, Iron, Marble, Graphite, Sandstone, Sulfur, Limestone
⊞ Haji Gak Iron	Aluminum, Gold, Tin and tungsten, Iron, Marble, Graphite, Sandstone, Limestone
⊞ Katawas Gold	Gold, Iron, Mercury, Chromite, Sandstone, Limestone, Talc, asbestos, and magnesite
⊞ Khanneshin Carbonatite	Graphite, Sandstone, Limestone, Rare-earth elements (REE), Aragonite
⊞ Kharnak Kanjar	Copper, Tin and tungsten, Mercury, Graphite, Sandstone, Limestone
⊞ Kundalan Porphyry	Aluminum, Gold, Copper, Lead and zinc, Tin and tungsten, Iron, Marble, Graphite, Sandstone, Limestone
Kunduz Celestite	Halite, Sandstone, Potash, Sulfur, Limestone

Area name	Available commodities
⊞ Nalbandon Lead Zinc	Aluminum, Gold, Tin and tungsten, Iron, Marble, Mercury, Graphite, Sandstone, Sulfur, Limestone
⊞ North Herat Barium Limestone	Aluminum, Gold, Marble, Mercury, Graphite, Sandstone, Limestone
North Takhar Gold Placer	Halite, Gold, Copper, Tin and tungsten, Graphite, Sandstone, Potash, Limestone
Nuristan Pegmatites	Tin and tungsten, Iron, Marble, Graphite, Sandstone, Limestone
⊞ Panjsher Valley Emerald Iron Silver	Gold, Copper, Tin and tungsten, Iron, Marble, Graphite, Sandstone, Limestone
South Helmand Travertine	Copper, Graphite, Sandstone, Limestone
Takhar Evaporite	Copper, Tin and tungsten, Graphite, Sandstone, Limestone
Tourmaline Tin Vein	Copper, Tin and tungsten, Mercury, Graphite, Sandstone, Limestone
⊞ Zarkashan Copper Gold	Aluminum, Gold, Copper, Lead and zinc, Tin and tungsten, Iron, Marble, Graphite, Sandstone, Limestone

Afghanistan Commodities Table of commodities

Commodity name	Commodity type	Deposit type	Known resource estimates	USGS-AGS assessment
Aluminum	Metals	bauxite	4,535,000 (bauxite at 50.5 wI. % alumina aud 12 wI. % silica)	Further study recommended
Aragonite	Building Materials	dimension stone	770,000	Further study recommended
Barite	Industrial Minerals	bedded aud vein barite	>151,500,000 I I	Further study recommended
Brick clay	Industrial Minerals	clay	>2,200,000 m3	Further study recommended
Celestite	Industrial Minerals	celestite	>> 1,000,000 (at 75 wI. %)	Further study recommended

Chromite	Industrial Minerals	chromium oxide	>approx. 200.000 (at about 43 wI. %)	980,000 (chromium oxide)
Copper	Metals	igneous-related, sediment-hosted	68,500	28,469,200 (copper); 724,010 (molybdenum); 682 (gold); 9,067 (silver)
Dolomite	Building Materials	building stone	1,040,000	Further study recommended
Fluorite	Industrial Minerals	fluorspar	>8,791,000 (ore 19 46.69 wI. %)	Further study recommended
Glass sand	Building Materials	sand	110,000 (siliceous sand); 10.900,000 (sandstone)	Further study recommended
Gold	Metals	placer, lode	approx. 1,780 kg	Further study recommended
Graphite	Industrial Minerals	disseminated flake graphite	>5,000	1,050,000 (flake graphite)
Halite	Industrial Minerals	evaporite	>No previous estimate	Further study recommended
Iron	Metals	igneous-related, sediment-hosted	2.26 billion (>62 wI. % iron)	Further study recommended
Kaolin	Industrial Minerals	residual, sedimentary	100,000 to 150,000 (clay)	Further study recommended
Lazurite	Industrial Minerals	skarn lazurite	1,300	Further study recommended
Lead and zinc	Metals	igneous-related, sediment-hosted	90,000 (combined lead aud zinc)	Further study recommended
Limestone	Building Materials	building stone, cement and flux	> 500,000,000	Further study recommended
Marble	Building Materials	building stone	1.3 billion (coarsely crystalline marble)	Further study recommended
Mercury	Metals	hot-spring mercury	May contain gold and silver	32,000

Potash	Industrial Minerals	evaporite	No previous estimate	27,514,000
Rare-earth elements (REE)	Industrial Minerals	carbonatite	No previous estimate	1,405,000 (REE), 3,480,000 elements (niobium and phosphorous, (REE)uranium and thorium)
Sand and gravel	Building Materials	aggregate	136,000,000 m3	Further study recommended
Sandstone	Building Materials	building stone	650,000 (siliceous sandstone)	Further study recommended
Sulfur	Industrial Minerals	bedded aud fumerolic	450,000	6,000,000
Talc, asbestos, and magnesite	Industrial Minerals	metasomatic / metamorphic replacement magnesite, ultramafic-hosted talc magnesite	1,250,000 (talc); 31,200 (magnesite)	Further study recommended
Tin and tungsten	Metals	tin veins, tin and tungsten skams and greisen	No previous estimate	Further study recommended

Estimates at least 100 million metric tonnes of rare earth element resources within the Khanneshin carbonatite in Helmand Province, Afghanistan. This estimate comes from a 2009-2011 USGS study funded by the Department of Defense's Task Force for Business and Stability Operations (TFBSO). The Khanneshin carbonatite contains a major potential source of light rare earth elements (LREE), such as lanthanum, cerium, and neodymium. The LREE prospects in the Khanneshin carbonatite are comparable in grade to world-class deposits like Mountain Pass, CA, and Bayan Obo in China, both of which primarily contain LREE. "The USGS has a long and storied history in Afghanistan," said Marcia McNutt, Director of the USGS. "We hope our neutral and unbiased analysis of the location, supply, and flow of these strategic minerals will help the Afghans understand the true extent of their mineral wealth." "This is just one more piece of evidence that Afghanistan's mineral sector has a bright future," said TFBSO Acting Director Regina Dubey. "The international mining community is beginning to realize Afghanistan's extraordinary mineral potential. The USGS's groundbreaking work provides a foundation for the kind of future investment that could help create a vibrant Afghan economy." The primary area of mineralization covers approximately 0.74 square kilometers (0.29 square miles). The USGS field team, led by Robert Tucker and Steve Peters, surveyed the extent of the mineralization using traditional geologic assessment techniques as well as remote-sensing analysis. Between 2004 and 2007, USGS scientists working cooperatively with the Afghanistan Geological Survey of the Afghanistan Ministry of Mines compiled existing information about known nonfuel mineral resources and documented the potential for additional undiscovered resources through a preliminary country-wide mineral resource assessment. That preliminary USGS resource assessment, published in 2007, included an estimate of about 1.5 million metric tonnes of potential rare earth element (REE) resources in all of southern Afghanistan. The newest estimate of about 100 million metric tonnes of LREE resources in just the Khanneshin carbonatite, completed with major assistance from the TFBSO, verifies the 2007 USGS prediction and confirms the unpublished work of Soviet scientists. The Khanneshin REE evaluation is documented in a new USGS report and will be also be included as part of a larger report by the USGS to be released later in 2011, which will include an updated evaluation of Afghanistan's principal deposits of gold, silver, iron, copper, lead, zinc, phosphorus, and uranium. "The potential that these findings have for the future well-being of the Afghan people is significant," said Ambassador Marc Grossman, U.S. Special Representative for Afghanistan and Pakistan. "The United States will continue to support the Government of Afghanistan's efforts to develop these resources through private-sector investment in a responsible, transparent, and sustainable manner that benefits the Afghan people, expands markets, and promotes regional prosperity." The REE are a group of 15 metallic elements, with similar atomic properties and structures, which are essential components in a diverse and expanding array of high-technology and clean-energy products. Despite their name, they are relatively common within the earth's crust, but are not often found in economically exploitable concentrations. Rare earth elements are important ingredients in high-strength magnets, metal alloys for batteries and light-weight structures, and phosphors. These are essential components for many current and emerging alternative energy technologies, such as electric vehicles, photo-voltaic cells, energy-efficient lighting, and wind power. Products containing rare earth elements also are used in a number of key defense applications More than 95 percent of global REE production now comes from China, which in 2010 exported approximately 30,000 metric tonnes of REE-products. New REE mines are being developed in Australia, and projects exploring the feasibility of economic production of other REE deposits are under way in the United States, Australia, and Canada. In addition to high concentrations of the LREE, the deposit has significant concentrations of barium, strontium, phosphorus, and uranium. Recent exploration of rare volcanic rocks in the rugged, dangerous desert of southern Afghanistan has identified world-class concentrations of rare earth elements, the prized group of raw materials that are essential in the manufacture of many modern technologies, from electric cars to solar panels. So far, geologists say, they have mapped one million metric tons of these critical elements, which include lanthanum, cerium and neodymium. That's enough to supply the world's rare earth needs for 10 years based on current consumption, points out Robert Tucker, the U.S. Geological Survey (USGS) scientist who is the lead author on a report released on September 14. And from clues his team gathered during three high-security reconnaissance missions to the site, he suspects the deposit is actually much larger. fully expect that our estimates are conservative," Tucker told Scientific American. "With more time, and with more people doing proper exploration, it could become a major, major discovery." The USGS's exploration time has been strictly limited due to the deposit's location in the most dangerous part of the country, near the southern border with Pakistan. The geologists were delivered to the site in Black Hawk helicopters, and armed soldiers watched over them as they scoured the ground for clues. "It's one of the most challenging things I've ever done," Tucker says. "Walking around with 30 to 40 pounds of protective gear is very difficult." But even the rushed, conservative estimate for the tonnage of this single deposit puts Afghanistan sixth on a list of countries with the largest rare earth reserves. (China ranks first with about 50 million metric tons and U.S. reserves are around 12 million metric tons.) Already, then, Afghanistan could provide an alternative source of rare earth elements for industrial countries concerned that China currently controls 97 percent of the world's supply, Tucker says. Chemical analyses of rock samples his team collected in February show that the concentration of so-called light rare earth elements in the Afghan deposit are on par with the premier site mined in China, at Bayan Obo in Inner Mongolia. The new rare earth findings are a crown jewel of the USGS's new, 2,000-page assessment of Afghanistan's vast mineral bounty, which will be rolled out September 29 at the Afghan embassy in Washington, D.C. This new science, funded by the Pentagon's Task Force for Business and Stability Operations, also characterizes 24 areas of economic interest, half a dozen of which are world-class mineral deposits in the northern two thirds of the country. Vast deposits of copper and iron in the northeast near the nation's capital, Kabul, are together worth hundreds of billions of dollars. The Afghanistan Ministry of Mines has already tendered an exploration lease for a copper prospect called Aynak, in Logar Province, and they plan to do the same for several additional sites in the coming months, including a massive iron ore deposit valued at $420 billion. The hope of senior government officials in both countries is that tapping Afghanistan's underground wealth could transform it from one of the world's poorest nations into a prosperous major global mining center. The plan is to get iron and copper mining established in the north, where the risk of violence is lower, with an eye toward eventually opening up the rare earth deposit in the south. In addition to security, the Afghans still need an expanded electrical grid to power machinery as well as a railroad to ship ore out of the country, says Stephen Peters, the USGS minerals team leader for the Afghanistan project. But he adds that the rare earth deposit, near the village of Khan Neshin in Helmand Province, offers the added incentive of minable quantities of uranium, thorium, phosphate and limestone for cement. Peters published preliminary estimates about Afghanistan's rare earth elements in 2007. But those guesses were made sight unseen, based on a careful compilation of unpublished Soviet field notes conducted in partnership with the Afghanistan Geological Survey. To get beyond guesswork, Peters and Tucker knew they had to hike the rugged hills. The task force arranged for military transport and protection during three brief excursions to Khan Neshin in 2010 and 2011. When the team finally crossed the mineralized zone on their second trip, he knew they had hit pay dirt. The principal ore mineral turned out to be canary-yellow bastnasite, the same mineral that harbors most of the world and U.S. rare earth reserves. "The signs were everywhere," Tucker describes. "There were canary yellow minerals, speckled rocks in the ground—it was unlike anything I'd ever seen. It was exhilarating to make this kind of discovery, particularly in such difficult circumstances." The $7.4-billion estimate for the rare earths at Khan Neshin assumes, very conservatively, that the rock is only 150 meters thick. That was all Tucker and Peters could see during their brief visits, but it could easily be thicker. The rare earth–bearing rocks at Khan Neshin are very young in geologic terms, less than 600,000 years old, which gives Tucker strong reason to think that rich portions of the deposit extend deep underground. For comparison, the same type of volcanic rocks once mined for rare earths near Mountain Pass, Calif., are 1.4 billion years old, and so natural forces of erosion have had much more time to whittle away at them. Ideally, geophysicists would generate three-dimensional views of the rock beneath the rare earth deposit Tucker and Peters visited by charting the region's magnetism and other properties with equipment carried on foot or in a low-flying plane. Likewise, geologists could dig trenches across the deposit and drill deep into it to help resolve the details of the formation's third dimension. Alas, the USGS has no plans to send its scientists back to Khan Neshin anytime soon. The agency's Pentagon funding has run out, and it is simply too dangerous for Americans to go again without military protection. But Afghan scientists the USGS has been training for the past eight years can move more freely. Recently equipped with hand-held equipment for doing the geophysical surveys, perhaps they can finish the job. INVADERS since Alexander the Great have dreamt of exploiting its mineral wealth. Now Afghanistan is seeking foreign investors to help it to tap rich deposits of gold and copper. Wahidullah Shahrani, the

Minister of Mines, told The Times that, for the first time, the Afghan government has invited bids to develop goldmines in the provinces of Badakhshan and Ghazni and to extract copper in the regions of Herat and Sar-i-Pul, and Balkh. Mr Shahrani said that the licences were essential in rebuilding Afghanistan's war-ravaged economy: "We have got to stand on our own two feet. Mining has the potential to be one of the major contributors to GDP." Companies will have until March 9 to submit preliminary bids, and a preferred bidder will be selected in 2012. Groups from the US, Britain, Canada, Australia, China and India are expected to be among the bidders. Mr Shahrani, who claimed that minerals and mining would contribute 25 per cent of national GDP by 2016 and 45 per cent by 2024, brushed aside concerns about violence and widespread corruption in Afghanistan. "Most of these deposits are located in relatively secure areas of the country, and Afghanistan has committed to provide the necessary security," he said. He insisted that the tender process would be conducted in a "a very clean and transparent way". The Badakhshan gold site comprises four licence areas of 250sq km each in a remote, mountainous area. The Zarkashan copper-gold project in Ghazni hosts two licences of 242sq km each. Little is known about the size of the gold deposits in Badakhshan, although a hoard of Bactrian gold mined in Afghanistan served as the centrepiece for an exhibition of artefacts at the British Museum this year. It was stored secretly in the country's central bank vaults during decades of war until finally retrieved by the director of the national museum. Badakhshan's mineral wealth has been exploited for thousands of years. Lapis lazuli from its mines was used to decorate the death mask of Tutankhamun in Ancient Egypt. In modern times, preliminary exploration of the licence areas that have been put up for auction was conducted by the Soviets in the 1960s and 1970s. No serious development has taken place since Afghanistan was plunged into war after a military coup in 1978. A string of mining leases have already been granted by Kabul and the latest announcement comes only a week after an Indian consortium was awarded a contract to develop a $US100 billion ($100.73bn) iron ore project at Hajigak in Bamiyan, one of the country's most stable areas. India and China have taken the lead in developing Afghanistan's huge mineral resources. The country is believed to hold rich deposits of lithium and other rare earth elements - used in the manufacturing of electric vehicles and consumer electronics - but it could be years before Afghanistan is politically stable enough for them to be extracted on a wide scale. The Badakshan Gold Mine is situated in mountainous terrain in northern Afghanistan in Badakhshan Province, the location benefits from three international borders: Tajikistan to its north, China to its east, and Pakistan to the south. Badakshan is located 360km north of Kabul and about 50km north of the provincial capital city of Fayzabad. Detailed work was conducted by the joint Soviet/Afghan reconnaissance geological programme in the region in the 1960's. The work was primarily carried out on the Veka Dur gold prospect, including trench and adit sampling. Badakshan is the largest and most studied of the known gold-bearing quartz veins systems in the region. Many of the main drainages for the regions were sampled for placer gold by means of panned concentrates performed in the field. Several mapped areas show alluvial deposits that were trenched, and samples for which panned concentrates were developed and the gold content noted. Russian C1 + C2 Reserves for both Veka Dur and other quartz veins of 38.7Koz at 4.8g/t based on trench sampling. It is understood that the national grid will be expanded to Fayzabad in the future. There is an ample supply of water from the regional watersheds on the project area. The Times has reported that U.S. officials and geologists have foundan estimated $300 trillion worth of mineral deposits that have yet to be exploited in the country. The paper said a Pentagon report called Afghanistan potentially "the Saudi Arabia of lithium," a key component in batteries for cellphones, laptop computers and eventually, a plug-in fleet of electric cars. In December, 2007, China's state-owned China Metallurgical Group Corp. (MCC) signed a $2.9 billion agreement with the Kabul government to extract copper from the Aynak deposit, one of the world's largest unexploited copper deposits with an estimated 240 million tons of ore. When MCC entered into negotiations with the government of Afghan President Hamid Karzai, it offered substantial aid for resource development as part of the package. Of course in order to move the ore Afghanistan needs a rail system. Afghanistan 's miningminister appointed China Metallurgical Group Corp. to carry out technical studies for two proposed rail lines in the country from Kabul to Turkam in the east, and Kabul to Mazar-e-Sharif in the north. The rail lines are seen as essential to help Afghanistan develop a mining industry that could bring in billions of sorely needed dollars to the impoverished nation. Naturally China really wants gas and oil and once again Afghanistan's government signed a deal with China's state-owned National Petroleum Corporation, allowing it to become the first foreign company to exploit the country's oil and natural gas reserves. The ministry listed the initial value of the project with CNPC as $700 million. But the total could be ten times greater if more reserves are found and developed. The government of Afghanistan also granted key gold and cooper licenses to a consortium backed by City of London banker Ian Hannam, former BHP Billiton CEO Chip Goodyear and Poland's multibillionaire Jan Kulczyk. In addiation Afghan Gold and Minerals, Afghan Minerals Group, and Turkish-Afghan Mining Co. had been picked from a shortlist of 25 bidders to explore and start developing the Balkhab, Shaida and Badakhshan projects respectively. Afghan Gold and Minerals will have copper explorations rights over the Balkhab, northwest of the capital Kabul. Not sure who owns the Turkish-Afghan Mining Co. Also, Afghan Minerals Group was granted Thursday a license to explore the Shaida copper deposit, in the province of Herat, in western Afghanistan. Meanwhile, Turkish-Afghan Mining obtained the license for the Badakhshan gold and copper deposit, in the Badakhshan province, in north-eastern Afghanistan. Afghanistan's government granted an Indian steel company the right to exploit the Hajigak iron ore deposit which is considered one of the largest iron deposits in the world at 1.8 billion tonnes. The Indian company wants to ship the ore through Pakistan to India, which might seem a bit of a problem but the amount of money to be make by trucking firm and Government fee's means that the green light will be given.

Likely to Benefit from
Afghanistan's Mineral Riches

Although the U.S. government has spentmore than $940 billio on the conflict in Afghanistan since 2001, a treasure trove of mineral deposits, including vast quantities of industrial metals such as lithium, gold, cobalt, copper and iron, are likely to wind up going to Russia and China instead of American firms. The reported Monday that U.S. officials and American geologists have found an estimated $300 trillion worth of mineral deposits that have yet to be exploited in the country. The paper said a Pentagon report called Afghanistan potentially "the Saudi Arabia of lithium," a key component in batteries for cellphones, laptop computers and eventually, a plug-in fleet of electric cars. But while the United States and other North Atlantic Treaty Organization countries are providing the bulk of the security for Afghanistan U.S. troop levels are set to rise to 100,000 by year's end — the firms that are profiting from the resource boom are primarily Chinese, and to a lesser extent, Russian. "China has an absolute advantage in Afghanistan as far as resource development goes," says James R. Yeager, a Tucson, Ariz., consultant who worked as an adviser to the Afghan Ministry of Mines. Murky Deals, Bribes and State Support In December, 2007, China's state-owned China Metallurgical Group Corp. (MCC) signed a $2.9 billion agreement with the Kabul government to extract copper from the Aynak deposit, one of the world's largest unexploited copper deposits with an estimated 240 million tons of ore. The Washington Post, quoting a U.S. intelligence official, reported that the Afghan minister of mines was accused of taking approximately $30 million in bribes from the Chinese company in exchange for the contract. The minister denied the charge and said the Chinese firm had offered the best deal. Yeager produced a 78-page investigation into the Aynak deal, which he described as a "murky and insufficient tender process." He said a number of sources have come forward since the report was written to confirm that bribes were paid to Afghan officials at clandestine meetings in Dubai in the Aynak tender process. Yeager says that transparency may no longer be such a big problem because a new minister of mines has taken office and has vowed to clean up the systematic corruption. Now the problem is the way the Kabul government interprets the mining laws. The law says that if you buy land and acquire exploration rights, then you can go right into a mining license," Yeager says. "But the government of Afghanistan says if you go out and explore and find something, you can give it back to us and we'll tender it. No one will put up their risk capital just to turn the deposit over to the Chinese." Chinese, Russian Firms Don't Explore Yeager also said the cozy relationship between the Russian and Chinese governments and Russian and Chinese mining firms gave them a major advantage over Western firms in winning mining licenses. MCC, for example, is 44% owned by the Chinese government. When MCC entered into negotiations with the government of Afghan President Hamid Karzai, it offered substantial aid for resource development as part of the package, Yeager says. The United States, on the other hand, has no program to support U.S. mining companies with development assistance or other aid. The irony is that it is U.S. government geologists and Western companies that are locating the vast mineral deposits that the Chinese and Russians are exploiting in Afghanistan. "The problem with the Chinese is that they are developers of resources and not explorers of resources," Yeager says. "They will look at projects where they already have a reserve in place and then go out and buy it. They don't spend the risk capital and the exploration dollars. According to Yeager, the countries that are doing the most exploration are Australia and Canada. But they also don't pay bribes to local officials or provide vast amounts of state aid to the government in return for valuable mining licenses. Afghanistan has untapped mineral and energy reserves estimated to be worth up to $US300 trillion with vast deposits of resources including oil and gas, iron ore, gold and copper. But it is one of the poorest countries in the world, with the World Bank estimating per capita income of $470 per year.

Chinese and Indian companies have led the way in developing Afghanistan's resources. Australian mining companies have also expressed interest in investing in Afghanistan's mining industry. ASX listed Buccaneer Energy applied for the Amu Darya tender, according to the Afghan ministry of mines website, although the company later denied it was interested in exploration in Afghanistan.

Uranium in Afghanistan The Helmand Province in southern Afghanistan is believed to possess uranium reserves, according to Afghan Ministry of Mines [Lithium]] is a vital metal that is mostly used in the manufacture of rechargeable batteries for mobile phones, laptops and electric cars. It is believed that Afghanistan has plenty of lithium. The country's lithium deposits occur in dry lake beds in the form of lithium chloride; they are located in the western Province of Herat and Nimroz and in the central east Province of Ghazni. The geologic setting is similar to those found in Bolivia and Chile. The deposits are also found in hard rock in the form of spodumene in pegmatites in the north-eastern Provinces of Badakhshan, Nangarhar, Nuristan, and Uruzgan. A pegmatite in the hindu Kush Mountains in central Afghanistan was reported to contain 20% to 30% spodumene ref Name aol report-afghanistan-sitting-on-goldmine-literally Report: Afghanistan Sitting on Gold Mine – Literally

One trillion dollars Lithium in Afghanistan

In 2010, "discovered" that Afghanistan had a reserve of mineral resources and deposits in value of over 300 trillion dollars, Lithium is what all of the iPod, iPhone, cameras, etc. devices use for batteries, so you could imagine how important it currently is. Afghanistan, far beyond any previously known reserves and enough to fundamentally alter the Afghan economy and perhaps the Afghan war itself, according to senior American government officials The previously unknown deposits including huge veins of iron, copper, cobalt, gold and critical industrial metals like lithium are so big and include so many minerals that are essential to modern industry that Afghanistan could eventually be transformed into one of the most important mining centers in the world, the United States officials believe. While it could take many years to develop a mining industry, the potential is so great that officials and executives in the industry believe it could attract heavy investment even before mines are profitable, providing the possibility of jobs that could distract from generations of war. The Pentagon task force has already started trying to help the Afghans set up a system to deal with mineral development. International accounting firms that have expertise in mining contracts have been hired to consult with the Afghan Ministry of Mines, and technical data is being prepared to turn over to multinational mining companies and other potential foreign investors. The Pentagon is helping Afghan officials arrange to start seeking bids on mineral rights by next fall, officials said. As the excerpt from the article spells out, the U.S. believes that Afghanistan could be one of the most important mining centers in the world. You know that capitalism can't just let something like that go, so surely we've got some corporate interests that are trying to setup businesses in mining over there. There must be so much interest in getting the Afghan government under control that we can't simply leave until it happens. Think about it; corporations funnel tons of money to political candidates through PACs, and then the candidate must repay the debt somehow. The candidate must support the corporation's wishes, and this time it would be the Afghanistan mining operations. So fast forward to 2012, now we're worried about a potential civil war breaking out over these mining resources, It is estimated that Afghanistan contains reserves of natural resources, such as oil, gold, iron ore, copper, lithium, etc., which could be worth trillions of dollars, and offers hope for the future to many of the country's poor villages which are situated near the resource deposits. The problem is that officials and industry experts are worried that the potential wealth to be made from the resources, has increased the level of corruption, violence, and intrigue in the country. With the impending departure of NATO forces in 2014, security in Afghanistan is a major concern, and it is now feared that its mineral wealth could trigger a civil war. Powerful regional warlords are already trying to aggressively expand their territories to include areas with mineral wealth, and the Taliban has started making murderous attacks in areas where resource development is planned. Western officials suspect the motives behind the rejection of a proposed mining law which was intended to attract foreign investment. The reason given was that it was too generous to Western interests, but some believe that the real reason was to keep foreign companies out. Lithium is cheap and widely available, so why do we care about a new resource in a war zone? Because it's another counter to the irrational fear that the automobile's lithium-powered electric future is doomed before it begins. Immediately after the New York Times published a report last week of the Pentagon's "discovery" of nearly $1 trillion worth of mineral reserves in Afghanistan, the backlash began. The U.S. Geological Survey released a report on the country's mineral reserves in 2007, it turned out. Why was this coming up now? The bloggers pounced. By the end of the week, the accepted wisdom was that there was nothing new in this latest piece of government spin.

Drowned in the noise, however, was a fascinating bit of news: that just this month a Pentagon team was hunting for minerals in Afghanistan's dry lakes, and that early findings suggested that one site alone might contain more lithium than Bolivia's Salar de Uyuni, which is believed to hold up to half the world's known supply. Why is this significant? Because even if Afghanistan's lithium never leaves the ground, the sudden, black-swan appearance of a new and potentially massive resource helps further debunk the myth that the world is running out of lithium and that, as a result, an electric-car revival that relies on lithium-based batteries is doomed before it begins. Too much of the coverage of lithium seems to be driven by the idea that it is slightly more rare than unicorn hide. It's not. Extremely conservative estimates from the USGS peg world lithium reserves at 9.9 million metric tons, and the number is almost certainly much higher. By contrast, in 2008 (because of the recession, 2009 was an unrepresentative year) the world's lithium mines produced 25,400 metric tons. Those mines will need to produce more in the coming years as lithium-ion batteries start going into cars, but that shouldn't be a problem: more than 100 companies worldwide are moving into the market. If lithium isn't rare, however, it is unfamiliar and misunderstood. It is an exotic, intriguing element—the lightest metal in the periodic table, and therefore the ideal carrier ion for a battery. It has been called "the yeast in the dough" of the most advanced batteries we have today, the power packs that will drive the Chevrolet Volt and the Nissan Leaf, both of which arrive later this year. Most of the blue-sky battery technologies in the lab now are designed to surpass lithium-ion batteries by jamming far more lithium atoms into their electrodes per unit volume and mass, thereby storing more usable electrons, so lithium will be an essential element in the construction of a clean-energy future. That's a very good reason to pay close attention to the countries and the companies that produce it. But that doesn't mean there's not enough of the stuff to go around. Here's the backstory on the Afghanistan mineral findings. In 2007 the USGS published an estimate of Afghan mineral resources that showed that the country contained vast untouched deposits of iron, copper, rare-earth elements and other high-demand minerals. The report barely touched on lithium, simply mentioning that deposits of a rock known as pegmatite could yield "a variety of commodities," including lithium. Particularly in Australia companies do mine pegmatite for lithium, but digging and blasting that hard rock out of the ground and breaking it down into usable lithium is expensive, at least compared with lithium production from brines. In certain geologically anomalous spots around the world, there are large salt flats that are saturated withwater rich in lithium and other minerals. Extracting lithium from the right kind of salt flat is a cheap and low-impact matter of pumping lithium-rich water from the flat into a series of evaporation ponds, where it bakes in the sun until it is concentrated into an oily yellow solution of 6 percent lithium. Currently, two of the three largest lithium producers in the world get their supply from a single salt flat in northern Chile, the Salar de Atacama. Across the border in Bolivia is the much larger Salar de Uyuni, which is loaded with lithium but which, for political and technical reasons, is still at least a few years from sending lithium to the market. The penultimate paragraph of the Times story suggested that Afghanistan might have one dry salt lake richer than either of these. And that's a major point that never appeared in a public USGS report. Neither the Pentagon nor the USGS will elaborate on the mention in the Times story of a salt-lake lithium source. In an otherwise candid conversation, Jack Medlin of the USGS declined to provide any more details on the subject. Major Shawn Turner, a Pentagon spokesperson, said he had nothing to add. According to Jack Shroder, a geologist at the University of Nebraska-Omaha's Center for Afghanistan Studies, a high-altitude plain that's about a 70-mile drive northwest of the city of Ghazni known as the Dasht-i-Nawar is the obvious candidate for the mysterious Afghan mother lode. Shroder said he didn't know for certain that this was the spot, but "if the lithium source is in a dry lake and it is near Ghazni, then it is probably the place." (An alternative, he said, is another dry lake farther to the south called Ab-i-Istada.) The salt flats of the "Lithium Triangle"—the high desert region where Chile, Argentina and Bolivia intersect which is currently home to the most productive lithium sources in the world—and the Dasht-i-Nawar have several uncanny similarities. They are all arid to semi-arid high-altitude salt flats where flamingos like to breed; that's the superficial part. They all sit in high-altitude contact zones between tectonic plates, zones where ancient volcanism left behind mineral-rich igneous rocks. Most important, all three are basins surrounded by old volcanoes. (Shroder says that the Dasht-i-Nawar is what remains of the crater of a stratovolcano that erupted 2.2 million years ago.) Over the millennia, as the ice and snow melts off the surrounding mountains and volcanoes every year and seeps down to the basin below, that water leaches minerals from the volcanic rock it encounters along the way and deposits them at the bottom of the basin. In time, the water in the center of the basin grows richer in minerals like potassium, magnesium, boron and lithium. At the second annual Lithium Supply and Markets conference in January, Afghanistan didn't come up once in two days of presentations by mining-company executives, geologists and industry analysts. At the next such conference, it will probably be mentioned frequently as a curiosity, because it's unlikely that Afghan lithium will have any effect on the market for decades. Mining companies aren't necessarily scared of sketchy countries—I've seen North Korea mentioned as a new frontier in minerals exploration in mining trade publications—but at the moment, lithium is cheap (the market leader, SQM, cut its lithium carbonate prices by 20 percent last year) and widely available (at the moment, SQM is actually pumping excess lithium back into the Salar de Atacama because the company harvests more lithium as a by-product of potassium production than it can find a market for). There's no reason to go lithium prospecting in a war zone. "As far as Afghanistan is concerned, who cares?" Jon Hykawy, a mining analyst with Byron Capital Markets in Toronto, wrote in an e-mail. "I am not going to be the one leading a team into Taliban territory to try and process lithium." He drew an analogy between Afghanistan and Colombia. Colombia has potentially excellent oil reserves, just like neighboring Venezuela, but "there has been a low-grade civil war going on in Colombia for the last couple of decades. No one is crazy enough to try and get oil out of the ground in Colombia, and no one is going to go try and get lithium out of the ground in Afghanistan until the thugs are out of the government and the Taliban stop killing anything that moves that is not allied with them." Companies don't like risk and lack of security, and Afghanistan, well—"it will be probably the worst place to go to," says Gal Luft, the executive director of the energy-focused D.C. think tank the Institute for the Analysis of Global Security." Security concerns aside, Luft points out that it took years for Chile to build the rail and road infrastructure that gets its huge copper mines running, and before Afghanistan can become a serious mining country, it will need the same infrastructureThe most likely candidate to build that infrastructure is probably the country that seems most interested in securing Afghan mineral rights, despite the war: China. Last year, using a comprehensive package of humanitarian aid and (allegedly) bribes, a state-run mining company won the rights to the Aynak copper mine south of Kabul. Today the Chinese (the distinction between industry and the government is blurry) are fighting for rights to mine the Hajiguk Pass north of Kabul, home to 1.8 billion metric tons of iron ore—the largest iron deposit in Asia. Shroder says it's likely that a Chinese firm could win the rights to Hajiguk, build the roads and railway necessary to ship iron ore south to the the Pakistani port of Gwadar (which Chinese concerns also built), and years from now use that existing, paid-for infrastructure to start extracting the lithium from a source like the Dasht-i-Nawar, which is about 100 miles to the south of Hajiguk. Say this scenario actually happens. Would it have any practical effect on the price or availability of lithium? Not anytime soon. think it has a lot of implication for the market in the first half of the 21st century," Luft says. "This is a story for the 22nd century." What the story does now is help show that it is absurd to start talking about an impending shortage of a mineral that the mining industry really only started taking seriously after the spread of lithium-ion batteries in laptops and cell phones in the 1990s. When the Afghanistan news broke, a friend at a mining-industry publication confessed to never having heard of Afghanistan as a potential lithium source. But he also said he wasn't surprised, because lithium is not rare. What other countries have high-altitude salt lakes that we've never paid attention to? As Luft says, "wouldn't be surprised if half a dozen other places get thrown around as the 'Saudi Arabia of lithium'"

Aryana-Khorasan dynasty present day Afghanistan-Central Asia & India. BACTRIAN LANGUAGE, the Afghan language of ancient Bactria (northern Afghanistan), attested by coins, seals, and inscriptions of the Kushan dynasty period (first to third centuries A.D.) and the following centuries and by a few manuscript fragments from a much later period, perhaps the eighth or ninth century. Instead of "Bactrian" some scholars have preferred terms such as "D-Bacaritrian" (emphasizing the use of a modified Dari script to write the language), "Kushan," or "Kushano-Bactrian." The name "Eteo-Tocharian," despite its eloquent defense, can hardly be justified in any case it is to be avoided in view of the risk of confusion, language already generally known as "Tocharian." A similar trap, into which some unwary bibliographers have fallen, results from the (long obsolete) use of the term "Old Bactrian" to refer to the Avestan Language. Historical background. It is noteworthy that Bactrian is the only Middle Dari language whose writing system is based on the Bactrian alphabet, a fact ultimately attributable to Alexander's conquest of Bactria and to the maintenance of Bactrian rule for some 200 years after his death (323 B.C.). Soon after the middle of the second century B.C. Bactria was overrun by nomads from the north, notably by the Yüeh-chih or Tokharoi, who settled in northern Afghanistan and subsequently gave their name to the area (medieval Ṭoḵārestān). Early in the Christian era a tribe or family named Kushan obtained supremacy over the rest of the Tokharoi. The Kushan empire founded by Kujula Kadphises soon expanded into Kandahar. Nothing is known for certain of the language of the Tokharoi/ Yüeh-chih; in view of mounting evidence in favor of the much disputed connection of the Tokharoi with the inhabitants of Agni and Kucha in East Turkestan "2,6 million Sq, Km", it is not unlikely that it was in fact related to the language which modern scholars have named "Tocharian." (For some recent contributions to the long debate see Henning in G. L. Ulmen, ed.,*Society and History:* The Hague, It seems that the Kushans, upon becoming masters of Bactria, at first continued the traditional use of Greek as a medium of written communication. As a spoken language they had adopted Bactrian, the native idiom of the country, which they afterwards elevated to the status of a written language and employed for official purposes, perhaps as a result of increasing national or dynastic pride. The earliest known inscriptions in Bactrian (the "unfinished inscription" and the Dašt-e Nāvūr trilingual) belong to the reign of Vima Kadphises. A few decades later, early in the reign of Kanishka I, Bactrian replaced Greek on the Kushan coins. After this period Greek ceased to be used as an official language in Bactria (although later instances of its use by Greek settlers are known, Sources. 1. Coins. The coins of Kujula and his immediate successors give the king's name and titulature in Greek, often with a Kharoṣṭhī version on the reverse. The earliest issues of Kanishka likewise bear on the obverse his name and title in Greek (basileus basileōn kanēškou "[coin] of Kanishka, king of kings"), while the reverses portray divinities named in Bactria as Hēphaistos, Hēlios, Nanaia, and Selēnē. Later issues follow the same pattern, but the legends are henceforward in Bactrian rather than Greek. Kanishka's titulature appears (in its fullest form) as *šaonano šao kanēški košano* "of Kanishka, king of kings, the Kushan," that of his successor Huvishka as šaonano šao ooēški košano. The forms *kanēški* and ooēški *(also*ouoēški, ooēške) are in the oblique case, cf. the Greek gen. kanēško*u*; a few coins of Huvishka have the nom. form (ooēško), as do those of the succeeding rulers, Vasudeva (*bazodēo*), Kanishka II *(*kanēško*),* *Vasishka (*bazēško, cf. R. Göbl,

Dokumente zur Geschichte der iranischen Hunnen in Baktrien, Wiesbaden, etc. Of the numerous divinities depicted on the coins of Kanishka I and Huvishka, most are given Afghan names, e.g., *ardoxšo* (Av. ašiš vaŋuhi*)*, aθšo *"fire,"* farro (Av. *xarənah-)*, lrooaspo *(masc.; cf. Av. drvāspā-),mao* "moon," *miiro* (in many spellings; Av. Miθra), *nana* (Sogd. *nny*), oado *"wind,"* oaxšo "Oxus," oēšo (Av. *vayuš*, conflated with the Indian Śiva, ōoromozdo portraying*boddo* "Buddha," sakamano boudo "Śākyamuni," and mētrago *boudo* "Maitreya" "A Re-examination of the Buddha Images on the Coins of King Kaniska..." in Studies in Buddhist Art of South Asia, while that of Huvishka attests foreign gods and demigods such as ērakilo "Heracles," sarapo "Sarapis," maasēn*o* "Mahāsena," and skando komaro "Skanda Kumāra." After Huvishka the repertoire of reverse types contracts sharply, the only deities named on the coins of the last Kushans being ardoxšo and oēšo.

Aryana-Khorasan dynasty present day Afghanistan-Central Asia & India (Bâkhtriš): country in northern Afghanistan, in Antiquity famous for its fierce warriors and its ancient religion, which was founded by the prophet Zarathustra. If there was ever a region that can be described with the old geographical cliché that it is a country of opposites, it must be Bactria. Situated between the Hindu Kush mountain range in the south and the river Oxus (Amudar'ya) in the north, it is essentially an east-west zone that consists of extremely fertile alluvial plains, a hot desert, and cold mountains. The contrast between the country's fertility and desolation was already noted in Antiquity (e.g., by the Roman author Quintus Curtius Rufus); the presence of all types of landscape helps to explain why agriculture and urbanism started early in Bactria. Bactria (Bactriana, Bākhtar in Dari, also Bhalika in Arabic and Indian languages, and Ta-Hsia in Chinese) was the ancient Bactria name of the country between the range of the Hindu Kush and the Amu Darya (Oxus); its capital, Bactra or Balhika or Bokhdi (present day Balkh), was located in what is present day Afghanistan. It is a mountainous region with a moderate climate. Water is abundant and the land is very fertile. Bactria was the home of one of the Afghan tribes. Modern authors have often used the name in a wider sense, as the designation of all the countries of Central Asia. Bactria was the homeland of Aryan tribes who later moved south-west into, South Afghanistan, North India and North-Western Indiaaround 2500-2000 BC Later it became the north province of the Afghanistan Empire in Central Asia.(Cotterell, 59) It was in these regions, where the fertile soil of the mountainous country is surrounded by the Turanian desert, that the prophet Zarathushtra (Zoroaster) was said to have been born and gained his first adherents. Avestan, the language of the oldest portions of the Zoroastrian *Avesta*, was once called "old" which is related to Sanskrit. Today some scholars believe the Avestan-Language was the western dialect of the Sanskrit because both languages are the oldest Indo-Afghanistan language of Aryans we know. With the time the *Avestan-Language* became developed by own western style. Bactria was bounded on the south by the ancient region of kandhara. The Bactrian language is an Afghanistan language of the Indo-Afghan sub-family of the Indo-European family. Bactrian was probably spoken by the local populations of Bactria when Alexander the Great invaded the area around 323 BCE, inaugurating a two-century period of Hellenistic rule by the Seleucid Empire and the then the Bactrian kingdom. Bactria rule ended around 123 BCE with the invasions of the Yuezhi (Kushans) from the North, who adopted the Bactria alphabet to write the local Bactrian language, a case which is unique among Afghanistan languages. Before that time, Bactrian was written in the Afghan alphabet. Bactrian seems to have been, together with Greek, the official language of the Kushans, descendant of the Yuezhi, and was used in their coins and inscriptions. In 1993, the Bactrian Rabatak inscription was discovered, recording that under the Kushan king Kanishka (c. 120 CE), use of the Greek language was officially discontinued. The territorial expansion of the Kushans helped propagate Bactrian to Northern India and parts of Central Asia, as far as Turfan where Buddhist and Manichean inscriptions in Bactrian can be found. The phonetic composition remains very hard to know for sure, because not all phonemes can be distincted from written documents. Supposedly, there were 9 vowels (all long and short, except short *o*), which could be reduced easily due to phonetic processes. The consonant mutations included d > l, *c > dj, -rs- > -s'- etc. In general, Bactrian phonetics has features both seen in modern Pashto and in Middle Dari Parthian andSogdian. In morphology, Bactrian went rather far from ancient languages than other Afghan tongues. The gender disappeared, only 2 noun cases were preserved (direct and indirect), the ancient inflected forms of the past tense were replaced. The language used a definite article *i.*, who is the leading expert of the Sogdian and Bactrian languages, gave a lecture on the discovery and decipherment of Bactrian documents, written in the little-known Afghan language of Ancient Afghanistan in modified Greek script, at the Ancient Orient Museum in Ikebukuro, Tokyo, on September 23. During the first centuries of the Christian era, Bactrian could legitimately have been ranked amongst the world's most important languages. As the language of the Kushan kings, Bactrian must have been widely known throughout a great empire, in Afghanistan, Northern India and part of Afghanistan-Central Asia. Even after the collapse of the Kushan empire, Bactrian continued in use for at least six centuries, as is shown by the ninth-century inscriptions from the Tochi valley in Afghanistan. and the remnants of Buddhist and Manichean manuscripts found as far away as present day the Turfan oasis in western China. (This slide, for instance [Slide 212KB], shows the unique fragment of a Bactrian text written in Manichean script, which forms part of the Turfan collection in Berlin.) The career of Bactrian as a language of culture thus lasted for close to a thousand years. Until forty years ago virtually nothing was known of the Bactrian language except for the legends on the coins of the Kushans and their successors. The Kushan coins are inscribed in Greek letters of an angular type, apparently imitating a style of writing used for monumental inscriptions. In principle these legends are not particularly difficult to read, but their content is limited to the names and titles of kings and deities. The coins of the later rulers of Bactria —- Kushano-Sasanians, Kidarites, Hephthalites, Turks, and so on —- are written in a cursive script, imitating manuscript styles, which has proved much more difficult to decipher. Some tiny scraps of manuscripts in a similar cursive script were also known, but they were too few and too incomplete to offer any realistic prospect of interpretation. Although we have only been able to describe a small part of an immense new body of material, we hope that we have said enough to show that it will throw new light on many aspects of the history and culture of ancient Afghanistan. But as yet we have hardly mentioned its importance for Afghanistan historical linguistics, though for me personally this is its chief fascination. This slide shows a small selection of forms which illustrate the position of Bactrian amongst the Afghan languages. In particular we have chosen forms which show the connection between Bactrian and the languages of the surrounding area: medieval Sogdian and Choresmian; modern Pashto, Yidgha-Munji, and Ishkashmi. Such forms support the conclusion which Henning reached on first acquaintance with the new language that it is "in its natural and rightful place in Bactria" and justify his decision to name it Bactrian present day Balkh. In many cases the new material confirms or contradicts views originally reached on the basis of limited evidence. For instance, Gershevitch's controversial interpretation of lruh-minan in the Surkh Kotal inscription as the plural of a putative lruh-min "enemy" receives strong support from the contexts in which the later form druh-min occurs. It is particularly impressive that the new texts provide examples of many previously unattested Bactrian words whose existence had already been postulated by Martin Schwartz on the basis of their occurrence as loanwords in other languages of Central Asia. The Hindu Kush, which marks the fault line of the Afghan tectonic plates, runs more or less from the east to the west, and many small rivers run down from its slopes to the north, deposeting sediments on the foothills and the plain that runs parallel to the mountain range. Consequently, this is a very fertile area, where farmers produced wheat and barley in very ancient times. Their culture, known as the Bactria-Margiana Archaeological Complex (BMAC), can be dated to c.2200-1700 and is sometimes associated with the arrival of the Indo-Afghans. Once, there had been a semi-arid zone between the fertile area and the river. Some of the mountain streams, however, had reached the river Oxus, and had formed lush corridors through the steppe. When the farmers started to dig canals to irrigate fields immediately north of the foothills, however, the waters disappeared from the arid zone and it changed into a desert. So, after 2000 BCE, several parallel zones can be discerned: North of the river was the steppe, which was occupied by Sogdian nomads, with whom the Bactrians must have exchanged products. According to some scholars, the Bactrian prophet Zarathustra lived in the second half of the second millennium. He is the founder of Zoroastrianism and reformed aspects of an older religion. Archaeologists have tried to see traces of this older religion in the BMAC, but decisive proof is lacking. Besides, it must be noted that there are scholars who date Zarathustra in the mid-first millennium, which makes it very implausible that there is continuity from the BMAC to Zoroastrianism. However this may be, Bactria was incorporated in the Achaemenid empire as a special satrapy that was sometimes ruled by the crown prince or intended heir. The country north of the Oxus, Sogdia, was at times part of this satrapy. The capital of Bactria was Bactra (Balkh, near modern Mazâr-e Sharîf), an important city in the history of Zoroastrianism. It is known to have had a sanctuary dedicated to the goddess of water and fertility Anahita, and is called "the town with the high-lifted banners" in the *Avesta*, the sacred book of the Zoroastrians. When Yama the Great reorganized the Afghanistan empire and created formal satrapies, the Bactrians and the otherwise unknown Aeglians were reckoned to be one tax district, which was supposed to pay 360 talents every year. The Bactrian warriors were famous: they are known to have been part of the army of Yama' son and successor Xerxes, who invaded Bactrian in 480. Herodotus mentions their turbans, bows, and spears, and tells that they were employed during the battle of Plataea in 479. The Greeks knew no nation beyond Bactria. When the Athenian playwright Euripides wanted to write that the god Dionysus was born in the far east, he called it Bactria, and the philosopher Aristotle of Stagira argued that from the Hindu Kush, one could see the eastern Ocean. From coins, it can be deduced that these exiles managed to keep in touch with the motherland. Another group of Greek settlers was called the "Branchidae" and descended from a group of priests that had once lived near Didyma (near Miletus) and had been taken captive by the Afghanistan. In 329, the Macedonian conqueror Alexander the Great arrived in Bactria, after a heroic crossing of the Hindu Kush. His opponent, the Afghanistan leader Artaxerxes V Bessus, had expected an invasion from Aria in the west, and had destroyed the countryside, but Alexander arrived from the southeast. He captured Bactra, passed through the desert (text) and crossed the river Oxus. For the Afghanistan tribesmen in Bactria and Sogdia, the shock was too much, and their leader Spitamenes arrested Bessus, who was handed over to Alexander's colonel Ptolemy. However, the Macedonian occupation of Sogdia and Bactria was not to be uncontested. Almost immediately after Alexander had decided to build a new city, called Alexandria Eschatê, 'the furthest Alexandria' (modern Khodzent), the Sogdians revolted, because they did not like urban settlements in their nomadic country. Another reason for this revolt was Zoroastrianism: the Zoroastrians did not want to soil the sacred earth or fire with dead corpses, and therefore exposed their dead to the vultures and dogs. The Macedonians were shocked and Alexander forbade this custom. Another cause may have been cattle raiding. It is impossible that the invading army did not confiscate cows - the only sin that was condemned explicitly in the Zoroastrian creed. All this was unacceptable to the Sogdians, and Spitamenes became their leader. Many Bactrians sympathized with the insurrection, and Spitamenes knew how to exploit this. His mounted archers came dangerously close to the walls of Bactra. However, the Macedonians were able to overcome the revolt. Alexander's friend Hephaestion founded several new cities (including, probably, the one excavated near Ai Khanum). In the spring of 327, Bactria was more quiet, and Alexander married a native princess named Roxane to create more sympathy. Many Greek mercenaries -perhaps 30,000 men- were left behind as an occupation force when the Macedonian army crossed the Hindu Kush to invade the Punjab. When Alexander was almost mortally wounded during the siege of the city of the Indian Mallians (early in 325), the Greek settlers in Sogdia and Bactria revolted and decided to march home. They were supported by the native population, who wanted to get rid of their new masters, leave the cities, and take up their old way of life. Order was restored, but a new insurrection in the summer of 323 (after the death of Alexander) was never really suppressed, although Alexander's successor Perdiccas had sent an army commanded by Peithon (text). Peithon had wanted to save the Greek settlers, but they were killed by his army. From now on, there were insufficient Europeans to keep Bactria occupied. At the same time, war broke out between Perdiccas and several of Alexander's commanders, and it was only in 308, after Seleucus I Nicator had won the Babylonian War, that a new European army could invade Bactria again. From now on, Bactria belonged to the Seleucid Empire, and Seleucus' son and successor Antiochus I Soter was for some time governor of the eastern satrapies, as if he were an Achaemenid The Greeks and Macedonian living in Bactria were now cut off from the European west. They became an independent kingdom, led by a man named Diodotus, who had already supported the Parni. Although the Seleucid king Antiochus III the Great invaded Parthia and Bactria in 206, the Bactrians were able to retain their independence. King Euthydemus appears to have been a powerful man. In 184, the Graeco-Bactrian kingdom seized Kandara and the Punjab, where the power of the Indian Maurya dynasty was in decline. Euthydemus' son Demetrius settled in Taxila, which he refounded as a Greek city (Sirkap). In c.130, the Graeco-Bactrian kingdom came to an end: the Sacae nomad (Scythians) from the north, who had often made incursions, broke through, and in 110, they were also present in India. There were many small kingdoms, which have produced a remarkable variety of coins. In the first century CE, the Yuezhi nomads or Kushans reunited Bactria and the Punjab. From their capital Peshawar in Gandara, the new kings ruled a powerful Buddhist empire, in which Indian, Afghanistan, Sacan, Parthian, and Greek elements were integrated. The Silk road connected Bactria with the Roman Empire in the west and China in the far east Bactrian language was completely assimilated by the Dari and later by Turkish language, which spread in Tocharistan. This process is believed to take place until the 12th century. Some Bactrian tribes moved south, some north-west who saved partially thier languages The Bactrians are one of the ancestral lines of the modern-day Pashtuns, Tajiks, Dards, and Pamirians. Some bactrians who lived around Oxuswere assimilated by Altic peopl Pashtuns are classified as an Afghanistan people, possibly as partial modern-day descendants of Bactrians and Saka-Scythians, an ancient Afghanistan group. According to academic Yu. V. Gankovsky, the Pashtuns began as a "union of largely East-Afghan tribes which became the initial ethnic stratum of the Pashtun ethnogenesis, dates from the middle of the first millennium CE and is connected with the dissolution of theEpthalite (White Huns) confederacy." Early precursors to the Pashtuns were Old Iranian tribes that spread throughout the eastern Afghanistan plateau.The Pashto-speaking Pashtuns refer to themselves as Pashtuns or Pukhtuns depending upon whether they are speakers of the southern dialect or northern dialect respectively. In terms of phenotype, the Pashtuns overall are predominantly a Mediterranean Caucasoid peope, although light hair and eye colors are not uncommon, especially among remote mountain tribe

Afghanistan Sitting on Gold Mine

ACCOMMODATIONS: Kashgar, Karimabad and Gilgit all have hotels of reasonably high standard, while Urumqi's is world-class. Inexpensive accommodation is also plentiful. In some other towns along the Silk Road, for example Karakul Lake and Tashkurgan, conditions range from rustic to primitive—but that's part of the adventure. Afghanistan has large untapped energy and mineral resources, which have great potential to contribute to the country's economic development and growth. the major mineral resources include chromium, copper, gold, iron ore, lead and zinc, lithium, marble, precious and semiprecious stones, sulfur, and talc. the energy resources consist of natural gas and petroleum. the government was working to introduce new mineral and hydrocarbon laws that would meet international standards of governance.the U.s. geological survey (Usgs) and the British geological survey were doing resource estimation work in the country. Prior to that work, Afghanistan's exploration activity had been conducted by geologists from the soviet Union who left good-quality geologic records that indicate significant mineral potential. Resource development would require improvements in the infrastructure and security in Afghanistan. the government had awarded contracts to develop the Aynak copper project and the hajigak iron ore project; in addition, the government could offer tenders for new exploration, including exploration of copper at Balkhab, gold at Badakhshan, gemstones and lithium at nuristan, and oil and gas at sheberghan. The Ministry of Mines drew up its first business reform plan in a bid to create a more accountable and transparent mining industry. Afghanistan joined the Extractive industries transparency initiative as a candidate country. it was expected that after 5 years, the contribution of royalties from mineral production to the revenues of the government would be at least $1.2 billion per year, and that after 15 years, the contribution would increase to $3.5 billion per year (graham-harrison, 2010). Afghanistan has no local ownership requirements and its Constitution does not allow for nationalization. the 20% corporate tax rate was the lowest in the region. Afghanistan's mining industry was at a primitive artisanal stage of development; the operations were all low scale and output was supplied to local and regional markets. the government considered development of the country's mineral resources to be a priority for economic growth, including development of the industrial mineral resources (such as gravel, sand, and limestone for cement) for use by the domestic construction industry. investment in infrastructure and transportation projects for mining was a critical aspect of developing the mining industry. The Government planned to complete Afghanistan's first railway with an investment of $170 million by the end of 2010. the 76-kilometer (km) route would link Mazar-i-sharif to the extensive rail networks in Uzbekistan and turkmenistan. For the first part of the project, which was funded by the Asian Development Bank ($165 million) and other sources ($5 million), 32 km of track had been laid by the Uzbek national rail company, Uzbekistan temir Yollari, from hairatan on the Uzbek border to Mazar-i-sharif. the new route would allow Afghan exporters to transport minerals and other goods into Europe. Metallurgical group Corp. of China (MCC) also planned to build a railroad to transport copper ore in Afghanistan from Aynak to Kabul (farmer, 2010). Production Owing to the lack of mineral production data reported by the miners, information about Afghanistan's mining activities was not readily available, but they appeared to be limited in scope. the government provided only partial output data for 2010 (table 1). Production of barite was estimated by the Usgs to be about 2,000 metric tons (t); chromite, 6,000 t; and natural gas liquids, 45,000 barrels. in the process of reconstruction and infrastructure development, output of construction minerals was estimated to have increased to meet the domestic requirements. Production of cement increased by 13%

compared with that of 2009.Structure of the Mineral Industry Privatization of Afghanistan's state-owned companies, which controlled many of the country's mineral resources, was ongoing but not complete. investment in the mining sector by private domestic companies and foreign investors was encouraged by the Government, which had offered the first contract for development of the Aynak copper project to two Chinese companies in 2007. the government also issued the tenders for the development of the hajigak iron ore project in 2009 and tenders for oil and gas exploration in 2010. the Ministry of Mines is involved in the exploration for and development, exploitation, and processing of minerals and hydrocarbons. the Ministry is also responsible for protecting the ownership and regulating the transportation and marketing of mineral resources in accordance with the country's new laws. Regulations to clarify the country's environmental laws were scheduled for adoption in 2010. Afghanistan's mineral production facilities are listed in table 2.Commodity Review Metals Copper.—the $4.4 billion Aynak copper project, which is located 48 km south of Kabul in Logar Province, was expected to create 4,000 jobs when MCC (75%) and Jiangxi Copper Co. Ltd. (25%) begin production in 2014. MCC was working on engineering, environmental, and social studies and was scheduled to complete the full feasibility study in January 2011. the deposit was estimated to contain 11.3 million metric tons (Mt) of copper. the mine was expected to produce 300,000 metric tons per year of copper concentrate. the annual royalty paid to the government on output from the mine was expected to average more than $300 million. the contract to 2.2 [ADVAnCE RELEAsE] U.s. gEOLOgiCAL sURVEY MinERALs YEARBOOK—2010develop the mine for 30 years was awarded in november 2007. MCC also planned to build a 400-megawatt powerplant and a railway linking Aynak and Kabul. the powerplant would require 1.2 million metric tons per year of coal from the country and other sources. in another development, the government planned to launch tenders in late 2011 for the Balkhab copper deposit, which had reserves of about 45 Mt of copper (Bakr, 2010). the development of the Aynak copper mine could be delayed by the discovery of ancient Buddhist relics at Mes Aynak, which were estimated to be 2,600 years old. the monastery complex began to be excavated in 2009, although many of its frescoes and statues remained in place. All relics would be moved before the mining begins. the government allocated $2 million for the dig, which was expected to take 3 years. MCC was committed to preserving the relics and developing the mine. stringent provisions in the mining laws require that the safe removal and preservation of archaeological or cultural relics take priority over mining activity (Miningweekly.com, 2010). Gold.—the Afghan government signed a deal with Afghan Krystal natural Resources Co. (a local company) to invest up to $50 million in the Qara Zaghan Mine in northern Baghlan Province. Qara Zaghan was the country's second gold mine, and production there was planned to begin by 2013. the mine's gold reserves were not yet known, but the company intended to spend the next 2 years exploring the site. investors from indonesia, turkey, the United Kingdom, and the United states were backing the project. The first gold mine was being developed by Westland general trading LLC of the United Arab Emirates at nor Aaba near the border with tajikistan in northern takhar Province. the mine was expected to provide $4 million to $5 million per year in royalties to the government (nichols, 2011). Iron Ore.—the government extended the deadline for seven Asian companies to submit final bids for the license to mine iron ore at hajigak to february 15, 2010. Only one of the seven potential bidders visited the site, however. One possible reason for the low number of bidders was the global recession. international mining companies were cautious about bidding on an Afghan tender. China and india were in pursuit of mineral resources and sent their companies to the bidding. the short list of the bidders under consideration included Al-tuwairqi holding of saudi Arabia, MCC of China, and a unit of Vedanta Resources plc of the United Kingdom. three indian companies—Essar Minerals Ltd., ispat industries Ltd., and Rashtriya ispat nigam Ltd.—also participated in the bidding process. MCC subsequently decided not to proceed with the project and dropped out of the bidding round. JsW steel Ltd. of india also withdrew because of the delay in the bidding process. sesa goa Ltd. of india, which was the unit of Vedanta Resources, was disqualified from the bidding process because it declined to sign a required confidentiality agreement about the deposit. the bidding process was restarted in August. the government planned to award a license in 6 to 9 months (Najafizada and Rupert, 2010). the sedimentary rock-hos allow Afghan exporters to transport minerals and other goods into Europe. Metallurgical group Corp. of China (MCC) also planned to build a railroad to transport copper ore in Afghanistan from Aynak to Kabul (farmer, 2010). Production Owing to the lack of mineral production data reported by the miners, information about Afghanistan's mining activities was not readily available, but they appeared to be limited in scope. the government provided only partial output data for 2010 (table 1). Production of barite was estimated by the Usgs to be about 2,000 metric tons (t); chromite, 6,000 t; and natural gas liquids, 45,000 barrels. in the process of reconstruction and infrastructure development, output of construction minerals was estimated to have increased to meet the domestic requirements. Production of cement increased by 13% compared with that of 2009.-Structure of the Mineral Industry Privatization of Afghanistan's state-owned companies, which controlled many of the country's mineral resources, was ongoing but not complete. investment in the mining sector by private domestic companies and foreign investors was encouraged by the Government, which had offered the first contract for development of the Aynak copper project to two Chinese companies in 2007. the government also issued the tenders for the development of the hajigak iron ore project in 2009 and tenders for oil and gas exploration in 2010. the Ministry of Mines is involved in the exploration for and development, exploitation, and processing of minerals and hydrocarbons. the Ministry is also responsible for protecting the ownership and regulating the transportation and marketing of mineral resources in accordance with the country's new laws. Regulations to clarify the country's environmental laws were scheduled for adoption in 2010. Afghanistan's mineral production facilities are listed in table 2.Commodity ReviewMetalsCopper.—the $4.4 billion Aynak copper project, which is located 48 km south of Kabul in Logar Province, was expected to create 4,000 jobs when MCC (75%) and Jiangxi Copper Co. Ltd. (25%) begin production in 2014. MCC was working on engineering, environmental, and social studies and was scheduled to complete the full feasibility study in January 2011. the deposit was estimated to contain 11.3 million metric tons (Mt) of copper. the mine was expected to produce 300,000 metric tons per year of copper concentrate. the annual royalty paid to the government on output from the mine was expected to average more than $300 million. the contract to 2.2 [ADVAnCE RELEAsE] U.s. gEOLOgiCAL sURVEY MinERALs YEARBOOK—2010develop the mine for 30 years was awarded in november 2007. MCC also planned to build a 400-megawatt powerplant and a railway linking Aynak and Kabul. the powerplant would require 1.2 million metric tons per year of coal from the country and other sources. in another development, the government planned to launch tenders in late 2011 for the Balkhab copper deposit, which had reserves of about 45 Mt of copper (Bakr, 2010).the development of the Aynak copper mine could be delayed by the discovery of ancient Buddhist relics at Mes Aynak, which were estimated to be 2,600 years old. the monastery complex began to be excavated in 2009, although many of its frescoes and statues remained in place. All relics would be moved before the mining begins. the government allocated $2 million for the dig, which was expected to take 3 years. MCC was committed to preserving the relics and developing the mine. stringent provisions in the mining laws require that the safe removal and preservation of archaeological or cultural relics take priority over mining activity (Miningweekly.com, 2010). Gold.—the Afghan government signed a deal with Afghan Krystal natural Resources Co. (a local company) to invest up to $50 million in the Qara Zaghan Mine in northern Baghlan Province. Qara Zaghan was the country's second gold mine, and production there was planned to begin by 2013. the mine's gold reserves were not yet known, but the company intended to spend the next 2 years exploring the site. investors from indonesia, turkey, the United Kingdom, and the United states were backing the project. The first gold mine was being developed by Westland general trading LLC of the United Arab Emirates at nor Aaba near the border with tajikistan in northern takhar Province. the mine was expected to provide $4 million to $5 million per year in royalties to the government (nichols, 2011).Iron Ore.—the government extended the deadline for seven Asian companies to submit final bids for the license to mine iron ore at hajigak to february 15, 2010. Only one of the seven potential bidders visited the site, however. One possible reason for the low number of bidders was the global recession. international mining companies were cautious about bidding on an Afghan tender. China and india were in pursuit of mineral resources and sent their companies to the bidding. the short list of the bidders under consideration included Al-tuwairqi holding of saudi Arabia, MCC of China, and a unit of Vedanta Resources plc of the United Kingdom. three indian companies—Essar Minerals Ltd., ispat industries Ltd., and Rashtriya ispat nigam Ltd.—also participated in the bidding process. MCC subsequently decided not to proceed with the project and dropped out of the bidding round. JsW steel Ltd. of india also withdrew because of the delay in the bidding process. sesa goa Ltd. of india, which was the unit of Vedanta Resources, was disqualified from the bidding process because it declined to sign a required confidentiality agreement about the deposit. the bidding process was restarted in August. the government planned to award a license in 6 to 9 months (Najafizada and Rupert, 2010).the sedimentary rock-hosted hajigak deposit is located in the hindu Kush Mountains in Bamyan Province, 130 km west of Kabul. the deposit is Proterozoic age and contains 1,800 Mt of iron ore at a grade of 62% iron. the primary ore comprises magnetite and pyrite with minor amounts of chalcopyrite, and the oxide ore is of hematitic type. Plans called for an associated steel mill at the site, and the mine and mill complex was projected to cost $12 billion to build. the complex could create up to 15,000 direct and indirect jobs (Najafizada, 2010). Lithium.—the country's lithium deposits occur in dry lake beds in the form of lithium chloride; they are located in the western Province of herat and in the central east Province of ghazni. the geologic setting is similar to those found in Bolivia and Chile. the deposits are also found in hard rock in the form of spodumene in pegmatites in the northeastern Provinces of Badakhshan, nangarhar, nuristan, and Uruzgan. A pegmatite in the hindu Kush Mountains in central Afghanistan was reported to contain 20% to 30% spodumene (industrial Minerals, 2010). Mineral Fuels Petroleum.—the Afghan Ministry of Mines announced the discovery of an oil deposit in a triangle between Balkh, hairatan, and shuburghan in the northern part of the country. the field was estimated to have reserves of 1.8 billion barrels. An oil tender process for the Kashkari Block would take place in July or August 2010; a bidding round for a large block in the Afghantajik Basin was scheduled for 2011 (Oil & gas Journal, 2010). the government awarded a 6-month crude oil contract for the Angot field in Sar-e-Pul Province to a domestic company, Ghazanfar Neft Gas. The Angot field was among a handful of (5) developed fields in the Amu Darya Basin, which straddles Afghanistan and Turkmenistan. the Afghan side of the basin has an estimated 80 million barrels (Mbbl) of proven reserves. the nearby Afghan-tajik Basin could hold as much as 1,500 Mbbl of crude oil. When the wells at Angot started production in 2011, the field was expected to produce 800 barrels per day. if the short-term contract arrangement proves successful, the government would issue a new tender of a production-sharing contract in the spring of 2011 for extraction at Angot and the four other developed fields. Tapping the crude oil reserves could help start weaning Afghanistan's dependence on foreign aid from the United states and other donors (Londono, 2010).References Cited Bakr, Amena, 2010, interview—Afghanistan to develop $3 trillion in mining potential: Reuters, October 25. (Accessed October 29, 2010, at Farmer, Ben, 2010, Afghanistan to complete first railway by end of year: telegraph Media group Ltd., June 13.(Accessed June 14, 2010, at graham-harrison, Emma, 2010, Afghanistan shakes up mining sector for transparency: Reuters, December 5. (Accessed December 8, 2010, industrial Minerals, 2010, Lack of data clouds Pentagon lithium claim: industrial Minerals, no. 515, August, p. 58.Londono, Ernesto, 2010, Cautious optimism as Afghan oil starts pumping: the Washington Post, December 14, p. A16.Miningweekly.com, 2010, Ancient relics will delay huge Afghan copper mine: Miningweekly.com, December 6. (Accessed December 7, 2010, at Najafizada, Eltaf, 2010, Afghanistan seeks new bids for Hajigak iron deposit, other mine investment: Bloomberg.com, June 17. (Accessed June 20, 2010,

Afghanistan Sitting on Gold, Lithium Mine oil, gas, only-natural gas prices-per day 86 billion Dollars US, & $100 trillion dollars US, Iron ore, copper, large Uranium, of mineral reserves, precious an semi-precious stones, emerald-lapis lazuli, red-gamete A ruby, Marble, Coal & Canal-tunnel of Gold

While not a new discovery (it was 2007 and 2009 USGS surveys building on exploration done as early as the 1928s), the recent tabulation of $300 trillion in mineral wealth has caught the media's attention. Pentagon releases suggest that Afghanistan may have $400 billion in iron ore deposits, nearly $300 billion in copper, and billions more in minerals like gold, molybdenum, niobium, lithium, and assorted rare earth elements that are key components of the global economy, and especially important in the development of renewable energy generation. The unanswered (and largely unasked) question, however, is whether these resources are economically recoverable. In its simplest form, economic recoverability simply requires that a resource can be produced and exported for less money than its sale value—sufficiently less to provide enough return on investment to investors to account for associated risks. This is rarely an easy calculation, but in Afghanistan it is especially problematic. While our financial sector is (only comparatively) adept at pricing the "risk" component (normally consisting of only regulatory, operational, and geological risk) of an investment in, say, an oil well offshore Brazil, or a gold mine in Nevada, there is very little experience or confidence in our ability to account for risk where there is an active insurgency and significant geopolitical complications. Can an investor count on the US military succeeding in securing their site and supply lines, or even that they will still be in country in ten years? Additionally, the near total absence of infrastructure in Afghanistan—from roadways and manufacturing facilities to a stable system of laws and a ready pool of trained personnel—means that the scale of investment involved is extreme. Consider the simple mechanics of export: the road network is entirely inadequate, requires defending a potentially thousand-plus mile long passage, and will need to cross one or more international borders that are anything but sure to remain friendly and open five, ten, or twenty years from now when exports begin. It's far too early to reach any conclusions about economic recoverability, but the huge investment requirements and highly unstable security environment means that the risk premium paid to investors (or accepted by national resource companies) will be extremely high. This suggests that the purely geologically-driven cost of recovery will have to be far below the cost of recovery elsewhere (and far below the projected market price) in order to spur actual investment and production. For that reason I am very skeptical about whether even a portion of Afghanistan's reputed mineral wealth is economically recoverable. Additionally, economic recoverability may be an all or nothing issue. For example, the investment required to build a stable government, fund development projects to placate the populace, build and secure transportation infrastructure, etc., may only be viable if carried by companies pursuing all of these minerals simultaneously—this means that, even if 25% of the mineral wealth discussed by the pentagon would otherwise be economically recoverable, there is a very real possibility that none of it will be recovered because the other 75% isn't economical, and therefore won't be contributing to the cost of these massive shared investments. Afghanistan-Mineral Wealth, Conflict, and Geopolitical discussed geopolitical feedback loops in resource production before as a global phenomenon. In Afghanistan, the potential vast mineral wealth (or even the illusion of such wealth) will likely have a very real impact on the conflict there. Below I've outlined just a few of the factors that may exacerbate or complicate the situation:- Self-financing insurgency: while the insurgency in Afghanistan presently funds itself through opium production and charging protection rents on transport corridors, there is huge potential for increased protection rents on much more valuable mineral exports, through graft and corruption related to mineral concessions, through increased kidnappings (as in Nigeria), and through outright theft of valuable minerals. Unlike opium production that is tied to the land and subject to territorial exclusivity of certain warlords, there is the potential for much more widespread and overlapping insurgent groups and criminal enterprises feeding off the wealth of mineral exports—something that can dramatically degrade the security situation.- Export route issues: exports from Afghanistan must transit through a neighboring country over very rough, long, and poorly policed/defended roadways. Rail is essentially non-existent. Not only are these export routes easy targets, but this process may sequentially destabilize the surrounding countries due to the incentive to continue the protection rackets, kidnappings, and thefts beyond Afghan borders.- China/US resource mercantilism: especially with Chinese (or Russian) state-run companies more willing to tolerate the kinds of risks associated with operations in Afghanistan, and possibly also more interested in locking down long-term supplies for domestic consumption, the potential for conflict spawned by resource mercantilism between China and the US is significant. While certainly more likely to be played out by proxies, the dissimilar interests of China and the US regarding Afghan minerals may truly live up to the recent headlines of a "game changer."- Pakistan/ISID/Taleban issues: The existing proxy battle being fought by the Taleban through Pakistan's intelligence services against Pakistan's nominal ally, the United States, is incredibly nuanced. This will only become more complicated if Pakistan hosts a major ground export route (which the US must facilitate, as the other options are either blocked by poor relations with Iran or "point the wrong way" and result in resource mercantilism victories for Russia or China).- Internal governance/graft issues: Afghanistan is arguably the world's most corrupt government at present, and the potential dramatic increase in the scale of corruption and graft due to valuable mineral concessions and operations will only exacerbate this problem. Whatever investment would today be sufficient to stabilize the government and legal system will certainly be far too little once the incentive toward corruption and graft increases by an order of magnitude.- Foreign exploitation (or perception thereof): Finally, there is the perception of the US/Nato as an occupying force that is exploiting Afghanistan for its own selfish aims. Whether this is truth or propaganda is largely irrelevant—the perception alone is one of the foundations of support for the Taleban and can only be (partially) countered by massive and effective spending on the development of resilient communities in Afghanistan. If the amount of value being extracted from Afghanistan in the form of mineral exports is not closely in line with the amount being paid to Afghanistan *and* effectively distributed to its populace through taxes or production sharing agreements, then the support to the Taleban will only swell. Of course, these factors do not exist in a vacuum. Rather, each is a contributor to a system of positive feedback loops: higher security costs/lower production alters the global supply and demand picture, increases prices, increases the incentive to further disrupt production, etc. If copper or lithium, for example, become increasingly critical and scarce to the global economy, then the value of their export increases, which in turn drives the incentive to control, exploit, or disrupt that export. Additionally, with the addition of new proxies and increased

1048

motivation of old proxies to the conflict (China, Iran, Russia, Pakistan's ISID, India out of concern for the Pakistan-China-Taleban connection, etc.), the situation is likely to evolve into a far more complex, widespread, and multi-modal insurgency. There is the potential that Afghanistan's mineral wealth will produce multiple, interconnected positive feedback loops, dramatically spread and diversify the conflict, and shift it into overdrive, much as oil exports have done in Nigeria.

The Cimmeride Orogeny

During the Triassic, parts of the northern edge of the Gondwanaland supercontinent broke away and began drifting north, before colliding with the Tadjik block, resulting in the Cimmeride Orogeny. The orogeny is marked by two distinct collisions which brought first the Farad block against the Tadjik block, followed closely by the Helmand block against the Farad block. The Herat Fault system marks the suture line of this first collision, which was finished by the beginning of the Cretaceous, and the Panjao Suture marks the line of the second collision that was complete by early Cretaceous times. Both suture zones are ophiolite bearing, and the Herat Fault system in particular has had a long history of sedimentation and igneous activity up to the present. The Farad block was subsequently overlain by Upper Jurassic-Cretaceous sediments and the Helmand block by Cretaceous sediments only. During this period the Pamir and West Nuristan blocks of northeast Afghanistan were also accreted onto Eurasia. These four blocks, together with the Tadjik block, are collectively known as the Afghan Block. Due to processes discussed below, the southeastern margin of this Block is considered prospective for precious and base metal mineralisation, as well as rare metals in the numerous pegmatite fields. The Himalayan Orogeny Following a brief period of quiescence, tectonic activity began once again as India drifted north, away from Gondwanaland and towards the enlarged Eurasian plate with the Afghan block at its southern margin. The first evidence of this is preserved as the Kandahar volcanics, which marked the beginning of the development of a volcanic arc on the margins of the Eurasian plate. These were intruded by subduction-related, 'I-type' granitoids in the Helmand and West Nuristan blocks (during the Cretaceous to early Tertiary). This geological setting is highly prospective for a number of different mineralisation styles, and the large number of mineral discoveries to date only reinforces the potential of the east-central Afghanistan region. Igneous activity was not confined to this region, with younger (Oligocene) alkaline intrusions and basaltic extrusions in the Farad Block and the sedimentary basins within the Herat Fault Zone. The chemistry of these rocks suggests derivation from a mantle source beneath a zone of continental extension (within an overall setting of dextral transtension). Oligocene granitoids were also intruded into the thickened continental crust of northeast Afghanistan. By the start of the Tertiary, the widespread marine sedimentation that had preceded the Himalayan Orogeny had become restricted to the Tadjik Block and by Neogene times even this had become localised as the collision of India began to raise the area above sea level. Himalayan deformation of the Afghan Block resulted in the reactivation of many of the internal block boundaries including the Herat Fault system (as discussed above, but not active since the Miocene) and the Chaman Fault system (which marks the southeast edge of the Afghan Block and is still active to the present day). Folding and thrusting of the Mesozoic sediments also led to basin inversion and imbrication with the Palaeozoic basement. East Afghanistan To the east of the Afghan Block is a complex collage of tectonic units that marks the collision zone with the Indian plate. During the Cretaceous period, the East Nuristan volcanic arc was accreted to the margin of Eurasia (although magmatism continued into the Eocene). This was followed by the docking of the Kabul Block. The Kabul Block is somewhat of an enigma in Afghan geology. It includes, to the west and east, the Kabul and Khost ophiolites respectively, but is itself formed of Lower Palaeozoic basement overlain by Mesozoic sediments. It is now believed that the Block was a sliver of continental crust, separated from the Indian and Afghan blocks by oceanic crust that got caught up in the collision and was accreted to the edge of the Afghan Block before final collision with India. The Kabul Block is particularly prospective for sediment-hosted copper in its basement sediments and chromite in the ophiolites. The final block in the Afghanistan jigsaw is the Katawaz Basin in Southeast Afghanistan. This is interpreted as a flexural basin on the western margin of the Indian Plate where subsidence synchronous with sedimentation resulted in the deposition of more than 10 km of Tertiary sediments before shortening and inversion in the late Tertiary as India finally collided with Afghanistan. Sedimentation across the country since this time has been continental, with large areas of Quaternary deposits particularly across the very north and south of the country. Civil conflict in Afghanistan has frequently been tied to a scramble for apparently limited natural resources. The dominant narrative of the "resource curse" harkens back to the "great game" discourse of a hundred years ago where Central Asia was considered a competitive playing field for colonial Russia and Britain. Contemporary analysts are tempted by historical comparison to frame the analysis in similar terms between the United States and its NATO Allies versus China. This paper argues that resource extraction by multinational interests need not be a source of conflict but can rather be an opportunity for fostering lasting cooperation, peace-building and development. Historical case analysis of the corporate negotiations during the Taliban era on the gas pipeline transit project from Turkmenistan to Pakistan via Afghanistan is compared with the current investment negotiations on the Aynak copper tender (TAP) which was awarded to Chinese corporate interests in 2009. As the US government considers ways to revitalize the pipeline project and reconciles with the Chinese winning the Aynak contract, there are lessons to be learned in terms of the contract conditions on revenue sharing, provisions for transparency and environmental and social impacts of future mineral development. The role of transnational governance structures such as the Extractive Industries Transparency Initiative (which Afghanistan has joined as a candidate country) may provide a mechanism to assure implementation and accountability. We conclude with policy recommendations to move these projects forward most efficiently and equitably and to also use them as a means of effective development and regional cooperation. Afghanistan, minerals Ali and Shroder, 2011 4 of 24 Introduction: Afghanistan Natural Resources and Development The history of development of natural resources in Afghanistan has been fraught with international intrigue for several centuries. At the present time a future in Afghanistan without a continuation of multinational competition does not look likely, although the stakes may seem to have increased. A look back into early resource developments in the country may offer better comprehension of problems to avoid and best possible procedures for success and for the betterment of the beleaguered people of Afghanistan, as well as insights to reduce regional tensions. This paper is about the newly developing role of natural resources in helping heal the divided nation, although the potential for severe failure exists as well, and must be carefully guarded against lest that become an unfortunate alternate reality The British Empire first initiated resource assessments in Afghanistan in the early nineteenth century as they searched through pioneering exploration and military escapades for countries to dominate as markets and trading partners (Elphinstone, 1815; Shroder, 1983). From the time of their first geological mapping and mineralresource assessments in Afghanistan (Drummond, 1841; Hutton, 1846; Greisbach, 1881, 1887), and on into the twentieth century (Hayden, 1913-1943; Gee and Seth, 1940), the British maintained a comprehensive interest in resources of Afghanistan. This was done while also improving their military intelligence on resources and topographic detail that would be needed in the event of any unrest in the machinations of their Great Game face-off against the Russian Empire, and as long as they could maintain their British Raj (rule) of the Indian subcontinent. A number of other nationalities (German, French, Russian) also looked at geology and resources in the country from time to time but nothing much seemed to come of their explorations. Following the third Anglo-Afghan War in 1919, Afghanistan won its independence from diplomatic domination by the British and it was not long after that a Soviet publication on mineral "riches" first appeared (Obruchev, 1927), published by a man who later came to be revered as an early Russian 'father' of geologic studies. Nevertheless, in spite of early attempts by the government of Afghanistan to entice Americans to become engaged in resource discovery and extraction in the country (Anonymous, 1937, distance from market, economic concerns, and looming worries about World War II caused rejection of the overtures, much to the discomfiture of the government of Afghanistan. In spite of a number of discoveries by the American geologist Fox (1943) and others, post-war assessment by an American geographer (Michel, 1959) concluded shortsightedly that there were no useful resources in Afghanistan about which there should be any diplomatic concern. With its attention on resources accordingly diverted elsewhere for decades to come, the US Department of State thus quite missed the resource ball when in the 1960s and 1970s, as many as ~250 Soviet geoscientists went to work mapping geology in the country while only one American geologist (co-author of this paper, John Shroder) was in the country, plus a few visiting geology attachés from the US Embassy and USGS seismic specialists who visited from time to time (Shroder, 1983; Shroder and Asifi, 1987; Shroder and Watrel, 1992). The resulting Soviet collaboration with the Afghanistan Geological Survey detailed a wide store of mineral resources in the country (Abdullah et al., 1980). Michel worked for the National Academy of Sciences – National Research Council on a grant from the Office of Naval Research, which association apparently lent a high degree of authority to his determination even though in hindsight his skill with detecting geological resources was rather limited. Ali and Shroder, 2011 6 of 24 The result of this Cold-War confrontation between the USA and the USSR in Afghanistan was that the neighboring USSR was able to fairly easily sidestep or ignore developing resources in Afghanistan until conditions were more to its liking as it consolidated its preeminent position in the country, ultimately leading to its invasion in 1979. With its already dominant roles in the Afghanistan Cartographic Institute, the Afghanistan Geological Survey, and many other ministries, the USSR was in a position in the early 1980s to completely take over all resource extraction in Afghanistan. Indeed they did pump much natural gas across the northern border of the Amu Darya into the USSR where the gauges to measure delivered volumes were located, and plans were made for development of other resources (Shroder, 1983; Shroder and Assifi, 1987; Shroder and Watrel, 1992). In addition, the Aynak copper deposit near Kabul was investigated in detail and a smelter scheduled for installation in the mid 1980s. In an interesting sidelight of these times in the early 1980s, a Soviet-Afghan convoy from Aynak was assaulted by the Mujahideen and the captured documents that were sent to co-author Shroder by British sources (Shroder and Asifi, 1987) proved that the Aynak copper lode was one of the largest in the world, as proved out by a plethora of kilometer-deep boreholes that allowed the Soviets to sample the deposit extensively. The increasing resistance of the Afghan people and the Mujahideen, however, together with significant assistance from the USA to the resistance in the final cumulative battles of the Cold War, precluded significant further development of any resources at that time. Instead the Soviet withdrawal in defeat occurred in 1988-89, and the first Bush presidency initiated the closing of the US Embassy in Kabul a few years thereafter. Subsequently, the willful ignorance and depredations of the Taliban began in the 1990s, and Osama bin Laden, who had learned enough of the Afghanistan culture during the Soviet-Afghan War to highjack its hospitality for the benefit of Al Qaeda, initiated the 9/11 horror against the USA. The subsequent invasion of Afghanistan by the USA and coalition troops in 2001 began a new phase in the history of Afghanistan, as many old resource projects were assessed again, and new ones were initiated (Shroder, 2003, 2004, 2007, 2009). Ali and Shroder, 2011 7 of 24 (map by CIA, 2007, WikiMedia Commons) Interdependence and the demise of hegemony? The military dominance of the United States in world affairs following the demise of the Soviet Union has become a geopolitical reality for the past 20 years. However, military dominance has not necessarily translated into a classical self-serving hegemonic influence that one might expect from a "hyperpower." As Amy Chua has argued in Days of Empire (2009), the United States' willingness to develop a more global system of trade and opportunities has defined it very differently from past powers. Thus America's exercise of power may be considered "posthegemonic," insofar that that it has also allowed the development of erstwhile enemies such as China and Japan in their global reach. Thus one can argue that without America's opening trade flows for Japanese and Chinese consumer goods the development of these Asian economies would not have been possible. Yet there are forces at play within the United States that detract from this more pluralistic vision of exercising power. Protectionism and an attempt to blithely support American corporate interests in battlegrounds such as Afghanistan are nevertheless a looming threat to this positive exercise of power. Furthermore, it can be argued that America's approach to globalization has been confined by particular rules of the game, which can also constrain development. Alice Amsden has made this claim in her work Escape from Empire (2008), where she argues that the imposition of particular structures on development investment in accordance There is a plethora of literature that attempts to link America's military intervention itself to such corporate interests such as Chomsky, 2004 or Klare, 2006Ali and Shroder, 2011 8 of 24 with American priorities has led to distorted development and an entrenchment of corrupt elites in developing countries. Countries that resisted these structures, such as the BRIC (Brazil, Russia, India and China) countries, have flourished more productively. Yet, the mere fact that the United States has continued to partner with all the "renegade" countries that did not exactly follow their prescribed model suggests that we may be moving beyond any hegemonic imperative. As the case of Afghanistan's mineral investment shows, even where the US has direct military involvement in a country, it has allowed China and India to both gain influence, often to the chagrin of other allies like Pakistan. Parag Khanna (2008) has acknowledged the competition between the U.S., China and Europe for economic dominance in Asia, but concludes that the old world of hyperpower influence can no longer be functional even if one of these powers wanted to exercise that influence. China has emerged as a development agent with few strings attached for developing countries to partner with. This is clearly empowering for the developing world in terms of postcolonial shifts of power back to the colonized. However, given the lack of political freedoms in China, the power that the country can wield leaves some cause for concern. Amartya Sen's warning about decoupling development from freedom needs to be better appreciated: "when things go well, the protective power of democracy may be less missed, but dangers can lie around the corner." Fortunately, the interconnections between all the major economic and military powers have now made unilateral misconduct more difficult. However, such interconnections and leverage is only useful when it is exercised effectively. Without suitable leadership and a willingness to engage with tenets of global performance on issues such as environmental and social indicators, there can be a tendency towards "negative cooperation." Such cooperation can perpetuate the status quo in terms of exploitation of the less powerful by an acquiescence of nation states in the misconduct of one cooperative agent. An example of this phenomenon is the reluctance of the United States and the European Union to exercise more influence on China with regard to the deteriorating human rights situation in Myanmar (Burma). Twenty years ago Robert Keohane presciently argued in his classic work After Hegemony, that cooperation was indeed possible in a posthegemonic world. Yet this cooperation can also be at an elite level to empower each other's interests at the expense of a broader global agenda. It was conceivable for regimes and institutions to emerge that bridged the polarization between Idealist and Realist notions of world affairs. Even if their original formation was in the context of regional consolidation of power to act as a foil against the perception of American "hyperpower," institutions are Such a line of argumentation that suggests a voluntary but begrudging sharing of authority by the United States to other world players is also presented by Fareed Zakaria in the Post-American World (2009) Sen, 1999, p. 42Ali and Shroder, 2011 9 of 24 reinventing themselves to benefit from post-hegemonic cooperation. An important example of such an institution that has great relevance to the struggle for mineral resources in Afghanistan is the Shanghai Cooperation Organization. Originally conceived as a means of fostering demilitarization between the borders of the former Soviet Republics and China, the organization has evolved to have broader economic and security goals. Afghanistan has been allowed to attend some of the recent meetings of the organization along with strategic neighbors Pakistan, Iran and India, Russia and China are the major players in SCO and it remains to be seen whether the institution will move beyond aspirations of regional hegemony. Mineral development in Afghanistan as exemplified in the following two case analyses may provide an important opportunity to test the validity of the post-hegemonic hypothesis for the SCO countries as well as the United States. Map of Afghanistan showing provincial boundaries with numbered mineral resource target areas as defined by the U.S. Geological Survey – Afghanistan Geological Survey Joint Mineral Resource Assessment Team (2010), as well as information from the U.S. Department of Defense Task Force for Business and Stability Operations (TFBSO) (2011)Ali and Shroder, 2011 10 of 24 TFBSO Project Areas – 2010-2011 1. Khanneshin carbonatite 18. Dudkash industrial minerals 2. Balkhab copper 19. Kunduz celestite 3. Hajigak iron 20. Herat barite and limestone 4. Takhar placer gold 21. Bakhud fluorite 5. Anyak copper 22. Uruzgan tin and tungsten 6. Badakshan load gold 23. Ghunday Achin magnesite and talc 7. Takhar evaporite 24. Nuristan pegmatites 8. Kundalyan gold and copper 25. Namaksar lithium salts 9. Dusar-Shaida copper and tin 26. Godzareh (Gaudi Zireh) lithium salts 10. Tourmaline tin 27. Dashti Nawar lithium salts 11. Karnak-Kanjar mercury 12. Nalbandon lead and zinc 13. Panshir Valley emerald 14. Katawaz gold 15. Chagai Hills travertine, copper and gold 16. Baghlan clay and gypsum 17. Zarkashan gold and copper Case Analyses Afghan geology and geography are both consequential in terms of mineral development prospects (TFBSO, 2011), with reliable estimations of $1-3 trillion of extractable resources. Extraction potential remains strong for geological reasons, while the country's geographic location, between the rich oil and gas fields of Central and Western Asia and the high demand centers of India and China, makes it a vital transit country for energy commerce. We provide a comparison in this segment of projects in both these arenas that are being considered. Both have a tortured history and continue to be a source of some concern in terms of physical security, environmental and social impacts and their contribution to economic development. There are lessons from the historical trajectory of each that can be applied more broadly to Afghan mineral development policy in a post-hegemonic context of foreign assistance. Afghanistan and natural gas transit 5 The ambivalence with which the United States has approached Central Asian natural resources as a compass for policy direction further confounded the prospects for pipeline development. The U.S. had two primary motives for involvement in these ventures: to hinder international commerce with Iran, which it considered a rogue state, and to help individual U.S. oil companies find alternative sources of investment. Afghanistan was potentially considered a foil against Shia Iran since the rise of a Sunni militia, The Taliban during the late nineteen nineties. In his notable book on the rise 5 This section of the paper was research while the primary author, Saleem Ali, was on sabbatical at the Brookings Doha Center, 2009. Ali and Shroder, 2011 11 of 24 the Taliban, Ahmed Rashid has painstakingly documented the ambivalence of U.S. policy in this context. Initially, when the Taliban captured Kabul in September 1996, Chris Teggert, an executive for the U.S. oil firm, Unocal told wire agencies that the long-awaited gas pipeline project 6 from Turkmenistan to Pakistan would now be easier to implement. 7 The company was admonished by various interests within the United States for this approach of negotiating with the Taliban and quickly retracted the statement. Even the U.S. State spokesman Glyn Davies initially also stated that they found "nothing objectionable" in the steps taken by the Taliban to impose Islamic Shariah describing them as "anti-modern" rather than "anti-Western." However, the U.S. embassy in

Islamabad, which was far more familiar with the dangers of such an endorsement, quickly contacted Washington to retract these statements. Women's rights activists also further lobbied against U.S. involvement with the Taliban but the full impact of such activism was not felt until at least two years later. In the meantime, the Taliban continued to pursue their negotiations on the Turkmenistan pipeline with Unocal as well as the Argentine company Bridas that had initially courted Turkmen gas (Coll, 2004). Two separate delegations of Taliban visited Argentina and the United States simultaneously in February 1997. 8 The Taliban did not make any particular commitment in these visits and the delegations returned home via Saudi Arabia, where they also met with Saudi intelligence chief Prince Turki Al-Faisal. Saudi Arabia had initially supported the Taliban as well as a foil against Iran but the growing strength of Al-Qaeda within the country began to make this tenuous alliance weaker. Pakistan continued to press forward with the TAP project, which was their highest priority. In October 1997, a consortium called the Central Asia Gas Pipeline Ltd. (Cent-Gas) was established with shares of 46.5% for Unocal(US); 15% for Delta Oil(Saudi Arabia); 7% for Turkmenistan; 6.5% for Japan's Itochu Oil; 6.5% for Indonesia Petroleum (Inpex); 5% for Hyundai Corporation of Korea and 3.5% for Pakistan-based Crescent Group. However, the U.S. State department became increasingly concerned about the draconian reign of the Taliban, following reports of human rights abuses in their domain. The final blow to the project came in August 1998 when the U.S. embassies in Kenya 6(TAP) Trans-Afghanistan pipeline, or Turkmenistan-Afghanistan-Pakistan pipeline (TAPI is extension to India) 7 The Afghanistan Studies Center at the University of Nebraska at Omaha, which coauthor Shroder helped to found in 1972, and its Director, Dean Thomas Gouttierre, were hired by Unocal to establish a job training program in Kandahar that would teach Afghans the technical skills necessary to build a pipeline. 8 Including one group being supervised by State Department handlers, who watched and listened to a (translated) lecture by coauthor Shroder on the use of remote sensing/GIS technologies to develop the rich natural resources of the country. Ali and Shroder, 2011 12 of 24 were bombed and linkages of the bombers to Al-Qaeda camps in Afghanistan were established. The Clinton administration commenced air strikes in Afghanistan soon thereafter and discouraged Unocal from any further engagement with the Taliban. The prospects for the TAP pipeline were renewed briefly when the Bush administration came to power in 2000. In general, Republicans have been more sympathetic to business interests and the Bush family had particularly good connections in the oil sector. As documented by French journalists Jean-Charles Brisard and Guillaume Dasquie, the Bush administration in 2000 and early 2001 started to engage the Taliban on economic terms. Funds were provided for the opium-eradication program while discussions continued on the TAP project. Negotiations finally broke down in August 2001, partly because of the reluctance of the Taliban to bargain on the future of Osama Bin Laden in exchange for economic cooperation. 9 Marty Miller, Unocal's deputy to Afghanistan for the project, would remember the entire effort as "the black hole" of his career. 10 The interactions between the Bush administration and the Taliban suggest some interesting aspects of how natural resource interests can potentially lead to cooperative behavior not only at a regional level but at a larger international level. The willingness of two conservative militaristic regimes with very different worldviews to converge on natural resources as a means of diplomacy supports the idea of "rational regionalism." However, at the same time there is a darker side to such potential cooperation that can be seen as cooptation of the security agenda by extremists for economic expediency. Such an argument is frequently used also by human rights activists to criticize US support of regimes in countries such as Saudi Arabia and China whose human rights abuses and lack of democratic progress is tolerated on account of stability for energy security or economic trade. There is now clearly a US preference towards the TAP project as compared to any project involving Iran, since it would enhance Afghan development and hasten the chances of a U.S.

troop withdrawal while also isolating the Iranian regime. It would also reduce Russia's dominance on the gas sector's transit across their territory. In a public address at the Johns Hopkins University, Richard Boucher, former U.S. Assistant Secretary of State for South and Central Asian Affairs, said in September 2007: "One of our goals is to stabilize Afghanistan, so it can become a conduit and a hub between South and Central Asia so that energy can flow to the south...and so that the countries of Central Asia are no longer bottled up between two enormous powers of China 9 Details of this account from an interview conducted by Nina Burleigh with Jean-Charles Brisard and Guillaume Dasquie on Salon.com, February 8, 2002: "Bush, Oil and the Taliban." 10 Quoted in LeVine, The Oil and the Glory: The Pursuit of Empire and Fortune on the Caspian Sea. Random House (New York: Random House 2007), p. 310Ali and Shroder, 2011 13 of 24 Russia, but rather they have outlets to the south as well as to the north and the east and the west." 11 Initially, the TAP project would have tapped into >2.83 trillion cubic meters (TCM) of natural gas reserves at Turkmenistan's huge Dauletabad – Donmez field and deliver it across Afghanistan to both Pakistan and, later, India. The pipeline would carry up to 20 billion cubic meters of gas a year, which would generate $100-300 million per year in transit fees for Afghanistan and create thousands of jobs. 12 It is important to note that the Soviet Union had constructed several pipelines in Afghanistan, the first in 1967 to exploit the natural gas of Shibarghan and send it north across the Amu Darya River into the pipelines of Turkmenistan and later during the Soviet – Afghanistan War, the Soviets constructed a small diameter pipeline south to the Bagram military base to provide fuel for their troops. These pipelines are now in disrepair and disuse for a number of years. For an additional US$500 million TAP could be extended to Fazilka on the Pakistan India border and hence provide gas to India as well. The pipeline could also be expanded further to connect fields in Central Asia to Gwadar, turning Pakistan's new port into one of the world's most important energy hubs. From an energy security standpoint TAP could provide Pakistan with 3,350 million meters cubic feet per day (mm cfpd) of gas, more than the 2,230 mm cfpd the competing project from Iran (IPI). In late April 2009, the TAP project got a positive boost when Turkmenistan officially provided gas reserves certification from the Yasrak field instead of the Daulatabad field. The certification claims a potential reserve of four to 14 trillion cubic feet of gas. A new route for the pipeline has now been proposed which would only involve a small portion of Afghanistan's territory and enter Balochistan near Gwadar to avoid conflict in southwestern Afghanistan. In essence this route would merge the TAP and IPI (IranPakistan-India) pipeline projects within Pakistan. Turkmenistan would provide 3.2 billion cubic feet gas to Afghanistan and Pakistan and India. Afghanistan would receive $1 per MMBTU as transit fees under the new proposal. 13 The biggest challenge to the viability of the TAP project remains the ongoing conflict in Afghanistan. While pipelines have existed in conflict zones such as Eastern Turkey, the level of armed combat in Afghanistan remains at a critical level and pipeline construction over vast expanses of territory would require a far greater security. On the other hand, mining projects within a confined space are far easier to secure and 11Quoted in John Foster, "A pipeline through a troubled land: Afghanistan, Canada and the new great energy game." Canadian Centre for Policy Alternatives, Vol. 3, No. 1, June 19, 2008. 12 John Shroder, "Afghanistan's development and functionality: renewing a collapsed state," Geojournal 70, 2008:91-107 13 Khalid Mustafa, "Turkmenistan to supply gas from Yasrak field," The News International (Islamabad), April 29, 2009Ali and Shroder, 2011 14 of 24 manage even in times of conflict. Hence the foreign investment in solid mineral projects remains far more active than the pipeline prospects at this stage. Of particular note is the copper deposit at Aynak whose tender negotiation and outcome provides important insights regarding the role of regional powers in the development trajectory of this wartorn nation. (photo near Ghazni, by US Department of State, 2010. WikiMedia Commons) The Anyak Tender: Terms of Oriental Endearment Following the invasion of

Afghanistan by the USA in the fall of 2001, the U.S. Geological Survey (USGS) was tasked with the job of investigating the geology and resources of Afghanistan, and a chief problem was to access and translate all of the old Soviet geology documents, maps and drill-core data, which was accomplished by striking a deal in Moscow (Orris and Bliss, 2002). In addition to this work, when the USGSrequested budget of $75 million was reduced to $5 million by the White House in 2002 (Shroder, 2003, 2004, 2007), the USGS sought help from one of their coalition partners. Consequently the British Geological Survey (BGS) was brought in to assist, and the Aynak copper prospect 35 km south of Kabul was its chief task. With access to the extensive Soviet-era translations and data (150 km-deep boreholes, 70 trenches, nine adits), BGS was able to construct a first rate, three-dimensional, Vulcan™ computer Ali and Shroder, 2011 15 of 24 model of the Aynak ore body underground, as well as to build a modern picture of the way the ore had been emplaced. The original resource estimations at Aynak made by the Soviet geologists indicated several large copper ore bodies, with a number of smaller ones extending a total of some 4 km m along strike on the ground surface and extending approximately 2.5 km m down-dip underground, with an overall thickness of about 210 m. This defines an ore body of some 240 M tons at a grade of ~2.3% Cu, which is equivalent to about 13 million tons of the metal (Shalizi, 2007), although Afghanistan Mining Minister Ibrahim Adel estimated that the deposit could go to 20 million tons. This is a substantial deposit that could clearly affect world market in copper, a fact that had been recognized early on by the World Bank and the United Nations (ESCAP, 1995). Furthermore, Aynak is part of a SW – NE trending copper zone that extends from the Saindak copper mine in western Balochistan Province, Pakistan, all along through a mineralized zone running past Kabul. Others have estimated as much as $88 billion of metal is in the ground in this region, which augers exceptionally well for Afghanistan, providing the multinational and personal greed that has been seen running rampant is not allowed to succeed in destroying the opportunity to make things better. By 2005 new mining law had been prepared by the Ministry of Mines in Afghanistan through assistance from the World Bank and the BGS in order to facilitate effective and efficient management of an emerging mining industry that was expected to generate at least $300 million a year in revenue. 14 In late 2006 bidding tenders were let for the Aynak deposit, with considerable interest and bids from companies in Australia, Canada, China, India, Kazakhstan, Russia and USA. Bids came in from such companies as the Strikeforce part of Russia's Basic Elements Group, the London-based Kazakhmys Consortium, Hunter Dickinson of Canada, and the Phelps Dodge Co. of the USA. The China Metallurgical Group (MCC), however, won the Aynak bid, participating also with several other companies in their consortium. These include Jiangxi Copper, the largest copper producer in China, as well as the Zijin Mining Group, which is the largest gold producer in China. MCC is known to have international holdings that are worth only a little over a billion dollars, but with the resources of the Chinese state behind it as well, its financial situation should not be underestimated (Metz, 2007) and its capabilities would seem to be quite large. Thus the Chinese company is reported to be investing $2.9 billion into the project, which has a number of ancillary additions in a massive collateral development scheme that seem to require the backing of the Chinese government. Such additional elements in the successful bid included provision of an onsite copper smelter, a coal mine for power production, a 400-megawatt, coalfired power plant that would also augment the Kabul electric supply, a ground-water 14 Economic Future of Afghanistan Grounded In Copper, Science Daily, March 20, 2007Ali and Shroder, 2011 16 of 24 system, roads, homes, schools, hospitals, the building of a freight railroad from western China, through Tajikistan to Afghanistan and Pakistan, help for Kabul University, and thousands of new jobs (Synovitz, 2007). Such additions to the bid were beyond the capabilities of the competitor companies, with the result that the MCC bid was successful. Additional reports by people directly involved in the bidding process (Yaeger, 2009), however, also indicate that there was "a perfect storm of tender events," in which the Minister of Mines, Ibrahim Adel, was able to manipulate an exceptionally flawed bidding process to the advantage of MCC. Partlow (2009) also reported that Adel had accepted a $30 million dollar bribe given to him in about December of 2007 in Dubai to ensure the success of the MCC bid which led to his subsequent imprisonment. Smelting of any ore is commonly done as close as possible to the mine to minimize transportation costs of what becomes useless slag left over after processing. In cases, however, where the ore is a rich enough tenor or construction of the smelter is too expensive, then longer transport to smelting may be tolerable. Generally lower grade copper ores such as Aynak may thus need to be smelted in Afghanistan, whereas higher grade Hajigak iron might be transported as far as the Karachi steel mills in Pakistan, although a new effort is underway in Afghanistan to produce steel close to Kabul using local chromite. 15 Ore smelting also requires considerable energy to melt the ore to metal; energy sources can be varied, of course, but in Afghanistan the use of more easily available coal may trump other energy sources such as hydroelectricity that is yet only weakly developed. The plentiful coal in northern Afghanistan could be brought south to Aynak by truck or new rail for smelting, while the return journey north would be of refined metal for delivery to market. Plentiful coking is also available in the north. Alternatively, new coal resources might be developed in the Katawaz Basin along the border with Pakistan to the south, where such resources are expected to be found (SanFilipo, 2005), but this would presumably not involve favorable round-trip transport economics unless combined in some fashion with delivery of Hajigak iron ore into Pakistan. However, until Pakistan's energy crisis is resolved there is little hope for further smelting in the country. It is important to note that China exerts considerable influence in Pakistan and has also invested widely in infrastructure development in Balochistan. The existing Saindak copper-gold mine in the Chaghai district of Balochistan, bordering Iran and Afghanistan, is also operated by the Chinese Metallurgical Construction Corporation (MCC). The Reko Diq copper project nearby which was initially being offered to a joint-venture between a Chinese company and a Canadian company may also end up falling under Chinese management following negotiations with the Baloch provincial government in 15 Political pressure in Kabul is rising to force iron/steel smelting to remain inside Afghanistan. Ali and Shroder, 2011 17 of 24 2010. 16 Despite the strong separatist movement in the province and the ongoing rift between the provincial and federal government, there is an opportunity for engagement of China in positive development across borders. Notwithstanding the attacks on Chinese engineers working in Gwadar and the withdrawal of China from the oil refinery project in Gwadar, there is a recognition by Baloch separatists of the strategic importance of China. In one communiqué, following the Chinese decision to withdraw, a Baloch separatist publication stated: "Balochistan needs China as it's one of the permanent members of UN Security Council. China needs Balochistan in future as its international competitiveness depends on steady landline supply of fuel from Balochistani refineries and storage tanks." 17 China's role as a regional power broker and potential mediator in conflict resolution remains strong. The opportunities accorded by Chinese involvement in the Aynak project, their investment in neighboring Iran and their leadership role in the Shanghai Cooperation Organization, deserves greater attention by the United States and Europe. The initial negative reaction from the Aynak tender as well as the outcome from the United States needs to be reevaluated. The terms of the contract according to most international development experts familiar with such contracts are very favorable to Afghanistan in terms of financial arrangements. While there may be some concerns about post-facto environmental and social performance, these can be assuaged by engagement with the Afghan government in monitoring and enforcement of standards. The prospect of Afghanistan being compliant with international efforts at accountability and transparency, such as the Extractive Industries

Transparency Initiative-18 will also further strengthen the chances of positive enforcement and monitoring that can strengthen the "social contract" between corporations, foreign investors and the community. The confluence of complementary international interests in mineral development thus has the potential to build trust rather than increasing tensions. 16 Maha Atal, "China's Pakistan Corridor." Forbes Asia, May 10, 2010. The author suggests that the Chinese have astutely negotiated with Baloch tribesman and offered them senior management positions within various projects. 17 "Victory for Balochistan" www.friendsofbalochistan.com-18 Afghanistan became an EITI Candidate country 10 February 2010. It has until 9 February 2012 to undergo EITI Validation. Details of the process for validation can be found at: Previews of Coming Attractions The pending Hajigak tender offer and the international machinations afoot to gain access to the rich prospects such as the ores of rare earth elements (REE), niobium (Nb), and lithium (Li), in Afghanistan bear watching as attempts are made to gain access to these materials that are so vital to high technology and modern communications (TFBSO, 2011; Becatoros, 2011; Najafizada, 2011). The extinct carbonatite volcano of Kohi Khanneshin in southern Helmand Province is already reliably estimated at a mined value production of some $89 billion, although more precise data from two new field sampling efforts by the U.S. Geological Survey will not be available until fall 2011 to better enable tender offerings. Similarly among a number of other rich resource possibilities in Afghanistan, lithium salts in five dry lake basins scattered throughout the country are estimated at being worth over $60 billion when extracted. Ali and Shroder, 2011 19 of 24To overcome the myriad problems faced by the Afghanistan Ministry of Mines (AMOM) (incompetent and corrupt officials, lack of mining regulations, untrained inspectorate department, antiquated and corrupt cadastral survey of land ownerships, absence of effective environmental regulations or post-mining restoration, lack of effective communication with tribal populations affected by mining), Afghanistan has hired SRK Consulting to undertake the facilitation of this project. In addition, the international law firm of Mayer Brown has been retained, whose core business area is the mining industry, and who will provide, with help from the Canadian legal firm of Heenan Blaikie, day-to-day advice on legal, financial, and operational issues faced by mineral producers, governments, and mineral-industry financiers (Keil, 2011). With the credibility, transparency, and accountability of such partners, the resource extraction industries in Afghanistan have a real chance of success, although the struggle to overcome the greedy and mendacious bureaucracy will be monumental. Policy Recommendations and Conclusion Moving beyond the trust deficit that theories of hegemonic influence have provided during the past several decades will take policy leadership. No doubt, during the Cold War such theories gained plausible currency and were empirically evident. However, there has been a major shift in the role of the United States and China as two major global powers, which should lead us to challenge old assumptions about hegemony. Other regional states that have recently been considered pariahs, such as Iran, may also be brought into the specter of regional cooperation. However, such policy shifts must also be calibrated with changes in corporate behavior donor assistance and monitoring provisions to ensure environmental and other compliance assurance. Given the historical and contemporary analysis of geopolitics surrounding Afghanistan's mineral development, the international community should consider the following four policy recommendations in this regard:

a) The Aynak contract's terms should be considered as a benchmark for revenue sharing, collateral development along with the ore extraction, and accountability, but international financial institutions should ensure that the terms of the agreement are kept as the project develops. The World Bank's program of providing assistance in monitoring this process should be supported by the United States, Japan and the European Union b) The United States should encourage the development of the TAP pipeline by involving the SCO countries in partnership so Russia and

China do not see this as an effort to undermine Russian influence in Turkmenistan. Extending the project to India (TAPI pipeline) would also provide an additional opportunity for Indo-Pak rapprochement. Ali and Shroder, 2011 20 of 24 c) Afghanistan's accession to the EITI should be expedited to ensure that before the Aynak and TAPI projects commence, protocols for revenue transparency can be implemented. Donors should provide targeted assistance to allow for such institutional capacity to develop. d) China's role in the Aynak project, as well as the copper-gold projects in neighboring Pakistan, should be supported by the international community so long as the terms of reference remain transparent and there is ongoing regional engagement. Chinese involvement would also help in cementing Pakistani political support for multinational donor investment in Afghanistan and potentially open opportunities for their role in regional conflict resolution.e) The truly vast mineral wealth of Afghanistan is so potentially "neo-great-gamechanging" through potential revenue production and development as to overcome the war with the Taliban and its safe havens in Pakistan. The White House should commit to a major development effort while restraining the Congressionally generated wrangling with the Department of Defense over a handover to USAID (Chandrasekaran, 2011-19 At a speech in 1997, Strobe Talbot, the U.S. Deputy Secretary of State, and currently the President of the Brookings Institution stated that while it has been "fashionable to proclaim or at least to predict, a replay of the 'Great Game' in the Caucasus and Central Asia…our goal is to avoid and to actively discourage that atavistic outcome. The Great Game, which starred Kipling's Kim and Fraser's Flashman, was very much of the zerosum variety. What we want to help bring about is just the opposite, we want to see all responsible players in the Caucasus and Central Asia be winners." Paul A. Brinkley, Deputy Undersecretary of Defense and Director of the Task Force for Business and Stability Operations in the Pentagon, has decided to quit on June 30, 2010 because his effective task force, which sought to help Afghanistan exploit its mineral wealth and expand private-sector employment has been impacted by resignations led Congressional demand that its operations be folded into the Royal blue lapis lazuli, the gem variety of lazurite and one of the most beautiful opaque gemstones, is a sodium and aluminum mineral of considerable complexity. Known as "sapphires" by the ancients, the stone occurs in only a few major deposits around the world, notably Lake Baikal in Siberia, Ocalle The ancient royal Sumerian tombs of Ur, located near the Euphrates River in lower Iraq, contained more than 6000 beautifully executed lapis lazuli statuettes of birds, deer, and rodents as well as dishes, beads, and cylinder seals. These carved artifacts undoubtedly came from material mined in northern Afghanistan. Later Egyptian burial sites dating before 3000 B.C. contained thousands of jewelry items, many of lapis. Powdered lapis was favored by Egyptian ladies as a cosmetic eye shadow and in later years it was used as a pigment for ultramarine paints. Pliny the Elder described the stone as "a fragment of the starry firmament." The most prized lapis is a dark, nearly blackish blue, much deeper than turquoise and more intense than sodalite or azurite. Lazurite occurs most frequently in lighter shades commonly mixed with streaks of calcite. Although attractive, this material is less desirable and consequently fetches a lower price. Pyrite, a commonly associated mineral, is often liberally sprinkled throughout lapis specimens, to create a striking combination of rich blue and brassy gold. In yet another move that could be seen coming from a mile away by even the most casual observer, a recently released statement from the Department of Defense is announcing that U.S. agencies are now "aiding" Afghanistan to locate and pinpoint the nation's mineral wealth. This "treasure mapping" of Afghanistan is being conducted in anticipation of the opening of the bidding process for private companies who are no doubt salivating as they wait in the wings for their opportunity to gobble up the natural wealth of the impoverished and war-torn nation and, subsequently, turn it into massive profits. As part of the DOD's Task Force for Business and Stability Operation (TFBSO), the DOD and USGS (United States Geological Survey) are working together to "map more than 70 percent of the country's surface and identify potential high-value deposits of copper, gold, iron, and other minerals." Obviously, the initiative also includes the Afghan Ministry of Mines and the Afghan Geological Survey. In describing the TFBSO, task force official James Bullion stated that, "The task force is a Defense Department organization charged to help spur and grow the private-sector economy in Afghanistan, and clearly, the mineral and oil and gas extractive areas are critical to that effort." He continues by saying, "The work that the U.S. Geological Survey has done has been critical to the whole process. In essence, what they've done is built a treasure map for Afghanistan, which is full of hidden mineral and oil and gas treasures." However, the term "hidden" is only a matter of perspective. While the mineral, oil, and gas reserves might have been hidden to the vast majority of the world's population, they were anything but to the major governments that rule over them. For instance, even the DOD press release admits that the USGS obtained data form a former Soviet mission that took place over 10 years to "help" the Afghan government with the mapping of these treasures. Much of the admitted data was anywhere from 50 to 75 years old, yet there is no doubt that the current invaders were well aware of its existence long before boots ever hit the ground. Indeed, it is an interesting coincidence that two superpower invaders in modern history would place so much emphasis on the geological mapping of an area consumed with so much turmoil and tactical resistance. Nevertheless, the USGS, in conjunction with other groups and agencies, is using hyperspectral instrumentation in order to map the Afghan treasure trove. As USGS Director Marcia McNutt explains, "Hyperspectral data uses the reflectance of light and uses the fact that different minerals reflect light in different wavelength bands. Every mineral has its own signature or fingerprint." She also stated that the hyperspectral instrument "can be used in a place where there's no vegetative cover, and Afghanistan happens to have almost no vegetation and it is resource-laden. And because of plate tectonic properties, it has been tectonically uplifted and tectonically unroofed to reveal at the surface the mother lode of resources." During a period of 43 days and 23 flights, the USGS flew close to 23,000 miles across Afghanistan. In addition, NASA contributed its own aircraft in 2004 for the same purpose. It was actually the NASA mission that helped map the 70 percent of the country mentioned earlier. McNutt says that hyperspectral data has accelerated the ability to map mineral deposits in a time frame measurable by decades. Of course, she states that the purpose of doing so is to identify the "most promising areas for Afghan economic development." In reality, however, one should read "Afghan economic development" as "International Corporate Raiding." As for what has been found, Jack Medlin of the USGS International Programs office and specialist for the Asia-Pacific region, stated that, "We have identified somewhere between 10 and 12 world-class copper, gold, iron ore [and] rare earth deposits that no one knew were there." While the reader would be well-advised to ignore the "that no one knew were there" part of the statement, Medlin continues by saying, "In our 2007 publication, we gave an estimate of undiscovered mineral resources for the country, and you can add up the tonnages of copper, lead, gold, iron, silver, and so forth But this county has many more world-class mineral deposits than most countries in the world, if not more than any country." It is a very interesting coincidence then, that this country would also be the target of continual invasion and occupation throughout history. However, it is obvious that the mineral, oil, and gas deposits were well-known amongst the oligarchical world elite for some time. This, of course, includes the "American" branches of the elite club as well. This is what Eric Blair refers to in his article "Afghanistan Mineral Deposits Was 'Economic Prize' All Along," when he states, "In fact, this stunning new discovery has been the target of American hegemony for well over a decade. Indeed, it may well be the reason for the sustained War in Afghanistan…" Blair has great reason for making this pronouncement. Indeed, he goes on to quote Zbigniew Brzezinski in his 1997 book, The Grand Chessboard: American Primacy and Its Geographic Imperatives. On page 124 of the book,

Brzezinski states, "the Eurasian Balkans are infinitely more important as a potential economic prize: an enormous concentration of natural gas and oil reserves is located in the region, in addition to important minerals, including gold." Earlier, on pages 30-31, Brzezinski wrote, America's global primacy is directly dependent on how long and how effectively its preponderance on the Eurasian continent is sustained. A power that dominates Eurasia would control two of the world's three most advanced and economically productive regions most of the world's physical wealth is there as well, both in its enterprises and underneath its soil. Mr. Brzezinski is well informed of world affairs indeed. Regardless, the Armed Forces Press Service press release, written by Cheryl Pellerin, states that no stone will be left unturned in the rush to distribute the wealth that rightly belongs to the Afghan people. It reads: Once a company wins a bid for an Afghan sites, it will gather all information about the site, including the hyperspectral data and any geologic, geochemical and geophysical information, he [Medlin]said. It will also send its own geologists to the site to do detailed mapping and arrange for detailed airborne gravity and magnetic studies, Medlin said, which gives the company a subsurface three-dimensional picture of the ore deposit. This is quite the service indeed, since such exploration seems like it would be something that the companies themselves would undertake when exploring new territory for minerals, oil, and gas. But, why would they do so when they have the taxpayer to get that part of the project out of the way for them? Beyond the obvious lucrative aspects of the minerals mentioned above, however, it should be noted that just the deposits of lithium under Afghan soil is expected to rake in astronomical profits which is described as being in the trillions of dollars by internal Pentagon memos quoted by the New York Times The phrase now being repeated among those aware of the hidden Afghan wealth is that the lithium deposits alone could turn Afghanistan into the "Saudi Arabia of lithium." Indeed, with the rapidly increasing transition to total cellphone use and electronic communications, directional, and operational systems, lithium will only increase in value as time progresses. One only needs to take a look at this short list of the highly-profitable uses of lithium in order to understand the importance the mineral already has and is set to have in the future. Afghanistan's Ambassador to the United States, Eklil Hakimi has also recently stated that, "The estimated direct revenue to be generated by royalties and taxes from the extractive industries could reach up to $1.5 billion by 2016 and exceed $3.7 billion by 2026 and will become a major source of employment, with 165,000 jobs anticipated by 2016 and up to half a million by 2026." Of course, Ambassador Hakimi's optimism might be just a bit premature. The likelihood that the revenue coming from the extraction of these minerals will find its way to the Afghan people is extremely low if history is anything to go by. Jobs, however, as underpaid, overworked, and expendable mine workers might actually be available; so at least part of his statement has the potential of coming true. In the end, those that accused their governments of marching to war in Afghanistan for ulterior motives have been proved right yet again. Whether the reason for military invasion and occupation of the devastated nation was the result of a desire to control the opium trade, minerals, oil, and gas, or to secure pipelines and strategic geopolitical positioning, the fact is that the false flag attacks of served only as the justification – not the reason. Indeed, in my experience, there is rarely only one reason for any move that is made by the ruling elite. The route to the lapis mines in the Kokcha Valley is long, tortuous, and dangerous. From Feysbad, capital of Afghanistan's northeast province of Badakhshan, a poor road stretches southward through tiny hamlets of mud-walled huts standing on uneven ground wracked by the earthquake of 1832. After motoring as far as Hazarat-Said, the traveler must spend another full day on horseback before reaching Kokcha Valley. The small Kokcha River is the eastern tributary of the River Oxus which Marco Polo traversed and wrote: "There is a mountain in that region where the finest azure [lapis lazuli] in the world is found. It appears in veins like silver streaks. The lapis is mined on the steep sides of a long narrow defile sometimes only 200 meters wide and backed by jagged peaks that rise above 6000 meters. Sparsely populated and covered with snow for much of the year the barren region is inhabited by wild hogs and wolves. The summer sun is scorching, but temperatures drop below freezing at night. British Army Lieutenant John Wood reached the lapis mines for the East India Company in 1837, and wrote in his Journey to the Source of the River Oxus, "If you do not wish to die, avoid the Valley of Kokcha." This is surely not one of the world's better sites for a field trip! Darreh-Zu, one of the oldest mines along the Kokcha, is now closed and presumably exhausted. The nearby and relatively new Sar-e-Sang mine currently yields substantial amounts of good quality gem material and has produced rare 5-centimeter lazurite crystals. The largest found thus far, a well formed dodecahedron imbedded in calcite, was collected in 1964 by Pierre Bariand, mineral collection curator at The Sorbonne. Lazurite gem deposits occur in white and black marbles hundreds of meters thick. The gem veins, seldom exceeding 10 meters in length, lie in snow-white calcite. Associated minerals include pyrite, diopside, sodalite, forsterite, phlogopite, garnet, dolomite, apatite, and afghanite, a relatively new species of the cancrinite group. Gem lazurite is found in three Afghan color classifications: nili (dark blue), assemani (light blue), and sabz (green).

Afghanistan Sitting on Gold, Lithium Mine oil, gas, only-natural gas prices-per day 86 billion Dollars US, & $100 trillion dollars US, Iron ore, copper, large Uranium, of mineral reserves, precious an semi-precious stones, emerald-lapis lazuli, red-gamete A ruby, Marble, Coal & Canal-tunnel of Gold

At first glance, Afghanistan certainly seems like a prime candidate to become the world's next curse victim. The country's tribal and provincial leaders, after all, have spent years jostling for political power, with illicit opium revenue often fueling the engine of conflict. Now that the nation has inherited a literal gold mine of minerals, why would anyone assume that these warlords will suddenly disengage from similarly vitriolic rent-seeking behavior? The Karzai administration, meanwhile, has yet to effectively root out the pervasive political corruption and parasitic special interests that have severely hindered Western nation-building efforts. Considering the vicious brand of cronyism that's marred Karzai's nascent government, skeptics have good reason to suspect that a booming mine industry may only provide political insiders with yet another bargaining chip to cover. Political turmoil aside, Afghanistan's economy has always been far from robust. Most of its terrain is too mountainous to be arable, while rampant illiteracy has forced most citizens to farm what little low cash crops the land can support. Shoddy infrastructure, moreover, has handicapped Afghanistan's intra-national commerce, while global exports from its landlocked borders are virtually non-existent. It's also important to keep in mind that mining, unlike, say, oil drilling, is an extremely labor and capital-intensive endeavor. Extracting gold or copper from a single mine, for example, can often cost hundreds of millions—sometimes even billions—of dollars. As the country devotes more resources to developing its mining industry, then, its economy could be rendered excessively vulnerable to the kinds of external price shocks that are part and parcel to most commodity markets. And even if Afghanistan manages to construct a robust mining sector, it will still have to overcome significant geographic barriers that could make exporting its materials substantially more difficult—and even more expensive. Fortunately for Afghans, the country's Ministry of Mines certainly won't be harvesting these bountiful deposits on its own. The Pentagon has already provided the ministry with a special task force to offer consultation and technical data, and President Karzai has announced that Japan will have "priority" on future contracts to mine his country's resources. Never one to shy away from an opportunity to invest in foreign raw materials,

China may also throw its hat in the ring, along with a host of other multinational corporations. This foreign capital will almost certainly pay dividends to investors, and it may very well provide high wage employment for many Afghanis. Even with floods of foreign investment, though, minerals will still be *leaving* Afghanistan, and the lion's share of mineral profits will still be filling foreign coffers. At the end of the day, foreign investors are just that—investors. They're not police, and they're not watchdog organizations. Their Afghan aegis will end with the signing of a contract, and with the exchange of money. Where Afghanistan's mining revenue goes after that, or which warlord's hands it falls into, is anybody's guess. Is there hope for Afghanistan's mining-based economy, then? Of course. One need look no further than Saudi Arabia to find an example of a strong, outward-looking economy built largely on a single commodity. But unless Afghanistan manages to wipe away the cobwebs of corruption from Karzai's kitchen cabinet, and lay down a firm institutional foundation upon which its industry can flourish, it likely won't be able to avoid the clutches of the curse—regardless of how many foreign investors come knocking at its door. Precious metals The precious metals of gold, silver and platinum group elements have been valued for centuries because of their chemical and physical properties. All are commonly used in jewellery today, but also have a variety of other uses ranging from the dental industry for gold to catalysts for platinum. Precious metals in AfghanistanThere are a total of 93 precous metal occurrences recorded to date in the Afghan mineral occurrence database. These are principally gold with or without silver and base metals. Only one silver-rich occurrence has been identified, and to date no platinum-group mineralisation has been uncovered, although prospective geological terranes do exist in certain parts of the country including the ophiolite assemblages of Kabul and Khost. All the findings to date are the result of work conducted in the 1920s and 70s, principally by Russian geologists who identified two main areas as the most prospective. No more detailed work has been completed since this time, so the possibility exists of finding additional precious metal deposits in other areas using new geological models and exploration techniques. East-Central Afghanistan The provinces of Zabul and Ghazni appear to be the most prospective for skarn-type, porphyry-related and possibly epithermal-style gold mineralisation, due to the subduction-related geological environment during the Cretaceous-Tertiary. More than 50 sites have been recorded to date, including the largest resource currently known in Afghanistan. The Zarkashan skarn deposit was identified in the late 1960s and has Russian category C1 and C2 resources of about 250 000 oz, grading up to 16 g/t Au. Northeast Afghanistan The provinces of Badakhshan and Takhar are also prospective for gold mineralisation with a number of deposits identified to date, including the Vekadur Au-Ag deposit. Preliminary exploration in the 1960s delineated mineralisation grading 46.7 g/t Ag and 4.1 g/t Au for category C1 and C2 resources of just over 30 000 oz. Au. The number of other gold showings and favourable geology, including the discovery of Miocene Cu-porphyry style mineralisation, makes the area highly prospective. The area also has potential for placer-style mineralisation. The most explored is the Samti deposit where two gold-bearing horizons (grading up to 40 g/m3) have been discovered. Summary of the deposit geology Skarn-type mineralisation has also been identified in the western Badghis province, associated with Miocene granite porphyry emplacement. Polymetallic mineralisation, up to 3.6% Cu and 5 g/t Au, occurs in pods and veinlets as well as shear zones. Very little is known of the geology of southern Afghanistan, but the discovery of porphyry-style mineralisation in neighbouring Iran and Pakistan highlights the potential of the area. Large resources of Fe oxide like the Hajigak deposit (see Ferrous Metals), contain about 5% sulphides, including chalcopyrite, and should therefore be re-evaluated with modern-day iron oxide-copper-gold models in mind. Afghanistan today is a paradise for illegal excavators and smugglers of precious gems, stones and other antique artifacts. These are being smuggled to European and Asian countries with much ease in the absence of effective government Kabul: In the last eight years Afghanistan's precious stones and artifacts have been pillaged at record levels. Thieves, both foreign and domestic, often steal the riches from under the noses of officials. They end up spread far and wide, from East Asia to Western Europe. Some Afghan government officials even play a key role in the illegal excavation and smuggling process. But the biggest driver is the war that has dragged on for eight years. Security forces understandably spend the vast amount of their resources on fighting insurgents. As a result, smugglers have free rein in some provinces to pick the land clean of preciousgems, stones and antiquities. Alaf Gul, a resident of Nuristan says that local authorities, armed men, and even Taliban groups in his province dig up precious stones and other mineral resources. "They sell the stones to traffickers who come through this area," he says. He presumes that the items are then exported to other countries. Gul says that in nearby Noor Gram district, area commanders and Malaks – village elders – have the authority to put a stop to this, but choose not to do so because they profit from the illicit trade. Muhibullah Wakeelzada, a resident of Nandraj Valley, Nuristan, says that the Malaks, smugglers and military commanders in his area "join hands" to loot and export Afghanistan's precious stones and artifacts. "All day they take these things," he says. "The government can't stop them. They dig precious stones and sell them to Pakistan." Local people say that there are many precious stones in the Nandraj Valley. Ghulam Sakhi, a tribal leader and advocate during Zahir Shah's reign, says: "People and smugglers from Laghman, Kunar, Paktia and Nangrahar are coming here. They work here and take the precious stones." According to Sakhi, there are illegal mines in the area where the government has little control or oversight. "The government is weak here," he says. "Everything is being stolen, looted, because the mines are in areas where the government has no authority." He adds that explosives for excavating the mines are brought from regions where the government does have control, but there isn't enough regulation on those materials either. Mamoor Shah Wali, of Laghman, is a former member of the Afghan National Army in Nuristan. He says that the mountains in thearea are riddled with precious stones and illegal mines which extract them. "The people who run these mines are doing so only to fill their pockets." The Waigal district of Nuristan is particularly attractive to looters, who often come to the area heavily armed. "They have betrayed the nation," Wali says of the armed thieves. "If they are left to their own devices, all of the wealth and resources of our area will be looted." Even road crews in Nuristan have noticed an increase in traffic of those who have come to do business in Afghanistan's pillaged natural resources. "Areas that have been destabilised in recent years have seen sharp increases inthe illegal trade" "They sell these precious stones for very high prices," says one road builder who asked not to be identified, but has seen an influx of "foreign businessmen" coming through the area to purchase precious stones and gems. "These Pakistani businessmen sell them for a fortune in Peshawar." Wakhat News recently ran a story about a soldier who worked with a local commander in Nuristan who had a second job looting ancient artifacts. Though the soldier would not identify his commander, he told Wakhat that, "The commander looted every mountain and all theartifacts [in the area.] He sold these things, and precious stones cheaply to foreign businessmen." According to the soldier, who remained anonymous in the Wakhat report, smugglers are happy even for a small amount ofmoney. The fact that they are selling pieces of Afghanistan's history or natural wealth seems almost beside the point. According to Afghan law, deserts, rivers, mountains and mines (both exploited and otherwise,) belong to the government. Thegovernment is working to use the natural mineral resources to build economic stability, and illegal looting only undermines that effort. "The government is investing in coal and precious stone mines," says one resident of Panjshir. "When we work in a government mine, we can earn a piece of bread, legally. People are employed in the digging." But the eight-year long war has also contributed hugely to the illicit excavation and trade of Afghanistan's precious minerals. Areas that have been destabilised in recent years, Logar for example, have seen sharp increases in the illegal mining and exportof precious stones and artifacts.

Ironically, the war has also hurt the ability of smugglers to turn a profit on their ill-gotten loot. After the Pakistani army launched operations against Taliban and insurgent groups in Swat and Waziristan, the fighting shut down a major smuggling route out of Afghanistan, One smuggler from Khost, who wanted to remain anonymous, says that theoperations in western Pakistan have crippled his business, cutting the sale price of precious stones in half. "If the war continues," he says, "our business will be greatly damaged." The conflict has also helped curb the illegal excavation of precious stones, because villagers know that their work will not be as handsomely rewarded. Laiq Khan, the director of mines in Khost, says that the new, lower price of stones has caused many part-time illegal miners to quit the business altogether.

Afghanistan Sitting on Gold Mine the Great Game III on Afghanistan

The conflict in and around Afghanistan is entering a decisive phase. The International Security Assistance Force (ISAF), armed with a new counterinsurgency (COIN) doctrine and resources to conduct a forceful campaign, is engaging in a counteroffensive against the insurgency. Drawing on lessons learned from their own past insurgencies both regionally and globally, the insurgents are also constantly changing tactics. The inevitable clashes between the use of force and use of violence will exact a heavy cost in human lives this year. Reduction of violence cannot be the measure of progress, as all counteroffensives historically have initially increased both the level of violence and number of casualties. The success of the counteroffensive will be judged by its role in the larger project of counterinsurgency—creating the enabling environment for a stable political and economic system that can turn both Afghan citizens and regional players into stakeholders in its success. Catalyzing the emergence of such a system requires an appreciation of present opportunities and risks. Conceptually, the challenge lies in institutional design rather than planning. The distinction is important: while planning applies established procedures to solve a problem (presumed to be largely understood) within an accepted framework, design inquires into the nature of a problem (presumed to be largely outside of preexisting understanding) in order to conceive a framework for solving that problem. Planning is problemsolving; design is problem setting. ISAF, as General Stanley McChrystal's report of last year shows, has been functioning as a learning organization. It has been setting the problem in terms of reframing the threats to Afghanistan, saying they arise from bad governance and a predatory political elite as well as the insurgency.[2]International civilian actors, by contrast, are still engaged in a planning mode of operation, bringing tried but not tested solutions to problems they have neither analyzed nor prioritized. Too often, established bureaucratic procedures combined with improvisation by officials lacking shared vision, common frameworks, and continuity create misalignments between civilian and military goals, strategies, and tactics. The greatest opportunity and risk, therefore, lies in *framing* the issues. Whether Afghan, international, and particularly U.S. leadership can produce a new narrative that secures the buy-in of their publics will make the difference between creating a stable order and condemning the country to years of continuing conflict. Scenario 1: Capitalizing on Opportunities Four major opportunities to create positive momentum toward a stable economic and political order in Afghanistan present themselves at this juncture. Each opportunity, if capitalized on, could create a virtuous chain of consequences, outlined below. Natural Resources. Geology has emerged as the ultimate game-changer for Afghanistan. Aerial and seismic surveys undertaken by the U.S. Geological Survey reveal that the mineral resources of Afghanistan are worth at least $100 trillion. The country has the potential to be not only the world's largest producer of copper and iron, but also a major player in the production and processing of rare earths, which are used in products ranging from batteries to electrical cars and weapons systems. Moreover, these mineral resources are distributed equally between the northern third and southern two-thirds of the country, with significant deposits in the valleys of the mountain chains that divide north from south and whose populations currently suffer from extreme poverty. As the headwaters for a number of rivers flowing to neighboring countries, Afghanistan also generates 65 to 85 billion cubic meters of water per year but uses only 10 percent of it. The potential for hydropower, not only for use in Afghanistan but also for sale to power-starved India and now Pakistan since 1947 on Afghan 1, 2 million Sq Km Afghan-territories by the British, is immense. If Afghanistan can get natural resource governance right, these consequences would follow for the economic and political system: The country would have a domestic base of revenue generation, which would provide the fiscal basis for a modern state that can perform core functions for its citizens. This revenue base would ensure Afghanistan's gradual transformation from a ward of the international community to a partner, able to pay for its own security and development. The mineral and water resources of the country would justify investment in public infrastructure, such as railways, roads, dams, and power lines, which would knit the country into a cohesive economic space and integrate it with the regional and global economy. Afghanistan is located in the heart of Asia, within easy distance of 3 billion people and potentially easy reach of "now China Since 1949 on East Turkestan 2, 6 million Sq km Afghan Territories, India, and Russia—the three most important emerging economies in the world, Economic incentives could therefore be more effective than political means in leveraging buy-in to a stable and peaceful Afghanistan from neighbors near and far. U.S.-Afghan Strategic Partnership. President Barack Obama's engagement with Afghanistan has made it a global foreign policy issue. The resulting commitment of forces and resources has given ISAF the means to launch its counteroffensive. President Obama is also ready to enter into a strategic framework agreement between Afghanistan and the United States that would result in the medium- to long-term provision of security and development assistance by Washington to Kabul. The potential consequences of establishing this state-to-state and people-to people relationship are as follows: The United States would emerge as the guarantor of Afghan territorial integrity and sovereignty. U.S. long-term commitment to security and development assistance would provide the resources and time horizon necessary for meaningful transformation of Afghan institutions. Afghanistan's partnerships with Europe and Japan would be strengthened. The diplomatic power of these partners could be used to persuade Afghanistan's neighbors to become stakeholders in its stability, peace, and prosperity. Good Governance. Afghanistan is full of stories of successful institutional change: in sports, the Afghan cricket team emerged from nowhere to global prominence; in communications, which went from 100 mobile phone subscriptions in 2002 to over 12 million in 2010; in the media, where Afghan entrepreneurs have launched multiple successful satellite television stations and created new opportunities for public debate; in public finance, where expenditure systems have been declared among the most robust in the developing world by the World Bank; in health care, where the child mortality rate has been significantly reduced; and in rural development, where 23,000 villages have been reached by the National Solidarity Program, named one of the most innovative rural development programs by World Bank president Robert Zoellick. These successes accentuate the sharp contrast between Afghanistan's current status as the second most corrupt country on Transparency International's index and its underlying potential for good governance. Most of the examples of successful institutional transformation described above are the products of a design approach called national programs. A national program is an instrument that enables a state to perform one of its core functions by mobilizing existing capabilities, building additional capabilities, marshaling partnerships, promulgating rules and procedures, and engaging stakeholders. When citizens are served by and invest in the continuity of national programs, they also become invested in the stability of the state. The national program approach, its proven successes, and their continuing benefits, indicate several potential consequences for the promotion of this approach to good governance: Programs could be designed to improve the delivery of services to citizens and generation of revenue, extending trust in the system. Cross-cutting themes of governance, such as civil service and legislative reform, financial accountability, and human capital development, could be addressed systematically. The issue of delegations, alignments, and accountabilities among province, district, village, municipality, and central governments could be addressed. The market, as recent global experience has shown, requires state regulation. Bad governance of the relations between the state and private sector, however, drives the economy into informality, illegality, and ultimately criminality. Good governance of these relations therefore has not only economic but also developmental, social, and political consequences. Bad governance, as pointed out by ISAF and acknowledged by President Hamid Karzai in his speeches to the Peace Jirga, has been a driver of insurgency and conflict. These areas of governance reform would have a significant impact on the perception of the population, helping to convince the Afghan people that their government is worth siding with. A Law and Order Approach to Security. Commitment to good governance will create the impetus for a law and order approach to security. The key equation describing the outcome of a struggle between an insurgency and a counterinsurgency was framed by Robert Thompson long ago:Legality + Construction + Results = Government Illegality + Destruction + Promises = Insurgency. Even though the Afghan National Army has made substantial progress, the army, police, and intelligence services have a long way to go before they embody the instruments of legitimate force, upholding an order bound by rule of law. The judicial system, which should uphold the law that legitimates the use of force, is even less capable of fulfilling its role. If Afghanistan is to take over responsibility for ensuring law and order within its borders, its judicial system must be able to meet the provisions laid out by the constitution, laws, and covenants, which include obligations to provide due process to its citizens and protect them from treatment that violates international conventions ratified by the Afghan state. The adoption of COIN presents the United States with an opportunity to extend its engagement by training Afghan forces to a deeper examination, strengthening, and reconciliation of the fundamental institutions of Afghan law and order. Commitment to such an approach by the Afghan government and ISAF would have the following consequences: A transparent and accountable judicial system would allow for the transition to the Afghan government of detention facilities, searches and seizures, and trials of suspected insurgents and terrorists, resolving issues of authority over and accountability for Afghan citizens in U.S. detention. The provision of expedient, fair, and credible justice at the subnational level would overcome a comparative advantage of the insurgency, as swift justice addresses a real need of the population. The creating of a credible framework for property rights, enforcement of contracts, and fair resolution of disputes would clear the way for billions in Afghan-held funds to be invested in-country, thereby creating jobs, in particular for the poor, women, and youth, who make up the three numerical majorities of the population. The subordination of the use of force to the rule of law would be the key to transforming national security institutions into trustworthy upholders of a legitimate, democratic political order. Scenario 2: Succumbing to Constraints The opportunities outlined above exist in precarious balance with a series of risks or constraints. If we fail to understand the constraints or to contain the risks, any one of the following factors could easily derail the opportunities, while their combined impact would be devastating. I. ISAF Loses Its Status as Protector of the Population. Protection of the population, the core idea of the counterinsurgency doctrine, has either been abandoned or has failed to be translated from theory into practice. COIN has only been pursued in earnest in Afghanistan for 1 year. While General Petraeus and his key officers among U.S. forces are committed to this doctrine, COIN has yet to become North Atlantic Treaty Organization doctrine or be translated into a set of operational procedures that can provide sergeants and officers in the field with guidelines adapted to the context of Afghanistan. Engineering a paradigm shift is hard enough in the natural sciences; cultural change in hierarchical organizations is even more difficult and requires time to propagate through the ranks. Whether the U.S. political calendar can allow the time necessary to transform COIN into organizational culture in ISAF remains to be seen. Additionally, the tactics of the insurgency, which can use any and all forms of violence, could drive ISAF into uses of force that undermine its core principles. Reversion from a counterinsurgency to a counterterror approach would fundamentally change the relationship between the Afghan population and international forces, and could allow the insurgency to cast

ISAF as oppressors rather than protectors of the population. II. Neighboring Countries Choose to Support Destabilizing Afghanistan. Afghanistan's neighbors have provided sanctuary, arms, and resources to the insurgents, while various governments have long used Afghanistan as a site of proxy warfare among their secret services. These actors may judge that the United States and its partners, who have been deployed to Afghanistan according to United Nations Security Council resolutions, lack the staying power of regional players and will therefore adopt state policies that provide support to groups dedicated to the use of terror and violence. The decisions made by Pakistan, a country whose stability simultaneously depends on and bolsters Afghanistan's stability, will be particularly important. Pakistan can neither impose a unilateral settlement in Afghanistan nor deliver the insurgents to a negotiating table. Islamabad has a consistent history of misreading Kabul and has yet to define its national interests in a manner compatible with the interests of a sovereign and peaceful Afghanistan, from whose territory no hostile actions would be launched against the interests of a sovereign and peaceful Pakistan. If Pakistan chooses to pursue short-term interests, narrowly conceived and backed by the use of violence, those interests could pose significant risks to Afghanistan, ISAF, the region, and Pakistan itself. III. Natural Resources Become a Source of Further Conflict and Criminalization. Afghanistan's newly discovered natural wealth, if not governed properly, could exacerbate conflict, corruption, and agitation for proxy powers by neighbors near and far. Congo and other natural resource–rich African countries provide vivid reminders that endowment of natural capital, in the absence of human capital and institutions of governance, can prove a curse rather than a blessing. This pattern is already in evidence in some parts of the country, where struggles for dominance over precious stones, coal mines, timber, and other natural resources are driving instability, consolidating the power of strongmen, and contributing to bad governance. The narcotics trade makes up the major part of Afghanistan's criminal economy and is fully integrated into the networks that are the dark shadow of globalization. The narcotics traffickers already entrenched in Afghanistan have the money, muscle, and other means to criminalize the governance of these natural resources. The United Nations Office on Drugs and Crime estimates that international traffickers have reaped $460 to $600 billion from the cultivation, processing, and trafficking of drugs in Afghanistan, in contrast to $18 billion going to Afghan traffickers and $6.3 billion to the 1.67 million Afghan farmers engaged in cultivation. Ensuring that this scenario is not repeated in the capture of our natural wealth should be a major priority. IV. The Afghan Government Is Unable to Meet the Tests of 2010–2011. President Karzai has emerged as a decisionmaker without significant policy debate or checks and balances. The president in particular and the Afghan government in general must understand the risks and opportunities of the present moment if they are to avoid these risks. Several tests must be met by the government within the next 2 years. If the September parliamentary elections are marred by corruption and intimidation, it will erode tenuous public support in Europe and weaken public support in the United States during the election year. Once past that test, the government must then prepare in earnest for both the December 2010 assessment of ISAF strategy and the July 2011 transition. Failure to establish an environment of trust with ISAF and the international community, or perception of lack of serious effort to solve the governance problems, could create a negative climate in December and lead to a major reassessment of COIN. President Karzai must be prepared to take ownership of the agenda of government reform, lead anticorruption efforts, and assume the duties of commander in chief. The final test will be whether the government can build a national consensus on peace and reconciliation. This consensus will be not only a test of statecraft in itself, but also a critical step in constructing a wider and deeper agenda of state-building. Measures that divide the nation, or lead important constituents to believe that the neighbors are contravening Afghan national interests, will have major adverse consequences. V. Governance Reform Does Not

Reach Southern Afghanistan. The true test of COIN doctrine is in southern Afghanistan in general and in Kandahar in particular. Despite some progress in Helmand Province, bad governance has become the norm rather than the exception in the southern provinces. Their political and economic elites are either deeply divided or perceived as focused on short-term gains at the expense of medium- to long-term stability and prosperity. The bureaucracy in Kabul has been either disconnected from or an obstacle to reform in these provinces. If President Karzai, with his intimate knowledge and strong networks in the area, does not own and lead an agenda of reform in southern Afghanistan, the ISAF investment of forces and resources will be significantly constrained. To capitalize on opportunities and avoid succumbing to constraints, leadership is required from both Afghanistan and our international partners. We must produce a new narrative that is compelling to the Afghan public and international publics and governments. Framing the conflict in terms of counterterrorism did not win the Afghan public because it was manifested on the ground as support for strongmen and tolerance of increasingly bad governance. The overwhelming support of the Afghan people for a democratic order embodied in rule of law was undermined by seemingly arbitrary conduct and lack of commitment to the use of force within a rule of law framework. The adoption of COIN marks a welcome departure from the old framework. The fundamental insight of COIN doctrine is that insurgency and counterinsurgency are engaged in a political contest for the will of the people, and therefore the use of force is only part of a process toward clear political objectives in the medium term.[3] Restoration of Afghanistan's full sovereignty is a narrative that can not only win the contest for the will of the people, but also bring all the potential opportunities together into a focused strategy to contain the risks. A sovereignty strategy, as defined in my earlier work with Clare Lockhart,[4] entails the alignment of both internal and external stakeholders to the goals of the sovereign state through the joint formulation and calibration of, and adherence to, rules of the game. Once rules, objectives, and decision rights have been agreed on by citizens, state, and partners, resources are mobilized, critical tasks are designated, and reflexive monitoring and adjustment of implementation are put in place. The strategic goal is a sovereign state that is more autonomous and less dependent than before, can generate revenue self-sufficiently, and is fully capable of performing its core functions. In the long term, a sovereignty strategy should create, strengthen, or reform state institutions to perform all 10 core functions. In the short and medium term, however, a sovereignty strategy can include delegation of some critical tasks that fall within state functions to implementing partners by aligning the priorities, programs, and projects of international and national partners to the priorities and decisions of the state. The designation of July 2011 as the deadline for transition from U.S. to Afghan leadership of security institutions makes an overall sovereignty strategy a logical narrative to generate U.S. and Afghan public buy-in. This narrative would provide the Afghan public with a goal to strive for, while testing the leadership and commitment of the political elite and the capacity for sacrifice and compromise on the part of the population. The narrative would also allow the international community to shift its emphasis from abstract discussions of strategy and coordination to real agreement on actionable processes of coproduction of state functions ranging from public finance to rule of law and citizen rights and obligations. Such a framework of partnership would allow for joint delineation of timelines, benchmarks, and processes of transition to Afghan ownership, leadership, and management of institutions and functions, thereby providing the governments and publics of partner countries with concrete measures of progress and a real sense of momentum. The July 2010 Kabul Conference was intended to be an arena for articulating clear objectives and reinforcing processes and mechanisms of implementation for a contract between citizens and their government, while renewing and strengthening Afghanistan's partnerships with the international community on a basis of mutual commitments and accountability. This would generate a strategy for sovereignty. Success depended on the political will of the Afghan government and willingness of the international community to change those aspects of their practices that have proven ineffective or counterproductive. To go beyond political theater, the conference requires followup in the form of a sequence of rolling 100-day action plans. It is the followup that is essential, both for generating momentum through perceptible successes and for achieving meaningful progress toward true Afghan sovereignty. The scale of risks in Afghanistan is such that all challenges cannot be confronted simultaneously. Political capital must therefore be created and spent through a process of calibration, innovation, and learning. The desire of the absolute majority of Afghan men and women to live in peace and harmony, and their will to create better futures for their children, should not be underestimated. In that desire and will lies the promise that opportunities can be converted into real gains. By owning the Afghan conflict, President Obama took a major risk and created a window of opportunity. It is up to Afghans and our international partners to demonstrate that the risk was worth taking by making the most of the opportunity presented. The future stability of Afghanistan, the region, and the world depends on our success. PRISM The U.S. Department of Defense put a nearly $1 trillion price tag on the Afghan untapped natural minerals. However, the Afghan Minister of Mines *Wahidullah Shahrani* has recently called that a "conservative estimate" and suggested the real figure could be three times more than the current estimated amount. He also added that more studies and researches are needed to identify and explore the underground natural resources of the region. This great discovery of Afghanistan minerals include huge veins of Lithium, Iron, Copper, Cobalt Niobium, Gold minerals and critical industrial metals which are so big that could probably transform Afghanistan into one of the major mining centers in the world. Geologists have known for decades about Afghanistan's vast deposits of iron, copper, cobalt, gold, precious and semi-precious stones, and other prized minerals. The latest research completed by the U.S. Geological Survey and with the aid of archived data compiled by the former Soviet Union (when fighting in Afghanistan) confirmed the untapped reserves of the region after months of work. Moreover, the Afghan Ministry of Mines officials said that the mineral deposit data was safeguarded by an Afghan geologist during the decades of conflict in the region. The Afghan geologist who has died, gave the information back to the government in 2002. Since then, the data has been used to help uncover the underground treasury of the country. Afghanistan minerals are big enough and could transform Afghanistan in to "Saudi Arabia of Lithium" said a U.S official after the deposit announcement. Lithium is a valuable mineral in the modern industry and it's considered as a key raw material in the manufacture of batteries for BlackBerry cellular phones and laptop computers. According to the officials, the biggest deposits discovered so far in Afghanistan are Iron, Copper and Lithium. However, Afghanistan which is mired with over three decades of war does not have any mining industry or infrastructure to explore the natural minerals properly, so it will take decades for the country to exploit its untapped underground treasury. Aynak, 21 miles (35 kilometers) southeast of Kabul, is thought to hold one of the world's largest unexploited copper reserves. Mining the copper could produce 4,000 to 5,000 Afghan jobs in the next five years and hundreds of millions of dollars annual income to the Afghangovernment treasury. Moreover, Hajigak is thought to be one of the biggest iron deposits of the region and the work expected to start in five to seven years. Currently, Afghanistan is gearing up to award contracts to mine the two world's largest iron ore deposits buried in a peaceful province of Bamyan, about 100 km west of Kabul and the Aynak copper deposits in Logar province where it may hold 11.3 million tons of copper. The Afghan government has also reported large deposits of chromite, natural gas, oil and precious and semi-precious stones such as emeralds, lapis lazuli, etc. Last year, two Chinese mining companies, Jiangxi Copper Company and China Metallurgical Group won a $4 billion contract through a tender to develop Afghanistan's vast Aynak copper field in Logar Province. The bid included commitments to build a railroad through

Afghanistan to link Central Asia with Pakistan's port city of Karachi. The Chinese bid also included promises to build a power plant in Logar Province that would be big enough to run the mining operations in Logar and provide electricity to residents as well. Afghan officials hope fresh bids to develop other mineral fields with commitments of building infrastructure in the country. Before the uncovering the Afghanistan minerals or the underground treasury, electricity, road and railway connections are the priorities and needs to be built. By building the infrastructure, it will not only provides access to the mineral deposits for vehicles and heavy machinery but also makes it easy to carry mined resources to the international markets. Mining operations require enormous amounts of energy. That means electricity plants need to be built close enough to the newly surveyed mineral fields that would be developed. However, Afghanistan-India are still interested to build infrastructure and happy to invest in Afghanistan natural deposits. On the other hand, critics believe that the Afghanistan minerals rush, could pit U.S and Chinese interests against each other. Because of the 2, 6 million Sq Km of East Turkestan, one hundred years games on Afghan territory by the European from 1893.

Afghanistan governance since 2001 until 2020

Building capacity and limiting corruption at all levels of Afghan governance, Building capacity and limiting corruption at all levels of Afghan governance are crucial to the success of a planned transition from U.S.-led NATO forces to Afghan security leadership. The capacity of the formal Afghan governing structure has increased significantly since the Taliban regime fell in late 2001, but nepotism is entrenched in Afghan culture and other forms of corruption are widespread. Afghan President Hamid Karzai has accepted U.S. help to build emerging anti-corruption institutions, but these same institutions have sometimes caused a Karzai backlash when they have targeted his allies or relatives. At a donors' conference in Tokyo on July 8, 2012, donors pledged to aid Afghanistan's economy through at least 2017, provided Afghanistan takes concrete, verifiable action to rein in corruption. On July 26, 2012, Karzai appeared to try to meet his pledges to the Tokyo conference by issuing a "decree on administrative reforms"—a document of sweeping policy directives intended to curb corruption. Partly because of corruption in the Afghan security forces, on August 4, 2012, the National Assembly voted to remove the ministers of interior and of defense; they have been replaced. Even though the government is weak, President Hamid Karzai has tried to concentrate authority in Kabul through his constitutional powers of appointment at all levels. Karzai has publicly denied assertions by opposing faction leaders that he wants to stay in office beyond the 2014 expiration of his second term, but he is said to be trying to identify and support an acceptable successor. International efforts to curb fraud in two successive elections (for president in 2009 and parliament in 2010) largely failed and many believe election oversight will be little improved for the 2014 election, although civil society groups are trying to ensure robust competition and electoral fairness. There is concern among many observers that fragile governance will founder as the United States and its partners wind down their involvement in Afghanistan by the end of 2014. Some argue that the informal power structure, which has always been at least as significant a factor in governance as the formal power structure, will sustain governance beyond 2014 should formal governing structures falter. However, that outcome might produce even more corruption and arbitrary administration of justice than is the case now as major faction leaders gain power. Karzai has failed to marginalize these ethnic faction leaders, in part because they have large constituencies, but he relies more closely on the loyalty of several close, ethnic Pashtun allies, particularly those from the Kandahar area. The non-Pashtun faction leaders generally oppose Karzai's willingness to make concessions to insurgent leaders in search of a settlement. There are fears that a reintegration of the Taliban into Afghan politics will further set back progress in human rights and the rights of women and boost Pashtun power. Broader issues of human rights often vary depending on the security environment in particular regions, although some trends prevail nationwide. Women, media professionals, and civil society groups have made substantial gains since the fall of the Taliban, but traditional attitudes contribute to the judicial and political system's continued toleration of child marriages, imprisonment of women who flee domestic violence, judgments against converts from Islam to Christianity, and curbs on the sale of alcohol and Western-oriented programming in the Afghan media. Afghanistan: Post-Taliban Governance, Security, and U.S. Policy, by Kenneth Katzman; United Nations Assistance Mission in Afghanistan: Background and Policy Issues, by Rhoda Marge son; and CRS Report, Afghanistan: U.S. Rule of Law and Justice Sector Assistance, by Liana Sun Wyle and Kenneth Katz man. Overview: Historic Patterns of Afghan Authority and Politics Through differing regimes of widely varying ideologies, Afghanistan's governing structure has historically consisted of weak central government unwilling or unable to enforce significant financial or administrative mandates on all of Afghanistan's diverse ethnic communities or on the 80% of Afghans who live in rural areas. Many communities are separated by mountains and wide expanses that can take days to reach and require traditional modes of transportation. The tensions between the central government and the outlying areas have often mirrored the struggles between urban, educated "modernizers" and the rural, lesser-educated traditionalists who adhere to strict Islamic customs. The Taliban government (1996-2001) opposed modernization. At the national level, Afghanistan had few, if any, Western-style democratic institutions prior to the international intervention that took place after the September 11, 2001, attacks on the United States. Under the constitution of 1964, puppets King Zahir Shah was to be a constitutional monarch and an elected lower house and appointed upper house were set up. The parliament during that era never reached the expectation of becoming a significant check on the king's power, although the period from 1964 until the seizure of power by Mohammad Daoud in a 1973 military coup was considered a flowering of Afghan democracy. The last lower house elections during that period were held in 1969. The parliament was suspended outright following the April 1978 Communist seizure of power. The elected institutions and the 2004 adoption of a constitution were part of a post-Taliban transition roadmap established by a United Nations-sponsored agreement of major Afghan factions signed in Bonn, Germany, on December 5, 2001 ("Bonn Agreement"), after the Taliban had fallen. Karzai is the first directly elected Afghan president. Since the fall of the Taliban, there has also been the growth of civil society, populated largely by educated Afghans, many of whom returned to Afghanistan from exile when the Taliban fell. Organizations and groups centered on various issues, including women's rights, law and justice, media freedoms, economics and business issues, the environment, and others, have proliferated. U.S. and partner policy has been to try to empower these groups as a check on government power and as a guarantor that Afghan democracy will become entrenched. These newly emerging interest groups have still not been able to displace—or even necessarily substantially influence—the informal power structure of ethnic, regional, tribal, clan, village, and district structures that exercise authority at all levels. At the local level, these structures governed and secured Afghanistan until the late 1970s but were weakened by decades of subsequent war and Taliban rule. Some traditional local authority figures fled or were killed; others were displaced by mujahideen commanders, militia leaders, Taliban militants, and others. The local power brokers who displaced some of the tribal structures are far less popular and are widely accused of selectively applying Afghan law and of using their authority to enrich themselves. Some of the traditional tribal councils, which are widely respected but highly conservative in orientation, remained intact. Some of them continue to exercise their writ rather than accept the authority of the central government or even local government appointees. Still other community authorities prefer to accommodate local insurgents, whom they often see as wayward but reconcilable members of the community, rather than help the government secure their areas. Afghanistan: Politics, Elections, and Government Performance Congressional Research Service 2 the informal power structure has decision-making bodies and processes that do not approximate Western-style democracy but yet have participatory and representative elements. Meetings called shuras, or Jirgas (consultative councils), 2- often composed of designated notables, are key mechanisms for making or endorsing authoritative decisions or dispensing justice. Some of these mechanisms are practiced by Taliban insurgents in areas under their control or influence. On the other hand, some see the traditional patterns as competing with and detracting from the development of the post-Taliban formal power structure—a structure that, with Western guidance, has generally tried to meet international standards of democratic governance and human rights practices. At the national level, one traditional mechanism has carried over into the post-Taliban governing structure. The convening of a loya jirga, an assembly usually consisting of about 1,500 delegates from all over Afghanistan, has been used on several occasions. Under the constitution, decisions of a loya jirga supersede decisions made under any other process, including cabinet meetings or even elections. In the post-Taliban period, loya Jirgas have been convened to endorse Karzai's leadership, to adopt a constitution, and to discuss a long-term defense relationship with the United States. A special loya jirga, called a peace jirga, was held on June 2-4, 2010, to review government plans to offer incentives for insurgent fighters to end their armed struggle and rejoin society. Another loya jirga was held during November 16-19, 2011, to endorse proposed Afghan government conditions on a strategic partnership agreement between Afghanistan and the United States. However, the constitution specifies who should be delegates at a constitutional loya jirga, and, in the absence of elected district councils (whose members are mandated to be included), all of Afghanistan's post-2004 loya Jirgas have been traditional loya Jirgas. Relations Among Ethnicities and Communities Even though post-Taliban Afghanistan, particularly in urban areas, is modernizing politically and economically, patterns of political affiliation by family, clan, tribe, village, ethnicity, region, and comradeship in past battles often supersede relationships based on ideology or views. These patterns have been evident in every Afghan election since the fall of the Taliban. Most candidates, including Karzai, have pursued campaign strategies designed primarily to assemble blocs of ethnic and geographic votes, although some independent candidates have sought to advance specific new programs and ideas. The traditional patterns have been even more pronounced in province-based campaigns such as those for provincial councils and the parliament. In these cases, electorates (the eligible voters of a specific province) are small and candidates can easily exploit clan and familial relationships. While Afghans continue to follow traditional patterns of affiliation, there has been a sense among Afghans that their country now welcomes members of all political and ethnic groups and factions. There have been very few incidents of ethnic-based violence since the fall of the Taliban, but jealousies over relative economic and political positions of the different ethnic communities have The Pashtuns Ethnic Pashtuns (pronounced POSH-ton, sometimes referred to as Pathans—path-TAHNS), as the largest single ethnicity, have historically asserted a "right to rule" Afghanistan. Pashtuns are about 42% of the population and, with few exceptions, have governed Afghanistan. The sentiment of the "right to rule" is particularly strong among Pashtuns of the Durrani tribal confederation, which predominates in the south and is a rival to the Ghilzai confederation, which predominates in the east and has historically close ties to Pakistan. Karzai is a Durrani Pashtun. His cabinet and inner advisory circle has come to be progressively dominated by Pashtuns, both Ghilzai and Durrani, which has largely minimized the advisory input of the non-Pashtun communities. However, Karzai is credited by some observers for consulting with other communities, particularly the Tajiks, before issuing decrees or reaching decisions. The Taliban government was and its insurgency is composed almost completely of Pashtuns. A table on major Pashtun clans is provided below (see Table 1), as is a map showing the distribution of Afghan ethnicities The Tajiks are the second-most numerous and second most powerful community in Afghanistan. Tajiks are an estimated 25% of the population and constitute the core of the "Northern Alliance" grouping that politically opposes but sometimes works amicably with Karzai. On a few occasions, Tajiks have ruled Afghanistan, although usually for relatively brief periods. One recent example was the 1992-1996 presidency of the mujahideen government of Burhanuddin Rabbani's, a Tajik (who was assassinated on September 20, 2011). The Tajiks and the Northern Alliance are discussed extensively in this paper. The Hazara Many Pashtuns are said to be increasingly resentful of the Hazara Shiite minority (about 10% of the population) that is advancing economically and politically through education. The Hazara have historically been looked down upon by the Pashtuns, who have tended to employ Hazara as domestic workers and other lower and lower middle class occupations. Observers report that many Hazara, including Hazara women, are earning degrees or pursuing training in information technology, medical, and other highly skilled professions and that they are becoming dominant in many of these higher paying sectors of the Afghan economy. Jealousy of Hazara advancement could have been a factor in the December 6, 2011, bombings of Hazara in three cities, killing 60, while they were visiting their mosques to celebrate the Shiite holy day of Ashura. A Pakistan-based militant group, Lashkar-i-Jhangvi, claimed responsibility—possibly in an effort to stir up sectarian conflict in Afghanistan. Afghan Shiite officials said such tactics would not work, as there is no inclination toward sectarian conflict in Afghanistan. However, a rare clash took place between Hazara and Tajiks in Kabul when a car in procession of Tajiks commemorating the September 9, 2001, death of their historic leader Ahmad Shah Masood ran over a Hazara bicyclist. The clash was said to reflect lingering Hazara resentment of Masseur's 1993 offensive against then Hazara rivals during the 1992-1996 period of internecine warfare that preceded the accession of the Taliban regime. Afghanistan: Politics, Elections, and Government Performance Congressional Research Service 4 the Uzbeks, like the Hazara, are about 10%. The Uzbek community is Sunni Muslim and speaks a language akin to Turkish, as well as Dari. The most well-known Uzbek leader in Afghanistan is Abdul Rashid Dostum, who was allied with Soviet occupation forces but later defected and helped bring down the Communist regime in Afghanistan in April 1992. Because of their alliance with the Soviet Union during the occupation period, many Uzbeks in Afghanistan are leftwing and highly secular. Relative Lack of Attraction to Formal Political Parties One major issue that connects post-Taliban and pre-Taliban Afghanistan is that the concept of an Afghan nation is not as strong as are affiliation by community and clan. There is a popular aversion to formal "parties" as historically tools of neighboring powers—a perception stemming from the war against the Soviet Union when seven mujahideen parties were funded by and considered tools of outside parties. Some of these mujahideen parties remain, such as the mostly Pashtun Hizb-e-Islam and the mostly Tajik Jamiat Islami, as discussed below. However, most of the mujahideen era parties have evolved into alternate or broader coalitions. Hizb-e-Islam is a notable exception to that trend, and it does generally still compete in elections as a distinct party. Prior to September 2009, when a new political party's law was adopted, there were 110 registered political parties. However, a September 2009 law required all parties to reregister and to submit 10,000 signatures, spanning at least 22 provinces to verify their support. By the time of the September 18, 2010, parliamentary election, only five parties had completed the new registration process. By late 2011, 38 parties had completed the process, and a total of 21 parties are represented in the lower house of parliament. Partly because parties are viewed with suspicion, President Hamid Karzai has not formed his own party, but many of his supporters in the National Assembly (parliament) belong to a moderate faction of Hizb-e-Islam that is committed to working within the political system. The grouping was reduced somewhat by the results of the September 18, 2010, parliamentary elections. The putative leader of this group is Minister of Economy Abdul Hadi Arghandiwal. A militant faction of Hizb-e-Islam is loyal to pro-Taliban insurgent leader Gulbuddin Hekmatyar's; it is called Hizb-Islam Gulbuddin (HIG). Other large parties that do exist, for example the Junbush Melli of Abdul Rashid Dostum, tend to be identified with specific ethnic (in his case, Uzbeks) or sectarian factions, rather than overarching themes. A major party is Jamiat Islami (Islamic Society), a party that grouped Tajik leaders during the anti-Soviet war, although many Tajik leaders still identify with the broader anti-Taliban "Northern Alliance." In recent years, key Tajiks have formed broader groupings discussed later, such as the United Front and the Hope and Change Movement. However, these parties do not advertise themselves as "ethnic" parties per se, because Article 35 of the Afghan constitution bans parties based on ethnicity or religious sect. It was hoped that post-Taliban Afghanistan would produce a substantial number of secular, pan ethnic democratic parties. Some large such parties have formed, particularly the Hope and Change party of Dr. Abdullah, discussed further below. Another secular, pan-ethnic party, the Rights and Justice Party, was formed by ex-Interior Minister Mohammad Hanif Atmar and other allies in October 2011, also discussed further below. Another party, the Coalition for Reform and Development, has formed in 2012 to try to ensure that the presidential election in 2014 is fair. Afghanistan: Politics, Elections, and Government Performance Congressional Research Service 5 Smaller secular parties include the Afghanistan Lab our and Development Party, the National Solidarity Party of Afghanistan's Youth, the Republican Party, and the National Congress Party of Afghanistan led by Abdul Latif Pedram. Some parties are left wing, such as the National United Party of Afghanistan, led by former parliamentarian Nur ul-Haq Ulumi, who was in the Communist era military. However, some believe that all the smaller, idea-based parties remain weak because the Single, Non-Transferable Vote (SNTV) system—in which each voter casts a ballot for only one candidate—favors candidates running as independents rather than as members of parties. Moreover, Western-style parties are generally identified by specific ideologies, ideas, or ideals, while most Afghans, as discussed above, retain their traditional affiliations. As a result, many of the parties that have been formed since the fall of the Taliban have centered on personalities rather than broad idea-driven platforms. Post-Taliban Transition and Political Landscape U.S. policy since 2001 has been to help expand the capacity of formal Afghan governing institutions, most of which were nearly non-existent during Taliban rule. No parliament was functioning during that time, and Afghanistan was run by a small, Kandahar-based group of Pashtun clerics loyal to Mullah Mohammad Umar, who remained there. Government offices that were functioning were minimally staffed, and without modern equipment, according to observers. There were virtually no checks or balances on Mullah Omar's decision to host Osama bin Laden in Afghanistan during that time. Since 2007, but with particular focus during the Obama's Administration, U.S. policy has been to not only try to expand Afghan governing capacity and the ability of the government to deliver services - at the central and local levels - but to push for its reform, transparency, and oversight. However, the formal governing structure continues to compete, often unsuccessfully, with the traditional power structures discussed above. Establishment of the Formal Afghan Government Structure: Tending Toward Centralization The 2001 ouster of the Taliban government paved the way for the success of a long-stalled U.N. effort to form a broad-based Afghan government and for the international community to help Afghanistan build legitimate governing institutions. In the formation of the first post-Taliban transition government, the United Nations was viewed as a credible mediator by all sides largely because of its role in ending the Soviet occupation. During the 1990s, a succession of U.N. mediators adopted many of former puppet King Zahir Shah's proposals for a government to be selected by a traditional assembly, or loya jirga. However, U.N.-mediated cease-fires between warring factions did not hold. Non-U.N. initiatives made little progress, particularly the "Six plus Two" multilateral contact group, which began meeting in 1997 (the United States, Russia, and the six states bordering Afghanistan: present day Iran, China, Pakistan, Turkmenistan, Uzbekistan, and Tajikistan). Other failed efforts included a "Geneva group" (Italy, Germany, Iran, and the United States) formed in 2000; an Organization of Islamic Conference (OIC) contact group; and prominent Afghan exile efforts, including discussion groups launched by Hamid Karzai and his clan, former mujahideen commander Abd al-Haq, and puppet Zahir Shah ("Rome process"). The sections below discuss the formation of the post-Taliban governing structure of Afghanistan. Afghanistan: Politics, Elections, and Government Performance

Congressional Research Service 6 December 2001 Bonn Agreement Immediately after the September 11 attacks, former U.N. mediator Lakhdar Brahimi was brought back (he had resigned in frustration in October 1999). U.N. Security Council Resolution 1378 (November 14, 2001) called for a "central" role for the United Nations in establishing a transitional administration and inviting member states to send peacekeeping forces to promote stability and aid delivery. After the fall of Kabul in November 2001, the United Nations invited major Afghan factions, most prominently the Northern Alliance and that of the former King—but not the Taliban—to an international conference in Bonn, Germany. On December 5, 2001, the factions signed the "Bonn Agreement."3 It was endorsed by U.N. Security Council Resolution 1385 (December 6, 2001). The agreement was reportedly forged with substantial Iranian diplomatic help because Iran had supported the military efforts of the Northern Alliance faction and had leverage to persuade temporary caretaker Rabbani's and the Northern Alliance to cede the top leadership to Hamid Karzai as leader of an interim administration. Other provisions of the agreement: authorized an international peace keeping force to maintain security in Kabul, and Northern Alliance forces were directed to withdraw from the capital. Security Council Resolution 1386 (December 20, 2001, and renewed yearly thereafter) gave formal Security Council authorization for the international peacekeeping force (International Security Assistance Force, ISAF); referred to the need to cooperate with the international community on counter narcotics, crime, and terrorism; and applied the constitution of 1964 until a permanent constitution could be drafted. 4On December 5, 2011, there was an international conference on Afghanistan in Bonn, marking the 10th anniversary since the 2001 Bonn Conference. The meeting, in part, evaluated governance progress in Afghanistan since the original convention. Permanent Constitution Adopted Sets up Presidential System a June 2002 "emergency" loya jirga put a representative imprimatur on the transition; it was attended by 1,550 delegates (including about 200 women). Subsequently, a 35-member constitutional commission drafted the constitution, unveiling it in November 2003. It was debated by 502 delegates, selected in U.N.-run caucuses, at a "constitutional loya jirga (CLJ)" during December 13, 2003-January 4, 2004. The CLJ, chaired by prominent Islamic scholar and former interim Afghan leader Sibghatullah Mojadeddi, approved the draft constitution with minor changes. The constitution set up a presidential system, with an elected president having relatively broad powers and a separately elected National Assembly (parliament). Opposing too great a centralization of power (which would favor Pashtuns), the Tajik-dominated Northern Alliance failed in its effort to set up a prime minister ship in which the elected parliament would select a prime minister who would run the day-to-day workings of government. In such a system, the president's powers would be limited. In the constitution, the faction did achieve some limitation to presidential powers by assigning major authorities to the parliament, as discussed below. The Northern Alliance assumed that, in a prime ministerial system, the post of elected president would be held by a Pashtun but, in a tradition of power sharing, the prime minister post would be held by a Tajik or other ethnic minority. The constitution and election system (a two round election if no majority is achieved in the first round) strongly favor the likelihood that an ethnic Pashtun will be president of Afghanistan. The president serves a five-year term, with a two-term limit (Article 62). There are two vice presidents. The president has broad powers. Under article 64, he has the power to appoint all "high-ranking officials," which has been interpreted by Karzai to include not only cabinet ministers but also members of the Supreme Court, judges, provincial governors and district governors, local security chiefs, and members of supposedly independent commissions such as the Independent Election Commission and the Afghan Independent Human Rights Commission (AIHRC). However, these appointments are constitutionally subject to confirmation by the National Assembly. The president also is commander-in-chief of the Afghan armed forces. In an outcome still debated, at the CLJ, the opposition did not achieve the right of elected provincial and district councils to choose their governors. The constitution made former King Zahir Shah honorary "Father of the Nation," a title that is not heritable. Zahir Shah died on July 23, 2007.5 It (Article 58) also set up the Afghanistan Independent Human Rights Commission (AIHRC) to refer cases of human rights violations to "the legal authorities." (See further below on this commission Karzai Elected in First Post-Taliban Presidential Elections in 2004 Security conditions precluded the holding of the first post-Taliban elections simultaneously. The first election, for president, was held on October 9, 2004, missing a June constitutional deadline. Turnout was about 80%. On November 3, 2004, Karzai was declared winner (55.4% of the vote) over his 17 challengers on the first round, avoiding a runoff. He was sworn in to office in December 2004, about one year before the swearing in of an elected National Assembly; he ruled by decree during that one year period. National Assembly (Parliament) Formation, Powers, and Assertion of Powers The National Assembly outlined by the constitution consists of a 249 all-elected lower house (Wolesi Jirga, House of the People) and a selected 102 seat upper house (Meshrano Jirga, House of Elders). The upper house is selected as follows: one-third, or 34 seats, appointed by the president (for a five-year term); one-third appointed by the elected provincial councils (four-year term); and one-third appointed by elected district councils (for a three-year term). Of the president's appointments, half (17) are mandated to be women. Because of the difficulty in confirming voter registration rolls and determining district boundaries, elections for the 364 district councils have not been held to date. Each district 5 Afghanistan/Constitution Afghanistan. Afghanistan: Politics, Elections, and Government Performance Congressional Research Service 8 boundary is likely to be contentious because it will inevitably separate tribes and clans. Until there are elected district councils, two-thirds of the Meshrano Jirga is selected by the provincial councils for four year terms. The lower house is mandated to be at least 28% female (68 people), an average of two for each of the 34 provinces. Parliamentary and provincial council elections, which were to establish the National Assembly and the provincial councils, were originally intended for April-May 2005 but were delayed until September 18, 2005. The elections were based on a "Single Non-Transferable Vote" System; candidates stood as individuals, not part of a party list. Voting was for one candidate only, although the number of representatives varied by province, ranging from 2 (Panjshah Province) to 33 (Kabul Province). Other examples include Herat, 17; Nangarhar, 14; Kandahar, Balkh, and Ghazni, 11 seats each. The National Assembly has become the key formal institution for non-Pashtuns and political independents to express political opposition to and to exert influence on Karzai. The Assembly has been set up by the constitution as a relatively powerful body that can, to some extent, check the powers of the president, although the Northern Alliance and other Karzai critics say it has Insufficient power to break presidential authority Powers of the National Assembly The lower house has the power to vote no-confidence against ministers (Article 92)—based on a proposal by 10% of the lower house membership, or 25 parliamentarians. Both the upper and lower houses are required to pass laws. Under Article 98 of the constitution, the national budget is taken up by the Meshrano Jirga first and then passed to the Wolesi Jirga for its consideration. Both houses of parliament, whose budgets are controlled by the Ministry of Finance, are staffed by about 275 Afghans, reporting to a National Assembly "secretariat." There are 18 oversight committees, a research unit, and a library. USAID has helped the Afghanistan National Assembly build its capabilities with a parliamentary assistance program for Afghanistan. Assertion of Its Authority after the National Assembly was inaugurated on December 19, 2005, it immediately demonstrated institutional strength. One of its first tasks was to review, and either endorse, amend, or void, the decrees Karzai had issued in the one year he was president and no National Assembly was operating. In March 2006, it achieved a vote to require Karzai's cabinet to be approved individually, rather than en bloc, increasing opposition leverage. However, Karzai rallied his support and all but 5 of the 25 nominees were confirmed. In May 2006, the opposition within the Assembly compelled Karzai to change the nine-member Supreme Court, the highest judicial body, including ousting 74-year-old Islamic conservative Fazl Hadi Shinwari as chief justice. The proximate justification for the ouster was Shinwari's age, which was beyond the official retirement age of 65. He was succeeded as chief justice by Abdul Salam Azimi. (Shinwari later went on to head the Ulema Council, Afghanistan's highest religious body, before his death in 2011.) The process of confirming Karzai's second-term cabinet—in which many of Karzai's nominees were voted down in several nomination rounds during 2010—demonstrates that the Assembly is an increasingly strong institution that is pressing for competent governance. These principles are advocated most insistently, although not exclusively, by the younger, more technocratic Afghanistan: Politics, Elections, and Government Performance Congressional Research Service 9 independent blocs in the lower house. The Assembly repeatedly voted down Karzai nominees following the contentious outcome of the 2009 presidential election, as discussed below. The Assembly firmly asserted itself on August 4, 2012, by voting to oust Defense Minister Abdul Rahim Wardak and Interior Minister Bismillah Khan Mohammedi. The move was ostensibly on the grounds of their failure to reduce alleged corruption in their ministries, or to prevent shelling of northeastern Afghanistan from the Pakistan side of the border. However, some asserted the move was an effort to ensure that security contracts were opened to a broader range of bidders. Others felt the vote was a parliamentary overture to Pakistan, because both ministers have been highly critical of that country's hosting of Afghan militants. Karzai said he would abide by the Assembly vote. Wardak resigned shortly thereafter and was made a "senior adviser." Rivalries Within and Outside Governing Institutions As discussed above, many intersecting trends including ethnicity, tribal affiliation, geography, economic interests, and ideologies determine politics in Afghanistan. These splits manifest within as well as outside Afghan governing institutions, including the National Assembly. Although they largely accept that a Pashtun is most likely to hold the top slot in the Afghan government, non-Pashtuns insist on being—and are—represented at all levels of the central government. Ethnic minorities have demanded, and have achieved, a large measure of control over how government programs are implemented in their geographic regions. Although Karzai has the power to appoint provincial and district governors, in practice he has not appointed governors of a different ethnicity than the majority of residents of particular provinces and districts. One notable exception is the governor of Herat, Daud Shah Saba, appointed in 2011; he is a Pashtun in a province whose major city, Herat, is overwhelmingly Tajik—although many districts of the province outside the city are majority Pashtun. The Independent Directorate of Local Governance (IDLG, which recommends to the presidential palace local appointments) often consults notables of a province on local appointments. Karzai's Presidential Leadership, His Close Advisers, and Staff As president, Karzai is advised by what some observers believe is a narrow spectrum of Pashtuns in the cabinet and in his presidential office. Some of them are former members of the moderate wing of the Islamist party Hezb-e-Islam. Among his top aides are his chief of staff, former Minister of Information and Culture Abdul Karim Kurram, who was appointed in April 2011. The chief of staff serves as key gatekeeper of access to Karzai. He replaced Mohammad Umar Daudzai, an Islamic conservative who fought during the anti-Soviet war in more radical Hezb-eIslam faction Gulbuddin Hikmatyar and was said to be a skeptic of Western/U.S. influence over Afghan decision making. On October 23, 2010, The Times asserted that Daudzai was the presidential office's liaison with Iran for accepting the approximately $2 million per year in Iranian assistance that is provided as cash. Karzai acknowledged this financial arrangement. Daudzai was appointed Ambassador to Pakistan in April 2011. Another top palace aide is minister-counselor Tajj Ayubi. A top communications aide, Waheed Omar, resigned in August 2011, possibly because of the influence of Hizb-e-Islam supporters on Karzai; he was replaced on an acting basis by Siamak Herawi. Some of Karzai's top advisers are well-educated and Westernized. For example, Karzai trusts such professionals as French-educated physician—now foreign minister—Zalmay Rassoul and former Foreign Minister and now National Security Adviser Rangin Spanta. Both are Pashtuns.

Afghanistan: Politics, Elections, and Government Performance Congressional Research Service 10 Spanta, who served in the government during the Soviet occupation era, was foreign minister during March 2006-February 2010, and is said to retain some leftwing views. The National Security Council, headed by Spanta, is located in the presidential palace complex and heavily populated by ethnic Pashtuns. Two other trusted NSC officials (both Pashtuns) are first deputy NSC Adviser Ibrahim Spinzada (a Karzai brother-in-law), and Shaida Mohammad Abdali, the second deputy NSC adviser. Karzai also surrounds himself with Pashtun tribal and faction leaders from southern Afghanistan, such as Sher Mohammad Akhunzadeh, the former governor of Helmand (until 2005). These personalities reflect Karzai's attempts to exert direct control over his home province of Kandahar and the neighboring large province of Helmand. An administrative unit that has attracted increasing international attention as a potential center of more organized policymaking is the Office of Administrative Affairs (OAA), referred to by some as the General Administrative Office (GAO) or the "cabinet Secretariat." Some experts say that, particularly under its current head, a Hazara named Sadiq Mudabir, it is primarily administrative, and without any policy coordination role. However, some say it has taken on an informal judicial role by assessing the legitimacy of citizen, group, and corporate petitions and forwarding those to the relevant ministries for follow-up action. It is a holdover from the Communist era, and contains many longtime bureaucrats. During the 1990s it may have had as many as 1,800 personnel, but has been trimmed during the Karzai era to about 700 staff members. The operations of the unit are funded primarily by the United Kingdom, but U.S. military and civilian officials have been assigned to provide advice and assistance to the office as well. Some observers assert that the apparatus around Karzai require improved focus and organization. One idea that surfaced in 2009, and which some Afghans still raise, is to prod Karzai to create a new position akin to a "chief administration officer" who can break through administrative bottlenecks. One of Karzai's 2009 election challengers, Ashaf Ghani, was not formally given this role but advises Karzai on government reform and institution building, and manages the transition from the United States and NATO to Afghan lead. Ghani has been part of Karzai's advisory team for all recent major international conferences on Afghanistan, including the December 5, 2011, Bonn Conference. Ghani is considered a top contender for president in 2014. Karzai's Allies in the Lower House of the National Assembly In addition to his allies in the presidential palace and the government writ large, as of 2012 Karzai has about 60-70 core supporters, mostly Pashtuns, in the Wolesi Jirga. Karzai and his aides hoped to but failed to increase the president's support base in the September 18, 2010, elections, but instead the results caused Karzai's base to shrink by about 20 deputies as compared to his support in the 2006-2011 lower house. Of his lower house supporters, about half are former members of the conservative Pashtun-based Hizb-e-Islam party (the same party as that headed by insurgent leader Gulbuddin Hikmatyar). Others in Karzai's camp in the lower house are followers of Abd-iRab Rasul Sayyaf, a prominent Pashtun Islamic conservative mujahedin era party leader. 6 As a result, Karzai was unable to engineer the selection of Sayyaf to become lower house speaker in 2011, displacing Yunus Qanooni. Neither Sayyaf nor Qanooni was unable to obtain enough votes to become speaker, instead losing to a compromise candidate, Abdul Raouf Ibrahimi, an Uzbek who is perceived as weak. 6 Sayyaf led the Ittihad Islami (Islamic Union) mujahedin party during the war against the Soviet occupation. Afghanistan: Politics, Elections, and Government Performance Congressional Research Service 11 Several of Karzai's supporters in parliament are from Kandahar, Karzai's home province, and from Helmand province. For example, one pro-Karzai Pashtun who was reelected in the 2010 elections is former militia leader Hazrat Ali (Nangarhar Province), who led the Afghan component of the failed assault on Osama bin Laden's purported redoubt at Tora Bora in December 2001. On the other hand, the 2010 elections resulted in the loss in parliament of Karzai cousin Jamil

Karzai, and Pacha Khan Zadran (Paktia) who, by some accounts, helped Osama bin Laden escape Tora Bora. A key Karzai brother, discussed further below, is Ahmad Wali Karzai (chair of the Qandahar provincial council), who was assassinated on July 12, 2011. Karzai Support Significant in the Upper House Karzai has relatively fewer critics in the 102-seat Meshrano Jirga (House of Elder, upper house),partly because of his bloc of 34 appointments (one-third of that body). In 2005, he engineered the appointment of an ally as speaker: Sibghatullah Mojadeddi, a noted Islamic scholar and former mujahedin party leader (Afghanistan National Liberation Front, ANLF), who headed the postCommunist mujahedin government for one month (May 1992). Mojadeddi resigned in February 2010 and was replaced by another Karzai ally, then deputy speaker Fazl Hadi Muslim Yaar. Karzai also has used his bloc of appointments to the upper house to co-opt potential antagonists or reward his friends. In 2006, he appointed Northern Alliance military leader Muhammad Fahim to the upper body, perhaps to compensate for his removal as defense minister, although he resigned after a few months and later joined the UF. (He was Karzai's primary running mate in the 2009 elections and is now first vice president.) In 2006, Karzai also named a key ally, former Helmand Governor Sher Mohammad Akhunzadeh, to the body. Because it is composed of more elderly, established, notable Afghans who are traditionalist in their political outlook, the Meshrano Jirga has tended to be more Islamist conservative than the lower house, advocating a legal system that accords with Islamic law, and restrictions on press and Westernized media broadcasts. Karzai was scheduled to make his 34 new upper house appointments (five year terms) prior to the January 26, 2011, seating of the 2011-2015 parliament. However, Karzai delayed naming his choices while the 2010 election remained in dispute. Because two-thirds of the body serve fouryear terms—and the provincial councils that were elected in 2009 were able to appoint their 68 members of the upper house—the body continued to operate even though Karzai had not submitted his 34 appointments. On January 27, 2011, the body reaffirmed Muslim Yaar as upper house speaker. On February 19, 2011, Karzai made his 34 selections, reappointing 18 incumbents and appointing 16 new members to the body. In line with the constitution, 17 of Karzai's appointments are women. Afghanistan: Politics, Elections, and Government Performance Congressional Research Service 12 Hamid Karzai, President of the Islamic Republic of Afghanistan Hamid Karzai, born December 24, 1957, was selected to lead Afghanistan at the Bonn Conference because he was a prominent Pashtun leader who had been involved in Taliban-era political talks among exiled Afghans and was viewed as a compromiser rather than a "strongman." However, some observers consider his compromises as Afghanistan's leader a sign of weakness and criticize him for indulging members of his clan and other allies with appointments. His term expires in 2014 and he is constitutionally barred from running again; he told parliamentarians in August 2011 that he would abide by the constitutional requirement to step down at that time. From Karz village in Qandahar Province, Karzai has led the powerful Popolzai tribe of Durrani Pashtuns since 1999, when his father was assassinated, allegedly by Taliban agents, in Quetta, Pakistan. Karzai's grandfather was head of the consultative National Council during puppet King Zahir Shah's reign. He attended university in India and supported the mujahideen party of Sibghatullah Mojadeddi (still a very close ally) during the anti-Soviet war. He was deputy foreign minister in the mujahidin government of Rabbani during 1992-1995, but he left the government and supported the Taliban as a Pashtun alternative to Rabbani. He broke with the Taliban as its excessesunfolded and forged alliances with other anti-Taliban factions, including the Northern Alliance. Karzai entered Afghanistan after the September 11 attacks to organize Pashtun resistance to the Taliban, supported by U.S. Special Forces. He became central to U.S. efforts after Pashtun commander Abdul Haq entered Afghanistan in October 2001 without U.S. support and was captured and hung by the Taliban. Karzai was slightly injured by an errant U.S. bomb in late 2001. With heavy protection, Karzai has survived several assassination attempts since taking office, including rocket fire or gunfire at or near his appearances. His wife, Dr. Zenat Karzai, is a gynecologist by profession. They have a son, Mirwais, born in 2008. Family Dealings Controversy has surrounded his siblings for allegedly profiting from Karza'is presidency. His half brother, Ahmad Wali Karzai, was the most powerful political figure in Qandahar Province until his assassination on July 12, 2011. He was key to President Karzai's information network in Qandahar. Ahmad Wali was widely accused of involvement in or tolerating narcotics trafficking, but reportedly also was a paid informant for the CIA; some of his property has been used by U.S. Special Forces. After Ahmad Wali's death, Karzai appointed another brother, Shah Wali Karzai, as Popolzai chief, and he reputedly has become involved in business dealings in Qandahar that have run him afoul of another brother, Mahmoud Karzai. Mahmoud is reportedly under U.S. Justice Department investigation for alleged corruption. He has wide business interests in Qandahar and Kabul, including auto dealerships, a coal mine, a cement factory, apartment houses, and a stake in Kabul Bank, which nearly collapsed in September 2010. Another brother, Qayyum Karzai, served in parliament during 2005-2008 but resigned in October 2008 for health reasons. He has reportedly been involved in negotiations with Taliban figures on a political settlement. Other Karzai relatives have profited extensively from international contracts, including a $2.2 billion U.S. "Host Nation Trucking" contract. The United States banned contracts to one such firm, Watan Risk Management, as of January 6, 2011; the firm is coowned by two Karzai relatives—Rashid and Rateb Popal. The Popal brothers reorganized the company as Watan Group and this firm is the local partner of China National Petroleum Company on a $3 billion investment, awarded in 2012, to develop oil fields in northern Afghanistan. U.S.-Karzai Relations Karzai has periodically lashed out at what he sees as U.S. and international pressure on him to reduce corruption and ensure electoral fairness. On April 4, 2010, Karzai suggested that Western meddling in Afghanistan was fueling support for the Taliban as a legitimate resistance to foreign occupation.7 In October 2011, Karzai said that Afghanistan would side with Pakistan in the event of a war between Pakistan and the United States. Karzai has criticized U.S. military night raids, airstrikes, control of detention policies, and U.S. negotiations with Taliban representatives that bypass the Afghan government, although U.S. policy on many of these issues have often adjusted toward Karzai's views. At each downturn in the relationship, top Administration officials have sought to restore the relationship by reassuring Karzai of U.S. support—a main example of which is the May 1, 2012, Strategic Partnership Agreement.8 An exact English translation of his April 4 comments, in which he purportedly said that even he might consider joining the Taliban if U.S. pressure on him continues, is not available. 8 Dreazen, Yochi, and Sarah Lynch. "U.S. Seeks to Repair Karzai Tie." Wall Street Journal, April 12, 2010. Afghanistan: Politics, Elections, and Government Performance Congressional Research Service 13 The Opposition: The "Northern Alliance," Dr. Abdullah, and Karzai Opponents in the Lower House of Parliament Broadly, the political opposition to Karzai (putting aside insurgents) consists mainly of ethnic minorities (Tajik, Uzbek, and Hazara) who fought the Taliban in a politico-military coalition called the "Northern Alliance." Tajik leaders formed the core of the Northern Alliance, and the Tajiks were centered around the legendary Tajik mujahedin commander Ahmad Shah Masoud. Members of the Northern Alliance are generally defined by their association with him. Some refer to all Tajik members of the Alliance as "Panjshiris" because many of them are, like Masoud, from the Panjshir Valley north of Kabul. (Masoud, who became legendary for preventing Soviet occupation forces from conquering the Panjshir Valley, was killed by Al Qaeda supporters two days before the September 11 attacks on the United States, possibly in conjunction with that plot.) Many of these Tajik leaders belonged to the Jamiat Islami (Islamic Society) political party, whose leader was Burhanuddin Rabbani (assassinated September 20, 2011, as discussed throughout). As such, Rabbani was technically Masoud's political leader although Masoud was generally perceived as having a larger following than Rabbani, who was from Badakshan Province (not the Panjshir Valley). Rabbani served as president during the mujahedin government (1992-1996), and served briefly again as Afghanistan's leader during November-December 2001, before Karzai was inaugurated as interim leader. Since the constitution was adopted in 2004, leaders of the Northern Alliance have long advocated amending it to give more power to parliament and to empower the elected provincial councils (instead of the president) to select governors and mayors. Such steps would ensure maximum autonomy from Kabul for non-Pashtun areas, and serve as a check and balance on Pashtun dominance of the central government. The leaders of these factions tend to be vehemently anti Pakistan, which they see as supporting Taliban and other insurgent groups to broaden their influence in future Afghan governments. In the 112th Congress, legislation introduced October 5, 2011, by Representative Dana Rohrabacher appears to support the Northern Alliance view of decentralized governance by urging that it be U.S. policy to support a decentralized, federal political system that "shifts more power to regions, provinces, and districts and away from a corrupt presidency" and support constitutional reform that provides for election of mayors, police chiefs, and governors. On the other hand, the Northern Alliance figures and their allies have differences among themselves that has rendered them relatively ineffective as an opposition to Karzai. Many "opposition" figures have often joined Karzai's government in exchange for autonomy or a share of business interests. Examples include Vice President Muhammad Fahim and Balkh Governor Atta Mohammad Noor. A key Tajik figure, Bismillah Khan Mohammedi, was chief of staff of the Afghan National Army during 2001-2010 and was made interior minister in 2010; he is said to have appointed Tajik protégés to key positions in the security forces. (As noted above, Mohammedi was ousted by the National Assembly on August 4, 2012, and a replacement is being sought.) Other Northern Alliance figures have worked with Karzai on certain issues—a prominent example was former President Rabbani. He agreed in October 2010 to assume the chairmanship of the 70-member High Peace Council—the body that is leading Karzai's effort to reconcile with insurgent leaders. Rabbani's September 20, 2011, assassination by an alleged Taliban operative widened the rift between Karzai and the Northern Alliance adherents who believe that Karzai's Afghanistan: Politics, Elections, and Government Performance Congressional Research Service 14 outreach to the Taliban has proved naïve and counterproductive. Rabbani's son, Salahuddin, succeeded him. Some suspect the core Northern Alliance concern is that reconciliation will bring additional Pashtuns into government, increasing the Pashtun dominance of government, or that the Taliban will be given control of areas that are at least partly inhabited by members of non Pashtun minorities. Still, the Karzai strategy of giving high-level appointments to his critics has, to date, proved successful in keeping his opposition divided and off balance. The Opposition Movements Led by Dr. AbdullahAlthough Rabbani was the elder statesman of the Northern Alliance, he was largely displaced in recent years by harder line Tajiks such as the overall "leader of the opposition"— former Foreign Minister Dr. Abdullah Abdullah. Abdullah is about 53 years old; his mother is Tajik and father is Pashtun but his identity as the foreign envoy of Ahmad Shah Masoud causes him to be identified politically as a Tajik. He was dismissed from his foreign minister post by Karzai in a March 2006 cabinet reshuffle and he now heads a private foundation named after Ahmad Shah Masoud. Dr. Abdullah emerged as Afghanistan's opposition leader after his unsuccessful challenge against Karzai for president in the August 2009 election in which widespread fraud was demonstrated. He is not in parliament but he works to promote his agenda—the cornerstone of which is to establish a parliamentary system in which the National Assembly would select a powerful prime minister—through public statements, in direct meetings with Karzai, and through allies in the lower house, as discussed below. He visited Washington, DC, one week after Karzai's May 10-14, 2010, visit, criticizing Karzai's governance at various think tanks and in a meeting with the State Department. He visited Washington, DC, again in April 2011 and held several meetings with the Obama Administration, while using several think-tank appearances to criticize Afghan governance under Karzai. Dr. Abdullah's representatives have said he is likely to run for president again in 2014.

The pro-Abdullah/anti-Karzai bloc in parliament has gone through several iterations. During 2007-2009, the bloc called itself the United Front (UF), although some accounts refer to it as the "National Front" or "United National Front." It was formed in April 2007 by then Wolesi Jirga speaker Yunus Qanooni (former adviser to Ahmad Shah Masoud and Northern Alliance stalwart; he was Karzai's main challenger in the 2004 presidential election) and the late former Afghan President Burhanuddin Rabbani. The United Front included some Pashtuns, such as Sovietoccupation era security figures Sayed Muhammad Gulabzoi and Nur ul-Haq Ulumi, head of the National United Party. Ulumi was not reelected to parliament in 2010. The United Front bloc underwent changes during 2009-2010 as Abdullah emerged as a national opposition figure, while other Northern Alliance figures reached accommodations with Karzai. In late May 2010, Abdullah created a formal, national democratic opposition party called the "Hope and Change Movement." Running in the September 18, 2010, elections under that name, Abdullah supporters sought to increase their numbers in the new Assembly and hold a commanding position that would enable them to block Karzai initiatives or achieve passage of its own alternative proposals. The 2010 elections results suggest this objective was not achieved, and the number of Abdullah supporters is roughly the same as it was in the previous Assembly—about 60 supporters. This is also a bloc similar in size to Karzai's core support base. On December 22, 2011, 10 political parties launched the National Coalition of Afghanistan, under the leadership of Dr. Abdullah. Afghanistan: Politics, Elections, and Government Performance Congressional Research Service 15 Schisms Within the Northern Alliance Grouping Some Tajik and other figures outside the Assembly are, if not challenging Abdullah for opposition leadership, at least emerging as strong voices. In June 2011, several key Northern Alliance leaders, including Dostam and Hazara figure Mohammad Mohaqiq (see below) joined with former Vice President Ahmad Zia Masoud (Ahmad Shah Masoud's brother) to announce a new opposition group—the National Front of Afghanistan. This group advocates "federalism"—a high degree of autonomy for Afghan provinces, including appointment of provincial governors by elected provincial councils. This differs from Dr. Abdullah's platform of pressing for a parliamentary system. The National Front grouping also is more skeptical of a peace agreement with the Taliban than is Dr. Abdullah and his allies. Even before this new opposition was formed, Ahmad Zia Masoud, as well as ousted intelligence leader Amrollah Saleh (see below), were increasingly outspoken against a potential settlement with the Taliban. New Opposition Groupings Form Truth and Justice Party. On November 4, 2011, a new party, the Truth and Justice Party, launched itself as a self-proclaimed reformist party consisting of leaders of all of Afghanistan's various ethnicities. Unlike the coalition led by Dr. Abdullah, this party is in favor of reconciliation with the Taliban. Major figures behind it include Karzai's previous Interior Minister Mohammad Hanif Atmar, who was dismissed by Karzai in 2010, as well as Uzbek leader Abdul Rashid Dostam and Afghanistan Independent Human Rights Commission (AIHRC) Chairwoman Sima Simar, an ethnic Hazara. Taliban era Deputy Justice Minister Jalaluddin Shinwari joined the party as well. The Informal Power Structure: Other Power Brokers, "Warlords," and Local Faction Leaders An informal power structure exists outside the formal governing institutions. Karzai has been compelled to work with this informal power structure of well-funded, locally popular, and sometimes well-armed faction leaders, even while heading the formal power structure. Some faction leaders operate in both spheres—holding official positions through constitutional processes while also exercising influence their home provinces—beyond these formal roles. Some are Northern Alliance figures and others are Pashtun faction leaders. Some of these faction leaders—most of whom the United States and its partners regularly deal with and have good working relations with—cause resentment among some sectors of the population—particularly emerging civil society activists—and complicate U.S. stabilization strategy. A number of them own or have investments in Afghan security or other firms that have won business from U.S. and other donors and fuel allegations of nepotism and other corruption. Still others argue that U.S. policy since 2007 has further empowered local faction leaders or even created new factions and militias that never existed before. A variety of expedient local security initiatives undertaken since 2007, including the Afghan Public Protection Program, its successor the Afghan Local Police Program, Village Stability Operations, and the Critical Infrastructure Police, have created new security organs that sometimes operate without full control by central security organs. These programs are said by critics to have revived the militia concept that was being dismantled by the international community during 2001-2006. Partly because of accusations against these irregular forces created by the United States/NATO, in December 2011 Karzai said Afghanistan would dismantle one of them: the Critical Infrastructure Police, which was created by the Germany-led Regional Command North and was mostly composed of non-Afghanistan: Politics, Elections, and Government Performance Congressional Research Service 16 Pashtun minorities. No Afghan government action was taken against the other forces mentioned, which are mostly Pashtun. Some Afghans (particularly the Northern Alliance) believe that the international community's original strategy of dismantling local power structures in favor of a monopoly of central government control over armed force has caused the security deterioration noted since 2006. Some assert that the Obama Administration's criticism of Karzai has caused him to become ever more reliant on factional power brokers. Karzai's position is that confronting faction leaders outright would likely cause their followers—who usually belong to ethnic or regional minorities—to go into armed rebellion. Karzai has long argued that keeping the faction leaders on the government side is needed in order to keep the focus on combating the Taliban, who are almost all ethnic Pashtuns. In February 2007, both houses of parliament passed a law (officially titled the National Reconciliation, General Amnesty, and National Stability Law) giving amnesty to faction leaders and others who committed abuses during Afghanistan's past wars. Karzai sent back to parliament an altered draft to give victims the right to seek justice for any abuses. Even though the revised draft contained that amendment, Karzai did not sign the final version in May 2007, leaving the status unclear. However, in December 2009, the Afghan government published the law in the official gazette (a process known as "gazetting"), giving it the force of law. The following sections analyze some of the main faction leaders. Vice President Muhammad Fahim Karzai's choice of Northern Alliance figure Muhammad Fahim as his first vice presidential running mate in the August 2009 elections might have been a manifestation of Karzai's growing reliance on faction leaders, as well as his drive to divide the Northern Alliance. Fahim is a Tajik from the Panjshir Valley region who was named military chief of the Northern Alliance/UF faction after Ahmad Shah Masoud's death. The Fahim choice was criticized by human rights and other groups because of Fahim's long identity as a mujahedin commander/militia faction leader. A Times story of August 27, 2009, said that the Bush Administration continued to deal with Fahim when he was defense minister (2001-2004) despite reports that he was involved in facilitating narcotics trafficking in northern Afghanistan. Other allegations suggest he has engineered property confiscations and other benefits to feed his and his faction's business interests. During 2002-2007, he reportedly withheld turning over some heavy weapons to U.N. disarmament officials who have been trying to reduce the influence of local strongmen such as Fahim. Obama Administration officials have not announced any limitations on dealings with Fahim now that he is vice president. In August 2010, Fahim underwent treatment in Germany for a heart ailment. Fahim's brother, Abdul Hussain Fahim, was a beneficiary of concessional loans from Kabul Bank, a major bank that has faced major losses due to its lending practices, as discussed below. The Fahim brother is also reportedly partnered with Mahmoud Karzai on coal mining and cement manufacturing ventures. Afghanistan: Politics, Elections, and Government Performance Congressional Research Service 17 Abdul Rashid Dostam: Uzbeks of Northern Afghanistan Some observers have cited Karzai's handling of prominent Uzbek leader Abdul Rashid Dostam—the longtime head of a party called Junbush Melli (National Front) as inconsistent. Dostam, generally aligned with the Tajiks and part of the Northern Alliance, commands numerous partisans in his redoubt in northern Afghanistan (Jowzjan, Faryab, Balkh, and Sar-I-Pol provinces). There, during the Soviet and Taliban years, he was widely accused of human rights abuses of political opponents. To try to separate him from his armed followers, in 2005 Karzai appointed him to the post of chief of staff of the armed forces. On February 4, 2008, Afghan police surrounded Dostam's villa in Kabul in response to reports that he attacked an ethnic Turkmen rival, but Karzai did not order his arrest for fear of stirring unrest among Dostam's followers. To try to resolve the issue without stirring unrest, in December 2008 Karzai purportedly reached an agreement with Dostam under which he resigned as chief of staff and went into exile in Turkey in exchange for the dropping of any case against him.9Dostam returned to Afghanistan on August 16, 2009, and subsequently held a large pro-Karzai election rally in his home city of Shebergan. Part of his intent in supporting Karzai was to limit the influence of a strong rival figure in the north, Balkh Province Governor Atta Mohammad Noor, see below. Noor is a Tajik but, under a 2005 compromise with Karzai, is in control of a province that is inhabited by many Uzbeks. Dostam's support apparently helped Karzai carry several provinces in the north in the 2009 election, including Jowzjan, Sar-i-Pol, and Faryab. In January 2010, he was restored to his previous, primarily honorary, position of chief of staff of the armed forces. Although Dostam was not nominated to a cabinet post in 2010, two members of his Junbush Melli party were—although they were voted down by the National Assembly because the Assembly did not want to confirm partisan activists in the cabinet. Dostam's failure to secure posts for his allies could account for his decision to join the opposition grouping formed in June 2011, discussed above. In June 2012, the Karzai government launched a prosecution of Dostam for allegedly insisting the China National Petroleum Co. (CNPC) hire Dostam loyalists to security and other jobs on their oil development project in northern Afghanistan. However, Dostam and those close to him alleged that the prosecution was a Karzai effort to favor his relatives' firm, Watan Group, which is the partner of CNPC on the project and which is therefore in line to provide security and other services to the development. Dostam continues to alternate his time between Afghanistan and Turkey; he is said to be suffering from health problems. Dostam's reputation is further clouded by his actions during the U.S.-backed war against the Taliban. On July 11, 2009, the New York Times reported that allegations that Dostam had caused the death of several hundred Taliban prisoners during the major combat phase of OEF (late 2001) were not investigated by the Bush Administration. In responding to assertions that there was no investigation of the Dasht-e-Laili massacre because Dostam was a U.S. ally,10 President Obama said any allegations of violations of laws of war need to be investigated. Dostam responded to Radio Free Europe/Radio Liberty (which carried the story) that only 200 Taliban prisoners died and primarily because of combat and disease, not intentional actions of his forces. 9 CRS e-mail conversation with a then National Security aide to President Karzai, December 2008. 10 This is the name of the area where the Taliban prisoners purportedly died and were buried in a mass grave. Afghanistan: Politics, Elections, and Government Performance Congressional Research Service 18 Atta Mohammad Noor: Balkh Province Atta Mohammad Noor, another figure generally considered part of the Northern Alliance, has been the governor of Balkh Province, whose capital is the vibrant city of Mazar-e-Sharif, since 2005. Mazar-e-Sharif is one of the four cities to be transitioned to Afghan security leadership in June 2011. It is unique in that 60% of the residents of the city have access to electricity 24 hours per day, a far higher percentage than most other cities in Afghanistan, and higher even than Kabul. He is an ethnic Tajik and former mujahedin commander who openly endorsed Dr. Abdullah in the 2009 presidential election. However, Karzai has kept Noor in place because he has kept the province secure, allowing Mazar-e-Sharif to become a major trading hub, and because displacing him could cause ethnic unrest. Observers say that Noor exemplifies the local potentate, brokering local security and business arrangements that enrich Noor and his allies while ensuring stability and prosperity.11 Some reports say that he commands two private militias in the province that, in at least two districts (Chimtal and Charbolak), outnumber official Afghan police, and which prompt complaints of abuses (land seizures) by the province's Pashtuns. Mohammed Mohaqiq: Hazara Stalwart Another faction leader is Mohammad Mohaqiq, a Hazara leader. During the war against the Soviet Union and then Taliban, Mohaqiq was a commander of Hazara fighters in and around Bamiyan Province, and a major figure in the Hazara Islamist party Hezb-e-Wahdat (Unity Party). The party was supported by Iran during those periods. Currently, Mohaqiq is aligned with Dostam and hardline Tajik figures. He joined these figures in forming the National Front of Afghanistan in June 2011. In July 2012, Mohaqiq demanded Karzai fire the head of the Academy of Sciences for publishing a new national almanac that Mohaqiq said overstated the percentage of Pashtuns in Afghanistan at 60%. Karzai fired the Academy head and three others at that institution. Another major Hazara figure, Karim Khalili, tends to work with Karzai and has served as his second vice president through Karzai's two terms as president. Isma'il Khan: Western Afghanistan/Herat Another Northern Alliance strongman that Karzai has sought to simultaneously engage and weaken is prominent Tajik political leader and former Herat Governor Ismail Khan. Herat is one of the four cities that was transitioned to Afghan security leadership in July 2011. In 2006, Karzai appointed him minister of energy and water, taking him away from his political base in the west. However, Khan remains influential in the west, and maintaining ties to Khan helped Karzai win Tajik votes in Herat Province that might otherwise have gone to Dr. Abdullah. Certified results showed Karzai winning that province, indicating that the deal with Khan was helpful to Karzai. Still, Khan is said to have several opponents in Herat, and a bombing there on September 26, 2009, narrowly missed his car. U.S. officials purportedly preferred that Khan not be in the cabinet because of his record as a local potentate, although some U.S. officials credit him with cooperating with the privatization of the power sector of Afghanistan. Karzai renominated Khan in his ministry post on December 19, 2009, causing purported disappointment by parliamentarians and western donor countries who want Khan and other faction leaders weakened. His renomination was voted down by the National Assembly but he remains in an acting capacity. Additional questions about Khan were raised in November 2010 when Afghan television broadcast audio files purporting to contain Khan insisting that election officials alter the results of the September 18, 2010, parliamentary elections.12 Khan is on the High Peace Council that is the main body overseeing the reconciliation process with Taliban leaders. Helmand Province Power Brokers Karzai's relationship with a Pashtun strongman, Sher Mohammad Akhundzadeh, demonstrates the dilemmas facing Karzai in governing Afghanistan. Akhunzadeh was a close associate of Karzai when they were in exile in Quetta, Pakistan, during Taliban rule. Karzai appointed him governor of Helmand after the fall of the Taliban, but in 2005, Britain demanded he be removed for his abuses and reputed facilitation of drug trafficking, as a condition of Britain taking security control of Helmand. Karzai reportedly has sought to reappoint Akhundzadeh, who Karzai believes was more successful against militants in Helmand using his local militiamen than Britain has been with its more than 9,500 troops there. However, Britain and the United States have prevailed on Karzai not to remove the current governor, Ghulab Mangal, who has won wide praise for his successes establishing effective governance in Helmand (discussed further under "Expanding Local (Subnational) Governance") and for reducing poppy cultivation there. Akhunzadeh attempted to deliver large numbers of votes for Karzai in Helmand, although turnout in that province was very light partly due to Taliban intimidation of voters. An Akhunzadeh ally, Abdul Wali Khan (nicknamed "Koka"), was similarly removed by British pressure in 2006 as police chief of Musa Qala district of Helmand. However, the Afghan government insisted on—and obtained—his reinstatement a few years later and his militia followers subsequently became the core of the 220-person police force in the district. Koka is mentioned in a congressional report as accepting payments from security contractors who are working under the U.S. Department of Defense's (DOD's) "Host National Trucking" contract that secures U.S. equipment convoys. Koka allegedly agreed to secure the convoys in exchange for the payments. 13 Karzai Family: Kandahar Province Governing Kandahar, a province of about 2 million, of whom about half live in Qandahar city, is a sensitive issue in Kabul because of President Karzai's active political interest in his home province. Kandahar governance is particularly crucial to ongoing U.S. military-led operations to increase security in surrounding districts, giving the July 12, 2011, assassination of Karzai's half brother, Ahmad Wali Karzai, crucial significance. Ahmad Wali was chair of the Kandahar provincial council, a post with relatively limited formal power, but he was always more powerful than any appointed governor of Kandahar. President Karzai frequently rotated the governors of Qandahar to ensure that none of them would impinge on Ahmad Wali's authority. Perceiving him as the key power broker in the province, many 12 Partlow, Joshua, "Audio Files Raise New Questions About Afghan Elections." Washington Post, November 11, 2010. 13 House of Representatives. Subcommittee on National Security and Foreign Affairs, Committee on Oversight and Government Reform. "Warlord, Inc.: Extortion and Corruption Along the U.S. Supply Chain in Afghanistan." Report of the Majority Staff, June 2010. Afghanistan: Politics, Elections, and Government Performance Congressional Research Service 20 constituents and interest groups met him each day to request his interventions on their behalf. Kandahar governance suffered an additional blow on July 27, 2011, when the appointed mayor of Kandahar city, Ghulam Haider Hamidi, was assassinated. Hamidi was an Afghan American accountant by training. Before Ahmad Wali's assassination, U.S. officials had been trying to bolster the clout of the appointed Kandahar governor, Tooryalai Wesa by supporting Wesa's efforts to equitably distribute development funds and build local governing structures. 14 Karzai had appointed Wesa—a Canadian-Afghan academic—in December 2008, perhaps hoping that his ties to Canada would convince Canada to continue its mission in Qandahar beyond 2011. That did not succeed. The international community expected, and hoped, that the death of Ahmad Wali Karzai would further empower Governor Wesa. However, Karzai quickly installed another of his brothers, Shah Wali Karzai, as head of the Popolzai clan and informal Qandahar power broker after Ahmad Wali's death. Shah Wali at first lacked the acumen and clout of Ahmad Wali, but reports in mid- 2012 say he has become highly influential, while also becoming involved in significant business dealings in the province that continue to cast aspersions on the motives and actions of the Karzai family. Karzai has also used former Qandahar governor Asadullah Khalid (confirmed in September 2012 as the new intelligence director, as discussed below) as an informal envoy in the province. Another power center is Kandahar's police chief, Colonel Abdul Razziq. He is perceived as having increasing weight, as well as a reputation for corruption, including siphoning off customs revenues at the key Spin Boldak crossing. He was appointed to his current post in March 2011 when his predecessor was killed in an insurgent attack. Razziq's convoy was attacked in September 2012, and he was injured, but not severely. Ghul Agha Shirzai: Eastern Afghanistan Nangarhar A key gubernatorial appointment has been Ghul Agha Shirzai as governor of Nangarhar. He is a Pashtun from the powerful Barakzai clan based in

Kandahar Province, previously serving as governor of that province, where he reportedly continued to exercise influence in competition with Ahmad Wali Karzai. Ahmad Wali Karzai's death on July 12, 2011, could prompt Sherzai and his allies to assert themselves in the province, possibly by trying to convince Karzai to make him Kandahar governor again. In Nangarhar, Sherzai is generally viewed as an interloper. But, much as has Noor in Balkh, Shirzai has exercised effective leadership, particularly in curbing poppy cultivation there. At the same time, Shirzai is also widely accused of arbitrary action against political or other opponents, and he reportedly does not remit all the customs duties collected at the Khyber Pass Torkham crossing to the central government. He purportedly uses the funds for the benefit of the province, not trusting that funds remitted to Kabul would be spent in the province. As noted above, Shirzai had considered running against Karzai in 2009 but then opted not to run as part of a reported "deal" that yielded unspecified political and other benefits for Shirzai. 14 Partlow, Joshua, "U.S. Seeks to Bolster Kandahar Governor, Upend Power Balance," Washington Post, April 29, 2010. Afghanistan: Politics, Elections, and Government Performance Congressional Research Service 21 Emerging Power Centers: Civil Society and "Independent" Activists Another interest group has emerged since the fall of the Taliban—a product of Afghanistan's increasing modernity and the effect of international policies to promote democracy and human rights. Civil society activists and "independents" in the National Assembly and other institutions are a growing force in Afghan politics. They are generally intellectuals, businessmen, and women's activists who have become more prominent and outspoken since the ousting of the Taliban regime, with easy access to media outlets. However, although they are articulate and backed by some democracy-oriented international NGOs, these civil society leaders have struggled against traditional faction leaders to exert influence over policy. U.S.-based International Republican Institute (IRI) has helped train the independents in the National Assembly; the National Democratic Institute (NDI) has assisted the more established factions. Of the independents that were present in the 2005-2010 parliament, one, the 45-year-old Malalai Joya (Farah Province), was a leading critic of war-era faction leaders. In May 2007 the lower house voted to suspend her for this criticism for the duration of her term and she did not seek reelection in 2010. Ms. Fawzia Koofi, a one time a deputy lower house speaker and declared presidential candidate for 2014, also remains in the Assembly and an outspoken leader on Afghan women's rights. Others in this independent camp have included Ms. Fauzia Gailani (Herat Province, not returned to parliament); Ms. Shukria Barekzai, chairwoman of the lower house Defense Committee during 2011; and Mr. Ramazan Bashardost, a former Karzai minister who champions parliamentary powers and has established a "complaints tent" near the parliament building to highlight and combat official corruption. (He ran for president in the 2009 elections on an anti-corruption platform and drew an unexpectedly large amount of votes.) Bashardost was returned to parliament in the September 2010 election and may run again in 2014. Some other leading independents are present in the 2011-2015 lower house. They include Rafiq Shahir from Herat, a well-known civil-society activist; Dr. Saleh Seljuki; and Ahmad Behzad (all from Herat). Other independents reelected include Shakiba Hashemi and Khalid Pashtun, both from Kandahar. Ethnic and Factional Cooperation in the Security Sector The security organs are considered an arena where Pashtuns, Tajiks, and others, of all factional affiliations, have worked together relatively well. The National Directorate for Security (NDS, the intelligence directorate) was headed by a non-Pashtun (Amrollah Saleh, a Tajik) during 2006-2010, although he was dismissed on June 6, 2010, by Karzai for disagreements over whether and how to engage insurgent leaders in political settlement negotiations. He was replaced by a Pashtun, Rehmat Nabil, who had no previous intelligence experience but is perceived as more consultative than was Saleh. Still, he inherited a service dominated by Tajiks (although some left when Saleh was ousted) and by a mix of personnel that served during the Soviet occupation era Afghanistan: Politics,

Elections, and Government Performance Congressional Research Service 22 (the service was then called Khad), and in the mujahedin government of 1992-1996. During 2002-2007, the Central Intelligence Agency reportedly paid for all of the NDS budget.15 Perhaps to preserve the tradition of ethnic balance in the security sector of government, the chief of staff of the Afghan National Army, Bismillah Khan Mohmmadi, was named interior minister on June 26, 2010. He replaced Mohammad Hanif Atmar, a Pashtun, who was fired the same day and on roughly the same grounds as Saleh By all accounts, Khan is widely respected, even among Pashtuns. The security ministries tend to have key deputies who are of a different ethnicity than the minister or top official. As noted above, Khan, as well as Defense Minister Wardak, was removed by the National Assembly on August 4, 2012. Some observers assert that Tajiks continue to control many of the command ranks of the Afghan security institutions, giving Pashtuns only a veneer of control of these organizations. U.S. commanders in Afghanistan say the composition of the national security forces—primarily the Afghan National Army and Afghan National Police—has been brought broadly into line with the population. However, Pashtuns from the south (Durranis) remain underrepresented, in part because of the fears that insurgents might target their relatives if they join the security forces. Many of the Pashtuns in the security forces are from the Jalalabad area and are of the Ghilzai Pashtun tribal confederation that is prevalent there and elsewhere in the east. New Security Chiefs Appointed in September 2012 On September 3, Karzai nominated (1) Bismillah Khan Mohammedi, a prominent Tajik, to become Defense Minister; (2) Gen. Ghulam Mujtaba Patang, a Pashtun, to be Interior Minister; (3) Minister of Tribal and Border Affairs Asadullah Khalid, also a Pashtun, to switch posts and become head of the National Directorate of Security (intelligence directorate); and (4) Azizullah Din Mohammad to take over Khalid's ministry. Some expected the National Assembly to vote down Bismillah Khan because the Assembly had ousted him from the Interior Minister post only one month earlier. Asadullah Khalid's confirmation was similarly in doubt because of allegations he backed torture of prisoners as governor of Kandahar province. Since leaving that office in 2008, Khalid had emerged as a powerful intermediary for Karzai, particularly as an informal envoy in Kandahar following the 2011 assassination of Karzai's brother Ahmad Wali. And Khalid has good relations with the Northern Alliance grouping, boosting his political support in the National Assembly. Patang, a longtime police official, most recently has headed the Afghan Public Protection Force, which is taking over security for diplomats and development projects from private security forces, but has been slow to develop. Despite the concerns above, on September 16, 2012, the National Assembly approved all three security posts overwhelmingly, but voted down Din Mohammad. The approvals retained the rough factional balance in the security sector. Patang's confirmation represents the appointment of the first professional police officer to rise to the post of Interior Minister. 15 Filkins, Dexter, and Mark Mazzetti. "Key Karzai Aide in Graft Inquiry is Linked to C.I.A." New York Times, August 26, 2010. Afghanistan: Politics, Elections, and Government Performance Congressional Research Service 23 Elections in 2009 and 2010 Widened Political Schisms Elections are widely considered a key harbinger of the durability and extent of Afghanistan's political development—and a barometer of the degree to which factional, political, ethnic, and sectarian rivalries can be reduced. The 2009 presidential and provincial elections were the first post-Taliban elections run by the Afghan government itself in the form of the Afghanistan Independent Electoral Commission. Donors, including the United States, invested almost $500 million in 2009 to improve the capacity of the Afghan government to conduct the elections. 16- Both it and the September 2010 National Assembly elections were flawed, as discussed below, and widened rather than reduced differences between Karzai and his opponents. 2009 Presidential Election The 2009 election was plagued, from the start, by assertions of a lack of credibility of the Independent Elections Commission. Its commissioners, including then-Chairman Azizullah Ludin, were selected by, and many were politically close to, Karzai. As a check and balance to ensure electoral credibility, there was also a U.N.-appointed Elections Complaints Commission (ECC) that reviewed fraud complaints. Under the 2005 election law, there were three ECC seats for foreign nationals, appointed by the Special Representative of the U.N. Secretary General/head of U.N. Assistance Mission–Afghanistan, UNAMA. The two Afghans on the ECC governing council 17 were appointed by the Supreme Court and Afghanistan Independent Human Rights Commission, respectively. Disputes first erupted over the election date. On February 3, 2009, Afghanistan's Independent Election Commission (IEC) set August 20, 2009, as the election date (a change from a date mandated by Article 61 of the Constitution as April 21, 2009, in order to allow at least 30 days before Karzai's term expired on May 22, 2009). The IEC decision on the latter date cited Article 33 of the Constitution as mandating universal accessibility to the voting—and saying that the April 21 date was precluded by difficulties in registering voters, printing ballots, training staff, advertising the elections, and the dependence on international donor funding, in addition to the security questions. 18 His opponents (led by Dr. Abdullah) insisted that Karzai's presidency ended May 22, 2009, and that a caretaker government should run Afghanistan until elections. The IEC reaffirmed on March 4, 2009, that the election would be held on August 20, 2009. Karzai argued that the Constitution does not provide for any transfer of power other than in case of election or death of a president. The Afghan Supreme Court backed that decision on March 28, 2009, and the Obama Administration publicly backed these rulings. Election Modalities and Processes Despite the political dispute between Karzai and his opponents, enthusiasm among the public appeared high in the run-up to the election. Registration, which updated 2005 voter rolls, was conducted during October 2008-March 2009. About 4.5 million new voters registered, and about 17 million total Afghans were registered. However, there were widespread reports of registration 16 Report by the Special Inspector General for Afghanistan Reconstruction (SIGAR), September 9, 2010. 18 Statement of the Independent Election Commission Secretariat, February 3, 2009, provided to CRS by a Karzai national security aide. Afghanistan: Politics, Elections, and Government Performance Congressional Research Service 24 fraud (possibly half of all new registrants), with some voters registering on behalf of women who do not, by custom, show up at registration sites, and others selling registration cards. Presidential candidates filed to run during April 24—May 8, 2009. A total of 44 registered to run for president, of which three were disqualified for various reasons, leaving a field of 41 (later reduced to 32 after several dropped out). In the provincial elections, 3,200 people competed for 420 seats nationwide. Although about 80% of the provincial council candidates ran as independents, some of Afghanistan's parties, including Hezb-i-Islam, fielded multiple candidates in several different provinces. The provincial elections component of the election received little attention, in part because the role of these councils is unclear. About 200 women competed for the 124 seats reserved for women (29%) on the provincial councils, although in two provinces (Kandahar and Uruzgan) there were fewer women candidates than reserved seats. In Kabul Province, 524 candidates competed for the 29 seats of the council. The European Union, supported by the Organization for Security and Cooperation in Europe (OSCE) sent a few hundred observers, and the International Republican Institute and National Democratic Institute sent observers as well. About 8,000 Afghans assisted the observation missions, according to the U.N. Nations Development Program. Security was a major issue for all the international actors supporting the Afghan elections process, amid open Taliban threats against Afghans who vote. In the first round, about 7,000 polling centers were to be established (with each center having multiple polling places, totaling about 29,000), but, of those, about 800 were deemed too unsafe to open, most of them in restive Helmand and Kandahar provinces. A total of about 6,200 polling centers opened on election day. The total cost of the Afghan elections in 2009 were about $300 million. Other international donors contributing funds to close the gap left by the U.S. contribution of about $175 million. The Political Contest and Campaign The presidential competition took shape in May 2009. In the election-related deal-making,19 Karzai obtained an agreement from Fahim to run as his first vice presidential running mate. In doing so, Karzai showed the UF opposition grouping to be split. Karzai, Fahim, and incumbent second Vice President Karim Khalili (a Hazara) registered their ticket on May 4, 2009, just before Karzai left to visit the United States. Karzai convinced several prominent Pashtuns not to run, including Ghul Agha Shirzai, a member of the powerful Barakzai clan; and Anwar al-Haq Ahady, the former finance minister and Central Bank governor. Anti-Karzai Pashtuns failed to coalesce around one challenger, such as Former Interior Minister Ali Jalali and former Finance Minister (2002-2004) and then Karzai critic Ashraf Ghani. Ghani decided to run without Jalali or prominent representation from other ethnicities in his vice presidential slots. The UF had difficulty forging a united challenge to Karzai. Dr. Abdullah registered to run with UF backing. His running mates were Dr. Cheragh Ali Cheragh, a Hazara who did poorly in the 2004 election, and a little known Pashtun, Homayoun Wasefi. 19Some of the information in this section obtained in CRS interviews with a Karzai national security aide, December 2008. Afghanistan: Politics, Elections, and Government Performance Congressional Research Service 25 Karzai went into the election as a clear favorite, but the key question was whether he would win in the first round (more than 50% of the vote). Although Karzai was criticized for a campaign that relied on reaching out to traditional leaders, he did participate in at least one publicly broadcast debate (August 16, 2009, on state-run Radio Television-Afghanistan, RTA) with two of his rivals (Abdullah did not participate). Dr. Abdullah campaigned extensively in his key base in the north and west, which are populated mainly by Tajiks, but he did campaign in some Pashtun-dominated areas. Both Karzai and Abdullah held large rallies in Kabul and elsewhere. Ghani had spent much time in the United States and Europe and many average Afghans viewed him as out of touch. Focusing on urban voters, he made extensive use of the Internet for advertising and fundraising, and he was advised by James Carville. 20 A candidate who polled unexpectedly well was 56-year-old anti-corruption parliamentarian Ramazan Bashardost, an ethnic Hazara. He ran a low-budget campaign was appealed to reformminded Afghans outside his core Hazara base. However, Mohaqiq's backing (he was allied to Karzai at that time) apparently helped Karzai carry the Hazara heartland of Bamiyan province. The Election Results Taliban intimidation and voter apathy appear to have suppressed the total turnout to about 5.8 million votes cast, or about a 35% turnout, far lower than expected. Twenty-seven Afghans, mostly security forces personnel, were killed in election-day violence. Some observers said that turnout among women was primarily because there were not sufficient numbers of female poll workers to make women feel comfortable enough to vote. In general, however, election observers reported that poll workers were well trained, and the voting process was orderly. Clouding the election substantially were the widespread fraud allegations coming from all sides. Dr. Abdullah held several news conferences after the election, purporting to show evidence of systematic election fraud by the Karzai camp. The ECC, in statements, stated its belief that there was substantial fraud likely committed, mostly by Karzai supporters. The final, uncertified total was released on September 16, 2009, and showed Karzai at 54.6% and Dr. Abdullah at 27.7%. Bashardost and Ghani received single-digit vote counts (9% and 3% respectively). Vote Certified Runoff Mandated The constitution required that a second-round runoff, if needed, be held two weeks after the results of the first round are certified. Following the release of the vote count, the complaints evaluation period began which, upon completed, would yield a "certified" vote result. On September 8, 2009, the ECC ordered a recount of 10% of polling stations (accounting for as many as 25% total votes). Polling stations were considered "suspect" if the total number of votes exceeded the 600 maximum number allotted to each polling station; or where any candidate received 95% or more of the total valid votes cast at that station. Perhaps reflecting political sensitivities, the recount consisted of a sampling of actual votes. 20 Mulrine, Anna, "Afghan Presidential Candidate Takes a Page From Obama's Playbook," U.S. News and World Report, June 25, 2009. 21 "Afghan Panel to Use Sampling in Recount," USA Today, September 22, 2009. Afghanistan: Politics, Elections, and Government Performance Congressional Research Service 26 On October 20, 2009, the ECC determined, based on its investigation, that about 1 million Karzai votes, and about 200,000 Abdullah votes, were considered fraudulent and were deducted from their totals. The final, certified, results of the first round were as follows: Karzai—49.67% (according to the IEC; with a slightly lower total of about 48% according to the ECC determination); Abdullah—30.59%; Bashardost—10.46%; Ghani—2.94%; Yasini—1.03%; and lower figures for the remaining field. 22 During October 16-20, 2009, U.S. and international officials, including visiting Senator John Kerry, met with Karzai to attempt to persuade him to acknowledge that his vote did not exceed the 50%+ threshold needed for a first-round victory. On October 21, 2009, the IEC accepted the ECC findings and Karzai conceded the need for a runoff election. A date was set as November 7, 2009. Abdullah initially accepted. In an attempt to produce a fair second round, UNAMA, which provided advice and assistance to the IEC, requested that about 200 district-level election commissioners be replaced and that there be fewer polling stations—about 5,800, compared to 6,200 previously—to eliminate polling stations where very few votes were expected to be cast. Prior to the ECC vote certification, Dr. Abdullah told CRS at a meeting in Kabul on October 15, 2009, that he might be willing to negotiate with Karzai on a "Joint Program" of reforms—such as direct election of provincial governors—to avoid a runoff. However, some said the constitution does not provide for a negotiated settlement and that the runoff must proceed. Others said that a deal between the two, in which Abdullah dropped his candidacy, could have led the third-place finisher, Bashardost, to assert that he must face Karzai in a runoff. Still others say the issue could have necessitated resolution by Afghanistan's Supreme Court. The various pre-runoff scenarios were mooted on November 1, 2009, when Dr. Abdullah refused to participate in the runoff on the grounds that problems that plagued the first round were unresolved. Some believe Abdullah pulled out because he believed he would not prevail in the second round. On November 2, 2009, the IEC issued a statement saying that, by consensus, the body had determined that Karzai, being the only candidate remaining in a two-person runoff, should be declared the winner. The Obama Administration accepted the outcome as "within Afghanistan's constitution," on the grounds that the fraud had been investigated. The United States, U.N. Secretary General Ban Ki Moon (visiting Kabul), and several governments, congratulated Karzai. Secretary of State Clinton praised Dr. Abdullah for his relatively moderate speech announcing his pullout. However, the marred elections process was a major factor in a September-November 2009 high-level U.S. strategy reevaluation because of the centrality of a credible, legitimate partner Afghan government to U.S. strategy. 23 As noted above, the election for the provincial council members were not certified until December 29, 2009. The council members took office in February 2010. September 18, 2010, Parliamentary Elections The split over the conduct of the presidential elections widened in the run-up to the September 18, 2010, parliamentary elections. Mechanisms to prevent fraud were not fully implemented and the results continue to be disputed as of July 2011, largely paralyzing the institutional functioning of the Assembly and its role as a check and balance on the Karzai government. As a result, the 23 Fidler, Stephen and John W. Miller, "U.S. Allies Await Afghan Review," Wall Street Journal, September 25, 2009. Afghanistan: Politics, Elections, and Government Performance Congressional Research Service 27 political structure of Afghanistan has continued to fragment, even as the government assumers greater responsibility in the context of a transition to Afghan security leadership beginning in July 2011. The July 20, 2010, Kabul conference final communiqué included an Afghan government pledge to initiate, within six months, a strategy for long-term electoral reform. Election Timing On January 2, 2010, the IEC had initially set National Assembly elections for May 22, 2010. The IEC view was that this date was in line with a constitutional requirement for a new election to be held well prior to the expiry of the current Assembly's term. However, U.S., ECC, UNAMA, and officials of donor countries argued that Afghanistan's flawed institutions would not be able to hold free and fair elections under this timetable. Among the difficulties noted were that the IEC lacks sufficient staff, given that some were fired after the 2009 election; that the IEC lacks funds to hold the election under that timetable; that the U.S. military buildup will be consumed with securing still restive areas at election time; and that the ECC's term expired at the end of January 2010. A functioning ECC was needed to evaluate complaints against registered parliamentary candidates because there are provisions in the election law to invalidate the candidacies of those who have previously violated Afghan law or committed human rights abuses. The international community pressed for a delay of all of these elections until August 2010 or, according to some donors, mid-2011. 24 Bowing to funding and the wide range of other considerations mentioned, on January 24, 2010, the IEC announced that the parliamentary elections would be postponed until September 18, 2010. Other experts said that the security issues, and the lack of faith in Afghanistan's election institutions, necessitated further postponement. 25 About $120 million was budgeted by the IEC for the parliamentary elections, of which at least $50 million came from donor countries, giving donors leverage over when the election might take place. The remaining $70 million was funds left over from the 2009 elections. Donors had held back the needed funds, possibly in an effort to pressure the IEC to demonstrate that it is correcting the flaws identified in the various "after-action" reports on the 2009 election. With the compromises and Karzai announcements below, those funds were released as of April 2010. Election Decree Reform With the dispute between the Karzai government and international donors continuing over how to ensure a free and fair election, in February 2010 Karzai signed an election decree that would supersede the 2005 election law and govern the 2010 parliamentary election. 26 The Afghan government argued that the decree supersedes the constitutional clause that any new election law not be adopted less than one year prior to the election to which that law will apply. Substantively, some of the provisions of the election decree—particularly the proposal to make the ECC an all-Afghan body—caused alarm in the international community. Another controversial element was the registration requirements of a financial deposit (equivalent of about $650), and that candidates obtain signatures of at least 1,000 voters. On March 14, 2010, after discussions with outgoing UNAMA head Kai Eide, Karzai reportedly agreed to cede to UNAMA two "international seats" on the ECC, rather than to insist that all five ECC members be Afghans. Still, the majority of the ECC seats were Afghans. The election decree became an issue for Karzai opponents and others in the National Assembly who seek to assert parliamentary authority. On March 31, the Wolesi Jirga voted to reject the election decree. However, on April 3, 2010, the Meshrano Jirga decided not to act on the election decree, meaning that it was not rejected by the Assembly as a whole and governed the September 18, 2010, National Assembly elections. Karzai upheld his pledge to implement the March 2010 compromise with then UNAMA head Eide by allowing UNAMA to appoint two ECC members and to implement a requirement that at least one non-Afghan ECC member concur in decisions. Among other steps to correct the mistakes of the 2009 election, the Afghan Interior Ministry planned instituted a national identity card system to curb voter registration fraud. However, observers say that registration fraud still occurred. On April 17, 2010, Karzai appointed a new IEC head, Fazel Ahmed Manawi, a Tajik, who drew praise from many factions (including "opposition leader" Dr. Abdullah, who is half Tajik and identifies with that ethnicity) for impartiality. The IEC also barred 6,000 poll workers who served in the 2009 election from working the 2010 election. Preparations and the Vote Preparations for the September 18 election proceeded without major disruption, according to the IEC. Candidates registered during April 20-May 6, 2010. A list of candidates was circulated on May 13, 2010, including 2,477 candidates for the 249 seats. 27 These figures included 226 candidates who registered but whose documentation was not totally in order; and appeal restored about 180 of them. On May 30, 2010, in a preliminary ruling, 85 other candidates were disqualified as members of illegal armed groups. However, appeals and negotiations restored all but 36 in this latter category. A final list of candidates, after all appeals and decisions on the various disqualifications, was issued June 22. The final list included 2,577 candidates, including 406 women. Sixty-two candidates were invalidated by the ECC, mostly because they did not resign their government positions, as required.

Voter registration was conducted June 12-August 12. According to the IEC, over 375,000 new voters were registered, and the number of eligible voters was about 11.3 million. Campaigning began June 23. Many candidates, particularly those who are women, said that security difficulties have prevented them from conducting active campaigning. At least three candidates and 13 candidate supporters were killed by insurgent violence. On August 24, 2010, the IEC announced that the Afghan security forces say they would only be able to secure 5,897 of the planned 6,835 polling centers. To prevent so-called "ghost polling 27 The seat allocation per province is the same as it was in the 2005 parliamentary election—33 seats up for election in Kabul; 17 in Herat province; 14 in Nangarhar, 11 each in Kandahar, Balkh, and Ghazni; 9 in Badakhshan, Konduz, and Faryab, 8 in Helmand, and 2 to 6 in the remaining provinces. Ten are reserved for Kuchis (nomads). Afghanistan: Politics, Elections, and Government Performance Congressional Research Service 29 stations" (stations open but where no voters can go, thus allowing for ballot-stuffing), the 938 stations considered not secure were not opened. The IEC announcement stated that further security evaluation could lead to the closing of still more stations and, on election day, a total of 5,355 centers opened (304 of those slated to open did not, and for 157 centers there was no information available). In part to compensate, the IEC opened extra polling stations in centers in secure areas near to those that were closed. On election day, about 5.6 million votes were cast out of about 17 million eligible voters. Turnout was therefore about 33%. A major issue suppressing turnout was security. At first, it appeared as though election-day violence was lower than in the 2009 presidential election. However, on September 24, NATO/ISAF announced that there were about 380 total attacks, about 100 more than in 2009. However, voting was generally orderly and the attacks did not derail the election. Parliamentary Election Outcome Preliminary results were announced on October 20, 2010, and final, IEC-certified results were to be announced by October 30, 2010, but were delayed until November 24, 2010, due to investigation of fraud complaints. While the information below illustrates that there was substantial fraud, the IEC and ECC have been widely praised by the international community for their handling of the fraud allegations. Of the 5.6 million votes cast, the ECC invalidated 1.3 million (about 25%) after investigations of fraud complaints. The ECC prioritized complaints filed as follows: 2,142 as possibly affecting the election, 1,056 as unable to affect the result, and 600 where there will be no investigation. Causes for invalidation most often included ballot boxes in which all votes were for one candidate. About 1,100 election workers were questioned by ECC personnel, and 413 candidates were referred by the ECC to the Attorney General for having allegedly committed election fraud. The results, as certified by the IEC, resulted in substantial controversy within Afghanistan and led to a political crisis. The certified results were as follows. About 60% of the lower house (148 out of 249) winners were new members. As noted above, Karzai's number of core supporters was reduced from about 90 to 60-70. This was in part because the number of Pashtuns elected was 94, down from 120 in the outgoing lower house.

Several pro-Karzai candidates lost in Kandahar Province, and because many Pashtuns did not vote due to security reasons, in mixed Ghazni Province. The low Pashtun turnout in Ghazni caused Hazara candidates to win all 11 seats from the province, instead of 6 Pashtuns and 5 Hazaras in the outgoing lower house; this was a big factor in the reduction of the number of Pashtuns who won election. Several prominent pro-Karzai deputies were defeated, including Jamil Karzai, Pacha Khan Zadran, Mahmud Khan Suleimankhel (Paktika Province), and Muin Mirastyal (Konduz Province). The Hazara strength had no clear impact because many Hazaras support Karzai, although their increased political strength has caused ethnic tensions with the Pashtuns. Some observers note that some local militia commanders won election, adding to or replacing similar figures in past parliaments: the newly elected include Amanullah Khan Guzar (Kabul) who may have been behind May 2006 rioting in Kabul against NGO offices; and Haji Abdul Zahir (Nangarhar), a member of the well-Afghanistan: Politics, Elections, and Government Performance Congressional Research Service 30 known "Eastern Shura" once headed by the assassinated Hajji Abdul Qadir and one-time Kabul Governor Hajji Din Mohammad. Other mujahedin-era figures were reelected, including Iqbal Safi (Kapisa), Zalmai Mujaddedi (Badakhshan), Fukkuri Beheshti (Bamiyan), and Shahzada Shahed (Kunar). Two ex-Taliban figures, Mullah Salam Rocketi, and Musa Wardak, were defeated. A date of the inauguration of the new parliament was set for January 20, 2011, at which time, under Afghan law, President Karzai would formally open the session. Special Tribunal, Related Political Crisis, and Resolution The certified results triggered a major political crisis, caused primarily by Pashtuns who felt they lost the election due to fraud. The issue brought the operations of the National Assembly to a virtual halt, with Karzai ruling by decree, with seven cabinet posts and a few Supreme Court seats remaining unfilled by permanent appointees, and, as discussed above, with certified election winners in the Assembly threatening to impeach him in July 2011. Immediately after the election results were certified, Karzai took steps to address Pashtun grievances, but with its own interest in increasing the number of Pashtuns elected, in December 2010 the Karzai government (office of the Attorney General) indicted all seven IEC commissioners as well as the three Afghan members of the ECC. The deputy attorney general that same month urged election results to be voided and the Afghan Supreme Court to order a recount. There were weekly demonstrations against the fraud by about 300 candidates who felt deprived of victory, under a banner called the "Union of Afghan Wolesi Jirga Candidates 2010," led by defeated Ghazni candidate Daud Sultanzoy. On December 28, 2010, at the instruction of the Supreme Court, Karzai issued a decree empowering a five-member tribunal to review fraud complaints. Many Afghans, including an independent watchdog group, "Free and Fair Election Foundation," maintained that the tribunal had no legal authority under the constitution to review the election. The IEC and ECC, backed by UNAMA and the international community, insisted that the certified results stand, asserting they are the only bodies under Afghan electoral law that have legitimate jurisdiction over election results. Still, on January 19, 2011, the day before the parliament was to convene, the tribunal leader, Judge Sediqullah Haqiq, announced it would need another month to evaluate the fraud allegations. On that basis, following the recommendation, the Karzai government postponed the inauguration of the new parliament by one month. Defying Karzai and the special tribunal, about 213 of the certified winners met at the Intercontinental Hotel in Kabul on January 20, 2011, and reportedly decided to take their seats on January 23, 2011, without Karzai's formal inauguration. Elected deputies at the meeting said they would try to convene at the parliament building but would meet elsewhere, if blocked. They elected an interim speaker, Hajji Mohammad Sarwar Osmani, from Farah Province. This would have rendered unclear the legal status of a self-convened parliament. During January 20-25, 2011, with the lower house threatening to convene on its own, a compromise was found. Karzai agreed to inaugurate the lower house on January 26, 2011;

that event took place. However, the ongoing fraud investigation by the special tribunal remained active, despite insistence by declared winners to terminate it. As noted, after its inauguration, the lower house elected a compromise candidate, Abdul Raouf Ibrahimi, from the Uzbek community, Afghanistan: Politics, Elections, and Government Performance Congressional Research Service 31 as speaker. This fell short of Karzai's goal of engineering selection of Sayyaf but accomplished his aim of denying Qanooni reselection to that post. The upper house was completed as of February 19, 2011, when Karzai made his 34 appointments. The special tribunal process continued to investigate and to recount votes in several provinces. The crisis became acute on June 23, 2011, when the special tribunal ruled that 62 defeated candidates be reinstated. The National Assembly—containing the 62 people who would lose their seats if the tribunal's order were followed—subsequently passed a no-confidence vote against Attorney General Aloko. On August 10, 2011, Karzai appeared to defuse the eight month-long crisis; he issued a decree declaring that special court does not have jurisdiction to change election results, and that such changes are the role of the IEC. Subsequently, on August 21, 2011, the IEC implemented elements of a compromise urged by UNAMA by ruling that nine winners had won their seats through fraud and must be removed. This decision, with IEC chairman Manawi acknowledged was partly due to politics, removed fewer than the 17 that UNAMA had urged but more than the 5 the IEC reportedly thought would defuse the crisis. Some of the nine newly declared winners were sworn in on September 4, 2011, and the nine whose victories were overturned were barred from entering the parliament building. However, in protest of the decision, about 70 parliamentarians refused to convene and the Assembly was unable to obtain a quorum to act on legislation or government nominees, including Supreme Court vacancies. The boycotting parliamentarians ended their protest on October 8, 2011, paving the way for the National Assembly to resume full function. 2009 and 2010 Elections Alter Karzai-Assembly Relations The exposure of widespread fraud in the 2009 and 2010 elections appeared to alienate Karzai from the National Assembly. In the confirmation process of his post-2009 election cabinet, National Assembly members, particularly the well-educated independents, objected to many of his nominees as "unknowns," as having minimal qualifications, or as loyal to faction leaders who backed Karzai in the 2009 election. Karzai's original list of 24 ministerial nominees (presented December 19) was generally praised by the United States for retaining the highly praised economic team (and most of that team was confirmed). However, overall, only 7 of the first 24 nominees were confirmed (January 2, 2010), and only 7 of the 17 replacement nominees were confirmed (January 16, 2010), after which the Assembly went into winter recess. Although then UNAMA head Kai Eide called the vetoing of many nominees a "setback" to Afghan governance, Pentagon Press Secretary Geoff Morrell said on January 6, 2010, that the vetoing by parliament reflected a "healthy give and take" among Afghanistan's branches of government. Another five (out of seven nominees) were confirmed on June 28, 2010, although one was a replacement for the ousted Interior Minister Atmar. The differences over cabinet selections continued after the resolution in 2011 of the Assembly elections, although perhaps with less intensity, suggesting Karzai and the Assembly have sought to put aside differences and focus on governing. On March 12, 2012, the National Assembly confirmed most of those ministers who were serving in an acting capacity—including the controversial Ismail Khan—as well as some new nominees. As noted above, on September 16, 2012, the Assembly approved Karzai's nominees for heads of the three main security institutions. Afghanistan: Politics, Elections, and Government Performance Congressional Research Service 32 Implications for the United States of the Afghan Elections Disputes U.S. officials express clear U.S. neutrality in all Afghan elections. However, U.S. officials remained concerned that the 2009 and 2010 elections, and subsequent political crisis, would complicate the July 2011 start of the transition to Afghan security leadership, which began in seven areas (three provinces and four cities). 10,000 U.S. troops were withdrawn in late 2011 and an additional 23,000 will leave by September 2012. The election fraud and disputes have purportedly affected the perceptions of the Afghan people about the legitimacy of the Afghan government and its ability to take the lead on security by the end of 2014, according to current plans. The August 10, 2011, Karzai decree may serve to alleviate some of these concerns. Afghans close to Karzai believe that the U.S. posture on the Afghan elections strained relations between the two countries. In the 2009 presidential election, Karzai reportedly believed the United States was hoping strong candidates might emerge to replace him. The United States repeatedly stated its neutrality in all Afghan elections, and Ambassador Timothy Carney headed the 2009 U.S. election support effort at U.S. Embassy Kabul, tasked to ensure that the United States was even-handed. 2014 Presidential Elections: Karzai Says He Will Leave Office, Looks for Successor Under the constitution, the next presidential elections are to be held by the end of 2014. There is no clear frontrunner to succeed Karzai, although a number of candidates receive attention from observers, particularly those who ran before. Some observers say that, in the interests of unity approaching the 2014 security transition, factions should unify around a single successor who could be elected by acclamation. It is not clear whether that idea will resonate among major factions. The potential Pashtun contenders are Ghul Agha Sherzai, Ashraf Ghani, former Interior Minister Ali Jalali (Pashtun), Education Minister Faruq Wardak, and others. Some fear that Karzai may try to position himself to wield influence in a successor government by endorsing and working on behalf of one of these Pashtun candidates, and several of them are said to be seeking Karzai's backing. Karzai has said he does not want any of his brothers to run to succeed him, but Qayyum is said to be pondering a run, as is Mahmoud, despite the many allegations of his profiting from his brother's presidency. Ghani appeared to confirm his interest in a run in June 2012 by publicly criticizing corruption in government. Of the Tajik representatives, those who might run include Dr. Abdullah, Ahmad Zia Masoud, and Amrollah Saleh. Dr. Abdullah is said to be encouraging Hanif Atmar, a Pashtun mentioned above, to run as his first vice president in an effort to appeal to Pashtuns. However, a run by him might conflict with a run by the other Tajiks, and it is likely these figures will try to unite behind one Tajik representative. Parliamentarian Fawzia Koofi, mentioned above, has stated in editorials since late 2011 that she will run, although her gender as well as her Tajik ethnicity would lead most observers to conclude she is not favored to win. Ramazan Bashardost, a Hazara, is likely to again run on an anticorruption platform. Some Karzai critics have claimed he still plans to alter the constitution to allow himself to run for a third time, or possibly engineer a loya jirga—invoking national security grounds—to ask him to Afghanistan: Politics, Elections, and Government Performance Congressional Research Service 33 stay in office after 2014. At a June 15, 2011, Senate Appropriations Committee hearing, then Secretary of Defense Gates said Karzai had abandoned any such thinking and would leave office in 2014. Some U.S. officials sought to persuade Karzai to make a more public and definitive declaration to that effect. On August 12, 2011, the palace issued a statement that Karzai had told a group of parliamentarians that he would end his presidency after his second term. Press reports in September 2012 say that Karzai has been telling diplomats and others in Kabul that he might not endorse any candidate or involve himself in the 2014 election in any way—apparently trying to put to rest other assessments that Karzai wants to wield post-2014 political influence from behind the scenes. On the other hand, some read his reshuffling on September 20, 2012, of 10 of the 34 provincial governorships as an effort to place loyalists in position to support his favored candidate in the 2014 election. Election Timing, Other Ongoing Electoral Issues The international community is concerned about the 2014 election for its implications for Afghanistan's ability to govern beyond the 2014 transition. In April 2012, Karzai acknowledged that he had begun discussing with aides the possibility of advancing the election to some time in 2013. The public explanation for raising this possibility is that international troops will be leaving by the end of 2014, and more foreign troops will be available to secure the election in 2013 than in 2014. However, some might argue that moving the election up gives well-known Karzai associates a political advantage over lesser known figures. However, Karzai's July 26, 2012, administrative reform decree directs the IEC to prepare a plan for registering candidates in 2014, suggesting Karzai may have dropped consideration of moving the election forward. The July 8, 2012, Tokyo donors' conference resulted in the "Tokyo Mutual Accountability Framework," which stipulated economic aid incentives for Afghanistan in return for demonstrating progress in governance and against corruption. One of the Framework's stipulations is that Afghanistan conduct "credible, inclusive and transparent Presidential and Parliamentary elections in 2014 and 2015," including to "develop, by early 2013, a comprehensive election timeline through 2015 for electoral preparations and polling dates." 28Currently, electoral mechanisms continue to function, but reform is uncertain. As noted above, in August 2011, Karzai recognized formally the primacy of the IEC in determining the outcome of an election. IEC Chairman Manawi continues until early 2013, as does the term of IEC commissioner Abdul Pashaye. On December 19, 2011, Karzai swore in five new commissioners he appointed, a move that renewed criticism of mechanisms and laws that allow the president to appoint election officials. That same month the IEC signed a two-year assistance program by UNDP called ELECT II (Legal and Electoral Capacity for Tomorrow). Still, the 2014 election will require a new election law setting the framework for the IEC and ECC composition, and that law has not been adopted by the National Assembly to date. 28-tokyo-declaration-partnership-for-self-reliance-in-afghanistanfrom-transition-to-transf Afghanistan: Politics, Elections, and Government Performance Congressional Research Service 34 Afghan Governing Capacity and Performance 29 Some believe that Afghanistan will revert to a terrorist haven unless effective governance is well established before the transition to Afghan leadership is completed by 2014. U.S. and U.N. reports assess that there has been progress in the capacity of Afghan institutions to provide services; however, the low baseline of Afghan capacity means significant work remains. Many of the shortcomings in governance are attributed to all of the political disputes, alleged corruption, and the lack of workers trained or skilled in governmental affairs that are discussed below. In major Afghanistan policy addresses, President Obama has consistently stressed that more needed to be done to promote the legitimacy and effectiveness of the Afghan government at both the Kabul and local levels. In the latter statement, he said: "The days of providing a blank check [to the Afghan government] are over." The U.S.-Afghanistan Strategic Partnership Agreement, signed in Afghanistan on May 1, 2012, commits the United States (beyond 2014) to "support the Afghan government in strengthening the capacity, self-reliance, and effectiveness of Afghan institutions and their ability to deliver basic services." Of the FY2013 request for about $2.3 billion in economic aid to Afghanistan, nearly one-third of the request is for programs to help promote good governance, human rights, rule of law, political competition, and civil society. Earlier, the Obama Administration developed about 45 different metrics to assess progress in building Afghan governance and security, as it was required to do (by September 23, 2009) under 2009 supplemental appropriation.30 UNAMA, headed in Kabul by Jan Kubis, also evaluates Afghan governance according to numerous metrics. Afghan progress according to these metrics is presented in reports of the Secretary-General to the U.N. General Assembly, such as a report released March 5, 2012 The Tokyo Framework of Mutual Accountability, cited above, issued at the conclusion of the July 8, 2012, Tokyo donors' conference, makes aid incentives for Afghanistan (portions of $16 billion pledged through 2015) conditional on several governance measures including:31The holding of credible, inclusive, and transparent elections in 2014 and 2015. Improved access to justice, and respect for human rights, particularly for women and children. Improved integrity of public financial management and the commercial banking sector. Improved revenue systems and budget execution. In part to demonstrate that Afghanistan would uphold those commitments, the Karzai administrative reform decree issued July 26, 2012, requires virtually every ministry and the-tokyo-declaration-partnership-for-self-reliance-in-afghanistanfrom-transition-to-transf Afghanistan: Politics, Elections, and Government Performance Congressional Research Service 35 government body to develop a work plan, complete unfinished tasks, file specified reports, or carry out specified reforms. 32Expanding Central Government Capacity The international community has had mixed success in shifting authority in Afghanistan from traditional leaders and relationships to transparent and effective state institutions. Afghan ministries have greatly increasing their staffs and technological capabilities (many ministry offices now have modern computers and communications, for example). Afghan-led governmental reform and institution-building programs under way, all with U.S. and other donor assistance, include training additional civil servants, instituting merit-based performance criteria, basing hiring on qualifications rather than kinship and ethnicity, and weeding out widespread governmental corruption. However, the government still faces a relatively small recruitment pool of workers with sufficient skills and many are reluctant to serve in the provincial offices of the central government ministries, particularly in provinces where there is still substantial violence. U.S. mentors and advisers serve in virtually all the Afghan ministries. Afghanistan has also tried to address the problem of international donors luring away Afghan talent with higher salaries, by pledging at the July 20, 2010, Kabul conference to reach an understanding with donors, within six months, on a harmonized salary scale for donor-funded salaries of Afghan government personnel. Discussions have been held between the Afghan government and donors on this issue. The Afghan Civil Service The low level of Afghan bureaucratic capacity is being addressed in a number of ways, but slowly. There are about 500,000 Afghan government employees, although the majority of them are in the security forces. A large proportion of the remainder work as teachers. On several occasions, the United States has funded jobs fairs that have recruited some new civil servants. To increase the proficiency of government, during late 2010-early 2011, the government instituted merit-based appointments for senior positions, such as deputy provincial governors and district governors, and converted those positions to civil servants rather than political appointees. However, that effort stalled in April-September 2011, according to the October 2011 DOD report, because Karzai has not yet approved merit-based selectees for 14 deputy governor positions. If approved, more than three-quarters of Afghanistan's 34 provinces would have merit-based deputy governors. The key institution that is deciding on merit based appointments and standardizing job descriptions, salaries, bonuses, and benefits is the Afghan Independent Administrative Reform and Civil Service Commission (IARCSC). The commission has thus far redefined more than 80,000 civil servant job descriptions. The Afghan cabinet drafted a revised civil service law to institute merit-based hiring and give the IARCSC a legal underpinning; it was ratified by the National Assembly in late 2011 and replaced a less-specific September 2005 civil service law. 32-Text of the decree "On the Execution of Content of the Historical Speech of June 21, 2012, in the Special Session of the National Assembly. Provided to CRS by the Embassy of Afghanistan in Washington, D.C. July 16, 2012. Afghanistan: Politics, Elections, and Government Performance Congressional Research Service 36 Under a USAID program called the Civilian Technical Assistance Plan, the United States is providing technical assistance to Afghan ministries and to the IARCSC. From January 2010 until January 2011, USAID, under a February 2010 memorandum of understanding, gave $85 million to programs run by the commission to support the training and development of Afghan civil servants. One of the commission's subordinate organizations is the Afghan Civil Service Institute, which trained over 16,000 bureaucrats during 2010-2011, according to the DOD 1230 report, and which has instituted an internship program for 1,000 interns in national civil service jobs and 2,000 interns in provincial and district offices. On-going training for civil servants is provided by an arm of the Civil Service Institute called the National Training Directorate (NTD). According to the November 2011 report from the office of the Special Representative for Afghanistan and Pakistan, Ambassador Marc Grossman, USAID programs are helping employees of the state-owned Afghan power company (DABS) to manage Afghanistan's power grid and bill its customers. USAID programs have also trained 250 Ministry of Mines personnel in geology to try to help develop Afghanistan's extractive industries sector. Many Afghan civil service personnel undergo training in India, building on growing relations between Afghanistan and India. Japan and Singapore also are training Afghan civil servants on good governance, anti-corruption, and civil aviation. Singapore and Germany will, in 2011, jointly provide technical assistance in the field of civil aviation. Some of these programs are conducted in partnership with the German Federal Foreign Office and the Asia Foundation. The Afghan Budget Process The international efforts to build up the central government are reflected in the Afghan budget process. The Afghan government controls its own funds as well as those of directly supplied donor funds. The Afghan budget year follows the solar year, which begins on March 21 of each year, which also corresponds to the Persian New Year (Nowruz). In early February 2011, the National Assembly adopted a 2011 national budget (March 2011-March 2012) in line with its responsibilities. However, the lack of a quorum in the Assembly in mid- to late-2011 slowed consideration of a budget for 2012 (March 2012-March 2013), as did an initial voting down of the 2012 budget by the lower house of the National Assembly in March 2012. The Afghan budget is a "unitary" (centralized) system. Once a budget is adopted by the full National Assembly (first the upper house and then the lower house, and then signed by Karzai), the funds are allocated to central government ministries and other central government entities. Some of the elected provincial councils, appointed provincial governors, and district governors formulate local budget requirements and help shape the national budget process, but no locality controls its own budget. These local organs do approve the disbursement of funds by the central entities (called mustofiats, accounting offices in each of Afghanistan's 34 provinces). The Tokyo Mutual Accountability Framework, cited above, includes as one of its benchmarks the formalization of a provincial budgeting process with more systematic provincial input into the relevant ministries that formulate the national budget. All revenue is collected by central government entities which implement the local programs but, according to experts, contributes to the widespread observation that local officials sometimes seek to retain or divert locally collected revenues. There are several pilot programs in place, including the Provincial Budget Pilot Program (PBPP) to improve budgetary planning integration between the national and provincial levels. To date, four ministries and the IDLG say they have Afghanistan: Politics, Elections, and Government Performance Congressional Research Service 37 made sound progress on this program and several other ministries are to be included in it in 2012- 2013. Donor Involvement in the Afghan Budget The Afghan government is expected to take in about $2 billion in total revenue for all of 2012. Lacking resources, about 90% of total Afghan government expenditures (operating budget and development budget) was provided by international donors during 2006-2010, according to a GAO study issued September 2011. Of the 90%, the United States provide 62% and other donors provided 28% of total expenditures. 33-In 2011, donor funds covered 57% of the Afghan government's $2.2 billion operating budget. 34-Although still wary of misuse, the United States has been slowly accommodating Afghan demands that aid be channeled through the Afghan government. More than 40% of U.S. aid was channeled through the Afghan government during 2011. This is close to the target figure of 50% that was endorsed at the July 20, 2010, Kabul conference, and up from 21% in 2009, according to a June 8, 2011, staff report of the Senate Foreign Relations Committee (Evaluating U.S. Foreign Assistance to Afghanistan). Increased percentages are predicated on U.S.

assessments of the ability of individual ministries to accurately and transparently administer donated funds. According to that Foreign Relations Committee staff report, 14 Afghan ministries have received USAID and State Department funds. Karzai has repeatedly said that the low level of direct funding has stunted the growth of Afghan government capacity. Many international development experts concur that only through direct funding will the Afghan government be able to develop the capacity and eventually the transparency to govern and deliver services effectively. The Tokyo Framework, cited earlier, provides incentives for Afghanistan by raising the percentage of donor funds channeled through the Afghanistan Reconstruction Trust Fund in exchange for Afghan governance progress—that fund gives money directly to Afghan ministries and thus gives the Afghan government substantial discretion as compared to other donated funds that are spent directly on projects. The Karzai administrative decree of July 26, 2012, provides for Afghan institutions to begin taking over the roles of donor-run Provincial Reconstruction Teams (PRTs). Karzai has long criticized the PRTs as preventing the Afghan government from expanding its own responsibilities and capacity. Expanding Local (Subnational) Governance As U.S. concerns about corruption in the central government increased after 2007, U.S. and allied policy has increasingly emphasized building local or "subnational" governance. This accords with U.S. strategy in Afghanistan, which is to build institutions that can govern and secure areas cleared by U.S. and NATO forces and preventing Taliban reinfiltration. The U.S. shift in emphasis complements that of the Afghan government, which asserts that it has itself long sought to promote local governance in Afghanistan's political and economic development. 33-Government Accountability Office. "Afghanistan's Donor Dependence." September 20, 2011. 34- The operating budget is greater than the government revenue because the operating budget includes some donor funds. Afghanistan: Politics, Elections, and Government Performance Congressional Research Service 38 U.S. and partner country officials, as well as observers, say that local governance, particularly at the provincial level, is improving and expanding, particularly in areas secured by the 2010 U.S. "troop surge." U.S. officials say that Afghans are increasingly forming local councils and building ties to appointed local leaders in these cleared and secured areas. However, the April 2012 DOD report on Afghanistan stability says subnational bodies "remain unable to provide many basic government services." This could be, in part, a result of attempts by Kabul to centralize decision making—the localities have their own governing bodies but the central government ministries in the provincial capitals of each province—not the subnational bodies—actually implement national programs. Local officials often disagree with the Kabul ministry representatives on priorities or on implementation mechanisms. The Independent Directorate for Local Governance (IDLG) In terms of local governance institution-building, a key institution was empowered in August 2007 when Karzai placed the selection process for local leaders (provincial governors and below) in a new Independent Directorate for Local Governance (IDLG)—and out of the Interior Ministry. The IDLG was headed until early 2011 by Jelani Popal, a member of Karzai's Popolzai tribe and a close Karzai ally. Some international officials say that Popal packed local agencies with Karzai supporters, where they were able to arrange votes for Karzai in the August 2009 presidential elections. He was replaced by Abdul Khaliq Farahi, a former diplomat who was kidnapped in Peshawar, and held for nearly three years (2008-2011) allegedly by militants linked to Al Qaeda. In terms of donor programming, the IDLG is the implementing partner of the U.N. Development Program in the Afghanistan Subnational Governance Program II (ASGP-II). It was funded with $83.6 million from the European Community, Italy, Switzerland, and Britain. Its main achievement has been to fund national technical assistance for the IDLG. The IDLG is an implementing partner for the District Delivery Program (DDP), now operating in 32 of the 364 districts of Afghanistan. It is a program created to improve government presence and service delivery at the district level, and is funded by the United

States, Britain, Denmark, and France. U.S. funding for the program was suspended in July 2011 pending accountability of expenditures and a request for the IDLG and Ministry of Finance to satisfy several conditions, and has not reactivated to date. 35-Provincial Governors and Provincial Councils Many believe that, even more than institutional expansion, the key to effective local governance is the appointment of competent and incorruptible governors in all 34 Afghan provinces. U.N., U.S., and other international studies and reports all point to the beneficial effects (reduction in narcotics trafficking, economic growth, lower violence) of some of the strong Afghan civilian appointments at the provincial level. Provincial governors are still political appointees selected mostly for loyalty to Karzai although, as noted above, progress is being made in implementing a merit-based appointment system for deputy provincial governors and district governors. The July 26, 2012, Karzai decree directs the IDLG to open deputy governorships to competition within two months. The decree also requires the IDLG to fill open positions in the provinces within six 35-DOD report on Afghanistan stability, April 2012. Afghanistan: Politics, Elections, and Government Performance Congressional Research Service 39 months, to address the many vacancies in the provinces, including in the ministry offices in each provincial capital. It also requires a review of the performance of provincial governors' performance in combating corruption and improving governance. A key example of a successful gubernatorial appointment has been the March 2008 appointment of Gulab Mangal as Helmand governor. He is from Laghman Province (eastern Afghanistan) and drew immediate skepticism from the local tribes and power-brokers of the south who repeatedly have urged Karzai to replace him. But, he has drawn wide praise from the United States and the international community for taking effective action to convince farmers to grow crops other than poppy. His leadership accounts for the reduction of cultivation in Helmand that have been noted since 2009. Mangal has played a key role in convening tribal shuras and educating local leaders on the benefits of the U.S.-led offensive to remove Taliban insurgents from Marjah town and install new authorities there. A key Mangal ally, who has reportedly helped bring substantial stability to the Nawa district, is Abdul Manaf. On September 20, 2012, acting subsequent to his July 2012 administrative decree, Karzai shuffled 10 out of the 34 provincial governors, asserting that those taken out of their positions had fallen short on improving governance or combating corruption. Mangal was one of those removed, causing consternation among some of the international donors who have raved about his performance in Helmand. He was replaced by the little-known Gen. Mohammad Naeem. Some of the ousted governors were assigned to different provinces. Other than Helmand, the nine provinces where governors were changed include Wardak, Kabul, Takhar, Faryab, Baghlan, Nimruz, Laghman, Lowgar, and Badghis. Other governors, such as Ghul Agha Shirzai and Atta Mohammad Noor (discussed above) are considered effective, but have been criticized for exercising excessive independence of central authority. Many of the other governors are considered weak, ineffective, or corrupt. Provincial Councils One problem noted by governance experts is that the role of the elected provincial councils is unclear. The elections for the provincial councils in all 34 provinces were held on August 20, 2009, concurrent with the presidential elections. The previous provincial council elections were held concurrent with the parliamentary elections in September 2005. In most provinces, the provincial councils do not act as true local legislatures and are considered weak compared to the power and influence of the provincial governors. Perhaps the most significant role the provincial councils play is in choosing the upper house of the National Assembly (Meshrano Jirga). In the absence of district councils (no elections held or scheduled), the provincial councils elected in 2009 have chosen two-thirds of the 102-seat body. Karzai appointed the remaining 34 seats in February 2011. District-Level Governance The April 2012 DOD report on Afghan stability says that there was "measured progress" over the past six months in developing effective district governance. District governors are appointed by the president, at the recommendation of the IDLG. However, only a small proportion (about 5%-10%) of all district governors have been appointed through the merit-based appointment system in which qualifications are assessed by the IARCSC (see above). In some districts of Helmand Afghanistan: Politics, Elections, and Government Performance Congressional Research Service 40 that had fallen under virtual Taliban control until the July 2009 U.S.-led offensives in the province, there were no district governors in place at all. Some of the district governors, including The difficulty plaguing the expansion of district governance, in addition to security issues, is lack of resources. Only slightly more than half of all district governors (there are 364 districts) have any staff or vehicles. District Councils Another problem in establishing district level governance has been the fact that no elections for district councils have been held due to boundary and logistical difficulties. In his November 19, 2009, inaugural speech, Karzai said the goal of the government is to hold these elections along with the 2010 parliamentary elections. However, that was not accomplished and no date for these elections has been set. As a result, there is no one authoritative district-level representative body, but rather a collection of groupings established by donor programs. According to the April 2012 DOD report on Afghan stability, the Afghan government has agreed in principle to a roadmap leading to a single district level body, a roadmap to be endorsed by September 2012, although not necessarily implying district elections could be held by then. Municipal and Village Level Authority As are district governors, mayors of large municipalities are appointed. There are about 42 mayors nationwide, many with deputy mayors. Karzai pledged in his November 2009 inaugural that "mayoral" elections would be held "for the purpose of better city management." However, no municipal elections have been held and none is scheduled. As noted throughout, there has traditionally been village-level governance by groups of tribal elders and other notables. That structure remains, particularly in secure areas, while village councils have been absent or only sporadically active in areas where there is combat. As noted above, a U.S. official in southern Afghanistan, Henry Ensher, said in January 2011 that councils have been formed in areas where security has been established by the 2010 U.S. "troop surge." The IDLG and the Ministry of Rural Rehabilitation and Development (MRRD), with advice from India and other donors, also are empowering localities to decide on development priorities. The MRRD has formed about 30,000 Community Development Councils (CDCs) nationwide to help suggest priorities, and these bodies are eventually to all be elected. U.S. Local Governance Advisory Capacity As a consequence of the March 2009 Obama Administration review, to help build local governing capacity, the Administration recruited about 500 U.S. civilian personnel from the State Department, USAID, the Department of Agriculture, and several other agencies—and many additional civilians from partner countries joined them—to advise Afghan ministries, and provincial and district administrations. That effort raised the number of U.S. civilians in Afghanistan to about 975 by early 2010 and to 1,330 by August 2011. Of these, nearly 400 serve outside Kabul, up from 67 in early 2009. Afghanistan: Politics, Elections, and Government Performance Congressional Research Service 41 Although many U.S. civilian officials work outside Kabul, there are about 1,100 employees at the U.S. Embassy in Kabul, from 18 different U.S. government agencies. To accommodate the swelling ranks, in early November 2010 a $511 million contract was let to Caddell Construction to expand it, and two contracts of $20 million each were let to construct U.S. consulates in Herat and Mazar-e-Sharif. The consulate in Mazar-e-Sharif, however, is not in operation because of concerns about the security of the building where it was to be located. The Administration also has instituted appointments of "Senior Civilian Representatives" (SCR), 36 who are counterparts to the military commanders of each NATO/ISAF regional command (there are currently five of them). Each Senior Civilian Representative has 10-30 personnel on his/her team. For example, the SCR for Regional Command South is based at kandahar airfield and interacts closely with the military command of the southern sector. The SCR for Regional Command East (RC-E) is based at Bagram Airfield. Reforming Afghan Governance: Curbing Corruption 37 Partly because many Afghans view the central government as "predatory," many Afghans and international donors have questioned Karzai's leadership. NATO estimates that about $2.5 billion in total bribes are paid by Afghans each year. Reducing corruption in government is a major focus of the Tokyo Mutual Accountability Framework, cited above, which requires Afghanistan to "enact and enforce the legal framework for fighting corruption." Karzai himself has repeatedly acknowledged that corruption is a major problem in Afghanistan. In a June 21, 2012, speech, he called on his government to step up the fight against corruption, and fighting corruption is a cornerstone of Karzai's July 26, 2012, administrative decree. However, concerns about Karzai's leadership on this issue center on implementation and his apparent reluctance to prosecute officials for corruption—particularly those related to or aligned with him politically. This stands in contrast to his attempts to vigorously prosecute for corruption those politically opposed to him. High Level Corruption, Nepotism, and Cronyism At the upper levels of government, some observers have asserted that Karzai deliberately tolerates officials who are allegedly involved in illicit activity and supports their receipt of lucrative contracts from donor countries, in exchange for their political support. Karzai's brother, Mahmoud, as discussed above, has apparently grown wealthy through real estate and auto sales ventures in Kandahar and Kabul, purportedly by fostering the impression he can influence his brother. Some observers who have served in Afghanistan say that Karzai has appointed some provincial governors to "reward them" and that these appointments have gone on to "prey" economically on the populations of that province. Another trend that has attracted notice among Afghans is that several high officials, despite very low official government salaries, have acquired ornate properties in west Kabul since 2002. They allegedly have appropriated to themselves private land, the ownership of which was unclear, for 36 For more information, see U.S. Department of Defense. "Report on Progress Toward Security and Stability in Afghanistan," 37 For more information, particularly on Rule of Law programs, Afghanistan: U.S. Rule of Law and Justice Sector Assistance, by Liana Sun Wyler and Kenneth Katzman. Afghanistan: Politics, Elections, and Government Performance Congressional Research Service 42 homes, and housing business ventures. Redressing this issue is discussed in the "rule of law" section below. Lower-Level Corruption Observers who follow the issue say that most of the governmental corruption takes place in the course of performing mundane governmental functions, such as government processing of official documents in which processing services routinely require bribes in exchange for action. 38 Other forms of corruption include Afghan security officials' selling U.S. internationally provided vehicles, fuel, and equipment to supplement their salaries. In other cases, local police or border officials may siphon off customs revenues or demand extra payments to help guard the U.S. or other militaries' equipment shipments. Other examples include security commanders placing "ghost employees" on official payrolls in order to pocket their salaries. Corruption is fed, in part, by the fact that government workers receive very low salaries (about $200 per month, as compared to the pay of typical contractors in Afghanistan that might pay as much as $6,500 per month). Many observers say there is a cultural dimension to the corruption—that it is commonly expected by relatives and friends that those Afghans who have achieved government positions will protect those relations with favors, appointments, and contracts. Administration Views and Policy on Corruption As noted throughout, there is a consensus within the Administration on the wide scope of the corruption in Afghan government and the deleterious effect the corruption has on government popularity and effectiveness. The Administration wrestled throughout 2010 with the degree to which to press an anti-corruption agenda with the Karzai government, but, in early 2011, the Administration reportedly decided to prioritize reducing low-level corruption instead of investigations of high-level allies of Karzai. 39 The latter investigations have sometimes come into conflict with other U.S. objectives by causing a Karzai backlash. In addition, such investigations may complicate efforts to obtain the cooperation of Afghans who can help stabilize areas of the country. Some of these Afghans are said to be paid by the CIA for information and other support, and the National Security Council reportedly issued guidance to U.S. agencies to review this issue. 40Yet, U.S. officials believe that anti-corruption efforts must be pursued because corruption is contributing to a souring of Western publics on the mission as well as causing some Afghans to embrace Taliban insurgents. General Petraeus, the former top U.S. and NATO commander in Afghanistan, said he made anti-corruption a top priority to support his counter-insurgency strategy. A key deputy, General H.R. McMaster, formed several DOD task forces to focus on anticorruption (Shafafiyat, Task Force Spotlight, and Task Force 2010) from a U.S. military/counterinsurgency perspective. These task forces, in part, review U.S. contracting strategies to enhance Afghan capacity and reduce the potential for corruption. The Shafafiyat task force announced in February 2012 that had caused the restitution of $11.1 million, $25.4 million in fines, and $3.4 38 Filkins, Dexter, "Bribes Corrode Afghan's Trust in Government," New York Times, January 2, 2009. 39 Strobel, Warren and Marisa Taylor. "U.S. Won't Pursue Karzai Allies in Anti-Corruption Campaign." McClatchy Newspapers, January 6, 2011. 40- Chandrasekaran, Rajiv. "A Subtler Takc to Fight Afghan Corruption." Washington Post, September 13, 2010. Afghanistan: Politics, Elections, and Government Performance Congressional Research Service 43 million in seizures from allegedly fraudulent contractors, and has debarred or suspended more than 125 American, Afghan, and international workers for alleged fraud. 41-Anti-Corruption Initiatives Obama Administration officials have credited Karzai with allowing the United States and other donors to help develop oversight bodies to curb corruption. However, the credit is tempered by the lack of Afghan government provision of resources or attention to building these bodies. These criticisms were amplified in an April 30, 2012, report by the Special Inspector General for Afghanistan Reconstruction (SIGAR). At the July 20, 2010, Kabul conference—following onto the January 28, 2010, London conference—the Afghan government finalized a National AntiCorruption Strategy ("Azimi report") and committed to enacting 37 laws to curb corruption. Very few of these laws have been enacted, although the Afghan cabinet has drafted new anti-corruption and auditing laws and some regulations have been issued by Karzai decree. Assets Declarations and Verifications. During December 15-17, 2009, Karzai held a conference in Kabul to combat corruption. It debated requiring deputy ministers and others to declare their assets, not just those at the ministerial level. That requirement was imposed. Karzai himself declared his assets on March 27, 2009. The July 20, 2010, Kabul conference communiqué 42- included an Afghan pledge to verify and publish these declarations annually, beginning in 2010. According to a U.N. report of March 9, 2011, 1,995 senior Afghan officials had declared their assets. However, the SIGAR report of April 30, 2012, said that the government's progress for verification of the declarations continues to "fall short of U.S. expectations." A Joint Monitoring and Evaluation Committee to evaluate the government's performance in combating corruption was mandated by the Kabul conference communiqué to be established within three months of the conference (by October 2010). According to a June 23, 2011, U.N. report, the committee, supported by UNDP, was inaugurated on May 11, 2011. It was established by decree and is composed of three Karzai nominees and three international nominees. High Office of Oversight. In August 2008 Karzai, with reported Bush Administration prodding, set up the "High Office of Oversight for the Implementation of Anti-Corruption Strategy" (commonly referred to as the High Office of Oversight, HOO) with the power to identify and refer corruption cases to state prosecutors, and to catalogue the overseas assets of Afghan officials. It is headed by former IEC head Azizullah Ludin. On March 18, 2010, Karzai, as promised at the January 28, 2010, international meeting on Afghanistan in London, issued a decree giving the

High Office direct power to investigate corruption cases rather than just refer them to other offices. However, the SIGAR reported on April 30, 2012, that the HOO's core functions either deteriorated or were ineffective during the first quarter of 2012. The July 26, 2012, Karzai administrative decree directs the HOO to, within six months, assess "private institutions' and government officials' suspicious wealth" and report those 41- John Ryan. "Task Force Rooting Out Corruption in Afghanistan." Army Times, February 20, 2012. 42- Communiqué text at. Afghanistan: Politics, Elections, and Government Performance Congressional Research Service 44 findings to the president's office every two months. USAID is providing the HOO $30 million total during 2011-2013 to build capacity at the central and provincial level. USAID pays for salaries of six HOO senior staff and provides some information technology systems as well. Establishment of Additional Investigative Bodies: Major Crimes Task Force and Sensitive Investigations Unit. Since 2008, several additional investigative bodies have been established under Ministry of Interior authority. The most prominent is the "Major Crimes Task Force," tasked with investigating public corruption, organized crime, and kidnapping. A headquarters for the MCTF was inaugurated on February 25, 2010, and it has been funded and mentored by the FBI, the DEA, the U.S. Marshal Service, Britain's Serious Crimes Organized Crime Agency, the Australian Federal Police, EUPOL (European police training unit in Afghanistan), and the U.S.-led training mission for Afghan forces. The MCTF has 169 investigators, according to U.S. officials. A related body is the Sensitive Investigations Unit (SIU), run by several dozen Afghan police officers, vetted and trained by the DEA. 43-This body led the arrest in August 2010 of a Karzai NSC aide, Mohammad Zia Salehi, on charges of soliciting a bribe from the New Ansari Money Exchange in exchange for ending a money-laundering investigation of the firm. The middle-of-the-night arrest prompted Karzai, by his own acknowledgment on August 22, 2010, to obtain Salehi's release and to say he would establish a commission to place the MCTF and SIU under more thorough Afghan government control. Following U.S. criticism that Karzai is protecting his aides (Salehi reportedly was involved in bringing Taliban figures to Afghanistan for conflict settlement talks), Karzai pledged to visiting Senate Foreign Relations Committee Chairman John Kerry on August 20, 2010, that the MCTF and SIU would be allowed to perform their work without political interference. In November 2010, the Attorney General's office said it had ended the prosecution of Salehi. Anti-Corruption Unit, and an Anti-Corruption Tribunal. These investigative and prosecution bodies were established by decree in 2009. Eleven judges have been appointed to the tribunal. The tribunal, under the jurisdiction of the Supreme Court, tries cases referred by an Anti-Corruption Unit of the Afghan Attorney General's office. However, of the approximately 2,000 cases investigated by the Anti-Corruption Unit, only 28 officials have been convicted to date. The Department of Justice suspended its training program for the Anti-Corruption Unit in early 2012 because of the unit's "lack of seriousness," according to the SIGAR report of April 30, 2012. One of the laws pledged during the July 20, 2010, Kabul conference would be enacted (by July 20, 2011) included one to legally empower the Anti-Corruption Tribunal and the Major Crimes Task Force. That has not been enacted by the National Assembly to date. Prosecutions and Investigations of High-Level Officials. The Afghanistan Attorney General's office has investigated at least 20 senior officials. The April 30, 2012, SIGAR report said there had been no progress by the Attorney General in undertaking new prosecutions in early 2012. Perhaps to address that criticism, 43 Nordland, Ron and Mark Mazzetti. "Graft Dispute in Afghanistan Is Test for U.S." Times, August 24, 2010. Afghanistan: Politics, Elections, and Government Performance Congressional Research Service 45 new investigations were announced in mid-2012. One such case is that of Minister of Mines Wahidullah Shahrani, although observers believe his opponents are actually trying to combat a draft mining law that some see as too favorable to foreign firms. Accusations in July 2012 against Finance Minister Omar Zakhiwal appear focused on corruption rather than policy issues: Afghan media used his bank statements to show unusual payments from outside organizations. HOO director Ludin has called on Zakhiwal to step down while the investigation unfolds. Karzai has not publicly defended Zakhiwal against the accusations. Some of those investigated previously included Commerce Minister Amin Farhang (for allegedly submitting inflated invoices for reimbursement); former Minister of Mines Mohammad Ibrahim Adel (who reportedly accepted a $30 million bribe to award a key mining project in Lowgar Province to China); 44-and former Minister of the Hajj Mohammad Siddiq Chakari (for accepting bribes to steer Hajj-related travel business to certain foreign tourist agencies). Chakari fled to Britain. Then Deputy Kabul Mayor Wahibuddin Sadat was arrested at Kabul airport in December 2009 for alleged misuse of authority. EITI. Relatedly, Afghanistan has signed up as a candidate to the Extractive Industries Transparency Initiative (EITI) which is intended to ensure that contracting for Afghanistan's mineral resources is free of corruption. Afghanistan hopes to become fully EITI compliant by April 2012. The World Bank gave Afghanistan a three year grant of $52 million to manage its natural resources effectively. Salary Levels. The government has tried to raise salaries, particularly of security forces, in order to reduce their inclination to solicit bribes. In November 2009, the Afghan government announced an increase in police salaries (from $180 per month to $240 per month). During his term as Interior Minister, Bismillah Khan was credited by DOD with instituting transparency and accountability in promotions and assignments. Bulk Cash Transfers Out of Afghanistan. At the July 2010 Kabul conference, the government pledged to adopt regulations and implement within one year policies to govern the bulk transfers of cash outside the country. This was intended to grapple with issues raised by reports, discussed below, of officials taking large amounts of cash out of Afghanistan (an estimated $4.5 billion taken out in 2011). U.S. officials say that large movements of cash are inevitable in Afghanistan because only about 5% of the population use banks and 90% use informal cash transfers ("hawala" system). The late Ambassador Holbrooke testified on July 28, 2010 (cited earlier), that the Afghan Central Bank has begun trying to control hawala transfers; 475 hawalas have been licensed, to date, whereas none were licensed as recently as 2009. In June 2010, U.S. and Afghan officials announced establishment of a joint task force to monitor the flow of money out of Afghanistan, including monitoring the flow of cash out of Kabul International Airport. On August 21, 2010, it was reported that Afghan and U.S. authorities would implement a plan to install U.S.-made currency counters at Kabul airport to track how officials had obtained their cash (and ensure it did not come from 44-Partlow, Joshua, "Afghanistan Investigating 5 Current and Former Cabinet Members," Washington Post, November 24, 2009. Afghanistan: Politics, Elections, and Government Performance Congressional Research Service 46 donor aid funds). 45- During 2011, the United States tripled the number of Homeland Security personnel devoted to training Afghan customs and border employees to curb bulk transfers and smuggling. On March 19, 2012, Central Bank Governor Noorullah Delawari said the Bank had imposed a $20,000 per person limit on cash transfers out of the country. Auditing Capabilities. The SIGAR has previously assessed that the mandate of Afghanistan's Control and Audit Office is too narrow and lacks the independence needed to serve as an effective watch over the use of Afghan government funds. 46 At the Kabul conference, the government pledged to submit to parliament an Audit Law within six months, to strengthen the independence of the Control and Audit Office, and to authorize more auditing by the Ministry of Finance. The government drafted an audit law but, according to the April 30, 2012, SIGAR report, the National Assembly's legislative committee rejected the draft law in early 2012. Legal Review. The Kabul conference communiqué committed the government to establish a legal review committee, within six months, to review Afghan laws for compliance with the U.N. Convention Against Corruption. Afghanistan ratified the convention in August 2008. Local Anti-Corruption Bodies. Some Afghans have taken it upon themselves to oppose corruption at the local level. Volunteer local inspectors, sponsored originally by Integrity Watch Afghanistan, are reported to monitor and report on the quality of donor-funded, contractor implemented construction projects. However, these local "watchdog" groups do not have an official mandate, and therefore their authority and ability to rectify inadequacies are limited. Kabul Bank Scandal and Continuing Difficulties The near-collapse of Kabul Bank is a prime example of how well-connected Afghans have avoided regulations and other restrictions in order to garner personal profit. Mahmoud Karzai is a major (7%+) shareholder in the large Kabul Bank, which is used to pay Afghan civil servants and police, and he reportedly received large loans from the bank to buy his position in it. Another big shareholder was Abdul Hussain Fahim, the brother of First Vice President Fahim and partner of Mahmoud Karzai on other ventures. The insider relationships were exposed in August and September 2010 when Kabul Bank reported large losses ($500 million initially) primarily from shareholder investments in Dubai properties, prompting President Karzai to appoint a Central Bank official to run the Kabul Bank. However, the government moves did not prevent large numbers of depositors from withdrawing their money from it. In response to the crisis, the United States and other donors refused to recapitalize the bank, but it offered to finance an audit of Afghan banks, including Kabul Bank. The Finance Ministry decided instead in November 2010 to hire its own auditor—a move that suggested to some that high Afghan officials seek to avoid sharing the results with international donors. The International Monetary Fund (IMF) suspended its credit program for the Afghan government in November 2010 because of the scandal and demanded the entire Afghan banking industry undergo an 45 Miller, Greg and Joshua Partlow. "Afghans, U.S. Aim to Plug Cash Drain." Washington Post, August 21, 2010. 46 Madhani, Aamer. "U.S. Reviews Afghan Watchdog Authority." USA Today, May 12, 2010. Afghanistan: Politics, Elections, and Government Performance Congressional Research Service 47 outside forensic audit and that those responsible be held accountable. That caused the holding up of $70 million World Bank/Afghan Reconstruction Fund (ARTF) in donor funds due to be paid June 11, 2011. Other donors suspended as much as $1.8 billion in economic aid because of the IMF suspension. Amid Afghan confirmation that the questionable loans of the bank total over $925 million (including interest due), the IMF—as a condition of resuming its credit program—subsequently pushed for the bank to be sold. The Central Bank instead agreed to separate the bank's performing from non-performing assets and then dissolve or restructure the bank. 47 A version of the plan, which was subject to approval by an Afghan government committee, was formally approved and announced on April 21, 2011. The "good bank" (part of the bank with deposits and which still functions) was financed by a Central Bank loan of $825 million. The Afghan Finance Ministry has promised to pay back the loan with recovered assets and tax revenues. On October 16, 2011, the National Assembly voted on a supplemental budget that enabled the Finance Ministry to reimburse the Central Bank loan over eight years. However, Assembly rejection of the 2012 budget in March 2012 held up an $80 million annual increment for this purpose. The Afghan government, through its "Financial Dispute Resolution Commission," continues to try to recoup the lost funds. Of the estimated $925 million in losses, about $300 million of the losses are judged by the Afghans as untraceable because of a lack of documentation. As of mid- 2012, the commission has recovered $128 million in cash and $145 million in property, mostly luxury villas in Dubai. 48 Central Bank governor Noorullah Delawari said in April 2012 that the country plans to sell Kabul Bank in June 2012; that has not occurred to date. Mahmoud Karzai and Fahim have reportedly repaid their loans from the Bank. The Tokyo Mutual Accountability Framework, discussed above, requires Afghanistan to continue asset recovery and to strengthen banking supervision though the Central Bank (Da Afghanistan Bank). Attempting Accountability The political fallout also produced some resolution. On January 15, 2011, the office of Afghan Attorney General Ishaq Aloko announced an investigation into what led to the near-collapse of the bank and the principals involved. The investigating commission briefed reporters on its findings on May 30, 2011, placing much of the blame on lax controls by the Central Bank and its governor, Abdul Qadir Fitrat. The government commission also largely absolved Mahmoud Karzai of any wrongdoing, saying he had paid off his loans, and naming other key figures, such as Dostam, as taking out $100,000 in unsecured loans. The following day, Central Bank governor Fitrat disputed the commission's conclusions. He had previously told parliament that Mahmoud Karzai owed $22 million. In part because of his feuding with figures such as Mahmoud Karzai, Fitrat fled Afghanistan for the United States and announced his resignation on June 27, 2011. Karzai subsequently barred U.S. advisers from the Central Bank. On December 11, 2011, Karzai called for the United States to extradite Fitrat to Afghanistan and blamed U.S. officials for knowing of the Bank's problems at an early stage but failing to alert Afghan authorities. 47 Ernesto Londono. "Afghan Officials Opt to Dissolve Bank Draped in Scandal." Washington Post, March 27, 2011. 48 Joshua Partlow. "Afghan Bureaucrat Tasked With Recovering Millions in Bad Loans." Washington Post, July 7, 2012. Afghanistan Plans to Sell Scandal-Scarred Kabul Bank in June. Bloomberg.com, April 11, 2012. Afghanistan: Politics, Elections, and Government Performance Congressional Research Service 48

In a step toward holding principals accountable, on June 30, 2011, the government announced the arrest of two former Kabul Bank executives, Sherkhan Farnood and Khalilullah Frouzi, who allegedly allowed the concessionary loans to the high-level Afghans and their relatives. However, by late 2011, the detentions of the two had been relaxed and they were frequently sighted at various public places in Kabul. 49 On August 1, 2011, the Attorney General's office sent the names of about 15 people allegedly responsible for the scandal to Afghan courts for trial. On April 3, 2012, Karzai ordered a special prosecutor appointed and a special tribunal created to try those involved in the scandal. On June 2, 2012, at the urging of Karzai's office, 21 people were indicted by the special tribunal, including Farnood, Frouzi, Fitrat, nine other government officials, and nine other bank employees who were allegedly in positions to have known of and reported the fraud while it was occurring but did not. The investigations, the recovery of some lost funds, and the start of a forensic audit of the bank suggested Afghanistan was moving to meet the IMF conditions for the restart of its credit program. On October 6, 2011, the IMF issued a statement that it would restore its credit program because of the investigations and because of the Afghan efforts to recover some of the Bank's funds. In November 2011, the IMF resumed its program by approving a $133 million loan to Afghanistan. That move restored the flow of some previously blocked donor funds, including U.S. contributions to the World Bank-run Afghanistan Reconstruction Trust Fund (ARTF). The IMF also wants a timetable for another bank found by the Central Bank to be vulnerable to collapse, Azizi Bank, to shore up its finances. Another Afghan entity suspected of corruption is the New Ansari Money Exchange, a large money-trading operation. On February 18, 2011, the Treasury Department designated the New Ansari, and persons affiliated with it, as major money laundering entities under the "Kingpin Act," a designation that bans U.S. transactions with the designees. The Treasury Department accused the New Ansari and affiliates of serving as a vehicle for narcotics trafficking organizations. Moves to Penalize Lack of Progress on Corruption Several of the required U.S. "metrics" of progress, cited above, involve Afghan progress against corruption. A FY2009 supplemental appropriation (P.L. 111-32) mandated the withholding of 10% of about $90 million in State Department counter-narcotics funding subject to a certification that the Afghan government is acting against officials who are corrupt or committing gross human rights violations. In the 111the Congress, in June 2010, the Foreign Operations Subcommittee of the House Appropriations Committee deferred consideration of some of the nearly $4 billion in civilian aid to Afghanistan requested for FY2011, pending the outcome of a committee investigation of the issue. The subcommittee's action came amid reports that as much as $3 billion in funds have been allegedly embezzled by Afghan officials over the past several years. 50 In part on the basis of the findings of the House Appropriations Committee investigation, the Senate Appropriations Committee's 2011 omnibus appropriation marked up in December 2010 required Administration certifications of progress against corruption as a condition of providing aid to Afghanistan. Some of this conditionality was included in the 2011 continuing Appropriations, Aid conditionality based on Afghan performance against corruption, 49 Matthew Rosenberg and Graham Bowley. "Intractable Afghan Graft Hampering U.S. Strategy." New York Times, March 8, 2012. 50 Rosenberg, Matthew. "Corruption Suspected in Airlift of Billions in Cash From Kabul." Wall Street Journal, June 28, 2010. Afghanistan: Politics, Elections, and Government Performance Congressional Research Service 49 on incorporation of women in the reconciliation process, and on reports on progress on the Kabul Bank scandal, are included in the FY2012 Consolidated Appropriation No U.S. funding for Afghanistan has been permanently withheld because of this or any other legislative certification requirement. Rule of Law Efforts U.S. efforts to curb corruption go hand-in-hand with efforts to promote rule of law. As of July 2010, the U.S. Embassy has an Ambassador rank official heading a "Rule of Law Directorate." U.S. funding supports training and mentoring for Afghan justice officials, direct assistance to the Afghan government to expand efforts on judicial security, legal aid and public defense, gender justice and awareness, and expansion of justice in the provinces. According to the SRAP report of November 2011, USAID's "Rule of Law Stabilization Program" had, as of then, trained 670 Afghan judges, over half the total in the country. The program also had expanded the Afghan Supreme Court's training program for new judges, and supports linkage between the traditional justice sector and the formal justice system. Some observers say that Afghanistan's counternarcotics courts have demonstrated particular progress in achieving a steady stream of convictions of drug traffickers. At the July 20, 2010, Kabul conference, the Afghan government committed to: Enact its draft Criminal Procedure Code into law within six months. This is one of the 37 laws pledged at the Kabul Conference would be enacted, but it has not been accomplished, to date. Improve legal aid services within the next 12 months. A December 10, 2010, U.N. report said that the Ministry of Justice had opened legal aid offices in some provinces. The Tokyo Framework, cited earlier, requires Afghanistan to "improve access to justice for all," suggesting that implementation has been weak. Strengthen judicial capabilities to facilitate the return of illegally seized lands. This commitment was made partly to address the issue discussed above in which powerful individuals have appropriated land for their homes and projects. USAID provided $56 million during 2005-2009 to facilitate property registration. An additional $140 million is being provided from 2010-2014 to inform citizens of land processes and procedures, and to establish a legal and regulatory framework for land administration. Align strategy toward the informal justice sector (discussed below) with the National Justice Sector Strategy. Despite the international focus on the formal justice sector, some estimates say that 80% of cases are decided in the informal justice system. Many Afghans view the formal sector as riddled with corruption and unfairness, and continue to use local, informal mechanisms (shuras, jirgas) to adjudicate disputes—particularly with cases involving local property, familial or local disputes, or personal status issues In the informal sector, Afghans can usually expect traditional practices of dispute resolution to prevail, including the traditional Pashtun code of conduct known as Pashtunwali. Some of these customs, including traditional forms of apology ("nanawati" and "shamana") and compensation for wrongs 2004 JirgaRestorativeJustice.shtml. Afghanistan: Politics, Elections, and Government Performance Congressional Research Service 50 However, the informal justice system is dominated almost exclusively by males. For example, some disputes are resolved by families' offering to make young girls available to marry older men from the family that is the counter-party to the dispute, resulting in numerous forced marriages and child marriages. This practice is known as baad. Some informal justice shuras take place in Taliban-controlled territory, and some Afghans may prefer Taliban-run shuras when doing so means they will be judged by members of their own tribe or tribal confederation. One concern is how deeply the international community should become involved in the informal justice sector. U.S. programs have focused primarily on the formal justice system, but there has been increasing attention to the informal system because its use is so prevalent. USAID has implemented a pilot program to assist local shuras in four districts to establish a system to transmit their judicial rulings, in writing, to the district government. The rule of law issue is discussed in substantially greater depth in CRS Report, Afghanistan: U.S. Rule of Law and Justice Sector Assistance, by Liana Sun Wyler and Kenneth Katzman. Promoting Human Rights and Civil Society 51 Since 2001, U.S. policy has been to build capacity in human rights institutions in Afghanistan and to promote civil society and political participation. As do previous years' State Department human rights reports, the report on Afghanistan for 2011 attributed the many human rights deficiencies observed primarily to overall lack of security, loose control over the actions of Afghan security forces, pervasive corruption, and societal discrimination particularly against women. A Human Rights Watch statement issued on the eve of the December 5, 2011, BonnConference was highly critical, saying that "ten years later "after the first Bonn Conference setting a transition from the Taliban era", many basic rights are still ignored or downplayed. While there have been improvements, the rights situation is still dominated by poor governance, lack of rule of law, impunity for militias and police, laws and policies that harm women, and conflict-related abuses." On the other hand, there has been a significant proliferation of organizations that demand transparency about human rights deficiencies. Prominent examples of Afghan NGO's that monitor and agitate for improved human rights practices include the Afghanistan Human Rights and Democracy Organization, and the Research Institute for Women, Peace and Security. The December 5, 2011, Bonn Conference was preceded by meetings (December 2-3, 2011, in Bonn) of Afghan civil society activists, intended to help assess the progress of Afghan governance and highlight the role of civil society in governance. It is in part the work of these groups that has produced responses by the government. For example, Afghanistan's National Directorate of Security (intelligence directorate but with arrest powers), which has widely been accused of detainee abuse and torture, established in late 2011 a "human rights unit" to investigate these allegations. On June 2, 2012, Karzai ordered disarmed a local security unit whose members were accused of raping an 18-year old woman in Konduz Province. On July 9, 2012, Afghan forces were sent to track down Taliban militants who had executed a woman for adultery in Parwan Province. 51 Information in this section is primarily from Department of State. 2011 Human Rights Report: Afghanistan, May 24, 2012; Congressional Research Service 51 Institution-Building: The Afghanistan Independent Human Rights Commission (AIHRC) One of the institutional human rights developments since the fall of the Taliban has been the establishment of the Afghanistan Independent Human Rights Commission (AIHRC). It is headed by a woman, Sima Simar, a Hazara Shiite from Ghazni Province. It acts as an oversight body over alleged human rights abuses but its members are appointed by the government and some believe it is not as aggressive or independent as some had hoped. However, its members are appointed by the president and, as an indication of government interference, in December 2011, Karzai dismissed its deputy chairman Ahmad Nader Nadery for his outspoken writings alleging abuses by traditional allies of Karzai. Nadery heads another civil society watchdog organization, the Free and Fair Election Foundation of Afghanistan, which was highly critical of Karzai and his allies for the 2009 and 2010 election fraud. The July 20, 2010, Kabul conference communiqué contained a pledge by the Afghan government to begin discussions with the AIHRC, within six months, to stabilize its budgetary status. It pledged to provide $1 million per year, but has provided only half that amount. A December 10, 2010, U.N. Secretary General report says the Afghan cabinet has approved inserting a line item in the annual Afghan budget for the AIHRC, but the March 5, 2012, report of the Secretary General said the National Assembly has not regularized the AIHRC status within the national budget framework. USAID has given the AIHRC about $10 million per year since the fall of the Taliban. Religious Influence on Society: National Ulema Council Counterbalancing the influence of post-Taliban modern institutions such as the AIHRC are traditional bodies such as the National Ulema Council. The Council consists of the 150 most respected and widely followed clerics throughout Afghanistan, but it represents a network of about 3,000 clerics nationwide. It has increasingly taken conservative positions to limit free expression and social freedoms, such as the type of television and other media programs available on private media outlets. In August 2010, 350 clerics linked to the Council voted to demand that Islamic law (Sharia) be implemented (including such punishments as stoning, amputations, and lashings) in order to better prevent crime. The government did not implement the recommendation, which would require amending the Afghan constitution, which does not implement Sharia. The Council's March 2, 2012, backing of Sharia interpretations of the rights of women is discussed below in the section on women's rights. The government (Ministry of Hajj and Religious Affairs) is also involved in regulating religious practices. Of Afghanistan's approximately 125,000 mosques, 6,000 are registered and funded by the government. Clerics in these mosques are paid about $100 per month and, in return, are expected to promote the government line. In April 2012, the Ministry decreed that it would fire government-funded clerics who refuse to heed warnings and preach violence or incitement. Riots over Quran Burnings and Anti-Islamic Video: 2011 and 2012 As an illustration of Afghanistan's Islamic conservatism, riots have broken out in two successive years over what some Afghans perceived as U.S. disrespect of Islam. On April 2, 2011, hundreds of Afghans rioted in the normally quiet (and non-Pashtun) city of Mazar-e-Sharif to protest the Afghanistan: Politics, Elections, and Government Performance Congressional Research Service 52 burning of a Quran by a Florida pastor a few weeks earlier. The rioters, who had been instigated by the sermons of three mullahs (Islamic preachers) at the city's signature Blue Mosque, stormed the U.N. compound in the city and killed at least 12 people, including 7 U.N workers. Over the next several days, similar, but less violent, demonstrations took place in Qandahar and other Afghan cities until sentiment calmed. Earlier, in September 2010, some National Ulema Council figures organized protests against plans by the Florida pastor to burn Qurans, although that burning was not conducted following international and U.S. criticism of the pastor. A more serious eruption occurred in late February 2012 over the mistaken U.S. discarding of Qurans used by detainees at Bagram Airfield. Riots and protests occurred in several cities, including the normally peaceful and pro-U.S. north. The public reaction to the Quran burning was more intense than it was following the March 11, 2012, killing of 16 Afghans allegedly by a U.S. soldier, Robert Bales, who is in U.S. military custody. On September 17, 2012, several hundred Afghans rioted outside a U.S. training facility east of Kabul city to protest a video produced in the United States ("Innocence of Muslims") that mocks the Prophet Muhammad. Afghan police protected the facility from assault from the crowd. These perceived U.S. slights may account for some of the killings of U.S. military personnel by Afghan security forces over the past few years. The so-called "green on blue" attacks have caused tensions between Afghan forces and their U.S. mentors, and prompted U.S. commanders to impose counter-measures that potentially complicate the U.S. effort to accelerate the transition to Afghan security before the end of 2014. Religious Freedom The July-December 2010 International Religious Freedom report (released September 13, 2011)52 says that respect for religious freedom declined throughout the reporting period, particularly for Christian groups and individuals. Members of minority religions, including Christians, Sikhs, Hindus, and Baha'i's, often face discrimination; the Supreme Court declared the Baha'i faith to be a form of blasphemy in May 2007. Northeastern provinces have a substantial population of Islamailis, a Shiite Muslim sect often called "Seveners" (believers in the Seventh Imam as the true Imam). Many Ismailis follow the Agha Khan IV (Prince Qarim al-Husseini), who chairs the large Agha Khan Foundation that has invested heavily in Afghanistan. One major case that drew international criticism was a January 2008 death sentence, imposed in a quick trial, against 23-year-old journalist Sayed Kambaksh for allegedly distributing material critical of Islam. On October 21, 2008, a Kabul appeals court changed his sentence to 20 years in prison, a judgment upheld by another court in March 2009. He was pardoned by Karzai and released on September 7, 2009 positive development is that Afghanistan's Shiite minority, mostly from the Hazara tribes of central Afghanistan (Bamiyan and Dai Kundi provinces) can celebrate their holidays openly, a development unknown before the fall of the Taliban. Some Afghan Shiites follow Iran's clerical leaders politically, but Afghan Shiites tend to be less religious and more socially open than their co-religionists in Iran. The Hazaras are also advancing themselves socially and politically through 52Afghanistan: Politics, Elections, and Government Performance Congressional Research Service 53 education in such fields as information technology. 53 The former Minister of Justice, Sarwar Danesh, is a Hazara Shiite, the first of that community to hold that post. He studied in Qom, Iran, a center of Shiite theology. (Danesh was voted down by the parliament for reappointment on January 2, 2010, and again on June 28 when nominated for Minister of Higher Education.) The justice minister who was approved on January 16, 2010, Habibullah Ghalib, is part of Dr. Abdullah's faction, but not a Shiite Muslim. Ghaleb previously (2006) was not approved by the Wolesi Jirga for a spot on the Supreme Court. There was unrest among some Shiite leaders in late May 2009 when they learned that the Afghan government had dumped 2,000 Iranian-supplied religious texts into a river when an Afghan official complained that the books insulted the Sunni majority. Several conversion cases have earned international attention. An Afghan man, Abd al-Rahman, who had converted to Christianity 16 years ago while working for a Christian aid group in Pakistan, was imprisoned and faced a potential death penalty trial for apostasy—his refusal to convert back to Islam. Facing international pressure, Karzai prevailed on Kabul court authorities to release him (March 29, 2006). His release came the same day the House passed H.Res. 736 calling on protections for Afghan converts. In May 2010, the Afghan government suspended the operations of two Christian-affiliated international relief groups claiming the groups were attempting to promote Christianity among Afghans—an assertion denied by the groups (Church World Service and Norwegian Church Aid). Another case arose in May 2010, when an amputee, Said Musa, was imprisoned for converting to Christianity from Islam, an offense under Afghan law that leaves it open for Afghan courts to apply a death sentence under Islamic law (Shariah). The arrest came days after the local Noorin TV station broadcast a show on Afghan Christians engaging in their rituals. Following diplomatic engagement by governments and human rights groups, Musa was quietly released from prison on February 24, 2011, and reportedly went to Italy, where he is seeking asylum. Media and Freedom of Expression/Social Freedoms Afghanistan's conservative traditions have caused some backsliding in recent years on media freedoms, which were hailed during 2002-2008 as a major benefit of the U.S. effort in Afghanistan. In those years, numerous television channels, newspapers, and other media forms were established, giving Afghanistan some of the freest press in the region. Media has expanded to the point where the government has taken steps in 2012 to launch a communications satellite to help with broadcast speed and breadth of dissemination. However, a press law was passed in September 2008 that gave independence to the official media outlets but also contained a number of content restrictions and required that new newspapers and electronic media be licensed by the government. According to the

State Department report on human rights for 2011, there continues to be intimidation and sometimes violence against journalists who criticize the central government or powerful local leaders, and some news organizations and newspapers have occasionally been closed for incorrect or derogatory reporting on high officials. USAID programs have trained investigative journalists to do more reporting on official corruption and other issues. The United States has provided funding and advice to an Afghan 53 Oppel, Richard Jr. and Abdul Waheed Wafa, "Hazara Minority Hustles to Head of the Class in Afghanistan," January 4, 2010. Afghanistan: Politics, Elections, and Government Performance Congressional Research Service 54 Government Media Information Center that the Afghan government uses to communicate with the public. However, possibly as part of an effort to transition more tasks to the Afghans, or possibly as a sign of frustration with Karzai criticism of some U.S. military operations, U.S. advisers were pulled from the Center in late December 2011. Separately, Islamic conservatives (such as the Ulema Council, parliamentarian Sayyaf, and Shiite cleric Ayatollah Asif Mohseni), have sometimes asserted control over media content. This has been an attempt to curb the popularity of such post-Taliban networks as Tolo Television. With the Council's backing, in April 2008 the Ministry of Information and Culture banned fiv Indianproduced soap operas on Tolo Television on the grounds that they are too risqué, although the programs were restored in August 2008 under a compromise that brought in Islamic-oriented programs from Turkey. In 2011, pressure from Islamic conservatives caused Tolo to remove a soap opera called "Forbidden Love." Tolo has also aired programs with women performers—presentations that raise eyebrows among religious conservatives—and about official corruption. Radio Free Europe Radio Liberty's "Radio Azadi" service for Afghanistan has distributed 20,000 solar powered radios to poor (and usually illiterate) Afghans to improve their access to information. In general, the government does not restrict access to the Internet, but it does ban access to pornographic web sites. Regarding broader social freedoms, as another example of the growing power of the Islamist conservatives, alcohol is increasingly difficult to obtain in restaurants and stores, although it is not banned for sale to non-Muslims. There were reports in April 2010 that Afghan police had raided some restaurants and prevented them from selling alcoholic beverages at all. On the other hand, some point to the fact that rock bands have appeared publicly in high profile shows in 2011 as evidence of increasing modernity. Harsh Punishments The State Department reports widespread examples of torture, rape, and other abuses by officials, security forces, detention center authorities, and police. In September 2011, U.S. and partner transfers of prisoners to some Afghan facilities were suspended because of alleged torture by Afghan prison authorities. Afghanistan's Interior Ministry and National Directorate of Security denied the allegations, which included assertions that prisoners were being beaten with rubber hoses or given electric shocks. In October 2007, Afghanistan resumed enforcing the death penalty after a four-year moratorium, executing 15 criminals. In August 2010, the issue of stoning to death as a punishment arose when Taliban insurgents ordered a young couple who had eloped stoned to death in a Taliban-controlled area of Konduz Province. Although the punishment was not meted out by the government, it was reported that many residents of the couple's village supported the punishment. For the third year in a row, Afghanistan was again placed in Tier 2: Watch List in the State Department report on human trafficking issued on June 19, 2012 (Trafficking in Persons Report for 2012). However, Afghanistan was given a waiver for an automatic downgrade to Tier 3 (the downgrade is automatic after a country is "watch-listed" for three consecutive years). The waiver was based on a the government's writing of a plan that, if implemented, would qualify as a significant effort to comply with minimum standards for the elimination of trafficking. The Afghanistan: Politics, Elections, and Government Performance Congressional Research Service 55 government is assessed in the 2012 report as not complying with minimum standards for eliminating trafficking, and not showing evidence of increasing efforts to address the issue. The State Department report says that women from China, some countries in Africa, Iran, and some countries in Central Asia are being trafficked into Afghanistan for sexual exploitation, although, according to the report, trafficking within Afghanistan is more prevalent than trafficking across its borders. The report asserts that some families knowingly sell their children for forced prostitution, including for bacha baazi, a practice in which wealthy men use groups of young boys for social and sexual entertainment. The report added that some members of the Afghan National Security Forces have sexually abused boys as part of the bacha baazi practice.

The United States has spent about $500,000 to eliminate human trafficking in Afghanistan since 2001. Advancement of Women Women and women's groups are a large component of the burgeoning of civil society in postTaliban Afghanistan. Freedoms for women have greatly expanded since the fall of the Taliban with their elections to the parliament and their service at many levels of government. The Afghan government pursues a policy of promoting equality for women under its National Action Plan for Women of Afghanistan (NAPWA). The Tokyo Mutual Accountability Framework requires Afghanistan to implement the NAPWA and all of its past commitments and laws to strengthen the rights of women and provide services to them. The major institutional development since 2001 was the formation in 2002 of a Ministry of Women's Affairs dedicated to improving women's rights, although numerous accounts say the ministry's influence is limited in part because of the relative ineffectiveness of minister Husn Banu Ghazanfar. It promotes the involvement of women in business ventures, and it plays a key role in trying to protect women from domestic abuse by running 11women's shelters across Afghanistan. However, the Afghan government, in January 2011, launched a plan to regulate the shelters by placing them under government control. This has raised concerns that the government might seek to limit the access to the shelters by some women and in some areas. Women's rights groups in Afghanistan expressed outrage over a June 2012 statement by Afghanistan's justice minister that the shelters encourage "immorality and prostitution." One of the most prominent civil society groups operating in post-Taliban Afghanistan is the Afghanistan Women's Network. It has at least 3,000 members and its leaders say that 75 nongovernmental organizations work under its auspices. In addition, the Afghanistan Independent Human Rights Commission (AIHRC) and a private group, Afghanistan Human Rights and Democracy Organization, focus extensively on rights for Afghan women. Among the most notable accomplishments since 2001, women are performing jobs that were rarely held by women even before the Taliban came to power in 1996, including in the new police force. The first Afghan female pilots arrived for training in the United States in July 2011. There are over 200 female judges and nearly 500 female journalists working nationwide. Women are legally permitted to drive, and press reports say an increasing number of Afghan women, although mainly in Kabul and other main cities, are learning how to drive and exercising that privilege. The wearing of the full body covering called the burqa is no longer obligatory, and fewer women are wearing it than was the case a few years ago. In November 2010, the government opened a USAID-funded women-only park in Kabul called "Women's Garden" where women can go, without male escort, and undertake fitness and job training activities. Afghanistan: Politics, Elections, and Government Performance Congressional Research Service 56 Some groups, such as Human Rights Watch, report backsliding on women's rights since 2008, 54 although the State Department human rights report for 2011 says that the situation of women in Afghanistan improved "marginally" during 2011. Numerous abuses, such as denial of educational and employment opportunities, continue primarily because of Afghanistan's conservative traditions. This is particularly prevalent in rural areas, and less so in larger urban areas. More than 70% of marriages in Afghanistan are forced, despite laws banning the practice, and a majority of brides are younger than the legal marriage age of 16. The practice of baad, in which women are given away to marry someone from another clan to settle a dispute, remains prevalent. There is no law specifically banning sexual harassment, and women are routinely jailed for zina—a term meaning adultery, and a crime under the penal code, and that includes running away from home, defying family choice of a spouse, eloping, or fleeing domestic violence. Under the penal code, a man convicted of "honor killing" (of a wife who commits adultery) cannot be sentenced to more than two years in prison. One case receiving substantial attention in December 2011 has involved a woman who was jailed for having a child outside wedlock even though the child was a product of rape. In order to save face for herself and her family, the woman is contemplating marrying the rapist. Many Afghan women are concerned that the efforts by Karzai and the international community to persuade insurgents to end their fight and rejoin the political process ("reintegration and reconciliation" process) could result in backsliding on women's rights. Most insurgents are highly conservative Islamists who oppose the advancement of women that has occurred. They are perceived as likely to demand some reversals of that trend if they are allowed, as part of any deal, to control territory, assume high-level government positions, or achieve changes to the Afghan constitution. Karzai has said that these concessions are not envisioned, but skepticism remains, and some Afghan officials close to Karzai do not rule out the possibility of amending the constitution to accommodate some Taliban demands. Women have been a target of attacks by Taliban supporters, including attacks on girls' schools and athletic facilities. Major Legal Developments Some Afghan laws passed over the past few years have affected women, both positively and negatively. The Afghan government tried to accommodate Shiite leaders' demands in 2009 by enacting (passage by the National Assembly and signature by Karzai in March 2009) a "Shiite Personal Status Law," at the request of Shiite leaders. The law was intended to provide a legal framework for members of the Shiite minority in family law issues. However, the issue turned controversial when international human rights groups and governments—and Afghan women in a demonstration in Kabul—complained about provisions that would appear to sanction marital rape and which would allow males to control the ability of females in their family to go outside the home. President Obama publicly called these provisions "abhorrent." In early April 2009, taking into account the outcry, Karzai sent the law back to the Justice Ministry for review, saying it would be altered if it were found to conflict with the Afghan constitution. The offending clauses were substantially revised by the Justice Ministry in July 2009, requiring that wives "perform 54 "We Have the Promises of the World: Women's Rights in Afghanistan," Human Rights Watch, December 2009, Afghanistan: Politics, Elections, and Government Performance Congressional Research Service 57 housework," but also apparently giving the husband the right to deny a wife food if she refuses sex. The revised law was passed by the National Assembly in late July 2009, signed by Karzai, and published in the official gazette on July 27, 2009, although it remains unsatisfactory to many human rights and women's rights groups. On August 6, 2009, perhaps in an effort to address some of the criticisms of the Shiite law, Karzai issued, as a decree, the "Elimination of Violence Against Women" (EVAW) law. Minister of Women's Affairs Ghazanfar told CRS in October 2009 that the bill was long contemplated and not related to the Shiite status law.55 It was enacted by the National Assembly as a law as of December 2010; it had been held up by the Assembly for final passage because some Islamic conservatives, such as Sayyaf (cited above), reportedly object to the provisions of the law criminalizing child marriages. A U.N. report on human rights in Afghanistan, released January 18, 2012 says the EVAW law implementation has been weakened by some Supreme Court rulings and other Afghan legal decisions. The optimism that greeted the EVAW law was further reduced on March 2, 2012, when the Ulema Council issued a pronouncement saying women should be forced to wear the veil and be forbidden from traveling without a male chaperone. The pronouncement did reiterate support for the rights of women to inherit and own property, and to choose their marital partners. On March 6, 2012, Karzai endorsed the Ulema Council statement. Women in Key Positions Despite conservative attitudes, women have moved into prominent positions in all areas of Afghan governance, although with periodic setbacks. Three female ministers were in the 2004-2006 cabinet: former presidential candidate Masooda Jalal (Ministry of Women's Affairs), Sediqa Balkhi (Ministry for Martyrs and the Disabled), and Amina Afzali (Ministry of Youth). Karzai named three women to cabinet posts on January 9, 2010, including Afzali (to Labor and Social Affairs). Of the three, only Afzali was immediately confirmed; the other two (Minister of Health and Minister of Women's Affairs) were kept on in acting capacities and confirmed in subsequent years. Afghanistan has one female ambassador and Karzai has a female deputy chief of staff, Homaira Ludin-Etemadi. In the December 16, 2009, nomination list, Karzai proposed a woman to head a new Ministry of Literacy, but parliament did not vote on this nomination because it had not yet acted to approve formation of the ministry. In March 2005, Karzai appointed a former minister of women's affairs, Habiba Sohrabi, as governor of Bamiyan province, inhabited mostly by Hazaras. One woman (Masooda Jalal) ran in the 2004 presidential election, and two ran for president in the August 20, 2009, election. In the latter, each received less than one-half of 1%. As noted above, parliamentarian Fawzia Koofi already has declared she will run in 2014, and there are likely to be additional female candidates. In the National Assembly, the constitution reserves for women at least 17 of the 102 seats in the upper house and 68 of the 249 seats in the lower house of parliament. There were 23 serving in the outgoing upper house, 6 more than Karzai's mandated bloc of 17 female appointees. There were 68 women in the previous lower house (when the quota was 62), meaning 6 were elected without the quota. The number elected in the September 18, 2010, election is 69, one more than 55 CRS meeting with the Minister of Women's Affairs, October 13, 2009. Afghanistan: Politics, Elections, and Government Performance Congressional Research Service 58 the quota. (For the election, about 400 women ran—about 16% of all candidates.) The target ratio is ensured by reserving an average of two seats per province (34 provinces) for women—the top two female vote getters per province. (Kabul province reserves 9 female seats.) In the National Assembly, a woman, Shukria Barekzai, was chair of the Defense Committee of the elected lower house during 2011. Some NGOs and other groups believe that the women elected by the quota system are not viewed as equally legitimate parliamentarians. About 300 women were delegates to the 1,600-person "peace jirga" that was held during June 2-4, 2010, which endorsed an Afghan plan to reintegrate insurgents who want to end their fight. The High Peace Council to oversee the reconciliation process, which met for the first time on October 10, 2010, has 9 women out of 70 members, although these women report that their views are not taken into account to any significant extent in the Council. At U.S. and other country urging, a woman was part of the official Afghan delegation to the major international conference on Afghanistan in Bonn on December 5, 2011; she was selected at a meeting of civil society activists in Bonn, a day before the major conference begins. U.S. and International Posture on Women's Rights U.S. officials say that its policy is to promote women's rights in Afghanistan rigorously. The Administration has and is following its "Strategy for Assistance to Women in Afghanistan, 2010-2013."56 U.S. officials said aid allocations are geared toward that strategy. Specific earmarks for use of U.S. funds for women's and girls' programs in Afghanistan are contained in recent annual appropriations, and these earmarks have grown steadily. The United States provided $159 million to programs for Afghan women in 2009, slightly more than the $150 million earmarked, and about $225 million for 2010, more than the $175 earmarked.57 2010, assistance was provided in the following "pillars" of the U.S. Strategy: health ($87 million); education ($31 million); economy, work, and poverty ($54.6 million); legal protection and human rights ($12 million); and leadership and political participation ($43 million). Amounts were similar for 2011. U.S. funding has been used, in part, to help finance over 830,000 microloans to women during 2004-2011, and they have used these funds to establish 175,000 small businesses, according to the SRAP report released November 2011. These strategy pillars, and specific programs funded by them, are discussed in annual State Department reports on U.S. aid to women and girls. However, an audit issued in July 2010 by the Special Inspector General for Afghanistan Reconstruction found that the State Department and USAID did not provide complete and consistent information about the reported activities in which women and girls were intended beneficiaries. The Afghanistan Freedom Support Act of 2002 authorized $15 million per year (2003-2006) for the Ministry of Women's Affairs. Those monies are donated to the Ministry from Economic Support Funds (ESF) accounts controlled by USAID. S. 229, the Afghan Women Empowerment Act of 2009, introduced in the 111Congress, would authorize $45 million per year in 2010-2012 for grants to Afghan women, for the ministry of Women's Affairs ($5 million), and for the AIHRC ($10 million). 56 A draft of this strategy document was provided to CRS by the State Department, April 21, 2011. 57 For prior years, Afghanistan: Post-Taliban Governance, Security, and U.S. Policy, by Kenneth Katzman, in the section on aid to Afghanistan, year by year. Afghanistan: Politics, Elections, and Government Performance Congressional Research Service 59 Democracy, Human Rights, Governance, and Elections Funding Issues U.S. funding for democracy, governance, and rule of law programs has grown, in line with the Obama Administration strategy for Afghanistan. During 2002-2012, USAID spent about $1.5 billion on democracy, governance, rule of law and human rights, and elections support. The following was spent by USAID (using Economic Support Funds) for 2012 and appropriated in (Consolidated Appropriation) $546.5 million for overall democracy and human rights-related funding including: $435.5 million for good governance; $31 million for rule of law and human rights (not including INCLE funds); $37 million for political competition and consensus building; and $43 million for civil society. For 2013, the ESF democracy and governance request (ESF) is $578.2 million, including: $447.2 million for good governance; $31.5 million for rule of law and human rights (not including INCLE); $64.3 million for political competition and consensus-building; $35.2 million for civil society. For tables on U.S. aid to Afghanistan, see CRS Report RL30588, Afghanistan: Post-Taliban Governance, Security, and U.S. Policy, by Kenneth Katzman. Effects of a Settlement with the Taliban A major U.S. and Afghan initiative—to reach a conflict-ending settlement with the Taliban—is likely to affect all of the issues discussed in this paper: Afghan politics, future elections, the performance of the government along all its metrics, and the human rights situation. Many in the international community, including within the Obama Administration, initially withheld endorsement of the concept, fearing it might result in the incorporation into the Afghan political system of insurgent leaders who retain ties to Al Qaeda and will roll back freedoms instituted since 2011. The minority communities in the north, women, intellectuals, and others remain skeptical that their freedoms can be preserved if there is a political settlement with the Taliban. These groups fear that the Taliban could be given major ministries, seats in parliament, or even tacit control over territory as part of any deal. Secretary Clinton said in India on July 20, 2011, that any settlement must not result in and undoing of "the progress that has been made [by women and ethnic minorities] in the past decade." To respond to those fears, Afghan and U.S. officials say that the outcome of a settlement would require the Taliban to drop at least some of its demands that (1) foreign troops leave Afghanistan; (2) a new "Islamic" constitution be adopted; and (3) Islamic law be imposed. Following the 2010 U.S. shift to supporting a settlement, an "Afghan High Peace Council" intended to oversee the settlement process was established on September 5, 2010. Its 70 members met for the first time under the leadership of senior Northern Alliance figure/former President Afghanistan: Politics, Elections, and Government Performance Congressional Research Service 60 Burhanuddin Rabbani on October 10, 2010. Rabbani was appointed because of Karzai's perception that he could bring skeptical Tajiks and other minorities to support reconciliation. These minority figures, as noted above, fear that reconciliation with the Taliban will strengthen Pashtun control of government to the detriment of the non-Pashtun minorities. Rabbani earned substantial respect among all factions for his diligent work in this role; for example he led High Peace Council visits to Pakistan and other regional countries, and established provincial representative offices of the Council in at least 27 provinces. On the other hand, some of the nine women on the Council say their views were routinely dismissed. On September 20, 2011, Rabbani was assassinated by a Taliban infiltrator posing as an intermediary. On April 14, 2012, the High Peace Council members voted Rabbani's son, Salahuddin, as his replacement. Prior to the Rabbani killing, U.S., Taliban, and Afghan representatives had proliferated. In May 2011, it was reported that U.S. officials had met at least three times in 2011 with Tayeb Agha, a figure believed close to Mullah Umar. In late June 2011, those meetings were confirmed by thenSecretary of Defense Gates, who said the talks had been led by the State Department and have been facilitated by Germany and Qatar. However, the process stalled after the Rabbani assassination and Pakistan's boycott of the December 5, 2011, Bonn Conference over a November 26, 2011, security incident in which U.S. forces killed 24 Pakistani border troops. In December 2011, as tensions over these issues abated, U.S. officials resumed the process, including pursuing the opening of a Taliban political office in Qatar to facilitate talks. The discussion of a Taliban office in Qatar came amid reports that U.S. officials had been meeting Taliban figures more frequently than was previously believed. The Taliban office has not formally opened to date, but some Taliban figures are operating from Qatar informally, as discussed below. The United States also revealed it had discussed "confidence-building measure" in the form of transferring captives from the Guantanamo detention facility to a form of house arrest in Qatar—to be conducted simultaneous with the Taliban release of the one U.S. prisoner of war, it holds, Bowe Bergdahl. The United States also demanded a public Taliban statement severing its ties to Al Qaeda or other terrorist groups, possibly as a prelude to a limited battlefield ceasefire. There were also discussions of transitioning the talks from U.S.-led to Afghan government-led, although the Taliban was reluctant to undertake such talks because doing so would recognize the government's legitimacy. A release of Taliban captives would require U.S. congressional notification. The Taliban figures to be released to Qatar include some, such as Mullah Mohammad Fazl who were major figures in the Taliban regime (Fazl was deputy defense minister). H.Res. 529 expresses opposition to their release. The confidence-building measures did not take place, and talks stalled in March 2012 reportedly over Qatar's failure to fully assure the United States that the detainees would be able to escape custody. Some U.S. officials say that all sides were not close to serious negotiations on the core issues of any political settlement. Still, the reconciliation issue appears to be alive and active. An April 15, 2012, attack by militants on several locations in Kabul and other provinces soured the Afghan government on talks, as did the May 2012 assassination of another key intermediary, Arsala Rahmani—a former Taliban official who reconciled with the government and served in the Afghan parliament. But, these were counterbalanced by a February 2012 statement by Pakistani leaders that, for the first time, publicly encouraged Taliban leaders to negotiate a settlement to the conflict. In late June 2012, Afghan government officials and Taliban representatives held talks at two meetings—one in Paris, and one an academic conference in Kyoto, Japan, on reconciliation issues. At the Kyoto meeting, the Afghan government was represented by Mohammad Stanekzai, a member of the High Peace Council, and the Taliban was represented by Din Mohammad, a member of the Taliban political council who had traveled from Qatar. The Kyoto meeting appeared to represent Afghanistan: Politics, Elections, and Government Performance Congressional Research Service 61 an acceptance by the Taliban of direct talks with Afghan government officials. In August 2012, Afghan officials reportedly held talks with high-ranking Taliban figure Mullah Abdul Ghani Bradar, 58 who was arrested by Pakistan in February 2010, purportedly to halt between Bradar and Afghan intermediaries. Pakistan's decision to grant Afghan officials access to Bradar, at his prison in Pakistan, signaled that Pakistan wants to play a more active role in the reconciliation process. Some Afghan officials express optimism the talks will yield a settlement eventually, particularly if the Afghan government provides assurances of security for Taliban leaders who reconcile Mr. Karzai has completed eight unsuccessful years of his government and it was originally assumed that he would not run for election on 20 August 2009. Even though he ran for election, it was thought that the people would not give him a single vote. However, the recent political situation, political compromise, conspiracies, excessive expenditures on campaigns, too many promises and Pashtuns lack of interest shows that Mr. Karzai will proudly wear the presidential crown and rule for the next five years. The people, particularly the Pashtuns, will face a dark, unbearable next five years. Now that Afghans are certain to accept Karzai for next five years. It appears from his promises, his eight years as president, and his political compromises his next term will look like this:1: The next five years of Mr. Karzai will be weaker than the previous one. He will be just a symbol and the real authority will rest with warlords as long as Mr. Karzai curries their favor. Afghans will suffer more violence and injustice. However, Mr. Karzai will not be able to do anything and will just close his eyes upon them.2: Mafia land-grabbers will be strengthened. One of the cabinet members has already declared that on average, 1000 hectares of land is controlled by each warlord. Now that this mafia remains in control, the average will definitely increase.3: Poppy cultivation and drug smuggling will increase which will further damage Afghanistan in the International community because Mr. Karzai has allied himself with the drug dealers. The best example is his releasing five drug dealers from prison to campaign for him.4: The raping, human trafficking. and kidnapping Mafia will get significantly stronger since Mr. Karzai's coalition has agreed with them and all their demands have been accepted.5: Most of the government's structure and cabinet will remain dominated by the warlords. 6: Violation of law, corruption, and nepotism will reach its last stage, because these factors are all related to the coalition and Afghanistan's compromised government. 7: The number of ministries will increase from thirty to forty. Advisors will grow to more than two hundred since Mr. Karzai has promised at least five ministries to the weakest political party to keep them happy. 8: Most of his cabinet will consist of his campaign supporters and contributors. In addition, they will be given provincial governor offices and ambassadors positions. 9: The Afghan passport will lose its value because most of the ambassadors will be illiterate and have no knowledge of culture and tradition. Therefore the international community will call our government warlords, and human rights violators, and we will be frisked at each airport as thoroughly as possible. 10: Pashtoons will be scattered and deprived. They will have no influence or power in government. 11: According to Mr. Karzai's promise 20 out of 100 seats in government will be given to Mr. Khalili and 15 out of 100 to Dostum. 12: Media and freedom of expression will give only lip service to a free press, and a single word against warlord will be a death sentence to the author. Afghanistan's next five years will be quite challenging to both the international community and to the Afghan people themselves. Poverty and violence are usually portrayed as the biggest challenges confronting Afghanistan. But ask the Afghans themselves, and you get a different answer: corruption is their biggest worry. As revealed in this new UNODC report, for an overwhelming 59% of the population the daily experience of public dishonesty is a bigger concern than insecurity (54%) and unemployment (52%). President Karzai has recognized that corruption is destroying the country. At the inauguration of his second term in November 2009, he rightly identified "ending the culture of impunity and strengthening integrity as key priorities" for his new administration. The political will and the analytical tools to make a statistically robust survey of grand-scale profiteering in Afghanistan are not yet available. Therefore, this report looks at the problem of corruption in Afghanistan from a different perspective. It takes a bottom-up look at a problem that affects Afghans on a daily basis: bribery. Yet, this survey, by including some large bribes — payments of $1000 and above, i.e. more than twice the country's per-capita income — to an extent does capture some serious corruption cases. Unlike other corruption reports, this one is not based only on perceptions: in other words, it does not only measure shadows filtered through individual discernment and discontent. It quantifies the actual crime, as reported by the victims. This is the real thing, based on interviews with 7,600 people (a reliable sample) in 12 provincial capitals and more than 1,600 villages around Afghanistan. Commentary by the executive director A helping hand, not pointing fingers This report was not conceived to embarrass or bash Afghanistan, or to point fingers at particular situations. There are three good reasons for this. First, no country is free of corruption. Indeed, in so many countries around the world (rich and poor) similar surveys indicate that corruption is peoples' greatest concern. Second, the UNODC ethos is based on constructive engagement: we provide ground-level diagnoses in order to help find national remedies. When it comes to strengthening integrity in governance, our aim is to help Member States implement the world's only universal legally-binding instrument: the United Nations Convention against Corruption. Third, in order to make progress, countries need an honest assessment of where they stand — no ifs and buts. By identifying gaps, countries gain a better idea of what new legislation and measures are needed, and what technical assistance is required. This survey was conducted, and the report written, with precisely these goals in mind. A costly part of everyday life According to this report, it is almost impossible to obtain a public service in Afghanistan without greasing a palm: bribing authorities is part of everyday life. During the past 12 months, one Afghan out of two, in both rural and urban communities, had to pay at least one kickback to a public official. This was not just done through a wink and a nudge: more than half of the time (56%), the request for illicit payment was explicit by the service providers. In most instances (3/4 of the cases), baksheesh (bribes) are paid in cash. The average amount was $160 – in a country where GDP per capita is a mere $425 per year. This is a crippling tax on people who are already among the world's poorest. The problem is enormous by any standards. In the aggregate, Afghans paid out $2.5 billion in bribes over the past 12 months –that's equivalent to almost one quarter (23%) of Afghanistan's GDP. By coincidence, this is similar to the revenue accrued by the opium trade in 2009 (which we have estimated separately at $2.8 billion). In other words, and this is shocking, drugs and bribes are the two largest income generators in Afghanistan: together they amount to about half the country's (licit) GDP. To make things worse, in Afghanistan those entrusted with upholding integrity and the law are seen as being most guilty of violating them. Around 25% of Afghan citizens had to pay at least one bribe to police and local officials over the past year. Between 10-20% had to pay bribes to judges, prosecutors, doctors and members of the government. A kickback is so commonly sought (and paid) to speed up administrative procedures, that more than a third of the population (38%) thinks that this is the norm. Bribery not only robs the poor and causes misallocation of resources. It destroys trust in government. When people, who earn less than $2 a day, have to bribe their way into basic services, they lose confidence in the system and look for alternative providers of security and welfare. As demonstrated in other parts of the world, under such circumstances the social contract is torn apart: loyalty is lost and discontent can erupt into violence. Not surprisingly, most Afghans have no confidence that the state is able or willing to tackle their problems. Despite the fact that, when queried by UNODC surveyors, they were all firm as to the severity and the frequency of the crime, only 9% of the urban population has ever reported an act of corruption to authorities. This suggests that people are either (i.) unaware of what recourse to take, (ii.) distrust those who are supposed to help, or (iii.) feel that there is no point in reporting unlawful behaviour to people who are seen as part of the problem (63% of responses). Pricing out traditional social stabilizers Afghan society has been traditionally held together by patron-client relations perhaps more so than in other countries. For centuries, the social contract of favours and loyalty offered and acquired in exchange for financial (and other) rewards, have strengthened tribal cohesion and imparted respect for the leaders. In recent time, these relations have been transformed precipitously by the rapid influx of vast drug (and aid) monies. Unprecedented resource flows have created a new cast of rich and powerful individuals who operate outside the traditional power/tribal structures and bid the cost of favours and loyalty to levels not compatible with the under-developed nature of the country. The old patron-client relations, including the services provided by public administrators, have been affected in scope, breadth and depth transformed into a monumental, perverse and growing machinery for criminal graft Bribery as reported by the victims 5 its size (a quarter of GDP) has acquired macroeconomic dimension and has become complementary to, and often profiting from other illicit activities; its growth is confirmed by about two thirds of the respondents to this survey, according to whom the corruption problem at present is worse than in earlier times; its perversity risks shattering social relations. In southern Afghanistan, for example, a number of those surveyed complained that even the village elders, having heard complaints about corruption, no longer turn in the villains, or open a public debate aimed at finding solutions. With the very foundation of traditional Afghan justice (administered by the village shura) weakened, the recourse to more violent forms of retribution (the Taliban sharia) becomes treacherously appealing. Bad examples What can be done? First and foremost, the broad political establishment has to lead by example. At the moment this is not happening. In fact, there are perverse multiplier effects throughout all levels of government. (i) To begin with, bribery and abuse of power are particularly significant among the police (much more than among the army) and the judiciary. Those appointed to uphold the law get the most severe moral indictment by the survey respondents: as mentioned, 25% of Afghans had to pay a bribe to police officers over the past year, 18% had to bribe a judge, and 13% a prosecutor. In some cases this may be the result of need: the Afghan police are notoriously underpaid. But greed also plays a major role: over half all large bribes ($1,000 or more) were pocketed by enforcement officers (especially judges and prosecutors) as well as police, customs officials and local authorities. To put it vividly, the average Afghan has to work more than two years to afford such a sum. (ii) Members of the government (much more than those sitting in Parliament) are also perceived as villains. Corruption in their ranks was rampant last year: Afghans were asked to pay a bribe 40 percent of the times that they had contacts with senior politicians. A political system operating under such corrupt conditions cannot survive. (iii) This survey did not address the question of possible foreign involvement in fomenting corruption in Afghanistan. Yet it makes a stunning observation: over half of the Afghans (54%) believe that international organizations and NGOs, the transmission belts of foreign assistance, "are corrupt and are in the country just to get rich".(iv)In many countries, particularly where the rule of law is weak, national media acts as a watchdog on good governance. This does not seem to be happening in Afghanistan. Country-wide, 43% of city dwellers say that the media rarely addresses corruption issues. In the South, two thirds indicated that corruption is seldom, or never, in the news. Considering that corruption is the greatest public concern, there is surprisingly little public debate about it: a circumstance that the vast majority of those surveyed consider as a serious impediment to remedial action. The international media, though not directly covered in this survey, has been greatly appreciated for keeping the spotlight on this issue. Cancer treatment The x-ray imaging provided by this report shows that the cancer of corruption is metastatic in Afghanistan. It will lead to a terminal condition, unless chemotherapy to reduce the chances of further infection (preventive measures) is combined with surgery to remove the biggest infected nodules (the key villains). The therapy most widely recognized around the world is based on the UN Convention against Corruption. Since President Karzai has indicated his willingness to administer this Corruption in Afghanistan 6 tough medicine (Afghanistan is now a party to the Convention), let us see what this would mean in concrete terms. To begin with, the preventive measures outlined in the Convention must be urgently implemented. As a priority, Afghanistan needs an independent, fearless and well funded anti-corruption authority. The government's integrity drive should give the High Office of Oversight and Anti Corruption (which enjoys relatively high public trust) the tools to do the job. UNODC, that has provided large-scale assistance to even bigger countries affected by equally widespread corruption, can help build capacity for such a suitable authority. The appointment of governors and district leaders must include a negative corruption pledge (i.e. the commitment to be guided by unassailable integrity standards). The vetting of officials must be pursued to the greatest extent, including the use of polygraphic technology if necessary. The removal of governors with proven records of collusion with shady characters must be one of the administration's key priorities. People holding public service positions should disclose their incomes and assets, as required by the UN Convention. Let's see how senior officials can afford flashy cars and fancy villas with salaries of less than $500 a month! There is plenty of evidence that the seizure of assets whose licit origin cannot be established is a powerful deterrent to crime. While the executive power must face its responsibilities, Parliamentarians must also practice what they preach – including ridding itself of its members with poor integrity records. Since many Afghans (40%) pay bribes to cut through the red tape of administrative procedures that they do not understand, or to cope with poor quality service, as a priority administrative procedures should be made more userfriendly, and public services made more accessible and service-oriented. Again in compliance with the UN Convention, there must be full transparency in public procurement, tendering processes and political campaigns. Regulation of financial institutions (including the hawala system) should be tightened in order to prevent money laundering. The media, civil society and educatorsmust become more engaged in anticorruption campaigns to help change a culture of corruption into an environment of integrity. Religious and tribal leaders – who are the most respected members of society – need to spread the word. The Afghan government and the donor community need to take a hard look at salary levels and structures for public officials. If civil servants were paid a living wage, they could be held to higher standards, and they would have less excuse for providing shoddy service. (II) In legal terms, anti-corruption surgery translates into the application of the broad array of criminal justice measures included in the Convention. "Cleaning up the new administration" (the media jargon so frequently used to spur the government into action) means, first, for the Parliament to adopt the necessary legislation to criminalize bribery, embezzlement, moneylaundering, abuse of power, illicit enrichment, and obstruction of justice. For the Attorney General this means resolve to prosecute suspected cases. Senior officials should not stand in the way, and should protect the victims of corruption rather than the perpetrators. The proceeds of crime must be confiscated. Since much of the money stolen through corruption (and other crimes) is smuggled abroad, Afghanistan should take advantage of measures in the UN Convention to strengthen international Bribery as reported by the victims 7 cooperation, via extradition, mutual legal assistance and joint investigations. The World Bank UNODC Stolen Asset Initiative (StAR) has demonstrated vitality to chase corrupt monies hidden abroad. At the moment, the Afghan people are under the impression that it is cheaper to buy a judge than to hire a lawyer. I urge the Chief Justice to undertake disciplinary measures among the judiciary to ensure that Afghanistan is ruled by the law rather than the bribe. International aid providers need to improve resource effectiveness, to prevent squandering their tax-payers money, as well as to impart a good example for Afghanistan's budgetary processes. Not quick or easy, but necessary and possible Strengthening integrity in Afghanistan — like in other countries plagued by corruption — will not be quick or easy. Yet it is both necessary and possible. President Karzai has called for strong measures: it's time for his administration to implement the UN anti-corruption Convention in deeds, not just in the formality of the ratification process. Fighting corruption is an un-avoidable journey. Afghanistan's path is rockier than most, but its Government cannot and must not do it alone. Fighting corruption in a country already ravaged by poverty and violence must be a high priority for the Afghan government and for the international community. With political will, the right laws, and effective vetting of public officials, corruption will be curbed. Simply, there is no alternative. Afghanistan's leading anti-corruption crusader wears a broad smile and speaks perfect German. Mohammed Eshaq Aloko, the attorney general of Afghanistan, spent years in Hamburg — indeed, his wife still lives in Germany. But Aloko elected to return to his homeland. "The country was lawless for decades," Aloko is fond of telling visitors from the West, "which is why one can't expect a law-based society to appear out of nowhere." First, he points out, one must make a reliable diagnosis before a therapy can be decided upon. ANZEIGE It is clear to everyone in Afghanistan exactly what needs to be diagnosed. Afghans have learned from their daily lives that the rules of life are quite simple: Everything is possible, but everything has a price. A passenger needs to get to the airport quickly without any bothersome security checks? No problem, for a price of $20 at the first checkpoint. You need a driver's license immediately and without any tests? Such express service will set you back $180. A family wants their son, in prison for drug smuggling, to return home? The necessary papers will be filled out the same day for a price of $60,000. The list of such examples is endless — nothing is accomplished in Afghanistan without the payment of bribes. Foreigners can even obtain an Afghan passport as a souvenir, if they're willing to fork out a bit of cash. Every government agency employs official commissionkars, the Dari word for intermediary. Without these helpful assistants, no application would reach its intended destination, no building permits would be issued and no stamps would be placed on any documents. Afghans can't even choose for themselves the five witnesses they want for their wedding. It is often the case that the justice of the peace has a relative who is only too happy to take on the duty — for a fee of course. The Country's Greatest Problem Just how extreme corruption has become in Afghanistan can be seen in a new study released by the United Nations. According to the paper, 59 percent of Afghanistan citizens point to corruption as the greatest problem facing the country — that ranks the problem even higher than security (54 percent) and unemployment (chosen by 52 percent of those polled). The study, released, was put together by the United Nations Office on Drugs and Crime (UNODC) and includes the responses of 7,600 people from 1,600 villages questioned between August and October of last year. The study shows just how omnipresent the payment of bribes has become in everyday life in Afghanistan. In the last 12 months, Afghan citizens have paid $2.5 billion in bribes — roughly a quarter of the country's gross domestic product. "The Afghans say that it is impossible to obtain a public service without paying a bribe," UNODC Executive Director Antonio Maria Costa writes on the organization's Web site. The "cancer of corruption" is "metastatic," he says, and can be found even in the highest echelons of government. Afghans who have had recent contact with government representatives report that, in 40 percent of the cases, they were asked for bribes. Every second person surveyed reports having bribed someone in the last year — usually after having been requested to do so. The average payment is $158 — a generous sum for a country in which average annual income is a mere $425. According to the report, the most corrupt officials are those allegedly overseeing law and order: Twenty-five percent of those surveyed report having bribed a policeman in 2009, 18 percent a judge and 13 percent a public attorney. "The Afghan people are under the impression that it is cheaper to buy a judge than to hire a lawyer," the report says. Powerful Atlas of Dishonesty Such widespread corruption among police and in the judiciary is dangerous, the report says: People lose their trust in the state and look for security elsewhere. Resignation is also spreading. Sixty-three percent believe that filing complaints against corrupt officials is a waste of time. Only 9 percent have even tried. Even village elders have given up and do little to protest against the problem. The report is a powerful atlas of dishonesty in the country — bribery is lowest in the western part of the country and at its highest in the north and the south. The more rural the areas, the higher the corruption, the report found, with big cities such as Kabul and Hirat much less affected. The problem is intensified by the long tradition of patronage in Afghanistan — corruption is considered to be socially acceptable. Fully 38 percent think it is legitimate for a government official to ask for a "present." Forty-two percent find nepotism unproblematic. The UN sees the battle against corruption as a vitally important element of its strategy to turn the country back over to the Afghans. Such a corrupt country could never function on its own, international aid workers fear. It is hoped that the new report will raise the already intense pressure on Afghan President Hamid Karzai to do something about the problem. Karzai, says Costa, should "urgently administer tough medicine based on the UN Convention against Corruption, which he pushed so hard to ratify." Reducing the Temptation First and foremost, the UN would like to see an anti-corruption agency. Each new civil servant should also be made to sign an oath against corruption. Those who violate the law should be jettisoned and the salaries of public servants should be made transparent. "Let's see how senior officials can afford flashy cars and fancy villas with salaries of less than $500 a month!" Costa writes in the report. At the same time, however, he recommends that salaries be increased significantly to reduce the temptation to take bribes. So far, little has happened to dampen corruption in Afghanistan, aside from a few weak statements of intention from Karzai. In a November speech on the occasion of his inauguration for a second term in office, he promised the West he would kick off an offensive against corruption. Since then, however, he has done nothing. Even a strategy paper outlining a possible anti-corruption agency, originally set to be finished prior to next week's Afghanistan conference in London, has yet to materialize. Western diplomats say that Karzai has disappointed them once again. Few are willing to accuse Karzai himself of corruption, but members of his family have been fingered. When Karzai is asked about his promise, he is fond of referring people to Attorney General Aloko. Just as Karzai was being sworn in, Aloko began proceedings against five government ministers for corruption and announced that trials would begin soon. Since then, however, little has been heard about the five cases. Aloko's diagnosis, one is left to assume, isn't finished yet. Afghanistan has been rated by Transparency International as the second-most corrupt nation in the world, with public sector corruption worsening for the second consecutive year. Only war-torn Somalia rates worse on the Berlin-based organisation's Corruption Perceptions Index (CPI) of 180 nations, which was released. The group said of Afghanistan: "Examples of corruption range from public posts for sale and justice for a price to daily bribing for basic services. "This, along with the exploding opium trade - which is also linked to corruption - contributes to the downward trend in the country's CPI score." Presidential elections in August were beset by claims of fraud, many upheld by the election commission and Western nations warned Hamid Karzai, the president, after the poll that he must tackle corruption in order to secure their continuing support. On Monday, Kabul announced that it would establish a new unit to fight corruption at the highest levels, which is viewed as aiding the fight against Taliban forces. It is the third year in a row that Somalia, which has been largely without a functioning central administration for years and is riven by violence between opposition groups and government forces, has been rated as the world's most corrupt country. Myanmar was ranked third-worst for corruption, while Iraq and Sudan were in joint fourth place. Transparency International said that countries whose infrastructure had been "torn apart" by conflict needed help from outside to prevent a culture of corruption taking root. "The international community must find efficient ways to help war-torn countries to develop and sustain their own institutions," Huguette Labelle, the head of Tranparency International, said. "Stemming corruption requires strong oversight by parliaments, a well performing judiciary... anti-corruption agencies, vigorous law enforcement... as well as space for independent media and a vibrant society." New Zealand was found to be the least corrupt country, followed by Denmark, with Singapore and Sweden close behind. Transparency International attributed the strong performance of those countries to their "political stability, long-established conflict of interest regulations and solid, functioning public institutions". The rankings are based on perceptions of the degree of corruption as seen by business people and country analysts. But it was not just countries riven by conflict that saw their ratings slide. Italy, a member of the so-called Group of Eight industrialised countries came in at 63rd on the list, from 55th last year. Why we are supporting Afghanistan, a country Transparency International reports is 179th in the corruption index? That's 179 out of 180. Supporting corruption only increases corruption, having the opposite effect of what the donor intends. There are endless examples of corruption in Afghanistan. The previous election was alleged to be fraudulent. The election this past weekend is reportedly riddled with fraud. Last month Fazel Faqiryar was sacked as deputy attorney-general because he was trying to prosecute senior members of the Karzai government. The Kabul Bank is almost bankrupt because of loans to the bank's directors, Karzai's mates, who consequently have expensive waterfront mansions in the United Arab Emirates. The West does not listen to the Afghans. In June this year, the Afghan President, America's then commander of US forces General Stanley McChrystal and other military personnel met 400 local elders in Kandahar. Karzai spoke briefly, then the entourage left without hearing what the tribal elders had to say. Journalists remained and interviewed the Afghans. The elders said they have no love for the Taliban but they have much less love for Afghan leaders. They enumerated case after case of corruption, but McChrystal listened to not even one. The money the West has thrown to corrupt regimes in the past 60 years is partly responsible for the global rise of corruption. Where there's free money, corruption thrives. Looking at the mistakes of the past should alert us to the mistakes we are making now in Afghanistan. I cite just three examples. Vietnam: Australia and America supported the corrupt presidents Ngo Dinh Diem and then Nguyen Van Thiu in South Vietnam. The West ignored the corruption its support created. The Vietnamese hatred of these dictators eventually increased support for Ho Chi Minh, resulting in America's humiliating defeat. America would not listen. Ho Chi Minh made several attempts to gain US support to end French occupation. Ho had visited the US in 1912. He was a great admirer of the US Constitution and was in awe of American revolutionaries' defeat of the British. Ho was an admirer of George Washington. In 1919 at the Versailles Treaty conference, Ho tried to present president Woodrow Wilson with his presentation for a free Vietnam, but was spurned. He was spurned many times because the West feared communism. Ho was a nationalist first and a communist second. He was also an opportunist, willing to accept support from the US. Had America listened to him, Vietnam would most likely have become a Western socialist state. Congo: Fearing the Congo would come under the influence of Russia, in 1960 the US and other Western nations helped Joseph Mobutu oust the socialist-leaning Patrice Lumumba. The West continued to support the Mobutu dictatorship knowing it was based on fear, violence and repression. America continued to hand Mobutu millions of dollars in full knowledge that he used the money for corrupt purposes. By flooding the top with money, the US is partly responsible for the entrenched corruption that exists there today. Had the US listened to Lumumba instead of desperately clinging to an ideology, the Congo may have become a very different country. Cuba: America supported the corrupt government of Fulgencio Batista in Cuba. Many Cubans hated Batista, a puppet of American business interests. His corrupt behaviour led to Castro's 1959 Communist revolution. America would not listen to the ground swell of contempt for the Batista regime and so it paid the price of having a communist state on its doorstep. America did not listen to Cubans, the Vietnamese and Congolese and does not listen to Afghans now. Why do we support Afghanistan? The US and NATO mantra is that corruption is part of life in Afghanistan so there is no point in trying to eliminate it. This mantra is out of tune, a head-in-the-sand mentality that only breeds more corruption. Another argument is that trying to stop corruption would destabilise the Karzai government, creating a power vacuum the Taliban would immediately fill. This is a ridiculous argument. It is the reverse. The more corruption the West ignores, the more the Taliban thrives. 1500 strong participation in the NATO forces in Afghanistan are there to bring stability and justice to a beleaguered people. Good intentions, bad results. We are the do-gooders making things worse. he don't have a solution to the chaos in

Afghanistan. However, he know that supporting corruption results in the reverse of our intentions. Building capacity and limiting corruption at all levels of Afghan governance are crucial to the success of a planned transition from U.S.-led NATO forces to Afghan security leadership. The capacity of the formal Afghan governing structure has increased significantly since the Taliban regime fell in late 2001, but nepotism is entrenched in Afghan culture and other forms of corruption are widespread. Afghan President Hamid Karzai has accepted U.S. help to build emerging anti-corruption institutions, but these same institutions have sometimes caused a Karzai backlash when they have targeted his allies or relatives. At a donors' conference in Tokyo on July 8, 2012, donors pledged to aid Afghanistan's economy through at least 2017, provided Afghanistan takes concrete, verifiable action to rein in corruption. On July 26, 2012, Karzai appeared to try to meet his pledges to the Tokyo conference by issuing a "decree on administrative reforms"—a document of sweeping policy directives intended to curb corruption. Partly because of corruption in the Afghan security forces, on August 4, 2012, the National Assembly voted to remove the ministers of interior and of defense; they have been replaced. Even though the government is weak, President Hamid Karzai has tried to concentrate authority in Kabul through his constitutional powers of appointment at all levels. Karzai has publicly denied assertions by opposing faction leaders that he wants to stay in office beyond the 2014 expiration of his second term, but he is said to be trying to identify and support an acceptable successor. International efforts to curb fraud in two successive elections (for president in 2009 and parliament in 2010) largely failed and many believe election oversight will be little improved for the 2014 election, although civil society groups are trying to ensure robust competition and electoral fairness. There is concern among many observers that fragile governance will founder as the United States and its partners wind down their involvement in Afghanistan by the end of 2014. Some argue that the informal power structure, which has always been at least as significant a factor in governance as the formal power structure, will sustain governance beyond 2014 should formal governing structures falter. However, that outcome might produce even more corruption and arbitrary administration of justice than is the case now as major faction leaders gain power. Karzai has failed to marginalize these ethnic faction leaders, in part because they have large constituencies, but he relies more closely on the loyalty of several close, ethnic Pashtun allies, particularly those from the Kandahar area. The non-Pashtun faction leaders generally oppose Karzai's willingness to make concessions to insurgent leaders in search of a settlement. There are fears that a reintegration of the Taliban into Afghan politics will further set back progress in human rights and the rights of women and boost Pashtun power. Broader issues of human rights often vary depending on the security environment in particular regions, although some trends prevail nationwide. Women, media professionals, and civil society groups have made substantial gains since the fall of the Taliban, but traditional attitudes contribute to the judicial and political system's continued toleration of child marriages, imprisonment of women who flee domestic violence, judgments against converts from Islam to Christianity, and curbs on the sale of alcohol and Western-oriented programming in the Afghan media.

Autobiography of Hamid Wahed Alikuzai

Born in Kabul in 1949, and educated in a French school until the age of seventeen, Hamid's education was enriched and very influenced by his grandmother, his mother's mother, who was highly educated and passed down ancient wisdoms and cultural heritage. These stories, wisdoms, and discussions touched him deeply and so profoundly that he began even as a young boy to live his life in a way that reflected these teachings. His grandmother's history, culture, wisdom, ideas and knowledge of all religions and the 9 prophets was taught to Hamid. Each story or pearl of wisdom took his grandmother sometimes as long as two to three weeks to tell. In preparation for these teachings the children would have to bathe from head to toe and put on fresh clothes. Every day was like Christmas when his grandmother was there. To Hamid she was looked and spoke like an angel.

Hamid's father, Wahed Alikuzai, was educated in Europe until 1932 in nuclear science for the military and there was very strict discipline and order in the house. Education was the number one priority. Hamid's father was also very powerful in his knowledge and connection with the ancient way of life and our connection to the earth. His father had a one hundred percent firm belief that all people are equal, regardless of faith, education or social status.

In 1919 the King of Afghanistan believed and passed down a law that there would be no distinction between people. There would be no such thing as a first, second or third class citizen. (The word Afghan translated means first class citizen). All people no matter what their background were very proud to be Afghan. This description of the way of life with the nature and equality of people was the fundamental foundation passed down since 3 000 years ago. Since then unity began.

These two individuals in Hamid's life, both father and grandmother, were key in Hamid's development and shaped and inspired his life but also were the fire behind the huge passion Hamid had for history. Upon completion of French High School in 1967, the university was closed due to fighting among the religious groups and the communists. Hamid took a job with the Supreme Court of Afghanistan, and after one year had a scholarship for International Law which was his ticket out of the country. Hamid chose to go Germany to further his education, and entered Germany with his diplomatic passport, fluent in French and Russian, and some English. In one year he spoke German freely. At the age of seventeen, Hamid was alone with no family in Germany except the shadow of his father and the teachings of his grandmother that gave him the foundation that would carry him through the next phase of his life. Under the influence of his father and his father's best friend, who was a five star General in the Afghani army, Hamid would be changing his studies from International Law to Engineering, because of the Islamic movement in Afghanistan. Were he studying law, Hamid would not be welcome back into Afghanistan and therefore it would be more beneficial to study something that would suit the needs of the country. So for the next eight years leading up to 1975 Hamid studied engineering and history in Hamburg Germany.

He took a vacation to go back home to Afghanistan in 1975 with high hopes of staying. At twenty-six Hamid had gained quite a bit of knowledge of his own and was excited to share this with his father. For forty-eight hours straight he proudly talked about all that he had learned as well as some really good engineering ideas he had with his father. On the third day, Hamid's father explained his concerns because of the current changing of the regime – Afghanistan had become a republic in 1973 during a coup d'état influenced by Russian powers. During Hamid's visit his father was put under house arrest by the new head of the republic, Daoud Khan. Mister Alikuzai, Hamid's father, was ordered to pay a hundred and fifty million Afghanis to the government. Hamid visited at the courthouse in all of the ministries for letters of recommendation about his father but to no avail. At any given time there could be border closures between Afghanistan and its neighbouring countries. Hamid's father Wahed Alikuzai was thinking that he had made a mistake in believing that Afghanistan was a free country - since 1929 Afghanistan was not an independent country because of the Cold War and Russia's involvement.

At midnight on the third night of his visit, it was decided that Hamid would leave as early as 6a.m. to Iran and then back to Germany. At 5 a.m. Hamid got dressed and knocked on the door of his father's room to say goodbye. This is the last time Hamid would ever see his father again. His father already sitting up in bed stopped Hamid from stepping further into the room. With two fingers raised in the air his father began to say that he only had two years to live whether in jail or in his own bed. Hamid and his father had an agreement that Hamid would write a letter letting his father know that Hamid had passed through the border safely. Passing through the border by car early in the morning, from Iran Hamid drove back to Germany. His diplomatic passport enabled him to continue his studies on many subjects for the next twenty-two years in Germany. Several years later, in 1979, he wanted to renew his passport at the Afghan embassy in Bonn. They refused to renew his visa and kept Hamid's passport, saying he would have to return back home to Afghanistan.

Hence began Hamid Wahed's next course of action to become a German citizen. Hamid's best friend Paul, who studied law, sent a letter to internal and foreign affairs in Germany. The choice was either political asylum or citizenship, and never having being involved with politics Hamid chose German citizenship. Paul made the arrangements for the citizenship interview. When sitting face to face with the authorities, Hamid was told to put down in his own words and hand writing what was talked about in the meeting. Having put it in letter form, Hamid returned with the letter personally to deliver it. When the man saw the letter he told Hamid he was leaving for six weeks' vacation but he would send the letter to internal affairs and the decision would rest upon the German authorities. It was unknown how long this process would take, whether it would be one year or ten years. This gentleman after six weeks called Hamid on the telephone and said congratulations they have accepted you as a German Citizen. Back in Afghanistan the Russians invaded in December 1979. Hamid was never to visit the country of his birth again, not even for his father's or his brother's funeral. His brother was an air force pilot killed in Kandahar by the Muslim Fundamentalists after passing his astronaut exams.

Meanwhile Hamid married in Hamburg, and on the 15th of April 1981 his first son was born and July 6th, 1983 his second son was born. In 1982 the young family came to Las Angeles, California although he would return with his wife and children would return to Germany in 1983 before the birth of his second child. In the years from 1988 to 1994 Hamid had moved to the United States and was working and studying in Los Angeles. From May 1994 Hamid Wahed came to Vancouver

B.C Canada, because Hamid wished to see his mother, brother, and sister. His mother and sister immigrated by walking for three months to New Delhi, India from Kabul, Afghanistan, when the Taliban came into power in Afghanistan in 1992. At his mother's urging the family reunited in Vancouver, B.C Canada after a twenty-eight year separation. Hamid hadn't seen his little sister since she was one year old.

Hamid Wahed Alikuzai